HOLT McDOUGAL

Earth SCIENCE

Mead A. Allison

Arthur T. DeGaetano

Jay M. Pasachoff

HOLT McDOUGAL
a division of Houghton Mifflin Harcourt

About the Authors

Mead A. Allison, Ph.D.
The University of Texas, Austin, Texas
Mead Allison received his Ph.D. in oceanography from State University of New York. Formerly a professor of Earth and environmental science at Tulane University in Louisiana, Dr. Allison is now a Senior Research Scientist at the Institute for Geophysics, Jackson School of Geosciences at The University of Texas at Austin.

Arthur T. DeGaetano, Ph.D.
Cornell University, Ithaca, New York
Arthur DeGaetano received his Ph.D. in meteorology from Rutgers University. He is a professor of Earth and atmospheric sciences at Cornell University in New York, where he teaches introductory climatology and upper-level courses in atmospheric thermodynamics and physical meteorology. Dr. DeGaetano is also the director of the Northeast Regional Climate Center.

Jay M. Pasachoff, Ph.D.
Williams College, Williamstown, Massachusetts
Jay Pasachoff received his Ph.D. in astronomy from Harvard University. He is the Field Memorial Professor of Astronomy and the director of the Hopkins Observatory at Williams College in Massachusetts, where he teaches introductory and upper-level courses in astronomy. In addition, Dr. Pasachoff has written several popular college-level astronomy textbooks and an astronomy field guide.

Printed in the U.S.A.

ISBN-13: 978-0-547-72497-3

3 4 5 6 7 8 9 10 0868 20 19 18 17 16 15 14 13 12
4500351161 A B C D E F G

HOLT McDOUGAL

Earth SCIENCE

TEACHER'S EDITION

Mead A. Allison, Ph.D. • Austin, Texas
Arthur T. DeGaetano, Ph.D. • Ithaca, New York
Jay M. Pasachoff, Ph.D. • Williamstown, Massachusetts

Student Edition Contents in Brief

Teacher's Edition Walk-Through

HOLT McDOUGAL
a division of Houghton Mifflin Harcourt

Discover the Earth and beyond

Students will investigate the core of the Earth and explore far-away planets with the comprehensive and up-to-date content of ***Holt McDougal Earth Science.*** Environmental science and other cross-disciplinary connections help students integrate Earth science with other studies and improve their critical-thinking skills. The engaging, easy-to-read text and vivid images encourage students to master science skills. Your teaching options will abound with engaging elements and versatile print and technology resources.

LEVELED ACTIVITIES MEET THE NEEDS OF ALL STUDENTS AND STRENGTHEN THEIR ANALYTICAL SKILLS.

- The accessible and engaging design and structure with abundant visuals ensures comprehension.
- Activities are labeled by ability level—**Basic, General,** or **Advanced**—in the **Chapter Planner** and in the ***Chapter Resource Files*** so you can easily assign exercises appropriate for each student.
- Exercises in the teacher's wrap address different **Learning Styles,** plus **Differentiated Instruction Strategies** are included so you can easily provide alternative teaching techniques.

A FLEXIBLE LAB PROGRAM GIVES STUDENTS HANDS-ON EXPERIENCES TO APPLY INQUIRY SKILLS.

- The extensive laboratory program includes leveled in-text **Chapter Labs,** two in-text **Quick Labs** and one in-text **Inquiry Lab** for each chapter, and additional labs in the ***Chapter Resource Files*** and on the ***Lab Generator CD-ROM.***
- The variety of chapter lab types—**Making Models, Inquiry,** and **Skills Practice**—meets the needs of your curriculum.
- All labs are tested by teachers for safety and efficiency, so you know they are reliable.

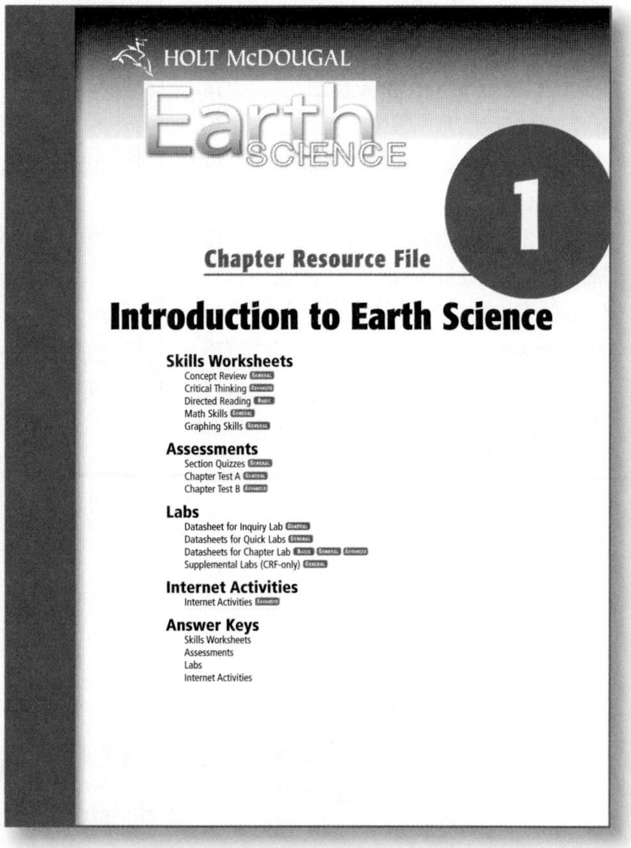

CUSTOMIZABLE, MULTI-LEVEL ASSESSMENTS KEEP STUDENTS ON TRACK.

- Comprehensive section and chapter assessments allow you to check students' progress while building their critical-thinking skills.
- The program helps prepare students for testing with **Standardized Test Prep** in each chapter in addition to reading, math, and interpreting graphics skills development throughout the program.
- Leveled assessments, such as **General** and **Advanced Chapter Tests,** allow you to tailor to students' varying abilities.
- The **ExamView® Version 6 Assessment Suite** on the ***Teacher One Stop™*** gives you the power to customize your own assessments, and post them to **Holt Online Assessment** for automatic grading and to track student progress.

INTEGRATED TECHNOLOGY AND ONLINE RESOURCES REINFORCE STUDENTS' COMPREHENSION OF SCIENCE.

- Students can easily study at home with the online edition ***ThinkCentral, Student Access*** or the interactive ***Student One Stop™.***
- The ***Teacher One Stop™*** makes planning a breeze with lesson plans, *Calendar Planner, PowerNotes® Presentations, Interactive Teacher's Edition,* PuzzlePro®, test generator, and more, all in one package.
- The new ***Lab Generator CD-ROM*** lets you search for labs by keywords, standards, and other criteria. You can also edit labs to meet your needs, create new labs, or add labs, and get a customized materials list instantly.

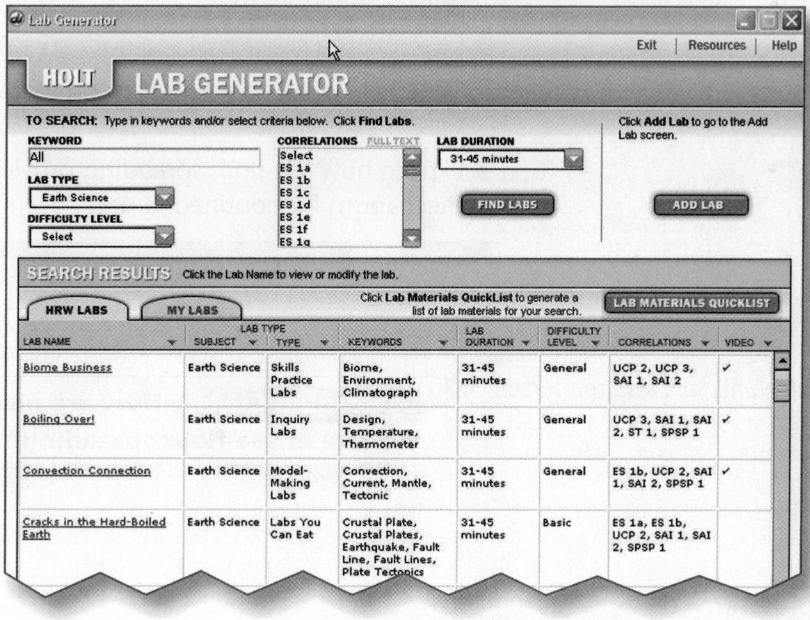

Reading Comprehension Tools

READING SUPPORT UNLOCKS SCIENCE CONTENT

Every chapter begins with tools such as **Graphic Organizers** or **FoldNotes** to help students access key science content. These tools are suggested again at point-of-use within the chapter. The first question in every **Chapter Review** provides practice using a **Reading Toolbox** application. Additionally, the *Teacher's Edition* provides toolbox suggestions in the margin wrap.

READING TOOLBOX These reading tools will help you learn the material in this chapter.

Word Parts

Prefixes Many scientific words are made up of word parts that come from Latin and Greek. You can figure out the meanings of unfamiliar science terms by looking at their word parts.

The words *Pangaea* and *Panthalassa* contain the prefix *pan-*. *Pan-* comes from a Greek word meaning "all." The root words *gaea* and *thalassa* come from Greek words meaning "land" and "ocean." *Pangaea* means "all lands," and *Panthalassa* means "all oceans."

Your Turn Prefixes found in this chapter include *paleo-*, *di-*, *trans-*, and *pan-*. As you read this chapter, make a table like the one started below. List words or terms that contain prefixes and give the meaning of each prefix.

WORD OR TERM	PREFIX	MEANING
paleomagetism	paleo-	
divergent boundary	di-	

Fact, Hypothesis, or Theory?

Recognizing Facts, Hypotheses, and Theories A fact is a statement about the world that is based on observation. A hypothesis is a possible explanation that can be tested. A scientific theory is a model or explanation that ties together many hypotheses and observations.

Your Turn Make a table like the one shown below. List statements of fact, hypotheses, and theories from Sections 1 and 2. Identify the type of statement, and write any language from the text that signals the type of statement.

STATEMENT	FACT, HYPOTHESIS, OR THEORY	KEY WORDS
	hypothesis	"proposed a hypothesis..."
	fact	"scientists found that..."
	theory	"lead to a theory called ________"

FoldNotes

Three-Panel Flip Chart FoldNotes are a fun way to help you learn and remember ideas that you encounter as you read. FoldNotes help you organize concepts and see the "big picture."

Your Turn Follow the instructions in **Appendix A** for making a three-panel flip chart. Label the first panel "Divergent boundary," the second "Convergent boundary," and the third "Transform boundary." Open the appropriate flap to take notes about each type of boundary discussed in Section 2 and make a sketch.

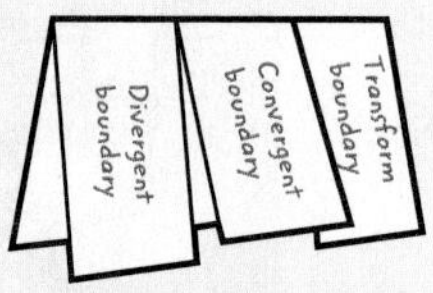

For more information on how to use these and other tools, see **Appendix A**.

Key Ideas

- Summarize Wegener's hypothesis of continental drift.
- Describe the process of sea-floor spreading.
- Identify how paleomagnetism provides support for the idea of sea-floor spreading.
- Explain how sea-floor spreading provides a mechanism for continental drift.

Each section begins with statements that guide students' reading and provide focus.

Important points are also reinforced with questions that check students' reading comprehension.

Reading Check **How are magnetic patterns in sea-floor rock evidence of sea-floor spreading?**

VOCABULARY BUILDS UNDERSTANDING

Longitude

The latitude of a particular place indicates only its position north or south of the equator. To determine the specific location of a place, you also need to know how far east or west that place is along its circle of latitude. East-west locations are established by using meridians. As **Figure 2** shows, a **meridian** is a semicircle (half of a circle) that runs from pole t...

By international agreement, one m... This meridian, called the *prime meridia*... England. **Longitude** is the angular di... east or west of the prime meridian.

meridian any semicircle that runs north and south around Earth from the geographic North Pole to the geographic South Pole; a line of longitude

longitude the angular distance east or west from the prime meridian; expressed in degrees

Academic Vocabulary

location (loh KAY shuhn) place or position

Key Terms are highlighted in context and defined in the margin for quick reference.

Academic Vocabulary provides definitions of terms that are frequently used in science.

ADDITIONALLY YOU'LL FIND:

Directed Reading Workbook helps students organize the main points of a lesson as they read.

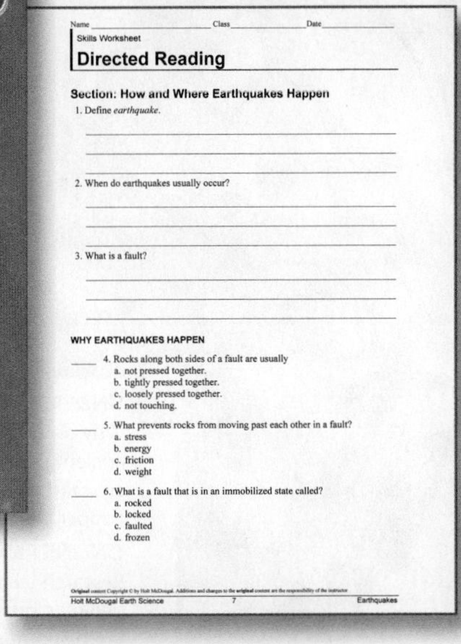
Name ______ Class ______ Date ______

Skills Worksheet

Directed Reading

Section: How and Where Earthquakes Happen

1. Define *earthquake*.

2. When do earthquakes usually occur?

3. What is a fault?

WHY EARTHQUAKES HAPPEN

____ 4. Rocks along both sides of a fault are usually
a. not pressed together.
b. tightly pressed together.
c. loosely pressed together.
d. not touching.

____ 5. What prevents rocks from moving past each other in a fault?
a. stress
b. energy
c. friction
d. weight

____ 6. What is a fault that is in an immobilized state called?
a. rocked
b. locked
c. faulted
d. frozen

Holt McDougal Earth Science 7 Earthquakes

Visual Concepts animations and videos are available online and on CD to reinforce key Earth Science concepts.

The **Guided Reading Audio Program** provides a direct read of the textbook. Files are available in MP3 format.

WHY IT MATTERS

Why It Matters

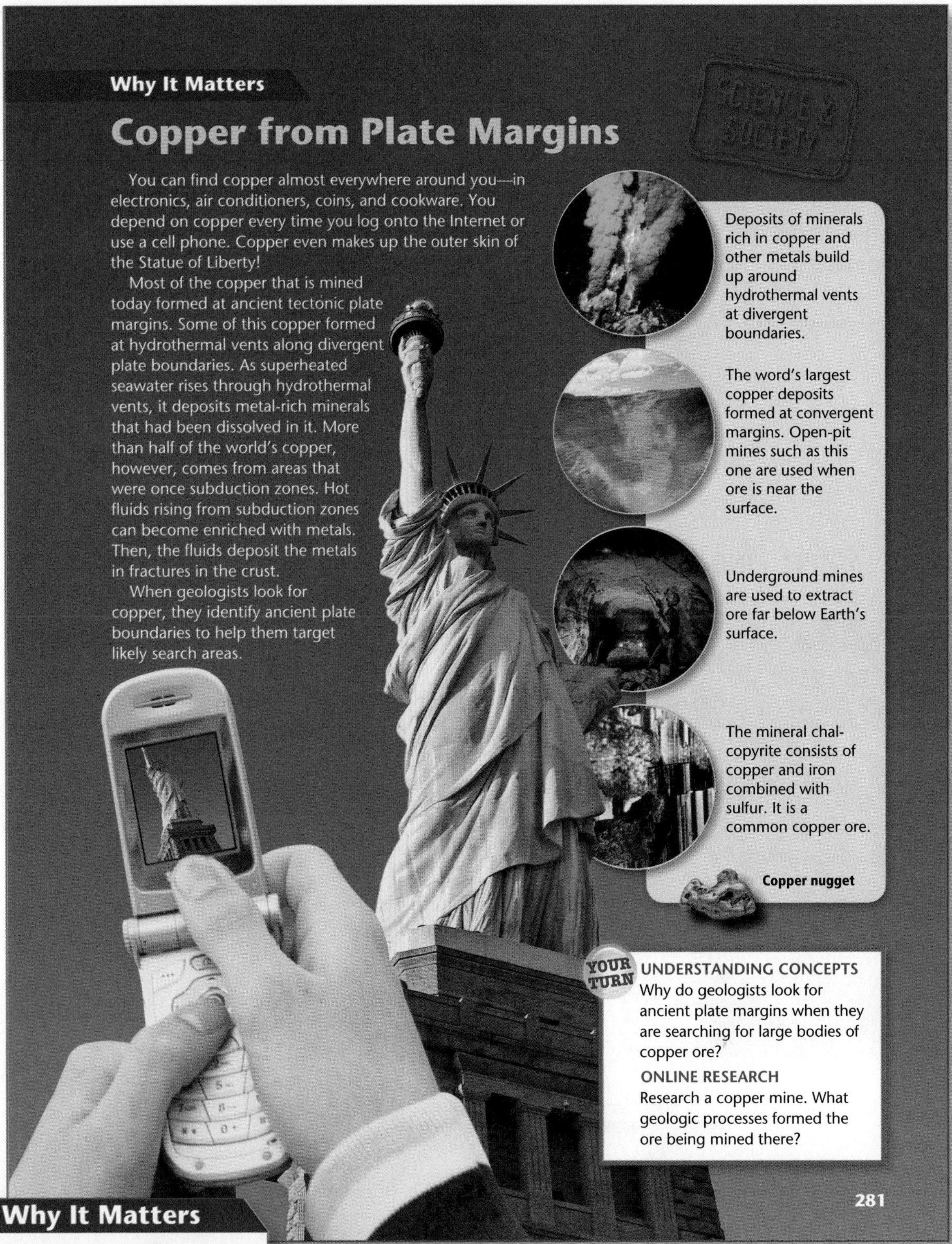

Why It Matters

Copper from Plate Margins

SCIENCE & SOCIETY

You can find copper almost everywhere around you—in electronics, air conditioners, coins, and cookware. You depend on copper every time you log onto the Internet or use a cell phone. Copper even makes up the outer skin of the Statue of Liberty!

Most of the copper that is mined today formed at ancient tectonic plate margins. Some of this copper formed at hydrothermal vents along divergent plate boundaries. As superheated seawater rises through hydrothermal vents, it deposits metal-rich minerals that had been dissolved in it. More than half of the world's copper, however, comes from areas that were once subduction zones. Hot fluids rising from subduction zones can become enriched with metals. Then, the fluids deposit the metals in fractures in the crust.

When geologists look for copper, they identify ancient plate boundaries to help them target likely search areas.

Deposits of minerals rich in copper and other metals build up around hydrothermal vents at divergent boundaries.

The word's largest copper deposits formed at convergent margins. Open-pit mines such as this one are used when ore is near the surface.

Underground mines are used to extract ore far below Earth's surface.

The mineral chalcopyrite consists of copper and iron combined with sulfur. It is a common copper ore.

Copper nugget

YOUR TURN

UNDERSTANDING CONCEPTS

Why do geologists look for ancient plate margins when they are searching for large bodies of copper ore?

ONLINE RESEARCH

Research a copper mine. What geologic processes formed the ore being mined there?

281

Why It Matters

Evidence for continental drift was found in Earth's natural magnetism. This magnetism not only supports scientists' hypotheses, it also protects us all from the dangers of solar radiation.

Designed more like a magazine layout than a textbook page, **Why It Matters** features capture students' interest and make science relevant in the context of real-world science, weird science, or science and society.

Each chapter and section also begins by emphasizing the relevance of the lesson content to student's everyday lives with **Why It Matters** explanations.

Skills Practice

MAPS *in Action*

Locations of Earthquakes in South America

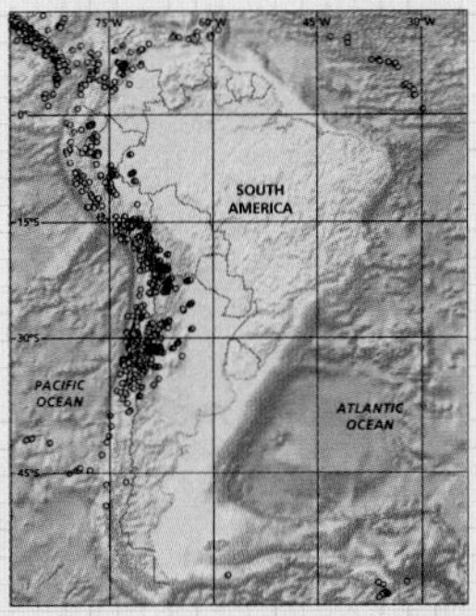

MAPS IN ACTION FEATURES SHARPEN STUDENT SKILLS

Maps in Action features, found in every chapter, help improve students' critical-thinking skills such as analyzing data, making comparisons, and inferring relationships. Corresponding transparencies and worksheets are found in *Teaching Transparencies.*

STUDENTS IMPROVE THEIR MATH SKILLS WHILE LEARNING SCIENCE

Math Skills

The Rate of Plate Movement Tectonic plates move slowly on Earth's surface. The rate of plate movement can be calculated by using the following equation:

$$rate = \frac{distance}{time}$$

In kilometers, how far would a plate that moves 4 cm per year move in 2 million years?

Math Skills features link mathematics directly to the science topic being covered.

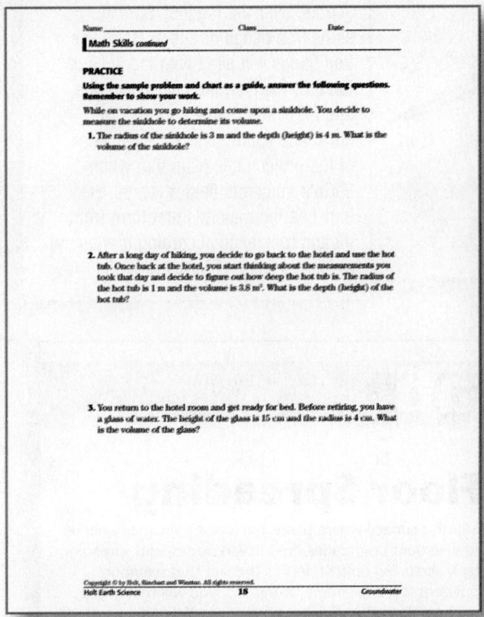

Name__________ Class________ Date________

Math Skills *continued*

PRACTICE

Using the sample problem and chart as a guide, answer the following questions. Remember to show your work.

While on vacation you go hiking and come upon a sinkhole. You decide to measure the sinkhole to determine its volume.

1. The radius of the sinkhole is 3 m and the depth (height) is 4 m. What is the volume of the sinkhole?

2. After a long day of hiking, you decide to go back to the hotel and use the hot tub. Once back at the hotel, you start thinking about the measurements you took that day and decide to figure out how deep the hot tub is. The radius of the hot tub is 1 m and the volume is 3.8 m^3. What is the depth (height) of the hot tub?

3. You return to the hotel room and get ready for bed. Before retiring, you have a glass of water. The height of the glass is 15 cm and the radius is 4 cm. What is the volume of the glass?

Copyright © by Holt, Rinehart and Winston. All rights reserved.
Holt Earth Science 18 Groundwater

Math Skills worksheets in the ***Chapter Resource Files*** hone students' math skills by providing challenging math exercises.

Skill Builder ADVANCED

Math The Atlantic Ocean is spreading at a rate of 1 to 2 cm per year, and the eastern Pacific sea floor is spreading between 3 and 8 cm per year. Have students use the average rate of spreading for the Atlantic Ocean to calculate how many years the sea floor of the Atlantic Ocean would take to spread 1 km. (1.5 cm/year; 1 km ÷ 0.000015 km/year = 66,667 years) Have students use the average rate of spreading of the Pacific Ocean to calculate how many years the sea floor of the Pacific Ocean would take to spread 1 km. (5.5 cm/year; 1 km ÷ 0.000055 km/year = 18,182 years) **LS Logical**

Skill Builder: Math in the teacher's wrap gives students another chance to integrate math with science.

WRITING EXERCISES REINFORCE STUDENTS' KNOWLEDGE OF SCIENCE

WRITING SKILLS

31. **Writing Persuasively** Imagine that you are Alfred Wegener. Write a persuasive essay to explain your idea of continental drift. Use only evidence originally used by Wegener to support his hypothesis.
32. **Communicating Main Ideas** Explain how the research of Wegener, Hess, and others led to the theory of plate tectonics.

Writing Skills questions in the Chapter Review allow students to practice their writing skills and develop clear and persuasive essays.

Skill Builder GENERAL

Writing Ask students to research a specific plate boundary and to write a short essay about that plate boundary. The report must include where the boundary is located, which plates meet at that boundary, and what type of boundary it is. Students may also include what geologic features are found near the boundary, such as mountain ranges or volcanoes, and how plate boundaries affect humans. **LS Verbal**

Skill Builder: Writing in the teacher's wrap gives students opportunities to apply writing skills using science topics.

Inquiry, Labs, and Hands-On Learning

IN-TEXT LABS AND ACTIVITIES IMPROVE STUDENTS' SCIENCE SKILLS.

Inquiry Lab

15 min

Reconstructing Landmasses

Draw a map of a large landmass on a piece of paper. Use colored pencils or markers to show geological features, such as mountain ranges and types of rock at the surface. Using scissors, cut your map into irregular pieces. Trade map pieces with another group, and then reconstruct the other group's landmass.

Questions to Get You Started

1. What features of the interiors of the pieces did you use to put the pieces back together?
2. What features of the edges of the pieces did you use for your reconstruction?

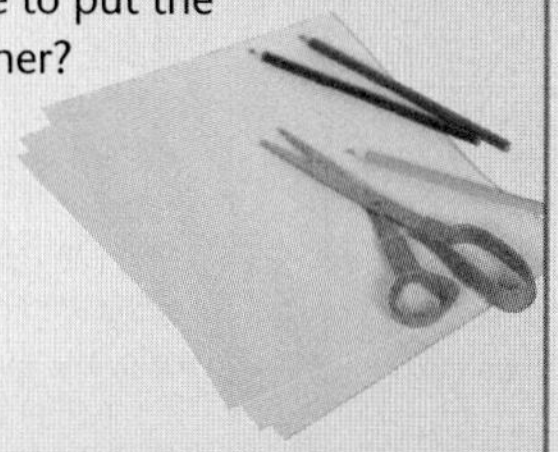

Chapters begin with an **Inquiry Lab** activity to get students thinking about the science content they are about to study.

Demonstration BASIC

Earth's Magnetic Field To help students visualize how iron-bearing minerals in molten rocks align with Earth's magnetic field, place a magnet in the center of an overhead projector so that the north pole faces the top of the projector. Place a sheet of clear acetate over the magnet. Sprinkle some iron filings on the acetate. The iron filings will align with the lines of force of the magnet. Lift the acetate, and move the magnet so that the north and south poles face the sides of the projector. Explain that when Earth's magnetic field reverses, the iron-bearing minerals that form from molten rock align according to the new magnetic field. **LS Visual**

Demonstrations for science concepts are located in the margin of the *Teacher's Edition.*

Making Models Lab

90 min

Sea-Floor Spreading

What You'll Do

› **Model** the formation of sea floor.

› **Identify** how magnetic patterns are caused by sea-floor spreading.

What You'll Need

marker
paper, unlined
ruler, metric
scissors or utility knife
shoebox

Safety

The places on Earth's surface where plates pull apart have many names. They are called divergent boundaries, mid-ocean ridges, and spreading centers. The term *spreading center* refers to the fact that sea-floor spreading happens at these locations. In this lab, you will model the formation of new sea floor at a divergent boundary. You will also model the formation of magnetic patterns on the sea floor.

Procedure

1. Cut two identical strips of unlined paper, each 7 cm wide and 30 cm long.
2. Cut a slit 8 cm long in the cent
3. Lay the strips of paper together end so that the ends line up. Pu slit in the shoe box, so that a fe of the slit.
4. Place the shoe box flat on a tab the ends of the paper strips are

Chapter Labs focus on experimental skills and test scientific principles through the use of scientific methods. Leveled datasheets for basic, general, and advanced learners are available for every chapter lab on the *Lab Generator CD-ROM* and in the *Chapter Resource Files.*

Quick Lab

10 min

Making Magnets

Procedure

1. Slide one end of a bar magnet down the side of a 5 inch iron nail 10 times. Always slide the magnet in the same direction.
2. Hold the nail over a small pile of steel paper clips. Record what happens.
3. Slide the bar magnet back and forth 10 times down the side of the nail. Repeat step 2.

Analysis

1. What was the effect of sliding the magnet down the nail in one direction? in different directions?
2. How does this lab demonstrate the idea of polarity?

Short, **Quick Labs** in every section highlight key science concepts with few demands on time and equipment.

ADDITIONAL LABS AND ACTIVITIES EXPAND YOUR OPTIONS

Lab Generator CD-ROM contains every lab in the *Student Edition,* as well as all additional labs included in the ***Chapter Resource Files,*** and additional environmental science labs. This time-saving resource allows you to:

- Search for labs by topic, difficulty level, lab duration, or **State Standard.**
- Edit labs to fit classroom needs.
- Develop new labs from our easy-to-use formatted template.
- Customize science kits and save time ordering materials using **Lab Materials QuickList Software.**

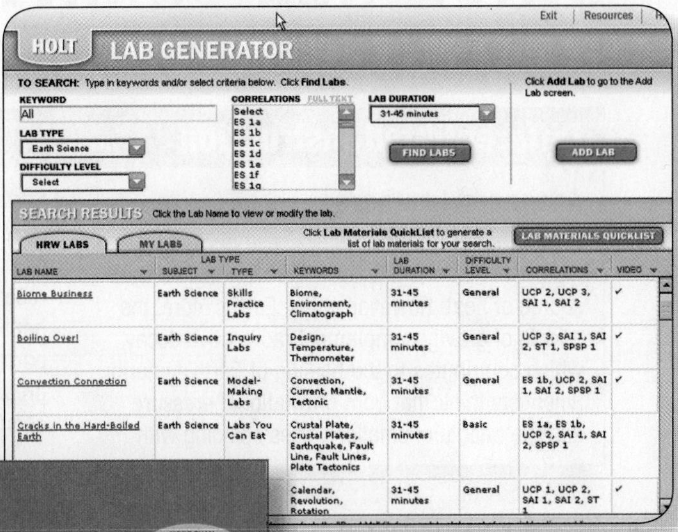

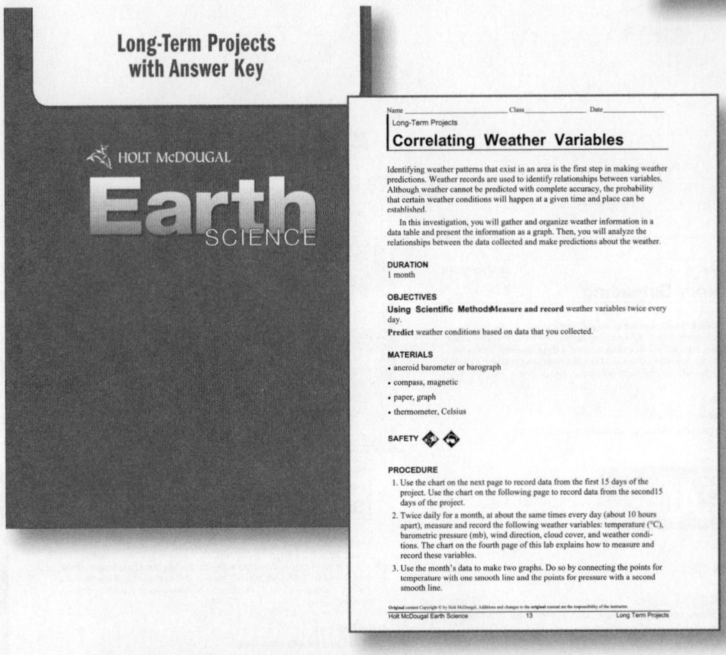

Name ____________ Class ________ Date ________

Long-Term Projects

Correlating Weather Variables

Identifying weather patterns that exist in an area is the first step in making weather predictions. Weather records are used to identify relationships between variables. Although weather cannot be predicted with complete accuracy, the probability that certain weather conditions will happen at a given time and place can be established.

In this investigation, you will gather and organize weather information in a data table and present the information as a graph. Then, you will analyze the relationships between the data collected and make predictions about the weather.

DURATION

1 month

OBJECTIVES

Using Scientific MethodsMeasure and record weather variables twice every day.

Predict weather conditions based on data that you collected.

MATERIALS

- aneroid barometer or barograph
- compass, magnetic
- paper, graph
- thermometer, Celsius

SAFETY

PROCEDURE

1. Use the chart on the next page to record data from the first 15 days of the project. Use the chart on the following page to record data from the second15 days of the project.
2. Twice daily for a month, at about the same times every day (about 10 hours apart), measure and record the following weather variables: temperature (°C), barometric pressure (mb), wind direction, cloud cover, and weather conditions. The chart on the fourth page of this lab explains how to measure and record these variables.
3. Use the month's data to make two graphs. Do so by connecting the points for temperature with one smooth line and the points for pressure with a second smooth line.

Original content Copyright © by Holt McDougal. Additions and changes to the original content are the responsibility of the instructor.

Holt McDougal Earth Science 13 Long Term Projects

Long-Term Projects workbook allows students to organize and conduct research on their own like actual scientists.

Virtual Investigations CD-ROM makes it easy for students to practice science skills without the expense. Students perform simulated lab experiments in a safe environment.

Differentiated Instruction

PLANNING FOR DIFFERENTIATED INSTRUCTION

Differentiated Instruction

Advanced Learners

Gravitational Heating Radioactive decay of material in Earth's interior is Earth's main internal source of heat. However, within Earths' core, the effects of gravity complement radioactive decay, which contributes to the heating of Earth's interior. Scientists think that both gravitational pressure and the effects of smaller bodies colliding with Earth accreted to form the primitive Earth, and they have used laboratory experiments and models to gain insights into these processes. Have students research theories of the causes of gravitational heating and how the scientific process has supported or discounted these theories. Students may present their research as a poster, a Web page, or a short essay. **LS Verbal/Logical**

The *Teacher's Edition* margin wrap provides strategies for differentiating instruction at point-of-use for important science content.

Differentiated datasheets are available on both the ***Lab Generator CD-ROM*** and the ***Teacher One Stop™,*** so all your students can perform the same lab, but work at their own level.

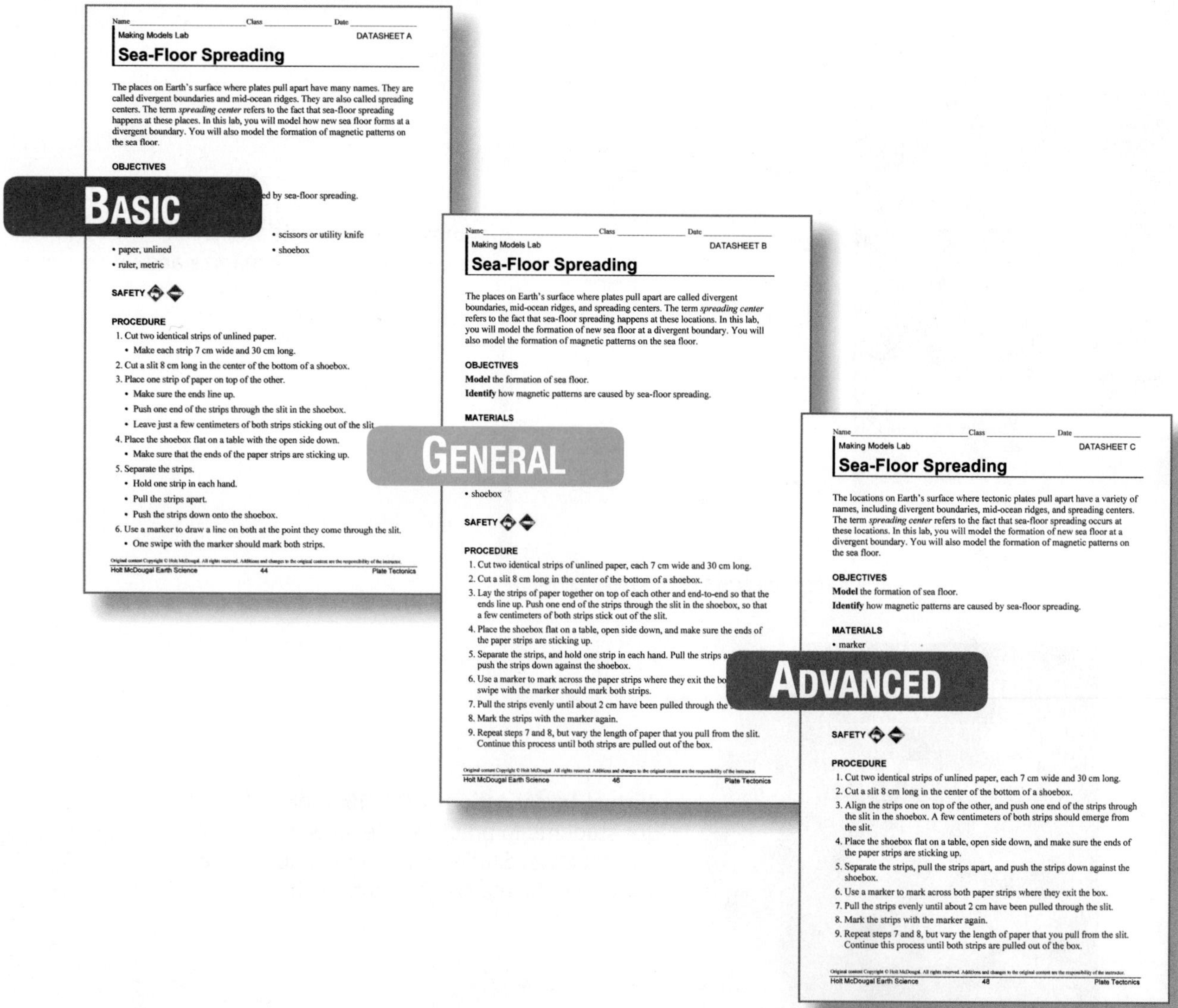

Name________ Class________ Date________

Making Models Lab DATASHEET A

Sea-Floor Spreading

The places on Earth's surface where plates pull apart have many names. They are called divergent boundaries and mid-ocean ridges. They are also called spreading centers. The term *spreading center* refers to the fact that sea-floor spreading happens at these places. In this lab, you will model how new sea floor forms at a divergent boundary. You will also model the formation of magnetic patterns on the sea floor.

OBJECTIVES

...ed by sea-floor spreading.

- scissors or utility knife
- shoebox
- paper, unlined
- ruler, metric

SAFETY

PROCEDURE

1. Cut two identical strips of unlined paper.
   - Make each strip 7 cm wide and 30 cm long.
2. Cut a slit 8 cm long in the center of the bottom of a shoebox.
3. Place one strip of paper on top of the other.
   - Make sure the ends line up.
   - Push one end of the strips through the slit in the shoebox.
   - Leave just a few centimeters of both strips sticking out of the slit.
4. Place the shoebox flat on a table with the open side down.
   - Make sure that the ends of the paper strips are sticking up.
5. Separate the strips.
   - Hold one strip in each hand.
   - Pull the strips apart.
   - Push the strips down onto the shoebox.
6. Use a marker to draw a line on both at the point they come through the slit.
   - One swipe with the marker should mark both strips.

Original content Copyright © Holt McDougal. All rights reserved. Additions and changes to the original content are the responsibility of the instructor.
Holt McDougal Earth Science 44 Plate Tectonics

Name________ Class________ Date________

Making Models Lab DATASHEET B

Sea-Floor Spreading

The places on Earth's surface where plates pull apart are called divergent boundaries, mid-ocean ridges, and spreading centers. The term *spreading center* refers to the fact that sea-floor spreading happens at these locations. In this lab, you will model the formation of new sea floor at a divergent boundary. You will also model the formation of magnetic patterns on the sea floor.

OBJECTIVES

Model the formation of sea floor.

Identify how magnetic patterns are caused by sea-floor spreading.

MATERIALS

- shoebox

SAFETY

PROCEDURE

1. Cut two identical strips of unlined paper, each 7 cm wide and 30 cm long.
2. Cut a slit 8 cm long in the center of the bottom of a shoebox.
3. Lay the strips of paper together on top of each other and end-to-end so that the ends line up. Push one end of the strips through the slit in the shoebox, so that a few centimeters of both strips stick out of the slit.
4. Place the shoebox flat on a table, open side down, and make sure the ends of the paper strips are sticking up.
5. Separate the strips, and hold one strip in each hand. Pull the strips a... push the strips down against the shoebox.
6. Use a marker to mark across the paper strips where they exit the bo... swipe with the marker should mark both strips.
7. Pull the strips evenly until about 2 cm have been pulled through the...
8. Mark the strips with the marker again.
9. Repeat steps 7 and 8, but vary the length of paper that you pull from the slit. Continue this process until both strips are pulled out of the box.

Original content Copyright © Holt McDougal. All rights reserved. Additions and changes to the original content are the responsibility of the instructor.
Holt McDougal Earth Science 46 Plate Tectonics

Name________ Class________ Date________

Making Models Lab DATASHEET C

Sea-Floor Spreading

The locations on Earth's surface where tectonic plates pull apart have a variety of names, including divergent boundaries, mid-ocean ridges, and spreading centers. The term *spreading center* refers to the fact that sea-floor spreading occurs at these locations. In this lab, you will model the formation of new sea floor at a divergent boundary. You will also model the formation of magnetic patterns on the sea floor.

OBJECTIVES

Model the formation of sea floor.

Identify how magnetic patterns are caused by sea-floor spreading.

MATERIALS

- marker

SAFETY

PROCEDURE

1. Cut two identical strips of unlined paper, each 7 cm wide and 30 cm long.
2. Cut a slit 8 cm long in the center of the bottom of a shoebox.
3. Align the strips one on top of the other, and push one end of the strips through the slit in the shoebox. A few centimeters of both strips should emerge from the slit.
4. Place the shoebox flat on a table, open side down, and make sure the ends of the paper strips are sticking up.
5. Separate the strips, pull the strips apart, and push the strips down against the shoebox.
6. Use a marker to mark across both paper strips where they exit the box.
7. Pull the strips evenly until about 2 cm have been pulled through the slit.
8. Mark the strips with the marker again.
9. Repeat steps 7 and 8, but vary the length of paper that you pull from the slit. Continue this process until both strips are pulled out of the box.

Original content Copyright © Holt McDougal. All rights reserved. Additions and changes to the original content are the responsibility of the instructor.
Holt McDougal Earth Science 48 Plate Tectonics

HELP FOR STRUGGLING AND RELUCTANT READERS

Guided Reading Audio Program provides a direct read of the textbook. Files are available in MP3 format.

ACCESSIBLE CONTENT FOR ENGLISH LANGUAGE LEARNERS

Support for **English-language learners** is unparalleled and includes:

- *Student Edition, Spanish*
- **Spanish Glossary** in both the English and Spanish *Student Editions*
- ***Review Guide, Spanish***
- ***Assessments, Spanish***
- ***Guided Reading Audio Program, Spanish***
- ***Strategies for English Language Learners***
- **ExamView Version 6 Assessment Suite** test questions available in Spanish on the ***Teacher One Stop Planner™***

DIFFERENTIATED INSTRUCTION

Meeting Individual Needs

Students have a wide range of abilities and learning exceptionalities. These pages show you how ***Holt McDougal Earth Science*** provides resources and strategies to help you tailor your instruction to engage every student in your classroom.

Learning exceptionality	Resources and strategies	
Learning Disabilities and Slow Learners Students who have dyslexia or dysgraphia, students reading below grade level, students having difficulty understanding abstract or complex concepts, and slow learners	• Inclusion Strategies labeled **Learning Disabled** • Activities labeled **Basic** • **Reteaching** activities • Activities labeled **Visual, Kinesthetic,** or **Auditory**	• Hands-on activities or projects • Oral presentations instead of written tests or assignments
Developmental Delays Students who are functioning far below grade level because of mental retardation, autism, or brain injury; goals are to learn or retain basic concepts	• Inclusion Strategies labeled **Developmentally Delayed** • Activities labeled **Basic**	• **Reteaching** activities • Project-based activities
Attention Deficit Disorders Students experiencing difficulty completing a task that has multiple steps, difficulty handling long assignments, or difficulty concentrating without sensory input from physical activity	• Inclusion Strategies labeled **Attention Deficit Disorder** • Activities labeled **Basic** • **Reteaching** activities • Activities labeled **Co-op Learning**	• Activities labeled **Visual, Kinesthetic,** or **Auditory** • Concepts broken into small chunks • Oral presentations instead of written tests or assignments
English as a Second Language Students learning English	• Activities labeled **English-Language Learners** • Activities labeled **Basic**	• **Reteaching** activities • Activities labeled **Visual**
Gifted and Talented Students who are performing above grade level and demonstrate aptitude in crosscurricular assignments	• Inclusion Strategies labeled **Gifted and Talented** • Activities labeled **Advanced**	• **Connection** activities • Activities that involve multiple tasks, a strong degree of independence, and student initiative

General Strategies The following strategies can help you modify instruction to help students who struggle with common classroom difficulties.

A student experiencing difficulty with...	May benefit if you...	
Beginning assignments	• Assign work in small amounts • Have the student use cooperative or paired learning • Provide varied and interesting activities	• Allow choice in assignments or projects • Reinforce participation • Seat the student closer to you
Following directions	• Gain the student's attention before giving directions • Break up the task into small steps • Give written directions rather than oral directions • Use short, simple phrases	• Stand near the student when you are giving directions • Have the student repeat directions to you • Prepare the student for changes in activity • Give visual cues by posting general routines • Reinforce improvement in or approximation of following directions
Keeping track of assignments	• Have the student use folders for assignments • Have the student use assignment notebooks	• Have the student keep a checklist of assignments and highlight assignments when they are turned in
Reading the textbook	• Provide outlines of the textbook content • Reduce the length of required reading • Allow extra time for reading • Have the students read aloud in small groups	• Have the student use peer or mentor readers • Have the student use books on tape or CD • Discuss the content of the textbook in class after reading
Staying on task	• Reduce distracting elements in the classroom • Provide a task-completion checklist • Seat the student near you	• Provide alternative ways to complete assignments, such as oral projects taped with a buddy
Behavioral or social skills	• Model the appropriate behaviors • Establish class rules, and reiterate them often • Reinforce positive behavior • Assign a mentor as a positive role model to the student • Contract with the student for expected behaviors • Reinforce the desired behaviors or any steps toward improvement	• Separate the student from any peer who stimulates the inappropriate behavior • Provide a "cooling off" period before talking with the student • Address academic/instructional problems that may contribute to disruptive behaviors • Include parents in the problem-solving process through conferences, home visits, and frequent communication
Attendance	• Recognize and reinforce attendance by giving incentives or verbal praise • Emphasize the importance of attendance by letting the student know that he or she was missed when he or she was absent	• Encourage the student's desire to be in school by planning activities that are likely to be enjoyable, giving the student a preferred responsibility to be performed in class, and involving the student in extracurricular activities • Schedule problem-solving meeting with parents, faculty, or both
Test-taking skills	• Prepare the student for testing by teaching ways to study in pairs, such as using flashcards, practice tests, and study guides, and by promoting adequate sleep, nourishment, and exercise • Decrease visual distraction by improving the visual design of the test through use of larger type, spacing, consistent layout, and shorter sentences	• During testing, allow the student to respond orally on tape or to respond using a computer; to use notes; to take breaks; to take the test in another location; to work without time constraints; or to take the test in several short sessions

Chapter Planner

Pacing Each **Chapter Planner** breaks down the chapter into instructional blocks. Each instructional block consists of sections and labs that you can cover in 45 or 90 minutes. The **Chapter Planner** also lists activities, demonstrations, and resources that are available to accompany each section.

Chapter Planner **10** **Plate Tectonics**

		Standards	Teach Key Ideas
Chapter Opener, pp. 256–257	45 min.	National Science Education Standards	
Section 1 Continental Drift, pp. 259–266 ❯ Wegener's Hypothesis ❯ Sea-Floor Spreading ❯ Paleomagnetism ❯ Wegener Redeemed	45 min.	SAI 2a, SAI 2e, HNS 3c, UC P1 ES 1b, ES 3c, UCP 3	■ ◆ **Bellringer,** p. 259 ■ **DI (Special Education Students):** Vocabulary Notebook, p. 260 ■ **Debate:** Wegener's Idea, p. 261 ■ **Discussion:** Making Predictions, p. 261 ■ **DI (Basic Learners):** Chain of Events, p. 263 ■ **Demonstration:** Earth's Magnetic Field, p. 264 ■ **DI (Special Education Students):** Magnetic Symmetry, p. 265 ◆ **Transparency:** 49 Sea-Floor Spreading ▲ **Visual Concepts:** Continental Drift (Pangaea) • Sea-Floor Spreading • Magnetic Reversals and Sea-Floor Spreading
Section 2 The Theory of Plate Tectonics, pp. 267–274 ❯ How Continents Move ❯ Tectonic Plates ❯ Types of Plate Boundaries ❯ Causes of Plate Motion	45 min.	UCP 1, UCP 2	■ ◆ **Bellringer,** p. 267 ■ **DI (English Learners):** Root Words, p. 268 ■ **Discussion:** Crustal Chemistry, p. 269 ■ **DI (Special Education Students):** Modeling Plate Boundaries, p. 270 ■ **DI (Struggling Readers):** Comprehension Strategy, p. 272 ◆ **Transparencies:** 50 Tectonic Plate Boundaries • 51 Types of Plate Boundaries • 52 Ridge Push and Slab Pull • 54 Locations of Earthquakes in South America ▲ **Visual Concepts:** Tectonic Plates and Plate Tectonics • Causes of Tectonic Plate Motion • Convergent Boundary • Subduction Zone • Divergent and Transform Boundaries
Section 3 The Changing Continents, pp. 275–280 ❯ Reshaping Earth's Crust ❯ Effects of Continental Change ❯ The Supercontinent Cycle	45 min.		■ ◆ **Bellringer,** p. 275 ■ **Demonstration:** Modeling Accretion, p. 276 ■ **DI (Advanced Learners):** Accreted Terranes, p. 276 ■ **Teaching Tip:** Connect to Prior Knowledge, p. 278 ■ **DI (Special Education Students):** Supercontinent Cycle, p. 278 ◆ **Transparency:** 53 The Supercontinent Cycle ▲ **Visual Concepts:** Continental Drift (Pangaea)
Chapter Wrap-Up, pp. 285–289	90 min.		**Chapter Summary,** p. 285

See also PowerNotes® Presentations

CHAPTER *Fast Track* *To shorten instruction because of time limitations, omit Section 3.*

256A Chapter 10 **Plate Tectonics**

Assessment Each chapter includes enough chapter assessment material to fill two 45-minute periods.

Compression In many cases, a chapter contains more material than you will have time to teach. The Compression Guide in each **Chapter Planner** suggests sections or labs you can omit if you are short on time. The sections or labs that can be omitted often contain advanced material. You may wish to also consider using the material suggested for omission as extension material for advanced students.

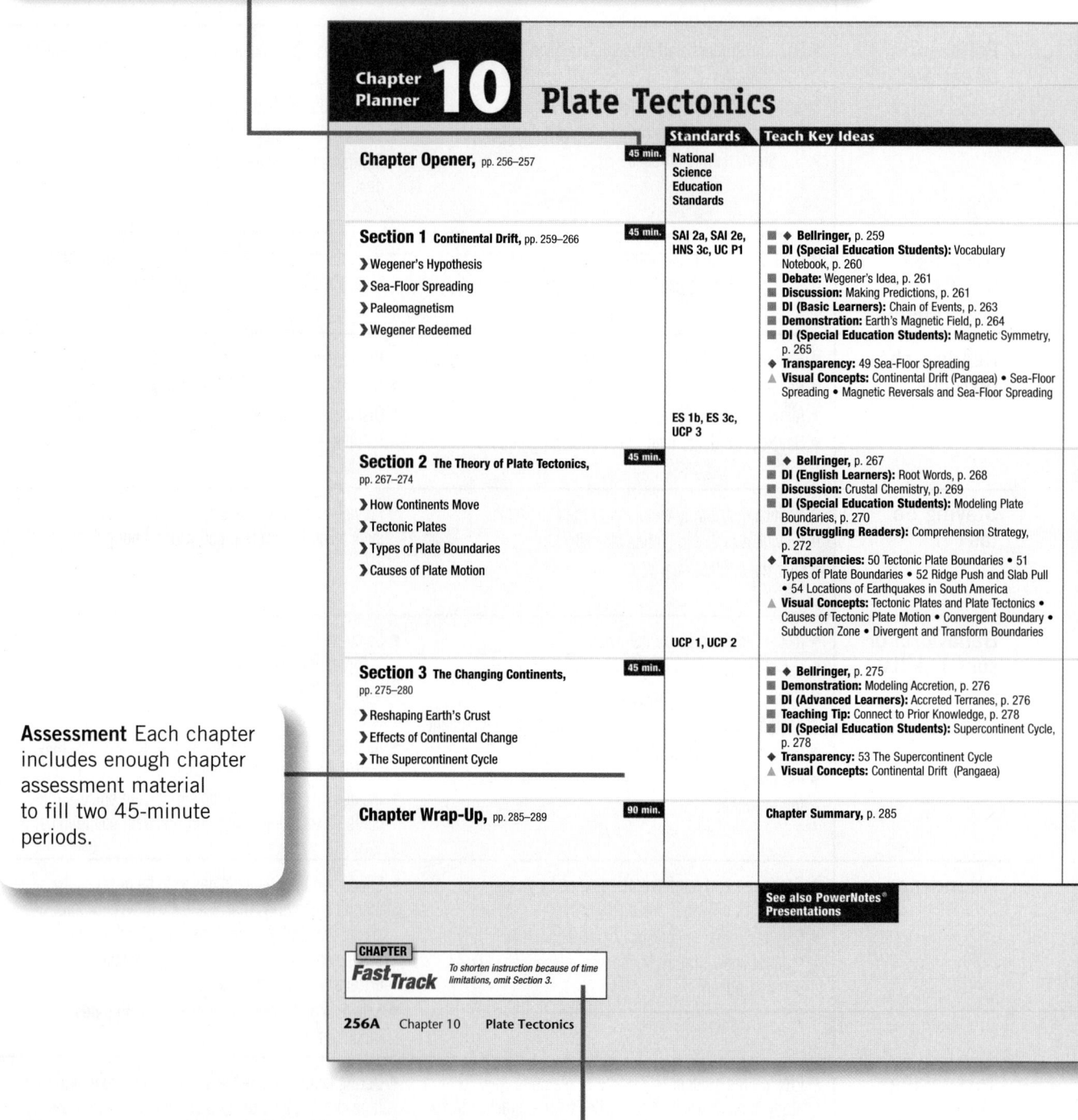

Key
Teacher's Edition ■ Teaching Transparencies ◆
Chapter Resource File ● Online Edition ▲

All resources listed below are also available on the Teacher One Stop™.

Why It Matters	Hands-On	Skills Development	Assessment
■ **Chapter Overview,** p. 256 ■ **Using the Figure:** Rifting in Iceland, p. 256	**Inquiry Lab:** Reconstructing Landmasses, p. 257	**Reading Toolbox,** p. 258	
■ **Section Overview,** p. 259 ■ **Using the Figure:** Continental Puzzles, p. 259 ■ **Using the Figure:** Mountain Ranges and Fossils, p. 260 ■ **History Connection:** Alfred Lothar Wegener, p. 261 ■ **Why It Matters:** Ridges and Rises, p. 262 ■ **Physics Connection:** Sonar, p. 262 ■ **Using the Figure:** Sea-Floor Formation, p. 263 **Our Own Space Shield,** p. 264	■ **Activity:** Sea-Floor Sediments, p. 262 **Quick Lab:** Making Magnets, p. 265 **Making Models Lab:** Sea-Floor Spreading, pp. 282–283	■ **Reading Skill Builder:** Paired Summarizing, p. 260 **Reading Toolbox:** Three-Panel Flip Chart, p. 261 ■ **Skill Builder:** Math, p. 263	**Reading Check,** p. 261 **Reading Check,** p. 263 **Reading Check,** p. 265 **Section Review,** p. 266 ■ **Reteaching,** p. 265 ■ **Quiz,** p. 265 ■ **DI (Alternative Assessment):** Persuasive Essay, p. 266 ● **Section Quiz**
■ **Section Overview,** p. 267 ■ **Physics Connection:** Earthquakes, p. 268 ■ **Chemistry Connection:** Plate Boundary Volcanoes, p. 270 ■ **Why It Matters:** Fracture Zones, p. 271 ■ **Teaching Tip:** Connect to Familiar Processes, p. 272 ■ **Using the Figure:** Mantle Convection, p. 272 ■ **Why It Matters:** Speeding Plates, p. 272	■ **Activity:** Jigsaw Puzzles, p. 267 **Quick Lab:** Tectonic Plate Boundaries, p. 273 ■ **Group Activity:** 3-D Model, p. 284 ● **Inquiry Lab:** Where Do Earthquakes Happen? ● **Making Models Lab:** Eggshell Tectonics	**Math Skills:** The Rate of Plate Movement, p. 268 ■ ● **Internet Activity:** Earthquakes, p. 268 ■ **Skill Builder:** Vocabulary, p. 269 **Reading Toolbox:** Prefixes, p. 270 ■ **Skill Builder:** Writing, p. 271 **Maps in Action:** Locations of Earthquakes in South America, p. 284 ● **Internet Activity:** The Heimaey Eruption	**Reading Check,** p. 268 **Reading Check,** p. 270 **Reading Check,** p. 273 **Section Review,** p. 274 ■ **Reteaching,** p. 273 ■ **Quiz,** p. 273 ● **Section Quiz**
■ **Section Overview,** p. 275 ■ **Using the Figure:** Accretion, p. 276 ■ **Biology Connection:** Extinction, p. 277 ■ **Environmental Connection:** Climate Changes, p. 277	■ **Activity:** Modeling Rifting, p. 275 ■ **Group Activity:** Responses to Climate Change, p. 277	■ **Skill Builder: Vocabulary,** p. 276 ■ **Reading Skill Builder:** Reading Organizer, p. 277 ■ ● **Internet Activity:** The Paleomap Project, p. 278 **Reading Toolbox:** Recognizing Facts, Hypotheses, and Theories, p. 280	**Reading Check,** p. 276 **Reading Check,** p. 279 **Section Review,** p. 280 ■ **Reteaching,** p. 279 ■ **Quiz,** p. 279 ■ **DI (Alternative Assessment):** Process Models, p. 280 ● **Section Quiz**
Copper from Plate Margins, p. 281		▲ **Super Summary** **Standardized Test Prep,** pp. 288–289	**Chapter Review,** p. 286–287 ■ **DI (Alternative Assessment):** Comparing Scientific Ideas, p. 285 ● **Chapter Tests**
	See also Lab Generator		**See also Holt Online Assessment Resources**

Assessment

CHAPTER ASSESSMENT WITHIN EACH LESSON HELPS MONITOR STUDENTS' PROGRESS

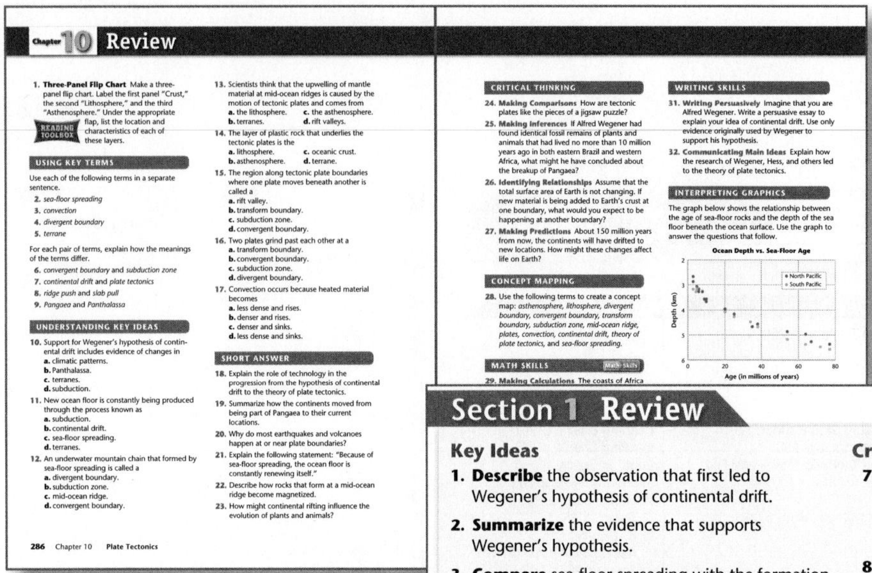

Section Reviews and **Chapter Reviews** provide a variety of question types that progress from simple concepts and alternative assessments to in-depth critical-thinking questions. The *Teacher's Edition* contains answers to all questions.

Section 1 Review

Key Ideas

1. **Describe** the observation that first led to Wegener's hypothesis of continental drift.
2. **Summarize** the evidence that supports Wegener's hypothesis.
3. **Compare** sea-floor spreading with the formation of mid-ocean ridges.
4. **Explain** how scientists know that Earth's magnetic poles have reversed many times during Earth's history.
5. **Identify** how magnetic symmetry can be used as evidence of sea-floor spreading.
6. **Explain** how scientists date sea-floor rocks.

Critical Thinking

7. **Making Inferences** How does evidence that rocks farther from a ridge are older than rocks closer to the ridge support the idea of spreading?
8. **Analyzing Ideas** Explain how sea-floor spreading provides an explanation for how continents move over Earth's surface.

Concept Mapping

9. Use the following terms to create a concept map: *continental drift, paleomagnetism, fossils, climate, sea-floor spreading, geologic evidence, supercontinent,* and *mid-ocean ridge.*

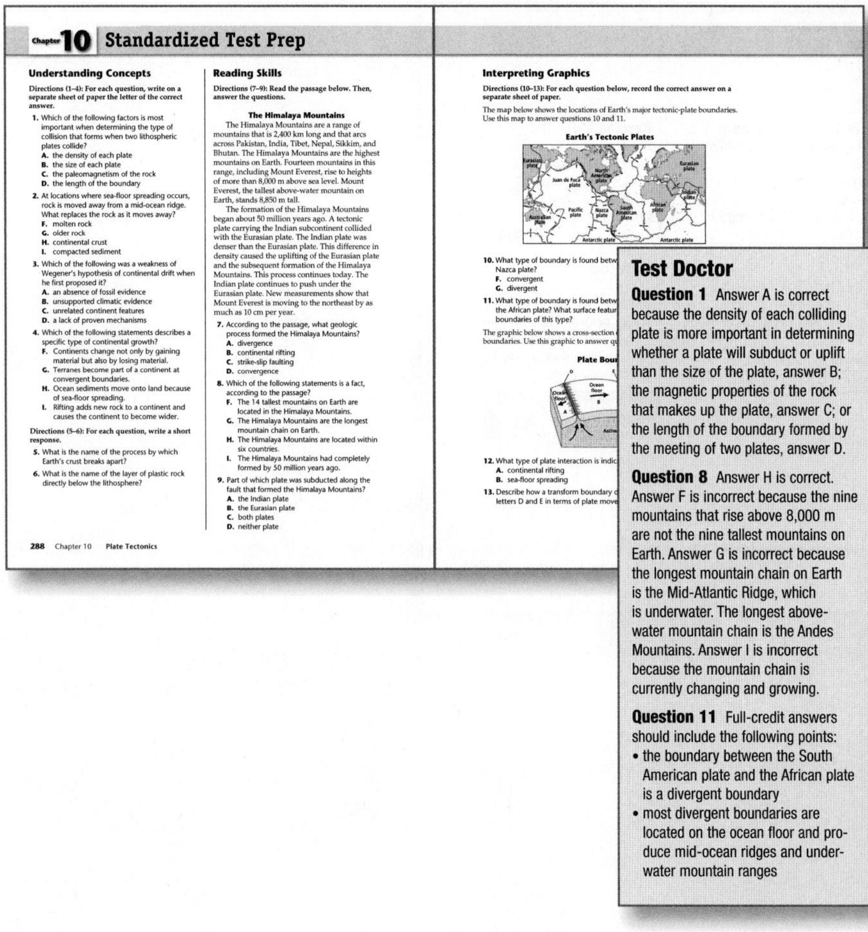

Integrated **Standardized Test Prep,** at the end of each chapter, focuses on mastery of key science concepts.

Test Doctor

Question 1 Answer A is correct because the density of each colliding plate is more important in determining whether a plate will subduct or uplift than the size of the plate, answer B; the magnetic properties of the rock that makes up the plate, answer C; or the length of the boundary formed by the meeting of two plates, answer D.

Question 8 Answer H is correct. Answer F is incorrect because the nine mountains that rise above 8,000 m are not the nine tallest mountains on Earth. Answer G is incorrect because the longest mountain chain on Earth is the Mid-Atlantic Ridge, which is underwater. The longest above-water mountain chain is the Andes Mountains. Answer I is incorrect because the mountain chain is currently changing and growing.

Question 11 Full-credit answers should include the following points:

- the boundary between the South American plate and the African plate is a divergent boundary
- most divergent boundaries are located on the ocean floor and produce mid-ocean ridges and underwater mountain ranges

The **Test Doctor**, located in the *Teacher's Edition* wrap, is a diagnostic tool that helps identify why a student might have answered a question incorrectly.

ASSESSMENT WITH INTERVENTION PUTS STUDENTS ON THE RIGHT PATH

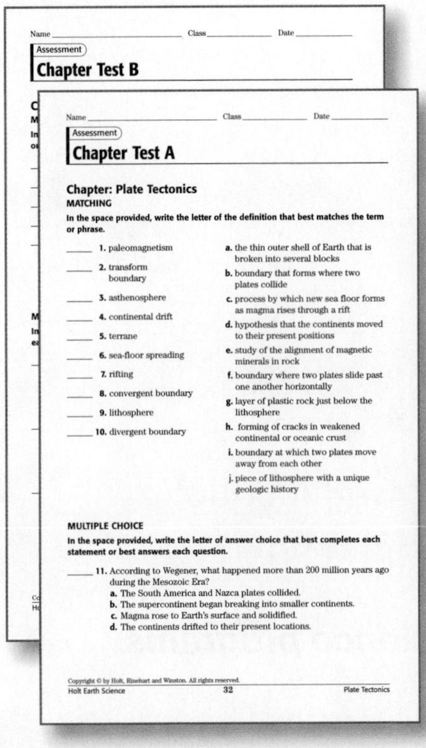
Name ____ Class ____ Date ____

Assessment

Chapter Test A

Chapter: Plate Tectonics

MATCHING

In the space provided, write the letter of the definition that best matches the term or phrase.

____ 1. paleomagnetism	a. the thin outer shell of Earth that is broken into several blocks
____ 2. transform boundary	b. boundary that forms where two plates collide
____ 3. asthenosphere	c. process by which new sea floor forms as magma rises through a rift
____ 4. continental drift	d. hypothesis that the continents moved to their present positions
____ 5. terrane	e. study of the alignment of magnetic minerals in rock
____ 6. sea-floor spreading	f. boundary where two plates slide past one another horizontally
____ 7. rifting	g. layer of plastic rock just below the lithosphere
____ 8. convergent boundary	h. forming of cracks in weakened continental or oceanic crust
____ 9. lithosphere	i. boundary at which two plates move away from each other
____ 10. divergent boundary	j. piece of lithosphere with a unique geologic history

MULTIPLE CHOICE

In the space provided, write the letter of answer choice that best completes each statement or best answers each question.

____ 11. According to Wegener, what happened more than 200 million years ago during the Mesozoic Era?
a. The South America and Nazca plates collided.
b. The supercontinent began breaking into smaller continents.
c. Magma rose to Earth's surface and solidified.
d. The continents drifted to their present locations.

Copyright © by Holt, Rinehart and Winston. All rights reserved.
Holt Earth Science 32 Plate Tectonics

Chapter Resource Files provide teachers with worksheets and additional **Section Quizzes** and **leveled Chapter Tests.** These Resources are also on the ***Teacher One Stop™.***

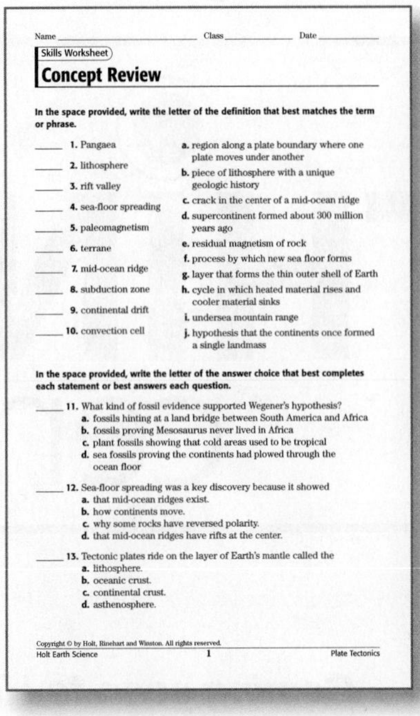
Name ____ Class ____ Date ____

Skills Worksheet

Concept Review

In the space provided, write the letter of the definition that best matches the term or phrase.

____ 1. Pangaea	a. region along a plate boundary where one plate moves under another
____ 2. lithosphere	b. piece of lithosphere with a unique geologic history
____ 3. rift valley	c. crack in the center of a mid-ocean ridge
____ 4. sea-floor spreading	d. supercontinent formed about 300 million years ago
____ 5. paleomagnetism	e. residual magnetism of rock
____ 6. terrane	f. process by which new sea floor forms
____ 7. mid-ocean ridge	g. layer that forms the thin outer shell of Earth
____ 8. subduction zone	h. cycle in which heated material rises and cooler material sinks
____ 9. continental drift	i. undersea mountain range
____ 10. convection cell	j. hypothesis that the continents once formed a single landmass

In the space provided, write the letter of the answer choice that best completes each statement or best answers each question.

____ 11. What kind of fossil evidence supported Wegener's hypothesis?
a. fossils hinting at a land bridge between South America and Africa
b. fossils proving Mesosaurus never lived in Africa
c. plant fossils showing that cold areas used to be tropical
d. sea fossils proving the continents had plowed through the ocean floor

____ 12. Sea-floor spreading was a key discovery because it showed
a. that mid-ocean ridges exist.
b. how continents move.
c. why some rocks have reversed polarity.
d. that mid-ocean ridges have rifts at the center.

____ 13. Tectonic plates ride on the layer of Earth's mantle called the
a. lithosphere.
b. oceanic crust.
c. continental crust.
d. asthenosphere.

Copyright © by Holt, Rinehart and Winston. All rights reserved.
Holt Earth Science 1 Plate Tectonics

Review Guide provides **Concept Review** worksheets that help students focus on key concepts and prepare them for assessment.

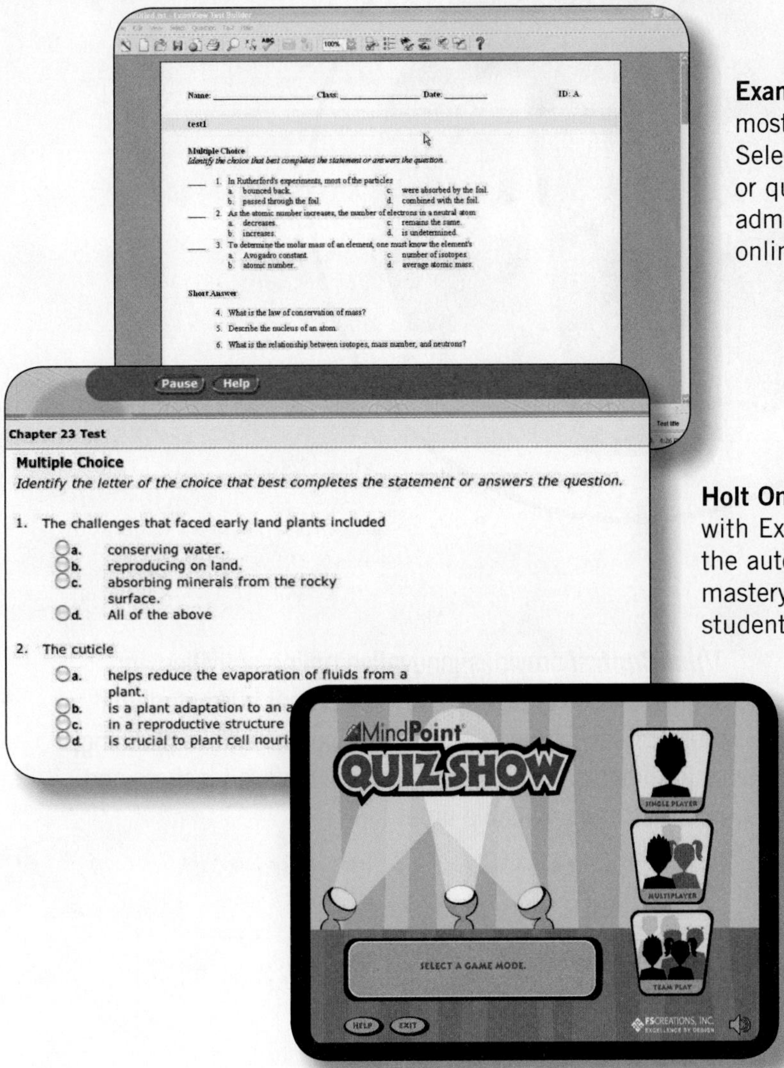

ExamView® Version 6 Assessment Suite is the most powerful assessment generator to date. Select assessment items by difficulty, standard or question type, edit them as you see fit, and administer them to students in either print or online format for automatic grading.

Holt Online Assessment is seamlessly integrated with ExamView®. Customize assignments, use the automatic grading system to quickly analyze mastery by topic or standard, and then offer students feedback or additional practice online.

MindPoint® ***Quiz Show*** on the ***Teacher One Stop™*** provides questions from **ExamView® Version 6 Assessment Suite** in an engaging, interactive quiz show format.

Introducing

THINK central

One location,
endless educational resources.

Coming soon to Holt McDougal Science programs.

ThinkCentral provides innovative **online** activities and simulations, extension opportunities that build students' problem-solving and critical-thinking, innovative planning, instructional, and assessment options save teachers and administrators valuable time!

INTERACTIVE MEDIA

Harness the power of the Web to help students learn and study in a whole new way. Engage all learners with cutting-edge video, audio, and animations.

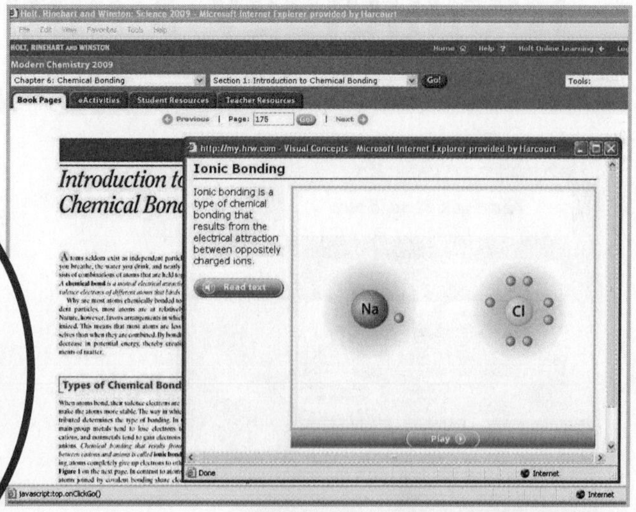

FULL PROGRAM RESOURCES

Find all of your program resources—for students and teachers—in an easy to navigate, online environment.

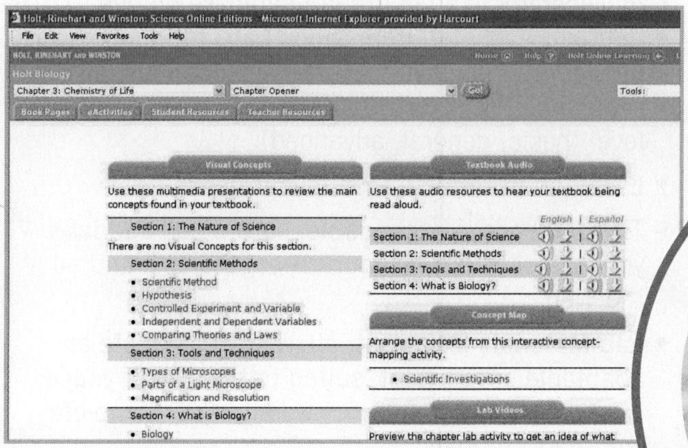

POWERFUL ASSESSMENTS

Quickly access assessment and standards-based reports to ensure students master content and standards.

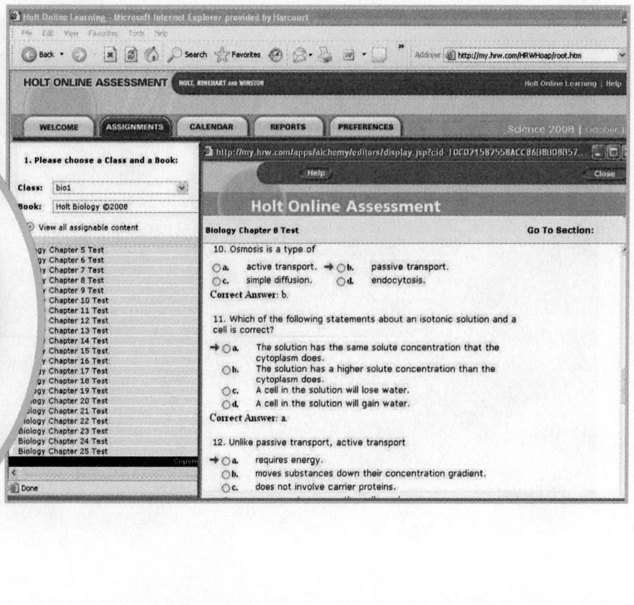

Technology Solutions

THREE DIGITAL COMPONENTS OF *HOLT MCDOUGAL EARTH SCIENCE* MAKE YOUR LIFE EASIER.

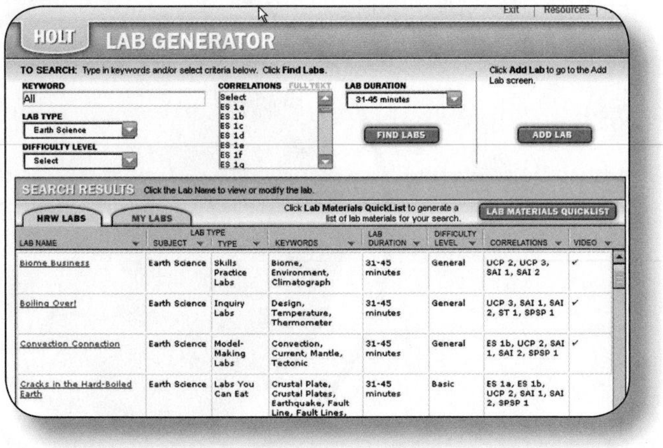

Teacher One Stop™ is an indispensable collection of resources, all in one place.

- Searchable, printable, and editable worksheets, lab sheets, assessments, and more.
- Digital transparencies of images from the textbook.
- Pre-built and editable **PowerNotes® Resources** complete with embedded animations and figures.
- Installers for teacher productivity software, such as **ExamView® Version 6 Assessment Suite, Calendar Planner,** and **Puzzle Pro®.**
- A link to download state-specific resources.

Lab Generator is an entire lab database on one CD.

- Contains every lab from **Quick Labs** to **Inquiry Labs,** plus additional environmental science labs, all searchable by criteria you choose, including ability level (basic, general, advanced).
- Every lab is editable to suit your needs.
- The database is expandable, so you can add labs you've received from your colleagues or found on the Web.
- **Lab Materials QuickList,** allows you to create an adaptable order sheet, suited to the size of your classes and the number of workgroups, complete with part numbers.

Student One Stop™ contains all student resources including:

- *Student Edition*
- Student worksheets for all consumable workbooks
- Tools to help review and practice
- Full text of *Student Edition* with audio recordings at point of use

Pacing Guide

Today's Earth science classroom often requires a more flexible curriculum. ***Holt McDougal Earth Science*** can help you meet a variety of needs and challenges you and your students face in the classroom. The **Pacing Guide** below shows a number of ways to adapt the program to your teaching schedule.

This **Pacing Guide** can be further adapted, allowing you to mix and match or compress the material so you can spend more time on select topics, or to allow for special projects and activities.

- **Basic** gives more time for the foundations of Earth science, especially mathematical problem-solving, with less emphasis on some advanced topics from later in the course.
- **General** provides the recommended course of study as indicated in the ***Teacher's Edition*** found in the individual chapter **Planning Guides** preceding each chapter.
- **Advanced** moves quickly through foundations of Earth science for students who may be comfortable with the basics, to provide additional time for advanced topics.
- **Heavy Lab/Activity** indicates ways to streamline "lecture" time to provide hands-on experience for more than a third of the blocks in the school year. (Note: even this approach does not cover all of the labs and activities that are available with ***Holt McDougal Earth Science*** and its ancillaries.)

Numbers indicate class periods recommended for the material within each chapter.	Basic	General	Advanced	Heavy Lab/ Activity
Chapter 1: Introduction to Earth Science	**6**	**5**	**4**	**0**
Section 1 What Is Earth Science?	1	1	1	0
Section 2 Science as a Process	2	2	1	0
Lab Experiments	1	0	0	0
Chapter Review and Assessment	2	2	2	0
Chapter 2: Earth as a System	**6**	**7**	**7**	**5**
Section 1 Earth: A Unique Planet	1	1	1	1
Section 2 Energy in the Earth System	2	2	2	2
Section 3 Ecology	0	1	1	0
Lab Experiments	1	1	1	0
Chapter Review and Assessment	2	2	2	2
Chapter 3: Models of the Earth	**8**	**6**	**6**	**6**
Section 1 Finding Locations on Earth	1	1	1	1
Section 2 Mapping Earth's Surface	2	1	1	0
Section 3 Types of Maps	2	1	1	1
Lab Experiments	1	1	1	2
Chapter Review and Assessment	2	2	2	2
Chapter 4: Earth Chemistry	**0**	**4**	**5**	**0**
Section 1 Matter	0	1	1	0
Section 2 Combinations of Atoms	0	1	1	0
Lab Experiments	0	0	1	0
Chapter Review and Assessment	0	2	2	0
Chapter 5: Minerals of Earth's Crust	**7**	**5**	**5**	**6**
Section 1 What Is a Mineral?	2	1	1	1
Section 2 Identifying Minerals	2	1	1	1
Lab Experiments	1	1	1	2
Chapter Review and Assessment	2	2	2	2
Chapter 6: Rocks	**9**	**7**	**7**	**8**
Section 1 Rocks and the Rock Cycle	1	1	1	1
Section 2 Igneous Rock	2	1	1	1
Section 3 Sedimentary Rock	2	1	1	1
Section 4 Metamorphic Rock	1	1	1	1
Lab Experiments	1	1	1	2
Chapter Review and Assessment	2	2	2	2

PACING GUIDE

Numbers indicate class periods recommended for the material within each chapter.

	Basic	General	Advanced	Heavy Lab/ Activity
Chapter 7: Resources and Energy	**8**	**7**	**7**	**7**
Section 1 Mineral Resources	1	1	1	0
Section 2 Nonrenewable Energy	2	1	1	1
Section 3 Renewable Energy	1	1	1	1
Section 4 Resources and Conservation	1	1	1	1
Lab Experiments	1	1	1	2
Chapter Review and Assessment	2	2	2	2
Chapter 8: The Rock Record	**7**	**4**	**6**	**4**
Section 1 Determining Relative Age	2	1	1	1
Section 2 Determining Absolute Age	2	1	1	1
Section 3 The Fossil Record	0	0	1	0
Lab Experiments	1	0	1	0
Chapter Review and Assessment	2	2	2	2
Chapter 9: A View of Earth's Past	**4**	**6**	**6**	**5**
Section 1 Geologic Time	1	1	1	1
Section 2 Precambrian Time and the Paleozoic Era	0	1	1	0
Section 3 The Mesozoic and Cenozoic Eras	0	1	1	0
Lab Experiments	1	1	1	2
Chapter Review and Assessment	2	2	2	2
Chapter 10: Plate Tectonics	**7**	**8**	**8**	**8**
Section 1 Continental Drift	2	2	2	2
Section 2 The Theory of Plate Tectonics	2	2	2	2
Section 3 The Changing Continents	0	1	1	0
Lab Experiments	1	1	1	2
Chapter Review and Assessment	2	2	2	2
Chapter 11: Deformation of the Crust	**0**	**5**	**6**	**5**
Section 1 How Rock Deforms	0	2	2	0
Section 2 How Mountains Form	0	1	1	1
Lab Experiments	0	0	1	2
Chapter Review and Assessment	0	2	2	2
Chapter 12: Earthquakes	**7**	**5**	**4**	**7**
Section 1 How and Where Earthquakes Happen	2	1	1	1
Section 2 Studying Earthquakes	1	1	1	1
Section 3 Earthquakes and Society	1	1	0	1
Lab Experiments	1	0	0	2
Chapter Review and Assessment	2	2	2	2
Chapter 13: Volcanoes	**7**	**4**	**4**	**6**
Section 1 Volcanoes and Plate Tectonics	2	1	1	1
Section 2 Volcanic Eruptions	2	1	1	1
Lab Experiments	1	0	0	2
Chapter Review and Assessment	2	2	2	2
Chapter 14: Weathering and Erosion	**9**	**7**	**7**	**9**
Section 1 Weathering Processes	2	1	1	1
Section 2 Rates of Weathering	1	1	1	1
Section 3 Soil	1	1	1	1
Section 4 Erosion	2	2	2	2
Lab Experiments	1	0	0	2
Chapter Review and Assessment	2	2	2	2

Numbers indicate class periods recommended for the material within each chapter.	Basic	General	Advanced	Heavy Lab/ Activity
Chapter 15: River Systems	**6**	**6**	**5**	**6**
Section 1 The Water Cycle	1	1	0	0
Section 2 Stream Erosion	1	1	1	1
Section 3 Stream Deposition	1	1	1	1
Lab Experiments	1	1	1	2
Chapter Review and Assessment	2	2	2	2
Chapter 16: Groundwater	**6**	**6**	**6**	**6**
Section 1 Water Beneath the Surface	2	2	2	2
Section 2 Groundwater and Chemical Weathering	1	1	1	0
Lab Experiments	1	1	1	2
Chapter Review and Assessment	2	2	2	2
Chapter 17: Glaciers	**7**	**6**	**6**	**8**
Section 1 Glaciers: Moving Ice	1	1	1	1
Section 2 Glacial Erosion and Deposition	2	2	2	2
Section 3 Ice Ages	1	1	1	1
Lab Experiments	1	0	0	2
Chapter Review and Assessment	2	2	2	2
Chapter 18: Erosion by Wind and Waves	**5**	**6**	**6**	**6**
Section 1 Wind Erosion	1	1	1	1
Section 2 Wave Erosion	1	1	1	1
Section 3 Coastal Erosion and Deposition	0	1	1	0
Lab Experiments	1	1	1	2
Chapter Review and Assessment	2	2	2	2
Chapter 19: The Atmosphere	**8**	**6**	**6**	**8**
Section 1 Characteristics of the Atmosphere	2	2	2	2
Section 2 Solar Energy and the Atmosphere	2	1	1	1
Section 3 Atmospheric Circulation	1	1	1	1
Lab Experiments	1	0	0	2
Chapter Review and Assessment	2	2	2	2
Chapter 20: Water in the Atmosphere	**0**	**5**	**5**	**7**
Section 1 Atmospheric Moisture	0	1	1	1
Section 2 Clouds and Fog	0	1	1	1
Section 3 Precipitation	0	1	1	1
Lab Experiments	0	0	0	2
Chapter Review and Assessment	0	2	2	2
Chapter 21: Weather	**7**	**7**	**7**	**6**
Section 1 Air Masses	1	1	1	0
Section 2 Fronts	1	1	1	1
Section 3 Weather Instruments	1	1	1	0
Section 4 Forecasting the Weather	1	1	1	1
Lab Experiments	1	1	1	2
Chapter Review and Assessment	2	2	2	2
Chapter 22: Climate	**7**	**5**	**5**	**7**
Section 1 Factors That Affect Climate	2	1	1	1
Section 2 Climate Zones	1	1	1	1
Section 3 Climate Change	1	1	1	1
Lab Experiments	1	0	0	2
Chapter Review and Assessment	2	2	2	2

Numbers indicate class periods recommended for the material within each chapter.	Basic	General	Advanced	Heavy Lab/ Activity
Chapter 23: The Ocean Basins	**6**	**6**	**5**	**4**
Section 1 The Water Planet	1	1	0	1
Section 2 Features of the Ocean Floor	1	1	1	1
Section 3 Ocean-Floor Sediments	1	1	1	0
Lab Experiments	1	1	1	0
Chapter Review and Assessment	2	2	2	2
Chapter 24: Ocean Water	**5**	**7**	**7**	**7**
Section 1 Properties of Ocean Water	1	2	2	2
Section 2 Life in the Oceans	0	1	1	0
Section 3 Ocean Resources	1	1	1	1
Lab Experiments	1	1	1	2
Chapter Review and Assessment	2	2	2	2
Chapter 25: Movements of the Ocean	**5**	**4**	**4**	**4**
Section 1 Ocean Currents	1	1	1	1
Section 2 Ocean Waves	0	0	0	0
Section 3 Tides	1	1	1	1
Lab Experiments	1	0	0	0
Chapter Review and Assessment	2	2	2	2
Chapter 26: Studying Space	**7**	**6**	**6**	**8**
Section 1 Viewing the Universe	2	2	2	2
Section 2 Movements of the Earth	2	2	2	2
Lab Experiments	1	0	0	2
Chapter Review and Assessment	2	2	2	2
Chapter 27: Planets of the Solar System	**7**	**7**	**7**	**9**
Section 1 Formation of the Solar System	1	1	1	1
Section 2 Models of the Solar System	0	1	1	1
Section 3 The Inner Planets	1	1	1	1
Section 4 The Outer Planets	2	2	2	2
Lab Experiments	1	0	0	2
Chapter Review and Assessment	2	2	2	2
Chapter 28: Minor Bodies of the Solar System	**6**	**8**	**8**	**4**
Section 1 Earth's Moon	1	1	1	1
Section 2 Movements of the Moon	0	2	2	0
Section 3 Satellites of Other Planets	1	1	1	0
Section 4 Asteroids, Comets, and Meteoroids	1	1	1	1
Lab Experiments	1	1	1	0
Chapter Review and Assessment	2	2	2	2
Chapter 29: The Sun	**5**	**5**	**5**	**5**
Section 1 Structure of the Sun	1	1	1	1
Section 2 Solar Activity	1	1	1	0
Lab Experiments	1	1	1	2
Chapter Review and Assessment	2	2	2	2
Chapter 30: Stars, Galaxies, and the Universe	**6**	**8**	**8**	**7**
Section 1 Characteristics of Stars	1	1	1	0
Section 2 Stellar Evolution	0	2	2	2
Section 3 Star Groups	1	1	1	1
Section 4 The Big Bang Theory	1	1	1	1
Lab Experiments	1	1	1	1
Chapter Review and Assessment	2	2	2	2
Total	**178**	**178**	**178**	**178**

Correlation of *Holt McDougal Virginia Earth Science* to the Virginia Science Standards of Learning and Curriculum Framework (2010)

Standards of Learning	*Holt McDougal Virginia Earth Science* Citations
ES.1 The student will plan and conduct investigations in which	
ES.1.a volume, area, mass, elapsed time, direction, temperature, pressure, distance, density, and changes in elevation/depth are calculated utilizing the most appropriate tools;	SE 37, 46-47, 74-75, 100-101, 121, 178, 334-335, 355, 380, 420-421, 444-445, 472-473, 517, 532-533, 560-561, 569, 584, 590, 608, 622-623, 639, 650-651, 659, 678-679, 834-835, 944-945, 950-953
ES.1.b technologies, including computers, probeware, and geospatial technologies, are used to collect, analyze, and report data and to demonstrate concepts and simulate experimental conditions;	SE 61, 72, 87, 334-335, 396, 397, 594-595, 603, 647, 706-707, 812-813, 940-943, 944-945, 946-949, 950-953, 954-957
ES.1.c scales, diagrams, charts, graphs, tables, imagery, models, and profiles are constructed and interpreted;	SE 46-47, 68, 74-75, 114, 124-125, 156-157, 165, 199, 218-219, 230, 273, 282-283, 294, 296, 308-309, 334-335, 358-359, 444-445, 472-473, 494, 532-533, 541, 552, 608, 622-623, 650-651, 706-707, 719, 747, 774-775, 812-813, 825, 868-869, 936-939, 940-943, 944-945, 946-949, 950-953, 954-957
ES.1.d maps and globes are read and interpreted, including location by latitude and longitude;	SE 57-60, 61-66, 67-72, 74-75, 76, 78-79, 81, 257, 594-595
ES.1.e variables are manipulated with repeated trials; and	SE 46-47, 650-651, 678-679, 843
ES.1.f current applications are used to reinforce Earth science concepts.	SE 17, 59, 123, 185, 209, 307, 592, 830, 867
Essential Knowledge and Skills (EKS) In order to meet this standard, it is expected that students will	
ES.1.EKS-1 measure mass and volume of regular and irregular shaped objects and materials using common laboratory tools, including metric scales and graduated cylinders.	SE 46-47, 100-101, 121
ES.1.EKS-2 apply the concept of mass per unit volume and calculate density without being given a formula.	SE 129 (#33), 678-679
ES.1.EKS-3 record data in systematic, properly-labeled, multicell tables, and using data, construct and interpret continuous line graphs, frequency distributions, bar graphs, and other explicating graphics that present a range of parameters, relationships, and pathways.	SE 46-47, 124-125, 156-157, 230, 296, 334-335, 444-445, 494, 532-533, 608, 622-623, 650-651, 678-679, 812-813, 936-939, 940-943, 944-945, 946-949, 950-953
ES.1.EKS-4 interpret data from a graph or table that shows changes in temperature or pressure with depth or altitude.	SE 518, 666 TE 666
ES.1.EKS-5 interpret landforms, water features, map scale, horizontal distance between points, elevation and elevation changes, latitude and longitude, human-made structures and other pertinent features on 7.5 minute quadrangles on topographic maps.	SE 920-921 TE 68

FULL STANDARD CORRELATION

Standards of Learning	*Holt McDougal Virginia Earth Science* Citations
ES.1.EKS-6 construct profiles from topographic contours.	SE 69 TE 67
ES.1.ESK-7 use latitude and longitude down to minutes, with correct north-south and east-west designations, to locate points on a map.	SE 922-923
ES.2 The student will demonstrate an understanding of the nature of science and scientific reasoning and logic. Key concepts include	
ES.2.a science explains and predicts the interactions and dynamics of complex Earth systems;	SE 5-8, 9-16, 18-19, 29-32, 33-40, 41-44, 46-47, 135-138, 203, 267-274, 275-290, 282-283, 293-300, 301-306, 308-309, 319-324, 345-350, 351-356, 358-359, 373-378, 387-388, 393-394, 407-409, 411-414, 415-416, 418, 434, 439-442, 459-466, 483-488, 489-492, 493-495, 521-526, 527-530, 532-533, 543, 549-551, 571-574, 575-579, 582, 689-694, 695-700
ES.2.b evidence is required to evaluate hypotheses and explanations;	SE 10-11, 16, 258
ES.2.c observation and logic are essential for reaching a conclusion; and	SE 3, 10, 11, 13, 16
ES.2.d evidence is evaluated for scientific theories.	SE 14-15, 16, 233, 259-266, 267
Essential Knowledge and Skills (EKS) In order to meet this standard, it is expected that students will	
ES.2.EKS-1 analyze how natural processes explain multiple aspects of Earth systems and their interactions (e.g., storms, earthquakes, volcanic eruptions, floods, climate, mountain chains and landforms, geological formations and stratigraphy, fossils) can be used to make predictions of future interactions and allow scientific explanations for what has happened in the past.	SE 27, 29-32, 33-40, 43-44, 46-47, 135-138, 203, 267-274, 275-290, 282-283, 293-300, 301-306, 308-309, 319-324, 345-350, 351-356, 358-359, 373-378, 387-388, 393-394, 407-409, 411-414, 415-416, 418, 434, 439-442, 459-466, 483-488, 489-492, 493-495, 521-526, 527-530, 532-533, 543, 549-551, 571-574, 575-579, 582, 689-694, 695-700
ES.2.EKS-2 make predictions, using scientific data and data analysis.	SE 18-19, 75, 166, 219, 498-499, 532-533, 650-651
ES.2.EKS-3 use data to support or reject a hypothesis.	SE 10-11, 16, 18-19, 100-101, 186-187, 420-421, 498-499, 532-533, 622-623, 678-679, 738-739
ES.2.EKS-4 differentiate between systematically-obtained, verifiable data and unfounded claims.	SE 10-15, 16, 18-19 TE 14
ES.2.EKS-5 evaluate statements to determine if systematic science is used correctly, consistently, thoroughly, and in the proper context.	SE 9-16, 18-19, 100-101, 186-187, 420-421, 498-499, 532-533, 622-623, 678-679, 738-739
ES.2.EKS-6 distinguish between examples of observations and inferences.	SE 74-75, 560-561, 594-595, 650-651, 678-679, 812-813
ES.2.EKS-7 explain how scientific methodology is used to support, refute, or improve scientific theories.	SE 9-15, 16, 23 TE 10
ES.2.EKS-8 contrast the formal, scientific use of the term "theory" with the everyday nontechnical usage of "theory."	SE 15, 16, 258, 844
ES.2.EKS-9 compare and contrast hypotheses, theories, and scientific laws. For example, students should be able to compare/contrast the Law of Superposition and the Theory of Plate Tectonics.	SE 10-11, 15, 23, 28, 203, 206, 258, 259-262, 266, 267, 280, 287, 789, 844 TE 15

Standards of Learning	*Holt McDougal Virginia Earth Science* Citations
ES.3 The student will investigate and understand the characteristics of Earth and the solar system. Key concepts include	
ES.3.a position of Earth in the solar system;	SE 747, 748, 755, 758
ES.3.b sun-Earth-moon relationships (seasons, tides, and eclipses);	SE 701-704, 711, 713, 734-736, 742, 745, 793-795, 798, 816
ES.3.c characteristics of the sun, planets and their moons, comets, meteors, and asteroids; and	SE 759-764, 765-772, 774-775, 778-779, 781, 785-788, 790, 799-804, 805-810, 812-813, 816-817, 821, 823-828, 829-832, 838-839
ES.3.d the history and contributions of space exploration.	SE 719, 721, 723-728, 759, 761, 764, 767, 768, 769m, 770, 773, 867
Essential Knowledge and Skills (EKS) In order to meet this standard, it is expected that students will	
ES.3..EKS-1 analyze the role of 1) the position of Earth in the Solar System; 2) the size of Earth and sun; and 3) Earth's axial tilt in affecting the evolution of the planet and life on the planet.	SE 734-736, 762, 764
ES.3..EKS-2 analyze historical explanations for the origin of the moon.	SE 789-790
ES.3.EKS-3 create a model showing the position of Earth, the moon, and the resulting moon phases.	TE 796 SE* 796-797 * Foundational
ES.3.EKS-4 explain why there is not a solar and lunar eclipse each month.	SE 795, 798
ES.3.EKS-5 create a model showing the position of Earth, moon, and sun during a solar and lunar eclipse.	SE 794
ES.3.EKS-6 differentiate between the inner (terrestrial) planets and the outer (gaseous) planets and their corresponding atmospheric characteristics.	SE 759-764, 765-772, 778-779
ES.3.EKS-7 compare and contrast the internal makeup of the four inner planets and explain why they vary so significantly.	SE 752, 759-764
ES.3.EKS-8 compare and contrast the atmospheres, planetary makeup, surface conditions, and rotation of the planets.	SE 759-764, 765-772
ES.3.EKS-9 compare the classification of the dwarf planet Pluto to the planets in relation to its orbit, and its similarity to other objects in the Kuiper Belt.	SE 771, 772
ES.3.EKS-10 compare and contrast the defining characteristics among moons, comets, meteoroids, and asteroids.	SE 785-788, 790, 799-804, 805-810, 812-813, 816-817, 819
ES.3.EKS-11 compare and contrast the characteristics of Venus, Earth, Mercury, and Mars, and interpret various reasons why each planet has such characteristics.	SE 752-754, 759-764

Standards of Learning	*Holt McDougal Virginia Earth Science* Citations
ES.3.EKS-12 predict what conditions we would need to have in place for another celestial object to support life.	SE 762, 772
ES.3.EKS-13 compare the various types of evidence obtained from the Apollo moon landings and other lunar exploration and how this is used to inform thinking about the moon.	SE 785-790
ES.3.EKS-14 analyze how the role of technology (Galileo's telescope, Hubble telescope, planetary orbiters, landers/ rovers) has contributed to social and scientific change and enlightenment.	SE 719, 721, 723-728, 759, 761, 764, 767, 768, 769m, 770, 773, 867
ES.3.EKS-15 create a timeline of key events in space exploration.	SE 730 TE 814
ES.4 The student will investigate and understand how to identify major rock-forming and ore minerals based on physical and chemical properties. Key concepts include	
ES.4.a hardness, color and streak, luster, cleavage, fracture, and unique properties; and	SE 109, 111-116, 117-122, 124-125, 128-129
ES.4.b uses of minerals.	SE 112, 169, 170
Essential Knowledge and Skills (EKS) In order to meet this standard, it is expected that students will	
ES.4.EKS-1 analyze why certain common metallic elements (iron, aluminum, silicon) are rarely, if ever, found in the native state.	SE 93, 167, C20
ES.4.EKS-2 analyze the distribution and persistence of minerals at or near Earth's surface in terms of Earth's general structure, plate tectonics, and chemical and physical weathering.	SE 126, 129, 167-168, 170
ES.4.EKS-3 analyze the relationship between the qualities of cleavage, fracture, and hardness and the molecular structure and chemistry of silicates, carbonates, and oxides.	SE 112-116, 118-119, 128
ES.4.EKS-4 identify minerals by their physical properties, such as hardness, color, luster, and streak.	SE 117-122, 124-125
ES.4.EKS-5 recognize some major rock-forming minerals such as quartz, feldspar, calcite, and mica.	SE 112, 142-144
ES.4.EKS-6 recognize ore minerals includeing pyrite, magnetite, hematite, galena, graphite, and sulfur.	SE 167-168, 170
ES.5 The student will investigate and understand the rock cycle as it relates to the origin and transformation of rock types and how to identify common rock types based on mineral composition and textures. Key concepts include	
ES.5.a igneous rocks;	SE 135, 138, 139-144, 156-157, 160
ES.5.b sedimentary rocks; and	SE 133, 135, 138, 145-150, 156-157, 160
ES.5.c metamorphic rocks.	SE 135, 138, 151-154, 156-157, 160
Essential Knowledge and Skills (EKS) In order to meet this standard, it is expected that students will	

Standards of Learning	*Holt McDougal Virginia Earth Science* Citations
ES.5.EKS-1 comprehend and identify various igneous rock textural features and mineral components with a hand sample or by description, and analyze the significance of these features in terms of mode of origin and history.	SE 139-141, 144, 156-157 TE 139
ES.5.EKS-2 analyze and identify various sedimentary rocks in terms of mode of origin and history, using sedimentary features (grain size, texture, and composition).	SE 145-150, 156-157
ES.5.EKS-3 analyze the major groups of metamorphic rocks for mineral composition and textural features and determine the potential parent rock and in terms of the rock cycle.	SE 151-154, 156-157
ES.5.EKS-4 analyze a sequence of rocks in terms of types, textures, composition, fossils, structural, and weathering features in order to infer the history of the sequence over time.	SE 148-149, 202-206
ES.5.EKS-5 integrate the rock cycle with Plate Tectonics Theory and determine how this is reflected in the geology of Virginia's five physiographic provinces.	SE 135-136, 138, 158, 163, C8
ES.5.EKS-6 classify the following rock types as igneous, metamorphic, or sedimentary: pumice, obsidian, basalt, granite, sandstone, conglomerate, shale, limestone, slate, schist, gneiss, marble, and quartzite.	SE 156-157
ES.5.EKS-7 differentiate between clastic and non-clastic sedimentary rocks.	SE 156-157
ES.5.EKS-8 compare and contrast distinguishing characteristics of the crystal structure and textures of extrusive and intrusive igneous rocks.	SE 140, 141, 144, 160
ES.5.EKS-9 describe the structure of foliated and unfoliated metamorphic rocks.	SE 153-154
ES.6 The student will investigate and understand the differences between renewable and nonrenewable resources. Key concepts include	
ES.6.a fossil fuels, minerals, rocks, water, and vegetation	SE 40, 126, 167-169, 170, 171-173, 176, 179, 190, 407-410
ES.6.b advantages and disadvantages of various energy sources;	SE 171, 173, 176, 177-180, 182, 184, 190-191, 419
ES.6.c resources found in Virginia; and	SE 126, 924, 971, 972
ES.6.d environmental costs and benefits.	SE 181-184, 419
Essential Knowledge and Skills (EKS) In order to meet this standard, it is expected that students will	
ES.6.EKS-1 analyze the formation of fossil fuels in terms of the rock cycle and Plate Tectonics Theory, and relate the formation of fossil fuels to ancient biologic and atmospheric conditions and changes and locations within Virginia.	SE 171-173, 176, 924, 925, C12

FULL STANDARD CORRELATION

Standards of Learning	*Holt McDougal Virginia Earth Science* Citations
ES.6.EKS-2 analyze how Virginia's production and use of various natural resources has changed over time. Define and cite differences over time especially in the last 150 years.	SE 126, 924, 971, 972, C18
ES.6.ESK-3 evaluate Virginia's potential as a producer of renewable energy sources.	SE C29
ES.6.EKS-4 assess the role of fossil fuels and renewable energy sources in the future and compare and contrast the environmental benefits and costs among the various options.	SE 173, 177-180, 185, 188
ES.6.EKS-5 analyze the advantages and disadvantages of various energy sources.	SE 171, 173, 176, 177-180, 182, 184, 190-191, 419
ES.6.ESK-6 analyze a range of emerging energy and mineral resources in Virginia in terms of costs and benefits.	SE C29
ES.6.EKS-7 determine the sources of clean water in their community and analyze consumption and supply data.	SE C29 TE 447
ES.7 The student will investigate and understand geologic processes including plate tectonics. Key concepts include	
ES.7.a geologic processes and their resulting features; and	SE 135-136, 138, 259-266, 275-280, 282-283, 286-287, 289, 291, 292, 293-300, 301-306, 308-309, 312-313, 317, 319-324, 345-350, 351-356, 358-359, 365
ES.7.b tectonic processes.	SE 267-274, 302-303, 315, 323, 324, 345-350
Essential Knowledge and Skills (EKS) In order to meet this standard, it is expected that students will	
ES.7.EKS-1 label on a map and recognize the major features of the physiographic provinces of Virginia.	SE 969, C8
ES.7.EKS-2 comprehend the topographic, rock-type and geologic-structural characteristics of each physiographic province of Virginia.	SE 158, C8 TE 68, 76
ES.7.EKS-3 analyze the geologic history of Virginia in terms of the structures, rock types, and topography represented in the five physiographic provinces.	SE 158, C8, C29 TE 68, 76
ES.7.EKS-4 integrate and interpret the rock cycle, plate tectonics, and Virginia's geology in an interacting diagram.	SE C15 TE 138
ES.7.EKS-5 analyze how multiple continental collisions and rifting events over the last billion years have created the current physiography of Virginia.	SE 260, 268, 270, 289
ES.7.EKS-6 comprehend and apply the details of Plate Tectonics Theory to the formation of continents, mountain chains, island arcs, deep open trenches, earthquake zones, and continental and mid-ocean volcanism.	SE 262-263, 267-274, 301-306, 308-309, 323, 324, 346-349, 350
ES.7.EKS-7 analyze the composition and structure of the continental and oceanic lithosphere in terms of topographic features, density, thickness, and rates of motion.	SE 30-31, 272-274, 282-283, 293, 307

Standards of Learning	*Holt McDougal Virginia Earth Science* Citations
ES.7.EKS-8 compare and contrast various types of volcanism and geothermal activity (i.e., Hawaii, Iceland, Mount St. Helens, Catoctin Greenstone, Tambora, the Deccan Traps, and Yellowstone).	SE 346-349, 350, 351-355, 356
ES.7.EKS-9 compare and contrast different types of current and ancient plate boundaries (i.e., Japan, California, New Madrid, Missouri, the Appalachian system, Iceland, and Tonga).	SE 268, 278-280
ES.7.EKS-10 analyze how seismic waves provide evidence of the structure of the deep Earth including the inner and outer core in terms of composition, density, and viscosity.	SE 322, 324
ES.7.EKS-11 analyze the body of evidence for Plate Tectonics Theory (i.e., seafloor age, magnetic information, seismic profiles, laser-measured motion studies, fossil evidence, rock types associated with particular tectonic environments).	SE 259-266
ES.7.EKS-12 analyze the various structures produced in convergent plate boundaries.	SE 270-271, 274, 301-304, 306, 346
ES.7.EKS-13 offer interpretations of the tectonic history of an area based on the range and type of rocks found in that area.	SE 151-152
ES.7.EKS-14 compare and contrast the tectonic activity of the east coast and the west coast of North America.	SE 304-305, 323, 346 TE 304
ES.8 The student will investigate and understand how freshwater resources are influenced by geologic processes and the activities of humans. Key concepts include	
ES.8.a processes of soil development;	SE 373-377, 378, 382, 383-385, 386
ES.8.b development of karst topography;	SE 439, 442, 448
ES.8.c relationships between groundwater zones, including saturated and unsaturated zones, and the water table;	SE 433-434
ES.8.d identification of sources of fresh water including rivers, springs, and aquifers, with reference to the hydrologic cycle;	SE 407-409, 410, 411, 414, 431-438, 444-445
ES.8.e dependence on freshwater resources and the effects of human usage on water quality; and	SE 409-410, 435, 446, 449
ES.8.f identification of the major watershed systems in Virginia, including the Chesapeake Bay and its tributaries.	SE C30 TE 411
Essential Knowledge and Skills (EKS) In order to meet this standard, it is expected that students will	
ES.8.EKS-1 interpret a simple groundwater diagram showing the zone of aeration, the zone of saturation, the water table, and an aquifer.	SE 433
ES.8.EKS-2 interpret a simple hydrologic cycle diagram, including evaporation, condensation, precipitation, and runoff.	SE 408, 451

FULL STANDARD CORRELATION

Standards of Learning	*Holt McDougal Virginia Earth Science* Citations
ES.8.EKS-3 locate the major Virginia watershed systems on a map (Chesapeake Bay, Gulf of Mexico, and North Carolina sounds).	SE C30 TE 411
ES.8.EKS-4 analyze the formation of karst in terms of rock type, solubility and permeability, uplift, the water table, and chemical and physical weathering.	SE 439, 442, 448
ES.8.EKS-5 analyze the presence of groundwater in various types of rock terrains, including areas found in each of the physiographic provinces of Virginia.	SE 431-435, 438, C17
ES.8.EKS-6 analyze the relationship between salt-water intrusion in the ground water in certain areas of eastern Virginia and buried crater structures.	SE C15
ES.9 The student will investigate and understand that many aspects of the history and evolution of Earth and life can be inferred by studying rocks and fossils. Key concepts include	
ES.9.a traces and remains of ancient, often extinct, life are preserved by various means in many sedimentary rocks;	SE 146, 213-216, 218-219, 222
ES.9.b superposition, cross-cutting relationships, index fossils, and radioactive decay are methods of dating bodies of rock;	SE 199, 201-206, 207-212, 213, 216, 222-223, 229-230, 246-247
ES.9.c absolute and relative dating have different applications but can be used together to determine the age of rocks and structures; and	SE 201-206, 207-212, 222-223, 246-247
ES.9.d rocks and fossils from many different geologic periods and epochs are found in Virginia.	SE 158, 247 TE 220
Essential Knowledge and Skills (EKS) In order to meet this standard, it is expected that students will	
ES.9.EKS-1 describe how life has changed and become more complex over geologic time.	SE 233-238, 239-244, 250
ES.9.EKS-2 interpret a simple geologic history diagram, using superposition and cross-cutting relations.	SE 223, 225, 246-247
ES.9.EKS-3 analyze how radioactive decay provides a reliable method to determine the age of many types of organic and inorganic materials.	SE 209-212, 222
ES.9.EKS-4 analyze the impact and role of global catastrophies (including asteroid/comet impacts, volcanism, continental collisions, climate collapse) on extinctions and evolution.	SE 238, 239, 241
ES.9.EKS-5 analyze and interpret complex cross sections using both relative and absolute dating to unravel and define the geologic history of the section.	SE 223, 246-247
ES.10 The student will investigate and understand that oceans are complex, interactive physical, chemical, and biological systems and are subject to long- and short-term variations. Key concepts include	

Standards of Learning	*Holt McDougal Virginia Earth Science* Citations
ES.10.a physical and chemical changes related to tides, waves, currents, sea level and ice cap variations, upwelling, and salinity variations;	SE 489-492, 493-495, 496, 498-499, 619, 664-667, 668, 670, 678-679, 682-683, 685, 687, 689-694, 695-700, 701-704, 710-711, 713, 754
ES.10.b importance of environmental and geologic implications;	SE 489-492, 493-495, 496, 498-499, 500, 505, 618-619, 621, 669-672, 673-676
ES.10.c systems interactions;	SE 579, 608-609, 610, 689-694, 695-700, 701-704
ES.10.d features of the seafloor as reflections of tectonic processes; and	SE 262, 270, 272, 641-644
ES.10.e economic and public policy issues concerning the oceans and the coastal zone including the Chesapeake Bay.	SE 496, 676, C16
Essential Knowledge and Skills (EKS) In order to meet this standard, it is expected that students will	
ES.10.EKS-1 identify the effects of human activities on the oceans.	SE 496, 675, 676
ES.10.EKS-2 analyze the potential impact of a major environmental disaster on the base of the food web and vertebrate organisms; economics; cultures; and future productivity.	SE 676, 683
ES.10.EKS-3 analyze the relationship between moving continents, the presence of ice caps, and ocean circulation over long periods of time.	SE 617, 277
ES.10.EKS-4 relate important ocean conditions, including El Niño, to weather on the continents.	SE 608-609
ES.10.EKS-5 evaluate the role of the marine environment in the extraction of carbon dioxide in carbonates and the production of oxygen.	SE 514, 662, 668, 669
ES.10.EKS-6 analyze the role of ocean currents in the distribution of heat from the equatorial regions to the poles, and predict what changes may occur as continents move and atmospheric conditions and climate vary.	SE 617, 691-693
ES.10.EKS-7 compare Atlantic Ocean and Gulf of Mexico water temperatures during the yearly cycle, and relate this to the formation of storms.	SE 579, 692
ES.10.EKS-8 describe how different types of pollution can pollute the Chesapeake Bay even though the pollutant source may be hundreds of miles from the Bay.	SW 676, C30
ES.11 The student will investigate and understand the origin and evolution of the atmosphere and the interrelationship of geologic processes, biologic processes, and human activities on its composition and dynamics. Key concepts include	
ES.11.a scientific evidence for atmospheric composition changes over geologic time;	SE 513-515, 520, 753-754
ES.11.b current theories related to the effects of early life on the chemical makeup of the atmosphere;	SE 753, 762, C10

FULL STANDARD CORRELATION

Standards of Learning	*Holt McDougal Virginia Earth Science* Citations
ES.11.c atmospheric regulation mechanisms including the effects of density differences and energy transfer; and	SE 521-526, 528-530, 532-533, 571, 575-576, 607
ES.11.d potential changes to the atmosphere and climate due to human, biologic, and geologic activity.	SE 515, 520, 618, 620
Essential Knowledge and Skills (EKS) In order to meet this standard, it is expected that students will	
ES.11.EKS-1 analyze the array of climate feedback mechanisms that control the Earth's temperature over time, and compare and contrast these feedback mechanisms to those operating on inner planets and the gas giants.	SE 521-526, 605-610, 622-623, 760, 766, 768, 769, 770
ES.11.EKS-2 analyze the evidence for atmospheric compositional change over geologic time including oxygen and carbon sinks and the role of photosynthetic organisms.	SE 753, 754, 762
ES.11.EKS-3 explain how volcanic activity or meteor impacts could affect the atmosphere and life on Earth.	SE 618, 753
ES.11.EKS-4 explain how biologic activity, including human activities, may influence global temperature and climate.	SE 618-619
ES.12 The student will investigate and understand that energy transfer between the sun and Earth and its atmosphere drives weather and climate on Earth. Key concepts include	
ES.12.a observation and collection of weather data;	SE 557, 560-561, 569, 583-586, 944-945
ES.12.b prediction of weather patterns;	SE 587-592, 594-595, 946-949
ES.12.c severe weather occurrences, such as tornadoes, hurricanes, and major storms; and	SE 578-579, 580-581, 582
ES.12.d weather phenomena and the factors that affect climate including radiation, conduction, and convection.	SE 521-526, 532-533, 605-610
Essential Knowledge and Skills (EKS) In order to meet this standard, it is expected that students will	
ES.12.EKS-1 identify and describe the direction of local winds (land, sea breezes and jet stream).	SE 529, 530
ES.12.EKS-2 read and interpret data from a thermometer, a barometer, and a psychrometer.	SE 516-517, 532-533, 547, 560-561, 590, 944-945
ES.12.EKS-3 predict weather based on cloud type, temperature, and barometric pressure.	SE 587-592, 594-595, 946-949
ES.12.EKS-4 read and interpret a weather map containing fronts, isobars, and isotherms.	SE 594-595, 944-948
ES.12.EKS-5 read and interpret weather station models.	SE 588, 594-595 TE 589
ES.12.EKS-6 identify types and origins of air masses, fronts and the accompanying weather conditions.	SE 571-574, 575-577, 582
ES.12.EKS-7 read and interpret climate graphs.	SE 950-953

Standards of Learning	*Holt McDougal Virginia Earth Science* Citations
ES.12.EKS-8 label a diagram of global climate zones and the surface movement of ocean currents.	SE 611-613, C2
ES.12.EKS-9 label a diagram that demonstrates the interaction of Earth's atmosphere and energy transfer (conduction, convection, and radiation).	SE 521, 526, C2
ES.12.EKS-10 analyze the impact of satellite technology on weather prediction and the tracking of severe storms, including hurricanes, and evaluate the cost and benefits of this technology in terms of lives and property saved. Predict the impact on storm preparedness if there were no weather satellites.	SE 586, C22
ES.13 The student will investigate and understand scientific concepts related to the origin and evolution of the universe. Key concepts include	
ES.13.a cosmology including the Big Bang theory; and	SE 863-866
ES.13.b the origin and evolution of stars, star systems, and galaxies.	SE 851-858, 860-862
Essential Knowledge and Skills (EKS) In order to meet this standard, it is expected that students will	
ES.13.EKS-1 contrast the life span and energy output of a blue giant star to that of the sun and relate this to the potential existence of life on planets in its orbit.	SE 772, 853, 854
ES.13.EKS-2 explain the potential origin and role of ultra massive black holes in the center of galaxies.	SE 858, 862
ES.13.EKS-3 using the Hertzsprung-Russell diagram, classify stars as to their place on the main sequence or in beginning or end points in their life cycles.	SE 851-858
ES.13.EKS-4 evaluate the probability of travel to nearby solar systems using current spacecraft speeds.	SE 848
ES.13.EKS-5 analyze the various fusion product of a blue giant star over its lifetime, and relate this to the presence and abundance of elements that make up our solar system and its contents, including living organisms.	SE 825 TE 90

Safety in Your Laboratory

Risk Assessment

MAKING YOUR LABORATORY A SAFE PLACE TO WORK AND LEARN

Concern for safety must begin before any activity in the classroom and before students enter the lab. A careful review of the facilities should be a basic part of preparation for each school term. You should investigate the physical environment, identify any safety risks, and inspect your work areas for compliance with safety regulations.

The review of the lab should be thorough, and all safety issues must be addressed immediately. Keep a file of your review, and add to the list each year. This will allow you to continue to raise the standard of safety in your lab and classroom.

Many classroom experiments, demonstrations, and other activities are classics that have been used for years. This familiarity may lead to a comfort that can obscure inherent safety concerns. Review all experiments, demonstrations, and activities for safety concerns before presenting them to the class. Identify and eliminate potential safety hazards.

1. Identify the Risks
Before introducing any activity, demonstration, or experiment to the class, analyze it and consider what could possibly go wrong. Carefully review the list of materials to make sure they are safe. Inspect the equipment in your lab or classroom to make sure it is in good working order. Read the procedures to make sure they are safe. Record any hazards or concerns you identify.

2. Evaluate the Risks
Minimize the risks you identified in the last step without sacrificing learning. Remember that no activity you perform in the lab or classroom is worth risking injury. Thus, extremely hazardous activities, or those that violate your school's policies, must be eliminated. For activities that present smaller risks, analyze each risk carefully to determine its likelihood. If the pedagogical value of the activity does not outweigh the risks, the activity must be eliminated.

3. Select Controls to Address Risks
Even low-risk activities require controls to eliminate or minimize the risks. Make sure that in devising controls you do not substitute an equally or more hazardous alternative. Some control methods include the following:

- Explicit verbal and written warnings may be added or posted.
- Equipment may be rebuilt or relocated, have parts replaced, or be replaced entirely by safer alternatives.
- Risky procedures may be eliminated.
- Activities may be changed from student activities to teacher demonstrations.

4. Implement and Review Selected Controls
Controls do not help if they are forgotten or not enforced. The implementation and review of controls should be as systematic and thorough as the initial analysis of safety concerns in the lab and laboratory activities.

SOME SAFETY RISKS AND PREVENTATIVE CONTROLS

The following list describes several possible safety hazards and controls that can be implemented to resolve them. This list is not complete, but it can be used as a starting point to identify hazards in your laboratory.

Identified risk	Preventative control
Facilities and Equipment	
Lab tables are in disrepair, room is poorly lighted and ventilated, faucets and electrical outlets do not work or are difficult to use because of their location.	Work surfaces should be level and stable. There should be adequate lighting and ventilation. Water supplies, drains, and electrical outlets should be in good working order. Any equipment in a dangerous location should not be used; it should be relocated or rendered inoperable.
Wiring, plumbing, and air circulation systems do not work or do not meet current specifications.	Specifications should be kept on file. Conduct a periodic review of all equipment, and document compliance. Damaged fixtures must be labeled as such and must be repaired as soon as possible.
Eyewash fountains and safety showers are present but no one knows anything about their specifications.	Ensure that eyewash fountains and safety showers meet the requirements of the ANSI standard (Z358.1).
Eyewash fountains are checked and cleaned once at the beginning of each school year. No records are kept of routine checks and maintenance on the safety showers and eyewash fountains.	Flush eyewash fountains for 5 min. every month to remove any bacteria or other organisms from pipes. Test safety showers (measure flow in gallons per min) and eyewash fountains every 6 months and keep records of the test results.
Labs are conducted in multipurpose rooms, and equipment from other courses remains accessible.	Only the items necessary for a given activity should be available to students. All equipment should be locked away when not in use.
Students are permitted to enter or work in the lab without teacher supervision.	Lock all laboratory rooms whenever a teacher is not present. Supervising teachers must be trained in lab safety and emergency procedures.
Safety equipment and emergency procedures	
Fire and other emergency drills are infrequent, and no records or measurements are made of the results of the drills.	Always carry out critical reviews of fire or other emergency drills. Be sure that plans include alternate routes. Don't wait until an emergency to find the flaws in your plans.
Emergency evacuation plans do not include instructions for securing the lab in the event of an evacuation during a lab activity.	Plan actions in case of emergency: establish what devices should be turned off, which escape route to use, and where to meet outside the building.
Fire extinguishers are in out-of-the-way locations, not on the escape route.	Place fire extinguishers near escape routes so that they will be of use during an emergency.
Fire extinguishers are not maintained. Teachers are not trained to use them.	Document regular maintenance of fire extinguishers. Train supervisory personnel in the proper use of extinguishers. Instruct students not to use an extinguisher but to call for a teacher.
Teachers in labs and neighboring classrooms are not trained in CPR or first aid.	Teachers should receive training. The American Red Cross and other groups offer training. Certifications should be kept current with frequent refresher courses.
Teachers are not aware of their legal responsibilities in case of an injury or accident.	Review your faculty handbook for your responsibilities regarding safety in the classroom and laboratory. Contact the legal counsel for your school district to find out the extent of their support and any rules, regulations, or procedures you must follow.

Identified risk	Preventative control
Safety equipment and emergency procedures *(continued)*	
Emergency procedures are not posted. Emergency numbers are kept only at the switchboard or main office. Instructions are given verbally only at the beginning of the year.	Emergency procedures should be posted at all exits and near all safety equipment. Emergency numbers should be posted at all phones, and a script should be provided for the caller to use. Emergency procedures must be reviewed periodically, and students should be reminded of them at the beginning of each activity.
Spills are handled on a case-by-case basis and are cleaned up with whatever materials happen to be on hand.	Have the appropriate equipment and materials available for cleaning up; replace them before expiration dates. Make sure students know to alert you to spilled chemicals, blood, and broken glass.
Work habits and environment	
Safety wear is only used for activities involving chemicals or hot plates.	Aprons and goggles should be worn in the lab at all times. Long hair, loose clothing, and loose jewelry should be secured.
There is no dress code established for the laboratory; students are allowed to wear sandals or open-toed shoes.	Open-toed shoes should never be worn in the laboratory. Do not allow any footwear in the lab that does not cover feet completely.
Students are required to wear safety gear but teachers and visitors are not.	Always wear safety gear in the lab. Keep extra equipment on hand for visitors.
Safety is emphasized at the beginning of the term but is not mentioned later in the year.	Safety must be the first priority in all lab work. Students should be warned of risks and instructed in emergency procedures for each activity.
There is no assessment of students' knowledge and attitudes regarding safety.	Conduct frequent safety quizzes. Only students with perfect scores should be allowed to work in the lab.
You work alone during your preparation period to organize the day's labs.	Never work alone in a science laboratory or a storage area.
Safety inspections are conducted irregularly and are not documented. Teachers and administrators are unaware of what documentation will be necessary in case of a lawsuit.	Safety reviews should be frequent and regular. All reviews should be documented, and improvements must be implemented immediately. Contact legal counsel for your district to make sure your procedures will protect you in case of a lawsuit.
Purchasing, storing, and using chemicals	
The storeroom is too crowded, so you decide to keep some equipment on the lab benches.	Do not store reagents or equipment on lab benches and keep shelves organized. Never place reactive chemicals (in bottles, beakers, flasks, wash bottles, etc.) near the edges of a lab bench.
You prepare solutions from concentrated stock to save money.	Reduce risks by ordering diluted instead of concentrated substances.
You purchase plenty of chemicals to be sure that you won't run out or to save money.	Purchase chemicals in class-size quantities. Do not purchase or have on hand more than one year's supply of each chemical.

Identified risk	Preventative control
Purchasing, storing, and using chemicals ***(continued)***	
You don't generally read labels on chemicals when preparing solutions for a lab, because you already know about a chemical.	Read each label to be sure it states the hazards and describes the precautions and first aid procedures (when appropriate) that apply to the contents in case someone else has to deal with that chemical in an emergency.
You never read the Material Safety Data Sheets (MSDSs) that come with your chemicals.	Always read the Material Safety Data Sheet (MSDS) for a chemical before using it and follow the precautions described. File and organize MSDSs for all chemicals where they can be found easily in case of an emergency.
The main stockroom contains chemicals that haven't been used for years.	Do not leave bottles of chemicals unused on the shelves of the lab for more than one week or unused in the main stockroom for more than one year. Dispose of or use up any leftover chemicals.
No extra precautions are taken when flammable liquids are dispensed from their containers.	When transferring flammable liquids from bulk containers, ground the container, and before transferring to a smaller metal container, ground both containers.
Students are told to put their broken glass and solid chemical wastes in the trash can.	Have separate containers for trash, for broken glass, and for different categories of hazardous chemical wastes.
You store chemicals alphabetically instead of by hazard class. Chemicals are stored without consideration of possible emergencies (fire, earthquake, flood, etc.), which could compound the hazard.	Use MSDSs to determine which chemicals are incompatible. Store chemicals by the hazard class indicated on the MSDS. Store chemicals that are incompatible with common fire-fighting media like water (such as alkali metals) or carbon dioxide (such as alkali and alkaline-earth metals) under conditions that eliminate the possibility of a reaction with water or carbon dioxide if it is necessary to fight a fire in the storage area.
Corrosives are kept above eye level, out of reach from anyone who is not authorized to be in the storeroom.	Always store corrosive chemicals on shelves below eye level. Remember, fumes from many corrosives can destroy metal cabinets and shelving.
Chemicals are kept on the stockroom floor on the days that they will be used so that they are easy to find.	Never store chemicals or other materials on floors or in the aisles of the laboratory or storeroom, even for a few minutes.

HOLT McDOUGAL

Earth SCIENCE

Mead A. Allison

Arthur T. DeGaetano

Jay M. Pasachoff

HOLT McDOUGAL

a division of Houghton Mifflin Harcourt

About the Authors

Mead A. Allison, Ph.D.
The University of Texas, Austin, Texas
Mead Allison received his Ph.D. in oceanography from State University of New York. Formerly a professor of Earth and environmental science at Tulane University in Louisiana, Dr. Allison is now a Senior Research Scientist at the Institute for Geophysics, Jackson School of Geosciences at The University of Texas at Austin.

Arthur T. DeGaetano, Ph.D.
Cornell University, Ithaca, New York
Arthur DeGaetano received his Ph.D. in meteorology from Rutgers University. He is a professor of Earth and atmospheric sciences at Cornell University in New York, where he teaches introductory climatology and upper-level courses in atmospheric thermodynamics and physical meteorology. Dr. DeGaetano is also the director of the Northeast Regional Climate Center.

Jay M. Pasachoff, Ph.D.
Williams College, Williamstown, Massachusetts
Jay Pasachoff received his Ph.D. in astronomy from Harvard University. He is the Field Memorial Professor of Astronomy and the director of the Hopkins Observatory at Williams College in Massachusetts, where he teaches introductory and upper-level courses in astronomy. In addition, Dr. Pasachoff has written several popular college-level astronomy textbooks and an astronomy field guide.

Printed in the U.S.A.

ISBN-13: 978-0-547-72497-3

3 4 5 6 7 8 9 10 0868 20 19 18 17 16 15 14 13 12
4500351161 A B C D E F G

Acknowledgments

Authors

Mead A. Allison, Ph.D.
Senior Research Scientist
Institute for Geophysics
Jackson School of Geosciences
The University of Texas
Austin, Texas

Arthur T. DeGaetano, Ph.D.
Director, Northeast Regional Climate Center
Professor
Department of Earth and Atmospheric Science
Cornell University
Ithaca, New York

Jay M. Pasachoff, Ph.D.
Director, Hopkins Observatory
Field Memorial Professor of Astronomy
Williams College
Williamstown, Massachusetts

Academic Reviewers

Paul Asimow, Ph.D.
Associate Professor of Geology and Geochemistry
Geological and Planetary Sciences
California Institute of Technology
Pasadena, California

Nolan Aughenbaugh
Professor
Department of Geology and Geological Engineering
The University of Mississippi
University, Mississippi

Loren E. Babcock, Ph.D.
Professor
School of Earth Sciences
The Ohio State University
Columbus, Ohio

John A. Brockhaus, Ph.D.
Professor & Program Director of Geospatial Information Science
Geospatial Information Science Program
United States Military Academy
West Point, New York

Jim Burt, Ph.D.
Professor of Geography
Department of Geography
University of Wisconsin-Madison
Madison, Wisconsin

Scott A. Darveau, Ph.D.
Professor of Chemistry
Chemistry Department
University of Nebraska at Kearney
Kearney, Nebraska
Faculty Associate
Nebraska Center for Materials and Nanoscience
University of Nebraska-Lincoln
Lincoln, Nebraska

Deborah Hanley, Ph.D.
Meteorologist
Florida Division of Forestry
Department of Agriculture and Consumer Services
Tallahassee, Florida

Brennan Jordan, Ph.D.
Assistant Professor
Department of Earth Sciences
University of South Dakota
Vermillion, South Dakota

Daniel Leavell, Ph.D.
Assistant Professor
Department of Geology
The Ohio State University at Newark
Newark, Ohio

Sten Odenwald, Ph.D.
Senior Astronomer/Author
Astronomy and Space Physics
NASA-Goddard Space Flight Center
Greenbelt, Maryland

Jim Price, Ph.D.
Senior Scientist
Physical Oceanography Department
Woods Hole Oceanographic Institution
Woods Hole, Massachusetts

Kenneth H. Rubin, Ph.D.
Professor
Department of Geology and Geophysics
School of Ocean and Earth Science
University of Hawaii
Honolulu, Hawaii

Dork Sahagian, Ph.D.
Director of Environmental Initiative
Professor of Earth and Environmental Sciences
Department of Earth and Environmental Sciences
Lehigh University
Bethlehem, Pennsylvania

Vatche P. Tchakerian, Ph.D.
Professor of Geology and Geophysics
Associate Dean for Academic Affairs
College of Geosciences
Texas A&M University
College Station, Texas

Teacher Reviewers

Lowell S. Bailey
Earth Science Educator
Bedford-North Lawrence High School
Bedford, Indiana

Daniel Brownstein, MAT/MA
Science Department Chair
Hastings High School
Hastings, New York

Jeanne Endrikat
Science Chair (Retired)
Lake Braddock Secondary School
Burke, Virginia

Anthony P. LaSalvia
Curriculum Coordinator and Science Teacher
New Lebanon Central Schools
New Lebanon, New York

Keith McKain
Earth Science Teacher
Colonel Richardson High School
Federalsburg, Maryland

Mike McKee
Program Director of The Greater Orlando Graduate Fellows in K-12 Education Program Director of Florida Science Olympiad
University of Central Florida
Orlando, Florida

Christine V. McLelland
Distinguished Earth Science Educator in Residence
Education and Outreach
Geological Society of America
Boulder, Colorado

Tammie Niffenegger
Science Chair and Teacher
Port Washington High School
Port Washington, Wisconsin

Scott Robertson
Earth Science and Physics Teacher
North Warren Central School District
Chestertown, New York

Sharon M. Stroud
Earth Science Teacher and Consultant
Colorado Springs, Colorado

Teresa Tucker
Earth Science Teacher and High School Science Curriculum Chair
Northwest Community Schools
Jackson, Michigan

Lab Reviewers

Randa Flinn, M.S.
Teacher and Science Curriculum Facilitator
Northeast High School
Broward County, Florida

Tammie Niffenegger
Science Chair and Teacher
Port Washington High School
Port Washington, Wisconsin

Scott Robertson
Earth Science and Physics Teacher
North Warren Central School District
Chestertown, New York

CONTENTS IN BRIEF

CONTENTS

Unit 1 Studying the Earth

Environmental Connection

Unit 2 Composition of the Earth

Unit 3 History of the Earth

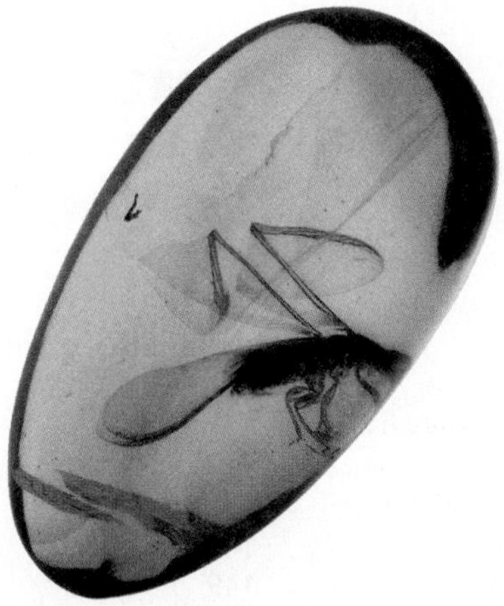

Environmental Connection

Unit 4 The Dynamic Earth

Unit 5 Reshaping the Crust

🌿 Environmental Connection

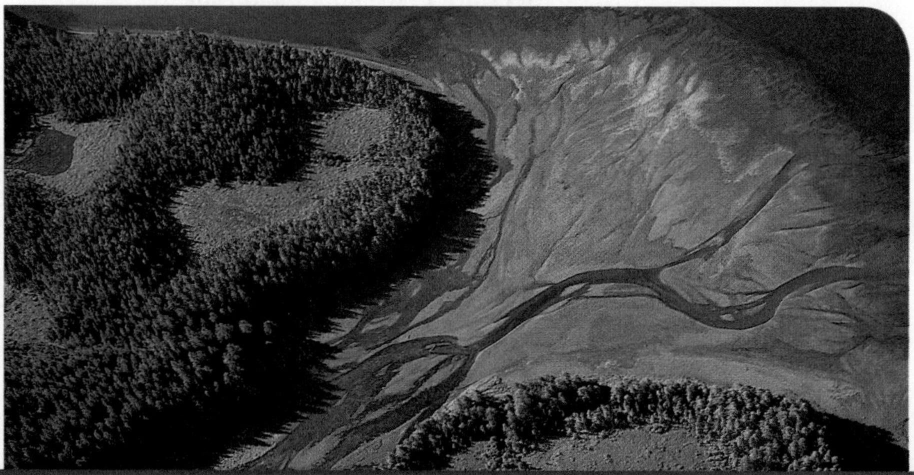

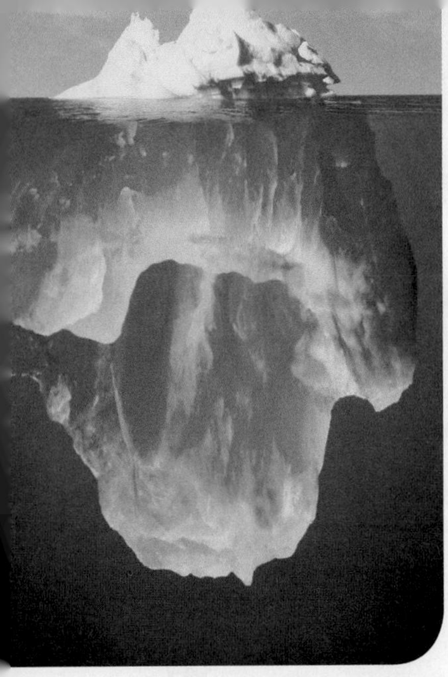

Unit 6 Atmospheric Forces

Environmental Connection

Unit 7 Oceans

Unit 8 Space

Environmental Connection

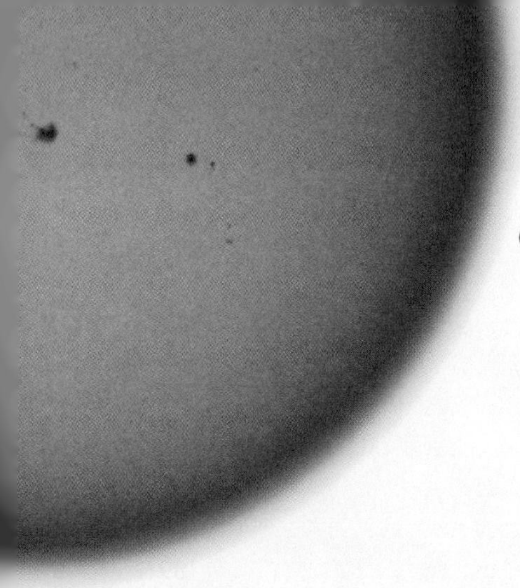

Reference

Labs

Short Labs

These short *Inquiry Labs* and *QuickLabs* are designed to be done quickly during any class period (or at home!) with simple materials.

Inquiry Labs

Quick Labs

Chapter Labs

Each chapter includes an in-depth, hands-on lab that lets you experience science first-hand.

Inquiry Labs

Skills Practice Labs

Making Models Labs

MAPS *in Action*

Maps are important tools of the Earth scientist. This collection of map-skills activities will help you read and understand a variety of maps.

READING TOOLBOX

Reading a textbook is different from reading a novel. The *Reading ToolBoxes* suggest ways to help you organize the concepts in each chapter to get the most out of your reading.

Why It Matters

Have you ever wondered why you need to learn science? Check out these short, interesting articles to learn how science relates to the world around you.

Real World

Weird Science

Forensic Science

Science & Society

Eye on the Environment

History in Science

LAB SAFETY

In the laboratory or in the field, you can engage in hands-on explorations, test your scientific hypotheses, and build practical lab skills. However, while you are working, it is your responsibility to protect yourself and your classmates by conducting yourself in a safe manner. You will avoid accidents by following directions, handling materials carefully, and taking your work seriously. Read the following safety guidelines before working in the lab or field. Make sure that you understand all safety guidelines before entering the lab or field.

Before You Begin

- **Read the entire activity before entering the lab.** Be familiar with the instructions before beginning an activity. Do not start an activity until you have asked your teacher to explain any parts of the activity that you do not understand.
- **Wear the right clothing for lab work.** Before beginning work, tie back long hair, roll up loose sleeves, and put on any required personal protective equipment as directed by your teacher. Remove your wristwatch and any necklaces or jewelry that could get caught in moving parts or contact electrical connections. Avoid or confine loose clothing that could knock things over, catch on fire, get caught in moving parts, contact electrical connections, or absorb chemical solutions. Wear pants rather than shorts or skirts. Nylon and polyester fabrics burn and melt more readily than cotton does. Protect your feet from chemical spills and falling objects. Do not wear open-toed shoes, sandals, or canvas shoes in the lab.
- **Know the location of all safety and emergency equipment used in the lab.** Know proper fire-drill procedures and the location of all fire exits. Ask your teacher where the nearest eyewash stations, safety blankets, safety shower, fire extinguisher, first-aid kit, and chemical spill kit are located. Be sure that you know how to operate the equipment safely.

While You Are Working

- **Always wear a lab apron and safety goggles.** Wear these items while in the lab, even if you are not working on an activity. Labs contain chemicals that can damage your clothing, skin, and eyes. Aprons and goggles also protect against many physical hazards. If your safety goggles cloud up or are uncomfortable, ask your teacher for help. Lengthening the strap slightly, washing the goggles with soap and warm water, or using an anti-fog spray may help the problem.
- **NEVER work alone in the lab.** Work in the lab only when supervised by your teacher.
- **NEVER leave equipment unattended while it is in operation.**
- **Perform only activities specifically assigned by your teacher.** Do not attempt any procedure without your teacher's direction. Use only materials and equipment listed in the activity or authorized by your teacher. Steps in a procedure should be performed only as described in the activity or as approved by your teacher.
- **Keep your work area neat and uncluttered.** Have only books and other materials that are needed to conduct the activity in the lab. Keep backpacks, purses, and other items in your desk, locker, or other designated storage areas.
- **Always heed safety symbols and cautions listed in activities, listed on handouts, posted in the room, provided on equipment or chemical labels (whether provided by the manufacturer or added later), and given verbally by your teacher.** Be aware of the potential hazards of the required materials and procedures, and follow all precautions indicated.
- **Be alert, and walk with care in the lab.** Be aware of others near you and your equipment and be aware of what they are doing.
- **Do not take food, drinks, chewing gum, or tobacco products into the lab.** Do not store or eat food in the lab. Either finish these items or discard them before coming into the lab or beginning work in the field.
- **NEVER taste chemicals or allow them to contact your skin.** Keep your hands away from your face and mouth, even if you are wearing gloves. Only smell vapors as instructed by your teacher and only in the manner indicated.

- **Exercise caution when working with electrical equipment.** Do not use electrical equipment with frayed or twisted wires. Check that insulation on wiring is intact. Be sure that your hands are dry before using electrical equipment. Do not let electrical cords dangle from work stations. Dangling cords can catch on apparatus on tables, can cause you to trip and can cause an electrical shock. The area under and around electrical equipment should be dry; cords should not lie in puddles of spilled liquid, under sink spigots, or in sinks themselves.
- **Use extreme caution when working with hot plates and other heating devices.** Keep your head, hands, hair, and clothing away from the flame or heating area. Remember that metal surfaces connected to the heated area will become hot by conduction. Gas burners should be lit only with a spark lighter, not with matches. Make sure that all heating devices and gas valves are turned off before you leave the lab. Never leave a heating device unattended when it is in use. Metal, ceramic, and glass items do not necessarily look hot when they are hot. Allow all items to cool before storing them.
- **Do not fool around in the lab.** Take your lab work seriously, and behave appropriately in the lab. Lab equipment and apparatus are not toys; never use lab time or equipment for anything other than the intended purpose. Be considerate and be aware of the safety of your classmates as well as your safety at all times.

Emergency Procedures

- **Follow standard fire-safety procedures.** If your clothing catches on fire, do not run; WALK to the safety shower, stand under it, and turn it on. While doing so, call to your teacher. In case of fire, alert your teacher and leave the lab.
- **Report any accident, incident, or hazard—no matter how trivial—to your teacher immediately.** Any incident involving bleeding, burns, fainting, nausea, dizziness, chemical exposure, or ingestion should also be reported immediately to the school nurse or to a physician. If you have a close call, tell your teacher so that you and your teacher can find a way to prevent it from happening again.
- **Report all spills to your teacher immediately.** Call your teacher rather than trying to clean a spill yourself. Your teacher will tell you whether it is safe for you to clean up the spill; if it is not safe, your teacher will know how to clean up the spill.
- **If you spill a chemical on your skin, wash the chemical off in the sink and call your teacher.** If you spill a solid chemical onto your clothing, using an appropriate container, brush it off carefully without scattering it onto somebody else and call your teacher. If you spill corrosive substances on your skin or clothing, use the safety shower or a faucet to rinse. Remove affected clothing while you are under the shower, and call to your teacher. (It may be temporarily embarrassing to remove clothing in front of your classmates, but failure to thoroughly rinse a chemical off your skin could result in permanent damage.)
- **If you get a chemical in your eyes, walk immediately to the eyewash station, turn it on, and lower your head so your eyes are in the running water.** Hold your eyelids open with your thumbs and fingers, and roll your eyeballs around. You have to flush your eyes continuously for at least 15 minutes. Call your teacher while you are doing this.

When You Are Finished

- **Clean your work area at the conclusion of each lab period as directed by your teacher.** Broken glass, chemicals, and other waste products should be disposed of in separate, special containers. Dispose of waste materials as directed by your teacher. Put away all material and equipment according to your teacher's instructions. Report any damaged or missing equipment or materials to your teacher.
- **Even if you wore gloves, wash your hands with soap and hot water after each lab period.** To avoid contamination, wash your hands at the conclusion of each lab period, and before you leave the lab.

SAFETY SYMBOLS

Before you begin working on an activity, familiarize yourself with the following safety symbols, which are used throughout your textbook, and the guidelines that you should follow when you see these symbols.

Eye Protection

- **Wear approved safety goggles as directed.** Safety goggles should be worn in the lab at all times, especially when you are working with a chemical or solution, a heat source, or a mechanical device.
- **If chemicals get into your eyes, flush your eyes immediately.** Go to an eyewash station immediately, and flush your eyes (including under the eyelids) with running water for at least 15 minutes. Use your thumb and fingers to hold your eyelids open and roll your eyeballs around. While doing so, call your teacher or ask another student to notify your teacher.
- **Do not look directly at the sun or any intense light source or laser.** Do not look at these through any optical device or lens system. Do not reflect direct sunlight to illuminate a microscope. Such actions concentrate light rays to an intensity that can severely burn your retinas, causing blindness.

Clothing Protection

- **Wear an apron or lab coat at all times in the lab to prevent chemicals or chemical solutions from contacting skin or clothes.**
- **Tie back long hair, secure loose clothing, and remove loose jewelry so that they do not knock over equipment, get caught in moving parts, or come into contact with hazardous materials or electrical connections.**
- **Do not wear open-toed shoes, sandals, or canvas shoes in the lab.** Splashed chemicals directly contact skin or quickly soak through canvas. Hard shoes will not allow chemicals to soak through as quickly and they provide more protection against dropped or falling objects.

Hand Safety

- **Do not cut an object while holding the object in your hand.** Cut objects on a suitable work surface. Always cut in a direction away from your body.
- **Wear appropriate protective gloves when working with an open flame, chemicals, solutions, or wild or unknown plants.** Your teacher will provide the type of gloves necessary for a given activity.
- **Use a heat-resistant mitt to handle resistors, light sources, and other equipment that may be hot.** Allow all equipment to cool before storing it.

Hygienic Care

- **Keep your hands away from your face, hair, and mouth while you are working on any activity.**
- **Wash your hands thoroughly before you leave the lab or when you finish any activity.**
- **Remove contaminated clothing immediately.** If you spill corrosive substances on your skin or clothing, use the safety shower or a faucet to rinse. Remove affected clothing while you are under the shower, and call to your teacher. (It may be temporarily embarrassing to remove clothing in front of your classmates, but failure to thoroughly rinse a chemical off your skin could result in permanent damage.)

Sharp-Object Safety

- **Use extreme care when handling all sharp and pointed instruments, such as scalpels, sharp probes, and knives.**
- **Do not cut an object while holding the object in your hand.** Cut objects on a suitable work surface. Always cut in a direction away from your body.
- **Do not use double-edged razor blades in the lab.**
- **Be aware of sharp objects or protrusions on equipment or apparatus.**

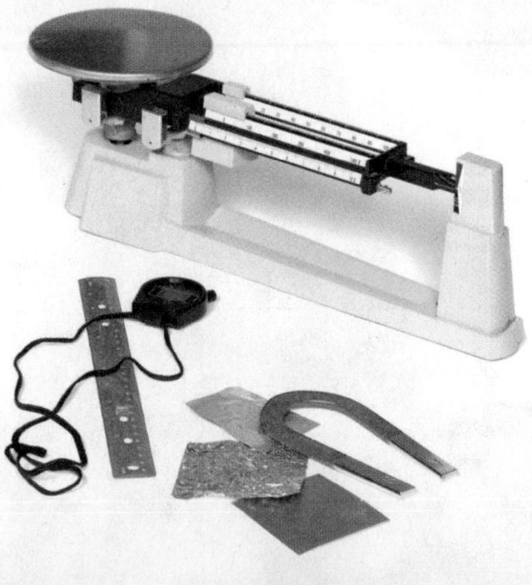

Glassware Safety

- **Inspect glassware before use; do not use chipped or cracked glassware.** Use heat-resistant glassware for heating materials or storing hot liquids, and use appropriate tongs or a heat-resistant mitt to handle this equipment.
- **Notify your teacher immediately if a piece of glassware or a light bulb breaks.** Do not attempt to clean up broken glass or remove broken bulbs unless your teacher directs you to do so.

Proper Waste Disposal

- **Clean and sanitize all work surfaces and personal protective equipment after each lab period as directed by your teacher.**
- **Dispose of contaminated materials (biological or chemical) in special containers only as directed by your teacher.** Never put these materials into a regular waste container or down the drain.
- **Dispose of sharp objects (such as broken glass) in the appropriate sharps or broken-glass container as directed by your teacher.**

Electrical Safety

- **Do not use equipment with frayed electrical cords or loose plugs.** Do not attempt to remove a plug tine if it breaks off in the socket. Notify your teacher and stay away from the outlet.
- **Fasten electrical cords to work surfaces by using tape.** Doing so will prevent tripping and will ensure that equipment will not be pulled or fall off the table.
- **Do not use electrical equipment near water or when your clothing or hands are wet.**
- **Hold the plug housing when you plug in or unplug equipment.** Do not touch the metal prongs of the plug, and do not unplug equipment by pulling on the cord.
- **Wire coils in circuits may heat up rapidly.** If heating occurs, open the switch immediately and use a hot mitt to handle the equipment.

Heating Safety

- **Be aware of any source of flames, sparks, or heat (such as open flames, electric heating coils, or hot plates) before working with flammable liquids or gases.**
- **Avoid using open flames.** If possible, work only with hot plates that have an on/off switch and an indicator light. Do not leave hot plates unattended. Do not use alcohol lamps. Turn off hot plates and open flames when they are not in use.
- **Never leave a hot plate unattended while it is turned on or while it is cooling off.**
- **Know the location of lab fire extinguishers and fire-safety blankets.**
- **Use tongs or appropriate insulated holders when handling heated objects.** Heated objects often do not appear to be hot. Do not pick up an object with your hand if it could be warm.
- **Keep flammable substances away from heat, flames, and other ignition sources.**
- **Allow all equipment to cool before storing it.**

Fire Safety

- **Know the location of lab fire extinguishers and fire-safety blankets.**
- **Know your school's fire-evacuation routes.** Always evacuate the building when the fire alarm is activated.
- **If your clothing catches on fire, walk (do not run) to the emergency lab shower to put out the fire.** If the shower is not working, STOP, DROP, and ROLL! Smother the fire by stopping immediately, dropping to the floor, and rolling until the fire is out.

Safety with Gases

- **Do not inhale any gas or vapor unless directed to do so by your teacher.** Never inhale pure gases.
- **Handle materials that emit vapors or gases in a well-ventilated area.** This work should be done in an approved chemical fume hood. Always work at least four to six inches inside the front edge of the hood.

Caustic Substances

- **If a chemical gets on your skin, on your clothing, or in your eyes, rinse it immediately (shower, faucet or eyewash fountain) and alert your teacher.**
- **If you spill a chemical on the floor or lab bench, alert your teacher, but do not clean it up yourself unless your teacher directs you to do so.**

How to Use Your Textbook

This textbook might seem confusing to you when you first look through it. But by reading the next few pages, you will learn how the different parts of this textbook will help you to become a successful science student. You may be tempted to skip this section, but you should read it. This textbook is an important tool in your exploration of science. Like any tool, the more you know about how to use this textbook, the better your results will be.

Step into Science

The beginning of each chapter is designed to get you involved with science. You will immediately see that science matters!

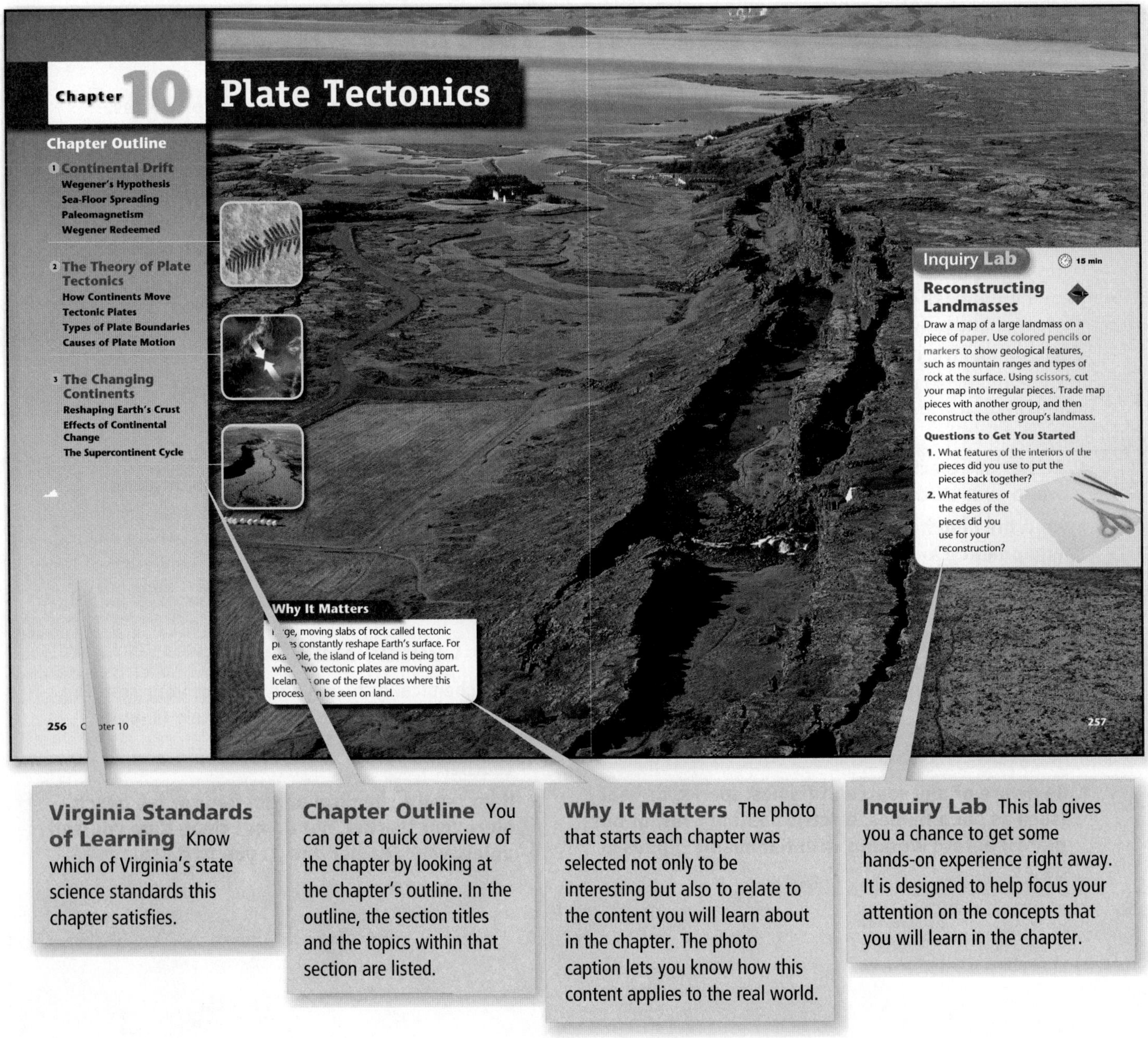

Virginia Standards of Learning Know which of Virginia's state science standards this chapter satisfies.

Chapter Outline You can get a quick overview of the chapter by looking at the chapter's outline. In the outline, the section titles and the topics within that section are listed.

Why It Matters The photo that starts each chapter was selected not only to be interesting but also to relate to the content you will learn about in the chapter. The photo caption lets you know how this content applies to the real world.

Inquiry Lab This lab gives you a chance to get some hands-on experience right away. It is designed to help focus your attention on the concepts that you will learn in the chapter.

Read for Meaning

At the beginning of each chapter you will find tools that will help you grasp the meaning of what you read. Each section also introduces what is important in that section and why.

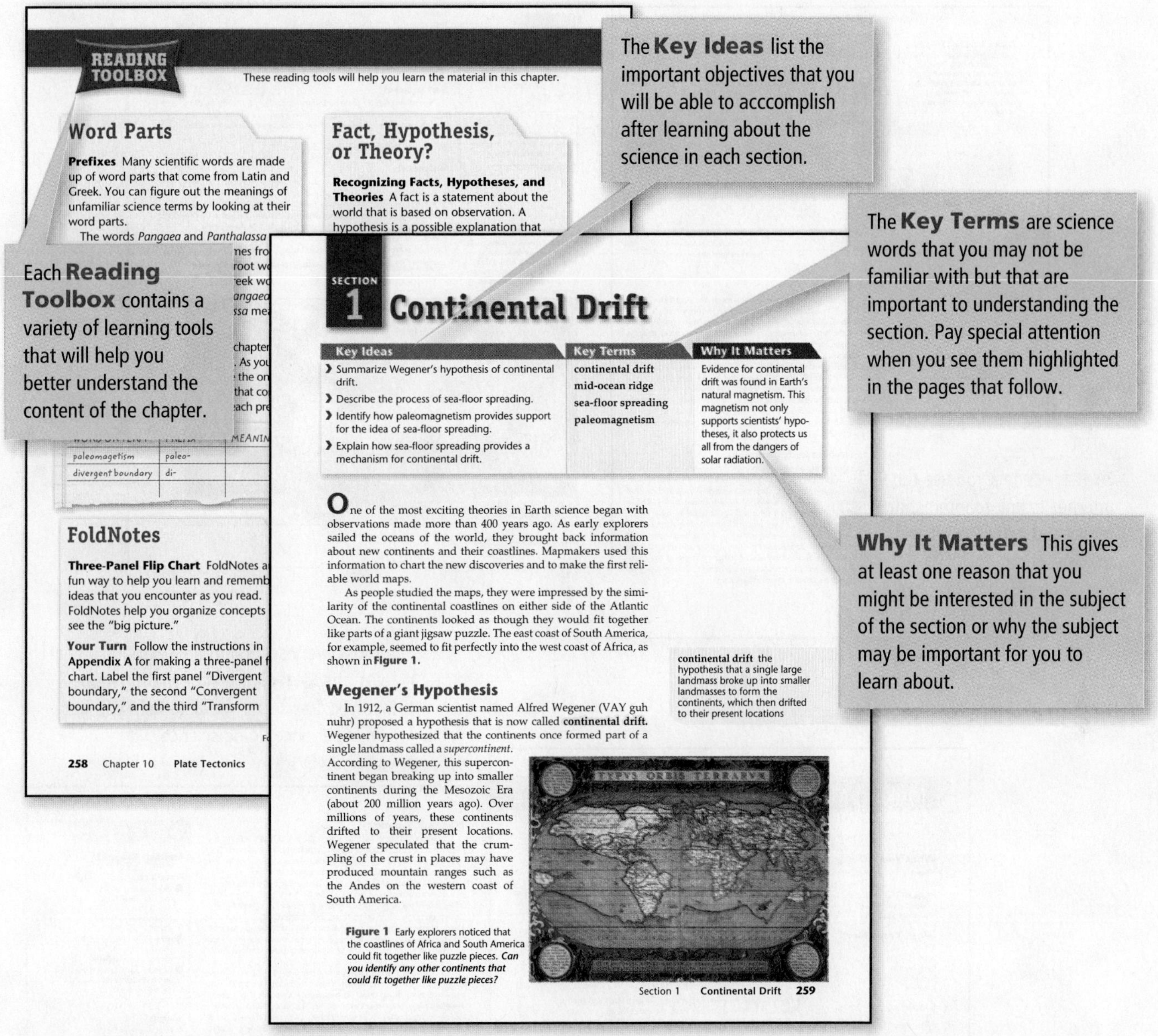

Keep an Eye on Headings

Notice that the headings in this textbook are different sizes and different colors. The headings help you organize your reading and form a simple outline, as shown below.

Blue: Section titles

Red: Main heading

Green: Sub-heading

Science Is Doing

You will get many opportunities throughout this textbook to actually do science. After all, doing is what science is about.

Build your reasoning and problem-solving skills by following the example problems in **Math Skills.**

Check your reading comprehension with the **Reading Check** questions. Answers are found in Appendix G.

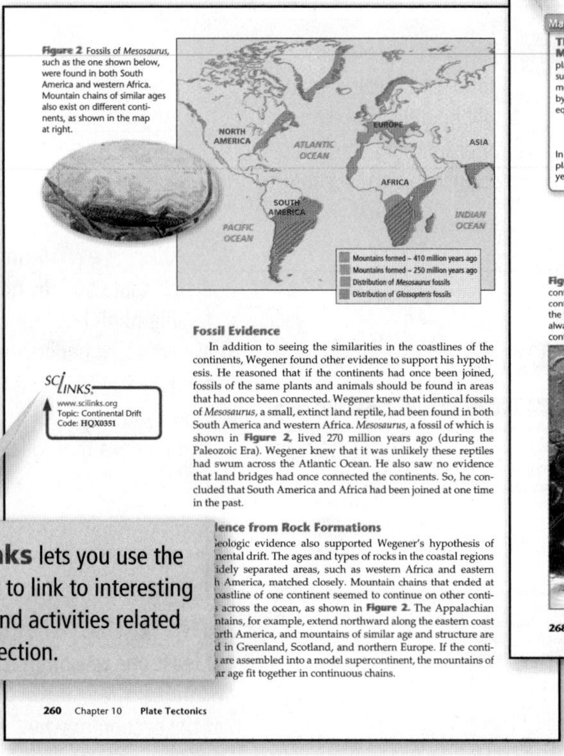

Figure 2 Fossils of *Mesosaurus*, such as the one shown below, were found in both South America and western Africa. Mountain chains of similar ages also exist on different continents, as shown in the map at right.

SCILINKS. www.scilinks.org Topic: Continental Drift Code: HQX0351

Fossil Evidence

In addition to seeing the similarities in the coastlines of the continents, Wegener found other evidence to support his hypothesis. He reasoned that if the continents had once been joined, fossils of the same plants and animals should be found in areas that had once been connected. Wegener knew that identical fossils of *Mesosaurus*, a small, extinct land reptile, had been found in both South America and western Africa. *Mesosaurus*, a fossil of which is shown in **Figure 2**, lived 270 million years ago (during the Paleozoic Era). Wegener knew that it was unlikely these reptiles had swum across the Atlantic Ocean. He also saw no evidence that land bridges had once connected the continents. So, he concluded that South America and Africa had been joined at one time in the past.

…lence from Rock Formations

…eologic evidence also supported Wegener's hypothesis of …nental drift. The ages and types of rocks in the coastal regions …idely separated areas, such as western Africa and eastern …h America, matched closely. Mountain chains that ended at …oastline of one continent seemed to continue on other conti…s across the ocean, as shown in **Figure 2**. The Appalachian …ntains, for example, extend northward along the eastern coast …rth America, and mountains of similar age and structure are …d in Greenland, Scotland, and northern Europe. If the conti…s are assembled into a model supercontinent, the mountains of …ar age fit together in continuous chains.

260 Chapter 10 Plate Tectonics

SciLinks lets you use the Internet to link to interesting topics and activities related to the section.

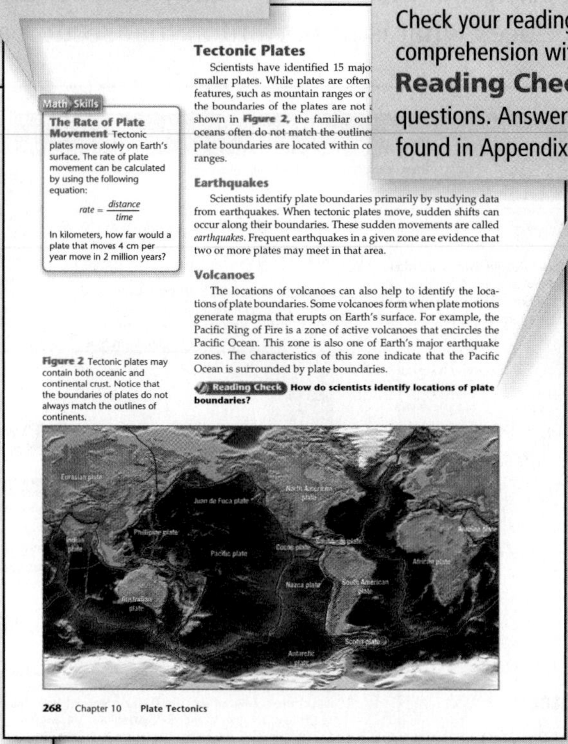

Tectonic Plates

Scientists have identified 15 majo… smaller plates. While plates are often … features, such as mountain ranges or … the boundaries of the plates are not … shown in **Figure 2**, the familiar outl… oceans often do not match the outline… plate boundaries are located within co… ranges.

Math Skills

The Rate of Plate Movement Tectonic plates move slowly on Earth's surface. The rate of plate movement can be calculated by using the following equation:

$$rate = \frac{distance}{time}$$

In kilometers, how far would a plate that moves 4 cm per year move in 2 million years?

Earthquakes

Scientists identify plate boundaries primarily by studying data from earthquakes. When tectonic plates move, sudden shifts can occur along their boundaries. These sudden movements are called *earthquakes*. Frequent earthquakes in a given zone are evidence that two or more plates may meet in that area.

Volcanoes

The locations of volcanoes can also help to identify the locations of plate boundaries. Some volcanoes form when plate motions generate magma that erupts on Earth's surface. For example, the Pacific Ring of Fire is a zone of active volcanoes that encircles the Pacific Ocean. This zone is also one of Earth's major earthquake zones. The characteristics of this zone indicate that the Pacific Ocean is surrounded by plate boundaries.

Reading Check **How do scientists identify locations of plate boundaries?**

Figure 2 Tectonic plates may contain both oceanic and continental crust. Notice that the boundaries of plates do not always match the outlines of continents.

268 Chapter 10 Plate Tectonics

Almost every section in the textbook has at least one **Quick Lab** or slightly more-involved **Inquiry Lab** to help you get real experience doing science.

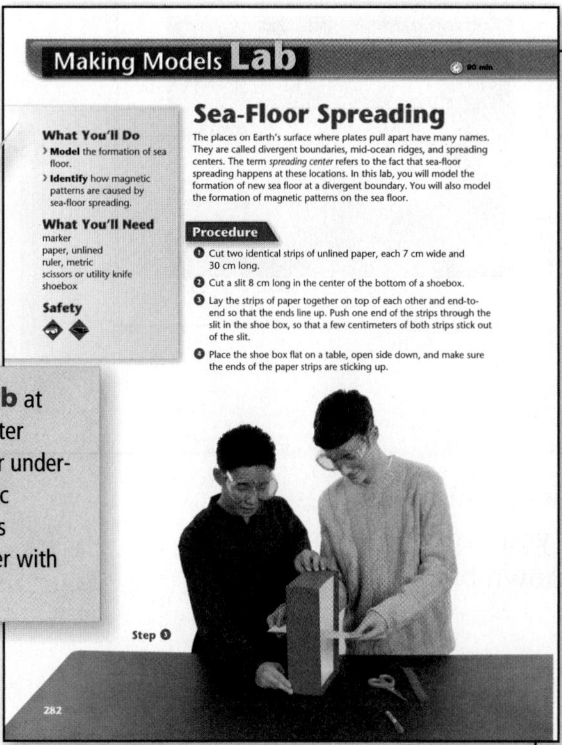

Making Models **Lab** 90 min

Sea-Floor Spreading

What You'll Do

- **Model** the formation of sea floor.
- **Identify** how magnetic patterns are caused by sea-floor spreading.

What You'll Need

marker
paper, unlined
ruler, metric
scissors or utility knife
shoebox

Safety

The places on Earth's surface where plates pull apart have many names. They are called divergent boundaries, mid-ocean ridges, and spreading centers. The term *spreading center* refers to the fact that sea-floor spreading happens at these locations. In this lab, you will model the formation of new sea floor at a divergent boundary. You will also model the formation of magnetic patterns on the sea floor.

Procedure

1. Cut two identical strips of unlined paper, each 7 cm wide and 30 cm long.
2. Cut a slit 8 cm long in the center of the bottom of a shoebox.
3. Lay the strips of paper together on top of each other and end-to-end so that the ends line up. Push one end of the strips through the slit in the shoe box, so that a few centimeters of both strips stick out of the slit.
4. Place the shoe box flat on a table, open side down, and make sure the ends of the paper strips are sticking up.

Step 3

282

The **Chapter Lab** at the end of the chapter helps you build your understanding of scientific methods. These labs reinforce the chapter with hands-on activity.

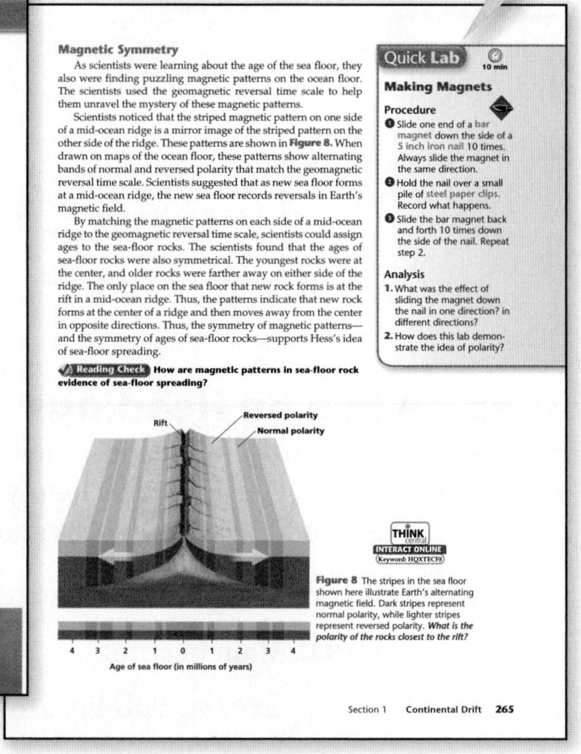

Magnetic Symmetry

As scientists were learning about the age of the sea floor, they also were finding puzzling magnetic patterns on the ocean floor. The scientists used the geomagnetic reversal time scale to help them unravel the mystery of these magnetic patterns.

Scientists noticed that the striped magnetic pattern on one side of a mid-ocean ridge is a mirror image of the striped pattern on the other side of the ridge. These patterns are shown in **Figure 8.** When drawn on maps of the ocean floor, these patterns show alternating bands of normal and reversed polarity that match the geomagnetic reversal time scale. Scientists suggested that as new sea floor forms at a mid-ocean ridge, the new sea floor records reversals in Earth's magnetic field.

By matching the magnetic patterns on each side of a mid-ocean ridge to the geomagnetic reversal time scale, scientists could assign ages to the sea-floor rocks. The scientists found that the ages of sea-floor rocks were also symmetrical. The youngest rocks were at the center, and older rocks were farther away on either side of the ridge. The only place on the sea floor that new rock forms is at the rift in a mid-ocean ridge. Thus, the patterns indicate that new rock forms at the center of a ridge and then moves away from the center in opposite directions. Thus, the symmetry of magnetic patterns—and the symmetry of ages of sea-floor rocks—supports Hess's idea of sea-floor spreading.

Reading Check **How are magnetic patterns in sea-floor rock evidence of sea-floor spreading?**

Quick **Lab** 10 min

Making Magnets

Procedure

1. Slide one end of a bar magnet down the side of a 5 inch iron nail 10 times. Always slide the magnet in the same direction.
2. Hold the nail over a small pile of steel paper clips. Record what happens.
3. Slide the bar magnet back and forth 10 times down the side of the nail. Repeat step 2.

Analysis

1. What was the effect of sliding the magnet down the nail in one direction? in different directions?
2. How does this lab demonstrate the idea of polarity?

Figure 8 The stripes in the sea floor shown here illustrate Earth's alternating magnetic field. Dark stripes represent normal polarity, while lighter stripes represent reversed polarity. ***What is the polarity of the rocks closest to the rift?***

Section 1 Continental Drift 265

Review What You Have Learned

You can't review too much when you are learning science. To help you review, a **Section Review** appears at the end of every section and a **Chapter Summary** and **Chapter Review** appear at the end of every chapter. These reviews not only help you study for tests but also help further your understanding of the content.

Just a few clicks away, each **Super Summary** gives you even more ways to review and study for tests using a computer and the Internet.

Be sure to read the **Key Ideas** to see how they all fit together. If you need to recall any of the **Key Terms,** the page number on which they appear is given.

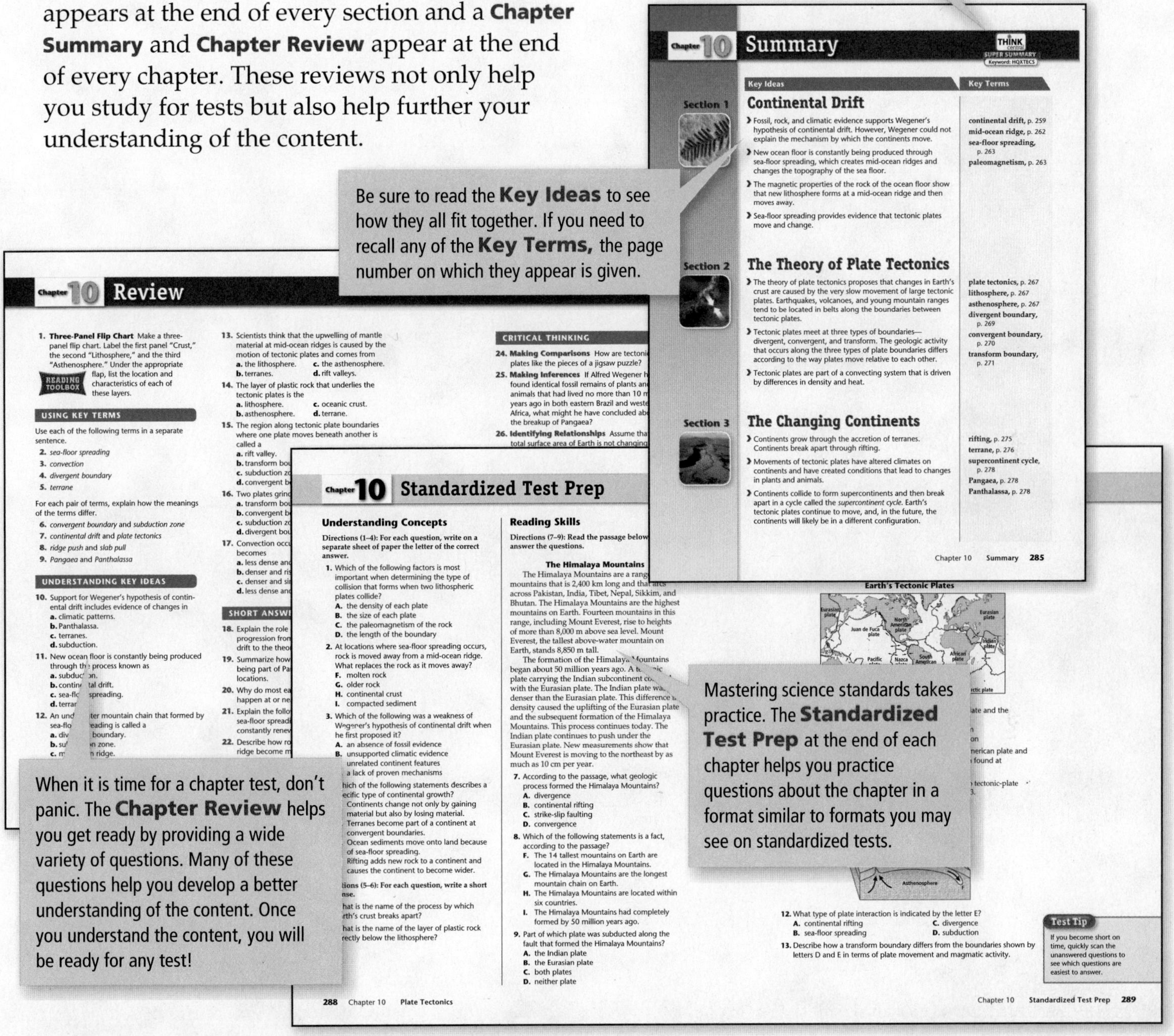

When it is time for a chapter test, don't panic. The **Chapter Review** helps you get ready by providing a wide variety of questions. Many of these questions help you develop a better understanding of the content. Once you understand the content, you will be ready for any test!

Mastering science standards takes practice. The **Standardized Test Prep** at the end of each chapter helps you practice questions about the chapter in a format similar to formats you may see on standardized tests.

Be Resourceful—Use the Web!

THINK central

Your Online Textbook

If your teacher gives you a special password to log onto the thinkcentral.com site, you will find your complete textbook on the Web in an online format. In addition, you will find some great learning tools and interactive materials. You can now access your textbook anywhere and anytime via the Internet.

Take a Test Drive

How well can you use this book now? Take Chapter 1 out for a spin and see how you do. Log onto thinkcentral.com and enter the keyword **HQX TEST DRIVE** for a short list of questions that will test your ability to navigate this book.

Unit 1 Studying the Earth

Chapter Planner 1

Introduction to Earth Science

	Standards	Teach Key Ideas
Chapter Opener, pp. 2–3 — 45 min.	National Science Education Standards	
Section 1 What Is Earth Science, pp. 5–8 — 45 min. ❯ The Scientific Study of Earth ❯ Branches of Earth Science ❯ The Importance of Earth Science	SAI 2a, SAI 2b, SAI 2c, SAI 2f, ST 2a, ST 2b, ST 2d, SPSP 6a, SPSP 6d, HNS 3c	■ ◆ **Bellringer,** p. 5 ■ **Discussion:** Creating Calendars, p. 5 ■ **DI (Special Education Students):** Outlining, p. 7 ◆ **Transparency:** 3 Geologic Features and Political Boundaries in Europe ▲ **Visual Concepts:** Earth Sciences
Section 2 Science as a Process, pp. 9–16 — 45 min. ❯ Behavior of Natural Systems ❯ Scientific Methods ❯ Scientific Measurements and Analysis ❯ Acceptance of Scientific Ideas ❯ Science and Society	SAI 2a, SAI 2b, SAI 2d, SAI 2e, SAI 2f, ST 2a, ST 2b, ST 2d, SPSP 6a, SPSP 6d, UCP 1	■ ◆ **Bellringer,** p. 9 ■ **Discussion:** Influences on Natural Systems, p. 9 ■ **Discussion:** Types of Reasoning, p. 10 ■ **DI (Advanced Learners):** Revised Scientific Theories, p. 10 ■ **Discussion:** Variables and Controls, p. 11 ■ **DI (Special Education Students):** Pacing, p. 13 ■ **Discussion:** Peer-Review Pressure, p. 14 ■ **DI (Advanced Learners):** Essay, p. 14 ■ **Debate:** Should Science Always Be Applied?, p. 15 ◆ **Transparencies:** 1 Scientific Methods • 2 The Importance of Interdisciplinary Science ▲ **Visual Concepts:** Scientific Method • Hypothesis • Controlled Experiment and Variable • Accuracy and Precision • Models • Physical, Mathematical, and Conceptual Models • Comparing Theories and Laws
Chapter Wrap-Up, pp. 21–25 — 90 min.		**Chapter Summary,** p. 21

See also PowerNotes® Presentations

CHAPTER Fast Track *To shorten instruction because of time limitations, omit the Chapter Lab.*

Key

Teacher's Edition ■	Teaching Transparencies ◆
Chapter Resource File ●	Online Edition ▲

All resources listed below are also available on the **Teacher One Stop™.**

Why It Matters	Hands-On	Skills Development	Assessment
■ **Chapter Overview,** p. 2 ■ **Using the Figure:** Racetrack Playa, p. 2	**Inquiry Lab:** How Observant Are You?, p. 3	**Reading Toolbox,** p. 4	
■ **Section Overview,** p. 5 ■ **Using the Figure:** Doing Science, p. 6 **More than a Pretty Picture,** p. 7 ■ **Environmental Connection:** Our Unique Planet, p. 7	■ **Activity:** Not Your Typical Office Job, p. 6 ■ **Group Activity:** Making Maps, p. 20	**Reading Toolbox:** Spider Map, p. 6 ■ ● **Internet Activity:** Ice Cores and Climates, p. 6 ■ **Skill Builder:** Vocabulary, p. 7 **Maps in Action:** Geologic Features and Political Boundaries in Europe, p. 20	**Reading Check,** p. 7 **Section Review,** p. 8 ■ **Reteaching,** p. 8 ■ **Quiz,** p. 8 ■ **DI (Alternative Assessment):** Role Play, p. 8 ● **Section Quiz**
■ **Section Overview,** p. 9 ■ **Using the Figure:** Scientific Methods, p. 10 ■ **Using the Figure:** Levels of Analysis, p. 13 ■ **Technology Connection:** Numbers Become Pictures, p. 13 ■ **Social Studies Connection:** Margin of Error, p. 13	**Quick Lab:** Making Observations, p. 11 ■ **Activity:** Precision and Accuracy, p. 12 **Quick Lab:** Sample Size and Accuracy, p. 12 **Inquiry Lab:** Scientific Methods, pp. 18–19 ● **Inquiry Lab:** What's Before Your Eyes ● **Skills Practice Lab:** Testing a Prediction	■ **Skill Builder:** Reading Organizer, p. 11 ■ **Skill Builder:** Math, p. 12 **Math Skills:** Percentage Error, p. 13 **Reading Toolbox:** Spider Map, p. 14 ■ ● **Internet Activity:** Limitations of Information Systems, p. 15 **Reading Toolbox:** Word Parts, p. 22	**Reading Check,** p. 10 **Reading Check,** p. 13 **Reading Check,** p. 14 **Section Review,** p. 16 ■ **Reteaching,** p. 15 ■ **Quiz,** p. 15 ■ **DI (Alternative Assessment):** Scientific Proposal, p. 16 ● **Section Quiz**
How Do Robots Go to Extremes?, p. 17		▲ **Super Summary** **Standardized Test Prep,** pp. 24–25	**Chapter Review,** pp. 22–23 ■ **DI (Alternative Assessment):** Frontiers of Earth Science, p. 21 ● **Chapter Tests**

See also Lab Generator

See also Holt Online Assessment Resources

Chapter Overview

This chapter introduces students to the branches of Earth science, scientific methods, and the methods of measurement and analysis that they will use in their study of Earth science. In addition, this chapter reminds students about the relationship between science and society.

Using the Figure GENERAL

Racetrack Playa Reinforce the idea that scientists still do not know how rocks, such as the one in the photo, move across the desert floor. Invite students to hypothesize how the rocks may move. Have them suggest ways that they could test their hypotheses. (Answers may vary. Accept all reasonable hypotheses and feasible suggestions for testing them.) LS **Logical**

Why It Matters

The movement of rocks, such as the one depicted here, in an area called *Racetrack Playa,* in California, has intrigued Earth scientists for years. There are many hypotheses as to how rocks that weigh over 320 kg can move more than 880 m; however, none of the hypotheses have been proven.

Chapter 1

Introduction to Earth Science

Chapter Outline

Virginia Standards of Learning
ES.1.f
ES.2.a
ES.2.b
ES.2.c
ES.2.d

Why It Matters

Scientists who study Earth explore the relationships among human society and the air, water, and soil of Earth. They also solve mysteries, such as how this heavy boulder moves on its own across a flat plain in Death Valley, California.

Chapter Correlations

Virginia Standards of Learning

ES.1.f current applications are used to reinforce Earth science concepts.
ES.2.a science explains and predicts the interactions and dynamics of complex Earth systems.
ES.2.b evidence is required to evaluate hypotheses and explanations.
ES.2.c observation and logic are essential for reaching a conclusion.
ES.2.d evidence is evaluated for scientific theories.

Inquiry Lab

15 min

How Observant Are You?

Working in groups, make and record as many observations about your classroom as you can in 10 min. Use a **magnifying glass**, a **thermometer**, and a **meterstick** to help you. Compare your observations with the observations made by other students.

Questions to Get You Started

1. Which of your observations were qualitative? Which were quantitative?
2. Think of a question about your classroom that could be answered by making more observations. What observations would you make to answer your question?

Inquiry Lab

Central Concept: Earth science requires scientists to make observations about the world around them. Every setting offers scope for observation. Students will become familiar with common tools that are used to observe the natural world.

Materials (per group)
- Magnifying glass
- Thermometer
- Meterstick

Skills Acquired
- Observation
- Measurement

Teacher's Notes: You may wish to assign each student in the group a role for the lab. Have one student responsible for each of the lab materials and one student act as the group record-keeper, to write down questions and answers.

Answers to Getting Started

1. Student answers will vary, but may include the following: number of ceiling tiles: quantitative; color of walls: qualitative; number of desks: quantitative; temperature beside window: quantitative.
2. Student answers will vary. Accept all reasonable answers that include a question and observations that might answer the question.

Using THINK central Resources

An online version of this chapter, as well as all the print and multimedia resources that accompany the program are available to registered teachers and their students. Log onto **www.thinkcentral.com** to access these materials and tools to organize your preparation and student learning.

READING TOOLBOX

These reading tools will help you learn the material in this chapter.

Word Parts

Suffixes When you add the suffix *-logy* to a root word or a prefix, you form a word that means "the science of." For example, when you combine *-logy* with the prefix *bio-* (which means "life"), you form the word *biology.* Biology is the study of life.

Your Turn Two key terms in Section 1 use the suffix *-logy.* (Key terms in sections are indicated by bold text with yellow highlights.) Copy the table below and add the second key term.

Key term	Root and its meaning	Suffix	Definition
geology	geo-, means "Earth"	-logy	the study of the origin, history, processes, and structure of the solid Earth

Graphic Organizers

Spider Maps Spider maps show how details are organized into categories that, in turn, are related to a main idea. To make a spider map, follow these steps.

1. For your title, write the main topic. Draw an oval around it.
2. From the oval, draw legs. Each leg represents a category of the main topic.
3. From each leg, draw horizontal lines. Write details about each category on these lines.

Your Turn As you read Section 2, complete a spider map like the one started here to organize the ideas you learn about scientific measurement.

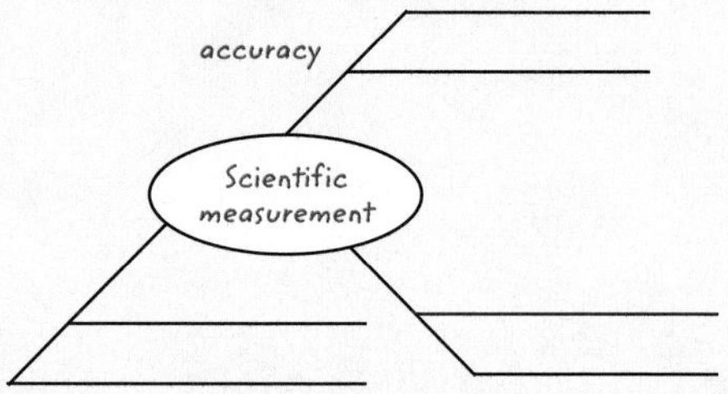

Finding Examples

Words That Signal Examples As you are reading, certain words or phrases can serve as signals that an example is about to be introduced. Two of these signal phrases are "for example" and "such as."

Your Turn In Chapter 1, there are ten sentences with examples that are signaled by "for example" and ten sentences with examples that are signaled by "such as." Search the chapter to find and record three sentences that use "for example" and four sentences that use "such as."

For more information on how to use these and other tools, see **Appendix A.**

READING TOOLBOX

Word Parts

Suffixes Meteorology, meteor+logy, is the study of the atmosphere of a planet, especially Earth, usually focusing on the weather.

Finding Examples

Words that Signal Examples

Sentences with "for example:"

For example, a volcanic eruption may bury a town under ash.

For example, changes in temperature and humidity can cause rain in one city, but the same changes in temperature and humidity may cause fog in another city.

The scientists in **Figure 1,** for example, are studying ice cores in Antarctica.

For example, to test how sunlight affects plants, a scientist would grow identical plants.

For example, a distance that is measured in millimeters is more precise than a distance that is measured in centimeters.

For example, imagine that the average length of all of the ears of corn in a field is 23 cm, and 90% of the ears are within 3 cm of the average length.

Sentences with "such as:"

By understanding how natural forces shape our environment, Earth scientists, such as those in **Figure 3,** can better predict potential disasters and help save lives and property.

The ability to make observations improves when technology, such as new processes or equipment, is developed.

These different results might be due to differences in the two cities or due to complex issues, such as differences in climate.

Simple questions such as these have fueled years of scientific research and have been investigated through scientific methods.

Scientists commonly present the results of their work in scientific journals or at professional meetings, such as the one shown in **Figure 6**.

DEPTHX, an underwater rover, can be lowered hundreds of meters into deep, uncharted sinkholes such as Zacatón cenote in central Mexico.

Graphic Organizers

Spider Map

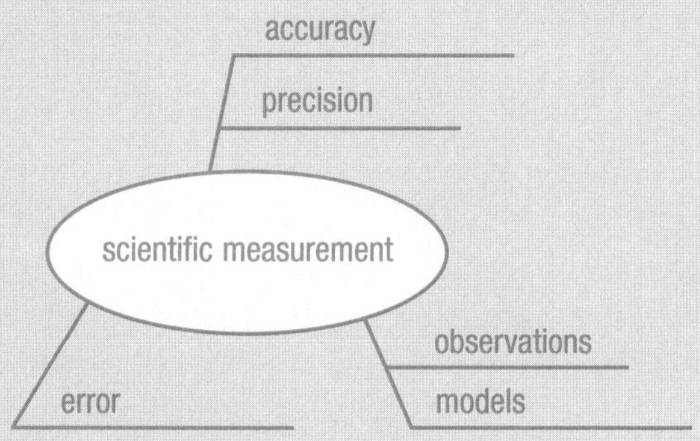

SECTION 1 What Is Earth Science?

Key Ideas	Key Terms	Why It Matters
❯ Describe two cultures that contributed to modern scientific study. ❯ Name the four main branches of Earth science. ❯ Discuss how Earth scientists help us understand the world around us.	Earth science geology oceanography meteorology astronomy	Earth scientists help us understand our place in Earth's history and in the universe. They can also help us gain access to Earth's resources and use these resources wisely.

For thousands of years, people have looked at the world around them and wondered what forces shaped it. Throughout history, many cultures have been terrified and fascinated by seeing volcanoes erupt, feeling the ground shake during an earthquake, or watching the sky darken during an eclipse.

Some cultures developed myths or stories to explain these events. Modern science searches for natural causes and uses careful observations to explain these same events and to understand Earth and its changing landscape.

The Scientific Study of Earth

Scientific study of Earth began with careful observations. Scientists in China began keeping records of earthquakes as early as 780 BCE. The ancient Greeks compiled a catalog of rocks and minerals around 200 BCE. Other ancient peoples, including the Maya, tracked the movements of the sun, the moon, and the planets at observatories like the one shown in **Figure 1.** The Maya used these observations to create accurate calendars.

For many centuries, scientific discoveries were limited to observations of phenomena that could be seen with the unaided eye. Then, in the 16th and 17th centuries, the inventions of the microscope and the telescope made seeing previously hidden worlds possible. Eventually, the body of knowledge about Earth became known as Earth science. **Earth science** is the study of Earth and of the universe around it. Earth science, like other sciences, assumes that natural events, or phenomena, can be explained through careful observation and experimentation.

Earth science the scientific study of Earth and the universe around it

Figure 1 El Caracol, an observatory built by the ancient Maya of Central America, is one of the oldest known observatories in the Americas. Mayan calendars include the celestial movements that the Maya tracked by using observatories.

Section 1

Focus

Overview

This section defines Earth science and describes its branches of study. This section also explains why the scientific study of Earth is important.

Bellringer

Ask students why it is important to study Earth science. (Answers may vary. Accept all reasonable answers.) **LS Logical/Verbal**

Motivate

Discussion — GENERAL

Creating Calendars The Maya, Chinese, and other early peoples created calendars based on observations of the sun, moon, planets, and stars. Have students discuss why humans create calendars and how having a calendar enhances a culture and helps people. (Answers may vary. Accept all reasonable answers. Sample answer: Calendars help with agriculture and provide an order for seasonal or religious rites and holidays.) **LS Logical/Verbal**

Key Resources

Chapter Resource File
- Directed Reading BASIC

Technology
- Transparencies
  Bellringer

Teach

Using the Figure ADVANCED

Doing Science Have students describe what each scientist in the figure at the bottom of the page is doing. Have them explain how technology is helping each scientist conduct his or her research. Interested students may research one type of technology shown in the figure and write about how it was developed and how it is used in Earth science. (Students should describe how each type of technology was developed and how scientists use it to gather information that may lead to new scientific discoveries.)
LS Logical/Visual

READING TOOLBOX

Spider Map
See p. 81A for sample answers.

Internet Activity ADVANCED

Ice Cores and Climate Have interested students use the Internet to research how ice-core research is used to study ancient Earth climates as a way to learn about climate change today. Students may write a report or present their findings to the class for discussion. A worksheet designed to direct student research on this topic can be found in the **Chapter Resource File** booklet or by visiting www.thinkcentral.com and entering the keyword **HQXIESX.**
LS Logical/Verbal

READING TOOLBOX

Spider Map
Create a spider map that summarizes the branches of Earth science. Use the green heads in this section as the legs of your spider map, and add one or two branches to each leg.

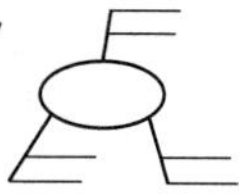

Branches of Earth Science

The ability to make observations improves when technology, such as new processes or equipment, is developed. Technology has allowed scientists to explore the ocean depths, Earth's unseen interior, and the vastness of space. Earth scientists have used technology and hard work to build an immense body of knowledge about Earth.

Most Earth scientists specialize in one of four major areas of study: the solid Earth, the oceans, the atmosphere, and the universe beyond Earth. Examples of Earth scientists working in these areas are shown in **Figure 2.**

Geology

geology the scientific study of the origin, history, and structure of Earth and the processes that shape Earth

oceanography the scientific study of the ocean, including the properties and movements of ocean water, the characteristics of the ocean floor, and the organisms that live in the ocean

The study of the origin, history, processes, and structure of the solid Earth is called **geology.** Geology includes many specialized areas of study. Some geologists explore Earth's crust for deposits of coal, oil, gas, and other resources. Other geologists study the forces within Earth to predict earthquakes and volcanic eruptions. Some geologists study fossils to learn more about Earth's past. Often, new knowledge forms new areas of study.

Oceanography

Academic Vocabulary
technology (tek NAHL uh jee) tools, including electronic devices

Oceans cover nearly three-fourths of Earth's surface. The study of Earth's oceans is called **oceanography.** Some oceanographers work on research ships that are equipped with special instruments for studying the sea. Other oceanographers study waves, tides, and ocean currents. Some oceanographers explore the ocean floor to obtain clues to Earth's history or to locate mineral deposits.

Figure 2 Fields of Study in Earth Science

Geologists who study volcanoes are called volcanologists. This volcanologist is measuring the properties of moving lava.

This astronomer is linking a telescope with a specialized instrument called a spectrograph. Information gathered will help her catalog the composition of more than 100 galaxies.

This meteorologist is studying ice samples to learn about past climate. Studying past climate patterns gives scientists information about possible future changes in climate.

Activity GENERAL

Not Your Typical Office Job Invite interested students to describe what it would be like to have a career in one of the branches of Earth science discussed in the text. Have students talk about whether this type of career would allow them to spend time outdoors, whether it would allow them to travel, and whether it would involve adventure or danger. Have students discuss why they would or would not be interested in learning about careers in a branch of Earth science. Explain to students that most jobs in science require advanced college degrees, although some technical jobs may not. Have interested students find out about the various careers available in a particular branch of Earth science, the training needed, and what the careers entail.
LS Intrapersonal

Why It Matters

More than a Pretty Picture

Scientists use a variety of instruments and methods to study Earth. For example, common methods for studying climate change include analyzing ice cores and tree rings. Now, one innovative scientist has turned instead to art. Scientists know that volcanic ash in the atmosphere blocks sunlight, which causes temperatures to drop. Could painting shed light on past temperatures?

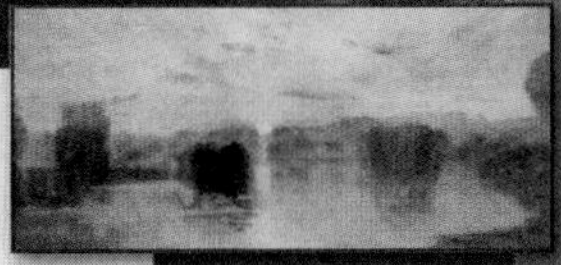

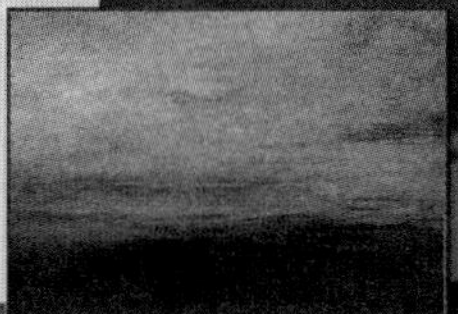

J.M.W. Turner made the top painting three years before a volcanic eruption in the Philippines in 1831. He made the bottom painting in 1833. The redder sunset in the bottom painting was caused by volcanic ash.

YOUR TURN CRITICAL THINKING
How could studying paintings by different artists affect scientists' conclusions?

Meteorology

The study of Earth's atmosphere is called **meteorology**. Using satellites, radar, and other technologies, meteorologists study the atmospheric conditions that produce weather. Many meteorologists work as weather observers and measure factors such as wind speed, temperature, and rainfall. This weather information is then used to prepare detailed weather maps. Other meteorologists use weather maps, satellite images, and computer models to make weather forecasts. Some meteorologists study *climate*, the patterns of weather that occur over long periods of time.

meteorology the scientific study of Earth's atmosphere, especially in relation to weather and climate

astronomy the scientific study of the universe

Astronomy

The study of the universe beyond Earth is called **astronomy.** Astronomy is one of the oldest branches of Earth science. In fact, the ancient Babylonians charted the positions of planets and stars nearly 4,000 years ago. Modern astronomers use Earth-based and space-based telescopes as well as other instruments to study the sun, the moon, the planets, and the universe. Technologies such as rovers and space probes have also provided astronomers with new information about the universe.

SCILINKS.
www.scilinks.org
Topic: Branches of Earth Science
Code: **HQX0191**

Reading Check **What information is used for weather maps?** (See Appendix G for answers to Reading Checks.)

Why It Matters

More than a Pretty Picture

The record for measurements of atmospheric phenomena related to climate change is not continuous. For example, direct measurement of carbon-dioxide concentrations in the atmosphere began in 1958. Climate change models depend heavily on proxy data, collected from natural sources such as ice cores, tree rings, and historical documents such as the logs of mariners and farmers. Dr. Christos Zerefos, a professor of atmospheric physics, has added art to the list of historical sources from which scientists can infer information about past climate conditions.

Zerefos measured the ratio of red-to-green used to paint sunsets in 554 paintings by 181 artists from 1500 to 1900—a period when 11 major volcanic eruptions took place. Zerefos classified 54 paintings, by 19 different artists, as "volcanic sunset paintings." In these paintings, the red-to-green ratio is higher than it is in "non-volcanic sunset paintings." Thus, art acts as a source of climate-related information.

Answer to Your Turn

Critical Thinking Different artists might interpret and/or represent color in their paintings in different ways, making the information unreliable for scientists.

Skill Builder — GENERAL

Vocabulary Point out that the names of some of the Earth sciences end with the suffix *-ology*. Tell students that this suffix comes from the Latin *logia*, which means "science (of)." Invite students to name as many fields of science that contain the suffix *-ology* as they can. (Answers may vary.) **LS Verbal**

Answer to Reading Check

Meteorologists use information gathered by satellites, radar, and other technologies on factors such as wind speed, temperature, and rainfall to create weather maps.

Differentiated Instruction

Special Education Students

Outlining Create an outline system appropriate for this chapter and set tabs at one-half inch. For example, Roman numerals could be used for section heads, capital letters could be used for large subheads, Arabic numbers could be used for small subheads, and lowercase letters could be used for additional notes. Have students who have handwriting issues type chapter notes on a computer instead of writing them by hand.
LS Visual

Environmental Connection

Our Unique Planet While Earth may seem to be so large that humans can have no major effect on it, human activities have been putting our environmental support system at risk. Because all of Earth's systems are related, small changes in one system may have drastic effects on other systems.

Close

Reteaching BASIC

Picture This Provide posters or magazines that show pictures of scientists engaged in each branch of Earth science. As students read, have them correlate what is shown in each picture to the Earth science described in the text. English Language Learners
LS **Visual**

Quiz GENERAL

1. What 17th century advances in technology helped advance scientific research? (the invention of the microscope and telescope)
2. What Earth processes do geologists study to try to save lives? (earthquakes and volcanoes)

Answers to Section Review

1. Answers may vary. Accept all reasonable answers.
2. geology, oceanography, astronomy, and meteorology
3. Answers may vary. Accept all reasonable answers.
4. Oceanographers study ocean currents, tides, and waves. Meteorologists study weather patterns and predict storms.
5. Telescopes, satellites, and space probes have expanded astronomers' view of the universe.
6. Earth scientists have helped us understand the forces that shape Earth and thus shape the environment we live in. Their understanding helps us predict geologic events and helps us find Earth resources we need.
7. Both are inhospitable environments for humans and require the use of special equipment for humans to study them.
8. *Earth science* includes the fields of *geology; meteorology,* which includes the study of *climate; environmental science; astronomy;* and *oceanography.*

Figure 3 These meteorologists are risking their lives to gather information about tornadoes. If scientists can better predict when tornadoes will occur, many lives may be saved each year.

Environmental Science and Earth Science

Some Earth scientists study the ways in which humans interact with their environment in a relatively new field of science called *environmental science*. Many fields of study, such as Earth science, biology, and the social sciences, contribute to environmental science. The goal of environmental science is to understand and solve problems that result from how we use natural resources and how our actions affect the environment.

The Importance of Earth Science

Natural forces not only shape Earth but also affect life on Earth. For example, a volcanic eruption may bury a town under ash. And an earthquake may produce huge ocean waves that destroy shorelines. By understanding how natural forces shape our environment, Earth scientists, such as those in **Figure 3,** can better predict potential disasters and help save lives and property.

The work of Earth scientists also helps us understand our place in the universe. Astronomers studying distant galaxies have come up with new ideas about the origins of our universe. Geologists studying rock layers have found clues to Earth's past environments and to the evolution of life on this planet.

Earth provides the resources that make life as we know it possible. Earth also provides the materials to enrich the quality of people's lives. The fuel that powers a jet, the metal used in surgical instruments, and the paper and ink in this book all come from Earth's resources. The study of Earth science can help people gain access to Earth's resources, but Earth scientists also strive to help people use those resources wisely.

Section 1 Review

Key Ideas

1. **Discuss** how one culture contributed to modern science.
2. **Name** the four major branches of Earth science.
3. **Describe** two specialized fields of geology.
4. **Describe** the work of oceanographers and meteorologists.
5. **Explain** how the work of astronomers has been affected by technology.

Critical Thinking

6. **Analyzing Ideas** How have Earth scientists improved our understanding of the environment?
7. **Analyzing Concepts** Give two examples of how exploring space and exploring the ocean depths are similar.

Concept Mapping

8. Use the following terms to create a concept map: *Earth science, geology, meteorology, climate, environmental science, astronomy,* and *oceanography.*

Differentiated Instruction

Alternative Assessment

Role Play Divide students into groups, and have each group role play being scientists in one branch of Earth science. Ask students to explain what they do and to bring in tools (or models and pictures of tools) that they would use. Encourage students to describe how their branch of Earth science helps people and expands human understanding of the world and the universe. LS **Kinesthetic**

SECTION 2
Science as a Process

Key Ideas

- Explain how science is different from other forms of human endeavor.
- Identify the steps that make up scientific methods.
- Analyze how scientific thought changes as new information is collected.
- Explain how science affects society.

Key Terms

observation
hypothesis
independent variable
dependent variable
peer review
theory

Why It Matters

Science helps us understand Earth, nature, and the universe. Science also helps us apply our knowledge to develop technologies which, in turn, help us solve problems and improve the condition of human society.

Art, architecture, philosophy, and science are all forms of human endeavor. Although artists, architects, and philosophers may use science in their work, science does not have the same goals as other human endeavors do.

The goal of science is to explain natural phenomena. Scientists ask questions about natural events and then work to answer those questions through experiments and examination. Scientific understanding moves forward through the work of many scientists, who build on the research of the generations of scientists before them.

Behavior of Natural Systems

Scientists start with the assumption that nature is understandable, and they expect that similar forces in a similar situation will cause similar results. But the forces involved in natural events are complex. For example, changes in temperature and humidity can cause rain in one city, but the same changes in temperature and humidity may cause fog in another city. These different results might be due to differences in the two cities or due to complex issues, such as differences in climate.

Scientists also expect that nature is predictable, which means that the future behavior of natural forces can be anticipated. So, if scientists understand the forces and materials involved in a process, they can predict how that process will evolve. The scientists in **Figure 1**, for example, are studying ice cores in Antarctica. Ice cores can provide clues to Earth's past climate changes. Because natural systems are complex, however, a high level of understanding and predictability can be difficult to achieve. To increase their understanding, scientists follow the same basic processes of studying and describing natural events.

Figure 1 Scientists use ice cores to study past compositions of Earth's atmosphere. This information can help scientists learn about past climate changes.

Section 2

Focus

This section describes scientific methods and analyzes how scientific thought changes as new data are uncovered. This section also describes how science and society are interrelated.

Bellringer

Ask students what they think are the goals of the following human endeavors: art, architecture, philosophy, sports, and politics. (Answers may vary. Accept all reasonable answers.)
LS Intrapersonal/Interpersonal

Motivate

Discussion GENERAL

Influences on Natural Systems
Ask students if they have ever planted seeds. Then ask them why different plants of the same species may grow at different rates. Have them list all the reasons they can think of. (Answers may vary. Students may suggest that environmental variables, such as soil, nutrients, water, air, and light, influence how well a plant grows.) **LS Logical**

Key Resources

Chapter Resource File
- Directed Reading BASIC
- Inquiry Lab: What's Before Your Eyes? GENERAL
- Skills Practice Lab: Testing a Prediction GENERAL

Technology
- Transparencies
  Bellringer

Teach

Using the Figure GENERAL

Scientific Methods Direct students' attention to the diagram at the bottom of the page, and emphasize that this is a basic flowchart to be used as a guideline for scientific inquiry. Have them review the steps. Ask students how it is possible to go from Drawing Conclusions back to Asking Questions within the steps. (Sometimes, experimentation leads to new questions.) **LS Logical/Verbal**

Discussion GENERAL

Types of Reasoning Explain to students that scientists use two types of reasoning to help them solve problems. Inductive reasoning involves starting from a specific fact or a single case and then forming a general conclusion. Deductive reasoning involves starting with a general, known principle and then drawing a conclusion about one particular case. Have students give examples of ways they might use each type of reasoning in their everyday lives. Then, guide students in a discussion about why both types of reasoning are useful in scientific investigations. **LS Verbal**

Answer to Reading Check

Observations may lead to interesting scientific questions and may help scientists formulate reasonable and testable hypotheses.

Scientific Methods

Over time, the scientific community has developed organized and logical approaches to scientific research. These approaches are known as *scientific methods.* Scientific methods are not a set of sequential steps that scientists always follow. Rather, these methods are guidelines to scientific problem solving. **Figure 2** shows a basic flowchart of scientific methods.

Ask a Question

observation the process of obtaining information by using the senses; the information obtained by using the senses

hypothesis a testable idea or explanation that leads to scientific investigation

Scientific methods often begin with observations. **Observation** is the process of using the senses of sight, touch, taste, hearing, and smell to gather information about the world. When you see thunderclouds form in the summer sky, you are making an observation. And when you feel cool, smooth, polished marble or hear the roar of river rapids, you are making observations.

Observations can often lead to questions. What causes tornadoes to form? Why is oil discovered only in certain locations? What causes a river to change its course? What causes some plants to grow faster than others? Simple questions such as these have fueled years of scientific research and have been investigated through scientific methods.

Form a Hypothesis

SCILINKS.
www.scilinks.org
Topic: Scientific Methods
Code: **HQX1359**

Once a question has been asked and basic information has been gathered, a scientist may propose a tentative answer, which is also known as a hypothesis (hie PAHTH uh sis). A **hypothesis** (plural, *hypotheses*) is a possible explanation or solution to a problem. Hypotheses can be developed through close and careful observation. Most hypotheses are based on known facts about similar events. One example of a hypothesis is that plants that are given a large amount of sunlight will grow faster than plants given a smaller amount of sunlight. This hypothesis could be made from observing how and where other plants grow.

Reading Check **Name two ways scientific methods depend on careful observations.**

Figure 2 Scientific Method Flowchart

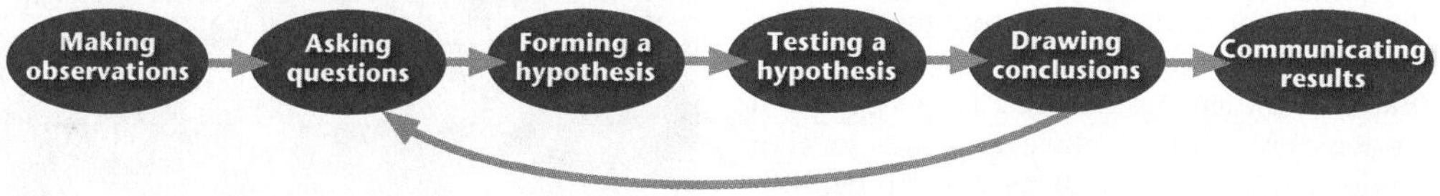

Key Resources

Technology

- Transparencies
  1 Scientific Methods

Differentiated Instruction

Advanced Learners

Revised Scientific Theories Have students research a scientific theory that is no longer accepted, such as a theory about Earth's shape or the phlogiston theory of combustion. Ask them to write a few paragraphs explaining why the theory was originally accepted, why it was later replaced, and what it was replaced by. **LS Verbal**

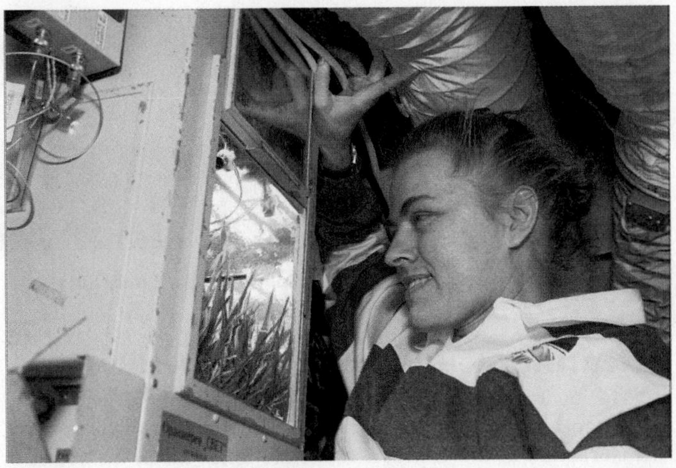

Figure 3 Astronaut Shannon Lucid observes wheat plants as a part of a controlled experiment in orbit around Earth.

independent variable in an experiment, the factor that is deliberately manipulated

dependent variable in an experiment, the factor that changes as a result of manipulation of one or more other factors (the independent variables)

Test the Hypothesis

After a hypothesis is proposed, it is often tested by performing experiments. An *experiment* is a procedure that is carried out according to certain guidelines. Factors that can be changed in an experiment are variables. **Independent variables** are factors that are changed by the person performing the experiment. **Dependent variables** are variables that change as a result of a change in independent variables.

In most experiments, only one independent variable is tested. For example, to test how sunlight affects plants, a scientist would grow identical plants. The plants would receive the same amount of water and fertilizer but different amounts of sunlight. Thus, sunlight would be the independent variable. How the plants respond to the different amounts of sunlight would be the dependent variable. Most experiments include a control group. A *control group* is a group that serves as a standard of comparison with another group to which the control group is identical except for one factor. In this experiment, the plants that receive a natural amount of sunlight would be the control group. An experiment that contains a control is called a *controlled experiment*. Most scientific experiments are controlled experiments. The "zero gravity" experiment shown in **Figure 3** is a controlled experiment.

Draw Conclusions

After many experiments and observations, a scientist may reach conclusions about his or her hypothesis. If the hypothesis fits the known facts, it may be accepted as true. If the experimental results differ from what was expected, the hypothesis may be changed or discarded. Expected and unexpected results lead to new questions and further study. The results of scientific inquiry may also lead to new knowledge and new methods of inquiry that further scientific aims.

Quick Lab 5 min

Making Observations

Procedure

1. Get an ordinary candle of any shape and color.
2. Record all the observations you can make about the candle.
3. Light the candle with a match, and watch it burn for 1 min.
4. Record as many observations about the burning candle as you can. When you are finished, extinguish the flame. Record any observations.

Analysis

1. Share your results with your class. How many things that your classmates observed did you not observe? Explain this phenomenon.

Discussion — GENERAL

Variables and Controls Have students discuss why it is important to study only one independent variable at a time in an experiment. Ask how having more than one independent variable or one experimental control would affect the results of the experiment. Ask why it is important to be able to compare results involving manipulated variables with an unmanipulated control. (Students should be aware that having too many variables makes identifying the source of a change difficult. A control shows whether the independent variable resulted in any observable difference from "normal.")

LS Logical/Verbal

Quick Lab

Skills Acquired

- Observing

Materials

- Candle
- Match

Teacher's Notes: You may want to explain to students that independent variables are also known as *manipulated variables* and dependent variables are also known as *responding variables*. Help students identify each during this Quick Lab.

Answer to Analysis

Answers may vary. Accept all reasonable answers. Differences in observations may be based on wick size, slight environmental differences in different parts of the room, and how closely students are watching.

Skill Builder — BASIC

Reading Organizer As students read about scientific methods, have them write an outline that lists all the steps discussed in this section and describes what each step involves. Later, students may use their outline as a study guide for assessments.

LS Verbal

Activity — BASIC

Precision and Accuracy Divide students into groups to measure their desktops. Each group should use a different method of measurement. Groups should use one of the following units: inches, millimeters, the length of the first thumb joint, or the length of a student's foot. Have groups share their measurements, and then discuss which units of measure are the most and least accurate and precise. (Most accurate and precise may vary, but should be millimeters or inches. Least accurate and precise should be foot and thumb-joint length.) **LS Logical**

Skill Builder — GENERAL

Math Have students measure the dimensions of objects in the classroom, such as a piece of notebook paper, the board, and a shoebox, using standard units. Then, have students use this table to convert the measurements to SI units:

1 inch = 2.54 cm
1 foot = 0.3048 m
1 yard = 0.91 m

You may want to have pairs of students measure the same objects and check their conversions against the measurements of other pairs of students.
LS Logical

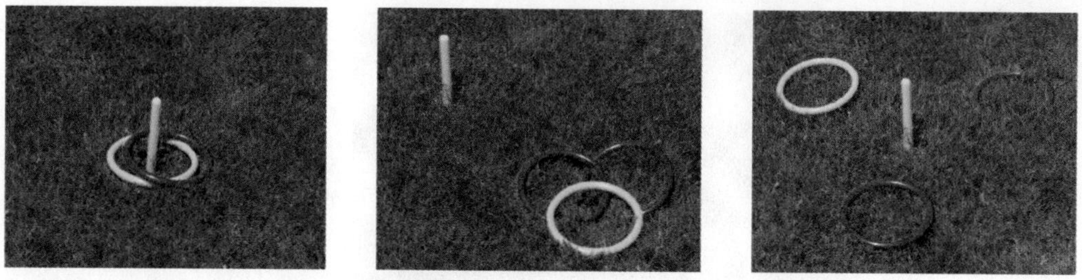

Good accuracy and good precision | **Poor accuracy but good precision** | **Good overall accuracy but poor precision**

Figure 4 Accuracy and Precision

THINK central
INTERACT ONLINE
Keyword: HQXIESF4

Scientific Measurements and Analysis

During an experiment, scientists must gather information. An important method of gathering information is measurement. Measurement is the comparison of some aspect of an object or event with a standard unit. Scientists around the world can compare and analyze each other's measurements because scientists use a common system of measurement called the *International System of Units*, or SI. This system includes standard measurements for length, mass, temperature, and volume. All SI units are based on intervals of 10. The Reference Tables section of the Appendix contains a chart of SI units.

Accuracy and Precision

Accuracy and precision are important in scientific measurements. *Accuracy* refers to how close a measurement is to the true value of the thing being measured. *Precision* is the exactness of the measurement. For example, a distance that is measured in millimeters is more precise than a distance that is measured in centimeters. Measurements can be precise and yet inaccurate. The relationship between accuracy and precision is shown in **Figure 4.**

Quick Lab — Sample Size and Accuracy

15 min

Procedure

1. Shuffle a deck of 52 playing cards eight times.
2. Lay out 10 cards. Record the number of red cards.
3. Reshuffle, and repeat step 2 four more times.
4. Which trials showed the highest number and lowest number of red cards? Calculate the total range of red cards by finding the difference between the highest number and lowest number.
5. Determine the mean number of red cards per trial by adding the number of red cards in the five trials and then dividing by 5.

Analysis

1. A deck of cards has 50% red cards. How close is your average to the percentage of red cards in the deck?
2. Pool the results of your classmates. How close is the new average to the percentage of red cards in the deck?
3. How does changing the sample size affect accuracy?

Quick Lab

Skills Acquired
- Observing
- Analyzing

Materials
- Deck of 52 playing cards

Teacher's Notes: You may want to have students work in pairs or in larger groups, depending on the number of card decks you have. However, the more groups that participate, the larger the sample size will be.

Answers to Analysis
1. Answers may vary.
2. Answers may vary, but the new average should be closer to 50%.
3. The larger the sample size is, the more accurate the results will be.

Error

Error is an expression of the amount of imprecision or variation in a set of measurements. Error is commonly expressed as percentage error or as a confidence interval. Percentage error is the percentage of deviation of an experimental value from an accepted value. A *confidence interval* describes the range of values for a set percentage of measurements. For example, imagine that the average length of all of the ears of corn in a field is 23 cm, and 90% of the ears are within 3 cm of the average length. A scientist may report that the average length of all of the ears of corn in a field is 23 ± 3 cm with 90% confidence.

Observations and Models

In Earth science, using controlled experiments to test a hypothesis is often impossible. When experiments are impossible, scientists make additional observations to gather evidence. The hypothesis is then tested by examining how well the hypothesis fits or explains all of the known evidence.

Scientists also use models to simulate conditions in the natural world. A *model* is a description, representation, or imitation of an object, system, process, or concept. Scientists use several types of models, two of which are shown in **Figure 5.** Physical models are three-dimensional models that can be touched. Maps and charts are examples of graphical models.

Conceptual models are verbal or graphical models that represent how a system works or is organized. Mathematical models are mathematical equations that represent the way a system or process works. Computer models are a kind of mathematical model that use the high speed and efficiency of a computer to make calculations and display results. After a good computer model has been created, scientists can perform experiments by manipulating variables much as they would when performing a physical experiment.

Reading Check **Name three types of models.**

Math Skills

Percentage Error
Percentage error is calculated by using the following equation:

$$\text{percent error} = \left[\frac{(\text{accepted value} - \text{experimental value})}{\text{accepted value}}\right] \times 100$$

If the accepted value for the weight of a gallon of water is 3.78 kg and the measured value is 3.72 kg, what is the percentage error for the measurement? Show your work.

Figure 5 Two models of Mount Everest are shown below. The computer model on the right is used to track erosion along the Tibetan Plateau. The model on the left is a physical model.

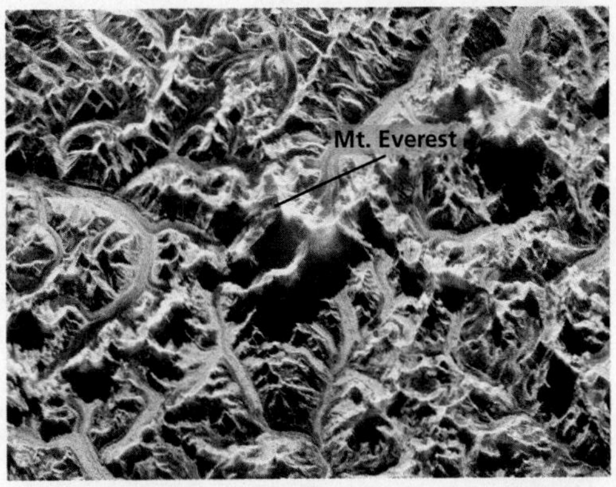

Math Skills

Answer

% error = [(accepted value − experimental value) ÷ accepted value] × 100

[(3.78 kg − 3.72 kg) ÷ 3.78 kg] × 100 = 1.59%

Social Studies Connection — GENERAL

Margin of Error Polls are often taken before elections to see which candidate people prefer and to attempt to forecast the outcome. As in scientific measurements, polls contain a percentage—or margin—of error. Ask students the following question: If 47% of people polled say they like candidate A and 44% say they like candidate B, and the margin of error is plus or minus 3%, which candidate will likely get elected? (You cannot tell because the margin of error makes them even.) Have students discuss why it is important to note the percentage of error in polls and other types of statistics they may come across in daily life. (Without understanding the percent error, the poll numbers may seem more conclusive than they really are.) **LS Logical**

Answer to Reading Check

Answers may vary but should include three of the following types of models: physical models, graphic models, conceptual models, computer models, and mathematical models.

Using the Figure — BASIC

Levels of Analysis Have students discuss the differences in scale they see in the two models shown in the figure. Ask students in what context each model would be more useful. (The physical model is more useful for smaller scale analysis of fine details of the mountain itself, while the satellite image is more useful in a larger context in which the subject, Mt. Everest, is seen relative to a wide area around it.) **LS Visual/Logical**

Technology Connection — GENERAL

Numbers Become Pictures Most computer models are visual representations of mathematical formulas. Data are entered into a formula, and a software program solves the equation. What is seen on the computer screen is a picture of how the data act within the equation. Even a graphic, such as the satellite image on this page, may be created from numerical data. Satellite equipment measures the heights of objects on Earth. These measurements may then be converted into an image that shows the relative heights of the objects.

Differentiated Instruction

Special Education Students

Pacing Some students can concentrate better on what they are reading if they walk while they read. Allow those who think best on the move to pace in the back of the room while reading the text. If too many students want to walk and read, or if the room is too small, ask students to read the text at home. Invite all students to try walking while they read. **LS Kinesthetic**

Teach, *continued*

READING TOOLBOX GENERAL

Spider Map See page 81A for sample answers.

MISCONCEPTION ALERT

Reproducible Truth Students may think that all scientific studies mentioned in the media are true and absolute. This is not the case. Sometimes, peer reviewers accept a scientific study because the methods were careful and correct, data were accurately analyzed, and findings were reasonable. However, this does not mean that the findings are necessarily true. A prime criterion for accepting any scientific findings is that the experiment or study be reproducible. Once a study is published, other scientists attempt to repeat the experiment. If many scientists get the same results, it is likely that the original findings were correct. But if some or many scientists do not get the same results, it is likely that the original findings were incorrect or incomplete. Many experiments must be performed with the same results before the findings are accepted. Thus, it should not be assumed that one study reveals an absolute scientific truth.

Answer to Reading Check

Scientists present the results of their work at professional meetings and in scientific journals.

Figure 6 Meteorologists at a conference in California are watching the "Science On a Sphere™" exhibit. They are wearing 3-D glasses to better see the complex and changing three-dimensional display of global temperatures.

READING TOOLBOX

Spider Map

Create a spider map that outlines the process that new scientific ideas go through before they are accepted by the scientific community. Label the center of your spider map "Acceptance of a new scientific idea," and create a leg for each part of the process. Add details about each part of the process to its corresponding leg.

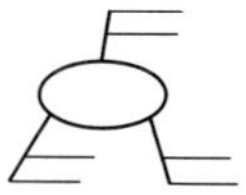

Acceptance of Scientific Ideas

When scientists reach a conclusion, they introduce their findings to the scientific community. New scientific ideas undergo review and testing by other scientists before the ideas are accepted.

Publication of Results and Conclusions

Scientists commonly present the results of their work in scientific journals or at professional meetings, such as the one shown in **Figure 6.** Results published in journals are usually written in a standard scientific format. Many journals are now being published online to allow scientists quicker access to the results of other scientists and to reduce the costs of printing journals.

Peer Review

Scientists in any one research group tend to view scientific ideas similarly. Therefore, they may be biased in their experimental design or data analysis. To reduce bias, scientists submit their ideas to other scientists for peer review. **Peer review** is the process in which several experts on a given topic review another expert's work on that topic before the work gets published. These experts determine if the results and conclusions of the study merit publication. Peer reviewers commonly suggest improvements to the study, or they may determine that the results or conclusions are flawed and recommend that the study not be published. Scientists follow an ethical code that states that only valid experimental results should be published. The peer review process serves as a filter that allows only well-supported ideas to be published.

peer review the process in which experts in a given field examine the results and conclusions of a scientist's study before that study is accepted for publication

Reading Check **Name two places scientists present the results of their work.**

Discussion GENERAL

Peer-Review Pressure Ask students which task they would give more careful attention to: a task that is to be handed in and graded or a task that no one will check. Invite students to apply this concept to peer review of scientific work. Have students talk about how peer review motivates scientists to be extremely careful, accurate, and thorough in experimental design, data collection, and reporting. Invite students to discuss whether peer review is more important in science than in other fields and to give reasons for their answers. LS **Interpersonal/Intrapersonal**

Differentiated Instruction

Advanced Learners

Essay Have students write an essay about the importance of the peer review process in the acceptance of scientific ideas. To help students focus their essays, suggest they start by using library and/or Internet resources to answer the following questions: What are the advantages of the peer review system? How does the peer review system help ensure that information reaching the public is accurate? What could happen if there was no peer review process?

Formulating a Theory

After results are published, they usually lead to more experiments, which are designed to test and expand the original idea. This process may continue for years until the original idea is disproved, is modified, or becomes generally accepted. Sometimes, elements of different ideas are combined to form concepts that are more complete.

When an idea has undergone much testing and reaches general acceptance, that idea may help form a theory. A **theory** is an explanation that is consistent with all existing tests and observations. Theories are often based on scientific laws. A *scientific law* is a general statement that describes how the natural world behaves under certain conditions and for which no exceptions have been found. Like theories, laws are discovered through scientific research. Theories and scientific laws can be changed if conflicting information is discovered in the future.

Academic Vocabulary

concept (KAHN sept) an idea or a thought

theory a system of ideas that explains many related observations and is supported by a large body of evidence acquired through scientific investigation

The Importance of Interdisciplinary Science

Scientists from many disciplines commonly contribute the information necessary to support an idea. The free exchange of ideas between fields of science allows scientists to identify explanations that fit a wide range of scientific evidence. When an explanation is supported by evidence from a variety of fields, the explanation is more likely to be accurate. New disciplines of science sometimes emerge as a result of new connections that are found between more than one branch of science. An example of the development of a widely accepted hypothesis that is based on interdisciplinary evidence is shown in **Figure 7.**

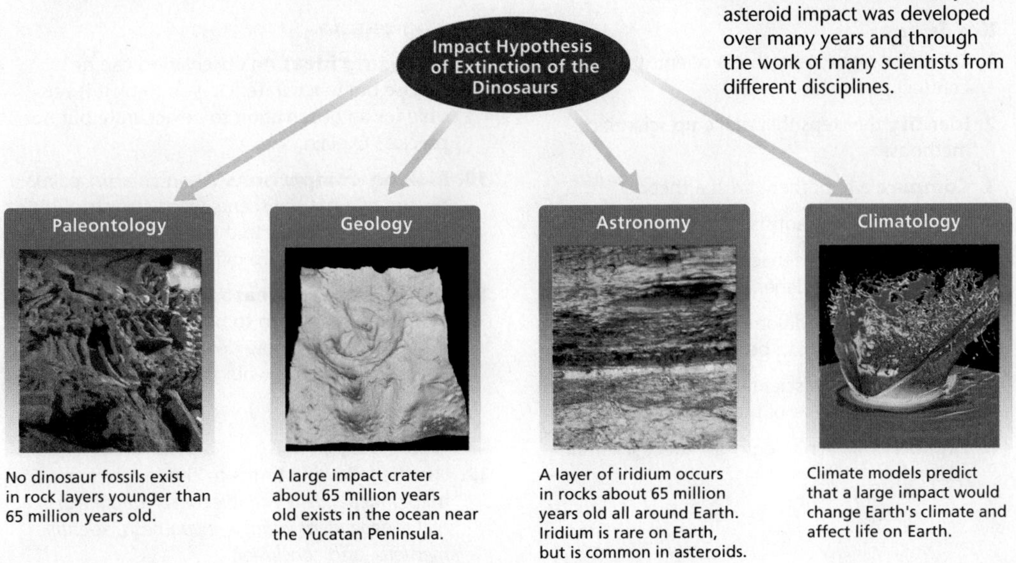
Impact Hypothesis of Extinction of the Dinosaurs
Paleontology
Geology
Astronomy
Climatology
No dinosaur fossils exist in rock layers younger than 65 million years old.
A large impact crater about 65 million years old exists in the ocean near the Yucatan Peninsula.
A layer of iridium occurs in rocks about 65 million years old all around Earth. Iridium is rare on Earth, but is common in asteroids.
Climate models predict that a large impact would change Earth's climate and affect life on Earth.

Figure 7 The hypothesis that the dinosaurs were killed by an asteroid impact was developed over many years and through the work of many scientists from different disciplines.

Debate — ADVANCED

Should Science Always Be Applied? Divide students into two groups: those who think that people should always or often apply scientific discoveries to everyday life and those who think that some consequences or side effects of knowledge gained from research should restrain people from applying findings swiftly. Have students use examples they are familiar with to support their view and counter the opposing view. **LS Verbal/Logical**

Close

Reteaching — BASIC

Chart of Scientific Methods Ask students to use poster-sized paper to create a chart of the different steps in scientific methods. Students should label each step and include details. They may draw or find pictures to illustrate each step as well. **LS Kinesthetic/Visual**

Quiz — GENERAL

1. What is the difference between a theory and a scientific law? (A theory is an explanation that best fits all of the data; a law is a general statement to which no known exceptions exist.)
2. Why do nearly all scientific experiments use a control? (The control allows scientists to determine whether a variable had an effect on the experimental subject.)

Internet Activity — GENERAL

Limitations of Information Systems Have students research common misconceptions in science, such as the following: "Earth's asthenosphere is molten," "raindrops are tear-shaped," and "clouds and steam are water vapor." Have students write a short paper that describes one misconception and then accurately explains the concept. Ask students to conclude their paper with a discussion of how the Internet can be used to disseminate both accurate and inaccurate information. Have them identify the limitations and impacts of information systems and explain how knowing the limitations allows for the effective use of these systems. A worksheet designed to direct student research on this topic can be found in the **Chapter Resource File** booklet or at www.thinkcentral.com, by entering the keyword **HQXIESX. LS Logical**

Key Resources

Technology

- Transparencies
  2 The Importance of Interdisciplinary Science

Close, *continued*

Answers to Section Review

1. to explain what causes some natural phenomenon or to answer a question
2. Ask a question, form a hypothesis, test the hypothesis or make observations, and draw conclusions.
3. A hypothesis is an idea based on observation that can be tested; a theory is an explanation based on testing and evidence that does not conflict with existing results or observations.
4. by following a designed experiment that usually contains one independent variable and a control
5. An independent variable can be changed by the experimenter; a dependent variable changes as a result of a change in an independent variable.
6. when information that conflicts with them is discovered
7. by forming a framework that all scientists follow to establish scientific truth
8. Technological development may lead to new and useful tools that help scientists explore areas they previously could not explore.
9. Sample answer: An observation that is accurate may be imprecise because the units of measurement may have been too large to identify small differences.
10. The artist is the same in that he or she observes nature carefully; the artist is different in that art is personal interpretation, not scientific measurement and reasoning.

Figure 8 The Alaskan pipeline has carried more than 15 billion barrels of oil since it was built in 1977. The pipeline has also sparked controversy about the potential dangers to nearby Alaskan wildlife.

Science and Society

Scientific knowledge helps us understand our world. The work of people, including scientists, is influenced by their cultural and personal beliefs. Science is a part of society, and advances in science can have important and long-lasting effects on both science and society. Examples of these far-reaching advances include the theory of plate tectonics, quantum mechanics, and the theory of evolution.

Science is also used to develop new technology, including new tools, machines, materials, and processes. Sometimes, technologies are designed to address a specific human need. In other cases, technology is an indirect result of science that was directed at another goal. For example, technology that was designed for space exploration has been used to improve computers, cars, medical equipment, and airplanes.

However, new technology may also create new problems. Scientists involved in research that leads to new technologies may or may not consider the possible negative effects of their work. Before making decisions about the technology they adopt, people should consider alternatives, risks, and costs and benefits to humans, to other life, and to Earth. Even after decisions are made, society often continues to debate them. For example, the Alaskan pipeline, part of which is shown in **Figure 8**, transports oil. But the transport of oil in the United States is part of an ongoing debate about how we use oil resources and how these uses affect our natural world.

SCILINKS.
www.scilinks.org
Topic: Careers in Earth Science
Code: **HQX0222**

Section 2 Review

Key Ideas

1. **Describe** one reason that a scientist might conduct research.
2. **Identify** the steps that make up scientific methods.
3. **Compare** a hypothesis with a theory.
4. **Describe** how scientists test hypotheses.
5. **Describe** the difference between a dependent variable and an independent variable.
6. **Describe** the conditions under which scientific laws and theories can be changed.
7. **Summarize** how scientific methods contribute to the development of modern science.
8. **Explain** how technology can affect scientific research.

Critical Thinking

9. **Analyzing Ideas** An observation can be precise but inaccurate. Do you think it is possible for an observation to be accurate but not precise? Explain.
10. **Making Comparisons** When an artist paints a picture of a natural scene, what aspects of his or her work are similar to the methods of a scientist? What aspects are different?
11. **Demonstrating Reasoned Judgment** A new technology is known to be harmful to a small group of people. How does this knowledge affect whether you would use this new technology? Explain.

Concept Mapping

12. Use the following terms to create a concept map: *independent variable, observation, experiment, dependent variable, hypothesis, scientific methods,* and *conclusion.*

11. Student responses may vary but should explain why the risk to this group is acceptable or not, based on the general value of the technology.
12. *Scientific methods* include making *observations*, forming a *hypothesis* that is tested by using an *experiment* that includes *independent variables* and *dependent variables*, and drawing *conclusions*.

Differentiated Instruction

Alternative Assessment

Scientific Proposal Have students write a proposal in which they describe a scientific question they would like to answer by performing an experiment. Have them identify the question, explain why it is important, summarize their hypothesis, describe how they would test their hypothesis, and identify the steps of the scientific method they would follow. **LS Logical**

Why It Matters

How Do Robots Go to Extremes?

Scientific observation is not always easy. Earth scientists often need to go to extreme places to make observations and gather data. But some places are too extreme, even for the most daring scientists. How can scientists gather data in places that are too cold, too hot, too deep, or too far away?

The answer, more and more often, is robots. Robots can be designed to withstand extreme conditions, such as intense cold. They also can be outfitted with special tools and abilities for their missions. For example, one robot, which was designed for research in Antarctica, hovers like a helicopter and flies at speeds up to 100 km/h. It uses a camera and infrared sensor to observe the ice below. Another robot is designed to glide across snowy slopes and icy crevasses.

Robovolc explores volcanoes and collects samples to analyze. Its six rugged wheels keep it stable on jagged volcanic terrain. Its gripper is engineered to pick up rock samples.

DEPTHX, an underwater rover, can be lowered hundreds of meters into deep, uncharted sinkholes such as El Zacatón cenote in central Mexico.

Mars Science Laboratory (MSL) is the next-generation Mars rover. Its lab equipment will help scientists study Mars's geology, and possible biology, in greater detail than ever before.

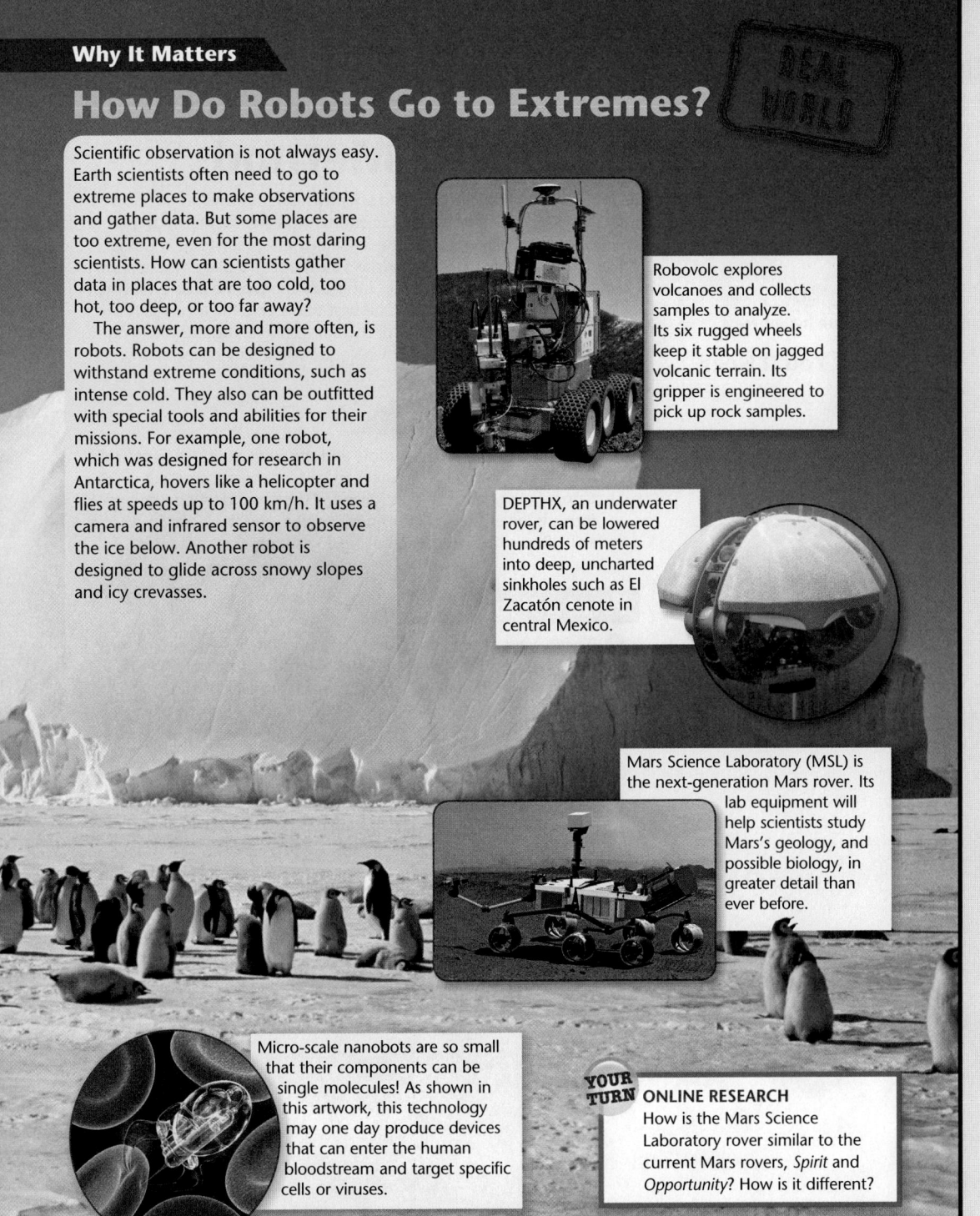

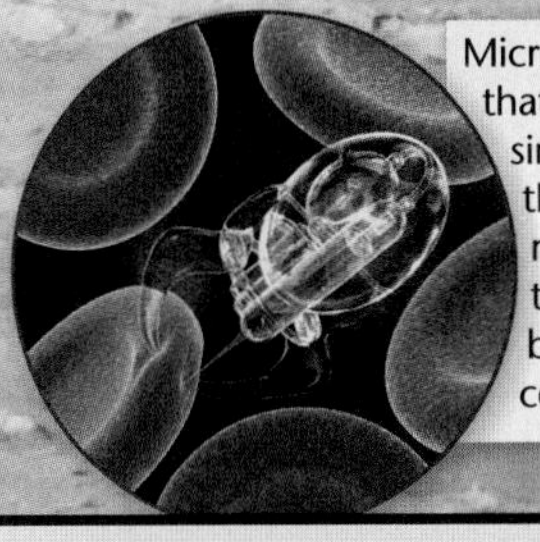

Micro-scale nanobots are so small that their components can be single molecules! As shown in this artwork, this technology may one day produce devices that can enter the human bloodstream and target specific cells or viruses.

YOUR TURN ONLINE RESEARCH

How is the Mars Science Laboratory rover similar to the current Mars rovers, *Spirit* and *Opportunity*? How is it different?

Why It Matters

Extreme Robots

Robots have a history of industrial, military, medical, transportation, and exploration applications. Of particular value to scientists are robots equipped to maneuver over, within, and through extreme environments and to gather data from and about those environments.

Some exploration robots, such as the International Space Station's double-arm robot, Dextre, mimic the shape and/or articulations of human appendanges. Other robots mimic the shape and/or articulations of all or parts of animals such as fish (e.g., RoboTuna), frogs (e.g., Frogbot), insects (e.g., Flybot), and spiders (e.g., spiderbot). There are also robotic transportation devices such as probes, rovers, and submersibles that may be outfitted with cameras, articulated appendages, and various types of sensors for gathering data both within and beyond the range of human sensory perception.

Answer to Your Turn

Online Research Student answers will vary. Similarities: The *MLS* will have six wheels. The *MLS* will have cameras on a mast. Differences: The *MLS* is twice as long and three times as heavy as the earlier Mars rovers. It is equipped to search for organic molecules, whereas the earlier rovers were equipped to search for water. The earlier rovers used solar panels to generate the electricity that runs them. The *MLS* will run on electricity generated by a nuclear reactor.

Inquiry Lab

Time Required

two 45-minute class periods

Lab Ratings

EASY → HARD

Teacher Preparation 2
Student Setup 1
Concept Level 1
Cleanup 1

Skills Acquired

- Observing
- Measuring
- Organizing and Analyzing Data
- Predicting
- Interpreting

Scientific Methods

In this lab, students will
- Make Observations
- Form a Hypothesis
- Test the Hypothesis
- Draw Conclusions

Materials

The materials listed are enough for groups of two to four students. You may wish to have students flag or otherwise mark the puddle they are studying so they can locate it easily on return trips.

Inquiry Lab

90 min

What You'll Do

- **Observe** natural phenomena.
- **Propose** hypotheses to explain natural phenomena.
- **Evaluate** hypotheses.

What You'll Need

hand lens
meterstick

Scientific Methods

Not all scientists think alike, and scientists don't always agree about various concepts. However, all scientists use scientific methods, part of which are the skills of observing, inferring, and predicting. In this lab, you will apply scientific methods as you examine a place where puddles often form after rainstorms. You can study the puddle area even when the ground is dry, but it would be best to observe the area again when it is wet. Because water is one of the most effective agents of change in our environment, you should be able to make many observations.

Make Observations

1. Examine the area of the puddle and the surrounding area carefully. Make a numbered list of what can be seen, heard, smelled, or felt. Sample observations are as follows: "The ground where the puddle forms is lower than the surrounding area, and there are cracks in the soil." Remember to avoid making any suggestions of causes.

Form a Hypothesis

2. Review your observations, and write possible hypotheses for those observations. A sample hypothesis might be "Cracks in the soil (Observation 2) may have been caused by a lack of rain (Observation 5)."
3. Review your observations and possible hypotheses, and place them into similar groups, if possible. Can one hypothesis or set of hypotheses explain several observations? Is each hypothesis reasonable when compared with the others? Does any hypothesis contradict any of the other observations?

Step 1

Tips and Tricks

You may wish to scout some areas for puddles before students do the lab. If you cannot locate a park or similar area near your school, you may find vacant lots or cracked sidewalks that tend to hold puddles.

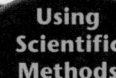

Test the Hypothesis

4. Based only on your hypotheses, make some predictions about what will happen at the puddle as conditions change. Describe the changes you expect and your reasoning. A sample prediction is the following: "If the puddle dries out, the crack will grow wider because of the loss of water."
5. Revisit the puddle several times to see if the changes that you observe match your predictions.

Step 2

Analyze the Results

1. **Evaluating Results** Which of your predictions were correct, and which predictions were incorrect?
2. **Analyzing Methods** Which of your senses did you use most to make your observations? How could you improve your observations by using this sense? by using other senses?
3. **Evaluating Methods** What could you have used to measure, or quantify, many of your observations? Is quantitative observation better than qualitative observation? Explain your answer.

Draw Conclusions

4. **Drawing Conclusions** Examine your incorrect predictions. What new knowledge have you gained from them?
5. **Analyzing Results** Reexamine your hypotheses. What can you say now about the ones that were correct?
6. **Drawing Conclusions** When knowledge is derived from observation and prediction, this process uses *scientific methods*. After reporting the results of a prediction, how might a scientist continue his or her research?

Extension

Designing Experiments Choose another small area to examine, but look for changes caused by a different factor, such as wind. Follow the steps outlined in this lab to predict changes that will occur in the area. Use scientific methods to design an experiment. Briefly describe your experiment, including how you would perform it.

Answers to Analyze the Results

1. Answers may vary. Accept all reasonable answers.
2. Answers may vary. Students may state that they used the sense of sight more than any other sense.
3. Answers may vary. Students could have measured the depth of the puddle and the degree of slope in the puddled area. They could have used these measurements to calculate the volume of water in the puddle and then to determine the rate at which the puddle disappeared.

Answers to Draw Conclusions

4. Answers may vary. Accept all reasonable answers.
5. Answers may vary. Accept all reasonable answers.
6. Students should recognize that after reporting the results of a prediction, a scientist would want to publish the results so other scientists could repeat the experiment to see if the results apply in all cases.

Answer to Extension

Answers may vary but should include an experiment that is reproducible and that uses scientific methods.

Geologic Features and Political Boundaries in Europe

Group Activity GENERAL

Making Maps Divide students into groups, and have each group create a map of one region of the United States. Students should research the boundaries, rivers, and topography of each state in their region. Students should use different colors or patterns to indicate rivers, boundaries, and various elevations. Have students present and explain their maps to the class.
LS Kinesthetic/Visual

Answers to Map Skills Activity

1. rivers
2. 29 countries (including the micro-states of Monaco, San Marino, and Vatican City)
3. Italy
4. rivers
5. mountains
6. Answers may vary. Surface features represent clear physical boundaries that can be easily seen and do not change.

MAPS in Action

Geologic Features and Political Boundaries in Europe

Map Skills Activity

This map shows the political boundaries of a part of Europe. The map also shows some surface features. Use the map to answer the questions below.

1. **Using a Key** What do the blue lines represent?
2. **Analyzing Data** How many countries are represented on the map?
3. **Examining Data** What country has two smaller countries within its borders?
4. **Applying Ideas** What type of surface features define the political boundary between Romania and Moldova and the political boundary between Switzerland and Germany?
5. **Applying Ideas** What type of surface feature defines the political boundary between Poland and Slovakia?
6. **Making Inferences** Why do you think that political boundaries commonly correspond with surface features?

Key Resources

Technology
- Transparencies
  3 Geologic Features and Political Boundaries in Europe

Chapter 1

Summary

THINK central SUPER SUMMARY Keyword: HQXIESS

Key Ideas | **Key Terms**

Section 1

What Is Earth Science?

- Many cultures, including the ancient Greeks and Maya, contributed to the development of modern scientific study.
- The four main branches of Earth science are geology, oceanography, meteorology, and astronomy.
- Earth scientists help us understand how Earth formed and the natural forces that affect human society.

Earth science, p. 5
geology, p. 6
oceanography, p. 6
meteorology, p. 7
astronomy, p. 7

Section 2

Science as a Process

- Science differs from other human endeavors by following a procedure of testing to help understand natural phenomena.
- The steps that make up scientific methods include asking questions, forming hypotheses, testing hypotheses, and drawing conclusions.
- New scientific thought undergoes review and testing by other scientists before new ideas are accepted.
- Science affects society by helping us understand our world. Science is also used to develop new technology that can help solve existing problems as well as create new problems that require solutions.

observation, p. 10
hypothesis, p. 10
independent variable, p. 11
dependent variable, p. 11
peer review, p. 14
theory, p. 15

Chapter Summary

Using THINK central Resources

Super Summary

Have students connect the major concepts in this chapter through an interactive Super Summary. Visit **www.thinkcentral.com** and type in the keyword **HQXIESS** to access the Super Summary for this chapter.

Differentiated Instruction

Alternative Assessment

Frontiers of Earth Science Have students think of one question they have about Earth science that could be answered by new research. Have students write down the question and the branches of Earth science (and other sciences, if appropriate) that could be involved in answering the question. Then, have students apply all the appropriate steps of scientific methods to answer their question. **LS Verbal/Logical**

Chapter Review

Assignment Guide	
Section	**Questions**
1	1, 6, 7, 9–14, 21, 25, 26, 35
2	2–5, 8, 15–20, 22–24, 27–30, 36–39
1 and 2	31–34

Reading Toolbox

1. Astronomy—the study of objects outside Earth's atmosphere; astro—relating to space or stars; nomos—rules or laws. Student answers for next two words will vary; accept any reasonable answers.

Using Key Terms

2–9. Answers may vary but should show that students understand the definitions of and differences between key terms.

Understanding Key Ideas

10. a
11. b
12. d
13. d
14. a
15. b
16. d
17. b
18. a

Short Answer

19. Accuracy is how close a measurement is to the true value; precision is the exactness of the measurement.
20. A control helps to identify the response of a subject to a variable.
21. astronomy and geology
22. Answers may vary. Scientific discoveries may lead to real-world applications, such as the development of new technological tools, which in turn help scientists make more new discoveries.
23. Some explanations require data and expertise from more than one scientific discipline. Other disciplines may help to support or provide evidence for findings in another field.
24. Peer review ensures that reported scientific findings were achieved through the use of correct scientific methods that can be tested by other scientists.
25. by developing myths and legends

Chapter 1 Review

1. **Word Parts** Write the word *astronomy* and its definition. Then use a dictionary to look up the meanings of *astro-* and *-nomy*. Do this for two more words that have the suffix *-nomy*.

READING TOOLBOX

USING KEY TERMS

Use each of the following terms in a separate sentence.

2. *observation*
3. *peer review*
4. *theory*

For each pair of terms, explain how the meanings of the terms differ.

5. *hypothesis* and *theory*
6. *geology* and *astronomy*
7. *oceanography* and *meteorology*
8. *dependent variable* and *independent variable*
9. *Earth science* and *geology*

UNDERSTANDING KEY IDEAS

10. The study of solid Earth is called
    a. geology. **b.** meteorology. **c.** oceanography. **d.** astronomy.
11. The Earth scientist most likely to study storms is a(n)
    a. geologist.
    b. meteorologist.
    c. oceanographer.
    d. astronomer.
12. The study of the origin of the solar system and the universe in general is
    a. geology.
    b. ecology.
    c. meteorology.
    d. astronomy.
13. How long ago were the first scientific observations about Earth made?
    a. a few years ago
    b. a few decades ago
    c. hundreds of years ago
    d. several thousand years ago
14. The Earth scientist most likely to study volcanoes is a(n)
    a. geologist.
    b. meteorologist.
    c. oceanographer.
    d. astronomer.
15. One possible first step in scientific problem solving is to
    a. form a hypothesis.
    b. ask a question.
    c. test a hypothesis.
    d. state a conclusion.
16. A possible explanation for a scientific problem is called a(n)
    a. experiment. **b.** theory. **c.** observation. **d.** hypothesis.
17. A statement that consistently and correctly explains a natural phenomenon is
    a. a hypothesis. **b.** a theory. **c.** an observation. **d.** a control.
18. When scientists pose questions about how nature operates and attempt to answer those questions through testing and observation, they are conducting
    a. research. **b.** predictions. **c.** examinations. **d.** peer reviews.

SHORT ANSWER

19. How does accuracy differ from precision in a scientific measurement?
20. Why do scientists use control groups in experiments?
21. A meteorite lands in your backyard. What two branches of Earth science would help you explain that natural event?
22. Write a short paragraph about the relationship between science and technology.
23. Give two reasons why interdisciplinary science is important to society.
24. Explain how peer review affects scientific knowledge.
25. How did some ancient cultures explain natural phenomena?

CRITICAL THINKING

26. Making Connections How could knowing how our solar system formed affect our understanding of the universe?

27. Evaluating Hypotheses Some scientists have hypothesized that meteorites have periodically bombarded Earth and caused mass extinctions every 26 million years. How might this hypothesis be tested?

28. Determining Cause and Effect Name some possible negative effects of a new technology that uses nuclear fuel to power cars.

29. Analyzing Ideas A scientist observes that each eruption of a volcano is preceded by a series of small earthquakes. The scientist then makes the following statement: "Earthquakes cause volcanic eruptions." Is the scientist's statement a hypothesis or a theory? Why?

30. Forming a Hypothesis You find a yellow rock and wonder if it is gold. How could you apply scientific methods to this problem?

CONCEPT MAPPING

31. Use the following terms to create a concept map: *control group, accuracy, precision, variable, technology, Earth science, experiment,* and *error.*

MATH SKILLS

Math Skills

32. Making Calculations One kilogram is equal to 2.205 lb at sea level. At the same location, how many kilograms are in 100 lb?

33. Making Calculations One meter is equal to 3.281 ft. How many meters are in 5 ft?

34. Making Calculations The accepted value of the average distance between Earth and the moon is 384,467 km. If a scientist measures that the moon is 384,476 km from Earth, what is the measurement's percentage error?

WRITING SKILLS

35. Expressing Original Ideas Imagine that you must live in a place that has all the benefits of only one of the Earth sciences. Which branch would you choose? Defend your choice in an essay.

36. Outlining Topics Explain the sequence of events that happens as a scientific hypothesis becomes a theory.

INTERPRETING GRAPHICS

The graph below shows error in measuring tectonic plate movements. The blue bars represent confidence intervals. Use this graph to answer the questions that follow.

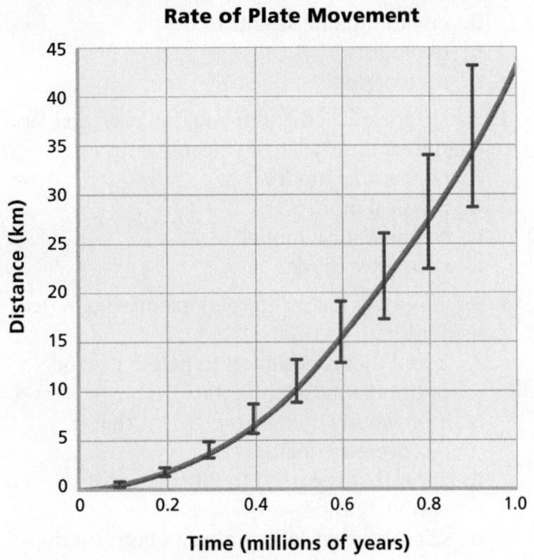

37. How much error is there in the smallest measurement of plate movement?

38. How much error is there in the largest measurement of plate movement?

39. How would you explain the difference between the error in the smallest measurement and the error in the largest measurement?

Chapter Review

Critical Thinking

26. Answers may vary. Knowing how our solar system formed helps us understand Earth's origin and how solar systems in other parts of the universe formed.

27. Answers may vary. This hypothesis might be tested by looking at ancient rocks to see if they contain evidence of meteorite material and by analyzing the fossil record to see if it supports this hypothesis.

28. Answers may vary. Possible negative effects might be leakage of radioactivity, especially in accidents, and the need to store consumed, but still dangerous, nuclear waste.

29. The scientist's statement is a hypothesis because it has not yet been tested.

30. Answers may vary. Sample answer: My hypothesis may be "This rock that has a gold color is gold." Then, I would design an experiment to measure the rock's density to determine if the rock is actually gold.

Concept Mapping

31. Answers may vary but should include all of the terms listed. Sample answers appear at the end of this unit on page 81B.

Math Skills

32. 100 kg ÷ 2.205 lb/kg = 45.35 kg

33. 5 ft ÷ 3.281 ft/m = 1.52 m

34. 384,467 km − 384,476 km = −9 km; −9 km ÷ 384,467 km = −0.00002 × 100 = −0.002%

Writing Skills

35. Answers may vary. Accept all reasonable answers.

36. Answers may vary. Accept all reasonable answers.

Interpreting Graphics

37. 1 km or less

38. about 15 km

39. Answers may vary. Sample answer: The older the rock is, the more difficult it is to measure the rate of movement at the time the rock formed, so the higher the error value is.

Standardized Test Prep

Estimated Time

To give students practice under more realistic testing conditions, allow them 30 minutes to answer all of the questions in this practice test.

Test Doctor

Question 2 Answer H is correct. Scientists should not force the results to match their assumptions, so answers F and I are incorrect. Greater precision will not necessarily result in a more accurate value, so answer G is incorrect. Scientists often reevaluate hypotheses and change them if the hypotheses do not fit the facts.

Question 5 Answer A is correct. Students should be clued to the fact that new technology is often designed for a specific purpose and may take the form of a tool or machine. Answer B is an advancement in science. Such an advancement may be aided by technology, but it is not an example of technology itself. Answer C demonstrates the way in which society may interact with science to help create new technologies, but a law is not an example of technology. Answer D may also be aided by technology and may represent new information, but recording observations is not an example of a new tool, process, or machine, and recording observations does not necessarily meet any human need.

Chapter 1 Standardized Test Prep

Understanding Concepts

Directions (1–5): For each question, write on a separate sheet of paper the letter of the correct answer.

1. A tested explanation of a natural phenomenon that has become widely adopted is a scientific
A. hypothesis.
B. law.
C. theory.
D. observation.

2. If experimental results do not match their predictions, scientists generally will
F. repeat the experiment until they do match.
G. make the measurements more precise.
H. revise their working hypothesis.
I. change their experimental results.

3. Scientists who study weather charts to analyze trends and to predict future weather events are
A. astronomers.
B. environmental scientists.
C. geologists.
D. meteorologists.

4. What type of model uses molded clay, soil, and chemicals to simulate a volcanic eruption?
F. conceptual model
G. physical model
H. mathematical model
I. computer model

5. Which of the following is an example of a new technology?
A. a tool that is designed to help a doctor better diagnose patients
B. a previously unknown element that is discovered in nature
C. a law that is passed to fund scientists conducting new experiments
D. scientists that record observations on the movement of a star

Directions (6–7): For each question, write a short response.

6. What is the term for the factors that change as a result of a scientific experiment?

7. Why do scientists often review one another's work before it is published?

Reading Skills

Directions (8–10): Read the passage below. Then, answer the questions.

Scientific Investigation

Scientists look for answers by asking questions. These questions are often answered through experimentation and observation. For example, scientists have wondered if there is some relationship between Earth's core and Earth's magnetic field.

To form their hypothesis, scientists started with what they knew: Earth has a dense, solid inner core and a molten outer core. They then created a computer model to simulate how Earth's magnetic field is generated. The model predicted that Earth's inner core spins in the same direction as the rest of Earth does but slightly faster than the surface does. If the hypothesis is correct, it might explain how Earth's magnetic field is generated. But how could the researchers test the hypothesis? Because scientists do not have the technology to drill to the core, they had to get their information indirectly. To do this, they decided to track the seismic waves that are created by earthquakes. These waves travel through Earth, and scientists can use them to infer information about the core.

8. The possibility of a connection between Earth's core and Earth's magnetic field formed the basis of the scientist's what?
F. theory
G. law
H. hypothesis
I. fact

9. To begin their investigation, the scientists first built a model. What did this model predict?
A. Earth's outer core is molten, and the inner core is solid.
B. Earth's inner core is molten, and the outer core is solid.
C. Earth's inner core spins in the same direction as the rest of Earth does.
D. Earth's outer core spins in the same direction as the rest of Earth does.

10. Why might the scientists have chosen to build a computer model of Earth, instead of a physical model of Earth?

Question 11 Answer G is correct. Meteorologists study the weather and atmosphere in area C. Answer F is incorrect because Earth's age is more easily determined by a geologist, who studies the history and structure of solid Earth in area A. Answer H is incorrect because the movement of waves and tides take place in area B, not area C. Answer I is incorrect because astronomers study the movement of stars across the sky in area D.

Question 12 Full-credit answers should include the following points:
- Students should demonstrate an understanding that scientific methods are logical ways of solving problems but are not sets of steps that are followed in an invariable sequence, leading to an invariable outcome.
- Possible outomes include new observations and data collection.
- Scientists analyze data to decide whether they support or disprove the hypothesis. If they disprove the hypothesis, the hypothesis is rethought.
- Not only do experimental results sometimes lead to a new hypothesis, but they also often open new avenues for investigation by suggesting new questions.

Interpreting Graphics

Directions (11–12): For each question below, record the correct answer on a separate sheet of paper.

The diagram below shows the four major areas studied by Earth scientists. Use this diagram to answer question 11.

Branches of Earth Science

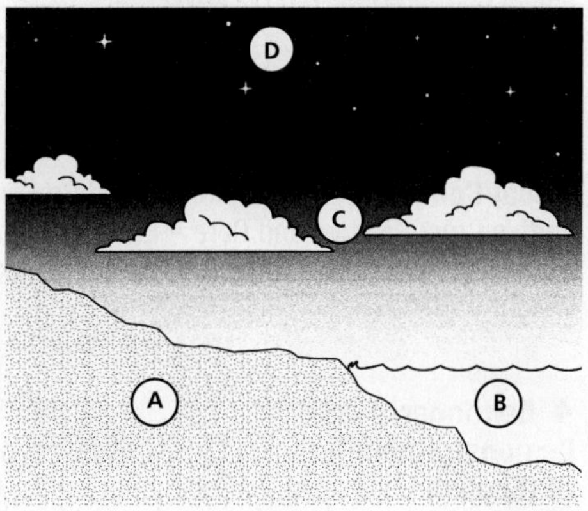

11. A scientist studying the events that take place in area C would be primarily concerned with which of the following?

F. Earth's age
G. Earth's weather
H. movement of waves and tides
I. movement of the stars across the sky

Use the flowchart below to answer question 12.

Using a Scientific Method

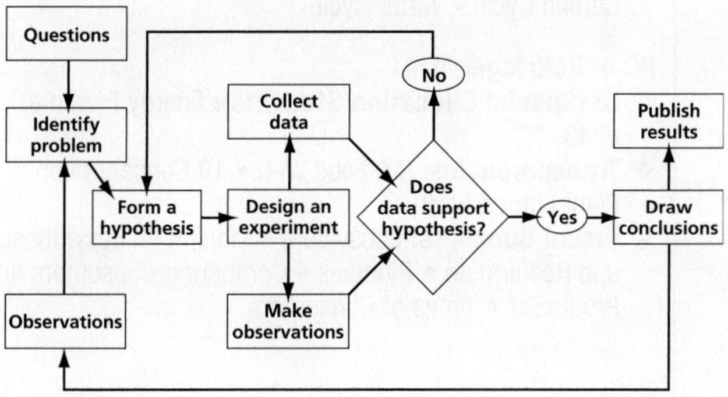

12. What are two possible outcomes of the experimental process? What would a scientist do with the information gathered during the experimental process?

Test Tip

If you are unsure of an answer, eliminate the answers that you know are wrong before choosing your response.

Standardized Test Prep

Using THINK central Resources

State Resources

- For specific resources for your state, visit www.thinkcentral.com and type in the keyword **HSHSTR.**

Answers

Understanding Concepts

1. C
2. H
3. D
4. G
5. A
6. dependent variables
7. to determine the validity of the results and conclusions

Reading Skills

8. H
9. C
10. Because of the complexity of the inner workings of Earth, a computer model would be more practical and accurate than a physical model in this case.

Interpreting Graphics

11. G
12. Answers may vary. See Test Doctor for a detailed scoring rubric.

Chapter Planner 2

Earth as a System

	Standards	Teach Key Ideas
Chapter Opener, pp. 26–27 (45 min)	National Science Education Standards	
Section 1 Earth: A Unique Planet, pp. 29–32 (45 min) ❯ Earth Basics ❯ Earth's Interior ❯ Earth as a Magnet ❯ Earth's Gravity	UCP 1, PS 4b	■ ◆ **Bellringer,** p. 29 ■ **Discussion:** Earth and Its Moon, p. 29 ◆ **Transparency:** 4 Earth's Interior ▲ **Visual Concepts:** Structure of the Earth • Formation of Earth's Crust, Mantle, and Core • Earth's Magnetic Field • Law of Universal Gravitation • Comparing Mass and Weight
Section 2 Energy in the Earth System, pp. 33–40 (45 min) ❯ Earth-System Science ❯ Earth's Four Spheres ❯ Earth's Energy Budget ❯ Cycles in the Earth System	UCP 1, PS 5a, PS 5d, LS 4a, LS 5a, LS 5b, LS 5e	■ ◆ **Bellringer,** p. 33 ■ **Demonstration:** Open and Closed Systems, p. 33 ■ **DI (English Learners):** Paired Summarizing, p. 34 ■ **DI (Special Education Students):** Word Associations, p. 35 ■ **DI (Advanced Learners):** Gravitational Heating, p. 37 ■ **DI (Struggling Readers):** Reading Hint, p. 38 ◆ **Transparencies:** 5 Open and Closed Systems • 6 Earth's Energy Budget • 7 The Nitrogen Cycle • 8 The Carbon Cycle ▲ **Visual Concepts:** Biosphere • The Nitrogen Cycle • Carbon Cycle • Water Cycle
Section 3 Ecology, pp. 41–44 (90 min) ❯ Ecosystems ❯ Balancing Forces in Ecosystems ❯ Energy Transfer ❯ Human Stewardship of the Environment	LS 4a, LS 4b, LS 4c, LS 4d, LS 4e, LS 5a, LS 5b, LS 5c, LS 5e	■ ◆ **Bellringer,** p. 41 ■ **DI (Special Education Students):** Energy Pyramid, p. 43 ◆ **Transparencies:** 9 A Food Web • 10 Concentration of Plant Life on Earth ▲ **Visual Concepts:** Ecosystem • Linking Photosynthesis and Respiration • Biomass • Comparing Consumers and Producers • Types of Consumers
Chapter Wrap-Up, pp. 49–53 (90 min)		**Chapter Summary,** p. 49 ■ **DI (English Learners):** Poster Project, p. 45

See also PowerNotes® Presentations

CHAPTER Fast Track *To shorten instruction because of time limitations, omit Section 3.*

Key

Teacher's Edition ■ | Teaching Transparencies ◆
Chapter Resource File ● | Online Edition ▲

All resources listed below are also available on the **Teacher One Stop™.**

Why It Matters	Hands-On	Skills Development	Assessment
■ **Chapter Overview,** p. 26 ■ **Using the Figure:** Energy Changes, p. 26	**Inquiry Lab:** Observing Water's Changes, p. 27	**Reading Toolbox,** p. 28	
■ **Section Overview,** p. 29 ■ **Using the Figure:** Earth's Interior, p. 30 ■ **Physics Connection:** Seismic Waves, p. 30		**Math Skills:** Speeding Waves, p. 30 **Reading Toolbox:** Generalizations, p. 31 ■ **Skill Builder:** Writing, p. 31	**Reading Check,** p. 30 **Section Review,** p. 32 ■ **Reteaching,** p. 31 ■ **Quiz,** p. 31 ■ **DI (Alternative Assessment):** Poster Project, p. 32 ● **Section Quiz**
■ **Section Overview,** p. 33 ■ **Using the Figure:** Overlapping of Spheres, p. 35 ■ **Space Science Connection:** Spheres of Other Planets and Moons, p. 35 ■ **Using the Figure:** Energy Budget, p. 36 ■ **Physics Connection:** The Laws of Thermodynamics, p. 36 ■ **Using the Figure:** Nitrogen Cycle, p. 38	**Quick Lab:** Effects of Solar Energy, p. 37 ■ **Group Activity:** Earth's Other Cycles, p. 39 **Skills Practice Lab:** Testing the Conservation of Mass, pp. 46–47 ● **Inquiry Lab:** Energy Transfer ● **Making Models Lab:** The Water Cycle	■ **Reading Toolbox:** Vocabulary, p. 35 **Reading Toolbox:** Outlining, p. 38	**Reading Check,** p. 34 **Reading Check,** p. 36 **Reading Check,** p. 38 **Section Review,** p. 40 ■ **Reteaching,** p. 39 ■ **Quiz,** p. 39 ■ **DI (Alternative Assessment):** Rates of Cycles, p. 40 ● **Section Quiz**
■ **Section Overview,** p. 41 ■ **Using the Figure:** Members of Ecosystems, p. 41 **How Does Life Form on Bare Rock?,** p. 42 ■ **Using the Figure:** Food Chains, p. 43	■ **Activity:** Poster Project, p. 42 **Quick Lab:** Studying Ecosystems, p. 43 ■ **Activity:** Ocean-Plant Distribution, p. 48	**Maps in Action:** Concentration of Plant Life on Earth, p. 48 ● **Internet Activity:** Health and Biological Clocks	**Reading Check,** p. 42 **Section Review,** p. 44 ■ **Reteaching,** p. 43 ■ **Quiz,** p. 43 ■ **DI (Alternative Assessment):** Modeling Ecosystems, p. 44 ● **Section Quiz**
Fish that Feed the Forest, p. 45		▲ **Super Summary** **Standardized Test Prep,** pp. 52–53	**Chapter Review,** pp. 50–51 ● **Chapter Tests**

See also Lab Generator

See also Holt Online Assessment Resources

Chapter Overview

Earth is a unique planet. It is also a system in which the amount of matter is relatively constant, but through which energy flows. Earth's four spheres—its atmosphere, its bodies of water, its land, and its living organisms—all interact. The transfer of energy and matter on Earth takes place through various cycles. Complex relationships exist between Earth's living inhabitants and their nonliving environment.

Using the Figure GENERAL

Energy Changes Explain that bears position themselves so that when salmon leap up the waterfall, the salmon can be easily caught. Ask students what energy changes take place when a salmon leaps upward. (Answers may vary. Sample answer: The salmon uses energy stored in its body to overcome gravity.) **LS Logical**

Why It Matters

The systems approach to studying Earth provides students and scientists with a way to conceptualize the interrelated nature of the physical, chemical, and biological forces on the planet. Brown bears, such as the one pictured here, gain energy and nutrients from salmon. Predators' consumption of prey represents one way that matter and energy move through Earth's systems. Invite students to brainstorm other ways that matter and energy move through Earth's systems.

Chapter 2 Earth as a System

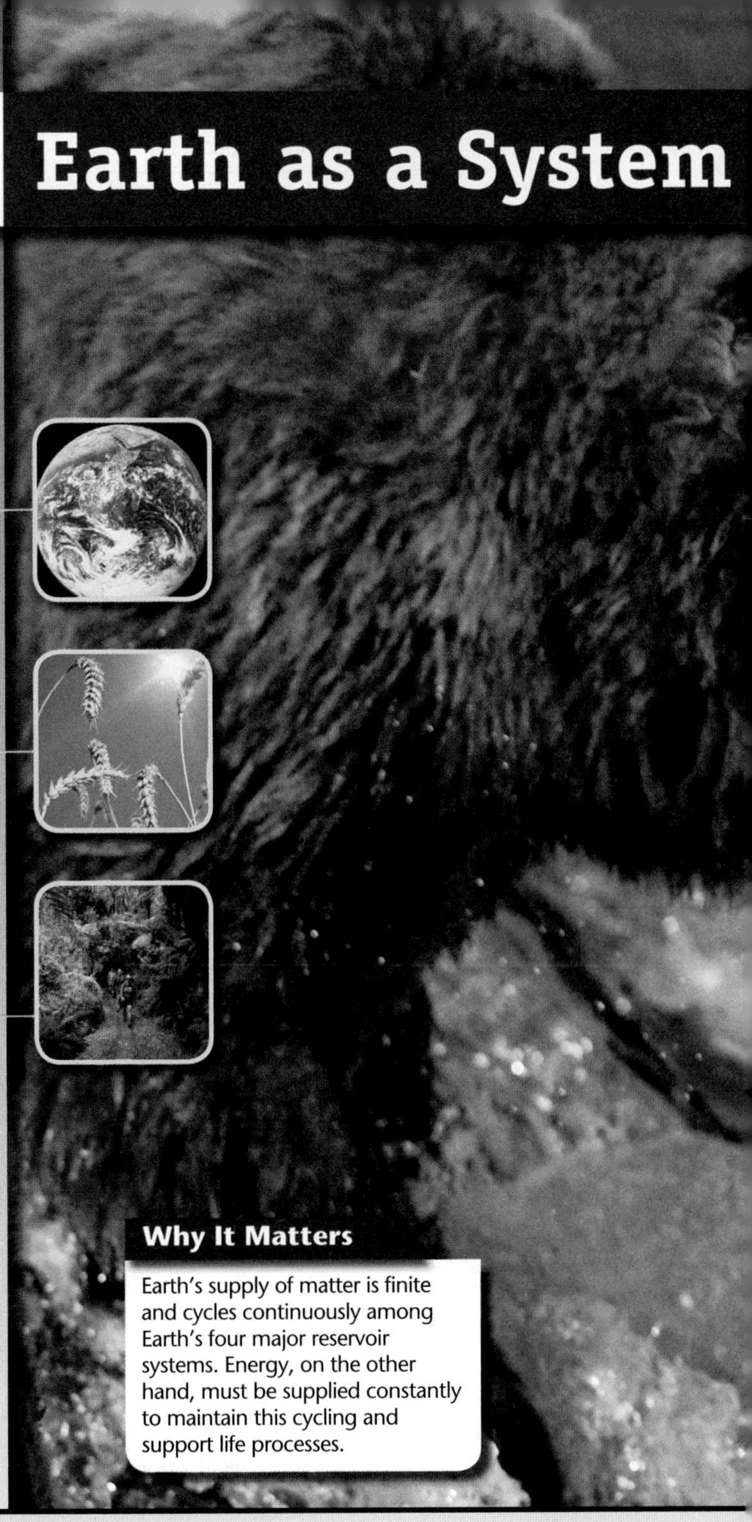

Chapter Outline

Virginia Standards of Learning
ES.1.a
ES.1.c
ES.1.e
ES.2.a
ES.6.a

Why It Matters

Earth's supply of matter is finite and cycles continuously among Earth's four major reservoir systems. Energy, on the other hand, must be supplied constantly to maintain this cycling and support life processes.

Chapter Correlations — *Virginia Standards of Learning*

ES.1.a volume, area, mass, elapsed time, direction, temperature, pressure, distance, density, and changes in elevation/depth are calculated utilizing the most appropriate tools.
ES.1.c scales, diagrams, charts, graphs, tables, imagery, models, and profiles are constructed and interpreted.
ES.1.e variables are manipulated with repeated trials.
ES.2.a science explains and predicts the interactions and dynamics of complex Earth systems.
ES.6.a fossil fuels, minerals, rocks, water, and vegetation

Inquiry Lab

15 min

Observing Water's Changes

Fill a jar with room-temperature water until it is nearly full. Place the lid upside down on top of the jar. Stack as many ice cubes as you can on top of the lid. Make and record observations for about 10 min.

Questions to Get You Started

1. What are the three states of water and all other kinds of matter?
2. Which states did you observe changing from one state to another?
3. How might this setup be used as a model for the water cycle?

Inquiry Lab

Central Concept: The total amount of water on Earth is finite. Water, like other essential substances such as nitrogen, carbon, and oxygen, cycles endlessly through the spheres of the Earth system.

Materials (per group)

- Jar with lid
- Room-temperature water
- Ice cubes

Skills Acquired

- Observation
- Prediction

Teacher's Notes: Inform students that water is the only common substance on Earth that is naturally present in all three of its states. Have students read the lab before starting, predict what they will observe, and identify the stages at which they will see each of water's states.

Answers to Getting Started

1. The three states are solid, liquid, and gas.
2. Students observed gaseous water vapor changing (condensing) to liquid water, and solid water changing (melting) to liquid water. In addition, students could infer (but not observe) that liquid water in the jar was changing (evaporating) to gaseous water vapor.
3. During the water cycle, the input of energy causes liquid water to evaporate and the removal of energy causes gaseous water vapor to condense and/or solidify. In this setup, the room-temperature water supplied the energy needed for the water to evaporate. The ice cubes were in contact with the jar lid, drawing heat from the lid by conduction. The removal of heat (energy) from the lid caused the water vapor in contact with the lid to condense.

Using THINK central Resources

An online version of this chapter, as well as all the print and multimedia resources that accompany the program are available to registered teachers and their students. Log onto www.thinkcentral.com to access these materials and tools to organize your preparation and student learning.

READING TOOLBOX

Generalizations

Characteristics of Earth Answers may vary. Sample answer:

Water covers most of Earth's surface.

"Most of" signals that water covers a large part of the surface, but not all.

The continental crust is 15 to 80 km thick.

This is a generalization because the thickness of the continental crust varies, increasing beneath high mountain ranges, but is generally between 15 to 80 km thick.

Fact, Hypothesis, or Theory?

Scientific Laws Answers may vary, but should list the three laws of thermodynamics and give an example of each law in action.

Note Taking

Outlining Answers may vary. All answers should include the following section titles:

I. Earth Basics
II. Earth's Interior
III. Earth as a Magnet
IV. Earth's Gravity

READING TOOLBOX

These reading tools will help you learn the material in this chapter.

Generalizations

Characteristics of Earth Generalizations are statements that apply to a large group of things (or people). Generalizations may be signaled by words, such as *most, mostly,* or *generally*, and by phrases, such as *in general* or *for the most part*. Many generalizations, however, are not signaled by any words or phrases.

Example of a generalization:
Earth is made mostly of rock.

This statement is a generalization because
- it applies to most—but not all—of Earth's matter
- water (which covers Earth's surface) and air (which surrounds Earth's surface) are exceptions.

Your Turn Record two statements in Section 2 or 3 that are generalizations. Give one or two reasons why each is a generalization.

Fact, Hypothesis, or Theory?

Scientific Laws A scientific law describes or summarizes a pattern in nature. Scientific theories are sometimes confused with scientific laws, but they are not the same thing. Theories explain. Laws describe. The following statements apply to scientific laws:
- They describe patterns in nature.
- They are different from theories.
- They have been confirmed by experiments, or they have been observed so often that they are assumed to be true.

Your Turn As you read Section 2, record the name of each law that is discussed. Also record the pattern that the law describes or summarizes. Include an example of a situation to which the law applies to help you remember it.

Note Taking

Outlining Outlining the content of a section or chapter is a simple and effective way to take notes. To make an outline, follow the steps below.

1. List each main idea or topic, such as a section title, after a Roman numeral.
2. Add major points that give you important information about the idea or topic. List these points after capitalized letters.
3. Add subpoints that describe or explain the major points. List these subpoints after numerals.
4. Add supporting details for each subpoint. List these details after lowercase letters.

Your Turn Use outlining to take notes for Section 1. The example below, for part of Section 1, can help you get started.

I. Earth's Gravity
A. Gravity: force of attraction between all matter
1. Law of Gravitation: The force of attraction depends on masses of objects and distance between objects.

For more information on how to use these and other tools, see **Appendix A.**

SECTION 1

Earth: A Unique Planet

Key Ideas	Key Terms	Why It Matters
› Describe the size and shape of Earth. › Describe the compositional and structural layers of Earth's interior. › Identify the possible source of Earth's magnetic field. › Summarize Newton's law of gravitation.	**crust** **mantle** **core** **lithosphere** **asthenosphere** **mesosphere**	Understanding Earth's structure and composition helps us not only study other bodies in the universe, but also appreciate the features that make our own planet unique.

Earth is unique for several reasons. It is the only known planet in the solar system that has liquid water on its surface and an atmosphere that contains a large proportion of oxygen. Earth is also the only planet—in our solar system or in any other solar system—that is known to support life. Scientists study the characteristics of Earth that make life possible in order to know what life-supporting conditions to look for on other planets.

Earth Basics

Earth is the third planet from the sun in our solar system. Earth formed about 4.6 billion years ago and is made mostly of rock. Approximately 71% of Earth's surface is covered by a relatively thin layer of salt water called the *global ocean*.

As viewed from space, Earth is a blue sphere covered with white clouds. Earth appears to be a perfect sphere but is actually an *oblate spheroid*, or slightly flattened sphere, as **Figure 1** shows. The spinning of Earth on its axis makes the polar regions flatten and the equatorial zone bulge. Earth's circumference from pole to pole is 40,007 km. Its equatorial circumference is 40,074 km.

Earth's surface is relatively smooth. That is, distances between surface high points and low points are small when compared with Earth's size. The difference between the height of the tallest mountain and the depth of the deepest ocean trench is about 20 km. This distance is small compared with Earth's average diameter of 12,756 km.

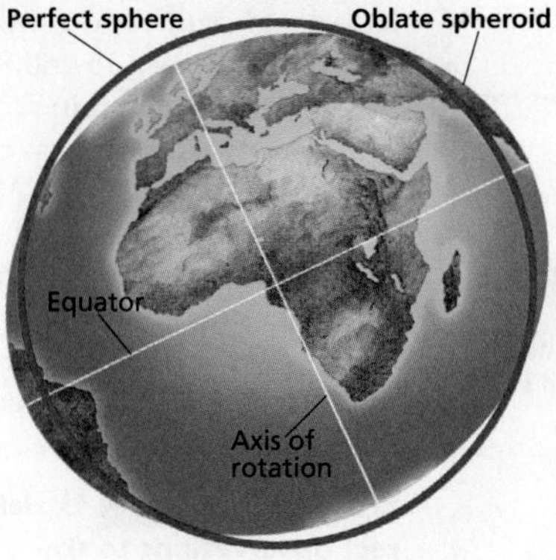

Figure 1 Although from afar Earth looks like a sphere (left), it is an oblate spheroid. In this illustration, Earth's shape has been exaggerated to show that Earth bulges at the equator.

Section 1

Focus

Overview

This section describes the structure of Earth, the basic surface features of Earth, and the nature of Earth's magnetic field.

Bellringer

Have students write down four features of Earth. These may include features not easily observed, such as the structural features of Earth's interior. (Sample answers: atmosphere, water, oceans that cover most of Earth's surface, extensive plant and animal life, icecaps, tropical rain forests, deserts, geologic activity as indicated by volcanoes and earthquakes, mountain ranges, and glaciers) **LS Verbal/Logical**

Motivate

Discussion — GENERAL

Earth and Its Moon On the board, make two columns labeled *Similarities* and *Differences*. Have students consider the differences between Earth and its moon and give ideas for each column. (Similarities may include their rocky surfaces, their spherical shapes, and the sun as an energy source. Differences may include the following: Earth has life, while the moon is lifeless; the moon has no water; and the moon has no atmosphere.) **LS Verbal/Logical**

Key Resources

Chapter Resource File
- Directed Reading BASIC

Technology
- Transparencies
  Bellringer

Teach

Using the Figure BASIC

Earth's Interior Have students examine the figure on this page. Explain to students that the specific pressures and temperatures of the interior determine whether a layer is solid or liquid. Higher temperatures tend to cause solids to melt and become liquid, but higher pressures may counter this effect and compress liquids into solids. Then, ask students which part of Earth's interior takes up the greatest volume. (the mantle) Ask which region takes up the smallest volume. (the crust) Have students use the text to create a depth scale for the layers in the figure. Ask students where the continental crust is thickest. (The crust is thickest beneath large mountain ranges.) **LS Visual**

Math Skills

time of travel for wave
$= \text{thickness of layer} \div \text{speed of wave}$
$= (35\text{ km} \div 8\text{ km/s}) + (2{,}900\text{ km} \div 12\text{ km/s}) + (2{,}250\text{ km} \div 9.5\text{ km/s}) + (1{,}228\text{ km} \div 10.5\text{ km/s})$
time of travel for wave
$= 4\text{ s} + 242\text{ s} + 237\text{ s} + 117\text{ s}$
$= 600\text{ s}$

Answer to Reading Check

Indirect observations are the only means available for exploring Earth's interior at depths too great to be reached by drilling.

Key Resources

Technology
- Transparencies
  4 Earth's Interior

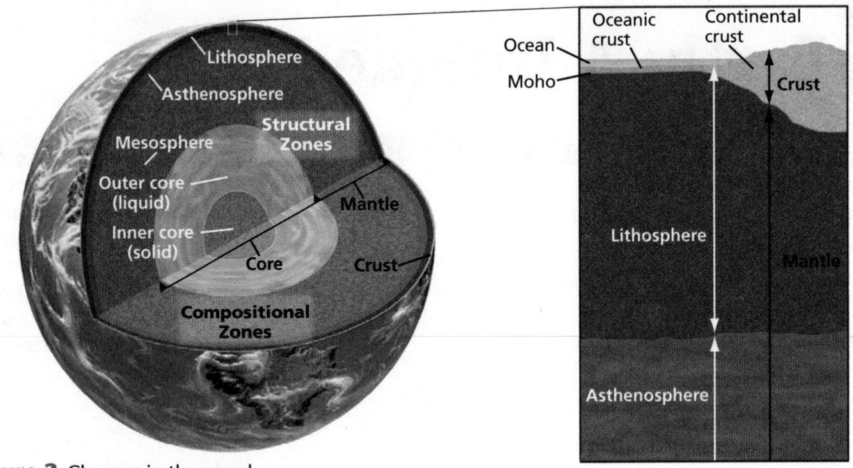

Figure 2 Changes in the speed and direction of seismic waves were used to determine the locations and properties of Earth's interior zones.

Math Skills

Speeding Waves Earth's layers are of the following average thicknesses: crust, 35 km; mantle, 2,900 km; outer core, 2,250 km; and inner core, 1,228 km. Estimate how long a seismic wave would take to reach Earth's center if the wave's average rate of travel was 8 km/s through the crust, 12 km/s through the mantle, 9.5 km/s through the outer core, and 10.5 km/s through the inner core.

Earth's Interior

Direct observation of Earth's interior has been limited to the upper few kilometers that can be reached by drilling. So, scientists rely on indirect methods to study Earth at greater depths. For example, scientists have made important discoveries about Earth's interior through studies of seismic waves. *Seismic waves* are vibrations that travel through Earth. Earthquakes and explosions near Earth's surface produce seismic waves. By studying these waves as they travel through Earth, scientists have determined that Earth is made up of three major compositional zones and five major structural zones, as shown in **Figure 2.**

Compositional Zones of Earth's Interior

The thin, solid, outermost zone of Earth is called the **crust.** The crust makes up only 1% of Earth's mass. The crust beneath the oceans is called *oceanic crust*. Oceanic crust is only 5 to 10 km thick. The part of the crust that makes up the continents is called *continental crust*. The continental crust varies in thickness and is generally between 15 and 80 km thick. Continental crust is thickest beneath high mountain ranges.

The lower boundary of the crust, which was named for its discoverer, is called the *Mohorovičić* (MOH hoh ROH vuh CHICH) *discontinuity*, or *Moho*. The **mantle,** the layer that underlies the crust, is denser than the crust. The mantle is nearly 2,900 km thick and makes up almost two-thirds of Earth's mass.

The center of Earth is a sphere whose radius is about 3,500 km. Scientists think that this center sphere, called the **core,** is composed mainly of iron and nickel.

Reading Check **Explain why scientists have to rely on indirect observations to study Earth's interior.** (See Appendix G for answers to Reading Checks.)

crust the thin and solid outermost layer of the Earth above the mantle

mantle in Earth science, the layer of rock between Earth's crust and core

core the central part of the Earth below the mantle

Physics Connection ADVANCED

Seismic Waves Scientists have learned about the physical structure of Earth's interior by measuring seismic waves. Seismic waves are an example of traveling waves, or mechanical waves that travel through a medium. Sound waves are the most familiar example of traveling waves. The speed of sound within a given medium depends on factors such as the density and compressibility of the medium. Seismic waves, however, differ from sound waves in that they consist of two different types: P waves (also called *primary* or *pressure waves*) and S waves (also called *secondary* or *shear waves*). One difference between these waves is that S waves do not travel through liquids, whereas P waves do, although more slowly than they travel through solids.

Have students research the differences between longitudinal (or compression) waves and transverse waves, and relate these differences to P waves and S waves. Students should present their findings in a short written report or oral presentation. **LS Verbal**

Structural Zones of Earth's Interior

The three compositional zones of Earth's interior are divided into five structural zones. The uppermost part of the mantle is cool and brittle. This part of the mantle and the crust above it make up the **lithosphere,** a rigid layer 15 to 300 km thick. Below the lithosphere is a less rigid layer, known as the **asthenosphere.** The asthenosphere is about 200 to 250 km thick. Because of enormous heat and pressure, the solid rock of the asthenosphere has the ability to flow. This ability to flow is called *plasticity*. Below the asthenosphere is a layer of solid mantle rock called the **mesosphere.**

At a depth of about 2,900 km lies the boundary between the mantle and the *outer core*. Scientists think that the outer core is a dense liquid. The inner core begins at a depth of 5,150 km. The inner core is a dense, rigid solid. The inner and outer core together make up nearly one-third of Earth's mass.

lithosphere the solid, outer layer of Earth that consists of the crust and the rigid upper part of the mantle

asthenosphere the solid, plastic layer of the mantle beneath the lithosphere; made of mantle rock that flows very slowly, which allows tectonic plates to move on top of it

mesosphere literally, the "middle sphere"; the strong, lower part of the mantle between the asthenosphere and the outer core

Earth as a Magnet

Earth has two magnetic poles. The lines of force of Earth's magnetic field extend between the North geomagnetic pole and the South geomagnetic pole. Earth's magnetic field, shown in **Figure 3,** extends beyond the atmosphere and affects a region of space called the *magnetosphere*.

The source of Earth's magnetic field may be the liquid iron in Earth's outer core. Scientists hypothesize that motions within the core produce electric currents that in turn create Earth's magnetic field. However, recent research indicates that the magnetic field may have another source. Scientists have learned that the sun and moon also have magnetic fields. Because the sun contains little iron and the moon does not have a liquid outer core, discovering the sources of the magnetic fields of the sun and moon may help identify the source of Earth's magnetic field.

READING TOOLBOX

Generalizations
Find at least two generalizations in Section 1. Record them in a list, and underline any words or phrases that signal the generalizations. As you read the rest of the chapter, find other generalizations and add them to your list.

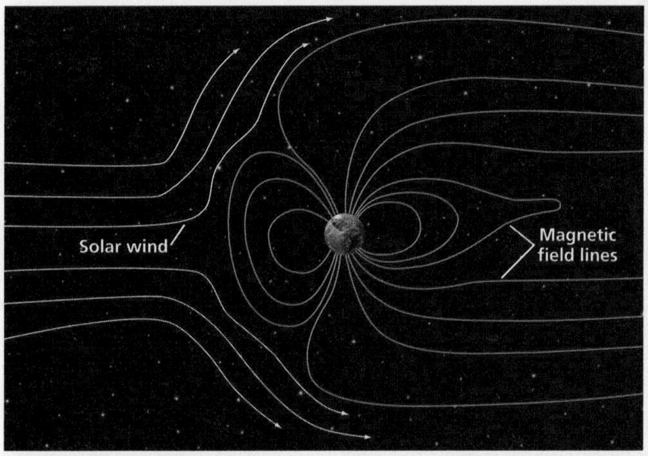

SciLinks®
www.scilinks.org
Topic: Zones of Earth
Code: HQX1684

Figure 3 The magnetic field lines around Earth show the shape of Earth's magnetosphere. Earth's magnetosphere is compressed and shaped by solar wind, which is the flow of charged particles from the sun.

READING TOOLBOX

Generalizations Refresh students' memories of words and phrases that may signal generalizations, such as *about, mostly, generally, in general,* or *for the most part.*

Answers may vary. Sentences that students find may include the following:
Earth formed about 4.6 billion years ago and is made mostly of rock.
Earth's surface is relatively smooth.
The continental crust varies in thickness and is generally between 15 to 80 km thick.
Scientists think that this center sphere, called the core, is composed mainly of iron and nickel.

Close

Reteaching — Basic

Earth's Interior Structure Draw a series of concentric circles on the board, making the two outer circles very close together and the second and third circles very far apart. To the side of the circles, write the words *crust, mantle, outer core,* and *inner core.* Have students indicate which region within the circles corresponds to each layer of Earth. **LS Visual**

Quiz — General

Determine whether each of the following statements is true or false.

1. Earth has the shape of a perfect sphere. (false)
2. The force of gravity on Earth's surface is greater at the poles than at the equator. (true)
3. Earth's core consists of two regions, one liquid and one solid. (true)

Teaching Tip — Basic

Connect to Familiar Processes Students may have difficulty visualizing the properties of the asthenosphere and how solid rock can also be fluid. Have students start by thinking of thick fluids that flow slowly, such as honey or syrup. Explain that some fluids are so thick that they cannot be observed flowing, except over long periods of time. Remind students that children's plastic putty has this property.

Skill Builder — Advanced

Writing Have students research and write an essay that compares and contrasts Earth's magnetic field with that of another planet in the solar system. Subtopics might include how each magnetic field is generated, how strong it is, and what effects it has on the planet and on the region of space that surrounds it. Encourage students to use a Venn diagram or a chart to help them organize and compare the information before they begin writing.
LS Verbal/Logical

Close, *continued*

Answers to Section Review

1. Earth is an oblate, or slightly flattened, spheroid with a polar circumference of 40,007 km and an equatorial circumference of 40,074 km.
2. Answers should include two of the following characteristics: Earth's surface is mostly covered by water; Earth has a thick atmosphere containing a large proportion of oxygen; and Earth supports life.
3. Scientists observe how seismic waves travel through Earth's interior to determine the physical states of Earth's deeper regions.
4. Earth's three compositional layers are the thin crust at the surface, the large mantle that lies beneath the crust, and the core, which lies at Earth's center. The five structural layers describe the interior in terms of physical properties. The crust and upper mantle make up the lithosphere of solid, rigid rock; beneath this lies the asthenosphere of solid but plastic rock; the mesosphere is the solid rock that makes up the rest of the mantle; the liquid outer core comes next; and the solid inner core is at Earth's center.
5. Motion within the liquid iron of Earth's outer core may produce electric currents, which in turn generate Earth's magnetic field.
6. The force of gravitational attraction between two objects increases as the masses of the objects increase and as the distance between the objects decreases.
7. My greater weight at the poles than at the equator suggests that the equator is farther from Earth's center than the poles are, and therefore Earth's shape is not perfectly spherical.
8. The asthenosphere is solid rock that is able to flow because of its plasticity; the mesosphere is solid rock that remains rigid.
9. On the mountain peak, I would be farther from Earth's center than at sea level, so the gravitational attraction would be slightly less. Therefore, I would weigh less.
10. Earth's interior has five compositional zones: the lithosphere, which consists of the crust and the rigid upper part of the mantle; the asthenosphere; the mesosphere; and the two regions of Earth's core, the liquid outer core and the solid inner core.

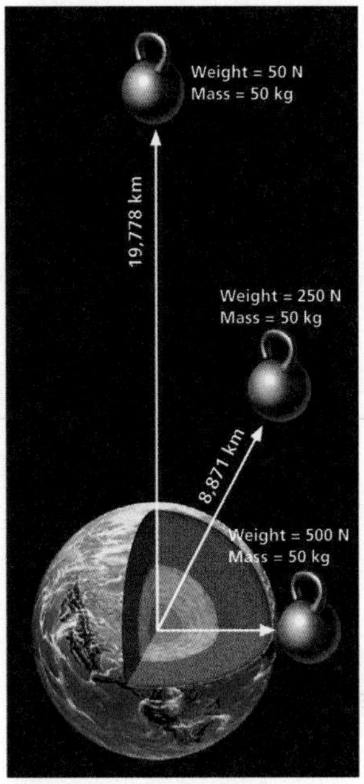

Figure 4 As the distance between an object and Earth's center changes, weight changes but mass remains constant.

THINK central
INTERACT ONLINE
(Keyword: HQXEASF4)

Earth's Gravity

Earth, like all objects in the universe, is affected by gravity. *Gravity* is the force of attraction that exists between all matter in the universe. The 17th-century scientist Isaac Newton was the first to explain the phenomenon of gravity. Newton described the effects of gravity in his *law of gravitation*. According to the law of gravitation, the force of attraction between any two objects depends on the masses of the objects and the distance between the objects. The larger the masses of two objects and the closer together that the two objects are, the greater the force of gravity between the objects will be.

Weight and Mass

Earth exerts a gravitational force that pulls objects toward the center of Earth. Weight is a measure of the strength of the pull of gravity on an object. The newton (N) is the SI unit used to measure weight. On Earth's surface, a kilogram of mass weighs about 10 N. The mass of an object does not change with location, but the weight of the object does. An object's weight depends on its mass and its distance from Earth's center. According to the law of gravitation, the force of gravity decreases as the distance from Earth's center increases, as shown in **Figure 4.**

Weight and Location

Weight varies according to location on Earth's surface. As you may recall, Earth spins on its axis, and this motion causes Earth to bulge near the equator. Therefore, the distance between Earth's surface and its center is greater at the equator than at the poles. This difference in distance means that your weight at the equator would be about 0.3% less than your weight at the North Pole.

Section 1 Review

Key Ideas

1. **Describe** the size and shape of Earth.
2. **Describe** two characteristics that make Earth unique in our solar system.
3. **Summarize** how scientists learn about Earth's interior.
4. **Compare** Earth's compositional layers with its structural layers.
5. **Identify** the possible source of Earth's magnetic field.
6. **Summarize** Newton's law of gravitation.

Critical Thinking

7. **Making Inferences** What does the difference between your weight at the equator and your weight at the poles suggest about Earth's shape?
8. **Making Comparisons** How does the asthenosphere differ from the mesosphere?
9. **Analyzing Ideas** Why would you weigh less on a high mountain peak than you would at sea level?

Concept Mapping

10. Use the following terms to create a concept map: *crust, mantle, core, lithosphere, asthenosphere, mesosphere, inner core,* and *outer core.*

Differentiated Instruction

Alternative Assessment

Poster Project Have students select one of the other planets in the solar system and develop a poster that compares the internal structures, shapes, surfaces, magnetic fields, and gravitational fields of the chosen planet and Earth.

LS Visual/Logical

SECTION 2

ENVIRONMENTAL CONNECTION

Energy in the Earth System

Key Ideas	Key Terms	Why It Matters
› Compare an open system with a closed system. › List the characteristics of Earth's four major spheres. › Identify the two main sources of energy in the Earth system. › Identify four processes in which matter and energy cycle on Earth.	system atmosphere hydrosphere geosphere biosphere	Viewing Earth as a system helps scientists study ways that matter and energy interact to create and support Earth's life forms and living conditions.

Traditionally, different fields of Earth science have been studied separately. Geologists studied Earth's rocks and interior, oceanographers studied the oceans, and meteorologists studied the atmosphere. But now, some scientists are combining knowledge of several fields of Earth science in order to study Earth as a system.

Earth-System Science

An organized group of related objects or components that interact to create a whole is a **system.** Systems vary in size from subatomic to the size of the universe. All systems have boundaries, and many systems have matter and energy that flow through them. Even though each system can be described separately, all systems are linked. A large and complex system, such as the Earth system, operates as a result of the combination of smaller, interrelated systems, as shown in **Figure 1.**

system a set of particles or interacting components considered to be a distinct physical entity for the purpose of study

The operation of the Earth system is a result of interaction between the two most basic components of the universe: matter and energy. *Matter* is anything that has mass and takes up space. Matter can be atoms or molecules, such as oxygen atoms or water molecules, and matter can be larger objects, such as rocks, living organisms, or planets. *Energy* is defined as the ability to do work. Energy can be transferred in a variety of forms, including heat, light, vibrations, or electromagnetic waves. A system can be described by the way that matter and energy are transferred within the system or to and from other systems. Transfers of matter and energy are commonly accompanied by changes in the physical or chemical properties of the matter.

Figure 1 This threadfin butterflyfish is part of a system that includes other living organisms, such as coral. Together, the organisms are part of a larger system, a coral reef system in Micronesia.

Section 2

Focus

Overview

This section explains open and closed systems and identifies how Earth is a type of open system. Earth's four spheres are identified, and Earth's energy budget is described. Finally, the cycles in the Earth system and the effects of human activity on these cycles are examined.

Bellringer

Have students write down how energy and matter are added to and removed from the Earth system. (Answers may vary. Sample answer: Energy is added by sunlight and from Earth's interior, and is removed by radiation into space. Matter is added when meteorites collide with Earth and is removed when spacecraft are launched. Matter is also removed by the steady loss of gases into space.) **LS Logical**

Motivate

Demonstration — GENERAL

Open and Closed Systems Boil water in a pan on a hot plate. When water vapor rises out of the pan, ask students if they think the pan, hot plate, and water represent an open or closed system, and why. (The system is open because water leaves the pan in the form of water vapor.) Place a lid on the pan. Ask students if the system is now open or closed. (The system is now closed because matter no longer leaves the system.) **LS Visual/Logical**

Key Resources

Chapter Resource File
- Directed Reading BASIC

Technology
- Transparencies
  Bellringer

Teach

Teaching Tip GENERAL

Connect to Prior Knowledge To help students determine whether a system is open or closed, have them ask themselves the question "Is matter in the form of a gas entering or leaving the system?" Many systems are actually open, but because the matter that is transferred between the system and its surroundings is in the form of gas atoms or molecules, the transfer is invisible and therefore may be overlooked. If students first think about whether gas is entering or leaving the system, it will be easier for them to determine whether the system is open or closed. English Language Learners
LS Logical

Homework GENERAL

Systems at Home Have students look for various systems in and around their own homes and compile a list of six to ten of these systems, noting whether the systems are open or closed and briefly explaining why. They may list such systems as a refrigerator (a closed system, if no food is added or removed), an automobile (an open system), an electric lamp (a closed system), and a washing machine (an open system). You may wish to have students describe one system from their list for the class.
LS Verbal/Logical

Answer to Reading Check
Dust and rock come to Earth from space, while hydrogen atoms in the atmosphere enter space from Earth.

Figure 2 Energy is exchanged in both the open system (left) and the closed system (right). In the open system, matter is also exchanged.

Open Systems

An *open system* is a system in which both energy and matter are exchanged with the surroundings. The open jar in **Figure 2** is an open system. A lake is also an open system. Water molecules enter a lake through rainfall and streams. Water exits a lake through streams, evaporation, and absorption by the ground. Sunlight and air exchange heat with the lake. Wind's energy is transferred to the lake as waves.

Closed Systems

A *closed system* is a system in which energy, but not matter, is exchanged with the surroundings. The sealed jar in **Figure 2** is a closed system. Energy in the form of light and heat can be exchanged through the jar's sides. But because the jar is sealed, matter cannot exit or enter the system. Most aquariums are open systems because oxygen and food must be added to them, but some are closed systems. Closed-system aquariums contain a variety of organisms: plants, which produce oxygen, and aquatic animals, some of which are food for others. Some of the animals feed on the plants. Animal wastes and organic matter nourish the plants. Only sunlight enters from the surroundings.

The Earth System

Technically, all systems that make up the Earth system are open. But the Earth system is almost a closed system because matter exchange is limited. Energy enters the system in the form of sunlight and is released into space as heat. Only a small amount of dust and rock from space enters the system, and only a fraction of the hydrogen atoms in the atmosphere escape into space.

Reading Check **What types of matter and energy are exchanged between Earth and space?**

Differentiated Instruction

English Learners

Paired Summarizing Group students into pairs, and have them read silently about open and closed systems. Then, have one student summarize how open and closed systems are similar and how they are different. The other student should listen to the retelling and should point out any inaccuracies or ideas that were left out. Allow students to refer to the text as needed. **LS Verbal**

Key Resources

Technology
- Transparencies
  5 Open and Closed Systems

Earth's Four Spheres

Matter on Earth is in solid, liquid, and gaseous states. The Earth system is composed of four "spheres" that are storehouses of all of the planet's matter. These four spheres are shown in **Figure 3.**

The Atmosphere

The blanket of gases that surrounds Earth's surface is called the **atmosphere.** The atmosphere provides the air that you breathe and shields Earth from the sun's harmful radiation. Earth's atmosphere is made up of 78% nitrogen and 21% oxygen. The remaining 1% includes other gases, such as argon, carbon dioxide, and helium.

The Hydrosphere

Water covers much of Earth's surface, and 97% of this water is contained in the salty oceans. The remaining 3% is fresh water. Fresh water can be found in lakes, rivers, and streams, frozen in glaciers and the polar ice sheets, and underground in soil and bedrock. All of Earth's water makes up the **hydrosphere.**

The Geosphere

The mostly solid part of Earth is known as the **geosphere.** This sphere includes all of the rock and soil on the surface of the continents and on the ocean floor. The geosphere also includes the solid and molten interior of Earth, which makes up the largest volume of matter on Earth. Natural processes, such as volcanism, bring matter from deep inside Earth's interior to the surface. Other processes move surface matter back into Earth's interior.

The Biosphere

Another one of the four subdivisions of the Earth system is the biosphere. The **biosphere** is composed of all of the forms of life in the geosphere, in the hydrosphere, and in the atmosphere. The biosphere also contains any organic matter that has not decomposed. Once organic matter has completely decomposed, it becomes a part of the other three spheres. The biosphere extends from the deepest parts of the ocean to the atmosphere a few kilometers above Earth's surface.

atmosphere a mixture of gases that surrounds a planet, moon, or other celestial body

hydrosphere the portion of the Earth that is water

geosphere the mostly solid, rocky part of the Earth; extends from the center of the core to the surface of the crust

biosphere the part of Earth where life exists; includes all of the living organisms on Earth

Figure 3 The Earth system is composed of the atmosphere, hydrosphere, geosphere, and biosphere. ***Can you identify elements of the four spheres in this photo?***

READING TOOLBOX

Vocabulary The names of Earth's four spheres are derived from ancient Greek. The Greek word for "ball" is *sphaira,* from which the word *sphere* is derived. The Greek roots *atmos, hydro, geo,* and *bios* mean "vapor," "water," "earth," and "life," respectively.
LS Verbal

Using the Figure — Basic

Overlapping of Spheres Have students look carefully at the figure on this page. Point out to them that the contents of the four spheres are not always separate, and that elements of one sphere may be found in another sphere. Thus, while water in the form of ice or liquid water is part of the hydrosphere, water in the form of water vapor is found in the atmosphere. Answer to caption question: The gases in the sky are parts of the atmosphere. The hydrosphere is represented by the lake, the snow on the mountains, and the clouds in the air. The field, forest, and mountains are parts of the geosphere, as well as the bottom of the lake on which the moose is standing. The moose in the foreground and the vegetation in the field and forest of the background are all parts of the biosphere. **LS Visual**

Space Science Connection — Advanced

Spheres of Other Planets and Moons Earth is the only known planet with a biosphere, but the other three spheres are found, to some degree, on other planets. Some planets, like the gas giant Jupiter, are almost entirely atmosphere. Other planets, like Mercury, may have a hydrosphere in the form of ice near the poles but are almost exclusively geospheres.

Have students research planets or large moons of planets, and whether they possess geospheres, hydrospheres, or atmospheres. Have students note unusual features of these spheres, compared with Earth. Students may then present their findings in a written report, oral presentation, or poster project.
LS Verbal

Differentiated Instruction

Special Education Students

Word Associations Many students struggle with larger words that are not in their day-to-day vocabularies. Give students the following word associations to help them understand and remember Earth's four spheres:

Atmosphere: air
Hydrosphere: H_2O
Geosphere: ground
Biosphere: bodies and bushes

Teach, *continued*

Using the Figure GENERAL

Energy Budget Point out to students that the energy distribution shown in the figure is for the whole Earth and that the percentages will vary for different specific locations. For instance, a desert will absorb and reflect a different amount of radiation than a forest or an ocean will. A greater quantity of carbon dioxide or water in the atmosphere will alter the absorbing properties of the atmosphere. Ask students, "How much of the total energy is reradiated into space?" (30%) "How much of this reflected energy is scattered by particles in the air?" (6%) Remind students that energy is conserved, so all the energy that enters Earth's spheres equals the total energy that is released by them. Ask students how much energy is not absorbed by water and land. (100% − 51% = 49%)
LS Visual/Logical

Answer to Reading Check

An energy budget is the total distribution of energy to, from, and between Earth's various spheres.

Key Resources

Technology
- Transparencies
  6 Earth's Energy Budget

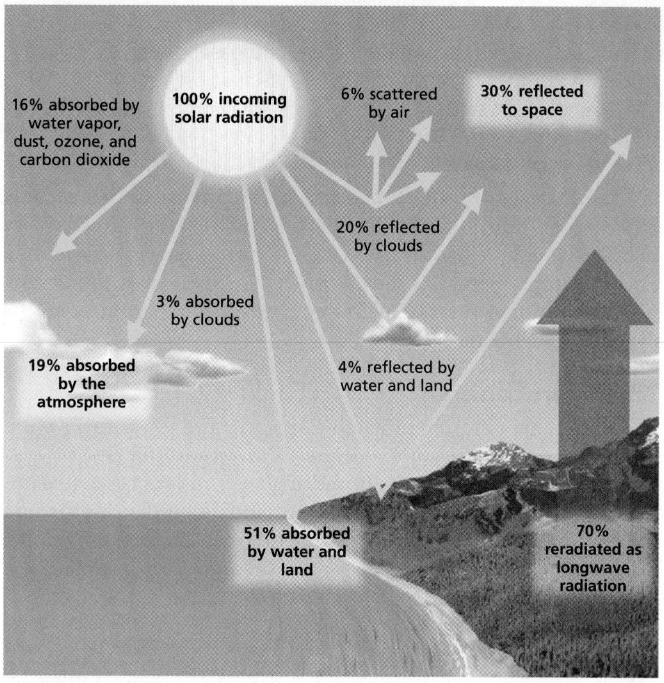

Figure 4 Incoming solar energy is balanced by solar energy reflected or reradiated by several of Earth's systems.

Earth's Energy Budget

Exchanges and flow of energy on Earth happen in predictable ways. According to the *first law of thermodynamics*, energy is transferred between systems, but it cannot be created or destroyed. The transfers of energy between Earth's spheres can be thought of as parts of an *energy budget*, in which additions in energy are balanced by subtractions. This concept is shown in **Figure 4,** which shows how solar energy is transferred through Earth's systems. Solar energy is absorbed and reflected in such a way that the solar energy input is balanced by the solar energy output. Like energy, matter can be transferred but cannot be created or destroyed.

The *second law of thermodynamics* states that when energy transfer takes place, matter becomes less organized with time. The overall effect of this natural law is that the universe's energy is spread out more and more uniformly over time.

Earth's four main spheres are open systems that can be thought of as huge storehouses of matter and energy. Matter and energy are constantly being exchanged between the spheres. This constant exchange happens through chemical reactions, radioactive decay, the radiation of energy (including light and heat), and the growth and decay of organisms.

Reading Check **Define *energy budget*.**

Physics Connection ADVANCED

The Laws of Thermodynamics The laws of thermodynamics were discovered in the 19th century as the nature of heat was understood. Heat was seen as energy that could be added to or removed from a system. Because different aspects of thermodynamics were of interest at different times, the discoveries of its principles occurred in a rather haphazard order. Thus, the second law of thermodynamics, which deals with how energy becomes less useful as it is spontaneously transferred from a higher-temperature object to a lower-temperature object, was discovered before the first law was conclusively proven. Have students research the historical development of the four laws of thermodynamics, and have them present their findings as a bulletin-board exhibit or as a Web page. **LS Verbal**

Internal Sources of Energy

When Earth formed about 4.6 billion years ago, its interior was heated by radioactive decay and gravitational contraction. Since that time, the amount of energy as heat generated by radioactive decay has declined. But the decay of radioactive atoms still generates enough energy to keep Earth's interior hot. Earth's interior also retains much of the energy from the planet's formation.

Because Earth's interior is warmer than its surface layers, hot materials move toward the surface in a process called *convection*. As material is heated, the material's density decreases, and the hot material rises and releases energy as heat. Cooler, denser material sinks and displaces the hot material. As a result, the energy in Earth's interior is transferred through the layers of Earth and is released at Earth's surface as heat. On a large scale, this process drives the motions in the surface layers of the geosphere that create mountain ranges and ocean basins.

External Energy Sources

In order for the life-supporting processes on Earth to continue operating for billions of years, energy must be added to the Earth system. Earth's most important external energy source is the sun. Solar radiation warms Earth's atmosphere and surface. This heating causes the movement of air masses, which generates winds and ocean currents. Plants, such as the wheat shown in **Figure 5,** use solar energy to fuel their growth. Because many animals feed on plants, plants provide the energy that acts as a base for the energy flow through the biosphere. Even the chemical reactions that break down rock into soil require solar energy. Another important external source of energy is gravitational energy from the moon and sun. The pull of the sun and the moon on the oceans, combined with Earth's rotation, generates tides that cause currents and drive the mixing of ocean water.

Quick Lab
10 min

Effects of Solar Energy

Procedure

1. Wrap one small glass jar with black construction paper so that no light can enter it. Get a second glass jar. Make sure that the second jar has a clean, transparent surface.
2. Use a hammer and large nail to punch a hole in each jar lid.
3. Place a thermometer through the hole in each jar lid. Place the lids tightly onto the jars.
4. Place the jars on the windowsill. Wait 5 min. Then, read the temperature from each jar's thermometer.

Analysis

1. Which jar had the higher temperature?
2. Which jar represents a system in which energy enters from outside the system?

Figure 5 Solar energy is changed into stored energy in the wheat kernels by chemical processes in the wheat plant. When the wheat is eaten, the stored energy is released from the wheat and used or stored by the consumer.

Quick Lab

Materials

- 2 glass jars with lids
- Black construction paper
- Hammer
- Nail
- Thermometer
- Towel

Skills Acquired

- Experimenting
- Constructing Models
- Observing
- Identifying and recognizing patterns

Teacher's Notes: Students should place a towel beneath the jar lids when punching holes to protect the table. The nail should have a smaller diameter than the thermometers, so the thermometers will fit securely in the lids. Be sure that the thermometers do not touch the walls or bottoms of the jars.

Answers to Analysis

1. the jar that is not covered by paper
2. the jar that is not covered by paper

Differentiated Instruction

Advanced Learners

Gravitational Heating Radioactive decay of material in Earth's interior is Earth's main internal source of heat. However, within Earths' core, the effects of gravity complement radioactive decay, which contributes to the heating of Earth's interior. Scientists think that both gravitational pressure and the effects of smaller bodies colliding with Earth accreted to form the primitive Earth, and they have used laboratory experiments and models to gain insights into these processes. Have students research theories of the causes of gravitational heating and how the scientific process has supported or discounted these theories. Students may present their research as a poster, a Web page, or a short essay. **LS Verbal/Logical**

READING TOOLBOX

Outlining Student outlines should list the red headings as main topics and the green subheadings as subtopics, and include one or two points from the text to explain or support the subtopics. Have students compare their outline with that of a partner, and explain to their partner why they chose the information they did.

Using the Figure — BASIC

Nitrogen Cycle Ask students in what general directions the arrows point in the figure. (In general, the arrows point from the air to the soil or water and from the soil or water to the air.) Point out that the main components in the nitrogen cycle are nitrogen in the air, which is absorbed by bacteria in the soil or water, and the chemical processes and bacteria that return the nitrogen to the air. Other components, such as animals and plants, are simply added links in this basic cycle and do not change its overall workings. Answer to caption question: Animals extract nitrogen from plants they eat and return the nitrogen to the soil through their wastes and when their bodies decompose. **LS Visual/Logical**

Answer to Reading Check
soil and plants

Key Resources

Technology
- Transparencies
  7 The Nitrogen Cycle
  8 The Carbon Cycle

Cycles in the Earth System

A *reservoir* is a place where matter or energy is stored. A *cycle* is a group of processes in which matter repeatedly moves through a series of reservoirs. Many elements on Earth cycle between reservoirs. These cycles rely on energy sources to drive them. The length of time that energy or matter spends in a reservoir can vary from a few hours to several million years.

READING TOOLBOX

Outlining
Use outlining to make notes about the main ideas in Section 2. Use the red- and green-colored topic headings to help you organize your notes. Trading outlines with other students can help you learn how to improve your outlining skills.

The Nitrogen Cycle

Organisms on Earth use the element nitrogen to build proteins, which are then used to build cells. Nitrogen gas makes up 78% of the atmosphere, but most organisms cannot use the atmospheric form of nitrogen. The nitrogen must be altered, or *fixed*, before organisms can use it. Nitrogen fixing is an important step in the *nitrogen cycle*, which is shown in **Figure 6.**

In the nitrogen cycle, nitrogen moves from air to soil, from soil to plants and animals, and back to air again. Nitrogen is removed from air mainly by the action of nitrogen-fixing bacteria. These bacteria live in soil and on the roots of certain plants. The bacteria chemically change nitrogen from air into nitrogen compounds, which are vital to the growth of all plants. When animals eat plants, nitrogen compounds in the plants become part of the animals' bodies. These compounds are returned to the soil by the decay of dead animals and in animals' excretions. After nitrogen compounds enter the soil, chemical processes release nitrogen back into the atmosphere. Water-dwelling plants and animals take part in a similar nitrogen cycle.

Reading Check **Identify two nitrogen reservoirs on Earth.**

Figure 6 The balance of nitrogen in the atmosphere and biosphere is maintained through the nitrogen cycle. ***What role do animals play in the nitrogen cycle?***

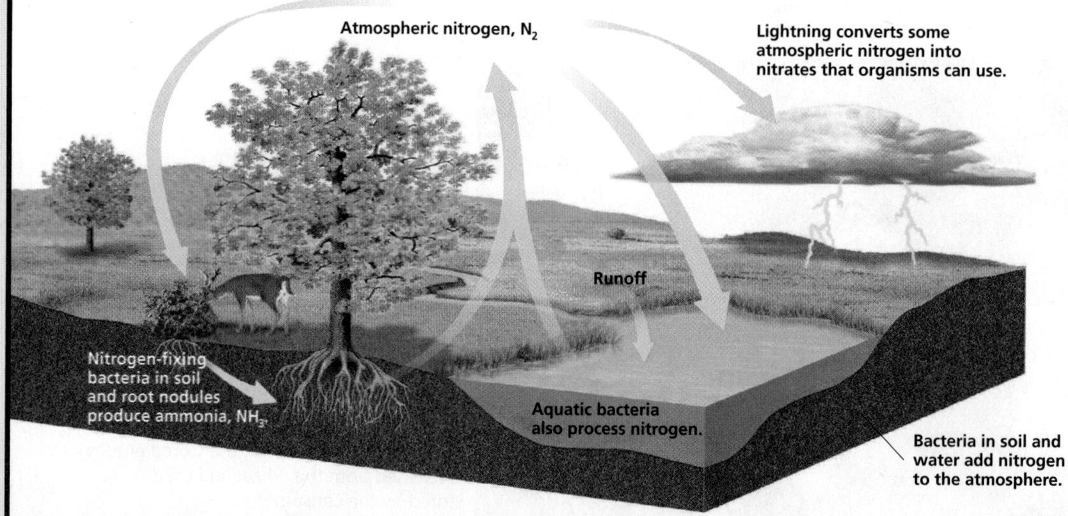
Atmospheric nitrogen, N_2
Lightning converts some atmospheric nitrogen into nitrates that organisms can use.
Runoff
Nitrogen-fixing bacteria in soil and root nodules produce ammonia, NH_3
Aquatic bacteria also process nitrogen.
Bacteria in soil and water add nitrogen to the atmosphere.

Differentiated Instruction

Struggling Readers

Reading Hint Before students read the passages under "Cycles in the Earth System," ask them to think of words that include the word *cycle*. *(bicycle, recycle, motorcycle)* Explain that the word *cycle* comes from the Greek word for "wheel" and, in general, refers to anything that returns to its starting place or repeats itself. Emphasize the word *cycle* in the passages on this page and the following page, and stress that students should be aware of how certain materials return to their initial states. **LS Verbal**

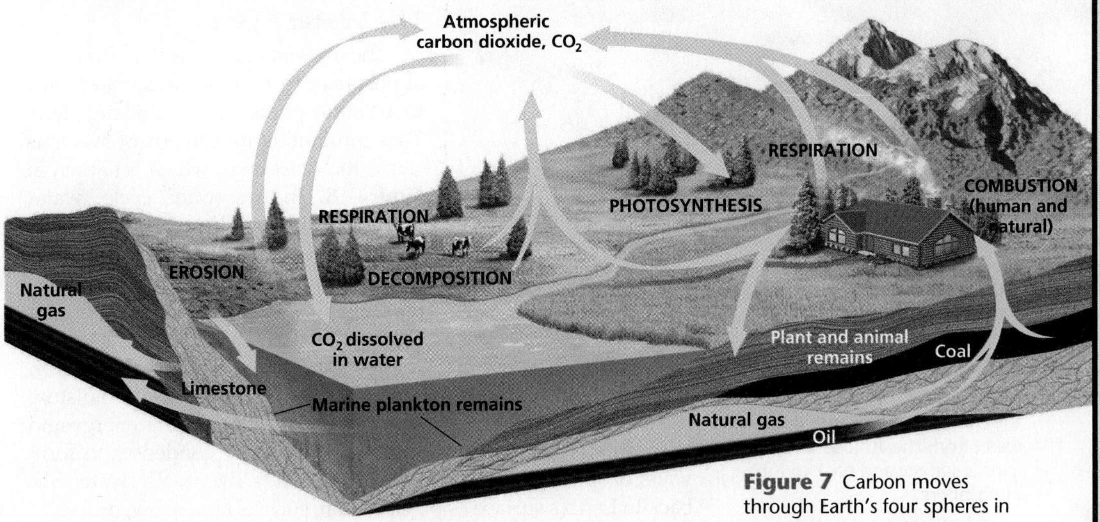

Figure 7 Carbon moves through Earth's four spheres in a combination of short-term and long-term cycles.

The Carbon Cycle

Carbon is an essential substance in the fuels used for life processes. Carbon moves through all four spheres in a process called the *carbon cycle*, as **Figure 7** shows. Part of the carbon cycle is a short-term cycle. In this short-term cycle, plants convert carbon dioxide, CO_2, from the atmosphere into carbohydrates, such as glucose, $C_6H_{12}O_6$. Then, organisms eat the plants and obtain the carbon from the carbohydrates. Next, organisms' bodies break down the carbohydrates and release some of the carbon back into the air as CO_2. Organisms also release carbon into the air through their organic wastes and by the decay of their remains, which release carbon into the air as CO_2 or as methane, CH_4.

Part of the carbon cycle is a long-term cycle in which carbon moves through Earth's four spheres over a very long time. Carbon is stored in the geosphere in buried plant or animal remains and in a type of rock called a *carbonate*, such as limestone. Carbonate forms from shells and bones of once-living organisms.

SCILINKS.
www.scilinks.org
Topic: Carbon Cycle
Code: **HQX0216**
Topic: Nitrogen Cycle
Code: **HQX1036**

The Phosphorus Cycle

The element phosphorus is part of some molecules that organisms need to build cells. During the *phosphorus cycle*, phosphorus moves through every sphere except the atmosphere, because phosphorus is rarely a gas. Phosphorus enters soil and water when rock breaks down and when phosphorus dissolves in water. Some organisms excrete their excess phosphorus in their waste, and this phosphorus may enter soil and water. Plants absorb this phosphorus through their roots. The plants then incorporate it into their tissues. Animals absorb the phosphorus when they eat the plants. When the animals die, the phosphorus returns to the environment through decomposition.

Close

Reteaching — BASIC

Open and Closed Systems Write the following descriptions on cards or on the board, or draw pictures to illustrate these descriptions: an air conditioner that changes warm air to cool air (open system), a water wheel that does work as water flows over it (open system), a closed refrigerator that cools the air inside by removing heat to the outside of the refrigerator (closed system), a pressure cooker in which water is boiled at high pressure (closed system). Have students identify which of these systems are open and which are closed. **LS Logical**

Quiz — GENERAL

1. What would you call a set of interacting components in which energy, but not matter, is exchanged with the surroundings? (a closed system)
2. What part of Earth contains all forms of water? (the hydrosphere)
3. What is the addition, removal, and transfer of energy between Earth's spheres an example of? (an energy budget)

Group Activity — ADVANCED

Earth's Other Cycles Have groups of three or four students research the oxygen, rock, and energy cycles within Earth's spheres. Students should describe and explain the basic steps of each cycle and note how the cycles affect processes in various spheres (for example, how the carbon cycle affects climate through the "greenhouse effect"). The groups that research the energy cycle should note its connection to the water cycle, its effects on weather, and how it differs from the cycles involving matter. Each group should report its findings in an oral presentation. **LS Verbal/Logical**

Close, *continued*

Answers to Section Review

1. because it consists of many interacting components
2. In an open system, matter and energy are added and removed. In a closed system, only energy enters or leaves.
3. The atmosphere contains gases that sustain life and shield Earth from harmful radiation. The hydrosphere covers more than 70% of Earth's surface and is made up of all the water on Earth. The geosphere consists of the rock and soil of Earth's crust and the solid and molten rock within Earth's interior. The biosphere contains all living organisms and extends from the deep ocean to the atmosphere.
4. Energy in Earth's system comes from the sun and from Earth's interior.
5. chemical reactions, radioactive decay, radiation of energy as heat and light, and the growth and decay of organisms
6. In the short-term cycle, CO_2 is absorbed from the atmosphere by plants, which produce carbohydrates that are consumed by organisms. Carbon is returned to the atmosphere mainly as CO_2 from animal and plant respiration and decay. In the long-term cycle, carbon also becomes buried in rock.
7. Nitrogen from the atmosphere is fixed by bacteria in the soil and water. This nitrogen is absorbed by plants, which are consumed by animals, and is returned to the soil or water when dead animals decompose. Other bacteria return nitrogen to the atmosphere.

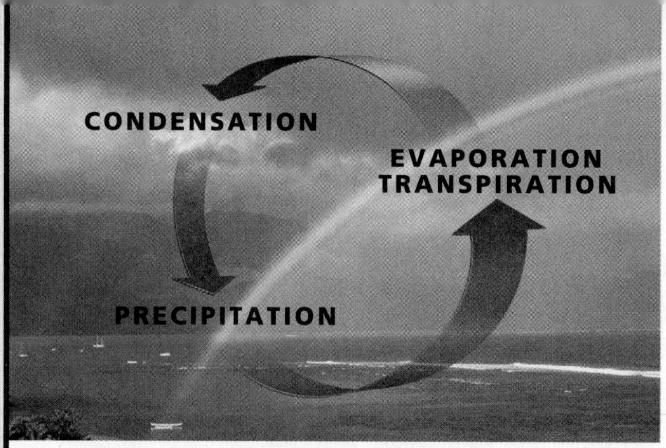

Figure 8 The water cycle is the continuous movement of water from the atmosphere to Earth's surface and back to the atmosphere.

The Water Cycle

The movement of water from the atmosphere to Earth's surface and back to the atmosphere is always taking place. This continuous movement of water is called the *water cycle*, which is shown in **Figure 8.** In the water cycle, water changes from liquid water to water vapor through the energy transfers involved in evaporation and transpiration. Evaporation occurs when energy is absorbed by liquid water and the energy changes the water into water vapor. Transpiration is the release of moisture from plant leaves. During these processes, water absorbs energy and changes state. When the water loses energy, it condenses to form water droplets, such as those that form clouds. Eventually, water falls back to Earth's surface as precipitation, such as rain, snow, or hail.

Humans and the Earth System

All natural cycles can be altered by human activities. The carbon cycle is affected when humans use fossil fuels. Fossil fuels form over millions of years. Carbon dioxide is returned to the atmospheric reservoir rapidly when humans burn these fuels. Also, both the nitrogen and phosphorus cycles are affected by agriculture. Some farming techniques can strip the soil of nitrogen and phosphorus. Many farmers replace these nutrients by using fertilizers, which can upset the balance of these elements in nature.

Section 2 Review

Key Ideas

1. **Explain** how Earth can be considered a system.
2. **Compare** an open system with a closed system.
3. **List** two characteristics of each of Earth's four major spheres.
4. **Identify** the two main sources of energy in Earth's system.
5. **Identify** four processes in which matter cycles on Earth.
6. **Explain** how carbon cycles in Earth's system.
7. **Explain** how nitrogen cycles in Earth's system.

Critical Thinking

8. **Identifying Relationships** For each of Earth's four spheres, describe one way that the water cycle affects the sphere.
9. **Determining Cause and Effect** What effect, if any, would you expect a massive forest fire to have on the amount of carbon dioxide in the atmosphere? Explain your answer.
10. **Analyzing Ideas** Early Earth was constantly being bombarded by meteorites, comets, and asteroids. Was early Earth an open system or a closed system? Explain your answer.
11. **Analyzing Relationships** Explain the role of energy in the carbon cycle.

Concept Mapping

12. Use the following terms to create a concept map: *closed system, system, open system, matter, atmosphere, biosphere, energy, geosphere,* and *hydrosphere.*

8. Water that evaporates into the atmosphere moderates the temperature of air; water as precipitation in the geosphere causes the weathering of rock; liquid water in the biosphere sustains life; and water as precipitation in the hydrosphere replenishes supplies of fresh water.
9. It would add carbon dioxide to the atmosphere, because when organisms such as trees burn, CO_2 is released.
10. an open system, because matter was being added to it

Answers continued on p. 81A

Differentiated Instruction

Alternative Assessment

Rates of Cycles Have students research the time required for the various steps to take place in the phosphorus, nitrogen, or long-term carbon cycles. Have students then describe each cycle in terms of how quickly each step in the cycle can occur and how long a given quantity of carbon, phosphorus, or nitrogen takes to go through the complete cycle. Students may present their findings as a written report, oral presentation, or poster. **LS Verbal/Logical**

ENVIRONMENTAL CONNECTION

SECTION 3 Ecology

Key Ideas	Key Terms	Why It Matters
❯ Define *ecosystem.* ❯ Identify three factors that control the balance of an ecosystem. ❯ Summarize how energy is transferred through an ecosystem. ❯ Describe one way that ecosystems respond to environmental change.	**ecosystem** **carrying capacity** **food web**	The study of ecology demonstrates, and helps us appreciate, the interconnectedness of all the Earth systems that support and sustain humans and all other living things.

One area of science in which life science and Earth science are closely linked is called *ecology*. Ecology is the study of the complex relationships between living things and their nonliving, or *abiotic,* environment. Some ecologists also investigate how communities of organisms change over time.

Ecosystems

Organisms on Earth inhabit many different environments. A community of organisms and the abiotic environment that the organisms inhabit is called an **ecosystem.** The terms *ecology* and *ecosystem* come from the Greek word *oikos*, which means "house." Each ecosystem on Earth is a distinct, self-supporting system. An ecosystem may be as large as an ocean or as small as a drop of water. The largest ecosystem is the entire biosphere.

ecosystem a community of organisms and their abiotic environment

Most of Earth's ecosystems contain a variety of plants and animals. Plants are important to an ecosystem because they use energy from the sun to produce their own food. Organisms that make their own food are called *producers*. Producers are a source of food for other organisms. *Consumers* are organisms that get their energy by eating other organisms. Consumers may get energy by eating producers or by eating other consumers, as the consumers shown in **Figure 1** are doing. Some consumers get energy by breaking down dead organisms. These consumers are called *decomposers*. To remain healthy, an ecosystem needs to have a balance of producers, consumers, and decomposers.

Figure 1 Vultures and a spotted hyena are feeding on an elephant carcass in Chobe National Park in Botswana. ***Name two consumers that are shown in this photo.***

Section 3

Focus

Overview

This section explains how ecosystems function, how interactions must maintain balance if an ecosystem is to thrive, and how human activities influence environmental conditions.

Bellringer

Have students write down what they think the words *ecosystem* and *ecology* mean. (Sample answer: An ecosystem is an environment in which various organisms depend on each other to exist. Ecology is the study of the function and preservation of ecosystems.) **LS Verbal**

Motivate

Using the Figure — GENERAL

Members of Ecosystems Point out that, as a general rule, plants are producers and animals are consumers. However, the roles of each kingdom, as well as the functions of fungi and single-celled organisms, blur the lines somewhat. Ask students to identify producers in the photograph and explain why they are producers. (The grasses, plants, and tree in the background are examples of producers, because they manufacture food for themselves.) Answer to caption question: The hyena and vultures are consumers. When alive, the elephant was a consumer. **LS Visual**

Key Resources

Chapter Resource File
- Directed Reading BASIC

Technology
- Transparencies
  Bellringer

Teach

Teaching Tip ADVANCED

Connect to Familiar Processes Explain to students that the idea of carrying capacity is related to the economic idea of supply and demand. Draw an analogy to a store that has 100 loaves of bread on the shelf at any given time. If each consumer requires one loaf of bread, the maximum number of consumers—the carrying capacity—will be 100. Just as the store cannot supply 101 customers with the minimum number of loaves that each needs, so an ecosystem cannot supply more organisms with food than its resources allow. **LS Logical**

Answer to Reading Check

The amount of matter and energy in an ecosystem can supply a population of a given size, and no larger. This maximum population is the carrying capacity of the ecosystem.

Activity GENERAL

Poster Project Have students research how predator populations increase and decrease with variations in the populations of their prey. Students may use the lemming example in the text, or you may suggest other examples, such as ringed seals and polar bears. Students should find maximum and minimum numbers for given populations of predators and prey over 20 to 50 years. Posters should show pictures and explanations of steps in the cycle. Have students explain their posters to the class. **LS Visual/Verbal**

Figure 2 The fur of this elk calf was singed in a forest fire in Yellowstone National Park.

Balancing Forces in Ecosystems

Organisms in an ecosystem use matter and energy. Because amounts of matter and energy in an ecosystem are limited, population growth within the ecosystem is limited, too. The largest population that an environment can support at any given time is called the **carrying capacity.** Carrying capacity depends on available resources. The carrying capacity of an ecosystem is also affected by how easily matter and energy are transferred between life-forms and the environment in that ecosystem. So, a given ecosystem can support only the number of organisms that allows matter and energy to be transferred efficiently through the ecosystem.

Ecological Responses to Change

Changes in any one part of an ecosystem may affect the entire system in unpredictable ways. However, in general, ecosystems react to changes in ways that maintain or restore balance in the ecosystem.

Environmental change in the form of a sudden disturbance, such as a forest fire, can greatly damage and disrupt ecosystems, as shown in **Figure 2.** But over time, organisms will migrate back into damaged areas in predictable patterns. First, grasses and fast-growing plants will start to grow. Then, shrubs and small animal species will return. Eventually, larger tree species and larger animals will return to the area. Ecosystems are resilient and tend to restore a community of organisms to a state like its original state unless the physical environment is permanently altered.

carrying capacity the largest population that an environment can support at any given time

Reading Check **Explain the relationship between carrying capacity and the amount of matter and energy in an ecosystem.**

Why It Matters

How Does Life Form on Bare Rock?

REAL WORLD

In 1963, scientists observed an underwater volcanic eruption off the south coast of Iceland create a new island, named Surtsey. Winds and ocean currents brought seeds to the fresh, bare rock, and plants soon became established. Insects, spiders, birds, and worms followed.

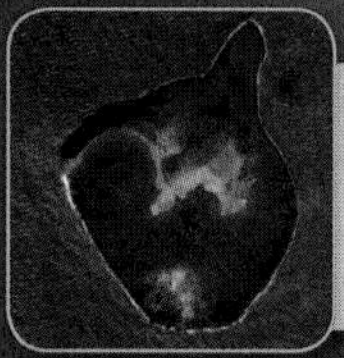

Notice the green patch in the south of this aerial view. The densest plant growth occurs here.

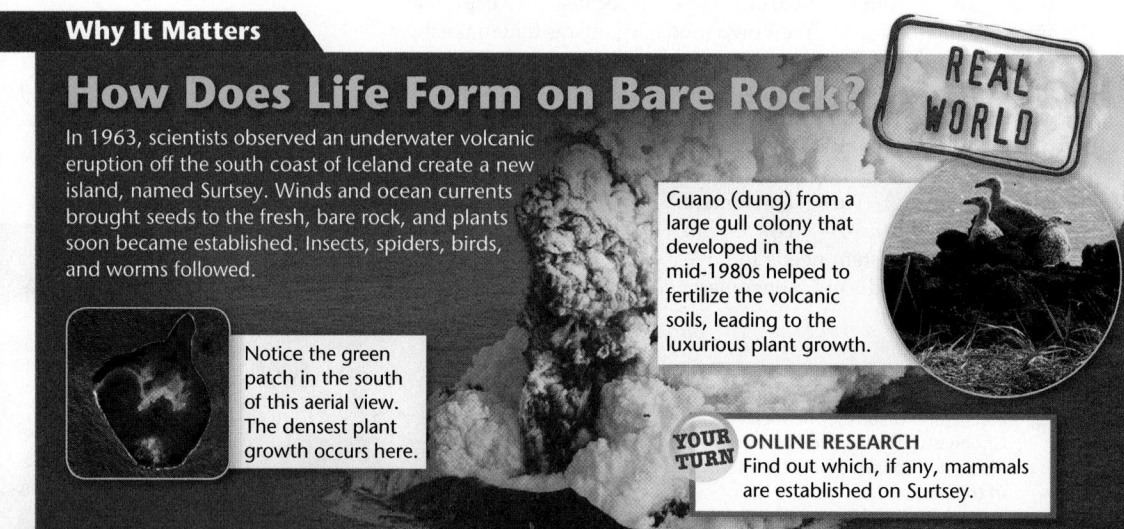

Guano (dung) from a large gull colony that developed in the mid-1980s helped to fertilize the volcanic soils, leading to the luxurious plant growth.

YOUR TURN **ONLINE RESEARCH** Find out which, if any, mammals are established on Surtsey.

Why It Matters

How Does Life Form on Bare Rock? The eruption that formed Surtsey ended in June 1967. When it was over, about 9% of the total island mass, nearly 3 km^2, rested above sea level.

Although lichens are often cited as initial colonizers of bare-rock environments, the earliest colonizers of the island were moss species. Currently, the island supports a variety of plants, fungi, birds, and invertebrate animals. Several seal species are the only mammals known to visit and breed on the island.

Answer to Your Turn

Online Research No mammals are established yet on the island. Breeding groups of seals use the island, but are not there year round.

Energy Transfer

The ultimate source of energy for almost every ecosystem is the sun. Plants capture solar energy by a chemical process called *photosynthesis*. This captured energy then flows through ecosystems from the plants, to the animals that feed on the plants, and finally to the decomposers of animal and plant remains. Matter also cycles through an ecosystem by this process.

As matter cycles and energy flows through an ecosystem, chemical elements are combined and recombined. Each chemical change results in either the temporary storage of energy or the loss of energy. One way to see how energy is lost as it moves through the ecosystem is to draw an energy pyramid. Producers form the base of the pyramid. Consumers that eat producers are the next level of the pyramid. Animals that eat those consumers form the upper levels of the pyramid. As you move up the pyramid, more energy is lost at each level. Therefore, the least amount of total energy is available to organisms at the top of the pyramid.

Food Chains and Food Webs

The sequence in which organisms consume other organisms can be represented by a *food chain*. However, ecosystems are complex and generally contain more organisms than are on a single food chain. In addition, many organisms eat more than just one other species. Therefore, a **food web,** such as the one shown in **Figure 3,** is used to represent the relationships between multiple food chains. Each arrow points to the organism that eats the organism at the base of the arrow.

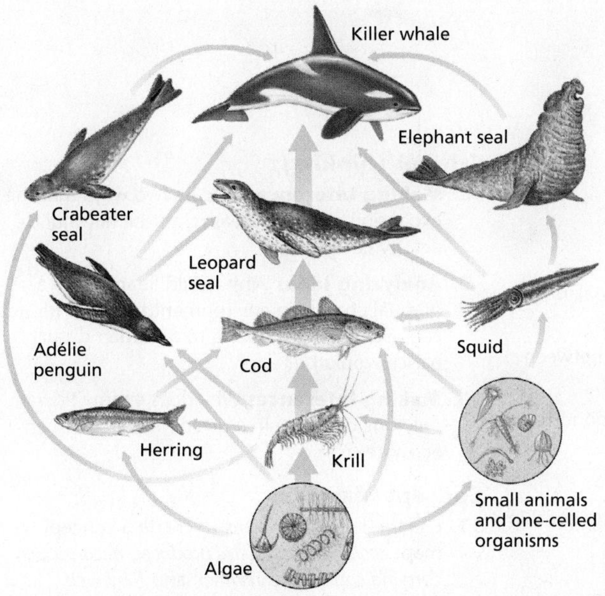

Figure 3 This food web shows how, in an ocean ecosystem, the largest organisms, such as killer whales, depend on the smallest organisms, such as algae. ***Which organisms would be near the top of a food pyramid?***

THINK central
INTERACT ONLINE
(Keyword: HQXEASF3)

Quick Lab 20 min

Studying Ecosystems

Procedure

1. Find a small natural area near your school.
2. Choose a 5 m by 5 m section of the natural area to study. This area may include the ground or vegetation such as trees or bushes.
3. Spend 10 min documenting the number and types of organisms that live in the area.

Analysis

1. How many kinds of organisms live in the area that you studied?
2. Draw a food web that describes how energy may flow through the ecosystem that you studied.

food web a diagram that shows the feeding relationships among organisms in an ecosystem

Quick Lab

Skills Acquired
- Identifying and Recognizing Patterns

Teacher's Notes: Separate students into groups of two or three, and assign each group a different ecosystem.

Answers to Analysis

1. Answers may vary depending on the ecosystem and the time of year in which it is studied.
2. Answers may vary. For example, students may indicate that insects feed on the remains of dead animals, that birds feed on insects, and that the energy is transferred from previous consumers to the organisms that consume them.

Key Resources

Technology
- Transparencies
  9 A Food Web

Close

Reteaching — BASIC

Food Chains Make a series of cards on which pictures and names of the following organisms are drawn or pasted: plant, caterpillar, spider, bird, cat. Have students indicate the order in which the organisms occupy the food chain, from the lowest-level producer to the highest-level consumer. (The organisms are listed above in the correct food chain sequence.) LS **Logical**

Quiz — GENERAL

1. How does an ecosystem typically react to changes? (The ecosystem responds to restore and maintain balance.)
2. What are the three kinds of organisms in an ecosystem? (producers, consumers, and decomposers)

Using the Figure — BASIC

Food Webs Have students examine the directions in which the arrows point in the figure. Ask students which organism has all arrows pointing away from it and what this means. (Algae; they are producers and the basic source of energy for the food web.) Ask students which organism has all arrows pointing toward it and what this means. (Killer whale; it is a consumer and eats more than one kind of organism.) Answer to caption question: Organisms near the top of a food pyramid would be the largest and strongest consumers. LS **Visual/Logical**

Differentiated Instruction

Special Education Students

Energy Pyramid Students with behavior control issues are more successful learners when they have hands-on involvement. Divide the class into small groups. Scatter students with such issues among the groups. Ask them to be the "writers" for their groups. Have each group create an energy pyramid, as described on this page. Have students use old science magazines as a source of pictures for their pyramids.

Close, *continued*

Answers to Section Review

1. An ecosystem is a community of organisms and the environment that the organisms inhabit.
2. The biosphere sustains organisms that interact and affect each other, providing an environment for all of them.
3. how matter and energy cycle through the ecosystem, how ecosystems respond to change, and how organisms in the ecosystem interact
4. The sun's energy is stored in carbohydrates that are produced by plants by photosynthesis. This energy is absorbed by consumers that eat the plants and is, in turn, absorbed by higher-level consumers. Energy from animal remains is transferred to decomposers.
5. Ecosystems generally respond to change in a way that restores balance within the ecosystem.
6. A food chain is a sequence in which an organism is consumed by another organism. In a food web, several organisms feed upon one type of organism, which are consumed by still other organisms that compete with each other, producing a more complex pattern of consumption.
7. Good stewardship helps to maintain balance within and between ecosystems, which helps to ensure their health and productivity.
8. The expansion of urban areas removes vegetation that helps to hold topsoil in place, otherwise leading to soil erosion; water pollution from street runoff affects the water supplies; animals may flee, disturbing neighboring ecosystems.

Figure 4 These hikers are acting responsibly by choosing to remain on marked trails in the rain forest. In this way, they are helping prevent ecological damage to the area.

Human Stewardship of the Environment

All of Earth's systems are interconnected, and changes in one system may affect the operation of other systems. Earth's ecosystems provide a wide variety of resources on which people depend. People need water and air to survive. Changes in ecosystems can affect the ability of an area to sustain a human population. For example, the quality of the atmosphere, the productivity of soils, and the availability of natural resources can affect the availability of food.

Ecological balances can be disrupted by human activity. Populations of plants and animals can be destroyed through overconsumption of resources. When humans convert large natural areas to agricultural or urban areas, natural ecosystems are often destroyed. Another serious threat to ecosystems is pollution. *Pollution* is the contamination of the environment with harmful waste products or impurities.

When people, such as those in **Figure 4**, strive to prevent ecological damage to an area, they are trying to be responsible stewards of Earth. To help ensure the ongoing health and productivity of the Earth system, many people work to use Earth's resources wisely. By using fossil fuels, land and water resources, and other natural resources wisely, many people are helping keep Earth's ecosystems in balance.

Section 3 Review

Key Ideas

1. **Define** *ecosystem.*
2. **Explain** why the entire biosphere is an ecosystem.
3. **Identify** three factors that control the balance of an ecosystem.
4. **Summarize** how energy is transferred between the sun and consumers in an ecosystem.
5. **Describe** one way that ecosystems respond to environmental change.
6. **Compare** a food chain with a food web.
7. **Summarize** the importance of good stewardship of Earth's resources.

Critical Thinking

8. **Making Inferences** Discuss two ways that the expansion of urban areas might be harmful to nearby ecosystems.
9. **Analyzing Ideas** Why would adapting to a gradual change in environment be easier for an ecosystem than adapting to a sudden disturbance would be?
10. **Making Inferences** Why does energy flow in only one direction in a given food chain of an ecosystem?

Concept Mapping

11. Use the following terms to create a concept map: *ecology, ecosystem, producer, decomposer, carrying capacity, consumer,* and *food web.*

9. An ecosystem can react to gradual changes by making small adjustments to maintain the overall balance of the system. Extreme environmental changes require dramatic adjustments by organisms and may result in permanent changes to some components of the ecosystem.
10. Energy flows from producers toward consumers that use more energy. Lower-level consumers rarely consume higher-level consumers. Producers do not consume at all.
11. *Ecology* is the study of *ecosystems,* which have a *carrying capacity* and contain a *food web* that has *producers, consumers,* and *decomposers.*

Differentiated Instruction

Alternative Assessment

Modeling Ecosystems Have students create a poster, diorama, or computer model showing the relationships between organisms in a small ecosystem they are familiar with, such as a pond or dead log near their home. The model should include producers, consumers, and decomposers. **LS Kinesthetic/Logical**

Why It Matters

Fish that Feed the Forest

Food webs and cycles can involve some unlikely participants. Did you know that salmon nourish the forests of North America's Pacific coast? Up to 77% of the nitrogen in coastal rain-forest trees comes from the ocean. Trees that grow close to inland salmon-spawning streams, such as Sitka spruce, grow faster than trees that do not. By understanding the links between different Earth systems, scientists have pieced together an unexpected relationship between nitrogen from the ocean, bears, salmon, and inland rain-forest trees.

Salmon spend most of their lives in the ocean. Before they die, they migrate from the ocean, up freshwater rivers and into inland streams to spawn. In the shallow waters of their spawning grounds, salmon are easy prey to predators, such as bears.

Bears often drag the salmon they catch into the forest. They often eat only their favorite parts of the fish and leave the rest to decay on the forest floor. The decaying nitrogen-rich carcasses become the fertilizer that ensures the health of the rain forest.

YOUR TURN

UNDERSTANDING CONCEPTS
How does nitrogen from the ocean end up in inland coastal trees?

CRITICAL THINKING
What could happen to the coastal rain forests if salmon populations decreased dramatically?

Why It Matters

Fish that Feed the Forest Nitrogen is a key nutrient for all plants and is one of the main ingredients of all plant fertilizers. Studies conducted between 1998 and 2002 provided evidence that spawning salmon were the main source of ocean-derived nitrogen that sustains riparian (riverbank) vegetation. Scientists can analyze the composition of wood from living trees to find the percentage of nitrogen that comes from the ocean and the percentage that comes from the atmosphere. On North America's Pacific coast, up to 77% of the nitrogen in riparian trees comes from the ocean. Bears appear to be a key vector—through their feces, for example, as well as the salmon carcasses they drag up to 300 m from spawning streams linking ocean nitrogen with riparian vegetation.

Answers to Your Turn

Understanding Concepts Nitrogen-rich salmon carcasses, left behind by bears, decay on the forest floor.

Critical Thinking If salmon populations decreased, the health of the vegetation in coastal rain forests could decrease. As a result, trees might experience stunted and/or sparser growth.

Differentiated Instruction

English Learners

Poster Project Have students select an ecosystem and research the interactions between various organisms within the ecosystem. Then, have students create a poster that shows both the energy budget for the ecosystem and the food web for the selected organisms. Students should include labels to identify the various interactions in each process. **LS Visual/Logical**

Skills Practice Lab

Time Required
one 45 min class period

Lab Ratings
EASY → HARD

Teacher Preparation
Student Setup
Concept Level
Cleanup

Skills Acquired
- Experimenting
- Measuring
- Observing
- Interpreting

Scientific Methods
In this lab, students will
- Make Observations
- Test the Hypothesis
- Analyze the Results
- Draw Conclusions

Materials
The materials listed are enough for groups of two students. If there are not enough beakers, graduated cylinders, or balances, have pairs or groups of students share these materials.

Skills Practice Lab

45 min

Testing the Conservation of Mass

What You'll Do
- **Measure** the masses of reactants and products in a chemical reaction.
- **Describe** how measuring masses of reactants and products can illustrate the law of conservation of mass.

What You'll Need
bag, plastic sandwich, zipper-type closure
baking soda (sodium bicarbonate)
balance (or scale), metric
beaker, 400 mL
cup, clear plastic, 150 mL (2)
graduated cylinder, 100 mL
paper, weighing (2 pieces)
twist tie
vinegar (acetic acid solution)
water

Safety

As matter cycles through the Earth system, the matter can undergo chemical changes that cause it to change its identity. However, although the matter may change, it is not destroyed. This principle is known as the *law of conservation of mass.* In this lab, you will cause two chemicals to react to form products that differ from the two reacting chemicals. Then, you will determine whether the amount of mass in the system (the experiment) has changed.

Procedure

1. On a blank sheet of paper, prepare a table like the one shown on the next page.
2. Place a piece of weighing paper on a balance. Place 4 to 5 g of baking soda on the paper. Carefully transfer the baking soda to a plastic cup.
3. Using a graduated cylinder, measure 50 mL of vinegar. Pour the vinegar into a second plastic cup.
4. Place both cups on the balance, and determine the combined mass of the cups, baking soda, and vinegar to the nearest 0.01 g. Record the combined mass in the first row of your table under "Initial mass."
5. Take the cups off the balance. Carefully and slowly pour the vinegar into the cup that contains the baking soda. To avoid splattering, add only a small amount of vinegar at a time. Gently swirl the cup to make sure that the reactants are well mixed.

Step 2

Tips and Tricks
Have extra reactants and weighing paper available in case students make mistakes or accidentally spill the reactants. Students should be sure that the reactions have reached completion before measuring the final masses of the products.

	Initial mass (g)	Final mass (g)	Change in mass (g)
Trial 1			
Trial 2			

6. When the reaction has finished, place both cups back on the balance. Determine the combined mass to the nearest 0.01 g. Record the combined mass in the first row of your table under "Final mass."
7. Subtract final mass from initial mass, and record the difference in the first row of your table under "Change in mass."
8. Repeat step 2, but carefully transfer the baking soda to one corner of a plastic bag rather than the cup.
9. To seal the baking soda in the corner of the bag, twist the corner of the bag above the baking soda and wrap the twist tie tightly around the twisted part of the bag.
10. Add 50 mL of vinegar to the bag. Zipper-close the bag so that the vinegar cannot leak out and the bag is airtight.
11. Place the bag in the beaker, and measure the mass of the beaker, the bag, and the reactants. Record the combined mass in the second row of your table under "Initial mass."
12. Remove the twist tie from the bag, and mix the reactants.
13. When the reaction has finished, repeat steps 6 and 7 by using the beaker, bag, twist tie, and products. Record the final mass and change in mass in the table's second row.

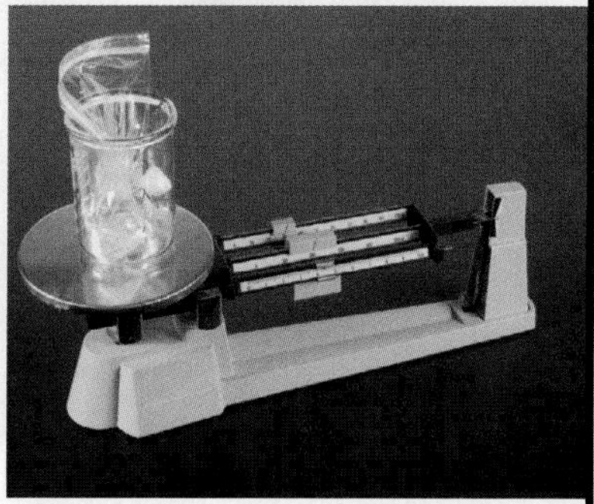

Step 11

Analysis

1. **Analyzing Data** Compare the change in mass that you calculated for the first trial with the change in mass that you calculated for the second trial. What evidence of the conservation of mass does the second trial show?
2. **Analyzing Results** Was the law of conservation of mass violated in the first trial? Explain your answer.
3. **Drawing Conclusions** Was the first trial an example of a closed system or an open system? Which type of system was the second trial? Explain your answer.

Extension

Designing an Experiment Brainstorm other ways to demonstrate the law of conservation of mass in a laboratory. Describe the materials that you would need, and describe any difficulties that you foresee.

Answers to Analysis

1. In the second trial, the mass of the reactants before the reaction took place equaled the mass of the products after the reaction.
2. No. The gas released during the reaction entered the atmosphere, and so was not weighed with the other reaction products.
3. The first trial was an example of an open system, because matter left the cup during the reaction, in the form of a gas. The second trial was an example of a closed system, because all matter remained inside the plastic bag before, during, and after the reaction.

Answer to Extension

Answers may vary. Accept all reasonable answers.

Concentration of Plant Life on Earth

Activity GENERAL

Ocean-Plant Distribution Have students research the types of plants that are found in the oceans. Have them use this research to explain the distribution of ocean plants shown on the map. Have students present their findings as a written report, an oral presentation, or a poster presentation. LS **Verbal/Visual**

Answers to Map Skills Activity

1. Concentrations of chlorophyll on land and in the oceans are indicated by reversed color scales. So, a high concentration in the oceans is indicated by the color red, while a high concentration on land is indicated by the color green.
2. Answers may vary. Sample answer: North Africa, central Australia, and the Arabian peninsula all have low concentrations of chlorophyll. All these areas are deserts, without much vegetation.
3. They are covered with ice.
4. The highest chlorophyll concentrations are found near the edges of continents, especially near major river mouths. These areas are rich in nutrients that organisms need to survive.
5. Days along the equator tend to be more uniform in length than days at higher latitudes, providing a more continuous level of sunlight and therefore a steadier growth of plant life. Also, sunlight is more direct to these regions.

MAPS in Action

Concentration of Plant Life on Earth

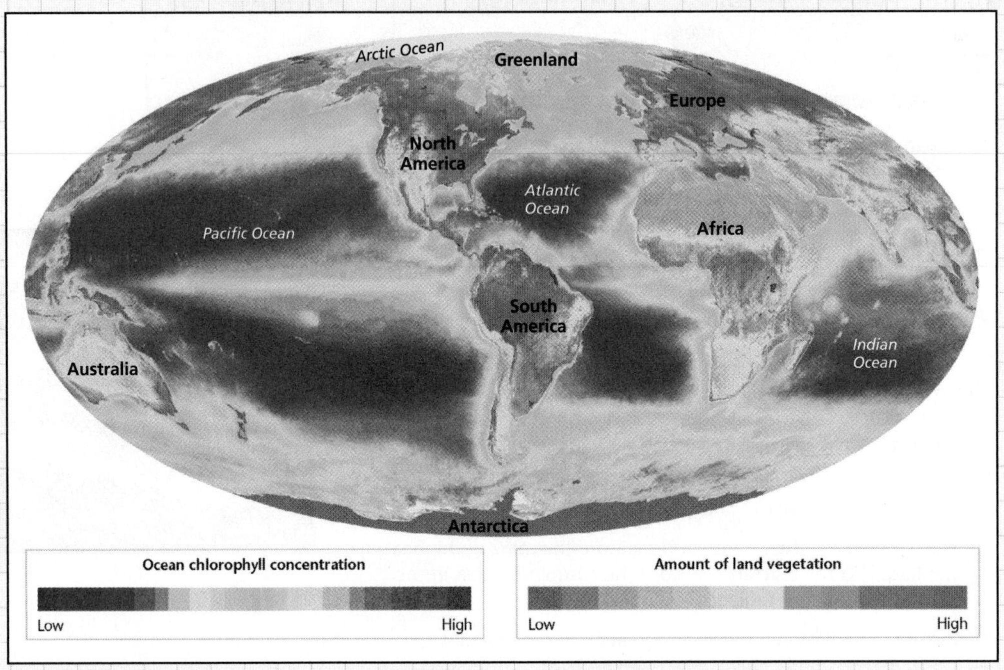

Map Skills Activity

This map shows the concentration of plant life on land and in the oceans. Each color in the key represents a concentration of plant life as indicated by the concentration of chlorophyll. The higher the concentration of chlorophyll is, the higher the concentration of plant life is. Use the map to answer the questions below.

1. **Using a Key** How can you distinguish between high chlorophyll concentration in the ocean and high chlorophyll concentration on land?
2. **Comparing Areas** List three areas that have very low chlorophyll concentration on land. What characteristics of these areas cause such low chlorophyll concentrations?
3. **Comparing Areas** Why do you think Antarctica, Greenland, and the Arctic Ocean lack chlorophyll?
4. **Identifying Trends** Where are the highest chlorophyll concentrations in the ocean located? Why do you think that these locations have high chlorophyll concentrations?
5. **Identifying Trends** Plants use sunlight and chlorophyll to produce energy. What can you infer about the amount of sunlight around the equator that could help explain why areas along the equator tend to have higher concentrations of chlorophyll than surrounding areas do?

Key Resources

Technology

- Transparencies
  10 Concentration of Plant Life on Earth

Chapter 2

Summary

THINK central SUPER SUMMARY Keyword: HQXEASS

Key Ideas | **Key Terms**

Section 1

Earth: A Unique Planet

- Earth is an oblate spheroid that has an average diameter of 12,756 km.
- The compositional layers of Earth's interior are the thin, solid outermost crust, the rocky mantle beneath the crust, and the central core. These layers are divided into five structural zones: lithosphere, asthenosphere, mesosphere, outer core, and inner core.
- Liquid iron in the outer core may be a source of Earth's magnetic field.
- Newton's law of gravitation states that the force of attraction between any two objects depends on their masses and the distance between them.

Key Terms: **crust,** p. 30; **mantle,** p. 30; **core,** p. 30; **lithosphere,** p. 31; **asthenosphere,** p. 31; **mesosphere,** p. 31

Section 2

Energy in the Earth System

- In an open system, both energy and matter enter and exit the system. In a closed system, energy enters and exits, but matter neither enters nor exits.
- The atmosphere is gaseous. The hydrosphere is mostly liquid water but may also appear in solid or vapor form. The geosphere is the solid part of Earth. The biosphere contains all the life in the other three spheres.
- The sun (external) and radioactive decay (internal) are the two main sources of energy in the Earth system.
- Matter moves through Earth systems in cycles such as the nitrogen, carbon, phosphorus, and water cycles.

Key Terms: **system,** p. 33; **atmosphere,** p. 35; **hydrosphere,** p. 35; **geosphere,** p. 35; **biosphere,** p. 35

Section 3

Ecology

- An ecosystem is a community of organisms and the environment that they inhabit.
- Carrying capacity, disturbance, and energy transfer are three factors that control the balance of an ecosystem.
- Energy is transferred through an ecosystem via feeding relationships.
- In general, an ecosystem responds to changes in ways that maintain or restore balance in the ecosystem.

Key Terms: **ecosystem,** p. 41; **carrying capacity,** p. 42; **food web,** p. 43

Chapter Summary

Using THINK central Resources

Super Summary

Have students connect the major concepts in this chapter through an interactive Super Summary. Visit www.thinkcentral.com and type in the keyword **HQXEASS** to access the Super Summary for this chapter.

Chapter Review

Assignment Guide	
Section	**Question**
1	4, 8, 10, 12, 19, 21, 33
2	2, 6, 7, 11, 13, 14, 16–18, 23, 25, 27, 35–38
3	3, 9, 15, 24, 26, 28, 30, 34
2 and 3	5, 20, 22, 29, 32
1–3	1, 31

Reading Toolbox

1. Sample answer: The law of gravitation is a law because it describes a pattern in nature that is observed so often it is assumed to be true. A theory explains a natural pattern.

Using Key Terms

2–9. Answers may vary but should show that students understand the definitions of and differences between key terms.

Understanding Key Concepts

10. b
11. b
12. a
13. d
14. b
15. d
16. c
17. c
18. b

Short Answer

19. the liquid iron in Earth's outer core
20. Decomposers break down organic matter and help to move carbon, phosphorus, and nitrogen through their cycles.
21. The mantle, or second compositional zone, is divided into three segments that form structural zones. The lithosphere is made up of the crust (the first compositional layer) and uppermost mantle; the asthenosphere is the next layer of the mantle; and the mesosphere is the lower part of the mantle. The third compositional zone, the core, is divided into two structural zones: the outer core and the inner core.
22. The first law of thermodynamics states that energy cannot be created or destroyed. This means that all ecosystems share, transfer, and convert energy, but they do not create or destroy it. The second law of thermodynamics states that energy becomes less organized with each process. This means that as energy is transferred within or between ecosystems, it becomes less useful. An example is loss of energy at each step up on the food pyramid.
23. Answers may vary. Sample answer: Drinking water temporarily removes it from the supply of liquid water. Breathing and perspiring introduce water vapor into the atmosphere.
24. It keeps ecosystems in balance, keeps the Earth system healthy and productive, and protects resources, organisms, and ecosystems that are essential for human survival.
25. The atmosphere weathers rock to form sand and soil, interacts with the geosphere to recycle carbon over long periods of time, and interacts with nitrogen-fixing bacteria to return nitrogen to the geosphere.

Chapter 2 Review

1. **Outlining** Choose one of the scientific laws in this chapter. Explain why it is an example of a scientific law rather than a scientific theory. Include an example of a scientific theory for comparison.

READING TOOLBOX

USING KEY TERMS

Use each of the following terms in a separate sentence.

2. *system*
3. *carrying capacity*
4. *lithosphere*

For each pair of terms, explain how the meanings of the terms differ.

5. *system* and *ecosystem*
6. *biosphere* and *geosphere*
7. *hydrosphere* and *atmosphere*
8. *mantle* and *asthenosphere*
9. *energy pyramid* and *food web*

UNDERSTANDING KEY IDEAS

10. The diameter of Earth is greatest at the
    a. poles.
    b. equator.
    c. oceans.
    d. continents.
11. The element that makes up the largest percentage of the atmosphere is
    a. oxygen.
    b. nitrogen.
    c. carbon dioxide.
    d. ozone.
12. The gravitational attraction between two objects is determined by the mass of the two objects and the
    a. distance between the objects.
    b. weight of the objects.
    c. diameter of the objects.
    d. density of the objects.
13. Energy can enter the Earth system from internal sources through convection and from external sources through
    a. radioactive decay. **c.** wind energy.
    b. wave energy. **d.** solar energy.
14. Closed systems exchange energy but do *not* exchange
    a. gravity. **c.** sunlight.
    b. matter. **d.** heat.
15. Which of the following is *not* an ecosystem?
    a. a lake **c.** a tree
    b. an ocean **d.** a population
16. Which of the following processes is *not* involved in the water cycle?
    a. evaporation
    b. transpiration
    c. combustion
    d. precipitation
17. A jar with its lid on tightly is one example of a(n)
    a. open system.
    b. biosphere.
    c. closed system.
    d. ecosystem.
18. Phosphorus cycles through all spheres except the
    a. geosphere.
    b. atmosphere.
    c. biosphere.
    d. hydrosphere.

SHORT ANSWER

19. What characteristic of Earth's interior is likely to be responsible for Earth's magnetic field?
20. What is the role of decomposers in the cycling of matter in the biosphere?
21. Corrolate the three compositional zones of Earth to the five structural zones of Earth.
22. Restate the first and second laws of thermodynamics, and explain how they relate to ecosystems on Earth.
23. Describe two ways that your daily activities affect the water cycle.

24. Explain three reasons that stewardship of Earth's resources is important.
25. Describe three ways in which the atmosphere interacts with the geosphere.
26. Identify two distinguishing factors of a nearby ecosystem, and name five kinds of organisms that live in that ecosystem.

CRITICAL THINKING

27. **Analyzing Ideas** What happens to the matter and energy in fossil fuels when the fuels are burned?
28. **Making Inferences** Draw an energy pyramid that includes the organisms shown in the food web diagram in this chapter.
29. **Making Predictions** How would the removal of decomposers from Earth's biosphere affect the carbon, nitrogen, and phosphorus cycles?
30. **Analyzing Relationships** Do you think that Earth has a carrying capacity for humans? Explain your reasoning.

CONCEPT MAPPING

31. Use the following terms to create a concept map: *biosphere, magnetosphere, mantle, atmosphere, geosphere, hydrosphere, ecosystem, crust,* and *core.*

MATH SKILLS

Math Skills

32. **Making Calculations** In one year, the plants in each square meter of an ecosystem obtained 1,460 kilowatt•hours (kWh) of the sun's energy by photosynthesis. In that year, each square meter of plants stored 237 kWh. What percentage of the sun's energy did the plants use for life processes in that year?
33. **Making Calculations** The average radius of Earth is 6,371 km. If the average thickness of oceanic crust is 7.5 km and the average thickness of continental crust is 35 km, what fraction of Earth's radius is each type of crust?

WRITING SKILLS

34. **Creative Writing** If you noticed that pollution was harming a nearby lake, how would you convince your community of the need to take action to solve the problem? Describe three research tools you would use to find materials that support your opinion.
35. **Communicating Main Ideas** Explain why closed systems typically do not exist on Earth. Suggest two examples of a closed system created by humans.

INTERPRETING GRAPHICS

The graphs below show the difference in energy consumption and population size in developed and developing countries. Use the graphs to answer the questions that follow.

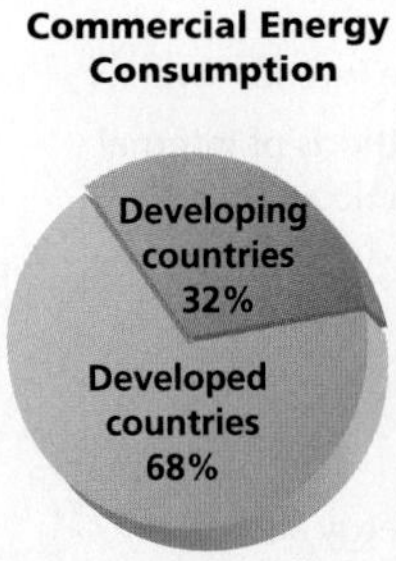

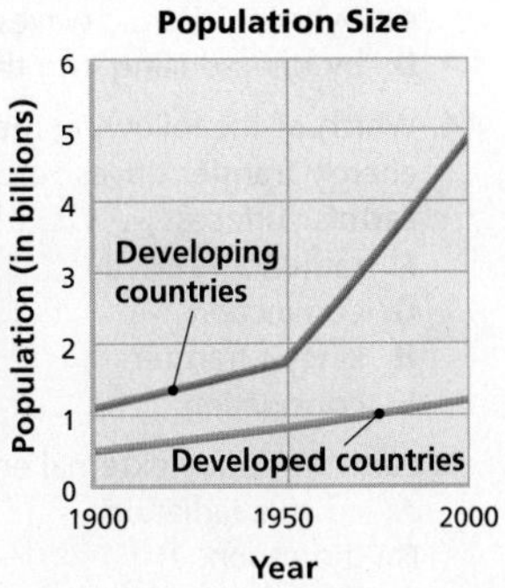

36. Describe the differences in energy consumption and population growth between developed and the developing countries.
37. Do you think that the percentage of commercial energy consumed by developing countries will increase or decrease? Explain your answer.
38. Why is information on energy consumption represented in a pie graph, while population size is shown in a line graph?

Chapter Review

26. Answers may vary. Sample answer: A pond contains water and has both producers and consumers to support aquatic life. Organisms may include fish, frogs, salamanders, underwater plants, and mosquitoes.

Critical Thinking

27. When fuel is burned, the products enter the atmosphere, hydrosphere, and/or geosphere. The stored energy is changed into heat or light, which may be used to do work or to provide warmth.
28. Student drawings should indicate that the smaller organisms form the base of the pyramid, while progressively larger organisms form higher layers. The killer whale should be at the top of the pyramid.
29. Because decomposers break down dead organisms, they help to transfer the organisms' carbon, nitrogen, and phosphorus to soil. Without decomposers, these cycles would be slowed down or would cease.
30. Yes. Earth is finite in size, and therefore has a finite amount of resources, many of which are nonrenewable. Humans require a minimum amount of certain resources to survive and remain healthy. Therefore, there is a maximum number of humans that Earth can sustain.

Concept Mapping

31. Answers may vary but should include all of the terms listed. Sample answers appear at the end of this unit on p. 81B.

Math Skills

32. energy used = 1,460 kWh − 237 kWh = 1,223 kWh; percentage of energy = (1,223 kWh ÷ 1,460 kWh) × 100 = 83.8%
33. percentage of radius that is oceanic crust = (7.5 km ÷ 6,371 km) × 100 = 0.12%

    percentage of radius that is continental crust = (35 km ÷ 6,371 km) × 100 = 0.55%

Writing Skills

34. Answers may vary. Accept all reasonable answers.
35. Answers may vary. Accept all reasonable answers.

Interpreting Graphics

36. Developing countries have a much higher rate of population growth than developed countries do. Developed countries use about twice as much energy as developing countries do, even though the populations of developed countries are much smaller.
37. Developing countries will probably consume a higher percentage of commercial energy over time, because population growth is increasing in developing countries.
38. The pie graph shows how separate amounts make up a total amount, while the line graph of population size shows change over time.

Estimated Time

To give students practice under more realistic testing conditions, allow them 30 minutes to answer all of the questions in this practice test.

Test Doctor

Question 3 Answer C is correct. Scientists use seismic waves to determine the composition and size of Earth's interior. Answers A and D are incorrect because scientists can drill only a few kilometers into Earth's crust, not enough to reach the interior layers or to directly observe them. Answer B is incorrect because rock samples at the surface tell us little about the interior of Earth.

Question 4 Answer G is correct. Convection causes materials of different temperatures and densities to rise and fall in the mantle. This movement drives volcanic activity at the surface. Answer F is incorrect because radioactive decay provides only a very small amount of Earth's internal energy. Answers H and I are similar forms of energy transfer that provide little energy transfer to the surface.

Question 11 Answer B is correct. Answer A is incorrect because the use of oil is predicted to stay about the same over the next 25 years. Answer C is incorrect because the use of coal is predicted to fall slightly over the next 25 years. Answer D is incorrect because the use of renewable energy sources is predicted to stay about the same.

Chapter 2 Standardized Test Prep

Understanding Concepts

Directions (1–5): For each question, write on a separate sheet of paper the letter of the correct answer.

1. The crust and the rigid upper part of the mantle are found in what part of the Earth?
   A. the asthenosphere
   B. the lithosphere
   C. the mesosphere
   D. the stratosphere
2. Because phosphorus rarely occurs as a gas, the phosphorus cycle mainly occurs between the
   F. biosphere, geosphere, and hydrosphere.
   G. biosphere, geosphere, and atmosphere.
   H. geosphere, hydrosphere, and atmosphere.
   I. biosphere, hydrosphere, and atmosphere.
3. How are scientists able to study the composition and size of the interior layers of Earth?
   A. by direct observation
   B. by analyzing surface rock samples
   C. by using seismic waves
   D. by deep-drilling into the interior layers
4. Which of the following methods of internal energy transfer drives volcanic activity on Earth's surface?
   F. radioactive decay
   G. convection
   H. kinetic transfer
   I. conduction
5. Earth's primary external energy source is
   A. cosmic radiation.
   B. the moon.
   C. distant stars.
   D. the sun.

Directions (6–7): For each question, write a short response.

6. What do decomposers break down to obtain energy?
7. What scientific principle states that energy can be transferred but that it cannot be created or destroyed?

Reading Skills

Directions (8–9): Read the passage below. Then, answer the questions.

Acid Rain

Acid rain is rain, snow, fog, dew, or sleet that has a pH that is lower than the pH of normal precipitation. Acid rain occurs primarily as a result of the combustion of fossil fuels—a process that produces, as byproducts, oxides of nitrogen and sulfur dioxide. When combined with water in the atmosphere, these compounds form nitric acid and sulfuric acid. When it falls to Earth, acid rain has profound effects. It harms forests by damaging tree leaves and bark, which leaves them vulnerable to weather, disease, and parasites. Similarly, it damages crops. And it damages aquatic ecosystems by causing the death of all but the hardiest species. Because of the extensive damage that acid rain causes, the U.S. Environmental Protection Agency limits the amount of sulfur dioxide and nitrogen oxides that can be emitted by factories, power plants, and motor vehicles.

8. According to the passage, which of the following contributes to the problem of acid rain?
   F. the use of fossil fuels in power plants and motor vehicles
   G. parasites and diseases that harm tree leaves and bark
   H. the release of nitrogen into the atmosphere by aquatic ecosystems
   I. damaged crops that release too many gases into the atmosphere
9. Which of the following statements can be inferred from the information in the passage?
   A. Acid rain is a natural problem that will correct itself if given enough time.
   B. Ecosystems damaged by acid rain adapt so that they will not be damaged in the future.
   C. Human activities are largely to blame for the problem of acid rain.
   D. Acid rain is a local phenomenon and only damages plants and animals near power plants or roadways.

Question 12 Full-credit answers should include the following points:

- Overall, general energy trends are predicted to remain the same over the next 25 years.
- Oil is predicted to continue to be the leading fuel source in the future.
- Natural gas is expected to overtake coal by 2010 as an energy source, and the difference between the use of the two sources is expected to continue to increase steadily through 2025.
- Nuclear power is predicted to remain the least-used energy source and is expected to slightly decrease in use.
- Fossil fuels are predicted to continue to outpace nuclear and renewable energy resources by a ratio of more than 4 to 1.

Interpreting Graphics

Directions (10–12): For each question below, record the correct answer on a separate sheet of paper.

The diagram below shows the interior layers of Earth. The layers in the diagram are representative of arrangement and are not drawn to scale. Use this diagram to answer question 10.

Structure of the Earth

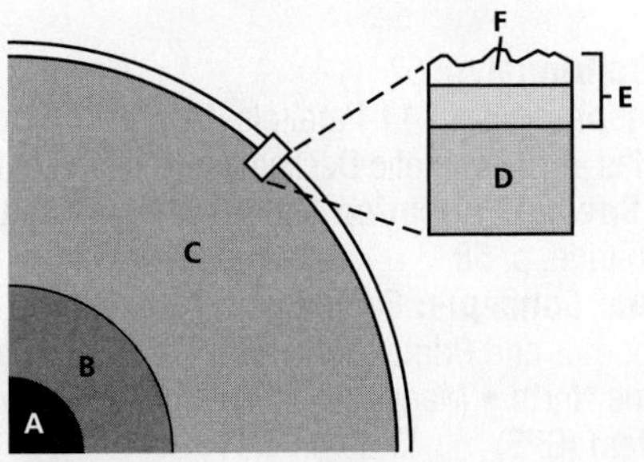

10. Which letter represents the layer of Earth known as the lithosphere?

F. layer E
G. layer D
H. layer C
I. layer A

Use the graph below, which shows predicted worldwide energy consumption by fuel type between the years 2001 and 2025, to answer questions 11 and 12.

Worldwide Energy Consumption By Source

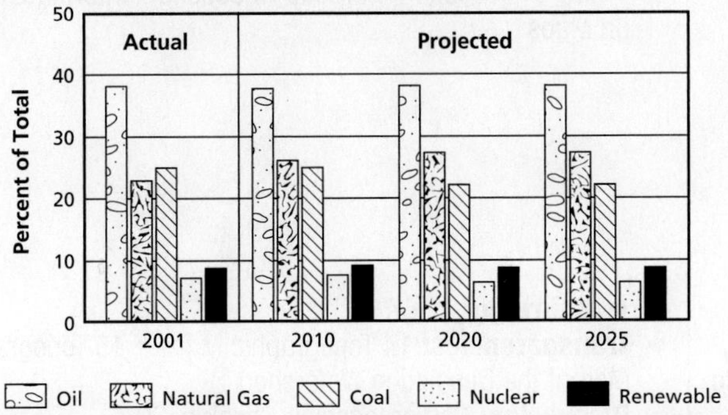

11. Which of the following sources of energy is predicted to see the greatest increase in usage between 2001 and 2025?

A. oil
B. natural gas
C. coal
D. renewable

12. What trends in energy consumption by fuel type will change over the 25 years shown on the graph above? What trends will stay the same?

Test Tip

If time permits, take short mental breaks during the test to improve your concentration.

Standardized Test Prep

Using THINK central Resources

State Resources

- For specific resources for your state, visit www.thinkcentral.com and type in the keyword **HSHSTR.**

Answers

Understanding Concepts

1. B
2. F
3. C
4. G
5. D
6. dead organisms
7. first law of thermodynamics

Reading Skills

8. F
9. C

Interpreting Graphics

10. F
11. B
12. Answers may vary. See Test Doctor for a detailed scoring rubric.

Chapter Planner 3 Models of the Earth

	Time	Standards	Teach Key Ideas
Chapter Opener, pp. 54–55	45 min.	National Science Education Standards	
Section 1 Finding Locations on Earth, pp. 57–60 › Latitude › Longitude › Great Circles › Finding Direction	45 min.	UCP 1, UCP 2, SAI 2c, SAI 2d, HNS 2a, HNS 3c, HNS 3d	■ ◆ **Bellringer,** p. 57 ◆ **Transparencies:** 11 Parallels, Meridians, and Great Circles • 12 Magnetic Declination of the United States ■ **DI (Special Education Students):** Finding Latitude and Longitude, p. 58 ▲ **Visual Concepts:** Comparing Latitude and Longitude • Equator and Prime Meridian • Earth's Magnetic Field • True North • Magnetic Declination • Global Positioning System (GPS)
Section 2 Mapping Earth's Surface, pp. 61–66 › How Scientists Make Maps › Map Projections › Reading a Map	45 min.	UCP 1, UCP 2, SAI 2c, SAI 2d, HNS 2a, HNS 3c	■ ◆ **Bellringer,** p. 61 ◆ **Transparency:** 13 Types of Map Projections ■ **Discussion:** Round Earth, Flat Maps p. 62 ■ **DI (Advanced Learners):** Cartography, p. 63 ■ **Demonstration:** Sun and Shadow, p. 64 ▲ **Visual Concepts:** Remote Sensing • Aerial Photograph • Map Projections • Cardinal Directions • Information on Maps
Section 3 Types of Maps, pp. 67–72 › Topographic Maps › Geologic Maps › Soil Maps › Other Types of Maps	90 min.	UCP 1, UCP 2, SAI 2c, SAI 2d, HNS 2a, HNS 3c	■ ◆ **Bellringer,** p. 67 ◆ **Transparencies:** 14 Topographic Maps • 15 Topographic Map of the Desolation Watershed ■ **Discussion:** Comprehension Check p. 69 ■ **DI (Basic Learners):** Topographic Knuckles, p. 69 ■ **Discussion:** Value of Geologic Maps p. 70 ▲ **Visual Concepts:** Topographic Maps and Contour Lines • Elevation • Index Contour, Contour Interval, and Relief • Contour Lines: The Golden Rules
Chapter Wrap-Up, pp. 77–81	90 min.		**Chapter Summary,** p. 77

See also PowerNotes® Presentations

CHAPTER *Fast Track*

To shorten instruction because of time limitations, omit Section 2.

Key
Teacher's Edition ■ Teaching Transparencies ◆
Chapter Resource File ● Online Edition ▲

All resources listed below are also available on the Teacher One Stop™.

Why It Matters	Hands-On	Skills Development	Assessment
■ **Chapter Overview,** p. 54 ■ **Using the Figure:** Topographic Map, p. 54	**Inquiry Lab:** Using a Compass, p. 55	**Reading Toolbox,** p. 56	
■ **Section Overview,** p. 57 **Longitude and Time Zones,** p. 58 **Geocaching,** p. 59 ■ **History Connection,** Early Cartographer, p. 58	■ **Activity:** On the Grid, p. 57	■ **Skill Builder:** Vocabulary, p. 58 ■● **Internet Activity:** Magnetic Declination, p. 59 **Reading Toolbox:** Everyday Words Used in Science p. 60	**Reading Check,** p. 58 **Section Review,** p. 60 ■ **Reteaching,** p. 59 ■ **Quiz,** p. 59 ■ **DI (Alternative Assessment):** Cartoons Around the Globe, p. 60 ● **Section Quiz**
■ **Section Overview,** p. 61 **Map Orientation,** p. 64 ■ **Using the Figure:** Planning a Trip, p. 65	■ **Group Activity:** School Map, p. 61 ■ **Activity:** Map A-Peel, p. 62 **Quick Lab:** Making Projections, p. 62 ■ **Group Activity:** Maps and Globes, p. 63 ■ **Group Activity:** Chart Your Course, p. 64 ● **Inquiry Lab:** Scale the School ● **Making Models Lab:** Remote Sensing	**Reading Toolbox:** Layered Book, p. 63 **Math Skills:** Determining Distance, p. 65	**Reading Check,** p. 62 **Reading Check,** p. 65 **Section Review,** p. 66 ■ **Reteaching,** p. 65 ■ **Quiz,** p. 65 ■ **DI (Alternative Assessment):** Treasure Hunt, p. 66 ● **Section Quiz**
■ **Section Overview,** p. 67 ■ **Geography Connection:** Quadrangles, p. 66 ■ **History Connection:** Public Lands, p. 69 ■ **Using the Figure:** Map Layers, p. 70 ■ **Environmental Connection:** Soil Surveys, p. 71	■ **Group Activity:** Terrain Models, p. 67 **Quick Lab:** Topographic Maps, p. 68 ■ **Group Activity:** Local Soil Maps, p. 71 **Making Models Lab:** Contour Maps: Island Construction, pp. 74–75 ■ **Activity:** Local Watershed, p. 76	■ **Skill Builder:** Math, p. 68 ■ **Reading Skill Builder:** Reading Hint, p. 69 **Reading Toolbox:** Layered Book, p. 70 **Maps in Action:** Topographic Map of the Desolation Watershed, p. 76	**Reading Check,** p. 69 **Reading Check,** p. 71 **Section Review,** p. 72 ■ **Reteaching,** p. 71 ■ **Quiz,** p. 71 ■ **DI (Alternative Assessment):** Song Lyrics, p. 72 ● **Section Quiz**
Is There Anywhere That Isn't Mapped? p. 73		▲ **Super Summary** **Standardized Test Prep,** pp. 80–81	**Chapter Review,** pp. 78–79 **DI (Alternative Assessment):** Mapmaker, Mapmaker, p. 77 ● **Chapter Tests**

See also Lab Generator

See also Holt Online Assessment Resources

Chapter Overview

This chapter explains how scientists map and locate features on Earth's surface, how elevation is shown on maps, and how maps convey information about Earth.

Using the Figure GENERAL

Topographic Map This satellite image shows the region of Southern Asia that includes India, Nepal, Tibet, and Sri Lanka. The red area north of the kite-shaped Indian subcontinent represents the Himalayas, the world's highest mountain range. The green areas represent lowlands and the yellow/orange areas represent mountains and highlands. Ask students what land feature the central area of the tear-shaped island of Sri Lanka represents. (a mountain, possibly volcanic) **LS Visual**

Why It Matters

Satellite data can be used to produce shaded relief maps like the one here. Topographic features are shown as if shaded by sunlight.

Chapter 3 Models of the Earth

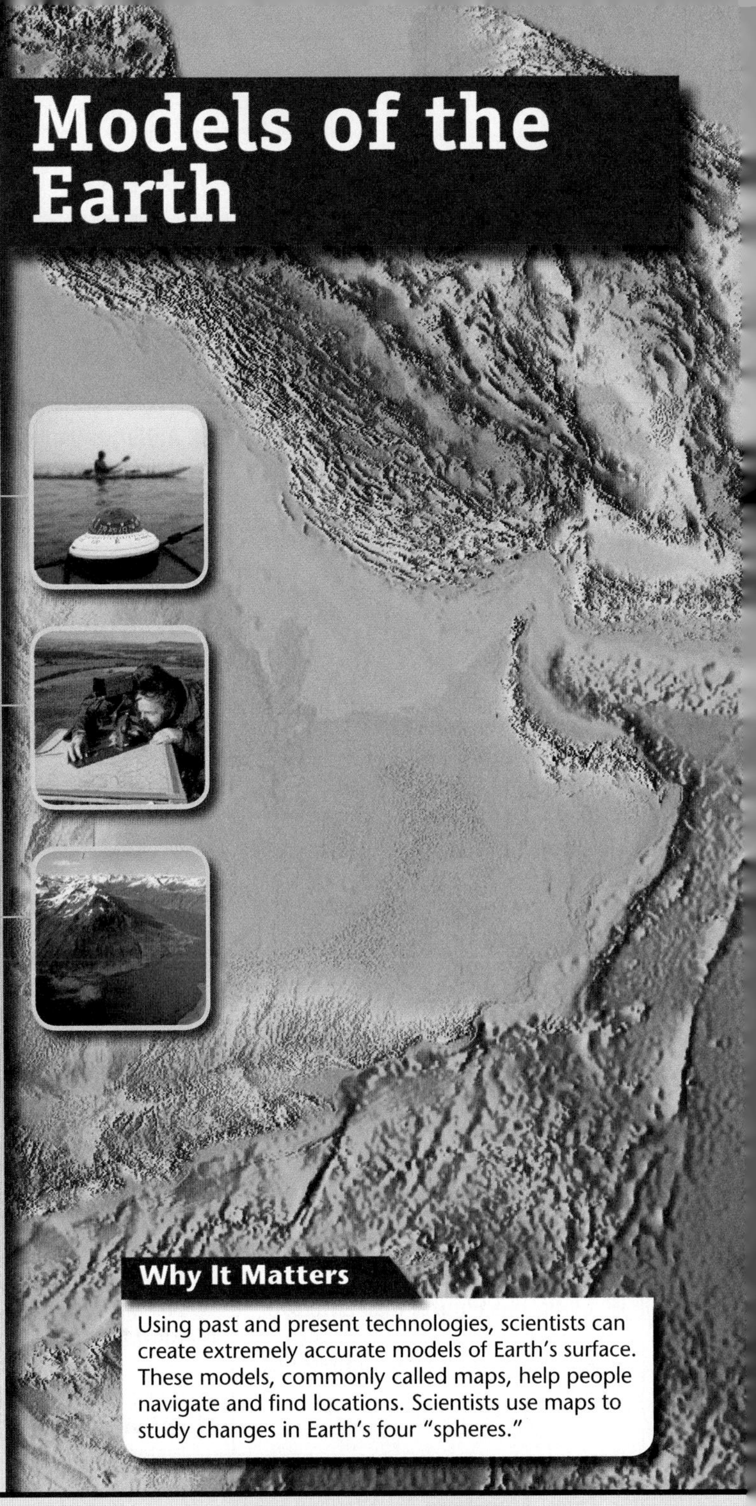

Chapter Outline

1 Finding Locations on Earth
- Latitude
- Longitude
- Great Circles
- Finding Direction

2 Mapping Earth's Surface
- How Scientists Make Maps
- Map Projections
- Reading a Map

3 Types of Maps
- Topographic Maps
- Geologic Maps
- Soil Maps
- Other Types of Maps

Virginia Standards of Learning
ES.1.a
ES.1.b
ES.1.c
ES.1.d
ES.1.f

Why It Matters

Using past and present technologies, scientists can create extremely accurate models of Earth's surface. These models, commonly called maps, help people navigate and find locations. Scientists use maps to study changes in Earth's four "spheres."

Chapter Correlations — *Virginia Standards of Learning*

ES.1.a volume, area, mass, elapsed time, direction, temperature, pressure, distance, density, and changes in elevation/depth are calculated utilizing the most appropriate tools.
ES.1.b technologies, including computers, probeware, and geospatial technologies, are used to collect, analyze, and report data and to demonstrate concepts and simulate experimental conditions.
ES.1.c scales, diagrams, charts, graphs, tables, imagery, models, and profiles are constructed and interpreted.
ES.1.d maps and globes are read and interpreted, including location by latitude and longitude.
ES.1.f current applications are used to reinforce Earth science concepts.

Inquiry Lab

30 min

Using a Compass

Working as a team, choose an object in your classroom. Use a **directional compass** to determine and record directions that another team could follow to arrive at the object you chose. Use cardinal directions (north, south, east, and west) and ordinal directions (northeast, northwest, southeast, and southwest). For example, you could write directions like these: "Stand with your back to the classroom door. Turn east, and walk five steps. Then walk three steps northeast." Trade directions with other teams.

Questions to Get You Started

1. In what direction does a compass needle always point?
2. How do you use the letters and numbers on a compass housing to adjust the compass?

Inquiry Lab

Central Concept: Students use a compass to help them model the process of creating and following navigational directions.

Teacher's Notes: Students who have orienteering experience could be asked to demonstrate the use of a compass to the class. Alternatively, selected students could be invited to prepare ahead of time to demonstrate the use of a compass to small groups.

Materials (per group)
- Directional compass

Skills Acquired
- Inferring
- Interpreting
- Communicating

Answers to Getting Started

1. A compass needle always points in the direction of the geomagnetic north pole.
2. To go in a certain direction, turn the compass housing so the direction-of-travel arrow points in that direction, indicated either by the letters or the numbers (whichever you are using). Then turn your body and the compass (but not the housing) until the compass needle lines up with the lines in the compass housing. Moving in the direction of the direction-of-travel arrow means you are going in your chosen direction.

Using THINK central Resources

An online version of this chapter, as well as all the print and multimedia resources that accompany the program are available to registered teachers and their students. Log onto www.thinkcentral.com to access these materials and tools to organize your preparation and student learning.

READING TOOLBOX

Science Terms

For their tables, students should choose everyday words that have a distinctly different scientific meaning. They also may choose words that are personally confusing to them, even if the everyday definition and the scientific definition are similar. The table shown below gives examples drawn from Section 2.

Term	Scientific context	Everyday meaning
legend	a list of map symbols and their meanings	a story that is handed down through the generations; a person whose accomplishments make him or her stand out (*a living legend*)
scale	the relationship between the distance shown on a map and the actual distance	an instrument used to weigh objects; the small plates that cover the bodies of fish and reptiles

READING TOOLBOX

These reading tools will help you learn the material in this chapter.

Science Terms

Everyday Words Used in Science All the key terms in this textbook are words that scientists use. Many words that are used in science are also used in everyday speech. You should pay attention to the definitions of these words so that you can use them correctly in scientific contexts.

Your Turn As you read Chapter 3, make a table like the one below for the terms *relief* and *projection* (from the key term *map projection*). Add other everyday words that are used by scientists as you find them in the chapter.

Term	Scientific context	Everyday meaning
relief	the difference between the highest and lowest elevations in a given area	a lessening or easing of a burden or anxiety, pain, or stress

Frequency

Always, Sometimes, or Never? Many statements include a word that tells you how often they are true. Examples include words such as *always, often, sometimes,* and *never*. Words such as *all, some, many,* and *most* tell you about frequency in number.

Your Turn As you read this chapter, make a list of statements that contain frequency words. For each statement in your list, underline the word or phrase that tells how frequently the statement is true. Here is an example: Air and sea routes often travel along great circles.

FoldNotes

Layered Book FoldNotes are a fun way to help you learn and remember ideas that you encounter as you read. You can use the four flaps of the layered book to divide the ideas into four categories.

Your Turn As you read Section 1, make a layered book, as described in **Appendix A**. Label the tabs of the layered book with "Latitude," "Longitude," "Great Circles," and "Finding Direction." Write notes on the appropriate layer as you read the section.

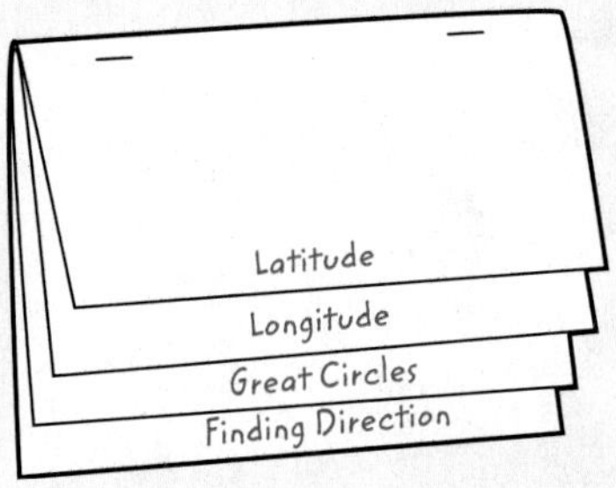

For more information on how to use these and other tools, see **Appendix A**.

Frequency

Students should create a list of sentences that contain frequency words, with the frequency words underlined. Sentences should be drawn from all three sections. Samples shown below.

Section 1

All locations east of the prime meridian have longitudes between 0° and 180° E.

However, all meridians meet at the poles.

A great circle is often used in navigation, especially by long-distance aircraft.

Answers continued on p. 81A

FoldNotes

Answers may vary. Students' notes should appear similar to the example shown. Notes on the "Latitude" page of the layered book should contain sections on degrees of latitude and minutes and seconds. The notes on the "Longitude" page of the layered book should contain sections on degrees of longitude and the distance between meridians. The notes on the "Finding Direction" page of the layered book should contain sections on magnetic declination and the global positioning system.

SECTION 1

Finding Locations on Earth

Key Ideas	Key Terms	Why It Matters
› Distinguish between latitude and longitude. › Explain how latitude and longitude can be used to locate places on Earth's surface. › Explain how a magnetic compass can be used to find directions on Earth's surface.	parallel latitude meridian longitude	Latitude and longitude form a frame of reference that is based on Earth's axis of rotation, making it possible to identify and locate any point on Earth.

The points at which Earth's axis of rotation intersects Earth's surface are used as reference points for defining direction. These reference points are the geographic North and South Poles. Halfway between the poles, a circle called the *equator* divides Earth into the Northern and Southern Hemispheres. A reference grid of additional circles is used to locate places on Earth's surface.

Latitude

One set of circles describes positions north and south of the equator. These circles are called **parallels** because they run east and west around the world, parallel to the equator. The angular distance north or south of the equator is called **latitude.**

parallel any circle that runs east and west around Earth and that is parallel to the equator; a line of latitude

latitude the angular distance north or south from the equator; expressed in degrees

Degrees of Latitude

Latitude is measured in degrees, and the equator is designated as 0° latitude. Because the distance from the equator to either of the poles is one-fourth of a circle, and a circle has 360°, the latitude of both the North Pole and the South Pole is one-quarter of 360°, or 90°, as shown in **Figure 1.** In actual distance, 1° of latitude equals 1/360 of Earth's circumference, or about 111 km. Parallels north of the equator are labeled N; those south of the equator are labeled S.

Minutes and Seconds

Each degree of latitude consists of 60 equal parts, called *minutes.* One minute (symbol: ') of latitude equals 1.85 km. In turn, each minute is divided into 60 equal parts, called *seconds* (symbol: "). So, the latitude of the center of Washington, D.C., could be expressed as 38°53'23"N.

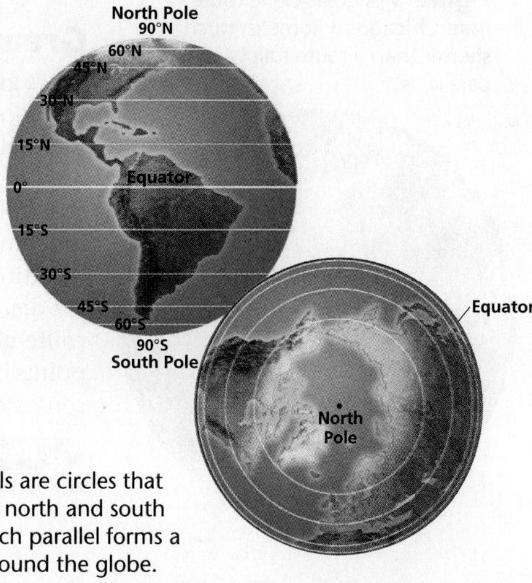

Figure 1 Parallels are circles that describe positions north and south of the equator. Each parallel forms a complete circle around the globe.

Section 1

Focus

Overview

This section explains how latitude and longitude, Earth's magnetism, and the Global Positioning System (GPS) are used to find locations on Earth.

Bellringer

Ask students to think about the route that they took to arrive at school in the morning. Have students write out a description so someone else could follow it, starting from the same location. (Answers may vary but students will probably use landmarks or cross-streets to describe their route.) **LS Verbal**

Motivate

Activity GENERAL

On the Grid Clear an area of the floor about 2 m^2. Use masking tape to lay down a series of grid lines and label them with sticky notes. Label one axis with letters and the other axis with numbers. Place objects, such as books or building blocks, within the grid. Give each student a sheet of graph paper. Have them make a map of the floor that shows the locations of all the objects. Ask students how the grid helped them map the location of objects. (The places where the grid lines cross provide reference points that can be used to describe where objects are.) **LS Visual**

Key Resources

Chapter Resource File
- Directed Reading BASIC

Technology
- Transparencies
  Bellringer
  11 Parallels, Meridians, and Great Circles
  12 Magnetic Declination of the United States

Teach

Reading Skill Builder — GENERAL

Vocabulary Lines of longitude are also known as *meridians*. The word comes from the Latin *meri-*, a variation of *medius*, which means "middle" and *dies*, meaning "day." The word once meant "noon," because all points on the same line of longitude experienced noon (and every other hour) at the same time, and therefore, were said to be located on the same meridian. Times of the day before noon were known as *ante meridian*, while times after it were *post meridian*. Today's abbreviations A.M. and P.M. come from these terms. English Language Learners
LS Verbal

Why It Matters

Longitude and Time Zones Local time is a measure of the position of the sun relative to a given location. Solar noon occurs when the sun is at the highest point in the sky. As Earth rotates, at any moment, it is solar noon along one meridian. The time-zone system divides the 360° of longitude into 24 time zones—one for each hour of the day, each 15° wide—and uses the spinning Earth as a giant clock.

Answer to Reading Check

because the equator is the only parallel that divides Earth into halves

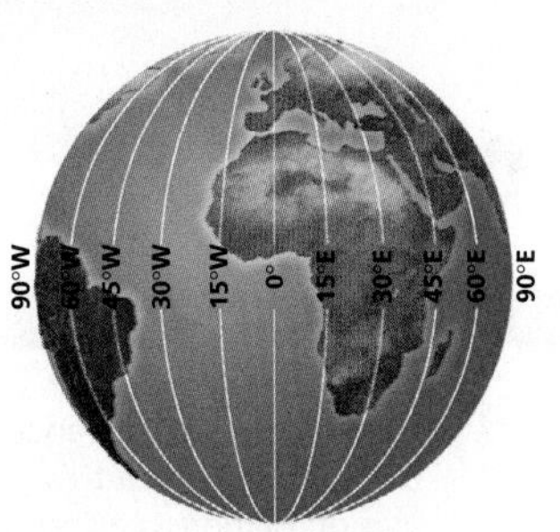

Figure 2 Meridians are semicircles reaching around Earth from pole to pole.

Longitude

The latitude of a particular place indicates only its position north or south of the equator. To determine the specific location of a place, you also need to know how far east or west that place is along its circle of latitude. East-west locations are established by using meridians. As **Figure 2** shows, a **meridian** is a semicircle (half of a circle) that runs from pole to pole.

By international agreement, one meridian was selected to be 0°. This meridian, called the *prime meridian*, passes through Greenwich, England. **Longitude** is the angular distance, measured in degrees, east or west of the prime meridian.

meridian any semicircle that runs north and south around Earth from the geographic North Pole to the geographic South Pole; a line of longitude

longitude the angular distance east or west from the prime meridian; expressed in degrees

Academic Vocabulary

location (loh KAY shuhn) place or position

Degrees of Longitude

Because a circle is 360°, the meridian opposite the prime meridian, halfway around the world, is labeled 180°. All locations east of the prime meridian have longitudes between 0° and 180°E. All locations west of the prime meridian have longitudes between 0° and 180°W. Washington, D.C., which lies west of the prime meridian, has a longitude of 77°W. Like latitude, longitude can be expressed in degrees, minutes, and seconds. So, a more precise location for Washington, D.C., is 38°53'23"N, 77°00'33"W.

Distance Between Meridians

The distance covered by a degree of longitude depends on where the degree is measured. At the equator, or 0° latitude, a degree of longitude equals approximately 111 km. However, all meridians meet at the poles. Because meridians meet, the distance measured by a degree of longitude decreases as you move from the equator toward the poles. At a latitude of 60°N, for example, 1° of longitude equals about 55 km. At 80°N, 1° of longitude equals only about 20 km.

Figure 3 A great-circle route from Chicago to Rome is much shorter than a route following a parallel is.

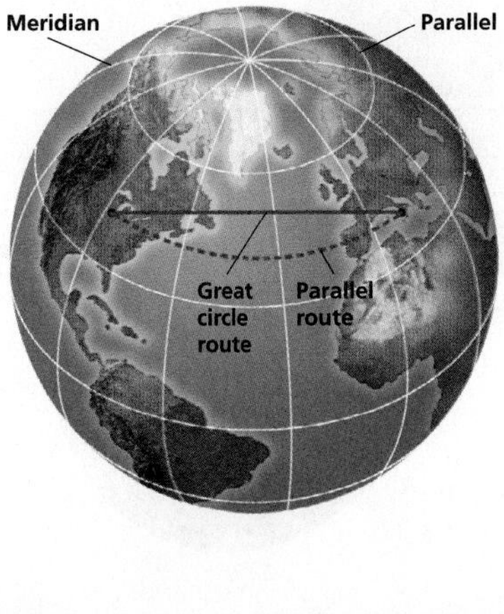

Great Circles

A great circle is often used in navigation, especially by long-distance aircraft. A *great circle* is any circle that divides the globe into halves, or marks the circumference of the globe. Any circle formed by two meridians of longitude that are directly across the globe from each other is a great circle. The equator is the only line of latitude that is a great circle. Great circles can run in any direction around the globe. Just as a straight line is the shortest distance between two points on a flat surface or plane, the route along a great circle is the shortest distance between two points on a sphere, as shown in **Figure 3.** As a result, air and sea routes often travel along great circles.

Reading Check **Why is the equator the only parallel that is a great circle?** (See Appendix G for answers to Reading Checks.)

History Connection — ADVANCED

Early Cartographer Explain that the method we use for dividing the degree into subdivisions—minutes and seconds—was introduced by the Roman scholar Claudius Ptolemy in his work called *Almagest* during the second century CE. Ptolemy also compiled one of the first collections of maps. He developed the coordinate system of latitude and longitude as a way of pinpointing locations. Unfortunately, Ptolemy's maps contained errors because the estimate of Earth's size that he used was too small. Invite students to learn more about Ptolemy's contributions to Earth science. Have them share what they learn with the class in oral or written presentations. **LS Verbal**

Differentiated Instruction

Special Education Students

Finding Latitude and Longitude One way of engaging students who have behavior control issues is to empower them by letting them make some decisions. Have students use a globe to find the latitude and longitude of major cities. Ask students to choose the cities either by thinking of them or by going to the globe and choosing them. Have students make a list of their cities and the latitude and longitude coordinates for each. **LS Logical**

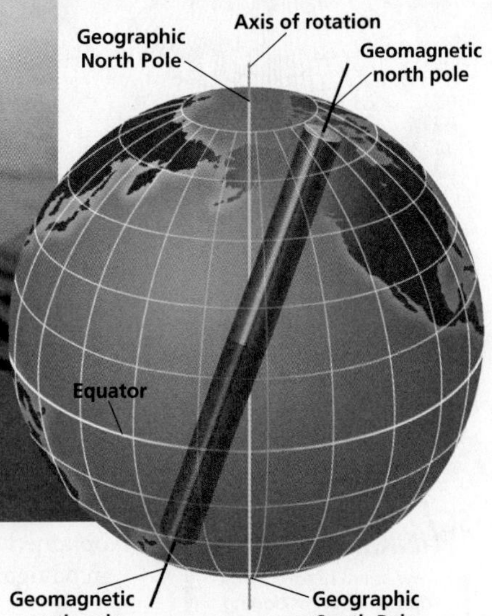

Figure 4 Earth's magnetic poles are at an angle to Earth's axis of rotation.

Finding Direction

One way to find direction on Earth is to use a magnetic compass. A magnetic compass can indicate direction because Earth has magnetic properties as if a powerful bar-shaped magnet were buried at Earth's center at an angle to Earth's axis of rotation, as shown in **Figure 4.**

The areas on Earth's surface where the poles of the imaginary magnet would be are called the *geomagnetic poles*. The geomagnetic poles and the geographic poles are different and are located in different places. The north end of a compass needle points in the direction of the geomagnetic north pole.

Why It Matters

Geocaching

SCIENCE & SOCIETY

Finding direction is not only for when you're lost. In geocaching, people hide a cache of "treasure" and post the coordinates (latitude and longitude) online. Other people then use GPS (Global Positioning System) receivers to find the cache.

People hide a cache of items, including a logbook, in a safe place.

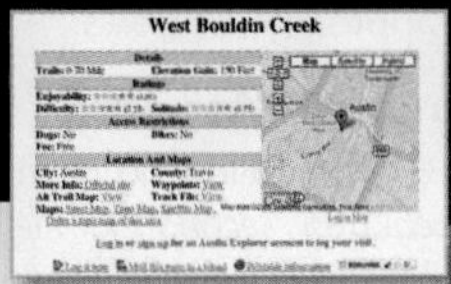

The cache's coordinates are posted on a geocaching Web site.

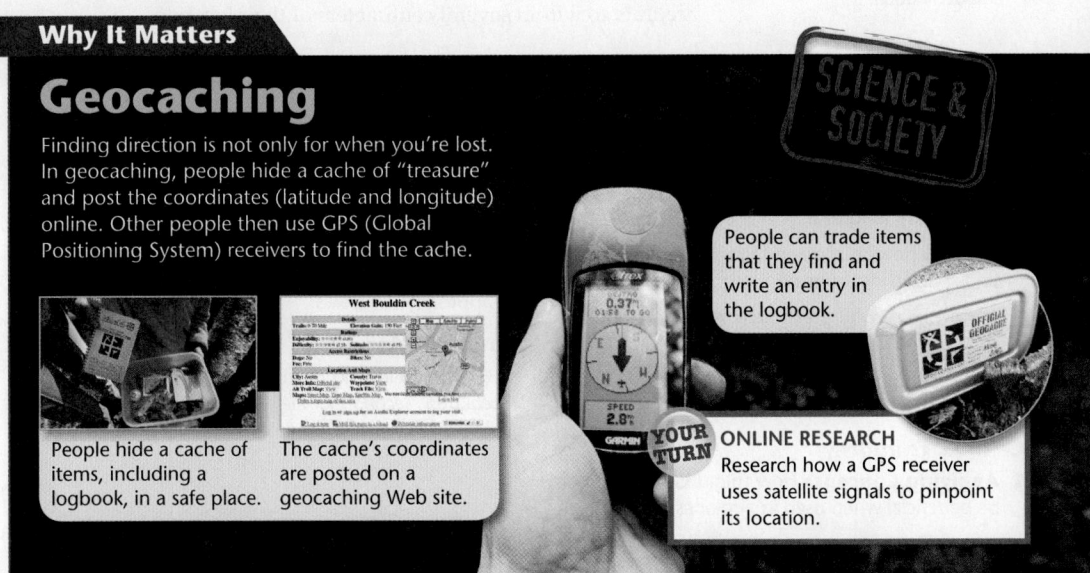

People can trade items that they find and write an entry in the logbook.

YOUR TURN ONLINE RESEARCH
Research how a GPS receiver uses satellite signals to pinpoint its location.

Why It Matters

Geocaching The first documented geocache was planted and discovered in 2000. The activity quickly caught on, and it is now played on every continent—even Antarctica. In addition to enjoyment, benefits include the encouragement of outdoor activity, such as hiking and exploration, as well as the development of orienteering skills. Since 2002, the geocaching community has supported an event called Cache In Trash Out (CITO), in which participants are encouraged to pick up litter while they look for cached treasure. CITO is practiced as an organized, annual event, but it is also recommended as common and courteous practice for any geocaching adventure.

Answer to Your Turn

Online Research A GPS receiver uses signals from at least three (of a global network of satellites) to calculate its distance from each satellite and, through triangulation, determine its own location.

Internet Activity — GENERAL

Magnetic Declination Have students use the latitude and longitude of your city or town to look up the geomagnetic declination of your location by using the National Geophysical Data Center Web site. A worksheet designed to direct student research on this topic can be found in the **Chapter Resource File** booklet or by visiting www.thinkcentral.com and entering the keyword **HQXMODX.** **LS Logical**

Close

Reteaching — BASIC

Global Grid Use a ball, rubber bands, and a marking pen. Put a rubber band around the center of the ball. Draw the circle representing the ball's equator. Make a series of parallel circles above and below the equator. Ask what the circles represent. (parallels) Put a second rubber band around the middle of the ball in the opposite direction. Draw the prime meridian. Make a series of circles running from one pole to the other. Ask what these circles represent. (meridians) Point out how distance between meridians decreases as you move from the equator to the poles. **LS Visual**

Quiz — GENERAL

1. Compare what happens to longitude near the poles with what happens to latitude. (The meridians of longitude meet at the poles, so the distance between them decreases. As the circles or parallels of latitude approach the poles, they get smaller in circumference. The distances between them stay the same.)
2. What does a magnetic compass use to indicate direction? (Earth's magnetic field and the magnetic properties of metals or some minerals) **LS Verbal**

READING TOOLBOX

Everyday Words Used in Science

Show students that words in the dictionary often have more than one meaning listed. Scientific meanings are often indicated by an abbreviation of a field of study, as in *Geol.* for *geology*. scientific meaning: "a bending in a downward direction;" everyday meaning: "declining to say, do, or accept something"

Close, *continued*

Answers to Section Review

1. latitude runs parallel to the equator; longitude runs pole to pole
2. The intersection of latitude and longitude lines pinpoint the locations of places on the globe in degrees, minutes, and seconds. Latitude marks position north or south of the equator, and longitude marks position east or west of the prime meridian.
3. because they represent the shortest distance between two points on the globe
4. The compass needle aligns itself in a north-south direction because it points toward the geomagnetic poles. The other directions on the dial are found by reading number of degrees east or west of north.
5. Because GPS technology can give locations that are accurate to within several centimeters, GPS can be used for navigation in airplanes or ships when using compasses or landmarks is difficult or impossible.

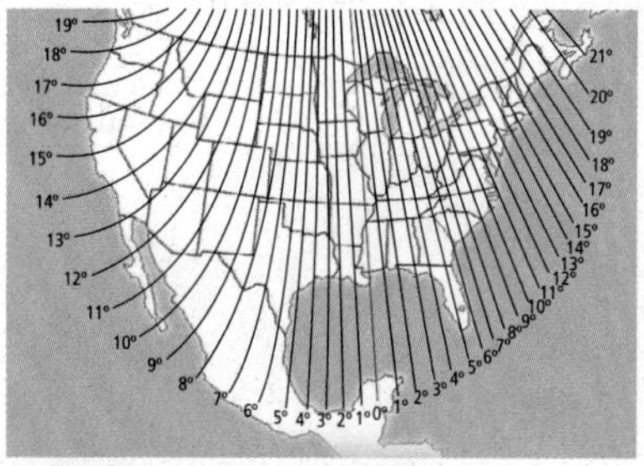

Figure 5 This map shows the pattern of magnetic declinations over North America. The lines connect points that have the same magnetic declination.

SCILINKS.
www.scilinks.org
Topic: Global Positioning System
Code: HQX0680

READING TOOLBOX

Everyday Words Used in Science

Use a dictionary to help you compare the scientific and everyday meanings of the term *declination.*

Magnetic Declination

The angle between the direction of the geographic pole and the direction in which the compass needle points is called *magnetic declination.* In the Northern Hemisphere, magnetic declination is measured in degrees east or west of the geographic North Pole. A compass needle will align with both the geographic North Pole and the geomagnetic north pole for all locations along the line of 0° magnetic declination, which is shown as the red line in **Figure 5.**

Magnetic declination has been determined for points all over Earth. However, because Earth's magnetic field is constantly changing, the magnetic declinations of locations around the globe also change constantly. **Figure 5** shows recent magnetic declinations for most of the United States. By using magnetic declination, a person can use a compass to determine geographic north for any place on Earth. Current declination at any location can be obtained from the Internet. Locating geographic north is important in navigation and in mapmaking.

The Global Positioning System

Another way people can find their location on Earth is by using the *global positioning system,* or *GPS.* GPS is a satellite navigation system that is based on a global network of satellites that transmit radio signals to Earth's surface. The first GPS satellite, known as NAVSTAR, was launched in 1978.

A GPS receiver held by a person on the ground receives signals from at least three satellites, which it uses to calculate the latitude, longitude, and altitude of the receiver on Earth. Personal GPS receivers are accurate to within 10 to 15 m of their position, but high-tech receivers designed for military or commercial use can be accurate to within several centimeters of their location.

Section 1 Review

Key Ideas

1. **Describe** the difference between lines of latitude and lines of longitude.
2. **Explain** how latitude and longitude are used to find specific locations on Earth.
3. **Summarize** why great-circle routes are commonly used in navigation.
4. **Explain** how a magnetic compass can be used to find directions on Earth.

Critical Thinking

5. **Applying Concepts** How might GPS technology be beneficial when used in airplanes or on ships?
6. **Making Comparisons** How do parallels differ from latitude?
7. **Identifying Patterns** Explain why the distance between parallels is constant but the distance between meridians decreases as the meridians approach the poles.

Concept Mapping

8. Use the following terms to create a concept map: *equator, second, parallel, degree, Earth, minute, longitude, meridian, prime meridian,* and *latitude.*

6. Parallels are imaginary circles parallel with the equator; latitude is angular distance (in degrees) north or south of the equator.

Answers continued on p. 81A

Key Resources

Technology

- Transparencies
  12 Magnetic Declination of the United States

Differentiated Instruction

Alternative Assessment

Cartoons Around the Globe Have students create cartoons or comic strips that focus on one of the key concepts in this section: how the system of circles is used to locate places, how magnetic compasses indicate direction, or how the GPS satellite network makes finding places in the modern world easier. Tell students to write captions that explain the drawings. Students could use explorers such as Columbus, Lewis and Clark, or astronauts to make cartoons concrete and relevant. **LS Visual**

SECTION 2

Mapping Earth's Surface

Key Ideas	Key Terms	Why It Matters
❯ Explain two ways that scientists get data to make maps. ❯ Describe the characteristics and uses of three types of map projections. ❯ Summarize how to use keys, legends, and scales to read maps.	remote sensing map projection legend scale isogram	Maps are models of Earth's surface that can be made or chosen to display characteristics for a specific purpose, such as plotting the best route for your next road trip.

A globe is a familiar model of Earth. Because a globe is spherical like Earth, a globe can accurately represent the locations, relative areas, and relative shapes of Earth's surface features. A globe is especially useful for studying large surface features, such as continents and oceans. But most globes are too small to show details of Earth's surface, such as streams and highways. For that reason, a great variety of maps have been developed for studying and displaying detailed information about Earth.

How Scientists Make Maps

The science of making maps, called *cartography*, is a subfield of Earth science and geography. Scientists who make maps are called *cartographers*.

Cartographers use data from a variety of sources to create maps. They may collect data by conducting a field survey, shown in **Figure 1.** During a field survey, cartographers walk or drive through an area to be mapped and make measurements of that area. The information they collect is then plotted on a map. Because surveyors cannot take measurements at every site in an area, they often use their measurements to make estimated measurements for sites between surveyed points.

remote sensing the process of gathering and analyzing information about an object without physically being in touch with the object

By using remote sensing, cartographers can collect information about a site without being at that site. In **remote sensing,** equipment on satellites or airplanes obtains images of Earth's surface. Maps are often made by combining information from images gathered remotely with information from field surveys.

Figure 1 Cartographers in the field use technology to enhance the precision of their measurements. Electronic devices can be used to measure the distance between an observer and a distant point with a high degree of accuracy.

Section 2

Focus

Overview

This section explains how cartographers obtain information to create maps, describes map projections, and explains how to use a compass rose, a legend, and scales.

Bellringer

Ask students to write a brief paragraph that summarizes different kinds of maps they have seen and what kinds of information each presents. (Students may describe floor plans of public buildings, bus or train maps, navigational charts, road maps, maps of the human body, weather maps, or maps of other planets.) LS **Verbal**

Motivate

Group Activity — GENERAL

School Map Have students work in groups to make a map of the classroom or of another area of the school. Ask them to start by making a sketch map of their area. Then, have them use tape measures, rulers, and triangles to make a more accurate map. Have them determine a scale for their map. Ask students how they think cartographers map larger areas of Earth. (Answers may vary. Students may mention field surveying, triangulating, taking aerial photographs, and using satellite images.) LS **Kinesthetic**

Key Resources

Chapter Resource File
- Directed Reading BASIC
- Inquiry Lab: Scale the School GENERAL
- Making Models Lab: Remote Sensing GENERAL

Technology
- Transparencies
  Bellringer

Teach

Activity — GENERAL

Map A-Peel Give students a large orange or grapefruit. Tell students to use a marking pen to draw latitude and longitude lines on the outside of the fruit skin. Then, have them draw the rough outlines of the continents. After the ink is dry, use a knife to free the skin near the stem of each fruit and make a single cut the length of the fruit from top to bottom. By carefully slipping their fingers under the skin, students should separate the peel from the fruit in one piece. Once the peel is free, have them flatten it out. They should make additional tears in the peel to make the "map" lie flat. Have students describe any distortions produced by flattening the fruit skin. (Sample answer: Parts of the continents became separated and gaps appeared in the map.) **LS Kinesthetic**

Discussion — GENERAL

Round Earth, Flat Maps Ask students why a globe is the only completely accurate map. (Sample answer: Because the globe is three-dimensional like Earth itself, it can show all the areas in the correct shapes and relative sizes; it can also show correct directions and relative distances. Flat maps always introduce distortions by stretching or flattening Earth's curved surface.) **LS Logical**

Answer to Reading Check

Because both the parallels and the meridians are equally spaced straight lines on a cylindrical projection, the parallels and meridians form a grid.

Quick Lab — 20 min

Making Projections

Procedure

1. Use a fine-tip marker to draw a variety of shapes on a small glass ivy bowl or clear plastic hemisphere.
2. Shine a flashlight through the bottom of the bowl.
3. Shape a piece of white paper into a cylinder around the bowl.
4. Trace the shapes projected from the bowl onto the paper.
5. Using a cone of paper, repeat steps 3 and 4.

Analysis

1. What type of projection did you create in steps 3 and 4? in step 5?
2. Compare the sizes of the shapes on the bowl with those on your papers. What areas did each projection distort?

map projection a flat map that represents a spherical surface

Map Projections

A map is a flat representation of Earth's curved surface. However, transferring a curved surface to a flat map results in a distorted image of the curved surface. An area shown on a map may be distorted in size, shape, distance, or direction. The larger the area being shown is, the greater the distortion tends to be. A map of the entire Earth would show the greatest distortion. A map of a small area, such as a city, would show only slight distortion.

Over the years, cartographers have developed several ways to transfer the curved surface of Earth onto flat maps. A flat map that represents the three-dimensional curved surface of a globe is called a **map projection.** No projection is an entirely accurate representation of Earth's surface. However, each kind of projection has certain advantages and disadvantages that must be considered when choosing a map.

Cylindrical Projections

Imagine Earth as a transparent sphere that has a light inside. If you wrapped a cylinder of paper around this lighted globe and traced the outlines of continents, oceans, parallels, and meridians, a *cylindrical projection,* shown in **Figure 2,** would result. Meridians on a cylindrical projection appear as straight, parallel lines that have an equal amount of space between them. On a globe, however, the meridians come together at the poles. A cylindrical projection is accurate near the equator but distorts distances and sizes near the poles.

Though distorted, cylindrical projections have some advantages. One advantage is that parallels and meridians form a grid, which makes locating positions easier. Also, the shapes of small areas are usually well preserved. When a cylindrical projection is used to map small areas, distortion is minimal.

Reading Check **Why do meridians and parallels appear as a grid when shown on a cylindrical projection?**

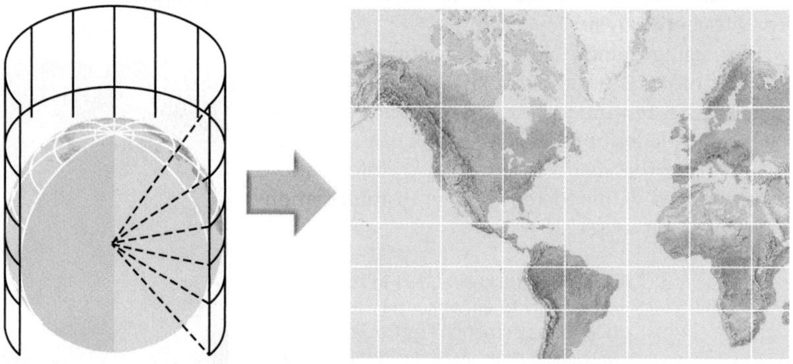

Figure 2 A light at the center of a transparent globe would project lines on a cylinder of paper (left) that would produce a cylindrical projection (right).

Quick Lab

Skills Acquired

- Recognizing patterns
- Constructing models

Materials

- Fine-tip marker
- Small glass ivy bowl or clear plastic hemisphere
- Flashlight
- Piece of white paper

Teacher's Notes: A goldfish bowl or clear plastic hamster ball can also be used. Students can add a grid to their map projections by shaping soft wire over the bowl to form latitude and longitude lines.

Key Resources

Technology

- Transparencies
  13 Types of Map Projections

Answers to Analysis

1. Steps 3 and 4 create a cylindrical projection. Step 5 creates a conic projection.
2. On the cylindrical projection, shapes and distances closer to the poles are distorted more than those near the equator. Shapes farthest from the place where the cone came into contact with the ball are distorted the most.

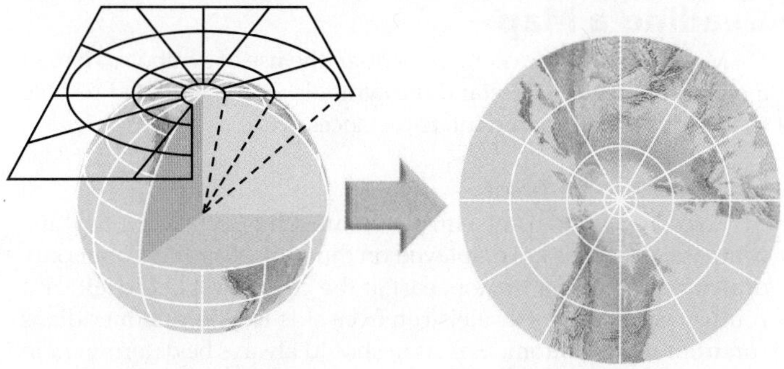

Figure 3 When a sheet of paper is placed so that it touches a lighted globe at only one point (left), the lines projected on the paper form an azimuthal projection (right).

Azimuthal Projections

A projection made by placing a sheet of paper against a transparent, lighted globe such that the paper touches the globe at only one point is called an *azimuthal* (AZ uh MYOOTH uhl) *projection,* as shown in **Figure 3.** On an azimuthal projection, little distortion occurs at the point of contact, which is commonly one of the poles. However, an azimuthal projection shows unequal spacing between parallels that causes a distortion in both direction and distance. This distortion increases as distance from the point of contact increases.

Despite distortion, an azimuthal projection is a great help to navigators in plotting routes used in air travel. As you know, a great circle is the shortest distance between any two points on the globe. When projected onto an azimuthal projection, a great circle appears as a straight line. Therefore, by drawing a straight line between any two points on an azimuthal projection, navigators can readily find a great-circle route.

Conic Projections

A projection made by placing a paper cone over a lighted globe so that the axis of the cone aligns with the axis of the globe is known as a *conic projection.* The cone touches the globe along one parallel of latitude. As shown in **Figure 4,** areas near the parallel where the cone and globe are in contact are distorted the least.

A series of conic projections may be used to increase accuracy by mapping a number of neighboring areas. Each cone touches the globe at a slightly different latitude. Fitting the adjoining areas together then produces a continuous map. Maps made in this way are called *polyconic projections.* The relative size and shape of small areas on the map are nearly the same as those on the globe.

READING TOOLBOX

Layered Book

Make a layered book FoldNote. Label the tabs with the three types of map projections. Write notes on the appropriate tab to list the advantages and disadvantages of each type of map projection.

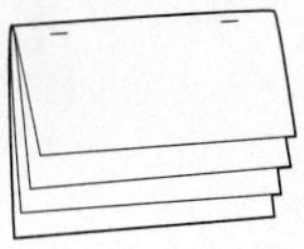

Academic Vocabulary

contact (KON takt) state of touching; coming together of objects or surfaces

Figure 4 A light at the center of a transparent globe would project lines on a paper cone (left) that would produce a conic projection (right).

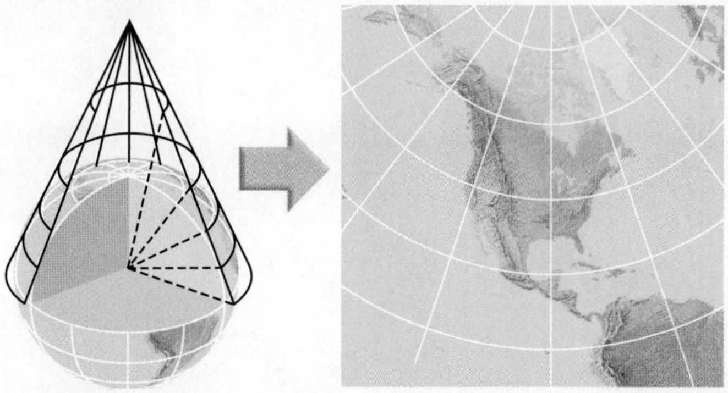

Group Activity — GENERAL

Maps and Globes Divide the class into small groups. Give each group a globe and several maps that use different projections. Have students compare the sizes of continents and large islands on different maps. Tell students to examine the shapes (curved or straight) and spacing of grid lines on different projections. Have them identify the kinds of distortions produced by different map projections. Bring groups together and have them discuss their conclusions. **LS Visual** Co-op Learning

READING TOOLBOX

Layered Book

Sample notes:

Cylindrical projection

- accurate near the equator but distorts distances and sizes near the poles
- parallels and meridians form a grid
- distortion is minimal when used to map small areas

Azimuthal projection

- little distortion occurs at point of contact used to project map, increasing with distance from point of contact
- shows unequal spacing between parallels that distorts direction and distance
- helpful for plotting air travel routes, because great circles appear as straight lines

Conic projection

- distortion is least where the cone touches the globe
- fairly accurate maps called polyconic projections are made using a series of conic projections

Differentiated Instruction

Advanced Learners

Cartography Ask students to go beyond the textbook and work together to learn more about cartographers. Tell them to create a questionnaire that has at least twelve questions they would like to ask about mapmaking. Then, have them use the Internet to find some companies that create maps and send their questionnaires to several of these firms. Ask them to compile any replies into an illustrated report for the class. **LS Verbal/Interpersonal**

MISCONCEPTION ALERT

Geographical Distortions Misconceptions about location and size of geographical features may be reinforced by common map projections. Cylindrical projections greatly stretch Canada and Greenland so that students may not be aware of their actual sizes. The misplacements of Europe close to the equator, of South America directly south of North America, and of most of Africa south of the equator are common geographical misconceptions.

Teach, *continued*

Demonstration GENERAL

Sun and Shadow Cardinal directions on Earth are determined relative to the sun. To help students associate direction with the sun, use a stick and its shadow to find directions. On a sunny day, place the stick vertically in the ground and mark the tip of its shadow with a chalk mark. Wait one hour, and again mark the tip of the shadow. A line drawn from the first mark to the second gives the approximate east/west axis. (The first mark is the west end of the line and the second is the east end.) Use those directions to determine north and south. Draw an appropriate compass rose. Invite students to check the results by using a magnetic compass.
LS Kinesthetic/Visual

Cultural Awareness BASIC

Map Orientation Point out that it is merely by convention that north is placed at the top of most modern maps. One explanation is that most of the world's landmasses are found in the Northern Hemisphere. In medieval Europe, many maps placed Jerusalem and the east at the top. Thus, the phrase "to orient" comes from the Latin *oriens,* meaning "rising sun" and "east." The Chinese, who invented magnetic compasses, thought of the compass needle as pointing south rather than north. In the Southern Hemisphere, maps that place south at the top are very popular.

SCI*LINKS*.
www.scilinks.org
Topic: Cartography
Code: **HQX0229**

Reading a Map

Maps provide information through the use of symbols. To read a map, you must understand the symbols on the map and be able to find directions and calculate distances.

Direction on a Map

To correctly interpret a map, you must first determine how the compass directions are displayed on the map. Maps are commonly drawn with north at the top, east at the right, west at the left, and south at the bottom. Parallels run from side to side, and meridians run from top to bottom. Direction should always be determined in relation to the parallels and meridians.

On maps published by the United States Geological Survey (USGS), such as the one shown in **Figure 5**, north is located at the top of the map and is marked by a parallel. The southern boundary, at the bottom of a map, is also marked by a parallel. At least two additional parallels are usually drawn in or indicated by cross hairs at 2.5' intervals. Meridians of longitude indicate the eastern and western boundaries of USGS maps. Additional meridians may also be shown. All parallels and meridians shown on these maps are labeled in degrees, minutes, and seconds.

Many maps also include a compass rose, as shown in **Figure 5**. A *compass rose* is a symbol that indicates the cardinal directions. The *cardinal directions* are north, east, south, and west. Some maps replace the compass rose with a single arrow that points to geographic north. This arrow is generally labeled and may not always point to the top of the map.

Figure 5 Maps may show locations by marking parallels and meridians. Direction is commonly shown with a compass rose (inset).

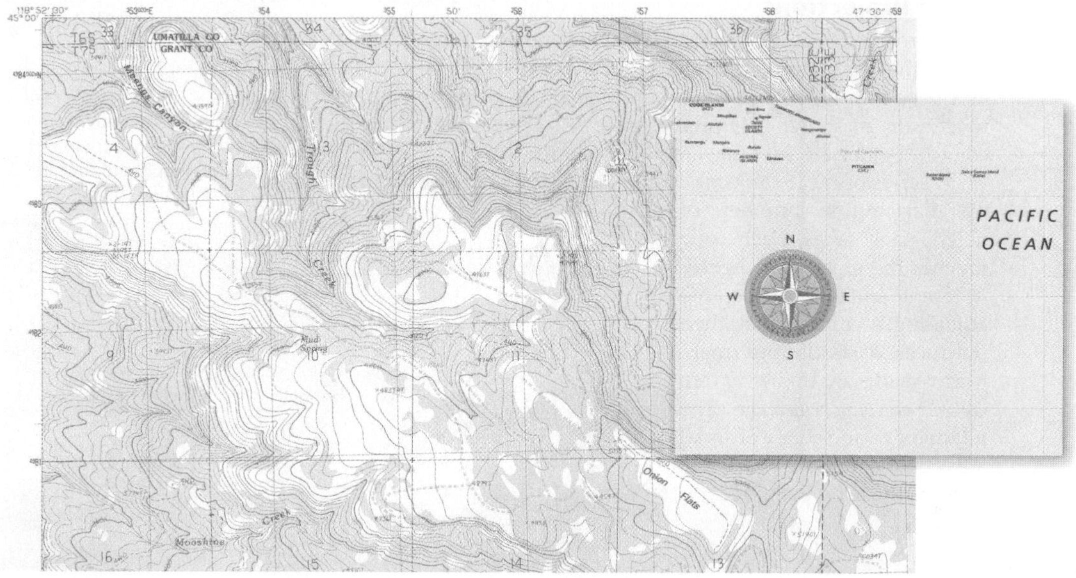

Group Activity ADVANCED

Chart Your Course Obtain a U.S. Geological Survey map of an area near your school. Distribute photocopies of the relevant part of the map to groups of students. Visit the site with the class. Have each group select a land feature as its destination. Tell groups to draw a line from their present location to their destination, extending the line to the map border. Center a compass over the line, align the axis N-S or E-W, and read the compass bearing of the destination. Have groups locate their destination in the field. **LS Kinesthetic**

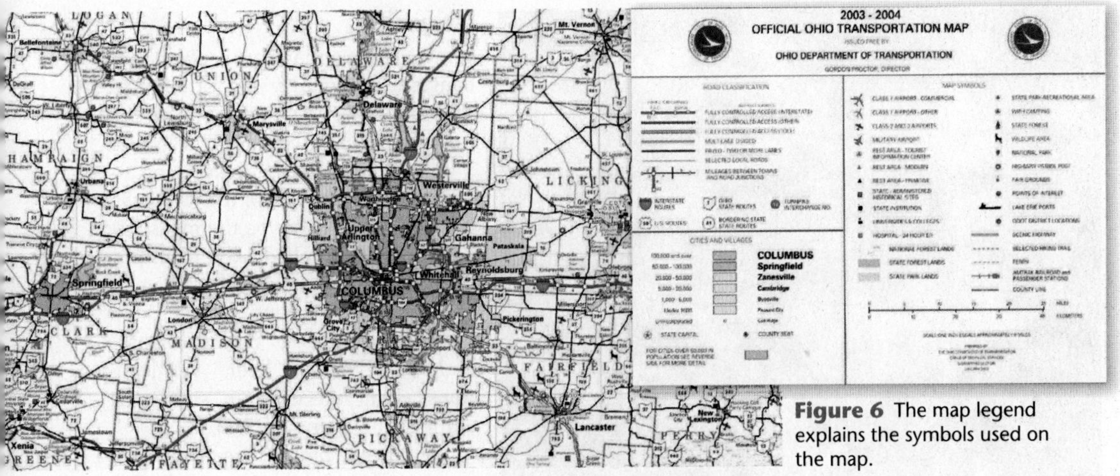

Figure 6 The map legend explains the symbols used on the map.

Symbols

Maps often have symbols for features such as cities and rivers. The symbols are explained in the map **legend,** a list of the symbols and their meanings, such as the one shown in **Figure 6.** Some symbols resemble the features that they represent. Others, such as those for towns and urban areas, are more abstract.

legend a list of map symbols and their meanings

scale the relationship between the distance shown on a map and the actual distance

Map Scales

To be accurate, a map must be drawn to **scale.** The scale of a map indicates the relationship between distance shown on the map and actual distance. A map scale can be expressed as a graphic scale, a fractional scale, or a verbal scale.

A *graphic scale* is a printed line that has markings on it that are similar to those on a ruler. The line represents a unit of measure, such as the kilometer or the mile. Each part of the scale represents a specific distance on Earth. To find the actual distance between two points on Earth, you first measure the distance between the points as shown on the map. Then, you compare that measurement with the map scale.

A second way of expressing scale is by using a ratio, or a *fractional scale.* For example, a fractional scale such as 1:25,000 indicates that 1 unit of distance on the map represents 25,000 of the same unit on Earth. A fractional scale remains the same with any system of measurement. In other words, the scale 1:100 could be read as 1 in. equals 100 in. or as 1 cm equals 100 cm.

A *verbal scale* expresses scale in sentence form. An example of a verbal scale is "One centimeter is equal to one kilometer." In this scale, 1 cm on the map represents 1 km on Earth.

Reading Check **Name three ways to express scale on a map.**

Math Skills

Determining Distance You notice that the scale on a map of the United States says, "One centimeter equals 120 kilometers." By measuring the straight-line distance between Brooklyn, New York, and Miami, Florida, you determine that the cities are about 14.5 cm apart on the map. What is the approximate distance in kilometers between the two cities?

Using the Figure GENERAL

Planning a Trip Invite students to use the map legend to plan a route that they would take if they were acting as navigators for a family automobile trip from Columbus, Ohio, to a nearby town shown on the map, such as London or Mechanicsburg.
LS Visual

Close

Reteaching BASIC

Using the Legend Give students several different maps of the same geographic area—a political map, a terrain map, a road map, and a weather map. Have students use the map legends to identify the symbols each map uses to convey information. Have them compare the scales and symbols on the maps and describe how the symbols convey the purpose of each map. **LS Visual**

Quiz GENERAL

1. What are flat maps that represent the three-dimensional spherical surface of Earth called? (map projections)
2. What part of a map explains the symbols used on that map? (the legend)
3. What is the chief advantage of a cylindrical map projection? (Parallels and meridians appear as a grid, which makes locating positions easy.)

Answer to Reading Check

by using a graphic scale, or a printed line divided into proportional parts that represent units of measure; a fractional scale, in which a ratio shows how distance on Earth relates to distance on a map; or a verbal scale, which expresses scale in sentence form

Math Skills

Answer

1 cm = 120 km; 14.5 cm × 120 km/cm = 1,740 km

Close, *continued*

Answers to Section Review

1. Cartographers obtain information to make maps by doing surveys and by remote sensing via satellites or aerial surveys.
2. Cylindrical projections are accurate near the equator but distort distances near the poles. The parallels and meridians make a grid that makes locating positions easy. Azimuthal projections distort direction and distance because of unequal spacing of parallels, but great circles form straight lines, so plotting air travel routes is easier. When conic projections are fitted together, they produce a continuous map and preserve the relative size and shape of small areas.
3. The process of transferring a curved surface onto a flat surface causes all flat maps to distort some aspect of size, shape, distance, or direction.
4. The legend can be used to interpret the map symbols, and the scale is used to determine the relationship between distances shown on the map and actual distances.
5. Isograms connect points of equal value; isograms can be used to represent a variety of different units of measure.
6. To show a small area in useful detail, a globe would have to be huge. A flat map of a small area would be compact and have only slight distortion.
7. Maps are commonly drawn with north at the top, west to the left, east to the right, and south at the bottom. A compass rose is often included on maps to indicate the cardinal directions. If parallels and meridians are shown, they can be used to determine direction.
8. A fractional scale should be used because the scale remains the same with any system of measurement.
9. If the cone used to make the conic projection touches the globe along a parallel close to the poles, there will be little distortion and the map will be more accurate. A cylindrical projection will distort sizes and distances most near the poles.
10. *Cartography* uses many different *map projections,* including *cylindrical projections, azimuthal projections,* and *conic projections* to produce *maps,* which you can read by using a *scale* to estimate distances and the *legend* to interpret the *symbols.*

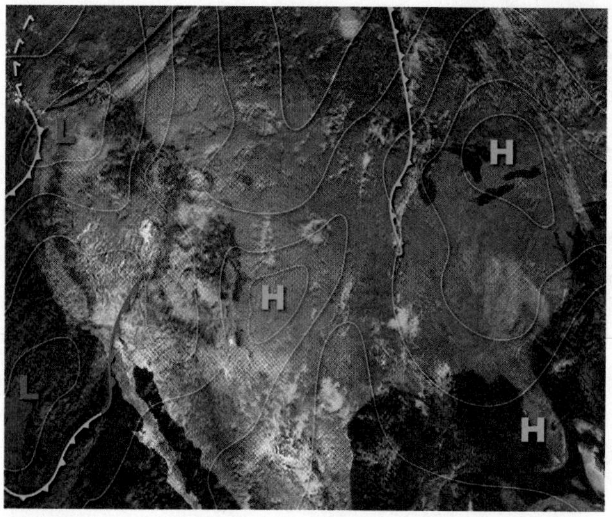

Figure 7 Areas connected by the isobars on the map share equal atmospheric pressure.

Isograms

A line on a map that represents a constant or equal value of a given quantity is an **isogram.** The prefix *iso-* is Greek for "equal." The second part of the word, *-gram,* means "drawing." This part of the word can be changed to describe the measurement being graphed. For example, when a line connects points of equal temperature, the line is called an *isotherm* because *iso-* means "equal" and *therm* means "heat." All locations along an isogram share the value that is being measured.

Isograms can be used to plot many types of data. Meteorologists use these lines to show changes in atmospheric pressure on weather maps. Isograms used for this purpose on a weather map are called *isobars,* as shown in **Figure 7.** All points along an isobar share the same pressure value. Because one location cannot have two air pressures, isobars never cross one another.

isogram a line on a map that represents a constant or equal value of a given quantity

Scientists can use isograms on a map to plot data that represent almost any type of measurement. Isograms are commonly used to show areas that have similar measurements of precipitation, temperature, gravity, magnetism, density, elevation, or chemical composition.

Section 2 Review

Key Ideas

1. **Identify** two methods that scientists use to get the data needed to make maps.
2. **Describe** three types of map projections in terms of their different characteristics and uses.
3. **Explain** why all maps are in some way inaccurate representations.
4. **Summarize** how to use legends and scales to read maps.
5. **Describe** what isograms show.
6. **Explain** why maps are more useful than globes are for studying small areas on the surface of Earth.
7. **Summarize** how to find directions on a map.

Critical Thinking

8. **Applying Concepts** If a cartographer is making a map for three countries that do not use a common unit of measurement, what type of scale should the cartographer use on the map? Explain your answer.
9. **Making Inferences** Why would a conic projection produce a better map for exploring polar regions than a cylindrical projection would?

Concept Mapping

10. Use the following terms to create a concept map: *cartography, map projection, cylindrical projection, azimuthal projection, conic projection, map, legend, scale,* and *symbol.*

Differentiated Instruction

Alternative Assessment

Treasure Hunt Assign groups of students to specific areas of the school. Have them hide small prizes on school grounds and make a scale map of the area, using a graphic or verbal scale. Have them create a legend by using colors for landscape features and provide a compass rose. Have them write brief instructions to help others locate the prizes. Ask groups to exchange maps and to find the objects hidden by the other group. **LS Kinesthetic**

SECTION
3 Types of Maps

Key Ideas	Key Terms	Why It Matters
❯ Explain how elevation and topography are shown on a map. ❯ Describe three types of information shown in geologic maps. ❯ Identify two uses of soil maps.	**topography** **elevation** **contour line** **relief**	Different types of maps enable scientists to display detailed three-dimensional information about the surface and below-surface features of Earth.

Earth scientists use a wide variety of maps that show many distinct characteristics of an area. Some of these characteristics include types of rocks, differences in air pressure, and varying depths of groundwater in a region. Scientists also use maps that show locations, elevations, and surface features of Earth.

Topographic Maps

One of the most widely used maps is called a *topographic map*. Topographic maps show the surface features, or **topography,** of Earth. Most topographic maps show both natural features, such as rivers and hills, and constructed features, such as buildings and roads. Topographic maps are made by using both aerial photographs and survey points collected in the field. A topographic map shows the **elevation,** or height above sea level, of the land. Elevation is measured from *mean sea level,* the point midway between the highest and lowest tide levels of the ocean. The elevation at mean sea level is 0.

topography the size and shape of the land surface features of a region, including its relief

elevation the height of an object above sea level

Advantages of Topographic Maps

An aerial view of an island is shown in **Figure 1.** Although the drawing shows the shape of the island, it does not indicate the island's size or elevation. A typical map projection would show the island's size and shape but would not show the island's topography. A topographic map provides more detailed information about the surface of the island than either the drawing or a projection map does. The advantage of a topographic map is that it shows the island's size, shape, and elevation.

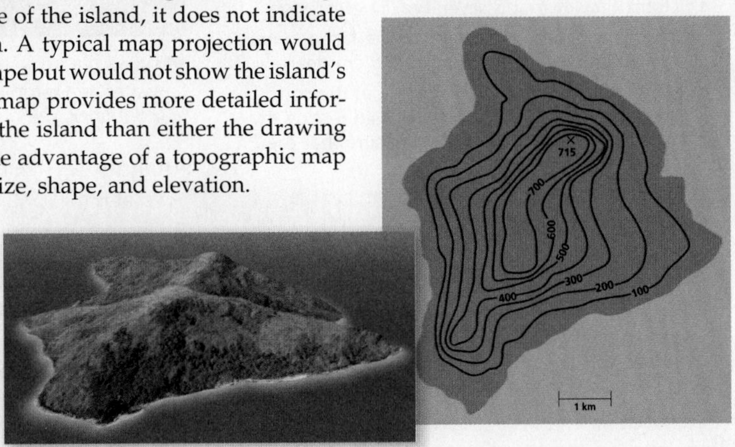

Figure 1 A drawing gives little information about the elevation of the island (left). In the topographic map (right), contour lines have been drawn to show elevation. An × marks the highest point on this map.

Section 3

Focus

Overview

This section explains how elevation and topographic features are shown on maps. The section also describes geologic maps, soil maps, and other kinds of maps used by Earth scientists.

Bellringer

Ask students to draw a picture of a hill, mountain, or valley in profile so that differences in elevation and depth are clear. Ask them how such differences might be pictured on a map. (Answers may vary. Accept all reasonable answers.) **LS Visual**

Motivate

Group Activity — GENERAL

Terrain Models Divide the class into small groups. Have them make a relief model of a familiar landform by using cardboard or foam pieces. Have them glue the layers together. Once the models are constructed, have students cover the models with papier-mâché or a flour and salt dough. Have them paint their models and add features such as roads or bridges for a more realistic effect. Ask students to compare the models they created to a topographic map. (Sample answer: The model has raised features like the surface of Earth it represents, but is more cumbersome to handle.) **LS Kinesthetic**

Key Resources

Chapter Resource File
- Directed Reading BASIC

Technology
- Transparencies
  Bellringer
  14 Topographic Maps

Teach

Geography Connection GENERAL

Quadrangles Topographic maps made by the United States Geological Survey (USGS) are called *topographic sheets* or *quadrangles*. The USGS began the project of mapping the United States in 1879. The earlier series of USGS maps represented quadrangles that covered 15′ of latitude and 15′ of longitude. The newer series of maps covers 7.5′ of latitude and 7.5′ of longitude—a smaller area, but in much greater detail. Invite interested students to check out the USGS National Map on the Internet to find a map of your local area. **LS Visual**

Skill Builder GENERAL

Math Tell students that the contour interval for a topographic map is 25 m. Ask them what their elevation would be if they started climbing at the bottom (0 m) and crossed 3 contour lines; 5 lines; 8 lines; and 10 lines. (3 lines: 3×25 m = 75 m; 5 lines: 5×25 m = 125 m; 8 lines: 8×25 m = 200 m; 10 lines: 10×25 m = 250 m) **LS Logical**

Figure 2 On a topographic map, the contour interval for this mountain would be very large because of the mountain's steep slope.

contour line a line that connects points of equal elevation on a map

relief the difference between the highest and lowest elevations in a given area

Elevation on Topographic Maps

On topographic maps, **contour lines** are used to show elevation. Each contour line is an isogram that connects points that have the same elevation. Because points at a given elevation are connected, the shape of the contour lines reflects the shape of the land.

The difference in elevation between one contour line and the next is called the *contour interval*. A cartographer chooses a contour interval suited to the scale of the map and the relief of the land. **Relief** is the difference in elevation between the highest and lowest points of the area being mapped. On maps of areas where the relief is high, such as the area shown in **Figure 2,** the contour interval may be as large as 50 or 100 m. Where the relief is low, the interval may be only 1 or 2 m.

To make reading the map easier, a cartographer makes every fifth contour line bolder than the four lines on each side of it. These bold lines, called *index contours*, are labeled by elevation. A point between two contour lines has an elevation between the elevations of the two lines. For example, if a point is halfway between the 50 and 100 m contour lines, its elevation is about 75 m. Exact elevations are marked by an × and are labeled.

Quick Lab Topographic Maps

20 min

Procedure

1. Make a model mountain that is 6 to 8 cm high out of modeling clay. Work on a flat surface, and smooth out the mountain's shape. Make one side of the mountain slightly steeper than the other side.
2. Run a paper clip down one side of the model to form a valley that is several millimeters wide.
3. Place the model in the center of a large waterproof container that is at least 8 cm deep.
4. Use tape to hold a ruler upright in the container. One end of the ruler should rest on the bottom of the container. Make sure that the container is level.
5. Using the ruler as a guide, add water to the container to a depth of 1 cm. Use a sharp pencil to inscribe the clay by tracing around the model along the waterline.
6. Raise the water level 1 cm at a time until you reach the top of the model. Each time you add water to the container, inscribe another contour line in the clay along the waterline.
7. When you have finished, carefully drain the water and remove the model from the container.

Analysis

1. What is the contour interval of your model?
2. Observe your model from directly above. Try to duplicate the size and spacing of the contour lines on a sheet of paper to create a topographic map.
3. Compare the contour lines on a steep slope with those on a gentle slope. How do they differ?
4. How is a valley represented on your topographic map?

Quick Lab

Skills Acquired
- Constructing Models
- Observing
- Analyzing Data

Materials
- Modeling clay
- Paper clip
- Large waterproof container
- Tape
- Ruler
- Water
- Sharp pencil

Teacher's Notes: Remind students to make the models no taller than the sides of the container.

Answers to Analysis
1. 1 cm
2. Maps may vary.
3. The steeper the slope is, the closer together the contour lines are. A gentler slope will have more widely spaced contour lines.
4. The valley on my topographic map is represented by V-shaped contour lines in which the tip of the V points upstream.

Mount St. Helens, Topographic Profile

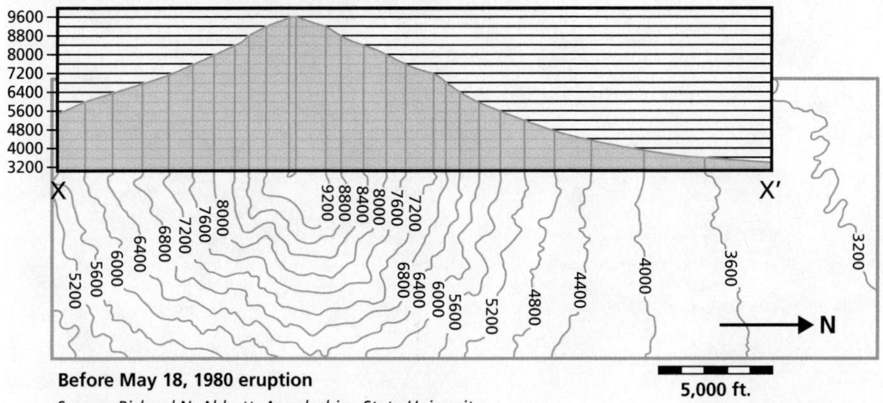

Before May 18, 1980 eruption

Source: *Richard N. Abbott, Appalachian State University*

Figure 3 This is a topographical profile of Mount St. Helens in Washington state before its cataclysmic eruption in May 1980. The elevation from the base of the mountain to the summit was approximately 1,850 m.

Landforms on Topographic Maps

As shown in **Figure 3,** the spacing and the direction of contour lines indicate the shapes of the landforms represented on a topographic map. Contour lines spaced widely apart indicate that the change in elevation is gradual and that the land is relatively level. Closely spaced contour lines indicate that the change in elevation is rapid and that the slope is steep.

A contour line that bends to form a V shape indicates a valley. The bend in the V points toward the higher end of the valley. If a stream or river flows through the valley, the V in the contour line will point upstream, the direction from which the water flows. A river always flows from higher to lower elevation. The width of the V formed by the contour line shows the width of the valley.

Contour lines that form closed loops indicate a hilltop or a depression. Generally, a depression is indicated by *depression contours,* which are closed-loop contour lines that have short, straight lines perpendicular to the inside of the loop. These short lines point toward the center of the depression.

Reading Check **Why do V-shaped contour lines along a river point upstream?**

Topographic Map Symbols

Symbols are used to show certain features on topographic maps. Symbol color indicates the type of feature. For example, constructed features, such as buildings, boundaries, roads, and railroads, are generally shown in black. Major highways are shown in red. Bodies of water are shown in blue, and forested areas are shown in green. Contour lines are brown or black. Often, areas whose map information has been updated based on aerial photography but not verified by field exploration are shown in purple. A key to common topographic map symbols is provided for your reference in Appendix E.

THINK central
INTERACT ONLINE
(Keyword: HQXMODF3)

SCILINKS.
www.scilinks.org
Topic: Topographic Maps
Code: **HQX1536**

Discussion — BASIC

Comprehension Check Invite students to summarize how color is used on topographic maps. (Sample answers: Contour lines are shown in brown, green is used for forested areas, blue is used for bodies of water, roadways are red, and human-built structures such as buildings or railroads are shown in black.) **LS Verbal**

Answer to Reading Check

Water moves from areas of higher elevation to areas of lower elevation. Because the V shape points toward higher elevation, it points upstream.

Reading Skill Builder — BASIC

Reading Hint Explain that the word *topography* comes from the Greek words *topos* and *graphein. Topos* means "place," and *graphein* means "to write." In biology, *topotype* refers to a typical specimen collected from a given locality; in literature, a *biography* describes someone's life. Similarly, a *topographer* describes the surface features of a specific place, and *topography* refers to the detailed mapping of the relief features of an area. English Language Learners **LS Verbal**

History Connection — ADVANCED

Public Lands The Land Ordinance System of 1785, which was signed into law by Thomas Jefferson, established the rectangular system of land survey in the Northwest Territory. Begun in Ohio and extended as the nation moved west, the survey system used latitude and longitude lines to divide public lands into townships and to subdivide townships into sections for settlement. Have students compare topographic maps of eastern states, such as Massachusetts or Virginia, that are unaffected by these practices with western states, such as Colorado or Kansas. Encourage students to look at boundaries, roads, and the grid patterns of city streets. **LS Visual**

Differentiated Instruction

Basic Learners

Topographic Knuckles Have students make a fist with one hand, knuckles pointing up. Tell students to imagine their knuckles are mountains. Have students draw two or three circles around their knuckles, one at the top, and the others moving down. Then, have students spread their hands flat. The flat hand is like a topographic map.

Teach, *continued*

Using the Figure GENERAL

Map Layers Point out that geologic maps are made by using a regular topographic map as a base and adding a layer of information about rock types. Ask students what symbols are used on geologic maps. (Answers may vary. Sample answer: Color is used to represent different rock types. The rock units are labeled with letters to indicate the geologic period when they formed. Lines show where geologic units meet. Special strike and dip symbols show angles of rock beds.) Tell students that because the geology of every area is different, geologic maps must have a legend that explains all of the colors and symbols used. In addition to the colors, the legend identifies any special geological information such as the location of fossils, faults or geologic hazards, or mineral resources.
LS Visual

Discussion GENERAL

Value of Geologic Maps Explain that geologic maps are important tools used by geologists, developers and planners, and engineers. Ask students to speculate how these people might use geologic maps. (Sample answers: These maps could be used to locate mineral deposits, energy resources, and sources of groundwater. They would also be useful in identifying potential hazards such as landslides, faults, or volcanoes, or to determine which areas are best suited to different land uses, construction projects, or urban developments.)
LS Interpersonal

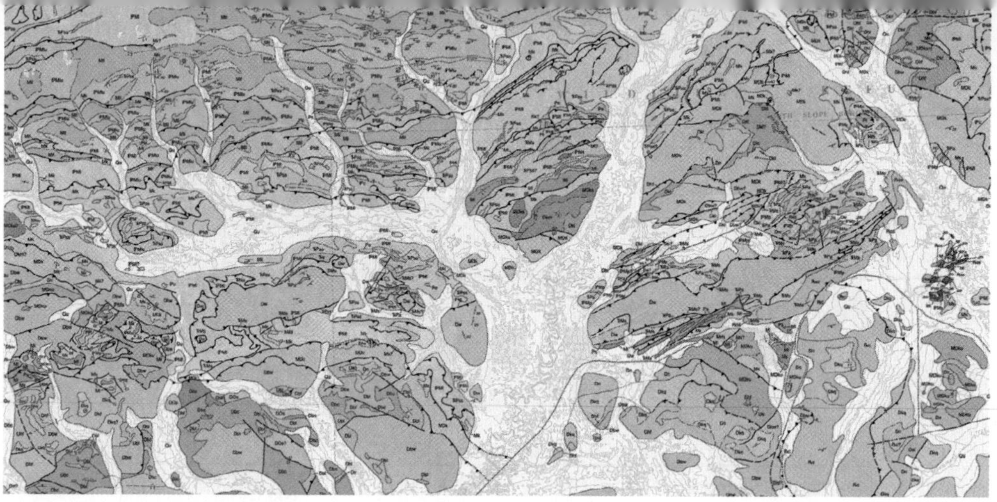

Figure 4 Each color on this geologic map represents a distinct type of rock and shows where in this region that type of rock occurs.

Geologic Maps

Geologic maps, such as the one shown in **Figure 4**, are designed to show the distribution of geologic features. In particular, geologic maps show the types of rocks found in a given area and the locations of faults, folds, and other structures.

Geologic maps are created on top of another map, called a *base map*. The base map provides surface features, such as topography or roads, to help identify the location of the geologic units. The base map is commonly printed in light colors or as gray lines so that the geologic information on the map is easy to read and understand.

READING TOOLBOX

Layered Book
Make a layered book FoldNote, and label the tabs "Topographic Maps," "Geologic Maps," "Soil Maps," and "Other Maps." Write notes on the appropriate layer as you read Section 3.

Rock Units on Geologic Maps

A volume of rock of a given age range and rock type is a *geologic unit*. On geologic maps, geologic units are distinguished by color. Units of similar ages are generally assigned colors in the same color family, such as different shades of blue. In addition to assigning a color, geologists assign a set of letters to each rock unit. This set of letters is commonly one capital letter followed by one or more lowercase letters. The capital letter symbolizes the age of the rock, usually by geologic period. The lowercase letters represent the name of the unit or the type of rock.

Other Structures on Geologic Maps

Other markings on geologic maps are contact lines. A *contact line* indicates places at which two geologic units meet, called *contacts*. The two main types of contacts are faults and depositional contacts. Depositional contacts show where one rock layer formed above another. Faults are cracks where rocks have moved past each other. Also on geologic maps are strike and dip symbols for rock beds. *Strike* indicates the direction in which the beds run, and *dip* indicates the angle at which the beds tilt.

READING TOOLBOX

Layered Book

Sample notes:

Topographic Maps
- show surface features (topography) of Earth
- show natural features (rivers) and constructed features (buildings)
- made by using aerial photographs and survey points
- contour lines show elevation
- *contour interval:* difference in elevation between one contour line and the next
- *relief:* difference in elevation between highest and lowest points being mapped
- *index contours:* the bolded fifth contour line, labeled by elevation
- spacing and direction of contour lines indicates shapes of landforms
- colored symbols are used to show certain features

Geologic Maps
- show the distribution of geologic features
- show types of rocks and faults, folds, and other structures
- created on top of base map, which shows surface features
- *geologic unit:* a volume of rock of a given age range and rock type

Answers continued on p. 81A

Soil Maps

Another type of map that is commonly used by Earth scientists is called a *soil map*. Scientists construct soil maps to classify, map, and describe soils. Soil maps are based on soil surveys that record information about the properties of soils in a given area. Soil surveys can be performed for a variety of areas, but they are most commonly performed for a county.

The government agency that is in charge of overseeing and compiling soil data is the Natural Resources Conservation Service (NRCS). The NRCS is part of the United States Department of Agriculture (USDA). The NRCS has been mapping the distribution of soils in the United States for more than a century.

Academic Vocabulary

distribution (DIS tri BYOO shuhn) relative arrangement of objects or organisms in time or space

Reading Check **Why do scientists create soil maps?**

Soil Surveys

A soil survey consists of three main parts: text, maps, and tables. The text of soil surveys includes general information about the geology, topography, and climate of the area being mapped. The tables describe the types and volumes of soils in the area. Soil surveys generally include two types of soil maps. The first type is a very general map that shows the approximate location of different types of soil within the area, such as the one shown in **Figure 5.** The second type shows detailed information about soils in the area.

Uses of Soil Maps

Soil maps are valuable tools for agriculture and land management. Knowing the properties of the soil in an area helps farmers, agricultural engineers, and government agencies identify ways to conserve and use soil and to plan sites for future development.

Figure 5 Scientists gather data to make a soil map by taking soil samples. Soil maps help scientists determine the potential abilities and limitations of the land to support development and agriculture.

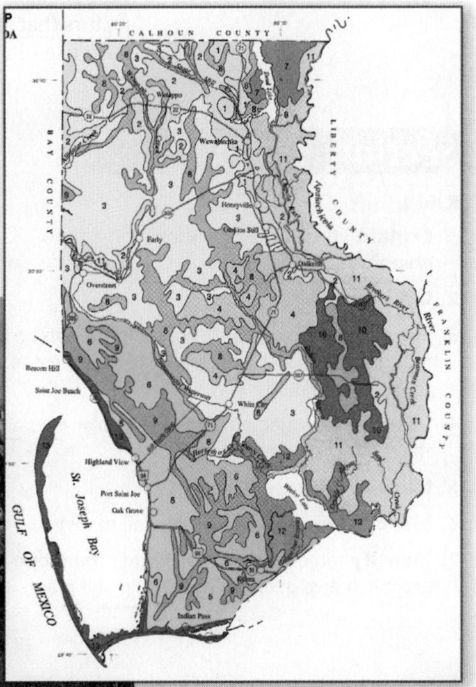

Environmental Connection

Soil Surveys Descriptions found in soil survey reports include the depth of each soil layer, how well water and plant roots penetrate the soil, the soil's pH, and how easily the soil can be eroded. Soil surveys describe not only the potential uses of soil but also the risks of damaging the soil or the environment. Where there is danger of erosion, a soil survey can point out how to control erosion and what plants are best for specific soils. In addition, soils are rated as to their suitability for recreational purposes, commercial uses, and habitats for wildlife.

Group Activity — ADVANCED

Local Soil Maps Divide students into groups and have each student collect soil samples from three different areas. Have them label each sample with its location. Allow the samples to dry, and have students group the soils according to particle size, color, or amount of organic matter. Next, have students create a base map by tracing the outline of a local map on paper. Invite students to pool their data and map locations of soil types, based on points where samples were collected, to see if there are any patterns.
LS Kinesthetic/Logical

Answer to Reading Check

Scientists create soil maps to classify, map, and describe soils.

Close

Reteaching — BASIC

Mapping Vocabulary Have students work in pairs to write definitions or to make an explanatory diagram for each of the key terms and italicized words in this section. Then, have them take turns quizzing each other to study for assessments. **LS Verbal/Visual**

Quiz — GENERAL

1. What mapping technique can be used to study changes in Earth's surface over time? (maps produced from satellite images)
2. What does the contour interval tell you about the slope of the land in a region being mapped? (The larger the contour interval the more mountainous or hilly the relief is. If a smaller interval can be used, the relief is lower.)
3. How would you plot points of equal temperature on weather maps? (by using isograms, in this case, isotherms)
4. What kind of map would you consult to determine the locations of mineral resources or natural hazards? (a geologic map)

Close, *continued*

Answers to Section Review

1. Contour lines connect points that have the same elevation.
2. the difference in elevation represented by the space between two adjacent contour lines
3. Contour lines that are spaced closely together indicate that the slope is steep, while those that are spaced farther apart indicate that the slope is flatter.
4. Geologic units of similar age are usually similar in color and are identified by letter symbols.
5. text: information on the geology, topography, and climate of an area; maps: the location and properties of soils found there; tables: types and volumes of soil within the area
6. to identify ways to conserve and use soil and to plan future land development
7. Sample answer: weather maps, maps of groundwater flow, and satellite maps that show changes in Earth over time
8. A V-shaped contour line indicates a valley. The bend of the V points toward higher elevation, and because water always flows from higher to lower elevation, the V points upstream.
9. Sample answer: In addition to locating rivers and roads, hikers in an unfamiliar area could easily find out where the ground is relatively level or where steep landforms are so they could plan a route.
10. A geologic map would indicate the location of any faults along which earthquakes may occur.
11. *Topographic maps* show *elevation* above the *mean sea level* and use *contour lines* and *index contours* to show elevation by using a set *contour interval*.

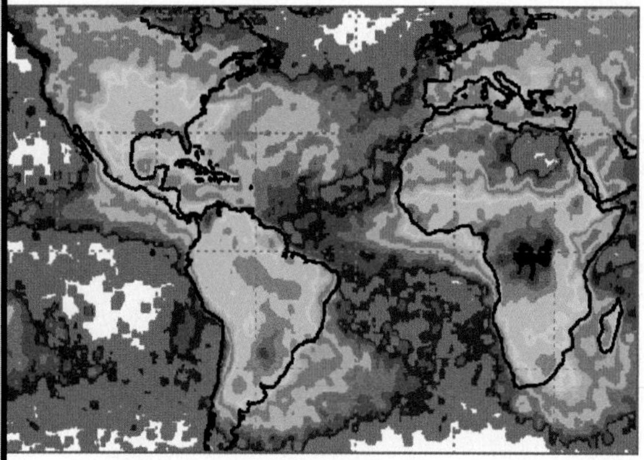

Figure 6 This map was created by using satellite data. The map shows the global distribution of lightning based on the average number of strikes per square kilometer. The highest frequency of strikes is shown in black, and the lowest frequency is shown in white.

Other Types of Maps

Earth scientists also use maps to show the location and flow of both water and air. These maps are commonly constructed by plotting data from various points around a region and then using isograms to connect the points whose data are identical.

Maps are useful to every branch of Earth science. For example, meteorologists use maps such as the one shown in **Figure 6** to record and predict weather events. Maps may be used to plot the amount of precipitation that falls in a given area. Maps are also used to show the locations of areas of high and low air pressure and the weather fronts that move across Earth's surface. These maps are updated constantly and are used by meteorologists to communicate to the public important information on daily weather conditions and emergency situations.

The location and direction of the flow of groundwater can be recorded on maps. Data from these maps can be used to determine where and when water shortages may occur. Scientists use map information to identify potential locations for power plants, waste disposal sites, and new communities.

Other types of Earth scientists use maps to study changes in Earth's surface over time. Such changes include changes in topography, changes in amounts of available resources, and changes in factors that affect climate. Maps generated by satellites are particularly useful for studying changes in Earth's surface.

Section 3 Review

Key Ideas

1. **Explain** how elevation is shown on a topographic map.
2. **Define** *contour interval.*
3. **Summarize** how you can use information on a topographic map to compare the steepness of slopes on the map.
4. **Describe** how geologic units of similar ages are shown on a geologic map.
5. **Identify** the three main parts of a soil survey.
6. **Identify** two primary uses for soil maps.
7. **Identify** three types of maps other than topographic maps, geologic maps, and soil maps.

Critical Thinking

8. **Applying Ideas** How can you use lines on a topographic map to identify the direction of river flow?
9. **Making Inferences** In what ways might topographic maps be more useful than simple map projections to someone who wants to hike in an area that he or she has never hiked in before?
10. **Identifying Patterns** What type of map would be the most useful to a scientist studying earthquake patterns: a geologic map or a topographic map?

Concept Mapping

11. Use the following terms to create a concept map: *topographic map, elevation, mean sea level, contour interval, contour line,* and *index contour.*

Differentiated Instruction

Alternative Assessment

Song Lyrics Have students write a song about the ways in which different types of maps convey information. They could write one verse about topographic maps, another about geologic maps, and a third on soil maps. Students may find it easier to write the words first, then experiment with the rhythm and beat. After students have composed the songs, invite them to perform their songs for the class or to create an audiotape or CD recording. **LS Auditory**

Why It Matters

Is There Anywhere That Isn't Mapped?

REAL WORLD

Lost in the city? Consult a map. Lost in the woods? Check your handy GPS receiver. With our ever-improving models of Earth, it is getting harder to "get lost"—harder, but not impossible. While much of Earth's surface is mapped, a detailed view of many features on and below its surface remains incomplete. Parts of rain forests around the world remain uncharted, and there are many kilometers of caves and sinkholes (cenotes) that no human has ever entered.

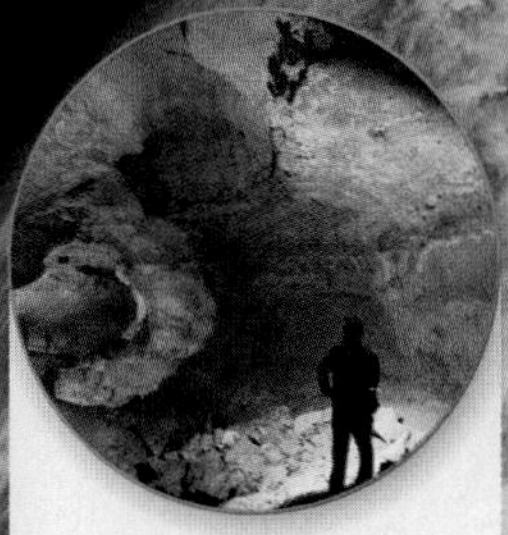

Mammoth Cave in Kentucky has more than 600 km of surveyed passages and perhaps twice as many that are still unmapped.

Inventor and explorer Bill Stone used a robotic submarine, DEPTHX, to survey Mexico's unexplored El Zacatón cenote in 2007. The same technology may one day be used to map the moons of the outer planets.

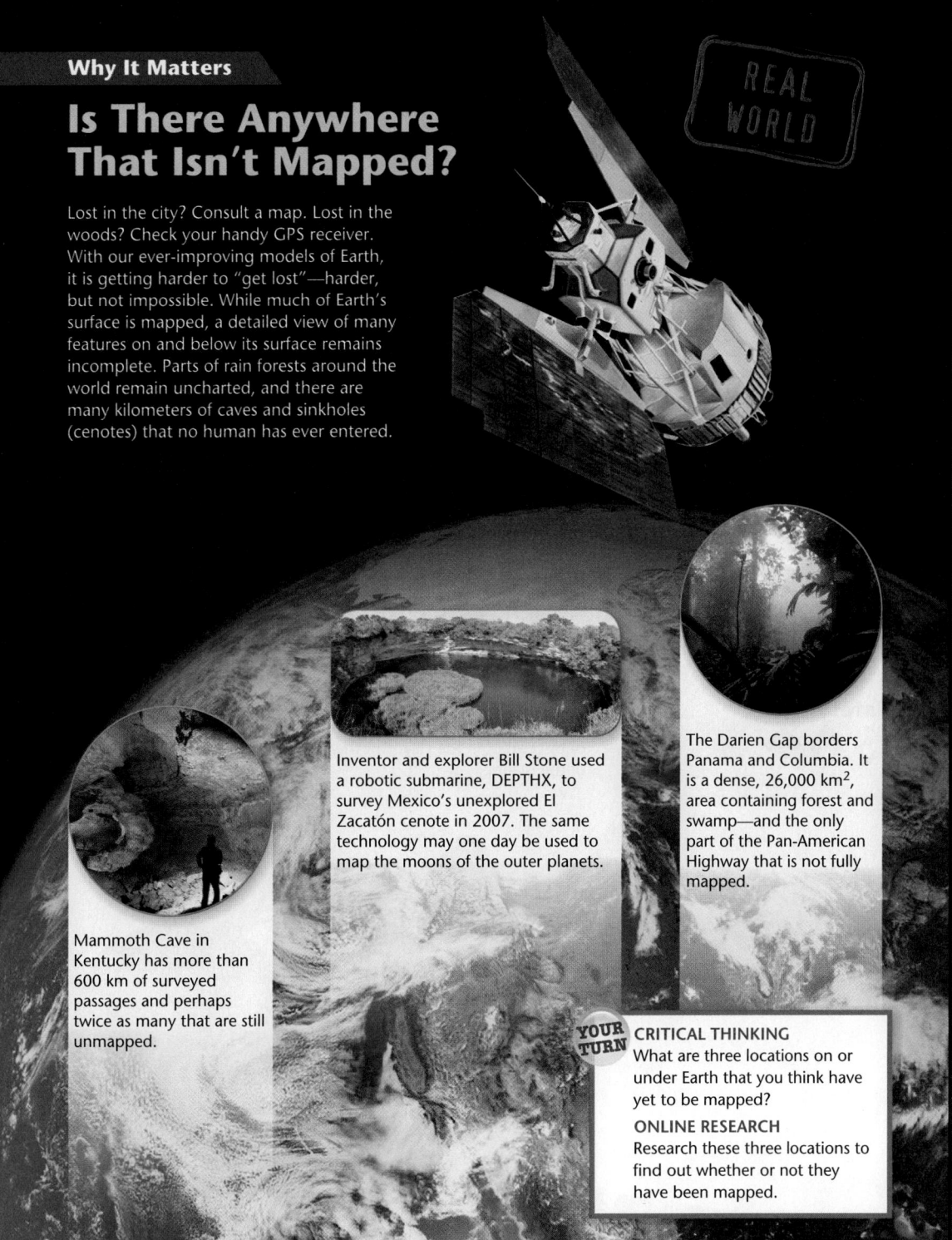

The Darien Gap borders Panama and Columbia. It is a dense, 26,000 km^2, area containing forest and swamp—and the only part of the Pan-American Highway that is not fully mapped.

YOUR TURN

CRITICAL THINKING
What are three locations on or under Earth that you think have yet to be mapped?

ONLINE RESEARCH
Research these three locations to find out whether or not they have been mapped.

Why It Matters

Is There Anywhere That Isn't Mapped?

People have been exploring and mapping Earth for thousands of years. While much of Earth's surface is mapped, a detailed view of many features below the surface remains incomplete. Technologies such as remotely controlled vehicles (often designed for underwater exploration) and imaging satellites (often designed for exploration of other planets and solar-system bodies) are helping to fill in some of the gaps.

Answers to Your Turn

Critical Thinking: Students might suggest locations such as underwater caverns or trenches, extreme environments such as the high Arctic and/or Antarctic, dense jungles of Africa or Central or South America—any location that seems remote or inaccessible.

Online Research: Answers will depend on locations chosen. Students likely will find that underwater locations and some jungle areas have not been mapped. Polar regions have been explored but not exhaustively mapped.

Time Required

two 45-minute class periods

Lab Ratings

Teacher Preparation 🧪🧪
Student Setup 🧪🧪
Concept Level 🧪🧪🧪
Cleanup 🧪🧪

Skills Acquired

• Constructing Models
• Identifying and Recognizing Patterns
• Interpreting
• Analyzing Data
• Measuring
• Communicating

Scientific Methods

In this lab, students will
• Make Observations
• Analyze Results
• Draw Conclusions

Materials

Materials listed are enough for groups of 2–4 students. Use waterproof clay for model construction so the model will not lose its shape when students add water.

Making Models **Lab**

 90 min

What You'll Do

> **Build** a scale model based on a map.
> **Identify** contour intervals and landscape features based on a map.

What You'll Need

basin, flat (or large pan), 8 cm deep
clay, modeling (4 lb)
dowel, thick wooden (or rolling pin)
knife, plastic
paper, white
pencil
ruler, metric
scissors
topographic map from Reference Tables section of the Appendix
water

Safety

Contour Maps: Island Construction

A map is a drawing that shows a simplified version of some detail of Earth's surface. There are many types of maps. Each type has its own special features and purpose. One of the most useful types of maps is the topographic map, or contour map. This type of map shows elevation and other important features of the landscape. Scientists make a contour map by using data obtained from a careful survey and photographic study of the area that the map represents.

Procedure

1 Study the topographic map in the Reference Tables section of the Appendix. Record the contour interval used on the island contour map. Then, count the number of contour lines that appear on the map.

2 Use the dowel to press out as many flat pieces of clay as there were contour lines counted in step 1. Each piece of clay should be 1 cm thick and large enough to cover the island shown on the map.

3 On a blank sheet of paper, trace the island contour map. Cut out the island from your copy of the contour map along the outermost contour line.

4 Place this cutout on top of one of the pieces of clay. Trace the edge of the cutout in the clay. Cut the piece of clay to match the shape of the island.

Step **2**

Tips and Tricks

An alternative approach is for students to sculpt the terrain from a mound of clay. If students try this, supply graph paper to serve as a grid under the map and under the plastic box so contours can be more accurately reconstructed.

Students could also build terrain models with other geologic formations such as lakes, volcanoes, or canyons and then trace the contour lines to investigate how their contours appear on topographic maps.

You may wish to have students calculate the gradient of different slopes on the model island. Provide protractors to measure the angle. Slope is measured by calculating the tangent of the surface. The tangent is calculated by dividing the vertical change in elevation by the horizontal distance. Gradient % = $100 \times \tan(\text{angle})$.

5. Cut the paper tracing along the next contour line, making sure not to damage the outer ring of paper as you cut.
6. Using the new paper shape and a new layer of clay, repeat step 4.
7. Place the paper ring from the first cut on the first clay shape that you cut out so that the outer edges of the paper ring line up with the edges of the clay. Stack the second layer of clay on the first layer so that the second layer fits inside the paper contour ring. This gives you the same contour spacing as shown on the map. Remove the paper ring.
8. Continue steps 4–7 for each of the contour layers.
9. Use leftover clay to smooth the terraced edges into a more natural profile.
10. Make a mark inside a pan approximately 1 cm down from the rim. Put the clay model of the island into the pan, and add water to a depth of 1 cm.
11. Compare the shoreline of the model with the lines on the contour map. Continue to add water at 1 cm intervals until the water reaches the mark on the pan.

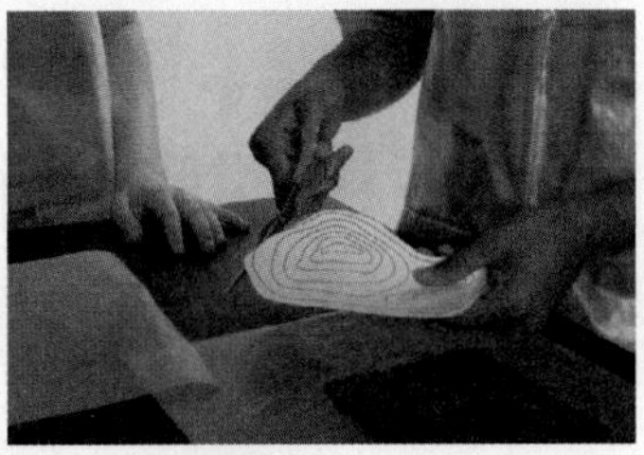

Step 5

Step 6

Analysis

1. **Making Inferences** What is the contour interval of your map?
2. **Understanding Relationships** How could you tell the steepest slope from the gentlest slope by observing the spacing of the contour lines?
3. **Analyzing Data** What is the elevation above sea level for the highest point of your model?
4. **Applying Ideas** How do you know if your model contains any areas that are below sea level? If there are any such areas, where are they and what are their elevations?
5. **Evaluating Models** What landscape feature is located at point C on your model, as indicated on the original map? What is the elevation of point B on your model?

Extension

Making Predictions From observations of your model, what conclusions can you make about where people might live on this island? Explain your answer.

Answers to Analysis

1. 10 meters
2. The contour lines on the steepest slope are closest together. This indicates a rapid rise in elevation over a short distance. The contour lines on the gentlest slope are spaced farther apart. This indicates a more gradual increase in elevation over a longer distance.
3. above 60 m but below 70 m
4. Near point A is an area marked by closed loops with short lines perpendicular to the inside of the loops. This indicates a depression. Because it occurs at the sea level elevation, it must extend below sea level; the elevation of the depression is at least 10 m but not greater than 20 m below mean sea level.
5. Point C represents a pass between two hills; Point B is between 20 m and 30 m above mean sea level.

Answer to Extension

Answers may vary. Sample answer: People would be more likely to live in the upland regions in the south-central part of the island beyond point C, where the higher elevations would be less affected by flooding from high tides or storm surges. The gentler slopes would be easier to cultivate and build upon.

Topographic Map of the Desolation Watershed

Activity — General

Local Watershed Obtain a topographic map of your area that includes a local watershed. Make copies of the map and laminate them. Have students locate a stream. Have them lay a transparency over the topographic map and trace the stream in blue. Then, have them locate familiar landmarks and mark their locations on the transparency. Have them copy the contour lines onto the transparency. Next, have students locate the highest points surrounding the body of water. Explain that the watershed is the drainage basin of the stream. Have students locate the watershed boundaries. If possible, take the class on a field trip and have them locate their stream.
LS Visual

Answers to Map Skills Activity

1. about 11,700 ft
2. southwest; The contours that cross the river valley make a V shape that points upstream.
3. the area around Bruin Creek; The contour lines near Bruin Creek are much closer together than the contour lines around Park Creek are.
4. 4,520 ft
5. All three creeks flow from higher elevation to lower elevation. Also, Park Creek and Bruin Creek join Desolation Creek and then flow north-northwest.
6. 200 ft

MAPS in Action

Topographic Map of the Desolation Watershed

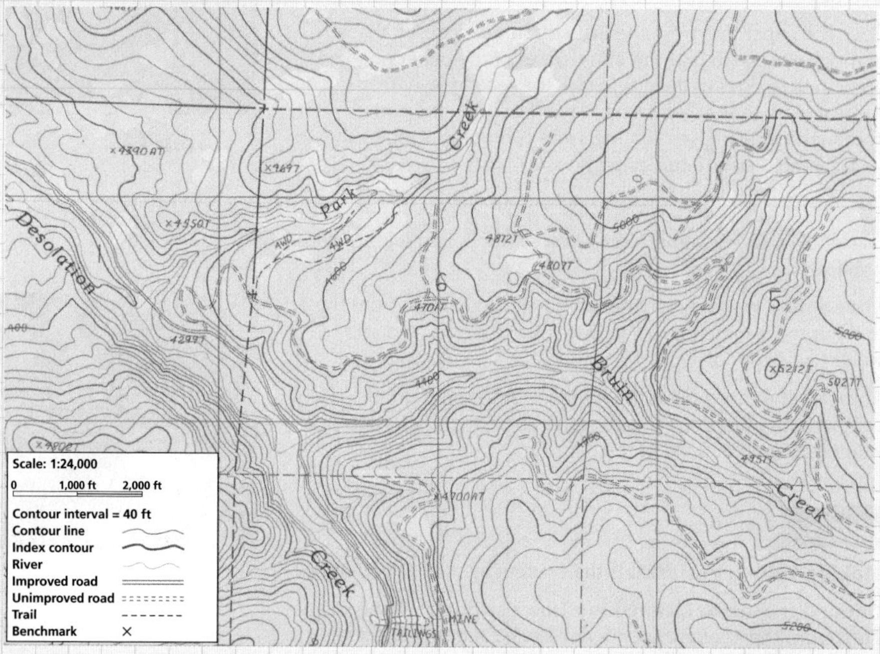

Map Skills Activity

This map, produced by the United States Geological Survey (USGS), shows the topography of the area around the Desolation watershed located in eastern Oregon. Note that the USGS uses English and metric units when measuring distance. Use the map to answer the questions below.

1. **Using a Key** What is the distance between the location on the northwest corner of the map labeled "4681T" and the location on the eastern side of the map labeled "5212T"?
2. **Analyzing Data** In what direction does Park Creek flow? How are you able to determine this information by looking at the map?
3. **Making Comparisons** Which area has the steeper slopes: the area around Park Creek or the area around Bruin Creek? How are you able to determine this information by looking at the map?
4. **Inferring Relationships** What is the elevation of the contour line that circles the point 4550T, located on the northwest of the map?
5. **Identifying Trends** Desolation Creek, Park Creek, and Bruin Creek enter the map from different geographic directions. Use the information on the map to determine what these creeks have in common in terms of their direction of flow.
6. **Analyzing Relationships** What is the total change in elevation between two index contours?

Key Resources

Workbooks

- Transparencies
  15 Topographic Map of the Desolation Watershed

Chapter 3 Summary

THINK central SUPER SUMMARY Keyword: HQXMODS

Key Ideas | **Key Terms**

Section 1

Finding Locations on Earth

- Lines of latitude are parallels that run east and west around Earth. Lines of longitude are meridians that run north and south from pole to pole.
- Lines of latitude and longitude form a system of intersecting lines (a grid system). The points at which lines intersect may be used to identify places on Earth's surface.
- The needle of a compass points to the geomagnetic north pole. Once north is located, south, east, and west may be determined.

parallel, p. 57
latitude, p. 57
meridian, p. 58
longitude, p. 58

Section 2

Mapping Earth's Surface

- Two ways that scientists get data to make maps are by using field surveys and by using images of Earth's surface obtained by remote sensing.
- For cylindrical projections, distances and sizes are accurate near the equator but distorted at the poles. Azimuthal projections are commonly used to map the poles, where distortion is minimal; distortion increases, however, farther from the poles. Conic projections are useful for mapping mid-latitude regions.
- The keys and legends of maps list map symbols and their meanings. Map scales show the relationship between distance shown on a map and actual distance.

remote sensing, p. 61
map projection, p. 62
legend, p. 65
scale, p. 65
isogram, p. 66

Section 3

Types of Maps

- Contour lines are used to show elevation and topography on a map.
- Geologic maps show the types and locations of rocks, faults, folds, and other geologic features.
- Soil maps are used to classify, map, and describe soils.

topography, p. 67
elevation, p. 67
contour line, p. 68
relief, p. 68

Chapter Summary

Using THINK central Resources

Super Summary

Have students connect the major concepts in this chapter through an interactive Super Summary. Visit www.thinkcentral.com and type in the keyword **HQXMODS** to access the Super Summary for this chapter.

Differentiated Instruction

Alternative Assessment

Mapmaker, Mapmaker Pose this scenario to students: "Suppose you want to meet a classmate at a movie theater or at a record store, but your friend is unfamiliar with your neighborhood. You decide to make a map to help your friend find the way."

Have students work with a partner to make a map that shows how to reach a destination they choose in their neighborhood. Students can measure distances by pacing or by using a large ball of string. They will also need blank or graph paper, pencils, and a compass or protractor for measuring angles. Tell students to choose an appropriate scale, to include a compass rose, and to label the streets and important landmarks. Students should include a map legend for any important symbols. Have them sketch a clear route from one of the landmarks to their chosen destination. Ask them to explain why the map is a more precise method of giving directions than a verbal description is.

LS Kinesthetic

Chapter Review

Assignment Guide	
Section	**Questions**
1	5, 6, 10–13, 18, 19, 24–26, 32–34
2	2, 3, 7, 14, 20–22, 31
3	4, 8, 9, 15–17, 23, 27, 28, 30, 35–37
1–3	1, 29

Reading Toolbox

1. Answers may vary. Students' notes should summarize the most important information in each of the chapter's three sections.

Using Key Terms

2–9. Answers may vary but should show that students understand the definitions of and differences between key terms.

Understanding Key Concepts

10. b 14. c
11. d 15. b
12. a 16. a
13. d 17. a

Short Answer

18. One minute of latitude is equal to 1.85 km, so 1 second of latitude would be 1/60 of that distance, or 0.0308 km, or 30.8 meters.

19. Latitude is the angular distance in degrees north or south of the equator, and longitude is the angular distance in degrees east or west of the prime meridian.

20. Three main map projections are cylindrical, azimuthal, and conic. They differ in the orientation of the surface on which the map is projected: cylinder, flat sheet, or cone (respectively), and the points of contact between the globe and map. This affects the amount and type of distortion, whether latitude and longitude lines are straight or curved, and whether great circles are straight lines.

21. In cylindrical projections, latitude and longitude lines form a rectangular grid, but distances and sizes near the poles are distorted. In azimuthal projections, great circle routes are straight lines so they are useful for navigation; map distortion increases the farther one moves from the point of contact. In conic projections, maps of neighboring areas can be fitted together to increase accuracy; areas farther from the parallel where the cone and globe contact are more distorted.

22. Legends help people understand the symbols used on maps. Scales help people calculate distances in the real world from distances on the map.

23. Contour lines connect points of equal elevation on the map. Every fifth line is labeled with the elevation. The spacing of contour lines indicates the slope, whether gradual or steep. V-shaped contour lines represent valleys.

Chapter 3 Review

1. **Layered Book** You have made a layered book for concepts within a section. Now make a layered book with the names of the three sections themselves and summarize the key ideas in the chapter. READING TOOLBOX

USING KEY TERMS

Use each of the following terms in a separate sentence.

2. *cartography*
3. *map projection*
4. *contour lines*

For each pair of terms, explain how the meanings of the terms differ.

5. *parallel* and *latitude*
6. *meridian* and *longitude*
7. *legend* and *scale*
8. *topography* and *relief*
9. *index contour* and *contour interval*

UNDERSTANDING KEY IDEAS

10. The distance in degrees east or west of the prime meridian is
 a. latitude.
 b. longitude.
 c. declination.
 d. projection.
11. The distance covered by a degree of longitude
 a. is 1/180 of Earth's circumference.
 b. is always equal to 11 km.
 c. increases as you approach the poles.
 d. decreases as you approach the poles.
12. The needle of a magnetic compass points toward the
 a. geomagnetic pole.
 b. geographic pole.
 c. parallels.
 d. meridians.
13. The shortest distance between any two points on the globe is along
 a. the equator.
 b. a line of latitude.
 c. the prime meridian.
 d. a great circle.
14. If 1 cm on a map equals 1 km on Earth, the fractional scale would be written as
 a. 1:1. **c.** 1:100,000.
 b. 1:100. **d.** 1:1,000,000.
15. On a topographic map, elevation is shown by means of
 a. great circles.
 b. contour lines.
 c. verbal scale.
 d. fractional scale.
16. What type of map is commonly used to locate faults and folds in beds of rock?
 a. geologic map
 b. topographic map
 c. soil map
 d. isogram map
17. The contour interval is a measurement of
 a. the change in elevation between two adjacent contour lines.
 b. the distance between mean sea level and any given contour line.
 c. the length of a contour line.
 d. the time needed to travel between any two contour lines.

SHORT ANSWER

18. How much distance on Earth's surface does one second of latitude equal?
19. What is the difference between latitude and longitude?
20. What are the three main types of map projections? How do they differ?
21. Compare the advantages and disadvantages of the three main types of map projections.
22. How do legends and scales help people interpret maps?
23. How do contour lines on a map illustrate topography?

CRITICAL THINKING

24. Applying Ideas What is wrong with the following location: 135°N, 185°E?

25. Identifying Trends As you move from point A to point B in the Northern Hemisphere, the length of a degree of longitude progressively decreases. In which direction are you moving?

26. Understanding Relationships Imagine that you are at a location where the magnetic declination is 0°. Describe your position relative to magnetic north and true north.

27. Making Inferences You examine a topographic map on which the contour interval is 100 m. In general, what type of terrain is probably shown on the map?

28. Applying Ideas A topographic map shows two hiking trails. Along trail A, the contour lines are widely spaced. Along trail B, the contour lines are almost touching. Which path would probably be easier and safer to follow? Why?

CONCEPT MAPPING

29. Use the following terms to create a concept map: *latitude, longitude, relief, map projection, cylindrical projection, elevation, map, azimuthal projection, contour line, conic projection, topography, legend,* and *scale.*

MATH SKILLS

Math Skills

30. Making Calculations A topographic map has a contour interval of 30 m. By how many meters would your elevation change if you crossed seven contour lines?

31. Applying Quantities A map has a fractional scale of 1:24,000. How many kilometers would 3 cm on the map represent?

32. Making Calculations A city to which you are traveling is located along the same meridian as your current position but is 11° of latitude to the north of your current position. About how far away is the city?

WRITING SKILLS

33. Writing from Research Research the navigation instrument known as the *sextant.* Make a diagram explaining how the sextant can be used to determine latitude.

34. Writing from Research Use the Internet and library resources to research global positioning systems. Write a short essay describing the different ways that GPS devices are currently being used in everyday situations. Then, make a prediction about how the technology might be used in the future.

INTERPRETING GRAPHICS

The map below shows contour lines of groundwater. The lines show elevation of the water table in meters above sea level. Use the map to answer the questions that follow.

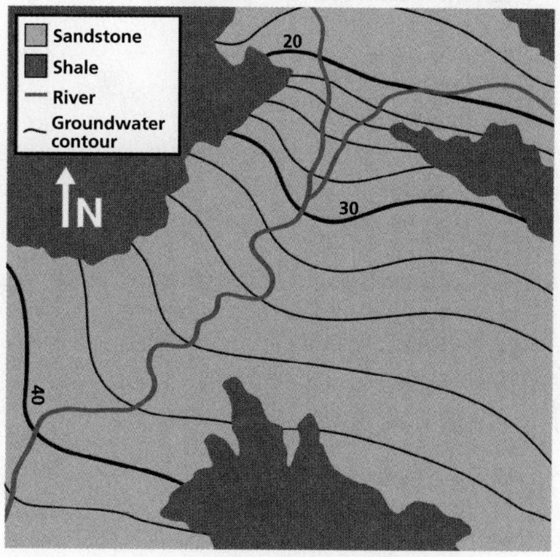

35. What is the contour interval for this map?

36. What is the highest measured level of the water table?

37. Groundwater flows from highest to lowest elevation. In which direction is the groundwater flowing?

Chapter Review

Critical Thinking

24. The latitude of the North Pole is 90°N. You cannot go any farther north than 90°. The meridian opposite the prime meridian (halfway around Earth) is 180°. At that point, the numbering starts over with W longitude. There is no such meridian as 185°E.

25. If the distance covered by a degree of longitude is decreasing from point A to point B, you are moving north toward the North Pole.

26. If you are located along a line of 0° magnetic declination, your position would be aligned with both the geomagnetic north pole and geographic north.

27. If the contour interval is as large as 100 m, the map probably represents fairly mountainous terrain.

28. Trail A, because the widely spaced contour lines indicate a gradual slope. The tightly spaced contour lines on Trail B indicate that the slope is very steep, and the path would be more dangerous.

Concept Mapping

29. Answers may vary but should include all of the terms listed. Sample answers appear at the end of this unit on p. 81B.

Math Skills

30. $30 \text{ m} \times 7 = 210 \text{ m}$

31. $100 \text{ cm/m} \times 1000 \text{m/km} = 100{,}000 \text{ cm/km}$; $24{,}000 \text{ cm} \times 3 \text{ cm} = 72{,}000 \text{ cm} \div 100{,}000 \text{ cm/km} = 0.72 \text{ km}$

32. $11 \times 111 \text{ km} = 1{,}221 \text{ km}$ north

Writing Skills

33. Answers may vary. Accept all reasonable answers.

34. Answers may vary. Accept all reasonable answers.

Interpreting Graphics

35. contour interval = 2 m

36. 42 m

37. The water is flowing northeast.

Estimated Time

To give students practice under more realistic testing conditions, allow them 30 minutes to answer all of the questions in this practice test.

Test Doctor

Question 1 Answer B is correct. Answer A is incorrect because V-shaped contour lines are more useful in determining the direction of a the flow of a river. Answer C is incorrect because short, straight lines inside a loop indicate a depression. Answer D is incorrect because tightly spaced lines are indicative of a steep slope, not a gradual slope.

Question 8 Answer F is correct. Students should recall that great circles are the shortest distance between two points on a globe. Because great circles appear as straight lines on a azimuthal projection, such maps are often used when plotting flight plans for airplanes. Answer G is incorrect because parallels would appear as circles on the type of projection described. Answer H is incorrect because the equator, while a great circle, would appear as a parallel, a large circle. Answer I is incorrect because coastlines would appear similar to their physical shapes, with distortion in size and shape increasing as they moved away from the North Pole.

Chapter 3 Standardized Test Prep

Understanding Concepts

Directions (1–5): For each question, write on a separate sheet of paper the letter of the correct answer.

1. How can you determine whether the contours on a topographic map show a gradual slope?
   A. Look for V-shaped contour lines.
   B. Look for widely spaced contour lines.
   C. Look for short, straight lines inside the loop.
   D. Look for tightly spaced, circular contour lines.
2. What is the difference in elevation between two successive index contours on a map with a contour interval of 5 m?
   F. 5 m
   G. 10 m
   H. 20 m
   I. 25 m
3. What part of a road map would you use in order to measure the distance from your current location to your destination?
   A. latitude lines
   B. map scale
   C. longitude lines
   D. map legend
4. For what reason do meteorologists use isobars on a weather map?
   F. to show differences in atmospheric air pressure
   G. to connect points of equal temperature
   H. to plot local precipitation data
   I. to show elevation above or below sea level
5. What is the angular distance, measured in degrees, east or west of the prime meridian?
   A. latitude
   B. longitude
   C. isogram
   D. relief

Directions (6–7): For each question, write a short response.

6. What is the longitude of the prime meridian?
7. What is the latitude of the North Pole?

Reading Skills

Directions (8–10): Read the passage below. Then, answer the questions.

Map Projections

Earth is a sphere, and thus its surface is curved. When a curved surface is transferred to a flat map, distortions in size, shape, distance, and direction occur. To limit these distortions, cartographers have developed many ways of transferring a three-dimensional curved surface to a flat map. On cylindrical projections, meridians and parallels appear as straight lines. These lines cross each other at 90° angles and form a grid. On azimuthal projections, there is little distortion at one contact point on the map, which is often one of the poles. But distortion in direction and distance increases as distance from the point of contact increases. On conic projections, the map is accurate along one parallel of latitude. Areas near this parallel are distorted the least. However, none of these maps is an entirely accurate representation of Earth's surface.

8. Which of the following appears as a straight line on an azimuthal projection, where the point of contact is the North Pole?
   F. great circles
   G. parallels
   H. the equator
   I. coastlines
9. Which of the following statements about cylindrical projections is true?
   A. Because latitude and longitude form a grid, plotting great circles can be done by using a straight-edged ruler.
   B. Because latitude and longitude form a grid, finding specific locations is easy on a cylindrical-projection map.
   C. Maps made by cylindrical projection often show the greatest distortion where the projection touched the globe.
   D. Cylindrical projections often show polar regions as being much smaller than they actually are.
10. Why does each map described display some sort of distortion?

Question 12 Full-credit answers should include the following points:
- students should correctly determine that the river is flowing from northwest to southeast
- students should cite the fact that the topographic lines near the river form V shapes
- the tips of these V's point upstream, which allows one to determine the direction in which the river is flowing

Question 14 In order to answer this question correctly, students must correctly calculate the number of degrees between points G and E. Common mistakes include arriving at the answer 222 km. Students may make this mistake if they calculate the difference using 2°. Though there are two increments of latitude between the locations, each increment represents 30° of distance, not 1°. Another common mistake is arriving at an answer of 3,330 km. Students may make this mistake when calculating the difference in the locations to be 30°. This is the angular distance of each location compared to the equator, but the total distance between the locations is 60°. The correct answer is 6,660 km, which is calculated by multiplying 111 km by 60.

Interpreting Graphics

Directions (11–14): For each question below, record the correct answer on a separate sheet of paper.

Use the topographic map below to answer questions 11 and 12.

Topographic Map of the Orr River

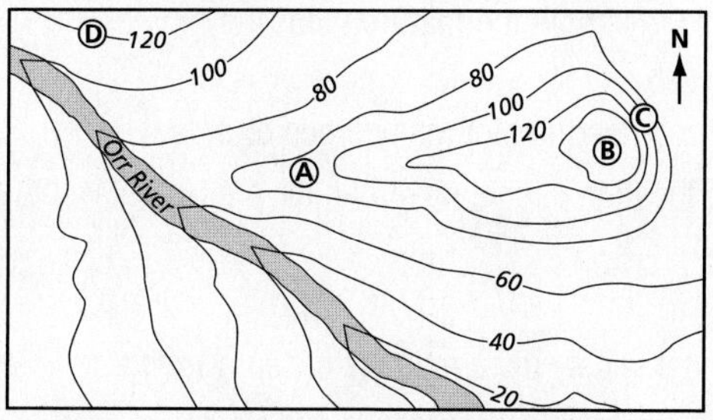

11. What location on the map has the steepest gradient?
F. location A
G. location B
H. location C
I. location D

12. In which direction is the river in the topographic map flowing? What information on the map helped you determine your answer?

The diagram below shows Earth's system of latitude and longitude lines. Lines are shown in 30° increments. Use this diagram to answer questions 13 and 14.

Latitude and Longitude

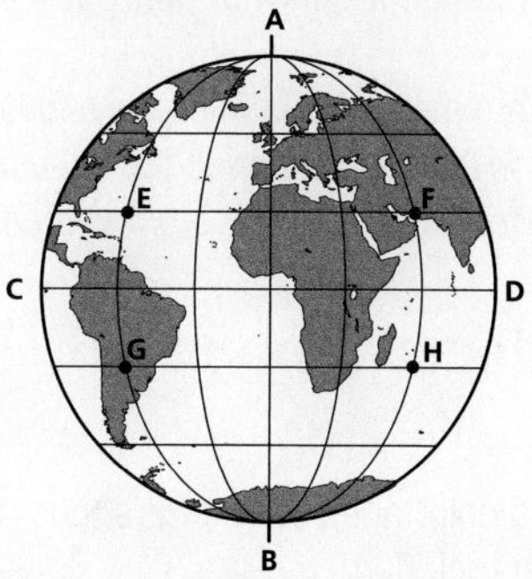

13. Which point is located at 30°N, 60°E?
A. point E
B. point F
C. point G
D. point H

14. The distance between two lines of parallel that are 1° apart is about 111 km. What is the approximate distance between points G and E?

Test Tip

Choose an answer to a question based on both what you already know as well as any information presented in the question.

Standardized Test Prep

Using THINK central Resources

State Resources

- For specific resources for your state, visit www.thinkcentral.com and type in the keyword **HSHSTR.**

Answers

Understanding Concepts

1. B
2. I
3. B
4. F
5. B
6. International Date Line
7. 90°N

Reading Skills

8. F
9. B
10. Any time a curved surface is mapped on a flat surface, distortion occurs. This distortion can take different forms and each map type produces different amounts of distortion.

Interpreting Graphics

11. H
12. Answers may vary. See Test Doctor for a detailed scoring rubric.
13. A
14. 6660 km

Answers continued from p. 6

Spider Map

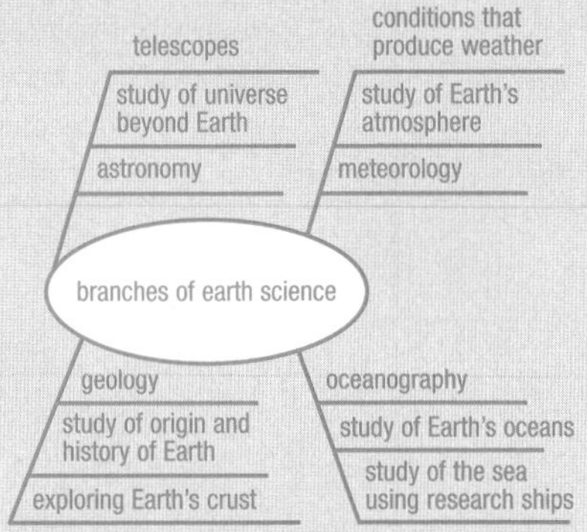

Answers continued from p. 14

Spider Map

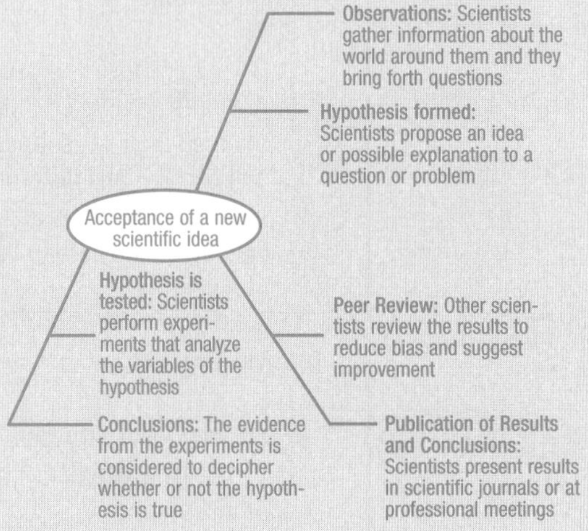

Answers continued from p. 40

Section Review

11. As carbon moves through the carbon cycle, it undergoes physical and chemical changes that involve transfers of energy.
12. A *system* may be a *closed system* or an *open system,* such as Earth in which both *matter* and *energy* are exchanged in the *atmosphere, hydrosphere, geosphere,* and *biosphere.*

Answers continued from p. 56

Frequency

Section 2

Direction should always be determined in relation to the parallels and meridians.

Some symbols resemble the features that they represent.

Isograms can be used to plot many types of data.

Because one location cannot have two air pressures, isobars never cross one another.

Section 3

One of the most widely used maps is called a *topographic map.*

A river always flows from higher to lower elevation.

Maps are useful to every branch of Earth science.

Answers continued from p. 60

Section Review

7. The circles that represent latitude are parallel and never cross one another. However, lines of longitude all pass through Earth's poles. Because Earth's circumference is greater at the equator than at the poles, the lines of latitude are farther apart at the equator than they are at the poles.
8. Locations on *Earth* are measured in *degrees, minutes,* and *seconds* by using lines of *latitude* that run *parallel* to the *equator,* and *meridians* that define lines of *longitude* and include the *prime meridian.*

Answers continued from p. 70

Layered Book

- geologists assign a color and set of letters (one capital, one or more lowercase) to each rock unit
- capital letter is age of rock by geologic period
- lowercase letters are name of unit or type of rock

Soil Maps

- used to classify, map, and describe soils
- based on soil surveys that show properties of soils
- Natural Resources Conservation Service (NRCS) in charge of compiling soil data
- text: discusses geology, topography, and climate of area
- tables: describes types and volumes of soils in area
- maps: (1) location of soils in area and (2) information on the soils
- soil maps help farmers, engineers, and the government conserve and use soil

Other Maps

- some maps show location and flow of water and air
- meteorologists use maps to record and predict weather (precipitation, air pressure, fronts, etc.)
- some Earth scientists use maps to study changes in Earth's surface over time (topography, resources, climate, etc.)

Sample Answers to Concept Maps from Chapter Reviews

Chapter 1 Introduction to Earth Science, p. 23

31.

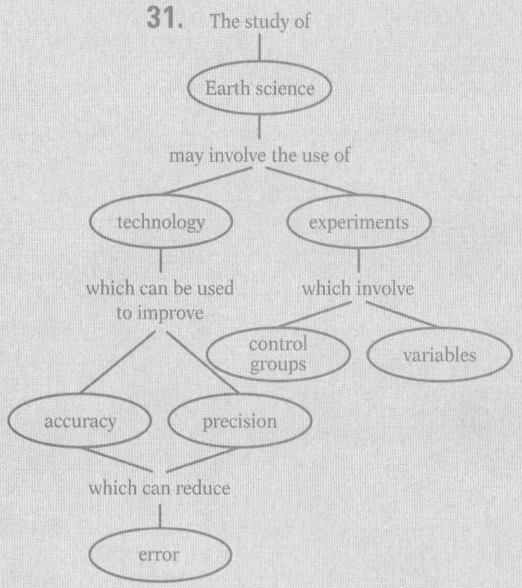

Chapter 2 Earth as a System, p. 51

31.

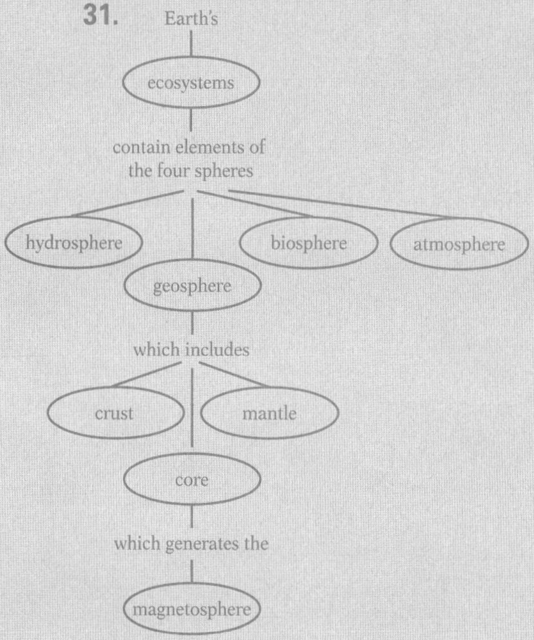

Chapter 3 Models of the Earth, p. 79

29.

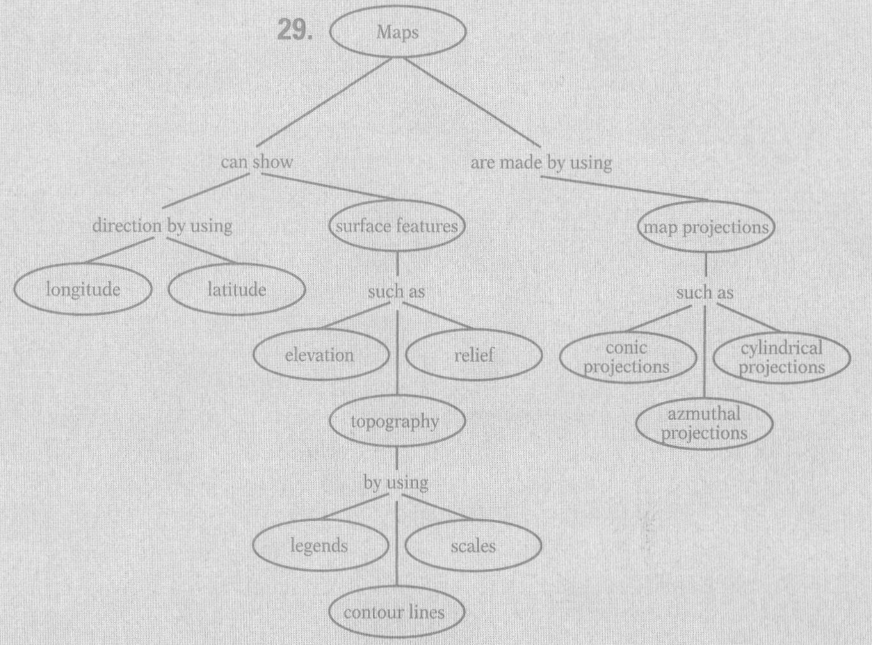

Unit 2 Composition of the Earth

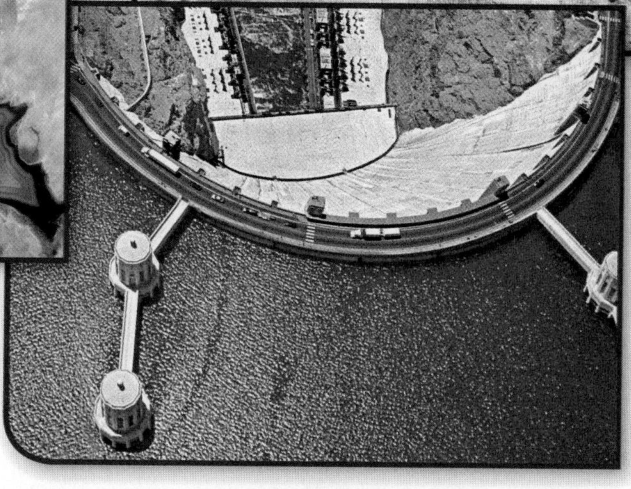

Chapter Planner 4 Earth Chemistry

	Standards	Teach Key Ideas
Chapter Opener, pp. 84–85 (45 min)	National Science Education Standards	
Section 1 Matter, pp. 87–92 (45 min) ❯ Properties of Matter ❯ Atomic Structure ❯ Atomic Number ❯ Atomic Mass ❯ The Periodic Table of Elements ❯ Valence Electrons and Periodic Properties	PS 1a, PS 1b, PS 2b, HNS 3c	■ ◆ **Bellringer,** p. 87 ■ **DI (Special Education Students):** Concept Map, p. 88 ◆ **Transparencies:** 16 The Periodic Table • 17 Atomic Number and Atomic Mass ▲ **Visual Concepts:** Matter • Comparing Physical and Chemical Properties • Element • Parts of the Atom • Electron Cloud • Atomic Number • Mass Number • Isotopes • Periodic Table Overview • Comparing Metals, Nonmetals, and Metalloids • Average Atomic Mass • Valence Electrons
Section 2 Combinations of Atoms, pp. 93–98 (45 min) ❯ Chemical Formulas ❯ Chemical Equations ❯ Chemical Bonds ❯ Mixtures	PS 2a, PS 2e	■ ◆ **Bellringer,** p. 93 ■ **DI (Special Education Students):** Modeling, p. 94 ◆ **Transparencies:** 18 Balancing Equations • 19 Ionic Bonds and Covalent Bonds • 20 Element Resources in the United States ▲ **Visual Concepts:** Compounds • Molecule • Chemical Formula • Reading Chemical Formulas • Signs of a Chemical Reaction • Chemical Equation • Symbols Used in Chemical Equations • Reading a Chemical Equation • Balancing a Chemical Equation by Inspection • Chemical Blend • Ion • Ionization • Ionic Bonding • Covalent Bonding • Comparing Polar and Nonpolar Covalent Bonds • Classification Scheme for Matter • Solutions • Solid, Liquid, and Gas
Chapter Wrap-Up, pp. 103–107 (90 min)		**Chapter Summary,** p. 103

See also PowerNotes® Presentations

CHAPTER Fast Track *To shorten instruction because of time limitations, omit the Chapter Lab.*

Key

Teacher's Edition ■ Teaching Transparencies ◆
Chapter Resource File ● Online Edition ▲

All resources listed below are also available on the **Teacher One Stop™.**

Why It Matters	Hands-On	Skills Development	Assessment
■ **Chapter Overview,** p. 84 ■ **Using the Figure:** Champagne Pool, p. 84	**Inquiry Lab:** Classifying Matter, p. 85	**Reading Toolbox,** p. 86	
■ **Section Overview,** p. 87 ■ **Using the Figure:** Earth's Elements, p. 87 ■ **Astronomy Connection:** Forming Elements, p. 90 ■ **Using the Figure:** Radioactive Elements, p. 91	**Quick Lab:** Using the Periodic Table, p. 89 ■ **Activity:** Poster Project, p. 89 **Inquiry Lab:** Physical Properties of Elements, pp. 100–101 ● **Skills Practice Lab:** Flame Tests	**Reading Toolbox:** Comparison Table, p. 88 **Maps in Action:** Element Resources in the United States, p. 102 ■ ● **Internet Activity:** High-Energy Physics, p. 88	**Reading Check,** p. 89 **Section Review,** p. 92 ■ **Reteaching,** p. 91 ■ **Quiz,** p. 91 ■ **DI (Alternative Assessment):** Quiz Show, p. 92 ● **Section Quiz**
■ **Section Overview,** p. 93 ■ **Using the Figure:** Describing Reactions, p. 94 **How Can Diamond and Graphite Both Be Carbon?** p. 95 ■ **Chemistry Connection:** Chemical Bonding, p. 95	■ **Activity:** Composition of Compounds, p. 93 **Quick Lab:** Compounds, p. 97 ● **Inquiry Lab:** Ionic and Covalent Conductivity	**Math Skills:** Balancing Equations, p. 94 ■ **Skill Builder:** Math, p. 96 **Reading Toolbox:** Double-Door Fold, p. 96	**Reading Check,** p. 95 **Reading Check,** p. 97 **Section Review,** p. 98 ■ **Reteaching,** p. 97 ■ **Quiz,** p. 97 ■ **DI (Alternative Assessment):** Balancing Chemical Equations, p. 98 ● **Section Quiz**
Not Such a Strange State, p. 99		▲ **Super Summary** **Standardized Test Prep,** pp. 106–107	**Chapter Review,** pp. 104–105 ■ **DI (Alternative Assessment):** Poster Project, p. 103 ● **Chapter Tests**

See also Lab Generator

See also Holt Online Assessment Resources

Chapter Overview

Matter consists of atoms, either of one type (elements), or in combination with other types (compounds). This chapter describes how electrons are arranged around an atom's nucleus, how atoms combine to form molecules, and the types of chemical bonds that hold molecules together.

Using the Figure GENERAL

Champagne Pool The geothermal pool in the figure is heated by volcanic activity on the North Island of New Zealand. Ask students if anything in the photograph indicates heating. (The steam rising from the pool indicates heating.) The orange color in the foreground is caused by arsenic sulfides. Although various elements are present in the water, they are not visible.
LS Visual

Why It Matters

Champagne Pool is named for the dissolved CO_2 that bubbles to the surface. Some dissolved elements, including gold, may precipitate, and a large gold deposit may exist beneath the pool. Other dissolved elements, such as arsenic and mercury, are toxic.

Chapter 4 Earth Chemistry

Chapter Outline

Virginia Standards of Learning
ES.1.a
ES.1.b

Why It Matters

New Zealand's geothermal Champagne Pool is steaming hot, at 74 °C. Its water contains dissolved elements, such as gold, silver, mercury, and arsenic. In fact, the entire Earth is made of chemical elements. Understanding the chemical structure of elements and molecules will help you understand the properties of the substances that make up Earth.

Chapter Correlations — *Virginia Standards of Learning*

ES.1.a volume, area, mass, elapsed time, direction, temperature, pressure, distance, density, and changes in elevation/depth are calculated utilizing the most appropriate tools.

ES.1.b technologies, including computers, probeware, and geospatial technologies, are used to collect, analyze, and report data and to demonstrate concepts and simulate experimental conditions.

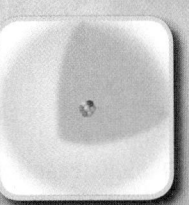

Inquiry Lab

20 min

Classifying Matter

Examine each of the six solids provided by your teacher, and record your observations. Consider properties such as mass, shininess, color, texture, size, and hardness. Determine whether the solids are made up of only one component, or two or more different components. Add each solid to a beaker with water, and observe how it behaves. Based on your observations, classify the solids into two or three groups.

Questions to Get You Started

1. Some properties help you distinguish one solid from another, and some do not. Explain which properties are the most and least helpful for developing a classification system.
2. How did you decide on your classification system? Explain your reasoning.
3. Compare your classification system with another group's classification system. Explain the similarities and differences.

Inquiry Lab

Central Concept: Scientists use physical and chemical properties to classify matter according to shared characteristics. Students will practice classifying matter and form rationales for their systems.

Teacher's Notes: You may wish to add additional solids for classification, including baking powder, chalk, iron, or others.

Materials (per group)

- Beaker
- Water
- Six solids (sand, copper wire, aluminum foil, cube of wood, piece of pyrite, salt)

Skills Acquired

- Observing
- Classifying

Answers to Getting Started

1. Answers will vary. Students may note that size and mass are not helpful for some items, because the same solid may occur in various sizes and masses. Hardness is a helpful property for some items, because it remains consistent for a certain solid.
2. Answers will vary. Students should include their rationale.
3. Answers will vary.

Using THINK central Resources

An online version of this chapter, as well as all the print and multimedia resources that accompany the program are available to registered teachers and their students. Log onto www.thinkcentral.com to access these materials and tools to organize your preparation and student learning.

READING TOOLBOX

FoldNotes

Section 1:

Element
- cannot be broken down into simpler, stable substance
- has a unique set of physical and chemical properties
- more than 90 elements occur naturally

Atom
- smallest unit of an element
- cannot be broken down into smaller particles with the same properties as the atom

Section 2:

Compound
- made of atoms of two or more elements joined by chemical bonds
- properties of a compound differ from those of the elements that make up the compound
- cannot be physically separated into parts

Mixture
- two or more substances that are not chemically combined
- substances that make up a mixture keep their individual properties
- can be physically separated into parts

READING TOOLBOX

These reading tools will help you learn the material in this chapter.

FoldNotes

Double-Door Fold This type of FoldNote can help you identify the similarities and differences between topics.

Your Turn Use a double-door fold to compare the terms *element* and *atom* in Section 1. For Section 2, compare the terms *compound* and *mixture*.

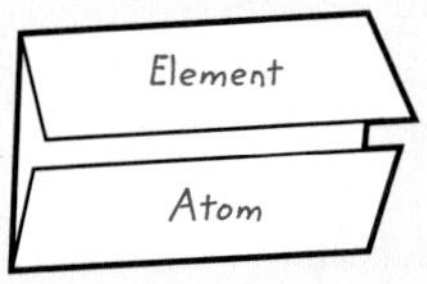

Note Taking

Comparison Table You can use a comparison table to organize your notes as you compare related terms or topics. A table that compares chemical and physical properties has been started for you below.

Your Turn As you read Section 1, complete a table like the one started here.

Type of Property	Physical	Chemical
How the property is observed	can be observed without changing the composition of the substance	
Examples		

Science Terms

Everyday Words Used in Science Many words that are used in science are also used in everyday speech. These words often have different or more precise meanings in science contexts than in everyday speech. Pay attention to the definitions of these words so that you can use them correctly in scientific contexts.

Your Turn As you read Chapter 4, complete a table like the one shown. For each term, write its everyday meaning and its scientific meaning.

Term	Everyday meaning	Scientific meaning
matter	a subject or problem	anything that takes up space and has mass
element	a piece or component of something	
compound		
mixture		
solution		

For more information on how to use these and other tools, see **Appendix A**.

Note Taking

Type of Property	Physical	Chemical
How the property is observed	can be observed without changing the composition of the substance	observed when composition of the substance changes
Examples	density, color, hardness, freezing point, boiling point	iron reacts with oxygen to form rust, helium is not reactive

Science Terms

See page 195A for answers to science terms.

SECTION 1

Matter

Key Ideas	Key Terms	Why It Matters
❯ Compare chemical properties and physical properties of matter. ❯ Describe the basic structure of an atom. ❯ Compare atomic number, mass number, and atomic mass. ❯ Define *isotope*. ❯ Describe the arrangement of elements in the periodic table.	matter element atom proton electron neutron isotope	To understand the world around you, it helps to understand what Earth is made of—matter. From Earth's rocks to the oceans and air (and even your own body), matter really matters.

Every object in the universe is made of particles of some kind of substance. Scientists use the word *matter* to describe the substances of which objects are made. **Matter** is anything that takes up space and has mass. The amount of matter in any object is its *mass*.

Properties of Matter

All matter has two types of distinguishing characteristics—physical properties and chemical properties. *Physical properties* can be observed without changing the composition of the substance. Physical properties include density, color, hardness, freezing point, boiling point, and the ability to conduct an electric current.

Chemical properties describe how a substance reacts with other substances. For example, a chemical property of iron is that iron reacts with oxygen to form rust. Understanding the chemical properties of a substance requires knowing some basic information about the particles that make up all substances.

matter anything that has mass and takes up space

element a substance that cannot be separated or broken down into simpler substances by chemical means

Elements

An **element** is a substance that cannot be broken down into simpler, stable substances by chemical means. Each element has physical and chemical properties that can be used to identify it. **Figure 1** shows common elements in Earth's crust. Approximately 90 elements occur naturally on Earth. Eight of these make up more than 98% of Earth's crust.

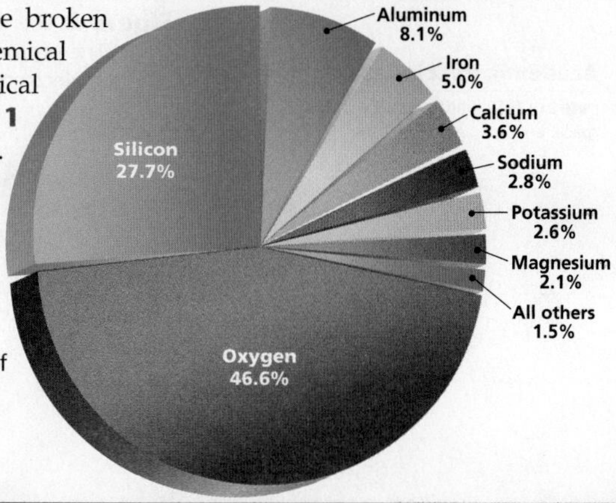

Figure 1 This graph shows the percentage of total mass that each common element makes up in Earth's continental crust.

Section 1

Focus

Overview

This section describes elements and their basic unit, the atom. Physical and chemical properties of matter are introduced, along with the structure of atoms and their relation to each other in the periodic table.

Bellringer

Tell students that we are completely surrounded by matter. Have students give examples of matter around them. Ask them to list some characteristics of matter. Then, have them name some things that are not matter. (Answers may vary. Accept all reasonable answers.) **LS Verbal**

Motivate

Using the Figure GENERAL

Earth's Elements Point out to students that while a number of the elements shown in the pie graph exist only as elements, most are combined with other elements to form chemical compounds, such as iron oxides, in which iron and oxygen are bonded together. Ask students to use the pie chart to identify the three most common elements in Earth's continental crust and their respective percentages. (oxygen, 46.6%; silicon, 27.7%; and aluminum, 8.1%) **LS Visual**

Key Resources

Chapter Resource File

- Directed Reading BASIC
- Skills Practice Lab: Flame Tests GENERAL

Technology

- Transparencies
  Bellringer

Teach

READING TOOLBOX GENERAL

Comparison Table

Particle	Proton	Electron	Neutron
Charge	positive (+)	negative (−)	neutral (no charge)
Location	nucleus	electron cloud (surrounding the nucleus)	nucleus

Internet Activity ADVANCED

High-Energy Physics Have students use the Internet to research the field of high-energy physics and the various types of particle accelerators used throughout the world to study subatomic particles. Students may check the Web sites of various facilities, such as the Stanford Linear Accelerator Center (SLAC) in California, Fermilab in Illinois, and CERN in Switzerland. Have students report their findings in a written report, oral presentation, or poster presentation. A worksheet designed to direct student research on this topic can be found in the **Chapter Resource File** booklet or by visiting www.thinkcentral.com and entering the keyword **HQXCHMX.** LS **Verbal**

READING TOOLBOX

Comparison Table
As you read this page, create a comparison table for the terms *proton, electron,* and *neutron.*

Atoms

Elements consist of atoms. An **atom** is the smallest unit of an element that has the chemical properties of that element. Atoms cannot be broken down into smaller particles that will have the same chemical and physical properties as the atom. A single atom is so small that its size is difficult to imagine. To get an idea of how small it is, look at the thickness of this page. About a million atoms lined up side by side would be equal to that thickness.

Atomic Structure

Even though atoms are very tiny, they are made up of even smaller parts called *subatomic particles.* The three major kinds of subatomic particles are protons, electrons, and neutrons. **Protons** are subatomic particles that have a positive charge. **Electrons** are subatomic particles that have a negative charge. **Neutrons** are subatomic particles that are neutral, which means that they have no charge.

atom the smallest unit of an element that maintains the chemical properties of that element

proton a subatomic particle that has a positive charge and that is located in the nucleus of an atom; the number of protons of the nucleus is the atomic number, which determines the identity of an element

electron a subatomic particle that has a negative charge

neutron a subatomic particle that has no charge and that is located in the nucleus of an atom

The Nucleus

As shown in **Figure 2,** the protons and neutrons of an atom are packed close to one another. Together they form the *nucleus,* which is a small region in the center of an atom. The nucleus has a positive charge because protons have a positive charge and neutrons have no charge.

The nucleus makes up most of an atom's mass but very little of an atom's volume. If an atom's nucleus were the size of a gumdrop, the atom itself would be as big as a football stadium.

The Electron Cloud

The electrons of an atom move in a certain region of space called an *electron cloud* that surrounds the nucleus. Because opposite charges attract each other, the negatively charged electrons are attracted to the positively charged nucleus. This attraction is what holds electrons in the atom.

Academic Vocabulary

region (REE juhn) a specific surface or space; an area

Figure 2 The nucleus of the atom is made up of protons and neutrons. The protons give the nucleus a positive charge. The negatively charged electrons are in the electron cloud that surrounds the nucleus.

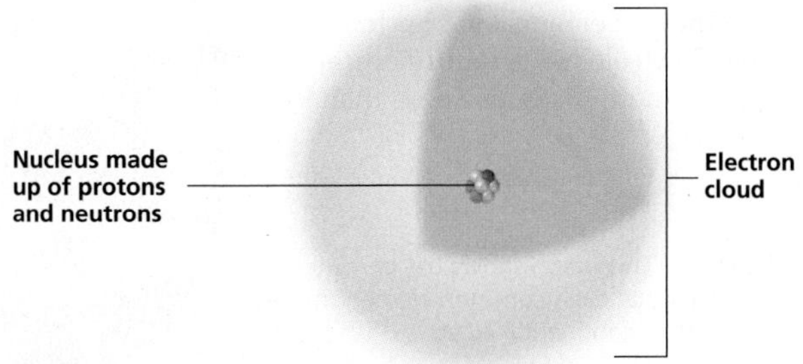

MISCONCEPTION ALERT

Electron Cloud Explain to students that an electron cloud is an idealized representation of where an electron may be found at a particular point in time. Matter the size of tiny atoms is described as having properties of both particles and waves. Thinking of an electron as if it were spread out like a cloud within a region around the nucleus helps students understand the extended wave-like properties. Have students visualize blades of a fan moving within a region around the fan's axis. While each blade is located in only one place, pinpointing the exact location at any given moment is difficult.

Differentiated Instruction

Special Education Students

Concept Map Many students better understand information when it is given visually. Help students understand the relationships among elements, atoms, electrons, protons, neutrons, and nuclei by creating a concept map.

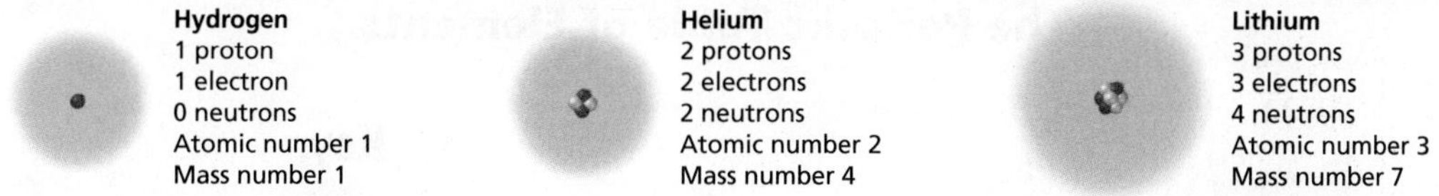

Figure 3 Hydrogen, helium, and lithium are unique, as indicated by their atomic numbers.

Atomic Number

The number of protons in the nucleus of an atom is called the *atomic number*. All atoms of any given element have the same atomic number. An element's atomic number sets the atoms of that element apart from the atoms of all other kinds of elements, as shown in **Figure 3.** Because an uncharged atom has an equal number of protons and electrons, the atomic number is also equal to the number of electrons in an atom of any given element.

Elements on the periodic table are ordered according to their atomic numbers. The *periodic table*, shown on the following pages, is a system for classifying elements. Elements in the same column on the periodic table have similar arrangements of electrons in their atoms. Elements that have similar arrangements of electrons have similar chemical properties.

Atomic Mass

The sum of the number of protons and neutrons in an atom is the *mass number*. The mass of a subatomic particle is too small to be expressed easily in grams. So, a special unit called the *unified atomic mass unit* (u) is used. Protons and neutrons each have an atomic mass that is close to 1 u. In contrast, electrons have much less mass than protons and neutrons do. The mass of 1 proton is equal to the combined mass of about 1,840 electrons. Because electrons add little to an atom's total mass, their mass can be ignored when calculating an atom's approximate mass.

Reading Check **What is the difference between atomic number, mass number, and unified atomic mass unit?** (See Appendix G for answers to Reading Checks.)

Isotopes

Although all atoms of a given element contain the same number of protons, the number of neutrons may differ. For example, while most helium atoms have two neutrons, some helium atoms have only one neutron. An atom that has the same number of protons (or the same atomic number) as other atoms of the same element do but has a different number of neutrons (and thus a different atomic mass) is called an **isotope** (IE suh TOHP).

A helium atom that has two neutrons is more massive than a helium atom that has only one neutron. Because of their different numbers of neutrons and their different masses, different isotopes of the same element have slightly different properties.

Quick Lab 10 min

Using the Periodic Table

Procedure

1. Use the periodic table to find the atomic numbers of the following elements: carbon, iron, molybdenum, and iodine.
2. Determine the number of protons and electrons that are in each neutral atom of the elements listed in step 1.
3. Find the average atomic masses of the elements listed in step 1.

Analysis

1. Use the atomic number and average atomic mass of each element to estimate the average number of neutrons in each atom of the elements listed in step 1 of this activity.
2. Which element has the largest difference between its average number of neutrons and the number of protons? Describe any trends that you observe.

isotope one of two or more atoms that have the same number of protons (atomic number) but different numbers of neutrons (atomic mass)

Quick Lab

Materials
Periodic table

Skills Acquired
- Collecting Data
- Classifying
- Identifying/Recognizing Patterns

Teacher's Notes: Instruct students to round the average atomic masses to a whole number to simplify their calculations.

Carbon: atomic number = 6, average atomic mass = 12 u
Iron: atomic number = 26, average atomic mass = 56 u
Molybdenum: atomic number = 42, average atomic mass = 96 u
Iodine: atomic number = 53, average atomic mass = 127 u

Answers to Analysis

1. Average number of neutrons:
   Carbon: 12 − 6 = 6
   Iron: 56 − 26 = 30
   Molybdenum: 96 − 42 = 54
   Iodine: 127 − 53 = 74
2. iodine; The larger the atom, the larger the difference between the number of protons and the number of neutrons.

Answer to Reading Check

The atomic number is the number of protons in an atom's nucleus. The mass number is the sum of the number of protons and the number of neutrons in an atom. The unified atomic mass unit is used to express the mass of subatomic particles or atoms.

Activity — BASIC

Poster Project Assign, or have each student select, an element as the subject of a poster project. Have students research the basic atomic properties of their element: atomic number, the number of electrons, mass number, number of neutrons in the most abundant isotope, and average atomic mass. Also have students list some of the element's uses and qualities. Students can give brief presentations. Alternatively, students can display posters throughout the classroom. **LS Visual**

Teach, *continued*

Homework ADVANCED

Naming the Elements Assign each student five elements from the periodic table. Have students research the origin and meaning of the names of each of their elements. Try to include in each student's list one element known since ancient or medieval times, three discovered in the nineteenth century, and one transuranium element. Have students present their findings in a short written report, an oral presentation, a poster, a skit, or a song. **LS Verbal/Auditory**

Cultural Awareness BASIC

Creating the Periodic Table The periodic table was first devised by the Russian chemist Dmitri Mendeleev in 1869. At the time, the atomic nature of matter was not widely accepted or well understood. Nevertheless, organizing elements by atomic weight and chemical properties enabled Mendeleev to discern a pattern in which elements with similar properties could be grouped together. Mendeleev even predicted the properties of the elements scandium, gallium, and germanium before they were discovered. The element mendelevium is named in his honor.

Key Resources

Technology

- Transparencies
  16 The Periodic Table

The Periodic Table of Elements

Key:

Atomic number	Symbol	Name	Average atomic mass
6	C	Carbon	12.0107

Period	Group 1	Group 2	Group 3	Group 4	Group 5	Group 6	Group 7	Group 8	Group 9
1	1 H Hydrogen 1.007 94								
2	3 Li Lithium 6.941	4 Be Beryllium 9.012 182							
3	11 Na Sodium 22.989 769 28	12 Mg Magnesium 24.3050							
4	19 K Potassium 39.0983	20 Ca Calcium 40.078	21 Sc Scandium 44.955 912	22 Ti Titanium 47.867	23 V Vanadium 50.9415	24 Cr Chromium 51.9961	25 Mn Manganese 54.938 045	26 Fe Iron 55.845	27 Co Cobalt 58.933 195
5	37 Rb Rubidium 85.4678	38 Sr Strontium 87.62	39 Y Yttrium 88.905 85	40 Zr Zirconium 91.224	41 Nb Niobium 92.906 38	42 Mo Molybdenum 95.96	43 Tc Technetium (98)	44 Ru Ruthenium 101.07	45 Rh Rhodium 102.905 50
6	55 Cs Cesium 132.905 4519	56 Ba Barium 137.327	57 La Lanthanum 138.905 47	72 Hf Hafnium 178.49	73 Ta Tantalum 180.947 88	74 W Tungsten 183.84	75 Re Rhenium 186.207	76 Os Osmium 190.23	77 Ir Iridium 192.217
7	87 Fr Francium (223)	88 Ra Radium (226)	89 Ac Actinium (227)	104 Rf Rutherfordium (261)	105 Db Dubnium (262)	106 Sg Seaborgium (266)	107 Bh Bohrium (264)	108 Hs Hassium (277)	109 Mt Meitnerium (268)

58 Ce Cerium 140.116	59 Pr Praseodymium 140.907 65	60 Nd Neodymium 144.242	61 Pm Promethium (145)	62 Sm Samarium 150.36
90 Th Thorium 232.038 06	91 Pa Protactinium 231.035 88	92 U Uranium 238.028 91	93 Np Neptunium (237)	94 Pu Plutonium (244)

* The systematic names and symbols for elements greater than 111 will be used until the approval of trivial names by IUPAC.

THINK central RESOURCES (Keyword: Holt Periodic)

Astronomy Connection ADVANCED

Forming Elements Hydrogen is the most abundant element in the universe. Scientists theorize that all of the hydrogen in the universe, along with some helium and lithium, was produced shortly after the Big Bang. Most other elements on Earth, however, are the products of exploding stars called *supernovas.* When stars that have masses more than 20 times that of the sun reach a certain point in their evolution, their cores collapse. Then, the outer layers of the star rapidly collapse inward as well, releasing a tremendous amount of energy in a short period of time. This energy passes outward through the star, heating and bombarding nuclear material to form the various elements in a process called *nucleosynthesis.* The star's nuclear material spreads outward from the star into interstellar space until it becomes part of new stars and their planets. Have students research the estimated amounts of certain stable elements that would be produced in an exploding supernova. Compare the results to the amounts of these elements on Earth. Have students calculate how many "Earths" could be constructed from the elements exploded outward from a supernova. **LS Logical**

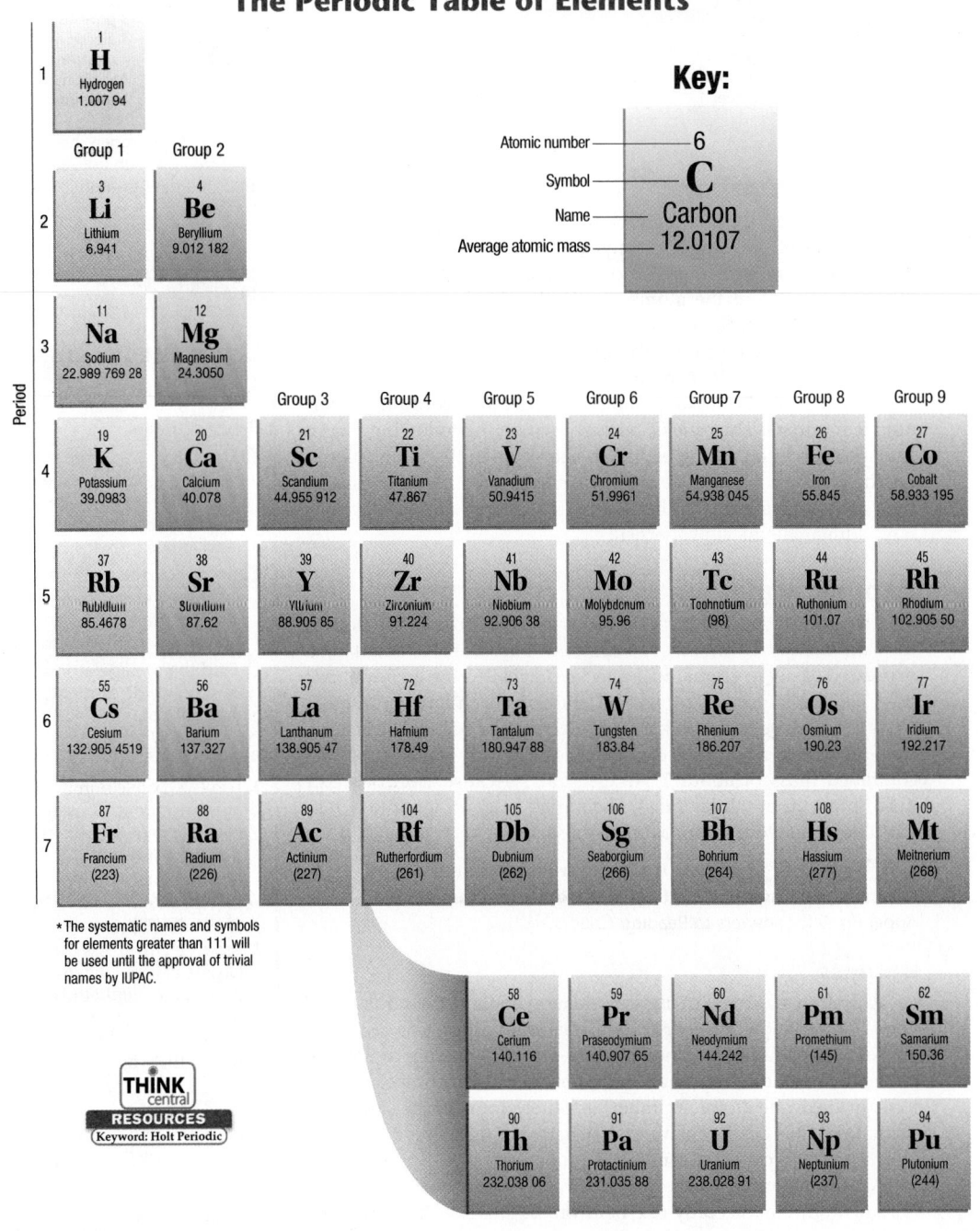

- Hydrogen
- Semiconductors (also known as metalloids)

Metals
- Alkali metals
- Alkaline-earth metals
- Transition metals
- Other metals

Nonmetals
- Halogens
- Noble gases
- Other nonmetals

Group 10	Group 11	Group 12	Group 13	Group 14	Group 15	Group 16	Group 17	Group 18
								2 **He** Helium 4.002 602
			5 **B** Boron 10.811	6 **C** Carbon 12.0107	7 **N** Nitrogen 14.0067	8 **O** Oxygen 15.9994	9 **F** Fluorine 18.998 4032	10 **Ne** Neon 20.1797
			13 **Al** Aluminum 26.981 5386	14 **Si** Silicon 28.0855	15 **P** Phosphorus 30.973 762	16 **S** Sulfur 32.065	17 **Cl** Chlorine 35.453	18 **Ar** Argon 39.948
28 **Ni** Nickel 58.6934	29 **Cu** Copper 63.546	30 **Zn** Zinc 65.38	31 **Ga** Gallium 69.723	32 **Ge** Germanium 72.64	33 **As** Arsenic 74.921 60	34 **Se** Selenium 78.96	35 **Br** Bromine 79.904	36 **Kr** Krypton 83.798
46 **Pd** Palladium 106.42	47 **Ag** Silver 107.8682	48 **Cd** Cadmium 112.411	49 **In** Indium 114.818	50 **Sn** Tin 118.710	51 **Sb** Antimony 121.760	52 **Te** Tellurium 127.60	53 **I** Iodine 126.904 47	54 **Xe** Xenon 131.293
78 **Pt** Platinum 195.084	79 **Au** Gold 196.966 569	80 **Hg** Mercury 200.59	81 **Tl** Thallium 204.3833	82 **Pb** Lead 207.2	83 **Bi** Bismuth 208.980 40	84 **Po** Polonium (209)	85 **At** Astatine (210)	86 **Rn** Radon (222)
110 **Ds** Darmstadtium (271)	111 **Rg** Roentgenium (272)	112 **Uub*** Ununbium (285)	113 **Uut*** Ununtrium (284)	114 **Uuq*** Ununquadium (289)	115 **Uup*** Ununpentium (288)	116 **Uuh*** Ununhexium (292)		118 **Uuo*** Ununoctium (294)

The discoveries of elements with atomic numbers 112 through 116 and 118 have been reported but not fully confirmed.

63 **Eu** Europium 151.964	64 **Gd** Gadolinium 157.25	65 **Tb** Terbium 158.925 35	66 **Dy** Dysprosium 162.500	67 **Ho** Holmium 164.930 32	68 **Er** Erbium 167.259	69 **Tm** Thulium 168.934 21	70 **Yb** Ytterbium 173.054	71 **Lu** Lutetium 174.9668
95 **Am** Americium (243)	96 **Cm** Curium (247)	97 **Bk** Berkelium (247)	98 **Cf** Californium (251)	99 **Es** Einsteinium (252)	100 **Fm** Fermium (257)	101 **Md** Mendelevium (258)	102 **No** Nobelium (259)	103 **Lr** Lawrencium (262)

The atomic masses listed in this table reflect the precision of current measurements. (Each value listed in parentheses is the mass number of that radioactive element's most stable or most common isotope.)

Using the Figure — GENERAL

Radioactive Elements Point out to students that some elements undergo radioactive decay, becoming other elements in the process. Ask students to find technetium, the lightest radioactive element, and give its atomic number. (atomic number 43) Ask students to give the average atomic mass, rounded to a whole number, of the element lead. (207 u)
LS Visual/Logical

Close

Reteaching — BASIC

Atomic and Mass Numbers
Write in a column on the board the mass numbers and atomic numbers for elements widely scattered about the periodic table. Obtain the mass numbers by rounding the average atomic mass values to the nearest whole numbers. Have students use the periodic table to identify the elements. Then, have them use the masses and atomic numbers to determine the number of protons, electrons, and neutrons in each element. **LS Logical**

Quiz — GENERAL

Determine whether each of the following statements is true or false.

1. An element is made up of only one kind of atom. (true)
2. The average atomic mass is equal to the number of neutrons in an atom. (false)
3. Atoms that have the same number of protons but different numbers of neutrons are called isotopes. (true)

Close, *continued*

Answers to Section Review

1. Physical properties are characteristics that can be observed without changing the composition of the substance. Chemical properties are characteristics that describe how a substance interacts with other substances to produce different kinds of matter.
2. Atoms consist of protons and neutrons in the nucleus and electrons that move in a cloud around the nucleus.
3. protons, neutrons, and electrons
4. Atomic number is the number of protons in the nucleus of an atom, as well as the number of electrons in the neutral form of the atom. Mass number is the total number of protons and neutrons in the nucleus of an atom. Average atomic mass is the weighted average of the atomic masses of the isotopes of an element.
5. Isotopes have the same number of protons as other atoms of the same element but have different numbers of neutrons.
6. The combination of atoms to form a new substance that has different properties is a result of the chemical properties of the elements.
7. Atoms of different elements have different numbers of protons in their nuclei.
8. *Matter* is made up of *atoms* that consist of *protons, neutrons,* and *electrons* and that may form *elements*, which are organized in the *periodic table* by their *atomic number.*

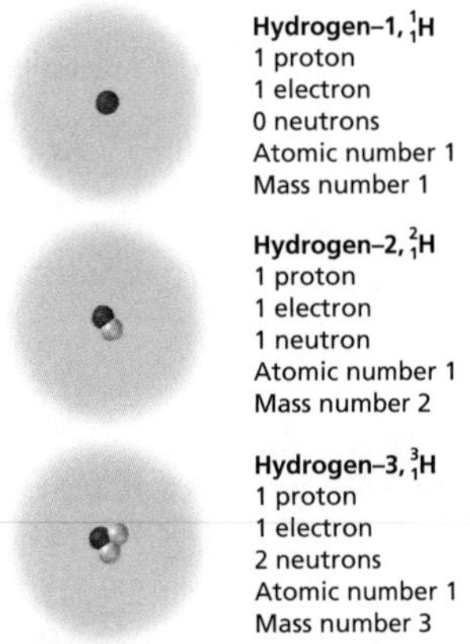

Figure 4 There are three naturally occurring isotopes of hydrogen. The main difference between these isotopes is their mass numbers.

SCILINKS
www.scilinks.org
Topic: Valence Electrons
Code: **HQX1591**

Average Atomic Mass

Because the isotopes of an element have different masses, the periodic table uses an average atomic mass for each element. The *average atomic mass* is the weighted average of the atomic masses of the naturally occurring isotopes of an element.

As shown in **Figure 4**, hydrogen has three isotopes. Each isotope has a different mass because each has a different number of neutrons. By calculating the weighted average of the atomic masses of the three naturally occurring hydrogen isotopes, you can determine the average atomic mass. As noted on the periodic table, the average atomic mass of hydrogen is 1.007 94 u.

Valence Electrons and Periodic Properties

Based on similarities in their chemical properties, elements on the periodic table are arranged in columns, which are called *groups*. An atom's chemical properties are largely determined by the number of the outermost electrons in an atom's electron cloud. These electrons are called *valence* (VAY luhns) *electrons*.

Within each group, the atoms of each element generally have the same number of valence electrons. For Groups 1 and 2, the number of valence electrons in each atom is the same as that atom's group number. Atoms of elements in Groups 3–12 have 2 or more valence electrons. For Groups 13–18, the number of valence electrons in each atom is the same as that atom's group number minus 10, except for helium, He. It has only two valence electrons. Atoms in Group 18 have 8 valence electrons. When an atom has 8 valence electrons, it is considered stable, or chemically unreactive. Unreactive atoms do not easily lose or gain electrons.

Elements whose atoms have only one, two, or three valence electrons tend to lose electrons easily. These elements have metallic properties and are generally classified as *metals*. Elements whose atoms have from four to seven valence electrons are more likely to gain electrons. Many of these elements, which are in Groups 13–17, are classified as *nonmetals*.

Section 1 Review

Key Ideas

1. **Compare** the physical properties of matter with the chemical properties of matter.
2. **Describe** the basic structure of an atom.
3. **Name** the three basic subatomic particles.
4. **Compare** atomic number, mass number, and atomic mass.
5. **Explain** how isotopes of an element differ from each other.

Critical Thinking

6. **Evaluating Data** Oxygen combines with hydrogen and becomes water. Is this combination a result of the physical or chemical properties of hydrogen?
7. **Making Comparisons** What sets an atom of one element apart from atoms of all other elements?

Concept Mapping

8. Use the following terms to create a concept map: *matter, element, atom, electron, proton, neutron, atomic number,* and *periodic table.*

Differentiated Instruction

Alternative Assessment

Quiz Show Have students create a game show in which contestants are given clues about different elements, and must identify the element. The fewer clues needed to answer correctly, the more points that are awarded. The game can be designed for individual competitors or for teams.
LS Interpersonal

Key Resources

Technology
- Transparencies
  17 Atomic Number and Atomic Mass

SECTION 2

Combinations of Atoms

Key Ideas

- Define *compound* and *molecule.*
- Interpret chemical formulas.
- Describe two ways that electrons form chemical bonds between atoms.
- Explain the differences between compounds and mixtures.

Key Terms

compound
molecule
ion
ionic bond
covalent bond
mixture
solution

Why It Matters

Most of the matter in the universe consists of a collection of electrons and ions. This state of matter, called plasma, is used in televisions, light bulbs, and other technologies.

Elements rarely occur in pure form in Earth's crust. They generally occur in combination with other elements. A substance that is made of two or more elements that are joined by chemical bonds between the atoms of those elements is called a **compound.** The properties of a compound differ from those of the elements that make up the compound, as shown in **Figure 1.**

The smallest unit of a compound that can exist by itself and retain all of the compound's chemical properties is a molecule. A **molecule** is made of atoms that are chemically bonded together.

Some elements occur naturally as *diatomic molecules,* which are molecules that are made up of only two atoms. For example, the oxygen in the air you breathe is the diatomic molecule O_2. The *O* in this notation is the symbol for oxygen. The subscript *2* indicates the number of oxygen atoms that are bonded together.

compound a substance made up of atoms of two or more different elements joined by chemical bonds

molecule a group of atoms that are held together by chemical forces

Chemical Formulas

In any given compound, the elements that make up the compound occur in the same relative proportions. Therefore, a compound can be represented by a chemical formula. A *chemical formula* is a combination of letters and numbers that shows which elements make up a compound. It also shows the number of atoms of each element that are required to make a molecule of a compound.

The chemical formula for water is H_2O, which indicates that each water molecule consists of two atoms of hydrogen and one atom of oxygen. In a chemical formula, the subscript that appears after the symbol for an element shows the number of atoms of that element that are in a molecule.

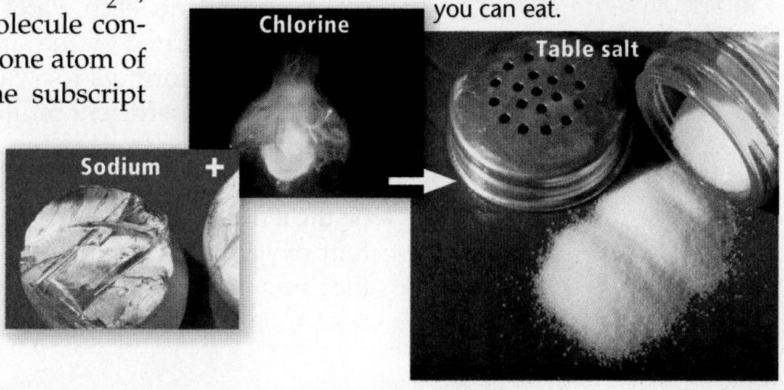

Figure 1 Sodium, a silvery metal, and chlorine, a poisonous, greenish-yellow gas, are both components of table salt, which you can eat.

Section 2

Focus

Overview

This section describes molecules, chemical formulas, and how the arrangement of electrons in atoms leads to the formation of compounds. It also explains the two main types of chemical bonds, as well as mixtures and solutions.

Bellringer

Have students list three familiar compounds that each consist of two elements. Point out that there may be more than two atoms in each compound. (Answers may vary. Three common examples are water, H_2O; table salt, NaCl; and carbon dioxide, CO_2.) **LS Logical**

Motivate

Activity — GENERAL

Composition of Compounds

Write a list of compounds on the board and have students use the periodic table to identify the elements in the compounds. Make sure the list contains at least one diatomic molecule, one compound composed of two elements, and one compound made of three or more elements. Point out that many element symbols contain two letters, and that the second letter is always lowercase. This convention is used to avoid confusion when writing a molecular formula, such as CO (carbon monoxide), or an element, such as Co (cobalt). **LS Visual/Logical**

Key Resources

Technology

- Transparencies
  Bellringer

Teach

Using the Figure GENERAL

Describing Reactions Have students study the diagram at the top of this page. Have students count the number of atoms of each element in each compound and compare that number to the number of atoms of each element in the chemical formulas below. Ask students how the chemical formulas relate to the illustration. (The chemical formulas describe the number of each type of element in the reaction.) Answer to caption question: There are four hydrogen atoms on each side of the equation. LS **Visual**

Math Skills
Answer
unbalanced: $Mg + O_2 \rightarrow MgO$
balanced: $2Mg + O_2 \rightarrow 2MgO$

Key Resources

Technology
- Transparencies
  18 Balancing Equations

Figure 2 Methane, CH_4, and oxygen gas, O_2, react during combustion to form the products carbon dioxide, CO_2, and water, H_2O. ***How many hydrogen atoms are on each side of this reaction?***

THINK central
INTERACT ONLINE
Keyword: HQXCHMF2

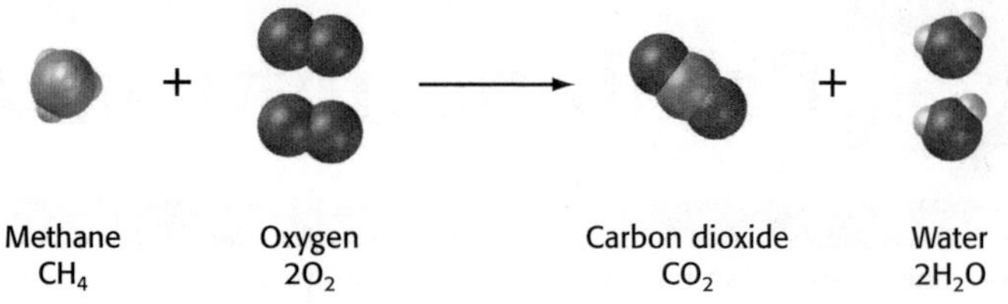

Chemical Equations

Elements and compounds often combine through chemical reactions to form new compounds. The reaction of these elements and compounds can be described in a *chemical equation.*

Equation Structure

In a chemical equation, such as the one shown below, the *reactants*, which are on the left-hand side of the arrow, form the *products*, which are on the right-hand side of the arrow. In a chemical equation, the arrow means "gives" or "yields."

$$CH_4 + 2O_2 \rightarrow CO_2 + 2H_2O$$

In this equation, one molecule of methane, CH_4, reacts with two molecules of oxygen, O_2, to yield one molecule of carbon dioxide, CO_2, and two molecules of water, H_2O, as shown in **Figure 2.**

Balanced Equations

Chemical equations are useful for showing the types and amounts of the products that could form from a particular set of reactants. However, the equation must be balanced to show this information. A chemical equation is balanced when the number of atoms of each element on the right side of the equation is equal to the number of atoms of the same element on the left side.

To balance an equation, you cannot change the chemical formulas. Changing the formulas would mean that different substances were in the reaction. To balance an equation, you must put numbers called *coefficients* in front of chemical formulas.

On the left side of the equation above, the methane molecule has four hydrogen atoms, which are indicated by the subscript 4. On the right side, each water molecule has two hydrogen atoms, which are indicated by the subscript 2. A coefficient of 2 is placed in front of the formula for water to balance the number of hydrogen atoms. A coefficient multiplies the subscript in a formula. For example, four hydrogen atoms are in the formula $2H_2O$.

A coefficient of 2 is also placed in front of the oxygen molecule on the left side of the equation so that both sides of the equation have four oxygen atoms. When the number of atoms of each element is the same on both sides of the equation, the equation is balanced.

Math Skills

Balancing Equations
Magnesium, Mg, reacts with oxygen gas, O_2, to form magnesium oxide, MgO. Write a balanced chemical equation for this reaction by placing the coefficients that are needed to obtain an equal number of magnesium and oxygen atoms on either side of the equation.

Differentiated Instruction

Special Education Students

Modeling Have students model balancing an equation. Have twelve students wear reversible basketball jerseys and pretend to be atoms of hydrogen and oxygen. Organize 4 students wearing dark jerseys (H) and 3 students wearing light jerseys (O) into the unbalanced equation: $H_2 + O_2 \rightarrow H_2O$. Have students not wearing jerseys place the remaining students who are wearing jerseys into the equation to balance it. Students may have to reverse their jerseys to have the correct number of atoms. The balanced equation is $2H_2 + O_2 \rightarrow 2H_2O$. LS **Kinesthetic** Co-op Learning

Chemical Bonds

The forces that hold together the atoms in molecules are called *chemical bonds*. Chemical bonds form because of the attraction between positive and negative charges. Atoms form chemical bonds by either sharing or transferring valence electrons from one atom to another. Transferring or sharing valence electrons from one atom to another changes the properties of the substance. Variations in the forces that hold molecules together are responsible for a wide range of physical and chemical properties.

As shown in **Figure 3**, scientists can study interactions of atoms to predict which kinds of atoms will form chemical bonds together. Scientists do this by comparing the number of valence electrons that are present in a particular atom with the maximum number of valence electrons that are possible. For example, a hydrogen atom has only one valence electron. But because hydrogen can have two valence electrons, it will give up or accept another electron to reach a more chemically unreactive state.

Reading Check **In what two ways do atoms form chemical bonds?**

Figure 3 Scientists sometimes make physical models of molecules to better understand how chemical bonds affect the properties of compounds.

Academic Vocabulary

transfer (TRANS fuhr) to carry or cause to pass from one thing to another

Why It Matters

How Can Diamond and Graphite Both Be Carbon?

Diamonds are valued for their sparkle, and diamond-coated blades can cut through granite. The soft black graphite in your pencil is also used in powdered form as an industrial lubricant. But diamonds and graphite are both made of pure carbon. The extreme differences in their properties are because of differences in how their carbon atoms are bonded together.

Graphite is made of carbon atoms arranged in layers, with weak bonds between the layers.

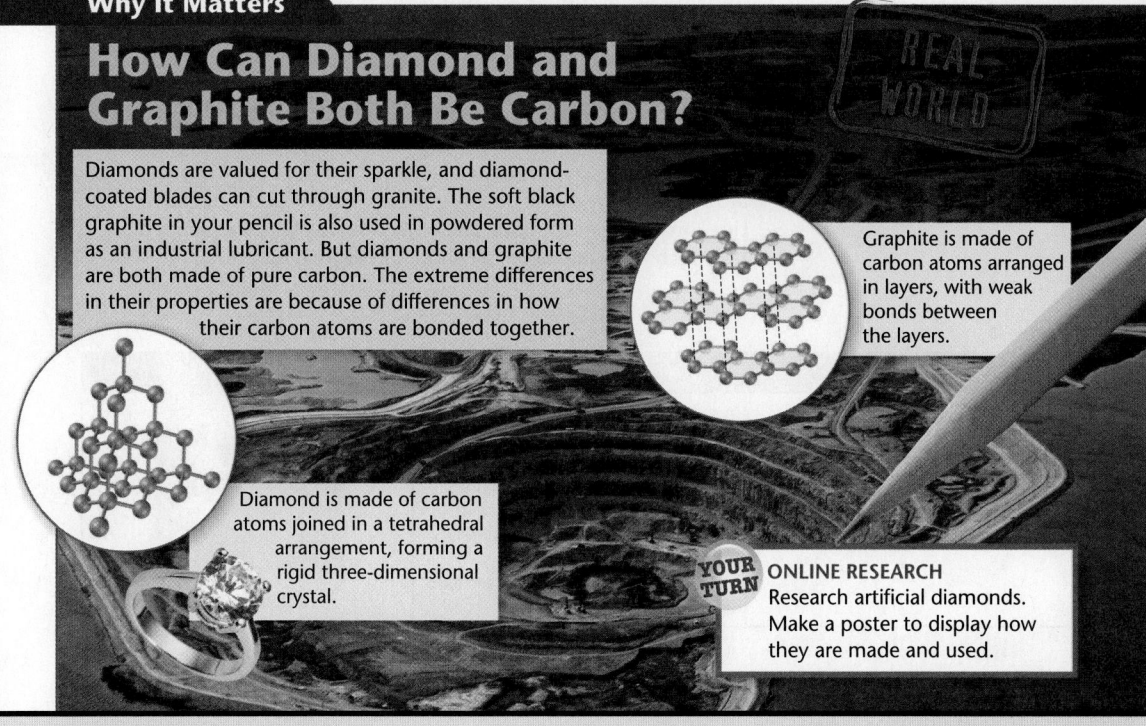

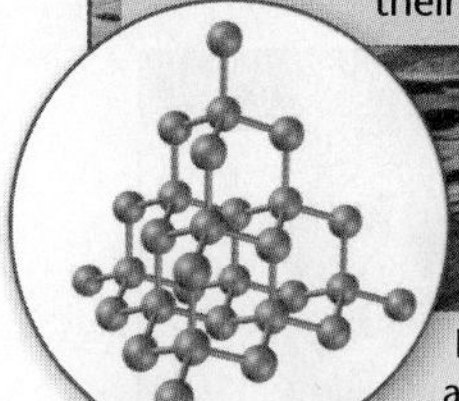

Diamond is made of carbon atoms joined in a tetrahedral arrangement, forming a rigid three-dimensional crystal.

YOUR TURN ONLINE RESEARCH
Research artificial diamonds. Make a poster to display how they are made and used.

MISCONCEPTION ALERT

Orbitals Students may think of an atom as electrons orbiting the nucleus, much like planets orbiting the sun. Explain that the term *orbital* refers just to the energy level occupied by certain electrons in an atom. Point out that while electrons possess properties similar to those of objects in orbital motion, they do not actually move in a circular or elliptical path around the nucleus.

Chemistry Connection

Chemical Bonding One of the earliest hypotheses of chemical bonding was developed by the Swedish chemist Jöns Jacob Berzelius (1779–1848). Berzelius hypothesized that all elements had either a positive or a negative charge and that only positive and negative elements would bond with each other.

Answer to Reading Check

Atoms form chemical bonds by transferring electrons or by sharing electrons.

Why It Matters

How Can Diamond and Graphite Both Be Carbon?

At extremely high temperatures and pressures, graphite can be converted into diamond in a laboratory. Most of these artificial diamonds—around 90%—are used for industrial purposes. As Earth's hardest natural material, diamonds are useful as industrial abrasives and blade coatings. Natural diamonds form deep underground, and may be transported to Earth's surface in volcanic eruptions.

Answer to Your Turn

Online Research Artificial diamonds are made under extreme heat and pressure, typically with a metallic catalyst. They are used as abrasives, for cutting, and for conducting heat.

Teach, *continued*

Skill Builder — ADVANCED

Math Reinforce the fact that the charge of an ion depends both on whether electrons are added to or removed from the neutral atom, and on how many electrons are involved in the transfer. Ions that give up electrons are always positively charged and are denoted by an *n*+ superscript, where *n* is the number of electrons lost. Ions that gain electrons are always negatively charged and are denoted by an *n*– superscript, where *n* is the number of electrons gained. Ask students to apply these rules, along with information from the periodic table, to identify the most stable ions for the following elements: K, Mg, Sr, Br, I, O, Mo, S. (K^+, Mg^{2+}, Sr^{2+}, Br^-, I^-, O^{2-}, Mo^{6+}, S^{2-}) LS **Logical**

READING TOOLBOX

Double-Door Fold

ionic bond
• results from the transfer of electrons from one atom to another
covalent bond
• results when atoms share electrons

MISCONCEPTION ALERT

Polyatomic Ions Students may think that ions consist of only single atoms. Explain that many ionic compounds are made up of two ions, one of which is polyatomic, or contains several atoms. Examples of polyatomic ions are OH^-, NO_3^-, CO_3^{2-}, and SO_4^{2-}. Polyatomic ions that are positively charged are less common, although the ammonium ion, NH_4^+, appears in some compounds.

ion an atom or molecule that has gained or lost one or more electrons and has a negative or positive charge

ionic bond the attractive force between oppositely charged ions, which form when electrons are transferred from one atom or molecule to another

SCILINKS®
www.scilinks.org
Topic: Covalent and Ionic Bonds
Code: **HQX0362**

READING TOOLBOX

Double-Door Fold
Create a double-door fold. Label one door "Ionic bond" and the other door "Covalent bond." Write notes about these terms behind each door.

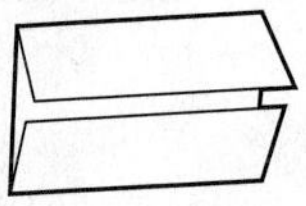

Ions

When an electron is transferred from one atom to another, both atoms become charged. A particle, such as an atom or molecule, that carries a charge is called an **ion.**

Neutral sodium atoms have 11 electrons. And because a sodium atom has 1 valence electron, sodium is a Group 1 element on the periodic table. If a sodium atom loses its outermost electron, the next 8 electrons in the atom's electron cloud become the outermost electrons. Because the sodium atom now has 8 valence electrons, it is unlikely to share or transfer electrons and, therefore, is stable.

However, the sodium atom is missing the 1 electron that was needed to balance the number of protons in the nucleus. When an atom no longer has equal numbers of positive and negative charges, it becomes an ion. The sodium atom became a positive sodium ion, Na^+, when the atom released its valence electron.

Suppose a chlorine atom accepts the electron that the above sodium atom lost. A chlorine atom has a total of 17 electrons, 7 of which are valence electrons. This chlorine atom now has a complete set of 8 valence electrons and is chemically stable. The extra electron, however, changes the neutral chlorine atom into a negatively charged chloride ion, Cl^-.

Ionic Bonds

The attractive force between oppositely charged ions that result from the transfer of electrons from one atom to another is called an **ionic bond.** A compound that forms through the transfer of electrons is called an *ionic compound*. Most ionic compounds form when electrons are transferred between the atoms of metallic and nonmetallic elements.

Sodium chloride, or common table salt, is an ionic compound. The positively charged sodium ions and negatively charged chloride ions attract one another because of their opposite charges. This attraction between the positive sodium ions and the negative chloride ions is an ionic bond. The attraction creates cube-shaped crystals, such as in the table salt shown in **Figure 4.**

Figure 4

Ionic Bonds

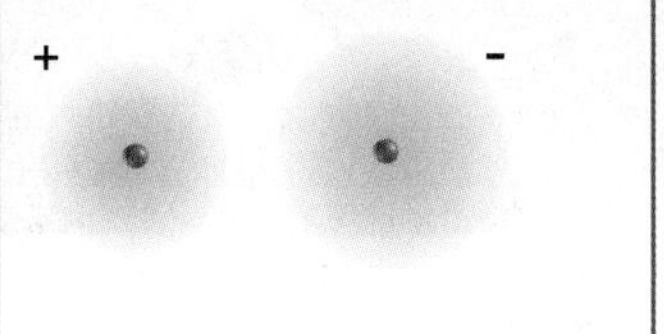

A sodium atom, Na, transfers an electron to a chlorine atom, Cl, to form table salt, NaCl. The chlorine atom with the added electron becomes a negatively charged ion, Cl^-, and the sodium atom, which lost the electron, becomes a positively charged ion, Na^+. The oppositely charged ions attract each other and form an ionic bond.

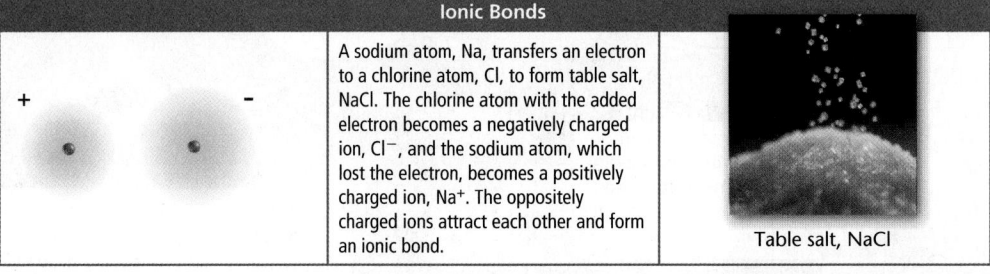

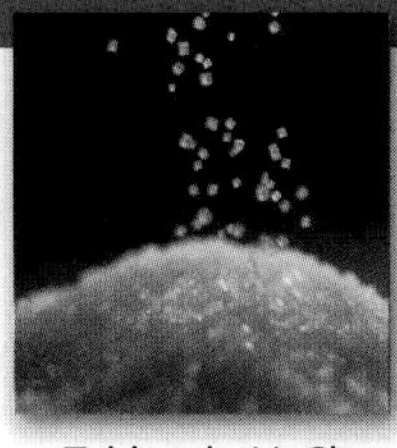

Table salt, NaCl

Homework — ADVANCED

Atomic and Ionic Radius The radii of atoms vary with the number of electrons in the atom's outer energy levels. For neutral atoms in a single period of the periodic table, the radius decreases as the number of electrons in the highest energy level increases. The atomic radii also increase as more high energy levels are filled.

The radius of a neutral atom is altered when that atom gives up or gains electrons to become an ion. Have students research atomic and ionic radii for a single period (row) of the periodic table. Have students then collect their findings and present them in a visual form so that comparisons between the radii of neutral and ionized atoms can be made. One way of doing this is to create a poster showing the same row of the periodic table twice, with one figure showing the radii for the neutral atoms and the other figure showing the radii for the ions. Three-dimensional or computer models can also be constructed for this purpose. LS **Kinesthetic**

Figure 5

Covalent Bonds		
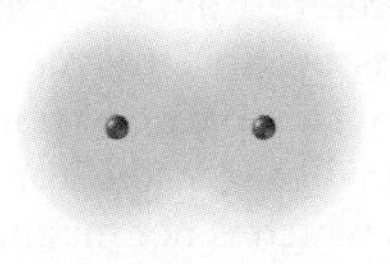	Covalent bonds form when atoms share one or more pairs of electrons. In a covalent compound, pairs of electrons are shared between most of the atoms that make up the compound. Some elements also contain covalent bonds. In molecules of chlorine, two chlorine atoms are bonded together by sharing electrons.	 Chlorine gas, Cl_2

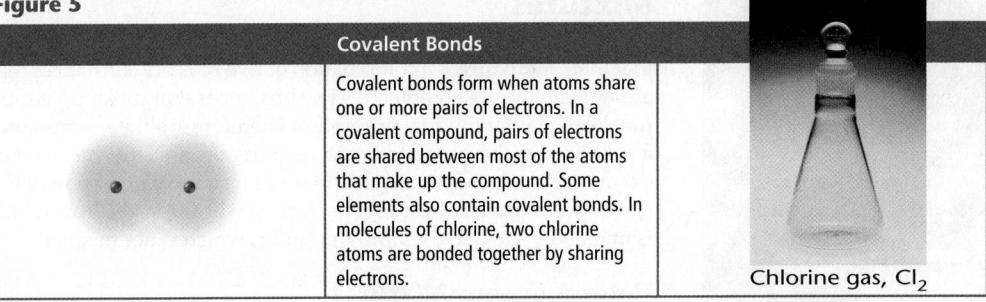

Covalent Bonds

A bond that is formed by the attraction between atoms that share electrons is a **covalent bond.** When atoms share electrons, the positive nucleus of each atom is attracted to the shared negative electrons, as shown in **Figure 5.** The pull between the positive and negative charges is the force that keeps these atoms joined.

Water is an example of a *covalent compound*—that is, a compound formed by the sharing of electrons. Two hydrogen atoms can share their single valence electrons with an oxygen atom that has six valence electrons. The sharing of electrons creates a bond and gives oxygen a stable number of eight outermost electrons. At the same time, the oxygen atom shares two of its electrons—one for each hydrogen atom—which gives each hydrogen atom a more stable number of two electrons. Thus, a water molecule consists of two atoms of hydrogen bonded with one atom of oxygen.

covalent bond a bond formed when atoms share one or more pairs of electrons

Polar Covalent Bonds

In many cases, atoms that are covalently bonded do not equally share electrons. The reason for this is that the ability of atoms of some elements to attract electrons from atoms of other elements differs. A covalent bond in which the bonded atoms have an unequal attraction for the shared electrons is called a *polar covalent bond*. Water is an example of a molecule that forms as a result of polar covalent bonds. Two hydrogen atoms bond covalently with an oxygen atom and form a water molecule. Because the oxygen atom has more ability to attract electrons than the hydrogen atoms do, the electrons are not shared equally between the oxygen and hydrogen atoms. Instead, the electrons remain closer to the oxygen nucleus, which has the greater pull. As a result, the water molecule as a whole has a slightly negative charge at its oxygen end and slightly positive charges at its hydrogen ends. The slightly positive ends of a water molecule attract the slightly negative ends of other water molecules.

Reading Check **Why do water molecules form from polar covalent bonds?**

Quick Lab

10 min

Compounds

Procedure

1. Place 4 g of compound A in a clear plastic cup.
2. Place 4 g of compound B in a second clear plastic cup.
3. Observe the color and texture of each compound. Record your observations.
4. Add 5 mL of vinegar to each cup. Record your observations.

Analysis

1. What physical and chemical differences between the two compounds did you record? How do physical properties and chemical properties differ?
2. Vinegar reacts with baking soda but not with powdered sugar. Which of these compounds is compound A, and which is compound B?

Quick Lab

Materials

- Compounds A and B (see Teacher's Notes below)
- Clear plastic cups
- Vinegar

Skills Acquired

- Experimenting
- Observing
- Inferring
- Interpreting
- Identifying/Recognizing Patterns

Teacher's Notes: Compound A is powdered sugar. Compound B is baking soda. Be sure that students follow the safety precautions and clean up quickly and completely.

Answers to Analysis

1. Answers may vary but physical differences should include that, when moistened, compound A is sticky, whereas compound B is not. Chemical properties include that compound B bubbles when it reacts with vinegar, whereas compound A does not. Chemical properties are properties that change as a result of chemical reactions.
2. Compound B is baking soda.

Close

Reteaching — Basic

Types of Compounds Write the following compound formulas on the board, and have students identify them as being ionic or covalent: CO_2, NaCl, LiBr, H_2, MgF_2, NH_3. (covalent, ionic, ionic, covalent, ionic, covalent)

LS Visual

Quiz — General

1. What type of compound contains elements that share electrons to form bonds? (a covalent compound)
2. What is the charge on the most stable magnesium ion? (2+)
3. What is the charge on the most stable fluorine ion? (1−)

Key Resources

Technology

- Transparencies
  19 Ionic Bonds and Covalent Bonds

Answer to Reading Check

The oxygen atom has a larger and more positively charged nucleus than the hydrogen atoms do. As a result, the oxygen nucleus pulls the electrons from the hydrogen atoms closer to it than the hydrogen nuclei pull the shared electrons from the oxygen. This unequal attraction forms a polar-covalent bond.

Close, *continued*

Answers to Section Review

1. A compound is a substance made up of atoms of two or more different elements joined by chemical bonds. A molecule is the smallest unit of a substance that consists of two or more atoms and that keeps all of the substance's chemical properties.
2. 6 carbon (C) atoms, 12 hydrogen (H) atoms, 6 oxygen (O) atoms
3. The electrical attraction between the nucleus of an atom and the outermost electrons of the other atom causes the atoms to bond, forming a molecule.
4. Ionic bonds form between oppositely charged ions. Covalent bonds form from the attraction between atoms that share electrons.
5. The greater positive charge of the oxygen nucleus exerts a stronger attraction on the electrons of the hydrogen atom than the hydrogen nuclei exert on the electrons of the oxygen atom.
6. A mixture contains two or more substances that are not chemically combined. A compound consists of several atoms that combine in exact proportions to form a substance that has unique chemical properties.
7. sea water (NaCl in solution) and alloys such as steel
8. The substance does not chemically combine when it forms a mixture, so its chemical properties remain the same.

Figure 6 The steel that is being smelted in this steel mill in Iowa is a solution of iron, carbon, and various other metals such as nickel, chromium, and manganese.

mixture a combination of two or more substances that are not chemically combined

solution a homogeneous mixture throughout which two or more substances are uniformly dispersed

Mixtures

On Earth, elements and compounds are generally mixed together. A **mixture** is a combination of two or more substances that are not chemically combined. The substances that make up a mixture keep their individual properties. Therefore, unlike a compound, a mixture can be separated into its parts by physical means. For example, you can use a magnet to separate a mixture of powdered sulfur, S, and iron, Fe, filings. The magnet will attract the iron, which is magnetic, and leave behind the sulfur, which is not magnetic.

Heterogeneous Mixtures

Mixtures in which two or more substances are not uniformly distributed are called *heterogeneous mixtures*. For example, the igneous rock granite is a heterogeneous mixture of crystals of the minerals quartz, feldspar, hornblende, and biotite.

Homogeneous Mixtures

In chemistry, the word *homogeneous* means "having the same composition and properties throughout." A homogeneous mixture of two or more substances that are uniformly dispersed throughout the mixture is a **solution.**

Any part of a given sample of the solution known as sea water, for example, will have the same composition. Sodium chloride, NaCl, (along with many other ionic compounds) is dissolved in sea water. The positive ends of water molecules attract negative chloride ions. And the negative ends of water molecules attract positive sodium ions. Eventually, all of the sodium and chloride ions become uniformly distributed among the water molecules.

Gases and solids can also be solutions. An *alloy* is a solution composed of two or more metals. The steel shown in **Figure 6** is an example of such a solution, both in liquid and solid states.

Section 2 Review

Key Ideas

1. **Define** the term *compound.*
2. **Determine** the number of each type of atom in the following chemical formula: $C_6H_{12}O_6$.
3. **Explain** why atoms join to form molecules.
4. **Describe** the difference between ionic and covalent bonds.
5. **Explain** why a water molecule has polar covalent bonds.
6. **Compare** compounds and mixtures.
7. **Identify** two common solutions.

Critical Thinking

8. **Applying Ideas** What happens to the chemical properties of a substance when it becomes part of a mixture?
9. **Evaluating Data** If you were given two mixtures and told that one is a solution, how might you determine which one is the solution?

Concept Mapping

10. Use the following terms to create a concept map: *compound, molecule, ionic compound, ionic bond, ion, covalent compound,* and *covalent bond.*

9. The solution would be a homogeneous mixture, so the composition of the solution would be the same throughout. This would not necessarily be true of the other mixture.
10. Two or more atoms combine to form a *molecule,* which is the basic unit for a *compound,* which may be either an *ionic compound,* in which each element is a charged *ion,* and is held to the other ion by an *ionic bond,* or a *covalent compound,* in which atoms share electrons to form a *covalent bond.*

Differentiated Instruction

Alternative Assessment

Balancing Chemical Equations Have students select, or select for them, several unbalanced chemical reactions. Then, have students show the steps to finding the coefficients to balance the equations. Be sure all numerical steps are shown. **LS Logical**

Why It Matters

Not Such a Strange State

In elementary school, you learned about the three states of matter. But over 99.9% of the matter in the universe is not in the gas, liquid, or solid state. Instead, it is in a state called *plasma.* Very large amounts of energy can split gaseous atoms apart. The resulting matter is plasma—a collection of negatively charged electrons and positively charged ions. All stars, including our sun, are giant plasmas. On Earth, natural plasmas are formed in very hot fires and during lightning. Artificial plasmas are used in fluorescent lamps and flat-screen televisions.

The huge current in a lightning bolt supplies the energy to heat the air to 30,000 °C, creating a plasma.

A high voltage in a noble gas, such as neon or xenon, produces the plasma in displays like this.

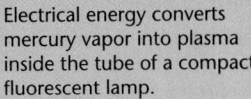

Electrical energy converts mercury vapor into plasma inside the tube of a compact fluorescent lamp.

YOUR TURN

UNDERSTANDING CONCEPTS
How is a gas different from a plasma?

ONLINE RESEARCH
Find out about other applications of plasma technology, besides televisions and lights. Describe at least two of these applications.

Why It Matters

A plasma is an ionized gas. A gas is considered "ionized" when heat or another energy source separates the electrons from the atoms' nuclei. The electrons and protons remain in proximity, but are sufficiently separated to make the plasma electrically charged. The term "plasma" was first applied to ionized gases in the 1920s, by the scientist Irving Langmuir. Evidently, the ionized gases he studied somehow reminded him of blood plasma. Plasma physics and technologies are active areas of research, with diverse applications.

Answers to Your Turn

Understanding Concepts Whole atoms make up a gas, while a plasma is a mixture of electrons and positively charged ions resulting from split-apart gaseous atoms.

Online Research Answers may vary, for example, toxic waste may be processed by plasma torches and engines may be powered by plasma.

Time Required

two 45-minute class periods

Lab Ratings

EASY ——————————→ HARD

Teacher Preparation 🧪🧪
Student Setup 🧪🧪🧪
Concept Level 🧪🧪🧪
Cleanup 🧪🧪

Skills Acquired

- Collecting Data
- Measuring
- Organizing and Analyzing Data
- Designing Experiments
- Interpreting
- Identifying and Recognizing Patterns

Scientific Methods

In this lab, students will
- Ask a Question
- Form and Test a Hypothesis
- Make Observations
- Analyze the Results
- Draw Conclusions

Materials

The materials listed on the page are enough for groups of two or three students. If students decide to test the heat conductivity of the metal, a hot-water bath should be set up in advance for students to use.

Inquiry **Lab**

 90 min

What You'll Do

> **Design** an experiment to test the physical properties of different metals.
> **Identify** unknown metals by comparing the data you collect and reference information.

What You'll Need

balance
beakers (several)
graduated cylinder
hot plate
magnet
metal samples, unknown, similarly shaped (several)
ruler, metric
stopwatch
water
wax

Safety

Physical Properties of Elements

In this lab, you will identify samples of various metals by collecting data and comparing the data with the reference information listed in the table below. Use at least two of the physical properties listed in the table to identify each metal.

Ask a Question

① How can you use an element's physical properties to identify the element?

Form a Hypothesis

② Use the table below to identify which physical properties you will test. Write a few sentences that describe your hypothesis and the procedure you will use to test those physical properties.

Test the Hypothesis

③ With your lab partner(s), decide how you will use the available materials to identify each metal that you are given. Because there are many ways to measure some of the physical properties that are listed in the table below, you may need to use only some of the materials that are provided.

④ Before you start to test your hypothesis, list each step that you will need to perform.

⑤ After your teacher approves your plan, perform your experiment. Keep in mind that the more exact your measurements are, the easier it will be for you to identify the metals that you have been provided.

⑥ Record all the data that you collect and any observations that you make.

Physical Properties of Some Metals

Metal	Density (g/cm³)	Relative hardness	Relative heat conductivity	Magnetic attraction
Aluminum, Al	2.7	28	100	No
Iron, Fe	7.9	50	34	Yes
Nickel, Ni	8.9	67	38	Slight
Tin, Sn	7.3	19	28	No
Tungsten, W	19.3	100	73	No
Zinc, Zn	7.1	28	49	No

Tips and Tricks

Students should use the same methods for measuring each sample. Students should recalibrate the balance after each weighing.

A computer component could be added to this lab by using probes to measure heat conductivity.

You may want to allow students to try brief experiments that they create, and then give students specific directions if they do not appear to have identified appropriate testing techniques. Students may encounter error in magnetism of nickel if the lab magnet is weak. Students may also encounter error in density measurements for very small volumes of metal.

How to Measure Physical Properties of Metals

Physical property	Description	How to measure the property
Density	mass per unit volume	If the metal is box-shaped, measure its length, height, and width, and then use these measurements to calculate the metal's volume. If the shape of the metal is irregular, add the metal to a known volume of water and determine what volume of water is displaced.
Relative hardness	how easy it is to scratch the substance	An object that has a high hardness value can scratch an object that has a lower value, but not vice versa.
Relative heat conductivity	how quickly a metal heats or cools	A metal that has a value of 100 will heat or cool twice as quickly as a metal that has a value of 50.
Magnetism	whether an object is magnetic	If a magnet placed near a metal attracts the metal, the metal is magnetic.

Analyze the Results

1. **Summarizing Data** Make a table that lists which physical properties you compared and what data you collected for each of the metals that you tested.
2. **Making Comparisons** Which physical properties were the easiest for you to measure and compare? Which were the most difficult to measure and compare? Explain why.
3. **Applying Ideas** What would happen if you tried to use zinc to scratch aluminum?

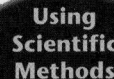

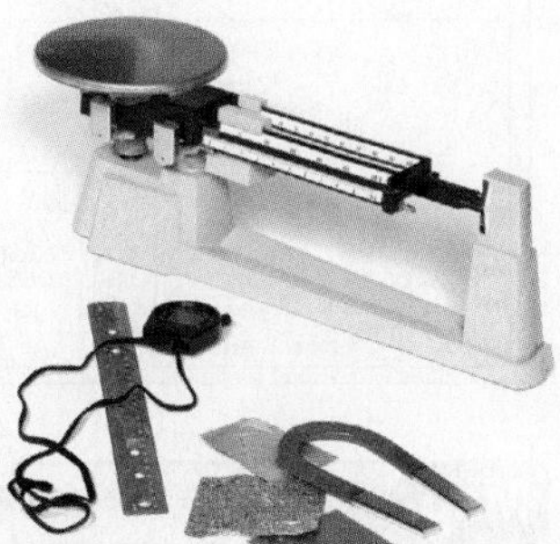

Draw Conclusions

4. **Summarizing Results** Which metals were given to you? Explain how you identified each metal.
5. **Analyzing Methods** Explain why you would have difficulty distinguishing between iron and nickel unless you were to measure each metal's density.

Extension

Evaluating Data Suppose you find a metal fastener that has a density of 7 g/cm^3. What are two ways to determine whether the unknown metal is tin or zinc?

Answers to Analyze the Results

1. Answers may vary but should be consistent with the physical properties of metals.
2. Answers may vary. However, magnetic properties should be easiest to test, followed by densities, which could be directly calculated. Hardness assessment calls for subjective judgments between the various metals tested. Heat conductivity is the most difficult, given the comparative nature of the measurements and the numerous variables, such as temperature, time, and mass of water used for cooling, that need to be controlled.
3. Because aluminum and zinc have the same hardness, neither metal would be scratched when rubbed against the other.

Answers to Draw Conclusions

4. Answers may vary but should be consistent with the materials provided to each student or group.
5. Because iron and nickel are both magnetic and have nearly the same hardness, only their densities make them easily distinguishable.

Answer to Extension

By testing the hardness of the fastener against a sample of zinc and a sample of tin or by comparing the fastener's heat conductivity with that of the two samples, the identity of the metal could be determined.

Answers to Map Skills Activity

1. Answers may vary but should correspond to the symbols shown within the borders of the correct state.
2. Lead and zinc deposits are commonly, though not always, close together. Lead is rarely far from a zinc deposit, though zinc deposits exist in some areas, such as KY and TN, without any nearby lead deposits.
3. no; The map indicates only the existence of deposits, not their size or the amount of each element that is extracted.
4. Silver recovery would be greatest in the western states that have more deposits of the other elements, including New Mexico, Arizona, California, Nevada, Washington, Idaho, Montana, Wyoming, Utah, Colorado, and Alaska.
5. Uranium can be found in Washington, Montana, Wyoming, Nebraska, Utah, Colorado, Arizona, New Mexico, and Texas.

MAPS in Action

Element Resources in the United States

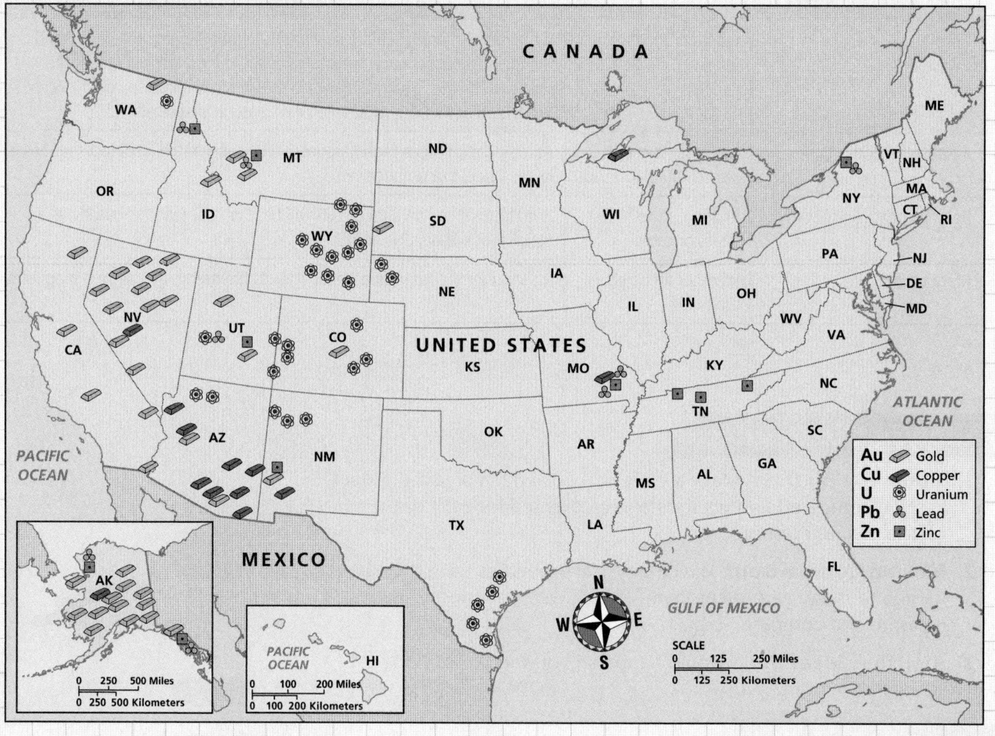

Map Skills Activity

This map shows the distribution of five elements that are used as resources in the United States. Use the map to answer the questions below.

1. **Using a Key** Use the map to locate the state in which you live. Are any of the elements from the key found in your state?
2. **Analyzing Relationships** Can you identify any relationship between the locations of lead deposits and the locations of zinc deposits? Explain your reasoning.
3. **Inferring Relationships** Is it possible to use this map to find out which states have the highest production of the mineral resources that are listed on the map? Why or why not?
4. **Inferring Relationships** Silver is mainly recovered as a byproduct of the bulk mining of other metals such as copper, lead, zinc, and gold. Where in the United States do you think silver recovery would happen?
5. **Using a Key** Use the map to identify the states where uranium can be found.

Key Resources

Technology

- Transparencies
  20 Element Resources in the United States

Chapter 4

Summary

THINK central
SUPER SUMMARY
Keyword: HQXCHMS

Key Ideas | **Key Terms**

Section 1

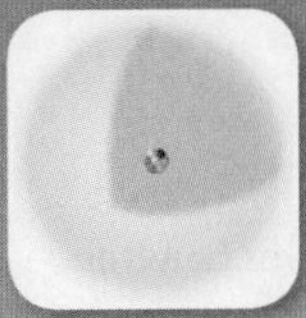

Matter

- A physical property of matter can be observed without changing the composition of the substance. In contrast, a chemical property describes how a substance reacts with other substances to produce different substances.
- An atom consists of electrons surrounding a nucleus that is made up of protons and neutrons.
- The atomic number of an atom is equal to the number of protons in the atom. The mass number is equal to the sum of the protons and neutrons in the atom. Atomic mass is the mass of an atom, expressed in atomic mass units (amu). Protons and neutrons each have an atomic mass that is close to 1 amu.
- An isotope is an atom that has the same number of protons as other atoms of the same element, but different numbers of neutrons.
- Elements on the periodic table are arranged in groups that are based on similarities in the chemical properties of the elements.

Key Terms

matter, p. 87
element, p. 87
atom, p. 88
proton, p. 88
electron, p. 88
neutron, p. 88
isotope, p. 89

Section 2

Combinations of Atoms

- A compound is a substance made up of atoms of two or more different elements joined by chemical bonds. A molecule is a group of atoms bonded together.
- A chemical formula describes which elements and how many atoms of each of those elements make up a molecule of a compound.
- Ionic bonds occur when electrons are transferred from one atom to another. Covalent bonds occur when electrons are shared between atoms.
- A compound is a made up of atoms of two or more different elements joined by chemical bonds. A mixture consists of two or more substances that are not chemically bonded.

Key Terms

compound, p. 93
molecule, p. 93
ion, p. 96
ionic bond, p. 96
covalent bond, p. 97
mixture, p. 98
solution, p. 98

Chapter Summary

Using THINK central Resources

Super Summary

Have students connect the major concepts in this chapter through an interactive Super Summary. Visit **www.thinkcentral.com** and type in the keyword **HQXCHMS** to access the Super Summary for this chapter.

Differentiated Instruction

Alternative Assessment

Poster Project Have students create a poster that shows the processes by which atoms bond together ionically and covalently. The poster should also depict how polar-covalent bonds form. Student illustrations should clearly show the basic nuclear structure of atoms and the correct number of electrons around the nucleus. Students should cover all relevant details in the poster. **LS Logical**

Chapter Review

Assignment Guide	
Section	**Question**
1	2, 3, 7, 10–15, 19–22, 24, 25, 34–37
2	1, 4, 8–9, 16–18, 23, 26–28, 32, 33
1 and 2	5, 6, 29–31

Reading Toolbox

1. Sample sentences with scientific meanings:
Some elements join with other elements to form compounds.
You can separate the parts of a mixture by physical means.

Sample sentences with everyday meanings:
That house is in the middle of a compound.
That salad is a mixture of lettuce, tomatoes, and cucumbers.

Using Key Terms

2–9. Answers may vary but should show that students understand the definitions of and differences between key terms.

Understanding Key Ideas

10. a 14. c
11. a 15. d
12. c 16. c
13. d 17. b

Short Answer

18. Chemical properties are characteristics that describe how a substance interacts with other substances; physical properties are characteristics that can be observed without changing the composition of a substance.
19. An element is a substance that cannot be broken down into a simpler substance by chemical means.
20. protons, neutrons, and electrons
21. Metallic elements tend to lose electrons easily because they have only 1, 2, or 3 valence electrons. Nonmetallic elements tend to gain electrons easily because they have 4–7 valence electrons.
22. covalent
23. NaCl contains one sodium (Na) atom and one chlorine (Cl) atom. H_2O_2 contains two hydrogen (H) atoms and two oxygen (O) atoms. Fe_3O_4 contains three iron (Fe) atoms and four oxygen (O) atoms. SiO_2 contains one silicon (Si) atom and two oxygen (O) atoms.

Chapter 4 Review

1. **Everyday Words Used in Science** The words *compound* and *mixture* have different meanings in science contexts than in everyday speech. Write one sentence using each term in its science context. Write another sentence using each term in an everyday context.

READING TOOLBOX

USING KEY TERMS

Use each of the following terms in a separate sentence.

2. *matter*
3. *neutron*
4. *ion*

For each pair of terms, explain how the meanings of the terms differ.

5. *atom* and *molecule*
6. *element* and *compound*
7. *proton* and *electron*
8. *compound* and *mixture*
9. *covalent bond* and *ionic bond*

UNDERSTANDING KEY IDEAS

10. Color and hardness are examples of a substance's
a. physical properties.
b. chemical properties.
c. atomic structure.
d. molecular properties.
11. Subatomic particles in atoms that do not carry an electric charge are called
a. neutrons.
b. protons.
c. nuclei.
d. ions.
12. Atoms of the same element that differ in mass are
a. ions.
b. neutrons.
c. isotopes.
d. molecules.
13. A combination of letters and numbers that indicates which elements make up a compound is a
a. coefficient.
b. reactant.
c. chemical bond.
d. chemical formula.
14. The type of chemical bond that forms between oppositely charged ions is a(n)
a. covalent bond.
b. mixture.
c. ionic bond.
d. solution.
15. Two or more elements whose atoms are chemically bonded form a(n)
a. mixture.
b. ion.
c. nucleus.
d. compound.
16. The outermost electrons in an atom's electron cloud are called
a. ions. **c.** valence electrons.
b. isotopes. **d.** neutrons.
17. A molecule of water, or H_2O, has one atom of
a. hydrogen. **c.** helium.
b. oxygen. **d.** osmium.

SHORT ANSWER

18. How do chemical properties differ from physical properties?
19. Define the term *element*.
20. Name three basic subatomic particles.
21. In terms of valence electrons, what is the difference between metallic elements and nonmetallic elements?
22. Which type of bonding includes the sharing of electrons?
23. Using the periodic table to help you to understand the following chemical formulas, list the name and number of atoms of each element in each compound: NaCl, H_2O_2, Fe_3O_4, and SiO_2.

CRITICAL THINKING

24. What sets an atom of one element apart from the atoms of all other elements?
25. **Applying Ideas** Is a diatomic molecule more likely to be held together by a covalent bond or by an ionic bond? Explain your answer.
26. **Making Inferences** Calcium chloride is an ionic compound. Carbon dioxide is a covalent compound. Which of these compounds forms as a result of the transfer of electrons from one atom to another? Explain your answer.
27. **Analyzing Relationships** What happens to the chemical properties of a substance when it becomes part of a mixture? Explain your answer.
28. **Classifying Information** Oxygen combines with hydrogen to form water. Is this process due to the physical or chemical properties of oxygen and hydrogen?

CONCEPT MAPPING

29. Use the following terms to create a concept map: *chemical property, element, atom, electron, proton, neutron, atomic number, mass number, isotope, compound,* and *chemical bond.*

MATH SKILLS

Math Skills

30. **Making Calculations** How many neutrons does a potassium atom have if its atomic number is 19 and its mass number is 39?
31. **Using Formulas** The covalent compound formaldehyde forms when one carbon atom, two hydrogen atoms, and one oxygen atom bond. Write a chemical formula for formaldehyde.
32. **Balancing Equations** Zinc metal, Zn, will react with hydrochloric acid, HCl, to produce hydrogen gas, H_2, and zinc chloride, $ZnCl_2$. Write and balance the chemical equation for this reaction.

WRITING SKILLS

33. **Organizing Data** Choose one of the eight most common elements in Earth's crust, and write a brief report on the element's atomic structure, its chemical properties, and its economic importance.
34. **Communicating Main Ideas** Write a brief essay that describes how an element's chemical properties determine what other elements are likely to bond with that element.
35. **Making Comparisons** Write a brief essay that describes the differences between atoms, elements, ions, and isotopes.

INTERPRETING GRAPHICS

The table below shows the average atomic masses and the atomic numbers of five elements. Use this table to answer the questions that follow.

Element	Symbol	Average atomic mass	Atomic number
Magnesium	Mg	24.3050	12
Tungsten	W	183.84	74
Copper	Cu	63.546	29
Silicon	Si	28.0855	14
Bromine	Br	79.904	35

36. If an atom of magnesium has 12 neutrons, what is its mass number?
37. Estimate the average number of neutrons in an atom of tungsten and in an atom of silicon.
38. Which element has the largest difference between the number of protons and the number of neutrons in the nucleus of one of its atoms? Explain your answer.

Chapter Review

Critical Thinking

24. The number of protons in an atom's nucleus distinguishes it from atoms of other elements.
25. If a diatomic molecule consists of atoms of one element, they will likely be bonded covalently, because both atoms are likely to have the same electrical charge.
26. Calcium chloride forms when electrons from a calcium atom transfer to two chlorine atoms, to form a calcium ion that has a +2 positive charge and two chloride ions that each have a −1 charge.
27. The chemical properties of a substance are unchanged by becoming part of a mixture, because the substance does not chemically react with the other substances in the mixture.
28. Water forms because of the chemical properties of oxygen and hydrogen.

Concept Mapping

29. Answers may vary but should include all of the terms listed. Sample answers appear at the end of this unit on page 195D.

Math Skills

30. 39 − 19 = 20 neutrons
31. CH_2O
32. $Zn + HCl \longrightarrow H_2 + ZnCl_2$; one Zn atom on each side of equation; HCl must be multiplied by 2 to give two Cl atoms and 2 H atoms on each side.
$Zn + 2HCl \longrightarrow H_2 + ZnCl_2$
one Zn atom, two Cl atoms, and two H atoms on each side of equation; equation is balanced

Writing Skills

33. Answers may vary. Accept all reasonable answers.
34. Answers may vary. Accept all reasonable answers.
35. Answers may vary. Accept all reasonable answers.

Interpreting Graphics

36. Mass number = number of protons (atomic number) + number of neutrons; for Mg: atomic number = 12; mass number for Mg = 12 + 12 = 24
37. Number of neutrons = mass number − atomic number; for W: 184 − 74 = 110 neutrons; for Si: 28 − 14 = 14 neutrons
38. tungsten; The average atomic mass is close to the mass number for the element, and the difference between the average atomic mass and the atomic number, which is a measure of the number of neutrons, is greatest for tungsten (110 neutrons − 74 protons = 36). The other elements have differences between the two types of particles of less than 10.

Estimated Time

To give students practice under more realistic testing conditions, allow them 30 minutes to answer all of the questions in this practice test.

Test Doctor

Question 1 Answer C is correct. Students should show an understanding that a mixture is a combination of two or more substances that are not chemically combined. Within a soil mixture, students may cite examples of elements and compounds, but these are usually isolated parts of a more comprehensive soil mixture that will be made of many types of compounds. Therefore, answers A, B, and D are incorrect.

Question 9 The correct answer is 12. Students should apply the rules explained in the passage about the placement of subscripts in order to correctly answer this question. Sulfur has two atoms so it has a subscript of 2 below and to the right of its chemical symbol. Flouride has 10 atoms so it has a subscript of 10 below and to the right of its chemical symbol. Students should add these numbers together to get the total number of atoms, 12, in one molecule of S_2F_{10}.

Chapter 4 Standardized Test Prep

Understanding Concepts

Directions (1–4): For each question, write on a separate sheet of paper the letter of the correct answer.

1. Soil is an example of
   A. a solution.
   B. a compound.
   C. a mixture.
   D. an element.
2. Isotopes are atoms of the same element that have different mass numbers. This difference is caused by
   F. a different number of electrons in the atoms.
   G. a different number of protons in the atoms.
   H. a different number of neutrons in the atoms.
   I. a different number of nuclei in the atoms.
3. Which of the following statements best describes the charges of subatomic particles?
   A. Electrons have a negative charge, protons have a positive charge, and neutrons have no charge.
   B. Electrons have a positive charge, protons have a negative charge, and neutrons have a positive charge.
   C. Electrons have no charge, protons have a positive charge, and neutrons have a negative charge.
   D. In neutral atoms, protons, neutrons, and electrons have no charges.
4. An element is located on the periodic table according to
   F. when the element was discovered.
   G. the letters of the element's chemical symbol.
   H. the element's chemical name.
   I. the element's chemical properties.

Directions (5–6): For each question, write a short response.

5. What is the name for an atom that has gained or lost one or more electrons and has acquired a charge?
6. Scientists use atomic numbers to help identify the atoms of different elements. How is the atomic number of an element determined?

Reading Skills

Directions (7–9): Read the passage below. Then, answer the questions.

Chemical Formulas

All substances can be formed by a combination of elements from a list of about 100 possible elements. Each element has a chemical symbol. A chemical formula is shorthand notation that uses chemical symbols and numbers to represent a substance. A chemical formula shows the amount of each kind of atom present in a specific molecule of a substance.

The chemical formula for water is H_2O. This formula tells you that one water molecule is composed of two atoms of hydrogen and one atom of oxygen. The 2 in the formula is a subscript. A subscript is a number written below and to the right of a chemical symbol in a formula. When a symbol, such as the O for oxygen in water's formula, has no subscript, only one atom of that element is present.

7. What does a subscript in a chemical formula represent?
   A. Subscripts represent the number of atoms of the chemical symbol they directly follow present in the molecule.
   B. Subscripts represent the number of atoms of the chemical symbol they directly precede present in the molecule.
   C. Subscripts represent the number of protons present in each atom's nucleus.
   D. Subscripts represent the total number of atoms present in a molecule.
8. Which of the following statements can be inferred from the information in the passage?
   F. Two atoms of hydrogen are always present in chemical formulas.
   G. A chemical formula indicates the elements that a molecule is made of.
   H. Chemical formulas can be used only to show simple molecules.
   I. No more than one atom of oxygen can be present in a chemical formula.
9. How many atoms would be found in a single molecule that has the chemical formula S_2F_{10}?

Question 12 The correct answer is 2. Students should understand that both protons and neutrons contribute equally to a neutral atom's mass, while electrons contribute little. Helium has an atomic mass of 4.00. This number is usually divided equally among protons and neutrons. Therefore, a helium atom contains two protons and two neutrons. Some students may answer 4. These students are most likely neglecting the role of neutrons in determining atomic mass.

Question 14 Full-credit answers should include the following points:

- students should demonstrate a conceptual understanding of the different properties of the three primary states of matter
- jar A has a compact, but unordered structure that fills the space in the bottom of the jar. Students should recognize this as a model of a liquid
- jar B has a definite and self-contained structure. The atoms are held in close, fixed positions. Students should recognize this as a model of solid matter
- jar C shows fast-moving atoms that have no structure and that are filling the entire space in the jar. The particles have no relationship with one another, and if the jar were not present, the distance between the particles would expand indefinitely. Students should recognize this as matter in a gaseous state

Interpreting Graphics

Directions (10–14): For each question below, record the correct answer on a separate sheet of paper.

The graphic below shows the upper right segment of the periodic table. Use this graphic to answer questions 10 through 12.

Segment of the Periodic Table

13	14	15	16	17	18
					2 **He** 4.00
5 **B** 10.81	6 **C** 12.01	7 **N** 14.01	8 **O** 16.00	9 **F** 19.00	10 **Ne** 20.18
13 **Al** 26.98	14 **Si** 28.09	15 **P** 30.97	16 **S** 32.07	17 **Cl** 35.45	18 **Ar** 39.95

10. Which pair of elements would most likely have a similar arrangement of outer electrons and have similar chemical behaviors?
- **A.** boron and aluminum
- **B.** helium and fluoride
- **C.** carbon and nitrogen
- **D.** chlorine and oxygen

11. What is the atomic mass of helium?
- **F.** 0.18
- **G.** 0.26
- **H.** 2.00
- **I.** 4.00

12. How many neutrons does the average helium atom contain?

The graphic below shows matter in three different states. Use this graphic to answer questions 13 and 14.

States of Matter

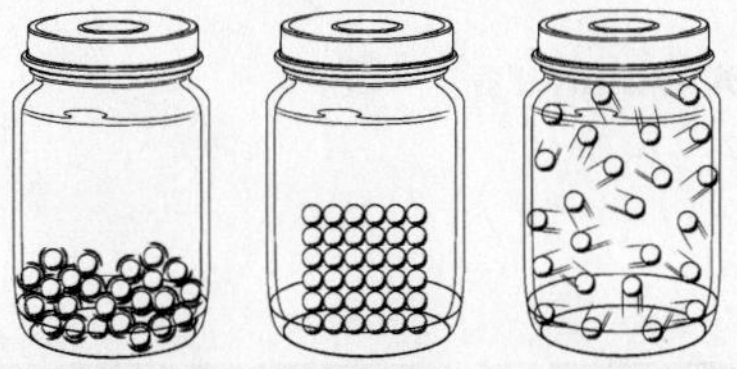

A B C

13. In what physical state is the matter in jar A?
- **A.** solid
- **B.** liquid
- **C.** gas
- **D.** plasma

14. Explain how the positions and motions of particles determine the characteristics of each state of matter.

Test Tip

Double check (with a calculator, if permitted) all mathematical computations involved in answering a question.

Using THINK central Resources

State Resources

- For specific resources for your state, visit www.thinkcentral.com and type in the keyword **HSHSTR.**

Answers

Understanding Concepts

1. C
2. H
3. A
4. I
5. an ion
6. by the number of protons in the atom

Reading Skills

7. A
8. G
9. 12

Interpreting Graphics

10. A
11. I
12. 2
13. B
14. Answers may vary. See Test Doctor for a detailed scoring rubric.

Chapter Planner 5 Minerals of Earth's Crust

	Time	Standards	Teach Key Ideas
Chapter Opener, pp. 108–109	45 min	**National Science Education Standards**	
Section 1 What Is a Mineral? pp. 111–116 ❯ Characteristics of Minerals ❯ Kinds of Minerals ❯ Crystalline Structure ❯ Crystalline Structure of Silicate Minerals ❯ Crystalline Structure of Nonsilicate Minerals	45 min	**PS 2c, PS 2f**	■ ◆ **Bellringer,** p. 111 ■ **DI (English Learners):** Matching Game, p. 113 ■ **DI (Special Education Students):** Drawing, p. 114 ◆ **Transparencies:** 21 Characteristics of Minerals • 22 Structures of Silicate Minerals • 25 Rock and Mineral Production in the United States ▲ **Visual Concepts:** Types of Crystals • Types of Basic Crystalline Systems • Comparing Crystalline and Amorphous Solids
Section 2 Identifying Minerals, pp. 117–122 ❯ Physical Properties of Minerals ❯ Special Properties of Minerals	90 min	**PS 2c, PS 2f**	■ ◆ **Bellringer,** p. 117 ■ **Demonstration:** The Same, But Different, p. 117 ■ **DI (Special Education Students):** Making Connections, p. 118 ■ **Discussion:** Crystal Powers, p. 120 ■ **DI (Advanced Learners):** Writing, p. 120 ◆ **Transparencies:** 23 Mohs Hardness Scale • 24 The Six Basic Crystal Systems ▲ **Visual Concepts:** Comparing Rocks and Minerals • Mineral Color, Luster, and Streak • Mineral Cleavage and Fracture • Mineral Density: Specific Gravity • Equation for Density
Chapter Wrap-Up, pp. 127–131	90 min		**Chapter Summary,** p. 127

See also PowerNotes® Presentations

CHAPTER Fast Track *To shorten instruction because of time limitations, omit the Chapter Lab.*

Key

Teacher's Edition ■ Teaching Transparencies ◆
Chapter Resource File ● Online Edition ▲

All resources listed below are also available on the Teacher One Stop™.

Why It Matters	Hands-On	Skills Development	Assessment
■ **Chapter Overview,** p. 108 ■ **Using the Figure:** Quartz Quest, p. 108	**Inquiry Lab:** Magnetic Minerals, p. 109	**Reading Toolbox,** p. 110	
■ **Section Overview,** p. 111 **A Mineral for Your Mouth,** p. 112 ■ **Biology Connection:** The Mineral Within, p. 113 ■ **Physics Connection:** X-Ray Crystallography, p. 115	■ **Group Activity:** Mineral—Yes or No? p. 111 ■ **Activity:** Acid Test, p. 113 **Quick Lab:** Modeling Tetrahedra, p. 114 ■ **Group Activity:** Growing Crystals, p. 114	■ ● **Internet Activity:** How Minerals Form, p. 112 **Reading Toolbox:** Key-Term Fold, p. 116 **Maps in Action:** Rock and Mineral Production in the United States, p. 126 ■ ● **Internet Activity:** Mining Impacts, p. 126	**Reading Check,** p. 113 **Reading Check,** p. 114 **Section Review,** p. 116 ■ **Reteaching,** p. 115 ■ **Quiz,** p. 115 ■ **DI (Alternative Assessment):** Flowchart, p. 116 ● **Section Quiz**
■ **Section Overview,** p. 117 **Gemstones,** p. 118 ■ **History Connection:** Hardness Scale, p. 119 ■ **Chemistry Connection:** Lighting Up, p. 121	● **Inquiry Lab:** Growing Crystals ■ **Activity:** Those Are the Breaks, p. 118 ■ **Activity:** Guest Speaker, p. 119 **Quick Lab:** Determining Density, p. 121 **Skills Practice Lab:** Mineral Identification, pp. 124–125	**Reading Toolbox:** Two-Column Notes, p. 119 **Math Skills:** Calculating Density, p. 120	**Reading Check,** p. 119 **Reading Check,** p. 121 **Section Review,** p. 122 ■ **Reteaching,** p. 121 ■ **Quiz,** p. 121 ■ **DI (Alternative Assessment):** Crystal Models, p. 122 ● **Section Quiz**
Know by the Glow, p. 123		▲ **Super Summary** **Standardized Test Prep,** pp. 130–131	**Chapter Review,** pp. 128–129 ■ **DI (Alternative Assessment):** Mineral Displays, p. 127 ● **Chapter Tests**

See also Lab Generator

See also Holt Online Assessment Resources

Chapter Overview

Minerals are used to make many familiar and not-so-familiar items, from jewelry to computers. This chapter compares the two main mineral groups—silicates and nonsilicates—and describes their chemical and physical properties.

Using the Figure GENERAL

Quartz Quest This photograph shows an agate (AG it), a form of the mineral chalcedony (kal SED uh nee). Chalcedony is a type of quartz. Chalcedony is microcrystalline, which means that the crystals are so small that they can be seen only by using a microscope, and commonly forms when the mineral is deposited by water. Agates, carnelian, tiger's eye, jasper, and chrysoprase are all varieties of microcrystalline quartz. Have interested students investigate the various forms of quartz and prepare posters that illustrate their findings.
LS Visual

Why It Matters

Chalcedony was an important material for early humans in what is now the United States. Weapons, such as knives and points, and decorative or ceremonial items, such as bowls and jewelry, were all made out of agate.

Chapter 5 Minerals of Earth's Crust

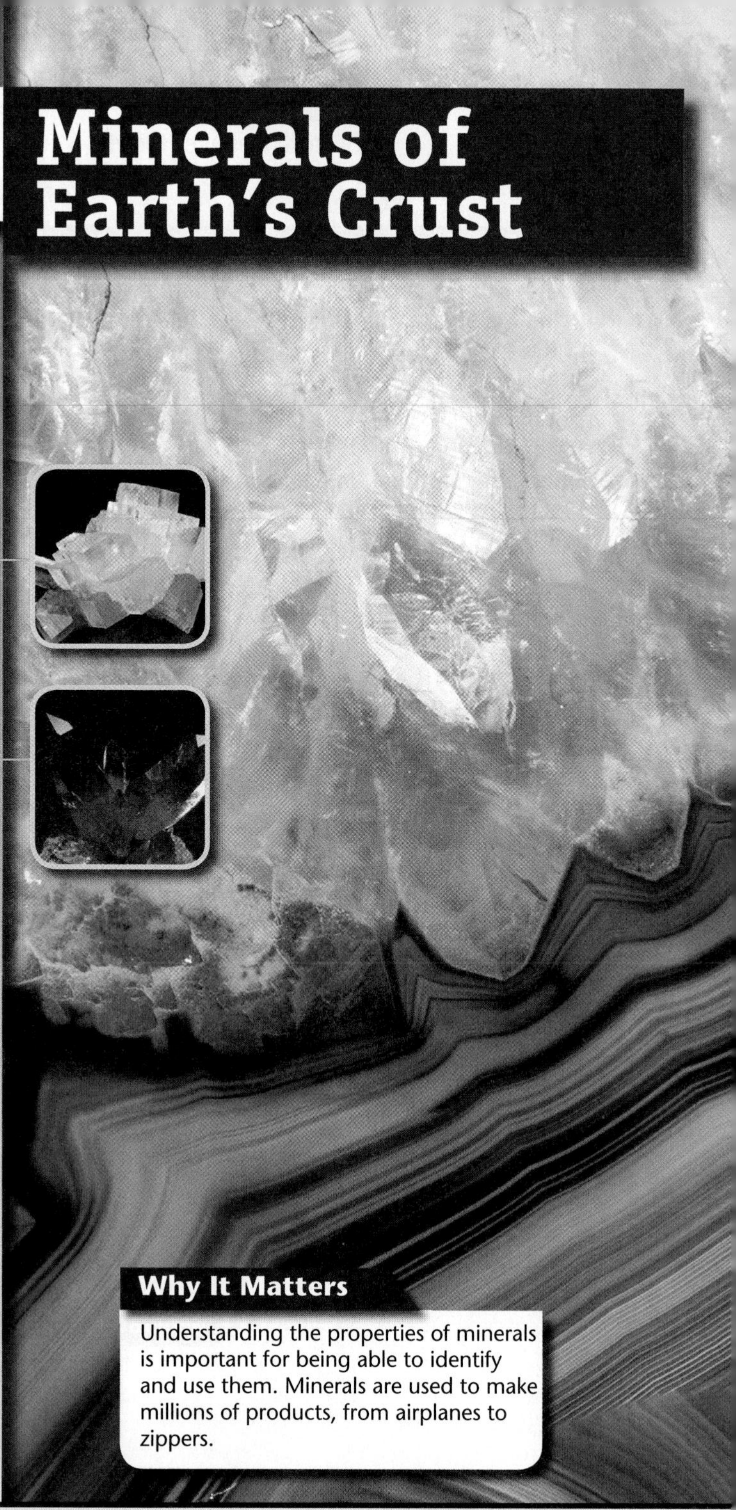

Chapter Outline

1 **What Is a Mineral?**
- Characteristics of Minerals
- Kinds of Minerals
- Crystalline Structure
- Crystalline Structure of Silicate Minerals
- Crystalline Structure of Nonsilicate Minerals

2 **Identifying Minerals**
- Physical Properties of Minerals
- Special Properties of Minerals

Virginia Standards of Learning
ES.1.a
ES.1.c
ES.1.f
ES.4.a
ES.4.b
ES.6.a
ES.6.c

Why It Matters

Understanding the properties of minerals is important for being able to identify and use them. Minerals are used to make millions of products, from airplanes to zippers.

Chapter Correlations — *Virginia Standards of Learning*

ES.1.a volume, area, mass, elapsed time, direction, temperature, pressure, distance, density, and changes in elevation/depth are calculated utilizing the most appropriate tools.
ES.1.c scales, diagrams, charts, graphs, tables, imagery, models, and profiles are constructed and interpreted.
ES.1.f current applications are used to reinforce Earth science concepts
ES.4.a hardness, color and streak, luster, cleavage, fracture, and unique properties
ES.4.b uses of minerals
ES.6.a fossil fuels, minerals, rocks, water, and vegetation
ES.6.c resources found in Virginia

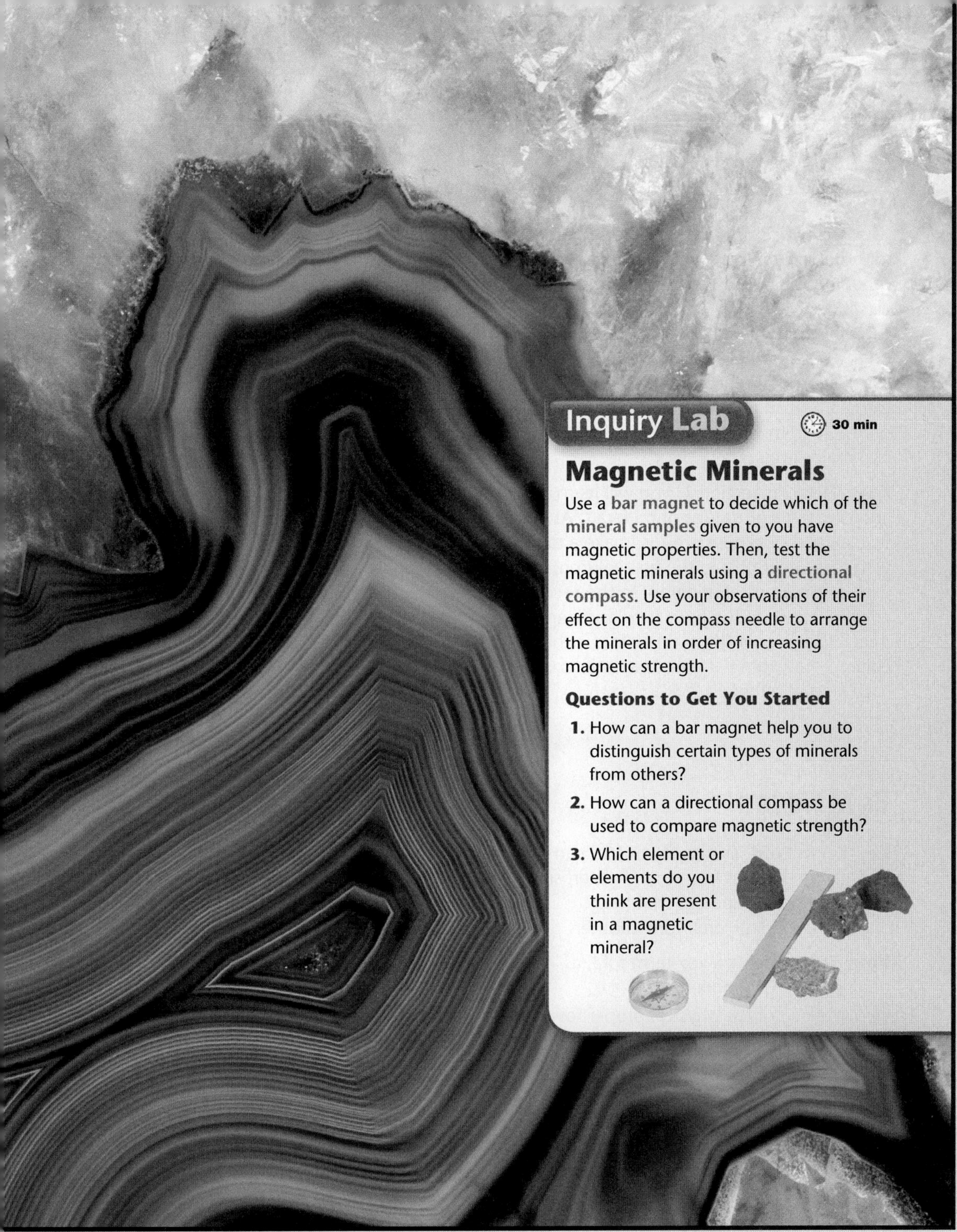

Inquiry Lab

30 min

Magnetic Minerals

Use a **bar magnet** to decide which of the **mineral samples** given to you have magnetic properties. Then, test the magnetic minerals using a **directional compass.** Use your observations of their effect on the compass needle to arrange the minerals in order of increasing magnetic strength.

Questions to Get You Started

1. How can a bar magnet help you to distinguish certain types of minerals from others?
2. How can a directional compass be used to compare magnetic strength?
3. Which element or elements do you think are present in a magnetic mineral?

Inquiry Lab

Central Concept: Some minerals contain magnetic elements. The magnetic properties of a mineral can be identified with a bar magnet. The magnetic strength of different magnetic minerals varies, depending on the mineral composition.

Teacher's Notes: A directional compass points to magnetic north, which is different from true north. Magnetic north is currently located in Northern Canada, but the precise location varies. It can move over 10 km each year.

Materials (per group)

- Bar magnet
- Mineral samples
- Directional compass

Skills Acquired

- Observing
- Recognizing Patterns

Answers to Getting Started

1. A bar magnet attracts the minerals with magnetic properties.
2. The greater the magnetic strength, the more an object will pull the compass needle.
3. Students will likely think of iron. Cobalt and nickel are also magnetic elements found in minerals.

Using THINK central Resources

An online version of this chapter, as well as all the print and multimedia resources that accompany the program are available to registered teachers and their students. Log onto www.thinkcentral.com to access these materials and tools to organize your preparation and student learning.

READING TOOLBOX

Classification

A sample classification table can be found on page 195A.

Note Taking

Answers may vary. Students' notes should appear similar to the example shown. The detailed notes in the second column should be written in students' own words.

FoldNotes

Students should consult Appendix A for tips on making a key-term fold. The information for this FoldNote can be found on page 195B.

READING TOOLBOX

These reading tools will help you learn the material in this chapter.

Classification

Kinds of Minerals Classification is a tool for organizing objects and ideas by grouping them into categories. Groups are classified by defining characteristics. One of the ways that minerals can be classified is on the basis of their composition. For example, some minerals contain the element silicon and others do not. Based on this fact, minerals can be classified into two major groups.

Your Turn In Section 1, you will learn about two major groups of minerals. As you learn about these groups, make a table with three columns. In the first column, list each of the kinds of minerals. In the second column, describe the basis for classifying minerals as one of these kinds. In the third column, list examples and descriptions of each kind of mineral.

Note Taking

Two-Column Notes Two-column notes can help you learn the key ideas from each section.

- Write the key ideas in the left column.
- In your own words, record notes and examples in the right column.

Your Turn Complete the two-column notes for Section 1, adding another row for each key idea.

KEY IDEA #1	A mineral is a solid that meets all four of these criteria:
Define mineral.	• It is inorganic. • It occurs naturally. • It is crystalline. • It has a consistent chemical composition.

FoldNotes

Key-Term Fold The key-term fold can help you learn key terms from this chapter, such as the physical properties that help distinguish one mineral from another.

Your Turn Create a key-term fold, as described in **Appendix A.**

1. Write one of the physical properties of minerals on the front of each tab.
2. Write a definition or description for each term under its tab.
3. Use this FoldNote to help you study the key terms in this chapter.

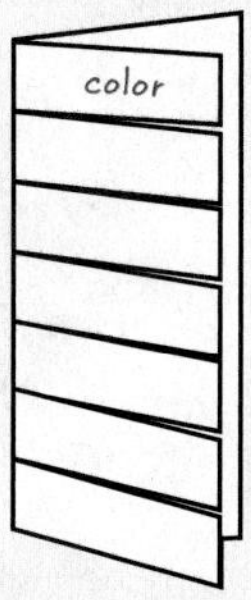

For more information on how to use these and other tools, see **Appendix A.**

SECTION 1

What Is a Mineral?

Key Ideas	Key Terms	Why It Matters
❯ Define *mineral*. ❯ Compare the two main groups of minerals. ❯ Identify the six types of silicate crystalline structures. ❯ Describe three common nonsilicate crystalline structures.	**mineral** **silicate mineral** **nonsilicate mineral** **crystal** **silicon-oxygen tetrahedron**	Almost everything you do each day—from brushing your teeth in the morning to setting your alarm clock at night—involves minerals in some way.

A ruby, a gold nugget, and a grain of salt look very different from one another, but they have one thing in common. They are minerals, the basic materials of Earth's crust. A **mineral** is a natural, usually inorganic solid that has a characteristic chemical composition, an orderly internal structure, and a characteristic set of physical properties.

Characteristics of Minerals

To determine whether a substance is a mineral or a nonmineral, scientists ask four basic questions, as shown in **Table 1.** If the answer to all four questions is yes, the substance is a mineral.

First, is the substance inorganic? An inorganic substance is one that is not made up of living things or the remains of living things. Coal, for example, is organic—it is composed of the remains of ancient plants. Thus, coal is not a mineral.

Second, does the substance occur naturally? Minerals form and exist in nature. Thus, a manufactured substance, such as steel or brass, is not a mineral.

Third, is the substance a solid in crystalline form? The volcanic glass obsidian is a naturally occurring substance. However, the atoms in obsidian are not arranged in a regularly repeating crystalline structure. Thus, obsidian is not a mineral.

Finally, does the substance have a consistent chemical composition? The mineral fluorite has a consistent chemical composition of one calcium ion for every two fluoride ions. Granite, however, can have a variety of substances. The ratio of these substances commonly varies in each sample of granite.

mineral a natural, usually inorganic solid that has a characteristic chemical composition, an orderly internal structure, and a characteristic set of physical properties

SCILINKS
www.scilinks.org
Topic: Minerals
Code: **HQX0966**

Table 1 Four Criteria for Minerals

Questions to Identify a Mineral	Coal	Brass	Obsidian	Basalt	Fluorite
Is it inorganic?	No	Yes	Yes	Yes	Yes
Does it occur naturally?		No	Yes	Yes	Yes
Is it a crystalline solid?			No	Yes	Yes
Does it have a consistent chemical composition?				No	Yes

Section 1

Focus

Overview

This section defines what a mineral is and reviews the two main groups of minerals, silicates and nonsilicates. It describes the six common crystalline structures of silicates. It also describes the six major classes of nonsilicates.

Bellringer

Ask students to define what a mineral is and give an example. (Answers may vary. Use definitions to identify misconceptions about what a mineral is and to introduce the four characteristics that all minerals must have.)
LS Logical

Motivate

Group Activity — GENERAL

Mineral—Yes or No? Organize students into small groups and give each group a set of samples that includes salt, sugar, ice, rock, and charcoal. Have students determine if each sample is a mineral, based on answers to the four questions scientists ask to determine if a substance is a mineral. Discuss identifications as a class. (Salt and ice are minerals. Sugar and charcoal are organic, and rock does not have a consistent chemical composition.) **LS Visual/Kinesthetic**

Key Resources

Chapter Resource File
- Directed Reading BASIC

Technology
- Transparencies
  Bellringer
  21 Characteristics of Minerals

Teach

Teaching Tip — BASIC

Connect to Real Life Remind students that we use minerals regularly in everyday life. They are found in computers, watches, emery boards, dentist drills, toothpaste, and more. Have students keep a journal for a week in which they record their use of or contact with minerals or mineral-containing products. At the end of the week, discuss what types of minerals they used most often. Interested students may wish to do more research. The United States Geological Survey Web site is a good place to start.
LS **Logical**

Internet Activity — ADVANCED

How Minerals Form Invite interested students to research the three basic ways minerals form: solidification of a melt; precipitation from solution; and solid-state diffusion. Guide students to research how scientists use these processes in laboratory settings to grow flawless synthetic minerals. Students may present their findings in a written or oral report to the class. A worksheet designed to direct student research on this topic can be found in the **Chapter Resource File** booklet or by visiting www.thinkcentral.com and entering the keyword **HQXMINX**.
LS **Logical**

Figure 1 Plagioclase feldspar (left), muscovite mica (center), and orthoclase feldspar (right) are 3 of the 20 common rock-forming minerals.

silicate mineral a mineral that contains a combination of silicon and oxygen and that may also contain one or more metals

Kinds of Minerals

Earth scientists have identified more than 4,000 minerals, but fewer than 20 of the minerals are common. The common minerals are called *rock-forming minerals* because they form the rocks that make up Earth's crust. Three of these minerals are shown in **Figure 1.** Of the 20 rock-forming minerals, about half are so common that they make up 90% of the mass of Earth's crust. These include quartz, orthoclase, plagioclase, muscovite, biotite, calcite, dolomite, halite, gypsum, and ferromagnesian minerals. All minerals, however, can be classified into two main groups—silicate minerals and nonsilicate minerals—based on the chemical compositions of the minerals.

Silicate Minerals

A mineral that contains a combination of silicon, Si, and oxygen, O, is a **silicate mineral.** The mineral quartz has only silicon and oxygen atoms. However, other silicate minerals have one or more additional elements. Feldspars are the most common silicate minerals. The type of feldspar that forms depends on which metal combines with the silicon and oxygen atoms. Orthoclase forms when the metal is potassium, K. Plagioclase forms when the metal is sodium, Na, calcium, Ca, or both.

In addition to quartz and the feldspars, ferromagnesian minerals—which are rich in iron, Fe, and magnesium, Mg—are silicates. These minerals include olivines, pyroxenes, amphiboles, and biotite. Silicate minerals make up 96% of Earth's crust. Feldspars and quartz alone make up more than 50% of the crust.

Why It Matters

A Mineral for Your Mouth

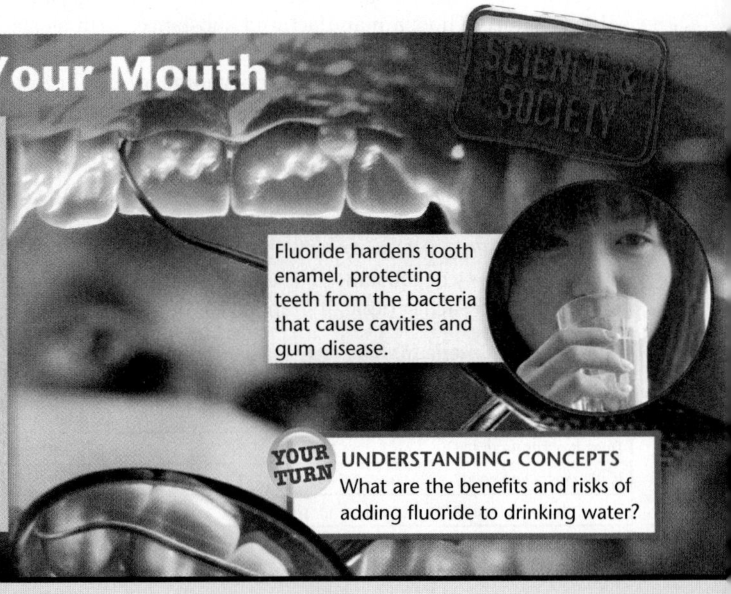

Fluoride is found in many non-silicate minerals. It is also a powerful ally in the battle against the bacteria that work 24/7 to decay your teeth. When fluoride is naturally present in drinking water, people develop fewer cavities, so fluoride is added to the water supply and to many dental products. About 60% of the U.S. population drink fluoridated water. Some people oppose its use, however, because too much fluoride can damage bones and discolor teeth.

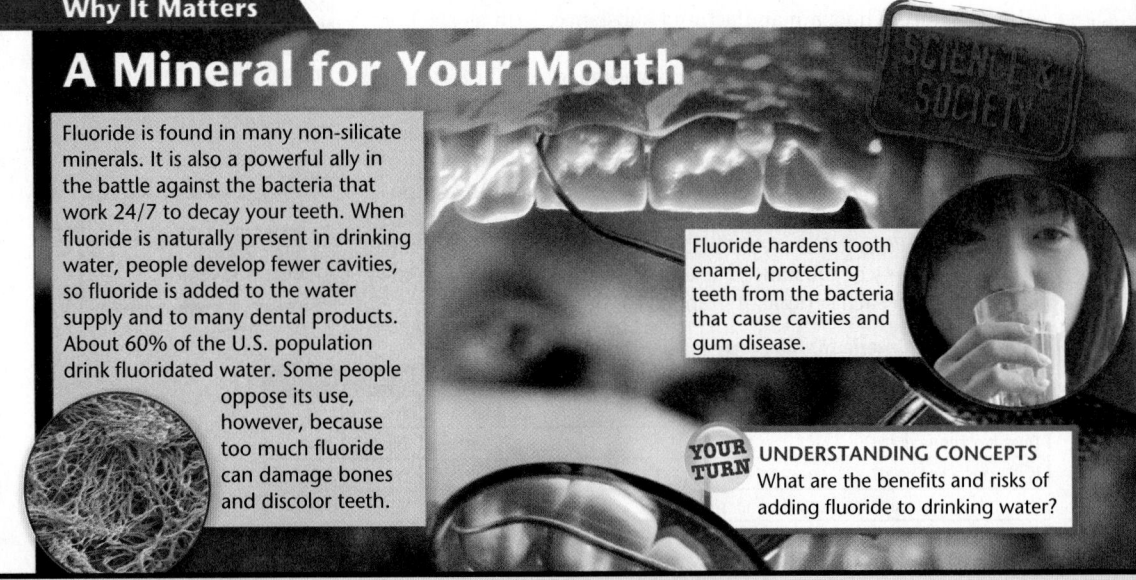

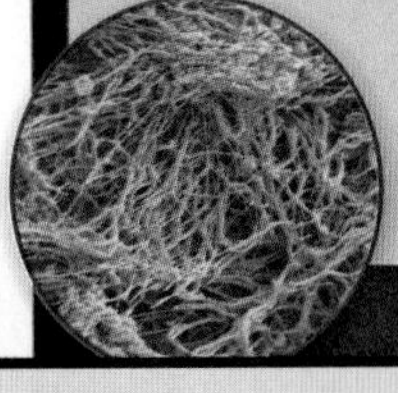

Fluoride hardens tooth enamel, protecting teeth from the bacteria that cause cavities and gum disease.

YOUR TURN UNDERSTANDING CONCEPTS
What are the benefits and risks of adding fluoride to drinking water?

Why It Matters

A Mineral for your Mouth In the early 1900s, Dr. Frederick McKay, practicing dentistry in Colorado Springs, noticed brown stains on children's teeth. Dr. McKay found that people with these stains had fewer cavities. By 1931, the brown stains were traced back to naturally occurring fluoride in the public water supply. As the water trickled through deposits of cryolite, it washed out fluoride ions.

Answer to Your Turn

Understanding Concepts Fluoride hardens tooth enamel, helping to prevent decay. Excess fluoride can discolor teeth and cause bone damage.

Table 2 Major Classes of Nonsilicate Minerals

Carbonates compounds that contain a carbonate group (CO_3)	 Dolomite, $CaMg(CO_3)_2$	 Calcite, $CaCO_3$
Halides compounds that consist of chlorine or fluorine combined with sodium, potassium, or calcium	 Halite, NaCl	 Fluorite, CaF_2
Native elements elements uncombined with other elements	 Silver, Ag	 Copper, Cu
Oxides compounds that contain oxygen and an element other than silicon	 Corundum, Al_2O_3	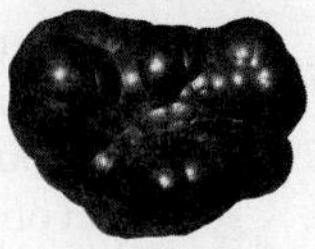 Hematite, Fe_2O_3
Sulfates compounds that contain a sulfate group (SO_4)	 Gypsum, $CaSO_4 \bullet 2H_2O$	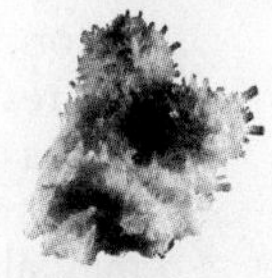 Anhydrite, $CaSO_4$
Sulfides compounds that consist of one or more elements combined with sulfur	 Galena, PbS	 Pyrite, FeS_2

Nonsilicate Minerals

Approximately 4% of Earth's crust is made up of minerals that do not contain compounds of silicon and oxygen, or **nonsilicate minerals. Table 2** organizes the six major groups of nonsilicate minerals by their chemical compositions: carbonates, halides, native elements, oxides, sulfates, and sulfides.

nonsilicate mineral a mineral that does not contain compounds of silicon and oxygen

Reading Check What compounds will you never find in a nonsilicate mineral? (See Appendix G for answers to Reading Checks.)

Homework ADVANCED

Mineral Names Some minerals are named after locations or scientists. Others are derived from a Greek or Latin word describing a characteristic of the mineral. Some are named after a myth or legend. Have students research the origin of two or three mineral names and present their findings to the class. **LS Verbal**

Activity BASIC

Acid Test Carbonates can be identified because they produce carbon dioxide gas when combined with an acid. Many carbonates will react with a weak acid such as vinegar. Provide students with a carbonate such as calcite, a noncarbonate, and strong vinegar. Have them drop the vinegar on each sample and identify which sample is the carbonate. They should see fizzing or bubbling on the surface of the carbonate but no reaction with the noncarbonate. Note that if a sulfide is used as the noncarbonate, it also may react, but the gas is hydrogen sulfide or sulfur dioxide and has a strong smell of rotten eggs. **LS Kinesthetic**

Biology Connection

The Mineral Within Although rare, phosphate minerals are important to animals that have bones. The nonliving part of our teeth and bones is made of microscopic calcium phosphate crystals laid down by cells within the bone (the osteocytes). Calcium phosphate may make up as much as 65% of an adult bone.

Answer to Reading Check

Nonsilicate minerals never contain compounds of silicon bonded to oxygen.

Differentiated Instruction

English Learners

Matching Game Photocopy this page. Cut along columns and rows to yield 18 "cards." Pair students to play a game matching nonsilicate minerals with classes. Lay the six cards with written descriptions face up, in front of student A. Lay the 12 cards with mineral photos face down. Student A must pick a card. Student B then looks at the card, without showing Student A. Student A will use the descriptions to ask yes or no questions to identify the class of mineral (e.g. does it contain a sulfate group?). Student B responds, based on the chemical formula of the mineral, and hands Student A the card when the correct class of mineral is identified. **LS Verbal/Auditory**

Teach, *continued*

Quick Lab

Skills Acquired
- Constructing Models

Materials
- Toothpicks
- Small marshmallows
- Large marshmallows

Teacher's Notes: You can also use plastic foam balls of different sizes to represent the silicon and oxygen. Using different colored marshmallows or plastic foam balls may help students visualize the different atoms better.

Answers to Analysis
1. The toothpicks represent the silicon-oxygen bonds.
2. Build a second tetrahedron using one of the large marshmallows on the first tetrahedron. This represents the sharing of oxygen atoms between tetrahedra.

Answer to Reading Check
The building block of the silicate crystalline structure is a four-sided structure known as the silicon-oxygen tetrahedron, which is one silicon atom surrounded by four oxygen atoms.

Quick Lab — 5 min

Modeling Tetrahedra

Procedure
1. Place four toothpicks in a small marshmallow. Evenly space the toothpicks as far from each other as possible.
2. Place four large marshmallows on the ends of the toothpicks.

Analysis
1. In your model, what do the toothpicks represent?
2. When tetrahedra form chains or rings, they share oxygen atoms. If you wanted to build a chain of tetrahedra, how would you connect two tetrahedra together?

Crystalline Structure

All minerals in Earth's crust have a crystalline structure. Each type of mineral crystal is characterized by a specific geometric arrangement of atoms. A **crystal** is a solid whose atoms, ions, or molecules are arranged in a regular, repeating pattern. A large mineral crystal displays the characteristic geometry of that crystal's internal structure. The conditions under which minerals form, however, often hinder the growth of single, large crystals. As a result, minerals are commonly made up of masses of crystals that are so small you can see them only with a microscope. But, if a crystal forms where the surrounding material is not restrictive, the mineral will develop as a single, large crystal that has one of six basic crystal shapes. Knowing the crystal shapes is helpful in identifying minerals.

One way that scientists study the structure of crystals is by using X rays. X rays that pass through a crystal and strike a photographic plate produce an image that shows the geometric arrangement of the atoms that make up the crystal.

Crystalline Structure of Silicate Minerals

Even though there are many kinds of silicate minerals, their crystalline structure is made up of the same basic building blocks. Each building block has four oxygen atoms arranged in a pyramid with one silicon atom in the center. **Figure 2** shows this four-sided structure, which is known as a **silicon-oxygen tetrahedron.**

Silicon-oxygen tetrahedra combine in different arrangements to form different silicate minerals. The various arrangements are the result of the kinds of bonds that form between the oxygen atoms of the tetrahedra and other atoms. The oxygen atoms of tetrahedra may be shared with those of neighboring tetrahedra. Bonds may also form between the oxygen atoms in the tetrahedra and other elements' atoms outside of the tetrahedra.

crystal a solid whose atoms, ions, or molecules are arranged in a regular, repeating pattern

silicon-oxygen tetrahedron the basic unit of the structure of silicate minerals; a silicon ion chemically bonded to and surrounded by four oxygen ions

Reading Check **What is the building block of the silicate crystalline structure?**

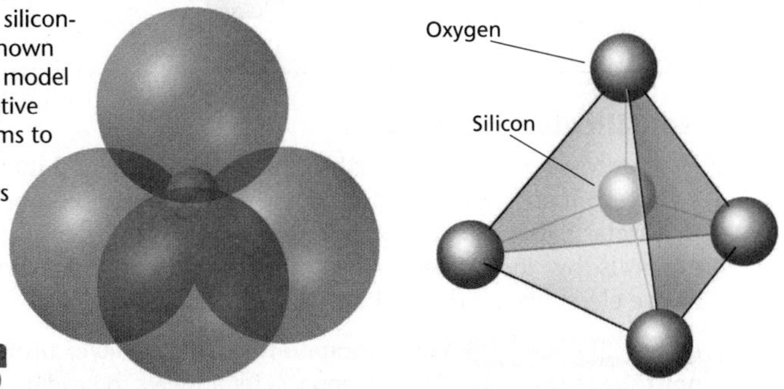

Figure 2 The structure of a silicon-oxygen tetrahedron can be shown by two different models. The model on the left represents the relative size and proximity of the atoms to one another in the molecule. The model on the right shows the tetrahedral shape of the molecule.

THINK central INTERACT ONLINE (Keyword: HQXMINF2)

Group Activity — BASIC

Growing Crystals Have students work in pairs to grow crystals of sodium carbonate (washing soda) or sodium chloride (rock salt). Fill a jar with very hot water. Stir in washing soda or salt until no more will dissolve. Tie a paperclip to a piece of string. Tie the other end of the string to a pencil. Place the pencil across the top of the jar to suspend the paperclip in the solution. Let the jar sit undisturbed for 24 hours or more. After crystals have grown, carefully remove them and observe them with a magnifying glass.
LS Visual

Differentiated Instruction

Special Education Students

Drawing Help students understand silicate-mineral arrangements by having them draw the structures. Give each student six sheets of graph paper. Have students use markers to create and label each silicate-mineral arrangement. Guide them to use the graph paper lines and intersections to make sure the triangles are even.

Isolated Tetrahedral Silicates and Ring Silicates

Six kinds of arrangements that tetrahedra form are shown in **Figure 3.** In minerals that have *isolated tetrahedra,* only atoms other than silicon and oxygen atoms link silicon-oxygen tetrahedra. For example, olivine is a mineral that forms when the oxygen atoms of tetrahedra bond to magnesium, Mg, and iron, Fe, atoms.

Ring silicates form when shared oxygen atoms join the tetrahedra to form three-, four-, or six-sided rings. The rings can align to create channels that can contain a variety of ions, molecules, and neutral atoms. Beryl and tourmaline are minerals that have ring-silicate structures.

Single-Chain Silicates and Double-Chain Silicates

In *single-chain silicates,* each tetrahedron shares corner oxygen atoms with two others. In *double-chain silicates,* two single chains of tetrahedra link to each other by sharing oxygen atoms. Most single-chain silicate minerals are called *pyroxenes,* and those made up of double chains are called *amphiboles.*

Sheet Silicates and Framework Silicates

In the *sheet silicates,* each tetrahedron shares three oxygen atoms with other tetrahedra. The unshared oxygen atoms bond with aluminum, Al, or magnesium atoms that hold other sheets of silicon-oxygen tetrahedra together. The mica minerals, such as muscovite and biotite, are examples of sheet silicates.

In the *framework silicates,* each tetrahedron shares all of its oxygen atoms with four neighboring tetrahedra to form a three-dimensional network. Frameworks that contain only silicon-oxygen tetrahedra form the mineral quartz. The chemical formula for quartz is SiO_2. Other framework silicates, such as the feldspars, contain some tetrahedra in which atoms of aluminum substitute for some of the silicon atoms.

Figure 3 Six Kinds of Silicate-Mineral Arrangements

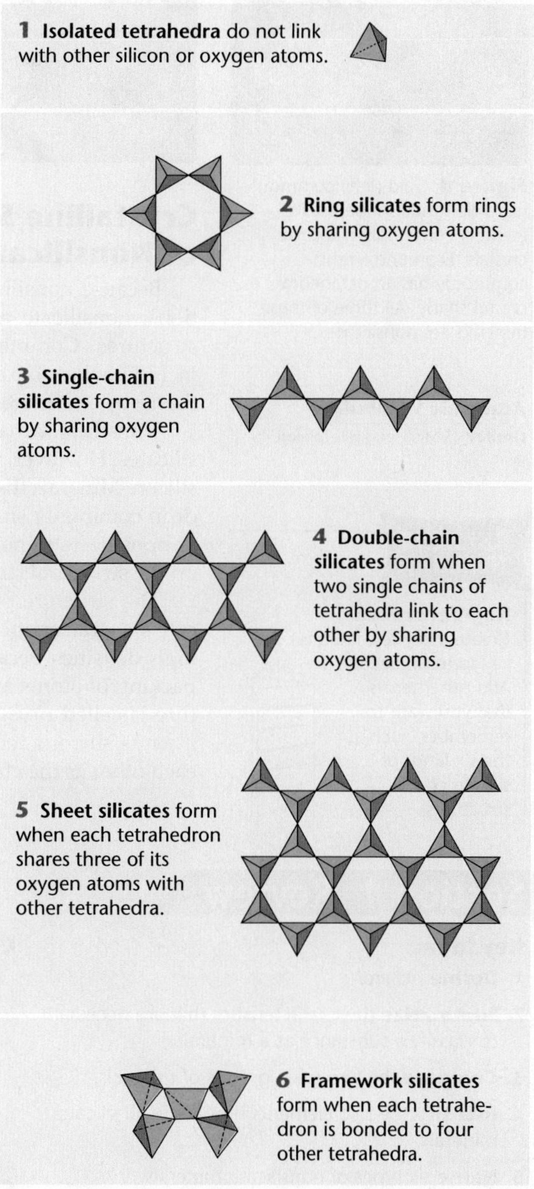

1 Isolated tetrahedra do not link with other silicon or oxygen atoms.
2 Ring silicates form rings by sharing oxygen atoms.
3 Single-chain silicates form a chain by sharing oxygen atoms.
4 Double-chain silicates form when two single chains of tetrahedra link to each other by sharing oxygen atoms.
5 Sheet silicates form when each tetrahedron shares three of its oxygen atoms with other tetrahedra.
6 Framework silicates form when each tetrahedron is bonded to four other tetrahedra.

Physics Connection

X-Ray Crystallography In 1912, German physicist Max von Laue passed an X-ray beam through a crystal. The beam was diffracted, creating a pattern of spots on a projection screen. Von Laue knew that diffraction occurs when X rays pass through materials that have regularly spaced obstacles. He proposed that regularly spaced atoms within crystals could explain the pattern. Today, X-ray crystallography has become an important tool in many fields and has even helped decipher the structure of DNA.

Close

Reteaching — BASIC

Name That Mineral Have students write characteristics of silicate and nonsilicate minerals on index cards. Have them work in pairs to quiz each other about the differences between the two groups by using the cards.
LS Visual/Logical

Quiz — GENERAL

1. What are three common crystal structures for nonsilicates? (cubes, prisms, and irregular masses)
2. What is a crystal? (a solid whose atoms, ions, or molecules are arranged in a regular, repeating pattern)
3. Name one method scientists use to study the structure of crystals? (They pass X rays through the crystals to produce an image of the geometric arrangement of the atoms in the crystal.)

Key Resources

Technology
- Transparencies
  22 Structures of Silicate Minerals

![READING TOOLBOX]

Key-Term Fold

Students should consult Appendix A for tips on making a key-term fold. The information for this FoldNote can be found on page 195B.

Close, *continued*

Answers to Section Review

1. a naturally occurring, inorganic, crystalline solid that has a consistent chemical composition and a characteristic set of physical properties
2. naturally occurring, inorganic, crystalline solid, with a consistent chemical composition
3. Silicates are composed of silicon-oxygen tetrahedra, sometimes combined with other elements. Nonsilicates do not contain silicon-oxygen compounds.
4. silicon and oxygen
5. carbonates, halides, oxides, sulfates, sulfides, and native elements
6. Isolated tetrahedra do not link with other silicon or oxygen atoms. Ring silicates form rings by sharing oxygen atoms. Single-chain silicates form a chain by sharing oxygen atoms. Double-chain silicates form when two single chains of tetrahedra bond together. Sheet silicates form when each tetrahedron shares three of its oxygen atoms with other tetrahedra. Framework silicates form when each tetrahedron bonds to four other tetrahedra.
7. because they have diverse chemical compositions and do not have to form tetrahedra.
8. It would not form tetrahedra. The Si-O compound would probably be more planar and would more likely form sheet structures when it combined.
9. Yes. It satisfies all four criteria that define a mineral.
10. *Minerals* are grouped into *silicate minerals*, which are composed of *silicon-oxygen tetrahedra* that can combine to form *single-chain silicates*, *ring silicates*, and *framework silicates*; and *nonsilicate minerals*, which form many types of *crystals*.

Figure 4 Gold (left) commonly has a dendritic shape. Halite (center) commonly has cubic crystals. Diamond (right) commonly has an octahedral crystal shape. All three of these minerals are nonsilicates.

Academic Vocabulary

similar (SIM uh luhr) alike; almost the same

READING TOOLBOX

Key-Term Fold

Create a key-term fold for the key terms in Section 1. Add other terms that you want to remember, such as the six kinds of silicate crystal structures.

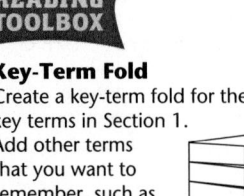

Crystalline Structure of Nonsilicate Minerals

Because nonsilicate minerals have diverse chemical compositions, nonsilicate minerals display a vast variety of crystalline structures. Common crystal structures for nonsilicate minerals include cubes, hexagonal prisms, and irregular masses. Some of these structures are shown in **Figure 4.**

Nonsilicates may form tetrahedra that are similar to those in silicates. However, the ions at the center of these tetrahedra are not silicon. Minerals that have the same ion at the center of the tetrahedron commonly share similar crystal structures. Thus, the classes of nonsilicate minerals can be divided into smaller groups based on the structural similarities of the minerals' crystals.

The structure of a nonsilicate crystal determines the nonsilicate's characteristics. For example, the native elements have very high densities because their crystal structures are based on the packing of atoms as close together as possible. This crystal structure is called *closest packing*. In this crystal structure, each metal atom is surrounded by 12 other metal atoms that are as close to each other as the charges of the atomic nuclei will allow.

Section 1 Review

Key Ideas

1. **Define** *mineral.*
2. **Summarize** the characteristics that are necessary to classify a substance as a mineral.
3. **Compare** the two main groups of minerals.
4. **Identify** the two elements that are in all silicate minerals.
5. **Name** six types of nonsilicate minerals.
6. **Describe** the six main crystalline structures of silicate minerals.
7. **Explain** why nonsilicate minerals have a wider variety of crystalline structures than silicate minerals do.

Critical Thinking

8. **Predicting Consequences** If silicon bonded with three oxygen atoms, how might the crystalline structures of silicate minerals be different?
9. **Applying Ideas** Gold is an inorganic substance that forms naturally in Earth's crust. Gold is also a solid and has a definite chemical composition. Is gold a mineral? Explain your answer.

Concept Mapping

10. Use the following terms to create a concept map: *mineral, crystal, silicate mineral, nonsilicate mineral, ring silicate, framework silicate, single-chain silicate,* and *silicon-oxygen tetrahedron.*

Differentiated Instruction

Alternative Assessment

Flowchart Have students work in small groups to design a flowchart that classifies and describes the two main groups of minerals and their major subgroups. **LS Visual/Logical**

SECTION 2

Identifying Minerals

Key Ideas	Key Terms	Why It Matters
❯ Describe seven physical properties that help to distinguish one mineral from another. ❯ List five special properties that may help to identify certain minerals.	mineralogist, streak, luster, cleavage, fracture, Mohs hardness scale, density	Some minerals glow in the dark; others are magnetic. The properties of minerals help people to identify and use them.

Earth scientists called **mineralogists** examine, analyze, and classify minerals. To identify minerals, mineralogists study the properties of the minerals. Some properties are simple to study, while special equipment may be needed to study other properties.

mineralogist a person who examines, analyzes, and classifies minerals

Physical Properties of Minerals

Each mineral has specific properties that are a result of its chemical composition and crystalline structure. These properties provide useful clues for identifying minerals. Many of these properties can be identified by simply looking at a sample of the mineral. Other properties can be identified through simple tests.

Color

One property of a mineral that is easy to observe is the mineral's color. Some minerals have very distinct colors. For example, sulfur is bright yellow, and azurite is deep blue. Color alone, however, is generally not a reliable clue for identifying a mineral sample. Many minerals are similar in color, and very small amounts of certain elements may greatly affect the color of a mineral. For example, corundum is a colorless mineral composed of aluminum and oxygen atoms. However, corundum that has traces of chromium, Cr, forms the red gem called *ruby*. Sapphire, which is a type of corundum, gets its blue color from traces of iron, Fe, and titanium, Ti. **Figure 1** compares colorless, pure quartz with purple amethyst. Amethyst is quartz that has manganese, Mn, and iron, Fe, which cause the purple color.

Color is also an unreliable identification clue because weathered surfaces may hide the color of minerals. For example, the golden color of iron pyrite ranges from dark yellow to black when iron pyrite is weathered. When examining a mineral for color, you should inspect only the mineral's freshly exposed surfaces.

Figure 1 Pure quartz (above) is colorless. Amethyst (right) is a variety of quartz that is purple because of the presence of small amounts of manganese and iron.

Section 2

Focus

Overview

This section identifies the major properties and crystal systems of minerals. It also explains special properties that help in the identification of minerals.

Bellringer

Ask students to list properties they might use to tell one mineral from another. Use student lists to introduce the characteristics that mineralogists use to identify minerals. (Answers may vary but could include color, hardness, shape, density, and transparency.)

Motivate

Demonstration — GENERAL

The Same, But Different Show students crystals of purple fluorite, amethyst, and rose quartz. Ask students to identify which two crystals are the same mineral. Use this demonstration to explain why using only color is not a good way to identify minerals. (Fluorite and amethyst are both purple, have the same nonmetallic glassy luster, and have white streaks, but they are not the same. Amethyst is purple quartz and is much harder than fluorite; quartz does not show any cleavage, while fluorite has perfect cleavage in four directions.) **LS Visual**

Key Resources

Chapter Resource File
- Directed Reading BASIC
- Inquiry Lab: Growing Crystals GENERAL

Technology
- Transparencies
  Bellringer

Teach

Activity — GENERAL

Those Are the Breaks Cement five or six craft sticks together sandwich style with a mixture of plaster of paris (2 Tbsp), white glue (1/2 tsp), and water (2 tsp). Allow the models to dry for one hour. When dry, have students try to break apart the sticks. The stack should break apart into thinner layers, modeling the way some minerals split along one cleavage plane. For example, mica has perfect cleavage in one plane and forms thin flakes as it is cleaved. Provide a piece of mica for students to examine. Challenge students to use the craft stick model to demonstrate cleavage in more than one plane.
LS Kinesthetic

Why It Matters

Gemstones When cutting gems, such as diamonds, emeralds, and rubies, a gem cutter, or *lapidary*, may break a large stone into smaller pieces by splitting it along a cleavage plane. The lapidary determines the crystal shape, then cuts facets and grinds and polishes them to make the gem sparkle. The largest diamond ever found, the Cullinan Diamond (initial weight: 3,106 carats, or 621 g) was cut into nine large gems and many smaller ones.

Figure 2 All minerals have either a metallic luster, as platinum does (top), or a nonmetallic luster, as talc does (bottom).

Streak

A more reliable clue to the identity of a mineral is the color of the mineral in powdered form, which is called the mineral's **streak.** The easiest way to observe the streak of a mineral is to rub some of the mineral against a piece of unglazed ceramic tile called a *streak plate*. The streak's color may differ from the color of the solid form of the mineral. Metallic minerals generally have a dark streak. For example, the streak of gold-colored pyrite is black. For most nonmetallic minerals, however, the streak is either colorless or a very light shade of the mineral's standard color. Minerals that are harder than the ceramic plate will leave no streak.

Luster

Light that is reflected from a mineral's surface is called **luster.** A mineral is said to have a *metallic luster* if the mineral reflects light as polished metal does, as shown in **Figure 2.** All other minerals have a *nonmetallic luster*. Mineralogists distinguish several types of nonmetallic luster. Transparent quartz and other minerals that look like glass have a glassy luster. Minerals that have the appearance of candle wax have a waxy luster. Some minerals, such as the mica minerals, have a pearly luster. Diamond is an example of a mineral that has a brilliant luster. A mineral that lacks any shiny appearance has a dull or earthy luster.

streak the color of a mineral in powdered form

luster the way in which a mineral reflects light

cleavage the tendency of a mineral to split along specific planes of weakness to form smooth, flat surfaces

fracture the manner in which a mineral breaks along either curved or irregular surfaces

Academic Vocabulary

specific (spuh SIF ik) unique; peculiar to or characteristic of; exact

Cleavage and Fracture

The tendency of a mineral to split along specific planes of weakness to form smooth, flat surfaces is called **cleavage.** When a mineral has cleavage, as shown in **Figure 3,** it breaks along flat surfaces that generally run parallel to planes of weakness in the crystal structure. For example, the mica minerals, which are sheet silicates, tend to split into parallel sheets.

Many minerals, however, do not break along cleavage planes. Instead, they **fracture,** or break unevenly, into pieces that have curved or irregular surfaces. Mineralogists describe a fracture according to the appearance of the broken surface. For example, a rough surface has an *uneven* or *irregular fracture*. A broken surface that looks like a piece of broken wood has a *splintery* or *fibrous fracture*. Curved surfaces are *conchoidal fractures* (kahng KOYD uhl FRAK chuhr), as shown in **Figure 3.**

Figure 3 Calcite is a mineral that cleaves in three directions. Quartz (right) tends to have a conchoidal fracture.

Differentiated Instruction

Special Education Students

Making Connections To help students organize the information necessary to identify minerals by their properties, guide students to associate each property with a familiar concept, object, or idea. Color: Associate sulfur's yellow with the sun or the blue of azurite with the sky. Streak: Make a streak on a piece of paper with a tube of lip balm. Luster: Feel a glass object (glassy) and a piece of talc (waxy). Cleavage and fracture: Feel a split piece of mica (cleavage) and the edges of a fractured rock (fracture). Hardness: Try to scratch a piece of wood and a rock by using a nail. Crystal shape: Feel wooden blocks that have the following shapes: square, rhombus, hexagon, and rectangle. Density: Hold a brick and a piece of plastic foam that have the same dimensions.

Table 1 Mohs Hardness Scale

Mineral	Hardness	Common test	Mineral	Hardness	Common test
Talc	1	easily scratched by fingernail	Feldspar	6	scratches glass, but does not scratch steel
Gypsum	2	can be scratched by fingernail	Quartz	7	easily scratches both glass and steel
Calcite	3	barely can be scratched by copper penny	Topaz	8	scratches quartz
Fluorite	4	easily scratched with steel file or glass	Corundum	9	scratches topaz
Apatite	5	can be scratched by steel file or glass	Diamond	10	scratches everything

Hardness

The measure of the ability of a mineral to resist scratching is called *hardness*. Hardness does not mean "resistance to cleavage or fracture." A diamond, for example, is extremely hard but can be split along cleavage planes more easily than calcite, a softer mineral, can be split.

To determine the hardness of an unknown mineral, you can scratch the mineral against those on the **Mohs hardness scale,** which is shown in **Table 1.** This scale lists 10 minerals in order of increasing hardness. The softest mineral, talc, has a hardness of 1. The hardest mineral, diamond, has a hardness of 10. The difference in hardness between two consecutive minerals is about the same throughout the scale except for the difference between the two hardest minerals. Diamond (10) is much harder than corundum (9), which is listed on the scale before diamond.

To test an unknown mineral for hardness, you must determine the hardest mineral on the scale that the unknown mineral can scratch. For example, galena can scratch gypsum but not calcite. Thus, galena has a hardness that ranges between 2 and 3 on the Mohs hardness scale. If neither of two minerals scratches the other, the minerals have the same hardness.

The strength of the bonds between the atoms that make up a mineral's internal structure determines the hardness of that mineral. Both diamond and graphite consist only of carbon atoms. However, diamond has a hardness of 10, while the hardness of graphite is between 1 and 2. A diamond's hardness results from a strong crystalline structure in which each carbon atom is firmly bonded to four other carbon atoms. In contrast, the carbon atoms in graphite are arranged in layers that are held together by much weaker chemical bonds.

Reading Check **What determines the hardness of a mineral?**

SCILINKS.
www.scilinks.org
Topic: Mineral Identification
Code: **HQX0965**

Mohs hardness scale the standard scale against which the hardness of minerals is rated

READING TOOLBOX

Two-Column Notes
Create two-column notes to outline all the physical properties of minerals, including special properties, that mineralogists can use to help them identify minerals. Put the physical properties in the first column, and add notes and examples in the second column.

History Connection

Hardness Scale The Mohs hardness scale is named after German mineralogist and professor Friedrich Mohs. In 1822, Mohs devised the scale by arranging ten minerals according to their resistance to being scratched, from softest to hardest. He used common minerals that were readily available to him. He assigned a value of 1 to the softest, talc, and a value of 10 to the hardest, diamond. The scale is not linear; diamond is many more than 10 times harder than talc is. While the Mohs hardness scale is very useful in mineral identification, when a material's hardness must be accurately measured, a device called a *sclerometer* is used. This device measures the force needed to scratch a material with diamond.

READING TOOLBOX

Two-Column Notes

Answers may vary. Students' notes should appear similar to the example shown in the Reading Toolbox at the beginning of the chapter. The notes in the second column should be written in students' own words.

Key Resources

Technology
- Transparencies
  23 Mohs Hardness Scale

Answer to Reading Check

The strength and geometric arrangement of the bonds between the atoms that make up a mineral's internal structure determine the hardness of a mineral.

Activity GENERAL

Guest Speaker Invite a rock or mineral collector to talk to your class. Rock and mineral collecting clubs exist in many cities around the country. Members are usually very willing to share their passion with others and to introduce others to the ins and outs of mineral collecting. The *Lapidary Journal* Web site has a page that lists local clubs by state. You could also check with a local geological survey bureau. LS **Visual/Verbal**

Discussion — General

Crystal Powers Since ancient times, crystals have been associated with magical powers. The ancient Greeks and Romans believed the future could be seen in quartz crystal balls. Emeralds were once believed to have the power to blind snakes, and rubies were thought to bring a wearer power and romance. In the 15th century, amethyst was thought to have the power to cure drunkenness. Even today, many ascribe healing powers to crystals. The Crystal Academy in Taos, New Mexico, explores the ancient art of crystal healing. Most geologists do not believe crystals have any special healing powers. Discuss crystal healing with students. What evidence would scientists need to accept that crystals have the power to heal? Have interested students research crystal healing further and report their findings to the class. **LS Interpersonal**

Math Skills

Answer

$85 \text{ g} \div 34 \text{ cm}^3 = 2.5 \text{ g/cm}^3$

Table 2 The Six Basic Crystal Systems

Isometric or Cubic System Three axes of equal length intersect at 90° angles. 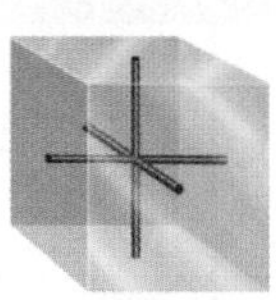	**Orthorhombic System** Three axes of unequal length intersect at 90° angles. 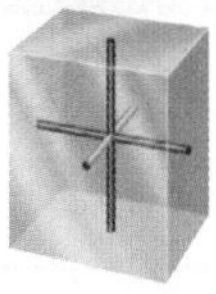
Tetragonal System Three axes intersect at 90° angles. The two horizontal axes are of equal length. The vertical axis is longer or shorter than the horizontal axes. 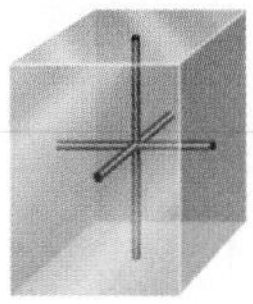	**Hexagonal System** Three horizontal axes of the same length intersect at 120° angles. The vertical axis is longer or shorter than the horizontal axes. 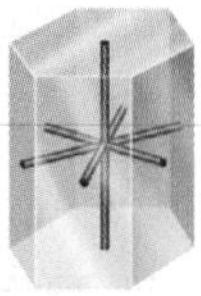
Monoclinic System Two of the three axes of unequal length intersect at 90° angles. The third axis is oblique to the others. 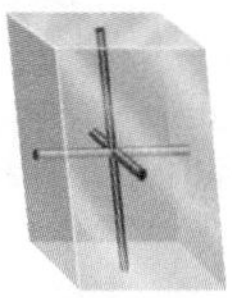	**Triclinic System** Three axes of unequal length are oblique to one another. 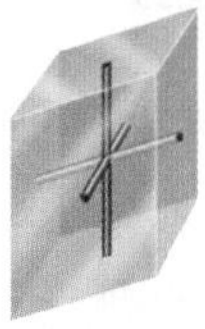

Math Skills

Calculating Density A mineral sample has a mass (m) of 85 g and a volume (V) of 34 cm^3. Use the equation below to calculate the sample's density (D).

$$D = \frac{m}{V}$$

density the ratio of the mass of a substance to the volume of the substance; commonly expressed as grams per cubic centimeter for solids and liquids and as grams per liter for gases

Crystal Shape

A mineral crystal forms in one of six basic shapes, as shown in **Table 2.** A certain mineral always has the same basic crystal system because the atoms that form its crystals always combine in the same geometric pattern. But the six basic shapes can become more complex as a result of environmental conditions during crystal growth, such as temperature and pressure.

Density

When handling equal-sized specimens of various minerals, you may notice that some feel heavier than others do. For example, a piece of galena feels heavier than a piece of quartz of the same size does. However, a more precise comparison can be made by measuring the density of a sample. **Density** is the ratio of the mass of a substance to the volume of the substance.

The density of a mineral depends on the kinds of atoms that the mineral has and on how closely the atoms are packed. Most of the common minerals in Earth's crust have densities between 2 and 3 g/cm^3. However, the densities of minerals that contain heavy metals, such as lead, uranium, gold, and silver, range from 7 to 20 g/cm^3. Thus, density helps identify heavier minerals more readily than it helps identify lighter ones.

Differentiated Instruction

Advanced Learners

Writing A mineral's habit is the way clusters of crystals grow together, creating a distinctive overall form and texture. Have students write an illustrated paper that describes some common mineral habits. **LS Verbal/Visual**

Key Resources

Technology

- Transparencies
  24 The Six Basic Crystal Systems

Special Properties of Minerals

All minerals exhibit the properties that were described earlier in this section. However, a few minerals have some additional, special properties that can help identify those minerals.

Fluorescence and Phosphorescence

The mineral calcite is usually white in ordinary light, but in ultraviolet light, calcite often appears red. This ability to glow under ultraviolet light is called *fluorescence*. Fluorescent minerals absorb ultraviolet light and then produce visible light of various colors, as shown in **Figure 4.**

When subjected to ultraviolet light, some minerals will continue to glow after the ultraviolet light is turned off. This property is called *phosphorescence*. It is useful in the mining of phosphorescent minerals such as eucryptite, which is an ore of lithium.

Chatoyancy and Asterism

In reflected light, some minerals display a silky appearance that is called *chatoyancy* (shuh TOY uhn see). This effect is also called the *cat's-eye effect*. The word *chatoyancy* comes from the French word *chat*, which means "cat," and from *oeil*, which means "eye." Chatoyancy is the result of closely packed parallel fibers within the mineral. A similar effect called *asterism* is the phenomenon in which a six-sided star shape appears when a mineral reflects light.

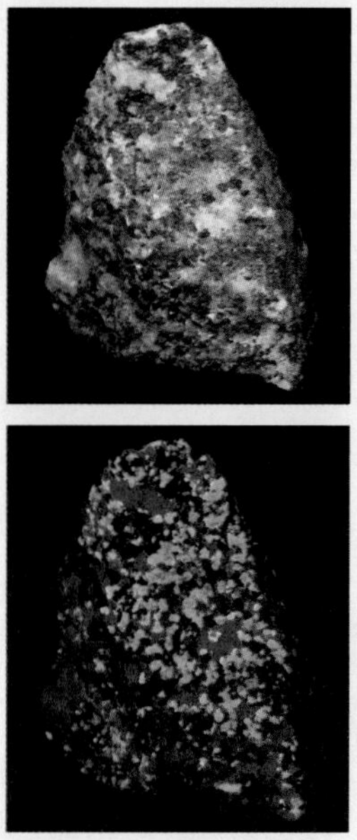

Figure 4 The fluorescent minerals calcite and willemite within this rock change colors as they are exposed to ordinary light (top) and ultraviolet light (bottom).

Reading Check **What is the difference between chatoyancy and asterism?**

Quick Lab

15 min

Determining Density

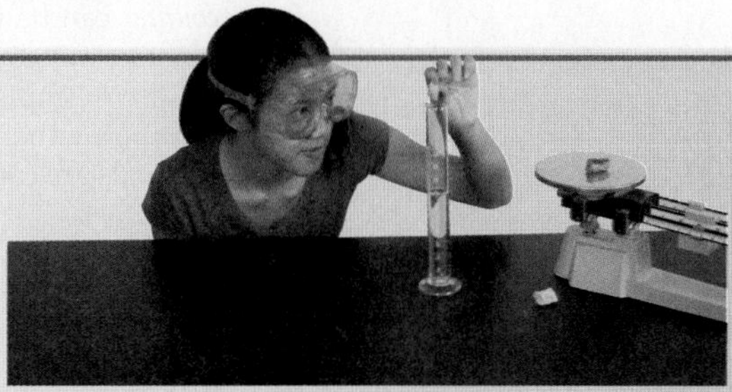

Procedure

1. Use a triple-beam balance to determine the mass of three similarly sized mineral samples that have different masses. Record the mass of each mineral sample.
2. Fill a graduated cylinder with 70 mL of water.
3. Add one mineral sample to the water in the graduated cylinder. Record the new volume after the mineral sample is added to the water.
4. Calculate the volume of the mineral sample by subtracting 70 mL from the new volume.
5. Repeat steps 3 and 4 for the other two mineral samples.
6. Convert the volume of the mineral samples that you calculated in step 4 from milliliters to cubic centimeters by using the conversion: 1 mL=1 cm^3.

Analysis

1. Calculate the density of each mineral sample by using the following equation:

   density = mass/volume

2. Compare the density of each mineral sample with the density of common minerals in Earth's crust. Compare the density of each mineral sample with minerals that contain a high percentage of heavy metals.
3. Do any of the mineral samples contain a high percentage of heavy metals? Explain your answer.

Chemistry Connection

Lighting Up Fluorescence occurs when light energy interacts with certain atoms, known as *activator elements*, in a crystal. When the atom's excited electrons fall back to their initial state, they release energy, emitting some in the form of light. Fluorescence stops once an energy source is gone. Phosphorescence continues after the light source is turned off because in some cases, excited electrons get trapped in the high-energy state. They eventually fall back to their initial energy state and give off light when they do.

Answer to Reading Check

Chatoyancy is the silky appearance of some minerals in reflected light. Asterism is the appearance of a six-sided star when a mineral reflects light.

Close

Reteaching — BASIC

Peer Reviewing Have students work in pairs to write three to five questions about the material in this section. Then, have students use their questions to quiz each other.

LS Interpersonal Co-op Learning

Quiz — GENERAL

1. What instrument can detect radioactive minerals? (Geiger counter)
2. What is the hardest substance on the Mohs scale? (diamond)
3. Amethyst is quartz with what impurities? (manganese and iron)

Quick Lab

Skills Acquired
- Collecting Data
- Classifying

Materials
- Triple-beam balance
- Mineral samples
- Graduated cylinder
- Water

Teacher's Notes: If possible, give the same specimen to more than one student and have students that have the same specimen compare observations. Students may also compare the densities they calculate with those listed in a field guide to minerals. For your records, number the samples and keep an answer key.

Answers to Analysis

1. Answers may vary depending on the samples used.
2. Answers may vary. Most common minerals have densities between 2 g/cm^3 and 3 g/cm^3. Minerals that contain heavy metals have densities between 7g/cm^3 and 20 g/cm^3.
3. Answers may vary. Mineral samples that contain a high percentage of heavy metals will have high densities.

Close, *continued*

Answers to Section Review

1. Color, streak, luster, cleavage and fracture, hardness, and density help distinguish one mineral from another.
2. metallic and nonmetallic
3. To determine hardness, scratch a mineral with the minerals on the Mohs hardness scale or with a fingernail, a penny, or a piece of glass. The hardness of the unknown mineral is greater than the hardness of a mineral it can scratch but is less than the hardness of a mineral that scratches it.
4. Color is not a very reliable clue to the identity of a mineral because small amounts of certain elements in a crystal can greatly alter color and because weathering can change a mineral's color.
5. Answers may vary but should include five of the following: fluorescence, phosphorescence, chatoyancy, asterism, double refraction, magnetism, and radioactivity.
6. Minerals that contain iron may be attracted to magnets. Some minerals, especially magnetite, act as magnets themselves.
7. The mineral is likely to be metallic because metals generally have dark streaks and high densities.
8. One could shine UV light in mines and identify places where rocks continue to glow after the light is turned off. Phosphorescent minerals could be used as a coating to make things glow in the dark.

Figure 5 Some forms of the mineral calcite exhibit double refraction when light rays enter the crystal and split.

Double Refraction

Light rays bend as they pass through transparent minerals. This bending of light rays as they pass from one substance, such as air, to another, such as a mineral, is called *refraction*. Crystals of calcite and some other transparent minerals bend light in such a way that they produce a double image of any object viewed through them, as shown in **Figure 5.** This property is called *double refraction*. Double refraction takes place because light rays are split into two parts as they enter the crystal.

Magnetism

Magnets may attract small particles of some minerals that contain iron. Those minerals are also sometimes magnetic. In general, nonsilicate minerals that contain iron, such as magnetite, are more likely to be magnetic than other nonsilicate minerals are. Lodestone is a form of magnetite. Like a bar magnet, some pieces of lodestone have a north pole at one end and a south pole at the other. The needles of the first magnetic compasses were made of tiny slivers of lodestone.

Radioactivity

Some minerals have a property known as *radioactivity*. The arrangement of protons and neutrons in the nuclei of some atoms is unstable. Radioactivity results as unstable nuclei decay over time into stable nuclei by releasing particles and energy. A *Geiger counter* can be used to detect the released particles and, thus, to identify minerals that are radioactive. Uranium, U, and radium, Ra, are examples of radioactive elements. Pitchblende is the most common mineral that contains uranium. Other uranium-bearing minerals are carnotite and autunite.

Section 2 Review

Key Ideas

1. **Describe** seven physical properties that help distinguish one mineral from another.
2. **Identify** the two main types of luster.
3. **Summarize** how you would determine the hardness of an unidentified mineral sample.
4. **Explain** why color is an unreliable clue to the identity of a mineral.
5. **List** five special properties that may help to identify certain minerals.
6. **Explain** how magnetism can be useful for identifying minerals.

Critical Thinking

7. **Evaluating Data** An unknown mineral has a black streak and a density of 18 g/cm^3. Is the mineral more likely to be metallic or nonmetallic?
8. **Analyzing Methods** Explain how phosphorescence is helpful in mining eucryptite. Describe other ways in which phosphorescent minerals might be used.

Concept Mapping

9. Use the following terms to create a concept map: *luster, streak, fracture, hardness, Mohs hardness scale, streak plate, nonmetallic luster, metallic luster,* and *conchoidal fracture.*

9. A mineral can be identified by using *luster*, which can be either *metallic luster* or *nonmetallic luster; streak*, which can be tested on a *streak plate; fracture*, which might be *conchoidal fracture*; and *hardness*, which is assessed by using the *Mohs hardness scale.*

Differentiated Instruction

Alternative Assessment

Crystal Models Have students build models of the six crystal shapes to understand the symmetrical features of crystals. For example, they could build stick models showing the axes of symmetry, clay models of the crystal shapes, 3-dimensional paper models, or some other model of their own design.
LS Visual/Kinesthetic

Why It Matters

Know by the Glow

FORENSIC SCIENCE

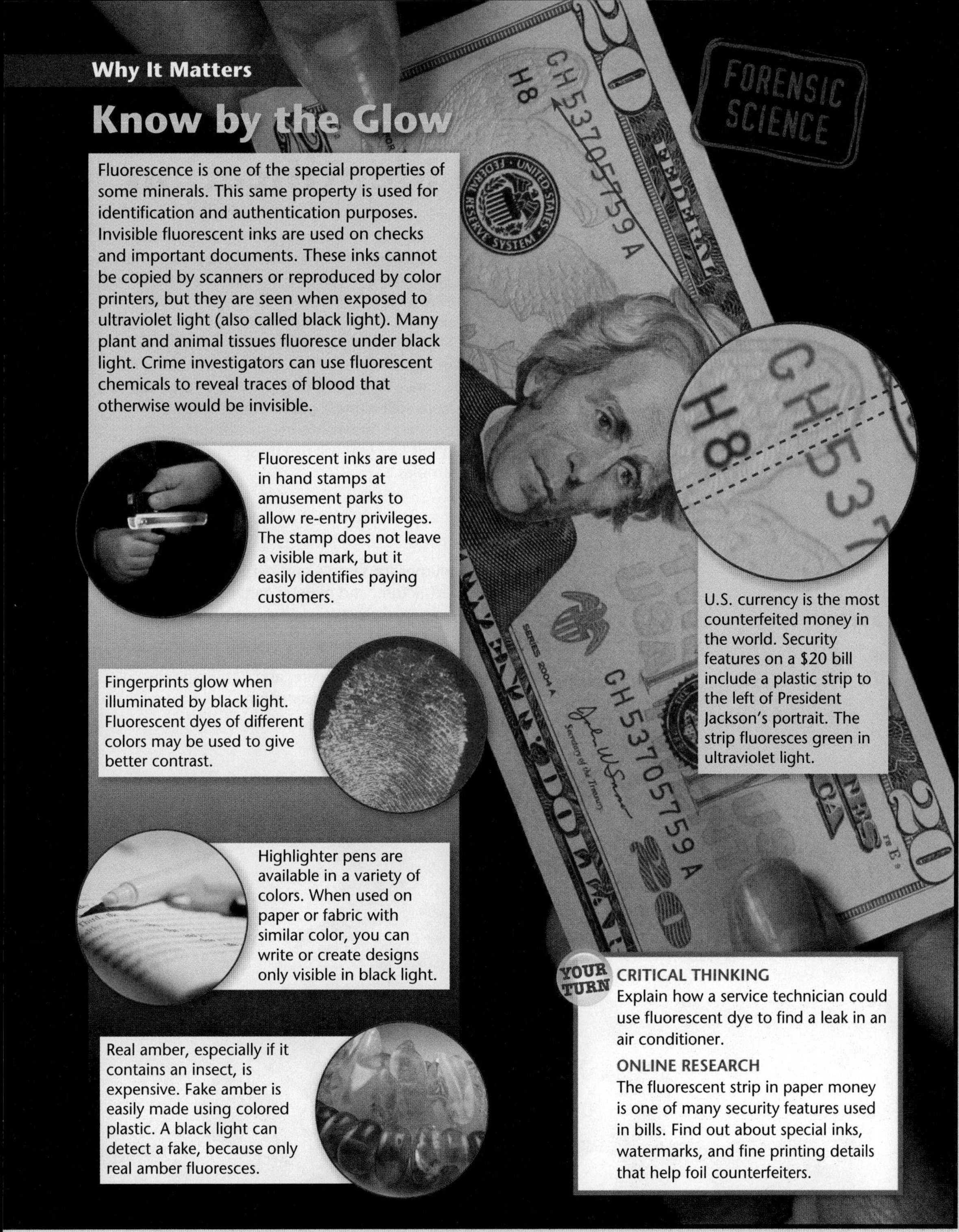

Fluorescence is one of the special properties of some minerals. This same property is used for identification and authentication purposes. Invisible fluorescent inks are used on checks and important documents. These inks cannot be copied by scanners or reproduced by color printers, but they are seen when exposed to ultraviolet light (also called black light). Many plant and animal tissues fluoresce under black light. Crime investigators can use fluorescent chemicals to reveal traces of blood that otherwise would be invisible.

Fluorescent inks are used in hand stamps at amusement parks to allow re-entry privileges. The stamp does not leave a visible mark, but it easily identifies paying customers.

Fingerprints glow when illuminated by black light. Fluorescent dyes of different colors may be used to give better contrast.

Highlighter pens are available in a variety of colors. When used on paper or fabric with similar color, you can write or create designs only visible in black light.

Real amber, especially if it contains an insect, is expensive. Fake amber is easily made using colored plastic. A black light can detect a fake, because only real amber fluoresces.

U.S. currency is the most counterfeited money in the world. Security features on a $20 bill include a plastic strip to the left of President Jackson's portrait. The strip fluoresces green in ultraviolet light.

YOUR TURN

CRITICAL THINKING

Explain how a service technician could use fluorescent dye to find a leak in an air conditioner.

ONLINE RESEARCH

The fluorescent strip in paper money is one of many security features used in bills. Find out about special inks, watermarks, and fine printing details that help foil counterfeiters.

Why It Matters

Know by the Glow

George Stokes coined the word "fluorescence" in 1852 to describe the emission of light he observed from fluorspar (calcium fluoride) and other minerals. Stokes also found that fluorescent materials absorb light at one wavelength and re-emit the energy at a longer wavelength. The absorbed light is often in the ultraviolet, and the emitted light is characteristic of the material illuminated. Inks that fluoresce are usually clear liquids, and thus invisible in ordinary light—and therefore undetectable by ordinary scanners. Their use adds a level of security to checks, bonds, and paper currency. Many biological tissues fluoresce, which is the basis of fluorescent microscopy that allows scientists to identify specific areas of cells. On TV shows, crime scene investigators are often seen using an ultraviolet light to detect bodily fluids.

Answers to Your Turn

Critical Thinking A service technician might add a fluorescent dye to the coolant in an air conditioner and illuminate the coils and compressor with an ultraviolet light to find the source of a leak.

Online Research Answers will vary. Paper currency uses many methods to foil counterfeiters, including magnetic and fluorescent inks, watermarks, security threads, and color-shifting ink. Students should describe one or more of these features. For example, the "20" in the lower right corner on the face of a twenty dollar bill changes color from copper to green when the bill is tilted. The bill is micro-printed with extremely fine lines and details that are impossible to duplicate using an ordinary scanner and printer.

Skills Practice Lab

Time Required
one 45-minute class period

Lab Ratings
EASY → HARD

Teacher Preparation: 2
Student Setup: 1
Concept Level: 2
Cleanup: 1

Skills Acquired
- Observing
- Measuring
- Collecting Data
- Organizing and Analyzing Data
- Identifying and Recognizing Patterns

Scientific Methods
In this lab, students will
- Make Observations
- Analyze Results
- Draw Conclusions
- Communicate Results

Materials
The materials listed on this page are enough for groups of two to four students.

Skills Practice Lab

45 min

Mineral Identification

A mineral identification key can be used to compare the properties of minerals so that unknown mineral samples can be identified. Mineral properties that are often used in mineral identification keys are color, hardness, streak, luster, cleavage, and fracture. Hardness is determined by a scratch test. The Mohs hardness scale classifies minerals from 1 (soft) to 10 (hard). Streak is the color of a mineral in a finely powdered form. The streak shows less variation than the color of a sample does and thus is more useful in identification. The luster of a mineral is either metallic (having an appearance of metals) or nonmetallic. Cleavage is the tendency of a mineral to split along a plane. Planes may be in several directions. Other minerals break into irregular fragments in a process called *fracture*. In this lab, you will use these properties to classify several mineral samples.

What You'll Do
- **Identify** several unknown mineral samples.
- **Evaluate** which properties of minerals are most useful in identifying mineral samples.

What You'll Need
file, steel
Guide to Common Minerals (in the Reference Tables section of the Appendix)
hand lens
mineral samples (5)
penny, copper
square, glass
streak plate

Safety

Procedure

1. Make a table with columns for sample number, color/luster, hardness, streak, cleavage/fracture, and mineral name.
2. Observe and record in your table the color of each mineral sample. Note whether the luster of each mineral is metallic or nonmetallic.
3. Rub each mineral against the streak plate, and determine the color of the mineral's streak. Record your observations.

Step 4

Tips and Tricks
You may want to have a field guide to minerals available for student use. Depending on the samples you provide, you could also have students perform other tests such as for magnetism, fluorescence/phosphorescence, or double refraction. Once students have tentatively identified their samples, have them compare their results with other groups and discuss any differences they find.

Sample number	Color/ luster	Hardness	Streak	Cleavage/ fracture	Mineral name
1					
2					
3					
4					
5					

4. Using a fingernail, copper penny, glass square, and steel file, test each mineral to determine its hardness based on the Mohs hardness scale. Arrange the minerals in order of hardness. Record your observations in your table.
5. Determine whether the surface of each mineral displays cleavage and/or fracture. Record your observations.
6. Use the Guide to Common Minerals in the Reference Tables section of the Appendix to help you identify the mineral samples. Remember that samples of the same mineral will vary somewhat.

Analysis

1. **Analyzing Results** For each mineral, compare the streak with the color of the mineral. Which minerals have the same color as their streak? Which do not?
2. **Classifying Information** Of the mineral samples you identified, how many were silicate minerals? How many were nonsilicate minerals?
3. **Analyzing Methods** Did you find any properties that were especially useful or especially not useful in identifying each sample? Identify these properties, and explain why they were or were not useful.
4. **Evaluating Methods** If you had to write a manual to explain, step by step, how to identify minerals, in what order would you test different properties? Explain your reasoning.

Extension

Understanding Relationships Corundum, rubies, and sapphires have different colors but are considered to be the same mineral. Diamonds and graphite are made of the element carbon but are not considered to be the same mineral. Research these minerals, and explain why they are classified in this way.

Answers to Analysis

1. Answers may vary depending on the samples provided to the students. In general, nonmetals have a streak similar to their color, while metals show a dark streak.
2. Answers may vary depending on samples provided to students.
3. Answers may vary depending on samples provided to students and students' observations. Accept all reasonable answers.
4. Answers may vary. Accept all reasonable answers.

Answer to Extension

Graphite and diamond are both composed of carbon atoms, but have different crystalline structures. They are known as polymorphs. In graphite, each carbon atom bonds to three other carbon atoms to form 2-dimensional sheets that are weakly bonded together. The weak bonding gives graphite flexibility and lubricating properties. In diamond, each carbon atom bonds to four other carbon atoms in a strong three-dimensional network, giving diamond its incredible strength and thermal stability. Corundum, ruby, and sapphire are all considered the same mineral, even though they are different colors, because they have the same chemical composition (Al_2O_3) and the same crystalline structure (trigonal). The color differences result from impurities in the crystal. Rubies are corundum with trace amounts of chromium, while sapphires are corundum with trace amounts of iron and titanium.

Rock and Mineral Production in the United States

Internet Activity GENERAL

Mining Impacts Mining can have serious effects on the environment. Have interested students investigate the past and present environmental effects of mining in your state or a nearby state. They may investigate reclamation efforts or the use of technology at current mines. Have students write a persuasive essay supporting or opposing continued mining in your region based on their findings. A worksheet designed to direct student research on this topic can be found in the **Chapter Resource File** booklet or by visiting www.thinkcentral.com and entering the keyword **HQXMINX.**

LS Logical/Interpersonal

Answers to Map Skills Activity

1. stone
2. (5.1 + 8.6 + 2.9 + 2.3) ÷ 55.6 × 100 = 34%; AK, AZ, CO, ID, MO, MT, NM, NV, SD, UT, and WA
3. Answers may vary.
4. (13.1 + 7.9) ÷ 55.6 × 100 = 38%.
5. the Rocky Mountains

MAPS in Action

Rock and Mineral Production in the United States

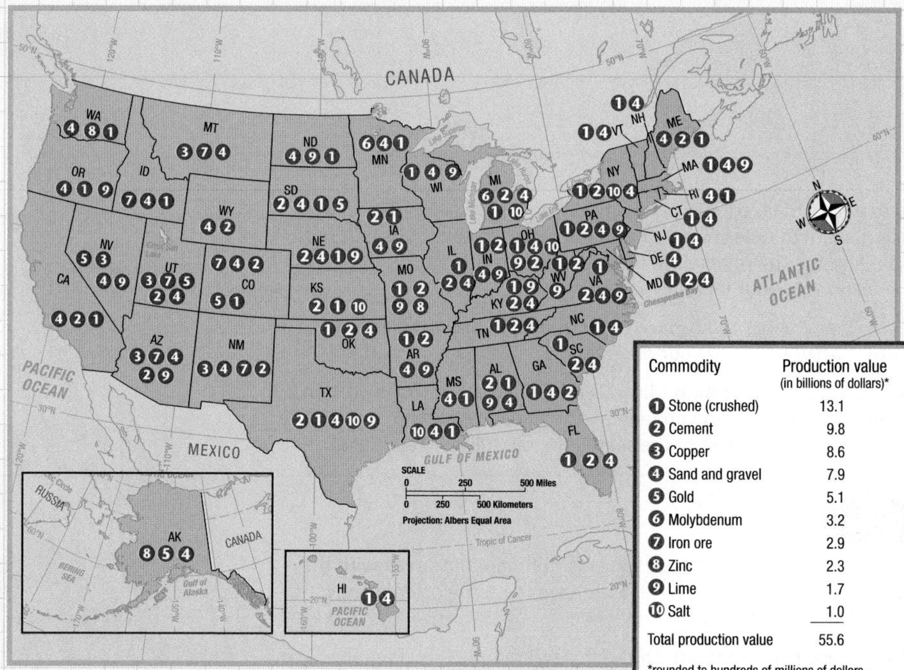

Commodity	Production value (in billions of dollars)*
❶ Stone (crushed)	13.1
❷ Cement	9.8
❸ Copper	8.6
❹ Sand and gravel	7.9
❺ Gold	5.1
❻ Molybdenum	3.2
❼ Iron ore	2.9
❽ Zinc	2.3
❾ Lime	1.7
❿ Salt	1.0
Total production value	55.6

*rounded to hundreds of millions of dollars

Map Skills Activity

This map shows the distribution of the top 10 rock and mineral commodities produced in the United States. The key provides production values for these commodities. Use the map to answer the questions below.

1. **Using a Key** According to the map, which commodity has the highest production value?
2. **Evaluating Data** Gold, copper, iron ore, and zinc are metals in the top 10 mineral commodities produced. What percentage of the total production value do these metals represent? Which of the states produce these metals?
3. **Using a Key** Find your state on the map. Which of the top 10 mineral commodities are produced in your state?
4. **Evaluating Data** Stone, sand, and gravel are collectively known as *aggregates*. What percentage of the total production value of the 10 commodities listed do aggregates represent?
5. **Analyzing Relationships** According to the map, the states that produce enough iron ore to make the top-10 list are located in the western part of the United States. What geologic feature do most of these states share?

Key Resources

Technology

- Transparencies
  25 Rock and Mineral Production in the United States

Chapter 5 **Summary**

THINK central SUPER SUMMARY Keyword: HQXMINS

Key Ideas

Section 1

What Is a Mineral?

- A mineral is a natural, usually inorganic solid that has a characteristic chemical composition, an orderly internal structure, and a characteristic set of physical properties.
- The two main types of minerals, silicates and nonsilicates, are classified based on differences in their composition. Silicates contain compounds of silicon and oxygen; nonsilicates do not.
- Six types of silicate crystalline structures are isolated tetrahedral, ring, single-chain, double-chain, sheet, and framework.
- The three common nonsilicate crystalline structures commonly include cubes, hexagonal prisms, and irregular masses, but may also include tetrahedrons.

Key Terms

mineral, p. 111
silicate mineral, p. 112
nonsilicate mineral, p. 113
crystal, p. 114
silicon-oxygen tetrahedron, p. 114

Section 2

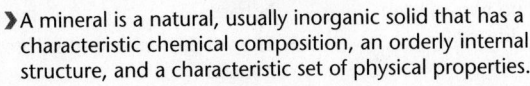

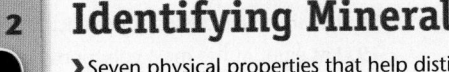

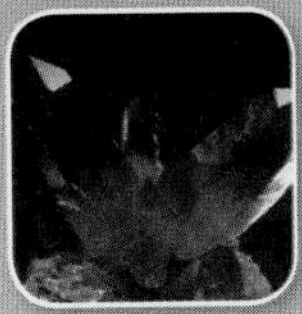

Identifying Minerals

- Seven physical properties that help distinguish one mineral from another are color, streak, luster, cleavage and fracture, hardness, crystal shape, and density.
- Special properties that can aid in identifying certain minerals include fluorescence and phosphorescence, chatoyancy and asterism, double refraction, magnetism, and radioactivity.

Key Terms

mineralogist, p. 117
streak, p. 118
luster, p. 118
cleavage, p. 118
fracture, p. 118
Mohs hardness scale, p. 119
density, p. 120

Chapter Summary

Using THINK central Resources

Super Summary

Have students connect the major concepts in this chapter through an interactive Super Summary. Visit **www.thinkcentral.com** and type in the keyword **HQXMINS** to access the Super Summary for this chapter.

Differentiated Instruction

Alternative Assessment

Mineral Displays Assign each student one of the classes of silicate or nonsilicate minerals to investigate. Have them create a poster that displays three to five of the common minerals in that class. The display should identify the chemical composition and structure of the minerals the student chose; each mineral's major characteristics and special features, if any; uses of the minerals; and anything else that might be of interest, such as origin of mineral names. Display the posters around your classroom and allow students to view each other's work. **LS Visual**

Chapter Review

Assignment Guide	
Section	**Questions**
1	2, 3, 6, 7, 10–13, 18–27, 31, 32, 35
2	4, 5, 8, 9, 14–17, 28, 29, 33
1 and 2	30, 34, 36–38

Reading Toolbox

1. Answers may vary. Students' notes should appear similar to the example shown on page 110. The notes in the second column should be written in students' own words.

Using Key Terms

2–9. Answers may vary but should show that students understand the definitions of and differences between key terms.

Understanding Key Ideas

10. a 14. a
11. b 15. b
12. b 16. b
13. d 17. c

Short Answer

18. carbonates, containing the CO_3 group; halides, consisting of chlorine or fluorine most commonly combined with sodium, potassium, or calcium; native elements, elements uncombined with other elements; oxides, compounds containing oxygen combined with elements other than silicon; sulfates containing the SO_4 group; and sulfides, compounds of elements combined with sulfur

Chapter 5 Review

1. **Two-Column Notes** You already have two-column notes for the Key Ideas of Section 1. Complete your notes for the whole chapter by creating two-column notes for the Key Ideas of Section 2.

READING TOOLBOX

USING KEY TERMS

Use each of the following terms in a separate sentence.

2. *silicon-oxygen tetrahedron*
3. *mineral*
4. *Mohs hardness scale*
5. *cleavage*

For each pair of terms, explain how the meanings of the terms differ.

6. *mineral* and *crystal*
7. *silicate mineral* and *nonsilicate mineral*
8. *luster* and *streak*
9. *fluorescence* and *phosphorescence*

UNDERSTANDING KEY IDEAS

10. The most common silicate minerals are the
    a. feldspars. **c.** carbonates.
    b. halides. **d.** sulfates.
11. Ninety-six percent of Earth's crust is made up of
    a. sulfur and lead.
    b. silicate minerals.
    c. copper and aluminum.
    d. nonsilicate minerals.
12. An example of a mineral that has a basic structure consisting of isolated tetrahedra linked by atoms of other elements is
    a. mica. **c.** quartz.
    b. olivine. **d.** feldspar.
13. When two single chains of tetrahedra bond to each other, the result is called a
    a. single-chain silicate.
    b. sheet silicate.
    c. framework silicate.
    d. double-chain silicate.
14. The words *waxy, pearly,* and *dull* describe a mineral's
    a. luster. **c.** streak.
    b. hardness. **d.** fluorescence.
15. The words *uneven* and *splintery* describe a mineral's
    a. cleavage. **c.** hardness.
    b. fracture. **d.** luster.
16. The ratio of a mineral's mass to its volume is the mineral's
    a. atomic weight. **c.** mass.
    b. density. **d.** weight.
17. Double refraction is a property of some crystals of
    a. mica. **c.** calcite.
    b. feldspar. **d.** galena.

SHORT ANSWER

18. List six major classes of nonsilicate minerals.
19. List eight of the most common rock-forming minerals.
20. Why do minerals that have the nonsilicate crystalline structure called *closest packing* have high density?
21. Which of the two main groups of minerals is more abundant in Earth's crust?
22. Which of the following mineral groups, if any, contain silicon: carbonates, halides, or sulfides?
23. Describe the tetrahedral arrangement of olivine.
24. Summarize the characteristics that a substance must have to be classified as a mineral.
25. How many oxygen ions and silicon ions are in a silicon-oxygen tetrahedron?

CRITICAL THINKING

26. **Classifying Information** Natural gas is a substance that occurs naturally in Earth's crust. Is it a mineral? Explain your answer.
27. **Making Comparisons** Which of the following are you more likely to find in Earth's crust: the silicates feldspar and quartz or the nonsilicates copper and iron? Explain your answer.

19. quartz, orthoclase, plagioclase, muscovite, biotite, calcite, dolomite, halite, gypsum, and ferromagnesian minerals
20. Nonsilicates that have the closest-packing structure have high densities because the atoms are packed as closely together as possible, and thus, the large mass takes up the least space or volume.
21. silicates
22. none; Carbonates, halides, and sulfides are all nonsilicates.
23. Olivine is composed of isolated SiO_4 tetrahedra. The oxygen atoms of the tetrahedra bond to magnesium and iron atoms.
24. To be classified as a mineral, a substance must be an inorganic, naturally occurring crystalline solid that has a consistent chemical composition.
25. There are four oxygen atoms and one silicon atom in each silicon-oxygen tetrahedron.

28. **Applying Ideas** Iron pyrite, FeS_2, is called *fool's gold* because it looks a lot like gold. What simple test could you use to determine whether a mineral sample is gold or pyrite? Explain what the test would show.

29. **Drawing Conclusions** Can you determine conclusively that an unknown substance contains magnetite by using only a magnet? Explain your answer.

CONCEPT MAPPING

30. Use the following terms to create a concept map: *mineral, silicate mineral, nonsilicate mineral, silicon-oxygen tetrahedron, color, density, crystal shape, magnetism, native element, sulfate,* and *phosphorescence.*

MATH SKILLS

Math Skills

31. **Applying Quantities** Hematite, Fe_2O_3, has three atoms of oxygen and two atoms of iron in each molecule. What percentage of the atoms in a hematite molecule are oxygen atoms?

32. **Making Calculations** A sample of olivine contains 3.4 billion silicon-oxygen tetrahedra. How many oxygen atoms are in the sample?

33. **Applying Quantities** A mineral sample has a mass of 51 g and a volume of 15 cm^3. What is the density of the mineral sample?

WRITING SKILLS

34. **Writing from Research** Use the Internet or your school library to find a mineral map of the United States. Write a brief report that outlines how the minerals in your state are discovered and mined.

35. **Communicating Main Ideas** Write and illustrate an essay that explains how six different crystal structures form from silicon-oxygen tetrahedra.

INTERPRETING GRAPHICS

This table provides information about the eight most abundant elements in Earth's crust. Use the table to answer the questions that follow.

The Eight Most Abundant Chemicals in Earth's Crust

Element	Chemical symbol	Weight (% of Earth's crust)	Volume (% of Earth's crust)*
Oxygen	O	46.60	93.8
Silicon	Si	27.72	0.9
Aluminum	Al	8.13	0.5
Iron	Fe	5.00	0.4
Calcium	Ca	3.63	1.0
Sodium	Na	2.83	1.3
Potassium	K	2.59	1.8
Magnesium	Mg	2.09	0.3
	Total	98.59	100.0

*The volume of Earth's crust comprised by all other elements is so small that it is essentially 0% when the numbers are rounded to the nearest tenth of a percent.

36. What percentage of the weight of Earth's crust is made of silicon?

37. Oxygen makes up 93.8% of Earth's crust by volume, but oxygen is only 46.60% of Earth's crust by weight. How is this possible?

38. By comparing the volume and weight percentages of aluminum and calcium, determine which element has the higher density.

Chapter Review

Critical Thinking

26. Natural gas is not a mineral because it is not a crystalline solid and because it is usually organic in origin.
27. You are more likely to find feldspar and quartz in Earth's crust because silicates make up 96% of the crust. Feldspar and quartz alone make up over 50% of the crust.
28. Streak and density would be very different for gold and pyrite. Pyrite has a green to black streak while gold has a gold streak. Gold is also much denser than pyrite is.
29. Because small particles of some minerals that contain iron may be attracted to a magnet, you cannot conclusively determine that an unknown substance contains magnetite.

Concept Mapping

30. Answers may vary but should include all of the terms listed. Sample answers appear at the end of this unit on page 195D.

Math Skills

31. 3 out of 5 atoms in a hematite molecule are oxygen.
$3/5 \times 100 = 60\%$
32. Olivine is composed of isolated tetrahedra, so each tetrahedron has 4 oxygen atoms; 3.4 billion tetrahedra × 4 O atoms/tetrahedron = 13.6 billion O atoms.
33. Density = mass / volume = 51 g ÷ 15 cm^3 = 3.4 g/cm^3

Writing Skills

34. Answers may vary. Accept all reasonable answers.
35. Answers may vary. Accept all reasonable answers.

Interpreting Graphics

36. 27.72%
37. Oxygen is not very dense, so it can take up a large volume without having a lot of weight.
38. Aluminum has a higher density than calcium does.

Estimated Time

To give students practice under more realistic testing conditions, allow them 30 minutes to answer all of the questions in this practice test.

Test Doctor

Question 1 Answer C is correct. An organic substance is one that is made up of living things or the remains of living things. Coal is made up of the remains of plants, so it is organic. Minerals are inorganic. Therefore, coal is organic and not a mineral. Students who miss this question may need to review the properties of minerals.

Question 3 Each mineral has specific properties that are a result of its chemical composition and crystal structure. These properties are color, streak, luster, cleavage and fracture, hardness, crystal shape, and density.

Question 11 Full-credit answers should include the following points:

- most early metals used by humans were soft metals that could be easily worked and shaped
- copper is relatively abundant in many areas. It is easy to mine and refine. Copper is a soft metal that is easily bent and shaped
- copper resists corrosion and can be polished to a shining finish
- copper weapons and tools were superior in strength and durability to previous tools

Chapter 5 Standardized Test Prep

Understanding Concepts

Directions (1–5): For each question, write on a separate sheet of paper the letter of the correct answer.

1. Coal is
   A. organic and a mineral.
   B. inorganic and a mineral.
   C. organic and not a mineral.
   D. inorganic and not a mineral.

2. Which of the following is one of the rock-forming minerals that make up 90% of the mass of Earth's crust?
   F. quartz
   G. fluorite
   H. copper
   I. talc

3. In many cases, minerals can be identified by all of the following properties *except*
   A. specimen color.
   B. specimen streak.
   C. specimen hardness.
   D. specimen luster.

4. All minerals in Earth's crust
   F. have a crystalline structure.
   G. are classified as ring silicates.
   H. are classified as pyroxenes or amphiboles.
   I. have no silicon in their tetrahedral structure.

5. Which mineral can be scratched by a fingernail, which has a hardness of 2.5 on the Mohs scale?
   A. diamond
   B. quartz
   C. topaz
   D. talc

Directions (6–8): For each question, write a short response.

6. Carbonates, halides, native elements, oxides, sulfates, and sulfides are classes of what mineral group?

7. What mineral is made up of *only* the elements oxygen and silicon?

8. What property is a mineral said to have when a person is able to view double images through it?

Reading Skills

Directions (9–11): Read the passage below. Then, answer the questions.

Native American Copper

In North America, copper was mined at least 6,700 years ago by the Native Americans who lived on Michigan's upper peninsula. Much of this mining took place on Isle Royale, an island located in the waters of Lake Superior.

These ancient people removed copper from the rock by using stone hammers and wedges. The rock was sometimes heated to make breaking it easier. Copper that was mined was used to make a wide variety of items for the Native Americans including jewelry, tools, weapons, fish hooks, and other objects. These objects were often marked with intricate designs. The copper mined at the Lake Superior site was traded over long distances along ancient trade routes. Copper objects from the region have been found in Ohio, Florida, the Southwest, and the Northwest.

9. According to the passage, Native Americans who mined copper
   F. used the mineral as a form of currency when buying goods from other tribes.
   G. traded copper objects with other Native American tribes over a large area.
   H. used the mineral to produce vastly superior weapons and armor.
   I. sold it to the Native Americans living around Lake Superior.

10. Which of the following statements can be inferred from the information in the passage?
    A. Copper is a very strong metal and can be forged into extremely strong items.
    B. Copper mining in the ancient world was only common in North America.
    C. Copper is a useful metal that can be forged into a wide variety of goods.
    D. Copper is a weak metal, and no items made by the ancient Native Americans remain.

11. What are some properties of copper that might have made the metal useful to Native Americans?

Question 13 Full-credit answers should include the following points:

- by weight, oxygen and silicon make up 74.3% of Earth's crust. Minerals that contain these elements are silicate minerals, which are the most abundant minerals in Earth's crust
- however, silicate minerals may also contain additional elements. These additional elements make the total weight of silicate minerals greater than the total weight of the two base elements of oxygen and silicon
- the silicate mineral quartz is made up of only oxygen and silicon, but other silicate minerals contain one or more other elements

Question 15 Full-credit answers should include the following points:

- olivines, pyroxenes, amphiboles, and biotite are ferromagnesian minerals
- ferromagnesian minerals are rich in both iron (Fe) and magnesium (Mg)
- due to the presence of these metallic elements, the minerals formed are often dark in color
- metallic lusters and high densities are common features of ferromagnesian minerals
- often, due to the high iron content, such minerals are also magnetic

Interpreting Graphics

Directions (12–15): For each question below, record the correct answer on a separate sheet of paper.

Base your answers to questions 12 and 13 on the figure below, which shows the abundance of various elements in Earth's crust.

Elements in Earth's Crust

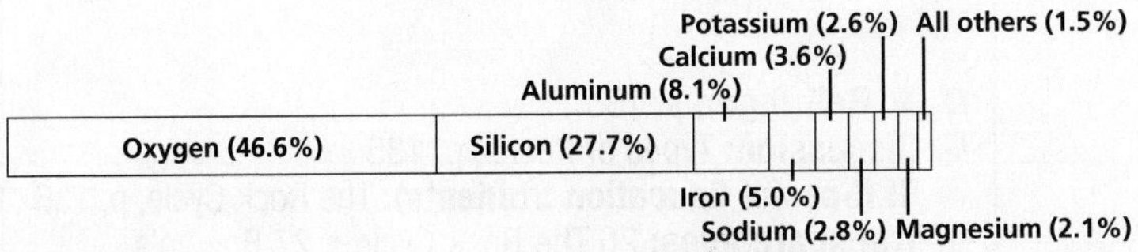

12. Which of these elements combines with oxygen to form hematite?

F. calcium
G. aluminum
H. sodium
I. iron

13. Silicate minerals make up about 95% of Earth's crust. However, the elements present in all minerals in this group, oxygen and silicon, make up a significantly smaller percentage of the weight of Earth's crust. How can this discrepancy be explained?

Base your answers to questions 14 and 15 on the table below, which provides information about silicate minerals.

Common Silicates

Mineral	Idealized formula	Cleavage
Olivine	$(Mg,Fe)_2SiO_4$	none
Pyroxene group	$(Mg,Fe)SiO_3$	two planes at right angles
Amphibole group	$Ca_2(Mg,Fe)_5Si_8O_{22}(OH)_2$	two planes at 60° and 120°
Micas, biotite	$K(Mg,Fe)_3AlSi_3O_{10}(OH)_2$	one plane
Micas, muscovite	$KAl_2(AlSi_3O_{10})(OH)_2$	one plane
Feldspars, orthoclase	$KAlSi_3O_8$	two planes at 90°
Feldspars, plagioclase	$(Ca,Na)AlSi_3O_8$	two planes at 90°
Quartz	SiO_2	none

14. How is the cleavage of amphibole minerals similar to that of feldspar minerals?

A. Both have two planes.
B. Both have one plane.
C. Both cleave at 60°.
D. Both cleave at 90°.

15. Which minerals are ferromagnesian? How can you identify these minerals? Predict how the chemical composition of ferromagnesian minerals affects the minerals' density and magnetic properties.

Test Tip

If a question or an answer choice contains an unfamiliar term, try to break the word into parts to determine its meaning.

Using THINK central Resources

State Resources

- For specific resources for your state, visit www.thinkcentral.com and type in the keyword **HSHSTR.**

Answers

Understanding Concepts

1. C
2. F
3. A
4. F
5. D
6. nonsilicate minerals
7. quartz
8. double refraction

Reading Skills

9. G
10. C
11. Answers may vary. See Test Doctor for a detailed scoring rubric.

Interpreting Graphics

12. I
13. Answers may vary. See Test Doctor for a detailed scoring rubric.
14. A
15. Answers may vary. See Test Doctor for a detailed scoring rubric.

Chapter Planner 6 Rocks

	Standards	Teach Key Ideas
Chapter Opener, pp. 132–133 **45 min.**	National Science Education Standards	
Section 1 Rocks and the Rock Cycle pp. 135–138 **45 min.** ❯ Three Major Types of Rock ❯ The Rock Cycle ❯ Properties of Rocks	ES 2b	■ ◆ **Bellringer,** p. 135 ■ **Discussion:** Types of Rocks, p. 135 ■ **DI (Special Education Students):** The Rock Cycle, p. 136 ◆ **Transparencies:** 26 The Rock Cycle • 27 Bowen's Reaction Series ▲ **Visual Concepts:** Types of Rock • Formation of Rock Types • Rock Cycle
Section 2 Igneous Rock pp. 139–144 **45 min.** ❯ The Formation of Magma ❯ Textures of Igneous Rocks ❯ Composition of Igneous Rocks ❯ Intrusive Igneous Rock ❯ Extrusive Igneous Rock	ES 2b	■ ◆ **Bellringer,** p. 139 ■ **Discussion:** Hand Samples, p. 139 ■ **Demonstration:** Partial Freezing, p. 140 ■ **DI (Struggling Readers):** Reading Organizer, p. 141 ■ **DI (English Learners):** Vocabulary, p. 143 ◆ **Transparency:** 28 Partial Melting and Fractional Crystallization ▲ **Visual Concepts:** Magma • Igneous Rock Texture • Intrusive Igneous Rock Formations • Comparing Intrusive and Extrusive Igneous Rock
Section 3 Sedimentary Rock pp. 145–150 **45 min.** ❯ Formation of Sedimentary Rocks ❯ Chemical Sedimentary Rock ❯ Organic Sedimentary Rock ❯ Clastic Sedimentary Rock ❯ Characteristics of Clastic Sediments ❯ Sedimentary Rock Features	ES 2b	■ ◆ **Bellringer,** p. 145 ■ **Demonstration:** Sedimentation, p. 145 ■ **Discussion:** Comprehension Check, p. 147 ■ **DI (English Learners):** Paired Summarizing, p. 147 ■ **DI (Special Education Students):** Sorting, p. 148 ◆ **Transparency:** 29 Organic Limestone Formation ▲ **Visual Concepts:** Sedimentary Rock Cycle • Types of Sedimentary Rock
Section 4 Metamorphic Rock pp. 151–154 **45 min.** ❯ Formation of Metamorphic Rocks ❯ Classification of Metamorphic Rocks	ES 2b	■ ◆ **Bellringer,** p. 151 ■ **Demonstration:** Metamorphism, p. 151 ■ **DI (Advanced Learners):** Anticipation Guide, p. 152 ◆ **Transparency:** 30 Indicators of Metamorphic Conditions ▲ **Visual Concepts:** Comparing Contact and Regional Metamorphism
Chapter Wrap-Up, pp. 159–163 **90 min.**		**Chapter Summary,** p. 159 ◆ **Transparency:** 31 Geologic Map of Virginia

CHAPTER Fast Track *To shorten instruction because of time limitations, omit the Chapter Lab.*

See also PowerNotes® Presentations

Key
Teacher's Edition ■ Teaching Transparencies ◆
Chapter Resource File ● Online Edition ▲

All resources listed below are also available on the **Teacher One Stop™.**

Why It Matters	Hands-On	Skills Development	Assessment
■ **Chapter Overview,** p. 132 ■ **Using the Figure:** Eagletail Peak, p. 132	**Inquiry Lab:** Sedimentary Sandwich, p. 133	**Reading Toolbox,** p. 134	
■ **Section Overview,** p. 135 ■ **Using the Figure:** The Rock Cycle, p. 136 **Lunar Rocks,** p. 136		**Reading Toolbox:** Chain-of-Events Chart, p. 137	**Reading Check,** p. 137 **Section Review,** p. 138 ■ **Reteaching,** p. 137 ■ **Quiz,** p. 137 ■ **DI (Alternative Assessment):** Rock Crystallization, p. 138 ● **Section Quiz**
■ **Section Overview,** p. 139 ■ **Using the Figure:** Fractional Crystallization, p. 140 ■ **Geology Connection:** Information from Igneous Rocks, p. 141 ■ **Using the Figure:** Intrusive Igneous Structures, p. 143	**Quick Lab:** Crystal Formation, p. 140 ■ **Group Activity:** Poster Project, p. 142	**Reading Toolbox:** Pyramid FoldNote, p. 142	**Reading Check,** p. 141 **Reading Check,** p. 143 **Section Review,** p. 144 ■ **Reteaching,** p. 143 ■ **Quiz,** p. 143 ■ **DI (Alternative Assessment):** Travel Brochures, p. 144 ● **Section Quiz**
■ **Section Overview,** p. 145 ■ **Using the Figure:** Organic Limestone Formation, p. 146	● **Inquiry Lab:** Sorting Sediments **Quick Lab:** Graded Bedding, p. 149	■ **Reading Toolbox:** Chain-of-Events Chart, p. 146 **Math Skills:** Sedimentation Rates, p. 147 ■ ● **Internet Activity:** Identifying Sedimentary Rock Features, p. 148	**Reading Check,** p. 147 **Reading Check,** p. 149 **Section Review,** p. 150 ■ **Reteaching,** p. 149 ■ **Quiz,** p. 149 ■ **DI (Alternative Assessment):** Modeling Sedimentation, p. 150 ● **Section Quiz**
■ **Section Overview,** p. 151 **Why Are Rubies so Rare?** p. 152	● **Making Models Lab:** Metamorphic Rocks ■ **Activity:** Poster Project, p. 152	**Reading Toolbox:** Summarizing Ideas, p. 153	**Reading Check,** p. 152 **Section Review,** p. 154 ■ **Reteaching,** p. 153 ■ **Quiz,** p. 153 ■ **DI (Alternative Assessment):** Metamorphic Chemistry, p. 154 ● **Section Quiz**
A Nuclear Waste Basket p. 155	**Skills Practice Lab:** Classification of Rocks, pp. 156–157	▲ **Super Summary** **Standardized Test Prep,** pp. 162–163 **Maps in Action:** Geologic Map of Virginia, p. 158	**Chapter Review,** pp. 160–161 ■ **DI (Alternative Assessment):** Bulletin Board Display, p. 159 ● **Chapter Tests**

See also Lab Generator

See also Holt Online Assessment Resources

Chapter Overview

Rocks are generally classified as igneous, sedimentary, or metamorphic. Rocks form in a variety of ways and have characteristic compositions and textures that help scientists classify the rocks.

Using the Figure GENERAL

Eagletail Peak Eagletail Peak is in the Eagletail Mountains, about 100 miles west of Phoenix, Arizona. These mountains are composed mainly of sedimentary rock. Explain to students that sedimentary rock can form from rock fragments that are deposited by wind or water. Then, ask students how the rock in the photograph could have formed. (Answers may vary. Students may note that the rock that makes up the formation was deposited in flat layers a long time ago. Since then, uplift and erosion caused the rock structures that exist today to form.) **LS Visual**

Why It Matters

In both natural and constructed settings, rocks form the literal and figurative building blocks of civilization as we know it. In natural settings, rocks provide clues to Earths' formation and age. Quarried and used, some rocks are very visible—in buildings, monuments, floors, and countertops, while others are less visible—in construction and manufacturing. Limestone (sedimentary), marble (metamorphic), and granite (igneous) are familiar rocks.

Chapter 6 Rocks

Chapter Outline

Virginia Standards of Learning

ES.1.c	ES.5.c
ES.2.a	ES.7.a
ES.5.a	ES.9.a
ES.5.b	ES.9.d

Why It Matters

The hundreds of different types of rocks on Earth can be classified into three main types: igneous, sedimentary, and metamorphic. This formation in Arizona is made of sedimentary rock. When you know the type of rock, you know something about how that rock formed.

Chapter Correlations — *Virginia Standards of Learning*

ES.1.c scales, diagrams, charts, graphs, tables, imagery, models, and profiles are constructed and interpreted.
ES.2.a science explains and predicts the interactions and dynamics of complex Earth systems.
ES.5.a igneous rocks
ES.5.b sedimentary rocks
ES.5.c metamorphic rocks
ES.7.a geologic processes and their resulting features
ES.9.a traces and remains of ancient, often extinct, life are preserved by various means in many sedimentary rocks.
ES.9.d rocks and fossils from many different geologic periods and epochs are found in Virginia.

Inquiry Lab Sedimentary Sandwich

15 min

Use **slices of different types of bread** to model layers of different types of sediment deposits. Next, put your model in a **plastic bag**. Place a **weight** on top of the bag to simulate the process of compacting sediment into rock. Then, use an empty **film canister** to obtain a core sample of the sedimentary sandwich. Trade samples with another group and observe the other group's sample. Identify the different layers of rock and determine if rock layers are the same thickness or if some are thicker than others.

Questions to Get You Started

1. Make a labeled diagram showing the rock layers in the sample you observed.
2. Which factors might affect the thickness of a rock layer in a real rock formation?
3. Your model has layers of different types of rocks. In a real formation, what might changes in rock type indicate about the formation's geological history?

Inquiry Lab

Central Concept: Sedimentary rocks form from depositional layers. Examining the layers of rock can provide evidence about conditions when the rock formed. Students will model sedimentary rock formation using bread slices.

Teacher's Notes: Use different types of bread, for example, pumpernickel, rye, white, wheat, and multigrain. Challenge students to model uplift and folding of rock layers. Ask students how they might determine the original order of deposition after the layers have been disturbed.

Materials (per group)
- Film canister
- Plastic bag
- Slices of different types of bread

Skills Acquired
- Making Models
- Interpreting Models

Answers to Getting Started

1. Students should draw a diagram of the sample they observed and label the different "rock" layers.
2. Answers may vary. Possible factors include the quantity of sediment deposited or the duration of deposition of the sediment.
3. A change in rock type indicates that a different type of sediment was deposited. For example, one layer may indicate that the area was under water at the time and a later layer may indicate that the area was no longer submerged. Fossils within the layers may give evidence of changes in the environment.

Using THINK central Resources

An online version of this chapter, as well as all the print and multimedia resources that accompany the program are available to registered teachers and their students. Log onto www.thinkcentral.com to access these materials and tools to organize your preparation and student learning.

READING TOOLBOX

FoldNotes

Students should consult Appendix A for tips on making a pyramid FoldNote. The information for this FoldNote can be found on page 195C, in the form of a table.

Graphic Organizer

Answers may vary. An example chain-of-events chart is shown below.

In a sediment deposit, there are open spaces between grains of sediment.

↓

New layers of sediment squeeze together, or compact, the sediment below.

↓

The rock that forms from the sediment layers has less volume and is less porous than the original sediment.

READING TOOLBOX

These reading tools will help you learn the material in this chapter.

FoldNotes

Pyramid Pyramid FoldNotes help you compare words or ideas in sets of three.

Your Turn Before you read this chapter, make a Pyramid FoldNote as described in **Appendix A.** Label the sides of the pyramid with "Igneous rock," "Sedimentary rock," and "Metamorphic rock." As you read the chapter, define each type of rock, and write characteristics of each type of rock on the appropriate side of the pyramid.

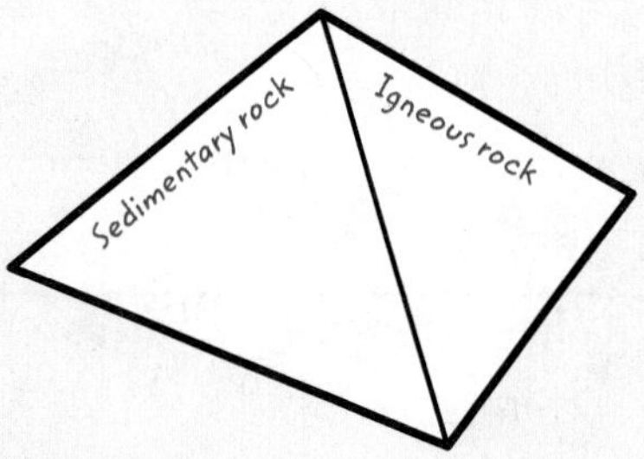

Graphic Organizer

Chain-of-Events Chart A chain-of-events chart is similar to a flow chart. A chain-of-events chart shows the order in which the steps of a process occur.

Your Turn In Section 3, you will read about the formation of sedimentary rocks. Make a chain-of-events chart like the one started below to describe *compaction,* one of the processes that form sedimentary rock. Use as many boxes as you need to record all steps of the process.

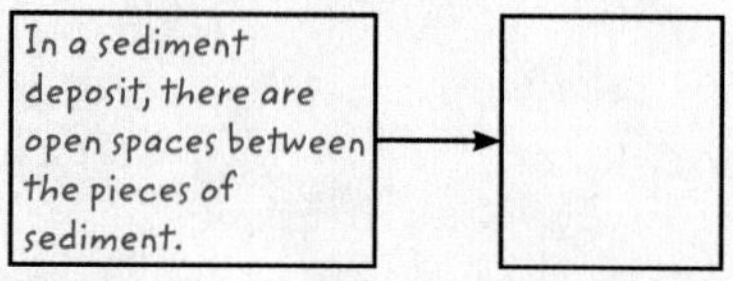

Note Taking

Summarizing Ideas Summarizing the content of each paragraph or set of paragraphs under a heading is a simple way to take notes. A few tips on summarizing are listed below.

1. Summary statements should be short, but fully express the idea.
2. Use the green subheadings for guidance in forming summary statements.
3. Many paragraphs start or end with a sentence that summarizes the main idea of the paragraph.

Your Turn As you read each section, take notes by summarizing the main ideas. You may add structure to your notes by also writing the section title and red headings in the appropriate places.

For more information on how to use these and other tools, see **Appendix A.**

Note Taking

Answers may vary. Students' notes should appear similar to the example shown below, which is a summary of Section 1.

Section 1 – Rocks and the Rock Cycle

- Rock is made of one or more minerals or of organic matter.

Three Major Types of Rock

- The three major types of rock are igneous rock, formed from magma, sedimentary rock, formed from sediment deposits, and metamorphic rock, formed when an existing rock is changed.

The Rock Cycle

- Each of the three types of rocks can change into any of the other types.
- The rock cycle includes the geological processes in which rock forms, changes into another type of rock, is destroyed, and then forms again.

Properties of Rocks

- Where and how a rock forms determines its physical and chemical properties.
- A mineral's chemical composition and melting point determines when it will crystallize from cooling magma. Bowen's reaction series illustrates the order in which minerals crystallize.
- Chemically stable minerals form at temperatures similar to those on Earth's surface. The physical stability of rocks depends on natural zones of weakness.

SECTION 1
Rocks and the Rock Cycle

Key Ideas	Key Terms	Why It Matters
❯ Identify the three major types of rock, and explain how each type forms. ❯ Summarize the steps in the rock cycle. ❯ Explain Bowen's reaction series. ❯ Summarize the factors that affect the stability of rocks.	**rock cycle** **Bowen's reaction series**	Some rocks crumble and others make for solid buildings. The physical and chemical properties of rock are determined by the conditions under which the rock forms.

The material that makes up the solid parts of Earth is known as *rock*. Rock can be a collection of one or more minerals, or rock can be made of solid organic matter. In some cases, rock is made of solid matter that is not crystalline, such as glass. Geologists study the forces and processes that form and change the rocks of Earth's crust. Based on these studies, geologists have classified rocks into three major types by the way the rocks form.

Three Major Types of Rock

Volcanic activity produces *igneous rock*. The word *igneous* is derived from a Latin term that means "from fire." Igneous rock forms when *magma*, or molten rock, cools and hardens. Magma is called *lava* when it is exposed at Earth's surface.

Over time, natural processes break down all types of rock into small fragments. Rocks, mineral crystals, and organic matter that have been broken into fragments are known as *sediment*. Sediment is carried away and deposited by water, ice, and wind. When these sediment deposits are compressed, cemented together, and harden, *sedimentary rock* forms.

Certain forces and processes, including tremendous pressure, extreme heat, and chemical processes, also can change the form of existing rock. The rock that forms when existing rock is altered is *metamorphic rock*. The word *metamorphic* means "changed form." **Figure 1** shows an example of each major type of rock.

Figure 1 These rocks are examples of the three major rock types.

Section 1

Focus

Overview

This section introduces the three basic types of rock, describes how rock changes form through the rock cycle, and describes Bowen's reaction series and the factors that affect the chemical and physical stability of rocks.

Bellringer

Have students list the names of five rocks with which they are familiar, and have them describe characteristics of the rock and identify how each type of rock is used. (Answers may vary.)

LS Verbal

Motivate

Discussion GENERAL

Types of Rocks Place on display for the class the igneous rocks pumice and granite, the sedimentary rocks sandstone and limestone, and the metamorphic rocks gneiss and schist. Ask students to note and discuss the common features of the two rocks of each type. (Answers may vary. Students may note that both limestone and sandstone have fine, grainy layers, that pumice is glassy and granite is made up of crystals, and that the schist and gneiss have bands of minerals or layers of crystals.)

LS Verbal/Visual

Key Resources

Chapter Resource File
- Directed Reading BASIC

Technology
- Transparencies
  Bellringer

Teach

Using the Figure GENERAL

The Rock Cycle Ask students to identify the processes that change each type of rock into another. (students should find the corresponding processes on the figure) LS Visual

Why It Matters

Lunar Rocks According to currently accepted theory, the moon formed as a result of the collision of a large body (perhaps as big as Mars) and the molten Earth about 4.6 billion years ago. This model is supported by, and accounts for, both the composition of lunar rock and its density, which is lower than Earth rock. Lunar rock came from the less dense material of Earth's surface and upper mantle. The smaller size of the moon allowed it to cool more rapidly than Earth has cooled. The absence of plate-tectonic activity and of an atmosphere has made the rock cycle of the moon much simpler and less dramatic than that of Earth.

Key Resources

Technology

- Transparencies
  - 26 The Rock Cycle
  - 27 Bowen's Reaction Series

Figure 2 The rock cycle illustrates the changes that igneous, sedimentary, and metamorphic rocks undergo.

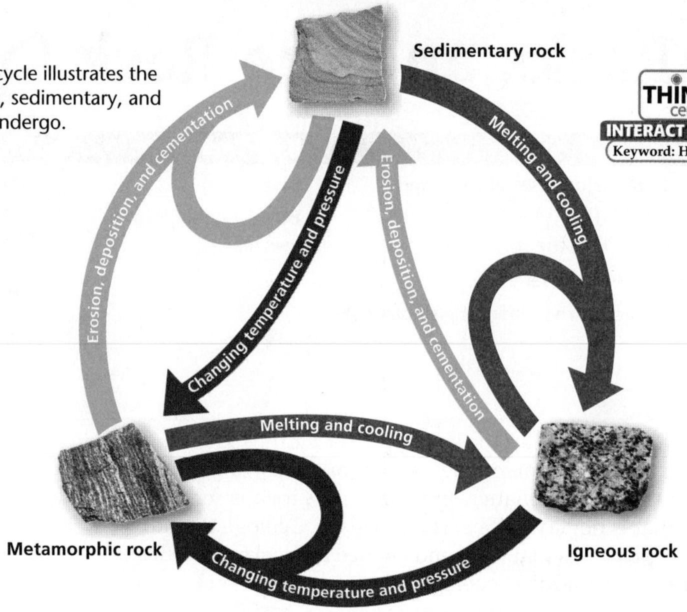

The Rock Cycle

Any of the three major types of rock can be changed into another of the three types. Geologic forces and processes cause rock to change from one type to another. This series of changes is called the **rock cycle,** which is shown in **Figure 2.**

rock cycle the series of processes in which rock forms, changes from one type to another, is destroyed, and forms again by geological processes

One starting point for examining the steps of the rock cycle is igneous rock. When a body of igneous rock is exposed at Earth's surface, a number of processes break down the igneous rock into sediment. When sediment from igneous rocks is compacted and cemented, the sediment becomes sedimentary rock. Then, if sedimentary rocks are subjected to changes in temperature and pressure, the rocks may become metamorphic rocks. Under certain temperature and pressure conditions, the metamorphic rock will melt and form magma. Then, if the magma cools, new igneous rock will form.

Much of the rock in Earth's continental crust has probably passed through the rock cycle many times during Earth's history. However, as **Figure 2** shows, a particular body of rock does not always pass through each stage of the rock cycle. For example, igneous rock may never be exposed at Earth's surface where the rock could change into sediment. Instead, the igneous rock may change directly into metamorphic rock while still beneath Earth's surface. Sedimentary rock may be broken down at Earth's surface, and the sediment may become another sedimentary rock. Metamorphic rock can be altered by heat and pressure to form a different type of metamorphic rock.

SCILINKS.
www.scilinks.org
Topic: The Rock Cycle
Code: **HQX1319**

Differentiated Instruction

Special Education Students

The Rock Cycle Many students can better understand an idea if they break it into individual parts. Help students to comprehend the rock cycle by asking them to write the possible changes that each type of rock can undergo. Ask them to divide a piece of paper into three parts and use each part for one type of rock. Help them get started with the sedimentary section by using the following prompts: 1: Sedimentary rock can be melted, cooled, and hardened to form igneous rock. 2: Sedimentary rock can undergo pressure and temperature changes or chemical processes to turn into ____. 3: Sedimentary rock can ____. Their responses will be repetitive, but repetitiveness will help to clarify that the same forces are acting on different types of rocks. LS Visual

Properties of Rocks

All rock has physical and chemical properties that are determined by how and where the rock formed. The physical characteristics of rock reflect the chemical composition of the rock as a whole and of the individual minerals that make up the rock. The rate at which rock weathers and the way that rock breaks apart are determined by the chemical stability of the minerals in the rock.

Bowen's Reaction Series

In the early 1900s, a Canadian geologist named N. L. Bowen began studying how minerals crystallize from magma. He learned that as magma cools, certain minerals tend to crystallize first. As these minerals form, they remove specific elements from the magma, which changes the magma's composition. The changing composition of the magma allows different minerals that contain different elements to form. Thus, different minerals form at different times during the solidification (cooling) of magma, and they generally form in the same order.

In 1928, Bowen proposed a simplified pattern that explains the order in which minerals form as magma solidifies. This simplified flow chart is known as **Bowen's reaction series** and is shown in **Figure 3.** According to Bowen's hypothesis, minerals form in one of two ways. The first way is characterized by a gradual, continuous formation of minerals that have similar chemical compositions. The second way is characterized by sudden, or discontinuous, changes in mineral types. As magma cools, the discontinuous and continuous reaction series occur simultaneously, or at the same time.

Reading Check **Summarize Bowen's reaction series.** (See Appendix G for answers to Reading Checks.)

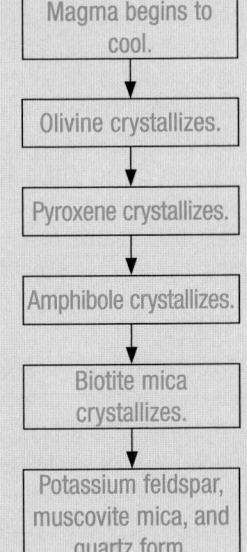

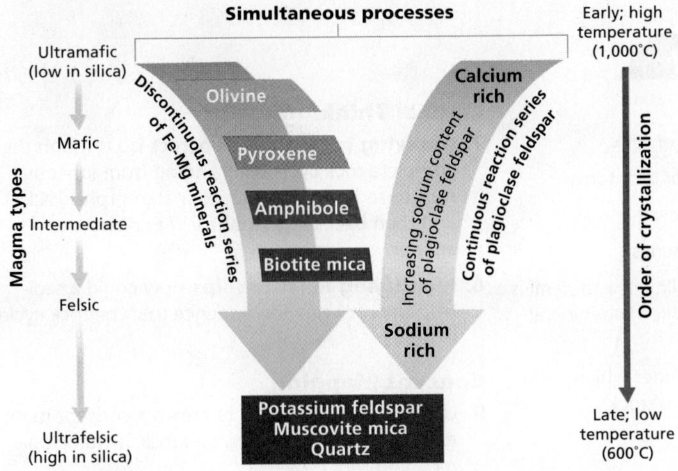

Figure 3 Different minerals crystallize at different times during the solidification of magma. Thus, as minerals crystallize from magma, the composition of the magma changes.

READING TOOLBOX

Chain-of-Events Chart
Make a chain-of-events chart to show each step of the discontinuous reaction series of Bowen's reaction series. Remember to use as many boxes as you need to show all steps.

Academic Vocabulary

remove (ri MOOV) to take away or eliminate

Bowen's reaction series the simplified pattern that illustrates the order in which minerals crystallize from cooling magma according to their chemical composition and melting point

READING TOOLBOX

Chain-of-Events Chart A sample chain-of-events chart is shown below.

Magma begins to cool.
↓
Olivine crystallizes.
↓
Pyroxene crystallizes.
↓
Amphibole crystallizes.
↓
Biotite mica crystallizes.
↓
Potassium feldspar, muscovite mica, and quartz form.

Close

Reteaching — BASIC

Rock Cycle Processes On the board, write the phrases "breaking down and compression," "changes in temperature and pressure," and "melting and cooling" on different lines. Have students indicate which processes apply to the formation of igneous, metamorphic, and sedimentary rocks. **LS Verbal/Visual**

Quiz — GENERAL

1. What type of rock forms when small rock fragments are cemented together? (sedimentary rock)
2. What happens to igneous rock if it is melted and cooled? (The rock forms a new igneous rock.)

Teaching Tip — BASIC

Connect to Familiar Processes To help students understand how the removal of a mineral from magma determines what minerals will form from the remaining magma, have them think of a soup with many ingredients. Removing water from the mixture causes the soup to be thicker and to have a stronger taste. If, for example, potatoes and carrots are removed at the start, the soup will take on more of the flavor of meat and the remaining vegetables. Be sure that students understand that soup is a mixture, so changes to it are not chemical, as changes to solidifying magma are. **LS Logical**

Answer to Reading Check
As magma cools and solidifies, minerals crystallize out of the magma in a specific order, that depends on their melting points.

Close, *continued*

Answers to Section Review

1. igneous, sedimentary, and metamorphic
2. Igneous rock forms when molten rock (magma) cools and hardens. When rock is broken down, small fragments are deposited and then compressed and cemented to form sedimentary rock. Rock that is subjected to changes in temperature or pressure or to chemical processes becomes metamorphic rock.
3. Answers may vary but should describe the formation of all three types of rock.
4. As the temperature of magma decreases, minerals crystallize out of the magma, depending on their melting points. This crystallization changes the chemical composition of the remaining magma, causing different minerals to form. This process can occur following either a continuous or a discontinuous path.
5. In general, the rocks that have the greatest chemical stability (those most resistant to weathering) are the rocks whose minerals have the greatest number of bonds between silicon and oxygen.
6. Rocks have zones of weakness determined by how and where they form. These zones may form between the layers in sedimentary rocks, or as joints in igneous rock. The rocks break more easily along these zones.
7. no; Rocks can move back and forth between any of the types of rock in the rock cycle. They may even reform as the same kind of rock for several cycles.

Figure 4 Devils Postpile National Monument in California is one of the world's finest examples of the igneous rock structures known as columnar joints.

Chemical Stability of Minerals

The rate at which a mineral chemically breaks down is dependent on the chemical stability of the mineral. *Chemical stability* is a measure of the tendency of a chemical compound to maintain its original chemical composition rather than break down to form a different chemical. In general, the minerals that are most stable are minerals that formed at the lowest temperatures, under conditions similar to those on Earth's surface. Minerals that formed at the highest temperatures, under conditions very different than those on Earth's surface, are least stable.

Physical Stability of Rocks

Rocks have natural zones of weakness that are determined by how and where the rocks form. For example, sedimentary rocks may form as a series of layers of sediment. These rocks tend to break between layers. Some metamorphic rocks also tend to break in layers that form as the minerals in the rocks align during metamorphism.

Massive igneous rock structures commonly have evenly spaced zones of weakness, called *joints,* that form as the rock cools and contracts. Devils Postpile, shown in **Figure 4**, is igneous rock that has joints that cause the rock to break into columns.

Zones of weakness may also form when the rock is under intense pressure inside Earth. When rock that formed under intense pressure is uplifted to Earth's surface, decreased pressure allows the joints and fractures to open. Once these weaknesses are exposed to air and water, chemical and physical processes begin to break down the rock.

Section 1 Review

Key Ideas

1. **Identify** the three major types of rock.
2. **Explain** how each major type of rock forms.
3. **Describe** the steps in the rock cycle.
4. **Summarize** Bowen's reaction series.
5. **Explain** how the chemical stability of a mineral is related to the temperature at which the mineral forms.
6. **Describe** how the conditions under which rocks form affect the physical stability of rocks.

Critical Thinking

7. **Applying Ideas** Does every rock go through the complete rock cycle by changing from igneous rock to sedimentary rock, to metamorphic rock, and then back to igneous rock? Explain your answer.
8. **Identifying Relationships** How could a sedimentary rock provide evidence that the rock cycle exists?

Concept Mapping

9. Use the following terms to create a concept map: *rock, igneous rock, sedimentary rock, metamorphic rock,* and *rock cycle.*

8. Answers may vary. Sample answer: If the sedimentary rock consists of fragments of igneous rock, this would indicate that the igneous rock broke down and changed through some process to become sedimentary rock.
9. *Rock* can be one of three main types—*igneous rock, sedimentary rock,* or *metamorphic rock*—and changes from one form to another through the *rock cycle.*

Differentiated Instruction

Alternative Assessment

Rock Crystallization Have students create 3-dimensional models of the rock cycle. Students may use any materials they want, as long as students can explain why they chose those materials. **LS Kinesthetic**

SECTION 2

Igneous Rock

Key Ideas	Key Terms	Why It Matters
❯ Summarize three factors that affect whether rock melts. ❯ Describe how the cooling rate of magma and lava affects the texture of igneous rocks. ❯ Classify igneous rocks according to their composition and texture. ❯ Describe intrusive and extrusive igneous rock.	**igneous rock** **intrusive igneous rock** **extrusive igneous rock** **felsic** **mafic**	The many different compositions and textures of igneous rocks make sense once you understand the processes by which they form. Useful applications of these properties include nuclear-waste disposal.

When magma cools and hardens, it forms **igneous rock.** Because minerals usually crystallize as igneous rock forms from magma, most igneous rock can be identified as *crystalline,* or made of crystals.

The Formation of Magma

Magma forms when rock melts. Rock melts when the temperature of the rock increases to above the melting point of minerals in the rock. The chemical composition of minerals determines their melting temperatures. In general, rock melts at lower temperatures under lower pressures. If excess pressure is removed from rock that is close to melting, the rock may melt. Hot rock may also melt when fluids such as water are added. The addition of fluids generally decreases the melting point of certain minerals in the rock, which can cause those minerals to melt.

igneous rock rock that forms when magma cools and solidifies

Partial Melting

Different minerals have different melting points, and minerals that have lower melting points are the first minerals to melt. When the first minerals melt, the magma that forms has a specific composition. As the temperature increases and as other minerals melt, the magma's composition changes. The process by which different minerals in rock melt at different temperatures is called *partial melting*. Partial melting is shown in **Figure 1.**

Figure 1 How Magma Forms by Partial Melting

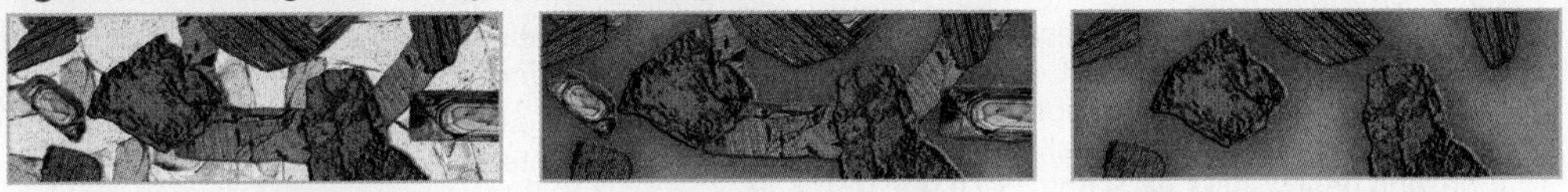

This solid rock contains the minerals quartz (yellow), feldspar (gray), biotite (brown), and hornblende (green).

The first minerals that melt are quartz and some types of feldspars. The orange background represents magma.

Minerals such as biotite and hornblende generally melt last, which changes the composition of the magma.

Key Resources

Chapter Resource File

- Directed Reading BASIC

Technology

- Transparencies
  Bellringer
  28 Partial Melting and Fractional Crystallization

Section 2

Focus

Overview

This section describes how igneous rocks form and what factors affect the texture and composition of igneous rocks. The section concludes with a description of igneous rock structures.

Bellringer

Have students write a short paragraph that explains where and why rock melts. (Answers may vary. Use students' answers to begin a discussion of how magma forms.) LS **Logical**

Motivate

Discussion — GENERAL

Hand Samples Show the class samples of the following igneous rocks: basalt, pumice, granite, and obsidian. Ask students what these four rocks of very different appearance have in common. (All are made of glassy or crystalline components.) Ask students how the textures of the rocks differ. (obsidian: very smooth, no crystals; basalt: tiny crystals; granite: large crystals; pumice: no crystals, large holes.) Point out that all of the rocks formed from molten rock but the conditions under which each rock formed account for their different appearances. LS **Kinesthetic/Visual**

Quick Lab

Skills Acquired
- Experimenting
- Predicting
- Identifying/Recognizing Patterns

Materials
- Three glasses
- Ice cubes
- Sauce pan
- Epsom salts
- Water
- Hot plate
- Spoon or stirring rod
- Funnel
- Three test tubes
- Tongs

Teacher's Notes: Be sure that students take extra care when pouring the melted Epsom salts. Clean up spills quickly.

Answers to Analysis

1. The crystals in the test tube cooled in the hot water will be largest.
2. The crystals in the test tube cooled in the ice water will be smallest.
3. The faster the liquid cools, the smaller the crystals will be.
4. Large crystals form from slowly cooling magma, and smaller crystals form from rapidly cooling magma.
5. by placing the test tube in water whose temperature is slightly lower than the temperature of the liquid Epsom salts

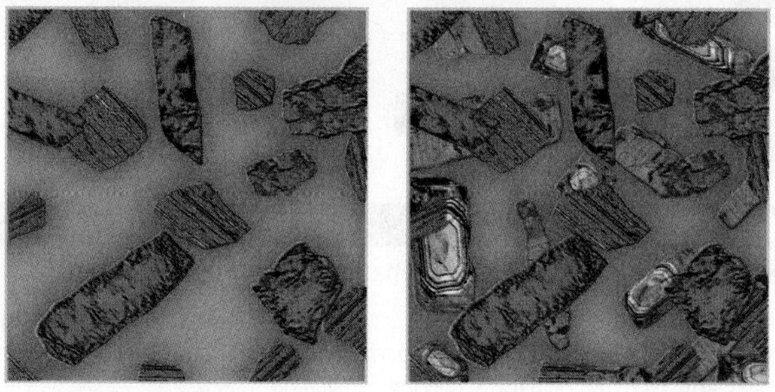

Figure 2 As the temperature decreases, the first minerals to crystallize from magma are minerals that have the highest freezing points. As the magma changes composition and cools, minerals that have lower freezing points form.

Fractional Crystallization

When magma cools, the cooling process is the reverse of the process of partial melting. Chemicals in magma combine to form minerals, and each mineral has a different freezing point. Minerals that have the highest freezing points crystallize first. As minerals crystallize, they remove specific chemicals from the magma. As the composition of the magma changes, new minerals begin to form. The crystallization and removal of different minerals from the cooling magma, as occurs in Bowen's reaction series, is called *fractional crystallization* and is shown in **Figure 2.**

Minerals that form during fractional crystallization tend to settle to the bottom of the magma chamber or to stick to the ceiling and walls of the magma chamber. Crystals that form early in the process are commonly the largest because they have the longest time to grow. In some crystals, the chemical composition of the inner part of the crystal differs from the composition of the outer parts of the crystal. This difference occurs because the magma's composition changed while the crystal was growing.

Quick Lab Crystal Formation

20 min

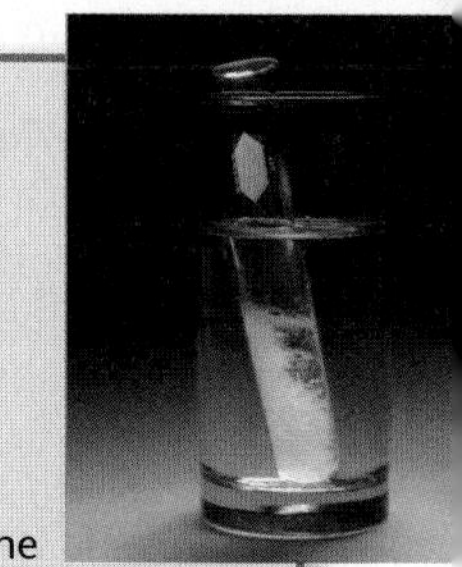

Procedure

1. Add the following until **three glasses** are 2/3 full: glass 1—water and **ice cubes;** glass 2—water at room temperature; and glass 3—hot tap water.
2. In a small **sauce pan,** mix **120 mL of Epsom salts** in **120 mL of water.** Heat the mixture on a **hot plate** over low heat. Do not let the mixture boil. Stir the mixture with a **spoon or stirring rod** until no more crystals dissolve.
3. Using a **funnel,** carefully pour equal amounts of the Epsom salts mixture into **three test tubes.** Use **tongs** to steady the test tubes as you pour. Drop a few crystals of Epsom salt into each test tube, and gently shake each one. Place one test tube into each glass.
4. Observe the solutions as they cool for 15 minutes. Let the glasses sit overnight, and examine the solutions again after 24 hours.

Analysis

1. In which test tube are the crystals the largest?
2. In which test tube are the crystals the smallest?
3. How does the rate of cooling affect the size of the crystals that form? Explain your answer.
4. How are the differing rates of crystal formation you observed related to igneous rock formation?
5. How would you change the procedure to obtain larger crystals of Epsom salts? Explain your answer.

Teach

Using the Figure — Basic

Fractional Crystallization Ask students how the process shown in the figure at the top of the page relates to the figure of partial melting at the bottom of the previous page. (The figure of fractional crystallization shows the reverse of the process of partial melting.) Ask students what a third illustration in this series would look like if it showed even cooler magma. (The amount of magma would be reduced, and more crystals, probably of different minerals, would be present.) **LS Visual/Logical**

Demonstration — General

Partial Freezing To help students visualize the process that occurs during fractional crystallization, prepare a mixture of 60 mL paraffin, 60 mL butter, and 60 mL water in a 250 mL beaker. Heat the mixture until the butter and paraffin melt. Then, place the beaker in a 1,000 mL beaker that is half full of an ice and water mixture. Have students watch the beaker and note that the wax solidifies before the butter does. Point out that if the mixture is cooled to a temperature below that of the icebath, the water will freeze. **LS Visual**

Textures of Igneous Rocks

Igneous rocks may form beneath Earth's surface or on Earth's surface. Magma that cools deep inside the crust forms **intrusive igneous rock.** The magma that forms these rocks intrudes, or enters, into other rock masses beneath Earth's surface. The magma then slowly cools and hardens. Lava that cools at Earth's surface forms **extrusive igneous rock.**

Intrusive and extrusive igneous rocks differ from each other not only in where they form but also in the size of their crystals or grains. The texture of igneous rock is determined by the size of the crystals in the rock. The size of the crystals is determined mainly by the cooling rate of the magma. Examples of different textures of igneous rocks are shown in **Figure 3.**

Coarse-Grained Igneous Rock

Intrusive igneous rocks commonly have large mineral crystals. The slow loss of heat allows the minerals in the cooling magma to form large, well-developed crystals. Igneous rocks that are composed of large mineral grains are described as having a *coarse-grained texture.* An example of a coarse-grained igneous rock is granite. The upper part of the continental crust is made mostly of granite.

Fine-Grained Igneous Rock

Many extrusive igneous rocks are composed of small mineral grains that cannot be seen by the unaided eye. Because these rocks form when magma cools rapidly, large crystals are unable to form. Igneous rocks that are composed of small crystals are described as having a *fine-grained texture.* Examples of common fine-grained igneous rocks are basalt and rhyolite (RIE uh LIET).

Other Igneous Rock Textures

Some igneous rock forms when magma cools slowly at first but then cools more rapidly as it nears Earth's surface. This type of cooling produces large crystals embedded within a mass of smaller ones. Igneous rock that has a mixture of large and small crystals has a *porphyritic texture* (POHR fuh RIT ik TEKS chuhr).

When a highly viscous, or thick, magma cools quickly, few crystals are able to grow. Quickly cooling magma may form a rock that has a *glassy* texture, such as obsidian. When magma contains a large amount of dissolved gases and cools rapidly, the gases become trapped as bubbles in the rock that forms. The rapid cooling process produces a rock full of holes called *vesicles,* such as those in pumice. This type of rock is said to have a *vesicular texture.*

Reading Check **What is the difference between fine-grained and coarse-grained igneous rock?**

intrusive igneous rock rock formed from the cooling and solidification of magma beneath Earth's surface

extrusive igneous rock rock that forms from the cooling and solidification of lava at Earth's surface

Figure 3 Igneous Rock Textures

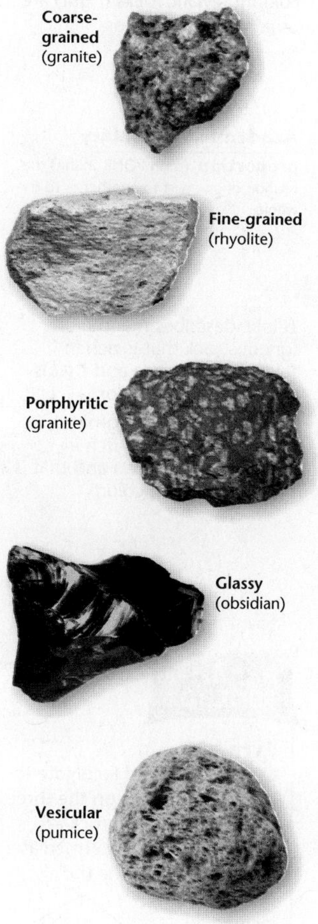

Geology Connection — ADVANCED

Information from Igneous Rocks

Igneous rocks are affected by where they form, their rate of cooling, the presence of dissolved gases, and their chemical composition. Because of this, information about specific geological processes can be obtained by studying different types of igneous rock.

For example, the basalts that are found in the ocean crust are low in the elements rubidium and thorium, while the basalts of the continental crust have higher amounts of these elements. This difference provides information about the mechanisms by which the continental crust forms and the rate at which it forms. Similarly, a lower concentration of silica, SiO_2, which is found in differing amounts in all igneous rocks, occurs in rocks near the summits of older volcanoes. These rocks are commonly an indicator of reduced volcanic activity. Have students research what geologic processes result in the different igneous rock textures. Students should present their findings to the class.

LS Verbal/Logical

Answer to Reading Check

Fine-grained igneous rock forms mainly from magma that cools rapidly; coarse-grained igneous rock forms mainly from magma that cools more slowly.

Differentiated Instruction

Struggling Readers

Reading Organizer Before students read this page, have them make a table that has three columns and six rows. Have them label the columns with "Texture," "Intrusive," and "Extrusive." In the "Texture" column, have students label the rows with "Coarse-grained," "Fine-grained," "Porphyritic," "Volcanic glass," and "Vesicular." As students read the page, have them insert in the correct box a brief description of the heat loss that takes place (for example, "slow heat loss" for "coarse-grained" in the "Intrusive" column), as well as whether gas is dissolved in the magma. Have students add the name of a type of igneous rock that fits each description. Later, students can use their charts as study guides for assessments.

LS Verbal

English Language Learners

Teach, *continued*

Group Activity — Advanced

Poster Project Divide the class into groups of three or four students, and have each group create a poster that lists the properties and provides examples of felsic, mafic, and intermediate rocks. The posters should include information about the chemical compositions, range of densities, range of melting temperatures, typical colors, and textures of each rock type, as well as common examples of each kind. Students should each do research on two or three different igneous rocks and then pool their information to create the poster. Have each group present their poster to the rest of the class. **LS Visual/Logical** Co-op Learning

READING TOOLBOX

Pyramid Students should consult Appendix A for tips on making a pyramid FoldNote. The information for this FoldNote is presented below.

The Three Families of Igneous Rock

Felsic: igneous rock that is rich in feldspars and silica; generally light in color; examples: granite, rhyolite, obsidian, pumice

Mafic: igneous rock that is rich in magnesium and iron; generally dark in color; examples: basalt, gabbro

Intermediate: igneous rock that is made up of plagioclase feldspar, hornblende, pyroxene, and biotite mica; examples: diorite, andesite

Figure 4 Felsic rocks, such as the outcropping and hand sample shown above (left), have light coloring. Mafic rocks (right) are usually darker in color.

Academic Vocabulary

proportion (proh POHR shuhn) the relation of one part to another or to the whole

felsic describes magma or igneous rock that is rich in feldspars and silica and that is generally light in color

mafic describes magma or igneous rock that is rich in magnesium and iron and that is generally dark in color

Composition of Igneous Rocks

The mineral composition of an igneous rock is determined by the chemical composition of the magma from which the rock formed. Each type of igneous rock has a specific mineral composition. Geologists divide igneous rock into three families—felsic, mafic (MAF ik), and intermediate. Each of the three families has a different mineral composition. Examples of rock from the felsic and mafic families are shown in **Figure 4.**

Felsic Rock

Rock in the **felsic** family forms from magma that contains a large proportion of silica. Felsic rock generally has the light coloring of its main mineral components, potassium feldspar and quartz. Felsic rock commonly also contains plagioclase feldspar, biotite mica, and muscovite mica. The felsic family includes many common rocks, such as granite, rhyolite, obsidian, and pumice.

Mafic Rock

Rock in the **mafic** family forms from magma that contains lower proportions of silica than felsic rock does and that is rich in iron and magnesium. The main mineral components of rock in this family are plagioclase feldspar and pyroxene minerals. Mafic rock may also include dark-colored *ferromagnesian minerals,* such as hornblende. These ferromagnesian components, as well as the mineral olivine, give mafic rock a dark color. The mafic family includes the common rocks basalt and gabbro.

Intermediate Rocks

Rocks of the intermediate family are made up of the minerals plagioclase feldspar, hornblende, pyroxene, and biotite mica. Rocks in the intermediate family contain lower proportions of silica than rocks in the felsic family do but contain higher proportions of silica than rocks in the mafic family contain. Rocks in the intermediate family include diorite and andesite.

READING TOOLBOX

Pyramid

Create a pyramid FoldNote to record your notes on the three families of igneous rock—felsic, mafic, and intermediate. For each term, write the definition and include an example of a rock from that family.

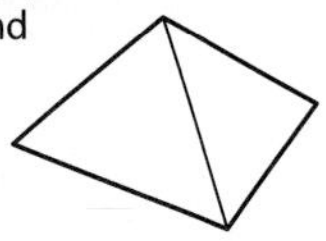

Teaching Tip

Use Technology Resources Plagioclase feldspars, which consist of aluminum silicates bound to either calcium or sodium ions, are found in both felsic and mafic rock. However, the percentage of plagioclase feldspar in magma in part determines whether the magma is felsic or mafic. Felsic magmas contain small amounts of plagioclase feldspar, and large amounts of orthoclase feldspar, or potassium aluminum silicate. Mafic magmas are made up of larger quantities of plagioclase feldspar, and contain no orthoclase feldspar, though their overall feldspar content is less than that of felsic magmas.

Encourage students to use the Internet to research the role of both kinds of feldspars in igneous rocks. A number of sites contain diagrams that show the proportions of different minerals in felsic, intermediate, and mafic magmas, as well as the olivine-rich magmas called *ultramafic.* **LS Logical**

Intrusive Igneous Rock

Igneous rock masses that form underground are called *intrusions*. Intrusions form when magma intrudes, or enters, into other rock masses and then cools deep inside Earth's crust. A variety of intrusions are shown in **Figure 5.**

Batholiths and Stocks

The largest of all intrusions are called *batholiths*. Batholiths are intrusive formations that spread over at least 100 km^2 when they are exposed on Earth's surface. The word *batholith* means "deep rock." Batholiths were once thought to extend to great depths beneath Earth's surface. However, studies have determined that many batholiths extend only several thousand meters below the surface. Batholiths form the cores of many mountain ranges, such as the Sierra Nevadas in California. The largest batholith in North America forms the core of the Coast Range in British Columbia. Another type of intrusion is called a *stock*. Stocks are similar to batholiths but cover less than 100 km^2 at the surface.

SCILINKS.
www.scilinks.org
Topic: Igneous Rock
Code: HQX0783

Laccoliths

When magma flows between rock layers and spreads upward, it sometimes pushes the overlying rock layers into a dome. The base of the intrusion is parallel to the rock layer beneath it. This type of intrusion is called a *laccolith*. The word *laccolith* means "lake of rock." Laccoliths commonly occur in groups and can sometimes be identified by the small dome-shaped mountains they form on Earth's surface. Many laccoliths are located beneath the Black Hills of South Dakota.

Reading Check What is the difference between stocks and batholiths?

Sills and Dikes

When magma flows between the layers of rock and hardens, a *sill* forms. A sill lies parallel to the layers of rock that surround it, even if the layers are tilted. Sills vary in thickness from a few centimeters to hundreds of meters.

Magma sometimes forces itself through rock layers by following existing vertical fractures or by creating new ones. When the magma solidifies, a *dike* forms. Dikes cut across rock layers rather than lying parallel to the rock layers. Dikes are common in areas of volcanic activity.

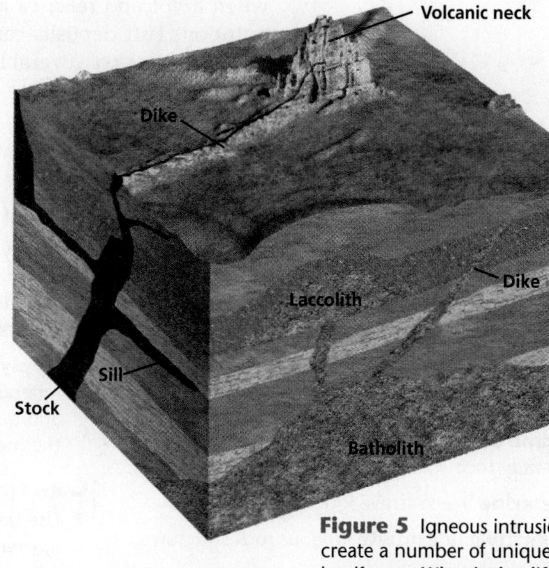

Figure 5 Igneous intrusions create a number of unique landforms. ***What is the difference between a dike and a sill?***

Using the Figure GENERAL

Intrusive Igneous Structures

Ask students to point out the main landforms shown in the figure and describe how they are caused by intrusions. (Answers may vary. Students should point out the volcanic neck, the ridges connected to the volcanic neck and the mound in the foreground. The volcanic neck and dikes at the surface formed when overlying, less-resistant rock was eroded and the harder intrusive rock was exposed. The mound in the foreground formed when magma in the laccolith pushed the overlying layers up.) Answer to caption question: A sill is parallel to the layers of rock that it intrudes. A dike cuts across the layers it intrudes. **LS Visual/Logical**

Answer to Reading Check

A batholith is an intrusive structure that covers an area of at least 100 km^2. A stock covers an area of less than 100 km^2.

Close

Reteaching BASIC

Igneous Rock Characteristics

Have students create a table that has two columns and four rows. Have students label the columns "Coarse-grained" and "Fine-grained." Have them label the rows "Mafic," "Felsic," "Intrusive," and "Extrusive." Then, have students fill in the table by using the names of igneous rocks or the structures that fit in each category.
LS Logical

Quiz GENERAL

Determine whether each of the following statements is true or false.

1. Fine-grained igneous rock results from rapid cooling. (true)
2. Mafic magmas generally produce light-colored rocks. (false)
3. During partial melting, minerals that have lower melting points melt first. (true)

MISCONCEPTION ALERT

Exposed Intrusive Structures Students may be confused about how intrusive structures that form below Earth's surface become exposed at the surface. Explain that parts or all of such structures are exposed when the structure is pushed up toward the surface by tectonic activity or when the material surrounding it is eroded.

Differentiated Instruction

English Learners

Vocabulary While some of the terms for intrusive igneous structures are Greek in origin, such as *batholith* and *laccolith*, many terms can be traced back to Old English. The word *stock* comes from the Old English word *stocc*, meaning "tree trunk," which these structures vaguely resemble. *Sill* comes from the Old English *syll*, meaning "threshold." The word *dike* derives from the Old English word for "ditch" or "trench." **LS Verbal**

Close, *continued*

Answers to Section Review

1. temperature, pressure, and the addition of fluids to the rock
2. Partial melting occurs when rock's temperature increases, causing minerals that have the lowest melting points to melt first. Fractional crystallization is the reverse process. As magma's temperature decreases, different minerals form as the composition of the magma changes.
3. When magma cools slowly, larger crystals may form, and the rock is coarse-grained. When magma cools rapidly, smaller crystals may form, and the rock is fine-grained.
4. felsic: high in potassium feldspar and quartz, with some plagioclase feldspar and mica; mafic: high in plagioclase feldspars, iron- and magnesium-rich minerals such as pyroxene and hornblende, and olivine; intermediate: plagioclase feldspar, hornblende, pyroxene, and biotite mica
5. *Batholiths* are large intrusive structures that cover an area of 100 km^2 or more. *Stocks* are intrusive structures that cover less than 100 km^2. *Laccoliths* are intrusions that push the overlying rock layers into domes and whose bases lie parallel to the rock layers beneath them. *Sills* are intrusions that are parallel to the surrounding rock layers. *Dikes* are intrusions that cut across surrounding rock layers.
6. volcanoes, volcanic necks, lava flows, lava plateaus, and tuffs
7. There can be several variables, but one that would work is to keep the rate of cooling of the magma from which crystals will form as slow as possible.
8. the felsic family, which includes potassium feldspar and quartz, and whose members are typically light in color
9. *Igneous rock* forms from *magma*, which may be *felsic*, *mafic*, or *intermediate*, and may be *coarse-grained* or *fine-grained*.

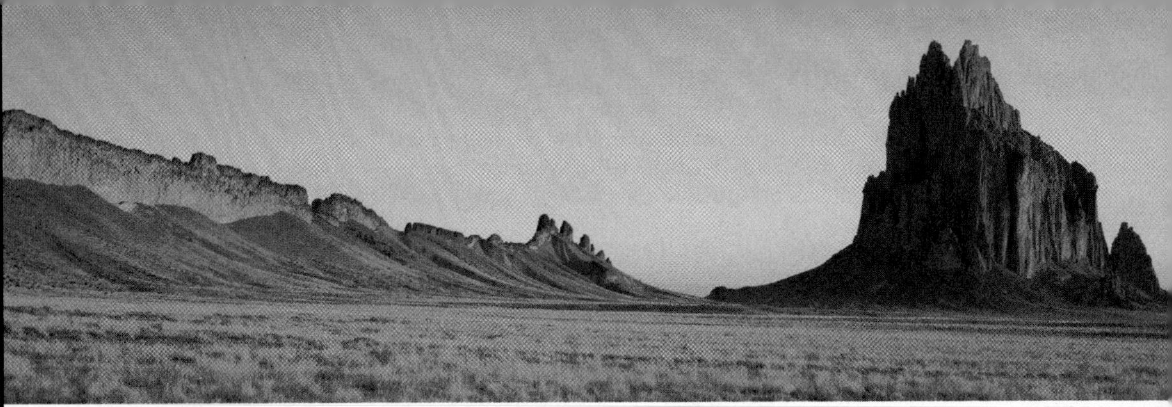

Figure 6 Shiprock, in New Mexico, is an example of a volcanic neck that was exposed by erosion.

Extrusive Igneous Rock

A *volcano* is a vent through which magma, gases, or volcanic ash is expelled. When a volcanic eruption stops, the magma in the vent may cool to form rock. Eventually, the soft parts of the volcano are eroded by wind and water, and only the hardest rock in the vent remains. The solidified central vent is called a *volcanic neck*. Narrow dikes that sometimes radiate from the neck may also be exposed. A dramatic example of a volcanic neck called Shiprock is shown in **Figure 6**.

Igneous rock masses that form on Earth's surface are called *extrusions*. Many extrusions are simply flat masses of rock called *lava flows*. A series of lava flows that cover a vast area with thick rock is known as a *lava plateau*. Volcanic rock called *tuff* forms when a volcano releases ash and other solid particles during an eruption. Tuff deposits can be several hundred meters thick and can cover areas of several hundred kilometers.

Section 2 Review

Key Ideas

1. **Summarize** three factors that affect the melting of rock.
2. **Contrast** partial melting and fractional crystallization.
3. **Describe** how the cooling rate of magma affects the texture of igneous rock.
4. **Name** the three families of igneous rocks, and identify their specific mineral compositions.
5. **Describe** five intrusive igneous rock structures.
6. **Identify** four extrusive igneous rock structures.

Critical Thinking

7. **Applying Ideas** If you wanted to create a rock that has large crystals in a laboratory, what conditions would you have to control? Explain your answer.
8. **Applying Ideas** An unidentified, light-colored igneous rock is made up of potassium feldspar and quartz. To what family of igneous rocks does the rock belong? Explain your answer.

Concept Mapping

9. Use the following terms to create a concept map: *igneous rock, magma, coarse grained, fine grained, felsic, mafic,* and *intermediate.*

Differentiated Instruction

Alternative Assessment

Travel Brochures Have students create travel brochures to five locations that have prominent exposed intrusive or extrusive igneous structures. The brochures should describe the kinds of igneous rock that make up each structure and the geological processes that formed the structure. Students should include drawings or photos of the structures. **LS Visual**

SECTION
3 Sedimentary Rock

Key Ideas	Key Terms	Why It Matters
❯ Explain the processes of compaction and cementation. ❯ Describe how chemical and organic sedimentary rocks form. ❯ Describe how clastic sedimentary rock forms. ❯ Identify seven sedimentary rock features.	**compaction** **cementation** **chemical sedimentary rock** **organic sedimentary rock** **clastic sedimentary rock**	Sedimentary rock is a common building material. Understanding its properties is crucial to public safety. The ways in which it is formed affects the rock's properties.

Loose fragments of rock, minerals, and organic material that result from natural processes, including the physical breakdown of rocks, are called *sediment*. Most sedimentary rock is made up of combinations of different types of sediment. The characteristics of sedimentary rock are determined by the source of the sediment, the way the sediment was moved, and the conditions under which the sediment was deposited.

Formation of Sedimentary Rocks

After sediments form, they are generally transported by wind, water, or ice to a new location. The source of the sediment determines the sediment's composition. As the sediment moves, its characteristics change as it is physically broken down or chemically altered. Eventually, the loose sediment is deposited.

Two main processes convert loose sediment to sedimentary rock—compaction and cementation. **Compaction,** as shown in **Figure 1,** is the process in which sediment is squeezed and in which the size of the pore space between sediment grains is reduced by the weight and pressure of overlying layers. **Cementation** is the process in which sediments are glued together by minerals that are deposited by water.

Geologists classify sedimentary rocks by the processes by which the rocks form and by the composition of the rocks. There are three main classes of sedimentary rocks—chemical, organic, and clastic.

compaction the process in which the volume and porosity of a sediment is decreased by the weight of overlying sediments as a result of burial beneath other sediments

cementation the process in which minerals precipitate into pore spaces between sediment grains and bind sediments together to form rock

Figure 1 Processes That Form Sedimentary Rock

When mud is deposited, there may be a lot of space between grains. During compaction, the grains are squeezed together, and the rock that forms takes up less space.

Overlying layers squeeze sediment.
50-60% water
10-20% water

When sand is deposited, there are many spaces between the grains. During cementation, water deposits minerals such as calcite or quartz in the spaces around the sand grains, which glues the grains together.

Pore spaces between sediment grains are empty.
Water moves through pore spaces.
Minerals deposited by water cement the grains together.

Section 3

Focus

Overview

This section explains how chemical, organic, and clastic sedimentary rocks form. It also explains how sediments change during transport and identifies seven features of sedimentary rocks.

Bellringer

Have students write down three features that they associate with sedimentary rock compared with other kinds of rock. (Answers may vary. Sample answers: Sedimentary rock may be layered, may be sandy or gritty, and may contain fossils.) **LS Verbal**

Motivate

Demonstration — GENERAL

Sedimentation Demonstrate the basic process of sedimentation by placing a few tablespoons of fine silt in a jar. Fill the jar with water, and place the lid tightly on the jar. Shake the jar, and while doing so, ask students what will happen when you set the jar down. (The silt will settle over time.) Set the jar down, and wait for two minutes. If the silt has not entirely settled, check back after 10 or 15 minutes.
LS Visual

Key Resources

Chapter Resource File
- Directed Reading BASIC
- Inquiry Lab: Sorting Sediments GENERAL

Technology
- Transparencies
  Bellringer

Teach

Homework GENERAL

Chemical Sedimentary Rock
Assign students to research different types of chemical sedimentary rock. Have students identify carbonate precipitates, such as calcite (chemical limestone, which is sometimes referred to as travertine). Have them also identify evaporates other than halite and gypsum (such as borax), as well as variant forms of gypsum (such as alabaster) and of halides (such as sylvite and hydrite). Students should also identify well-known locations where these various types of rock can be found. (for instance, Death Valley National Park, White Sands National Monument, and Carlsbad Caverns National Park) LS **Logical**

Using the Figure GENERAL

Organic Limestone Formation
Have students study the diagrams at the bottom of the page. Ask students if the process by which the shells become limestone is better described as compaction or cementation. (compaction) Ask students to explain their answer. (The microscopic shells are much like tiny particles of mud that can be compacted to take up less space. However, some cementation probably also occurs.) Ask students what grain size they would expect limestone to have, given this information. (Limestone should have grains the size of fine sand or grit.) LS **Logical**

chemical sedimentary rock sedimentary rock that forms when minerals precipitate from a solution or settle from a suspension

organic sedimentary rock sedimentary rock that forms from the remains of plants or animals

READING TOOLBOX

Chain-of-Events Chart
Make a chain-of-events chart to show the steps in the formation of organic sedimentary rocks. Write the first step of the process in a box. Add boxes with additional steps, and connect the boxes with arrows.

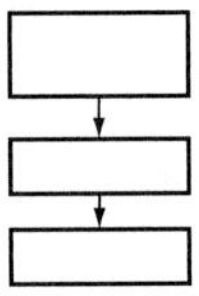

Chemical Sedimentary Rock

Minerals made up of ions such as calcium, potassium, and chloride can dissolve in water. **Chemical sedimentary rock** forms when the ions from dissolved minerals precipitate out of water because of changing concentrations of chemicals.

One reason minerals precipitate is due to evaporation. When water evaporates, the minerals that were dissolved in the water are left behind. Eventually, the concentration of minerals in the remaining water becomes high enough to cause minerals to precipitate out of the water. The minerals left behind form rocks called *evaporites*. Gypsum and halite, or rock salt, are two examples of evaporites. The Bonneville Salt Flats near the Great Salt Lake in Utah are a good example of evaporite deposits.

Organic Sedimentary Rock

The second class of sedimentary rock is **organic sedimentary rock.** Organic sedimentary rock is rock that forms from the remains of living things. Coal and some limestones are examples of organic sedimentary rocks. Coal forms from plant remains that are buried before they decay and are then compacted into matter that is composed mostly of carbon.

While chemical limestones precipitate from chemicals dissolved in water, organic limestones form when marine organisms, such as coral, clams, oysters, and plankton, remove the chemical components of the minerals calcite and aragonite from sea water. These organisms make their shells from these minerals. When they die, their shells eventually become limestone. This process of limestone formation is shown in **Figure 2.** Chalk is one example of limestone made up of the shells of tiny, one-celled marine organisms that settle to the ocean floor.

Figure 2 **Organic Limestone Formation**

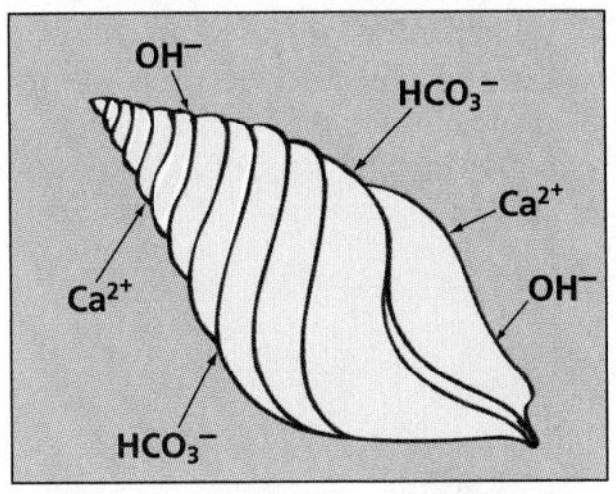

Organisms that live in lakes or oceans take chemicals from the water and produce the mineral calcium carbonate, $CaCO_3$. They use the $CaCO_3$ to build their shells or skeletons.

When the organisms die, the hard remains that are made of $CaCO_3$ settle to the lake or ocean floor.

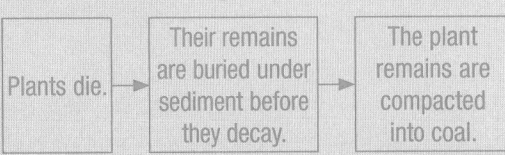

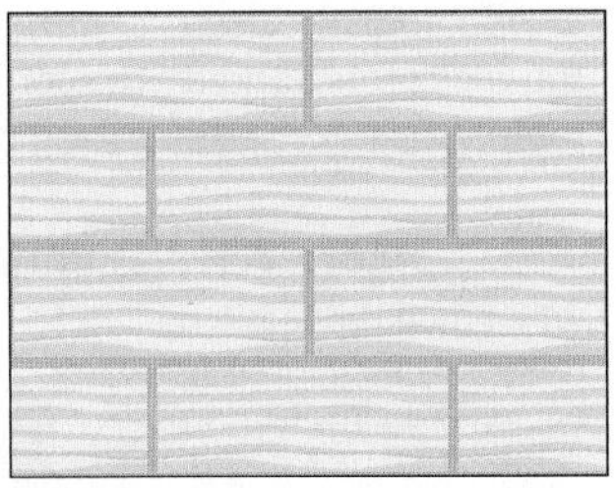

The shells of the dead organisms pile up. Eventually, the layers are compacted and cemented to form limestone.

READING TOOLBOX

Chain-of-Events Chart A sample chain-of-events chart for the formation of coal is shown here. Students may also show the formation of organic limestone.

Plants die. → Their remains are buried under sediment before they decay. → The plant remains are compacted into coal.

Key Resources

Technology

- Transparencies
  29 Organic Limestone Formation

Figure 3 Types of Clastic Sedimentary Rock

Conglomerate is composed of rounded, pebble-sized fragments that are held together by a cement.

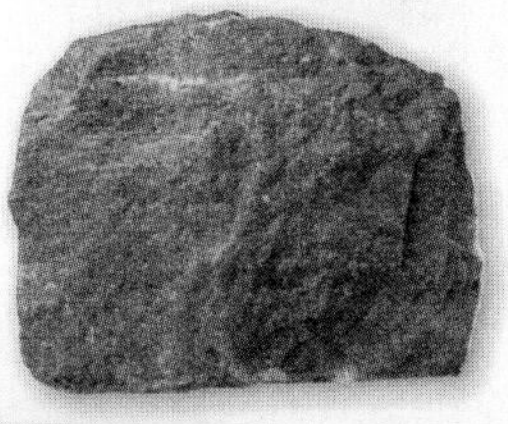

Sandstone is made of small mineral grains that are cemented together.

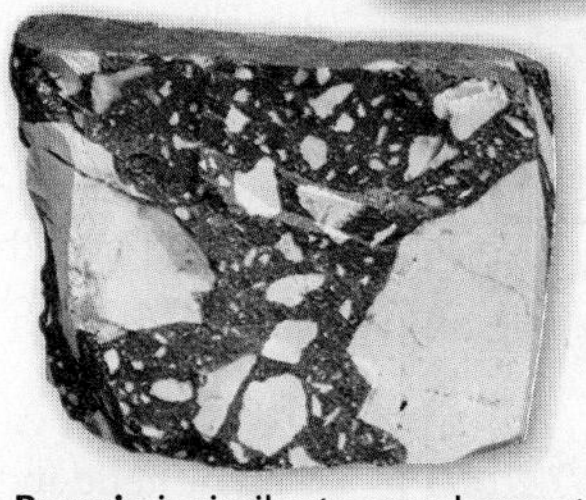

Breccia is similar to conglomerate, but breccia contains angular fragments.

Shale is made of flaky clay particles that compress into flat layers.

Clastic Sedimentary Rock

The third class of sedimentary rock is made of rock fragments that are carried away from their source by water, wind, or ice and left as deposits. Over time, the individual fragments may become compacted and cemented into solid rock. The rock formed from these deposits is called **clastic sedimentary rock.**

clastic sedimentary rock sedimentary rock that forms when fragments of preexisting rocks are compacted or cemented together

Clastic sedimentary rocks are classified by the size of the sediments they contain, as shown in **Figure 3.** One group consists of large fragments that are cemented together. Rock that is composed of rounded fragments that range in size from 2 mm to boulders is called a *conglomerate.* If the fragments are angular and have sharp corners, the rock is called a *breccia* (BRECH ee uh). In conglomerates and breccias, the individual pieces of sediment can be easily seen.

Another group of clastic sedimentary rocks is made up of sand-sized grains that have been cemented together. These rocks are called *sandstone.* Quartz is the major component of most sandstones. Many sandstones have pores between the sand grains through which fluids, such as groundwater, natural gas, and crude oil, can move.

A third group of clastic sedimentary rocks, called *shale,* consists of clay-sized particles that are cemented and compacted. The flaky clay particles are usually pressed into flat layers that will easily split apart.

Reading Check **Name three groups of clastic sedimentary rock.**

Math Skills

Sedimentation Rates The rate at which sediment accumulates is called the *sedimentation rate.* The sedimentation rate of an area is 1.5 mm per year. At this rate, how many years must pass for 10 cm of sediment to be deposited?

Math Skills

Answer

$1.5 \text{ mm/year} + x \text{ years} = 10 \text{ cm}$

$1.5 \text{ mm} = 0.15 \text{ cm}$

$x \text{ years} = 10 \text{ cm} \div 0.15 \text{ cm}$

$= 67 \text{ years}$

Answer to Reading Check

Three groups of clastic sedimentary rock are conglomerates and breccias, sandstones, and shales.

Discussion — GENERAL

Comprehension Check Ask students how texture in each of the three groups of clastic sedimentary rock indicates whether the group formed by cementation or by compaction. (The larger the clasts, or particles, in the rock, the less likely they are able to stick together without cement.) Present to students this scenario: "You find a piece of sedimentary rock in a high mountain valley. The rock has a sandy texture and no signs of internal layering. What type of rock is it? On what evidence do you base your answer?" (Answers may vary. Most likely the rock is a clastic sedimentary rock of the sandstone group. If the rock is made of tiny particles of sand or rock, the rock must be clastic. The fine grain eliminates conglomerate or breccia, and the coarseness of the grains eliminates shale.) LS **Logical**

Differentiated Instruction

English Learners

Paired Summarizing Group students into pairs and have them read silently about the three groups of clastic sedimentary rock. Then, have one student summarize the features of the rocks in each group. The other student should listen to the retelling and point out any inaccuracies or ideas that were left out. Allow students to refer to the text as needed.
LS **Verbal** Co-op Learning English Language Learners

Cultural Awareness — BASIC

Sacred Rocks The sedimentary rock forms produced by weathering and erosion commonly inspire awe. Many native peoples throughout the world consider the rock forms of their region sacred. For example, the Navajo of North America ascribe supernatural powers to the sandstone buttes and spires of Monument Valley, their tribal park in Utah and Arizona. The Aborigines of central Australia regard the vast sandstone monolith Uluru, also known as "Ayres Rock," as having an underground energy source called the "dream time," a term that also refers to a record of ancestors' activities.

Teaching, *continued*

Teaching Tip — BASIC

Connect to Familiar Processes
To help students understand the process of sediment sorting, draw an analogy between sorting in a moving medium (air or water) and passing sediments through a screen. If a box with a screen bottom is used to scoop up a mixture of sand, gravel, and silt, only the sand and silt will pass through the screen, while the larger gravel remains in the box. If the sand and silt mixture is put into another box with a finer screen, the silt will pass through the screen, leaving the sand behind. In the natural process of sorting, the mass of each fragment is important, in addition to its size. Also, the speed at which the wind or water moves the particles functions as the screens do. Larger particles are gradually left behind, while smaller ones are moved farther until only the finest grains remain. Sediments become better sorted the longer the sorting process continues. You may want to perform this activity as a demonstration
LS Logical

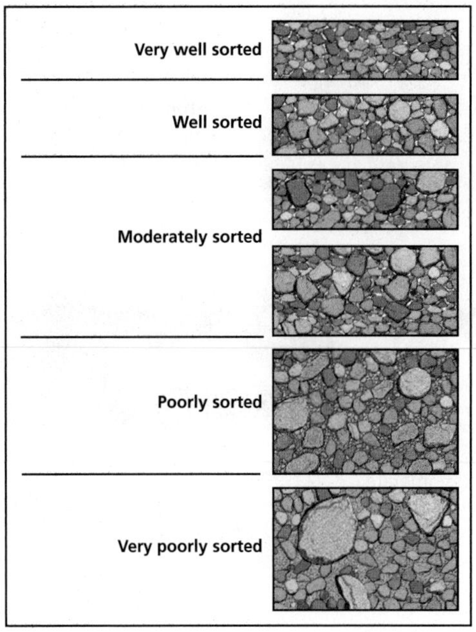

Figure 4 Sorting of Sediments

Characteristics of Clastic Sediments

The physical characteristics of sediments are determined mainly by the way sediments were transported to the place where they are deposited. Sediments are transported by four main agents: water, ice, wind, and the effects of gravity. The size of sediment particles that can be carried and the distance that the particles will move depends on the speed with which the sediment is moved. In general, both the distance the sediment is moved and the agent that moves the sediment determine the characteristics of that sediment.

Sorting

The tendency for currents of air or water to separate sediments according to size is called *sorting*. Sediments can be very well sorted, very poorly sorted, or somewhere in between, as shown in **Figure 4.** In well-sorted sediments, all of the grains are roughly the same size and shape. Poorly sorted sediment consists of grains that are many different sizes. The sorting of a sediment is the result of changes in the speed of the agent that is moving the sediment. For example, when a fast-moving stream enters a lake, the speed of the water decreases sharply. Because large grains are too heavy for the current to carry, these grains are deposited first. Fine grains can stay suspended in the water for much longer than large grains can. So, fine particles are commonly deposited farther from shore or on top of coarser sediments.

Academic Vocabulary
transport (trans POHRT) to carry from one place to another

Angularity

As sediment is transported from its source to where it is deposited, the particles collide with each other and with other objects in their path. These collisions can cause the particles to change size and shape. When particles first break from the source rock, they tend to be angular and uneven. Particles that have moved long distances from the source tend to be more rounded and smooth. In general, the farther sediment travels from its source, the finer and smoother the particles of sediment become.

SCILINKS.
www.scilinks.org
Topic: Sedimentary Rock
Code: **HQX1365**

Sedimentary Rock Features

The place or setting in which sediment is deposited is called a *depositional environment*. Common depositional environments include rivers, deltas, beaches, and oceans. Each depositional environment has different characteristics that create specific structures in sedimentary rock. These features allow scientists to identify the depositional environment in which the rock formed.

Internet Activity — GENERAL

Identifying Sedimentary Rock Features
Have students use the Internet to locate an example of each of the sedimentary rock features described on the next page. Students may find information and photographs at Web sites for the National Park Service and the United States Geological Survey. Have students compile their findings in a written report. A worksheet designed to direct student research on this topic can be found in the **Chapter Resource File** booklet or by visiting www.thinkcentral.com and entering the keyword **HQXRXSX. LS Visual**

Differentiated Instruction

Special Education Students

Sorting Help students understand the concept of sorting by using mixtures of actual objects. Use objects such as marbles, bottle caps, ball bearings, and beads. Make mixtures that fit into each category, from very well sorted to very poorly sorted. Let students feel each mixture and match it to the correct category. **LS Visual/Kinesthetic**

Stratification

Layering of sedimentary rock, as shown in **Figure 5,** is called *stratification.* Stratification occurs when the conditions of sediment deposition change. The conditions may vary when there is a change in sediment type or of depositional environment. For example, a rise in sea level may cause an area that was once a beach to become a shallow ocean, which changes the type of sediment that is deposited in the area.

Stratified layers, or *beds,* vary in thickness depending on the length of time during which sediment is deposited and how much sediment is deposited. *Massive beds,* or beds that have no internal structures, form when similar sediment is deposited under similar conditions for long periods of time or when a large amount of sediment is deposited at one time.

Cross-beds and Graded Bedding

Some sedimentary rocks are characterized by slanting layers called *cross-beds* that form within beds. Cross-beds, which generally form in sand dunes or river beds, are shown in **Figure 5.**

When various sizes and kinds of materials are deposited within one layer, a type of stratification called *graded bedding* may occur. Graded bedding occurs when different sizes and shapes of sediment settle to different levels. Graded beds commonly transition from largest grains on the bottom to smallest grains on the top. However, certain depositional events, such as some mudflows, may cause *reverse grading,* in which the smallest grains are on the bottom and the largest grains are on top.

Reading Check **What is graded bedding?**

Quick Lab

10 min

Graded Bedding

Procedure

1. Place 20 mL of water into a small glass jar.
2. Pour 10 mL of poorly sorted sediment into the jar. Place a lid securely on the jar.
3. Shake the jar vigorously for 1 min, and then let it sit still for 5 min.
4. Observe the settled sediment.

Analysis

1. Describe any sedimentary structures you observed.
2. Name two factors responsible for the sedimentary structures you observed.

Figure 5 Examples of Sedimentary Rock Structures

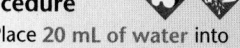

Answer to Reading Check

Graded bedding is a type of stratification in which different sizes and types of sediments settle to different levels.

Quick Lab

Skills Acquired
- Experimenting
- Identifying/Recognizing Patterns
- Predicting

Materials
- Water
- Small glass jar with lid
- Poorly sorted sediment

Teacher's Notes: You may want to use plastic jars, to prevent students from breaking glass jars.

Answers to Analysis

1. The sediment shows graded bedding; the largest fragments lie on the bottom, over which lie the next largest, and so forth up to the top where the finest sediments are located.
2. The size and density of sediment grains cause these structures to form.

Close

Reteaching BASIC

Sedimentary Rocks On the board, write *limestone, sandstone, breccia, evaporites,* and *shale* in one column. Write *chemical, clastic,* and *organic* in another column. Have students match the appropriate terms in the two columns. **LS Logical/Verbal**

Quiz GENERAL

1. What reduces the angularity of clastic sediments? (The continual transport of those sediments over long periods of time causes the sediments to become rounded and smooth.)
2. What is the compound in the shells of marine animals that makes up limestone? (calcium carbonate, or $CaCO_3$)

Close, *continued*

Answers to Section Review

1. During compaction, fine grains are squeezed together and the rock that forms takes up less space. During cementation, minerals that are deposited by water glue sediments together.
2. Chemical sedimentary rocks form when chemicals in solution precipitate out of the solution and form deposits at the bottom of the body of water. Examples include gypsum and halite. Organic sedimentary rocks form when the remains of plants and animals are gradually compacted or cemented together. Examples include limestone and coal.
3. Clastic rock forms from rock fragments that were transported away from their source by wind, water, gravity, or ice, rather than by chemical processes.
4. The farther sediment is transported and the longer the transport takes, the more well-sorted and less angular the fragments become.
5. Stratification, cross-beds, graded bedding, ripple marks, mud cracks, fossils, and concretions are all features that provide information about how sediment was deposited.
6. Smooth, small rocks have probably been transported farther or for a longer period of time than angular, uneven rocks have.
7. A slow-moving stream sorts sediments more effectively because it cannot carry larger or heavier sediments as easily as it carries smaller or lighter sediments.

Figure 6 This dry and mud-cracked river bed is in Nagasaki, Japan.

Ripple Marks

Some sedimentary rocks clearly display *ripple marks*. Ripple marks are caused by the action of wind or water on sand. When the sand becomes sandstone, the ripple marks may be preserved. When scientists find ripple marks in sedimentary rock, the scientists know that the sediment was once part of a beach or a river bed.

Mud Cracks

The ground in **Figure 6** shows mud cracks, which are another feature of sedimentary rock. Mud cracks form when muddy deposits dry and shrink. The shrinking causes the drying mud to crack. A river's flood plain or a dry lake bed is a common place to find mud cracks. Once the area is flooded again, new deposits may fill in the cracks and preserve their features when the mud hardens to solid rock.

Fossils and Concretions

The remains or traces of ancient plants and animals, called *fossils,* may be preserved in sedimentary rock. As sediments pile up, plant and animal remains are buried. Hard parts of these remains may be preserved in the rock. More often, even the hard parts dissolve and leave only impressions in the rock. Sedimentary rocks sometimes contain lumps of rock that have a composition that is different from that of the main rock body. These lumps are known as *concretions*. Concretions form when minerals precipitate from fluids and build up around a nucleus. Groundwater sometimes deposits dissolved minerals inside cavities in sedimentary rock. The minerals may crystallize inside the cavities to form a special type of rock called a *geode*.

Section 3 Review

Key Ideas

1. **Explain** how the processes of compaction and cementation form sedimentary rock.
2. **Describe** how chemical and organic sedimentary rocks form, and give two examples of each.
3. **Describe** how clastic sedimentary rock differs from chemical and organic sedimentary rock.
4. **Explain** how the physical characteristics of sediments change during transport.
5. **Identify** seven features that you can use to identify the depositional environment in which sedimentary rocks formed.

Critical Thinking

6. **Making Comparisons** Compare the histories of rounded, smooth rocks and angular, uneven rocks.
7. **Identifying Relationships** Which of the following would most effectively sort sediments: a fast-moving river or a small, slow-moving stream? Explain your answer.

Concept Mapping

8. Use the following terms to create a concept map: *cementation, clastic sedimentary rock, sedimentary rock, chemical sedimentary rock, compaction,* and *organic sedimentary rock.*

8. *Sedimentary rock,* is classified as *chemical sedimentary rock, organic sedimentary rock,* and *clastic sedimentary rock,* and may form by *cementation* and *compaction.*

Differentiated Instruction

Alternative Assessment

Modeling Sedimentation Have students create a computer model or a series of detailed diagrams that show the various stages in the formation of sedimentary rock. Students should model both compaction and cementation. The models should show all of the steps that lead to the formation of sedimentary rock from deposited materials. **LS Kinesthetic/Logical**

SECTION 4

Metamorphic Rock

Key Ideas	Key Terms	Why It Matters
❯ Describe the process of metamorphism. ❯ Explain the difference between regional and contact metamorphism. ❯ Distinguish between foliated and nonfoliated metamorphic rocks, and give an example of each.	**metamorphism** **contact metamorphism** **regional metamorphism** **foliation** **nonfoliated**	Metamorphism can produce marble and gemstones, such as rubies. Materials such as these are important to civilization, both ancient and modern.

The process by which heat, pressure, or chemical processes change one type of rock to another is called **metamorphism.** Most metamorphic rock, or rock that has undergone metamorphism, forms deep within Earth's crust. All metamorphic rock forms from existing igneous, sedimentary, or metamorphic rock.

Formation of Metamorphic Rocks

During metamorphism, heat, pressure, and hot fluids cause some minerals to change into other minerals. Minerals may also change in size or shape, or they may separate into parallel bands that give the rock a layered appearance. Hot fluids from magma may circulate through the rock and change the mineral composition of the rock by dissolving some materials and by adding others. All of these changes are part of metamorphism.

The type of rock that forms because of metamorphism can indicate the conditions that were in place when the original rock changed, as shown in **Figure 1.** The composition of the rock being metamorphosed, the amount and direction of heat and pressure, and the presence or absence of certain fluids cause different combinations of minerals to form.

Two types of metamorphism occur in Earth's crust. One type occurs when small volumes of rock come into contact with magma. The second type occurs when large areas of Earth's crust are affected by the heat and pressure that is caused by the movement and collisions of Earth's giant tectonic plates.

metamorphism the process in which one type of rock changes into metamorphic rock because of chemical processes or changes in temperature and pressure

Figure 1 Indicators of Metamorphic Conditions

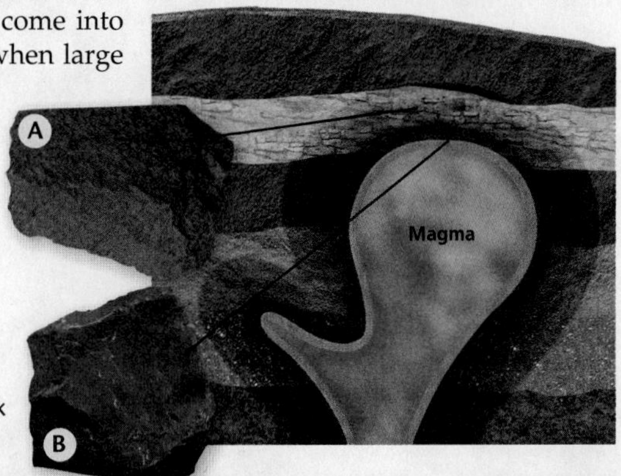

Slate (A) is a metamorphic rock that commonly forms in the outer zone of metamorphism around a body of magma where clay-rich rock is exposed to relatively small amounts of heat.
Hornfels (B) is a metamorphic rock that forms in the innermost zone of metamorphism, where clay-rich rock is exposed to large amounts of heat from the magma.

Section 4

Focus

Overview

This section describes how temperature and pressure changes and chemical processes change one type of rock to another. The section also explains the difference between regional and contact metamorphism and distinguishes between foliated and nonfoliated metamorphic rock.

Bellringer

Ask students to list items that change from one form to another. (Sample answers: Caterpillars become butterflies; nuts or seeds become trees; superheroes change from their secret identities; and liquid water freezes to become ice.) LS **Verbal**

Motivate

Demonstration GENERAL

Metamorphism Sometimes, metamorphism changes a rock without changing its bulk chemical composition. Show the class samples of granite and gneiss and of limestone and marble. Have students observe similarities and differences. (Granite and gneiss may both be made of quartz and feldspars, but gneiss has bands of minerals. Marble and limestone are both composed of calcium carbonate, but marble appears to be crystalline.) LS **Visual**

Key Resources

Chapter Resource File
- Directed Reading BASIC
- Making Models Lab: Metamorphic Rocks GENERAL

Technology
- Transparencies
  Bellringer
  30 Indicators of Metamorphic Conditions

Teach

Activity — ADVANCED

Poster Project Have interested students research an area in which contact or regional metamorphism is occurring. Have students identify the specific causes of the metamorphism, as well as the types of rock before and after the metamorphism takes place. Students should also infer whether the stresses on the rock are applied to large areas or small areas. Students should organize their findings and present them as a poster or series of posters. **LS Logical/Visual**

Why It Matters

Why Are Rubies so Rare? Pure corundum is rare in nature, and colorless. Trace amounts of certain elements give corundum different colors. The majority of rubies are found in patches of marble deposits along the southern slope of the Himalaya mountain range. The temperature and pressure deep inside the earth during mountain formation provided the conditions to make rubies, alongside metamorphic rocks. Synthetic rubies are now used in many applications, including the laser scanner at supermarket checkouts, and for bearings where their greater hardness compared with steel bearings is an advantage.

Answer to Your Turn

Comparing Processes Natural and synthetic rubies are both made from similar chemicals at high temperatures. They are very similar and only an expert can tell the difference.

contact metamorphism a change in the texture, structure, or chemical composition of a rock due to contact with magma

regional metamorphism a change in the texture, structure, or chemical composition of a rock due to changes in temperature and pressure over a large area, generally as a result of tectonic forces

Academic Vocabulary

generate (JEN uhr AYT) to bring about; to produce

Contact Metamorphism

When magma comes into contact with existing rock, heat from the magma can change the structure and mineral composition of the surrounding rock by a process called **contact metamorphism.** This process forms the hornfels shown on the previous page. During contact metamorphism only a small area of rock that surrounds the hot magma is changed by the magma's heat. Hot chemical fluids moving through fractures may also cause changes in the surrounding rock during contact metamorphism.

Regional Metamorphism

Metamorphism sometimes occurs over an area of thousands of square kilometers during periods of high tectonic activity, such as when mountain ranges form. The type of metamorphism that occurs over a large area is called **regional metamorphism.**

Tectonic activity generates tremendous heat and pressure, which cause chemical changes in the minerals of rock. Most metamorphic rock forms as a result of regional metamorphism. However, volcanism and the movement of magma often accompany tectonic activity. Thus, rocks that are formed by contact metamorphism are also commonly discovered in locations where regional metamorphism has occurred.

Reading Check How are minerals affected by regional metamorphism?

Why It Matters

Why Are Rubies so Rare?

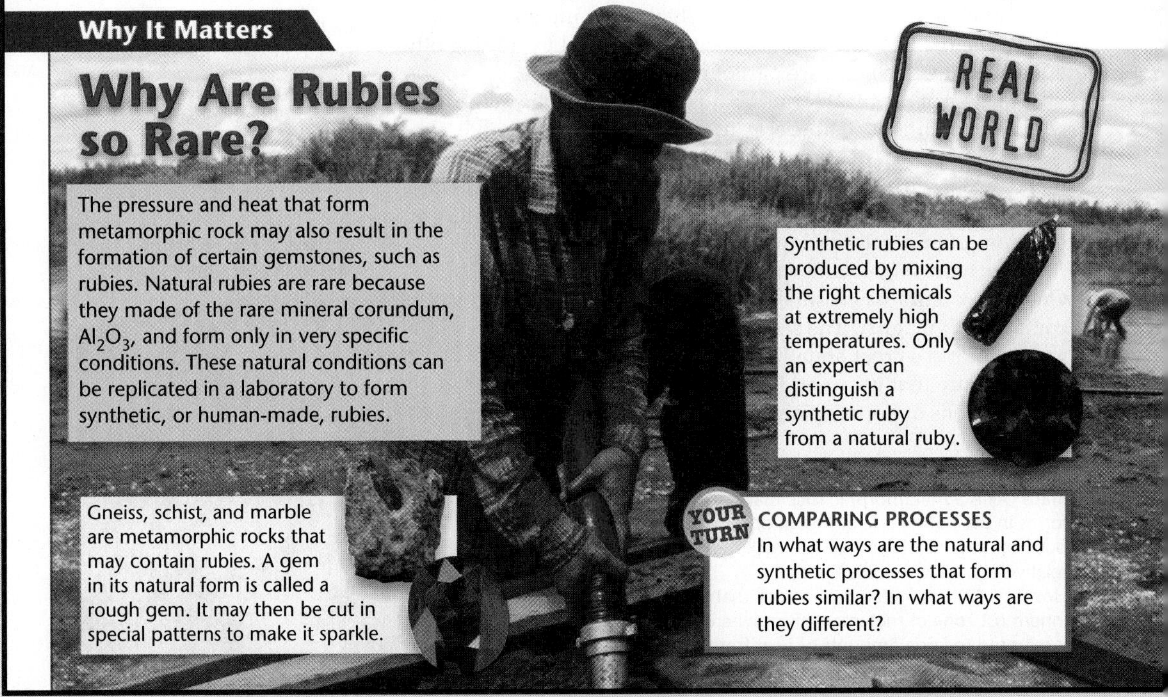

The pressure and heat that form metamorphic rock may also result in the formation of certain gemstones, such as rubies. Natural rubies are rare because they made of the rare mineral corundum, Al_2O_3, and form only in very specific conditions. These natural conditions can be replicated in a laboratory to form synthetic, or human-made, rubies.

Synthetic rubies can be produced by mixing the right chemicals at extremely high temperatures. Only an expert can distinguish a synthetic ruby from a natural ruby.

Gneiss, schist, and marble are metamorphic rocks that may contain rubies. A gem in its natural form is called a rough gem. It may then be cut in special patterns to make it sparkle.

YOUR TURN COMPARING PROCESSES
In what ways are the natural and synthetic processes that form rubies similar? In what ways are they different?

Answer to Reading Check

The high pressures and temperatures that result from the movements of tectonic plates may cause chemical changes in the minerals.

Differentiated Instruction

Advanced Learners

Anticipation Guide Before students read this page, ask them to predict the difference between contact metamorphism and regional metamorphism. Have students write down their predictions, and then read the page to find out if their predictions were accurate. **LS Logical**

Classification of Metamorphic Rocks

Minerals in the original rock help determine the mineral composition of the metamorphosed rock. As the original rock is exposed to changes in heat and pressure, the minerals in the original rock often combine chemically to form new minerals. While metamorphic rocks are classified by chemical composition, they are first classified according to their texture. Metamorphic rocks have either a foliated texture or a nonfoliated texture.

READING TOOLBOX

Summarizing Ideas
As you read this page and the next, summarize the main ideas about the classification of metamorphic rocks. Include a summary of the differences between foliated and nonfoliated rocks.

Foliated Rocks

The metamorphic rock texture in which minerals are arranged in planes or bands is called **foliation.** Foliated rock can form in one of two ways. Extreme pressure may cause the mineral crystals in the rock to realign or regrow to form parallel bands. Foliation also occurs as minerals that have different compositions separate to produce a series of alternating dark and light bands.

foliation the metamorphic rock texture in which mineral grains are arranged in planes or bands

Foliated metamorphic rocks include the common rocks slate, schist, and gneiss (NIES). Slate forms when pressure is exerted on the sedimentary rock shale, which contains clay minerals that are flat and thin. The fine-grained minerals in slate are compressed into thin layers, which split easily into flat sheets. Flat sheets of slate are used in building materials, such as roof tiles or walkway stones.

When large amounts of heat and pressure are exerted on slate, a coarse-grained metamorphic rock known as *schist* may form. Deep underground, intense heat and pressure may cause the minerals in schist to separate into bands as the minerals recrystallize. The metamorphosed rock that has bands of light and dark minerals is called *gneiss*. Gneiss is shown in **Figure 2.**

SCILINKS.
www.scilinks.org
Topic: Metamorphic Rock
Code: HQX0949

Figure 2 Large amounts of heat and pressure may change rock into the metamorphic rock gneiss, which shows pronounced foliation.

READING TOOLBOX

Summarizing Ideas

Answers may vary. A sample summary is shown here.

Metamorphic rocks are classified by texture (foliated or nonfoliated) and chemical composition. The minerals in foliated rocks, such as slate, schist, and gneiss, appear in planes or bands, while the minerals in metamorphic nonfoliated rocks, such as quartzite and marble, do not.

Close

Reteaching — BASIC

Metamorphic Rocks On the board, write the words "foliated" and "nonfoliated." In a side column, write the names "slate," "quartzite," "schist," "gneiss," and "marble." Have students indicate which of the rocks fall under the first two headings. **LS Logical**

Quiz — GENERAL

1. What are the two types of metamorphism? (contact metamorphism and regional metamorphism)
2. Why do minerals in some metamorphic rocks separate into compositional bands? (Intense heat and pressure cause different minerals to separate as they recrystallize.)
3. How are marble and limestone similar? How are they different? (They have the same chemical composition. Marble is a nonfoliated metamorphic rock. Limestone, from which marble forms, is an organic sedimentary rock.)

MISCONCEPTION ALERT

Physical Separation Emphasize that foliation is a physical property of rock and not a chemical change. Minerals may become aligned as the crystals reform in a direction perpendicular to the stress, without changing chemical composition. Separation of minerals into compositional bands may result as minerals recrystallize under conditions of great heat and pressure. In both cases, changes are because of the physical properties and not a change in composition.

Homework — ADVANCED

Degrees of Metamorphism Have students research metamorphic grades of rock. Students should choose a sedimentary or igneous rock and then research the temperature and pressure conditions required to transform that rock into several different forms. Have students present their findings in a short oral report. **LS Auditory**

Close, *continued*

Answers to Section Review

1. Metamorphism is the process by which one rock changes into another kind of rock because of chemical processes or changes in temperature and pressure.
2. Contact metamorphism occurs in a small region where rock comes in contact with magma. Regional metamorphism occurs over a large area, and is generally the result of tectonic forces.
3. Foliated metamorphic rock has a texture in which mineral grains are arranged in planes or bands, whereas the texture of nonfoliated metamorphic rock does not have minerals arranged in planes or bands.
4. Slate and schist are foliated metamorphic rocks, while quartzite and marble are nonfoliated metamorphic rocks.
5. Both a butterfly and metamorphic rock undergo a change from an earlier form (a caterpillar in the case of the butterfly; a different type of rock in the case of the rock) to a new form.
6. Both rocks formed when clay-rich rock underwent contact metamorphism, but the rock that formed slate was farther from the magma than the rock that formed hornfels was.
7. Regional metamorphism is occurring where the two tectonic plates collide to uplift the Himalayas. Therefore, most metamorphism will be widespread.
8. *Metamorphic rock* forms as a result of *contact metamorphism* or *regional metamorphism*, and may be *foliated* or *nonfoliated.*

Figure 3 Marble is a nonfoliated metamorphic rock that is used as building and sculpting material.

nonfoliated the metamorphic rock texture in which mineral grains are not arranged in planes or bands

Nonfoliated Rocks

Rocks that do not have bands or aligned minerals are **nonfoliated.** Most nonfoliated metamorphic rocks share at least one of two main characteristics. First, the original rock that is metamorphosed may contain grains of only one mineral or contains very small amounts of other minerals. Thus, the rock does not form bands of different mineral compositions when it is metamorphosed. Second, the original rock may contain grains that are round or square. Because the grains do not have some long and some short sides, these grains do not change position when exposed to pressure in one direction.

Quartzite is one common nonfoliated rock. Quartzite forms when quartz sandstone is metamorphosed. Quartzite is very hard and does not wear away easily. For this reason, quartzite remains after weaker rocks around it have worn away and may form hills or mountains.

Marble, the beautiful stone that is used for building monuments and statues, is a metamorphic rock that forms from the compression of limestone. The Parthenon, which is shown in **Figure 3,** has been standing in Greece for more than 1,400 years. However, the calcium carbonate in marble reacts with acid rain, which is caused by air pollution. Many ancient marble structures and sculptures are being damaged by acid rain.

Section 4 Review

Key Ideas

1. **Describe** the process of metamorphism.
2. **Explain** the difference between regional and contact metamorphism.
3. **Distinguish** between foliated and nonfoliated metamorphic rocks.
4. **Identify** two foliated metamorphic rocks and two nonfoliated metamorphic rocks.

Critical Thinking

5. **Analyzing Relationships** What do a butterfly and metamorphic rock have in common?
6. **Making Comparisons** If you have samples of the two metamorphic rocks slate and hornfels, what can you say about the history of each rock?
7. **Identifying Relationships** The Himalaya Mountains are located on a boundary between two colliding tectonic plates. Would most of the metamorphic rock in that area occur in small patches or in wide regions? Explain your answer.

Concept Mapping

8. Use the following terms to create a concept map: *contact metamorphism, foliated, regional metamorphism, metamorphic rock,* and *nonfoliated.*

Differentiated Instruction

Alternative Assessment

Metamorphic Chemistry Have students research the exact geological and chemical processes required for forming one of the following gemstones: sapphires, jade, and star sapphires. Students should present their findings in a short written report. **LS Verbal/Logical**

Why It Matters

A Nuclear Waste Basket

EYE ON THE ENVIRONMENT

Each day, about 6 tons of highly reactive used fuel rods from nuclear reactors are added to the 30,000 tons held at various sites across the country. These rods and other radioactive waste must be stored for thousands of years, away from people and water. But where? One solution is to place the waste 300 m below ground, in the very stable rock under Yucca Mountain in Nevada.

Used fuel rods are only part of the nuclear waste problem. A large volume of low- and medium-level radioactive waste is piling up in drums like these.

Nuclear waste will be placed in containers for transportation to Yucca Mountain. Tens of thousands of truck and train shipments will be required.

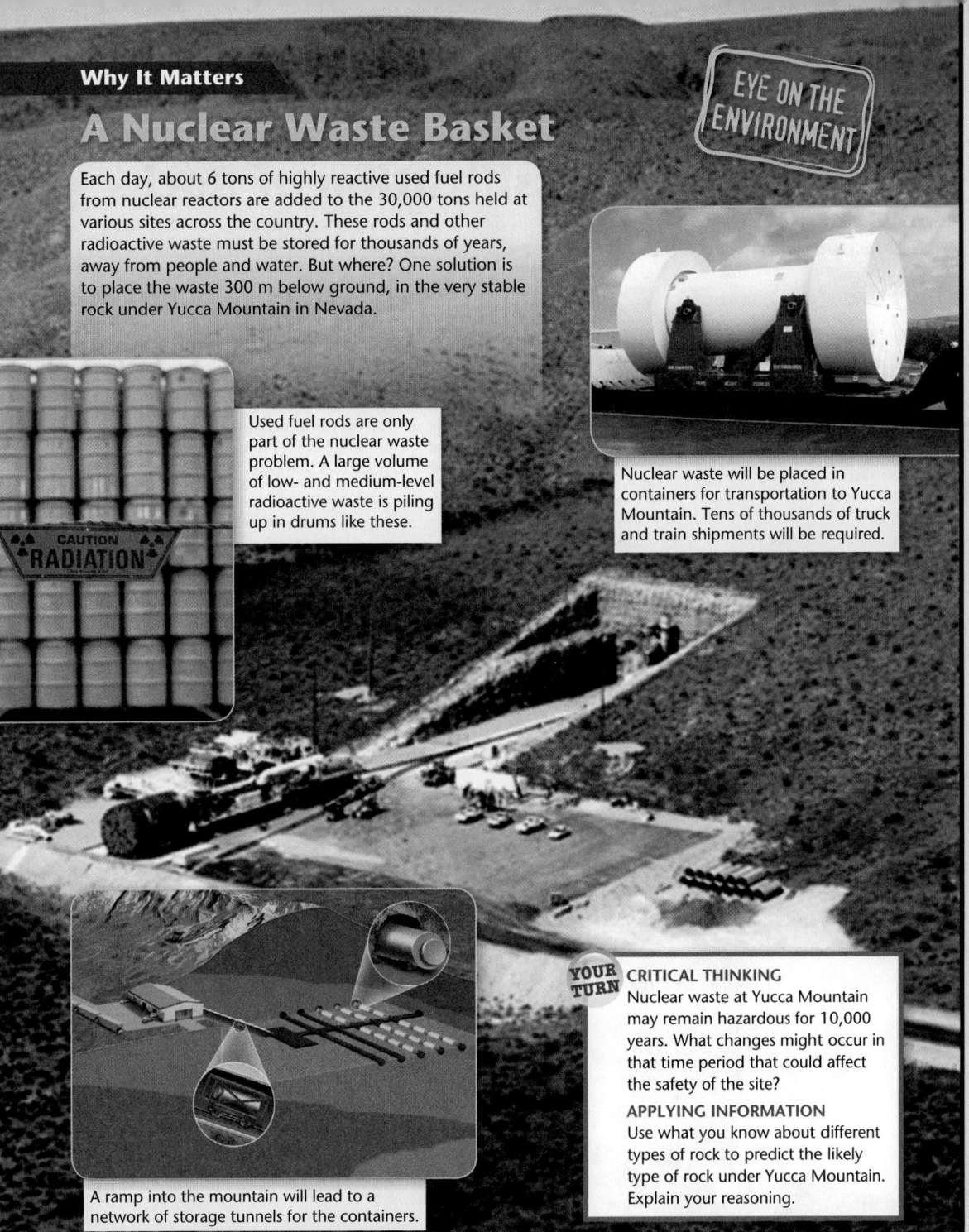

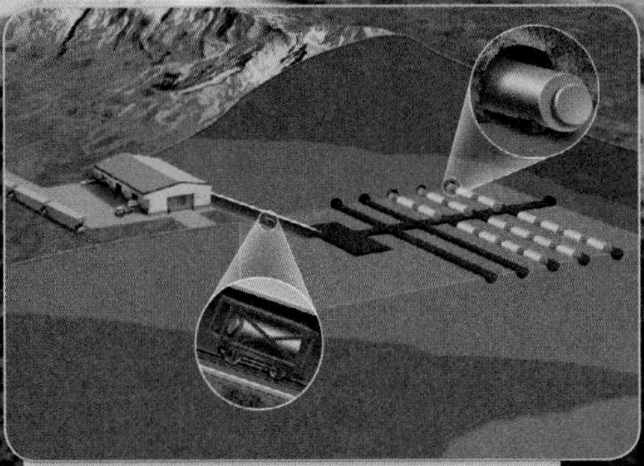

A ramp into the mountain will lead to a network of storage tunnels for the containers.

YOUR TURN

CRITICAL THINKING
Nuclear waste at Yucca Mountain may remain hazardous for 10,000 years. What changes might occur in that time period that could affect the safety of the site?

APPLYING INFORMATION
Use what you know about different types of rock to predict the likely type of rock under Yucca Mountain. Explain your reasoning.

Why It Matters

Nuclear waste must be stored somewhere. The Yucca Mountain storage space has been in planning for decades, and is scheduled to open in less than 10 years. Yucca Mountain is considered a relatively safe place to store nuclear waste because of its location, the type of rock, and the absence of water. The water table is 600 m below ground, and the site is far from aquifers used for water supplies. Some geologists are concerned that earthquakes or volcanic activity could disturb the depository and release radioactive material. There is also concern that materials could move through fractures in the tuff, the rock that makes up the repository. The U.S. Department of Energy believes that the repository could withstand significant disruption, but debate continues about the safety of the site.

Answers to Your Turn

Critical Thinking Answers may vary. Students may suggest that the rock could be disturbed by earthquakes or volcanic activity.

Applying Information Answers may vary. Students may reason that it is not sedimentary rock, because a porous or permeable rock would be unsuitable. They may reason that the rock is metamorphic or igneous because the formation of Yucca Mountain may have involved volcanic activity and metamorphism.

Skills Practice Lab

Time Required
two 45-minute class periods

Lab Ratings
EASY → HARD

Teacher Preparation: 2
Student Setup: 1
Concept Level: 2
Cleanup: 2

Skills Acquired
- Experimenting
- Collecting Data
- Organizing and Analyzing Data
- Classifying
- Identifying and Recognizing Patterns

Scientific Methods
In this lab, students will
- Make Observations
- Analyze the Results
- Draw Conclusions

Materials
The materials listed on the page are enough for groups of two students. If two hand lenses are provided for each workstation, students could work in groups of four. You may want to use lemon juice in place of the acid.

Skills Practice Lab

90 min

Classification of Rocks

What You'll Do
- **Observe** the characteristics of common rocks.
- **Compare and contrast** the features of igneous, sedimentary, and metamorphic rocks.
- **Identify** igneous, sedimentary, and metamorphic rocks.

What You'll Need
hand lens
hydrochloric acid, 10% dilute
medicine dropper
rock samples

Safety

There are many different types of igneous, sedimentary, and metamorphic rocks. Therefore, it is important to know distinguishing features of the rocks to identify the rocks. The classification of rocks is generally based on the way in which they formed, their mineral composition, and the size and arrangement (or texture) of their minerals.

Igneous rocks differ in the minerals they contain and the sizes of their crystals. Metamorphic rocks often look similar to igneous rocks, but they may have bands of minerals. Most sedimentary rocks are made of fragments of other rocks that are compressed and cemented together. Some common features of sedimentary rocks are parallel layers, ripple marks, cross-bedding, and the presence of fossils. In this lab, you will use these features to identify various rock samples.

Procedure

1. In your notebook, make a table that has columns for sample number, description of properties, rock class, and rock name. List the numbers of the rock samples you received from your teacher.
2. Examine the rocks carefully. You can use a hand lens to study the fine details of the rock samples. Look for characteristics such as the shape, size, and arrangement of the mineral grains. For each sample, list in your table the distinguishing features that you observe.

Step 2

Tips and Tricks
Students should visually identify the rocks before performing the acid test. When students test the rocks for acid reactivity, they should test all of the samples in sequence at the same time. This will reduce the number of times students will have to work with the acid, and thus reduce the chance of accidents. Make sure students wash their hands thoroughly when they are finished with the acid.

3. Refer to the Guide to Common Rocks in the Reference Tables section of the Appendix. Compare the properties for each rock sample that you listed with the properties listed in the identification table. If you are unable to identify certain rocks, examine these rock samples again.

Sample	Descriptions of Properties	Rock Class	Rock Name

4. Certain rocks react with acid, which indicates that they are composed of calcite. If a rock contains calcite, the rock will bubble and release carbon dioxide. Using a medicine dropper and 10% dilute hydrochloric acid, test various samples for their reactions. **CAUTION** Wear goggles, gloves, and an apron when you work with hydrochloric acid. Rinse each sample and wash your hands thoroughly afterward.

5. Complete your table by identifying the class of rock—igneous, sedimentary, or metamorphic—that each sample belongs to, and then name the rock.

Analysis

1. **Analyzing Methods** Which properties were most useful and least useful in identifying each rock sample? Explain.
2. **Evaluating Results** Were there any samples that you found difficult to identify? Explain.
3. **Making Comparisons** Describe any characteristics common to all of the rock samples.
4. **Evaluating Ideas** How can you distinguish between a sedimentary rock and a foliated metamorphic rock if both have observable layering?

Extension

Applying Conclusions Collect a variety of rocks from your area. Use the Guide to Common Rocks to see how many you can classify. How many igneous rocks did you collect? How many sedimentary rocks did you collect? How many metamorphic rocks did you collect? After you identify the class of each rock, try to name the rock.

Answers to Analysis

1. Answers will vary with each student or group. Possible answers will be rock textures; the clear presence of crystals; and bands, layers, or internal structures of the rock. Least useful properties will probably include color and shape.
2. Answers will vary with each student or group. The presence of crystals, especially fine-grained ones, may make certain igneous rock difficult to identify. Nonfoliated metamorphic rock may be hard to identify. Some sedimentary rocks, though usually classifiable through their cemented texture, may not be easy to identify by name.
3. Answers will vary with each student or group. Most structural features will be common to two groups, but not to all three. Rocks of all three types may have similar chemical compositions.
4. Sedimentary rocks are made of grains that are cemented together, while foliated metamorphic rocks are made of crystals.

Answer to Extension

Answers will depend on the number and types of rocks collected by each student and on the ease with which they can be identified. You may want to contact the United States Geological Survey or a local geologist or bureau of geology to determine the types of rocks found in your area.

Geologic Map of Virginia

MISCONCEPTION ALERT

Variations in Dates The dates given for geologic time intervals on this map are based on the ages of the rocks in the region. These dates may not match the dates in other geologic time scales because most time scales represent compiled data for several areas and include a variety of sources.

Answers to Map Skills Activity

1. Paleozoic Era, Cambrian Period
2. Charlottesville and Roanoke
3. Norfolk
4. Water in rivers and along the coastline contributed to deposition of material in the Holocene Epoch.
5. All of the Precambrian rocks formed at roughly the same time next to or on top of each other, so they are exposed near each other. The Precambrian rocks that are represented by the color tan are slightly metamorphosed rocks. The Precambrian rocks represented by the color brown are all metamorphic rocks. The Precambrian rocks represented by the patterned rock are igneous and metamorphic rocks that are older than the other two types of rock.
6. The oldest igneous rock formed between 1,400 million and 980 million years ago. The oldest metamorphic rock formed between 750 million and 550 million years ago. The oldest sedimentary rock formed between 550 million and 500 million years ago.

MAPS in Action

Geologic Map of Virginia

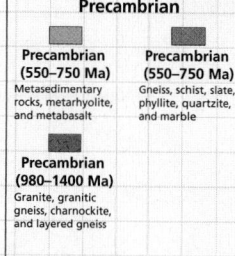

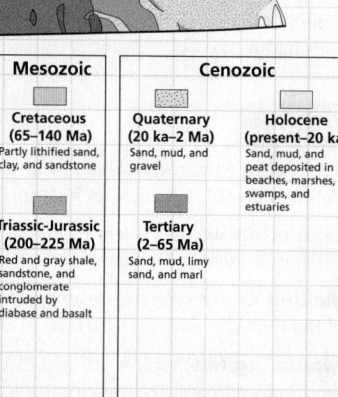

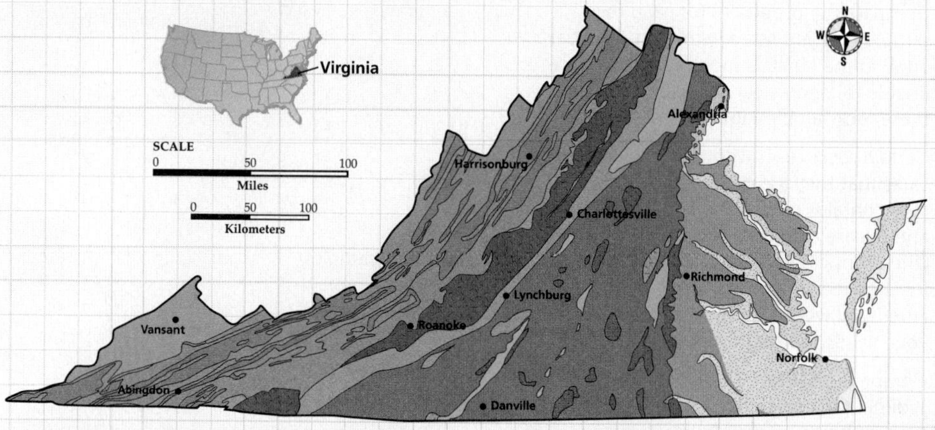

Precambrian

- **Precambrian (550–750 Ma)** Metasedimentary rocks, metarhyolite, and metabasalt
- **Precambrian (550–750 Ma)** Gneiss, schist, slate, phyllite, quartzite, and marble
- **Precambrian (980–1400 Ma)** Granite, granitic gneiss, charnockite, and layered gneiss

Paleozoic

- **Cambrian (500–550 Ma)** Dolomite, limestone, shale, and sandstone
- **Mississippian-Devonian (320–410 Ma)** Sandstone and shale with minor gypsum and coal
- **Silurian-Ordovican (410–500 Ma)** Limestone, dolomite, shale, and sandstone
- **Pennsylvanian (290–320 Ma)** Sandstone, shale, and coal
- **Paleozoic (300–500 Ma)** Granite and other felsic igneous rocks
- **Paleozoic (300–500 Ma)** Gabbro and other mafic igneous rocks

Mesozoic

- **Cretaceous (65–140 Ma)** Partly lithified sand, clay, and sandstone
- **Triassic-Jurassic (200–225 Ma)** Red and gray shale, sandstone, and conglomerate intruded by diabase and basalt

Cenozoic

- **Quaternary (20 ka–2 Ma)** Sand, mud, and gravel
- **Holocene (present–20 ka)** Sand, mud, and peat deposited in beaches, marshes, swamps, and estuaries
- **Tertiary (2–65 Ma)** Sand, mud, limy sand, and marl

Map Skills Activity

The colors on this map of Virginia represent rocks that formed at different times in Earth's past. These time spans are divisions of the geologic time scale, which divides Earth's history into eons, eras, periods, and epochs. Use the map to answer the questions below.

1. **Using a Key** From what geologic era and period are rocks found in Roanoke, Virginia?
2. **Analyzing Data** Near which cities in Virginia are the oldest rocks in the state found?
3. **Analyzing Data** Near which city in Virginia are the youngest rocks in the state found?
4. **Inferring Relationships** Some of the youngest sediments in Virginia are found along rivers. What do you think might explain this pattern?
5. **Identifying Trends** What are the differences between the three types of Precambrian rocks found in Virginia? Why do you think they are all located near each other?
6. **Analyzing Relationships** What are the age ranges of the oldest of each of the three rock types—igneous, metamorphic, and sedimentary—found in Virginia?

Key Resources

Technology

- Transparencies
  31 Geologic Map of Virginia

Chapter 6

Summary

THINK central SUPER SUMMARY Keyword: HQXRXSS

Key Ideas | **Key Terms**

Section 1

Rocks and the Rock Cycle

- The three major types of rock are igneous rock, sedimentary rock, and metamorphic rock.
- The rock cycle describes the natural processes through which each type of rock can change into any other type of rock.
- Bowen's reaction series describes the order in which different minerals form as magma cools.
- Chemical factors, such as mineral make up, and physical factors, such as joints and fractures, affect the stability of rocks.

Key Terms:
rock cycle, p. 136
Bowen's reaction series, p. 137

Section 2

Igneous Rock

- Three factors that affect whether rock melts are temperature, pressure, and the presence of fluids in the rock.
- The rate at which magma cools determines the texture of the igneous rock that forms.
- Igneous rocks may be classified according to their composition and their texture.
- Intrusive igneous rock structures form underground and extrusive igneous rock structures form above ground.

Key Terms:
igneous rock, p. 139
intrusive igneous rock, p. 141
extrusive igneous rock, p. 141
felsic, p. 142
mafic, p. 142

Section 3

Sedimentary Rock

- Compaction and cementation are two main processes that form sedimentary rock.
- Chemical sedimentary rock forms from minerals that were once dissolved in water, and organic sedimentary rocks form from the remains of living things.
- Clastic sedimentary rock forms from fragments of preexisting rocks that get compacted and cemented together.
- Seven sedimentary rock features are stratification, cross-beds, graded bedding, ripple marks, mud cracks, fossils, and concretions.

Key Terms:
compaction, p. 145
cementation, p. 145
chemical sedimentary rock, p. 146
organic sedimentary rock, p. 146
clastic sedimentary rock, p. 147

Section 4

Metamorphic Rock

- Metamorphism changes one type of rock into another.
- Regional metamorphism occurs over a large geographic area. Contact metamorphism occurs in a small area near magma.
- Foliated metamorphic rocks have minerals arranged in bands, while nonfoliated metamorphic rocks do not.

Key Terms:
metamorphism, p. 151
contact metamorphism, p. 152
regional metamorphism, p. 152
foliation, p. 153
nonfoliated, p. 154

Chapter Summary

Using THINK central Resources

Super Summary

Have students connect the major concepts in this chapter through an interactive Super Summary. Visit www.thinkcentral.com and type in the keyword **HQXRXSS** to access the Super Summary for this chapter.

Differentiated Instruction

Alternative Assessment

Bulletin Board Display Have students create a display on a bulletin board that shows the processes by which rocks form and transform into other rocks. The basic form of the display should resemble the figure of the rock cycle, but students may modify the layout and the size to include other details, such as the rate of cooling and the magma type for igneous rocks, the properties of the classes of sedimentary rocks, and the textures of metamorphic rocks. **LS Logical/Visual**

Chapter Review

Assignment Guide	
Section	**Questions**
1	2–4, 18, 20, 21, 32
2	6, 10–13, 17, 22, 25, 30, 31, 34, 35
3	7, 14, 15, 19, 24, 26, 27
4	8, 9, 16, 23, 28
2 and 4	5
1–4	1, 29, 33

Reading Toolbox

1. Answers will vary. Students' summaries should include the main concepts from each section.

Using Key Terms

2–9. Answers may vary but should show that students understand the definitions of and differences between key terms.

Understanding Key Ideas

10. c
11. c
12. d
13. d
14. c
15. a
16. d

Short Answer

17. In partial melting, as the temperature of a rock increases, the minerals that have the lowest melting point melt first. Fractional crystallization works in the opposite way. As the temperature of molten rock decreases, crystals of minerals with high freezing points form first.
18. Igneous rock forms when magma cools. Sedimentary rock forms when rock fragments are compressed and cemented together or by chemical or organic processes. Metamorphic rock forms when a rock is subjected to temperature and pressure changes or to chemical processes.
19. Clastic sedimentary rocks form from fragments of other rocks. Chemical and organic sedimentary rock form through chemical or organic processes.
20. Bowen's reaction series is a simplified pattern that shows the order in which minerals crystallize from cooling magma according to their chemical compositions and melting points.

Chapter 6 Review

1. **Summarizing Ideas** Look back at your summaries of each section. Now, summarize your summaries. For each section, write one or two sentences that summarize the main ideas of the whole section. READING TOOLBOX

USING KEY TERMS

Use each of the following terms in a separate sentence.

2. *rock cycle*
3. *Bowen's reaction series*
4. *sediment*

For each pair of terms, explain how the meanings of the terms differ.

5. *igneous rock* and *metamorphic rock*
6. *intrusive igneous rock* and *extrusive igneous rock*
7. *chemical sedimentary rock* and *organic sedimentary rock*
8. *contact metamorphism* and *regional metamorphism*
9. *foliated* and *nonfoliated*

UNDERSTANDING KEY IDEAS

10. Intrusive igneous rocks are characterized by a coarse-grained texture because they contain
    a. heavy elements.
    b. small crystals.
    c. large crystals.
    d. fragments of different sizes and shapes.
11. Light-colored igneous rocks are generally part of the
    a. basalt family.
    b. intermediate family.
    c. felsic family.
    d. mafic family.
12. Magma that solidifies underground forms rock masses that are known as
    a. extrusions.
    b. volcanic cones.
    c. lava plateaus.
    d. intrusions.
13. One example of an extrusion is a
    a. stock.
    b. dike.
    c. batholith.
    d. lava plateau.
14. Sedimentary rock formed from rock fragments is called
    a. organic.
    b. chemical.
    c. clastic.
    d. granite.
15. One example of chemical sedimentary rock is
    a. an evaporite.
    b. coal.
    c. sandstone.
    d. breccia.
16. The splitting of slate into flat layers illustrates its
    a. contact metamorphism.
    b. formation.
    c. sedimentation.
    d. foliation.

SHORT ANSWER

17. Describe partial melting and fractional crystallization.
18. Name and define the three main types of rock.
19. How do clastic sedimentary rocks differ from chemical and organic sedimentary rocks?
20. What is Bowen's reaction series?
21. What factors affect the chemical and physical stability of rock?
22. Describe three factors that affect whether rock melts.
23. Why are some metamorphic rocks foliated while others are not?
24. How does transport affect the size and shape of sediment particles?

21. Strength of the chemical bonds between atoms in minerals affects the chemical stability of rock. Physical stability is affected by natural zones of weakness in rocks. Examples of these zones include areas between layers in sedimentary and metamorphic rock, joints formed by the cooling and contracting of igneous rock, and exfoliation layers formed by changes in pressure as rock is uplifed to Earth's surface.
22. The temperature, pressure, and presence of fluids within rock all determine the melting point of rock.
23. Foliation occurs when a rock contains two or more minerals that have grains that are neither round nor square. These conditions allow the crystals to realign under pressure or cause the minerals to separate into compositional bands. Foliation does not occur when rock is composed mainly of a single mineral.
24. As sediment particles are transported, they undergo additional weathering. The longer the transport process takes, the finer the particles become. Their shapes also become rounder and smoother as transport continues.

CRITICAL THINKING

25. Making Inferences A certain rock is made up mostly of plagioclase feldspar and pyroxene minerals. It also includes olivine and hornblende. Will the rock have a light or dark coloring? Explain your answer.

26. Classifying Information Explain how metamorphic rock can change into either of the other two types of rock through the rock cycle.

27. Applying Ideas Imagine that you have found a piece of limestone, which is a sedimentary rock, that has strange-shaped lumps on it. Will the lumps have the same composition as the limestone? Explain your answer.

28. Analyzing Ideas Which would be easier to break, the foliated rock slate or the nonfoliated rock quartzite? Explain your answer.

CONCEPT MAPPING

29. Use the following terms to create a concept map: *rock cycle, foliated, igneous rock, intrusive, sedimentary rock, clastic sedimentary rock, metamorphic rock, chemical sedimentary rock, extrusive, organic sedimentary rock,* and *nonfoliated.*

MATH SKILLS

Math Skills

30. Making Calculations The gram formula weight (weight of one mole) of the mineral quartz is 60.1 g, and the gram formula weight of magnetite is 231.5 g. If you had 4 moles of magnetite, how many moles of quartz would be equal to the weight of the magnetite?

31. Making Calculations The gram formula weight (weight of one mole) of the mineral hematite, Fe_2O_3, is 159.7 g, and the gram formula weight of magnetite, Fe_3O_4, is 231.5 g. Which of the following would weigh more: half a mole of hematite or one-third of a mole of magnetite?

WRITING SKILLS

32. Outlining Topics Outline the essential steps in the rock cycle.

33. Writing from Research Find out what types of rock are most abundant in your state. Research the geologic processes that form those types of rock, and write a brief report that describes how the rocks in your state most likely formed.

INTERPRETING GRAPHICS

The graph below is a ternary diagram that shows the classification of some igneous rocks. Refer to Graphing Skills in Appendix B for instructions on how to read a ternary diagram. Use the diagram to answer the questions that follow.

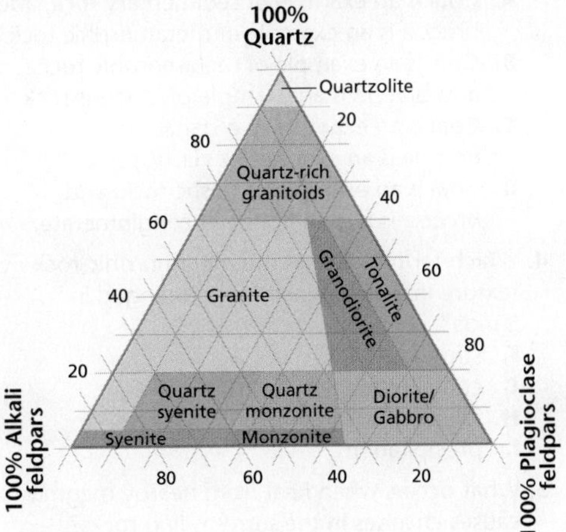

34. What is the maximum amount of quartz in a quartz syenite?

35. What would a rock that contains 30% quartz, 20% alkali feldspar, and 50% plagioclase feldspar be called?

Chapter Review

Critical Thinking

25. The minerals pyroxene, olivine, and hornblende are ferromagnesian minerals. The rock probably formed from mafic magma and will be dark in color.

26. If metamorphic rock is uplifted to Earth's surface and is exposed to air and water, it may break down into sediment that becomes sedimentary rock. If metamorphic rock is melted and then cools, igneous rock will form.

27. The lumps are probably concretions that formed around some type of nucleus. They will not have the same composition as the limestone.

28. The slate would be more easily broken, because the grains in slate are aligned in thin layers that have weak areas between them. Nonfoliated rocks, like quartzite, do not form layers and thus do not have those zones of weakness.

Concept Mapping

29. Answers may vary but should include all of the terms listed. Sample answers appear at the end of this unit on p. 195D.

Math Skills

30. (231.5 g/mol ÷ 60.1 g/mol) × 4 mol = 15.4 mol; or (231.5 g/mol × 4 mol) ÷ 60.1 g/mol = 15.4 mol

31. 159.7 g of hematite ÷ 2 = 79.9 g; 231.5 g of magnetite ÷ 3 = 77.2 g; The sample of hematite weighs more.

Writing Skills

32. Answers may vary. Accept all reasonable answers.

33. Answers may vary. Accept all reasonable answers.

Interpreting Graphics

34. 20%

35. granodiorite

Estimated Time

To give students practice under more realistic testing conditions, allow them 30 minutes to answer all of the questions in this practice test.

Test Doctor

Question 1 Answer B is correct. Answer A is incorrect because organic remains would not withstand the high temperature conditions that produce magma, from which igneous rocks form. Answer C is incorrect because it is unlikely that organic remains would withstand the massive heat and pressure that change existing rocks into metamorphic rocks. Answer D is incorrect because felsic rock is one of the families of igneous rock. Fossils and organic remains are typically found in sedimentary rock.

Question 4 Answer H is correct. Answer F is incorrect because rocks that form last, at the lowest temperatures, tend to withstand weathering the longest. Answer G is incorrect because rocks that form first are the least stable. Answer I is incorrect because Bowen's Reaction series not only accounts for the production of different rocks from the same magma but also explains how some rocks weather faster than others. The rocks that form last are also the most chemically stable.

Chapter 6 Standardized Test Prep

Understanding Concepts

Directions (1–5): For each question, write on a sheet of paper the letter of the correct answer.

1. A rock that contains a fossil is most likely
- **A.** igneous.
- **B.** sedimentary.
- **C.** metamorphic.
- **D.** felsic.

2. The large, well-developed crystals found in some samples of granite are a sign that
- **F.** the magma from which it formed cooled rapidly.
- **G.** the magma contained a lot of dissolved gases.
- **H.** the magma from which it formed cooled slowly.
- **I.** water deposited minerals in the rock cavities.

3. How does coal differ from breccia?
- **A.** Coal is an example of sedimentary rock, and breccia is an example of metamorphic rock.
- **B.** Coal is an example of metamorphic rock, and breccia is an example of igneous rock.
- **C.** Coal is an example of organic rock, and breccia is an example of clastic rock.
- **D.** Coal is an example of clastic rock, and breccia is an example of a conglomerate.

4. Which term describes the metamorphic rock texture in which minerals are arranged in bands?
- **F.** stratification
- **G.** cementation
- **H.** foliation
- **I.** precipitation

5. What occurs when heat from nearby magma causes changes in the surrounding rocks?
- **A.** contact metamorphism
- **B.** fluid metamorphism
- **C.** intrusive metamorphism
- **D.** regional metamorphism

Directions (6–7): For each question, write a short response.

6. What type of sedimentary rock is formed when angular clastic materials cement together?

7. What type of rock is formed when heat, pressure, and chemical processes change the physical properties of igneous rock?

Reading Skills

Directions (8–10): Read the passage below. Then, answer the questions.

Igneous and Sedimentary Rocks

Scientists think that Earth began as a melted mixture of many different materials. These materials underwent a physical change as they cooled and solidified. These became the first igneous rocks. Igneous rock continues to form today. Liquid rock changes from a liquid to a solid, when lava that is brought to Earth's surface by volcanoes hardens. This process can also take place far more slowly, when magma deep beneath the Earth's surface changes to a solid.

At the same time that new rocks are forming, old rocks are broken down by other processes. Weathering is the process by which wind, water, and gravity break up rock. During erosion, broken up pieces of rock are carried by water, wind, or ice and deposited as sediments elsewhere. These pieces pile up and, under heat and pressure, form sedimentary rock—rock composed of cemented fragments of older rocks.

8. Which of the following statements about the texture of sedimentary rock is most likely true?
- **F.** Sedimentary rocks are always lumpy and made up of large pieces of older rocks.
- **G.** Sedimentary rocks all contain alternating bands of lumpy and smooth textures.
- **H.** Sedimentary rocks are always smooth and made up of small pieces of older rocks.
- **I.** Sedimentary rocks have a variety of textures that depend on the size and type of pieces that make up the rock.

9. Which of the following statements can be inferred from the information in the passage?
- **A.** Igneous rocks are the hardest form of rock.
- **B.** Sedimentary rocks are the final stage in the life cycle of a rock.
- **C.** Igneous rocks began forming early in Earth's history.
- **D.** Sedimentary rocks are not affected by weathering.

10. Is igneous rock or sedimentary rock more likely to contain fossils? Explain your answer.

Question 12 Full-credit answers should include the following points:
- students should be able to recognize different types of rocks by the physical characteristics of the rocks
- rock D is a sedimentary rock
- the presence of fossils or embedded seashells is a clear clue that this is a sedimentary rock
- students should demonstrate an understanding that sedimentary rocks are composed of many parts and particles that have been cemented together

Questions 13 Full-credit answers should include the following points:
- students should demonstrate an understanding that most rocks are combinations of one or more minerals
- the rock described in the table appears to be made up of more than one type of substance, so it is most likely not made of only a single mineral

Interpreting Graphics

Directions (11–13): For each question below, record the correct answer on a separate sheet of paper.

The diagram below shows the rock cycle. Use this diagram to answer question 11.

The Rock Cycle

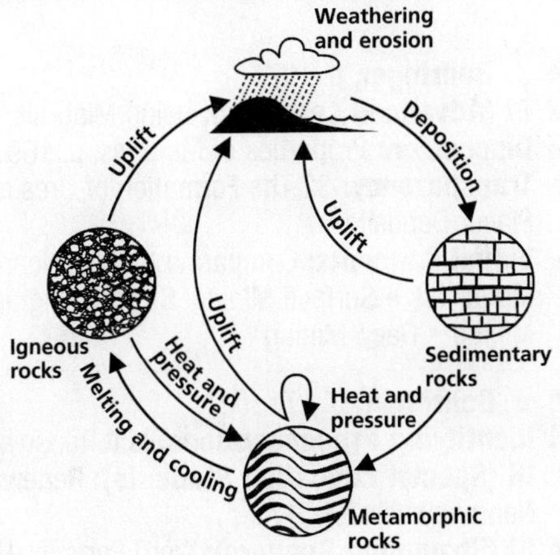

11. Which of the following processes brings rocks to Earth's surface, where weathering and erosion occur?
F. deposition
G. heat and pressure
H. melting and cooling
I. uplift

Use this table to answer questions 12 and 13.

Rock Types

Rock sample	Characteristics
Rock A	multiple compacted, round, gravel-sized fragments
Rock B	coarse, well-developed, crystalline mineral grains
Rock C	small, sand-sized grains, tan coloration
Rock D	gritty texture; many small, embedded seashells

12. Is rock D igneous, sedimentary, or metamorphic? Explain the evidence that supports this classification.

13. Is rock A made up of only one mineral or more than one mineral? Explain the evidence supporting this classification.

Test Tip

When several questions refer to the same graph, table, or diagram, or text passage, answer the questions you are sure of first.

Standardized Test Prep

Using THINK central Resources

State Resources

- For specific resources for your state, visit **www.thinkcentral.com** and type in the keyword **HSHSTR.**

Answers

Understanding Concepts

1. B
2. H
3. C
4. H
5. A
6. breccias
7. metamorphic rock

Reading Skills

8. I
9. C
10. sedimentary rock; Sedimentary rocks are made up of pieces of older rocks and may contain fossils. Fossils in the original material of an igneous rock would have been destroyed when melted.

Interpreting Graphics

11. I
12. Answers may vary. See Test Doctor for a detailed scoring rubric.
13. Answers may vary. See Test Doctor for a detailed scoring rubric.

Chapter Planner 7

Resources and Energy

	Standards	Teach Key Ideas
Chapter Opener, pp. 164–165 **45 min.**	**National Science Education Standards**	
Section 1 Mineral Resources, pp. 167–170 **45 min.** ❯ Ores ❯ Uses of Mineral Resources ❯ Mineral Exploration and Mining	**PS 3a, PS 3b, SPSP 3a**	■ ▲ **Bellringer,** p. 167 ■ **DI (Advanced Learners):** Using Minerals, p. 168 ■ **Discussion:** Properties of Minerals, p. 169 ◆ **Transparency:** 32 The Formation of Ores and Placer Deposits ▲ **Visual Concepts:** Comparing Metals, Nonmetals, and Metalloids • Surface Mining: Strip Mining and Open-Pit Mining • Deep Mining
Section 2 Nonrenewable Energy, pp. 171–176 **45 min.** ❯ Fossil Fuels ❯ Fossil-Fuel Supplies ❯ Nuclear Energy	**PS 1c, PS 2f, PS 3a, PS 3b, PS 3c, LS 4a, LS 4e, SPSP 3a**	■ ◆ **Bellringer,** p. 171 ■ **Identifying Preconceptions:** Is It Renewable?, p. 171 ■ **DI (Special Education Students):** Renewable or Nonrenewable?, p. 171 ■ **DI (Struggling Readers):** Word Parts, p. 173 ■ **Demonstration:** Chain Reaction, p. 174 ■ **Debate:** Pros and Cons, p. 175 ■ **DI (Advanced Learners):** Fudging Fusion?, p. 175 ◆ **Transparencies:** 33 Types of Coal • 34 Oil Traps • 35 A Nuclear Fission Reaction • 36 How a Nuclear Power Plant Generates Electricity ▲ **Visual Concepts:** Energy Resources • Fossil Fuels • Coal Formation • Petroleum and Gas Formation • Nuclear Energy • Nuclear Fission • Nuclear Chain Reaction • Parts of a Nuclear Reactor • Nuclear Fusion
Section 3 Renewable Energy, pp. 177–180 **90 min.** ❯ Geothermal Energy ❯ Solar Energy ❯ Energy from Moving Water ❯ Energy from Biomass ❯ Energy from Wind	**PS 3a, PS 3b, SPSP 3a**	■ ◆ **Bellringer,** p. 177 ■ **DI (English Learners):** Vocabulary, p. 178 ◆ **Transparencies:** 37 How a Hydroelectric Dam Generates Electricity • 38 Wind Power in the United States ▲ **Visual Concepts:** Renewable Energy Resources • Tidal Energy • Biomass as an Energy Resource • Biomass
Section 4 Resources and Conservation, pp. 181–184 **45 min.** ❯ Environmental Impacts of Mining ❯ Fossil Fuels and the Environment ❯ Conservation	**PS 3c, LS 4a, SPSP 3a**	■ ◆ **Bellringer,** p. 181 ■ **Discussion:** Mining, p. 181 ■ **DI (Struggling Readers):** Educating the Public, p. 182 ▲ **Visual Concepts:** Conservation • Recycling
Chapter Wrap-Up, pp. 189–193 **90 min.**		**Chapter Summary,** p. 189

CHAPTER Fast Track *To shorten instruction because of time limitations, omit Section 1.*

See also PowerNotes® Presentations

Key
Teacher's Edition ■ Teaching Transparencies ◆
Chapter Resource File ● Online Edition ▲

All resources listed below are also available on the **Teacher One Stop™.**

Why It Matters	Hands-On	Skills Development	Assessment
■ **Chapter Overview,** p. 164 ■ **Using the Figure:** Hoover Dam, p. 164	**Inquiry Lab:** Modeling Mining, p. 165	**Reading Toolbox,** p. 166	
■ **Section Overview,** p. 167 ■ **Using the Figure:** Slowing Water Flow, p. 168 ■ **Why It Matters:** Alloys, p. 169 ■ **Environmental Connection:** Mountaintop Removal, p. 169	■ **Activity:** Minerals at Work, p. 167 ■ **Group Activity:** Mineral Use, p. 169 ● **Skills Practice Lab:** Determination of Carbonate in Ore	**Reading Toolbox:** Chain-of-Events Chart, p. 168 ■ **Reading Skill Builder:** Reading Organizer, p. 168	**Reading Check,** p. 168 **Section Review,** p. 170 ■ **Reteaching,** p. 170 ■ **Quiz,** p. 170 ■ **DI (Alternative Assessment):** Chart, p. 170 ● **Section Quiz**
■ **Section Overview,** p. 171 ■ **Using the Figure:** Rock Layers and Density, p. 173 ■ **Why It Matters:** Hydrocarbon Use, p. 173 ■ **History Connection:** Nuclear Theory, p. 174 ■ **Using the Figure:** Electricity from Nuclear Fission, p. 175	■ **Group Activity:** Purifying with Pressure, p. 172	■ ● **Internet Activity:** Resource Locations, p. 172 **Math Skills:** Coal Reserves, p. 172 ■ **Skill Builder:** Vocabulary, p. 174 **Reading Toolbox:** Chain-of-Events Chart, p. 175	**Reading Check,** p. 173 **Reading Check,** p. 174 **Section Review,** p. 176 ■ **Reteaching,** p. 176 ■ **Quiz,** p. 176 ■ **DI (Alternative Assessment):** Letter to the Editor, p. 176 ● **Section Quiz**
■ **Section Overview,** p. 177 ■ **Using the Figure:** Natural Hot Tub, p. 177 ■ **Environmental Connection:** Impact of Dams, p. 178 ■ **Why It Matters:** Favorable Winds, p. 179	**Quick Lab:** Solar Collector, p. 178 **Inquiry Lab:** Blowing in the Wind, pp. 186–187 ● **Inquiry Lab:** Generation of Natural Gas from Biomass	**Reading Toolbox:** Everyday Words Used in Science, p. 178 ■ ● **Internet Activity:** Biomass Potential, p. 179 **Maps in Action:** Wind Power in the United States, p. 188 ■ ● **Internet Activity:** Alternative Energy Use in Your State, p. 188	**Reading Check,** p. 179 **Section Review,** p. 180 ■ **Reteaching,** p. 179 ■ **Quiz,** p. 180 ■ **DI (Alternative Assessment):** Tour Brochure, p. 180 ● **Section Quiz**
■ **Section Overview,** p. 181 ■ **Using the Figure:** Raw Recyclables, p. 183 **Disposing of Electronic Waste,** p. 183 ■ **Environmental Connection:** The Cost of Energy Conservation, p. 183	**Quick Lab:** Reclamation, p. 182	■ **Reading Skill Builder:** Reading Hint, p. 182 **Reading Toolbox:** The Language of Prediction, p. 184	**Reading Check,** p. 182 **Section Review,** p. 184 ■ **Reteaching,** p. 183 ■ **Quiz,** p. 183 ■ **DI (Alternative Assessment):** Survey, p. 184 ● **Section Quiz**
What Does Your Dream Car Run On?, p. 185		▲ **Super Summary** **Standardized Test Prep,** pp. 192–193	**Chapter Review,** pp. 190–191 ■ **DI (Alternative Assessment):** Keeping Track, p. 189 ● **Chapter Tests**

See also Lab Generator

See also Holt Online Assessment Resources

Chapter Overview

Earth's resources provide the energy required for animal, plant, and human life to exist. This chapter describes Earth's resources and the sources of renewable and nonrenewable energy. It also explores how humans obtain resources and the resulting impact on the environment.

Using the Figure GENERAL

Hoover Dam Tell students that Hoover Dam was built across the Colorado River near Las Vegas, Nevada, in the 1930s to provide water and electricity to people moving into arid lands. Explain that, while the dam provides energy, it also affects the environment. Discuss with students what changes may occur when a dam is built. (The river's normal flow is disrupted; the reservoir behind the dam floods land that people or wildlife lived on; areas downstream from the dam may be deprived of water.) **LS Interpersonal**

Why It Matters

About seven percent of the power produced in the United States comes from hydroelectricity. Because hydroelectric dams rely on gravity to move water through them, they are built in areas of high topographic relief. Most of the good locations for large hydroelectric dams are already being used. In the future, smaller hydroelectric dams are likely to be built to supply electricity to individual communities.

Chapter 7 Resources and Energy

Chapter Outline

Virginia Standards of Learning
ES.1.a
ES.1.c
ES.1.f
ES.4.b
ES.6.a
ES.6.b
ES.6.d

Chapter Correlations — *Virginia Standards of Learning*

ES.1.a volume, area, mass, elapsed time, direction, temperature, pressure, distance, density, and changes in elevation/depth are calculated utilizing the most appropriate tools.
ES.1.c scales, diagrams, charts, graphs, tables, imagery, models, and profiles are constructed and interpreted.
ES.1.f current applications are used to reinforce Earth science concepts.
ES.4.b uses of minerals
ES.6.a fossil fuels, minerals, rocks, water, and vegetation
ES.6.b advantages and disadvantages of various energy sources
ES.6.d environmental costs and benefits

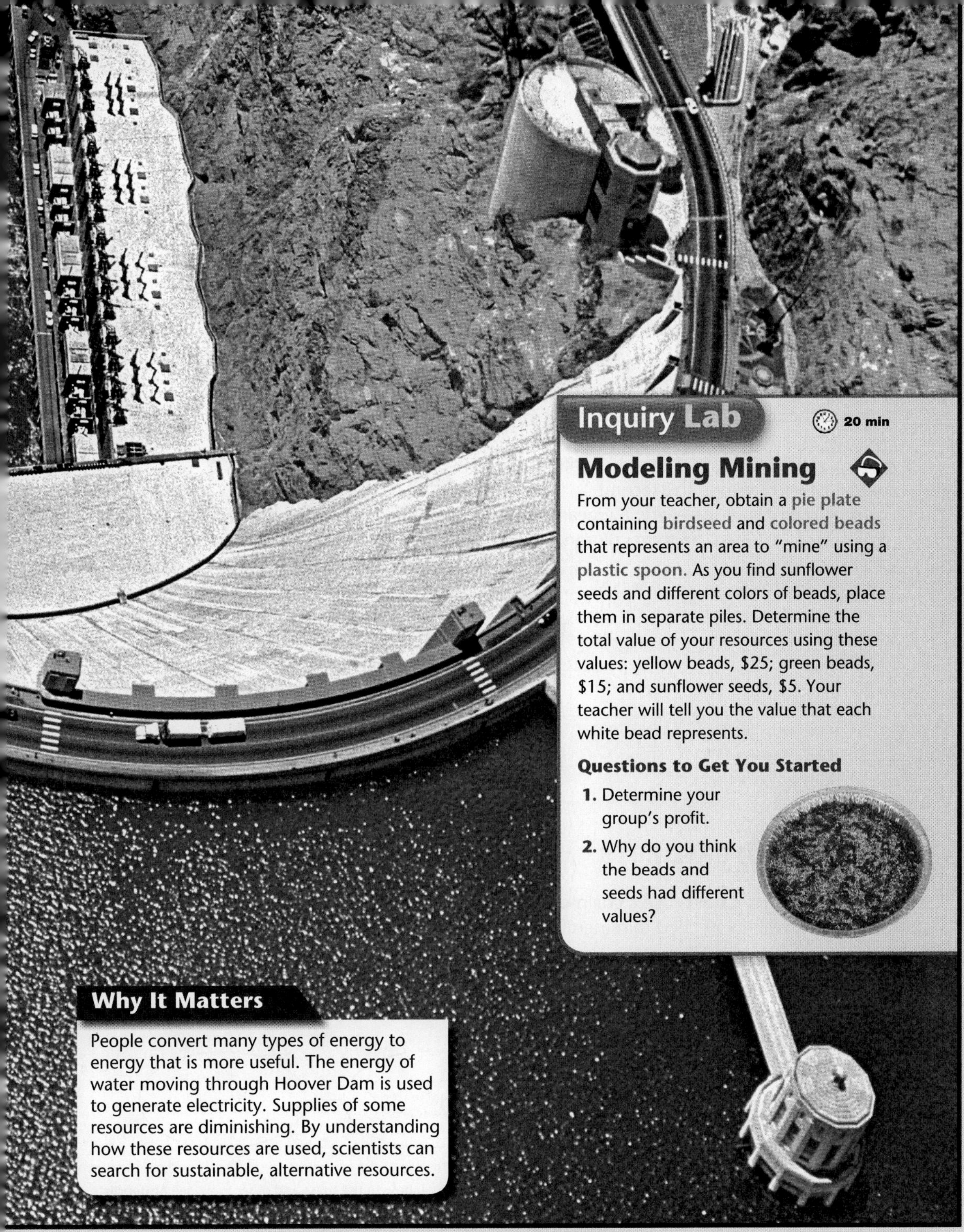

Inquiry Lab

20 min

Modeling Mining

From your teacher, obtain a **pie plate** containing **birdseed** and **colored beads** that represents an area to "mine" using a **plastic spoon.** As you find sunflower seeds and different colors of beads, place them in separate piles. Determine the total value of your resources using these values: yellow beads, $25; green beads, $15; and sunflower seeds, $5. Your teacher will tell you the value that each white bead represents.

Questions to Get You Started

1. Determine your group's profit.

2. Why do you think the beads and seeds had different values?

Why It Matters

People convert many types of energy to energy that is more useful. The energy of water moving through Hoover Dam is used to generate electricity. Supplies of some resources are diminishing. By understanding how these resources are used, scientists can search for sustainable, alternative resources.

Inquiry Lab

Central Concept: Students model how mining processes recover a small amount of valuable minerals from a large volume of rock, and they explore the economics of mining and land restoration.

Teacher's Notes: You may wish to assign one student in each group to count the number of seeds and types of beads, one student to calculate profit (or loss), and one student to record questions and answers. After students have finished mining and calculated their gross profit, tell them to subtract $50 for each white bead to represent the cost of land restoration. You may wish to impose environmental impact "fines" for needlessly messy mining.

Materials (per group)
- Pie plate or shallow pan
- Birdseed mix that contains sunflower seeds
- 6 small yellow beads
- 15 small green beads
- 2 medium white beads

Skills Acquired
- Interpreting models
- Calculating
- Inferring

Answers to Getting Started

1. Answers may vary.
2. Answers may vary. Example: "The yellow beads represent a rare ore such as a gold ore, the green beads represent a more common ore, such as a copper ore, and the sunflower seeds represent a common ore, such as an iron ore."

Using THINK central Resources

An online version of this chapter, as well as all the print and multimedia resources that accompany the program are available to registered teachers and their students. Log onto www.thinkcentral.com to access these materials and tools to organize your preparation and student learning.

READING TOOLBOX

Everyday Words Used in Science

Term	Scientific Context	Everyday Meaning
placer deposit	material concentrated in one place by the movement of wind, water, or ice	deposit—a partial payment; putting money in a bank
native element	metallic minerals such as gold, silver, and copper; can form nuggets of pure metal	native—belonging to a place because one was born or grew up there
hydrothermal solution	hot fluids that can dissolve minerals from surrounding rock	solution—the answer to a problem

Prediction Statements

Answers may vary. Check to make sure students correctly identify prediction statements and underline words indicating that predictions are being made.

READING TOOLBOX

These reading tools will help you learn the material in this chapter.

Science Terms

Everyday Words Used in Science Many words used in science are familiar words from everyday speech. However, when these words are used in science, their meanings are often different from the everyday meanings.

Your Turn As you read Section 1, make a table like the one below for the terms *placer deposit, native element,* and *hydrothermal solution*. Write the scientific context of each term in the second column. Then, write the everyday meaning of each word listed in the third column.

Term	Scientific Context	Everyday Meaning
placer deposit		deposit—
native element		native—
hydrothermal solution		solution—

Predictions

The Language of Prediction Scientific theories can be used to explain things that happened in the past. They can also be used to make predictions about what will happen in the future. To recognize a statement of prediction, look for words such as these:

- the word *will* before a verb
- words such as *might* or *may*
- the word *if* followed first by a condition and then by a result

Your Turn As you read Sections 2 and 3, make a list of statements of prediction. In each statement, underline the key words that tell you the statement is a prediction. Some examples are given below.

Prediction Statements

- If a fission reaction is allowed to continue uncontrolled, the reaction will escalate quickly and may result in an explosion.
- If a nucleus is struck by a free neutron, however, the nucleus of the atom may split.

Graphic Organizers

Chain-of-Events Chart Use a chain-of-events chart when you need to remember the steps in a process.

Your Turn As you read Section 2, complete the chain-of-events chart that outlines the formation of coal.

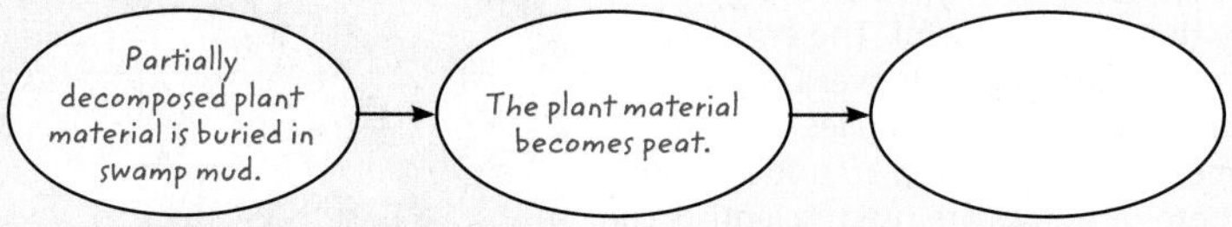

Partially decomposed plant material is buried in swamp mud.
The plant material becomes peat.

For more information on how to use these and other tools, see **Appendix A.**

Chain-of-Events Chart

Example:

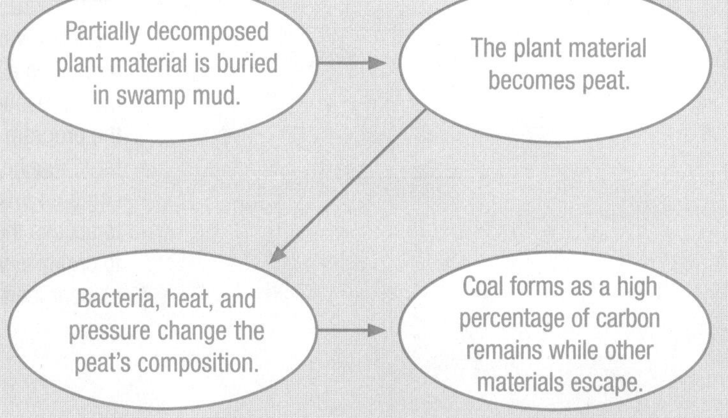

Partially decomposed plant material is buried in swamp mud.
The plant material becomes peat.
Bacteria, heat, and pressure change the peat's composition.
Coal forms as a high percentage of carbon remains while other materials escape.

SECTION 1

Mineral Resources

ENVIRONMENTAL CONNECTION

Key Ideas	Key Terms	Why It Matters
❯ Explain what ores are and where they form. ❯ Identify why mineral resources are important. ❯ Describe four methods by which humans obtain mineral resources.	ore lode placer deposit gemstone	Minerals are sources of many types of useful materials. People use various mining techniques to obtain minerals.

Earth's crust contains useful mineral resources. The processes that formed many of these resources took millions of years. Many of these mineral resources are mined for human use. Mineral resources can be either *metals*, such as gold, Au, silver, Ag, and aluminum, Al, or *nonmetals*, such as sulfur, S, and quartz, SiO_2.

Ores

Metallic minerals, such as gold, silver, and copper, Cu, are called *native elements* and can exist in Earth's crust as nuggets of pure metal. But most other minerals in Earth's crust are *compounds* of two or more elements. Mineral deposits from which metals and nonmetals can be removed profitably are called **ores**. For example, the metal iron, Fe, can be removed from naturally occurring deposits of the minerals magnetite and hematite. Mercury, Hg, can be separated from cinnabar. Aluminum can be separated from bauxite.

ore a natural material whose concentration of economically valuable minerals is high enough for the material to be mined profitably

Ores Formed by Cooling Magma

Ores form in a variety of ways, as shown in **Figure 1.** Some ores, such as ores of chromium, Cr, nickel, Ni, and lead, Pb, form within cooling magma. As the magma cools, dense metallic minerals sink. As the minerals sink, layers of these minerals accumulate at the bottom of the magma chamber to form ore deposits.

Figure 1 The Formation of Ores

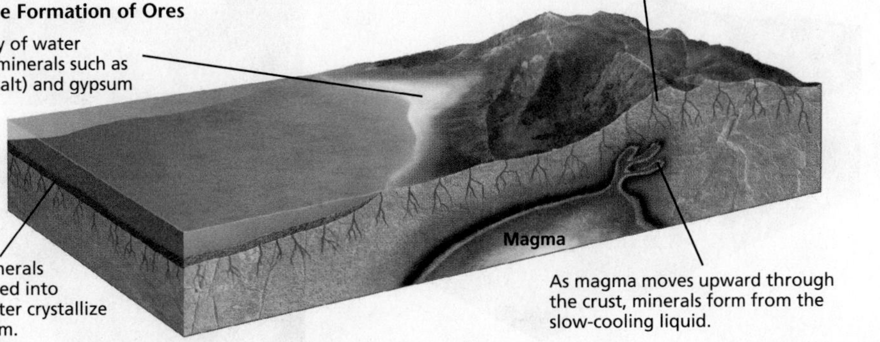

Groundwater moving downward through rock is heated by magma. Dissolved metals crystallize out of the hot fluid to form new minerals.
When a body of water evaporates, minerals such as halite (rock salt) and gypsum crystallize.
Magma
Dissolved minerals that are carried into bodies of water crystallize on the bottom.
As magma moves upward through the crust, minerals form from the slow-cooling liquid.

Section 1

Focus

Overview

This section summarizes Earth's mineral resources and describes how minerals are removed from ore compounds. The section also describes how humans use mineral resources.

Bellringer

Ask students to define *mineral.* (a natural, inorganic solid that has a characteristic chemical composition, an orderly internal structure, and a characteristic set of physical properties) Have them name five common minerals. (Answers may vary. Sample answers: quartz, silver, gold, salt, clay, and graphite) LS **Verbal**

Motivate

Activity — GENERAL

Minerals at Work Have students list objects in the room or other common objects that are made from minerals. Ask them to identify those that are metallic or nonmetallic, those that are pure minerals, and those that are mixed with other components. (Answers may vary. Accept all reasonable answers.) LS **Visual/Logical**

Key Resources

Chapter Resource File

- Directed Reading BASIC
- Skills Practice Lab: Determination of Carbonate in Ore GENERAL

Technology

- Transparencies
  Bellringer
  32 The Formation of Ores and Placer Deposits

Teach

READING TOOLBOX

Chain-of-Events Chart You may wish to use this activity to assess students' prior knowledge before beginning discussion of contact metamorphism.

Using the Figure — GENERAL

Slowing Water Flow Have students study the figure on this page. Ask them to describe where the ore deposits occur in each picture and then relate the locations of deposits to the stream features—the pool at the base of the waterfall and the bend. Discuss with students why these features cause the stream to deposit its load of ore fragments. (These features slow the rate of water flow. When the water slows, it can no longer carry heavy mineral particles, which sink due to gravity and collect in low areas.) LS **Visual/Logical**

Reading Skill Builder — BASIC

Reading Organizer Create a two-column chart to help students understand and remember the chemical abbreviations for elements discussed in this section. In one column, have students write the English word for an ore or element, and in the other column, have them write the chemical abbreviation for the element. English Language Learners
LS **Verbal**

READING TOOLBOX

Chain-of-Events Chart
Create a chain-of-events chart to describe the process of contact metamorphism.

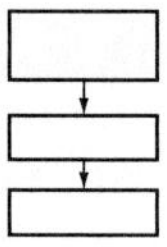

Ores Formed by Contact Metamorphism

Some ores of lead, copper, and zinc, Zn, form through the process of contact metamorphism. *Contact metamorphism* is a process that occurs when magma comes into contact with existing rock. Heat and chemical reactions with hot fluids from the magma can change the composition of the existing rock. These changes sometimes form ores.

Contact metamorphism can also form ore deposits when hot fluids called *hydrothermal solutions* move through small cracks in a large mass of rock. In this process, minerals from the surrounding rock dissolve into the hydrothermal solution. Over time, new minerals precipitate from the solution and form narrow zones of rock called *veins.* Veins commonly consist of ores of valuable heavy minerals, such as gold, tin, Sn, lead, and copper. When many thick mineral veins form in a relatively small region, the ore deposit is called a **lode.** Stories of a "mother lode" kept people coming to California during the California gold rush in the late 1840s and 1850s.

lode a mineral deposit within a rock formation

placer deposit a deposit that contains a valuable mineral that has been concentrated by mechanical action

Ores Formed by Moving Water

The movement of water helps to form ore deposits. First, tiny fragments of native elements, such as gold, are released from rock as it breaks down by weathering. Then, streams carry the fragments until the currents become too weak to carry these dense metals. Finally, because of the mechanical action of the stream, the fragments become concentrated at the bottom of stream beds in **placer deposits.** A placer deposit is shown in **Figure 2.**

Academic Vocabulary
release (ri LEES) to set free; to let go

Reading Check **Name two ways water creates ore deposits.** (See Appendix G for answers to Reading Checks.)

Figure 2 Placer deposits may occur at a river bend (left) or in holes downstream from a waterfall (right). Gold is a mineral that is commonly found in placer deposits. A stream carries heavy gold grains and nuggets, and then drops them where the current is weak.

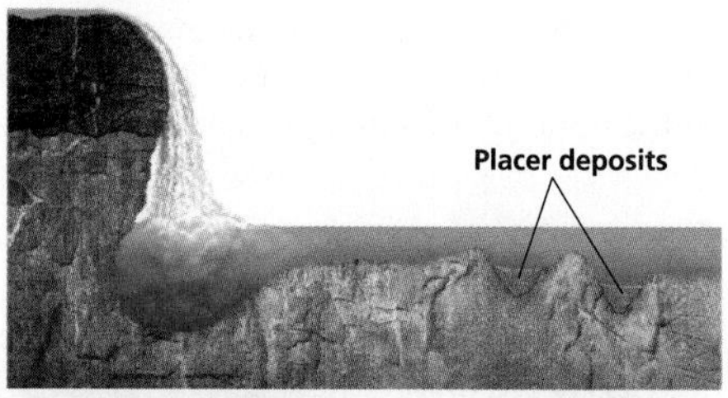

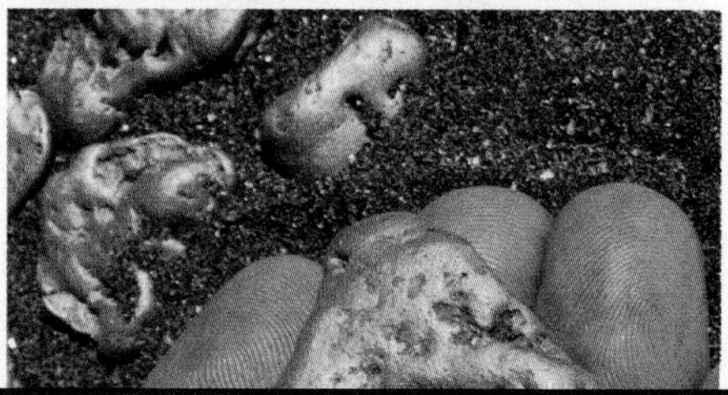

Answer to Reading Check
Water creates ore deposits by eroding rock and releasing minerals and by carrying the mineral fragments and depositing them in streambeds.

Differentiated Instruction

Advanced Learners

Using Minerals Invite students to do further research on various uses for individual minerals. Have each student research one mineral and try to find at least five common—or not so common—uses. Students may present their findings to the class in an oral report or as a poster or other display. LS **Verbal**

Table 1 Minerals and Their Uses

Metallic minerals	Uses
Hematite and magnetite (iron)	for making steel
Galena (lead)	in car batteries; in solder
Gold, silver, and platinum	in electronics and dental work; as objects such as coins, jewelry, eating utensils, and bowls
Chalcopyrite (copper)	as wiring; in coins and jewelry; as building ornaments
Sphalerite (zinc)	for making brass and galvanized steel
Nonmetallic minerals	**Uses**
Diamond (carbon)	in drill bits and saws (industrial grade); in jewelry (gemstone quality)
Graphite (carbon)	in pencils, paint, lubricants, and batteries
Calcite	in cement; as building stone
Halite (salt)	for food preparation and preservation
Kaolinite (clay)	in ceramics, paper, cement, and bricks
Quartz (sand)	in glass and computer chips
Sulfur	in gunpowder, medicines, and rubber
Gypsum	in plaster and wallboard

Uses of Mineral Resources

Some metals, such as gold, platinum, Pt, and silver, are prized for their beauty and rarity. Metallic ores are sources of these valuable minerals and elements. Certain rare nonmetallic minerals called **gemstones** display extraordinary brilliance and color when they are specially cut for jewelry. Other nonmetallic minerals, such as calcite and gypsum, are used as building materials. **Table 1** shows some metallic and nonmetallic minerals and their common uses.

gemstone a mineral, rock, or organic material that can be used as jewelry or an ornament when it is cut and polished

Mineral Exploration and Mining

Companies that mine and recover minerals are often looking for new areas to mine. These companies identify areas that may contain enough minerals for economic recovery through mineral exploration. In general, an area is considered for mining if it has at least 100 to 1,000 times the concentration of minerals that are found elsewhere.

During mineral exploration, people search for mineral deposits by studying local geology. Airplanes that carry special equipment are used to measure and identify patterns in magnetism, gravity, radioactivity, and rock color. Exploration teams collect and test rock samples to determine whether the rock contains enough metal to make a mine profitable.

SciLinks
www.scilinks.org
Topic: Using Mineral Resources
Code: HQX1587
Topic: Mining Minerals
Code: HQX0968

Discussion — Advanced

Properties of Minerals Have students review the different methods used in mineral exploration, as described in the last paragraph. Challenge students to suggest what mineral property each type of exploration is designed to detect. (Answers may vary. Examples: magnetism—minerals found in rocks that contain magnetized mineral grains, which generally consist of iron; gravity—minerals that are denser or less dense than surrounding rock; radioactivity—radioactive minerals or those found in rocks that contain radioactive materials; color—minerals that have a distinctive color or that commonly form in rocks that have a distinctive color.) **LS Logical**

Environmental Connection

Mountaintop Removal Discuss with the class what impact each type of mining described may have on the environment, such as the disruption of ecosystems and the pollution of water resources. Have interested students then research mountaintop-removal mining. Guide students to compare the effects of this type of mining on the environment to the effects of other mining methods. Students may present findings to the class by using pictures, drawings, or a model. **LS Verbal**

Why It Matters

Alloys An alloy is a solid mixture of two or more metals, or of a metal and a nonmetal, that are fused when melted together. Common alloys include bronze, which is an alloy of copper and tin, and pewter, which is made of tin and lead or other metals. An example of an alloy of a metal and a nonmetal is steel, which is a combination of iron and up to 2% carbon. Steel may also contain other metals and nonmetals.

Group Activity — General

Mineral Use Divide the class into three groups and have each group research the specific minerals and gemstones that are used in a variety of everyday objects, such as cell phones, televisions, and soup cans. Guide students to use the library, the Internet, or both for their research. Have each group create a multimedia presentation and present their findings to the class. **LS Logical/Visual**

Close

Reteaching — BASIC

Ore Minerals Have students make a table that lists commonly used metals and minerals, identifies how they are used, and predicts how they may be mined. **LS Logical**

Quiz — GENERAL

1. Why would mineral exploration teams be interested in identifying lodes? (Lodes are small regions of rich ore deposits that could potentially be mined easily for great profit because they are near the surface.)
2. What minerals are found as nodules in the ocean? (iron, manganese, and nickel)

Answers to Section Review

1. An ore is a mineral deposit from which metals or nonmetals can be removed profitably.
2. Deposits form from cooling magma, contact metamorphism, or stream deposition.
3. Sulfur is used in medicine and rubber. Copper is used in wire and in coins. Diamond is used in jewelry and in saws.
4. Subsurface mining involves working underground to mine ore. Surface mining involves the removal of surface material to reach ore. Placer mining involves dredging ore from stream or lake beds. Undersea mining involves recovering ore from the ocean floor.
5. Gold and copper are good conductors of electricity, and they can be easily shaped.

Figure 3 With a rim diameter of 4 km and a depth of almost 1 km, the Bingham Canyon Mine in Utah is the largest copper mine in the world.

Subsurface Mining

Many mineral deposits are located below Earth's surface. These minerals are mined by miners who work underground to recover the deposits. This type of mining is called *subsurface mining*.

Surface Mining

When mineral deposits are located close to Earth's surface, they may be mined by using *surface mining* methods. In these methods, the overlying rock material is stripped away to reveal the mineral deposits. A large openpit copper mine is shown in **Figure 3.**

Placer Mining

Minerals in placer deposits are mined by dredging. In placer mining, large buckets are attached to a floating barge. The buckets scoop up the sediments in front of the barge. Dense minerals from placer deposits are separated from the surrounding sediments. Then, the remaining sediments are released into the water.

Undersea Mining

The ocean floor also contains mineral resources. *Nodules* are lumps of minerals on the deep-ocean floor that contain iron, manganese, Mn, and nickel, and that could become economically important if they could be recovered efficiently. However, because of their location, these deposits are very difficult to mine. Mineral deposits on land can be mined less expensively than deposits on the deep-ocean floor can.

Section 1 Review

Key Ideas

1. **Define** *ore.*
2. **Describe** three ways that ore deposits form.
3. **Identify** two uses for each of the following minerals: sulfur, copper, and diamond.
4. **Summarize** the four main types of mining.

Critical Thinking

5. **Applying Ideas** Which properties of gold and copper make these metals suitable for use in electronics?
6. **Understanding Relationships** Why are dense minerals more likely to form placer deposits than less dense minerals are?
7. **Making Inferences** Why do you think that mining on land is less costly than mining in the deep ocean is?

Concept Mapping

8. Use the following terms to create a concept map: *mineral, ore, magma, contact metamorphism, vein, lode, placer deposit,* and *mine.*

6. Denser minerals are more likely to settle out of slowly moving water.
7. The ocean bottom can be reached only by using specialized technology and has conditions to which humans are not well adapted and for which mining procedures have not been developed.
8. A *mine* may be located over a *lode*, which is an area that is rich in *ores*, which are concentrations of *minerals* that form by stream deposition, which causes *placer deposits*, or by *contact metamorphism* or by the cooling of *magma*, both of which may form *veins*.

Differentiated Instruction

Alternative Assessment

Chart Have students create a flowchart by using boxes and arrows to show how a mineral of their choice becomes part of a deposit, is mined, and then is used to make a useful object. **LS Logical/Visual**

ENVIRONMENTAL CONNECTION

SECTION 2 Nonrenewable Energy

Key Ideas	Key Terms	Why It Matters
› Explain why coal is a fossil fuel. › Describe the formation of petroleum and natural gas. › Describe how fossil fuels are used today. › Explain how nuclear fission generates electricity.	**nonrenewable resource** **fossil fuel** **nuclear fission** **nuclear fusion**	Nonrenewable resources, such as fossil fuels, are limited in supply. People use fossil fuels as an energy resource. People use nuclear energy to generate electricity.

Many of Earth's resources are used to generate energy. Energy is used for transportation, manufacturing, and countless other activities that are important to society as we know it. Energy resources that exist in limited amounts and cannot be replaced quickly once they are used are examples of **nonrenewable resources.**

Fossil Fuels

Some of the most important nonrenewable resources are buried within Earth's crust. These natural resources—coal, petroleum, and natural gas—formed from the remains of living things. Because of their organic origin, coal, petroleum, and natural gas are called **fossil fuels.** Fossil fuels consist primarily of compounds of carbon and hydrogen called *hydrocarbons*. These compounds contain stored energy originally obtained from sunlight by plants and animals that lived millions of years ago. When hydrocarbons are burned, the formation of chemical bonds with oxygen (oxidation) releases energy as heat and light. Much of the energy humans use every day comes from the burning of fossil fuels.

nonrenewable resource a resource that forms at a rate that is much slower than the rate at which the resource is consumed

fossil fuel a nonrenewable energy resource formed from the remains of organisms that lived long ago

Formation of Coal

The most commonly burned fossil fuel is coal. The coal deposits of today are the remains of plants that have undergone a complex process called *carbonization*. Carbonization occurs when partially decomposed plant material is buried in swamp mud and becomes peat. Bacteria consume some of the peat and release the gases methane, CH_4, and carbon dioxide, CO_2. As gases escape, the chemical content of the peat gradually changes until mainly carbon remains. The complex chemical and physical changes that produce coal happen only if there is no oxygen in the swamp. If the conditions are not right for carbonization or if the time required for coal formation has not elapsed, peat remains. Peat can also be used as an energy source, as shown in **Figure 1.**

Figure 1 Some people in Ireland and Scotland heat their houses with peat.

Section 2

Focus

Overview

This section describes how fossil fuels—coal, petroleum, and natural gas—form and are acquired by humans. The section also explains nuclear processes and how nuclear fission can be used to generate electricity.

Bellringer

Ask students: "What would your life be like without electricity or gasoline?" (Answers may vary. Accept all reasonable answers.) **LS Intrapersonal**

Motivate

Identifying Preconceptions GENERAL

Is It Renewable? Present students with the following list: coal, water, oil, wind, wood, sunlight, and soil. Have students identify whether each resource is renewable or nonrenewable. (Coal is nonrenewable, oil is nonrenewable, wind is renewable, wood is renewable, sunlight is renewable, and soil is nonrenewable. Students may disagree about whether water is renewable.) Use students' responses to tailor your discussion of nonrenewable resources. **LS Logical**

Key Resources

Chapter Resource File
- Directed Reading BASIC

Technology
- Transparencies
  Bellringer

Differentiated Instruction

Special Education Students

Renewable or Nonrenewable? Show developmentally delayed students objects or pictures of objects. Have them name each object and tell you whether it's made from renewable or nonrenewable resources.

Teach

Group Activity GENERAL

Purifying with Pressure This activity shows how pressure removes impurities from coal. Organize students into small groups and provide each group a basin, a towel, a measuring cup, water, and several weights, such as bricks. Have students perform the following steps:

1. Fold the towel into a square and place it in the basin.
2. Fill the measuring cup with water.
3. Slowly pour the water onto the towel to saturate it, without allowing water to accumulate in the basin. Record how much water is used.
4. Place one brick on the towel, leave for one minute, and then remove.
5. Pour the water out of the basin and measure the amount of water.
6. Repeat steps 4 and 5 twice more, once using 2 bricks and once using 3 bricks.
7. Compare the amount of water that is removed from the towel by 1, 2, and 3 bricks.

Discuss with students how increasing pressure removes impurities from the compressed substance. (The greater the pressure, the more impurities are removed.) LS **Kinesthetic/Logical**

Math Skills

Answer

At a rate of 4.5 billion tons/year, the coal will last about 222 years (1,000 billion tons ÷ 4.5 billion tons/year). At a rate of 10 billion tons/year, the coal will last about 100 years (1,000 billion tons ÷ 10 billion tons/year).

Figure 2 Types of Coal

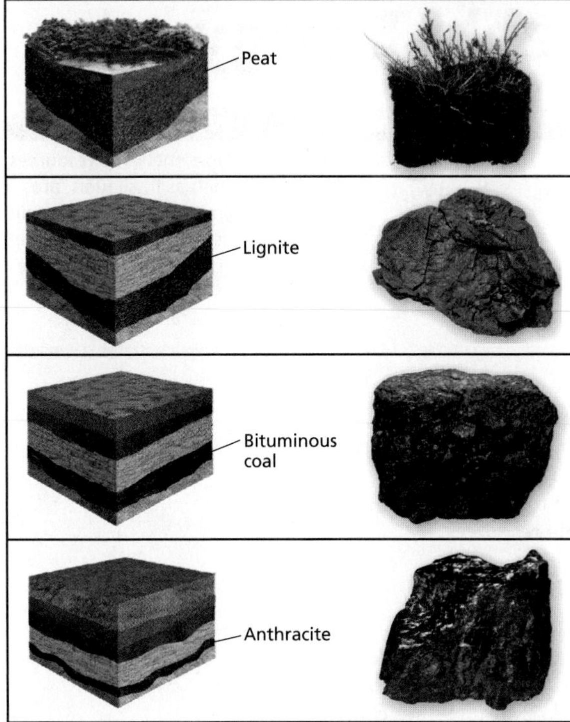

Stage 1: Peat

The partial decomposition of plant remains forms a brownish-black material called *peat.*

Stage 2: Lignite

Peat is buried by other sediment. As heat and pressure increase, peat becomes lignite. Lignite is also called *brown coal.*

Stage 3: Bituminous Coal

Increased temperature and pressure turn lignite into bituminous coal, which is 80% carbon. Bituminous coal is also called *soft coal.*

Stage 4: Anthracite

Under high temperature and pressure conditions, bituminous coal eventually becomes anthracite, which is the hardest form of coal.

Math Skills

Coal Reserves There is thought to be more than 1,000 billion tons of coal on Earth that can be mined. If 4.5 billion tons are used worldwide every year, for how many years will Earth's coal reserves last? If coal use increases to 10 billion tons per year, for how many years will Earth's coal reserves last?

Types of Coal Deposits

As peat is covered by layers of sediments, the weight of these sediments squeezes out water and gases. A denser material called *lignite* forms, as shown in the second stage of **Figure 2.** The increased temperature and pressure of more sediments compacts the lignite and forms *bituminous coal.* Bituminous coal is the most abundant type of coal. Where the folding of Earth's crust produces high temperatures and pressure, bituminous coal changes into *anthracite,* the hardest form of coal. Bituminous coal is made of 80% carbon, and anthracite is made of 90% carbon. Both release large amounts of energy as heat when they burn.

Formation of Petroleum and Natural Gas

When microorganisms and plants died in shallow prehistoric oceans and lakes, their remains accumulated on the ocean floor and lake bottoms and were buried by sediment. As more sediments accumulated, heat and pressure increased. Over millions of years, the heat and pressure caused chemical changes to convert the remains into petroleum and natural gas.

Petroleum and natural gas are mixtures of hydrocarbons. Petroleum, which is also called *oil,* is made of liquid hydrocarbons. Natural gas is made of hydrocarbons in the form of gas.

Internet Activity GENERAL

Resource Locations Have students use the Internet to find maps that show where significant deposits of coal occur on Earth. Students may share their findings with the class. A worksheet designed to direct student research on this topic can be found in the **Chapter Resource File** booklet or by visiting www.thinkcentral.com and entering the keyword **HQXRENX.** LS **Visual/Logical**

Key Resources

Technology
- Transparencies
  33 Types of Coal

Petroleum and Natural Gas Deposits

Petroleum and natural gas are very important sources of energy for transportation, farming, and many other industries. Because of their importance, petroleum and natural gas deposits are valuable and are highly sought after. Petroleum and natural gas are most often mined from permeable sedimentary rock. *Permeable rocks* have interconnected spaces through which liquids can easily flow.

As sediments accumulate and sedimentary rock forms, pressure increases. This pressure forces fluids, including oil and gas, out of the pores and up through the layers of permeable rock. The fluids move upward until they reach a layer of *impermeable rock,* or rock through which liquids cannot flow, called *cap rock*. Petroleum that accumulates beneath the cap rock fills all the spaces to form an oil reservoir. Because petroleum is less dense than water, petroleum rises above any trapped water. Similarly, natural gas rises above petroleum, because natural gas is less dense than both oil and water.

Figure 3 Oil Traps

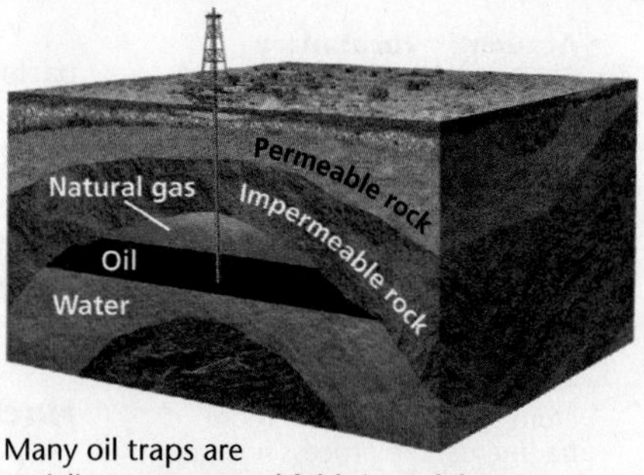

Many oil traps are anticlines, or upward folds in rock layers.

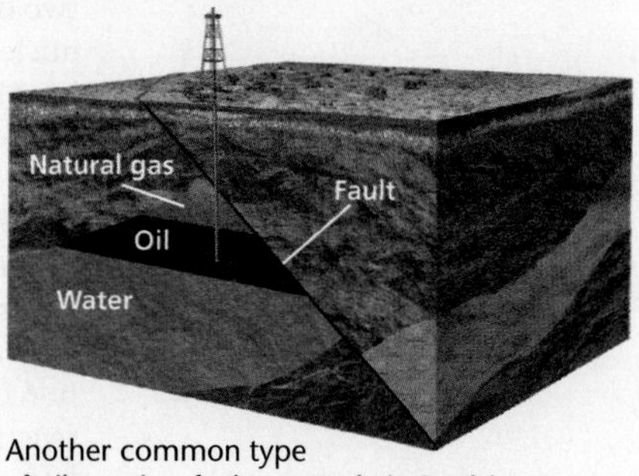

Another common type of oil trap is a fault, or crack, in Earth's crust that seals the oil- or gas-bearing formation.

Oil Traps

Geologists explore Earth's crust to discover the kinds of rock structures that may trap oil or gas. They look for oil trapped in places such as the ones shown in **Figure 3.** When a well is drilled into an oil reservoir, the petroleum and natural gas often flow to the surface. When the pressure of the overlying rock is removed, fluids rise up and out through the well.

Fossil-Fuel Supplies

Fossil fuels, like minerals, are nonrenewable resources. Globally, fossil fuels are one of the main sources of energy. *Crude oil,* or unrefined petroleum, is also used in the production of plastics, synthetic fabrics, medicines, waxes, synthetic rubber, insecticides, chemical fertilizers, detergents, shampoos, and many other products.

Coal is the most abundant fossil fuel in the world. Every continent has coal, but almost two-thirds of known deposits occur in three countries—the United States, Russia, and China. Scientists estimate that most of the petroleum reserves in the world have been discovered. However, scientists think that there are undiscovered natural gas reserves. There is also a relatively abundant material called *oil shale* that contains petroleum. But the cost of mining oil from shale is far greater than the present cost of recovering oil from other sedimentary rocks.

Reading Check **What is cap rock?**

SCILINKS.
www.scilinks.org
Topic: Nonrenewable Resources
Code: **HQX1044**
Topic: Fossil Fuels
Code: **HQX0614**

Using the Figure — GENERAL

Rock Layers and Density Have students study the figures that illustrate oil traps. Have students describe the characteristics of the rock layers above and below the fluids. Discuss the role that density plays in the formation of oil and natural gas deposits. Challenge students to explain how relative densities contribute to an oil "gusher." (Because the oil and natural gas cannot move through the overlying rock, as more oil and natural gas migrate up through the rock, pressure builds up. When the overlying rock is removed, the pressure causes the oil or natural gas to rush upward.) **LS Visual/Logical**

Answer to Reading Check

Cap rock is a layer of impermeable rock at the top of an oil- or natural gas-bearing formation through which fluids cannot flow.

Why It Matters

Hydrocarbon Use In the United States, the hydrocarbon most commonly used in power plants that generate electricity is bituminous coal. The purest coal, anthracite, burns more cleanly but is more expensive. In parts of Eastern Europe, lignite is the most commonly used type of coal. It has created air pollution problems in some areas. Other hydrocarbons commonly used worldwide are octane, diesel fuel, propane, oil, and butane.

Key Resources

Technology

- Transparencies
  34 Oil Traps

MISCONCEPTION ALERT

Petroleum Deposits Students may think that petroleum and natural gas deposits are "lakes" of liquid petroleum that floats freely through empty spaces underground. Explain that petroleum and natural gas exist as liquid or gas that is held in and moves through interconnected pores and cracks in underground rocks.

Differentiated Instruction

Struggling Readers

Word Parts Help students remember the meanings of the words *permeable* and *impermeable* by doing a word-part analysis. *Permeable* comes from the Latin word parts *per-*, meaning "through," and *meare*, meaning "to go, pass." *Impermeable* contains the prefix *im-*, meaning "not."

Teach, *continued*

Demonstration BASIC

Chain Reaction To help students understand a chain reaction, have all of the students in the class stand up. Shake the hand of one student. That student should then shake hands with two other students. These two each shake the hand of two more students. The process should continue, with each student shaking the hand of two other students, until all students have joined the chain. This process should not take long. Point out that each handshake is like a neutron striking an atomic nucleus in a chain reaction, which grows rapidly unless carefully controlled. **LS Kinesthetic**

Skill Builder GENERAL

Vocabulary Explain that the words *nucleus* and *nuclear* derive from the Latin word forms *nuc–* and *nux–*, which mean "kernel," or "nut." Discuss with students why this is an appropriate, or inappropriate, word root for the term that describes the nucleus of an atom. **LS Verbal**

Answer to Reading Check

As neutrons strike neighboring nuclei, the nuclei split and release additional neutrons that strike other nuclei and cause the chain to continue.

Key Resources

Technology

- Transparencies
  35 A Nuclear Fission Reaction
  36 How a Nuclear Power Plant Generates Electricity

Academic Vocabulary

fundamental (FUHN duh MENT'l) basic

nuclear fission the process by which the nucleus of a heavy atom splits into two or more fragments; the process releases neutrons and energy

SCILINKS.
www.scilinks.org
Topic: Nuclear Energy
Code: HQX1047

Nuclear Energy

When scientists discovered that atoms had smaller fundamental parts, scientists wondered if atoms could be split. In 1919, Ernest Rutherford first studied and explained the results of bombarding atomic nuclei with high-energy particles. In the 30 years that followed his research, scientists developed nuclear (NOO klee uhr) technologies that allowed atomic weapons to be made and allowed nuclear reactions to be used to generate electricity. Energy that is produced by using these technologies is called *nuclear energy*.

Nuclear Fission

One form of nuclear energy is produced by splitting the nuclei of heavy atoms. This splitting of the nucleus of a large atom into two or more smaller nuclei is called **nuclear fission.** The process of nuclear fission is shown in **Figure 4.**

The forces that hold the nucleus of an atom together are more than 1 million times stronger than the strongest chemical bonds between atoms. If a nucleus is struck by a free neutron, however, the nucleus of the atom may split. When a large nucleus splits, it releases additional neutrons as well as energy. The newly released neutrons strike other nearby nuclei, which causes those nuclei to split and to release more neutrons and more energy. A chain reaction occurs as more neutrons strike neighboring nuclei. If a fission reaction is allowed to continue uncontrolled, the reaction will escalate quickly and may result in an explosion. However, controlled fission produces heat that can be used to generate electricity.

Reading Check What causes a chain reaction during nuclear fission?

THINK central
INTERACT ONLINE
(Keyword: HQXRENF4)

Figure 4 An Example of a Nuclear Fission Reaction

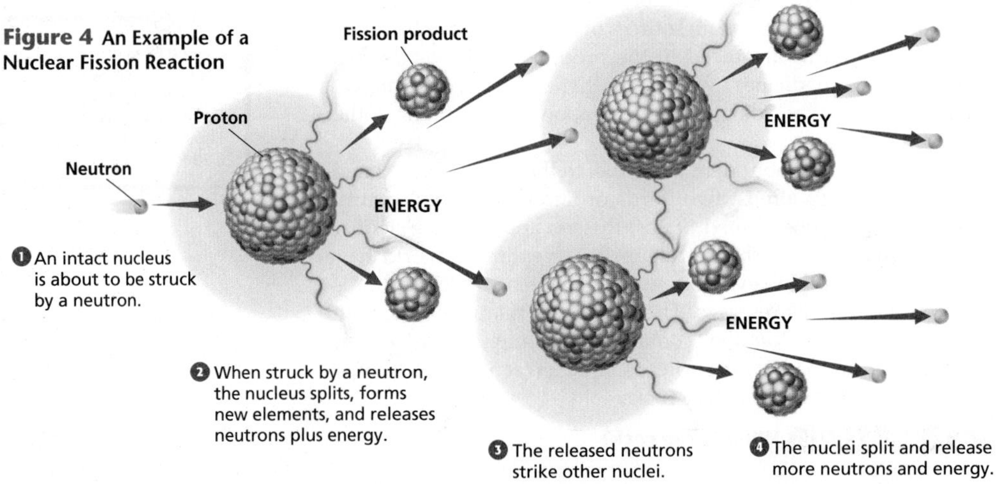

Fission product
Proton
Neutron
ENERGY
ENERGY
ENERGY
1 An intact nucleus is about to be struck by a neutron.
2 When struck by a neutron, the nucleus splits, forms new elements, and releases neutrons plus energy.
3 The released neutrons strike other nuclei.
4 The nuclei split and release more neutrons and energy.

History Connection ADVANCED

Nuclear Theory The discovery of radioactivity by chemists Pierre and Marie Curie in the late nineteenth century led to greater understanding of atoms and atomic structure. Invite interested students to learn more about important scientists whose work led to the development of nuclear theory—and to Nobel Prizes for some. In addition to the Curies, you may suggest Ernest Rutherford, James Chadwick, J.J. Thomson, Albert Einstein, Enrico Fermi, and Niels Bohr.

Guide students to understand how each scientist's work advanced knowledge about nuclear theory and how consequences of the discoveries have impacted people's lives. Students may work individually or in small groups and should present their findings to the class in a brief oral report. Groups may wish to divide tasks, such as research, writing, and presentation of results. **LS Verbal** Co-op Learning

Figure 5 How a Nuclear Power Plant Generates Electricity

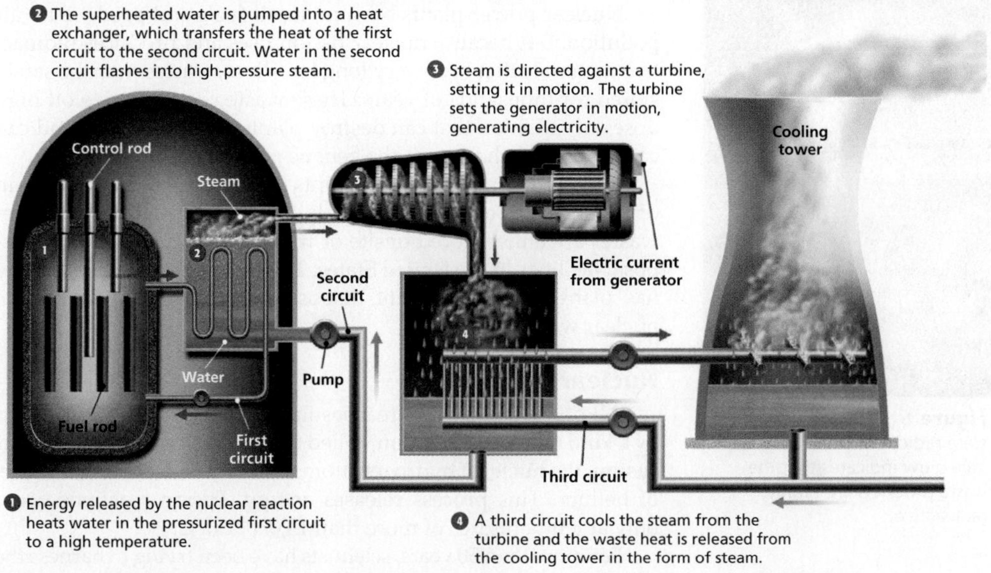

2 The superheated water is pumped into a heat exchanger, which transfers the heat of the first circuit to the second circuit. Water in the second circuit flashes into high-pressure steam.
3 Steam is directed against a turbine, setting it in motion. The turbine sets the generator in motion, generating electricity.
Cooling tower
Control rod
Steam
Second circuit
Electric current from generator
Pump
Water
Fuel rod
First circuit
Third circuit
1 Energy released by the nuclear reaction heats water in the pressurized first circuit to a high temperature.
4 A third circuit cools the steam from the turbine and the waste heat is released from the cooling tower in the form of steam.

How Fission Generates Electricity

When a nuclear power plant is working correctly, the chain reaction that occurs during nuclear fission is controlled. The flow of neutrons into the fission reaction is regulated so that the reaction can be slowed down, speeded up, or stopped as needed. The specialized equipment in which controlled nuclear fission is carried out is called a *nuclear reactor*.

During fission, a tremendous amount of heat energy is released. This heat energy can, in turn, be used to generate electricity. **Figure 5** shows how nuclear fission inside a nuclear reactor can be used to generate electricity. Currently, only one kind of naturally occurring element is used for nuclear fission. It is a rare isotope of the element uranium called *uranium-235*, or ^{235}U. Because ^{235}U is rare, the ore that is mined is processed into fuel pellets that have a high ^{235}U content. After this process is complete, the fuel pellets are said to be uranium-enriched pellets.

These enriched fuel pellets are placed into rods to make *fuel rods*. Bundles of these fuel rods are then bombarded by neutrons. When struck by a neutron, the ^{235}U nuclei in the fuel rods split and release neutrons and energy. The resulting chain reaction causes the fuel rods to become very hot.

Water is pumped around the fuel rods to absorb and remove the heat energy. The water is then pumped into a second circuit, where the water becomes steam. The steam turns the turbines that provide power for electric generators. A third water circuit carries away excess heat and releases it into the environment.

READING TOOLBOX

Chain-of-Events Chart
Create a chain-of-events chart to describe the process by which fission is used to generate electricity.

Debate — GENERAL

Pros and Cons Explain that radioactivity is harmful to human health and to the environment. Have students debate whether the risks of nuclear power are acceptable for the benefit of generating electricity. Encourage students to explore the health and environmental reasons for both sides of the argument. **LS Verbal/Logical**

Using the Figure — GENERAL

Electricity from Nuclear Fission Use the figure on this page to lead a discussion of each step in the process of using nuclear fission to generate electricity. Ask them to discuss why the fuel rods are housed in a large, massively reinforced structure. Have them explain why such a structure is necessary to contain the fuel rods. (A massive structure is needed to contain radioactivity in the event of a nuclear accident or other mishap.) **LS Visual/Logical**

READING TOOLBOX

Chain-of-Events Chart

You may wish to use this activity to assess students' prior knowledge before beginning a discussion of the process by which electricity is generated with nuclear power. You may also choose to use a similar activity as a quiz to assess students' knowledge of nuclear fission reactions or to assess students' knowledge after students have read this page.

Differentiated Instruction

Advanced Learners

Fudging Fusion? Have students research the claim made by scientists in 1989 that they had achieved "cold fusion," the fusion of hydrogen atoms at room temperature. Have students report to the class how the scientific method—specifically the requirement that all experiments be reproducible—revealed the claim to be false. Have students explain the difference between "hot" and "cold" fusion. **LS Verbal**

Close

Reteaching — BASIC

Flashcards Have students make flashcards that have a main idea about one form of energy resource on one side and details on the other side. Students may work in pairs to use the flashcards to reinforce the content of this section. **LS Visual**

Quiz — GENERAL

1. What form of coal has the highest percentage of carbon? (anthracite)
2. At what temperatures do nuclear fusion reactions take place? (greater than 15 million °C)

Answers to Section Review

1. because they formed from the remains of organisms that died millions of years ago
2. All three form from the remains of living things that undergo chemical changes when under intense pressure and heat inside Earth. Coal forms from plant remains. Oil and natural gas commonly form from the remains of marine organisms.
3. Petroleum may be trapped in porous rocks located in anticlines, under impermeable rock layers, or by faults.
4. uranium-235
5. A nuclear chain reaction generates a large amount of energy as heat. This heat boils water, which creates steam, which turns a turbine, which generates electricity.
6. Nuclei of hydrogen atoms combine to form the larger nuclei of helium, releasing energy in the process.
7. because only in the last 50 years have we better understood atomic structure and developed technology to control an atomic reaction and to dispose of radioactive waste adequately
8. No, because radioactive contamination would affect the environment and kill or harm aquatic life and affect humans who eat the organisms that live in the water
9. In fission, atomic nuclei are broken apart; in fusion, the nuclei are joined together.
10. *Nonrenewable resources* include *fossil fuels* such as *petroleum*, *natural gas*, and *coal*, which forms by *carbonization* and includes *peat*, *lignite*, *bituminous coal*, and *anthracite coal*.

Figure 6 These water pools store radioactive wastes. The blue glow indicates that the waste products are highly radioactive.

Advantages and Disadvantages of Nuclear Fission

Nuclear power plants burn no fossil fuels and produce no air pollution. But because nuclear fission uses and produces radioactive materials that have very long half-lives, wastes must be safely stored for thousands of years. These waste products give off high doses of radiation that can destroy plant and animal cells and can cause harmful changes in the genetic material of living cells.

Currently, nuclear power plants store their nuclear wastes in dry casks or in onsite water pools, as shown in **Figure 6.** Other wastes are either stored onsite or transported to one of three disposal facilities in the United States. The U.S. Department of Energy has plans for a permanent disposal site for highly radioactive nuclear wastes.

Nuclear Fusion

nuclear fusion the process by which nuclei of small atoms combine to form a new, more massive nucleus; the process releases energy

All of the energy that reaches Earth from the sun is produced by a kind of nuclear reaction, called nuclear fusion. During **nuclear fusion,** the nuclei of hydrogen atoms combine to form larger nuclei of helium. This process releases energy. Fusion reactions occur only at temperatures of more than 15,000,000 °C.

For more than 50 years, scientists have been trying to harness the energy released by nuclear fusion to produce electricity. More research is needed before a commercial fusion reactor can be built. If such a reactor could be built in the future, hydrogen atoms from ocean water might be used as the fuel. With ocean water as fuel, the amount of energy available from nuclear fusion would be almost limitless. Scientists also think that wastes from fusion would be much less dangerous than wastes from fission. The only byproducts of fusion are helium nuclei, which are harmless to living cells.

Section 2 Review

Key Ideas

1. **Explain** why coal, petroleum, and natural gas are called *fossil fuels*.
2. **Compare** how coal, petroleum, and natural gas form.
3. **Describe** the kinds of rock structures in which petroleum reservoirs form.
4. **Identify** the naturally occurring element that is used for nuclear fission.
5. **Explain** how nuclear fission generates electricity.
6. **Summarize** the process of nuclear fusion.

Critical Thinking

7. **Analyzing Relationships** Why have we been able to build nuclear power plants for only the last 50 years?
8. **Recognizing Relationships** Can the waste products of nuclear fission be safely disposed of in rivers or lakes? Explain your answer.
9. **Making Comparisons** How do the processes of nuclear fusion and nuclear fission differ?

Concept Mapping

10. Use the following terms to create a concept map: *nonrenewable resource, fossil fuel, coal, carbonization, peat, lignite, bituminous coal, anthracite coal, petroleum,* and *natural gas.*

Differentiated Instruction

Alternative Assessment

Letter to the Editor Have students write a letter to the editor of a local newspaper in which they advocate the use of either fossil fuels or nuclear energy. Students should argue for one type of energy by comparing it with the other. **LS Logical/Verbal**

ENVIRONMENTAL CONNECTION

SECTION 3

Renewable Energy

Key Ideas	Key Terms	Why It Matters
› Explain how geothermal energy may be used as a substitute for fossil fuels. › Describe two methods for harnessing energy from the sun. › Describe four sources of renewable alternative energy.	renewable resource geothermal energy solar energy hydroelectric energy biomass	Sources of renewable energy can be replaced quickly. Using renewable energy sources reduces pollution caused by the burning of fossil fuels.

If current trends continue and worldwide energy needs increase, the world's supply of fossil fuels may be used up in the next 200 years. Nuclear energy does not use fossil fuels, but numerous safety concerns are associated with it. Therefore, many nations are researching alternative energy sources to ensure that safe energy resources will be available far into the future. Resources that can be replaced within a human life span or as they are used are called **renewable resources.**

Geothermal Energy

In many locations, water flows far beneath Earth's surface. This water may flow through rock that is heated by nearby magma or by hot gases that are released by magma. This water becomes heated as it flows through the rock. The hot water, or the resulting steam, is the source of a large amount of heat energy. This heat energy is called **geothermal energy,** which means "energy from the heat of Earth's interior."

renewable resource a natural resource that can be replaced at the same rate at which the resource is consumed

geothermal energy the energy produced by heat within Earth

Engineers and scientists have harnessed geothermal energy by drilling wells to reach the hot water. Sometimes, water is first pumped down into the hot rocks if water does not already flow through them. The resulting steam and hot water can be used as a source of heat. The steam and hot water also serve as sources of power to drive turbines, which generate electricity.

The city of San Francisco, for example, obtains some of its electricity from a geothermal power plant located in the nearby mountains. In Iceland, 85% of the homes are heated by geothermal energy. Italy and Japan have also developed power plants that use geothermal energy. A geothermal power plant is shown in **Figure 1.**

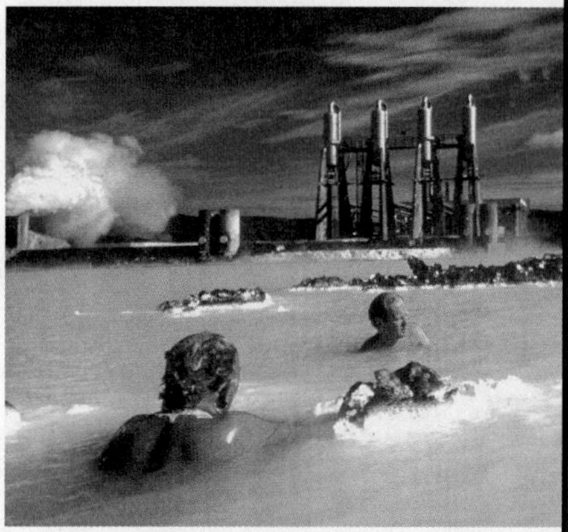

Figure 1 These swimmers are enjoying the hot water near a geothermal power plant in Svartsbening, Iceland.

Section 3

Focus

Overview

This section describes sources of renewable energy and how each source can substitute for fossil fuels.

Bellringer

Ask students to list things that they can renew. (Sample answers: memberships, library cards, interests, friendships) Ask them to use their list to help them write a definition of the term *renewable.* (Answers may vary.)
LS Logical

Motivate

Using the Figure GENERAL

Natural Hot Tub Have students study the photo at the bottom of the page. Ask students how they can tell that the water in the photo is hot. (Steam is rising from the water in the background.) Tell them that the water is a milky turquoise color because of the minerals in the water and the bacteria that live in the warm water.
LS Visual

Key Resources

Chapter Resource File

- Directed Reading BASIC
- Inquiry Lab: The Generation of Natural Gas from Biomass GENERAL

Technology

- Transparencies
  Bellringer

Teach

READING TOOLBOX

Everyday Words Used in Science

Answers may vary. Check to make sure students give correct meanings for scientific terms and everyday words.

Quick Lab

Skills Acquired

- Experimenting
- Organizing and Analyzing Data

Materials

- Small, shallow pan
- Black plastic
- Tape
- Thermometer
- Room-temperature water
- Plastic wrap
- Rubber band
- Stopwatch

Teacher's Notes: If your classroom has no sunny windows, you may use heat lamps.

Answers to Analysis

1. The variables are the pan lining and covering, time, and temperature. The first trial had the greatest temperature change. The last trial had the smallest temperature change.
2. The black plastic likely had the most dramatic effect on temperature change.
3. Answers may vary but should include a pan or box of water or other fluid and a lid that admits light and traps thermal energy.

Solar Energy

solar energy the energy received by Earth from the sun in the form of radiation

Another source of renewable energy is the sun. Every 15 minutes, Earth receives enough energy from the sun to meet the energy needs of the world for one year. Energy from the sun is called **solar energy.** The challenge engineers face is how to capture even a small part of the energy that travels to Earth from the sun.

Converting sunshine into heat energy can be done in two ways. A house that has windows facing the sun collects solar energy through a *passive system.* The system is passive because it does not use moving parts. Sunlight enters the house and warms the building material, which stores some heat for the evening. An *active system* includes the use of solar collectors. One type of *solar collector* is a box that has a glass top. The box is commonly placed on the roof of a building. Water circulates through tubes within the box. The sun heats the water as it moves through the tubes, which provides heat and hot water. On cloudy days, however, there may not be enough sunlight to heat the water. So, the system must use heat that was stored from previous days.

Photovoltaic cells are another active system that converts solar energy directly into electricity. Photovoltaic cells work well for small objects, such as calculators. Producing enough electricity from these cells to power cities is under investigation.

READING TOOLBOX

Everyday Words Used in Science

As you read this section, make a list of scientific terms that contain the word *energy* or *system*. Then, compare the familiar meaning of the words with the scientific meaning of the terms.

Quick Lab Solar Collector

30 min

Procedure

1. Line the inside of a **small, shallow pan** with **black plastic.** Use **tape** to attach a **thermometer** to the inside of the pan. Fill the pan with enough **room-temperature water** to cover the end of the thermometer. Fasten **plastic wrap** over the pan with a **rubber band.** Be sure you can read the thermometer.
2. Place the pan in a sunny area. Use a **stopwatch** to record the temperature every 5 min until the temperature stops rising. Discard the water.
3. Repeat steps 1 and 2, but do not cover the pan with plastic wrap.
4. Repeat steps 1 and 2, but do not line the pan with black plastic.
5. Repeat steps 1 and 2. But do not line the pan with black plastic, and do not cover the pan with plastic wrap.
6. Calculate the rate of temperature change for each trial by subtracting the beginning temperature from the ending temperature. Divide your result by the number of minutes the temperature increased to find the rate of temperature change.

Analysis

1. What are the variables in this investigation? Which trial had the greatest rate of temperature change? the smallest rate of temperature change?
2. Which variable that you tested has the most significant effect on temperature change?
3. What materials would you use to design and build an efficient solar collector? Explain your answer.

Environmental Connection

Impact of Dams Explain that even renewable energy sources may have some negative environmental effects. For example, when rivers are blocked or altered and land behind a dam is flooded to form a reservoir, water temperature may change and land and aquatic habitats may be damaged. Guide students to weigh the advantages (electricity, recreation) and disadvantages (environmental change) of hydroelectric dams. **LS Logical**

Differentiated Instruction

English Learners

Vocabulary Tell students that the prefix *photo-* means "light." Have students use this information to predict what the words *photosynthesis, photovoltaic,* and *photograph* mean. (the process of making something by using light, having the ability to generate electricity from light, and an image made by using light) **LS Verbal**

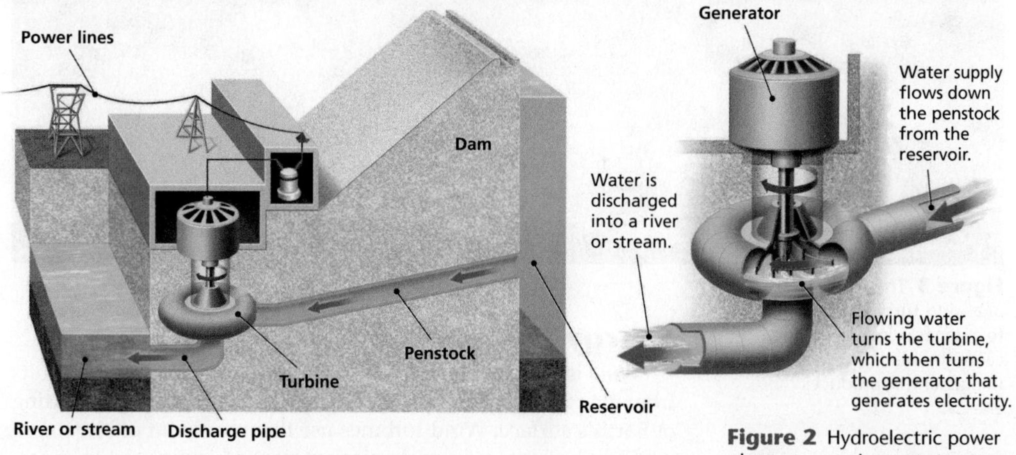

Power lines
Dam
Generator
Water supply flows down the penstock from the reservoir.
Water is discharged into a river or stream.
Penstock
Turbine
Reservoir
River or stream
Discharge pipe
Flowing water turns the turbine, which then turns the generator that generates electricity.

Figure 2 Hydroelectric power plants use moving water to turn turbines. The movement of each turbine powers a generator that generates electricity.

Energy from Moving Water

One of the oldest sources of energy comes from moving water. Energy can be harnessed from the running water of rivers and streams or from ocean tides. In some areas of the world, energy needs can be met by **hydroelectric energy,** or the energy produced by running water. Today, 6% of the electricity in the United States comes from hydroelectric power plants. At a hydroelectric plant, massive dams hold back running water and channel the water through the plant. Inside the plant, the water spins turbines, which turn generators that produce electricity. An example of a hydroelectric plant is shown in **Figure 2.**

Another renewable source of energy that comes from moving water is the tides. Tides are the rising and falling of sea level at certain times of the day. To make use of this tidal flow, people have built dams to trap the water at high tide and then release it at low tide. As the water is released, it turns the turbines within the dams.

hydroelectric energy electrical energy produced by the flow of water

biomass plant material, manure, or any other organic matter that is used as an energy source

Energy from Biomass

Other renewable resources are being exploited to help supply our energy needs. Renewable energy sources that come from plant material, manure, and other organic matter, such as sawdust or paper waste, are called **biomass.** Biomass is a major source of energy in many developing countries. More than half of all trees that are cut down are used as fuel for heating or cooking. Bacteria that decompose the organic matter produce gases, such as methane, that can also be burned. Liquid fuels, such as ethanol, also form from the action of bacteria on biomass. All of these resources can be burned to generate electricity.

Reading Check **Name three sources of renewable energy.**

Academic Vocabulary

exploit (EKS PLOYT) to use to the greatest possible advantage

SCILINKS.
www.scilinks.org
Topic: Renewable Resources
Code: **HQX1291**

Internet Activity — ADVANCED

Biomass Potential Have students use the Internet to find out how much organic waste, such as wood and other plant materials, paper, and agricultural waste, Americans discard each year. Have students learn about how this waste could be used to generate power. Students should then use their findings to create a proposal for how to use America's waste to generate electricity. A worksheet designed to direct student research on this topic can be found in the **Chapter Resource File** booklet or by visiting www.thinkcentral.com and entering the keyword **HQXRENX.**
LS Verbal

Close

Reteaching — BASIC

Energy in Action Have students demonstrate types of renewable energy by performing the following activities: solar: put a shallow bowl of water in the sun and allow the water to evaporate; wind: provide a pinwheel, and let the wind or a person's breath turn it; hydroelectric: have students hold the pinwheel upside down under a running faucet so that the flowing water turns the pinwheel. **LS Visual**

Answer to Reading Check

Answers may vary but should include three of the following: geothermal, solar, hydroelectric, and biomass.

Key Resources

Technology
- Transparencies
  37 How a Hydroelectric Dam Generates Electricity

Why It Matters

Favorable Winds The best areas for wind energy production have winds that blow steadily at between 12.8–16 km/h. High ridges and offshore regions are often good locations for wind farms. Tell students that for efficient electricity production, the blades on wind turbines may be more than 80 m long. You may want to use the Internet to find photos of wind turbines to illustrate their massive size.

Close, *continued*

Quiz GENERAL

1. Why might wind energy production be unsuitable for some locations? (Some sites have weak or unreliable winds.)
2. If you were to design a house, what would you include to promote passive solar heating? (large, south-facing windows that get lots of sun)

Answers to Section Review

1. because nonrenewable energy sources are running out
2. Heat from magma or rock heats water and produces steam that is used to boil water. The steam turns turbines that generate electricity.
3. Passive solar systems have no moving parts. Most active solar systems have pumps with moving parts and may use moving water.
4. Water released from a reservoir is channeled through turbines that turn generators to produce electricity.
5. Biomass may be burned, or it may be decomposed by bacteria to produce liquid or gas fuels that can be burned.
6. Wind and water move the blades of a turbine. The mechanical energy produced generates electricity.
7. Fossil fuels develop slowly over millions of years, while biomass can be regrown in a short time, such as a few years.
8. Answers may vary but should reflect knowledge of resources available and rationales for using them.
9. Types of *renewable resources* include *solar energy*, which may use a passive system or an *active system*, such as a *solar collector*; *geothermal energy*; *hydroelectric energy*; *biomass*; and *wind energy*.

Figure 3 The spinning blades of a wind turbine are connected to a generator. When winds cause the blades to spin faster, the generator produces more energy.

Energy from Wind

Wind is the movement of air over Earth's surface. Wind results from air-pressure differences caused by the sun's uneven heating of Earth's surface. Wind turbines use the movement of air to convert wind energy into mechanical energy, which is used to generate electricity.

Wind energy is now being used to produce electricity in locations that have constant winds. Small, wind-driven generators are used to meet the energy needs of individual homes. *Wind farms*, such as the one shown in **Figure 3,** may have hundreds of giant wind turbines that can produce enough energy to meet the electricity needs of entire communities. However, wind generators are not practical everywhere. Even in the most favorable locations, such as in windy mountain passes, the wind does not always blow. Because the wind does not always blow, wind energy cannot be depended on as the only energy source for most locations.

Section 3 Review

Key Ideas

1. **Explain** why many nations are researching alternative energy resources.
2. **Explain** how geothermal energy may be used as a substitute for fossil fuels.
3. **Describe** both passive and active methods of harnessing energy from the sun.
4. **Summarize** how electrical energy is generated from running water.
5. **Describe** how biomass can be used as fuel to generate electricity.
6. **Explain** how water and wind can be harnessed to generate electricity.

Critical Thinking

7. **Making Comparisons** Both fossil fuels and biomass fuels come from plant and animal matter. Why are fossil fuels considered to be nonrenewable, while biomass fuels are considered to be renewable?
8. **Demonstrating Reasoned Judgment** If you were asked to construct a power plant that uses only renewable energy sources in your area, what type of energy would you use? Explain.

Concept Mapping

9. Use the following terms to create a concept map: *renewable resource, solar collector, geothermal energy, solar energy, passive system, active system, hydroelectric energy, biomass,* and *wind energy.*

Differentiated Instruction

Alternative Assessment

Tour Brochure Have students write and illustrate a brochure about alternative energy use in different parts of the United States. The brochure should picture and describe each renewable energy source and explain why it is appropriately located. Students may use magazines or the Internet to find information and pictures.
LS Verbal/Visual

SECTION 4

ENVIRONMENTAL CONNECTION

Resources and Conservation

Key Ideas	Key Terms	Why It Matters
❯ Describe the importance of using fossil fuels wisely. ❯ Explain how the environmental impacts of mining can be reduced. ❯ Identify how conservation protects natural resources.	**conservation** **recycling**	The supply of fossil fuels is limited. Wise use of natural resources decreases waste and helps to protect the environment.

Scientists estimate that worldwide coal reserves will last about 200 years at the present rate of use. Many scientists also think that humans have already used half of Earth's oil supply. This limited supply of fossil fuels and other traditional energy resources has inspired research into possible new energy sources.

Scientists are also studying how the use of traditional energy sources affects Earth's ecosystems. We have learned that mining can damage or destroy fragile ecosystems. Fossil fuels and nuclear power generation may add pollution to Earth's air, water, and soil. However, people can reduce the environmental impact of their resource use. Many governments and public groups have worked to create and enforce policies that govern the use of these natural resources.

Environmental Impacts of Mining

Mining for minerals can cause a variety of environmental problems. Mining may cause both air and noise pollution. Nearby water resources may also be affected by water that carries toxic substances from mining processes. Surface mining is particularly destructive to wildlife habitats. For example, surface mining often uses controlled explosions to remove layers of rock and soil, as shown in **Figure 1.** Some mining practices cause increased erosion and soil degradation. Regions above subsurface mines may sink, or subside, because of the removal of the materials below. This sinking results in the formation of sinkholes. Fires in coal mines are also very difficult to extinguish and are commonly left to burn out, which may take several decades or centuries.

Figure 1 The surface of this gold mine in Nevada is being blasted to remove layers of rock.

Section 4

Focus

Overview

This section describes the environmental impacts of mining and laws that help mitigate that impact. The section also covers the effects of fossil fuels on the environment and explains resource conservation, including recycling.

Bellringer

Ask students to write a paragraph that explains which renewable forms of energy they think should be developed in case a growing human population makes it likely that the world will run out of crucial resources within the next century. (Accept all reasonable answers.) **LS Logical**

Key Resources

Chapter Resource File
- Directed Reading BASIC

Technology
- Transparencies
  Bellringer

Motivate

Discussion GENERAL

Mining Some students may think of mining as an activity that occurs only underground. Explain that today, most mining, especially of coal, is done on the surface. Invite students to talk about the impact of surface mining on the people who live near the mine. Ask them: "What problems do you think these people have to deal with every day? What advantages could there be to having a mining operation in their area?" (Accept all reasonable answers.)
LS Interpersonal

Teach

Quick Lab

Skills Acquired
- Modeling
- Calculating

Materials
- Plastic spoon
- Multi-layered gelatin dessert cup
- Small bowl

Teacher's Notes: You may also use chocolate chip cookies in place of gelatin cups, and have students attempt to remove the chips with as little damage as possible to the rest of the cookie. Have students relate the damage done to the cookie to the damage done by surface mining.

Answers to Analysis
1. reclaimed surface land
2. Answers may vary but should indicate that the uppermost layer is probably jumbled and ragged rather than smooth.
3. Answers may vary but should indicate that there will most likely be long-term damage to the area before the ecosystem can be restored.

Answer to Reading Check
The use of fossil fuels affects the environment when coal is mined from the surface, which destroys the land. When fossil fuels are burned, they affect the environment by creating air pollution.

Quick Lab — 30 min

Reclamation

Procedure
1. Use a plastic spoon to remove the first layer of gelatin from a multi-layered gelatin dessert cup into a small bowl.
2. Remove the next layer of gelatin, and discard it.
3. Restore the dessert cup by replacing the first layer of gelatin.

Analysis
1. What does the first layer of gelatin on the restored dessert cup represent?
2. Does the "reclaimed" dessert cup resemble the original, untouched dessert cup?
3. What factors would you address to make reclamation more successful?

Mining Regulations

In the United States, federal and state laws regulate the operation of mines. These laws are designed to prevent mining operations from contaminating local air, water, and soil resources. Some of these federal laws include the Clean Water Act; the Safe Drinking Water Act; and the Comprehensive Environmental Response, Compensation, and Liability Act. All mining operations must also comply with the federal Endangered Species Act, which protects threatened or endangered species and their habitats from being destroyed by mining practices.

Mine Reclamation

To reduce the amount of damage done to ecosystems, mining companies are required to return mined land to its original condition after the mining has been completed. This process, called *reclamation*, helps reduce the long-lasting environmental impact of mining. In addition to reclamation, some mining operations work hard to reduce environmental damage through frequent inspections and by using processes that reduce environmental impacts.

Fossil Fuels and the Environment

Fossil-fuel procurement affects the environment. Strip mining of coal can leave deep holes where coal was removed. Without plants and topsoil to protect it, exposed land often erodes quickly. When rocks that are exposed during mining get wet, they can weather to form acids. If runoff carries the acids into nearby rivers and streams, aquatic life may be harmed.

Fossil-fuel use also contributes to air pollution. The burning of coal that has a high sulfur content releases large amounts of sulfur dioxide, SO_2, into the atmosphere. When SO_2 combines with water in the air, acid precipitation forms. When petroleum and natural gas are burned, they also release pollutants that can damage the environment. The burning of gasoline in cars is a major contributor to air pollution. But emissions testing, which is shown in **Figure 2**, and careful maintenance help reduce the amount of pollutants released into the air. Emissions testing and maintenance include the testing of a car's catalytic converter, a device that removes numerous pollutants from the exhaust before the exhaust leaves the car.

Reading Check **Name two ways the use of fossil fuel affects the environment.**

Academic Vocabulary
procure (proh KYUR) to get as a result of effort; obtain or acquire

Figure 2 Emissions testing and maintenance of pollution-reducing devices in today's vehicles can help reduce air pollution.

Reading Skill Builder — Basic

Reading Hint Write the words *conserve* and *recycle* on the board. Invite a volunteer to define each term. Ask students to relate the meaning of the word *conserve* ("to save") to the term *conservation*. Have them define the prefix *re-* ("again") and the word *cycle* ("a regular course of events that begin and end at the same point") and then apply these meanings to the meaning of the term *recycle*. **LS Verbal**

Differentiated Instruction

Struggling Readers

Educating the Public Ask students to design educational flyers titled "Energy Conservation: What's Your Contribution?" to distribute to classes in the school. The flyers should include examples and ideas of what students and their families can do to conserve energy and to reduce pollution and waste in their community. The ideas and examples should make students and teachers aware of things they can do at school and at home.

Conservation

Many people and businesses around the world have adopted practices that help reduce the negative effects of the burning of fossil fuels and the use of other natural resources. This preservation and wise use of natural resources is called **conservation.** By conserving natural resources, people can ensure that limited natural resources last longer. Conservation can also help reduce the environmental damage and amount of pollution that can result from the mining and use of natural resources.

Mineral Conservation

Earth's mineral resources are being used at a faster rate each year. Every new person added to the world's population represents a need for additional mineral resources. In developing countries, people are using more mineral resources as their countries become more industrialized. This increased demand for minerals has led many scientists to look for ways to conserve Earth's minerals.

One way to conserve minerals is to use other abundant or renewable materials instead of scarce or nonrenewable minerals. Another way to conserve minerals is by recycling them. **Recycling** is the process of using materials more than once. Some metals, such as iron, copper, and aluminum, are often recycled, as shown in **Figure 3.** Glass and many building materials can also be efficiently recycled. Recycling does require energy, but recycling uses less energy than the mining and manufacturing of new resources does.

Figure 3 These cubes are made up of metals that have been compacted and are being sent to a recycling plant. ***Can you identify the source of these metals?***

conservation the preservation and wise use of natural resources

recycling the process of recovering valuable or useful materials from waste or scrap; the process of reusing some items

Why It Matters

Disposing of Electronic Waste

EYE ON THE ENVIRONMENT

Consumers purchase millions of cell phones, MP3 players, and computers every year, often to replace broken or slightly outdated equipment. But electronic devices contain toxic materials such as heavy metals. Recycling electronics instead of throwing them in the trash prevents toxins from entering the environment.

HEAVY METALS
PLAY FOREVER.
Don't dump lead and mercury—
recycle your electronics.
www.RecycleWorks.org

Some recycled electronics can be reused or repaired. Others can be taken apart to recover components and materials.

YOUR TURN ONLINE RESEARCH
Where in your area can you recycle electronic waste?

Using the Figure — GENERAL

Raw Recyclables Have students describe the metal cubes in the figure. Invite them to discuss what processes the recycled metal must likely undergo before it is ready to be used again in products. Answer to caption question: The source of the metals is largely aluminum soda cans. LS **Visual**

Close

Reteaching — BASIC

Materials We Use Have students collect pictures from magazines that illustrate each material discussed in this section. Have students create posters that categorize the pictures as relevant to Mining, Fossil Fuels, or Recycling and Conservation.
LS **Visual/Kinesthetic**

Quiz — GENERAL

1. How can fossil fuels damage the ocean environment? (through oil spills)
2. How does an expanding human population affect resource use? (More people will need and demand more goods and services that use resources.)

Environmental Connection

The Cost of Energy Conservation Many people think that making a home energy efficient is expensive. Although some measures, such as buying new appliances, are expensive, many are free or inexpensive. Turning off unused lights, cleaning refrigerator coils, and air-drying clothes cost nothing. The following methods are inexpensive and will pay for themselves in less than one year: wrapping your hot water heater ($12), installing a programmable thermostat ($25), changing air filters on heating and cooling systems ($12).

Why It Matters

Disposing of Electronic Waste Most discarded computers, monitors, and televisions end up in landfills rather than in recycling programs. Although e-waste only makes up about 2% of the landfill material in the United States, it makes up about 70% of the toxic waste, including lead, mercury, and cadmium. Recycling programs stop the release of toxic materials into the environment.

Answer to Your Turn

Answers may vary but should indicate where electronic waste can be recycled locally.

READING TOOLBOX

The Language of Prediction
Check to make sure students correctly identify prediction statements and underline words indicating that predictions are being made. Words that signal predictions include *if, must,* and *will.*

Close, *continued*

Answers to Section Review

1. destruction of wildlife habitats and pollution of air
2. by establishing and enforcing laws that reduce environmental impacts and by land reclamation
3. because fossil fuels cause environmental damage and are nonrenewable resources
4. Answers may vary but should say that reclamation is the restoration of land to its original condition.
5. Answers may vary. Sample answer: Use recycled paper and low-flow water fixtures, and bike instead of driving.
6. Recycling saves the energy that would be used to obtain resources from nature.
7. Answers may vary. Sample answer: Mining of coal may leave soil vulnerable to erosion and contamination. Spills from oil wells and pipelines can contaminate soil.
8. Energy is required both to mine minerals or cut down trees and to process these resources. Recycling uses energy mainly for processing.

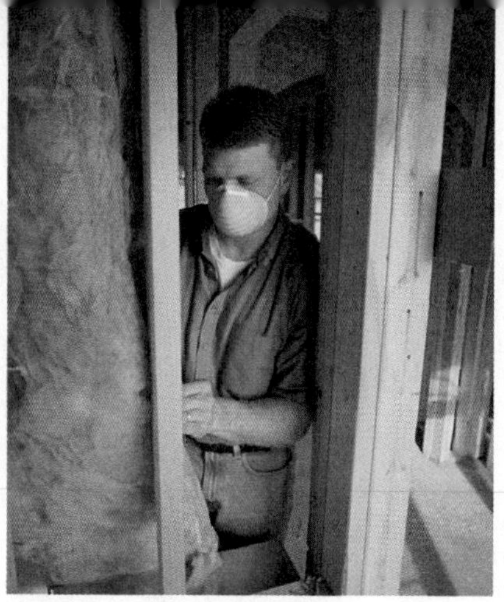

Figure 4 Fiberglass insulation is used in homes to reduce the energy required for heating and cooling.

Fossil-Fuel Conservation

Fossil fuels can be conserved by reducing the amount of energy used every day. If less energy is used, fewer fossil fuels must be burned every day to supply the smaller demand for energy. Energy can be conserved in many ways. **Figure 4** shows insulation being installed into a new house to reduce the amount of energy that will be needed for cooling and heating. Using energy-efficient appliances also reduces the amount of electricity used every day. In addition, simple actions, such as turning off lights when you leave a room and washing only full loads of laundry and dishes will reduce energy use.

Reducing the amount of driving you do also conserves fossil fuels. There is evidence that an average car produces more than 8 kg of carbon dioxide for every 3.8 L (1 gal) of gasoline burned. Even fuel-efficient and hybrid cars release some pollutants into the air. When making short trips, consider walking or riding a bicycle. If you need to use a car, combine errands so that you can make fewer trips.

READING TOOLBOX

The Language of Prediction
As you read this page, make a list of statements of prediction. Underline the key words that tell you each statement is a prediction.

Conservation of Other Natural Resources

Conservation is important for other natural resources, such as water. Some scientists estimate that by the year 2025, the world will have a critical shortage of freshwater resources because of the increased need by a larger human population. Water can be conserved by using water-saving shower heads, faucets, and toilets. By turning off the faucet as you brush your teeth, you can conserve up to 1 gallon of water every day. If you have a garden, you can help to conserve water by watering plants in the morning or at night and by planting native plants.

Section 4 Review

Key Ideas

1. **Name** two environmental problems associated with the mining and use of coal.
2. **Explain** two ways the environmental impacts of mining can be reduced.
3. **Describe** two reasons why scientists are looking for alternatives to fossil fuels.
4. **Define** the term *reclamation* in your own words.
5. **Identify** three ways that you can conserve natural resources every day.
6. **State** one way that recycling can help conserve energy.

Critical Thinking

7. **Analyzing Concepts** How do you think fossil-fuel use affects soil resources?
8. **Applying Ideas** Why does recycling require less energy than developing a new resource does?
9. **Drawing Conclusions** List 10 ways a small community can conserve energy and resources.

Concept Mapping

10. Use the following terms to create a concept map: *recycling, conservation, alternative energy source, renewable energy source, environmental impact, acid precipitation,* and *reclamation.*

9. Sample answer: establish a recycling facility; buy products made from recycled materials; establish bike lanes; promote carpooling; encourage the use of public transportation; use alternative-fuel buses; encourage the use of low-flow water fixtures; encourage the use of energy-efficient appliances; urge homeowners to install insulation; and educate people about conservation
10. Ways to reduce dependence on fossil fuels, which may cause *acid precipitation* and other harmful *environmental impacts*, include *conservation, recycling, reclamation*, using *renewable energy sources*, and finding *alternate energy sources.*

Differentiated Instruction

Alternative Assessment

Survey Tell students that recycling is only half the story and that conservation also includes buying products that contain recycled material. Have groups of students visit different types of stores and identify products that contain recycled materials. Students should make a list of the products that have the highest percentage of recycled content, then report back to the class.
LS Intrapersonal

Why It Matters

REAL WORLD

What Does Your Dream Car Run On?

Why pay lots of money for fuel that pollutes the environment? Scientists are developing cleaner alternatives to fossil fuels. One day you may be able to drive a zero-emission solar vehicle. People now build and race solar-powered cars, but the cars are not practical for day-to-day use. Adding features to the cars for safety and comfort would add too much weight and make the cars unacceptably slow. Right now, however, some mass-produced vehicles use hybrid technologies that reduce their need for fossil fuels.

Alternative-fuel vehicles

Because golf carts are lightweight, low-speed vehicles, **solar cells** can provide enough energy to run them.

Biofuels, such as the biodiesel this bus runs on, are made from plant and animal wastes.

Hybrid cars use two or more power sources. They produce fewer emissions than cars that run only on gasoline.

Cars that run mainly on **compressed air** are being developed. They produce little to no pollution.

YOUR TURN
UNDERSTANDING CONCEPTS
What are advantages of using alternatives to fossil fuels?

Why It Matters

What Does Your Dream Car Run On?

As the price of oil rises, the pressure to find viable alternatives to fossil fuels increases. Solar-powered cars are not yet practical for mass production, but scientists continue to work on developing them because they produce no carbon dioxide or other pollutants when operating. Hybrid vehicles using a combination of traditional and alternative fuels produce fewer emissions than traditional gasoline-powered vehicles. Today, the most commonly available hybrids are gasoline-electric hybrids. However, fuel-cell-gasoline hybrids, air-gasoline hybrids, and solar-electric hybrids are in development. Biofuels provide another alternative. They produce carbon dioxide as they are burned. However, as crops grow to produce the feedstocks for making the biofuel, they absorb carbon dioxide from the atmosphere, which offsets emissions. At this stage, it is difficult to predict which fuel or combination of fuels we will be using in the next ten years. Nonetheless, it appears that the traditional gasoline-powered engine is in for some tough competition.

Answer to Your Turn

Understanding Concepts Answers may vary but should include that fossil fuels are nonrenewable and that alternative fuels are more environmentally friendly.

Inquiry Lab

Time Required
two 45-minute class periods

Lab Ratings
EASY → HARD

Teacher Preparation
Student Setup
Concept Level
Cleanup

Skills Acquired
- Constructing Models
- Communicating
- Designing Experiments

Scientific Methods
In this lab, students will
- Ask a Question
- Form a Hypothesis
- Test the Hypothesis
- Evaluate Results

Materials
The materials listed are enough for groups of up to six students.

Inquiry Lab

90 min

What You'll Do
- **Prepare** a detailed sketch of your solution to the design problem.
- **Design and build** a functional windmill that lifts a specific weight as quickly as possible.

What You'll Need
blow-dryer, 1,500 W
dowel or smooth rod
foam board
glue, white
paper clips, large (30)
paper cup, small
spools of thread, empty (2)
string, 50 cm
optional materials for windmill blades:
foam board, paper plates, paper cups, or any other lightweight materials

Safety

Blowing in the Wind

MEMO

To: Division of Research and Development

Quixote Alternative Energy Systems is accepting design proposals to develop a windmill that can be used to lift window washers to the tops of buildings. As part of the design engineering division, your team has been asked to develop a working model of such a windmill. Your task is to design and build a model that can lift 30 large paper clips a vertical distance of 50 cm. The job will be given to the team whose model can lift the paper clips the fastest.

Ask a Question

1. What is the best windmill design?

Form a Hypothesis

2. Brainstorm with a partner or small group of classmates to design a windmill using only the objects listed in the materials list. Sketch your design, and write a few sentences about how you think your windmill will perform.

Test the Hypothesis

3. Have your teacher approve your design before you begin construction. Build the base for your windmill by using glue to attach the two spools to the foam board. Pass a dowel rod through the center of the spools. Make sure the spools are parallel and the dowel can rotate freely before you glue the spools. Attach one end of the string securely to the dowel between the two spools.

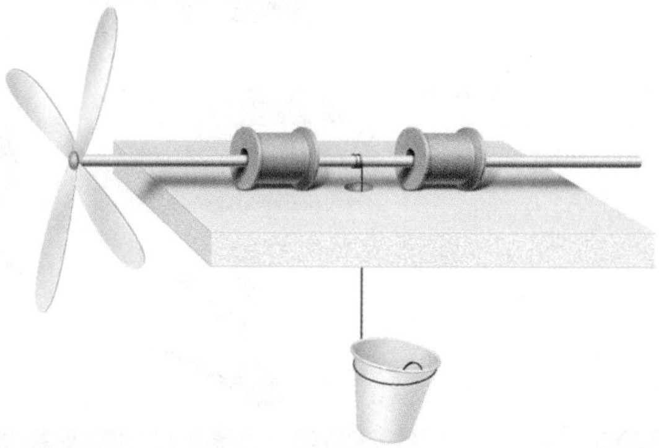

Step 3

Tips and Tricks
If enough time or materials are not available, have student groups draw their designs. Then, have all the students in the class evaluate each design for its potential success and choose the one they think will work best. Then, have students build the chosen design, or assign the construction of several models as homework, and have the class test the models in the next class period.

4 Poke a hole through the middle of the foam board to allow the string to pass through. Place your windmill base between two lab tables or in any area that will allow the string to hang freely.

5 After you have decided on your final design, attach the windmill blades to the base.

6 If you have time, you may want to try using different materials to construct your windmill blades. Test the various blades to determine whether they improve the original design. You may also want to vary the number and size of the blades on your windmill.

7 Attach the cup to the end of the string. Fill the cup with 30 paper clips. Turn on the blow-dryer, and measure the time it takes for your windmill to lift the cup.

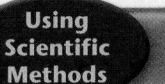

Step 2
Sample windmill blade designs

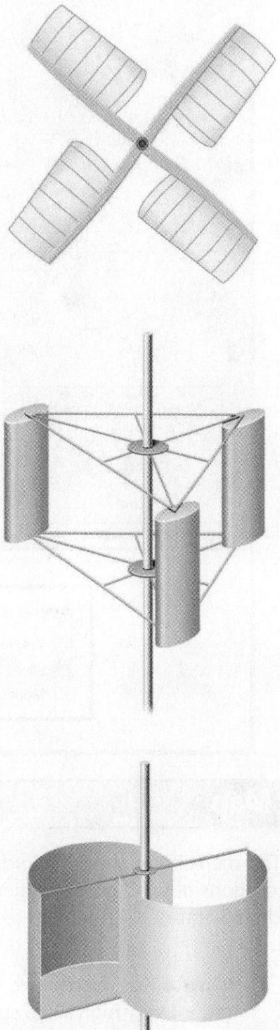

Analysis and Conclusion

1. **Evaluating Methods** As a class, test all the designs to determine which design takes the shortest amount of time to lift the cup with the paper clips. What elements of the design do you think made the winning design the fastest?
2. **Evaluating Models** Describe how you would change your design to make your windmill work better or faster.

Extension

Research Windmills have been used for more than 2,000 years. Research the three basic types of vertical axis machines and the applications in which they are used. Prepare a report of your findings.

Making Models Adapt your design to make a water wheel. You will find that a water wheel can lift much more weight than a windmill can. Find designs on the Internet for micro-hydropower water wheels, such as the Pelton wheel, and use the designs as inspiration for your model. You can even design your own dam and reservoir.

Answers to Analysis and Conclusion

1. Answers may vary but should include the reasons that students thought a particular design was the most effective.
2. Answers may vary. Accept all reasonable answers.

Answers to Extension

Research Answers may vary.
Making Models Designs may vary. Students may wish to build a model of the Pelton wheel. If students choose to draw a design for a dam and reservoir, have them explain to the class what design changes were needed to convert a wind-power design to a water-power design.

Wind Power in the United States

Internet Activity GENERAL

Alternative Energy Use in Your State Have students use the Internet to find national or state organizations that promote or have information about alternative energy. Have them find out what types of alternative energy are used in your state and where in the state they are used. Have them write a letter to the company, town, or county that is using the alternative energy and ask for more information about conditions at the site, how the energy is used, the technology behind the energy, and how it saves both money and resources. A worksheet designed to direct student research on this topic can be found in the **Chapter Resource File** booklet or by visiting **www.thinkcentral.com** and entering the keyword **HQXRENX.** **LS Verbal**

Answers to Map Skills Activity

1. Answers may vary. States include AK, CA, CO, ID, MT, NM, NV, TX, UT, and WY.
2. CA and MN
3. No; by 2008, TX ranked first and CA ranked second.
4. WY
5. the Rocky Mountains
6. CO, HI, ID, IL, KS, ME, MO, MT, ND, NE, NM, NY, OK, OR, PA, SD, TN, TX, WA, WV
7. The comparison means that these states could be a major source of wind energy, much as Saudi Arabia is a major source of oil.

MAPS in Action

Wind Power in the United States

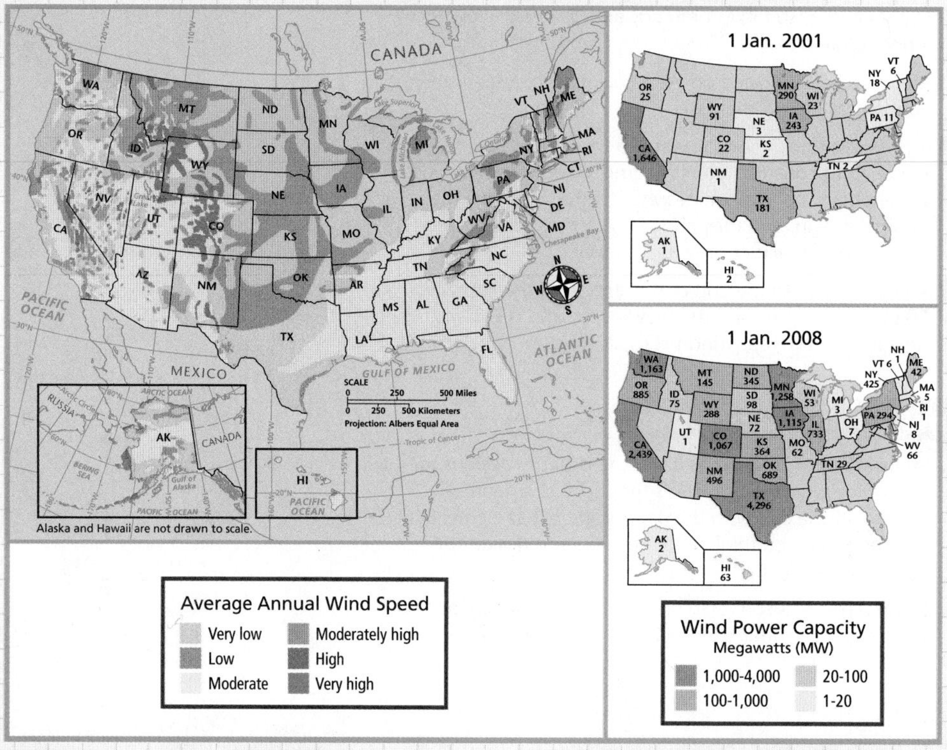

Map Skills Activity

This map shows average wind speeds and the locations of wind power projects throughout the United States. Use the map to answer the questions below.

1. **Using a Key** Name two states that have areas of very high wind speed.
2. **Using a Key** Which two states had the most wind power capacity in 2001?
3. **Making Comparisons** Did the two states with the most wind power capacity in 2001 still hold that rank in 2008? Explain.
4. **Analyzing Data** According to the map, which state has an area with the highest average annual wind speed?
5. **Inferring Relationships** Examine Idaho, Wyoming, Montana, and Colorado. What landscape feature might account for the strong winds in those states?
6. **Identifying Trends** Which states increased their wind power capacity by at least 10 times between 2001 and 2008?
7. **Making Comparisons** Because of their potential for wind power projects, the Great Plains states (MT, WY, CO, ND, SD, NE, KS, OK, TX, MN, and IA) have been called the "Saudi Arabia of wind energy." Why do you think this comparison has been made?

Key Resources

Technology

- Transparencies
  38 Wind Power in the United States

Chapter 7

Summary

THINK central
SUPER SUMMARY
Keyword: HQXRENS

Key Ideas	Key Terms

Section 1

Mineral Resources

- Ores are mineral deposits in Earth's crust from which metallic and nonmetallic minerals can be profitably removed.
- Minerals are important sources of many useful and valuable materials.
- Humans obtain mineral resources through subsurface, surface, placer, and undersea mining.

Key Terms: **ore,** p. 167; **lode,** p. 168; **placer deposit,** p. 168; **gemstone,** p. 169

Section 2

Nonrenewable Energy

- Chemical and physical processes changed the remains of ancient plants into coal.
- Petroleum and natural gas formed from the remains of ancient microorganisms.
- Today, fossil fuels provide much of the world's energy.
- The energy released by nuclear fission—the splitting of the nuclei of heavy atoms—can be used to generate electricity.

Key Terms: **nonrenewable resource,** p. 171; **fossil fuel,** p. 171; **nuclear fission,** p. 174; **nuclear fusion,** p. 176

Section 3

Renewable Energy

- Geothermal energy is energy from the heat of Earth's interior. Unlike fossil fuels, it can be replaced as it is used.
- Solar energy from the sun can be harnessed by both passive and active methods.
- Alternative sources of renewable energy include hydroelectric, tidal, solar, and wind energy.

Key Terms: **renewable resource,** p. 177; **geothermal energy,** p. 177; **solar energy,** p. 178; **hydroelectric energy,** p. 179; **biomass,** p. 179

Section 4

Resources and Conservation

- Fossil fuels are nonrenewable resources. Once a nonrenewable resource is depleted, the resource may take millions of years to be replenished.
- Responsible mining operations work hard to return mined land to good condition through reclamation.
- Conservation is the preservation and wise use of natural resources to ensure that they last longer.

Key Terms: **conservation,** p. 183; **recycling,** p. 183

Chapter Summary

Using THINK central Resources

Super Summary

Have students connect the major concepts in this chapter through an interactive Super Summary. Visit www.thinkcentral.com and type in the keyword **HQXRENS** to access the Super Summary for this chapter.

Differentiated Instruction

Alternative Assessment

Keeping Track Have students prepare a chart that has four columns labeled, left to right, "Object/Activity," "Materials/Components," "Energy Used," and "Conservation." As students go through the day, tell them to record the following items in the appropriate columns of their chart: the objects they use and/or activities they engage in; the materials or components of the objects and how these components are obtained; the energy sources required to make and use the object; and ways in which they can conserve resources. Because their lists could be very large, consider limiting the list to a period of time or one location, such as breakfast at home or gym period at school. Have students discuss their lists with the class. **LS Logical/Interpersonal**

Chapter Review

Assignment Guide	
Section	**Questions**
1	2, 6, 10, 17, 19, 24, 25
2	7, 12–14, 20, 26, 28
3	3, 8, 9, 15, 16, 21, 23, 30, 33
4	1, 4, 18, 22, 31, 32
2 and 3	5, 27, 34–36
1–4	29

Reading Toolbox

1. Check to make sure students correctly rephrase, in their own words, the effects of fossil fuels on the environment as statements of prediction.

Using Key Terms

2–9. Answers may vary but should show that students understand the definitions of and differences between key terms.

Understanding Key Concepts

10. c 14. b
11. d 15. c
12. c 16. a
13. b

Short Answer

17. As magma cools, dense metallic minerals crystallize and sink to form deposits. When magma contacts surrounding rock, chemical reactions occur that form an ore. Water weathers and erodes rock and then carries minerals downstream, where they may be dropped where currents slow to form placer deposits.

Chapter 7 Review

1. **The Language of Prediction** In your own words, rephrase in the form of statements of prediction the explanation in Section 4 of how obtaining and using fossil fuels affect the environment. READING TOOLBOX

USING KEY TERMS

Use each of the following terms in a separate sentence.

2. *placer deposit*
3. *solar energy*
4. *conservation*

For each pair of terms, explain how the meanings of the terms differ.

5. *renewable resource* and *nonrenewable resource*
6. *ore* and *lode*
7. *nuclear fission* and *nuclear fusion*
8. *fossil fuel* and *biomass*
9. *geothermal energy* and *hydroelectric energy*

UNDERSTANDING KEY IDEAS

10. Metals are known to
    a. have a dull surface.
    b. provide fuel.
    c. conduct heat and electricity well.
    d. occur only in placer deposits.
11. Energy resources that formed from the remains of once-living things are called
    a. minerals. **c.** metals.
    b. gemstones. **d.** fossil fuels.
12. Impermeable rock that occurs at the top of an oil reservoir is called
    a. coal.
    b. peat.
    c. cap rock.
    d. water.
13. Plastics, synthetic fabrics, and synthetic rubber are composed of chemicals that are derived from
    a. anthracite. **c.** peat.
    b. petroleum. **d.** minerals.
14. The splitting of the nucleus of an atom to produce energy is called
    a. geothermal energy.
    b. nuclear fission.
    c. nuclear fusion.
    d. hydroelectric power.
15. Energy experts have harnessed geothermal energy by
    a. building dams.
    b. building wind generators.
    c. drilling wells.
    d. burning coal.
16. In a hydroelectric power plant, running water produces energy by spinning a
    a. turbine.
    b. windmill.
    c. fan.
    d. reactor.

SHORT ANSWER

17. Compare the three ways that ores commonly form.
18. Name two regulations that mining operations must follow to reduce the impact they have on the environment.
19. Identify and describe the uses for three mineral resources.
20. Describe one advantage and one disadvantage of obtaining energy from nuclear fission.
21. Describe one advantage and one disadvantage of the use of solar energy.
22. Identify two ways recycling can reduce energy use.
23. Explain two ways that moving water can be used to generate electricity.
24. Compare two types of mining, and describe the possible environmental impact of each type.

18. Mines must follow the Clean Water Act and the Endangered Species Act.
19. Sample answer: Aluminum is used to make cans, gold is used for jewelry, and copper is used to make pots and pans.
20. advantage: no air pollutants; disadvantage: radioactive waste
21. advantage: It is a renewable resource; disadvantage: Solar energy systems may not produce as much energy when there is little sunlight.
22. Recycling a material takes less energy than mining new materials does. Also, recycling used materials takes less energy than manufacturing the same product using newly mined resources.
23. Hydroelectric dams produce electricity from moving water. Ocean tides may also be harnessed to produce energy.
24. Answers may vary. Sample answer: Subsurface mining removes ores from underground and does relatively little damage to the surface. Surface mining may disturb large areas of land and cause environmental damage by removing topsoil and vegetation. If dumped into streams, topsoil and rock may block the flow of water and upset aquatic ecosystems.

CRITICAL THINKING

25. Applying Ideas You learn that the price of iron is higher than it has been in 20 years. Do you think it might be profitable for a company to mine hematite? Explain your answer.

26. Understanding Relationships A certain area has extensive deposits of shale. Why might a petroleum geologist be interested in examining the area?

27. Identifying Trends Hybrid cars have efficient gasoline and electric motor combinations. They have other design elements that make them extremely fuel efficient. Do you expect that there will be more or fewer hybrid cars on the road in the future? Explain.

28. Making Inferences A certain company in your area produces ^{235}U pellets and fuel rods. With which energy source is the company involved? Explain.

CONCEPT MAPPING

29. Use the following terms to create a concept map: *resource, renewable, nonrenewable, fossil fuel, nuclear energy, geothermal energy, solar energy, hydroelectric energy,* and *conservation.*

MATH SKILLS

Math Skills

30. Making Calculations In one year, the United States produced 95,000 megawatts of power from renewable energy sources. If 3% of this power came from wind energy, how much energy did wind power produce that year?

31. Making Calculations A water-efficient washing machine uses 16 gallons of water per load of laundry. Older washing machines use more than 40 gallons of water per load of laundry. If you wash an average of 10 loads of laundry a month, how many gallons of water would you save in a year if you switched to the water-efficient washer?

WRITING SKILLS

32. Researching Information A debate surrounds municipal recycling programs. Do some research, and write a paragraph explaining each side of the debate. Write another paragraph explaining your view on whether recycling programs should be continued.

33. Writing Persuasively Research the pros and cons of building dams to harness energy. Write a letter to the editor of a local newspaper to express your opinion about whether dams should be used for generating electricity.

INTERPRETING GRAPHICS

The graph below shows the different contributions of various fuels to the U.S. energy supply since 1850. Use this graph to answer the questions that follow.

Energy Use in the United States

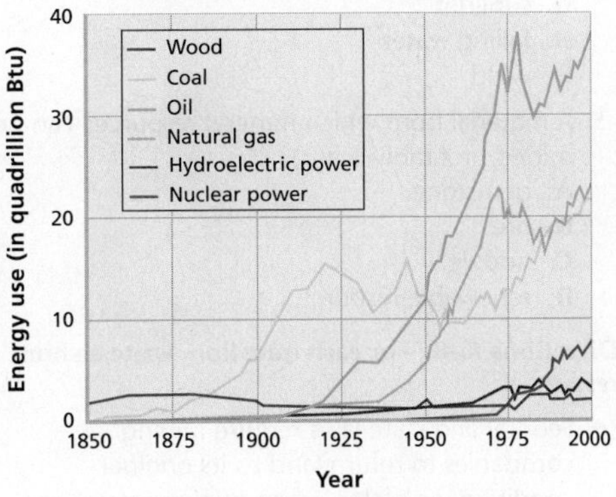

34. What were the two main energy sources used in 1875?

35. When did oil first become a more widely used energy source than coal?

36. The use of oil and natural gas rise and fall together. How do you explain this pattern?

Chapter Review

Critical Thinking

25. Answers may vary but should show that students understand the supply and demand for resources. If the rise in the price of iron were due to increased market demand, it would most likely be profitable to mine hematite. However, a price increase due to scarcity of hematite and/or increased costs to mine scarce materials may offset the potential for higher pricing due to scarcity alone. Thus, mining hematite may be less profitable.

26. The shale may be oil shale, a form of petroleum deposit, from which shale oil could be obtained by heating. Also, shale is commonly impermeable, so there may be oil trapped beneath the shale.

27. Answers may vary but should indicate that students understand that as petroleum becomes more scarce, gasoline prices may rise, causing some people to seek more fuel-efficient cars.

28. The company is involved in the nuclear energy business. Uranium is used in nuclear fission reactions.

Concept Mapping

29. Answers may vary but should include all of the terms listed. Sample answers appear at the end of this unit on p. 195D.

Math Skills

30. 95,000 MW × 0.03 = 2,850 MW

31. 40 gal/load − 16 gal/load = 24 gal/load × 10 loads/month = 240 gallons of water saved per month × 12 months/year = 2,880 gallons/year

Writing Skills

32. Answers may vary. Accept all reasonable answers.

33. Answers may vary. Accept all reasonable answers.

Interpreting Graphics

34. wood and coal

35. 1950

36. Answers may vary but should indicate that oil and natural gas commonly occur together in the same deposits. Thus, they would be available from the same sources and their prices would be stable relative to each other. Therefore, it is reasonable that oil and natural gas would be used in similar quantities during the same time periods.

Estimated Time

To give students practice under more realistic testing conditions, allow them 30 minutes to answer all of the questions in this practice test.

Test Doctor

Question 2 Answer G is correct. Scientists estimate that worldwide coal reserves will last about 200 years. Answer F refers to a possible shortage of freshwater resources and is incorrect. Answer H is incorrect because it is inconsistent with present rates of coal use. Answer I is incorrect because it applies only to renewable resources.

Question 3 Answer C is correct. A lode is formed from a large number of thick veins. Veins form when hot mineral solutions spread through small cracks in a large mass of rock. Answer A refers to placer deposits formed in moving water and is incorrect. Answer B is incorrect because it describes ores formed within cooling magma. Answer D refers to nodules on the ocean floor.

Question 11 Full-credit answers should include the following points:
- because the process to replenish petroleum and natural gas takes millions of years, these resources are considered nonrenewable
- nonrenewable resources are resources that form at a much slower rate than the rate at which they are consumed

Chapter 7 Standardized Test Prep

Understanding Concepts

Directions (1–5): For each question, write on a separate sheet of paper the letter of the correct answer.

1. Which of the following is an example of a nonmetal mineral resource?
A. gold
B. quartz
C. aluminum
D. copper

2. Scientists estimate that worldwide coal reserves will last
F. less than 20 years.
G. about 200 years.
H. about 1,000 years.
I. indefinitely.

3. A mineral deposit called a *lode* is formed by
A. metal fragments deposited in stream beds.
B. layers accumulating in cooling magma.
C. hot mineral solutions in cracks in rock.
D. precipitation of minerals from seawater.

4. Which of the following is an example of a nonrenewable resource?
F. natural gas
G. sunlight
H. falling water
I. wind

5. A material from which mineral resources can be mined profitably is a(n)
A. gemstone.
B. ore.
C. nodule.
D. renewable resource.

Directions (6–8): For each question, write a short response.

6. Federal and state laws require mining companies to return land to its original condition, or better, when mining operations have been completed. What is this process called?

7. What are the three forms of fossil fuels, and what form does each one take?

8. Name three common items that may be recycled to save energy and natural resources.

Reading Skills

Directions (9–11): Read the passage below. Then, answer the questions.

Fossil Fuels

All fossil fuels form from the buried remains of ancient organisms. But different types of fossil fuels form in different ways and from different types of organisms. Petroleum and natural gas form mainly from the remains of microscopic sea life. When these organisms die, their remains collect on the ocean floor, where they are buried by sediment. Over time, the sediment slowly becomes rock and traps the organic remains. Through physical and chemical changes over millions of years, the remains become petroleum and natural gas. Gradually, more rocks form above the rocks that contain the fossil fuels. Under the pressure of overlying rocks and sediments, the fossil fuels are able to move through permeable rocks. Permeable rocks are rocks that allow fluids, such as petroleum and natural gas, to move through them. These permeable rocks become reservoirs that hold petroleum and natural gas.

9. What process causes organic remains to turn into fossil fuels?
F. pressure caused by overlying rocks and sediments
G. the constant layering of remains from microscopic sea life
H. millions of years of physical and chemical changes
I. the movement of fluids through layers of permeable rock

10. Which of the following statements can be inferred from the information in the passage?
A. Fossil fuel formation is ongoing, and current remains may become petroleum in the future.
B. Fossil fuel formation happened millions of years ago and no longer takes place today.
C. Current petroleum and natural gas reservoirs are found only beneath the ocean floor.
D. Permeable rocks are also a good place to find other fossil fuels, such as coal.

11. Why do we consider petroleum and natural gas to be nonrenewable resources?

Question 13 Full-credit answers should include the following points:
- students should demonstrate an understanding that technology carries both benefits and risks
- students should realize that nuclear power is a powerful, but controversial, energy source
- nuclear power has dangerous, long-lasting byproducts and the potential for serious accidents
- nuclear power produces radioactive waste, which remains hazardous for thousands of years
- nuclear power also creates the potential for a nuclear meltdown, which could release radioactivity into the atmosphere. Besides having a direct and detrimental effect on the health of local populations, radioactivity could be moved around the world by global weather patterns
- safer, cleaner, renewable resources are currently not as effective as nuclear power in many situations. As renewable resources become more efficient, they are predicted to replace nuclear power

Interpreting Graphics

Directions (12–14): For each question below, record the correct answer on a separate sheet of paper.

The graph below illustrates the sources of energy used in the United States since 1850. Future statistics are predicted based on current trends and technology development. Use this graph to answer questions 12 and 13.

U.S. Energy Use from 1850 to 2100

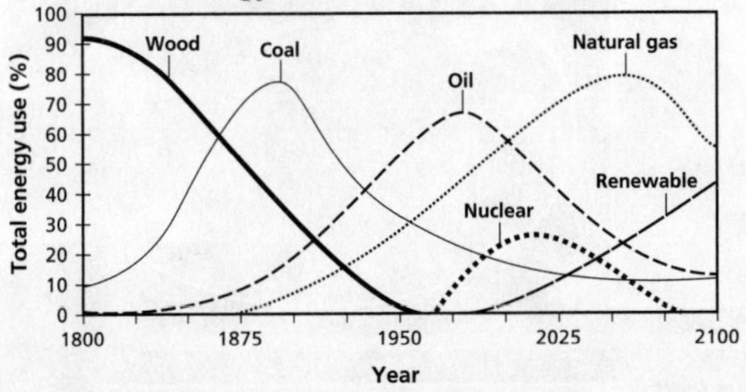

12. Which of the following is the main reason that coal became a more widely used energy source than wood in the mid-1800s?
- **F.** Coal burns easier than wood does.
- **G.** Coal is renewable resource, unlike wood.
- **H.** Coal is a more efficient energy producer than wood.
- **I.** Coal produces fewer byproducts and waste than wood does.

13. Evaluate reasons why nuclear power is predicted to peak in usage around the year 2025, and then steadily decline in usage.

The table below shows common minerals and their uses. Use this table to answer question 14.

Minerals and Their Uses

Minerals	Uses
Gold	electronics, coins, dental work, and jewelry
Galena	solder and batteries
Quartz	glass
Sulfur	medicines, gunpowder, and rubber
Graphite	pencils, paint, and lubricants
Hematite	steel
Chalcopyrite	coins, jewelry, and cables

14. Use your everyday knowledge of automobiles to describe the part of an automobile for which each mineral listed in the table may be used.

Test Tip

When a question refers to a graph, study the data plotted on the graph to determine any trends or anomalies before you try to answer the question.

Standardized Test Prep

Using THINK central Resources

State Resources
- For specific resources for your state, visit www.thinkcentral.com and type in the keyword **HSHSTR.**

Answers

Understanding Concepts
1. B
2. G
3. C
4. F
5. B
6. reclamation
7. coal: solid, petroleum: liquid, and natural gas: gas
8. Answers may vary but may include glass, paper, plastic, aluminum, and rubber.

Reading Skills
9. H
10. A
11. Answers may vary. See Test Doctor for a detailed scoring rubric.

Interpreting Graphics
12. H
13. Answers may vary. See Test Doctor for a detailed scoring rubric.
14. All of the minerals listed might be used in the car manufacturing as follows: gold for computers and electronics, galena for car batteries, quartz for windows or light coverings, sulfur for tires, graphite for paint, hematite for the body and framework, and chalcopyrite for wiring.

Why It Matters

Geology Connections

Tell students that the arrows show broad connections between events, not direct cause-and-effect relationships.

Students often forget that famous scientists were influenced by the social and political events of their time. The following information will help students connect the scientists to the time periods in which they lived.

Although Henry Bessemer was born in England, he worked for the Paris mint as a young man. While living in France, he established himself as an inventor and engineer. In 1848, he was forced to return to England because of the French Revolution. In England, he invented several processes and machines that earned him a small fortune. He used his fortune to fund additional experimentation and invention, such as the furnaces that led to his famous Bessemer process for the mass production of steel.

Joseph Monier was a gardener who was dissatisfied with the fragility of his clay and wooden flowerpots. As a result, he began to experiment with cement flowerpots. He embedded metal wire mesh into the cement to enhance the strength of the cement. He unveiled his invention at the Paris Exposition of 1867 and was awarded a patent for "Iron-Reinforced Troughs for Horticulture." In 1875, the first iron-reinforced cement bridge in the world was built in France. Monier had designed it.

When Karl Benz was two years old, his father, a locomotive engineer, was killed in a train accident. Although Benz was very poor as a child, he excelled in school and studied mechanical engineering, following in his father's footsteps. After graduating at the age of 19, Benz had a variety of jobs. As he pedaled his bicycle to and from work, he imagined designs for horseless carriages. Benz introduced the first commercial automobile, the Motorwagon, in 1885. He founded Benz & Company, which later became Daimler-Benz and Daimler-Chrysler.

Why It Matters

Geology Connections

Science, technology, and society are closely linked. This flowchart shows just a few of the connections in the history of geology.

359–299 Ma Forests, swamps, and oceans cover large areas of Earth's surface during the warm, humid Carboniferous Period.

8,000 B.C.E. Stone-age people in what is now China begin to mine coal for fuel use.

1751 Benjamin Franklin publishes his theory of electricity.

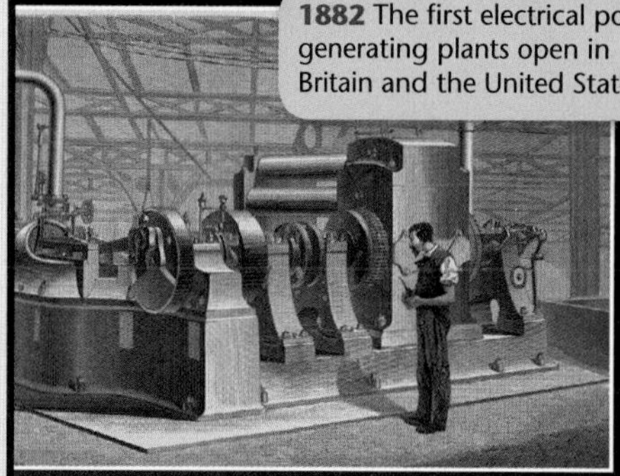

1882 The first electrical power generating plants open in Britain and the United States.

1200 B.C.E. The Iron Age begins in India, Greece, and the Near East. Early steel is produced in Africa.

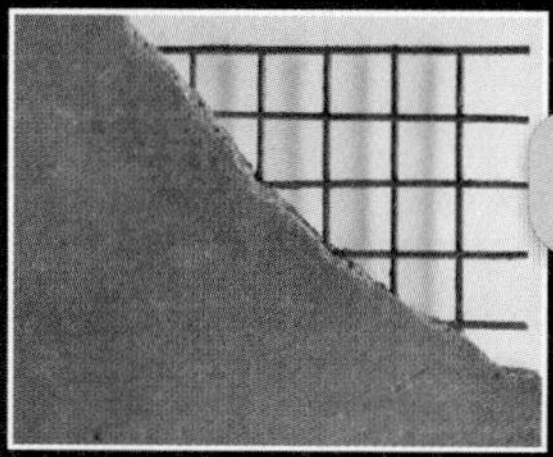

1849 Frenchman Joseph Monier invents steel-reinforced concrete.

300 B.C.E. Roman builders add volcanic ash to cement, building structures that still exist today.

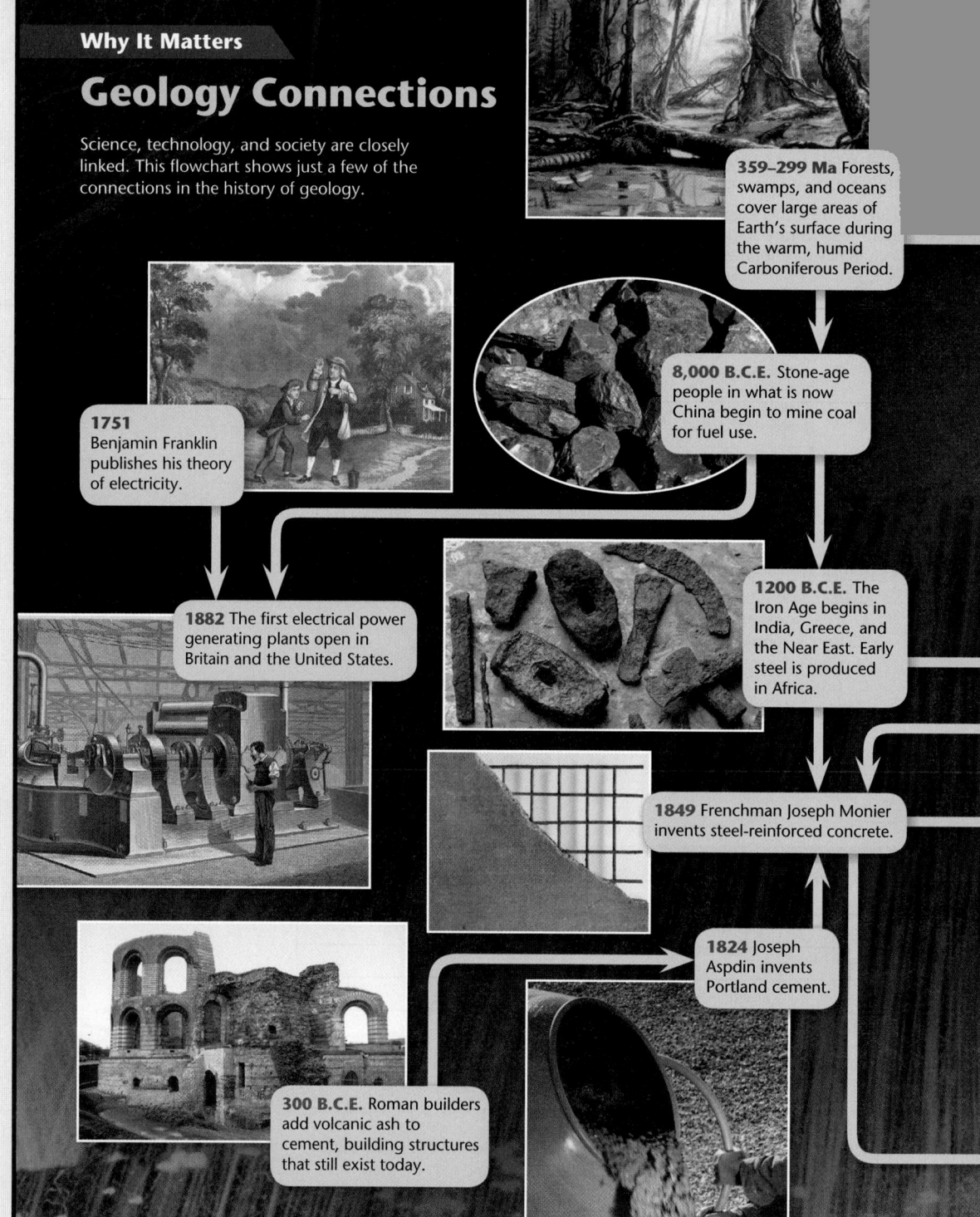

1824 Joseph Aspdin invents Portland cement.

Reading Skill Builder BASIC

Visual Literacy The image of Solar One shows the mirrors reflecting sunlight onto the tower. Solar One, the first large-scale solar power plant, began operation near Barstow, California, in 1982. It used 1,818 sun-tracking mirrors to focus solar energy on a tower, where a receiver absorbed the energy. The energy was used to heat water, which formed steam that powered a series of turbines.

HISTORY IN SCIENCE

1859 Edwin Drake drills the first oil well in Western Pennsylvania, which leads to the growth of the modern oil industry in the Americas.

1886 Karl Benz receives a patent for inventing the first gasoline-fueled car.

2006 The Venturi *Astrolab* becomes the world's first commercially available solar-electric hybrid car.

1855 The Bessemer process makes steel abundant and inexpensive.

GAS SHORTAGE!
Sales Limited to
10 GALS. OF GAS.
PER CUSTOMER

1970s Oil shortages promote interest in conservation and alternative energy resources.

1935 Hoover Dam is the world's first major dam to be constructed from concrete.

1982 Solar One, the first large-scale solar power plant, begins operation near Barstow, California.

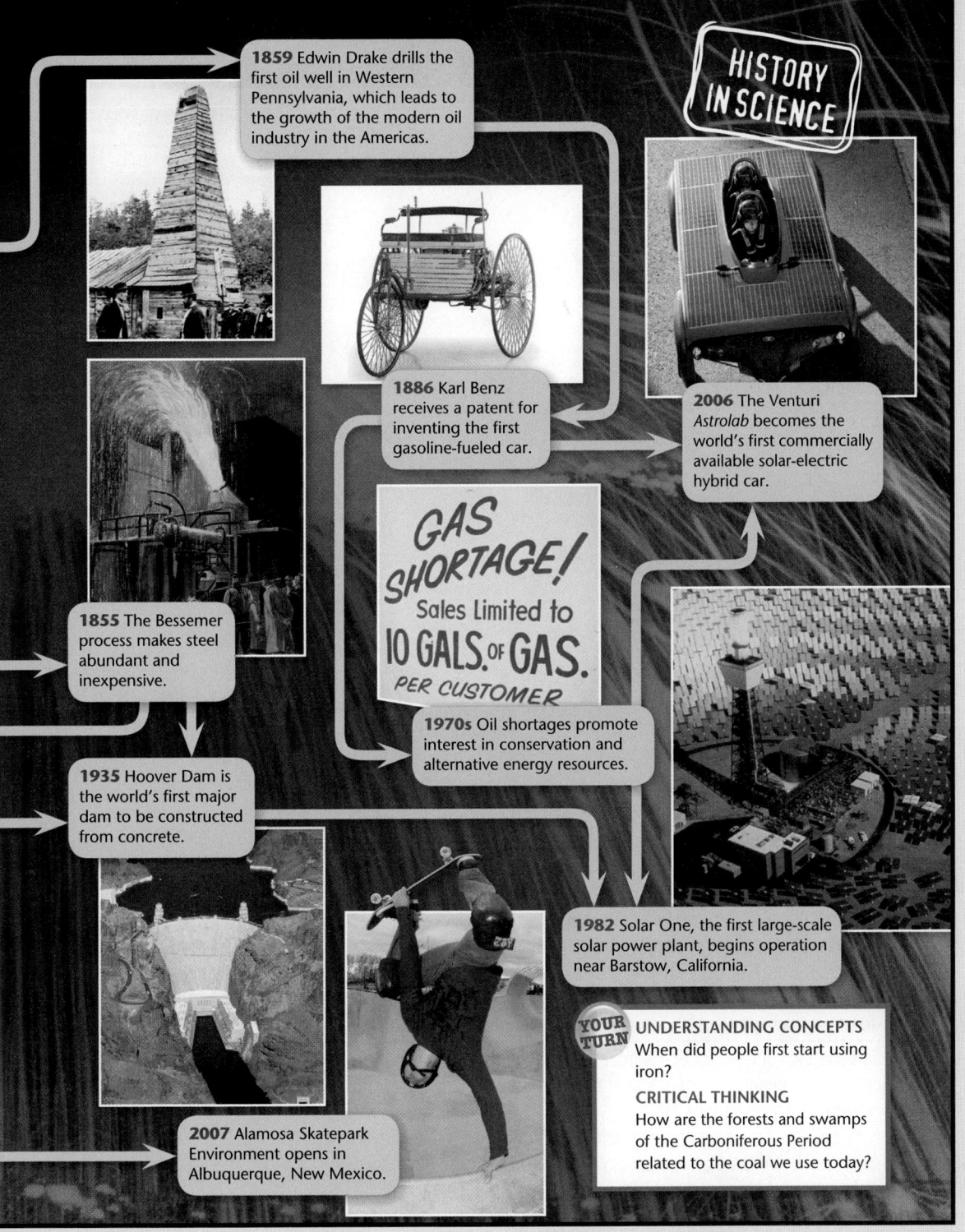

2007 Alamosa Skatepark Environment opens in Albuquerque, New Mexico.

YOUR TURN

UNDERSTANDING CONCEPTS
When did people first start using iron?

CRITICAL THINKING
How are the forests and swamps of the Carboniferous Period related to the coal we use today?

Answers to Your Turn

Understanding Concepts Humans first started to use iron around 1200 BCE, or about 3,200 years ago.

Critical Thinking The plant matter in the forests and swamps was buried by sediment before it decomposed. Over millions of years, heat and pressure below Earth's surface changed the plant matter to coal.

Why It Matters

The Bessemer Process In 1855, Henry Bessemer introduced the first industrial process for mass producing steel from molten iron. The Bessemer process lowered the cost of producing steel. As a result, steel became abundant and inexpensive enough to use for major construction. Before this, engineers and construction companies had been using less expensive but inferior materials to construct bridges and buildings. The Bessemer process paved the way for the construction of many of the world's famous steel structures.

Why It Matters

Oil in the Early 1970s In 1973, OPEC chose to reduce and halt shipments of oil to countries that had supported Israel during the Yom Kippur War. OPEC also used its leverage to raise oil prices. As a result, countries around the world adopted measures to reduce their oil dependence. These measures included researching renewable energy sources, such as solar and wind energy; expanding drilling for oil resources in North America; increasing the use of coal and nuclear energy; and initiating and increasing mass transit systems.

Answers continued from p. 86

Science Terms

Term	Everyday meaning	Scientific meaning
matter	a subject or problem	anything that takes up space and has mass
element	a piece or component of something	a substance that cannot be separated or broken down into simpler substances by chemical means
compound	a group of buildings within an enclosed space	a substance made up of atoms of two or more different elements joined by chemical bonds
mixture	a combination of ingredients, as in cooking	a combination of two or more substances that are not chemically combined
solution	the answer to a problem	a homogeneous mixture of two or more substances that are uniformly dispersed throughout the mixture

Answers continued from p. 110

Classification

Kind of Mineral	Basis for Classification	Examples and Descriptions
silicate	contains a combination of silicon and oxygen	- quartz: has only silicon and oxygen atoms - orthoclase: type of feldspar that forms when potassium combines with silicon and oxygen - plagioclase: type of feldspar that forms when sodium, calcium, or both combine with silicon and oxygen - ferromagnesian minerals: rich in iron and magnesium (olivines, pyroxenes, amphiboles, biotite)
nonsilicate	does not contain compounds of silicon and oxygen	- carbonates: compounds that contain a carbonate group (dolomite, calcite) - halides: compounds that consist of chlorine or fluorine combined with sodium, potassium, or calcium (halite, fluorite) - native elements: elements uncombined with other elements (silver, copper) - oxides: compounds that contain oxygen and an element other than silicon - sulfates: compounds that contain a sulfate group (gypsum, anhydrite) - sulfides: compounds that consist of one or more elements combined with sulfur (galena, pyrite)

FoldNotes

Physical Property	Definition/Description
color	Some minerals have very distinct colors. However, color alone is not a reliable way to identify a mineral, because many minerals are similar in color, very small amounts of certain elements can alter a mineral's color, and weathered surfaces may hide a mineral's color.
streak	It's the color of a mineral in powdered form. Streak is a more reliable method of identification. Rub a mineral on a *streak plate* to get a streak.
luster	It's the way in which a mineral reflects light. A mineral has a *metallic luster* if it reflects light the way polished metal does. All other minerals have a *nonmetallic luster*.
cleavage	It's the tendency of a mineral to split along specific planes of weakness to form smooth, flat surfaces.
fracture	It's the manner in which a mineral breaks along either curved or irregular surfaces. Minerals that don't break along cleavage planes fracture, or break unevenly.
hardness	It's the measure of the ability of a mineral to resist scratching. To determine the hardness of an unknown mineral, you can scratch the mineral against those on the *Mohs hardness scale*.
crystal shape	A mineral crystal forms in one of six basic shapes. A certain mineral always has the same general shape. But the six basic shapes can become more complex as a result of environmental conditions.
density	It's the ratio of the mass of a substance to the volume of the substance.
fluorescence	It's the ability of a mineral to glow under ultraviolet light. Only a few minerals have this physical property.
phosphorescence	When subjected to ultraviolet light, some minerals will continue to glow after the ultraviolet light is turned off. Only a few minerals have this physical property.
chatoyancy	In reflected light, some minerals display a silky appearance, also called the *cat's eye effect*. Only a few minerals have this physical property.
asterism	It's the phenomenon in which a six-sided star shape appears when a mineral reflects light. Only a few minerals have this physical property.
double refraction	Some minerals bend light in such a way that they produce a double image of any object viewed through them. Only a few minerals have this physical property.
magnetism	Magnets may attract small particles of some minerals that contain iron. Those minerals are also sometimes magnetic. Only a few minerals have this physical property.
radioactivity	The arrangement of protons and neutrons in the nuclei of some atoms is unstable. Radioactivity results as unstable nuclei decay over time into stable nuclei by releasing particles and energy. A *Geiger counter* can be used to detect the released particles. Only a few minerals have this physical property.

Answers continued from p. 116

Key-Term Fold

Key Term (or other important term)	Definition/Description
mineral	a natural, usually inorganic solid that has a characteristic chemical composition, an orderly internal structure, and a characteristic set of physical properties
silicate mineral	a mineral that contains a combination of silicon and oxygen, and that may also contain one or more metals
nonsilicate mineral	a mineral that does not contain compounds of silicon and oxygen
crystal	a solid whose atoms, ions, or molecules are arranged in a regular, repeating pattern
silicon-oxygen tetrahedron	the basic unit of the structure of silicate minerals; a silicon ion chemically bonded to and surrounded by four oxygen ions
isolated tetrahedra	do not link with other silicon or oxygen atoms
ring silicates	form rings by sharing oxygen atoms
single-chain silicates	form a chain by sharing oxygen atoms
double-chain silicates	form when two single-chains of tetrahedra bond to each other
sheet silicates	form when each tetrahedron shares three of its oxygen atoms with other tetrahedra
framework silicates	form when each tetrahedron bonds to four other tetrahedra

Answers continued from p. 134

FoldNotes

Igneous rock	Sedimentary rock	Metamorphic rock
- forms when magma cools and solidifies	- forms from sediment deposits that are compressed (compaction) and cemented together (cementation)	- has undergone metamorphism, the process in which one type of rock changes into metamorphic rock because of chemical processes or changes in temperature and pressure
- called crystalline because minerals crystallize as magma hardens into igneous rock	- characteristics determined by source of sediment, the way the sediment was moved, and the conditions under which it was deposited	- contact metamorphism is a change in the texture, structure, or chemical composition of a rock due to contact with magma.
- has different textures determined by size of crystals, which is determined by rate at which magma cools	- chemical sedimentary rock, such as gypsum and halite, forms when ions from dissolved minerals separate from water.	- regional metamorphism is a change in the texture, structure, or chemical composition of a rock due to changes in temperature and pressure over a large area, generally as a result of tectonic forces.
- textures include coarse-grained, fine-grained, porphyritic (mixture of large and small crystals), glassy (only a few crystals), and vesicular (rock full of holes).	- organic sedimentary rock, such as coal and chalk, forms from the remains of plants and animals.	- foliated metamorphic rocks contain planes or bands of minerals, while nonfoliated metamorphic rocks do not.
- mineral composition (felsic, mafic, intermediate) depends on chemical composition of magma	- clastic sedimentary rock—including the types called conglomerate, sandstone, and shale—forms from fragments of preexisting rocks.	
- intrusive rock masses: batholiths, stocks, laccoliths, sills, dikes	- Some sedimentary rock features that form in different depositional environments are stratification, cross-beds, graded bedding, ripple marks, mud cracks, fossils, and concretions.	
- extrusive rock masses: lava flows, lava plateaus, tuffs		

Sample Answers to Concept Maps from Chapter Reviews

Chapter 4 Earth Chemistry, p. 105

29.

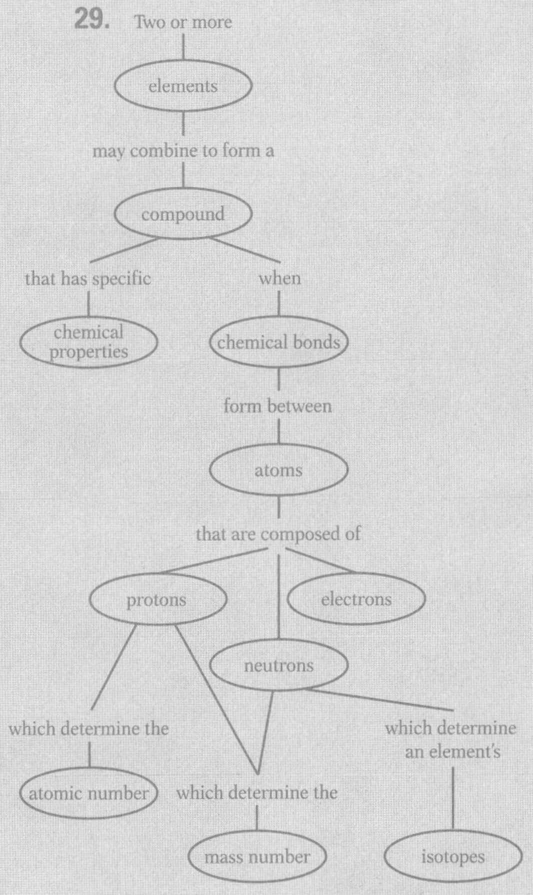

Chapter 5 Minerals of Earth's Crust, p. 129

30.

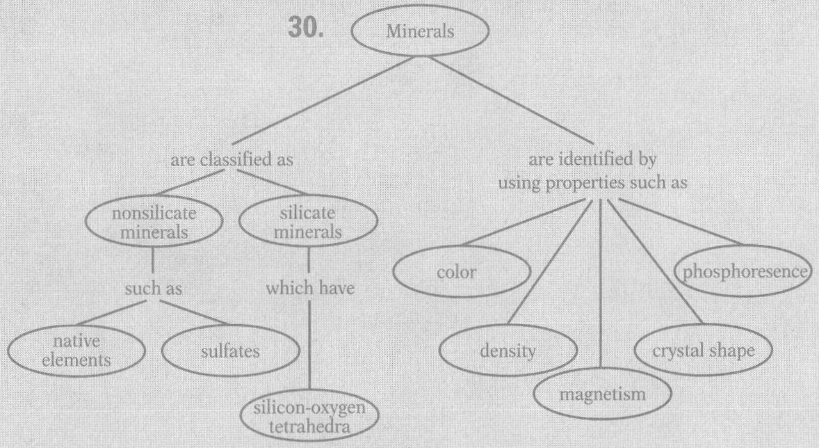

Chapter 6 Rocks, p. 161

29.

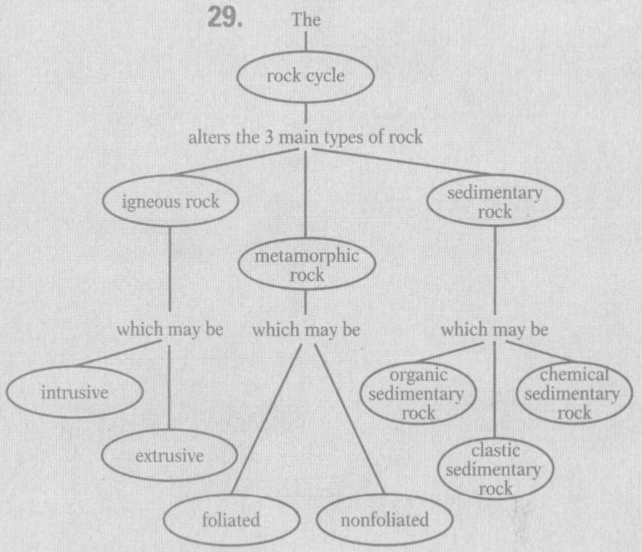

Chapter 7 Resources and Energy, p. 191

29.

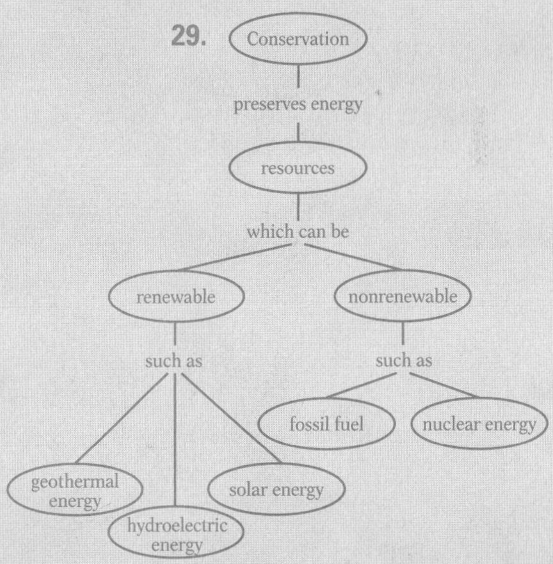

Unit 3 History of the Earth

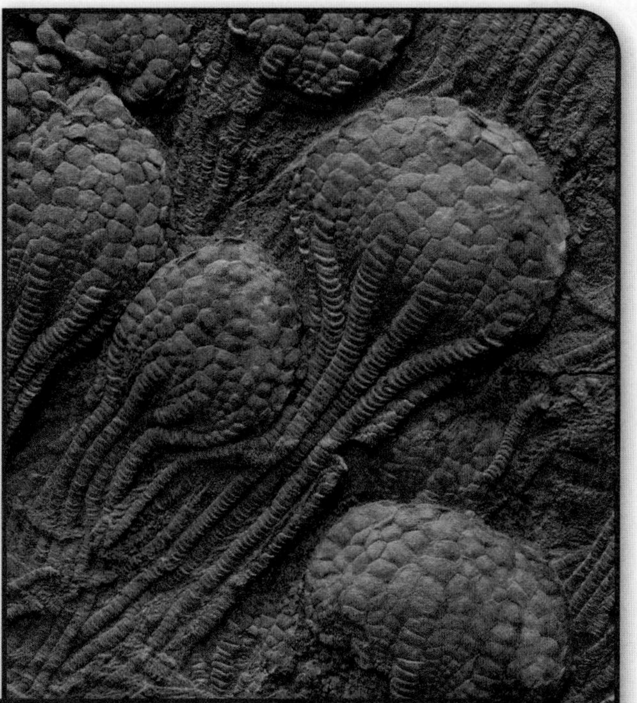

Chapter Planner 8

The Rock Record

	Standards	Teach Key Ideas
Chapter Opener, pp. 198–199 **45 min.**	**National Science Education Standards**	
Section 1 Determining Relative Age, pp. 201–206 **45 min.** › Uniformitarianism › Relative Age › Law of Superposition › Principle of Original Horizontality › Unconformities	**ES 3b, HNS 3c, UCP 4**	■ ▲ **Bellringer,** p. 201 ■ **Discussion:** Rock Layers, p. 201 ■ **DI (Special Education Students):** Key Terms, p. 202 ■ **Discussion:** Making Predictions, p. 203 ■ **DI (Basic Learners):** Illustrations, p. 204 ■ **DI (Special Education Students):** Unconformity Story, p. 205 ◆ **Transparencies** 39 Law of Superposition • 40 Types of Unconformities • 41 Crosscutting Relationships • 43 Geologic Map of Bedrock in Ohio ▲ **Visual Concepts:** Uniformitarianism and Catastrophism • Law of Superposition • Unconformities • Types of Unconformities
Section 2 Determining Absolute Age, pp. 207–212 **45 min.** › Absolute Dating Methods › Radiometric Dating › Carbon Dating	**ES 3b, HNS 3c, UCP 4, PS 1d**	■ ◆ **Bellringer,** p. 207 ■ **Discussion:** Measuring Decay, p. 209 ■ **DI (Advanced Learners):** Radioactive Decay of Uranium, p. 209 ■ **DI (Struggling Readers):** Summarizing, p. 211 ◆ **Transparency** 42 Radioactive Decay and Half-Life ▲ **Visual Concepts:** Isotopes • Half-Life • Decay Series • Radiometric Dating
Section 3 The Fossil Record, pp. 213–216 **90 min.** › Interpreting the Fossil Record › Fossilization › Types of Fossils › Index Fossils › Index Fossils and Absolute Age	**ES 3b, HNS 3c, UCP 4, LS 3a, LS 3b**	■ ◆ **Bellringer,** p. 213 ■ **Demonstration:** Learning Earth's History, p. 213 ■ **DI (Special Education Students):** Summarizing, p. 214 ■ **Discussion:** Handprint History, p. 214 ▲ **Visual Concepts:** Index Fossil
Chapter Wrap-Up, pp. 221–225 **90 min.**		**Chapter Summary,** p. 221

See also PowerNotes® Presentations

CHAPTER Fast Track

To shorten instruction because of time limitations, omit the Chapter Lab.

Key

Teacher's Edition ■ Teaching Transparencies ◆
Chapter Resource File ● Online Edition ▲

All resources listed below are also available on the Teacher One Stop™.

Why It Matters	Hands-On	Skills Development	Assessment
■ **Chapter Overview** p. 198 ■ **Using the Figure:** Fossil Forms, p. 198	**Inquiry Lab:** Modeling Rock Layers, p. 199	**Reading Toolbox,** p. 200	
■ **Section Overview,** p. 201 ■ **Using the Figure:** The Law of Superposition, p. 203 ■ **Using the Figure:** Comparing Sedimentary Rock, p. 204 ■ **Using the Table:** Analyzing Unconformities, p. 205	**QuickLab:** What's Your Relative Age?, p. 202 ■ **Group Activity:** Creating Layers, p. 204 ● **Skills Practice Lab:** Determining the Relative Age of Rock Strata	■ **Skill Builder:** Vocabulary, p. 203 ■ **Reading Skill Builder:** Reading Hint, p. 203 **Reading Toolbox:** Cause and Effect, p. 204 **Maps in Action:** Geologic Map of Bedrock in Ohio, p. 220	**Reading Check,** p. 202 **Reading Check,** p. 204 **Section Review,** p. 206 ■ **Reteaching,** p. 205 **Quiz,** p. 205 ■ **DI (Alternative Assessment):** Methods to Determine Relative Age, p. 206 ● **Section Quiz**
■ **Section Overview,** p. 207 ■ **Using the Figure:** Erosion Rate, p. 207 ■ **Geology Connection:** Glacial Lakes, p. 208 **Exposing a Fake Mummy,** p. 209 ■ **Using the Figure:** Counting Decay, p. 210 ■ **Environmental Connection:** Radioactive Waste, p. 210 ■ **Using the Table:** Methods for Dating Rocks, p. 211	■ **Activity:** Modeling Varves, p. 208 **QuickLab:** Radioactive Decay, p. 210	**Math Skills:** Deposition, p. 208 **Reading Toolbox:** Key-Term Fold, p. 208 ■ **Skill Builder:** Vocabulary, p. 209	**Reading Check,** p. 208 **Reading Check,** p. 211 **Section Review,** p. 212 ■ **Reteaching,** p. 211 ■ **Quiz,** p. 212 ■ **DI (Alternative Assessment):** Dating Rock, p. 212 ● **Section Quiz**
■ **Section Overview,** p. 213 ■ **Biology Connection:** Dinosaurs and Birds, p. 215	■ **Group Activity:** Fossils in Many Forms, p. 214 ■ **Activity:** Spacing Footprints, p. 215 **Making Models Lab:** Types of Fossils, pp. 218–219 ● **Inquiry Lab:** Got Fossils?	**Reading Toolbox:** Outlining, p. 214	**Reading Check,** p. 215 **Section Review,** p. 216 ■ **Reteaching,** p. 215 ■ **Quiz,** p. 216 ■ **DI (Alternative Assessment):** Captioned Pictures, p. 216 ● **Section Quiz**
A Record of Yellowstone's Explosive Past, p. 217		▲ **Super Summary** **Standardized Test Prep,** pp. 224–225	**Chapter Review,** pp. 222–223 ● **Chapter Tests**

See also Lab Generator

See also Holt Online Assessment Resources

Chapter Overview

This chapter describes the geologic record of rocks. The chapter introduces methods of dating rocks relatively and absolutely. The fossil record, processes of fossilization, and the types and importance of fossils are also covered.

Using the Figure GENERAL

Fossil Forms Ask students what the photo shows. (fossils of organisms called *crinoids*) Point out that the detail of this fossil slab is so distinct, it looks like a sculpture, but it is, in fact, sedimentary rock. Have students speculate about how this fossil formed. (As layers of sediment rapidly accumulated over the dead bodies of these marine organisms, the sediment filled in empty spaces and preserved the details. The fossil was preserved when the sediment layers were compacted and cemented into stone.) **LS Visual**

Why It Matters

The crinoid fossils depicted here give information about the marine environment in which the organisms lived. Crinoids are animals related to starfish and sea urchins. Modern species of crinoids provide clues about how ancient crinoid species functioned.

Chapter 8 The Rock Record

Chapter Outline

1 Determining Relative Age
- Uniformitarianism
- Relative Age
- Law of Superposition
- Principle of Original Horizontality
- Unconformities

2 Determining Absolute Age
- Absolute Dating Methods
- Radiometric Dating
- Carbon Dating

3 The Fossil Record
- Interpreting the Fossil Record
- Fossilization
- Types of Fossils
- Index Fossils
- Index Fossils and Absolute Age

Virginia Standards of Learning
ES.1.c
ES.1.f
ES.2.a
ES.9.a
ES.9.b
ES.9.c

Why It Matters

Rocks contain clues that show how and when they formed. Scientists study these clues to learn about Earth's history. Scientists also study fossils, such as the crinoids shown here. These animals have been living in aquatic environments on Earth for almost 490 million years.

Chapter Correlations

Virginia Standards of Learning

ES.1.c scales, diagrams, charts, graphs, tables, imagery, models, and profiles are constructed and interpreted.
ES.1.f current applications are used to reinforce Earth science concepts.
ES.2.a science explains and predicts the interactions and dynamics of complex Earth systems.
ES.9.a traces and remains of ancient, often extinct, life are preserved by various means in many sedimentary rocks.
ES.9.b superposition, cross-cutting relationships, index fossils, and radioactive decay are methods of dating bodies of rock.
ES.9.c absolute and relative dating have different applications but can be used together to determine the age of rocks and structures.

Inquiry Lab

10 min

Modeling Rock Layers

Use several types of small items to make layers in a beaker or jar. Each layer should be made up of only one type of item. Sketch the beaker or jar and the layers it contains.

Questions to Get You Started

1. Compare your sketch with other groups' sketches. Identify the oldest layer and the youngest layer. How can you tell?
2. Can you tell at what time each layer was made? Explain.

Inquiry Lab

Central Concept: Students make observations about layers they create to develop a beginning understanding of the law of superposition and the concepts of relative and absolute age.

Materials (per group)

- Small, clear jar or beaker
- 3–5 groups of items such as paper clips, erasers, beads, pebbles, or marbles

Skills Acquired

- Analyzing Relationships
- Inferring
- Recognizing Patterns

Teacher's Notes: You may wish to assign one student in each group to be responsible for lab materials, one student to be the sketch artist, and one student to record questions and answers.

Answers to Getting Started:

1. Student answers should state that the oldest layer formed first, so it is at the bottom, and the youngest layer formed last, so it is at the top.
2. Student answers should state that there is no way to tell by looking at the sketches the exact time at which the layers were formed.

Using THINK central Resources

An online version of this chapter, as well as all the print and multimedia resources that accompany the program are available to registered teachers and their students. Log onto www.thinkcentral.com to access these materials and tools to organize your preparation and student learning.

READING TOOLBOX

Key-Term Fold

Students should write key terms for the chapter on the front of the tabs of the key-term fold. Each term should be defined under the appropriate tab. The key terms for this chapter are *uniformitarianism, relative age, law of superposition, unconformity, law of crosscutting relationships, absolute age, varve, radiometric dating, half-life, fossil, paleontology, trace fossil,* and *index fossil.*

Signal Words

Students' tables should include cause-and-effect pairs and their markers (if any), drawn from the text of all three of the chapter's sections.

Outlining

Answers may vary. Students' notes should be in outline format as shown in this sample from Section 1.

READING TOOLBOX

These reading tools will help you learn the material in this chapter.

FoldNotes

Key-Term Fold A key-term fold can help you learn the key terms in this chapter.

Your Turn Create a key-term fold, as described in **Appendix A**.

1. Write one key term from the Summary page on the front of each tab.
2. As you read the chapter, write the definition of each term under its tab.
3. Use this FoldNote to study the key terms.

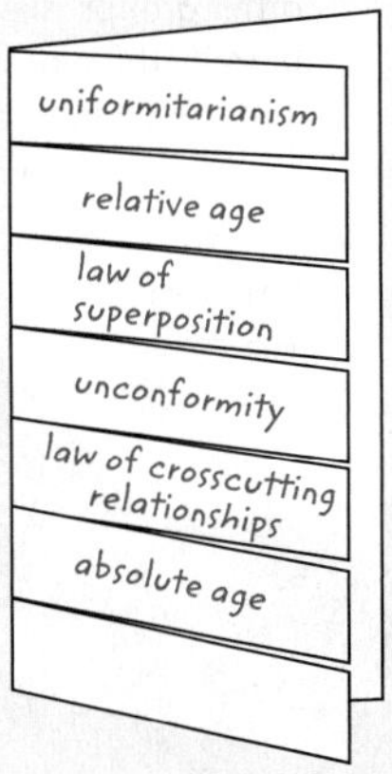

Cause and Effect

Signal Words Certain words or phrases can signal cause-and-effect relationships. Words and phrases that signal causes include *cause, affect,* and *because.* Words and phrases that signal effects include *therefore, results in,* and *thus.* Sentences can also express cause-and-effect relationships without using explicit markers.

Your Turn In this chapter, you will read about cause-and-effect relationships that allow scientists to draw conclusions about the ages of rock layers and structures. Complete a table of cause-and-effect pairs like the table below.

CAUSE	EFFECT	MARKER(S)
movements of Earth's crust	Buried rock layers can be lifted up and exposed to erosion.	(none)

Note Taking

Outlining Taking notes in outline form can help you see how information is organized in a chapter. You can use your outline notes to review the chapter before a test.

Your Turn As you read through this chapter, make notes about the chapter in outline form. An example from Section 1 is shown on the right to help you get started.

1. DETERMINING RELATIVE AGE
   A. Uniformitarianism
      1. The principle of uniformitarianism states that current geologic processes are the same ones that operated in the past.
         a. Uniformitarianism was developed by James Hutton in the 18th century.
         b. Uniformitarianism is one of the basic foundations of geology.
      2. Geologists after Hutton noted that, although geologic processes are the same through time, their rates may vary.

For more information on how to use these and other tools, see **Appendix A.**

SECTION 1

Determining Relative Age

Key Ideas	Key Terms	Why It Matters
❯ State the principle of uniformitarianism. ❯ Explain how the law of superposition can be used to determine the relative ages of rocks. ❯ Compare three types of unconformities. ❯ Apply the law of crosscutting relationships to determine the relative ages of rocks.	**uniformitarianism** **relative age** **law of superposition** **unconformity** **law of crosscutting relationships**	By determining the relative ages of rock layers and structures, we can better understand the processes that shape the world around us.

Geologists estimate that Earth is about 4.6 billion years old. The idea that Earth is billions of years old originated with the work of James Hutton, an 18th-century Scottish physician and farmer. Hutton, who is shown in **Figure 1**, wrote about agriculture, weather, climate, physics, and even philosophy. Hutton was also a keen observer of the geologic changes taking place on his farm. Using scientific methods, Hutton drew conclusions based on his observations. Today, he is most famous for his ideas and writings about geology.

Uniformitarianism

Hutton concluded that the same forces that changed the landscape of his farm had changed Earth's surface in the past. He thought that by studying the present, people could learn about Earth's past. Hutton's principle of **uniformitarianism** is that current geologic processes, such as volcanism and erosion, are the same processes that were at work in the past. This principle is one of the basic foundations of the science of geology. Geologists later refined Hutton's ideas by pointing out that although the processes of the past and present are the same, the rates of the processes may vary over time.

uniformitarianism a principle that geologic processes that occurred in the past can be explained by current geologic processes

Figure 1 James Hutton (left) thought that studying the present is the key to understanding the past. This modern-day geologist (right) is looking for clues to Earth's past.

Section 1

Focus

Overview

This section describes the process for determining the relative age of rocks and some processes that resulted in the modern rock record. The section also covers uniformitarianism, the law of superposition, the principle of original horizontality, and unconformities in rock layers.

Bellringer

Ask students, "What are five visual clues that help you determine if someone is older or younger than you are?" List student responses on the board. (Answers may vary but may include color of hair, wrinkles in skin, height, general demeanor, and style of dress.) **LS Interpersonal**

Motivate

Discussion GENERAL

Rock Layers Show students some pictures of sedimentary rock formations in which horizontal layers of rock are clearly visible. Tell them that each layer in the pictures may represent thousands of years of rock formation. Ask students which layers are the youngest and which the oldest. (The youngest layers are probably at the top, and the oldest are probably at the bottom.) **LS Visual/Logical**

Key Resources

Chapter Resource File
- Directed Reading BASIC
- Skills Practice Lab: Determining the Relative Age of Rock Strata GENERAL

Technology
- Transparencies
  Bellringer

Teach

Quick Lab

Skills Acquired
- Observing
- Designing Experiments
- Inferring
- Organizing Data

Teacher's Notes: You may want to ensure that the groups have a mix of boys and girls who have different physical characteristics and who have different birth dates, if possible.

Analysis
1. Students should use their birth dates to determine relative age.
2. The relative ages should correspond to absolute ages.
3. Unlike people, rocks may be dated according to their physical characteristics and relative positions.

Answer to Reading Check
Hutton reasoned that the extremely slow-working forces that changed the land on his farm had also slowly changed the rocks that make up Earth's crust. He concluded that large changes must happen over a period of millions of years.

Quick Lab — 20 min

What's Your Relative Age?

Procedure
1. Form a group with 5 to 10 of your classmates.
2. Work together to arrange group members in order from oldest to youngest.

Analysis
1. How did you determine your classmates' relative ages?
2. How did the relative ages compare to the absolute ages of your classmates?
3. How is this process of determining relative and absolute age different from the way scientists date rocks?

Earth's Age

Before Hutton's research was undertaken, many people thought that Earth was only about 6,000 years old. They also thought that all geologic features had formed at the same time. Hutton's principle of uniformitarianism raised some serious questions about Earth's age. Hutton observed that the forces that changed the land on his farm operated very slowly. He reasoned that millions of years must be needed for those same forces to create the complicated rock structures observed in Earth's crust. He concluded that Earth must be much older than previously thought. Hutton's observations and conclusions about the age of Earth encouraged other scientists to learn more about Earth's history. One way to learn about Earth's past is to determine the order in which rock layers and other rock structures formed.

Reading Check **What evidence did Hutton propose to show that Earth is very old?** (See Appendix G for answers to Reading Checks.)

Relative Age

In the same way that a history book shows an order of events, layers of rock, called *strata,* show the sequence of events that took place in the past. Using a few basic principles, scientists can determine the order in which rock layers formed. Once they know the order, a relative age can be determined for each rock layer. **Relative age** indicates that one layer is older or younger than another layer but does not indicate the rock's age in years.

Various types of rock form layers. Igneous rocks form layers when successive lava flows stack on top of each other. Metamorphic rocks that formed from layered rocks can have layers. To determine the relative ages of rocks, however, scientists commonly study the layers in sedimentary rocks, such as those shown in **Figure 2.**

Academic Vocabulary
sequence (SEE kwuhns) the order in which things come or events happen

relative age the age of an object in relation to the ages of other objects

Figure 2 The layers of sedimentary rock that make up this butte near Caineville, Utah were deposited over millions of years.

Differentiated Instruction

Special Education Students

Key Terms Some students need additional assistance to retain the pronunciations and meanings of the key terms presented in the section. For each of the five key terms, have students work with partners to complete the following steps:
1. Write the term at the top of a sheet of paper.
2. Write a pronunciation guide under the term.
3. Write the sentence from the textbook that first uses the term.
4. Write a new sentence that uses the term.
5. Draw a picture that shows what the term describes.
6. Share sentences and pictures with the group.

LS Verbal/Visual

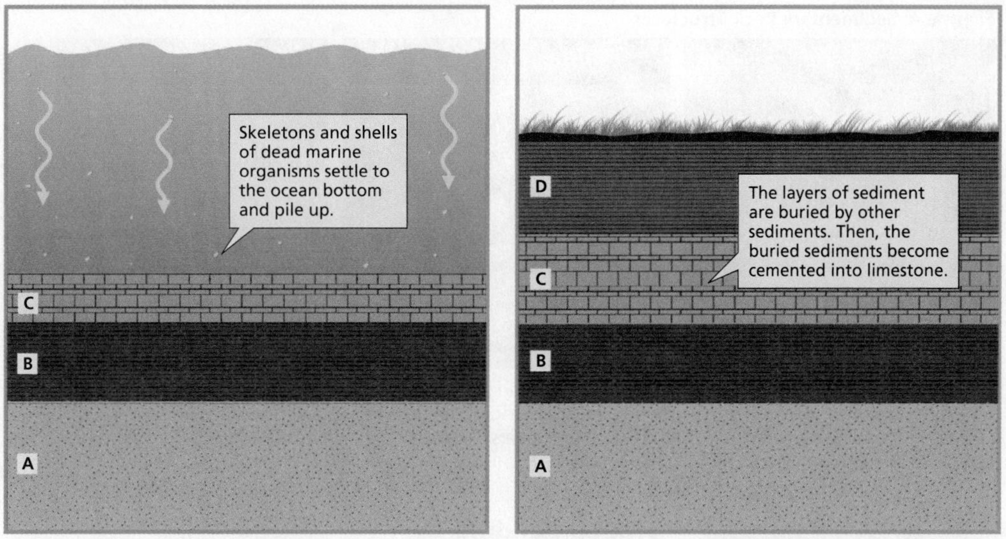

Skeletons and shells of dead marine organisms settle to the ocean bottom and pile up.
C
B
A
D
The layers of sediment are buried by other sediments. Then, the buried sediments become cemented into limestone.
C
B
A

Figure 3 By applying the law of superposition, geologists are able to determine that layer D is the youngest bed in this rock section. ***According to the law of superposition, is layer B older or younger than layer C?***

Law of Superposition

Sedimentary rocks form when new sediments are deposited on top of old layers of sediment. As the sediments accumulate, they are compressed and become naturally cemented into sedimentary rock layers that are called *beds*. The boundary between two beds is called a *bedding plane*.

Scientists use a basic principle called the law of superposition to determine the relative age of a layer of sedimentary rock. The **law of superposition** states that an undeformed sedimentary rock layer is older than the layers above it and younger than the layers below it. According to the law of superposition, layer A, shown in **Figure 3,** was the first layer deposited, and thus it is the oldest layer. The last layer deposited was layer D, and thus it is the youngest layer.

law of superposition the principle that a sedimentary rock layer is older than the layers above it and younger than the layers below it if the layers are not disturbed

Principle of Original Horizontality

Scientists also know that sedimentary rock generally forms in horizontal layers. The *principle of original horizontality* states that sedimentary rocks left undisturbed will remain in horizontal layers. Therefore, scientists can assume that sedimentary rock layers that are not horizontal have been tilted or deformed by crustal movements that happened after the layers formed.

In some cases, tectonic forces push older layers on top of younger layers or overturn a group of rock layers. In such cases, the law of superposition cannot be easily applied. So, scientists must look for clues to the original position of layers and then apply the law of superposition.

SCILINKS.
www.scilinks.org
Topic: Law of Superposition
Code: HQX0858

Using the Figure — GENERAL

The Law of Superposition Have students look carefully at the two diagrams in the figure and describe what material overlies layer C on the left. (seawater) Point out that over millions of years, the conditions shown on the left become the conditions shown on the right, and what was once sea becomes land. Answer to caption question: Layer B is older than layer C because B is below C and was deposited earlier. **LS Logical/Visual**

Discussion — GENERAL

Making Predictions Before students read the section on original horizontality, have them discuss what might disturb the layers of rock described in the section on superposition. Then, have them read the passage and determine whether their predictions were correct. **LS Verbal**

Skill Builder — BASIC

Vocabulary Tell students that the word *superposition* uses the prefix *super-*, which means "above." Ask students how knowing the meaning of this prefix can help them understand or remember the law of superposition. (The law of superposition states that rock layers on the bottom are older than those "above" or on top.)
LS Verbal English Language Learners

Key Resources

Technology
- Transparencies
  39 Law of Superposition

Reading Skill Builder — BASIC

Reading Hint Tell students to look for word roots, small words, and compound words as they read this section. Finding and understanding smaller words, such as *uniform, horizontal, cross,* and *conform,* within larger words will help students understand the content. Have students work in pairs to recognize and say word roots and smaller words they find in big words.
LS Verbal /Auditory English Language Learners

Teach, *continued*

Using the Figure GENERAL

Comparing Sedimentary Rock Have students examine and describe each photo at the top of this page. For Graded Bedding, ask students why large particles are found at the bottom of the layer. (Gravity causes heavier particles to settle faster, so the larger particles are at the bottom of the layer.) For Cross-Beds, have students identify the strata of which the cross-beds are a part. (Each set of slanted cross-beds is part of a larger layer. Cross-bedded layers are cut off by a flat plane at the top of the layer.) For Ripple Marks, ask students to identify the direction the water moved over the sediment that became this rock. (If the peaks of ripples point in the direction of flow, the water was flowing either from the bottom right toward the top left or from the top left to the bottom right.) **LS Visual**

READING TOOLBOX GENERAL

Cause and Effect Students' tables should list cause-and-effect pairs as well as any words or phrases that signal them. Causes should be in the first column, effects should be in the second column, and markers (if any) should be in the third column.

Answer to Reading Check

Because ripple marks form at the top of a rock layer, scientists can use the orientation of the ripple marks to determine which direction was "up" when the rock layers formed.

Figure 4 Sedimentary Rock Structures

Graded Bedding Heavy particles settle to the bottom of a lake or river faster than smaller particles do and create graded beds like these.

Cross-Beds As sand slides down the slope of a large sand dune, the sand forms slanting layers like the ones shown here.

Ripple Marks When waves move back and forth on a beach, ripple marks like these commonly form.

READING TOOLBOX

Cause and Effect Many factors give clues about the original position of rock layers. As you read this page and the previous page, look for multiple causes and multiple effects that allow scientists to recognize which layers formed above earlier layers.

Graded Bedding

One possible clue to the original position of rock layers is the size of the particles in the layers. In some depositional environments, the largest particles of sediment are deposited in the bottom layers, as shown in **Figure 4.** The arrangement of layers in which coarse and heavy particles are located in the bottom layers is called *graded bedding*. If larger particles are located in the top layers, the layers may have been overturned by tectonic forces.

Cross-Beds

Another clue to the original position of rock layers is in the shape of the bedding planes. When sand is deposited, sandy sediment forms beds at an angle to the bedding plane. These beds are called *cross-beds* and are shown in **Figure 4.** The tops of these layers commonly erode before new layers are deposited. So, the sediment appears to be curved at the bottom of the layer and to be cut off at the top. By studying the shape of the cross-beds, scientists can determine the original position of these layers.

Ripple Marks

Ripple marks are small waves that form on the surface of sand because of the action of water or wind. When the sand becomes sandstone, the ripple marks may be preserved, as shown in **Figure 4.** In undisturbed sedimentary rock layers, the crests of the ripple marks point upward. By examining the orientation of ripple marks, scientists can establish the original arrangement of the rock layers. The relative ages of the rocks can then be determined by using the law of superposition.

Reading Check **How can ripple marks indicate the original position of rock layers?**

Group Activity GENERAL

Creating Layers Give groups of students a variety of small pebbles, some sand, a plastic jar with a lid, and water. Have them shake up the sand and pebbles in the jar. Then, have them add enough water to the jar to cover the sediment, shake the jar vigorously, and let it sit for 15 minutes or more. Students should note the order in which particles settled at the bottom. Have students discuss how the experiment relates to the graded bedding of sedimentary rock. (Pebbles should form the bottom layer, with sand on top of it, and finer particles at the top.) **LS Kinesthetic**

Differentiated Instruction

Basic Learners

Illustrations Have students illustrate each type of rock formation they read about in this section. Students should label and write a brief description next to each picture. **LS Visual/Verbal**

Unconformities

Movements of Earth's crust can lift up rock layers that were buried and expose them to erosion. Then, if sediments are deposited, new rock layers form in place of the eroded layers. The missing rock layers create a break in the geologic record in the same way that pages missing from a book create a break in a story. A break in the geologic record is called an **unconformity.** An unconformity shows that deposition either stopped for a period of time, or rock may have been removed by erosion before deposition resumed.

As shown in **Table 1,** there are three types of unconformities. An unconformity in which stratified rock rests upon unstratified rock is called a *nonconformity*. The boundary between a set of tilted layers and a set of horizontal layers is called an *angular unconformity*. The boundary between horizontal layers of old sedimentary rock and younger, overlying layers that are deposited on an eroded surface is called a *disconformity*. According to the law of superposition, all rocks beneath an unconformity are older than the rocks above the unconformity.

unconformity a break in the geologic record created when rock layers are eroded or when sediment is not deposited for a long period of time

Table 1 Types of Unconformities

Type	Example	Description
Nonconformity	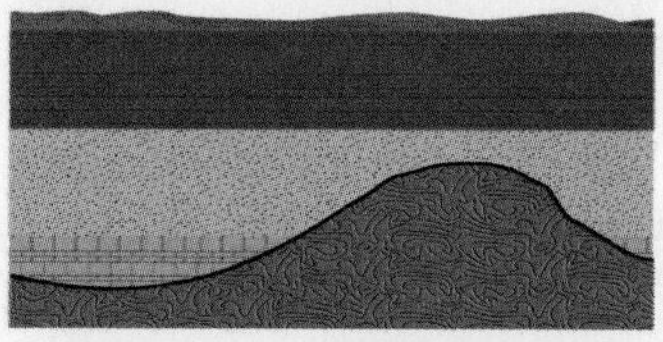	Unstratified igneous or metamorphic rock may be uplifted to Earth's surface by crustal movements. Once the rock is exposed, it erodes. Sediments may then be deposited on the eroded surface. The boundary between the new sedimentary rock and the igneous or metamorphic rock is a *nonconformity*. The boundary represents an unknown period of time during which the older rock was eroded.
Angular unconformity	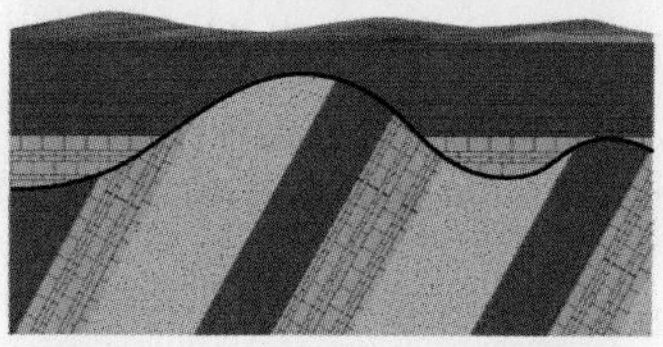	An angular unconformity forms when rock deposited in horizontal layers is folded or tilted and then eroded. When erosion stops, a new horizontal layer is deposited on top of a tilted layer. When the bedding planes of the older rock layers are not parallel to those of the younger rock layers deposited above them, an angular unconformity results.
Disconformity	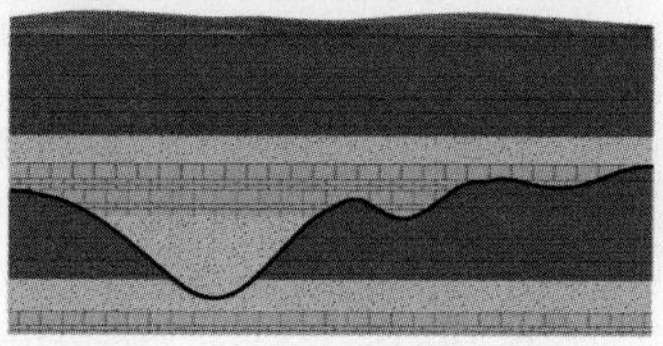	Sometimes, layers of sediments are uplifted without folding or tilting and are eroded. Eventually, the area subsides and deposition resumes. The layers on either side of the boundary are deposited horizontally. Although the rock layers look as if they were deposited continuously, a large time gap exists where the upper and lower layers meet. This gap is known as a *disconformity*.

Using the Table — ADVANCED

Analyzing Unconformities Have students study the table of unconformities. Then, have students explain which rocks are older: the rocks above or below the unconformity. (below) Ask students to summarize the differences between the types of unconformities. (The differences are based on the rocks below the unconformities. Nonconformities are underlain by metamorphic or igneous rock. Angular unconformities are underlain by tilted rock layers, while disconformities are underlain by rock layers that are parallel to the layers above the unconformity.)
LS Visual

Close

Reteaching — BASIC

Changing Rocks Have students use clay of different colors to model the rock structures they learned about in this section. Students may use tools to indicate ripples and should manipulate the clay to demonstrate the forces that cause changes in rock layers. As students work with their models, ask them about the relative ages of the "rocks," or clay layers they are manipulating. English Language Learners
LS Kinesthetic

Quiz — GENERAL

1. In graded bedding, what material would you find at the bottom if the rock were undisturbed? (large, heavy particles or pebbles)
2. What does the principle of original horizontality state? (Sedimentary rocks form in horizontal layers and undisturbed rock layers remain horizontal.)

Key Resources

Technology
- Transparencies
  40 Types of Unconformities

Differentiated Instruction

Special Education Students

Unconformity Story To help students understand unconformities, ask them to choose one type of unconformity. Have students write a story about geological events in an area that result in the formation of the unconformity. Then, have students share their stories with students who wrote about a different type of unconformity.

Close, *continued*

Answers to Section Review

1. so they can understand the age and history of Earth
2. Answers may vary. Accept all reasonable answers.
3. According to the law, a rock layer is always younger than the rock layer below it if the layers are undisturbed.
4. An unconformity is a break in the rock record; a nonconformity is a kind of unconformity in which metamorphic or igneous rock layers are overlain by sedimentary rock layers.
5. In an angular unconformity, tilted rock layers are overlain by horizontal rock layers. In a disconformity, the rock layers above and below the unconformity are parallel.
6. The law of crosscutting relationships helps scientists understand that a body of rock or a fault is always younger than any other body of rock that it cuts through.
7. A disconformity would be harder to recognize because it has horizontal layers on both sides of the boundary. A nonconformity could be identified by the metamorphic or igneous rock below the unconformity.
8. If the fault does not cut through the unconformity, the fault is older than the layers deposited above the unconformity.
9. The *relative age* of rocks can be determined by using the *principle of original horizontality* and the *law of superposition* or by using *graded bedding, cross-beds,* and *ripple marks* to establish the original arrangement of layers.

Figure 5 The law of crosscutting relationships can be used to determine the relative ages of rock layers and the faults and intrusions within them.

THINK central
INTERACT ONLINE
(Keyword: HQXRECF5)

Crosscutting Relationships

law of crosscutting relationships the principle that a fault or body of rock is younger than any other body of rock that it cuts through

When rock layers have been disturbed by faults or intrusions, determining relative age may be difficult. A *fault* is a break or crack in Earth's crust along which rocks shift their position. An *intrusion* is a mass of igneous rock that forms when magma is injected into rock and then cools and solidifies. In such cases, scientists may apply the law of crosscutting relationships. The **law of crosscutting relationships** is that a fault or igneous intrusion is always younger than the rock layers it cuts through. If a fault or intrusion cuts through an unconformity, the fault or intrusion is younger than all the rocks it cuts through above and below the unconformity.

Figure 5 shows a series of rock layers that contains both a fault and an igneous intrusion. As you can see, an intrusion cuts across layers A, B, and C. According to the law of crosscutting relationships, the intrusion is younger than layers A, B, and C. The fault is younger than the intrusion and all four layers.

Section 1 Review

Key Ideas

1. **Explain** why it is important for scientists to be able to determine the relative ages of rocks.
2. **State** the principle of uniformitarianism in your own words.
3. **Explain** how the law of superposition can be used to determine the relative age of sedimentary rock.
4. **Explain** the difference between an unconformity and a nonconformity.
5. **Compare** an angular unconformity with a disconformity.
6. **Describe** how the law of crosscutting relationships helps scientists determine the relative ages of rocks.

Critical Thinking

7. **Making Comparisons** Which would be more difficult to recognize: a nonconformity or a disconformity? Explain your answer.
8. **Analyzing Relationships** Suppose that you find a series of rock layers in which a fault ends at an unconformity. Explain how you could apply the law of crosscutting relationships to determine the relative age of the fault and of the rock layers that were deposited above the unconformity.

Concept Mapping

9. Use the following terms to create a concept map: *principle of original horizontality, relative age, graded bedding, law of superposition, cross-bed,* and *ripple mark.*

Key Resources

Technology

- Transparencies
  41 Crosscutting Relationships

Differentiated Instruction

Alternative Assessment

Methods to Determine Relative Age Have students make a table that gives information about methods to determine relative age. Along the top, have them write *Graded Bedding, Cross-Beds, Ripple Marks,* and *Crosscutting Relationships.* Along the sides, have them write *Characteristics* and *Sketch.* As they review this section, have students add information and sketches to their tables.

SECTION 2
Determining Absolute Age

Key Ideas	Key Terms	Why It Matters
❯ Summarize the limitations of using the rates of erosion and deposition to determine the absolute age of rock formations. ❯ Describe the formation of varves. ❯ Explain how the process of radioactive decay can be used to determine the absolute ages of rocks.	**absolute age** **varve** **radiometric dating** **half-life**	The absolute age of a rock can be determined using radioactive elements. This information helps us understand how our planet formed and continues to change.

Relative age indicates only that one rock formation is younger or older than another rock formation. To learn more about Earth's history, scientists often need to determine the numeric age, or **absolute age,** of a rock formation.

Absolute Dating Methods

Scientists use a variety of methods to measure absolute age. Some methods involve geologic processes that can be observed and measured over time. Other methods involve the chemical composition of certain materials in rock.

Rates of Erosion

One way to estimate absolute age is to study rates of erosion. For example, if scientists measure the rate at which a stream erodes its bed, they can estimate the age of the stream. But determining absolute age by using the rate of erosion is practical only for geologic features that formed within the past 10,000 to 20,000 years. One example of such a feature is Niagara Falls, which is shown in **Figure 1.** For older surface features, such as the Grand Canyon, which formed over millions of years, the method is less dependable because rates of erosion may vary greatly over millions of years.

absolute age the numeric age of an object or event, often stated in years before the present, as established by an absolute-dating process, such as radiometric dating

Academic Vocabulary
estimate (ES tuh MAYT) to calculate approximately

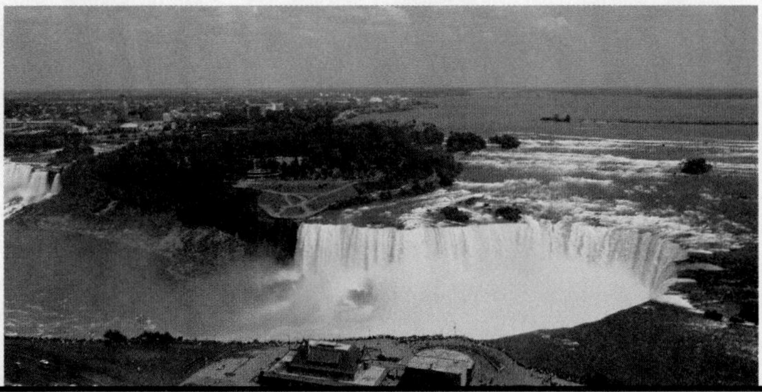

Figure 1 The rocky ledge that forms Niagara Falls has been eroding at a rate of about 1.3 m per year for nearly 9,900 years. ***How many kilometers has the ledge been eroded in the last 9,900 years?***

Section 2

Focus

Overview

This section explains the methods used to calculate the absolute age of rocks. These methods include using erosion and deposition rates, glacial lake deposits, and radiometric dating techniques. The concepts of radioactive decay and half-life are also presented.

Bellringer

Ask students to list the ways they know to determine the exact, or absolute, age of a person or object. (Answers may vary. For a person, they can ask the person, or see a birth certificate. For an object, they may see dates stamped or printed; experts may recognize a manufacture date; or various scientific techniques may be used.) **LS Interpersonal**

Motivate

Using the Figure — GENERAL

Erosion Rate Have students use the cars and buildings in the foreground of the photo at the bottom of the page to appreciate the size of the Canadian portion of Niagara Falls. Answer to caption question: Almost 13 km of ledge has been eroded ($9,900 \text{ y} \times 1.3 \text{ m/y} = 12,870 \text{ m} \div 1,000 = 12.87 \text{ km}$). **LS Logical/Visual**

Key Resources

Chapter Resource File
- Directed Reading BASIC

Technology
- Transparencies
  Bellringer

Teach

Math Skills

Answer

10 m = 1,000 cm; 1,000 cm ÷ 30 cm = 33.33 × 1,000 years = 33,330 years

READING TOOLBOX

Key-Term Fold Answers may vary. Students should write methods for determining absolute age (rates of erosion, rates of deposition, and varve count) on the front of the tabs of the key-term fold. Students should write three facts about each method under the appropriate tab.

Activity — BASIC

Modeling Varves Have students read the text under the heading "Varve Count" on this page. Divide the class into groups. Provide each group with a glass cylinder; coarse, light-colored sand; and fine, dark-colored sand. Have students model several varves by layering sand in the cylinder. When the groups are finished, ask students to explain what the layers represent. (Each pair of layers represents a varve, or an annual deposit of sediment in a glacial lake.) Ask them why each varve has two bands. (The lower band of coarse sediment is deposited in summer as a result of the coarse sediment carried into a lake by melting snow and ice. The upper layer of finer sediment is laid down in winter when the fine sediment particles finally settle out of the water.) LS **Kinesthetic/Visual**

Math Skills

Deposition If 30 cm of sediments are deposited every 1,000 years, how long would 10 m of sediments take to accumulate?

READING TOOLBOX

Key-Term Fold
Make a FoldNote for methods that can be used to determine absolute age. List each method and give three facts about how it is used.

varve a pair of sedimentary layers (one coarse, one fine) that is deposited in an annual cycle, commonly in glacial lakes, and that can be used to determine absolute age

Rates of Deposition

Another way to estimate absolute age is to calculate the rate of sediment deposition. By using data collected over a long period of time, geologists can estimate the average rates of deposition for common sedimentary rocks such as limestone, shale, and sandstone. In general, about 30 cm of sedimentary rock are deposited over a period of 1,000 years. However, any given sedimentary layer that is being studied may not have been deposited at an average rate. For example, a flood can deposit many meters of sediment in just one day. In addition, the rate of deposition may change over time. Therefore, this method of determining absolute age is not always accurate; it merely provides an estimate.

Varve Count

You may know that a tree's age can be estimated by counting the growth rings in its trunk. Scientists have devised a similar method for estimating the age of certain sedimentary deposits. Some sedimentary deposits show definite annual layers, called **varves,** that consist of a light-colored band of coarse particles and a dark band of fine particles.

Varves generally form in glacial lakes. During the summer, when snow and ice melt rapidly, a rush of water can carry large amounts of sediment into a lake. Most of the coarse particles settle quickly to form a layer on the bottom of the lake. With the coming of winter, the surface of the lake begins to freeze. Fine clay particles still suspended in the water settle slowly to form a thin layer on top of the coarse sediments. A coarse summer layer and the overlying, fine winter layer make up one varve. Thus, each varve represents one year of deposition. Some varves are shown in **Figure 2.** By counting the varves, scientists can estimate the age of the sediments.

Reading Check **How are varves like tree rings?**

Figure 2 Varves (below), which form in glacial lakes (right), can be counted to determine the absolute age of sediments.

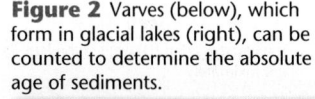

Geology Connection — GENERAL

Glacial Lakes Tell students that most glacial lakes formed after continental glaciers retreated at the end of the last glacial period. When snow and ice from the glacier melts and flows down into the lake, the meltwater carries large amounts of sediment with it. Have students do research to find out more about the formation and characteristics of glacial lakes. Ask them to contribute to a class bulletin board about these lakes. LS **Visual**

Answer to Reading Check

Varves are like tree rings in that varves are laid down each year. Thus, counting varves can reveal the age of sedimentary deposits.

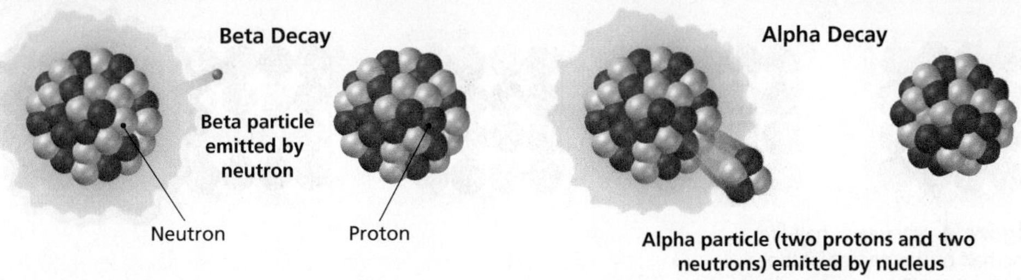

Figure 3 Beta decay and alpha decay are two forms of radioactive decay. In all forms of radioactive decay, an atom emits particles and energy.

Radiometric Dating

Rocks generally contain small amounts of radioactive material that can act as natural clocks. Atoms of the same element that have different numbers of neutrons are called *isotopes. Radioactive isotopes* have nuclei that emit particles and energy at a constant rate regardless of surrounding conditions. **Figure 3** shows two of the ways that radioactive isotopes decay. During the emission of the particles, large amounts of energy are released. Scientists use this natural breakdown of isotopes to accurately measure the absolute age of rocks. The method of using radioactive decay to measure absolute age is called **radiometric dating.**

As an atom emits particles and energy, the atom changes into a different isotope of the same element or an isotope of a different element. Scientists measure the concentrations of the original radioactive isotope, or *parent isotope,* and of the newly formed isotopes, or *daughter isotopes*. Using the known decay rate, the scientists compare the proportions of the parent and daughter isotopes to determine the absolute age of the rock.

radiometric dating a method of determining the absolute age of an object by comparing the relative percentages of a radioactive (parent) isotope and a stable (daughter) isotope

Why It Matters

Exposing a Fake Mummy

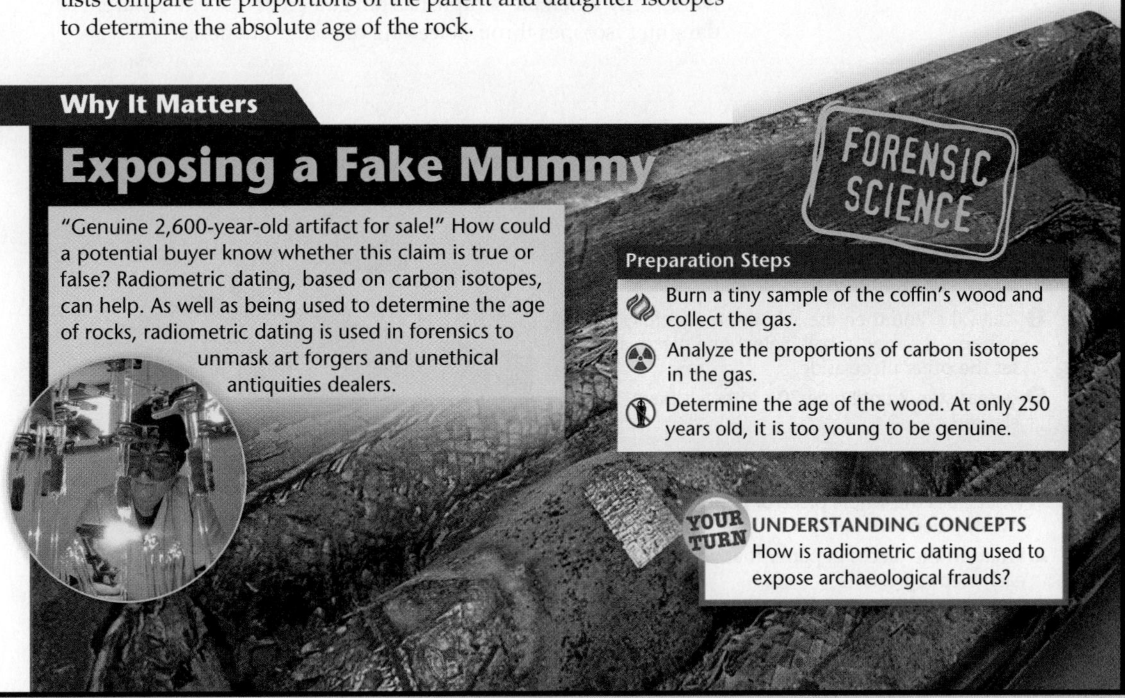

"Genuine 2,600-year-old artifact for sale!" How could a potential buyer know whether this claim is true or false? Radiometric dating, based on carbon isotopes, can help. As well as being used to determine the age of rocks, radiometric dating is used in forensics to unmask art forgers and unethical antiquities dealers.

Preparation Steps

- Burn a tiny sample of the coffin's wood and collect the gas.
- Analyze the proportions of carbon isotopes in the gas.
- Determine the age of the wood. At only 250 years old, it is too young to be genuine.

YOUR TURN UNDERSTANDING CONCEPTS
How is radiometric dating used to expose archaeological frauds?

Key Resources

Technology

- Transparencies
  42 Radioactive Decay and Half-Life

Differentiated Instruction

Advanced Learners

Radioactive Decay of Uranium Have students research all the steps of the decay of uranium-238 into other elements, ending with lead-206. Students may use the Internet or other sources to find this information. Have students create a poster that shows how uranium-238 decays. (Example: Title: "Radioactive Decay of Uranium"; decay series: "uranium-238, thorium-234, protactinium-234, uranium-234, thorium-230, radium-226, radon-222, polonium-218, lead-214, bismuth-214, polonium-214, lead-210, bismuth-210, polonium-210, lead-206.")

Discussion — GENERAL

Measuring Decay Have students talk about why knowing the rate of radioactive decay of different elements is crucial to scientists who use radiometric dating methods to date rocks. (The age of rocks is calculated using decay rates of the radioactive elements they contain.) **LS Logical**

Why It Matters

Exposing a Fake Mummy

Archaeologists use their knowledge of the period to support or refute the alleged age of an artifact. In the case of the Persian princess, archaeologists noted that mummification was not practiced in Iran during the alleged time the mummy was made. Also, the inscription on the mummy's plaque and coffin were inconsistent with the form of language used at that time, and it contained references to events that took place after the supposed mummification. Radiometric dating determined the age of the coffin to be approximately 250 years old. The mummy itself was less than two years old.

Answer to Your Turn

Radiometric dating is used to determine the age of an artifact by burning a small sample and analyzing the gas produced. If the parent-daughter isotopic ratio in the gas does not support the stated age, the artifact is likely to be fraudulent.

Skill Builder — ADVANCED

Vocabulary Tell students that the word *isotope* comes from the Greek *iso-* meaning "similar" or "identical," and *topos,* which means "place." Isotopes are forms of an element that have the same atomic number, but different mass numbers. The isotopes of an element have identical or very similar chemical properties. Because of this close similarity, all isotopes of an element occupy the same place on the periodic table of the elements. **LS Verbal**

Teach, *continued*

Using the Figure — BASIC

Counting Decay To reinforce the concept of half-life, have students determine the amount of the parent isotope in each square in the figure by counting out loud the number of circles shown in each square. Ask students to identify the color of the parent isotope in the figure (red) and the color of the daughter isotope (blue). Then, have them count the number of red circles in each subsequent square and tell the fraction of parent isotope and daughter isotope in each. **LS Logical/Auditory**

MISCONCEPTION ALERT

Radioactive Rocks Students may think that the radioactive isotopes found in most rocks pose a significant health threat. Tell students that most radioactive materials in rocks occur in extremely minute quantities that pose little danger to living things. Radioactive decay and isotopes are all around us, but for the most part do little harm.

Environmental Connection — ADVANCED

Radioactive Waste Discuss the fact that uranium used in nuclear power plants eventually becomes unusable, though still highly radioactive. This radioactive waste must be stored where it will not harm people or the environment. There have been proposals to store this waste under Yucca Mountain in Nevada, but some studies indicate that the area may be prone to earthquakes and the radioactivity may contaminate groundwater. Invite interested students to research the problem of radioactive waste storage and to debate the issue of nuclear power. **LS Logical**

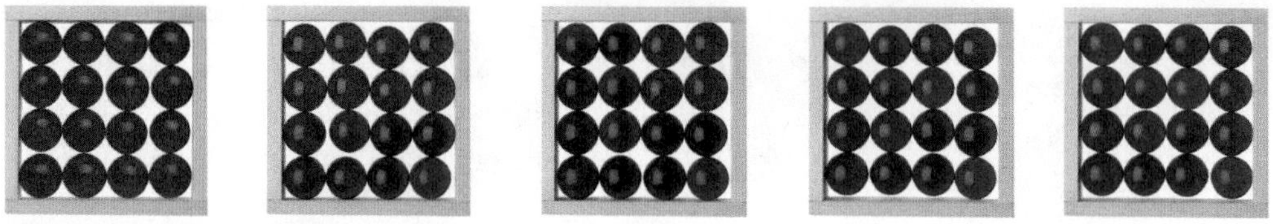

Figure 4 After each half-life, one-half of the parent isotope (shown in red) is converted into a daughter isotope (shown in blue). After four half-lives, only 1/16 of the parent isotope remains.

half-life the time required for half of a sample of a radioactive isotope to break down by radioactive decay to form a daughter isotope

Half-Life

Radioactive decay happens at a relatively constant rate that is not changed by temperature, pressure, or other environmental conditions. Scientists have determined that the time required for half of any amount of a particular radioactive isotope to decay is always the same and can be determined for any isotope. Therefore, a **half-life** is the time it takes half the mass of a given amount of a radioactive parent isotope to decay into its daughter isotopes. If you began with 10 g of a parent isotope, you would have 5 g of that isotope after one half-life of that isotope. At the end of a second half-life, one-fourth, or 2.5 g, of the original isotope would remain. Three-fourths of the sample would now be the daughter isotope. This process is shown in **Figure 4.**

By comparing the amounts of parent and daughter isotopes in a rock sample, scientists can determine the age of the sample. The greater the percentage of daughter isotopes present in the sample, the older the rock is. But comparing parent and daughter isotopes works only when the sample has not gained or lost either parent or daughter isotopes through leaking or contamination.

Quick Lab — Radioactive Decay

10 min

Procedure

1. Use a clock or watch that has a second hand to record the time.
2. Wait 20 s, and then use scissors to carefully cut a sheet of paper in half. Select one piece, and set the other piece aside.
3. Repeat step 2 until nine 20 s intervals have elapsed.

Analysis

1. What does the whole piece of paper used in this investigation represent?
2. What do the pieces of paper that you set aside in each step represent?
3. What is the half-life of your paper isotope?
4. How much of your paper isotope was left after the first three intervals? after six intervals? after nine intervals? Express your answers as percentages.
5. What two factors in your model must remain constant so that your model is accurate? Explain your answer.

Quick Lab

Skills Acquired

- Constructing Models
- Observing
- Drawing Conclusions

Materials

- Clock or watch with second hand
- Scissors
- Sheet of paper

Teacher's Notes: You may want to be timekeeper and announce each 20 s interval. Or, you may have students work in pairs, with one student keeping time and the other cutting the paper.

Analysis

1. The whole piece of paper represents the radioactive element, or parent isotope, before it begins to decay.
2. The pieces of paper set aside represent the fraction of the parent isotope that has decayed into daughter isotopes.
3. 20 seconds
4. 12.5%; 1.5625%; 0.1953125%
5. The length of the "half-life" interval and the fraction of the paper cut off each time (exactly 1/2) must remain constant.

Table 1 Radiometric Dating Methods

Radiometric dating methods	Parent isotope	Daughter isotope	Half-life	Effective dating range
Radiocarbon dating	carbon-14, ^{14}C	nitrogen-14, ^{14}N	5,730 years	less than 70,000 years
Argon-argon dating, $^{39}Ar/^{40}Ar$	potassium-40, ^{40}K irradiated to form argon-39, ^{39}Ar	argon-40, ^{40}Ar	1.25 billion years	10,000 to 4.6 billion years
Potassium-argon dating, $^{40}K/^{40}Ar$	potassium-40, ^{40}K	argon-40, ^{40}Ar	1.25 billion years	50,000 to 4.6 billion years
Rubidium-strontium dating, $^{87}Rb/^{87}Sr$	rubidium-87, ^{87}Rb	strontium-87, ^{87}Sr	48.1 billion years	10 million to 4.6 billion years
Uranium-lead dating, $^{235}U/^{207}Pb$	uranium-235, ^{235}U	lead-207, ^{207}Pb	704 million years	10 million to 4.6 billion years
Uranium-lead dating, $^{238}U/^{206}Pb$	uranium-238, ^{238}U	lead-206, ^{206}Pb	4.5 billion years	10 million to 4.6 billion years
Thorium-lead dating $^{232}Th/^{208}Pb$	thorium-232, ^{232}Th	lead-208, ^{208}Pb	14.0 billion years	greater than 200 million years

Radioactive Isotopes

The amount of time that has passed since a rock formed determines which radioactive element will give a more accurate age measurement. If too little time has passed since radioactive decay began, there may not be enough of the daughter isotope for accurate dating. If too much time has passed, there may not be enough of the parent isotope left for accurate dating.

Uranium-238, ^{238}U (which is read as "U two thirty-eight"), has an extremely long half-life of 4.5 billion years. ^{238}U is most useful for dating geologic samples that are more than 10 million years old, as long as they contain uranium. In addition to ^{238}U, several other radioactive isotopes are used to date rock samples. One such isotope is potassium-40, ^{40}K, which has a half-life of 1.25 billion years. ^{40}K occurs in mica, clay, and feldspar and is used to date rocks that are between 50,000 and 4.6 billion years old. Rubidium-87, ^{87}Rb, has a half-life of about 48 billion years. ^{87}Rb, which commonly occurs in minerals that contain ^{40}K, can be used to verify the age of rocks previously dated by using ^{40}K. **Table 1** provides a list of other radiometric dating methods.

Reading Check **How does the half-life of an isotope affect the accuracy of the radiometric dating method?**

SCILINKS
www.scilinks.org
Topic: Radiometric Dating
Code: **HQX1261**

Using the Table — GENERAL

Methods for Dating Rocks Have students study the table on this page. Ask students to identify the parent isotope and its daughter isotope in each method. Have students determine which isotope should be used for dating the oldest rocks (those with half-lives of billions of years) and for dating the youngest rocks (those with shorter half-lives). Have students discuss why scientists must know the composition of a rock before choosing a method of dating. (Because different rocks contain different isotopes, scientists need to choose a dating method that matches the isotopes they expect to find in the rock.) LS **Logical**

Close

Reteaching — BASIC

Half-Life Provide groups of students with 40 pennies. Have the groups shake the pennies and then spill them into a large shallow box or tray on a table. Then, students should remove all of the coins that show "heads." Have them record this number. Have students repeat the process until all of the pennies are gone. Ask them to graph their data and to compare their data with the data from the figure that illustrates half-life on the previous page. Have them point out any inaccuracies of the model. (The data should roughly correlate with the figure. Students should recognize that heads come up statistically about half the time, so the pennies should be removed at a rate of approximately half of the pennies with each turn. In the case of the coins, each spill represents an approximate "half-life." However, the rate of radioactive decay is constant and exactly 50% of the parent material decays each half-life.) LS **Kinesthetic/Logical**

Differentiated Instruction

Struggling Readers

Summarizing Have students silently read the text under the headings "Half-Life" and "Radioactive Isotopes." After a designated time, assign students to cooperative pairs. Have one student summarize what he or she read while the other student listens. The listener should point out inaccuracies and mention concepts that the other left out. Both students should work together during the final clarification process, referring to the text as needed.

Answers to Reading Check

An isotope that has an extremely long half-life will not show significant or measurable changes in a young rock. In a very old rock, an isotope that has a short half-life may have decayed to the point at which too little of the isotope is left to give an accurate age measurement. So, the estimated age of the rock must be correlated to the dating method used.

Close, *continued*

Quiz GENERAL

1. What are radioactive isotopes? (forms of elements with nuclei that emit particles and energy at a constant rate, regardless of surrounding conditions)
2. What must be present in rock for scientists to date it using radiocarbon dating? (organic material that is less than 70,000 years old)

Answers to Section Review

1. Relative age is the age of an object in relation to the age of other objects. Absolute age is the numeric age of an object.
2. The rate at which sediment is deposited or eroded can vary.
3. Varves are layers of sediment that consist of one layer of coarse particles covered by one layer of fine particles, that are deposited at the bottom of glacial lakes, and that represent one year of deposition.
4. By comparing the relative percentages of a radioactive (parent) isotope and a stable (daughter) isotope in a sample of rock, based on the known rate of decay of the parent, scientists can calculate the length of time since the rock formed.
5. Half-life is the time one half of a sample of a radioactive isotope takes to break down by radioactive decay to form a daughter substance. The number of half-lives that have passed can be used to determine absolute age.
6. Answers may vary but should reflect information from the table in this section.

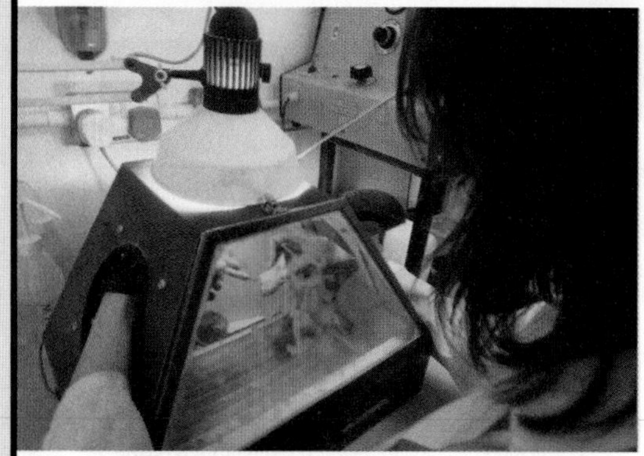

Figure 5 This scientist is preparing a mammoth's tooth for carbon-14 dating, which will determine the tooth's absolute age.

Carbon Dating

Younger rock layers may be dated indirectly by dating organic material found within the rock. The ages of wood, bones, shells, and other organic remains that are included in the layers and that are less than 70,000 years old can be determined by using a method known as *carbon-14 dating,* or *radiocarbon dating,* as shown in **Figure 5.** The isotope carbon-14, ^{14}C, combines with oxygen to form radioactive carbon dioxide, CO_2. Most CO_2 in the atmosphere contains nonradioactive carbon-12, ^{12}C. Only a small amount of CO_2 in the atmosphere contains ^{14}C.

Plants absorb CO_2, which contains either ^{12}C or ^{14}C, during photosynthesis. Then, when animals eat the plants or the plant-eating animals, the ^{12}C and ^{14}C become part of the animals' body tissues. Thus, all living organisms contain both ^{12}C and ^{14}C.

To find the age of a small amount of organic material, scientists first determine the ratio of ^{14}C to ^{12}C in the sample. Then, they compare that ratio with the ratio of ^{14}C to ^{12}C known to exist in a living organism. While organisms are alive, the ratio of ^{12}C to ^{14}C remains relatively constant. When a plant or an animal dies, however, the ratio begins to change. The half-life of ^{14}C is only about 5,730 years. Because the organism is dead, it no longer absorbs ^{12}C and ^{14}C, and the amount of ^{14}C in the organism's tissues decreases steadily as the radioactive ^{14}C decays to nonradioactive nitrogen-14, ^{14}N.

Section 2 Review

Key Ideas

1. **Differentiate** between relative and absolute age.
2. **Summarize** why calculations of absolute age based on rates of erosion and deposition can be inaccurate.
3. **Describe** varves, and describe how and where they form.
4. **Explain** how radiometric dating is used to estimate absolute age.
5. **Define** half-life, and explain how it helps determine an object's absolute age.
6. **List** three methods of radiometric dating, and explain the age range for which they are most effective.

Critical Thinking

7. **Demonstrating Reasoned Judgment** Suppose you have a shark's tooth that you suspect is about 15,000 years old. Would you use ^{238}U or ^{14}C to date the tooth? Explain your answer.
8. **Making Inferences** You see an advertisement for an atomic clock. You also know that radioactive decay emits harmful radiation. Do you think the atomic clock contains decaying isotopes? Explain.

Concept Mapping

9. Use the following terms to create a concept map: *absolute age, varve, radiometric dating, parent isotope, daughter isotope,* and *carbon dating.*

7. You would use radiocarbon dating because the object is organic and because it is too young to be accurately dated by using ^{238}U.
8. Answers may vary. Accept all reasonable answers. Atomic clocks are not radioactive.
9. The *absolute age* of a rock can be determined by counting *varves* or by *radiometric dating,* in which the percentages of *parent isotopes* and *daughter isotopes* are compared, and which includes *carbon dating.*

Differentiated Instruction

Alternative Assessment

Dating Rock Have students imagine that they have been given three rock samples to date: one sample contains ^{238}U; the second is a core from a lake bed that shows many sediment layers; the third is a young rock containing bits of bone. Have students write a description of the method they would use to date each sample and explain how the method works. LS **Logical/Verbal**

SECTION 3

The Fossil Record

Key Ideas	Key Terms	Why It Matters
❯ Describe four ways in which entire organisms can be preserved as fossils. ❯ List five examples of fossilized traces of organisms. ❯ Describe how index fossils can be used to determine the age of rocks.	fossil paleontology trace fossil index fossil	Fossils give information about the ages of rocks. They also give information about changes in life forms and the environment throughout time.

The remains or traces of animals or plants that lived in a previous geologic time are called **fossils.** Fossils, such as the one shown in **Figure 1,** are an important source of information for finding the relative and absolute ages of rocks. Fossils also provide clues to past geologic events, climates, and the evolution of living things over time. The study of fossils is called **paleontology.**

Almost all fossils are discovered in sedimentary rock. The sediments that cover the fossils slow or stop the process of decay and protect the body of the dead organism from damage. Fossils are rare in igneous rock or highly metamorphosed rock because intense heat, pressure, and chemical reactions that occur during the formation of these rock types destroy all organic structures.

fossil the trace or remains of an organism that lived long ago, most commonly preserved in sedimentary rock

paleontology the scientific study of fossils

Interpreting the Fossil Record

The fossil record provides information about the geologic history of Earth. By revealing how organisms have changed throughout the geologic past, fossils provide important clues to the environmental changes that occurred in Earth's past. For example, fossils of marine animals and plants have been discovered in areas far from any ocean. These fossils tell us that such areas were covered by an ocean in the past. Scientists can use this information to learn about how environmental changes have affected living organisms.

Figure 1 Paleontologists are unearthing the remains of rhinoceroses that are 10 million years old at this site in Orchard, Nebraska.

Section 3

Focus

Overview

This section describes the fossil record and how it is interpreted. The section also covers fossil formation and the different types of fossils, and describes index fossils and their relation to the absolute age of specific rock layers.

Bellringer

Have students draw or describe the process by which they think fossils form. (Answers and drawings may vary. You may use students' answers to begin a discussion of how fossils form.) LS **Logical**

Motivate

Demonstration — GENERAL

Learning Earth's History Before students read this page, show them a piece of limestone with fossil shells imbedded in it or a fossil of a fish from a place that is dry land today. Ask students what the fossil reveals about the history of the area where it was found. (that the area was once underwater) Have students discuss how fossils help scientists understand the geologic history of Earth. LS **Logical/Visual**

Key Resources

Chapter Resource File
- Directed Reading BASIC
- Inquiry Lab: Got Fossils? GENERAL

Technology
- Transparencies
  Bellringer

Teach

Outlining Answers may vary, but outlines should include key ideas, key terms, and topic headings. Students can consult Appendix A for tips on outlining.

Group Activity — GENERAL

Fossils in Many Forms Divide the class into five groups, and assign one of the five ways fossils form to each group. Have some students in each group use the Internet or library resources to collect information about how their particular type of fossil forms and under what conditions. They may also research where specimens of their specific type of fossil have been found. Ask other students to research the types of organisms most commonly preserved in that particular way. Have other students collect pictures of the fossilized organisms and use them to create a poster or to make models, if possible. (Note: Students working on mummification should concentrate on natural preservation, not artificial mummification.) Have students work together in their groups to write an oral presentation of their findings for the class. **LS Visual/Verbal** Co-op Learning

Fossilization

Normally, dead plants and animals are eaten by other animals or decomposed by bacteria. If left unprotected, even hard parts such as bones decay and leave no record of the organism. Only dead organisms that are buried quickly or protected from decay can become fossils. Generally, only the hard parts of organisms, such as wood, bones, shells, and teeth, become fossils. In rare cases, an entire organism may be preserved. In some types of fossils, only a replica of the original organism remains. Other fossils merely provide evidence that life once existed. **Table 1** describes different ways that fossils can form.

Academic Vocabulary
evidence (EV uh duhns) information showing whether an idea is true or valid

READING TOOLBOX

Outlining
Create an outline using the main ideas from this section. Include all key ideas, key terms, and red topic headings. Use your outline to review the material.

Table 1 How Fossils Form

Mummification Mummified remains are often found in very dry places, because most bacteria, which cause decay, cannot survive in these places. Some ancient civilizations mummified their dead by carefully extracting the body's internal organs and then wrapping the body in carefully prepared strips of cloth.

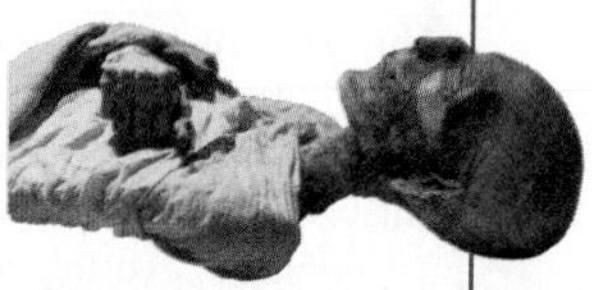

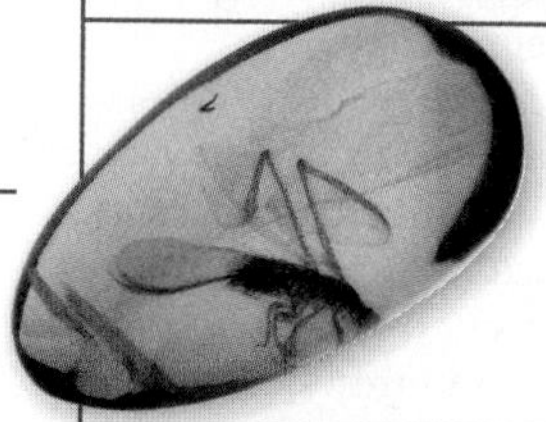

Amber Hardened tree sap is called *amber*. Insects become trapped in the sticky sap and are preserved when the sap hardens. In many cases, delicate features such as legs and antennae have been preserved. In rare cases, DNA has been recovered from amber.

Tar Seeps When thick petroleum oozes to Earth's surface, the petroleum forms a tar seep. Tar seeps are commonly covered by water. Animals that come to drink the water can become trapped in the sticky tar. Other animals prey on the trapped animals and can also become trapped. The remains of the trapped animals are covered by the tar and preserved.

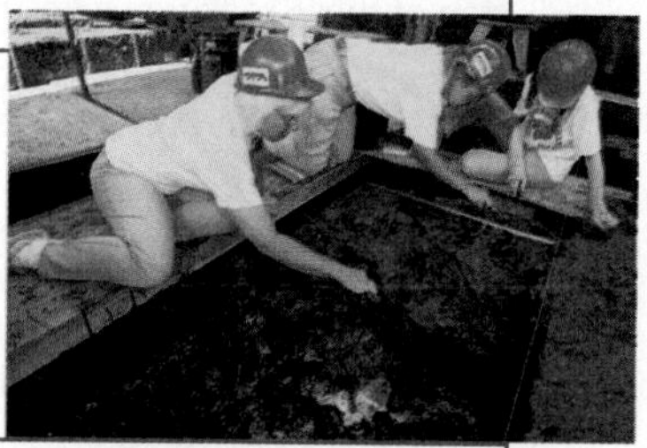

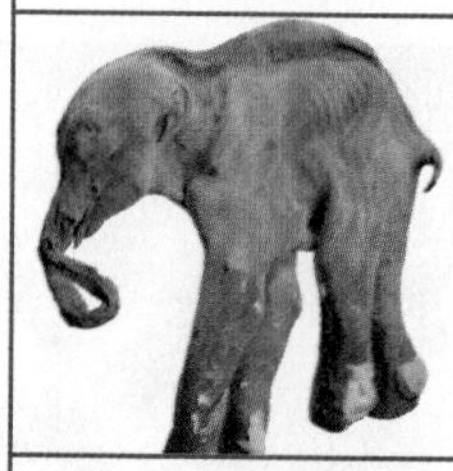

Freezing The low temperatures of frozen soil and ice can protect and preserve organisms. Because most bacteria cannot survive freezing temperatures, organisms that are buried in frozen soil or ice do not decay.

Petrification Minerals that precipitate from groundwater solutions replace original organic materials that have been buried under layers of sediment. Some common petrifying minerals are silica, calcite, and pyrite. The substitution of minerals for organic material often results in the formation of a nearly perfect mineral replica of the original organism.

Discussion — GENERAL

Handprint History Have students imagine that every year, on their birthday, they pour a layer of cement into a bucket and make a handprint in it. Ask students what the layers of cement record. (Students should recognize that the layers record how their hand changes over time.) If, after 1,000 years, someone could examine the layers, what changes would they note in each handprint? (The handprints grew for a while, then stayed the same for a long time, and finally shrank or became crooked as the maker of the handprint aged.) **LS Logical**

Differentiated Instruction

Special Education Students

Summarizing Have the class read the mummification information in the table on this page as a group. Discuss the information and then ask each student to write one sentence—in his or her own words—to explain mummification and fossils. Repeat with each of the other four rows of the table. **LS Auditory**

Table 2 Types of Fossils

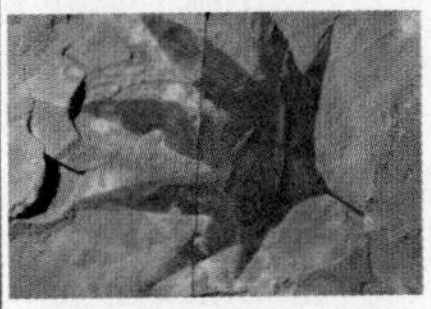

Carbon films Carbonized residue of leaves, stems, flowers, and fish have been found preserved in sedimentary rock made of soft mud or clay. When original organic material partially decays, it leaves behind a carbon-rich film that displays the surface features of the organism.

Molds and Casts Shells often leave empty spaces called *molds* within hardened sediment. When a shell is buried, its remains eventually dissolve and leave an empty space. When sand or mud fills a mold and turns into rock, a natural cast forms. A cast is a replica of the original organism.

Coprolites Fossilized dung or waste materials from ancient animals are called *coprolites.* They can be cut into thin sections and observed through a microscope. The materials identified in these sections reveal the feeding habits of ancient animals, such as dinosaurs.

Gastroliths Some dinosaurs had stones in their digestive systems to help grind their food. In many cases, these stones, which are called *gastroliths,* survive as fossils. Gastroliths can often be recognized by their smooth, polished surfaces and by their close proximity to dinosaur remains.

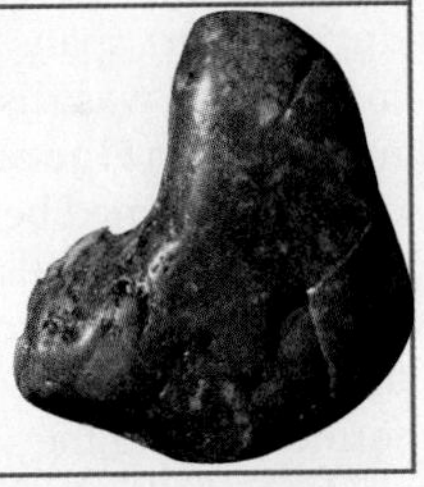

Types of Fossils

Fossils can show a remarkable amount of detail about ancient organisms. **Table 2** describes some of these fossils. In some cases, no part of the original organism survives in fossil form. But **trace fossils,** or fossilized evidence of past animal movement such as tracks, footprints, borings, and burrows, can still provide information about prehistoric life.

A trace fossil, such as the footprint of an animal, is an important clue to the animal's appearance and activities. Suppose that a giant dinosaur left deep footprints in soft mud. Sand or silt may have blown or washed into the footprint so gently that the footprints remained intact. Then, more sediment may have been deposited over the prints. As time passed, the mud containing the footprints turned into sedimentary rock and preserved the footprints. Scientists have discovered ancient footprints of reptiles, amphibians, birds, and mammals.

Reading Check **What is a trace fossil?**

trace fossil a fossilized mark that formed in sedimentary rock by the movement of an animal on or within soft sediment

SCILINKS.
www.scilinks.org
Topic: Fossil Record
Code: HQX0615

Activity — GENERAL

Spacing Footprints The distance between fossilized footprints can tell paleontologists how fast an ancient animal moved. Invite a few students to walk at a normal pace from one end of the classroom to the other, while other students make a chalk mark or drop a marker next to each footstep. Then, have the students run from one end of the room to the other, again marking their footsteps. Have students measure and record the distance between each set of footsteps. Ask students to draw a conclusion based on the data they've collected. (Students should conclude that the faster the movement, the farther apart the footprints are.)
LS Kinesthetic

Close

Reteaching — BASIC

Listing Make three columns on the board, and label the columns with the following heads: How Fossils Form, Types of Fossils, and Index Fossils. Have students review the text and tell you under what heads to write the information as they read it. At the end of the chapter, have students look at the three lists and describe the differences between the categories and the usefulness of each category to scientists. English Language Learners
LS Verbal

Biology Connection — ADVANCED

Dinosaurs and Birds Ask students which type of modern animal routinely consumes small pebbles that it stores in its gizzard to aid digestion. (many types of birds) The finding of gastroliths suggests that dinosaurs did this too. In fact, paleontologists cite gastroliths as evidence of an evolutionary connection between dinosaurs and birds. Invite interested students to research other evidence for the connection between birds and dinosaurs. Have them make a poster that illustrates their findings.
LS Logical/Visual

Answer to Reading Check
A trace fossil is fossilized evidence of past animal movement, such as tracks, footprints, borings, or burrows, that can provide information about prehistoric life.

Close, *continued*

Quiz — GENERAL

1. Why must an index fossil be clearly distinguishable from other fossils? (so that it is never confused with a fossil that may have lived in a different time period)
2. Why are index fossils useful for dating rocks? (They lived for only short spans of geologic time and exist over a large area.)
3. What is paleontology? (It is the scientific study of fossils.)

Answers to Section Review

1. An entire organism may be preserved as a fossil if it is mummified, trapped in amber or in tar seeps, frozen, or petrified.
2. Four types of fossils that can be used to provide indirect evidence of organisms are molds and casts, coprolites, and gastroliths.
3. When scientists know the time interval during which a specific organism lived, they can use the presence of those fossils to date sedimentary rock layers that contain those fossils.
4. Mummification occurs in very dry regions, where bacteria cannot decay the body. Thus, much of it remains unchanged. Petrification occurs in areas where mineral solutions replace the buried organic materials with new materials, such as silica and calcite.
5. Index fossils are fossils of distinct organisms that lived during short spans of geologic time. Any rocks that contain index fossils can be given an absolute age.
6. The environment preserved the dead organisms from decay.
7. You know that the rock layers are the same age because the index fossil they contain lived only during a short span of time. The index fossil gives you the absolute age of the layers.
8. *Fossils* form when an organism is preserved through *mummification, freezing,* or *petrification* or is trapped in *amber* or in a *tar seep.*

Figure 2 If you discovered fossils such as these ammonites, you would know that the surrounding rock formed between 180 million and 206 million years ago.

Index Fossils

Paleontologists can use fossils to determine the relative ages of the rock layers in which the fossils are located. Fossils that occur only in rock layers of a particular geologic age are called **index fossils.** To be an index fossil, a fossil must meet certain requirements. First, it must be present in rocks scattered over a large region. Second, it must have features that clearly distinguish it from other fossils. Third, the organisms from which the fossil formed must have lived during a short span of geologic time. Fourth, the fossil must occur in fairly large numbers within the rock layers.

index fossil a fossil that is used to establish the age of rock layers because it is distinct, abundant, and widespread and existed for only a short span of geologic time

Index Fossils and Absolute Age

Scientists can use index fossils to estimate absolute ages of specific rock layers. Because organisms that formed index fossils lived during short spans of geologic time, the rock layer in which an index fossil was discovered can be dated accurately. The ammonite fossils in **Figure 2** show that the rock in which the fossils were observed formed between 180 million and 206 million years ago.

Scientists can also use index fossils to date rock layers in separate areas. So, an index fossil discovered in rock layers in different areas of the world indicates that the rock layers in these areas formed during the same time period.

Geologists also use index fossils to help locate rock layers that are likely to contain oil and natural gas deposits. These deposits form from plant and animal remains that change by chemical processes over millions of years.

Section 3 Review

Key Ideas

1. **Describe** four ways in which an entire organism can be preserved as a fossil.
2. **List** four types of fossils that can be used to provide indirect evidence of organisms.
3. **Explain** how geologists use fossils to date sedimentary rock layers.
4. **Compare** the process of mummification with the process of petrification.
5. **Describe** how index fossils can be used to determine the ages of rocks.

Critical Thinking

6. **Applying Ideas** What characteristic do all good sources of animal fossils have in common?
7. **Identifying Relationships** If a rock layer in Mexico and a rock layer in Australia contain the same index fossil, what do you know about the absolute ages of the layers in both places? Explain your answer.

Concept Mapping

8. Use the following terms to create a concept map: *fossils, mummification, amber, tar seep, freezing,* and *petrification.*

Differentiated Instruction

Alternative Assessment

Captioned Pictures Ask students to create an illustrated booklet about how fossils form, types of fossils, and index fossils. Students may draw or find pictures of each category and should write an informative caption next to each picture. **LS Visual/Verbal**

Why It Matters

A Record of Yellowstone's Explosive Past

SCIENCE & SOCIETY

Would you feel safe camping on top of an active volcano with a destructive past? At Yellowstone National Park, people do, every day! Yellowstone's geysers are perched on one of Earth's largest active volcanoes. The rock record shows that three giant eruptions took place at Yellowstone, throwing massive amounts of volcanic ash into the air between 2.1 million and 640,000 years ago.

As a geyser's water heats up, pressure mounts underground, eventually forcing water high into the air.

Yellowstone's largest eruption created the Huckleberry Ridge ash bed, which formed this hillside.

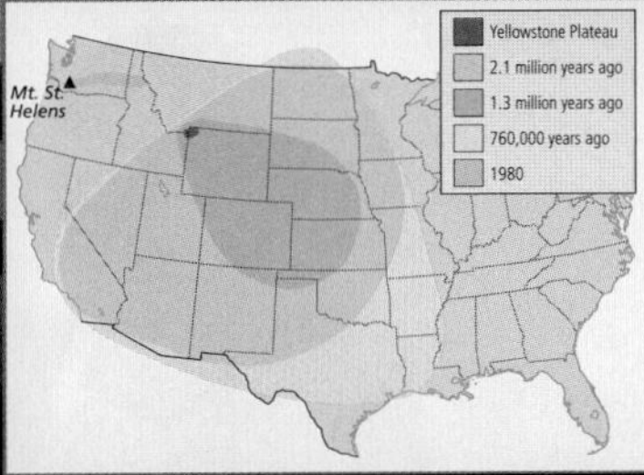

Ash deposits from a Yellowstone eruption have been identified more than 2,000 km away from the eruption site!

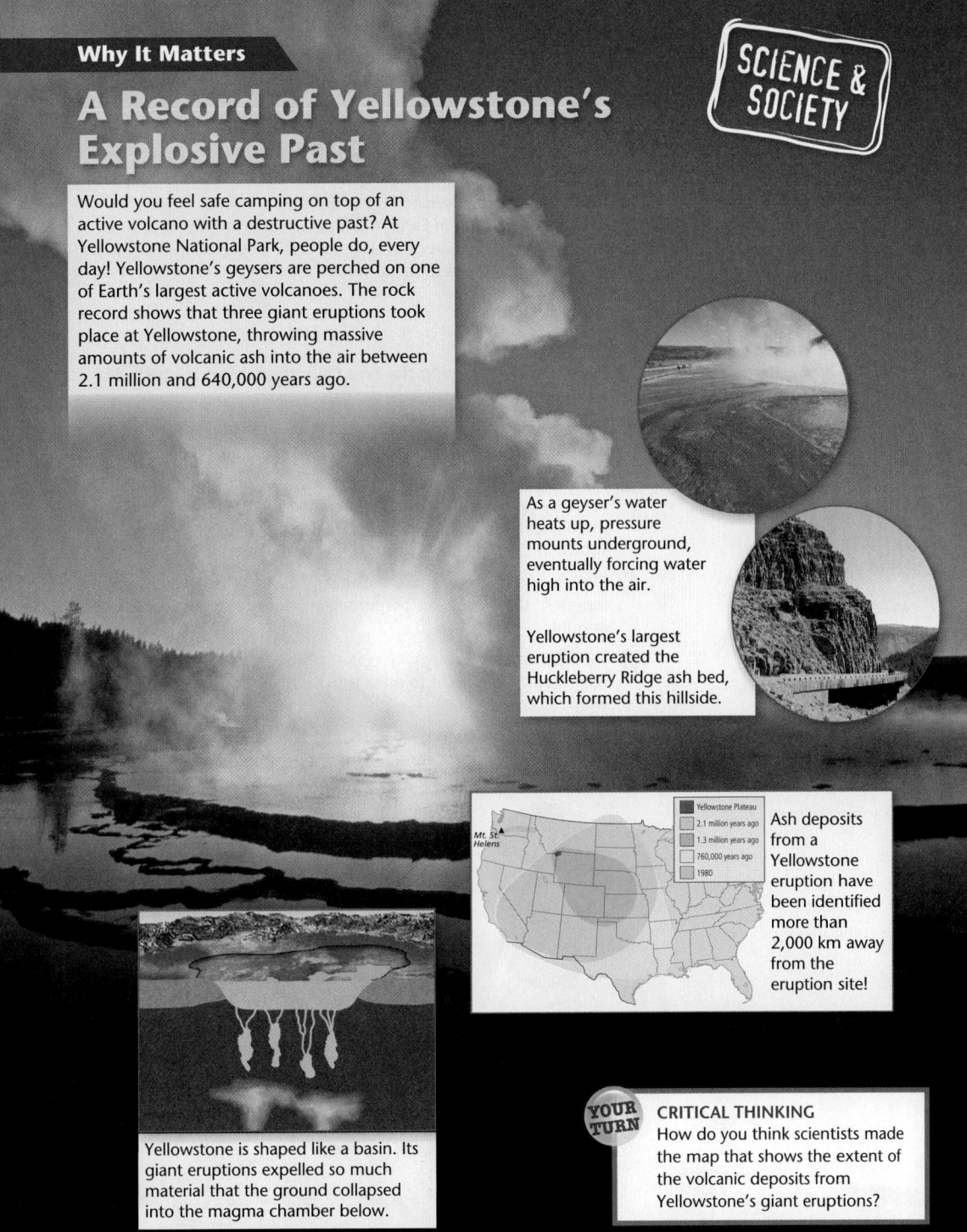

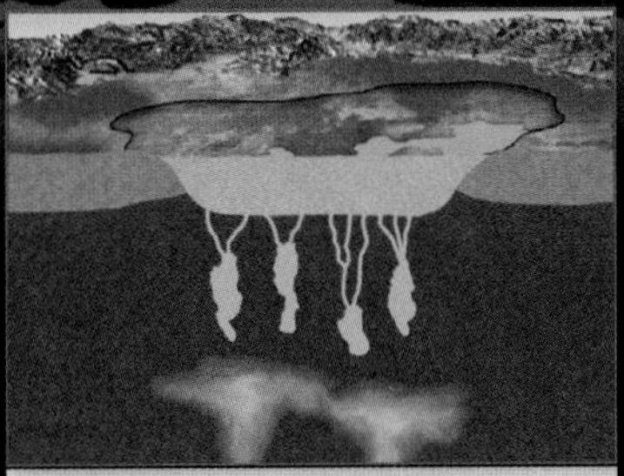

Yellowstone is shaped like a basin. Its giant eruptions expelled so much material that the ground collapsed into the magma chamber below.

YOUR TURN

CRITICAL THINKING

How do you think scientists made the map that shows the extent of the volcanic deposits from Yellowstone's giant eruptions?

Why It Matters

A Record of Yellowstone's Explosive Past

The explosive volcanic activity that has shaped Yellowstone's landscape began when the movement of the North American plate carried the area over a hot spot in Earth's mantle. The first giant eruption occurred about 2.1 million years ago and produced a crater, or caldera, larger than the state of Rhode Island. Another eruption occurred some 1.2 million years ago and formed the Henrys Fork Caldera. The latest giant eruption, about 640,000 years ago, formed the present-day Yellowstone Caldera. Combined, the three eruptions expelled enough magma to fill the Grand Canyon. Although another eruption of this magnitude is unlikely in the near future, the Yellowstone region remains geologically active. Every year, several thousand small earthquakes occur. Hydrothermal activity at Yellowstone, including geysers, hot springs, fumaroles, and mud pots, draws millions of visitors to the park every year.

Answer to Your Turn

Answers may vary but should include such concepts as the geographical extent of ash deposits, the composition of the ash from each eruption, and radiometric dating of ash deposits.

Skills Practice Lab

Time Required

one 45-minute class period

Lab Ratings

EASY → HARD

Teacher Preparation 2/4

Student Setup 2/4

Concept Level 2/4

Cleanup 3/4

Skills Acquired

- Constructing Models
- Classifying
- Interpreting Models

Scientific Methods

In this lab, students will

- Make Observations
- Analyze the Results
- Draw Conclusions

Materials

The materials listed are enough for groups of two to four students. You may have your first-period students leave all fresh materials prepared for the rest of your classes.

Making Models Lab

45 min

Types of Fossils

Paleontologists study fossils to find evidence of the kinds of life and conditions that existed on Earth in the past. Fossils are the remains of ancient plants and animals or evidence of their presence. In this lab, you will use various methods to make models of fossils.

What You'll Do

› **Model** how different types of fossils form.

› **Demonstrate** how certain types of fossils form.

What You'll Need

clay, modeling
container, plastic
hard objects such as a shell, key, paper clip, or coin
leaf
newspaper
paper, carbon, soft
paper, white (1 sheet)
pencil (or wood dowel)
plaster of Paris
spoon, plastic
tweezers
water
wax paper

Safety

Procedure

1. Place a ball of modeling clay on a flat surface that is covered with wax paper.
2. Press the clay down to form a flat disk about 8 cm in diameter. Turn the clay over so that the smooth, flat surface is facing up.
3. Choose a small, hard object. Press the object onto the clay carefully so that you do not disturb the indentation. Is the indentation left by the object a mold or a cast? What features of the object are best shown in the indentation? Sketch the indentation.
4. On a second piece of smooth, flat clay, make a shallow imprint to represent the burrow or footprint of an animal. Sketch your fossil imprint.
5. Fill the plastic container with water to a depth of 1 to 2 cm. Stir in enough plaster of Paris to make a paste that has the consistency of whipped cream.
6. Using the plastic spoon, fill both indentations with plaster. Allow excess plaster to run over the edges of the imprints. Let the plaster set for about 15 min, until it hardens.

Step 3

Tips and Tricks

To save time, you may wish to divide the class into three groups, with each group making only one type of fossil and then displaying and discussing it with the whole class. Or, you may want to prepare a batch of plaster of Paris for the whole class to use while the students are working on the first part of the lab. Keep the bucket of plaster moist and covered until the students are ready to use it.

7. After the plaster has hardened, remove both pieces of plaster from the clay. Do the pieces of hardened plaster represent molds or casts?

8. Place the carbon paper on a flat surface with the carbon facing up. Gently place the leaf on the carbon paper, and cover it with several sheets of newspaper. Roll the pencil or wooden dowel back and forth across the surface of the newspaper several times, and press firmly to bring the leaf into full contact with the carbon paper.

9. Remove the newspaper. Lift the leaf by using the tweezers, and place it on a clean sheet of paper with the carbon-coated side facing down. Cover the leaf with clean wax paper, and roll your pencil across the surface of the wax paper.

10. Remove the wax paper and leaf. Observe and describe the carbon film left by the leaf.

Step 6

Step 9

Analysis

1. **Analyzing Results** Look at the molds and casts made by others in your class. Identify as many of the objects used to make the molds and casts as you can.
2. **Making Comparisons** How does the carbon film you made differ from an actual carbonized film fossil?
3. **Applying Ideas** Trace fossils are evidence of the movement of an animal on or within soft sediment. Why are carbon films, molds, and casts not considered trace fossils?

Extension

Making Predictions Which organism—a rabbit, a housefly, an earthworm, or a snail—would be most likely to form fossils? Which of these organisms would leave trace fossils? Explain.

Answers to Procedure

3. The indentation left by the object is a mold.
7. The pieces of hardened plaster represent casts.

Answers to Analysis

1. Student responses may vary depending on the objects used, but students should be encouraged to notice details in the molds and casts that give clues to the identity of the object.
2. An actual carbon film fossil is made from the carbon contained in the organism itself.
3. Carbon films, molds, and casts are not trace fossils because they are fossils of an organism that formed after the organism has died. Trace fossils are marks left while the organism was alive and moving.

Answer to Extension

Answers may vary, but students should recognize that an organism with a hard shell, like the snail, or one with bones, like the rabbit, would be most likely to form a fossil. The fly might leave a fossil in amber. All of the organisms may leave trace fossils in soft sediment. The earthworm is most likely to leave a trace fossil of its movement through soil.

Geologic Map of Bedrock in Ohio

Group Activity ADVANCED

Map Making Have groups of students make maps of your state's bedrock geology, using the map on this page as a model. Student maps need not be highly detailed. If your state has a complex bedrock geology, tell students to map the most prominent or abundant types of bedrock, or have them concentrate on the bedrock beneath your county or region. **LS Visual**

Answers to Map Skills Activity

1. the Permian, Pennsylvanian, Mississippian, Devonian, Silurian, and Ordovician
2. The youngest bedrock is in the southeastern part of the state; the oldest bedrock is in the southwestern part of the state.
3. In traveling east to west, the bedrock would generally become older.
4. The bedrock layers are tilted upwards. The more horizontal surface of Earth cuts across the angled layers and thus exposes them. If the layers were horizontal, only the top, or youngest, layer would be exposed.
5. because Mississippian rock was formed in the Mississippian Period just after the rock formed in the Devonian Period
6. To find early reptile fossils, you'd look in Pennsylvanian rock, represented by the color blue, which occurs in a large stripe extending to the southwest from eastern Ohio.

MAPS in Action

Geologic Map of Bedrock in Ohio

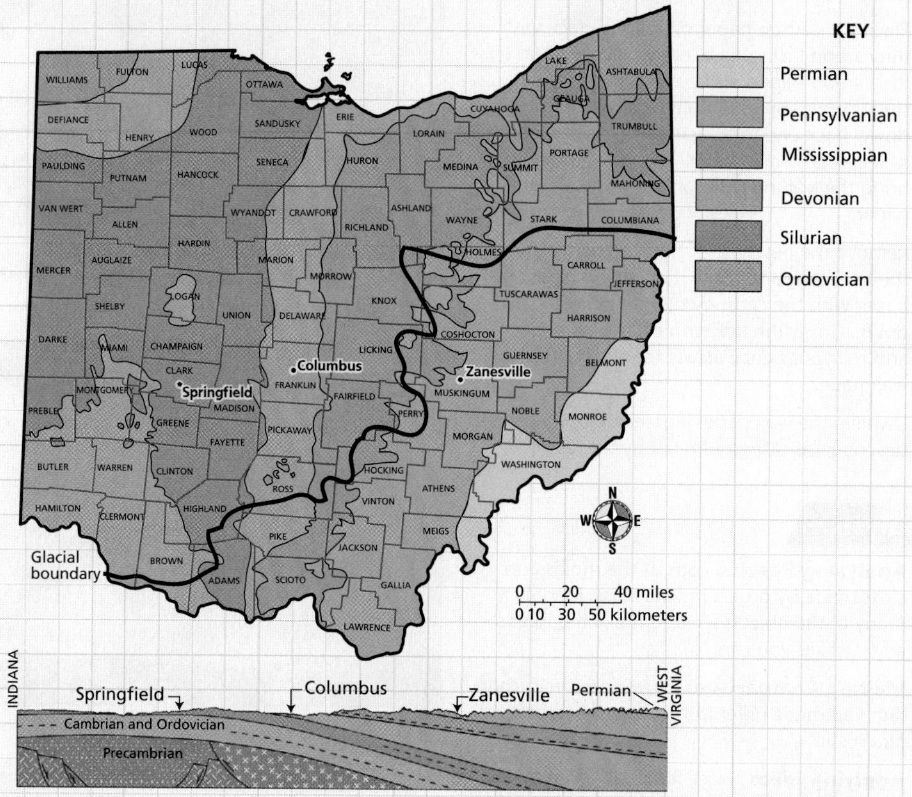

Map Skills Activity

This map shows the ages of the bedrock in Ohio. Bedrock is the solid rock that lies underneath all surface soil and other loose material. Use the map to answer the questions below.

1. **Using a Key** What geologic periods are represented by the bedrock in Ohio?
2. **Analyzing Data** Where is the youngest bedrock in Ohio? Where is the oldest bedrock in Ohio?
3. **Identifying Trends** If you traveled from east to west across Ohio, how would the ages of the rock beneath you change?
4. **Analyzing Relationships** Based on the geologic cross section, how does the shape of the rock beds cause rocks of different ages to be exposed at different places in Ohio?
5. **Identifying Relationships** Why is Mississippian rock likely to be located next to Devonian rock?
6. **Using a Key** The first reptiles appeared in the fossil record during the Pennsylvanian Period. If you wanted to look for fossils of these reptiles in Ohio, in what part of the state would you look? Explain your answer.

Key Resources

Technology

- Transparencies
  43 Geologic Map of Bedrock in Ohio

Chapter 8 # Summary

THINK central
SUPER SUMMARY
Keyword: HQXRECS

Key Ideas | **Key Terms**

Section 1

Determining Relative Age

- According to the principle of uniformitarianism, the forces that are changing Earth's surface today are the same forces that changed Earth's surface in the past.
- In undeformed rock layers, the youngest layer is on the top and the oldest layer is on the bottom, according to the law of superposition.
- Nonconformities, angular unconformities, and disconformities are interruptions in the sequence of rock layers and are collectively known as unconformities.
- According to the law of crosscutting relationships, a geologic feature is always younger than the rock it cuts through.

Key Terms

uniformitarianism, p. 201
relative age, p. 202
law of superposition, p. 203
unconformity, p. 205
law of crosscutting relationships, p. 206

Section 2

Determining Absolute Age

- Because rates of erosion and deposition can change over time, they are imprecise methods for determining absolute ages of rocks.
- Varves are layers of sediment that form in glacial lakes as a result of the annual cycle of freezing and thawing of the glacier.
- Radioactive elements decay at constant and measurable rates and can be used to determine absolute age.

Key Terms

absolute age, p. 207
varve, p. 208
radiometric dating, p. 209
half-life, p. 210

Section 3

The Fossil Record

- Entire organisms may be preserved in amber, in tar seeps, or through freezing or mummification.
- Fossilized evidence of organisms includes trace fossils, carbon films, molds, casts, coprolites, and gastroliths.
- Index fossils occur only in rock layers of a particular geologic age, and they can help geologists estimate the age of rock formations.

Key Terms

fossil, p. 213
paleontology, p. 213
trace fossil, p. 215
index fossil, p. 216

Chapter Summary

Using THINK central Resources

Super Summary

Have students connect the major concepts in this chapter through an interactive Super Summary. Visit www.thinkcentral.com and type in the keyword **HQXRECS** to access the Super Summary for this chapter.

Chapter Review

Assignment Guide	
Section	**Questions**
1	2, 7, 10, 11, 13, 16–18, 23–25, 32, 34–36
2	3–5, 9, 12, 19, 20, 26, 29–31, 33
3	8, 14, 15, 21, 22, 27
1 and 2	6
1–3	1, 28

Reading Toolbox

1. Answers may vary. Students' sentences should use key terms accurately.

Using Key Terms

2–8. Answers may vary but should show that students understand the definitions of and differences between key terms.

Understanding Key Concepts

9. b
10. b
11. c
12. d
13. c
14. b
15. a

Short Answer

16. He noticed geologic changes occurring on his farm and assumed the same forces had changed Earth's surface in the past.
17. The law of superposition helps scientists determine rocks' relative ages because older rocks are at the bottom of undisturbed strata and younger rocks are at the top.

Chapter 8 Review

1. **Key-Term Fold** Use the FoldNote that you made at the beginning of the chapter to study the key terms for this chapter. See if you know all of the definitions. When you have reviewed the terms, use each term in a sentence.

READING TOOLBOX

USING KEY TERMS

Use each of the following terms in a separate sentence.

2. *uniformitarianism*
3. *varve*
4. *radiometric dating*
5. *half-life*

For each pair of terms, explain how the meanings of the terms differ.

6. *relative age* and *absolute age*
7. *law of superposition* and *law of crosscutting relationships*
8. *trace fossil* and *index fossil*

UNDERSTANDING KEY IDEAS

9. Varves are layers of
   a. limestone mixed with coarse sediments.
   b. alternating coarse and fine sediments.
   c. fossils.
   d. sediments that have gaps that represent missing time in the rock sequence.
10. An unconformity that results when new sediments are deposited on eroded horizontal layers is a(n)
   a. angular unconformity.
   b. disconformity.
   c. crosscut unconformity.
   d. nonconformity.
11. A fault or intrusion is younger than the rock it cuts through, according to the
   a. type of unconformity.
   b. law of superposition.
   c. law of crosscutting relationships.
   d. principle of uniformitarianism.
12. The age of a rock in years is the rock's numerical age, or
   a. index age. **c.** half-life age.
   b. relative age. **d.** absolute age.
13. A gap in the sequence of rock layers is a(n)
   a. bedding plane.
   b. varve.
   c. unconformity.
   d. uniformity.
14. The process by which the remains of an organism are preserved by drying is called
   a. petrification. **c.** erosion.
   b. mummification. **d.** superposition.
15. Molds that fill with sediment sometimes produce
   a. casts. **c.** coprolites.
   b. gastroliths. **d.** carbon films.

SHORT ANSWER

16. What prompted James Hutton to formulate the principle of uniformitarianism?
17. Describe how the law of superposition helps scientists determine relative age.
18. Compare and contrast the three types of unconformities.
19. How do scientists use radioactive decay to determine absolute age?
20. Besides radiometric dating, what are three other methods of estimating absolute age?
21. List and describe five ways that organisms can be preserved.
22. List the four characteristics that define an index fossil.

CRITICAL THINKING

23. **Making Inferences** James Hutton developed the principle of uniformitarianism by observing geologic changes on his farm. What changes might he have observed?
24. **Applying Ideas** How might a scientist determine the original positions of the sedimentary layers beneath an angular unconformity?

18. All are breaks in the geologic record. A nonconformity is the boundary between new sedimentary rock on top of uplifted and eroded igneous or metamorphic rock. An angular unconformity occurs when horizontal rock layers are tilted and eroded. The layers below the unconformity are not parallel to rock layers above the unconformity. A disconformity is an unconformity in which the layers below the unconformity are parallel to the layers above the unconformity.
19. Scientists know the half-life (rate of decay) of radioactive isotopes. By comparing the relative percentages of a radioactive (parent) isotope in a rock and a stable (daughter) isotope they can calculate the time at which the rock formed.
20. Three other methods of estimating absolute age are using rates of erosion, using rates of deposition, and counting varves.
21. Organisms can be preserved by mummification, or drying; by being trapped in tree sap, which hardens into amber; by being trapped and preserved in a tar seep; by freezing in ice or soil; or by petrification, a process in which minerals in groundwater replace original organic material and solidify into rock.
22. An index fossil must occur in rocks spread over a wide area; it must have features that distinguish it clearly from other fossils; it must have existed during a relatively short geologic time span; and it must occur in large numbers.

25. **Analyzing Relationships** One intrusion cuts through all the rock layers. Another intrusion is eroded and lies beneath several layers of sedimentary rock. Which intrusion is younger? Explain your answer.
26. **Analyzing Concepts** A fossil that has unusual features is found in many areas on Earth. It represents a brief period of geologic time but occurs in small numbers. Would this fossil make a good index fossil? Explain.
27. **Making Comparisons** Compare the processes of mummification and freezing.

CONCEPT MAPPING

28. Use the following terms to create a concept map: *relative age, law of superposition, unconformity, law of crosscutting relationships, absolute age, radiometric dating, carbon dating,* and *index fossil.*

MATH SKILLS

Math Skills

29. **Making Calculations** Scientists know that 1 million grams of ^{238}U will undergo radioactive decay to produce 1/7,600 g of ^{206}Pb per year. How many grams of ^{238}U would be left after 1 million years?
30. **Applying Quantities** A sample contains 1,000 g of an isotope that has a half-life of 500 years. How many half-lives will have to pass before the sample contains less than 10 g of the parent isotope?
31. **Making Calculations** The half-life of ^{238}U is 4.5 billion years. How many years would 16 g of ^{238}U take to decay into 0.5 g of ^{238}U and 15.5 g of daughter products?

WRITING SKILLS

32. **Writing Persuasively** Imagine that you are James Hutton. Write a letter to a fellow scientist to convince him or her of the validity of the principle of uniformitarianism.
33. **Outlining Topics** Describe what happens to the amount of an isotope as it undergoes radioactive decay through three half-lives.

INTERPRETING GRAPHICS

The illustration below shows crosscutting relationships in an outcrop of rock. Use this illustration to answer the questions that follow.

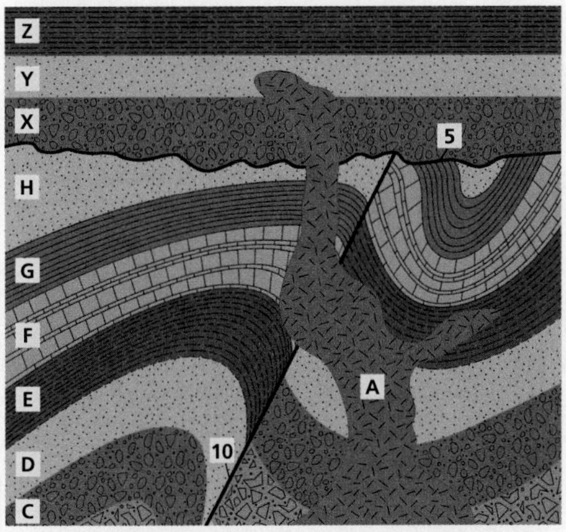

34. Is intrusion A older or younger than fault 10? Explain your answer.
35. What type of unconformity does feature 5 represent? Explain your answer.
36. Which rock formation is older: layer X or layer Y? Explain your answer.

Chapter Review

Critical Thinking

23. Answers may vary. Sample answer: He may have observed erosion and deposition over the years on his farm. He might also have noticed rock strata and concluded that they resembled layers of sediment that he saw building up through deposition.
24. Answers may vary but should state that scientists know that the rocks were originally deposited in horizontal layers and that structures such as cross-beds, ripple marks, and graded bedding can help them identify the original orientation of the layers.
25. The intrusion that cuts through all the rock layers is younger according to the law of crosscutting relationships. The other intrusion is older because it has eroded and more layers have been deposited above it.
26. Answers may vary. Sample answer: If the fossil was rare and could not be found easily in rock in different areas, it would not make a good index fossil.
27. Mummification and freezing are similar in that in both the whole body is preserved and does not decay because bacteria cannot decompose the body. However, mummification tends to occur in hot, dry regions, and freezing occurs in cold, dry regions.

Concept Mapping

28. Answers may vary but should include all of the terms listed. Sample answers appear at the end of this unit on page 253A.

Math Skills

29. 1/7,600 g/y × 1,000,000 y = 1,000,000 y/7,600 y/g = 131.58 g of ^{238}U has decayed; 1,000,000 g − 131.58 g = 999,868.42 g of ^{238}U remains
30. 7 half-lives or 3,500 years
31. Five half-lives, or 5 × 4.5 billion years = 22.5 billion years

Writing Skills

32. Answers may vary. Accept all reasonable answers.
33. Answers may vary. Accept all reasonable answers.

Interpreting Graphics

34. The intrusion is younger because it cuts through the fault.
35. angular unconformity; The layers below the unconformity are folded and are tilted where they are cut by the unconformity.
36. Layer X is older, because layer Y is on top of it.

Estimated Time

To give students practice under more realistic testing conditions, allow them 30 minutes to answer all of the questions in this practice test.

Test Doctor

Question 2 Answer F is correct. To answer correctly, students must recall the difference between the different types of fossils. Direct evidence of dietary habits can be found in coprolites—the fossilized dung from ancient animals.

Question 3 Answer B is correct. To answer correctly, students must recall the difference between absolute age and relative age. Answers A, C, and D are incorrect because they focus on finding the relative age of rock, not the absolute age of rock.

Question 10 Full-credit answers should include the following points:

- fossils that include the soft parts of animals are rare and may include impressions of organs or muscles
- scientists can use these animal parts to learn more about the internal structures and body systems of ancient animals
- scientists can compare the internal systems of ancient animals to the internal systems of modern animals in order to see how different animals and body systems have changed over time

Chapter 8 Standardized Test Prep

Understanding Concepts

Directions (1–5): For each question, write on a separate sheet of paper the letter of the correct answer.

1. A scientist used radiometric dating during an investigation. The scientist used this method because she wanted to determine the
 A. relative ages of rocks.
 B. absolute ages of rocks.
 C. climate of a past era.
 D. fossil types in a rock.

2. Fossils that provide direct evidence of the feeding habits of ancient animals are known as
 F. coprolites.
 G. molds and casts.
 H. carbon films.
 I. trace fossils.

3. One way to estimate the absolute age of rock is
 A. nonconformity.
 B. varve count.
 C. the law of superposition.
 D. the law of crosscutting relationships.

4. To be an index fossil, a fossil must
 F. be present in rocks that are scattered over a small geographic area.
 G. contain remains of organisms that lived for a long period of geologic time.
 H. occur in small numbers within the rock layers.
 I. have features that clearly distinguish it from other fossils.

5. Which of the following statements best describes the relationship between the law of superposition and the principle of original horizontality?
 A. Both describe the deposition of sediments in horizontal layers.
 B. Both conclude that Earth is more than 100,000 years old.
 C. Both indicate the absolute ages of layers of rock.
 D. Both recognize that the geologic processes in the past are the same as those at work now.

Directions (6): Write a short response to this question.

6. What is the name of a type of fossil that can be used to establish the age of rock?

Reading Skills

Directions (7–10): Read the passage below. Then, answer the questions on a separate sheet of paper.

Illinois Nodules

Around 300 million years ago, the region that is now Illinois had a very different climate. Swamps and marshes covered much of the area. Scientists estimate that no fewer than 500 species lived in this ancient environment. Today, the remains of these organisms are found preserved within structures known as nodules. Nodules are round or oblong structures that are usually composed of cemented sediments. Sometimes, these nodules contain the fossilized hard parts of plants and animals. The Illinois nodules are extremely unusual because many contain finely detailed impressions of the soft parts of the organisms together with the hard parts. Because they are rare, these nodules are desired for their incredible scientific value and may be found in fossil collections around the world.

7. According to the passage above, which of the following statements about nodules is correct?
 F. Nodules are rarely round or oblong.
 G. Nodules are usually composed of cemented sediments.
 H. Nodules are rarely found outside of Illinois.
 I. Nodules always contain fossils.

8. What is the most unusual feature of the nodules found in modern-day Illinois?
 A. their bright coloration
 B. the fact that they come in many more unusual shapes that other nodules
 C. the fact that they contain both the soft and hard parts of animals
 D. their extremely heavy weight

9. Which of the following statements can be inferred from the information in the passage?
 F. Illinois nodules are sought by scientists.
 G. Nodules can be purchased from the state.
 H. Similar nodules can be found in nearby Iowa.
 I. Nodules contain dinosaur fossils.

10. What might scientists learn from a nodule that contains the soft and hard parts of an animal?

Question 11 Answer B is correct. Students should be able to apply their own knowledge of how half-lives work to the chart to determine that it will take 2 half-lives for the number of daughter atoms to be 3 times the number of parent atoms. As the chart shows, after one half-life the amounts of daughter and parent atoms will be equal. After two half-lives the parent atoms atoms will have lost 75% of their original total, making up only 25% of the sample.

Question 13 Full-credit answers should include the following points:

- structure X is a simple fault—which, by definition, is younger than the rock it cuts through
- rock layer B must have formed before fault X occurred
- rock layer A is the youngest structure shown on the diagram. The unbroken layer on top is the youngest structure shown in the diagram. This layer must have formed after the fault. If it had formed before the fault, it would be broken in the same way that the other rock layers were broken

Interpreting Graphics

Directions (11–13): For each question below, record the correct answer on a separate sheet of paper.

The graph below shows the rate of radioactive decay. Use this graph to answer question 11.

Radioactive Decay

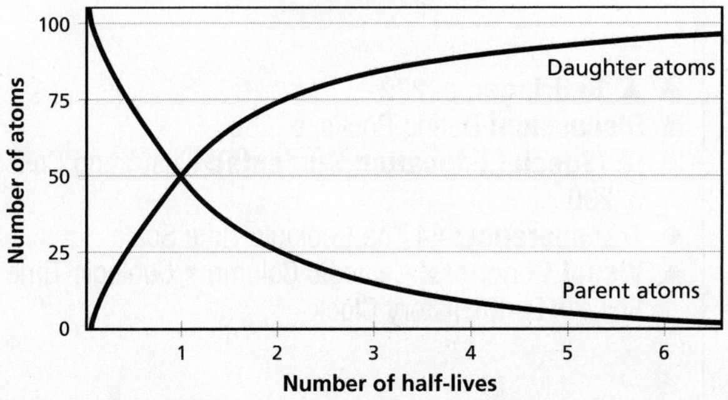

11. How many half-lives have passed when the number of daughter atoms is approximately three times the number of parent atoms?

A. one
B. two
C. three
D. four

The diagram below shows crosscutting taking place in layers of rock. Use this diagram to answer questions 12 and 13.

Layers of Rock with a Crosscutting Fault

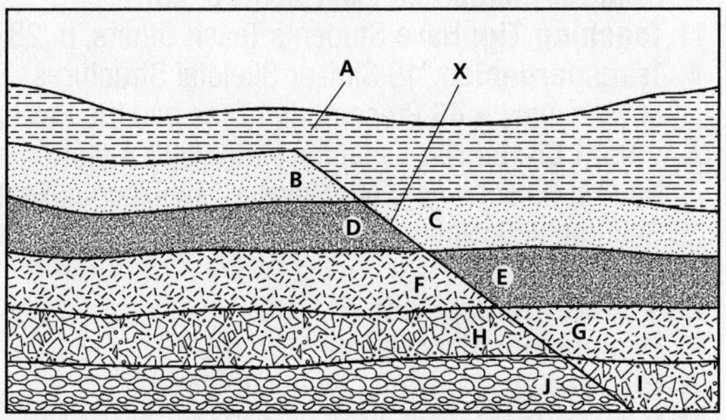

12. Which two layers belonged to the same layer of rock before the fault disrupted the layer?

F. C and D
G. C and F
H. G and I
I. G and F

13. Which is older, structure B or structure X? Explain your answer. What structure shown on the diagram is the youngest?

Test Tip

If time permits, take short mental breaks to improve your concentration during a test.

Using THINK central Resources

State Resources

- For specific resources for your state, visit www.thinkcentral.com and type in the keyword **HSHSTR.**

Answers

Understanding Concepts

1. C
2. F
3. B
4. I
5. A
6. index fossil

Reading Skills

7. G
8. C
9. F
10. Answers may vary. See Test Doctor for a detailed scoring rubric.

Interpreting Graphics

11. B
12. I
13. Answers may vary. See Test Doctor for a detailed scoring rubric.

Chapter Planner 9 A View of Earth's Past

	Standards	Teach Key Ideas
Chapter Opener, pp. 226–227 **45 min.**	National Science Education Standards	
Section 1 Geologic Time, pp. 229–232 **45 min.** ❯ The Geologic Column ❯ Divisions of Geologic Time	HNS 3c, ES 3b, ES 3d, SAI 2c, LS 3a, LS 3b, LS 3c	■ ▲ **Bellringer,** p. 229 ■ **Discussion:** Dating Rocks, p. 230 ■ **DI (Special Education Students):** Illustrating Concepts, p. 230 ◆ **Transparency:** 44 The Geologic Time Scale ▲ **Visual Concepts:** Geologic Column • Geologic Time Scale • Earth-History Clock
Section 2 Precambrian Time and the Paleozoic Era, pp. 233–238 **45 min.** ❯ Evolution ❯ Precambrian Time ❯ The Paleozoic Era	ES 3d, LS 3a, LS 3b, LS 3c	■ ◆ **Bellringer,** p. 233 ■ **DI (Special Education Students):** Geologic Timeline, p. 234 ■ **Discussion:** Drawing Conclusions, p. 235 ■ **DI (Advanced Learners):** Survivor: The Real Story, p. 235 ■ **Discussion:** Body of Evidence, p. 236 ■ **DI (Basic Learners):** Paleozoic Life-Forms, p. 236 ■ **Debate:** The Current Extinction?, p. 237 ■ **Teaching Tip:** Have Students Teach Others, p. 237 ◆ **Transparencies:** 45 Similar Skeletal Structures of Mammals • 46 Precambrian Time and the Paleozoic Era ▲ **Visual Concepts:** Evolution • Darwin's Theories • Natural Selection in Four Steps • Homologous Features • Geographic Isolation
Section 3 The Mesozoic and Cenozoic Eras, pp. 239–244 **45 min.** ❯ The Mesozoic Era ❯ The Cenozoic Era	LS 3c	■ ◆ **Bellringer,** p. 239 ■ **Discussion:** More Resources?, p. 239 ■ **Discussion:** Flowering Plants, p. 241 ■ **Debate:** Dinosaur Extinction, p. 241 ■ **DI (Struggling Readers):** Word Parts, p. 241 ■ **DI (Struggling Readers/Basic Learners):** Pattern Puzzles, p. 242 ■ **Homework:** Horse History, p. 243 ◆ **Transparencies:** 47 The Mesozoic and Cenozoic Eras • 48 Fossil Evidence for Gondwanaland ▲ **Visual Concepts:** Mass Extinction
Chapter Wrap-Up, pp. 249–253 **90 min.**		**Chapter Summary,** p. 249

See also PowerNotes® Presentations

CHAPTER Fast Track *To shorten instruction because of time limitations, omit Sections 2 and 3.*

Key
Teacher's Edition ■ Teaching Transparencies ◆
Chapter Resource File ● Online Edition ▲

All resources listed below are also available on the **Teacher One Stop™.**

Why It Matters	Hands-On	Skills Development	Assessment
■ **Chapter Overview,** p. 226 ■ **Using the Figure:** *Hypacrosaurus*, p. 226	**Inquiry Lab:** Exploring Geologic Evidence, p. 227	**Reading Toolbox,** p. 228	
■ **Section Overview,** p. 229 ■ **Using the Figure:** Rock Layers, p. 229	**QuickLab:** Geologic Time Scale, p. 230 **Skills Practice Lab:** History in the Rocks, pp. 246–247 ● **Making Models Lab:** Future Earth	**Reading Toolbox:** Temporal Language, p. 230 ■ **Skill Builder:** Vocabulary, p. 231 ■ ● **Internet Activity:** Extinct Organisms, p. 231 ● **Internet Activity:** Imaging Technologies	**Reading Check,** p. 229 **Section Review,** p. 232 ■ **Reteaching,** p. 231 ■ **Quiz,** p. 232 ■ **DI (Alternative Assessment):** Descriptive Essay, p. 232 ● **Section Quiz**
■ **Section Overview,** p. 233 ■ **Using the Figure:** Comparing Bones, p. 233 ■ **Using the Figure:** Geologic Time, p. 234 ■ **Environmental Connection:** Marine Mammal Evolution, p. 234 **Long-Term Survivors,** p. 234 ■ **Using the Figure:** Sea to Land, p. 237	**QuickLab:** Chocolate Candy Survival, p. 235	**Reading Toolbox:** Spider Map, p. 237 ■ ● **Internet Activity:** Supercontinents, p. 236	**Reading Check,** p. 234 **Reading Check,** p. 236 **Section Review,** p. 238 ■ **Reteaching,** p. 237 ■ **Quiz,** p. 238 ■ **DI (Alternative Assessment):** Television Script, p. 238 ● **Section Quiz**
■ **Section Overview,** p. 239 ■ **Using the Figure:** Comparing Characteristics, p. 240 ■ **Why It Matters:** The Dinosaur in the Birdcage?, p. 240 ■ **Using the Figure:** Mammal Characteristics, p. 242 ■ **Biology Connection:** Primitive Mammals, p. 242 ■ **Why It Matters:** Circumpolar Waters, p. 243	■ **Group Activity:** Dinosaur Map, p. 248 ● **Inquiry Lab:** Dinosaur Hunt	■ **Reading Skill Builder:** Reading Organizer, p. 240 ■ ● **Internet Activity:** Online Museums, p. 241 **Reading Toolbox:** Prefixes, p. 242 ■ **Skill Builder:** Math, p. 242 **Maps in Action:** Fossil Evidence for Gondwanaland, p. 248	**Reading Check,** p. 240 **Reading Check,** p. 243 **Section Review,** p. 244 ■ **Reteaching,** p. 243 ■ **Quiz,** p. 243 ■ **DI (Alternative Assessment):** Timeline, p. 244 ● **Section Quiz**
Reconstructing the Past, p. 245		▲ **Super Summary** **Standardized Test Prep,** pp. 252–253	**Chapter Review,** pp. 250–251 ■ **DI (Alternative Assessment):** Science Consultants, p. 249 ● **Chapter Tests**

See also Lab Generator

See also Holt Online Assessment Resources

Chapter Overview

Earth is billions of years old, and its changes and the evolution of its life-forms have been divided into time periods. This chapter explains geologic time and describes how Earth and its life forms have changed over geologic time.

Using the Figure GENERAL

Hypacrosaurus This illustration shows what one type of dinosaur that lived more than 65 million years ago may have looked like. Ask students how the artist knew what colors to use for the dinosaurs' skin. (The artist did not know the skin color for sure. This type of illustration requires some artistic freedom.) LS **Visual/Logical**

Why It Matters

Artists base their concepts of a dinosaur's appearance on the fossil record. Fossilized bones allow reconstruction of the skeleton. Muscle attachment scars on the bones allow reconstruction of a dinosaur's musculature. However, the colors and patterns of the dinosaur's skin remain unknown.

Chapter 9 A View of Earth's Past

Chapter Outline

1 **Geologic Time**
- The Geologic Column
- Divisions of Geologic Time

2 **Precambrian Time and the Paleozoic Era**
- Evolution
- Precambrian Time
- The Paleozoic Era

3 **The Mesozoic and Cenozoic Eras**
- The Mesozoic Era
- The Cenozoic Era

Virginia Standards of Learning
ES.1.c
ES.2.d
ES.9.b
ES.9.c
ES.9.d

Why It Matters

The rock and fossil records show that Earth's surface is constantly changing. Fossils provide valuable information about extinct organisms. This illustration shows an artist's idea of how a mother *Hypacrosaurus* might have looked as she fed her hatchlings. Because fossils do not record such characteristics as skin color, they are left to our imagination.

Chapter Correlations — *Virginia Standards of Learning*

ES.1.c scales, diagrams, charts, graphs, tables, imagery, models, and profiles are constructed and interpreted.
ES.2.d evidence is evaluated for scientific theories.
ES.9.b superposition, cross-cutting relationships, index fossils, and radioactive decay are methods of dating bodies of rock.
ES.9.c absolute and relative dating have different applications but can be used together to determine the age of rocks and structures.
ES.9.d rocks and fossils from many different geologic periods and epochs are found in Virginia.

Inquiry Lab

20 min

Exploring Geologic Evidence

Obtain a **box** from your teacher. Use a **spoon** to dig carefully through the layers in the box to find "fossils." Transfer material removed from the box to a sheet of **newspaper**. Record the layer in which each fossil was found. Sketch the layers, including the number and type of each fossil found, to produce a geologic history.

Questions to Get You Started

1. Which fossils are the oldest? How do you know?
2. Which fossils are found only in older layers? What are possible reasons for this distribution?

Inquiry Lab

Central Concept: Students model a paleontological dig using a shoebox pre-prepared with layers of material containing small objects that represent fossils. Students use their data to construct a geologic column.

Teacher's Notes: When preparing the boxes, place the "fossils" in the layers in a way that represents the extinction of older species and the appearance of newer ones. You may wish to assign one student in each group to be responsible for digging, one student to sketch the layers, and one student to record types of fossils in the layers.

Materials: (per group)
- Pre-prepared box with layers containing objects to represent fossils
- spoon
- sheet of newspaper

Skills Acquired
- Analyzing Relationships
- Interpreting Models
- Communicating

Answers to Getting Started
1. The oldest fossils are in the bottom layer, because that layer formed first.
2. Answers may vary but may include the organism's extinction or moving away from the area.

Using THINK central Resources

An online version of this chapter, as well as all the print and multimedia resources that accompany the program are available to registered teachers and their students. Log onto www.thinkcentral.com to access these materials and tools to organize your preparation and student learning.

READING TOOLBOX

Prefixes

Term	Prefix	Meaning of Prefix
Mesozoic	meso-	in the middle; intermediate
Cenozoic	ceno-	recent
Proterozoic	protero-	before; earlier; former
Phanerozoic	phanero-	visible; manifest; open

Temporal Language

Answers may vary. Temporal words and phrases indicating a specific time include *542 million years ago* and *today*; indicating duration, *during that time* and *several hundred million years*; indicating frequency, *rate* and *rarely*; and indicating sequence, *timeline* and *first.*

READING TOOLBOX

These reading tools will help you learn the material in this chapter.

Word Parts

Prefixes Many scientific words contain prefixes or suffixes that come from Latin and Greek. You can use the meanings of prefixes and suffixes to help you figure out the meanings of science terms.

The term *Paleozoic Era* contains the prefix *paleo-*, from the Greek word *palaio,* meaning "ancient," and the suffix *-zoic,* from the Greek word *zoe,* meaning "life." The Paleozoic Era is the time in which many early forms of life became abundant.

Your Turn As you read this chapter, make a table of terms containing a prefix and the suffix *-zoic*. Using a dictionary, enter the meanings of the prefixes in the table.

TERM	PREFIX	MEANING OF PREFIX
Paleozoic Era	paleo-	ancient
Mesozoic Era	meso-	
Cenozoic Era		

Describing Time

Temporal Language Temporal language is language that is used to describe time. Paying careful attention to temporal language can help you understand events and processes in the environment.

Your Turn Make a two-column table. As you read this chapter, look for words and phrases that refer to time. Write these words and phrases in the first column of your table. In the second column, write whether each word or phrase describes a specific time, duration, frequency, or sequence of events.

TEMPORAL WORD	DESCRIBES...
19th century	specific time
timeline	sequence
rate	frequency

Graphic Organizers

Spider Maps Spider maps show how details are organized into categories that relate to a main idea.

To make a spider map, follow these steps.

1. Write a main topic title, and draw an oval around it.
2. From the oval, draw legs. Each leg represents a category of the main topic.
3. From each leg, draw horizontal lines. Write details about each category on these lines.

Your Turn As you read Section 1, complete a spider map like the one started here to organize the ideas you learn about the geologic column.

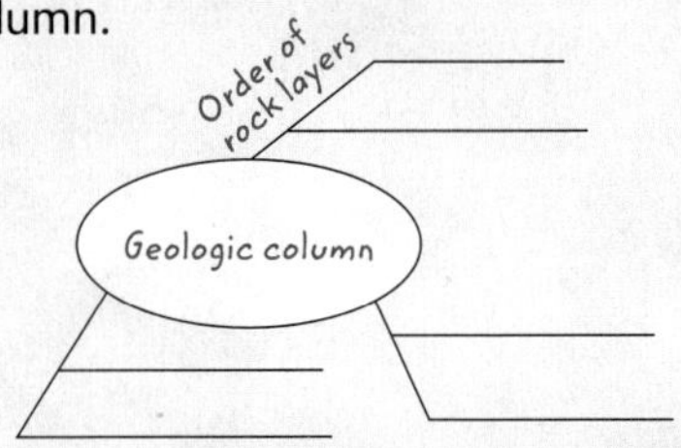

For more information on how to use these and other tools, see **Appendix A.**

Spider Map

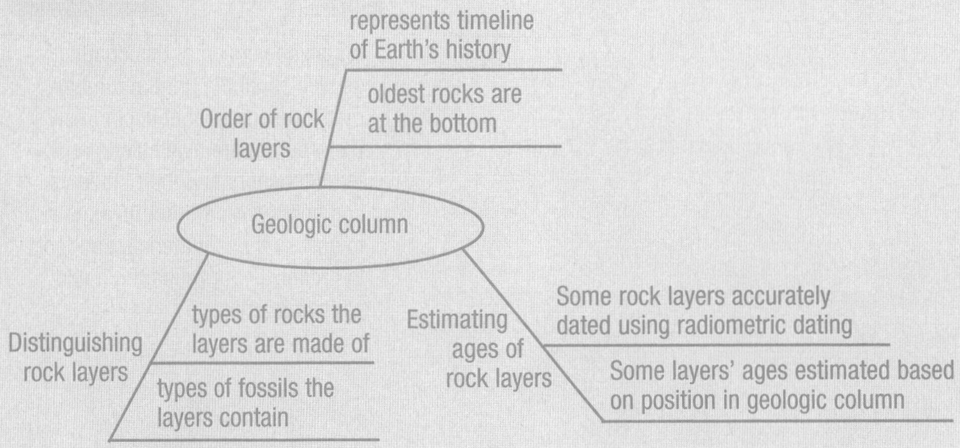

SECTION 1

Geologic Time

Key Ideas	Key Terms	Why It Matters
❯ Summarize how scientists worked together to develop the geologic column. ❯ List the major divisions of geologic time.	**geologic column** **era** **period** **epoch**	The geologic time scale provides a framework for understanding the geologic processes that shape our planet.

Earth's surface is constantly changing. Mountains form and erode; oceans rise and recede. As conditions on Earth's surface change, some organisms flourish and then later become extinct. Evidence of these changes is recorded in the rock layers of Earth's crust. To describe the sequence and length of these changes, scientists have developed a *geologic time scale*. This scale outlines the development of Earth and life on Earth.

The Geologic Column

By studying fossils and applying the principle that old layers of rock are below young layers, 19th-century scientists determined the relative ages of sedimentary rock in different areas around the world. No single area on Earth contained a record of all geologic time. So, scientists combined their observations to create a standard arrangement of rock layers. As shown in the example in **Figure 1,** this ordered arrangement of rock layers is called a **geologic column.** A geologic column represents a timeline of Earth's history. The oldest rocks are at the bottom of the column.

Rock layers in a geologic column are distinguished by the types of rock the layers are made of and by the kinds of fossils the layers contain. Fossils in the upper, more-recent layers resemble modern plants and animals. Most of the fossils in the lower, older layers are of plants and animals that are different from those living today. In fact, many of the fossils discovered in old layers are from species that have been extinct for millions of years.

geologic column an ordered arrangement of rock layers that is based on the relative ages of the rocks and in which the oldest rocks are at the bottom

THINK central INTERACT ONLINE (Keyword: HQXVEPF1)

Reading Check **Where would you find fossils of extinct animals on a geologic column?**
(See Appendix G for answers to Reading Checks.)

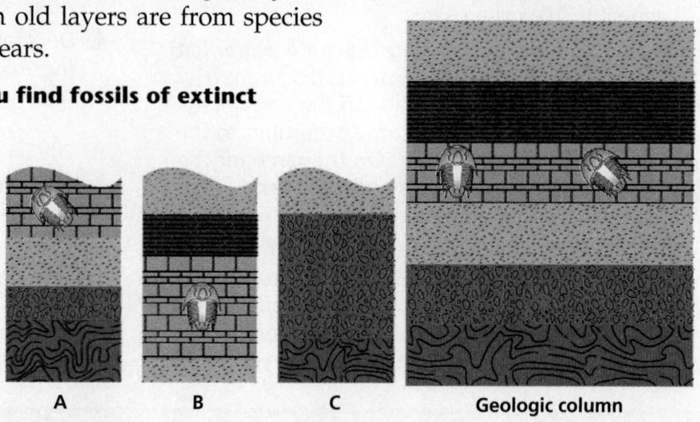

Figure 1 By combining observations of rock layers in areas A, B, and C, scientists can construct a geologic column. ***Why is relative position important for determining the ages of rock layers?***

Section 1

Focus

Overview

This section describes what geologic time is and how scientists divide geologic time.

Bellringer

Ask students to think about and list or describe what types of changes they think might have taken place on Earth during its more than 4-billion-year history. (Answers may vary. Accept all reasonable answers.) LS **Verbal**

Motivate

Using the Figure GENERAL

Rock Layers Have students examine and talk about the figure on this page. Then, use the question in the caption as the starting point for a discussion about geologic time. Answer to caption question: Relative position can tell you the relative ages of rock layers. LS **Visual**

Answer to Reading Check

You would find fossils of extinct animals in older layers of a geologic column.

Key Resources

Chapter Resource File

- Directed Reading BASIC
- Making Models Lab: Future Earth GENERAL

Technology

- Transparencies
  Bellringer

Teach

Discussion ADVANCED

Dating Rocks Tell students that, over time, Earth processes move and fold rocks. Have students discuss why radiometric dating technology is so useful to paleontologists. (It allows them to give numeric dates to rock layers.)

READING TOOLBOX

Temporal Language
Answers may vary. Temporal words and phrases include *after*, *lasted*, and *65 million years ago*.

Quick Lab

Skills Acquired
- Measuring
- Identifying and Recognizing Patterns

Materials
- Paper
- 5-m strip of adding-machine paper
- Meterstick
- Metric ruler
- Pencil
- Colored pencils

Teacher's Notes: You may wish to review with students how to use a scale in which one measure represents another, in this case, a period of time.

Answers to Analysis
1. Humans first appeared in the Pleistocene Epoch. The scale length is less than 2 mm.
2. The Paleozoic, Mesozoic, and Cenozoic Eras cover about 542 million years, or about 12% of geologic time. The Precambrian Era represents about 88% of geologic time.

Figure 2 This scientist is collecting rock samples that contain fossilized fungal spores that date the rock to the Triassic Period.

Academic Vocabulary
investigate (in VES ti geyt) to examine or study an object in detail in an attempt to learn the facts about it

READING TOOLBOX

Temporal Language
As you read in this section about the various divisions of geologic time, make a table that describes the temporal language that is used.

Using a Geologic Column

When the first geologic columns were being developed, scientists estimated the ages of rock layers by using factors such as the average rates of sediment deposition. The development of radiometric dating methods, however, allowed scientists to determine the absolute ages of rock layers with more accuracy.

Scientists can now use geologic columns to estimate the ages of rock layers that cannot be dated radiometrically. To determine the age of a given rock layer, scientists compare the rock layer with a similar layer in a geologic column that contains the same fossils or that has the same relative position. If the two layers match, they likely formed at about the same time. The scientist in **Figure 2** is investigating the ages of sedimentary rocks.

Divisions of Geologic Time

The geologic history of Earth is marked by major changes in Earth's surface, climate, and types of organisms. Geologists use these indicators to divide the geologic time scale into smaller units. Rocks grouped within each unit contain similar fossils. In fact, a unit of geologic time is generally characterized by fossils of a dominant lifeform. A simplified geologic time scale is shown in **Table 1.**

Because Earth's history is so long, geologists commonly use abbreviations when they discuss geologic time. For example, Ma stands for *mega-annum*, which means "million years."

Quick Lab 30 min

Geologic Time Scale

Procedure

1. Copy the table shown at right onto a piece of **paper**.
2. Complete the table by using the scale 1 cm is equal to 10 million years.
3. Lay a **5-m strip of adding-machine paper** flat on a hard surface. Use a **meterstick**, a **metric ruler**, and a **pencil** to mark off the beginning and end of Precambrian time according to the time scale you calculated. Do the same for the three eras. Label each time division, and color each a different color with **colored pencils**.
4. Pick two periods from the geologic time scale. Using the same scale that was used in step 2, calculate the scale length for each period listed. Mark the boundaries of each period on the paper strip, and label the periods on your scale.

Era	Length of time (years)	Scale length
Precambrian	4,058,000,000	
Paleozoic	291,000,000	DO NOT WRITE
Mesozoic	185,500,000	IN THIS BOOK
Cenozoic	65,500,000 (to present)	

5. Decorate your strip by adding names or drawings of the organisms that lived in each division of time.

Analysis

1. When did humans appear? What is the scale length from that time to the present?
2. Add the lengths of the Paleozoic, Mesozoic, and Cenozoic Eras. What percentage of the geologic time scale do these combined eras represent? What percentage of the geologic time scale does Precambrian time represent?

Differentiated Instruction

Special Education Students

Illustrating Concepts Have students draw and label pictures to accompany the text. Students should use all of the key terms that appear in bold type throughout the chapter as labels. They may also write descriptions on their pictures that help them remember key concepts in the chapter. **LS Visual/Verbal**

Table 1 Geologic Time Scale

Era	Period	Epoch	Beginning of interval in Ma	Characteristics from geologic and fossil evidence
Cenozoic	**Quaternary**	**Holocene**	0.0115	The last glacial period ends; complex human societies develop.
		**Pleistocene**	1.8	Woolly mammoths, rhinos, and humans appear.
	Tertiary	**Pliocene**	5.3	Large carnivores (bears, lions) appear.
		Miocene	23.0	Grazing herds are abundant; raccoons and wolves appear.
		Oligocene	33.9	Deer, pigs, camels, cats, and dogs appear.
		Eocene	55.8	Horses, flying squirrels, bats, and whales appear.
		Paleocene	65.5	Age of mammals begins; first primates appear.
Mesozoic	**Cretaceous**		146	Flowering plants and modern birds appear; mass extinctions mark the end of the Mesozoic Era.
	**Jurassic**		200	Dinosaurs are the dominant life-form; primitive birds and flying reptiles appear.
	Triassic		251	Dinosaurs appear; ammonites are common; cycads and conifers are abundant; mammals appear.
Paleozoic	**Permian**		299	Pangaea comes together; mass extinctions mark the end of the Paleozoic Era.
	**Carboniferous**	**Pennsylvanian Period**	318	Giant cockroaches and dragonflies are common; coal deposits form; reptiles appear.
		Mississippian Period	359	Amphibians flourish; brachiopods are common in oceans; forests and swamps cover most land.
	Devonian		416	Age of fishes begins; amphibians appear; giant horsetails, ferns, and seed-bearing plants develop.
	Silurian		444	Eurypterids, land plants and animals appear.
	Ordovician		488	Echinoderms appear; brachiopods increase; trilobites decline; graptolites flourish.
	Cambrian		542	Shelled marine invertebrates appear; trilobites and brachiopods are common; first vertebrates appear; atmosphere reaches modern O_2-rich state.
Precambrian time			4,600	Earth forms; continental shields appear; fossils are rare; cyanobacteria are the most common organism.

MISCONCEPTION ALERT

The Human Time Frame Some students may be under the impression that humans coexisted with dinosaurs, or with even earlier life-forms. Explain to students that hominids have been on Earth for less than 2 million years and that the dinosaurs became extinct 65 million years ago.

Skill Builder — GENERAL

Vocabulary Tell students that the suffix *-zoic* is related to the word "zoo." The suffix *-zoic* refers to the life-forms that existed during a specific geologic time. Many geologic time periods are named after the organisms that were common on Earth during that time.
LS Verbal/Auditory English Language Learners

Close

Reteaching — BASIC

Relative Time Have the class make a large poster or mural that shows the relative scale of each geologic eon and era they learn about in this chapter. The project will help them understand that each division is defined, not by a given time (that is, all eons or eras are not of equal length), but by the organisms that dominated during that time period. Students may label and describe each geologic time period on the poster or mural. **LS Visual/Kinesthetic**

Key Resources

Technology
- Transparencies
  44 The Geologic Time Scale

Internet Activity — GENERAL

Extinct Organisms Have students work in groups to find pictures of organisms that were common during one geologic period. Each group member may look for pictures of one organism or one class of organisms. Have students create posters that show the life-forms they researched. Invite advanced students to write about the characteristics of organisms from their time period. A worksheet designed to direct student research on this topic can be found in the **Chapter Resource File** booklet or by visiting www.thinkcentral.com and entering the keyword **HQXVEPX.** **LS Visual/Verbal** Co-op Learning

Close, *continued*

Quiz GENERAL

1. In a geologic column, where would you expect to find the oldest fossils? (in the older rock layers)
2. On what are most geologic time divisions based? (on the organisms that dominated in that time period)
3. Why do scientists use radiometric dating for rocks? (It provides an absolute, or numerical, age.)

Answers to Section Review

1. They had to work together because different rocks occur in different parts of the world.
2. Answers may vary. Sample answer: In the Devonian period, fishes dominated Earth and amphibians first appeared.
3. A geologic column is useful because it shows the relative ages of rocks and fossils.
4. year, age, epoch, period, era, eon
5. Paleozoic Era: 291 million years; Mesozoic Era: 186 million years; Cenozoic Era: 65.5 million years
6. The geologic column follows geologic time in that it consists of the rocks that formed during each division of geologic time.
7. The scientist would want to know the age of the rock in which the fossil was found.
8. It would change because we would have to rethink the entire evolution of animals and of conditions on Earth back to the Paleozoic.
9. *Geologic time* can be divided into *Precambrian time*, the *Paleozoic Era*, the *Mesozoic Era*, and the *Cenozoic Era*, which are each divided into shorter time units called *periods*, which include even shorter time units called *epochs*.

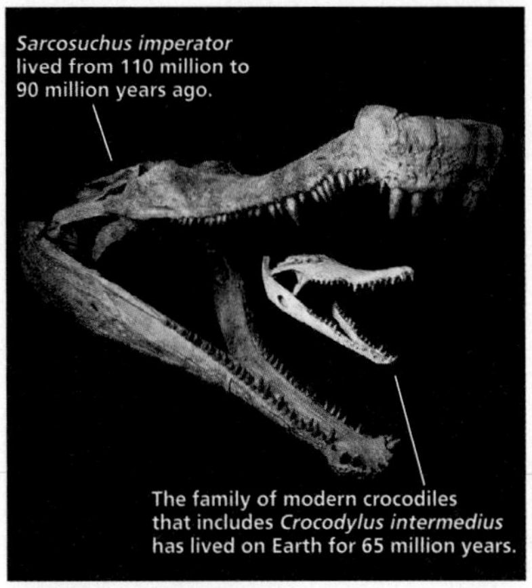

Sarcosuchus imperator lived from 110 million to 90 million years ago.
The family of modern crocodiles that includes *Crocodylus intermedius* has lived on Earth for 65 million years.

Figure 3 Crocodilians have lived on Earth for more than two geologic eras without major anatomical changes.

Eons and Eras

The largest unit of geologic time is an *eon*. Geologic time is divided into four eons: the Hadean Eon, the Archean Eon, the Proterozoic Eon, and the Phanerozoic Eon. The first three eons of Earth's history are part of a time interval commonly known as *Precambrian time*. This 4-billion-year interval contains most of Earth's history. Very few fossils exist in early Precambrian rocks, so dividing Precambrian time into smaller time units is difficult.

After Precambrian time, the Phanerozoic Eon began. This eon, as well as most eons, is divided into smaller units of geologic time called **eras.** The first era of the Phanerozoic Eon was the *Paleozoic Era,* which lasted about 291 million years. Paleozoic rocks contain fossils of a wide variety of marine and terrestrial life-forms. After the Paleozoic Era, the *Mesozoic Era* began and lasted about 186 million years. Mesozoic fossils include early forms of birds and reptiles, such as the giant crocodilian shown in **Figure 3.** The present geologic era is the *Cenozoic Era*, which began about 65 million years ago. Fossils of mammals are common in Cenozoic rocks.

Periods and Epochs

era a unit of geologic time that includes two or more periods

period a unit of geologic time that is longer than an epoch but shorter than an era

epoch a subdivision of geologic time that is longer than an age but shorter than a period

Eras are divided into shorter time units called **periods.** Each period is characterized by specific fossils and is usually named for the location in which the fossils were first discovered. Where the rock record is most complete and least deformed, a detailed fossil record may allow scientists to divide a period into shorter time units called **epochs.** An epoch may be divided into smaller units of time called *ages*. Ages are defined by the occurrence of distinct fossils in the fossil record.

Section 1 Review

Key Ideas

1. **Summarize** the reasons why many scientists had to work together to develop the geologic column.
2. **Describe** the major events in any one period of geologic time.
3. **Explain** why constructing geologic columns is useful to Earth scientists.
4. **List** the following units of time in order of length from shortest to longest: *year, period, era, eon, age,* and *epoch.*
5. **Name** the three eras of the Phanerozoic Eon, and identify how long each one lasted.
6. **Compare** geologic time with the geologic column.

Critical Thinking

7. **Analyzing Relationships** When a scientist discovers a new type of fossil, what characteristic of the rock around the fossil would he or she want to learn first?
8. **Predicting Consequences** How would our understanding of Earth's past change if a scientist discovered a mammal fossil from the Paleozoic Era?

Concept Mapping

9. Use the following terms to create a concept map: *geologic time, Precambrian time, Paleozoic Era, Mesozoic Era, Cenozoic Era, period,* and *epoch.*

Differentiated Instruction

Alternative Assessment

Descriptive Essay Have students use the time scale table as a starting point to write an essay that describes the history of life on Earth.
LS **Verbal/Logical**

SECTION 2

Precambrian Time and the Paleozoic Era

Key Ideas	Key Terms	Why It Matters
› Summarize how evolution is related to geologic change. › Identify two characteristics of Precambrian rock. › Identify one major geologic and two major biological developments during the Paleozoic Era.	**evolution** **Precambrian time** **Paleozoic Era**	The rock and fossil records show that Earth changes over time. One of these changes allowed the oxygen we breathe to begin accumulating in the atmosphere.

History is a record of past events. Just as the history of civilizations is written in books, the geologic history of Earth is recorded in rock layers. The types of rock and the fossils that occur in each layer reveal information about the environment when the layer formed. For example, the presence of a limestone layer in an area indicates that the area was once covered by water.

Evolution

Fossils indicate the kinds of organisms that lived when rock formed. By examining rock layers and fossils, scientists have discovered evidence that species of living things have changed over time. Scientists call this process evolution. **Evolution** is the gradual development of new organisms from preexisting organisms. Scientists think that evolution occurs by means of natural selection. Evidence for evolution includes the similarity in skeletal structures of animals, as shown in **Figure 1.** The theory of evolution by natural selection was proposed in 1859 by Charles Darwin, an English naturalist.

evolution the process of change by which new species develop from preexisting species over time

Evolution and Geologic Change

Major geologic and climatic changes can affect the ability of some organisms to survive. For example, dramatic changes in sea level greatly affect organisms that live in coastal areas. By using geologic evidence, scientists try to determine how environmental changes affected organisms in the past. The fossil record shows that some organisms survived environmental changes, while other organisms disappeared. Scientists use fossils to learn why some organisms survived long periods of time without changing, while other organisms changed or became extinct.

Figure 1 Bones in the front limbs of these animals are similar, even though the limbs are used in different ways. Similar structures indicate a common ancestor.

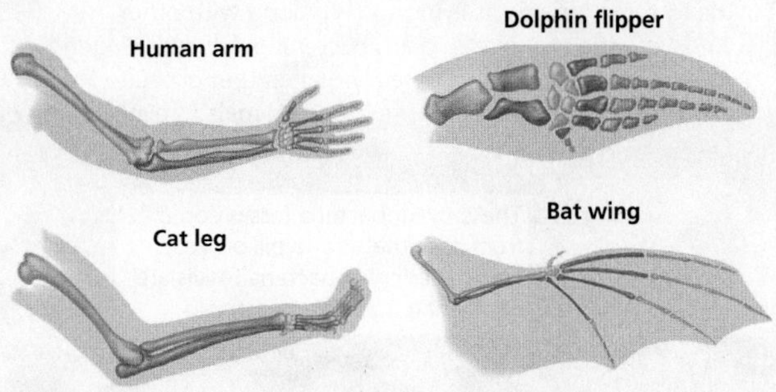

Section 2

Focus

Overview

This section describes how biological evolution is related to geologic changes. It also describes the evolution of life forms during Precambrian time and the Paleozoic Era.

Bellringer

Invite students to speculate how changing conditions on Earth, such as an ice age or rising sea levels, would lead to physical changes in plants and animals. Invite students to use their imaginations in describing these changes. (Answers may vary. Accept all reasonable answers.) **LS Logical/Verbal**

Motivate

Using the Figure — GENERAL

Comparing Bones Have students examine the front limb bones shown in the figure. Ask them to describe the similarities and differences in the bones of the four animals. Ask students to describe any evidence that indicates that these animals had a common ancestor. (Students may point out differences in bone length, but should also describe similarities in the number of bones and their placement in each of the front limb skeletons.)
LS Visual/Logical

Key Resources

Chapter Resource File
- Directed Reading BASIC

Technology
- Transparencies
  Bellringer
  45 Similar Skeletal Structures of Mammals

Teach

Using the Figure GENERAL

Geologic Time Tell students that the timescale at the top of the page shows the relative lengths of the eras to scale. To answer the caption question, students will have to calculate the distance represented by an interval of time, such as 2 mm = 65 million years. Answer to caption question: 3,650 million years ago (3.65 billion years ago) **LS Visual/Logical**

Why It Matters

Long-Term Survivors

Cyanobacteria often grow in colonies and secrete a substance forming a thick cell wall. These characteristics aid the trapping of sediment, which can enhance fossilization. In addition to helping to add free oxygen to Earth's early atmosphere, cyanobacteria formed a symbiotic relationship with eukaryotic cells, leading to the evolution of both chloroplasts and mitochondria.

Answer to Your Turn

Cyanobacteria and other early photosynthetic organisms added oxygen to the atmosphere.

Answer to Reading Check

Earth is approximately 4.6 billion years old.

Key Resources

Technology

- Transparencies
  46 Precambrian Time and the Paleozoic Era

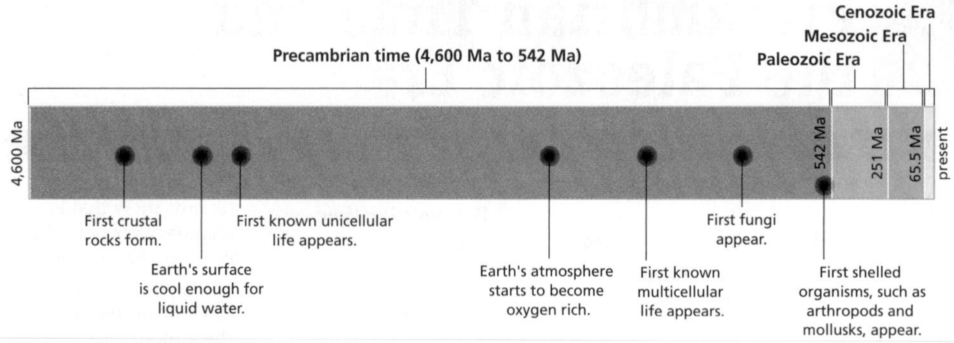

Cenozoic Era
Mesozoic Era
Precambrian time (4,600 Ma to 542 Ma)
Paleozoic Era
4,600 Ma
542 Ma
251 Ma
65.5 Ma
present
First crustal rocks form.
First known unicellular life appears.
Earth's surface is cool enough for liquid water.
Earth's atmosphere starts to become oxygen rich.
First known multicellular life appears.
First fungi appear.
First shelled organisms, such as arthropods and mollusks, appear.

Figure 2 Precambrian Timeline *How many million years ago did the first unicellular life appear?*

Precambrian time the interval of time in the geologic time scale from Earth's formation to the beginning of the Paleozoic era, from 4.6 billion to 542 million years ago

Precambrian Time

Most scientists agree that Earth formed about 4.6 billion years ago as a large cloud, or *nebula*, spun around the newly formed sun. As material spun around the sun, particles of matter began to clump together and eventually formed Earth and the other planets of the solar system. The time interval that began with the formation of Earth and ended about 542 million years ago is known as **Precambrian time.** This division of geologic time makes up about 88% of Earth's history, as shown in **Figure 2.**

Even though Precambrian time makes up such a large part of Earth's history, we know relatively little about what happened during that time. We lack information partly because the Precambrian rock record is difficult to interpret. Most Precambrian rocks have been so severely deformed and altered by tectonic activity that the original order of rock layers is rarely identifiable.

Reading Check **How old is Earth?**

Why It Matters

Long-Term Survivors

EYE ON THE ENVIRONMENT

Some species alive today have survived for billions of years. Cyanobacteria—sometimes called blue-green bacteria—are one important example. Earth's early atmosphere contained no free oxygen, so it would be toxic to most organisms living today. Along with other photosynthetic organisms, cyanobacteria produced oxygen that built up in the atmosphere. This alteration of the atmosphere allowed oxygen-breathing animals to evolve.

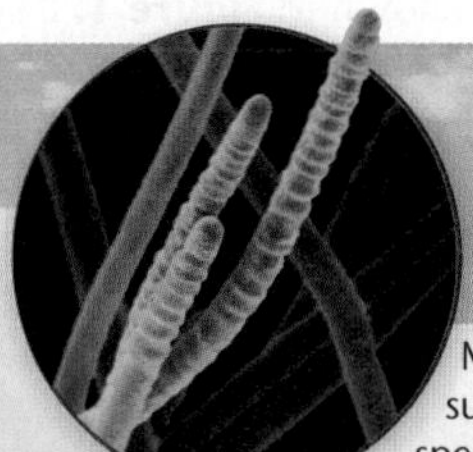

Modern cyanobacteria such as these belong to species that have survived essentially unchanged through the vast span of geologic time.

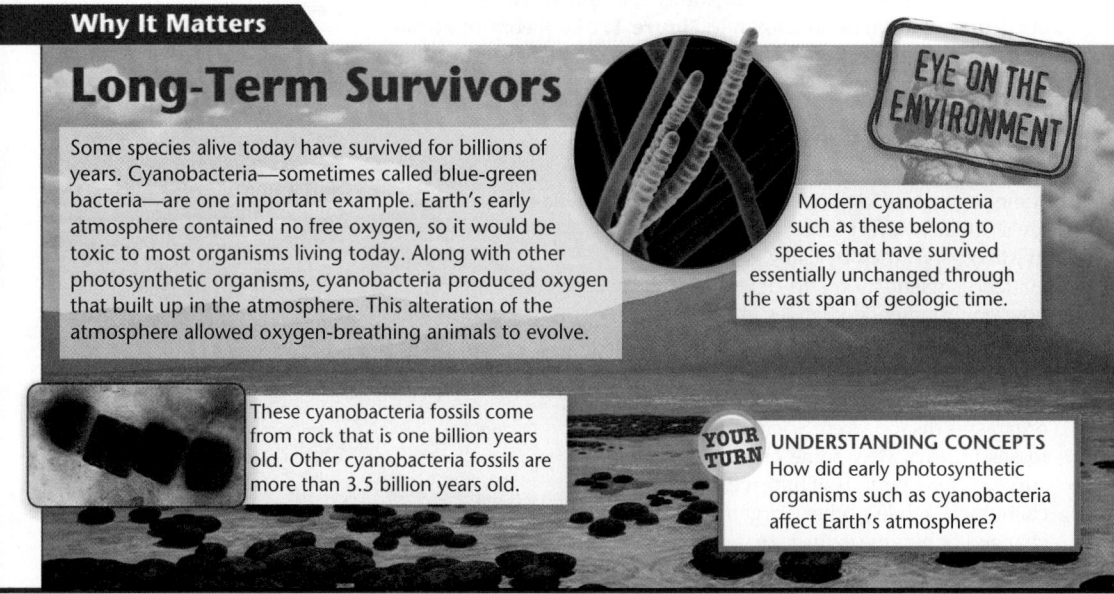

These cyanobacteria fossils come from rock that is one billion years old. Other cyanobacteria fossils are more than 3.5 billion years old.

YOUR TURN UNDERSTANDING CONCEPTS
How did early photosynthetic organisms such as cyanobacteria affect Earth's atmosphere?

Environmental Connection

Marine Mammal Evolution Scientists think that about 50 million years ago, the land environment changed and less food was available to land herbivores. As a result, ancient relatives of today's hoofed mammals, which likely resembled modern pigs or cows, increasingly sought food along the seashore. As more of these ancient animals came to the seaside to feed, competition may have forced some to swim farther out and to dive deeper in the water to find food. Marine mammals evolved from these ancient ungulates in less than 8 million years.

Differentiated Instruction

Special Education Students

Geologic Timeline Pair each visually impaired student with a non-visually impaired student. Have the sighted student tape a toothpick above the time division lines on a copy of the geologic timeline. As the visually impaired student runs a finger over the timeline, the sighted student explains what time period the space between the toothpicks represents. Have students discuss the relative lengths of time periods based on the space between the toothpicks. **LS Kinesthetic**

Precambrian Rocks

Large areas of exposed Precambrian rocks, called *shields*, exist on every continent except Antarctica. Precambrian shields are the result of several hundred million years of volcanic activity, mountain building, sedimentation, and metamorphism. After they were metamorphosed and deformed, the rocks of North America's Precambrian shield were uplifted and exposed at Earth's surface. Nearly half of the valuable mineral deposits in the world occur in the rocks of Precambrian shields. These valuable minerals include nickel, iron, gold, and copper.

Figure 3 Stromatolites contain layers of sediments that are cemented together by mats of cyanobacteria. Cyanobacteria are the most common Precambrian fossils.

Precambrian Life

Fossils are rare in Precambrian rocks, probably because Precambrian life-forms lacked bones, shells, or other hard parts that commonly form fossils. Also, Precambrian rocks are extremely old. Some date back nearly 3.9 billion years. Over this long period of time, volcanic activity, erosion, and extensive crustal movements, such as folding and faulting, probably destroyed most of the fossils that may have formed during Precambrian time.

Of the few Precambrian fossils that have been discovered, the most common are cyanobacteria in *stromatolites*, or layered, reef-like deposits. Stromatolites form today in warm, shallow waters, as shown in **Figure 3.** The presence of stromatolites in Precambrian rocks indicates that shallow seas covered much of Earth during intervals of Precambrian time. Fossils of marine worms, jellyfish, and single-celled organisms have also been discovered in rocks from late Precambrian time.

Academic Vocabulary

expose (eks POHZ) to present to view; to reveal; to uncover

Quick Lab — Chocolate Candy Survival

10 min

Procedure

1. Lay a piece of colorful cloth on a table.
2. Randomly sprinkle a handful of candy-coated chocolate bits on the cloth.
3. Look away for 1 min; then look back.
4. For 10 s, pick up chocolate bits one at a time. Record the colors of candy you picked up.
5. Repeat steps 1–4 with a piece of colorful cloth that has a different pattern.

Analysis

1. What colors were you more likely to pick up in the first trial? What about those candies made you pick them up?
2. When you changed the color of the cloth, did the color of the candies you picked up change?
3. How could camouflage help an organism survive?

Quick Lab

Skills Acquired

- Observing
- Analyzing

Materials

- 2 pieces of colorful cloth with different patterns
- Candy-coated chocolate bits

Teacher's Notes: You may want to make sure that the cloths closely match at least one color of candy-coated chocolate bits or that the cloth has a colorful and busy pattern. This lab can also be performed by using circles of construction paper instead of candy and extending the time in step 4 to 20 s.

Answers to Analysis

1. Students are more likely to pick up the candy that did not match the cloth color because it was most easily seen.
2. Students likely picked up different color candy when it was on a different color cloth.
3. By blending into the background (the cloth), the camouflaged candy was not eaten. This applies to prey animals in the wild; camouflage helps them avoid predators.

Differentiated Instruction

Advanced Learners

Survivor: The Real Story Have students research cyanobacteria to find out what makes these life-forms so successful at survival and to find out where stromatolites are forming on Earth today. Have students prepare an illustrated report to present to the class.

Discussion — GENERAL

Drawing Conclusions Have a group discussion with students about why cyanobacteria in stromatolites are the most abundant Precambrian fossils. Invite students to refer to the figure to draw conclusions about the physical characteristics that enable stromatolites to fossilize. Have students talk about how stromatolites are similar to and different from the coral reefs that occur in today's oceans. (Stromatolites are produced by cyanobacteria that form sticky mats, which trap carbonate mud. These structures may be preserved.) LS **Verbal/Visual**

Teach, continued

Internet Activity — ADVANCED

Supercontinents Have groups of interested students use the Internet to research supercontinents that preceded Pangaea. Invite one group to research the events that led to the creation of Rodinia (the name is Russian for "homeland"), a supercontinent that existed from 1.1 billion to 750 million years ago. Have students in this group create a map and locate today's continents as they existed in Rodinia. A second group of students should map the opening of the Panthalassic Ocean, the separation of Pannotia and the Congo craton, and the formation of Laurentia, Gondwana, and Baltica. Again, students may want to find current continents in these prehistoric landforms. Have groups present their findings to the class.
A worksheet designed to direct student research on this topic can be found in the **Chapter Resource File** booklet or by visiting www.thinkcentral.com and entering the keyword **HQXVEPX.**
LS Verbal/Logical

Answer to Reading Check

Answers may vary but should include three of the following: trilobites, brachiopods, jellyfish, worms, snails, and sponges.

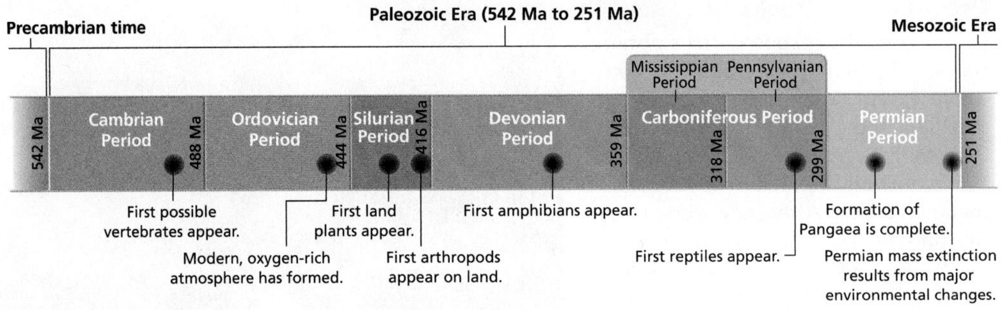

Figure 4 Paleozoic Timeline

The Paleozoic Era

Paleozoic Era the geologic era that followed Precambrian time and that lasted from 542 million to 251 million years ago

As shown in **Figure 4,** the geologic era that began about 542 million years ago and ended about 251 million years ago is called the **Paleozoic Era.** At the beginning of the Paleozoic Era, Earth's landmasses were scattered around the world. By the end of the Paleozoic Era, these landmasses had collided to form the supercontinent Pangaea. This tectonic activity created new mountain ranges and lifted large areas of land above sea level.

Unlike Precambrian rocks, Paleozoic rocks hold an abundance of fossils. The number of plant and animal species on Earth increased dramatically at the beginning of the Paleozoic Era. Because of this rich fossil record, North American geologists have divided the Paleozoic Era into six periods.

The Cambrian Period

The Cambrian Period is the first period of the Paleozoic Era. A variety of marine life-forms appeared during this period. These Cambrian life-forms were more advanced than previous life-forms and quickly displaced the primitive organisms as the dominant life-forms. The explosion of Cambrian life may have been partly due to the warm, shallow seas that covered much of the continents during the time period. Marine *invertebrates,* or animals that do not have backbones, thrived in the warm waters. The most common of the Cambrian invertebrates were *trilobites,* such as the one shown in **Figure 5.** Scientists use many trilobites as *index fossils* to date rocks to the Cambrian Period.

Figure 5 During the early Paleozoic Era, various types of trilobites, such as this fossilized trilobite of the genus *Modocia,* flourished in the warm, shallow seas.

Another group of common animals in the Cambrian Period were the *brachiopods,* which are shelled animals. Fossils indicate that at least 15 different families of brachiopods existed during this period. A few kinds of brachiopods exist today, but modern brachiopods are rare. Other Cambrian invertebrates included worms, jellyfish, snails, and sponges. However, little evidence of land-dwelling plants or animals has been discovered in Cambrian rocks.

Reading Check **Name three common invertebrates from the Cambrian Period.**

Discussion — BASIC

Body of Evidence Have students discuss why the bodies of some ancient animals, such as shelled invertebrates, are well fossilized, while those of other animals, such as non-shelled invertebrates are not, or are poorly fossilized. Ask students what key body characteristic increases an organism's likelihood of being fossilized. (Animals that have hard body parts, such as shells, teeth, or bones, are far more likely to be preserved as fossils than animals whose bodies are entirely soft. Soft tissue decays far more readily and rapidly than shell or bone does.) **LS Verbal**

Differentiated Instruction

Basic Learners

Paleozoic Life-Forms Have students choose a Paleozoic organism to research. Then, have them create a poster or brochure describing the organism and the environment in which it lived. Have students present their posters or brochures to the class.

Figure 6 During the Silurian Period, eurypterids lived in shallow lagoons. Eurypterids had one pair of legs for swimming and had four or five pairs for walking.

The Ordovician Period

During the Ordovician (AWR duh VISH uhn) Period, the number of trilobite species began to shrink. Brachiopods, bryozoans, and cephalopod mollusks became the dominant invertebrate lifeforms. Large numbers of corals appeared. Colonies of tiny invertebrates called *graptolites* also flourished in the oceans, and primitive fish appeared. By this period, *vertebrates*, or animals that have backbones, had appeared. The most primitive vertebrates were fish. Unlike modern fish, Ordovician fish did not have jaws or teeth, and their bodies were covered with thick, bony plates. During the Ordovician Period, as during the Cambrian Period, there was little plant life on land.

The Silurian Period

Vertebrate and invertebrate marine life continued to thrive during the Silurian Period. Echinoderms, relatives of modern sea stars, and corals became more common. Scorpion-like sea creatures called *eurypterids* (yoo RIP tuhr IDZ), such as the one shown in **Figure 6,** also existed during the Silurian Period. Fossils of giant eurypterids about 2 m long have been discovered in western New York. Near the end of this period, the earliest vascular land plants as well as animals, such as scorpions, evolved on land.

The Devonian Period

The Devonian Period is called the *Age of Fishes* because fossils of many bony fishes were discovered in rocks of this period. One type of fish, called a *lungfish,* had the ability to breathe the air. Other air-breathing fish, called *rhipidistians* (RIE puh DIS tee uhnz), had strong fins that may have allowed them to crawl onto the land for short periods of time. Early amphibians probably evolved from rhipidistians. *Ichthyostega* (IK thee oh STEG uh), early amphibians that resembled huge salamanders, are thought to be the ancestors of modern amphibians such as frogs and toads. During the Devonian Period, land plants, such as giant horsetails, ferns, and seed-bearing plants, also began to develop. In the sea, brachiopods and mollusks continued to thrive.

READING TOOLBOX

Spider Map
Make a spider map that has six legs and several lines on each leg. Use the map to describe the six periods in the Paleozoic Era.

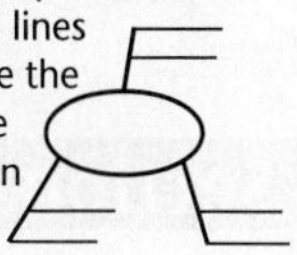

Using the Figure — GENERAL

Sea to Land Have students describe the eurypterid shown in the figure. Then, show students a large picture of a modern scorpion (with its legs apparent). Ask students what similarities they see in the two animals. Ask them to generate a hypothesis about why legs developed on the Silurian eurypterids, and then to speculate how this adaptation likely led to the emergence of the earliest scorpion-like animals on land. (Answers may vary. Eurypterids likely developed legs for moving around on the sea bottom or in shallow water. The evolution of legs used in the water enabled the first arthropods that left the water to move around on land.) **LS Visual/Logical**

READING TOOLBOX

Answers may vary. Students' spider maps should have legs for and details about the Cambrian, Ordovician, Silurian, Devonian, Carboniferous, and Permian Periods.

Close

Reteaching — BASIC

Life in the Paleozoic Tape a large, long sheet of paper to the board to represent the Paleozoic Era. Have students divide the paper into periods and then draw organisms that lived during each period. Students should label each period and each animal they draw. **LS Visual/Kinesthetic**

Debate — ADVANCED

The Current Extinction? Some scientists today think that 50% of all modern species will be extinct in a matter of a few centuries, which could make this event the worst mass extinction ever. Divide students into two groups. Have one group research and support the idea that a mass extinction is *not* occurring at this time. Have the other group research and support the idea that the worst mass extinction in Earth's history *is* occurring now. Then, have the groups debate in front of the class. **LS Verbal**

Teaching Tip — ADVANCED

Have Students Teach Others The evolution of lungs, which enabled animal life to thrive on land, is one of the major steps in the evolution of life on Earth. Have students research the evolution of lungs from gills. Invite them to give an illustrated presentation to the class to explain how this evolutionary change occurred. **LS Verbal**

Close, *continued*

Quiz GENERAL

1. What is an index fossil? (a common fossil that defines a geologic time interval)
2. What is the origin of most of the coal we use today? (compacted plants of the Carboniferous Period)
3. When did the first primitive lungs develop in animals? (in the Devonian Period)

Answers to Section Review

1. Geologic changes result in changing environmental conditions. As a result, populations either evolve or become extinct.
2. Most Precambrian rocks are highly deformed and contain few fossils.
3. Most Precambrian organisms were tiny and soft bodied. Also, the rocks are highly deformed and altered from their original state.
4. Cambrian: trilobites; Ordovician: mollusks; Silurian: echinoderms; Devonian: fishes; Carboniferous: amphibians; Permian: reptiles
5. Many types of fossil fishes have been found in rocks from this period.
6. Life-forms that became extinct during the Permian Period include many types of marine invertebrates.
7. When Pangaea formed, inland seas disappeared and organisms that lived in those seas evolved or became extinct.
8. The fossil record of Precambrian time contains few organisms.
9. The fossil record shows that life-forms from later geologic times have physical characteristics that could have resulted from the adaptation of organisms from earlier geologic times. Also, as the environment changed, new organisms appeared and others became extinct.
10. The *Paleozoic Era* is divided into seven periods, including the *Cambrian Period*, during which invertebrates dominated; the *Ordovician Period*, during which vertebrates became dominant; and the *Silurian Period*.

Figure 7 During the Carboniferous Period, crinoids, such as the one shown here, were common in the oceans. Crinoids are thought to be ancestors of modern animals called sea lillies.

The Carboniferous Period

During the Carboniferous Period, the climate was generally warm, and the humidity was at times very high over most of the world. Forests and swamps covered much of the land. Coal deposits in Pennsylvania, Ohio, and West Virginia are the fossilized remains of these forests and swamps. During this period, the rock in which some major oil deposits occur also formed. *Carboniferous* means "carbon bearing." In North America, the Carboniferous Period is divided into the Mississippian and Pennsylvanian Periods.

Amphibians and fish continued to flourish during the Carboniferous Period. *Crinoids*, like the one shown in **Figure 7**, were common in the oceans. Insects, such as giant cockroaches and dragonflies, were common on land. Toward the end of the Carboniferous Period, vertebrates that were adapted to life on land appeared. These early reptiles resembled large lizards.

The Permian Period

The Permian Period marks the end of the Paleozoic Era. A *mass extinction* of a large number of Paleozoic life-forms occurred at the end of the Permian Period. The continents had joined to form the supercontinent Pangaea. The collision of tectonic plates created the Appalachian Mountains. On the northwest side of the mountains, areas of desert and dry savanna climates developed. The shallow inland seas that had covered much of Earth disappeared. As the seas retreated, many species of marine invertebrates, including trilobites and eurypterids, became extinct. However, fossils indicate that reptiles and amphibians survived the environmental changes and dominated Earth in the millions of years that followed the Paleozoic Era.

Section 2 Review

Key Ideas

1. **Summarize** how evolution is related to geologic change.
2. **Identify** two characteristics of most Precambrian rocks.
3. **Explain** why fossils are rare in Precambrian rocks.
4. **Identify** one life-form from each of the six periods of the Paleozoic Era.
5. **Explain** why the Devonian Period is commonly called the *Age of Fishes*.
6. **Describe** the kinds of life-forms that became extinct during the mass extinction at the end of the Permian Period.

Critical Thinking

7. **Drawing Conclusions** Identify one way in which the formation of Pangaea affected Paleozoic life.
8. **Identifying Relationships** Why is Precambrian time—about 88% of geologic time—not divided into smaller units based on the fossil record?
9. **Analyzing Processes** Explain two ways in which the geologic record of the Paleozoic Era supports the theory of evolution.

Concept Mapping

10. Use the following terms to create a concept map: *Paleozoic Era, invertebrate, Cambrian Period, Ordovician Period, vertebrate,* and *Silurian Period.*

Differentiated Instruction

Alternative Assessment

Television Script Have students write a television script for a show about conditions and life during the Paleozoic Era. Students may read their scripts aloud to the class.
LS **Verbal/Auditory**

SECTION 3 The Mesozoic and Cenozoic Eras

Key Ideas	Key Terms	Why It Matters
❯ List the periods of the Mesozoic and Cenozoic Eras. ❯ Identify two major geologic and biological developments during the Mesozoic Era. ❯ Identify two major geologic and biological developments during the Cenozoic Era.	**mass extinction** **Mesozoic Era** **Cenozoic Era**	The movement of tectonic plates and the evolution and extinction of organisms have shaped the world we live in today. Our world continues to change as these processes continue.

At the end of the Permian Period, 90% of marine organisms and more than 70% of land organisms died. This episode during which an enormous number of species died, or **mass extinction,** left many resources available for the surviving life-forms. Because resources and space were readily available, an abundance of new life-forms appeared. These new life-forms evolved, and some flourished while others eventually became extinct.

The Mesozoic Era

As shown in **Figure 1,** the geologic era that began about 251 million years ago and ended about 65 million years ago is called the **Mesozoic Era.** Earth's surface changed dramatically during the Mesozoic Era. As Pangaea broke into smaller continents, the tectonic plates drifted and collided. These collisions uplifted mountain ranges such as the Sierra Nevada in California and the Andes in South America. Shallow seas and marshes covered much of the land. In general, the climate was warm and humid.

Conditions during the Mesozoic Era favored the survival of reptiles. Lizards, turtles, crocodiles, snakes, and a variety of dinosaurs flourished during the Mesozoic Era. Thus, this era is also known as the *Age of Reptiles*. The Mesozoic Era has a rich fossil record and is divided into three periods.

mass extinction an episode during which large numbers of species become extinct

Mesozoic Era the geologic era that lasted from 251 million to 65.5 million years ago; also called the *Age of Reptiles*

Figure 1 Mesozoic Timeline

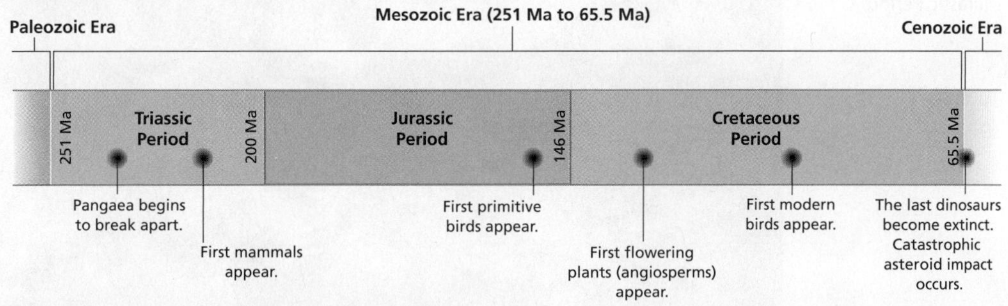

Paleozoic Era
Mesozoic Era (251 Ma to 65.5 Ma)
Cenozoic Era
251 Ma
Triassic Period
200 Ma
Jurassic Period
146 Ma
Cretaceous Period
65.5 Ma
Pangaea begins to break apart.
First mammals appear.
First primitive birds appear.
First flowering plants (angiosperms) appear.
First modern birds appear.
The last dinosaurs become extinct. Catastrophic asteroid impact occurs.

Section 3

Focus

Overview

This section describes the conditions and the organisms of the Mesozoic Era and introduces the concept of mass extinction. The section discusses the life-forms of the Cenozoic Era and its periods and epochs, including the emergence of humans.

Bellringer

Ask students to identify movies, TV shows, or books in which dinosaurs or the Mesozoic Era have been portrayed. Have students decide whether they think the movie, TV show, or book was a realistic representation of the time period. (Answers may vary. Accept all reasonable answers.)

Motivate

Discussion — GENERAL

More Resources? Invite students to discuss why there would be more, not fewer, resources available after a mass extinction or after a period during which a large percentage of species died out. (The resources previously used by all of the extinct species now would become available to other organisms.) **LS Logical/Verbal**

Key Resources

Chapter Resource File

- Directed Reading BASIC
- Inquiry Lab: Dinosaur Hunt GENERAL
- Internet Activity: Online Museums GENERAL

Technology

- Transparencies
  Bellringer
  47 The Mesozoic and Cenozoic Eras

Teach

Using the Figure GENERAL

Comparing Characteristics Have students examine the picture of the *Archaeopteryx* on this page. Invite them to describe the physical characteristics of this Jurassic animal. Ask them to explain the similarities they observe between the *Archaeopteryx* and modern birds. (Students should note the similarities in head and beak shape, eye placement, the bones of the wings, and the preserved image of the feathers extending from the skeleton.)
LS Visual/Verbal

Reading Skill Builder BASIC

Reading Organizer Have students make a three-column chart. Have them label the columns with "Period," "Life-Forms," and "Characteristics." Have students fill in the chart as they read this page and the next page, listing the life-forms and their unique characteristics for each period of the Mesozoic Era. Students may also draw pictures of the life-forms and their characteristics in the appropriate column, next to the written description. English Language Learners
LS Verbal/Visual

Answer to Reading Check
Answers may vary but could include *Archaeopteryx*, pterosaurs, *Apatosaurus*, and *Stegosaurus*.

Figure 2 A group of dinosaurs of the genus *Coelophysis* race through a Triassic conifer forest in what is now New Mexico.

The Triassic Period

Dinosaurs flourished during the Triassic Period of the Mesozoic Era. Some dinosaurs were the size of squirrels. Others weighed as much as 15 tons and were nearly 30 m long. However, most of the dinosaurs of the Triassic Period were about 2 m to 5 m long and moved very quickly. As shown in **Figure 2,** these dinosaurs roamed through lush forests of cone-bearing trees and *cycads*, which are thick-stemmed plants with crowns of fern-like leaves.

Reptiles called *ichthyosaurs* lived in the Triassic oceans. New forms of marine invertebrates also evolved. The most distinctive was the ammonite, a type of shellfish that is similar to the modern nautilus. Ammonites serve as Mesozoic index fossils. The first mammals, small rodent-like forest dwellers, also appeared.

Academic Vocabulary
dominant (DAHM uh nuhnt) having the greatest effect; most numerous

The Jurassic Period

Dinosaurs became the dominant life-form during the Jurassic Period. Fossil records indicate that two major groups of dinosaurs evolved. These groups are distinguished by their hip-bone structures. One group, called *saurischians*, or "lizard-hipped" dinosaurs, included herbivores, which are plant eaters, and carnivores, which are meat eaters. Among the largest saurischians were herbivores of the genus *Apatosaurus*, once known as *Brontosaurus*, which weighed up to 50 tons and grew up to 25 m long.

The other major group of Jurassic dinosaurs, called *ornithischians*, or "bird-hipped" dinosaurs, were herbivores. Among the best known of the ornithischians were herbivores of the genus *Stegosaurus*, which were about 9 m long and about 3 m tall at the hips. In addition, flying reptiles called *pterosaurs* were common during the Jurassic Period. Like modern bats, pterosaurs flew on skin-covered wings. Fossils of the earliest birds, such as the one shown in **Figure 3,** also occur in Jurassic rocks.

Reading Check **Name two fossils that were discovered in the fossil record of the Jurassic Period.**

Figure 3 The *Archaeopteryx* (AWR kee AUP tuhr IKS) was one of the first birds that appeared during the Jurassic Period.

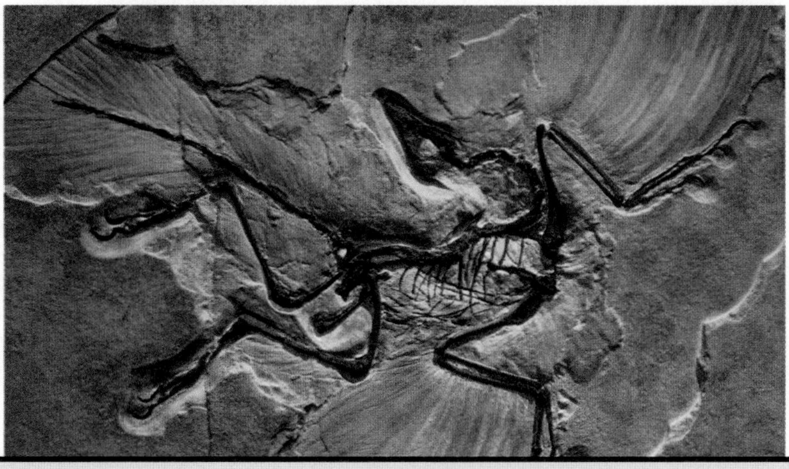

Why It Matters

The Dinosaur in the Birdcage? Though still hotly debated, there is some evidence that birds are the descendents of dinosaurs—that, in effect, dinosaurs did not die out, because some evolved into birds. The most compelling evidence of this connection is the morphological similarity between dinosaurs and birds. In addition, some dinosaur species formed huge nesting colonies, as do many of today's birds. Young hatched from eggs, and recent evidence suggests that dinosaur parents raised their young in the nest, bringing them food until they grew old enough to leave the nest. This behavior is common among birds but not among modern reptiles, whose young generally fend for themselves once they hatch. In contrast, many scientists doubt the bird-dinosaur connection and think that dinosaurs formed a third group, unlike either modern reptiles or birds.

Figure 4 This 12.5-m-long *Tyrannosaurus rex* was discovered near Faith, South Dakota. This specimen, named Sue, was displayed in the Field Museum in Chicago in 2000.

The Cretaceous Period

Dinosaurs continued to dominate Earth during the Cretaceous Period. Among the most spectacular dinosaurs was the carnivore *Tyrannosaurus rex*, such as the one shown in **Figure 4.** The *Tyrannosaurus rex* stood nearly 6 m tall and had huge jaws with sharp teeth that were up to 15 cm long. Also, among the common Cretaceous dinosaurs were the armored *ankylosaurs*, horned dinosaurs called *ceratopsians*, and duck-billed dinosaurs called *hadrosaurs*.

Plant life had become very sophisticated by the Cretaceous Period. The earliest flowering plants, or *angiosperms*, appeared during this period. The most common of these plants were trees such as magnolias and willows. Later, trees such as maples, oaks, and walnuts became abundant. Angiosperms became so successful that they are the dominant type of land plant today.

The Cretaceous-Tertiary Mass Extinction

The Cretaceous Period ended in another mass extinction. No dinosaur fossils have been found in rocks that formed after the Cretaceous Period. Some scientists think that this extinction was caused by environmental changes resulting from the movement of continents and increased volcanic activity.

However, many scientists accept the *impact hypothesis* as the explanation for the extinction of the last dinosaurs. This hypothesis is that about 65 million years ago, an asteroid crashed into Earth. The impact of the collision raised enough dust to block the sun's rays for many years. As Earth's climate became cooler, plant life began to die, and many animal species became extinct. As the dust settled over Earth, the dust formed a layer of iridium-laden sediment. Iridium is a chemical element that is uncommon in rocks on Earth but that is common in meteorites.

SCILINKS.
www.scilinks.org
Topic: Mass Extinctions
Code: **HQX0916**
Topic: Geologic Time Scale
Code: **HQX0669**

Internet Activity — GENERAL

Online Museums Have students use an Internet search engine to locate the Web sites of museums that have online exhibits about dinosaurs. Students may want to check Web sites of the Smithsonian Institution, the American Museum of Natural History, or the Museum of Paleontology at the University of California at Berkeley, for example. After students view an online exhibit, have them write a report that describes the exhibit or a museum guide to the exhibit, or have them create a poster or other artwork that illustrates what they learned about dinosaurs. A worksheet designed to direct student research on this topic can be found in the **Chapter Resource File** booklet or by visiting **www.thinkcentral.com** and entering the keyword **HQXVEPX.**
LS Visual/Verbal

Discussion — GENERAL

Flowering Plants Tell students that, although the Cretaceous Period is most famous for its dinosaurs, the advent of flowering plants is even more significant. Have students list flowering plants they know about and the animals that depend on them. (Students should list grasses and grains and include humans in the list of dependent animals.) Have students speculate about when these species of animals must have evolved. (after angiosperms evolved) You may also discuss the intimate connection between some angiosperms and their pollinators and how they must have evolved together. (for example, the yucca plant and yucca moth)
LS Logical/Verbal

Differentiated Instruction

Struggling Readers

Word Parts Explain to students that *dino-* comes from the Greek adjective *deinos,* which means "terrifying." The Greek word *sauros,* which means "lizard," is the source for *-saur.* Thus, *dinosaur* means "terrible lizard." Lizards are reptiles and in many ways resemble dinosaurs, which thrived in the Age of Reptiles. Ask students how this information can help them remember that the Mesozoic Era is the "Age of Reptiles." **LS Verbal/Logical**

Debate — ADVANCED

Dinosaur Extinction Have students form two groups to debate the causes of the mass extinction at the end of the Cretaceous Period. Ask one group of students to research and present evidence supporting the idea that climate/environmental changes caused the extinction. Have the other group research and support the impact hypothesis. After the debate, invite all students to ask questions of the debaters, to comment on the different points of view, and to offer their own viewpoints on the topic. **LS Logical/Verbal**

Teach, *continued*

READING TOOLBOX

Students's tables should list the epochs of the Cenozoic Era, their prefixes, and the meanings of the prefixes. Sample answer: "Paleocene, paleo-, ancient; Eocene, eo-, earliest, oldest; Oligocene, oligo-, few, little; Miocene, mio-, lesser; Pliocene, plio-, more; Pleistocene, pleisto-, most; Holocene, holo-, whole; entire."

Biology Connection ADVANCED

Primitive Mammals Tell students that some types of primitive mammals still exist today. *Monotremes,* such as today's platypus, lay eggs and produce milk through their skin pores. *Marsupials,* including the kangaroo and the opossum, have live young that undergo most of their development in the mother's exterior pouch. Invite students to learn about the evolution of these mammal groups and about how they differ from placental mammals such as humans. Have them present their findings as oral reports to the class. **LS Verbal**

Using the Figure GENERAL

Mammal Characteristics Have students describe the mammalian characteristics of the tarsier shown on this page. (The tarsier is covered with hair.) Tell students that the characteristics that they can't see include that its body contains fat as insulation, the tarsier is warm-blooded, and its body produces milk to feed its offspring. Answer to caption question: Hair and fat help mammals survive in cool climates. Because mammals are warm-blooded, they do not need to absorb heat from their environment. **LS Logical/Verbal**

Skill Builder BASIC

Math The earliest mammals were tiny and rodent-like and appeared in the Mesozoic Era around the time of the first dinosaurs, about 200 million years ago. The great explosion of mammal diversity and dominance on Earth did not begin until about 65 million years ago. How long did mammals exist on Earth before they began to assume a dominant role? (200 million years − 65 million years = 135 million years) **LS Logical**

Figure 5 Cenozoic Timeline

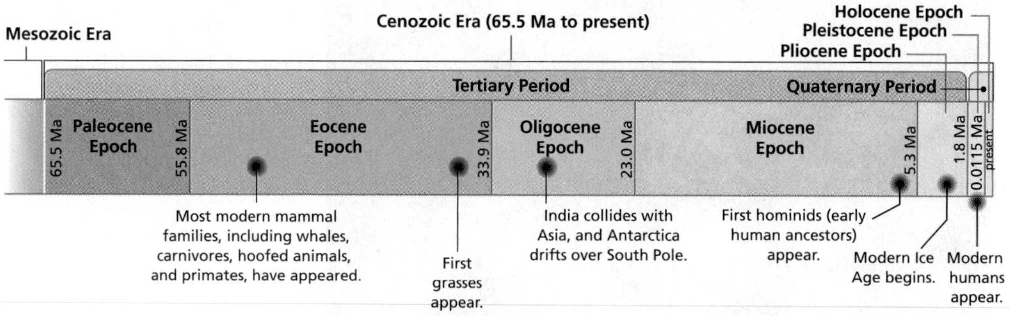

The Cenozoic Era

Cenozoic Era the current geologic era, which began 65.5 million years ago; also called the *Age of Mammals*

As shown in **Figure 5,** the **Cenozoic Era** is the division of geologic time that began about 65 million years ago and that includes the present period. During this era, the continents moved to their present-day positions. As tectonic plates collided, huge mountain ranges, such as the Alps and the Himalayas in Eurasia, formed.

During the Cenozoic Era, dramatic changes in climate have occurred. At times, continental ice sheets covered nearly one-third of Earth's land. As temperatures decreased during the ice ages, new species that were adapted to life in cooler climates appeared. Mammals became the dominant life-form and underwent many changes. The Cenozoic Era is thus commonly called the *Age of Mammals.*

READING TOOLBOX

Prefixes
Make a table that lists the names of the epochs of the Cenozoic Era. Give the meaning of each prefix attached to the suffix *-cene.*

The Tertiary and Quaternary Periods

The Cenozoic Era is divided into two periods. The Tertiary Period includes the time before the last ice age. The Quaternary Period began with the last ice age and includes the present. These periods have been divided into seven epochs. The Paleocene, Eocene, Oligocene, Miocene, and Pliocene Epochs make up the *Tertiary Period.* The Pleistocene and Holocene Epochs make up the *Quaternary Period.*

Figure 6 The *tarsier* is the sole modern survivor of a group of primates common during the earlier Cenozoic Era. ***Why are mammals better suited to cool climates than reptiles are?***

The Paleocene and Eocene Epochs

The fossil record indicates that during the Paleocene Epoch, many new mammals, such as small rodents, evolved. The first primates also evolved during the Paleocene Epoch. A modern survivor of an early primate group is shown in **Figure 6.**

Other mammals, including the earliest known ancestor of the horse, evolved during the Eocene Epoch. Fossil records indicate that the first whales, flying squirrels, and bats appeared during this epoch. Small reptiles continued to flourish. Worldwide, temperatures dropped by about 4 °C at the end of the Eocene Epoch.

Differentiated Instruction

Struggling Readers/Basic Learners

Pattern Puzzles Have students write each of the events and time intervals shown on the timeline in **Figure 5** on index cards. Have students arrange the time-interval cards in the proper hierarchy and sequence. Then, have students match events to the correct interval.

The Oligocene and Miocene Epochs

During the Oligocene Epoch, the Indian subcontinent began to collide with the Eurasian continent, which caused the uplifting of the Himalayas. The worldwide climate became significantly cooler and drier. This change in climate favored grasses as well as cone-bearing and hardwood trees. Many early mammals became extinct. However, large species of deer, pigs, horses, camels, cats, and dogs flourished. Marine invertebrates, especially clams and snails, also continued to flourish.

During the Miocene Epoch, circumpolar currents formed around Antarctica, and the modern Antarctic icecap began to form. By the late Miocene Epoch, tectonic forces and dropping sea levels caused the Mediterranean Sea to dry up and refill several times. The largest known land mammals existed during this epoch. Miocene rocks contain fossils of horses, camels, deer, rhinoceroses, pigs, raccoons, wolves, foxes, and the earliest saber-toothed cats, which are now extinct. The earliest human ancestors may date to this epoch.

SCILINKS.
www.scilinks.org
Topic: Geologic Periods and Epochs
Code: HQX0667

The Pliocene Epoch

During the Pliocene Epoch, predators—including members of the bear, dog, and cat families—evolved into modern forms. Herbivores, such as the giant ground sloth shown in **Figure 7**, flourished. The first modern horses also appeared in this epoch.

Toward the end of the Pliocene, dramatic climatic changes occurred, and the continental ice sheets began to spread. With more and more water locked in ice, sea level fell. The Bering land bridge appeared between Eurasia and North America. Changes in Earth's crust between North America and South America formed the Central American land bridge. Various species migrated between the continents across these two land bridges.

Reading Check **Why did sea level fall in the Pliocene Epoch?**

Figure 7 Giant ground sloths lived during the late Pliocene in parts of North America and South America. These slow-moving leaf-eaters could grow as large as an African bull elephant and weigh as much as 5 tons.

Homework — ADVANCED

Horse History Scientists think that today's horse is one of a small number of remnants of an evolutionary line that once included many species. Invite students to research the evolution of the horse and other members of the genus *Equus*, such as zebras, bringing in drawings of early and intermediate forms between *Eohippus* and modern horses. Students may offer their own explanations about why so few *Equus* species remain today while so many became extinct. **LS Visual/Logical**

Answer to Reading Check

During ice ages, water from the ocean was frozen as ice on the continents, so the amount of water in the seas decreased and sea level fell.

Close

Reteaching — BASIC

Create a Brochure Organize students into groups. Have each group create a travel brochure for one of the geologic periods or epochs in this section. Direct students to divide up the tasks of designing, writing, and illustrating the brochure. Brochures should include information about environmental conditions and the animals and plants of the time. Post the brochures in the class where all students can see and read them. **LS Verbal/Visual**
Co-op Learning

Quiz — GENERAL

1. What effect did the land bridges have on animal distribution during the ice ages? (They allowed animals to move from one continent to another.)
2. What is one possible cause of the mass extinction during the Cretaceous Era? (One possible cause is an asteroid impact.)

Why It Matters

Circumpolar Waters One of the reasons Antarctica is the coldest place on Earth is because it is completely encircled by the Southern Ocean, which blocks warmer ocean currents from approaching the contintent. About 25 million years ago, shifting tectonic plates caused a cold, deep-ocean belt of water to form around the Antarctic continent. The belt of cold water flows continuously around Antarctica, isolating it from warmer ocean currents. Only the deepest, coldest waters from currents north of the Antarctic penetrate the Southern Ocean, and then only at great depth. Most of the water that rises to the Southern Ocean surface is not warmed; instead it is chilled by freezing Antarctic air masses, and sinks again to the cold Antarctic Bottom Water.

Close, *continued*

Answers to Section Review

1. Triassic: ammonites; Jurassic: dinosaurs; Cretaceous: flowering plants
2. Geologic: The breakup of Pangaea began, and an asteroid collided with Earth. Biological: Birds appeared, and flowering plants appeared.
3. Tertiary Period: Paleocene Epoch: rodents, Eocene Epoch: horses, Oligocene Epoch: cats, Miocene Epoch: grazing herds, Pliocene Epoch: bears; Quaternary Period: Pleistocene Epoch: mammoths, Holocene Epoch: humans
4. Geologic: The continents moved to their present locations and ice sheets advanced and retreated several times. Biological: Mammals became dominant, and humans developed.
5. Ice ages led to the rise of hairy, warm-blooded mammals that could survive the cold.
6. We are living in the Cenozoic Era, the Quaternary Period, and the Holocene Epoch.
7. A combination of environmental changes and an asteroid impact caused the extinction of the dinosaurs and many other organisms, leaving many niches open for mammalian species to fill. Mammals were able to survive worldwide cooling and the following ice ages.
8. Scientists probably used evidence of the last ice age to divide the Cenozoic Era into the Tertiary and Quaternary Periods.
9. I would look for evidence of the asteroid impact that happened at that time.
10. The *Mesozoic Era* is known as the *Age of Reptiles*, included the *Triassic Period*, the *Jurassic Period*, and the *Cretaceous Period*, and was followed by the *Cenozoic Era*, which is known as the *Age of Mammals*, and included the *Tertiary Period* and the *Quaternary Period*.

Figure 8 This painting from the Stone Age was made by early humans between 15,000 and 13,000 years ago in a cave in Lascaux, France.

The Pleistocene Epoch

The Pleistocene Epoch began 1.8 million years ago. In Eurasia and North America, ice sheets advanced and retreated several times. Some animals had characteristics that allowed them to endure the cold climate, such as the thick fur that covered woolly mammoths and woolly rhinoceroses. Many other species survived by moving to warmer regions. Some species, such as giant ground sloths and dire wolves, became extinct.

Fossils of the earliest modern humans (*Homo sapiens*) were discovered in Pleistocene sediments. Evidence of modern humans, such as the cave painting shown in **Figure 8,** indicates that early humans may have been hunters.

The Holocene Epoch

The Holocene Epoch, which includes the present, began about 11,500 years ago, as the last glacial period ended. As the ice sheets melted, sea level rose about 140 m, and the coastlines took on their present shapes. The North American Great Lakes also formed as the last ice sheets retreated. During the early Holocene Epoch, modern humans developed agriculture and began to make and use tools made of bronze and iron.

Human history is extremely brief. If you think of the entire history of Earth as one year, the first multicellular organisms would have appeared in September. The dinosaurs would have disappeared at 8 P.M. on December 26. Modern humans would not have appeared until 11:48 P.M. on December 31.

Section 3 Review

Key Ideas

1. **List** the periods of the Mesozoic Era, and describe one major life-form in each period.
2. **Identify** two major geologic and two major biological developments of the Mesozoic Era.
3. **List** the periods and epochs of the Cenozoic Era, and describe one major life-form in each division.
4. **Identify** two major geologic and two major biological developments of the Cenozoic Era.
5. **Explain** how the ice ages affected animal life during the Cenozoic Era.
6. **Identify** the era, period, and epoch we are in today.
7. **Describe** the worldwide environmental changes that set the stage for the Age of Mammals.

Critical Thinking

8. **Drawing Conclusions** Explain the criteria that scientists may have used to divide the Cenozoic Era into the Tertiary and Quaternary Periods.
9. **Identifying Relationships** Suppose that you are a geologist who is looking for the boundary between the Cretaceous and Tertiary Periods in an outcrop. What characteristics would you look for to determine the location of the boundary? Explain your answer.

Concept Mapping

10. Use the following terms to create a concept map: *Mesozoic Era, Age of Reptiles, Jurassic Period, Triassic Period, Cretaceous Period, Cenozoic Era, Age of Mammals, Tertiary Period,* and *Quaternary Period.*

Differentiated Instruction

Alternative Assessment

Timeline Have pairs of students work together to produce their own timeline of the Mesozoic and Cenozoic Eras. Students should label each era and epoch, and list or draw the dominant animals and plants of the time. **LS Verbal/Visual**

Why It Matters

Reconstructing the Past

HISTORY IN SCIENCE

From films and books, most people can visualize the walk and long, swaying neck of an *Apatosaurus,* such as the one shown reaching for tree leaves. Dinosaurs became extinct millions of years ago. How do we know so much about them? Scientists use fossil evidence to reconstruct the bodies and lives of dinosaurs.

Scanning technology lets scientists analyze fossil evidence in a new way. By digitizing bones using CT and X-ray scanners, researchers can build detailed computer models of dinosaur skeletons. These models show how dinosaur bones functioned in living animals, helping us understand how dinosaurs looked and behaved, without resorting to cutting or slicing up the specimens.

Scientists have digitized a *Triceratops* skeleton for study and to replace missing bones.

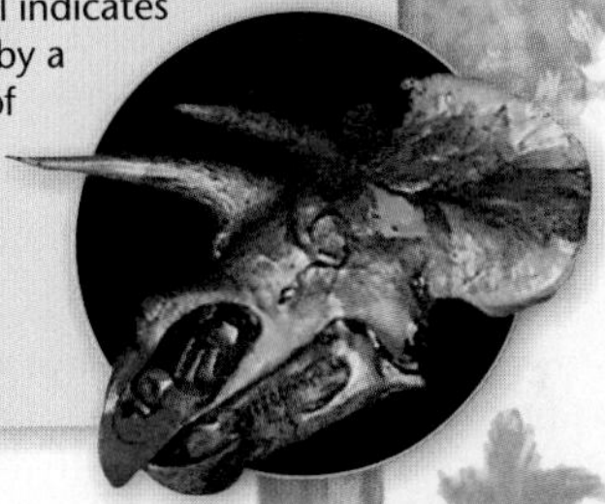

Each color of the digital *Triceratops* skull indicates data collected by a different pass of a 3D surface scanner. The passes were combined to "build" a complete skull.

Fossilized dinosaur tracks show that *Apatosaurus* behaved like modern herd animals, with the youngest animals in the center for protection.

Scientists use a digitized *Triceratops* skeleton to study the mechanics of this huge creature. This sequence shows how *Triceratops* moved as it walked.

YOUR TURN

UNDERSTANDING CONCEPTS
How has technology aided in the study of dinosaurs?

ONLINE RESEARCH
Research techniques used to digitize a *Triceratops* at the National Museum of Natural History. Describe the importance of this work.

Why It Matters

Reconstructing the Past

Although *Triceratops* lived 68 million to 65 million years ago, advances in technology allow scientists to use principles of biomechanics to model its movement and some of its behavior. For example, studies of *Triceratops'* leg joints show that these joints could lock in place so the animal could sleep while standing, much as modern cows and horses do. Scientists also found that the skull of a *Triceratops* was extremely well balanced on the spinal column, allowing a surprising degree of flexibility. It is likely *Triceratops* could precisely maneuver its horns when fighting for territory or defending itself from a predatory *Tyrannosaurus rex.*

Answer to Your Turn

Understanding Concepts Technology has allowed scientists to model dinosaur movements that could not be duplicated without the use of computers.

Online Research Answers may vary. Accept any reasonable response. Student answers might include the study of dinosaurs, evolution, or environmental change.

Skills Practice Lab

Time Required
one 45-minute class period

Lab Ratings
EASY → HARD

Teacher Preparation: 1 of 4
Student Setup: 1 of 4
Concept Level: 3 of 4
Cleanup: 1 of 4

Skills Acquired
- Identifying
- Analyzing
- Recognizing Patterns
- Interpreting Models

Scientific Methods
In this lab, students will
- Observe and Compare
- Analyze Data
- Determine Relationships
- Draw Conclusions

Materials
The materials listed are enough for individual students.

Skills Practice Lab

45 min

What You'll Do
- **Apply** the law of superposition to sample rock columns.
- **Demonstrate** the use of index fossils for determining relative and absolute ages.
- **Evaluate** the usefulness of different methods for determining relative and absolute ages.

What You'll Need
paper
pencil

History in the Rocks

Geologists have discovered much about the geologic history of Earth by studying the arrangement of fossils in rock layers, as well as by studying the arrangement of the rock layers themselves. Fossils provide clues about the environment in which the organisms that formed the fossils existed. Scientists can determine the age of the rocks in which fossils occur because the ages of many fossils have been determined by radiometric dating of associated igneous rocks. Radiometric dating, fossil age, and rock arrangement are all used to determine changes that have occurred in the arrangement of the rock layers through geologic time. In this lab, you will discover how the geologic history of an area can be determined by examining the arrangement of fossils and rock layers.

Figure A

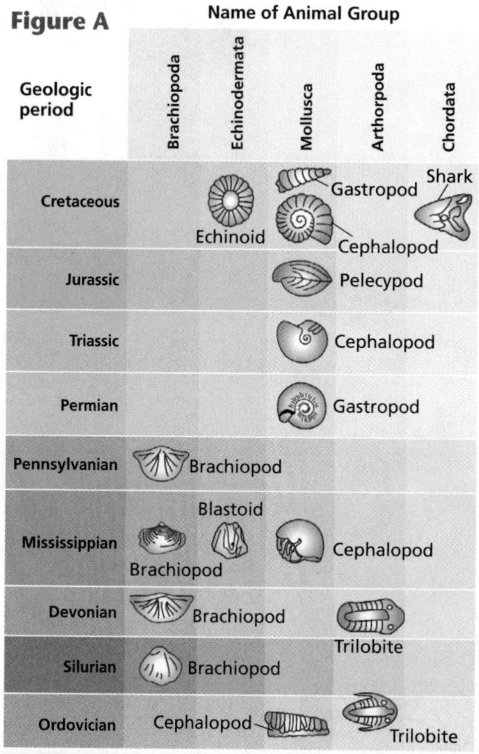

Procedure

1. Study the index fossils shown in **Figure A.** Note their placement in related groups and the geologic periods in which they lived.
2. Select one of the four rock columns shown in **Figure B.** This figure shows how some of these fossils may occur in a series of rock layers. Record the number of the arrangement that you are using.
3. Using **Figure A,** identify all the fossils in your column and the geologic time in which the organisms that formed the fossils lived.
4. List the fossil names in order from bottom to top.
5. Do the fossils in your column appear in the order of geologic time?
6. Do the fossils in your column show a complete sequence of geologic periods? If not, which periods are missing?
7. Repeat steps 2–6 with each of the other three rock columns.

Tips and Tricks
You may wish to have pairs of students work together to discuss their analysis of the fossil record as given in the lab. The following list describes the order of layers in each column of Figure B, from bottom to top:

Column 1: limestone, sandstone with Ordovician cephalopod, shale with Mississippian blastoid, limestone with Cretaceous echinoid, sandstone with Pennsylvanian brachiopod, shale with Triassic cephalopod.

Column 2: shale with Ordovician trilobite, shale with Silurian brachiopod, limestone with Devonian trilobite, shale with Cretaceous gastropod, shale with Cretaceous shark tooth, limestone with Cretaceous cephalopod.

Column 3: shale with Silurian brachiopod, limestone with Devonian brachiopod, shale with no fossils, sandstone with Pennsylvanian brachiopod, limestone with Devonian trilobite, shale with Ordovician trilobite.

Column 4: metamorphic rock (no fossils), limestone with no fossils, shale with Ordovician trilobite, sandstone with Mississippian cephalopod, shale with Triassic cephalopod, limestone with Cretaceous echinoid.

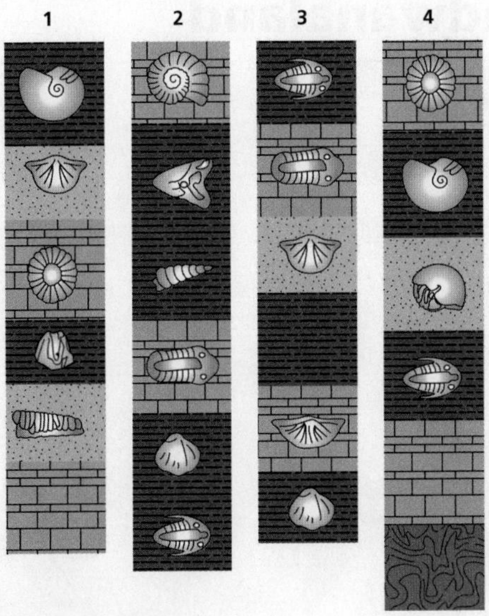

Figure B

Analysis

1. **Analyzing Processes** What processes or events might explain the order of the fossils in each of the rock columns?
2. **Evaluating Assumptions** Based on your observations in the procedure, why is it necessary that a fossil be found in a wide variety of geographic areas for it to be considered an index fossil?
3. **Explaining Events** Study arrangement 3 in **Figure B**. Note that there is a rock layer that contains no fossils between two rock layers that contain fossils. How might this have occurred?

Extension

Examining Data Collect fossils in your area. Identify the fossils you have collected, and describe what your area was like when the organisms existed.

Research Find out how index fossils are used to help petroleum geologists locate oil reservoirs. Then, use that information to give an oral report to your class.

Answers to Procedure

5. Column 1: no; Column 2: yes; Column 3: no; Column 4: yes
6. Column 1: no, missing periods: Silurian, Devonian, Permian, and Jurassic; Column 2: no, missing periods: Mississippian, Pennsylvanian, Permian, Triassic, and Jurassic; Column 3: no, missing periods: Mississippian, Permian, Triassic, Jurassic, and Cretaceous; Column 4: no, missing periods: Silurian, Devonian, Pennsylvanian, Permian, and Jurassic

Answers to Analysis

1. Deformation, including faulting or folding, of rocks in which fossils occur might explain an apparently out-of-order fossil.
2. If a fossil is found only in a small area, it cannot be used to date rocks in other areas of the world.
3. The rock may have formed in a depositional environment in which organisms did not thrive or in which the remains of organisms were not preserved.

Answers to Extension

Examining Data Answers may vary. Accept all reasonable answers. Students may find a variety of fossils in their area.

Research Answers may vary. Accept all reasonable answers. Many of the index fossils that are used by petroleum geologists are microscopic or must be viewed with some magnification.

Fossil Evidence for Gondwanaland

Group Activity GENERAL

Dinosaur Map Divide the class into three groups. Have each group of students research the species and distribution of dinosaurs in North America, Europe, or Asia. Students may divide up project tasks, and have some students do the research online, some research in the library, and others make a map with pictures of each dinosaur species at the site where that species' fossils were found. Students should indicate on their map the geologic time period during which each dinosaur species lived at that site. Ask each group to make an oral presentation to the class, using its map to illustrate major points. LS **Visual/Logical** Co-op Learning

Answers to Map Skills Activity

1. South America, Africa, Australia, Asia (India), and Antarctica
2. Africa, Asia (India), and Antarctica
3. *Mesosaurus*
4. South America, Antarctica, Asia (India), and Australia were likely touching Africa.
5. Africa, Australia, and Asia (India) were likely touching Antarctica.
6. Answers may vary. Sample answer: The organisms did not appear in other parts of the world that were not part of the Gondwanaland section of Pangaea. Thus, it is more likely that they evolved in the same area at the same time.

MAPS in Action

Fossil Evidence for Gondwanaland

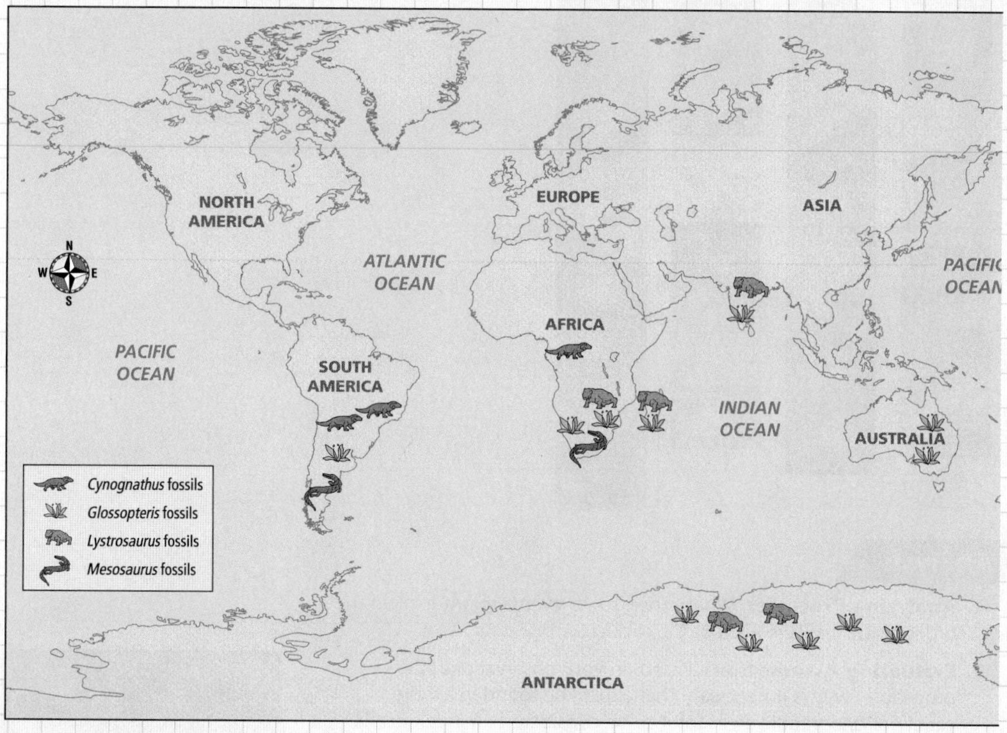

Map Skills Activity

This map shows areas where selected fossils have been found. Use the map to answer the questions below.

1. **Using a Key** On which continents have fossils of plants of the genus *Glossopteris* been found?
2. **Using a Key** On which continents have fossils of organisms of the genus *Lystrosaurus* been found?
3. **Making Comparisons** Which fossil shown on the map was spread over the smallest area?
4. **Inferring Relationships** Based on the map, which continents were connected to Africa when the continents formed a supercontinent?
5. **Inferring Relationships** Based on the map, which continents were connected to Antarctica when the continents formed a supercontinent?
6. **Analyzing Relationships** How would you argue against a claim that plants of the genus *Glossopteris* evolved independently on separate continents or were transported between continents that were not connected? Explain your answer.
7. **Identifying Trends** If the continents were to continue the motion they have had since the time when they formed Gondwanaland, would you expect the east coast of South America and the west coast of Africa to be moving closer together or farther apart? Explain your answer.

7. Answers may vary. Students may state that because the trend has been for the continents to separate, they would likely continue to move farther apart.

Key Resources

Technology

- Transparencies
  48 Fossil Evidence for Gondwanaland

Chapter 9

Summary

THINK central
SUPER SUMMARY
Keyword: HQXVEPS

Key Ideas	Key Terms

Section 1

Geologic Time

› Scientists developed the geologic column based on observations of the relative ages of rock layers throughout the world.

› Scientists used major changes in Earth's climate and extinctions recorded in the fossil record to divide the geologic time scale into smaller units. Geologic time is subdivided into eons, eras, periods, epochs, and ages.

Key Terms: **geologic column,** p. 229; **era,** p. 232; **period,** p. 232; **epoch,** p. 232

Section 2

Precambrian Time and the Paleozoic Era

› Evolution is the gradual development of organisms from other organisms. Evidence for the theory of evolution occurs throughout the fossil record.

› Precambrian rock contains valuable minerals but few fossils.

› The rock record reveals the formation of Pangaea and the evolution of marine invertebrates and vertebrates during the Paleozoic Era.

Key Terms: **evolution,** p. 233; **Precambrian time,** p. 234; **Paleozoic Era,** p. 236

Section 3

The Mesozoic and Cenozoic Eras

› The periods of the Mesozoic Era are the Triassic, Jurassic, and Cretaceous Periods; the periods of the Cenozoic Era are the Tertiary and Quaternary Periods.

› During the Mesozoic Era, Pangaea began to break apart, mountain ranges such as the Sierra Nevada formed, and the first mammals and flowering plants appeared.

› During the Cenozoic Era, India collided with Asia, Antarctica moved over the South Pole, and most modern mammal families, including humans, appeared.

Key Terms: **mass extinction,** p. 239; **Mesozoic Era,** p. 239; **Cenozoic Era,** p. 242

Chapter Summary

Using THINK central Resources

Super Summary

Have students connect the major concepts in this chapter through an interactive Super Summary. Visit www.thinkcentral.com and type in the keyword **HQXVEPS** to access the Super Summary for this chapter.

Differentiated Instruction

Alternative Assessment

Science Consultants Have students pretend that they have been hired by a theme-park owner to produce four new theme parks. The owner wants to create a theme park for every geologic era from Precambrian time through the Cenozoic Era (but not including the Holocene Epoch). Each theme park will feature the plants and animals of the era divided into periods and epochs, with informational displays and activities for visitors. Have students write a proposal and draw a plan for each theme park, detailing its features, displays, and activities. Students may wish to create a model. Students may work in groups, with each group covering one era. Groups should present their plans and illustrations to the class.

LS Verbal/Visual/Kinesthetic

Chapter Review

Assignment Guide	
Section	**Questions**
1	2–6, 8–12, 21
2	13, 14, 23, 25
3	7, 10, 15–18, 20, 24, 27
2 and 3	1, 19, 26
1–3	22, 28–34

Reading Toolbox

1. Answers may vary. Students should include details about the Permian mass extinction and the Cretaceous-Tertiary mass extinction.

Using Key Terms

2–8. Answers may vary but should show that students understand the definitions of and differences between key terms.

Understanding Key Concepts

9. b
10. b
11. a
12. b
13. b
14. d
15. b
16. c
17. a
18. d

Short Answer

19. Cyanobacteria, or blue-green bacteria, were among the early photosynthetic organisms that lived in the oceans during Precambrian time. During the Silurian and Devonian Periods of the Paleozoic Era, land plants such as ferns and seed-bearing plants developed. By the Carboniferous Period, forests of such plants covered the land. During the Cretaceous Period of the Mesozoic Era, the earliest flowering plants, or angiosperms, developed. They were very successful and are the dominant land plants today.

20. Answers may vary but may cite the ideas that climate change caused the extinctions or that an asteroid impact led to the Cretaceous-Tertiary extinction. Evidence for the asteroid impact theory includes iridium-rich rock layers and evidence of a crater in the ocean near the Yucatan peninsula that are the right age.

21. Scientists use rock types to distinguish the layers, as well as the kinds of fossils found in the layers.

22. Answers may vary. Sample answer: fish and reptiles; Their long-term success may be due to their ability to adapt to changing conditions.

Chapter 9 Review

1. **Spider Map** Make a spider map for mass extinctions. Add one leg for the Permian mass extinction and one leg for the Cretaceous-Tertiary mass extinction. To each leg, add details about the mass extinction. READING TOOLBOX

USING KEY TERMS

Use each of the following terms in a separate sentence.

2. *evolution*
3. *geologic column*
4. *period*

For each pair of terms, explain how the meanings of the terms differ.

5. *era* and *epoch*
6. *period* and *era*
7. *Mesozoic Era* and *Cenozoic Era*
8. *Precambrian time* and *Paleozoic Era*

UNDERSTANDING KEY IDEAS

9. The geologic time scale is a
   a. scale for weighing rocks.
   b. scale that divides Earth's history into time intervals.
   c. rock record of Earth's past.
   d. collection of the same kind of rocks.
10. Scientists are able to determine the absolute ages of most rock layers in a geologic column by using
   a. the law of superposition.
   b. radiometric dating.
   c. rates of deposition.
   d. rates of erosion.
11. To determine the age of a specific rock, scientists might correlate it with a layer in a geologic column that has the same relative position and
   a. fossil content.
   b. weight.
   c. temperature.
   d. density.
12. Geologic periods can be divided into
   a. eras. **c.** days.
   b. epochs. **d.** months.
13. Precambrian time ended about
   a. 4.6 billion years ago.
   b. 542 million years ago.
   c. 65 million years ago.
   d. 25 thousand years ago.
14. The most common fossils that occur in Precambrian rock are
   a. graptolites. **c.** eurypterids.
   b. trilobites. **d.** cyanobacteria.
15. The first vertebrates appeared during
   a. Precambrian time. **c.** the Mesozoic Era.
   b. the Paleozoic Era. **d.** the Cenozoic Era.
16. The *Age of Reptiles* is the name commonly given to
   a. Precambrian time. **c.** the Mesozoic Era.
   b. the Paleozoic Era. **d.** the Cenozoic Era.
17. The first flowering plants appeared during the
   a. Cretaceous Period.
   b. Triassic Period.
   c. Carboniferous Period.
   d. Ordovician Period.
18. The *Age of Mammals* is the name commonly given to
   a. Precambrian time. **c.** the Mesozoic Era.
   b. the Paleozoic Era. **d.** the Cenozoic Era.

SHORT ANSWER

19. Write a short paragraph describing the evolution of plants that is indicated by the fossil record.
20. Describe the events that may have led to the Cretaceous-Tertiary mass extinction. What evidence have scientists discovered that supports their hypothesis?
21. Describe the criteria that scientists use to divide a geologic column into different layers.
22. Identify two organisms that are found in the fossil record of a different geologic era but that are still living on Earth today. Identify what characteristic(s) have given them their long-term success.

CRITICAL THINKING

23. **Analyzing Ideas** Why can Precambrian time not be divided into periods by using fossils?
24. **Applying Ideas** Many coal and oil deposits formed during the Carboniferous Period. What element would you expect to find in both oil and coal?
25. **Identifying Relationships** What information in the geologic record might lead scientists to infer that shallow seas covered much of Earth during the Paleozoic Era?
26. **Making Comparisons** Compare the causes of the Permian mass extinction with those of the Cretaceous mass extinction.

CONCEPT MAPPING

27. Use the following terms to create a concept map: *geologic time, Paleozoic Era, Mesozoic Era, stromatolite, Precambrian time, eurypterid, crinoid, Cenozoic Era, trilobite, saurischian, ornithischian, dinosaur, mammal,* and *human.*

MATH SKILLS

Math Skills

28. **Scientific Notation** Write the beginning and end dates of each geologic era in scientific notation.
29. **Making Calculations** The Methuselah tree in California is 4.6×10^3 years old. How many times older than this tree is Earth ?

WRITING SKILLS

30. **Creative Writing** Write an essay about a trip back in time. Include descriptions of the organisms that lived during one of the geologic periods described in this chapter.
31. **Writing from Research** Research the discoveries made by British anthropologists Louis S.B. Leakey and Mary Leakey in Olduvai Gorge in Tanzania, Africa. Write a report about your findings.

INTERPRETING GRAPHICS

The graph below shows average global temperatures since Precambrian time. Use this graph to answer the questions that follow.

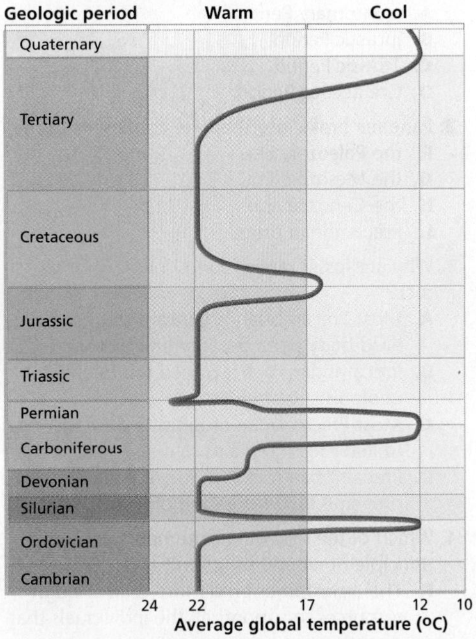

32. During which two periods was Earth's average global temperature the highest?
33. During which periods did Earth's average global temperature decrease?
34. Based on the graph, could long-term climate change have caused the Permian mass extinction? Is long-term climate change a likely cause of the mass extinction at the Cretaceous-Tertiary boundary? Explain your answer.

Chapter Review

Critical Thinking

23. Most Precambrian rocks have been so greatly changed by tectonic activity that it is difficult to identify the original order of layers. This same activity may have destroyed fossils, leaving too few to help scientists divide Precambrian time into periods. In addition, many Precambrian organisms may have lacked the hard parts that usually form fossils.

24. You would expect to find the element carbon in these deposits.

25. If scientists find fossils of marine organisms in rocks from all over the world and from places where no seas exist today, they might infer that seas were once more widespread on Earth.

26. The Permian mass extinction was likely caused by environmental changes that resulted from the formation of Pangaea, whereas the Cretaceous extinction was likely caused by an asteroid impact or by climate change.

Concept Mapping

27. Answers may vary but should include all of the terms listed. Sample answers appear at the end of this unit on p. 253A.

Math Skills

28. Precambrian time began 4.6×10^9 years ago and ended 5.42×10^8 years ago. The Paleozoic Era began 5.42×10^8 years ago and ended 2.51×10^8 years ago. The Mesozoic Era began 2.51×10^8 years ago and ended 6.55×10^7 years ago. The Cenozoic Era began 6.55×10^7 years ago and has not ended.

29. $4.6 \times 1,000 = 4,600$ years. Earth is 4.6 billion years old, so Earth is 1,000,000 times older than the Methuselah tree.

Writing Skills

30. Answers may vary. Accept all reasonable answers.

31. Answers may vary. Accept all reasonable answers.

Interpreting Graphics

32. Permian and Triassic

33. Ordovician, Devonian, Carboniferous, Triassic, Jurassic, and Tertiary

34. Answers may vary, but should state that climate change is a possible cause of the mass extinction at the Permian-Triassic boundary because the temperature changed so significantly at the end of the Permian Period. However, temperature did not change significantly at the Cretaceous-Tertiary boundary, and therefore is not as likely a cause of that extinction event.

Estimated Time

To give students practice under more realistic testing conditions, allow them 30 minutes to answer all of the questions in this practice test.

Test Doctor

Question 1 Answer B is correct. According to the scant fossil record, life on Earth during Precambrian time was primitive, so answer A is incorrect. Dinosaurs first appeared during the Triassic Period but were not the primary life-form, so answer C is incorrect. Though they continued to dominate during the Cretaceous Period, answer D, dinosaurs did not become the dominant life form until the Jurassic Period.

Question 4 Answer G is the best answer choice. Answer F is incorrect because ecosystems have limited carrying capacities. Answer H is incorrect because individuals in a population are not identical and, in fact, similarity does not foster natural selection. Answer I is incorrect because only some offspring live until maturity.

Question 9 Answer G is correct. Speed might be determined by fossilized footprints, not by teeth. The color of the dinosaur's skin would require a frozen sample, but even then, the color would be difficult to determine. Teeth would not help when determining the dinosaur's mating habits.

Chapter 9 Standardized Test Prep

Understanding Concepts

Directions (1–4): For each question, write on a separate sheet of paper the letter of the correct answer.

1. Dinosaurs first became the dominant life-forms during which geologic period?
A. Quaternary Period
B. Jurassic Period
C. Triassic Period
D. Cretaceous Period

2. Pangaea broke into separate continents during
F. the Paleozoic Era.
G. the Mesozoic Era.
H. the Cenozoic Era.
I. Precambrian time.

3. Why are fossils rarely found in Precambrian rock?
A. Most Precambrian organisms did not have hard body parts that commonly form fossils.
B. Precambrian rock is buried too deeply for geologists to study it.
C. Most Precambrian organisms were too small to leave fossil remains.
D. Precambrian rock is made of a material that prevented the formation of fossils.

4. Which of the following statements describes a principle of natural selection?
F. The environment has more than enough resources to support all the individuals that are born in a given ecosystem.
G. Only individuals well suited to the environment are likely to survive and reproduce.
H. Individuals in a healthy population are identical and have the same traits.
I. Most species produce plentiful offspring that will all live until maturity and reproduce.

Directions (5–7): For each question, write a short response.

5. What is the term for the largest unit of geologic time?

6. What is the term for the gradual development of organisms from other organisms by means of natural selection?

7. Why is the Cenozoic Era also known as the *Age of Mammals*?

Reading Skills

Directions (8–11): Read the passage below. Then, answer the questions.

The Discovery of a Dinosaur

In 1995, paleontologist Paul Sereno was working in a previously unexplored region of Morocco when his team made an astounding discovery—an enormous dinosaur skull. The skull was nearly 1.6 m long. Given the size of the skull, Sereno concluded that the skeleton of the animal it came from must have been about 14 m long—about as long as a full-sized school bus. The dinosaur was even larger than the *Tyrannosaurus rex.* The newly discovered dinosaur was thought to be 90 million years old. It most likely chased other dinosaurs by running on large, powerful hind legs, and its bladelike teeth must have meant certain death for its prey.

8. Which of the following is evidence that the dinosaur described in the passage above was most likely a predator?
A. It had sharp, bladelike teeth.
B. It had a large skeleton and powerful hind legs used for running.
C. It was found next to the bones of a smaller animal.
D. It was more than 90 million years old.

9. What types of information do you think fossilized teeth provide about an organism?
F. the color of its skin
G. the types of food it ate
H. the speed at which it ran
I. the mating habits it had

10. According to the passage, which of the following statements is true?
A. This dinosaur was most likely a predator.
B. This skull belonged to a large *Tyrannosaurus rex.*
C. This dinosaur had powerful arms.
D. This dinosaur ate mainly plants and berries.

11. What are some methods that scientists might have used to determine that the dinosaur skull was 90 million years old?

Question 11 Full-credit answers should include the following points:
- an understanding that scientists not only can, but usually do, use multiple means of authentication when dating the remains of ancient plants and animals
- scientists could also use nearby index fossils and stratigraphic layers

Question 13 Answer A is correct. To answer this question correctly, a student needs to divide 65 million years (the length of the Cenozoic era) by 4.6 billion years (the age of Earth). To save room on the calculator screen, some students may find it easier to drop the extra zeroes and simply divide 65 by 4,600. The answer is then multiplied by 100 to convert it to a percentage. The correct answer is 1.5%.

Interpreting Graphics

Directions (12–15): For each question below, record the correct answer on a separate sheet of paper.

The timeline below shows the time divisions of the Mesozoic and Cenozoic Eras. Use this timeline to answer questions 12 through 14.

The Mesozoic and Cenozoic Eras

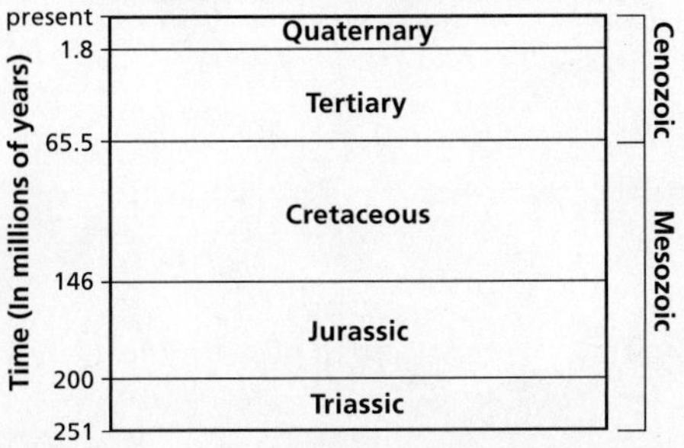

12. Human civilization developed during which of the following periods of time?
- **F.** Triassic Period
- **G.** Jurassic Period
- **H.** Tertiary Period
- **I.** Quaternary Period

13. If Earth formed about 4.6 billion years ago, what percentage of Earth's total history has the Cenozoic Era filled?
- **A.** about 1.5%
- **B.** about 10.5%
- **C.** about 15%
- **D.** about 50%

14. Which event coincides with the start of the Cenozoic Era?

The graph below shows data on global temperature changes during the last millennium. Use this graph to answer question 15.

The Medieval Warm Period and the Little Ice Age

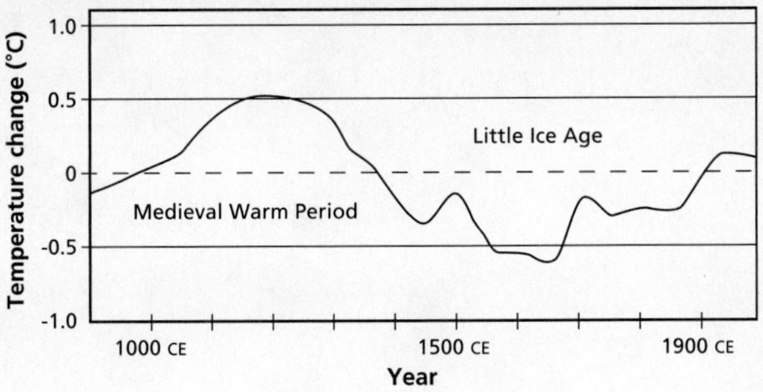

15. How do you think the temperature changes during the Little Ice Age of the Middle Ages affected the freezing and thawing of global waters? Explain your answer.

Test Tip

Simply keeping a positive attitude during any test will help you focus on the test and likely improve your score.

Using THINK central Resources

State Resources
- For specific resources for your state, visit www.thinkcentral.com and type in the keyword **HSHSTR.**

Answers

Part A

1. B
2. G
3. A
4. G
5. an era
6. evolution
7. Mammals became the dominant life-forms and underwent many evolutionary changes during this era.

Part B

8. A
9. G
10. A
11. Answers may vary. See Test Doctor for a detailed scoring rubric.

Part C

12. I
13. A
14. the mass extinction of the dinosaurs
15. During the Little Ice Age, glaciers did not increase in size by very much, but local freezing dates came earlier and thawing dates came later.

Sample Answers to Concept Maps from Chapter Reviews

Chapter 8 The Rock Record, p. 223

28.

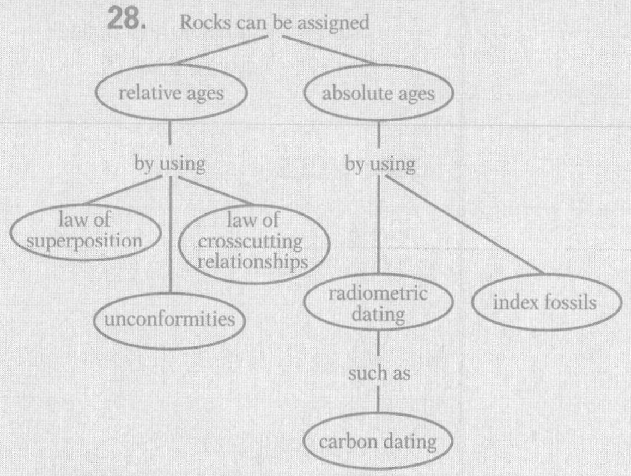

Chapter 9 A View of Earth's Past, p. 251

27.

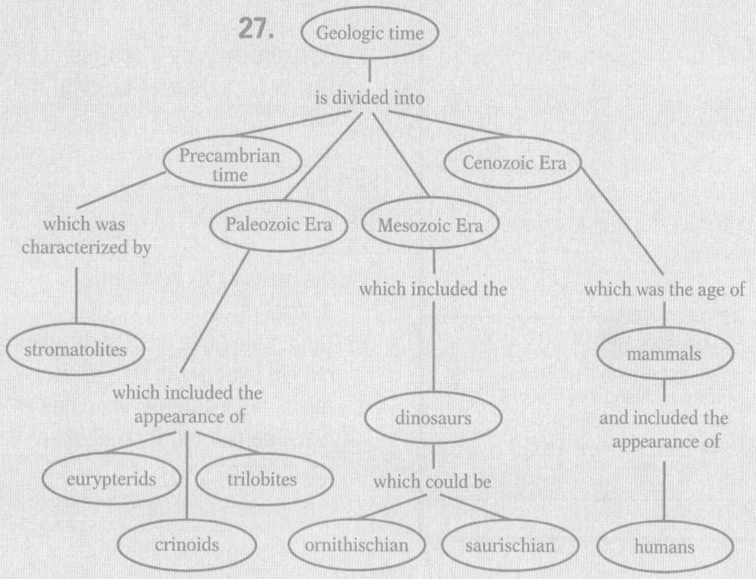

Unit 4 The Dynamic Earth

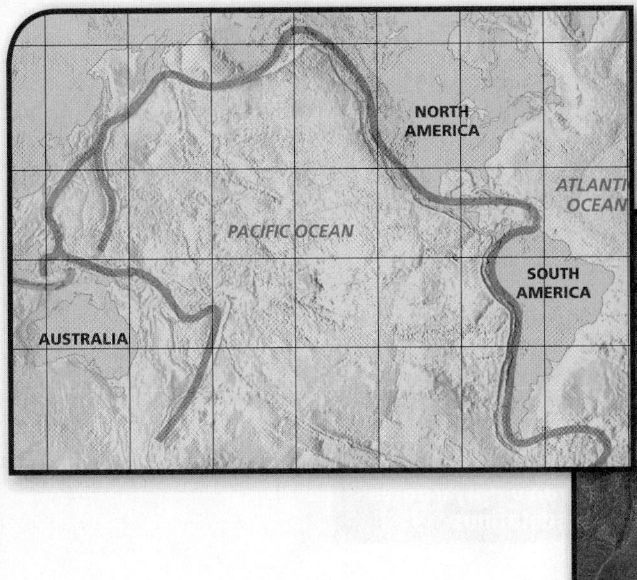

Chapter Planner 10

Plate Tectonics

	Standards	Teach Key Ideas
Chapter Opener, pp. 256–257 **45 min.**	National Science Education Standards	
Section 1 Continental Drift, pp. 259–266 **45 min.** ❯ Wegener's Hypothesis ❯ Sea-Floor Spreading ❯ Paleomagnetism ❯ Wegener Redeemed	SAI 2a, SAI 2e, HNS 3c, UC P1	■ ◆ **Bellringer,** p. 259 ■ **DI (Special Education Students):** Vocabulary Notebook, p. 260 ■ **Debate:** Wegener's Idea, p. 261 ■ **Discussion:** Making Predictions, p. 261 ■ **DI (Basic Learners):** Chain of Events, p. 263 ■ **Demonstration:** Earth's Magnetic Field, p. 264 ■ **DI (Special Education Students):** Magnetic Symmetry, p. 265 ◆ **Transparency:** 49 Sea-Floor Spreading ▲ **Visual Concepts:** Continental Drift (Pangaea) • Sea-Floor Spreading • Magnetic Reversals and Sea-Floor Spreading
Section 2 The Theory of Plate Tectonics, pp. 267–274 **45 min.** ❯ How Continents Move ❯ Tectonic Plates ❯ Types of Plate Boundaries ❯ Causes of Plate Motion	ES 1b, ES 3c, UCP 3	■ ◆ **Bellringer,** p. 267 ■ **DI (English Learners):** Root Words, p. 268 ■ **Discussion:** Crustal Chemistry, p. 269 ■ **DI (Special Education Students):** Modeling Plate Boundaries, p. 270 ■ **DI (Struggling Readers):** Comprehension Strategy, p. 272 ◆ **Transparencies:** 50 Tectonic Plate Boundaries • 51 Types of Plate Boundaries • 52 Ridge Push and Slab Pull • 54 Locations of Earthquakes in South America ▲ **Visual Concepts:** Tectonic Plates and Plate Tectonics • Convergent Boundary • Subduction Zone • Divergent and Transform Boundaries • Causes of Tectonic Plate Motion
Section 3 The Changing Continents, pp. 275–280 **45 min.** ❯ Reshaping Earth's Crust ❯ Effects of Continental Change ❯ The Supercontinent Cycle	UCP 1, UCP 2	■ ◆ **Bellringer,** p. 275 ■ **Demonstration:** Modeling Accretion, p. 276 ■ **DI (Advanced Learners):** Accreted Terranes, p. 276 ■ **Teaching Tip:** Connect to Prior Knowledge, p. 278 ■ **DI (Special Education Students):** Supercontinent Cycle, p. 278 ◆ **Transparency:** 53 The Supercontinent Cycle ▲ **Visual Concepts:** Continental Drift (Pangaea)
Chapter Wrap-Up, pp. 285–289 **90 min.**		**Chapter Summary,** p. 285

See also PowerNotes® Presentations

CHAPTER Fast Track *To shorten instruction because of time limitations, omit Section 3.*

Key

Teacher's Edition ■	Teaching Transparencies ◆
Chapter Resource File ●	Online Edition ▲

All resources listed below are also available on the **Teacher One Stop™.**

Why It Matters	Hands-On	Skills Development	Assessment
■ **Chapter Overview,** p. 256 ■ **Using the Figure:** Rifting in Iceland, p. 256	**Inquiry Lab:** Reconstructing Landmasses, p. 257	**Reading Toolbox,** p. 258	
■ **Section Overview,** p. 259 ■ **Using the Figure:** Continental Puzzles, p. 259 ■ **Using the Figure:** Mountain Ranges and Fossils, p. 260 ■ **History Connection:** Alfred Lothar Wegener, p. 261 ■ **Why It Matters:** Ridges and Rises, p. 262 ■ **Physics Connection:** Sonar, p. 262 ■ **Using the Figure:** Sea-Floor Formation, p. 263 **Our Own Space Shield,** p. 264	■ **Activity:** Sea-Floor Sediments, p. 262 **Quick Lab:** Making Magnets, p. 265 **Making Models Lab:** Sea-Floor Spreading, pp. 282–283	■ **Reading Skill Builder:** Paired Summarizing, p. 260 **Reading Toolbox:** Three-Panel Flip Chart, p. 261 ■ **Skill Builder:** Math, p. 263	**Reading Check,** p. 261 **Reading Check,** p. 263 **Reading Check,** p. 265 **Section Review,** p. 266 ■ **Reteaching,** p. 265 ■ **Quiz,** p. 265 ■ **DI (Alternative Assessment):** Persuasive Essay, p. 266 ● **Section Quiz**
■ **Section Overview,** p. 267 ■ **Physics Connection:** Earthquakes, p. 268 ■ **Chemistry Connection:** Plate Boundary Volcanoes, p. 270 ■ **Why It Matters:** Fracture Zones, p. 271 ■ **Teaching Tip:** Connect to Familiar Processes, p. 272 ■ **Using the Figure:** Mantle Convection, p. 272 ■ **Why It Matters:** Speeding Plates, p. 272	■ **Activity:** Jigsaw Puzzles, p. 267 **Quick Lab:** Tectonic Plate Boundaries, p. 273 ■ **Group Activity:** 3-D Model, p. 284 ● **Inquiry Lab:** Where Do Earthquakes Happen? ● **Making Models Lab:** Eggshell Tectonics	**Math Skills:** The Rate of Plate Movement, p. 268 ■ ● **Internet Activity:** Earthquakes, p. 268 ■ **Skill Builder:** Vocabulary, p. 269 **Reading Toolbox:** Prefixes, p. 270 ■ **Skill Builder:** Writing, p. 271 **Maps in Action:** Locations of Earthquakes in South America, p. 284 ● **Internet Activity:** The Heimaey Eruption	**Reading Check,** p. 268 **Reading Check,** p. 270 **Reading Check,** p. 273 **Section Review,** p. 274 ■ **Reteaching,** p. 273 ■ **Quiz,** p. 273 ● **Section Quiz**
■ **Section Overview,** p. 275 ■ **Using the Figure:** Accretion, p. 276 ■ **Biology Connection:** Extinction, p. 277 ■ **Environmental Connection:** Climate Changes, p. 277	■ **Activity:** Modeling Rifting, p. 275 ■ **Group Activity:** Responses to Climate Change, p. 277	■ **Skill Builder: Vocabulary,** p. 276 ■ **Reading Skill Builder:** Reading Organizer, p. 277 ■ ● **Internet Activity:** The Paleomap Project, p. 278 **Reading Toolbox:** Recognizing Facts, Hypotheses, and Theories, p. 280	**Reading Check,** p. 276 **Reading Check,** p. 279 **Section Review,** p. 280 ■ **Reteaching,** p. 279 ■ **Quiz,** p. 279 ■ **DI (Alternative Assessment):** Process Models, p. 280 ● **Section Quiz**
Copper from Plate Margins, p. 281		▲ **Super Summary** **Standardized Test Prep,** pp. 286–287	**Chapter Review,** pp. 286–287 ■ **DI (Alternative Assessment):** Comparing Scientific Ideas, p. 285 ● **Chapter Tests**

See also Lab Generator

See also Holt Online Assessment Resources

Chapter Overview

Earth is composed of layers of rock that have different compositions, structural features, and densities. Changes that occur at Earth's surface are driven by processes inside Earth that result from the transfer of energy as heat and from differences in density.

Using the Figure — GENERAL

Rifting in Iceland This photograph shows the axis of the Mid-Atlantic Ridge as it tears apart the island of Iceland. New crust forms along the spreading center of the Mid-Atlantic Ridge. Ask students to use the buildings in the background to estimate the size of the rift. The steam in the background may be from a geothermal power plant. Ask students to determine why Iceland has so many geothermal power plants. (Because new crust forms here, magma transfers a lot of heat to the surrounding rock. Also, the new crust is thin.)

Why It Matters

The island of Iceland straddles the Mid-Atlantic Ridge, allowing scientists to study on land the processes occurring at divergent boundaries. These processes usually take place at spreading centers submerged below kilometers of seawater.

Chapter 10 Plate Tectonics

Chapter Outline

Virginia Standards of Learning
ES.1.c
ES.1.d
ES.2.a
ES.2.b
ES.2.d
ES.7.a
ES.7.b
ES.10.d

Why It Matters

Huge, moving slabs of rock called tectonic plates constantly reshape Earth's surface. For example, the island of Iceland is being torn where two tectonic plates are moving apart. Iceland is one of the few places where this process can be seen on land.

Chapter Correlations — *Virginia Standards of Learning*

ES.1.c scales, diagrams, charts, graphs, tables, imagery, models, and profiles are constructed and interpreted.
ES.1.d maps and globes are read and interpreted, including location by latitude and longitude.
ES.2.a science explains and predicts the interactions and dynamics of complex Earth systems.
ES.2.b evidence is required to evaluate hypotheses and explanations.
ES.2.d evidence is evaluated for scientific theories.
ES.7.a geologic processes and their resulting features
ES.7.b tectonic processes
ES.10.d features of the seafloor as reflections of tectonic processes

Inquiry Lab

15 min

Reconstructing Landmasses

Draw a map of a large landmass on a piece of **paper**. Use **colored pencils** or **markers** to show geological features, such as mountain ranges and types of rock at the surface. Using **scissors**, cut your map into irregular pieces. Trade map pieces with another group, and then reconstruct the other group's landmass.

Questions to Get You Started

1. What features of the interiors of the pieces did you use to put the pieces back together?
2. What features of the edges of the pieces did you use for your reconstruction?

Inquiry Lab

Central Concept: Students use various types of evidence to reconstruct a landmass. Students model the process used by scientists in developing the concept of continental drift, which led to the theory of plate tectonics.

Teacher's Notes: You may wish to assign one student in each group to be responsible for lab materials, one student to be the map artist, and one student to record questions and answers. You may also wish to establish a maximum number of pieces into which the map may be cut.

Materials (per group)
- Paper
- Colored pencils or markers
- Scissors

Skills Acquired
- Analyzing
- Constructing Models
- Interpreting Models

Answers to Getting Started

1. Student answers may vary but may mention such features as mountain ranges and rock belts.
2. Student answers may vary but should cite the shapes of the map pieces.

Using THINK central Resources

An online version of this chapter, as well as all the print and multimedia resources that accompany the program are available to registered teachers and their students. Log onto www.thinkcentral.com to access these materials and tools to organize your preparation and student learning.

READING TOOLBOX

Prefixes

Word or Term	Prefix	Meaning of Prefix
paleomagnetism	paleo-	ancient
Paleozoic	paleo-	ancient
different	di-	apart
divergent boundary	di-	apart
three-dimensional	di	off, from
distance	di-	apart
differs	di-	apart
transform boundary	trans-	across, through
transfer	trans-	across, through
Pangaea	pan-	all, every
Panthalassa	pan-	all, every

Recognizing Facts, Hypotheses, and Theories

Answers may vary. Check to make sure students correctly classify statements as facts, hypotheses, or theories in their tables.

Three-Panel Flip Chart

Answers may vary but should accurately describe each kind of plate boundary. Students' notes and sketches should be under the appropriate tabs of the flip chart.

READING TOOLBOX

These reading tools will help you learn the material in this chapter.

Word Parts

Prefixes Many scientific words are made up of word parts that come from Latin and Greek. You can figure out the meanings of unfamiliar science terms by looking at their word parts.

The words *Pangaea* and *Panthalassa* contain the prefix *pan-*. *Pan-* comes from a Greek word meaning "all." The root words *gaea* and *thalassa* come from Greek words meaning "land" and "ocean." *Pangaea* means "all lands," and *Panthalassa* means "all oceans."

Your Turn Prefixes found in this chapter include *paleo-*, *di-*, *trans-*, and *pan-*. As you read this chapter, make a table like the one started below. List words or terms that contain prefixes and give the meaning of each prefix.

WORD OR TERM	PREFIX	MEANING
paleomagetism	paleo-	
divergent boundary	di-	

Fact, Hypothesis, or Theory?

Recognizing Facts, Hypotheses, and Theories A fact is a statement about the world that is based on observation. A hypothesis is a possible explanation that can be tested. A scientific theory is a model or explanation that ties together many hypotheses and observations.

Your Turn Make a table like the one shown below. List statements of fact, hypotheses, and theories from Sections 1 and 2. Identify the type of statement, and write any language from the text that signals the type of statement.

STATEMENT	FACT, HYPOTHESIS, OR THEORY	KEY WORDS
	hypothesis	"proposed a hypothesis..."
	fact	"scientists found that..."
	theory	"lead to a theory called ______"

FoldNotes

Three-Panel Flip Chart FoldNotes are a fun way to help you learn and remember ideas that you encounter as you read. FoldNotes help you organize concepts and see the "big picture."

Your Turn Follow the instructions in **Appendix A** for making a three-panel flip chart. Label the first panel "Divergent boundary," the second "Convergent boundary," and the third "Transform boundary." Open the appropriate flap to take notes about each type of boundary discussed in Section 2 and make a sketch.

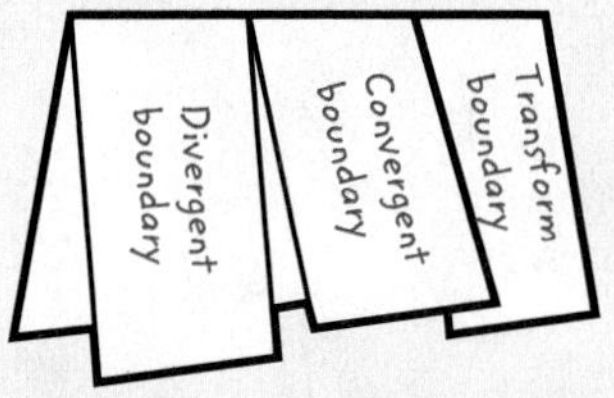

For more information on how to use these and other tools, see **Appendix A.**

SECTION 1

Continental Drift

Key Ideas	Key Terms	Why It Matters
❯ Summarize Wegener's hypothesis of continental drift. ❯ Describe the process of sea-floor spreading. ❯ Identify how paleomagnetism provides support for the idea of sea-floor spreading. ❯ Explain how sea-floor spreading provides a mechanism for continental drift.	**continental drift** **mid-ocean ridge** **sea-floor spreading** **paleomagnetism**	Evidence for continental drift was found in Earth's natural magnetism. This magnetism not only supports scientists' hypotheses, it also protects us all from the dangers of solar radiation.

One of the most exciting theories in Earth science began with observations made more than 400 years ago. As early explorers sailed the oceans of the world, they brought back information about new continents and their coastlines. Mapmakers used this information to chart the new discoveries and to make the first reliable world maps.

As people studied the maps, they were impressed by the similarity of the continental coastlines on either side of the Atlantic Ocean. The continents looked as though they would fit together like parts of a giant jigsaw puzzle. The east coast of South America, for example, seemed to fit perfectly into the west coast of Africa, as shown in **Figure 1**.

continental drift the hypothesis that a single large landmass broke up into smaller landmasses to form the continents, which then drifted to their present locations

Wegener's Hypothesis

In 1912, a German scientist named Alfred Wegener (VAY guh nuhr) proposed a hypothesis that is now called **continental drift.** Wegener hypothesized that the continents once formed part of a single landmass called a *supercontinent*. According to Wegener, this supercontinent began breaking up into smaller continents during the Mesozoic Era (about 200 million years ago). Over millions of years, these continents drifted to their present locations. Wegener speculated that the crumpling of the crust in places may have produced mountain ranges such as the Andes on the western coast of South America.

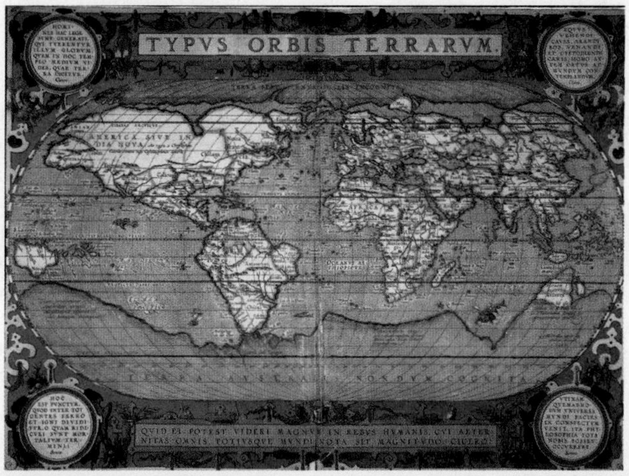

Figure 1 Early explorers noticed that the coastlines of Africa and South America could fit together like puzzle pieces. ***Can you identify any other continents that could fit together like puzzle pieces?***

Section 1

Focus

Overview

This section describes the idea of continental drift. The section describes evidence for continental drift, the process of sea-floor spreading, and flaws of the hypothesis of continental drift.

Bellringer

Propose the following scenario to students: "Two islands are 1,000 km apart. The rocks on both islands have the same mineral composition, the same rare fossils, and mountains of identical age and structure." Ask students to suggest a hypothesis to explain these similarities. (Students may hypothesize that the two islands were once joined but then split apart and somehow moved to their present locations.) **LS Logical**

Motivate

Using the Figure GENERAL

Continental Puzzles Use the question in the caption for the figure on this page as the starting point for a discussion. Answer to caption question: Other locations that may appear to fit like puzzle pieces include east Africa and the Arabian peninsula, and Madagascar and east Africa.
LS Logical

Key Resources

Chapter Resource File
- Directed Reading BASIC

Technology
- Transparencies
  Bellringer

Teach

Using the Figure ADVANCED

Mountain Ranges and Fossils Have students study the map on this page. Have them identify the ages of mountain ranges in the Northern Hemisphere that match. Have them identify the ranges of the organisms identified in the Southern Hemisphere. Then, have them draw a diagram that shows how the continents may have looked when they were connected. They can use the mountain ranges and distribution of organisms as a guide. (Students' drawings should show Greenland connected to Scandinavia and northern Britain, the east coast of North America connected to Europe and northwestern Africa, and South America connected to Africa, Madagascar, and India.) LS **Visual**

Reading Skill Builder BASIC

Paired Summarizing Group students into pairs, and have them read silently about the evidence for continental drift. Then, have one student summarize the idea of continental drift. The other student should listen to the retelling and should point out any inaccuracies or ideas that were left out. Allow students to refer to the text as needed. LS **Verbal/Auditory** English Language Learners

Figure 2 Fossils of *Mesosaurus*, such as the one shown below, were found in both South America and western Africa. Mountain chains of similar ages also exist on different continents, as shown in the map at right.

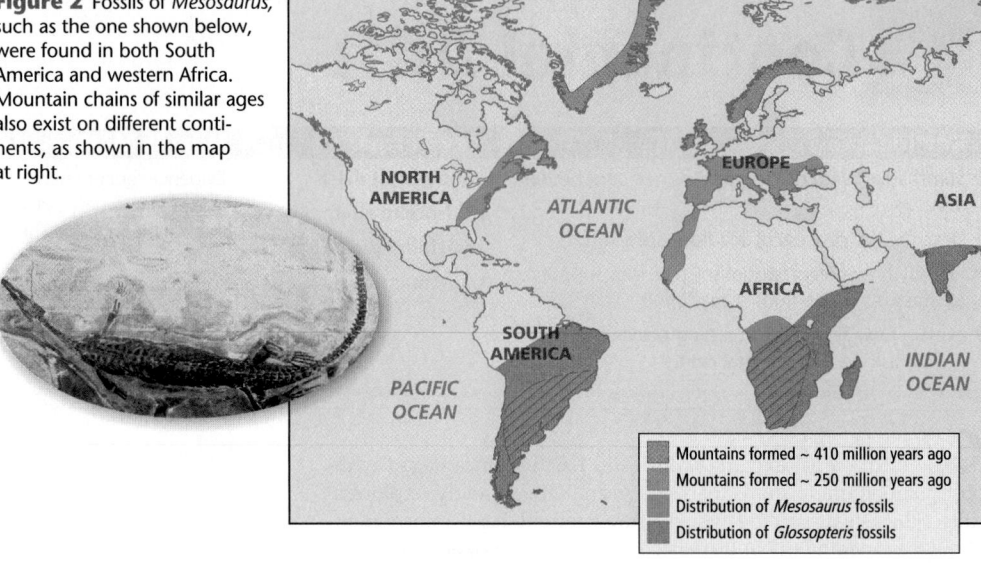

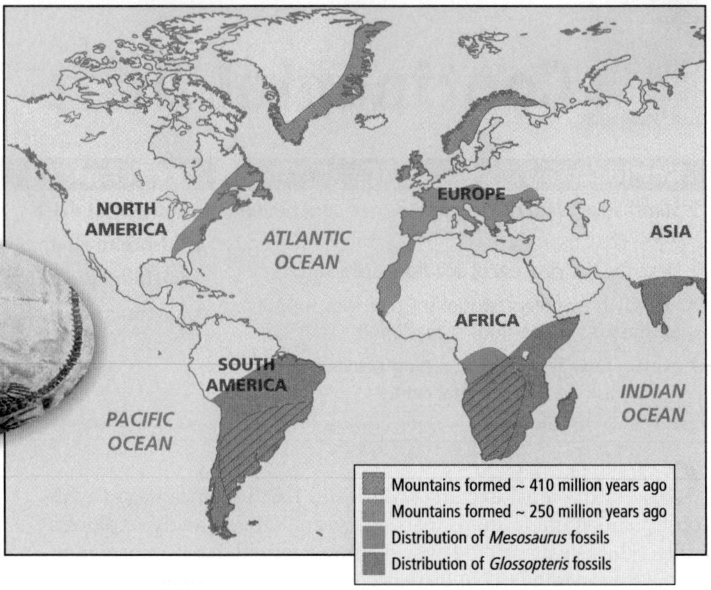

SCILINKS.
www.scilinks.org
Topic: Continental Drift
Code: HQX0351

Fossil Evidence

In addition to seeing the similarities in the coastlines of the continents, Wegener found other evidence to support his hypothesis. He reasoned that if the continents had once been joined, fossils of the same plants and animals should be found in areas that had once been connected. Wegener knew that identical fossils of *Mesosaurus,* a small, extinct land reptile, had been found in both South America and western Africa. *Mesosaurus,* a fossil of which is shown in **Figure 2**, lived 270 million years ago (during the Paleozoic Era). Wegener knew that it was unlikely these reptiles had swum across the Atlantic Ocean. He also saw no evidence that land bridges had once connected the continents. So, he concluded that South America and Africa had been joined at one time in the past.

Evidence from Rock Formations

Geologic evidence also supported Wegener's hypothesis of continental drift. The ages and types of rocks in the coastal regions of widely separated areas, such as western Africa and eastern South America, matched closely. Mountain chains that ended at the coastline of one continent seemed to continue on other continents across the ocean, as shown in **Figure 2.** The Appalachian Mountains, for example, extend northward along the eastern coast of North America, and mountains of similar age and structure are found in Greenland, Scotland, and northern Europe. If the continents are assembled into a model supercontinent, the mountains of similar age fit together in continuous chains.

Differentiated Instruction

Special Education Students

Vocabulary Notebook Ask students to copy all key terms that appear in bold type throughout the chapter into a Vocabulary Notebook. Students should also copy the margin definitions next to each key term. They can copy the sentence in which each key term appears to help them understand the word in the context of the chapter. The notebooks can be used for independent study. LS **Verbal**

Climatic Evidence

Changes in climatic patterns provided more evidence that the continents have not always been located where they are now. Geologists discovered layers of debris from ancient glaciers in southern Africa and South America. Today, those areas have climates that are too warm for glaciers to form. Other fossil evidence—such as the plant fossil shown in **Figure 3**—indicated that tropical or subtropical swamps covered areas that now have much colder climates. Wegener suggested that if the continents were once joined and positioned differently, evidence of climatic differences would be easy to explain.

Missing Mechanisms

Despite the evidence that supported the hypothesis of continental drift, Wegener's ideas were strongly opposed. Other scientists of the time rejected the mechanism proposed by Wegener to explain how the continents moved. Wegener suggested that the continents plowed through the rock of the ocean floor. However, this idea was shown to be physically impossible. Wegener spent the rest of his life searching for a mechanism that would gain scientific consensus. Unfortunately, Wegener died in 1930 before he identified a plausible explanation.

Reading Check **Why did many scientists reject Wegener's hypothesis of continental drift?** (See Appendix G for answers to Reading Checks.)

Figure 3 The climate of Antarctica was not always as harsh and cold as it is today. When the plant that became this fossil lived, the climate of Antarctica was warm and tropical.

READING TOOLBOX

Three-Panel Flip Chart
Make a three-panel flip chart. Label the panels "Fossil evidence," "Evidence from rock formations," and "Climatic evidence." Open the appropriate flap to take notes about evidence Wegener used to support his hypothesis.

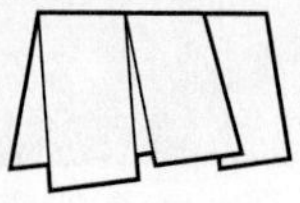

Academic Vocabulary

mechanism (MEK uh NIZ uhm) any system or means by which something gets done

READING TOOLBOX

Three-Panel Flip Chart Answers may vary, but students' flip charts should accurately describe evidence from fossils, rock forma and climatic data that Wegener used to support his hypothesis.

Debate — ADVANCED

Wegener's Idea Have students form two groups to debate the merits and flaws of Wegener's hypothesis. Have one group of students research and present specific examples of evidence that supports the idea of continental drift. Have the other students identify weaknesses of the hypothesis and present alternative explanations for the evidence suggested by the first group. **LS Logical/Verbal**
Co-op Learning

Discussion — GENERAL

Making Predictions Have a discussion about mechanisms for continental drift. Have students suggest possible mechanisms that may drive the movement of continents. Try to get students to imagine the amount of force needed to move an object as massive as a continent by comparing the size and mass of a continent to the size and mass of aircraft carriers (about 100,000 metric tons) and space vehicles (launch mass = 2,040,000 kg; launch thrust = 34,677 kN).
LS Verbal

Answer to Reading Check
Many scientists rejected Wegener's hypothesis because the mechanism that Wegener suggested was physically impossible.

History Connection

Alfred Lothar Wegener Alfred Wegener was born in Germany in 1880. He received a doctorate of astronomy in 1905 and served at the aeronautical observatory at Lindenberg early in his scientific career. He joined the German army at the outbreak of World War I but was injured shortly after joining. After the war, he did research in meteorology in Hamburg, Germany, for the German government. He was a professor of meteorology at the University of Graz in Austria from 1924 to 1930. He went on four polar expeditions between 1906 and 1930. On the last of these expeditions, he visited Greenland to try to determine the thickness of the Greenland ice sheet and the rate of drift of Greenland. At the end of that expedition, he died while rescuing some colleagues.

Teach, *continued*

Activity — GENERAL

Sea-Floor Sediments Have pairs of students model the depth of sea-floor sediments by following these simple steps.

1. Place a piece of paper on a flat surface.
2. Hold a shoe box of confetti so that confetti falls from one side rather than from a corner.
3. While moving the piece of paper, slowly sprinkle the confetti over the paper in a single line.
4. Measure the thickness of the confetti at different points along the line. Where is it thinnest? (nearest where you stopped sprinkling) Where is it thickest? (farther from where you stopped sprinkling) Why? (because it fell on the thickest point for the longest time)

LS **Kinesthetic/Visual**

Physics Connection

Sonar Researchers used sonar to discover that the ocean floor is not flat. In the 1950s, scientists broadcast sound waves toward the sea floor and measured how long the waves took to return. The echoes revealed the existence of oceanic valleys and mountains. In short, the ocean floors turned out to be as varied as the continents! Scientists were most amazed to find a chain of undersea mountains snaking thousands of kilometers around the globe—the mid-ocean ridges.

Figure 4 Black smokers are vents on the sea floor that form as hot, mineral-rich water rushes from the hot rock at mid-ocean ridges and mixes with the surrounding cold ocean water. This photo was taken from a submersible.

Mid-Ocean Ridges

The evidence that Wegener needed to support his hypothesis was discovered nearly two decades after his death. The evidence lay on the ocean floor. In 1947, a group of scientists set out to map the Mid-Atlantic Ridge. The Mid-Atlantic Ridge is part of a system of **mid-ocean ridges,** which are undersea mountain ranges through the center of which run steep, narrow valleys. A special feature of mid-ocean ridges is shown in **Figure 4.** While studying the Mid-Atlantic Ridge, scientists noticed two surprising trends. First, they noticed that the sediment that covers the sea floor is thinner closer to a ridge than it is farther from the ridge. This evidence suggests that sediment has been settling on the sea floor farther from the ridge for a longer time than it has been settling near the ridge. Scientists then examined the remains of tiny ocean organisms found in the sediment to date the sediment. The distribution of these organisms showed that the closer the sediment is to a ridge, the younger the sediment is. This evidence indicates that rocks closer to the ridge are younger than rocks farther from the ridge, as shown in **Figure 5.**

Second, scientists learned that the ocean floor is very young. While rocks on land are as much as 4 billion years old, none of the oceanic rocks are more than 200 million years old. Radiometric dating also showed evidence that sea-floor rocks closer to a mid-ocean ridge are younger than sea-floor rocks farther from a ridge.

mid-ocean ridge a long, undersea mountain chain that has a steep, narrow valley at its center, that forms as magma rises from the asthenosphere, and that creates new oceanic lithosphere (sea floor) as tectonic plates move apart

Figure 5 Rocks closer to a mid-ocean ridge are younger than rocks farther from the ridge. In addition, rocks closer to the ridge are covered with less sediment, which indicates that sediment has had less time to settle on them.

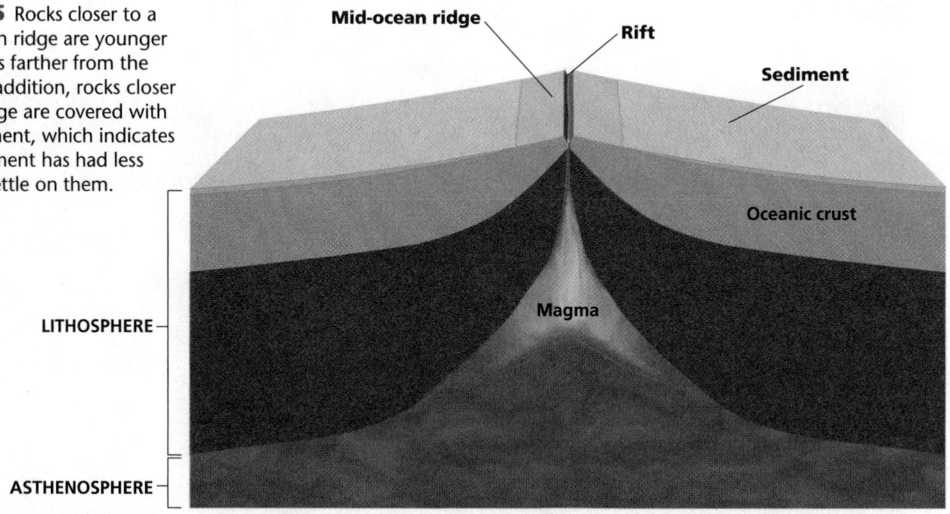

Why It Matters

Ridges and Rises At the Mid-Atlantic Ridge, approximately 2.5 to 5 cm of new sea floor forms each year. At a ridge, the topography is rough because a chain of small volcanoes is linked by fissure eruptions. At the East Pacific Rise, as much as 15 cm of new sea floor forms each year. At a rise, the topography is smoother because the crust is made of flat lava flows that erupt from large, long fissures.

Sea-Floor Spreading

In the late 1950s, a geologist named Harry Hess suggested a new hypothesis. He proposed that the valley at the center of the ridge was a crack, or *rift,* in Earth's crust. At this rift, molten rock, or *magma,* from deep inside Earth rises to fill the crack. As the ocean floor moves away from the ridge, rising magma cools and solidifies to form new rock that replaces the ocean floor. This process is shown in **Figure 6.** During this process, named **sea-floor spreading** by geologist Robert Dietz, new ocean lithosphere forms as magma rises to Earth's surface and solidifies at a mid-ocean ridge. Hess suggested that if the ocean floor is moving, the continents might be moving, too. Hess thought that sea-floor spreading was the mechanism that Wegener had failed to find.

Still, Hess's ideas were only hypotheses. More evidence for sea-floor spreading would come years later, in the mid-1960s. This evidence would be discovered through **paleomagnetism,** the study of the magnetic properties of rocks.

Reading Check **How does new sea floor form?**

sea-floor spreading the process by which new oceanic lithosphere (sea floor) forms when magma rises to Earth's surface at mid-ocean ridges and solidifies, as older, existing sea floor moves away from the ridge

paleomagnetism the study of the alignment of magnetic minerals in rock, specifically as it relates to the reversal of Earth's magnetic poles; *also* the magnetic properties that rock acquires during formation

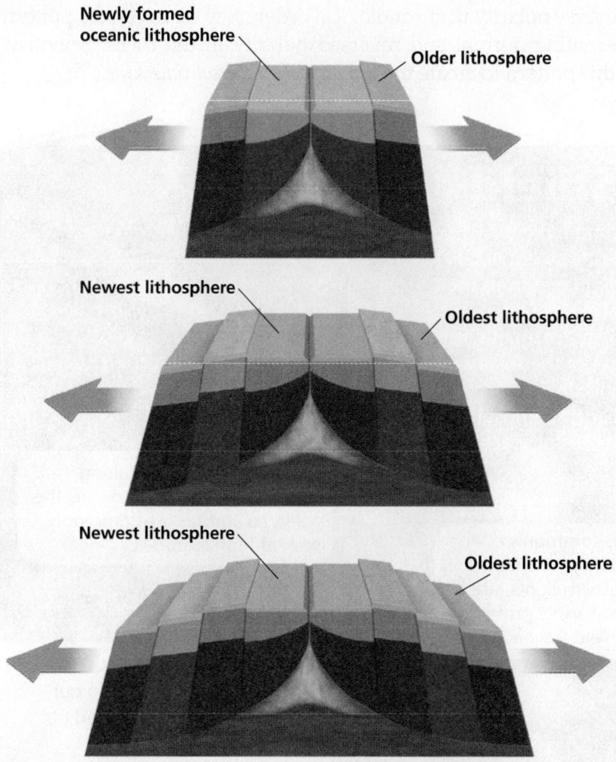

Figure 6 As the ocean floor spreads apart at a mid-ocean ridge, magma rises to fill the rift and then cools to form new rock. As this process is repeated over millions of years, new sea floor forms.

Using the Figure — BASIC

Sea-Floor Formation Have students analyze the figure that illustrates sea-floor spreading. Have students identify the relative age of each block in each diagram by following the green block through the frames. Ask students to write a list of steps that describe the process of sea-floor spreading. (1. Ocean floor pulls apart. 2. New sea floor forms in the crack. 3. Ocean floor pulls apart again, and the process repeats.) **LS Visual**

Answer to Reading Check

New sea floor forms as magma rises to fill the rift that forms when two plates pull apart at a divergent boundary.

Skill Builder — ADVANCED

Math The Atlantic Ocean is spreading at a rate of 1 to 2 cm per year, and the eastern Pacific sea floor is spreading between 3 and 8 cm per year. Have students use the average rate of spreading for the Atlantic Ocean to calculate how many years the sea floor of the Atlantic Ocean would take to spread 1 km. (1.5 cm/year; 1 km ÷ 0.000015 km/year = 66,667 years) Have students use the average rate of spreading of the Pacific Ocean to calculate how many years the sea floor of the Pacific Ocean would take to spread 1 km. (5.5 cm/year; 1 km ÷ 0.000055 km/year = 18,182 years) **LS Logical**

Differentiated Instruction

Basic Learners

Chain of Events Have students make a three-box chain-of-events chart as described in **Appendix A.** Then, ask students to fill in the chart with details about each step of sea-floor spreading. (Example: Box 1: "Magma rises and fills the rift at the center of the ridge," Box 2: The magma cools and forms new rock," Box 3: "More magma rises as sea-floor spreading carries the new rock away from the ridge.")

Key Resources

Technology

- Transparencies
  49 Sea-Floor Spreading

Teach, *continued*

Demonstration BASIC

Earth's Magnetic Field To help students visualize how iron-bearing minerals in molten rocks align with Earth's magnetic field, place a magnet in the center of an overhead projector so that the north pole faces the top of the projector. Place a sheet of clear acetate over the magnet. Sprinkle some iron filings on the acetate. The iron filings will align with the lines of force of the magnet. Lift the acetate, and move the magnet so that the north and south poles face the sides of the projector. Explain that when Earth's magnetic field reverses, the iron-bearing minerals that form from molten rock align according to the new magnetic field. **LS Visual**

Why It Matters

Our Own Space Shield Earth's magnetic field shields our planet from the solar wind, even though it can at times interfere with electrical systems. Particles from the solar wind are channeled down Earth's magnetic field lines to the poles, where they collide with nitrogen and oxygen atoms to produce heat and displays of light called auroras. The streamers of light shift and change as they interact with the solar wind. They are a sign that Earth's protective space shield is working.

Answer to Your Turn

Earth's atmosphere would be slowly lost to space.

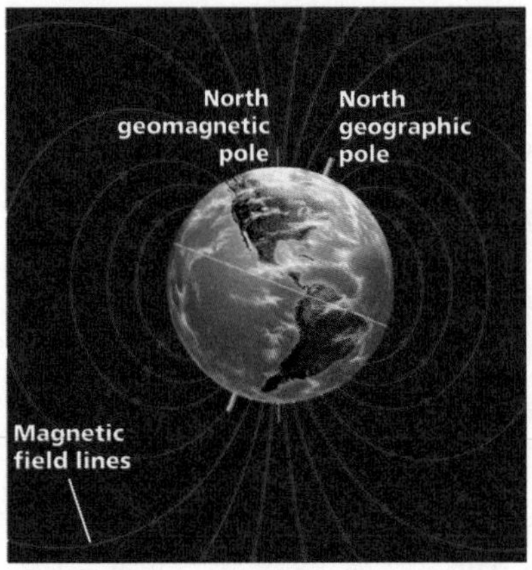

Figure 7 Earth acts as a giant magnet because of currents in Earth's core.

Paleomagnetism

If you have ever used a compass to determine direction, you know that Earth acts as a giant magnet. Earth has north and south geomagnetic poles, as shown in **Figure 7.** The compass needle aligns with the field of magnetic force that extends from one pole to the other.

As magma solidifies to form rock, iron-rich minerals in the magma align with Earth's magnetic field in the same way that a compass needle does. When the rock hardens, the magnetic orientation of the minerals becomes permanent. This residual magnetism of rock is called *paleomagnetism.*

Magnetic Reversals

Geologic evidence shows that Earth's magnetic field has not always pointed north, as it does now. Scientists have discovered rocks whose magnetic orientations point opposite to Earth's current magnetic field. Scientists have dated rocks of different magnetic polarities. All rocks with magnetic fields that point north, or *normal polarity,* are classified in the same time intervals. All rocks with magnetic fields that point south, or *reversed polarity,* also fall into specific time intervals. When scientists placed these periods of normal and reverse polarity in chronological order, they discovered a pattern of alternating normal and reversed polarity in the rocks. Scientists used this pattern to create the *geomagnetic reversal time scale.*

Why It Matters

Our Own Space Shield

WEIRD SCIENCE

Earth's magnetic field is not just an interesting topic for scientists. It makes life on Earth possible. Earth's magnetic field acts like a giant space shield, protecting our planet from the solar wind — electrically charged particles that stream away from the sun in all directions. Even with Earth's magnetic field in place, temporary increases in the strength of the solar wind can disrupt telecommunications systems and disable electric power grids. Without the magnetic field, Earth's atmosphere would be gradually swept away into the depths of space.

The solar wind moves along Earth's magnetic field toward the poles, so auroras are commonly seen at high latitudes.

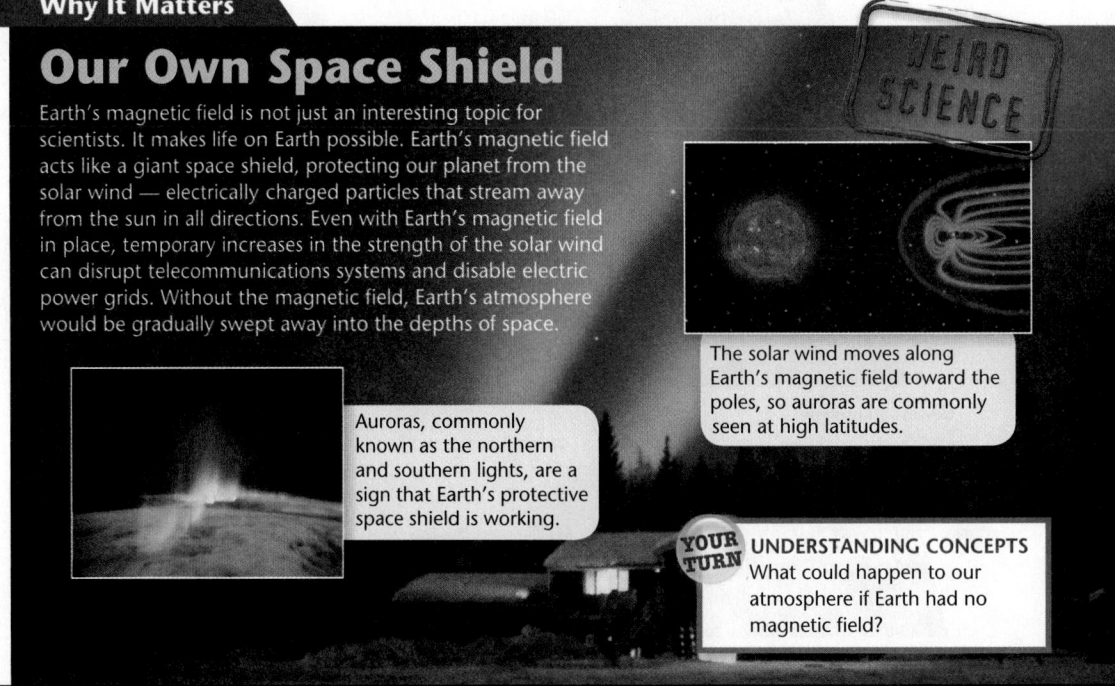

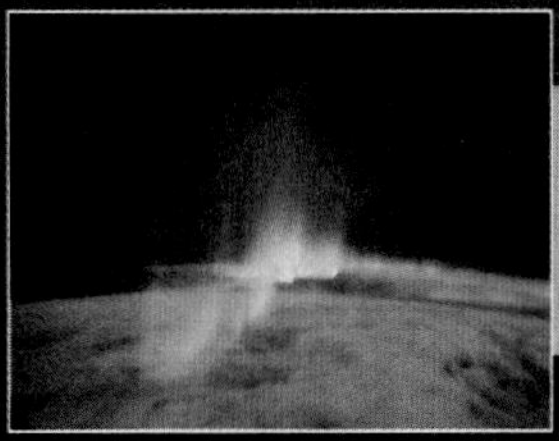

Auroras, commonly known as the northern and southern lights, are a sign that Earth's protective space shield is working.

YOUR TURN **UNDERSTANDING CONCEPTS**
What could happen to our atmosphere if Earth had no magnetic field?

MISCONCEPTION ALERT

Mineral Magnetism Students may think that crystals of magnetic minerals can change their alignments easily. Explain to students that as igneous rock forms at a mid-ocean ridge, minerals form in such a way that the magnetic fields of the minerals are aligned with Earth's magnetic field. Some students may ask why the magnetic fields of the minerals do not realign themselves when the next magnetic reversal occurs. The answer is that the rock must be heated beyond the mineral's Curie point for the mineral to lose its original magnetism. The Curie point is the temperature at which the electron orbitals in the atoms in a mineral no longer overlap because the crystal lattice has expanded too much. When the orbitals no longer overlap, the spin moments of the electrons do not align, and magnetism is lost. Unless magnetized rock is heated to a temperature above its Curie point, it will hold onto its original magnetism. The Curie temperature for the mineral magnetite is ~580 °C.

Magnetic Symmetry

As scientists were learning about the age of the sea floor, they also were finding puzzling magnetic patterns on the ocean floor. The scientists used the geomagnetic reversal time scale to help them unravel the mystery of these magnetic patterns.

Scientists noticed that the striped magnetic pattern on one side of a mid-ocean ridge is a mirror image of the striped pattern on the other side of the ridge. These patterns are shown in **Figure 8.** When drawn on maps of the ocean floor, these patterns show alternating bands of normal and reversed polarity that match the geomagnetic reversal time scale. Scientists suggested that as new sea floor forms at a mid-ocean ridge, the new sea floor records reversals in Earth's magnetic field.

By matching the magnetic patterns on each side of a mid-ocean ridge to the geomagnetic reversal time scale, scientists could assign ages to the sea-floor rocks. The scientists found that the ages of sea-floor rocks were also symmetrical. The youngest rocks were at the center, and older rocks were farther away on either side of the ridge. The only place on the sea floor that new rock forms is at the rift in a mid-ocean ridge. Thus, the patterns indicate that new rock forms at the center of a ridge and then moves away from the center in opposite directions. Thus, the symmetry of magnetic patterns—and the symmetry of ages of sea-floor rocks—supports Hess's idea of sea-floor spreading.

Reading Check **How are magnetic patterns in sea-floor rock evidence of sea-floor spreading?**

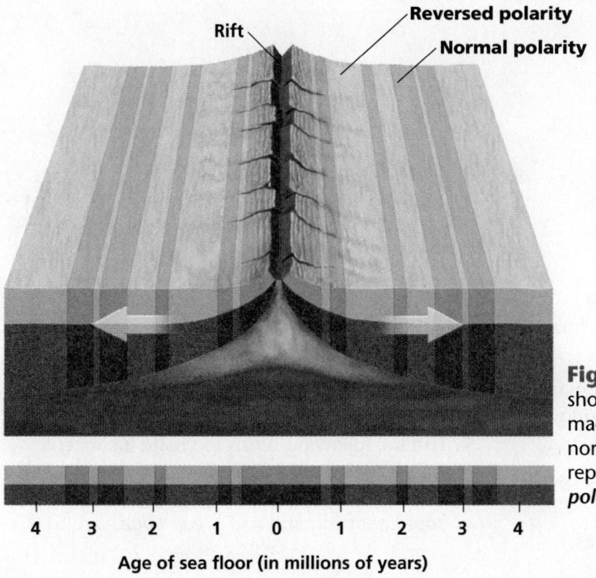

THINK central INTERACT ONLINE (Keyword: HQXTECF8)

Figure 8 The stripes in the sea floor shown here illustrate Earth's alternating magnetic field. Dark stripes represent normal polarity, while lighter stripes represent reversed polarity. ***What is the polarity of the rocks closest to the rift?***

Quick Lab — 10 min

Making Magnets

Procedure

1. Slide one end of a bar magnet down the side of a 5 inch iron nail 10 times. Always slide the magnet in the same direction.
2. Hold the nail over a small pile of steel paper clips. Record what happens.
3. Slide the bar magnet back and forth 10 times down the side of the nail. Repeat step 2.

Analysis

1. What was the effect of sliding the magnet down the nail in one direction? in different directions?
2. How does this lab demonstrate the idea of polarity?

Quick Lab

Skills Acquired
- Experimenting
- Observing

Materials
- Bar magnet
- 5-inch iron nail
- Steel paper clips

Teacher's Notes: You may want to check the nails before class to make sure that they are not magnetized before the lab. Tell students not to drop the nails; otherwise, the nails may lose their magnetism.

Answers to Analysis

1. Sliding the magnet down the nail in one direction magnetized the nail. Sliding the magnet in different directions demagnetized the nail.
2. Using the magnet can cause the nail's magnetic properties to change.

Close

Reteaching — BASIC

Evidence for Continental Drift Ask students to build a small model of the ocean floor. Then, have students use paint, colored pencils, or markers to draw magnetic polarity stripes on the sea floor. On the sea floor, students should make symmetrical stripes that mirror each other on either side of the mid-ocean ridges. **LS Kinesthetic**

Quiz — GENERAL

Determine whether each of the following statements is true or false.

1. Evidence for the hypothesis of continental drift includes land bridges between continents. (false)
2. Many scientists rejected the hypothesis of continental drift because it did not explain how continents move. (true)
3. Continental drift can be partially explained by sea-floor spreading. (true)

Differentiated Instruction

Special Education Students

Magnetic Symmetry To help visually impaired students understand magnetic patterns in sea-floor rocks, make a model of the ocean floor on either side of a mid-ocean ridge. Attach toothpicks to a piece of paper to form raised areas separated by non-raised areas. Vary the widths of the areas but make sure the widths are symmetrical about the ridge. Tell students the raised and non-raised areas represent rock of different polarities. Have students match the patterns on either side of the ridge to identify areas that represent rock of the same age.

Answer to Reading Check

The symmetrical magnetic patterns in sea-floor rocks show that rock formed at one place (at a ridge) and then broke apart and moved away from the center in opposite directions.

Close, *continued*

Answers to Section Review

1. The coastlines of the continents seem to fit together like pieces of a jigsaw puzzle.
2. The hypothesis of continental drift is supported by evidence from fossils, rock formations, locations of mountain ranges, and climatic evidence.
3. At rifts in Earth's crust along mid-ocean ridges, magma from the mantle rises to Earth's surface and cools to form new rock. As that rock cools, it moves away from the rift, and new magma rises to fill the empty space.
4. Rocks with normal polarity formed during distinct time spans, which differ from the time spans in which rocks with reverse polarity formed. Because these same patterns are found all over the planet, scientists agree that Earth's magnetic field must have reversed at various times in Earth's history.
5. The patterns of magnetic reversals are mirrored on both sides of a mid-ocean ridge, which indicates that the magma hardened to rock at the center and then moved away from the center through sea-floor spreading.
6. Scientists use radiometric dating, sediment thickness, fossil evidence in sediments, and magnetic reversal patterns to date sea-floor rocks.
7. As new rock forms at the mid-ocean ridge, the existing rock moves farther from the ridge. Thus, the rock at the ridge is the youngest, and the rock farthest from the ridge is the oldest.
8. As new sea floor forms, the older sea floor moves away from the spreading center. As the sea floor moves, it carries continents along with it.
9. *Sea-floor spreading* is the mechnism by which new ocean floor forms at *mid-ocean ridges*; was identified by using *paleomagnetism*; and is a mechanism that could drive *continental drift*, which could form *supercontinents* and is supported by evidence from studying *fossils, climate*, and *geologic evidence*.

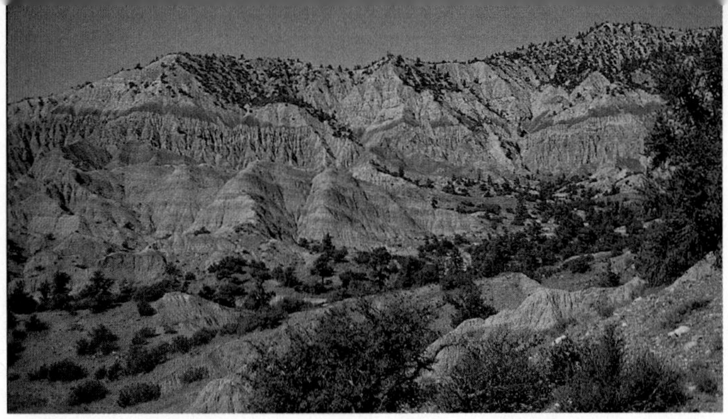

Figure 9 Scientists collected samples of these sedimentary rocks in California and used the magnetic properties of the samples to date the rocks by using the geomagnetic reversal time scale.

Wegener Redeemed

Another group of scientists discovered that the reversal patterns seen in rocks on the sea floor also appeared in rocks on land, such as those shown in **Figure 9.** The reversals in the land rocks matched the geomagnetic reversal time scale. Because the same pattern occurs in rocks of the same ages on both land and the sea floor, scientists became confident that magnetic patterns show changes over time. Thus, the idea of sea-floor spreading gained further favor in the scientific community.

Scientists reasoned that sea-floor spreading provides a way for the continents to move over Earth's surface. Continents are carried by the widening sea floor in much the same way that objects are carried by a conveyor belt. The molten rock from a rift cools, hardens, and then moves away in opposite directions on both sides of the ridge. Here, at last, was the mechanism that verified Wegener's hypothesis of continental drift.

Section 1 Review

Key Ideas

1. **Describe** the observation that first led to Wegener's hypothesis of continental drift.
2. **Summarize** the evidence that supports Wegener's hypothesis.
3. **Compare** sea-floor spreading with the formation of mid-ocean ridges.
4. **Explain** how scientists know that Earth's magnetic poles have reversed many times during Earth's history.
5. **Identify** how magnetic symmetry can be used as evidence of sea-floor spreading.
6. **Explain** how scientists date sea-floor rocks.

Critical Thinking

7. **Making Inferences** How does evidence that rocks farther from a ridge are older than rocks closer to the ridge support the idea of spreading?
8. **Analyzing Ideas** Explain how sea-floor spreading provides an explanation for how continents move over Earth's surface.

Concept Mapping

9. Use the following terms to create a concept map: *continental drift, paleomagnetism, fossils, climate, sea-floor spreading, geologic evidence, supercontinent,* and *mid-ocean ridge.*

Differentiated Instruction

Alternative Assessment

Persuasive Essay Have students write a persuasive essay that describes their stance on sea-floor spreading as a mechanism for continental drift. Students can choose to support sea-floor spreading as a mechanism, or they may argue against it. Whichever stance each student chooses, he or she must provide supporting reasoning and evidence. **LS Logical**

SECTION 2

The Theory of Plate Tectonics

Key Ideas	Key Terms	Why It Matters
❯ Summarize the theory of plate tectonics. ❯ Identify and describe the three types of plate boundaries. ❯ List and describe three causes of plate movement.	plate tectonics lithosphere asthenosphere divergent boundary convergent boundary transform boundary	Plate tectonics is not just a scientific theory. Because of plate tectonics, you are able to enjoy the use of a cell phone, MP3 player, or any number of other electronic devices.

By the 1960s, evidence supporting continental drift and sea-floor spreading led to the development of a theory called *plate tectonics.* **Plate tectonics** is the theory that explains why and how continents move and is the study of the formation of features in Earth's crust.

How Continents Move

Earth's crust and the rigid, upper part of the mantle form a layer of Earth called the **lithosphere.** The lithosphere forms the thin outer shell of Earth. It is broken into several blocks, called *tectonic plates,* that ride on a deformable layer of the mantle called the *asthenosphere* in much the same way that blocks of wood float on water. The **asthenosphere** (as THEN uh sfir) is a layer of "plastic" rock just below the lithosphere. Plastic rock is a solid, not a liquid, but it is so hot that it flows very slowly, like putty does. **Figure 1** shows what tectonic plates may look like.

Earth's crust is classified into two types—*oceanic crust* and *continental crust*. Oceanic crust is dense and is made of rock that is rich in iron and magnesium. Continental crust has a low density and is made of rock that is rich in silica. Tectonic plates can include continental crust, oceanic crust, or both. The crust is carried along on the moving tectonic plates in the same way that passengers are carried by a bus.

plate tectonics the theory that explains how large pieces of the lithosphere, called *plates,* move and change shape

lithosphere the solid, outer layer of Earth that consists of the crust and the rigid upper part of the mantle

asthenosphere the solid, plastic layer of the mantle beneath the lithosphere

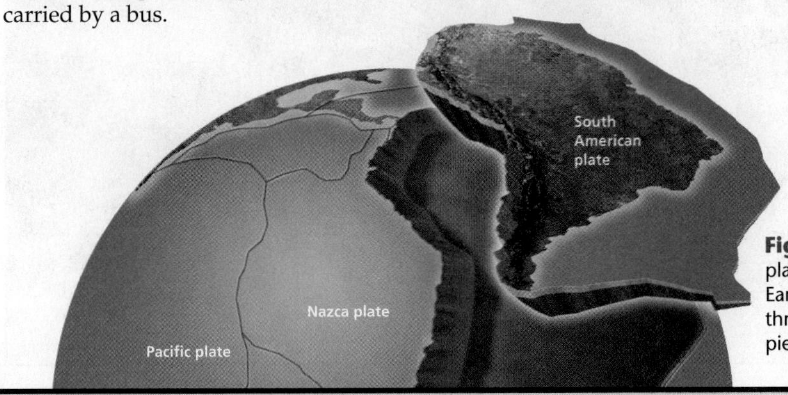

Figure 1 Tectonic plates fit together on Earth's surface like three-dimensional puzzle pieces.

Section 2

Focus

Overview

In this section, students learn about the theory of plate tectonics. The section describes the movements of tectonic plates, types of plate boundaries, and driving forces of plate tectonics.

Bellringer

Ask students how many continents exist on Earth's surface, and have them list the continents. (six: Australia, Antarctica, North America, South America, Eurasia, and Africa) Explain to students that scientists have identified at least 30 tectonic plates—10 to 15 major plates and many smaller subplates. **LS Logical**

Motivate

Activity — GENERAL

Jigsaw Puzzles Bring a 25-piece jigsaw puzzle to class, and challenge students to put the puzzle together. Explain to students that Earth's surface is like a spherical jigsaw puzzle, but instead of being small pieces of cardboard, the pieces are giant slabs of rock that are millions of square kilometers in area and billions of tons in weight. **LS Visual/Kinesthetic**

Key Resources

Chapter Resource File
- Directed Reading BASIC
- Inquiry Lab: Where Do Earthquakes Happen? GENERAL
- Making Models Lab: Eggshell Tectonics GENERAL
- Internet Activity: The Heimaey Eruption BASIC

Technology
- Transparencies
  Bellringer

Math Skills

Answer

rate = distance ÷ time;
1 cm = 0.00001 km;
0.00004 km/1 year = *x* km = 2,000,000 years; *x* km = 0.00004 km/year × 2,000,000 years = 80 km

Internet Activity — BASIC

Earthquakes Students may be interested in knowing what areas of Earth's surface have the most earthquakes each day, month, and year. The Incorporated Research Institutions for Seismicity has an online service known as the Seismic Monitor. This site constantly updates a global map of recent earthquake activity. Students can visit this site to learn where the most recent large earthquakes have occurred. A worksheet designed to direct student research on this topic can be found in the **Chapter Resource File** booklet or by visiting www.thinkcentral.com and entering the keyword **HQXTECX.**
LS Visual

Answer to Reading Check

Scientists use the locations of earthquakes, volcanoes, trenches, and mid-ocean ridges to outline tectonic plates.

Physics Connection

Earthquakes An earthquake creates a series of seismic waves that radiate outward in all directions from the point where the rocks move. Scientists use the behavior of seismic waves to study the structure of Earth's interior. Students may better understand this process if it is compared to shaking a wrapped gift to get clues about what's inside it.

Math Skills

The Rate of Plate Movement Tectonic plates move slowly on Earth's surface. The rate of plate movement can be calculated by using the following equation:

$$rate = \frac{distance}{time}$$

In kilometers, how far would a plate that moves 4 cm per year move in 2 million years?

Tectonic Plates

Scientists have identified 15 major tectonic plates and many smaller plates. While plates are often bordered by major surface features, such as mountain ranges or deep trenches in the oceans, the boundaries of the plates are not always easy to identify. As shown in **Figure 2**, the familiar outlines of the continents and oceans often do not match the outlines of plate boundaries. Some plate boundaries are located within continents far from mountain ranges.

Earthquakes

Scientists identify plate boundaries primarily by studying data from earthquakes. When tectonic plates move, sudden shifts can occur along their boundaries. These sudden movements are called *earthquakes*. Frequent earthquakes in a given zone are evidence that two or more plates may meet in that area.

Volcanoes

The locations of volcanoes can also help to identify the locations of plate boundaries. Some volcanoes form when plate motions generate magma that erupts on Earth's surface. For example, the Pacific Ring of Fire is a zone of active volcanoes that encircles the Pacific Ocean. This zone is also one of Earth's major earthquake zones. The characteristics of this zone indicate that the Pacific Ocean is surrounded by plate boundaries.

Reading Check **How do scientists identify locations of plate boundaries?**

Figure 2 Tectonic plates may contain both oceanic and continental crust. Notice that the boundaries of plates do not always match the outlines of continents.

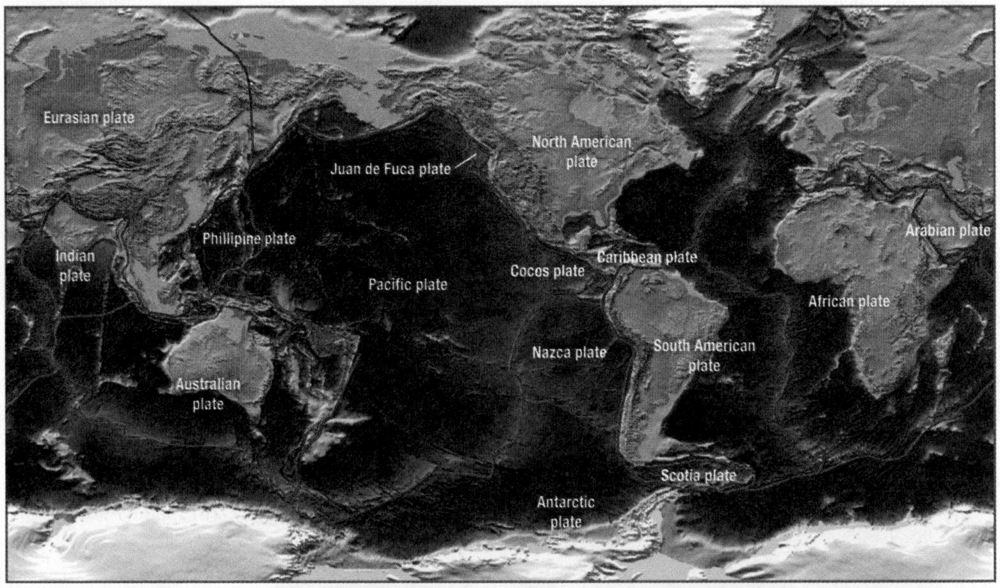

Key Resources

Technology

- Transparencies
  50 Tectonic Plate Boundaries

Differentiated Instruction

English Learners

Root Words Tell students the word *tectonics* is from the Greek word *tektonikos*, which means "construction." Tectonics is the study of the formation of features in Earth's crust. Ask students to explain how this root word can help them understand the geologic features that result from plate tectonics.

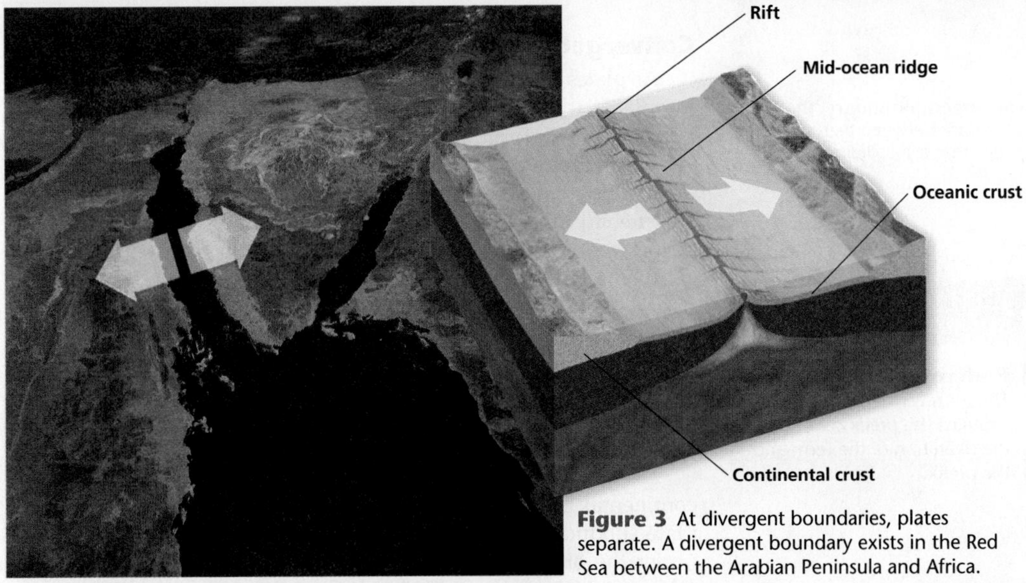

Figure 3 At divergent boundaries, plates separate. A divergent boundary exists in the Red Sea between the Arabian Peninsula and Africa.

Types of Plate Boundaries

Some of the most dramatic changes in Earth's crust, such as earthquakes and volcanic eruptions, happen along plate boundaries. Plate boundaries may be in the middle of an ocean basin, around the edges of continents, or even within continents. There are three types of plate boundaries. These plate boundaries are: divergent boundaries, convergent boundaries, and transform boundaries. Each type of plate boundary is associated with a characteristic type of geologic activity.

Divergent Boundaries

The way that plates move relative to each other determines how the plate boundary affects Earth's surface. At a **divergent boundary,** two plates move away from each other. A divergent boundary is illustrated in **Figure 3.**

At divergent boundaries, magma from the asthenosphere rises to the surface as the plates move apart. The magma then cools to form new oceanic lithosphere. The newly formed rock at the ridge is warm and light. This warm, light rock sits higher than the surrounding sea floor because it is less dense. This rock forms undersea mountain ranges known as *mid-ocean ridges*. Along the center of a mid-ocean ridge is a *rift valley,* a narrow valley that forms where the plates separate.

Most divergent boundaries are located on the ocean floor. However, rift valleys may also form where continents are separated by plate movement. For example, the Red Sea occupies a huge rift valley formed by the separation of the African plate and the Arabian plate, as shown in **Figure 3.**

divergent boundary the boundary between tectonic plates that are moving away from each other

Discussion — BASIC

Crustal Chemistry Tell students that oceanic crust is composed mainly of mafic rock, or rock that has a lot of heavy, iron- and magnesium-rich minerals. Tell students that continental crust is composed of lighter, silica-rich minerals. Ask students to think about a heavy china plate and a plastic foam plate floating on water. Ask them which plate is likely to sink beneath the other plate. (The china plate is more likely to sink, and the plastic foam plate is more likely to float.) Ask students to think about how this analogy could help them understand convergent boundaries. **LS Logical**

Skill Builder — BASIC

Vocabulary The word *divergent* is derived from the Latin *dis-*, which means "apart," and v*ergere*, which means "to turn." Discuss with students the definitions of other words that begin with the prefix dis-, such as *distant* (the condition of being separated in space or time), *distinguish* (to separate or tell apart by differences), *distribute* (to divide and give out in shares), or *distract* (to draw attention away).
LS Verbal English Language Learners

Key Resources

Technology

- Transparencies
  51 Types of Plate Boundaries

MISCONCEPTION ALERT

Shape of Divergent Boundaries Students may think of divergent boundaries as continuous, open cracks in Earth's surface. However, divergent boundaries are generally a series of smaller, offset cracks. The magma that rises at a rift flows upward through a series of small, vertical vents rather than flowing as a giant mass through a large, wide crack in the ocean floor.

Teach, *continued*

READING TOOLBOX

Prefixes A *convergent boundary* is a boundary that forms where two tectonic plates collide. The prefix *con-* means "with, together."

Chemistry Connection

Plate Boundary Volcanics The composition of igneous rock varies at different plate boundaries. In general, mafic and ultramafic rocks, or rocks that have very high iron and magnesium content, form at divergent plate boundaries. At convergent boundaries, igneous rocks that have intermediate compositions, or rocks with moderate amounts of both iron and silicate minerals, form. These differences are the result of the type of rock that melted to form the magma. At divergent boundaries, magma rises from the iron-rich mantle. At convergent boundaries, the crust of the overriding plate undergoes partial melting to form magma. Because continental crust and seafloor sediments are generally high in silica, this chemical makes up more of the magma at convergent boundaries than at divergent boundaries.

Answer to Reading Check

Collisions at convergent boundaries can happen between two oceanic plates, between two continental plates, or between one oceanic plate and one continental plate.

convergent boundary the boundary between tectonic plates that are colliding

READING TOOLBOX

Prefixes

The term *convergent boundary* contains the prefix *con-*. Give the definition of the term and the prefix.

Convergent Boundaries

As plates pull apart at one boundary, they push into neighboring plates at other boundaries. **Convergent boundaries** are plate boundaries that form where two plates collide.

Three types of collisions can happen at convergent boundaries. One type happens when oceanic lithosphere collides with continental lithosphere, as shown in **Figure 4.** Because oceanic lithosphere is denser, it *subducts,* or sinks, under the less dense continental lithosphere. The region along a plate boundary where one plate moves under another plate is called a *subduction zone.* Deep-ocean trenches form at subduction zones. As the oceanic plate subducts, it heats up and releases fluids into the mantle above it. The addition of these fluids causes material in the overlying mantle to melt to form magma. The magma rises to the surface and forms volcanic mountains.

A second type of collision happens when two plates made of continental lithosphere collide. In this type of collision, neither plate subducts because neither plate is dense enough to subduct under the other plate. Instead, the colliding edges crumple and thicken, which causes uplift that forms large mountain ranges. The Himalaya Mountains formed in this type of collision.

The third type of collision happens between two plates that are made of oceanic lithosphere. One plate subducts under the other plate, and a deep-ocean trench forms. Fluids released from the subducted plate cause mantle rock to melt and form magma. The magma rises to the surface to form an *island arc,* which is a chain of volcanic islands. Japan is an example of an island arc.

Reading Check **Describe the three types of collisions that happen at convergent boundaries.**

Figure 4 Plates collide at convergent boundaries. The islands of Japan are formed by the subduction of the Pacific plate and the Philippine plate under the Eurasian plate.

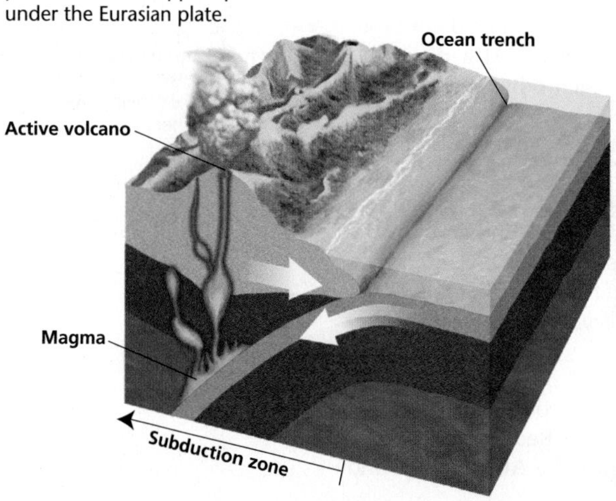

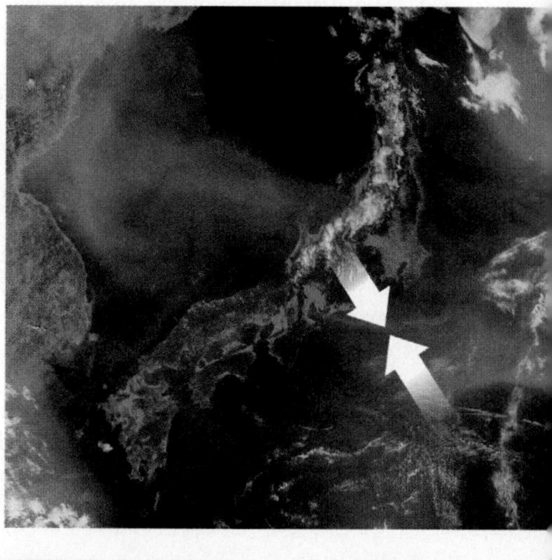

Differentiated Instruction

Special Education Students

Modeling Plate Boundaries Ask students to model the types of plate boundaries by using their hands. Have students place the index fingers of their hands together. Then, have them slide one hand under the other hand to model a convergent boundary. Have students model divergent boundaries by pulling their hands apart from the starting position. **LS Kinesthetic**

Figure 5 Plates slide past each other at transform boundaries. The course of the stream in the photo changed because the plates moved past each other at the San Andreas Fault in California.

Transform Boundaries

The boundary at which two plates slide past each other horizontally, as shown in **Figure 5,** is called a **transform boundary.** However, the plate edges usually do not slide along smoothly. Instead, they scrape against each other in a series of sudden spurts of motion that are felt as earthquakes. Unlike other types of boundaries, transform boundaries do not produce magma. The San Andreas Fault in California is a major transform boundary between the North American plate and the Pacific plate.

Transform motion also occurs along mid-ocean ridges. Short segments of a mid-ocean ridge are connected by transform boundaries called *fracture zones.*

Table 1 summarizes the three types of plate boundaries. The table also describes how each type of plate boundary changes Earth's surface and includes examples of each type of plate boundary.

transform boundary the boundary between tectonic plates that are sliding past each other horizontally

Table 1 Plate Boundary Summary

Type of boundary	Description	Example
Divergent	plates moving away from each other to form rifts and mid-ocean ridges	North American and Eurasian plates at the Mid-Atlantic Ridge
Convergent	plates moving toward each other and colliding to form ocean trenches, mountain ranges, volcanoes, and island arcs	South American and Nazca plates at the Chilean trench along the west coast of South America
Transform	plates sliding past each other while moving in opposite directions	North American and Pacific plates at the San Andreas Fault in California

Why It Matters

Fracture Zones Oceanic fracture zones are ocean-floor valleys that horizontally offset segments of mid-ocean ridges. Some of these zones are hundreds to thousands of kilometers long. Examples of large fracture zones include the Blanco, Mendocino, Murray, and Molokai Fracture Zones off the coast of California and Mexico. These zones are presently inactive, but the offsets of the patterns of magnetic striping provide evidence of previous transform-fault activity. The San Andreas Fault, one of the few transform faults exposed on land, connects a short segment of the South Gorda–Juan de Fuca–Explorer Ridge in the Pacific Ocean to a segment of the East Pacific Rise in the Gulf of California.

MISCONCEPTION ALERT

Plate-Boundary Zones Not all plate boundaries are as simple as the main types discussed in this section. In some places, the boundaries are not well defined because the deformation that accompanies the plate movement extends over a broad belt, called a *plate-boundary zone.* Plate-boundary zones commonly involve at least two large plates and one or more *microplates,* smaller fragments of plates between the larger plates. These zones tend to have complicated geological structures and earthquake patterns. Examples of plate-boundary zones include the Mediterranean-Alpine region between the Eurasian and African Plates and the Himalayan region between the Eurasian and Indian plates.

Skill Builder — GENERAL

Writing Ask students to research a specific plate boundary and to write a short report about that plate boundary. The report must include where the boundary is located, which plates meet at that boundary, and what type of boundary it is. Students may also include what geologic features are found near the boundary, such as mountain ranges or volcanoes, and how plate boundaries affect humans.
LS Verbal

Teach, *continued*

Teaching Tip BASIC

Connect to Familiar Processes Students may comprehend the process of mantle convection better if you compare the process of mantle convection with a process with which students may be familiar—boiling water. Ask students to think about how convection currents work in a pot of water on the stove. (As water heats up from the bottom, some of the hot water rises over the center of heat. The heated water is commonly seen as rising bubbles. When some water rises over the center of heat, cooler water from other parts of the pan sink and replace the rising water. This water is heated in turn, and the process repeats.)

LS **Verbal** English Language Learners

Using the Figure GENERAL

Mantle Convection Ask students to analyze the relationship between where lithosphere dives into the mantle and where colder mantle material sinks. (Lithosphere sinks into the asthenosphere near where colder mantle material sinks.) Answer to caption question: Divergent boundaries form where rising mantle material reaches the lithosphere. LS **Verbal**

Academic Vocabulary

process (PROH ses) a set of steps, events, or changes

Causes of Plate Motion

The movement of tectonic plates is part of the mantle convection system. *Convection* is the movement of heated material due to differences in density that are caused by differences in temperatures. This process can be modeled by boiling water in a pot on a stove. As the water at the bottom of the pot is heated, it expands and becomes less dense than the cooler water above it. The cooler, denser water sinks, and the warmer water rises to the surface to create a cycle called a *convection cell*.

Mantle Convection

Scientists think that Earth is also a convecting system. Energy generated by Earth's core and radioactivity within the mantle heat mantle material. This heated material rises through the cooler, denser material around it. As the hot material rises, the cooler, denser material flows away from the hot material and sinks into the mantle to replace the rising material. As the mantle material moves, the overlying tectonic plates move along with it, as shown in **Figure 6.**

Convection currents and the resulting movement of tectonic plates can explain many aspects of plate movement. But scientists have identified two specific mechanisms of convection that help to drive the process of plate motion.

Figure 6 Scientists think that tectonic plates are part of a convection system. ***How is the rising of hot material related to the location of divergent boundaries?***

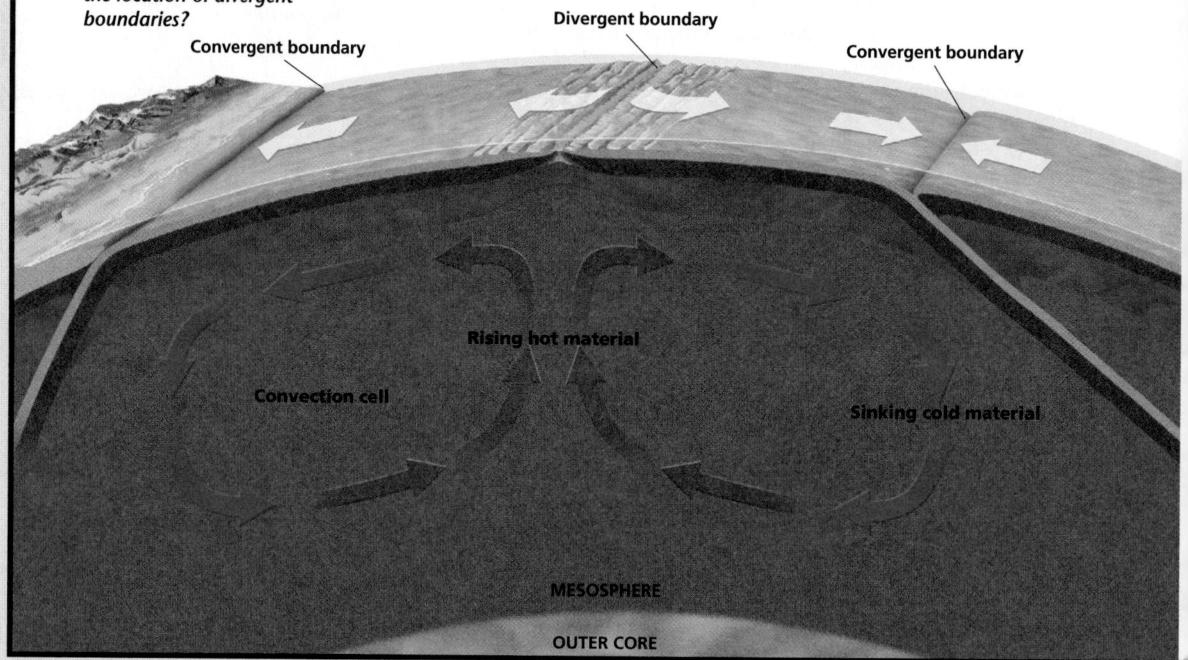

Why It Matters

Speeding Plates Tectonic plates that have the largest proportion of their boundaries subducting under other plates tend to be the fastest-moving tectonic plates. This relationship supports the idea that slab pull is a major factor in the movement of tectonic plates.

Differentiated Instruction

Struggling Readers

Comprehension Strategy To help students comprehend the text on this page, use **Figure 6**. As they read each sentence under the heading *Mantle Convection*, have them find the part of Figure 6 that the text is describing. For example, the red and blue arrows show the convecting system described by the first sentence under *Mantle Convection.*

Ridge Push

Newly formed rock at a mid-ocean ridge is warmer and less dense than older rock nearby. The warmer, less dense rock is elevated above nearby rock, and older, denser rock slopes downward away from the ridge. As the newer, warmer rock cools and becomes denser, it begins to slide down the slope between the lithosphere and the asthenosphere.

As the cooling rock slides down the slope of the ridge, it exerts force on the rest of the plate. This force is called *ridge push*. This force pushes the rest of the plate away from the mid-ocean ridge. Ridge push is illustrated in **Figure 7**.

Scientists think that ridge push may help to drive plate motions. However, most scientists agree that ridge push is not the main driving force of plate motion. So, scientists looked to convergent boundaries for other clues about forces that drive plate motion.

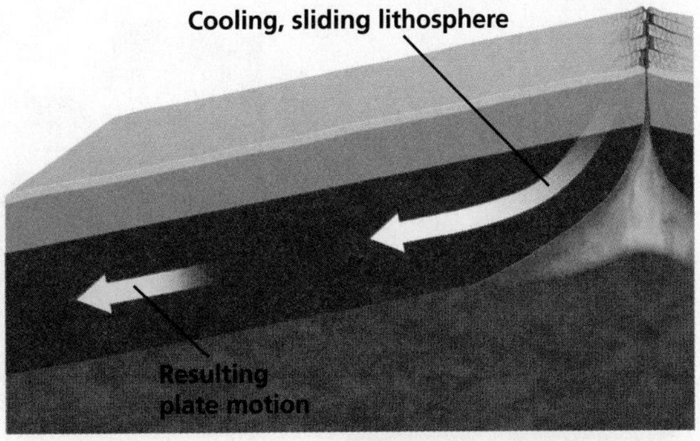

Figure 7 As the cooling lithosphere slides down the slope formed by the elevation of the mid-ocean ridge, it pushes on the rest of the plate. This process contributes to the movement of the entire plate.

Reading Check **How may density differences in the rock at a mid-ocean ridge help to drive plate motion?**

Quick Lab

30 min

Tectonic Plate Boundaries

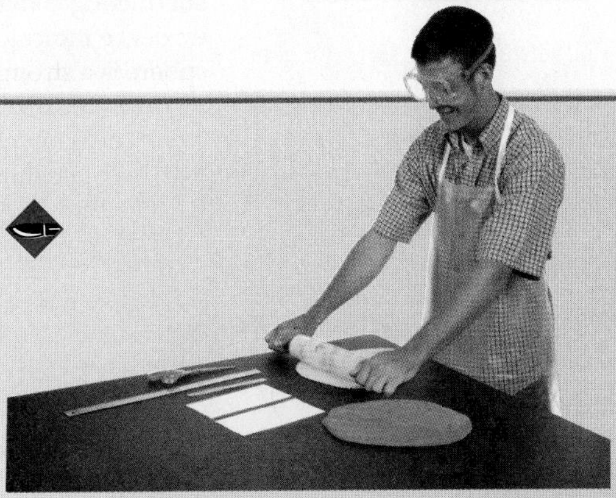

Procedure

1. Using a ruler, draw two 7 cm × 12 cm rectangles on a piece of paper. Cut them out with scissors.
2. Use a rolling pin to flatten two different-colored pieces of clay to about 0.5 cm thick.
3. Use a plastic knife to cut each piece of clay into a 7 cm × 12 cm rectangle. Place a paper rectangle on each piece of clay.
4. Place the two clay models side by side on a flat surface, paper side down.
5. Place one hand on each piece of clay, and slowly push the blocks together until the edges begin to buckle and rise off the surface of the table.
6. Turn the clay models around so that the unbuckled edges are touching each other.
7. Place one hand on each clay model. Apply slight pressure toward the plane where the two blocks meet. Slide one clay model forward 7 cm and the other model backward about 7 cm.

Analysis

1. What type of plate boundary are you modeling in step 5?
2. What type of plate boundary are you modeling in step 7?
3. How do you think the processes you modeled in this activity might affect the appearance of Earth's surface?

Answer to Reading Check

When denser lithosphere sinks into the asthenosphere, the asthenosphere must move out of the way. As the asthenosphere moves, it drags or pushes on other parts of the lithosphere, which causes movement.

Close

Reteaching — BASIC

Tectonic Processes Reinforce the idea of tectonic processes by having students build a small model of two tectonic plates by using clay. Have students model divergent plates or convergent plates that result in either subduction or mountain building. Then, have students identify plates that are currently undergoing these processes.

LS Kinesthetic

Quiz — GENERAL

1. How are tectonic plate boundaries related to earthquakes? (Most earthquakes happen as plates move at plate boundaries.)
2. What are the three types of plate boundaries? (convergent, divergent, and transform)
3. What is the main driving force of plate tectonics? (convection)

Quick Lab

Skills Acquired

- Modeling
- Inferring

Materials

- Ruler
- Piece of paper
- Scissors
- Two different colored pieces of clay
- Plastic knife

Teacher's Notes: You may want to prepare the models before class to save time. Students should line tables or desks with wax paper or newspaper before using clay.

Answers

1. convergent
2. transform
3. Convergent boundaries may cause mountains to form. Rocks at transform boundaries may get deformed by the plate motion.

Key Resources

Technology

- Transparencies
  52 Ridge Push and Slab Pull

Close, *continued*

Answers to Section Review

1. Earth's surface is covered by plates of solid lithosphere that move around on the plastic rock of the asthenosphere. The tectonic plates move as a result of convection in Earth's mantle.
2. Earthquakes occur when tectonic plates suddenly shift relative to each other. When plates interact, magma may form and rise to the surface to form volcanoes.
3. Convergent plate boundaries form where two plates collide as they move toward each other. Divergent plate boundaries form where two plates pull apart from each other. Transform boundaries form where two plates move past each other horizontally in opposite directions.
4. Convergent boundaries usually cause deep-ocean trenches, mountains, and volcanoes. Divergent boundaries are characterized by mid-ocean ridges.
5. As hot mantle material rises, cooler, denser mantle material flows away from the hot material and sinks to replace the rising material. As the mantle material moves, the overlying lithosphere moves with it as part of the convection cell.
6. As cooling rock slides down the ridge, it "pushes" on the rest of the plate in front of it. In slab pull, the leading edge of a subducting plate sinks and pulls the rest of the plate along behind it.
7. As one plate subducts, fluids from the plate cause partial melting of the mantle. The resulting magma rises to the surface and forms volcanoes.
8. As hot material moves toward Earth's surface through convection currents in the mantle, thermal energy is transferred toward the outer parts of Earth. This convection drives plate tectonics.
9. *Tectonic plates* meet at three types of *boundaries*—*convergent*, which form *subduction zones*; *divergent*, which form *mid-ocean ridges*; and *transform*—as they move over Earth's surface as a result of *convection*, which includes *slab pull* and *ridge push*.

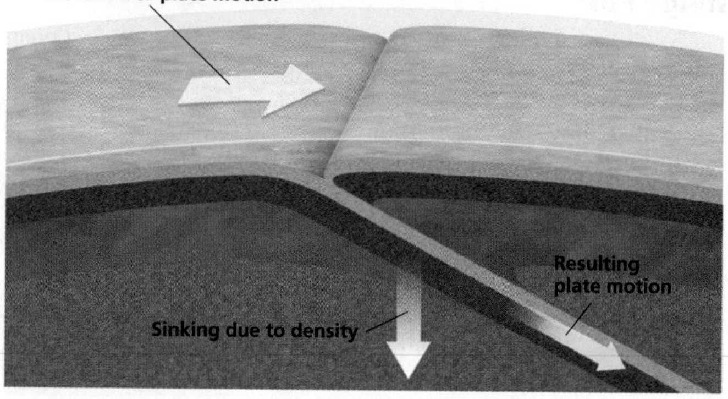

Figure 8 The leading edge of the subducting plate pulls the rest of the subducting plate into the astheno-sphere in a process called *slab pull.*

Slab Pull

Where plates pull away from each other at mid-ocean ridges, magma from the asthenosphere rises to the surface. The magma then cools to form new lithosphere. As the lithosphere moves away from the mid-ocean ridge, the lithosphere cools and becomes denser. Where the lithosphere is dense enough, it begins to subduct into the asthenosphere. As the leading edge of the plate sinks, it pulls the rest of the plate along behind it, as shown in **Figure 8.** The force exerted by the sinking plate is called *slab pull.* In general, plates that are subducting move faster than plates that are not subducting. This evidence indicates that the downward pull of the subducting lithosphere is a strong driving force for tectonic plate motion.

All three mechanisms of Earth's convecting system—movement as part of a convection cell, ridge push, and slab pull—work together to drive plate motions. These mechanisms form a system that makes Earth's tectonic plates move constantly.

SCILINKS®
www.scilinks.org
Topic: Plate Tectonics
Code: **HQX1171**

Section 2 Review

Key Ideas

1. **Summarize** the theory of plate tectonics.
2. **Explain** why most earthquakes and volcanoes happen along plate boundaries.
3. **Identify** and describe the three major types of plate boundaries.
4. **Compare** the changes in Earth's surface that happen at a convergent boundary with those that happen at a divergent boundary.
5. **Describe** the role of convection currents in plate movement.
6. **Describe** how ridge push and slab pull contribute to the movement of tectonic plates.

Critical Thinking

7. **Making Inferences** How do convergent boundaries add material to Earth's surface?
8. **Determining Cause and Effect** Explain how the outward transfer of energy as heat from inside Earth drives the movement of tectonic plates.

Concept Mapping

9. Use the following terms to create a concept map: *tectonic plate, divergent, convergent, convection, transform, ridge push, slab pull, subduction zone,* and *mid-ocean ridge.*

Differentiated Instruction

Alternative Assessment

Tectonic Art Have students draw examples of the three types of plate boundaries and label all of the components. Next to each drawing, students should list the geologic features that are common at each boundary. Encourage students to include these features as part of their drawings. **LS Visual**

SECTION 3

The Changing Continents

Key Ideas	Key Terms	Why It Matters
❯ Identify how movements of tectonic plates change Earth's surface. ❯ Summarize how movements of tectonic plates have influenced climates and life on Earth. ❯ Describe the supercontinent cycle.	rifting terrane supercontinent cycle Pangaea Panthalassa	Global warming is a big concern in today's world. But movements of Earth's tectonic plates have had an effect on climates both past and present.

The continents did not always have the same shapes that they have today. And geologic evidence indicates that they will not remain the same shapes forever. In fact, the continents are always changing. Slow movements of tectonic plates change the sizes and shapes of the continents over millions of years.

Reshaping Earth's Crust

All the continents that exist today contain large areas of stable rock, called *cratons,* that are older than 540 million years. Rocks within the cratons that have been exposed at Earth's surface are called *shields.* Cratons represent ancient cores around which the modern continents formed.

Rifting and Continental Breakup

One way that continents change shape is by breaking apart. **Rifting** is the process by which a continent breaks apart. New, smaller continents may form as a result of this process. The reason that continents rift is not entirely known. Because continental crust is thick and has a high silica content, continental crust acts as an insulator. This insulating property prevents heat in Earth's interior from escaping. Scientists think that as heat from the mantle builds up beneath the continent, continental lithosphere becomes thinner and begins to weaken. Eventually, a rift forms in this zone of weakness, and the continent begins to break apart, as shown in **Figure 1.**

rifting the process by which Earth's crust breaks apart; can occur within continental crust or oceanic crust

Figure 1 The East African Rift Valley formed as Africa began rifting about 30 million years ago.

Section 3

Focus

Overview

In this section, students learn about past and future movements of the continents. The section describes how continents change by rifting and accretion and how continental change affects climate and life on Earth.

Bellringer

Have students answer the following questions:

1. What might the United States be like if it were centered over the equator? (Major climate zones would range from tropical to subtropical.)
2. What might the United States be like if it were centered over the North Pole? (Temperatures would be much colder, and many mountains would be glaciated.) LS **Logical**

Motivate

Activity GENERAL

Modeling Rifting Have students flatten a piece of clay or plastic play putty until it is about 2 cm thick. Then, have students hold the edges of the clay or putty in their hands and pull apart slowly. The center of the clay or putty should thin and eventually pull apart. Explain to students that as continents rift, the crust in the rift zone thins and then eventually separates. LS **Kinesthetic/Visual**

Key Resources

Chapter Resource File
- Directed Reading BASIC

Technology
- Transparencies
  Bellringer

Teach

Demonstration GENERAL

Modeling Accretion Create a "continent" from one color of clay. Create several smaller "terranes" from other colors of clay. Place all of the terranes on a piece of wax paper at various intervals. Hold the continent just off the edge of a table, and pull the wax paper under the continent so that the terranes move toward the continent. Each terrane should collide with the continent to form several terranes of different colors at the edge of the continent. LS Visual

Using the Figure GENERAL

Accretion Have students analyze the figure that shows how terranes accrete. Have students make a drawing that shows what the continent would look like when the remaining oceanic crust has subducted. (Drawings should show that Terrane B has also become part of the continent.) Answer to caption question: Most of the sediment on the subducting plate gets scraped off and added to the edge of a continent. Some of the sediment is subducted along with the plate. LS Visual

Answer to Reading Check

As a plate subducts beneath another plate, islands and other land features on the subducting plate are scraped off the subducting plate and become part of the overriding plate.

terrane a piece of lithosphere that has a unique geologic history and that may be part of a larger piece of lithosphere, such as a continent

Terranes and Continental Growth

Continents change not only by breaking apart but also by gaining material. Most continents consist of cratons surrounded by a patchwork of terranes. A **terrane** is a piece of lithosphere that has a unique geologic history that differs from the histories of the surrounding lithosphere. A terrane can be identified by three characteristics. First, a terrane contains rock and fossils that differ from the rock and fossils of neighboring terranes. Second, there are major faults at the boundaries of a terrane. Third, the magnetic properties of a terrane generally do not match those of neighboring terranes.

Terranes become part of a continent at convergent boundaries. When a tectonic plate carrying a terrane subducts under a plate made of continental crust, the terrane is scraped off the subducting plate, as shown in **Figure 2.** The terrane then becomes part of the continent. Some terranes may form mountains, while other terranes simply add to the surface area of a continent. The process in which a terrane becomes part of a continent is called *accretion* (uh KREE shuhn).

A variety of materials can form terranes. Terranes may be small volcanic islands or underwater volcanoes called *seamounts.* Small coral islands, or *atolls,* that form on top of seamounts can also become terranes. And large chunks of continental crust can be terranes. When large terranes and continents collide, major mountain chains often form. For example, the Himalaya Mountains formed when India began colliding with Asia about 50 million years ago (during the Cenozoic Era).

Reading Check **Describe the process of accretion.**

Figure 2 As oceanic crust subducts, a terrane is scraped off the ocean floor and becomes part of the continental crust. ***What would you expect to happen to sediments on the sea floor when the plate they are on subducts?***

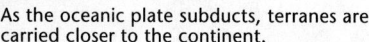

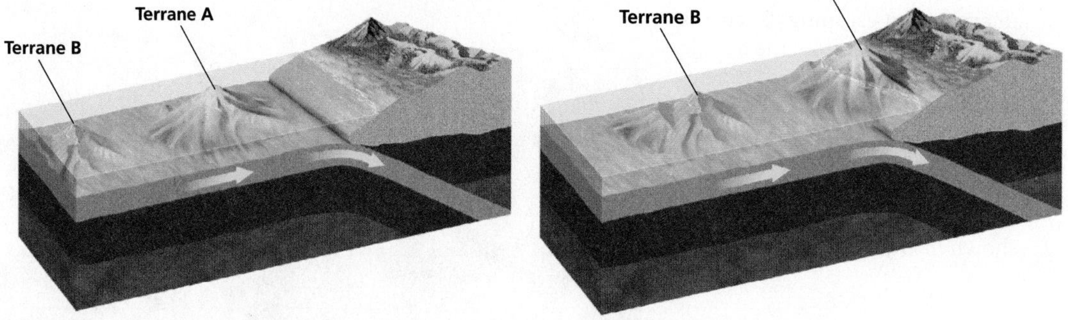

As the oceanic plate subducts, terranes are carried closer to the continent.

When the terrane reaches the subduction zone, the terrane is scraped off the subducting plate and added to the edge of the continent.

Skill Builder ADVANCED

Vocabulary The word *accrete* means "to grow by being added to." It comes from the Latin *accrescere,* which means "to increase or to grow." Ask students how knowing the etymology of *accrete* can help them understand the process of accretion. (Accretion is the process by which a continent grows when smaller pieces are added to it.) English Language Learners LS Verbal

Differentiated Instruction

Advanced Learners

Accreted Terranes Have students check library or Internet resources to identify areas of western North America that are composed of accreted terranes. Have them make a poster showing major terranes and their origins.

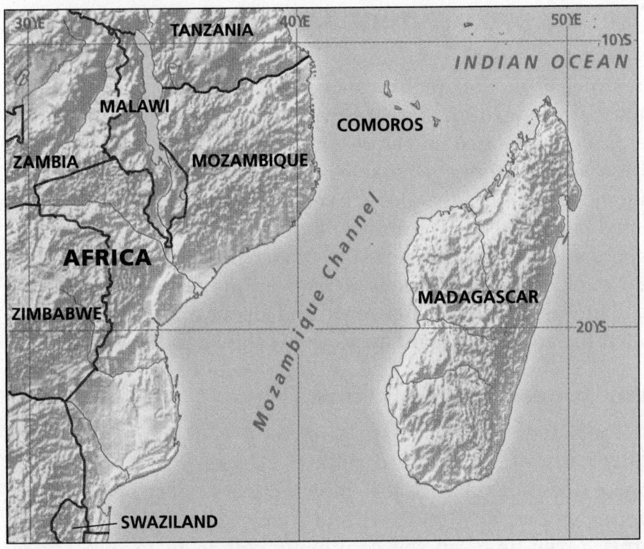

Figure 3 Madagascar separated from Africa about 165 million years ago and separated from India about 88 million years ago. This separation isolated the plants and animals on the island of Madagascar. As a result, unique species of plants and animals evolved on Madagascar. These species, such as the fossa (below), are found nowhere else on Earth.

Effects of Continental Change

Modern climates are a result of past movements of tectonic plates. A continent's location in relation to the equator and the poles affects the continent's overall climate. A continent's climate is also affected by the continent's location in relation to oceans and other continents. Mountain ranges affect air flow and wind patterns around the globe. Mountains also affect the amount of moisture that reaches certain parts of a continent. When continents move, the flow of air and moisture around the globe changes and causes climates to change.

Changes in Climate

Between 450 and 430 million years ago, the movement of continental plates placed North Africa near the position of the South Pole. The low level of sunlight at this latitude produced temperatures that were cold enough for a thick ice sheet, estimated to be 8 million km^2, to form. In addition, the nearness of the ocean ensured that there was enough humidity to produce large winter snowfall amounts. The grooves and furrows caused by moving ice that are found in the surface rock of the Sahara Desert provide evidence of this ancient North African ice sheet.

Changes in Life

As continents rift or as mountains form, populations of organisms are separated. When populations are separated, new species may evolve from existing species. Sometimes, isolation protects organisms from competitors and predators, and may allow the organisms to evolve into unique organisms, as shown in **Figure 3.**

Group Activity — ADVANCED

Responses to Climate Change Organize the class into four groups of students. Have all students stand together in the center of the room as if they were a population of one species that lives on one continent. Tell the students that parts of the continent are rifting apart, and tell them which groups of students should separate from the main group and move to another part of the room. Tell one group that the new climate is very cold. Tell another group that the climate is very dry, and tell a third group that the environment is now swampy. Have each group identify how its population may change to adapt to the new climates. (Cold-climate organisms may develop thick fur, small pine-like needles, or a light coloring. Dry-climate organisms may develop thick skins, nocturnal habits, or other means of preserving water. Swampy-environment organisms may adapt to a more aquatic lifestyle.) **LS Kinesthetic**

Reading Skill Builder — BASIC

Reading Organizer As students read this section, encourage them to take notes as described in Appendix A. Later, students can use these notes as a study guide for assessments or as a place to start when doing independent research for class projects or reports. **LS Logical**

Biology Connection

Extinction One of the assumptions of evolution by natural selection is that organisms are adapted to their environment. Because of this adaptation, changes in the environment affect the organisms. Only those organisms that can adapt to the environmental changes will survive. Organisms that cannot survive—in other words, those that are unfit to live and reproduce in the changing environment—become extinct.

Environmental Connection

Climate Changes Increased public concern about global warming has prompted much research into the environmental factors that may cause global warming. By studying climatic changes that occurred in Earth's geologic past, scientist hope to understand changes that are occurring in Earth's present climate.

Teach, *continued*

Teaching Tip GENERAL

Connect to Prior Knowledge
Complete the concept of the supercontinent cycle by asking students to draw on prior knowledge about continental drift. Ask students what evidence of continental drift can also be used to reconstruct the past positions of continents. (matching mountain ranges and rock types, matching fossils, and climatic evidence) Ask students how magnetic reversals and sea-floor spreading can be used to reconstruct the movements of continents over time. (Continents move away from each other during sea-floor spreading. Using the rates of sea-floor spreading based on the magnetic reversal patterns, scientists can show the relative positions of continents at specific points in the past.) **LS Logical**

Internet Activity BASIC

The Paleomap Project The Paleomap Project Web site offers a variety of maps, graphs, and animations that illustrate the movement of continents throughout Earth's history and into Earth's projected future. The site also includes data about changes in Earth's climate. Ask students to browse the Paleomap Project site. Have them report on some aspect of the site that interests them. A worksheet designed to direct student research on this topic can be found in the **Chapter Resource File** booklet or by visiting www.thinkcentral.com and entering the keyword **HQXTECX.**
LS Visual

The Supercontinent Cycle

Using evidence from many scientific fields, scientists can construct a general picture of continental change throughout time. Scientists think that, at several times in the past, the continents were arranged into large landmasses called *supercontinents.* These supercontinents broke apart to form smaller continents that moved around the globe. Eventually, the smaller continents joined again to form another supercontinent. When the last supercontinent broke apart, the modern continents formed. A new supercontinent is likely to form in the future. The process by which supercontinents form and break apart over time is called the **supercontinent cycle** and is shown in **Figure 4.**

supercontinent cycle the process by which supercontinents form and break apart over millions of years

Pangaea the supercontinent that formed 300 million years ago and that began to break up 200 million years ago

Panthalassa the single, large ocean that covered Earth's surface during the time the supercontinent Pangaea existed

Why Supercontinents Form

The movement of plates toward convergent boundaries eventually causes continents to collide. Because continental lithosphere does not subduct, the convergent boundary between two continents becomes inactive, and a new convergent boundary forms. Over time, all the continents collide to form a supercontinent. Then, heat from Earth's interior builds up under the supercontinent, and rifts form in the supercontinent. The supercontinent breaks apart, and plates carrying separate continents move around the globe.

Formation of Pangaea

The supercontinent **Pangaea** (pan JEE uh) formed about 300 million years ago (during the Paleozoic Era). As the continents collided to form Pangaea, mountains formed. The Appalachian Mountains of eastern North America and the Ural Mountains of Russia formed during these collisions. A body of water called the Tethys Sea cut into the eastern edge of Pangaea. The single, large ocean that surrounded Pangaea was called **Panthalassa.**

Figure 4 Over millions of years, supercontinents form and break apart in a cycle known as the *supercontinent cycle.*

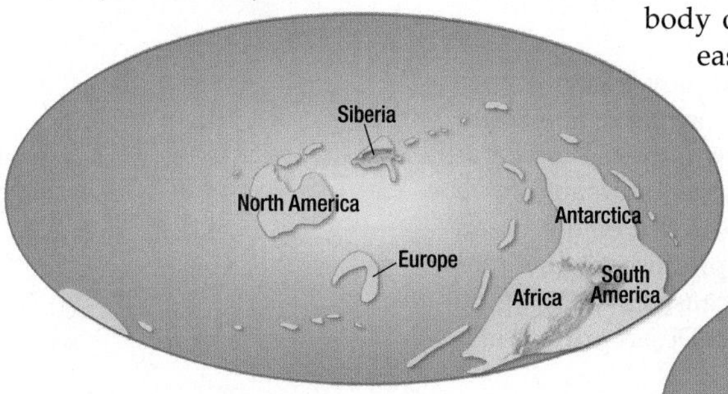

About 450 million years ago Earth's continents were separated, as they are today.

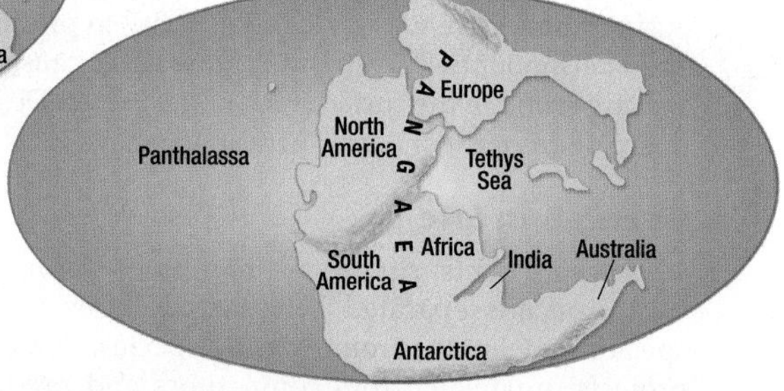

225 million to 200 million years ago Pangaea had formed and was beginning to break apart.

Key Resources

Technology
- Transparencies
  53 The Supercontinent Cycle

Differentiated Instruction

Special Education Students

Supercontinent Cycle Show developmentally delayed students a series of illustrations showing Pangaea, its breakup, and the movement of continents to their modern locations. Ask students to put the pictures in chronological order.

Breakup of Pangaea

About 200 million years ago (during the Mesozoic Era), Pangaea began to break into two continents—*Laurasia* and *Gondwanaland*. A large rift split the supercontinent from east to west. Then, Laurasia began to drift northward and rotate slowly, and a new rift formed. This rift separated Laurasia into the continents of North America and Eurasia, and eventually formed the North Atlantic Ocean. The rotation of Laurasia also caused the Tethys Sea to shrink, leaving a remnant that eventually became the Mediterranean Sea.

As Laurasia began to break apart, Gondwanaland also broke into two continents. One of these continents broke apart to become the continents of South America and Africa. About 150 million years ago (during the Mesozoic Era), a rift between Africa and South America opened to form the South Atlantic Ocean. The other continent separated to form India, Australia, and Antarctica. As India broke away from Australia and Antarctica, it started moving northward toward Eurasia. About 50 million years ago (during the Cenozoic Era), India collided with Eurasia, and the Himalaya Mountains began to form.

SciLinks
www.scilinks.org
Topic: Pangaea
Code: HQX1105

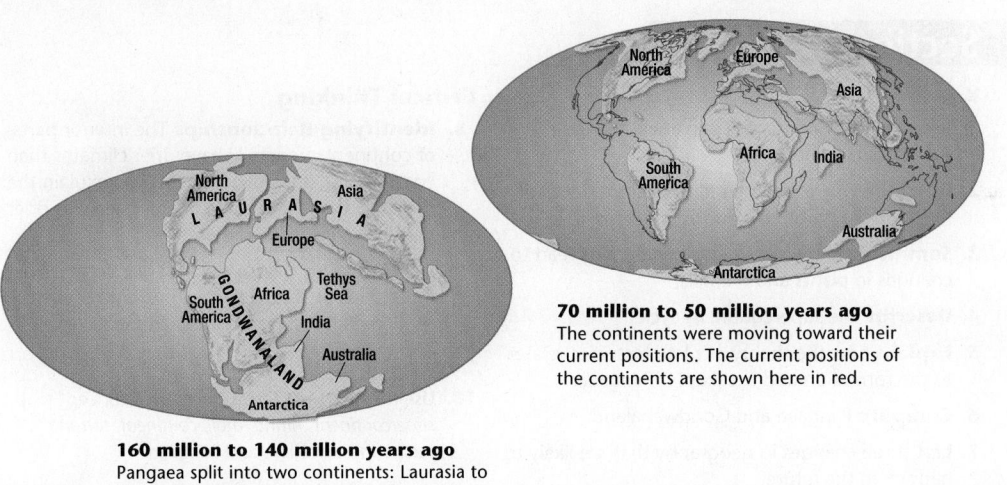

The Modern Continents

Slowly, the continents moved into their present positions. As the continents drifted, they collided with terranes and other continents. These collisions welded new crust onto the continents and uplifted the land. Mountain ranges, such as the Rocky Mountains, the Andes, and the Alps, formed. Tectonic plate motion also caused new oceans to open up and caused others to close.

Reading Check **What modern continents formed from Gondwanaland?**

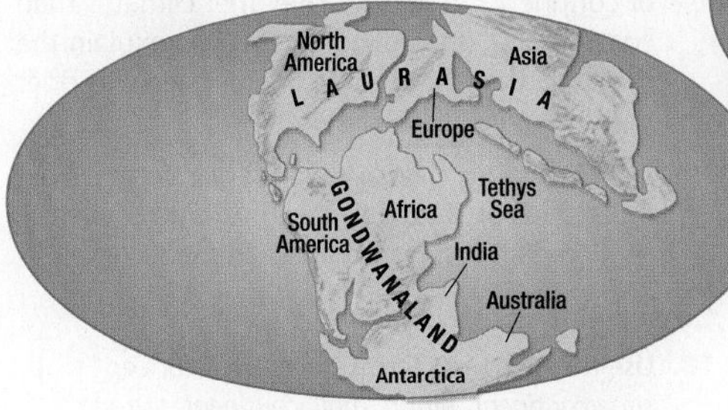

160 million to 140 million years ago
Pangaea split into two continents: Laurasia to the north and Gondwanaland to the south.

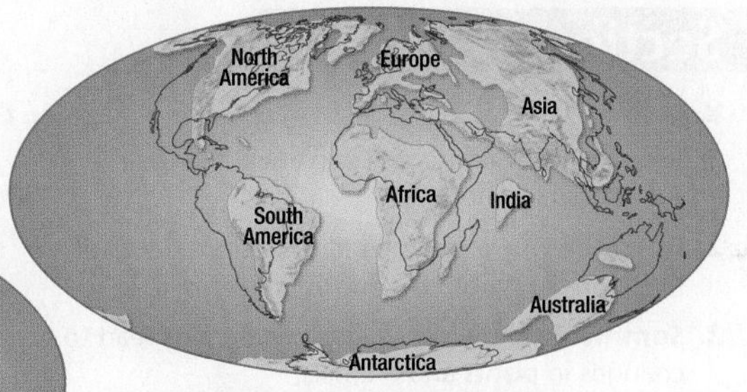

70 million to 50 million years ago
The continents were moving toward their current positions. The current positions of the continents are shown here in red.

Answer to Reading Check
The continents Africa, South America, Antarctica, and Australia formed from Gondwanaland. The subcontinent of India was also part of Gondwanaland.

Close

Reteaching — BASIC

Peer Reviewing Divide the class into pairs or small groups of students. Have each student write five questions that can be answered by reading the section. Have students use the questions to quiz each other on the information in the section.
LS Interpersonal

Quiz — GENERAL

1. By what process do continents break apart? (rifting)
2. How does mountain formation cause changes in climate? (Mountain ranges affect air flow and wind patterns around the globe as well as the amount of moisture in an area.)
3. What was the name of the last supercontinent? When did it form, and when did it begin to break apart? (Pangaea; about 300 million years ago; about 200 million years ago)

MISCONCEPTION ALERT

Supercontinents Students may think that Pangaea was the only supercontinent in the past or that all supercontinents were called Pangaea. In fact, scientists think that at least five supercontinents have existed at different times since the first crust formed on Earth. The supercontinent Rodinia broke apart about 750 million years ago. It later reassembled to form the supercontinent Pannotia, which broke apart about 540 million years ago. Pangaea assembled from the scattered continental fragments a few hundred million years later. Scientists do not call the landmasses that became the modern continents by their modern names, either. Previous continents included Congo, Laurentia, Gondwana, Cimmeria, and Baltica.

Close, *continued*

READING TOOLBOX

Recognizing Facts, Hypotheses, and Theories Check to make sure students have correctly classified facts, hypotheses, and theories in their tables.

Answers to Section Review

1. Continents get smaller as they break apart during rifting. Continents get larger as smaller pieces of crust collide during accretion.
2. A terrane is a piece of lithosphere that has a unique geologic history but has become part of a continent through accretion.
3. As continents rift apart or as mountain chains form, populations of plants and animals become separated and evolve in different ways in response to their changing environments.
4. Over time, movements of the tectonic plates cause all of the continents to collide to form a supercontinent and then break apart to form individual continents. This repeated pattern is called the *supercontinent cycle.*
5. Pangaea was a supercontinent that formed when all of the continents of Earth collided more than 300 million years ago. Continuing movements of the plates resulted in the breakup of Pangaea.
6. Pangaea was the supercontinent that formed about 300 million years ago. Gondwanaland was the large continent that broke away from Pangaea and eventually split to form Africa, South America, Australia, and Antarctica.
7. In about 150 million years, Africa will collide with Eurasia, as will North and South America. In 250 million years, a new supercontinent will form.
8. Because Pangaea was made of all of the continents combined, the area of the continent must have been much larger than any single continent today. Thus, the interior of the continent was larger, and the climate was drier.
9. Marine fossils formed on the ocean floor. Then, that part of the ocean became part of a convergent boundary, and the sea floor became part of the continent during accretion.
10. *Supercontinents*, such as *Pangaea*, form as *continents* collide with *terranes*, such as *seamounts* and *atolls*, in the process of *accretion*, and break apart as a result of *rifting*.

Geography of the Future

As tectonic plates continue to move, Earth's geography will change dramatically. If plate movements continue at current rates, in about 150 million years, Africa will collide with Eurasia, and the Mediterranean Sea will close. New subduction zones will form off the east coast of North and South America after North America collides with Eurasia. North and South America will then move east across the Atlantic Ocean. The Atlantic Ocean will close as North and South America collide with Africa.

In North America, Mexico's Baja Peninsula and the part of California that is west of the San Andreas Fault will move to where Alaska is today. If this plate movement occurs as predicted, Los Angeles will be located north of San Francisco's current location. Scientists predict that, in 250 million years, the continents will come together again to form a new supercontinent, as shown in **Figure 5.**

READING TOOLBOX

Recognizing Facts, Hypotheses, and Theories
Make a three-column table. In the first column, list statements from this page and the preceding page about the past and future positions of continents. In the second column, identify whether each is a fact, hypothesis, or theory. In the third column, write any language from the text that signals which type of statement each is.

Academic Vocabulary
predict (pree DIKT) to tell in advance

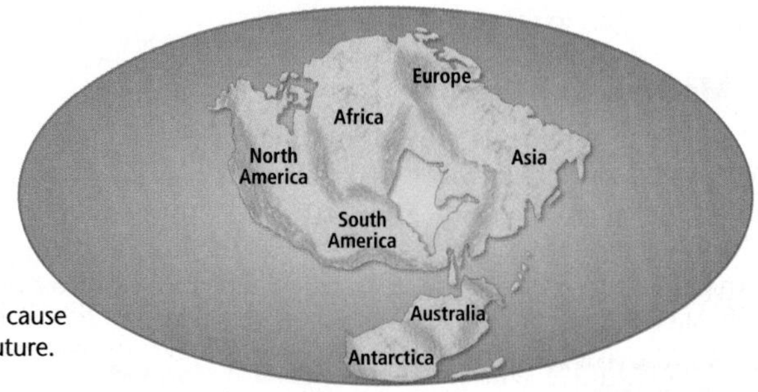

Figure 5 Scientists predict that movements of tectonic plates will cause a supercontinent to form in the future.

Section 3 Review

Key Ideas

1. **Identify** how rifting and accretion change the shapes of continents.
2. **Describe** why a terrane has a different geologic history from that of the surrounding area.
3. **Summarize** how continental rifting may lead to changes in plants and animals.
4. **Describe** the supercontinent cycle.
5. **Explain** how the theory of plate tectonics relates to the formation and breakup of Pangaea.
6. **Compare** Pangaea and Gondwanaland.
7. **List** three changes in geography that are likely to happen in the future.

Critical Thinking

8. **Identifying Relationships** The interior parts of continents generally have drier climates than coastal areas do. How does this fact explain the evidence that the climate on Pangaea was drier than many modern climates?
9. **Determining Cause and Effect** Explain how mountains on land can be composed of rocks that contain fossils of marine animals.

Concept Mapping

10. Use the following terms to create a concept map: *supercontinent, rifting, atoll, continent, terrane, seamount, accretion,* and *Pangaea.*

Differentiated Instruction

Alternative Assessment

Process Models Have students create models that illustrate the process of rifting or the process of accretion. The model should show steps in the process rather than just the final result of the process. Therefore, the models should be easy to reset to the original position or able to work in reverse. Students may wish to create computer models or animations for this purpose.
LS Kinesthetic

Why It Matters

Copper from Plate Margins

SCIENCE & SOCIETY

You can find copper almost everywhere around you—in electronics, air conditioners, coins, and cookware. You depend on copper every time you log onto the Internet or use a cell phone. Copper even makes up the outer skin of the Statue of Liberty!

Most of the copper that is mined today formed at ancient tectonic plate margins. Some of this copper formed at hydrothermal vents along divergent plate boundaries. As superheated seawater rises through hydrothermal vents, it deposits metal-rich minerals that had been dissolved in it. More than half of the world's copper, however, comes from areas that were once subduction zones. Hot fluids rising from subduction zones can become enriched with metals. Then, the fluids deposit the metals in fractures in the crust.

When geologists look for copper, they identify ancient plate boundaries to help them target likely search areas.

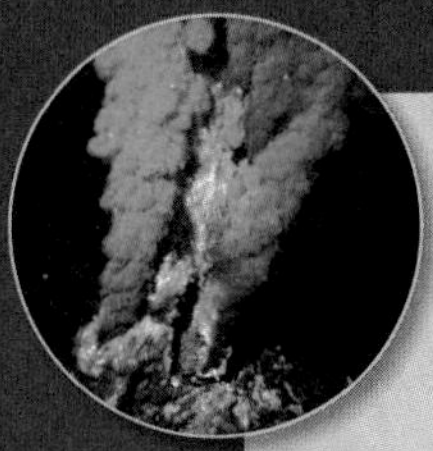

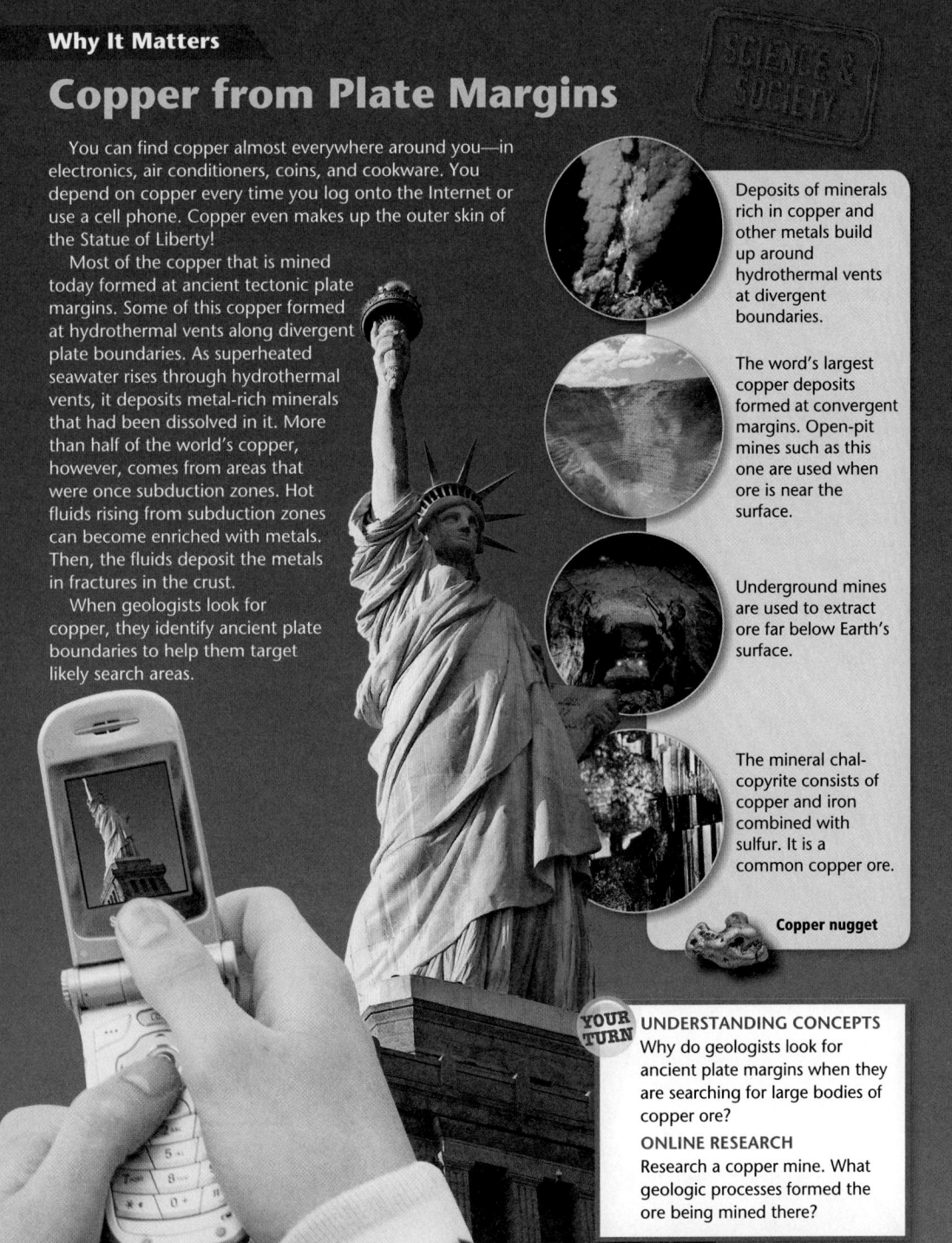

Deposits of minerals rich in copper and other metals build up around hydrothermal vents at divergent boundaries.

The word's largest copper deposits formed at convergent margins. Open-pit mines such as this one are used when ore is near the surface.

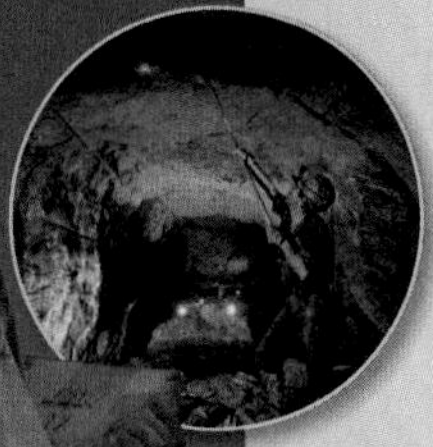

Underground mines are used to extract ore far below Earth's surface.

The mineral chalcopyrite consists of copper and iron combined with sulfur. It is a common copper ore.

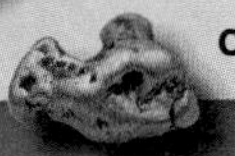

Copper nugget

YOUR TURN

UNDERSTANDING CONCEPTS
Why do geologists look for ancient plate margins when they are searching for large bodies of copper ore?

ONLINE RESEARCH
Research a copper mine. What geologic processes formed the ore being mined there?

Why It Matters

Copper from Plate Margins

Ancient plate margins are good locations to find economically valuable metals. Geologists use characteristics of modern convergent and divergent margins to identify ancient tectonic boundaries. For example, a rock assemblage typical of a mid-ocean ridge indicates an area was once a divergent margin. Along mid-ocean ridges, seawater infiltrates the hot volcanic rock and dissolves metals from it. Superheated seawater rises up through seafloor vents and deposits metal-rich chimneys around the vents. Subduction zones along convergent margins are also important settings for ore formation. Metals such as copper can become concentrated in fluids associated with magma rising from the subduction zone. The metals are deposited in fractures around and within the cooling magma body. By understanding the tectonic setting of the type of ore deposit they seek, geologists narrow their search areas. They save time and money, and they increase their chances of success.

Answers to Your Turn

Understanding Concepts Large copper deposits are commonly found in areas that were once mid-ocean ridges or subduction zones.

Online Research Answers may vary depending on which copper mine students research.

Time Required

two 45-minute class periods

Lab Ratings

EASY → HARD

Teacher Preparation
Student Setup
Concept Level
Cleanup

Skills Acquired

- Constructing Models
- Observing
- Identifying and Recognizing Patterns
- Interpreting Models

Scientific Methods

In this lab, students will
- Make Observations
- Analyze the Results
- Draw Conclusions

Materials

The materials listed are enough for groups of two to four students. If you have your first-period students prepare the shoe boxes, use the same shoe boxes for the rest of your classes.

Making Models Lab

90 min

Sea-Floor Spreading

What You'll Do

- **Model** the formation of sea floor.
- **Identify** how magnetic patterns are caused by sea-floor spreading.

What You'll Need

marker
paper, unlined
ruler, metric
scissors or utility knife
shoebox

Safety

The places on Earth's surface where plates pull apart have many names. They are called divergent boundaries, mid-ocean ridges, and spreading centers. The term *spreading center* refers to the fact that sea-floor spreading happens at these locations. In this lab, you will model the formation of new sea floor at a divergent boundary. You will also model the formation of magnetic patterns on the sea floor.

Procedure

1. Cut two identical strips of unlined paper, each 7 cm wide and 30 cm long.
2. Cut a slit 8 cm long in the center of the bottom of a shoebox.
3. Lay the strips of paper together on top of each other and end-to-end so that the ends line up. Push one end of the strips through the slit in the shoe box, so that a few centimeters of both strips stick out of the slit.
4. Place the shoe box flat on a table, open side down, and make sure the ends of the paper strips are sticking up.

Step 3

Tips and Tricks

Students may also wish to tape the trailing ends of the paper strips together to ensure that the strips are pulled equally. However, because rock at many divergent boundaries does not break down the center, students may try pulling one strip slightly faster than the other to make a more realistic model.

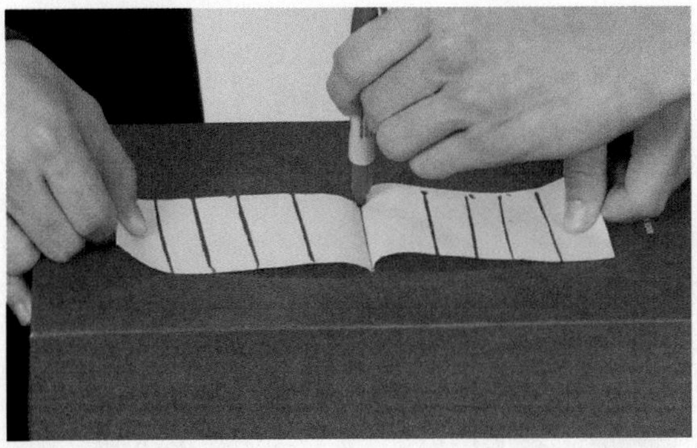

Step 6

5. Separate the strips, and hold one strip in each hand. Pull the strips apart. Then, push the strips down against the shoe box.
6. Use a marker to mark across the paper strips where they exit the box. One swipe with the marker should mark both strips.
7. Pull the strips evenly until about 2 cm have been pulled through the slit.
8. Mark the strips with the marker again.
9. Repeat steps 7 and 8, but vary the length of paper that you pull from the slit. Continue this process until both strips are pulled out of the box.

Analysis

1. **Evaluating Models** How does this activity model sea-floor spreading?
2. **Analyzing Models** What do the marker stripes in this model represent?
3. **Analyzing Methods** If each 2 cm on the paper is equal to 3 million years, how could you use your model to determine the age of certain points on the sea floor?
4. **Applying Conclusions** Suppose that you are given paper strips with marks already drawn on them. How would you use the paper strips to reconstruct the way in which the sea floor formed?

Extension

Making Models Design a model that shows what happens at a convergent boundary and what happens at a transform boundary. Present these models to the class.

Answers to Analysis

1. The paper strips represent magma that rises to the surface between plates that are moving apart. The slit in the shoe box represents the mid-ocean ridge.
2. The marker stripes represent the magnetic orientation of the rock.
3. Sample answer: I could measure the length of the strip in centimeters from the "spreading center" to the point I want to date. Then, I could multiply the number of centimeters by 3 to get the age in millions of years.
4. Sample answer: I could use the symmetry of the marker stripes to match the magnetic patterns of the "sea floor." The stripes will tell me the order in which each part of the sea floor formed.

Answer to Extension

Answers may vary. Accept all reasonable answers. Students may use a variety of materials to build their models.

Locations of Earthquakes in South America

Group Activity ADVANCED

3-D Model Have groups of students use the information in the map to make a three-dimensional model of the South American plate boundary. The model should have two tectonic plates, asthenosphere, and mesosphere. It should show the depth and thickness of each component to the same vertical and horizontal scale. Students may wish to research the thickness and geometry of the South American plate to make their model more realistic.
LS Kinesthetic/Visual

Answers to Map Skills Activity

1. about 11
2. shallow earthquakes
3. In the time period shown, no earthquakes with magnitude greater than 5.0 occurred on the east coast, but many occurred on the west coast.
4. along the western coast of South America
5. Most deep earthquakes happen toward the center of the continent. As you move east from the west coast, the earthquakes tend to get deeper.
6. The plate boundary on the west coast of South America is probably a convergent boundary (subduction zone). The subducting plate is moving eastward under the continent. As the subducting plate moves down under the continent, the earthquakes get deeper because the plate boundary is deeper.

MAPS *in Action*

Locations of Earthquakes in South America

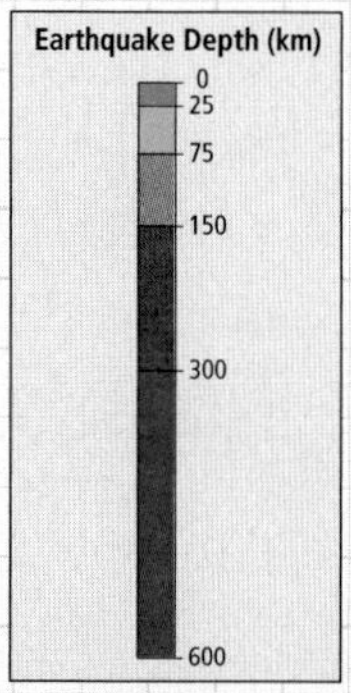

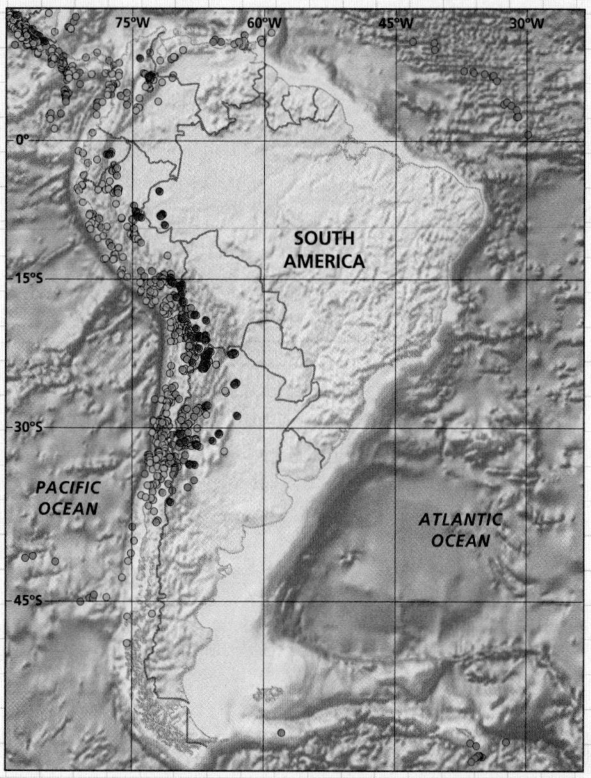

Map Skills Activity

This map shows the locations and depths of earthquakes that registered magnitudes greater than 5 and that happened in South America over a recent one-year span. Use the map to answer the questions below.

1. **Using a Key** How many earthquakes happened at a depth greater than 300 km?
2. **Analyzing Data** Deep earthquakes are earthquakes that happen at a depth greater than 300 km. Which earthquakes happen more frequently: deep earthquakes or shallow earthquakes?
3. **Making Comparisons** How does the earthquake activity on the eastern edge of South America differ from the earthquake activity on the western edge?
4. **Inferring Relationships** The locations of earthquakes and plate boundaries are related. Where would you expect to find a major plate boundary?
5. **Identifying Trends** In what part of South America do most deep earthquakes happen? What relationships do you see between the locations of shallow earthquakes and deep earthquakes in South America?
6. **Analyzing Relationships** Most deep earthquakes happen where subducting plates move deep into the mantle. What type of plate boundary is indicated by the earthquake activity in South America? Explain your answer.

Key Resources

Technology

- Transparencies
  54 Locations of Earthquakes in South America

Chapter 10

Summary

THINK central SUPER SUMMARY Keyword: HQXTECS

Key Ideas | **Key Terms**

Section 1

Continental Drift

- Fossil, rock, and climatic evidence supports Wegener's hypothesis of continental drift. However, Wegener could not explain the mechanism by which the continents move.
- New ocean floor is constantly being produced through sea-floor spreading, which creates mid-ocean ridges and changes the topography of the sea floor.
- The magnetic properties of the rock of the ocean floor show that new lithosphere forms at a mid-ocean ridge and then moves away.
- Sea-floor spreading provides evidence that tectonic plates move and change.

continental drift, p. 259
mid-ocean ridge, p. 262
sea-floor spreading, p. 263
paleomagnetism, p. 263

Section 2

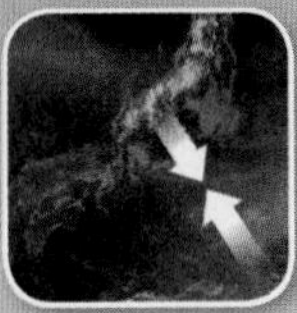

The Theory of Plate Tectonics

- The theory of plate tectonics proposes that changes in Earth's crust are caused by the very slow movement of large tectonic plates. Earthquakes, volcanoes, and young mountain ranges tend to be located in belts along the boundaries between tectonic plates.
- Tectonic plates meet at three types of boundaries—divergent, convergent, and transform. The geologic activity that occurs along the three types of plate boundaries differs according to the way plates move relative to each other.
- Tectonic plates are part of a convecting system that is driven by differences in density and heat.

plate tectonics, p. 267
lithosphere, p. 267
asthenosphere, p. 267
divergent boundary, p. 269
convergent boundary, p. 270
transform boundary, p. 271

Section 3

The Changing Continents

- Continents grow through the accretion of terranes. Continents break apart through rifting.
- Movements of tectonic plates have altered climates on continents and have created conditions that lead to changes in plants and animals.
- Continents collide to form supercontinents and then break apart in a cycle called the *supercontinent cycle.* Earth's tectonic plates continue to move, and, in the future, the continents will likely be in a different configuration.

rifting, p. 275
terrane, p. 276
supercontinent cycle, p. 278
Pangaea, p. 278
Panthalassa, p. 278

Chapter Summary

Using THINK central Resources

Super Summary

Have students connect the major concepts in this chapter through an interactive Super Summary. Visit www.thinkcentral.com and type in the keyword **HQXTECS** to access the Super Summary for this chapter.

Differentiated Instruction

Alternative Assessment

Comparing Scientific Ideas Have students create a table that compares Wegener's hypothesis of continental drift with the modern theory of plate tectonics. Students should include as much detail in each column as possible. When students have completed their tables, have them write a paragraph that explains how the hypothesis of continental drift provided a base that scientists worked from to develop the theory of plate tectonics. LS **Verbal**

Chapter Review

Assignment Guide	
Section	**Questions**
1	2, 10–13, 21, 22, 25, 31, 33–36
2	1, 3, 4, 6, 8, 14–17, 20, 24, 26
3	5, 9, 19, 23, 27
1 and 2	7, 18, 32
2 and 3	29, 30
1–3	28

Reading Toolbox

1. Answers may vary, but students' flip charts should accurately describe properties of the crust, lithosphere, and asthenosphere.

Using Key Terms

2–9. Answers may vary but should show that students understand the definitions of and differences between key terms.

Understanding Key Concepts

10. a
11. c
12. c
13. c
14. b
15. c
16. a
17. a

Short Answer

18. As scientists developed technology, such as sonar and magnetic sensing devices, to study the ocean floor, they became able to identify features of the ocean floor that helped identify plate boundaries and explain how plates move.
19. Pangaea rifted apart to form several smaller continents. Over many millions of years, the continents moved as a result of interactions of the plates until the continents reached their present locations.
20. Most earthquakes are sudden movements of crust that occur as tectonic plates grind past each other. Most volcanoes form as a result of upwelling magma at divergent boundaries or the interaction of fluids and heat at convergent plate boundaries.
21. During sea-floor spreading, new sea floor forms. At convergent boundaries, sea floor is destroyed. Thus, sea-floor spreading continually makes new sea floor to replace the old sea floor.
22. As rocks cool, the magnetic fields of some minerals in the rocks align with Earth's magnetic field. When the rocks are solid, the minerals hold that magnetic orientation.
23. As continents separate, populations of organisms are separated. These populations then change in different ways to adapt to their new and changing environments.

Critical Thinking

24. Tectonic plates fit together to form a connected pattern on Earth's surface.
25. He may have suggested that the continents had not separated until after 10 million years ago—otherwise, the same fossils would not be in both places.

Chapter 10 Review

1. **Three-Panel Flip Chart** Make a three-panel flip chart. Label the first panel "Crust," the second "Lithosphere," and the third "Asthenosphere." Under the appropriate flap, list the location and characteristics of each of these layers. **READING TOOLBOX**

USING KEY TERMS

Use each of the following terms in a separate sentence.

2. *sea-floor spreading*
3. *convection*
4. *divergent boundary*
5. *terrane*

For each pair of terms, explain how the meanings of the terms differ.

6. *convergent boundary* and *subduction zone*
7. *continental drift* and *plate tectonics*
8. *ridge push* and *slab pull*
9. *Pangaea* and *Panthalassa*

UNDERSTANDING KEY IDEAS

10. Support for Wegener's hypothesis of continental drift includes evidence of changes in
    a. climatic patterns.
    b. Panthalassa.
    c. terranes.
    d. subduction.
11. New ocean floor is constantly being produced through the process known as
    a. subduction.
    b. continental drift.
    c. sea-floor spreading.
    d. terranes.
12. An underwater mountain chain that formed by sea-floor spreading is called a
    a. divergent boundary.
    b. subduction zone.
    c. mid-ocean ridge.
    d. convergent boundary.
13. Scientists think that the upwelling of mantle material at mid-ocean ridges is caused by the motion of tectonic plates and comes from
    a. the lithosphere. **c.** the asthenosphere.
    b. terranes. **d.** rift valleys.
14. The layer of plastic rock that underlies the tectonic plates is the
    a. lithosphere. **c.** oceanic crust.
    b. asthenosphere. **d.** terrane.
15. The region along tectonic plate boundaries where one plate moves beneath another is called a
    a. rift valley.
    b. transform boundary.
    c. subduction zone.
    d. convergent boundary.
16. Two plates grind past each other at a
    a. transform boundary.
    b. convergent boundary.
    c. subduction zone.
    d. divergent boundary.
17. Convection occurs because heated material becomes
    a. less dense and rises.
    b. denser and rises.
    c. denser and sinks.
    d. less dense and sinks.

SHORT ANSWER

18. Explain the role of technology in the progression from the hypothesis of continental drift to the theory of plate tectonics.
19. Summarize how the continents moved from being part of Pangaea to their current locations.
20. Why do most earthquakes and volcanoes happen at or near plate boundaries?
21. Explain the following statement: "Because of sea-floor spreading, the ocean floor is constantly renewing itself."
22. Describe how rocks that form at a mid-ocean ridge become magnetized.
23. How might continental rifting influence the evolution of plants and animals?

CRITICAL THINKING

24. **Making Comparisons** How are tectonic plates like the pieces of a jigsaw puzzle?
25. **Making Inferences** If Alfred Wegener had found identical fossil remains of plants and animals that had lived no more than 10 million years ago in both eastern Brazil and western Africa, what might he have concluded about the breakup of Pangaea?
26. **Identifying Relationships** Assume that the total surface area of Earth is not changing. If new material is being added to Earth's crust at one boundary, what would you expect to be happening at another boundary?
27. **Making Predictions** About 150 million years from now, the continents will have drifted to new locations. How might these changes affect life on Earth?

CONCEPT MAPPING

28. Use the following terms to create a concept map: *asthenosphere, lithosphere, divergent boundary, convergent boundary, transform boundary, subduction zone, mid-ocean ridge, plates, convection, continental drift, theory of plate tectonics,* and *sea-floor spreading.*

MATH SKILLS

Math Skills

29. **Making Calculations** The coasts of Africa and South America began rifting about 150 million years ago. Today, the coast of South America is about 6,660 km from the coast of Africa. Using the equation *velocity* = *distance* ÷ *time,* determine how fast the continents moved apart, in millimeters per year.
30. **Using Equations** Assume that scientists know the rate at which the North American and Eurasian plates are moving away from each other. If t = time, d = distance, and v = velocity, what equation can they use to determine when North America separated from Eurasia during the breakup of Pangaea?

WRITING SKILLS

31. **Writing Persuasively** Imagine that you are Alfred Wegener. Write a persuasive essay to explain your idea of continental drift. Use only evidence originally used by Wegener to support his hypothesis.
32. **Communicating Main Ideas** Explain how the research of Wegener, Hess, and others led to the theory of plate tectonics.

INTERPRETING GRAPHICS

The graph below shows the relationship between the age of sea-floor rocks and the depth of the sea floor beneath the ocean surface. Use the graph to answer the questions that follow.

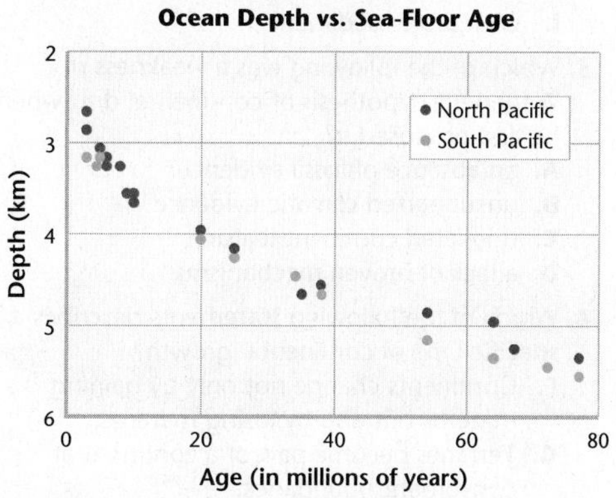

33. How old is the sea floor at a depth of 4 km?
34. Approximately how deep is the sea floor when it is 55 million years old?
35. What can you infer about the age of very deep sea floor from the data in the graph?
36. The ridge in the South Pacific Ocean is spreading faster than the ridge in the North Pacific Ocean. If this graph showed the depth of the sea floor in relation to the distance from the ridge, how would graphs for the North Pacific and South Pacific ridges differ?

Chapter Review

26. Sample answer: For the same surface area to be maintained, the same amount of material that is created must be destroyed. I would expect to find material being destroyed at other plate boundaries.
27. As the continents move, they affect climate. Thus, the climates of the various continents and of Earth as a whole would change. Also, rifting and collisions between continents would cause environmental changes that would cause species to change or become extinct.

Concept Mapping

28. Answers may vary but should include all of the terms listed. Sample answers appear at the end of this unit on p. 367A.

Math Skills

29. 1,000 m/km × 100 cm/m × 10 mm/cm = 1,000,000 mm/km; 6,660 km × 1,000,000 mm/1 km = 6,660,000,000 mm; 6,660,000,000 mm ÷ 150,000,000 years = 44.4 mm/year
30. *time* = *distance* ÷ *velocity* ($t = d/v$)

Writing Skills

31. Answers may vary. Accept all reasonable answers.
32. Answers may vary. Accept all reasonable answers.

Interpreting Graphics

33. 20 million years
34. 5 km
35. that the sea floor is very old
36. The graph of the North Pacific would have a steeper slope than the graph of the South Pacific would, because the sea floor closer to the North Pacific ridge would be older and thus deeper than sea floor at the same distance from the South Pacific ridge.

Estimated Time

To give students practice under more realistic testing conditions, allow them 30 minutes to answer all of the questions in this practice test.

Test Doctor

Question 1 Answer A is correct because the density of each colliding plate is more important in determining whether a plate will subduct or uplift than the size of the plate, answer B; the magnetic properties of the rock that makes up the plate, answer C; or the length of the boundary formed by the meeting of two plates, answer D.

Question 8 Answer H is correct. Answer F is incorrect because the nine mountains that rise above 8,000 m are not the nine tallest mountains on Earth. Answer G is incorrect because the longest mountain chain on Earth is the Mid-Atlantic Ridge, which is underwater. The longest above-water mountain chain is the Andes Mountains. Answer I is incorrect because the mountain chain is currently changing and growing.

Question 11 Full-credit answers should include the following points:
- the boundary between the South American plate and the African plate is a divergent boundary
- most divergent boundaries are located on the ocean floor and produce mid-ocean ridges and underwater mountain ranges

Chapter 10 Standardized Test Prep

Understanding Concepts

Directions (1–4): For each question, write on a separate sheet of paper the letter of the correct answer.

1. Which of the following factors is most important when determining the type of collision that forms when two lithospheric plates collide?
   A. the density of each plate
   B. the size of each plate
   C. the paleomagnetism of the rock
   D. the length of the boundary
2. At locations where sea-floor spreading occurs, rock is moved away from a mid-ocean ridge. What replaces the rock as it moves away?
   F. molten rock
   G. older rock
   H. continental crust
   I. compacted sediment
3. Which of the following was a weakness of Wegener's hypothesis of continental drift when he first proposed it?
   A. an absence of fossil evidence
   B. unsupported climatic evidence
   C. unrelated continent features
   D. a lack of proven mechanisms
4. Which of the following statements describes a specific type of continental growth?
   F. Continents change not only by gaining material but also by losing material.
   G. Terranes become part of a continent at convergent boundaries.
   H. Ocean sediments move onto land because of sea-floor spreading.
   I. Rifting adds new rock to a continent and causes the continent to become wider.

Directions (5–6): For each question, write a short response.

5. What is the name of the process by which Earth's crust breaks apart?
6. What is the name of the layer of plastic rock directly below the lithosphere?

Reading Skills

Directions (7–9): Read the passage below. Then, answer the questions.

The Himalaya Mountains

The Himalaya Mountains are a range of mountains that is 2,400 km long and that arcs across Pakistan, India, Tibet, Nepal, Sikkim, and Bhutan. The Himalaya Mountains are the highest mountains on Earth. Fourteen mountains in this range, including Mount Everest, rise to heights of more than 8,000 m above sea level. Mount Everest, the tallest above-water mountain on Earth, stands 8,850 m tall.

The formation of the Himalaya Mountains began about 50 million years ago. A tectonic plate carrying the Indian subcontinent collided with the Eurasian plate. The Indian plate was denser than the Eurasian plate. This difference in density caused the uplifting of the Eurasian plate and the subsequent formation of the Himalaya Mountains. This process continues today. The Indian plate continues to push under the Eurasian plate. New measurements show that Mount Everest is moving to the northeast by as much as 10 cm per year.

7. According to the passage, what geologic process formed the Himalaya Mountains?
   A. divergence
   B. continental rifting
   C. strike-slip faulting
   D. convergence
8. Which of the following statements is a fact, according to the passage?
   F. The 14 tallest mountains on Earth are located in the Himalaya Mountains.
   G. The Himalaya Mountains are the longest mountain chain on Earth.
   H. The Himalaya Mountains are located within six countries.
   I. The Himalaya Mountains had completely formed by 50 million years ago.
9. Part of which plate was subducted along the fault that formed the Himalaya Mountains?
   A. the Indian plate
   B. the Eurasian plate
   C. both plates
   D. neither plate

Question 13 Full-credit answers should include the following points:
- students should demonstrate a conceptual understanding that, unlike the plates at a convergent boundary, shown by letter E, or divergent boundary, shown by letter D, plates at a transform boundary move past one another, not into or away from one another
- transform boundaries produce a number of earthquakes, but they do not produce magma or cause mountain formation

Interpreting Graphics

Directions (10–13): For each question below, record the correct answer on a separate sheet of paper.

The map below shows the locations of Earth's major tectonic-plate boundaries. Use this map to answer questions 10 and 11.

Earth's Tectonic Plates

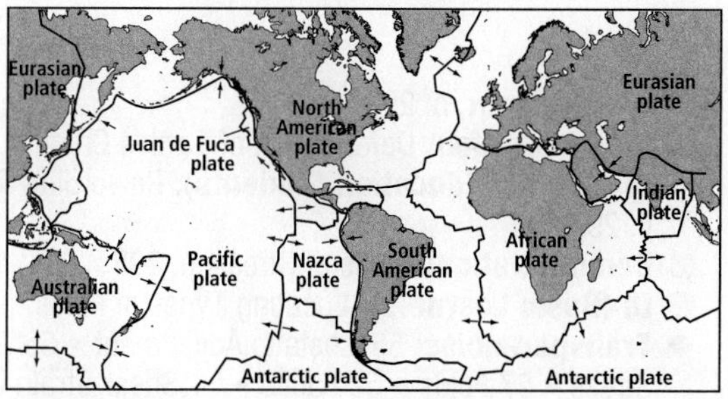

10. What type of boundary is found between the Pacific plate and the Nazca plate?
F. convergent
G. divergent
H. transform
I. subduction

11. What type of boundary is found between the South American plate and the African plate? What surface features are most often found at boundaries of this type?

The graphic below shows a cross-section of Earth with two tectonic-plate boundaries. Use this graphic to answer questions 12 and 13.

Plate Boundaries

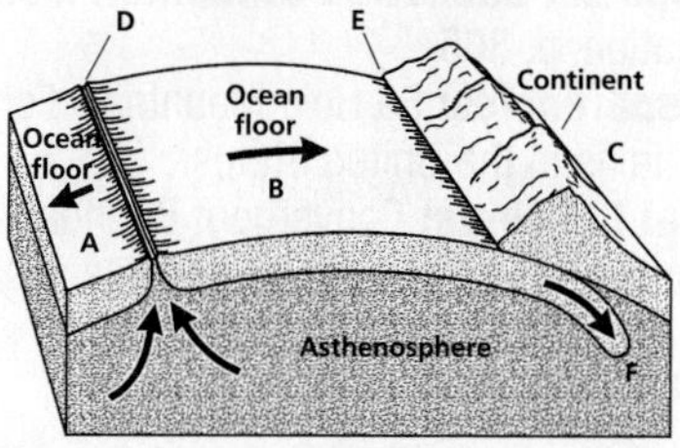

12. What type of plate interaction is indicated by the letter E?
A. continental rifting
B. sea-floor spreading
C. divergence
D. subduction

13. Describe how a transform boundary differs from the boundaries shown by letters D and E in terms of plate movement and magmatic activity.

Test Tip

If you become short on time, quickly scan the unanswered questions to see which questions are easiest to answer.

Standardized Test Prep

Using THINK central Resources

State Resources

- For specific resources for your state, visit www.thinkcentral.com and type in the keyword **HSHSTR.**

Answers

Understanding Concepts

1. A
2. F
3. D
4. G
5. rifting
6. the asthenosphere

Reading Skills

7. D
8. H
9. D

Interpreting Graphics

10. G
11. Answers may vary. See Test Doctor for a detailed scoring rubric.
12. D
13. Answers may vary. See Test Doctor for a detailed scoring rubric.

Chapter 11 Planner

Deformation of the Crust

	Standards	Teach Key Ideas
Chapter Opener, pp. 290–291 **45 min.**	**National Science Education Standards**	
Section 1 How Rock Deforms, pp. 293–300 **45 min.** ❯ Isostasy ❯ Stress ❯ Strain ❯ Folds ❯ Faults	**ES 1b, HNS 2a, UCP 3**	■ ▲ **Bellringer,** p. 293 ■ **Demonstration:** Deformation of Earth's Crust, p. 293 ■ **DI (Special Education Students):** Rewording Text, p. 294 ■ **Demonstration:** Types of Stress, p. 295 ■ **DI (Basic Learners):** Locating Types of Folds, p. 298 ◆ **Transparencies:** 55 Isostatic Adjustment • 56 Types of Stress • 57 Folds • 58 Faults • 61 Shear Strain in New Zealand ▲ **Visual Concepts:** Buoyant Force on Floating Objects • Stress • Types of Rock-Layer Folding • Hanging Walls and Footwalls • Types of Faults
Section 2 How Mountains Form, pp. 301–306 **90 min.** ❯ Mountain Ranges and Systems ❯ Plate Tectonics and Mountains ❯ Types of Mountains	**ES 1b, ES 3c, HNS 2a, UCP 3, UCP 4**	■ ◆ **Bellringer,** p. 301 ■ **Discussion:** Mountain Features, p. 301 ■ **DI (Basic Learners/Struggling Readers):** Mountain-Range Postcards, p. 302 ■ **DI (Special Education Students):** Modeling Mountain Formation, p. 305 ◆ **Transparencies:** 59 How Mountains Form • 60 Types of Mountains in the United States ▲ **Visual Concepts:** Convergent Boundary • Volcano Formation at Convergent Boundaries • Types of Mountains
Chapter Wrap-Up, pp. 311–315 **90 min.**		**Chapter Summary,** p. 311

See also PowerNotes® Presentations

CHAPTER Fast Track *To shorten instruction because of time limitations, omit Section 1.*

Key

Teacher's Edition ■ Teaching Transparencies ◆
Chapter Resource File ● Online Edition ▲

All resources listed below are also available on the **Teacher One Stop™.**

Why It Matters	Hands-On	Skills Development	Assessment
■ **Chapter Overview,** p. 290 ■ **Using the Figure:** Road Cuts, p. 290	**Inquiry Lab:** Types of Deformation, p. 291	**Reading Toolbox,** p. 292	
■ **Section Overview,** p. 293 ■ **Physics Connection:** Archimedes' Principle, p. 294 ■ **Physics Connection:** Elastic Modulus, p. 296 ■ **Using the Figure:** Identifying Limbs and Hinges, p. 297 **Which Features are Fit to Climb?** p. 298	**QuickLab:** Modeling Isostasy, p. 294 **QuickLab:** Modeling Stress and Strain, p. 296 ■ **Activity:** Folded Art, p. 297 ■ **Group Activity:** It's Your Fault, p. 299 ■ **Activity:** Geophysics of New Zealand, p. 310 ● **Inquiry Lab:** Rock Deformation ● **Skills Practice Lab:** Hooke's Law	**Reading Toolbox:** Cause and Effect Map, p. 296 **Math Skills:** Units of Stress, p. 297 ■ **Reading Skill Builder:** Reading Organizer, p. 298 **Maps in Action:** Shear Strain in New Zealand, p. 310	**Reading Check,** p. 295 **Reading Check,** p. 297 **Reading Check,** p. 299 **Section Review,** p. 300 ■ **Reteaching,** p. 299 **Quiz,** p. 299 ■ **DI (Alternative Assessment):** Modeling Isostasy, p. 300 ● **Section Quiz**
■ **Section Overview,** p. 301 ■ **Using the Figure:** Lithospheric Collisions and Mountain Types, p. 302 ■ **Why It Matters:** High Volcanoes, p. 303	■ **Group Activity:** Plates and Mountain Formation, p. 304 ■ **Homework:** Valleys, Plateaus, and Grabens, p. 304 **Making Models Lab:** Continental Collisions, pp. 308–309	**Reading Toolbox:** Analyzing Comparisons, p. 302 ■ **Skill Builder:** Writing, p. 302 ■ **Reading Skill Builder:** Discussion, p. 304 ■ ● **Internet Activity:** "Dead" Grabens, p. 304	**Reading Check,** p. 303 **Reading Check,** p. 305 **Section Review,** p. 306 ■ **Reteaching,** p. 305 ■ **Quiz,** p. 305 ■ **DI (Alternative Assessment):** Modeling Plate Interactions, p. 306 ● **Section Quiz**
Spying on Earth's Movements, p. 307		▲ **Super Summary** **Standardized Test Prep,** pp. 314–315	**Chapter Review,** pp. 312–313 ■ **DI (Alternative Assessment):** Poster Project, p. 311 ● **Chapter Tests**

See also Lab Generator

See also Holt Online Assessment Resources

Chapter Overview

The rock of Earth's crust deforms when the weight above the crust changes, as well as when tectonic plates collide. The results of the stress applied to rock are folds or faults. Deformation processes lead to the formation of mountains, and the type of mountain formed depends on the type of stress and the resulting strain.

Using the Figure GENERAL

Road Cuts Point out to students that places where highways have been cut through rock often reveal the geological processes that have taken place there. Ask students what structures indicate the type of rock that is shown in the figure. (The layers in the rock indicate that the rock may be sedimentary.) **LS Visual**

Why It Matters

Hillsides made of fractured, crumpled rock are more likely to experience landslides than are hillsides made of solid rock. The angle and composition of rock layers also affect the stability of slopes. If processes that caused crustal deformation in an area are ongoing, then structures should be constructed to resist the types of damage that can occur in tectonically active areas.

Chapter 11 Deformation of the Crust

Chapter Outline

Virginia Standards of Learning
ES.1.c
ES.1.f
ES.2.a
ES.7.a
ES.7.b

Why It Matters

Understanding how rock deforms by bending or breaking helps us understand the processes that shape Earth's surface. When building Highway 14 in California, construction crews cut through this hill. The exposed rock layers were folded by stress that was caused by movement along the nearby San Andreas fault.

Chapter Correlations — *Virginia Standards of Learning*

ES.1.c scales, diagrams, charts, graphs, tables, imagery, models, and profiles are constructed and interpreted.
current applications are used to reinforce Earth science concepts.

ES.2.a science explains and predicts the interactions and dynamics of complex Earth systems.
ES.7.a geologic processes and their resulting features
ES.7.b tectonic processes

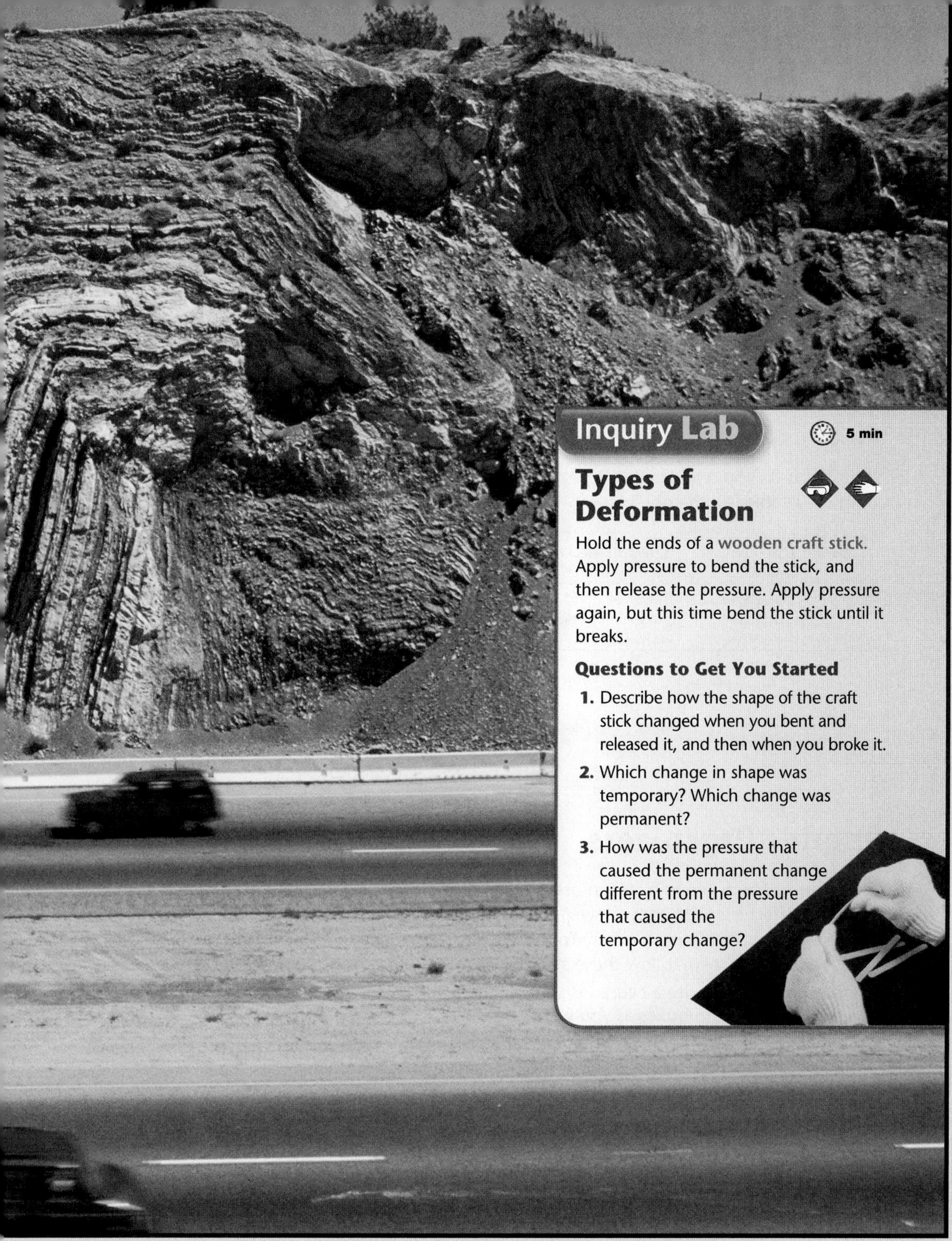

Inquiry Lab

5 min

Types of Deformation

Hold the ends of a wooden craft stick. Apply pressure to bend the stick, and then release the pressure. Apply pressure again, but this time bend the stick until it breaks.

Questions to Get You Started

1. Describe how the shape of the craft stick changed when you bent and released it, and then when you broke it.
2. Which change in shape was temporary? Which change was permanent?
3. How was the pressure that caused the permanent change different from the pressure that caused the temporary change?

Inquiry Lab

Central Concept: Students analyze how the application of pressure at different rates results in non-permanent (elastic) deformation and permanent (brittle) deformation of a material.

Teacher's Notes: You may wish to assign one student in each group to apply pressure to the craft stick and one student to record results of each pressure trial.

Materials (per group)
- wooden craft stick

Skills Acquired
- Observing
- Analyzing
- Interpreting Results

Answers to Getting Started

1. Student answers may vary but should mention that, when bent and released, the stick returned to nearly its original shape, but when bent more strongly, the stick broke.
2. Bending and releasing resulted in a change that was mostly temporary; breaking resulted in a permanent change.
3. The pressure that caused permanent change was stronger and applied at a faster rate; the pressure that caused a mainly temporary change was gentler and applied more slowly.

Using THINK central Resources

An online version of this chapter, as well as all the print and multimedia resources that accompany the program are available to registered teachers and their students. Log onto www.thinkcentral.com to access these materials and tools to organize your preparation and student learning.

READING TOOLBOX

Everyday Words Used in Science

Word	Everyday meaning	Scientific meaning
stress	an emphasis; a state of anxiety	the amount of force per unit area that acts on a rock
strain	make an intense effort	any change in a rock's shape or volume caused by stress
fault	responsi-bility for something wrong; a flaw; an error; a mistake	a fracture in Earth's crust along which one block of rock moves relative to another

Analyzing Comparisons

Answers may vary. Check to make sure students' tables contain accurate comparisons.

READING TOOLBOX

These reading tools will help you learn the material in this chapter.

Science Terms

Everyday Words Used in Science Many words that are used in science are also used in everyday speech. When these words are used in science, however, their meanings are often different from their everyday meanings, or more precise. Pay special attention to the definitions of such words so that you use the words correctly in scientific contexts.

Your Turn As you read Section 1, complete a table like the one below.

Word	Everyday meaning	Scientific meaning
stress	an emphasis; a state of anxiety	the amount of force per unit area that acts on a rock
strain	make an intense effort	
fault		

Comparisons

Analyzing Comparisons When you compare two things, you describe how they are similar or different. Words that may signal comparisons include *like*, *unlike*, *more*, and *less*, as well as words formed by using the suffixes *-er* and *-est*.

Your Turn Make a table like the one below. As you read the chapter, list the two things being compared in the first two columns. In the third column, describe how they are similar or different. In the last column, note any words or phrases that signal the comparison. The sample entry below is for the sentence "Like folds, faults vary greatly in size."

First thing	Second thing	Similarity or difference	Signaling word or phrase
folds	faults	Both can be very small or very large.	like

Graphic Organizers

Cause-and-Effect Maps You can use cause-and-effect maps to show how processes are related to each other. To make a cause-and-effect map, follow these steps.

1. Draw a box, and write a cause inside it. Add as many cause boxes as you want.
2. Draw another box to represent an effect. Add as many effect boxes as you want.
3. Connect each cause box to one or more effect boxes with arrows.
4. An effect can be the cause of one or more other effects. You may want to connect an effect box to one or more other effect boxes.

Your Turn As you read Section 1, use a separate sheet of paper to complete the cause-and-effect map started below. Add at least two more effects.

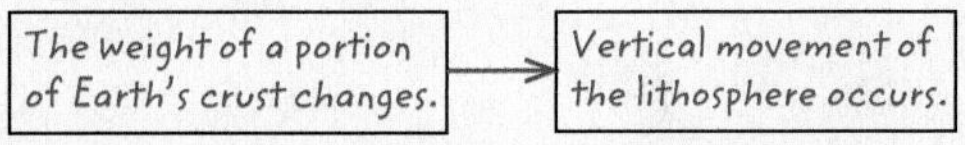

The weight of a portion of Earth's crust changes.
Vertical movement of the lithosphere occurs.

For more information on how to use these and other tools, see **Appendix A.**

Cause-and-Effect Map

Answers may vary. Sample answer:

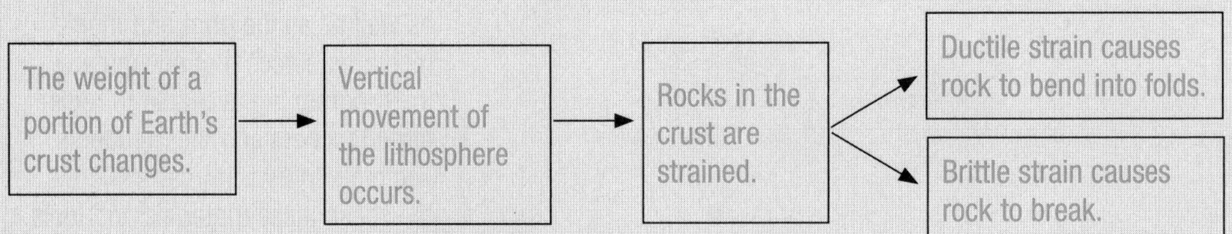

SECTION 1

How Rock Deforms

Key Ideas	Key Terms	Why It Matters
❯ Summarize the principle of isostasy. ❯ Identify the three main types of stress. ❯ Compare folds and faults.	deformation isostasy stress strain fold fault	Both folding and faulting can create tall mountains and deep valleys. Understanding how deformed rock behaves can help engineers determine how stable a hillside or a cliff is.

Mountain ranges are visible reminders that the shape of Earth's surface is constantly changing. These changes result from **deformation,** or the bending, tilting, and breaking of Earth's crust.

Isostasy

Deformation sometimes occurs because the weight of some part of Earth's crust changes. When the lithosphere (of which the crust is a part) thickens and becomes heavier, it sinks deeper into the asthenosphere. If the lithosphere thins and becomes lighter, it rises higher in the asthenosphere.

Vertical movement of the lithosphere depends on two opposing forces. One force is the force due to gravity, or weight, of the lithosphere pressing down on the asthenosphere. The other force is the buoyant force of the asthenosphere pressing up on the lithosphere. When these two forces are balanced, the lithosphere and asthenosphere are in a state called **isostasy.** However, when the weight of the lithosphere changes, the lithosphere sinks or rises until a balance of the forces is reached again. One type of this isostatic adjustment is shown in **Figure 1.** As these adjustments occur, areas of the crust are bent up and down. This bending causes rock in these areas to deform.

deformation the bending, tilting, and breaking of Earth's crust; the change in the shape of rock in response to stress

isostasy a condition of gravitational and buoyant equilibrium between Earth's lithosphere and asthenosphere

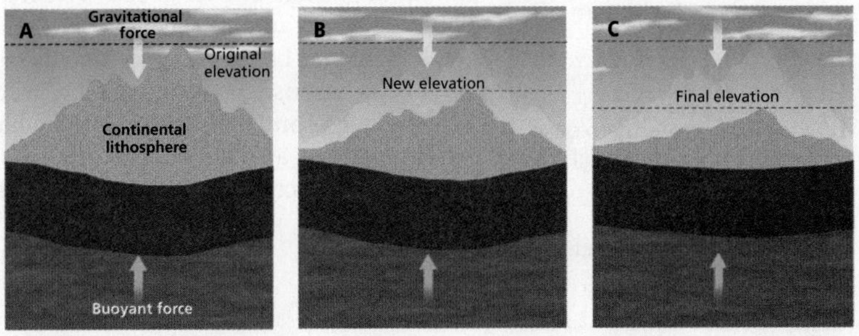

Figure 1 (A) When gravitational and buoyant forces are equal, a state of isostasy exists. (B) As erosion wears away the crust, the lithosphere becomes lighter and rises. (C) As erosion continues, the isostatic adjustment also continues.

Section 1

Focus

Overview

This section describes how changes in the weight of Earth's crust causes deformation. The section also explains how stress causes the bending and breaking of rock.

Bellringer

Have students imagine that they placed a bowling ball on a soft pillow. What would happen to the ball and to the pillow? (The ball would sink into the pillow, changing the pillow's shape.) **LS Verbal**

Motivate

Demonstration — GENERAL

Deformation of Earth's Crust Fill a large, clear container halfway with a mud or plaster thick enough so that a brick placed in it will sink very slowly, or sink only partway into the mixture. Level the top of the mixture, and then place a brick on top of the mixture. Ask students to describe what happens. (The mixture beneath the brick is pressed down, while the mixture around the brick rises up.) Point out that isostatic adjustment involves a similar process. **LS Visual**

Key Resources

Chapter Resource File
- Directed Reading BASIC
- Inquiry Lab: Rock Deformation GENERAL
- Skills Practice Lab: Hooke's Law GENERAL

Technology
- Transparencies
  Bellringer
  55 Isostatic Adjustment

Teach

Quick Lab

Skills Acquired
- Observing
- Interpreting

Materials
- 1 L beaker
- 500 mL water
- Wooden block
- 2 grease pencils
- Small mass

Teacher's Notes: Be sure that students do not break the glass beaker. Spills should be cleaned up quickly and completely. Students should wait for the water levels to become steady before making marks with the grease pencils.

Analysis
1. The block sinks deeper into the water.
2. The model depicts the type of isostatic adjustment that occurs when lithosphere gets heavier, such as when mountains form or when glaciers or ice sheets form.

Figure 2 Mt. Katahdin in Baxter State Park, Maine, has been worn down by weathering and erosion. As the mountain shrinks, the crust underneath it is uplifted.

Mountains and Isostasy

In mountainous regions, isostatic adjustments constantly occur. Over millions of years, the rock that forms mountains is worn away by the erosive actions of wind, water, and ice. This erosion can significantly reduce the height and weight of a mountain range, such as the one shown in **Figure 2.** As a mountain becomes smaller and lighter, the area may rise by isostatic adjustment in a process called *uplift*.

Deposition and Isostasy

Another type of isostatic adjustment occurs in areas where rivers carrying large amounts of mud, sand, and gravel flow into larger bodies of water. When a river flows into the ocean, most of the material that the river carries is deposited on the nearby ocean floor. The added weight of the deposited material causes the ocean floor to sink by isostatic adjustment in a process called *subsidence*. This process is occurring in the Gulf of Mexico at the mouth of the Mississippi River, where a thick accumulation of deposited materials has formed.

Glaciers and Isostasy

Isostatic adjustments also occur as a result of the growth and retreat of glaciers and ice sheets. When a large amount of water is held in glaciers and ice sheets on land, the weight of the ice causes the lithosphere beneath the ice to sink. Simultaneously, the ocean floor rises because the weight of the overlying ocean water is less. When glaciers and ice sheets melt, the land that was covered with ice slowly rises as the weight of the crust decreases. As the water returns to the ocean, the ocean floor sinks.

Quick Lab — 5 min

Modeling Isostasy

Procedure

1. Fill a 1 L beaker with 500 mL of water.
2. Place a wooden block in the water. Use a grease pencil to mark on the side of the beaker the levels of the top and the bottom of the block.
3. Place a small mass, of about 1 g, on the wooden block. Use a second grease pencil to mark the levels of the top and the bottom of the block.

Analysis

1. What happens to the block of wood when the weight is added?
2. What type of isostatic adjustment does this activity model?

Physics Connection

Archimedes' Principle Archimedes' principle states that the weight of a displaced fluid equals the buoyant force on the object displacing the fluid. If the object is less dense than the fluid, the displaced fluid will weigh more than the object. The buoyant force will be greater than the object's weight and will push the object upward until the two forces are balanced. Thus, the object will float. When the liquid is less dense than the object, the weight of the displaced fluid is less than the weight of the object, and the object will sink.

Differentiated Instruction

Special Education Students

Rewording Text Text with large words is often hard for students with reading delays to understand. The description of isostasy is an example. Help students understand these paragraphs by using this procedure: Read the first sentence aloud. Reword the sentence, replacing large words with definitions. Type or write the reworded sentence on a piece of paper. Repeat these steps with the remaining sentences. Make a copy of the reworded text for each student. **LS Verbal**

Stress

As Earth's lithosphere moves, the rock in the crust is squeezed, stretched, and twisted. These actions exert force on the rock. The amount of force that is exerted on each unit of area is called **stress.** For example, during isostatic adjustments, the lithosphere sinks and rises atop the asthenosphere. As the lithosphere sinks, the rock in the crust is squeezed and the direction of stress changes. As the lithosphere rises, the rock in the crust is stretched and the direction of stress changes again. Similarly, stress occurs in Earth's crust when tectonic plates collide, separate, or scrape past each other. **Figure 3** shows the three main types of stress.

stress the amount of force per unit area that acts on a rock

Compression

The type of stress that squeezes and shortens a body, such as rock, is called *compression*. Compression can reduce the amount of space that rock occupies. More commonly, however, compression changes the shape of the rock while pushing it higher up or deeper down into the crust. Much of the stress that occurs at or near convergent boundaries, where tectonic plates collide, is compression.

Tension

Another type of stress is tension. *Tension* is stress that stretches and pulls a body apart. When rock is pulled apart by tension, it tends to become thinner. Much of the stress that occurs at or near divergent boundaries, where tectonic plates pull apart, is tension.

THINK central
INTERACT ONLINE
(Keyword: HQXDEFF3)

Figure 3 Types of Stress

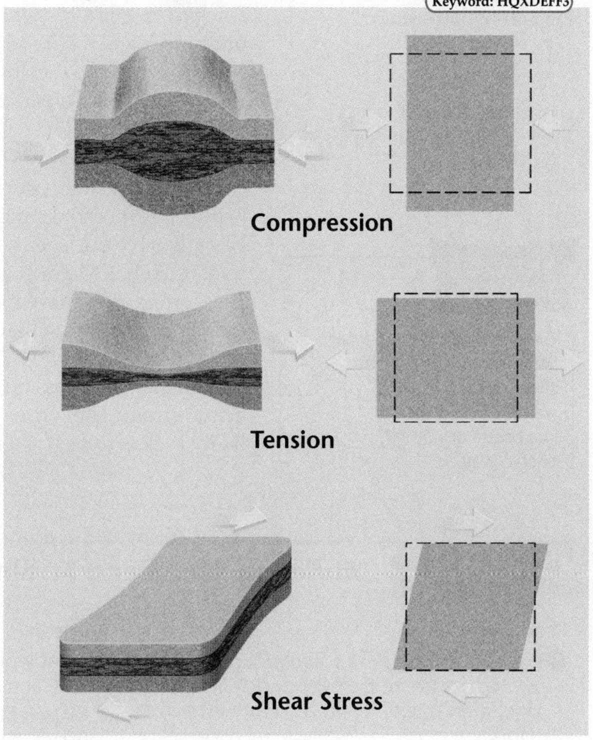

Shear Stress

The third type of stress is shear stress. *Shear stress* distorts a body by pushing parts of the body in opposite directions. Sheared rock bends, twists, or breaks apart as it slides past neighboring rock. Shear stress is common at transform boundaries, where tectonic plates slide horizontally past each other. However, each type of stress occurs at or near all types of plate boundaries and in various other regions of the crust, too.

Academic Vocabulary
distort (di STOHRT) to change the natural appearance of something

Reading Check **Which two kinds of stress pull rock apart?**
(See Appendix G for answers to Reading Checks.)

Demonstration — Basic

Types of Stress To help students visualize the different kinds of stress, take a block of clay about 5 cm long, 5 cm wide, and 3 cm thick. Demonstrate compression by pushing on the short sides of the block. Have students note that you pushed your hands toward each other and that the clay thickened in the middle. Reshape the clay block or use another, identical block to demonstrate tension by slowly pulling the sides of the block in opposite directions. Again, have students note that you moved your hands away from each other and that the clay thinned in the center. Return the clay to its original shape, or use a third identical block to demonstrate shear stress by placing your hands flat on opposite sides of the clay block, then moving your hands in opposite directions. Have students note that you moved your hands in opposite directions past each other and that the clay deformed by becoming offset at the edges.
LS **Visual**

Answer to Reading Check
Tension and shear stress can both pull rock apart.

Key Resources

Technology
- Transparencies
  56 Types of Stress

MISCONCEPTION ALERT

Ductility Students may be confused as to how a solid and seemingly rigid substance like rock can undergo deformation without breaking. Explain that all solid materials possess a property called *ductility*, which is a measure of how much the shape or volume of a solid can be changed without causing the substance to break. Ductility differs from elasticity, in that an elastic material will return to its original shape once the stress that deforms it has been removed. A ductile material does not break, but it will not return to its original shape when the stress is removed. An example of this difference is the difference between a rubber band and a piece of copper wire. When the rubber band is stretched and then released, it regains its original shape. When wire is bent or stretched and then released, the wire will stay bent or stretched. The ductility of rock varies with its composition and structure.

Teach, *continued*

READING TOOLBOX

Cause-and-effect map

Answers may vary. Sample answer:

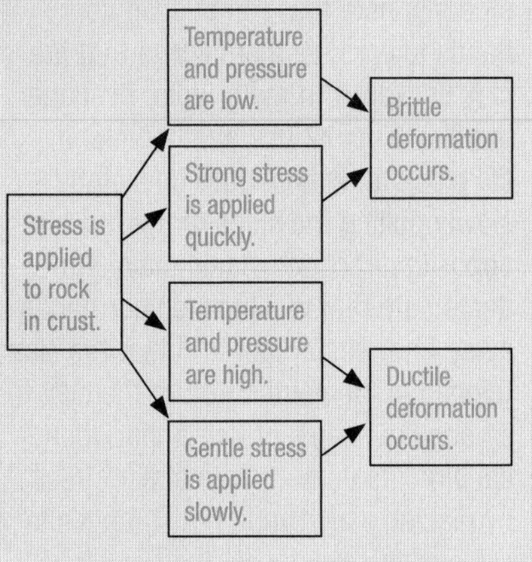

Physics Connection ADVANCED

Elastic Modulus Different materials respond differently to a given amount of stress—some recover completely from the stress, others show permanent deformation, and still others break under the stress. A measure of a material's elasticity is given by the ratio of the stress on a material to the amount of strain it exhibits. In general, this ratio is called the *elastic modulus* of the substance. Have students research the kinds of elastic modulus—stretch modulus, shear modulus, and bulk modulus—and relate them to the kinds of stress that rock undergoes. **LS Verbal**

Figure 4 This rock deformation in Kingman, Arizona, is an example of brittle strain.

strain any change in a rock's shape or volume caused by stress

READING TOOLBOX

Cause-and-Effect Map
Make a cause-and-effect map to show why rock deforms in a brittle or ductile way.

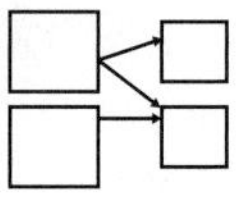

Strain

When stress is applied to rock, rock may deform. Any change in the shape or volume of rock that results from stress is called **strain**. When stress is applied slowly, the deformed rock may regain its original shape when the stress is removed. However, the amount of stress that rock can withstand without permanently changing shape is limited. This limit varies with the type of rock and the conditions under which the stress is applied. If a stress exceeds the rock's limit, the rock's shape permanently changes.

Types of Permanent Strain

Materials that respond to stress by breaking or fracturing are *brittle*. Brittle strain appears as cracks or fractures, as **Figure 4** shows. *Ductile* materials respond to stress by bending or deforming without breaking. Ductile strain is a change in the volume or shape of rock in which the rock does not crack or fracture. Brittle strain and ductile strain are types of permanent strain.

Factors That Affect Strain

The composition of rock determines whether rock is ductile or brittle. Temperature and pressure also affect how rock deforms. Near Earth's surface, where temperature and pressure are low, rock is likely to deform in a brittle way. At higher temperature and pressure, rock is more likely to deform in a ductile way.

The type of strain that stress causes is determined by the amount and type of stress and by the rate at which stress is applied to rock. The greater the stress on rock is, the more likely rock is to undergo brittle strain. The more quickly stress is applied to rock, the more likely rock is to respond in a brittle way.

Quick Lab — Modeling Stress and Strain

15 min

Procedure

1. Put on a pair of **gloves**, and pick up a 5 cm × 5 cm square of **frozen plastic play putty**. Hold one edge of the frozen putty in each hand.
2. Try to pull the putty apart by pulling the edges away from each other.
3. Push the edges of the frozen putty toward each other. (You may have to reshape the putty between steps.)
4. Push one edge of the frozen putty away from you, and pull the other edge toward you.
5. Repeat steps 2–4, but use a 5 cm × 5 cm square of **warm plastic play putty**.

Analysis

1. What types of stress did you model in steps 2, 3, and 4?
2. Make a table that lists the characteristics of the two substances that you modeled, the stresses that you modeled, and the resulting strain on each model.
3. How does the frozen putty respond to the stress? How does the warm putty's response to the stress differ from the frozen putty's response?

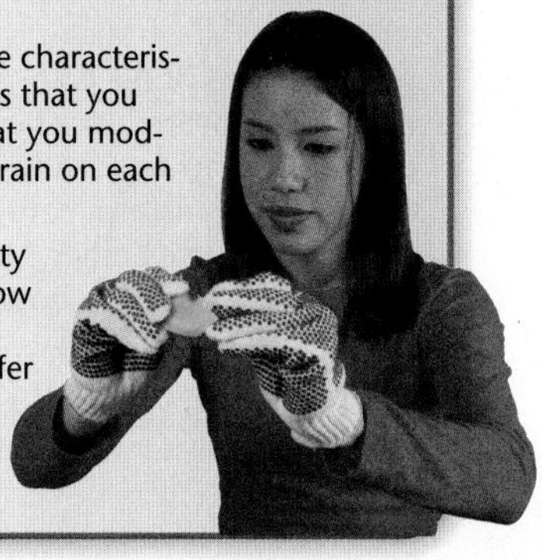

Quick Lab

Skills Acquired
- Experimenting
- Observing
- Identifying/Recognizing Patterns
- Interpreting

Materials
- Gloves
- Frozen plastic play putty
- Warm plastic play putty

Teacher's Notes Be sure that the frozen putty is not too cold, so that students are not accidentally "burned" by it. Students should make the observations of the frozen putty quickly, before it becomes too warm and pliable.

Analysis
1. tension, compression, and shear stress, respectively
2. Answers may vary. Accept all reasonable answers.
3. Answers may vary depending on the stresses applied. In general, the frozen putty should respond in a brittle way and the warm putty should respond in a ductile way.

Folds

When rock responds to stress by deforming in a ductile way, folds commonly form. A **fold** is a bend in rock layers that results from stress. A fold is most easily observed where flat layers of rock were compressed or squeezed inward. As stress was applied, the rock layers bent and folded. Cracks sometimes appear in or near a fold, but most commonly the rock layers remain intact. Although a fold commonly results from compression, it can also form as a result of shear stress.

fold a form of ductile strain in which rock layers bend, usually as a result of compression

Anatomy of a Fold

Folds have features by which they can be identified. Scientists use these features to describe folds. The main features of a fold are shown by the illustration in **Figure 5.** The sloping sides of a fold are called *limbs*. The limbs meet at the bend in the rock layers, which is called the *hinge*. Some folds also contain an additional feature. If a fold's structure is such that a plane could slice the fold into two symmetrical halves, the fold is symmetrical. The plane is called the fold's *axial plane*. However, the two halves of a fold are rarely symmetrical.

Many folds bend vertically, but folds can have many other shapes, as shown by the photograph in **Figure 5.** Folds are usually asymmetrical. Sometimes, one limb of a fold dips more steeply than the other limb does. If a fold is *overturned,* the fold appears to be lying on its side. Folds can have open shapes or be as tight as a hairpin. A fold's hinge can be a smooth bend or may come to a sharp point. Each fold is unique because the combination of stresses and conditions that caused the fold was unique.

Math Skills

Units of Stress Two units are commonly used to describe stress or pressure. One unit is the pascal (Pa). A pascal is a measure of force (in newtons) divided by area (in square meters). The other unit of stress is the pound per square inch (psi). If the pressure in a region of Earth's crust is measured as 25 MPa (megapascals) and as 3,626 psi, how many pounds per square inch does 1 MPa equal? (Note: 1 MPa = 1,000,000 Pa)

Reading Check **Name two features of a fold.**

Figure 5 Although folds are rarely symmetrical, every fold has a hinge and limbs. ***Can you identify the limbs and hinge of each fold in the photo?***

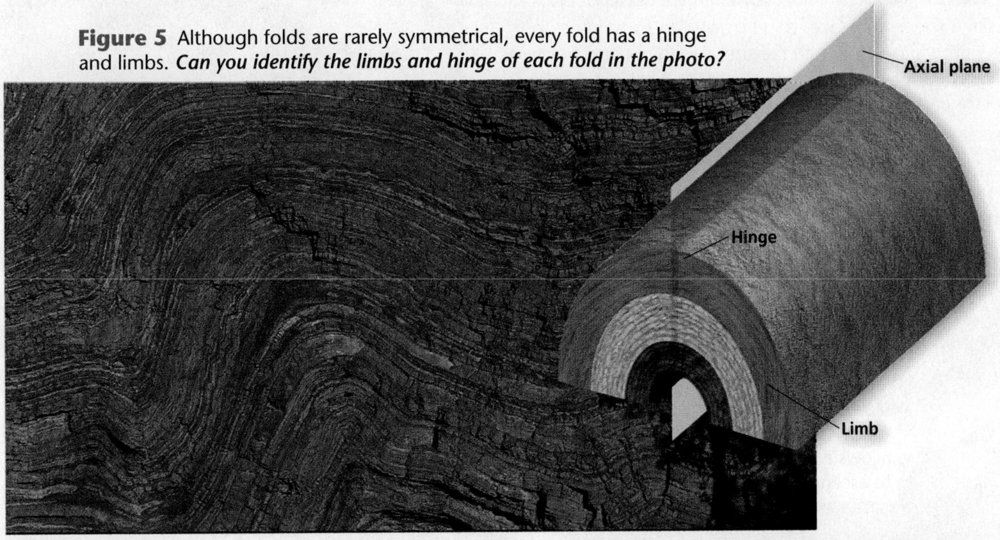

Math Skills

Answer

$x = (3{,}626 \text{ psi} \div 25 \text{ MPa}) \times 1 \text{ MPa} = 145 \text{ psi}$

Answer to Reading Check

limbs and hinges

Using the Figure — GENERAL

Identifying Limbs and Hinges Explain to students that limbs of two folds meet at a point called an *inflection point.* At this point, the limbs that slant away from one hinge change direction slightly as they slant toward a different hinge. The two limbs on either side of the inflection point are counted as separate limbs because they are part of separate folds. Ask students how many hinges and limbs they see in the diagram. (one hinge and two limbs) Ask students how many hinges and limbs extend from the folds in the upper left corner of the photograph. (two hinges and four limbs) Answer to caption question: The rock in the photo shows three clear hinges. The first is pointed toward the top of the photo at the lower left corner. The second is slightly to the right of the first hinge and points downward and slightly to the right. The third is the large hinge that points toward the upper left of the photo and is located at the center of the photo. The limbs are on either side of these hinges. **LS Visual**

Activity — ADVANCED

Folded Art Have interested students create drawings, paintings, or sculptures that represent symmetric and asymmetric folds. Students could also research and include art of isoclinal, overturned, recumbant, and chevron folds.
LS Visual/Kinesthetic

Key Resources

Technology

- Transparencies
  57 Folds

Teach, *continued*

Reading Skill Builder — Basic

Reading Organizer Before students read this page, have them make a table that has three columns and four rows. Have students label the columns with "Direction of curve" and "Location of oldest rock." Have students label the rows with "Anticline," "Syncline," and "Monocline." Then, have students read the page and insert into the table the correct information for each type of fold. Students should keep these tables as study guides for later assessments. English Language Learners
LS Verbal

Why It Matters

If a rock face provides enough natural weathering or deformation features, skilled climbers can free climb. They use rope and other equipment for safety but do not use devices to provide artificial holds or ledges. If a rock formation lacks sufficient natural features, climbers practice aid climbing, in which they move upward with the help of devices attached to the rock. Many climbers are now practicing clean climbing techniques that leave no sign of their presence behind.

Answer to Your Turn

Answers will vary. The photograph shows a spring-loaded camming device; other devices include carabiners, pitons, rock bolts, and chocks.

Figure 6 The three major types of folds are anticlines (top), synclines (middle), and monoclines (bottom).

Types of Folds

To categorize a fold, scientists study the relative ages of the rocks in the fold. The rock layers of the fold are identified by age from youngest to oldest. An *anticline* is a fold in which the oldest layer is in the center of the fold. Anticlines are commonly arch shaped. A *syncline* is a fold in which the youngest layer is in the center of the fold. Synclines are commonly bowl shaped. A *monocline* is a fold in which both limbs are horizontal or almost horizontal. Monoclines form when one part of Earth's crust moves up or down relative to another part. The three major types of folds are shown in **Figure 6.**

Sizes of Folds

Folds, which appear as wavelike structures in rock layers, vary greatly in size. Some folds are small enough to be contained in a hand-held rock specimen. Other folds cover thousands of square kilometers and can be seen only from the air.

Sometimes, a large anticline forms a ridge. A *ridge* is a large, narrow strip of elevated land that can occur near mountains. Nearby, a large syncline may form a valley. Over time, however, the varying resistance to erosion of rock in anticlines and synclines can change this simple landscape pattern.

Why It Matters

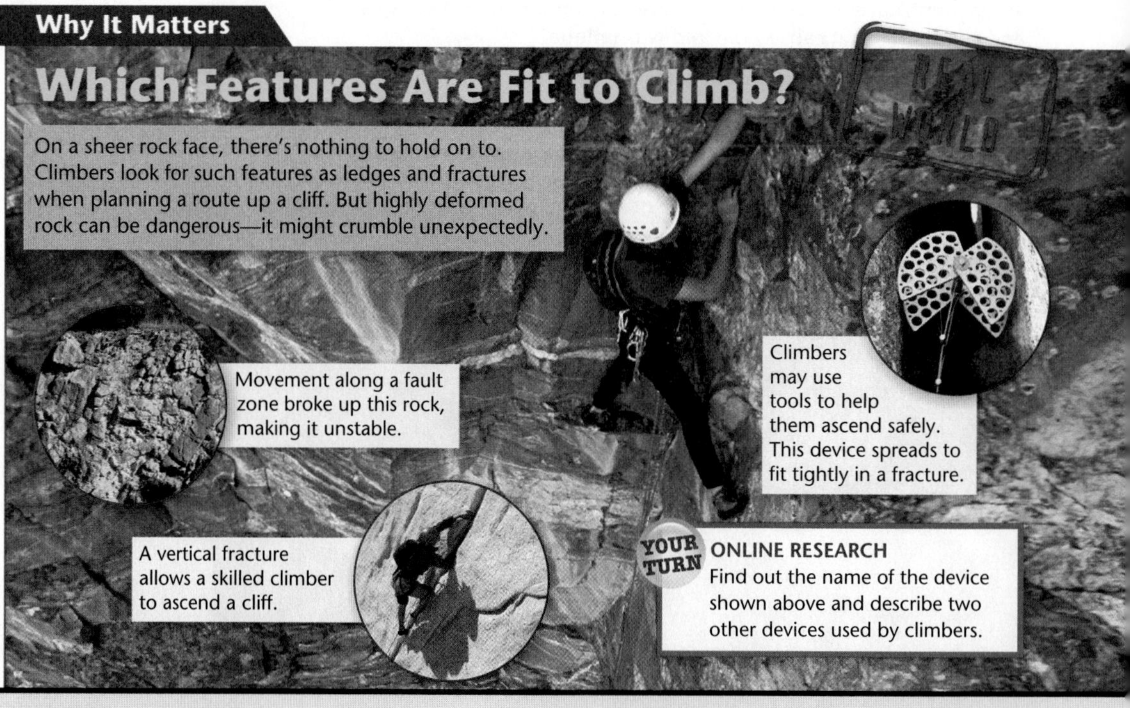

Which Features Are Fit to Climb?
On a sheer rock face, there's nothing to hold on to. Climbers look for such features as ledges and fractures when planning a route up a cliff. But highly deformed rock can be dangerous—it might crumble unexpectedly.
Movement along a fault zone broke up this rock, making it unstable.
Climbers may use tools to help them ascend safely. This device spreads to fit tightly in a fracture.
A vertical fracture allows a skilled climber to ascend a cliff.
YOUR TURN
ONLINE RESEARCH
Find out the name of the device shown above and describe two other devices used by climbers.

Differentiated Instruction

Basic Learners

Locating Types of Folds Have students research areas of the United States in which each of the three types of folds are common. Students should note the geographical location of the folds, the general size of the folds, and whether they appear in ridges or valleys. Students should then compile their findings into a short, written and illustrated report. Encourage students to use creativity in the style of their writing. **LS Verbal**

Figure 7 Normal and Reverse Faults

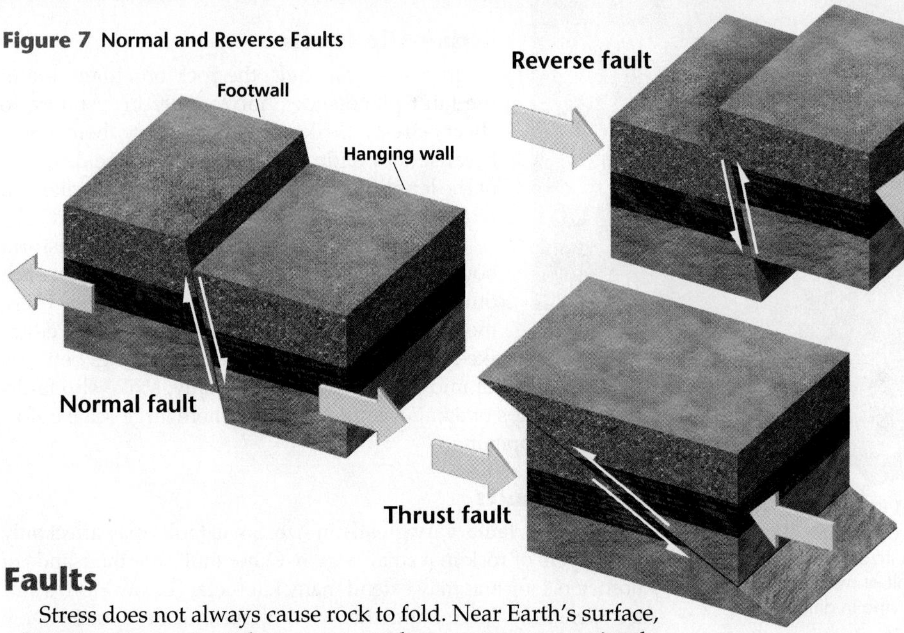

Faults

Stress does not always cause rock to fold. Near Earth's surface, where temperatures and pressure are low, stresses may simply cause rock to break. Breaks in rock are divided into two categories. A break along which there is no movement of the surrounding rock is called a *fracture*. A break along which the surrounding rock moves is called a **fault.** The surface or plane along which the motion occurs is called the *fault plane*. In a nonvertical fault, the *hanging wall* is the rock above the fault plane. The *footwall* is the rock below the fault plane.

fault a break in a body of rock along which one block slides relative to another; a form of brittle strain

Normal Faults

As shown in **Figure 7,** a *normal fault* is a fault in which the hanging wall moves downward relative to the footwall. Normal faults commonly form at divergent boundaries, where the crust is being pulled apart by tension. Normal faults may occur as a series of parallel fault lines, forming steep, steplike landforms. The Great Rift Valley of East Africa formed by large-scale normal faulting.

Reverse Faults

When compression causes the hanging wall to move upward relative to the footwall, also shown in **Figure 7,** a *reverse fault* forms. A *thrust fault* is a special type of reverse fault in which the fault plane is at a low angle or is nearly horizontal. Because of the low angle of the fault plane, the rock of the hanging wall is pushed up and over the rock of the footwall. Reverse faults and thrust faults are common in mountain ranges, such as the Rockies and the Alps, that formed mainly due to compression.

Reading Check **How does a thrust fault differ from a reverse fault?**

SCILINKS.
www.scilinks.org
Topic: Folding and Faulting
Code: **HQX0589**

Answer to Reading Check
A thrust fault is a type of reverse fault in which the fault plane is at a low angle relative to the surface.

Close

Reteaching BASIC

Deformation Flashcards Make a set of flashcards, and draw on each card a picture of either a type of stress (compression, tension, or shear stress) or a type of strain (different types of folds and faults). Show the cards rapidly to students, and have them identify whether the card illustrates stress or strain, what type of fold or fault is shown, and how that structure forms.
LS Visual

Quiz GENERAL

1. What happens to lithosphere when large amounts of mud, sand and gravel are deposited onto it? (It sinks deeper in the asthenosphere.)
2. What type of fault commonly forms at transform boundaries? (strike-slip)
3. What type of stress commonly results in folds? (compression)

Key Resources

Technology
- Transparencies
  58 Faults

Group Activity ADVANCED

It's Your Fault Separate the class into four or five groups of three or four students, and have each group research the major faults on one of the continents. Each student within the group should examine a region within the group's continent; locate any faults within the area; identify each fault as normal, reverse (or thrust), or strike-slip; and describe how the fault has contributed to the topography of the region. Have each group present their findings as a group to the rest of the class.
LS Verbal Co-op Learning

Close, *continued*

Answers to Section Review

1. Isostatic adjustments cause the lithosphere to rise or sink until the weight of the lithosphere equals the buoyant force from the asthenosphere and the two layers reach isostasy.
2. *Compression* is stress that squeezes and shortens a body. *Tension* is stress that stretches and thins a body. *Shear stress* is stress that acts by pushing different parts of a body in opposite directions.
3. *Stress* is the force applied per unit area on a rock or other material, whereas *strain* is the change in the shape or volume of rock that is affected by stress.
4. Folds are a type of ductile strain.
5. All folds have hinges and limbs. Folds that are symmetrical have axial planes.
6. A *normal fault* occurs when the hanging wall moves downward relative to the footwall. A *reverse fault* occurs when the hanging wall moves upward relative to the footwall. A *thrust fault* is a reverse fault that has a very low angle. A *strike-slip fault* occurs when the fault blocks slide horizontally past each other.
7. Folding is an example of ductile strain. Faulting is an example of brittle strain.
8. Rock temperatures and pressures are lower near Earth's surface, so the rock tends to be more brittle.
9. When glaciers melt, the continental crust becomes lighter and the lithosphere rises upward. Where material is deposited from a river into the ocean, the weight of the crust increases, and the lithosphere sinks.
10. The fold is a monocline, which formed when part of the rock had undergone vertical stress but the rest of the rock had not.
11. Because the rock is being heated, it is probably becoming more ductile. As a result, the rock is more likely to fold than to fracture.
12. *Stress*, such as *compression*, *tension*, and *shear stress*, may result in *strain*, such as *folds* and *faults*.

Figure 8 The San Andreas fault system stretches more than 1,200 km across California and is the result of two tectonic plates moving in different directions.

Strike-Slip Faults

In a *strike-slip fault*, the rock on either side of the fault plane slides horizontally in response to shear stress. Strike-slip faults got their name because they slide, or *slip*, parallel to the direction of the length, or *strike*, of the fault. Some strike-slip fault planes are vertical, but many are sloped.

Strike-slip faults commonly occur at transform boundaries, where tectonic plates grind past each other as they move in opposite directions. These motions cause shear stress on the rocks at the edges of the plates. Strike-slip faults also occur at fracture zones between offset segments of mid-ocean ridges. Commonly, strike-slip faults occur as groups of smaller faults in areas where large-scale deformation is happening.

Sizes of Faults

Like folds, faults vary greatly in size. Small faults may affect only a few layers of rock in a small region. Other faults are thousands of kilometers long and may extend many kilometers below Earth's surface. Generally, large faults that cover thousands of kilometers are composed of systems of many smaller, related faults, rather than a single fault. The San Andreas fault in California, shown in **Figure 8**, is an example of a large fault system.

Section 1 Review

Key Ideas

1. **Summarize** how isostatic adjustments affect isostasy.
2. **Identify and describe** three types of stress.
3. **Compare** stress and strain.
4. **Describe** one type of strain that results when rock responds to stress by permanently deforming without breaking.
5. **Identify** features that all types of folds share and features that only some types of folds have.
6. **Describe** four types of faults.
7. **Compare** folding and faulting as responses to stress.

Critical Thinking

8. **Applying Ideas** Why is faulting most likely to occur near Earth's surface and not deep within Earth?
9. **Making Comparisons** How would the isostatic adjustment that results from the melting of glaciers differ from the isostatic adjustment that may occur when a large river empties into the ocean?
10. **Analyzing Relationships** You are examining a rock outcrop that shows a fold in which both limbs are horizontal but occur at different elevations. What type of fold does this outcrop show, and what can you say about the type of stress that the rock underwent?
11. **Predicting Consequences** You are watching a lab experiment in which a rock sample is being gently heated and slowly bent. Would you expect the rock to fold or to fracture? Explain your reasoning.

Concept Mapping

12. Use the following terms to create a concept map: *stress, compression, strain, tension, shear stress, folds,* and *faults.*

Differentiated Instruction

Alternative Assessment

Modeling Isostasy Assign a particular isostatic adjustment to students, and have them create a series of models to demonstrate the changes that occur during the adjustment. The models can be physical models or computer models. The models should show at least four of the steps that take place during the isostatic adjustment. **LS Kinesthetic/Logical**

SECTION 2

How Mountains Form

Key Ideas	Key Terms	Why It Matters
❯ Identify the types of plate collisions that form mountains. ❯ Identify four types of mountains. ❯ Compare how folded and fault-block mountains form.	**mountain range** **folded mountain** **fault-block mountain** **dome mountain**	Many mountain ranges and volcanoes are growing taller. Scientists can measure the rate at which Earth's surface is moving and deforming.

Many mountains form due to extreme deformation. Mount Everest, whose elevation is more than 8 km above sea level, is Earth's highest mountain. Forces inside Earth cause Mount Everest to grow taller every year. Some mountains form by volcanic activity. Mount St. Helens is a volcano that captured the world's attention in 1980 when its explosive eruption devastated the surrounding area.

Mountain Ranges and Systems

A group of adjacent mountains that are related to each other in shape and structure is called a **mountain range.** Mount Everest is part of the Great Himalaya Range, and Mount St. Helens is part of the Cascade Range. A group of adjacent mountain ranges is called a *mountain system*. In the eastern United States, for example, the Great Smoky, Blue Ridge, Cumberland, Green, and White mountain ranges make up the Appalachian mountain system.

mountain range a series of mountains that are closely related in orientation, age, and mode of formation

The largest mountain systems are part of two larger systems called *mountain belts*. Earth's two youngest major mountain belts, the circum-Pacific belt and the Eurasian-Melanesian belt, are shown in **Figure 1.**

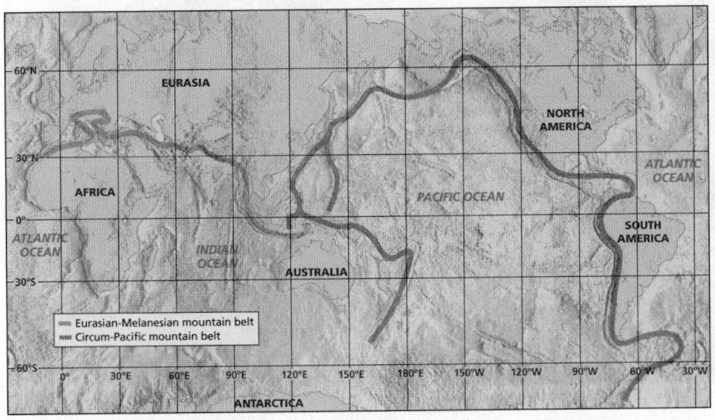

Figure 1 Most tall, young mountain ranges lie along either the Eurasian-Melanesian mountain belt or the circum-Pacific mountain belt.

Section 2

Focus

Overview

This section describes the types of plate collisions that form mountains, and compares the ways that four different types of mountains form.

Bellringer

Have students list as many mountain ranges as they can and name the continents on which the ranges are located. (Answers may vary.) **LS Verbal**

Motivate

Discussion GENERAL

Mountain Features Show students pictures of mountains or ask them to describe any mountains they may have visited. Discuss what features impressed students most. (Answers may vary. Students may note the height, steepness of the sides, their massiveness, how smooth and weathered the range was, or what types of vegetation grew there.) Point out that the features of each mountain range depend on a number of factors, including the material from which the mountains formed and how old the range is. **LS Verbal/Intrapersonal**

Key Resources

Chapter Resource File
- Directed Reading BASIC

Technology
- Transparencies
  Bellringer

Teach

READING TOOLBOX

Analyzing Comparisons Answers may vary. Students should correctly compare characteristics of various mountain ranges and mountain belts.

Using the Figure BASIC

Lithospheric Collisions and Mountain Types Have students examine the figures of three different ways that mountain ranges form. Point out that although two plates collide in each case, different types of mountains form because the composition of the crust on each plate is different. Ask students to explain how the collision that formed the Himalayas differs from the collisions that formed the Andes Mountains and the Mariana Islands. (In the Himalayas, after the brief subduction of oceanic crust, there is little subduction at all, but rather the pushing upward of two continental crusts.) Ask students which surface features result from the subduction of oceanic crust. (volcanoes and trenches)
LS Verbal/Logical

Key Resources

Technology

- Transparencies
  59 How Mountains Form

Academic Vocabulary
collision (kuh LIZH uhn) the event in which two bodies merge or combine; the act of colliding

Plate Tectonics and Mountains

Both the circum-Pacific and the Eurasian-Melanesian mountain belts are located along convergent plate boundaries. The location of these two mountain belts provides evidence that most mountains form as a result of collisions between tectonic plates. Some mountains, such as the Appalachians, do not lie along active convergent plate boundaries. However, evidence indicates that the places at which these ranges formed were previously active plate boundaries.

READING TOOLBOX

Analyzing Comparisons
As you read about different mountain ranges and belts, look for comparisons among them. Make a table of their similarities and differences.

Collisions Between Continental and Oceanic Crust

Some mountains form when oceanic lithosphere and continental lithosphere collide at convergent plate boundaries. When the moving plates collide, the oceanic lithosphere subducts beneath the continental lithosphere, as shown in **Figure 2.** This type of collision produces such large-scale deformation of rock that high mountains are uplifted. In addition, the subduction of the oceanic lithosphere causes partial melting of the overlying mantle and crust. This melting produces magma that may eventually erupt to form volcanic mountains on Earth's surface. The mountains of the Cascade Range in the northwest region of the United States formed in this way. The Andes mountains on the western coast of South America are another example of mountains that formed by this type of collision.

Some mountains at the boundary between continental lithosphere and oceanic lithosphere may form by a different process. As the oceanic lithosphere subducts, pieces of crust called *terranes* are scraped off. These terranes then become part of the continent and may form mountains.

Figure 2 The Andes, shown below, are being uplifted as the Pacific plate subducts beneath the South American plate.

Skill Builder GENERAL

Writing Mountains have inspired many writers. For example, Hiram Bingham's *Lost City of the Incas* told of the rediscovery after 400 years of Machu Picchu in the Andes Mountains. Fiction writers Thornton Wilder and H. G. Wells wrote stories set in the Andes. Have students read other mountain-inspired writings and write a book report or make an oral report. Encourage students to pay close attention to the author's knowledge of mountains and the role the mountainous setting had on plot, outcome, or character development. **LS Verbal**

Differentiated Instruction

Basic Learners/Struggling Readers

Mountain-Range Postcards Have students use index cards to make postcards showing mountain ranges. Students should include a description of the mountain range, its location, and the processes by which it formed. On the postcard, students can draw a picture of the mountain range, or they can include pictures from discarded magazines or from the Internet. Make a classroom display of students' postcards.

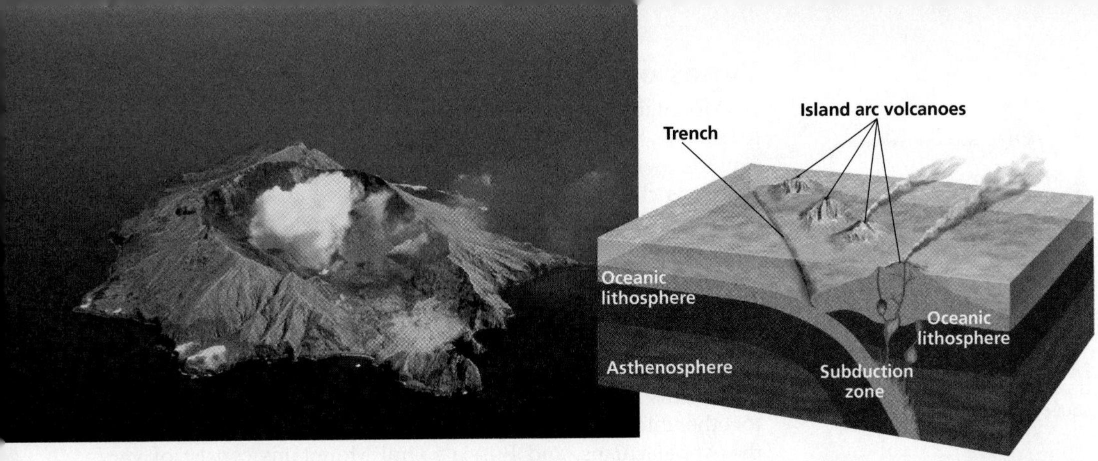

Figure 3 The Mariana Islands in the North Pacific Ocean are volcanic mountains that formed by the collision of two oceanic plates.

Collisions Between Oceanic Crust and Oceanic Crust

Volcanic mountains commonly form where two plates whose edges consist of oceanic lithosphere collide. In this collision, the denser oceanic plate subducts beneath the other oceanic plate, as shown in **Figure 3.** As the denser oceanic plate subducts, fluids from the subducting lithosphere cause partial melting of the overlying mantle and crust. The resulting magma rises and breaks through the oceanic lithosphere. These eruptions of magma form an arc of volcanic mountains on the ocean floor. The Mariana Islands are the peaks of volcanic mountains that rose above sea level.

Collisions Between Continents

Mountains can also form when two continents collide, as **Figure 4** shows. The Himalaya Mountains formed from such a collision. About 165 million years ago, India broke apart from Africa and Antarctica and became a separate continent. The Indian plate then began moving north toward Eurasia. The oceanic lithosphere of the Indian plate subducted beneath the Eurasian plate. This subduction continued until the continental lithosphere of India collided with the continental lithosphere of Eurasia. Because the two continents have equally dense lithosphere, subduction stopped but the collision continued. The intense deformation that resulted from the collision uplifted the Himalayas. Because the plates are still colliding, the Himalayas are still growing taller.

Reading Check **Why are the Himalayas growing taller today?**

Figure 4 The Himalayas formed when India collided with Eurasia.

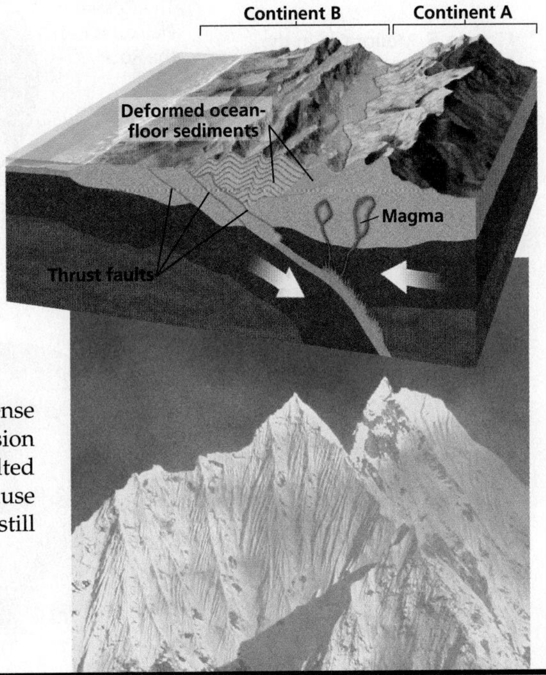

Why It Matters

High Volcanoes While the Andes and Himalayan mountain ranges contain the highest mountains in the world, the two ranges are dramatically different in one respect: there are numerous volcanoes, both active and extinct, in the Andes, whereas there are very few in the Himalayas. This difference has resulted from the nature of the tectonic forces that formed the two ranges. The volcanoes of the Andes result from the subduction of dense oceanic crust. The Himalayan range formed when the continental crust of the Indian subcontinent collided with the continental crust of Asia. Once the two continental plates collided, their similar densities prevented either plate from subducting. Instead, the plates pushed each other upward. This process did not generate the melted rock that occurs in subduction, so no significant volcanic activity occurred.

Answer to Reading Check

The Himalayas are growing taller because the two plates are still colliding and causing further compression of the rock, which further uplifts the mountains.

MISCONCEPTION ALERT

Diverging Plates Students may think that all mountain ranges are produced by collisions between tectonic plates. Remind students that large amounts of lava erupt onto Earth's surface on the ocean floor where two plates diverge. From such lava, volcanic mountain ranges form. Point out that one of the most extensive mountain ranges on Earth, the Mid-Atlantic Ridge, lies mostly underwater, with only a few peaks extending above the surface as islands. Also note that mountain ranges can also form on dry land from the divergence of plates, as is the case in the East African Rift. A range of volcanoes, extending from Malawi in southern Africa to Ethiopia, has formed as a result of lava produced by the separation of the Somali and African plates. The East African Rift Valley is an example of a graben surrounded by fault-block mountains.

Teach, *continued*

Group Activity — GENERAL

Plates and Mountain Formation Assign a small group of students to research the specific processes that formed each of the following mountain ranges: the Alps, the Himalayas, the Appalachians, and the Urals. Have students find out what plates interacted to form that particular range; when the range began forming; if and when formation ended; and, if applicable, what major processes have altered the mountains since the end of their growth. Students may present the results of their findings in a short written report, an oral presentation, or as a poster project. **LS Verbal**

Homework — GENERAL

Valleys, Plateaus, and Grabens The formation of mountains causes other geologic features to form in the same area. Have students research the following features, noting what type of features they are, where they are located, when they formed, how they formed, and any mountains in the region that formed from similar tectonic forces: Massif Central, Great Rift Valley, Altiplano, and Rhine Valley. Students may present findings in a brief written report, an oral presentation, or as a poster project. **LS Logical**

Key Resources

Technology

- Transparencies
  60 Types of Mountains in the United States

SCILINKS.
www.scilinks.org
Topic: Types of Mountains
Code: **HQX1568**

folded mountain a mountain that forms when rock layers are squeezed together and uplifted

Types of Mountains

Mountains are more than just elevated parts of Earth's crust. Mountains are complicated structures whose rock formations provide evidence of the stresses that created the mountains. Scientists classify mountains according to the way in which the crust was deformed and shaped by mountain-building stresses. Examples of several types of mountains are shown in **Figure 5.**

Folded Mountains and Plateaus

Many of the highest mountain ranges in the world consist of folded mountains that form when continents collide. **Folded mountains** form when tectonic movements squeeze rock layers together into accordion-like folds. Parts of the Alps, the Himalayas, the Appalachians, and Russia's Ural Mountains consist of very large and complex folds.

The same stresses that form folded mountains also uplift plateaus. *Plateaus* are large, flat areas of rock high above sea level. Most plateaus form when thick, horizontal layers of rock are slowly uplifted so that the layers remain flat instead of faulting and folding. Most plateaus are located near mountain ranges. For example, the Tibetan Plateau is next to the Himalaya Mountains, and the Colorado Plateau is next to the Rockies. Plateaus can also form when layers of molten rock harden and pile up on Earth's surface or when large areas of rock are eroded.

Figure 5 Mountains in the United States

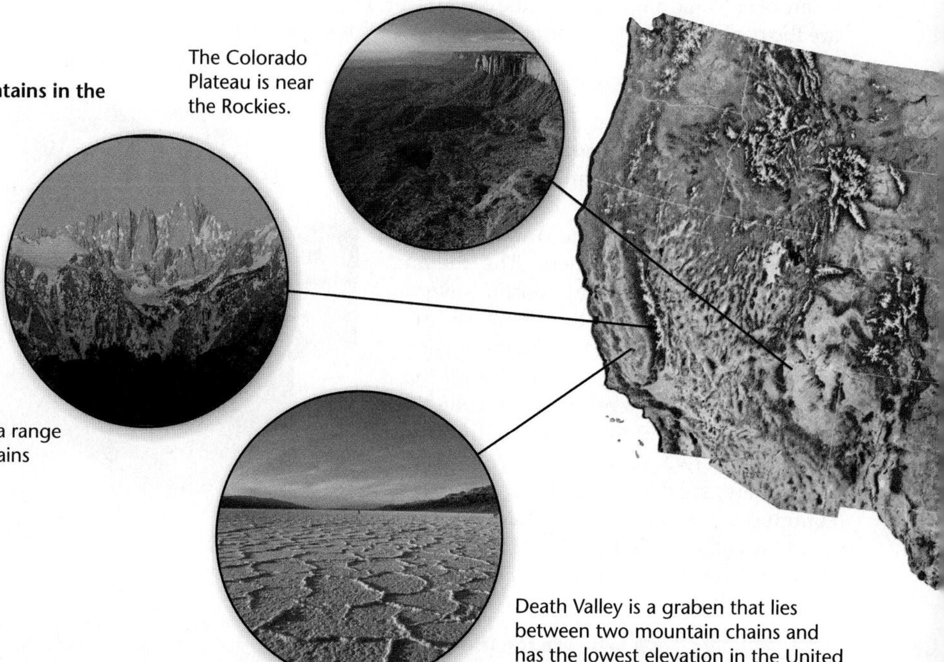

The Colorado Plateau is near the Rockies.

The Sierra Nevada range in California contains many fault-block mountains.

Death Valley is a graben that lies between two mountain chains and has the lowest elevation in the United States.

Internet Activity — ADVANCED

"Dead" Grabens The structural geology of Death Valley in California and of the Dead Sea in Israel is strikingly similar—both exist at low elevation and have an evaporating body of water. However, these two regions also display geologic differences. Have students research Death Valley and the Dead Sea and report on the similarities and differences between them. A worksheet designed to direct student research on this topic can be found in the **Chapter Resource File** booklet or by visiting **www.thinkcentral.com** and entering the keyword **HQXDEFX. LS Verbal**

Reading Skill Builder — BASIC

Discussion Geologic evidence indicates that the Appalachian Mountains formed between 390 and 210 million years ago, and that they are folded mountains, which tend to be very high. Ask students to explain why the Appalachians are not a higher range, like the Himalayas or Urals. (The Appalachians are relatively old mountains, and have had time for weathering and erosion to reduce their relief. Tell students that weathering is also indicated by sedimentary rock deposits east and west of the Appalachians.) **LS Logical**

Fault-Block Mountains and Grabens

Where parts of Earth's crust have been stretched and broken into large blocks, faulting may cause the blocks to tilt and drop relative to other blocks. The relatively higher blocks form **fault-block mountains.** The Sierra Nevada range of California consists of many fault-block mountains.

The same type of faulting that forms fault-block mountains also forms long, narrow valleys called *grabens*. Grabens develop when steep faults break the crust into blocks and one block slips downward relative to the surrounding blocks. Grabens and fault-block mountain ranges commonly occur together. For example, the Basin and Range Province of the western United States consists of grabens separated by fault-block mountain ranges.

fault-block mountain a mountain that forms where faulting breaks Earth's crust into large blocks, which causes some blocks to drop down relative to other blocks

dome mountain a circular or elliptical, almost symmetrical elevation or structure in which the stratified rock slopes downward gently from the central point of folding

Dome Mountains

A less common type of mountain forms when magma rises through the crust and pushes up the rock layers above the magma. The result is a **dome mountain,** a circular structure made of rock layers that slope gently away from a central point. Dome mountains may also form when tectonic forces gently uplift rock layers. The Black Hills of South Dakota and the Adirondack Mountains of New York are examples of dome mountains.

Reading Check **Name three types of mountains found in the United States.**

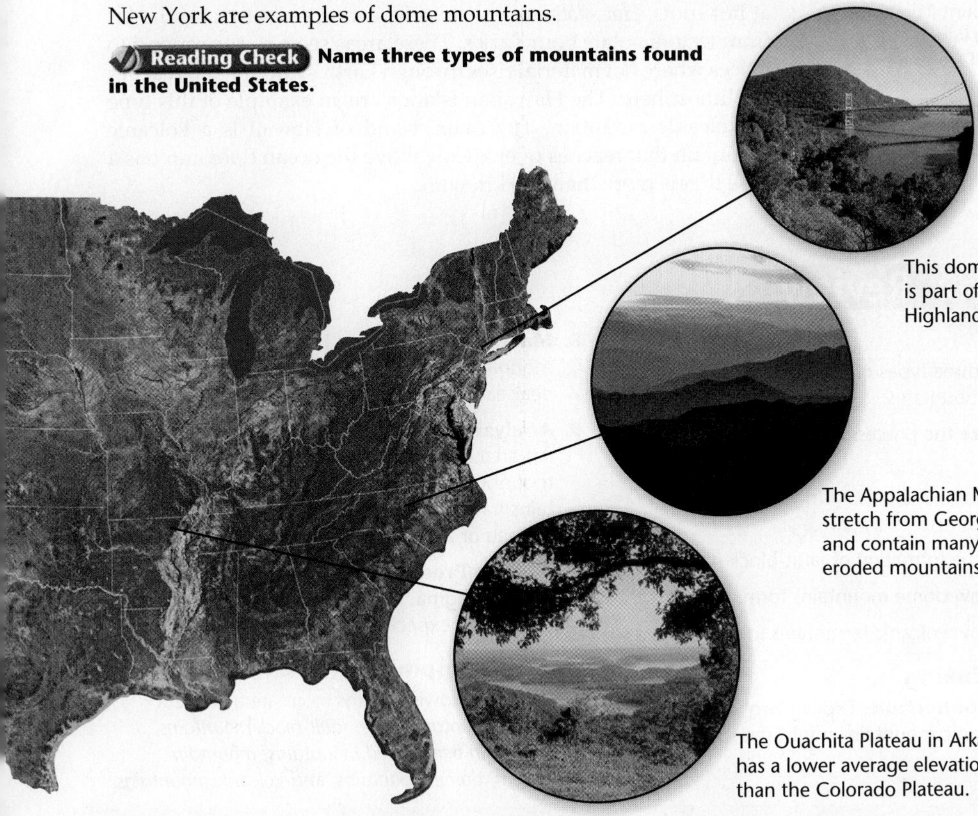

This dome mountain is part of the Hudson Highlands in New York.

The Appalachian Mountains stretch from Georgia to Canada and contain many older, more eroded mountains.

The Ouachita Plateau in Arkansas has a lower average elevation than the Colorado Plateau.

Answer to Reading Check

Answers may include three of the following: folded mountains, fault-block mountains, dome mountains, and volcanic mountains.

Close

Reteaching BASIC

Mountain Formation Processes On the board, list the four main types of mountains. In another column, write descriptions of how each type of mountain forms. Have students indicate which items in the first column are described by the items in the second column. **LS Logical**

Quiz GENERAL

Determine whether each of the following statements is true or false.

1. The Eurasian-Melanesian belt is one of Earth's two major mountain belts. (true)
2. Volcanic mountains form when continental crust collides with continental crust. (false)
3. Terranes are the remains of fault-block mountain formation. (false)

Differentiated Instruction

Special Education Students

Modeling Mountain Formation To show how converging plates form mountains, perform this small-group activity. Give each group two paper plates, two 8 1/2 × 11-inch pieces of paper, and tape. Have each group perform the following steps: "Tape the two pieces of paper together to form one 11 × 17-inch paper. Place the two paper plates side-by-side on the desk, and place the taped paper on top of the two paper plates. Hold the paper to the edges of the paper plates with your thumbs, and slide one plate over the top of the other." The taped paper should buckle upward, simulating mountain formation.
LS Verbal

Close, *continued*

Answers to Section Review

1. When an oceanic plate collides with a continental plate, the denser oceanic plate subducts. When an oceanic plate collides with another oceanic plate, the denser plate subducts. In both of these cases, magma rising from the subduction zone forms volcanic mountains. When a continental plate collides with another continental plates, mountains are pushed up, but no volcanoes form.
2. When a continental plate collides with other plate, the continental crust folds and forms mountains.
3. Plateaus have been uplifted by the same stresses that form folded mountains. However, plateaus are flat layers of slowly uplifted rock that are not folded.
4. Faulting in Earth's crust causes large blocks of the crust that have been broken to tilt and drop. The higher blocks make up fault-block mountains.
5. Magma beneath the crust pushes up the rock layers that lie over the magma.
6. Volcanic mountains form and grow as magma erupts onto Earth's surface.
7. Volcanic mountains could become smaller during explosive eruptions that destroy part of a volcano or by erosion and weathering.
8. Grabens are regions where blocks of Earth's crust have dropped between faults. Crustal blocks on either side of grabens form fault-block mountains. The two features are part of the same process.

Figure 6 Mount St. Helens (front) and Mount Rainier (back) in the Cascade Range of the western United States are volcanic mountains that formed along a convergent boundary.

Volcanic Mountains

Mountains that form when magma erupts onto Earth's surface are called *volcanic mountains*. Volcanic mountains commonly form along convergent plate boundaries. The Cascade Range of Washington, Oregon, and northern California is composed of this type of volcanic mountain, two of which are shown in **Figure 6.**

Some of the largest volcanic mountains are part of the mid-ocean ridges along divergent plate boundaries. Magma rising to Earth's surface at divergent boundaries makes mid-ocean ridges volcanically active areas. The peaks of these volcanic mountains sometimes rise above sea level to form volcanic islands, such as the Azores in the North Atlantic Ocean.

Other large volcanic mountains form at hot spots. *Hot spots* are volcanically active areas that can lie far from tectonic plate boundaries. These areas seem to correspond to places where hot material rises through Earth's interior and reaches the lithosphere. The Hawaiian Islands are an example of this type of volcanic mountain. The main island of Hawaii is a volcanic mountain that reaches over 10 km above the ocean floor and has a base that is more than 160 km wide.

Section 2 Review

Key Ideas

1. **Describe** three types of tectonic plate collisions that form mountains.
2. **Summarize** the process by which folded mountains form.
3. **Compare** how plateaus form with how folded mountains form.
4. **Describe** the formation of fault-block mountains.
5. **Explain** how dome mountains form.
6. **Explain** how volcanic mountains form.

Critical Thinking

7. **Making Connections** Explain two ways in which volcanic mountains might get smaller.
8. **Making Connections** Explain why fault-block mountains and grabens are commonly found near each other.
9. **Analyzing Ideas** You are standing on a large, flat area of land and are examining the nearby mountains. You notice that many of the mountains have large folds. Are you standing on a plateau or a graben? Explain your answer.
10. **Making Predictions** Igneous rocks form from cooled magma. Near what types of mountains would you expect to find new igneous rocks?

Concept Mapping

11. Use the following terms to create a concept map: *mountain range, fault-block mountains, mountain belt, folded mountains, mountain system, dome mountains,* and *volcanic mountains.*

9. Plateaus often form by the same processes that form folded mountains. Grabens form by the same processes that form fault-block mountains. Because the nearby mountains have large folds, the flat area is likely a plateau.
10. volcanic mountains
11. A *mountain range,* which can include *folded mountains, fault-block mountains, dome mountains,* and *volcanic mountains,* may be part of a *mountain system,* which is part of a *mountain belt.*

Differentiated Instruction

Alternative Assessment

Modeling Plate Interactions Have students create models to show how interactions between different tectonic plates cause different types of mountains to form. The models can be physical or computer models. The models should show at least four steps during the plate collision. **LS Kinesthetic/Logical**

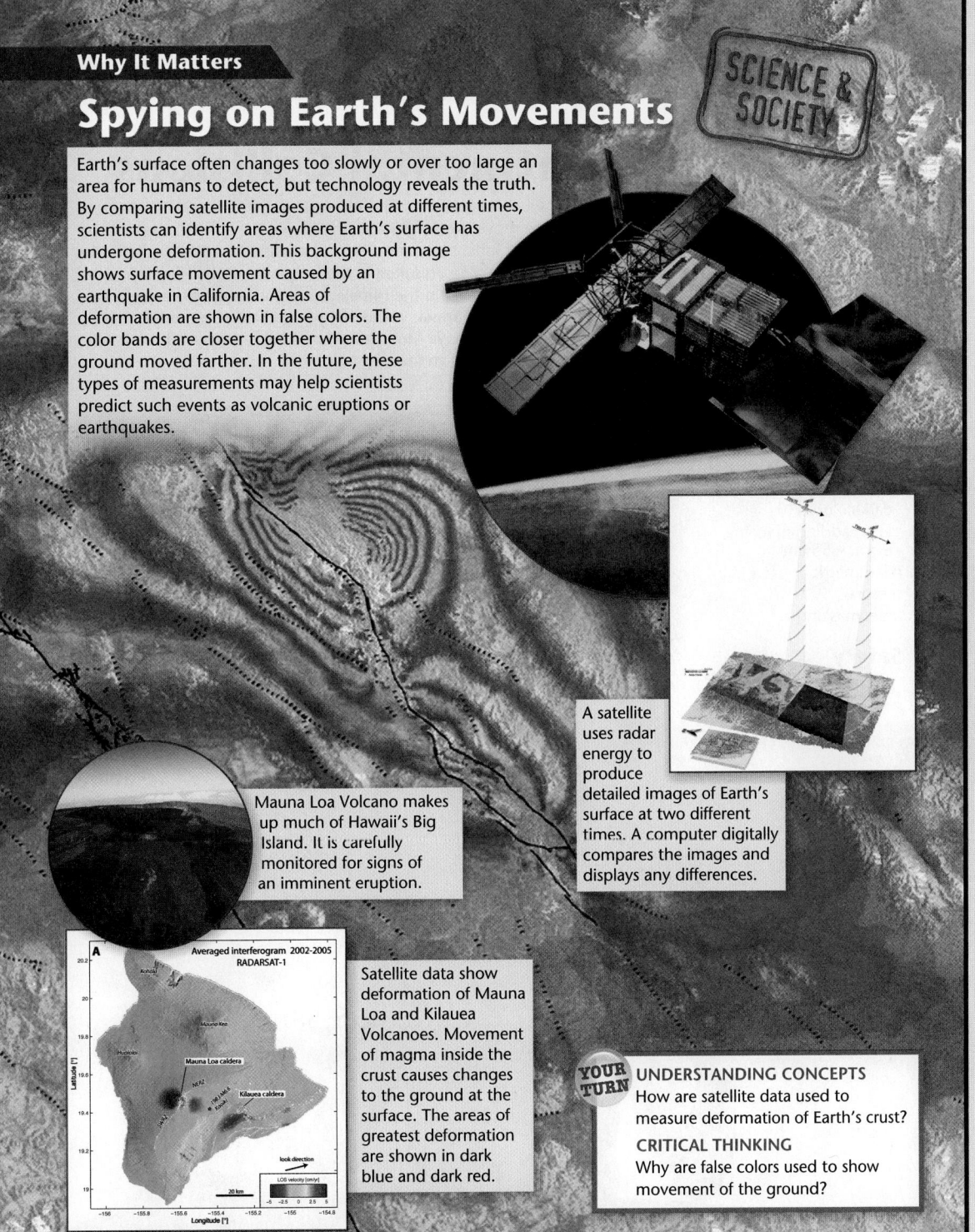

Why It Matters

Spying on Earth's Movements

SCIENCE & SOCIETY

Earth's surface often changes too slowly or over too large an area for humans to detect, but technology reveals the truth. By comparing satellite images produced at different times, scientists can identify areas where Earth's surface has undergone deformation. This background image shows surface movement caused by an earthquake in California. Areas of deformation are shown in false colors. The color bands are closer together where the ground moved farther. In the future, these types of measurements may help scientists predict such events as volcanic eruptions or earthquakes.

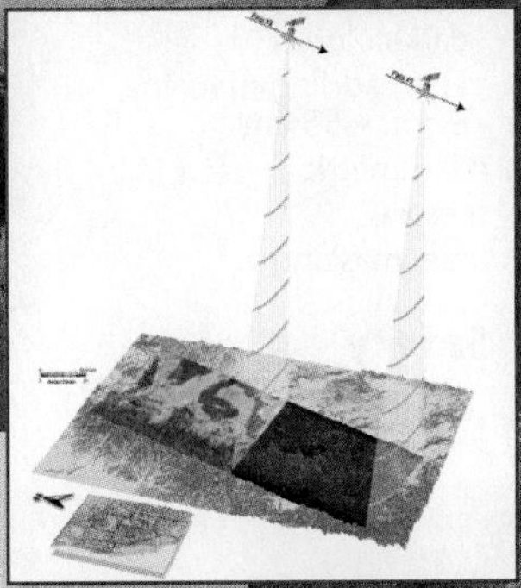

A satellite uses radar energy to produce detailed images of Earth's surface at two different times. A computer digitally compares the images and displays any differences.

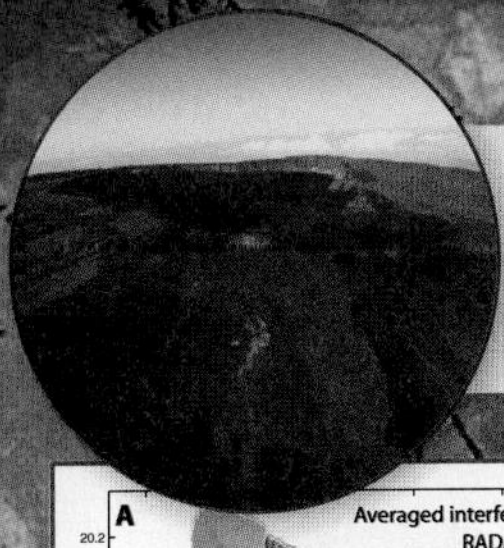

Mauna Loa Volcano makes up much of Hawaii's Big Island. It is carefully monitored for signs of an imminent eruption.

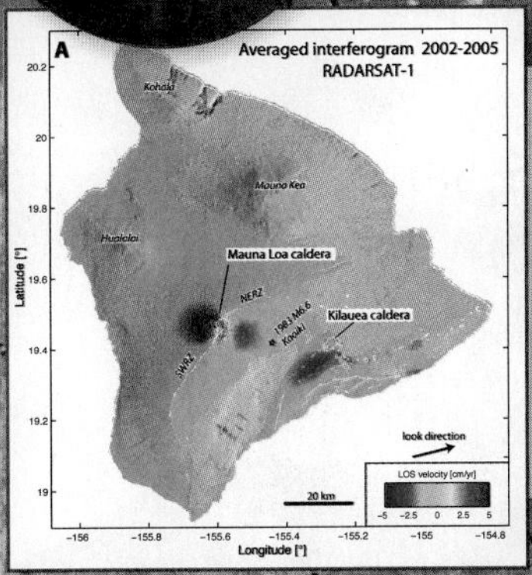

Satellite data show deformation of Mauna Loa and Kilauea Volcanoes. Movement of magma inside the crust causes changes to the ground at the surface. The areas of greatest deformation are shown in dark blue and dark red.

YOUR TURN

UNDERSTANDING CONCEPTS
How are satellite data used to measure deformation of Earth's crust?

CRITICAL THINKING
Why are false colors used to show movement of the ground?

Why It Matters

Spying on Earth's Movements

Active deformation of Earth's surface is often a slow process that occurs over a large area. It is difficult for humans to directly observe such processes. Satellites are one tool that people can use to identify "big picture" changes in Earth's crust over time. Computers can compare satellite images collected at different times to not only identify vertical movements of the ground, but also horizontal movements, which can be recognized by comparing images collected at an angle. Satellite imaging is already used to monitor volcanic activity. One day, it might be used to help predict earthquakes by measuring deformation of Earth's surface before a fault actually ruptures.

Answers to Your Turn

Understanding Concepts Comparing satellite images collected at different times of the same area allows scientists to measure deformation.

Critical Thinking Because changes resulting from deformation are usually small, false colors make the changes much easier to see.

Time Required

two 45-minute class periods

Lab Ratings

EASY ———————————➤ HARD

Teacher Preparation 🧪🧪
Student Setup 🧪🧪🧪
Concept Level 🧪🧪
Cleanup 🧪🧪

Skills Acquired

- Experimenting
- Constructing Models
- Predicting
- Interpreting
- Identifying and Recognizing Patterns

Scientific Methods

In this lab, students will
- Make Observations
- Test the Hypothesis
- Analyze the Results
- Draw Conclusions

Materials

The materials listed are enough for groups of two students. Tissue paper can be used in place of napkins. Napkins or tissue paper can be of any color.

Making Models Lab

Making Models Lab

🕐 **90 min**

What You'll Do

> **Model** collisions between continents.

> **Explain** how mountains form at convergent boundaries.

What You'll Need

blocks, wooden, 3 cm × 3 cm × 6 cm
bobby pins, long (5)
cardboard, thick, 15 cm × 30 cm
napkins, paper, light- and dark-colored
paper, adding-machine, 6 cm × 35 cm
ruler, metric
scissors
tape, masking

Safety

◆ ◆

Continental Collisions

When the subcontinent of India broke away from Africa and Antarctica and began to move northward toward Eurasia, the oceanic crust on the northern side of India began to subduct beneath the Eurasian plate. The deformation of the crust resulted in the formation of the Himalaya Mountains. Earthquakes in the Himalayan region suggest that India is still pushing against Eurasia. In this lab, you will create a model to help explain how the Himalaya Mountains formed as a result of the collision of the Indian and Eurasian tectonic plates.

Procedure

1 To assemble the continental-collision model, cut a 7-cm slit in the cardboard. The slit should be about 6 cm from (and parallel to) one of the short edges of the cardboard. Cut the slit wide enough such that the adding-machine paper will feed through the slit without being loose.

2 Securely tape one wood block along the slit between the slit and the near edge of the cardboard. Tape the other block across the paper strip about 6 cm from one end of the paper. The blocks should be parallel to one another, as shown in the illustration on the next page.

Step **8**

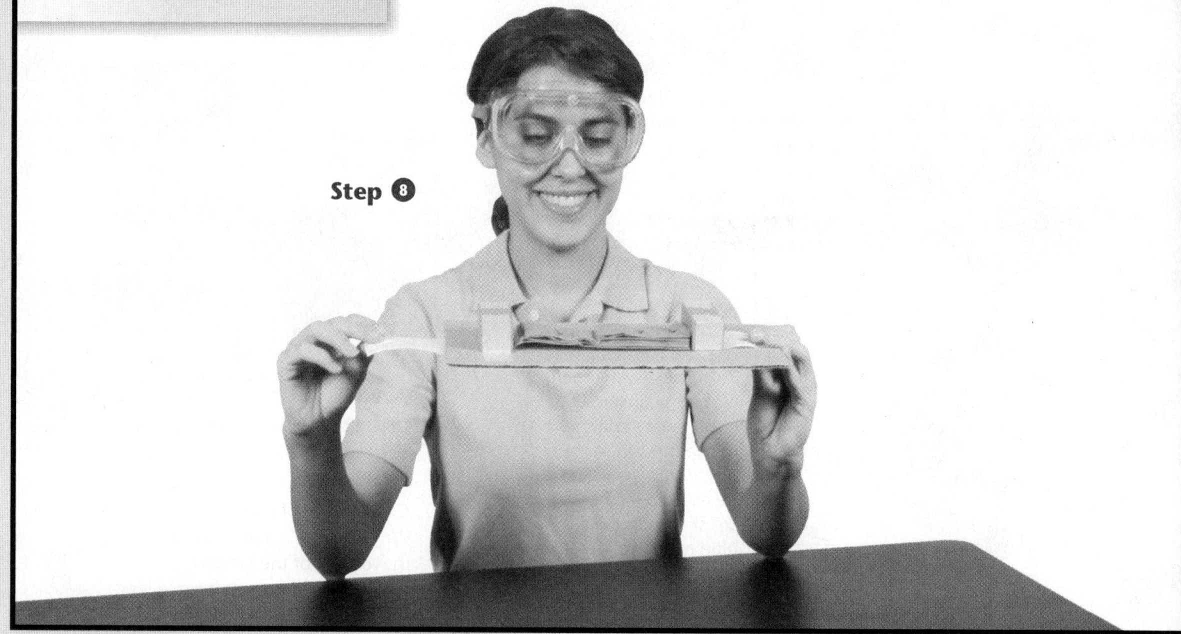

Tips and Tricks

Students should make sure that the strip of paper moves easily through the slit before proceeding to step 2. In step 6, students should be sure that the napkins are securely attached to the paper strip. In step 8, one student can hold the cardboard, while the other student pulls the paper strip.

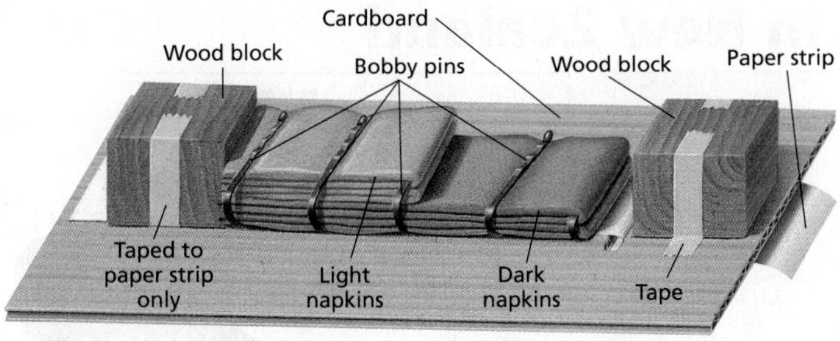

3. Cut two strips of the light-colored paper napkin that are about 6 cm wide and 16 cm long. Cut two strips of the dark-colored paper napkin that are about 6 cm wide and 32 cm long. Fold all four strips in half along their width.
4. Stack the napkin strips on top of each other such that all of the folds are along the same side. Place the two dark-colored napkins on the bottom.
5. Place the napkin strips lengthwise on the paper strip. The nonfolded ends of the napkin strips should be butted up against the wood block that is taped to the paper strip.
6. Using the bobby pins, attach the napkins to the paper strip, as shown in the illustration above.
7. Push the long end of the paper strip through the slit in the cardboard until the first fold of the napkin rests against the fixed wood block.
8. Hold the cardboard at about eye level, and pull down gently on the paper strip. You may need a partner's help. Observe what happens as the dark-colored napkins contact the fixed wood block and as you continue to pull down on the paper strip. Stop pulling when you feel resistance from the strip.

Analysis

1. **Evaluating Methods** Explain what is represented by the dark napkins, the light napkins, and the wood blocks.
2. **Analyzing Processes** What plate-tectonics process is represented by the motion of the paper strip in the model? Explain your answer.
3. **Applying Ideas** What type of mountain would result from the kind of collision shown by the model?
4. **Evaluating Models** Explain how the process modeled here differs from the process that formed the Himalaya Mountains.

Extension

Analyzing Data Obtain a world map of earthquake epicenters. Study the map. Describe the pattern of epicenters in the Himalayan region. Does the pattern suggest that the Himalaya Mountains are still rising?

Writing from Research Read about the breakup of Gondwanaland and the movement of India toward the Northern Hemisphere. Write about stages in India's movement. List the time frame in which each important event occurred.

Answers to Analysis

1. The dark napkins represent oceanic crust, the light napkins represent continental crust, and the wood blocks represent the mass of the rock in the two colliding plates.
2. The motion of the paper strip represents the subduction of the oceanic lithosphere into the asthenosphere.
3. Folded mountains would result from this type of collision.
4. In the model, the light napkins represent the material in one plate that is compressed. In the actual formation of the Himalayas, two continental plates collided, and rock from both continents deformed.

Answers to Extension

Analyzing Data Answers should indicate that the Himalayan Mountains are still growing.

Writing from Research Answers may vary. The essay should indicate that the Indian plate broke away from Africa about 165 million years ago and broke away from Madagascar about 88 million years ago. The Indian plate rotated as it traveled northward at a rate of about 15 cm/year. It collided with the Eurasian plate about 40 to 50 million years ago.

Shear Strain in New Zealand

Activity — GENERAL
Geophysics of New Zealand
Have students research New Zealand's geology, notably the volcanic activity that exists on the North Island and the absence of such activity on the South Island. Have students predict what New Zealand may look like in 1 million years, given that its two islands are on separate plates. **LS Verbal/Visual**

Answers to Map Skills Activity
1. 0.4 ppm/yr
2. The area of highest shear strain lies between 169° and 174° east longitude, and between 42° and 44° south latitude.
3. The area of maximum shear strain is approximately 400 km long.
4. The plate boundary is a convergent boundary that is bordered by a trough, which forms when an ocean plate subducts beneath another plate.
5. Compressional stress should be located near the convergent boundaries.
6. The Alpine Fault is most likely a strike-slip fault. The area surrounding the Alpine Fault has very high rates of shear strain, which indicates that the lithosphere is moving in opposite directions in that region.
7. Answers may vary. Sample answer: The compression and shear stress in this region would most likely result in the formation of folded mountains.

MAPS *in Action*

Shear Strain in New Zealand

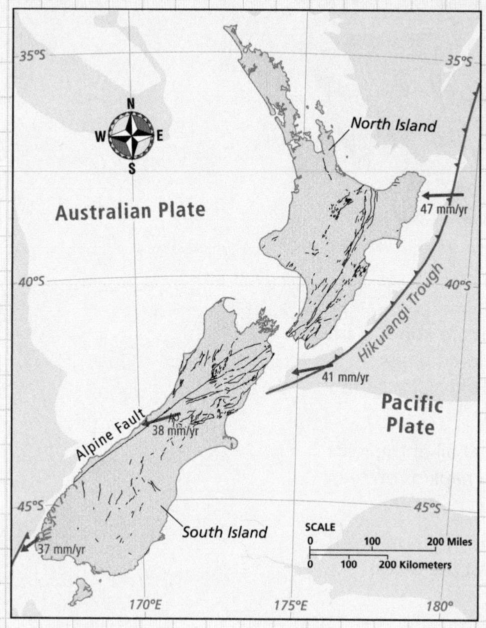

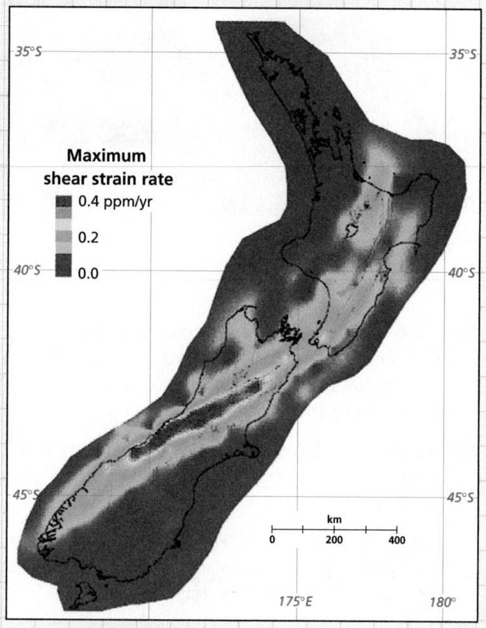

Map Skills Activity

The map above shows the plate boundary zone of New Zealand. In this region, the Australian plate is moving north, while the Pacific plate is moving west. These complex plate movements create areas of tension, compression, and shear stress, which result in strain. Strain is measured in parts per million (ppm) per year (yr). The map on the right shows strain in New Zealand. Use the two maps to answer the questions below.

1. **Using a Key** What is the highest amount of shear strain shown in the map on the right?
2. **Identifying Locations** Using latitude and longitude, describe the location of the area that has the highest amount of shear strain.
3. **Using a Key** What is the approximate length of the area of maximum shear strain?
4. **Understanding Relationships** What type of plate boundary is located along the east coast of the North Island? Explain your answer.
5. **Comparing Areas** In what areas might you expect to find compression? Explain your answer.
6. **Making Inferences** What type of fault is the Alpine Fault? Explain your answer.
7. **Drawing Conclusions** A mountain range known as the Southern Alps runs through the center of the South Island. What type of mountains do you think the Southern Alps are? Explain your answer.

Key Resources

Technology
- Transparencies
  61 Shear Strain in New Zealand

Chapter 11

Summary

THINK central
SUPER SUMMARY
Keyword: HQXDEFS

Key Ideas | **Key Terms**

Section 1

How Rock Deforms

- Isostasy occurs when there is a balance between the gravitational force of the lithosphere pressing downward and the buoyant force of the asthenosphere pressing upward.
- The three main types of stress are compression, which squeezes rock together; tension, which pulls rock apart; and shear stress, which bends and twists rock.
- Folds form when rock is bent without breaking. Faults form when a block of rock on one side of a fracture moves relative to the block on the other side.

Key Terms

deformation, p. 293
isostasy, p. 293
stress, p. 295
strain, p. 296
fold, p. 297
fault, p. 299

Section 2

How Mountains Form

- Collisions that form mountains can occur between an oceanic plate and a continental plate, between an oceanic plate and another oceanic plate, or between two continental plates.
- Four types of mountains are folded mountains, fault-block mountains, dome mountains, and volcanic mountains.
- Folded mountains form as tectonic movements squeeze Earth's crust into folds. Faulted mountains form as large blocks of crust tilt and move relative to other blocks of crust.

Key Terms

mountain range, p. 301
folded mountain, p. 304
fault-block mountain, p. 305
dome mountain, p. 305

Chapter Summary

Using THINK central Resources

Super Summary

Have students connect the major concepts in this chapter through an interactive Super Summary. Visit www.thinkcentral.com and type in the keyword **HQXDEFS** to access the Super Summary for this chapter.

Differentiated Instruction

Alternative Assessment

Poster Project Have students create a poster that shows the processes that rocks undergo that produce different types of mountains. Have students depict a given stress, show how the stress results from tectonic plate interaction, identify the resulting strain, and then show the final form that the mountain takes. Students should include labels to identify features and steps involved in each process.
LS Visual/Logical

Chapter Review

Assignment Guide	
Section	**Questions**
1	2–7, 10–16, 19, 20, 23, 25–27, 29, 31–36
2	1, 8, 9, 17, 18, 21, 22, 24, 28, 30

Reading Toolbox

1. Answers may vary. Have students work as a class to write all the meanings of *range* they can find on a poster. In everyday speech, meanings of *range* include "to roam about," "to vary between certain limits," and "oven." In biology, a species' range is the area to which it is native. In geology, a range is a series of adjacent mountains with similar age and processes of formation.

Using Key Terms

2–9. Answers may vary but should show that students understand the definitions of and differences between key terms.

Understanding Key Concepts

10. a
11. d
12. a
13. d
14. a
15. c
16. c
17. c
18. d

Short Answer

19. Folds and faults are two types of deformation in Earth's crust. When rock is ductile, it is able to bend with applied stress, so it folds. When rock is brittle, it breaks under stress, so it forms faults or fractures.

Chapter 11 Review

1. **Everyday Words Used in Science** The word *range* is used to describe mountains that are related by size and structure. What does the word *range* mean in everyday speech? What does it mean in a scientific context?

READING TOOLBOX

USING KEY TERMS

Use each of the following terms in a separate sentence.

2. *isostasy*
3. *compression*
4. *shear stress*

For each pair of terms, explain how the meanings of the terms differ.

5. *stress* and *strain*
6. *fold* and *fault*
7. *syncline* and *monocline*
8. *dome mountains* and *volcanic mountains*
9. *folded mountains* and *fault-block mountains*

UNDERSTANDING KEY IDEAS

10. When the weight of an area of Earth's crust increases, the lithosphere
 a. sinks.
 b. melts.
 c. rises.
 d. collides.
11. The force per unit area that changes the shape and volume of rock is
 a. footwall.
 b. isostasy.
 c. rising.
 d. stress.
12. Shear stress
 a. bends, twists, or breaks rock.
 b. causes isostasy.
 c. causes rock to melt.
 d. causes rock to expand.
13. When stress is applied under conditions of high pressure and high temperature, rock is more likely to
 a. fracture. **c.** fault.
 b. sink. **d.** fold.
14. Folds in which both limbs remain horizontal are called
 a. monoclines. **c.** synclines.
 b. fractures. **d.** anticlines.
15. When a fault is not vertical, the rock above the fault plane makes up the
 a. tension. **c.** hanging wall.
 b. footwall. **d.** compression.
16. A fault in which the rock on either side of the fault plane moves horizontally in nearly opposite directions is called a
 a. normal fault. **c.** strike-slip fault.
 b. reverse fault. **d.** thrust fault.
17. The largest mountain systems are part of still larger systems called
 a. continental margins.
 b. ranges.
 c. belts.
 d. synclines.
18. Large areas of flat-topped rock high above the surrounding landscape are
 a. grabens. **c.** hanging walls.
 b. footwalls. **d.** plateaus.

SHORT ANSWER

19. Name two types of deformation in Earth's crust, and explain how each type occurs.
20. Explain how to identify an anticline.
21. Identify the two major mountain belts on Earth.
22. Describe how the various types of mountains are categorized.
23. Identify the two forces that are kept in balance by isostatic adjustments.
24. Compare the features of dome mountains with those of fault-block mountains.

20. In an anticline, the outermost layers of the fold have the youngest rock. An anticline fold may be arch shaped.
21. The mountain belts are the circum-Pacific belt and the Eurasian-Melanesian belt.
22. Mountains are categorized as folded mountains, which commonly form when two continental plates collide; fault-block mountains, which commonly form when broken blocks of crust fall away from other blocks that become the mountains; dome mountains, which form when magma pushes upward on overlying rock, forming dome-like structures; and volcanic mountains, which form when magma erupts onto Earth's surface and accumulates to form a mountain.
23. gravitational force and buoyant force
24. Dome mountains are round or elliptical and have gentle slopes that descend symmetrically from the mountain's central peak. Fault-block mountains form from the broken blocks that lie between faults and have not dropped down or tilted. These blocks are relatively higher than the surrounding blocks.

CRITICAL THINKING

25. **Evaluating Ideas** If thick ice sheets covered large parts of Earth's continents again, how would you expect the lithosphere to respond to the added weight of the continental ice sheets? Explain your answer.
26. **Analyzing Relationships** When the Indian plate collided with the Eurasian plate and produced the Himalaya Mountains, which type of stress most likely occurred? Which type of stress is most likely occurring along the Mid-Atlantic Ridge? Which type of stress would you expect to find along the San Andreas fault? Explain your answers.
27. **Making Predictions** If the force that causes a rock to deform slightly begins to ease, what may happen to the rock? What might happen if the force causing the deformation becomes greater?
28. **Analyzing Processes** Why do you think that dome mountains do not always become volcanic mountains?

CONCEPT MAPPING

29. Use the following terms to create a concept map: *stress, strain, brittle, ductile, folds, faults, normal fault, reverse fault, thrust fault,* and *strike-slip fault.*

MATH SKILLS

Math Skills

30. **Making Calculations** Scientists calculate that parts of the Himalayas are rising at a rate of 6.1 mm per year. At this rate, in how many years will the Himalayas be 1 m taller than they are today?
31. **Analyzing Data** Rock stress is measured as 48 MPa at point A below Earth's surface. At point B nearby, stress is measured as 12 MPa. What percentage of the stress at point A is the stress at point B equal to?

WRITING SKILLS

32. **Creative Writing** Write a short story from the perspective of a rock that is being deformed. Describe the stresses that are affecting the rock and the final result of the stress.
33. **Writing from Research** Look for photos or illustrations of folding and faulting in a particular area. Then, research the geologic history of the area, and write a report based on your findings. Use any photos or drawings that you find to illustrate your report.

INTERPRETING GRAPHICS

The diagram below shows a fault. Use this diagram to answer the questions that follow.

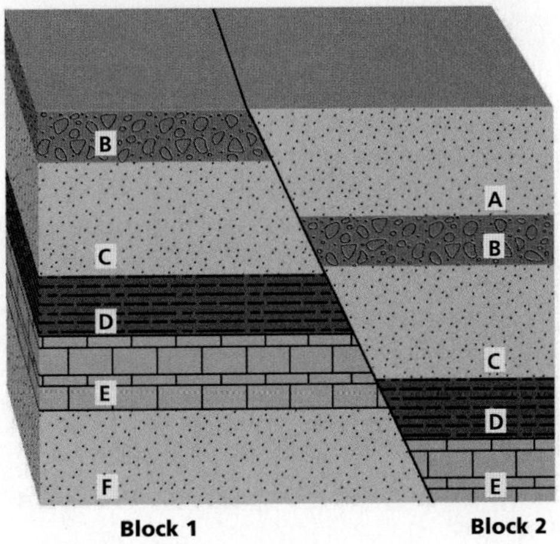

34. Is Block 2 a footwall or a hanging wall? Explain your answer.
35. What type of fault is illustrated? Explain your answer.
36. What type of stress generally causes this type of fault?

Chapter Review

Critical Thinking

25. The lithosphere under the continents would sink under the added weight of the continental ice sheets. The reduced amount of water in the oceans would reduce the weight over the lithosphere under the oceans, so that portion of the lithosphere would rise.
26. The collision between the Indian and Eurasian plates mainly involved compression. The plates that meet at the Mid-Atlantic Ridge are separating and are affected mainly by tension. The blocks on either side of the San Andreas fault are moving in opposite directions, which causes shear stress.
27. If the force is reduced, the rock may return to its original condition. If the force is increased, the rock may permanently deform by folding or by faulting or fracturing.
28. The properties of the rock overlying the magma are such that the rock does not melt, and the magma is unable to seep upward through it. Thus, the magma is only able to lift the rock upward, forming the dome mountain.

Concept Mapping

29. Answers may vary but should include all of the terms listed. Sample answers appear at the end of this unit on p. 367A.

Math Skills

30. number of years = increase in height ÷ amount of growth per year = [1 m ÷ (6.1 mm/year)] × 1000 mm/m = 164 years
31. percentage stress = (stress at B ÷ stress at A) × 100; percentage stress = (12 MPa/48 MPa) × 100 = 25%

Writing Skills

32. Answers may vary. Accept all reasonable answers.
33. Answers may vary. Accept all reasonable answers.

Interpreting Graphics

34. Block 2 is a hanging wall, because the rock lies above the fault plane.
35. A normal fault is shown, because the hanging wall has moved downward relative to the footwall.
36. tension

Estimated Time

To give students practice under more realistic testing conditions, allow them 30 minutes to answer all of the questions in this practice test.

Test Doctor

Question 4 Answer H describes a type of isostatic adjustment that occurs when a river that is carrying mud, sand, and gravel flows into the ocean. The added weight of this material, when deposited on the ocean floor, causes the floor to sink—not form mountains. Answers F, G, and I all describe situations in which mountain formation may occur.

Question 9 Answer G is correct. Answer F is incorrect because it describes flat, smooth surfaces, which are not produced by stress. Students who choose answer H may have a misunderstanding of the anology. Answer I is one example of stress. Students should assume by the wording in the passage that rocks undergo stress at other times.

Chapter 11 Standardized Test Prep

Understanding Concepts

Directions (1–4): For each question, write on a separate sheet of paper the letter of the correct answer.

1. Where are most plateaus located?
   A. near mountain ranges
   B. bordering ocean basins
   C. beneath grabens
   D. alongside diverging boundaries
2. Which of the following features form where parts of the crust have been broken by faults?
   F. monoclines
   G. plateaus
   H. synclines
   I. grabens
3. Which of the following statements describes the formation of rock along strike-slip faults?
   A. Rock on either side of the fault plane slides vertically.
   B. Rock on either side of the fault plane slides horizontally.
   C. Rock in the hanging wall is pushed up and over the rock of the footwall.
   D. Rock in the hanging wall moves down relative to the footwall.
4. Which does not result in mountain formation?
   F. collisions between continental and oceanic crust
   G. subduction of one oceanic plate beneath another oceanic plate
   H. deposition and isostasy
   I. deformation caused by collisions between two or more continents

Directions (5–7): For each question, write a short response.

5. What is the term for a condition of gravitational equilibrium in Earth's crust?
6. What is the term for a type of stress that squeezes and shortens a body?
7. As a volcanic mountain range forms, what does isostatic adjustment cause the crust beneath the mountain range to do?

Reading Skills

Directions (8–10): Read the passage below. Then, answer the questions.

Stress and Strain

Stress is defined as the amount of force per unit area on a rock. When enough stress is placed on a rock, the rock becomes strained, usually by bending and breaking. For example, if you put a small amount of pressure on the ends of a drinking straw, the straw may not bend—even though you have put stress on it. However, when you put enough pressure on it, the straw bends, or becomes strained.

One example of stress is when tectonic plates collide. When plates collide, a large amount of stress is placed on the rocks that make up the plates, especially the rocks at the edges of the plates involved in the collision. Because of the stress, these rocks become extremely strained. In fact, even the shapes of the tectonic plates can change as a result of these powerful collisions.

8. Based on the passage, which of the following statements is not true?
   A. Strain can cause rock to deform by bending or breaking.
   B. Rocks, like drinking straws, will not bend when pressure is applied to them.
   C. Stress is defined as amount of force per unit area that is put on rock.
   D. A large amount of stress is placed on the rocks involved in tectonic plate collisions.
9. Which of the following statements can be inferred from the information in the passage?
   F. The stress of tectonic plate collisions often creates large, smooth plains of rock.
   G. The stress of tectonic plate collisions often creates large mountain chains.
   H. Bending a drinking straw requires the same amount of pressure that is needed to bend a rock.
   I. The only time that rock has stress is when the rock is involved in a tectonic collision.
10. What happens to rocks when plates collide?

Question 12 Full-credit answers should include the following points:

- subduction causes partial melting of the overlying mantle, which produces magma that may erupt to form volcanic mountains
- as the oceanic plate is subducted by the denser continental plate, the oceanic plate heats up and releases water
- the water causes a partial melting of the mantle, which changes rock into magma
- this magma rises to the surface and forms volcanic mountains

Question 14 Full-credit answers should include the following points:

- when stress is applied, a rock can respond with brittle or ductile strain
- ductile strain is common in rock that is hot or in which pressure is evenly exerted
- ductile strain results in change in volume or shape without breaking
- ductile strain commonly results in bending or folding

Interpreting Graphics

Directions (11–14): For each question below, record the correct answer on a separate sheet of paper.

The diagrams below show a divergent and a convergent plate boundary. Use these diagrams to answer questions 11 and 12.

Divergent and Convergent Plate Boundaries

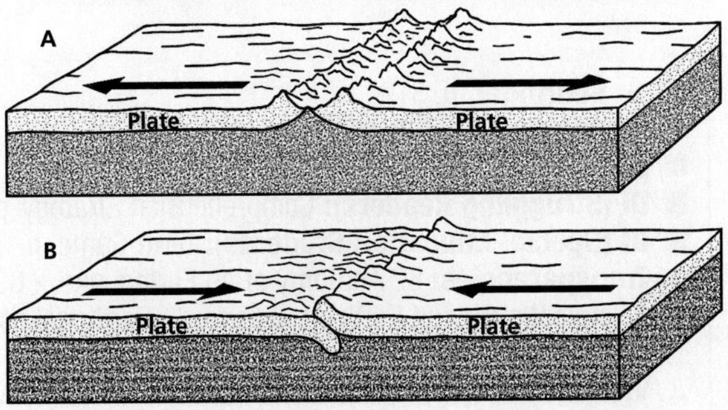

11. Which of the following is not likely to be found at or occur at the boundary shown in diagram A?

A. volcanoes
B. lava flows
C. earthquakes
D. subduction

12. How does the subduction of the oceanic crust shown in diagram B produce volcanic mountains?

The diagram below shows two possible outcomes when pressure, which is represented by the large arrows, is applied to the rock on the left. Use this diagram to answer questions 13 and 14.

Rock Deformation

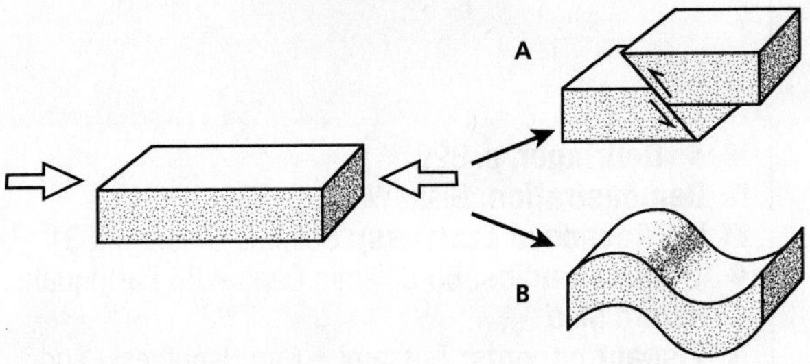

13. What type of deformation is seen in rock A?

F. brittle
G. ductile
H. folding
I. monocline

14. Describe the type of rock deformation shown in rock B. Under what conditions is this type of deformation likely to occur?

Test Tip

Carefully study all of the details of a diagram before answering the question or questions that refer to it.

Standardized Test Prep

Using THINK central Resources

State Resources

- For specific resources for your state, visit www.thinkcentral.com and type in the keyword **HSHSTR.**

Answers

Understanding Concepts

1. A
2. I
3. B
4. H
5. isostasy
6. compression
7. sink

Reading Skills

8. A
9. G
10. Rocks suffer severe stress in a tectonic collision, and they are usually deformed by the extremely high amounts of pressure generated.

Interpreting Graphics

11. D
12. Answers may vary. See Test Doctor for a detailed scoring rubric.
13. F
14. Answers may vary. See Test Doctor for a detailed scoring rubric.

Chapter Planner 12

Earthquakes

	Standards	Teach Key Ideas
Chapter Opener, pp. 316–317 (45 min.)	National Science Education Standards	
Section 1 How and Where Earthquakes Happen, pp. 319–324 (45 min.) ❯ Why Earthquakes Happen ❯ Seismic Waves and Earth's Interior ❯ Earthquakes and Plate Tectonics ❯ Fault Zones	PS 6, PS 6a, SPSP 5c, ES 3c	■ ▲ **Bellringer,** p. 319 ■ **Demonstration:** Elastic Rebound, p. 319 ■ **Discussion:** Surface Waves, p. 321 ■ **DI (Struggling Readers):** Comprehension Strategy, p. 321 ■ **DI (Special Education Students):** Term Game, p. 322 ◆ **Transparencies:** 62 Anatomy of an Earthquake • 63 Seismic Waves and Earth's Interior • 64 Earthquakes and Tectonic Plate Boundaries ▲ **Visual Concepts:** Elastic Deformation and Elastic Rebound • Body Waves: S Waves and P Waves • Seismic Waves: Surface Waves • Structure of the Earth • Seismographs and Mapping Earth's Layers • Mohos and Shadow Zones • Plate Motion and Earthquake Characteristics
Section 2 Studying Earthquakes, pp. 325–328 (90 min.) ❯ Recording Earthquakes ❯ Locating an Earthquake ❯ Earthquake Measurement	PS 6, PS 6a, SPSP 5c, UCP 3	■ ◆ **Bellringer,** p. 325 ■ **DI (Special Education Students):** Diagramming Information, p. 326 ▲ **Visual Concepts:** S-P-Time Method: Finding an Epicenter • Richter Scale
Section 3 Earthquakes and Society, pp. 329–332 (45 min.) ❯ Tsunamis ❯ Destruction to Buildings and Property ❯ Earthquake Safety ❯ Earthquake Warnings and Forecasts	PS 6, ST 1, SPSP 5, SPSP 5a, SPSP 5c, UCP 3	■ ◆ **Bellringer,** p. 329 ■ **Demonstration:** Giant Wave, p. 329 ■ **DI (Advanced Learners):** Seismic Creep, p. 331 ◆ **Transparencies:** 65 Seismic Gaps • 66 Earthquake Hazard Map ▲ **Visual Concepts:** Tsunami • Gap Hypothesis and Seismic Gaps • Earthquake-Hazard Level
Chapter Wrap-Up, pp. 337–341 (90 min.)		**Chapter Summary,** p. 337

See also PowerNotes® Presentations

CHAPTER Fast Track

To shorten instruction because of time limitations, omit the Chapter Lab.

Key
Teacher's Edition ■ Teaching Transparencies ◆
Chapter Resource File ● Online Edition ▲

All resources listed below are also available on the **Teacher One Stop™.**

Why It Matters	Hands-On	Skills Development	Assessment
■ **Chapter Overview,** p. 316 ■ **Using the Figure:** The Kobe Quake, p. 316	**Inquiry Lab:** Modeling Earthquake Waves, p. 317	**Reading Toolbox,** p. 318	
■ **Section Overview,** p. 319 ■ **Technology Connection:** Seismic Profiling, p. 321 **Do All Seismic Waves Come from Earthquakes?** p. 321 ■ **History Connection:** Moho Discontinuity, p. 322	■ **Group Activity:** Modeling Locked Faults, p. 320 ● **Inquiry Lab:** Simulating Earthquakes	■ **Skill Builder:** Vocabulary, p. 320 ■ ● **Internet Activity:** Distribution Patterns, p. 320 **Reading Toolbox:** Classification, p. 323	**Reading Check,** p. 321 **Reading Check,** p. 322 **Section Review,** p. 324 ■ **Reteaching,** p. 323 **Quiz,** p. 323 ■ **DI (Alternative Assessment):** Earthquake Patterns, p. 324 ● **Section Quiz**
■ **Section Overview,** p. 325 ■ **Why It Matters:** Largest Earthquakes, p. 327	■ **Group Activity:** Model Seismograph, p. 325 **QuickLab:** Seismographic Record, p. 326 **Skills Practice Lab:** Finding an Epicenter, pp. 334–335	■ **Reading Skill Builder:** Reading Organizer, p. 326 **Reading Toolbox:** Layered Book, p. 327 **Math Skills:** Magnitudes, p. 327 ■ **Skill Builder:** Graphing, p. 327	**Reading Check,** p. 327 **Section Review,** p. 328 ■ **Reteaching,** p. 327 ■ **Quiz,** p. 327 ■ **DI (Alternative Assessment):** Sizing Up Quakes, p. 328 ● **Section Quiz**
■ **Section Overview,** p. 329 ■ **Using the Figure,** p. 330	**QuickLab:** Earthquake-Safe Buildings, p. 330 ■ **Group Activity:** Earthquake Safety, p.330 ● **Skills Practice Lab:** Earthquakes and Soil	■ **Reading Skill Builder:** Paired Summarizing, p. 330 **Reading Toolbox:** Root Words, p. 331 **Maps in Action:** Earthquake Hazard Map, p. 336 ■ **Internet Activity:** Hazards in the Americas, p. 336 ● **Internet Activity:** Hazards in the Americas **Reading Toolbox:** Layered Book, p. 338	**Reading Check,** p. 331 **Section Review,** p. 332 ■ **Reteaching,** p. 331 ■ **Quiz,** p. 331 ■ **DI (Alternative Assessment):** Making Models, p. 332 ● **Section Quiz**
Detecting Earthquakes, p. 333		▲ **Super Summary** **Standardized Test Prep,** pp. 340–341	**Chapter Review,** pp. 338–339 ■ **DI (Alternative Assessment):** News Broadcast, p. 337 ● **Chapter Tests**

See also Lab Generator

See also Holt Online Assessment Resources

Chapter Overview

This chapter describes the causes of earthquakes and the tectonic settings where earthquakes are most likely to happen. The chapter also examines how earthquakes are measured and how earthquakes affect humans.

Using the Figure ___ GENERAL

The Kobe Quake During the earthquake that caused the damage in the photo, over 5,000 people lost their lives. Part of the Nojima Fault, which ruptured during the Kobe earthquake, lies directly beneath the city. Stresses in the region come from the junction of the Pacific, Eurasian, and Philippine plates. Ask students to speculate what effect damage to power lines, water mains, rail lines, and highways would have during a disaster of this magnitude. (Accept all reasonable answers.)
LS Interpersonal

Why It Matters

Kobe, an important port city in Japan, experienced a devastating earthquake in 1995. The elevated Hanshin Expressway collapsed. Port and wharf facilities were severely damaged by liquefaction, a process by which water-saturated, sandy soil flows like quicksand when shaken by an earthquake.

Chapter 12 Earthquakes

Chapter Outline

1 How and Where Earthquakes Happen
- Why Earthquakes Happen
- Seismic Waves and Earth's Interior
- Earthquakes and Plate Tectonics
- Fault Zones

2 Studying Earthquakes
- Recording Earthquakes
- Locating an Earthquake
- Earthquake Measurement

3 Earthquakes and Society
- Tsunamis
- Destruction to Buildings and Property
- Earthquake Safety
- Earthquake Warnings and Forecasts

Virginia Standards of Learning
ES.1.a
ES.1.b
ES.1.c
ES.2.a
ES.7.a
ES.7.b

Why It Matters

Understanding how, where, and why earthquakes happen can help scientists and engineers reduce earthquake damage and save lives. This expressway in Kobe, Japan, was toppled by an earthquake that caused the ground to shake for 20 s.

Chapter Correlations — *Virginia Standards of Learning*

ES.1.a volume, area, mass, elapsed time, direction, temperature, pressure, distance, density, and changes in elevation/depth are calculated utilizing the most appropriate tools.
ES.1.b technologies, including computers, probeware, and geospatial technologies, are used to collect, analyze, and report data and to demonstrate concepts and simulate experimental conditions.
ES.1.c scales, diagrams, charts, graphs, tables, imagery, models, and profiles are constructed and interpreted.
ES.2.a science explains and predicts the interactions and dynamics of complex Earth systems.
ES.7.a geologic processes and their resulting features
ES.7.b tectonic processes

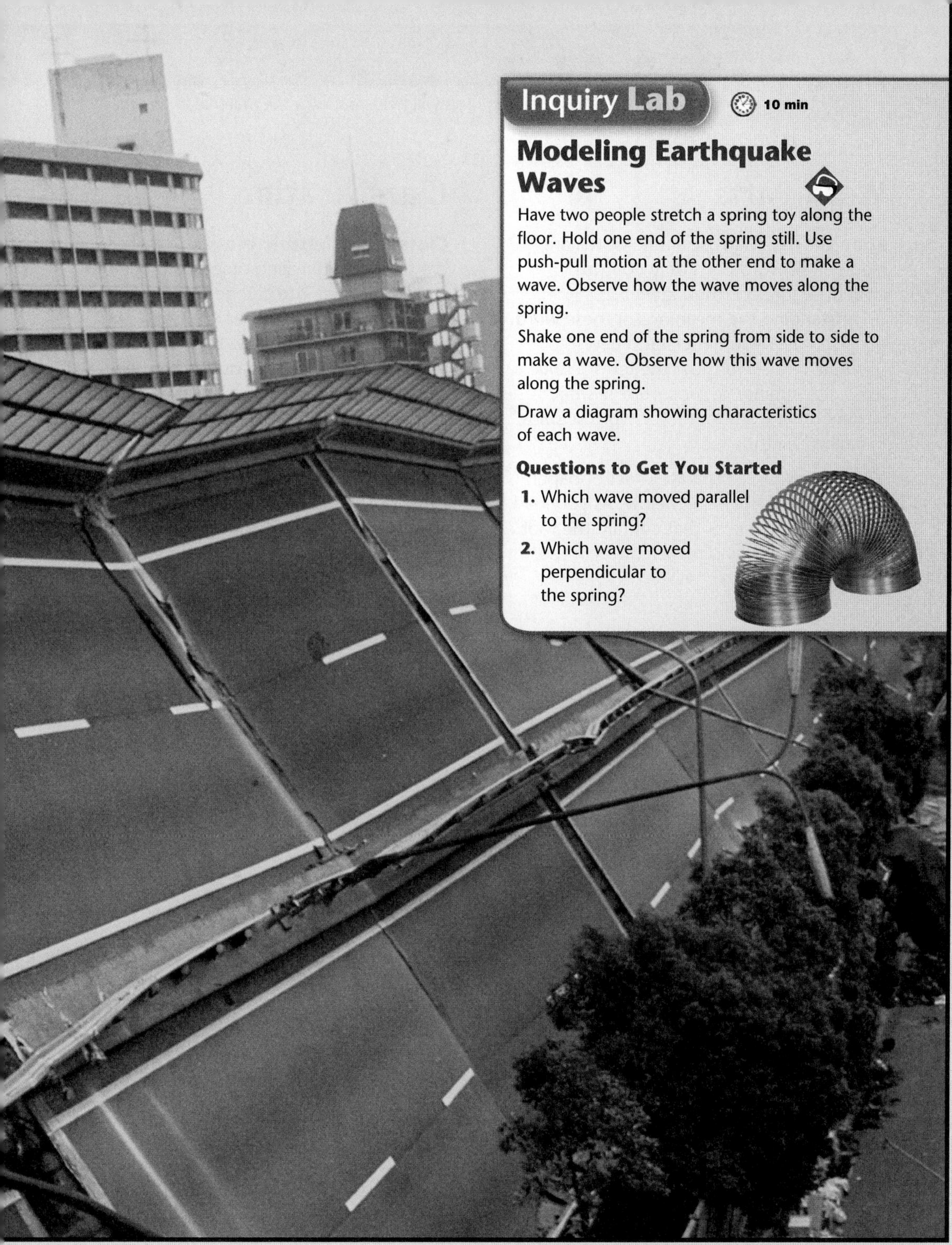

Inquiry Lab

10 min

Modeling Earthquake Waves

Have two people stretch a spring toy along the floor. Hold one end of the spring still. Use push-pull motion at the other end to make a wave. Observe how the wave moves along the spring.

Shake one end of the spring from side to side to make a wave. Observe how this wave moves along the spring.

Draw a diagram showing characteristics of each wave.

Questions to Get You Started

1. Which wave moved parallel to the spring?
2. Which wave moved perpendicular to the spring?

Inquiry Lab

Central Concept: Students use a spring toy to model the movement of compression waves (P waves) and shear waves (S waves) through a solid medium.

Teacher's Notes: You may wish to assign two students in each group to hold either end of the spring, one student to draw the diagrams, and one student to record questions and answers.

Materials: (per group)
- Spring toy

Skills Acquired
- Observing
- Interpreting Models
- Communicating

Answers to Getting Started

1. The push-pull motion caused a wave that moved parallel to the spring.
2. The side-to-side motion caused a wave that moved perpendicular to the spring.

Using THINK central Resources

An online version of this chapter, as well as all the print and multimedia resources that accompany the program are available to registered teachers and their students. Log onto www.thinkcentral.com to access these materials and tools to organize your preparation and student learning.

READING TOOLBOX

Root Words

Word or Term	Root	Definition
seismic wave	seism-	vibration that travels through Earth
seismology	seismo-	the study of earthquakes and seismic waves
seismograph	seismo-	an instrument that records ground vibrations
seismogram	seismo-	recording of ground motion made by a seismograph
seismologist	seismo-	scientist who studies earthquakes and seismic waves

READING TOOLBOX

These reading tools will help you learn the material in this chapter.

Word Parts

Root Words Many scientific words are made up of word parts derived from ancient or foreign languages. Understanding the meanings of these word parts can help you understand new scientific terms. Consider the term *seismic wave.* It contains the root word *seism-,* which comes from the Greek word *seismos,* meaning "earthquake."

Your Turn On a separate sheet of paper, start a table like the one below. As you read Section 2, find words that contain the root *seismo-* or *seism-* and make entries in the table for them.

Word or Term	Root	Definition
seismic wave	seism-	vibration that travels through Earth; often caused by an earthquake
seismology	seismo-	
seismograph		

Classification

Classifying Seismic Waves Classification is a tool for organizing objects and ideas by grouping them into categories. Groups are classified by defining characteristics. For example, the table below shows how seismic waves can be classified by their speed and type of movement they cause in Earth's crust.

Your Turn As you read Section 1, make a table like the one below for the following classes of seismic waves: P waves, S waves, Love waves, and Rayleigh waves.

CLASS	DEFINING CHARACTERISTICS
P waves	a type of body wave; fastest seismic wave; causes particles to travel in a direction parallel to the direction of travel of the wave
S waves	

FoldNotes

Layered Book FoldNotes are a fun way to help you learn and remember ideas that you encounter as you read.

Your Turn Make a layered book, as described in **Appendix A.** Label the tabs of the layered book with "Causes of Earthquakes," "Locating an Epicenter," and "Earthquake Safety." Write notes on the appropriate layer as you read the chapter.

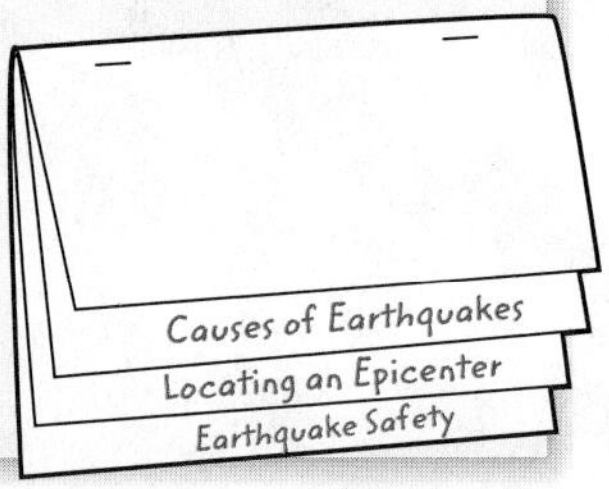

For more information on how to use these and other tools, see **Appendix A.**

Classifying Seismic Waves

Answers may vary. Students' tables should identify P waves and S waves as types of body waves and Love waves and Rayleigh waves as types of surface waves. In addition, tables should correctly describe other characteristics of each type of seismic wave.

Layered Book

Answers may vary but should provide correct information for each of the three topics. Students can consult Appendix A for tips on making layered books.

SECTION 1

How and Where Earthquakes Happen

Key Ideas	Key Terms		Why It Matters
❯ Describe elastic rebound. ❯ Compare body waves and surface waves. ❯ Explain how the structure of Earth's interior affects seismic waves. ❯ Explain why earthquakes generally occur at plate boundaries.	earthquake elastic rebound focus epicenter body wave	surface wave P wave S wave shadow zone fault zone	Understanding earthquakes helps people limit the destruction and loss of life that earthquakes can cause. Studying earthquakes also helps scientists understand Earth's interior.

Earthquakes are one of the most destructive natural disasters. A single earthquake can kill many thousands of people and cause billions of dollars in damage. **Earthquakes** are defined as movements of the ground that are caused by a sudden release of energy when rocks along a fault move. Earthquakes usually occur when rocks under stress suddenly shift along a fault. A *fault* is a break in a body of rock along which one block slides relative to another.

Why Earthquakes Happen

The rocks along both sides of a fault are commonly pressed together tightly. Although the rocks may be under stress, friction prevents them from moving past each other. In this immobile state, a fault is said to be *locked*. Parts of a fault remain locked until the stress becomes so great that the rocks suddenly slip past each other. This slippage causes the trembling and vibrations of an earthquake.

Elastic Rebound

Earthquakes are a result of elastic rebound. **Elastic rebound** is the sudden return of elastically deformed rock to its undeformed shape. This process is shown in **Figure 1.**

earthquake a movement or trembling of the ground that is caused by a sudden release of energy when rocks along a fault move

elastic rebound the sudden return of elastically deformed rock to its undeformed shape

Figure 1 Elastic Rebound

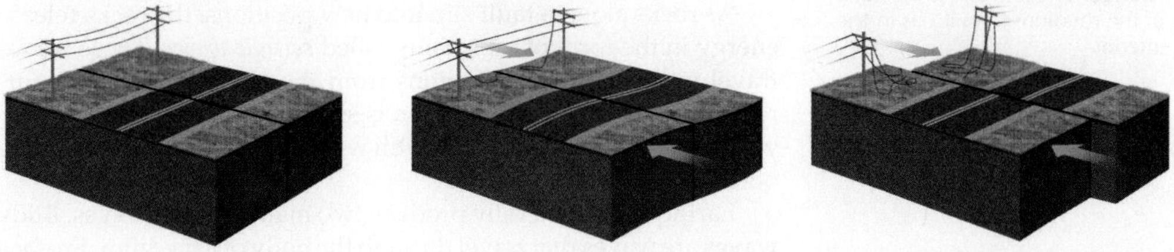

Two blocks of crust pressed against each other at a fault are under stress but do not move because friction holds them in place.

As stress builds up at the fault, the crust deforms. When rock is stressed past the point at which it can maintain integrity, it fractures.

When the rock fractures, it separates at the weakest point and snaps back, or *rebounds,* to its original shape, which causes an earthquake.

Section 1

Focus

Overview

This section explains the concept of elastic rebound and describes different types of seismic waves. It also explains how Earth's structure affects seismic waves and why earthquakes commonly occur at plate boundaries.

Bellringer

Have students describe what happens when a rock is thrown into a pond. Ask them to explain how this might be similar to an earthquake. (Sample answer: In each case, waves spread out from the source. However, the ripples you see on a pond's surface are two dimensional.) LS Visual

Motivate

Demonstration GENERAL

Elastic Rebound Take one end of a plastic ruler in each hand. Push down on the ends to form an arc. Then, stop pushing down and have students observe the rebounding motion of the ruler. Take a tongue depressor and bend it until it snaps. Explain that bending stores energy in the stick. That energy is released when the ruler rebounds or when the stick snaps. LS Visual

Key Resources

Chapter Resource File
- Directed Reading BASIC
- Inquiry Lab: Simulating Earthquakes GENERAL

Technology
- Transparencies
  Bellringer

Teach

Group Activity — GENERAL

Modeling Locked Faults Cover pairs of wood blocks with sandpaper. Use masking tape to hold the sandpaper in place. Have students hold one block in each hand. Tell them to push the sandpaper-covered edges of the blocks tightly together. While continuing to push the blocks together, have them try to slide the blocks in different directions. Ask someone to describe what happens. (The blocks lock and then move forward with a jerky motion.) Ask students how the model is like what happens during earthquakes. (Sample answer: The blocks are like rocks under stress. Friction prevents them from moving until suddenly they slip past each other and create the vibrations of an earthquake.)
LS Kinesthetic

Skill Builder — GENERAL

Vocabulary Point out that *center* refers to the source of an event or phenomenon. Explain that the Greek prefix *epi-* is used to mean "above" or "on the surface." For example, the *epidermis* is the outer part of the skin. Similarly, the *epicenter* is the point located on the surface of Earth directly above the focus of the earthquake. The Greek prefix *hypo-* means "under." The focus of an earthquake is sometimes called the *hypocenter*. It is the point below the surface at which the earthquake originated. English Language Learners
LS Verbal

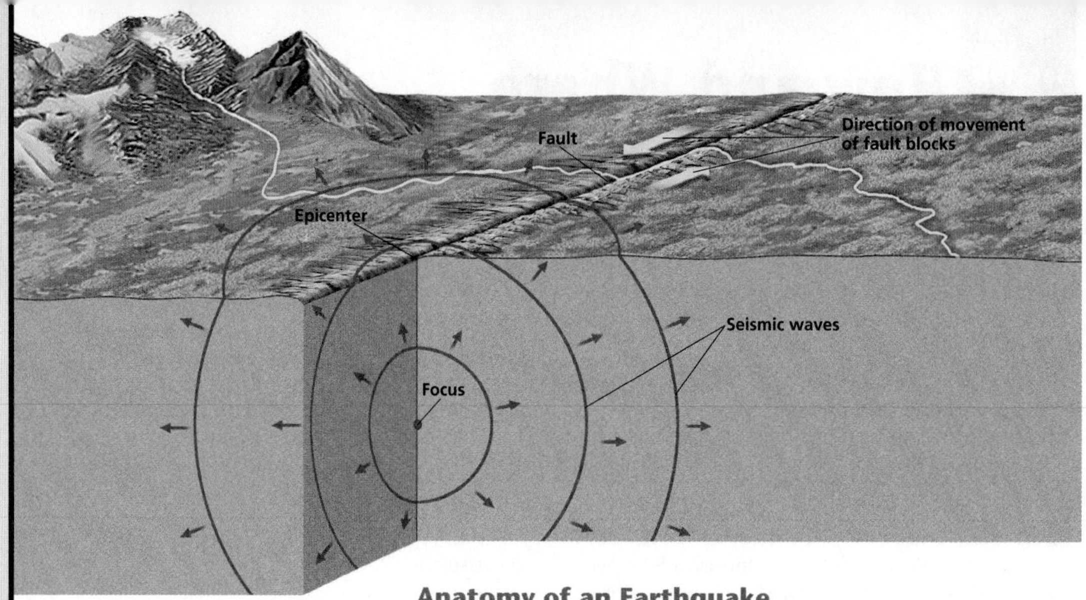

Figure 2 The epicenter of an earthquake is the point on the surface directly above the focus.

focus the location within Earth along a fault at which the first motion of an earthquake occurs

epicenter the point on Earth's surface directly above an earthquake's starting point, or focus

body wave a seismic wave that travels through the body of a medium

surface wave a seismic wave that travels along the surface of a medium and that has a stronger effect near the surface of the medium than it has in the interior

Anatomy of an Earthquake

The location within Earth along a fault at which the first motion of an earthquake occurs is called the **focus** (plural, *foci*). The point on Earth's surface directly above the focus is called the **epicenter** (EP i SENT uhr), as shown in **Figure 2.**

Although the focus depths of earthquakes vary, about 90% of continental earthquakes have shallow foci. Earthquakes that have shallow foci take place within 70 km of Earth's surface. Earthquakes that have intermediate foci take place at depths between 70 km and 300 km. Earthquakes that have deep foci take place at depths between 300 km and 650 km. Earthquakes that have deep foci usually occur in subduction zones and occur farther from the surface location of the plate boundary than shallower earthquakes do.

By the time the vibrations from an earthquake that has an intermediate or deep focus reach the surface, much of their energy has dissipated. For this reason, the earthquakes that cause the most damage usually have shallow foci.

Seismic Waves

As rocks along a fault slip into new positions, the rocks release energy in the form of vibrations called *seismic waves*. These waves travel outward in all directions from the focus through the surrounding rock. This wave action is similar to what happens when you drop a stone into a pool of still water and circular waves ripple outward from the center.

Earthquakes generally produce two main types of waves. **Body waves** are waves that travel through the body of a medium. **Surface waves** travel along the surface of a body rather than through the middle. Each type of wave travels at a different speed and causes different movements in Earth's crust.

Internet Activity — GENERAL

Distribution Patterns Ask students why shallow-focus earthquakes cause the greatest damage. (because their energy is released closer to Earth's surface) Invite interested students to research how earthquake foci are distributed relative to plate boundaries and to identify the most seismically active areas of North America. A worksheet designed to direct student research on this topic can be found in the **Chapter Resource File** booklet or by visiting www.thinkcentral.com and entering the key word **HQXEQKX. LS Visual**

Key Resources

Technology
- Transparencies
  62 Anatomy of an Earthquake

Body Waves

Body waves can be placed into two main categories: P waves and S waves. **P waves,** also called *primary waves* or *compression waves,* are the fastest seismic waves and are always the first waves of an earthquake to be detected. P waves cause particles of rock to move in a back-and-forth direction that is parallel to the direction in which the waves are traveling, as shown in **Figure 3.** P waves can move through solids, liquids, and gases. The more rigid the material is, the faster the P waves travel through it.

S waves, also called *secondary waves* or *shear waves,* are the second-fastest seismic waves and arrive at detection sites after P waves. S waves cause particles of rock to move in a side-to-side direction that is perpendicular to the direction in which the waves are traveling. Unlike P waves, however, S waves can only travel through solid material.

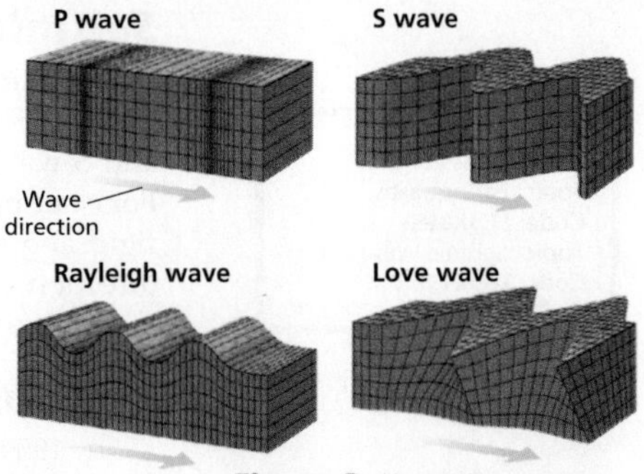

Figure 3 The different types of seismic waves cause different rock movements, which have different effects on Earth's crust.

Surface Waves

Surface waves form from motion along a shallow fault or from the conversion of energy when P waves and S waves reach Earth's surface. Although surface waves are the slowest-moving waves, they may cause the greatest damage during an earthquake. The two types of surface waves are Love waves and Rayleigh waves. *Love waves* cause rock to move side to side and perpendicular to the direction in which the waves are traveling. *Rayleigh waves* cause the ground to move with an elliptical, rolling motion.

P wave a primary wave, or compression wave; a seismic wave that causes particles of rock to move in a back-and-forth direction parallel to the direction in which the wave is traveling

S wave a secondary wave, or shear wave; a seismic wave that causes particles of rock to move in a side-to-side direction perpendicular to the direction in which the wave is traveling

Reading Check **Describe the two types of surface waves.**
(See Appendix G for answers to Reading Checks.)

Why It Matters

Do All Seismic Waves Come from Earthquakes?

REAL WORLD

Have you felt the ground shake as a large truck rumbles past? Seismic waves are produced not only by earthquakes but also by such events as explosions and even the movement of heavy equipment.

This meteorite impact in Peru produced measurable seismic waves.

Landslides produce seismic waves as large quantities of soil and rock suddenly collapse downhill.

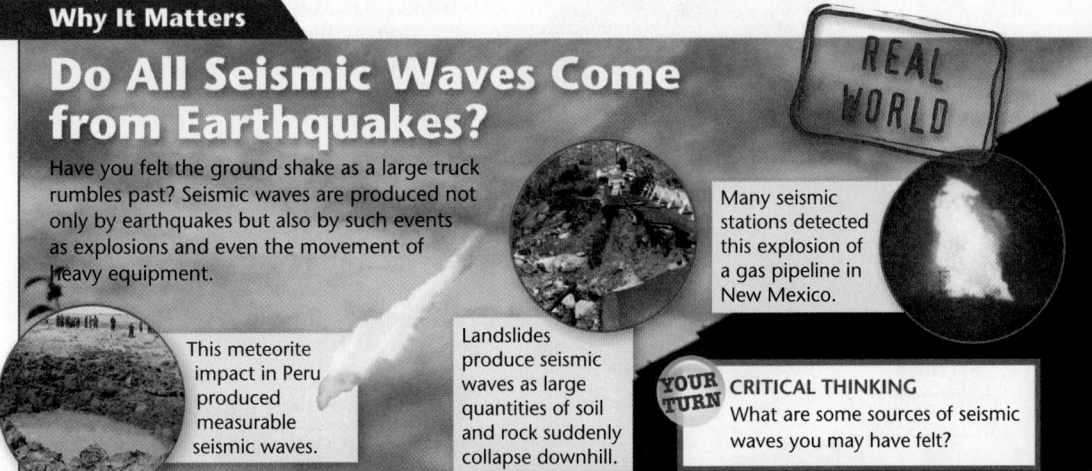

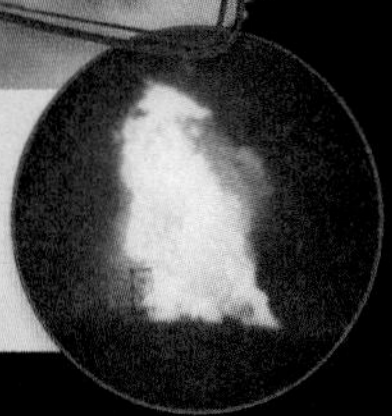

Many seismic stations detected this explosion of a gas pipeline in New Mexico.

YOUR TURN **CRITICAL THINKING**
What are some sources of seismic waves you may have felt?

Technology Connection — GENERAL

Seismic Profiling Oceanographers use a technique called *seismic profiling* to build a picture of the sea bottom that shows the thickness and geometry of layers of sediment. Oil companies looking for offshore oil pioneered the method, in which a compressed-air gun directs a sound pulse at the sea floor and an array of listening devices called *hydrophones* record the returning sound waves. These hydrophones are similar to the geophones used to map features of the underground surface. Invite interested students to create models or diagrams of how this technique works.
LS **Kinesthetic/Visual**

Discussion — BASIC

Surface Waves Ask students to describe the effects of the two different types of surface waves on Earth's surface. (Sample answer: Rayleigh waves cause the ground to move with a rolling motion like ocean waves. Love waves cause the ground to move horizontally and perpendicular to the direction the wave is traveling.) Next, ask students why surface waves may cause the most extensive damage even though they travel much slower than body waves do. (because their energy is concentrated at the surface)
LS **Verbal**

Answer to Reading Check

Rayleigh waves cause the ground to move in an elliptical, rolling motion. Love waves cause rock to move side-to-side and perpendicular to the direction the waves are traveling.

Differentiated Instruction

Struggling Readers

Comprehension Strategy To help students comprehend the difference between body waves and surface waves, use **Figure 3.** Have students identify depth-related differences between depictions of ground motions in the two upper panels and the two lower panels. Example: "The upper panels show that motion does not change with depth, but the lower panels show that motion is greatest at the surface and dies out with depth."

Why It Matters

Seismic waves are part of everyday experience even in areas not prone to earthquakes. The movement of heavy trucks generates seismic waves. They are also caused by such events as detonations associated with mining or construction and sonic booms in the atmosphere caused by fast-moving aircraft. Governments monitor seismic waves around the world for evidence of explosions associated with nuclear testing.

Answer to Your Turn

Answers will vary. Accept any reasonable response.

Teach, *continued*

History Connection — GENERAL

Moho Discontinuity The Croatian scientist Andrija Mohorovičić discovered the boundary layer between Earth's mantle and crust by analyzing the change in speed of seismic waves as they passed through different materials. The boundary layer was named the "Mohorovičić Discontinuity," or the "Moho," in his honor. He also contributed to our understanding of earthquakes' effects on buildings, location of earthquake epicenters, and Earth models. Invite students to investigate the work of this scientist, who also increased our knowledge of the energy of winds, and report back to the class. **LS Verbal**

Answer to Reading Check

The speed of seismic waves changes as they pass through different layers of Earth.

Key Resources

Technology

- Transparencies
  63 Seismic Waves and Earth's Interior

SciLinks.
www.scilinks.org
Topic: Earthquakes
Code: **HQX0453**
Topic: Seismic Waves
Code: **HQX1371**

Seismic Waves and Earth's Interior

Seismic waves are useful to scientists who are exploring Earth's interior. The composition of the material through which P waves and S waves travel affects the speed and direction of the waves. For example, P waves travel fastest through materials that are very rigid and are not easily compressed. By studying the speed and direction of seismic waves, scientists can learn more about the makeup and structure of Earth's interior.

Earth's Internal Layers

In 1909, Andrija Mohorovičić (MOH hoh ROH vuh CHICH), a Croatian scientist, discovered that the speed of seismic waves increases abruptly at about a 30-km depth beneath the surface of continents. The location at which the speed of the waves increases marks the boundary between the crust and the mantle. The depth of this boundary varies from about 10 km below the oceans to about 30 km below continents. This increase in speed takes place because the mantle is denser than the crust. By studying the speed of seismic waves, scientists have been able to locate boundaries between other internal layers of Earth. The three main compositional layers of Earth are the *crust,* the *mantle,* and the *core.* Earth is also composed of five mechanical layers—the *lithosphere,* the *asthenosphere,* the *mesosphere,* the *outer core,* and the *inner core.*

shadow zone an area on Earth's surface where no direct seismic waves from a particular earthquake can be detected

Shadow Zones

Recordings of seismic waves around the world reveal shadow zones. **Shadow zones** are locations on Earth's surface where no body waves from a particular earthquake can be detected. Shadow zones exist because the materials that make up Earth's interior are not uniform in rigidity. When seismic waves travel through materials of differing rigidities, the speed of the waves changes. The waves also bend and change direction as they pass through different materials.

As shown in **Figure 4,** a large S-wave shadow zone covers the side of Earth that is opposite an earthquake. S waves do not reach the S-wave shadow zone because they cannot pass through the liquid outer core. Although P waves can travel through all of the layers, the speed and direction of the waves change as the waves pass through each of Earth's layers. The waves bend in such a way that P-wave shadow zones form.

Reading Check **What causes the speed of a seismic wave to change?**

Figure 4 P waves and S waves behave differently as they pass through different structural layers of Earth.

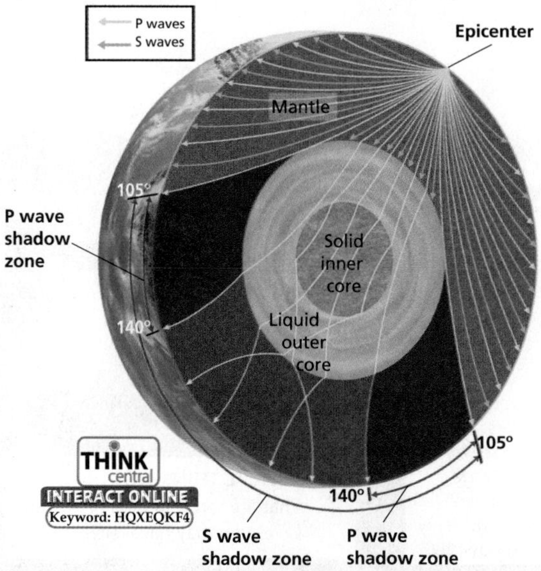

Differentiated Instruction

Special Education Students

Term Game Use the following game to help students review material in this section: Divide the class into groups of three or four students. Assign each team one term or concept from the section. Have each team plan to act out the assigned term silently. When they are ready, have them write three terms on the board for the class to guess—only one of which is the correct answer. After a team acts out its term, have the class vote on which of the three terms the team was depicting. **LS Kinesthetic**

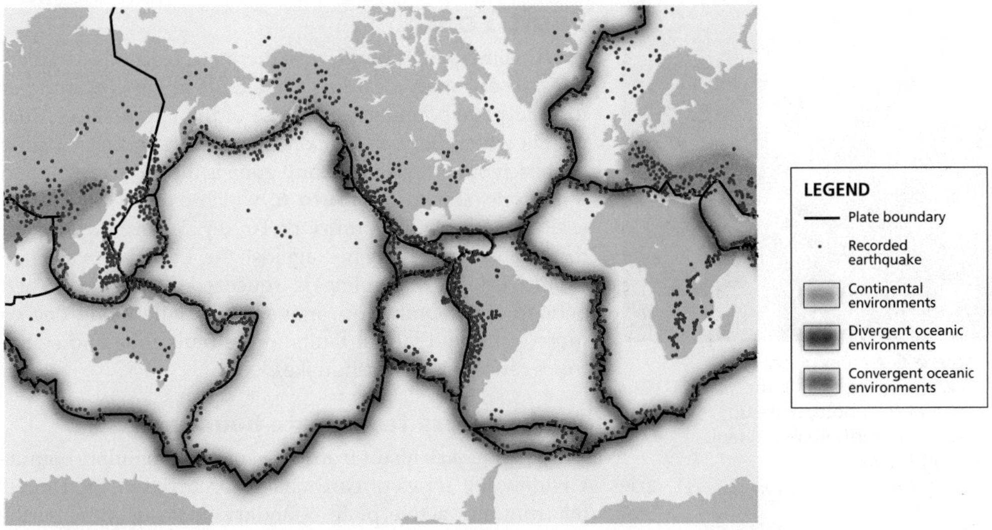

Figure 5 Earthquakes are the result of tectonic stresses in Earth's crust and occur in three main tectonic environments: mid-ocean ridges, subduction zones, and continental collisions.

Earthquakes and Plate Tectonics

Earthquakes are the result of stresses in Earth's lithosphere. Most earthquakes occur in three main tectonic environments, as shown in **Figure 5**. These environments are generally located at or near tectonic plate boundaries, where stress on the rock is greatest.

Convergent Oceanic Environments

At convergent plate boundaries, plates move toward each other and collide. The plate that is denser subducts, or sinks into the asthenosphere below the other plate. As the plates move, the overriding plate scrapes across the top of the subducting plate, and earthquakes occur. Convergent oceanic boundaries can occur between two oceanic plates or between one oceanic plate and one continental plate.

Divergent Oceanic Environments

At the divergent plate boundaries that make up the mid-ocean ridges, plates are moving away from each other. Earthquakes occur along mid-ocean ridges because oceanic lithosphere is pulling away from both sides of each ridge. This spreading motion causes earthquakes along the ocean ridges.

Continental Environments

Earthquakes also occur at locations where two continental plates converge, diverge, or move horizontally in opposite directions. As the continental plates interact, the rock surrounding the boundary experiences stress. The stress may cause mountains to form and also causes frequent earthquakes.

READING TOOLBOX

Classification
As you read about the three main tectonic environments in which earthquakes occur, make a table classifying the direction of movement of tectonic plates in each environment.

READING TOOLBOX

Classification Answers will vary. Example: "Convergent oceanic environments: Plates push together, and the denser plate subducts. The upper plate scrapes across the top of the subducting plate; Divergent oceanic environments: Plates move away from each other; Continental environments: Plates converge, diverge, or slide horizontally past each other."

Close

Reteaching — BASIC

Earthquake Maps Have students create a flip-book that illustrates the process of elastic rebound. The book should show how the fault blocks change before the earthquake and how the blocks respond to the earthquake. Books should include at least 10 drawings. **LS Visual**

Quiz — GENERAL

1. Why do earthquakes occur along plate boundaries? (As plates separate, collide, or grind past each other, they jerk suddenly as they move.)
2. What causes seismic waves to change direction within Earth? (Differences in the composition of the layers cause the waves to bend and travel in a different direction or to be reflected.)

Key Resources

Technology
- Transparencies
  64 Earthquakes and Tectonic Plate Boundaries

MISCONCEPTION ALERT

Earthquake Locations Students may think that earthquakes occur only at faults or at places where tectonic plates are colliding or subducting. However, volcanically active areas are also the sites of many shallow, small-magnitude earthquakes that are associated with volcanic eruptions and the movement of magma. As magma moves, surrounding rocks crack as a result of changes in temperature and pressure. This cracking causes earthquakes.

Close, *continued*

Answers to Section Review

1. the sudden return of deformed rock back to its original shape
2. The focus is located within Earth. The epicenter is a point on the surface above the focus.
3. Body waves travel through Earth's interior, while surface waves travel only along the outer surface.
4. Seismic waves behave differently as they pass through layers composed of different materials. These differences help create a picture of Earth's interior.
5. When seismic waves reach boundaries between rock layers, their speed changes. They are reflected or change direction as they pass through layers of different composition.
6. Earthquakes result from stress within the lithosphere. They commonly occur at plate boundaries because stress on rock is greatest near plate boundaries, which may be faulted, and thus weaker than plate interiors.
7. A fault zone is a region of numerous, closely spaced faults. When enough stress builds in the zone, movement occurs along one or more of the faults in the fault zone.
8. within about 70 km of Earth's surface
9. If the seismologic station records no S waves, you could conclude that the location of the epicenter was on the opposite side of Earth, because the S waves could not pass through the liquid outer core.
10. Because the center of Brazil is far away from any plate boundaries, you might conclude that a major fault zone lies deep below the region.
11. *Earthquakes* produce two types of *seismic waves*: *body waves*, which consist of *P waves* and *S waves*; and *surface waves*, which consist of *Rayleigh waves* and *Love waves*.

Figure 6 A series of parallel transform faults, seen in the center of this photo, make up part of the North Anatolian fault zone in Turkey.

fault zone a region of numerous, closely spaced faults

Academic Vocabulary

series (SEER eeze) a number of related events or objects coming one after another in succession

Fault Zones

At some plate boundaries, there are regions of numerous, closely spaced faults called **fault zones.** Fault zones form at plate boundaries because of the intense stress that results when the plates separate, collide, subduct, or slide past each other. One such fault zone is the North Anatolian fault zone, shown in **Figure 6,** which extends almost the entire length of the country of Turkey. Where the edge of the Arabian plate pushes against the Eurasian plate, the small Turkish microplate is squeezed westward. When enough stress builds up, movement occurs along one or more of the individual faults in the fault zone and sometimes causes major earthquakes.

Earthquakes Away from Plate Boundaries

Not all earthquakes result from movement along plate boundaries. A widely felt series of earthquakes occurred in the United States far from any active plate boundary. Instead, these earthquakes occurred in the middle of the continent, near New Madrid, Missouri, in 1811 and 1812. The vibrations from the earthquakes that rocked New Madrid were so strong that they caused damage as far away as South Carolina.

It was not until the late 1970s that studies of the Mississippi River region revealed an ancient fault zone deep within Earth's crust. This zone is thought to be part of a major fault zone in the North American plate. Scientists have determined that the fault formed at least 600 million years ago and that it was later buried under many layers of sediment and rock.

Section 1 Review

Key Ideas

1. **Describe** elastic rebound.
2. **Explain** the difference between the epicenter and the focus of an earthquake.
3. **Compare** body waves and surface waves.
4. **Explain** how seismic waves help scientists learn about Earth's interior.
5. **Explain** how the structure of Earth's interior affects seismic wave speed and direction.
6. **Explain** why earthquakes generally take place at plate boundaries.
7. **Describe** a fault zone, and explain how earthquakes occur along fault zones.

Critical Thinking

8. **Applying Ideas** In earthquakes that cause the most damage, at what depth would movement along a fault most likely occur?
9. **Identifying Patterns** If a seismologic station measures P waves but no S waves from an earthquake, what can you conclude about the earthquake's location?
10. **Making Inferences** If an earthquake occurs in the center of Brazil, what can you infer about the geology of that area?

Concept Mapping

11. Use the following terms to create a concept map: *earthquake, seismic wave, body wave, surface wave, P wave, S wave, Rayleigh wave,* and *Love wave.*

Differentiated Instruction

Alternative Assessment

Earthquake Patterns Give students a map of recent earthquake activity in the United States. Have students look for patterns in the data that indicate where the most earthquakes occurred or where the largest-magnitude earthquakes occurred. Have them explain the patterns they identify in terms of tectonic activity or the location of major fault zones. **LS Visual**

SECTION 2

Studying Earthquakes

Key Ideas	Key Terms	Why It Matters
❯ Describe the instrument used to measure and record earthquakes. ❯ Summarize the method scientists use to locate an epicenter. ❯ Describe the scales used to measure the magnitude and intensity of earthquakes.	**seismograph** **seismogram** **magnitude** **intensity**	Determining an earthquake's location and intensity allows aid to be sent quickly after a significant earthquake occurs.

The study of earthquakes and seismic waves is called *seismology*. Many scientists study earthquakes because earthquakes are the best tool available for investigating Earth's internal structure and dynamics. These scientists have developed special sensing equipment to record, locate, and measure earthquakes.

Recording Earthquakes

Vibrations in the ground can be detected and recorded by using an instrument called a **seismograph** (SIEZ MUH graf), such as the one shown in **Figure 1.** A modern three-component seismograph consists of three sensing devices. One device records the vertical motion of the ground. The other two devices record horizontal motion—one for east-west motion and the other for north-south motion. Seismographs record motion by tracing wave-shaped lines on paper or by translating the motion into electronic signals. The electronic signals can be recorded on magnetic tape or can be loaded directly into a computer that analyzes seismic waves. A tracing of earthquake motion that is recorded by a seismograph is called a **seismogram.**

seismograph an instrument that records vibrations in the ground

seismogram a tracing of earthquake motion that is recorded by a seismograph

Because P waves are the fastest-moving seismic waves, they are the first waves to be recorded by a seismograph. S waves travel much slower than P waves. Therefore, S waves are the second waves to be recorded by a seismograph. Surface waves are the slowest-moving waves and are the last waves to be recorded by a seismograph.

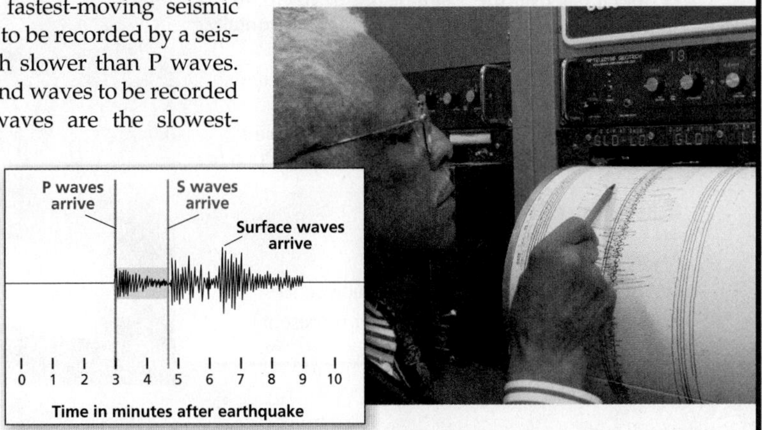

Figure 1 A seismograph station has banks of seismographs to record earthquakes. Each type of seismic wave leaves a unique "signature" on a seismogram (inset).

Section 2

Focus

Overview

This section describes the tools scientists use to measure earthquakes. The section explains how the source of an earthquake is identified and how its strength and destructiveness are measured.

Bellringer

Ask students to write down what information they would want to know if they were measuring or describing a major earthquake. (Accept all reasonable answers.) **LS Verbal**

Motivate

Group Activity — GENERAL

Model Seismograph Divide the class into groups of three. Tell each group to tape a sheet of paper around the cylinder of a rolling pin and secure it with a rubber band. Next, have them cut two notches in the sides of a shoebox to hold the ends of the roller and insert the drum into the notches. Tape the box securely to a table. Have one student hold a marking pen steady against the paper drum while the second turns the drum. The third student should shake the end of the table to simulate an earthquake. Have them compare the tracings from several tests. **LS Kinesthetic**

Key Resources

Chapter Resource File
- Directed Reading BASIC

Technology
- Transparencies
  Bellringer

Teach

Quick Lab

Skills Acquired
- Making Models
- Observing
- Analyzing

Materials
- Shoe box
- Plastic bag
- Sand
- Felt-tip pen
- Rubber band
- Pad of paper
- Ball
- Newspaper

Teacher's Notes: Remind students to move the paper slowly at a steady rate of speed. You could have students compare the effects of waves traveling through other materials by filling the bag with gravel or water, or stuffing the box with aluminum foil or foam peanuts.

Answers to Analysis
1. a graph of motion vs. time
2. different types of materials that make up Earth's crust
3. The sand vibrated less than the paper. The sand is more rigid than the crumpled paper and therefore vibrated less when the ball struck it.
4. They might deflect or change the speed of the waves.
5. The farther the waves have to travel, the more energy may dissipate.

Academic Vocabulary
analyze (AN uh LIEZ) study in detail

Locating an Earthquake

To determine the distance to an epicenter, scientists analyze the arrival times of the P waves and the S waves. The longer the lag time between the arrival of the P waves and the arrival of the S waves is, the farther away the earthquake occurred. Scientists use computers to calculate how far an earthquake is from a given seismograph station. Before computers were widely available, scientists consulted a lag-time graph. This graph translates the difference in arrival times of the P waves and S waves into distance from the epicenter to each station. The start time of the earthquake can also be determined by using this graph.

To locate the epicenter of an earthquake, scientists use computers to perform complex triangulations based on information from several seismograph stations. An earlier technique was simpler but less precise. On a map, scientists drew circles around at least three seismograph stations that recorded vibrations from the earthquake. The radius of each circle represented the distance from that station to the earthquake's epicenter. The point at which all of the circles intersected indicated the location of the epicenter of the earthquake.

SCILINKS.
www.scilinks.org
Topic: Earthquake Measurement
Code: HQX0452

Quick Lab — Seismographic Record

20 min

Procedure

1. Line a shoe box with a plastic bag. Fill the box to the rim with sand. Put on the lid.
2. Mark an X near the center of the lid.
3. Fasten a felt-tip pen to the lid of the box with a tight rubber band so that the pen extends slightly beyond the edge of the box.
4. Have a partner hold a pad of paper so that the paper touches the pen.
5. Hold a ball over the X at a height of 30 cm. As your partner slowly moves the paper horizontally past the pen, drop the ball on the X.
6. Label the resulting line with the type of material in the box.
7. Replace about 2/3 of the sand with crumpled newspaper. Put on the lid, and fasten the pen to the lid with the rubber band.
8. Repeat steps 4–6.

Analysis

1. What do the lines on the paper represent?
2. What do the sand and newspaper represent?
3. Compare the lines made in steps 4–6 with those made in step 8. Which material vibrated more when the ball was dropped on it? Explain why one material might vibrate more than the other.
4. How might different types of crustal material affect seismic waves that pass through it?
5. How might the distance of the epicenter of an earthquake from a seismograph affect the reading of a seismograph?

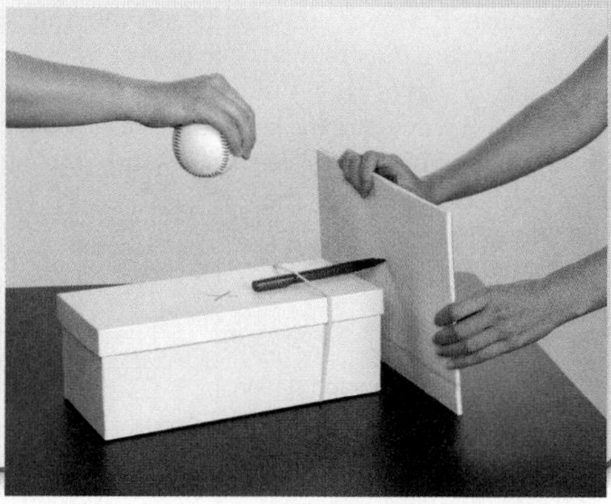

Reading Skill Builder — BASIC

Reading Organizer As students read this section, encourage them to outline the way scientists record and identify the source and measure the strength and intensity of an earthquake. They can use the section subheads as major outline heads and record details under each head. Later, students can use these outlines as a study guide for assessments. English Language Learners
LS Verbal

Differentiated Instruction

Special Education Students

Diagramming Information Ask volunteers to use text circles and lines to diagram groups of information on the board, such as:
1. Earthquake intensity: magnitude, extent of affected area from epicenter, local geology, and duration
2. Magnitude: Richter Scale, moment magnitude scale, used for most of last century, preferred by scientists now

Figure 2 The 2005 earthquake in northern Pakistan had a moment magnitude of 7.6, killed more than 86,000 people, and left about 3 million people homeless.

Earthquake Measurement

Scientists who study earthquakes are interested in the amount of energy released by an earthquake. Scientists also study the amount of damage done by the earthquake. These properties are studied by measuring magnitude and intensity.

Magnitude

The measure of the strength of an earthquake is called **magnitude.** Magnitude is determined by measuring the amount of ground motion caused by an earthquake. Seismologists express magnitude by using a magnitude scale, such as the Richter scale or the moment magnitude scale.

The *Richter scale* measures the ground motion from an earthquake to find the earthquake's strength. While the Richter scale was widely used for most of the 20th century, scientists now prefer the moment magnitude scale. *Moment magnitude* is a measurement of earthquake strength based on the size of the area of the fault that moves, the average distance that the fault blocks move, and the rigidity of the rocks in the fault zone. Although the moment magnitude and the Richter scales provide similar values for small earthquakes, the moment magnitude scale is more accurate for large earthquakes, such as the one shown in **Figure 2.**

The moment magnitude of an earthquake is expressed by a number. The larger the number, the stronger the earthquake. The largest earthquake that has been recorded (in Chile) registered a moment magnitude of 9.5. The earthquake in China in 2008 had a moment magnitude of 7.9 and devastated the country just before it hosted the Olympic Games that year. Earthquakes that have moment magnitudes of less than 2.5 usually are not felt by people.

Reading Check **What is the difference between the Richter scale and the moment magnitude scale?**

READING TOOLBOX

Layered Book
Make a layered book, and label the tabs with "Richter Scale," "Moment Magnitude Scale," and "Modified Mercalli Intensity Scale." Write notes on the appropriate tab as you read this section.

magnitude a measure of the strength of an earthquake

Math Skills

Magnitudes On both the moment magnitude scale and the Richter scale, the energy of an earthquake increases by a factor of about 30 for each increment on the scale. Thus, a magnitude 4 earthquake releases 30 times as much energy as a magnitude 3 earthquake does. How much more energy does a magnitude 6 earthquake release than a magnitude 3 earthquake does?

READING TOOLBOX

Layered Book Answers may vary. Students' notes should correctly distinguish among the three scales.

Answer to Reading Check
Moment magnitude is more accurate for larger earthquakes than the Richter scale is. Moment magnitude is directly related to rock properties and so is more closely related to the cause of the earthquake than the Richter scale is.

Math Skills

Answer
$30 \times 30 \times 30 = 27,000$ times as much energy

Close

Reteaching — BASIC

Earthquake Posters Have students draw a series of pictures to illustrate the increasing levels of damage represented by earthquakes of different intensities. For example, they could show objects swaying, bookcases toppling, cracks appearing in structures, and so on. Tell them to label their earthquake scale with phrases that describe the effects at each level. **LS Visual**

Quiz — GENERAL

1. Describe the sensing equipment used to record earthquakes. (Seismographs use sensing devices to record the vibrations of the ground.)
2. Compare the Richter scale with the Mercalli scale in describing an earthquake. (The Richter scale gives a numerical value to the amount of ground motion. The Mercalli scale describes the earthquake's intensity, including its effects on an area.) **LS Verbal**

Skill Builder — ADVANCED

Graphing Have students graph the seismic data for these earthquakes: 8.1: New Madrid, MO (1811); 2.2: Pyrenees (2004); 9.5: Chile (1960); 6.9: Loma Prieta, CA (1989); 4.5: Honshu, Japan (2004); 7.9: Gulf of Alaska (1987); 1.5: Straits of Gibraltar (2004); 8.6: Anchorage, AK (1960); 5.8: Jabalpur, India (1997). Place the magnitude on the horizontal axis and the approximate energy level represented by the magnitude of each event on the vertical axis. Have students compare the magnitude of New Madrid with one or more recent seismic events. **LS Logical/Visual**

Why It Matters

Largest Earthquakes The Great Alaskan Earthquake of 1964 was the largest earthquake in U.S. history, with an estimated magnitude of 9.2. The quake destroyed buildings and railroads and caused land to drop by more than 3 m. The largest earthquake of the last century was the Chilean earthquake of 1960, with an estimated magnitude of 9.5. It unleashed a tsunami that crossed the Pacific and devastated parts of Hawaii and Japan.

Close, *continued*

Answers to Section Review

1. A seismograph consists of three sensing devices that record ground motion: one records vertical motion, one records horizontal east-west motion, and the third records horizontal north-south motion.
2. A seismograph is the sensing device. The seismogram is the tracing of earthquake motion made by the seismograph.
3. Scientists drew circles on a map around three seismograph stations. They used the lag time between the arrival of the P waves and the S waves to determine the distance between each site and the epicenter. The epicenter was located where the three circles intersected.
4. The Richter scale determines earthquake strength based on ground motion and adjusts for distance. Moment magnitude measures earthquake strength based on the size of the area of the fault that moves, the average distance the fault blocks move, and the rigidity of the rocks in the fault zone.
5. Magnitude is the measure of an earthquake's strength. Intensity a measure of the effects of an earthquake on a particular area.
6. because the two circles representing the distance of two locations from the epicenter would intersect at two points, while three circles would intersect at only one point
7. Intensity depends on the local geology, the distance from the epicenter, and the earthquake's duration, as well as magnitude.
8. *Seismographs* record *P waves* and *S waves* to make *seismograms*, which can be used to determine an earthquake's *magnitude, intensity*, and location of the *epicenter*.

Table 1 Modified Mercalli Intensity Scale

Intensity	Description
I	is not felt except by very few under especially favorable conditions
II	is felt by only few people at rest; delicately suspended items may swing
III	is felt by most people indoors; vibration is similar to the passing of a large truck
IV	is felt by many people; dishes and windows rattle; sensation is similar to a building being struck
V	is felt by nearly everyone; some objects are broken; unstable objects are overturned
VI	is felt by all people; some heavy objects are moved; causes very slight damage to structures
VII	causes slight to moderate damage to ordinary buildings; some chimneys are broken
VIII	causes considerable damage (including partial collapse) to ordinary buildings
IX	causes considerable damage (including partial collapse) to earthquake-resistant buildings
X	destroys some to most structures, including foundations; rails are bent
XI	causes few structures, if any, to remain standing; bridges are destroyed and rails are bent
XII	causes total destruction; distorts lines of sight; objects are thrown into the air

Intensity

Before the development of magnitude scales, the size of an earthquake was determined based on the earthquake's effects. A measure of the effects of an earthquake is the earthquake's **intensity.** The modified *Mercalli scale,* shown in **Table 1,** expresses intensity in Roman numerals from I to XII and provides a description of the effects of each earthquake intensity. The highest-intensity earthquake is designated by Roman numeral XII and is described as total destruction. The intensity of an earthquake depends on the earthquake's magnitude, the distance between the epicenter and the affected area, the local geology, the earthquake's duration, and human infrastructure.

intensity in Earth science, the amount of damage caused by an earthquake

Section 2 Review

Key Ideas

1. **Describe** the instrument that is used to record seismic waves.
2. **Compare** a seismograph and a seismogram.
3. **Summarize** the method that scientists used to identify the location of an earthquake before computers became widely used.
4. **Describe** the scales that scientists use to measure the magnitude of an earthquake.
5. **Explain** the difference between magnitude and intensity of an earthquake.

Critical Thinking

6. **Analyzing Methods** Explain why it would be difficult for scientists to locate the epicenter of an earthquake if they have seismic wave information from only two locations.
7. **Evaluating Data** Explain why an earthquake with a moderate magnitude might have a high intensity.

Concept Mapping

8. Use the following terms to create a concept map: *seismograph, seismogram, epicenter, P wave, S wave, magnitude,* and *intensity.*

Differentiated Instruction

Alternative Assessment

Sizing Up Quakes Cover a workspace with a drop cloth. Fill a box lid with popped corn or salt. Have pairs of students drop the lid from several heights and compare the amount of disturbance produced by the model earthquakes. Have students devise a scale to measure the magnitude of their quakes. Then, have them compare their scale with the existing measurement scales.
LS Kinesthetic/Verbal

SECTION 3

Earthquakes and Society

Key Ideas	Key Terms	Why It Matters
❯ Discuss the relationship between tsunamis and earthquakes. ❯ Describe two possible effects of a major earthquake on buildings. ❯ List three safety techniques to prevent injury caused by earthquake activity. ❯ Identify four methods scientists use to forecast earthquake risks.	tsunami seismic gap	Knowing where powerful earthquakes are likely to occur and preparing for them in advance can save many lives, perhaps your own. Several safety rules should be followed by those living in areas prone to earthquakes.

Movement of the ground during an earthquake seldom directly causes many deaths or injuries. Instead, most injuries result from the collapse of buildings and other structures or from falling objects and flying glass. Other dangers include landslides, fires, explosions caused by broken electric and gas lines, and floodwaters released from collapsing dams.

Tsunamis

An earthquake whose epicenter is on the ocean floor may cause a giant ocean wave called a **tsunami** (tsoo NAH mee), which may cause serious destruction if it crashes into land. A tsunami may begin to form when a sudden drop or rise in the ocean floor occurs because of faulting associated with undersea earthquakes. The drop or rise of the ocean floor causes a large mass of sea water to also drop or rise suddenly. This movement sets into motion a series of long, low waves that increase in height as they near the shore. These waves are tsunamis.

tsunami a giant ocean wave that forms after a volcanic eruption, submarine earthquake, or landslide

Destruction to Buildings and Property

Most buildings are not designed to withstand the swaying motion caused by earthquakes. Buildings whose walls are weak may collapse completely. Very tall buildings may sway so violently that they tip over and fall onto lower neighboring structures, as shown in **Figure 1**.

The type of ground beneath a building can affect the way in which the building responds to seismic waves. During an earthquake, the loose soil and rock can vibrate like jelly. Buildings constructed on top of this kind of ground experience exaggerated motion and sway violently.

Figure 1 Rescue workers surround a building that toppled in Taipei, Taiwan, during the earthquake of 1999.

Section 3

Focus

Overview

This section describes the damage caused by earthquakes. The section also explains earthquake safety procedures and how scientists are attempting to forecast future earthquake events.

Bellringer

Have students think about disaster movies, news footage, or documentaries that include scenes of earthquakes. Have them write a brief description of some earthquake effects. (Answers may vary but can be used to identify preconceptions about earthquake damage.) **LS Verbal**

Motivate

Demonstration — GENERAL

Giant Wave Model how a tsunami forms. Cut a round hole about 10 cm in diameter in the bottom of a foil cake pan. Cover the hole with plastic wrap and tape it so that it is watertight. Fill the pan with water. Tap gently in the bottom of the plastic wrap. Then, increase the strength of the tap. Ask students to describe what happens. (Sample answer: The mass of water rises and falls as it adjusts to the change in water level produced by the force from below.) **LS Visual**

Key Resources

Chapter Resource File
- Directed Reading BASIC
- Skills Practice Lab: Earthquakes and Soil GENERAL
- Internet Activity: Hazards in the Americas GENERAL

Technology
- Transparencies Bellringer

Teach

Using the Figure BASIC

Direct students' attention to the photo showing the disaster control center. Explain that the items shown are sold in Japan for earthquake preparedness. Ask students to identify the items in the figure and explain how they would be useful during or after an earthquake. (Sample answer: The padded headgear would be useful in avoiding bumps from falling debris; the fire extinguishers would be used to put out fires caused by broken gas mains or electric lines.) **LS Verbal**

Quick Lab

Skills Acquired
- Modeling
- Observing
- Analyzing

Materials
- Building blocks
- Rubber bands

Teacher's Notes: Using small plastic tables or empty cardboard boxes as building surfaces will allow several groups to work at the same location. Rubber hammers would provide a more steady, even source of vibrations.

Answers to Analysis
1. The model building that was held together by rubber bands was more resistant to damage by the model earthquake.
2. Structures will be safer from earthquake damage if weak points are reinforced.

Figure 2 In Tokyo, Japan—an area that has a high earthquake-hazard level—earthquake safety materials are available at disaster control centers.

Quick Lab 10 min

Earthquake-Safe Buildings

Procedure
1. On a tabletop, build a structure by stacking **building blocks** on top of each other.
2. Pound gently on the side of the table. Record what happens to the structure.
3. Using **rubber bands,** wrap sets of three blocks together. Build a second structure by using these blocks.
4. Repeat step 2.

Analysis
1. Which of your structures was more resistant to damage caused by the "earthquake"?
2. How could this model relate to building real structures, such as elevated highways?

Earthquake Safety

A destructive earthquake may take place in any region of the United States. However, destructive earthquakes are more likely to occur in certain geographic areas, such as California or Alaska. People who live near active faults should be ready to follow a few simple earthquake safety rules. These safety rules may help prevent death, injury, and property damage.

Before an Earthquake

Before an earthquake occurs, be prepared. Keep on hand a supply of canned food, bottled water, flashlights, batteries, and a portable radio. Some safety materials are shown in **Figure 2.** Plan what you will do if an earthquake strikes while you are at home, at school, or in a car. Discuss these plans with your family. Learn how to turn off the gas, water, and electricity in your home.

During an Earthquake

When an earthquake occurs, stay calm. During the few seconds between tremors, you can move to a safer position. If you are indoors, protect yourself from falling debris by standing in a doorway or crouching under a desk or table. Stay away from windows, heavy furniture, and other objects that might topple over. If you are in school, follow the instructions given by your teacher or principal. If you are in a car, stop in a place that is away from tall buildings, tunnels, power lines, or bridges. Then, remain in the car until the tremors cease.

Academic Vocabulary
instruction (in STRUHK shun) information given; a direction

After an Earthquake

After an earthquake, be cautious. Check for fire and other hazards. Always wear shoes when walking near broken glass, and avoid downed power lines and objects touched by downed wires.

Group Activity GENERAL

Earthquake Safety Have students work in groups to explore ways of staying safe during an earthquake. One group could interview local officials regarding disaster relief plans in your community. Another could do library or Internet research about earthquake hazards in the region. Still others could develop a poster that outlines earthquake safety guidelines. The entire class can put its knowledge to work by conducting a mock earthquake safety drill. **LS Kinesthetic** Co-op Learning

Reading Skill Builder BASIC

Paired Summarizing Group students into pairs and have them read silently about earthquake warnings and forecasts. Then, have one student summarize the methods scientists have used to forecast earthquakes. The other student should listen to the retelling and point out any inaccuracies or ideas that were left out. Allow students to refer to the text as needed.
LS Verbal/Auditory English Language Learners

Earthquake Warnings and Forecasts

Humans have long sought methods by which to predict earthquakes. Accurate earthquake predictions could help prevent injuries and deaths that result from earthquakes.

Today, scientists study past earthquakes to predict where future earthquakes are most likely to occur. Using records of past earthquakes, scientists can make approximate forecasts of future earthquake risks. However, there is currently no reliable way of predicting exactly when or where an earthquake will occur. Even the best forecasts may be off by several years.

To make forecasts that are more accurate, scientists are trying to detect changes in Earth's crust that can signal an earthquake. Faults near many population centers have been located and mapped. Instruments placed along these faults measure small changes in rock movement around the faults and can detect an increase in stress. Currently, however, these methods cannot provide reliable or accurate predictions of earthquakes.

Seismic Gaps

Scientists have identified zones of low earthquake activity, or seismic gaps, along some faults. A **seismic gap** is an area along a fault where relatively few earthquakes have occurred recently but where strong earthquakes occurred in the past. Some scientists think that seismic gaps are likely locations of future earthquakes. Several gaps that exist along the San Andreas Fault zone may be sites of major earthquakes in the future. A couple of seismic gaps in California are illustrated in **Figure 3.**

Reading Check **Why do scientists think that seismic gaps are areas where future earthquakes are likely to occur?**

READING TOOLBOX

Root Words
Explain how you can use the meaning of the root word *seism-* to understand the term *seismic gap.*

seismic gap an area along a fault where relatively few earthquakes have occurred recently but where strong earthquakes are known to have occurred in the past

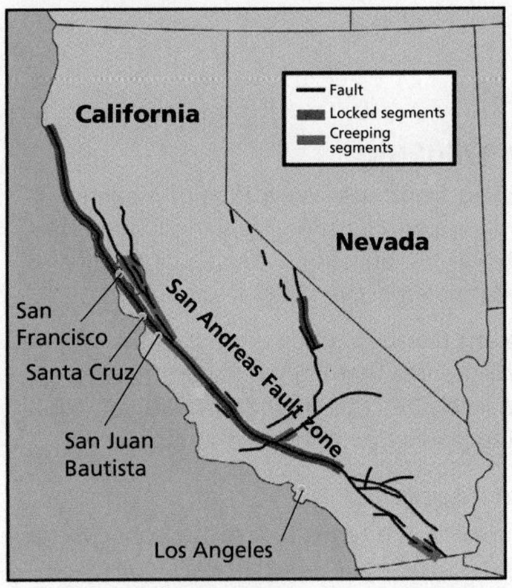

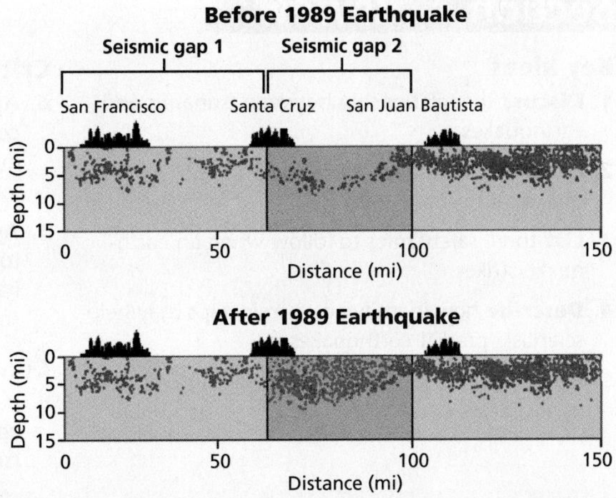

Figure 3 Each red dot in the cross sections of the San Andreas Fault represents an earthquake or aftershock before the 1989 Loma Prieta earthquake. Note how seismic gap 2 was filled by the 1989 earthquake and its aftershocks, which are represented by the blue dots.

READING TOOLBOX

Root Words Seism- comes from the Greek word seismos, meaning "earthquake." Gap means "a hole or opening." Therefore, the term seismic gap refers to a break in the occurrence of earthquakes in an area.

Answer to Reading Check
Scientists think that stress on a fault builds up to a critical point and is then released as an earthquake. Seismic gaps are areas in which no earthquakes have happened in a long period of time and thus are likely to be under a high amount of stress.

Close

Reteaching — BASIC

Questions Divide the class into small groups. Have students write questions on index cards about how earthquakes affect society. Invite a volunteer to act as host for a quiz game based on the questions and answers. **LS Verbal**

Quiz — GENERAL

1. Why might tsunamis accompany undersea earthquakes? (Faults along the sea bottom or undersea landslides cause the ocean floor to drop or change suddenly. As a result, the water creates giant waves that cross the ocean.)
2. What causes most of the injuries associated with earthquakes? (collapsing structures, falling objects, landslides, fires, and flooding)
3. How are geologists attempting to forecast future earthquakes? (They study past earthquakes, place instruments in fault zones to identify changes in rock motion, map seismic gaps, and look for signs of future seismic activity.)

Key Resources

Technology
- Transparencies
  65 Seismic Gaps

Differentiated Instruction

Advanced Learners

Seismic Creep Have students research seismic creep (constant, slow movement along a fault) to find out how it affects the buildup of stress along a fault. Have students prepare an illustrated report to present to the class.

Close, *continued*

Answers to Section Review

1. Undersea earthquakes cause sudden changes in the level of the ocean floor. This makes the water above drop or rise and sets in motion a series of long, low waves.
2. They may sway with the force of the earthquake so that they tip over onto nearby structures or they may collapse.
3. Remain calm and move to a safe position between tremors; stand in a doorway or crouch under a desk to avoid falling debris; stay away from windows or large objects that may fall; in a car, avoid buildings, power lines, or bridges.
4. Locations where relatively few earthquakes have occurred recently but have occurred in the past may be sites of future earthquakes if stress builds up there.
5. ground tilt, cracks in rocks caused by stress, changes in water content that could alter the rock's magnetic or electrical properties, or gas seepage
6. Sample answer: Buildings or dams should be constructed on solid rock. Plans should be approved by experts to ensure that buildings are constructed from materials that won't loosen and fall off and that they are designed to withstand the motion of the ground during an earthquake. Utility lines and cables should be protected to prevent fires and explosions.
7. Sample answer: I would map and locate all faults near population centers, place instruments along faults to measure changes in rock movements and increases in stress, identify seismic gaps, and monitor changes in nearby rock.
8. *Earthquake hazard levels* are assigned according to the number and size of *earthquakes*, the likelihood of *tsunamis*, and the type of *damage* that may occur, which can be reduced by following *safety* rules and setting up earthquake *prediction* programs.

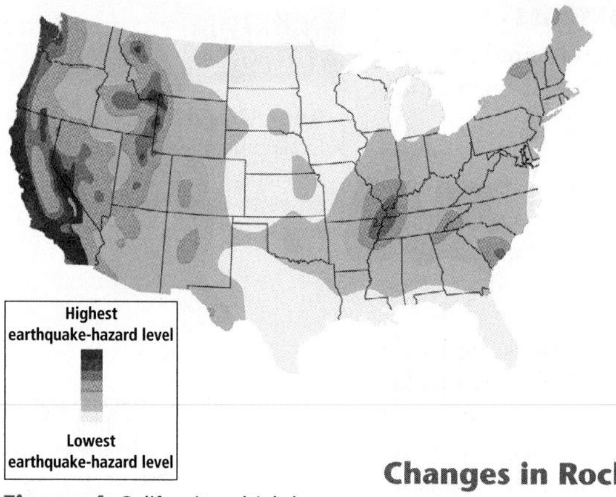

Figure 4 California, which has experienced severe earthquakes recently, has the highest earthquake-hazard level in the contiguous United States.

SCILINKS®
www.scilinks.org
Topic: Earthquakes and Society
Code: **HQX0455**

Foreshocks

Some earthquakes are preceded by little earthquakes called *foreshocks*. Foreshocks can precede an earthquake by a few seconds or a few weeks. In 1975, geophysicists in China recorded foreshocks near the city of Haicheng, which had a history of earthquakes. The city was evacuated the day before a major earthquake. The earthquake caused widespread destruction, but few lives were lost thanks to the warning. However, the Haicheng earthquake is the only example of a successful prediction made by using this method.

Changes in Rocks

Scientists use a variety of sensors to detect slight tilting of the ground and to identify the strain and cracks in rocks caused by the stress that builds up in fault zones. When cracks in rocks are filled with water, the magnetic and electrical properties of the rocks may change. Scientists also monitor natural gas seepage from rocks that are strained or fractured from seismic activity. Scientists hope that they will one day be able to use these signals to predict earthquakes.

Reliability of Earthquake Forecasts

Unfortunately, not all earthquakes have foreshocks or other precursors. Earthquake prediction is mostly unreliable. However, scientists have been able to determine areas that have a high earthquake-hazard level, as shown in **Figure 4.** Scientists continue to study seismic activity so that they may one day make accurate forecasts and save more lives.

Section 3 Review

Key Ideas

1. **Discuss** the relationship between tsunamis and earthquakes.
2. **Describe** two possible effects of a major earthquake on buildings.
3. **List** three safety rules to follow when an earthquake strikes.
4. **Describe** how identifying seismic gaps may help scientists predict earthquakes.
5. **Identify** changes in rocks that may signal earthquakes.

Critical Thinking

6. **Applying Concepts** What type of building construction and location regulations should be included in the building code of a city that is located near an active fault?
7. **Applying Concepts** You are a scientist assigned to study an area that has a high earthquake-hazard level. Describe a program that you could set up to predict potential earthquakes.

Concept Mapping

8. Use the following terms to create a concept map: *earthquake, earthquake-hazard level, damage, tsunami, safety,* and *prediction.*

Differentiated Instruction

Alternative Assessment

Making Models Give students shoeboxes, construction paper, scissors, tape, containers, rulers, small objects, and human figures. Have them construct dioramas and working models to demonstrate the effects of earthquakes on structures, how to remain safe during seismic events, or some of the methods used for earthquake forecasting, such as tiltmeters. They should supplement their models with explanatory labels and diagrams. **LS Visual**

Why It Matters

Detecting Earthquakes

The first known seismic wave detector was invented in China by Zhang Heng in 132 A.D. During an earthquake, a pendulum inside a large urn would move, causing one of eight dragons to drop a ball into the mouth of a frog below. The first "modern" seismograph was installed by Luigi Palmieri on Mount Vesuvius, Italy, in 1856. Today, the Global Seismographic Network has seismic detection stations around the world. Rapid detection of earthquakes allows tsunami warnings to be issued and aid efforts to be started quickly.

The direction of ground movement determined which dragon released its ball into the frog's mouth.

1. Palmieri's electromagnetic seismograph could measure both horizontal and vertical ground motions as well as duration and magnitude. **2.** This Global Seismographic Network station in Antarctica is part of the worldwide monitoring network. **3.** Early warning systems that alert commuter transit systems to slow down or stop at the first signs of shaking could help to save lives.

YOUR TURN CRITICAL THINKING
What is the relationship between detecting earthquakes and quickly issuing tsunami warnings?

Why It Matters

Detecting Earthquakes

Although reliable methods of earthquake prediction remain elusive, inventors over the centuries have devised various instruments to detect earthquakes. Zhang Heng's original seismograph has not survived to the present day; the urn in the photograph is a reproduction. In Luigi Palmieri's seismograph, pencils attached to metal rods recorded ground movements on a moving strip of paper, and a clock showed the time that shaking started. The modern Global Seismographic Network obtains high-quality digital data. Many of the stations in or near the ocean are part of a tsunami warning system. In earthquake-prone regions, early-warning systems are being installed. Even a few seconds' warning might allow industries to shut down pipelines for natural gas or toxic chemicals, or, after a major earthquake, allow rescuers working in unstable rubble to move to a safer location because of an imminent aftershock.

Answer to Your Turn

Critical Thinking Large earthquakes in the ocean floor can generate devastating tsunami waves that can race across an ocean basin.

Skills Practice Lab

Time Required
one 45-minute class period

Lab Ratings
EASY → HARD

Teacher Preparation: 1 flask
Student Setup: 1 flask
Concept Level: 2 flasks
Cleanup: 1 flask

Skills Acquired
- Experimenting
- Constructing Models
- Organizing and Analyzing Data
- Measuring
- Interpreting
- Communicating

Scientific Methods
In this lab, students will
- Ask a Question
- Test the Hypothesis
- Analyze Results
- Communicate Results

Materials
Because the materials required for this investigation are relatively simple, students could work alone or in pairs.

Skills Practice Lab

45 min

Finding an Epicenter

What You'll Do
- **Analyze** P waves and S waves to determine the distance from a city to the epicenter of an earthquake.
- **Determine** the location of an earthquake epicenter by using the distance from three different cities to the epicenter.

What You'll Need
calculator
drawing compass
ruler

An earthquake releases energy that travels through Earth in all directions. This energy is in the form of waves. Two kinds of seismic waves are P waves and S waves. P waves travel faster than S waves and are the first to be recorded at a seismograph station. The S waves arrive after the P waves. The time difference between the arrival of the P waves and the arrival of the S waves increases as the waves travel farther from their origin. This difference in arrival time, called *lag time,* can be used to find the distance to the epicenter of the earthquake. Once the distance from three different locations is determined, scientists can find the approximate location of the epicenter.

Procedure

1. The average speed of P waves is 6.1 km/s. The average speed of S waves is 4.1 km/s. Calculate the lag time between the arrival of P waves and S waves over a distance of 100 km.
2. The graph below shows seismic records made in three cities following an earthquake. The records begin at the left. The arrows indicate the arrival of the P waves. The beginning of the next wave on each record indicates the arrival of the S wave. Use the time scale to find the lag time between the P waves and the S waves for each city. Draw a table similar to **Table 1.**
3. Record the lag time for each city in your table.
4. Use the lag times found in step 2 and the lag time per 100 km found in step 1 to calculate the distance from each city to the epicenter of the earthquake by using the equation below.

$$distance = \frac{measured\ lag\ time\ (s) \times 100\ km}{lag\ time\ for\ 100\ km}$$

Seismograms

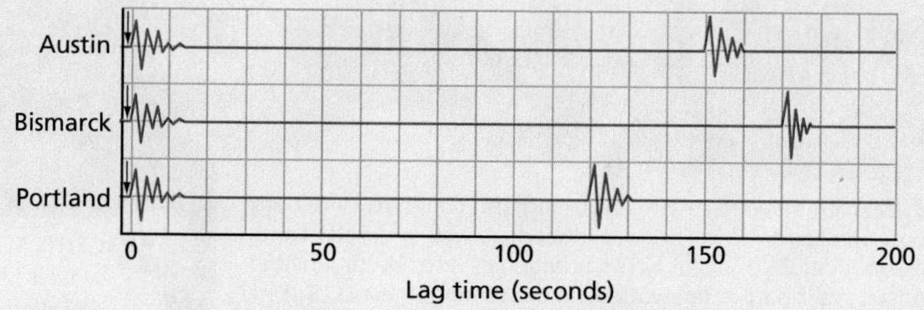

Tips and Tricks
If you choose to have students work in pairs, try to pair a student who is proficient in math with one who is not as adept.

Table 1

City	Lag time (seconds)	Distance from city to epicenter
Austin		
Bismarck		
Portland		

5. Record the distances in your table.
6. Copy the map below, which shows the location of the three cities. Using the map scale on your copy of the map, adjust the compass so that the radius of the circle with Austin at the center represents the distance calculation for Austin from step 4. Put the point of the compass on Austin. Draw a circle on your copy of the map.
7. Repeat step 6 for Bismarck and for Portland. The epicenter of the earthquake is located near the point at which the three circles intersect.

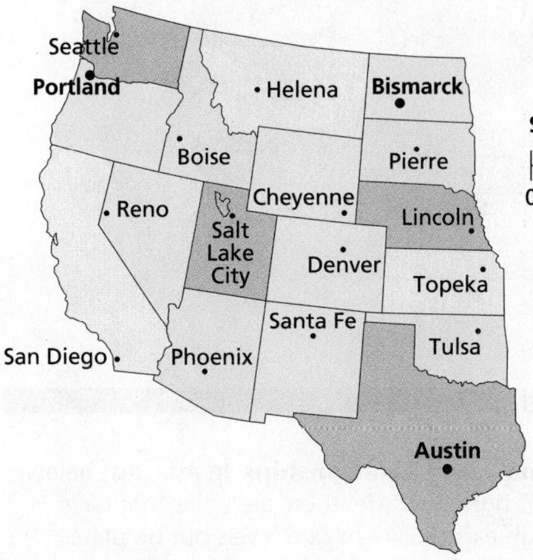

Scale

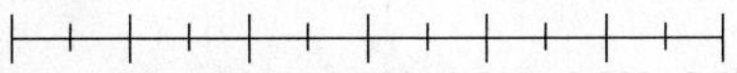

Analysis

1. **Evaluating Data** Describe how to locate an earthquake's epicenter. The epicenter that you found is closest to which city?
2. **Analyzing Processes** Why must measurements from three locations be used to find the epicenter of an earthquake?

Extension

Evaluating Data Research earthquakes in the United States. What is the probability of a major earthquake occurring in the area where you live? If an earthquake did occur in your area, what would most likely cause the earthquake?

Answers to Procedure

1. P wave: 100 km ÷ 6.1 km/s = 16.4 s; S wave: 100 km ÷ 4.1 km/s = 24.4 s; lag time = 24.4 s − 16.4 s = 8 s
2. Lag times for the cities: Austin, 150 s; Bismarck, 170 s; Portland, 120 s
4. Computed distance for each station: Austin: (150 s × 100 km) ÷ 8 s = 15,000 km ÷ 8 = 1,875 km; Bismarck: (170 s × 100 km) ÷ 8 s = 17,000 km ÷ 8 = 2,125 km; Portland: (120 s × 100 km) ÷ 8 s = 12,000 km ÷ 8 = 1,500 km.

Answers to Analysis

1. Draw a circle whose radius represents distance from the epicenter around each seismograph station. The three circles intersect at the epicenter. The closest city is San Diego, California.
2. Three locations are necessary because two of the circles can intersect at more than one point. The third circle intersects the other two at only one point, providing a clearer result.

Answer to Extension

Answers may vary depending on location. Common causes would be living near a major fault or rift zone. In the central United States, earthquakes could result from an old, buried fault being reactivated or the rebound of land from the retreat of a glacier.

Earthquake Hazard Map

Internet Activity GENERAL

Hazards in the Americas Give students an outline map of North and South America. Have them go to the USGS Earthquake Hazards Program Web site for real-time earthquake information. Have students plot recent earthquakes on the regional map, using the map on this page as a model. Ask them to include earthquakes that are magnitude 5.0 or larger and color code the earthquakes by magnitude. Have them sketch the tectonic plate boundaries on their map. A worksheet designed to direct student research on this topic can be found in the **Chapter Resource File** booklet or by visiting www.thinkcentral.com and entering keyword **HQXEQKX.** LS **Visual**

Answers to Map Skills Activity

1. Eurasia north of the Indian and Saudi Arabian peninsulas, Japan, and Indonesia
2. the continent of Africa, northern Europe, and most of central Russia
3. southern Asia, just north of India, just northeast of Saudi Arabia, and off the west coast near Japan; the Mediterranean region of Europe, and Indonesia.
4. Old rifts or other areas of weakness may exist in these regions.
5. The earthquakes generally are not particularly powerful because they occur along a mid-ocean ridge at a divergent plate boundary.
6. in East Africa, parallel to the eastern coast; The entire region represents a moderate hazard zone.

MAPS in Action

Earthquake Hazard Map

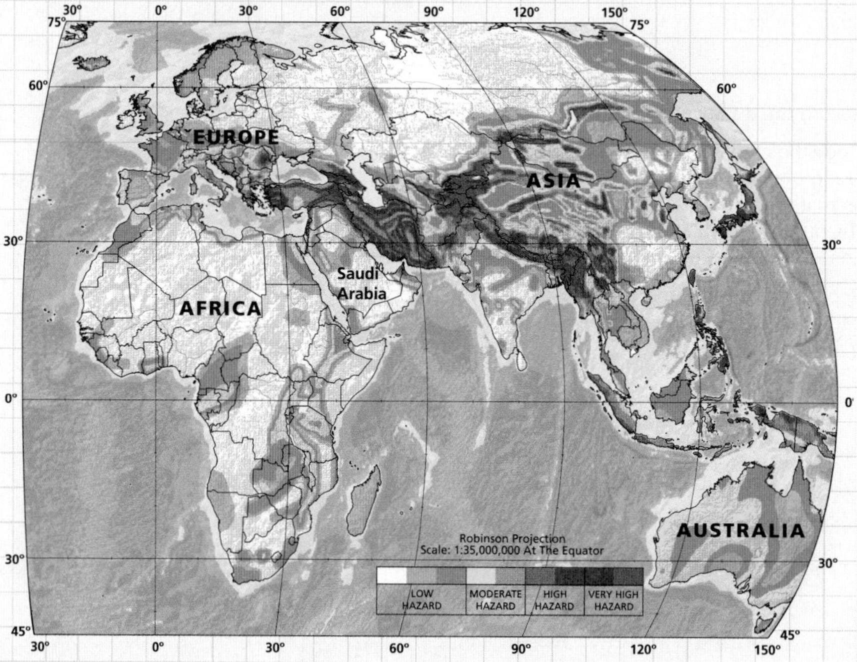

Map Skills Activity

This map shows the earthquake-hazard levels for Europe, Asia, Africa, and Australia. Use the map to answer the questions below.

1. **Using a Key** Which areas of the map have a very high earthquake-hazard level?
2. **Using a Key** Which areas of the map have very low earthquake-hazard levels?
3. **Inferring Relationships** Most earthquakes take place near tectonic plate boundaries. Based on the hazard levels, describe the areas of the map where you think tectonic plate boundaries are located.
4. **Analyzing Relationships** In Asia, just below 60° north latitude, there are areas that have high earthquake-hazard levels but no plate boundaries. Explain why these areas might experience earthquakes.
5. **Forming a Hypothesis** There is a tectonic plate boundary between Africa and Saudi Arabia. However, the earthquake-hazard level in that region is low. Explain the low earthquake-hazard level.
6. **Analyzing Relationships** A divergent plate boundary began to tear apart the continent of Africa about 30 million years ago. Where on the continent of Africa would you expect to find landforms created by this boundary? Explain your answer.

Key Resources

Technology

- Transparencies
  66 Earthquake Hazard Map

Chapter 12

Summary

THINK central SUPER SUMMARY Keyword: HQXEQKS

Key Ideas | **Key Terms**

Section 1

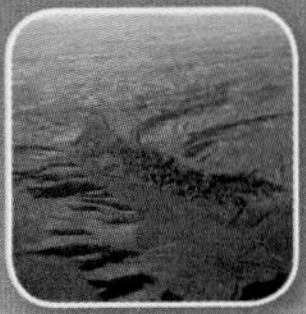

How and Where Earthquakes Happen

- In the process of elastic rebound, stress builds in rocks along a fault until they break and spring back to their original shape.
- The two major types of seismic waves are body waves, which travel through a medium, and surface waves, which travel along the surface of a medium.
- Different seismic waves act differently depending on the material of Earth's interior through which they pass.
- Most earthquakes occur near tectonic plate boundaries, because stress on rock is highest in these areas.

earthquake, p. 319
elastic rebound, p. 319
focus, p. 320
epicenter, p. 320
body wave, p. 320
surface wave, p. 320
P wave, p. 321
S wave, p. 321
shadow zone, p. 322
fault zone, p. 324

Section 2

Studying Earthquakes

- Seismographs are instruments that record earthquake vibrations.
- The difference in the times that P waves and S waves take to arrive at a seismograph station helps scientists locate the epicenter of an earthquake.
- Earthquake magnitude scales describe the strength of an earthquake. Intensity is a measure of the effects of an earthquake.

seismograph, p. 325
seismogram, p. 325
magnitude, p. 327
intensity, p. 328

Section 3

Earthquakes and Society

- Tsunamis often are caused by ocean-floor earthquakes.
- During a major earthquake, buildings can sway violently or collapse.
- Earthquake safety techniques include developing a safety plan before an earthquake, moving to a safer location during an earthquake, and avoiding downed power lines after an earthquake.
- Seismic gaps, tilting ground, foreshocks, and variations in rock properties are some of the changes in Earth's crust that scientists use when trying to predict earthquakes.

tsunami, p. 329
seismic gap, p. 331

Chapter Summary

Using THINK central Resources

Super Summary

Have students connect the major concepts in this chapter through an interactive Super Summary. Visit www.thinkcentral.com and type in the keyword **HQXEQKS** to access the Super Summary for this chapter.

Differentiated Instruction

Alternative Assessment

News Broadcast Have students work in small groups to write a script and perform a mock radio or TV broadcast that describes the effects of an earthquake on a local community. They may wish to include an interview with a "geologist," who could describe the seismic event and its cause; an interview with an "engineer," who could detail the effects on structures; safety bulletins issued by local officials or Red Cross personnel; or first-person accounts by individuals who experienced the disaster. Students could create animations, plan sound effects, or compile video sequences to lend realism to their broadcast simulation. LS **Verbal/Auditory**

Co-op Learning

Chapter Review

Assignment Guide	
Section	**Questions**
1	2, 3, 5–7, 10–15, 18, 19, 25
2	8, 9, 20, 21, 29–32
3	1, 4, 16, 17, 22–24, 27
1 and 2	34–37
2 and 3	26, 33
1–3	1, 28

Reading Toolbox

1. Answers may vary. Students' layered books should accurately describe aspects of the three topics involving earthquake prediction.

Using Key Terms

2–9. Answers may vary but should show that students understand the definitions of and differences between key terms.

Understanding Key Concepts

10. b 14. c
11. a 15. c
12. c 16. a
13. c 17. b

Short Answer

18. Scientists can learn about the composition and structure of Earth's interior by studying changes in the speed and direction of seismic waves.
19. The S-wave shadow zone covers a larger area on the opposite side of Earth from the epicenter because S waves cannot travel through the liquid outer core as P waves do.

Chapter 12 Review

1. **Layered Book** Make a layered book, and label the tabs with "Seismic Gaps," "Changes in Rocks," and "Earthquake Hazard Levels." **READING TOOLBOX** Write notes on the appropriate tab to summarize your understanding of earthquake prediction.

USING KEY TERMS

Use each of the following terms in a separate sentence.

2. *elastic rebound*
3. *fault zone*
4. *seismic gap*

For each pair of terms, explain how the meanings of the terms differ.

5. *focus* and *epicenter*
6. *body wave* and *surface wave*
7. *P wave* and *S wave*
8. *seismograph* and *seismogram*
9. *intensity* and *magnitude*

UNDERSTANDING KEY IDEAS

10. Vibrations in Earth that are caused by the sudden movement of rock are called
 a. epicenters.
 b. earthquakes.
 c. faults.
 d. tsunamis.
11. In the process of elastic rebound, as rock becomes stressed, it first
 a. deforms.
 b. melts.
 c. breaks.
 d. shrinks.
12. Earthquakes that cause severe damage are likely to have what characteristic?
 a. a deep focus
 b. an intermediate focus
 c. a shallow focus
 d. a deep epicenter
13. Most earthquakes occur
 a. in mountains.
 b. along major rivers.
 c. at plate boundaries.
 d. in the middle of tectonic plates.
14. P waves travel
 a. only through solids.
 b. only through liquids and gases.
 c. through solids, liquids, and gases.
 d. only through liquids.
15. S waves cannot pass through
 a. solids.
 b. the mantle.
 c. Earth's outer core.
 d. the asthenosphere.
16. Most injuries during earthquakes are caused by
 a. the collapse of buildings.
 b. cracks in Earth's surface.
 c. the vibration of S waves.
 d. the vibration of P waves.
17. Which of the following is not a method used to forecast earthquake risks?
 a. identifying seismic gaps
 b. determining moment magnitude
 c. recording foreshocks
 d. detecting changes in rock

SHORT ANSWER

18. How do seismic waves help scientists understand Earth's interior?
19. Why is the S-wave shadow zone larger than the P-wave shadow zones are?
20. How do scientists determine the location of an earthquake's epicenter?
21. Why do scientists prefer the moment magnitude scale to the Richter scale?
22. How might tall buildings respond during a major earthquake?
23. What should you do if you are in a car when an earthquake happens?
24. List three changes in rock that may one day be used to help forecast earthquakes.

20. Scientists use computers to perform triangulations from several seismograph stations to locate the epicenters of earthquakes.
21. because the moment magnitude scale is more closely related to the cause of earthquakes and is more accurate for larger earthquakes
22. by swaying so violently that they topple and fall over onto neighboring structures
23. Park away from tall buildings, tunnels, power lines, or bridges and stay there until the tremors stop.
24. Answers may vary but should include three of the following changes: changes in the tilt of the ground, the appearance of cracks, changes in water content that can affect rock's magnetic or electrical properties, and natural gas leakage from fractures.

Critical Thinking

25. because they are most powerful at the surface of Earth where structures are plentiful, and their energy has not dissipated as a result of traveling through the layers of Earth
26. Sample answer: At VI on the intensity scale there is only slight damage to structures, while at VIII there is considerable damage, including the collapse of some buildings. Thus, the city that experienced greater maximum intensity had higher damage costs.
27. no; The Colorado Rockies are located within the North American continent, far from the ocean. Tsunamis result from underwater earthquakes and other disturbances on the ocean floor.

CRITICAL THINKING

25. Understanding Relationships Why might surface waves cause the greatest damage during an earthquake?

26. Determining Cause and Effect Two cities are struck by the same earthquake. The cities are the same size, are built on the same type of ground, and have the same types of buildings. The city in which the earthquake produces a maximum intensity of VI on the Mercalli scale suffers $1 million in damage. The city in which the earthquake produces a maximum intensity of VIII on the Mercalli scale suffers $50 million in damage. What might account for this great difference in the costs of the damage?

27. Recognizing Relationships Would an earthquake in the Rocky Mountains in Colorado be likely to cause a tsunami? Explain your answer.

CONCEPT MAPPING

28. Use the following terms to create a concept map: *earthquake, elastic rebound, surface wave, body wave, seismic wave, tsunami, seismograph, magnitude, intensity, moment magnitude scale,* and *Richter scale.*

MATH SKILLS

Math Skills

29. Making Calculations If a P wave traveled 6.1 km/s, how long would the P wave take to travel 800 km?

30. Using Equations An earthquake with a magnitude of 3 releases 30 times more energy than does an earthquake with a magnitude of 2. How much more energy does an earthquake with a magnitude of 8 release than an earthquake with a magnitude of 6 does?

31. Making Calculations Of the approximately 420,000 earthquakes recorded each year, about 140 have a magnitude greater than 6. What percentage of all earthquakes have a magnitude greater than 6?

WRITING SKILLS

32. Writing from Research Find out how and why the worldwide network of seismograph stations was formed. Also, find out how all the stations in the network work together. Prepare a report about your findings.

33. Communicating Main Ideas Find out which earthquake registered the highest intensity in history. Write a brief report that describes the effects of this earthquake.

INTERPRETING GRAPHICS

The graph below shows three seismograms from a single earthquake. Use the graph to answer the questions that follow.

Seismic Wave Lapse Time

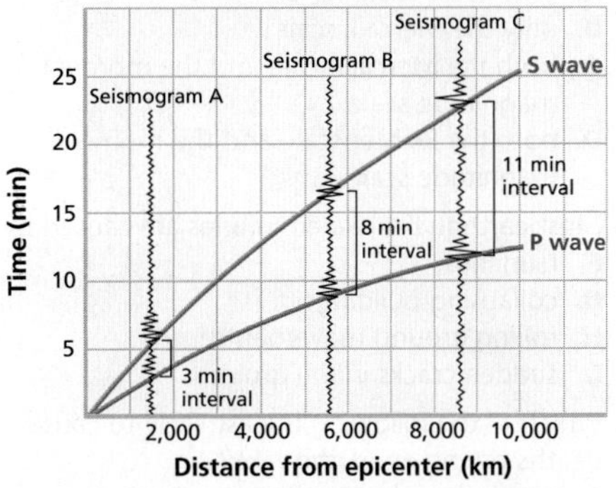

34. How far from the epicenter is seismograph B?

35. How far from the epicenter is seismograph C?

36. Which seismograph is farthest from the epicenter?

37. Why is there an 8 min interval between P waves and S waves in seismogram B but an 11 min interval between P waves and S waves in seismogram C?

Chapter Review

Concept Mapping

28. Answers may vary but should include all of the terms listed. Sample answers appear at the end of this unit on p. 367A.

Math Skills

29. 800 km ÷ 6.1 km/s = 131 s

30. 30 × 30 = 900; The magnitude 8 earthquake releases 900 times as much energy as the magnitude 6 earthquake does.

31. 140 ÷ 420,000 = 0.00033 × 100 = 0.033%

Writing Skills

32. Answers may vary. Accept all reasonable answers. Funding for the worldwide network came about partly because of the cold war. Western powers wanted to be able to detect Soviet nuclear test sites. The scientific community supported the project because it furthered earthquake research.

33. Answers may vary. Accept all reasonable answers. Some remarkable effects were reported during the Assam India earthquake in 1897 and during the April 1868 Hawaii earthquake.

Interpreting Graphics

34. 5,500 km

35. 8,600 km

36. seismograph C

37. There is a larger gap between the P-wave and the S-wave arrival times at seismograph C because the waves had to travel farther from the epicenter.

Estimated Time

To give students practice under more realistic testing conditions, allow them 30 minutes to answer all of the questions in this practice test.

Test Doctor

Question 3 Answer D is correct. The Mercalli scale measures the intensity of an earthquake rather than its magnitude, so answers B and C are incorrect. The Richter scale expresses the magnitude of an earthquake, but it is not the only scale to do so, so answer A is incorrect.

Question 5 Answer C is correct. Students can eliminate answers A, B, and D by carefully reading the question. People suffer more harm from the damage that is done to human-built structures than from the movement of the ground.

Question 9 Answer I is correct. Students should use their knowledge of the different types of seismic waves when answering this question. P and S waves are specific types of body waves and cause little surface damage. So, answers F, G, and H are incorrect. The passage describes destruction on the surface, which is most likely caused by the powerful surface waves.

Chapter 12 Standardized Test Prep

Understanding Concepts

Directions (1–5): For each question, write on a separate sheet of paper the letter of the correct answer.

1. Energy waves that produce an earthquake begin at what location on or within Earth?
A. the epicenter
B. the seismic gap
C. the focus
D. the shadow zone

2. The fastest-moving seismic waves produced by an earthquake are called
F. P waves.
G. S waves.
H. Rayleigh waves.
I. surface waves.

3. The magnitude of an earthquake can be expressed numerically by using
A. only the Richter scale.
B. only the Mercalli scale.
C. both the Mercalli scale and the moment magnitude scale.
D. both the Richter scale and the moment magnitude scale.

4. Most earthquake-related injuries are caused by
F. tsunamis.
G. collapsing buildings.
H. rolling ground movements.
I. sudden cracks in the ground.

5. Which of the following is least likely to cause deaths during an earthquake?
A. floodwaters from collapsing dams
B. falling objects and flying glass
C. actual ground movement
D. fires from broken electric and gas lines

Directions (6–8): For each question, write a short response.

6. What is the name of the instrument that is used to detect and record seismic waves?

7. What is the term for waves that move through a medium instead of along its surface?

8. How can the type of ground beneath a building affect the building's response to seismic waves?

Reading Skills

Directions (9–11): Read the passage below. Then, answer the questions.

The Loma Prieta Earthquake

At 5:04 P.M. on October 17, 1989, life in California's San Francisco Bay Area seemed relatively normal. While more than 62,000 excited fans filled Candlestick Park to watch the third game of baseball's World Series, other people were still rushing home from a long day's work or picking their children up from extracurricular activites. By 5:05 P.M., the situation had changed drastically. The area was rocked by the Loma Prieta earthquake, which was 6.9 on the moment magnitude scale. The earthquake lasted 20 seconds and caused 62 deaths, 3,757 injuries, and the destruction of more than 1,000 homes and businesses. By midnight, the city was fighting more than 20 large structural fires resulting from the earthquake. People suffered injuries from collapses in weakened structures for days following the initial earthquake. Considering that the earthquake was of such a high magnitude and that it happened during the busy rush hour, it is amazing that more people were not injured or killed.

9. What type of waves are the most likely to have caused the damage described during the Loma Prieta earthquake?
F. P waves
G. S waves
H. body waves
I. surface waves

10. Which of the following statements can be inferred from the information in the passage?
A. *Loma Prieta* is the Spanish term for "deadly earthquake."
B. The damage caused by the earthquake continued even after the waves had passed.
C. There were fewer people injured in this earthquake than in most earthquakes.
D. The Loma Prieta earthquake has the highest magnitude of any earthquake ever recorded.

11. The 6.9 rating of the Loma Prieta earthquake is a rating on what measurement scale?

Question 13 Full-credit answers should include the following points:
- letter C shows the surface waves of an earthquake
- these waves are generated when the potential energy of P and S waves are converted into kinetic energy
- surface waves are the last waves to form, they are slower-moving than P or S waves, and they produce the strongest vibrations
- surface waves cause the most damage to surface features and human constructions

Question 14 Full-credit answers should include the following points:
- students should carefully examine the illustration in order to determine the dangers present in the situation
- immediate hazards that non-rescue personnel should avoid include downed power lines, fires, and structural damage
- because this setting is near the ocean, hidden or delayed dangers may include flooding or tsunamis, so people should move inland and find higher ground
- people in earthquake-prone areas should always have emergency plans in place that may include pre-arranged meeting places for family members and friends, emergency supplies for dealing with power outages or injuries, and pre-determined evacuation routes

Interpreting Graphics

Directions (12–14): For each question below, record the correct answer on a separate sheet of paper.

The diagram below shows a recording of data by a seismograph. Use this diagram to answer questions 12 and 13.

Reading a Seismogram

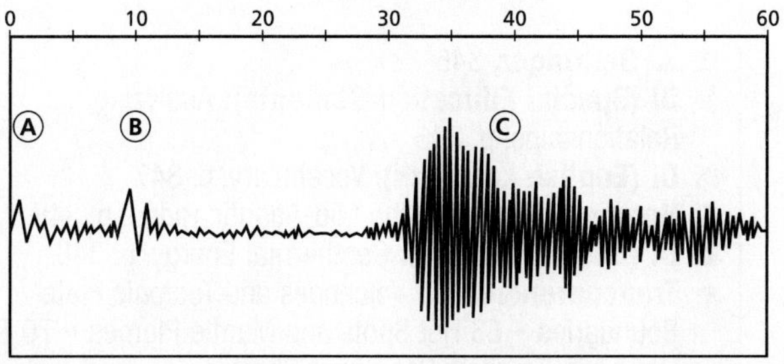

12. What type of seismic waves are indicated by the points on the seismogram marked by the letter A?

F. Love waves
G. Rayleigh waves
H. P waves
I. S waves

13. What type of seismic waves are indicated by the point on the seismogram marked by the letter C? How are these waves connected to the smaller waves that preceded them?

The illustration below shows the damage caused by an earthquake. Objects shown in this illustration are not drawn to scale. Use this illustration to answer question 14.

Earthquake Damage

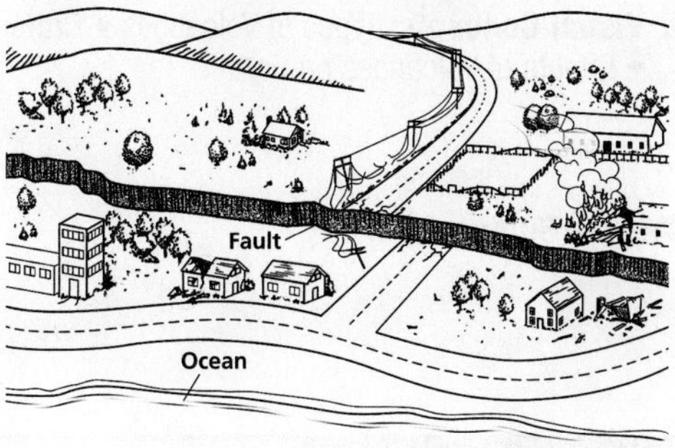

14. What safety hazards can you identify in this scene? What safety advice would you give to someone approaching this scene? How should people prepare for dealing with such post-earthquake safety hazards?

Test Tip

Always read the full question to make sure you understand what is being asked before you look at the answer choices.

Using THINK central Resources

State Resources

- For specific resources for your state, visit www.thinkcentral.com and type in the keyword **HSHSTR.**

Answers

Understanding Concepts

1. C
2. F
3. D
4. G
5. C
6. seismograph
7. body waves
8. The Ring of Fire surrounds the Pacific Ocean.

Reading Skills

9. I
10. B
11. the moment magnitude scale

Interpreting Graphics

12. H
13. Answers may vary. See Test Doctor for a detailed scoring rubric.
14. Answers may vary. See Test Doctor for a detailed scoring rubric.

Chapter Planner 13 Volcanoes

	Time	Standards	Teach Key Ideas
Chapter Opener, pp. 342–343	45 min	**National Science Education Standards**	
Section 1 Volcanoes and Plate Tectonics, pp. 345–350 ❯ Formation of Magma ❯ Volcanism ❯ Major Volcanic Zones ❯ Intrusive Activity	45 min	**ES 3c, UCP 4, ST 1e**	■ ▲ **Bellringer,** 345 ■ **DI (Special Education Students):** Analyzing Relationships, p. 346 ■ **DI (English Learners):** Vocabulary, p. 347 ■ **Homework:** Touring the Mid-Atlantic Ridge, p. 348 ■ **DI (Basic Learners):** Geothermal Energy, p. 348 ◆ **Transparencies:** 67 Volcanoes and Tectonic Plate Boundaries • 68 Hot Spots and Mantle Plumes • 70 The Hawaiian-Emperor Seamount Chain ▲ **Visual Concepts:** Magma Formation • Magma and Vents • Ring of Fire • Volcano Formation at Convergent Boundaries • Subduction Zone • Hot Spots and Mantle Plumes
Section 2 Volcanic Eruptions, pp. 351–356 ❯ Types of Eruptions ❯ Types of Pyroclastic Material ❯ Types of Volcanoes ❯ Calderas ❯ Predicting Volcanic Eruptions	90 min	**ES 3c, SPSP 5a, UCP 2, ST 1e**	■ ◆ **Bellringer,** p. 351 ■ **Demonstration:** Viscosity, p. 351 ■ **Discussion:** Mount St. Helens, p. 353 ■ **DI (English Learners):** Reading Hint, p. 354 ■ **DI (Special Education Students):** Volcano Characteristics, p. 354 ◆ **Transparency:** 69 Types of Volcanoes ▲ **Visual Concepts:** Types of Volcanoes • Crater • Calderas • Effects of Volcanoes on Earth
Chapter Wrap-Up, pp. 361–365	90 min		**Chapter Summary,** p. 361

See also PowerNotes® Presentations

CHAPTER *Fast Track* *To shorten instruction because of time limitations, omit the Chapter Lab.*

Key
Teacher's Edition ■ | Teaching Transparencies ◆
Chapter Resource File ● | Online Edition ▲

All resources listed below are also available on the **Teacher One Stop™.**

Why It Matters	Hands-On	Skills Development	Assessment
■ **Chapter Overview,** p. 342 ■ **Using the Figure:** Forming Islands, p. 342	**Inquiry Lab:** Temperature and Flow Properties, p. 343	**Reading Toolbox,** p. 344	
■ **Section Overview,** p. 345 ■ **Using the Figure:** Pressure and Magma Formation, p. 345 ■ **Using the Figure:** Volcano Locations, p. 346 **Energy Underfoot,** p. 348	**Quick Lab:** Changing Melting Point, p. 347 ■ **Group Activity:** Charting Volcanic Activity, p. 360 ● **Making Models Lab:** Magma in Earth's Crust	**Reading Toolbox:** Some, Many, or Most, p. 346 ■ **Reading Skill Builder:** Reading Organizer, p. 346 ■ **Skill Builder:** Graphing, p. 349 **Maps in Action:** The Hawaiian-Emperor Seamount Chain, p. 360	**Reading Check,** p. 347 **Reading Check,** p. 349 **Section Review,** p. 350 ■ **Reteaching,** p. 349 ■ **Quiz,** p. 349 ■ **DI (Alternative Assessment):** Modeling Volcanic Processes, p. 350 ● **Section Quiz**
■ **Section Overview,** p. 351 ■ **Using the Figure:** Lava Flows, p. 352 ■ **Astronomy Connection:** Extraterrestrial Volcanoes, p. 353 ■ **Using the Figure:** Volcano Types, p. 354	■ **Activity:** Poster Project, p. 353 **Quick Lab:** Volcanic Cones, p. 355 **Making Models Lab:** Volcano Verdict, pp. 358–359 ● **Inquiry Lab:** Lava Flows	**Math Skills:** A Lot of Lava, p. 352 **Reading Toolbox:** Summarizing Ideas, p. 353 ● **Internet Activity:** The Carbon Cycle	**Reading Check,** p. 352 **Reading Check,** p. 355 **Section Review,** p. 356 ■ **Reteaching,** p. 355 ■ **Quiz,** p. 355 ■ **DI (Alternative Assessment):** Modeling Volcano Formation, p. 356
Just How Dangerous Are Volcanoes?, p. 357		▲ **Super Summary** **Standardized Test Prep,** pp. 364–365	**Chapter Review,** pp. 362–363 ■ **DI (Alternative Assessment):** Catastrophic Eruptions, p. 361 ● **Chapter Tests**

See also Lab Generator

See also Holt Online Assessment Resources

Chapter Overview

This chapter describes the ways in which volcanoes form, the different types of volcanoes, and the causes of different types of volcanic eruptions.

Using the Figure GENERAL

Forming Islands The photograph shows lava from Puu Oo (POO oo OH oh), a volcanic opening in Hawaii Volcanoes National Park. The lava flows to the southeastern coast of the island of Hawaii. Ask students what details of the photograph indicate that lava is hot, flowing rock. (The red glow of the lava in the foreground and the steam in the background indicate that the material is hot, while the smooth shape of the rock suggests that the lava flows like a thick liquid.) Ask how the lava becomes solid land. (The hot lava cools on contact with air or water. It solidifies and adds land to the island.) **LS Visual**

Why It Matters

Volcanic rock often breaks down into fertile soil. Following eruptions, many areas around volcanoes show rapid recovery of plant growth. The rate of soil formation depends in large part on climate and rock composition. Lava flows in 1960 near Hilo, Hawaii, showed plant growth in just six years.

Chapter 13 Volcanoes

Chapter Outline

Virginia Standards of Learning
ES.1.a
ES.1.c
ES.2.a
ES.7.a
ES.7.b

Why It Matters

Volcanic eruptions can build landforms such as mountains and islands. Volcanic eruptions can also be dangerous to human life and property. Learning about volcanoes helps scientists better predict eruptions and warn people to leave an area where an eruption is likely.

Chapter Correlations

Virginia Standards of Learning

ES.1.a volume, area, mass, elapsed time, direction, temperature, pressure, distance, density, and changes in elevation/depth are calculated utilizing the most appropriate tools.
ES.1.c scales, diagrams, charts, graphs, tables, imagery, models, and profiles are constructed and interpreted.
ES.2.a science explains and predicts the interactions and dynamics of complex Earth systems.
ES.7.a geologic processes and their resulting features
ES.7.b tectonic processes

Inquiry Lab

⏱ 20 min

Temperature and Flow Properties

Put one teaspoon of corn syrup into each of two small beakers. Place one beaker into a hot-water bath, and place the other beaker into a cold-water bath. Leave the beakers in the water baths for ten min.

Make a ramp by leaning a piece of stiff cardboard against some blocks. Pour the hot and cold syrup side by side on the ramp at the same time. Observe the speed and shape of the two flows of syrup.

Questions to Get You Started

1. How did temperature affect the speed and shape of the syrup flows?
2. How might your observations apply to other fluids?

Inquiry Lab

Central Concept: Students explore how temperature affects the viscosity and speed of flow of a fluid.

Materials (per group)

- Teaspoons, 2
- Small beakers, 2
- Corn syrup
- Cold-water bath
- Hot-water bath
- Stiff cardboard
- Blocks

Skills Acquired

- Experimenting
- Analyzing
- Inferring

Teacher's Notes: You may wish to assign one student in each group to be responsible for lab materials, one student to pour the different-temperature syrup simultaneously, and one student to record questions and answers.

Answers to Getting Started

1. The shapes of the flows were similar, but the warm syrup flowed much more quickly than the cold syrup.
2. Student answers will vary but should include that many fluids are likely to flow more readily when they are warmer.

Using THINK central Resources

An online version of this chapter, as well as all the print and multimedia resources that accompany this program, are available to registered teachers and their students. Log onto www.thinkcentral.com to access these materials and tools to organize your preparation and student learning.

READING TOOLBOX

Everyday Words Used in Science

Term	Scientific Context	Everyday Meaning
volcanic ash	pyroclastic particles that are less than 2 mm in diameter	ash—the powder that is left after something is burned
volcanic dust	volcanic ash that is less than 0.25 mm in diameter	dust—fine bits of matter small enough to be suspended in air
volcanic bombs	large, hot blobs of ejected lava that cool while still in the air	bombs—explosive devices that can be thrown or detonated
volcanic blocks	largest pyroclastic materials; formed as an eruption blasts solid rock from a vent	blocks—square, three-dimensional objects; children's toys

Frequency

Answers may vary. Check to make sure students correctly identify statements of frequency and underline the word indicating how frequently a statement is true.

READING TOOLBOX

These reading tools will help you learn the material in this chapter.

Science Terms

Everyday Words Used in Science Many words used in science are familiar words from everyday speech. However, when these words are used in science, their meanings are often different from the everyday meanings. Knowing the definitions of such words lets you use them correctly in scientific contexts.

Your Turn As you read Section 2, make a table like the one below for the terms *volcanic ash, volcanic dust, volcanic bombs,* and *volcanic blocks.* Include the scientific context of the term and the everyday meaning of the word that comes after the word *volcanic.*

Term	Scientific Context	Everyday Meaning
volcanic ash	pyroclastic particles that are less than 2 mm in diameter	ash—the powder that is left after something is burned

Frequency

Some, Many, or Most? Many statements include a word that tells you how often the statement is true. Examples of frequency words are *sometimes, commonly,* and *usually.* Words such as *some, many,* and *most* tell you about frequency in number.

Your Turn As you read Section 2, make a list of statements that contain frequency words. For each statement in your list, underline the word or phrase that tells how frequently the statement is true. An example is given below.

Frequency Statement:
Most volcanic dust and ash settles on the land that immediately surrounds the volcano.

Note Taking

Summarizing Ideas Summarizing the text under a heading is a simple way to take notes. Tips on summarizing are listed below.

1. Summary statements should be short but should fully express the idea.
2. Many paragraphs start or end with a sentence that summarizes the main idea of the paragraph.
3. In some cases, you may need more than one sentence to summarize a paragraph.

Your Turn Use summarizing to take notes for Section 1. Include the section titles and red or green headings. The example below can help you get started.

Section 1—Volcanoes and Plate Tectonics
- Many volcanic eruptions are caused by the movement of tectonic plates.

Formation of Magma
- Rock can melt into magma when the rock's temperature rises, the pressure on the rock is lowered, or fluids are added.

For more information on how to use these and other tools, see **Appendix A**.

Note Taking

Answers may vary. Students' summaries should be similar to the example shown. Students can consult **Appendix A** for tips on summarizing.

SECTION 1

Volcanoes and Plate Tectonics

Key Ideas	Key Terms	Why It Matters
› Describe the three conditions under which magma can form. › Explain what volcanism is. › Identify three tectonic settings where volcanoes form. › Describe how magma can form plutons.	magma volcanism lava volcano hot spot	The heat associated with volcanic activity can be used as a source of nonpolluting geothermal energy. Volcanoes are a window into this underground resource.

Volcanic eruptions can cause some of the most dramatic changes to Earth's surface. Some eruptions can be more powerful than the explosion of an atomic bomb. The cause of many of these eruptions is the movement of tectonic plates. The movement of tectonic plates is driven by Earth's internal heat.

By studying temperatures within Earth, scientists can learn more about volcanic eruptions. **Figure 1** shows estimates of Earth's inner temperatures and pressures. The combined temperature and pressure in the lower part of the mantle keeps the rocks below their melting point.

Formation of Magma

Despite the high temperature in the mantle, most of this zone remains solid because of the large amount of pressure from the surrounding rock. Sometimes, however, solid mantle and crust melt to form **magma,** or liquid rock that forms under Earth's surface.

Magma can form under three conditions. First, if the temperature of rock rises above the melting point of the minerals the rock is composed of, the rock will melt. Second, if enough pressure is removed from the rock, the melting point will decrease and the rock will melt. Third, the addition of fluids, such as water, may decrease the melting point of some minerals in the rock and cause the rock to melt.

magma liquid rock produced under Earth's surface

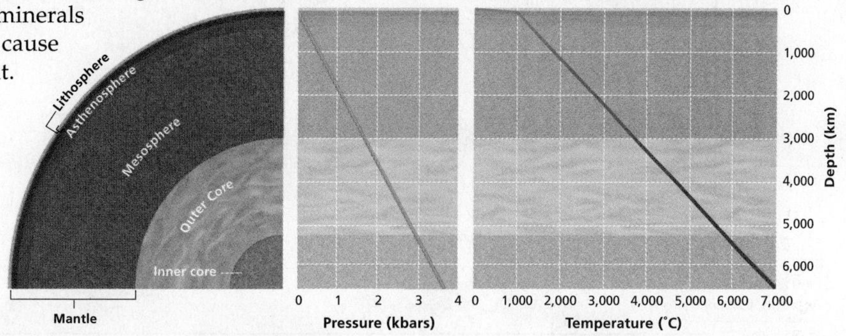

Figure 1 Temperature and pressure increase as depth beneath Earth's surface increases. So, rock in the lower mantle stays below its melting point.

Section 1

Focus

Overview

This section describes how plate tectonics affects the formation of volcanoes. This section also describes how different types of activities between and within lithospheric plates produce magma and how magma forms different types of volcanoes and intrusions.

Bellringer

Have students describe what they think of when they hear the terms *volcano* and *volcanic eruption.* Ask students to explain how and where volcanoes form. (Answers may vary. You may want to use students' answers to address misconceptions about volcanoes.)

LS Intrapersonal

Motivate

Using the Figure — GENERAL

Pressure and Magma Formation Explain that pressure keeps heated rock in a solid state. Reducing pressure causes the rock to melt without an increase in temperature. Ask students to look at the figure and explain why the rock in the mantle is solid. (Pressure from the overlying layers of rock keeps the mantle solid.)

LS Visual/Logical

Key Resources

Chapter Resource File

- Directed Reading BASIC
- Making Models Lab: Magma in Earth's Crust GENERAL

Technology

- Transparencies
  Bellringer

Teach

READING TOOLBOX

Some, Many, or Most? Check students' lists to make sure that students correctly identify statements of frequency.

Using the Figure — GENERAL

Volcano Locations Have students note where most of the active volcanoes are located on the map, and have them identify five regions that have high concentrations of active volcanoes. (Lists may include the following regions: Indonesia, the western Pacific Rim, Alaska and the Aleutian Islands, Central America, the west coast of South America, Iceland, and eastern Africa.) **LS Visual**

Reading Skill Builder — BASIC

Reading Organizer Have students make a concept map that relates volcanism to the movement of magma, the increase in the amount of magma as it rises to Earth's surface, and the difference between magma and lava. Students can later use the concept map as a study guide. **LS Logical** English Language Learners

volcanism any activity that includes the movement of magma toward or onto Earth's surface

lava magma that flows onto Earth's surface; the rock that forms when lava cools and solidifies

volcano a vent or fissure in Earth's surface through which magma and gases are expelled

Academic Vocabulary

expel (ek SPEL) to eliminate or drive out a contained substance

Volcanism

Any activity that includes the movement of magma onto Earth's surface is called **volcanism.** Magma rises upward through the crust because the magma is less dense than the surrounding rock. As bodies of magma rise toward the surface, they can become larger in two ways. First, because they are so hot, they can melt some of the surrounding rock. Second, as the magma rises, it is forced into cracks in the surrounding rock. This process causes large blocks of overlying rock to break off and melt. Both of these processes add material to the magma body.

When magma erupts onto Earth's surface, the magma is then called **lava.** As lava flows from an opening, or *vent*, it might build up as a cone of material that eventually forms a mountain. The vent in Earth's surface through which magma and gases are expelled is called a **volcano.**

READING TOOLBOX

Some, Many, or Most?
As you read this section, make a list of frequency statements that describe volcanism.

Major Volcanic Zones

If you were to plot the locations of the volcanoes that have erupted in the past 50 years, you would see that the locations form a pattern across Earth's surface. Like earthquakes, most active volcanoes occur in zones near both convergent and divergent boundaries of tectonic plates, as shown in **Figure 2.**

A major zone of active volcanoes encircles the Pacific Ocean. This zone, called the Pacific Ring of Fire, is formed by the subduction of plates along the Pacific coasts of North America, South America, Asia, and the islands of the western Pacific Ocean. The Pacific Ring of Fire is also one of Earth's major earthquake zones.

Figure 2 This map shows the locations of major tectonic plate boundaries and active volcanoes.

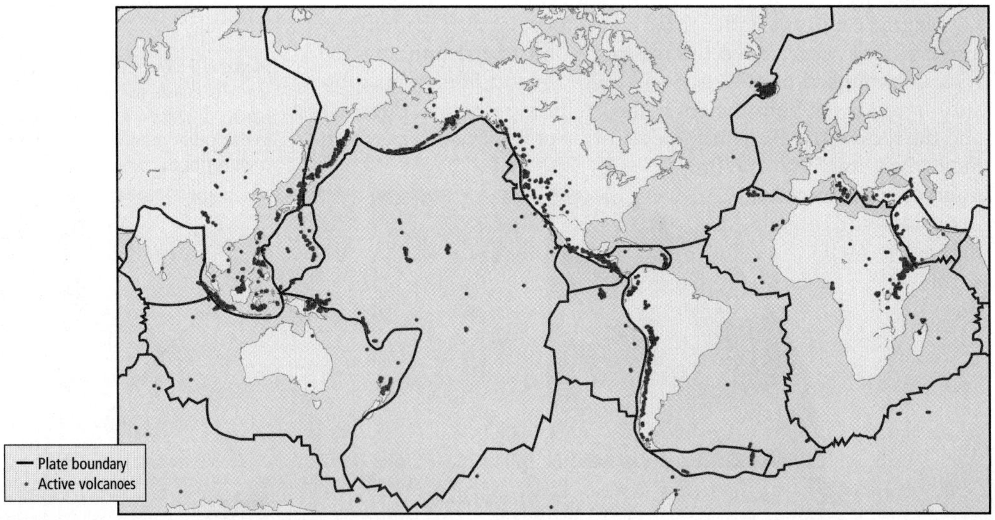

Differentiated Instruction

Special Education Students

Analyzing Relationships Tell students to mark answers to these three directives by using sticky notes as they read the section:

1. Find the relationship between volcanoes and mountains.
2. Find out how deep trenches sometimes form on the ocean floor.
3. Decide if "Devils Tower" is a good name for a pluton. **LS Logical**

Key Resources

Technology

- Transparencies
  67 Volcanoes and Tectonic Plate Boundaries

Subduction Zones

Many volcanoes are located along *subduction zones*, where one tectonic plate moves under another. When a plate that consists of oceanic lithosphere meets a plate that consists of continental lithosphere, the denser oceanic lithosphere moves beneath the continental lithosphere. A deep *trench* forms on the ocean floor along the edge of the continent where the plate is subducted. The plate that consists of continental lithosphere buckles and folds to form a line of mountains along the edge of the continent.

As the oceanic plate sinks into the asthenosphere, fluids such as water from the subducting plate combine with crust and mantle material. These fluids decrease the melting point of the rock and cause the rock to melt and form magma. When the magma rises through the lithosphere and erupts on Earth's surface, lines of volcanic mountains form along the edge of the tectonic plate.

If two plates that have oceanic lithosphere at their boundaries collide, one plate subducts, and a deep trench forms. As when oceanic lithosphere collides with continental lithosphere, magma forms as fluids are introduced into the mantle. Some of the magma breaks through the overriding plate to Earth's surface. Over time, a string of volcanic islands, called an *island arc*, forms on the overriding plate, as shown in **Figure 3.** The early stages of this type of subduction produce an arc of small volcanic islands, such as the Aleutian Islands, which are in the North Pacific Ocean and between Alaska and Siberia. As more magma reaches the surface, the islands become larger and join to form one landmass, such as the volcanic islands that joined to form present-day Japan.

Reading Check **When a plate that consists of oceanic crust and a plate that consists of continental crust meet, which plate subducts beneath the other plate?** (See Appendix G for answers to Reading Checks.)

Quick Lab

5 min

Changing Melting Point

Procedure

1. Place a piece of ice on a small paper plate.
2. Wait 1 min, and observe how much ice has melted. Remove the meltwater from the plate.
3. Pour 1/4 teaspoon of salt onto a second piece of ice.
4. Wait 1 min, and observe how much ice has melted.

Analysis

1. What happened to the rate of melting when you added salt to the ice?
2. In this model, what is represented by the ice? by the salt?

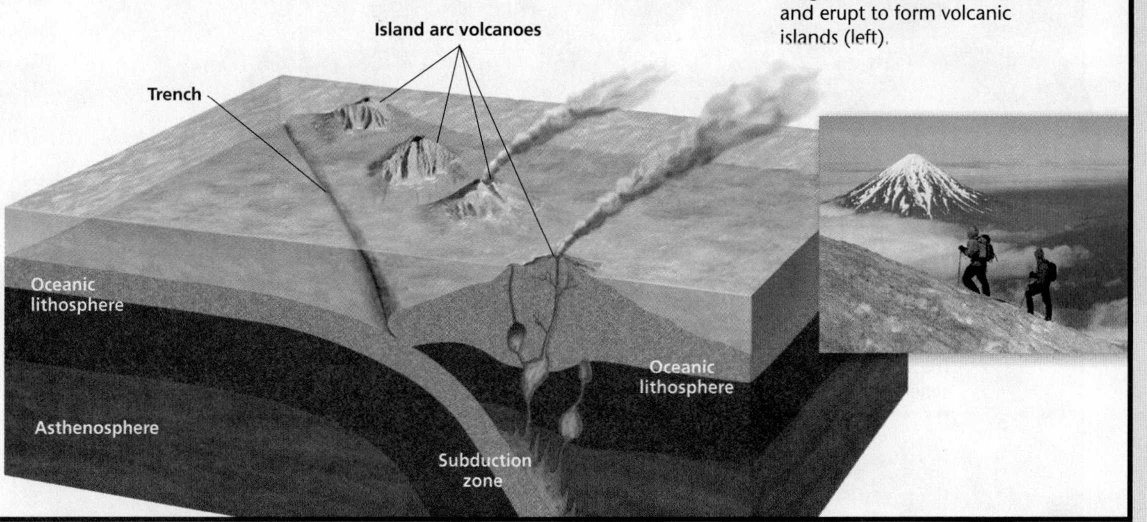

Figure 3 The Aleutian Islands (below) formed when oceanic lithosphere subducted beneath oceanic lithosphere and caused magma to rise to the surface and erupt to form volcanic islands (left).

Quick Lab

Skills Acquired

- Experimenting
- Observing
- Interpreting
- Inferring

Materials

- Ice, pieces, 2
- Paper plate, small
- Salt, 1/4 tsp

Teacher's Notes: Be sure that both pieces of ice are initially the same size and that both are equally unmelted at the beginning of each observation.

Answers to Analysis

1. The rate of melting increased.
2. The ice represents solid rock. The salt represents fluids that were added to the rock.

Answer to Reading Check

The denser plate of oceanic lithosphere subducts beneath the less dense plate of continental lithosphere.

Differentiated Instruction

English Learners

Vocabulary Many of the early terms that relate to volcanism are Latin in origin. The word *volcano* is derived from the name of the volcanic island *Vulcano,* which the Romans believed to be the home of the fire god Vulcan. The word *lava,* although it originates from the Latin *lavare* (to wash), means "a stream caused suddenly by rain." Living near Vesuvius, which was frequently active, the Neapolitans applied this word to the sudden streams of molten rock that flowed down the volcano. **LS Verbal**

Cultural Awareness — BASIC

Geomyths Have interested students research the various "geomyths" that different cultures have created to explain volcanoes and volcanic eruptions. Have students explore the role of these natural events in the cultures. Native Americans of the Pacific Northwest, the Polynesians of Hawaii, and the inhabitants of Iceland are examples of cultures that have developed volcano mythology. Students may work individually or in groups. They may present their findings to the class as an oral report, a skit, or a song. **LS Kinesthetic/Auditory**

Teach, *continued*

MISCONCEPTION ALERT

Expanding Earth Students may think of mid-ocean ridges forming in isolation. If that were the case, the continuing growth of the ocean floor would cause Earth to expand. Ask students to consider what would happen if Earth were to grow continually. (Earth's diameter would get larger.) Then, point out that Earth has remained a fairly constant size because as new lithosphere forms at a mid-ocean ridge, an equivalent amount of lithosphere is consumed by subduction or is crumpled up during mountain formation. Because these processes are linked, the surface area of Earth remains constant.

Homework ADVANCED

Touring the Mid-Atlantic Ridge Suggest that students plan a "tour" of the longest mountain range in the world—the Mid-Atlantic Ridge. Have students research the highest peaks in the range and identify the islands to which these peaks correspond. Have them indicate the distances between peaks, as well as which parts of the ridge are most volcanically active. Students should then compile their findings in a short, written report. Encourage students to use creativity in the style of their writing. LS Verbal

Figure 4 When water rapidly cools hot lava, a hard, pillow-shaped crust forms. As the crust cools, it contracts and cracks. Hot lava flows through the cracks in the crust and then cools quickly to form another pillow-shaped structure.

Mid-Ocean Ridges

The largest amount of magma comes to the surface where plates are moving apart at mid-ocean ridges. Thus, the interconnected mid-ocean ridges that circle Earth form a major zone of volcanic activity. As plates pull apart, magma flows upward along the rift zone. The upwelling magma adds material to the mid-ocean ridge and creates new lithosphere along the rift. This magma erupts to form underwater volcanoes. **Figure 4** shows pillow lava, an example of volcanic rock that forms underwater at a mid-ocean ridge. Pillow lava is named for its pillow shape, which is caused by the water that rapidly cools the outer surface of the lava.

Most volcanic eruptions that happen along mid-ocean ridges are unnoticed by humans because the eruptions take place deep in the ocean. An exception is found on Iceland. Iceland is one part of the Mid-Atlantic Ridge that is above sea level. One-half of Iceland is on the North American plate and is moving westward. The other half is on the Eurasian plate and is moving eastward. The middle of Iceland is cut by large *fissures*, which are cracks through which lava flows to Earth's surface.

Why It Matters

Energy Underfoot

Volcanic activity and heat go together! People can harness this energy as a clean and renewable power source. Iceland, a volcanic island, is rich in geothermal resources. Swimmers enjoy Iceland's Blue Lagoon, formed by water released from a geothermal power plant. Using geothermal energy decreases the need for oil and other fuels.

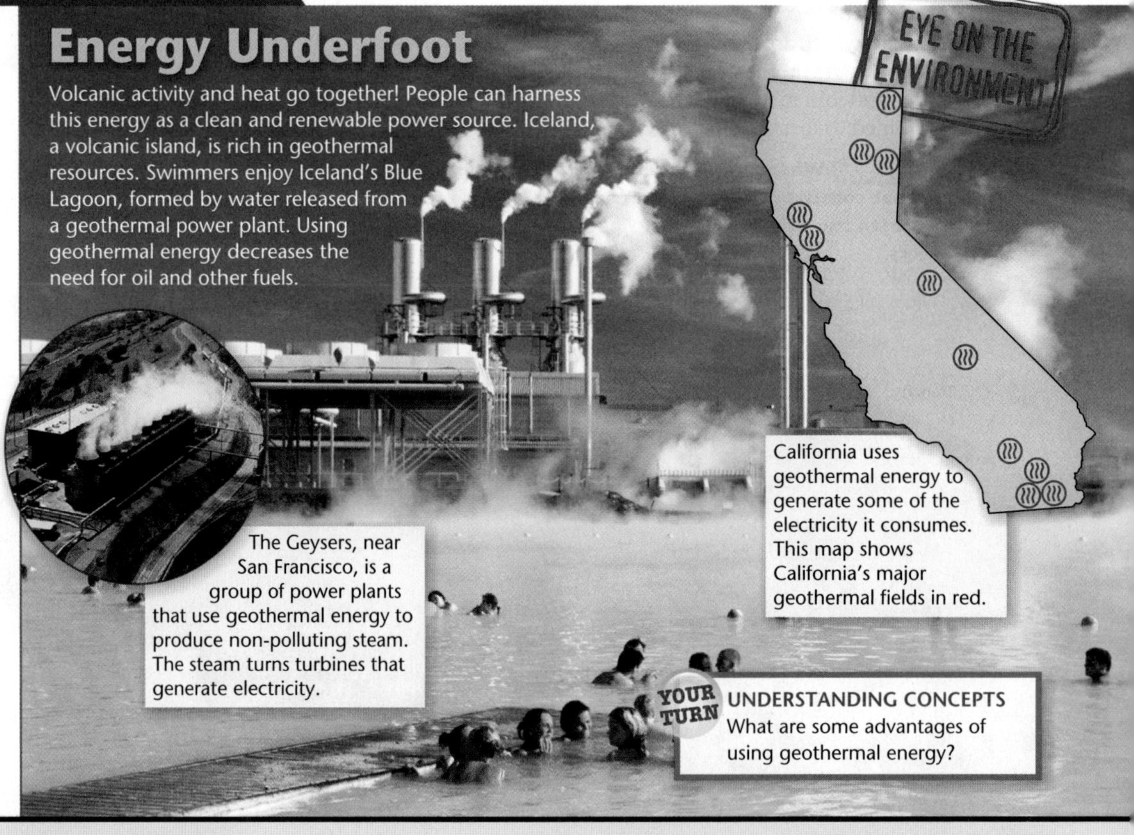

The Geysers, near San Francisco, is a group of power plants that use geothermal energy to produce non-polluting steam. The steam turns turbines that generate electricity.

California uses geothermal energy to generate some of the electricity it consumes. This map shows California's major geothermal fields in red.

YOUR TURN UNDERSTANDING CONCEPTS What are some advantages of using geothermal energy?

Why It Matters

Iceland, one of the most volcanically active areas along the Mid-Atlantic Ridge, has been using geothermal energy for decades. In the United States, California is a major developer of geothermal energy resources. In 2006, geothermal power plants in California produced almost 5 percent of the state's electrical energy.

Answer to Your Turn

Answers may vary but should include decreased reliance on fossil fuels and cleaner production of electricity.

Differentiated Instruction

Basic Learners

Geothermal Energy Tell students that bodies of groundwater indirectly heated by magma beneath the surface of Iceland have provided the island with hot water for heating since 1930. Steam from some of these hot springs is used to generate electric power, which has been done at the capital, Reykjavik, since 1964. Have students research and write a short report on other locations where volcanic activity is used for public benefit. LS Verbal

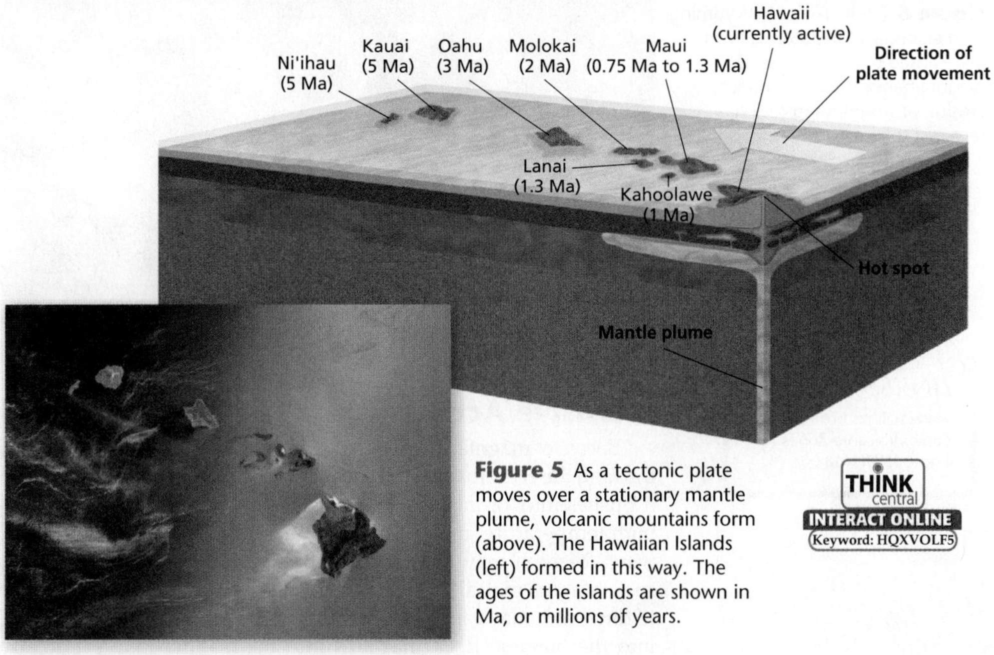

Figure 5 As a tectonic plate moves over a stationary mantle plume, volcanic mountains form (above). The Hawaiian Islands (left) formed in this way. The ages of the islands are shown in Ma, or millions of years.

THINK central INTERACT ONLINE (Keyword: HQXVOLF5)

Hot Spots

Not all volcanoes develop along plate boundaries. Areas of volcanism within the interiors of lithospheric plates are called **hot spots.** Most hot spots form where columns of solid, hot material from the deep mantle, called *mantle plumes*, rise and reach the lithosphere. When a mantle plume reaches the lithosphere, the plume spreads out. As magma rises to the surface, it breaks through the overlying crust. Volcanoes can then form in the interior of a tectonic plate, as shown in **Figure 5.**

hot spot a volcanically active area of Earth's surface, commonly far from a tectonic plate boundary

Mantle plumes appear to remain nearly stationary. However, the lithospheric plate above a mantle plume continues to drift slowly. So, the volcano on the surface is eventually carried away from the mantle plume. The activity of the volcano stops because it has moved away from the hot spot that supplied it with magma. A new volcano forms, however, at the point on the plate's surface that is now over the mantle plume.

Some mantle plumes are long and linear. As magma generated by these plumes rises through cracks in Earth's crust, a line of hot-spot volcanoes forms. Unlike volcanoes that form individually as a plate moves over a mantle plume, hot-spot volcanoes that form in lines over a long plume do not have any particular age relationship to each other.

Reading Check **Explain how one mantle plume can form several volcanic islands.**

Answer to Reading Check

As the lithosphere moves over the mantle plume, older volcanoes move away from the mantle plume. A new hot spot forms in the lithosphere above the mantle plume as a new volcano begins to form. In addition, a long plume can produce several volcanoes at once.

Skill Builder — ADVANCED

Graphing Have students research hot-spot activity in the Yellowstone National Park area. Have them learn the locations and dates of volcanic activity, and have them graph their results to show the direction and speed that the North American plate is moving. **LS Logical/Visual**

Close

Reteaching — BASIC

Volcanic Settings On the board, draw three diagrams to illustrate the separation of two lithospheric plates, the subduction of one plate below another, and a mantle plume rising to a hot spot. Then, write the terms *hot spot, mid-ocean ridge,* and *subduction zone* in a column to the side. Have students indicate which term goes with each image. **LS Visual**

Quiz — GENERAL

1. What happens to solid rock in the upper mantle and crust when pressure drops? (The rock melts, forming magma.)
2. Which tectonic setting that may result in volcanoes is not at a plate boundary? (hot spots)
3. What are structures that form when magma solidifies beneath Earth's surface called? (plutons)

Key Resources

Technology

- Transparencies
  68 Hot Spots and Mantle Plumes

MISCONCEPTION ALERT

Mantle Plumes and Hot Spots Students may think that mantle plumes are melted rock. Stress that the hot rock in the mantle plume, like all the rock in the mantle, is solid. The plume spreads out as it rises to the lithosphere, but it remains solid until the pressure decreases and some of the rock melts to form magma. The resulting volcanoes on the surface, not the plume, are the hot spot.

Close, *continued*

Answers to Section Review

1. Magma forms when the temperature of the rock rises above the melting point of the minerals that compose it, when the pressure of the rock decreases faster than its temperature does, or when it is mixed with fluids that decrease its melting point.
2. Magma reaches Earth's surface by rising through less dense rock in the crust.
3. Magma is melted rock beneath Earth's surface; lava is magma that erupts onto Earth's surface.
4. The denser, subducted plate releases fluids to the surrounding crust and mantle materials, thus lowering their melting points and causing magma to form.
5. subduction zones, mid-ocean ridges, and hot spots
6. A hot spot lies above a column of solid, hot material from the mantle. When the mantle material spreads out at the top of the plume, its pressure drops and the rock melts. The resulting magma forms volcanoes at the hot spot.
7. Dikes are small plutons that are tabular in shape and may be only a few centimeters wide. Batholiths are much larger plutons that are exposed on Earth's surface over an area of at least 100 km^2.
8. Ocean water in crustal rock can lower the melting point of the rock and aid the formation of magma.
9. The volcanic activity in Yellowstone National Park is due to a mantle plume that caused a hot spot within the continental crust.
10. *Volcanism* is the movement of *magma,* which may reach Earth's surface through a *vent,* which is the center of a *volcano,* at a *subduction zone* or a *hot spot,* or may cool under Earth's surface to form a *pluton,* such as a *dike.*

Figure 6 Devils Tower in Wyoming is an example of a pluton, a formation caused by the cooling of magma beneath Earth's surface. Erosion of surrounding rock has revealed this igneous formation.

SCILINKS. www.scilinks.org
Topic: Volcanic Zones
Code: **HQX1618**

Intrusive Activity

Because magma is less dense than solid rock, magma rises through the crust toward the surface. As the magma moves upward, it pushes into, or *intrudes*, the overlying rock. Because of magma's high temperature, magma affects surrounding rock in a variety of ways. Magma may melt surrounding rock, or it may change the rock. Magma may also fracture surrounding rock and cause fissures to form, or it may cause the surrounding rock to break apart and fall into the magma. Rock that falls into the magma may eventually melt, or the rock may be included as foreign pieces within the new *igneous rock*, which is rock that forms when the magma cools.

When magma does not reach Earth's surface, the magma may cool and solidify inside the crust. This process results in large formations of igneous rock called *plutons*, as shown in **Figure 6.** Plutons can vary greatly in size and shape. Small plutons called *dikes* are tabular in shape and may be only a few centimeters wide. *Batholiths* are large plutons that cover an area of at least 100 km^2 when they are exposed on Earth's surface.

Section 1 Review

Key Ideas

1. **Describe** three conditions that affect whether magma forms.
2. **Explain** how magma reaches Earth's surface.
3. **Compare** magma with lava.
4. **Describe** how subduction produces magma.
5. **Identify** three tectonic settings where volcanoes commonly occur.
6. **Summarize** the formation of hot spots.
7. **Describe** two igneous structures that form under Earth's surface.

Critical Thinking

8. **Identifying Relationships** Describe how the presence of ocean water in crustal rock might affect the formation of magma.
9. **Applying Ideas** Yellowstone National Park in Wyoming is far from any plate boundary. How would you explain the volcanic activity in the park?

Concept Mapping

10. Use the following terms to create a concept map: *magma, volcanism, vent, volcano, subduction zone, hot spot, dike,* and *pluton.*

Differentiated Instruction

Alternative Assessment

Modeling Volcanic Processes Have students create a computer model or a series of diagrams that shows the various stages in which a volcano forms by one of the three processes discussed in this section. The models should show the dynamic steps that lead to the formation of magma and its movement through the crust. **LS Kinesthetic/Visual**

SECTION 2

Volcanic Eruptions

Key Ideas	Key Terms	Why It Matters
❯ Explain how the composition of magma affects volcanic eruptions and lava flow. ❯ Describe the five major types of pyroclastic material. ❯ Identify the three main types of volcanic cones. ❯ Describe how a caldera forms. ❯ List three events that may signal a volcanic eruption.	**mafic** **felsic** **pyroclastic material** **caldera**	Understanding factors that lead to a quiet or explosive volcanic eruption lets scientists determine hazards associated with a particular volcano. By recognizing signs that an eruption may soon occur, scientists can issue warnings and save lives.

Volcanoes can be thought of as windows into Earth's interior. Lava that erupts from them provides an opportunity for scientists to study the nature of Earth's crust and mantle. By analyzing the composition of volcanic rocks, geologists have concluded that there are two general types of magma. **Mafic** (MAF ik) describes magma or rock that is rich in magnesium and iron and is commonly dark in color. **Felsic** (FEL sik) describes magma or rock that is rich in light-colored silicate materials. Mafic rock commonly makes up the oceanic crust, whereas felsic rock is more common than mafic rock in continental crust.

Types of Eruptions

The *viscosity*, or resistance to flow, of magma affects the force with which a particular volcano will erupt. The viscosity of magma is determined by the magma's composition. Because mafic magmas produce runny lava that has a low viscosity, they typically cause quiet eruptions. Because felsic magmas produce sticky lava that has a high viscosity, they typically cause explosive eruptions. Magma that contains large amounts of trapped, dissolved gases is more likely to produce explosive eruptions than is magma that contains small amounts of dissolved gases.

mafic describes magma or igneous rock that is rich in magnesium and iron and that is generally dark in color

felsic describes magma or igneous rock that is rich in feldspars and silica and that is generally light in color

Quiet Eruptions

Oceanic volcanoes commonly form from mafic magma. Because of mafic magma's low viscosity, gases can easily escape from mafic magma. Eruptions from oceanic volcanoes, such as those in Hawaii, shown in **Figure 1**, are usually quiet.

Figure 1 Lava flows from a quiet eruption like a red-hot river would flow. This lava flowed several miles from the Kilauea volcano to the sea.

Section 2

Focus

Overview

This section describes the effect of composition on the viscosity of magma, the types of pyroclastic materials, and the three main types of volcanoes. This section also describes how calderas form and how eruptions are predicted.

Bellringer

Have students draw a picture of a volcanic eruption. Use the pictures to start a discussion of the factors that determine the characteristics of an eruption. **LS Visual**

Motivate

Demonstration — GENERAL

Viscosity Wear a lab apron and goggles, and cover a table with newspapers. Be sure students observe from more than three feet away. Obtain three 400 mL beakers. Place the beakers on the newspapers. Fill one beaker with 100 mL of water, the second with 100 mL of cooking oil, and the third with 100 mL of honey. Using a drinking straw, blow bubbles gently into each of the liquids. Have students note which liquid traps the most bubbles. (honey) Explain that more viscous fluids trap more gases. The increased pressure of trapped gases causes more violent eruptions. **LS Visual**

Key Resources

Chapter Resource File
- Directed Reading BASIC
- Inquiry Lab: Lava Flows GENERAL
- Internet Activity: The Carbon Cycle GENERAL

Technology
- Transparencies
  Bellringer

Teach

Using the Figure BASIC

Lava Flows Emphasize to students that these flows apply specifically to mafic magma. Help students remember the names by noting the smooth, flowing sound of the word *pahoehoe* is like the smooth, flowing look of that rock. The word *aa* has a broken, abrupt sound, like the broken, sharp rock of that name. Point out that blocky lava is rougher and larger than aa lava, as if made of aa blocks. **LS Visual**

Math Skills

Answer

number of years for lava flow = 2003 − 1986 = 17 years

$(2.5\ km^3/17\ years) \times (1{,}000{,}000{,}000\ m^3/km^3) = 2{,}500{,}000{,}000\ m^3/17\ years = 147\ million\ m^3/year$

Answer to Reading Check

The faster the rate of flow is and the higher the gas content is, the more broken up and rough the resulting cooled lava will be.

Figure 2 Types of Mafic Lava Flows

Pahoehoe is the least viscous type of mafic lava. It forms wrinkly volcanic rock when it cools.

Aa lava is more viscous than pahoehoe lava and forms sharp volcanic rock when it cools.

Blocky lava is the most viscous type of mafic lava and forms chunky volcanic rock when it cools.

Lava Flows

When mafic lava cools rapidly, a crust forms on the surface of the flow. If the lava continues to flow after the crust forms, the crust wrinkles to form a volcanic rock called *pahoehoe* (pah HOH ee HOH ee), which is shown in **Figure 2.** Pahoehoe forms from hot, fluid lava. As it cools, it forms a smooth, ropy texture. Pahoehoe actually means "ropy" in Hawaiian.

If the crusted-over surface of the lava deforms rapidly or grows too thick to form wrinkles, the surface breaks into jagged chunks to form *aa* (AH AH). Aa forms from lava that has the same composition as pahoehoe lava. Aa lava's texture results from differences in gas content and in the rate and slope of the lava flow.

Blocky lava has a higher silica content than aa lava does, which makes blocky lava more viscous than aa lava. The high viscosity causes the cooled lava at the surface to break into large chunks, while the hot lava underneath continues to flow. This process gives the lava flow a blocky appearance.

Math Skills

A Lot of Lava Since late 1986, Kilauea volcano in Hawaii has been erupting mafic lava. In 2003, the total volume of lava that had been produced by this eruption was $0.6\ mi^3$, or $2.5\ km^3$. Calculate the average amount of lava, in cubic meters, that erupts from Kilauea each year.

Reading Check **How do flow rate and gas content affect the appearance of lavas?**

Explosive Eruptions

Unlike the fluid lavas produced by oceanic volcanoes, the felsic lavas of continental volcanoes, such as Mount St. Helens, tend to be cooler and stickier. Felsic lavas also contain large amounts of trapped gases, such as water vapor and carbon dioxide. When a volcano erupts, the dissolved gases within the lava escape and send molten and solid particles shooting into the air. So, felsic lava tends to explode and throw pyroclastic material into the air. **Pyroclastic material** consists of fragments of rock that form during a volcanic eruption.

pyroclastic material fragments of rock that form during a volcanic eruption

Cultural Awareness GENERAL

Vesuvius—Then and Now An eruption of Vesuvius, a volcano near what is now Naples, Italy, destroyed the thriving Roman towns of Pompeii and Herculaneum. In a short time, tons of erupted material buried people and animals alive. The eruption also engulfed—and preserved—public buildings, homes, and important art and engineering works. Scholars have excavated the sites and studied the artifacts. Today, visitors can stroll through parts of preserved 2,000-year-old homes, markets, and public baths. Colorful painted murals, mosaics, and statuary reflect how people lived. An archaeological museum holds many additional artifacts. Have interested students research what kind of eruption buried these towns, how volcanic ash preserves objects, how the sites were excavated, and what types of information scholars have learned. Students may work individually or in groups, and should prepare a written or oral report or create a diorama. **LS Verbal/Kinesthetic**

Types of Pyroclastic Material

Some pyroclastic materials form when magma breaks into fragments during an eruption because of the rapidly expanding gases in the magma. Other pyroclastic materials form when fragments of erupting lava cool and solidify as they fly through the air.

Scientists classify pyroclastic materials according to the sizes of the particles, as shown in **Figure 3.** Pyroclastic particles that are less than 2 mm in diameter are called *volcanic ash*. Volcanic ash that is less than 0.25 mm in diameter is called *volcanic dust*. Usually, most volcanic ash settles on the land surrounding the volcano. However, some of the smallest dust particles may travel around Earth in the upper atmosphere.

Large pyroclastic particles that are less than 64 mm in diameter are called *lapilli* (luh PIL ie), which is from a Latin word that means "little stones." Lapilli generally fall near the vent.

Large clots of lava may be thrown out of an erupting volcano while they are red-hot. As they spin through the air, they cool and develop a round or spindle shape. These pyroclastic particles are called *volcanic bombs*. The largest pyroclastic materials, known as *volcanic blocks*, form from solid rock that is blasted from the vent. Some volcanic blocks are the size of a small house.

READING TOOLBOX

Summarizing Ideas
As you read about types of pyroclastic material, summarize their characteristics.

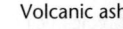

Figure 3 During an explosive eruption, like this one at Mount St. Helens, ash, blocks, and other pyroclastic materials are ejected violently from the volcano.

READING TOOLBOX

Summarizing Ideas Check to make sure students accurately and briefly summarize characteristics of the types of pyroclastic material discussed on this page.

Activity — ADVANCED

Poster Project Have interested students research the classification system for volcanic explosivity—the Volcano Explosivity Index (VEI)—developed by geologists C. G. Newhall and Steven Self in 1982. Students should report the various eruption properties, such as amount of material ejected and height of eruptive column, that contribute to the number assigned to a type of eruption. The roles of qualitative description and the Mercalli eruption classification system in the VEI should be included. Have students present their findings on a poster or make a report to the class. **LS Verbal/Visual**

Discussion — GENERAL

Mount St. Helens Have students research the 2004 eruption of Mount St. Helens. Have students determine what tectonic setting led to the formation of this volcano. Have them determine whether the eruption was explosive or quiet, list the types of materials that were expelled from the volcano, and describe how the eruption affected people in the surrounding area. **LS Verbal/Interpersonal**

Astronomy Connection — ADVANCED

Extraterrestrial Volcanoes Volcanic formations and ancient lava flows have been identified on the planets Mars and Venus. In fact, Mars boasts the largest volcano in the solar system: Olympus Mons. This shield volcano has a base of nearly 300,000 km^2 and a summit that rises 24 km above the surrounding surface. Jupiter's moon Io and Neptune's moon Triton also exhibit volcanic-like behaviors. Have interested students research volcanic activity on other planets and moons. Students should present their findings in a written or oral report. **LS Verbal**

Teach, *continued*

Using the Figure GENERAL

Volcano Types Explain that the three cross-sectional models of volcanoes shown are not to the same scale. Because a shield volcano is produced from lava that flows over a large area, the ratio of its height to the area of its base is small. The pyroclastic material that forms a cinder cone is ejected into the air and falls close to the vent, so the ratio of the height to the base is large. Ask students what they would expect the ratio of height to base area to be for a composite volcano, compared with the ratios for a shield volcano and a cinder cone. (The height to base area ratio for a composite volcano would be larger than for a shield volcano, but smaller than for a cinder cone.) Answer to caption question: A cinder cone forms from highly viscous lava. LS Visual

Key Resources

Technology

- Transparencies
  69 Types of Volcanoes

Academic Vocabulary

variety (vuh RIE uh tee) a collection of things that are very different from each other; diversity

Types of Volcanoes

Volcanic activity produces a variety of characteristic features that form during both quiet and explosive eruptions. The lava and pyroclastic material that are ejected during volcanic eruptions build up around the vent and form volcanic cones. There are three main types of volcanic cones, as described in **Table 1.**

The funnel-shaped pit at the top of a volcanic vent is known as a *crater*. The crater forms when material is blown out of the volcano by explosions. A crater usually becomes wider as weathering and erosion break down the walls of the crater and allow loose materials to collapse into the vent. Sometimes, a small cone forms within a crater. This formation occurs when subsequent eruptions cause material to build up around the vent.

Table 1 Volcanic cones are classified into three main categories. ***Which type of volcano would form from lava that is highly viscous?***

Types of Volcanoes

Shield Volcanoes Volcanic cones that are broad at the base and have gently sloping sides are called *shield volcanoes*. A shield volcano covers a wide area and generally forms from quiet eruptions. Layers of hot, mafic lava flow out around the vent, harden, and slowly build up to form the cone. The Hawaiian Islands are a chain of shield volcanoes that built up from the ocean floor at a hot spot, forming the largest volcanoes on Earth.

Cinder Cones A type of volcano that has very steep slopes is a cinder cone. The slope angles of cinder cones can be close to 40°, and the cones are rarely more than a few hundred meters high. Cinder cones form from small explosive eruptions and are made of pyroclastic material. Cinder cones are usually quite small in comparison to shield volcanoes or composite volcanoes.

Composite Volcanoes Composite volcanoes are made of alternating layers of hardened lava flows and pyroclastic material. During a quiet eruption, lava flows cover the sides of the cone. Then, when an explosive eruption occurs, large amounts of pyroclastic material are deposited around the vent. The explosive eruption is followed again by quiet lava flows. Composite volcanoes, also known as *stratovolcanoes*, commonly develop to form large volcanic mountains.

Differentiated Instruction

English Learners

Reading Hint Help students remember which types of lavas form which types of volcanoes. They can remember shield volcanoes by thinking of the flat sheets of rock that are layered, like the sheets of metal or leather on a shield. A cinder cone is made up of ash, which is another word for cinders. A *com*posite volcano is a *com*bination of both kinds of volcanic material. English Language Learners LS Verbal/Visual

Differentiated Instruction

Special Education Students

Volcano Characteristics Ask each student to choose three (no duplicates) active or once-active volcanoes and create a poster that shows which of the following attributes apply to each volcano: quiet eruptions, explosive eruptions, pahoehoe, aa, mafic lava, felsic lava, caldera, shield volcano, cinder cone, composite volcano, ash, and pyroclastic material. LS Logical

Figure 4 Formation of a Caldera

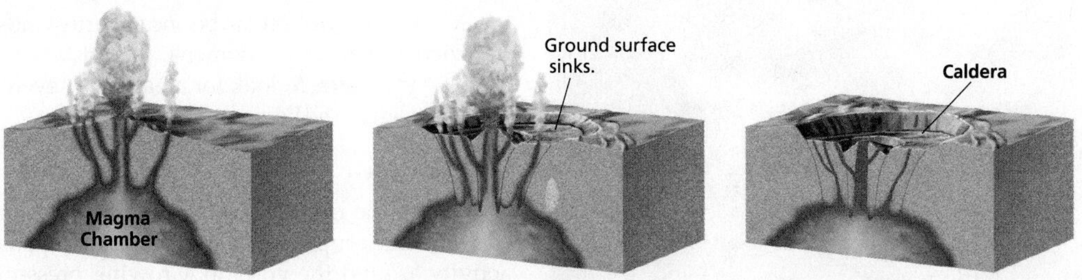

A cone forms from volcanic eruptions. Volcanic eruptions partially empty the magma chamber. The top of the cone collapses inward to form a caldera.

Calderas

When the magma chamber below a volcano empties, the volcanic cone may collapse and leave a large, basin-shaped depression called a **caldera** (kal DER uh). The process of caldera formation is shown in **Figure 4.**

Eruptions that discharge large amounts of magma can also cause a caldera to form. Krakatau, a volcanic island in Indonesia, is an example of this type of caldera. When the volcanic cone exploded in 1883, a caldera with a diameter of 6 km formed.

Calderas may later fill with water to form lakes. Thousands of years ago, the cone of Mount Mazama in Oregon collapsed during a massive eruption and formed a caldera. The caldera eventually filled with water and is now called Crater Lake.

caldera a large, circular depression that forms when the magma chamber below a volcano partially empties and causes the ground above to sink

Reading Check **Describe two ways that calderas form.**

Quick Lab Volcanic Cones

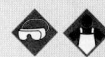

25 min

Procedure

1. Pour 1/2 cup (about 4 oz) of dry plaster of Paris into a measuring cup.
2. Use a graduated cylinder to measure 60 mL of water, and add the water to the dry plaster in the measuring cup. Use a mixing spoon to blend the mixture until it is smooth.
3. Hold the measuring cup about 2 cm over a paper plate. Pour the contents slowly and steadily onto the center of the plate. Allow the plaster to dry.
4. On a clean paper plate, pour dry oatmeal or potato flakes slowly until the mound is approximately 5 cm high.
5. Without disturbing the mound, use a protractor to measure its slope.
6. When the plaster cone is hardened, remove it from the plate. Measure the average slope angle of the cone.

Analysis

1. Which cone represents a cinder cone? Which cone represents a shield volcano? Compare the slope angles formed by these cones.
2. How would the slope be affected if the oatmeal were rounder? How would the slope be affected if the oatmeal were thicker?
3. How would you use the same supplies to model a composite volcano?

Answer to Reading Check
A caldera may form when a magma chamber empties or when large amounts of magma are discharged, causing the ground to collapse.

Close

Reteaching BASIC

Volcanoes, Magma, and Eruptions Make several cards with one of the following terms on each: *mafic magma, felsic magma, quiet eruption, explosive eruption, shield volcano,* and *cinder cone.* Have students combine the cards to form two groups containing three cards that describe one type of volcano. **LS Verbal**

Quiz GENERAL

1. What can you tell about the viscosity of the magma that formed a steep volcano of ash and blocks? (The magma was very viscous.)
2. How would you describe the slope of a mountain that formed from smooth lava flows? (The slope would be gentle with a low incline.)

Quick Lab

Skills Acquired

- Observing
- Classifying
- Interpreting
- Constructing Models

Materials

- Plaster of Paris, dry, 1/2 cup
- Cup, measuring
- Graduated cylinder
- Water, 60 mL
- Spoon, mixing
- Plate, paper
- Flakes, potato or oatmeal, dry
- Protractor

Teacher's Notes: Be sure that the plaster of Paris is not too thick, so that it pours easily.

Answers to Analysis

1. The oatmeal represents a cinder cone. The plaster represents a shield volcano. The cinder cone has a steeper slope than the shield volcano does.
2. The oatmeal would spread out more if its pieces were more round. It would form a steeper cone if it were thicker.
3. The plaster and oatmeal would be applied in alternating layers to model a composite volcano.

Close, *continued*

Answers to Section Review

1. Mafic magma has more magnesium and iron, is darker, and is less viscous than felsic magma, which is rich in silica and feldspars.
2. More viscous magma traps gases more easily than less viscous magma, which may lead to more explosive eruptions.
3. Pahoehoe is smooth, ropy lava rock. When the same magma flows at a different rate or has a different gas content, it may break into jagged chunks called aa. If the magma is more viscous than aa lava, the resulting large chunks are called *blocky lava.*
4. Pyroclastic material consists of fragments of rock that form during an explosive eruption, such as volcanic dust, volcanic ash, lapilli, volcanic bombs, and volcanic blocks.
5. shield volcanoes, cinder cones, and composite volcanoes
6. A caldera forms when the magma chamber of a volcano empties, causing the volcanic cone to collapse in upon it, or when magma is ejected violently and the cone is destroyed.
7. Earthquake activity may increase, rock temperatures may increase, and the volcano's surface may begin to bulge.
8. Explosive eruptions are more likely to increase the steepness of a volcano because the pyroclastic materials rise upward and fall close to the volcanic vent.
9. Sudden earthquake activity could be caused by magma moving upward through the rock around the volcano.

Figure 5 These scientists are sampling gases emitted from the fumarole field on Vulcano Island in Italy.

Predicting Volcanic Eruptions

A volcanic eruption can be one of Earth's most destructive natural phenomena. Scientists, such as those in **Figure 5,** look for a variety of events that may signal the beginning of an eruption.

Earthquake Activity

One of the most important warning signals of a volcanic eruption is a change in earthquake activity around the volcano. Growing pressure on the surrounding rock from magma that is moving upward causes small earthquakes. Temperature changes within the rock and fracturing of the rock around a volcano also cause small earthquakes. An increase in the strength and frequency of earthquakes may be a signal that an eruption is about to occur.

Patterns in Activity

Before an eruption, the upward movement of magma beneath the surface may cause the surface of the volcano to bulge outward. Special instruments can measure small changes in the tilt of the ground surface on the volcano's slopes.

Predicting the eruption of a particular volcano also requires some knowledge of its previous eruptions. Scientists compare the volcano's past behavior with current daily measurements of earthquakes, surface bulges, and changes in the amount and composition of the gases that the volcano emits. Unfortunately, only a few of the active volcanoes in the world have been studied by scientists long enough to establish any activity patterns. Also, volcanoes that have been dormant for long periods of time may, with little warning, suddenly become active.

SCILINKS.
www.scilinks.org
Topic: Predicting Volcanic Eruptions
Code: HQX1209

Section 2 Review

Key Ideas

1. **Summarize** the difference between mafic and felsic magma.
2. **Explain** how the composition of magma affects the force of volcanic eruptions.
3. **Compare** three major types of lava flows.
4. **Define** *pyroclastic material,* and list three examples.
5. **Identify** the three main types of volcanic cones.
6. **Describe** how calderas form.
7. **List** three events that may precede a volcanic eruption.

Critical Thinking

8. **Applying Ideas** Would quiet eruptions or explosive eruptions be more likely to increase the steepness of a volcanic cone? Explain your answer.
9. **Drawing Conclusions** Why would a sudden increase in earthquake activity around a volcano indicate a possible eruption?

Concept Mapping

10. Use the following terms to create a concept map: *mafic lava, felsic lava, pahoehoe, aa, shield volcano, pyroclastic material, lapilli, volcanic bomb, volcanic block, volcanic ash,* and *volcanic dust.*

10. Volcanoes form from *mafic lava,* which produces *shield volcanoes* from *pahoehoe* and *aa,* or from *felsic lava,* which produces *pyroclastic material* such as *volcanic dust, volcanic ash, lapilli, volcanic blocks,* and *volcanic bombs.*

Differentiated Instruction

Alternative Assessment

Modeling Volcano Formation Have students create a model that shows the process of volcano formation or the process of caldera collapse. The model should show several stages. It may be made of plaster, papier mâché, or clay, or it may be a computer model.
LS Kinesthetic

Why It Matters

Just How Dangerous Are Volcanoes?

Lava flows can be devastating, but volcanoes have many other powerful ways to cause death and destruction. For example, the 1980 eruption of Mount St. Helens included the initial landslide and explosion followed by heavy falls of volcanic ash and mudflows. Mount St. Helens is one of thirteen active volcanoes in the Cascade Range. Eruptions of Cascade volcanoes tend to be extremely explosive. In addition to other hazards, such eruptions can also produce pyroclastic flows—fast-moving flows of glowing-hot volcanic material mixed with deadly volcanic gases.

A volcanic mudflow partly buried these mailboxes. Many Cascade volcanoes are topped with ice and snow that can melt during an eruption. The water then mixes with volcanic ash to form mudflows resembling fast-moving rivers of cement.

More than one million people live in the Seattle-Tacoma area near Mount Rainier, an active volcano.

A scientist monitors one of the Three Sisters volcanoes in Oregon for signs of an eruption or landslide.

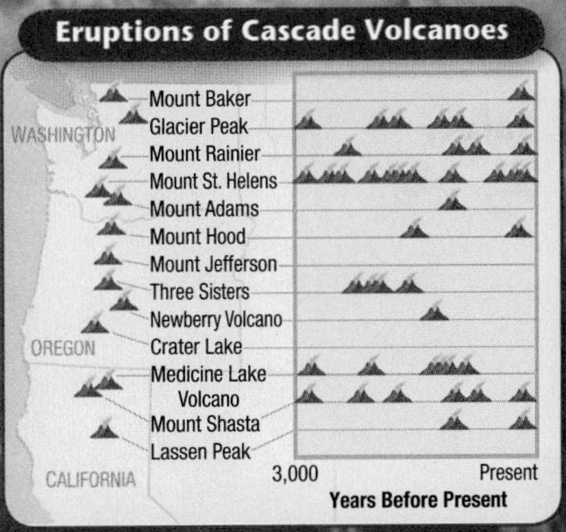

YOUR TURN

UNDERSTANDING CONCEPTS
What dangers are associated with explosive volcanic eruptions?

CRITICAL THINKING
What dangers are associated with volcanoes do not erupt explosively?

Why It Matters

Just How Dangerous Are Volcanoes? The Cascade Range is a 1,000-mile-long mountain chain stretching from northern California to southern British Columbia, near the western edge of North America. Many Cascade volcanoes have erupted in the geologically recent past. More eruptions are expected to occur in the next few decades to centuries. After the 1980 eruption of Mount St. Helens, the Cascades Volcano Observatory was established in Vancouver, Washington. The observatory's scientists and staff monitor volcanoes for signs of activity, assess hazards—which include not only volcanic eruptions but also earthquakes, landslides, and debris flows—and issue warnings as necessary. The scientists and staff also study environmental issues, such as how volcanic gases affect the atmosphere and how increased sediment transport related to volcanic activity affects streams and the organisms that rely on the streams.

Answers to Your Turn

Understanding Concepts Dangers associated with explosive eruptions include the blast of the eruption, heavy ash falls, mudflows, and pyroclastic flows.

Critical Thinking Dangers associated with non-explosive volcanic eruptions include lava flows and emissions of dangerous volcanic gases.

Making Models Lab

Time Required
one 45-min class period

Lab Ratings
EASY → HARD

Teacher Preparation 3
Student Setup 3
Concept Level 2
Cleanup 3

Skills Acquired
- Constructing Models
- Observing
- Designing Experiments
- Identifying and Recognizing Patterns
- Inferring

Scientific Methods
In this lab, students will
- Make Observations
- Analyze the Results
- Draw Conclusions

Materials
The materials listed are enough for groups of two to four students. You may wish to have your first-period students prepare the clay plugs and straws, and then use the same plugs for all of the following classes.

The limewater mixture should be made by adding 1.40 g of $Ca(OH_2)$ to 1 L of water. Using bromothymol blue instead of limewater may provide a more easily-seen reaction.

Making Models Lab

45 min

Volcano Verdict

You will need to have a partner for this lab. You and your partner will act as geologists who work in a city located near a volcano. City officials are counting on you to predict when the volcano will erupt next. You and your partner have decided to use limewater as a gas-emissions tester. You will use this tester to measure the levels of carbon dioxide emitted from a simulated volcano. The more active the volcano is, the more carbon dioxide it releases.

What You'll Do
- **Create** a working apparatus to test carbon dioxide levels.
- **Analyze** the levels of carbon dioxide emitted from a model volcano.
- **Predict** the possibility of an eruption from a model volcano.

What You'll Need
baking soda, 15 cm^3
drinking bottle, 16 oz
box or stand for plastic cup
clay, modeling
coin
cup, clear plastic, 9 oz
graduated cylinder
limewater, 1 L
straw, drinking, flexible
tissue, bathroom (2 sheets)
vinegar, white, 140 mL
water, 100 mL

Safety

Procedure

1. Carefully pour limewater into the plastic cup until the cup is three-fourths full. Place the cup on a box or stand. This will be your gas-emissions tester.
2. Now, build a model volcano. Begin by pouring 50 mL of water and 70 mL of vinegar into the drink bottle.
3. Form a plug of clay around the short end of the straw. The clay plug must be large enough to cover the opening of the bottle. Be careful not to get the clay wet.

Step 6

Tips and Tricks
Students should be sure that the clay plug is tightly and completely sealed in steps 5, 9, and 10. This will ensure that differences in results are due to different amounts of carbon dioxide being produced, not to stray leaks. Students should also be sure that the end of the straw is submerged at the bottom of the glass of limewater.

4. Sprinkle 5 cm^3 of baking soda along the center of a single section of bathroom tissue. Then, roll the tissue, and twist the ends so that the baking soda cannot fall out.
5. Drop the tissue into the drink bottle, and immediately put the short end of the straw inside the bottle and make a seal with the clay.
6. Put the other end of the straw into the limewater.
7. Record your observations. You have just taken your first measurement of gas levels from the volcano.
8. Imagine that it is several days later and that you need to test the volcano again to collect more data. Before you continue, toss a coin. If it lands heads up, go to step 9. If it lands tails up, go to step 10. Write down the step that you follow.
9. Repeat steps 1–7. But use 2 cm^3 of baking soda in the tissue in step 4 instead of 5 cm^3. (Note: You must use fresh water, vinegar, and limewater.) Record your observations.
10. Repeat steps 1–7. But use 8 cm^3 of baking soda in the tissue in step 4 instead of 5 cm^3. (Note: You must use fresh water, vinegar, and limewater.) Record your observations.

Mount Usu, 770 kilometers from Tokyo in Japan, erupted on March 31, 2000.

Analysis

1. **Explaining Events** How do you explain the difference in the appearance of the limewater from one trial to the next?
2. **Recognizing Patterns** What does the data that you collected tell you about the activity in the volcano?
3. **Evaluating Results** Based on your results in step 9 or 10, do you think it would be necessary to evacuate the city?
4. **Applying Conclusions** How would a geologist use a gas-emissions tester to predict volcanic eruptions?

Extension

Evaluating Data Scientists base their predictions of eruptions on a variety of evidence before recommending an evacuation. What other forms of evidence would a scientist need to know to predict an eruption?

Answers to Analysis

1. The difference in the limewater's appearance results from different amounts of carbon dioxide being added to the limewater by the baking soda.
2. The greater the activity of the volcano, the more carbon dioxide that is released by the volcano. A decrease in baking soda decreases the amount of carbon dioxide produced, whereas an increase in baking soda results in a greater release of carbon dioxide.
3. Results will vary with the coin toss. If step 9 is followed, evacuation is probably not necessary. If step 10 is followed, evacuation would be strongly advised.
4. Rapid increases in gas emissions would be an indicator of increased volcanic activity.

Answer to Extension

Ground temperature in the vicinity of the volcano, tilt of the ground indicating bulges due to rising magma, and increased earthquake activity would also be used to predict an eruption.

The Hawaiian-Emperor Seamount Chain

Group Activity — ADVANCED
Charting Volcanic Activity
Organize the class into groups of three or four students, and have each group study a geophysical map that shows an area with long-term volcanic activity. The Yellowstone hot spot, the Mid-Atlantic Ridge, and the Aleutian Islands arc are three possible areas. Students should obtain information about the ages of the various volcanic features. From this information, they should determine the speed at which the tectonic plate is moving. **LS Visual/Interpersonal**

Answers to Map Skills Activity
1. Kilauea
2. Suiko 2
3. Seamounts; they would be reduced in size by erosion.
4. Daikakuji; It is located at the end of the southbound Emperor chain and at the beginning of the southeast-bound Hawaiian chain.
5. northwest
6. about 43 million years ago
7. distance traveled by Emperor chain = 1,500 km; distance traveled by Hawaiian chain = 3,000 km; total distance = 1,500 km + 3,000 km = 4,500 km; average speed of plate = total distance/time; average speed of plate = 4,500 km/65,000,000 y × 1,000 m/km × 100 cm/m = 6.92 cm/y
8. At 6.92 cm/y × 1,000,000 y, Kilauea would move 69.2 km to the northwest, and a new volcano would form at Kilauea's present location.

MAPS in Action

The Hawaiian-Emperor Seamount Chain

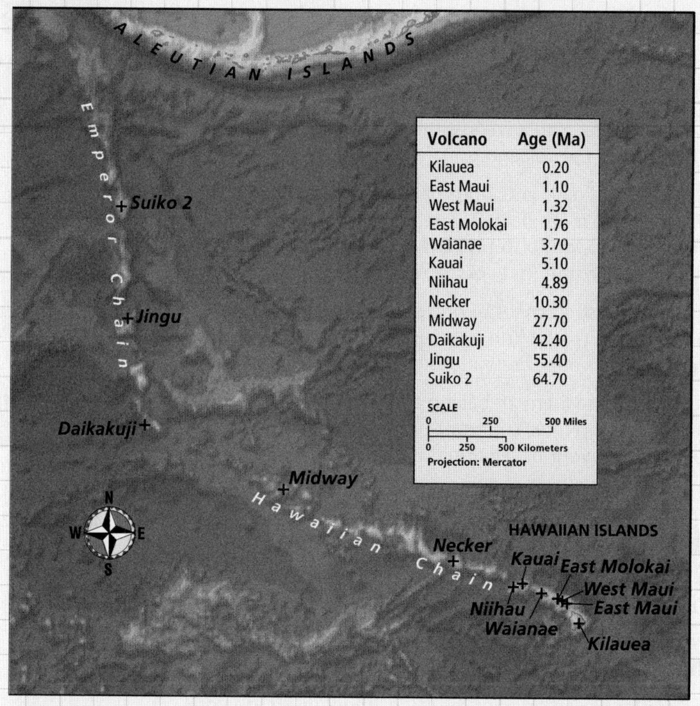

Volcano	Age (Ma)
Kilauea	0.20
East Maui	1.10
West Maui	1.32
East Molokai	1.76
Waianae	3.70
Kauai	5.10
Niihau	4.89
Necker	10.30
Midway	27.70
Daikakuji	42.40
Jingu	55.40
Suiko 2	64.70

Map Skills Activity

This map shows the locations and ages of islands and seamounts in the Hawaiian-Emperor seamount chain, which is located in the Pacific Ocean. Use the map to answer the questions below.

1. **Inferring Relationships** Under which volcano is the hot spot presently located?
2. **Using a Key** Which volcano is the oldest?
3. **Evaluating Data** A seamont is a submarine volcanic mountain. Would you expect older volcanoes to be seamounts or islands? Explain your answer.
4. **Analyzing Data** Which island signifies a change in direction of the movement of the Pacific plate? Explain your answer.
5. **Identifying Trends** In which direction has the Pacific plate been moving since the formation of the islands in the seamount chain changed direction?
6. **Analyzing Relationships** How many years ago did the Pacific plate change its direction?
7. **Analyzing Data** What is the average speed of the Pacific plate over the last 65 million years?
8. **Predicting Consequences** Where would you expect a new volcano to form 1 million years from now?

Key Resources

Technology
- Transparencies
  70 The Hawaiian-Emperor Seamount Chain

Chapter 13 **Summary**

THINK central SUPER SUMMARY Keyword: HQXVOLS

Key Ideas | **Key Terms**

Section 1

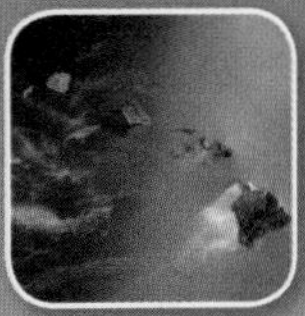

Volcanoes and Plate Tectonics

- Magma can form when temperature increases in or pressure decreases on mantle rock. Magma also may form when water is added to hot rock.
- Volcanism is any activity that includes the movement of magma toward or onto Earth's surface.
- Volcanism is common at convergent and divergent boundaries between tectonic plates. Hot spots are areas of volcanic activity that are located over rising mantle plumes, which can exist far from tectonic plate boundaries.
- Magma that cools below Earth's surface forms intrusive igneous rock bodies called plutons.

magma, p. 345
volcanism, p. 346
lava, p. 346
volcano, p. 346
hot spot, p. 349

Section 2

Volcanic Eruptions

- Hotter, less viscous, mafic lava commonly causes quiet eruptions. Cooler, more viscous, felsic lava commonly causes explosive eruptions, especially if it contains trapped gases.
- The five major types of pyroclastic materials are, from smallest to largest, volcanic dust, volcanic ash, lapilli, volcanic bombs, and volcanic blocks.
- Volcanic cones are classified into three categories—shield volcanoes, cinder cones, and composite volcanoes—based on composition and form.
- A caldera forms where a volcanic cone collapses during a massive eruption and leaves a large, basin-shaped depression.
- Events that might signal a volcanic eruption include changes in earthquake activity, changes in the volcano's shape, changes in composition and amount of gases emitted, and changes in the patterns of the volcano's normal activity.

mafic, p. 351
felsic, p. 351
pyroclastic material, p. 352
caldera, p. 355

Chapter Summary

Using THINK central Resources

Super Summary

Have students connect the major concepts in this chapter through an interactive Super Summary. Visit www.thinkcentral.com and type in the keyword **HQXVOLS** to access the Super Summary for this chapter.

Differentiated Instruction

Alternative Assessment

Catastrophic Eruptions Have students work in small groups to research a volcanic eruption, such as Santorini, Vesuvius, Tambora, Krakatau, Pelée, or Mount St. Helens. One or two students can research what made the event catastrophic, such as caldera collapse, heavy fall of ash, or pyroclastic flows. Another student can report the effects on nearby populations. The remaining student can research the effects at greater distances, such as the effect on climate and on coastal areas affected by tsunamis.
LS **Verbal** Co-op Learning

Chapter Review

Assignment Guide	
Section	**Questions**
1	2, 3, 10, 11, 17–20, 25, 26, 34
2	4–9, 12–16, 21–24, 27, 29, 31–33, 35–37
1 and 2	1, 28, 30

Reading Toolbox

1. The word *mantle* can refer to a cloak or to the portion of Earth's interior between the crust and core. The word *plume* can refer to a column. A *mantle plume* is a rising column of solid, hot mantle material that spreads out when it reaches the lithosphere.

Using Key Terms

2–8. Answers may vary but should show that students understand the definitions of and differences between key terms.

Understanding Key Ideas

9. b
10. d
11. a
12. b
13. b
14. b
15. b
16. b

Short Answer

17. Magma becomes lava when it erupts onto Earth's surface.
18. Tectonic movement can increase the temperature of rock, reduce the pressure on rock, or add fluids to rock, causing the rock to melt. This molten rock, or magma, rises through the crust to form volcanoes.
19. volcanism

Chapter 13 Review

1. **Everyday Words Used in Science** Find the everyday meanings of the words *mantle* and *plume*. Then, compare the everyday meanings of these words with the scientific meaning of *mantle plume*.

READING TOOLBOX

USING KEY TERMS

Use each of the following terms in a separate sentence.

2. *volcanism*
3. *hot spot*
4. *pyroclastic material*

For each pair of terms, explain how the meanings of the terms differ.

5. *magma* and *lava*
6. *mafic* and *felsic*
7. *shield volcano* and *composite volcano*
8. *crater* and *caldera*

UNDERSTANDING KEY IDEAS

9. A characteristic of lava that determines the force of a volcanic eruption is
   a. color.
   b. viscosity.
   c. density.
   d. age.
10. Island arcs form when oceanic lithosphere subducts under
    a. continental lithosphere.
    b. calderas.
    c. volcanic bombs.
    d. oceanic lithosphere.
11. Areas of volcanism within tectonic plates are called
    a. hot spots.
    b. cones.
    c. calderas.
    d. fissures.
12. Explosive volcanic eruptions commonly result from
    a. mafic magma.
    b. felsic magma.
    c. aa lava.
    d. pahoehoe lava.
13. Pyroclastic materials that form rounded or spindle shapes as they fly through the air are called
    a. ash.
    b. volcanic bombs.
    c. lapilli.
    d. volcanic blocks.
14. A cone formed by only solid fragments built up around a volcanic opening is a
    a. shield volcano.
    b. cinder cone.
    c. composite volcano.
    d. stratovolcano.
15. The depression that results when a volcanic cone collapses over an emptying magma chamber is a
    a. crater.
    b. caldera.
    c. vent.
    d. fissure.
16. Scientists have discovered that before an eruption, earthquakes commonly
    a. stop.
    b. increase in number.
    c. have no relationship with volcanism.
    d. decrease in number.

SHORT ANSWER

17. At what point does magma become lava?
18. Describe how tectonic movement can form volcanoes.
19. Name the process that includes the movement of magma onto Earth's surface.
20. What may happen to magma that does not reach Earth's surface?
21. How is the composition of magma related to the force of volcanic eruptions?
22. List and describe the major types of pyroclastic material.
23. Compare the three main types of volcanic cones.
24. What signs can scientists study to try to predict volcanic eruptions?

20. Magma that does not reach Earth's surface may solidify beneath the surface, resulting in a formation called a *pluton*.
21. Composition affects magma's viscosity. Lower viscosity magma causes quiet eruptions; more viscous magma causes explosive eruptions.
22. Small pyroclastic material (less than 2 mm in diameter) consists of volcanic ash and volcanic dust. Pyroclastic material less than 64 mm in diameter but greater than 2 mm in diameter is called *lapilli*. The largest pyroclastic materials are volcanic bombs and volcanic blocks.
23. Shield volcanoes are large, gently sloping mountains that form from layers of low-viscosity lava. Cinder cones are volcanoes that have steep sides made of accumulated pyroclastic material. Composite volcanoes consist of alternating layers of lava flows and pyroclastic material.
24. increasing earthquake activity, rising rock temperature, and bulging of the volcano's surface

CRITICAL THINKING

25. **Analyzing Ideas** Why is most lava that forms on Earth's surface unnoticed and unobserved?
26. **Identifying Relationships** The Pacific Ring of Fire is a zone of major volcanic activity because of tectonic plate boundaries. Identify another area of Earth where you might expect to find volcanic activity.
27. **Analyzing Processes** Why does felsic lava tend to form composite volcanoes and cinder cones rather than shield volcanoes?
28. **Making Inferences** How might geologists distinguish an impact crater on Earth, such as Meteor Crater in Arizona, from a volcanic crater?
29. **Making Comparisons** Sinkholes form when the roof of an underground cave is not supported by groundwater. Compare this process to the process by which calderas form.

CONCEPT MAPPING

30. Use the following terms to create a concept map: *magma, lava, volcano, pluton, mafic lava, felsic lava, pyroclastic material, volcanic ash, volcanic dust, lapilli, volcanic bomb, volcanic block, volcanic cone, shield volcano, cinder cone,* and *composite volcano.*

MATH SKILLS

Math Skills

31. **Making Calculations** On day 1, a volcano expelled 5 metric tons of sulfur dioxide. On day 2, the same volcano expelled 12 metric tons of sulfur dioxide. What is the percentage increase in sulfur dioxide expelled from day 1 to day 2?
32. **Interpreting Statistics** A lava flow traveled for 7.3 min before it flowed into the ocean. The speed of the lava was 3 m/s. How far did the lava flow travel?

WRITING SKILLS

33. **Outlining Topics** Outline the essential steps in the process of caldera formation.
34. **Communicating Main Ideas** Write an essay describing the formation of a volcano.

INTERPRETING GRAPHICS

The graphs below show data about earthquake activity; the slope angle, or *tilt*, of the ground; and the amount of gas emitted for a particular volcano over a period of 10 days. Use the graphs to answer the questions that follow.

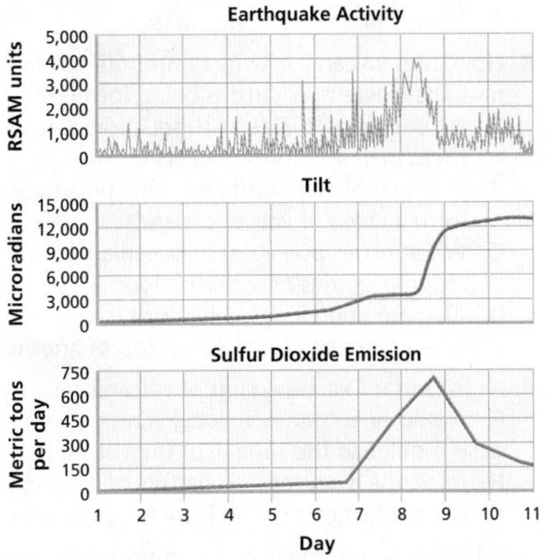

35. On what day did the volcano erupt? Explain your answer.
36. For how many days before the eruption did gas emission increase?
37. Why do you think the slope angle of the ground did not return to its original angle after the eruption?

Chapter Review

Critical Thinking

25. Most lava comes to Earth's surface where two oceanic plates diverge, deep under the ocean surface. The lava is therefore unobserved.
26. Answers may vary. Sample answer: The Mid-Atlantic Ridge, the Mediterranean fault zone, the rift zone along eastern Africa, and the hot spot near Yellowstone National Park are all locations of volcanic activity.
27. Lava from felsic magma is too viscous to flow smoothly and form shield volcanoes. Gas trapped in the felsic magma contributes to explosive eruptions, which form the pyroclastic materials found in cinder cones and composite volcanoes.
28. An impact crater would not have the large amounts of lava flows or pyroclastic materials that would be found in a volcanic crater.
29. Both sinkholes and calderas form when there is no fluid to support the ground above the empty underground chamber.

Concept Mapping

30. Answers may vary but should include all of the terms listed. Sample answers appear at the end of this unit on p. 367B.

Math Skills

31. percent increase = [(new amount − old amount)/old amount] × 100; percent increase = [(12 metric tons − 5 metric tons)/5 metric tons] × 100 = 140%
32. distance = velocity × time; distance = 3 m/s × 7.3 min × 60 s/min = 1,314 m, or 1.314 km

Writing Skills

33. Answers may vary. Accept all reasonable answers.
34. Answers may vary. Accept all reasonable answers.

Interpreting Graphics

35. The volcano erupted in the middle of the eighth day, when earthquake activity, slope, and gas emission increased suddenly.
36. 2 days
37. The ground surrounding the volcano may have been permanently distorted or changed by the eruption, either by being covered with new lava or pyroclastic materials, or by being blasted away by the eruption.

Estimated Time

To give students practice under more realistic testing conditions, allow them 30 minutes to answer all of the questions in this practice test.

Test Doctor

Question 1 Answer B is correct. Answers A and D are incorrect because basalt and mafic magma make up most of Earth's *oceanic* crust. Answer C is incorrect because although limestone is a common crustal rock, it is formed from sediments and is not volcanic in origin.

Question 10 Full-credit answers should include the following points:
- erupting volcanoes throw out dust, ash, fragments of rock, and lava, as well as dissolved CO_2 gas and sulphur compounds
- eruptions can send gases and volcanic dust high into the atmosphere, where they are able to travel all over the world
- volcanic particles could contribute to global warming by providing surfaces for ozone reactions or by adding CO_2, a greenhouse gas, to the air
- multiple large-scale eruptions over a short period of time would be required to produce longer-term effects to the climate
- if dust blocked sunlight for a long period of time, a reduction in plant growth could lead to ecological imbalances, possibly long-term

Chapter 13 Standardized Test Prep

Understanding Concepts

Directions (1–5): For each question, write on a separate sheet of paper the letter of the correct answer.

1. What type of volcanic rock commonly makes up much of the continental crust?
   A. basalt rock that is rich in olivines
   B. felsic rock that is rich in silicates
   C. limestone that is rich in calcium carbonate
   D. mafic rock that is rich in iron and magnesium
2. Which of the following formations results from magma that cools before it reaches Earth's surface?
   F. batholiths
   G. mantle plumes
   H. volcanic blocks
   I. aa lava
3. How does volcanic activity contribute to plate margins where new crust is being formed?
   A. Where plates collide at subduction zones, rocks melt and form pockets of magma.
   B. Between plate boundaries, hot spots may form a chain of volcanic islands.
   C. When plates pull apart at oceanic ridges, magma creates new ocean floor.
   D. At some boundaries, new crust is formed when one plate is forced on top of another.
4. An important warning sign of volcanic activity
   F. would be a change in local wind patterns.
   G. is a bulge in the surface of the volcano.
   H. might be a decrease in earthquake activity.
   I. is a marked increase in local temperatures.
5. Which aspect of mafic lava is important in the formation of smooth, ropy pahoehoe lava?
   A. a fairly high viscosity
   B. a fairly low viscosity
   C. rapidly deforming crust
   D. rapid underwater cooling

Directions (6–7): For each question, write a short response.

6. What is the name of rounded blobs of lava formed by the rapid, underwater cooling of lava?
7. Where is the Ring of Fire located?

Reading Skills

Directions (8–10): Read the passage below. Then, answer the questions.

Volcanoes That Changed the Weather

In 1815, Mount Tambora in Indonesia erupted violently. Following this eruption, one of the largest recorded weather-related disruptions of the last 10,000 years occurred throughout North America and Western Europe. The year 1816 became known as "the year without a summer." Snowfalls and a killing frost occurred during the summer months of June, July, and August of that year. A similar, but less severe episode of cooling followed the 1991 eruption of Mount Pinatubo. Eruptions such as these can send gases and volcanic dust high into the atmosphere. Once in the atmosphere, the gas and dust travel great distances, block sunlight, and cause short-term cooling over large areas of the globe. Some scientists have even suggested a connection between volcanoes and the ice ages.

8. What can be inferred from the passage?
   F. Earthquakes can create the same atmospheric effects as volcanoes do.
   G. Volcanic eruptions can have effects far beyond their local lava flows.
   H. Major volcanic eruptions are common events.
   I. The year 1815 also had a number of earthquakes and other natural disasters.
9. According to the passage, which of the following statements is false?
   A. The year 1816 became known as "the year without a summer."
   B. The world experienced a period of unusually warm weather after Mount Pinatubo erupted.
   C. Mount Pinatubo erupted in 1991.
   D. Eruptions send gas and dust into the atmosphere, where they travel around the globe.
10. The eruptions described in the passage changed the weather briefly. Some scientists believe that periods of severe volcanic activity can produce long-term changes in climate. Suggest one specific way in which the materials sent into the atmosphere by volcanoes might cause long-term changes in global climate and temperature.

Question 11 Full-credit answers should include the following points:
- students should understand that where the oceanic crust of the Juan de Fuca plate meets the continental crust of the North American plate, a deep-ocean trench forms. Along this trench, the Juan de Fuca plate subducts beneath the North American plate
- the subducting oceanic crust and some continental material melt and supply mixed mafic and felsic magma
- the magma rises through the crust to form the volcanoes of the Cascade Range

Question 13 Full-credit answers should include the following points:
- students should show a conceptual understanding that volcanoes can form in several different ways and that the way in which a volcano forms determines the shape of the cone and type of volcanic structure
- the diagram shows alternating layers and a cone with a steep angle
- the shape and layered composition of the volcano indicate that this volcano formed over a long period of time as different eruptions caused cooled lava and other pyroclastic materials to build up
- composite volcanoes form in this manner

Interpreting Graphics

Directions (11–13): For each question below, record the correct answer on a separate sheet of paper.

Base your answers to question 11 on the cross section below, which shows volcanic activity in the Cascade region of the Pacific West Coast.

Cross Section of the Juan de Fuca Ridge

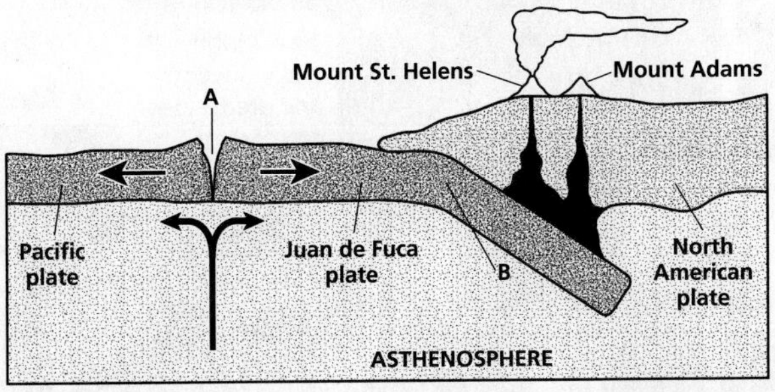

11. Explain how the tectonic activity near point B causes the volcanic activity at Mount St. Helens and Mount Adams in the Cascade Range.

Base your answers to questions 12 and 13 on the diagram of the interior of a volcano shown below.

Interior of a Volcano

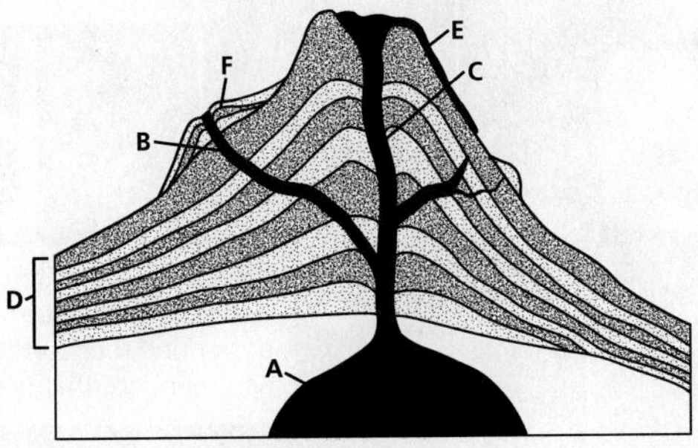

12. What is the term for the underground pool of molten rock, marked by the letter A, that feeds the volcano?
F. fissure
G. intrusion
H. lava pool
I. magma chamber

13. Letter D shows alternating layers in the volcanic cone. What are these layers made of, and what does this lead you to believe about the type of volcano that is represented in the diagram above?

Test Tip

When using a diagram to answer questions, carefully study each part of the diagram as well as any lines or labels used to indicate parts of the diagram.

Standardized Test Prep

Using THINK central Resources

State Resources

- For specific resources for your state, visit www.thinkcentral.com and type in the keyword **HSHSTR.**

Answers

Understanding Concepts

1. B
2. F
3. C
4. G
5. B
6. pillow lava
7. The Ring of Fire surrounds the Pacific Ocean.

Reading Skills

8. G
9. B
10. Answers may vary. See Test Doctor for a detailed scoring rubric.

Interpreting Graphics

11. Answers may vary. See Test Doctor for a detailed scoring rubric.
12. I
13. Answers may vary. See Test Doctor for a detailed scoring rubric.

Why It Matters

Geology Connections

Remind students that the arrows show broad connections between events, not direct cause-and-effect relationships.

Students often forget that famous scientists were influenced by the social and political events of their time. The following information will help students connect the scientists to the time periods in which they lived.

In 79 BCE, Pliny the Younger was visiting his uncle, Pliny the Elder, who was a Roman naval commander. Pliny the Elder's ships were stationed at Misenum, across the Bay of Naples, approximately 35 km from Mount Vesuvius. When Mount Vesuvius erupted violently, Pliny the Elder launched his ships and crossed the bay to rescue his friends and other people on the opposite shore. Although Pliny the Elder died that day, presumably from suffocation as a result of the ash fall, Pliny the Younger witnessed the eruption from Misenum and wrote a valuable first-hand account of what he had seen.

John Milne was a British geologist who was hired as a foreign advisor and professor of mining and geology at the Imperial College of Engineering in Tokyo, Japan. In 1880, Milne and two other British scientists who were working in Japan began to focus on seismology after a large earthquake struck Yokohama, Japan. They founded the Seismological Society of Japan, which funded the investigations that resulted in the invention of seismographs. Although the two other scientists worked closely with Milne, Milne is credited with having created the predecessor to modern seismographs.

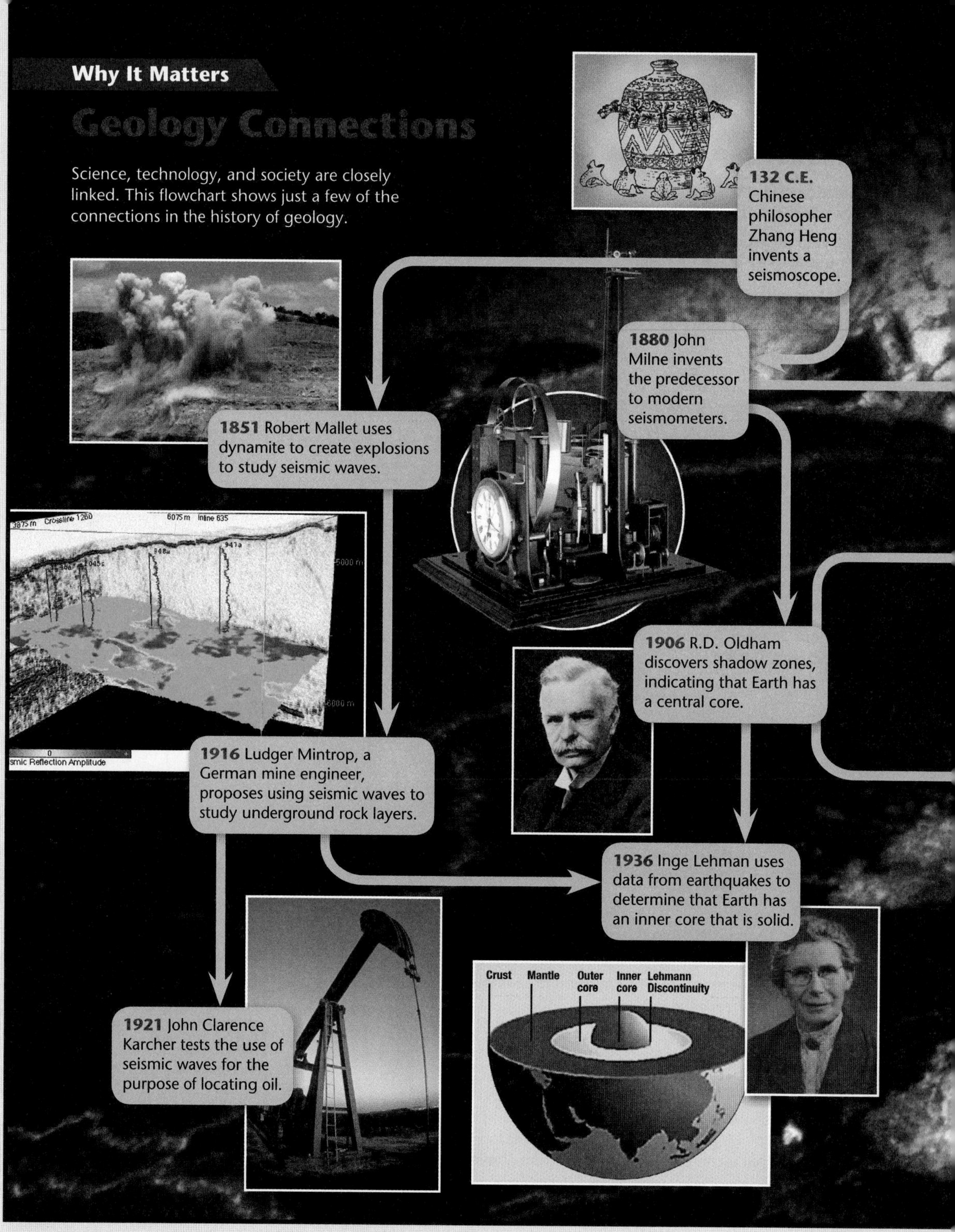

Why It Matters

Geology Connections

Science, technology, and society are closely linked. This flowchart shows just a few of the connections in the history of geology.

132 C.E. Chinese philosopher Zhang Heng invents a seismoscope.

1880 John Milne invents the predecessor to modern seismometers.

1851 Robert Mallet uses dynamite to create explosions to study seismic waves.

1906 R.D. Oldham discovers shadow zones, indicating that Earth has a central core.

1916 Ludger Mintrop, a German mine engineer, proposes using seismic waves to study underground rock layers.

1936 Inge Lehman uses data from earthquakes to determine that Earth has an inner core that is solid.

1921 John Clarence Karcher tests the use of seismic waves for the purpose of locating oil.

Inge Lehman was born in Denmark and raised in Copenhagen. She was educated at a school run by Hannah Adler, the aunt of the famous physicist Niels Bohr. She studied math and, after landing a job as the assistant to a geodesist, began to set up seismological observatories in Denmark and Greenland. Her love of seismology led her to discover Earth's inner core was solid.

Reading Skill Builder — Basic

Visual Literacy The seismic reflection map on the left-hand page shows how computers can model the shapes of rock layers underground. The reflectivity of underground surfaces allows scientists to get a good picture of where and how the rock layers change. Because different types of rock have different characteristics, they reflect seismic waves differently, enabling scientists to identify some of the rock layers. These unique images allow scientists to locate oil and natural gas reservoirs.

79 C.E Pliny the Younger describes the eruption of Mt. Vesuvius.

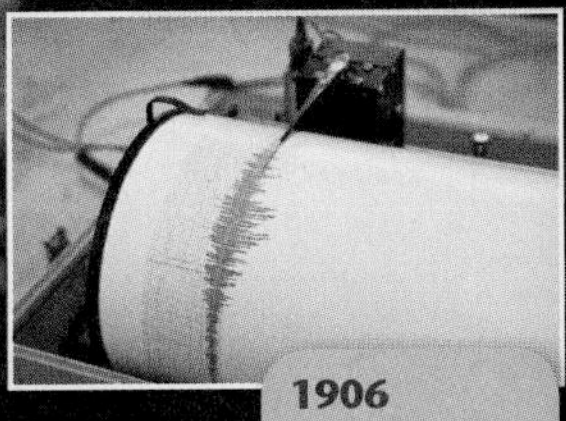

1906 Seismometers all around the world record an earthquake in California.

1912 The Hawaiian Volcano Observatory is formed at Kilauea.

1960 A magnitude 9.5 earthquake in Chile causes a tsunami that strikes Hawaii.

HISTORY IN SCIENCE

1968 The Pacific Tsunami Warning and Mitigation System is established.

TSUNAMI HAZARD ZONE
IN CASE OF EARTHQUAKE, GO TO HIGH GROUND OR INLAND

1985 Nevada del Ruiz erupts, killing 25,000 people in Colombia.

1986 The U.S. forms the Volcano Disaster Assistance Program (V.D.A.P.).

1991 The V.D.A.P. successfully predicts the eruption of Mt. Pinatubo.

2004 A tsunami in the Indian Ocean prompts the development of a tsunami warning system in the Indian Ocean.

2006 Thirty nations participate in a test of the Pacific Tsunami Warning System.

YOUR TURN

UNDERSTANDING CONCEPTS

For how many years have people been studying earthquakes?

CRITICAL THINKING

How did John Milne help save thousands of lives in 1991 when Mt. Pinatubo erupted?

Answers to Your Turn

Understanding Concepts People have been studying earthquakes for almost 2,000 years, since at least 132 BCE.

Critical Thinking John Milne invented the modern seismograph. The VDAP uses seismographs to monitor volcanic activity. The device John Milne invented in 1880 helped scientists predict the eruption of Mount Pinatubo and evacuate 75,000 local people in 1991.

Why It Matters

The Great Chilean Earthquake

The Great Chilean Earthquake of 1960 was the strongest earthquake ever recorded. The earthquake, with a magnitude of 9.5, sent tsunamis racing across the Pacific Ocean. Waves as tall as 25 m crashed into the southern coast of Chile. In Hilo, Hawaii, about 10,000 km away, 10 m waves destroyed the waterfront and devastated the eastern coast of the Big Island of Hawaii. As a result, the Pacific Tsunami Warning Center in Iwo Beach, Oahu, and the Alaska Regional Tsunami Warning System in Alaska were founded in 1967 and 1968. These centers monitor ocean surface movement throughout the Pacific basin by using buoys that track wave heights and wavelengths in open water.

Why It Matters

The Volcano Disaster Assistance Program In 1985, 25,000 Colombians died when the volcano Nevada del Ruiz erupted. Intense heat from pyroclastic flows melted the snow and ice at the top of the volcano, causing lahars, or mudslides. Lahars as thick as 50 m raced down the slope of the volcano and spread as far as 100 km. The town of Armero was completely buried and destroyed by the lahars. In 1986, the United States Geological Survey partnered with the U.S. Office of Foreign Disaster Assistance to form the Volcano Disaster Assistance Program (VDAP). The mission of the VDAP is to assess volcanic hazards around the world and respond to selected volcanic crises, helping to save lives and property and to reduce economic loss. In 1991, the VDAP successfully predicted the eruption of Mount Pinatubo in the Philippines. The VDAP's warning led to the evacuation of 75,000 people from the danger zone and helped to prevent the destruction of about $350 million in equipment.

Sample Answers to Concept Maps from Chapter Reviews

Chapter 10 Plate Tectonics, p. 287

28.

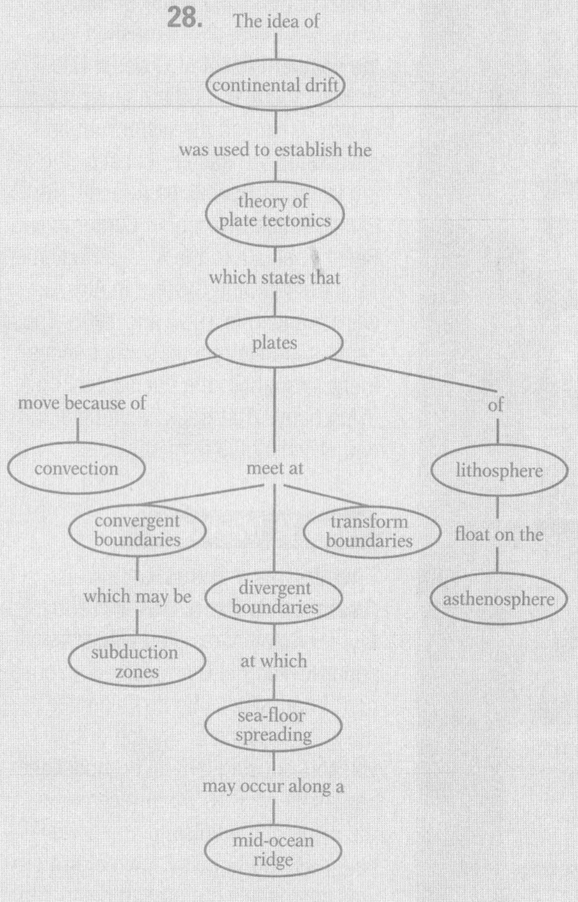

Chapter 11 Deformation of the Crust, p. 313

29.

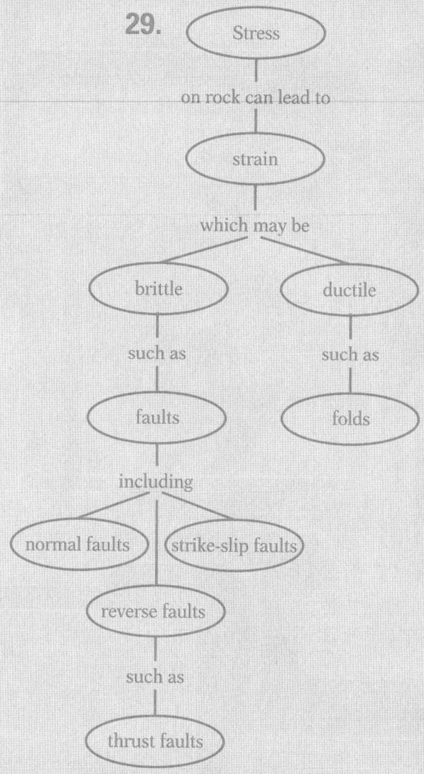

Chapter 12 Earthquakes, p. 339

28.

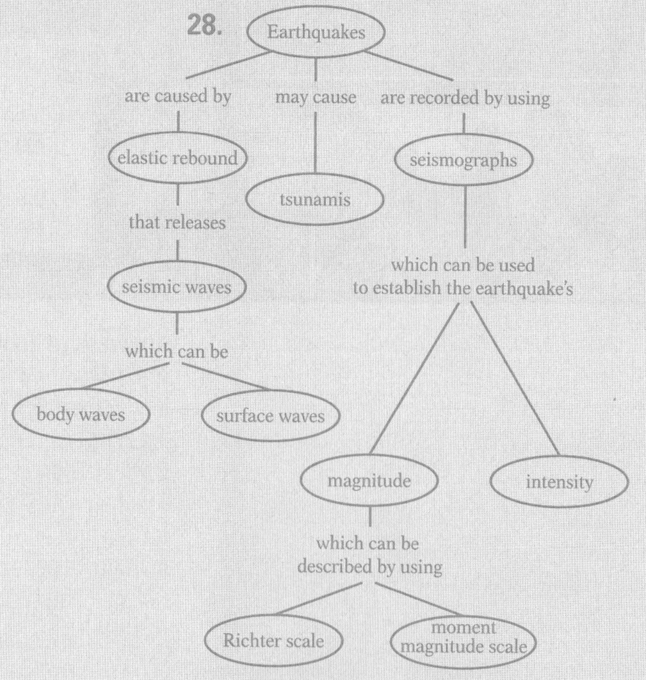

Sample Answers to Concept Maps from Chapter Reviews

Chapter 13 Volcanoes, p. 363

30.

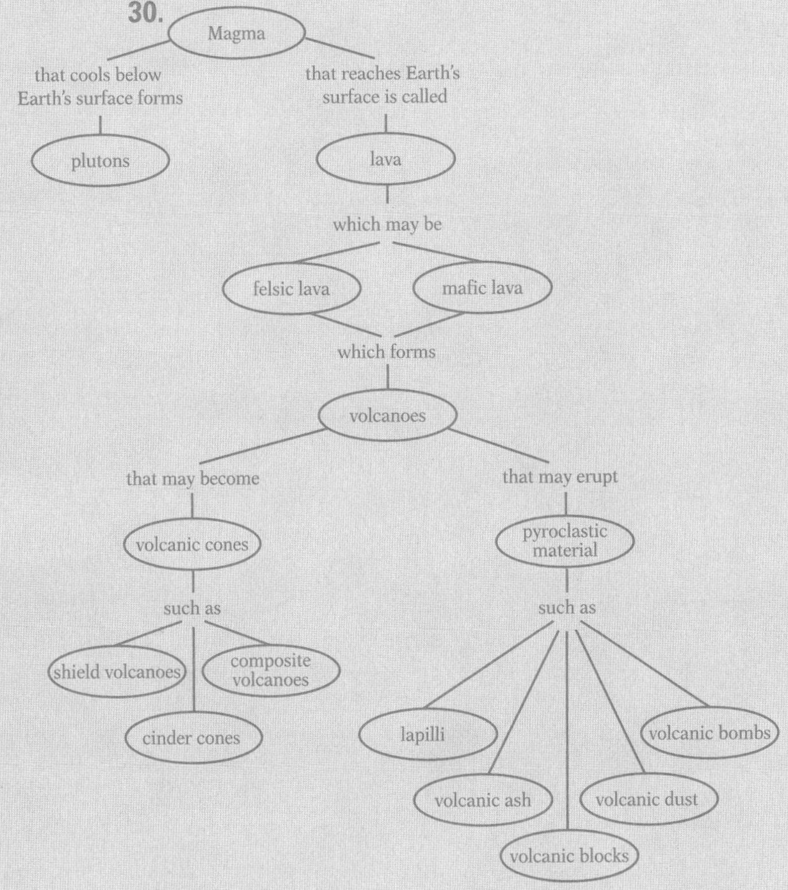

Unit 5 Reshaping the Crust

Chapter Planner 14

Weathering and Erosion

		Standards	Teach Key Ideas
Chapter Opener, pp. 370–371	45 min.	National Science Education Standards	
Section 1 Weathering Processes, pp. 373–378 ❯ Mechanical Weathering ❯ Chemical Weathering	45 min.	ES 3c, UPC 3, UPC 4	■ ◆ **Bellringer,** p. 373 ■ **DI (Special Education Students):** Communication, p. 374 ■ **Demonstration:** Rusting, p. 376 ■ **Discussion:** Weathering on the Moon, p. 376 ◆ **Transparency** 71 Chemical Weathering ▲ **Visual Concepts:** Mechanical Weathering • Ice Wedging • Chemical Weathering • Oxidation • Acid Precipitation
Section 2 Rates of Weathering, pp. 379–382 ❯ Differential Weathering ❯ Rock Composition ❯ Amount of Exposure ❯ Climate ❯ Topography and Elevation ❯ Human Activities ❯ Plant and Animal Activities	45 min.	ES 3c, SPSP 4a, UPC 3, UPC 4	■ ◆ **Bellringer,** p. 379 ◆ **Transparency** 72 Surface Area ▲ **Visual Concepts:** Differential Weathering • Rates of Weathering
Section 3 Soil, pp. 383–386 ❯ Soil Characteristics ❯ Soil Profile ❯ Soil and Climate ❯ Soil and Topography	90 min.	ES 3c, SPSP 4a, UPC 3, UPC 4	■ ◆ **Bellringer,** p. 383 ■ **Discussion:** Local Soils, p. 398 ◆ **Transparencies** 73 Soil Horizons of Residual Soils • 75 Soil Map of North Carolina ▲ **Visual Concepts:** Residual and Transported Soil • Topsoil, Subsoil, and Soil Horizons • Leaching • Soils and the Effects of Climate
Section 4 Erosion, pp. 387–394 ❯ Soil Erosion ❯ Soil Conservation ❯ Gravity and Erosion ❯ Erosion and Landforms	45 min.	ES 3c, SPSP 4a, SPSP 5c, UPC 3, UPC 4	■ ◆ **Bellringer,** p. 387 ■ **DI (Basic Learners):** Make Concepts Relevant, p. 389 ■ **Demonstration:** Soil Conservation, p. 390 ■ **Discussion:** Protecting Against Mass Movements, p. 391 ■ **Demonstration:** Solifluction, p. 392 ■ **DI (Special Education Students):** Erosion, p. 392 ◆ **Transparency** 74 Soil Erosion Vulnerability Map ▲ **Visual Concepts:** Erosion • Rapid Mass Movement • Creep
Chapter Wrap-Up, pp. 399–403	90 min.		**Chapter Summary,** p. 399

CHAPTER Fast Track
To shorten instruction because of time limitations, omit the Chapter Lab.

See also PowerNotes® Presentations

Key
Teacher's Edition ■ Teaching Transparencies ◆
Chapter Resource File ● Online Edition ▲

All resources listed below are also available on the Teacher One Stop™.

Why It Matters	Hands-On	Skills Development	Assessment
■ **Chapter Overview,** p. 370 ■ **Using the Figure:** Uluru, p. 370	**Inquiry Lab:** A Disappearing Act, p. 371	**Reading Toolbox,** p. 372	
■ **Section Overview,** p. 373 ■ **Earth Movers,** p. 375 ■ **Chemistry Connection:** Redox Reactions, p. 376 ■ **Environmental Connection:** Acid from the Sky, p. 377	■ **Activity:** Weathering Walk, p. 373 ■ **Activity:** Ice Wedging, p. 374 ■ **Group Activity:** Finding Evidence, p. 375 **Quick Lab:** Mechanical Weathering, p. 375 ■ **Activity:** Chalk Sculptures, p. 377	**Math Skills:** Rates of Weathering, p. 376 **Reading Toolbox:** Finding Examples, p. 377	**Reading Check,** p. 374 **Reading Check,** p. 376 **Section Review,** p. 378 ■ **Reteaching,** p. 377 ■ **Quiz,** p. 377 ■ **DI (Alternative Assessment):** Table, p. 377 ● **Section Quiz**
■ **Section Overview,** p. 379 ■ **Environmental Connection:** Off-Road Damage, p. 381	**Quick Lab:** Surface Areas, p. 380 ■ **Activity:** Create a Cave, p. 380	■ ● **Internet Activity:** National Parks, p. 379 **Reading Toolbox:** Spider Map, p. 381	**Reading Check,** p. 380 **Section Review,** p. 382 ■ **Reteaching,** p. 381 ■ **Quiz,** p. 381 ■ **DI (Alternative Assessment):** Concept Collage, p. 382 ● **Section Quiz**
■ **Section Overview,** p. 383 ■ **Using the Figure:** Soil Horizons, p. 384 ■ **Slash and Burn,** p. 384 ■ **Environmental Connection:** Acid Rain and Soil, p. 385	■ **Group Activity:** What Is Soil?, p. 383 **Skills Practice Lab:** Soil Chemistry, pp. 396–397 ● **Inquiry Lab:** Acid Rain and Soils ● **Making Models Lab:** Soil Profiles	■ **Skill Builder:** Math, p. 384 **Reading Toolbox:** Tri-Fold, p. 385 **Maps in Action:** Soil Map of North Carolina, p. 398	**Reading Check,** p. 385 **Section Review,** p. 386 ■ **Reteaching,** p. 385 ■ **Quiz,** p. 385 ■ **DI (Alternative Assessment):** Soil Profiles, p. 386 ● **Section Quiz**
■ **Section Overview,** p. 387 ■ **Using the Figure:** Local Vulnerability, p. 387 ■ **Worldwide Soil Losses,** p. 388 ■ **History Connection:** The Dust Bowl, p. 388 ■ **Geography Connection:** The Badlands, p. 388 **Putting Worms to Work,** p. 389 ■ **Environmental Connection:** Land Degradation, p. 389 ■ **Social Studies Connection:** The Hills of Southern California, p. 391 ■ **Creeping Trees,** p. 392 ■ **Geology Connection:** What Goes Up, p. 393	■ **Activity:** Plants and Soil, p. 393	■ **Skill Builder:** Math, p. 389 **Reading Toolbox:** Spider Map, p. 390 ■ ● **Internet Activity:** NRCS, p. 390 ■ **Skill Builder:** Writing, p. 391	**Reading Check,** p. 388 **Reading Check,** p. 391 **Reading Check,** p. 393 **Section Review,** p. 394 ■ **Reteaching,** p. 393 ■ **Quiz,** p. 393 ■ **DI (Alternative Assessment):** Conservation Plans, p. 394 ● **Section Quiz**
Living on the Edge, p. 395	■ **Activity:** Life as a Rock, p. 399	▲ **Super Summary** **Standardized Test Prep,** pp. 402–403	**Chapter Review,** pp. 400–401 ● **Chapter Tests**

See also Lab Generator

See also Holt Online Assessment Resources

Chapter Overview

Weathering and erosion are major forces that change Earth's surface over time. Chemical and mechanical weathering break down rock and help form one of our most important natural resources—soil.

Using the Figure GENERAL

Uluru This photograph shows Ayers Rock, also known as *Uluru* by aboriginal peoples, located in central Australia. Uluru towers 360 m above the desert plain and was originally part of a large mountain composed of beds of sandstone. The sandstone of Uluru resisted erosion over the years, while sandstone in the other beds did not. All that remains of the mountain are Uluru and the adjacent Olgas. Ask students if they have seen other landforms that illustrate differential weathering. (Answers may vary. Accept all reasonable answers.) **LS Logical**

Why It Matters

The terms *weathering* and *erosion* are often confused. Weathering is the breakdown of rock, while erosion is the movement of the resulting sediment. These natural processes form soil. Soil erosion accelerated by human activity is considered a critical global issue.

Chapter 14 Weathering and Erosion

Chapter Outline

Virginia Standards of Learning
ES.1.a
ES.1.b
ES.2.a
ES.8.a

Why It Matters

This red rock formation in Australia—like Earth's entire surface—is shaped by the processes of weathering and erosion. These processes are essential to the formation of soil, from which the food you eat grows.

Chapter Correlations — *Virginia Standards of Learning*

ES.1.a volume, area, mass, elapsed time, direction, temperature, pressure, distance, density, and changes in elevation/depth are calculated utilizing the most appropriate tools.
ES.1.b technologies, including computers, probeware, and geospatial technologies, are used to collect, analyze, and report data and to demonstrate concepts and simulate experimental conditions.
ES.2.a science explains and predicts the interactions and dynamics of complex Earth systems.
ES.8.a processes of soil development

Inquiry Lab

15 min

A Disappearing Act

Place two pieces of **limestone** and two pieces of **granite** in four separate labeled **beakers.** Pour a small amount of **vinegar** into one of the beakers with limestone and one of the beakers with granite. Record your observations. Next, pour **water** into the remaining two beakers, and observe.

Questions to Get You Started

1. What happens to the materials in vinegar? In water?
2. In general, which type of rock do you predict weathers more rapidly: limestone or granite? Explain.
3. What effect might acid rain have on the rate at which rock weathers? Explain.
4. What is one additional factor that could affect the rate at which rock weathers?

Inquiry Lab

Central Concept: Multiple factors affect the rate at which rock weathers, including rock type, climate, acidity of rainfall, and the exposed surface area of rock. Students will examine how two rock samples react with water and vinegar, and consider factors that affect weathering.

Materials (per group)
- Two small pieces of granite
- Two small pieces of limestone
- Four beakers
- Water
- Vinegar

Skills Acquired
- Predicting
- Inferring

Teacher's Notes: Make sure that students understand that vinegar could represent acid rain. You may wish to review the concept of the pH scale.

Answers to Getting Started

1. Granite does not change discernibly in water or vinegar. Limestone will react with vinegar but not with water.
2. Limestone, because it reacted with vinegar. It also is more brittle than the granite.
3. Acid rain might accelerate the rate of weathering, particularly with limestone, which reacted to vinegar, which is acidic.
4. Accept all reasonable answers. Sample answer: size of rock or surface area exposed.

Using THINK central Resources

An online version of this chapter, as well as all the print and multimedia resources that accompany the program are available to registered teachers and their students. Log onto www.thinkcentral.com to access these materials and tools to organize your preparation and student learning.

READING TOOLBOX

Finding Examples

Types of mechanical weathering	Examples	Signal words
exfoliation	overlying rocks erode, granite epands; joints form	for example
ice wedging	in the United States	such as
abrasion	caused by gravity, ice, running water, and wind	(none)
organic activity	roots grow and expand	as

READING TOOLBOX

These reading tools will help you learn the material in this chapter.

Finding Examples

Examples of Mechanical Weathering Examples can help you picture an idea or concept. Certain words or phrases can serve as signals that an example is about to be introduced. Such signals include

- *for example*
- *such as*
- *for instance*

Your Turn As you read Section 1, make a list of different types of mechanical weathering. See the sample list below to help you get started. Add examples for each type of mechanical weathering. If a word or phrase in the text signals the example, add that word or phrase.

Types of mechanical weathering	Examples	Signal words
exfoliation	overlying rocks erode, granite expands; joints form	for example
ice wedging		
abrasion		

FoldNotes

Tri-Fold A tri-fold can help you track your progress through the process of KWL. The letters KWL stand for "what I **K**now, what I **W**ant to know, and what I **L**earned." These notes help you relate new ideas to those you already know. This can help make new ideas easier to understand.

Your Turn Make a tri-fold FoldNote. In the left column, write what you already know about weathering and erosion. In the middle column, write what you want to know about weathering and erosion. In the right column, write what you learn as you read the chapter.

Know	Want to Know	Learned
Weathering is an important part of soil formation.	What else makes up soil besides weathered rock?	Soil is a combination of weathered rock, water, gases, and organic material.

Graphic Organizers

Spider Maps A spider map divides a topic into ideas and details.

To make a spider map, follow these steps:

1. For your title, write the main topic. Draw an oval around it.
2. From the oval, draw legs. Each leg represents a category of the main topic.
3. From each leg, draw horizontal lines. Write details about each category on these lines.

Your Turn As you read Section 4, complete a spider map like the one started here to organize the ideas you learn about gravity and erosion.

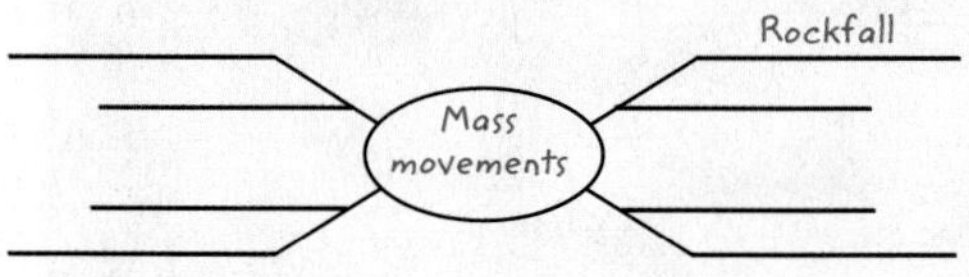

For more information on how to use these and other tools, see **Appendix A.**

Graphic Organizers

Spider Maps

Students' maps should have "mass movements" in the center. The main branches should include rockfall, landslides, mudflows, slump, solifluction, and creep. Details might include descriptions of each type of movement, whether they are fast or slow events, and what causes or contributes to their occurrence.

FoldNotes

Tri-Fold You may use student responses for "what I want to know" to make a master list for the class. After you have discussed the chapter in class, go back to that list and have students compare what they wanted to know with what they learned. Answers will vary

SECTION 1

Weathering Processes

Key Ideas	Key Terms		Why It Matters
❯ Identify three agents of mechanical weathering. ❯ Compare mechanical and chemical weathering processes. ❯ Describe four chemical reactions that decompose rock.	weathering mechanical weathering abrasion chemical weathering	oxidation hydrolysis carbonation acid precipitation	Although we say that something that does not change is "like a rock," rocks actually do change over time, through the processes of weathering. These processes also affect buildings, monuments, and other structures made of stone.

Most rocks deep within Earth's crust formed under conditions of high temperature and pressure. When these rocks are uplifted to the surface, they are exposed to much lower temperature and pressure. Uplifted rock is also exposed to the gases and water in Earth's atmosphere.

Because of these environmental factors, surface rocks undergo changes in their appearance and composition. The physical breakdown or chemical decomposition of rock materials exposed at Earth's surface is called **weathering.** There are two main types of weathering: mechanical weathering and chemical weathering. Each type of weathering has different effects on rock.

Mechanical Weathering

The process by which rock is broken down into smaller pieces by physical means is **mechanical weathering.** Mechanical weathering is strictly a physical process and does not change the composition of the rock. Common agents of mechanical weathering are ice, plants and animals, gravity, running water, and wind.

Physical changes within the rock also affect mechanical weathering. For example, when overlying rocks are eroded, granite that formed deep beneath Earth's surface can be exposed, decreasing the pressure on the granite. As a result of the decreasing pressure, the granite expands. Long, curved cracks, called *joints,* develop in the rock. When the joints are parallel to the surface of the rock, the rock breaks into curved sheets that peel away from the underlying rock in a process called *exfoliation.* One example of granite exfoliation is shown in **Figure 1.**

weathering the natural process by which atmospheric and environmental agents, such as wind, rain, and temperature changes, disintegrate and decompose rocks

mechanical weathering the process by which rocks break down into smaller pieces by physical means

Figure 1 This formation in Kings Canyon National Park is a dome of granite that is shedding large sheets of rock through the process of exfoliation.

Section 1

Focus

Overview

This section explains the processes of mechanical and chemical weathering. Wind, water, ice, gravity, and living organisms are all weathering agents.

Bellringer

Show students a large rock. Ask them to list some natural agents that might be able to break the rock into smaller pieces. (Answers may vary. Possible answers include other rocks, changes in temperature, wind, water, and chemical reactions.) LS **Logical**

Motivate

Activity — GENERAL

Weathering Walk Have students walk around the school or their home neighborhood to look for examples of weathering. Students should make a list of what they find. As a class, have them discuss their findings, try to determine the weathering agent, and classify their examples as mechanical or chemical weathering. As an extension, students could return to their sites days or weeks later to observe how much has changed.
LS **Visual/Kinesthetic**

Key Resources

Chapter Resource File
- Directed Reading BASIC

Technology
- Transparencies
  Bellringer

Teach

Teaching Tip — GENERAL

Connect to Familiar Processes Students may be familiar with potholes in streets. Street potholes form by thermal expansion and contraction of asphalt or concrete. Potholes may also form by the abrasive actions of pebbles and other materials that swirl around in natural depressions. These processes are similar to those that weather rock. Potholes may be especially bad in regions that have pronounced seasonal variation in temperature. **LS Logical/Visual**

Activity — GENERAL

Ice Wedging Divide the class into pairs. Have each pair moisten some clay with water and roll it into two balls. Wrap both in plastic wrap. Put one ball in the freezer and keep the other at room temperature. After 24 hours, unwrap both balls and compare them. Students should notice that the frozen clay ball has small cracks. The other ball should remain smooth and intact. Sometimes it takes two cycles of freezing to see changes.
LS Kinesthetic

Answer to Reading Check

Two forms of mechanical weathering are ice wedging and abrasion. Ice wedging is caused by water that seeps into cracks in rock and freezes. When water freezes, it expands and creates pressure on the rock, which widens and deepens cracks. Abrasion is the grinding away of rock surfaces by other rocks or sand particles. Abrasive agents may be carried by gravity, water, and wind.

Figure 2 Water flows into a crack in a rock's surface. When the water freezes, it expands and causes the crack to widen. Ice wedging is responsible for most of the cracks shown in this photo.

SciLinks
www.scilinks.org
Topic: Weathering
Code: HQX1648

Ice Wedging

Another form of mechanical weathering is called *ice wedging*. Ice wedging occurs when water seeps into cracks in rock and then freezes. When the water freezes, its volume increases by about 10% and creates pressure on the surrounding rock. Every time the ice thaws and refreezes, cracks in the rock widen and deepen. This process eventually splits the rock apart, as shown in **Figure 2.** Ice wedging commonly occurs at high elevations and in cold climates. It also occurs in climates where the temperature regularly rises above and then falls below freezing, such as in the northern United States.

Abrasion

abrasion the grinding and wearing away of rock surfaces through the mechanical action of other rock or sand particles

The collision of rocks that results in the breaking and wearing away of the rocks is a form of mechanical weathering called **abrasion.** Abrasion is caused by gravity, ice, running water, and wind. Gravity causes loose soil and rocks to move down the slope of a hill or mountain. Rocks break into smaller pieces as they fall and collide. Running water can carry sand or rock particles that scrape against each other and against stationary rocks. Thus, exposed surfaces are weathered by abrasion.

Wind is another agent of abrasion. When wind lifts and carries small particles, it can hurl them against surfaces, such as rock. As the airborne particles strike the rock, they wear away the surface in the same way that a sandblaster would.

Reading Check **Describe two forms of mechanical weathering.** (See Appendix G for answers to Reading Checks.)

Differentiated Instruction

Special Education Students

Communication Being able to see the face of a speaker helps others to understand what that person is saying. This communication aid is especially helpful for students who have hearing impairments. Divide the class into groups of five to eight students. Have each group sit so each person can see everyone else. Ask each group to read the subheadings in this section and discuss the content under each subheading.
LS Interpersonal

Figure 3 This gray wolf (left) is burrowing into soil to make a den. Prairie dogs also dig into soil to form extensive burrows, where an entire prairie dog community may live.

Plant and Animal Activity

Plants and animals are important agents of mechanical weathering. As plants grow, their roots grow and expand, creating pressure that wedges rock apart. The roots of small plants cause small cracks to form in the rocks. Eventually, the roots of larger plants and trees can fit in the cracks and make the cracks bigger.

The digging activities of burrowing animals, shown in **Figure 3**, affect the rate of weathering. Common burrowing animals include ground squirrels, prairie dogs, ants, earthworms, coyotes, and rabbits. Earthworms and other animals that move soil expose new rock surfaces to both mechanical and chemical weathering. Animal activities and plants can increase the rate of weathering dramatically over a long period of time.

Academic Vocabulary

agent (AY juhnt) a substance or living organism that has an impact on an ecological process

Quick Lab Mechanical Weathering

15 min

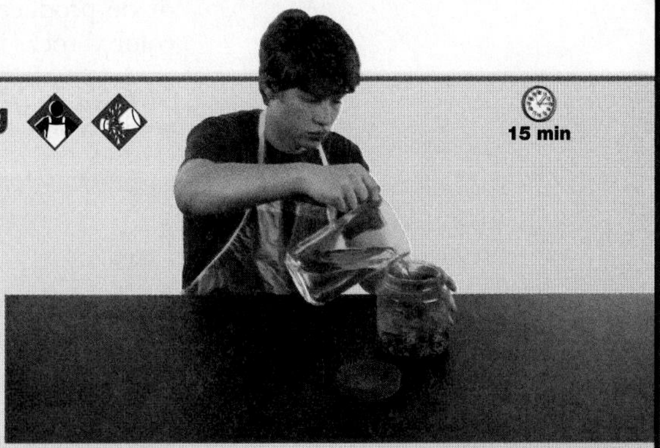

Procedure

1. Examine some silicate rock chips by using a hand lens. Observe the shape and surface texture.
2. Fill a plastic container that has a tight-fitting lid about half full of rock chips. Add water to just cover the chips.
3. Tighten the lid, and shake the container 100 times.
4. Hold a strainer over another container. Pour the water and rock chips into the strainer.
5. Move your finger around the inside of the empty container. Describe what you feel.
6. Use the hand lens to observe the rock chips.
7. Pour the water into a glass jar, and examine the water with the hand lens.
8. Put the rock chips and water back into the container that has the lid. Repeat steps 3 to 7.
9. Repeat step 8 two more times.

Analysis

1. Did the amount and particle size of the sediment that was left in the container change during your investigation? Explain your answer.
2. How did the appearance of the rock chips change? How did the appearance of the water change?
3. How does the transport of rock particles by water, such as in a river, affect the size and shape of the rock particles?

Group Activity — General

Finding Evidence As a class, visit a local park and look for examples of weathering caused by plants and animals. Look for plants wedging rocks apart, animal burrows, anthills and other plant and animal activities. Ask students to consider if human activities may also be contributing to weathering in the park. (Answers may vary. Students may notice that human activities, such as hiking, biking, and off-roading in the park may be contributing to weathering processes.)

LS Visual

Quick Lab

Skills Acquired

- Experimenting
- Interpreting

Materials

- Silicate rock chips
- Hand lens
- Plastic container with lid
- Water
- Strainer
- Glass jar

Teacher's Notes: Make sure students firmly secure lids before shaking the jar.

Answers to Analysis

1. Because of the abrasive effect of the rocks on each other, there should be more and finer sediment in the container after each time it is shaken.
2. The rock chips should become smoother and smaller as they are worn down. The water will likely become more clouded with sediment particles.
3. Rocks will likely become smoother, more rounded and smaller as they are transported by water in a river.

Why It Matters

Earth Movers Earthworms dig through soil looking for food. As they burrow, they bring rock and mineral particles to the surface for further weathering. Their tunnels aerate the soil and allow water to percolate to rocks below the soil surface. Earthworms have voracious appetites. They eat and digest about half their body weight each day. In the northern U.S., native earthworms were extirpated during the last glaciation. Today, nearly all earthworms in northern states are actually European species that arrived with settlers. Although earthworms contribute to soil formation, they can also interfere with the ecosystems they have colonized. For example, worms may eat through leaf litter in northern forests, interfering with native plant growth.

Math Skills

Answer

0.2 cm = 0.002 m

15 m ÷ 0.002 m/100 y = 750,000 y

Chemistry Connection ADVANCED

Redox Reactions Chemically speaking, oxidation is not just the process of elements combining with oxygen. By definition, oxidation is the loss of electrons from a substance. Some substance must accept the electrons and in the process is reduced, which is why these reactions are often called *redox reactions*. In many cases, oxygen accepts the electrons lost by the substance, which is why loss of electrons is called *oxidation*. Iron is easily oxidized and forms several different oxides, depending on how many electrons it loses. These oxides include FeO, Fe_2O_3 and Fe_3O_4. LS **Logical**

Answer to Reading Check

Two effects of chemical weathering are changes in the chemical composition and changes in the physical appearance of a rock.

chemical weathering the process by which rocks break down as a result of chemical reactions

oxidation the process by which a metallic element combines with oxygen

Chemical Weathering

The process by which rock is broken down because of chemical interactions with the environment is **chemical weathering.** Chemical weathering, or decomposition, occurs when chemical reactions act on the minerals in rock. Chemical reactions commonly occur between rock, water, carbon dioxide, oxygen, and acids. Acids are substances that form *hydronium ions,* H_3O^+, in water. Hydronium ions are electrically charged and can pull apart the chemical bonds of the minerals in rock. Bases can also chemically weather rock. Bases are substances that form *hydroxide ions,* OH^-, in water. Chemical reactions with either acids or bases can change the structure of minerals, which leads to the formation of new minerals. Chemical weathering changes both the chemical composition and physical appearance of rock.

Math Skills

Rates of Weathering
Limestone is dissolved by chemical weathering at a rate of 0.2 cm every 100 years. At this rate, after how many years would a layer of limestone 15 m thick completely dissolve?

Oxidation

The process by which elements combine with oxygen is called **oxidation.** Oxidation commonly occurs in rock that has iron-bearing minerals, such as hematite and magnetite. In this rock, iron, Fe, combines quickly with oxygen, O_2, that is dissolved in water to form rust, or iron oxide, Fe_2O_3:

$$4Fe + 3O_2 \rightarrow 2Fe_2O_3$$

The red color of much of the soil in the southeastern United States, as shown in **Figure 4,** is mainly due to the presence of iron oxide produced by oxidation. Similarly, the color of many red-colored rocks is caused by oxidized, iron-rich minerals.

Reading Check **Describe two effects of chemical weathering.**

Figure 4 The red color of the soil surrounding this farmhouse in Georgia is caused by the chemical interaction of iron-bearing minerals in the soil with oxygen in the atmosphere.

Demonstration GENERAL

Rusting Place a pad of steel wool moistened with water in a dish. Cover it with a glass and observe daily. The steel wool should turn reddish in a few days and crumble when touched as the iron oxidizes. Ask students if they can think of ways to prevent oxidation. (Answers may vary. Students may notice that the steel wool was not rusted to begin with. Iron in dry air is not easily oxidized. Painting protects steel from water and helps prevent rust and corrosion.) LS **Visual**

Discussion GENERAL

Weathering on the Moon Ask students to consider whether the surface of the moon has been weathered mechanically and/or chemically. (Mechanical weathering occurs when meteorites hit the moon surface, creating craters. But mechanical weathering by wind, water, and ice is absent because the moon has no water and no atmosphere. Similarly, chemical weathering is unlikely because the moon lacks water, an atmosphere, and life.) LS **Visual**

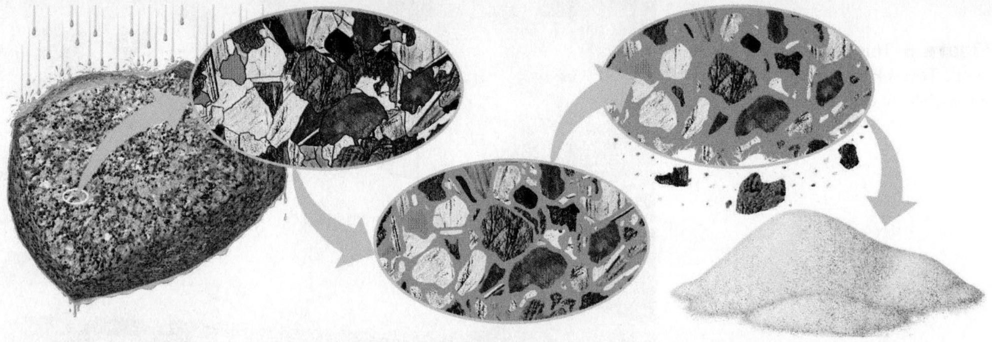

Rain, weak acids, and air chemically weather rock.

The bonds between mineral grains weaken as weathering proceeds.

Sediment forms from the weathered rock.

Figure 5 Thousands of years of chemical weathering processes, such as hydrolysis and carbonation, can turn even a hard rock into sediment.

Hydrolysis

Water plays a crucial role in chemical weathering, as shown in **Figure 5.** The change in the composition of minerals when they react chemically with water is called **hydrolysis.** For example, a type of feldspar combines with water and produces a common clay called *kaolin*. In this reaction, hydronium ions displace the potassium and calcium atoms in the feldspar crystals, which changes the feldspar into clay.

Minerals that are affected by hydrolysis often dissolve in water. Water can then carry the dissolved minerals to lower layers of rock in a process called *leaching*. Ore deposits, such as bauxite, the aluminum ore, sometimes form when leaching causes a mineral to concentrate in a thin layer beneath Earth's surface.

hydrolysis a chemical reaction between water and another substance to form two or more new substances

carbonation the conversion of a compound into a carbonate

Carbonation

When carbon dioxide, CO_2, from the air dissolves in water, H_2O, a weak acid called *carbonic acid*, H_2CO_3, forms:

$$H_2O + CO_2 \rightarrow H_2CO_3$$

Carbonic acid has a higher concentration of hydronium ions than pure water does, which speeds up the process of hydrolysis. When certain minerals come in contact with carbonic acid, they combine with the acid to form minerals called carbonates. The conversion of minerals into a carbonate is called **carbonation.**

One example of carbonation occurs when carbonic acid reacts with calcite, a major component of limestone, and converts the calcite into calcium bicarbonate. Calcium bicarbonate dissolves easily in water, so the limestone eventually weathers away.

READING TOOLBOX

Finding Examples
As you read, find examples of each form of chemical weathering. Don't forget to use signal words as clues. Record the examples in a table. See the Reading Toolbox at the beginning of this chapter if you need help getting started.

Organic Acids

Acids are produced naturally by certain living organisms. Lichens and mosses grow on rocks and produce weak acids that can weather the surface of the rock. The acids seep into the rock and produce cracks that eventually cause the rock to break apart.

Activity — GENERAL

Chalk Sculptures Have students make a statue by carving a piece of chalk. Then, use a small bit of clay to stand the statue upright in a dish. Have students put on goggles, spray their statues with white vinegar, and observe what happens. The statues should begin wearing away because chalk is calcium carbonate. Vinegar contains acetic acid, a weak acid that can eat away carbonates. Have students write a brief paragraph that describes how accurately this activity models the effects of acid rain.
LS **Visual/Verbal**

Close

Reteaching — BASIC

Weathering Processes Have students write descriptions of various types of mechanical and chemical weathering processes on index cards. Have them work in pairs to use the cards to quiz each other about weathering processes. LS **Visual/Logical**

Quiz — GENERAL

1. What kinds of animals can cause weathering? (Burrowing animals such as coyotes, foxes, rabbits, squirrels, earthworms and ants may contribute to weathering.)
2. Why is acid precipitation decreasing in some areas? (because of pollution controls required by the Clean Air Act)

Environmental Connection

Acid From the Sky Despite the Acid Rain Control Program, acid precipitation still occurs in parts of the United States and around the world. Vehicles remain a major source of nitrogen oxides and sulfur dioxides. At times, precipitation as acidic as the acid in a car battery (pH 2) has been recorded. This can weather rocks and damage forests, bodies of water, and buildings. Have interested students investigate where acid rain remains a problem and what solutions have been proposed to remedy it. They can report their findings to the class. LS **Verbal/Logical**

READING TOOLBOX

Finding Examples See p. 507A for sample answers.

Key Resources

Technology
- Transparencies
  71 Chemical Weathering

Close, *continued*

Answers to Section Review

1. wind, water, and temperature change
2. Water that seeps into cracks freezes and expands, which widens and deepens cracks with each freeze/thaw cycle.
3. Plant roots grow and expand, physically wedging rocks apart. Animal dig and burrow, which exposes new rock to weathering.
4. Mechanical weathering is a purely physical process, breaking large rocks into smaller rocks of the same chemical composition. Chemical weathering involves chemical reactions that break down rocks.
5. Oxidation: iron-bearing minerals combine with oxygen to form iron oxide. Hydrolysis: water and other substances react chemically to form new substances. Carbonation: carbonic acid converts minerals into carbonates.
6. Oxidation, hydrolysis and carbonation are all chemical processes that weather rocks. Water plays a role in both hydrolysis and carbonation and it can speed up oxidation. Oxidation involves elements combining with oxygen. Hydrolysis changes the composition of minerals that react with water. Carbonation occurs when minerals react with carbonic acid.
7. Acid precipitation forms when nitrogen oxides and sulfur dioxide released during fossil fuel combustion combine with water in the atmosphere to produce nitric, nitrous, or sulfuric acid. When these acids fall back to Earth, they are called *acid precipitation.*

Figure 6 This stone lion sits outside Leeds Town Hall in England. It was damaged by acid precipitation.

SciLinks® www.scilinks.org Topic: Acid Precipitation Code: **HQX1690**

acid precipitation
precipitation, such as rain, sleet, or snow, that contains a high concentration of acids, often because of the pollution of the atmosphere

Acid Precipitation

Natural rainwater is slightly acidic because it combines with small amounts of carbon dioxide. But when fossil fuels, especially coal, are burned, nitrogen oxides and sulfur dioxides are released into the air. These compounds combine with water in the atmosphere to produce nitric acid, nitrous acid, or sulfuric acid. When these acids fall to Earth, they are called **acid precipitation.**

Acid precipitation weathers some rock faster than ordinary precipitation does. In fact, many historical monuments and sculptures have been damaged by acid precipitation, as shown in **Figure 6.** Between 1940 and 1990, acid precipitation fell regularly in some cities in the United States. In 1990, the Acid Rain Control Program was added to the Clean Air Act of 1970. This program's regulations gave power plants 10 years to decrease sulfur dioxide emissions. The occurrence of acid precipitation has been greatly reduced since power plants have installed scrubbers that remove much of the sulfur dioxide before it can be released.

Section 1 Review

Key Ideas

1. **Identify** three agents of mechanical weathering.
2. **Describe** how ice wedging weathers rock.
3. **Explain** how two activities of plants or animals help weather rocks or soil.
4. **Compare** mechanical and chemical weathering processes.
5. **Identify** and describe three chemical processes that weather rock.
6. **Compare** hydrolysis, carbonation, and oxidation.
7. **Summarize** how acid precipitation forms.

Critical Thinking

8. **Making Connections** Which two agents of weathering would be rare in a desert? Explain your reasoning.
9. **Understanding Relationships** Automobile exhaust contains nitrogen oxides. How might these pollutants affect chemical weathering processes?

Concept Mapping

10. Use the following terms to create a concept map: *weathering, oxidation, mechanical weathering, ice wedging, hydrolysis, abrasion, chemical weathering, carbonation,* and *acid precipitation.*

8. Answers may vary. Sample answer: Running water and vegetation are agents of weathering that would rarely occur in a desert. Rainfall is low in desert areas, so fewer streams and rivers exist to erode valley areas.
9. Nitrogen oxides from exhaust could lead to the formation of acid precipitation and to an increase in chemical weathering.
10. *Weathering* includes *mechanical weathering,* such as *ice wedging* and *abrasion,* and *chemical weathering,* caused by *oxidation, hydrolysis, carbonation,* and *acid precipitation.*

Differentiated Instruction

Alternative Assessment

Table Have students create a table that compares mechanical and chemical weathering. Students should include as much detail as possible in each column, including the agents of weathering and the various types of weathering processes. Students should summarize the table by writing a brief paragraph noting the similarities and differences between mechanical and chemical weathering. **LS Logical/Verbal**

SECTION 2

Rates of Weathering

Key Ideas	Key Terms	Why It Matters
❯ Explain how rock composition affects the rate of weathering. ❯ Discuss how surface area affects the rate at which rock weathers. ❯ Describe the effects of climate and topography on the rate of weathering.	**differential weathering**	Learning about the different factors that affect weathering can help you understand how your own activities may impact the environment.

The processes of mechanical and chemical weathering generally work very slowly. For example, carbonation dissolves limestone at an average rate of only about one-twentieth of a centimeter (0.05 cm) every 100 years. At this rate, it could take up to 30 million years to dissolve a layer of limestone that is 150 m thick.

The pinnacles in Nambung National Park in Australia are shown in **Figure 1.** Most of the limestone was weathered away by agents of both chemical and mechanical weathering until only the pinnacles remained. The rate at which rock weathers depends on a number of factors, including rock composition, climate, and topography.

Differential Weathering

The composition of rock greatly affects the rate at which rock weathers. The process by which softer, less weather-resistant rock wears away and leaves harder, more resistant rock behind is called **differential weathering.** When rocks that are rich in the mineral quartz are exposed on Earth's surface, they remain basically unchanged, even after all the surrounding rock has weathered away. They remain unchanged because the chemical composition and crystal structure of quartz make quartz resistant to chemical weathering. These characteristics also make quartz a very hard mineral, so it resists mechanical weathering.

differential weathering the process by which softer, less weather-resistant rocks wear away at a faster rate than harder, more weather-resistant rocks do

Rock Composition

Limestone and other sedimentary rocks that contain calcite weather rapidly because they commonly undergo carbonation. Other sedimentary rocks are affected mainly by mechanical weathering processes. The rates at which these rocks weather depend mostly on the material that holds the sediment grains together. For example, shales and sandstones that are not firmly cemented gradually break up to become clay and sand particles. However, conglomerates and sandstones that are strongly cemented by silicates resist weathering longer than some igneous rocks do.

Figure 1 Different rates of weathering formed these limestone pinnacles at Nambung National Park in Australia over millions of years.

Section 2

Focus

Overview

This section describes how composition, exposure, climate, topography, and plant, animal, and human activities affect rates of weathering.

Bellringer

Ask students, "Do all rocks weather at the same rate? What factors might affect rates of weathering?" (Answers may vary but students may answer that some rocks weather more easily than others. Students may indicate that rock composition, surface area, temperature, and precipitation affect rates of weathering.) LS **Verbal**

Motivate

Internet Activity GENERAL

National Parks Have students visit the National Park Service Web site and choose one park in which weathering has played a role in the formation of the park's landforms. Students should present their findings to the class. A worksheet designed to direct student research on this topic can be found in the **Chapter Resource File** booklet or by visiting www.thinkcentral.com and entering the keyword **HQXWAEX.**
LS **Verbal**

Key Resources

Chapter Resource File
- Directed Reading BASIC

Technology
- Transparencies
  Bellringer

Teach

Quick Lab

Skills Acquired
- Experimenting
- Collecting Data
- Measuring
- Interpreting

Materials
- Two small containers
- Water
- Sugar cube
- Granulated sugar
- Two spoons
- Stopwatch

Teacher's Notes: This activity will work well as a demo. Using warm water will speed up dissolution of the sugar.

Answers to Analysis
1. The granulated sugar should dissolve more quickly than the cube sugar because it has a much greater surface area.
2. If both rocks have the same composition and are exposed to the same weathering processes, the smaller rock should wear away faster because it has a larger surface area to its volume.

Answer to Reading Check
Fractures and joints in a rock increase surface area and allow weathering to occur more rapidly.

Key Resources

Technology
- Transparencies
  72 Surface Area

Figure 2 The Ratio of Total Surface Area to Volume

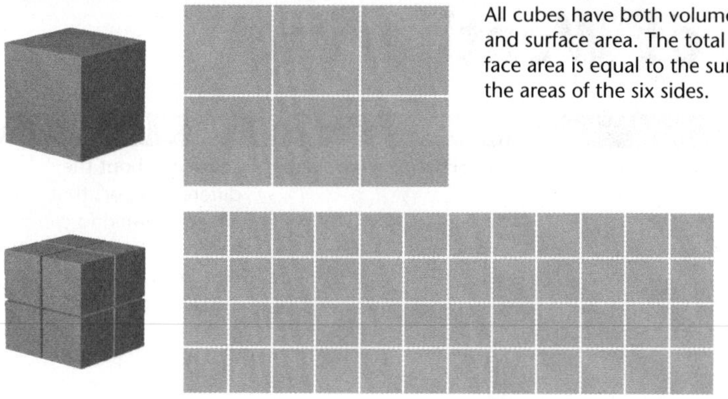

All cubes have both volume and surface area. The total surface area is equal to the sum of the areas of the six sides.

THINK central
INTERACT ONLINE
Keyword: HQXWAEF2

If you split the first cube into eight smaller cubes, you have the same amount of material (volume), but double the surface area. If you split each of the eight small cubes into eight even smaller cubes, the original surface area is doubled again.

Academic Vocabulary
factor (FAK tuhr) a condition or event that brings about or contributes to a result

Quick Lab — 10 min

Surface Areas

Procedure
1. Fill two small containers about half full with water.
2. Add one sugar cube to one container.
3. Add 1 tsp of granulated sugar to the other container.
4. Use two different spoons to stir the water and sugar in each container at the same rate.
5. Use a stopwatch to measure how long the sugar in each container takes to dissolve.

Analysis
1. Did the sugar dissolve at the same rate in both containers?
2. Which do you think would wear away faster—a large rock or a small rock? Explain your answer.

Amount of Exposure

The more exposure to weathering agents that a rock receives, the faster the rock will weather. The amount of time that the rock is exposed and the amount of the rock's surface area that is available for weathering are important factors in determining the rate of weathering.

Surface Area

Both chemical and mechanical weathering may split rock into a number of smaller rocks. The part of a rock that is exposed to air, water, and other agents of weathering is called the rock's *surface area*. As a rock breaks into smaller pieces, the surface area that is exposed increases. For example, imagine a block of rock as a cube that has six sides exposed. Splitting the block into eight smaller blocks, as shown in **Figure 2,** doubles the total surface area available for weathering.

Fractures and Joints

Most rocks on Earth's surface contain natural fractures and joints. These fractures and joints are natural zones of weakness within the rock. They increase the surface area of a rock and allow weathering to take place more rapidly. They also form natural channels through which water flows. Water may penetrate the rock through these channels and break the rock by ice wedging. As water moves through these channels, it chemically weathers the rock that is exposed in the fracture or joint. The chemical weathering removes rock material and makes the jointed or fractured area weaker.

Reading Check **How do fractures and joints in a rock affect surface area?**

Activity — General

Create a Cave Have students pour about an inch of sand in the bottom of a tall, clear plastic cup and place a layer of sugar cubes on top of the sand. Then, ask them to cover the cubes with wood glue, making sure it seeps down into the cracks between the cubes. When the glue is dry, have students add a layer of sand and then poke a hole in the bottom of the cup with a nail. Have them place the cup in a dish and slowly pour warm water over the sand layer. As water seeps through the sand, it will dissolve the sugar but not the wood glue. "Caverns" will be left in the cup. LS **Kinesthetic**

Figure 3 The photo on the left shows Cleopatra's Needle before it was moved to New York City. The photograph on the right shows the 3,000-year-old carvings after only one century in New York City.

Climate

In general, climates that have alternating periods of hot and cold weather allow the fastest rates of weathering. Freezing and thawing can cause the mechanical breakdown of rock by ice wedging. Chemical weathering can then act quickly on the fractured rock. When the temperature rises, the rate at which chemical reactions occur accelerates. In warm, humid climates, chemical weathering is also fairly rapid. The constant moisture is highly destructive to exposed surfaces.

The slowest rates of weathering occur in hot, dry climates. The lack of water limits many weathering processes, such as carbonation and ice wedging. Weathering is also slow in very cold climates.

The effects of climate on weathering rates can be seen on Cleopatra's Needle, which is shown in **Figure 3.** Cleopatra's needle is an obelisk that is made of granite. For 3,000 years, the obelisk remained in Egypt, where the hot, dry climate scarcely changed its surface. Then, in 1880, Cleopatra's Needle was moved to New York City. After only 130 years, the moisture, ice wedging, and pollution, such as acid precipitation, caused more weathering than was caused in the preceding 3,000 years in the Egyptian desert.

Topography and Elevation

Topography, or the elevation and slope of the land surface, also influences the rate of weathering. Because temperatures are generally cold at high elevations, ice wedging is more common at high elevations than at low elevations. On steep slopes, such as mountainsides, weathered rock fragments are pulled downhill by gravity and washed out by heavy rains. As the rock fragments slide down the mountain or are carried away by mountain streams, they smash against each other and break apart. As a result of the removal of these surface rocks, new surfaces of the mountain are continually exposed to weathering.

SCILINKS
www.scilinks.org
Topic: Rates of Weathering
Code: **HQX1269**

READING TOOLBOX

Spider Map
Create a spider map and label the center oval "Factors that affect the rate of weathering." Then, fill in the map with at least four factors presented in this section.

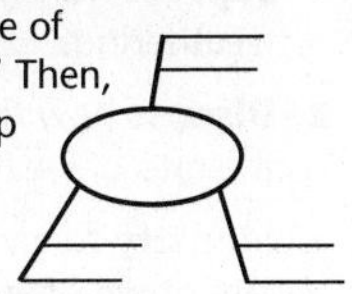

Homework — GENERAL

Research Paper Have interested students research efforts to preserve and restore famous monuments from the effects of weathering. Have them present their findings in a research paper or newspaper-style article highlighting preservation and restoration methods. **LS Logical/Verbal**

READING TOOLBOX

Spider Map
Students' maps should have "Factors that affect the rate of weathering" in the center. The main branches should include at least four of the following: rock composition, amount of exposure, climate, topography and elevation, human activities, plant and animal activities. Details should describe how each factor affects the rate of weathering.

Close

Reteaching — BASIC

Peer Reviewing Have students work in pairs to write three to five questions about the material in this section. Then, have students quiz each other. **LS Verbal/Interpersonal**
Co-op Learning

Quiz — GENERAL

1. What is the name of the process by which softer, less weather-resistant rock wears away, leaving harder, more resistant rock behind? (differential weathering)
2. Where do the slowest rates of weathering occur? (in hot, dry climates)

Environmental Connection

Off-Road Damage Riding off-road vehicles (ORVs), such as all-terrain vehicles and motorbikes, in backcountry areas is an increasingly popular recreational activity. However, it can dramatically increase weathering and threaten certain landscapes. When ORVs leave established roads and trails, they make ruts and expose rocks and soil. Have interested students research current regulation of ORV use on public lands and report their findings to the class. **LS Verbal/Logical**

Close, *continued*

Answers to Section Review

1. Rocks that contain calcite or other soft minerals weather rapidly. Rocks that are rich in quartz or other hard minerals weather slowly.
2. Increased surface area can lead to increased weathering because more areas are exposed to agents of weathering.
3. Climates that have alternating periods of hot and cold increase weathering rates because they allow for ice wedging. Warm, humid climates increase rates of weathering because the constant moisture wears away rock surfaces.
4. Ice wedging is more common at higher elevation because the temperature is colder. With steep topography, weathered rock is more easily pulled down by gravity and washed away by water. As a result, new rocks are continually exposed to weathering on steep mountain slopes.
5. Mining exposes rock surfaces to agents of weathering and may add strong chemicals to increase the rate. Construction removes soil and exposes rock surfaces. Recreational activities such as hiking, biking, and using all-terrain vehicles remove soil and expose previously unexposed rock.
6. Burrowing animals can expose rock surfaces to weathering agents. Animal waste can accelerate chemical weathering and attract small animals to a site, further speeding up the weathering process.

Figure 4 All-terrain vehicles and recreational activities can cause mechanical weathering of exposed rock. These activities may also expose new rock surfaces to chemical weathering.

Human Activities

Rock can be chemically and mechanically broken down by the action of humans. Mining and construction often expose rock surfaces to agents of weathering. Mining also exposes rock to strong acids and other chemical compounds that are used in mining processes. Construction often removes soil and exposes previously unexposed rock surfaces. Recreational activities, such as hiking and riding all-terrain vehicles, as shown in **Figure 4,** can also speed up weathering by exposing new rock surfaces. Rock that is disturbed or broken by human activities weathers more rapidly than undisturbed rock does.

Plant and Animal Activities

Rock that is disturbed or broken by plants or animals also weathers more rapidly than undisturbed rock does. The roots of plants and trees often break apart rock. Burrowing animals dig holes, exposing new rock surfaces. Some biological wastes of animals can cause chemical weathering. For example, caves that have large populations of bats also have large amounts of bat guano on the cave floors. Bat guano attracts insects, such as millipedes and beetles. The presence of these insects speeds up mechanical weathering, and the presence of the guano increases the rate of certain chemical weathering processes.

Section 2 Review

Key Ideas

1. **Explain** how rock composition affects the rate of weathering.
2. **Discuss** how the surface area of a rock can affect the rate of weathering.
3. **Identify** two ways that climate can affect the rate of weathering.
4. **Describe** two ways that the topography of a region can affect the rate of weathering.
5. **Summarize** three ways that human actions can affect the rate of weathering.
6. **Explain** two ways that animals can affect the rate of weathering.

Critical Thinking

7. **Applying Concepts** Imagine that there is an area of land where mechanical weathering has caused damage. Describe two ways to reduce the rate of mechanical weathering.
8. **Identifying Relationships** How would Cleopatra's Needle probably have been affected if it had been in the cold, dry climate of Siberia for 130 years?

Concept Mapping

9. Use the following terms to create a concept map: *composition, exposure, precipitation, surface area, climate, temperature, topography, weathering, elevation,* and *human activities.*

7. Reducing the rate of mechanical weathering might involve restoring soil and/or vegetation cover to the area, keeping humans and animals away, and protecting the area from too much water.
8. Cleopatra's Needle would probably have suffered less damage in Siberia because in a cold, dry climate weathering is slow compared to the wet, temperate climate of New York.
9. Factors that can affect *weathering* include rock *composition; surface area,* which determines amount of *exposure; climate,* which includes *temperature* and *precipitation* patterns; *topography,* or *elevation*; and *human activities.*

Differentiated Instruction

Alternative Assessment

Concept Collage Have students collect pictures or photographs that illustrate differential weathering and factors that affect rates of weathering. Have students use the pictures to create a visual concept map of the key points in this section.
LS Visual/Logical

SECTION

3 Soil

Key Ideas	Key Terms	Why It Matters
› Summarize how soils form. › Explain how the composition of parent rock affects soil composition. › Describe the characteristic layers of mature residual soils. › Predict the type of soil that will form in arctic and tropical climates.	soil soil profile horizon humus	Nearly all the food you eat was grown in soil. Earth scientists study the characteristics of soil to gain a better understanding of how to conserve and use this critical natural resource.

One result of weathering is the formation of *regolith,* the layer of weathered rock fragments that covers much of Earth's surface. *Bedrock* is the solid, unweathered rock that lies beneath the regolith. The lower regions of regolith are partly protected by those above and thus do not weather as rapidly as the upper regions do. The uppermost rock fragments weather to form a layer of very fine particles. This layer of small rock particles provides the basic components of soil. **Soil** is a complex mixture of minerals, water, gases, and the remains of dead organisms.

soil a loose mixture of rock fragments and organic material that can support the growth of vegetation

Soil Characteristics

The characteristics of soil depend largely on the rock from which the soil was weathered, which is called the soil's *parent rock.* Soil that forms and stays directly over its parent rock is called *residual soil.* However, the weathered mineral grains within soil may be carried away from the location of the parent rock by water, wind, or glaciers. Soil that results from the deposition of this material is called *transported soil,* and it may have different characteristics than the bedrock on which it rests.

Soil Composition

Parent rock that is rich in feldspar or other minerals that contain aluminum weathers to form soils that contain large amounts of clay. Parent rock that contains large amounts of quartz, such as granite, weathers to form sandy soils. Soil composition refers to the materials of which it is made. The color of soil is related to the composition of the soil. Black soils are commonly rich in organic material, while red soils may form from iron-rich parent rock. Soil moisture can also affect color, as shown in **Figure 1.**

Figure 1 These soil scientists are testing soil moisture to determine whether irrigation will be needed. Moister soils are generally darker than drier soils are.

Section 3

Focus

Overview

This section summarizes how soil forms and describes the characteristic layers of soils. It also explains how soil composition is affected by parent rock, climate, and topography.

Bellringer

Ask students to define *soil.* (Answers may vary.) LS **Verbal**

Motivate

Group Activity GENERAL

What Is Soil? Have groups of students do the following: Dig up and weigh a sample of soil from the school grounds. Then, spread the soil out on newspaper and break up large clumps. Examine the soil with a magnifying glass. Pick out animals and plants (alive or dead) and set aside. Sift the remaining soil through a wide mesh sieve, collecting what goes through on another sheet of newspaper. Observe and weigh what remains in the sieve (coarse soil). Sift the soil on the newspaper through fine mesh, collecting what goes through (fine soil). The soil that remains in the sieve is medium. Observe and weigh both samples. Have students make a graph that shows the composition of the soil and discuss what soil is. LS **Kinesthetic**

Key Resources

Chapter Resource File
- Directed Reading BASIC
- Inquiry Lab: Acid Rain and Soils GENERAL
- Making Models Lab: Soil Profiles GENERAL

Technology
- Transparencies
  Bellringer

Teach

Using the Figure GENERAL

Soil Horizons The descriptions on the left side of the figure provide the more thorough horizon classification used by soil scientists (OAEBCR). O = surface litter, or the organic layer; A = topsoil; E = zone of leaching; B = subsoil; C = rock particles; R = bedrock. Not all soils show all horizons. For example, agricultural soil often has little or no O horizon because plant remains are removed from fields. The E horizon is found only in heavily leached soils. Have interested students create a profile for soil on your school grounds by digging a hole and measuring the depths of the various layers.
LS Visual/Logical

Skill Builder BASIC

Math Forming soil takes an enormous amount of time. Estimates for forming 2.5 cm of topsoil range from 200 to 1,000 years, depending on various climatic and geographic factors. Have students determine the range in rates of soil formation in mm/year.

1 cm = 10 mm; 2.5 cm = 25 mm
25 mm ÷ 200 y = 0.125 mm/y
25 mm ÷ 1000 y = 0.025 mm/y;
range in mm/y = 0.025 to 0.125 mm/y **LS Logical**

Key Resources

Technology
- Transparencies
  73 Soil Horizons of Residual Soils

Soil Texture

Rock material in soil can be grouped into three main sizes: clay, silt, and sand. Clay particles have a diameter of less than 0.002 mm. Silt particles have diameters from 0.002 to 0.05 mm. Silt particles are too small to be seen easily, but they make soil feel gritty. Sand particles have diameters from 0.05 to 2 mm. The proportion of clay, silt, and sand in soil determines a soil's texture.

Soil Profile

Transported soils are commonly deposited in unsorted masses by water or wind. However, residual soils commonly develop distinct layers over time. To determine a soil's composition, scientists study a soil profile. A **soil profile** is a cross section of the soil and its bedrock. The different layers of soil are called **horizons.**

soil profile a vertical section of soil that shows the layers, or horizons

horizon a horizontal layer of soil that can be distinguished from the layers above and below it

humus dark, organic material formed in soil from the decayed remains of plants and animals

Residual soils generally consist of three main horizons. The *A horizon,* or *topsoil,* is a mixture of organic materials and small rock particles. Almost all organisms that live in soil inhabit the A horizon. As organisms die, their remains decay and produce **humus,** a dark, organic material. The A horizon is also the layer from which surface water leaches minerals. The *B horizon,* or *subsoil,* contains the minerals leached from the topsoil, clay, and sometimes humus. In dry climates, the B horizon also may contain minerals that accumulate as water in the soil evaporates. The *C horizon* consists of partially weathered bedrock. The first stages of mechanical and chemical change happen in this bottom layer. **Figure 2** shows the relationships between the three soil horizons.

Figure 2 Soil Horizons of Residual Soils

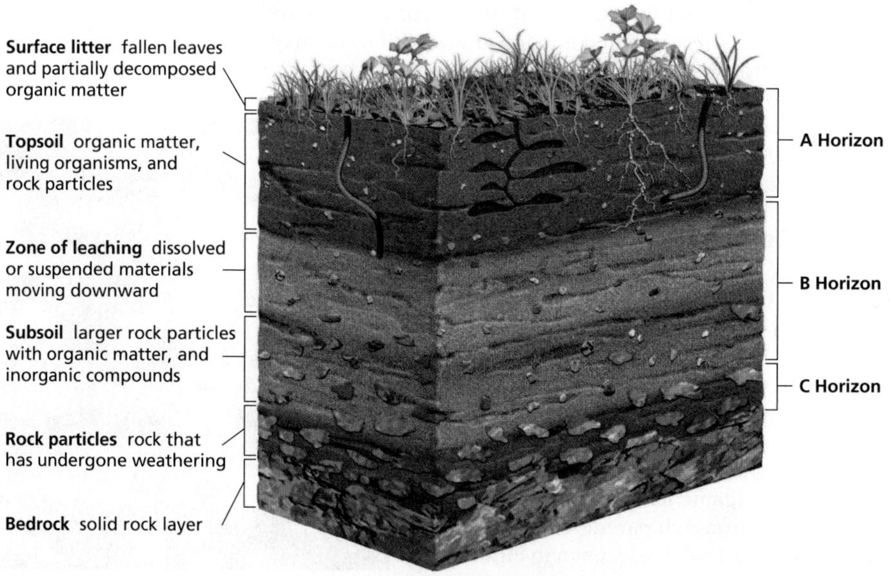

Why It Matters

Slash and Burn Although tropical soils are thick, they are not particularly fertile. Plant and animal remains quickly decay in the moist environment and are taken back up by plant roots. Most nutrients in a rainforest are locked up in the trees, and farming this soil is difficult. Using a practice called *shifting agriculture,* or "slash and burn," indigenous peoples have farmed the rainforests for thousands of years with little harm. They clear and burn small plots of forest and then farm for a few years, until nutrients are depleted. Then, they move on to a new patch, allowing forest to regrow on the old plot. On a small scale this worked well, but with growing populations, it contributes to deforestation. About half of tropical deforestation is related to this subsistence farming, and up to 12% of the plots are cleared not to raise food for locals, but to raise cattle for export to the developed world!

Soil and Climate

Climate is one of the most important factors that influence soil formation. Climate determines the weathering processes that occur in a region. These weathering processes, in turn, help to determine the composition of soil.

Tropical Soils

In humid tropical climates, where much rain falls and where temperatures are high, chemical weathering causes thick soils to develop rapidly. These thick, tropical soils, called *laterites* (LAT uhr IETS), contain iron and aluminum minerals that do not dissolve easily in water. Leached minerals from the A horizon sometimes collect in the B horizon. Heavy rains, which are common in tropical climates, cause a lot of leaching of the topsoil, and thus keep the A horizon thin. But because of the dense vegetation in humid, warm climates, organic material is continuously added to the soil. As a result, a thin layer of humus usually covers the B horizon, as shown in **Figure 3.**

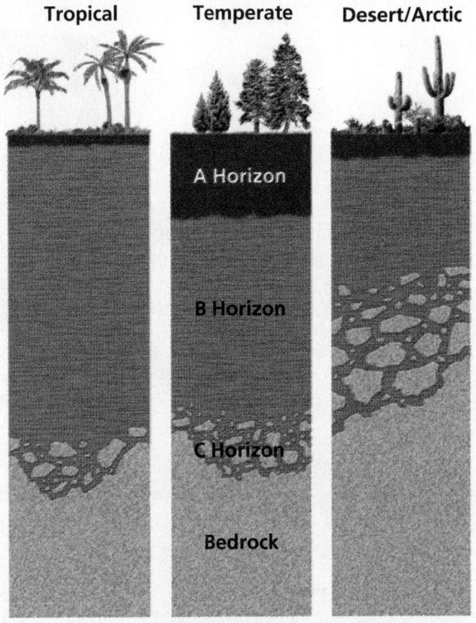

Figure 3 Tropical climates produce thick, infertile soils. Temperate climates produce thick, fertile soils. Desert and arctic climates produce thin soils.

Temperate Soils

In temperate climates, where temperatures range between cool and warm, and where rainfall is not excessive, both mechanical and chemical weathering occur. Temperate soils have the thickest A horizon, as shown in **Figure 3.**

Two main soil types form in temperate climates. In areas that receive more than 65 cm of rain per year, a type of soil called *pedalfer* (pi DAL fuhr) forms. Pedalfer soil contains clay, quartz, and iron compounds. The Gulf Coast states and states east of the Mississippi River have pedalfer soils. In areas that receive less than 65 cm of rain per year, a soil called *pedocal* (PED oh KAL) forms. Pedocal soil contains large amounts of calcium carbonate, which makes it very fertile and less acidic than pedalfer soil. The southwestern states and most states west of the Mississippi River have pedocal soils.

Academic Vocabulary

determine (dee TUHR muhn) to define or decide

Reading Check **Compare the formation of tropical soils and temperate soils.**

Desert and Arctic Soils

In desert and arctic climates, rainfall is minimal and chemical weathering occurs slowly. As a result, the soil is thin and consists mostly of regolith—evidence that the soil in these areas forms mainly by mechanical weathering. Also, desert and arctic climates are often too warm or too cold to sustain life, so their soils have little humus.

READING TOOLBOX

Tri-Fold

Create a tri-fold FoldNote to compare soil types in different climates. In the first column, write the type of soil. In the second column, describe the climate. In the third column, describe the soil.

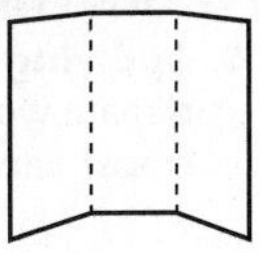

READING TOOLBOX

Tri-Fold Students should consult Appendix A for tips on making a Tri-Fold. The information for this Tri-Fold is shown in table form below.

Type of soil	Description of climate	Description of soil
laterites	tropical (humid, warm heavy rains)	- thick soils but thin A horizon
pedalfer pedocal	temperate (temperatures range between cool and warm, rainfall is not excessive)	- thick A horizon - pedalfer forms where there is high rainfall, pedocal where low rainfall - pedocal is more fertile and less acidic than pedalfer
regolith (layer of weathered rock fragments)	desert and arctic (very warm or very cold, rainfall is minimal)	- thin, with little humus

Close

Reteaching — BASIC

Flipbook Have students write the main soil types on index cards with a description of their soil profile and the factors that influence their formation. Students can also illustrate the cards. Have students bind the cards together with string or a binder ring and use them for review. **LS Visual**

Quiz — GENERAL

1. What type of parent rock forms sandy soil? (one with large amounts of quartz)
2. What is regolith? (the layer of weathered rock fragments that covers much of Earth's surface)

Answer to Reading Check

Large amounts of rainfall and high temperatures cause thick soils to form in both tropical and temperate climates. Tropical soils have thin A horizons because of the continuous leaching of topsoil. Temperate soils have three thick layers, because leaching of the A horizon in temperate climates is much less than leaching of the A horizon in tropical climates.

Environmental Connection

Acid Rain and Soil Not only does acid rain have an impact on weathering, it can affect fertility by altering soil chemistry. Excess acid washes some essential nutrients from soil, such as calcium and magnesium, but it can also make other minerals, such as manganese and aluminum, more available. Aluminum in high doses is toxic to plants. Vegetation shows more adverse effects from acid precipitation in some areas than in others. Have students hypothesize why this may be. (Pedocal soils in the west, for example, are alkaline and thus are more able to buffer the effects of acid precipitation. Pedalfer soils in the east are already acidic.) **LS Logical**

Close, *continued*

Answers to Section Review

1. Soils form by the mechanical and chemical weathering of rocks to form regolith. When the finer particles of regolith mix with organic matter and water, soil forms.
2. Soil composition, color, and texture are determined by parent rock composition.
3. The A horizon, or topsoil, is a mixture of small rock particles and organic matter. The B horizon, or subsoil, contains clay and minerals leached from the topsoil. The C horizon is partially weathered bedrock.
4. Thin soil, consisting mostly of regolith with little organic matter, will form in arctic climates. In the tropics, thick soils with thin A horizons will form.
5. A temperate climate would be ideal because it has well-developed soils with thick A horizons.
6. Sample answer: Crop growth would probably be more successful on level ground because the soil depth is thicker on level ground than it is on slopes.
7. Tropical soil has too thin an A horizon to be good for sustained farming. Crop plants rapidly use nutrients in the thin topsoil and good harvests cannot be sustained for long.
8. Arctic and desert soils are similar because of low rainfall, which reduces the rate of chemical weathering. In addition, both climates support fewer life forms, so humus is lacking in both soil types.
9. *Soil* is a mixture of *regolith* and *humus* and is classified as either *transported soil*, which is often different from the *bedrock* on which it rests, or *residual soil* which is greatly influenced by its *parent rock*, *climate*, and *topography* and develops a characteristic *soil profile* with distinct *horizons*.

Figure 4 Soil is thick at the top and bottom of a slope. Soil is thin along the slope.

Soil and Topography

The shape of the land, or topography, also affects soil formation. Because rainwater runs down a slope, much of the topsoil of the slope washes away. Therefore, as shown in **Figure 4,** the soil at the top and bottom of a slope tends to be thicker than the soil on the slope.

One study of soil in Canada showed that A horizons on flat areas were more than twice as thick as those on 10° slopes. Topsoil that remains on a slope is often too thin to support dense plant growth. The lack of vegetation contributes to the development of a poor-quality soil that lacks humus. The soils on the sides of mountains are commonly thin and rocky, with few nutrients. Lowlands that retain water tend to have thick, wet soils with a high concentration of organic matter, which forms humus. A fairly flat area that has good drainage provides the best surface for the formation of thick, fertile layers of residual soil.

SCILINKS.
www.scilinks.org
Topic: Soil
Code: HQX1407

Section 3 Review

Key Ideas

1. **Summarize** how soils form.
2. **Explain** how the composition of the parent rock affects soil composition.
3. **Describe** the three horizons of a residual soil.
4. **Predict** the type of soil that will form in arctic and tropical climates.

Critical Thinking

5. **Applying Ideas** What combination of soil and climate would be ideal for growing deep-rooted crops? Explain your answer.
6. **Analyzing Relationships** Would you expect crop growth to be more successful on a farm that has an uneven topography or on a farm that has level land? Explain your answer.
7. **Analyzing Ideas** Why would tropical soil not be good for sustained farming?
8. **Making Comparisons** Although desert and arctic climates are extremely different, their soils may be somewhat similar. Explain why.

Concept Mapping

9. Use the following terms to create a concept map: *soil, bedrock, regolith, humus, parent rock, residual soil, transported soil, horizon, soil profile, climate,* and *topography.*

Differentiated Instruction

Alternative Assessment

Soil Profiles Have students create a model soil profile for the climate of their choice. They should use a glass jar, organic litter, soil, and rock samples. Have them write a brief paragraph that describes their soil and the factors that influence its formation. **LS Visual**

ENVIRONMENTAL CONNECTION

SECTION 4
Erosion

Key Ideas	Key Terms	Why It Matters
❯ Define erosion, and list four agents of erosion. ❯ Identify four farming methods that conserve soil. ❯ Discuss two ways that gravity contributes to erosion. ❯ Describe the three major landforms shaped by weathering and erosion.	**erosion** **sheet erosion** **mass movement** **solifluction** **creep** **landform**	Erosion destroys homes, buildings, and lives every year—sometimes through dramatic events such as landslides. By understanding the factors involved in erosion, some of these consequences may be avoided.

When rock weathers, the resulting rock particles do not always stay near the parent rock. Various forces may move weathered fragments of rock away from where the weathering occurred. The process by which the products of weathering are transported is called **erosion.** The most common agents of erosion are gravity, wind, glaciers, and water. Water can move weathered rock in several different ways, including by ocean waves and currents, by streams and runoff, and by the movements of groundwater.

Soil Erosion

As rock weathers, it eventually becomes very fine particles that mix with water, air, and humus to form soil. The erosion of soil occurs worldwide and is normally a slow process. Ordinarily, new soil forms about as fast as existing soil erodes. However, some forms of land use and unusual climatic conditions can upset this natural balance. Once the balance is upset, soil erosion often accelerates.

Soil erosion is considered by some scientists to be the greatest environmental problem that faces the world today. As shown in **Figure 1,** vulnerability to erosion affects fertile topsoil around the world. This erosion prevents some countries from growing the crops needed to prevent widespread famine.

erosion a process in which the materials of Earth's surface are loosened, dissolved, or worn away and transported from one place to another by a natural agent, such as wind, water, ice, or gravity

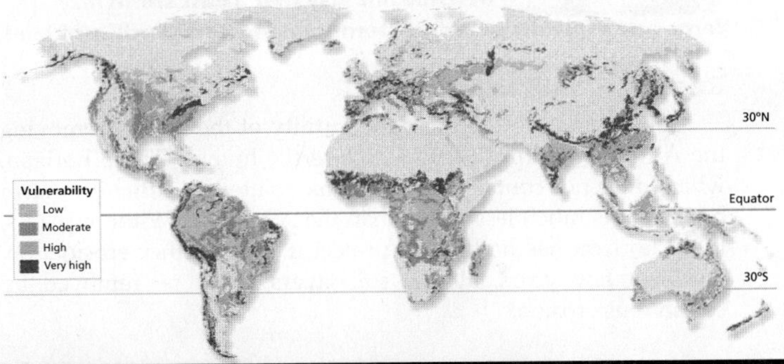

Figure 1 This map shows the vulnerability of soils to erosion by water.

Section 4

Focus

Overview

This section defines erosion, introduces agents of erosion, describes the basic landforms that are shaped by weathering and erosion, and explains soil conservation practices to reduce erosion. The section also describes mass movements and the catastrophic nature of rapid mass movement.

Bellringer

Ask students, "Why do the Rocky Mountains have jagged, rugged peaks, while the Appalachian Mountains have more rounded, gentle slopes?" (The Rocky Mountains are much younger than the Appalachian Mountains and have not undergone as many years of weathering and erosion that wear down rugged peaks to gentle slopes.)
LS Logical

Motivate

Using the Figure — GENERAL

Local Vulnerability Have students look at the world map that shows vulnerability of soils worldwide to erosion by water. Have them determine the vulnerability in your area. Discuss with students why your area may or may not be vulnerable to erosion by water and what conservation practices might be implemented to reduce or prevent erosion. **LS Visual**

Key Resources

Chapter Resource File
- Directed Reading BASIC

Technology
- Transparencies
  Bellringer
  74 Soil Erosion Vulnerability Map

Teach

History Connection

GENERAL

The Dust Bowl From 1930 to 1937, drought spread across the Great Plains from Mexico into Canada. In the years before the drought, native prairie grasses had been plowed under and replaced with wheat. The hardy native grasses could have withstood the drought, but the wheat could not. Repeated crop failure left the soil completely exposed. Winds swept across barren soils, causing massive dust storms and eroding millions of acres of topsoil. More than 74 million acres of land were severely damaged during the Dust Bowl years. *The Grapes of Wrath* by John Steinbeck and *Out of the Dust* by Karen Hesse movingly capture the plight of families living through this disaster. Have students read excerpts from these books and/or visit the PBS Web site, *Surviving the Dust Bowl*, to help them understand the impact of soil erosion.

LS Interpersonal

Answer to Reading Check

Dust storms may form during droughts when the soil is made dry and loose by lack of moisture and wind-caused sheet erosion carries it away in clouds of dust. If all the topsoil is removed, the remaining subsoil will not contain enough nutrients to raise crops.

Figure 2 This land in Madagascar can no longer be used for farming because of a form of rapid erosion called *gullying*.

SCILINKS®
www.scilinks.org
Topic: Soil Erosion
Code: HQX1410
Topic: Soil Conservation
Code: HQX1409

Gullying and Sheet Erosion

One farming technique that can accelerate soil erosion is the improper plowing of furrows, or long, narrow rows. Furrows that are plowed up and down slopes allow water to run swiftly over soil. As soil is washed away with each rainfall, the furrows become larger and form small gullies. Eventually, the land can become covered with deep gullies. This type of accelerated soil erosion is called *gullying*. The farmland shown in **Figure 2** has been ruined by gullying.

Another type of soil erosion strips away layers of topsoil. Eventually, erosion can expose the surface of the subsoil. This process is called **sheet erosion.** Sheet erosion may occur where continuous rainfall washes away layers of the topsoil. Wind also can cause sheet erosion during unusually dry periods. The soil, which is made dry and loose by a lack of moisture, is carried away by the wind as clouds of dust and drifting sand. These wind-borne particles may produce large dust storms.

sheet erosion the process by which water flows over a layer of soil and removes the topsoil

Reading Check **Describe one way that a dust storm may form, and explain how a dust storm can affect the fertility of land.**

Results of Soil Erosion

Constant erosion reduces the fertility of the soil by removing the A horizon, which contains the fertile humus. The B horizon, which does not contain much organic matter, is difficult to farm because it is much less fertile than the A horizon. Without plants, the B horizon has nothing to protect it from further erosion. So, within a few years, all the soil layers could be removed by continuous erosion.

Why It Matters

Worldwide Soil Losses Estimates indicate that we lose topsoil at a rate of 25 to 75 billion metric tons a year globally. This costs the global economy a staggering $400 billion dollars a year! Loss of topsoil reduces crop yield significantly because crops cannot be grown successfully if topsoil is too thin. In some areas, productivity has declined up to 50% due to erosion and desertification.

Geography Connection

The Badlands In South Dakota, gully erosion helped create the rugged sandstone peaks of Badlands National Park. The Sioux tribes named the area *malosche shica*–"bad land." French trappers called the region *mauvaises terres a traverser*–"bad lands to cross." Sudden rainstorms that cut deep into sandstone and soil created these rugged peaks. After the rain, the soil dries out quickly only to undergo the same process with the next storm. Over time, this process has created the deep gullies separated by sharp peaks.

Soil Conservation

Figure 3 Urban development and agriculture both contribute to the erosion of topsoil.

Erosion rates are affected not only by natural factors but also by human activities. Certain farming and grazing techniques and construction projects can also increase the rate of erosion. In developing urban areas, vegetation is removed to build houses and roads, such as those shown in **Figure 3.** This land clearing removes protective ground-cover plants and accelerates topsoil erosion. In some areas, such as deserts and mountainous regions, it may take hundreds or thousands of years for the topsoil to be replenished.

But rapid, destructive soil erosion can be prevented by soil conservation methods. People, including city planners and some land developers, have begun to recognize the environmental impact of land development and are beginning to implement soil conservation measures. Some land development projects are leaving trees and vegetation in place whenever possible. Other projects are planting cover plants to hold the topsoil in place. Farmers are also looking for new ways to minimize soil erosion and thus preserve fertile topsoil.

Why It Matters

Putting Worms to Work

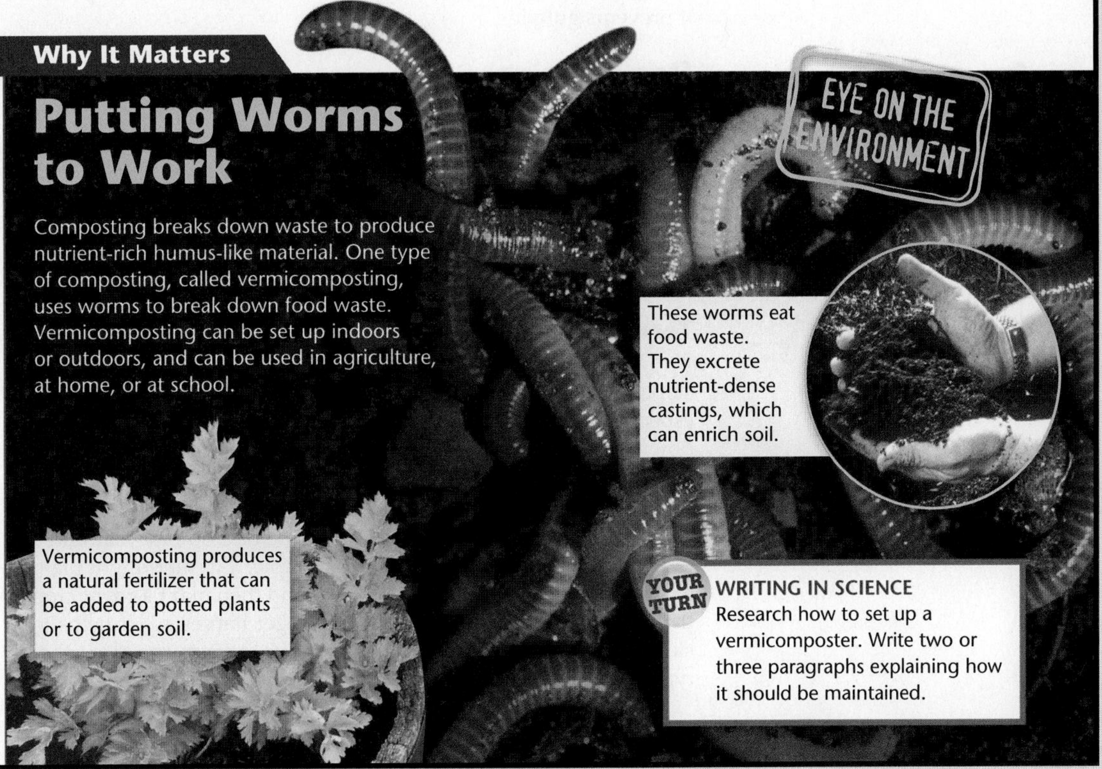

Composting breaks down waste to produce nutrient-rich humus-like material. One type of composting, called vermicomposting, uses worms to break down food waste. Vermicomposting can be set up indoors or outdoors, and can be used in agriculture, at home, or at school.

These worms eat food waste. They excrete nutrient-dense castings, which can enrich soil.

Vermicomposting produces a natural fertilizer that can be added to potted plants or to garden soil.

YOUR TURN **WRITING IN SCIENCE** Research how to set up a vermicomposter. Write two or three paragraphs explaining how it should be maintained.

Skill Builder — GENERAL

Math A severe rainstorm may wash away 1 mm of soil. Over a 20 yr period, this loss can add up to 2.5 cm. If 1 mm of soil from 1 hectare of land weighs 13 metric tons, how much topsoil may be lost in 20 years?
2.5 cm = 25 mm; 25 mm × 13 metric tons/mm = 325 metric tons
LS Logical

Why It Matters

Putting Worms to Work Red wrigglers are typically used for vermicomposting. In an established worm bin, different stages of the worm lifecycle are visible, including small ovate cocoons, which contain 1–3 tiny worms. Compost consisting of worm castings (manure) is very nutrient-rich. The nutrients are in a form that is highly available to plants.

Answer to Your Turn

Writing in Science Sample answer: A vermicomposter needs holes or openings to allow oxygen inside. The bin should be kept at a moderate temperature and should protect the worms from light. Bedding, such as shredded newspaper, is used in the bin to help trap moisture. The best foods for vermicomposting include vegetables and fruits, grains, coffee grounds, and other organic wastes. It is useful to add ground eggshells and gritty soil.

Differentiated Instruction

Basic Learners

Make Concepts Relevant Students may be unfamiliar with farming practices to reduce erosion, but they may have seen urban examples of erosion control. At construction sites, fabric fences, straw bales, slope regrading, groundcover planting on steep slopes, and detention ponds are just a few examples of methods used in urban settings to reduce erosion. Ask students to describe urban erosion control techniques they have seen. If possible, visit a local construction site to observe techniques.
LS Logical/Visual English Language Learners

Environmental Connection

Land Degradation As global population rises, we must find a way to feed, clothe, and shelter these future generations. At the same time, urbanization, deforestation, overgrazing, desertification, and other processes are degrading land around the world.

The biggest challenge of the 21st century may be feeding the world without destroying the land on which we depend. Have students look up the UN Global Assessment of Soil Degradation on the Internet for further information. **LS Logical/Verbal**

Teach, *continued*

READING TOOLBOX

Spider Map

Students' maps should have "Soil conservation methods" in the center. The main branches should include at least four of the following: using cover plants, leaving vegetation during construction, contour plowing, strip-cropping, terracing, and crop rotation. Details might describe each method and how it contributes to soil conservation.

Demonstration BASIC

Soil Conservation Fill two pans with packed soil. Raise one end of each pan with books. Make furrows across the slope of one pan to model contour plowing. Sprinkle both pans with water from a sprinkling can and observe what happens. The water should erode soil and wash it away, but the pan with furrows across the slope should experience less erosion. Challenge students to use the setup to model gullying and terracing.
LS Visual/Kinesthetic

Contour Plowing These fields were plowed in contours (or curves) that follow the shape of the land.

Strip-Cropping These fields were planted with alternating strips of different crops.

Terracing These terraced fields help slow runoff and prevent rapid soil erosion.

Figure 4 **Soil Conservation Methods**

Contour Plowing

Farmers in countries around the world use different planting methods to reduce soil erosion. In one method, called *contour plowing,* soil is plowed in curved bands that follow the contour, or shape, of the land. This method of planting, shown in the first part of **Figure 4,** prevents water from flowing directly down slopes, so it prevents gullying.

READING TOOLBOX

Spider Map
Create a spider map and label the center oval "Soil conservation methods." Then, fill in the map with at least four methods for soil conservation.

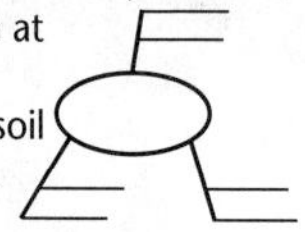

Strip-Cropping

In *strip-cropping,* crops are planted in alternating bands, also shown in **Figure 4.** A crop planted in rows, such as corn, may be planted in one band, and another crop that fully covers the surface of the land, such as alfalfa, will be planted next to it. The *cover crop* protects the soil by slowing the runoff of rainwater. Strip-cropping is often combined with contour plowing. The combination of these two methods can reduce soil erosion by 75%.

Terracing

The construction of steplike ridges that follow the contours of a sloped field is called *terracing,* as shown in **Figure 4.** Terraces, especially those used for growing rice in Asia, prevent or slow the downslope movement of water and thus prevent rapid erosion.

Crop Rotation

In *crop rotation,* farmers plant one type of crop one year and a different type of crop the next. For example, a farmer might plant a crop that will be harvested one year, and then plant a cover crop the next year. The cover crop does not get harvested. It helps to slow runoff and hold the soil in place. The main purpose of other types of crop rotation is to help maintain soil fertility.

Internet Activity GENERAL

NRCS The Natural Resources Conservation Service (NRCS) of the U.S. Department of Agriculture works with farmers and landowners to prevent loss of topsoil. Have students use the NRCS Web site to learn about soil conservation programs in your area and their effectiveness. A worksheet designed to direct student research on this topic can be found in the **Chapter Resource File** booklet or by visiting www.thinkcentral.com and entering the keyword **HQXWAEX.** **LS Verbal**

Gravity and Erosion

Gravity causes rock fragments to move down a slope. This movement of fragments down a slope is called **mass movement.** Some mass movements occur rapidly, and others occur very slowly.

mass movement the movement of a large mass of sediment or a section of land down a slope

Rockfalls and Landslides

The most dramatic and destructive mass movements occur rapidly. The fall of rock from a steep cliff is called a *rockfall.* A rockfall is the fastest kind of mass movement. Rocks in rockfalls often range in size from tiny fragments to giant boulders.

When masses of loose rock combined with soil suddenly fall down a slope, the event is called a *landslide.* Large landslides, in which loosened blocks of bedrock fall, generally occur on very steep slopes. You may have seen a small landslide on cliffs and steep hills overlooking highways, such as the one shown in **Figure 5.** Heavy rainfall, spring thaws, volcanic eruptions, and earthquakes can trigger landslides.

Academic Vocabulary

dramatic (druh MAT ik) vivid or striking

Reading Check **What is the difference between a rockfall and a landslide?**

Mudflows and Slumps

The rapid movement of a large amount of mud creates a *mudflow.* Mudflows occur in mountainous regions during sudden, heavy rainfall or as a result of volcanic eruptions. Mud churns and tumbles as it moves down slopes and through valleys, and it frequently spreads out in a large fan shape at the base of the slope. The mass movements that sometimes occur in hillside communities, such as the one shown in **Figure 5,** are often referred to as landslides, but they are actually mudflows.

Sometimes, a large block of soil and rock becomes unstable and moves downhill in one piece. The block of soil and rock then slides along the curved slope of the surface. This type of movement is called a *slump.* Slumping occurs along very steep slopes. Saturation by water and loss of friction with underlying rock causes loose soil and rock to slip downhill over the solid rock.

Figure 5 An earthquake in El Salvador caused this dramatic landslide (left). Heavy rains in the Philippines caused this destructive mudflow (right).

Skill Builder — Advanced

Writing Have students research a major landslide, mudflow, slump or other mass movement event that has occurred recently. Have students write a newspaper style article that describes the event and the conditions that contributed to its occurrence.
LS Verbal

Answer to Reading Check

Landslides are masses of loose rock combined with soil that suddenly fall down a slope. A rockfall consists of rock falling from a steep cliff.

Discussion — General

Protecting Against Mass Movements Although some mass movements are unpredictable and therefore unpreventable, others can be avoided. Geologists locate areas where mass movements have occurred, try to identify landforms and soils prone to mass movement, and look for signs of potential slump, creep, or other movement. Ask students to name landforms and soils prone to mass movement (clays, alpine and tundra soils, steep slopes, barren slopes, saturated soils) and signs of movement that geologists may look for. (tilted utility lines, cracks in building foundations, deep ridges and cracks in soil) Geologists use this information to create landslide potential maps that show regions susceptible to mass movement. If signs of movement are detected or land is prone to movement, common sense suggests not building there. If the area is already developed, steps can be taken to restabilize the slope. Ask students to discuss ways of doing this. (Answers may vary. Sample answers: replanting barren slopes, regrading slopes, terracing slopes, constructing retaining walls and other safety enclosures.) **LS Interpersonal**

Social Studies Connection — General

The Hills of Southern California The hills of southern California are extremely prone to mass movements of a catastrophic nature for several reasons. The region is hot and dry in the summer and supports mainly scrub and desert vegetation. Wildfires occur frequently leaving steep hillsides barren. When occasional heavy rains come, water quickly sinks into the sparsely covered hills, adding weight to the slopes, and making them unstable. Southern California also lies along an active plate boundary, the San Andreas fault. Numerous small earthquakes rock the area and shake those unstable masses free. Many Californians pay huge sums to live in the hills along the Pacific coast, even with the ever-present risk of mass movements that may destroy their homes. Over the years, homeowners and insurance companies have lost millions of dollars just to have "a room with a view." Have students debate the value of building in scenic areas that are prone to mass movements.
LS Verbal/Logical

Teach, *continued*

Demonstration — BASIC

Solifluction Build a slope out of modeling clay along one side of an aquarium or deep tray. Pour fine, dry sand over the slope, and then spray water on the sand until it becomes saturated. Have students describe what happens to the sand. (As the sand becomes saturated, it will slowly slip down the slope.) How does this model solifluction? (The clay subsoil is impermeable to water, so the sand above becomes saturated and slowly flows down the slope.) LS **Visual**

Why It Matters

Creeping Trees While you may not notice soil creep, other objects do. As soil slowly moves down slopes, power poles and gravestones tilt, fences and walls bend and crack, building foundations sink, and, believe it or not, trees bend. Trees that continue to grow on creeping soil have a pronounced curve at their base, as if they are trying to remain upright in opposition to the slide downhill!

solifluction the slow, downslope flow of soil saturated with water in areas surrounding glaciers at high elevations

creep the slow downhill movement of weathered rock material

Solifluction

Although most slopes appear to be unchanging, some slow mass movement commonly occurs. Catastrophic landslides are the most hazardous mass movement. However, more rock material is moved by the greater number of slow mass movements than by catastrophic landslides.

One form of slow mass movement is called solifluction. **Solifluction** is the process by which water-saturated soil slips over hard or frozen layers. Solifluction occurs in arctic and mountainous climates, where the subsoil is permanently frozen. In spring and summer, only the top layer of soil thaws. The moisture from this layer cannot penetrate the frozen layers beneath. So, the surface layer becomes muddy and slowly flows downslope, or downhill. Solifluction can also occur in warmer regions, where the subsoil consists of hard clay. The clay layer acts like the frozen subsoil in arctic climates by forming a waterproof barrier.

Creep

The extremely slow downhill movement of weathered rock material is known as **creep.** Soil creep moves the most soil of all types of mass movements. But creep may go unnoticed unless buildings, fences, or other surface objects move along with soil.

Many factors contribute to soil creep. Water separates rock particles, which allows them to move freely. Growing plants produce a wedgelike pressure that separates rock particles and loosens the soil. The burrowing of animals and repeated freezing and thawing loosen rock particles and allow gravity to slowly pull the particles downhill.

As rock fragments accumulate at the base of a slope, they form piles called *talus* (TAY luhs), as shown in **Figure 6.** Talus weathers into smaller fragments, which move farther down the slope. The fragments wash into gullies, are carried into successively larger waterways, and eventually flow into rivers.

Figure 6 The movement of rock fragments downslope formed these talus cones at the base of the Canadian Rockies.

Differentiated Instruction

Special Education Students

Erosion Use the following procedure to help students understand the idea of erosion:

1. Collect about 20 L of dirt, about 16 L of water, a 1 L plastic container, a sprinkling can, and an 8-1/2" × 11" piece of cardboard.
2. Divide the class into three teams. Assign a section of sidewalk to each team.
3. Have each team spread a thin layer of dirt about 1 m^3 in size.
4. Ask each team to simulate one of the following: blowing wind (fan with cardboard), gentle rain (water from the sprinkling can), or gushing rain (water from the plastic container).
5. Compare and contrast the effects of each of the three forms of erosion.
6. Clean up the sidewalk. LS **Kinesthetic**

Figure 7 The mountains in the Patagonian Andes, shown on the left, are still being uplifted and are more rugged than the more eroded Appalachian mountains on the right.

Erosion and Landforms

Through weathering and erosion, Earth's surface is shaped into different physical features, or **landforms.** There are three major landforms that are shaped by weathering and erosion: *mountains, plains,* and *plateaus.* Minor landforms that are shaped by weathering and erosion include hills, valleys, and dunes. The shapes of landforms are also influenced by rock composition.

All landforms are subject to two opposing sets of processes. One set of processes bends, breaks, and lifts Earth's crust and thus creates elevated, or uplifted, landforms. The other set of processes includes weathering and erosion, which wear down land surfaces.

landform a physical feature of Earth's surface

Erosion of Mountains

During the early stages in the history of a mountain, the mountain undergoes uplift. Generally, while tectonic forces are uplifting the mountain, it rises faster than it is eroded. Mountains that are being uplifted tend to be rugged and have sharp peaks and deep, narrow valleys. When forces stop uplifting the mountain, weathering and erosion wear down the rugged peaks to rounded peaks and gentle slopes. The formations in **Figure 7** show how the shapes of mountains are influenced by uplift and erosion.

Over millions of years, mountains that are not being uplifted become low, featureless surfaces. These areas are called *peneplains* (PEE nuh PLAYNZ), which means "almost flat." A peneplain commonly has low, rolling hills, as seen in New England.

Reading Check Describe how a mountain changes after it is no longer uplifted.

Geology Connection — General

What Goes Up There is a limit to how high mountains on Earth can grow for two basic reasons. First, as soon as mountains uplift, weathering and erosion start to attack and wear them down. Second, rocks are not infinitely strong. The weight of uplifted rock weighs down on rock buried deep below. The buried rocks gradually warm, soften, and flow. Mountains essentially begin to collapse under their own weight in a process geologists call *orogenic collapse.*

Activity — Basic

Plants and Soil To demonstrate the importance of plant cover in reducing soil erosion have students observe the root system of a potted plant. Run a knife around the edge of the pot to loosen the plant. Have students turn the pot upside down to remove the plant. Ask students to observe how the roots hold the soil together in a compact mass. If possible, have students observe the root system of grasses in a piece of sod. Have students write a brief paragraph that explains why strip-cropping and crop rotation are effective soil conservation methods. **LS Visual**

Answer to Reading Check

When a mountain is no longer being uplifted, weathering and erosion wear down its jagged peaks to low, featureless surfaces called *peneplains.*

Close

Reteaching — Basic

Section Summary Have students work in small groups to summarize the main points under each heading. After the groups have finished their summaries, quiz students orally to ensure their understanding. **LS Verbal**

Quiz — General

1. Where is solifluction most likely to occur? (in arctic or mountain climates where the subsoil remains permanently frozen or in regions where the subsoil is hard clay)
2. What is talus? (piles of rock fragments that accumulate at the base of a slope)

Close, *continued*

Answers to Section Review

1. Erosion is the process by which materials of Earth's surface are loosened, dissolved, or worn away and transported from one place to another by natural agents.
2. wind, water, glaciers, and gravity
3. Answers may vary. Sample answer: Gullying occurs when furrows are plowed up and down a slope. Rainfall runs swiftly through the furrows widening and deepening them. Sheet erosion occurs when water or wind flows over soil and removes the top layers in entire sheets.
4. contour plowing, strip cropping, terracing, and crop rotation
5. Gravity causes water to move down slopes and carry away topsoil. It also causes mass movements of rocks and soil.
6. Rapid mass movements include rockfalls, landslides, mudflows, and slumping and can be catastrophic in nature. Creep and solifluction are slow mass movements, and while they usually are not catastrophic, over time they can move more material than rapid movement does.
7. Mountains are eroded from rugged peaks into rounded gentle slopes over millions of years. Plains are flat landforms near sea level and that are usually not subject to as much erosion as plateaus are. Plateaus, broad flat landforms with a high elevation, may erode into mesas and buttes over time.

Figure 8 Ancient rivers carved plateaus into mesas, which eventually eroded into the buttes of Monument Valley in Arizona.

Erosion of Plains and Plateaus

A *plain* is a relatively flat landform near sea level. A *plateau* is a broad, flat landform that has a high elevation. A plateau is subject to much more erosion than a plain. Young plateaus, such as the Colorado Plateau in the southwestern United States, commonly have deep stream valleys that separate broad, flat regions. Older plateaus, such as those in the Catskill region in New York State, have been eroded into rugged hills and valleys.

The effect of weathering and erosion on a plateau depends on the climate and the composition and structure of the rock. In dry climates, resistant rock produces plateaus that have flat tops. As a plateau ages, erosion may dissect the plateau into smaller, tablelike areas called *mesas* (MAY suhz). Mesas ultimately erode into small, narrow-topped formations called *buttes* (BYOOTS). In dry areas, such as in the area shown in **Figure 8**, mesas and buttes have steep walls and flat tops. In areas that have wet climates, humidity and precipitation weather landforms into round shapes.

Section 4 Review

Key Ideas

1. **Define** erosion.
2. **List** four agents of erosion.
3. **Summarize** two processes of soil erosion.
4. **Identify** four farming methods that result in soil conservation.
5. **Discuss** two ways gravity contributes to erosion.
6. **Compare** rapid mass movements with slow mass movements.
7. **Describe** the erosion of the three major landforms.

Critical Thinking

8. **Analyzing Relationships** Describe an experiment that could help you determine whether a nearby hill is undergoing creep.
9. **Applying Ideas** Suppose that you wanted to grow grapevines on a hillside in Italy. What farming methods would you use? Explain your answer.
10. **Predicting Consequences** Describe two ways that a small butte would change if it was in a wet climate, rather than a dry climate.
11. **Drawing Conclusions** A hillside community has asked you to help brainstorm ways to prevent future mudflows. Describe three of your ideas.

Concept Mapping

12. Use the following terms to create a concept map: *erosion, gullying, sheet erosion, landslide, mudflow, slump, solifluction, creep, talus, landform, mountain, plain, plateau, mesa,* and *butte.*

8. Sample answer: Place a stick or pole in the ground on the slope and monitor its position over time.
9. contour planting with strip cropping between the rows of vines or terracing to reduce hillside erosion
10. The butte would probably have shallower slopes and a more rounded top.

Answers continued on page 507A

Differentiated Instruction

Alternative Assessment

Conservation Plans Have students work in groups to develop a conservation plan to reduce weathering and erosion around their school or home. Have each group prepare a poster or pamphlet that illustrates their plan and the steps they would take to implement it. The Natural Resources Conservation Service Web site has information that may help students develop their plans. **LS Visual/Verbal**

Why It Matters

Living on the Edge

Weathering and erosion are natural processes that reshape Earth's surface. Mass movements are characteristic of steep hills and shorelines—landforms that humans value, and on which homes are often built. About 25% of the homes and buildings within 150 m of the U.S. coastline and shores of the Great Lakes will be lost due to erosion within the next 60 years, according to the Federal Emergency Management Agency.

Erosion barriers, like these, are intended to slow the movement of sediment. These barriers must be maintained, replaced, and repaired regularly.

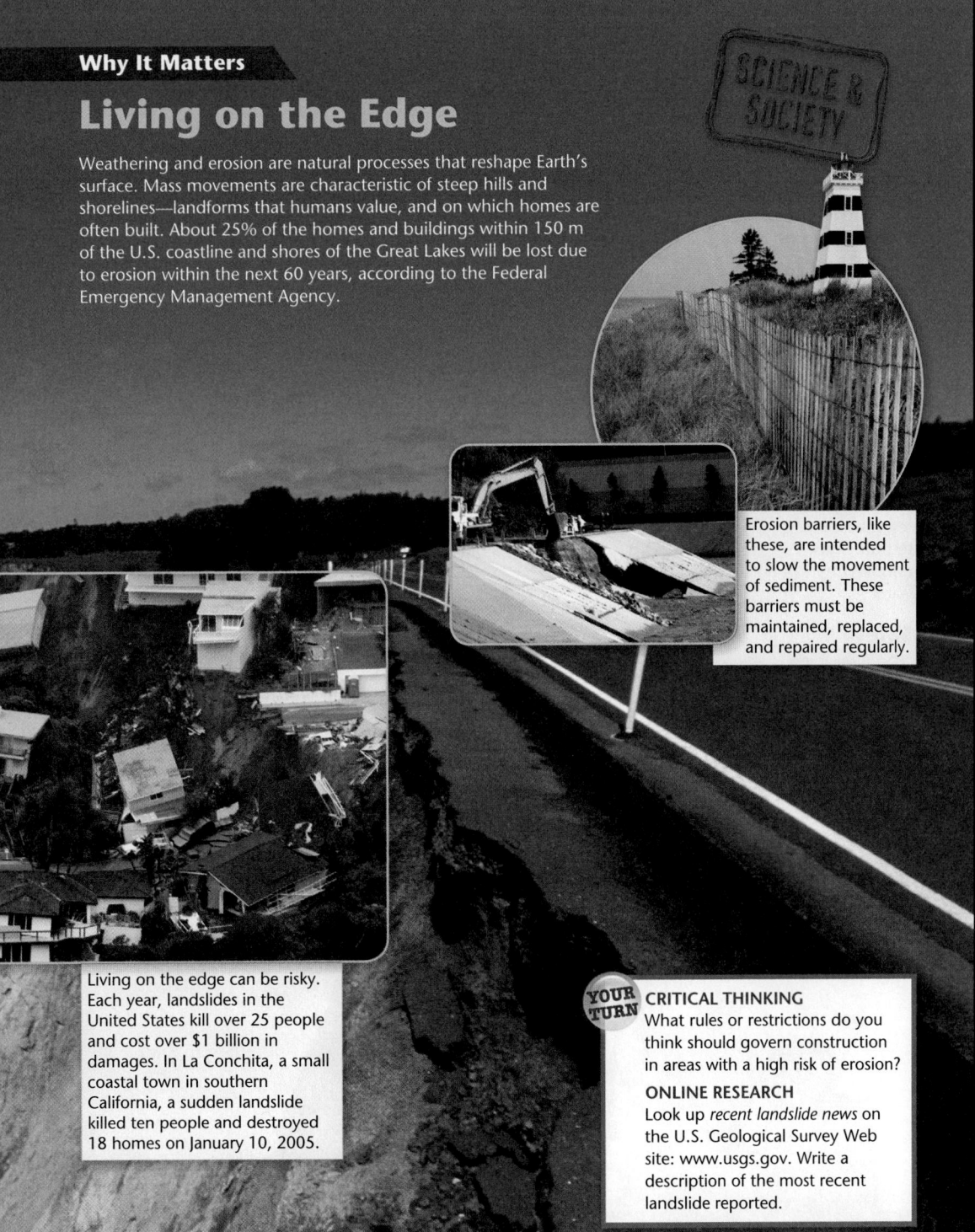

Living on the edge can be risky. Each year, landslides in the United States kill over 25 people and cost over $1 billion in damages. In La Conchita, a small coastal town in southern California, a sudden landslide killed ten people and destroyed 18 homes on January 10, 2005.

YOUR TURN

CRITICAL THINKING
What rules or restrictions do you think should govern construction in areas with a high risk of erosion?

ONLINE RESEARCH
Look up *recent landslide news* on the U.S. Geological Survey Web site: www.usgs.gov. Write a description of the most recent landslide reported.

Why It Matters

Living on the Edge

The number of people threatened by landslides increases each year because of the popularity of residential development on coasts and hillsides. The loss of homes from erosion is highest along the coast of the Atlantic Ocean and the Gulf of Mexico. Homes built on hillsides in tectonically active southern California are threatened by destruction from landslides. Not building on coasts and hillsides is the only way to eliminate the risk. Other measures, such as stabilizing slopes to prevent the rising of groundwater, directing water away from buildings, construction of retaining structures, and removing mass from the top of slopes, can reduce the risk of erosion and landslides.

Answers to Your Turn

Critical Thinking Student answers will vary. Construction in areas with a high risk of erosion could be subject to zoning restrictions and inspections by experts, such as engineering geologists. Landowners could also be required to purchase insurance to cover the cost of destruction caused by erosion and landslides.

Online Research The U.S. Geological Survey Web site (www.usgs.gov) provides monthly descriptions of landslides that have occurred around the world. Students should identify and describe the most recent landslide listed.

Skill Practice **Lab**

Time Required
one 45-minute class period

Lab Ratings
EASY → HARD

Teacher Preparation (2 of 4)
Student Setup (3 of 4)
Concept Level (2 of 4)
Cleanup (2 of 4)

Skills Acquired
- Measuring
- Collecting Data
- Predicting
- Organizing and Analyzing Data

Scientific Methods
In this lab, students will
- Make Observations
- Analyze Results
- Draw Conclusions
- Communicate Results

Materials
The materials listed on this page are enough for groups of two to four students.

Skills Practice **Lab**

45 min

Soil Chemistry

Different soil types contain different kinds and amounts of minerals. To support plant life, soil must have a proper balance of mineral nutrients. For plants to take in the nutrients they need, the soil must also have the proper acidity.

Acidity is measured on a scale called the *pH scale*. The pH scale ranges from 0 (acidic) to 14 (alkaline). A pH of 7 is neutral (neither acidic nor alkaline). In this lab, you will test the acidity of soil samples.

What You'll Do
- **Test** the acidity of soil samples.
- **Identify** the composition of soil samples.

What You'll Need
ammonia solution
stoppers, cork (9)
hydrochloric acid, dilute
medicine dropper
pH probe
subsoil sample (B and C horizons)
test tubes, 9
test-tube rack
topsoil sample (A horizon)
water

Safety

Procedure

1. Place the tip of the pH probe in the tap water. Look at the pH readout. What is the pH of the tap water?
2. Put some topsoil in a clean test tube until it is one-eighth full. Add water to the test tube until it is three-quarters full. Place a cork stopper on the test tube, and shake the test tube.
3. Set the soil and water mixture aside in the test-tube rack to settle. When the water is fairly clear, test it with a piece of pH paper. What is the pH of the soil sample? Is the soil acidic or alkaline?
4. Repeat steps 2 and 3 with the subsoil sample.
5. Pedalfer soils tend to be acidic. Pedocal soils tend to be alkaline. Based on the pH results in steps 3 and 4, predict whether your soil is pedalfer or pedocal.

Tips and Tricks
Make sure students are familiar with the safety precautions required when working with acids and bases. They should wear a lab apron and goggles throughout the entire period. Make sure students understand pH and how to read pH paper. Remind students to review the differences between pedalfer and pedocal soils so that they understand why they are performing steps 6–11.

6. To test your prediction, you will need to test the soil's composition. Take five rock particles from the subsoil sample. Place each particle in a separate test tube. Use the dropper to add two drops of hydrochloric acid, HCl, to the test tubes. **CAUTION** If you spill any acid on your skin or clothing, rinse immediately with cool water and alert your teacher.

7. HCl has little or no effect on silicates, but HCl reacts with calcium carbonate and causes CO_2 gas to bubble out of solution. How many of the rock particles were silicates? How many were calcium carbonate?

8. Put some of the subsoil in another test tube until it is one-eighth full. Slowly add HCl to the test tube until it is about two-thirds full. Cork the test tube, and gently shake it. **CAUTION** Always shake the test tube by pointing it away from yourself and other students.

9. After shaking the test tube, remove the stopper and set the test tube in the rack. Record your observations. After the mixture has settled, draw the test tube and its contents. Label each layer. If iron is present, the solution may look brown. What color is the liquid above the soil sample?

10. Use a medicine dropper to place 10 drops of the liquid in a clean test tube. Carefully add 12 drops of ammonia to the test tube. Test the pH of the solution. If the pH is greater than 8, any iron should settle out as a reddish-brown residue. The remaining solution will be colorless.

11. If the pH is less than 8, add two more drops of ammonia and test the pH again. Continue adding ammonia until the pH reaches 8 or higher. Record your observations, and draw a diagram of the test tube. Label each layer of material in the test tube.

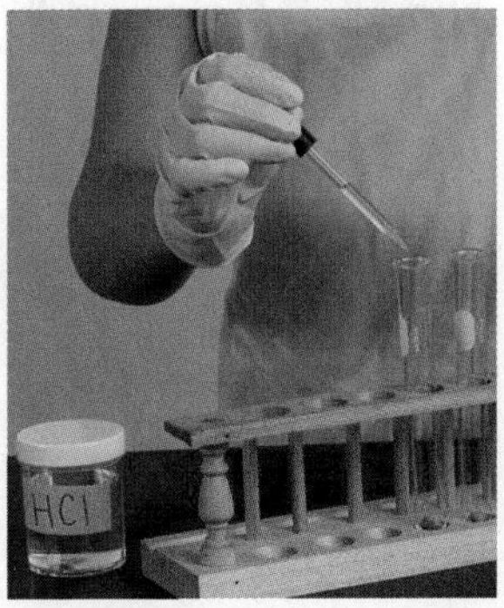

Step 6

Analysis

1. **Analyzing Results** Is your soil sample most likely pedalfer or pedocal? Explain your answer.
2. **Drawing Conclusions** What type of soil, pedalfer or pedocal, would you treat with acidic substances, such as phosphoric acid, sulfur, and ammonium sulfate, to help plant growth? Explain your answer.
3. **Recognizing Relationships** Explain why acidic substances are usually spread on the surface of the soil.

Extension

Research Use a library or the Internet to learn why the use of phosphate and nitrate detergents has been banned in some areas. Report your findings to the class.

Answers to Analysis

1. Answers may vary depending on the samples provided and the results of the tests. Pedalfer soil should be acidic and have silicates and iron. Pedocal should be alkaline and be composed mainly of carbonates.
2. Pedocal soils tend to be alkaline. They would be treated with acidic substances to reduce their pH, bringing it closer to neutral, which helps make certain minerals more available for plant uptake.
3. Acidic substances are spread on the surface of the soil because as water percolates through the soil, the acids will dissolve in the water and will aid in making certain minerals and nutrients found in the topsoil more available for plant uptake.

Answer to Extension

Answers may vary. Accept all reasonable answers. Students will likely find that phosphate detergents are banned in some areas because they run off into waterways and promote algae growth and cultural eutrophication of streams and lakes. Fertilizers contain nitrates and phosphates. When too much fertilizer is applied to soils, the excess may runoff in streams, rivers and lakes, promoting eutrophication. Phosphates and nitrates promote algae growth because they contain phosphorus and nitrogen, which (along with potassium) are the primary nutrients needed for plant growth.

Soil Map of North Carolina

Discussion GENERAL

Local Soils Obtain a map of your state that identifies the various soil types in your region. Discuss with students the various soil types and the conditions that led to their development. Discuss which, if any, regions in your state are most fertile, whether the area is currently used for food production, and whether it is threatened by land degradation. LS **Visual**

Answers to Map Skills Activity

1. 4
2. Large River Valleys and Flood Plain Systems; Outer Banks System; Brackish and Freshwater Marsh Systems; Organic Soil System; Lower Coastal Plain—Pamlico System; and Lower Coastal Plain—Wicomico and Talbot System
3. Answers may vary. Both Fayetteville and Wilmington are located within the "Large River Valleys and Flood Plain System" of soils, which indicates that they are located near a river.
4. mountains; Asheville is surrounded by the mountain soil region.
5. The Brackish and Freshwater Marsh Systems are located where major rivers empty into the ocean.
6. The average elevation would decrease from west to east, as you move from the mountains, through the piedmont (or foothills), and into the coastal plains. This trend is indicated both by the locations of the mountain, piedmont, and coastal plain soil regions and by the flow of the rivers eastward toward the ocean.

MAPS *in Action*

Soil Map of North Carolina

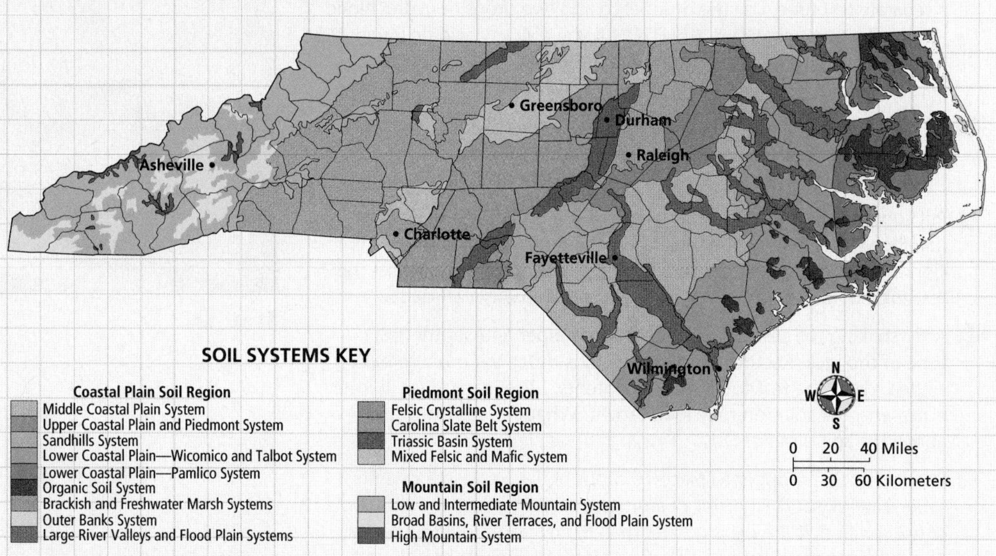

Map Skills Activity

This map shows soil systems in the state of North Carolina, including the Outer Banks barrier island system. Use the map to answer the questions below.

1. **Using a Key** How many colors on the map represent soil systems in the Piedmont Soil Region?
2. **Using a Key** Which soil systems are present along the eastern shore of North Carolina?
3. **Analyzing Data** Which city is located on the banks of a large river or in a river valley? Explain your answer.
4. **Inferring Relationships** What landforms would you expect to surround the town of Asheville? Explain your answer.
5. **Analyzing Relationships** Brackish water is water that is somewhat salty but not as salty as sea water. How does this fact explain the location of the Brackish and Freshwater Marsh soil systems?
6. **Identifying Trends** How would you describe the change in elevation of North Carolina, from west to east, based on the locations of soil systems? Explain your answer.

Key Resources

Technology

- Transparencies
  75 Soil Map of North Carolina

Chapter 14

Summary

THINK central
SUPER SUMMARY
Keyword: HQXWAES

Key Ideas | **Key Terms**

Section 1

Weathering Processes

- Ice, plants and animals, gravity, running water, and wind are all agents of mechanical weathering.
- Mechanical weathering physically breaks down rock. Chemical weathering changes the chemical composition of rock.
- Oxidation, hydrolysis, carbonation, and acid precipitation are four chemical reactions that decompose rock.

Key Terms:
weathering, p. 373
mechanical weathering, p. 373
abrasion, p. 374
chemical weathering, p. 376
oxidation, p. 376
hydrolysis, p. 377
carbonation, p. 377
acid precipitation, p. 378

Section 2

Rates of Weathering

- Softer rock weathers more rapidly than harder rock.
- Rock weathers faster when more surface area is exposed.
- Rock weathers fastest in climates with alternating hot and cold weather and steady moisture. Higher elevations may have more ice wedging. Gravity affects slopes.

Key Terms:
differential weathering, p. 379

Section 3

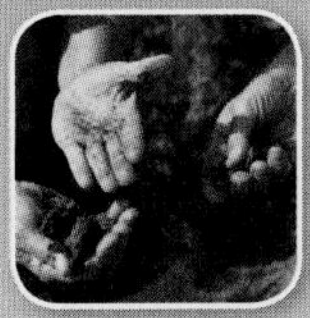

Soil

- Weathered rock, water, gases, and organic material form soils.
- The composition of parent rock determines the proportion of clay, sand, and silt in the resulting soil.
- Mature residual soils contain three layers: the A horizon, B horizon, and C horizon.
- Thick soils form in tropical and temperate climates. Thin soils form in arctic and desert climates, where rainfall is minimal.

Key Terms:
soil, p. 383
soil profile, p. 384
horizon, p. 384
humus, p. 384

Section 4

Erosion

- Erosion transports weathered rock. Gravity, wind, glaciers, and water are four agents of erosion.
- Contour plowing, strip-cropping, terracing, and crop rotation are four farming methods that conserve soil.
- Gravity contributes to erosion through rapid mass movements, such as rockfalls, and through slow mass movements, such as creep.
- Mountains, plains, and plateaus are three major landforms shaped by weathering and erosion.

Key Terms:
erosion, p. 387
sheet erosion, p. 388
mass movement, p. 391
solifluction, p. 392
creep, p. 392
landform, p. 393

Chapter Summary

Using THINK central Resources

Super Summary

Have students connect the major concepts in this chapter through an interactive Super Summary. Visit www.thinkcentral.com and type in the keyword **HQXWAES** to access the Super Summary for this chapter.

Activity — ADVANCED

Life as a Rock Have students write the life story of a rock. They should include details such as the landform where it originated; how it has been weathered, eroded, and transported; and whether it has become part of the soil. Students can illustrate their story if they wish. Some may want to write their stories as children's books. Encourage creativity, but make sure the stories are factually possible.
LS Verbal

Chapter Review

Assignment Guide	
Section	**Questions**
1	2, 6, 7, 10, 11, 18, 20
2	12, 13, 19, 25, 28, 30
3	3, 8, 14, 15, 37, 38
4	1, 4, 9, 16, 17, 21–23, 26, 29, 33–35
2 and 4	5, 24, 31
1 and 2	27, 36
1–4	32

Reading Toolbox

1. **Finding Examples** Practices that increase soil erosion include improper plowing of furrows, leaving bare soil, certain grazing techniques, not rotating crops, and not using methods to slow run-off. Practices that help conserve soil include contour plowing, strip-cropping, terracing, and crop rotation. Accept other reasonable examples.

Using Key Terms

2–9. Answers may vary but should show that students understand the definitions of and differences between key terms.

Understanding Key Ideas

10. b
11. b
12. d
13. d
14. c
15. a
16. d
17. d
18. c
19. c

Short Answer

20. Natural rain is slightly acidic due to the dissolution of carbon dioxide in water to create weak carbonic acid. Acid precipitation is considerably more acidic and contains nitric, nitrous, and sulfuric acids.
21. Answers may vary. Sample answer: Soil conservation is important to retain soil fertility mainly found in the A horizon and to avoid complete removal of all soil layers.
22. A mountain changes from a rugged mountain to gently rounded hills and finally to low, featureless surfaces called *peneplains* through processes of weathering and erosion over millions of years.
23. mountains, plains (flat landforms near sea level), and plateaus (broad, flat landforms with high elevation)
24. Weathering breaks down rocks into material that can be easily eroded, and both weathering and erosion are involved in shaping Earth's landforms.
25. Climates with wide seasonal variation in temperature have higher rates of weathering because of numerous freeze/thaw cycles. Warm, humid climates increase rates of chemical weathering because of the constant exposure to moisture. Lack of water in deserts and cold, dry climates decreases rates of weathering.
26. plateaus, mesas, and buttes

Chapter 14 Review

1. **Finding Examples** Review Section 4. As you review, list four examples of farming practices that increase soil erosion and four examples of farming methods that help to conserve soil. (READING TOOLBOX)

USING KEY TERMS

Use each of the following terms in a separate sentence.

2. *abrasion*
3. *humus*
4. *landform*

For each pair of terms, explain how the meanings of the terms differ.

5. *weathering* and *erosion*
6. *mechanical weathering* and *chemical weathering*
7. *oxidation* and *carbonation*
8. *soil profile* and *horizon*
9. *solifluction* and *creep*

UNDERSTANDING KEY IDEAS

10. A common kind of mechanical weathering is called
    a. oxidation. **c.** carbonation.
    b. ice wedging. **d.** leaching.
11. Oxides of sulfur and nitrogen that combine with water vapor cause
    a. hydrolysis.
    b. acid rain.
    c. mechanical weathering.
    d. carbonation.
12. The surface area of rocks exposed to weathering is increased by
    a. burial. **c.** leaching.
    b. accumulation. **d.** jointing.
13. Chemical weathering is most rapid in
    a. hot, dry climates.
    b. cold, dry climates.
    c. cold, wet climates.
    d. hot, wet climates.
14. The chemical composition of soil depends to a large extent on
    a. topography.
    b. the soil's A horizon.
    c. the parent material.
    d. the soil's B horizon.
15. The soil in tropical climates is often
    a. thick. **c.** dry.
    b. thin. **d.** fertile.
16. All of the following farming methods prevent gullying, *except*
    a. terracing. **c.** contour plowing.
    b. strip-cropping. **d.** irrigation.
17. The type of mass movement that moves the most soil is
    a. a landslide. **c.** a rockfall.
    b. a mudflow. **d.** creep.
18. The grinding away of rock surfaces through the mechanical action of rock or sand particles is called
    a. carbonation. **c.** abrasion.
    b. hydrolysis. **d.** erosion.
19. The process by which softer rock wears away and leaves harder rock behind is
    a. chemical weathering.
    b. mechanical weathering.
    c. differential weathering.
    d. erosion.

SHORT ANSWER

20. What is the difference between natural rain and acid precipitation?
21. Explain two reasons why soil conservation is important.
22. Describe how a mountain changes from a rugged mountain to a peneplain.
23. Describe three landforms that are shaped by weathering and erosion.
24. Explain two ways that weathering and erosion are related.
25. Identify three ways that climate affects the rate of weathering.
26. Name three landforms that you would expect to find in a desert.

CRITICAL THINKING

27. **Making Comparisons** Compare the weathering processes that affect a rock on top of a mountain with those that affect a rock beneath the ground surface.
28. **Understanding Relationships** Which do you think would weather faster, a sculpted marble statue or a smooth marble column? Explain your answer.
29. **Making Inferences** Mudflows in the southern California hills are usually preceded by a dry summer and widespread fires, which are followed by torrential rainfall. Explain why these phenomena are followed by mudflows.
30. **Evaluating Ideas** How can differential weathering help you determine whether a rock is harder or softer than the rock that surrounds it?
31. **Inferring Relationships** Suppose that a mountain has been wearing down at the rate of about 2 cm per year for 10 years. After 10 years, scientists find that the mountain is no longer losing elevation. Why do you think the mountain is no longer losing elevation?

CONCEPT MAPPING

32. Use the following terms to create a concept map: *composition, mechanical weathering, chemical weathering, topography, erosion, conservation, exposure, weathering, surface area,* and *climate.*

MATH SKILLS

Math Skills

33. **Making Calculations** A group of scientists calculates that an acre of land has crept 18 cm in 15 years. What is the average rate of creep in millimeters per year?
34. **Making Calculations** For a given area of land, the average rate of creep is 14 mm per year. How long will it take the area to move 1 m?

WRITING SKILLS

35. **Writing from Research** Research a mudslide or landslide that occurred in the past. Describe the conditions that led to this mass movement and the impact it had.
36. **Communicating Ideas** You are in charge of preserving a precious marble statue. Write a paragraph that describes how you would protect the statue from weathering.

INTERPRETING GRAPHICS

The graph below shows land use in the United States. Use this graph to answer the questions that follow.

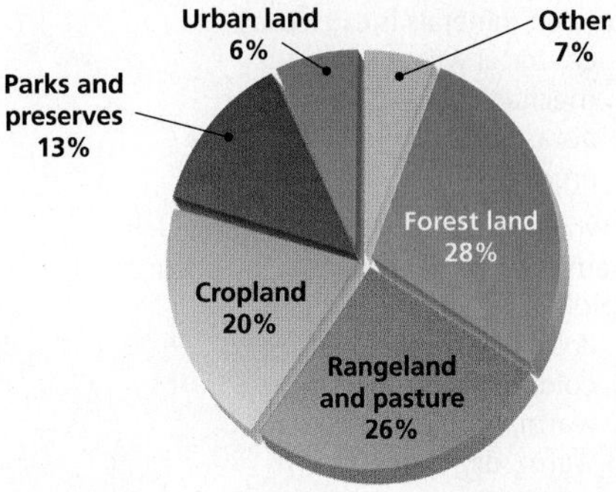

37. How much more land is rangeland and pasture than is urban land?
38. If cropland increased to 25% and all the other categories remained the same, except for forests, what would the percentage of forests be?

Chapter Review

Critical Thinking

27. A rock at the top of a mountain would be greatly affected by gravity and might be involved in rockslides. It would also be mechanically and chemically weathered because of exposure. A rock beneath the ground surface might be mechanically and chemically weathered by water seeping down to it through joints and fractures in the overlying ground, but lack of exposure to the atmosphere might prevent much weathering.
28. Assuming the two structures are located in the same climate, a sculpted marble statue would probably weather faster because it would have more surface area and cracks and crevices than a smooth marble column would.
29. Dry summers and wildfires strip hillsides of vegetation that could hold the soil in place. Then, heavy rains saturate the soils, creating heavy, runny mud that can suddenly slip down slopes.
30. Hard rock weathers less readily than softer rock does. So, if a rock layer sticks out above surrounding layers, it is harder than surrounding layers. A relatively soft rock layer will be surrounded by protruding layers.
31. Answers may vary. Accept all reasonable answers. Sample answers: The mountain is undergoing a new cycle of uplifting. Rocks now exposed to weathering are harder and less susceptible to the effects of weathering and erosion. Climate conditions may be changing.

Concept Mapping

32. Answers may vary but should include all of the terms listed. Sample answers appear at the end of this unit on p. 507C.

Math Skills

33. 18 cm = 180 mm
    180 mm/15 y = 12 mm/y
34. 1 m = 1,000 mm,
    1,000 mm ÷ 14 mm/y = 71 y

Writing Skills

35. Answers may vary. Accept all reasonable answers.
36. Answers may vary. Accept all reasonable answers.

Interpreting Graphics

37. 26% − 6% = 20%; Twenty percent more of the total land is rangeland and pasture than is urban land.
38. 25% − 20% = 5%; 28% − 5% = 23%; Forests must lose 5%, so they would account for 23% of land use in the United States.

Standardized Test Prep

Estimated Time

To give students practice under more realistic testing conditions, allow them 30 minutes to answer all of the questions in this practice test.

Test Doctor

Question 3 Answer A is correct. The reddish color is due to chemical processes. Mechanical weathering, answer B, abrasion, answer C, and erosion, answer D, are all physical processes and do not change the chemical composition of rocks and soil minerals.

Question 4 Answer H is correct. The chemical reactions involved in weathering are generally accelerated at higher temperatures, so answers F and G are incorrect. Many chemical and mechanical weathering processes are associated with the presence of water, so answer I is incorrect.

Question 10 Full-credit answers should include the following points:

- almost any activity initiated by a living organism that exposes rock and soil to wind or water would be an acceptable answer
- construction by humans breaks up rocks and creates quarries, which contribute to weathering
- tunneling animals, other than worms, churn and expose rocks in soil to the surface
- rotting vegetation and animal waste may release acids that can help destroy rocks when the acids are mixed with ground-water

Chapter 14 Standardized Test Prep

Understanding Concepts

Directions (1–5): For each question, write on a separate sheet of paper the letter of the correct answer.

1. The processes of physical weathering and erosion shape Earth's landforms by
A. expanding the elevation of Earth's surface.
B. decreasing the elevation of Earth's surface.
C. changing the composition of Earth's surface.
D. bending rock layers near Earth's surface.

2. Which of the following rocks is most likely to weather quickly?
F. a buried rock in a mountain
G. an exposed rock on a plain
H. a buried rock in a desert
I. an exposed rock on a slope

3. The red color of rocks and soil containing iron-rich minerals is caused by
A. chemical weathering.
B. mechanical weathering.
C. abrasion.
D. erosion.

4. In which of the following climates does chemical weathering generally occur most rapidly?
F. cold, wet climates
G. cold, dry climates
H. warm, humid climates
I. warm, dry climates

5. Which of the following has the greatest impact on soil composition?
A. the activities of plants and animals
B. the characteristics of the parent rock
C. the amount of precipitation
D. the shape of the land

Directions (6–7): For each question, write a short response.

6. In what type of decomposition reaction do hydrogen ions from water displace elements in a mineral?

7. What form of mechanical weathering is caused by sand carried by wind?

Reading Skills

Directions (8–10): Read the passage below. Then, answer the questions.

How Rock Becomes Soil

Earthworms are crucial for forming soil. As they search for food by digging tunnels, they expose rocks and minerals to the effects of weathering. Over time, this process creates new soil.

Worms are not the only living things that help to create soil. Plants also play a part in the weathering process. As the roots of plants grow and seek out water and nutrients, they help to break large rock fragments into smaller ones. Have you ever seen a plant growing in a sidewalk? As the plant grows, its roots spread into tiny cracks in the sidewalk. These roots apply pressure to the cracks, and, over time, the cracks become larger. As the plants make the cracks larger, ice wedging can occur more readily. As the cracks expand, more water can flow into them. When the water freezes, it expands and presses against the walls of the cracks, which makes the cracks larger. Over time, the weathering caused by water, plants, and worms helps to form soil.

8. Which of the following statements can be inferred from the passage?
F. Weathering can occur only when water freezes in cracks in rocks.
G. Only large plants have roots that are powerful enough to increase the rate of weathering.
H. Local biological activity may increase the rate of weathering in a given area.
I. Plant roots often prevent weathering by filling cracks and keeping water out of cracks.

9. Ice wedging, as described in the passage, is an example of which of the following?
A. oxidation
B. mechanical weathering
C. chemical weathering
D. hydrolysis

10. What are some ways, not mentioned in the passage, in which the activity of biological organisms may increase weathering?

Question 13 Full-credit answers should include the following points:

- the eight small blocks in part C will weather most rapidly
- students should relate the rate of weathering to the amount of exposed surface area available
- students should examine the diagram and consider that the total surface area of each rectangular solid, or cube, is equal to the sum of the areas of each of the cube's six sides. The block shown in figure A has far less exposed surface than the blocks shown in figures B or C. If all conditions are equal, the more surface area that is available to experience weathering, the faster weathering will occur
- even though the figures show the same volume and type of rock, the blocks of figure C would weather at the fastest rate due to their larger total surface area. The blocks of figure A would weather at the slowest rate

Interpreting Graphics

Directions (11–13): For each question below, record the correct answer on a separate sheet of paper.

The diagram below shows the soil profile of a mature soil. Use this diagram to answer questions 11 and 12.

Mature Soil Profile

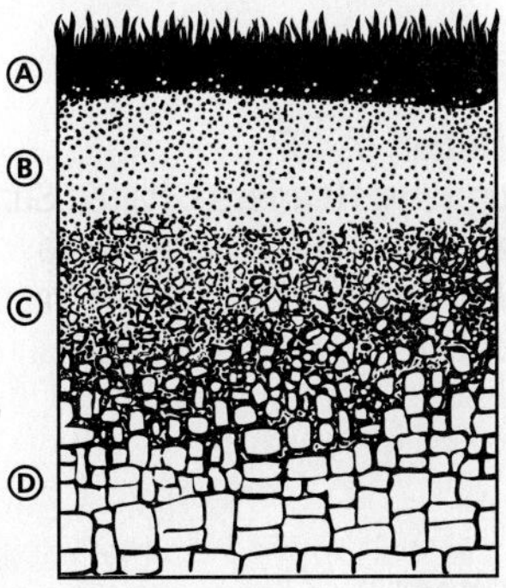

11. Which layer in the soil profile contains the greatest number of soil organisms?

F. layer A
G. layer B
H. layer C
I. layer D

12. Which two layers in the soil profile are least likely to contain the dark, organic material humus?

A. layers A and B
B. layers B and C
C. layers C and D
D. layers A and D

Use the diagrams of stone blocks below to answer question 13.

Blocks of Identical Volume

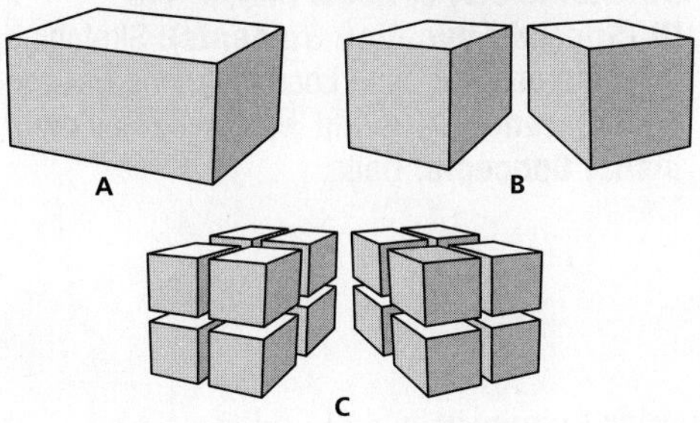

13. If the blocks shown in diagrams A, B, and C have the same volume and are made of the same types of minerals, will they weather at the same rate? Explain your answer.

Test Tip

Whenever possible, highlight or underline numbers or words that are important for correctly answering a question.

Standardized Test Prep

Using THINK central Resources

State Resources

- For specific resources for your state, visit www.thinkcentral.com and type in the keyword **HSHSTR.**

Answers

Understanding Concepts

1. B
2. I
3. A
4. H
5. B
6. hydrolysis
7. abrasion

Reading Skills

8. H
9. B
10. Answers may vary. See Test Doctor for a detailed scoring rubric.

Interpreting Graphics

11. F
12. C
13. Answers may vary. See Test Doctor for a detailed scoring rubric.

Chapter Planner **15**

River Systems

	Time	Standards	Teach Key Ideas
Chapter Opener, pp. 404–405	45 min.	National Science Education Standards	
Section 1 The Water Cycle, pp. 407–410 › Movement of Water on Earth › Water Budget	45 min.	SPSP 3c, UCP 4, ES 3c	■ ◆ **Bellringer,** p. 407 ■ **DI (Struggling Readers):** Paired Summarizing, p. 408 ◆ **Transparency:** 76 The Water Cycle ▲ **Visual Concepts:** Water Cycle • Vaporization and Condensation • Water Use in Households
Section 2 Stream Erosion, pp. 411–414 › Parts of a River System › Channel Erosion › Development of River Channels	90 min.	SPSP 5c, UCP 4	■ ◆ **Bellringer,** p. 411 ■ **Teaching Tip:** Make Concepts Relevant, p. 413 ◆ **Transparency:** 77 Stream Gradient and Channel Erosion ▲ **Visual Concepts:** Tributary, River System, and Drainage Basin • Divide • Types of Load • Discharge • Gradient • Youthful and Mature Rivers • Old and Rejuvenated Rivers
Section 3 Stream Deposition, pp. 415–418 › Deltas and Alluvial Fans › Floodplains › Human Impacts on Flooding › Flood Control › The Life Cycle of Lakes	45 min.	SPSP 5c, UCP 4	■ ◆ **Bellringer,** p. 415 ■ **Demonstration:** Changing Land Use, p. 415 ■ **Debate:** To Stay or Not to Stay, p. 416 ■ **DI (Special Education Students):** Sketching, p. 416 ■ **Discussion:** Sediment Load and Land Use, p. 422 ◆ **Transparency:** 78 World Watershed Sediment Yield ▲ **Visual Concepts:** Delta
Chapter Wrap-Up, pp. 423–427	90 min.		**Chapter Summary,** p. 423

See also PowerNotes® Presentations

CHAPTER Fast Track *To shorten instruction because of time limitations, omit Section 1.*

Key

Teacher's Edition ■ Teaching Transparencies ◆
Chapter Resource File ● Online Edition ▲

All resources listed below are also available on the **Teacher One Stop™.**

Why It Matters	Hands-On	Skills Development	Assessment
■ **Chapter Overview,** p. 404 ■ **Using the Figure:** Developing Wilderness, p. 404	**Inquiry Lab:** Building a Dam, p. 405	**Reading Toolbox,** p. 406	
■ **Section Overview,** p. 407 ■ **Environmental Connection:** Water Conservation, p. 409	■ **Group Activity:** Modeling the Water Cycle, p. 407 **Quick Lab:** Modeling the Water Cycle, p. 409 ● **Skills Practice Lab:** Stream Quality Monitoring	**Reading Toolbox:** Venn Diagram, p. 408	**Reading Check,** p. 408 **Section Review,** p. 410 ■ **Reteaching,** p. 409 ■ **Quiz,** p. 409 ■ **DI (Alternative Assessment):** Skit, p. 410 ● **Section Quiz**
■ **Section Overview,** p. 411 ■ **Art Connection:** The Big Muddy, p. 412	■ **Group Activity:** Field Trip, p. 412 **Inquiry Lab:** Sediments and Water, pp. 420–421	■ ● **Internet Activity:** Watersheds, p. 411 **Math Skills:** Water Discharge of a River, p. 412 ■ **Skill Builder:** Vocabulary, p. 413 **Reading Toolbox:** Cause-and-Effect Map, p. 414	**Reading Check,** p. 413 **Section Review,** p. 414 ■ **Reteaching,** p. 413 ■ **Quiz,** p. 413 ■ **DI (Alternative Assessment):** Build a Watershed, p. 414 ● **Section Quiz**
■ **Section Overview,** p. 415 **Uncovering Lost Streams,** p. 416	**Quick Lab:** Soil Erosion, p. 417	■ **Skill Builder:** Writing, p. 416 **Reading Toolbox:** Suffixes, p. 417 **Maps in Action:** World Watershed Sediment Yield, p. 422	**Reading Check,** p. 417 **Section Review,** p. 418 ■ **Reteaching,** p. 417 ■ **Quiz,** p. 417 ■ **DI (Alternative Assessment):** Sediment Stories, p. 418 ● **Section Quiz**
The Three Gorges Dam, p. 419		▲ **Super Summary** **Standardized Test Prep,** pp. 426–427	**Chapter Review,** pp. 424–425 ■ **DI (Alternative Assessment):** Biography of a River, p. 423 ● **Chapter Tests**

See also Lab Generator

See also Holt Online Assessment Resources

Chapter Overview

This chapter describes how water moves continuously between land, oceans, and atmosphere through the water cycle. The chapter also explains how rivers shape the land by erosion and deposition.

Using the Figure GENERAL

Developing Wilderness This photograph shows the Copper River delta in Alaska's Chugach National Forest, one of the most beautiful and untamed wetlands in the world. Some groups want more roads built to open the area for mining, logging, oil and gas exploration, and other activities. Lead a discussion exploring the impact of development on the river. (Possible adverse impacts include reducing wildlife populations, damaging scenic beauty, and increasing river pollution. Benefits may include better access to important natural resource deposits and improved local economy.)

LS Logical

Why It Matters

Around the globe, cities and towns are clustered along rivers, and have been since the earliest days of human society. Throughout history, rivers have furnished fresh water for drinking, agriculture, and irrigation, as well as transportation and food. Humanity has harnessed and changed rivers, constructing irrigation channels and building dams. The longest river in the U.S. is the Missouri River, which starts in Montana and flows into the Mississippi River near St. Louis.

Chapter 15 River Systems

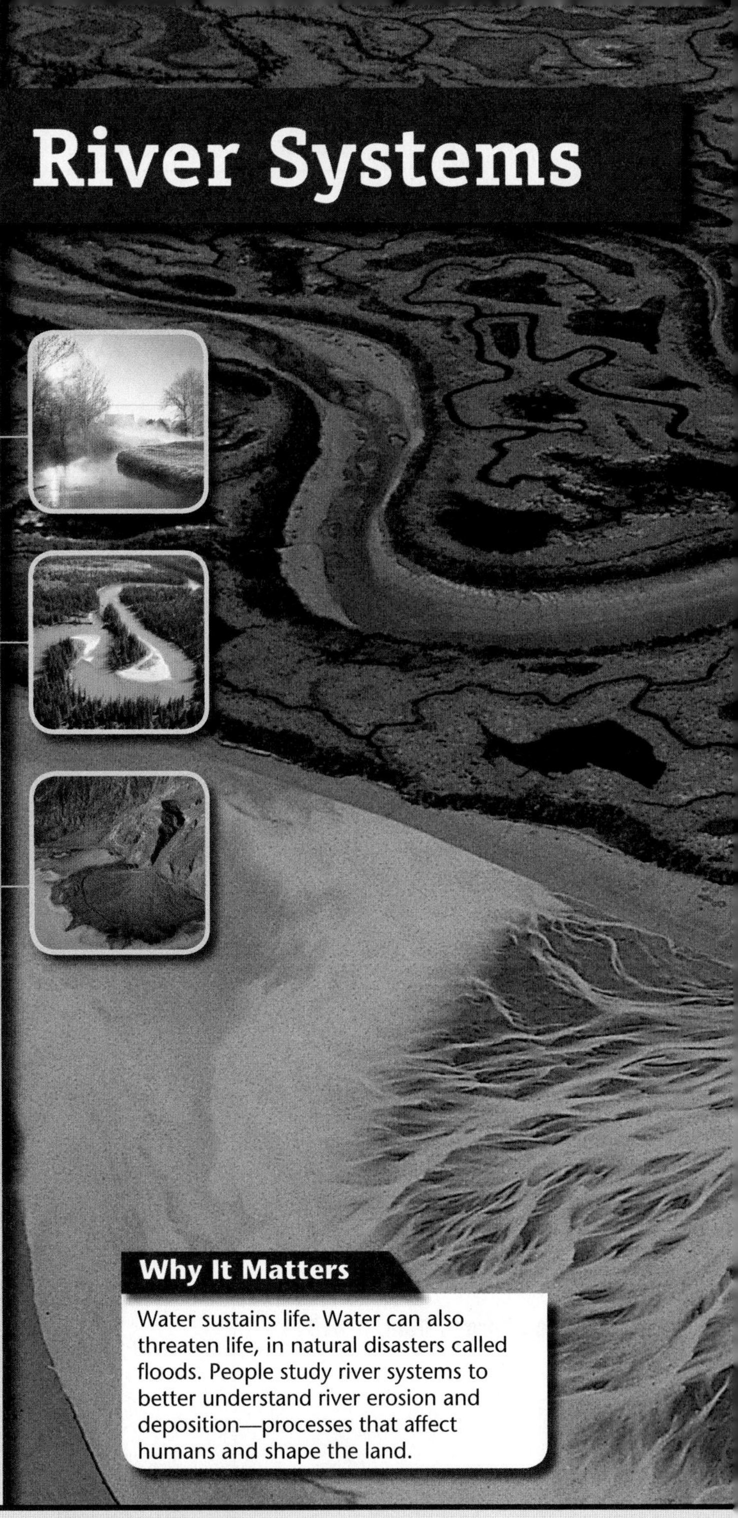

Chapter Outline

Virginia Standards of Learning
ES.1.a
ES.2.a
ES.6.a
ES.6.b
ES.6.d
ES.8.d
ES.8.e

Why It Matters

Water sustains life. Water can also threaten life, in natural disasters called floods. People study river systems to better understand river erosion and deposition—processes that affect humans and shape the land.

Chapter Correlations — *Virginia Standards of Learning*

ES.1.a volume, area, mass, elapsed time, direction, temperature, pressure, distance, density, and changes in elevation/depth are calculated utilizing the most appropriate tools.
ES.2.a science explains and predicts the interactions and dynamics of complex Earth systems/
ES.6.a fossil fuels, minerals, rocks, water, and vegetation
ES.6.b advantages and disadvantages of various energy sources
ES.6.d environmental costs and benefits.
ES.8.d identification of sources of fresh water including rivers, springs, and aquifers, with reference to the hydrologic cycle
ES.8.e dependence on freshwater resources and the effects of human usage on water quality

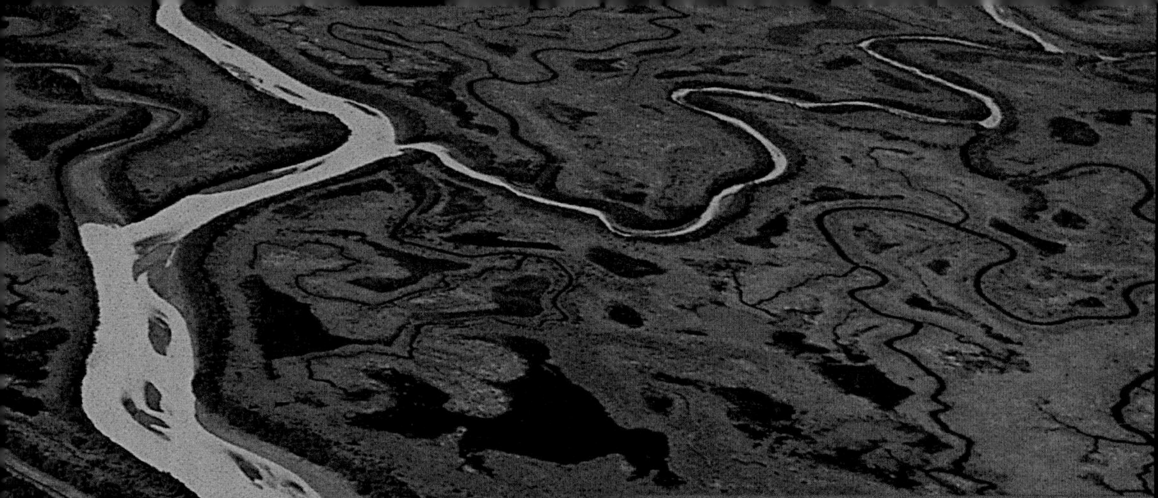

Inquiry Lab

30 min

Building a Dam

Use clay, sand, soil, and pebbles to build a small model of a landscape with hills and valleys in a large aluminum pan. Gently "rain" water onto your landscape, and observe the flow of the water. Find a place in your landscape that would be suitable for a dam. Use clay to build a dam. Then "rain" water onto your landscape again. Pay attention to how the flow of the water changes and where the water builds up.

Questions to Get You Started

1. Make a labeled diagram to show the paths that the water took as it flowed over your model landscape.
2. When a dam is built, a new lake forms. Describe how and where the lake forms, based on your model.

Inquiry Lab

Central Concept: Dams are used to control water flow along rivers and prevent flooding. The reservoir formed by the dam may be used for recreation, municipal and industrial applications, and irrigation of regional cropland. In this lab, students will construct a model dam and observe the resulting reservoir.

Teacher's Notes: Look online to locate a nearby dam as a real-world example.

Materials (per group)

- Clay
- Pan
- Pebbles
- Sand
- Soil
- Water
- Water container

Skills Acquired

- Making Models
- Observing

Answers to Getting Started

1. Students should make a labeled diagram of the paths of water on their model landscape.
2. The lake forms behind the dam. The dam prevents water flow and the water builds up, forming a reservoir. The exact location of the lake will vary, depending on the model.

Using THINK central Resources

An online version of this chapter, as well as all the print and multimedia resources that accompany the program are available to registered teachers and their students. Log onto www.thinkcentral.com to access these materials and tools to organize your preparation and student learning.

READING TOOLBOX

Word Parts

Key Term	Related Verb	Definition of Verb
condensation	condense	to change from a gas to a liquid
precipitation	precipitate	to fall from clouds, as rain or snow
desalination	desalinate	to remove salt from something
evaporation	evaporate	to change from liquid to gas
transpiration	transpire	to give off water

Graphic Organizers

Sample information for the Venn diagram is show below.

Delta: Occurs in water, when a stream empties into an ocean or lake.

Both: Formed by sediment deposited when a stream slows down.

Alluvial fan: Occurs on land, when a stream reaches a flat plain.

READING TOOLBOX

These reading tools will help you learn the material in this chapter.

Word Parts

Suffixes The suffixes *-ion* and *-ation* turn verbs into nouns. For example, the verb *cooperate* means "to work together." Adding the suffix *-ion* forms *cooperation,* a noun that means "the process of working together."

Your Turn In Section 1, the key terms *condensation, precipitation,* and *desalination* contain the suffix *-ion* or *-ation*. Identify the verb that each term came from, and write its definition. Record your notes in a table like the one started below. The key term *evapotranspiration* also contains the suffix *-ation*. Split this key term into its component words—*evaporation* and *transpiration*—and add these words to your table.

KEY TERM	RELATED VERB	DEFINITION OF VERB
condensation		
precipitation		
desalination	desalinate	to remove salt from something

Graphic Organizers

Venn Diagram A Venn diagram is useful for showing characteristics that topics share and characteristics that are unique to each topic. As you read, look for topics that have both shared and unique characteristics, and draw a Venn diagram to show how the topics are related.

Your Turn In Section 3, you will read about deltas and alluvial fans. Make a Venn diagram like the one started below, and fill it in with shared and unique characteristics of these two types of sediment deposits.

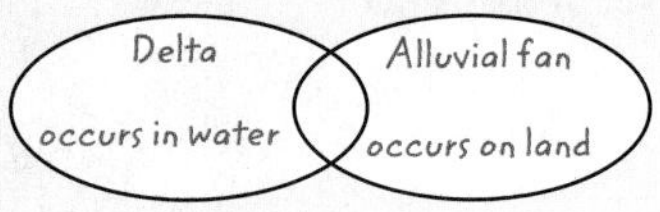

Graphic Organizers

Cause-and-Effect Maps A cause-and-effect map can help you illustrate how, when, or why one event causes another event.

Your Turn As you read Section 3, create a cause-and-effect map like the one started below to help you study the causes and effects of flooding. Remember that you may include as many cause boxes and as many effect boxes as you need.

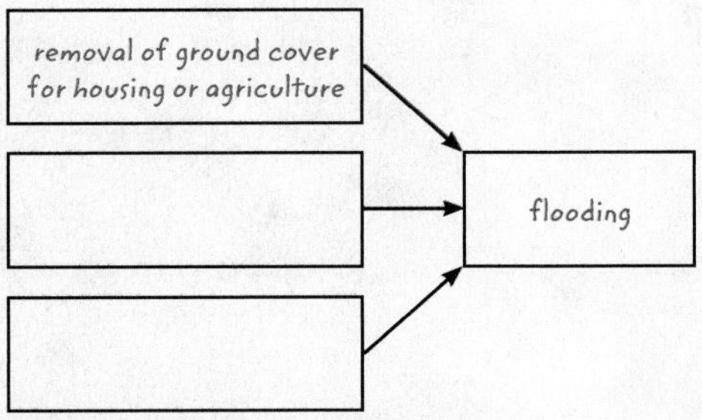

For more information on how to use these and other tools, see **Appendix A**.

Graphic Organizers

Sample information for the cause-and-effect map is shown below.

Cause boxes may include: removal of ground cover for housing, logging, and agriculture; increase in stream volume due to rainfall or snowmelt; natural events such as forest fires.

Effect boxes may include: flooding; property damage; formation of natural levees; rich floodplain soils form

SECTION 1
The Water Cycle

Key Ideas	Key Terms	Why It Matters
❯ Outline the stages of the water cycle. ❯ Describe factors that affect a water budget. ❯ List two approaches to water conservation.	water cycle evapotranspiration condensation precipitation desalination	Your survival depends on water, which makes up about two-thirds of your body. When you breathe out, you release water vapor, which becomes part of the water cycle.

The origin of Earth's water supply has puzzled people for centuries. Aristotle and other ancient Greek philosophers believed that rivers such as the Nile and the Danube could be supplied by rain and snow alone. It was not until the middle of the 17th century that scientists could accurately measure the amount of water received on Earth and the amount flowing in rivers. These measurements showed that Earth's surface receives up to 5 times as much water as rivers carry off. So, a more puzzling question than "Where does Earth's water come from?" is "Where does the water go?"

Movement of Water on Earth

Water is essential for humans and all other organisms. Its availability in different forms is critical for the continuation of life on Earth. More than two-thirds of Earth's surface is covered with water. Water flows in streams and rivers. It is held in lakes, oceans, and icecaps at Earth's poles. It even flows through the rock below Earth's surface as groundwater. Water is found not only in these familiar bodies of water but also in the tissues of all living creatures. In the atmosphere, water occurs as an invisible gas. This gas is called *water vapor*. Liquid water also exists in the atmosphere as small particles in clouds and fog, as shown in **Figure 1.**

Earth's water is constantly changing from one form to another. Water vapor falls from the sky as rain. Glaciers melt to form streams. Rivers flow into oceans, where liquid water escapes into the atmosphere as water vapor. This continuous movement of water on Earth's surface from the atmosphere to the land and oceans and back to the atmosphere is called the **water cycle.**

water cycle the continuous movement of water between the atmosphere, the land, and the oceans

Figure 1 The snow, the fog, and the river water in this photo are three of the forms that water takes on Earth. Invisible water vapor is also present in the air.

Section 1

Focus

Overview

This section describes the processes of the water cycle: evapotranspiration, condensation, and precipitation. It explains water budgets and local factors that affect them, and describes methods of water conservation.

Bellringer

Have students list as many properties and characteristics of water as they can think of. (Answers may vary. Accept all reasonable answers.) **LS Logical**

Motivate

Group Activity — GENERAL

Modeling the Water Cycle Have students work in small groups to build a terrarium in a jar to model the water cycle. Students should fill the bottom of their jar with soil and plants. A small plastic cup filled with water can model a lake. When their terrarium is complete, students should spray the soil with water and put a lid on the jar. Place the terrariums in a sunny window or near lights. Have each group observe what happens in their jar. Challenge students to keep their terrariums alive and active as long as possible. **LS Kinesthetic**

Key Resources

Chapter Resource File
- Directed Reading BASIC
- Skills Practice Lab: Stream Quality Monitoring GENERAL

Technology
- Transparencies
  Bellringer

Teach

READING TOOLBOX

Venn Diagram

Sample information for the Venn diagram is shown below.

Transpiration: occurs with water in plants

Both: releases water vapor into the air

Evaporation: occurs with liquid water in the ocean, lakes, streams, and soil

MISCONCEPTION ALERT

Water, Water Anywhere?

Students may not realize how little water is available as freshwater for human consumption. Ninety-seven percent of Earth's water exists as undrinkable saltwater in the oceans. The remaining 3% is freshwater. A little more than 2% is in glaciers, and thus is fairly inaccessible. Less than one half of 1% of all the water on Earth is readily available for human use as surface water in streams, rivers, and lakes.

Answer to Reading Check

Precipitation is any form of water that falls to Earth from the clouds, including rain, snow, sleet, and hail.

READING TOOLBOX

Venn Diagram
Make a Venn diagram with two circles. Label one circle "Transpiration" and the other circle "Evaporation." In the area where the circles overlap, write shared characteristics. In each of the other areas, write characteristics that are unique to each process.

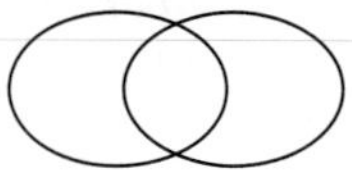

Evapotranspiration

The process by which liquid water changes into water vapor is called *evaporation*. Each year, about 500,000 km^3 of water evaporates into the atmosphere. About 86% of this water evaporates from the ocean. The remaining water evaporates from lakes, streams, and the soil. Water vapor also enters the air by *transpiration*, the process by which plants release water vapor into the atmosphere. The total loss of water from an area, which equals the sum of the water lost by evaporation from the soil and other surfaces and the water lost by transpiration from organisms, is called **evapotranspiration.** Evapotranspiration is one part of the water cycle, which is shown in **Figure 2.**

Condensation

Another process of the water cycle is *condensation*. **Condensation** is the change of state from a gas to a liquid. When air rises in the atmosphere, it expands and cools. As the air cools, the water vapor it contains becomes cooler, and some of it condenses, or changes into tiny liquid water droplets, forming clouds.

Precipitation

The third major process of the water cycle is *precipitation*, the process by which water falls from the clouds. **Precipitation** is any form of water that falls to Earth's surface from the clouds and includes rain, snow, sleet, and hail. More than 75% of all precipitation falls on Earth's oceans. The rest falls on land and becomes runoff or groundwater. Eventually, almost all of this water returns to the atmosphere by evapotranspiration, condenses, and falls back to Earth's surface to begin the cycle again.

Reading Check **List the forms of precipitation.** (See Appendix G for answers to Reading Checks.)

evapotranspiration the total loss of water from an area, which equals the sum of the water lost by evaporation from the soil and other surfaces and the water lost by transpiration from organisms

condensation the change of state from a gas to a liquid

precipitation any form of water that falls to Earth's surface from the clouds; includes rain, snow, sleet, and hail

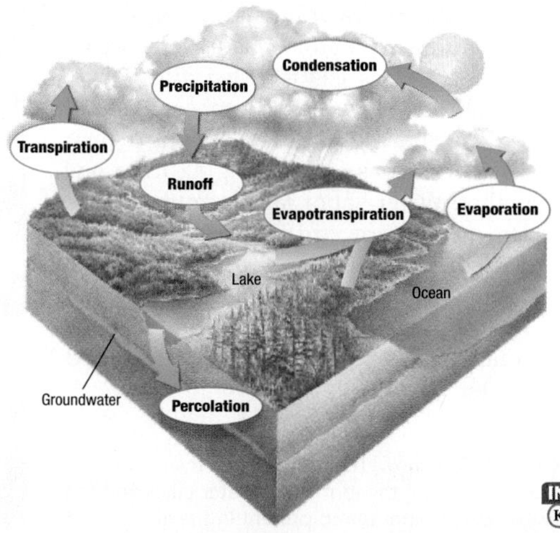

Figure 2 Evapotranspiration, condensation, and precipitation make up a continuous process called the *water cycle*.

THINK central
INTERACT ONLINE
(Keyword: HQXRVSF2)

Differentiated Instruction

Struggling Readers

Paired Summarizing Group students into pairs and have them read silently about evapotranspiration, condensation, and precipitation. Then, have one student summarize the role of these processes in the water cycle. The other student should listen to the retelling and point out any inaccuracies or ideas that were left out. Allow students to refer to the text as needed. **LS Verbal** Co-op Learning

English Language Learners

Key Resources

Technology

- Transparencies
  76 The Water Cycle

Water Budget

The continuous cycle of evapotranspiration, condensation, and precipitation establishes Earth's *water budget.* A financial budget is a statement of expected income—money coming in—and expenses—money going out. In Earth's water budget, precipitation is the income. Evapotranspiration and runoff are the expenses. The water budget of Earth as a whole is balanced because the amount of precipitation is equal to the amount of evapotranspiration and runoff. However, the water budget of a particular area, called the *local water budget,* usually is not balanced.

Figure 3 Tropical rain forests, such as the one in Queensland, Australia (top photo), receive large amounts of rainfall annually. Deserts, such as the Mojave Desert in California (bottom photo), receive small amounts of rainfall each year.

Factors That Affect the Water Budget

Factors that affect the local water budget include temperature, vegetation, wind, and the amount of rainfall. When precipitation exceeds evapotranspiration and runoff in an area, the result is moist soil and possible flooding. When evapotranspiration exceeds precipitation, the soil becomes dry and irrigation may be necessary. Vegetation reduces runoff in an area but increases evapotranspiration. Wind increases the rate of evapotranspiration.

The factors that affect the local water budget vary geographically. For example, the Mojave Desert in California receives much less precipitation than do the tropical rain forests of Queensland, Australia, as **Figure 3** shows.

In most areas of Earth, the local water budget also changes with the seasons. In general, cooler temperatures slow the rate of evapotranspiration. During the warmer months, evapotranspiration increases. As a result, streams generally transport more water in cooler months than they do in warmer months.

Quick Lab — Modeling the Water Cycle

35 min

Procedure

1. Place a short glass inside a large plastic mixing bowl. Add cold water to the mixing bowl until about three-fourths of the glass is covered with water. Make sure to keep the inside of the glass dry.
2. Add drops of food coloring (red, blue, or green) to the water in the bowl until the water has a strong color.
3. Now, add about 1 cup of dry soil to the water,and stir gently until the water is muddy as well as colored.
4. Cover the bowl tightly with a piece of plastic wrap secured to the bowl with a rubber band, and place a coin or stone in the middle of the plastic wrap above the glass.
5. Set the bowl in the sun or under a heat lamp for 30 minutes to several hours. Then, observe the water that has collected in the glass.

Analysis

1. What are the processes that have taken place to allow water to collect in the glass?
2. Why is the water in the glass not muddy?
3. Is the water in the glass colored? What does this say about pollutants in water systems and the water cycle?

Environmental Connection

Water Conservation The World Health Organization of the United Nations states that severe water shortages affecting 400 million people today will affect 2.7 billion people by 2025 and 4 billion by 2050 if the world continues to consume water at the current rate. States with little precipitation, such as Arizona in the southwestern U.S., will face severe freshwater shortages by 2025.

Close

Reteaching — BASIC

Water Budget Diagram Provide students with photos or figures of a tropical rainforest, arctic tundra, deserts and/or other areas. Have students draw arrows on the photos that show each of the four processes in the water cycle. The size of the arrows in each figure should represent the relative contribution of each process to the region's overall water budget. Have students explain whether each regional water budget is balanced or not.
LS Visual/Logical

Quiz — GENERAL

1. Why is desalination currently not a widely used method of obtaining freshwater? (At this time, it is too expensive on a large scale.)
2. In Earth's water budget, what processes are losses, or expenses? (evapotranspiration and runoff)

Quick Lab

Skills Acquired
- Observing
- Analyzing

Materials
- Short glass
- Large plastic mixing bowl
- Water, cold
- Food coloring
- Soil, dry
- Plastic wrap
- Rubber band
- Coin or stone
- Heat lamp

Teacher's Notes: This apparatus is called a solar still.

Answers to Analysis
1. evaporation and condensation
2. As the sun heats the water, the water turns to vapor, and the mud is left behind.
3. The dye molecules may or may not evaporate with the water. Evaporation can purify water of some dissolved pollutants but not all.

Close, *continued*

Answers to Section Review

1. Water reaches the ocean from rivers and from precipitation.
2. Evapotranspiration is loss of water due to the combined effects of evaporation from surfaces and transpiration by plants and animals. Condensation occurs when water changes state from gaseous water vapor to liquid water. Precipitation occurs when water falls to Earth's surface.
3. Condensation occurs when water vapor changes to liquid water droplets as it cools. These droplets can form clouds and the water may fall back to Earth as precipitation.
4. Most local water budgets are not balanced because precipitation and evapotranspiration vary seasonally and geographically. Sometimes, precipitation will exceed evapotranspiration, leading to excess water and possible flooding. At other times and places, the opposite may occur.
5. Vegetation reduces runoff but may increase evapotranspiration. Precipitation increases available water and leads to excess moisture and to possible flooding, especially if vegetation is lacking.
6. Two ways to ensure continued water are to conserve water and to find alternative sources of freshwater.
7. Answers may vary but may include taking shorter showers, recycling water, turning off water when brushing teeth, using low water-use landscaping and low flow toilets and showers, and using front-loading washing machines.

Figure 4 Waste from a paper mill has polluted the Qingai River in China.

Water Use

On average, each person in the United States uses about 95,000 L (20,890.5 gal) of water each year. Water is used for bathing, washing clothes and dishes, watering lawns, carrying away wastes, and drinking. Agriculture and industry also use large amounts of water. As the population of the United States increases, so does the demand for water.

About 90% of the water used by cities and industry is returned to rivers or to the oceans as wastewater. Some of this wastewater contains harmful materials, such as toxic chemicals and metals, as shown in **Figure 4.** These toxic materials can pollute rivers and can harm plants and animals in the water.

Conservation of Water

While Earth holds a lot of water, only a small percentage of that water is fresh water that can be used by humans. Scientists have identified two ways to ensure that enough fresh water is available today and in the future. One way is through conservation, or the wise use of water resources. Individuals can conserve water by limiting their water use as much as possible. Governments can help conserve water by enforcing conservation laws and antipollution laws that prohibit the dumping of waste into bodies of water.

A second way to protect the water supply is to find alternative methods of obtaining fresh water. One such method is called **desalination,** which is the process of removing salt from ocean water. However, this method is expensive and is impractical for supplying water to large populations. Currently, the best way of maintaining an adequate supply of fresh water is the wise use and conservation of the fresh water that is now available.

Academic Vocabulary

method (METH uhd) a way of doing something

desalination a process of removing salt from ocean water

Section 1 Review

Key Ideas

1. **List** two ways in which water reaches the oceans.
2. **Outline** the major stages of the water cycle.
3. **Explain** the difference between condensation and precipitation.
4. **Explain** why most local water budgets are not balanced.
5. **Describe** how vegetation and rainfall affect the local water budget.
6. **List** two ways to ensure the continued supply of fresh water.

Critical Thinking

7. **Applying Concepts** Describe five ways that you can conserve water at home.
8. **Analyzing Processes** Why are the oceans the location of most evaporation and precipitation?

Concept Mapping

9. Use the following terms to create a concept map: *water cycle, evaporation, transpiration, evapotranspiration, condensation, precipitation,* and *water budget.*

8. because oceans cover more than 70% of Earth's surface and oceans have a large water surface that is exposed to the atmosphere
9. The local *water budget* is controlled by the *water cycle,* which includes *condensation, precipitation,* and *evapotranspiration,* which is the sum of *evaporation* and *transpiration.*

Differentiated Instruction

Alternative Assessment

Skit Have students work in small groups to act out key processes in the water cycle. Students should play the role of water in its various states and depict evapotranspiration, condensation, and precipitation. Different groups can model how water budgets differ in a tropical region versus a desert. **LS Kinesthetic**

SECTION 2

Stream Erosion

Key Ideas	Key Terms		Why It Matters
❯ Summarize how a river develops. ❯ Describe the parts of a river system. ❯ Explain factors that affect the erosive ability of a river. ❯ Describe how erosive factors affect the development of a river channel.	**tributary** **watershed** **stream load** **discharge**	**gradient** **meander** **braided stream**	Rivers change course over time. Because they also often form political boundaries, such change can cause problems for people living on both sides of the river.

A river system begins to form when precipitation exceeds evapotranspiration in a given area. Excess water then moves downslope as runoff. As runoff moves across the land surface, it erodes rock and soil and eventually may form a narrow ditch, called a *gully*. Eventually, the processes of precipitation and erosion form a fully developed valley with a permanent stream.

Parts of a River System

A river system is made up of a main stream and **tributaries,** which are all of the feeder streams that flow into the main stream. The land from which water runs off into these streams is called a **watershed.** The ridges or elevated regions that separate watersheds are called *divides*. A river system is shown in **Figure 1.**

The relatively narrow depression that a stream follows as it flows downhill is called its *channel*. The edges of a stream channel that are above water level are called the stream's *banks*. The part of the stream channel that is below the water level is called the stream's *bed*. A stream channel gradually becomes wider and deeper as it erodes its banks and bed.

tributary a stream that flows into a lake or into a larger stream

watershed the area of land that is drained by a river system

Figure 1 The tributaries that run into this river are fed by runoff from surrounding land. All of the land that drains into a single river makes up the watershed of the river.

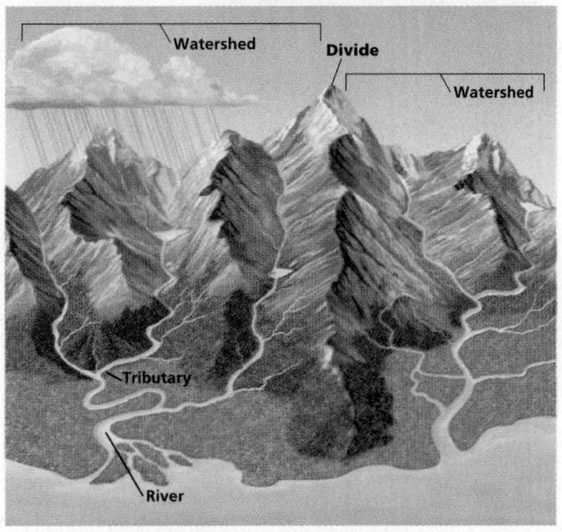

Channel Erosion

River systems change continuously because of erosion. In the process of *headward erosion*, channels lengthen and branch out at their upper ends, where runoff enters the streams. Erosion of the slopes in a watershed can also extend a river system and can add to the area of the watershed. In the process known as *stream piracy*, a stream from one watershed is "captured" by a stream from another watershed that has a higher rate of erosion. The captured stream then drains into the river system that has done the capturing.

Section 2

Focus

Overview

This section explains how a river develops and describes the parts of a river system. It explains the factors that affect the erosive capability of a river and how these factors influence the development of a river.

Bellringer

Ask students to make a list of words that describe rivers. The words can describe the shape of the river, how it affects the surrounding landscape, or the water in the river. (Answers may vary. Accept all reasonable answers.)
LS Verbal

Motivate

Internet Activity — GENERAL

Watersheds Have students identify the watershed in which they live by using the Environmental Protection Agency's "Surf Your Watershed" Web site. Ask them to investigate ways to preserve and protect the watershed. A worksheet designed to direct student research on this topic can be found in the **Chapter Resource File** booklet or by visiting www.thinkcentral.com and entering the keyword **HQXRVSX.**
LS Verbal

Key Resources

Chapter Resource File
- Directed Reading BASIC

Technology
- Transparencies
  Bellringer

Teach

Group Activity — GENERAL

Field Trip Visit a local stream or river. Have students walk along the channel and note stream gradient and flow, water quality, composition of stream bed, presence of meandering, bank erosion, sediment bars, flooding, evidence of human activities, human channel modifications, and other features. Have students make sketches, take notes, and/or take photographs.

To measure the speed of the stream, have students mark off a section of known distance, drop a leaf or other floating object near the stream center, and measure the time the object takes to travel the distance. For example, if the object travels 60 m in 20 s, the stream's surface speed is 60 m/20 s, or 3 m/s. To calculate an average speed for the stream as a whole, multiply by 0.8, because water flows faster near the surface of the stream and slower near the bottom. If possible, visit the site again after a heavy rainfall, and have students note changes in the stream. Have small groups of students design posters that illustrate the key characteristics of that section of the watershed. LS **Visual**

Math Skills

Answer

Discharge = speed × area

Discharge = 1.5 m/s × 520 m^2 = 780 m^3/s

Key Resources

Technology

- Transparencies
  77 Stream Gradient and Channel Erosion

stream load the materials other than the water that are carried by a stream

discharge the volume of water that flows within a given time

gradient the change in elevation over a given distance

Math Skills

Water Discharge of a River River channels can carry an enormous volume of water. The water that rivers discharge can be calculated by using the following equation:

discharge = *speed of the water* × *cross-sectional area of the river channel*

In cubic meters per second (m^3/s), what is the discharge of water carried by a river that moves 1.5 m/s through a cross-sectional area of 520 m^2?

Stream Load

A stream transports soil, loose rock fragments, and dissolved minerals as it flows downhill. The materials carried by a stream are called the **stream load.** Stream load takes three forms: suspended load, bed load, and dissolved load. The *suspended load* consists of particles of fine sand and silt. The speed, or rate of downstream travel, of the water keeps these particles suspended, so they do not sink to the stream bed. The *bed load* is made up of larger, coarser materials, such as coarse sand, gravel, and pebbles. This material moves by sliding and jumping along the bed. The *dissolved load* is mineral matter transported in liquid solution.

Stream Discharge

The volume of water moved by a stream in a given time period is the stream's **discharge.** The faster a stream flows, the higher its discharge and the greater the load that the stream can carry. Thus, a swift stream carries more sediment and larger particles than a slow stream does. A stream's speed also affects how the stream cuts down and widens its channel. Swift streams erode their channels more quickly than slow-moving streams do.

Stream Gradient

The speed of a stream depends mainly on gradient. **Gradient** is the change in elevation of a stream over a given horizontal distance. In other words, gradient is the steepness of the stream's slope. Near the *headwaters*, or the beginning of a stream, the gradient generally is steep. This area of the stream has a high rate of flow, which causes rapid channel erosion. As the stream nears its *mouth*, where the stream enters a larger body of water, its gradient often becomes flatter. As a result, the river's speed and erosive power decrease. The stream channel eventually is eroded to a nearly flat gradient by the time the stream channel reaches the sea. Streams with different gradients are shown in **Figure 2.**

Figure 2 Streams that have steep gradients, such as the stream on the left, have a higher speed than streams that have low gradients, such as the stream on the right, do.

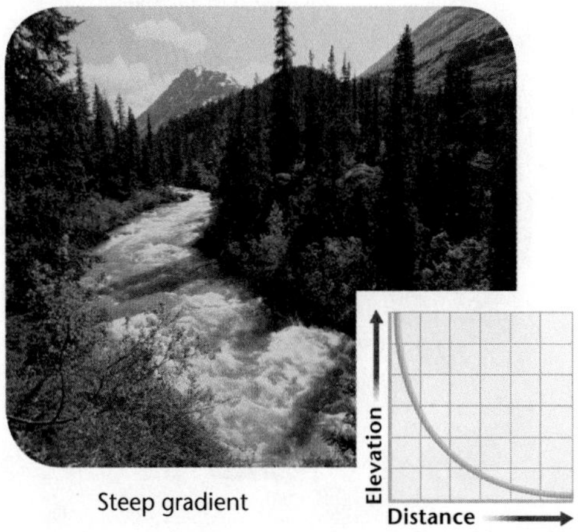

Steep gradient

Low gradient

Art Connection — ADVANCED

The Big Muddy The Mississippi River has had a profound effect on American culture, inspiring classic works of literature and art. The celebrated American writer Mark Twain chronicled river life and culture in *The Adventures of Huckleberry Finn, The Adventures of Tom Sawyer,* and *Life on the Mississippi.* The Mississippi River delta is also the birthplace of a uniquely American form of music—the blues. The main action of *Showboat,* America's first important musical drama, which is an original American art form, took place along the Mississippi. Have students read passages of Mark Twain's works and listen to blues music and songs from *Showboat,* including "Ol' Man River." The PBS Web site "River of Song" is a good source for information about blues music. Discuss with students why the Mississippi River plays such an important role in American life and culture. LS **Auditory/Verbal**

Figure 3 Decreased speed on the inside of a river's curve leads to the deposition of sediment, as this photo of a river in the Banff National Park in Alberta, Canada, shows.

Development of River Channels

As the stream's load, discharge, and gradient decrease, the erosive power of the stream decreases, which influences the development of the stream's channel. Over time, as the channel erodes, it becomes wider and deeper. When the stream becomes longer and wider, it is called a *river*.

Meandering Channels

As a river develops, it may form curves and bends. A river that has a low gradient tends to have more bends than a river that has a steep gradient does. A winding pattern of wide curves, called **meanders,** develops because as the gradient decreases, the speed of the water decreases. When the speed of the water decreases, the river is less able to erode down into its bed. As the water flows through the channel, more energy is directed against the banks, which causes erosion of the banks.

When a river rounds a bend, the speed of the water on the outside of the curve increases. The fast-moving water on the outside of a river bend erodes the outer bank of that bend. However, on the inside of the curve, the speed of the water decreases. This decrease in speed leads to the formation of a *bar* of deposited sediment, such as sand or gravel, as shown in **Figure 3.**

As this process continues, the curve enlarges while further sediment deposition takes place on the opposite bank, where the water is moving more slowly. Meanders can become so curved that they almost form a loop, separated by only a narrow neck of land. When the river cuts across this neck, the meander can become isolated from the river, and an *oxbow lake* forms.

Reading Check **How would you describe the gradient of a river that has meanders?**

meander one of the bends, twists, or curves in a low-gradient stream or river

SCILINKS
www.scilinks.org
Topic: River Systems
Code: **HQX1314**

Skill Builder — BASIC

Vocabulary The word *tributary* comes from the Latin *tribuere,* which means "to pay or contribute." Feeder streams, or tributaries, contribute their flow to the main river. The word *meander* comes from the Latin *maeander,* which means "circuitous winding." The Maeander River in Phyrgia, an ancient country in Asia Minor, was famous for its winding course. Have students think of other uses for the base root meanings of tributary and meander. (Answers may vary. Volunteer contributions help pay for charitable projects. People meander aimlessly in the park.) LS **Verbal** English Language Learners

Teaching Tip — BASIC

Make Concepts Relevant
Students may understand the erosive power of river systems if you show them examples of landforms carved by rivers. Show students a picture of the Grand Canyon with the Colorado River flowing through it. Ask them to think about how the action of river water could form something as vast and deep as the Grand Canyon. (Over millions of years, the relentless action of the river eroded the land, gradually cutting deeper into the rock to create steep canyons.) LS **Visual**

Answer to Reading Check
A river that has meanders probably has a low gradient.

Close

Reteaching — BASIC

Flowchart Have students construct a flowchart of the stages in the evolution of a stream. Have them identify factors that play a role in the features of the stream. LS **Visual**

Quiz — GENERAL

1. What separates one watershed from another? (ridges or elevated regions called *divides*)
2. What is a bar? (an area in a river channel where sediments, such as sand and gravel, have been deposited)
3. What is a watershed? (the area of land that is drained by a water system)

READING TOOLBOX

Cause-and-Effect Map

Sample information for the cause-and-effect map is shown below.

Cause boxes (meandering channels): low gradient, low velocity of water.

Cause boxes (braided streams): high gradient; large sediment load.

Close, *continued*

Answers to Section Review

1. When precipitation exceeds evapotranspiration, water that does not soak into the soil runs off, eroding rock and soil and forming a narrow gully. Gradually, the gully enlarges to form a channel that has a permanent stream.
2. A river system consists of the main stream, all of its tributaries, and their watersheds.
3. Headward erosion occurs when a stream lengthens and branches out at its upper end. If headward erosion cuts through a divide between watersheds, piracy, in which a stream captures water from another watershed, can occur.
4. suspended load, bed load, and dissolved load
5. A stream with a high discharge can carry a higher load and thus erodes its channel more quickly than slow-moving streams do. The steeper the gradient is, the faster a stream flows and the more it erodes its channel.
6. Braided rivers occur when streams have large sediment loads, especially coarse sand and gravel. The river cannot move all of the load and deposits it as bars along the bottom, dividing the river into multiple channels. A low gradient tends to cause meanders because, as its speed slows, water is less able to erode the riverbed but can still erode the banks.
7. Meanders can become so curved that the banks of the river are separated only by a narrow neck of land. If the river cuts across the neck, the loop may become isolated from the main channel, forming an oxbow lake.

Answers continued on page 507A

Figure 4 Braided streams, such as the Chisana River in Alaska, divide into multiple channels.

READING TOOLBOX

Cause-and-Effect Map
Make a cause-and-effect map that is similar to the one you made at the beginning of this chapter. Label the effects "meandering channels" and "braided streams." Then fill in the map with causes of meandering channels and braided streams. Add details about the causes and effects.

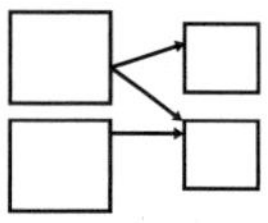

Academic Vocabulary
available (uh VAYL uh buhl) able to be used

braided stream a stream or river that is composed of multiple channels that divide and rejoin around sediment bars

Braided Streams

Most rivers are single channels. However, under certain conditions, the presence of sediment bars between a river's banks can divide the flow of the river into multiple channels. A stream or river that is composed of multiple channels that divide and rejoin around sediment bars is called a **braided stream.** Braided streams are a direct result of a high gradient and a large sediment load, particularly when a high percentage of the load is composed of coarse sand and gravel. The bars form on the channel floor when the river is unable to move all of the available load.

Although braided streams, such as those in **Figure 4,** look very different from meandering channels, they can cause just as much erosion. The channel location shifts constantly such that bars between channels erode and new bars form. Sometimes, a single river can change from a braided stream to a meandering stream as the gradient and discharge change.

Section 2 Review

Key Ideas

1. **Summarize** how a river develops.
2. **Describe** the parts of a river system.
3. **Explain** the processes of headward erosion and stream piracy.
4. **List** the three types of stream load.
5. **Explain** how stream discharge and gradient affect the erosive ability of a river.
6. **Describe** the factors that control whether a river is braided or meandering.
7. **Summarize** the process that forms an oxbow lake.

Critical Thinking

8. **Predicting Consequences** If geologic forces were to cause an uplift of the land surface, what would the effect on stream channel erosion be?
9. **Analyzing Processes** Explain how the speed of a stream affects the suspended load.

Concept Mapping

10. Use the following terms to create a concept map: *braided channels, stream load, suspended load, dissolved load, bed load, meanders, stream gradient,* and *headwaters.*

Differentiated Instruction

Alternative Assessment

Build a Watershed Have students work in small groups to build a model of a watershed out of sand and clay in a plastic container. Have students use clay to create the underlying structure, then layer sand over the clay. The model should show the slope of the watershed, the main channel, and several tributaries. Have students demonstrate the flow of runoff in their watershed by simulating rain with a spray bottle or by using a watering can. **LS Kinesthetic**

SECTION 3 Stream Deposition

Key Ideas	Key Terms	Why It Matters
❯ Explain the two types of stream deposition. ❯ Describe one advantage and one disadvantage of living in a floodplain. ❯ Identify three methods of flood control. ❯ Describe the life cycle of a lake.	**delta** **alluvial fan** **floodplain**	Building a dam involves risks, but *not* building a dam also has risks. An understanding of floodplains is critical for making good decisions about whether or not to build a dam.

The total load that a stream can carry is greatest when a large volume of water is flowing swiftly. When the speed of the water decreases, the ability of the stream to carry its load decreases. As a result, part of the stream load is deposited as sediment.

Deltas and Alluvial Fans

A stream may deposit sediment on land or in water. For example, the load carried by a stream can be deposited when the stream reaches an ocean or a lake. As a stream empties into a large body of water, the speed of the stream decreases sharply. The load is usually deposited at the mouth of the stream in a triangular shape. A triangular-shaped deposit that forms where the mouth of a stream enters a larger body of water is called a **delta.** The exact shape and size of a delta are determined by waves, tides, offshore depths, and the sediment load of the stream.

When a stream descends a steep slope and reaches a flat plain, the speed of the stream suddenly decreases. As a result, the stream deposits some of its load on the level plain at the base of the slope. A fan-shaped deposit called an **alluvial fan** forms on land, and its tip points upstream. In arid and semiarid regions, temporary streams commonly form alluvial fans. Alluvial fans differ from deltas in that alluvial fans form on land instead of being deposited in water. This difference is shown in **Figure 1.**

delta a fan-shaped mass of rock material deposited at the mouth of a stream

alluvial fan a fan-shaped mass of rock material deposited by a stream when the slope of the land decreases sharply

Figure 1 A delta, such as this one in Alaska's Prince William Sound (above), forms when a stream deposits sediment into another body of water. An alluvial fan, such as this one in California's Death Valley (right), forms when a stream deposits sediment on land.

Section 3

Focus

Overview

This section explains sediment deposition in deltas and alluvial fans. The section also describes floodplains and flood control and the life cycle of lakes.

Bellringer

Ask students to write a short paragraph that describes what they think happens to all of the sediment eroded and carried by a river. (Sediments are deposited when the water slows down or when the river reaches the ocean.) **LS Verbal**

Motivate

Demonstration — GENERAL

Changing Land Use Have students use a stream table or model watershed to investigate how land development may affect runoff. First, have students cover the banks of their stream with leaves to simulate vegetation. Then, have students make rain by using a watering can. Next, have students remove the vegetation and repeat the rain. Finally, have students cover the banks with plastic wrap or aluminum foil to simulate paving and repeat the rain. Discuss why flooding may become more frequent as a watershed is developed. **LS Kinesthetic**

Key Resources

Chapter Resource File
- Directed Reading BASIC

Technology
- Transparencies
  Bellringer

Teach

Debate — ADVANCED

To Stay or Not to Stay Have students debate this issue: Should communities be allowed to rebuild in an area prone to repeated and severe flooding? Have students investigate the pros and cons of living in a floodplain. Have students consider the costs of protecting, insuring, and rebuilding homes and businesses versus the costs of relocating the community. Students may wish to address who should pay for those costs. Have students present their views to the class, allowing time for questions, answers, and rebuttals.
LS Interpersonal/Logical

Why It Matters

Uncovering Lost Streams
Los Angeles is an example of a North American city that buried most of its streams to control flooding. The city experienced major flooding in the early 1900s. Ninety-four percent of the city's streams have been buried or diverted.

Streams are natural water-treatment systems. They slow the movement of run off. The Sun's ultraviolet rays can kill viruses in the water and soil can filter bacteria. Vegetation around streams can also take up pollutants, helping to clean the water. Daylighting aims to restore these natural systems.

Answer to Your Turn
Online Research Benefits of daylighting streams include their natural water-treatment effects, increased habitats for wildlife, and creation of greenspace for recreation.

Figure 2 Raised on stilts, houses in the Tonle Sap Floodplain in Cambodia stay dry during frequent flooding.

floodplain an area along a river that forms from sediments deposited when the river overflows its banks

Floodplains

The volume of water in nearly all streams varies depending on the amount of rainfall and snowmelt in the watershed. A dramatic increase in volume can cause a stream to overflow its banks and to wash over the valley floor. The part of the valley floor that may be covered with water during a flood is called a **floodplain.**

Natural Levees

When a stream overflows its banks and spreads out over the floodplain, the stream loses speed and deposits its coarser sediment load along the banks of the channel. The accumulation of these deposits along the banks eventually produces raised banks, called *natural levees.*

Finer Flood Sediments

Not all of the load deposited by a stream in a flood will form levees. Finer sediments are carried farther out into the floodplain by the flood waters and are deposited there. A series of floods produces a thick layer of fine sediment, which becomes a source of rich floodplain soils. Swampy areas are common on floodplains because drainage is usually poor in the area between the levees and the outer walls of the valley. Despite the hazards of periodic flooding, people choose to live on floodplains, as shown in **Figure 2.** Floodplains provide convenient access to the river for shipping, fishing, and transportation. The rich soils, which are good for farming, also draw people to live on floodplains.

Why It Matters

Uncovering Lost Streams

EYE ON THE ENVIRONMENT

Waterways in urban areas have been dramatically altered over time. Buried streams flow unseen in pipes beneath many North American cities. Some cities, however, are working to re-establish or "daylight" lost streams because of the environmental benefits. Daylighting returns a buried stream to its place above ground. Reestablished streams provide new habitats and beautify neighborhoods.

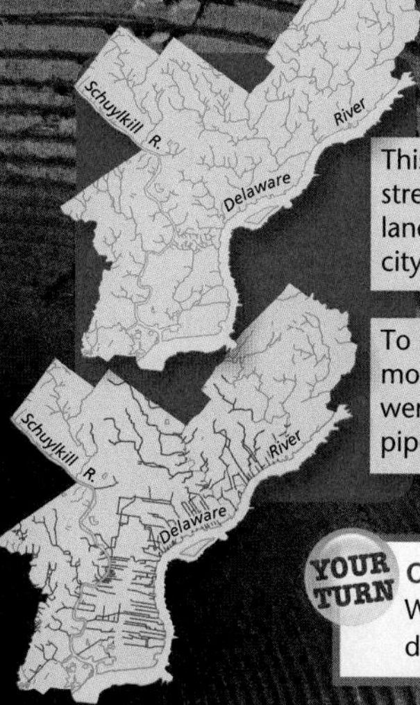

This map shows the many streams that flowed over the land that is now covered by the city of Philadelphia.

To make way for development, most of Philadelphia's streams were rerouted in underground pipes (shown in red).

YOUR TURN ONLINE RESEARCH
What is Philadelphia doing to daylight its streams?

Differentiated Instruction

Special Education Students

Sketching Have students join with a partner. Ask the partners to take turns reading alternate paragraphs aloud quietly. Then, have the students discuss what the paragraph means and draw a simple sketch that goes with the paragraph. When pairs are finished, ask partners to share their favorite sketches with the class.
LS Auditory/Verbal

Skill Builder — ADVANCED

Writing Have interested students research a historic U.S. flood, such as the 1889 Johnstown flood, the 1927 or the 1993 Mississippi River flood, or the 1976 Big Thompson Canyon flood. Have students write a newspaper style article that reports on the flood, its causes and consequences, and its aftermath. **LS Verbal**

Quick Lab Soil Erosion

40 min

Procedure

1. Fill a 23 cm × 33 cm pan about half full with moist, fine sand.
2. Place the pan in a sink so that one end of the pan is resting on a brick and is under the water faucet.
3. Position an additional pan or container such that it catches any sand and water that flow out of the first pan.
4. Slowly open the faucet until a gentle trickle of water falls onto the sand in the raised end of the pan. Let the water run for 15 to 20 s.
5. Turn off the water, and draw the pattern of water flow over the sand in your notebook.
6. Press the sand back into place, and carefully smooth the surface by using a ruler. Repeat steps 4 and 5 three more times. Each time, increase the rate of water flow slightly without splashing the sand.

Analysis

1. Describe how the rate of water flow affects erosion.
2. How does the rate of water flow affect gullies?
3. How could erosion on a real hillside be reduced without changing the rate of water flow?
4. How does the shape of a river bend change as water flows?

Human Impacts on Flooding

Human activity can contribute to the size and number of floods in many areas. Vegetation, such as trees and grass, protects the ground surface from erosion by taking in much of the water that would otherwise run off. Where this natural ground cover is removed, water can flow more freely across the surface. As a result, the likelihood of flooding increases. Logging and the clearing of land for agriculture or housing development can increase the volume and speed of runoff, which leads to more frequent flooding. Natural events, such as forest fires, can also increase the likelihood of flooding.

READING TOOLBOX

Suffixes
Add the words *accumulation, transportation,* and *conservation* to the suffix table you started at the beginning of this chapter. Remember to write the verb that each *-ation* word came from, as well as the verb's definition.

Flood Control

Indirect methods of flood control include forest and soil conservation measures that prevent excess runoff during periods of heavy rainfall. More-direct methods include the building of artificial structures that redirect the flow of water.

The most common method of direct flood control is the building of *dams*. The artificial lakes that form behind dams act as reservoirs for excess runoff. The stored water can be used to generate electricity, supply fresh water, and irrigate farmland. Another direct method of flood control is the building of *artificial levees*. However, artificial levees must be protected against erosion by the river. As **Figure 3** shows, when artificial levees break, flooding and property damage can result. Permanent overflow channels, or *floodways*, can also help prevent flooding. When the volume of water in a river increases, floodways carry away excess water and keep the river from overflowing.

Reading Check **Describe two ways that floods can be controlled.**

Figure 3 This levee near New Orleans broke as a result of Hurricane Katrina, allowing the Mississippi River through.

READING TOOLBOX

Suffixes

Key Term	Related Verb	Definition of Verb
accumulation	accumulate	to gather together
transportation	transport	to move something
conservation	conserve	to save or protect

Answer to Reading Check
Floods can be controlled indirectly through forest and soil conservation measures that reduce or prevent runoff, or directly by building artificial structures, such as dams, levees, and floodways, to redirect water flow.

Close

Reteaching BASIC

Peer Reviews Have students work in pairs to write three to five questions about the material in this section. Then, have students use their questions to quiz each other. **LS Interpersonal** Co-op Learning

Quiz GENERAL

1. What is a *floodway*? (a permanent overflow channel that diverts excess water at times of high river volume)
2. Define *natural levee.* (a raised bank of coarse sediments that are deposited when water speed decreases as a stream overflows its banks)

Quick Lab

Skills Acquired
- Observing
- Identifying/Recognizing Patterns

Materials
- 23 cm × 33 cm pan
- Moist fine sand
- Sink
- Brick
- Additional pan or container
- Ruler

Teacher's Notes: Use a stream table to further investigate streams.

Answers to Analysis
1. As the rate of flow increases, erosion should increase.
2. The faster water flow increases the size of gullies and the rate of gully formation.
3. by planting natural ground cover, such as trees and grass, or by constructing barriers to water flow
4. Answers may vary. As the channel gets deeper, it may also get wider or begin to meander a little.

Close, *continued*

Answers to Section Review

1. A delta forms where a stream or river enters a larger body of water, such as a lake or ocean. An alluvial fan forms on land where a steep stream reaches a flat plain.
2. Deltas and alluvial fans are triangle-shaped because the flow is no longer confined by a channel. When rivers overflow their banks, coarse sediments are deposited along the banks as natural levees, but finer sediments are carried farther out onto the floodplain and form rich, thick soils.
3. The disadvantage of living on a floodplain is that frequent flooding damages homes and businesses. But living on a floodplain provides convenient access to rivers for shipping, fishing, and transportation. The fertile soils of most floodplains are also very good for farming.
4. When humans remove natural ground cover for agricultural or urban development or pave areas, runoff increases, which can lead to more frequent and intense flooding. Humans can restore ground cover to reduce runoff and the potential for flooding.
5. Methods of flood control include forest and soil conservation and building dams, artificial levees, and floodways.
6. Lakes are usually short-lived because water drains away or evaporates faster than it is replenished. They also fill in with sediments carried by streams, rivers, and overland runoff.

Precipitation collects in a depression and forms a lake.

A lake loses its water as the water drains away or evaporates.

As water is lost, the lake basin may eventually become dry land.

Figure 4 Compared to rivers, lakes are short lived, and some lakes may eventually dry up.

SCILINKS.
www.scilinks.org
Topic: Flooding and Society
Code: **HQX0585**
Topic: Stream Deposition
Code: **HQX1457**

Academic Vocabulary
exceed (ek SEED) to be more than

The Life Cycle of Lakes

Not all streams flow from the land to the ocean. Sometimes, water from streams collects in a depression in the land and forms a lake. Most lakes are located at high latitudes and in mountainous areas. Most of the water in lakes comes from precipitation and the melting of ice and snow. Springs, rivers, and runoff coming directly from the land are also sources of lake water.

Most lakes are relatively short lived in geologic terms. Many lakes eventually disappear because too much of their water drains away or evaporates, as shown in **Figure 4.** A common cause of excess drainage is an outflowing stream that erodes its bed below the level of a lake basin. Lakes may also lose water if the climate becomes drier and evaporation exceeds precipitation.

Lake basins may also disappear if they fill with sediments. Streams that feed a lake deposit sediments in the lake. Sediments also are carried into the lake by water that runs off the land but does not enter a stream. Most of these sediments are deposited near the shore. These sediments build up over time, which creates new shorelines and gradually fills in the lake. Organic deposits from vegetation also may accumulate in the bottom of a shallow lake. As these deposits grow denser, a bog or swamp may form. The lake basin may eventually become dry land.

Section 3 Review

Key Ideas

1. **Identify** the differences between a delta and an alluvial fan.
2. **Explain** the differences between the deposition of sediment in deltas and alluvial fans with the deposition of sediment on a floodplain.
3. **Describe** the advantages and disadvantages of living in a floodplain.
4. **Summarize** how human activities can affect the size and number of floods.
5. **Identify** three methods of flood control.
6. **Explain** why lakes are usually short lived.

Critical Thinking

7. **Analyzing Ideas** Why are spring floods common in rivers where the headwaters are in an area of cold, snowy winters?
8. **Making Inferences** If you were picking a material to make an artificial levee, what major characteristic would you look for? Explain your answer.

Concept Mapping

9. Use the following terms to create a concept map: *stream deposition, delta, alluvial fan, floodplain, natural levee, dam, artificial levee,* and *lake.*

7. Answers may vary. When snow melts in the spring, a large amount of water flows through the area. The soil cannot soak up the water, so it runs off into stream channels that cannot hold all of the excess water.
8. Answers may vary. Artificial levees should be constructed of materials that are hard to erode, otherwise they will quickly be breached by floodwaters.
9. *Stream deposition* can fill in a *lake*, or may form *deltas, alluvial fans,* or *natural levees* in a *floodplain,* which can be protected from floods by *artificial levees* and *dams.*

Differentiated Instruction

Alternative Assessment

Sediment Stories Have students create a collage of photos of river deposits, floods, floodplains and lakes to illustrate the places where and ways in which rivers deposit their sediment loads. **LS Visual**

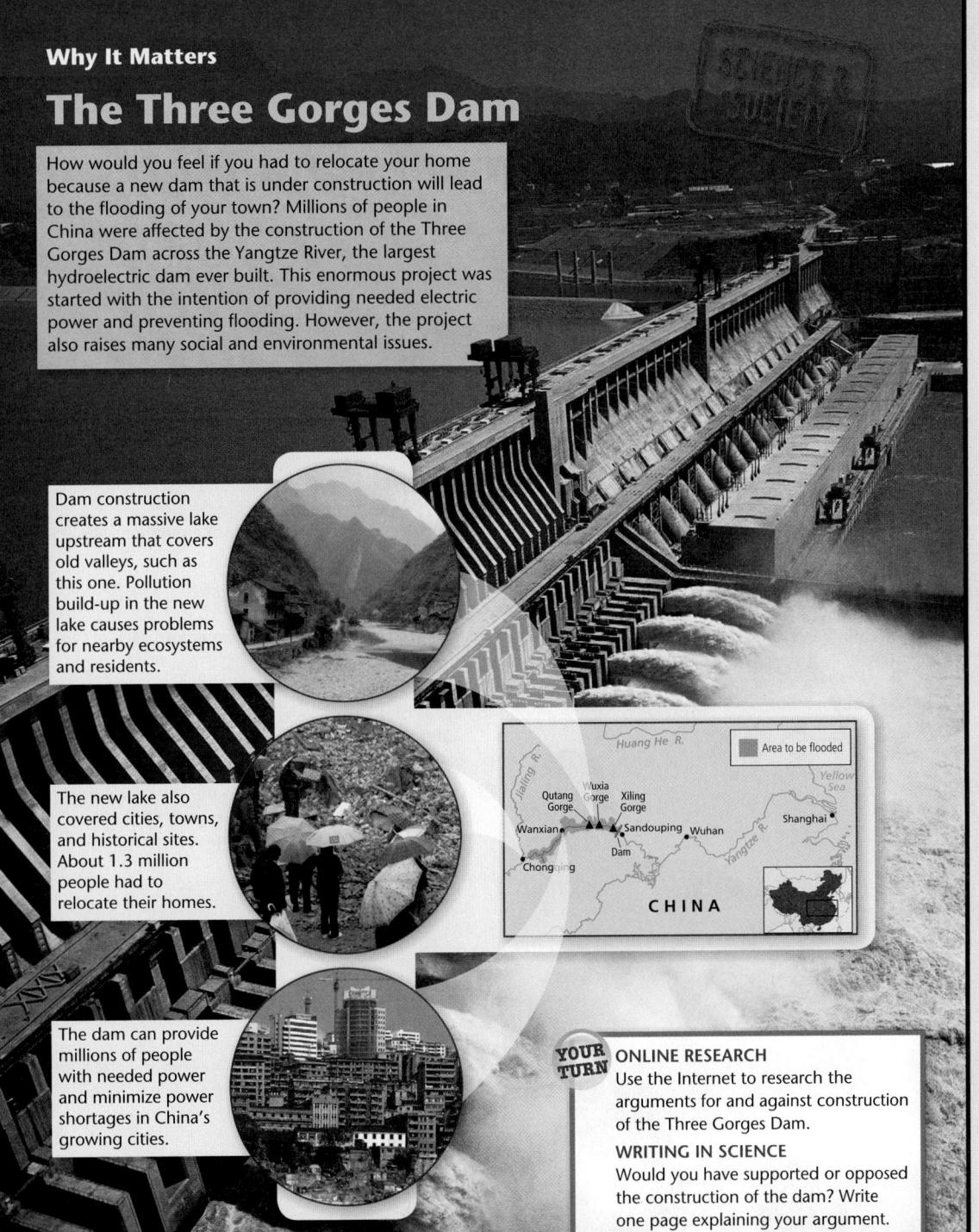

Why It Matters

The Three Gorges Dam

How would you feel if you had to relocate your home because a new dam that is under construction will lead to the flooding of your town? Millions of people in China were affected by the construction of the Three Gorges Dam across the Yangtze River, the largest hydroelectric dam ever built. This enormous project was started with the intention of providing needed electric power and preventing flooding. However, the project also raises many social and environmental issues.

Dam construction creates a massive lake upstream that covers old valleys, such as this one. Pollution build-up in the new lake causes problems for nearby ecosystems and residents.

The new lake also covered cities, towns, and historical sites. About 1.3 million people had to relocate their homes.

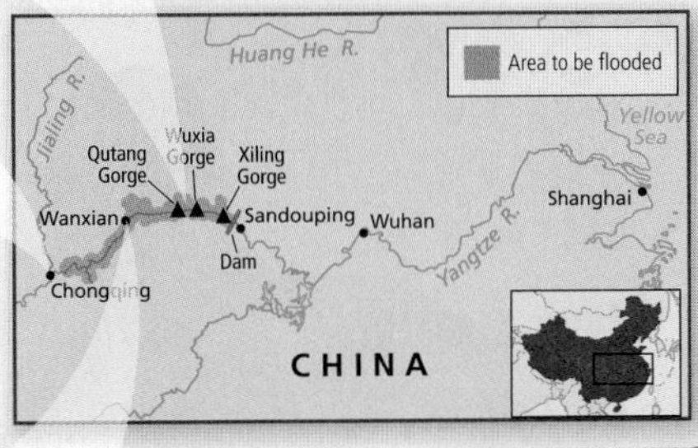

The dam can provide millions of people with needed power and minimize power shortages in China's growing cities.

YOUR TURN

ONLINE RESEARCH
Use the Internet to research the arguments for and against construction of the Three Gorges Dam.

WRITING IN SCIENCE
Would you have supported or opposed the construction of the dam? Write one page explaining your argument.

Why It Matters

The Three Gorges Dam

About one million people have died because of flooding along the Yangtze River in the past 100 years. The Three Gorges Dam may prevent flooding from the Yangtze River and provide millions of people with hydroelectric power. However, the dam is a controversial project. Some politicians who originally supported the dam are now stating that measures need to be taken to prevent a disaster. Because the dam lies over a fault, some scientists believe it is possible for the dam to be destroyed by an earthquake. If the dam burst, towns and cities downstream of the dam would be destroyed and many people would be killed.

Answers to Your Turn

Online Research Because the dam is such a massive and controversial project, it has been featured prominently in the media. Arguments for the dam include the provision of electricity to millions of people, the prevention of loss due to the flooding, and increased trade for China because the dam makes the river deep enough for large ships to move through it. The disadvantages include the relocation of more than one million people from their homes, the loss of ecosystems and historical sites, increased pollution in the river, and the potential for a major disaster because the dam lies over a fault line.

Writing In Science Student answers will vary and should be supported by some of the advantages or disadvantages listed above.

Inquiry Lab

Time Required
one 45-minute class period

Lab Ratings
EASY → HARD

Teacher Preparation (1 of 4)
Student Setup (2 of 4)
Concept Level (2 of 4)
Cleanup (2 of 4)

Skills Acquired
- Observing
- Measuring
- Experimenting
- Predicting
- Inferring
- Collecting Data
- Organizing and Analyzing Data

Scientific Methods
In this lab, students will
- Make Observations
- Ask Questions
- Test a Hypothesis
- Analyze the Results
- Draw Conclusions
- Communicate Results

Materials
The materials listed on this page are enough for groups of two to four students. You may want to ask students to bring in juice containers from home.

Inquiry Lab

45 min

Sediments and Water

Running water erodes some types of soil more easily than it erodes others. How rapidly a soil erodes depends on how well the soil holds water. In this lab, you will determine the erosive effect of water on various types of sediment.

What You'll Do
- **Measure** the amount of water that sediment can hold.
- **Identify** the properties that affect how sediment interacts with water.

What You'll Need
graduated cylinder, 100 mL
grease pencil
juice containers, 12 oz (2)
metric ruler
nail, large
pan, 23 cm × 33 cm × 5 cm or larger
sand, dry and coarse
silt, dry
stopwatch or clock with second hand
water

Safety

Ask a Question
1. Which type of soil would hold more water: sandy soil or silty soil? Which soil would water flow through faster and therefore would erode more rapidly: sandy soil or silty soil?

Form a Hypothesis
2. Write a hypothesis that is a possible answer to the questions above.

Test the Hypothesis
3. Use a graduated cylinder to pour 300 mL of water into each of two juice containers.
4. Place the containers on a flat surface. Using a grease pencil, draw a line around the inside of the containers to mark the height of the water. Label one container "A" and the other "B." Empty and dry the containers.
5. Using silt, fill container A up to the line drawn inside the container. Tap the container gently to even out the surface of the sediment. Repeat this step for container B, but use sand.

Step 5

Tips and Tricks
Have students observe the sediments with a magnifying glass or dissecting microscope. Students can also use the sediments in a stream table setup to see how resistant each type is to erosion under different conditions.

6 Fill the graduated cylinder with 100 mL of water. Slowly pour the water into container A. Stop every few seconds to allow the soil to absorb the water. Continue pouring until a thin film of water forms on the surface of the sediment. If more than 100 mL of water is needed, refill the graduated cylinder and continue this step.

7 Record the volume of water poured into the container.

8 Using container B, repeat steps 6 and 7. Record your observations.

Step 8

9 Use a metric ruler to measure 1 cm above the surface of the sediment in each container. Using the grease pencil, draw a line to mark this height on the inside of each container. Pour water from the graduated cylinder into containers A and B until the water reaches the 1 cm mark.

10 Poke a nail through the very bottom of the side of container A. Place the container inside the pan. At the same time, start recording the time by using a stopwatch and pull the nail out of the container.

11 Observe the water level, and record the amount of time that the water takes to drop to the sediment surface.

12 Using container B, repeat steps 10 and 11. Record your observations.

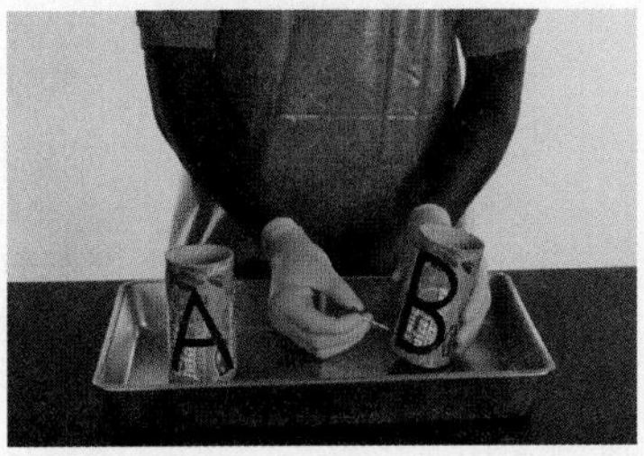

Step 12

Analyze the Results

1. **Analyzing Results** In step 8, which type of sediment held more water?
2. **Analyzing Results** Which type of sediment was the water able to flow through faster?
3. **Summarizing Results** What properties of the sediment do you think affected how the water flowed through the sediment? Explain your answer.

Draw Conclusions

4. **Analyzing Results** On the basis of your answers to the questions above, which would water erode more quickly: an area of silt or an area of sand? Explain your answer.
5. **Drawing Conclusions** In which sediment do you think a deep stream channel is most likely to form? In which sediment is a meandering stream likely to form? Explain your answers.

Extension

Applying Conclusions Describe three ways to make slopes covered with soil more resistant to erosion.

Answers to Analyze the Results

1. Silt should hold more water than sand.
2. Water should flow faster through the sand than through the silt.
3. The size of the particles and the spaces between particles influence how fast water flows through the sediments. Sand is coarser than silt and will have much larger pore spaces for water to flow through than silt does.

Answers to Draw Conclusions

4. Answers may vary. Because water can soak into and flow more quickly through the sand, there is less run-off to cause erosion. Because silt is finer than sand and because water cannot flow through silt as easily, the water would erode and carry away the silt.
5. Deep stream channels would most likely form in silty soils because water can erode the stream bed easily. Meandering streams are more likely to form in sandy sediments because the stream bed is less easily eroded.

Answer to Extension

Planting ground cover, building barriers, reducing the steepness of the slope, terracing, and contour planting can all slow runoff and make an area more resistant to soil erosion.

World Watershed Sediment Yield

Discussion GENERAL

Sediment Load and Land Use Draw students' attention to the relatively high sediment yields in Southeast Asia around Indonesia, Thailand, Myanmar, Bangladesh, and Malaysia. Have students propose a hypothesis to explain the high loads that come from this area. (Answers may vary; possibilities include high precipitation rates, high topographic relief, regular flooding during the monsoon season, and extensive loss of rainforests leading to increased runoff.) LS **Visual/Logical**

Answers to Map Skills Activity

1. Southeast Asia, around Indonesia (3,000 million tons)
2. less than 10 tons to 500 tons per square kilometer
3. 1,311 + 150 + 18 + 154 + 28 = 1,661 million tons.
4. Southeast Asia appears to have higher relief than Africa. Sediment yields in Southeast Asia tend to be more than 1,000 tons per square kilometer compared to less than 100 tons per square kilometer in Africa.
5. The total area of land in the Amazon basin is much larger (3 to 4 times greater) than the area of land in the Indian basin, which would explain why the total yield per year is so much larger in the Amazon basin. In addition, the Amazon basin receives a large part of its sediment load from the Andes Mountains, while most of the high relief areas in northern India drain east.

MAPS in Action

World Watershed Sediment Yield

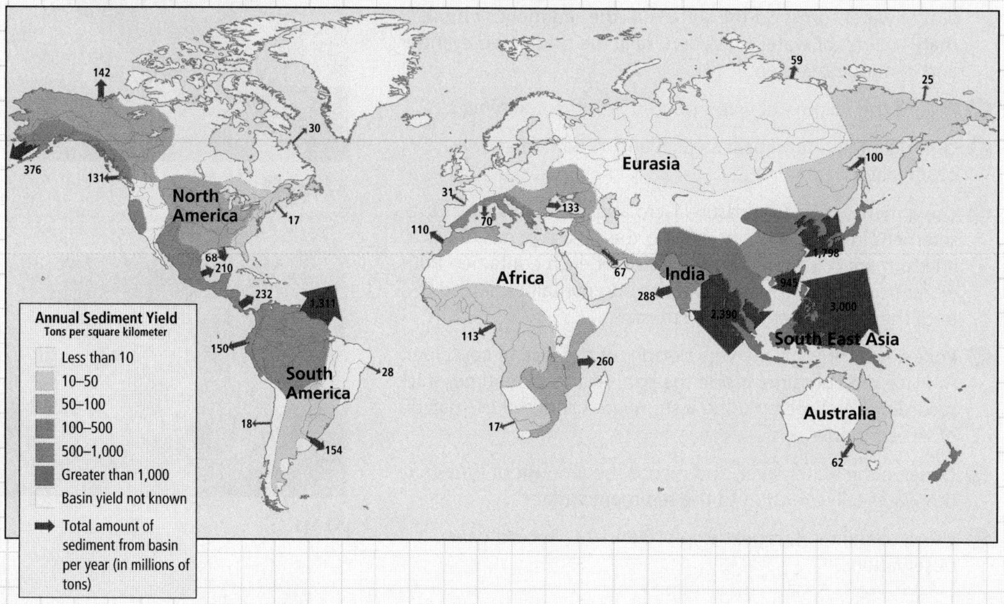

Map Skills Activity

This map shows the world's watersheds and identifies the sediment yield of each watershed basin in tons per square kilometer and the total amount of sediment that each basin dumps into the ocean in millions of tons per year. Use the map to answer the questions below.

1. **Using a Key** Which area has the highest total annual sediment yield from one basin?
2. **Using a Key** What is the range of the annual sediment yield in tons per square kilometer for the United States, excluding Alaska?
3. **Analyzing Data** What is the total amount of sediment that basins in South America yield per year?
4. **Analyzing Relationships** Areas that have high relief (where the range of elevations is great) tend to have higher sediment yields than do areas of low relief (where the topography is flatter). Which area would you conclude has higher relief: Africa or South East Asia? Explain your answer.
5. **Making Comparisons** Both the Amazon basin, which is in northern South America, and the India basin have an annual sediment yield range of 100 to 500 tons per square kilometer. However, the total amount of sediment per year from the Amazon basin is 1,311 million tons, while the total amount of sediment per year from the India basin is 288 million tons. Explain why these two basins differ so significantly in their total sediment yield per year.

Key Resources

Technology

- Transparencies
  78 World Watershed Sediment Yield

Chapter 15 Summary

THINK central SUPER SUMMARY
Keyword: HQXRVSS

Key Ideas | **Key Terms**

Section 1

The Water Cycle

- The water cycle involves the processes of evapotranspiration, condensation, and precipitation.
- A region's water budget is affected by temperature, vegetation, wind, and the amount of rainfall.
- Water can be conserved by individuals limiting water use and by governments enforcing conservation laws and antipollution laws.

Key Terms:
water cycle, p. 407
evapotranspiration, p. 408
condensation, p. 408
precipitation, p. 408
desalination, p. 410

Section 2

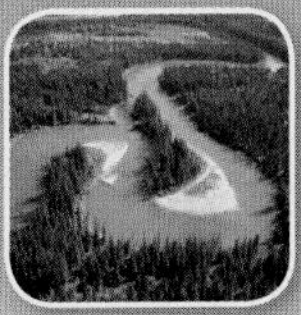

Stream Erosion

- A river develops over time, through the processes of precipitation and erosion.
- A river system consists of a main stream and tributaries.
- The erosive ability of a river is affected by stream load, stream discharge, and stream gradient.
- Erosive factors, such as gradient and discharge, can affect the development of a river channel, forming meanders and braided streams.

Key Terms:
tributary, p. 411
watershed, p. 411
stream load, p. 412
discharge, p. 412
gradient, p. 412
meander, p. 413
braided stream, p. 414

Section 3

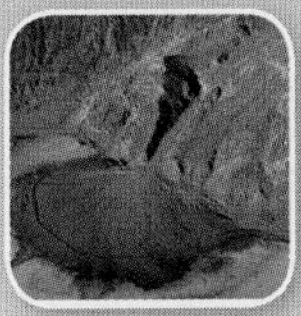

Stream Deposition

- Two types of stream deposition are deltas, which form in water, and alluvial fans, which form on land.
- Living in a floodplain has advantages, such as access to a river and rich soil, but the risk of flooding is a disadvantage.
- Three methods of flood control include forest and soil conservation, dams, and artificial levees.
- Over time, a lake may lose its water or fill with sediment and become dry land.

Key Terms:
delta, p. 415
alluvial fan, p. 415
floodplain, p. 416

Chapter Summary

Using THINK central Resources

Super Summary

Have students connect the major concepts in this chapter through an interactive Super Summary. Visit www.thinkcentral.com and type in the keyword **HQXRVSS** to access the Super Summary for this chapter.

Differentiated Instruction

Alternative Assessment

Biography of a River Have students research the history and development of one river and write its story. The biography should include an explanation of when and where the river formed, what its original course was, and how it has changed over time; a map of the river that notes major cities and land uses along its route; a list of historical events or people of importance to the river; and a description of past and current uses of the river and any environmental challenges it is facing. **LS Verbal/Visual**

Chapter Review

Assignment Guide	
Section	**Questions**
1	2, 4, 6, 10, 11, 18, 19, 24, 25, 30, 31
2	1, 3, 7, 8, 12–14, 20, 26, 29, 33–36
3	5, 9, 15–17, 22–23, 32
2 and 3	21
1–3	27, 28

Reading Toolbox

1. Sample information for the Venn diagram is shown below.

   Meandering channels: low speed; low gradient; winding pattern of wide curves; single channel.

   Both: types of rivers

   Braided streams: high gradient; large sediment load; braided pattern; multiple channels.

Using Key Terms

2–9. Answers may vary but should show that students understand the definitions of and differences between key terms.

Understanding Key Ideas

10. d 14. d
11. a 15. d
12. b 16. b
13. a 17. a

Short Answer

18. The water budget of Earth as a whole is balanced, but local water budgets commonly are not balanced.

Chapter 15 Review

1. **Venn Diagram** Make a Venn diagram with two circles. Label one circle "Meandering channel" and the other circle "Braided stream." In the area where the circles overlap, write shared characteristics. In each of the other areas, write characteristics that are unique to each type of river. READING TOOLBOX

USING KEY TERMS

Use each of the following terms in a separate sentence.

2. *water cycle*
3. *gradient*
4. *evapotranspiration*
5. *floodplain*

For each pair of terms, explain how the meanings of the terms differ.

6. *condensation* and *precipitation*
7. *watershed* and *tributary*
8. *stream load* and *discharge*
9. *delta* and *alluvial fan*

UNDERSTANDING KEY IDEAS

10. The change of water vapor into liquid water is called
    a. runoff.
    b. desalination.
    c. evaporation.
    d. condensation.
11. In a water budget, the income is precipitation and the expense is
    a. evapotranspiration and runoff.
    b. condensation and saltation.
    c. erosion and conservation.
    d. conservation and sedimentation.
12. The land area from which water runs off into a stream is called a
    a. tributary. **c.** divide.
    b. watershed. **d.** gully.
13. Tributaries branch out and lengthen as a river system develops by
    a. headward erosion.
    b. condensation.
    c. saltation.
    d. runoff.
14. The stream load that includes gravel and large rocks is the
    a. suspended load. **c.** dissolved load.
    b. runoff load. **d.** bed load.
15. A fan-shaped formation that develops when a stream deposits its sediment at the base of a steep slope is called a(n)
    a. delta.
    b. meander.
    c. oxbow lake.
    d. alluvial fan.
16. The part of a valley floor that may be covered during a flood is the
    a. floodway.
    b. floodplain.
    c. meander.
    d. artificial levee.
17. One way to control floods indirectly is through
    a. soil conservation.
    b. dams.
    c. floodways.
    d. artificial levees.

SHORT ANSWER

18. How does a local water budget differ from the water budget of the whole Earth?
19. How is reducing the pollution in streams and groundwater linked to water conservation?
20. Describe how bank erosion can cause a river to meander.
21. Why do most rivers that have a large sediment load also have a fast flow of water?
22. Describe how lakes fill with sediment.
23. What is the difference between direct and indirect methods of flood control?

19. Conservation of water means wise use of water. Polluting surface and ground water makes it unfit for many uses. Preventing pollution will keep existing water supplies fit for most uses, so we do not have to find other sources of freshwater.
20. As a river slows down it cannot erode its bed as effectively, but it still can erode its banks. At curves, along the outside bank, speed is highest, causing increased erosion in that area. Along the inside of the curve, the speed is slower, and sediment loads are deposited as bars of sand and gravel. Over time, the process continues and curves enlarge and progress along the length of the stream.
21. Sediment load is a function of the volume of water a stream carries and the stream's speed. Thus, to carry a large suspended and dissolved sediment load, a river needs a high volume of water or a high speed.
22. Streams that feed lakes deposit their sediment load into the lake. Water that runs off land but does not enter streams also can deposit sediments into lakes. Over time, the lake is gradually filled in and may become a swamp, bog, or even dry land.
23. Indirect methods of flood control try to prevent excess runoff during periods of high rainfall to avoid flooding. Direct methods try to redirect the flow during a flood to reduce damage from floodwaters.

CRITICAL THINKING

24. Evaluating Ideas How would Earth's water cycle be affected if a significant percentage of the sun's rays were blocked by dust or other contaminants in the atmosphere?

25. Making Comparisons Use an atlas to determine the geographic location of Kolkata, India, and Stockholm, Sweden. How might the local water budgets of these two cities differ? Explain your answer.

26. Making Inferences The Colorado River is usually grayish brown as it flows through the Grand Canyon. What causes this color?

27. Making Predictions What do you think would happen to cities in the southwestern United States if rivers in that area could not be dammed?

CONCEPT MAPPING

28. Use the following terms to create a concept map: *water vapor, condensation, precipitation, channel, stream load, bar, alluvial fan, delta, divides, watersheds, tributaries, floodplains, dams,* and *artificial levees.*

MATH SKILLS

29. Making Calculations If a river is 3,705 km long from its headwaters to its delta and the average speed of its water is 250 cm/s, use the equation *time = distance ÷ speed* to determine how many days a water molecule takes to make the trip.

30. Using Equations You wish to examine the annual water budget for the state of Colorado. If p = total precipitation, e = total evapotranspiration, r = total stream runoff, and g = total water soaking into the ground, what equation will allow you to determine whether Colorado experiences a net loss or net gain of water over the course of a year?

WRITING SKILLS

31. Writing Persuasively Write a persuasive essay of at least 300 words that suggests ways in which your community can conserve water and reduce water pollution.

32. Communicating Main Ideas Discuss the dangers and advantages of living in a river floodplain. Outline the options for adapting to living in a river floodplain.

INTERPRETING GRAPHICS

The graph below shows the gradients of several rivers of the United States. Use the graph to answer the questions that follow.

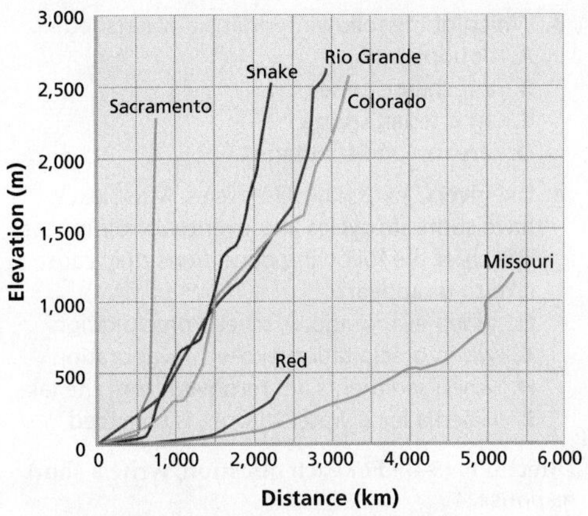

33. Which river has the shallowest average gradient over its entire course?

34. Which river has the steepest average gradient over its entire course?

35. Based only on gradient, how would the speed of the Snake River compare with the speed of the Missouri River?

36. Which end of each line on the graph represents the headwaters of the river system? Explain your answer.

Chapter Review

Critical Thinking

24. If the sun's rays were blocked by dust or other contaminants, the amount of evapotranspiration on Earth would be reduced. Less water in the atmosphere would mean less precipitation. But overall, Earth's water budget would remain balanced.

25. Kolkata, India, is much more tropical than Stockholm, Sweden. Evapotranspiration would likely be higher in Kolkata, while precipitation may be less frequent in Stockholm.

26. Sediments from upstream give the river its grayish-brown color.

27. If rivers in desert areas of the U.S. could not be dammed, much of the western U.S. would have significantly lower population densities and reduced agriculture. Cities such as Phoenix, Las Vegas, and others would be much smaller, and farming would be very difficult without irrigation.

Concept Mapping

28. Answers may vary but should include all of the terms listed. Sample answers appear at the end of this unit on p. 507C.

Math Skills

29. 100,000 cm = 1 km, so 250 cm/s = 0.0025 km/s time = distance/speed = 3,705 km ÷ 0.0025 km/s = 1,500,000 s; 1 day = 24 h × 60 min × 60 s = 86,400 s,

so $\frac{1{,}500{,}000 \text{ s}}{86{,}400 \text{ s/day}} = 17$ days

30. net budget = $(p + g) - (e + r)$

Writing Skills

31. Answers may vary. Accept all reasonable answers.

32. Answers may vary. Accept all reasonable answers.

Interpreting Graphics

33. The Red River has the shallowest average gradient (0.2 m/km) over its course.

34. The Sacramento River has the steepest gradient (3.1 m/km) over its course.

35. Based only on gradient, the Snake River would have a higher speed than the Missouri River does.

36. The headwaters of each river are represented by the point on each line that is at the highest elevation and that is farthest from the origin of the graph.

Estimated Time

To give students practice under more realistic testing conditions, allow them 30 minutes to answer all of the questions in this practice test.

Test Doctor

Question 4 Answer F is correct. Answer G is incorrect because excessive precipitation would keep a lake full and may even cause the lake to grow in size. Answer H is incorrect because sediments may actually be harmful to a lake if they build up. Removing sediments will often extend the lifespan of a lake. Answer I is incorrect because a balanced water budget would keep the lake's size stable.

Question 9 Answer C is correct. Students who do not thoroughly read the passage may choose answer A. They may think that half of the river, not the wetlands, has been lost.

Question 11 Full-credit answers should include the following points:
- the river was altered to accommodate human society and human inventions, such as boats
- students should realize that the river was being altered to benefit humans and that any attempts to alter nature in order to benefit human society may have unexpected—and unwanted—consequences

Chapter 15 Standardized Test Prep

Understanding Concepts

Directions (1–4): For each question, write on a separate sheet of paper the letter of the correct answer.

1. Condensation is often triggered as water vapor rising in the atmosphere
   - **A.** cools.
   - **B.** warms.
   - **C.** contracts.
   - **D.** breaks apart.
2. The continuous movement of water from the ocean, to the atmosphere, to the land, and back to the ocean is
   - **F.** condensation.
   - **G.** the water cycle.
   - **H.** precipitation.
   - **I.** evapotranspiration.
3. Which of the following drains a watershed?
   - **A.** floodplains
   - **B.** a recharge zone
   - **C.** an artesian spring
   - **D.** streams and tributaries
4. Like rivers, lakes have life cycles. Most lakes have short life cycles and eventually disappear. Which of the following conditions may cause a lake to disappear?
   - **F.** when evaporation exceeds precipitation
   - **G.** when precipitation exceeds evaporation
   - **H.** when sediments are removed from the lake
   - **I.** when a local water budget is balanced

Directions (5–8): For each question, write a short response.

5. What is the term for a volume of water that is moved by a stream during a given amount of time?
6. The gradient of a river is defined as a change in what over a given distance?
7. Streams are said to have varying loads. What makes up a stream's load?
8. Desalination removes what naturally occurring compound from ocean water?

Reading Skills

Directions (9–11): Read the passage below. Then, answer the questions.

The Mississippi Delta

In the Mississippi River Delta, long-legged birds step lightly through the marsh and hunt fish or frogs for breakfast. Hundreds of species of plants and animals start another day in this fragile ecosystem. This delta ecosystem, like many other ecosystems, is in danger of being destroyed.

The threat to the Mississippi River Delta ecosystem comes from efforts to make the river more useful. Large parts of the river bottom have been dredged to deepen the river for ship traffic. Underwater channels were built to control flooding. What no one realized was that the sediments that once formed new land now pass through the channels and flow out into the ocean. Those river sediments had once replaced the land that was lost every year to erosion. Without them, the river could no longer replace land lost to erosion. So, the Mississippi River Delta began shrinking. By 1995, more than half of the wetlands were already gone—swept out to sea by waves along the Lousiana coast.

9. Based on the passage, which of the following statements about the Mississippi River is true?
   - **A.** The Mississippi River never floods.
   - **B.** The Mississippi River is not wide enough for ships to travel on it.
   - **C.** The Mississippi River's delicate ecosystem is in danger of being lost.
   - **D.** The Mississippi River is disappearing.
10. Based on the passage, which of the following statements is true?
    - **F.** By 1995, more than half of the Mississippi River was gone.
    - **G.** Underwater channels may control flooding.
    - **H.** Channels help form new land.
    - **I.** Sediment cannot replace lost land.
11. The passage mentions that damage to the ecosystem came from efforts to make the river more useful. For who or what was the river being made more useful?

Question 13 Full-credit answers should include the following points:
- water flows from the left to the right in the diagram. This flow can be deduced from the difference in water levels
- students should understand that water naturally seeks to equalize the levels of the two pools and that, in situations such as those shown in the graphic, the water in the deeper pool will move into the shallower pool, if possible
- water is propelled from the deep reservoir on the left through the penstock by gravity and into the more shallow reservoir on the right

Question 15 Full-credit answers should include the following points:
- water on the outside edges of the river bend flows faster, which erodes the banks, and makes the meander wider
- students should know that meanders form when fast-moving water that is opposite to a bar deposition erodes the adjacent bank
- when meanders become so curved that they form a loop, the river may reconnect to itself and the meander may become isolated from the river, which forms an oxbow lake
- the faster the flow of water is, the faster this process of erosion and meander growth occurs

Interpreting Graphics

Directions (12–15): For each question below, record the correct answer on a separate sheet of paper.

The diagram below shows how a hydroelectric power plant works. Use this diagram to answer questions 12 and 13.

Hydroelectric Power Plant

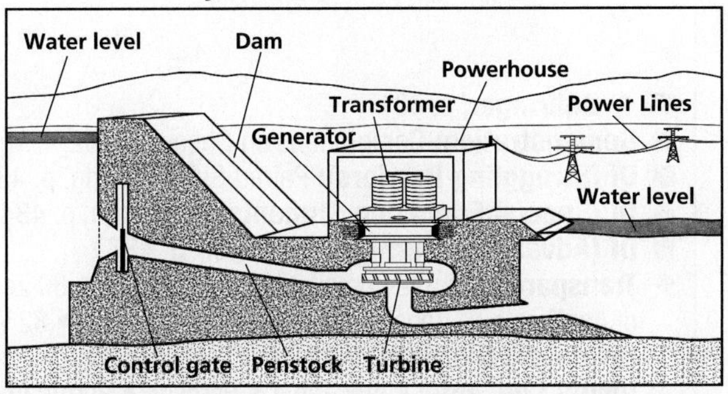

12. Hydroelectric dams are used to generate electricity for human use. As water rushes past the machinery inside, an electric current is generated. What does water rush past to turn the generator, which produces the current?

A. a transformer
B. the control gate
C. an intake
D. a turbine

13. Look at the diagram above. What direction does the water flow? What makes the water flow in this direction?

The graphic below shows the formation of an oxbow lake. Use this graphic to answer questions 14 and 15.

Formation of an Oxbow Lake

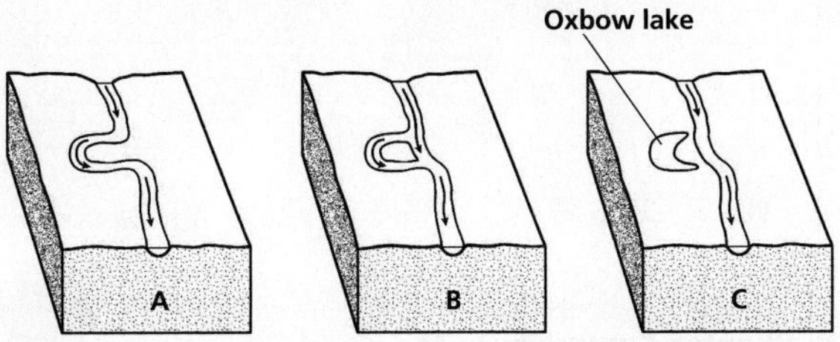

14. What is the term for the wide curves whose development causes the formation of oxbow lakes?

F. wanders
G. meanders
H. bows
I. loops

15. How does the speed at which the water flows contribute to the process of forming an oxbow lake?

Test Tip

If you are permitted to, draw a line through each incorrect answer choice as you eliminate it.

Standardized Test Prep

Using THINK central Resources

State Resources

- For specific resources for your state, visit www.thinkcentral.com and type in the keyword **HSHSTR.**

Answers

Understanding Concepts

1. A
2. G
3. D
4. F
5. discharge
6. elevation
7. small particles and dissolved minerals
8. salt

Reading Skills

9. C
10. G
11. Answers may vary. See Test Doctor for a detailed scoring rubric.

Interpreting Graphics

12. D
13. Answers may vary. See Test Doctor for a detailed scoring rubric.
14. G
15. Answers may vary. See Test Doctor for a detailed scoring rubric.

Chapter Planner 16 Groundwater

	Standards	Teach Key Ideas
Chapter Opener, pp. 428–429 (45 min.)	National Science Education Standards	
Section 1 **Water Beneath the Surface,** pp. 431–438 (45 min.) › Properties of Aquifers › Zones of Aquifers › Movement of Groundwater › Topography and the Water Table › Conserving Groundwater › Wells and Springs › Hot Springs › Geysers	LS 4e, SPSP 6b, UCP 1, ES 2b	■ ◆ **Bellringer,** p. 431 ■ **Demonstration:** Comprehension Check, p. 432 ■ **DI (Struggling Readers):** Paired Summarizing, p. 433 ■ **DI (Special Education Students):** Research, p. 434 ■ **DI (Advanced Learners):** Research, p. 437 ◆ **Transparencies:** 79 Porosity and Permeability • 80 Zones of Aquifers • 81 Topography and the Water Table • 82 Water Level in the Southern Ogallala ▲ **Visual Concepts:** Water Table • Porosity • Permeable and Impermeable Rocks • Groundwater • Well • Aquifer Recharge Zone • Aquifers and Artisan Springs
Section 2 **Groundwater and Chemical Weathering,** pp. 439–442 (45 min.) › Results of Weathering by Groundwater › Karst Topography	PS 3c, UCP 3, UCP 4	■ ◆ **Bellringer,** p. 439 ■ **DI (Special Education Students):** Chart, p. 441 ▲ **Visual Concepts:** Chemical Weathering
Chapter Wrap-Up, pp. 447–451 (90 min.)		**Chapter Summary,** p. 447

See also PowerNotes® Presentations

CHAPTER Fast Track

To shorten instruction because of time limitations, omit Section 2.

Key
Teacher's Edition ■
Chapter Resource File ●
Teaching Transparencies ◆
Online Edition ▲

All resources listed below are also available on the **Teacher One Stop™.**

Why It Matters	Hands-On	Skills Development	Assessment
■ **Chapter Overview,** p. 428 ■ **Using the Figure:** Warmth in a Cold Climate, p. 428	**Inquiry Lab:** Growing Stalactites, p. 429	**Reading Toolbox,** p. 430	
■ **Section Overview,** p. 431 ■ **Using the Figure:** Compare, p. 431 ■ **Using the Figure:** Replenishing Groundwater, p. 432 ■ **Using the Figure:** Extreme Conditions, p. 433 ■ **Using the Figure:** Going Down the Drain, p. 435 ■ **Environmental Connection:** Munching Microbes, p. 435 ■ **Using the Figure:** Slope, p. 437	**Quick Lab:** Permeability, p. 432 ■ **Group Activity:** Model an Aquifer, p. 433 **Skills Practice Lab:** Porosity, pp. 444–445 ● **Making Models Lab:** Making a Classroom Geyser	**Math Skills:** Rate of Groundwater Depletion, p. 434 ■ ● **Internet Activity:** Your Watershed, p. 434 **Reading Toolbox:** Venn Diagrams, p. 436 **Maps in Action:** Water Level in the Southern Ogallala, p. 446 ■ ● **Internet Activity:** Agriculture and the Ogallala Aquifer, p. 446	**Reading Check,** p. 433 **Reading Check,** p. 434 **Reading Check,** p. 437 **Section Review,** p. 438 ■ **Reteaching,** p. 437 ■ **Quiz,** p. 437 ■ **DI (Alternative Assessment):** Assessing Groundwater, p. 438 ● **Section Quiz**
■ **Section Overview,** p. 439 ■ **Using the Figure:** Cave Formations, p. 440 **Life in the Dark,** p. 440	**Quick Lab:** Chemical Weathering, p. 439 ● **Inquiry Lab:** Cave Formations and Ecology	■ ● **Internet Activity:** Sinkholes, p. 440 ■ **Skill Builder:** Writing, p. 441 **Reading Toolbox:** Venn Diagrams, p. 442	**Reading Check,** p. 441 **Section Review,** p. 442 ■ **Reteaching,** p. 441 ■ **Quiz,** p. 441 ■ **DI (Alternative Assessment):** Guided Tour, p. 442 ● **Section Quiz**
Is it Possible to Drown in Quicksand?, p. 443		▲ **Super Summary** **Standardized Test Prep,** pp. 450–451	**Chapter Review,** pp. 448–449 ■ **DI (Alternative Assessment):** The Water Beneath Your Feet, p. 447 ● **Chapter Tests**

See also Lab Generator

See also Holt Online Assessment Resources

Chapter Overview

Groundwater is water that seeps through soil and flows beneath Earth's surface. Water reaches the surface through wells and springs. Hot springs and geysers occur when hot, subsurface rock heats groundwater. As groundwater seeps through the ground, the water may react chemically with rock to form caverns and other geological formations.

Using the Figure GENERAL

Warmth in a Cold Climate Ask students to look at the background in the photograph and use it to describe the winter climate in this part of Japan. Ask students to explain how a hot spring can occur in such a cold climate. (A hot spring can occur in a cold climate because the water is heated by hot rocks or magma beneath Earth's surface.) **LS Logical**

Why It Matters

Geothermal steam can be used to produce electricity. The world's largest geothermal energy complex, called The Geysers, is located in California. This complex produces the majority of northern California's electricity.

Chapter 16 Groundwater

Chapter Outline

Virginia Standards of Learning
ES.1.a
ES.1.c
ES.2.a
ES.8.b
ES.8.c
ES.8.d
ES.8.e

Why It Matters

Groundwater is a major source of fresh water for humans. Where molten rock in Earth's crust heats groundwater and surrounding rock, hot springs form. These macaque monkeys bathe in hot springs in Jigokudani National Park in Japan.

Chapter Correlations — *Virginia Standards of Learning*

ES.1.a volume, area, mass, elapsed time, direction, temperature, pressure, distance, density, and changes in elevation/depth are calculated utilizing the most appropriate tools.
ES.1.c scales, diagrams, charts, graphs, tables, imagery, models, and profiles are constructed and interpreted.
ES.2.a science explains and predicts the interactions and dynamics of complex Earth systems.
ES.8.b development of karst topography
ES.8.c relationships between groundwater zones, including saturated and unsaturated zones, and the water table
ES.8.d identification of sources of fresh water including rivers, springs, and aquifers, with reference to the hydrologic cycle
ES.8.e dependence on freshwater resources and the effects of human usage on water quality

Inquiry Lab Growing Stalactites

15 min

Place two jars on a piece of cardboard. Fill each jar two-thirds full of Epsom salts. Then, fill with warm water to the top of the salt and stir to make a thick solution. Soak a 40 cm piece of twine in the solution until it is thoroughly wet. Then tie a weight onto each end of the twine. Place one end of the twine in each jar. The middle of the twine should hang between the two jars, lower than the water levels, but should not touch the cardboard. Place your set-up somewhere where it will not be disturbed. Observe what happens to the twine over several days.

Questions to Get You Started

1. Describe the formation that appears on the twine. How do you think this formed?
2. How is the formation on the twine similar to the natural formation called a stalactite?

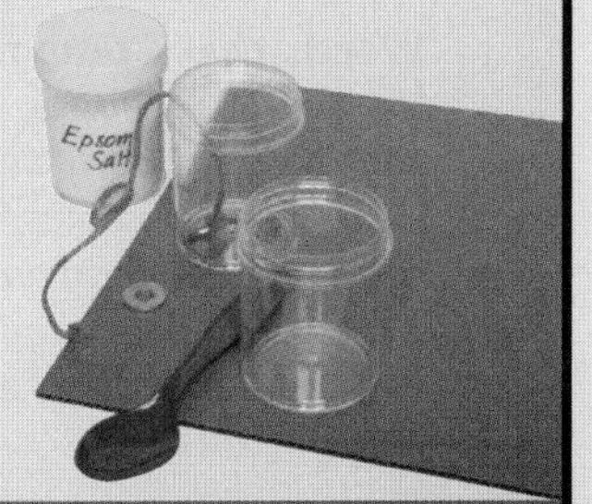

Inquiry Lab

Central Concept: Students will model the formation of stalactites and stalagmites.

Teacher's Notes: Make sure to use brown hemp twine for this activity. Other types of string may not work.

Materials (per group)

- Two jars
- Cardboard
- Epsom salts
- Warm water
- 40 cm piece of twine
- Two washers (used as weights)

Skills Acquired

- Making Models
- Observing

Answers to Getting Started

1. Sample answer: A long rippled cone-shaped solid, like a stalactite, formed hanging down from the twine. Beneath it, a mounded structure formed like a stalagmite. These formed as the water dripped from the twine and Epsom salts precipitated out of the solution.
2. Just like a stalactite forms as water with dissolved minerals drips through a cave, the formation on the twine formed as water with dissolved minerals dripped from the twine.

Using THINK central Resources

An online version of this chapter, as well as all the print and multimedia resources that accompany the program are available to registered teachers and their students. Log onto www.thinkcentral.com to access these materials and tools to organize your preparation and student learning.

READING TOOLBOX

Word Origins

Term	Definition	Etymology (Word Origin)
artesian wells	a well through which water flows freely without being pumped	from the French *artésian,* based on the place name *Artois,* a former province in northern France, where many wells of that type were used

Describing Time

Three examples are shown in the chart below. Students' charts may include many more examples.

Time Reference	Context of Time Reference
slowly	how carbonic acid dissolves limestone
often	when stalactites and stalagmites grow together to form columns
eventually	when a natural bridge may collapse

READING TOOLBOX

These reading tools will help you learn the material in this chapter.

Word Origins

Words that Come from Place Names In Section 2, you will learn about *karst topography,* a landscape characterized by caverns, sinkholes, and underground drainage. The term *karst topography* comes from *Karst,* the German name for a region of Slovenia, formerly a part of Yugoslavia, known for its caves.

Your Turn In Section 1, you will learn about *artesian wells.* Use a dictionary or the Internet to learn how these wells got their name. Create a table like the one below and use the information you find to fill it in.

Term	Definition	Etymology (Word Origin)
Artesian wells		

Describing Time

Temporal Language The word *temporal* means "related to time." Temporal language is language that is used to describe time. Paying careful attention to temporal language can help you understand the temporal nature of events and processes.

Your Turn As you read Section 2, make a two-column table. In the first column, write words or phrases in the text that refer to time. In the second column, note the context of the time reference.

Time Reference	Context of Time Reference
slowly	how carbonic acid dissolves limestone
often	when stalactites and stalagmites grow together to form columns

Graphic Organizers

Venn Diagrams A Venn diagram is a graphic representation of the relationships between similar things or ideas. See Appendix A for instructions for making a Venn diagram.

Your Turn As you read Section 2, complete a Venn diagram to represent the relationships between different features formed by chemical weathering.

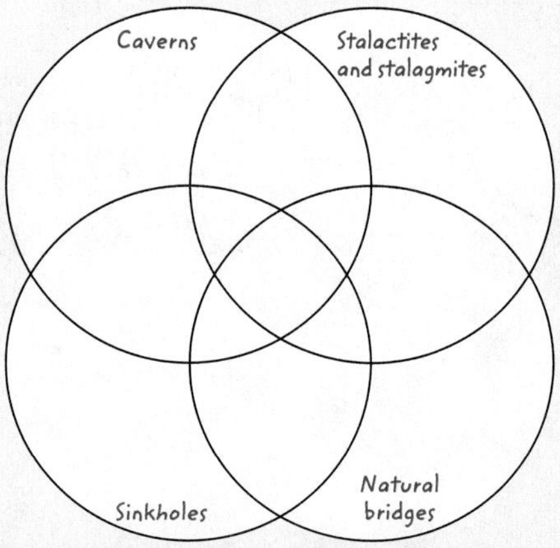

For more information on how to use these and other tools, see **Appendix A.**

Graphic Organizers

Answers will vary. Where all circles overlap, students should write characteristics common to all features. For example: all features are formed by chemical weathering and are common in areas of Karst topography. In overlaps of adjacent circles, students should write characteristics common to the two features from the overlapping circles. In the parts of the circles that do not overlap, students should write characteristics particular to each feature.

SECTION 1

Water Beneath the Surface

Key Ideas	Key Terms	Why It Matters
❯ Identify properties of aquifers that affect the flow of groundwater. ❯ Describe the water table and its relationship to the land surface. ❯ Compare wells, springs, and artesian formations. ❯ Describe two land features formed by hot groundwater.	groundwater aquifer porosity permeability water table artesian formation	Almost one-fourth of all fresh water used in the United States comes from groundwater sources. Understanding how water and the ground interact may affect the way you treat the environment.

Surface water that does not run off into streams and rivers may seep down through the soil into the upper layers of Earth's crust. There, the water fills spaces, or *pores,* between rock particles. Water may also fill fractures or cavities in rock that were caused by erosion. Water that fills and moves through these spaces in rock and sediment is called **groundwater.**

Properties of Aquifers

A body of rock or sediment in which large amounts of water can flow and be stored is called an **aquifer.** For water to flow freely through an aquifer, the pores or fractures in the aquifer must be connected. The ease with which water flows through an aquifer is affected by many factors, including porosity and permeability.

groundwater the water that is beneath Earth's surface

aquifer a body of rock or sediment that stores groundwater and allows the flow of groundwater

porosity the percentage of the total volume of a rock or sediment that consists of open spaces

Porosity

In a set volume of rock or sediment, the percentage of the rock or sediment that consists of open spaces is **porosity.** One factor that affects porosity is sorting. *Sorting* is the amount of uniformity in the size of the rock or sediment particles, as **Figure 1** shows. Most particles in a well-sorted sediment are about the same size. Poorly sorted sediment contains particles of many sizes. Small particles fill the spaces between large particles, which makes the rock less porous. Particle packing also affects porosity. Loosely packed particles leave many open spaces that can store water, so the rock has high porosity. Rock that has tightly packed particles contains few open spaces and thus has low porosity. Grain shape also affects porosity. In general, the more irregular the grain shape is, the more porous the rock or sediment is.

Figure 1 Differences in Porosity

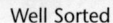

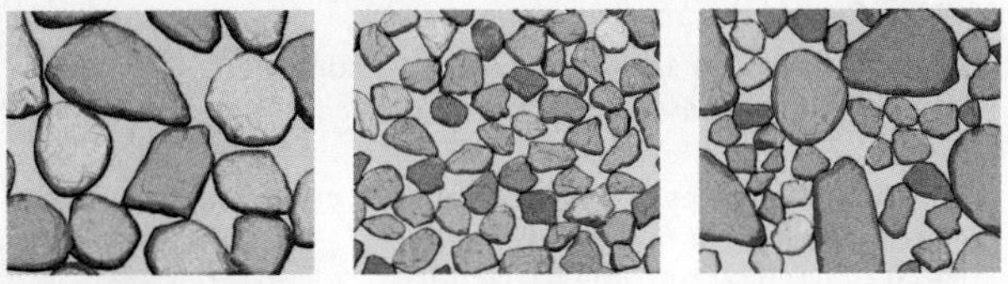

Section 1

Focus

Overview

This section describes aquifers, how water enters aquifers, aquifer porosity, permeability, and zonation. The section describes groundwater movement, water table levels, wells and springs, as well as the formation of hot springs and geysers.

Bellringer

Ask students where the water that flows from the faucets in their home comes from. (In most locations, the water that is used by humans comes from groundwater. In other locations, it may be purified surface water.)
LS Logical

Motivate

Using the Figure — GENERAL

Compare Have students describe the three types of sediment shown in the figure at the bottom of the page. Have them think about what may happen when grains of many sizes occur together. Ask them to hypothesize why poorly sorted sediment that has grains of different sizes has low porosity. (When grains of many sizes occur together, small grains may become trapped or compacted between large grains, thereby reducing porosity.)
LS Visual

Key Resources

Chapter Resource File
- Directed Reading BASIC
- Making Models Lab: Making a Classroom Geyser GENERAL

Technology
- Transparencies
  Bellringer
  79 Porosity and Permeability

Teach

Using the Figure GENERAL

Replenishing Groundwater Have students describe the differences they see between the porous rock and the permeable rock shown in the figure at the top of this page. Ask students to speculate on how water is replenished in porous rock (by precipitation only) as compared with permeable rock. (Water may flow from one water-filled space to another.) LS **Visual**

Quick Lab

Skills Acquired

- Measuring
- Calculating
- Observing

Materials

- Sharpened pencil
- Three paper or plastic cups
- Cheesecloth
- Rubber band
- Three thread spools
- Saucer or pie pan
- Sand
- Water
- Stopwatch
- Measuring cup
- Soil
- Gravel

Teacher's Notes: You may wish to try this lab ahead of time with the materials students will be using to determine the permeability of the soil.

Answers to Analysis

1. the gravel sample
2. Answers may vary. Gravel should be the most permeable; the sand or soil should be the least permeable.

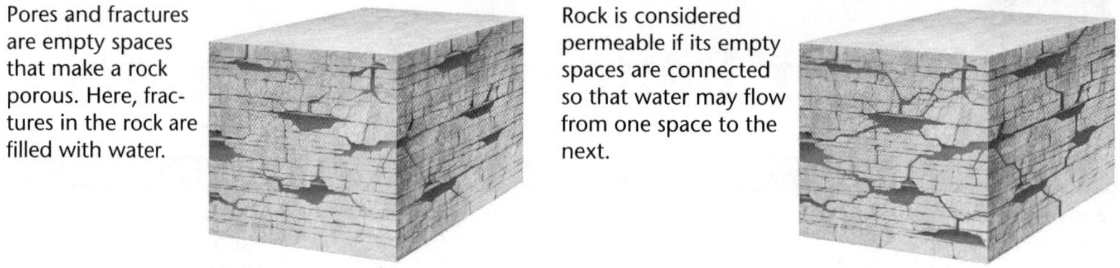

Pores and fractures are empty spaces that make a rock porous. Here, fractures in the rock are filled with water.
Rock is considered permeable if its empty spaces are connected so that water may flow from one space to the next.

Figure 2 Porous rocks do not make good aquifers unless water can move freely through the rocks.

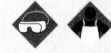

permeability the ability of a rock or sediment to let fluids pass through its open spaces, or pores

Permeability

The ease with which water passes through a porous material is called **permeability.** For a rock to be permeable, the open spaces must be connected, as shown in **Figure 2.** Rock that has high porosity is not permeable if the pores or fractures are not connected. Permeability is also affected by the size and sorting of the particles that make up the rock or sediment. The larger and better sorted the particles are, the more permeable the rock or sediment tends to be. The most permeable rock, such as sandstone, is composed of coarse particles. Other types of rock, such as limestone, may be permeable if they have interconnected cracks. Clay is a sediment composed of flat, very fine-grained particles. Because of this characteristic composition, clay is essentially *impermeable,* which means that water cannot flow through it.

Quick Lab Permeability

20 min

Procedure

1. With a sharpened pencil, make seven tiny holes in the bottom of each of three paper or plastic cups. Stretch cheesecloth tightly over the bottom of each cup. Secure the cloth with a rubber band.
2. Mark a line 2 cm from the top of one cup. Stand the cup on three thread spools in a saucer or pie pan, and fill the cup to the line with sand.
3. Pour 120 mL of water into the cup. Use a stopwatch to time how long the water takes to drain.
4. Pour the water from the saucer into a measuring cup. Record the amount of water.
5. Repeat steps 2 to 4 with the two other cups, but fill one cup with soil and one with gravel, not sand.
6. Calculate the rates of drainage for each cup by dividing the amount of water that drained by the time the water took to drain.
7. For each cup, calculate the percentage of water retained by subtracting the amount of water drained from 120 mL. Divide this volume by 120.

Analysis

1. Which cup had the highest drainage rate?
2. A sample with a high drainage rate and a low percentage of water retained is highly permeable. Which sample was the most permeable? Which sample was the least permeable?

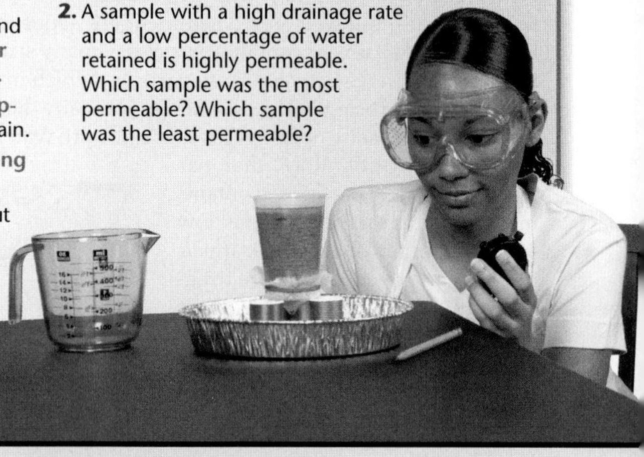

Demonstration GENERAL

Comprehension Check Demonstrate the concepts of permeability and impermeability. Get two shallow bowls or cups. In one bowl, press potters' clay around the bottom and up the sides to a height of 2.5 cm; put 2.5 cm of loose potting soil in the other bowl. Have students watch what happens as you pour about 60 mL of water into each bowl. The water should sit atop the clay because the clay is impermeable. The water should enter the soil because the soil is permeable. LS **Visual** English Language Learners

MISCONCEPTION ALERT

Underwater Lakes and Rivers Many students think of groundwater as an underground lake or as a river of water that flows through large open channels in rock. Explain to students that while groundwater does form underground lakes or rivers in some places, in most cases, groundwater flows slowly through tiny spaces between rock particles. The rate at which water flows depends on the permeability of the rock or sediment.

Zones of Aquifers

Soil particles attract water molecules and hold water in the soil. When there is more water than the soil can hold, gravity pulls water down through the rock layers until it reaches impermeable rock. As more water soaks into the ground, the water level rises underground and forms two distinct zones of groundwater, as shown in **Figure 3.**

Zone of Saturation

The layer of an aquifer in which the pore space is completely filled with water is the *zone of saturation*. The term *saturated* means "filled to capacity." The zone of saturation is the lower of the two zones of groundwater. The upper surface of the zone of saturation is called the **water table.**

water table the upper surface of underground water; the upper boundary of the zone of saturation

Zone of Aeration

The zone that lies between the water table and Earth's surface is called the *zone of aeration*. The uppermost region of the zone of aeration holds soil moisture—water that forms a film around grains of topsoil. The bottom region, just above the water table, is the capillary fringe. Water is drawn up from the zone of saturation into the capillary fringe by capillary action. *Capillary action* is caused by the attraction of water molecules to other materials, such as soil. For example, when a paper towel soaks up a spill, capillary action draws moisture into the towel. Between the soil moisture region and the capillary fringe is a region that contains both air and water in its pores.

SCILINKS®
www.scilinks.org
Topic: Groundwater
Code: HQX0699

Reading Check **What are the two zones of groundwater?**
(See Appendix G for answers to Reading Checks.)

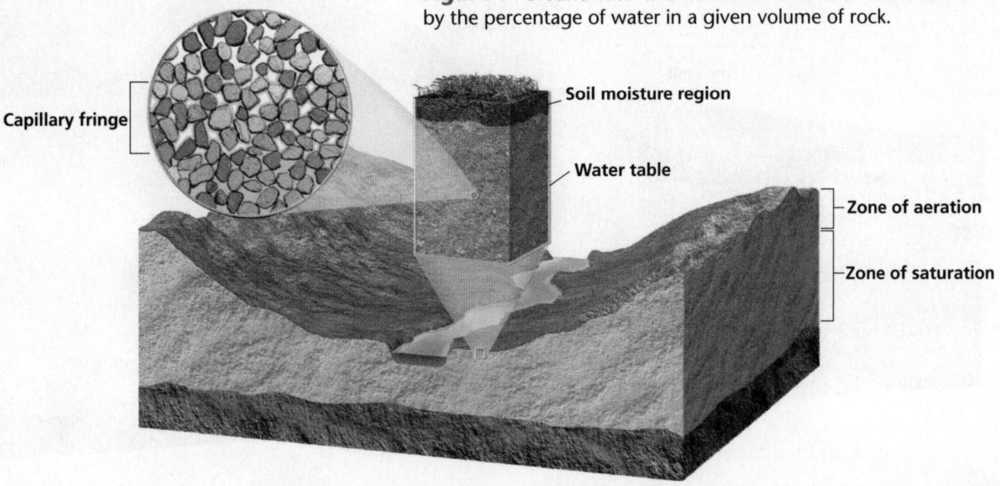

Figure 3 Groundwater is divided into zones that are defined by the percentage of water in a given volume of rock.

Using the Figure — GENERAL

Extreme Conditions Have students look at the illustration of the zones of groundwater. Have students identify and describe each layer shown. Ask students to identify the lowest layer, which is not labeled in the diagram. (the impermeable layer) Then, have students draw cross sections of an aquifer under two extreme conditions—during a drought and during an extended, heavy rain. Ask them to refer to their drawing to explain how each condition affects the zones of the aquifer. (During a drought, the water table is lower and the dry region expands; during a period of heavy rain, the water table rises and the dry region and the soil moisture layer may become saturated.) **LS Visual**

Answer to Reading Check

The two zones of groundwater are the zone of saturation and the zone of aeration.

Group Activity — GENERAL

Model an Aquifer Organize the class into groups of 5 or 6 students. Provide each group with a clear glass bowl or shallow jar, clay, small pebbles, soil, and a small amount of water. Have students create a model of an aquifer. Students should observe the water and then describe how their model is like an aquifer. (In the models, the water should collect on top of the impermeable clay and be stored in the empty spaces in the layer of pebbles.) **LS Kinesthetic**

Key Resources

Technology

- Transparencies
  80 Zones of Aquifers

Differentiated Instruction

Struggling Readers

Paired Summarizing Group students into pairs and have them read silently about the zones of aquifers. Then, have one student summarize the ideas of the zone of saturation and the zone of aeration. The other student should listen to the retelling and should point out any inaccuracies or ideas that were left out. Allow students to refer to the text as needed.
LS Verbal English Language Learners Co-op Learning

Math Skills

Answer

1,500 million m^3/y − 575 million m^3/y = 925 million m^3/y; The yearly loss of groundwater is 925 million m^3.
6,475 million m^3 ÷ 925 million m^3/y = 7 y; The aquifer should be depleted in 7 years.

Answer to Reading Check

The depth of a water table depends on topography, aquifer permeability, the amount of rainfall, and the rate at which humans use the groundwater.

Internet Activity — ADVANCED

Your Watershed Have students visit the Web site of the U.S. Environmental Protection Agency and go to their watershed page. Here, students can locate and learn what watershed your area is part of and find out about both surface water and groundwater resources. By analyzing the areas overlying the watershed, students can speculate about what types of contaminants enter surface water and groundwater and how these pollutants might affect the overall water supply. Have a group of students report to the class about what they learned. A worksheet designed to direct student research on this topic can be found in the **Chapter Resource File** booklet or by visiting www.thinkcentral.com and entering the keyword **HQXGWEX.** LS **Logical**

Math Skills

Rate of Groundwater Depletion In some areas, more groundwater is removed than is naturally replaced. In one area, for example, 575 million cubic meters of water enters the rock every year, while 1,500 million cubic meters of water is removed each year. What is the rate of groundwater depletion in that area? The total amount of groundwater available is 6,475 million cubic meters. If groundwater use continues at the current rate, in how many years will the water be completely depleted?

Movement of Groundwater

Like water on Earth's surface, groundwater flows downward in response to gravity. Water passes quickly through highly permeable rock and slowly through rock that is less permeable. The rate at which groundwater flows horizontally depends on both the permeability of the aquifer and the gradient of the water table. *Gradient* is the steepness of a slope. The speed of groundwater increases as the water table's gradient increases.

Topography and the Water Table

The depth of the water table below the ground surface depends on surface topography, the permeability of the aquifer, the amount of rainfall, and the rate at which humans use the water. Generally, shallow water tables match the contours of the surface, as shown in **Figure 4.** During periods of prolonged rainfall, the water table rises. During periods of drought, the water table falls and flattens because water that leaves the aquifer is not replaced.

Only one water table exists in most areas. In some areas, however, a layer of impermeable rock lies above the main water table. This rock layer prevents water from reaching the main zone of saturation. Water collects on top of this upper layer and creates a second water table, which is called a *perched water table.*

Reading Check **What four factors affect the depth of a water table?**

Figure 4 The water table generally mirrors surface topography. A perched water table lies above the main water table.

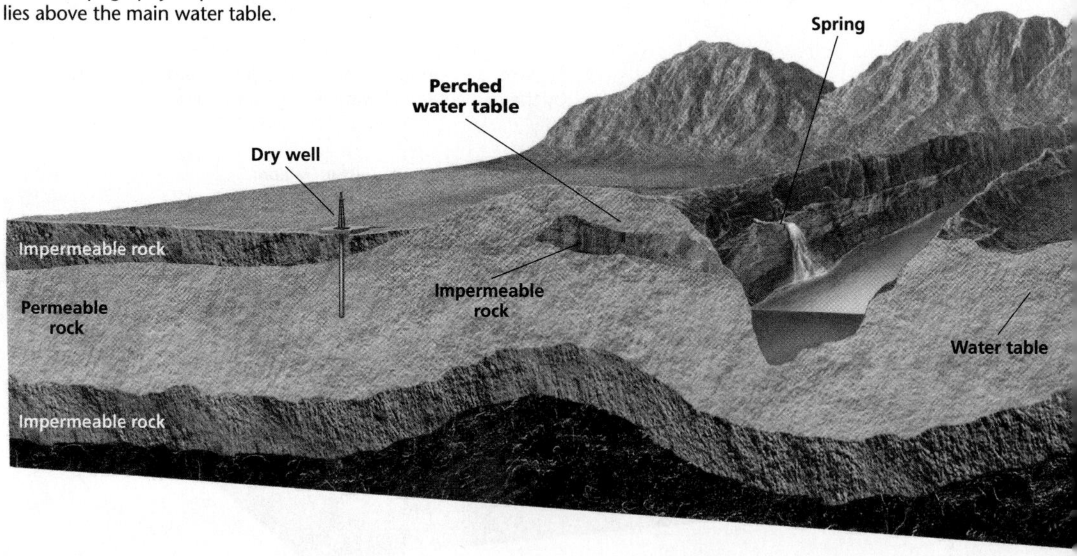

Differentiated Instruction

Special Education Students

Research Many students, especially those who are gifted and talented, find textbook material more interesting and meaningful if they extrapolate through research. Have students use the library, interviews, or the Internet to find the following details: 1–The names of the aquifers that supply water to the state you live in, 2–Other states that receive water from the same aquifer system, 3–The total number of aquifer systems that supply water to the United States.

Key Resources

Technology

- Transparencies
  81 Topography and the Water Table

Conserving Groundwater

In many communities, groundwater is the only source of fresh water. Although groundwater is renewable, its long renewal time limits its supply. Groundwater collects and moves slowly, and the water taken from aquifers may not be replenished for hundreds or thousands of years. Communities often regulate the use of groundwater to help conserve this valuable resource. They can monitor the level of the local water table and discourage excess pumping. Some communities recycle used water. This water is purified and may be used to replenish the groundwater supply.

Surface water enters an aquifer through an area called a recharge zone. A *recharge zone* is anywhere that water from the surface can travel through permeable rock to reach an aquifer, as shown in **Figure 4.** Recharge zones are environmentally sensitive areas because pollution in the recharge zone can enter the aquifer. Therefore, recharge zones are often labeled by signs like the one shown in **Figure 5.** Pollution can enter an aquifer from waste dumps and underground storage tanks for toxic chemicals, from fertilizers and pesticides used in agriculture and on lawns, or from leaking sewage systems. If too much groundwater is pumped from an aquifer that is near the ocean, salt water from the ocean can then flow into the aquifer and contaminate the groundwater supply.

Figure 5 Water that enters this drain runs off into the Charles River and surrounding aquifers in Massachusetts.

Identifying Preconceptions GENERAL

What Gets into Groundwater Perform this exercise before students begin to read this page. Supply students with a list of substances and ask them to determine whether or not each one enters the groundwater. These items may include lawn weedkiller, dog droppings, oil leaks from cars, discarded medications, and household waste from landfills. After students have discussed the items on the list, invite them to consider how all of these items, and countless others, do end up in groundwater as they wash off streets or leach through landfills.
LS Verbal/Logical

Environmental Connection

Munching Microbes Once pollutants get into groundwater, removing the pollutants is extremely difficult because groundwater is so inaccessible. In addition, the aquifer material may get coated with pollutants such as oil, which remain for a long time and recontaminate the water. Biologists are continuing to search for and find bacteria that "eat" groundwater pollutants. The bacteria they have in mind would ingest a contaminant and render it harmless. Experiments so far are promising, but scientists must make sure the bacteria are not harmful. Have students do research to find out more details about such experiments, including what kinds of pollution the bacteria ingest and how they make the pollutants harmless. Have them write a report presenting their findings.
LS Verbal

Using the Figure BASIC

Going Down the Drain Invite a volunteer to read the sign painted on the sidewalk in the photo at the top of the page. Ask students to identify the location of this drain. (It is on the curb next to the gutter and a storm drain.) Invite students to discuss why the sign just above the drain is probably insufficient to keep all contaminants out of the drain and thus out of groundwater. (When it rains, everything on the street will wash into the drain, even if nothing is deliberately dumped into it.) **LS Visual**

READING TOOLBOX

Venn Diagrams
Answers will vary. Sample information for the Venn diagram is given below.

Ordinary wells: water must be pumped

Both: bring groundwater to the surface; draw water from permeable rock

Artesian wells: water flows without being pumped

Teaching Tip ADVANCED

Make Concepts Relevant Tell students that when a new well is dug for a home, the well driller is required by law to test to see how much water the well can supply per minute. Ask students to discuss why this information is one of many factors that is important to the homeowner and why it might also be important to neighbors. (The homeowner must understand how much water can be used without depleting the well. Neighbors may wish to know because one neighbor could lower the overall water table and cause surrounding wells to go dry.)
LS **Interpersonal**

Wells and Springs

Groundwater reaches Earth's surface through wells and springs. A *well* is a hole that is dug to below the level of the water table and through which groundwater is brought to Earth's surface. A *spring* is a natural flow of groundwater to Earth's surface in places where the ground surface dips below the water table. Wells and springs are classified into two groups—ordinary and artesian.

READING TOOLBOX

Venn Diagrams
Draw a Venn diagram with two circles. Label one circle "Ordinary wells" and the other circle "Artesian wells." In the area where the circles overlap, write shared characteristics. In each of the other areas, write characteristics that are unique to each type of well.

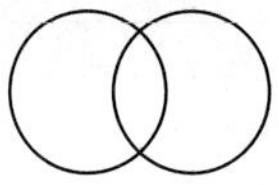

Ordinary Wells and Springs

Ordinary wells work only if they penetrate highly permeable sediment or rock below the water table. If the rock is not permeable enough, groundwater cannot flow into the well quickly enough to replace the water that is withdrawn.

Pumping water from a well lowers the water table around the well and forms a *cone of depression,* as shown in **Figure 6.** If too much water is taken from a well, the cone of depression may drop to the bottom of the well and the well will go dry. The lowered water table may extend several kilometers around the well and may cause surrounding wells to become dry.

Ordinary springs are usually found in rugged terrain where the ground surface drops below the water table. These springs may not flow continuously if the water table in the area has an irregular depth as a result of variable rainfall. Springs that form from perched water tables that intersect the ground surface are very sensitive to the amount of local precipitation. Thus, these springs may go dry during dry seasons or severe droughts.

Figure 6 A cone of depression develops in the water table around a pumping well.

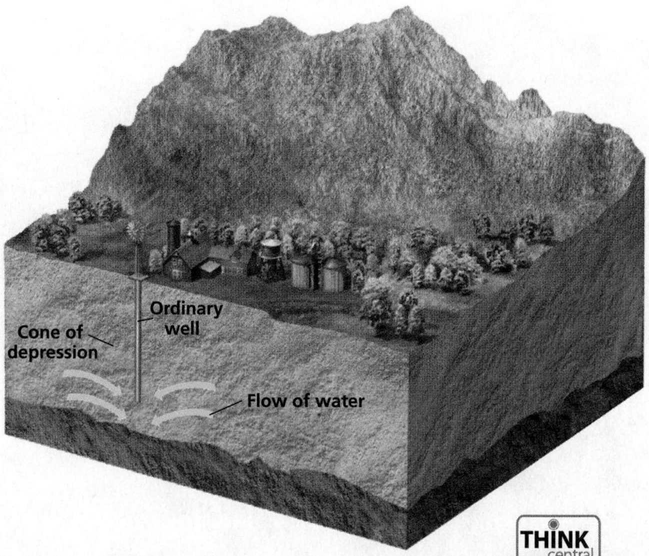

THINK central INTERACT ONLINE (Keyword: HQXGWEF6)

Homework GENERAL

Home Water Use Tell students that no matter the immediate source of their own water supply, conserving water is crucial. Because fresh water supplies replenish slowly, if present usage patterns continue, the water supply will be lower in the future than it is now. Have students create a checklist of fixtures and appliances in their homes that use water. Have them check which ones are designed to use "less" water and which are not. Students may also make a checklist of water wasting at home, such as taking long showers, running half-loads of laundry or of dishes in the dishwasher, and leaving the water running when they brush their teeth. Then, have students create a plan for conserving water at home. LS **Logical**

Figure 7 The aquifer in an artesian formation dips under the impermeable caprock. When a well is drilled into an artesian aquifer, pressure is released and the water rushes upward. These men are testing the quality of water from an artesian well in Pakistan.

Artesian Wells and Springs

The groundwater that supplies many wells comes from local precipitation. However, the water in some wells may come from as far away as hundreds of kilometers. Water may travel through an aquifer to a distant location. Because the aquifer is so extensive, it may become part of an artesian formation, an arrangement of permeable and impermeable rock.

An **artesian formation** is a sloping layer of permeable rock that is sandwiched between two layers of impermeable rock, as shown in **Figure 7.** The permeable rock is the aquifer, and the top layer of impermeable rock is called the *caprock*. Water enters the aquifer at a recharge zone and flows downhill through the aquifer. As the water flows downward, the weight of the overlying water causes pressure in the aquifer to increase. Because the water is under pressure, when a well is drilled through the caprock, the water quickly flows up through the well and may even spout from the surface. An *artesian well* is a well through which water flows freely without being pumped.

Artesian formations are also the source of water for some springs. When cracks occur naturally in the caprock, water from the aquifer flows through the cracks. This flow forms *artesian springs*.

Reading Check **What is the difference between ordinary springs and artesian springs?**

artesian formation a sloping layer of permeable rock sandwiched between two layers of impermeable rock and exposed at the surface

Academic Vocabulary

source (SOHRS) the thing from which something else comes

Using the Figure ADVANCED

Slope Have students study the diagram of an artesian formation. Ask them to speculate about why the slope enhances the formation. Have them describe how the angle of slope would affect the rate of release of the water at the surface. (The slope causes water to flow downward more quickly, which adds greater pressure to the water accumulated at the base. The greater the slope, the more pressure builds up at the base. Therefore, water emerges faster from an artesian well or spring at the base of a steep slope.)
LS Visual/Logical

Close

Reteaching BASIC

Diagrams Have students make sketches or diagrams of the different formations that hold groundwater. Have them label all of the layers, zones, and surface features. **LS Visual**

Quiz GENERAL

1. What type of sediment has the lowest porosity and therefore is able to hold the least amount of water? (poorly sorted sediment)
2. How does a water table's gradient affect the flow of groundwater? (the steeper the gradient, the faster the movement of groundwater)
3. What is travertine, and how does it form? (Travertine is the form of calcite that is deposited when hot spring waters cool as they reach the surface.)

Answer to Reading Check

Ordinary springs occur where the ground surface drops below the water table. An artesian spring occurs where groundwater flows to the surface through natural cracks in the overlying caprock.

Differentiated Instruction

Advanced Learners

Research Have students go beyond the text to research regional and national efforts to protect groundwater. Ask students to prepare a poster or a presentation to summarize their findings.
LS Verbal

Close, *continued*

Answers to Section Review

1. Porosity is the percentage of open space in rock or sediment. Permeability refers to the ease with which water passes through a porous material. The more permeable the rock is, the more easily groundwater flows through the rock.
2. The zone of saturation is completely filled with water. The zone of aeration lies above the zone of saturation and is composed of the soil water region, a dry region, and the capillary fringe.
3. The contours of a shallow water table generally match the land's topography.
4. because they depend on the amount of local precipitation
5. A cone of depression is an area where the water table is lowered as a result of the withdrawal of water from a well.
6. In an ordinary aquifer the rock layers may be horizontal and lack an impermeable cap. In an artesian formation the permeable rock layer slopes and is covered by an impermeable layer called the *caprock*.
7. In an ordinary well, the water is mechanically pumped to the surface; in an artesian well, natural pressure pushes the water to the surface.
8. Answers may vary. An artesian well may provide a more constant water source, because it is not subject to local weather conditions.
9. Pollutants produced in a recharge zone will likely find their way into the aquifer below.
10. Shallow pools do not erupt because the water is not under pressure, so it boils before it can reach the superheated state that causes a geyser to erupt.
11. The *water table* separates the *zone of aeration* from the *zone of saturation*, which stores *groundwater*.

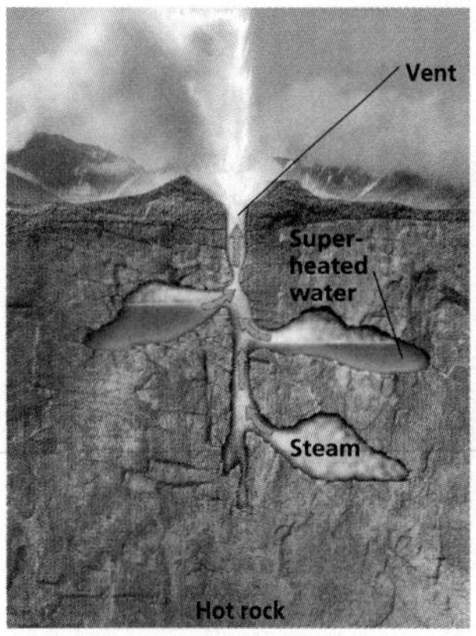

Figure 8 The vent and underground chambers of a geyser enable water to become superheated and to eventually erupt to the surface.

Hot Springs

Groundwater is heated when it passes through rock that has been heated by magma. Hot groundwater that is at least 37 °C and that rises to the surface before cooling produces a *hot spring*. When water in a hot spring cools, the water deposits minerals around the spring's edges. The deposits form steplike terraces of calcite called *travertine*. *Mud pots* form when chemically weathered rock mixes with hot water to form a sticky, liquid clay that bubbles at the surface. Mud pots are called *paint pots* when the clay is brightly colored by minerals or organic materials.

Geysers

Hot springs that periodically erupt from surface pools or through small vents are called *geysers*. A geyser consists of a narrow vent that connects one or more underground chambers with the surface. The hot rocks that make up the chamber walls superheat the groundwater. The water in the vent exerts pressure on the water in the chambers, which keeps the water in the chambers from boiling for a time. When the water in the vent finally begins to boil, the boiling water produces steam that pushes the water above it to the surface. Release of the water near the top of the vent relieves the pressure on the superheated water farther down. With the sudden release of pressure, the superheated water changes into steam and explodes toward the surface, as shown in **Figure 8.** The eruption continues until most of the water and steam are emptied from the vent and chambers. After the eruption, groundwater begins to collect again and the process is repeated, often at regular intervals.

Section 1 Review

Key Ideas

1. **Identify** the difference between porosity and permeability, and explain how permeability affects the flow of groundwater.
2. **Name and describe** the two zones of groundwater.
3. **Describe** how the contour of a shallow water table compares with the local topography.
4. **Explain** why ordinary springs often flow intermittently.
5. **Define** the term *cone of depression.*
6. **Compare** the rock layers in an artesian formation with those in an ordinary aquifer.
7. **Compare** artesian wells and ordinary wells.

Critical Thinking

8. **Making Inferences** Which type of well would provide a community with a more constant source of water: an ordinary well or an artesian well? Explain your answer.
9. **Identifying Relationships** Why is protecting the environment from pollution important for communities in recharge zones?
10. **Analyzing Ideas** Why don't shallow pools of hot water erupt the way that geysers erupt?

Concept Mapping

11. Use the following terms to create a concept map: *groundwater, water table, zone of saturation,* and *zone of aeration.*

Differentiated Instruction

Alternative Assessment

Assessing Groundwater Have students imagine they are experts charged with assessing groundwater resources in one region of your state. Have them make a list of criteria that they would study in preparing a report about groundwater resources. Students may create an illustration or diagram to accompany their checklist. **LS Logical/Visual**

SECTION 2

Groundwater and Chemical Weathering

Key Ideas	Key Terms	Why It Matters
❯ Describe how water chemically weathers rock. ❯ Explain how caverns and sinkholes form. ❯ Identify two features of karst topography.	**cavern** **sinkhole** **karst topography**	Water underground causes problems as well as opportunities for adventure and discovery.

As groundwater passes through permeable rock, minerals in the rock dissolve. The warmer the rock is and the longer it is in contact with water, the greater the amount of dissolved minerals in the water. Water that contains relatively high concentrations of dissolved minerals, especially minerals rich in calcium, magnesium, and iron, is called *hard water*. Water that contains relatively low concentrations of dissolved minerals is called *soft water*.

Many people think that using hard water is unappealing. For example, more soap is needed to produce suds in hard water than in soft water. Also, many people prefer not to drink hard water because of its metallic taste. Some household appliances or fixtures may be damaged by the buildup of mineral deposits from hard water. **Figure 1** shows some results of the long-term presence of hard water.

Results of Weathering by Groundwater

One way that minerals become dissolved in groundwater is through chemical weathering. As water moves through soil and other organic materials, the water combines with carbon dioxide to form carbonic acid. This weak acid chemically weathers the rock that the acid passes through by breaking down and dissolving the minerals in the rock.

Figure 1 Soap scum forms when soap reacts with calcium carbonate in hard water (inset). During high-water stages, hard water deposited a residue of calcium carbonate on the canyon walls that border this creek.

Quick Lab — 25 min

Chemical Weathering

Procedure

1. Place **limestone, granite, pyrite,** and **chalk chips** into separate **small beakers.**
2. Cover the rocks in **1% HCl solution.**
3. After 20 min, observe the rocks.

Analysis

1. How have the rocks changed?
2. How is this process of change like the process of chemical weathering by groundwater?

Key Resources

Chapter Resource File
- Directed Reading BASIC
- Inquiry Lab: Cave Formations and Ecology GENERAL

Technology
- Transparencies
  Bellringer

Section 2

Focus

Overview

This section explains the weathering of rock by groundwater, and the formations that result.

Bellringer

Ask students to describe how minerals in water can affect objects that are in extensive contact with the water. (Students may think of mineral buildup in pipes or rusty stains under water faucets.) **LS Visual**

Motivate

Quick Lab

Skills Acquired
- Observing

Materials
- Limestone
- Granite
- Pyrite
- Chalk chips
- Small beakers
- 1% HCl solution

Teacher's Notes: Instruct students on the correct handling and disposal of the acid. You can use lemon juice instead of 1% HCl solution.

Answers to Analysis
1. The limestone and chalk became pitted and/or reduced in size.
2. The HCl is like the carbonic acid in groundwater that chemically weathers rock.

Teach

Using the Figure GENERAL

Cave Formations Tell students a simple mnemonic to remember cave formations: stalactites hold tight to the ceiling and stalagmites might grow up there some day. Answer to caption question: Stalagmites are the upward-pointing cones on the floor of a cave. **LS Visual**

Cultural Awareness GENERAL

Prehistoric Cave Art Display pictures of prehistoric cave art, such as the cave art at Lascaux, France. Discuss with students how early humans painted the walls of caves with remarkable pictures of animals and other objects. Invite interested students to read about prehistoric cave art and to report to the class on how cave painting was done and what its significance may have been to prehistoric people. **LS Visual/Interpersonal**

Internet Activity GENERAL

Sinkholes Have students research occurrences of sinkholes that have caused property damage, as in Florida in recent years. They may search area newspapers to find out what caused the sinkholes and what is being done to prevent others. A worksheet designed to direct student research on this topic can be found in the **Chapter Resource File** booklet or by visiting www.thinkcentral.com and entering the keyword **HQXGWEX. LS Verbal**

Figure 2 The formations in Carlsbad Caverns in New Mexico are made of calcite. ***Which formations in this photo are stalagmites?***

cavern a natural cavity that forms in rock as a result of the dissolution of minerals; also a large cave that commonly contains many smaller, connecting chambers

Caverns

Rocks that are rich in the mineral calcite, such as limestone, are especially vulnerable to chemical weathering. Although limestone is not porous, vertical and horizontal cracks commonly cut through limestone layers. As groundwater flows through these cracks, carbonic acid slowly dissolves the limestone and enlarges the cracks. Eventually, a cavern may form. A **cavern** is a large cave that may consist of many smaller connecting chambers. Carlsbad Caverns in New Mexico is a good example of a large limestone cavern, as shown in **Figure 2.**

Stalactites and Stalagmites

Although a cavern that lies above the water table does not fill with water, water still passes through the rock surrounding the cavern. When water containing dissolved calcite drips from the ceiling of a limestone cavern, some of the calcite is deposited on the ceiling. As this calcite builds up, it forms a suspended, cone-shaped deposit called a *stalactite* (stuh LAK TIET). When drops of water fall on the cavern floor, calcite builds up to form an upward-pointing cone called a *stalagmite* (stuh LAG MIET). Often, a stalactite and a stalagmite will grow until they meet and form a calcite deposit called a *column*.

Why It Matters

Life in the Dark

WEIRD SCIENCE

Thousands of species of animals live their entire lives deep in the darkest crevices of caves, without sunlight and with very little food. These animals, called troglobites, have special adaptations for living in the dark.

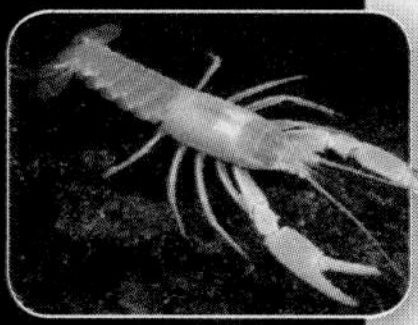

Many troglobites have slow metabolisms, or body functions, that help them cope with scarce food supplies. A slow metabolism can mean a long life.

Some troglobites, including some species of salamanders, spiders, and fish, do not have eyes, and have evolved other means of sensing their environment.

Because there is no advantage to being a specific color in a dark environment, many troglobites do not have pigment and are colorless.

YOUR TURN UNDERSTANDING CONCEPTS
What are three adaptations of cave-dwelling animals?

Why It Matters

Life in the Dark The slow metabolisms of troglobites can mean a long life. A cave-dwelling crayfish species *Orconectes australis,* found in Alabama caves, can live for 175 years. The organisms pictured here are troglobites—organisms that live only in caves and nowhere else. *Troglophiles,* such as some rodents, can live their entire lives in caves but may also be found outside of caves. *Trogloxenes,* such as bats, use caves for part of their life cycle but must leave the cave to find food.

Answer to Your Turn

Understanding Concepts Three adaptations of cave-dwelling animals are slow metabolisms, special means of sensing the environment in the dark, and a lack of pigment.

Sinkholes

A circular depression that forms at the surface when rock dissolves, when sediment is removed, or when caves or mines collapse is a **sinkhole.** Most sinkholes form by dissolution, in which the limestone or other rock dissolves where weak areas in the rock, such as fractures, previously existed. The dissolved material is carried away from the surface, and a small depression forms. *Subsidence sinkholes* form by a similar process except that as rock dissolves, overlying sediments settle into cracks in the rock and a depression forms.

Figure 3 When land overlying a cavern collapses to form a sinkhole, human-made structures, such as this highway, can be damaged.

Collapse sinkholes may form when sediment below the surface is removed and an empty space forms within the sediment layer. Eventually, the overlying sediments collapse into the empty space below. Collapse sinkholes may also form during dry periods, when the water table is low and caverns are not completely filled with water. Because water no longer supports the roof of the cavern, the roof may collapse. Collapse sinkholes may develop abruptly and cause extensive damage. A collapse sinkhole is shown in **Figure 3.**

sinkhole a circular depression that forms when rock dissolves, when overlying sediment fills an existing cavity, or when the roof of an underground cavern or mine collapses

Natural Bridges

When the roof of a cavern collapses in several places, a relatively straight line of sinkholes forms. The uncollapsed rock between each pair of sinkholes forms an arch of rock called a *natural bridge,* such as the one shown in **Figure 4.** When a natural bridge first forms, it is thick, but erosion causes the bridge to become thinner. Eventually, the natural bridge may collapse.

Reading Check **How are sinkholes related to natural bridges?**

Figure 4 This natural bridge near San Antonio, Texas, formed when the roof of a large cavern room collapsed.

Answer to Reading Check
A natural bridge may form when two sinkholes form close to each other. The bridge is the uncollapsed rock between the sinkholes.

Skill Builder — ADVANCED

Writing Ask students to imagine they live on a street where a sinkhole "swallowed" several cars and damaged some homes. Have students write a letter to the editor of the local newspaper to explain how they feel about the situation and what, if anything, they think should be done to prevent future occurrences. **LS Intrapersonal**

Close

Reteaching — BASIC

Illustrating Cave Formation
Have students draw illustrations showing how water flows through rock to create the caves and cave formations, as well as the sinkholes and natural bridges, covered in the section. Student pictures should show direction of water flow and label the formation of features (e.g., stalactites and stalagmites) within caves. Students may create their pictures as they read through the section. **LS Visual**

Quiz — GENERAL

1. What is the difference between hard water and soft water? (Hard water has more minerals dissolved in it than soft water does.)
2. How does a subsidence sinkhole form? (Rock dissolves and overlying sediments settle into cracks in the rock. Eventually, a depression forms at the surface.)

Differentiated Instruction

Special Education Students

Chart Many students learn better if they have a chance to move around. Give these students a chance to get out of their seats by having them fill in an empty chart you have drawn on the board. Use these column headings: Caverns, Stalactites and Stalagmites, Sinkholes, and Natural Bridges. Use these questions as row labels: Caused by rock dissolving? Caused by rock building up? Usually seen above ground? Takes years to form? (Caverns—yes, no, no, yes; Stalactites and Stalagmites—yes, yes, no, yes; Sinkholes: yes, no, yes, no; Natural Bridges: yes, no, yes, no) **LS Logical/Visual**

READING TOOLBOX

Venn Diagrams

Answers will vary. Sample information for the Venn diagram is given below.

Karst in humid climate: typical location for karst topography

Both: may contain caverns, sinkholes, and disappearing streams

Karst in dry climate: may contain dramatic arches and spires from closely clustered sinkholes

Close, *continued*

Answers to Section Review

1. Water that moves through soil combines with CO_2 to form carbonic acid. This acid breaks down and dissolves minerals in the rock.
2. Caverns form when groundwater flows through cracks in limestone. Over time, the limestone dissolves and large, open spaces form.
3. Stalactites form as calcite precipitates from water that drips down from the cavern ceiling. Stalagmites build up as calcite precipitates from water that drips onto the floor of a cavern.
4. Three common features of karst topography are many closely spaced sinkholes, many caverns, and disappearing and emerging streams.
5. A natural bridge may form when the roof of a cavern collapses in several places. Natural bridges may also form from uncollapsed rock between two sinkholes.
6. Caverns are empty spaces within rock that form as a result of chemical weathering. Sinkholes are circular depressions that form when rock dissolves or when the roofs of caverns collapse.
7. Answers may vary but may include that karst topography may form in a dry climate where the water table has fallen and caused sinkholes to form.
8. Answers may vary. Sample answer: Limestone layers are commonly aquifers. Anywhere the water table reaches the surface, you would expect to find a spring.
9. *Groundwater* erodes limestone to form *caverns* that have *stalactites* on the ceilings and *stalagmites* on the ground, and dissolves rock to form *sinkholes*, which may leave a *natural bridge*.

Figure 5 The Stone Forest in Yunnan, China, is a dramatic example of karst topography.

READING TOOLBOX

Venn Diagrams

Draw a Venn diagram with two circles, and title it "Karst Topography." Label one circle "Humid climate" and the other circle "Dry climate." In each circle, write characteristics that are unique to the landscape in each type of climate. In the area where the circles overlap, write shared characteristics.

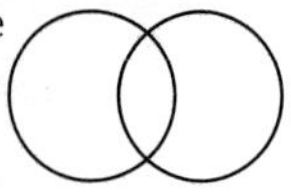

Karst Topography

Irregular topography caused by the chemical weathering of limestone or other soluble rock by groundwater is called **karst topography.** Common features of karst topography include many closely spaced sinkholes and caverns. In karst regions, streams often disappear into cracks in the rock and then emerge in caves or through other cracks many kilometers away. In the United States, there is extensive karst topography in Kentucky, Tennessee, southern Indiana, northern Florida, and Puerto Rico.

Generally, karst topography forms in regions where the climate is humid and where limestone formations exist at or near the surface. The plentiful precipitation in these regions commonly becomes groundwater. The groundwater flows through the limestone and reacts chemically with the calcite in the limestone. As the groundwater dissolves the limestone, cracks in the rock enlarge to form cave systems. Features of karst topography can form in relatively dry regions, too. In these areas, sinkholes may form very close together and leave dramatic arches and spires, as shown in **Figure 5.** Karst topography in these regions may indicate that the climate is becoming drier.

karst topography a type of irregular topography that is characterized by caverns, sinkholes, and underground drainage and that forms on limestone or other soluble rock

Academic Vocabulary

feature (FEE chuhr) the shape or form of a thing; characteristic

Section 2 Review

Key Ideas

1. **Describe** how water chemically weathers rock.
2. **Explain** how caverns form.
3. **Explain** the difference between stalactites and stalagmites.
4. **Identify** three common features of karst topography.
5. **Describe** two ways in which a natural bridge might form.
6. **Compare** sinkholes and caverns.

Critical Thinking

7. **Making Inferences** If an area has a dry climate, how can the area have karst topography?
8. **Identifying Relationships** Why might you expect to find springs in regions that have karst topography?

Concept Mapping

9. Use the following terms to create a concept map: *groundwater, stalagmite, stalactite, natural bridge, cavern,* and *sinkhole.*

Differentiated Instruction

Alternative Assessment

Guided Tour Have students pretend that they are guides who lead visitors through a cavern. Have them write a brochure, which they may illustrate, that describes the cavern's history and all of the features that visitors will see when they tour the cavern. **LS Visual/Verbal**

Why It Matters

Is it Possible to Drown in Quicksand?

REAL WORLD

In certain areas where groundwater is near the land surface, quicksand can form. Quicksand is made of fine grains of sand and clay saturated with water. When a person steps on quicksand, the pressure causes water below the sand to move up, turning the sand into a thick jelly-like substance.

Have you ever seen a movie where a character falls into quicksand and completely disappears? This could not actually happen. A person can sink in quicksand, but only to the waist, because humans are not as dense as quicksand.

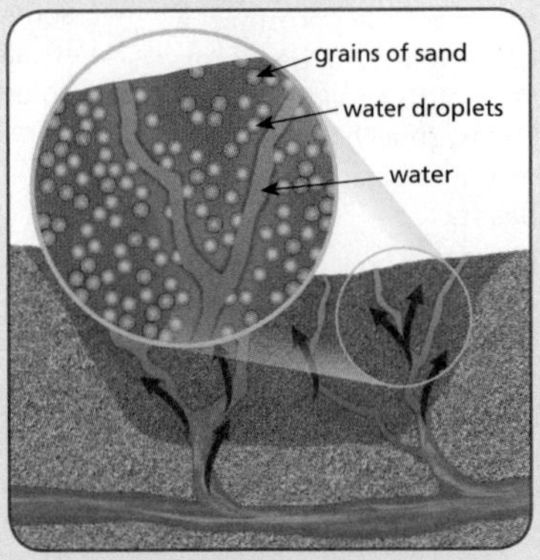

When force is applied to quicksand, groundwater moves up, resulting in a thick and sandy fluid.

It is easy, however, to become trapped in quicksand. If you were stuck in quicksand, you could not simply be pulled out. Instead, you should wiggle your legs to slowly make a space around your body. Water can flow into this space and let you pull yourself free.

YOUR TURN

UNDERSTANDING CONCEPTS
What happens when someone steps on quicksand?

APPLYING INFORMATION
Describe the porosity and permeability of quicksand.

Why It Matters

Is it Possible to Drown in Quicksand?

A human cannot sink completely into quicksand but a person can become stuck. Researchers have estimated that pulling a person's foot out of quicksand at speed of 1 cm/s would require the same amount of force as lifting a medium-sized car. Slow, deliberate movements will, however, allow a person to get out of quicksand. The only way a person might actually drown in quicksand is if they sunk headfirst or they got stuck in the quicksand during a low tide and were unable to remove themselves before high tide.

Answers to Your Turn

Understanding Concepts When a person steps on quicksand, the pressure causes groundwater below the sand to move up. The sand becomes a thin jelly-like substance.

Applying Information Quicksand is both porous and highly permeable. Water moves quickly and easily through quicksand sediment.

45 min

Time Required

one 45-minute class period

Lab Ratings

EASY ———————————→ HARD

Teacher Preparation
Student Setup
Concept Level
Cleanup

Skills Acquired

- Constructing Models
- Measuring
- Observing
- Interpreting Data

Scientific Methods

In this lab, students will
- Construct Models
- Make Observations
- Interpret Data
- Analyze Data
- Draw Conclusions

Materials

The materials listed on the page are enough for groups of two to four students. This activity could also work with different sized marbles or with well-sorted pebbles.

What You'll Do

> **Measure** the porosity of a given volume of beads for each of three samples: large beads, small beads, and a mix of large and small beads.

> **Describe** how particle size and sorting of a material affect porosity.

What You'll Need

beads, plastic, 4 mm (400)
beads, plastic, 8 mm (200)
beaker, 100 mL
graduated cylinder, 100 mL

Safety

Porosity

Whether soil is composed of coarse pieces of rock or very fine particles, some pore space remains between the pieces of solid material. Porosity is calculated by dividing the volume of the pore space by the total volume of the soil sample. Thus, if 50 cm³ of soil contains 5.0 cm³ of pore space, the porosity of the soil sample is

$$5.0 \text{ cm}^3/50 \text{ cm}^3 = 0.10 \times 100 = 10\%.$$

The result is generally written as a percentage. In this lab, you will measure and compare the porosity of three samples that represent rock particles.

Procedure

1. Fill a beaker to the top with water. Pour the water into a graduated cylinder and record the volume of water.

2. Dry the beaker, and fill it to the top with large (8 mm) plastic beads. Gently tap the beaker to settle and compact the beads. Add more beads to fill the beaker until the beads are level with the top. Record the total volume of the beads, which includes the pore space volume.

3. Fill the graduated cylinder with water to the top mark, and record the volume of water. Carefully pour the water from the cylinder into the beaker filled with the large beads until the water level just reaches the top of the beads.

Step ❸

Tips and Tricks

You may wish to have students take turns, with one actively doing one step of the lab while the other records the data. Then, have the students exchange roles.

4. To determine the amount of water that you added to the beaker, subtract the volume of water in the graduated cylinder from the volume that you recorded in step 3. This difference is the volume of the pore space between the beads. Record the volume of the pore space.
5. Calculate the porosity of the beads. Record the porosity as a decimal and as a percentage.
6. Repeat steps 2 to 5 using small (4 mm) beads.
7. Drain and dry both sets of beads. Mix together equal volumes of the small and large beads. Using the mixed-size beads, repeat steps 2 to 5.

Step 4

Analysis

1. **Analyzing Methods** Do the 8 mm beads in step 2 represent well-sorted large rock particles, well-sorted small rock particles, or unsorted rock particles?
2. **Analyzing Methods** Do the 4 mm beads in step 6 represent well-sorted large rock particles, well-sorted small rock particles, or unsorted rock particles?
3. **Analyzing Methods** Do the mixed beads in step 7 represent well-sorted or unsorted rock particles?
4. **Making Graphs** Compare your measurements of the porosity of the large beads with your measurements of the porosity of the small beads. Make a graph that shows bead size on the *x*-axis and porosity on the *y*-axis.
5. **Drawing Conclusions** In well-sorted sediment, does porosity depend on particle size? Explain your answer.
6. **Determining Cause and Effect** How did mixing the bead sizes affect the porosity? Explain the effect.

Extension

Designing Experiments How would mixing coarse gravel with fine sand affect the porosity of the gravel? Conduct an experiment to find out if your answer is correct.

Answers to Analysis

1. The 8 mm beads represent well-sorted large rock particles.
2. The 4 mm beads represent well-sorted small rock particles.
3. The mixed beads represent unsorted rock particles.
4. Graphs may vary slightly but should show that 4 mm and 8 mm beads have basically the same porosity.
5. If you have well-sorted sediment, both coarse- and fine-grained sediment will have the same porosity.
6. Mixing the two bead sizes together lowers the porosity because the smaller beads fill in some of the spaces between the bigger beads.

Answer to Extension

Sand would reduce the porosity of the gravel because some of the sand grains fill in the spaces between the gravel.

Maps in Action

Water Level in the Southern Ogallala

Internet Activity GENERAL

Agriculture and the Ogallala Aquifer Most of the Ogallala aquifer (or High Plains aquifer) underlies agricultural land. Divide the class into two groups to do Internet or library research about this aquifer. One group should research the effects of center-pivot irrigation on withdrawal rates from the aquifer and on conservation of the Ogallala's water resources. The other group should research the amounts of pesticides and other agricultural chemicals applied to land overlying the aquifer and their effects on groundwater and drinking water in the region. Have students prepare a presentation, with illustrations, for the class when their research is complete. A worksheet designed to direct student research on this topic can be found in the **Chapter Resource File** booklet or by visiting **www.thinkcentral.com** and entering the keyword **HQXGWEX.**
LS Verbal

Answers to Map Skills Activity

1. Two states had a decline in water level of more than 150 ft.
2. Six states had water levels that rose.
3. More areas have seen a decline in water level than an increase.
4. Answers may vary. The trend may be related to increases in population in the region, to increased water use on agricultural land, or to changes in rainfall.
5. Answers may vary.

MAPS in Action

Water Level in the Southern Ogallala

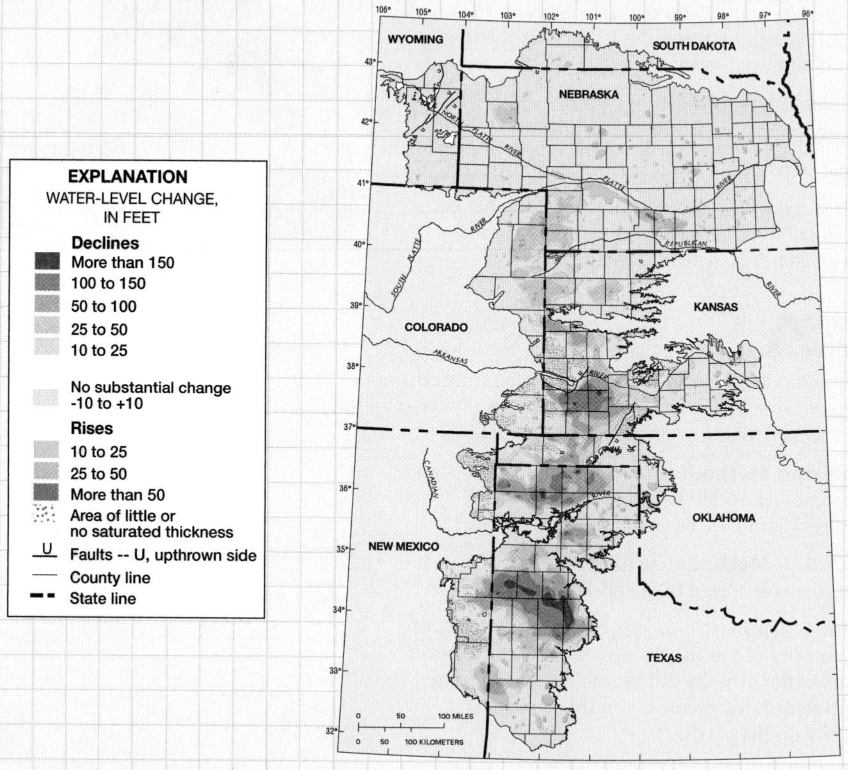

Map Skills Activity

This map shows water-level change from predevelopment to 2005 in regions of the Ogallala Aquifer, which supplies much of the drinking water in the midwestern United States. Use the map to answer the questions below.

1. **Using a Key** From predevelopment to 2005, how many states had areas in which the water level declined more than 150 feet?
2. **Using a Key** From predevelopment to 2005, how many states had areas in which the water level rose?
3. **Identifying Trends** How has the water level changed overall, from predevelopment to 2005?
4. **Analyzing Relationships** What may have caused the trend that you identified in question 3?
5. **Making Predictions** How do you think the aquifer's overall water level will change over the next 50 years? Explain.

Key Resources

Technology

- Transparencies
  82 Water Level in the Southern Ogallala

Chapter 16 Summary

THINK central
SUPER SUMMARY
Keyword: HQXGWES

Key Ideas	Key Terms
Section 1  **Water Beneath the Surface** › The porosity and permeability of an aquifer affect the flow of groundwater. › The water table is the upper surface of the zone of saturation, beneath the land surface and the zone of aeration. › A well is a hole dug to below the water table, while a spring is a natural flow of groundwater to Earth's surface. Water also may flow naturally to Earth's surface through artesian formations. › Hot springs and geysers are two land features formed by hot groundwater.	**groundwater,** p. 431 **aquifer,** p. 431 **porosity,** p. 431 **permeability,** p. 432 **water table,** p. 433 **artesian formation,** p. 437
Section 2  **Groundwater and Chemical Weathering** › Water combines with carbon dioxide to form carbonic acid, which breaks down and dissolves minerals in rock that the water passes through. › Caverns and sinkholes form as limestone or other rock is slowly dissolved by chemical weathering. › Features of karst topography include caverns, sinkholes, and underground drainage.	**cavern,** p. 440 **sinkhole,** p. 441 **karst topography,** p. 442

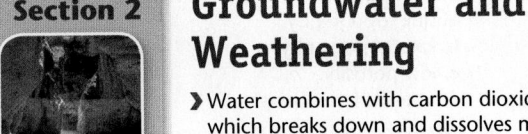

Chapter Summary

Using THINK central Resources

Super Summary

Have students connect the major concepts in this chapter through an interactive Super Summary. Visit www.thinkcentral.com and type in the keyword **HQXGWES** to access the Super Summary for this chapter.

Differentiated Instruction

Alternative Assessment

The Water Beneath Your Feet Have students work in groups to research the groundwater resources and characteristics in your region or your state. Have one group of students identify and map aquifers in your area. A second group should research and map wells and springs. A third group may find out how to test local water for pH and hardness and conduct the tests. A fourth group should research and map or illustrate any caves or caverns in your region or state. Students may also research groundwater's effects on limestone in your area. If caves do occur, have students in this group find out how they formed and what physical characteristics they have. Students may put all of their research and materials together to give a class demonstration and "teach-in" on groundwater in your area.

LS Visual/Kinesthetic
Co-op Learning

Chapter Review

Assignment Guide	
Section	**Questions**
1	1–3, 5–8, 10–15, 19, 20, 22–24, 26–30, 32–39
2	4, 9, 16–18, 21, 25, 31

Reading Toolbox

1. Answers may vary. For example, students may include "periodically" (time reference) and "when geysers erupt" (context) in their chart.

Using Key Terms

2–9. Answers may vary but should show that students understand the definitions of and differences between key terms.

Understanding Key Ideas

10. b
11. d
12. a
13. a
14. a
15. a
16. c
17. b
18. a
19. d

Short Answer

20. lakes, rivers, and swamps
21. As groundwater drips from the ceiling to the floor of a cavern, calcite is left behind to form stalactites and stalagmites. Icicles form in a similar process.
22. A mud pot forms when chemically weathered rock mixes with hot water to form a sticky liquid clay that bubbles at the surface.

Chapter 16 Review

1. **Temporal Language** Create a temporal language table for the page in Section 1 that discusses hot springs and geysers. Find at least five words or phrases that refer to time and record them in the table. Use the table shown in the Reading Toolbox at the beginning of the chapter as a model. READING TOOLBOX

USING KEY TERMS

Use each of the following terms in a separate sentence.

2. *groundwater*
3. *water table*
4. *karst topography*

For each pair of terms, explain how the meanings of the terms differ.

5. *geyser* and *hot spring*
6. *porosity* and *permeability*
7. *well* and *spring*
8. *ordinary well* and *artesian well*
9. *stalactite* and *stalagmite*

UNDERSTANDING KEY IDEAS

10. Any body of rock or sediment in which water can flow and be stored is called a(n)
    a. well.
    b. aquifer.
    c. sinkhole.
    d. artesian formation.
11. The percentage of open space in a given volume of rock is the rock's
    a. viscosity.
    b. capillary fringe.
    c. permeability.
    d. porosity.
12. The ease with which water can pass through a rock or sediment is called
    a. permeability. **c.** porosity.
    b. carbonation. **d.** velocity.
13. The slope of a water table is called the
    a. gradient. **c.** permeability.
    b. porosity. **d.** aquifer.
14. A natural flow of groundwater that has reached the surface is a(n)
    a. spring. **c.** aquifer.
    b. well. **d.** travertine.
15. Pumping water from a well causes a local lowering of the water table known as a
    a. cone of depression.
    b. horizontal fissure.
    c. hot spring.
    d. sinkhole.
16. Calcite formations that hang from the ceiling of a cavern are called
    a. stalagmites.
    b. sinks.
    c. stalactites.
    d. aquifers.
17. Caverns and sinkholes are typical in areas of
    a. sink topography.
    b. karst topography.
    c. low porosity.
    d. artesian formations.
18. When the roofs of several caverns collapse, the uncollapsed rock between sinkholes can form
    a. natural bridges.
    b. stalactites.
    c. limestone topography.
    d. artesian formations.
19. A layer of permeable rock that is sandwiched between layers of impermeable rock is called
    a. a natural bridge.
    b. karst topography.
    c. limestone topography.
    d. an artesian formation.

SHORT ANSWER

20. In regions where the water table is at the surface of the land, what type of terrain would you expect to find?
21. Explain the process that forms stalactites and stalagmites. Name another process in nature that produces shapes similar to the shapes of stalactites.
22. How does a mud pot form?

23. In an aquifer, the zone in which the pore spaces are completely filled with water is the zone of saturation. The zone of aeration is the zone that contains dry soil and the capillary fringe and that lies between the ground surface and the zone of saturation.
24. Groundwater may reach the surface through wells or through springs.
25. Both caverns and sinkholes result from the weathering of rock by groundwater or surface water.
26. A geyser erupts when magma or hot rock superheats water and causes steam to push the water to the surface.
27. Groundwater moves slowly through rock and is replenished very slowly by rain.

23. Describe the zones of an aquifer.

24. What are two ways that groundwater reaches Earth's surface?

25. How are caverns and sinkholes related?

26. What causes a geyser to erupt?

27. Why does it take a long time to replenish a depleted aquifer?

CRITICAL THINKING

28. **Making Inferences** In what type of location might pumping too much water from an aquifer lead to contamination of the groundwater supply? Explain how the water becomes contaminated.

29. **Analyzing Relationships** Describe an artesian formation, and explain how the water in an artesian well may have entered the ground many hundreds of kilometers away.

30. **Analyzing Ideas** Explain how a rock can be both porous and impermeable.

31. **Identifying Relationships** Do you think that an area that has karst topography would have many surface streams or few surface streams? Explain your answer.

CONCEPT MAPPING

32. Use the following terms to create a concept map: *porosity, sorting, permeability, ordinary well, artesian formation, highly permeable rock,* and *impermeable rock.*

MATH SKILLS

Math Skills

33. **Evaluating Data** People in Oklahoma use 11 billion gallons of water every day. The renewable water supply in Oklahoma is 68.7 billion gallons per day. What percentage of the renewable water supply do Oklahomans use every day?

34. **Making Conversions** In an average aquifer, groundwater moves about 50 m per year. At this rate, how long would the groundwater take to flow 1 km?

WRITING SKILLS

35. **Writing Persuasively** Write a persuasive essay about the importance of conserving groundwater.

36. **Communicating Main Ideas** Explain how overpumping at one well can affect groundwater availability in surrounding areas.

INTERPRETING GRAPHICS

The graph below shows the average annual decline in water level for the Ogallala Aquifer over 30 years. Use the graph below to answer the questions that follow.

Average Annual Rate of Decline by Decade for the Ogallala Aquifer, 1969–1999

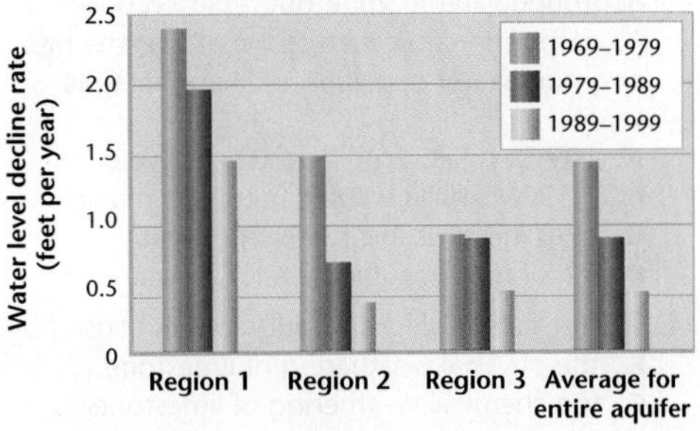

37. Which region had the highest rate of decline from 1969 to 1999?

38. Over which decade did the aquifer have the lowest rate of decline?

39. Which years would you expect to have a higher rate of decline: the years 1999 to 2009 or the years 1989 to 1999? Explain your answer.

Chapter Review

Critical Thinking

28. In areas near the ocean, pumping too much groundwater may cause an influx of saltwater from the sea.

29. The water in an artesian formation may have entered the aquifer far away and then traveled a long distance down the slope of the aquifer. The water in an artesian formation can emerge only when the overlying impermeable rock layer is cracked or drilled.

30. If the open spaces in a porous rock are not connected, the rock will not be very permeable.

31. Karst areas have few surface streams because there are so many cracks into which streams may disappear.

Concept Mapping

32. Answers may vary but should include all of the terms listed. Sample answers appear at the end of this unit on p. 507C.

Math Skills

33. 11 billion gal $\div$ 68.7 billion gal $=$ $0.16 \times 100 = 16\%$

34. 50 m $=$ 0.050 km/y; 1 km $\div$ 0.050 km/y $=$ 20 y

Writing Skills

35. Answers may vary. Accept all reasonable answers.

36. Answers may vary. Accept all reasonable answers.

Interpreting Graphics

37. Region 1

38. 1989–1999

39. Answers may vary. Sample answer: I would expect 1989–1999 to have a greater rate of decline because the overall trend is decreasing.

Standardized Test Prep

Estimated Time

To give students practice under more realistic testing conditions, allow them 30 minutes to answer all of the questions in this practice test.

Test Doctor

Question 1 Answer C is false. Gravity pulls water down through soil and rock layers, which causes the underground water level to rise and form *two* distinct zones of groundwater: the zone of saturation and the zone of aeration.

Question 3 Answer D is correct. Simple subtraction can be used to determine that groundwater was depleted at a rate of 82.28 million cubic meters in 2002.

Question 4 Answer G is correct. In a region where there is plentiful precipitation, groundwater flows through limestone and dissolves it. This chemical reaction results in the enlargement of cracks in the rock to form cave systems. Answers F and H therefore describe the process of karst topography formation in *humid* regions. Answer I is not applicable to karst topography, which is due to chemical weathering, not physical weathering.

Chapter 16 Standardized Test Prep

Understanding Concepts

Directions (1–5): For each question, write on a separate sheet of paper the letter of the correct answer.

1. Which of the following statements is false?
- **A.** Permeability affects flow through an aquifer.
- **B.** Groundwater can be stored in an aquifer.
- **C.** Aquifers are always a single rock layer.
- **D.** Well-sorted sediment holds the most water.

2. The amount of surface water that seeps into the pores between rock particles is influenced by which of the following factors?
- **F.** rock type, land slope, and climate
- **G.** rock type, land slope, and capillary fringe
- **H.** rock type, land slope, and sea level
- **I.** rock type, land slope, and recharging

3. Shanghai removed 96.03 million cubic meters of groundwater in 2002 but replaced only 13.75 million cubic meters. What was the rate of groundwater depletion in Shanghai that year?
- **A.** 109.78 million cubic meters per year
- **B.** 1,320.41 million cubic meters per year
- **C.** 6.98 million cubic meters per year
- **D.** 82.28 million cubic meters per year

4. The formation of karst topography is caused by
- **F.** the physical weathering of limestone.
- **G.** the chemical weathering of limestone.
- **H.** closely spaced sinkholes.
- **I.** irregular topography.

5. What quality distinguishes an ordinary well from an artesian well?
- **A.** Water flows freely from an ordinary well.
- **B.** Water is pressurized in an ordinary well.
- **C.** Water must be pumped from an ordinary well.
- **D.** Water comes from rainfall in an ordinary well.

Directions (6–7): For each question, write a short response.

6. What is a watershed?

7. What is the term for a local lowering of the water table caused by the pumping of water from a well?

Reading Skills

Directions (8–10): Read the passage below. Then, answer the questions.

Land Subsidence

Land subsidence is the settling or sinking of earth in response to the movement of materials under its surface. The greatest contributor to land subsidence is aquifer depletion. As groundwater is removed, the surface above may sink. Rocks may settle and pores may close, which leaves less area for water to be stored. In areas where aquifers are replenished, the surface of Earth may subside and then return almost to its previous level. However, in areas where water is not pumped back into aquifers, subsidence is substantial and whole regions may sink. Human activites can contribute to land subsidence. These activities include the pumping of water, gas, and oil from underground reservoirs and the collapse of mine tunnels.

8. According to the passage, which of the following statements is not true?
- **F.** Land subsidence is the settling or sinking of earth.
- **G.** As groundwater is removed, the earth above may sink.
- **H.** The greatest contributor to land subsidence is aquifer depletion.
- **I.** Rocks settle and pores close, which leaves more area for water to be stored.

9. Which of the following statements can be inferred from the information in the passage?
- **A.** Subsidence sinkholes occur most often in rural areas.
- **B.** The majority of all subsidence sinkholes are formed through natural processes.
- **C.** Subsidence sinkholes form both naturally and because of the activities of humans.
- **D.** Older sinkholes are easily recovered by refilling the area with water.

10. Subsidence due to groundwater depletion may occur slowly or very abruptly. Which type of subsidence presents a greater chance for recovery? Why?

Question 12 Students should bring to this test item the ability to propose creative and viable solutions for implementation.

Full-credit answers should include the following points:
- toilet flushing is the largest use of indoor water
- an understanding that toilets are a necessity, but may be made more water-efficient.
- suggested solutions may include using low-flow toilets, not flushing items such as tissue unnecessarily, and keeping toilets in good working order to help reduce the need for water

Question 13 Full-credit answers should include the following points:
- students should estimate the percentage of water used for the two largest uses of indoor water, toilet flushing (40%) and bathing (32%). Rounded to the nearest 10, these uses account for 70% of water usage
- proposed suggestions for conservation that target the largest uses of water first
- students may connect ecological benefits of water conservation to the economic benefits of water conservation
- students may suggest that people may be more easily convinced to reduce water usage if they are shown how much that usage costs them

Interpreting Graphics

Directions (11–13): For each question below, record the correct answer on a separate sheet of paper.

This graphic shows an example of the water cycle. Use this graphic to answer question 11.

The Water Cycle

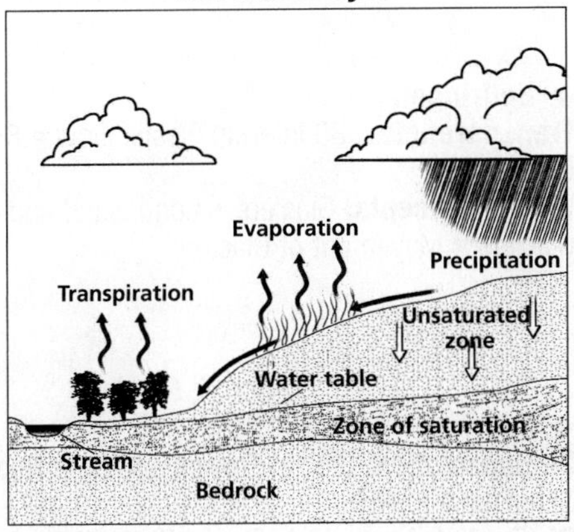

11. Which process occurs where the water table intersects the surface?
F. stream formation
G. runoff
H. groundwater movement
I. saturation

The graph below shows indoor water use for a typical family in the United States. Use this graph to answer questions 12 and 13.

Water Use for a Family of Four

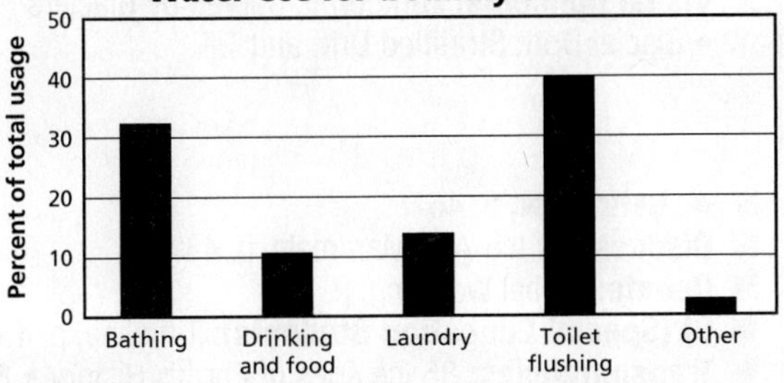

12. According to the graph, what is the largest use of indoor water for a family in the United States? Name some ways that people can reduce the amount of water consumed by this task.

13. What total percentage of household indoor water is consumed by the two largest uses of indoor water? Round your answer to the nearest 10. How could this knowledge be used to help people reduce water usage?

Test Tip

Remember that if you can eliminate two of four answer choices, your chances of choosing the correct answer will double.

Standardized Test Prep

Using THINK central Resources

State Resources

- For specific resources for your state, visit www.thinkcentral.com and type in the keyword **HSHSTR.**

Answers

Understanding Concepts

1. C
2. F
3. D
4. G
5. C
6. the area of land that is drained by a river
7. a cone of depression

Reading Skills

8. I
9. C
10. Abrupt subsidence may involve greater compression of pore space and leave less chance for recovery.

Interpreting Graphics

11. F
12. Answers may vary. See Test Doctor for a detailed scoring rubric.
13. Answers may vary. See Test Doctor for a detailed scoring rubric.

Chapter Planner **17**

Glaciers

	Standards	Teach Key Ideas
Chapter Opener, pp. 452–453 **45 min.**	National Science Education Standards	
Section 1 Glaciers: Moving Ice, pp. 455–458 **45 min.** ❯ Formation of Glaciers ❯ Types of Glaciers ❯ Movement of Glaciers ❯ Features of Glaciers	UCP 4, SPSP 5c	■ ◆ **Bellringer,** p. 455 ◆ **Transparencies:** 83 Internal Plastic Flow • 88 Gulkana Glacier ▲ **Visual Concepts:** Glaciers • Continental and Alpine Glaciers • Movement of Glaciers
Section 2 Glacial Erosion and Deposition, pp. 459–466 **90 min.** ❯ Glacial Erosion ❯ Glacial Deposition ❯ Glacial Lakes	UCP 4, SPSP 5c	■ ◆ **Bellringer,** p. 459 ■ **Demonstration:** Glacial Erosion and Deposition Simulation, p. 459 ■ **DI (English Learners):** Glacial Deposition and Erosion Gallery, p. 460 ■ **Discussion:** Comprehension Check, p. 462 ■ **DI (Special Education Students):** Defining Terms, p. 463 ◆ **Transparencies:** 84 Landforms Created by Glacial Erosion • 85 Features of Glacial Deposition ▲ **Visual Concepts:** Landforms Carved by Glaciers • Glacial Drift: Stratified Drift and Till
Section 3 Ice Ages, pp. 467–470 **90 min.** ❯ Glacial and Interglacial Periods ❯ Causes of Glaciation	UCP 4, SPSP 5c, ES 3c	■ ◆ **Bellringer,** p. 467 ■ **Discussion:** Ice-Age Mammals, p. 467 ■ **Debate:** Global Warming, p. 468 ■ **DI (Special Education Students):** Timeline, p. 468 ◆ **Transparencies:** 86 Ice Ages of Earth's History • 87 The Milankovitch Theory ▲ **Visual Concepts:** Ice Age • Milankovitch Theory
Chapter Wrap-Up, pp. 475–479 **90 min.**		**Chapter Summary,** p. 475

See also PowerNotes® Presentations

CHAPTER Fast Track *To shorten instruction because of time limitations, omit the Chapter Lab.*

Key

Teacher's Edition ■ | Teaching Transparencies ◆
Chapter Resource File ● | Online Edition ▲

All resources listed below are also available on the **Teacher One Stop™.**

Why It Matters	Hands-On	Skills Development	Assessment
■ **Chapter Overview** p. 452 ■ **Using the Figure:** Blue and White Ice, p. 452	**Inquiry Lab:** Iceberg in a Glass, p. 453	**Reading Toolbox,** p. 454	
■ **Section Overview,** p. 455 ■ **Glacier Classification,** p. 456	■ **Activity:** Modeling Glacial Ice Formation, p. 455 **Quick Lab:** Slipping Ice, p. 457	■ ● **Internet Activity:** Glacial Sounds, p. 456 **Reading Toolbox:** Classification, p. 456 **Maps in Action:** Gulkana Glacier, p. 474 ■ ● **Internet Activity:** Gulkana Glacier, p. 474	**Reading Check,** p. 456 **Section Review,** p. 458 ■ **Reteaching,** p. 457 ■ **Quiz,** p. 457 ■ **DI (Alternative Assessment):** Glacial Variety and Features, p. 458 ● **Section Quiz**
■ **Section Overview,** p. 459 ■ **Using the Figure:** Comprehension Check, p. 460 ■ **Glacier Flour and Milk,** p. 462 ■ **Using the Figure:** Describing Glacial Landforms, p. 463 ■ **Geography Connection:** Local Glacial Formations, p. 464 **Can You Drink a Glacier?,** p. 465	**Quick Lab:** Glacial Erosion, p. 461 ■ **Activity:** Glacial Erosion Theories, p. 461 ■ **Activity:** Effects of Glacial Erosion and Deposition, p. 464 ■ **Group Activity:** Types of Glacial Lakes, p. 464 ● **Inquiry Lab:** Glacial Deposition ● **Making Models Lab:** Melted Glacier Formations	■ **Skill Builder:** Vocabulary, p. 460 **Reading Toolbox:** Word Families, p. 463 ■ ● **Internet Activity:** More Glacial Landforms and Features, p. 464	**Reading Check,** p. 460 **Reading Check,** p. 463 **Reading Check,** p. 464 **Section Review,** p. 466 ■ **Reteaching,** p. 465 ■ **Quiz,** p. 465 ■ **DI (Alternative Assessment):** Modeling Glacial Landforms, p. 466 ● **Section Quiz**
■ **Section Overview,** p. 467 ■ **Environmental Connection:** Climate Change, p. 468	**Making Models Lab:** Glaciers and Sea-Level Change, pp. 472–473	■ ● **Internet Activity:** Vanishing Ice Caps, p. 468 **Reading Toolbox:** Booklet FoldNote, p. 468 **Math Skills:** Earth's Tilt, p. 469	**Reading Check,** p. 468 **Section Review,** p. 470 ■ **Reteaching,** p. 469 ■ **Quiz,** p. 469 ■ **DI (Alternative Assessment):** Poster Project, p. 470 ● **Section Quiz**
Watermelon Ice, p. 471		▲ **Super Summary** **Standardized Test Prep,** pp. 478–479	**Chapter Review,** pp. 476–477 ● **Chapter Tests**
	See also Lab Generator		**See also Holt Online Assessment Resources**

Chapter Overview

This chapter discusses the nature of glaciers and their effect on Earth's surface. The chapter explains how glaciers act as indicators of climate change and concludes with an explanation of Earth's glacial cycles.

Using the Figure ADVANCED

Blue and White Ice Over time, compression forces the air from between the ice grains in glaciers. This loss of air makes the ice very dense. When light travels into the ice, the ice grains scatter the blue light and absorb the red light. As a result, glaciers appear blue. Unlike glaciers, the ice in icebergs contains many different-sized air bubbles that are very close together in the ice. This causes all of the colors of light to scatter, making icebergs appear white. Ask students why the ice on a pond or skating rink does not appear blue. (The ice is not thick and heavy enough to produce the density of grains necessary to scatter the blue light.) **LS Visual**

Why It Matters

Alaska's Mendenhall glacier, pictured here, began melting faster than accumulating in the mid-1700s. Today, melting continues, causing the ice to retreat at a rate of about 30 to 46 m/yr.

Chapter 17 Glaciers

Chapter Outline

Virginia Standards of Learning
ES.1.a
ES.1.c
ES.2.a

Why It Matters

Glaciers—huge masses of slowly moving ice—reshape Earth's surface by carving valleys, forming lakes, and moving sediment. Glaciers provide information about past and present climates, and they are key indicators of current climate changes.

Chapter Correlations

Virginia Standards of Learning

ES.1.a volume, area, mass, elapsed time, direction, temperature, pressure, distance, density, and changes in elevation/depth are calculated utilizing the most appropriate tools.

ES.1.c scales, diagrams, charts, graphs, tables, imagery, models, and profiles are constructed and interpreted.

ES.2.a science explains and predicts the interactions and dynamics of complex Earth systems.

Inquiry Lab

⏱ 20 min

Iceberg in a Glass

Find the volume of an ice cube. Place your "iceberg" in a glass that is two-thirds full of water. Determine the volume of the ice that is floating above the water and the volume of the ice that is below the water. Without disturbing the glass, observe what happens as the ice melts. Record your observations.

Fill another glass two-thirds full of water. Add salt, stirring until no more salt dissolves. Find the volume of a new ice cube. Place your new "iceberg" in the glass with the salt water. Determine the volume of the ice above and below the water. Record your observations as the ice melts.

Calculate the percentage of the iceberg that is above the water in each glass.

Questions to Get You Started

1. If a rectangular iceberg with a volume of 60,000 m^3 is floating in the ocean, what volume of ice is above the surface of the water? Explain your answer.
2. Describe what happened as the ice melted in each glass. What accounts for any differences between the two glasses?

Inquiry Lab

Central Concept: Most of an iceberg is underwater, with only the tip emerged—hence the phrase "the tip of the iceberg," which refers to something that is only a small bit of the whole. Students will observe this phenomenon, and observe that the iceberg meltwater is less dense than salt water.

Teacher's Notes: Prepare ice cubes using water dyed with blue food coloring. The coloring will help students to see the meltwater in contrast to the water in the glass. The ice cube floats only millimeters higher in the salt water than in the fresh water so have students measure carefully. Remind students to calculate volume using $l \times w \times h$.

Materials (per group)
- Two ice cubes
- Two glasses
- Water
- Salt
- Spoon
- Metric ruler

Skills Acquired
- Making Models
- Measuring

Answers to Getting Started

1. Answers may vary. Accept all reasonable answers in which students apply their calculations of the percentage of the volume of the model iceberg that was above water to find the above-water volume of a 60,000 m^3 iceberg.
2. The water from the melting ice in the glass with fresh water tended to sink, but the water from the melting ice in the glass with salt water remained in a layer on the surface. In the first glass, cold, fresh water from the melted ice was denser than the fresh water in the glass. In the second glass, cold, fresh water from the melted ice was less dense than the salt water.

Using THINK central Resources

An online version of this chapter, as well as all the print and multimedia resources that accompany the program are available to registered teachers and their students. Log onto www.thinkcentral.com to access these materials and tools to organize your preparation and student learning.

READING TOOLBOX

Word Families

Student answers may vary, especially in the third column. Go over students' definitions with them and correct any inaccuracies or misconceptions. An example chart can be found on page 507B.

Classification

See page 507A for a sample chart.

FoldNotes

Answers may vary. Students should consult Appendix A for tips on making a booklet FoldNote. Students' booklets should devote a page to each of the main topics in Sections 1 and 2.

READING TOOLBOX

These reading tools will help you learn the material in this chapter.

Word Families

Glacier In this chapter, you will learn many two-word terms, including *alpine glacier* and *glacial drift*, that contain the word *glacier* or *glacial*. Both *glacier* and *glacial* come from the Latin word *glacies,* meaning "ice."

Your Turn As you read this chapter, make a table like the one below. In the first column, write all the terms that include either *glacier* or *glacial*. In the second column, define the other word in each term. Then write your own definition of the whole two-word term.

Term	Definition of second word	Definition of whole two-word term
alpine glacier	*alpine* = of or like mountains	
continental glacier	continent =	
glacial drift	drift =	
glacial period	period =	

Classification

Classifying Glacial Depositions
Classification is a tool for organizing objects and ideas by grouping them into categories. The categories are based on defining characteristics of the objects and ideas. For example, the following table shows how landforms produced by glacial erosion can be classified by their shape and location.

Landform produced by glacial erosion	Shape	Location
cirque	bowl-shaped depression	floor of a valley
arête	sharp, jagged ridge	between cirques

Your Turn As you read Section 2, create a table like the one above to show how glacial depositions can be classified by their composition and by where and how they are deposited.

FoldNotes

Booklet FoldNote A booklet is a useful tool for taking notes as you read a chapter. Each page of the booklet can be used to record details about one of the main topics in the chapter.

Your Turn Create a booklet FoldNote as described in Appendix A. On each page of the booklet, write one of the main topics in Sections 1 and 2: Formation of Glaciers, Types of Glaciers, Movement of Glaciers, Features of Glaciers, Glacial Erosion, Glacial Deposition, and Glacial Lakes. As you read, take notes about each main topic on the appropriate page of your booklet.

For more information on how to use these and other tools, see **Appendix A.**

SECTION 1

Glaciers: Moving Ice

ENVIRONMENTAL CONNECTION

Key Ideas	Key Terms	Why It Matters
❯ Describe how glaciers form. ❯ Compare two main kinds of glaciers. ❯ Explain two processes by which glaciers move. ❯ Describe three features of glaciers.	**glacier** **alpine glacier** **continental glacier** **basal slip** **internal plastic flow** **crevasse**	Because the size of glaciers depends on climate, glaciers are also an indicator of climate change. Understanding how glaciers form and move can help us make predictions about climate.

A single snowflake is lighter than a feather. However, if you squeeze a handful of snow, you make a firm snowball. In a process similar to making a snowball, natural forces compact snow to make a large mass of moving ice called a **glacier.**

Formation of Glaciers

At high elevations and in polar regions, snow may remain on the ground all year and form an almost motionless mass of permanent snow and ice called a *snowfield*. Snowfields form as ice and snow accumulate above the snowline. The *snowline* is the elevation above which ice and snow remain throughout the year, as shown in **Figure 1.**

Average temperatures at high elevations and in polar regions are always near or below the freezing point of water. So, snow that falls there accumulates year after year. Cycles of partial melting and refreezing change the snow into grainy ice called *firn*.

In deep layers of snow and firn, the pressure of the overlying layers flattens the ice grains and squeezes the air from between the grains. The continued buildup of snow and firn forms a glacier that moves downslope or outward under its own weight.

The size of a glacier depends on the amount of snowfall received and the amount of ice lost. When new snow is added faster than ice and snow melt, the glacier gets bigger. When the ice melts faster than snow is added, the glacier gets smaller. Small differences in average yearly temperatures and snowfall may upset the balance between snowfall and ice loss. Thus, changes in the size of a glacier may indicate climatic change.

Figure 1 The snowline on the Grand Teton Mountains at Grand Teton National Park, Wyoming, is more than 3,000 m above sea level.

glacier a large mass of moving ice

SCILINKS.
www.scilinks.org
Topic: Glaciers
Code: **HQX0675**

Section 1

Focus

Overview

This section explains the nature of glaciers, the types of glaciers, and the features of glaciers. It also explains, how glaciers form and how they move.

Bellringer

Ask students what they know about ice and glaciers. (Answers may vary. Students may mention that glaciers consist of heavy, thick areas of ice and snow, are found at the poles, and move.)

Motivate

Activity GENERAL

Modeling Glacial Ice Formation

Give each student a square-shaped piece of white paper and scissors. Tell them to make a paper snowflake by following this process: "Fold the paper in half diagonally and in half again. Next, fold the paper in thirds. Then, cut several small areas from each of the three edges and unfold." Tell students that a snowflake contains 90–95% air; firn contains 20–30% air, and glacial ice contains less than 10% air. Have students model glacial ice formation by crushing the paper snowflake in their hands first into golf ball size to represent firn and then into as small and compact a ball as possible to represent glacial ice. **LS Visual/Kinesthetic**

Key Resources

Chapter Resource File
- Directed Reading BASIC

Technology
- Transparencies
  Bellringer

Teach

Environmental Connection

Harvesting Glacial Ice Alaska's glaciers cover 75,000 km^2. Seventy-five percent of its water is stored in these glaciers. Alaska issues permits, allowing companies to take more than 18 metric tons of glacier ice. Have students research glacier harvesting and write an essay that discusses its potential positive and negative environmental impacts.

Internet Activity GENERAL

Glacial Sounds Ask students what sounds they think glaciers make and what might cause them. Then, listen to audio files of glacier ice popping; glaciers calving, or losing material; and icebergs cracking. Discuss how the actual sounds compared to the students' predictions. A worksheet designed to direct student research on this topic can be found in the **Chapter Resource File** booklet or by visiting www.thinkcentral.com and entering the keyword **HQXGLAX.** **LS Auditory**

Answer to Reading Check

Continental glaciers exist only in Greenland and Antarctica.

READING TOOLBOX

Classification

Type of glacier	Characteristics	Examples
alpine	form in mountainous regions; relatively small	in Alaska, Himalaya Mountains, Andes, Alps, and New Zealand.
continental	massive sheets of ice; relatively large	in Greenland and Antarctica

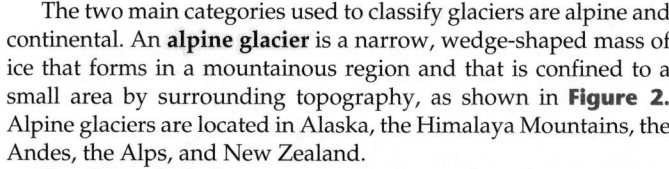

Figure 2 An alpine glacier (above) descends through Thompson Pass in Alaska. A continental glacier (right) covers much of the land surface in Greenland.

alpine glacier a narrow, wedge-shaped mass of ice that forms in a mountainous region and that is confined to a small area by surrounding topography

continental glacier a massive sheet of ice that may cover millions of square kilometers, that may be thousands of meters thick, and that is not confined by surrounding topography

Types of Glaciers

The two main categories used to classify glaciers are alpine and continental. An **alpine glacier** is a narrow, wedge-shaped mass of ice that forms in a mountainous region and that is confined to a small area by surrounding topography, as shown in **Figure 2.** Alpine glaciers are located in Alaska, the Himalaya Mountains, the Andes, the Alps, and New Zealand.

Continental glaciers are massive sheets of ice that may cover millions of square kilometers, that may be thousands of meters thick, and that are not confined by surrounding topography, as shown in **Figure 2.** Today, continental glaciers, also called *ice sheets*, exist only in Greenland and Antarctica. The Antarctic ice sheet covers an area of more than 13 million km^2 and is more than 4,000 m thick in some places. The Greenland ice sheet covers 1.7 million km^2 of land, and its maximum thickness is more than 3,000 m. If these ice sheets melted, the water they contain would raise the worldwide sea level by more than 50 m.

Reading Check **Where can you find continental glaciers today?** (See Appendix G for answers to Reading Checks.)

READING TOOLBOX

Classification
As you read this page, create a classification table like the one at the beginning of this chapter. List the two main types of glaciers, describe their characteristics, and give examples.

Movement of Glaciers

Glaciers are sometimes called "rivers of ice." Gravity causes both glaciers and rivers to flow downward. However, glaciers and rivers move in different ways. Unlike water in a river, glacial ice cannot move rapidly or flow easily around barriers. In a year, some glaciers may travel only a few centimeters, while others may move a kilometer or more. Glaciers move by two basic processes—basal slip and internal plastic flow.

Why It Matters

Glacier Classification Glaciers are sometimes classified by their environments. There are three glacial environments: polar, subpolar, and temperate.

Polar environments have cold temperatures, little glacial melting, and a permanent ice pack. Summer temperatures are below 0 °C. Antarctica and Northern Greenland are examples of polar environments.

In subpolar environments, the temperatures in summer are less than 10 °C, but are warm enough for some vegetation to grow. Moderate summer rain causes some glacial surface melting. Southern Greenland and Iceland have subpolar environments.

In temperate environments, summer temperatures are higher than 10 °C, and considerable melting and precipitation occur. The glaciers in Patagonia, New Zealand, and Alaska are in temperate environments.

Basal Slip

One way that glaciers move is by slipping over a thin layer of water and sediment that lies between the ice and the ground. The weight of the ice in a glacier exerts pressure that lowers the melting point of ice. As a result, the ice melts where the glacier touches the ground. The water mixes with sediment at the base of the glacier. This mixture acts as a lubricant between the ice and the underlying surface. The process that lubricates a glacier's base and causes the glacier to slide forward is called **basal slip.**

Basal slip also allows a glacier to work its way over small barriers in its path by melting and then refreezing. For example, if the ice pushes against a rock barrier, the pressure causes some of the ice to melt. The water from the melted ice travels around the barrier and freezes again as the pressure is removed.

basal slip the process that causes the ice at the base of a glacier to melt and the glacier to slide

internal plastic flow the process by which glaciers flow slowly as grains of ice deform under pressure and slide over each other

Internal Plastic Flow

Glaciers also move by a process called **internal plastic flow.** In this process, pressure deforms grains of ice under a glacier. As the grains deform, they slide over each other and cause the glacier to flow slowly. However, the rate of internal plastic flow varies for different parts of a glacier, as shown in **Figure 3.** The slope of the ground and the thickness and temperature of the ice determine the rate at which ice flows at a given point. The edges of a glacier move more slowly than the center because of friction with underlying rock. For this same reason, a glacier moves more quickly near its surface than near its base.

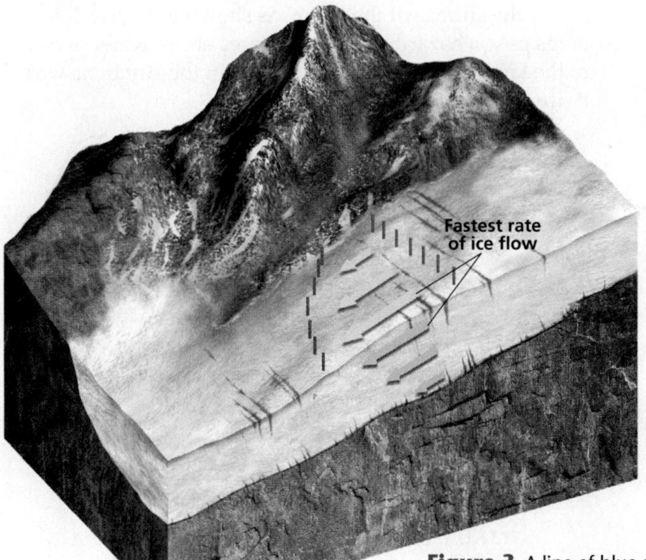

Figure 3 A line of blue stakes driven into an alpine glacier moves to the position of the red stakes as the glacier flows. This measurement shows that the central part of the glacier moves faster than its edges.

Quick Lab — 15 min

Slipping Ice

Procedure

1. Squeeze flat a handful of snow or shaved ice until you notice a change in the particles.
2. Place the squeezed ice on a tray. Place a heavy weight on the squeezed ice.
3. Lift one end of the tray to a 30° incline, and record your observations.

Analysis

1. What does squeezing do to the particles of snow or ice?
2. How is squeezing the snow or ice similar to the formation of a glacier?
3. What did you observe when you placed the squeezed ice on the tray? What glacial movement process is modeled here?

Key Resources

Technology

- Transparencies
  83 Internal Plastic Flow

Quick Lab

Skills Acquired

- Observing
- Identifying/Recognizing Patterns

Materials

- Snow or shaved ice
- Tray
- Heavy weight

Teacher's Notes: Caution students to squeeze the ice strongly but briefly and into a flat shape that can accommodate a weight.

Answers to Analysis

1. Squeezing removes air from between the particles and compacts the ice.
2. Glaciers form when pressure flattens ice grains and squeezes air out.
3. At first, the ice did not move. A little while after the weight was placed on the ice, the ice started to slide. Basal slip is being modeled.

Close

Reteaching — BASIC

Glacial Movement Have students work in pairs to review the steps of both types of glacial movement. Have one student write each step of basal slip on an index card and have the other student write each step of internal plastic flow. Next, have students shuffle their sets of cards and exchange them. Then have students put the sets of cards in the correct order. English Language Learners

LS Verbal/Logical
Co-op Learning

Quiz — GENERAL

1. What factors affect the size of a glacier? (the amounts of snowfall received and of ice lost due to raised temperature)
2. What is another name for an ice sheet? (continental glacier)
3. What is firn and how does it form? (Firn is grainy ice that forms by the melting and refreezing of snow.)

Close, *continued*

Answers to Section Review

1. Snow accumulates year after year at high elevations and in polar regions.
2. The pressure from overlying snow flattens the snow into grains of ice and squeezes out the air. As snow and firn build up, a glacier forms.
3. An alpine glacier is narrow and wedge-shaped. It forms in mountainous areas and is confined by the surrounding topography. A continental glacier is a massive sheet of ice that is not confined by surrounding topography and may cover large expanses of land.
4. In internal plastic flow, the glacier's interior moves as grains of ice deform under pressure and slip over each other. In basal slip, the entire glacier moves by slipping over a thin layer of water and sediment at the glacier's base.
5. Answers may vary. Sample answer: Crevasses are large cracks on the surface of a glacier. Ice shelves are part of a continental glacier that has moved out over the ocean.
6. A snowfield is a nearly motionless mass of permanent snow and ice that forms as ice and snow accumulate above the snowline. A glacier is a moving mass of snow and firn whose ice crystals have been flattened and compacted by the pressure of overlying layers of firn and ice.
7. Tension and compression under the surface of a glacier caused by uneven flow make the glacier's brittle surface crack, forming crevasses.

Figure 4 Crevasses (right) are large cracks in a glacier. The composite image below shows what an iceberg might look like if you could see the entire iceberg.

crevasse in a glacier, a large crack or fissure that results from ice movement

Features of Glaciers

While the interior of a glacier moves by internal plastic flow and the entire glacier moves by basal slip, the low pressure on the surface ice causes the surface ice to remain brittle. The glacier flows unevenly beneath the surface, and regions of tension and compression build under the brittle surface. As a result, large cracks, called **crevasses** (kruh VAS uhz), form on the surface, as shown in **Figure 4.** Some crevasses may be as deep as 50 m!

Continental glaciers move outward in all directions from their centers toward the edges of their landmasses. Some parts of the ice sheets may move out over the ocean and form *ice shelves*. When the tides rise and fall, large blocks of ice, called *icebergs*, may break from the ice shelves and drift into the ocean. Because most of an iceberg is below the surface of the water, as shown in Figure 4, icebergs pose a hazard to ships. The area above water of one of the largest icebergs ever observed in the Antarctic was twice the size of Connecticut!

Section 1 Review

Key Ideas

1. **Identify** two regions in which snow accumulates year after year.
2. **Describe** the process by which glaciers form.
3. **Compare** an alpine glacier and a continental glacier.
4. **Explain** how internal plastic flow and basal slip move glaciers.
5. **Describe** two features of glaciers.
6. **Compare** a glacier and a snowfield.
7. **Explain** how a crevasse forms.

Critical Thinking

8. **Making Inferences** If glaciers could move only by internal plastic flow, what might happen to the rate at which glaciers move? Explain your answer.
9. **Identifying Relationships** How can changes in the size of a glacier indicate climate change?
10. **Analyzing Ideas** If icebergs are visible at sea level, why do they pose a hazard to ships?

Concept Mapping

11. Use the following terms to create a concept map: *glacier, firn, snowline, snowfield, alpine glacier, continental glacier, basal slip, internal plastic flow, ice shelf, iceberg,* and *crevasse.*

8. Answers may vary. Sample answer: All glaciers would move more slowly because moving by internal flow is more complex and gradual than moving by basal slip.
9. Small differences in average yearly temperatures and snowfall amounts affect the size of the glacier. If average temperatures go up, a glacier may get smaller. If average temperatures drop, a glacier may get larger.
10. Most of the ice in an iceberg is underwater and cannot be easily seen.
11. *Glaciers* form from *firn* in *snowfields* above the *snowline*; form features such as *ice shelves*, *icebergs*, and *crevasses*; may be *alpine glaciers* or *continental glaciers*; and move by *internal plastic flow* and *basal slip*.

Differentiated Instruction

Alternative Assessment

Glacial Variety and Features Have students make a slide presentation that shows images of different glacial types and features. Tell students to identify the type of glacier or feature and the location of the glacier. The Web site of the United States Geological Survey has many images of glaciers. **LS Visual/Verbal**

SECTION 2 Glacial Erosion and Deposition

Key Ideas	Key Terms		Why It Matters
❯ Describe the landscape features that are produced by glacial erosion. ❯ Name and describe five features formed by glacial deposition. ❯ Explain how glacial lakes form.	cirque arête horn erratic glacial drift	till moraine kettle esker	While glaciers have only affected the surface of the northern part of the United States, they are responsible for many of our nation's natural wonders.

Many of the landforms in Canada and in the northern United States were created by glaciers. Large lakes, solitary boulders on flat plains, and jagged ridges are just a few examples of landforms created by glaciers. Glaciers created these landforms through the processes of erosion and deposition.

Glacial Erosion

Like rivers, glaciers are agents of erosion. Both a river and a glacier can pick up and carry rock and sediment. However, because of the size and density of glaciers, landforms that result from glacial action are very different from those that rivers form. For example, deep depressions in rock form when a moving glacier loosens and dislodges, or plucks, a rock from the bedrock at the base or side of the glacier. The rock plucked by the glacier is then dragged across the bedrock and causes abrasions. As shown in **Figure 1,** long parallel grooves in the bedrock are left behind and show the direction of the glacier's movement.

Figure 1 As a glacier moves, it picks up and carries rocks from the bedrock. These grooves at Kelly's Island in Ohio were carved by a glacier 35,000 years ago.

Section 2

Focus

Overview

This section describes the different features that are produced by glacial erosion and deposition and how glacial lakes form.

Bellringer

Ask students to describe the actions of a steam shovel, a chisel, sandpaper, and a conveyor belt. Then, ask them to predict how glaciers behave like each of these objects. (Answers may vary. Accept all reasonable answers.)
LS Logical

Motivate

Demonstration — GENERAL

Glacial Erosion and Deposition Simulation Before class, prepare about 50 mL of a mixture of table salt, coarse salt, and a small amount of rock salt and spread it evenly over a sheet of paper. Cover a 3 × 5 index card with double-sided tape; and, with the sticky side facing down, move the index card across the length of the paper exerting even pressure on the card. Ask students to describe how the salt mixture and the card look after the card has moved across the paper. Ask students what effect the movement of glaciers has on the land. (Glaciers remove material by picking it up, they leave grooves on the land, and they push material to another place.)
LS Visual/Verbal

Key Resources

Chapter Resource File
- Directed Reading BASIC
- Inquiry Lab: Glacial Deposition GENERAL
- Making Models Lab: Melted Glacier Formations GENERAL

Technology
- Transparencies Bellringer

Teach

Skill Builder GENERAL

Vocabulary The word *arête* comes from the Old French *areste*, which means "fishbone spine." Ask students to explain how this information may help them remember the meaning of the term *arête*. (English Language Learners)
LS Verbal

Using the Figure GENERAL

Comprehension Check Tell students that scientists study landforms created by glaciers to learn more about the path and action of glaciers. Ask students why one side of a *roche moutonnée* is steep and jagged and what *roches moutonnées* reveal about the movement of a glacier. (One side is steep and jagged because rock was pulled away as the glacier passed. The smooth, sloping side faces the direction from which the glacier came.) Answer to caption question: The jagged ridge that separates cirques are called *arêtes*. **LS Logical**

Teaching Tip BASIC

Connect to Prior Knowledge Obtain a photograph of the Matterhorn. Show students the photograph. Suggest that they may be familiar with this well-known mountain peak because "horn" is part of its name. Ask students to name the mountain peak. (the Matterhorn)
LS Visual

Answer to Reading Check
A moving glacier forms a cirque by pulling blocks of rock from the floor and walls of a valley and leaving a bowl-shaped depression.

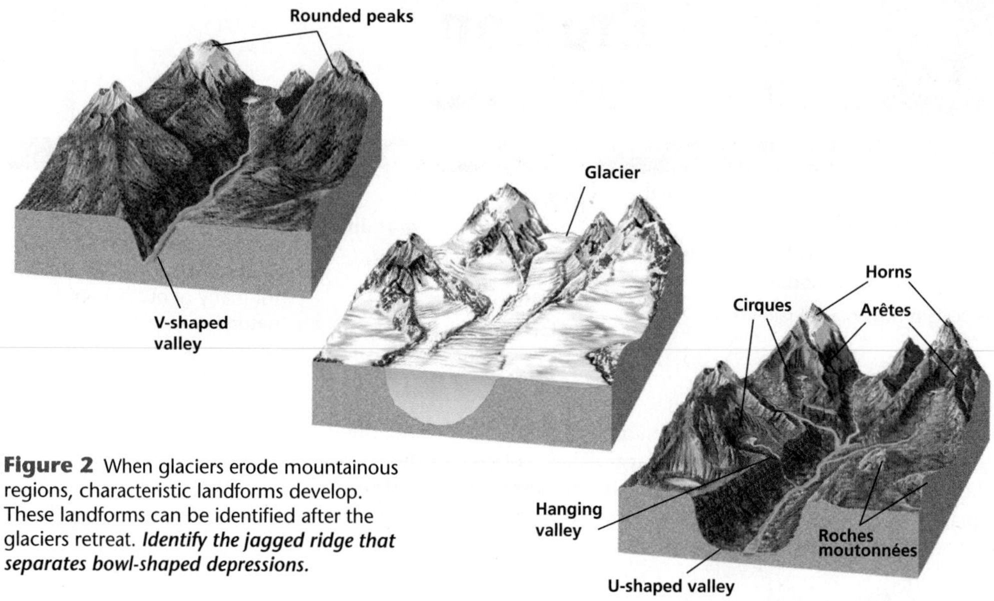

Figure 2 When glaciers erode mountainous regions, characteristic landforms develop. These landforms can be identified after the glaciers retreat. ***Identify the jagged ridge that separates bowl-shaped depressions.***

Landforms Created by Glacial Erosion

Glaciers have shaped many mountain ranges and have created unique landforms by erosive processes. The glacial processes that change the shape of mountains begin in the upper end of the valley where an alpine glacier forms. As a glacier moves through a narrow, V-shaped river valley, rock from the valley walls breaks off and the walls become steeper. The moving glacier also pulls blocks of rock from the floor of the valley. These actions create a bowl-shaped depression called a **cirque** (SUHRK). A sharp, jagged ridge called an **arête** (uh RAYT) forms between cirques. When several arêtes join, they form a sharp, pyramid-like peak called a **horn,** as shown in **Figure 2.**

cirque a deep and steep bowl-like depression produced by glacial erosion

arête a sharp, jagged ridge that forms between cirques

horn a sharp, pyramid-like peak that forms because of the erosion of cirques

As the glacier flows down through an existing valley, the glacier picks up large amounts of rock. These rock fragments, which range in size from microscopic particles to large boulders, become embedded in the ice.

Rock particles embedded in the ice may polish solid rock as the ice moves over the rock. Large rocks carried by the ice may gouge deep grooves in the bedrock. Glaciers may also round large rock projections. These rounded projections usually have a smooth, gently sloping side facing the direction from which the glacier came. The other side is steep and jagged because rock is pulled away as the ice passes. The resulting rounded knobs of rock are called *roches moutonnées* (ROHSH MOO tuh NAY), which means "sheep rocks" in French.

Academic Vocabulary
projection (proh JEK shuhn) an extension or a structural outgrowth

Reading Check **How does a glacier form a cirque?**

Differentiated Instruction

English Learners

Glacial Deposition and Erosion Gallery As students read this section, direct them to make a scrapbook of photos or drawings, from the Internet or magazines, that show the different effects of glacial erosion. Tell students to include labels with every photo that identify the landform in the photo, as well as the location of the landform and any other information they can find about the location. **LS Visual/Verbal**

Key Resources

Technology
- Transparencies
  84 Landforms Created by Glacial Erosion

U-Shaped Valleys

A stream forms the V shape of a valley. As a glacier scrapes away a valley's walls and floor, this original V shape becomes a U shape, as shown in **Figure 3.** Because glacial erosion is the only way by which U-shaped valleys form, scientists can use this feature to determine whether a valley has been glaciated in the past.

Small tributary glaciers in adjacent valleys may flow into a main alpine glacier. Because a small tributary glacier has less ice and less cutting power than the main alpine glacier does, the small glacier's U-shaped valley is not cut as deeply into the mountains. When the ice melts, the tributary valley is suspended high above the main valley floor and is called a *hanging valley*. When a stream flows from a hanging valley, a waterfall forms.

Figure 3 Jollie Valley, a U-shaped glaciated valley, is located in the Southern Alps of New Zealand.

Erosion by Continental Glaciers

The landscape eroded by continental glaciers differs from the sharp, rugged features eroded by alpine glaciers. Continental glaciers erode by leveling landforms to produce a smooth, rounded landscape. Continental glaciers smooth and round exposed rock surfaces in a way similar to the way that bulldozers flatten landscapes. Rock surfaces are also scratched and grooved by rocks carried at the base of the ice sheet. These scratches and grooves are parallel to the direction of glacial movement.

Quick Lab Glacial Erosion

25 min

Procedure

1. Put a mixture of sand, gravel, and rock in the bottom of a 15 cm × 10 cm × 5 cm plastic container. Fill the container with water to a depth of about 4 cm. Freeze the container until the water is solid. Remove the ice block from the container.
2. Use a rolling pin or large dowel to flatten some modeling clay into a rectangle about 20 cm × 10 cm × 1 cm.
3. Grasp the ice block firmly with a hand towel. Place the block with the gravel-and-rock side down at one end of the clay. Press down on the ice block, and push it along the length of the flat clay surface.
4. Sketch the pattern made in the clay by the ice block.
5. Next, press a 2 cm layer of damp sand into the bottom of a shallow, rectangular box. As in step 3, push the ice block along the surface of the sand, but press down lightly.

6. Repeat steps 3 and 4, but use a soft, wooden board in place of the clay.

Analysis

1. Describe the effects of the ice block on the clay, on the sand, and on the wood.
2. Did any clay, sand, or wood become mixed with material from the ice block? Did the ice deposit material on any surface?
3. What glacial land features are represented by the features of the clay model? the sand model? the wood model?

Quick Lab

Skills Acquired
- Constructing Models
- Observing

Materials
- Mixture of sand, gravel, and rock
- 15 cm × 10 cm × 5 cm plastic container
- Damp sand
- Ice block
- Hand towel
- Modeling clay
- Rolling pin or large dowel
- Shallow, rectangular box
- Soft wooden board
- Water

Teacher's Notes: Prepare the sand, gravel, rock, and ice and freeze them before class. If possible, use an ice block fresh from the freezer for each part of the lab. You may wish to conduct this lab as a demonstration and have students collect and analyze the data.

Answers to Analysis

1. Students should describe the depressions and grooves that the ice block makes in each.
2. None of the clay or wood mixed with the ice block, but some of the sand did. The ice deposited the most material on the sand.
3. The clay represents a smooth, rounded landscape. The sand and the wood represent a rock surface with scratches and grooves.

Homework GENERAL

Fiord Formation Tell students that a fiord forms when a narrow U-shaped valley that extends to a coastline becomes partly flooded by sea water after the glacier melts. Have students research the Harriman Fiord in Alaska, which was discovered in 1899. Ask students to imagine that they were participants in the Harriman expedition. Have each student write a series of journal entries that describe the days leading up to the discovery and the day of the discovery itself. **LS Verbal/Intrapersonal**

Activity ADVANCED

Glacial Erosion Theories Direct interested students to research the historical development of glacial erosion hypotheses up through the most recent. Have students use their research results to write an essay in which they explain each hypothesis and describe how past hypotheses helped lead to modern understanding of glaciers. **LS Logical**

Teach, *continued*

Discussion GENERAL

Comprehension Check Tell students to imagine that they have discovered a large boulder in a local park. It is approximately 3 m high, has scratches on one side, and is uncharacteristic of the rocks found in the area. Ask students to identify the glacial deposit that they have discovered and to explain what the rock tells them about the area. (The rock is an erratic. It tells us that a glacier once covered the area but dropped the rock as it melted.) LS **Visual/Kinesthetic**

MISCONCEPTION ALERT

Different Drifts Students may confuse *glacial drift* and *snowdrift* because they sound similar and both involve cold conditions. Explain that each term involves a different substance and is a result of a different process. A snowdrift is the result of wind blowing snow into a mound. Glacial drift is sediment, such as sand, rocks, or gravel, that has been carried and deposited by glaciers.

erratic a large rock transported from a distant source by a glacier

glacial drift rock material carried and deposited by glaciers

till unsorted rock material that is deposited directly by a melting glacier

Glacial Deposition

Glaciers are also agents of deposition. Deposition occurs when a glacier melts. A glacier will melt if it reaches low, warm elevations or if the climate becomes warmer. As the glacier melts, it deposits all of the material that it has accumulated, which may range in size from fine sediment to large rocks.

Large rocks that a glacier transports from a distant source are called **erratics.** Because a glacier carries an erratic a long distance, the composition of an erratic usually differs from that of the bedrock over which the erratic lies.

Various other landforms develop as glaciers melt and deposit sediment, as shown in **Figure 4.** The general term for all sediments deposited by a glacier is **glacial drift.** Unsorted glacial drift that is deposited directly from a melting glacier is called **till.** Till is composed of sediments from the base of the glacier and is commonly left behind when glacial ice melts. Another type of glacial drift is *stratified drift.* Stratified drift is material that has been sorted and deposited in layers by streams flowing from the melted ice, or *meltwater*.

Figure 4 Moraines, glacial lakes, drumlins, meltwater streams, and outwash plains are some examples of landforms created by glacial deposition.

Key Resources

Technology

- Transparencies
  85 Features of Glacial Deposition

Why It Matters

Glacier Flour and Milk Glacier flour forms when a glacier's drift grinds against Earth's rocky surface. Glacier flour, which consists of very finely ground rock, silt, and clay, is washed out of glaciers in meltwater. The sediment-laden meltwater is called *glacier milk* and often is white in color.

Till Deposits

Landforms that result when a glacier deposits till are called *moraines*. **Moraines** are ridges of unsorted sediment on the ground or on the glacier itself. There are several types of moraines, as shown in **Figure 4.** A *lateral moraine* is a moraine that is deposited along the sides of an alpine glacier, usually as a long ridge. When two or more alpine glaciers join, their adjacent lateral moraines combine to form a *medial moraine*.

The unsorted material left beneath the glacier when the ice melts is the *ground moraine*. The soil of a ground moraine is commonly very rocky. An ice sheet may mold ground moraine into clusters of drumlins. *Drumlins* are long, low, tear-shaped mounds of till. The long axes of the drumlins are parallel to the direction of glacial movement.

Terminal moraines are small ridges of till that are deposited at the leading edge of a melting glacier. These moraines have many depressions that may contain lakes or ponds. Large terminal moraines, some of which are more than 100 km long, can be seen across the Midwest, especially south of the Great Lakes.

Reading Check Which glacial deposit is a tear-shaped mound of sediment?

moraine a landform that is made from unsorted sediments deposited by a glacier

READING TOOLBOX

Word Families
Many two-word terms on this page include the key term *moraine*. Make a table for this family of words, similar to the one at the beginning of this chapter. Use a dictionary to find definitions for the words *lateral, medial, ground,* and *terminal.* Then, write your own definition of each two-word term.

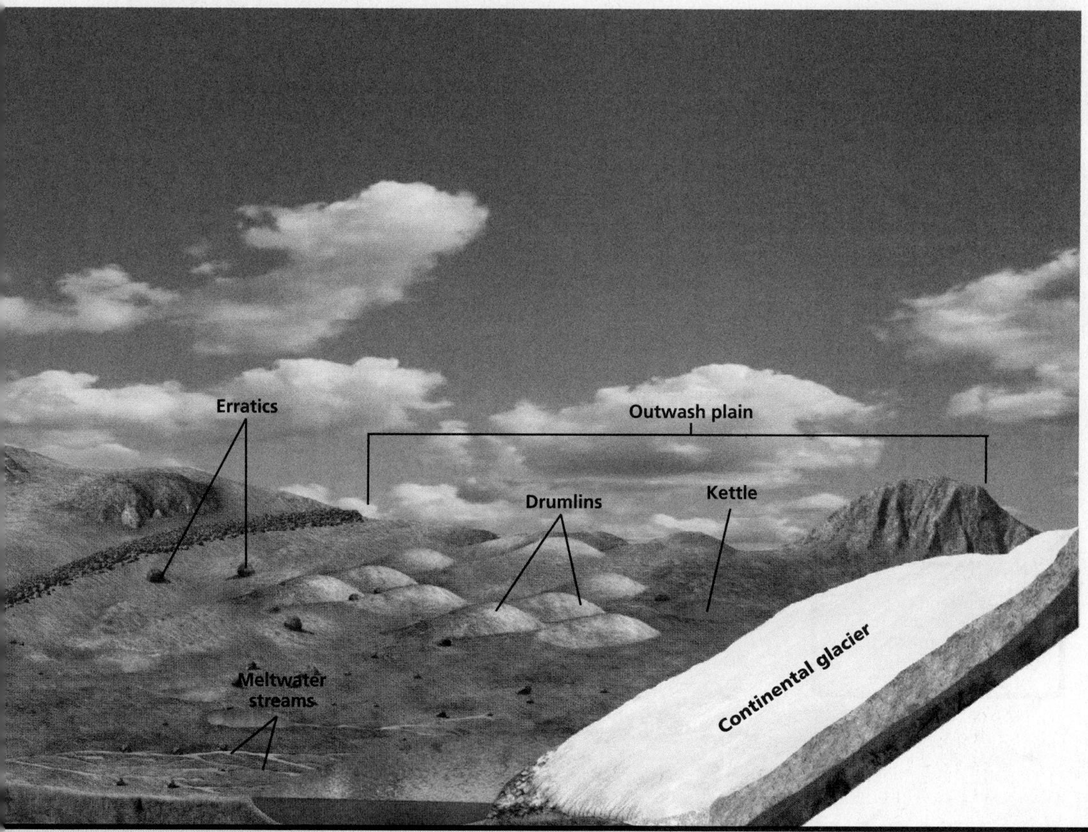

READING TOOLBOX

Word Families

Term	Definition of second word	Definition of whole term
lateral moraine	lateral: on the side	moraine on the side of a glacier
medial moraine	medial: in the middle	moraine in the middle of glaciers
ground moraine	ground: Earth surface	moraine beneath the glacier
terminal moraine	terminal: at the end	moraine at the end of a glacier

Answer to Reading Check
A drumlin is a long, low, tear-shaped mound of till.

Using the Figure GENERAL

Describing Glacial Landforms
Direct students to list each glacial landform that is labeled in the figure on the bottom of these pages. Then, have students write a description of the feature and an explanation of how that feature formed. (Medial moraines form when two adjacent lateral moraines combine. Lateral moraines are unsorted sediment that is deposited along the sides of a glacier. Terminal moraines are small ridges of till that are deposited at the leading edge of a melting glacier. Erratics are large rocks that were transported from a distant source by a glacier and that were deposited when the glacier melted. Meltwater streams are streams that flow from the melted ice of a glacier. Outwash plains are areas of stratified drift deposited by meltwater in front of terminal moraines. Kettles are depressions in glacial drift that form when chunks of ice buried in the drift melt. Drumlins are long, low, tear-shaped mounds of till.) LS **Visual/Verbal**

Differentiated Instruction

Special Education Students

Defining Terms Divide the class into small groups. Have each group choose one or more paragraphs from the text. Help them to identify in these paragraphs words (other than ones that are defined and explained) that they don't understand. Have each group rewrite their paragraphs using definitions or synonyms in place of the identified words. Ask groups to read their new paragraphs to the class. LS **Verbal**

Teach, *continued*

Activity — BASIC

Effects of Glacial Erosion and Deposition Have students make a table that has two columns. Have them label one column "Erosion" and the other column "Deposition." Have them label the rows "Continental glacier" and "Alpine glacier." Tell students to list the landforms that result from each process in the appropriate row. **LS Verbal**

Internet Activity — GENERAL

More Glacial Landforms and Features Have interested students use the Internet to research topographical features formed by glacial deposition, such as chatter scratches, kames, scours, whale-backs, and braided streams. Direct students to write descriptions of the appearance and formation of each feature. A worksheet designed to direct student research on this topic can be found in the **Chapter Resource File** booklet or by visiting www.thinkcentral.com and entering the keyword **HQXGLAX. LS Verbal**

Answer to Reading Check

Eskers form when meltwater from receding continental glaciers flows through ice tunnels and deposits long, winding ridges of gravel and sand.

Figure 5 This kettle lake in Saskatchewan, Canada, formed as a result of glacial deposition.

Outwash Plains

When a glacier melts, streams of meltwater flow from the edges, the surface, and beneath the glacier. Glacial meltwater may have beautiful colors, such as milky white, emerald green, or turquoise blue, because it carries very fine sediment. The meltwater carries drift as well as rock particles and deposits them in front of the glacier as a large outwash plain. An *outwash plain* is a deposit of stratified drift that lies in front of a terminal moraine and is crossed by many meltwater streams.

kettle a bowl-shaped depression in a glacial drift deposit

esker a long, winding ridge of gravel and coarse sand deposited by glacial meltwater streams

Kettles

Most outwash plains are pitted with depressions called **kettles.** A kettle forms when a chunk of glacial ice is buried in drift. As the ice melts, a cavity forms in the drift. The drift collapses into the cavity and produces a depression. Kettles commonly fill with water to form kettle lakes, such as the one shown in **Figure 5.**

SCILINKS.
www.scilinks.org
Topic: Glaciers and Landforms
Code: **HQX0676**

Eskers

When continental glaciers recede, **eskers** (ES kuhrz)—long, winding ridges of gravel and sand—may be left behind. These ridges consist of stratified drift deposited by streams of meltwater that flow through ice tunnels within the glaciers. Eskers may extend for tens of kilometers, like raised, winding roadways.

Reading Check **How do eskers form?**

Geography Connection — ADVANCED

Local Glacial Formations Tell students that glaciers significantly changed the surface of large parts of Europe, Asia, and North America. Have students work in pairs to research the glacial history of the continents. Tell students to make a map of one continent that shows the location of different glacial formations. Students should use a different symbol to indicate each type of landform or deposit. **LS Visual**

Group Activity — GENERAL

Types of Glacial Lakes Tell students that there are three types of glacial lakes: kettle lakes, cirque lakes, and moraine-formed lakes. Organize the class into three groups. Have each group research one type of glacial lake and create a poster or multimedia presentation that describes how that type of lake forms and what its characteristics are. **LS Verbal**

Glacial Lakes

Lake basins commonly form where glaciers erode surfaces and leave depressions in the bedrock. Thousands of lake basins in Canada and the northern United States were gouged from solid rock by a continental glacier. Thousands of other glacial lakes form as a result of deposition rather than as a result of erosion. Many lakes form in the uneven surface of ground moraine deposited by glaciers. These lakes exist in many areas of North America and Europe.

Long, narrow *finger lakes,* such as those in western New York, form where terminal and lateral moraines block existing streams. The area south of the Great Lakes, from Minnesota to Ohio, has belts of moraines and lakes. Minnesota, also called the "Land of 10,000 Lakes," was completely glaciated and has evidence of all types of glacial lakes.

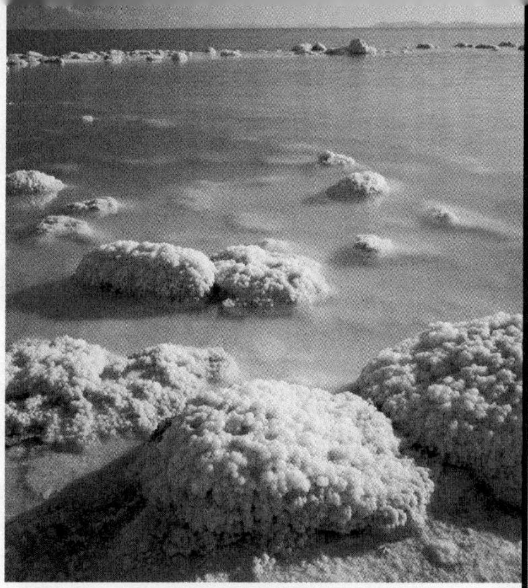

Figure 6 Many streams and rivers carry dissolved minerals to the Great Salt Lake in Utah. However, because there is no outlet, the lake becomes concentrated with these minerals as continual evaporation removes water.

Formation of Salt Lakes

Many lakes existed during the last glacial advance. But because of topographic and climatic changes, outlet streams no longer leave these lakes. Water leaves the lakes only by evaporation. When the water evaporates, salt that was dissolved in the water is left behind, which makes the water increasingly salty. Salt lakes, such as the one shown in **Figure 6,** commonly form in dry climates, where evaporation is rapid and precipitation is low.

Why It Matters

Can You Drink a Glacier?

Over 7 billion gallons of bottled water are sold each year in the United States. Companies that bottle water from glacial streams claim that their water is purer than other bottled water because it has been trapped in ice for centuries. Some companies use images of glaciers on their bottles, even if their water does not actually come from glaciers.

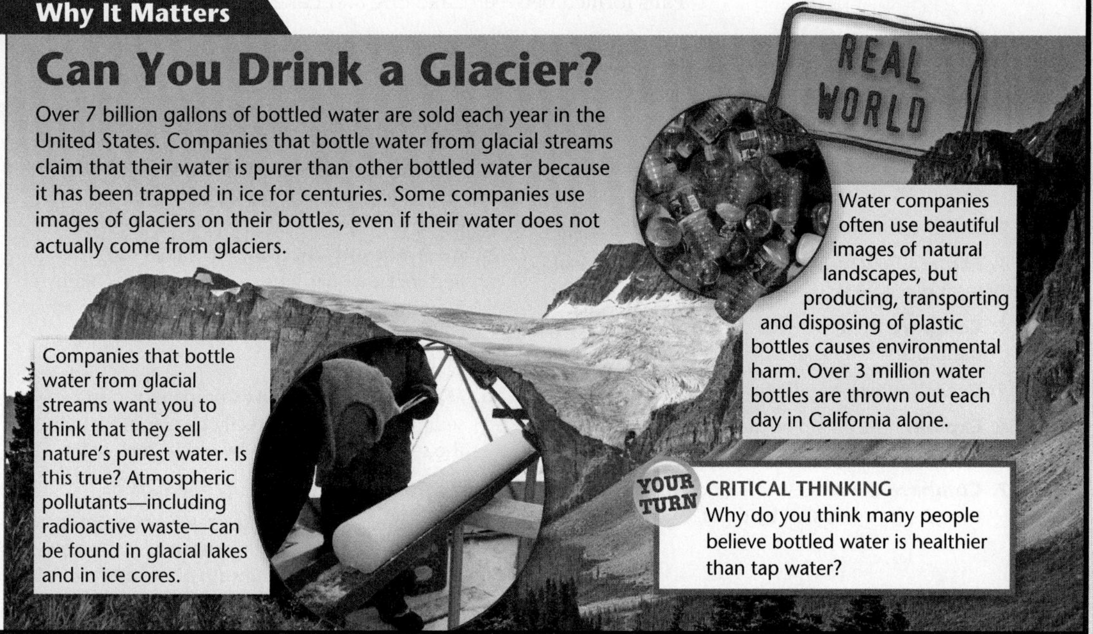

Water companies often use beautiful images of natural landscapes, but producing, transporting and disposing of plastic bottles causes environmental harm. Over 3 million water bottles are thrown out each day in California alone.

Companies that bottle water from glacial streams want you to think that they sell nature's purest water. Is this true? Atmospheric pollutants—including radioactive waste—can be found in glacial lakes and in ice cores.

YOUR TURN **CRITICAL THINKING**
Why do you think many people believe bottled water is healthier than tap water?

Why It Matters

Pollutants can travel long distances in the atmosphere and end up in the precipitation that forms glaciers. Even radioactive waste has been detected in glaciers. Nevertheless, glaciers are an often-used symbol of purity. Despite the image of health, recent studies confirm that bottled water is no healthier than tap water.

Answer to Your Turn

Critical Thinking Answers will vary. Students may note the role of marketing.

Close

Reteaching — BASIC

Chart Glacial Landforms Make a class chart of glacial landforms. Divide the class into three groups. Ask students in one group to provide the names of different types of glacial landforms. Make a list of them on the board. Have the second group come up with a description for each landform. Add the descriptions to the board. Ask the third group to indicate whether each landform results from glacial erosion or deposition. Record their answers on the chart. Students may make copies of the finished chart to help them study glacial landforms.
LS Verbal Co-op Learning

Quiz — GENERAL

1. How does a hanging valley form and what happens when a stream flows from it? (A hanging valley forms when a tributary glacier cuts a shallower valley than the main valley glacier. The tributary valley is suspended above the floor of the main valley. A waterfall forms when a stream flows from a hanging valley.)
2. What is meltwater? (Meltwater is the stream of melted ice that flows from a receding glacier.)
3. Why do salt lakes most commonly form in dry climates? (Evaporation is rapid and precipitation is low in dry climates. Dissolved salt remains behind as water evaporates from lakes.)

Close, *continued*

Answers to Section Review

1. A cirque is a deep, steep bowl-shaped depression produced by glacial erosion. An arête is a sharp, jagged ridge that forms between cirques. A horn is a sharp, jagged ridge that forms when several arêtes are joined.
2. Features formed by glacial deposition include erratics, drumlins, moraines, outwash plains, kettles, eskers, glacial lakes, and meltwater streams.
3. Long narrow lakes form when terminal and lateral moraines block existing streams.
4. Glacial deposition occurs as a glacier melts and deposits material it has collected. Glacial erosion occurs when a glacier carries material away, leaving depressions in the bedrock, and when this material is dragged, causing abrasions in the rock.
5. A kettle forms when a chunk of glacial ice that has been buried in drift melts. A cavity forms in the drift, which collapses into the cavity to produce a depression.
6. An alpine glacier erodes mountainous regions, creating landforms such as cirques, arêtes, and hanging valleys.
7. Both rivers and glaciers pick up and carry rocks and other sediment. However, while rivers create V-shaped valleys and floodplains, glaciers, because of their size and density, form unique landforms, such as U-shaped valleys, horns, and cirques.

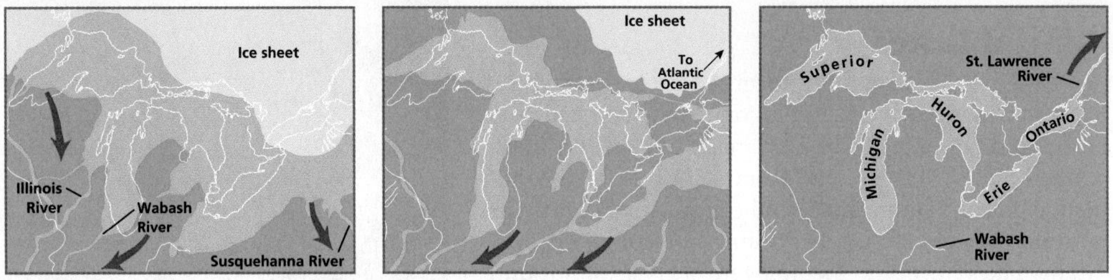

Early Ice Retreat The ice sheet that covered much of North America formed enormous lakes.

Late Ice Retreat As the ice sheet retreated, the lakes became smaller and the drainage pattern changed.

Today's Great Lakes Uplifting of the land reduced the Great Lakes to their present sizes.

Figure 7 The Great Lakes in the northern United States were formed by a massive continental glacier.

History of the Great Lakes

The Great Lakes of North America formed as a result of erosion and deposition by a continental glacier, as shown in **Figure 7.** Glacial erosion widened and deepened existing river valleys. Moraines to the south blocked off the ends of these valleys. As the ice sheet melted, the meltwater was trapped in the valleys by the moraines, and lakes formed.

In their early stages, the lakes emptied to the south into the Wabash and Illinois Rivers, which flowed into the Mississippi River. Later, the lakes grew larger and also drained into the Atlantic Ocean through the Susquehanna, Mohawk, and Hudson River valleys.

After the glacial period, the crust rose as the weight of the ice was removed. The lake beds uplifted and shrank. The uplift of the land caused the lakes to drain to the northeast through the St. Lawrence River. As a result of this northeasterly flow, Niagara Falls formed between Lake Erie and Lake Ontario.

Section 2 Review

Key Ideas

1. **Describe** the following landscape features: a cirque, an arête, and a horn.
2. **List** five features that form by glacial deposition.
3. **Explain** how terminal and lateral moraines can form glacial lakes.
4. **Compare** the process of glacial deposition with the process of glacial erosion.
5. **Describe** how a kettle forms.
6. **Explain** how an alpine glacier can change the topography of a mountainous area.
7. **Compare** the process of erosion by glaciers with the process of erosion by rivers.

Critical Thinking

8. **Making Comparisons** Compare the processes that form ground moraines with the processes that form eskers.
9. **Analyzing Predictions** On a field trip, you find rock that has long, parallel grooves. Form a hypothesis that explains this feature. What other landforms would you try to find to test this hypothesis?
10. **Making Comparisons** Compare glacial sediment deposited directly by glacial ice with the sediment deposited by glacial meltwater.

Concept Mapping

11. Use the following terms to create a concept map: *cirque, stratified drift, roches moutonnées, moraine, till, glacial drift, kettle, outwash plains,* and *glacier.*

8. A ground moraine is the rocky, unsorted material left beneath the glacier when the ice melts. An esker is long winding ridge of gravel and sand that is deposited by melt water streams.
9. Answers may vary. Sample answer: The hypothesis is that a glacier once moved across the area. I would try to find erratics, eskers, kettle lakes, and drumlins.

Answers continued on page 507B

Differentiated Instruction

Alternative Assessment

Modeling Glacial Landforms Direct students to make a three-dimensional model, using clay, papier-mâché, or plaster of Paris, that shows different landforms created by glaciation. Tell them to label each landform. **LS Kinesthetic/Visual**

SECTION 3

Ice Ages

ENVIRONMENTAL CONNECTION

Key Ideas	Key Terms	Why It Matters
❯ Describe glacial and interglacial periods within an ice age. ❯ Summarize the theory that best accounts for the ice ages.	**ice age** **Milankovitch theory**	Given global warming, an advance of glaciation seems remote, but it's only a matter of time.

Today, continental glaciers are located mainly in latitudes near the North and South Poles. However, thousands of years ago, ice sheets covered much more of Earth's surface. An **ice age** is a long period of climatic cooling during which the continents are glaciated repeatedly. Several major ice ages have occurred during Earth's geologic history, as shown in **Figure 1.** The earliest known ice age began about 800 million years ago. The most recent ice age began about 4 million years ago. The last advance of this ice age's massive ice sheets reached its peak about 18,000 years ago. Ice ages probably begin with a long, slow decrease in Earth's average temperatures. A drop in average global temperature of only about 5 °C may be enough to start an ice age.

ice age a long period of climatic cooling during which the continents are glaciated repeatedly

Glacial and Interglacial Periods

Continental glaciers advance and retreat several times during an ice age. The ice sheets advance during colder periods and retreat during warmer periods. A period of cooler climate that is characterized by the advancement of glaciers is called a *glacial period*. A period of warmer climate that is characterized by the retreat of glaciers is called an *interglacial period*. Currently, Earth is in an interglacial period of the most recent ice age.

Ice age
Glacial period
Interglacial period

Figure 1 Glacial and Interglacial Periods

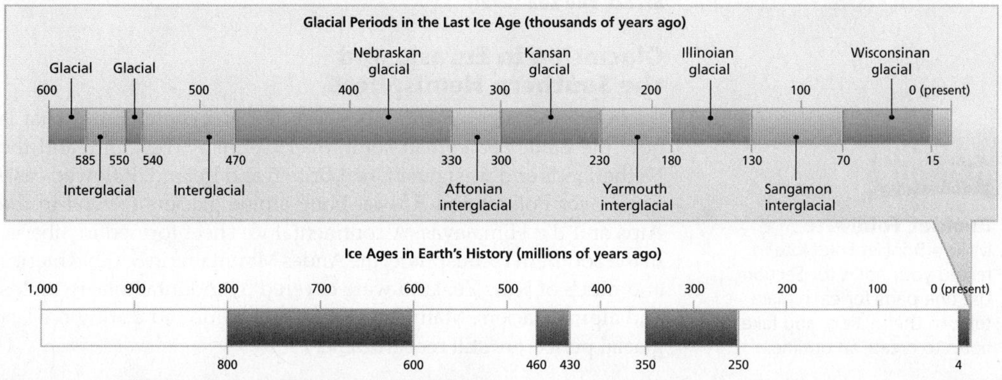

Section 3

Focus

Overview

This section describes the history and effect of Earth's ice ages, the difference between glacial and interglacial periods, and hypotheses about the causes of ice ages.

Bellringer

Ask students to describe what they think Earth would be like during an ice age. (Answers may vary. Students may describe a snow-covered landscape populated by woolly mammoths and other animals from the last ice age.)
LS Verbal

Motivate

Discussion — GENERAL

Ice-Age Mammals Show images of ice-age animals such as saber-toothed cats, woolly rhinos, mammoths, and giant ground sloths. Images can be found at the Web site of the National Museum of Natural History in Washington, D.C. Explain that about 80 species of mammals became extinct at the end of the last ice age and that there are several hypotheses about the cause. Have students suggest reasons why these mammals may have become extinct. (Answers may vary. Current hypotheses include climate change, human hunting, disease, and a combination of these factors.)
LS Logical

Key Resources

Chapter Resource File
- Directed Reading BASIC

Technology
- Transparencies
  Bellringer
  86 Ice Ages of Earth's History

Teach

Environmental Connection

Climate Change Earth is currently in the middle of an interglacial period. The last massive ice sheets started to retreat about 15,000 years ago. Since then, the climate slowly warmed, with shorter periods of cooling. The American Association for the Advancement of Science, the Intergovernmental Panel on Climate Change, and other major science organizations agree that human activities have contributed to warming trends in the last 150 years.

Debate — ADVANCED

Global Warming Have interested students research and debate whether global warming might stall the next glacial period. You may wish to assign students to prepare arguments for and against this hypothesis. **LS Verbal/Logical**

Internet Activity — GENERAL

Vanishing Ice Caps Tell students that recent research has found that Greenland's ice cap is thinning. Direct students to view NASA Goddard Space Flight Center's Scientific Visualization Studio Web site. Have students present a summary of the significance and implications of Greenland's vanishing ice. A worksheet designed to direct student research on this topic can be found in the **Chapter Resource File** booklet or by visiting www.thinkcentral.com and entering the keyword **HQXGLAX. LS Verbal**

Answer to Reading Check

The sea level was up to 140 m lower than it is now.

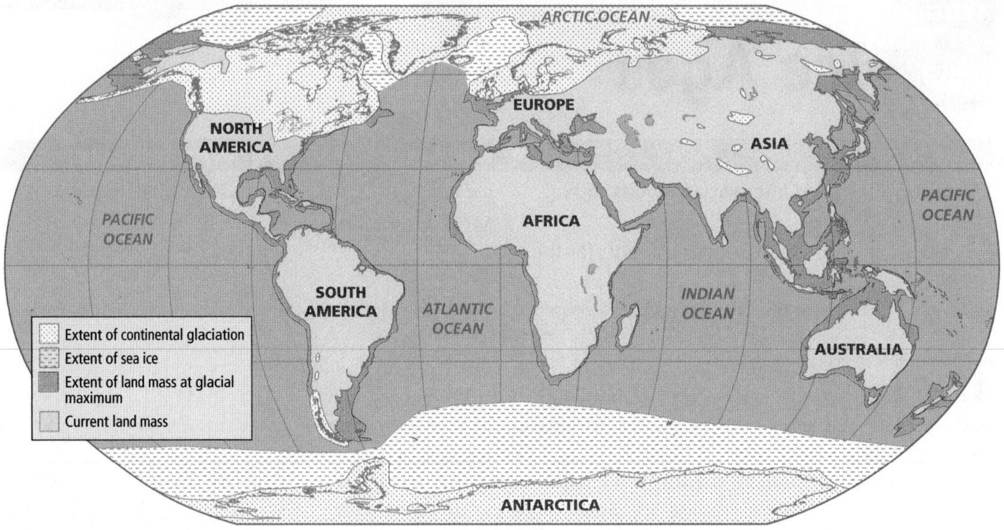

Figure 2 During the last glacial period, about 30% of Earth's surface was covered with ice.

Glaciation in North America

Glaciers covered about one-third of Earth's surface during the last glacial period. Most glaciation took place in North America and Eurasia. In some parts of North America, the ice was several kilometers thick. So much water was locked in ice during the last glacial period that sea level was as much as 140 m lower than it is today. As a result, the coastlines of the continents extended farther than they do today, as shown in **Figure 2.**

Canada and the mountainous regions of Alaska were buried under ice. In the mountains of the western United States, numerous small alpine glaciers joined to form larger glaciers. These large glaciers flowed outward from the Rocky Mountains and the Cascade and Sierra Nevada Ranges. A great continental ice sheet that was centered on what is now the Hudson Bay region of Canada spread as far south as the Missouri and Ohio Rivers.

Reading Check How did glaciation in the last glacial period affect the sea level?

Academic Vocabulary

period (PIR ee uhd) an interval or unit

SCILINKS.
www.scilinks.org
Topic: Ice Ages
Code: HQX0781

Glaciation in Eurasia and the Southern Hemisphere

In Europe, a continental ice sheet that was centered on what is now the Baltic Sea spread south over Germany, Belgium, and the Netherlands and west over Great Britain and Ireland. It flowed eastward over Poland and Russia. Long alpine glaciers formed in the Alps and the Himalayas. A continental ice sheet formed in Siberia. In the Southern Hemisphere, the Andes Mountains in South America and much of New Zealand were covered by mountainous ice fields and alpine glaciers. Many land features that formed during the last glacial period are still recognizable.

READING TOOLBOX

Booklet FoldNote
Make a Booklet FoldNote to record your notes for Section 3. Use one page for each main topic in the section, and take notes to create an outline.

READING TOOLBOX

Booklet FoldNote

Answers will vary. Students should consult Appendix A for tips on making a booklet FoldNote. Students' booklets should devote a page to each of the main topics in Section 3.

Differentiated Instruction

Special Education Students

Timeline To help students understand the idea of a geologic timeline, ask them to make a timeline of their own lives. Ask students to draw a one-pointed arrow that starts at the left edge of the paper and points right. Then have them divide the arrow into equal parts with 20 short lines, labeled from 1 to 20 years. Tell them to plot the following important life events under the correct years: I was born, I learned to walk, I started school, and Today. Then, ask them to add three important events that they choose themselves. **LS Logical**

Causes of Glaciation

The repeated glaciation of Earth's surface is caused by a variety of complex factors. These factors range from very rapid events to very slow processes. For example, the movement of tectonic plates happens very slowly but can cause changes in global circulation patterns of air and ocean water. These changes may lead to ice ages. Scientists have also proposed a number of ideas to explain glacial and interglacial periods. The leading explanation is the Milankovitch theory.

The Milankovitch Theory

A Serbian scientist named Milutin Milankovitch proposed a theory to explain the cause of glacial periods. Milankovitch noticed that climate change occurs in cycles. He thought that these cycles could be linked to cycles in Earth's movement relative to the sun. The **Milankovitch theory** is the theory that cyclical changes in Earth's orbit and in the tilt of Earth's axis occur over thousands of years and cause climatic changes.

Three periodic changes occur in the way that Earth moves around the sun, as **Figure 3** shows. First, the shape of Earth's orbit, or *eccentricity*, changes from nearly circular to elongated and back to nearly circular every 100,000 years. The second change occurs in the tilt of Earth's axis. Every 41,000 years, the tilt of Earth's axis varies between about 22.2° and 24.5°. A third periodic change is caused by the circular motion, or *precession*, of Earth's axis. Precession causes the axis to change its position, which is often described as a wobble. The axis of Earth traces a complete circle every 25,700 years.

Milankovitch calculated how these three factors may affect the distribution of solar energy that reaches Earth's surface. Changes in the distribution of solar energy affects global temperatures, which may cause periods of glacial advance and retreat.

Math Skills

Earth's Tilt The current angle of Earth's tilt is 23.5°. That angle is decreasing. If the tilt moves from 24.5° to 22.2° over 41,000 years, estimate how many years will pass before Earth's current tilt reaches 22.2°.

Milankovitch theory the theory that cyclical changes in Earth's orbit and in the tilt of Earth's axis occur over thousands of years and cause climatic changes

Figure 3 According to the Milankovitch theory, the distribution of solar radiation that Earth receives varies because of three kinds of changes in Earth's position relative to the sun.

THINK central
INTERACT ONLINE
(Keyword: HQXGLAF3)

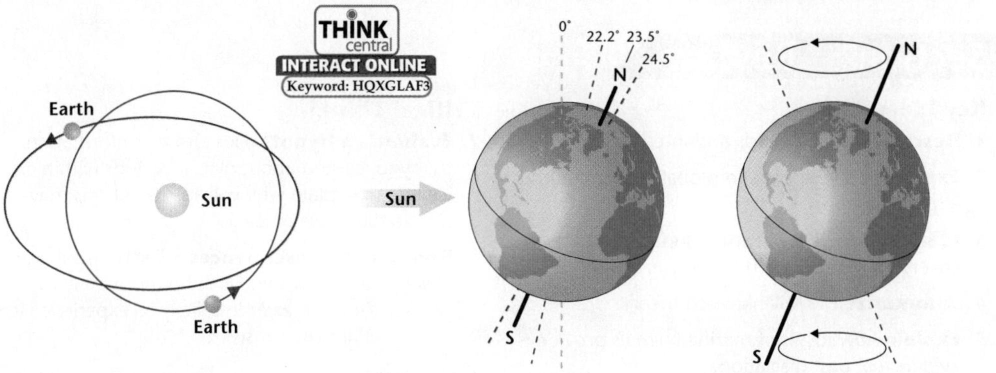

Eccentricity Changes in orbital eccentricity cause an increase in seasonality in one hemisphere and reduce seasonality in the other hemisphere.

Tilt Over a period of 41,000 years, the tilt of Earth's axis varies between 22.2° and 24.5°. The poles receive more solar energy when the tilt angle is greater.

Precession A gradual change, or "wobble," in the orientation of Earth's axis affects the relationship between Earth's tilt and eccentricity.

Math Skills

Answer

24.5° − 22.2° = 2.3°
23.5° − 22.2° = 1.3°
(41,000 years/2.3°) ×
1.3° = 23,000 years

Close

Reteaching — BASIC

Reading Organizer Have students outline the chapter material using the section headings and subheadings. Then, have students fill in the outline by providing additional detail for each heading. **LS Verbal**

Quiz — GENERAL

1. What is an ice age? (An ice age is a long period of climatic cooling during which the continents are glaciated repeatedly.)
2. How much of Earth's surface was covered by ice during the last glacial period? (one-third)
3. Explain the differences among Earth's eccentricity, tilt, and precession. (Eccentricity is the shape of Earth's orbit. Tilt is the angle of Earth's axis. Precession is the circular motion of Earth's axis.)

Key Resources

Technology

- Transparencies
  87 The Milankovitch Theory

Career

Glaciologist Glaciologists are scientists who study the physical properties of snow and ice. You might call them "ice experts." These scientists design experiments to learn more about global sea level and climate changes. Glaciologists also monitor ice movement and changes in elevation; they measure ice markers, take ice cores, and analyze trapped atmospheric gases from ancient times to gain information. Glaciologists have a college degree in geology.

Close, *continued*

Answers to Section Review

1. A glacial period is a period in which the climate is cooler and glaciers advance. An interglacial period is a period in which the climate is warmer and glaciers retreat.
2. The sea level decreases during a glacial period because more water is stored in glacial ice.
3. In North America: Canada, the mountainous region of Alaska, the Rocky Mountains, the Cascade and Sierra Nevada ranges, and from the Canadian border to the Missouri and Ohio rivers in the United States; in Europe and Asia: Belgium, the Netherlands, Great Britain, Poland, Russia, Siberia, the Tibetan Plateau, the mountains of Asia, and from the Baltic Sea to over Germany; and parts of South America, Africa, and New Zealand
4. The Milankovitch theory states that Earth's eccentricity, tilt, and precession affect the distribution of solar energy to Earth's surface. When the intensity of solar energy that reaches Earth is less, global temperature decreases, which can cause a glacial period.
5. Because the shells of Foraminifera curl to the right instead of to the left when they live in water warmer than 8 °C, scientists can determine the temperature of the water when the sediment layer containing Foraminifera fossils formed.
6. Glacial periods may start when dust from volcanic eruptions blocks the sun's rays. Glacial periods may be caused by a change the amount of solar energy that the sun produces.

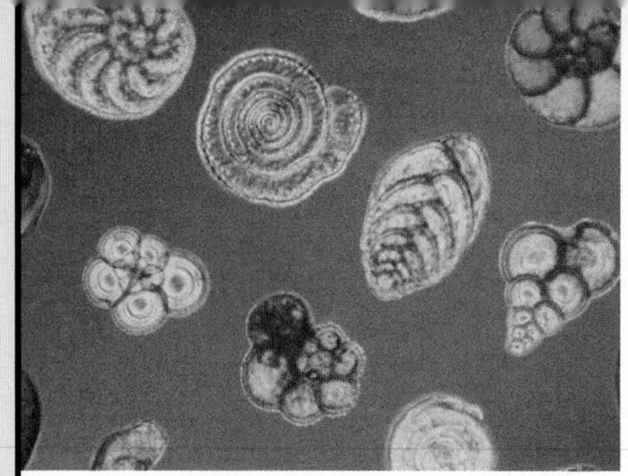

Figure 4 The microscopic shells of organisms from the order Foraminifera give clues to climate change.

Biological Evidence of Glaciation

Evidence for past glaciation has been discovered in the shells of dead marine animals found on the ocean floor. The formation of the shells of organisms from the order Foraminifera, shown in **Figure 4,** is affected by the temperature of the ocean water. Temperature of the ocean water affects the amount of oxygen that the water dissolves. The amount of oxygen in turn affects how these organisms form their shells. In addition, organisms that lived in ocean waters that were warmer than 8 °C coiled their shells to the right. Organisms that lived in ocean waters that were much cooler coiled their shells to the left.

By studying Foraminifera shells in the layers of sediment on the ocean floor, scientists have discovered evidence of different glacial periods. Scientists have found that the record of changes in marine sediments closely follows the cycle of cooling and warming predicted by the Milankovitch theory.

Other Explanations for Glaciation

Other explanations for the causes of glacial periods have been suggested. Most of these explanations indicate that the glacial periods were caused by changes in the amount of solar energy that reached Earth's surface that were not caused by changes in Earth's position relative to the sun. Some scientists propose that changes in solar energy are caused by varying amounts of energy produced by the sun. Other scientists suggest that glacial periods start when volcanic dust blocks the sun's rays. Volcanic dust in Earth's atmosphere prevents solar radiation from reaching Earth's surface. As a result, Earth's average global temperature drops.

Section 3 Review

Key Ideas

1. **Describe** glacial periods and interglacial periods.
2. **Explain** what happens to global sea level during a glacial period.
3. **Identify** the areas of Earth's surface that were covered by ice during the last glacial period.
4. **Summarize** the Milankovitch theory.
5. **Explain** how fossils of marine animals provide evidence of past glaciation.
6. **Describe** two explanations for glacial periods other than the Milankovitch theory.

Critical Thinking

7. **Evaluating Hypotheses** Use the information that you learned about glacial periods within an ice age to explain why volcanic eruptions may not be the cause of ice ages.
8. **Predicting Consequences** If Earth's orbit were always circular, would Earth be more likely to experience ice ages or less likely to experience ice ages? Explain your answer.

Concept Mapping

9. Use the following terms to create a concept map: *ice age, glacial period, interglacial period, Milankovitch theory, eccentricity, tilt, volcanic eruption,* and *precession.*

7. Volcanic eruptions have a short-term effect on Earth's atmosphere, so they are not likely to cause long ice ages.
8. Answers may vary. Sample answer: If Earth's orbit were circular, Earth would be less likely to have ice ages because when Earth's orbit is more circular, Earth receives more energy from the sun.
9. An *ice age* has *glacial periods* and *interglacial periods* and may be caused by *volcanic eruptions* or by changes in Earth's *eccentricity, precession,* and *tilt,* which are described in the *Milankovitch theory.*

Differentiated Instruction

Alternative Assessment

Poster Project Direct students to make a three-panel poster that shows Earth's ice ages and glacial and interglacial periods, the areas of Earth covered by ice during the last glacial period, and the various explanations about what causes the start of an ice age. **LS Verbal/Visual**

Watermelon Ice

WEIRD SCIENCE

Believe it or not, glacial ice is home to hundreds of different organisms, including over 60 different species of snow algae in the United States. One type of red snow algae forms the base of the glacial food web. These algae cause pink snow, known as "watermelon ice." When a person walks on the pink snow, the crushed algae release a compound that smells like watermelon!

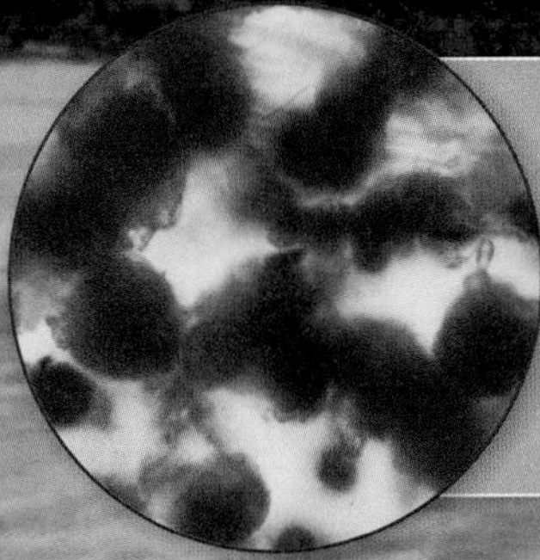

These red snow algae contain carotene—the pigment found in carrots, oranges, flowers, and flamingoes. Carotene helps another pigment, chlorophyll, in the process of photosynthesis and protects the organism from intense exposure to the sun.

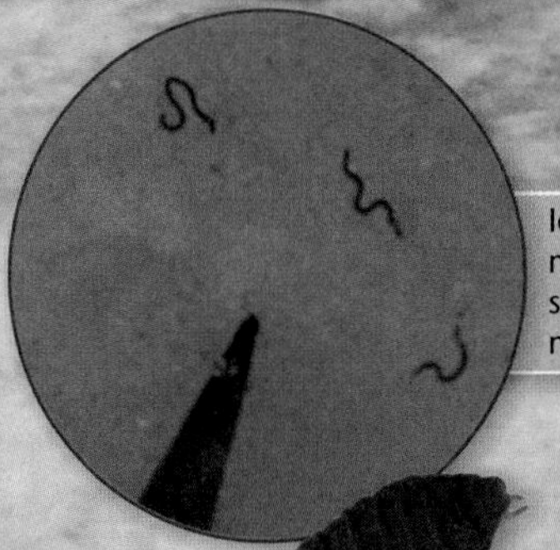

Ice worms come out by the millions at night. They eat snow algae and other microscopic organisms.

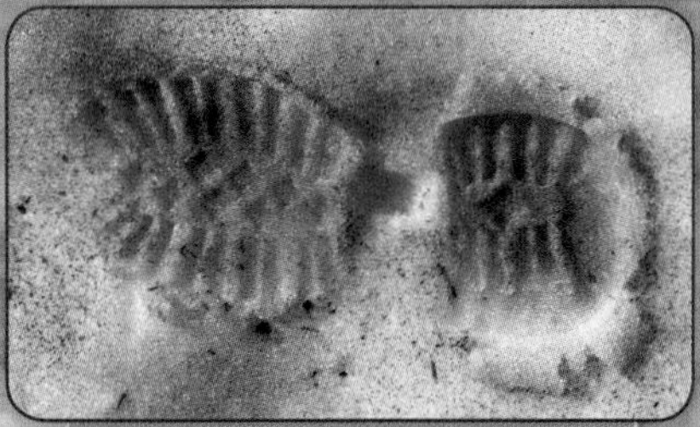

Walking on watermelon ice can stain the soles of a person's shoes.

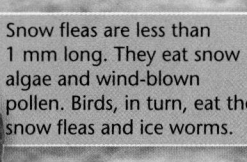

Snow fleas are less than 1 mm long. They eat snow algae and wind-blown pollen. Birds, in turn, eat the snow fleas and ice worms.

YOUR TURN

UNDERSTANDING CONCEPTS
How does the color of red snow algae help them survive the glacial environment?

ONLINE RESEARCH
Use the Internet to find out more about one of the organisms described above. Write a one-page summary to describe your findings.

Watermelon Ice

Glaciers are sometimes thought to be lifeless deserts of ice and snow with conditions too hostile to support any life. The reality is that glacial ice is home to hundreds of different organisms that use the sun's energy and the glacial meltwater to create habitats that influence foodchains on the glacier and beyond. Various forms of bacteria and cyanobacteria (blue-green bacteria) grow in the upper layers of the glacial ice and result in "carpets" of colourful ice that are commonly called "watermelon ice".

In addition to acting as sunscreen, carotene is an accessory pigment used in photosynthesis. Carotene absorbs different wavelenghts of sunlight than does chlorphyll.

Answers to Your Turn

Understanding Concepts The red pigment helps protect the algae from the intense sunlight.

Online Research Answers will vary. Students should summarize what they learn about red snow algae, ice worms, or snow fleas.

Making Models Lab

Time Required
two 45-minute class periods

Lab Ratings
EASY → HARD

Teacher Preparation 3
Student Setup 1
Concept Level 3
Cleanup 4

Skills Acquired
- Constructing Models
- Observing
- Measuring
- Collecting Data
- Analyzing Models
- Interpreting Models

Scientific Methods
In this lab, students will
- Make Observations
- Analyze the Results
- Draw Conclusions

Materials
The materials listed on the page are enough for groups of two to four students. Blocks of ice must be prepared prior to the day the lab is conducted to allow sufficient time for the water to freeze.

Making Models Lab

90 min

Glaciers and Sea-Level Change

What You'll Do
- **Model** the melting of an ice sheet.
- **Analyze** the effects of melting ice on sea level.

What You'll Need
block, ice, 5 cm × 5 cm × 5 cm
block, wooden, 5 cm × 5 cm × 5 cm
pan, 30 cm × 40 cm × 10 cm
pebbles (1 kg)
ruler, metric
sand (1 kg)
water

Safety

Today, glaciers hold only about 2% of Earth's water. But if the polar ice sheets melted, the coastal areas of many countries would flood. Many major cities, such as New York, New Orleans, Houston, and Los Angeles, would flood if the sea level rose only a few meters. In this lab, you will construct a model to simulate what would happen if the Antarctic ice sheet melted.

Procedure

1. Calculate and record the approximate surface area of the bottom of the pan. Area (A) is equal to length (l) times width (w), or $A = l \times w$, and is expressed in square units.
2. Calculate and record the overall volume of the ice block and the area of one side of the ice block. Volume (V) is equal to length (l) times width (w) times height (h), or $V = l \times w \times h$, and is expressed in cubic units.
3. Add the sand and small pebbles to one end of the pan so that they cover about half of the area of the pan and slope toward the middle of the pan. Use the wooden block to elevate the end of the pan containing the sand and pebbles.
4. Slowly add water to the opposite end of the pan. Be sure that the water does not cover the sand and pebbles and touches only the edge of the sand.

Step 3

Tips and Tricks
To speed up the melting of the ice block, you may wish to use a hair drier or other safe heat source. This lab also can be done as a classroom demonstration. Tell the students to record the measurements as you make them.

5 Measure and record the depth of the water at the deepest point.

6 Measure and record the distance from the end of the pan covered with sand to the point where the sand touches the water.

7 Place the block of ice in the pan on top of the sand. Calculate and record the percentage of the total area of the pan that is covered by ice.

8 As the ice begins to melt, pick up the ice block. Note the appearance of the bottom of the ice block and the appearance of the sand under the ice block. Record what is happening to the ice block and what is happening to the sand under the ice block. Place the ice block back on the sand.

9 While the ice is melting, calculate the expected rise in the pan's water level by using the following formula:

$$\text{rise in water level} = \frac{\text{volume of water in ice block}}{\text{area of pan covered by water}}$$

10 When the ice is completely melted, measure and record the depth of water at the deepest point.

11 Measure and record the distance from the end of the pan covered with sand to the point where the sand touches the water.

Step 4

Analysis

1. **Making Comparisons** Compare the depth of the water at the beginning of the lab with the depth at the end of the lab. Explain any differences.
2. **Analyzing Results** How did the distance from the end of the pan covered with sand to the point where the sand touches the water change? Explain your answer.
3. **Compare and Contrast** How does the ice-block model differ from a glacier on Earth?
4. **Drawing Conclusions** How does the ice-block model represent what would happen on Earth if the Antarctic polar ice sheet melted?

Extension

Evaluating Models In this lab, you used a physical model to simulate an occurrence in nature. In what other ways do scientists use models? What kinds of errors can occur when models are used?

Answers to Analysis

1. The depth of the water is greater at the end of the exercise than at the beginning because the ice melted.
2. The distance decreased because the surface of the liquid water increased.
3. Answers may vary. Sample answer: The ice-block model does not have all of the physical features of a glacier on Earth. For example, the ice in the model has not undergone the compression of a real glacier. Therefore, the volume of water in the ice block is less than the volume of water in actual glacier ice.
4. The water on Earth would enter the ocean, which would cause sea levels to rise and to cover land just as the water covered some of the sand in the model.

Answer to Extension

Answers may vary. Sample answer: Scientists study the universe by making models of things that are too large or too small to be easily observed in nature. Models can be simpler than an actual item or situation or they can be out of proportion. These factors can cause errors.

Gulkana Glacier

Internet Activity GENERAL

Gulkana Glacier Have students compare photographs of the Gulkana Glacier with the topographic map. The Gulkana Glacier home page of the United States Geological Survey Web site contains aerial photographs and other images of the glacier. Have students write a short essay that describes the Gulkana landscape. A worksheet designed to direct student research on this topic can be found in the **Chapter Resource File** booklet or by visiting **www.thinkcentral.com** and entering the keyword **HQXGLAX.**

LS Visual

Answers to Map Skills Activity

1. about 6.25 km
2. 63° 16.9'N latitude 145° 21'W longitude
3. northwest
4. southwest
5. Answers may vary. Sample answer: The movement of the glacier is toward the lower elevation. For measurement stake A, the elevation becomes lower toward the southwest; for measurement stake B, the elevation becomes lower toward the south. The direction of flow is constrained by surrounding topography.
6. Answers may vary: Sample answer: Scientists are probably measuring the rate at which the glacier is flowing.

MAPS *in Action*

Gulkana Glacier

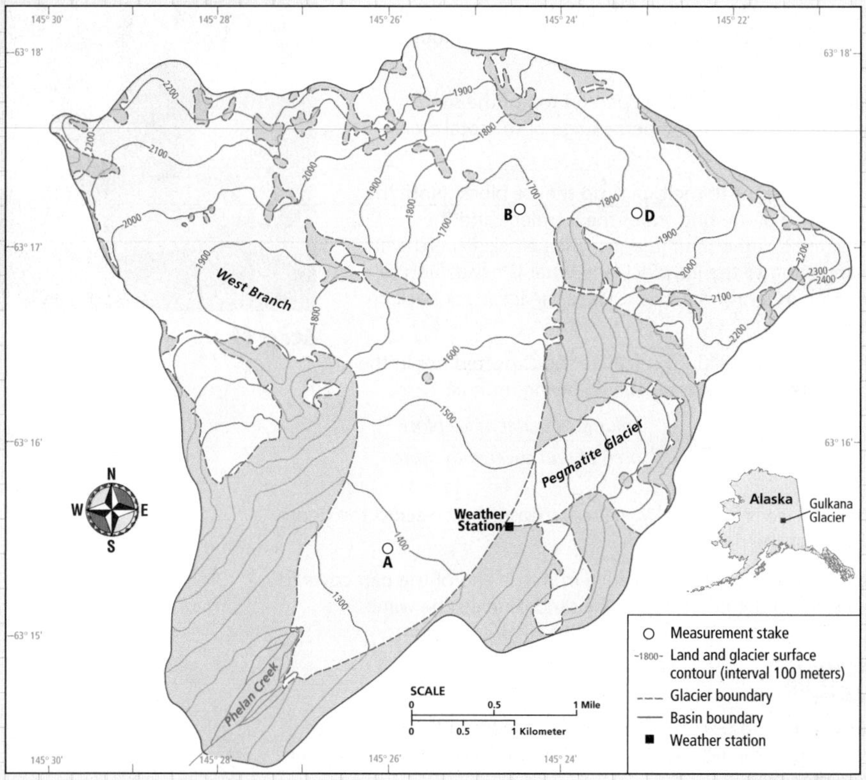

Map Skills Activity

This contour map shows the elevation and boundaries of the Gulkana Glacier located in Alaska. Use the map to answer the questions below.

1. **Using a Key** Estimate the length of the Gulkana Glacier from its northernmost point to its southernmost point.
2. **Analyzing Data** Estimate the latitude and longitude of the glacier's highest point.
3. **Identifying Trends** In which direction do you think Gulkana Glacier is moving at measurement stake D?
4. **Identifying Trends** In which direction do you think Gulkana Glacier is moving at measurement stake A?
5. **Predicting Consequences** Why might you think that the glacier moves in different directions at measurement stake A and measurement stake B?
6. **Analyzing Data** What do you think the scientists are measuring at the measurement stakes?

Key Resources

Technology

- Transparencies
  88 Gulkana Glacier

Chapter 17

Summary

THINK central
SUPER SUMMARY
Keyword: HQXGLAS

Key Ideas

Section 1

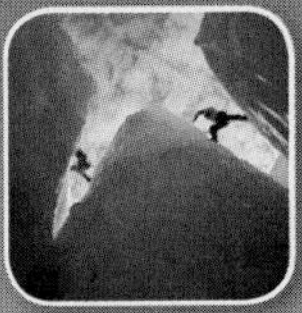

Glaciers: Moving Ice

- Glaciers form at high elevations and in polar regions as layers of snow and ice build up.
- The two main types of glaciers are alpine glaciers, which form in mountainous areas and are relatively small, and continental glaciers, which are massive ice sheets that cover millions of square kilometers.
- Glaciers move by basal slip, sliding over the thin layer of water and sediment that separates the ice from the ground, and internal plastic flow, the process by which grains of ice deform under pressure and slide over each other.
- Three features of glaciers are large cracks called crevasses, ice sheets that extend out over the ocean called ice shelves, and large pieces of ice that break off into the ocean called icebergs.

Key Terms

glacier, p. 455
alpine glacier, p. 456
continental glacier, p. 456
basal slip, p. 457
internal plastic flow, p. 457
crevasse, p. 458

Section 2

Glacial Erosion and Deposition

- Features produced by glacial erosion include U-shaped valleys, hanging valleys, bowl-shaped depressions called cirques, sharp ridges called arêtes, pointed peaks called horns, and rounded rocks called roches moutonnées.
- Features formed by glacial deposition include large transported rocks called erratics, depressions called kettles, ridges called eskers, mounds of till called drumlins, and ridges of sediment called moraines.
- Glaciers may form lake basins by eroding the land or by depositing sediments.

Key Terms

cirque, p. 460
arête, p. 460
horn, p. 460
erratic, p. 462
glacial drift, p. 462
till, p. 462
moraine, p. 463
kettle, p. 464
esker, p. 464

Section 3

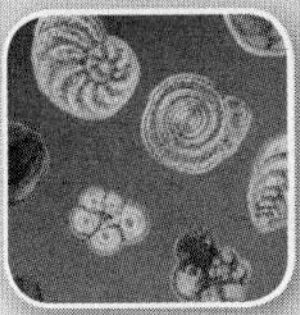

Ice Ages

- During an ice age, cooler glacial periods, characterized by the advancement of glaciers, alternate with warmer interglacial periods, characterized by the retreat of glaciers.
- The Milankovitch theory best accounts for the ice ages. It suggests that glacial periods are caused by changes in the distribution of solar energy Earth receives. These changes are caused by regular changes in the eccentricity of Earth's orbit, the tilt of Earth's axis, and precession.

Key Terms

ice age, p. 467
Milankovitch theory, p. 469

Chapter Summary

Using THINK central Resources

Super Summary

Have students connect the major concepts in this chapter through an interactive Super Summary. Visit www.thinkcentral.com and type in the keyword **HQXGLAS** to access the Super Summary for this chapter.

Chapter Review

Assignment Guide	
Section	**Questions**
1	1–3, 5, 7, 10–13, 22, 24, 27
2	6, 8, 14, 15, 19–21
3	4, 9, 16–18, 25, 31–34
1 and 2	26
1–3	23, 28–30

Reading Toolbox

1. Sample information for students' charts follows. Basal slip: occurs where the glacier touches the ground; glacier's weight causes the basal ice to melt, allowing the glacier to slide over the ground. Internal plastic flow: occurs throughout the glacier, from deformation of ice grains; the edges move more slowly than the center.

Using Key Terms

2–9. Answers may vary but should show that students understand the definitions of and differences between key terms.

Understanding Key Ideas

10. b
11. a
12. a
13. b
14. a
15. b
16. a
17. c

Short Answer

18. The climate cools during an ice age.

Chapter 17 Review

1. **Classification** Make a three-column table to classify the two main ways that glaciers move. Label the first column "Type of movement," the second column "Where movement occurs on glacier," and the third column "Description of movement." Fill in your table with details about basal slip and internal plastic flow.

READING TOOLBOX

USING KEY TERMS

Use each of the following terms in a separate sentence.

2. *glacier*
3. *crevasse*
4. *ice age*

For each pair of terms, explain how the meanings of the terms differ.

5. *alpine glacier* and *continental glacier*
6. *till* and *moraine*
7. *basal slip* and *internal plastic flow*
8. *cirque* and *arête*
9. *glacial period* and *interglacial period*

UNDERSTANDING KEY IDEAS

10. Glaciers that form in mountainous areas are called
    a. continental glaciers.
    b. alpine glaciers.
    c. icebergs.
    d. ice shelves.
11. A glacier will move by sliding when the base of the ice and the underlying rock are separated by a thin layer of
    a. water and sediment.
    b. snow.
    c. pebbles.
    d. drift.
12. What part of a glacier moves fastest when the glacier moves by internal plastic flow?
    a. The center of the glacier moves fastest.
    b. The bottom of the glacier moves fastest.
    c. The edges of the glacier move fastest.
    d. The whole ice mass moves at the same speed.
13. Icebergs form when ice breaks off of a(n)
    a. crevasse.
    b. ice shelf.
    c. alpine glacier.
    d. esker.
14. As a glacier moves through a valley, it carves out a(n)
    a. U shape.
    b. esker.
    c. V shape.
    d. moraine.
15. A deposit of stratified drift is called a(n)
    a. drumlin.
    b. outwash plain.
    c. ground moraine.
    d. roche moutonnée.
16. One component of the Milankovitch theory is
    a. the circular motion of Earth's axis.
    b. continental drift.
    c. volcanic activity.
    d. landslide activity.
17. Which of the following is not a theory for the cause of ice ages?
    a. volcanic eruptions
    b. variations in Earth's orbit
    c. Foraminifera shell coils
    d. changes in Earth's axial orientation

SHORT ANSWER

18. How does climate change during an ice age?
19. What are the four types of moraines, and how are they different from each other?
20. Identify three types of landforms created by alpine glaciers.
21. In what two ways do glacial lakes form?
22. How do the processes of basal slip and internal plastic flow differ?

19. A *lateral moraine* is sediment deposited along the sides of a valley glacier. A *medial moraine* is a combination of two adjacent lateral moraines that occurs when two or more valley glaciers join. A *ground moraine* is the unsorted material left when the ice melts. A *terminal moraine* is a small ridge of till deposited at the leading edge of a melting glacier.
20. Students should identify three of the following landforms: cirques, or bowl-shaped depressions; arêtes, or sharp, jagged ridges between cirques; horns, or sharp, pyramid-like peaks that form when several arêtes are joined; and hanging valleys, tributary valleys suspended on mountains high above the main valley floor.
21. Some glacial lakes form when glaciers erode surfaces and leave depressions. Others form in the uneven surfaces of ground moraine deposits.
22. Basal slip is the process by which an entire glacier moves by slipping over a thin layer of water and sediment that is the result of the melting of the ice that is in contact with the ground. Internal plastic flow is the process by which the interior of a glacier moves as grains of ice deform under pressure and slip over each other.

CRITICAL THINKING

23. Identifying Relationships Why is it important for scientists to monitor and study the continental ice sheets that cover Greenland and Antarctica?

24. Applying Concepts Antarctic explorers need special training to travel safely over the ice sheet. Besides the cold, what structural aspects of the glaciers may be dangerous?

25. Evaluating Data What phenomenon other than decreased temperature and increased snowfall might signal the beginning of a glacial period?

CONCEPT MAPPING

26. Use the following terms to create a concept map: *snowfield, erosion, deposition, glacier, horn, arête, kettle, moraine, basal slip,* and *internal plastic flow.*

MATH SKILLS

Math Skills

27. Using Equations The area of Earth's surface that is covered with water is 361,000,000 km^2. The volume of water locked in ice in the Antarctic ice sheet is about 26,384,368 km^3. Use the following equation to find the average worldwide rise in sea level, in meters, that would occur if the Antarctic ice sheet melted.

$$\textit{rise in water level} = \frac{\textit{volume of water in ice sheet}}{\textit{area of Earth covered by water}}$$

28. Evaluating Data New York City has an average elevation of 27 m above sea level. Although highly unlikely, what would happen to the city if the Antarctic ice sheet suddenly melted and raised the worldwide sea level by 50 m?

WRITING SKILLS

29. Writing Persuasively Write a research proposal to the National Science Foundation that details a plan of action and reasons for studying the ice sheet in Greenland.

30. Writing from Research Research how ocean currents affect the polar icecaps. Write a short essay that describes global ocean currents and explains how they affect the formation and advancement of polar icecaps.

INTERPRETING GRAPHICS

The graph below shows the relationship between cycles of eccentricity, tilt, and precession. Use the graph to answer the questions that follow.

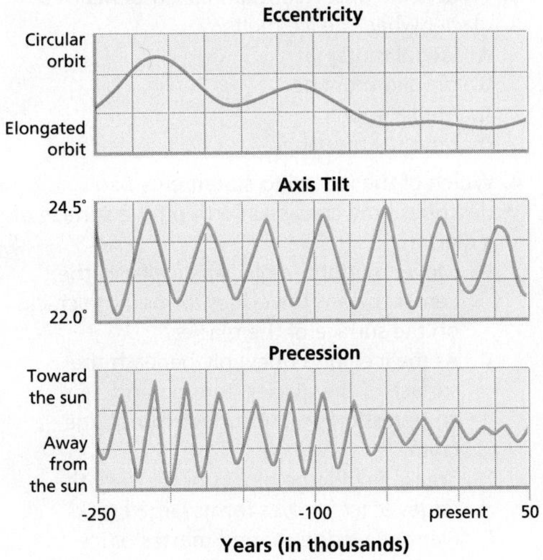

31. What was the angle of Earth's tilt 50,000 years ago?

32. Describe the shape of Earth's orbit 200,000 years ago.

33. How would the seasons 50,000 years from now be different from the seasons 50,000 years ago?

Chapter Review

Critical Thinking

23. If these ice sheets melted, the worldwide sea level could rise and could flood many coastal cities.
24. The surface of a glacier is brittle, which causes crevasses to form. Large pieces of an ice shelf may break off to form an iceberg.
25. The advancement of ice sheets and a drop in sea levels may be indications of the beginning of a glacial period.

Concept Mapping

26. Answers may vary but should include all of the terms listed. Sample answers appear at the end of this unit on p. 507D.

Math Skills

27. 26,384,368 km^3 ÷ 361,000,000 km^2 = 0.073 km = 73 m
28. Because the average water level would rise 50 m, New York would be 23 m under water (50 m − 27 m = 23 m).

Writing Skills

29. Answers may vary. Accept all reasonable answers.
30. Answers may vary. Accept all reasonable answers.

Interpreting Graphics

31. approximately 24.3°
32. more circular than now
33. There will be less seasonality 50,000 years from now than there was 50,000 years ago. There will be less snow melt in summer and more snowfall in winter. Although Earth's orbit and precession will be about the same as they were then, the tilt of the axis will be much less.

Estimated Time

To give students practice under more realistic testing conditions, allow them 30 minutes to answer all of the questions in this practice test.

Test Doctor

Question 1 Answer C is correct. Though glaciers are sometimes called *rivers of ice,* frozen water moves differently than water in its liquid state. So answer D is incorrect. Glacial ice cannot flow rapidly or move around obstacles easily, so answers A and B are incorrect. Both ice and water, however, do flow downward in response to gravity.

Question 4 Answer G is correct. Outward movement of ice sheets forms *ice shelves,* so answer answer F is incorrect. The breakage of large blocks of ice from the edges of ice shelves forms *icebergs,* so answer H is incorrect. Narrow, wedge-shaped masses of ice confined to small areas by the surrounding topography are *alpine glaciers,* so answer I is incorrect.

Question 8 From the information in the passage, the best choice is answer I. The text does not discuss how often ice ages occur, so students can rule out answer F. Answers G and H use the word *always,* which should serve as a warning flag to students. The text describes one instance but does not discuss what always happens.

Chapter 17 Standardized Test Prep

Understanding Concepts

Directions (1–4): For each question, write on a separate sheet of paper the letter of the correct answer.

1. Which statement *best* compares the movement of glacial ice to the movement of river water?
- **A.** Glacial ice moves more rapidly than water.
- **B.** Glacial ice cannot easily flow around barriers.
- **C.** Glacial ice moves in response to gravity.
- **D.** Glacial ice moves in the same way as water.

2. What landforms created by glaciers have bowl-like shapes?
- **F.** cirques
- **G.** arêtes
- **H.** horns
- **I.** roches moutonnées

3. What is the unsorted material left beneath a glacier when the ice melts?
- **A.** lateral moraine
- **B.** ground moraine
- **C.** medial moraine
- **D.** terminal moraine

4. Which of the following statements *best* describes how crevasses form on the surface of a glacier?
- **F.** Movement of the glacier's ice from the center toward the edges forms large cracks on the surface of the glacier.
- **G.** As the ice flows unevenly beneath the surface of the glacier, tension and compression on the surface form large cracks.
- **H.** Breakage of large blocks of ice from the edges of ice shelves forms large cracks.
- **I.** Narrow, wedge-shaped masses of ice confined to a small area form large cracks.

Directions (5–6): For each question, write a short response.

5. What is the term for all types of sediments deposited by a glacier?

6. What is the name of a jagged ridge that is formed between two or more cirques that cut into the same mountain?

Reading Skills

Directions (7–9): Read the passage below. Then, answer the questions.

Glacial and Interglacial Periods

Ice ages are periods during which ice collects in high latitudes and moves toward lower latitudes. During an ice age, there are periods of cold and of warmth. These periods are called *glacial* and *interglacial periods.* During glacial periods, enormous sheets of ice advance, grow bigger, and cover a large area. Because a large amount of sea water is frozen during glacial periods, the sea level around the world drops.

Warmer time periods that occur between glacial periods are known as interglacial periods. During an interglacial period, the large ice sheets begin to melt and the sea levels begin to rise again. Scientists believe that the last interglacial period began approximately 10,000 years ago and is still happening. For nearly 200 years, scientists have been debating what the current interglacial period might mean for humans and the possibility of a future glacial period.

7. According to the passage, which of the following statements is true?
- **A.** The last interglacial period began approximately 1,000 years ago.
- **B.** Scientists have been thinking about the next glacial period for two centuries.
- **C.** Ice ages are periods during which ice collects in the lower latitudes and moves toward higher latitudes.
- **D.** During glacial periods, enormous sheets of ice tend to melt, so they become smaller and cover less area.

8. Which of the following statements can be inferred from the information in the passage?
- **F.** On average, ice ages occur every 50,000 years and always start with a glacial period.
- **G.** Interglacial periods always last 10,000 years.
- **H.** Glacial periods always last 10,000 years.
- **I.** The current interglacial period will likely be followed by a glacial period.

9. If a new glacial period began tomorrow, what might happen to coastal cities?

Question 11 Full-credit answers should include the following points:
- as pressure builds up, heat energy is created which causes the ice to melt
- meltwater acts as a lubricant, decreasing friction between the glacier and the underlying obstacle, and allows the glacier to slide over obstacles
- once past the obstacle, the pressure decreases and the meltwater refreezes

Question 13 Answer F is the correct choice. Speed is the ratio between the distance moved and the time taken to move that distance. Students can use the following equation to find the answer:

$$x = 36 \text{ m} \div 180 \text{ days}$$

Students should arrive at an answer of 0.20 meters per day.

Interpreting Graphics

Directions (10–13): For each question below, record the correct answer on a separate sheet of paper.

Base your answers to questions 10 and 11 on the diagram below.

Basal Slip

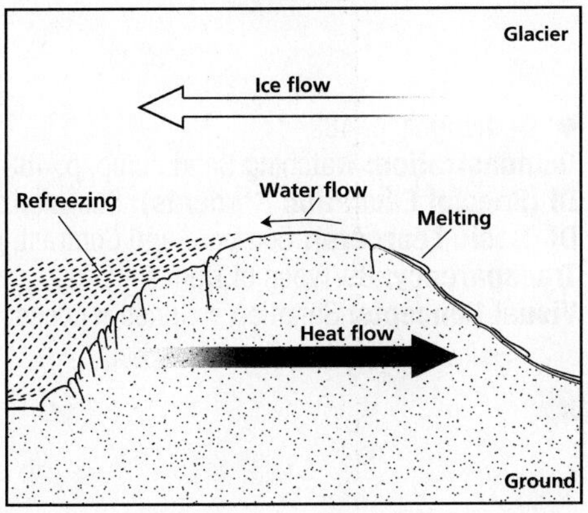

10. What causes the ice to melt in the diagram above?
A. Pressure decreases the melting point of the ice.
B. Pressure increases the melting point of the ice.
C. The ground heats the ice until it melts.
D. Ice at the base of a glacier does not melt.

11. How does meltwater influence basal slip?

Base your answer to question 12 on the table below.

World Cities and Their Elevations

City	Elevation (m)
New York City	27
Kiev, Ukraine	168
Buenos Aires, Argentina	25
Amsterdam, Netherlands	2

12. Although unlikely, what would happen to each of the cities listed in the table if the Antarctic ice sheet were to melt and raise the sea level by 50 m?

13. The movement of a glacier was recorded over a period of 180 days. During that time, the glacier moved a total of 36 m. What was the average speed of the glacier each day?
F. 0.20 m/day
G. 0.50 m/day
H. 2.00 m/day
I. 5.00 m/day

Test Tip

For a group of questions that refer to a diagram, graph, or table, read all of the questions quickly to determine what information you will need to glean from the graphic.

Standardized Test Prep

Using THINK central Resources

State Resources

- For specific resources for your state, visit www.thinkcentral.com and type in the keyword **HSHSTR.**

Answers

Understanding Concepts

1. C
2. F
3. B
4. G
5. glacial drift
6. arêtes

Reading Skills

7. B
8. I
9. As sea levels decreased, some coastal cities might become land-locked. Due to the withdrawal of ocean water, they may also experience changes in local wind and weather patterns.

Interpreting Graphics

10. A
11. Answers may vary. See Test Doctor for a detailed scoring rubric.
12. Only Kiev would remain above sea level. The other cities would be below sea level by as few as 23 m (New York) and as much as 48 m (Amsterdam).
13. F

Chapter Planner **18**

Erosion by Wind and Waves

	Standards	Teach Key Ideas
Chapter Opener, pp. 480–481 **45 min.**	National Science Education Standards	
Section 1 Wind Erosion, pp. 483–488 **45 min.** ❯ How Wind Moves Sand and Dust ❯ Effects of Wind Erosion ❯ Wind Deposition ❯ Loess	ES 3c, SPSP 5c, UCP 3, UCP 4	■ ◆ **Bellringer,** p. 483 ■ **Demonstration:** Watching Sand Jump, p. 483 ■ **DI (Special Education Students):** Summarizing, p. 484 ■ **DI (Basic Learners):** Compare and Contrast, p. 486 ◆ **Transparency:** 89 Types of Dunes ▲ **Visual Concepts:** Saltation • Dunes • Loess
Section 2 Wave Erosion, pp. 489–492 **90 min.** ❯ Shoreline Erosion ❯ Beaches ❯ Longshore-Current Deposits	ES 3c, SPSP 5c, UCP 3, UCP 4	■ ◆ **Bellringer,** p. 489 ■ **DI (Special Education Students):** Shoreline Features, p. 490 ◆ **Transparency:** 90 Wave Erosion and Landforms ▲ **Visual Concepts:** Ocean Wave Energy • Shorelines and Beaches • Longshore Current
Section 3 Coastal Erosion and Deposition, pp. 493–496 **45 min.** ❯ Absolute Sea-Level Changes ❯ Relative Sea-Level Changes ❯ Preserving the Coastline	ES 3c, SPSP 5c, SAI 1a, SAI 1f, ST 1e, UCP 2, UCP 3, UCP 4	■ ◆ **Bellringer,** p. 493 ■ **DI (Advanced Learners):** Coastal Features, p. 494 ■ **Homework:** Coastal Landforms, p. 500 ◆ **Transparencies:** 91 Submergent Coastlines • 92 Coastal Erosion Near the Beaufort Sea ▲ **Visual Concepts:** Estuary
Chapter Wrap-Up, pp. 501–505 **90 min.**		**Chapter Summary,** p. 501

See also PowerNotes® Presentations

CHAPTER *Fast Track*

To shorten instruction because of time limitations, omit Section 3.

Key
Teacher's Edition ■ | Teaching Transparencies ◆
Chapter Resource File ● | Online Edition ▲

All resources listed below are also available on the Teacher One Stop™.

Why It Matters	Hands-On	Skills Development	Assessment
■ **Chapter Overview,** p. 480 ■ **Using the Figure:** Rock Formation, p. 480	**Inquiry Lab:** Shake It Up, p. 481	**Reading Toolbox,** p. 482	
■ **Section Overview,** p. 483 ■ **Sand Blasting,** p. 485 ■ **Using the Figure:** Dune Formation, p. 485 ■ **History Connection:** Dust Bowl, p. 485 ■ **Dune Movement,** p. 486 ■ **Using the Figure:** Dune Migration, p. 487	■ **Activity:** Shaping, p. 485 **Quick Lab:** Modeling Desert Winds, p. 487 ● **Inquiry Lab:** Soil Erosion	■ ● **Internet Activity:** Great Lakes Dunes, p. 486 **Reading Toolbox:** Root Words, p. 488	**Reading Check,** p. 484 **Reading Check,** p. 486 **Section Review,** p. 488 ■ **Reteaching,** p. 487 ■ **Quiz,** p. 487 ■ **DI (Alternative Assessment):** Landform Description, p. 488 ● **Section Quiz**
■ **Section Overview,** p. 489 ■ **Using the Figure:** Breaking Waves, p. 489	**Inquiry Lab:** Beaches, pp. 498–499	■ ● **Internet Activity:** Landform Photographs, p. 490 **Reading Toolbox:** Four-Corner Fold, p. 490 **Math Skills:** Wave Depth, p. 491 ■ **Skill Builder:** Writing, p. 491	**Reading Check,** p. 490 **Section Review,** p. 492 ■ **Reteaching,** p. 491 ■ **Quiz,** p. 491 ■ **DI (Alternative Assessment):** Landform Identification, p. 492 ● **Section Quiz**
■ **Section Overview,** p. 493 ■ **Using the Figure:** Sea-Level Changes, p. 493 **Wave Power,** p. 495	**Quick Lab:** Graphing Tides, p. 494 ● **Making Models Lab:** Erosion of a Submerging Coastal Profile	**Maps in Action:** Coastal Erosion Near the Beaufort Sea, p. 500	**Reading Check,** p. 495 **Section Review,** p. 496 ■ **Reteaching,** p. 495 ■ **Quiz,** p. 495 ■ **DI (Alternative Assessment):** Landform Description, p. 496 ● **Section Quiz**
Where Did All This Sand Come From?, p. 497		▲ **Super Summary** **Standardized Test Prep,** pp. 504–505	**Chapter Review,** pp. 502–503 ■ **DI (Alternative Assessment):** Quiz Show, p. 501 ● **Chapter Tests**

See also Lab Generator

See also Holt Online Assessment Resources

Chapter Overview

This chapter describes the powerful influence of wind and waves on Earth's surface. Agents of erosion constantly modify the appearance of coastlines and challenge humans to find creative solutions to protect coastal lands.

Using the Figure GENERAL

Rock Formation Ask students if they have seen rock formations similar to the one in the photo. Have students describe where they saw these formations and what the rock looked like. Provide pictures of rock formations, coastline erosion, dunes, and oceans to demonstrate the power of erosion by wind and water. **LS Visual**

Why It Matters

In the United States and around the world, humans live in high densities near the seashore. In these areas, the natural processes of erosion by wind and waves shape shoreline features—sometimes dramatically, as during Hurricane Katrina.

Chapter 18 Erosion by Wind and Waves

Chapter Outline

Virginia Standards of Learning
ES.1.c
ES.2.a
ES.10.a
ES.10.b
ES.10.e

Why It Matters

Wind and waves are powerful forces of erosion. Wind may carry away soil that is needed for farming. Waves may wash away coastlines, which are important economic areas. This curved and pitted rock, on Kangaroo Island off the southern shore of Australia, was shaped by wind and waves.

Chapter Correlations

Virginia Standards of Learning

ES.1.c scales, diagrams, charts, graphs, tables, imagery, models, and profiles are constructed and interpreted.
ES.2.a science explains and predicts the interactions and dynamics of complex Earth systems.
ES.10.a physical and chemical changes related to tides, waves, currents, sea level and ice cap variations, upwelling, and salinity variations
ES.10.b importance of environmental and geologic implications
ES.10.e economic and public policy issues concerning the oceans and the coastal zone including the Chesapeake Bay

Inquiry Lab

20 min

Shake It Up

Use a magnifying glass or dissecting microscope to observe the samples of shoreline sediment provided by your teacher. Record your observations, noting similarities and differences among the samples. Place all of the samples in the same jar, add water until the jar is three-quarters full, and seal the jar. Shake the jar for 1 min to represent shoreline wave action. Then let the jar rest, and observe the rates of deposition for different-sized particles. Record your observations.

Questions to Get You Started

1. Describe the relationship between particle size and rate of deposition in the jar.
2. Based on your observations, how would you expect different-sized particles to settle on a real shoreline?

Inquiry Lab

Central Concept: Particle size affects the length of time that a particle will remain suspended in water.

Teacher's Notes: It may take longer than 30 min for the sediment to settle completely. Have students leave the jars undisturbed, and look again at the jars at the end of class. Remind students that wave action is continuous on shorelines, unlike in this jar model.

Materials (per group)
- Magnifying glass
- Dissecting microscope
- Shoreline sediment
- Jar
- Water

Skills Acquired
- Making Models
- Observing

Answers to Getting Started

1. The larger the particles, the faster they settle. The smallest particles remain suspended for a very long time.
2. Answers may vary. Students should logically connect their observations of the jar to a shoreline setting.

Using THINK central Resources

An online version of this chapter, as well as all the print and multimedia resources that accompany the program are available to registered teachers and their students. Log onto www.thinkcentral.com to access these materials and tools to organize your preparation and student learning.

READING TOOLBOX

Word Parts

Students should include at least four terms from Sections 1 and 2 in a chart like the one here.

Term	Root Word	Definition of Root Word	Definition of Term
deflation	inflatus (Latin)	to blow into, inflate	wind erosion in which fine particles are blown away
tombolo	tumulus (Latin)	a mound	beach deposit that connects an offshore island to the mainland

Mnemonics

Answers will vary. Students' mnemonics should help them remember the definitions of the key terms in the chapter.

FoldNotes

Answers will vary. Student's four-corner folds should include notes about the four types of dunes (barchan, parabolic, transverse, and longitudinal) under the appropriate flaps.

READING TOOLBOX

These reading tools will help you learn the material in this chapter.

Word Parts

Root Words The word *saltation,* a key term in Section 1, may remind you of the salt that you sprinkle on food. Actually, *saltation* is from the Latin word *saltatio,* which means "a dancing" or "dance." This Latin root makes sense, because saltation is the way that wind and water move sand—by bounces and jumps.

Your Turn Choose four key terms or italicized terms in Sections 1 and 2. Using print or online sources, research the root word of each term. Record your findings in a table like the one below.

Term	Root Word	Definition of Root Word	Definition of Term
(desert or stone) pavement	pavimentum (Latin)	beaten floor	a surface of closely packed small rocks

Mnemonics

Longshore Current A mnemonic is a sentence or phrase that can help you remember specific information. For example, a longshore current is a water current that travels near and parallel to the shoreline. You can use the following mnemonic to help you remember the direction and location of a longshore current:

A longshore current flows **along** the shoreline.

Your Turn Say this mnemonic a few times to help you learn and remember the direction in which a longshore current flows. Find the other key terms in the chapter, and make up mnemonics that will help you remember their definitions.

FoldNotes

Four-Corner Fold A four-corner fold is useful when you want to compare the characteristics of four topics. You can organize the characteristics of the four topics side by side under the flaps.

Your Turn As you read about dunes in Section 1, make a four-corner fold by following the instructions in **Appendix A.** Label the four outer flaps with the names of the four types of dunes: barchan dunes, parabolic dunes, transverse dunes, and longitudinal dunes. Take notes about each type of dune underneath the appropriate flap.

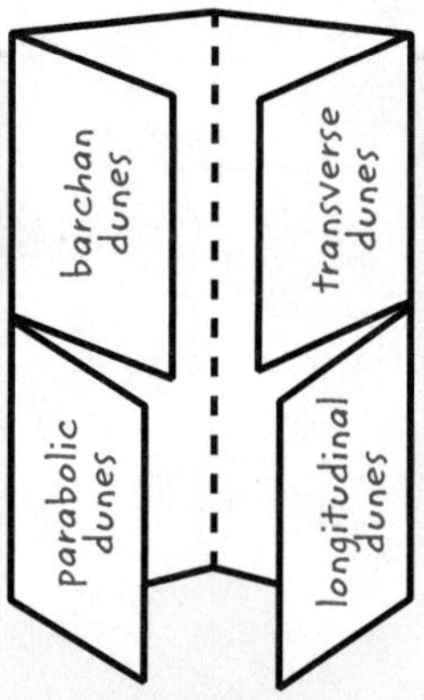

For more information on how to use these and other tools, see **Appendix A.**

SECTION

1 Wind Erosion

Key Ideas	Key Terms	Why It Matters
› Describe two ways that wind erodes land. › Compare the two types of wind deposits.	saltation, dune, deflation, loess, ventifact	Blowing wind moves sand, soil, dust, and other particles all over Earth. As a result, wind helps to shape the land, which can be a benefit to those who live there.

Wind contains energy. Some of this energy can move a sailboat or turn a wind turbine, but this energy can also erode the land. As wind passes over the land, the wind can carry sand or dust. Sand is loose fragments of weathered rocks and minerals. Most grains of sand are made of quartz. Other common minerals that make up sand are mica, feldspar, and magnetite.

Dust consists of particles that are smaller than the smallest sand grain. Most dust particles are microscopic fragments of rocks and minerals that come from the soil or volcanic eruptions. Other sources of dust are plants, animals, bacteria, pollution from the burning of fuels, and certain manufacturing processes.

How Wind Moves Sand and Dust

Wind cannot keep sand aloft. Instead, sand grains are rolled by the wind along the ground (surface creep) or are moved by a series of jumps and bounces called **saltation.** Saltation occurs when rolling sand grains collide and some bounce up, as shown in **Figure 1.** Once in the air, a sand grain moves ahead a short distance and then falls. As a sand grain falls, it strikes other sand grains. Saltating sand grains move in the same direction that the wind blows. However, the grains rarely rise more than 1 m above the ground, even in very strong winds.

saltation the movement of sand or other sediments by short jumps and bounces that is caused by wind or water

Because dust particles are very small and light, even gentle air currents can keep dust particles suspended in the air. Dust from volcanic eruptions can remain in the atmosphere for several years. Strong winds may lift large amounts of dust and create dust storms, such as the one shown in **Figure 1.** Some dust storms cover hundreds of square kilometers and darken the sky for several days.

Wind direction
Smaller particles are lifted and carried by the wind.
Larger particles bounce and skip along the ground.

Figure 1 Heavy sand gains move by rolling or by making low, arcing jumps when blown by the wind (left). Dust is light enough to be suspended for days, as shown in this dust storm in Phoenix, Arizona (right).

Section 1

Focus

Overview

This section explains how wind moves sand and dust. It also describes the effects of wind erosion and wind deposition, as well as the creation of dunes, dune migration, and the deposition of loess.

Bellringer

Ask students how something as tiny as sand or dust can erode hard surfaces. (Over long periods of time wind-borne particles of sand or dust become abrasive against solid objects by breaking off tiny pieces.) LS **Logical**

Motivate

Demonstration GENERAL

Watching Sand Jump Place a wood block at the end of an ice cube tray. Spoon a mixture of fine and coarse sand onto the block in the shape of a dune and blow the sand into the tray. The finer sand should travel farthest. Have students observe the remains of the sand dune and the sand particles that traveled into the tray. The heaviest particles will remain closest to the dune and the lightest particles will travel the farthest distance. LS **Visual**

Key Resources

Chapter Resource File
- Directed Reading BASIC
- Inquiry Lab: Soil Erosion GENERAL

Technology
- Transparencies
  Bellringer

Teach

Answer to Reading Check

Moisture makes soil heavier, so the soil sticks and is more difficult to move. Therefore, erosion happens faster in dry climates.

Homework BASIC

Soil Conservation The process of producing rich fertile soil takes hundreds or thousands of years, but soil can be depleted of its nutrients or washed away in just a few years. Farming practices that have not taken this problem into consideration have caused losses of millions of acres of soil. Ask students to research some of the unsound agricultural methods that have caused such erosion. (over-tilling, plowing without regard to contours, cutting down trees, overgrazing herds of cattle) Have students research ways that farmers prevent soil erosion. (wind breaks, ground cover, contour plowing, and terracing) Have them make a poster that shows what the technique looks like, describes what the technique does, and identifies why and where the technique is used.
LS Logical/Visual

Figure 2 Desert pavement, such as this example in Calico Hills, California, prevents erosion of the material beneath it.

SCI LINKS
www.scilinks.org
Topic: Wind Erosion
Code: **HQX1669**

Effects of Wind Erosion

While wind erosion happens everywhere there is wind, the landscapes that are most dramatically shaped by wind erosion are deserts and coastlines. In these areas, fewer plant roots anchor soil and sand in place to reduce the amount of wind erosion. Also, in the desert, where there is little moisture, soil layers are thin and are likely to be swept away by the wind. Moisture makes soil heavy and causes some soil and rock particles to stick together, which makes them difficult to move.

Reading Check **Why does wind erosion happen faster in dry climates than in moist climates?** (See Appendix G for answers to Reading Checks.)

Desert Pavement

deflation a form of wind erosion in which fine, dry soil particles are blown away

One common form of wind erosion is deflation. **Deflation** is the process by which wind removes the top layer of fine, very dry soil or rock particles and leaves behind large rock particles. Deflation is one of many processes that may form a surface of closely packed small rocks called *desert pavement*, or *stone pavement*, as shown in **Figure 2.** Desert pavement protects the underlying land from erosion by forming a protective barrier over underlying soil.

Deflation Hollows

Deflation is a serious problem for farmers because it blows away the best soil for growing crops. Deflation may form shallow depressions in areas where the natural plant cover has been removed. As the wind strips off the topsoil, a shallow depression called a *deflation hollow* forms. A deflation hollow may expand to a width of several kilometers and to a depth of 5 to 20 m.

Differentiated Instruction

Special Education Students

Summarizing Many students with special needs have trouble organizing and summarizing information while they read. Ask students to physically organize and summarize the section by using the following procedure: Start with a blank piece of paper. Write "Wind Erosion" (the section heading) at the top left. Skip three lines. Indent one inch and write "How Wind Moves Sand and Dust" (first red subheading). Skip three lines. In line with the first red heading, write "Effects of Wind Erosion" (second red subheading). Skip three lines. Indent two inches and write "Desert Pavement" (first green subheading). Skip three lines. Continue in this fashion until all remaining subheadings are included and are arranged correctly. Then, under each heading, write one sentence that summarizes the information in that part of the text. **LS Logical**

Ventifacts

When pebbles and small stones in deserts and on beaches are exposed to wind abrasion, the surfaces of the rocks become flattened and polished on two or three sides. Rocks that have been pitted or smoothed by wind abrasion are called **ventifacts.** The word *ventifact* comes from the Latin word *ventus*, which means "wind." The direction of the prevailing wind in an area can be determined by the appearance of ventifacts.

Scientists once thought that large rock structures, such as desert basins, natural bridges, rock pinnacles, and rocks perched on pedestals, were formed by wind erosion. However, scientists now think that it is more likely that such large features were produced by erosion due to surface water and weathering. Erosion of large masses of rock by wind-blown sand happens very slowly and happens only close to the ground, where saltation occurs.

ventifact any rock that is pitted, grooved, or polished by wind abrasion

dune a mound of wind-deposited sand that moves as a result of the action of wind

Wind Deposition

The wind drops particles when it slows down and can no longer carry them. These deposited particles are continually covered by additional deposits. Eventually, cementation and pressure from overlying layers bind the fragments together. This process is one way that sedimentary rocks form.

Academic Vocabulary

fragment (FRAG muhnt) a particle or piece that has broken off or been detached from something larger

Dunes

The best-known wind deposits are **dunes,** which are mounds of wind-deposited sand. Dunes form where the soil is dry and unprotected and where the wind is strong, such as in deserts and along the shores of oceans and large lakes. A dune begins to form when a barrier slows the speed of the wind. When wind speed slows, sand accumulates on both sides of the barrier, as shown in **Figure 3.** As more sand is deposited, the dune itself acts as a barrier, grows, and buries the original barrier.

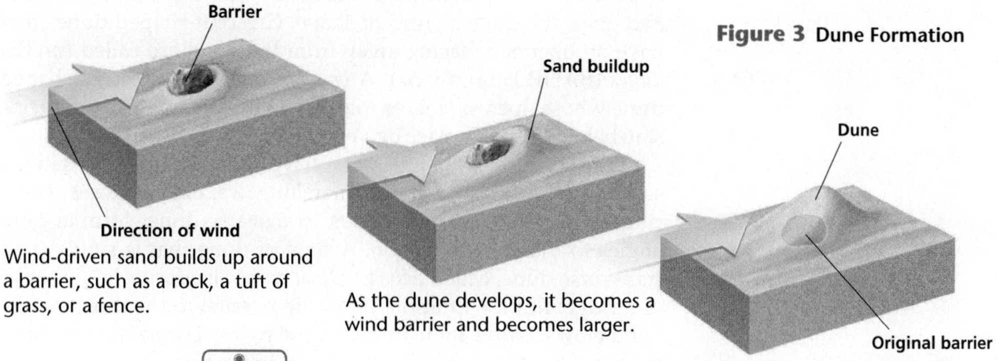

Figure 3 Dune Formation

Wind-driven sand builds up around a barrier, such as a rock, a tuft of grass, or a fence.

As the dune develops, it becomes a wind barrier and becomes larger.

The fully formed dune covers the original barrier.

THINK central INTERACT ONLINE (Keyword: HQXEWWF3)

Activity GENERAL

Shaping Take an emery board and rub it back and forth across the ridges of a six-sided pencil. What happens to the pencil? (The ridges are worn down.) As the file moves back and forth across the pencil, its rough grainy surface cuts tiny pieces from the pencil. Ask students: How is this process like abrasion by blowing sand? (Grains of sand act like a file as they cut away surfaces of rocks, pitting and polishing the rock.) LS Visual

History Connection ADVANCED

Dust Bowl The Great Plains of the U.S. were covered with grassland before World War I. Over the following decade, grasslands were plowed to make room for wheat crops. A severe drought in the early 1930s caused topsoil to be blown into huge dust storms. Have students research the Dust Bowl and make a presentation to the class. Students' reports should include answers to the following questions: Why did the dust storms occur? What was done to stop them? What damage did they cause? Are similar dust storms a threat today? LS Verbal

Using the Figure BASIC

Dune Formation Use the figure on this page to lead a discussion of how dunes form. Ask students to explain the steps in the process and to identify the most important factor in dune formation. (a barrier that slows the speed of the wind and lets sand accumulate around it) LS Visual

Why It Matters

Sand Blasting Sand blasting, or sand abrasion, is a type of wind erosion in which blown sand grains work like tiny chisels, eventually grinding down even the hardest materials. Glass bottles have been worn down to look dull and frosted. Cars caught in sandstorms for less than half an hour have had all of the paint worn off and the windshields permanently frosted. Even wooden telephone poles can be worn away by sand blasting.

Teach, *continued*

Identifying Preconceptions BASIC

Living and Dead Dunes To assess students' ideas regarding the movement of dunes, ask them: What do you think is the difference between a living dune and a "dead" dune? Can a dead dune come back to life?

The four types of dunes discussed in the Student Edition are called *living dunes,* which means that they continue to move under the action of the wind. Once a dune is invaded by vegetation, it can become dead, or stabilized. When a dune is dead, the wind does not affect it. However, if the vegetation is destroyed, erosion begins again and the dune is revitalized. **LS Verbal**

Answer to Reading Check

Barchan dunes are crescent shaped; transverse dunes form linear ridges.

Why It Matters

Dune Movement All living dunes move in some manner. How fast and how far they move depends on wind strength, wind direction, and the size of the dune. Most dunes travel from about 1 to 20 m per year. Generally, the larger the dune is, the more slowly it moves, but large barchan dunes are among the fastest moving dunes, traveling up to 30 m per year.

Key Resources

Technology

- Transparencies
  89 Types of Dunes

Table 1 Types of Dunes

Barchan dunes
When sand is limited, strong winds form these crescent-shaped dunes.

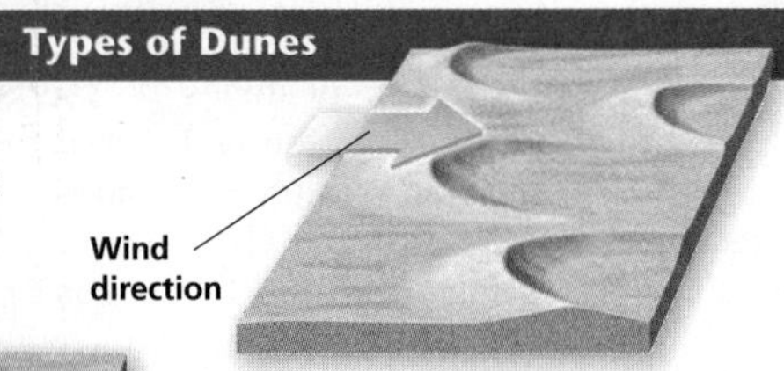

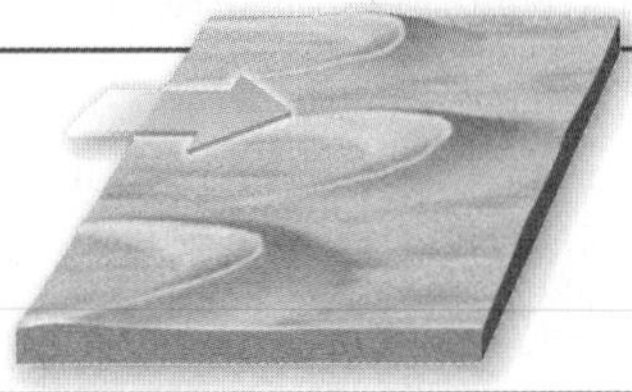

Parabolic dunes
U-shaped parabolic dunes can form when plants anchor the edges of barchan dunes and invert their shape.

Transverse dunes
When sand is plentiful, barchan dunes can join together in long ridges to form transverse dunes.

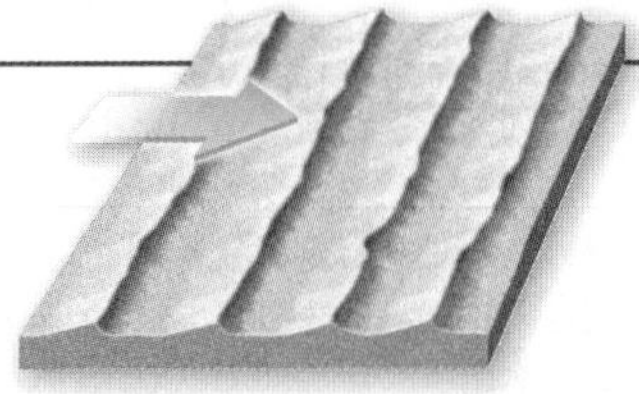

Longitudinal dunes
These dunes are similar to transverse dunes except they lie parallel to the direction of the wind.

Types of Dunes

The force and direction of the wind shapes sand dunes. Commonly, the gentlest slope of a dune is the side that faces the wind. Sand that is blown over the crest of the dune tumbles down the opposite side, which is called the *slipface*. The slipface has a steeper slope than the windward side does. Two long, pointed extensions may form as wind sweeps around the ends of the dune and gives the dune a crescent shape. Crescent-shaped dunes that have an open side facing away from the wind are called *barchan dunes* (BAHR kahn doonz). A *parabolic dune* is a crescent-shaped dune whose open side faces into the wind. The long crescent ends stay behind, held in place by vegetation.

In desert or coastal areas that have a large amount of sand, a series of ridges of sand may form in long, wavelike patterns. These ridges are called *transverse dunes*. Transverse dunes form at right angles to the wind direction. A type of dune that is similar to a transverse dune, called a *longitudinal dune,* also forms in the shape of a ridge. But longitudinal dunes lie parallel to the direction the wind blows. **Table 1** illustrates several types of dunes and explains how the shape of dunes relates to wind direction.

Reading Check **How do barchan dunes differ from transverse dunes?**

Differentiated Instruction

Basic Learners

Compare and Contrast In pairs, have students compare and contrast the four types of dunes. Students should summarize the information in a one-page format of their choosing—notes, a chart, or other visual. Then, have pairs of students trade papers. Encourage students to add any missing information to the other pair's paper. **LS Verbal/Visual**

Internet Activity ADVANCED

Great Lakes Dunes Great Lakes Shoreline Geography is a Web site that offers a wealth of information about how the sand dunes formed around the North American Great Lakes. Ask students to research the history of the dunes. Have students identify some of the problems people in that area have with dune migration and the solutions they have used to combat this problem. A worksheet designed to direct student research on this topic can be found in the **Chapter Resource File** booklet or by visiting www.thinkcentral.com and entering the keyword **HQXEWWX. LS Verbal**

Figure 4 Wind erodes sand from the windward side of the dune and deposits it on the slipface. ***Which direction is this sand dune migrating?***

Dune Migration

The movement of dunes is called *dune migration*. If the wind usually blows from the same direction, dunes will move downwind. Dune migration occurs as sand is blown over the crest from the windward side and builds up on the slipface, as shown in **Figure 4**. In mostly level areas, dunes migrate until they reach a barrier. To prevent dunes from drifting over highways and farmland, people often build fences or plant grasses, trees, and shrubs.

Quick Lab **Modeling Desert Winds**

20 min

Procedure

1. Spread a mixture of dust, sand, and gravel on a table placed outdoors.
2. Place an electric fan at one end of the table.
3. Put on safety goggles and a filter mask. Aim the fan across the sediment you have laid out. Start the fan on the lowest speed. Record any observations.
4. Turn the fan to medium speed and record any observations. Then, turn the fan to its highest speed to imitate a desert windstorm. Record any observations.

Analysis

1. In what direction did the sediment move?
2. What was the relationship between the wind speed and the sediment size that was moved?
3. How does the remaining sediment compare to desert pavement?
4. How did the sand move in this activity? How do your observations relate to dune migration?
5. Using the same materials, how would you model dune migration? How would you model the formation of the different kinds of dunes?

Using the Figure — Basic

Dune Migration Have students study the photograph at the top of the page. Ask them to identify which direction the wind is blowing. (The wind is blowing to the right.) Answer to caption question: The sand dune is moving from left to right in the picture. LS **Visual**

Close

Reteaching — Basic

Crossword Puzzle Have students create a crossword puzzle that uses all of the vocabulary words from this section. Provide graph paper so that students can place words in a grid format and then write the clues to match. Students should work in pairs and then switch papers with another pair to fill in the puzzle and to check for any inaccuracies. LS **Logical**

Quiz — General

1. What is deflation? (a form of wind erosion in which fine, dry soil particles are blown away)
2. What is the composition of loess? (very fertile, fine sediments of quartz, feldspar, hornblende, and mica)

Quick Lab

Skills Acquired
- Experimenting
- Constructing Models

Materials
- Dust, sand, and gravel
- Electric fan
- Safety goggles
- Filter mask

Teacher's Notes: If possible, conduct this lab outdoors, using an extension cord. Caution students to stand away from blowing sand. Also, make sure students stand away from blowing sand.

Answers to Analysis
1. away from the fan
2. The higher the wind speed, the larger the sediment that was moved.
3. It is similar to desert pavement. Particles that remain are too large for the wind to move.
4. The sand moves with a skipping motion. The sand would form a dune when the sand is stopped by a barrier.
5. Answers may vary. Accept all resonable answers.

Close, *continued*

READING TOOLBOX

Root Words

Term	Root Word	Definition of Root Word	Definition of Term
loess	lösen (German)	to loosen	fine-grained sediments deposited by the wind

Answers to Section Review

1. Sand grains move by jumps and bounces, colliding with other grains.
2. Deflation is a form of wind erosion in which dry soil particles are blown away, leaving a shallow depression called a *deflation hollow*.
3. Ventifacts form as wind abrades rocks, making the surfaces smoothed or pitted.
4. Dunes form where sediment is dry and unprotected and where the wind is strong. A barrier slows the speed of the wind, and the sand accumulates on both sides of the barrier, eventually burying it. Dune migration occurs as the sand is blown over the crest of the dune and builds up on the slipface.
5. Wind carries loess by suspending it in the air.
6. There are few plants and roots in the desert to anchor the soil and sand, and the dry, thin soil is easily swept away by the wind.
7. Barchan and parabolic dunes are crescent shaped. Barchan dunes have an open side that faces away from the wind, and parabolic dunes have an open side that faces the wind. Transverse and longitudinal dunes are ridge-shaped. Transverse dunes form at right angles to the wind direction, and longitudinal dunes form parallel to the wind direction.
8. by blowing away the top layer of fine, dry soil, and leaving behind a surface of closely packed small rocks
9. They provide a barrier to stop the wind from carrying dune material onto and across a road.
10. Dunes move continuously.
11. Wind can move sediment by *deflation*, which lifts dust from the *top soil layer* and forms *desert pavement* and *deflation hollows*; and by *saltation*, which moves *sand particles* and may form *dunes* that move by *migration*.

Figure 5 These loess deposits are located in Vicksburg, Mississippi. Much of the surrounding land is fertile farmland.

READING TOOLBOX

Root Words
Use print or online sources to research the root word of *loess*. Add your findings to the table you started at the beginning of the chapter.

Loess

The wind carries dust higher and much farther than it carries sand. Fine dust may be deposited in such thin layers that it is not noticed. However, thick deposits of yellowish, fine-grained sediment, called **loess** (LOH ES), can form by the accumulation of windblown dust. Although loess is soft and easily eroded, it sometimes forms steep bluffs, such as those shown in **Figure 5.**

loess fine-grained sediments of quartz, feldspar, hornblende, mica, and clay deposited by the wind

A large area in northern China is covered in a deep layer of loess. The material in this deposit came from the Gobi Desert, in Mongolia. Deposits of loess are also located in central Europe. In North America, loess is located in the midwestern states, along the eastern border of the Mississippi River valley, and in eastern Oregon and Washington State. These deposits probably formed as dust from dried beds of glacial lakes and from outwash plains blew across the region. Loess deposits are extremely fertile and provide excellent soil for grain-growing regions.

Section 1 Review

Key Ideas

1. **Describe** how wind transports sediment by saltation.
2. **Define** *deflation*, and explain how *deflation hollows* form.
3. **Describe** how ventifacts form.
4. **Describe** how sand dunes form and how dunes migrate.
5. **Explain** how the wind moves loess.
6. **Identify** two reasons why wind erosion has a major effect on deserts.
7. **Compare** the four main shapes of dunes.

Critical Thinking

8. **Analyzing Processes** Explain how wind erosion might contribute to the formation of desert pavement.
9. **Determining Cause and Effect** Why does planting grass, trees, or shrubs help prevent dunes from covering roads?
10. **Analyzing Processes** Explain why the position of dunes would not be helpful for navigation in the desert.

Concept Mapping

11. Use the following terms to create a concept map: *saltation, deflation, dune, deflation hollow, desert pavement, wind, sand particle, top soil layer,* and *migration.*

Differentiated Instruction

Alternative Assessment

Landform Description Have students pretend that they are flying over a desert to get to the coast. Ask them to describe the landforms they would see that were created by wind erosion and deposition. They must describe at least two features of each landform and explain how each feature formed. **LS Verbal**

SECTION 2

Wave Erosion

Key Ideas	Key Terms	Why It Matters
❯ Compare the formation of six features produced by wave erosion. ❯ Explain how beaches form. ❯ Describe the features produced by the movement of sand along a shore.	**headland** **beach** **longshore current**	The endless pounding of the surf produces spectacular shorelines, which, themselves, never stay the same.

As wind moves over the ocean, the wind produces waves and currents that erode the coastline. Wave erosion changes the shape of shorelines, the places where the ocean and the land meet.

Shoreline Erosion

The power of waves striking rock along a shoreline can sometimes shake the ground as much as a small earthquake would. The great force of waves may break off pieces of rock and throw the pieces back against the shore. These sediments grind together in the tumbling water. This abrasive action, which is known as *mechanical weathering*, eventually reduces most of the rock fragments to small pebbles and sand grains.

Much of the erosion along a shoreline takes place during storms, which cause large waves that release tremendous amounts of energy, as shown in **Figure 1**. A severe storm can noticeably change the appearance of a shoreline in a single day.

Chemical weathering also affects the rock along a shoreline. The waves force salt water and air into small cracks in the rock. Chemicals in the air and water react with the rock and enlarge the cracks. Enlarged cracks expose more of the rock to mechanical and chemical weathering.

Figure 1 Large waves break apart rock on shorelines and change the shoreline's appearance. ***Where is erosion occurring in the photo shown here?***

Section 2

Focus

Overview

This section describes and compares six coastal features produced by wave erosion and explains how these features form. It also explains how beaches form and what features form when longshore currents transport sand along the shoreline.

Bellringer

Show students a picture of a coastline with steep cliffs. Have students draw pictures of what they think the shoreline will look like in 50 years and in 500 years. Students can share their drawings with each other. (Answers may vary.) LS Visual

Motivate

Using the Figure GENERAL

Breaking Waves Have students study the photograph at the bottom of this page. Ask students to imagine the force with which the waves are striking the rock in the foreground. Answer to caption question: Erosion is occurring in the cracks and on the surface of the rock in the foreground where the water strikes the rock. LS Visual

Key Resources

Chapter Resource File
- Directed Reading BASIC

Technology
- Transparencies
  Bellringer

Teach

Internet Activity GENERAL

Landform Photographs Have students search the Internet for examples, descriptions, and photos of the shoreline feature formations caused by wave erosion. Have them search by using either the name of the formation or the broad heading of wave erosion. Some sites have short movies that show how wave erosion has changed coastlines over time. A worksheet designed to direct student research on this topic can be found in the **Chapter Resource File** booklet or by visiting www.thinkcentral.com and entering the keyword **HQXEWWX.** **LS Visual**

READING TOOLBOX

Four-Corner Fold

Answers will vary. Student's four-corner folds should include notes about the four land features that are formed by wave erosion (sea cliffs, sea caves, sea arches, and sea stacks) under the appropriate flaps.

Answer to Reading Check

Answers should include three of the following: sea cliffs, sea caves, sea arches, sea stacks, wave-cut terraces, and wave-built terraces.

Key Resources

Technology

- Transparencies
  90 Wave Erosion and Landforms

headland a high and steep formation of rock that extends out from shore into the water

READING TOOLBOX

Four-Corner Fold

Make a four-corner fold. Label the outer flaps with the names of four land features that are formed by wave erosion: Sea Cliffs, Sea Caves, Sea Arches, and Sea Stacks. Take notes about each type of land feature under the appropriate flap.

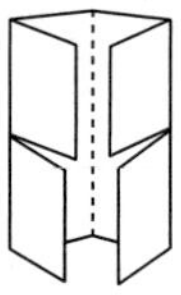

Sea Cliffs

In places where waves strike directly against rock, the waves slowly erode the base of the rock. The waves cut under the overhanging rock, until the rock eventually collapses to form a steep sea *cliff.* The rate at which sea cliffs erode depends on the amount of wave energy and on the resistance of the rock along the shoreline. Soft rock, such as limestone, erodes very rapidly. Harder rock, such as granite, shows little change over hundreds of years. Resistant rock formations that project out from shore are called **headlands.** Areas that have less resistant rock form *bays.* **Figure 2** shows bays and several other coastal landforms produced by wave erosion.

Sea Caves, Arches, and Stacks

Waves often cut deep into fractured and weak rock along the base of a cliff to form a large hole, or a *sea cave.* When waves cut completely through a headland, a *sea arch* forms. Offshore columns of rock that once were connected to a sea cliff or headland, are called *sea stacks.*

Terraces

As a sea cliff is worn, a nearly level platform, called a *wave-cut terrace,* usually remains beneath the water at the base of the cliff. Eroded material may be deposited offshore to create an extension to the wave-cut terrace called a *wave-built terrace.*

Reading Check **List three features that are caused by shoreline erosion.**

Figure 2 Wave erosion of sea cliffs causes cliff retreat and forms isolated sea stacks. Sea cliffs develop where waves strike directly against rock that is along a shoreline.

Teaching Tip GENERAL

Connect to Prior Knowledge Ask students to recall visits to lake and/or ocean beaches. Have them describe landscapes and landforms around the beaches they have seen. After they listen to other students' descriptions, have them discuss the similarities and differences between ocean shoreline formations and features found around lakes. **LS Verbal**

Differentiated Instruction

Special Education Students

Shoreline Features Students can work in small groups or pairs to demonstrate different shore formations by using their hands. For example, a sideways-cupped hand with a hand over the top represents a cave. Or, have students sculpt formations with modeling clay, based on verbal descriptions or from feeling the hands or models of others. **LS Kinesthetic**

Beaches

Waves create features by eroding the land and depositing sediment. A deposit of sediment along an ocean or lake shore is called a **beach.** Beaches form where more sediment is deposited than is removed. After a beach forms, the rate at which sediment is deposited and the rate at which sediment is removed may vary.

beach an area of the shoreline that is made up of deposited sediment

Composition of Beaches

The sizes and kinds of materials that make up beaches vary. In general, the smaller the particle is, the farther it traveled before it was deposited. The composition of beach materials depends on the minerals in the source rock. Some beaches may consist of fragments of shells and coral that are washed ashore. In other locations, sand beaches form from sediment deposited by rivers or glaciers. Other beaches are composed of large pebbles.

The Berm

Each wave that reaches the shore moves sand slightly. The sand piles up to produce a sloping surface. During high tides or large storms, sand is deposited at the back of this slope. So, most beaches have a raised section called the *berm*, as shown in **Figure 2.** The berm is high and steep during the winter because large storms remove sand from the beach on the seaward side of the berm. The sand that is removed may be deposited offshore to form a long underwater ridge called a *sand bar*. In the summer, waves may move the sand back to the shore to widen the beach.

Math Skills

Wave Depth A wave will break when the depth of the wave is equal to one and a half times the height of the water column. This statement can be represented by the following formula.

$$D = \frac{3}{2}H$$

If the tallest wave in a specific area is 6 m, what is the maximum depth at which wave erosion would occur in that area?

Math Skills

Answer

$$D = \frac{3}{2}H$$

If the tallest wave is 6 m, then the maximum depth at which wave erosion would occur is

$$\frac{3}{2} \times 6\text{ m} = 9\text{ m}$$

Close

Reteaching — BASIC

Vocabulary Flash Cards Have students make vocabulary and picture flashcards of the different landforms described in the section. Have students write the term on one side of the card and place a description and picture of the landform on the other side. Students can use the cards to quiz each other on identifying the formations. **LS Visual**

Quiz — GENERAL

1. How is mechanical weathering different from chemical weathering? (Mechanical weathering is the abrasive action that occurs when waves break off pieces of rock and they tumble against each other. Chemical weathering occurs when chemicals in air and water react with rock to break the rock down.)
2. Name two sand deposits formed by longshore currents. (spits and tombolos)
3. Describe how a sea cliff forms. (When waves strike directly against rock, the base of the rock erodes, or wears away. Eventually the overlying rock collapses and a steep sea cliff remains.)

Homework — ADVANCED

Beach Composition Have students research the composition of sand beaches in different locations around the world. Students should report what minerals are found in each beach and the color of each beach. Students should learn that the color of sand on a beach depends on the rock that was eroded to produce the sand. For example, white sand commonly forms from coral and seashells, pale yellow sand commonly forms from quartz, black sand commonly forms from basaltic lava, and green sand commonly forms from the mineral olivine. **LS Verbal**

Skill Builder — BASIC

Writing After students read the paragraphs that explain beaches, ask them to write a short story about a grain of sand or a pebble that becomes part of a beach. The story should be an adventure story that describes where the particle came from and how the particle reaches the beach. Students may choose to write the story in the first person or in the third person. **LS Verbal**

Close, *continued*

Answers to Section Review

1. Sea cliffs form when water erodes the base of a rock and the rock collapses. Sea caves form when waves cut a large hole into the base of a cliff. Sea arches form when waves cut through a headland. Sea stacks form when part of a sea cliff becomes isolated by water. A wave-cut terrace is a flat platform that forms when a sea cliff is worn down. A wave-built terrace is an extension to a wave-cut terrace that is made of deposited material.
2. the composition of the source rock and the distance that the particles travel
3. Beaches form where more sediment is deposited than is removed by wave action.
4. A sea cave is a cave at the base of a headland. When waves cut a hole completely through the headland, an arch is made. When the arch collapses to leave a column of rock surrounded by water, a sea stack has formed.
5. A beach is an area of the shoreline made of deposited sediment. A spit is a long, narrow deposit of sand connected at one end to the shore. Tombolos are ridges of sand that connect an island to the mainland.
6. During winter, large storms remove sand from the beach on the seaward side of the berm. In summer, waves move the sand toward the land, widening the beach.
7. Only very rapidly moving water can carry large particles. When the speed of the water decreases, the water is able to move only smaller particles, so it deposits the larger particles. Very fine particles are deposited only in very still water.
8. Wave action causes *shoreline erosion,* which can result in a *sea cliff,* a *sea arch,* a *sea cave,* or a *terrace,* which could be a *wave-cut terrace* or a *wave-built terrace.*

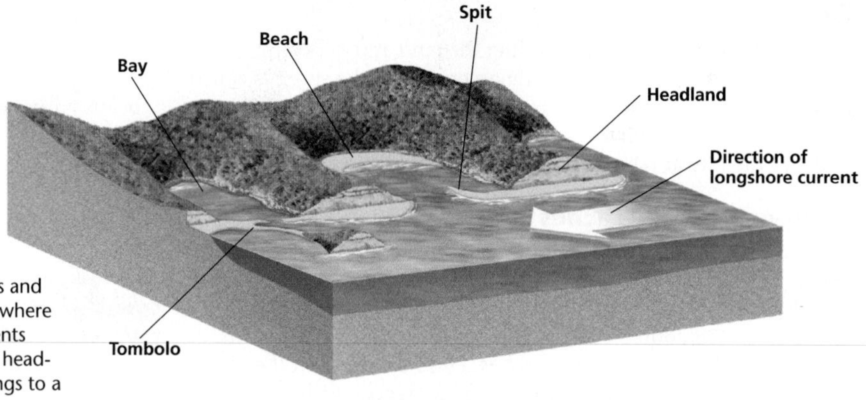

Figure 3 Spits and tombolos form where longshore currents deposit sand at headlands, at openings to a bay, or on offshore islands.

Academic Vocabulary

individual (IN duh VIJ oo uhl) existing as a single, separate entity; particular

longshore current a water current that travels near and parallel to the shoreline

Longshore-Current Deposits

The direction in which a wave approaches the shore determines how the wave will move sediment. Most waves approach the beach at an angle and retreat in a direction that is more perpendicular to the shore. So, waves move individual sand grains in a zig-zag motion. The general movement of sand along the beach is in the direction in which the waves strike the shore.

Waves moving at an angle to the shoreline often create longshore currents. A **longshore current** is a movement of water parallel to and near the shoreline. Longshore currents transport sand parallel to the shoreline, as shown in **Figure 3.**

Along a relatively straight coastline, sand keeps moving until the shoreline changes direction at bays and headlands. The longshore current slows, and sand is deposited at the far end of the headland. A long, narrow deposit of sand connected at one end to the shore is called a *spit*. Currents and waves may curve the end of a spit into a hook shape. Beach deposits may also connect an offshore island to the mainland. Such connecting ridges of sand are called *tombolos*.

Section 2 Review

Key Ideas

1. **Compare** the formation of six features that are produced by shoreline erosion.
2. **Identify** two factors that determine the composition of beach materials.
3. **Explain** how beaches form.
4. **Compare** sea arches, sea caves, and sea stacks.
5. **Describe** three features produced by the movement of sand along a shore.

Critical Thinking

6. **Making Inferences** How do seasonal changes affect beaches?
7. **Identifying Relationships** How does the speed at which water moves affect the deposition of materials of differing sizes?

Concept Mapping

8. Use the following terms to create a concept map: *shoreline erosion, sea arch, sea cave, sea cliff, wave-cut terrace, wave-built terrace,* and *terrace.*

Differentiated Instruction

Alternative Assessment

Landform Identification Show students photographs of coastal formations. Have students identify the formations and describe how they formed. **LS Visual**

SECTION 3

Coastal Erosion and Deposition

ENVIRONMENTAL CONNECTION

Key Ideas	Key Terms	Why It Matters
❯ Explain how changes in sea level affect coastlines.	estuary	The same wave energy that erodes shorelines can be harnessed to produce electricity.
❯ Describe the features of a barrier island.	barrier island	
❯ Analyze the effect of human activity on coastal land.	lagoon	

The boundaries between land and the ocean are among the most rapidly changing parts of Earth's surface. Coastal areas extend from relatively shallow water to several kilometers inland. Coastlines are affected by the long-term rise and fall of sea level and by the long-term uplifting or sinking of the land that borders the water. These and other more rapid processes, such as wave erosion and deposition, constantly change the appearance of coastlines.

Absolute Sea-Level Changes

A change in the amount of ocean water causes sea level to rise or fall, so coastlines are covered or exposed. During the last glacial period, which ended about 15,000 years ago, some of the water that is now in the ocean existed as continental ice sheets. Scientists estimate that the ice sheets held about 70 million cubic kilometers of ice. Now, the ice sheets in Antarctica and Greenland hold only about 25 million cubic kilometers of ice.

During the last glacial period, the water that made up the additional 45 million cubic kilometers of ice is thought to have come from the oceans. As a result, sea level was as much as 140 m lower during the last glacial period than it is today. Since the last glacial period, the ice sheets have been melting, as shown in **Figure 1.** Over the last 5,000 years, sea level has been rising at a rate of about 1 mm per year. If, in the distant future, the polar icecaps were to melt completely, the oceans would rise over 50 m and submerge low-lying coastal regions. The locations of many large cities, such as New York, Los Angeles, Miami, and Houston would be submerged.

Figure 1 This graph shows how sea level has changed during the past 35,000 years.

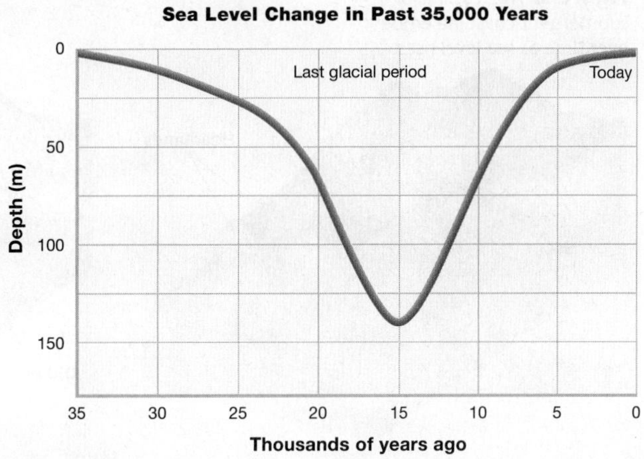

Section 3

Focus

Overview

This section distinguishes between submergent and emergent coastlines and describes the formation of barrier islands and lagoons and the effects of human activities on coastlines.

Bellringer

Ask students to imagine how life on Earth would be different if the sea level was 140 m (420 feet) lower than it is today. Ask them: What would the land look like? How would plant and animal life change? (Answers may vary.)
LS Logical

Motivate

Using the Figure — GENERAL

Sea-Level Changes Use the figure on this page to lead a discussion about sea-level changes. Global warming increases the melting of the polar ice caps and glaciers, but thermal expansion of the water may be a greater factor affecting sea-level changes. As the water in Earth's oceans warms, it becomes less dense and expands. In addition, ice sheets melt and break off faster than new ice can form. Ask students what they know about global warming and how it would affect sea-level changes and consequently coastal erosion. **LS Verbal/Logical**

Key Resources

Chapter Resource File
- Directed Reading BASIC
- Making Models Lab: Erosion of a Submerging Coastal Profile GENERAL

Technology
- Transparencies
  Bellringer

Quick Lab

Skills Acquired
- Collecting Data
- Identifying Patterns
- Organizing and Analyzing Data

Teacher's Notes: Tidal data may be found on the Internet. If data are already graphed, have students use the graphs. Students should plot the daily range between high and low tides on a graph and compare that information with the phases of the moon.

Answers to Analysis

1. Answers may vary but should accurately reflect the data.
2. Tides represent relative sea-level changes.
3. At first and last quarter moons, the sun, the moon, and Earth are at right angles and neap tides occur, when the tidal range is the smallest. At new and full moons, the sun, the moon, and Earth are in alignment and spring tides occur, when the tidal range is greatest.

Key Resources

Technology
- Transparencies
 91 Submergent Coastlines

Quick Lab 35 min

Graphing Tides

Procedure

1. Research the daily tidal data for a certain area for one calendar month.
2. Graph the tide measurements on a line graph.

Analysis

1. When was high tide? When was low tide?
2. What kind of sea-level changes do tides represent?
3. Research the full and new moon dates for the time period you graphed. How does the moon correspond with your high and low tides?

Relative Sea-Level Changes

Absolute sea level changes when the amount of water in the ocean changes. Relative sea level changes when the land or features near the coast change. These changes can be caused by large-scale geologic processes or by localized coastal changes. For example, movements of Earth's crust can cause coastlines to sink or to rise. Coastlines near a tectonic plate boundary may change as tectonic plates move. When coastlines change, the relative sea level of that area also changes.

Submergent Coastlines

When sea level rises or when land sinks, a *submergent coastline* forms. Divides between neighboring valleys become headlands separated by bays and inlets, and submerged peaks may form offshore islands, as shown in **Figure 2.** Beaches are generally short, narrow, and rocky. When U-shaped glacial valleys become flooded with ocean water as sea level rises, spectacular narrow, deep bays that have steep walls, called *fiords* (FYAWRDZ), form.

The mouth of a river valley that is submerged by ocean water may become a wide, shallow bay that extends far inland. This type of bay, where salt water and fresh water mix, is called an **estuary** (ES tyoo er ee).

estuary an area where fresh water from rivers mixes with salt water from the ocean; the part of a river where the tides meet the river current

Emergent Coastlines

When the land rises or when sea level falls, an *emergent coastline* forms. If an emergent coastline has a steep slope and is exposed rapidly, the coastline will erode to form sea cliffs, narrow inlets, and bays. A series of wave-cut terraces may be exposed as well.

A gentle slope forms when part of the continental shelf is slowly lifted and exposed. The gentle slope forms a smooth coastal plain that has few bays or headlands and that has many long, wide beaches.

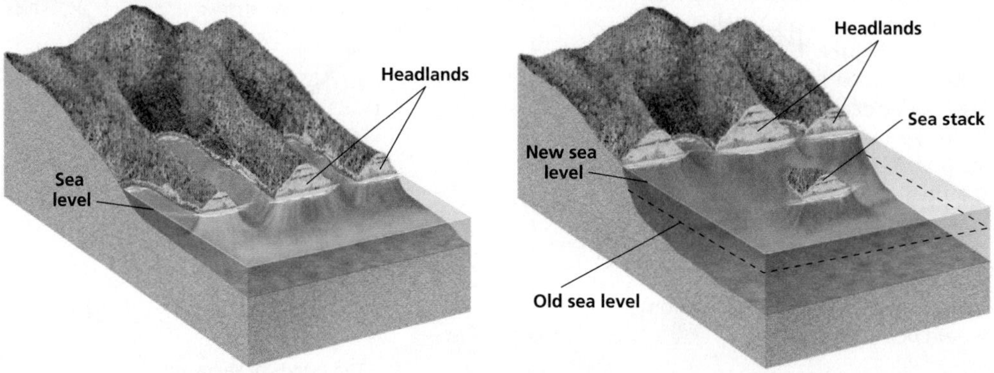

Figure 2 The features of a submergent coastline erode over time as sea level rises.

Cultural Awareness GENERAL

Tides Before students perform the Quick Lab, ask them what they know about tides. Then, tell them that ancient people came up with their own ideas and explanations for tides. Chinese people believed that a huge Earth monster was breathing in and out, making the tides rise and fall. In Scandinavian legends, Thor, the god of aerial forces, was believed to make the tides as he blew on the waters of the sea and then let them recede.

Differentiated Instruction

Advanced Learners

Coastal Features Have students research fiords, estuaries, and lagoons and create posters that show examples of each feature from different parts of the world. Ask students to identify whether these three features are related geographically in any way and how each feature forms. LS **Visual**

Barrier Islands

As sea level rises over a flat coastal plain, the shoreline moves inland and isolates dunes from the old shoreline to form barrier islands, such as the one shown in **Figure 3.** **Barrier islands** are long, narrow ridges of sand that lie nearly parallel to the shoreline. Barrier islands can be 3 to 30 km offshore and can be more than 100 km long. Between a barrier island and the shoreline is a narrow region of shallow water called a **lagoon.**

Figure 3 Santa Rosa Island is a long, narrow barrier island that is located off the coast of Florida.

Barrier islands also form when sand spits are separated from the land by storms or when waves pile up ridges of sand that were scraped from the shallow, offshore sea bottom. These deposits are then moved toward the shore by waves, currents, and winds. This motion causes most barrier islands to migrate toward the shoreline. Winds blowing toward the land often create a line of dunes that are 3 to 6 m high on the side of the island that faces the shore.

Large waves from storms, especially waves from hurricanes, may severely erode barrier islands. During a storm, sand washes from the ocean side toward the inland side of the island. Some barrier islands are eroding at a rate of about 20 m per year.

barrier island a long ridge of sand or narrow island that lies parallel to the shore

lagoon a small body of water separated from the sea by a low, narrow strip of land

Reading Check **How do barrier islands form?**

Why It Matters

Wave Power

EYE ON THE ENVIRONMENT

What if we could capture the ocean's energy and use it in our homes? Ocean waves may one day provide trillions of watts of power. Like solar power and wind power, wave power can produce electricity without pollution. This machine, called Pelamis, converts wave energy into electricity.

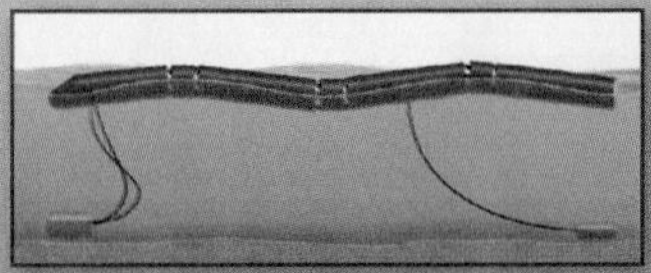

YOUR TURN CRITICAL THINKING
On which shorelines is wave power possible? Explain why.

Answer to Reading Check
As sea levels rise over a flat coastal plain, the shoreline moves inland and isolates dunes from the old shoreline. These dunes become barrier islands.

Close

Reteaching — BASIC

Organizing Ideas Ask students to re-read the text under the heading "Relative Sea-Level Changes" and create a chart with the following headings: "Sea-Level Change," "Resulting Coastline," and "Formations." Under the first heading should be two entries—"Increasing" and "Decreasing." Have students summarize what happens in each situation. (Increasing–submergent—fiords, estuaries, barrier islands, and lagoons. Decreasing–emergent—if steep, sea cliffs, narrow inlets, and bays; if gently sloping, few bays or headlands and long, wide beaches.)
LS Logical

Quiz — GENERAL

1. What effect would the melting of polar ice caps have on coastlines around the world? (Absolute sea level would rise and submergent coastlines would form.)
2. What landforms result from the formation of an emergent coastline? (If steep slopes are present and the coastline is exposed rapidly, then sea cliffs, narrow bays, and inlets will form. If an emergent coastline forms slowly, then a gently-sloping coastal plain that has few headlands and bays and many wide beaches forms.)

Why It Matters

Like solar power or wind power, wave power can produce electricity without pollution. An ocean area used to harness wave energy is called a wave farm.

A variety of devices may be used to capture wave energy, and convert it into electricity that gets sent in an underwater cable back to the shore. These devices must be very sturdy, and endure strong ocean wind, waves, and storms.

The commercial use of wave energy is a very new field. Research and development continues in the effort to build a durable and affordable system.

Answer to Your Turn
Critical Thinking Wave power would be possible on shorelines that have reliable and strong wave action. These shorelines would have lots of ocean energy which could be captured.

Close, *continued*

Answers to Section Review

1. Changes in sea level affect how waves and currents erode the land and deposit sediment. These changes alter the appearance of the shoreline.
2. A submergent coastline forms when the sea level rises or land sinks. An emergent coastline forms when sea level falls or land rises.
3. A barrier island is a long narrow ridge of sand that lies parallel to the shore and is separated from the shore by a narrow region of shallow water.
4. Barrier islands are sensitive to erosion because they are made of sand and they are exposed to the full force of the ocean.
5. Oil spills and garbage and sewage from towns and industries affect coastlines.
6. A season of heavy storms would severely erode or possibly destroy a barrier island by removing much of the sand.
7. Sea levels would drop and emergent coastlines would form.
8. A *coastline* is a boundary between land and the ocean, and may be a *submergent coastline*, or an *emergent coastline*, or may include a *barrier island* that is isolated from the main shoreline by a *lagoon*.

Figure 4 This beach area near Biloxi, Mississippi was devastated by Hurricane Katrina.

Preserving the Coastline

Coastal lands are used for commercial fishing, shipping, industrial and residential development, and recreation. While development of coastal areas is economically important, it can also damage coastal areas in several ways. Pollution is a serious threat to coastal resources. Oil spills are a threat because tankers travel near shorelines and because oil wells are drilled offshore. Garbage, pollution from industry, and sewage from towns on the coast can pollute the coastline. This pollution can damage habitats and kill marine birds and other animals.

Beaches damaged by hurricanes such as Katrina in 2005 will require years of rebuilding, as shown in **Figure 4.** To preserve the coastal zone, private owners and government agencies often work together to set guidelines for coastal protection. Coastal development in some environmentally sensitive areas, such as the North Carolina coast, has been slowed or stopped completely in an attempt to protect these important areas.

Academic Vocabulary
economic (ek uh NAHM ik) relating to commerce

SCILINKS.
www.scilinks.org
Topic: Coastal Changes
Code: HQX0307

Section 3 Review

Key Ideas

1. **Explain** how changes in sea level affect coastlines.
2. **Explain** how the formation of a submergent coastline differs from the formation of an emergent coastline.
3. **Describe** two features of a barrier island.
4. **Explain** why barrier islands are particularly sensitive to erosion.
5. **Describe** two ways in which human activity affects coastlines.

Critical Thinking

6. **Making Predictions** Predict the effect that a season of heavy storms would have on a barrier island.
7. **Identifying Relationships** If Earth were to enter a new glacial period, how might coastlines around the world change?

Concept Mapping

8. Use the following terms to create a concept map: *coastline, emergent coastline, submergent coastline, barrier island,* and *lagoon.*

Differentiated Instruction

Alternative Assessment

Landform Description Ask students to read the imaginary headlines below and write the news story that would accompany each. Students should include a description of the landscapes formed and how humans, animals, and plants would be affected.

1. Polar Ice Caps Melt!—Ocean Levels Rise 60 Meters! (submergent coastline)
2. Lake Michigan Rises Unexpectedly: Sand Dunes Surrounded by Water! (barrier island and lagoon) LS **Verbal**

Why It Matters

Where Did All This Sand Come From?

It is hard to make a mountain move, but it is just as hard to make a sand dune stop moving. Over decades and centuries, sand dunes have buried many towns and structures. Today, sand dunes threaten to blanket towns and cities in parts of Northern China, Saharan Africa, and the Middle East. The rate of a dune's movement depends on the dune's size and location, as well as wind patterns. Scientists study the movement of dunes to better understand dune migration and to help manage dunes in areas where they threaten human populations.

This house is in a Namibian village built in the early 1900s. Today, the town is covered in sand.

This Danish lighthouse was fully functional in 1900. It was closed in the 1960s, taken over by coastal erosion.

Dunes loom over Nouakchott, Mauritania—the largest city in Saharan Africa. Sooner or later, the dunes will move in on the city.

YOUR TURN

UNDERSTANDING CONCEPTS
List three factors that affect the rate at which a sand dune moves.

ONLINE RESEARCH
Sand dunes move through the process of *granular flow*. Use the Internet to learn more about this process. Write a one-page summary of what you learn.

Why It Matters

Where Did All This Sand Come From?

In Northern China, dunes are moving approximately 20 m each year, threatening smaller towns. Dunes also threaten towns and agriculture in regions of Africa and the Middle East. Current efforts to control the movement of sand dunes include the use of fences and barriers. In some cases, sand dunes have been covered in oil to inhibit movement. This practice, however, has significant environmental drawbacks. Control of dunes is difficult, in part because the movement of sand dunes is hard to predict and poorly understood. Sand dunes do not move like solids, liquids, or gases—substances with physical properties we understand fairly well. Physical scientists are working to understand the movement of sand dunes and other granular materials, called granular flow.

Answers to Your Turn

Understanding Concepts Size, location, and wind patterns affect the rate at which a dune moves.

Online Research Answers will vary. Sand dunes, powders, and other granular materials exhibit granular flow. Granular flow is a poorly-understood type of movement, different from the movement of solids, liquids, or gases. Three components of granular flow are saltation, described in this chapter, sheet flows, in which a larger mass of sand grains move together, and avalanches, in which an entire dune moves.

Inquiry Lab

Time Required
one 45-minute class period

Lab Ratings
EASY ——— HARD

Teacher Preparation
Student Setup
Concept Level
Cleanup

Skills Acquired
- Constructing Models
- Observing
- Predicting
- Collecting Data
- Experimenting
- Interpreting
- Organizing and Analyzing Data
- Inferring
- Communicating

Scientific Methods
In this lab, students will
- Make Observations
- Ask Questions
- Form and Test Hypotheses
- Analyze Results
- Draw Conclusions
- Communicate

Materials
Have extra containers available for students to store the sandy water after the activity. Use plastic toy shovels or large serving spoons to help scoop the sand out of the containers.

Inquiry Lab

45 min

Beaches

What You'll Do
› **Model** the effects of wave action and longshore currents on a beach.

› **Identify** ways to decrease the effects of wave action on beach sand.

What You'll Need
block, plaster (2)
block, wooden, large
container, plastic, large
pebbles
ruler, metric
sand, 5 to 10 lb
water

Safety

Coastal management is a growing concern because beaches are increasingly used for resources and recreation. The supply of sand for many beaches has been cut off by dams built on rivers and streams that would otherwise carry sand to the shoreline. Waves generated by storms also continuously wear away beaches. In some places, breakwaters have been built offshore to protect beaches from washing away. In this lab, you will examine how wave action may change the shape of beaches and how these changes can be reduced.

Ask a Question
1. How does wave action affect the amount of sand on a beach? How can these effects be reduced?

Form a Hypothesis
2. Form a hypothesis that answers your question. Explain your reasoning.

Test the Hypothesis
3. Make a beach in a large, shallow container by placing a mixture of sand and small pebbles at one end of the container. The beach should occupy about one-fourth of the length of the container.
4. In front of the sand, add water to a depth of 2 to 3 cm. Record what happens.
5. Use the large wooden block to generate several waves by moving the block up and down in the water at the end of the container opposite the beach. Continue this wave action until about half the beach has moved. Describe the beach after this wave action has taken place.

Step 5

Tips and Tricks
Organizing students into groups of three would allow each student to contribute one breakwater design in step 7. Make a mark on the large plastic containers to indicate water level. Encourage students to create a data table that describes the shore before waves and after each type of breakwater is constructed.

Have students communicate the results of their designs with the class. Each student or group can share their drawings with the class to see other students' designs. Show actual pictures of breakwater designs to compare with those the students designed.

6. Remove the sand, and rebuild the beach.
7. Design three breakwaters that change the flow of water along the beach. Draw your designs on a piece of paper. The two top photos at right are samples of some break-water arrangements.
8. Have your teacher approve your designs before you build them into your model beach.
9. Use the two plaster blocks to model the first breakwater that you designed. Use a wooden block to generate waves as in step 5. Record your observations.
10. Use the wooden block to generate waves that move parallel to the beach. Record your observations.
11. Repeat steps 9 and 10 for each of your other two designs. Record your observations.

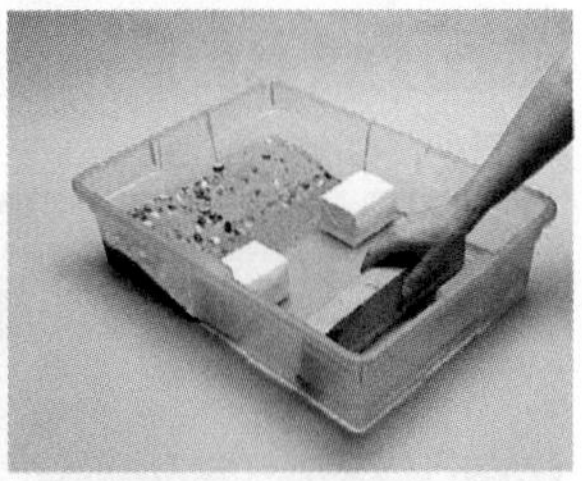
Step 7

Step 7

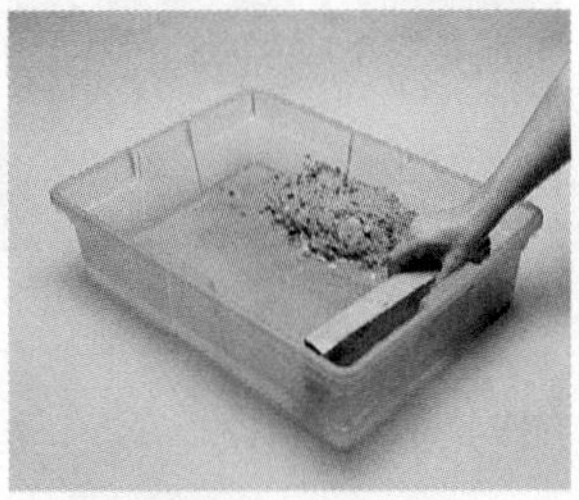
Step 10

Analyze the Results

1. **Making Comparisons** How does wave action build up a beach? How does wave action wear away a beach?
2. **Explaining Events** Describe how the sand moved when the waves ran parallel to the beach in step 10.
3. **Analyzing Results** How do breakwaters modify the effect that longshore currents have on the shape of a beach?

Draw Conclusions

4. **Making Predictions** Predict what will happen to a beach that is affected by wave action if it had no source of additional sand.
5. **Drawing Conclusions** What effect would a series of jetties have on a beach?

Extension

Research and Communications Research what can be done to preserve a recreational beach from erosion that is caused by excessive use by people. Write a letter to a local authority outlining a plan of action to protect that beach.

Answers to Analyze the Results

1. Beaches form where more sediment is deposited than is removed. Wave action during storms or high tides generally carries sediment onto the beach.
2. Answers may vary. Waves should transport sand parallel to the "shore."
3. Answers may vary. Breakwaters should reduce the amount of sand that longshore currents remove from the beach.

Answers to Draw Conclusions

4. Answers may vary. The beach, over time, would lose sediment and would disappear or would become covered with water.
5. Sample answer: A series of jetties would impede movement of sand along the beach, which would cause sand to accumulate on the side of the jetty that faces the current and to be carried away from the back side of the jetty.

Answer to Extension

Answers may vary. Accept all reasonable answers.

Coastal Erosion Near the Beaufort Sea

Homework ADVANCED

Coastal Landforms Coastal landforms can be classified as erosional or depositional. Many coasts are a combination of both, to varying degrees. Each type of coastal landform has defining characteristics. Have students research the characteristics of both erosional and depositional coastal landforms. They should identify the rock formations and beach composition as well as places in the United States where each type is located. After students present their research, ask them to use the clues in the map to identify the type of coastal region depicted in the map. **LS Visual**

Answers to Map Skills Activity

1. 11
2. Most areas show no detectable erosion.
3. The estimated overall shoreline change shows a negative value, indicating erosion.
4. The coastal area toward the south shows more erosion.
5. The area appears to be more affected by waves along the shoreline than by depositional actions of rivers entering the ocean. Many areas show moderate to rapid erosion. The areas of deposition are fewer, smaller, and located only in sheltered areas.
6. Answers may vary. Sample answer: The islands would be eroded more drastically over time and may eventually disappear.

MAPS in Action

Coastal Erosion Near the Beaufort Sea

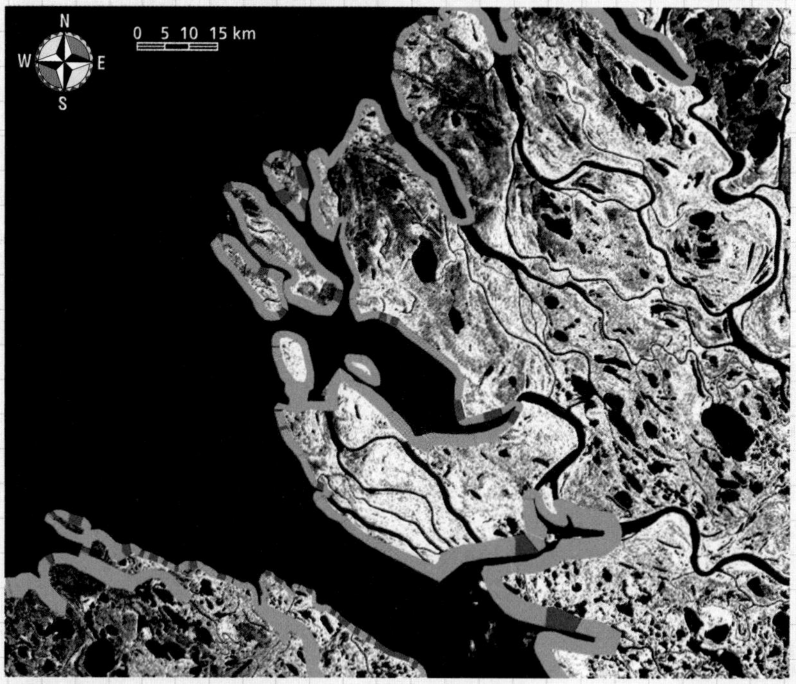

Rapid erosion (>5 m/per year)

Moderate erosion (1 to 5 m/per year)

No detectable erosion (–1 to 1 m/per year)

Deposition (<–1 m/per year)

Areas of accretion are shown in purple. Accretion occurs when more material is deposited than is eroded.

Map Skills Activity

This map shows the coastline of the Beaufort Sea in Canada along with computed amounts of shoreline erosion and accretion. Use the map to answer the questions below.

1. **Using a Key** How many areas of accretion are shown on the map?
2. **Using a Key** What is the level of erosion that is present in most areas shown?
3. **Analyzing Data** Is the estimated overall shoreline change for the entire area shown a positive value (accretion) or a negative value (erosion)?
4. **Making Comparisons** Is there more erosion on the coastal area toward the north or on the area toward the south?
5. **Inferring Relationships** Is the area shown in the map more significantly affected by the effects of waves along the shoreline or by the depositional actions of rivers that enter the ocean? Explain your answer.
6. **Identifying Trends** If present conditions remain the same, what would you expect to happen to the five small islands that are located on the northwest area of the map?

Key Resources

Technology

- Transparencies
  92 Coastal Erosion Near the Beaufort Sea

Chapter 18

Summary

THINK central
SUPER SUMMARY
Keyword: HQXEWWS

Key Ideas | **Key Terms**

Section 1

Wind Erosion

- Saltation and deflation are two ways that wind erodes land. Saltation is the movement of particles by a series of jumps or bounces. Deflation is a form of erosion in which dry soil or rock particles are removed by the wind while larger rock particles are left behind.
- The two types of wind deposits are dunes, which are generally made of sand, and loess, which is made of dust particles.

Key Terms: **saltation,** p. 483; **deflation,** p. 484; **ventifact,** p. 485; **dune,** p. 485; **loess,** p. 488

Section 2

Wave Erosion

- Wave erosion produces many shoreline features, including steep rock cliffs called *sea cliffs*, holes at the bases of cliffs called *sea caves,* rock bridges called *sea arches,* rock columns called *sea stacks*, flat platforms at the bases of cliffs called *terraces*, and sediment deposits along the shore called *beaches*.
- Beaches form from the deposition of sediments by waves.
- Longshore currents carry sand parallel to the shoreline, forming narrow deposits of sand called *spits*, and ridges of sand that connect islands to the shore called *tombolos*.

Key Terms: **headland,** p. 490; **beach,** p. 491; **longshore current,** p. 492

Section 3

Coastal Erosion and Deposition

- Coastlines migrate as sea level changes.
- Barrier islands are long, narrow offshore ridges of sand.
- Human activities, including development and pollution, threaten coastal resources and habitat.

Key Terms: **estuary,** p. 494; **barrier island,** p. 495; **lagoon,** p. 495

Chapter Summary

Using THINK central Resources

Super Summary

Have students connect the major concepts in this chapter through an interactive Super Summary. Visit www.thinkcentral.com and type in the keyword **HQXEWWS** to access the Super Summary for this chapter.

Differentiated Instruction

Alternative Assessment

Quiz Show To see how students have grasped the ideas from the chapter, set up a quiz-style game. Categories can include:

- Name that Formation (show a picture of a landform and have students name it)
- Match the Process (describe an erosional process and have students name it)
- Wind or Wave? (list a process or formation and have students identify whether it forms as a result of wind or wave action)
- Spelling Bee (have students spell vocabulary terms)
- Dunes Day (have students identify characteristics of the different dunes)

One variation of the game may be to divide the class into teams and have each student take a turn choosing a question. Students can use their notes and teammates to find answers.

LS Verbal/Auditory

Chapter Review

Assignment Guide	
Section	**Questions**
1	2, 4, 5, 8–11, 20, 22, 23, 29–33
2	3, 6, 12–14, 19, 24, 25, 27
3	7, 15–18, 21, 26
1–3	1, 28

Reading Toolbox

1. Answers will vary. Student's four-corner folds should include notes, under the appropriate flaps, that describe how erosion by wind and water affects different types of landscapes.

Using Key Terms

2–7. Answers may vary but should show that students understand the definitions of and differences between key terms.

Understanding Key Ideas

8. c
9. a
10. b
11. b
12. a
13. a
14. b
15. d
16. d

Short Answer

17. An emergent coastline forms when the sea level falls or land rises. A submergent coastline occurs when the sea level rises or when land sinks.
18. If shoreline resources are not protected, then habitats can be damaged and shoreline birds and other animals killed.

Chapter 18 Review

1. **Four-Corner Fold** Make a four-corner fold. Label the outer flaps with the names of different types of landscapes: Coastlines and Beaches, Deserts, Cities and Towns, and Farmland. Under the appropriate flap, describe how erosion from wind and water affects each type of landscape. READING TOOLBOX

USING KEY TERMS

Use each of the following terms in a separate sentence.

2. *ventifact*
3. *longshore current*
4. *loess*

For each pair of terms, explain how the meanings of the terms differ.

5. *saltation* and *deflation*
6. *headland* and *beach*
7. *barrier island* and *lagoon*

UNDERSTANDING KEY IDEAS

8. Wind forms desert pavement by removing fine sediment and by leaving large rocks behind in a process called
   a. saltation.
   b. abrasion.
   c. deflation.
   d. ventifact.
9. Wind moves sand by
   a. saltation.
   b. emergence.
   c. abrasion.
   d. depression.
10. Dunes move primarily by the process called
   a. abrasion.
   b. migration.
   c. deflation.
   d. submergence.
11. Thinly layered, yellowish, fine-grained deposits are called
   a. beaches.
   b. loess.
   c. dunes.
   d. desert pavement.
12. The most important erosion agent on shorelines is
   a. wave action. **c.** wind.
   b. weathering. **d.** the tide.
13. Which of the following shoreline features is *not* produced by wave erosion of sea cliffs?
   a. spits
   b. sea stacks
   c. wave-cut terraces
   d. sea arches
14. Longshore-current deposition of sand at the end of a headland produces a
   a. sand bar. **c.** dune.
   b. spit. **d.** sea cliff.
15. Over the last 5,000 years, sea level has changed by
   a. no significant amount.
   b. falling about 1 mm per year.
   c. rising about 1 cm per year.
   d. rising about 1 mm per year.
16. Barrier islands tend to migrate
   a. away from the shore.
   b. along the shore.
   c. in the summer.
   d. toward the shore.

SHORT ANSWER

17. What is the difference between an emergent coastline and a submergent coastline?
18. Explain what may happen if shoreline resources are not protected.
19. What factors affect the composition of a beach?
20. Explain the difference between the four main types of dunes.
21. Explain the difference between absolute sea-level change and relative sea-level change.

CRITICAL THINKING

22. **Identifying Relationships** The deserts of the southwestern United States contain many tall, sculpted rock formations. Was wind or water erosion the most likely agent responsible for these formations? Explain.

19. The factors that determine the composition of a beach are the composition of the source rock and the distance the particles travel before being deposited.
20. Barchan and parabolic dunes are both crescent shaped. However, the center of a Barchan dune faces away from the wind, and the center of a parabolic dune faces into the wind. Transverse and longitudinal dunes take the shape of ridges in long wavelike patterns. Transverse dunes form perpendicular to the direction of the wind, while longitudinal dunes form parallel to the direction of the wind.
21. Absolute sea level changes when the amount of water in the ocean changes. Relative sea level changes when the land or features near the shore change.

23. **Making Inferences** Suppose that one time each month for a year a satellite orbiting Earth takes a photograph of the same sandy, 1 km^2 area of the Sahara. Would the surface features shown in these 12 photographs remain essentially the same, or would they vary? Explain your answer.

24. **Inferring Relationships** Wave energy decreases when waves travel through shallow water. Based on this information, what effect do you think development of a wave-built terrace has on erosion of the shoreline? Explain your answer.

CONCEPT MAPPING

25. Use the following terms to create a concept map: *wave erosion, beaches, spit, berm,* and *tombolos.*

MATH SKILLS

Math Skills

26. **Making Calculations** Suppose it was possible for the sea level to continuously rise at the rate of 1 mm per year and that other factors affecting the coastlines do not change. How many kilometers would the sea level rise in 1 million years?

27. **Applying Quantities** Every year, 25 km^3 of sand is deposited on a beach by a nearby river, and 28 km^3 of sand is removed by wave action. Is the size of the beach increasing or decreasing? Explain.

WRITING SKILLS

28. **Creative Writing** Imagine that you are a newspaper reporter who has traveled to another planet. Scientists know that, at one time, both wind and water eroded the surface of the planet. Prepare a news release that describes the landscape you see and explains the processes that produced it.

29. **Writing Persuasively** You have learned that beautifully colored sunsets and sunrises are the result of dust in the atmosphere. Write a letter or essay to your doubting friend to convince him or her that sunsets and sunrises are caused by dust. Use the evidence that remarkable sunsets were visible around the world for two years after the 1883 eruption of Krakatau, a volcanic island in Indonesia, in your essay.

INTERPRETING GRAPHICS

The graph below shows soil erosion in the United States by wind and water from 1987 to 2003. Use this graph to answer the questions that follow.

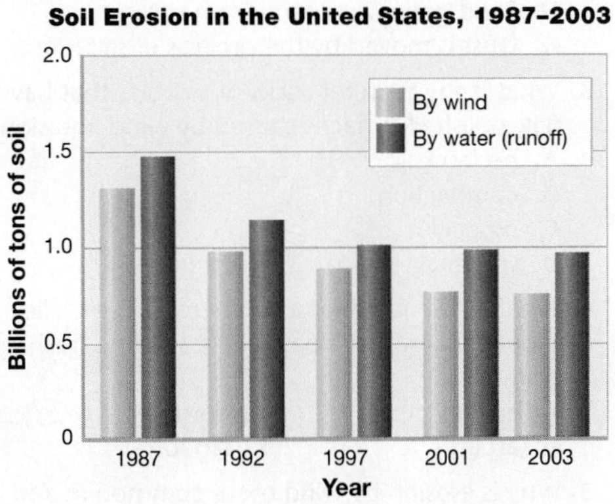

30. Which year had the most combined soil erosion?

31. Which year had the most soil erosion due to water?

32. Do you predict more or less soil erosion by wind in future years? Explain your answer.

33. Would you expect that the amount of soil erosion in the United States would ever be zero? Explain your answer.

Chapter Review

Critical Thinking

22. Sample answer: The tall, sculpted rock formations were most likely produced by water erosion because most wind erosion occurs very close to the ground.
23. Sample answer: Photos taken of the same area of the Sahara Desert over a year's time would vary because the sand dunes would migrate and change shape slightly over that time.
24. The wave-built terrace would make the depth of water decrease closer to the shore. If wave energy decreases through shallow water, then the development of wave-built terraces would slow the effects of erosion on the coastline.

Concept Mapping

25. Answers may vary but should include all of the terms listed. Sample answers appear at the end of this unit on p. 507D.

Math Skills

26. 1 mm/y × 1,000,000 y = 1,000,000 mm; 1,000,000 mm × 1 m/1,000 mm = 1,000 m; 1,000 m × 1 km/1,000 m = 1 km
27. The beach is gradually getting smaller by 3 km^3 each year: 25 km^3 – 28 km^3 = –3 km^3.

Writing Skills

28. Answers may vary. Accept all reasonable answers.
29. Answers may vary. Accept all reasonable answers.

Interpreting Graphics

30. 1987
31. 1987
32. Sample answer: less; the downward trend indicates that efforts are being made to control soil erosion, and the trend should continue.
33. Sample answer: no; soil erosion could never be completely stopped, but the amount of soil eroded could remain relatively stable if conservation methods are employed and no extreme weather conditions occur.

Estimated Time

To give students practice under more realistic testing conditions, allow them 30 minutes to answer all of the questions in this practice test.

Test Doctor

Question 2 Answer G is correct. Dust particles are much smaller than sand grains. Answer F is incorrect because most sand particles are not lifted high but move by short jumps along the ground. Answer H is incorrect because both dust and sand are composed of rock fragments. Answer I is incorrect because sand, not dust, is moved by saltation.

Question 10 Full-credit answers should include the following points:
- the dust came from topsoil that was loosened by overworking
- clearing land for planting removes plant roots that hold the soil in place. The over plowed, overgrazed, and overworked lands were devastated by erosion
- without rain, soil drys out, is lifted up by high winds, is suspended in the air, and forms dark dust clouds
- when the dust fell, it suffocated crops that had survived the drought

Chapter 18 Standardized Test Prep

Understanding Concepts

Directions (1–5): For each question, write on a separate sheet of paper the letter of the correct answer.

1. Which of the following factors most affects the rate at which waves erode land features along the shore?
   A. temperature of the waves
   B. direction in which waves approach shores
   C. shape of the rock formation
   D. compostion of the rock formation
2. Why are dust particles more likely to remain in the atmosphere longer and travel farther than sand particles?
   F. Sand grains are carried higher and fall.
   G. Dust particles are smaller and lighter.
   H. Sand grains are made from rocks.
   I. Dust is moved by the process of saltation.
3. What is the term for rocks or pebbles that have flat, polished surfaces caused by wind abrasion?
   A. bedrock
   B. compaction
   C. pinnacles
   D. ventifacts
4. What is the name for a submerged river valley mouth that forms a bay where salt and fresh water mix?
   F. estuary   **G.** fiord
   H. atoll   **I.** lagoon
5. Why is erosion by wind more common in arid climates than in other regions of the world?
   A. Arid climates have much thicker soil layers.
   B. Arid climates have less frequent dust storms.
   C. Arid climates have less plant cover to anchor soil.
   D. Arid climates have more moisture to hold soil.

Directions (6–7): For each question, write a short response.

6. What is the term for dune movement?
7. What factor is most important in determining the composition of beach materials?

Reading Skills

Directions (8–10): Read the passage below. Then, answer the questions.

Black Blizzards

The area that covers parts of Colorado, Kansas, New Mexico, Oklahoma, and Texas had been converted from natural grassland to farmland in the early 1900s. Many of the plants brought in to replace the natural prairie grasses had shallow root systems that could not hold soil in place. Much of the rest of the grassland was turned over to grazing land for hungry livestock.

During the 1930s, a long period of drought set in and the already dry soil turned to dust. In the spring of 1934, high winds blew black dust clouds across the dry wheat fields of these states. Some of the dust settled only when it reached Boston and New York City. The sky turned black at mid-day. And when the dust fell, houses were coated with thick layers of dust. Roads and fences were covered by dust. The remaining crops that had survived the droughts suffocated on the ground as the dust blocked the sunlight and other nutrients. Millions of people left their farms in search of a better life.

8. According to the passage, how far did some of the dust travel during the dust storms of 1934?
   F. all the way to the Pacific Ocean
   G. all the way to the Atlantic Ocean
   H. only as far as the Rocky Mountains
   I. only as far as the Great Smokey Mountains
9. Which of the following statements can be inferred from the information in the passage?
   A. The dust storms from the 1930s continued well into the 1940s.
   B. Black blizzards are common occurrences in the states of Texas and Colorado.
   C. One of the main causes of the dust storms of the 1930s was misuse of land by humans.
   D. Damage from the dust storms of the 1930s can still be seen today in states such as Texas and Oklahoma.
10. Briefly describe how high winds and an extensive drought could combine to produce the terrible conditions seen during the 1930s.

Question 12 Full-credit answers should include the following points:
- students must use critical-thinking skills and their knowledge of deposition to answer this question
- an understanding that under natural conditions, rivers dump tons of sediment in the areas where they meet the ocean
- under natural circumstances, the rate of this deposition may effectively balance the rate of erosion in the area. Currents that run parallel to the shore carry deposited sediments that replace sand lost to erosion
- as humans build dams that slow the flow of water and filter sediments, less deposition takes place in the mouth of the stream. The amount of sediment that reaches the Gulf of Mexico is decreased significantly
- erosion happens faster than deposition under these circumstances
- other human activities, such as construction and the pumping of oil and groundwater, also contribute to the problem by weakening the shoreline's physical integrity

Interpreting Graphics

Directions (11–12): For each question below, record the correct answer on a separate sheet of paper.

Base your answer to question 11 on the image of an eroding sea cliff below. The projecting headland of the cliff is composed of granite, and the hillside below it is made of limestone.

Erosion of a Sea Cliff

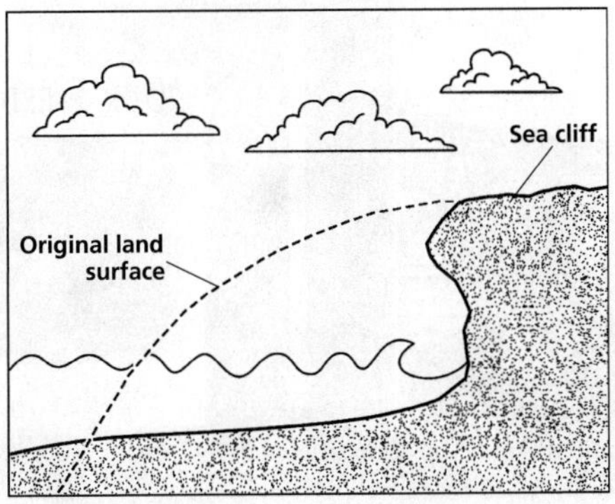

11. The coastal landforms shown were most likely formed as a result of the action of

F. glacial movements.
G. seismic activity.
H. sea level changes.
I. waves and weathering.

Base your answer to question 12 on the map below, which shows shoreline changes across parts of the United States.

Map of Coastal Erosion Patterns

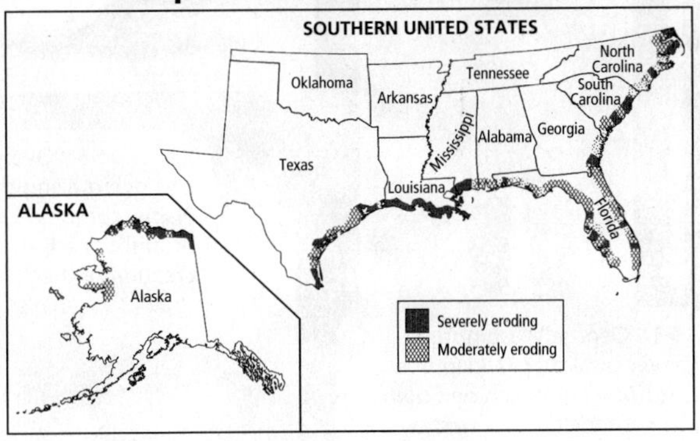

12. How might human activities along the rivers that empty into the Gulf of Mexico and the coastal shoreline play a part in the increasing rate of erosion that is affecting the region?

Test Tip

Do not spend a long period of time on any single question. Mark a question that you cannot answer quickly, and come back to it.

Standardized Test Prep

Using THINK central Resources

State Resources

- For specific resources for your state, visit www.thinkcentral.com and type in the keyword **HSHSTR.**

Answers

Understanding Concepts

1. D
2. G
3. D
4. F
5. C
6. migration
7. the source rock

Reading Skills

8. G
9. C
10. Answers may vary. See Test Doctor for a detailed scoring rubric.

Interpreting Graphics

11. I
12. Answers may vary. See Test Doctor for a detailed scoring rubric.

Why It Matters

Geology Connections

Remind students that the arrows show broad connections between events, not direct cause-and-effect relationships.

Students often forget that famous scientists were influenced by the social and political events of their time. The following information will help students connect the scientists to the time periods in which they lived.

Cyrus McCormick was born in 1809 in Rock Bridge County, Virginia, and grew up farming. His father tried for 28 years to build a reaper. Working with his father's designs, McCormick completed a successful design in only 18 months.

Charles "Turnip" Townshend was a government official who saw agriculture as a hobby. He introduced four-field crop rotation to Europe in the 18th century. Before that time, most of Europe had used three-crop rotation. Townshend suggested rotating wheat, barley, turnips, and clover to improve the quality of the soil.

George Washington Carver was born before slavery was abolished in the United States, but he lived most of his life as a free man after the Civil War. In the South, the soil had been depleted by the exclusive farming of cotton over many years. Carver devoted his life to developing techniques for replenishing the soil and to teaching others about these methods. He focused on crops that restore soil nutrients, such as soybeans, sweet potatoes, and peanuts. Carver published articles and spoke with former slaves about farming techniques that would allow them to grow their own food and achieve self-sufficiency, while maintaining healthy soil.

Why It Matters

Geology Connections

Science, technology, and society are closely linked. This flowchart shows just a few of the connections in the history of geology.

9,500 B.C.E. Systematic farming begins in the Fertile Crescent.

1620 The *Mayflower* carries 102 passengers to Plymouth, Massachusetts.

1790 Farmers make up 90% of the labor force in the United States.

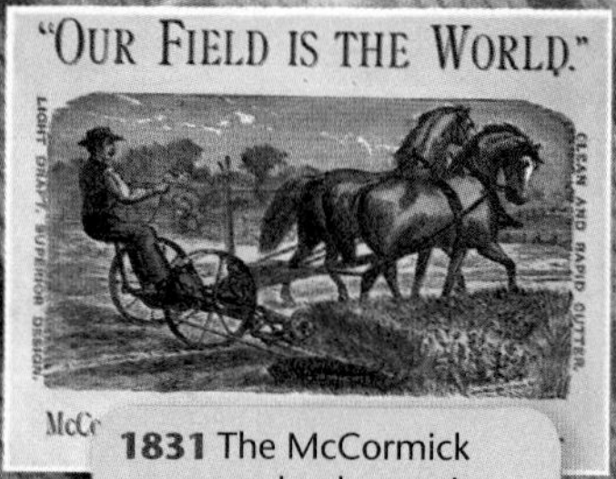

1831 The McCormick reaper makes harvesting grain much more efficient.

1730s Charles "Turnip" Townshend introduces the 4-year crop rotation method.

1916 George Washington Carver publishes *Help for the Hard Times* in which he outlines soil conservation suggestions.

1837 John Deere invents a steel walking plow with a curved blade.

1935–1938 Overplowing and overgrazing the Great Plains, combined with drought, leads to the creation of the "Dust Bowl."

Reading Skill Builder

BASIC

Visual Literacy The map of the Ogallala aquifer shows the size and shape of the aquifer relative to the states that it underlies. As you can see, the aquifer lies mainly under Nebraska and Kansas, the panhandles of Texas and Oklahoma, and the boundaries of New Mexico, Colorado, Wyoming, and South Dakota. The regions of Nebraska, Kansas, Oklahoma, and Texas that draw water from the aquifer are intensely farmed and, therefore, draw much of the water for irrigation.

800 B.C.E. Farmers in the Persian empire develop the *qanat* irrigation system.

312 B.C.E. The Romans build the *Aqua Appia,* the first of eleven major aqueducts.

1900 American farmers first use sprinkler irrigation systems.

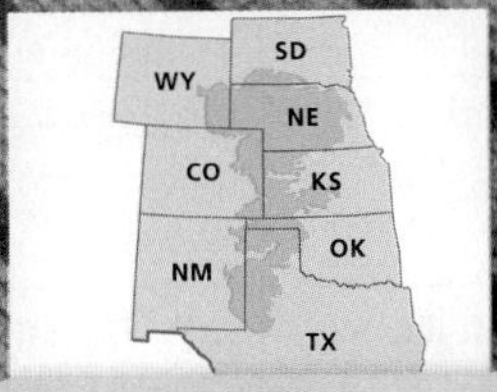

1911 The Ogallala aquifer in the Midwestern United States is first tapped for irrigation.

1935 The Natural Resource Conservation Service is established.

1954 More farms use tractors than animals, such as horses or mules, for farm production processes.

2000 Every day, 17 billion gallons of water from the Ogallala aquifer are used for irrigation.

2004 Global sales of bottled water exceed $100 billion per year.

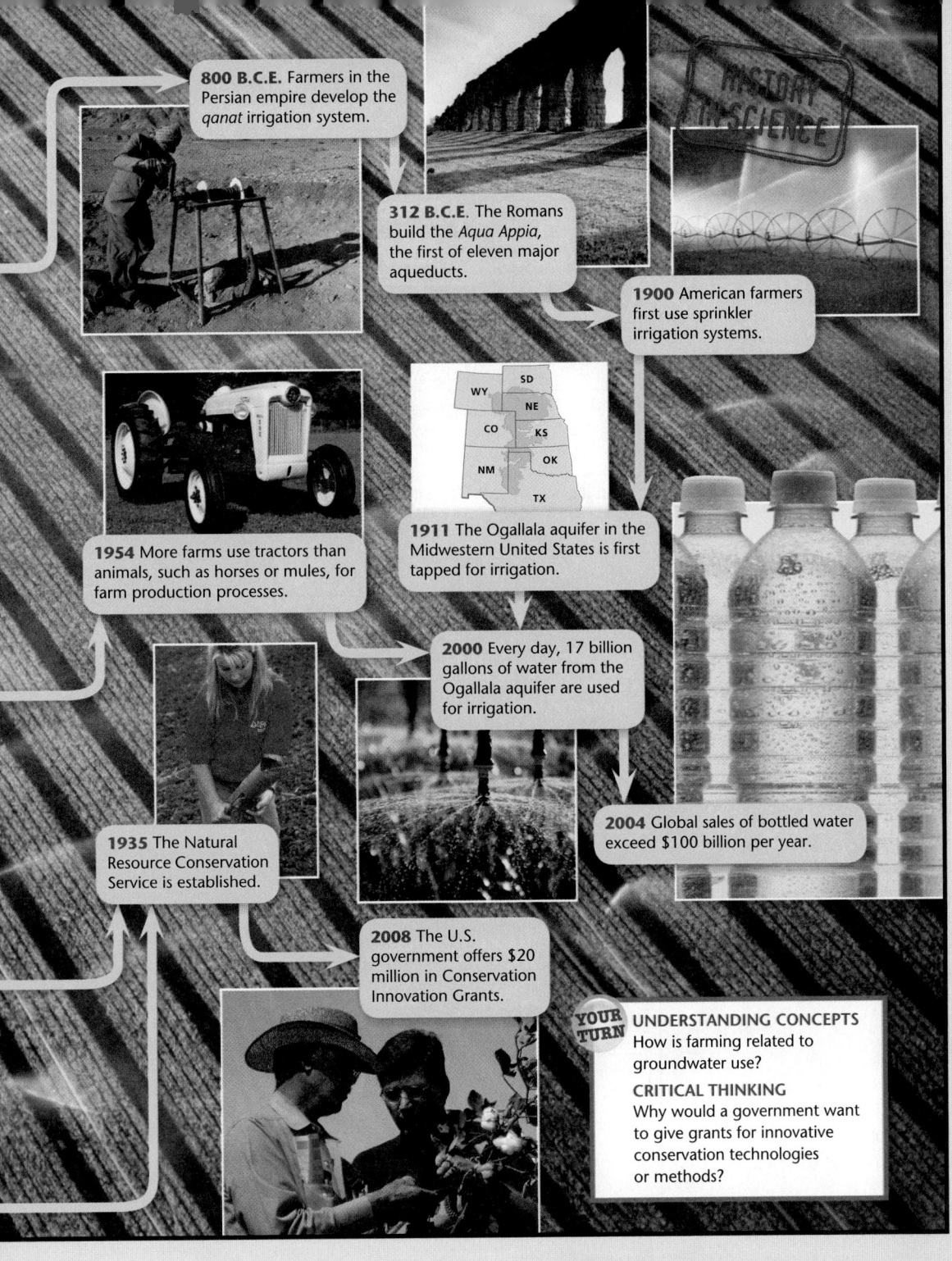

2008 The U.S. government offers $20 million in Conservation Innovation Grants.

YOUR TURN

UNDERSTANDING CONCEPTS
How is farming related to groundwater use?

CRITICAL THINKING
Why would a government want to give grants for innovative conservation technologies or methods?

Answers to Your Turn

Understanding Concepts Farming affects groundwater by withdrawing water from aquifers for irrigation. Farming also affects groundwater by causing non-point source pollution, such as fertilizers and pesticides that run off the fields and may enter aquifers.

Critical Thinking The government wants to promote conservation and protect the quality of soil and water in the nation. These grants help people develop and produce technologies and methods for this purpose.

Why It Matters

Qanat Irrigation Around 800 BCE, farmers in the Persian Empire developed the qanat irrigation system, which is still used today. This irrigation system reliably supplies water to desert regions without using pumps. The technology involves a series of vertical well-like shafts that tap into an upland aquifer and are connected by gently sloping tunnels. The destination for the water is generally lower than the source, so the water runs downhill, powered only by gravity.

Why It Matters

The Steel Walking Plow In 1837, John Deere invented the steel walking plow. While steel plows had been used before, the highly polished surface and uniquely curved shape of Deere's plow allowed the sticky clay soil of the prairies to slide off the plow. Deere's plow made the previously untilled soil of the American Great Plains easier to cultivate.

Why It Matters

The Ogallala Aquifer The Ogallala aquifer is the largest aquifer in the United States and one of the largest aquifers in the world. It lies beneath eight states in the middle of the United States and supplies the drinking water for 82% of the population that lives over it. Although the area covered by the aquifer is vast, the depth of the aquifer is shallow. It was first tapped for irrigation in 1911. By 2000, 17 billion gallons of water were being pumped from it every day for irrigation. It is currently being depleted at the rate of 12 billion cubic meters per year. At this rate of depletion, the Ogallala aquifer could be dry within 25 years. Depletion of the Ogallala aquifer could result in the desertification of the central Great Plains of the United States.

Answers continued from p. 377

Finding Examples

Types of chemical weathering	Examples	Signal words
oxidation	red-colored rocks from iron oxide, rust	(none)
hydrolysis	kaolin (type of clay produced by feldspar combining with water)	for example
carbonation	calcium bicarbonate from reaction of carbonic acid with calcite	one example
organic acids	rocks cracked by acid from lichen and mosses	(none)
acid precipitation	many historical monuments and sculptures	in fact

Answers continued from p. 394

Section Review

11. Answers may vary. Possible answers include improving ground cover so soils are held by roots and do not become saturated with heavy rains, preventing or containing wildfires so slopes do not become empty of vegetation during the dry season, building retaining walls, regrading the hillside, or forbidding further building on the hillside.
12. *Landforms* such as *mountains*, *plains*, and *plateaus*, which erode into *mesas* and *buttes*, are shaped by *erosion* processes, such as *gullying*, *sheet erosion*, *landslides*, *mudflows*, *slump*, *solifluction*, and *creep*, which produces rock piles called *talus*.

Answers continued from p. 414

Section Review

8. If uplift occurred, the gradient of the stream would increase, causing an increase in stream speed and channel erosion.
9. The higher the speed is, the more sediment and larger particles a stream can carry.
10. At the *headwaters*, the *stream gradient* is steep, so *stream load*, composed of *bed load*, *suspended load*, and *dissolved load*, is high, but *meanders* and *braided channels* develop as gradient and load change.

Answers continued from p. 454

Word Families

Term	Definition of second word	Definition of whole two-word term
alpine glacier	alpine—of or like mountains	a glacier in the mountains
continental glacier	continental—of or characteristic of a continent	a glacier that spreads over a large area
tributary glacier	tributary—a smaller one flowing into a larger one (stream, river, etc.)	a small glacier that flows into a larger glacier
glacial ice	ice—frozen water	ice that is part of a glacier
glacial movement	movement—the act of moving	the movements of a glacier
glacial drift	drift—moving aimlessly, being carried along	rock material carried and deposited by a glacier
glacial period	period—a certain length of time	a certain length of time when glaciers are prevalent
interglacial period	period—a certain length of time	the time between times when glaciers are prevalent
glacial erosion	erosion—being worn away	when glaciers erode rock and other matter
glacial deposition	deposition—being deposited	when glaciers deposit sediment
glacial lake	lake—a body of water, larger than a pond and smaller than an ocean	a lake formed by a glacier
glacial stream	stream—a body of running water, smaller than a river	a stream formed by a glacier
glacial meltwater	meltwater—water that has melted from snow or ice	water that comes from the melting of a glacier
glacial sediment	sediment—matter, such as dirt and eroded rock	sediment that is eroded by a glacier
glacial advance	advance—to move forward	when glaciers get larger
glacial retreat	retreat—to move backward	when glaciers melt

Classification

Glacial deposition or landform produced by glacial deposition	Composition	Where and how deposited
erratic	different from that of the nearby bedrock	carried over a long distance by a glacier; deposited when a glacier melts
glacial drift	all sediments deposited by a glacier	deposited when glacier melts
till	unsorted sediments from the base of a glacier	left behind when glacial ice melts
stratified drift	material that is sorted into layers	sorted and deposited in layers by streams flowing from melted ice
moraine	till	deposited as ridges on the ground or the glacier itself
lateral moraine	till	deposited along the sides of an alpine glacier, usually as a long ridge
medial moraine	till	formed by adjacent lateral moraines when two or more alpine glaciers join
ground moraine	till	left beneath a glacier when the ice melts
drumlins	till	long, low, tear-shaped mounds; sometimes made when an ice sheet molds ground moraine into clusters
terminal moraines	till	small ridges deposited at the leading edge of a melting glacier;
outwash plain	stratified drift	lies in front of a terminal moraine
kettle	drift	formed when a chunk of glacial ice is buried in drift; as ice melts, a cavity forms in the drift
esker	stratified drift (gravel and sand)	long, winding ridges left behind when continental glaciers recede; material deposited by streams of meltwater that flow through ice tunnels within the glaciers
meltwater stream	meltwater from glaciers; sediment; drift; rock particles	formed when glaciers melt
glacial lake	meltwater	sometimes form in the uneven surface of ground moraine deposited by melting glaciers

Answers continued from p. 466

Section Review

10. The glacial sediment deposited by glacial ice is called till, which is unsorted sand and rock. The glacial sediment deposited by glacial meltwater is stratified drift, which is sorted and deposited in layers.

11. A *glacier* erodes land, forming *cirques* and *roches moutonnées*, and deposits *glacial drift*, such as *till*, *moraines*, and *stratified drift*, on *outwash plains* that are commonly pitted with *kettles*.

Sample Answers to Concept Maps from Chapter Reviews

Chapter 14 Weathering and Erosion, p. 401

32.

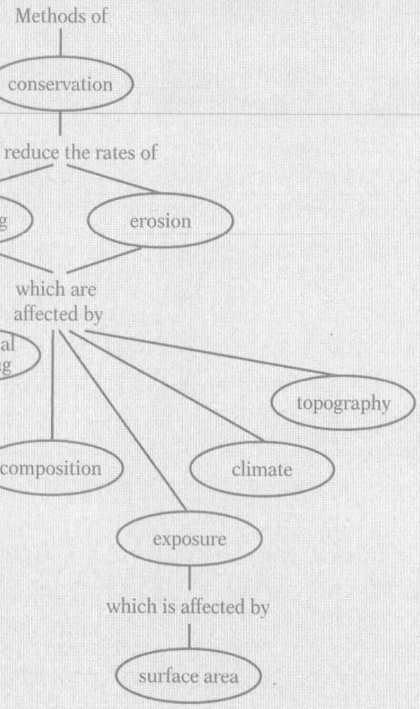

Chapter 16 Groundwater, p. 449

32.

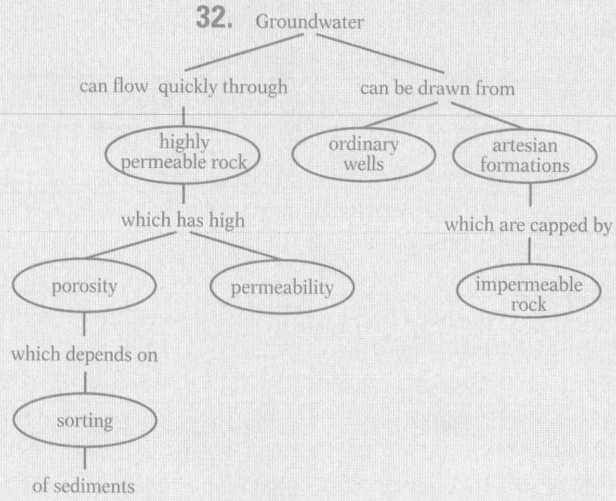

Chapter 15 River Systems, p. 425

28.

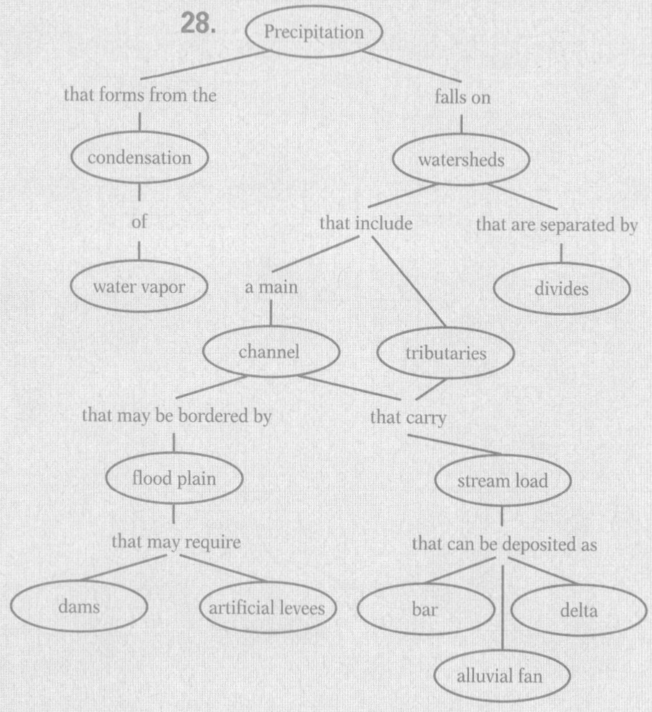

Sample Answers to Concept Maps from Chapter Reviews

Chapter 17 Glaciers, p. 477

26.

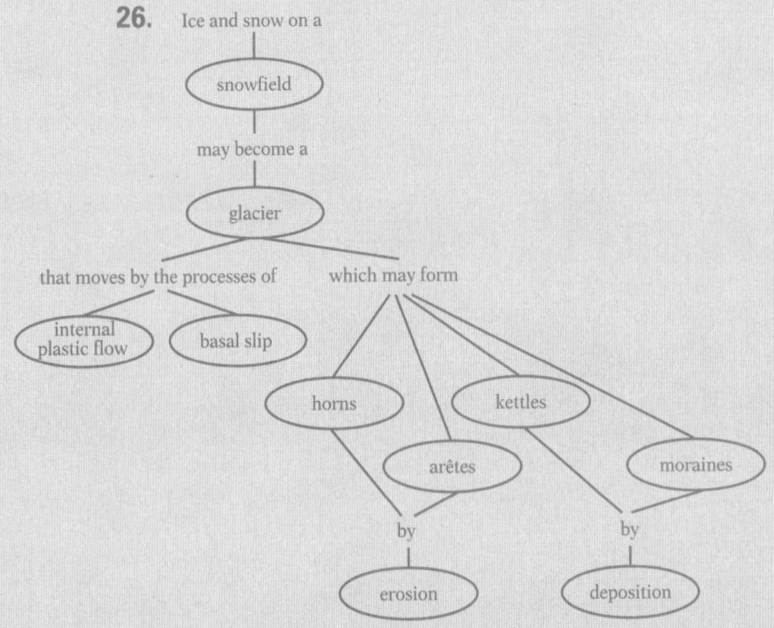

Chapter 18 Erosion by Wind and Waves, p. 503

25.

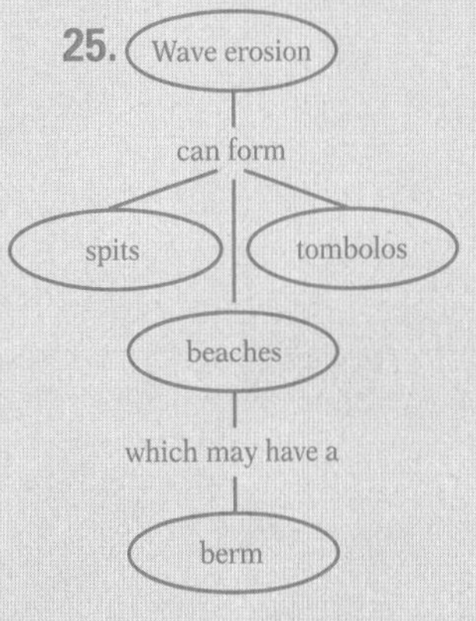

Unit 6 Atmospheric Forces

Chapter Planner **19**

The Atmosphere

	Standards	Teach Key Ideas
Chapter Opener, pp. 510–511 **45 min.**	National Science Education Standards	
Section 1 Characteristics of the Atmosphere pp. 513–520 **45 min.** ❯ Composition of the Atmosphere ❯ Atmospheric Pressure ❯ Measuring Atmospheric Pressure ❯ Layers of the Atmosphere ❯ Temperature Inversions	SAI 2c, ES 2b	■ ◆ **Bellringer,** p. 513 ■ **Demonstration:** Air Force, p. 513 ■ **DI (English Learners):** Paired Summarizing, p. 514 ■ **DI (Advanced Learners):** High Altitude, p. 516 ■ **DI (Special Education Students):** Layers of the Atmosphere, p. 518 ◆ **Transparency:** 93 Layers of the Atmosphere ▲ **Visual Concepts:** Biogeochemical Cycle • Photosynthesis • Linking Photosynthesis and Respiration • Ozone and Ozone Holes • Ozone and Ecosystems • Atmospheric Pressure • Barometer • Layers of the Atmosphere • Altitude and Air Pressure • Temperature Inversion • Smog
Section 2 Solar Energy and the Atmosphere pp. 521–526 **90 min.** ❯ Radiation ❯ The Atmosphere and Solar Radiation ❯ Absorption and Infrared Energy ❯ Variations in Temperature ❯ Conduction ❯ Convection	SAI 2c, ES 1c, ES 1d, PS 6a, PS 6b	■ ◆ **Bellringer,** p. 521 ■ **DI (Struggling Readers):** Radiation, p. 521 ■ **DI (Advanced Learners):** CFCs, p. 523 ■ **DI (Basic Learners):** The Greenhouse Effect, p. 524 ■ **Discussion:** The Tropics, p. 534 ◆ **Transparencies:** 94 The Electromagnetic Spectrum • 95 The Greenhouse Effect and Latitude and Season • 98 Absorbed Solar Radiation ▲ **Visual Concepts:** Electromagnetic Spectrum • Radiation Balance • Greenhouse Effect • Atmospheric Heating: Radiation, Conduction, and Convection • Comparing Convection, Conduction, and Radiation
Section 3 Atmospheric Circulation pp. 527–530 **45 min.** ❯ The Coriolis Effect ❯ Global Winds ❯ Local Winds	UCP 4, ES 1c, ES 1d	■ ◆ **Bellringer,** p. 527 ■ **Demonstration:** Modeling the Coriolis Effect, p. 527 ■ **DI (Struggling Readers):** Reading Organizer, p. 527 ■ **DI (Special Education Students):** Science Vocabulary, p. 528 ◆ **Transparencies:** 96 The Coriolis Effect • 97 Global Wind Belts ▲ **Visual Concepts:** Coriolis Effect • Pressure Belts and Convection Cells • Wind • Types of Wind • Prevailing Winds • Local Winds
Chapter Wrap-Up, pp. 535–539 **90 min.**		**Chapter Summary,** p. 535

See also PowerNotes® Presentations

CHAPTER Fast Track *To shorten instruction because of time limitations, omit the Chapter Lab.*

Key

Teacher's Edition ■ | Teaching Transparencies ◆
Chapter Resource File ● | Online Edition ▲

All resources listed below are also available on the Teacher One Stop™.

Why It Matters	Hands-On	Skills Development	Assessment
■ **Chapter Overview,** p. 510 ■ **Using the Figure:** Storm Watch, p. 510	**Inquiry Lab:** Colorful Currents, p. 511	**Reading Toolbox,** p. 512	
■ **Section Overview,** p. 513 ■ **Biology Connection:** The Breath of Life, p. 514 ■ **Environmental Connection:** Ozone, Good or Bad?, p. 515 ■ **History Connection:** Incontestable Experiment, p. 516 ■ **Using the Figure:** Mercurial Barometers, p. 517 ■ **Gas Mass,** p. 518 ■ **Radio Waves,** p. 519 ■ **Environmental Connection:** Deadly Blankets of Smog, p. 519	■ **Activity:** Dust Collectors, p. 515 ■ **Activity:** Create a Vacuum, p. 516 ■ **Activity:** Weather Maps, p. 517 **QuickLab:** Barometric Pressure, p. 517	**Reading Toolbox:** Signal Words, p. 514 **MathPractice:** Force of the Air, p. 516	**Reading Check,** p. 514 **Reading Check,** p. 517 **Reading Check,** p. 519 **Section Review,** p. 520 ■ **Reteaching,** p. 519 ■ **Quiz,** p. 519 ■ **DI (Alternative Assessment):** Modeling, p. 520 ● **Section Quiz**
■ **Section Overview,** p. 521 **Gardens in the Sky,** p. 522 ■ **Using the Figure:** Phantom Images, p. 523 ■ **Environmental Connection:** CO_2 Concentrations, p. 524	■ **Activity:** Magic with Beads, p. 521 **Activity:** Blue and Red Skies, p. 522 ■ **Group Activity:** Comparing Albedos, p. 523 **QuickLab:** Light and Latitude, p. 525 **Inquiry Lab:** Energy Absorption and Reflection, pp. 532–533 ● **Inquiry Lab:** Ultraviolet Protection	**Reading Toolbox:** Prefixes, p. 523 ■ **Skill Builder:** Vocabulary, p. 523 ● ■ **Internet Activity:** Global Warming, p. 524 **Maps in Action:** Absorbed Solar Radiation, p. 534	**Reading Check,** p. 525 **Section Review,** p. 526 ■ **Reteaching,** p. 525 ■ **Quiz,** p. 525 ■ **DI (Alternative Assessment):** The Spectrum of Life, p. 526 ● **Section Quiz**
■ **Section Overview,** p. 527 ■ **Using the Figure:** Coriolis Effect, p. 528 ■ **The Horse Latitudes,** p. 529	■ **Group Activity:** It's a Breeze, p. 528 ● **Making Models Lab:** Global Air Movement	■ **Reading Toolbox:** Layered Book, p. 529 ● **Internet Activity:** Harnessing Wind	**Reading Check,** p. 528 **Section Review,** p. 530 ■ **Reteaching,** p. 529 ■ **Quiz,** p. 529 ■ **DI (Alternative Assessment):** Wind and Solar Energy, p. 530 ● **Section Quiz**
Chasing Rainbows and Sundogs, p. 531		▲ **Super Summary** **Standardized Test Prep,** p. 538–539	**Chapter Review,** pp. 536–537 ● **Chapter Tests**

See also Lab Generator

See also Holt Online Assessment Resources

Chapter Overview

The atmosphere is the protective blanket of gases that surrounds Earth. The atmosphere not only contains the oxygen we breathe, but makes life on Earth possible by protecting us from harmful solar radiation and by moderating global temperatures.

Using the Figure — GENERAL

Storm Watch Point out how the clouds in the photo seem to top out at a certain level—the tropopause. This is the boundary between the troposphere, the atmospheric layer closest to Earth, and the stratosphere. Most clouds form in the troposphere. However, the storm at the center of the photo rises through the tropopause. Ask students why many pilots prefer to fly at or above the tropopause. (fewer clouds, better visibility, less likely to encounter storms and other adverse weather conditions) **LS Logical**

Why It Matters

Without the particular composition and thickness of Earth's atmosphere, life as we know would not be possible. The atmospheres of other planets are vastly different from Earth's atmosphere. Mars, the planet most like Earth, has a thin atmosphere that contains virtually no oxygen and provides only a weak greenhouse effect. The thick atmosphere of Venus consists mostly of carbon dioxide and traps heat so well the average temperature on Venus is about 450 °C; too hot to support life as we know it.

Chapter 19 The Atmosphere

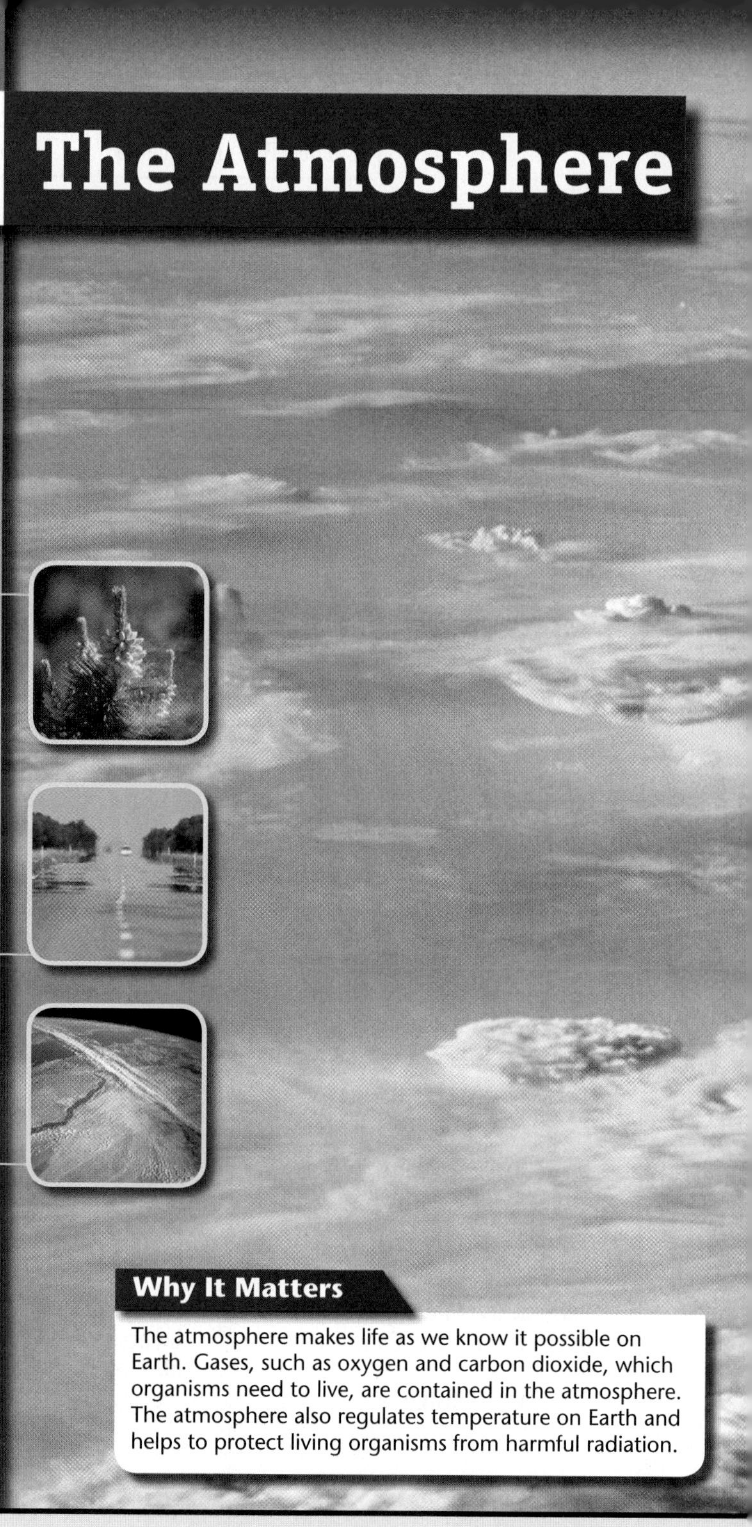

Chapter Outline

1 Characteristics of the Atmosphere
- Composition of the Atmosphere
- Atmospheric Pressure
- Measuring Atmospheric Pressure
- Layers of the Atmosphere
- Temperature Inversions

2 Solar Energy and the Atmosphere
- Radiation
- The Atmosphere and Solar Radiation
- Absorption and Infrared Energy
- Variations in Temperature
- Conduction
- Convection

3 Atmospheric Circulation
- The Coriolis Effect
- Global Winds
- Local Winds

Virginia Standards of Learning
ES.1.a
ES.1.c
ES.2.a
ES.11.a
ES.11.c
ES.11.d
ES.12.d

Why It Matters

The atmosphere makes life as we know it possible on Earth. Gases, such as oxygen and carbon dioxide, which organisms need to live, are contained in the atmosphere. The atmosphere also regulates temperature on Earth and helps to protect living organisms from harmful radiation.

Chapter Correlations — *Virginia Standards of Learning*

ES.1.a volume, area, mass, elapsed time, direction, temperature, pressure, distance, density, and changes in elevation/depth are calculated utilizing the most appropriate tools.
ES.1.c scales, diagrams, charts, graphs, tables, imagery, models, and profiles are constructed and interpreted.
ES.2.a science explains and predicts the interactions and dynamics of complex Earth systems.
ES.11.a scientific evidence for atmospheric composition changes over geologic time
ES.11.c atmospheric regulation mechanisms including the effects of density differences and energy transfer
ES.11.d potential changes to the atmosphere and climate due to human, biologic, and geologic activity
ES.12.d weather phenomena and the factors that affect climate including radiation, conduction, and convection

Inquiry Lab

15 min

Colorful Currents

Pour hot water into two beakers, so that the beakers are three-fourths full. To one beaker, add a chunk of dyed ice. To the second beaker, add a chunk of dyed ice that contains a short length of metal chain or several large paper clips strung together. Observe the beakers. Record your observations at 0 min, 1 min, and 5 min.

Questions to Get You Started

1. What is happening in the beakers at 0 min? What is happening at 1 min and at 5 min?
2. What type of energy transfer explains the effect that you see in the first beaker? How can you tell?
3. What type of energy transfer explains the effect that you see in the second beaker? How can you tell?

Inquiry Lab

Central concept: Energy transfer occurs in the atmosphere through radiation, conduction, and convection. This lab allows students to observe and compare energy transfer via conduction and convection.

Teacher's notes: You may wish to review the concepts of conduction and convection before beginning the lab. Conduction is the transfer of energy as heat from one object to another by direct contact. Convection is the process by which air or other matter rises and sinks because of differences in temperature.

Materials (per group)

- Hot water
- Two beakers
- Two chunks of dyed ice
- A short length of metal chain or several large paper clips

Skills Acquired

- Observing
- Interpreting

Answers to Getting Started

1. Possible answer: In Beaker 1, the ice chunk floated and the food coloring sank. As the ice melted, it rolled. In Beaker 2, the ice chunk sank. The food coloring stayed near the bottom. The ice took longer to melt than the chunk in Beaker 1.
2. Energy was transferred by convection. I could see the convection current rotating the ice chunk.
3. Energy was transferred by conduction. I could see the food coloring right around the ice chunk, coming into contact with the rest of the water.

Using THINK central Resources

An online version of this chapter, as well as all the print and multimedia resources that accompany the program are available to registered teachers and their students. Log onto www.thinkcentral.com to access these materials and tools to organize your preparation and student learning.

READING TOOLBOX

Word Parts

Prefixes Completed tables should contain the following information: Layer: troposphere, Prefix: tropo-, Meaning: change; Layer: stratosphere, Prefix: strato-, Meaning: spread out; Layer: mesosphere, Prefix: meso-, Meaning: in the middle; Layer: thermosphere, Prefix: thermo-, Meaning: heat

Cause and Effect

Signal Words Possible answers: Cause: scattering, Effect: sunlight that reaches Earth comes from all directions, Marker: as a result; Cause: the intensity and amount of time a surface material receives radiation, Effect: how much energy is reflected or absorbed, Marker: affects; Cause: tilt of Earth's axis, Effect: seasonal temperature variation, Marker: because of

FoldNotes

Layered Book FoldNotes Students should write notes about the characteristics of each layer of the atmosphere. Characteristics can include altitude reached and how temperature changes with altitude.

READING TOOLBOX

These reading tools will help you learn the material in this chapter.

Word Parts

Prefixes You can figure out the meanings of many unfamiliar science terms by looking at their word parts. For example, the word *atmosphere* is formed by combining the prefix *atmos-* with the root *sphere. Atmos* comes from the Greek word for "vapor" and means "air." *Sphere* is used because the atmosphere is shaped like a sphere around Earth.

Your Turn As you read Section 1, make a table like the one started below. List the layers of the atmosphere, the prefix in the name of each layer, and your guess for the meaning of the prefix. After you have finished, look up the prefixes in a dictionary and correct your table as necessary.

Layer	Prefix	Meaning
troposphere	tropo-	
stratosphere		

Cause and Effect

Signal Words Certain words and phrases signal cause-and-effect relationships. These signal words and phrases are called *cause-and-effect markers.*

Cause markers	Effect markers
cause	therefore
affect	thus
produce	as a result of
as a result of	is an effect of
due to	results from
because	consequently

Your Turn Complete a table of cause-and-effect markers, like the one started below, as you read this chapter.

Cause	Effect	Marker(s)
convection	heating of the lower atmosphere of Earth	the result of; because

Fold Notes

Layered Book FoldNotes are a fun way to help you learn and remember ideas that you encounter as you read. You can use the flaps of the layered book to summarize information you learn into categories.

Your Turn Make a layered book, as described in **Appendix A**. Label the tabs of the layered book

"Troposphere," "Stratosphere," "Mesosphere," and "Thermosphere."

Write notes on the appropriate layers as you read Section 1.

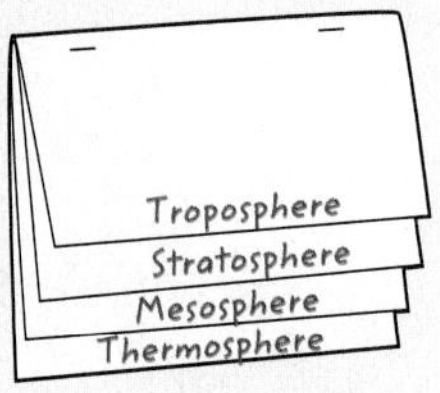

For more information on how to use these and other tools, see **Appendix A**.

SECTION 1

Characteristics of the Atmosphere

Key Ideas	Key Terms	Why It Matters
❯ Describe the composition of Earth's atmosphere. ❯ Explain how two types of barometers work. ❯ Identify the layers of the atmosphere. ❯ Identify two effects of air pollution.	atmosphere ozone atmospheric pressure troposphere stratosphere mesosphere thermosphere	Certain characteristics of the atmosphere have a direct effect on your health and well-being. Whether it's the gases that make up air or the way that it is structured, without the atmosphere, life as we know it would be impossible.

The layer of gases that surrounds Earth is called the **atmosphere.** The atmosphere is made up of a mixture of chemical elements and compounds that is commonly called *air*. The atmosphere protects Earth's surface from the sun's radiation and helps to regulate the temperature of Earth's surface.

Composition of the Atmosphere

As the graph in **Figure 1** shows, the most abundant elements in air are the gases nitrogen, oxygen, and argon. The composition of dry air is nearly the same everywhere on Earth's surface and up to an altitude of about 80 km. The two most abundant compounds in air are the gases carbon dioxide, CO_2, and water vapor, H_2O. In addition to containing gaseous elements and compounds, the atmosphere commonly carries various kinds of tiny solid particles, such as dust and pollen.

atmosphere a mixture of gases that surrounds a planet, moon, or other celestial body

Nitrogen in the Atmosphere

Nitrogen makes up about 78% of Earth's atmosphere. Nitrogen in the atmosphere is maintained through a process called the *nitrogen cycle.* During the nitrogen cycle, nitrogen moves from air to the soil and then to plants and animals, and eventually returns to the air.

Nitrogen is removed from the air mainly by the action of nitrogen-fixing bacteria. These microscopic organisms live in the soil and on the roots of certain plants. The bacteria chemically change nitrogen from the air into nitrogen compounds that are vital to the growth of all plants. When animals eat plants, nitrogen compounds enter the animals' bodies. Nitrogen compounds are then returned to the soil through animal wastes or by the decay of dead organisms. Decay releases nitrogen back into the atmosphere. A similar nitrogen cycle takes place between marine organisms and ocean water.

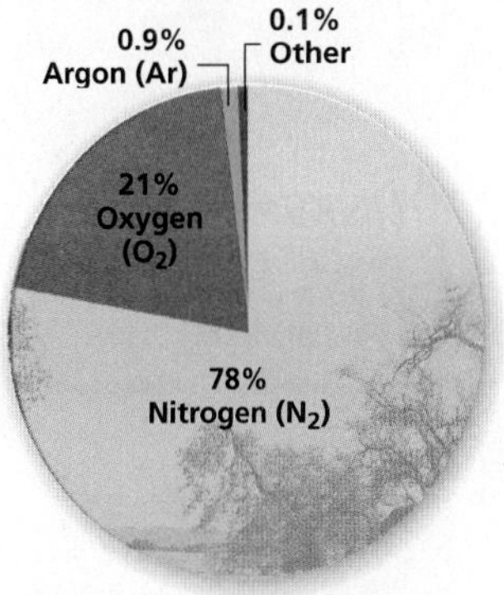

Figure 1 This pie graph shows the composition of dry air by volume at sea level.

Section 1

Focus

Overview

This section explains the major components and the four layers of Earth's atmosphere. It describes ways to measure atmospheric pressure and describes air pollution and its effects on people, animals, plants, and property.

Bellringer

Have students predict what will happen to a lighted candle that is covered by a glass jar. (Combustion will use up the oxygen in the jar, and the candle will go out.)

Motivate

Demonstration GENERAL

Air Force Demonstrate air pressure using a 600 mL glass milk bottle or similar glass bottle with an opening of about 4 cm and a peeled hard-boiled egg. Make sure the egg can sit on the opening of the bottle without falling in. Light three matches at once and drop them quickly into the bottle. Then, immediately set the egg on the opening. The egg will be forced into the bottle. Ask students why they think this happened. (The burning matches caused a partial vacuum inside the bottle, which decreased the air pressure in the bottle. The greater pressure of the outside air pushed the egg into the bottle.) **LS Visual**

Key Resources

Chapter Resource File
- Directed Reading BASIC

Technology
- Transparencies
  Bellringer

Teach

Teaching Tip — BASIC

Connect to Prior Knowledge Ask students where the water in a puddle that forms after a rain shower comes from. (Some water came from the sky as rain. Some water ran into the puddle from the surrounding ground.) Ask them what happens to the puddle after a few hot, dry days. (The puddle shrinks and the water disappears. This happens as the water evaporates.) Explain to students that water cycles between the land, ocean, and atmosphere through the water cycle.
LS Logical

READING TOOLBOX

Signal Words Students should include the following examples: Cause: photosynthesis, Effect: oxygen produced and released, Marker: produced; Cause: amount of oxygen produced by plants is about equal to the amount consumed by animal life processes, Effect: oxygen content in air remains about 21% of Earth's atmosphere, Marker: thus; Cause: amount of water vapor in air varies, Effect: composition of the atmosphere is usually given as that of dry air, Marker: because

Answer to Reading Check
Transpiration increases the amount of water vapor in the atmosphere.

Figure 2 Several processes interact to maintain stable amounts of oxygen, carbon dioxide, and water in the atmosphere.

Oxygen in the Atmosphere

Oxygen makes up about 21% of Earth's atmosphere. As shown in **Figure 2,** natural processes maintain the chemical balance of oxygen in the atmosphere. Animals, bacteria, and plants remove oxygen from the air as part of their life processes. Forest fires, the burning of fuels, and the weathering of some rocks also remove oxygen from the air. These processes would quickly use up most atmospheric oxygen if various processes that add oxygen to the air did not take place.

Land and ocean plants produce large quantities of oxygen in a process called *photosynthesis*. During photosynthesis, plants use sunlight, water, and carbon dioxide to produce their food, and they release oxygen as a byproduct. The amount of oxygen produced by plants each year is about equal to the amount consumed by all animal life processes. Thus, the oxygen content of the air remains at about 21% of Earth's atmosphere.

READING TOOLBOX

Signal Words
Locate the signal words that indicate cause-and-effect relationships on this page. Use a table with three columns to record the causes, the effects, and their markers.

Water Vapor in the Atmosphere

As water evaporates from oceans, lakes, streams, and soil, it enters air as the invisible gas *water vapor*. Plants and animals release water vapor during the life processes of transpiration or respiration, as shown in **Figure 2.** But as water vapor enters the atmosphere, it is removed by the processes of condensation and precipitation. The percentage of water vapor in the atmosphere varies depending on factors such as time of day, location, and season. Because the amount of water vapor in air varies, the composition of the atmosphere is usually given as that of dry air. Dry air has less than 1% water vapor. Moist air may contain as much as 4% water vapor.

SCILINKS.
www.scilinks.org
Topic: The Atmosphere
Code: HQX0112

Reading Check **Does transpiration increase or decrease the amount of water vapor in the atmosphere?** (See Appendix G for answers to Reading Checks.)

Differentiated Instruction

English Learners

Paired Summarizing Group students into pairs, and have them read silently about oxygen and water vapor in the atmosphere. Then, have one student summarize the processes that maintain stable amounts of these gases in the atmosphere. The other student should listen to the retelling and point out any inaccuracies or ideas that were left out. Allow students to refer to the text as needed. **LS Verbal**

Biology Connection — GENERAL

The Breath of Life Respiration is the process by which our bodies use oxygen to convert the energy stored in the chemical bonds of carbohydrates, fats, and proteins into ATP, a compound the cells can use for energy. Without oxygen, the cells would become starved for the energy needed to carry out all of our bodies' functions, and we would quickly die. Invite interested students to research this process and make diagrams that illustrate it. **LS Logical**

Ozone in the Atmosphere

Although it is present only in small amounts, a form of oxygen called **ozone** is an important component of the atmosphere. The oxygen that we breathe, O_2, has two atoms per molecule, but ozone, O_3, has three atoms. Ozone in the upper atmosphere forms the *ozone layer*, which absorbs harmful ultraviolet radiation from the sun. Without the ozone layer, living organisms would be severely damaged by the sun's ultraviolet rays. Unfortunately, a number of human activities damage the ozone layer. Compounds known as *chlorofluorocarbons*, or CFCs, which were previously used in refrigerators and air conditioners, and exhaust compounds, such as nitrogen oxide, break down ozone and have caused parts of the ozone layer to weaken, as **Figure 3** shows.

ozone a gas molecule that is made up of three oxygen atoms

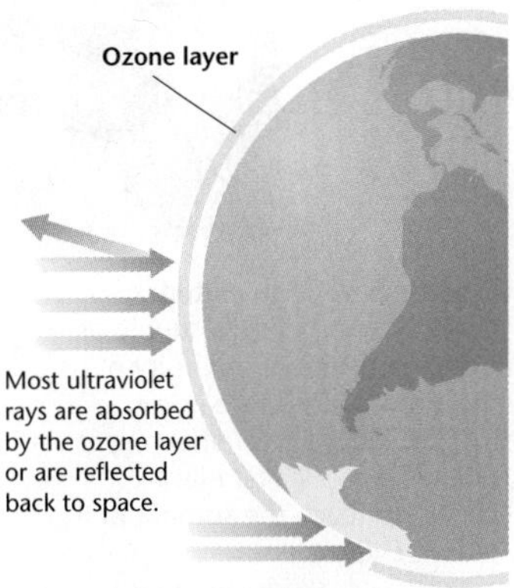

Ozone layer
Most ultraviolet rays are absorbed by the ozone layer or are reflected back to space.
More ultraviolet rays penetrate to Earth's surface through the weakened ozone layer.

Figure 3 Harmful ultraviolet radiation can reach Earth's surface through the weakened ozone layer over Antarctica.

Particulates in the Atmosphere

In addition to gases, the atmosphere contains various tiny solid and liquid particles, called *particulates*. Particulates can be volcanic dust, ash from fires, microscopic organisms, or mineral particles lifted from soil by winds. Pollen from plants and particles from meteors that have vaporized are also particulates. When tiny drops of ocean water are tossed into the air as sea spray, the drops evaporate. Left behind in the air are tiny crystals of salt, another type of particulate. Four common sources of particulates are shown in **Figure 4**. Large, heavy particles remain in the atmosphere only briefly, but tiny particles can remain suspended in the atmosphere for months or years.

Figure 4 Sources of Particulates

Volcanic ash and dust can remain in the atmosphere for months.

The wind carries pollen from plant to plant.

Tornadoes and windstorms carry dirt and dust high into the atmosphere.

As seaspray evaporates, salt particles are left in the atmosphere.

Environmental Connection

Ozone, Good or Bad? While stratospheric ozone is essential to life on Earth, in the troposphere ozone is a pollutant. Have students research the effects of ground-level ozone. Have them prepare a brochure that explains how ground-level ozone forms; how it affects humans, animals, and plants; and what actions can be taken to reduce it. **LS Verbal/Visual**

Activity — BASIC

Dust Collectors Have students coat one side of several glass slides with petroleum jelly. Have them place the slides outdoors for 24 hours in various locations. Then, have students view the slides under a microscope and describe what they see to the class. Discuss which locations are "dirtiest" and the possible sources of airborne particulates. **LS Visual/Kinesthetic**

Teaching Tip — GENERAL

Make Concepts Relevant For every 1% loss of ozone, the amount of UV radiation that reaches the ground increases by 2%. The increase in exposure to UV radiation is linked to greater incidence of skin cancers and immune system suppression. Have interested students research local, regional, and global efforts to protect the ozone layer. Have them make an oral report to the class. **LS Logical**

MISCONCEPTION ALERT

The Ozone Hole Most of the ozone molecules in the atmosphere are located in a layer between 10 and 40 km above Earth's surface. During the Antarctic winter, a vortex of atmospheric circulation results in many ozone molecules being destroyed. So, the "ozone hole" is, in actuality, an area that has fewer ozone molecules in that layer. Because Antarctica is largely uninhabited by humans, students might assume that this phenomenon could not affect them. But at times the thinning has extended over parts of South America, Australia, and New Zealand. Furthermore, recent studies show that over much of the United States and most of the middle latitudes around the world, ozone levels have declined 5% in the summer and up to 10% in the winter, compared to pre-1980 levels. There is good news: the level of CFCs in the stratosphere seems to have peaked, so some scientists think that the ozone layer will recover within 40 to 50 years.

Teach, *continued*

Math Skills

Answer

If the force exerted on Earth's surface by a column of air that has a base of 1 m^2 = 101,325 N, then the force exerted by a column of air that has a base of 3 m^2 = 101,325 $N/m^2 \times 3\ m^2$ = 303,975 N

Activity — BASIC

Create a Vacuum Have students fill a plastic soda bottle half full with hot water and screw the top on. Then, have them place the bottle in a pan. Have them cover the bottle with ice and cold water and observe what happens. (The hot water vapor cools and condenses, forming a partial vacuum in the bottle. The bottle is crushed because the air pressure is greater outside than inside the bottle.)

LS Visual/Kinesthetic

History Connection

Incontestable Experiment In 1643, Galileo asked his assistant, Evangelista Torricelli, to find out why water could never be pumped higher than 33 ft (10 m). Torricelli conducted experiments using a tube filled not with water, but with mercury, the heaviest liquid. As a result of his experiments, Torricelli developed a precursor to the mercurial barometer. He also established that "We live submerged at the bottom of an ocean of elementary air, which is known by incontestable experiments to have weight."

Figure 5 At high altitudes, many climbers carry a supply of oxygen because the density of the atmosphere there is very low. In 2001, Eric Weihenmeyer (above) was the first blind person to reach the summit of Mount Everest.

Atmospheric Pressure

Gravity holds the gases of the atmosphere near Earth's surface. As a result, the air molecules are compressed together and exert force on Earth's surface. The pressure exerted on a surface by the atmosphere is called **atmospheric pressure.** Atmospheric pressure is exerted equally in all directions—up, down, and sideways.

atmospheric pressure the force per unit area that is exerted on a surface by the weight of the atmosphere

Earth's gravity keeps 99% of the total mass of the atmosphere within 32 km of Earth's surface. The remaining 1% extends upward for hundreds of kilometers but gets increasingly thinner at high altitudes, as shown in **Figure 5.** Because there is less weight pressing down from above at higher altitudes, the air molecules are farther apart and exert less pressure on each other at higher altitudes. Thus, atmospheric pressure decreases as altitude increases.

Atmospheric pressure also changes as a result of differences in temperature and in the amount of water vapor in the air. In general, as temperature increases, atmospheric pressure at sea level decreases. The reason is that molecules move farther apart when the air is heated. So, fewer particles exert pressure on a given area, and the pressure decreases. Similarly, air that contains a lot of water vapor is less dense than drier air because water vapor molecules have less mass than nitrogen or oxygen molecules do. The lighter water vapor molecules replace an equal number of heavier oxygen and nitrogen molecules, which makes the volume of the air less dense.

Math Skills

Force of the Air On average, a column of air 1 m^2 at its base that reaches upward from sea level has a mass of 10,300 kg and exerts a force of 101,325 N (newtons) on the ground. So, at sea level, on every square meter of Earth's surface, the atmosphere presses down with an average force of 101,325 N. What would the average force of a column of air that has a 3 m^2 base be?

Measuring Atmospheric Pressure

Meteorologists use three units for atmospheric pressure: atmospheres (atm), millimeters or inches of mercury, and millibars (mb). *Standard atmospheric pressure,* or 1 atm, is equal to 760 mm of mercury, or 1,000 mb. The average atmospheric pressure at sea level is 1 atm. Meteorologists measure atmospheric pressure by using an instrument called a *barometer.*

Differentiated Instruction

Advanced Learners

High Altitude Cooking at altitudes above 1.5 km often calls for changes to recipes. Have students research how and why higher altitude affects cooking. Have students write a short report on the differences between cooking at sea level and cooking at high altitudes. Students should include specific examples of how recipes change or how timing in the cooking process is affected.

Mercurial Barometers

Meteorologists use two main types of barometers. One type is the *mercurial barometer*, a model of which is shown in **Figure 6.** Atmospheric pressure presses on the liquid mercury in a well at the base of the barometer. The pressure holds the mercury up to a certain height inside a tube. The height of the mercury inside the tube varies with the atmospheric pressure. The greater the atmospheric pressure is, the higher the mercury rises.

Aneroid Barometers

The type of barometer most commonly used today is called an *aneroid barometer*. Inside an aneroid barometer is a sealed metal container from which most of the air has been removed to form a partial vacuum. Changes in atmospheric pressure cause the sides of the container to bend inward or bulge out. These changes move a pointer on a scale. Aneroid barometers can be constructed to keep a continuous record of atmospheric pressure.

An aneroid barometer can also measure altitude above sea level. When used for this purpose, an aneroid barometer is called an *altimeter*. The scale on an altimeter registers altitude instead of pressure. At high altitudes, the atmosphere is less dense and has less pressure exerted on it from above than at low altitudes. So, a lowered pressure reading can be interpreted as an increased altitude reading.

Reading Check **What is inside an aneroid barometer?**

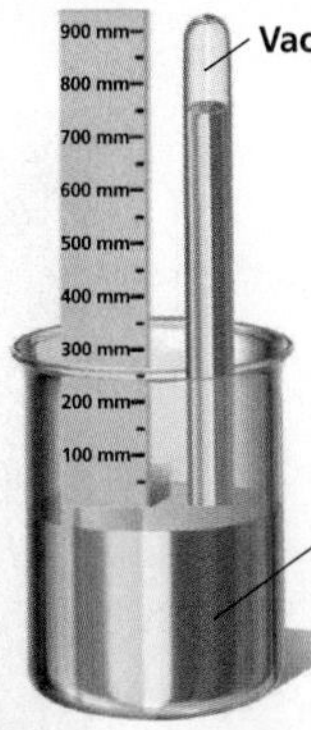

Figure 6 The height of the mercury in this mercurial barometer indicates barometric pressure. ***What is the barometric pressure shown?***

Academic Vocabulary

interpret (in TUHR pruht) figure out the meaning of

Quick Lab: Barometric Pressure

25 min (over 5 days)

Procedure

1. Use a rubber band to secure plastic wrap tightly over the open end of a coffee can.
2. Use tape to secure one end of a 10 cm drinking straw onto the plastic wrap near the center of the can.
3. Use scissors and a metric ruler to cut a piece of cardboard 10 cm wide. The cardboard should also be at least 13 cm taller than the can.
4. Fold the cardboard so that it stands upright and extends at least 3 cm above the top of the straw.
5. Place the cardboard near the can so that the free end of the straw just touches the front of the cardboard. Mark an *X* where the straw touches.
6. Draw three horizontal lines on the cardboard: one that is level with the *X*, one that is 2 cm above the *X*, and one that is 2 cm below the *X*.
7. Position the cardboard so that the straw touches the *X*. Tape the base of the cardboard in place.
8. Observe the level of the straw at least once per day over a 5-day period. Record any changes that you see.

Analysis

1. What factors affect how your model works? Explain.
2. What does an upward movement of the straw indicate? What does a downward movement indicate?
3. Compare your results with the barometric pressures listed in your local newspaper. What may have caused your results to differ from the newspaper's?

Activity — GENERAL

Weather Maps Have students bring in current weather maps from the DataStreme Atmosphere Web site, posted by the American Meteorological Society, or from other sources. Discuss with students how to read these maps. In a high-pressure area, the number increases as you move toward the center of the circles; lows are the opposite. The spacing of the isobars indicates the pressure gradient, or change in pressure over a given distance. The closer the spacing is, the steeper the pressure gradient is and the stronger the winds associated with a weather system are. Concentric rings of isobars indicate high and low pressure systems. **LS Visual/Logical**

Using the Figure — BASIC

Mercurial Barometers Have students study the diagram of a mercurial barometer. Ask students: "If a low pressure system moved into the area, what would happen to the height of the mercury column in this figure?" (The height of the mercury in the vacuum would drop to lower than 750 mm of Hg.) Answer to caption question: The barometric pressure shown is 750 mm of Hg. **LS Logical**

Answer to Reading Check

An aneroid barometer contains a sealed metal container that has a partial vacuum.

Quick Lab

Skills Acquired

- Observing
- Analyzing

Materials

- Rubberband
- Plastic wrap
- Coffee can
- Tape
- 10 cm drinking straw
- Scissors
- Metric ruler
- Cardboard

Teacher's notes: Tell students that this apparatus is a "Cape Cod Barometer," which measures air density. A balloon can also be used in place of the plastic wrap. Make sure that the temperature remains constant. Students also may find weather data on the Internet.

Answers to Analysis

1. The can must be well sealed and remain at about the same temperature.
2. upward: increasing pressure is pushing down on the plastic; downward: decreasing pressure causes the plastic to bulge up
3. Answers may vary. Possible reasons for differences: different instruments are used; the model uses a relative scale; and instruments are in different locations.

Teach, *continued*

Teaching Tip — GENERAL

Connect to Prior Knowledge Most students have probably seen a thunderstorm developing or pictures of thunderstorm clouds. Tell students that the anvil-shaped, flat top of storm clouds is due to the tropopause. As the cumulonimbus thunderclouds build up in the atmosphere, fed by warm, moist air, they rise and eventually reach the tropopause. Because the atmosphere in the tropopause is extremely stable and does not tend to move up or down, the cloud spreads out horizontally, which accounts for its flat top. Occasionally a very strong thunderstorm can break through the tropopause, and a bulge of clouds may protrude above the flat top. Bring in photos of thunderclouds or search the Internet for photos of thunderstorms. **LS Visual**

Why It Matters

Gas Mass The troposphere has about 80% of the gases of the atmosphere by mass. The stratosphere contains about 19%, and the mesosphere and thermosphere each have less than 1% of the atmosphere's gases by mass.

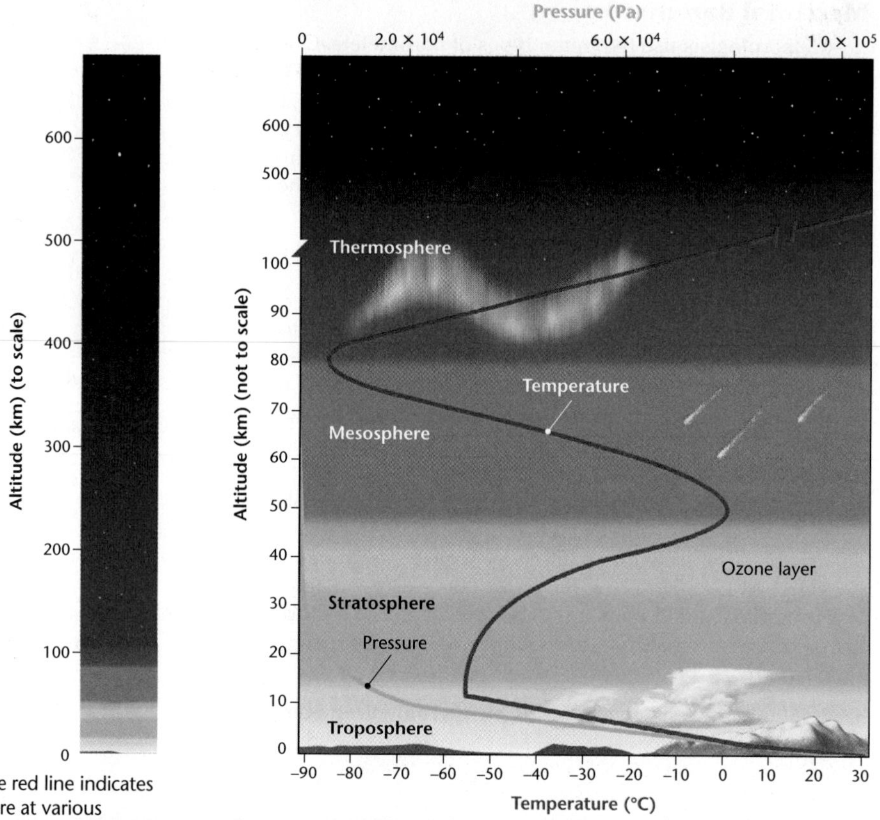

Figure 7 The red line indicates the temperature at various altitudes in the atmosphere. The green line indicates atmospheric pressure at various altitudes.

Layers of the Atmosphere

Earth's atmosphere has a distinctive pattern of temperature changes with increasing altitude, as shown in **Figure 7.** The temperature differences mainly result from how solar energy is absorbed as it moves through the atmosphere. Scientists identify four main layers of the atmosphere based on these differences.

The Troposphere

troposphere the lowest layer of the atmosphere, in which temperature drops at a constant rate as altitude increases; the part of the atmosphere where weather conditions exist

The atmospheric layer that is closest to Earth's surface and in which nearly all weather occurs is called the **troposphere.** Almost all the water vapor and carbon dioxide in the atmosphere is found in this layer. Temperature within the troposphere decreases as altitude increases because air in this layer is heated from below by thermal energy that radiates from Earth's surface. The temperature within the troposphere decreases at the average rate of 6.5 °C per kilometer as the distance from Earth's surface increases. However, at an average altitude of 12 km, the temperature stops decreasing. This zone is called the *tropopause* and represents the upper boundary of the troposphere. The altitude of this boundary varies with latitude and season.

Key Resources

Technology
- Transparencies
  93 Layers of the Atmosphere

Differentiated Instruction

Special Education Students

Layers of the Atmosphere Use tactile skills to help students better understand the layers of the atmosphere. Gather a supply of fabrics and papers that have different textures. Divide the class into groups of three to five students. Have each group use the different textured materials to make a poster that shows the different layers of the atmosphere. Students who have visual impairments should feel the poster elements to understand the order and altitudes of the layers.

The Stratosphere

The layer of the atmosphere called the **stratosphere** extends from the tropopause to an altitude of nearly 50 km. Almost all the ozone in the atmosphere is concentrated in this layer. In the lower stratosphere, the temperature is almost –60 °C. In the upper stratosphere, the temperature increases as altitude increases because air in the stratosphere is heated by absorption of solar radiation by ozone. The temperature of the air in this layer rises steadily to a temperature of about 0 °C at an altitude of about 50 km above Earth's surface. This zone, called the *stratopause*, marks the upper boundary of the stratosphere.

stratosphere the layer of the atmosphere that lies between the troposphere and the mesosphere and in which temperature increases as altitude increases; contains the ozone layer

mesosphere the coldest layer of the atmosphere, between the stratosphere and the thermosphere, in which temperature decreases as altitude increases

thermosphere the uppermost layer of the atmosphere, in which temperature increases as altitude increases; includes the ionosphere

The Mesosphere

Located above the stratopause and extending to an altitude of about 80 km is the **mesosphere.** In this layer, temperature decreases as altitude increases. The upper boundary of the mesosphere, called the *mesopause*, has an average temperature of nearly –90 °C, which is the coldest temperature in the atmosphere. Above this boundary, temperatures again begin to increase.

The Thermosphere

The atmospheric layer above the mesopause is called the **thermosphere.** In the thermosphere, temperature increases steadily as altitude increases because nitrogen and oxygen atoms absorb solar radiation. Because air particles in the thermosphere are very far apart, they do not strike a thermometer often enough to produce an accurate temperature reading. Therefore, special instruments are needed. These instruments have recorded temperatures of more than 1,000 °C in the thermosphere.

The lower region of the thermosphere, at an altitude of 80 to 400 km, is commonly called the *ionosphere*. In the ionosphere, solar radiation that is absorbed by atmospheric gases causes the atoms of gas molecules to lose electrons and to produce ions and free electrons. Interactions between solar radiation and the ionosphere cause the phenomena known as *auroras*, which are shown in **Figure 8.**

There are not enough data about temperature changes in the thermosphere to determine its upper boundary. However, above the ionosphere is the region where Earth's atmosphere blends into the almost complete vacuum of space. This zone of indefinite altitude, called the *exosphere*, extends for thousands of kilometers above the ionosphere.

Reading Check **What is the lower region of the thermosphere called?**

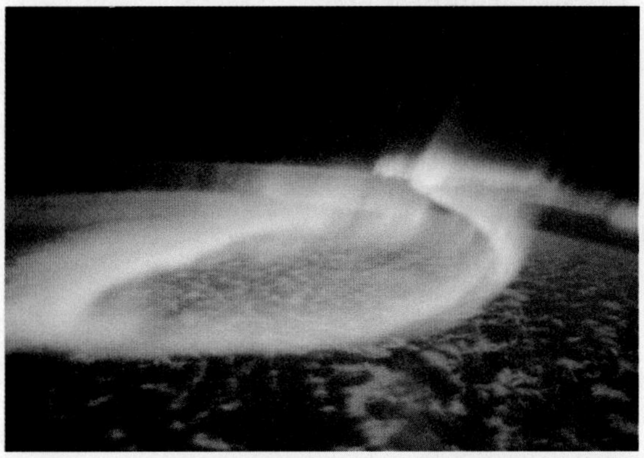

Figure 8 Auroras can be seen from space as well as from the ground.

Answer to Reading Check

The lower region of the thermosphere is called the *ionosphere.*

Environmental Connection

Deadly Blankets of Smog One fall evening in 1948, dirty fog crept into the small industrial valley town of Donora, Pennsylvania. Due to thermal inversion, the smog stayed for several days. More than 7,000 people were hospitalized with breathing difficulties. In London, about 4,000 people died in one week due to "the Great Smog" in 1952. Instances such as these led to the passage of clean air laws in the United States, culminating in the federal Clean Air Act of 1970.

Close

Reteaching — BASIC

Name that Sphere Have students write characteristics of the atmospheric layers on index cards. Have them work in pairs, using the cards to quiz each other about the atmosphere.
LS Visual/Logical

Quiz — GENERAL

1. What are auroras? (Interactions between solar radiation and the ionosphere create displays of light in the night sky.)
2. What layer of Earth's atmosphere blends into space? (the exosphere)
3. What units are used to measure atmospheric pressure? (atmospheres, millimeters or inches of mercury, and millibars)

Why It Matters

Radio Waves The ionosphere makes worldwide radio communication possible. Tiny, charged particles act as transmitters, bouncing radio waves back to Earth. On the ground, the signals are received and can be transmitted back up to the ionosphere. Thus, radio signals can be sent around Earth without the satellites or cable required for higher frequency television transmissions.

Close, *continued*

Answers to Section Review

1. 78% nitrogen (N_2), 21% oxygen (O_2), 0.9% argon (Ar), and less than 0.1% other gases such as carbon dioxide
2. nitrogen, oxygen, water vapor, ozone, and particulates
3. Atmospheric pressure is caused by the weight of atmospheric gases as a result of gravity pulling the gas molecules toward Earth.
4. Atmospheric pressure pushes on liquid mercury in a well at the base of a mercurial barometer. This holds the mercury in a tube at a height that varies with pressure. Changes in air pressure cause the sides of a sealed metal container that holds a partial vacuum to bend inward or bulge outward, moving the pointer on a scale of an aneroid barometer.
5. the troposphere
6. Answers may vary but should reflect the information about composition, altitude, temperature, and pressure that is presented in this section.
7. troposphere and thermosphere
8. because molecules move farther apart when they are heated, so there are fewer particles in a given area to exert pressure
9. 9 km × 6.5 °C/km = 58.5 °C; Temperature on Mount Everest is about 58.5 °C colder than on the coast.
10. A city on the Great Plains would have fewer problems with temperature inversions because the topography is flatter, allowing air to circulate more readily and not be trapped in valleys or against the mountains.
11. Answers may vary. Sample answer: First, temperatures at that altitude are relatively cold and air pressure relatively low, which could make breathing difficult. Second, he would have to find a way to land his lawn chair safely.
12. The *atmosphere* is a mixture of gases commonly referred to as *air* that includes *nitrogen, oxygen,* and *ozone;* compounds such as *water vapor;* and tiny particles called *particulates.*

Figure 9 During a temperature inversion, polluted cool air becomes trapped beneath a warm-air layer.

Temperature Inversions

Any substance that is in the atmosphere and that is harmful to people, animals, plants, or property is called an *air pollutant*. Today, the main source of air pollution is the burning of fossil fuels, such as coal and petroleum. As these fuels burn, they may release harmful chemical substances, such as sulfur dioxide gas, hydrocarbons, nitrogen oxides, carbon monoxide, and lead, into the air.

Certain weather conditions can make air pollution worse. One such condition is a *temperature inversion*, the layering of warm air on top of cool air. Warm air, which is less dense than cool air is, can trap cool, polluted air beneath it. In some areas, topography may make air pollution even worse by keeping the polluted inversion layer from dispersing, as **Figure 9** shows. Under conditions in which air cannot circulate up and away from an area, trapped automobile exhaust can produce *smog*, a general term for air pollution that is a combination of smoke and fog.

Air pollution can be controlled only by preventing the release of pollutants into the atmosphere. International, federal, and local laws have been passed to reduce the amount of air pollutants produced by automobiles and industry.

Section 1 Review

Key Ideas

1. **Describe** the composition of dry air at sea level.
2. **Identify** five main components of the atmosphere.
3. **Explain** the cause of atmospheric pressure.
4. **Explain** how the two types of barometers measure atmospheric pressure.
5. **Identify** the layer of the atmosphere in which weather occurs.
6. **Compare** the four main layers of the atmosphere.
7. **Identify** the two atmospheric layers that contain air as warm as 25 °C.

Critical Thinking

8. **Drawing Conclusions** Why is atmospheric pressure generally lower beneath a mass of warm air than beneath a mass of cold air?
9. **Making Calculations** How much colder is the air at the top of Mount Everest, which is almost 9 km above sea level, than the air at the Indian coastline? (Hint: On average, the temperature in the troposphere decreases by 6.5 °C per kilometer of altitude.)
10. **Applying Ideas** Which industrial city would have fewer air-pollution incidents related to temperature inversions: one on the Great Plains or one near the Rocky Mountains? Explain your answer.
11. **Applying Concepts** In 1982, Larry Walters rose to an altitude of approximately 4,900 m on a lawn chair attached to 45 helium-filled weather balloons. Give two reasons why Walters' trip was dangerous.

Concept Mapping

12. Use the following terms to create a concept map: *oxygen, atmosphere, air, nitrogen, water vapor, ozone,* and *particulates.*

Differentiated Instruction

Alternative Assessment

Modeling Have students work in small groups to design a model of Earth's atmosphere. The model should demonstrate the layers of Earth's atmosphere and how temperature, pressure, and chemical composition vary in the different layers. LS **Kinesthetic**

SECTION 2

Solar Energy and the Atmosphere

Key Ideas	Key Terms	Why It Matters
❯ Explain how radiant energy reaches Earth. ❯ Describe how visible light and infrared energy warm Earth. ❯ Summarize the processes of radiation, conduction, and convection.	**electromagnetic spectrum** **albedo** **greenhouse effect** **conduction** **convection**	By understanding what happens to solar radiation in the atmosphere, scientists can learn more about how the actions of humans affect the atmosphere.

Earth's atmosphere is heated by the transfer of energy from the sun. Some of the heat in the atmosphere comes from the absorption of the sun's rays by gases in the atmosphere. Some heat enters the atmosphere indirectly as ocean and land surfaces absorb solar energy and then give off this energy as heat.

Radiation

All of the energy that Earth receives from the sun travels through space between Earth and the sun as radiation. *Radiation* includes all forms of energy that travel through space as waves. Visible light is the form of radiation that human eyes can detect. However, there are many other forms of radiation that humans cannot see, such as ultraviolet light, X rays, and radio waves.

Radiation travels through space in the form of waves at a very high speed—approximately 300,000 km/s. The distance from any point on a wave to the identical point on the next wave, for example, from crest to crest, is called the *wavelength* of a wave. The various types of radiation differ in the length of their waves. Visible light, for example, consists of waves with various wavelengths that are seen as different colors. The wavelengths of ultraviolet rays, X rays, and gamma rays are shorter than those of visible light. Infrared waves and radio waves have relatively long wavelengths. The waves that make up all forms of radiation are called electromagnetic waves. Almost all the energy that reaches Earth from the sun is in the form of *electromagnetic waves*. The **electromagnetic spectrum,** shown in **Figure 1**, consists of the complete range of wavelengths of electromagnetic waves.

electromagnetic spectrum all of the frequencies or wavelengths of electromagnetic radiation

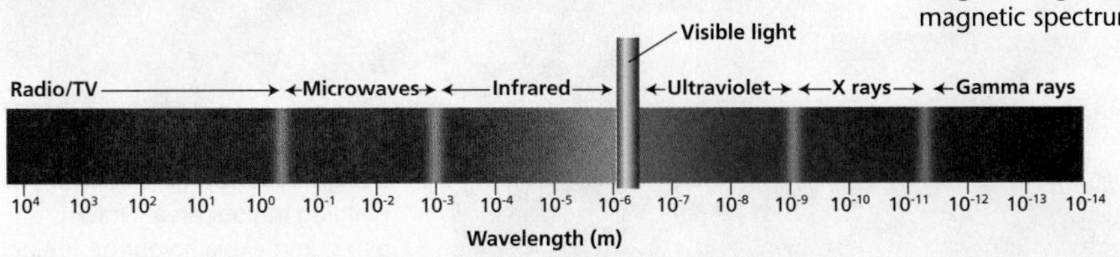

Figure 1 The sun emits radiation whose wavelengths range throughout the electromagnetic spectrum.

Section 2

Focus

Overview

This section explains how radiant energy from the sun interacts with Earth and its atmosphere. The section reviews the processes of conduction and convection and explains the greenhouse effect.

Bellringer

Ask students to describe what effect the sun has on Earth. (Answers may vary. The sun warms Earth's surface and provides light and energy.)

Motivate

Activity — GENERAL

Magic with Beads Use ultraviolet sensing beads (small beads that change color when exposed to UV light) to demonstrate how sunlight differs from indoor light. These beads are available through science supply catalogs. Have students expose the beads to light from an incandescent light bulb and then to sunlight and observe what happens. (The beads should change color only in the sun because light from the bulb does not have UV.) Then, have students use a prism and sunlight to create a spectrum. Place beads just outside the red and blue ends. In what regions do the beads change color? (only in the region just beyond the violet end of the spectrum, the UV region) **LS Visual**

Key Resources

Chapter Resource File

- Directed Reading BASIC
- Inquiry Lab: Ultraviolet Protection GENERAL

Technology

- Transparencies
  Bellringer
  94 The Electromagnetic Spectrum

Differentiated Instruction

Struggling Readers

Radiation Have students reread the passage about radiation sentence by sentence. As they read each sentence, have them stop and restate the meaning in their own words to check for comprehension. Students can write and draw their interpretations of sentences in the passage.

Teach

Activity — GENERAL

Blue and Red Skies Skies appear blue because the gases and dust in the atmosphere scatter blue light most. Sunsets are commonly yellow or red because the sun is low on the horizon and the light has to travel through so much of the atmosphere that only red and yellow light make it through without being scattered. To model this effect, have students shine a flashlight at different angles through a glass of water that has about half a teaspoon of milk in it. The milk acts like the dust and gases in the atmosphere that scatter light. The color changes are subtle and best viewed in a darkened room. Have students add more milk, a teaspoon at a time, and see how this affects color. **LS Visual/Logical**

Why It Matters

Gardens in the Sky Rooftop gardens can help mitigate the heat island effect, in which the temperature of the air and surfaces in urban and suburban areas is higher than the temperature of surrounding rural areas. Regular rooftops can be hotter than the surrounding air, but green roofs are often cooler than the air. Green roofs provide the benefits of shade from trees and of evapotranspiration from trees and plants.

Answer to Your Turn

Answers will vary. Students' plans should include an explanation of how their rooftop gardens will benefit the environment.

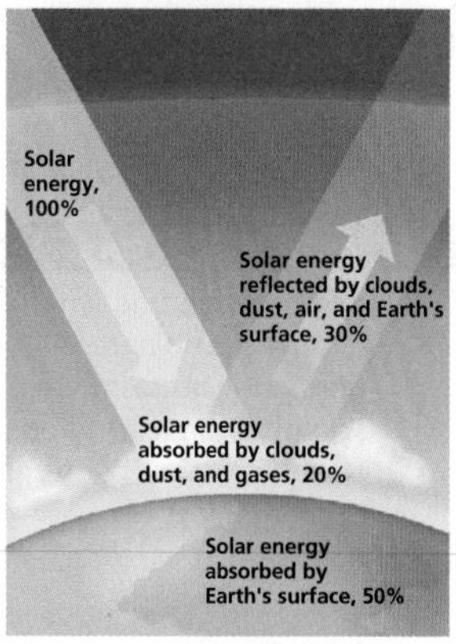

Figure 2 About 70% of the solar energy that reaches Earth is absorbed by Earth's land and ocean surfaces and by the atmosphere. The remainder is reflected back into space.

The Atmosphere and Solar Radiation

As solar radiation passes through Earth's atmosphere, the atmosphere affects the radiation in several ways. The upper atmosphere absorbs almost all radiation that has a wavelength shorter than the wavelengths of visible light. Molecules of nitrogen and oxygen in the thermosphere and mesosphere absorb the X rays, gamma rays, and ultraviolet rays. In the stratosphere, ultraviolet rays are absorbed and act upon oxygen molecules to form ozone.

Most of the solar rays that reach the lower atmosphere, such as visible and infrared waves, have longer wavelengths. Most incoming infrared radiation is absorbed by carbon dioxide, water vapor, and other complex molecules in the troposphere. As visible light waves pass through the atmosphere, only a small amount of this radiation is absorbed. **Figure 2** shows the percentage of solar energy that is reflected and absorbed by the atmosphere.

Scattering

Clouds, dust, water droplets, and gas molecules in the atmosphere disrupt the paths of radiation from the sun and cause scattering. Scattering occurs when particles and gas molecules in the atmosphere reflect and bend the solar rays. This deflection causes the rays to travel out in all directions without changing their wavelengths. Scattering sends some of the radiation back into space. The remaining radiation continues toward Earth's surface. As a result of scattering, sunlight that reaches Earth's surface comes from all directions. In addition, scattering makes the sky appear blue and makes the sun appear red at sunset.

Why It Matters

Gardens in the Sky

Rooftop gardens—such as this one on top of Chicago's City Hall—harness solar radiation, which helps the environment and cuts energy costs. While concrete roofs absorb only 55 to 65% of solar radiation, plants on "green roofs" absorb 75 to 95%. The plants help to decrease indoor temperatures in the summer, which means less air conditioning is needed. In addition, plants filter air pollution and muffle street noise, and provide a habitat for animals such as birds.

The layers of a rooftop garden absorb rainwater, which helps to prevent flooding of the sewage system in the city below.

YOUR TURN WRITING IN SCIENCE
Design a rooftop garden for a building in your area. Draw plans, and explain your design.

Table 1 Reflection and Absorption Rates of Various Materials

	Percentage of Solar Radiation	
Surface	Reflected	Absorbed
Soil (dark colored)	5–10	90–95
Desert	20–40	60–80
Grass	5–25	75–95
Forest	5–10	90–95
Snow	50–90	10–50
Water (high sun angle)	5–10	90–95
Water (low sun angle)	50–80	20–50

READING TOOLBOX

Prefixes
The prefix ab- in *absorb* means "from" while the prefix re- in *reflect* means "back." Explain how these prefixes give you a clue to the direction of solar radiation when it is absorbed or reflected by different surfaces.

Reflection

When solar energy reaches Earth's surface, the surface either absorbs or reflects the energy. The amount of energy that is absorbed or reflected depends on characteristics such as the color, texture, composition, volume, mass, transparency, state of matter, and specific heat of the material on which the solar radiation falls. The intensity and amount of time that a surface material receives radiation also affects how much energy is reflected or absorbed.

The fraction of solar radiation that is reflected by a particular surface is called the **albedo.** Because 30% of the solar energy that reaches Earth's atmosphere is either reflected or scattered, Earth is said to have an albedo of 0.3. **Table 1** shows the amount of incoming solar radiation that is absorbed and reflected by various surfaces.

albedo the fraction of solar radiation that is reflected off the surface of an object

Absorption and Infrared Energy

The sun constantly emits radiation. Solar radiation that is not reflected is absorbed by rocks, soil, water, and other surface materials. When Earth's surface absorbs solar radiation, the radiation's short-wavelength infrared rays and visible light heat the surface materials. Then, the heated materials convert the energy into infrared rays with longer wavelengths and reemit the energy at those wavelengths. Gas molecules, such as water vapor and carbon dioxide, in the atmosphere absorb the infrared rays. The absorption of thermal energy from the ground heats the lower atmosphere and keeps Earth's surface much warmer than it would be if there were no atmosphere. Sometimes, warm air near Earth's surface bends light rays to produce an effect called a *mirage*, as **Figure 3** shows.

Figure 3 Hot air near the surface of this road bends light rays. ***What objects in this photo appear to be reflected?***

Group Activity GENERAL

Comparing Albedos Have students work in small groups to fill two jars with dry sand and to cover the top of one jar with white paper and the other jar with black paper. Have students seal both jars by using tape. Have students place the jars side by side in the sun. After about a half an hour, have students measure the temperature just above the surface of the paper and just below the surface of the sand. Have each group explain their observations based on what they know about albedo. **LS Kinesthetic**

Using the Figure GENERAL

Phantom Images Mirages form when light passes through layers of air that have different densities. The light is refracted, and forms an image above or below an object's true location. The mirage in this figure is an inferior mirage because it forms below the object's true location. Inferior mirages are most likely to form above hot land surfaces such as deserts or highways. Superior mirages form above an object's true location, most often above large bodies of water or fields of ice and snow. While mirages may seem to be delusions of the mind, they are real and can be photographed, as this figure shows. Answer to caption question: The sky and the poles appear to be reflected in this photo.
LS Visual/Logical

READING TOOLBOX

Prefixes Solar radiation coming from the sun is absorbed by different surfaces on Earth. Some solar radiation is reflected back toward the sun by these surfaces.

Differentiated Instruction

Advanced Learners

CFCs Have students investigate the history of chlorofluorocarbons (CFCs) and their effects on the atmosphere. Students should prepare a report that includes information on the chemicals being used in place of CFCs and compares the substitute products to CFCs in terms of use, cost, and possible adverse environmental effects.

Skill Builder BASIC

Vocabulary The term *albedo* comes from the Latin, *albedo,* which means "whiteness." Objects that are white tend to reflect light, so a surface that has high albedo reflects much of the sunlight it receives. Snow and ice, for example, have a very high albedo. English Language Learners
LS Verbal

Teach, *continued*

Internet Activity GENERAL

Global Warming Many scientists are concerned that the global climate is warming due to a human-enhanced greenhouse effect. Have students investigate the causes and potential impact of an enhanced greenhouse effect on Earth, as well as the controversies that surround predictions of global warming. A worksheet designed to direct student research on this topic can be found in the **Chapter Resource File** booklet or by visiting www.thinkcentral.com and entering the keyword **HQXATMX**. **LS Verbal**

Environmental Connection

CO_2 Concentrations The CO_2 concentration has risen from 0.028% to over 0.036% since 1860, which is commonly considered to be the beginning of the Industrial Age. Burning fossil fuels in vehicles and power plants contributes significantly to greenhouse gas emissions.

MISCONCEPTION ALERT

Greenhouse Goofs A common misconception is that the greenhouse effect has only negative effects to life on Earth. The greenhouse effect is actually essential to life on Earth. Without the greenhouse effect, scientists estimate that Earth would be 15.5 °C (60 °F) cooler, and life on Earth would be very different. On the other hand, too much of a greenhouse effect would make Earth much like Venus—too hot to support life as we know it.

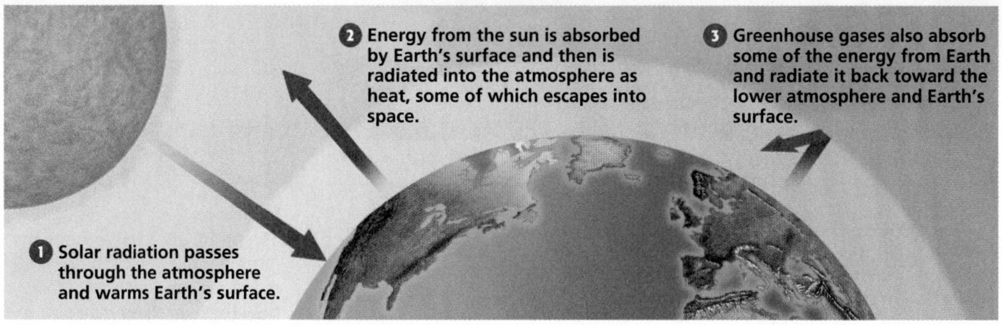

1 Solar radiation passes through the atmosphere and warms Earth's surface.
2 Energy from the sun is absorbed by Earth's surface and then is radiated into the atmosphere as heat, some of which escapes into space.
3 Greenhouse gases also absorb some of the energy from Earth and radiate it back toward the lower atmosphere and Earth's surface.

Figure 4 One process that helps to heat Earth's atmosphere is similar to the process that heats a greenhouse.

THINK central INTERACT ONLINE (Keyword: HQXATMF4)

The Greenhouse Effect

One of the ways in which the gases of the atmosphere absorb and reradiate infrared rays, shown in **Figure 4,** can be compared to the process that keeps a greenhouse warm. The glass of a greenhouse allows visible light and infrared rays from the sun to pass through and warm the surfaces inside the greenhouse. But the glass prevents the infrared rays that are emitted by the warmed surfaces within the greenhouse from escaping quickly. Similarly, Earth's atmosphere reduces the escape of energy that radiates from Earth's surface. Because this process is similar to the process that heats a greenhouse, it is called the **greenhouse effect.**

greenhouse effect the warming of the surface and lower atmosphere of Earth that occurs when carbon dioxide, water vapor, and other gases in the air absorb and reradiate infrared radiation

Human Impact on the Greenhouse Effect

Generally, the amount of solar energy that enters Earth's atmosphere is about equal to the amount that escapes into space. However, human activities, in addition to natural causes, are changing this balance and are causing the average temperature of the atmosphere to increase. For example, measurements indicate that the amount of carbon dioxide in the atmosphere has been increasing in recent years. These increases have been attributed to the burning of more fossil fuels and seem likely to continue in the future. Increases in the amount of carbon dioxide may intensify the greenhouse effect and may cause Earth to become warmer.

SCILINKS. www.scilinks.org
Topic: Greenhouse Effect
Code: **HQX0694**

Variations in Temperature

Radiation from the sun does not heat Earth equally at all places at all times. In addition, a slight delay occurs between the absorption of energy and an increase in temperature. Earth's surface must absorb energy for a time before enough heat has been absorbed and reradiated from the ground to change the temperature of the atmosphere. For a similar reason, the warmest hours of the day are usually mid- to late afternoon even though solar radiation is most intense at noon. The temperature of the atmosphere in any region on Earth's surface depends on several factors, including latitude, surface features, and the time of year and day.

Differentiated Instruction

Basic Learners

The Greenhouse Effect Have students think about what happens to the temperature on the inside of a closed car on a hot, sunny day. Have them explain how this is analogous to the greenhouse effect of Earth's atmosphere. Encourage students to draw a diagram as part of their explanations.

Key Resources

Technology

- Transparencies
  95 The Greenhouse Effect and Latitude and Season

Latitude and Season

Latitude is the primary factor that affects the amount of solar energy that reaches any point on Earth's surface. Because Earth is a sphere, the sun's rays do not strike all areas at the same angle, as shown in **Figure 5.** The rays of the sun strike the ground near the equator at an angle near 90°. At the poles, the sunlight strikes the ground at a much smaller angle. When sunlight hits Earth's surface at an angle smaller than 90°, the energy is spread out over a larger area and is less intense. Thus, the energy that reaches the equator is more intense than the energy that strikes the poles, so average temperatures are higher near the equator than near the poles.

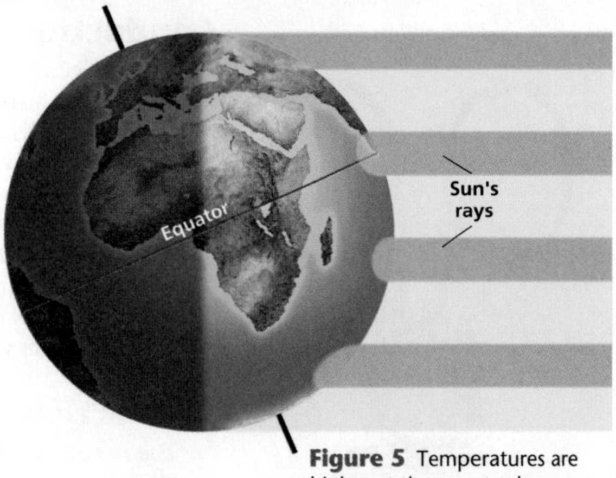

Figure 5 Temperatures are higher at the equator because solar energy is concentrated in a small area. Farther north and south, the same amount of solar energy is spread out over a larger area.

Temperature varies seasonally because of the tilt of Earth's axis. As Earth revolves around the sun once each year, the portion of Earth's surface that receives the most intense sunlight changes. For part of the year, the Northern Hemisphere is tilted toward the sun and receives more direct sunlight. During this time of year, temperatures are at their highest. For the other part of the year, the Southern Hemisphere is tilted toward the sun. During this time, the Northern Hemisphere receives less direct sunlight, and the temperatures there are at their lowest.

Academic Vocabulary

primary (PRIE MER ee) highest in rank or importance

Water in the Air and on the Surface

Because water vapor stores energy, the amount of water in the air affects the temperature of a region. The thinner air at high elevations contains less water vapor and carbon dioxide to absorb heat energy. As a result, those areas become warm during the day but cool very quickly at night. Similarly, desert temperatures may vary widely between day and night because little water vapor is present to hold the heat of the day.

Land areas close to large bodies of water generally have more moderate temperatures. In other words, these areas will be cooler during the day and warmer at night than inland regions that have the same general weather conditions. The reason for these moderate temperatures is that water heats up and cools down slower than land does, so the temperature of water changes less than the temperature of land does.

The wind patterns in an area also affect temperature. A region that receives winds off the ocean has more moderate temperatures than a similar region in which the winds blow from the land.

Reading Check **Why are deserts generally colder at night than other areas are?**

Quick Lab 5 min

Light and Latitude

Procedure

1. Hold a **flashlight** so that the beam shines directly down on a **white piece of paper.** Use a **pencil** to trace the outline of the beam of light.
2. Move the flashlight so that the light shines on the paper at an angle. Trace the outline of the beam of light.

Analysis

1. How does the area of the direct beam differ from the area of the angled beam?
2. How does this lab illustrate how latitude affects incoming solar radiation?

Answer to Reading Check

Deserts are colder at night than other areas are because the air in deserts contains little water vapor that can absorb heat during the day and release heat slowly at night.

Quick Lab

Skills Acquired
- Observing
- Analyzing

Materials
- Flashlight
- Piece of white paper
- Pencil

Teacher's notes: Make sure the height of the flashlight does not change when students change the angle of the flashlight.

Answers to Analysis
1. The area of the direct beam is smaller than the area of the angled beam.
2. At the equator, energy from the sun hits Earth at a 90° angle, so the energy is concentrated on a small area. At latitudes far north and south of the equator, sunlight hits Earth at angles less than 90°. The same amount of energy is spread out over a greater area. Therefore, each square unit of surface receives less energy.

Close

Reteaching BASIC

Peer Reviewing Have students work in pairs to write three to five questions about the material in this section. Then, have students use their questions to quiz each other.
LS Interpersonal Co-op Learning

Quiz BASIC

1. What property makes a substance a good conductor? (molecules that are close together, such as in solid metals
2. What may happen to Earth's climate if the amount of carbon dioxide in the air continues to increase? (The greenhouse effect may intensify and the average annual temperature of most areas will be warmer.)
3. What is the main cause of increasing carbon dioxide concentrations in the atmosphere? (The burning of fossil fuels.)

Close, *continued*

Answers to Section Review

1. Radiation from the sun travels through space in the form of electromagnetic waves.
2. long wavelength waves: radio/TV, microwaves, infrared, and visible light; short wavelength waves: UV rays, X rays, and gamma rays
3. Nitrogen, oxygen, and ozone in the upper atmosphere absorb most radiation that has a wavelength shorter than that of visible light. In the lower atmosphere, carbon dioxide and water vapor absorb infrared radiation. About 50% of solar energy reaches Earth's surface. Clouds, particulates, and gases in the lower atmosphere scatter and reflect much of the light.
4. Infrared and visible light that reach Earth's surface are absorbed. The heated surfaces radiate heat back into the air, where greenhouse gases absorb some of the heat.
5. If the sunlight is concentrated over a small area, as happens near the equator, the sun's energy is more intense and the surface becomes hotter. When sunlight is spread over a larger area, as happens at higher latitudes, the sun's energy and the resulting heat are less intense.
6. Conduction is the transfer of energy from one substance to another by direct contact. Convection is the transfer of energy through movement of matter due to differences in density as a result of temperature differences.
7. Scientists study the entire electromagnetic spectrum because Earth is affected by radiation of all of the wavelengths in the spectrum.
8. In convection ovens, the fan mixes the air, so that hot or cold spots are less likely to form, resulting in more even cooking.
9. The hottest hours of the day will probably be in the late afternoon when Earth's surface has had time to absorb and reradiate energy and when convection is at its peak.
10. The atmosphere interacts with *electromagnetic waves* from the sun, such as *ultraviolet waves*, *visible light* and *infrared waves*, by *scattering* or *absorption*, which is part of the *greenhouse effect*.

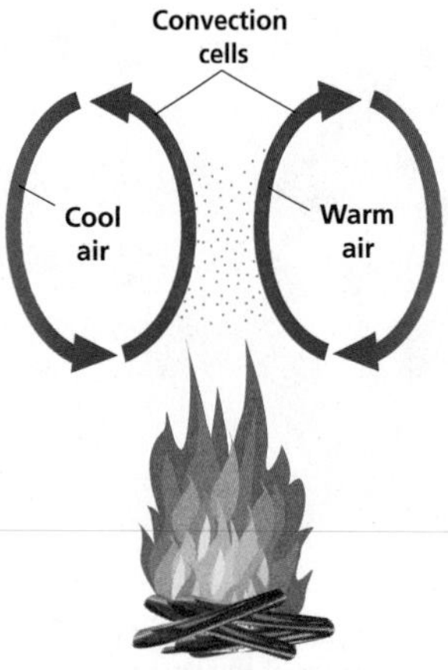

Figure 6 During convection, energy is carried away by heated air as it rises above cooler, denser air.

Conduction

The molecules in a substance move faster as they become heated. These fast-moving molecules cause other molecules to move faster. Collisions between the particles result in the transfer of energy, which warms the substance. The transfer of energy as heat from one substance to another by direct contact is called **conduction.** Solid substances, in which the molecules are close together, make relatively good conductors. Because the molecules of air are far apart, air is a poor conductor. Thus, conduction heats only the lowest few centimeters of the atmosphere, where air comes into direct contact with the warmed surface of Earth.

conduction the transfer of energy as heat through a material

convection the movement of matter due to differences in density that are caused by temperature variations; can result in the transfer of energy as heat

Convection

The heating of the lower atmosphere is primarily the result of the distribution of heat through the troposphere by convection. **Convection** is the process by which air, or other matter, rises or sinks because of differences in temperature. Convection occurs when gases or liquids are heated unevenly. As air is heated by radiation or conduction, it becomes less dense and is pushed up by nearby cooler air. In turn, this cooler air becomes warmer, and the cycle repeats, as shown in **Figure 6.**

The continuous cycle in which cold air sinks and warm air rises warms Earth's atmosphere. Because warm air is less dense than cool air is, warm air exerts less pressure than the same volume of cooler air does. So, the atmospheric pressure is lower beneath a mass of warm air. As dense, cool air moves into a low-pressure region, the less dense, warmer air is pushed upward. These pressure differences, which are the result of the unequal heating that causes convection, create winds.

Section 2 Review

Key Ideas

1. **Explain** how radiant energy reaches Earth.
2. **List and describe** the types of electromagnetic waves.
3. **Describe** how gases and particles in the atmosphere interact with light rays.
4. **Describe** how visible light and infrared energy warm Earth.
5. **Explain** how variations in the intensity of sunlight can cause temperature differences on Earth's surface.
6. **Summarize** the processes of conduction and convection.

Critical Thinking

7. **Making Inferences** Why do scientists study all wavelengths of the electromagnetic spectrum?
8. **Applying Concepts** Explain how fans in convection ovens help to cook food more evenly.
9. **Applying Conclusions** You decide not to be outside during the hottest hours of a summer day. When will the hottest hours probably be? How do you know?

Concept Mapping

10. Use the following terms to create a concept map: *electromagnetic waves, infrared waves, greenhouse effect, ultraviolet waves, visible light, scattering,* and *absorption.*

Differentiated Instruction

Alternative Assessment

The Spectrum of Life Have students keep an "electromagnetic journal" for one week. They should record each time they observe or encounter electromagnetic radiation. The record should include the types of radiation, explanations of their encounters, and what type of radiation they encounter most. **LS Verbal**

SECTION 3

Atmospheric Circulation

Key Ideas	Key Terms	Why It Matters
❯ Explain the Coriolis effect. ❯ Describe the global patterns of air circulation, and name three global wind belts. ❯ Identify two factors that form local wind patterns.	**Coriolis effect** **trade winds** **westerlies** **polar easterlies** **jet stream**	Understanding how wind works was important to early travelers. Such understanding has practical advantages even today.

Air near Earth's surface generally flows from the poles toward the equator. The reason for this flow is that air moves from high-pressure regions to low-pressure regions. High-pressure regions form where cold air sinks toward Earth's surface. Low-pressure regions form where warm air rises away from Earth's surface.

The Coriolis Effect

The circulation of the atmosphere and the oceans is affected by the rotation of Earth on its axis. Because each point on Earth makes one complete rotation every day, points near the equator travel farther and faster in a day than points closer to the poles do. When air moves toward the poles, it travels east faster than the land beneath it does. As a result, the air follows a curved path. The tendency of a moving object to follow a curved path rather than a straight path because of the rotation of Earth is called the **Coriolis effect,** which is shown in **Figure 1.**

Coriolis effect the curving of the path of a moving object from an otherwise straight path due to Earth's rotation

The Coriolis effect deflects a moving object along a path that depends on the speed, latitude, and direction of the object. Objects are deflected to the right in the Northern Hemisphere and are deflected to the left in the Southern Hemisphere.

The faster an object travels, the greater the Coriolis effect on the object is. The Coriolis effect also noticeably changes the paths of large masses that travel long distances, such as air and ocean currents. In general, the Coriolis effect is detectable only on objects that move very fast or that travel over long distances.

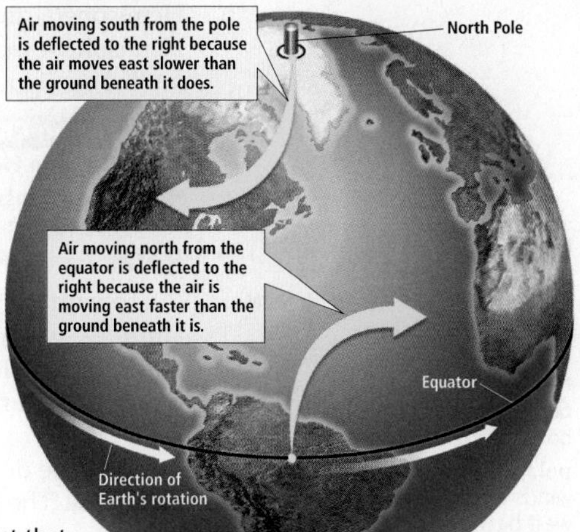

Air moving south from the pole is deflected to the right because the air moves east slower than the ground beneath it does.
North Pole
Air moving north from the equator is deflected to the right because the air is moving east faster than the ground beneath it is.
Equator
Direction of Earth's rotation

Figure 1 Because of Earth's rotation, an object that travels north from the equator will curve to the east. This curving is called the *Coriolis effect.*

Section 3

Focus

Overview

This section explains the Coriolis effect and global patterns of air circulation that result from pressure differences in Earth's atmosphere. It also describes the local winds that result from land features such as mountains and bodies of water.

Bellringer

Ask students to describe what causes air to move. (Answers may vary. Use student answers to begin a discussion of the causes of winds.) **LS Logical**

Motivate

Demonstration GENERAL

Modeling the Coriolis Effect Center a paper plate on a turntable or "lazy susan." Draw a straight line from the center of the plate to the outside edge without spinning the turntable. Then, spin the turntable counterclockwise (the direction that Earth rotates), and draw another line from the center to the edge of the plate. Because the paper is spinning, the second line will spiral around the plate to the right. Ask students what the spinning plate and curved line model. (The spinning plate models the rotation of Earth on its axis; the curved line models the Coriolis effect on air in the Northern Hemisphere.) **LS Visual**

Key Resources

Chapter Resource File
- Directed Reading BASIC
- Making Models Lab: Global Air Movement GENERAL
- Internet Activity: Harnessing Wind GENERAL

Technology
- Transparencies
  Bellringer
  96 The Coriolis Effect

Differentiated Instruction

Struggling Readers

Reading Organizer As students read this section, encourage them to take notes as described in Appendix A. Later students can use these notes as a study guide for assessments. **LS Verbal**

Teach

Using the Figure ADVANCED

Coriolis Effect Explain to students that the convection cells from the equator to the subtropics are known as *Hadley cells*, after George Hadley, a lawyer, who in 1735 proposed a partially correct explanation for the direction of the trade winds. The convection cells from the subtropics to the subpolar regions are known as *Ferrell cells*, after William Ferrell, an American schoolteacher, who in 1855 correctly proposed the three-cell model that accounts for the global wind belts. Answer to caption question: Winds curve clockwise in the Northern Hemisphere. **LS Visual**

Group Activity GENERAL

It's a Breeze Have students work in small groups to fill one baking dish with sand and warm it up in an oven on low heat. Have them fill another baking pan with ice and place the pans side by side. Have students make a screen 20–25 cm high out of cardboard and use it to surround the pans on three sides. Then, have them light an incense stick and hold it between the two pans. Ask students to describe and explain what happens. (The sand warms the air above it, making the air rise. The air above the ice is cold and dense and flows in to take the place of the warm air rising above the sand, creating a breeze.) **LS Verbal/Visual**

Answer to Reading Check

They flow in opposite directions from each other, and they occur at different latitudes.

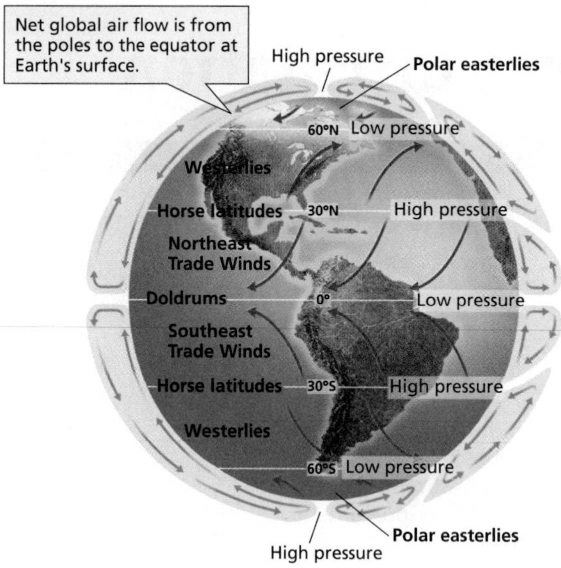

Figure 2 Each hemisphere has three wind belts. Wind belts are the result of pressure differences at the equator, the subtropics, the subpolar regions, and the poles. Winds in the belts curve because of the Coriolis effect. ***Do winds in the Northern Hemisphere curve clockwise or counterclockwise?***

Global Winds

The air that flows from the poles toward the equator does not flow in a single, straight line. Each hemisphere contains three looping patterns of flow called *convection cells.* Each convection cell correlates to an area of Earth's surface, called a *wind belt,* that is characterized by winds that flow in one main direction. These winds are called *prevailing winds.* All six wind belts are shown in **Figure 2.**

Trade Winds

In both hemispheres, the winds that flow toward the equator between 30° and 0° latitude are called **trade winds.** Like all winds, the trade winds are named according to the direction from which they flow. In the Northern Hemisphere, the trade winds flow from the northeast and are called the *northeast trade winds.* In the Southern Hemisphere, the trade winds are called the *southeast trade winds.* These wind belts are called *trade winds* because many trading ships sailed on these winds from Europe in the 18th and 19th centuries.

Westerlies

Between 30° and 60° latitude, air moving toward the poles is deflected by the Coriolis effect. This flow creates the **westerlies,** which exist in another wind belt in each hemisphere. In the Northern Hemisphere, the westerlies are southwest winds. In the Southern Hemisphere, they are northwest winds. The westerlies blow throughout the contiguous United States.

Reading Check **Name two ways in which the trade winds of the Northern Hemisphere differ from the westerlies of the Northern Hemisphere.**

trade winds prevailing winds that blow from east to west from 30° latitude to the equator in both hemispheres

westerlies prevailing winds that blow from west to east between 30° and 60° latitude in both hemispheres

polar easterlies prevailing winds that blow from east to west between 60° and 90° latitude in both hemispheres

Polar Easterlies

Toward the poles, or poleward, of the westerlies—at about 60° latitude—is a zone of low pressure. This zone of low pressure separates the westerlies from a third wind belt in each hemisphere. Over the polar regions themselves, descending cold air creates areas of high pressure. Surface winds created by the polar high pressure are deflected by the Coriolis effect and become the **polar easterlies.** The polar easterlies are strongest where they flow off Antarctica. Where the polar easterlies meet warm air from the westerlies, a stormy region known as a *front* forms.

Differentiated Instruction

Special Education Students

Science Vocabulary Students with disabilities may learn the terminology of science lessons more easily by using this method: Divide the class into three teams. Assign one of the three sections to each team. Ask each team to divide up the list of terms and create drawings that depict the terms. Have teams display their drawings. **LS Visual/Verbal**

Key Resources

Technology

- Transparencies
  97 Global Wind Belts

The Doldrums and Horse Latitudes

As **Figure 2** shows, the trade wind systems of the Northern Hemisphere and Southern Hemisphere meet at the equator in a narrow zone called the *doldrums*. In this warm zone, most air movement is upward and surface winds are weak and variable. As the air approaches 30° latitude, it descends and a high-pressure zone forms. These subtropical high-pressure zones are called the *horse latitudes*. Here, too, surface winds are weak and variable.

Wind and Pressure Shifts

As the sun's rays shift 23.5° northward and southward during the changing seasons of the year, the positions of the pressure belts and wind belts shift in response. Although the area that receives direct sunlight can shift by up to 47°, the average shift for the pressure belts and wind belts is only about 10° of latitude. However, even this small change causes some areas of Earth's surface to be in different wind belts during different times of the year. In southern Florida, for example, westerlies prevail in the winter, but trade winds dominate in the summer.

Jet Streams

Narrow bands of high-speed winds that blow in the upper troposphere and lower stratosphere are **jet streams.** These winds exist in the Northern Hemisphere and Southern Hemisphere.

One type of jet stream is a polar jet stream. Polar jet streams form as a result of density differences between cold polar air and the warmer air of the middle latitudes. These bands of winds, which are about 100 km wide and 2 to 3 km thick, are located at altitudes of 10 to 15 km. Polar jet streams can reach speeds of over 400 km/h and can affect airline routes and the paths of storms.

Another type of jet stream is a subtropical jet stream. In the subtropical regions, very warm equatorial air meets the cooler air of the middle latitudes, and *subtropical jet streams* form. Unlike polar jet streams, subtropical jet streams do not change much in speed or position. A subtropical jet stream is shown in **Figure 3.**

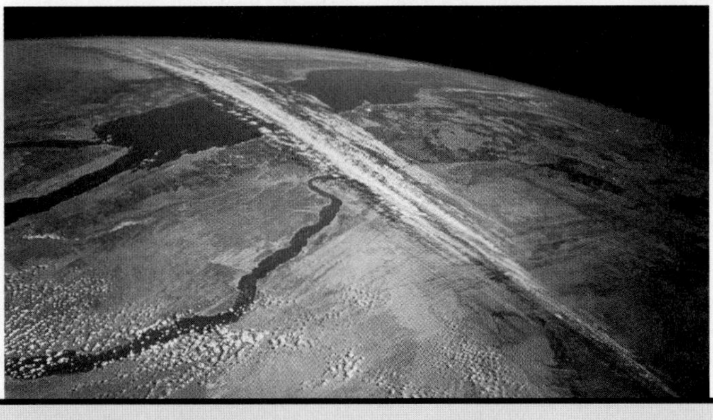

Figure 3 Clouds indicate the path of a jet stream traveling high over Egypt.

READING TOOLBOX

Layered Book
Make a layered book FoldNote, and label the tabs "Trade Winds," "Westerlies," "Polar Easterlies," and "Doldrums and Horse Latitudes." Write notes on the appropriate layers as you read this section.

jet stream a narrow band of strong winds that blow in the upper troposphere

READING TOOLBOX

Layered Book Students should include characteristics of these belts, such as the latitude at which they occur, the direction in which the wind blows, and what causes the winds to form.

Close

Reteaching — BASIC

Labeling Have students use a laminated map or a globe to identify the location and prevailing direction of the major wind belts. **LS Visual**

Quiz — GENERAL

1. What are the doldrums? (a region of low pressure near the equator where the trade wind systems meet and surface winds are very weak and variable)
2. What is a convection cell? (a vertical looping pattern of air flow that corresponds to the global wind belts)
3. What is a breeze? (wind that blows at speeds of less than 50 km/h)

Why It Matters

The Horse Latitudes The region where trade winds and the westerlies diverge, at about 30° North latitude, got its name for a macabre reason. Here, winds are light or even calm over vast areas of the ocean. Ships sailing to the New World often were becalmed here for weeks at a time. When food and water ran low, horses carried as cargo were tossed overboard to conserve remaining supplies. Their carcasses floated around these waters, a grim reminder for the next passing ship.

Close, *continued*

Answers to Section Review

1. Air moves from regions of high pressure toward regions of low pressure.
2. The Coriolis effect causes winds to curve because the rate at which the air travels differs from the rate of travel of the ground beneath the air. In the Northern Hemisphere, winds curve to the right; in the Southern Hemisphere, they curve to the left.
3. Polar easterlies are prevailing winds that blow from east to west between 60° and 90° latitude in both hemispheres. The westerlies are winds that blow from the southwest in the Northern Hemisphere and from the northwest in the Southern Hemisphere in the belts between 30° and 60° latitude. The trade winds are prevailing winds that blow from the northeast from 30°N to the equator and from the southeast from 30°S to the equator.
4. Jet streams are narrow bands of high-speed winds that blow in the upper troposphere and lower stratosphere. They are important because they can affect the paths of storms and airline routes.
5. Temperature differences between land and sea and between mountains and valleys influence local wind patterns.
6. Wind moving southward from the equator will curve to the east because of the Coriolis effect.
7. The air in my lungs has lower pressure. Because air moves from regions of higher pressure to areas of lower pressure, the air pressure in my lungs must be lower than the pressure outside my body.
8. Because sea breezes blowing from the water to land generally form in the afternoon, I would walk into the wind to reach the ocean.
9. *Winds* may be *global winds,* such as *polar easterlies, westerlies,* and *trade winds,* or *local winds,* such as *sea breezes, land breezes, mountain breezes,* and *valley breezes.*

Figure 4 Sea breezes keep these kites aloft during the afternoon.

Local Winds

Winds also exist on a scale that is much smaller than a global scale. Movements of air are influenced by local conditions, and local temperature variations commonly cause local winds. Local winds are not part of the global wind belts. Winds that blow at speeds of less than 50 km/h are called *breezes.*

Academic Vocabulary
influence (IN floo uhns) the effect of one thing on another

Land and Sea Breezes

Equal areas of land and water may receive the same amount of energy from the sun. However, land surfaces heat up faster than water surfaces do. Therefore, during daylight hours, a sharp temperature difference develops between a body of water and the land along the water's edge. This temperature difference is apparent in the air above the land and water. The warm air above the land rises, creating low pressure. Then, cool air from above the water moves in to replace the warm air. A cool wind moving from water to land, called a *sea breeze,* generally forms in the afternoon, as shown in **Figure 4.** Overnight, the land cools more rapidly than the water does, and the sea breeze is replaced by a *land breeze.* A land breeze flows from the cool land toward the warmer water.

Mountain and Valley Breezes

During the daylight hours in mountainous regions, a gentle valley breeze blows upslope. This *valley breeze* forms when warm air from the valleys moves upslope. At night, the mountains cool more quickly than the valleys do, and cool air descends from the mountain peaks to create a *mountain breeze.* Areas near mountains may experience a warm afternoon that turns into a cold evening soon after sunset. This evening cooling happens because cold air flows down mountain slopes and settles in valleys.

Section 3 Review

Key Ideas

1. **Describe** the pattern of air circulation between an area of low pressure and an area of high pressure.
2. **Explain** how the Coriolis effect affects wind flow.
3. **Name and describe** Earth's three global wind belts.
4. **Summarize** the importance of jet streams.
5. **Identify** two factors that create local wind patterns.

Critical Thinking

6. **Applying Concepts** Determine whether wind moving south from the equator will curve eastward or westward because of the Coriolis effect.
7. **Inferring Relationships** Which has a lower pressure: the air in your lungs as you inhale or the air outside your body? Explain.
8. **Applying Ideas** While visiting the Oregon coast, you decide to hike toward the ocean, but you are not sure of the direction. The time is 4:00 P.M. How might the breeze help you find your way?

Concept Mapping

9. Use the following terms to create a concept map: *wind, sea breeze, global winds, trade winds, westerlies, local winds, polar easterlies, land breeze, mountain breeze,* and *valley breeze.*

Differentiated Instruction

Alternative Assessment

Wind and Solar Energy Ask students to write a short essay that explains why it is correct to say that wind energy is related to solar energy.
LS Verbal/Logical

Why It Matters

Chasing Rainbows and Sundogs

WEIRD SCIENCE

The interplay of sunlight or moonlight and airborne water droplets, ice crystals, or particulates can create amazing, short-lived effects known collectively as atmospheric optics. Long before computer programs could manipulate images to produce new and surprising versions of reality, atmospheric optics were producing astounding light effects in the sky. Rainbows are the most well-known of these effects. Rainbows are formed when the sun's rays are refracted as they pass through spherical raindrops, causing the white light to split into the colors of the visible spectrum.

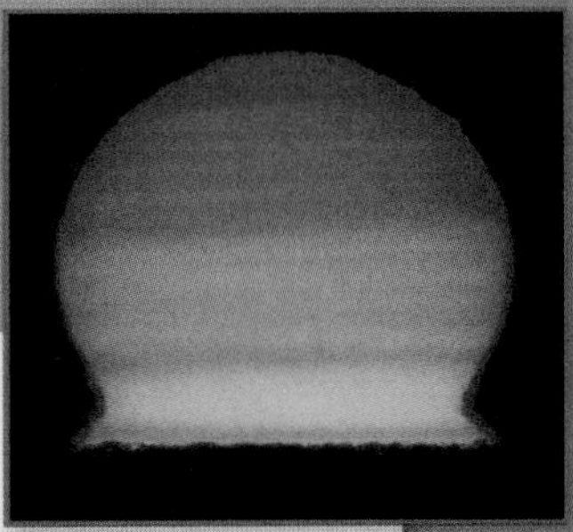

Sunset mirages are caused when the rays of the setting sun are refracted through layers of air that are different temperatures.

Crepuscular rays are rays of sunlight that stream through gaps between clouds and alternate with shadowy areas. They are formed when sunlight is partially blocked by clouds, mountains, or anything else that casts a shadow, and then scattered as it hits airborne particulates, water droplets, or ice crystals.

Circumzenithal arcs, which appear as upside-down rainbows, are formed by the refraction of sunlight through horizontally oriented ice crystals. Sunlight enters the top face of an ice crystal and exits through a vertical side face.

Sundogs (also called *parhelia*) are two bright spots that appear on either side of the sun just after sunrise or just before sunset. They are formed when hexagonal, horizontally oriented ice crystals refract sunlight.

YOUR TURN

UNDERSTANDING CONCEPTS
Compare and contrast rainbows and circumzenithal arcs.

ONLINE RESEARCH
Find and describe another example of an atmospheric optic. What causes it to form?

Why It Matters

Chasing Rainbows and Sundogs

Rainbows have many variations. One of the rarest is the moonbow (also known as a lunar rainbow). Conditions have to be just right for a moonbow to appear. The moon must be nearly full and not too high in the sky, it must be raining in the opposite direction from where the moon is rising, and the sky must be dark (so that the viewer sees colors and not grey streaks). Often, even if the sky is dark the viewer sees grey streaks instead of the moonbow's colors, because the human eye cannot perceive the colors in such faint light.

Answer to Your Turn

Understanding Concepts Rainbows arch upward, while circumzenithal arcs appear as upside-down rainbows. Rainbows are formed when sunlight is refracted through spherical raindrops, while circumzenithal arcs are formed when sunlight is refracted through horizontally-oriented ice crystals, entering the top face of the crystal and exiting through a vertical side face.

Online Research Answers may vary. Students may describe a wide range of atmospheric optics, from glories to coronas. Sample answer: Fogbows are nearly white, with light tinges of red on the outside edges and light smears of blue on the inside. They form in much the same way that rainbows form. But the raindrops that create rainbows are large, while the cloud and fog droplets that create fogbows are quite small. Diffraction caused by these small drops of water causes the colors of the spectrum to overlap and appear mostly white.

Inquiry Lab

Time Required
one 45-minute class period

Lab Ratings
EASY → HARD

Teacher Preparation: 1 flask
Student Setup: 2 flasks
Concept Level: 3 flasks
Cleanup: 2 flasks

Skills Acquired
- Predicting
- Experimenting
- Observing
- Measuring
- Collecting Data
- Organizing and Analyzing Data
- Inferring

Scientific Methods
In this lab, students will
- Ask Questions
- Form and Test a Hypothesis
- Make Observations
- Analyze the Results
- Draw Conclusions
- Communicate Results

Materials
The materials listed on this page are enough for groups of two to four students.

Inquiry Lab

45 min

Energy Absorption and Reflection

What You'll Do
- **Determine** which material would keep the inside of a house the coolest.
- **Explain** which properties of this material determine whether it is a conductor or an insulator.

What You'll Need
cardboard, 4 cm × 4 cm × 1 cm (4 pieces)
paint, black, white, and light blue tempera
metal, 4 cm × 4 cm × 1 cm
rubber, beige or tan, 4 cm × 4 cm × 1 cm
sandpaper, 4 cm × 4 cm × 1 cm
thermometers, Celsius (4)
watch or clock
wood, beige or tan, 4 cm × 4 cm × 1 cm

Safety

When solar energy reaches Earth's surface, the energy is either reflected or absorbed by the material that the surface is made of. Whether the material absorbs or reflects energy, and the amount of energy that is reflected or absorbed, depends on several characteristics of the material. These characteristics include the material's composition, its color and texture, how transparent the material is, the mass and volume of the material, and the specific heat of the material. In this lab, you will study these characteristics to determine which material is best suited for use as roofing material.

Ask a Question
1. Which material will keep the interior of a house the coolest?

Form a Hypothesis
2. Identify the material that you think will keep the inside of a house the coolest. List the characteristics of this material that caused you to choose it.

Test the Hypothesis
3. Brainstorm with a partner or with a small group of classmates to design a procedure that will help you determine which materials absorb the most energy and which materials keep the surface below them the coolest. You do not have to test all the materials, if you can explain why you think those materials would not be the coolest. Write down your experimental procedure.
4. Have your teacher approve your experimental design.

Step 3

Tips and Tricks
You may want to limit the number of materials that students can use for this activitiy. Have all materials cut to the appropriate size before students begin to use them. To save time, you may want to paint materials before students arrive.

5. Create a table like the one shown on the right. Use this table to record the data you collect as you perform your experiment.

6. Following your design, measure the temperatures that the materials and the surfaces beneath them reach.

Material	Color	Surface temperature (°C)	Temperature below material (°C)
Cardboard	white		
Rubber	beige		
Sandpaper	beige		

Analyze the Results

1. **Graphing Data** Use the data you collected to create a bar graph. Label the *x*-axis with the materials you tested and the *y*-axis with a range of temperatures.
2. **Analyzing Data** Which material reached the highest temperature on its surface? Which material caused the surface below it to reach the highest temperature?
3. **Analyzing Data** Which material stayed the lowest temperature at its surface? Which material kept the temperature of the surface beneath it the lowest?
4. **Evaluating Results** Did the color of the materials affect whether they absorbed or reflected solar energy? Explain your answer.

Draw Conclusions

5. **Drawing Conclusions** Based on your results, which material would you use for the roof of a house? Did your experimental results support your original hypothesis?
6. **Inferring Relationships** What properties of the material you identified in question 5 do you think make it best for this purpose? Explain your answer.
7. **Making Predictions** Do you think the material you chose would keep the inside of a house warm in colder weather? Explain your answer.
8. **Analyzing Methods** Name two changes in your experimental design that you would make if you were going to repeat the experiment. Explain why you would make each change.

Extension

Applying Ideas Use the materials you tested in the experiment to create a model of Earth's surface that represents how different parts of Earth's surface absorb or reflect solar energy. Which areas of Earth's surface absorb the least energy?

Answers to Analyze the Results

1. Graphs may vary.
2. Answers may vary but should accurately reflect student data.
3. Answers may vary but should accurately reflect student data.
4. Answers may vary. In general, darker colors will absorb more energy than lighter colors will.

Answers to Draw Conclusions

5. Answers may vary. Accept all reasonable answers.
6. Answers may vary. Accept all reasonable answers.
7. Answers may vary. Accept all reasonable answers.
8. Answers may vary. Accept all reasonable answers.

Answer to Extension

Models may vary. The areas of Earth's surface that absorb the least amount of energy are the oceans and icecaps.

Maps in Action

Absorbed Solar Radiation

Discussion GENERAL

The Tropics Draw students' attention to the relatively low amounts of absorbed radiation in both January and July at both poles. Why would the poles tend not to absorb radiation very well? (They have high albedo because of ice and snow cover throughout the year, especially in the Antarctic.) Discuss with students the effects global warming might have on the albedo in these regions and how those effects might affect the regional climate. (Global warming could cause the snow and ice in these areas to melt and be replaced with a surface that has lower albedo. This would result in higher absorption and higher temperatures.) **LS Visual/Logical**

Answers to Map Skills Activity

1. In January, the highest amount of absorbed solar radiation is at about 30°S in bands on the Pacific, Atlantic, and Indian Oceans.
2. In July, the highest amount of absorbed solar radiation is at about 30°N, 20°E, in the Mediterranean Sea just north of Libya and Egypt.
3. Southern Australia
4. The amount of radiation absorbed is least changed from January to July at the equator, 0° latitude.
5. In the Northern Hemisphere in January, when absorbed solar radiation is very low, temperatures are low, and winter is occurring. In the Northern Hemisphere in July, absorbed radiation is much higher, so temperatures are higher, and summer occurs.

MAPS in Action

Absorbed Solar Radiation

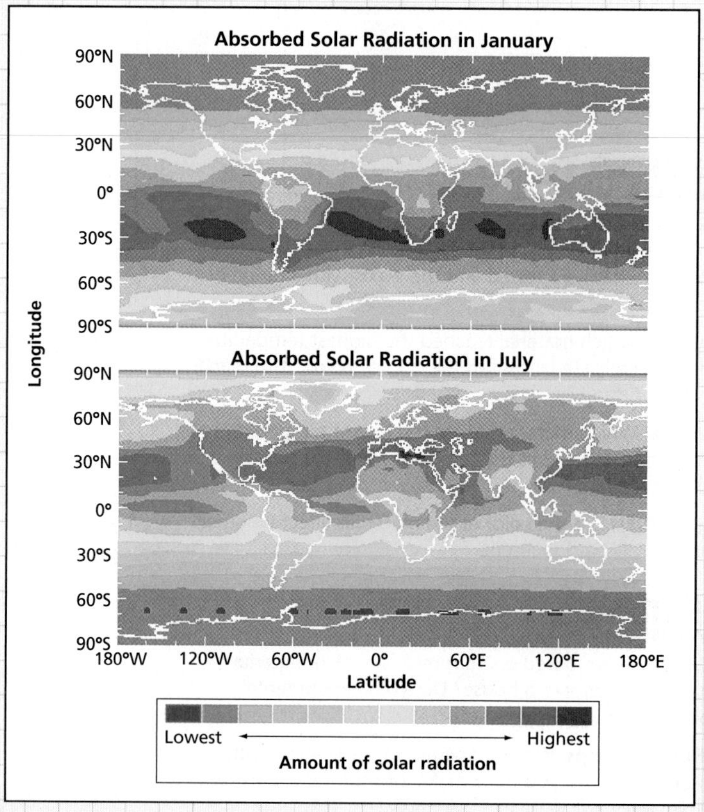

Map Skills Activity

These maps show the total amount of solar radiation that is absorbed by Earth in January and July. Use the maps to answer the questions below.

1. **Using a Key** In January, which region has the highest amount of absorbed solar radiation?
2. **Using a Key** In July, which region has the highest amount of absorbed solar radiation?
3. **Comparing Areas** Which area has the greatest difference between the amount of absorbed solar radiation in January and in July: southern Australia or northeastern South America?
4. **Analyzing Data** At what latitudes are January's and July's amounts of absorbed solar radiation similar?
5. **Inferring Relationships** How do these maps explain the differences between the Northern Hemisphere's weather in January and in July?

Key Resources

Technology

- Transparencies
  98 Absorbed Solar Radiation

Chapter 19

Summary

THINK central
SUPER SUMMARY
Keyword: HQXATMS

Key Ideas | Key Terms

Section 1

Characteristics of the Atmosphere

- Earth's atmosphere is the mixture of gases, called *air*, that surrounds Earth. Solid and liquid particles, called *particulates*, are mixed with the gases that make up air.
- Mercury inside a mercurial barometer rises or sinks as air pressure increases or decreases. In an aneroid barometer, changes in air pressure cause a metal container inside the barometer to bend inward or bulge outward. This moves a pointer on a scale.
- The atmosphere is divided into four main layers: the troposphere, the stratosphere, the mesosphere, and the thermosphere.
- Air pollution can be harmful to people, animals, plants, and property.

atmosphere, p. 513
ozone, p. 515
atmospheric pressure, p. 516
troposphere, p. 518
stratosphere, p. 519
mesosphere, p. 519
thermosphere, p. 519

Section 2

Solar Energy and the Atmosphere

- Most of the energy that reaches Earth from the sun is in the form of electromagnetic radiation.
- Visible light and infrared rays from the sun penetrate Earth's atmosphere and heat materials on Earth's surface.
- The upper atmosphere is heated by absorption of radiation from the sun. The lower atmosphere is heated by conduction from Earth's surface and by convection of air.

electromagnetic spectrum, p. 521
albedo, p. 523
greenhouse effect, p. 524
conduction, p. 526
convection, p. 526

Section 3

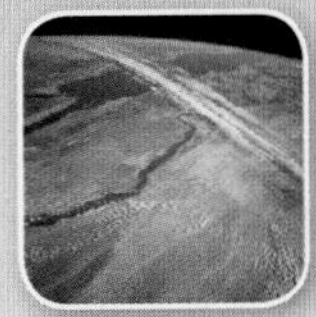

Atmospheric Circulation

- The Coriolis effect is the tendency of a moving object to follow a curved path rather than a straight path because of the rotation of Earth.
- Each hemisphere contains three convection cells that circulate air. Net global airflow near Earth's surface is from the poles toward the equator. The three global wind belts are the trade winds, the westerlies, and the polar easterlies.
- A surface feature, such as a body of water, a mountain, or a valley, can influence local wind patterns.

Coriolis effect, p. 527
trade winds, p. 528
westerlies, p. 528
polar easterlies, p. 528
jet stream, p. 529

Chapter Summary

Using THINK central Resources

Super Summary
Have students connect the major concepts in this chapter through an interactive Super Summary. Visit www.thinkcentral.com and type in the keyword **HQXATMS** to access the Super Summary for this chapter.

Differentiated Instruction

Alternative Assessment

Life's a Gas Have students imagine that they are one of the main gases in the atmosphere (N_2, O_2, Ar, H_2O, ozone, or CO_2) and have them write a story that describes their life by using words and illustrations. They should identify what gas they are, what layers of the atmosphere they have resided in, and what has happened to them during their life in the atmosphere. Students may want to describe whether they have cycled through living or nonliving things on Earth, interacted with solar radiation, or reacted with pollutants in the air. Encourage creativity and accept all reasonable answers but make sure their stories and illustrations are factually possible. **LS Verbal/Visual**

Chapter Review

Assignment Guide	
Section	**Questions**
1	2, 5, 6, 10–13, 18–22, 34
2	1, 3, 7, 14, 15, 23–26, 33, 35, 37
3	4, 8, 9, 16, 17, 27–31, 36, 38–40
1 and 2	32

Reading Toolbox

1. Seasons occur because of Earth's tilt. For part of the year, the Northern Hemisphere is tilted toward the sun and, as a result, receives more direct sunlight. During this time, temperatures are at their highest. For the other part of the year the Northern Hemisphere is tilted away from the sun. Thus, temperatures during this time are at their lowest.

Using Key Terms

2–9. Answers may vary but should show that students understand the definitions of and differences between key terms.

Understanding Key Concepts

10. a 15. d
11. b 16. b
12. a 17. c
13. c 18. a
14. a 19. d

Short Answer

20. nitrogen, oxygen, and argon
21. Atmospheric pressure is the force per unit area exerted on a surface by the weight of the atmosphere. It is measured by using a barometer.

Chapter 19 Review

1. **Cause and Effect** Use cause-and-effect signal words to explain the link between Earth's tilt and the seasons. READING TOOLBOX

USING KEY TERMS

Use each of the following terms in a separate sentence.

2. *atmosphere*
3. *electromagnetic spectrum*
4. *Coriolis effect*

For each pair of terms, explain how the meanings of the terms differ.

5. *troposphere* and *stratosphere*
6. *mesosphere* and *thermosphere*
7. *conduction* and *convection*
8. *trade winds* and *westerlies*
9. *polar easterlies* and *westerlies*

UNDERSTANDING KEY IDEAS

10. During one part of the nitrogen cycle, nitrogen is removed from the air mainly by nitrogen-fixing
 a. bacteria.
 b. waves.
 c. minerals.
 d. crystals.
11. The atmosphere contains tiny solid particles called
 a. gases.
 b. particulates.
 c. meteors.
 d. nitrogen.
12. A barometer measures
 a. atmospheric pressure.
 b. wind speed.
 c. ozone concentration.
 d. wavelengths.
13. Almost all the water and carbon dioxide in the atmosphere is in the
 a. exosphere. **c.** troposphere.
 b. ionosphere. **d.** stratosphere.
14. The process by which the atmosphere reduces Earth's loss of heat to space is called the
 a. greenhouse effect.
 b. Coriolis effect.
 c. doldrums.
 d. convection cell.
15. Energy as heat can be transferred within the atmosphere in three ways: radiation, conduction, and
 a. transpiration.
 b. temperature inversion.
 c. weathering.
 d. convection.
16. A vertical looping pattern of airflow is known as
 a. the Coriolis effect.
 b. a convection cell.
 c. a trade wind.
 d. a westerly.
17. Wind with a speed of less than 50 km/h is called
 a. a jet stream.
 b. the doldrums.
 c. a breeze.
 d. a trade wind.
18. Which of the following layers of the atmosphere is closest to the ground?
 a. troposphere
 b. thermosphere
 c. mesosphere
 d. exosphere
19. Which of the following layers of the atmosphere is closest to space?
 a. troposphere
 b. ionosphere
 c. mesosphere
 d. exosphere

SHORT ANSWER

20. List the three main elemental gases that compose the atmosphere.
21. What is atmospheric pressure, and how is it measured?
22. List and describe the four main layers of the atmosphere.

22. The *troposphere* is the lowest layer of the atmosphere and is the place where most weather occurs. Temperature decreases with altitude in the troposphere, until the tropopause, or boundary between the troposphere and the *stratosphere*, is reached. In the stratosphere, temperature increases with increasing altitude as solar radiation is absorbed by ozone. Almost all of the ozone in the atmosphere is concentrated in this layer, which extends to an altitude of about 50 km. The *mesosphere*, extending to an altitude of about 80 km, is the coldest layer of the atmosphere. Temperature decreases with increasing altitude. In the *thermosphere*, temperature increases with increasing altitude.
23. Visible light that enters the atmosphere is reflected, absorbed, or scattered by the atmosphere and by Earth's surface.
24. by radiation, conduction, and convection
25. Because Earth is a sphere, sunlight does not hit the surface at the same angle all over the globe. When sunlight hits Earth's surface at angles less than 90°, as at high latitudes, its energy is spread out over a larger area and thus is less intense and temperatures are lower.
26. The greenhouse effect warms Earth's lower atmosphere as carbon dioxide, water vapor and other greenhouse gases absorb and reradiate infrared radiation, which slows the escape of heat from Earth.

23. What happens to visible light that enters Earth's atmosphere?

24. How is heat energy transferred by Earth's atmosphere?

25. How does latitude affect the temperature of a region?

26. Explain how the greenhouse effect helps to warm the atmosphere.

27. What causes the Coriolis effect?

28. Name and describe the three main wind belts in both hemispheres.

29. How do surface features influence local wind patterns?

CRITICAL THINKING

30. **Making Inferences** If a breeze is blowing from the ocean to the land on the coast of Maine, about what time of day is it? Explain your answer.

31. **Evaluating Ideas** What effect might jet streams have on airplane travel?

32. **Inferring Relationships** Most aerosol sprays that contain CFCs have been banned in the United States. Which of the four layers of the atmosphere does this ban help to protect? Explain your answer.

33. **Evaluating Information** You hear a report about Earth's weather. The reporter says that visible light rays coming from Earth's surface heat the atmosphere in a way similar to the way a greenhouse is heated. Explain why the reporter's statement is incorrect.

CONCEPT MAPPING

34. Use the following terms to create a concept map: *atmosphere, troposphere, stratosphere, temperature, mesosphere, thermosphere, atmospheric pressure, altitude,* and *exosphere.*

MATH SKILLS

Math Skills

35. **Applying Quantities** The albedo of the moon is 0.07. What percentage of the total solar radiation that reaches the moon is reflected?

36. **Making Calculations** Maximum local wind speeds for each of the last seven days were 12 km/h, 20 km/h, 11 km/h, 6 km/h, 8 km/h, 19 km/h, and 17 km/h. What was the average maximum wind speed?

WRITING SKILLS

37. **Writing from Research** Research the debate about global warming. Write one paragraph about evidence that supports global warming and one paragraph about evidence that does not support global warming.

INTERPRETING GRAPHICS

The graph below shows how the Coriolis effect changes as latitude and wind speed change. Use this graph to answer the questions that follow.

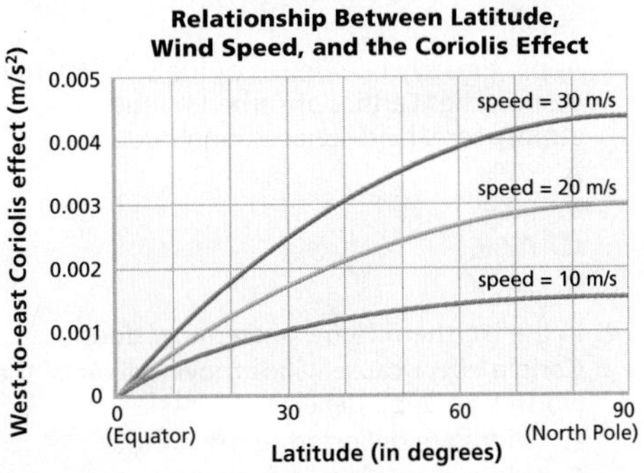

38. At what wind speed is the Coriolis effect the greatest?

39. At what latitude is the Coriolis effect the smallest?

40. At 90° latitude, is there a direct relationship between the Coriolis effect and wind speed?

Chapter Review

27. the rotation of Earth
28. The trade winds are prevailing winds that blow from the northeast from 30° North latitude to the equator and southeast from 30° South latitude to the equator. The westerlies are winds that blow from west to east in the belt between 30° and 60° North and South latitude. Polar easterlies are prevailing winds that blow from east to west between 60° and 90° North and South latitudes.
29. Surface features, such as bodies of water, mountains, and valleys, create local winds as a result of uneven heating and cooling of the ground surface.

Critical Thinking

30. It is most likely afternoon, because warm air above the land rises and is replaced by cool air from the ocean.
31. Because jet streams influence storm paths, airplanes might tend to avoid the jet streams when major storms are brewing. On the other hand, pilots may "ride" jet streams in fair weather to take advantage of tailwinds by cutting fuel costs and flight times.
32. The ban on CFCs helps protect the stratosphere, the location of most of the ozone in the atmosphere, because CFCs destroy ozone.
33. Infrared rays, not visible light rays, radiate from Earth's surface and are trapped by gases in the atmosphere much as heat is trapped in a greenhouse.

Concept Mapping

34. Answers may vary but should include all of the terms listed. Sample answers appear at the end of this unit on p. 631B.

Math Skills

35. Albedo is the fraction of solar radiation that is reflected off the surface of an object, and the moon's albedo is 0.07, 7% of solar radiation that reaches the moon is reflected. ($0.07 \times 100 = 7\%$)
36. Average maximum wind speed = sum of maximum wind speed each day ÷ number of days = $(12 + 20 + 11 + 6 + 8 + 19 + 17) \div 7 = 13$ km/h

Writing Skills

37. Answers may vary. Accept all reasonable answers.

Interpreting Graphics

38. The Coriolis effect is greatest at the highest wind speed, 30 m/s.
39. The Coriolis effect is smallest at 0°, the equator.
40. yes; For every 10 m/s rise in wind speed, the Coriolis effect increases by 0.0015 m/s^2.

Standardized Test Prep

Estimated Time

To give students practice under more realistic testing conditions, allow them 30 minutes to answer all of the questions in this practice test.

Test Doctor

Question 1 Answer D is correct. Students should understand that oxidation, respiration, and combustion are processes that consume, not produce, oxygen. So, answers A, B, and C are incorrect.

Question 9 Full-credit answers should include the following points:

- students should demonstrate an understanding that chinook winds are warm, dry winds that occur mostly in the winter
- chinook winds can affect the temperature down a mountainside drastically and quickly, such as raising winter temperatures from −4 ºF to 45 ºF in a matter of minutes
- chinook winds can melt large amounts of snow in just a few hours

Question 10 Answer A is correct. Students should know that as air becomes warmer and less dense, it rises. Some students may mistakenly select answer B by following the arrows in a circle until the air sinks back toward Earth. However, the air sinks only after cooling again.

Chapter 19 Standardized Test Prep

Understanding Concepts

Directions (1–4): For each question, write on a separate sheet of paper the letter of the correct answer.

1. Which of the following processes is the source of the oxygen gas found in Earth's atmosphere?
A. oxidation
B. combustion
C. respiration
D. photosynthesis

2. Which of the following statements best describes the relationship of atmospheric pressure to altitude?
F. The atmospheric pressure increases as the altitude increases.
G. The atmospheric pressure increases as the altitude decreases.
H. The atmospheric pressure varies unpredictably at different altitudes.
I. The atmospheric pressure is constant at all altitudes.

3. Approximately how much of the solar energy that reaches Earth is absorbed by the atmosphere, land surfaces, and ocean?
A. 30%
B. 50%
C. 70%
D. 100%

4. In the Northern Hemisphere, how does the Coriolis effect cause winds moving toward the North Pole to be deflected?
F. Winds are deflected to the right.
G. Winds are deflected to the left.
H. Winds are deflected in unpredictable patterns.
I. Winds are not deflected by the Coriolis effect.

Directions (5–6): For each question, write a short response.

5. What is the most abundant gas in Earth's atmosphere?

6. In which atmospheric layer do interactions between gas molecules and solar radiation produce the aurora borealis?

Reading Skills

Directions (7–9): Read the passage below. Then, answer the questions.

The Snow Eater

The chinook, or "snow eater," is a dry wind that blows down the eastern side of the Rocky Mountains from New Mexico to Canada. Chinooks have the ability to melt large amounts of snow very quickly. Chinooks form when moist air is forced over a mountain range. The air cools as it rises. As the air cools, it releases moisture in the form of rain or snow, which nourishes the local flora. As the dry air flows over the mountaintop, it descends, compressing and heating the air below. The warm, dry wind that results can melt half of a meter of snow in just a few hours.

The temperature change caused when a chinook rushes down a mountainside can be dramatic. On January 22, 1943, in Spearfish, South Dakota, the temperature at 7:30 A.M. was –4 °F. But only two minutes later, a chinook caused the temperature to soar to 45 °F.

7. Why are the chinook winds of the Rocky Mountains called "snow eaters"?
A. Chinook winds pick up snow and carry it to new locations.
B. Chinook winds drop all their snow on the western side of the mountains.
C. Chinook winds cause the temperature to decrease, which causes snow to accumulate.
D. Chinook winds cause the temperature to increase rapidly, which causes snow to melt.

8. Which of the following statements can be inferred from the information in the passage?
F. Chinook winds are a relatively new phenomenon related to global warming.
G. Chinook winds occur during the winter.
H. The only type of wind that blows down from mountaintops are chinook winds.
I. When they blow up the western side of the Rocky Mountains, chinook winds are very hot.

9. How do chinook winds affect weather on the eastern side of the Rocky Mountains?

Question 12 Full-credit answers should include the following points:

- students should demonstrate a conceptual understanding that the directions of local winds would be different at this location during the night from those during the day
- students should also demonstrate an understanding that the sun will heat land and water at different rates. This concept should lead students to the idea that temperature and density differences will exist in the air masses above the land and the water
- during the day, solar radiation will heat the land faster than it will heat the ocean. This will produce a wind that moves from the ocean to the land as warm land air rises
- just as land warms quicker during the day than water, land cools more quickly at night than ocean water does
- at night, cool air from the land moves seaward as warmer ocean air rises

Interpreting Graphics

Directions (10–12): For each question below, record the correct answer on a separate sheet of paper.

The diagram below shows global wind belts and convection cells at different latitudes. Use this diagram to answer questions 10 and 11.

Global Wind Belts

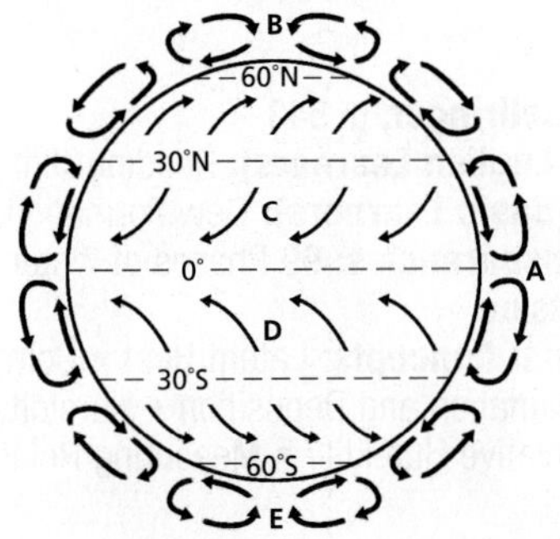

10. What happens to the air around location A as the air warms and decreases in density?

A. It rises.
B. It sinks.
C. It stagnates.
D. It contracts.

11. Compare and contrast the wind patterns in the global wind belts labeled C and D. Why do the winds move in the directions shown?

The graphic below shows a typical coastal area. Use this graphic to answer question 12.

Coastal Land Area on a Summer Day

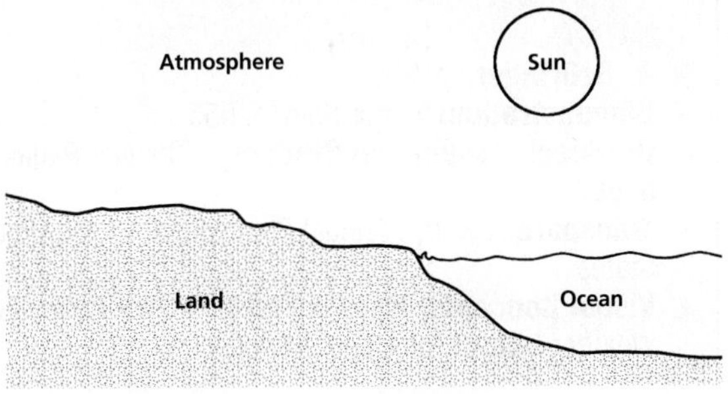

12. Would the direction of local winds be the same during the night as they would during the day in this location? Explain your answer in terms of the direction and cause of the winds during the day and during the night.

Test Tip

Do not be fooled by answers that may seem correct just because they contain unfamiliar words.

Standardized Test Prep

Using THINK central Resources

State Resources

- For specific resources for your state, visit www.thinkcentral.com and type in the keyword **HSHSTR.**

Answers

Understanding Concepts

1. D
2. G
3. C
4. F
5. nitrogen
6. ionosphere

Reading Skills

7. D
8. G
9. Answers may vary. See Test Doctor for a detailed scoring rubric.

Interpreting Graphics

10. A
11. Location C has northeast winds. Location D has southeast winds. Cool air flows toward low pressure caused by rising warm air near the equator. Both winds are somewhat easterly because of Earth's rotation.
12. Answers may vary. See Test Doctor for a detailed scoring rubric.

Chapter Planner 20

Water in the Atmosphere

	Time	Standards	Teach Key Ideas
Chapter Opener, pp. 540–541	45 min.	**National Science Education Standards**	
Section 1 Atmospheric Moisture, pp. 543–548 ❯ Changing Forms of Water ❯ Humidity ❯ Measuring Humidity	45 min.	**ES 2b, ES 1c, ES 1d**	■ ◆ **Bellringer,** p. 543 ■ **DI (English Learners):** Reading Hint, p. 545 ■ **DI (Basic Learners):** Dew Formation, p. 546 ◆ **Transparencies:** 99 Phases of Water • 100 Vapor Pressure ▲ **Visual Concepts:** Latent Heat • Comparing Sublimation and Deposition • Humidity • Dew Point • Relative Humidity • Measuring Relative Humidity
Section 2 Clouds and Fog, pp. 549–554 ❯ Cloud Formation ❯ Adiabatic Cooling ❯ Mixing ❯ Lifting ❯ Advective Cooling ❯ Classification of Clouds	45 min.	**ES 2b, ES 1c, ES 1d, PS 2d**	■ ◆ **Bellringer,** p. 549 ■ **Demonstration:** Condensation Nuclei, p. 549 ■ **DI (English Learners):** Visual Literacy, p. 549 ■ **DI (Special Education Students):** Appearance of Clouds, p. 551 ◆ **Transparencies:** 101 Formation of a Water Droplet • 102 Classification of Clouds ▲ **Visual Concepts:** Formation of Clouds and Precipitation • Types of Clouds
Section 3 Precipitation, pp. 555–558 ❯ Forms of Precipitation ❯ Causes of Precipitation ❯ Measuring Precipitation ❯ Weather Modification	45 min.	**ES 2b, ES 1c, LS 4e**	■ ◆ **Bellringer,** p. 555 ■ **Demonstration:** Indoor Rain, p. 555 ■ **DI (Special Education Students):** Doppler Radar, p. 557 ◆ **Transparency:** 103 Annual Precipitation in the United States ▲ **Visual Concepts:** Types of Precipitation • Collecting Weather Data in the Upper Atmosphere
Chapter Wrap-Up, pp. 563–567	90 min.		**Chapter Summary,** p. 563

See also PowerNotes® Presentations

CHAPTER Fast Track *To shorten instruction because of time limitations, omit the Chapter Lab.*

Key
Teacher's Edition ■
Chapter Resource File ●
Teaching Transparencies ◆
Online Edition ▲

All resources listed below are also available on the **Teacher One Stop™.**

Why It Matters	Hands-On	Skills Development	Assessment
■ **Chapter Overview,** p. 540 ■ **Using the Figure:** Clouds and Weather, p. 540	**Inquiry Lab:** Average Precipitation, p. 541	**Reading Toolbox,** p. 542	
■ **Section Overview,** p. 543 **Why Does Humid Air Feel Hotter?** p. 544 ■ **Chemistry Connection:** Hidden Energy, p. 544 ■ **Biology Connection:** Desert Survival, p. 546	■ **Activity:** Cooling Effect, p. 543 ■ **Activity:** Scientific Instruments, p. 546 **Quick Lab:** Dew Point, p. 547 **Skills Practice Lab:** Relative Humidity, pp. 560–561	**Reading Toolbox:** Two-Panel Flip Chart, p. 545 **Math Skills:** Relative Humidity, p. 546	**Reading Check,** p. 544 **Reading Check,** p. 546 **Section Review,** p. 548 ■ **Reteaching,** p. 547 ■ **Quiz,** p. 547 ■ **DI (Alternative Assessment):** Song Lyrics, p. 548 ● **Section Quiz**
■ **Section Overview,** p. 549 ■ **Using the Figure:** Discussion, p. 550 ■ **Geology Connection:** Rain Shadow, p. 551 ■ **Using the Figure:** Cloud Bulletin Board, p. 552	**Quick Lab:** Cloud Formation, p. 552	■ **Skill Builder:** Math, p. 550 ■ ● **Internet Activity:** Latent Heat and Thunderstorms, p. 550 ■ **Skill Builder:** Vocabulary, p. 552 ■ **Reading ToolBox:** Analyzing Comparisons, p. 553	**Reading Check,** p. 550 **Reading Check,** p. 553 **Section Review,** p. 554 ■ **Reteaching,** p. 553 ■ **Quiz,** p. 553 ■ **DI (Alternative Assessment):** Cloud Atlas, p. 554 ● **Section Quiz**
■ **Section Overview,** p. 555 ■ **Environmental Connection:** Climate and Precipitation, p. 556	■ **Group Activity:** Supercooled: Test-Tube Hail, p. 556 ● **Inquiry Lab:** How Big Is a Raindrop? ● **Making Models Lab:** What Is the Shape of a Raindrop?	■ **Reading ToolBox:** Suffixes, p. 557 **Maps in Action: Annual Precipitation in the United States,** p. 562 ■ ● **Internet Activity:** Climate and Precipitation, p. 562	**Reading Check,** p. 557 **Section Review,** p. 558 ■ **Reteaching,** p. 557 ■ **Quiz,** p. 557 ■ **DI (Alternative Assessment):** Instruction Manuals, p. 558 ● **Section Quiz**
Ice Storms, p. 559		▲ **Super Summary** **Standardized Test Prep,** pp. 566–567	**Chapter Review,** pp. 564–565 ■ **DI (Alternative Assessment):** Water Cycle Skit, p. 563 ● **Chapter Tests**

See also Lab Generator

See also Holt Online Assessment Resources

Chapter Overview

This chapter describes how moisture in the atmosphere is described and measured. The chapter also explains how clouds form and what causes precipitation.

Using the Figure GENERAL

Clouds and Weather Unlike other aspects of weather, clouds can easily be seen and studied. Different types of clouds can indicate approaching weather systems. The leading edge of the clouds in the photo is a squall line that indicates approaching storms. Ask students what types of weather they associate with particular clouds. (Sample answers: Dark clouds bring lightning, thunder, and heavy rain. High, layered clouds may mean rain is coming.) **LS Visual**

Why It Matters

Water vapor in the atmosphere is a critical component of the water cycle. The evaporation and condensation of water in the atmosphere transfers energy as heat through the atmosphere. Condensation of water vapor leads to the formation of clouds and eventually precipitation, returning water to Earth's surface.

Chapter 20 Water in the Atmosphere

Chapter Outline

1 Atmospheric Moisture
- Changing Forms of Water
- Humidity
- Measuring Humidity

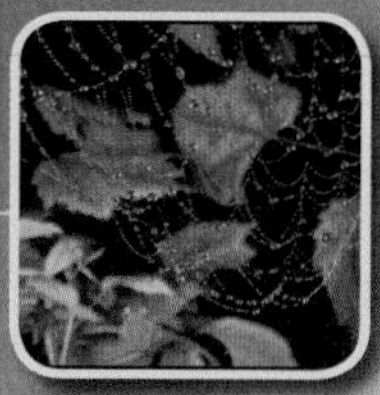

2 Clouds and Fog
- Cloud Formation
- Adiabatic Cooling
- Mixing
- Lifting
- Advective Cooling
- Classification of Clouds

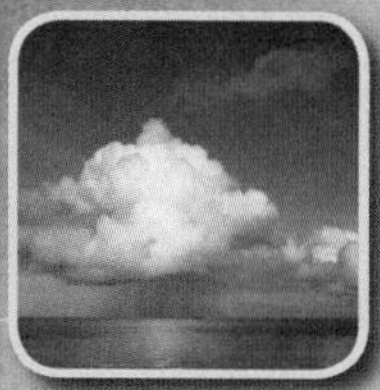

3 Precipitation
- Forms of Precipitation
- Causes of Precipitation
- Measuring Precipitation
- Weather Modification

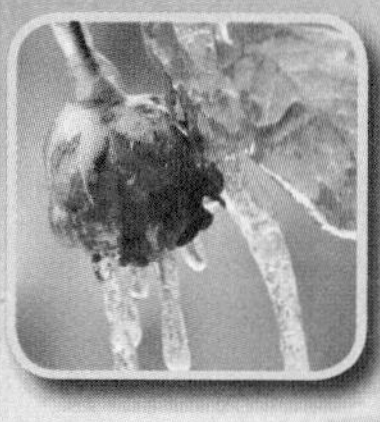

Virginia Standards of Learning
ES.1.a
ES.1.c
ES.2.a
ES.12.a

Why It Matters

Understanding how water moves through the atmosphere provides a basis for understanding how heat is transferred around the globe and for predicting the weather.

Chapter Correlations

Virginia Standards of Learning

ES.1.a volume, area, mass, elapsed time, direction, temperature, pressure, distance, density, and changes in elevation/depth are calculated utilizing the most appropriate tools.

ES.1.c scales, diagrams, charts, graphs, tables, imagery, models, and profiles are constructed and interpreted.

ES.2.a science explains and predicts the interactions and dynamics of complex Earth systems.

ES.12.a observation and collection of weather data

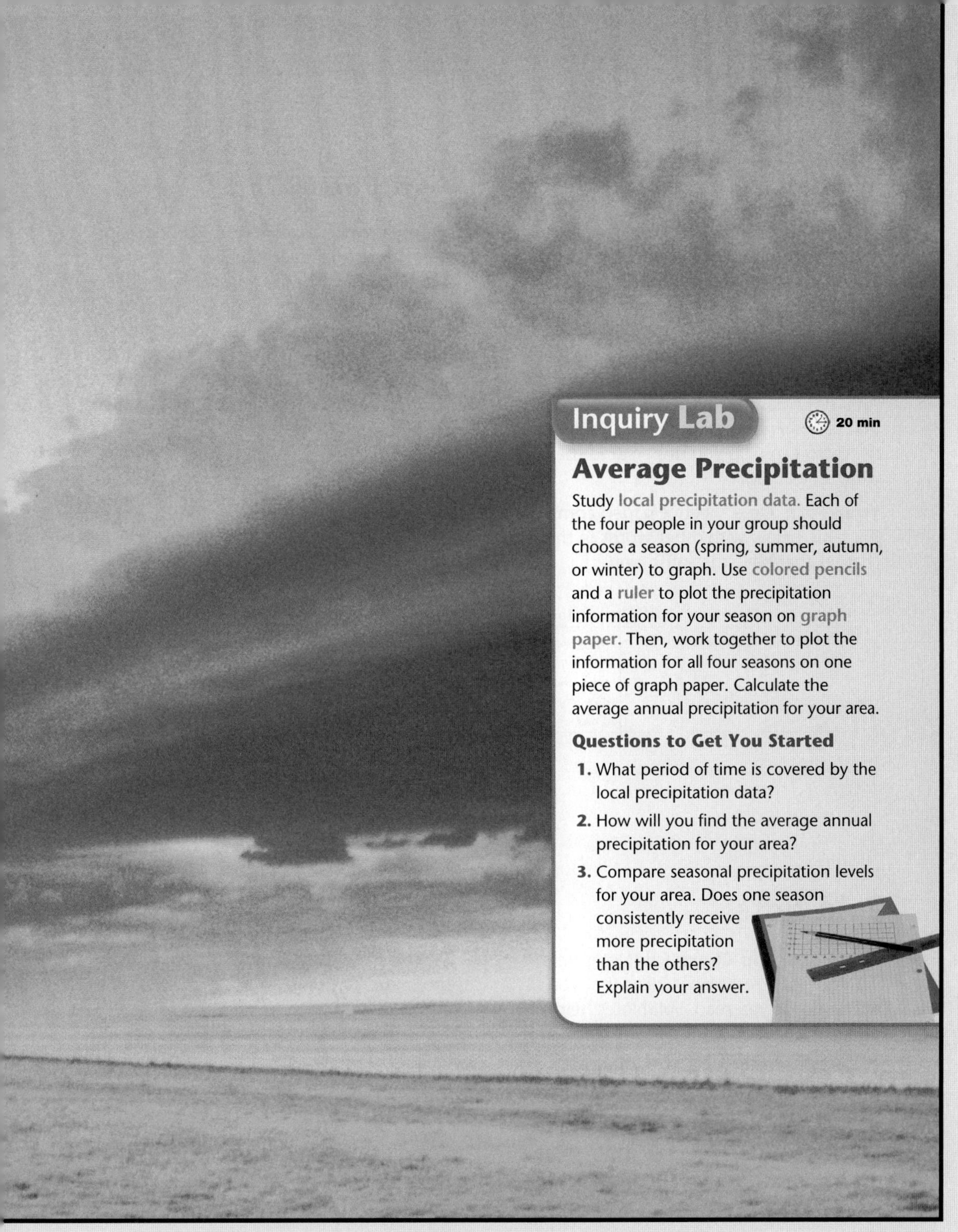

Inquiry Lab

20 min

Average Precipitation

Study local precipitation data. Each of the four people in your group should choose a season (spring, summer, autumn, or winter) to graph. Use colored pencils and a ruler to plot the precipitation information for your season on graph paper. Then, work together to plot the information for all four seasons on one piece of graph paper. Calculate the average annual precipitation for your area.

Questions to Get You Started

1. What period of time is covered by the local precipitation data?
2. How will you find the average annual precipitation for your area?
3. Compare seasonal precipitation levels for your area. Does one season consistently receive more precipitation than the others? Explain your answer.

Inquiry Lab

Central Concept: Students will graph and analyze precipitation data as an introduction to water in the atmosphere and how it is monitored.

Teacher's Notes: Obtain precipitation data prior to lab. You may want to have each group use data from a different region and have students compare data.

Materials (per group)

- Precipitation data
- Colored pencils
- Ruler
- Graph paper

Skills Acquired

Organizing and Analyzing Data

Answers to Getting Started

1. Answers will vary. Students should indicate the time period covered by the graph, such as from January to December of 2009.
2. Add the data from each month together and divide the sum by the number of months.
3. Answers will vary depending on location.

Using THINK central Resources

An online version of this chapter, as well as all the print and multimedia resources that accompany the program are available to registered teachers and their students. Log onto www.thinkcentral.com to access these materials and tools to organize your preparation and student learning.

READING TOOLBOX

Word Parts

Suffixes Completed tables may contain the following examples: precipitation, precipitate, -ion, moisture that falls to Earth's surface; evaporation, evaporate, -ion, the process by which a liquid changes into a gas; saturation, saturate, -ion, the act of being saturated

Comparisons

Analyzing Comparisons Possible examples: First thing: frost, Second thing: frozen dew, Similarities or Differences: Frozen dew forms as clear beads of ice, Signal Word or Phrase: unlike; First thing: clouds, Second thing: fog, Similarities and Differences: Fog and clouds result from the condensation of water vapor in the air, Signal Word or Phrase: like

FoldNotes

Two-Panel Flip Chart Students should write notes about cloud formation and precipitation. Students may draw a sketch of the different types of clouds or how the process by which different types of precipitation form.

READING TOOLBOX

These reading tools will help you learn the material in this chapter.

Word Parts

Suffixes The suffix *–ion* usually changes verbs into nouns to denote a process. For example, *combination* is a noun formed from the verb *combine.* It means "the result of combining." The suffix *-ly* changes a noun, an adjective, or a verb to an adverb. It means "in the manner of." *Slowly* means "in a slow manner." When you see a word that uses one of these suffixes, the root of the word can help you understand the word's meaning.

Your Turn On a sheet of paper, complete the table below with other words in the chapter that have the suffix *–ion.*

Word	Root	Suffix	Definition
sublimation	sublimate	- ion	the process by which a solid changes directly into a gas
		- ion	

Comparisons

Analyzing Comparisons Comparisons are often signaled by the use of a few key words. The words *like* and *unlike* can tell you whether a comparison is focused on similarities or differences. Comparative words can be formed by using the suffixes *-er* and *-est*. Comparative phrases can be formed by using the words *more* and *less*.

Your Turn As you read this chapter, fill out a table of comparisons like the one below. The entry is for the sentence "Unlike nimbostratus clouds, which produce heavy precipitation, altostratus clouds produce very little precipitation."

First thing	Second thing	Similarities or differences	Signal words or phrases
nimbostratus clouds	altostratus clouds	nimbostratus: heavy precipitation, altostratus: little precipitation	unlike

Fold Notes

Two-Panel Flip Chart FoldNotes help you learn and remember ideas that you encounter as you read. FoldNotes help you organize concepts and see the "big picture."

Your Turn Follow the instructions in **Appendix A** for making a two-panel flip chart. Label the panels as shown here.

Open the appropriate flap to take notes about each topic and draw a sketch.

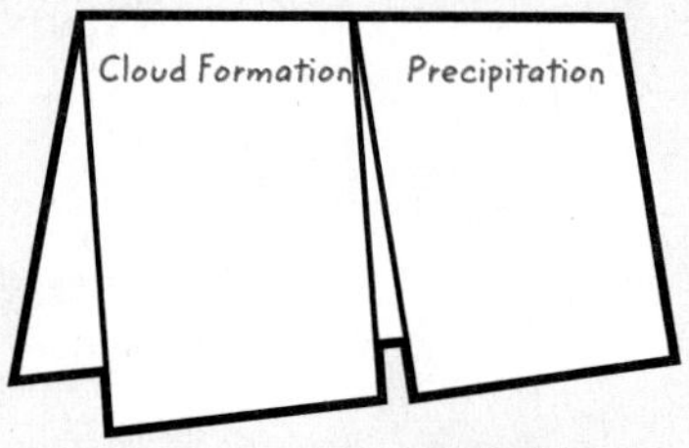

For more information on how to use these and other tools, see **Appendix A.**

SECTION 1

Atmospheric Moisture

Key Ideas	Key Terms	Why It Matters
› Explain how heat energy affects the changing phases of water. › Explain what absolute and relative humidity are, and describe how they are measured. › Describe what happens when the temperature of air decreases to the dew point or below.	**latent heat** **sublimation** **dew point** **absolute humidity** **relative humidity**	When the air is humid, you feel warmer than you would if the air were dry, even if the temperature is the same. The humidity affects your body's ability to cool itself by sweating.

Water in the atmosphere exists in three states, or *phases.* One phase is a gas known as *water vapor.* The other two phases of water are the solid phase known as *ice* and the liquid phase known as *water.*

Changing Forms of Water

Water changes from one phase to another when heat energy is absorbed or released, as shown in **Figure 1.** Molecules of ice are held almost stationary in a definite crystalline arrangement. However, when energy is absorbed by the ice, the molecules move more rapidly. They break from their fixed positions and slide past each other in the fluid form of a liquid.

When more energy is absorbed by liquid water, the water changes from a liquid to a gas. Because the additional energy causes the movement of the molecules in liquid water to speed up, the molecules collide more frequently with each other. Such collisions can cause the molecules to move so rapidly that the fastest-moving molecules escape from the liquid to form invisible water vapor in a process called *evaporation.*

latent heat the heat energy that is absorbed or released by a substance during a phase change

Latent Heat

The heat energy that is absorbed or released by a substance during a phase change is called **latent heat.** When liquid water evaporates, the water absorbs energy from the environment. This energy becomes potential energy between the molecules. When water vapor changes back into a liquid through the process of *condensation,* energy is released to the surrounding air and the molecules move closer together. Likewise, latent heat is absorbed when ice thaws, and latent heat is released when water freezes.

Figure 1 Water exists in three states, called *phases.* As it changes from one phase to another, water either absorbs or releases heat energy.

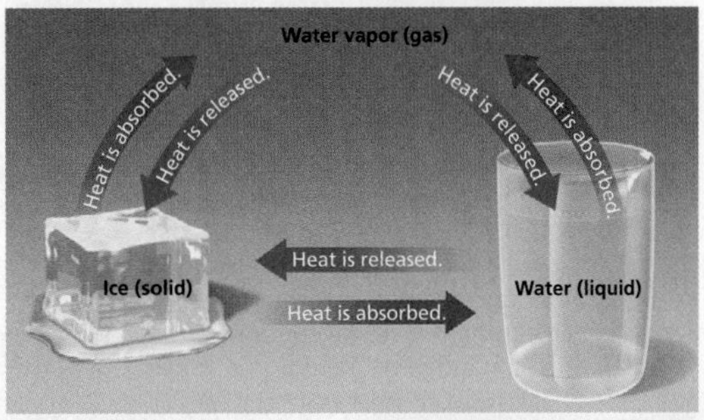

Section 1

Focus

Overview

This section explains the phases of water, the concepts of absolute and relative humidity and how they are measured, and the effects of temperature changes on moisture in the air.

Bellringer

Ask students to describe what must happen to ice to cause it to melt and what must happen to water to cause it to boil. (Temperature must increase, or more thermal energy must be added to the system.) LS **Visual**

Motivate

Activity GENERAL

Cooling Effect Divide the class into pairs and distribute isopropyl alcohol swabs to each team. Explain that alcohol evaporates quickly. Have students rub the alcohol swab on a patch of skin. (Caution students not to participate if they have skin allergies.) Ask students to describe how the swabbed skin feels, and why. (cool; Because energy is required to change the liquid to a gas, heat leaves the skin during evaporation. This process leaves the skin feeling cooler.) LS **Kinesthetic**

Key Resources

Chapter Resource File
- Directed Reading BASIC

Technology
- Transparencies
  Bellringer
  99 Phases of Water

Teach

Chemistry Connection — GENERAL

Hidden Energy Water's unusual properties and behavior, including its high latent heat value, are largely due to its chemical structure. Water is a V-shaped polar molecule arranged so the oxygen side has a slight negative charge and the hydrogen side has a slight positive charge. This arrangement allows each hydrogen atom to share electrons with the oxygen atom through a stable covalent bond. In addition, a force called *hydrogen bonding* exists between water molecules. Water's latent heat results from hydrogen bonding. In the solid state, water molecules are bound together in a crystal lattice. In liquid water, they are arranged more irregularly but are able to glide past each other. In water vapor, the hydrogen bonds between the molecules are broken, and water exists as separate molecules. The energy used to create and maintain the separation between the water molecules is latent heat.

Answer to Reading Check

When the air is very dry and the temperature is below freezing, ice and snow change directly into water vapor by sublimation.

Evaporation

Most water enters the atmosphere through the process of evaporation. Because the largest amounts of solar energy reach Earth near the equator, most evaporation takes place over the oceans of the equatorial region. However, water vapor also enters the atmosphere by evaporation from lakes, ponds, streams, and soil. Plants release water into the atmosphere in a process called transpiration. Volcanoes and burning fuels also release small amounts of water vapor into the atmosphere.

Sublimation

sublimation the process in which a solid changes directly into a gas (the term is sometimes also used for the reverse process)

Ice commonly changes into a liquid before changing into a gas. However, in some cases, ice can change directly into water vapor without becoming a liquid. The process by which a solid changes directly into a gas is called **sublimation.** When the air is dry and the temperature is below freezing, ice and snow may sublimate into water vapor. Water vapor can also turn directly into ice without becoming a liquid.

Reading Check **Summarize the conditions under which sublimation commonly occurs.** (See Appendix G for answers to Reading Checks.)

Why It Matters

Why Does Humid Air Feel Hotter?

REAL WORLD

You probably have heard people say, "It's not the heat—it's the humidity." When relative humidity is high, the day feels hotter than the temperature you read on the thermometer. Why? Evaporation of sweat is a main mechanism by which the body regulates temperature. Sweat does not evaporate when relative humidity is about 80 percent or higher. When sweat doesn't evaporate, the body does not cool as efficiently.

Smog is worsened by high humidity. Not only do you feel hotter, smog aggravates emphysema, asthma, and other respiratory problems. People can protect themselves by checking the pollution index before going outside.

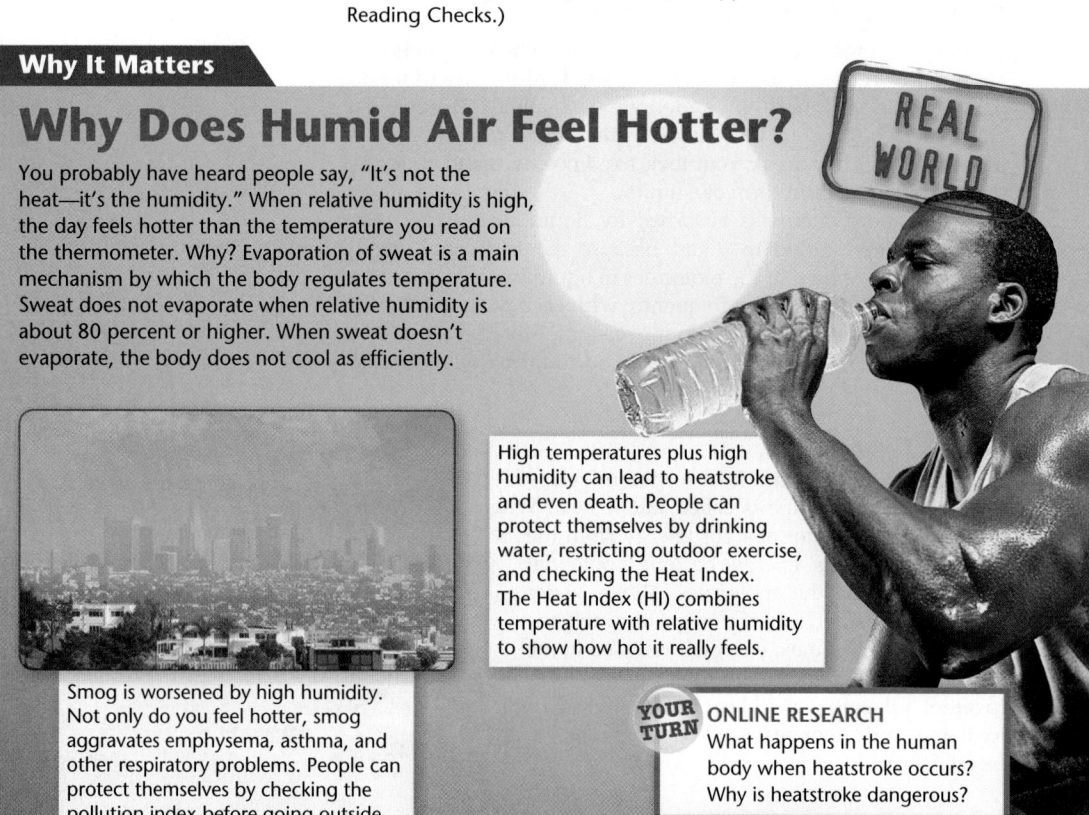

High temperatures plus high humidity can lead to heatstroke and even death. People can protect themselves by drinking water, restricting outdoor exercise, and checking the Heat Index. The Heat Index (HI) combines temperature with relative humidity to show how hot it really feels.

YOUR TURN **ONLINE RESEARCH**
What happens in the human body when heatstroke occurs? Why is heatstroke dangerous?

Why It Matters

Why Does Humid Air Feel Hotter? Heatstroke is only one of several heat-related illnesses and conditions, including heat exhaustion and heat cramps. Heat exhaustion can happen when people overexert themselves in hot weather and don't stay hydrated. Symptoms include heavy sweating and cool, moist skin, headache, nausea, a slight fever, and a rapid pulse. Heat cramps also occur during heavy exercise without adequate hydration in hot weather. When a person is suffering from heat cramps, muscles in the legs, arms, or back tighten and won't relax.

Answer to Your Turn

Online Research Heatstroke causes the body to stop sweating. Since sweating is the body's way of cooling itself, if it does not sweat, its internal temperature rises quickly to 105° F and higher. The patient's skin will be red, hot, and dry, and the pulse and breathing will be rapid. He or she may feel dizzy or confused and may faint or become unconscious. The high body temperature can cause brain damage and even death unless the patient is rapidly cooled.

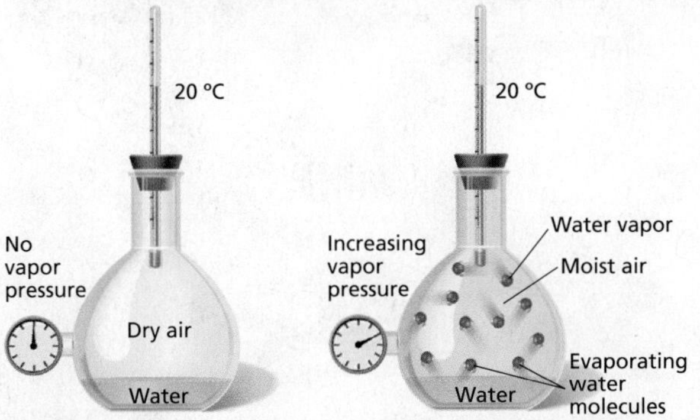

THINK central
INTERACT ONLINE
(Keyword: HQXWIAF2)

Figure 2 When water comes into contact with dry air, some of the water molecules evaporate into the dry air. The addition of the water molecules to the air causes the air pressure to increase. This increase in pressure is due to vapor pressure.

Humidity

Water vapor in the atmosphere is known as *humidity*. Humidity is controlled by rates of condensation and evaporation. The rate of evaporation is determined by the temperature of the air. The higher the temperature is, the higher the rate of evaporation is. The rate of condensation is determined by *vapor pressure.* Vapor pressure is the part of the total atmospheric pressure that is caused by water vapor, as shown in **Figure 2.** When vapor pressure is high, the condensation rate is high.

When the rate of evaporation and the rate of condensation are in equilibrium, the air is said to be "saturated." The temperature at which the condensation rate equals the evaporation rate is called the **dew point.** At temperatures below the dew point, net condensation occurs, and liquid water droplets form.

dew point at constant pressure and water vapor content, the temperature at which the rate of condensation equals the rate of evaporation

absolute humidity the mass of water vapor per unit volume of air that contains the water vapor, usually expressed as grams of water vapor per cubic meter of air

Absolute Humidity

One way to express the amount of moisture in the air is by absolute humidity. **Absolute humidity** is the mass of water vapor contained in a given volume of air. In other words, absolute humidity is a measure of the actual amount of water vapor in the air. Absolute humidity is calculated by using the following equation:

$$\textit{absolute humidity} = \frac{\textit{mass of water vapor (grams)}}{\textit{volume of air (cubic meters)}}$$

However, as air moves, its volume changes as a result of temperature and pressure changes. Therefore, meteorologists prefer to describe humidity by using the mixing ratio of air. The *mixing ratio* is the mass of water vapor in a unit of air relative to the mass of the dry air. For example, the very moist air in tropical regions might have 18 g of water vapor in 1 kg of air, or a mixing ratio of 18 g/kg. On the other hand, the cold, dry air in polar regions commonly has a mixing ratio of less than 1 g/kg. Because this measurement uses only units of mass, it is not affected by changes in temperature or pressure.

SCILINKS.
www.scilinks.org
Topic: Atmospheric Moisture
Code: HQX0113

READING TOOLBOX

Two-Panel Flip Chart
Make a two-panel flip chart. Label the first panel "Humidity" and the second panel "Measuring Humidity." Inside each panel, write key ideas about the corresponding topics.

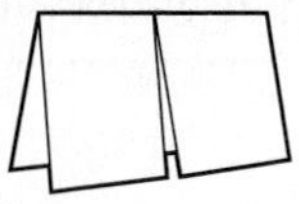

MISCONCEPTION ALERT

Holding Capacity of Air Students may think that air has an inherent capacity for holding water that is dependent on temperature. They also may think that condensation occurs (dew point is reached) when air holds as much water as possible. However, there is no inherent limit to how much water air can hold. Water molecules are constantly moving back and forth between solid, liquid, and gas phases. If more molecules leave the water's surface than enter the water, the evaporation rate exceeds the condensation rate. Warm air tends to "hold" more water than cooler air does because the evaporation rate is usually greater than the condensation rate in warm air. LS Verbal

Teaching Tip GENERAL

Make Concepts Relevant Discuss some of the effects of humidity on humans. For example, when humidity is high, sweat does not evaporate easily, and people have difficulty cooling their bodies. Invite students to describe some of the effects of low humidity. (Sample answers: Skin becomes drier. Drier nasal passages make it easier for germs to enter the body. Forest fires are more common when dry conditions persist for a long time.) LS Verbal

Differentiated Instruction

English Learners

Reading Hint Before students read this page and the next, ask them to think about occasions when they have heard relative humidity discussed in weather reports. Ask them how humidity level relates to physical comfort. (Sample answers: When the humidity is high, especially during summer, people may feel hot and "sticky." Sometimes in the winter when humidity is low, and the air is very dry, some people may have trouble breathing.) Explain that this section describes what determines the moisture content of the air. LS Verbal

READING TOOLBOX

Two-Panel Flip Chart Students should include key ideas such as definitions of terms, differences between absolute humidity and relative humidity, what happens when air temperature reaches and then drops below the dew point, and instruments used to measure humidity.

Key Resources

Technology
- Transparencies
  100 Vapor Pressure

Teach, *continued*

Biology Connection — ADVANCED

Desert Survival Southwest Africa's Namib Desert is one of the hottest and driest places on Earth. This region is home to a dazzling variety of creatures with unusual adaptations to help them survive in this harsh environment. Like other places around the globe, dawn in the Namib is a time when moisture condenses and collects on desert vegetation. There is no rain, but warm air from the Atlantic Ocean regularly sweeps over the cold waters of the Benguela current, creating thick coastal fogs. Creatures such as the long-legged beetle, dune ants, desert crickets, and the side-winder snake all have special ways to get water from condensation. Ask students to research these creatures' ingenious survival methods and report their findings to the class. **LS Logical**

Math Skills

Answer

10 g/kg ÷ 14 g/kg = 0.71 × 100 = 71%

Answer to Reading Check

Dew is liquid moisture that condenses from air on cool objects when the air is nearly saturated and the temperature drops. Frost is water vapor that condenses as ice crystals onto a cool surface directly from the air when the dew point is below freezing.

Figure 3 Dew forms on surfaces such as grass and spider webs when the temperature of the air drops lower than the dew point.

relative humidity the ratio of the amount of water vapor in the air to the amount of water vapor needed to reach saturation at a given temperature

Relative Humidity

A more common way to express the amount of water vapor in the atmosphere is by *relative humidity*. **Relative humidity** is a ratio of the actual water vapor content of the air to the amount of water vapor needed to reach saturation. In other words, relative humidity is a measure of how close the air is to reaching the dew point. For example, at 25 °C, air is saturated when it contains 20 g of water vapor per 1 kg of air. If air that is 25 °C contains 5 g of water vapor, the relative humidity is expressed as 5/20, or 25%.

If the temperature does not change, the relative humidity will increase if moisture enters the air. Relative humidity can also increase if the moisture in the air remains constant but the temperature decreases. If the temperature increases as the moisture in the air remains constant, the relative humidity will decrease.

Math Skills

Relative Humidity
Relative humidity can be calculated by using the following equation:

$$\text{relative humidity} = \left[\frac{\text{amount of water vapor in air}}{\text{amount of water vapor needed to reach saturation}}\right] \times 100$$

Air at 20 °C is saturated when it contains 14 g/kg of water vapor. What is the relative humidity of a volume of air that is 20 °C and contains 10 g/kg of water vapor?

Reaching the Dew Point

When the air is nearly saturated with a relative humidity of almost 100%, only a small temperature drop is needed for the air to reach its dew point. Air may cool to its dew point by conduction when the air comes in contact with a cold surface. During the night, grass, leaves, and other objects near the ground lose heat. Their surface temperatures often drop to the dew point of the surrounding air. Air, which normally remains warmer than surfaces near the ground do, cools to the dew point when it comes into contact with cooler objects, such as grass. When the temperature of air cools below the dew point, condensation, shown in **Figure 3,** called *dew* forms. Dew is most likely to form on cool, clear nights when there is little wind.

If the dew point falls below the freezing temperature of water, water vapor may change directly into solid ice crystals, or *frost*. Because frost forms when water vapor turns directly into ice, frost is not frozen dew. Frozen dew is relatively uncommon. Unlike frost, frozen dew forms as clear beads of ice.

Reading Check **How does dew differ from frost?**

Activity — GENERAL

Scientific Instruments Bring in real meteorological instruments for measuring relative humidity, such as dew cells, psychrometers, or hair and electric hygrometers, so students can see how the tools work. Set up the instruments in workstations and allow students to rotate though the stations. Have volunteers demonstrate and explain the use of each tool. **LS Kinesthetic**

Differentiated Instruction

Basic Learners

Dew Formation Have students reread the passage about how dew forms. Have students draw a diagram that shows the steps involved in dew formation. Encourage students to include speech bubbles to explain what is occurring in each step.

Measuring Humidity

Meteorologists are interested in measuring humidity so that they can better predict weather conditions. Relative humidity can be measured by using a variety of instruments, such as an electrical hygrometer, a psychrometer, a dew cell, and a hair hygrometer.

Using an Electrical Hygrometer

Humidity is commonly measured by an electrical hygrometer that uses a *thin polymer film*. The relative humidity of the surrounding air affects the ability of the thin polymer film to absorb or release water vapor. The amount of water vapor that the thin polymer film contains changes the film's ability to conduct electricity. The polymer film's ability to conduct electricity is affected by the relative humidity of the surrounding air. Thus, by measuring the polymer film's ability to conduct electricity, relative humidity can be determined.

Using a Psychrometer

A *psychrometer*, shown in **Figure 4**, is another instrument that is used to measure relative humidity. It consists of two identical thermometers. The bulb of one thermometer is covered with a damp wick, while the bulb of the other thermometer remains dry. When the psychrometer is held by a handle and whirled through the air, the air circulates around both thermometers. As a result, the water in the wick of the wet-bulb thermometer evaporates. Evaporation requires energy, so energy as heat is released by the thermometer. Consequently, the temperature of the wet-bulb thermometer is lower than that of the dry-bulb thermometer. The difference between the dry-bulb temperature and the wet-bulb temperature is used to calculate relative humidity. If there is no difference between the wet-bulb temperature and dry-bulb temperature, no water evaporated from the wet-bulb thermometer. Thus, the air is saturated and the relative humidity is 100%.

Quick Lab 10 min

Dew Point

Procedure

1. Pour room-temperature water into a glass container, such as a drinking glass, until the water level is near the top of the cup.
2. Observe the outside of the glass container, and record your observations.
3. Add one or two ice cubes to the container of water.
4. Watch the outside of the container for 5 min for any changes.

Analysis

1. What happened to the outside of the container?
2. What is the liquid on the container?
3. Where did the liquid come from? Explain your answer.

Academic Vocabulary

instrument (IN struh muhnt) a mechanical or electronic measuring device

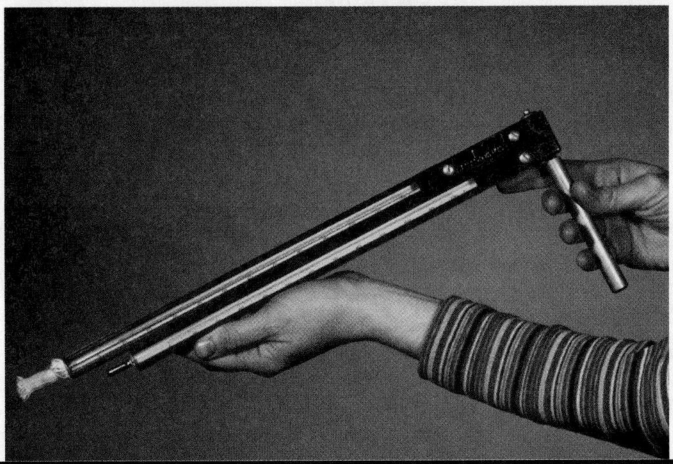

Figure 4 A psychrometer shows differences between wet-bulb and dry-bulb temperatures that can be used to determine relative humidity.

Quick Lab

Skills Acquired
- Experimenting
- Observing
- Analyzing

Materials
- Water
- Glass container
- Two ice cubes

Teacher's Notes: Tell students to record the starting air temperature next to the glass and the temperature when dew forms on the outside of the container.

Answers to Analysis

1. Moisture appeared on the outside of the container.
2. water
3. from the surrounding air; The ice lowered the temperature of the air to below the dew point, which caused the water vapor in the air to condense on the cool surface of the container.

Close

Reteaching — BASIC

Making Diagrams Have pairs of students create diagrams with labels and captions to illustrate chapter concepts such as latent heat in phase changes, dew point and vapor pressure, and humidity. After students have completed their diagrams, invite them to take turns using the diagrams to explain the illustrated concepts to each other. **LS Visual/Auditory**

Quiz — GENERAL

1. How is thermal energy involved in the evaporation of water? (Water absorbs heat energy from the environment, energizing the molecules to break the bonds holding them together.)
2. What happens to water in the air when the rate of condensation exceeds the rate of evaporation? (Net condensation results in visible moisture condensing out of the air.)
3. How is thermal energy involved in the condensation of water? (The heat energy is released into the surrounding air as molecules come closer together.)
4. What forms when water vapor changes directly into solid form? (frost)

Close, *continued*

Answers to Section Review

1. When water absorbs heat energy, the energy causes the molecules to move so rapidly that they escape the liquid and enter the air.
2. the oceans in the equatorial region
3. sublimation
4. Humidity is water vapor in the atmosphere.
5. Absolute humidity is the mass of water vapor per unit volume of air and represents a measure of the actual amount of water in the air. Relative humidity is the ratio of the amount of water vapor in the air compared with the amount of water vapor needed to reach saturation at a given temperature.
6. As air temperature drops, the rate of condensation increases, and the rate of evaporation decreases. At the dew point, the rates of condensation and evaporation are equal. Below the dew point, net condensation occurs, and visible water droplets form on surfaces.
7. dew cells, psychrometers, hair hygrometers, and polymer films
8. The rate of condensation would increase.
9. Because the solar energy that reaches Earth's surface at the equator is more intense than the energy that reaches the poles, the equatorial region would probably have a higher overall absolute humidity than polar regions, because evaporation is higher where temperature is higher.
10. *Water vapor* in the air is known as *humidity,* which can be expressed as *absolute humidity* or *relative humidity,* which can be measured by using a *dew cell,* a *hygrometer,* or a *psychrometer;* and which is controlled by rates of *condensation* and *evaporation,* which determine the *dew point.*

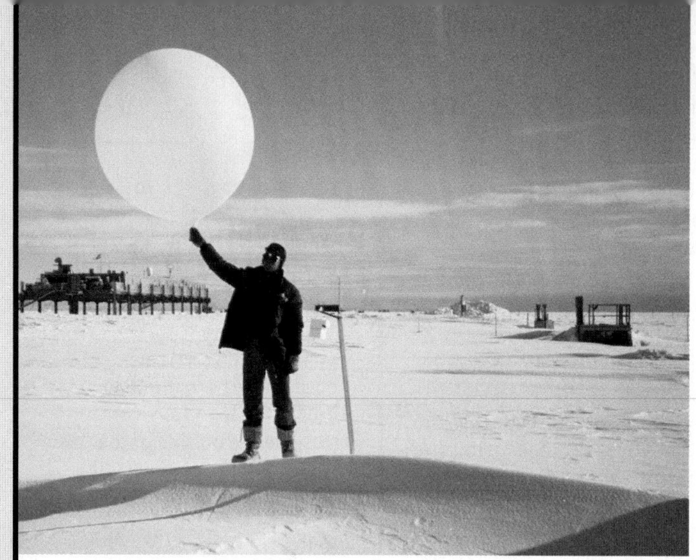

Figure 5 Scientists use weather balloons, such as this one in Antarctica, to send electrical hygrometers into the high altitudes of the atmosphere.

Other Methods for Measuring Humidity

Another instrument that has been used to measure relative humidity is a *dew cell.* A dew cell consists of a ceramic cylinder with electrodes attached to it and treated with lithium chloride, LiCl. When LiCl absorbs water from the air, the dew cell's ability to conduct electricity increases. By detecting the electrical resistance of LiCl as it is heated and cooled, the dew cell can determine the dew point.

A *hair hygrometer* determines relative humidity based on the principle that hair becomes longer as relative humidity increases. As relative humidity decreases, hair becomes shorter.

Measuring Humidity at High Altitudes

To measure humidity at high altitudes, scientists use an electrical hygrometer. The hygrometer may be carried up into the atmosphere in an instrument package known as a *radiosonde.* The radiosonde is attached to a weather balloon, such as the one shown in **Figure 5.** The electrical hygrometer is triggered by passing an electric current through a moisture-attracting chemical substance. The amount of moisture changes the electrical conductivity of the chemical substance. The change can then be expressed as the relative humidity of the surrounding air.

Section 1 Review

Key Ideas

1. **Explain** how most water vapor enters the air.
2. **Identify** the principal source from which most water vapor enters the atmosphere.
3. **Identify** the process by which ice changes directly into a gas.
4. **Define** *humidity.*
5. **Compare** relative humidity with absolute humidity.
6. **Describe** what happens when the temperature of air decreases to the dew point or below the dew point.
7. **Identify** four instruments that are used to measure relative humidity.

Critical Thinking

8. **Predicting Consequences** Explain what would happen to a sample of air whose relative humidity is 100% if the temperature decreased.
9. **Identifying Relationships** Which region of Earth would you expect to have a higher absolute humidity: the equatorial region or the polar regions?

Concept Mapping

10. Use the following terms to create a concept map: *humidity, water vapor, dew point, absolute humidity, dew cell, psychrometer, hygrometer, evaporation, condensation,* and *relative humidity.*

Differentiated Instruction

Alternative Assessment

Song Lyrics Have students compose a song about energy and phase changes. The completed songs should include at least two verses and a chorus and should incorporate what students have learned about such processes as evaporation and condensation. Remind students that song lyrics are similar to a poem, except that they are set to music. One way to get started is to use a children's tune (such as Pop Goes the Weasel or Three Blind Mice), keep the music, and change the words. A rhyming dictionary can be helpful in composing the lyrics. Students may want to perform their songs for the class and make a video or an audio recording. LS **Verbal/Auditory**

SECTION 2
Clouds and Fog

Key Ideas	Key Terms	Why It Matters
› Describe the conditions that are necessary for clouds to form. › Explain the four processes of cooling that can lead to the formation of clouds. › Identify the three major types of clouds, noting their characteristic shapes and the altitudes at which they generally form. › Describe four ways in which fog can form.	**cloud** **condensation nucleus** **adiabatic cooling** **advective cooling** **stratus cloud** **cumulus cloud** **cirrus cloud** **fog**	Often you do not have access to the local weather report. Understanding how clouds form and being able to recognize different cloud types will help you make your own weather predictions and might save you from a drenching.

A **cloud** is a collection of small water droplets or ice crystals in the air. People commonly think that clouds are high in the sky and fog is close to the ground. However, clouds are not limited to high altitudes. Fog is actually a cloud that forms near or on Earth's surface.

Cloud Formation

For water vapor to condense and form a cloud, a solid surface on which condensation can take place must be available. The lowest layer of the atmosphere, the *troposphere*, contains millions of particles of ice, salt, dust, and other materials that serve as solid surfaces. These particles are so small—less than 0.001 mm in diameter—that they remain suspended in the atmosphere for a long time. The suspended particles that provide the surfaces necessary for water vapor to condense are called **condensation nuclei.** As water molecules collect on the nuclei, water droplets form, as **Figure 1** shows.

In addition, for clouds to form, the air must be "saturated" with water vapor. When the temperature of the air drops, condensation occurs more rapidly than evaporation does. As a result of this net condensation, clouds begin to form. Because the rate of evaporation decreases as temperature decreases, the cooling of air may lead to net condensation.

cloud a collection of small water droplets or ice crystals suspended in the air, which forms when the air is cooled and condensation occurs

condensation nucleus a solid particle in the atmosphere that provides the surface on which water vapor condenses

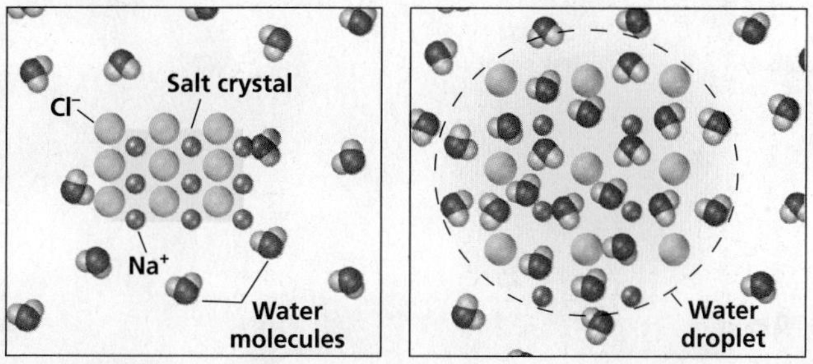

Figure 1 Water molecules are attracted to the sodium and chloride ions in a salt crystal, forming a solution. Additional water molecules are attracted to the solution and the droplet gets bigger.

Section 2

Focus

Overview

This section describes the conditions necessary for cloud formation and the processes that cause clouds and fog to form. The section also explains how clouds are classified.

Bellringer

Ask students to think about kinds of clouds they have seen. Then, have them write brief descriptions or draw sketches of the different cloud formations. (Answers may vary. Accept all reasonable answers.) **LS Visual**

Motivate

Demonstration GENERAL

Condensation Nuclei Put a few grains of salt on a glass microscope slide. Place the slide in a petri dish and use several bent paper clips to elevate the slide above the bottom of the dish. Add just enough water to wet the bottom of the dish without wetting the slide. Ask someone to describe the shape of the salt grains. (cubes) Cover the petri dish. Point out that the closed container has a very high relative humidity. After 15 to 20 minutes, invite students to describe what happened. (The water evaporates from the bottom of the dish, dissolves the grains of salt, and forms droplets of water on the slide.) **LS Visual**

Key Resources

Chapter Resource File
- Directed Reading BASIC

Technology
- Transparencies
  Bellringer
  101 Formation of a Water Droplet

Differentiated Instruction

English Learners

Visual Literacy Have students use **Figure 1** to explain how a water droplet forms around a salt crystal. (Sample answer: Water molecules are attracted to the sodium and chloride ions in the salt crystal. The water molecules and salt ions bind to each other. More water molecules are attracted to the salt and water solution. The droplet gets bigger.)

Teach

Internet Activity GENERAL

Latent Heat and Thunderstorms

Latent heat plays a critical role in many weather processes, including the development of thunderstorms and tornadoes. As a result of rising and expanding, lifting air begins to cool. At a certain elevation, air cools below the dew point, resulting in condensation and cloud formation. This condensation releases huge quantities of latent heat into the air, and produces further uplift, which helps fuel the developing thunderstorm. Invite interested students to do further Internet research into the role of latent heat in these exceptional weather patterns. Have them create diagrams that help explain the processes. A worksheet designed to direct student research on this topic can be found in the **Chapter Resource File** booklet or by visiting www.thinkcentral.com and entering the keyword **HQXWIAX.** **LS Logical**

Using the Figure BASIC

Discussion Direct students' attention to the diagram of dew-point temperature versus cloud height on this page. Point out that the flat bottom of the clouds indicates the altitude of the condensation level, where net condensation begins. Ask students at what temperature the dew point and the atmospheric temperature are equal. (at 10 °C) **LS Logical**

Adiabatic Cooling

As a mass of air rises, the surrounding atmospheric pressure decreases. Because of the lower pressure, the molecules in the rising air move farther apart. Thus, fewer collisions between the molecules happen. The resulting decrease in the amount of energy that is transferred between molecules decreases the temperature of the air. The process by which the temperature of a mass of air decreases as the air rises and expands is called **adiabatic cooling** (AD ee uh BAT ik KOOL ing).

adiabatic cooling the process by which the temperature of an air mass decreases as the air mass rises and expands

Adiabatic Lapse Rate

The rate at which the temperature of a parcel of air changes as the air rises or sinks is called the *adiabatic lapse rate*. The adiabatic lapse rate for clear air is about –1°C for every 100 m that the air rises. Air that is below the dew point—and thus is cloudy—cools more slowly, however. The average adiabatic lapse rate for cloudy air varies between –0.5°C and –0.9°C per 100 m that the air rises. The slower rate of cooling of moist air results from the release of latent heat as the water condenses.

Academic Vocabulary
expand (ek SPAND) to enlarge

Condensation Level

The process through which clouds form by adiabatic cooling is shown in **Figure 2.** Earth's surface absorbs energy from the sun and then reradiates that energy as heat. The air close to Earth's surface absorbs the heat. As the air warms, it rises, expands, and then cools. When the air cools to a temperature that is below the dew point, net condensation causes clouds to form. The altitude at which this net condensation begins is called the *condensation level*. The condensation level is marked by the base of the clouds. Further condensation allows clouds to rise and expand above the condensation level.

Reading Check **What is the source of energy that warms the air and leads to cloud formation?**

Figure 2 Notice in this illustration that temperature and dew point are the same at an altitude of 1,000 m. Above that altitude, condensation begins and clouds, such as the clouds in the image on the right, form.

Skill Builder GENERAL

Math Tell students that the adiabatic lapse rate for the dew point in a cloud is −0.2 °C per 100 m. Have them calculate how much the dew point would drop for elevation heights of 300 m, 500 m and, 1,500 m. (For 300 m: −0.2 °C/100 m × 300 m = −0.2 °C × 3 = −0.6 °C. For 500 m: −0.2 °C/100 m × 500 m = −0.2 °C × 5 = −1 °C. For 1,500 m: −0.2 °C/100 m × 1,500 m = −0.2 °C × 15 = −3 °C.) **LS Logical**

Answer to Reading Check
The source of energy that warms the air and leads to cloud formation is solar energy that is reradiated as heat by Earth's surface. As the process continues, latent heat released by the condensation may allow the clouds to expand beyond the condensation level.

Figure 3 Clouds can form as air is pushed up along a mountain slope and is cooled to below the dew point.

Mixing

Some clouds form when one body of moist air mixes with another body of moist air that has a different temperature. The combination of the two bodies of air causes the temperature of the air to change. This temperature change may cool the combined air to below its dew point, which results in cloud formation.

SCILINKS.
www.scilinks.org
Topic: Clouds and Fog
Code: **HQX0304**

Lifting

The forced upward movement of air commonly results in the cooling of air and in cloud formation. Air can be forced upward when a moving mass of air meets sloping terrain, such as a mountain range. As the rising air expands and cools, clouds form. As **Figure 3** shows, entire mountaintops can be covered with clouds that formed in this way.

The large cloud formations that are associated with storm systems also form by lifting. These clouds form when a mass of cold, dense air enters an area and pushes a less dense mass of warmer air upward.

Advective Cooling

Another cooling process that is associated with cloud formation is advective cooling. **Advective cooling** is the process by which the temperature of an air mass decreases as the air mass moves over a cold surface, such as a cold ocean or land surface. As air moves over a surface that is colder than the air is, the cold surface absorbs heat from the air and the air cools. If the air cools to below its dew point, clouds form.

advective cooling the process by which the temperature of an air mass decreases as the air mass moves over a cold surface

Geography Connection — GENERAL

Rain Shadow Deserts form on the leeward side of mountain ranges due to the rain shadow effect. A rain shadow is one result of the effect topography has on weather. The phenomenon occurs when moisture-rich air moves inland from the ocean, is lifted over a coastal mountain range, and cools. Clouds build up along the windward side of the mountain range, and when the atmosphere becomes saturated, rain occurs. Once the air reaches the other side of the mountain, the cloud no longer contains enough moisture to produce rain. One example of this effect in the United States is the Sierra Nevada range in California and the deserts of Nevada and Arizona. The Andes Mountains of Chile also produce a rain shadow that affects the Atacama Desert. Have students research the rain shadow effect and find other examples. Have them draw diagrams that explain the process. **LS Visual**

Differentiated Instruction

Special Education Students

Appearance of Clouds Help students with visual impairments understand the appearance of stratus, cumulus, and cirrus clouds by using cotton balls, glue, and a piece of corrugated cardboard (10" × 10") for each type of cloud. On the cardboard, shape the cotton to resemble the appropriate cloud. Glue the cloud shapes in place. Ask students to feel and experience the different clouds.

Teaching Tip — GENERAL

Connect to Familiar Processes Help students understand the process of cloud formation better by comparing cloud formation to the cloud that forms when you boil a kettle of water on the stove. The mist that comes out of the spout is popularly called "steam," but it is really a mixed cloud composed of water droplets, not water vapor. Another example of cloud formation is the cloud that forms when you exhale on a cold day. **LS Verbal/Visual**

Teach, *continued*

Quick Lab

Skills Acquired
- Experimenting
- Observing
- Analyzing

Materials
- Bottle opener
- Glass jar with metal lid
- 1 mL of water
- Ice cube

Teacher's Notes: Substitute a metal dish for the jar lid, and use additional ice cubes to chill the air above the water's surface more rapidly.

Answers to Analysis

1. Evaporation takes place near the water's surface, where latent heat is absorbed. Condensation in the form of a cloud forms at the top of the jar, where latent heat is released.
2. The conversion of liquid water to a gas requires energy to break the attractive forces between water molecules. When the process is reversed, the energy reenters the air.

Key Resources

Technology
- Transparencies
  102 Classification of Clouds

Quick Lab 15 min

Cloud Formation

Procedure

1. Use a bottle opener to puncture one or two holes into the metal lid of a glass jar.
2. Pour 1 mL of hot water into the jar, then secure the lid on the jar.
3. Place an ice cube over the holes in the lid of the jar. Make sure that the holes are completely covered.
4. Observe the changes that occur within the jar.

Analysis

1. Draw a diagram of the jar. Label the areas of the diagram where evaporation and condensation take place. Also, label areas where latent heat is released and absorbed.
2. Explain why latent heat was released and absorbed in the areas that you labeled on your diagram.

Classification of Clouds

Clouds are classified by their shape and their altitude. The three basic cloud types are stratus clouds, cumulus clouds, and cirrus clouds. There are also three altitude groups: low clouds (0 to 2,000 m), middle clouds (2,000 to 6,000 m), and high clouds (above 6,000 m). This classification system is shown in **Figure 4.**

Stratus Clouds

Clouds that have a flat, uniform base and that begin to form at very low altitudes are called **stratus clouds.** *Stratus* means "sheet-like" or "layered." The base of stratus clouds is low and may almost touch Earth's surface. Stratus clouds form where a layer of warm, moist air lies above a layer of cool air. When the overlying warm air cools below its dew point, wide clouds appear. Stratus clouds cover large areas of sky and often block out the sun. Usually, very little precipitation falls from most types of stratus clouds.

Two variations of stratus clouds are known as *nimbostratus* and *altostratus*. The prefix *nimbo-* and the suffix *-nimbus* mean "rain." Unlike other stratus clouds, the dark nimbostratus clouds can cause heavy precipitation. Altostratus clouds form at the middle altitudes and usually produce very little precipitation.

stratus cloud a gray cloud that has a flat, uniform base and that commonly forms at very low altitudes

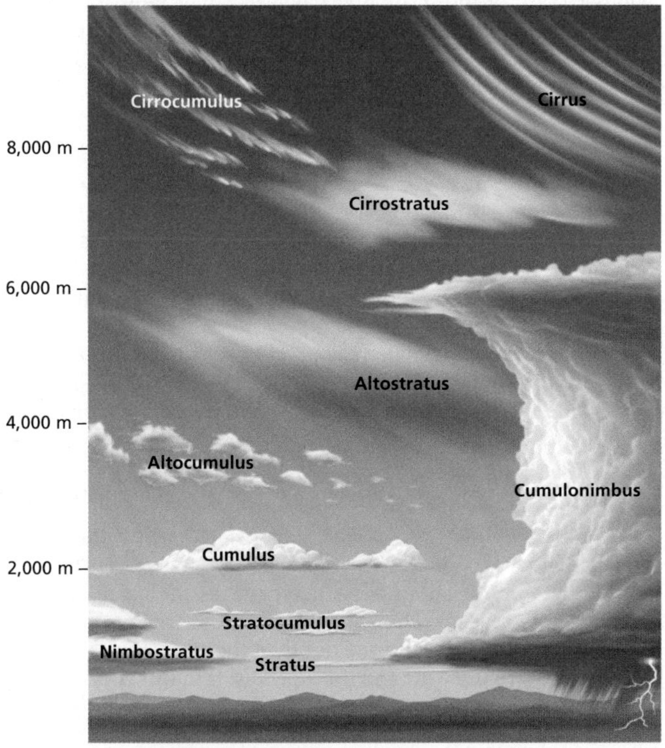

Figure 4 A variety of cloud types can be identified by their altitude and shape. ***What cloud types form at or above 6,000 m?***

Using the Figure — GENERAL

Cloud Bulletin Board The figure summarizes the basic cloud types and the altitudes at which they form. Invite interested students to use this diagram to make a bulletin board that shows different cloud types. Students should use a background of blue construction paper and pictures of clouds cut from magazines or photos of clouds. Answer to caption question: Above 6,000 m, cirrus, cirrostratus, and cirrocumulus clouds form. **LS Visual**
Co-op Learning

Skill Builder — GENERAL

Vocabulary The names assigned to the three basic cloud shapes have Latin roots. The name *cumulus* comes from *cumulo-*, which means "piled" or "heaped." The term *stratus* comes from *stratum*, which means "layered," and the word *cirrus* comes from *cirro-*, which means "hair" or "curl." The word *nimbus*, meaning "rain," is used to describe the dark clouds that bring heavy rains. The name *alto*, from *altus*, meaning "high," describes the height of the cloud base. Various combinations of these prefixes and suffixes give the ten basic cloud groupings. English Language Learners
LS Verbal

Figure 5 Cumulus clouds (left) are puffy, vertically growing clouds, while cirrus clouds (right) are wispy.

Cumulus Clouds

Low-altitude, billowy clouds that commonly have a top that resembles cotton balls and a dark bottom are called **cumulus clouds.** *Cumulus* means "piled" or "heaped." Cumulus clouds usually look fluffy, as shown in **Figure 5.** These clouds form when warm, moist air rises and cools. As the cooling air reaches its dew point, the clouds form. The flat base that is characteristic of most cumulus clouds represents the condensation level.

The height of a cumulus cloud depends on the stability of the troposphere, which is the layer of the atmosphere that touches Earth's surface, and on the amount of moisture in the air. On hot, humid days, cumulus clouds reach their greatest heights. High, dark storm clouds known as *cumulonimbus clouds*, or thunderheads, are often accompanied by rain, lightning, and thunder. If the base of cumulus clouds begins at middle altitudes, the clouds are called *altocumulus clouds*. Low clouds that are a combination of stratus and cumulus clouds are called *stratocumulus clouds*.

cumulus cloud a low-level, billowy cloud that commonly has a top that resembles cotton balls and a dark bottom

cirrus cloud a feathery cloud that is composed of ice crystals and that has the highest altitude of any cloud in the sky

Cirrus Clouds

Feathery clouds that are composed of ice crystals and that have the highest altitude of any cloud in the sky are **cirrus clouds.** Cirrus clouds are also shown in **Figure 5.** *Cirro-* and *cirrus* mean "curly." Cirrus clouds form at altitudes above 6,000 m. These clouds are made of ice crystals because the temperatures are low at such high altitudes. Because these clouds are thin, light can easily pass through them.

Cirrocumulus clouds are high-altitude, billowy clouds composed entirely of ice crystals. Cirrocumulus clouds commonly appear just before a snowfall or a rainfall. Long, thin clouds called *cirrostratus clouds* form a high, transparent veil across the sky. A halo may appear around the sun or moon when either is viewed through a cirrostratus cloud. This halo effect is caused by the bending of light rays as they pass through the ice crystals.

Reading Check **Why are cirrus clouds commonly composed of ice crystals?**

READING TOOLBOX

Analyzing Comparisons
As you read about cumulus clouds and cirrus clouds, look for comparisons between them. Create a table of their similarities and differences.

Answer to Reading Check
because cirrus clouds form at very high altitudes where air temperature is low

Close

Reteaching — BASIC

Cloud Lingo Have students work in pairs to write on index cards key terms and italicized words from the section. They can write the word on one side of the card and write a definition or draw an explanatory diagram on the back. Then, bring the groups together to play a game that uses the cards to review the vocabulary words. **LS Auditory**

Quiz — GENERAL

1. Why are condensation nuclei necessary for cloud formation? (The suspended particles provide a surface on which water droplets can form.)
2. How is advective cooling involved in cloud and fog formation? (As the air moves over the cooler surface, the surface absorbs heat from the air, and cools the air to below the dew point.)

READING TOOLBOX

Analyzing Comparisons Tables may include the following examples: Similarities: Both form combinations with other cloud types; Differences: Cumulus clouds are low-altitude clouds that are billowy. Cirrus clouds are high-altitude clouds that are wispy.

Close, *continued*

Answers to Section Review

1. There must be suspended particles around which water droplets can form, and the temperature of the saturated air must be below the dew point so that the rate of evaporation is slower than the rate of condensation.
2. rising and expansion of an air mass (adiabatic); mixing of moist air with another air mass at a different temperature; forced upward movement of air as it moves over sloped terrain; and an air mass moving over a cooler surface (advective)
3. cirrus and cirrocumulus
4. Stratus clouds are layered and form when warm moist air lies above a layer of cooler air. Cumulus clouds are puffy, vertically growing clouds. Cirrus clouds are wispy, high-altitude clouds composed of ice crystals.
5. cumulonimbus
6. Both form as a result of condensation of water vapor in the air. Fog occurs near the surface of Earth, while clouds occur at higher altitudes.
7. Radiation fog occurs as a result of the nightly cooling of Earth when the layer of air in contact with the ground is chilled. Advection fog occurs when warm moist air moves across a cold surface, as when air moves from water to flow over cooler land. Upland fog forms when moist air rises over a slope. Steam fog forms when cool air moves over a warm body of water such as a river.

Figure 6 Steam fog covers the Yakima River in Washington.

Fog

Like clouds, **fog** is the result of the condensation of water vapor in the air. The obvious difference between fog and clouds is that fog is very near the surface of Earth. However, fog also differs from clouds because of how fog forms.

Radiation Fog

One type of fog forms from the nightly cooling of Earth. The layer of air in contact with the ground becomes chilled to below the dew point, and the water vapor in that layer condenses into droplets. This type of fog is called *radiation fog* because it results from the loss of heat by radiation. Radiation fog is thickest in valleys and low places because dense, cold air sinks to low elevations. Radiation fog is often quite thick around cities, where smoke and dust particles act as condensation nuclei.

Other Types of Fog

fog water vapor that has condensed very near the surface of Earth because air close to the ground has cooled

Another type of fog, *advection fog*, forms when warm, moist air moves across a cold surface. Advection fog is common along coasts, where warm, moist air from above the water moves in over a cooler land surface. Advection fog forms over the ocean when warm, moist air is carried over cold ocean currents.

An *upslope fog* forms by the lifting and cooling of air as the air rises along land slopes. *Steam fog* is a shallow layer of fog that forms when cool air moves over an inland warm body of water, such as a river, as shown in **Figure 6.**

Section 2 Review

Key Ideas

1. **Describe** the conditions that are necessary for clouds to form.
2. **Explain** the four processes of cooling that can lead to cloud formation.
3. **Identify** the cloud types that form at 8,000 m.
4. **Compare** cirrus, cumulus, and stratus clouds.
5. **Identify** the type of cloud that is known for causing thunderstorms.
6. **Compare** clouds with fog.
7. **Describe** four ways in which fog can form.

Critical Thinking

8. **Applying Ideas** Explain why air expands when it rises.
9. **Making Predictions** How might an increase in pollution affect cloud formation?
10. **Making Comparisons** Which type of cloud has the lowest condensation level? Which type has the highest condensation level?

Concept Mapping

11. Use the following terms to create a concept map: *cloud, cirrus, condensation level, advective cooling, adiabatic cooling, stratus, cumulus,* and *fog.*

8. When air rises, it enters an area of lower pressure. The lower pressure allows the air molecules to move farther apart.
9. Sample answer: The pollutants would provide additional surfaces on which water droplets can condense.
10. Stratus clouds condense at the lowest altitudes. Cirrus clouds condense at the highest altitudes, above 6,000 m.
11. *Fog* and *clouds,* such as *stratus, cirrus,* and *cumulus,* can form through *adiabatic cooling* or *advective cooling* at different *condensation levels.*

Differentiated Instruction

Alternative Assessment

Cloud Atlas Have students create a Cloud Atlas based on the modern cloud classification system. Students can illustrate the atlas and guide to cloud types by using photos or drawings of the common types of clouds and fog, giving the cloud names, and showing the altitude and general appearance of each cloud. They should include details about how the clouds form and what weather conditions are related to the clouds. **LS Visual**

SECTION 3

Precipitation

ENVIRONMENTAL CONNECTION

Key Ideas	Key Terms	Why It Matters
❯ Identify the four forms of precipitation. ❯ Compare the two processes that cause precipitation. ❯ Describe two ways that precipitation is measured. ❯ Explain how rain can be produced artificially.	**precipitation** **coalescence** **supercooling** **cloud seeding**	You may not appreciate the rain when you need to go outside. But rain and other forms of precipitation are an essential part of the water cycle.

Any moisture that falls from the air to Earth's surface is called **precipitation.** The four major types of precipitation are rain, snow, sleet, and hail.

Forms of Precipitation

Rain is liquid precipitation. Normal raindrops are between 0.5 and 5 mm in diameter. They may vary from a fine mist to large drops in a torrential rainstorm. If the raindrops are smaller than 0.5 mm in diameter, the rain is called *drizzle*. Drizzle results in only a small amount of total precipitation.

The most common form of solid precipitation is *snow*, which consists of ice particles. These particles may fall as small pellets, as individual crystals, or as crystals that combine to form snowflakes. Snowflakes tend to be large at temperatures near 0°C and become smaller at lower temperatures.

precipitation any form of water that falls to Earth's surface from the clouds; includes rain, snow, sleet, and hail

When rain falls through a layer of freezing air near the ground, clear ice pellets, called *sleet*, can form. In some cases, the rain does not freeze until it strikes a surface near the ground. There, it forms a thick layer of ice called *glaze ice*, as shown in **Figure 1.** The condition in which glaze ice is produced is commonly referred to as an *ice storm*.

Hail is solid precipitation in the form of lumps of ice. The lumps can be either spherical or irregularly shaped. Hail usually forms in cumulonimbus clouds. Convection currents within the clouds carry raindrops to high levels, where the raindrops freeze before they fall. If the frozen raindrops are carried upward again, they can accumulate additional layers of ice until they are too heavy for the convection currents to carry them. Then they fall to the ground. Large hailstones can damage crops and property.

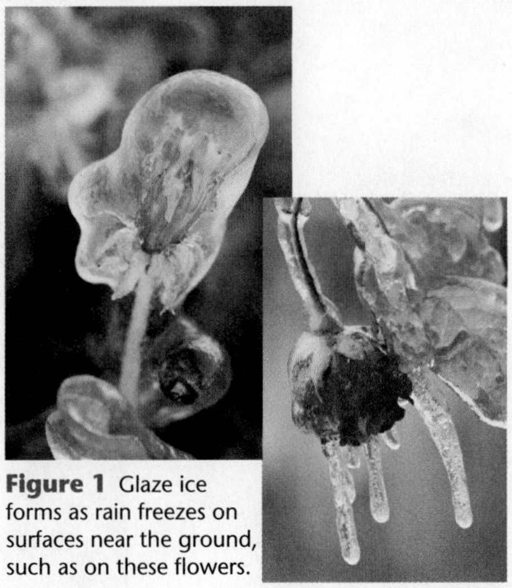

Figure 1 Glaze ice forms as rain freezes on surfaces near the ground, such as on these flowers.

Section 3

Focus

Overview

This section describes precipitation and how it forms. The section also explains how rain and snow are measured and describes cloud seeding.

Bellringer

Ask students why they think the water droplets that form clouds often fall to Earth as rain or other forms of precipitation.

Motivate

Demonstration — GENERAL

Indoor Rain You will need a hot plate, a wide-mouth jar, ice cubes, a zip-top plastic bag, and aluminum foil. Heat some water to the boiling point on a hot plate. Pour about a cup of the hot water into the jar and cover it tightly with aluminum foil. Put ice cubes into the zip-top bag and place the bag on top of the foil. Have students observe for a few minutes. Invite a volunteer to describe what happens. (Sample answer: Water evaporates from the hot water, and condenses on the cool surface of the aluminum foil. Water droplets fall back down into the jar, simulating rain.) **LS Visual**

Key Resources

Chapter Resource File

- Directed Reading BASIC
- Inquiry Lab: How Big Is a Raindrop? GENERAL
- Making Models Lab: What Is the Shape of a Raindrop? GENERAL

Technology

- Transparencies
  Bellringer

Teach

Group Activity — GENERAL

Supercooled: Test-Tube Hail You will need beakers, clean test tubes, thermometers, crushed ice, and salt. Divide the class into small groups. Have students fill beakers about three-quarters full with ice and cold water and add salt to the mixture until no more salt will dissolve. Ask students to fill the test tube with cold water so that when it is placed in the beaker the water levels of the beaker and the tube will be the same. Have students place the test tubes and thermometers into the beakers and take the starting temperature, then watch for ten minutes. Then, have them gently remove the test tube and immediately drop a piece of ice into it. Have someone describe what happens when the ice is dropped into the test tube. (Ice immediately begins to form.) Ask students why it was important that the test tube be clean. (If there were particles in the test tube, ice would form before the ice crystal was added and before the water became supercooled.) LS **Visual/Kinesthetic**

MISCONCEPTION ALERT

Shape of Raindrops Although in popular culture raindrops are often visualized as tear-shaped, small raindrops (less than 1 mm) are actually spherical. As they get larger they take on a flattened shape, something like a hamburger bun. When they become larger than 4.5 mm, raindrops assume a bag-like shape and then split into smaller drops.

Figure 2 During coalescence, cloud droplets collide and combine with smaller droplets as they fall. The resulting larger droplets fall as rain.

Causes of Precipitation

Most cloud droplets have a diameter of about 20 μm (micrometers), which is smaller than the period at the end of this sentence. Droplets of this size fall very slowly through the air. A droplet must increase in diameter by about 100 times to fall as precipitation. Two natural processes cause cloud droplets to grow large enough to fall as precipitation: coalescence and supercooling.

Coalescence

The formation of a large droplet by the combination of smaller droplets is called **coalescence** (KOH uh LES uhnts) and is shown in **Figure 2.** Large droplets fall much faster through the air than small droplets do. As these larger droplets drift downward, they collide and combine with smaller droplets. Each large droplet continues to coalesce until it contains a million times as much water as it did originally.

Supercooling

Precipitation also forms by the process of supercooling. **Supercooling** is a condition in which a substance is cooled to below its freezing point, condensation point, or sublimation point without changing state. Supercooled water droplets may have a temperature as low as –40 °C. Yet even at this low temperature, the water droplets do not freeze. They cannot freeze because too few *freezing nuclei* on which ice can form are available. Freezing nuclei are solid particles that are suspended in the air and that have structures similar to the crystal structure of ice. Most water from the supercooled water droplets evaporates. The water vapor then condenses on the ice crystals that have formed on the freezing nuclei. The ice crystals rapidly increase in size until they gain enough mass to fall as snow, as shown in **Figure 3.** If the ice crystals melt and turn into rain as they pass through air whose temperature is above freezing, they form the big raindrops that are common in summer thunderstorms.

coalescence the formation of a large droplet by the combination of smaller droplets

supercooling a condition in which a substance is cooled below its freezing point, condensation point, or sublimation point without going through a change of state

Figure 3 Most of the rain and snow in the middle and high latitudes of Earth are the result of the formation of ice crystals in supercooled clouds.

Environmental Connection

Climate and Precipitation The global water cycle lies at the heart of Earth's climate system. A study by scientists at NASA's Goddard Flight Center suggests that a 20-year warming trend may accelerate patterns of evaporation and precipitation and lead to increased warm rain over tropical oceans. The study found that warm rains account for over 30 percent of global rainfall and play a critical role in the overall water cycle. Scientists think that warm tropical rains deplete clouds of rain with more efficiency than cold rains do. The information on liquid water and precipitation rates was gathered by a variety of space satellites used to collect data on cloud heights and temperatures and to monitor tropical rainfall patterns. The NASA scientists think that the warmer climate may be associated with a more vigorous water cycle and more extreme weather patterns. Invite interested students to learn more about precipitation rates and climate and about the satellite imaging programs (GPM and TRMM) designed to collect data on rainfall over oceans.

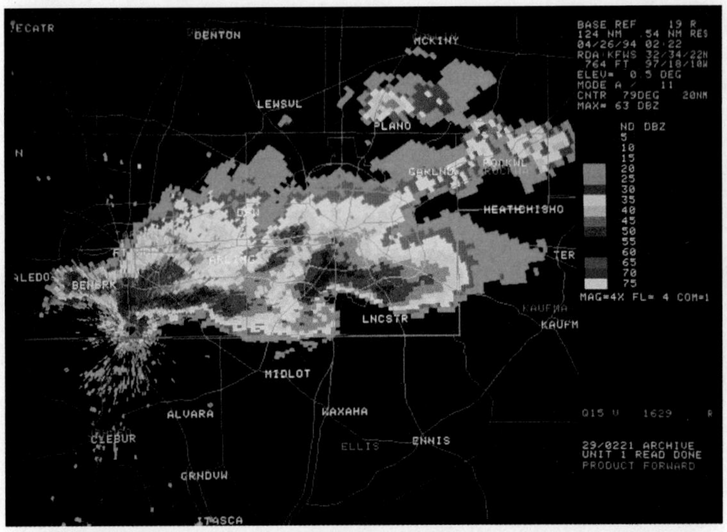

Figure 4 Doppler radar helps meteorologists track storms, such as this large thunderstorm system over North Texas. The colors represent the intensity of rainfall. Reds and yellows indicate areas of heaviest rainfall, while blues and greens denote areas of lighter rainfall.

Measuring Precipitation

Meteorologists use a variety of instruments to measure precipitation. For example, a *rain gauge* may be used to measure rainfall.

Amount of Precipitation

In one type of rain gauge, rainwater passes through a funnel into a calibrated container, where the amount of rainfall can then be measured. In another type of rain gauge, rain caught in a funnel fills a bucket. Each time the bucket fills with a given amount of rainwater, the bucket tips and sets off an electrical device that records the amount. As the bucket tips, it activates a switch that releases the water from the bucket.

Snow depth is simply determined with a measuring stick. The water content of the snow is determined by melting a measured volume of snow and by measuring the amount of water that results. On average, 10 cm of snow will melt to produce about 1 cm of water.

Doppler Radar

The intensity of precipitation can be measured using Doppler radar. Doppler radar images, such as the one in **Figure 4**, are commonly used by meteorologists for communicating weather forecasts. Doppler radar works by bouncing radio waves off rain or snow. By timing how long the wave takes to return, meteorologists can detect the location, direction of movement, and intensity of the precipitation. This information is extremely valuable for saving lives because people can be warned of an approaching storm.

Reading Check **What aspects of precipitation can Doppler radar measure?**

READING TOOLBOX

Suffixes
Find two adverbs that end in the suffix *-ly* on this page. Identify which adjective forms the root of each adverb, and give the meaning of the adverb.

SCILINKS.
www.scilinks.org
Topic: Precipitation
Code: **HQX1202**

Academic Vocabulary
detect (dee TEKT) to discover the presence of something

Answer to Reading Check
Doppler radar measures the location, direction of movement, and intensity of precipitation.

READING TOOLBOX

Suffixes Students should include two of the following examples: simply, root word is simple, means clearly or plainly; commonly, root word is common, means occurring frequently; extremely, root word is extreme, means in an extreme manner

Close

Reteaching — BASIC

Comparison Table Divide students into pairs. Have students create a comparison table to compare the different forms of precipitation according to their mode of formation, their state of matter, their shape or structure, and the means of measurement. **LS Logical**

Quiz — GENERAL

1. Compare how sleet forms with how hail forms. (Sleet forms from raindrops falling through a layer of freezing air near the ground. Hail forms when raindrops are carried by convection currents in clouds to high levels where they freeze before they fall.)
2. How is precipitation by supercooling similar to the formation of clouds? (Both processes require solid nuclei on which water vapor can condense.)
3. Explain why large raindrops are often the result of freezing. (Large ice crystals form as a result of supercooling. If the crystals melt as they pass through warmer air, they will fall as large rain drops.)

Differentiated Instruction

Special Education Students

Doppler Radar Students who have behavior control issues and learning disabilities will better understand how Doppler radar works if they watch actual screens in motion. Ask students to record Doppler radar reports from news shows on their televisions at home. Have them bring their recordings to school and show them to the class. Have the class watch the reports and discuss the information given by each. **LS Visual**

Homework — GENERAL

Measuring Rainfall Have students make a simple rain gauge from a clean, empty 2-liter plastic bottle. Have students cut off the top of the bottle to use as a funnel. Have them make a scale on the outside by taping a thin plastic ruler to the bottle. They should put marbles inside the bottle to add stability and insert the funnel upside-down into the mouth of the rain gauge. Tell students to find a secure place in the open for the instrument. Ask them to record the daily rainfall amounts for at least a week and graph their results. **LS Kinesthetic**

Close, *continued*

Answers to Section Review

1. rain, snow, sleet, and hail
2. Coalescence is the combination of many smaller droplets into a larger drop. Supercooling is the cooling of water to below its freezing point without a change of state until the water encounters freezing nuclei and forms ice crystals.
3. a rain gauge
4. Snow depth is determined by using a measuring stick. Melting a measured volume of snow, and then measuring the amount of water that forms from the melted snow determines the water content of the snow.
5. Doppler radar works by bouncing radio waves off rain or snow. By measuring the waves that return, the intensity of the precipitation can be determined.
6. Precipitation can be stimulated artificially by introducing condensation nuclei in the form of dry ice or other chemical crystals into a cloud.
7. Because there are generally too few freezing nuclei on which snow crystals can form naturally, if water could not be supercooled below its freezing point, much of the precipitation in colder climates would be in the form of sleet or hail.
8. It might result in severe storms, or it might actually decrease precipitation.
9. *Precipitation,* such as *rain, sleet, snow, hail, drizzle,* and *glaze ice,* results from the processes of *coalescence* and *super-cooling,* which involves *freezing nuclei.*

Figure 5 Special equipment attached to the wings of cloud-seeding planes releases freezing nuclei into clouds. Meteorologists hope that cloud seeding will induce rain to fall on drought-stricken areas.

Weather Modification

In areas suffering from drought, scientists may attempt to induce precipitation through cloud seeding, as shown in **Figure 5. Cloud seeding** is the process of introducing freezing nuclei or condensation nuclei into a cloud to cause rain to fall.

cloud seeding the process of introducing freezing nuclei or condensation nuclei into a cloud in order to cause rain to fall

Methods of Cloud Seeding

One method of cloud seeding uses silver iodide crystals, which resemble ice crystals, as freezing nuclei. The silver iodide is released from burners on the ground or from flares dropped from aircraft. Another method of cloud seeding uses powdered dry ice, which is dropped from aircraft to cool cloud droplets and to cause ice crystals to form. As the ice crystals fall, they may melt to form raindrops.

Improving Cloud Seeding

In some cases, seeded clouds produce more precipitation than unseeded clouds do. In other cases, cloud seeding does not cause a significant increase in precipitation. Sometimes, cloud seeding appears to cause less precipitation. Thus, meteorologists have concluded that cloud seeding may increase precipitation under some conditions but decrease it under others. Research is underway to identify the conditions that cause increased precipitation. Eventually, cloud seeding may become a way to overcome many drought-related problems. In theory, cloud seeding could also help to control a severe storm by releasing precipitation from clouds before the storm can become too large. But scientific experiments have so far failed to prove this.

Section 3 Review

Key Ideas

1. **Identify** four forms of precipitation.
2. **Compare** coalescence and supercooling.
3. **Identify** the instrument that measures amounts of rainfall.
4. **Describe** how the amount of snowfall can be measured.
5. **Explain** how Doppler radar can be used to measure the intensity of precipitation.
6. **Describe** how precipitation can be induced or increased artificially.

Critical Thinking

7. **Predicting Consequences** If water could not remain liquid during supercooling, how would the potential for precipitation in colder climates be affected?
8. **Making Inferences** Explain how cloud seeding could be dangerous if it is not done properly.

Concept Mapping

9. Use the following terms to create a concept map: *precipitation, rain, snow, glaze ice, hail, coalescence, supercooling, freezing nucleus, sleet,* and *drizzle.*

Differentiated Instruction

Alternative Assessment

Instruction Manuals Have students write an instruction manual on how to form rain, snow, sleet, and hail in the atmosphere. Students should include information about how to measure these types of precipitation. **LS Logical**

Why It Matters

Ice Storms

Beautiful but dangerous, ice storms are one of weather's most sudden phenomena. Ice storms occur when falling snow, passing through a layer of warmer air, melts into rain. At ground level, the rain then passes through a layer of colder air and freezes when it makes contact with a solid object, coating the object in ice. The rain does not have time to form sleet or snow before it hits Earth's surface because the layer of cold air is very close to the ground.

Ice storms can cover roads with ice in a matter of minutes, causing traffic accidents, as surprised motorists are unable to control their cars. Ice coats power lines and utility poles, which can break when the ice becomes too heavy, causing massive power outages that deprive homes of heat during the coldest part of the year.

People can prepare for ice storms by listening to the radio or watching television for news of winter storm watches, warnings, and advisories. They should have extra food and water at home, plus other supplies such as flashlights, batteries, and a first aid kit.

YOUR TURN

UNDERSTANDING CONCEPTS
Why does freezing rain coat Earth's surface with ice instead of falling as sleet?

WRITING IN SCIENCE
Create a pamphlet that explains what people should do in the event of an ice storm.

Why It Matters

Ice Storms

One of the dangers of ice storms is the fact that power lines coated with ice may break and fall, cutting off electricity to homes. Many homes have heaters that run on electricity, so a power outage means that these homes have no heat. In these conditions, hypothermia can be a danger, especially for elderly people. A person has hypothermia if the body temperature is 95° F (35° C) or lower. Symptoms of hypothermia include slurred speech, confusion, shivering, clumsiness, and sleepiness. Hypothermia is very dangerous because the symptoms appear gradually, and often a victim does not realize what is happening. Hypothermia will eventually cause death if not treated, because the low body temperature will cause the heart and lungs to stop working.

Answer to Your Turn

Understanding Concepts Freezing rain doesn't have time to form sleet because just before it hits the ground, it passes through a layer of cold air and freezes, coating whatever surface it hits with ice.

Writing in Science Answers will vary. Students' pamphlets should include sections about getting weather updates from radio or television; stocking extra food and water; gathering useful supplies such as flashlights and a first aid kit; dressing properly for winter weather; and having a plan if people should find themselves caught outside or in a vehicle during an ice storm.

Skills Practice **Lab**

 45 min

Time Required

one 45-minute class period

Lab Ratings

EASY ——————————→ HARD

Teacher Preparation
Student Setup
Concept Level
Cleanup

Skills Acquired

• Predicting
• Experimenting
• Collecting Data
• Interpreting Results

Scientific Methods

In this lab, students will
• Make Observations
• Analyze Results
• Communicate Results

Materials

The materials listed are enough for groups of 2 to 4 students. A rubber band or piece of string will keep the cloth securely fastened around the wet-bulb thermometer. If ring stands are unavailable, thermometers can also be securely mounted on a piece of stiff poster board by using tape. This also makes transporting and using the psy-chrometer later in an outside weather shelter easier.

What You'll Do

> **Measure** humidity in the classroom.
> **Determine** relative humidity.

What You'll Need

cloth, cotton, at least
 8 cm × 8 cm
container, plastic
piece of paper
ring stand with ring
rubber band
string
thermometer, Celsius (2)
water

Safety

Relative Humidity

Earth's atmosphere acts as a reservoir for water that evaporates from Earth's surface. However, the amount of water vapor in the atmosphere depends on the relative rates of condensation and evaporation. When the rates of condensation and evaporation are equal, the air is said to be "saturated." When the rate of condensation exceeds the rate of evapo-ration, water droplets begin to form in the air or on nearby surfaces. The point at which the condensation rate equals the evaporation rate is called the *dew point* and depends on the temperature of the air and on the atmospheric pressure.

 Relative humidity is the ratio of the amount of water vapor in the air to the amount of water vapor that is needed for the air to become saturated. This ratio is most commonly expressed as a percentage. When the air is saturated, the air is said to have a relative humidity of 100%. In this lab, you will use wet-bulb and dry-bulb thermometer readings to determine the relative humidity of the air in your classroom.

Procedure

❶ Hang two thermometers from a ring stand, as shown in the photo below.

❷ Using a rubber band, fasten a piece of cotton cloth around the bulb of one thermometer. Adjust the length of the string so that only the cloth, not the thermometer bulb, is immersed in the water. By using this setup, you can measure both the air temperature and the cooling effect of evaporation.

Step ❷

Tips and Tricks

The wet bulb is chilled because it releases heat to the evaporating water. The drier the air is, the faster the water will evaporate, and the more the bulb will be chilled.

 Students will need to take readings from both bulbs to obtain the relative humidity from the Relative Humidity Table in Appendix E on p. 966.

3. Predict whether the two thermometers will have the same reading or which thermometer will have the lower reading.

4. Using a piece of paper, fan both thermometers rapidly until the reading on the wet-bulb thermometer stops changing. Read the temperature on each thermometer.
   - **a.** What is the temperature on the dry-bulb thermometer?
   - **b.** What is the temperature on the wet-bulb thermometer?
   - **c.** What is the difference in the two temperature readings?

5. Use the table entitled "Relative Humidity" in the Reference Tables section of the Appendix to find the relative humidity based on your temperature readings in step 4. Look at the left-hand column labeled "Dry-Bulb Temperature." Find the temperature that you recorded in step 4a. Then, find the difference in temperature that you recorded in step 4c along the top row of the table. Locate the intersection of the row and column you have identified. The number shown, expressed as a percentage, is the relative humidity. What is the relative humidity of the air in your classroom?

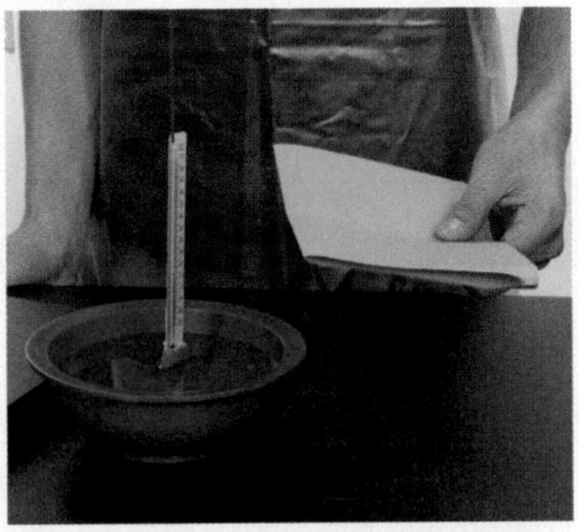

Step 4

Analysis

1. **Drawing Conclusions** On the basis of the relative humidity you determined, is the air in your classroom close to or far from the dew point? Explain your answer.
2. **Applying Conclusions** If you wet the back of your hand, would the water evaporate and cool your skin?

Extension

Making Inferences Suppose that you exercise in a room in which the relative humidity is 100%.

- **a.** Would the moisture on your skin from perspiration evaporate easily?
- **b.** Would you be able to cool off readily? Explain your answer.

Applying Ideas Suppose that you have just stepped out of a swimming pool. The relative humidity is low, about 30%. Would you feel warm or cool? Explain your answer.

Answers to Procedure

3. Answers may vary.
4a–c. Answers may vary.
5. Answers may vary.

Answers to Analysis

1. Answers may vary depending on how close the relative humidity is to 100%.
2. Unless the relative humidity is 100%, at which point the net condensation equals evaporation, yes.

Answers to Extension

Making Inferences **a.** no **b.** no; Because the air is saturated, no more water will evaporate from the skin and, thus, there would be little cooling effect.

Applying Ideas cool; Because the relative humidity is low, rapid evaporation would cause the skin to cool.

Annual Precipitation in the United States

Internet Activity GENERAL

Climate and Precipitation Have students research the annual rates of two forms of precipitation for one region of the United States. Have them identify what factors, such as presence of large bodies of water, elevations, or air temperature, have led to this pattern of precipitation. A worksheet designed to direct student research on this topic can be found in the **Chapter Resource File** booklet or by visiting www.thinkcentral.com and entering the keyword **HQXWIAX.** **LS Visual**

Answers to Map Skills Activity

1. Answers may vary.
2. the Pacific Northwest
3. More moisture is in the air in coastal areas that are bordered by mountains.
4. Answers may vary. Sample answers: rain: Oregon; snow or freezing rain: Northeast or Midwest
5. southwestern states such as Nevada, Utah, Arizona, and New Mexico
6. southern and southwestern states
7. the Pacific Northwest and the Gulf coast states

MAPS in Action

Annual Precipitation in the United States

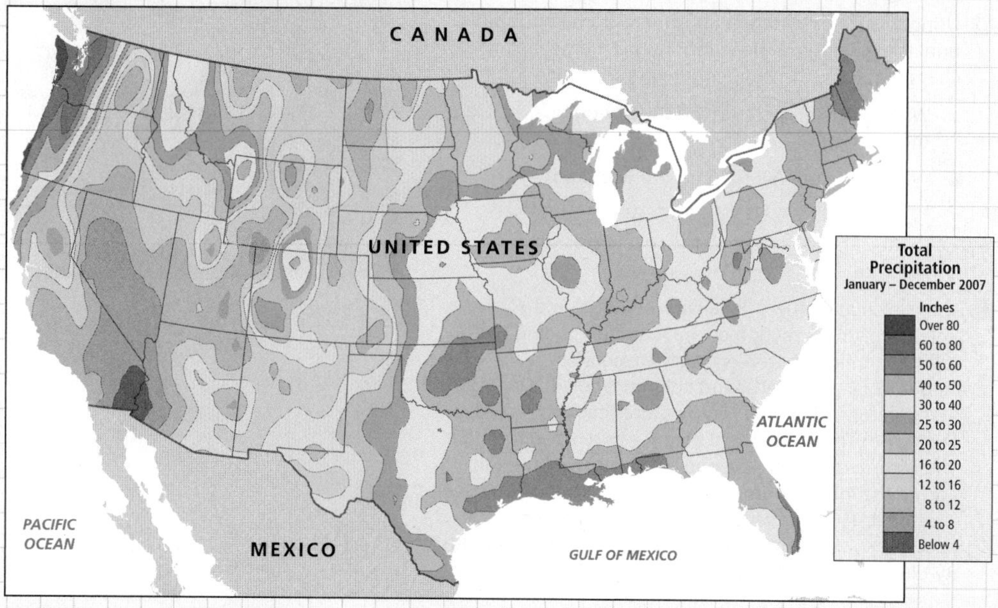

Map Skills Activity

This map shows the total precipitation for the continental United States in 2007. Use the map to answer the questions below.

1. **Using a Key** What is the highest total amount of precipitation for any area in your state?
2. **Making Comparisons** Which area of the United States has the highest total annual precipitation?
3. **Analyzing Methods** Using what you have learned about the formation of precipitation, explain why one area of the United States might have a higher total annual precipitation than another area has.
4. **Making Inferences** List the forms of precipitation that occur in the United States. Identify areas of the United States where you would likely encounter each form.
5. **Evaluating Data** Describe the area of the United States that might be classified as desert.
6. **Making Comparisons** Describe the area of the United States that might have the highest rate of evaporation.
7. **Making Comparisons** Describe the area of the United States that you think might have the highest relative humidity.

Key Resources

Technology

- Transparencies
  103 Annual Precipitation in the United States

Chapter 20

Summary

THINK central SUPER SUMMARY Keyword: HQXWIAS

Key Ideas | **Key Terms**

Section 1

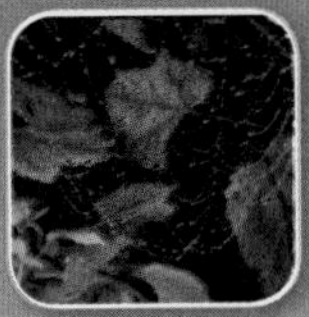

Atmospheric Moisture

- Latent heat is released or absorbed when water changes from one state to another.
- Absolute humidity is the mass of water vapor contained in a given volume of air. Relative humidity is a ratio of the actual amount of water vapor in the air to the amount of water vapor needed to reach saturation. Humidity can be measured using a variety of instruments, including an electrical hygrometer, a psychrometer, a dew cell, and a hair hygrometer.
- When air reaches the dew point, the rate of condensation equals the rate of evaporation. Below the dew point, net condensation or deposition causes dew or frost to form.

Key Terms

latent heat, p. 543
sublimation, p. 544
dew point, p. 545
absolute humidity, p. 545
relative humidity, p. 546

Section 2

Clouds and Fog

- Clouds form when water vapor cools and condenses on condensation nuclei.
- Water vapor can cool and condense by adiabatic cooling, by the mixing of two bodies of moist air that have different temperatures, by the lifting of air, and by advective cooling.
- The three major types of clouds are stratus clouds, cumulus clouds, and cirrus clouds.
- Fog forms when air near Earth's surface is chilled below the dew point. Fog can form due to heat loss through radiation, advective cooling, the lifting and cooling of air along land slopes, or when cool air moves over an inland body of warm water.

Key Terms

cloud, p. 549
condensation nucleus, p. 549
adiabatic cooling, p. 550
advective cooling, p. 551
stratus cloud, p. 552
cumulus cloud, p. 553
cirrus cloud, p. 553
fog, p. 554

Section 3

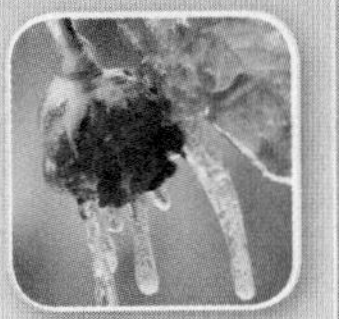

Precipitation

- The major forms of precipitation are rain, snow, sleet, and hail.
- Coalescence and supercooling are two processes by which cloud droplets become large enough to fall as precipitation.
- A rain gauge is used to measure liquid precipitation. Snow is measured by its depth and water content.
- Meteorologists utilize cloud seeding to try to induce precipitation.

Key Terms

precipitation, p. 555
coalescence, p. 556
supercooling, p. 556
cloud seeding, p. 558

Chapter Summary

Using THINK central Resources

Super Summary

Have students connect the major concepts in this chapter through an interactive Super Summary. Visit www.thinkcentral.com and type in the keyword **HQXWIAS** to access the Super Summary for this chapter.

Differentiated Instruction

Alternative Assessment

Water Cycle Skit Invite students to write and perform a skit in which they explain how water moves around Earth through the water cycle. Students can take on the roles of water in the ocean, and in different types of clouds, and the various forms of precipitation—rain, sleet, dew, snowflakes, frost, and hail. They can make props, scenery, and include diagrams to make their explanations clearer or more convincing.

LS Kinesthetic

Chapter Review

Assignment Guide	
Section	**Questions**
1	2, 8, 10, 19–22, 26, 27, 33, 36–40
2	3, 6, 7, 9, 11–15, 25, 28, 30, 34
3	1, 4, 5, 16–18, 23, 24, 29, 32
2 and 3	35
1–3	31

Reading Toolbox

1. Tables may include the following information: Rain is liquid precipitation. Snow is solid precipitation that consists of ice particles. Sleet starts as rain, but hits the ground as ice pellets. Hail is solid precipitation that begins as rain but freezes when the drops are carried to high altitudes by convection currents in clouds.

Using Key Terms

2–9. Answers may vary but should show that students understand the definitions of and differences between key terms.

Understanding Key Concepts

10. d
11. c
12. a
13. b
14. c
15. c
16. b
17. d
18. a
19. d

Chapter 20 Review

1. **Comparisons** READING TOOLBOX Create a table of the similarities and differences among the different types of precipitation.

USING KEY TERMS

Use each of the following terms in a separate sentence.

2. *latent heat*
3. *condensation nucleus*
4. *precipitation*

For each pair of terms, explain how the meanings of the terms differ.

5. *coalescence* and *supercooling*
6. *stratus cloud* and *cumulus cloud*
7. *adiabatic cooling* and *advective cooling*
8. *relative humidity* and *absolute humidity*
9. *cloud* and *fog*

UNDERSTANDING KEY IDEAS

10. When the temperature of the air decreases, the rate of evaporation
   a. increases.
   b. varies.
   c. stays the same.
   d. decreases.
11. The type of fog that results when moist air moves across a cold surface is
   a. radiation fog.
   b. ground fog.
   c. advection fog.
   d. steam fog.
12. Changes in temperature that result from the cooling of rising air or the warming of sinking air are
   a. adiabatic.
   b. relative.
   c. advective.
   d. latent.
13. Clouds form when the water vapor in air condenses as
   a. the air is heated.
   b. the air is cooled.
   c. snow falls.
   d. the air is superheated.
14. The prefix *nimbo-* and the suffix *-nimbus* mean
   a. high. **c.** rain.
   b. billowy. **d.** layered.
15. The fog that results from the nightly cooling of Earth is called
   a. steam fog. **c.** radiation fog.
   b. upslope fog. **d.** advection fog.
16. Rain that freezes when it strikes a surface produces
   a. sleet. **c.** hail.
   b. glaze ice. **d.** frost.
17. Clouds in which the water droplets remain liquid below 0 °C are said to be
   a. saturated. **c.** superheated.
   b. supersaturated. **d.** supercooled.
18. In one method of cloud seeding, silver iodide crystals are used as
   a. freezing nuclei. **c.** dry ice.
   b. cloud droplets. **d.** latent heat.
19. An instrument that uses the electrical conductance of the chemical lithium chloride to measure relative humidity is the
   a. hygrometer. **c.** psychrometer.
   b. rain gauge. **d.** dew cell.

SHORT ANSWER

20. Explain how the transfer of energy affects the changing forms of water.
21. Explain how a psychrometer measures humidity.
22. Describe how frost forms.
23. Describe how precipitation is measured.
24. Describe how cloud seeding may increase precipitation.
25. Explain how clouds are classified.

Short Answer

20. Water changes from one phase to another when energy is transferred. When energy is absorbed by liquid water, the water changes to a gas. When water vapor condenses back into a liquid form, energy is released back into the surrounding air.
21. A pychrometer consists of two identical thermometers. The bulb of one thermometer is covered with a damp cloth. They are whirled through the air, which causes the water surrounding the wet bulb to evaporate rapidly. Heat leaves as water evaporates from the wet bulb. The difference in the temperature between the two thermometer readings is used to calculate relative humidity.
22. Frost forms when the dew point temperature is below freezing and water vapor changes directly to solid ice crystals on a cold surface.
23. Precipitation is measured by using a calibrated container in which the amount of rainfall can be directly measured or by using an electrical device that records the amount of precipitation that tips into a divided bucket. The water content of snow is measured by melting, or is directly measured by using a meter stick to determine the snowfall depth.
24. Cloud seeding increases precipitation by artificially introducing condensation nuclei or freezing nuclei on which the water droplets or ice crystals may form.

CRITICAL THINKING

26. **Making Inferences** Where would air contain more water vapor: over Panama or over Antarctica? Explain your answer.
27. **Identifying Relationships** One body of air has a relative humidity of 97%. Another has a relative humidity of 44%. At the same temperature, which body of air is closer to its dew point? Explain your answer.
28. **Applying Ideas** Why would polluted air be more likely to form fog than clean air would?
29. **Analyzing Relationships** In tropical regions, surface temperatures are very high. However, some precipitation in these regions forms by supercooling. Why might this happen?
30. **Predicting Consequences** How would a significant decrease in condensation nuclei in the world's atmosphere affect cloud formation and climate?

CONCEPT MAPPING

31. Use the following terms to create a concept map: *hygrometer, condensation nucleus, stratus, cirrus, cloud, cumulus, precipitation, relative humidity, saturated, rain, supercooling, snow, sleet, coalescence, dew cell,* and *psychrometer.*

MATH SKILLS

Math Skills

32. **Applying Quantities** One day in January, 6 cm of snow falls on your area. If all this snow melts quickly, how deep will the water from the melted snow be? Explain your answer.
33. **Making Calculations** At 15 °C, air reaches saturation when it contains 10 g of water vapor per 1 kg of air. What is the relative humidity of air at 15 °C if the air contains 7 g of water vapor per 1 kg of air?

WRITING SKILLS

34. **Writing from Research** Write a report that describes weather conditions necessary to form each type of cloud. Propose regions and describe climates where each cloud type is most likely to be found.
35. **Outlining Topics** Create an outline of how clouds form and a separate outline of how precipitation forms. Then, explain how the two differ.

INTERPRETING GRAPHICS

The graph below shows variations in temperature and humidity over a 24 h period. Use this graph to answer the questions that follow.

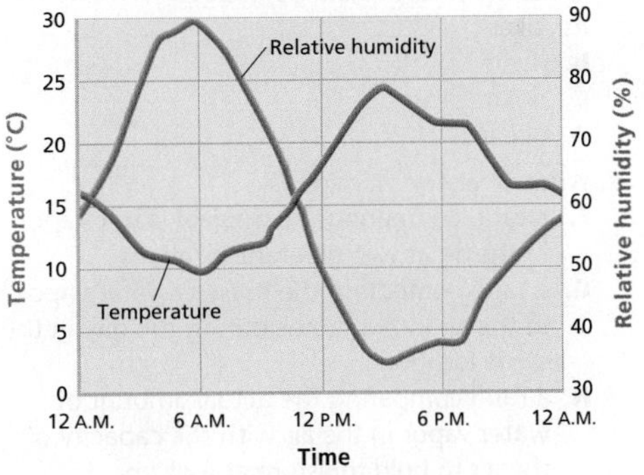

36. Estimate the relative humidity at 6:00 A.M.
37. Estimate the temperature at 6:00 A.M.
38. Explain why relative humidity might be the highest at 6:00 A.M.
39. When is relative humidity the lowest?
40. How does humidity vary relative to temperature?

Chapter Review

25. Clouds are classified by both their appearance and their height above Earth's surface.

Critical Thinking

26. Air would be likely to contain more water vapor over Panama, because it is located near the equator where more solar energy reaches Earth's surface to cause evaporation of the ocean water.
27. The air that has a relative humidity of 97% is closer to its dew point because it is nearly saturated. Only a small increase in moisture or a small drop in temperature is needed for the air to reach its dew point.
28. Polluted air has smoke, dust, and chemicals that can serve as condensation nuclei for fog formation.
29. Supercooling happens at high altitudes where air temperatures are low. If the air rises quickly and there are not enough freezing nuclei, supercooling will occur.
30. Answers may vary. Sample answer: Cloud formation would decrease, and possibly worldwide precipitation would also change. This might sharply increase drought conditions temporarily or contribute to desertification.

Concept Mapping

31. Answers may vary but should include all of the terms listed. Sample answers appear at the end of this unit on p. 631B.

Math Skills

32. On average, 10 cm of snow melts to produce 1 cm of water. 6 cm/10 cm = 0.6 × 1 cm = 0.6 cm of water
33. relative humidity = (amount of H_2O in air ÷ amount needed to reach saturation) × 100; relative humidity = 7 g/kg ÷ 10 g/kg = 7/10 or 0.7 × 100 = 70%

Writing Skills

34. Answers may vary. Accept all reasonable answers.
35. Answers may vary. Accept all reasonable answers.

Interpreting Graphics

36. 89%
37. 10°C
38. Relative humidity is highest in the early morning when temperature is lowest because the air is close to the dew point. Evaporation is slowest compared to condensation.
39. at about 3 P.M.
40. Relative humidity seems to have an inverse relationship to temperature. Humidity tends to decrease during the day when temperatures are higher and to increase at night when the air temperature is cooler.

Standardized Test Prep

Estimated Time

To give students practice under more realistic testing conditions, allow them 30 minutes to answer all of the questions in this practice test.

Test Doctor

Question 2 Answer G is correct. A greater area of Earth's surface is covered by water than by ice, so answer F is incorrect. Advective cooling, answer H, and convective cooling, answer I, do not produce water vapor.

Question 4 Answer H is correct. Relative humidity is a measurement of the moisture in the atmosphere at a given time in one location. Answers F, G, and I do not accurately describe this measurement.

Question 9 Answer F is correct. Answer G is incorrect because, while some species may adapt to low acidic levels, acid rain is destructive to most plant and animal species. Answer H is incorrect because the acid in precipitation raises the acidic levels of lakes and streams, it is not neutralized. Answer I is incorrect because the text does not describe the number of points on the pH scale.

Chapter 20 Standardized Test Prep

Understanding Concepts

Directions (1–4): For each question, write on a separate sheet of paper the letter of the correct answer.

1. Which type of fog is formed when cool air moves across a warm river or lake?
   - **A.** radiation fog
   - **B.** advection fog
   - **C.** upslope fog
   - **D.** steam fog
2. Which of the following processes produces most of the water vapor in the atmosphere?
   - **F.** sublimation
   - **G.** evaporation
   - **H.** advective cooling
   - **I.** convective cooling
3. Which of the following is the main source of moisture in Earth's atmosphere?
   - **A.** lakes
   - **B.** rivers
   - **C.** polar icecaps
   - **D.** oceans
4. What is relative humidity?
   - **F.** a ratio comparing the mass of water vapor in the air at two different locations
   - **G.** a ratio comparing the mass of water vapor in the air at two times during the day in the same location
   - **H.** a ratio comparing the actual amount of water vapor in the air with the capacity of the air to hold moisture at a given temperature
   - **I.** a ratio comparing the mass of water vapor that air can hold at two different altitudes at noon and at midnight

Directions (5–7): For each question, write a short response.

5. What instrument is used to measure atmospheric pressure?
6. Particles called condensation nuclei, which are suspended in the atmosphere, are necessary in allowing what process to take place?
7. What does water vapor turn into when the dew point falls below the freezing point of water?

Reading Skills

Directions (8–9): Read the passage below. Then, answer the questions.

Acid Precipitation

Thousands of lakes thoughout the world are affected by acid precipitation, often known simply as acid rain. Acid precipitation is precipitation, such as rain, sleet, or snow, that contains high concentrations of acids. When fossil fuels are burned, they release oxides of sulfur and nitrogen. When the oxides combine with water in the atmosphere, they form sulfuric acid and nitric acid, which fall as precipitation. This acidic water flows over and through the ground, and then flows into lakes, rivers, and streams. Acid precipitation can kill living things and can result in the decline or loss of some local animal and plant populations.

A pH (power of hydrogen) number is a measure of how acidic or basic a substance is. The lower the number on the pH scale is, the more acidic a substance is; the highter a pH number is, the more basic a substance is. Each whole number on the pH scale indicates a tenfold change in acidity.

8. According to the passage, which of the following statements is true?
   - **A.** Acid precipitation always falls as rain.
   - **B.** Acid precipitation seeps into local water supplies and may pose a danger to living things in the area.
   - **C.** Sulfur and nitrogen mix with oxygen in the atmosphere and become acids.
   - **D.** The amount of acidic precipitation is balanced in nature by an equal amount of basic precipitation.
9. Which of the following statements can be inferred from the information in the passage?
   - **F.** A reduction in the use of fossil fuels may help to alleviate the problem of acid rain.
   - **G.** Local animal and plant species will most likely adapt to acid rain.
   - **H.** The acid in precipitation is effectively neutralized once it is in a lake or stream.
   - **I.** The amount of acid in a substance can be measured by using a 10-point scale.

Questions 10 and 11 For question 10, answer B is correct. For question 11, answer F is correct. Students can use the diagram to determine that air is forced upward or downward at the specified locations. Students should demonstrate an understanding of the adiabatic temperature changes that result from expansion or compression of air. As the air rises between points A and B, it loses energy and undergoes adiabatic cooling. As the air falls from point B toward point C, it gains energy and undergoes adiabatic warming.

Question 14 Full-credit answers should include the following points:

- dew point temperature and relative humidity are calculated through dry-bulb and wet-bulb temperature readings
- dry-bulb temperature readings indicate air temperature; wet-bulb temperature readings indicate the cooling effect of evaporation
- these readings indicate the evaporation rate at the current temperature

Interpreting Graphics

Directions (10–14): For each question below, record the correct answer on a separate sheet of paper.

The diagram below shows the direction of air movement over a mountain. Use this diagram to answer questions 10 through 12.

Movement of Air over a Mountain

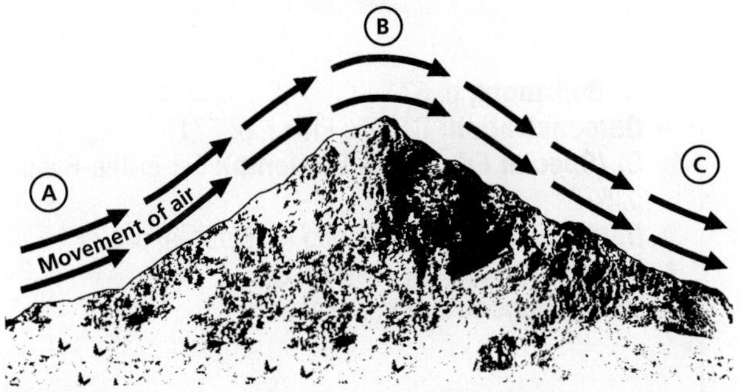

10. As air moves from point A to point B, the air temperature
- **A.** increases.
- **B.** decreases.
- **C.** stays the same.
- **D.** is impossible to predict.

11. Air moving from point B to point C will become compressed and gain energy as it moves down the mountain, which will cause the air to undergo
- **F.** adiabatic warming.
- **G.** adiabatic cooling.
- **H.** condensation.
- **I.** sublimation.

12. If moist air moves up the mountain from point A, what process is likely to occur when the moist air moves near point B?

The diagram below shows the parts of a psychrometer. Use this diagram to answer questions 13 and 14.

Parts of a Psychrometer

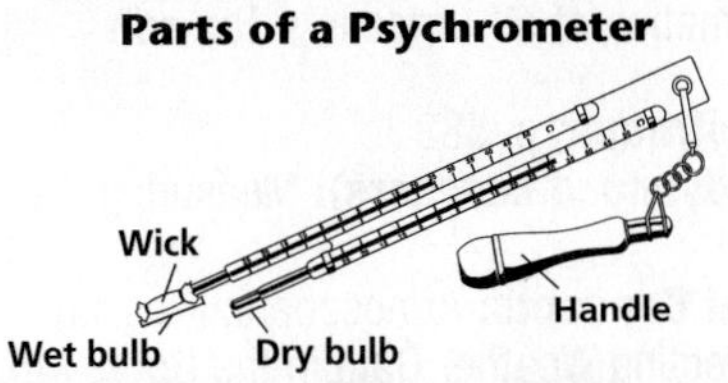

13. How does a meteorologist use a psychrometer, such as the one shown in the diagram above?
- **A.** It is placed in a pan of water and exposed to the air for 1 h.
- **B.** The handle is used to dip it into a body of water, such as a lake.
- **C.** It is held by the handle and twirled in the air.
- **D.** It is held until the readings on both thermometers are equal.

14. Why is it necessary to obtain two readings? What measurements of atmospheric moisture can be determined from these readings?

Test Tip

If you are not sure of an answer, go to the next question, but remember to skip that number on your answer sheet.

Standardized Test Prep

Using THINK central Resources

State Resources
- For specific resources for your state, visit www.thinkcentral.com and type in the keyword **HSHSTR.**

Answers

Understanding Concepts

1. D
2. G
3. D
4. H
5. barometer
6. cloud formation
7. frost

Reading Skills

8. B
9. F

Interpreting Graphics

10. B
11. F
12. cloud formation
13. C
14. Answers may vary. See Test Doctor for a detailed scoring rubric.

Chapter Planner 21

Weather

		Standards	Teach Key Ideas
Chapter Opener, pp. 568–569	45 min.	National Science Education Standards	
Section 1 Air Masses, pp. 571–574 ❯ How Air Moves ❯ Formation of Air Masses ❯ Types of Air Masses ❯ North American Air Masses	45 min.	SAI 2a, HNS 2a, UCP 2, UCP 3	■ ◆ **Bellringer,** p. 571 ■ **Demonstration:** Coriolis Effect, p. 571 ■ **DI (Special Education Students):** Fill-in-the-Blank, p. 572 ■ **Demonstration:** Comparing Air Masses, p. 572 ◆ **Transparency:** 104 Air Masses ▲ **Visual Concepts:** Air Masses
Section 2 Fronts, pp. 575–582 ❯ Types of Fronts ❯ Polar Fronts and Midlatitude Cyclones ❯ Severe Weather	45 min.	SAI 2a, HNS 2a, UCP 2, UCP 3	■ ◆ **Bellringer,** p. 575 ■ **Demonstration:** Make a Cold Front, p. 575 ■ **DI (Basic Learners):** Fronts, p. 575 ■ **DI (English Learners):** Paired Summarizing, p. 576 ■ **Discussion:** Highs and Lows, p. 577 ■ **Demonstration:** Spiraling Winds, p. 577 ■ **Demonstration:** Updrafts, p. 578 ◆ **Transparencies:** 105 Types of Fronts • 106 Stages of a Midlatitude Cyclone • 107 Anatomy of a Hurricane • 110 Weather-Related Disasters ▲ **Visual Concepts:** Types of Fronts • Cyclones and Anticyclones • Thunderstorms • Lightning and Thunder • Formation of a Hurricane • Tornado
Section 3 Weather Instruments, pp. 583–586 ❯ Measuring Lower-Atmospheric Conditions ❯ Measuring Upper-Atmospheric Conditions	45 min.	SAI 2a, HNS 2a, UCP 1, UCP 2, UCP 3	■ ◆ **Bellringer,** p. 583 ■ **DI (Advanced Learners):** Measuring Weather Variables, p. 584 ▲ **Visual Concepts:** Atmospheric Pressure • Anemometer • Collecting Weather Data in the Upper Atmosphere
Section 4 Forecasting the Weather, pp. 587–592 ❯ Global Weather Monitoring ❯ Weather Maps ❯ Weather Forecasts ❯ Controlling the Weather	90 min.	SAI 2a, SPSP 1a, HNS 2a, UCP 1, UCP 2, UCP 3	■ ◆ **Bellringer,** p. 587 ■ **Discussion:** Weather Lore, p. 587 ■ **Discussion:** Comprehension Check, p. 588 ■ **Discussion:** Barometric Pressure, p. 588 ■ **Discussion:** Isotherms, p. 589 ■ **DI (Basic Learners):** Station Models, p. 589 ■ **DI (Advanced Learners):** Weather Station, p. 590 ■ **Debate:** Weather Modification, p. 591 ◆ **Transparencies:** 108 Weather Symbols • 109 Weather Map of the United States ▲ **Visual Concepts:** Station Model • Isobar
Chapter Wrap-Up, pp. 597–601	90 min.		**Chapter Summary,** p. 597

CHAPTER Fast Track

To shorten instruction because of time limitations, omit Sections 1 and 3.

See also PowerNotes® Presentations

Key

Teacher's Edition ■ Teaching Transparencies ◆
Chapter Resource File ● Online Edition ▲

All resources listed below are also available on the **Teacher One Stop™.**

Why It Matters	Hands-On	Skills Development	Assessment
■ **Chapter Overview,** p. 568 ■ **Using the Figure:** Light Show, p. 568	**Inquiry Lab:** Build a Wind Vane, p. 569	**Reading Toolbox,** p. 570	
■ **Section Overview,** p. 571	■ **Activity:** Air on the Move, p. 572 ■ **Activity:** Bulletin Board Project, p. 573	**Reading Toolbox:** Generalizations, p. 572	**Reading Check,** p. 573 **Section Review,** p. 574 ■ **Reteaching,** p. 573 ■ **Quiz,** p. 573 ■ **DI (Alternative Assessment):** Electronic Quiz Game, p. 574 ● **Section Quiz**
■ **Section Overview,** p. 575 ■ **History Connection:** Pioneer Meteorologist, p. 576 ■ **Physics Connection:** Lightning Discharge, p. 578 **Hurricane Katrina** pp. 580–581	■ **Group Activity:** Weather Front Pop-Ups, p. 576	■ **Reading ToolBox:** Two-Column Notes, p. 576 ■ **Skill Builder:** Vocabulary, p. 577 **Math Skills:** Thunderstorm Distance, p. 578 **Maps in Action:** Weather-Related Disasters, p. 596	**Reading Check,** p. 577 **Reading Check,** p. 579 **Section Review,** p. 582 ■ **Reteaching,** p. 579 ■ **Quiz,** p. 579 ■ **DI (Alternative Assessment):** Radio Play, p. 582 ● **Section Quiz**
■ **Section Overview,** p. 583 **How Does Wind Affect Flight?** p. 585	■ **Group Activity:** Simple Thermometer, p. 583 **Quick Lab:** Wind Chill, p. 584 ● **Inquiry Lab:** Building a Weather Station	■ **Skill Builder:** Graphing, p. 584 ■ **Reading ToolBox:** Two-Column Notes, p. 585 ■ ● **Internet Activity:** Weather Images, p. 585	**Reading Check,** p. 584 **Section Review,** p. 586 ■ **Reteaching,** p. 585 ■ **Quiz,** p. 585 ■ **DI (Alternative Assessment):** Weather Riddles, p. 586 ● **Section Quiz**
■ **Section Overview,** p. 587 ■ **Using the Figure:** Classroom Station Model, p. 588 ■ **Using the Figure:** Isobars, p. 589 ■ **Literature Connection:** The Perfect Storm, p. 590	■ **Group Activity:** Cloud Cover, p. 588 ■ **Activity:** Local Weather Maps, p. 589 **Quick Lab:** Gathering Weather Data, p. 590 ■ **Group Activity:** Weather Safety Project, p. 591 **Skills Practice Lab:** Weather Map Interpretation, pp. 594–595 ● **Making Models Lab:** Blowing in the Wind	■ **Reading ToolBox:** Prefixes, Suffixes, and Roots Words, p. 591	**Reading Check,** p. 589 **Reading Check,** p. 590 **Section Review,** p. 592 ■ **Reteaching,** p. 591 ■ **Quiz,** p. 591 ■ **DI (Alternative Assessment):** Weather Forecast, p. 592 ● **Section Quiz**
When Lightning Strikes, p. 593	■ **Activity:** Weatherwise Museum, p. 597	▲ **Super Summary** **Standardized Test Prep,** p. 600	**Chapter Review,** pp. 598–599 ● **Chapter Tests**

See also Lab Generator

See also Holt Online Assessment Resources

Chapter Overview

This chapter describes how air masses affect weather and how fronts produce severe weather. The chapter also explains how scientists measure atmospheric conditions and forecast weather.

Using the Figure GENERAL

Light Show Cumulonimbus clouds discharge lightning to balance electrical charges. Ice crystals at the top of the clouds are positively charged; rain near the bottom becomes negatively charged. As a result of this charge separation, the ground below also becomes positively charged. When the difference in charge is great enough, an electric spark flows between the cloud and the ground. Thunder is the sound of rapidly expanding gases from the channel of the lightning. Ask students why thunder always follows lightning. (Sound and light travel at different speeds.) **LS Visual**

Why It Matters

Weather affects our lives every day. We decide what to wear and make plans based on the weather forecast. Meteorologists study weather data in order to make the most accurate forecast possible. An accurate forecast, with warnings for severe weather, can save lives.

Chapter 21 Weather

Chapter Outline

Virginia Standards of Learning
ES.1.a
ES.1.b
ES.1.d
ES.1.f
ES.2.a
ES.10.c
ES.11.c
ES.12.a
ES.12.b
ES.12.c

Why It Matters

Weather—both mild and severe—affects our daily lives. Scientists use weather data and weather patterns to help predict and forecast the weather.

Chapter Correlations — *Virginia Standards of Learning*

ES.1.a volume, area, mass, elapsed time, direction, temperature, pressure, distance, density, and changes in elevation/depth are calculated utilizing the most appropriate tools/
ES.1.b technologies, including computers, probeware, and geospatial technologies, are used to collect, analyze, and report data and to demonstrate concepts and simulate experimental conditions.
ES.1.d maps and globes are read and interpreted, including location by latitude and longitude.
ES.1.f current applications are used to reinforce Earth science concepts.
ES.2.a science explains and predicts the interactions and dynamics of complex Earth systems.
ES.10.c systems interactions
ES.11.c atmospheric regulation mechanisms including the effects of density differences and energy transfer
ES.12.a observation and collection of weather data
ES.12.b prediction of weather patterns
ES.12.c severe weather occurrences, such as tornadoes, hurricanes, and major storms

Inquiry Lab

20 min

Build a Wind Vane

Use **scissors** to cut a piece of **thin cardboard** or **manila paper** into a triangular arrowhead, 5 cm long, and a rectangular tail, 7 cm long. Make parallel cuts at both ends of a **drinking straw** about 2 cm long, and slide in the arrowhead and the tail. Push a **straight pin** through the balance point of the straw and into the eraser end of a **pencil.** Then push the pointed end of the pencil vertically through the center of an **aluminum pie plate** and into a lump of **modeling clay.** Place the clay in center of a heavy **paper plate** and press down, forming a sandwich of clay between the two plates. (You may also want to steady the pin with a small piece of clay.) Mark the directions N, S, E, and W around the edges of the pie plate with a **marker.** Place your wind vane in front of a **fan** and turn the fan on low speed. Observe what happens.

Questions to Get You Started

1. What does a wind vane measure?
2. How does the design of your wind vane make the arrow point upwind?
3. How is wind direction described? Is it described as the direction from which the wind blows or the direction in which the wind is blowing?

Inquiry Lab

Central Concept: Students will build and test a wind vane.

Teacher's Notes: Prepare ahead of time several templates of the arrow-head and tail for students to trace. Tell students to make sure the straight pin is straight up and down when they push it through the straw. If the vanes are not turning, try lubricating the pin by sticking it through a bar of soap.

Materials (per group)

- Scissors
- Cardboard or manila paper
- Drinking straw
- Straight pin
- Pencil
- Modeling clay
- Marker
- Paper plate
- Aluminum pie plate
- Electric fan

Skills Acquired

- Making Models
- Observing

Answers to Getting Started

1. wind direction
2. Wind vanes have a smaller end (the front arrow) and a larger end (the tail). The smaller end will turn into the wind.
3. Wind direction is described as the direction from which the wind blows.

Using THINK central Resources

An online version of this chapter, as well as all the print and multi-media resources that accompany the program are available to registered teachers and their students. Log onto www.thinkcentral.com to access these materials and tools to organize your preparation and student learning.

READING TOOLBOX

Word Parts

Prefixes, Suffixes, and Root Words Accept all reasonable answers. Sample answer: Maritime: Definition: air masses that form over the sea, Root: time: from Indo-European base da-, meaning "cut up, divide," Prefix: mari-: from Latin word mare, meaning "sea" (Latin), Suffix: none; Thermometer: Definition: an instrument that measures and indicates temperature, Root: none, Prefix: thermo-: from the Greek word, *thermé,* meaning "heat," Suffix: -meter: from the Greek word *metron,* meaning "measure."

Generalizations

Properties of Severe Weather Answers may vary. Sample answers include: Sentence: Large cumulus and cumulonimbus clouds typically form along fast-moving cold fronts, Signal Word: typically, Explanation: The statement applies to most, but not all, cumulus and cumulonimbus clouds; Sentence: In North America, midlatitude cyclones generally travel about 45 km/h in an easterly direction as they spin counterclockwise, Signal Word: generally, Explanation: The statement applies to most, but not all, midlatitude cyclones in North America.

READING TOOLBOX

These reading tools will help you learn the material in this chapter.

Word Parts

Prefixes, Suffixes, and Root Words The prefix *iso-* is from the Greek word *isos,* meaning "equal." When added to the root word *therm,* which means "heat," you have the word *isotherm,* which means "a line on a weather map that connects points of equal temperature."

Your Turn On a separate sheet of paper, complete a table like the one below with key terms or italicized words from this chapter that contain prefixes, suffixes, or word roots. Use a dictionary or the Internet to find the meanings of the word parts.

Word	Definition	Root	Prefix	Suffix
isobar	a line on a weather map that connects points of equal atmospheric pressure	bar: from the Greek word baros, meaning "weight"	iso: from the Greek word isos, meaning "equal"	

Generalizations

Properties of Severe Weather When you make a generalization, you make a statement that applies to a large group of things or people. If you say, "Most students studied for the test," you are saying that most, but not all, students studied for the test. Words such as *most, usually, typically, commonly,* and *generally,* and phrases such as *in general* and *for the most part,* signal generalizations. Some generalizations do not have a word or phrase signal.

Your Turn As you read Section 2, complete a table like the one below to list the generalizations that you find.

Sentence	Word or phrase that signals generalization	Explanation of why sentence is a generalization
Tornadoes generally cover paths not more than 100 m wide.	generally	The statement applies to most, but not all, tornadoes.

Note Taking

Two-Column Notes Two-column notes can help you learn the key terms, italicized words, and main ideas as you read.

Your Turn Complete two-column notes for Sections 1 and 4.

1. Write one key term, italicized word, or main idea in each row of the left-hand column.
2. Add definitions, details, and examples in the right-hand column.

Key term, italicized word, or main idea	Definitions, details, and examples
maritime	• on or near the ocean
maritime air masses	• air masses that form over the ocean • take on the characteristics of the water over which they form (moist, humid) • usually bring precipitation and fog

For more information on how to use these and other tools, see **Appendix A.**

Note Taking

Two-Column Notes Answers may vary. Students should consult Appendix A for tips on taking two-column notes. Students' two-column notes should cover the key terms, italicized terms, and main ideas of Sections 1 and 4.

SECTION 1

Air Masses

Key Ideas	Key Terms	Why It Matters
› Explain how an air mass forms. › List the four main types of air masses. › Describe how air masses affect the weather of North America.	**air mass**	You may not think about air masses very often, but they influence weather across North America every day.

Differences in air pressure are caused by unequal heating of Earth's surface. The region along the equator receives more solar energy than the regions at the poles do. The heated equatorial air rises and creates a low-pressure center. Conversely, cold air near the poles sinks and creates high-pressure centers. Differences in air pressure at different locations on Earth create wind patterns.

How Air Moves

Air moves from areas of high pressure to areas of low pressure. Therefore, there is a general, worldwide movement of surface air from the poles toward the equator. At high altitudes, the warmed air flows from the equator toward the poles. Temperature and pressure differences on Earth's surface create three wind belts in the Northern Hemisphere and three wind belts in the Southern Hemisphere. These wind belts are influenced by the *Coriolis effect,* which occurs when winds are deflected by Earth's rotation. The processes that affect air movement also influence storms, such as the one shown in **Figure 1.**

air mass a large body of air throughout which temperature and moisture content are similar

Formation of Air Masses

When air pressure differences are small, the air remains relatively stationary. If the air remains stationary or moves slowly over a uniform region, it takes on the characteristic temperature and humidity of that region. A large body of air throughout which temperature and moisture are similar is called an **air mass.** Air masses that form over frozen polar regions are very cold and dry. Air masses that form over tropical oceans are warm and moist.

Figure 1 The motion of Earth's atmosphere can lead to the formation of powerful storms, such as Hurricane Katrina.

Key Resources

Chapter Resource File
- Directed Reading BASIC

Technology
- Transparencies
  Bellringer

Section 1

Focus

Overview

This section tells how air masses form, introduces the four main types of air masses, and explains how they affect the weather patterns of North America.

Bellringer

Ask students to compare what they know about characteristics of land air and ocean air, and characteristics of polar air and tropical air. (Land air is dry and ocean air is humid; polar air is cold and tropical air is warm.)
LS Verbal

Motivate

Demonstration GENERAL

Coriolis Effect Gather the class around a globe. Ask a student to draw a straight chalk line from the North Pole to the equator. Ask the class to imagine what would happen to the line if the globe were spinning. Then, have the volunteer repeat the experiment while you spin the globe slowly from west to east. What happens to the chalk line? (The line curves to the right) Earth's rotation causes winds to move in curved paths around the surface of Earth. These curving wind patterns create massive, twisting storms such as the one shown on this page.
LS Visual

Teach

Demonstration GENERAL

Comparing Air Masses To model the formation of air masses on a small scale, fill two dishpans with about 2.5 cm of water to represent oceans. Place wet-dry bulb hygrometers on trays to keep them dry. Put them inside the pans so the wet and dry temperatures (or humidity of the air) can be compared. Cover the pans with plastic wrap and label them as indicated. Put one in the sun (mT) and the other in the shade (mP). After 1/2 hour, measure the temperature and humidity of each air mass. Dry out the pans to represent continents, and repeat the set-up. Put one in the sun (cT) and the other in the shade (cP). Repeat the measurements. Ask students to explain how stable air masses form, and have them compare the characteristics of the different air masses. (Sample answer: When air remains over an area, it takes on the temperature and humidity of the region; mP is cool and moist; mT is warm and moist; cT is dry and warm; and cP is dry and cool.) **LS Kinesthetic**

READING TOOLBOX

Generalizations Accept all reasonable responses. Sample answer: Sentence: When these very moist masses of air travel to a new location, they commonly bring more precipitation and fog, Signal Word: commonly, Explanation: The statement applies to most, but not all, maritime air masses.

Table 1 Air Masses

Source region	Type of air	Symbol
Continental	dry	c
Maritime	moist	m
Tropical	warm	T
Polar	cold	P

Types of Air Masses

Air masses are classified according to their source regions. The source regions determine the temperature and the humidity of the air masses. The source regions for cold air masses are polar areas. The source regions for warm air masses are tropical areas. Air masses that form over oceans are called *maritime*. Air masses that form over land are called *continental*. Maritime air masses are moist, and continental air masses are dry. Air masses and the symbols used to designate them are listed in **Table 1.** The combination of tropical or polar air and continental or maritime air results in air masses that have distinct characteristics.

Continental Air Masses

Continental air masses form over large landmasses, such as northern Canada, northern Asia, and the southwestern United States. Because these air masses form over land, the level of humidity is very low. An air mass may remain over its source region for days or weeks. However, the air mass will eventually move into other regions because of global wind patterns. In general, continental air masses bring dry weather conditions when they move into another region. There are two types of continental air masses: *continental polar* (cP) and *continental tropical* (cT). Continental polar air masses are cold and dry. Continental tropical air masses are warm and dry.

READING TOOLBOX

Generalizations
As you read Section 1, look for sentences that contain generalizations. List them in a table like the one shown at the beginning of this chapter. Remember that some generalizations are not signaled by a word or phrase.

Maritime Air Masses

Maritime air masses form over oceans and other large bodies of water. These air masses take on the characteristics of the water over which they form. The humidity in these air masses tends to be higher than that of continental air masses. When these very moist air masses travel to a new location, they commonly bring precipitation and fog, as shown in **Figure 2.**

The two types of maritime air masses are *maritime polar* (mP) and *maritime tropical* (mT). Maritime polar air masses are moist and cold. Maritime tropical air masses are moist and warm.

Figure 2 A maritime air mass brings fog that rolls in off the coast of California.

Activity GENERAL

Air on the Move Give students the following instructions: "On an outline map of North America, use a blue pencil to draw an air mass moving south over the northern U.S. from Canada. Label it *Air mass 1*. Use a red pencil to draw a second air mass moving northeast from the south Pacific. Label it *Air mass 2*." Ask students to describe the characteristics of each air mass. (Sample answer: Air mass 1 is continental polar, dry and cold; Air mass 2 is maritime tropical, warm and moist). **LS Visual**

Differentiated Instruction

Special Education Students

Fill-in-the-Blank Use the following activity to encourage some student movement. On the board, write numbered sentences with fill-in blanks related to section content. Assign numbers to specific students. Ask the students to read to find the answers for their assigned sentences, and then to go to the board and fill in the blanks. **LS Kinesthetic/Verbal**

North American Air Masses

The four types of air masses that affect the weather of North America come from six locations. These air masses, their source locations, their movements, and the weather they bring are summarized in **Table 2.** The general directions of the air masses' movements are shown in **Figure 3.** An air mass usually brings the weather of its source location, but an air mass may change as it moves away from its source location. For example, cold, dry air may become warmer and more moist as it moves from land to a warm ocean. As the lower layers of the air are warmed, the air rises. This warmed air may then create clouds and precipitation.

Table 2 Air Masses of North America

Air mass	Source location	Movement	Weather
cP	polar regions in Canada	south-southeast	cold and dry
mP	polar Pacific; polar Atlantic	southeast; southwest-south	cold and moist
cT	U.S. southwest	north-northeast	warm and dry
mT	tropical Pacific; tropical Atlantic	northeast; north-northwest	warm and moist

Academic Vocabulary
summarize (SUHM uh RIEZ) explain in a brief way

Tropical Air Masses

Continental tropical air masses form over the deserts of the southwestern United States. These air masses bring dry, hot weather in the summer. They do not form in the winter. Maritime tropical air masses form over the warm water of the tropical Atlantic Ocean, the Caribbean Sea, and the Gulf of Mexico. They bring mild, often cloudy weather to the eastern United States in the winter. In the summer, they bring hot, humid weather and thunderstorms. Maritime tropical air masses also form over warm areas of the Pacific Ocean. But these air masses do not usually reach the Pacific coast. In the winter, maritime tropical air masses bring moderate precipitation to the coast and the southwestern deserts.

SCILINKS. www.scilinks.org
Topic: Air Masses
Code: HQX0031

Reading Check **Which air mass brings dry, hot weather in the summer?** (See Appendix G for answers to Reading Checks.)

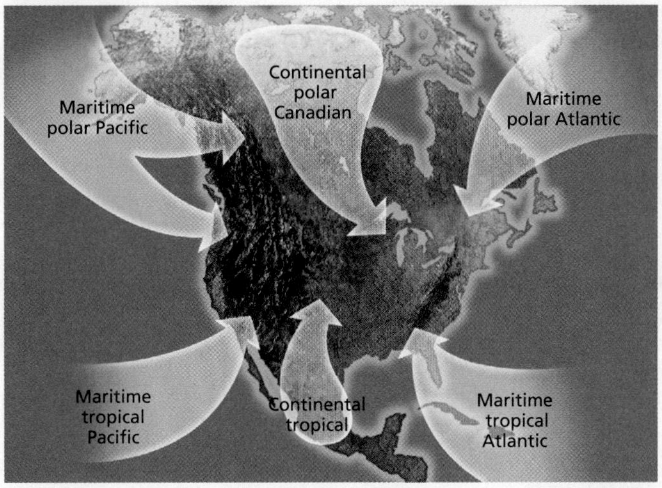

Figure 3 The four types of air masses that influence the weather in North America come from six locations and are named according to their source locations.

Answer to Reading Check
a continental tropical air mass

Close

Reteaching — BASIC

Spider Maps Have students create a spider map around the concept of air masses. Have them create a leg for each type of air mass and fill in the branches with details about its source and direction of movement and about the type of weather associated with each air mass. Students can use these graphic organizers to study for assessments. LS **Visual**

Quiz — GENERAL

1. What determines the distinct characteristics of an air mass? (the region over which it forms)
2. What type of air mass forms over the Gulf of Mexico and the warm waters of the Atlantic Ocean in summer? What kind of weather does it bring when it travels northward? (maritime tropical; hot, humid weather and thunderstorms)
3. What are the properties of a continental polar air mass? Identify a place where this air mass is likely to form. (cold and dry; over northern Canada)
4. What type of air mass develops over the North Pacific Ocean? How might the character of this air mass change as it moves inland over the central United States? (maritime polar; It might lose some of its moisture and warm slightly.)

Activity — GENERAL

Bulletin Board Project Have interested students create a weather bulletin board using the information on North American air masses and their associated weather phenomena. They can place a large map in the center and use colored yarn to connect the source region of each air mass to poems or drawings that describe the weather it brings. As students learn more, they can add additional information about weather fronts and storm systems, weather instruments, and weather forecasting to the bulletin board. LS **Visual**

Key Resources

Technology
- Transparencies
  104 Air Masses

Close, *continued*

Answers to Section Review

1. a large body of air that has the same temperature and moisture content throughout
2. When differences in air pressure are small, air remains stationary or moves very slowly and takes on the characteristics of the region.
3. over land in a polar region
4. continental polar, continental tropical, maritime polar, and maritime tropical
5. continental polar: cool, dry weather in summer and cold weather in the north in winter; maritime polar: rain and snow along the Pacific coast in winter and cool, foggy weather in summer; continental tropical: hot, dry weather; Atlantic maritime tropical: hot, humid weather or thunderstorms in summer and mild, cloudy weather in winter; Pacific maritime tropical: moderate precipitation
6. The maritime tropical air mass that forms over the Atlantic is warm and moist. The symbol is mT.
7. Warm, moist air of a maritime tropical air mass would be replaced with cool, dry air.
8. Answers may vary. Sample answer: A tropical air mass near the coast of Europe would have originated in the South Atlantic Ocean and moved north and east. I would expect the air mass to continue in the same direction, moving across continental Europe. The tendency of colder air from the North Pole to move into the low-pressure area and push the warm air south would be offset by the Coriolis effect.
9. *Air masses* may be polar which includes *maritime polar*, such as *maritime polar Pacific* and *maritime polar Atlantic*, or *continental polar*, which includes *continental polar Canadian*.

Figure 4 Maritime polar Atlantic air masses can bring heavy snowfall, such as this snowstorm that hit New York City in 2003.

Polar Air Masses

Polar air masses from three regions—northern Canada and the northern Pacific and Atlantic Oceans—influence weather in North America. Continental polar air masses form over ice- and snow-covered land. These air masses move into the northern United States and can occasionally reach as far south as the Gulf Coast of the United States. In summer, these air masses usually bring cool, dry weather. In winter, they bring very cold weather to the northern United States.

Maritime polar air masses form over the North Pacific Ocean and are very moist, but they are not as cold as continental polar Canadian air masses. In winter, maritime polar Pacific air masses bring rain and snow to the Pacific Coast. In summer, they bring cool, often foggy weather. As they move inland and eastward over the Cascades, the Sierra Nevada, and the Rocky Mountains, these cold air masses lose much of their moisture and warm slightly. Thus, they may bring cool and dry weather by the time they reach the central United States.

Maritime polar Atlantic air masses generally move eastward toward Europe, but they sometimes move westward over New England and eastern Canada. In winter, they can bring cold, cloudy weather and snow, as shown in **Figure 4.** In summer, these air masses can produce cool weather, low clouds, and fog.

Section 1 Review

Key Ideas

1. **Define** *air mass.*
2. **Explain** how an air mass forms.
3. **Identify** the location where a cold, dry air mass would form.
4. **List** the four main types of air masses.
5. **Describe** how the four main types of air masses affect the weather of North America.
6. **Describe** the air mass that forms over the warm water of the Atlantic Ocean. What letters designate the source region of this air mass?

Critical Thinking

7. **Making Predictions** How do temperature and humidity change when a maritime tropical air mass is replaced by a continental polar air mass?
8. **Recognizing Relationships** In which direction would you expect a tropical air mass near the coast of Europe to travel? Explain your answer.

Concept Mapping

9. Use the following terms to create a concept map: *maritime polar Pacific, maritime polar, continental polar Canadian, air mass, continental polar,* and *maritime polar Atlantic.*

Differentiated Instruction

Alternative Assessment

Electric Quiz Game Invite groups of students to create a homemade, electric match game about the characteristics of air masses. Students may use a string of tree lights, tag board, 2 C batteries in a battery holder, paper clips, a hole punch, strips of aluminum foil, and electrical tape. Students can either enlarge the map of North America or use a question and answer format so that a bulb will light up when a paper clip switch touches items that match. Tell them to mix up the questions and answers so that they are not lined up. **LS Kinesthetic**

SECTION 2 Fronts

Key Ideas	Key Terms		Why It Matters
❯ Compare the characteristic weather patterns of cold fronts with those of warm fronts. ❯ Describe how a midlatitude cyclone forms. ❯ Describe the development of hurricanes, thunderstorms, and tornadoes.	cold front warm front stationary front occluded front midlatitude cyclone	thunderstorm hurricane tornado	You've probably heard a weather forecaster use the term *front* and perhaps say that a cold front would pass through your area. Tracking the movement of fronts helps us forecast the weather.

When two unlike air masses meet, density differences usually keep the air masses separate. A cool air mass is dense and does not mix with the less-dense air of a warm air mass. Thus, a boundary, called a *front,* forms between air masses. A typical front is several hundred kilometers long. However, some fronts may be several thousand kilometers long. Changes in middle-latitude weather usually take place along the various types of fronts. Fronts do not exist in the tropics because no air masses that have significant temperature differences exist there.

Types of Fronts

For a front to form, one air mass must collide with another air mass. The kind of front that forms is determined by how the air masses move in relationship to each other.

Cold Fronts

When a cold air mass overtakes a warm air mass, a **cold front** forms. The moving cold air lifts the warm air. If the warm air is moist, clouds will form. Large cumulus and cumulonimbus clouds typically form along fast-moving cold fronts, as shown in **Figure 1.** Storms that form along cold fronts are usually short-lived and are sometimes violent. A long line of heavy thunderstorms, called a *squall line,* may occur in the warm, moist air just ahead of a fast-moving cold front. A slow-moving cold front lifts the warm air ahead of it more slowly than a fast-moving cold front does. A slow-moving cold front typically produces weaker storms and lighter precipitation than a fast-moving cold front does.

cold front the front edge of a moving mass of cold air that pushes beneath a warmer air mass like a wedge

Figure 1 As a cold air mass overtakes a warm air mass, a line of thunderstorms called a *squall line* forms.

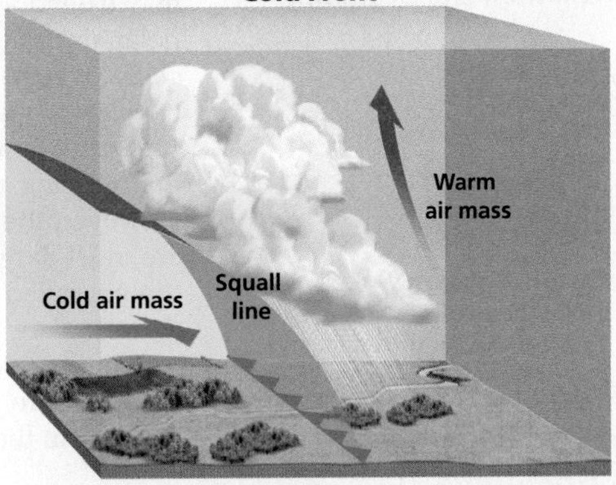

Section 2

Focus

Overview

This section explains what happens when air masses collide and describes different kinds of fronts. The section also describes cyclones and anticyclones and violent weather systems.

Bellringer

Provide the following list: blizzard, thunderstorm, drought, hurricane, thunderstorm, and tornado. Have students select a weather condition from the list and write a paragraph that describes how it affects people.
LS Verbal/Interpersonal

Motivate

Demonstration GENERAL

Make a Cold Front You can demonstrate the effects of meeting air masses by using liquids. Fill an empty jar two-thirds full with warm water. Then, pour cold milk gently down the side of the jar. Ask students to describe what happens. (The cold milk stays at the bottom and the warm water remains on top. It takes some time before the liquids start to mix.) Have them repeat the experiment using cold milk and cold tap water. Ask what happens now. (The liquids should mix fairly quickly.) **LS Visual**

Key Resources

Chapter Resource File
- Directed Reading BASIC

Technology
- Transparencies
  Bellringer
  105 Types of Fronts

Differentiated Instruction

Basic Learners

Fronts Give students figures, with no captions or other explanation, of the four different types of fronts. Have students explain what is happening in each figure and then write a caption for the figure. **LS Visual/Verbal**

Teach

Group Activity — GENERAL

Weather Front Pop-Ups Have students work in small groups to create booklets or cards using pop-up folds and 3-D effects to show what happens when cold, warm, stationary, or occluded fronts form. Provide stiff cards, scissors, glue, and reference materials with basic instructions for paper-engineering projects. You may want to show students samples of pop-up books or cards. Tell students to write captions to explain what is happening in their paper models. After they construct their models, students can display them in the classroom. Discuss the weather patterns associated with each front. LS **Kinesthetic**

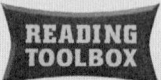

READING TOOLBOX

Two-Column Notes Student answers will vary. Accept all reasonable answers.

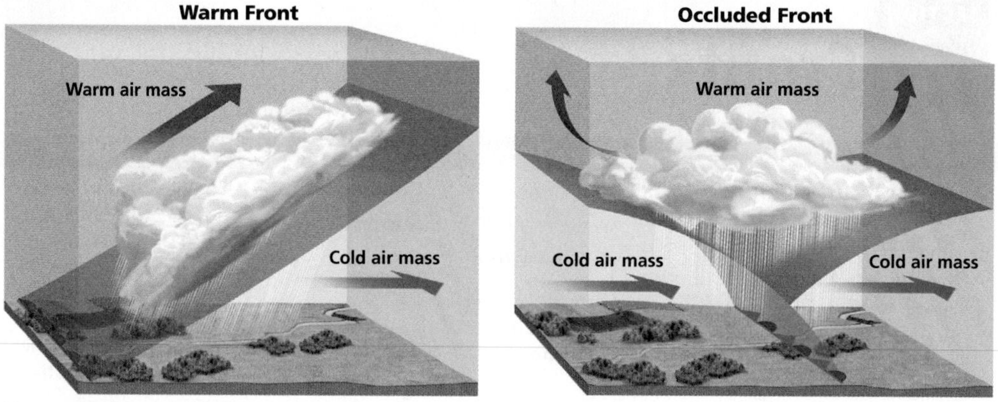

Figure 2 As a warm air mass rises over a cold air mass (left), a warm front forms at the boundary of the two air masses. An occluded front (right) forms when a cold air mass lifts a warm air mass off the ground.

warm front the front edge of an advancing warm air mass that replaces colder air with warmer air

stationary front a front of air masses that moves either very slowly or not at all

occluded front a front that forms when a cold air mass overtakes a warm air mass and lifts the warm air mass off the ground and over another air mass

midlatitude cyclone an area of low pressure that is characterized by rotating wind that moves toward the rising air of the central low-pressure region

Warm Fronts

When a warm air mass overtakes a cold air mass, a **warm front** forms. The less dense warm air rises over the cooler air. The slope of a warm front is gradual, as shown in **Figure 2.** Because of this gentle slope, clouds may extend far ahead of the surface location, or *base,* of the front. A warm front generally produces precipitation over a large area and may occasionally cause violent weather.

Stationary and Occluded Fronts

Sometimes, when two air masses meet, the air moves parallel to the front and neither air mass is displaced. A front at which air masses move either very slowly or not at all is called a **stationary front.** The weather produced by a stationary front is similar to the weather produced by a warm front. An **occluded front** usually forms when a fast-moving cold front overtakes a warm front and lifts the warm air off the ground completely, as shown in **Figure 2.**

Polar Fronts and Midlatitude Cyclones

Over each of Earth's polar regions is a dome of cold air that may extend as far as 60° latitude. The boundary where this cold polar air meets the tropical air mass of the middle latitudes, especially over the ocean, is called the *polar front*. Waves commonly develop along the polar front. A *wave* is a bend that forms in a cold front or a stationary front. This wave is similar to the waves that moving air produces when it passes over a body of water. However, the waves that form in a cold front or stationary front are much larger. They are the beginnings of low-pressure storm centers called midlatitude cyclones or *wave cyclones*. **Midlatitude cyclones** are areas of low pressure that are characterized by rotating wind, which moves toward the rising air of the central, low-pressure region. These cyclones strongly influence weather patterns in the middle latitudes.

READING TOOLBOX

Two-Column Notes
Use the two-column table that you started at the beginning of the chapter as a model to review the main ideas about fronts in this section.

History Connection — ADVANCED

Pioneer Meteorologist The Norwegian scientist Vilhelm Bjerknes was one of the founders of the field of meteorology and weather forecasting. A professor at Stockholm University, he studied the circulation of the atmosphere and the oceans. Together with his son Jacob, Bjerknes developed the theory of air masses and fronts. Encourage students to learn more about the contributions of this family of meteorologists to the science of predicting the weather. Invite them to share their discoveries through oral and written reports. LS **Verbal**

Differentiated Instruction

English Learners

Paired Summarizing Group students into pairs, and have them read silently about cold, warm, stationary, and occluded fronts. Then, have one student summarize the definitions and effects of these fronts, while the other student listens to the retelling and points out any inaccuracies or ideas that were left out. Allow students to refer to the text as needed. LS **Verbal/Auditory**

Stages of a Midlatitude Cyclone

A midlatitude cyclone usually lasts several days. The stages of formation and dissipation of a midlatitude cyclone are shown in **Figure 3.** In North America, midlatitude cyclones generally travel about 45 km/h in an easterly direction as they spin counterclockwise. They follow several storm tracks, or routes, as they move from the Pacific coast to the Atlantic coast. As they pass over the western mountains, they may lose their moisture and energy.

Anticyclones

Unlike the air in a midlatitude cyclone, the air in an *anticyclone* sinks and flows outward from a center of high pressure. Because of the Coriolis effect, the circulation of air around an anticyclone is clockwise in the Northern Hemisphere. Anticyclones bring dry weather, because their sinking air does not promote cloud formation. If an anticyclone stagnates over a region for a few days, it may cause air pollution problems. After being stationary for a few weeks, an anticyclone may cause a drought.

Reading Check **How is the air of an anticyclone different from the air of a midlatitude cyclone?**

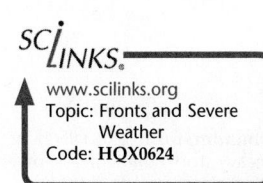

SCILINKS.
www.scilinks.org
Topic: Fronts and Severe Weather
Code: **HQX0624**

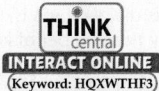

THINK central
INTERACT ONLINE
(Keyword: HQXWTHF3)

Figure 3 Stages of a Midlatitude Cyclone

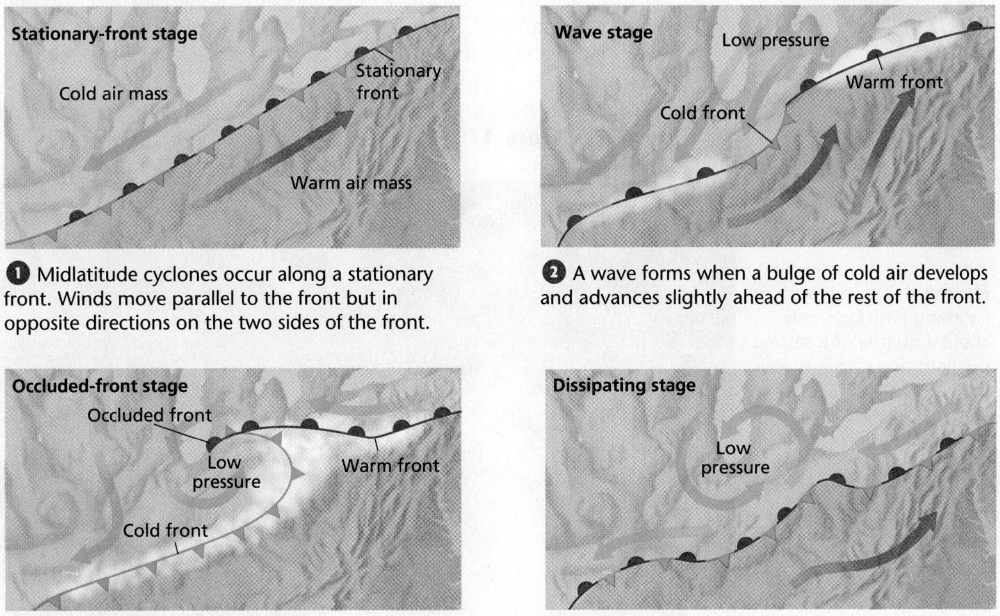

1 Midlatitude cyclones occur along a stationary front. Winds move parallel to the front but in opposite directions on the two sides of the front.

2 A wave forms when a bulge of cold air develops and advances slightly ahead of the rest of the front.

3 As the fast-moving part of the cold front overtakes the warm front, an occluded front forms and the storm reaches its highest intensity.

4 Eventually, the system loses most of its energy and the midlatitude cyclone dissipates.

Demonstration — General

Spiraling Winds Set a pan of tap water over a hot plate. Heat the water until it steams gently. While the water heats, draw a circle 7.5 cm in diameter on a sheet of printer paper. Cut out the circle to form a spiral shape. Tape a 30 cm length of thread to the center of the paper spiral. Hold the free end of the thread so that the paper spiral hangs about 5 cm above the pan of hot water. Invite students to describe what happens to the paper spiral. Ask them what causes the paper to move and where it gets its energy. (The paper model swirls around with a circular motion. Rising air currents strike the paper model, causing it to turn. The energy comes from the heat of the water.) **LS Visual**

Discussion — General

Highs and Lows Remind students that cold air masses are normally associated with high pressure because cold air is denser. Thus, the air pressure is higher. In contrast, warmer air masses are associated with low-pressure areas. Point out that cyclones are low-pressure areas (rising air), whereas anticyclones are high-pressure areas (sinking air). Ask students how these facts can help them remember the characteristics of cyclones and anticyclones. (Sample answers: With cyclones, air flows counterclockwise into the low-pressure zone. As this air rises, it cools. The moisture in the air condenses to form clouds and often violent storms. In an anticyclone, the air flows in the opposite direction, clockwise (in the Northern Hemisphere). As the air sinks around the high-pressure area, it warms, which inhibits the formation of clouds. This is why highs bring fair weather and lows tend to bring storms.) **LS Verbal/Logical**

Skill Builder — Basic

Vocabulary Explain to students that the word *cyclone* comes from the Greek word *kyklos,* which means "a circle." Winds form a circle around a low-pressure area. This root word was combined with the prefix *anti-* meaning "the opposite of," to describe the wind pattern that forms around a high-pressure area. Invite students to name other science words that use this prefix. (Sample answers: antibiotic, antibody, antidote, antigravity, and antigen) **LS Verbal** English Language Learners

Answer to Reading Check

The air of an anticyclone sinks and flows outward from a center of high pressure. The air of a midlatitude cyclone rotates toward the rising air of a central low-pressure region.

Key Resources

Technology

- Transparencies
  106 Stages of a Midlatitude Cyclone

Teach, *continued*

Demonstration GENERAL

Updrafts To help students visualize the lifting power of winds within severe storms, invite a student to balance a table tennis ball in the airstream produced by an upturned hair dryer. With a little practice, the ball will be supported. Now, have the volunteer try the experiment with a tennis ball. Compare the tennis ball to a growing raindrop or hailstone. **LS Visual**

Math Skills GENERAL

Thunderstorm Distance Explain to students that they can use the difference in speed between thunder and lightning to determine not only approximately how far the thunderstorm is from them, but also whether it is moving toward them or away. Suggest that they try this activity the next time they are indoors during a storm. Have them estimate the storm's distance for several successive lightning flashes and thunder crashes by dividing the lapse time (in seconds) by 3 s/km to obtain the distance in kilometers. If the distance increases, the storm is moving away. If the distance decreases, the storm is approaching their location. **LS Logical**

Math Skills

Answer

thunderstorm distance =
27 s ÷ 3 s/km = 9 km

Severe Weather

Severe weather is weather that may cause property damage or loss of life. Severe weather may include large quantities of rain, lightning, hail, strong winds, or tornadoes. This type of weather causes billions of dollars in damage each year.

Thunderstorms

thunderstorm a usually brief, heavy storm that consists of rain, strong winds, lightning, and thunder

A heavy storm that is accompanied by rain, thunder, lightning, and strong winds is called a **thunderstorm.** Thunderstorms develop in three distinct stages. In the first stage, or *cumulus stage,* warm, moist air rises, and the water vapor within the air condenses to form a cumulus cloud. In the next stage, called the *mature stage,* condensation continues as the cloud rises and becomes a dark cumulonimbus cloud. Heavy, torrential rain and hailstones may fall from the cloud. While strong updrafts continue to rise, downdrafts form as the air is dragged downward by the falling precipitation. During the final stage, or *dissipating stage,* the strong downdrafts stop air currents from rising. The thunderstorm dissipates as the supply of water vapor decreases.

Math Skills

Thunderstorm Distance The time between when you see a lightning strike and when you hear thunder indicates how far away the lightning bolt was from you. Sound travels approximately 1 km in 3 s. The lapse time in seconds divided by 3 is roughly the number of kilometers between you and the lightning. If 27 s pass between a flash of lightning and the sound of thunder, how far away was the lightning strike from you?

Lightning

During a thunderstorm, clouds discharge electricity in the form of *lightning*. The released electricity heats the air, and the air expands rapidly and produces the loud noise known as *thunder*. For lightning to occur, the clouds must have areas that carry distinct electrical charges. The upper part of a cloud usually carries a positive charge, while the lower part usually carries a negative charge. Lightning is a huge spark that travels within the cloud, or between the cloud and the ground, to equalize the electrical charges. **Figure 4** shows an example of lightning.

Figure 4 The average lightning flash lasts only about a quarter of a second, but lightning causes more than $330,000,000 in damage per year in the United States.

Physics Connection

Lightning Discharge Air currents cause friction among ice particles within clouds. Ice crystals splinter, and the smaller outer shells with positive charges are carried upward while the heavier negatively charged inside portions of the crystal fall to the bottom of the cloud. Positively charged particles build up at the top of cloud layers, and heavier, negatively charged particles collect at the bottom. A charge separation occurs on Earth as well. When the difference between the charges becomes strong enough to overcome the insulating properties of the air, electrons jump the gap. A giant spark is produced as this difference in charge is transformed into electrical energy in the cloud and then into light, sound, and heat energy. Lightning can flash in three ways: within clouds, between clouds, and between a cloud and the ground. Only about 20% of lightning strikes are cloud to ground. Lightning rods are tall pointed conductors attached to the tops of buildings and grounded to Earth. Because they are made of materials that conduct electricity, lightning rods provide a safe, direct path for the static electricity to travel harmlessly to Earth.

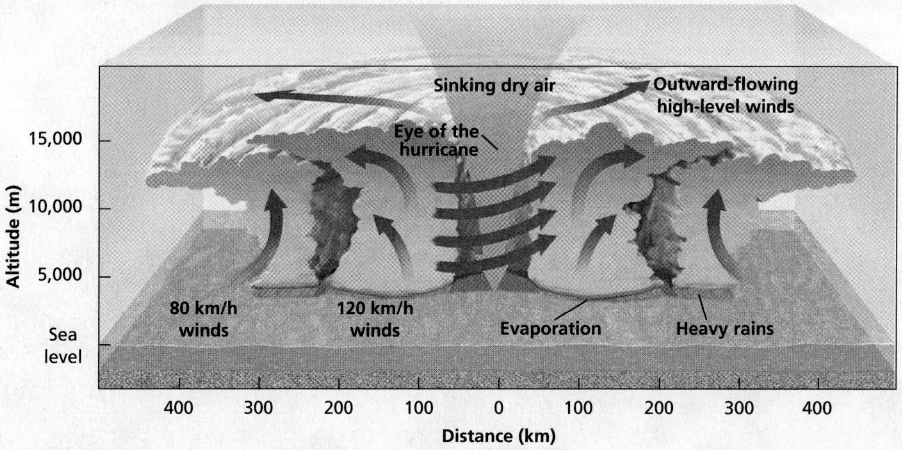

Figure 5 Although hurricanes are the most destructive storms, the eye at the center of a hurricane is relatively calm.

Hurricanes

Tropical storms differ from midlatitude cyclones in several ways. Tropical storms are concentrated over a smaller area. They lack warm and cold fronts. Also, they are usually much more violent and destructive than midlatitude cyclones. A tropical storm with wind speeds of 120 km/h or more that spiral in toward an intense low-pressure center is called a **hurricane.**

hurricane a severe storm that develops over tropical oceans and whose strong winds of more than 120 km/h spiral in toward the intensely low-pressure storm center

Hurricanes develop over warm, tropical oceans. A hurricane begins when warm, moist air over the ocean rises rapidly. When moisture in the rising warm air condenses, a large amount of energy in the form of latent heat is released. *Latent heat* is heat energy that is absorbed or released during a phase change. This heat increases the strength of the rising air.

A fully developed hurricane consists of a series of thick cumulonimbus cloud bands that spiral upward around the center of the storm, as shown in **Figure 5.** Winds increase toward the center, or eye, of the storm and reach speeds of up to 275 km/h along the eyewall. The eye itself, however, is a region of calm, clear, sinking air.

With a range in diameter of 400 to 800 km, hurricanes are the most destructive storms that occur on Earth. The most dangerous aspect of a hurricane is a rising sea level with large waves, called a *storm surge.* A storm surge can flood vast low-lying coastal areas. This flooding is the reason why most deaths during hurricanes are caused by drowning.

Every hurricane is categorized on the *Saffir-Simpson scale* by using several factors. These factors include central pressure, wind speed, and storm surge. The Saffir-Simpson scale has five categories. Category 1 storms cause the least damage. Category 5 storms can result in catastrophic damage.

Reading Check **Where do hurricanes develop?**

Close

Reteaching — BASIC

Game Show Have groups of students brainstorm a series of 4 or 5 clues or phrases that describe each of the weather patterns associated with warm or cold fronts, cyclones or anticyclones, and severe weather systems such as thunderstorms, hurricanes, or tornadoes. Have them write their clues on cards—one card for each weather pattern. Shuffle the cards and have teams try to guess the weather pattern from as few clues as possible. **LS Verbal**

Quiz — GENERAL

1. What is a front? (the boundary between two colliding air masses)
2. What is the Saffir-Simpson scale? (a scale used to classify the destructiveness of hurricanes based on pressure, wind speed, and storm surge)
3. Compare the characteristics of a midlatitude cyclone with those of an anticyclone. (cyclone: Air moves counterclockwise toward the low-pressure center, often bringing stormy weather. anticyclone: Air moves outward from the high-pressure center, often bringing fair weather.)

Answer to Reading Check
over warm tropical seas

Key Resources

Technology
- Transparencies
  107 Anatomy of a Hurricane

Why It Matters

New Orleans and Sea Level

New Orleans was founded by the French in 1718 as a port city to handle the merchant traffic along the Mississippi River. Situated on rare high ground in the Mississippi Delta, the city grew along the gently sloping natural levees formed by the Mississippi River's annual flood cycle. In 1722, however, a hurricane blew down most of the structures in the infant city. During reconstruction, city officials enforced a grid structure for roads. This plan can still be seen in the French Quarter today. By the middle of the 19th century, New Orleans was a thriving merchant city. Because of its precarious position, with much of its habitable land below sea level, a series of levees was constructed to keep the ocean from overwhelming the city. Flood waters have breached these levees several times throughout the city's history.

Why It Matters

Hurricane Katrina

Hurricane Katrina came marching in to New Orleans, Louisiana, on August 28, 2005. She was accompanied by torrential rain, sustained winds of 282 km/h, and storm surges of up to 8.5 meters. This event taught Americans many lessons about storm preparedness.

Katrina Approaches

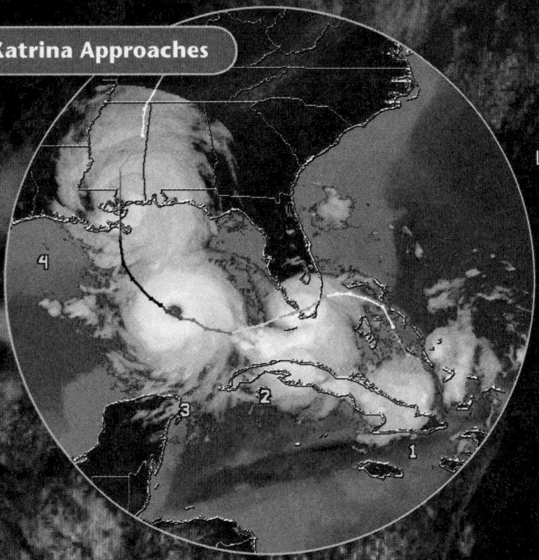

Large areas of New Orleans are below sea level. Therefore, city officials were concerned when the hurricane's path turned northward and the storm intensified as it moved toward the coast.

Thousands Homeless

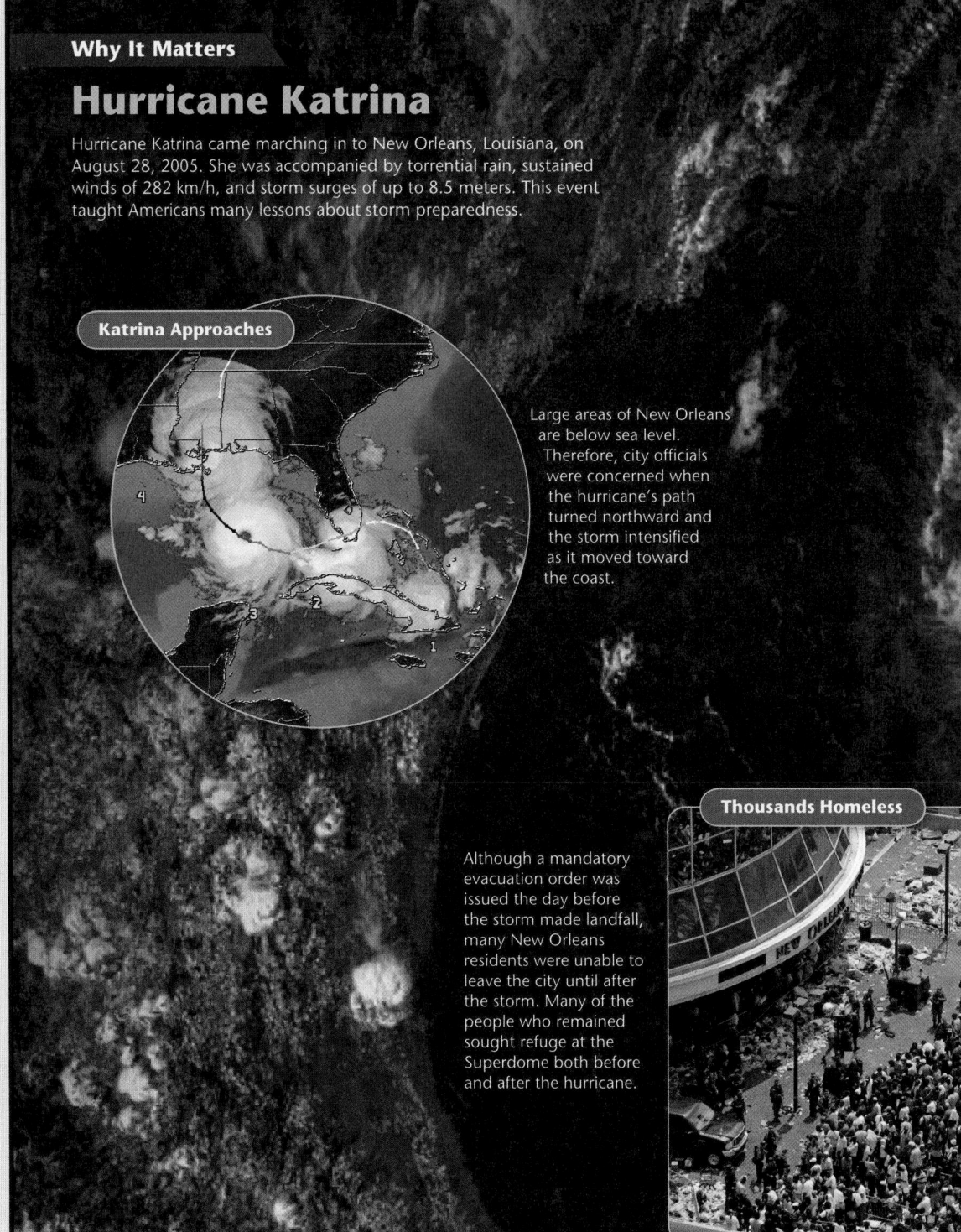

Although a mandatory evacuation order was issued the day before the storm made landfall, many New Orleans residents were unable to leave the city until after the storm. Many of the people who remained sought refuge at the Superdome both before and after the hurricane.

Reading Skill Builder — Basic

Visual Literacy The map showing the approach of Hurricane Katrina includes several visual elements that can help students understand the storm's progression. The map shows Katrina's location at five different times, from the storm's early formation in the Atlantic Ocean to after it made landfall. The curved line shows the location and movement of the center of the storm. The shapes of the storm at different locations show how the storm changed in both size and strength as it moved. The presence of the dark center circle in the fourth location shows that the storm had organized and had a clearly defined eye—a hallmark of a powerful hurricane.

Preventing Future Disasters

In the aftermath of the storm, teams of engineers and scientists reviewed the performance of the city's levees. These teams recommended ways to construct more storm-resistant levees.

Because of Hurricane Katrina, Hurricane Rita—which followed Hurricane Katrina by less than a month—was tracked very carefully, and evacuation orders were issued days in advance.

YOUR TURN

UNDERSTANDING CONCEPTS
Why did Hurricane Katrina particularly endanger New Orleans?

CRITICAL THINKING
What did scientists and government officials learn from Hurricane Katrina?

Answers to Your Turn

Understanding Concepts Large areas of New Orleans are located below sea level and are protected from flooding by levees. Intense storm surges from a strong hurricane can overrun or break the levees and cause widespread damage to the city.

Critical Thinking Scientists, engineers, and government officials learned how to build stronger, more storm-resistant levees. They also learned valuable lessons about tracking storms, preparing for storms, and evacuating endangered areas.

Why It Matters

The Variable Storm Four days before Katrina made landfall in New Orleans on August 28, 2005, it was upgraded from a tropical storm to a hurricane. Katrina was a category 1 hurricane as it moved over southern Florida. Two days later, scientists changed the projected path of the hurricane from the western Gulf of Mexico to Louisiana and Mississippi. One day before its projected landfall, Katrina was upgraded to a category 5 hurricane. Projections indicated that the eye would make landfall within 120 km of New Orleans.

Why It Matters

Overtopping the Levees Most of the city's levees were designed and built in the 1960s by the U.S. Army Corps of Engineers. Hurricane Katrina's storm surges overwhelmed the levees by overtopping them, or rising above the tops of the levees and eroding their bases on the landward side as the water rushed over the embankments. These breaches were responsible for most of the flooding. By August 31, 2005, 80% of New Orleans was underwater. In some places, the water was up to 4.5 meters deep.

Why It Matters

Government Preparedness The extreme destruction and loss of life caused by Hurricane Katrina was met by support and aid from across the United States and around the world. Government preparedness and emergency planning for a natural disaster the size of Hurricane Katrina, however, underwent intense scrutiny. As a result, government officials and scientists were more cautious and proactive when preparing people for Hurricane Rita, which followed Hurricane Katrina by less than a month. Evacuation orders were issued days in advance of the storm's arrival. The state of Texas provided the use of school buses and city buses to increase the ability of citizens in coastal areas to evacuate. The state also created relief shelters in sports stadiums, arenas, and convention centers in other Texas cities and suspended the collection of hotel and motel taxes from the victims of Hurricane Rita.

Close, *continued*

Answers to Section Review

1. *Cold fronts* form when a cold air mass pushes beneath a warm air mass. A *warm front* is the leading edge of an advancing warm air mass that replaces colder air. *Stationary fronts* move slowly or not at all. An *occluded front* occurs when cold air overtakes warm air, lifting the warm air over another cold air mass.
2. Storms along cold fronts are short-lived. A warm front generally produces precipitation over a wider area. Both may produce violent weather.
3. a fast-moving cold front
4. Midlatitude cyclones form along cold or stationary fronts. Winds move parallel to the front, but in opposite directions on each side. A wave of rotating air forms around the central low-pressure region as cold air advances ahead of the rest of the front. An occluded front forms as the cold front overtakes the warm front.
5. Warm, moist air rises and condenses, forming clouds. Condensation continues, and the clouds rise, changing into cumulonimbus clouds. Strong updrafts continue to rise and downdrafts form. Heavy rain and hailstones fall. Strong downdrafts stop air currents from rising, and so the storm's energy dissipates.
6. Warm, moist air rises rapidly over the oceans. Latent heat is released as moisture in the warm air condenses. This feeds development of cumulonimbus clouds and winds spiraling around a calm region.

Figure 6 A powerful tornado in Texas embedded this bucket in a wooden door (inset).

tornado a destructive, rotating column of air that has very high wind speeds and that may be visible as a funnel-shaped cloud

Tornadoes

The smallest, most violent, and shortest-lived severe storm is a tornado. A **tornado** is a destructive, rotating column of air that has very high wind speeds and that is visible as a funnel-shaped cloud, as shown in **Figure 6.**

A tornado forms when a thunderstorm meets high-altitude, horizontal winds. These winds cause the rising air in the thunderstorm to rotate. A storm cloud may develop a narrow, funnel-shaped, rapidly spinning extension that reaches downward and may or may not touch the ground. If the funnel does touch the ground, it generally moves in a wandering, haphazard path. Frequently, the funnel rises and touches down again a short distance away. Tornadoes generally cover paths not more than 100 m wide. Usually, however, everything in that path is destroyed. Tornadoes occur in many locations, but they are most common in *Tornado Alley* in the late spring or early summer. Tornado Alley stretches from Texas up through the midwestern United States.

The destructive power of a tornado is due to mainly the speed of the wind in the funnel. This wind may reach speeds of more than 400 km/h. Most injuries and deaths caused by tornadoes occur when people are trapped in collapsing buildings or are struck by objects blown by the wind.

Section 2 Review

Key Ideas

1. **Describe** the four main types of fronts.
2. **Compare** the characteristic weather patterns of cold fronts with those of warm fronts.
3. **Identify** the type of front that may form a squall line.
4. **Summarize** how a midlatitude cyclone forms.
5. **Describe** the stages in the development of a thunderstorm.
6. **Describe** the stages in the development of a hurricane.
7. **Explain** why tornadoes are so destructive.

Critical Thinking

8. **Evaluating Methods** What areas of Earth should meteorologists monitor to detect developing hurricanes? Explain your answer.
9. **Making Comparisons** Compare the destructive power of midlatitude cyclones, hurricanes, and tornadoes in terms of size, wind speed, and duration.

Concept Mapping

10. Use the following terms to create a concept map: *tornado, hurricane, warm front, squall line, cold front, severe weather, stationary front, front, midlatitude cyclone,* and *occluded front.*

7. because the funnel may touch the ground with winds that may reach speeds of more than 400 km/h
8. Scientists should monitor storms developing over warm tropical seas, where hurricanes start. The tropical air would flow north toward the continent from the ocean, and the Coriolis effect would deflect the air to the right, or east.

Answers continued on p. 631A

Differentiated Instruction

Alternative Assessment

Radio Play Divide the class into small groups. Have groups develop a short radio script that describes the development of a complex weather system such as a midlatitude cyclone, a thunderstorm, a hurricane, or a tornado. Tell them to include a description of each stage in the process. When they have completed writing the scripts, have each group perform its play for the class or create an audio recording of the performance. They can use simple props to create sound effects. **LS Auditory**

SECTION 3

Weather Instruments

Key Ideas	Key Terms	Why It Matters
❯ Identify four instruments that measure lower-atmospheric weather conditions. ❯ Describe how scientists measure conditions in the upper atmosphere. ❯ Explain how computers help scientists understand weather.	thermometer barometer anemometer wind vane radiosonde radar	When you look at a weather forecast, you see lots of numbers, including temperature, air pressure, and humidity data. These measurements help meteorologists track weather.

Weather observations are based on a variety of measurements, including atmospheric pressure, humidity, temperature, wind speed, and precipitation. These measurements are made with special instruments. Meteorologists then use these measurements to forecast weather patterns.

Measuring Lower-Atmospheric Conditions

During the course of a day, the lower-atmospheric conditions at a given location can change drastically. Meteorologists use the magnitude and speed of these changes to predict future weather events. To obtain accurate data from the lower atmosphere, scientists use instruments such as those shown in **Figure 1.**

Air Temperature

An instrument that measures and indicates temperature is called a **thermometer.** A common type of thermometer uses a liquid—usually mercury or alcohol—sealed in a glass tube to indicate temperature. A rise in temperature causes the liquid to expand and fill more of the tube. A drop in temperature causes the liquid to contract and fill less of the tube. A scale marked on the glass tube indicates the temperature.

Another type of thermometer is an *electrical thermometer*. As the temperature rises, the electric current that flows through the material of the electrical thermometer increases and is translated into temperature readings. A *thermistor*, or thermal resistor, is a type of electrical thermometer that responds very quickly to temperature changes. For this reason, thermistors are extremely useful where temperature change occurs rapidly.

thermometer an instrument that measures and indicates temperature

Figure 1 Weather instruments, such as these at Elk Mountain weather research facility in Wyoming, indicate wind speed and direction.

Key Resources

Chapter Resource File
- Directed Reading BASIC
- Inquiry Lab: Building a Weather Station GENERAL

Technology
- Transparencies
  Bellringer

Section 3

Focus

Overview

This section explains how meteorologists measure weather conditions.

Bellringer

Have students brainstorm a list of weather conditions that scientists monitor. (Sample answers: temperature, wind direction, and precipitation) LS **Visual**

Motivate

Group Activity GENERAL

Simple Thermometer Have students work in pairs. Provide empty water bottles, see-through straws, rubbing alcohol, clay, and food color. Have students fill the bottles one quarter full with equal parts rubbing alcohol and water, and then add a few drops of food color. Have them put the straw in the bottle and seal the neck with the clay so the straw stays in place. Have them cut two slits in a piece of paper and slip the paper over the straw and tape it in place. Have students mark the present level of the liquid in the straw, and then observe what happens to the level of the liquid. Ask them to explain why, as air temperature changes, the level rises or falls. (Sample answer: Heat makes the liquid expand and rise. A decrease in temperature makes the liquid contract and fall.) LS **Kinesthetic**

Teach

Quick Lab

Skills Acquired
- Experimenting
- Observing
- Analyzing

Materials
- 23 cm x 33 cm pan
- Water
- Thermometer
- Electric fan

Teacher's Notes: Small portable desk fans will work for this activity. If you are not able to obtain enough fans for a small group activity, present this lab as a demonstration. Assign student assistants to perform the demonstration for the class.

Answers to Analysis
1. The temperature of the water decreases.
2. The wind from the fan increases the rate of evaporation of the water. Evaporation takes heat from the water, decreasing the temperature.
3. Answers may vary. Sample answer: minimize the effects of wind chill by exposing as little skin as possible.

Answer to Reading Check
A barometer is used to measure atmospheric pressure.

Figure 2 A meteorologist uses an anemometer during Hurricane Luis to measure wind speed.

barometer an instrument that measures atmospheric pressure

anemometer an instrument used to measure wind speed

wind vane an instrument used to determine the direction of the wind

Air Pressure

Changes in air pressure affect air masses at certain locations. The approach of a front is usually indicated by a drop in air pressure. Scientists use instruments called **barometers** to measure atmospheric pressure.

Wind Speed

An instrument called an **anemometer** (AN uh MAHM uht uhr) measures wind speed. A typical anemometer consists of small cups that are attached by spokes to a shaft that rotates freely. The wind pushes against the cups and causes them to rotate, as shown in **Figure 2.** This rotation triggers an electrical signal that registers the wind speed in meters per second or in miles per hour.

Wind Direction

The direction of the wind is determined by using an instrument called a **wind vane.** The wind vane is commonly an arrow-shaped device that turns freely on a pole as the tail catches the wind. Wind direction may be described by using one of 16 compass directions, such as north-northeast. Wind direction also may be described in degrees by moving clockwise, beginning with 0° at the north. Thus, east is 90°, south is 180°, and west is 270°.

Reading Check **Which instrument is used to measure air pressure?**

Quick Lab Wind Chill

15 min

Procedure

1. Place a 23 cm × 33 cm pan on a level table. Fill the pan to a depth of 1 cm with room-temperature water.
2. Lay a thermometer in the center of the pan, with the bulb submerged. After 5 min, record the water temperature. Do not touch the thermometer.
3. Place an electric fan facing the pan and a few centimeters from the pan. Turn on the fan at a low speed. **CAUTION** Do not get the fan or cord wet.
4. Record the water temperature every minute until the temperature remains constant.

Analysis

1. How does the moving air affect the temperature of the water?
2. If the moving air is the same temperature as the still air in the room, what causes the water temperature to change?
3. How would you dress on a cool, windy day to stay comfortable? Explain your answer.

Skill Builder — GENERAL

Graphing Have students use a mercury or alcohol thermometer to take hourly air temperature readings from 9 A.M. to 6 P.M. You may want to assign this project as weekend homework. Have students make a simple line graph of their temperature data and identify temperature patterns. When is air temperature highest? When is it lowest? (Temperatures generally peak in mid-afternoon and get lower toward evening.) **LS Logical**

Differentiated Instruction

Advanced Learners

Measuring Weather Variables Have students track daily local atmospheric pressure, humidity, temperature, wind speed, and precipitation. Also have students record the weather for each day—cloudy or sunny, rain or snow, or no precipitation. Then, have students create graphs that show the relationships of the measurements to the weather. **LS Logical**

Why It Matters

How Does Wind Affect Flight?

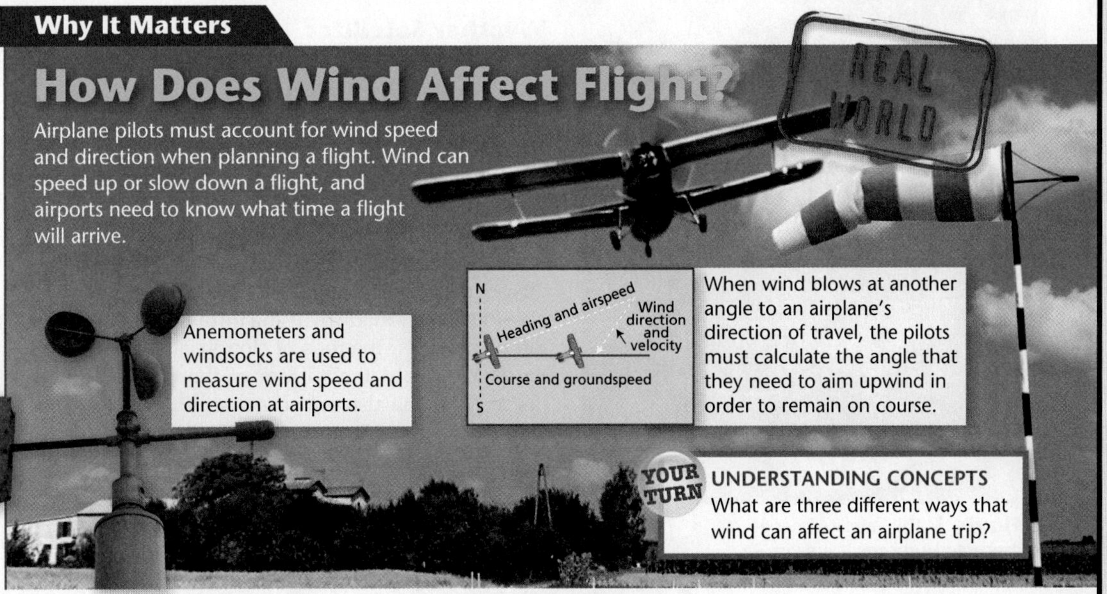

REAL WORLD
Airplane pilots must account for wind speed and direction when planning a flight. Wind can speed up or slow down a flight, and airports need to know what time a flight will arrive.
Anemometers and windsocks are used to measure wind speed and direction at airports.
N
Heading and airspeed
Wind direction and velocity
Course and groundspeed
S
When wind blows at another angle to an airplane's direction of travel, the pilots must calculate the angle that they need to aim upwind in order to remain on course.
YOUR TURN
UNDERSTANDING CONCEPTS
What are three different ways that wind can affect an airplane trip?

Measuring Upper-Atmospheric Conditions

Conditions of the atmosphere near Earth's surface are only part of the complete weather picture. Scientists use several instruments to measure conditions in the upper atmosphere, to obtain a better understanding of local and global weather patterns.

Radiosonde

An instrument package that is carried high into the atmosphere by a helium-filled weather balloon to measure relative humidity, air pressure, and air temperature is called a **radiosonde.** A radiosonde sends measurements as radio waves to a receiver that records the information. The path of the balloon is tracked to determine the direction and speed of high-altitude winds. When the balloon reaches a very high altitude, the balloon expands and bursts, and the radiosonde parachutes back to Earth.

Radar

Another instrument for determining weather conditions in the atmosphere is radar. **Radar,** which stands for **ra**dio **d**etection **a**nd **r**anging, is a system that uses reflected radio waves to determine the velocity and location of objects. For example, large particles of water in the atmosphere reflect radar pulses. Thus, precipitation and storms, such as thunderstorms, tornadoes, and hurricanes, are visible on a radar screen. The newest Doppler radar can indicate the precise location, movement, and extent of a storm. It can also indicate the intensity of precipitation and wind patterns within a storm.

radiosonde a package of instruments that is carried aloft by a balloon to measure upper atmospheric conditions, including temperature, dew point, and wind velocity

radar a system that uses reflected radio waves to determine the velocity and location of objects

READING TOOLBOX

Two-Column Notes
Create two-column notes to review the main ideas about weather instruments in this section. Put the main ideas in the left column. Add details and examples, in your own words, in the right column.

Why It Matters

How Does Wind Affect Flight Wind can affect scheduling at busy airports, fuel economy and resultant cost savings, and safety. Busy airports must know exactly when a plane will arrive, so understanding the effects of wind on travel time is essential for flight scheduling. Depending upon whether planes are traveling in the same direction as the jet stream or against it, they can choose to fly in it or avoid it, thereby cutting down on fuel consumption. Wind has the greatest affect on airplanes during take-off and landing. A wind blowing crossway to the runway makes landing difficult, and if the crosswind is too strong then planes cannot land safely at all.

Answers to Your Turn

Understanding Concepts Wind can affect a plane trip by slowing it down, speeding it up, or influencing the course.

READING TOOLBOX

Two-Column Notes Student answers will vary. Accept all reasonable answers.

Internet Activity — GENERAL

Weather Images Two kinds of satellites monitor weather conditions from orbit. Geostationary satellites orbit the equator at speeds that match Earth's rotation. Polar orbiting satellites orbit Earth, passing over the North and South Poles. Students may visit the National Weather Service Web site and report on an aspect that interests them. A worksheet designed to direct student research on this topic can be found in the **Chapter Resource File** booklet or by visiting www.thinkcentral.com and entering the keyword **HQXWTHX.**
LS Visual

Close

Reteaching — BASIC

Tools of the Trade Have students work in pairs to create a poster that illustrates what instruments scientists use to measure weather variables and how each tool works. The poster should be divided into surface and upper atmosphere conditions. It should include a picture or sketch of each instrument and a diagram or verbal description of how each instrument is used. **LS Visual**

Quiz — GENERAL

1. How may temperature changes be used to predict weather? (Sample answer: A sharp drop in temperature may signal the arrival of a cold front, which may produce precipitation.)
2. What devices do scientists use to measure wind direction and speed? (Scientists use wind vanes to determine wind direction and anemometers to measure wind speed.)
3. What kinds of information do weather balloons help scientists collect? (air pressure, temperature, humidity at different altitudes, and the direction and speed of high-altitude winds)

Close, *continued*

Answers to Section Review

1. thermometer, barometer, anemometer, and weather vane
2. Upper-level atmospheric conditions affect local and global weather patterns.
3. Answers may vary but should accurately describe radiosondes, radar, and weather satellites.
4. Meteorologists use helium-filled balloons to carry instrument packages into the upper atmosphere. Their paths can be tracked using radio signals. At high altitudes, the balloon bursts and the package parachutes back to Earth.
5. Satellites provide images and information that cannot be obtained from the ground, such as wind speed and direction within clouds, temperatures at the tops of clouds, and observations of ocean currents and wave heights.
6. Computers can be used to model the behavior of weather conditions that require complex equations. They can also store weather records for rapid retrieval and help improve weather forecasts.
7. That is the direction from which developing weather systems will come.
8. Sample answers: Air pressure would go down at the higher elevation. Air temperature would be lower, and wind speed readings would increase. In the valley, the instruments were protected from upper-level wind patterns.
9. *Weather instruments* that measure conditions in the *lower atmosphere*, such as *thermometers*, *barometers*, and *anemometers*; and in the *upper atmosphere*, such as *radar*, *satellites*, and *radiosondes*, provide weather data to scientists.

Figure 3 This satellite image captured Hurricane Wilma in 2005 as it approached Florida.

Weather Satellites

Instruments carried by weather satellites also collect important information about the atmosphere. Satellite images, such as the one shown in **Figure 3,** provide weather information for regions where observations cannot be made from the ground.

The direction and speed of the wind at the level of the clouds can be measured by examining a continuous sequence of cloud images. For night monitoring, satellite images made by using infrared energy reveal temperatures at the tops of clouds, at the surface of the land, and at the surface of the ocean. Satellite instruments can also measure marine conditions. For example, the instruments on satellites can measure the temperature and flow of ocean currents and the height of ocean waves. In addition, satellites can measure land temperatures and soil moisture conditions at remote locations on Earth.

SCILINKS.
www.scilinks.org
Topic: Weather Instruments
Code: **HQX1646**

Computers

Meteorologists use supercomputers to understand the weather. Before computers were available, solving the mathematical equations that describe the behavior of the atmosphere was very difficult, and sometimes impossible. In addition to solving many of these equations, computers can store weather data from around the world. These data can provide information that is useful in forecasting weather changes. Computers can also store weather records for quick retrieval. In the future, powerful computers may greatly improve weather forecasts and provide a much better understanding of the atmosphere.

Section 3 Review

Key Ideas

1. **Identify** four instruments that scientists use to measure lower-atmospheric conditions.
2. **Explain** why scientists are interested in weather conditions in the upper atmosphere.
3. **Describe** the instruments used to measure conditions in the upper atmosphere.
4. **Explain** how meteorologists send weather instruments into the upper atmosphere.
5. **Summarize** how satellites help meteorologists study weather.
6. **Summarize** how computers help scientists study weather.

Critical Thinking

7. **Recognizing Relationships** Wind is named according to the direction from which it blows. Why would a meteorologist need to know the direction that wind is blowing from?
8. **Making Inferences** If weather instruments were moved from a valley to the top of a hill, what changes would you expect in the data? Explain your answer.

Concept Mapping

9. Use the following terms to create a concept map: *thermometer, barometer, anemometer, radar, radio-sonde, satellite, upper atmosphere, lower atmosphere,* and *weather instruments.*

Differentiated Instruction

Alternative Assessment

Weather Riddles Have students create a booklet from construction paper in which they write and illustrate a set of riddles, each of which describes a different weather instrument. Have them exchange riddle books and try to solve each others' word puzzles. **LS Verbal/Visual**

SECTION 4

Forecasting the Weather

Key Ideas	Key Terms	Why It Matters
❯ Explain how weather stations communicate weather data. ❯ Explain how a weather map is created. ❯ Explain how computer models help meteorologists forecast weather. ❯ List three types of weather that meteorologists have attempted to control.	station model	Early warnings of severe weather can reduce damage and save lives. Understanding weather information will help you take warnings seriously.

Predicting the weather has challenged people for thousands of years. People in many early civilizations attributed control of weather conditions, such as wind, rain, and thunder, to gods. Some people attempted to forecast the weather by using the positions of the stars and the moon as the basis for their predictions.

Scientific weather forecasting began with the invention of basic weather instruments, such as the thermometer and the barometer. The invention of the telegraph in 1844 enabled meteorologists to share information about weather conditions quickly and led to the creation of national weather services.

Global Weather Monitoring

Weather observers at stations around the world report weather conditions frequently, often several times per hour. They record the barometric pressure and how it has changed, as well as the speed and direction of surface wind. They measure precipitation, temperature, and humidity. They note the type, amount, and height of cloud cover. Weather observers also record visibility and general weather conditions. Similar data are gathered continuously by automated observing systems. Each station in the system sends its data to a collection center. Weather centers around the world exchange the weather information they have collected.

The World Meteorological Organization (WMO) sponsors a program called *World Weather Watch* to promote the rapid exchange of weather information. This organization helps developing countries establish or improve their meteorological services, as shown in **Figure 1.** It also offers advice on the effect of weather on natural resources and on human activities, such as farming and transportation.

Figure 1 One major role of the World Meteorological Organization is to train professionals to use weather instruments, such as this Dobson spectrophotometer installed at Maun, Botswana.

Section 4

Focus

Overview

This section explains how global weather is monitored, how maps display data, and how computers are used. The section also provides weather safety tips.

Bellringer

Have students think about weather reports they have seen or heard. Have them write down the kinds of information they expect a complete weather forecast to include. (Sample answers: cloud coverage, temperature data, expected precipitation, wind speed, highs and lows, wind chill factor, and humidity levels) **LS Verbal**

Motivate

Discussion — GENERAL

Weather Lore Discuss with students stories and sayings from other cultures about the weather. For example, some sayings claim that the color of the evening and morning sky can be used to predict weather. Tell students that many myths and folk tales attempt to explain powerful natural forces. **LS Interpersonal**

Key Resources

Chapter Resource File
- Directed Reading BASIC
- Making Models Lab: Blowing in the Wind GENERAL

Technology
- Transparencies
  Bellringer

Teach

Using the Figure — GENERAL

Classroom Station Model Invite interested students to use the chart of meteorological symbols to create a large Classroom Station Model as part of a Weather Bulletin Board. Have students make the model with symbols that they can move around on the board. Assign students to change the classroom station model as outside weather conditions change. **LS Kinesthetic**

Discussion — BASIC

Comprehension Check Direct students' attention to the temperature data contained in the station model on this page. Ask students how they could use the current temperature and the dew point to determine the likelihood of precipitation. (Sample answer: The closer the dew-point temperature is to the air temperature, the greater the likelihood of fog, rain, or snow.) **LS Verbal**

Key Resources

Technology

- Transparencies
  108 Weather Symbols

Academic Vocabulary

communicate (kuh MYOO ni KAYT) make known; tell

station model a pattern of meteorological symbols that represents the weather at a particular observing station and that is recorded on a weather map

Weather Maps

The data that weather stations collect are transferred onto weather maps. Weather maps allow meteorologists to understand the current weather and to predict future weather events. To communicate weather data on a weather map, meteorologists use symbols and colors. These symbols and colors are understood and used by meteorologists around the world.

Weather Symbols

On some weather maps, clusters of meteorological symbols show weather conditions at the locations of weather stations. Such a cluster of symbols is called a **station model.** Common weather symbols describe cloud cover, wind speed, wind direction, and weather conditions, such as type of precipitation and storm activity. These symbols and a station model are shown in **Figure 2.** Notice that the symbols for cloud cover, wind speed, and wind direction are combined in one symbol in the station model.

Other information included in the station model are the air temperature and the dew point. The *dew point* is the temperature at which the rate of condensation equals the rate of evaporation. The dew point indicates how high the humidity of the air is.

The station model also includes the atmospheric pressure, indicated by a three-digit number in the upper right-hand corner. The digits show pressure to the nearest tenth of a millibar (mb). Therefore you would add a 9 or a 10 to the beginning of the three-digit number to get the number nearest 1,000. For example, a value of 021 would be understood as 1,002.1 mb. A value of 987 would be understood as 998.7 mb. The position of a straight line under this figure—horizontal or angled up or down—shows whether the atmospheric pressure is steady or is rising or falling.

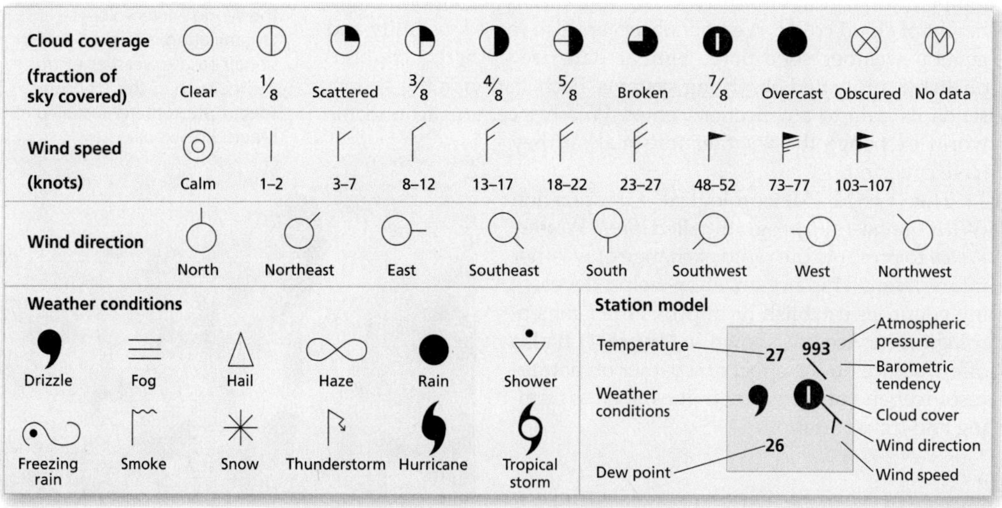

Figure 2 Meteorologists use symbols to indicate weather conditions. The station model (lower right) shows an example of conditions around a weather station.

Group Activity — GENERAL

Cloud Cover Divide a mirror into a grid by using a ruler and a wax crayon. Mark the cardinal points of the compass on the outside edges of the mirror. When the sky is partly covered with clouds, put the mirror on the ground outside, and position it with N facing north. Have groups of students count the number of squares covered by clouds and divide by the total number of squares to determine the percentage of the sky that is covered by clouds. Use the motion of the clouds across the mirror to determine upper atmospheric wind direction. **LS Visual**

Discussion — GENERAL

Barometric Pressure A change in the barometric tendency—the line angled up or down under the number that indicates pressure—generally predicts a change in the weather pattern. Ask students what a falling barometric reading would indicate. (Because warm air accompanies low-pressure systems, a drop in barometric pressure indicates that a warm front may be approaching, which may lead to precipitation.) Ask students what rising barometric pressure indicates. (High pressure is associated with colder air, which may be associated with clear weather.) **LS Verbal**

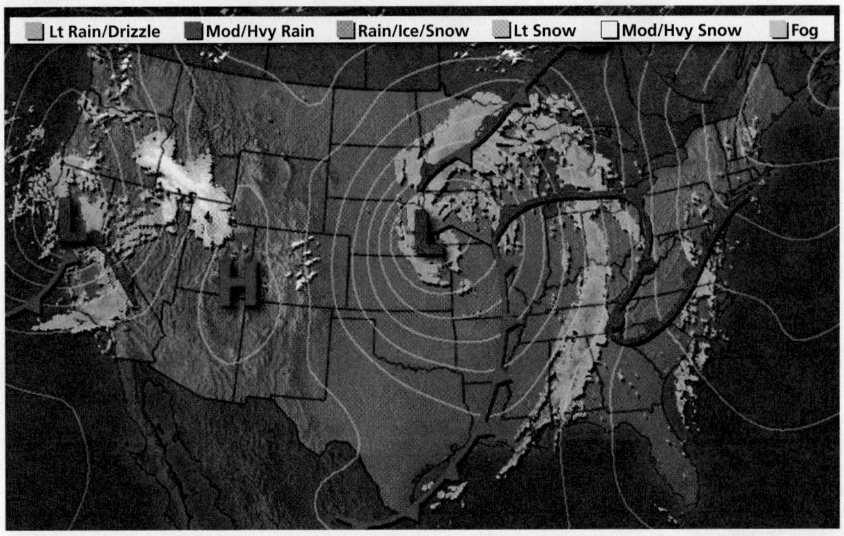

Figure 3 A typical weather map shows isobars, highs and lows, fronts, and precipitation. ***In what parts of the United States are low-pressure areas located?***

Plotting Temperature and Pressure

Scientists use lines on weather maps to connect points of equal measurement. Lines that connect points of equal temperature are called *isotherms*. Lines that connect points of equal atmospheric pressure are called *isobars*. The spacing and shape of the isobars help meteorologists interpret their observations about the speed and direction of the wind. Closely spaced isobars indicate a rapid change in pressure and high wind speeds. Widely spaced isobars generally indicate a gradual change in pressure and low wind speeds. Isobars that form circles indicate centers of high or low air pressure. Centers that are marked with an *H* represent high pressure, as you can see in **Figure 3.** Centers that are marked with an *L* represent low pressure.

Plotting Fronts and Precipitation

Most weather maps mark the locations of fronts and areas of precipitation. The weather map in **Figure 3** shows examples of a warm front, a cold front, an occluded front, and a stationary front. Fronts are identified by sharp changes in wind speed and direction, temperature, or humidity.

Areas of precipitation are commonly marked with colors or symbols. Different forms of precipitation are represented by different colors or symbols. For example, the weather map in **Figure 3** indicates light rain by using light green, and snow by using gray and white. Some weather maps use colors to represent different amounts of precipitation so the amounts of precipitation that fall in different areas can be compared.

Reading Check **How do meteorologists mark precipitation on a weather map?**

SCILINKS.
www.scilinks.org
Topic: Weather Maps
Code: **HQX1647**
Topic: Weather Forecasting
Code: **HQX1645**

Using the Figure — GENERAL

Isobars Explain that weather maps with isobars allow us to identify low- and high-pressure areas. Isobars are typically spaced at intervals of 4 millibars (mb) apart. Ask how this pressure data helps forecast the weather. (Sample answer: High-pressure regions are commonly associated with dry weather, and low-pressure centers bring precipitation.) Ask students to identify the precipitation pattern associated with the low in the midwestern part of the United States. (light rain and drizzle) Answer to caption question: There are low-pressure areas centered over eastern Nebraska and northern California. **LS Visual**

Discussion — BASIC

Isotherms Isotherms connect areas of equal temperature and are typically spaced at intervals of 2 °C apart. Ask students what key weather characteristic maps with isotherms would help to locate. (Sample answer: where large air masses with similar weather conditions are, and how quickly temperature changes can be expected) **LS Verbal**

Answer to Reading Check

Areas of precipitation are marked by using colors or symbols.

Career

Meteorologist Meteorology is the science of the atmosphere. Meteorologists work in fields such as atmospheric research, weather forecasting, and classroom teaching. They study pollution, the behavior of tornadoes and hurricanes, and global climate change, among many other weather phenomena. Their tools range from basic weather instruments to research aircraft and satellites with remote-sensing capabilities. A career in meteorology requires a bachelor's degree or higher, including courses in chemistry, physics, mathematics, and other fields.

Key Resources

Technology
- Transparencies
  109 Weather Map of the United States

Activity — GENERAL

Local Weather Maps Have students bring in weather maps from local newspapers for two or more days. Tell students to make a list of the symbols they find. Explain that meteorologists around the globe use the same symbols. Ask students to identify symbols for cold and warm fronts. (cold fronts: triangles connected by a line representing the front boundary; warm fronts: half circles connected by a boundary line) Have students compare the previous day's weather map with the current one to see if the forecast was accurate. **LS Verbal**

Differentiated Instruction

Basic Learners

Station Models Obtain a local weather report. Remove the weather map or graphics. Have students create a station model to record the weather data. Have them include sky conditions, wind direction and speed, temperature, dew point, barometric pressure and the pressure tendency, precipitation, and any other recorded weather conditions. **LS Visual**

Teach, *continued*

Literature Connection GENERAL

The Perfect Storm The storm described in Sebastian Junger's best-selling book *The Perfect Storm* resulted from a collision between a cold high-pressure system from Canada; a low-pressure system moving east; and the warm, moist air from a dying hurricane. Share excerpts from this exciting narrative with the class, or invite interested students to read the book and make a written or oral presentation. LS **Verbal**

Quick Lab

Skills Acquired
- Experimenting
- Measuring
- Observing
- Analyzing

Materials
- Thermometer
- Magnetic compass

Teacher's Notes: You may have students monitor other conditions such as barometric pressure. They can use instruments they have already made or commercial instruments you have access to. You can have them use the Beaufort wind scale to estimate wind speed.

Answers to Analysis
1. Answers will vary depending on conditions.
2. Answers may vary but should use recognized weather symbols.

Figure 4 With the help of Doppler radar, meteorologists can track severe storms from radar stations, such as this one in Kansas.

Quick Lab 10 min

Gathering Weather Data

Procedure

1. Select an area that is outside your school building, in the shade and away from buildings and pavement.
2. Use a **thermometer** to measure the air temperature.
3. Estimate the percentage of cloud cover.
4. Estimate the wind speed. Use a **magnetic compass** to estimate the wind direction.

Analysis

1. What are the current weather conditions outside your school?
2. Using the data you collected, create a station model that describes the weather at your school.

Weather Forecasts

To forecast the weather, meteorologists use computers to plot the intensity and path of weather systems on maps. Meteorologists then study the most recent weather map and compare it with maps from previous hours. This comparison allows them to follow the progress of large weather systems. By following the progress of weather systems, meteorologists can forecast the weather.

Weather Data

Doppler radar, shown in **Figure 4,** and satellite images supply important information, such as intensity of precipitation. Meteorologists input these data into computers to create weather models. Computer models can show the possible weather conditions for several days. However, meteorologists must carefully interpret these models because computer predictions are based on generalized descriptions.

Some computer models may be better at predicting precipitation for a particular area, while other computer models may be better at predicting temperature and pressure. Comparing models helps meteorologists better predict weather. If weather information on two or more models is similar, a meteorologist will be more confident about a weather prediction. By using all the weather data available, meteorologists can issue an accurate forecast of the weather.

Temperature, wind direction, wind speed, cloudiness, and precipitation can usually be forecast accurately. But it is often difficult to predict precisely the time when precipitation will occur or the exact amount. By using computers, scientists can manipulate data on temperature and pressure to simulate errors in measuring these data. Forecasts are then compared to see if slight data changes cause substantial differences in forecasts. From what they learn, meteorologists can make more accurate forecasts.

Reading Check **Why do meteorologists compare models?**

Answer to Reading Check
Meteorologists compare computer models because different models are better at predicting different weather variables. If information from two or more models matches, scientists can be more confident of their predictions.

Differentiated Instruction

Advanced Learners

Weather Station Invite groups of interested students to build a class weather station that consists of homemade weather instruments. Store equipment out of direct sunlight. Encourage students to make simple observational equipment such as a rain gauge or a weather vane. Assign students to keep a weekly chart of weather observations, and have them graph the data collected. After reviewing their data, have them forecast the weather and then compare their predictions with the actual weather. LS **Kinesthetic/Logical**

Types of Forecasts

Meteorologists make four types of forecasts. *Nowcasts* mainly use radar and enable forecasters to focus on timing precipitation and tracking severe weather. *Daily forecasts* predict weather conditions for a 48-h period. *Extended forecasts* look ahead 3 to 5 days. *Medium-range forecasts* look ahead 3 to 7 days. *Long-range forecasts* look ahead at least 7 days and may cover monthly and seasonal periods.

Accurate weather forecasts can be made for 0 to 5 days. However, accuracy decreases with each day. Extended forecasts are made by computer analysis of slowly changing large-scale movements of air. These changes help meteorologists predict the general weather pattern. For example, the changes indicate if temperature will be warmer or cooler than normal or if conditions will be dry or wet.

READING TOOLBOX

Prefixes, Suffixes, and Root Words
The word *forecast* is part of several italicized terms on this page. It contains the prefix *fore-* and the root word *cast*. Use print or online sources to find the meanings of these word parts, and add the meanings to the table you started at the beginning of the chapter.

Severe Weather Watches and Warnings

One main goal of meteorology is to reduce the amount of destruction caused by severe weather by forecasting severe weather early. When meteorologists forecast severe weather, they issue warnings and watches. A *watch* is issued when the conditions are ideal for severe weather. A *warning* is given when severe weather has been spotted (thunderstorms or tornadoes) or is expected within 24 h (snowstorms or hurricanes). Meteorologists use these alerts to provide people in areas facing severe weather with instructions on how to be safer during the event. **Table 1** lists some safety tips to follow for different types of severe weather.

Table 1 Severe Weather Safety Tips

Type of weather	How to prepare	Safety during the event
Thunderstorm	Have a storm preparedness kit that includes a portable radio, fresh batteries, flashlights, rain gear, blankets, bottled water, canned food, and medicines.	Listen to weather updates. Stay or go indoors. Avoid electrical appliances, running water, metal pipes, and phone lines. If outside, avoid tall objects, stay away from bodies of water, and get into a car, if possible.
Tornado	Have a storm preparedness kit as described above. Plan and practice a safety route.	Listen to weather updates. Stay or go indoors. Go to a basement, storm cellar, or small, inner room, closet, or hallway that has no windows. Stay away from areas that are likely to have flying debris or other dangers. If outside, lie in a low-lying area. Protect your head and neck.
Hurricane	Have a storm preparedness kit as described above. Secure loose objects, doors, and windows. Plan and practice an evacuation route.	Listen to weather updates. Be prepared to follow instructions and planned evacuation routes. Stay indoors and away from areas that are likely to have flying debris or other dangers.
Blizzard	Have a storm preparedness kit as described above. Make sure that you have a way to make heat safely, in the event of power outages.	Listen to weather updates. Stay or go indoors. Dress warmly. Avoid walking or driving in icy conditions.

READING TOOLBOX

Prefixes, Suffixes, and Root Words For the term *forecast*, the root word *cast* means to give forth or project, to calculate; the prefix *fore* means before; there is no suffix.

Close

Reteaching — BASIC

Matching Game Have pairs of students make drawings of meteorological symbols on index cards with an identifying label. The cards are shuffled and placed face down. Students take turns turning over cards and trying to match the weather symbols. The object of the game is to find all the matching pairs of cards. As they play, students will familiarize themselves with the weather symbols. **LS Kinesthetic**

Quiz — GENERAL

1. Which organization helps developing countries improve their weather data collection? (the World Meteorological Organization)
2. How do meteorologists present a cluster of weather information from one location on weather maps? (They use a station model to record weather data.)
3. What are the circles on weather maps formed by isobars? (low- or high-pressure areas)
4. What safety precautions should you take during thunderstorms? (Avoid tall objects such as trees and electrical wiring or metals; remain indoors; and listen for updates.)
5. How reliable are extended weather forecasts? (Weather forecasting requires the correlation of so many variables that accuracy declines with each added day.)

Group Activity — GENERAL

Weather Safety Project Divide the class into groups, and assign each group a different type of weather. Have students explore ways of remaining safe during weather emergencies. Some students could do library or Internet research to identify the hazards associated with the assigned weather condition. Another student could interview local officials regarding your community's disaster plan. Other students could develop posters to heighten awareness of safety guidelines. Groups could plan and conduct safety drills. **LS Interpersonal** Co-op Learning

Debate — ADVANCED

Weather Modification Have interested students research and debate the ethical and environmental issues surrounding weather modification experiments. For example, could cloud seeding potentially cause harm by changing the direction of hurricane wind patterns, cause unexpected flooding, or even aggravate drought conditions if not done properly? Also, what are the potential long-term effects on the environment? You may wish to assign students to prepare arguments for or against the use of weather modification practices. **LS Verbal/Logical**

Close, *continued*

Answers to Section Review

1. Weather stations record precipitation, temperature, humidity, changes in air pressure, wind speed and direction, cloud cover, and visibility. Some functions are automated. Weather data collected is exchanged all over the world.
2. The data collected at local weather stations are transferred to weather maps in the form of meteorological symbols. Clusters are plotted around a station model.
3. Closely spaced isobars would indicate strong winds.
4. Answer should include 6 of the following: cloud cover, wind speed, wind direction, temperature, barometric pressure, dew point, pressure tendency
5. Comparison of new weather data with old weather maps allows meteorologists to follow changing weather systems and forecast future conditions.
6. Meteorologists input data into computers to create weather models and accurately predict temperature, wind direction, wind speed, and precipitation for a particular area. Computers allow them to manipulate the data, but they must make use of experience to interpret the results and make their forecasts.
7. precipitation levels, storm intensity or wind strength, and lightning
8. Cloud seeding may reduce the amount of moisture in air to prevent hailstones from forming.

Figure 5 An outdoor ultra-high-voltage laboratory generates artificial lightning to test its effects on electrical utility equipment.

Controlling the Weather

Some meteorologists are investigating methods of controlling rain, hail, and lightning. Currently, the most researched method for producing rain has been *cloud seeding*. In this process, particles are added to clouds to cause the clouds to precipitate. Cloud seeding can also be used to prevent more-severe precipitation. Scientists in Russia have used cloud seeding, with some success, on potential hail clouds by causing rain, rather than hail, to fall.

Hurricane Control

Hurricanes have also been seeded with freezing nuclei in an effort to reduce their intensity. During Project Stormfury, which took place from 1962 to 1983, four hurricanes were seeded, and the project had mixed results. Scientists have, for the most part, abandoned storm and hurricane control because it is not an attainable goal with existing technology. They do, however, continue to seed clouds to cause precipitation.

Lightning Control

Attempts have also been made to control lightning. Seeding of potential lightning storms with silver-iodide nuclei has seemed to modify the occurrence of lightning. However, no conclusive results have been obtained. Researchers have generated artificial lightning at research facilities to learn more about lightning and how it affects objects it strikes. An example of one of these facilities is shown in **Figure 5.**

Section 4 Review

Key Ideas

1. **Summarize** how global weather is monitored.
2. **Explain** how a weather map is made.
3. **Explain** which would show stronger winds: widely spaced isobars or closely spaced isobars.
4. **List** six different pieces of information that you can obtain from a station model.
5. **Explain** why meteorologists compare new weather maps with weather maps that are 24 h old.
6. **Describe** how computer models help meteorologists forecast weather.
7. **List** three types of weather that meteorologists have tried to control.

Critical Thinking

8. **Making Inferences** Why might cloud seeding reduce the amount of hail from a storm?
9. **Making Reasoned Judgment** Seeding hurricanes may or may not yield positive results. Each attempt costs a lot of money. If you were in charge of deciding whether to seed a potentially dangerous hurricane, what factors would you consider when deciding what to do? Explain your answer.

Concept Mapping

10. Use the following terms to create a concept map: *isobar, isotherm, weather map, forecast, watch, warning, station model,* and *meteorological symbol.*

9. Answers may vary, but should indicate well-reasoned solutions based upon risks, benefits, and costs to individuals, government, and businesses.
10. Meteorologists create *weather maps* containing *isobars*, *isotherms*, and *station models*, which are clusters of *meteorological symbols*, in order to *forecast* severe weather and issue weather *warnings* and *watches*.

Differentiated Instruction

Alternative Assessment

Weather Forecast Have interested students play the role of a meteorologist and present the class with a weather forecast. Encourage students to use real weather data in their forecast, perhaps that they have interpreted themselves to make predictions. Students should include a daily forecast and an extended forecast in their presentation.

Why It Matters

When Lightning Strikes!

HISTORY IN SCIENCE

For thousands of years, most people believed that lightning was caused by the activities of various gods. American inventor Benjamin Franklin was the first person to propose that lightning was actually a giant electrical spark. In the 1750s, Franklin conducted several famous experiments, which involved flying kites in thunderstorms, to test his hypothesis.

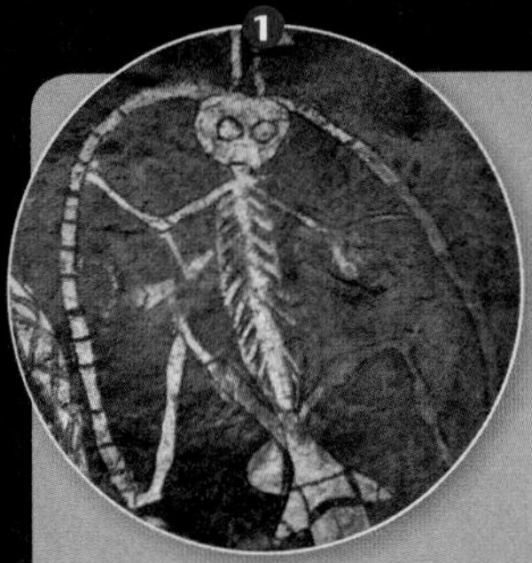

1. In the mythology of the Aboriginals of northern Australia, Namarrgon the Lightning Man is a Creation Ancestor. The band from Namarrgon's head to his ankles represents the lightning he creates. **2.** Early sailors noticed a bluish glow, which they called St. Elmo's Fire, coming from the masts on their boats. The glow appeared before or after lightning storms. **3.** Franklin invented the first U.S. lightning rod. Placed on tall buildings, lightning rods channel electricity into the ground, keeping the building and the people inside safe.

YOUR TURN

UNDERSTANDING CONCEPTS
Who was the first person to relate lightning to electricity?

ONLINE RESEARCH
What is St. Elmo's Fire, and what causes it to form?

Why It Matters

When Lightning Strikes! Prior to Benjamin Franklin's experiments and western society's scientific explanations of lightning and electricity, many other cultures around the world developed mythologies about lightning and thunder. In Scandinavian mythology, Thor was the god of thunder and lightning. In fact, the word "thunder" is derived from the name "Thor." In Greek and Roman mythology, the thunderbolt is the weapon that the Cyclops gave to the god Zeus (Greek) and Jupiter (Roman).

St. Elmo's Fire is a bluish glow caused by the ionization of air particles. It typically appears at the end of pointed objects when there is a difference in charge between the air and the ground, such as during thunderstorms. Since it appears around points, it was most often seen at the ends of ships' masts. Ancient Greek sailors observed it, as did many famous explorers such as Magellan and Columbus. St. Elmo's Fire is still seen today, often on the tips of airplane wings.

Answer to Your Turn

Understanding Concepts Benjamin Franklin

Online Research St. Elmo's Fire is caused when air molecules at the end of a metal rod are charged. These molecules discharge and give off a faint glow of light that can be seen at night. When clouds that are charged are overhead, St. Elmo's Fire can be seen at the top of a ship's mast at night.

Skills Practice Lab

Time Required
one 45-minute class period

Lab Ratings
EASY → HARD

Teacher Preparation 1
Student Setup 1
Concept Level 3
Cleanup 1

Skills Acquired
- Collecting Data
- Organizing and Analyzing Data
- Identifying and Recognizing Patterns
- Interpreting
- Communicating

Scientific Methods
In this lab, students will
- Make Observations
- Analyze Results
- Draw Conclusions

Materials
Students can either do this investigation alone or with a partner. Students should make an enlarged photocopy of the weather map from the Reference Tables section of the Appendix.

Tips and Tricks
To read this weather map, students must be familiar with the meanings of the map symbols.

Skills Practice Lab

45 min

What You'll Do
- **Construct** a pressure and temperature map.
- **Interpret** a weather map.
- **Explain** how weather patterns are related to pressure systems.

What You'll Need
paper
pencil
pencils, red and blue

Weather Map Interpretation

Weather maps use various map symbols and lines to illustrate the weather conditions in an area at a given time. In this lab, you will study the symbols used on a weather map to gain an understanding of the relationships between temperature, pressure, and winds.

Procedure

1. Make a copy of the weather map on the following page. You may want to copy a larger version of this map, which can be found in Appendix E. You will use the map symbols on the same page of the Appendix to interpret the weather map. The number on the right of each station on the map represents atmospheric pressure. The number on the left represents temperature.
2. On your copy of the weather map, find stations that have a temperature of 10.0 °C. Use a red pencil to draw a light line through these stations. If two adjacent stations have temperatures above and below 10 °C, there is an estimated point between them that is 10.0 °C. Draw a line through these estimated points to connect the stations that have temperatures of 10.0 °C with an isotherm. Label the isotherm 10 °C.
3. Using the same method as in step 2, draw isotherms for every two degrees of temperature. Examples are isotherms of 12.0 °C, 14.0 °C, and 16.0 °C. Label each isotherm with the temperature it represents.

Step 2

4. Find a station that has a barometric pressure of 1,001.2 mb (millibars), marked 012. Use a blue pencil, and follow the same method that you used in step 2 to create a 1,001.2 mb isobar.

5. Using the same method as in step 3, lightly draw isobars for every few millibars of pressure. Examples are isobars of 1,000.6 mb, 1,000.4 mb, and 994 mb. Label each isobar with the pressure it represents.

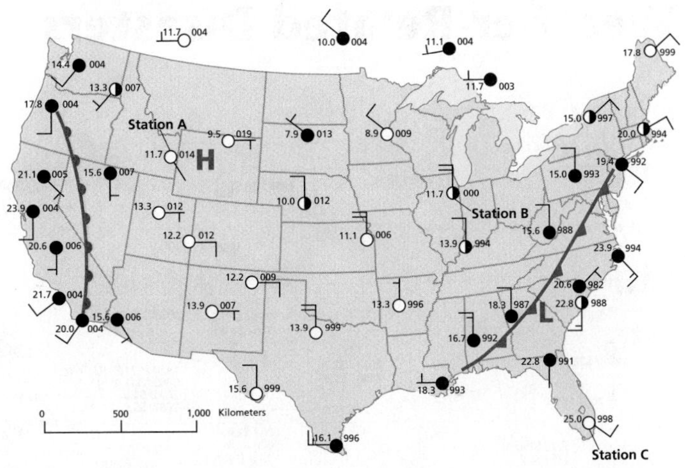

Analysis

1. **Identifying Trends** What is the lowest temperature for which you have drawn an isotherm? What is the highest temperature for which you have drawn an isotherm? Is either isotherm a closed loop? If so, which one?
2. **Making Inferences** Is the air mass that is identified by the closed isotherm a cold air mass or a warm air mass? Explain your answer.
3. **Analyzing Data** Is there a shift in wind direction associated with either front shown on your map? Describe the shift.
4. **Identifying Trends** What is the value of the lowest-pressure isobar that you drew? What is the value of the highest-pressure isobar that you drew? Is either isobar a closed loop? If so, which one?
5. **Drawing Conclusions** At the time that the map represents, were there any areas of low pressure? Were there any areas of high pressure? Identify these areas. What weather conditions would you expect to find in these areas?

Extension

Making Predictions Predict the weather conditions at Station A 24 h after the observations for your map were made. Record your predictions in a table with columns for pressure, wind direction, wind speed, temperature, and sky condition. Also, make and record predictions for Station B and Station C.

Answers to Analysis

1. Accept all reasonable answers. The lowest temperature isotherm is 10.0 °C and the highest temperature isotherm is 16.0 °C. The lowest isotherm was a closed loop.
2. cold; Low temperatures are associated with cold air masses.
3. yes; The winds ahead of the cold front shift from a south-southeasterly direction to a northerly direction as the front passes, but the winds ahead of the warm front show little or no shift in direction.
4. Accept all reasonable answers. The lowest pressure isobar is 998.8 mb. The highest pressure isobar is 1001.2 mb. Both form closed loops.
5. There is a high-pressure area over Wyoming and a low-pressure area over the Carolinas. The high-pressure area is associated with clear weather. Rain, clouds, rapid temperature changes, and wind shifts occur in low-pressure areas.

Answer to Extension

Answers may vary. Accept all reasonable predictions based on the weather data.

Maps in Action

Weather-Related Disasters

Answers to the Map Skills Activity

1. eleven
2. floods
3. western U.S.: primarily fires and floods; eastern U.S.: mixture of tropical storms, hurricanes, ice and snow; The convergence of 2 polar and 2 maritime air masses over the eastern U.S. and the general west to east movement of weather systems may help account for the difference.
4. Icy conditions are not common in southern states so they are not prepared with the proper equipment to deal with them.
5. The Atlantic Ocean and Gulf of Mexico are the sources of maritime tropical air masses that form hurricanes.
6. Snow and ice that fall in the winter melt to form water that may cause flooding. If more ice and snow fell than normal, the spring meltwaters would be higher than normal as well.
7. Lightning strikes from electrical storms may cause brush fires that destroy acres of forested land.

MAPS in Action

Weather-Related Disasters

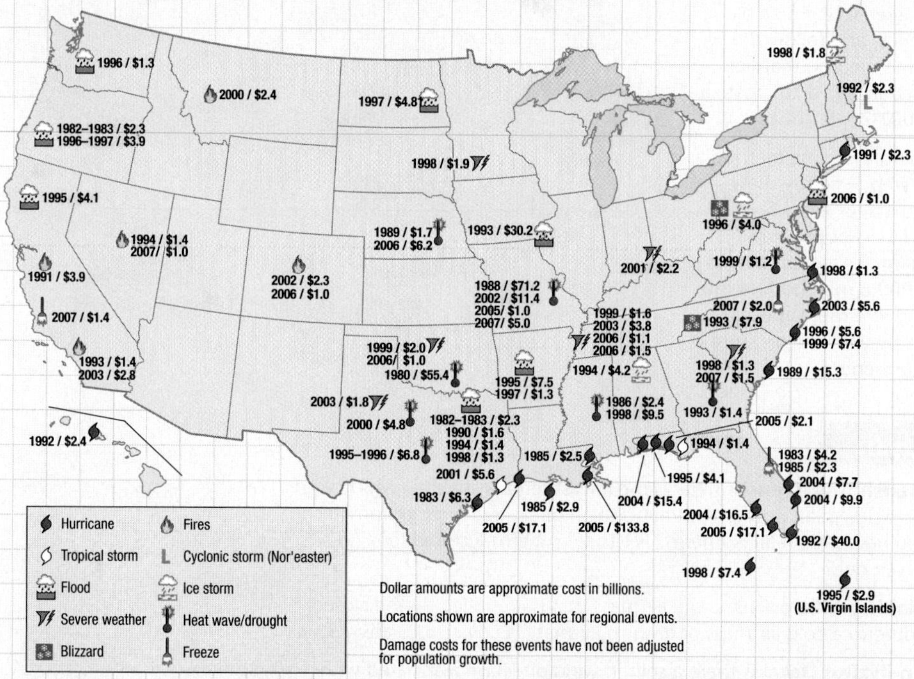

Map Skills Activity

This map shows the types and locations of weather disasters that caused at least $1 billion in damage in the United States. Use the map to answer the questions below.

1. **Using a Key** According to the map, how many severe weather events caused more than $10 billion in damage?
2. **Analyzing Data** Which type of weather disaster is more common: floods or fires?
3. **Making Comparisons** How do the types of disasters that happen in the western United States differ from the types of disasters that happen in the eastern United States? Explain why this difference exists.
4. **Inferring Relationships** Why might an ice storm in Alabama cause more damage than an ice storm in Maine?
5. **Identifying Trends** Almost all hurricane damage during this period happened along the coasts of the Atlantic Ocean and the Gulf of Mexico. Explain why.
6. **Analyzing Relationships** In 1996, a blizzard and floods caused $4.0 billion in damage in Ohio, Pennsylvania, and West Virginia. How might these events be related? Explain your answer.
7. **Analyzing Processes** Explain why fires are included in this map of weather-related disasters.

Key Resources

Technology

- Transparencies
  110 Weather-Related Disasters

Chapter 21 Summary

THINK central
SUPER SUMMARY
Keyword: HQXWTHS

Key Ideas | **Key Terms**

Section 1

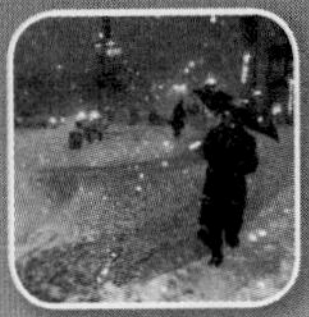

Air Masses

- An air mass forms when air remains stationary or moves slowly over a uniform region, taking on the characteristic temperature and humidity of that region.
- The four main types of air masses are polar, tropical, continental, and maritime.
- Air masses affect the weather by bringing air that is warm or cold, and dry or moist, to a region. Tropical air masses bring mild weather in the winter, and polar air masses bring cool weather in the summer.

Key Terms:
air mass, p. 571

Section 2

Fronts

- Cold fronts usually produce short-lived storms. Warm fronts usually produce precipitation over a large area.
- A midlatitude cyclone forms along a cold or stationary front, in which rotating wind moves toward a low-pressure center.
- Thunderstorms and tornadoes are caused by the interaction of air masses that have different properties. Hurricanes develop when warm, moist air over the ocean rises rapidly.

Key Terms:
cold front, p. 575
warm front, p. 576
stationary front, p. 576
occluded front, p. 576
midlatitude cyclone, p. 576
thunderstorm, p. 578
hurricane, p. 579
tornado, p. 582

Section 3

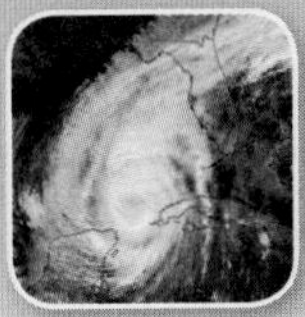

Weather Instruments

- Thermometers, barometers, anemometers, and wind vanes measure lower-atmospheric weather conditions.
- Radiosondes, radar, and satellite equipment measure upper-atmospheric weather conditions.
- Computers are used to solve complicated mathematical equations that describe weather.

Key Terms:
thermometer, p. 583
barometer, p. 584
anemometer, p. 584
wind vane, p. 584
radiosonde, p. 585
radar, p. 585

Section 4

Forecasting the Weather

- Each weather station sends data to a collection center.
- Meteorologists prepare weather maps that are based on information from weather stations around the world.
- Computer models predict weather conditions for several days.
- Meteorologists have attempted to control rain, hurricanes, and lightning with only limited success.

Key Terms:
station model, p. 588

Chapter Summary

Using THINK central Resources

Super Summary

Have students connect the major concepts in this chapter through an interactive Super Summary. Visit www.thinkcentral.com and type in the keyword **HQXWTHS** to access the Super Summary for this chapter.

Activity — GENERAL

Weatherwise Museum Divide the class into working groups of 3 or 4 students. Have each group create models, diagrams, demonstrations, and hands-on activities that will help visitors to a weather museum understand the following ideas: (1) how air masses form and which air masses affect weather in North America,
(2) how interactions between weather fronts cause cyclones, storms, and other severe weather systems, and
(3) how scientists forecast the weather and warn people about hazardous atmospheric conditions. Students can use any working models that they have made of weather instruments. Suggest that students label the parts of the exhibits and displays they create, and provide simple instructions for any activities that they set up. Remind them to think about safety precautions.
LS Kinesthetic Co-op Learning

Chapter Review

Assignment Guide	
Section	**Questions**
1	2, 11, 24, 33
2	3, 5, 8, 12–16, 19–21, 25, 31, 32, 34–36
3	6, 7, 9, 17, 23, 28, 30
4	4, 10, 18, 22, 27
2 and 4	26
1–3	29
1–4	1

1. Sample answer: I think these word parts were used so often in this chapter because they have to do with natural phenomena (thermé, anemos), with measuring (da-, metron, baros), with the shapes or attitude of things (kyklos, anti), and with places (mare). All of these things have to do with the weather.

Using Key Terms

2–9. Answers may vary but should show that students understand the definitions of and differences between the key terms.

Understanding Key Ideas

10. c
11. a
12. a
13. b
14. c
15. b
16. c
17. d
18. a

Chapter 21 Review

1. **Prefixes, Suffixes, and Root Words** Look over the table of prefixes, suffixes, and root words that you made while reading this chapter. Identify the word parts that were used most often. Why were these word parts used so often in this chapter? READING TOOLBOX

USING KEY TERMS

Use each of the following terms in a separate sentence.

2. *air mass*
3. *stationary front*
4. *station model*

For each pair of terms, explain how the meanings of the terms differ.

5. *midlatitude cyclone* and *hurricane*
6. *wind vane* and *anemometer*
7. *radiosonde* and *radar*
8. *cold front* and *warm front*
9. *thermometer* and *barometer*

UNDERSTANDING KEY IDEAS

10. Which of the following is information you would not find in a station model?
a. precipitation **c.** front
b. cloud cover **d.** wind speed
11. Continental polar Canadian air masses generally move
a. southeasterly. **c.** northeasterly.
b. northerly. **d.** westerly.
12. The type of front that forms when two air masses move parallel to the front between them is called
a. stationary. **c.** polar.
b. occluded. **d.** warm.
13. The type of front that forms when warm air is completely lifted off the ground by cold air is called
a. cold. **c.** polar.
b. occluded. **d.** warm.
14. The eye of a hurricane is a region of
a. hailstorms. **c.** calm, clear air.
b. torrential rainfall. **d.** strong winds.
15. The wind of a midlatitude cyclone blows in a circular path around a
a. front.
b. low-pressure center.
c. high-pressure center.
d. jet stream.
16. In the mature stage of a thunderstorm, a cumulus cloud grows until it becomes a
a. stratocumulus cloud.
b. altocumulus cloud.
c. cumulonimbus cloud.
d. cirrocumulus cloud.
17. An instrument package attached to a weather balloon is
a. an anemometer. **c.** a thermograph.
b. a wind vane. **d.** a radiosonde.
18. The lines that connect points of equal atmospheric pressure on a weather map are called
a. isobars. **c.** highs.
b. isotherms. **d.** lows.

SHORT ANSWER

19. Describe the weather before and after an occluded front.
20. What causes lightning?
21. What is the most likely location for hurricane development? Explain your answer.
22. How could a meteorologist use a station model to determine whether a cold front is approaching?
23. Identify the wind direction of wind given as 315°. What direction would a wind vane point in this case?
24. Identify the type of air mass that is most likely responsible if the air in your area is warm and dry. What letters designate this air mass?

Short Answer

19. Before the occluded front forms, a fast moving cold front overtakes a warm front. These conditions often produce cumulonimbus clouds and a line of heavy thunderstorms called a *squall line*. After the occluded front forms, the storm reaches its highest intensity. Then, the system loses its energy and dissipates within 24 hours.
20. Lightning is caused by electrical differences within clouds or between the ground and a cloud.
21. Hurricanes develop over warm tropical oceans away from the equator during intense tropical storms. Latent heat released during the formation of storm clouds increases the force of the rising air, generating powerful rotating winds.
22. The barometric tendency indicates whether pressure is rising or falling. Falling pressure may indicate the approach of a front. The station models could be compared to nearby and previous ones to identify patterns in pressure, temperature, wind direction, and wind speed.
23. northwest; The wind vane would point to the northwest.
24. continental tropical air mass (cT)

CRITICAL THINKING

25. Making Predictions Suppose that people on Vancouver Island, off the west coast of Canada, hear reports of a midlatitude cyclone in the Gulf of Alaska. Is it likely that this midlatitude cyclone will reach their area? Explain why.

26. Making Inferences Suppose that a hurricane is passing over a Caribbean island. Suddenly, the rain and wind stop and the air becomes calm and clear. Can a person living on that island safely go outside? Explain your answer.

27. Applying Ideas Is it safe to be in an automobile during a tornado? Explain your answer.

28. Making Inferences An air traffic controller is monitoring nearby airplanes by radar. The controller warns an incoming pilot of a storm that is a few miles away. How did radar help the controller detect the storm?

CONCEPT MAPPING

29. Use the following terms to create a concept map: *air mass, front, warm front, cold front, cyclone, thunderstorm, thermometer, hurricane, barometer,* and *anemometer.*

MATH SKILLS

Math Skills

30. Making Calculations The temperature at a weather station is given as 47°F. Using the equation °C = 5/9 × (°F − 32), find the temperature in degrees Celsius.

31. Making Calculations An average of 124 tornadoes occur each year in Texas. If this is equivalent to 4.7 tornadoes per 10,000 square miles, what is the area of Texas in square miles?

WRITING SKILLS

32. Creative Writing Imagine that you are traveling with friends through the desert in the southwestern United States and a thunderstorm occurs. You tell your friends about the type of front that may have brought the storm. Describe what the stages might look like by types of clouds formed, types of precipitation, and sky color.

33. Communicating Main Ideas Explain how cP and mT air masses travel across the United States, and explain why this information helps meteorologists make forecasts.

INTERPRETING GRAPHICS

The graph below shows the average number of tornadoes that generally occur at different times of day. Use this graph to answer the questions that follow.

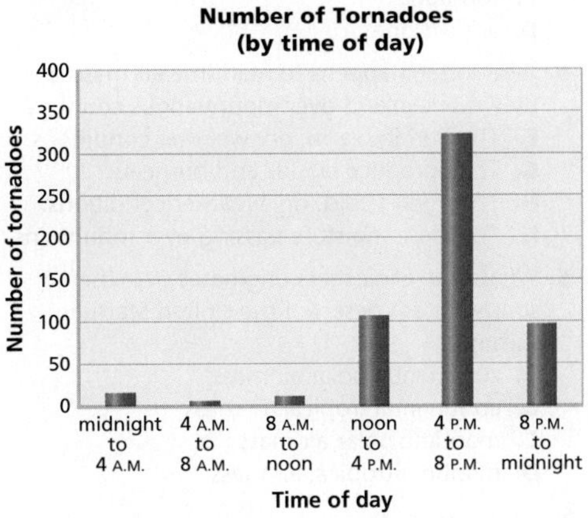

34. During which time of day do the least tornadoes occur?

35. Would students be more likely to experience a tornado while they are at school or while they are at home?

36. During which time of day do most tornadoes occur? Why would most tornadoes occur at this time of day?

Chapter Review

Critical Thinking

25. Sample answer: Maritime polar air masses form over the North Pacific Ocean. They move southeasterly and do bring rain and snow to the Pacific coast. In all probability, if a midlatitude cyclone forms over the Gulf of Alaska and travels at about 45 km/h, much of the storm's energy will probably dissipate before the storm reaches Vancouver Island (over 1,800 km away).

26. Sample answer: The center of a hurricane is a region of calm air. The eye of the storm might be passing directly overhead. The hurricane could be up to 700 km in diameter and its violent winds could easily pick up again. The person should remain indoors, away from flying debris.

27. Sample answer: no; An automobile would not provide adequate protection from the violent winds. It is best to remain indoors in a basement or underground shelter away from flying debris or from windows that could break.

28. The air traffic controller could see the approaching thunderstorms on the radar screen and estimate how far away they were from the airplanes he was monitoring.

Concept Mapping

29. Answers may vary but should include all of the terms listed. Sample answers appear at the end of this unit on p. 631B.

Math Skills

30. °C = 5/9 × (°F − 32) = 5/9 × (47 °F − 32) = 5/9 × 15° = 75/9 = 8.3 °C

31. area of Texas = 124 ÷ 4.7 = 26 × 10,000 mi^2 = 260,000 mi^2

Writing Skills

32. Answers may vary. Accept all reasonable answers. Answers should include the fact that maritime tropical air masses bring moderate precipitation to the southwestern desert.

33. Answers may vary. Accept all reasonable answers. Answers should include the facts that air masses bring the weather of the source region and that the general direction of movement of the air masses is known.

Interpreting Graphics

34. between 4 A.M. and 8 A.M.

35. at home; More tornadoes occur during the period from 4 P.M. to 8 A.M. than between 8 A.M. and 4 P.M.

36. Most tornadoes occur between 4 P.M. and 8 P.M. because daily temperatures tend to peak during mid-afternoon hours, which is necessary for the development of the strong updrafts that produce destructive wind patterns.

Estimated Time

To give students practice under more realistic testing conditions, allow them 30 minutes to answer all of the questions in this practice test.

Test Doctor

Question 2 Answer I is correct. Answer F is incorrect because in an occluded front, warm air is lifted up and cut off by cold air. Answer G is incorrect because polar fronts form at the boundary between a dome of cold air and warm air. Answer H is incorrect because in a warm front, warm air rises over cool air.

Question 4 Answer I is correct. Air masses that rise over mountains often lose moisture through precipitation. Answers F and H are incorrect because most air masses bring weather from their source region. Maritime air masses are most likely to bring wet conditions because they form over water. Answer G is incorrect. Though maritime air masses may spawn hurricanes, the formation of these storms is not triggered by the air mass moving over mountainous terrain.

Question 11 Answer I is correct. The symbols for cloud cover, wind direction, and wind speed are combined in one symbol. The cloud cover circle on the station model, which is indicated by the letter A, is mostly darkened to show an overcast sky. This symbol shows that 70% to 80% of the sky is covered. The temperature, shown by letter B, is 35°C; the dew point, shown by letter C, is 34°C. Letter D shows the barometric reading, which is 999.8 mb. The wind barb, which is indicated by the letter E, points in the direction the wind is coming from. In this case, the wind is coming from the south.

Question 14 Full-credit answers should include the following points:
- as the cups on the anemometer catch the wind, the device begins to rotate
- the speed of this rotation, usually given in revolutions per minute, and the circumference of the circle made by the cups are used to calculate wind speed
- rudimentary devices rely on the user to count the revolutions per minute of the device and to perform the necessary math to determine the wind speed
- in modern computerized devices, a number of factors may be considered to obtain the most accurate measurement possible. These factors include the circumference of the device, friction of the air, and drag

Chapter 21 Standardized Test Prep

Understanding Concepts

Directions (1–5): For each question, write on a separate sheet of paper the letter of the correct answer.

1. What tool do meteorologists use to analyze particle movements within storms?
A. an anemometer
B. a radiosonde
C. doppler radar
D. satellite imaging

2. What kind of front forms when two air masses move parallel to the boundary located between them?
F. an occluded front
G. a polar front
H. a warm front
I. a stationary front

3. Which of the following weather systems commonly forms over warm tropical oceans?
A. midlatitude cyclones
B. hurricanes
C. tornadoes
D. anticyclones

4. What often happens to maritime air masses as they move inland over mountainous country?
F. They bring warm, dry weather conditions.
G. They produce clouds and hurricanes.
H. They bring cold, dry weather conditions.
I. They lose moisture passing over mountains.

5. What type of air mass originates over the southwestern desert of the United States in summer?
A. continental polar air mass
B. continental tropical air mass
C. maritime polar air mass
D. maritime tropical air mass

Directions (6–7): For each question, write a short response.

6. What type of front is formed when a warm air mass is overtaken by a cold air mass, which causes the warm air to lift above the cold air?

7. What do closely spaced isobars indicate about the wind on a weather map?

Reading Skills

Directions (8–10): Read the passage below. Then, answer the questions.

Tornado Alley

Although tornadoes are not unique to the area, the violent, rotating, funnel-shaped clouds and their trails of destruction are so common in the central United States that the area is called Tornado Alley. Severe thunderstorms and the super-cell tornadoes that they spawn are formed when warm, moist air from the Gulf of Mexico becomes trapped beneath hot, dry air from the southwest desert region. Above the hot, dry air, cold, dry air sweeps in from the Rocky Mountains. The interaction between high-altitude winds and thunderstorms creates the funnel-shaped vortex of high-speed winds known as a tornado.

The largest outbreak of tornadoes in this region occurred in April of 1974. Before the storms ended, 148 separate tornadoes roared through 13 different states. More than 300 people lost their lives, and another 5,000 people were injured. More than 1,300 buildings were destroyed.

8. Why is the central part of the United States known as Tornado Alley?
F. Tornadoes in this part of the country move in straight lines known as alleys.
G. The destruction left by tornadoes makes this part of the country look like an unkempt alley.
H. Areas between buildings are the safest places to be during of a tornado.
I. Tornadoes are a common occurrence in this part of the country.

9. Which of the following statements can be inferred from the information in the passage?
A. In the United States, tornadoes are more common in some areas than in other areas.
B. Tornadoes can form only in the area near the Rocky Mountains.
C. All tornadoes cause injuries to humans.
D. Multiple tornadoes are a rare occurrence.

10. What makes tornadoes so much more difficult to predict than other severe weather systems?

Interpreting Graphics

Directions (11–14): For each question below, record the correct answer on a separate sheet of paper.

The diagram below shows a station model. Use this diagram to answer questions 11 and 12.

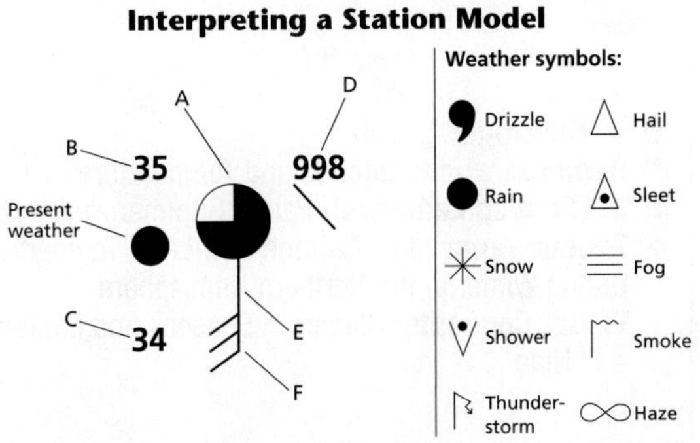

11. What letter in the station model represents the current barometric reading?

F. letter A
G. letter B
H. letter C
I. letter D

12. What weather information do the symbols indicated by the letters E and F provide? Interpret this part of the station model.

The diagram below shows a home weather station. Use this diagram to answer questions 13 and 14.

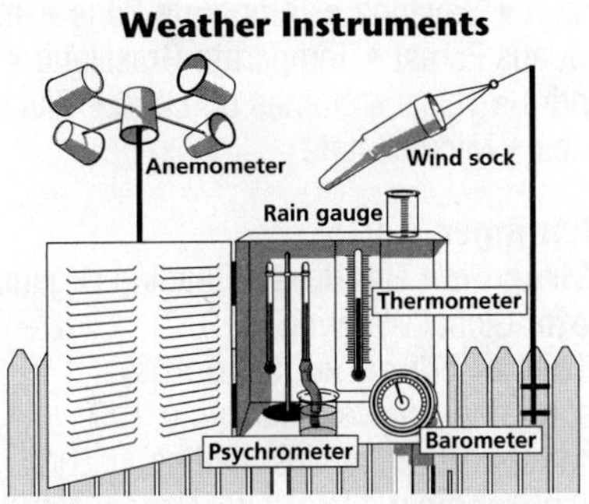

13. Which of the following weather instruments shown measures atmospheric pressure?

A. a rain gauge
B. a barometer
C. a wind sock
D. a thermometer

14. Describe how an anemometer is used to calculate wind speed.

Test Tip

Sometimes, only one part of a diagram, graph, or table is needed to answer a question. In such cases, focus on only that information to answer the question.

Standardized Test Prep

Using THINK central Resources

State Resources

- For specific resources for your state, visit www.thinkcentral.com and type in the keyword **HSHSTR.**

Answers

Understanding Concepts

1. C
2. I
3. B
4. I
5. B
6. cold front
7. high-speed winds

Reading Skills

8. I
9. A
10. Tornadoes are difficult to predict because they form suddenly from unstable conditions.

Interpreting Graphics

11. I
12. E is wind direction, and F is wind speed; Currently the station model is showing a 30-knot wind that is blowing in from south.
13. B
14. Answers may vary. See Test Doctor for a detailed scoring rubric.

Chapter Planner 22 Climate

	Time	Standards	Teach Key Ideas
Chapter Opener, pp. 602–603	45 min.	National Science Education Standards	
Section 1 Factors That Affect Climate, pp. 605–610 ❯ Temperature and Precipitation ❯ Latitude ❯ Heat Absorption and Balance ❯ Topography	45 min.	ES 1d	■ ◆ **Bellringer,** p. 605 ■ **Demonstration:** Latitude and Temperature, p. 606 ■ **DI (English Learners):** Paired Summarizing, p. 606 ◆ **Transparency:** 111 Average Sea-Level Temperatures During Winter in the Northern Hemisphere ▲ **Visual Concepts:** Climate • Seasons and Latitude • El Niño
Section 2 Climate Zones, pp. 611–614 ❯ Tropical Climates ❯ Middle-Latitude Climates ❯ Polar Climates ❯ Local Climates	45 min.	ES 1d, SPSP 5b	■ ◆ **Bellringer,** p. 611 ■ **Discussion:** Climate Classification, p. 624 ■ **Discussion:** Name That Climate, p. 611 ◆ **Transparencies:** 112 Tropical Climates • 113 Middle-Latitude Climates • 114 Polar Climates ▲ **Visual Concepts:** Tropical Zone • Tropical Rain Forest • Desert • Savanna • Temperate Zone •Temperate Deciduous Forest • Temperate Grassland • Polar Zone • Tundra • Taiga • Biomes on Land • Climate and Species • Microclimate
Section 3 Climate Change, pp. 615–620 ❯ Studying Climate Change ❯ Potential Causes of Climate Change ❯ Potential Impacts of Climate Change ❯ What Humans Can Do	45 min.	ES 1d, SPSP 4a, SPSP 4b, SPSP 4c, SPSP 5a, SPSP 5b, SPSP 5d, UCP 2	■ ◆ **Bellringer,** p. 615 ■ **DI (Struggling Readers):** Reading Organizer, p. 615 ■ **Debate:** Global Warming, p. 617 ■ **DI (Special Education Students):** Question-and-Answer Session, p. 617 ■ **Demonstration:** Icecaps Melting, p. 619 ◆ **Transparencies:** 115 Orbital Changes and Climate • 116 Climates of the World ▲ **Visual Concepts:** Milankovitch Theory • Effects of Volcanoes on Earth • Global Warming • Greenhouse Effect
Chapter Wrap-Up, pp. 625–629	90 min.		**Chapter Summary,** p. 625

See also PowerNotes® Presentations

CHAPTER Fast Track *To shorten instruction because of time limitations, omit the Chapter Lab.*

Key
Teacher's Edition ■ Teaching Transparencies ◆
Chapter Resource File ● Online Edition ▲

All resources listed below are also available on the **Teacher One Stop™.**

Why It Matters	Hands-On	Skills Development	Assessment
■ **Chapter Overview,** p. 602 ■ **Using the Figure:** Life Adapts, p. 602	**Inquiry Lab:** Calculating Average and Yearly Temperatures, p. 603	**Reading Toolbox,** p. 604	
■ **Section Overview,** p. 605 ■ **Using the Figure:** Temperature Ranges, p. 605 ■ **Environmental Connection:** As Earth Tilts, p. 606 ■ **Using the Figure:** Shifting Winds, p. 607 ■ **Deep Ocean Currents and Climate,** p. 607 ■ **Physics Connection:** Latent Heat, p. 608	**Quick Lab:** Evaporation, p. 608 ■ **Activity:** El Niño, p. 609 **Inquiry Lab:** Factors That Affect Climate, pp. 622–623	■ **Reading Toolbox:** Key-Term Fold, p. 607 **Math Skills:** Specific Heat, p. 608	**Reading Check,** p. 607 **Reading Check,** p. 608 **Section Review,** p. 610 ■ **Reteaching,** p. 609 ■ **Quiz,** p. 610 ■ **DI (Alternative Assessment):** Graphing, p. 609 ● **Section Quiz**
■ **Section Overview,** p. 611 ■ **Environmental Connection:** The North American Rain Forest, p. 613	■ **Activity:** Adaptations, p. 612 ● **Skills Practice Lab:** Microclimates	■ **Reading ToolBox:** Cause-and-Effect Map, p. 612 ■ **Skill Builder:** Math, p. 612 **Maps in Action:** Climates of the World, p. 624	**Reading Check,** p. 612 **Section Review,** p. 614 ■ **Reteaching,** p. 613 ■ **Quiz,** p. 613 ■ **DI (Alternative Assessment):** Travel Agent, p. 614 ● **Section Quiz**
■ **Section Overview,** p. 615 **Ice Tells a Story,** p. 616 ■ **The Little Ice Age,** p. 617 ■ **Astronomy Connections:** A Variable Star, p. 617 ■ **Using the Figure:** Rising Seas, p. 619	■ **Activity:** Tree Rings, p. 615 **Quick Lab:** Hot Stuff, p. 618 ● **Inquiry Lab:** Particulates in the Atmosphere	■ ● **Internet Activity:** Climate Models, p. 616 ■ **Reading ToolBox:** Temporal Language, p. 617	**Reading Check,** p. 616 **Reading Check,** p. 618 **Section Review,** p. 620 ■ **Reteaching,** p. 619 ■ **Quiz,** p. 619 ■ **DI (Alternative Assessment):** Global Warming in the News, p. 620 ● **Section Quiz**
Polar Bears on Thin Ice p. 621	■ **Activity:** Subclimate Story, p. 625	▲ **Super Summary** **Standardized Test Prep,** pp. 628–629	**Chapter Review,** pp. 626–627 ● **Chapter Tests**

See also Lab Generator

See also Holt Online Assessment Resources

Chapter Overview

Many factors help shape climates, and latitude plays a key role in controlling climate. Climates change over time for various reasons. Scientists study past climate changes to better understand the effects climate change may have on life on Earth.

Using the Figure GENERAL

Life Adapts In all environments, plants and animals adapt to the climate. For example, polar bears can live in the icy Arctic realm because they have traits that allow them to thrive in the cold. Discuss with students how plants and animals adapt to their surroundings. Ask students whether humans adapt in the same ways. (Answers may vary. Accept all reasonable answers.) **LS Logical**

Why It Matters

Recently, attention has been focused on the link between climate change and human activities. Scientists use information about past climate changes to help understand more about how human activities affect climate conditions.

Chapter 22 Climate

Chapter Outline

1 Factors That Affect Climate
- Temperature and Precipitation
- Latitude
- Heat Absorption and Balance
- Topography

2 Climate Zones
- Tropical Climates
- Middle-Latitude Climates
- Polar Climates
- Local Climates

3 Climate Change
- Studying Climate Change
- Potential Causes of Climate Change
- Potential Impacts of Climate Change
- What Humans Can Do

Virginia Standards of Learning
ES.1.a
ES.1.b
ES.1.c
ES.10.a
ES.10.b
ES.10.c
ES.11.c
ES.11.d
ES.12.d

Why It Matters

By learning about climate, we can understand more about the atmospheric conditions of Earth in the past and how human activities may affect atmospheric conditions in the future.

Chapter Correlations — *Virginia Standards of Learning*

ES.1.a volume, area, mass, elapsed time, direction, temperature, pressure, distance, density, and changes in elevation/depth are calculated utilizing the most appropriate tools.
ES.1.b technologies, including computers, probeware, and geospatial technologies, are used to collect, analyze, and report data and to demonstrate concepts and simulate experimental conditions.
ES.1.c scales, diagrams, charts, graphs, tables, imagery, models, and profiles are constructed and interpreted/
ES.10.a physical and chemical changes related to tides, waves, currents, sea level and ice cap variations, upwelling, and salinity variations
ES.10.b importance of environmental and geologic implications
ES.10.c systems interactions
ES.11.c atmospheric regulation mechanisms including the effects of density differences and energy transfer
ES.11.d potential changes to the atmosphere and climate due to human, biologic, and geologic activity
ES.12.d weather phenomena and the factors that affect climate including radiation, conduction, and convection

Inquiry Lab

30 min

Calculating Average and Yearly Temperatures

Use the **Internet** or the **library** to research the average monthly temperatures for the area in which you live. Using **graph paper**, construct a graph of the average monthly temperatures, with the temperatures on the *y*-axis and the months on the *x*-axis. Next, find the average yearly temperature by calculating the average of the monthly temperatures you used to make the graph. Finally, find the yearly temperature range by determining the difference between the highest average monthly temperature and the lowest average monthly temperature.

Questions to Get You Started

1. How does the temperature change throughout the year in your area?
2. Why is it important to know the average yearly temperature and the yearly temperature range of an area?

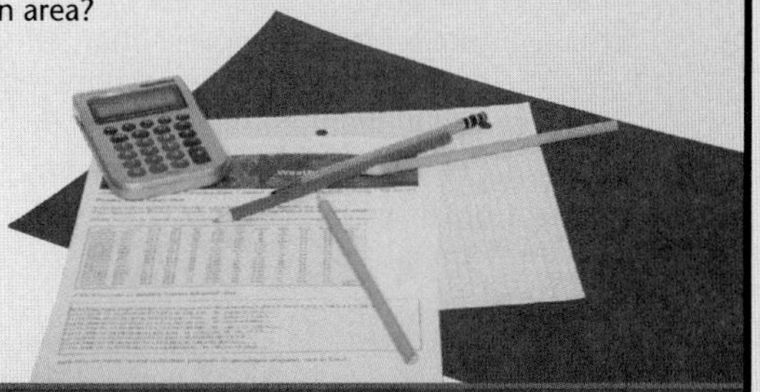

Inquiry Lab

Central Concept: The two main variables used to describe climate are temperature and precipitation. Graphing and calculating average temperatures helps students become familiar with the data scientists use to analyze climate and climate change.

Teacher's Notes: You may wish to assign each group to find and work with data from a different region, then have groups compare results. You may want to have some data ready to hand out if students do not have on-site Internet access.

Materials: (per group)
- Internet access
- Graph paper

Skills Acquired
Analyzing Data
Calculating

Answers to Getting Started

1. Student answers will vary based on geographic location. Continental climates will have higher temperatures in the summer and cooler temperatures in the winter.
2. Possible answer: Scientists use temperature data to define different climates worldwide. Monitoring temperature data helps scientists track changes in climate.

Using THINK central Resources

An online version of this chapter, as well as all the print and multimedia resources that accompany the program are available to registered teachers and their students. Log onto **www.thinkcentral.com** to access these materials and tools to organize your preparation and student learning.

READING TOOLBOX

FoldNotes

Key-Term Fold Encourage students to use their completed key-term fold to review for quizzes and tests.

Describing Time

Temporal Language Students should find the following examples: daily—specific time; yearly—specific time; seasonally—specific time; millions of years—duration; a few weeks—duration

Graphic Organizers

Cause and Effect Maps Students should find at least three of the following causes: changes in the shape of Earth's orbit; changes in Earth's tilt; changes in the wobble of Earth's axis; human activities (burning fossil fuels, deforestation); volcanic activities

READING TOOLBOX

These reading tools will help you learn the material in this chapter.

FoldNotes

Key-Term Fold A key-term fold can help you learn the key terms in this chapter.

Your Turn Create a key-term fold as described in **Appendix A.**

1. Write one key term from the Chapter Summary on the front of each tab.
2. As you read the chapter, write the definition of each term under its tab.
3. Use this FoldNote to study the key terms.

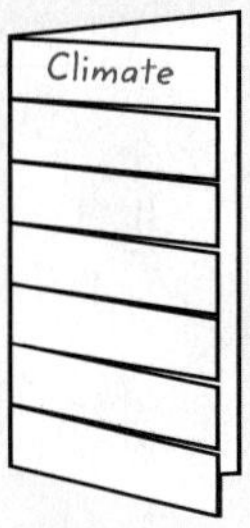

Describing Time

Temporal Language *Temporal language* is language that is used to describe time. Paying careful attention to temporal language can help you understand events and processes in the environment.

Your Turn Make a two-column table. As you read this chapter, write words or phrases that refer to time in the first column of your table. In the second column, write whether the word or phrase describes a specific time, duration, frequency, or sequence of events.

Temporal word or phrase	Describes
over millions of years	duration
today	specific time

Graphic Organizers

Cause-and-Effect Maps You can use cause-and-effect maps to show visually how physical processes depend on one another. To make a cause-and-effect map, follow these steps:

1. Draw a box, and write a cause inside the box. You can have as many cause boxes as you want.
2. Draw another box to represent an effect of the cause. You can have as many effect boxes as you want.
3. Connect each cause box to one or more effect boxes with an arrow.
4. If an effect is also the cause of another effect, you may connect the effect box to another effect box.

Your Turn On a separate sheet of paper, complete the cause-and-effect map started below about the causes of climate change. Add at least three more causes.

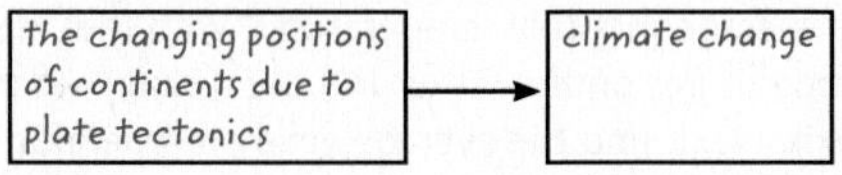

For more information on how to use these and other tools, see **Appendix A.**

SECTION 1

ENVIRONMENTAL CONNECTION

Factors That Affect Climate

Key Ideas	Key Terms	Why It Matters
❯ Identify two major factors used to describe climate. ❯ Explain how latitude determines the amount of solar energy received on Earth. ❯ Describe how the different rates at which land and water are heated affect climate. ❯ Explain the effects of topography on climate.	**climate** **specific heat** **El Niño** **monsoon**	Climate change is big in the news these days. Understanding the factors that affect climate can help us evaluate the news and make informed decisions about our role in climate change.

The weather conditions for an area over a long period of time are referred to as **climate.** Climate is different from weather in that weather is the condition of the atmosphere at a particular time. Weather conditions vary from day to day. Climate is a pattern that varies on a much longer basis.

Temperature and Precipitation

Climates are chiefly described by using average temperature and precipitation. To estimate the average daily temperature, add the high and low temperatures of the day and divide by two. The monthly average is the average of all the daily averages for a given month. The yearly average temperature can be found by averaging the 12 monthly averages. However, using only average temperatures to describe climate can be misleading. As you can see in **Figure 1,** areas that have similar average temperatures may have very different temperature ranges. Another way scientists describe climate is by using the *yearly temperature range,* or the difference between the highest and lowest monthly averages.

Precipitation is also described by using monthly and yearly averages, as well as ranges. As with temperature, average yearly precipitation alone is not enough to describe climate. The months that have the largest amount of precipitation are also important. When describing climate, extremes of temperature and precipitation, as well as averages, have to be considered. The factors that have the greatest influence on both temperature and precipitation are latitude, heat absorption and release, and topography.

climate the weather conditions in an area over a long period of time

Figure 1 Both St. Louis and San Francisco have the same average yearly temperature. However, St. Louis (right) has a climate of cold winters and hot summers, while San Francisco (left) has a generally mild climate all year.

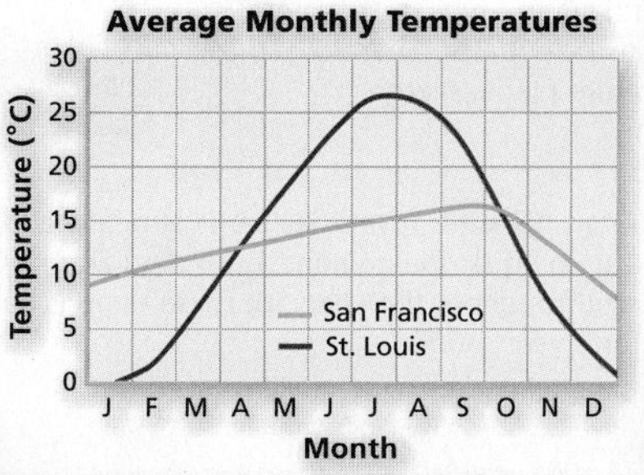

Section 1

Focus

Overview

This section presents temperature and precipitation as the two major factors used to describe climate. The section also explains how latitude, proximity to large bodies of water, and topography affect climate.

Bellringer

Ask students, "What is the difference between weather and climate?" (Weather is the day-to-day variations in temperature, humidity, wind, and precipitation. Climate is the weather conditions for an area over a long period.) **LS Logical**

Motivate

Using the Figure GENERAL

Temperature Ranges Have students use the figure that shows the average monthly temperatures of St. Louis and San Francisco to determine and compare the average yearly temperatures of the two cities. Then, have them determine the yearly temperature range in the two cities. Students will find that, while the average yearly temperature is similar, (about 13 °C) the temperature range for St. Louis is much greater than that for San Francisco. (about 28 °C for St. Louis and about 8 °C for San Francisco) **LS Logical/Visual**

Key Resources

Chapter Resource File
- Directed Reading BASIC

Technology
- Transparencies
  Bellringer

Teach

Teaching Tip GENERAL

Make Concepts Relevant Remind students that the tilt of Earth's axis determines the seasons. In December, the northern end of the axis is tilted away from the sun, so the Northern Hemisphere receives less solar energy than at other times of the year, and the Northern Hemisphere experiences winter. At the same time, the Southern Hemisphere receives more solar energy than at other times of the year, and the Southern Hemisphere experiences summer. In June the opposite occurs: the Northern Hemisphere begins to experience summer and the Southern Hemisphere begins its winter. **LS Logical/Visual**

Environmental Connection

As Earth Tilts While most people understand that seasons are due to the tilt of Earth's axis, it is less well-known that the degree of tilt changes from 22.2° to 24.5° every 41,000 years. As the angle decreases, temperature differences between the seasons at high latitudes reduces (because the intensity of the solar energy at Earth's surface does not vary as much with the seasons).

Key Resources

Technology

- Transparencies
  111 Average Sea-Level Temperatures During Winter in the Northern Hemisphere

Latitude

One of the most important factors that determines a region's climate is latitude. Different latitudes on Earth's surface receive different amounts of solar energy. Solar energy determines the temperature and wind patterns of an area, which influence the average annual temperature and precipitation.

SCILINKS.
www.scilinks.org
Topic: What Affects Climate?
Code: HQX1652

Solar Energy

The higher the latitude of an area is, the smaller the angle at which the sun's rays hit Earth is and the smaller the amount of solar energy received by the area is. At the equator, or 0° latitude, the sun's rays hit Earth at a 90° angle. So, temperatures at the equator are high. Nearer the poles, the sun's rays hit Earth at a smaller angle, and solar energy is spread over a larger area. So, temperatures at the poles are low.

Because Earth's axis is tilted, the angle at which the sun's rays hit an area changes as Earth orbits the sun. During winter in the Northern Hemisphere, the northern half of Earth is tilted away from the sun. Thus, light that reaches the Northern Hemisphere hits Earth's surface at a smaller angle than it does in summer, when the axis is tilted toward the sun. Because of the tilt of Earth's axis during winter in the Northern Hemisphere, areas of Earth at higher northern latitudes directly face the sun for less time than during summer. As a result, the days are shorter and the temperatures are lower during the winter months than during the summer months. **Figure 2** describes these effects.

Figure 2 Average Sea-Level Temperatures During Winter in the Northern Hemisphere

❶ In polar regions, the amount of daylight varies from 24 h of daylight in the summer to 0 h in the winter. Thus, the annual temperature range is very large, but the daily temperature ranges are very small.

❷ At middle latitudes, the sun's rays strike Earth at an angle of less than 90°. The energy of the rays is spread over a large area. Thus, average yearly temperatures at middle latitudes are lower than those at the equator. The lengths of days and nights vary more than they do at the equator. Therefore, the yearly temperature range is large.

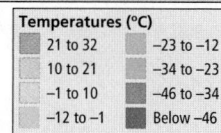

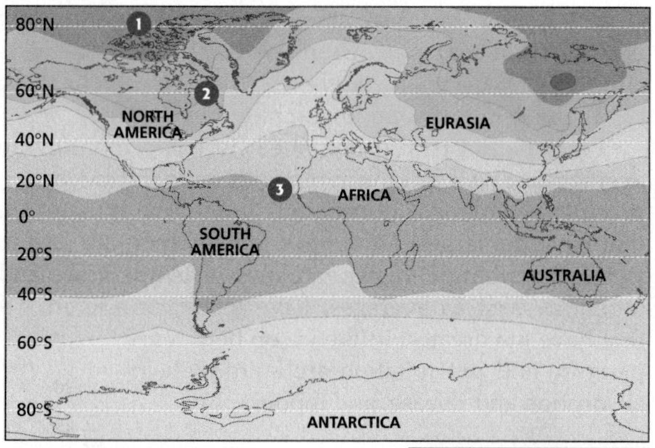

Temperatures (°C)

21 to 32	−23 to −12
10 to 21	−34 to −23
−1 to 10	−46 to −34
−12 to −1	Below −46

❸ At the equator, the sun's rays strike Earth at nearly a 90° angle for much of the year. In equatorial regions, both days and nights are about 12 h long throughout the year. So, these regions have steady, high temperatures year-round.

Differentiated Instruction

English Learners

Paired Summarizing Have students join with a partner and read silently about how the tilt of Earth's axis affects the amount of solar energy Earth receives. Then, have one student summarize the effect of the axial tilt on temperatures in the Northern Hemisphere over the course of the year. The other student should listen to the retelling and point out any inaccuracies or ideas that were left out. Allow students to refer to the text as needed. **LS Verbal**

Demonstration GENERAL

Latitude and Temperature Place three thermometers at angles of 0°, 45°, and 90° at the same distance from a light source. Record the temperature of each thermometer. Have students predict which will show the greatest rise in temperature. At the end of class, record the temperatures. Discuss the results and how they relate to the effect of latitude on Earth's temperatures. (The one at 0° represents the poles and should show the least change; the one at 90° represents the equator and should show the greatest increase.) **LS Visual**

Global Wind Patterns

Because Earth receives different amounts of solar energy at different latitudes, belts of cool, dense air form at latitudes near the poles, while belts of warm, less dense air form near the equator. Because cool air is dense, it forms regions of high pressure, while warm air forms regions of low pressure. Differences in air pressure create wind. Because air pressure is affected by latitude, the atmosphere is made up of global wind belts that run parallel to lines of latitude. Winds affect many weather conditions, such as precipitation, temperature, and cloud cover. Thus, regions that have different global wind belts often have different climates.

In the equatorial belt of low pressure, called the *doldrums,* the air rises and cools, and water vapor condenses. Thus, this region generally has large amounts of precipitation. The amount of precipitation generally decreases as latitude increases. In the regions between about 20° and 30° latitude in both hemispheres, or the *subtropical highs,* the air sinks, warms, and decreases in relative humidity. Thus, little precipitation occurs in these regions. Most of the world's deserts are located in these regions. In the middle latitudes, at about 45° to 60° latitude in both hemispheres, warm tropical air meets cold polar air, which leads to belts of greater precipitation. In the high-pressure areas, above 60° latitude, the air masses are cold and dry, and average precipitation is low.

As seasons change, global wind belts shift in a north or south direction, as shown in **Figure 3.** As the wind and pressure belts shift, the belts of precipitation associated with them also shift.

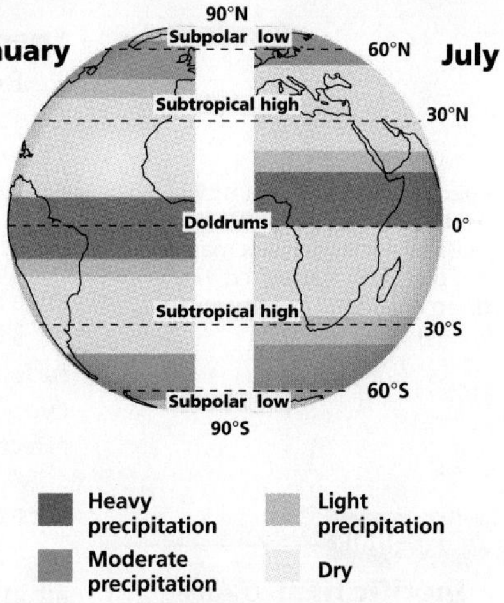

Figure 3 During winter in the Northern Hemisphere, global wind and precipitation belts shift to the south.

Academic Vocabulary

area (ER ee uh) the measure of the size of a surface or region

Heat Absorption and Balance

Latitude and cloud cover affect the amount of solar energy that an area receives. However, different areas absorb and release energy differently. Land heats faster than water and thus can reach a higher temperature in the same amount of time. One reason for this difference is that the land surface is opaque and unmoving. Surface ocean water, on the other hand, is transparent and moves continuously. Waves, currents, and other movements continuously replace warm surface water with cooler water from the ocean depths. This action prevents the surface temperature of the water from increasing rapidly. However, the surface temperature of the land can continue to increase as more solar energy is received. In turn, the temperature of the land or ocean influences the amount of heat that the air above the land or ocean absorbs or releases. The temperature of the air then affects the climate of the area.

Reading Check **How do wind and ocean currents affect the surface temperature of oceans?** (See Appendix G for answers to Reading Checks.)

READING TOOLBOX

Key-Term Fold

Make a FoldNote for terms related to how climate is affected by the temperature differences between land and water. List each term, and explain its effect on climate.

Using the Figure — ADVANCED

Shifting Winds The figure at the top of this page shows how global wind and precipitation belts shift south during winter in the Northern Hemisphere. The shift occurs because in the winter, a very strong high-pressure system develops over Asia and a weaker high-pressure system develops over North America. These systems push global wind belts and the doldrums, or the Intertropical Convergence Zone, south. As the continents warm in the summer, low-pressure systems develop, especially in India and to a lesser extent in the southwestern United States, pushing the wind belts back north. Ask students to explain why climates near the equator may not have temperature-based seasons, but commonly do have wet and dry seasons. (The intensity of radiation from the sun does not vary much throughout the year at the equator. Therefore, temperature does not change significantly. However, as the wind belts shift north and south over the course of the year, some regions will experience changes in precipitation, such as in the central part of Africa [about 15°N] and in South America [about 15°S]) **LS Visual**

READING TOOLBOX

Key-Term Fold

Students may include the terms *specific heat* and *monsoons.* Since the specific heat of water is higher than that of land, differences in the temperature of air above land and the air above water leads to wind. Winds blowing from the ocean affect coastal climates, including creating monsoon climates.

Answer to Reading Check

Waves, currents, and other water motions continually replace warm surface waters with cooler water from the ocean depths, which keeps the surface temperature of the water from increasing rapidly.

Why It Matters

Deep-Ocean Currents and Climate Water circulates deep within the ocean because of differences in density, which in turn are the result of differences in temperature and salinity. Cold, salty water tends to sink because it is denser than warm, less salty water. Water near the poles is cold; it is also very saline because as water freezes salts remain behind in the water. Cold, dense water in the Arctic and Antarctic regions sinks and travels toward the equator along the ocean floor. Near the equator, these waters rise and join surface currents in a global conveyor belt that circulates water through the ocean. Water may take several hundred to thousands of years to complete a circuit. This global conveyer belt influences climate because the deep ocean currents act as a reservoir for carbon dioxide and for thermal energy.

Teach, *continued*

Math Skills

Answer

6 °C = 279 K

$(4{,}186\ J/kg{*}K) \times 200\ kg \times 279\ K$
$= 23{,}357{,}888{,}000\ J = 2.34 \times 10^{10}\ J$

Quick Lab

Skills Acquired

- Measuring
- Analyzing

Materials

- Piece of paper
- Ring stand
- Table
- Meterstick
- Clamp lamp
- Incandescent bulb
- Three Petri dishes or watch glasses
- Three thermometers
- Stopwatch
- 30 mL of water
- Graduated cylinder

Teacher's Notes: Position the lamp on a separate support. Lamps may have to be turned off overnight for safety or insurance reasons. If so, similar results can be achieved by using the lamp for two school days. If the lamp is turned off, cover dishes to prevent evaporation overnight.

Answers to Analysis

1. The most water evaporated from the dish closest to the lamp. The least evaporated from the dish at the base of the stand.
2. As temperature increases, rate of evaporation increases.
3. Water evaporates more quickly from puddles in summer because the air and the water are warmer in summer than in fall or winter.

Specific Heat and Evaporation

Even if not in motion, water warms more slowly than land does. Water also releases heat energy more slowly than land does. This is because the specific heat of water is higher than that of land. **Specific heat** is the amount of energy needed to change the temperature of 1 g of a substance by 1 °C. A given mass of water requires more energy than land of the same mass does to experience an increase in temperature of the same number of degrees.

The average temperatures of land and water at the same latitude also vary because of differences in the loss of heat through evaporation. Evaporation affects water surfaces much more than it affects land surfaces.

specific heat the quantity of heat required to raise a unit mass of homogeneous material 1 K or 1 °C in a specified way, given constant pressure and volume

Math Skills

Specific Heat Use the following equation to calculate the amount of energy needed to heat 200 kg of water 6 °C, given that the specific heat of water is 4,186 J/kg•K.

energy = specific heat × mass × temperature change

Ocean Currents

The temperature of ocean currents that come in contact with the air influences the amount of heat absorbed or released by the air. If winds consistently blow toward shore, ocean currents have a strong effect on air masses over land. For example, the combination of a warm Atlantic current and steady westerly winds gives northwestern Europe a high average temperature for its latitude. In contrast, the warm Gulf Stream has little effect on the eastern coast of the United States. This is because westerly winds usually blow the Gulf Stream and its warm tropical air away from the coast.

Reading Check **Why does land heat faster than water does?**

Quick Lab — Evaporation

30 min

Procedure

1. On a **piece of paper,** make a data table similar to the one shown here.
2. Assemble a **ring stand** on a **table.** Use a **meterstick** to place the support rings at heights of 20 cm and 40 cm above the base. Position a **portable clamp lamp that has an incandescent bulb** directly over the rings, at a height of 60 cm.
3. Place **three Petri dishes** or **watch glasses** as follows: one on the base of the stand and one on each of the two rings.
4. Take **three thermometers,** and lay one across each dish. Turn on the lamp. Use a **stopwatch** to record the temperature every 3 min for 9 min.
5. Remove the thermometers, and add **30 mL of water** to each of the three dishes.
6. Keep the lamp on and over the dishes for 24 h.

Dish	Temperature	Amount of water evaporated
1		
2		
3		

7. Turn off the lamp. Carefully pour the water from the first dish into a **graduated cylinder,** and record any change in volume. Repeat this process for the other two dishes.

Analysis

1. At what distance from the lamp did the most water evaporate? the least water evaporate?
2. Explain the relationship between temperature and the rate of evaporation.
3. Explain why puddles of water dry out much more quickly in summer than they do in fall or winter.

Answer to Reading Check

The temperature of land increases faster than that of water because the specific heat of land is lower than that of water, and thus the land requires less energy to heat up than the water does.

Physics Connection GENERAL

Latent Heat Much of the thermal energy absorbed by water is used not to increase temperature but to increase the motion of the water molecules, allowing them to escape the water surface. When the higher-temperature molecules escape as water vapor, they leave cooler molecules (molecules that are vibrating less rapidly) behind, which is why evaporation has a cooling effect.

El Niño–Southern Oscillation

The *El Niño–Southern Oscillation*, or *ENSO*, is a cycle of changing wind and water-current patterns in the Pacific Ocean. Every 3 to 10 years, **El Niño,** which is the warm-water phase of the ENSO, causes surface-water temperatures along the west coast of South America to rise. The event changes the interaction of the ocean and the atmosphere, which can change global weather patterns. During El Niño, an increase in typhoons, cyclones, and floods may occur in the Pacific Ocean region. Droughts may strike other areas around the world, such as Indonesia and Australia. The ENSO has a cool-water phase, called *La Niña,* as well. La Niña also affects weather patterns, such as increasing the number of Atlantic hurricanes.

El Niño the warm-water phase of the El Niño–Southern Oscillation; a periodic occurrence in the eastern Pacific Ocean in which the surface-water temperature becomes unusually warm

monsoon a seasonal wind that blows toward the land in the summer, bringing heavy rains, and that blows away from the land in the winter, bringing dry weather

Seasonal Winds

Temperature differences between the land and the ocean sometimes cause winds to shift seasonally in some regions. During the summer, the land warms more quickly than the ocean. The warm air rises and is replaced by cool air from the ocean. Thus, the wind moves toward the land. During the winter, the land loses heat more quickly than the ocean does, and the cool air flows away from the land. Thus, the wind moves seaward. Such seasonal winds are called **monsoons.**

Monsoon climates, such as that in southern Asia, are caused by heating and cooling of the northern Indian peninsula. In the winter, continental winds bring dry weather and sometimes drought. In the summer, winds carry moisture to the land from the ocean and cause heavy rainfall and flooding, as shown in **Figure 4.** Monsoon conditions also occur in eastern Asia and affect the tropical regions of Australia and East Africa.

Figure 4 Effects of Monsoon Climates

Because monsoon rains cause regular flooding, such as this flood in eastern India, people who live in monsoon regions have adapted to living in flood conditions.

People who live in monsoon climates must adjust to periodic droughts, such as the drought that affected this cropland in southern India.

Activity — GENERAL

El Niño Ask interested students to research recent El Niño events, how they are predicted, and their effects on wildlife and on weather patterns around the world. Some students may also want to research La Niña. Have students prepare a poster that illustrates their findings to display for the class. **LS Visual/Verbal**

Close

Reteaching — BASIC

Climate Factors Have students write a brief description on index cards of major factors that affect climate. Have them work in pairs using the cards to quiz one another. **LS Visual/Logical**

Quiz — GENERAL

1. Why does northwestern Europe have a milder climate than its latitude would indicate? (A warm Atlantic current [the Gulf Stream] and steady westerly winds moderate its climate.)
2. Where are most of the world's deserts located? (in the region of the subtropical highs, 20° to 30° N and S latitude)

Cultural Awareness — ADVANCED

Climates and Culture Climate has a profound effect on people's clothing, housing, food, and customs. Have students work in small groups to study a specific culture. They may choose a traditional or a modern culture anywhere in the world. Have them research how climate has shaped the culture they have chosen. Groups should prepare a creative presentation that illustrates the culture and the effects of climate on the culture of the people they studied. **LS Visual/Verbal**

Close, *continued*

Answers to Section Review

1. temperature and precipitation
2. The higher the latitude, the smaller the angle at which the sun's rays hit Earth and the smaller the amount of solar energy an area receives.
3. Because Earth receives different amounts of solar energy at different latitudes, belts of air of different densities form, with cool, dense air at the poles and warm, less dense air at the equator. These differences in air pressure create winds. Global wind belts run roughly parallel to lines of latitude.
4. Land heats and cools faster than water does. If a large body of water is nearby, the temperature range will likely be smaller.
5. El Niño is the warm-water phase of the ENSO that periodically warms surface water along the west coast of South America. This warming changes atmospheric and oceanic interactions, which can affect global weather patterns.
6. In summer, winds blow from the ocean, as air warmed by the land is replaced by air cooled by the ocean. These winds carry moisture to the land and bring heavy rain. In the winter, winds blow from the cooler land, bringing dry weather.
7. Temperature decreases with increasing altitude, so even mountain peaks at the equator can be covered with snow.

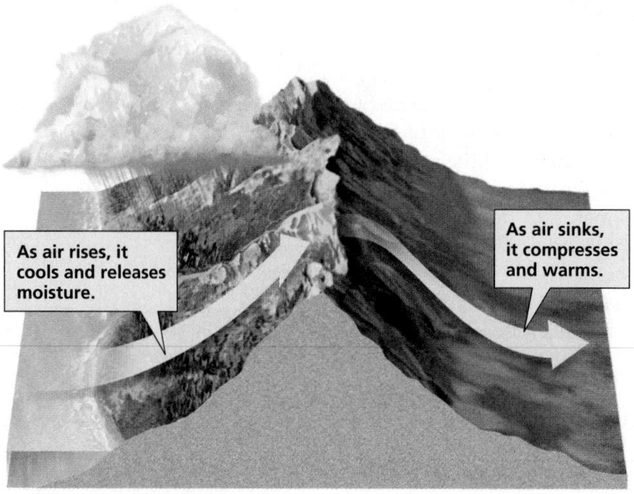

As air rises, it cools and releases moisture.
As air sinks, it compresses and warms.

Figure 5 Mountains cause air to rise, cool, and lose moisture as the air passes over them. This process affects the climate on both sides of the mountains.

Topography

The surface features of the land, or *topography*, also influence climate. Topographical features, such as mountains, can control the flow of air through a region.

Elevation

The elevation, or height of landforms above sea level, produces distinct temperature changes. Temperature generally decreases as elevation increases. For example, for every 100 m increase in elevation, the average temperature decreases by 0.7 °C. Even along the equator, the peaks of high mountains can be cold enough to be covered with snow.

Rain Shadows

When a moving air mass encounters a mountain range, the air mass rises, cools, and loses most of its moisture through precipitation, as shown in **Figure 5.** As a result, the air that flows down the other side of the range is usually warm and dry. This effect is called a *rain shadow*. One type of warm, dry wind that forms in this way is the *foehn* (FAYN), a dry wind that flows down the slopes of the Alps. Similar dry, warm winds that flow down the eastern slopes of the Rocky Mountains are called *chinooks*.

Section 1 Review

Key Ideas

1. **Identify** two factors that are used to describe climate.
2. **Explain** how latitude determines the amount of solar energy received on Earth.
3. **Describe** how latitude determines wind patterns.
4. **Describe** how the different rates at which land and water are heated affect climate.
5. **Explain** the El Niño–Southern Oscillation cycle.
6. **Summarize** the conditions that cause monsoons.
7. **Explain** how elevation affects climate.
8. **Describe** a rain shadow and the resulting local winds.

Critical Thinking

9. **Making Inferences** If land and water had the same specific heat, how might climate be different around the world?
10. **Analyzing Processes** On a mountain, are you likely to find more vegetation on the side facing prevailing winds or on the side facing away from them?
11. **Recognizing Relationships** Why might you find snow-capped mountains in Hawaii even though Hawaii is closer to the equator than Florida is?

Concept Mapping

12. Use the following terms to create a concept map: *climate, temperature range, wind, doldrums, subtropical high, monsoon, El Niño,* and *topography.*

8. When an air mass reaches a mountain, it rises and cools. The water vapor it contains condenses and falls as precipitation. Air flowing down the other side of the slope, in the rain shadow, is dry and warms up as it sinks.
9. Climate would be less varied. There would be fewer differences in air pressure and thus fewer winds. The moderating effect of bodies of water on climate would be lost.
10. I would expect more vegetation on the side facing the prevailing winds because that side receives the most precipitation.

Answers continued on p. 631A

Differentiated Instruction

Alternative Assessment

Graphing Have students graph the monthly average precipitation (noting if and when it is snow) and the high and low temperatures for a city of their choice over the last year. Then, have them write a short description of that climate and the factors that influence it. **LS Logical**

SECTION 2

Climate Zones

ENVIRONMENTAL CONNECTION

Key Ideas	Key Terms	Why It Matters
› Describe the three types of tropical climates. › Describe the five types of middle-latitude climates. › Describe the three types of polar climates. › Explain why city climates may differ from rural climates.	**tropical climate** **middle-latitude climate** **polar climate** **microclimate**	Identifying and studying the different types of climates on Earth helps you better understand the factors that influence the climate where you live.

Earth has three major types of climate zones—tropical, middle-latitude, and polar—each with distinct temperature characteristics. Each zone also has several types of climates because the amount of precipitation within each zone varies.

Tropical Climates

Climates characterized by high temperatures and located in the equatorial region are referred to as **tropical climates.** These climates have an average monthly temperature of at least 18 °C, even during the coldest months. Within the tropical zone, there are three types of tropical climates, as shown in **Table 1.**

tropical climate a climate characterized by high temperatures and heavy precipitation during at least part of the year

Tropical rain-forest climates are humid and warm. Central Africa, the Amazon River basin of South America, Central America, and Southeast Asia have areas with tropical rain-forest climates.

Tropical desert climates receive very little precipitation. The largest belt of tropical deserts extends across north Africa and southwestern Asia.

Savanna climates are located in South America, Africa, Southeast Asia, and northern Australia. These climates are described in **Table 1.**

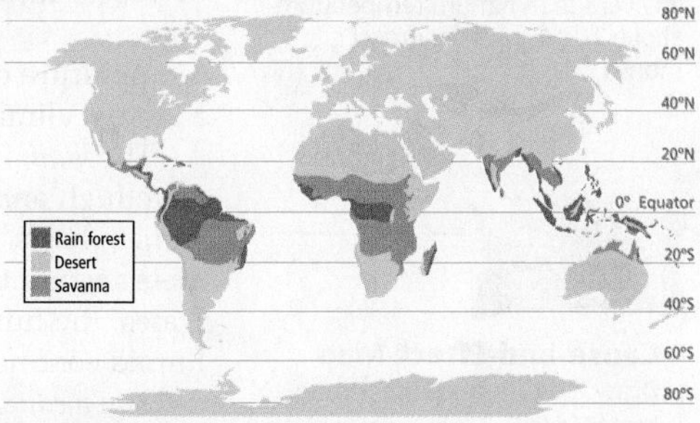

Table 1 Tropical Climates

Climate	Temperature and precipitation	Description
Rain forest	small temperature range; annual rainfall of 200 cm	characterized by dense, lush vegetation; broadleaf plants; and high biodiversity
Desert	large temperature range, with hot days and cold nights; annual rainfall of less than 25 cm	characterized by little to no vegetation and organisms adapted to dry conditions
Savanna	small temperature range; annual rainfall of 50 cm; alternating wet and dry periods	characterized by open grasslands that have clumps of drought-resistant shrubs

Section 2

Focus

Overview

This section describes the three major climate zones and the subclimate zones within them. The section also explains factors that may alter local climates.

Bellringer

Ask students to describe the climate and physical features of the region where they live and to identify any other regions of the world that have similar climates. (Answers may vary. Accept all reasonable answers.)
LS Verbal

Motivate

Discussion GENERAL

Name That Climate Ask students to name and briefly describe as many climates as they can think of that exist on Earth. Use student responses to address misconceptions about climate zones and introduce the major climates and their subclimates.
LS Verbal/Logical

Key Resources

Chapter Resource File
- Directed Reading BASIC

Technology
- Transparencies
  Bellringer
  112 Tropical Climates

Teach

Activity — GENERAL

Adaptations Collect photos of a variety of leaves and/or plants from various climates around the world, such as cacti, jade plants, grasses, bromeliads, orchids, sedges, mosses, lichens, ferns, conifers, and deciduous trees. (If it is possible, collect actual plants.) Have students observe the plants and try to determine under what conditions the plant is most likely to grow. Then, lead a discussion about the adaptations of the various plants and how the traits enable the plants to thrive in their home climate. **LS Visual**

Skill Builder — GENERAL

Math Have students use the table and text that describe middle-latitude climates to convert temperature and precipitation values from SI units to English units for one of the subclimates. Have students use the following conversion factors: °F = (°C × 1.8) + 32, and 1 in. = 2.54 cm.

Sample answer—marine west coast: summer temp = (20 °C × 1.8) + 32 = 68 °F
winter temp = (7 °C × 1.8) + 32 = 45 °F
precipitation range = (60 cm ÷ 2.54 cm/in.) to (150 cm ÷ 2.54 cm/in.) = 24 to 59 in.
LS Logical

Answer to Reading Check

marine west coast, humid continental, and humid subtropical

Table 2 Middle-Latitude Climates

Climate	Temperature and precipitation	Description
Marine west coast	small annual temperature range; frequent rainfall throughout the year	characterized by deciduous trees and dense forests; mild winters and summers
Steppe	large annual temperature range; annual precipitation of less than 40 cm	characterized by drought-resistant vegetation; cold, dry winters and warm, wet summers
Humid continental	large annual temperature range; annual precipitation of greater than 75 cm	characterized by a wide variety of vegetation and evergreen trees; variable weather
Humid subtropical	large annual temperature range; annual precipitation of 75 to 165 cm	characterized by broadleaf and evergreen trees; high humidity
Mediterranean	small annual temperature range; average annual precipitation of about 40 cm	characterized by broadleaf and evergreen trees; long, dry summers and mild, wet winters

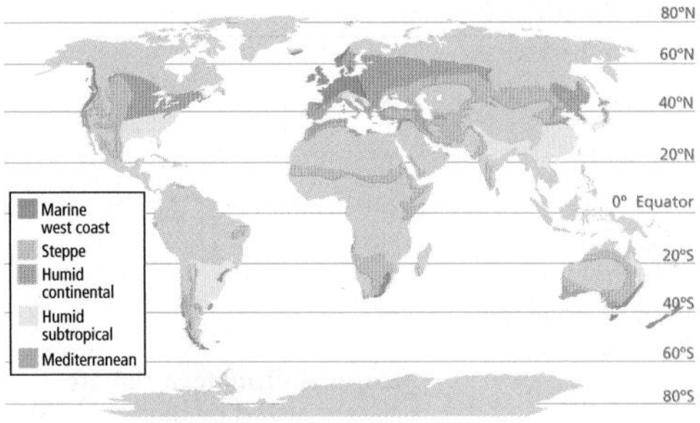

Middle-Latitude Climates

Climates that have an average maximum temperature below 18 °C in the coldest month and an average minimum temperature above 10 °C in the warmest month are referred to as **middle-latitude climates.** There are five middle-latitude climates, which are described in **Table 2.**

middle-latitude climate a climate that has an average maximum temperature below 18 °C in the coldest month and an average minimum temperature above 10 °C in the warmest month

Marine west coast climates receive about 60 to 150 cm of precipitation annually. The average temperature is 20 °C in the summer and 7 °C in the winter. The Pacific Northwest of the United States has a marine west coast climate.

Steppe climates are dry climates that receive less than 40 cm of precipitation per year. The average summer temperature is about 23 °C. The winters are very cold and have an average temperature of −1 °C. The Great Plains of the United States has a steppe climate.

The *humid continental climate* and *humid subtropical climate* both have high annual precipitation. However, the humid continental climate has a much greater temperature range between the summers and winters than the humid subtropical climate. In the United States, the humid subtropical climate is in the southeast and the humid continental climate is in the northeast.

The *mediterranean climate* is a mild climate that has a small temperature range between summer and winter. This climate is named after the sea between Africa and Europe, where this climate is located. However, this climate is also found along the coast of central and southern California.

READING TOOLBOX

Cause-and-Effect Map
Draw a cause-and-effect map that shows how different climate conditions affect vegetation.

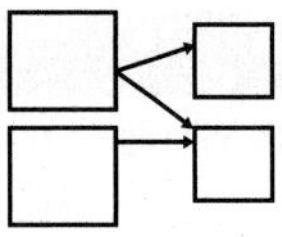

Reading Check **Which subclimates have high annual precipitation?**

READING TOOLBOX

Cause-and-Effect Map Answers will vary but could include: Cause: desert climate, no rain; Effect: little or no vegetation; Cause: steppe climate, less than 40 cm of rain per year; Effect: drought-resistant vegetation

Key Resources

Technology

- Transparencies
  113 Middle-Latitude Climates
  114 Polar Climates

Figure 1 Subarctic climates, as shown here at Tombstone Valley in Yukon, Canada, support sparse tree growth.

SCI LINKS.
www.scilinks.org
Topic: Polar Climates
Code: **HQX1175**

Polar Climates

The climates of the polar regions are referred to as the **polar climates.** There are three types of polar climates: the subarctic climate, shown in **Figure 1,** the tundra climate, and the polar icecap climate. The *subarctic climate* has the largest annual temperature range of all climates. The difference between summer and winter temperatures in the subarctic climate has been as much as 63 °C. The *tundra climate* has a smaller annual temperature range than the subarctic climate does. However, the average temperature of the tundra climate is colder than that of the subarctic climate. In the *polar icecap climate,* most of the land surface and much of the ocean are covered in thick sheets of ice year-round. The average temperature never rises above freezing. The polar climates are described in **Table 3.**

polar climate a climate that is characterized by average temperatures that are near or below freezing

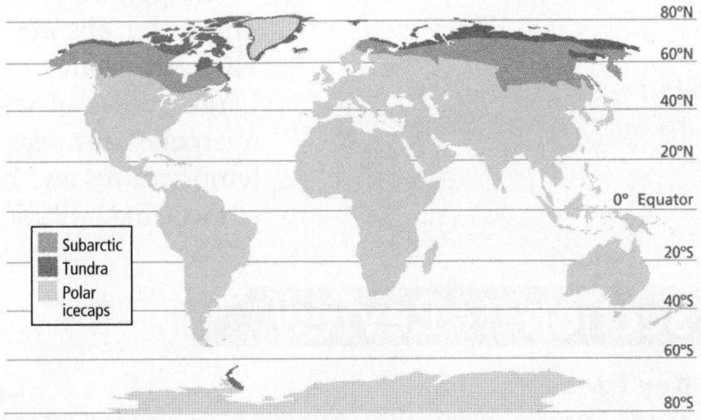

Table 3 Polar Climates

Climate	Temperature and precipitation	Description
Subarctic	largest annual temperature range (63 °C); annual precipitation of 25 to 50 cm	characterized by evergreen trees; brief, cool summers and long, cold winters
Tundra	average temperature below 4 °C; annual precipitation of 25 cm	characterized by treeless plains; nine months of temperatures below freezing
Polar icecap	average temperature below 0 °C; low annual precipitation	characterized by little or no life; temperatures below freezing year-round and high winds

Close

Reteaching BASIC

Flipbook Have students write all the subclimates on index cards with a description of temperature, precipitation, and other characteristics. Have them organize the subclimates into major climate zones and connect the cards together by using a binder ring. Students can illustrate the cards and use them for review. **LS Visual**

Quiz GENERAL

1. What is a highland climate? (A highland climate is located in the mountains and has large variations in temperature and precipitation over short distances because of changes in elevation.)
2. What is a heat island? (an area that shows a higher temperature than surrounding areas; The rise in temperature commonly occurs over cities, where buildings and pavement absorb and reradiate a lot of heat.)

Environmental Connection

The North American Rain Forest Olympic National Park in Washington is home to a rain forest. In this long stretch of coast, the prevailing winds blow humid air onshore from the Pacific Ocean. As winds hit the coastal mountains, the air rises and dumps large amounts of rain and snow throughout the year. Thick forests of Sitka spruce, Douglas fir, Western cedar, and giant redwoods grow in this lush, mild region. Have students identify the other areas with marine west coast climates and whether rain forests occur in these places. (southern Australia, much of western Europe, tip of South America; Rain forests have largely disappeared as a result of development and logging.)

Close, *continued*

Answers to Section Review

1. tropical, middle-latitude, and polar
2. rain forest: small temperature range, annual precipitation of 200 cm, lush, dense vegetation and high biodiversity; desert: large temperature range, precipitation less than 25 cm, little vegetation; savanna: small temperature range, alternating dry and wet periods with precipitation of 50 cm, open grasslands
3. marine west coast: small temperature range, frequent rainfall, mild winters and summers, dense forests; steppe: large temperature range, low precipitation, drought-resistant vegetation, cold, dry winters, and warm, wet summers; humid continental: large temperature range, precipitation greater than 75 cm, diverse vegetation, variable weather; humid subtropical: large temperature range, high precipitation, broadleaf and evergreen trees, high humidity; mediterranean: small temperature range, precipitation about 40 cm, broadleaf and evergreens, long, dry summers and mild, wet winters
4. subarctic: largest temperature range, precipitation of 25 to 50 cm, evergreen trees, cool summers and long, cold winters; tundra: average temp below 4 °C, 9 months below freezing, precipitation of 25 cm, treeless plains; polar icecaps: average temp below 0 °C, low annual precipitation, high winds, little or no life
5. vegetation, elevation, and proximity to bodies of water
6. City climates have surfaces, such as pavement and buildings, that absorb and reradiate large amounts of heat, so temperatures may be several degrees warmer than in surrounding rural areas.
7. Temperatures would be higher because pavement absorbs and reradiates more heat than vegetation does.
8. Climate zones do not always line up with latitude because of the effect of prevailing winds, elevation, and proximity to oceans and other large bodies of water.

Answers continued on p. 631A

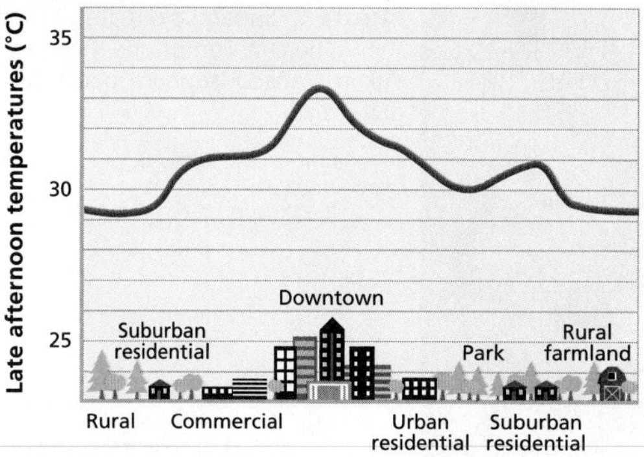

Figure 2 The less vegetation and more pavement and buildings an area has, the higher the temperatures in the area tend to be.

Local Climates

The climate of a small area is called a **microclimate.** Microclimates are influenced by density of vegetation, by elevation, and by proximity to large bodies of water and structures built by humans. For example, in a city, pavement and buildings absorb solar energy and then reradiate that energy as heat, which raises the temperature of the air above and creates a "heat island," as shown in **Figure 2.** As a result, the average temperature may be a few degrees higher in the city than it is in surrounding rural areas. In contrast, vegetation in rural areas does not reradiate as much energy, so temperatures in those areas are lower.

microclimate the climate of a small area

Effects of Elevation

Elevation also may affect local climates. As elevation increases, temperature decreases and the climate changes. For example, the *highland climate* is characterized by large variations in temperature and precipitation over short distances because of changes in elevation. Highland climates are commonly located in mountainous regions—even in tropical areas.

Academic Vocabulary

variation (VER ee AY shuhn) a difference in the usual form or function

Effects of Large Bodies of Water

Large bodies of water, such as lakes, influence local climates. The water absorbs and releases heat slower than the land does. Thus, the water moderates the temperature of the nearby land. Large bodies of water can also increase precipitation. Therefore, microclimates near large bodies of water have a smaller range of temperatures and higher annual precipitation than other locations at the same latitude do.

Section 2 Review

Key Ideas

1. **Identify** the three types of climate zones.
2. **Describe** the three types of tropical climates.
3. **Describe** the five types of middle-latitude climates.
4. **Describe** the three types of polar climates.
5. **Identify** three factors that influence microclimates.
6. **Explain** why city climates may differ from rural climates.

Critical Thinking

7. **Making Inferences** What would happen to the temperature of a rural location if the vegetation were replaced with a parking lot?
8. **Compare and Contrast** Compare latitude lines with the boundaries of major climate zones. Why do they align in some regions but not in others?

Concept Mapping

9. Use the following terms to create a concept map: *tropical climate, subarctic, tundra, steppe, polar icecap, mediterranean, middle-latitude climate, rain forest, savanna, desert,* and *polar climate.*

Differentiated Instruction

Alternative Assessment

Travel Agent Have students pretend they are travel agents. They should choose a travel destination and prepare a brochure that describes the destination, its climate, what types of wildlife lives there, and what travelers should pack for their trip. Encourage students to be creative and to use photos or illustrations in their brochure. They might also describe side trips to destinations that have different climates.
LS Verbal/Visual

SECTION 3

Climate Change

ENVIRONMENTAL CONNECTION

Key Ideas	Key Terms	Why It Matters
❯ Compare four methods used to study climate change. ❯ Describe four factors that may cause climate change. ❯ Identify potential impacts of climate change. ❯ Identify ways that humans can minimize their effect on climate change.	**climatologist** **global warming**	There's no doubt that climate changes. Understanding how and why it changes will help guide your response to issues like global warming.

Scientists who study and compare past and present climates are called **climatologists.** Climatologists look at past climates to find patterns in the changes that occur. Identifying those patterns allows the scientists to make predictions about future climates.

Studying Climate Change

When trying to learn about factors that influence climate change, scientists study the evidence left by past climates. This evidence can be left in the remains of plants and animals from earlier time periods. For example, *fossils* of a plant or animal may show adaptations to a particular environment that can reveal clues about the environment's climate. Even polar icecaps contain evidence of past climates. By studying the concentration of gases trapped within *ice cores,* scientists can learn about the gas composition of the atmosphere thousands of years ago. **Table 1** describes some of the methods used to study past climates.

climatologist a scientist who gathers data to study and compare past and present climates and to predict future climate change

Table 1 Methods of Studying Past Climates

Method	What is measured	What is indicated	Length of time measured
Ice cores	concentrations of gases in ice and meltwater	High levels of CO_2 indicate warmer climate; ice ages accompany decreases in CO_2.	hundreds of thousands of years
Sea-floor sediment	concentration of ^{18}O in shells of microorganisms	High ^{18}O levels indicate cool water; lower ^{18}O levels indicate warm water.	hundreds of thousands of years
Fossils	pollen types, leaf shapes, and animal body adaptations	Flower pollens and broad leaves indicate warm climates; evergreen pollens and small, waxy leaves indicate cool climates. Animal fossils show adaptations to climate changes.	millions of years
Tree rings	ring width	Thin rings indicate cool weather and/or less precipitation.	hundreds to thousands of years
Speleothems	concentrations of ^{13}C and ^{18}O in stalagmites	High levels of ^{13}C indicate El Niño events. Low levels of ^{18}O record individual hurricanes.	weeks to hundreds of years

Key Resources

Chapter Resource File

- Directed Reading BASIC
- Inquiry Lab: Particulates in the Atmosphere GENERAL

Technology

- Transparencies Bellringer

Differentiated Instruction

Struggling Readers

Reading Organizer As students read this section, encourage them to outline or take notes as described in Appendix A. Later students can used these notes as a study guide for assessments. LS **Verbal**

Section 3

Focus

Overview

This section explains how scientists study past climate change and model future climate change. It describes natural factors and human activities that may alter climate and ways to minimize human effects on climate.

Bellringer

Have students imagine that the climate of the area in which they live has changed so that it is now colder than it used to be. Have students write down five different ways that they think the area would be affected by cooler temperatures. LS **Logical**

Motivate

Activity GENERAL

Tree Rings Obtain a cross-section of a tree trunk. Have students look closely at the rings. Ask, "Are all of the rings the same thickness?" (no) Have students discuss under what conditions growth rings might be thicker or thinner. (Thicker rings grow during years that have good growing conditions, thinner rings form during years that have poor growing conditions. Tree rings show more about short-term climate changes than long-term climate changes. Tree rings also reveal the history of forest fires, disease, and weather.) LS **Visual**

Teach

Internet Activity — GENERAL

Climate Models Have interested students visit Web sites of government agencies, such as NASA's Goddard Institute for Space Studies and the University Corporation for Atmospheric Research, that use general circulation models (GCMs). Have them investigate the history of GCMs, how they are set up, what variables they incorporate, what predictions they make, and what limitations they have. Have students present their findings in a short oral report. A worksheet designed to direct student research on this topic can be found in the **Chapter Resource File** booklet or by visiting www.thinkcentral.com and entering the keyword **HQXCLIX.** **LS Verbal**

Answer to Reading Check

Scientists use computer models to incorporate as much data as possible to sort out the complex variables that influence climate and to make predictions about climate.

Figure 1 Scientists need to use powerful computers to process the amount of data required to study climates.

Modeling Climates

Because so many factors influence climate, studying climate change is a complicated process. Currently, scientists use computers to create models to study climate, as shown in **Figure 1.** These models incorporate millions of pieces of data and help sort the complex sets of variables that influence climate. They are called *general circulation models,* or *GCMs.* GCMs simulate changes in one variable when other variables are unchanged. For example, if the sulfur dioxide level is raised in a particular model, the model indicates a decrease in incoming solar radiation because sulfur dioxide reflects sunlight.

Climate models simulate many factors of climate, including temperature, precipitation, wind patterns, and sea-level changes. These computer models are complex because they model interactions between oceans, wind, land, clouds, and vegetation. As computers become more powerful, computer-generated climate models will provide greater detail about the global climate system and will help scientists better understand climate change.

Reading Check **Why do scientists use computers to model climate?**

Why It Matters

Ice Tells a Story

EYE ON THE ENVIRONMENT

Have you ever had a frozen treat with several layers that were different colors or textures? You probably inferred that each layer would have a different flavor. Similarly, each layer of ice in the Arctic and Antarctica was formed under different conditions, such as temperature, wind patterns, and amount of precipitation. Scientists study layers of ice in ice cores and make inferences about the conditions under which each layer formed. Ice cores are obtained by drilling thousands of meters down into polar ice. Ice cores can help scientists understand past climate change and develop models to predict future climate change.

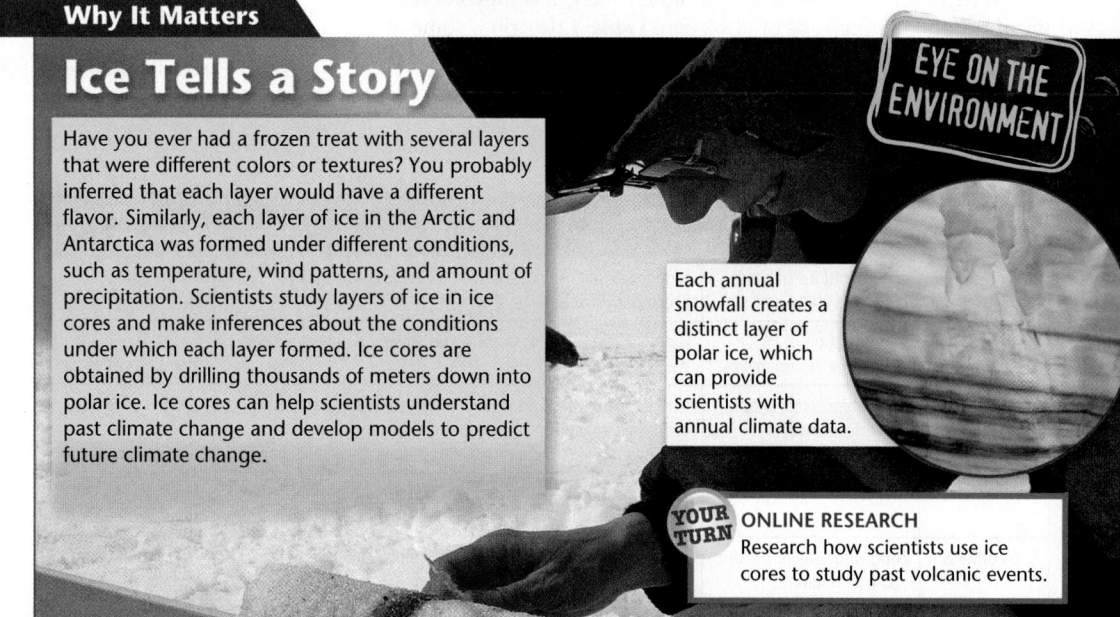

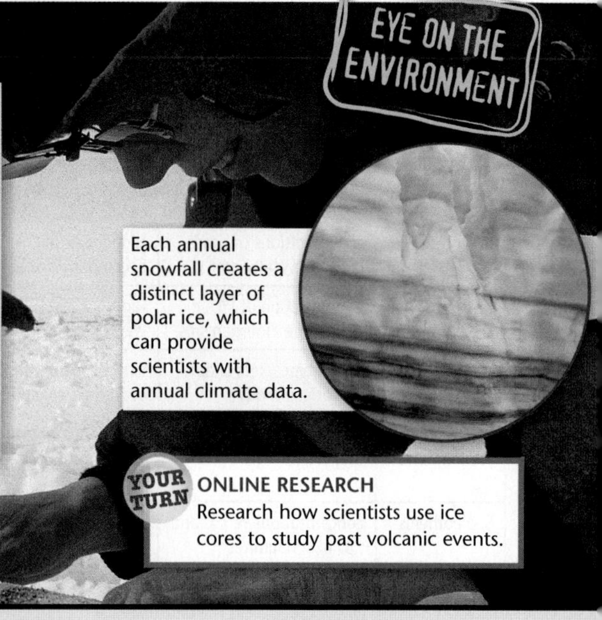

Each annual snowfall creates a distinct layer of polar ice, which can provide scientists with annual climate data.

YOUR TURN ONLINE RESEARCH
Research how scientists use ice cores to study past volcanic events.

Why It Matters

Ice Tells a Story Snow that falls near the poles does not melt; it accumulates over hundreds of thousands of years. As it accumulates each year, the new snow puts pressure on the layers below, and the deeper layers turn to ice. Scientists can determine past air temperatures by finding the ratio of oxygen isotopes in the layers. Layers that fell during colder temperatures have lower concentrations of the heavy oxygen isotope (oxygen-18).

Answers to Your Turn

Ash from volcanoes can become trapped in ice layers. Scientists can study the ash to learn about past wind patterns and volcanic eruptions.

Potential Causes of Climate Change

By studying computer-generated climate models, scientists have determined several potential causes of climate change. Factors that might cause climate change include the movement of tectonic plates, changes in Earth's orbit, human activity, and atmospheric changes.

Plate Tectonics

The movement of continents over millions of years caused by tectonic plate motion may affect climate change. The changing position of the continents changes wind flow and ocean currents around the globe. These changes affect the temperature and precipitation patterns of the continents and oceans. Thus, the climate of any particular continent is not the same as it was millions of years ago.

Orbital Changes

Periodic changes in the shape of Earth's orbit, changes in Earth's tilt, and the wobble of Earth on its axis can lead to climate change, as shown in **Figure 2.** The combination of these factors is described by the *Milankovitch theory*. Each change of motion has a different effect on climate. Variation in the shape of Earth's orbit, from elliptical to more circular, affects Earth's distance from the sun. Earth's distance from the sun affects the temperature of Earth and therefore affects the climate. Decreasing tilt decreases temperature differences between seasons. The wobble of Earth on its axis changes the direction of Earth's tilt and can reverse the seasons. These changes occur in cycles of 100,000, 41,000, and 26,000 years respectively.

READING TOOLBOX

Temporal Language
As you read about climate change, make a table that describes the temporal language that is used.

THINK central
INTERACT ONLINE
(Keyword: HQXCLIF2)

Figure 2 Earth's Orbital Changes

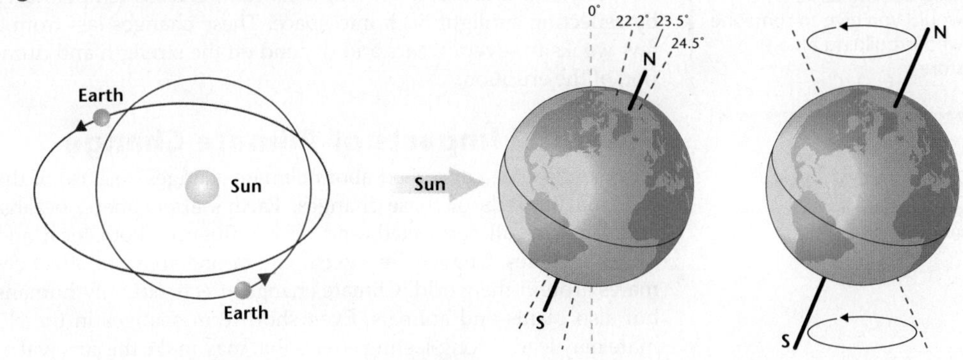

Eccentricity Earth encounters more variation in the energy that it receives from the sun when Earth's orbit is elongated than it does when Earth's orbit is more circular.

Tilt The tilt of Earth's axis varies between 22.2° and 24.5°. The greater the tilt angle is, the more solar energy the poles receive.

Precession A gradual change, or "wobble," in the orientation of Earth's axis affects the relationship between Earth's tilt and eccentricity.

READING TOOLBOX

Temporal Language Students should include words and phases such as hundreds of thousands of years, millions of years, hundreds to thousands of years, currently, a few weeks to several years, short-term changes, long-term effects, and during this century.

Debate — ADVANCED

Global Warming While many climatologists think that human activities are inducing global warming, some remain skeptical. Given the variety of other factors known to influence climate and the evidence that climates have changed in the past without human influence, these scientists do not think that increasing greenhouse gases are solely responsible for the temperature increases during the last century. Have interested students research different sides of this issue and present a debate to the class. **LS Verbal/Logical**

Why It Matters

The Little Ice Age While the last glacial period ended more than 15,000 years ago, many parts of the world experienced what is known as the "Little Ice Age" between the 15th and the mid-19th centuries. In Europe, winters were harsh, springs and summers were cold and wet, crops failed, growing seasons were shorter, and mountain glaciers advanced. North America and China experienced similar trends. Around 1900, temperatures started rising again and continued to rise through the 20th century.

Differentiated Instruction

Special Education Students

Question-and-Answer Session To help students stay involved with the text, ask them to think of and write possible test questions while they are reading the text. Then, have students review by asking other students their questions. After the question-and-answer session, collect all of the questions. Tell students you are going to use some of their questions for a test or quiz—and do so. **LS Verbal**

Astronomy Connection

A Variable Star The sun is a variable star; its energy output varies over time. During the last 200 to 300 years, the sun's brightness has increased about 0.4 percent. According to studies, this increase is too weak to explain global warming. However, changes in the number and duration of sunspots—the dark, cooler regions on the surface of the sun—also correlate with changes in Earth's temperature. Current climate changes may be the result of both natural events and human activities.

Key Resources

Technology
- Transparencies
  115 Orbital Changes and Climate

Teach, *continued*

Homework ADVANCED

Volcanoes and Climate Volcanic eruptions can have dramatic effects on climates around the world. In June 1991, Mount Pinatubo erupted, spewing millions of tons of soot and ash into the atmosphere. Within a year, average global temperatures dropped about 0.5 °C and many regions experienced a harsher winter and cooler summer. Other eruptions have had similar effects, perhaps most notably, the "year without a summer" that followed the 1815 eruption of Mount Tambora in Indonesia. Have interested students investigate major volcanic eruptions throughout history and prepare a timeline documenting the effects on climate. LS **Verbal**

Answers to Reading Check

Climate change influences humans, plants, and animals. It also affects nearby climates, sea level, and precipitation rates.

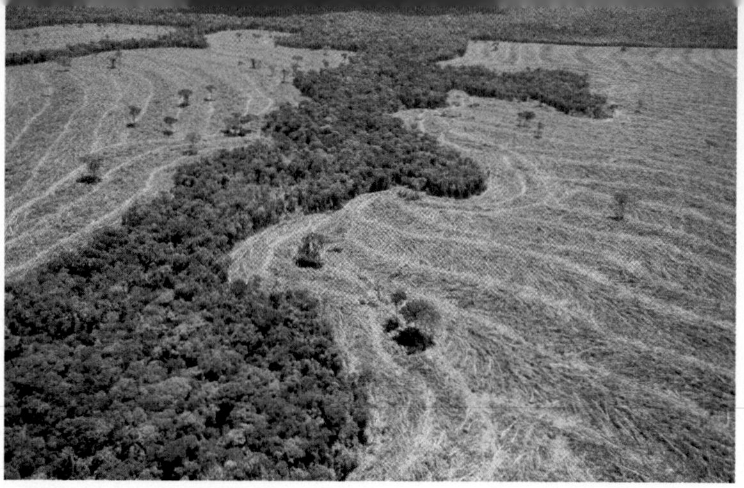

Figure 3 Most deforestation in Brazil is caused by farmers who clear the land for planting crops.

Quick Lab 15 min

Hot Stuff

Procedure

1. In mid-afternoon, use a thermometer to measure the air temperature over a grassy field or other vegetated area. Make sure to shield the thermometer from direct sunlight.
2. Measure the air temperature over a parking lot. Take the measurement at the same height above the surface as the height of the measurement over the vegetated area. Again, make sure that the thermometer is not directly in the sunlight.

Analysis

1. How did the results differ for each location?
2. How would you explain the difference in the results?
3. What suggestion for how to keep cooling costs low would you give to someone who is building a new store?

Academic Vocabulary

impact (IM PAKT) the effect of one thing on another

Human Activity

Human activity affects climate through emissions and land use. Pollution from transportation and industry releases carbon dioxide, CO_2, into the atmosphere. Increases in CO_2 concentrations may lead to global warming, an increase in temperatures around Earth. CO_2 is also released into the atmosphere when trees are burned to provide land for agriculture and urban development. Because vegetation uses CO_2 to make food, deforestation, as shown in **Figure 3,** also affects one of the natural ways of removing CO_2 from the atmosphere. As scientists continue to study climate, they will learn more about how human activity affects climate and about how changes in climate may affect us.

Volcanic Activity

Large volcanic eruptions can influence climates around the world. Sulfur and ash from eruptions can decrease temperatures by reflecting sunlight back into space. These changes last from a few weeks to several years and depend on the strength and duration of the eruption.

Potential Impacts of Climate Change

Scientists are concerned about climate changes because of the potential impacts of these changes. Earth's atmosphere, oceans, and land are all connected, and each influences both local and global climates. Changes in the climate of one area can affect climates around the world. Climate change affects not only humans but also plants and animals. Even short-term changes in the climate may lead to long-lasting effects that may make the survival of life on Earth more difficult for both humans and other species. Some of these potential climate changes include global warming, sea-level changes, and changes in precipitation.

Reading Check **What things are influenced by climate change?**

Quick Lab

Skills Acquired
- Measuring
- Analyzing

Materials
- Thermometer

Teacher's Notes: Make sure the thermometer is not directly in the sun and that students measure temperature at the same height over the grass and the pavement.

Answers to Analysis

1. The temperature should be hotter over the pavement.
2. Pavement absorbs and reradiates more heat than a grassy field does, heating the air above it to a higher temperature.
3. Make sure to have some trees and other landscaping around the new store and not just a massive expanse of parking lot.

Global Warming

Global temperatures have increased approximately 1 °C over the last 100 years. Researchers are trying to determine if this increase is a natural variation or the result of human activities, such as deforestation and pollution. A gradual increase in average global temperatures is called **global warming.** This process may result from an increase in the concentration of greenhouse gases, such as CO_2, in the atmosphere.

global warming a gradual increase in the average global temperature

An increase in global temperature can lead to an increase in evaporation. Increased evaporation could cause some areas to become drier than they are now. Some plants and animals would not be able to live in these drier conditions. An increase in evaporation in other areas could cause crops to suffer damage. However, an increase in temperatures due to global warming might improve conditions for crops in colder, northern regions.

An increase in global temperatures could also cause ice at the poles to melt. If a significant amount of ice melts, sea levels around the world could rise. This rise in sea levels would cause flooding around coastlines, where many cities are located.

SciLINKS
www.scilinks.org
Topic: Global Warming
Code: HQX0681

Sea-Level Changes

Using computer models, some scientists have predicted an increase in global temperature of 2 to 4 °C during this century. An increase of only a few degrees worldwide could melt the polar icecaps and raise sea level by the addition of water to the oceans and by thermal expansion of the ocean water itself. On a shoreline that has a gentle slope, the shoreline could shift inland many miles, as shown in **Figure 4.** Many coastal inhabitants would be displaced, and freshwater and agricultural land resources would be diminished. Because approximately 50% of the world's population lives near coastlines, this sea-level rise would have devastating effects.

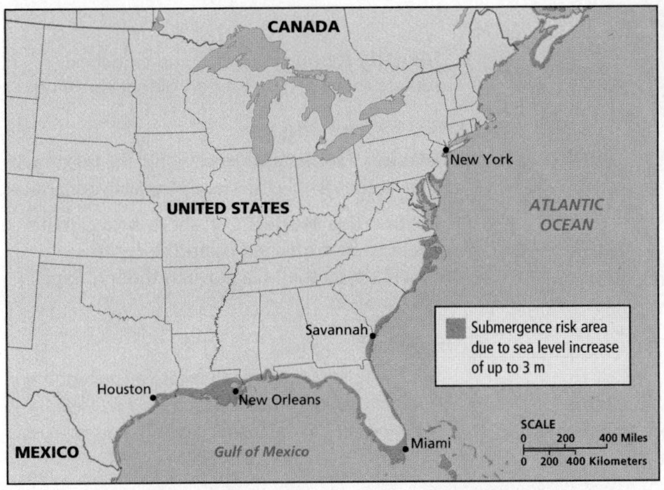

Figure 4 As sea level rises, shorelines could shift inland many miles. ***Which two states would lose the most area if sea level were to rise by 3 m?***

Demonstration — BASIC

Icecaps Melting Sea levels may rise if icecaps melt but only if those icecaps cover land, as the Antarctic ice sheet does. Fill a bowl with water, and add a few ice cubes to simulate floating icecaps. Mark the water level, and then let the ice melt, observing any changes as the ice melts. (The water level should stay the same.) Repeat with the same level of water, but with an island made of clay in the bowl. Place the ice cubes on the clay, and mark the water level. Let the ice melt, and observe how the water level rises. **LS Visual**

Using the Figure — GENERAL

Rising Seas If global warming continues, rising sea levels pose real threats to more than half of the world's people, those who live near coastlines. Recent estimates indicate that sea levels could rise almost a meter by 2100. Cities along coasts would be prone to flooding. Some islands might disappear. Bangladesh could lose up to 18% of its land, displacing millions of people. Have students investigate the causes and consequences of rising sea levels. Answer to caption question: Louisiana and Florida **LS Interpersonal**

Close

Reteaching — BASIC

Peer Reviewing Have students work in pairs to write three to five questions about the material in this section. Then, have students quiz each other by using the questions they wrote. **LS Interpersonal** Co-op Learning

Quiz — GENERAL

1. What does a climatologist do? (studies and compares past and present climates to help predict future climate changes)
2. What is a hybrid car and how can its use reduce pollution? (A hybrid car uses both gasoline and electricity. It releases less CO_2 into the atmosphere.)

Law Connection — ADVANCED

Kyoto Protocol In 1997, 160 nations met in Japan to negotiate a treaty limiting greenhouse gas emissions in an effort to forestall climate change. The nations agreed to reduce emissions from 1990 levels by an average of 5.2%. However, not all of the countries ended up ratifying the treaty. Have interested students investigate the status of the treaty and the position of the United States. Have them present findings in a poster or oral report. **LS Logical/Verbal**

Close, *continued*

Answers to Section Review

1. Student answers should contain four of the following methods: ice cores: measure concentrations of CO_2 in ice and meltwater; sea-floor sediments: measure concentrations of oxygen isotopes in microorganism shells; fossils: measure changes in pollen types, leaf shapes, and animal adaptations; tree rings: measure ring widths; speleotherms: measure isotopes of oxygen. Speleotherms help climatologists assess climate change over weeks to hundreds of years. Tree rings help climatologists assess climate change over hundreds and thousands of years. Ice cores and sea-floor sediments help climatologists assess climate change over hundreds of thousands of years, while fossils help climatologists reconstruct changes over millions of years.
2. movement of continents due to plate tectonics; changes in Earth's orbit and tilt; volcanic activity; human activity
3. When Earth's orbit is elliptical, Earth encounters more variation in energy from the sun. The tilt of the Earth's axis also changes. When tilt decreases, temperature differences between seasons decreases. Wobble changes the direction of tilt and can reverse the seasons.
4. Carbon dioxide is a greenhouse gas that absorbs heat radiated by Earth's surface. Increasing carbon dioxide could increase the greenhouse effect and lead to global warming.

Figure 5 People from the Wangari Maathai Green Belt Movement in Kenya, Africa, prepare seedlings for planting.

What Humans Can Do

Many countries are working together to reduce the potential effects of global warming. Treaties and laws have been passed to reduce pollution. Industrial practices are being monitored and changed. Even community projects to reforest areas, such as the one shown in **Figure 5,** have been developed on a local level.

Individual Efforts

Each individual person can also help to reduce pollution that is caused by the burning of fossil fuels, such as running automobiles and using electricity. These activities increase CO_2 concentrations in the atmosphere. Therefore, humans can have a significant effect on pollution rates by turning lights off when they are not in use, by turning down the heat in the winter, and by reducing air conditioner use in the summer. Recycling is also helpful because less energy is needed to recycle some products than to create them.

Transportation Solutions

Using public transportation and driving fuel-efficient vehicles can also help to release less CO_2 into the atmosphere. All vehicles burn fuel more efficiently when they are properly tuned and the tires are properly inflated. Driving at a consistent speed also allows a vehicle to burn fuel efficiently. Car manufacturers have been developing cars that are more fuel efficient. For example, *hybrid cars* use both gasoline and electricity. These cars release less CO_2 into the atmosphere from burning fuel than other cars do.

Section 3 Review

Key Ideas

1. **Compare** four methods that climatologists use to study climate.
2. **Identify** four factors that may cause climate change.
3. **Describe** how orbital changes may affect climate.
4. **Explain** how changes in CO_2 concentrations affect global temperatures.
5. **Explain** one potential negative impact of global warming.
6. **Identify** two ways that countries can work together to reduce their impact on, and the potential effects of, global warming.
7. **Identify** four ways that an individual can reduce their own impact on global warming.

Critical Thinking

8. **Making Predictions** How would the melting of small icebergs affect sea level? Explain your answer.
9. **Evaluating Models** Can short-term climate changes be explained using the cycles described by the Milankovitch theory? Explain your answer.

Concept Mapping

10. Use the following terms to create a concept map: *climatologist, general circulation models, global warming, ice cores, tree rings, fossils,* and *isotopes.*

5. Answers may vary. Sample answer: One potential negative impact of global warming would be the flooding of coastal communities caused by rising sea levels as polar icecaps melt.
6. Treaties and laws aimed at reducing pollution can help countries reduce their impacts on global warming. Monitoring of industrial practices can also play a role in reducing those impacts.
7. By turning off lights, reducing heating and cooling, recycling, and using mass transportation, individuals can reduce their impacts on global warming.

Answers continued on p. 631A

Differentiated Instruction

Alternative Assessment

Global Warming in the News Have students write a newspaper style article about global warming. The article should describe how scientists study and model past and present climate change and what their models predict for the future. **LS Verbal**

Why It Matters

SCIENCE & SOCIETY

Polar Bears on Thin Ice

What would you do if a corner store, where you bought milk, juice, and snacks, became farther away each day? What would you do if a trip to this store involved not only a longer distance but also more difficult conditions, which you were not adapted to?

As the ice cover in the Arctic decreases, polar bears are facing these kinds of challenges in their search for food. Many researchers predict that, if climate models are correct, at least two-thirds of the polar bear population will be gone by 2050 and the species will not survive the century.

Some polar bears have drowned trying to travel longer and longer distances between ice floes.

Polar bears depend on ice as a platform from which to hunt seals. With less ice, some bears are starving to death.

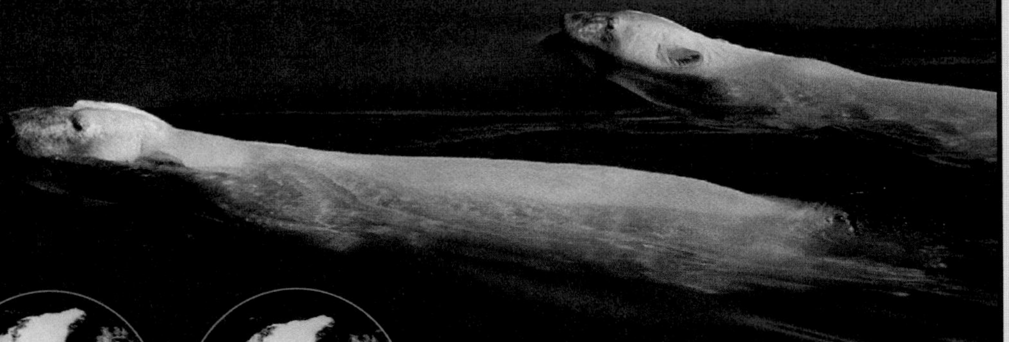

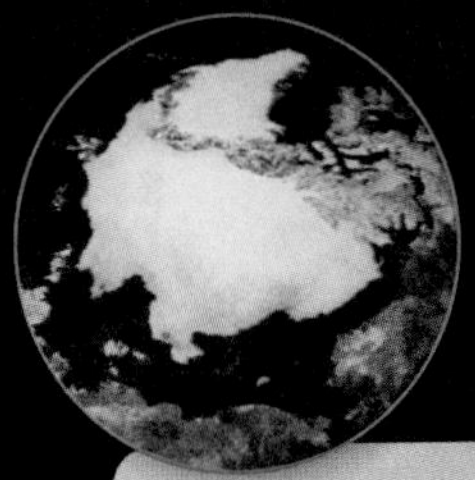

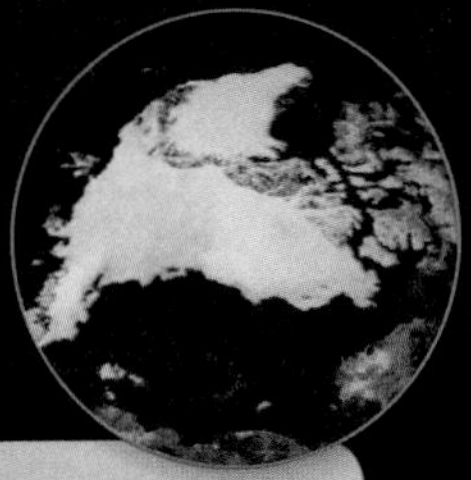

2005 2007

Sea ice in the Arctic has been decreasing dramatically as temperatures rise.

YOUR TURN

CRITICAL THINKING

Why do you think polar bears are often used to symbolize climate change?

UNDERSTANDING CONCEPTS

Seals give birth and nurse their young on ice. How might this further affect polar bears as the ice cover in the Arctic decreases?

Why It Matters

Are Polar Bears on Thin Ice?

The plight of the polar bear is often used to illustrate the impact of climate change on our natural world. The potential loss of polar bear populations will also directly affect human populations. Some Arctic peoples hunt and depend on polar bears for food and livelihood. If polar bears disappear these people will lose a traditional source of food and an important part of their culture.

Answer to Your Turn

Critical Thinking The decrease in ice cover in the polar regions is the most visible result of climate change today, and polar bears rely on ice for survival. Polar bears are a popular symbol of the north and nature. They are often seen as majestic and powerful animals.

Understanding Concepts Seals are the main source of food for polar bears. As the ice cover in the Arctic decreases, seals have to compete for fewer and fewer appropriate places to have their young. This competition will result in a decrease in the seal population. With fewer seals, polar bears will have less to eat and their populations will also decrease.

Inquiry Lab
 45 min

Time Required

one 45-minute class period

Lab Ratings

EASY ——————————→ HARD

Teacher Preparation △

Student Setup △△

Concept Level △△

Cleanup △△

Skills Acquired

- Observing
- Measuring
- Experimenting
- Predicting
- Collecting Data
- Organizing and Analyzing Data

Scientific Methods

In this lab, students will
- Ask Questions
- Form and Test a Hypothesis
- Make Observations
- Analyze the Results
- Draw Conclusions

Materials

The materials listed on this page are enough for groups of two to four students.

What You'll Do

> **Determine** whether land or water absorbs heat faster.

> **Explain** how the properties of land and water affect climate.

What You'll Need

container (2)
heat lamp
meterstick
soil
thermometer, Celsius (2)
water

Safety

Factors That Affect Climate

Many factors affect climate. One of the most significant factors that influence climate is the distribution of land and water. Because land and water absorb and release thermal energy (or energy as heat) differently, they affect the atmosphere differently. In turn, the differences between land and water affect climate. In this lab, you will explore how the properties of land and water affect climate.

Ask a Question

❶ How do the properties of land and water affect climate?

Form a Hypothesis

❷ On a separate piece of paper, write a hypothesis that is a possible answer to the question above.

Test the Hypothesis

❸ Fill one container with soil and the other container with water. Place both containers on a flat surface next to each other.

Step ❺

Tips and Tricks

Make sure that the two containers are the same size and shape and that the lamp is positioned so that it shines evenly on both containers. The thermometers should be positioned the same distance below the surface of the soil and the water, and the same volume of soil and water should be used in the containers. Also, make sure that the soil is dry. Have students predict the results of this activity if they used different soil types or sand or gravel.

4. Place the thermometer in the soil, as shown below. The bulb of the thermometer should be covered by no more than 0.5 cm of soil. Record the temperature.
5. Place the second thermometer in the container of water, as shown in the photo on the previous page. Make sure that the bulb of the thermometer is covered by no more than 0.5 cm of water.
6. Place the heat lamp 25 cm above both containers. Turn on the heat lamp.
7. Create a data table like the one at the right. In your table, record the temperature of each sample at 1, 3, 5, and 10 min intervals.
8. Disconnect the lamp, and move it aside. Record the temperature of the soil and water after 5 min. **CAUTION** Be sure to let the heat lamp cool before storing it.

Data Table

Time (min)	Temperature of soil (°C)	Temperature of water (°C)
1		
3		
5		
10		
5 (after light off)		

Analyze the Results

1. **Analyzing Data** Which substance absorbed more thermal energy: water or soil?
2. **Analyzing Results** Which substance lost thermal energy faster when the heat source was turned off: water or soil?

Draw Conclusions

3. **Evaluating Conclusions** What conclusion can you draw about how land and water on Earth are heated by the sun?
4. **Analyzing Methods** Does this experiment describe how proximity to a body of water affects the temperature of a region? If so, explain your answer. If not, how could you test that variable?

Extension

Applying Ideas Repeat this experiment, but modify the angle at which the light strikes the surface of the soil and the water. How do your results differ from the results of the original experiment? How does the angle of the light affect temperature change in water and soil?

Answers to Analyze the Results

1. The soil absorbed more energy than the water did.
2. The soil lost energy faster than the water did.

Answers to Draw Conclusions

3. The sun heats the land faster than it does the water. The water, on the other hand, will retain heat from the sun longer than the land does and the water will cool down more slowly.
4. While this experiment provides evidence that proximity to a body of water might have an effect on the temperature of a region, it does not really test that variable specifically. One way to test that variable would be to take measurements of soil temperatures in areas near a large body of water and away from the water at various times on a sunny day and again at different times throughout the following night.

Answer to Extension

At angles of less than 90°, the soil and water should not heat up as much or as quickly as they did in the original experiment. The smaller the angle at which the light strikes the soil and water, the smaller the temperature increase should be. Nevertheless, similar differences between the soil and water should be evident.

Climates of the World

Discussion GENERAL

Climate Classification Discuss with students the fact that classification schemes are the product of human ideas and are not natural phenomena. The value of a system is determined by how it is used. A classification system may be useful for one purpose and of no use for others. Have interested students investigate other climate classification systems and their uses or devise their own system. **LS Logical**

Answers to Map Skills Activity

1. about 15°N to 30°N
2. The eastern coast has a different climate than the western coast because a warm current flows northward along the Atlantic coast, while a cold current flows southward along the Pacific coast.
3. If the current on the west coast of Australia were a warm current, the climate of western Australia would probably be wetter and more like the climate on the eastern coast of Australia.
4. Monsoons are located from about 0° (the equator) to 40°N, near India and Southeast Asia.
5. The western coast of South America is desert because the cold ocean current that flows along the coast chills and stabilizes air masses, preventing rainfall. Prevailing winds also blow away from the continent. The inland part of the continent at the same latitude is humid because the trade winds blow across warm Atlantic currents, bringing the region large amounts of precipitation.

MAPS in Action

Climates of the World

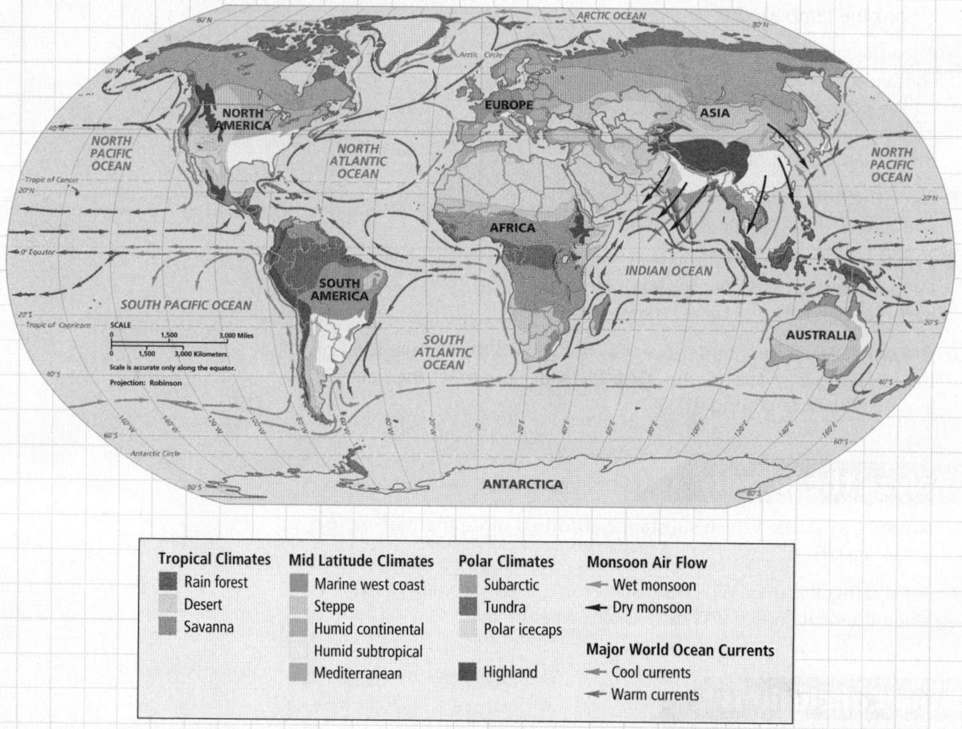

Map Skills Activity

This map shows the climate regions of Earth and the locations of warm and cold ocean currents. Use the map to answer the questions below.

1. **Analyzing Data** Estimate the latitude range for the desert climate of northern Africa.
2. **Making Comparisons** Why does the eastern coast of the United States have a different climate than the western coast does, even though the coasts are at similar latitudes?
3. **Analyzing Ideas** If the ocean current that flows off the western coast of Australia were a warm current, how would it affect the climate of western Australia?
4. **Using a Key** Identify the latitudes where monsoons are located.
5. **Evaluating Data** Explain why the western coast of South America is desert while the inland part of the continent at the same latitude is humid.

Key Resources

Technology

- Transparencies
  116 Climates of the World

Chapter 22

Summary

THINK central SUPER SUMMARY Keyword: HQXCLIS

Key Ideas	Key Terms

Section 1

Factors That Affect Climate

- The climate of a region is described by the region's temperature and precipitation.
- Latitude determines the angle at which the sun's rays hit Earth. At higher latitudes, the angle is smaller so areas receive less solar energy. At lower latitudes, the angle is larger so areas receive more solar energy.
- The temperature of land or water influences the amount of heat that the air above the land or water can absorb or release. The temperature of the air then affects the climate of the area.
- Topography affects climate by causing temperature variations due to elevation and by creating rain shadows.

climate, p. 605
specific heat, p. 608
El Niño, p. 609
monsoon, p. 609

Section 2

Climate Zones

- The three tropical climates, which are located near the equator, are tropical rain forest, tropical desert, and savanna climates.
- The five middle-latitude climates are marine west coast, steppe, humid continental, humid subtropical, and mediterranean climates.
- The three polar climates are subarctic, tundra, and polar icecap climates.
- Due to the heat island effect, the average temperature in a city is a few degrees higher than it is in surrounding rural areas.

tropical climate, p. 611
middle-latitude climate, p. 612
polar climate, p. 613
microclimate, p. 614

Section 3

Climate Change

- By using ice cores, sea-floor sediment, fossils, tree rings, and speleothems, scientists have been able to study past climates.
- Natural processes and human activity may be causing changes in Earth's climate, including global warming.
- One potential effect of climate change is a rise in sea levels, which could lead to flooding around coastlines.
- Humans can minimize their contribution to climate change by reducing pollution from burning fossil fuels, recycling, and using public transportation.

climatologist, p. 615
global warming, p. 619

Chapter Summary

Using THINK central Resources

Super Summary

Have students connect the major concepts in this chapter through an interactive Super Summary. Visit www.thinkcentral.com and type in the keyword **HQXCLIS** to access the Super Summary for this chapter.

Activity — GENERAL

Subclimate Story Have students choose a subclimate other than their own and write a story about a family that lives in that subclimate. The family should include at least one teenager. The story plot may be in the form of "a day in the life" of the family or something more complex. The story should include references to the factors that have shaped the climate, adaptations people make to the climate in their daily lives, and how climate change might alter this climate and its inhabitants. Allow students time for additional research. Have volunteers read their stories aloud to the class.
LS Verbal/Interpersonal

Chapter Review

Assignment Guide	
Section	**Questions**
1	2, 6, 8, 10–13, 23, 25
2	1, 3, 7, 14–16, 19, 21, 28
3	4, 9, 17, 18, 26, 27, 29–31
1 and 2	5, 22
1–3	20, 24

Reading Toolbox

1. Cause—air temperature decreases as altitude increases; Effect—climates at high altitudes are cooler

Using Key Terms

2–7. Answers may vary but should show that students understand the definitions of and differences between key terms.

Understanding Key Concepts

8. b
9. b
10. a
11. b
12. c
13. c
14. c
15. a
16. b

Short Answer

17. The Milankovitch theory proposes that cyclic changes in Earth's orbit from circular to elliptical and changes in the tilt and wobble of Earth's axis can lead to climate change by altering the amount of energy Earth receives from the sun. Changes to incoming solar energy would affect Earth's temperature and thus could cause some climate changes.

Chapter 22 Review

1. **Cause-and-Effect Map** Draw a cause-and-effect map that shows how elevation affects climate. READING TOOLBOX

USING KEY TERMS

Use each of the following terms in a separate sentence.

2. *specific heat*
3. *microclimate*
4. *climatologist*

For each pair of terms, explain how the meanings of the terms differ.

5. *climate* and *microclimate*
6. *El Niño* and *monsoon*
7. *tropical climate* and *polar climate*

UNDERSTANDING KEY IDEAS

8. At the equator, the sun's rays always strike Earth
   a. at a low angle.
   b. at nearly a 90° angle.
   c. 18 h each day.
   d. no more than 8 h each day.
9. Which of the following is *not* used as evidence of past climates?
   a. ice cores
   b. general circulation models
   c. tree rings
   d. fossils
10. Water cools
    a. more slowly than land does.
    b. more quickly than land does.
    c. only during evaporation.
    d. during global warming.
11. Ocean currents influence temperature by
    a. eroding shorelines.
    b. heating or cooling the air.
    c. washing warm, dry sediments out to sea.
    d. dispersing the rays of the sun.
12. Winds that blow in opposite directions in different seasons because of the differential heating of the land and the oceans are called
    a. chinooks.
    b. foehn.
    c. monsoons.
    d. El Niño.
13. When a moving air mass encounters a mountain range, the air mass
    a. stops moving.
    b. slows and sinks.
    c. rises and cools.
    d. reverses its direction.
14. In regions that have a mediterranean climate, almost all of the yearly precipitation falls
    a. during monsoons.
    b. in the summer.
    c. in the winter.
    d. during hurricanes.
15. The climate that has the largest annual temperature range is the
    a. subarctic climate.
    b. middle-latitude desert climate.
    c. mediterranean climate.
    d. humid continental climate.
16. The pavement and buildings in cities affect the local climate by
    a. decreasing the temperature.
    b. increasing the temperature.
    c. increasing the relative humidity.
    d. decreasing the precipitation.

SHORT ANSWER

17. Describe the Milankovitch theory, including how it may explain some climate changes.
18. What are the possible effects of global warming?
19. Compare marine west coast and humid continental climates.

---

18. Answers may vary. Accept all reasonable answers. The possible effects of global warming include changes in global precipitation patterns; melting of polar icecaps and rising sea levels, leading to coastal flooding; and changes in agricultural production.
19. The marine west coast climate has less seasonal temperature fluctuation than the humid continental climate does. Both receive significant amounts of precipitation throughout the year. Marine west coast climates are characterized by mild winters and summers, while humid continental climates have variable weather.

Critical Thinking

20. If all of the trees in California were cut down, the climate might be significantly warmer during the day because vegetation absorbs solar energy but does not reradiate as much energy as bare ground does. Vegetation also moderates night temperatures, so nights might be colder. Precipitation would likely decrease because of the decrease in transpiration.
21. Vegetation in the tundra is sparse because the temperature is so cold (<4 °C) almost all of the time. Some layers of the soil are permanently frozen, and few plants can survive these cold conditions.

CRITICAL THINKING

20. **Making Predictions** Describe how the climate in California might be affected if all of the trees in California were cut down.

21. **Making Inferences** Explain why the vegetation in areas that have a tundra climate is sparse even though these areas receive enough precipitation to support plant life.

22. **Analyzing Ideas** Explain why climates cannot be classified only by latitude.

23. **Predicting Consequences** How would global climate be affected if Earth were not tilted on its axis? Explain your reasoning.

CONCEPT MAPPING

24. Use the following terms to create a concept map: *fossil, ice cores, climate, polar climate, climatologist, steppe, temperature range, tropical climate, middle-latitude climate,* and *savanna.*

MATH SKILLS

Math Skills

25. **Using Equations** Temperature generally decreases about 6.5 °C for every kilometer above sea level. If T_N = temperature at a new altitude, a = altitude in kilometers, and T_I = initial temperature at sea level, what equation can be used to find the temperature at a given altitude?

26. **Making Calculations** From 1970 to 2005, nitrogen-oxide, NO_x, emissions in the United States decreased from about 26.9 million to about 19.0 million tons per year. By what percentage did NO_x emissions decrease over these years?

WRITING SKILLS

27. **Researching Topics** Research greenhouse gases to determine how they are produced. Then, write a brief essay that outlines how they can be reduced.

28. **Communicating Main Ideas** Imagine that you are going to build a vacation house. Research three locations where you would like to build your vacation house, and outline the climate features that would make each location ideal.

INTERPRETING GRAPHICS

The pie graphs below show world emissions of carbon dioxide, CO_2, in 1995 and predict emissions in 2035. Use these graphs to answer the questions that follow.

Total World Emissions of Carbon Dioxide

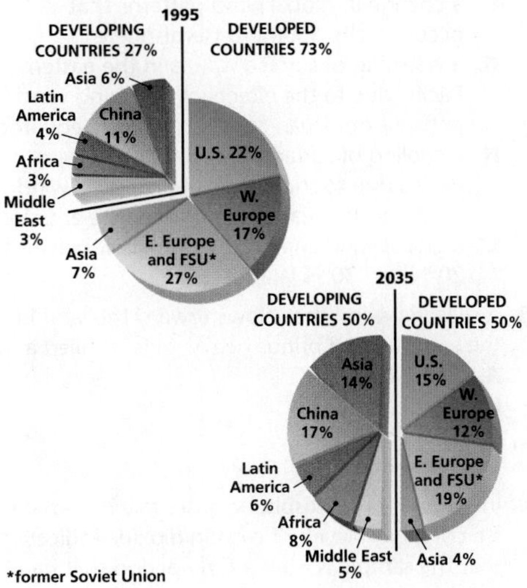

*former Soviet Union

29. In 1995, which country or region emitted the most CO_2? Which emitted the least CO_2?

30. What percentage of the total CO_2 was emitted by developing countries in 1995?

31. Why do you think researchers predict that CO_2 emissions of developing countries will equal those of developed countries by 2035?

Chapter Review

22. Climates cannot be classified by latitude alone because land features such as mountains, dense vegetation, proximity to large bodies of water, and ocean currents can greatly affect climate.
23. If Earth were not tilted on its axis, there would be no seasons in the Northern and Southern Hemispheres. Seasons result from the tilt of Earth's axis. The tilt causes changes in the angle at which the sun's rays hit Earth as the planet orbits the sun. In winter, the northern part of the axis tilts away from the sun, the angle at which sunlight strikes the Northern Hemisphere is smaller, and the sun's energy is weaker at higher latitudes of the Northern Hemisphere. In summer, the opposite occurs.

Concept Mapping

24. Answers may vary but should include all of the terms listed. Sample answers appear at the end of this unit on p. 631B.

Math Skills

25. $T_N = T_I - (6.5\ °C \times a)$
26. Percentage decrease = [(26.9 million − 19.0 million) ÷ 26.9 million] × 100 = 29%

Writing Skills

27. Answers may vary. Accept all reasonable answers.
28. Answers may vary. Accept all reasonable answers.

Interpreting Graphics

29. Eastern Europe and the former Soviet Union emitted the most CO_2 in 1995 (27%), though the United States emitted the most of any single country (22%). Africa and the Middle East emitted the least (3% each).
30. Developing countries emitted 27% of total CO_2 emissions in 1995.
31. Answers may vary. Possible answers include rapid population growth and/or rapid economic development in developing countries, both of which will require higher energy consumption. Also, many developed countries are attempting to reduce their CO_2 emissions.

Estimated Time

To give students practice under more realistic testing conditions, allow them 30 minutes to answer all of the questions in this practice test.

Test Doctor

Question 1 Answer B is correct. Water has a higher specific heat than land, which means that if both are exposed to the same amount of solar energy, the temperature of the water will increase less. Therefore, answers A, C, and D are incorrect.

Question 2 Answer G is correct. The El Niño–Southern Oscillation is a complex phenomenon that involves *both* winds and ocean currents, so answers F and I are incorrect. As wind patterns change at the equator, the movement of surface water warmed, not cooled, by the sun changes, so answer H is incorrect.

Question 8 Answer I is correct. Answer F is incorrect because, while the greenhouse effect has been amplified by the use of fossil fuels by humans, it did not necessarily cause humans to increase the use of such fuels. Answer G is incorrect because humans did not create the greenhouse effect. Answer H is incorrect because humans are not the only producers of greenhouse gases.

Chapter 22 Standardized Test Prep

Understanding Concepts

Directions (1–4): For each question, write on a separate sheet of paper the letter of the correct answer.

1. Which statement best compares how land and water are heated by solar energy?
- **A.** Water heats up faster and to a higher temperature than land does.
- **B.** Land heats up faster and to a higher temperature than water does.
- **C.** Water heats up more slowly but reaches a higher temperature than land does.
- **D.** Land heats up more slowly and reaches a lower temperature than water does.

2. Which of the following statements best describes the El Niño–Southern Oscillation?
- **F.** a change in global wind patterns that occurs in the Southern Hemisphere
- **G.** a warming of surface waters in the eastern Pacific due to the effects of changing wind patterns on ocean currents near the equator
- **H.** a cooling of surface waters in the eastern Pacific due to the effects of changing wind patterns on ocean currents near the equator
- **I.** a global wind and precipitation belt between 20°N and 30°N latitude

3. A seasonal wind that blows toward the land in the summer and brings heavy rains is called a
- **A.** trade wind.
- **B.** jet stream.
- **C.** doldrum.
- **D.** monsoon.

4. In samples of atmospheric gases taken from an ice core, high levels of carbon dioxide indicate that the sample is from a time period that had
- **F.** a warm climate.
- **G.** a cool climate.
- **H.** high amounts of precipitation.
- **I.** low amounts of precipitation.

Directions (5–6): For each question, write a short response.

5. What is the term for the area around a mountain that receives warm, dry winds?

6. What is the term for the weather conditions in an area over a long period of time?

Reading Skills

Directions (7–9): Read the passage below. Then, answer the questions.

The Greenhouse Effect

The greenhouse effect is Earth's natural heating process, in which gases in the atmosphere trap thermal energy. Earth's atmosphere acts like the glass windows of a car. Imagine that it is a hot day and that you are about to get inside a car. You immediately notice that it feels hotter inside the car than it does outside the car.

Many scientists hypothesize that the rise in global temperatures is due to an increase in carbon dioxide that is produced as a result of human activity. Most evidence indicates that the increase in carbon dioxide is caused by the burning of fossil fuels that release carbon dioxide into the atmosphere. Fossil fuels are organic compounds that are formed from the buried remains of ancient plants and animals. These fuels are used by humans for many things, such as heating homes and providing fuel for automobiles.

7. Based on the passage, which of the following statements is not true?
- **A.** The way that the atmosphere of Earth traps thermal energy is similar to the way that car windows keep the interior of a car warm.
- **B.** The greenhouse effect is a natural heating process for Earth.
- **C.** Earth absorbs sunlight and reradiates it as carbon dioxide.
- **D.** Human activity is one producer of the greenhouse gas carbon dioxide.

8. Which of the following statements can be inferred from the information in the passage?
- **F.** The greenhouse effect is responsible for an increase in the use of fossil fuels by humans.
- **G.** Humans created the greenhouse effect by burning coal for industrial uses.
- **H.** Human activity is the only producer of gases that create the greenhouse effect.
- **I.** Human activity may play a role in amplifying the natural process of the greenhouse effect.

9. Name some fossil fuels that are contributors to the production of carbon dioxide.

Question 10 Answer A is correct. Students should understand that city A is located inland, far from the ocean. Students that miss this question may not understand that land absorbs and releases heat more rapidly than water does. This produces a larger temperature range around the location city A than the temperature range at the location of city B.

Question 13 Full-credit answers should include the following points:
- students can locate summer and winter months on the x-axis of each climatogram and use the temperature and precipitation data for these months to start their analyses
- locations that have large amounts of consistent rainfall are likely to be lush year-round. Cities that have more-distinct seasons are more likely to have deciduous forest vegetation
- climatogram A shows a climate that has warm, humid summers and cold winters
- the area near climatogram A likely has deciduous forest vegetation
- climatogram B shows a climate that is hot and rainy all year
- the area near climatogram B likely has tropical rain-forest vegetation

Interpreting Graphics

Directions (10–13): For each question below, record the correct answer on a separate sheet of paper.

The diagram below shows the locations of two cities at the same latitude. Use this diagram to answer questions 10 and 11.

Two Cities Separated by Coastal Mountains

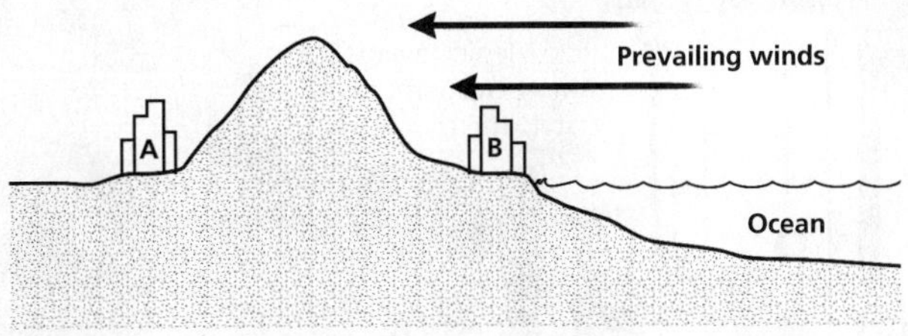

10. Which city is most likely to have the largest yearly temperature range?
- **A.** City A would likely have the largest yearly temperature range.
- **B.** City B would likely have the largest yearly temperature range.
- **C.** Both cities would likely have the same temperature range.
- **D.** There is not enough information to answer the question.

11. Which city is most likely to have a dry climate? Explain what would cause this city's climate to be drier than the other city's climate.

The climatograms below summarize average monthly precipitation and temperature data measured in two locations over a period of one year. Use these climatograms to answer questions 12 and 13.

Climatograms for Two Cities

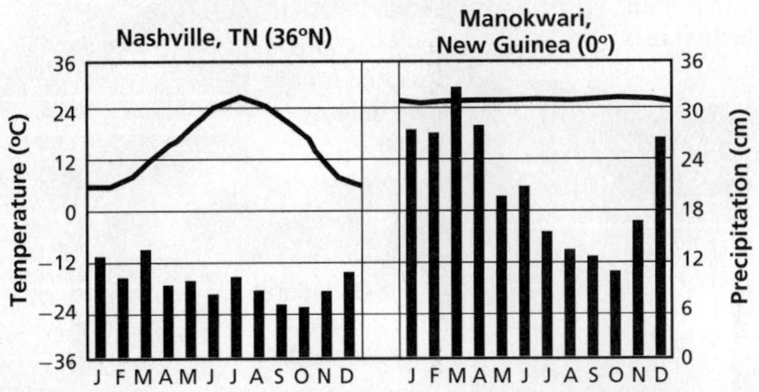

12. Which month shows the most rainfall for both climates in the climatograms?
- **F.** March
- **G.** June
- **H.** September
- **I.** December

13. Based on the data in the climatograms, write a description of the climate in each location and the type of vegetation that is likely to occur as a result of the climate.

Test Tip

Read all the information, including the heads, in a table or chart before answering the questions that refer to it.

Standardized Test Prep

Using THINK central Resources

State Resources
- For specific resources for your state, visit www.thinkcentral.com and type in the keyword **HSHSTR.**

Answers

Understanding Concepts
1. B
2. G
3. D
4. F
5. rain shadow
6. climate

Reading Skills

7. C
8. I
9. coal, natural gas, and oil

Interpreting Graphics

10. A
11. city A; City A is located in the rain shadow of a mountain range.
12. F
13. Answers may vary. See Test Doctor for a detailed scoring rubric.

Why It Matters

Meteorology Connections

Be sure students realize that the arrows show broad connections between events but do not indicate direct cause-and-effect relationships.

Students often forget that famous scientists were influenced by the social and political events of their time. Below are some events to help students connect the scientists to the time periods in which they lived.

Because Aristotle's father was a personal physician to King Amyntas of Macedon, Aristotle received the education of a noble. As a young man, he traveled to Athens, where he became a student of Plato. In the middle of his life, he tutored Alexander the Great in rhetoric and literature. Later in his life, Aristotle established his own school in Athens, where he studied and published works on every imaginable subject. After the death of Alexander, anti-Macedonian sentiments rose in Athens. Aristotle fled the city and died within the same year.

Robert Goddard was a pioneer in the field of liquid-fueled rocketry. He developed an interest in flight at a young age when he began flying kites and balloons. When he was 16 years old, he became interested in space after reading H.G. Wells's *War of the Worlds.* In the early 1940s, after studying physics, Goddard took his ideas to the U.S. Army, but the Army did not see the military applications. In Germany, however, Werner von Braun used Goddard's ideas to construct the A1 and A2 prototype rockets, and the subsequent rocket known as the V2. These rockets became an integral part of Germany's arsenal during the later years of World War II. In 1959, NASA named its Goddard Space Flight Center after Robert Goddard. NASA also named a crater on the moon after Goddard.

Although German physicist Heinrich Hertz died at the age of 36, he was the first person to demonstrate conclusively the existence of electromagnetic waves. During his short lifetime, the second Industrial Revolution caused a volatile economic situation in Germany. Economic highs fueled massive investment in the research and development of electrical equipment. Because Germany produced about half of the world's electrical equipment, engineering became extremely important.

Why It Matters

Meteorology Connections

Science, technology, and society are closely linked. This flowchart shows just a few of the connections in the history of meteorology.

340 B.C.E. Aristotle describes weather patterns in his book titled *Meteorologica.*

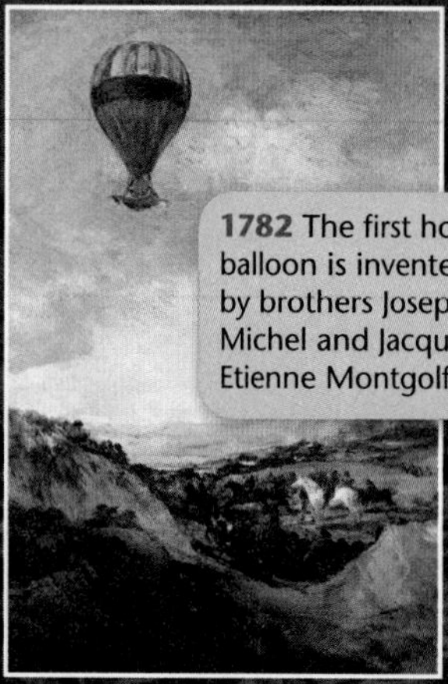

1782 The first hot-air balloon is invented by brothers Joseph-Michel and Jacques-Etienne Montgolfier.

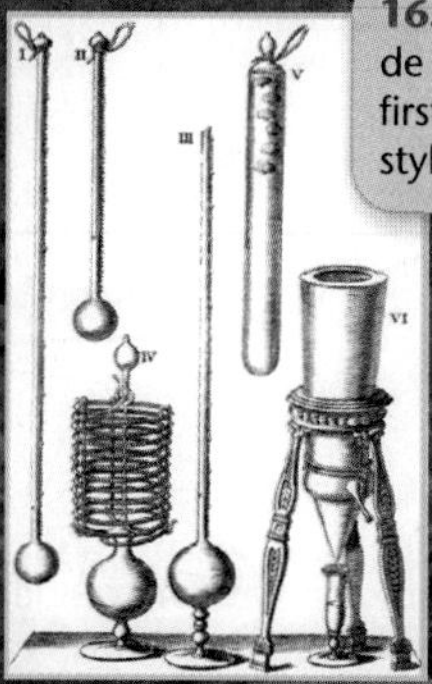

1654 Ferdinando II de Medici invents the first sealed, modern-style thermometer.

1887 Heinrich Hertz experiments with creating radio waves in his laboratory.

1930 The first radiosonde is launched, attached to a weather balloon.

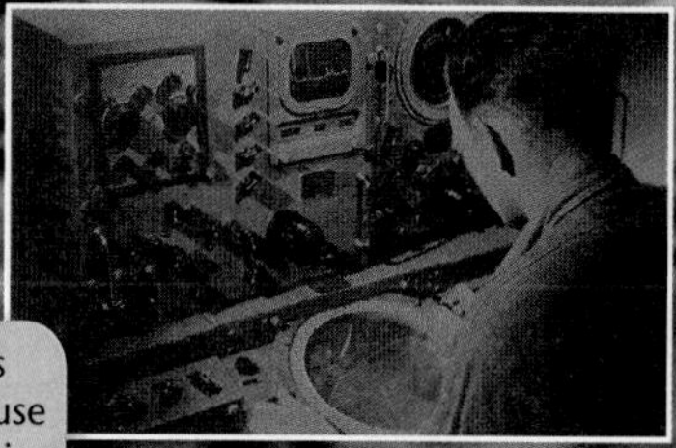

1935 Radar is designed for use in air defense in Britain.

1943 Radar is first used for storm tracking.

1946 A radar air-traffic control system is used experimentally.

2007 The Hartsfield-Jackson International Airport in Atlanta, Georgia, manages 994,346 flights.

Reading Skill Builder — Basic

Visual Literacy The image of Hurricane Rita shows the path of the storm over several days. Meteorologists use maps like this one to project the path of a storm and to estimate the location, date, and time at which the storm will make landfall. The speed and size of the storm can also be tracked, and scientists can easily see any important changes in the storm.

HISTORY IN SCIENCE

1926 Robert Goddard invents the first practical liquid-fueled rocket.

1939 World War II breaks out in Europe.

1946 Scientists develop the first computer, ENIAC.

1957 The Soviet Union launches *Sputnik I,* the first orbital satellite.

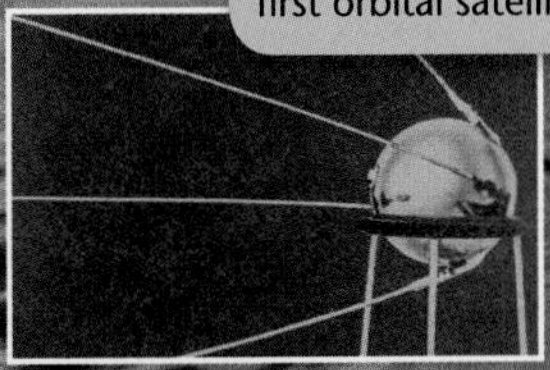

1960 The first successful weather satellite, *TIROS,* is launched from Cape Canaveral.

1969 The first "Internet," ARPANET, becomes functional.

1988 The National Weather Service initiates a nationwide Doppler radar system.

2002 The *Aqua* satellite gathers data about Earth's surface and atmosphere.

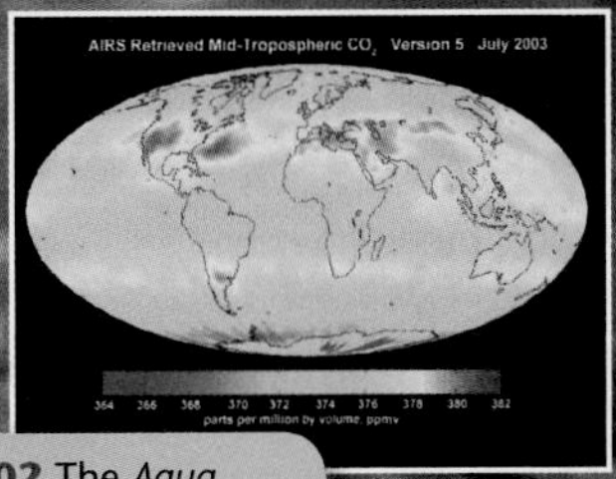

2005 Accurate prediction of the path of Hurricane Rita allows for evacuations.

2007 Local weather information is available for almost any place on Earth.

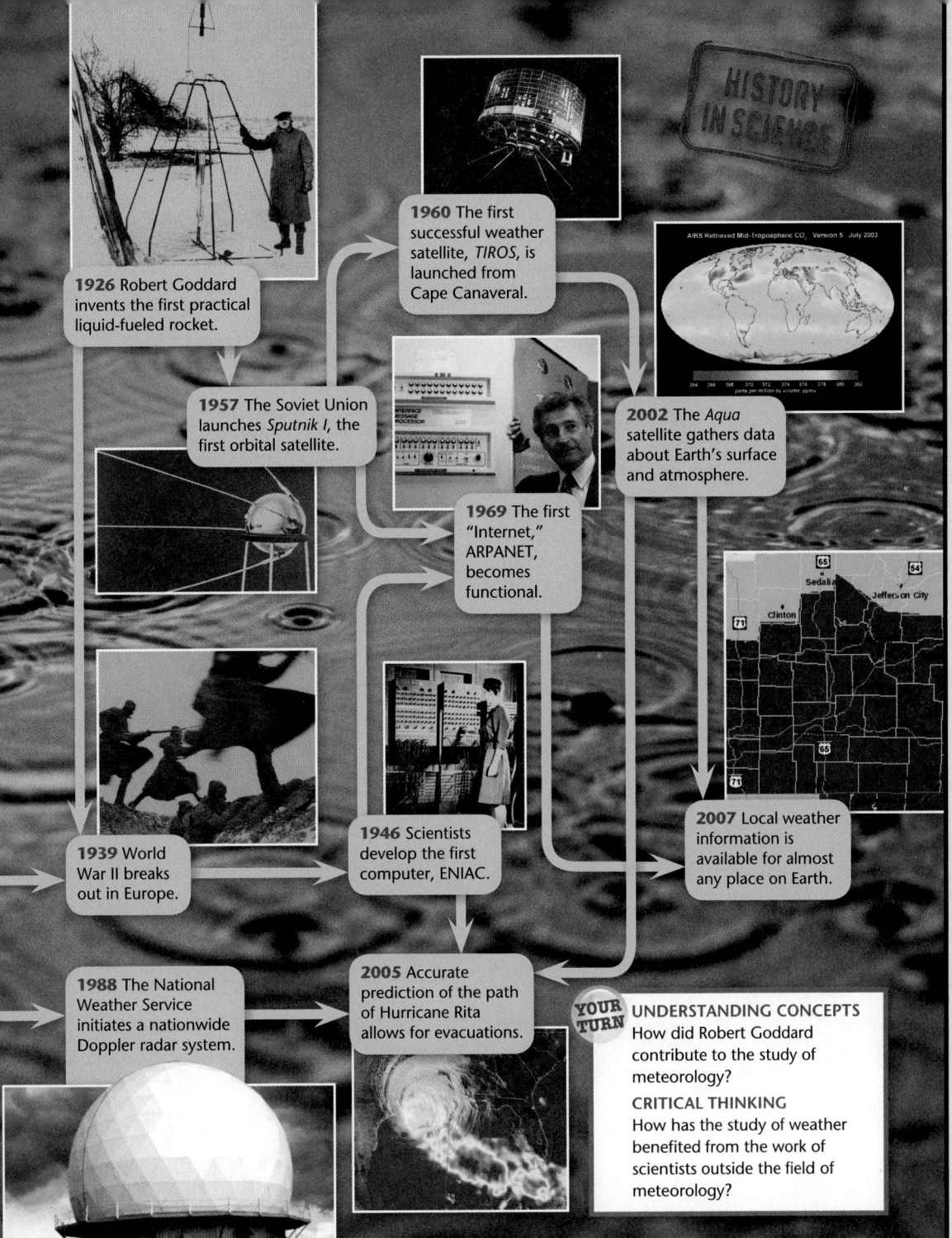

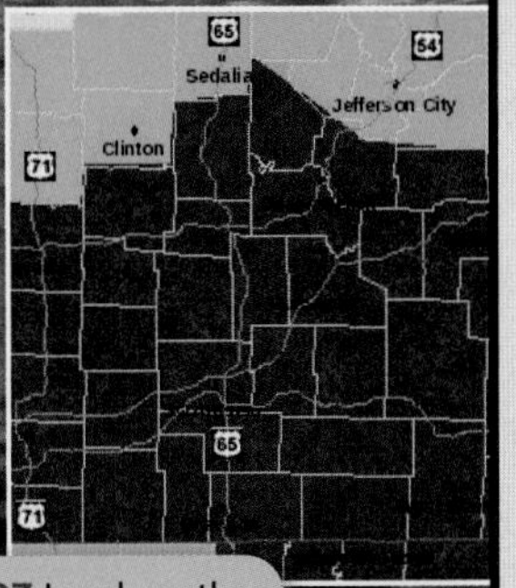

YOUR TURN

UNDERSTANDING CONCEPTS
How did Robert Goddard contribute to the study of meteorology?

CRITICAL THINKING
How has the study of weather benefited from the work of scientists outside the field of meteorology?

Why It Matters

The Space Race The launch of *Sputnik I* in 1957 was the beginning of the space age. *Sputnik I* was the first object ever launched into orbit. It spent about three months in orbit, before burning up on reentry into the atmosphere. This sphere, only 58.5 cm in diameter, began the space race that occupied the imaginations of millions and the engineers of both the Soviet Union and the United States.

Why It Matters

NASA's Aqua Mission In 2002, NASA launched *Aqua,* the second of three Earth Observing System (EOS) satellites, to study of the evaporation and precipitation of water on Earth. (The other two satellites are *Terra* and *Aura.*) The Aqua mission is an example of multinational cooperation, with special equipment provided by Japan and Brazil. Aqua contains six instruments to study water on Earth's surface and in the atmosphere. These instruments measure cloud properties, sea surface temperatures, near-surface wind speed, radioactive energy flux, surface water, ice and snow, aerosol properties, and land-cover and land-use changes, as well as many other features of Earth's water cycle.

Why It Matters

ENIAC The development of computers, such as ENIAC, allowed mathematical models to be used for processing large amounts of data. ENIAC was first constructed by the University of Pennsylvania for the U.S. Army. It was designed to calculate artillery firing tables for the army. It was the first computer that was reprogrammable for other uses, however, and it was upgradeable. This advancement led to the development of other general-use computers.

Answers to Your Turn

Understanding Concepts Robert Goddard's rockets made it possible for scientists to launch orbital satellites that record weather data.

Critical Thinking Scientists in the field of physics have contributed radar and rocketry to the field of meteorology. The development of computers and the Internet allow for the rapid collection, analysis, and sharing of weather data around the world.

Answers continued from p. 582

Section Review

9. Midlatitude cyclones produce storms that generally travel about 45 km/h in an easterly direction as they spin counterclockwise. Hurricanes and tropical storms produce wind speeds of 120–275 km/h. They can be as large as 700 km in diameter. Tornados have narrow paths generally no more than 100 m wide, but wind speeds as high as 400 km/h. Increasing storm diameter means a greater area may be damaged. Higher winds increase the potential for damage. Rain may lead to flooding.
10. Weather, which includes *severe weather* such as *tornadoes, hurricanes*, and *midlatitude cyclones*, is caused by the movement of *fronts*, such as *warm fronts, stationary fronts, occluded fronts, and cold fronts* that may be preceded by *squall lines.*

Answers continued from p. 610

Section Review

11. Snow-capped mountains occur in Hawaii because temperature decreases with altitude.
12. *Climate* is described by using *temperature range* and precipitation, and is affected by *topography* and *winds*, which can be global, which cause the *doldrums* and *subtropical highs*; and seasonal, such as *monsoons* and *El Niño.*

Answers continued from p. 614

Section Review

9. Climate zones include *tropical climates*, such as *rain forests, savannas,* and *deserts; middle-latitude* climates, such as *mediterranean* climates and *steppes;* and *polar climates*, such as the *subarctic, tundra,* and *polar icecap* climates.

Answers continued from p. 620

Section Review

8. The melting of small icebergs would not affect sea level because they are floating in the ocean water. They displace the same amount of water as their volume.
9. Short-term climate changes could not be explained by the Milankovitch theory because these orbital changes occur on cycles of 21,000 to 100,000 years.
10. A *climatologist* may study *fossils*, *tree rings*, *ice cores*, oxygen *isotopes* in sea-floor sediments, and *general circulation models* to study climate change and *global warming.*

Sample Answers to Concept Maps from Chapter Reviews

Chapter 19 The Atmosphere, p. 537

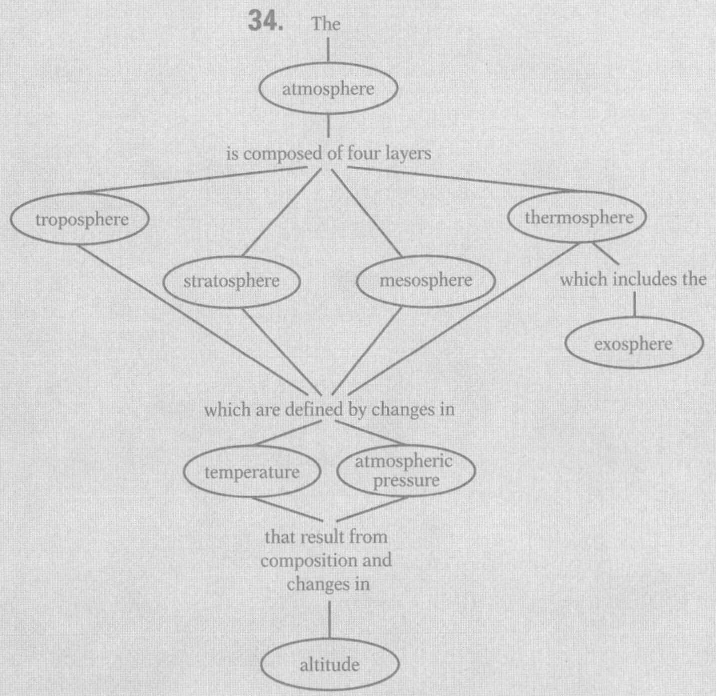

Chapter 20 Water in the Atmosphere, p. 565

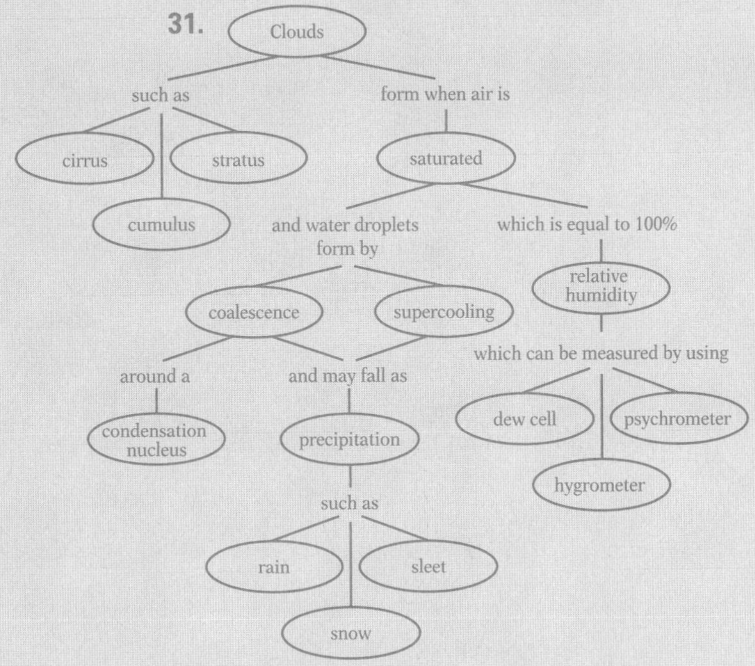

Chapter 21 Weather, p. 599

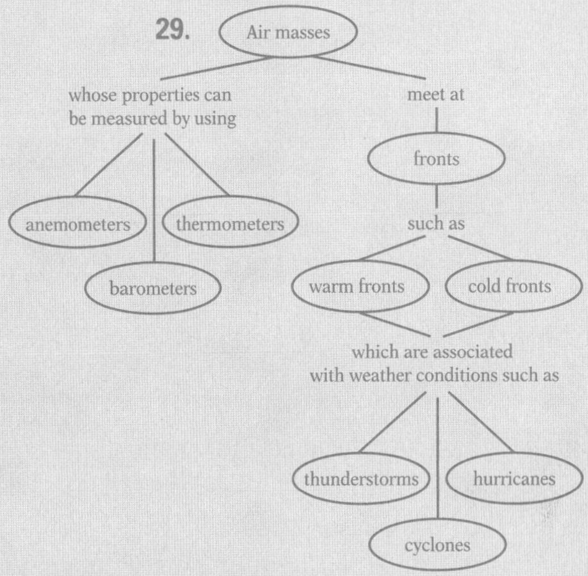

Chapter 22 Climate, p. 627

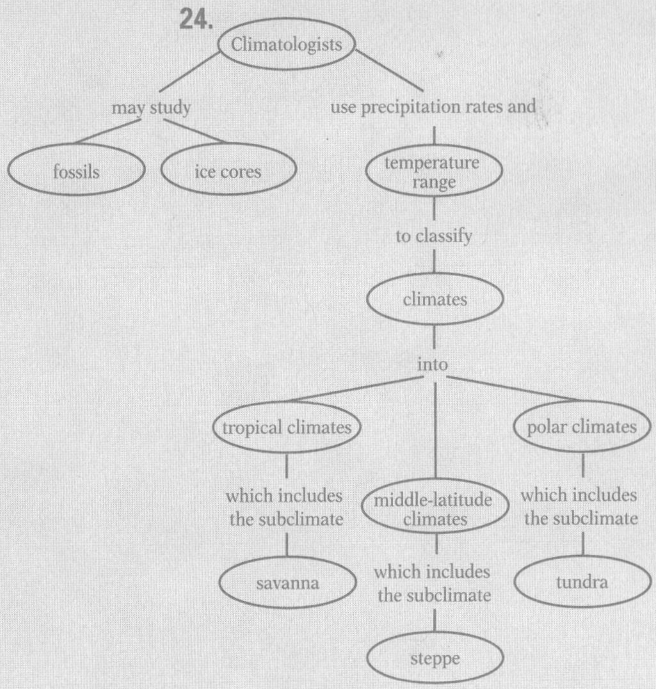

Unit 7 Oceans

Chapter Planner 23

The Ocean Basins

	Time	Standards	Teach Key Ideas
Chapter Opener, pp. 634–635	45 min.	National Science Education Standards	
Section 1 The Water Planet, pp. 637–640 › Divisions of the Global Ocean › Exploration of the Ocean	45 min.	SAI 2c	■ ◆ **Bellringer,** p. 637 ■ **DI (English Learners):** Summarizing, p. 638 ◆ **Transparency:** 117 The Global Ocean ▲ **Visual Concepts:** Divisions of the Global Ocean • Sonar
Section 2 Features of the Ocean Floor, pp. 641–644 › Continental Margins › Deep-Ocean Basins	45 min.		■ ◆ **Bellringer,** p. 641 ■ **Identifying Preconceptions:** Where Do the Continents End?, p. 642 ■ **DI (Special Education Students):** Modeling the Ocean Floor, p. 642 ◆ **Transparency:** 118 Features of the Ocean Floor ▲ **Visual Concepts:** The Ocean Floor
Section 3 Ocean-Floor Sediments, pp. 645–648 › Sources of Deep Ocean-Basin Sediments › Physical Classification of Sediments	90 min.	SAI 2c UCP 4	■ ◆ **Bellringer,** p. 645 ■ **Demonstration:** Sediments Sinking, p. 645 ■ **DI (Special Education Students):** Ocean-Basin Sediments, p. 645 ■ **Demonstration:** Turbidity Currents and Submarine Canyons, p. 646 ◆ **Transparency:** 119 Total Sediment Thickness of Earth's Oceans
Chapter Wrap-Up, pp. 653–657	90 min.		**Chapter Summary,** p. 653

See also PowerNotes® Presentations

CHAPTER Fast Track *To shorten instruction because of time limitations, omit Section 3.*

Key
Teacher's Edition ■
Chapter Resource File ●
Teaching Transparencies ◆
Online Edition ▲

All resources listed below are also available on the Teacher One Stop™.

Why It Matters	Hands-On	Skills Development	Assessment
■ **Chapter Overview,** p. 634 ■ **Using the Figure:** The Ora Verde, p. 634	**Inquiry Lab:** Sink or Float? p. 635	**Reading Toolbox,** p. 636	
■ **Section Overview,** p. 637 ■ **Using the Figure:** Global Oceans, p. 637 ■ **Language Arts Connection:** 20,000 Leagues Under the Sea Today, p. 638 ■ **Biology Connection:** Seeing with Sound, p. 639	**QuickLab:** Sonar, p. 639	■ **Skill Builder:** Writing, p. 638 ■ **Skill Builder:** Math, p. 639 **Reading Toolbox:** Classification, p. 639	**Reading Check,** p. 638 **Section Review,** p. 640 ■ **Reteaching,** p. 640 ■ **Quiz,** p. 640 ■ **DI (Alternative Assessment):** Oceanographic Interview, p. 640 ● **Section Quiz**
■ **Section Overview,** p. 641 ■ **Using the Figure:** Modeling the Ocean Floor, p. 641 ■ **Ridges and Rises,** p. 642	● **Making Models Lab:** Island to Guyot	■ **Reading ToolBox:** Everyday Words Used in Science, p. 642	**Reading Check,** p. 642 **Section Review,** p. 644 ■ **Reteaching,** p. 643 ■ **Quiz,** p. 643 ■ **DI (Alternative Assessment):** Deep-Sea Tour, p. 644 ● **Section Quiz**
■ **Section Overview,** p. 645 **How Do You Turn Mud into Money?** p. 646	**Quick Lab:** Diatoms, p. 647 **Inquiry Lab:** Ocean-Floor Sediments, pp. 650–651	**Math Skills:** Ocean-Floor Sediments, p. 647 ■ **Reading ToolBox:** Spider Maps, p. 648 **Maps in Action:** Total Sediment Thickness of Earth's Oceans, p. 652 ■ ● **Internet Activity:** Deep-Sea Sediment Core Samples, p. 652	**Reading Check,** p. 647 **Section Review,** p. 648 ■ **Reteaching,** p. 647 ■ **Quiz,** p. 648 ■ **DI (Alternative Assessment):** Comparing and Contrasting Sediments, p. 648 ● **Section Quiz**
Underwater Aliens, p. 649		▲ **Super Summary** **Standardized Test Prep,** pp. 656–657	**Chapter Review,** pp. 654–655 ● **Chapter Tests**

See also Lab Generator

See also Holt Online Assessment Resources

Chapter Overview

This chapter describes how scientists study the deep trenches, huge mountain ranges, submarine canyons, and the abyssal plains of the ocean basins. This chapter also describes ocean-floor sediments.

Using the Figure GENERAL

The Ora Verde This photograph shows the Ora Verde, a ship lost off the Grand Cayman Islands. With advances in undersea exploration, scientists and adventurers are uncovering more and more shipwrecks. Have students discuss some difficult issues that may arise from exploring shipwrecks. (Answers may vary but may include: showing respect for the dead; deciding who owns the site and who should profit from salvaged "treasures"; and undertaking dangerous expeditions solely for profit.) LS **Interpersonal**

Why It Matters

Oceans influence life on Earth in many ways. The ocean plays a vital role in the water cycle and the interaction between the ocean and the atmosphere helps shape global climate. Half of the oxygen in the atmosphere is produced by marine phytoplankton, which also form the base of the food chain in the ocean. Many resources used by humans come from the ocean, including minerals and food.

Chapter 23 The Ocean Basins

Chapter Outline

Virginia Standards of Learning
ES.1.a
ES.1.b
ES.1.c
ES.1.e
ES.10.d

Why It Matters

Oceans cover more than 70 percent of Earth's surface. Oceans interact with the atmosphere to influence weather and climate. Exploring and analyzing data about the chemistry of ocean water, the geology of the ocean floor, marine ecosystems, and the physics of water movement is critical to understanding natural processes on Earth.

Chapter Correlations — *Virginia Standards of Learning*

ES.1.a volume, area, mass, elapsed time, direction, temperature, pressure, distance, density, and changes in elevation/depth are calculated utilizing the most appropriate tools.
ES.1.b technologies, including computers, probeware, and geospatial technologies, are used to collect, analyze, and report data and to demonstrate concepts and simulate experimental conditions.
ES.1.c scales, diagrams, charts, graphs, tables, imagery, models, and profiles are constructed and interpreted.
ES.1.e variables are manipulated with repeated trials
ES.10.d features of the seafloor as reflections of tectonic processes

Inquiry Lab

20 min

Sink or Float?

Fill the **bottom half of 3-L soda bottle** with **water** to within about 3 inches from the top and place it on a **plastic** or **metal tray** to catch any spills. Using small **(3-oz) plastic cups,** with some **paper clips** and **metal nuts** for ballast, see if you can get a cup to sink with air still trapped inside, simulating a submersible. You may need something pointed to make holes in the cups.

Questions to Get You Started

1. What is buoyancy and why is it so important for maritime travel?
2. Compare techniques for sinking the cup. Does one method consistently work better than others?
3. What challenges do engineers face when designing submersibles?

Using THINK central Resources

An online version of this chapter, as well as all the print and multimedia resources that accompany the program are available to registered teachers and their students. Log onto **www.thinkcentral.com** to access these materials and tools to organize your preparation and student learning.

Inquiry Lab

Central Concept: Students will experiment with buoyancy and how it is related to submersibles and other vessels used to explore the ocean.

Teacher's Notes: Cut the tops off of the soda bottles prior to the lab. You may want to place tape around edge of the bottle to avoid exposing students to sharp edges. Encourage students to be creative with their designs.

Materials (per group)
- Bottom half of a 3-L soda bottle
- Water
- Plastic or metal tray
- 2 3 oz. plastic cups
- Small and large paper clips
- Metal nuts
- Hole puncher

Safety
Students should wear gloves and goggles.

Skills Acquired
- Experimenting
- Observing
- Interpreting Results

Answers to Getting Started

1. Buoyancy is the upward force exerted on an object by a fluid. If there is not enough buoyancy to counteract gravity (which is a downward force), a ship or submersible will sink. Being able to regulate buoyancy in a submersible allows the vessel to move higher or lower in the water column.
2. Answers will vary. Students may find that taping two cups end-to-end, then filling one cup with nuts is an effective design.
3. Answers will vary. Students may include ideas such as how to design a submersible to withstand high pressure and low temperatures, and how to provide a safe atmosphere for humans inside the vessel.

READING TOOLBOX

Science Terms

Everyday Words Used in Science Possible answers: Informal definition: Margin is the space at the edge of a piece of paper. Scientific definition: The shallow part of the ocean floor made of continental crust and sediment. Sample sentences: I wrote some notes in the margin of the book pages. The continental margin has high biodiversity.

Classification

Classifying Sediments Biogenic Characteristics: Sediments that are produced by living organisms, such as the remains of marine plants and animals. Mostly made of silica and calcium carbonate. Chemical Characteristics: Formed when substances dissolved in ocean water crystallize. Examples include nodules made of manganese, nickel, copper, and iron.

Graphic Organizers

Spider Maps Continental Margin: continental shelf, continental slope, continental rise; Deep Ocean: trenches, abyssal plains, mid-ocean ridges, seamounts

READING TOOLBOX

These reading tools will help you learn the material in this chapter.

Science Terms

Everyday Words Used in Science Many words used in science are familiar words from everyday speech. However, the meanings of these everyday words are often different from their meanings in scientific contexts.

Your Turn Before you read this chapter, write down an informal definition of what the word *margin* means to you. As you come across this word in the chapter, write the scientific definition next to your informal definition. For each definition, write a sentence that uses the word *margin* correctly.

Classification

Classifying Sediments Classification is a tool for organizing objects and ideas by grouping them into categories. Groups are classified by defining characteristics. For example, the table below shows how sediments can be classified by their composition.

Your Turn As you read the chapter, complete a table like the one shown here for the three types of sediments described in Section 3.

Type of Sediment	Characteristics
Inorganic	Carried from land to ocean by rivers, wind, and icebergs
Biogenic	
Chemical	

Graphic Organizers

Spider Maps Spider maps show how details are organized into categories, which in turn are related to a main idea. To make a spider map, follow the steps.

1. Write a main topic title, and draw an oval around it.
2. From the oval, draw legs. Each leg represents a category of the main topic.
3. From each leg, draw horizontal lines. Write details about each category on these lines.

Your Turn As you read Section 2, use a spider map to organize the information that you learn about features of the ocean floor.

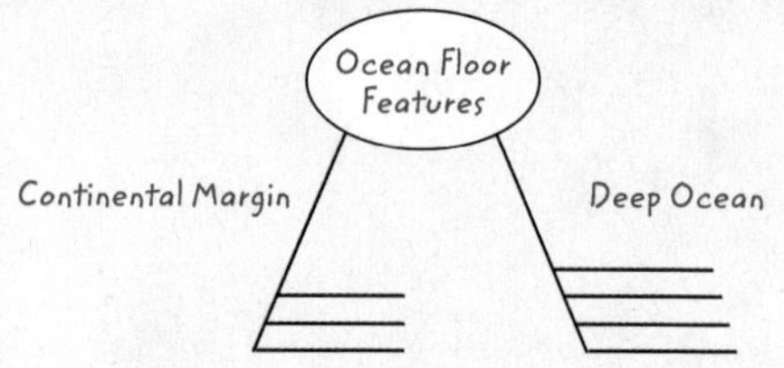

For more information on how to use these and other tools, see **Appendix A**.

SECTION 1

The Water Planet

Key Ideas	Key Terms	Why It Matters
› Name the major divisions of the global ocean. › Describe how oceanographers study the ocean. › Explain how sonar works.	**global ocean** **sea** **oceanography** **sonar**	New ways to explore the cold, dark ocean depths have revealed to us the bizarre life forms that thrive there.

Nearly three-quarters of Earth's surface lies beneath a body of salt water called the **global ocean.** No other known planet has a similar covering of liquid water. Only Earth can be called the *water planet*.

The global ocean contains more than 97% of all of the water on or near Earth's surface. Although the ocean is the most prominent feature of Earth's surface, the ocean is only about 1/4,000 of Earth's total mass and only 1/800 of Earth's total volume.

Divisions of the Global Ocean

As shown in **Figure 1**, the global ocean is divided into five major oceans. These major oceans are the Atlantic, Pacific, Indian, Arctic, and Southern Oceans. Each ocean has special characteristics. The Pacific Ocean is the largest ocean on Earth's surface. It contains more than one-half of the ocean water on Earth. With an average depth of 4.3 km, the Pacific Ocean is also the deepest ocean. The next largest ocean is the Atlantic Ocean. The Atlantic Ocean has an average depth of 3.9 km. The Indian Ocean is the third-largest ocean and has an average depth of 3.9 km. The Southern Ocean is the fourth-largest ocean and extends from the coast of Antarctica to 60°S latitude. The Arctic Ocean is the smallest ocean, and it surrounds the North Pole.

A **sea** is a body of water that is smaller than an ocean and that may be partially surrounded by land. Examples of major seas include the Mediterranean Sea, the Caribbean Sea, and the South China Sea.

global ocean the body of salt water that covers nearly three-fourths of Earth's surface

sea a large, commonly saline body of water that is smaller than an ocean and that may be partially or completely surrounded by land

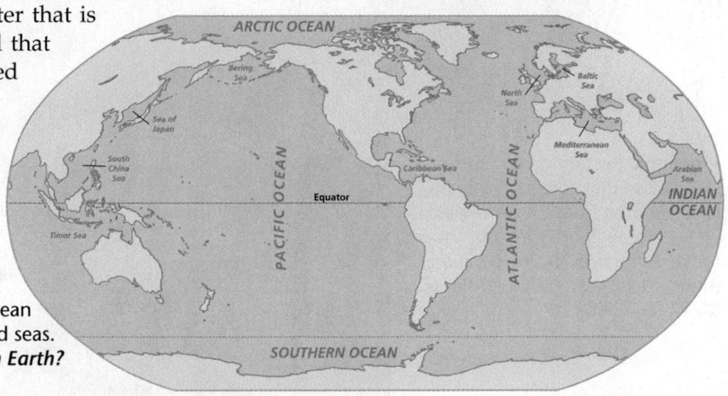

Figure 1 The global ocean is divided into oceans and seas. *How many oceans are on Earth?*

Section 1

Focus

Overview

This section reviews the major divisions of the global ocean differentiates between oceans and seas, and describes how oceanographers study the ocean by using sonar and submersibles for underwater research.

Bellringer

Ask students why they think the famous science fiction novelist Arthur C. Clarke once remarked: "How inappropriate to call this planet Earth, when clearly it is Ocean." (More than 70% of Earth's surface is covered with water. It is known as the global ocean.)
LS Logical

Motivate

Using the Figure — GENERAL

Global Oceans The map at left shows the divisions of the global ocean. Have students use this map to determine the area of Earth covered by the various oceans. Have students trace the map onto graph paper and count the number of squares covered by all of the oceans compared to the total number of squares covered by the map. (The area of the oceans should equal about 70% of the total area of the map.) Answer to caption question: five **LS Visual**

Key Resources

Technology

- Transparencies
  Bellringer
  117 The Global Ocean

Teach

Skill Builder ADVANCED

Writing Have students visit the Web site of the Woods Hole Oceanographic Institution, the home of *Alvin.* Have them find information about one of *Alvin*'s expeditions and write a short newspaper-style article about the expedition's findings. LS **Verbal**

Teaching Tip BASIC

Make Concepts Relevant Invite students to discuss why studying the ocean is important. (Answers will vary but could include: the importance of understanding the influence of oceans on weather and climate change; the importance of understanding life in the oceans; and the importance of exploring for natural resources.) LS **Logical**

Answer to Reading Check

Oceanographers study the physical characteristics, chemical composition, and life forms of the ocean.

oceanography the scientific study of the ocean, including the properties and movements of ocean water, the characteristics of the ocean floor, and the organisms that live in the ocean

SCILINKS.
www.scilinks.org
Topic: The Oceans
Code: HQX1069

Academic Vocabulary
research (REE SUHRCH) a careful search for and study of information

Exploration of the Ocean

The study of the physical and geological characteristics, chemical composition, and life-forms of the ocean is called **oceanography.** Although some ancient civilizations studied the ocean, modern oceanography did not begin until the 1850s.

The Birth of Oceanography

An American naval officer named Matthew F. Maury used records from navy ships to learn about ocean currents, winds, depths, and weather conditions. In 1855, he published these observations as one of the first textbooks about the oceans. Then, from 1872 to 1876, a team of scientists aboard the British Navy ship HMS *Challenger* crossed the Atlantic, Indian, and Pacific Oceans. The scientists measured water temperatures at great depths and collected samples of ocean water, sediments, and thousands of marine organisms. The voyages of the HMS *Challenger* laid the foundation for the modern science of oceanography.

Today, many ships perform oceanographic research. In the 1990s and in the beginning of the 21st century, the research ship *JOIDES Resolution* was the world's largest and most sophisticated scientific drilling ship. Samples drilled by *JOIDES Resolution,* shown in **Figure 2,** provide scientists with valuable information about plate tectonics and the ocean floor. The Japanese ship *CHIKYU,* which is operated by the Integrated Ocean Drilling Program, is one of the most advanced drilling ships now in use.

Reading Check **List three characteristics of the ocean that oceanographers study.** (See Appendix G for answers to Reading Checks.)

Figure 2 Reentry cones (above) are used so that core samples can later be taken from the same place on the ocean floor. Scientists aboard the research ship *JOIDES Resolution* (right) perform scientific studies of the ocean floor.

Language Arts Connection ADVANCED

20,000 Leagues Under the Sea Today In 1870, Jules Verne published *20,000 Leagues Under the Sea*, a science fiction account of the adventures of Captain Nemo as he piloted the deep-sea vehicle *Nautilus.* In many ways, this story was visionary. Have students read excerpts from the book. Then, have students write an updated version of an important scene, using information about modern methods of undersea exploration. LS **Verbal**

Differentiated Instruction

English Learners

Summarizing Have students read about the tools oceanographers use to study the oceans, then have them summarize the ideas of sonar and submersibles, either orally or in writing. Check for comprehension by looking for inaccuracies or ideas that were left out. Allow students to refer to the text as needed.

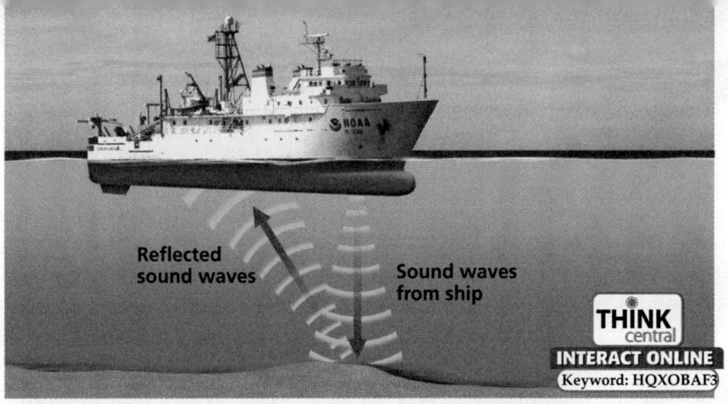

Figure 3 Active sonar sends out a pulse of sound. The pulse, called a *ping* because of the way it sounds, reflects when it strikes a solid object.

READING TOOLBOX

Classification
Classify each type of tool used to collect data from oceans, including records from ships, samples taken from ships, sonar, and submersibles, as surface tools or deep-ocean tools.

Sonar

Oceanographic research ships are often equipped with sonar. **Sonar** is a system that uses acoustic signals and returned echoes to determine the location of objects or to communicate. Sonar is an acronym for ***so****und* ***n****avigation* ***a****nd* ***r****anging.* A sonar transmitter sends out a continuous series of sound waves from a ship to the ocean floor, as shown in **Figure 3.** The sound waves travel at about 1,500 m/s through sea water and bounce off the solid ocean floor. The waves reflect back to a receiver. Scientists measure the time that the sound waves take to travel from the transmitter, to the ocean floor, and to the receiver in order to calculate the depth of the ocean floor. Scientists then use this information to make maps and profiles of the ocean floor.

sonar *sound navigation and ranging,* a system that uses acoustic signals and returned echoes to determine the location of objects or to communicate

Quick Lab Sonar

30 min

Procedure

1. Use **heavy string** to tie one end of a **spring** securely to a **doorknob.** Pull the spring taut and parallel to the floor. You will need to keep the tension of the spring constant throughout the lab.
2. Use **masking tape** to mark the floor directly beneath the hand that is holding the spring taut. Use a **meterstick** to measure and record the distance from that hand to the doorknob.
3. Note the time on a **stopwatch or clock with a second hand.** Hold the spring taut, and hit the spring horizontally to create a compression wave.
4. Check the time again to see how long the pulse takes to travel to the doorknob and back to your hand. Record the time.
5. Repeat steps 2 to 4 three times. Each time, hold the spring 60 cm closer to the doorknob. Keep tension constant by gathering coils as necessary.
6. Calculate the rate of travel for each trial by multiplying the distance between your hand and the doorknob by 2. Then, divide by the number of seconds the pulse took to travel to the doorknob and back.

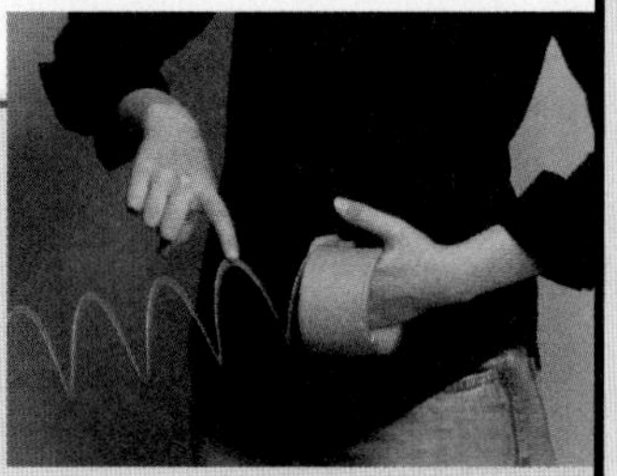

Analysis

1. Did the rate the pulse traveled change during the course of the investigation?
2. If a pulse took 3 s to travel to the doorknob and back to your hand, what is the distance from the doorknob to your hand?
3. How is the apparatus you used similar to sonar? How is the apparatus different than sonar? Explain.

READING TOOLBOX

Classification Surface: records from ships; Deep Ocean: data collected by ships, sonar, submersibles

Skill Builder — Basic

Math Sound waves travel 1,500 m/s in sea water. Calculate the depth of the ocean floor if a sonar ping takes 10 s to return to a research vessel.

$$\text{depth} = \frac{\text{rate} \times \text{time}}{2 \text{ (to account for time to the ocean floor and back)}}$$

$$\text{depth} = \frac{1{,}500 \text{ m/s} \times 10 \text{ s}}{2}$$

$$\text{depth} = 7{,}500 \text{ m}$$ **LS Logical**

Biology Connection — General

Seeing with Sound Sonar is like "seeing" with sound. Explain to students that some animals use sonar, or *echolocation,* to navigate and to find prey. Whales can locate objects, such as krill schools or members of the pod, by echolocation. Using low and high frequency clicks, whales can precisely map size, shape, speed, distance, and density of objects. Bats are well known for their echolocation abilities. They produce frequency-modulated ultrasound to find and track insect prey and to navigate at night.

Quick Lab

Skills Acquired
- Measuring
- Calculating

Materials
- Heavy string
- Spring
- Doorknob
- Masking tape
- Meterstick
- Stopwatch or clock with a second hand

Teacher's Notes: Make sure that students strike the spring in a horizontal direction to form a compression wave and that they keep the tension on the spring constant by pulling the coil taut as they shorten the distance to the doorknob.

Answers to Analysis

1. If the spring tension is kept constant, the rate should not change.
2. Answer will depend on the rate calculated. Sample answer: If the rate is 100 cm/s, then 100 cm/s × 3 s = 300 cm to doorknob and back, distance to doorknob is 150 cm (300 ÷ 2).
3. They both use waves to measure distances. Sonar uses sound waves, while the spring model uses a compression wave.

Close

Reteaching BASIC

Outline Have students make a brief timeline of advances in oceanographic research techniques, identifying important vessels and methods. **LS Visual**

Quiz GENERAL

1. How is a bathyscaph different from a bathysphere? (A bathyscaph is self-propelled and free moving. A bathysphere is tethered to a research ship for communications and life support.)
2. Where have strange life forms, such as giant clams and tube-worms, been discovered? (near hydrothermal vents along mid-ocean ridges)
3. When did modern oceanography start? (in the 1850s)

Answers to Section Review

1. The five major divisions of the global ocean are the Atlantic, the Pacific, the Indian, the Arctic, and the Southern oceans.
2. A sea is a body of water that is smaller than the ocean, and that may be partially surrounded by land.
3. Oceanography is the study of the physical, chemical, geological, and biological characteristics of the ocean.
4. Oceanographers use sonar and submersibles to study the ocean.
5. Sonar uses acoustic signals and returned echoes to determine the position of objects or the depth of the ocean floor.
6. Submersibles can collect samples from the ocean floor and take photographs of the ocean floor.
7. The bathyscaph and the bathysphere are both piloted by humans. Submarine robots are remotely operated.
8. Answers may vary but should explain how sonar waves bounce off objects in a vessel's path, which allows the vessel to move around any obstacles.
9. Answers may vary. Sample answer: Submarine robots can stay in the ocean depths for much longer periods than human-piloted submersibles can.
10. The science of *oceanography* uses *sonar* and *submersibles* such as *bathyspheres, bathyscaphs,* and *robot submersibles.*

Figure 4 The submersible *Nautile* (top) carries enough oxygen to keep a three-person crew underwater for more than five hours. Deep-sea submersibles have discovered many strange organisms in the deep ocean, such as this angler fish (bottom).

Submersibles

Underwater research vessels, called *submersibles,* also enable oceanographers to study the ocean depths. Some submersibles are piloted by people. One such submersible is the *bathysphere,* a spherical diving vessel that remains connected to the research ship for communications and life support. Another type of piloted submersible, called a *bathyscaph,* is a self-propelled, free-moving submarine. One of the most well-known bathyscaphs is the *Alvin.* Another modern submersible, called *Nautile* (NOH teel), is shown in **Figure 4.**

Other modern submersibles are submarine robots. They can take photographs, collect mineral samples from the ocean floor, and perform many other tasks. These robotic submersibles are remotely piloted and allow oceanographers to study the ocean depths for long periods of time.

Underwater Research

Submersibles have helped scientists make exciting discoveries about the deep ocean. During one dive in a submersible, startled oceanographers saw communities of unusual marine life living at depths and temperatures where scientists thought that almost no life could exist. Giant clams, blind white crabs, and giant tube worms were some of the strange life-forms that were discovered. Many of these life-forms have unusual adaptations that allow them to live in hostile environments. The angler fish, shown in **Figure 4,** can produce its own light, which attracts prey.

Section 1 Review

Key Ideas

1. **Name** the five major divisions of the global ocean.
2. **Explain** the difference between an ocean and a sea.
3. **Define** *oceanography.*
4. **Describe** two ways that oceanographers study the ocean.
5. **Explain** how sonar works.
6. **Describe** two aspects of the ocean that submersibles are used to study.
7. **List** three types of submersibles.

Critical Thinking

8. **Evaluating Ideas** Most submarines use sonar as a navigation aid. How would sonar enable an underwater vessel to move through the ocean depths?
9. **Analyzing Methods** Why are submarine robots more practical for deep-ocean research than submersibles designed to carry people are?

Concept Mapping

10. Use the following terms to create a concept map: *oceanography, submersible, bathysphere, bathyscaph, robot submersible,* and *sonar.*

Differentiated Instruction

Alternative Assessment

Oceanographic Interview Have students form pairs and pretend that one of them is a journalist and the other is an oceanographer who is being interviewed for a magazine article. The interviewer should ask, "What is the most important advance in oceanographic research in the last 100 years? What is the most important future oceanographic question to address?" When one student has answered, have students switch roles. **LS Verbal/Interpersonal**

SECTION 2

Features of the Ocean Floor

Key Ideas	Key Terms	Why It Matters
› Describe the main features of the continental margins. › Describe the main features of the deep-ocean basin.	**continental margin** **deep-ocean basin** **trench** **abyssal plain**	Shelves and basins are features not just of your kitchen but of the ocean floor—home to the tallest mountains and flattest plains on Earth.

The ocean floor can be divided into two major areas, as shown in **Figure 1.** The **continental margins** are shallow parts of the ocean floor that are made of continental crust and a thick wedge of sediment. The other major area is the **deep-ocean basin,** which is made of oceanic crust and a thin sediment layer. It forms the deep part of the ocean beyond the continental margin.

Continental Margins

The line that divides the continental crust from the oceanic crust is not abrupt or distinct. Shorelines are not the true boundaries between the oceanic crust and the continental crust. The boundaries are actually some distance offshore and beneath the ocean and the thick sediments of the continental margin.

Continental Shelf

Continents are outlined in most places by a zone of shallow water where the ocean covers the edge of the continent. The part of the continent that is covered by water is called a *continental shelf.* The shelf usually slopes gently from the shoreline and drops about 0.12 m every 100 m. The average depth of the water covering a continental shelf is about 60 m. Though underwater, a continental shelf is part of the continental margin, not the deep-ocean basin.

Changes in sea level affect the continental shelves. During glacial periods, continental ice sheets hold large amounts of water. So, sea level falls and exposes more of the continental shelf to weathering and erosion. But if ice sheets melt adding water to the oceans, sea level rises and covers the continental shelf.

continental margin the shallow sea floor that is located between the shoreline and the deep-ocean bottom

deep-ocean basin the part of the ocean floor that is under deep water beyond the continent margin and that is composed of oceanic crust and a thin layer of sediment

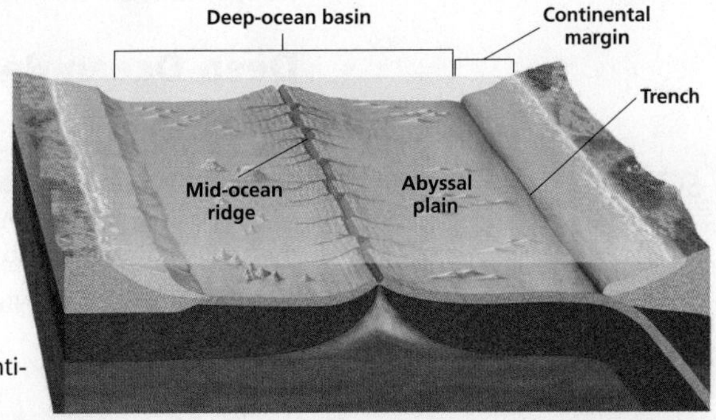

Figure 1 The ocean floor includes the continental margins and the deep-ocean basin.

Section 2

Focus

Overview

This section reviews the features of the ocean floor. It describes the continental margin, including the continental shelf, slope, and rise. It explains features of the deep ocean basins, such as trenches, abyssal plains, mid-ocean ridges, and seamounts.

Bellringer

Have students make a quick sketch of what they think the ocean floor looks like from the mid-Atlantic United States to Spain. (Sketches may vary but can be used to start a discussion of the ocean floor.) **LS Visual**

Motivate

Using the Figure GENERAL

Modeling the Ocean Floor The diagram at left shows the features of the ocean floor. Have students work in groups to build a model ocean floor out of modeling clay in a plastic tub. Have students cover the top and walls of the tub with black paper so that the ocean floor cannot be seen. Have groups exchange models and try to map the model ocean floor by using a dowel or craft stick to measure depths at various locations. **LS Kinesthetic/Visual**

Key Resources

Chapter Resource File
- Directed Reading BASIC
- Making Models Lab: Island to Guyot GENERAL

Technology
- Transparencies
  Bellringer

Teach

Identifying Preconceptions GENERAL

Where Do the Continents End?
Perform this exercise before students begin to read this section. On a map of the eastern continental margin of North America, have students mark where they think the continental crust ends and the oceanic crust begins. Students may place the boundary right at the shoreline. While presenting this section, emphasize that the boundary is some distance offshore and is not necessarily abrupt or distinct. **LS Verbal/Visual**

READING TOOLBOX

Everyday Words Used in Science
shelf: a flat, narrow piece of material fastened horizontally to a wall, used to hold objects; slope: a degree of inclination; The continental shelf is the part of the continent is covered by water. The continental slope is a steeper slope at the seaward edge of the continental shelf.

Answer to Reading Check
Trenches; broad, flat plains; mountain ranges; and submerged volcanoes are part of the deep-ocean basins.

Key Resources

Technology
- Transparencies
  118 Features of the Ocean Floor

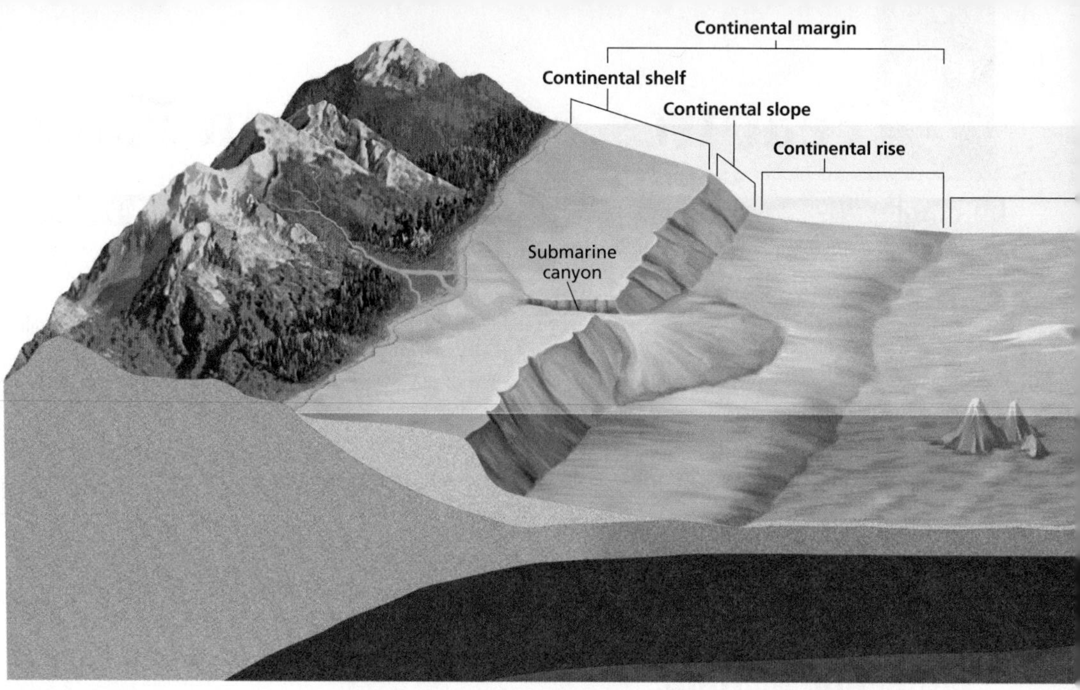

Figure 2 The ocean floor is made of distinct areas and features.

READING TOOLBOX

Everyday Words Used in Science
Use a dictionary to write alternate definitions for the multiple meaning words *shelf* and *slope*. Compare these definitions to the scientific definitions used here.

Continental Slope and Continental Rise

At the seaward edge of a continental shelf is a steeper slope called a *continental slope*. The boundary between the continental crust and the oceanic crust is located at the base of the continental slope. Along the continental slope, the ocean depth increases by several thousand meters within an average distance of about 20 kilometers, as shown in **Figure 2.** The continental shelf and continental slope may be cut by deep V-shaped valleys. These deep valleys are called *submarine canyons*. These deep canyons are often found near the mouths of major rivers. Other canyons may form over time as very dense currents called *turbidity currents* carry large amounts of sediment down the continental slopes. Turbidity currents form when earthquakes cause underwater landslides or when large sediment loads run down a slope. These sediments form a wedge at the base of the continental slope called a *continental rise*.

Deep-Ocean Basins

Deep-ocean basins also have distinct features, as shown in **Figure 2.** These features include broad, flat plains; submerged volcanoes; gigantic mountain ranges; and deep trenches. In the deep-ocean basins, the mountains are higher and the plains are flatter than any features found on the continents.

Reading Check **What features are located in the deep-ocean basins?**

SCILINKS
www.scilinks.org
Topic: Ocean-Floor Features
Code: HQX1067

Why It Matters

Ridges and Rises At the slow-moving Mid-Atlantic Ridge, only approximately 3 cm of new sea floor forms each year. The topography is rough because the magma supply does not keep up with spreading, creating rift valleys and faults. In contrast, as much as 8 cm of new sea floor forms each year at the East Pacific Rise. Here the topography is smoother because magma supply keeps up with extension, so less faulting occurs.

Differentiated Instruction

Special Education Students

Modeling the Ocean Floor Work with students to build a replica of the different levels of the ocean floor that are pictured in the figures on the first three pages of this section. Shape modeling clay to show elevation changes, ridges, seamounts, trenches, and abyssal plains that they can touch with their hands. Let the clay dry overnight. **LS Kinesthetic**

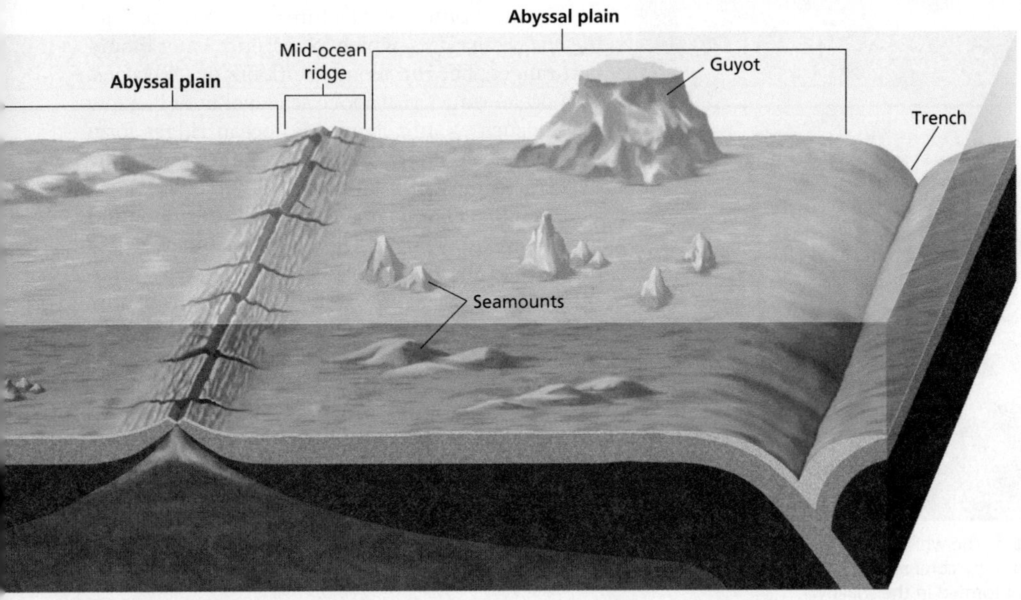

Trenches

Long, narrow depressions located in the deep-ocean basins are called **trenches.** At more than 11,000 m deep, the Mariana Trench, in the western Pacific Ocean, is the deepest place in Earth's crust. Trenches form where one tectonic plate subducts below another plate. Earthquakes occur near trenches. Volcanic mountain ranges and volcanic island arcs also form near trenches.

trench a long, narrow, and steep depression that forms on the ocean floor as a result of subduction of a tectonic plate, that runs parallel to the trend of a chain of volcanic islands or the coastline of a continent, and that may be as deep as 11 km below sea level; also called an *ocean trench* or a *deep-ocean trench*

abyssal plain a large, flat, almost level area of the deep-ocean basin

Abyssal Plains

The vast, flat areas of the deep-ocean basins where the ocean is more than 4 km deep are called **abyssal plains** (uh BIS uhl PLAYNZ). Abyssal plains cover about half of the deep-ocean basins and are the flattest regions on Earth. In some places, the ocean depth changes less than 3 m over more than 1,300 km.

Layers of fine sediment cover the abyssal plains. Ocean currents and wind carry some sediments from the continental margins. Other sediment is made when organisms that live in the ocean settle to the ocean floor when they die.

The thickness of sediments on the abyssal plains is determined by three factors. The age of the oceanic crust is one factor. Older crust is generally covered with thicker sediments than younger crust is. The distance from the continental margin to the abyssal plain also determines how much sediment reaches the plain from the continent. Third, the sediment cover on abyssal plains that are bordered by trenches is generally thinner than the sediment cover on abyssal plains that are not bordered by trenches.

Academic Vocabulary

layer (LAY uhr) a separate or distinct portion of matter that has thickness

MISCONCEPTION ALERT

Lifeforms on Abyssal Plains Many creatures, such as sea urchins, sea cucumbers, clams, and mussels, live in and feed on the sediments of the abyssal plains. In the 1980s, a team of scientists studying deep-ocean sediments off the eastern United States found 90,677 individual organisms from 798 species in an area of only 54 km^2. Sixty percent of these organisms were new to humans. Based on their results, the scientists estimated that a new species might be found in every square kilometer of deep-sea floor—100 million more species to be discovered!

Teaching Tip — GENERAL

Connect to Prior Knowledge

Remind students that plate tectonics is a theory that explains how continents and ocean basins form and change over time. Trenches result when one plate slides beneath another. As a result, earthquakes and volcanic activity are frequent in these areas. The Peru-Chile trench, resulting from the Nazca plate's subduction beneath the South American plate, is an example of a trench that formed along a continental margin. **LS Logical**

Close

Reteaching — BASIC

Diagram Have students label an ocean floor diagram with the various features discussed in the section. **LS Visual**

Quiz — GENERAL

1. Is the shoreline generally the boundary between the continental crust and the oceanic crust? (No, the shoreline is a boundary between land and water. The boundary between continental and oceanic crust is generally some distance offshore at the base of the continental slope.)
2. Where are submarine canyons commonly located? (near the mouths of major rivers)
3. What regions of the ocean basin are the flattest places on Earth? (the abyssal plains)
4. Where do seamounts form? (near hot spots, or regions of the oceanic crust that have increased volcanic activity)

Close, *continued*

Answers to Section Review

1. The continental shelf is the part of the continent submerged underwater. The continental slope is the steep, seaward edge of the continental shelf. The continental rise is a wedge of sediment at the base of the continental slope.
2. The boundary between the continental crust and the oceanic crust is generally offshore, at the base of the continental slope.
3. Submarine canyons commonly form where large loads of sediment run down a slope as part of turbidity currents.
4. Trenches are very deep and form where one tectonic plate subducts under another. Abyssal plains are vast flat areas of the ocean more than 4 km deep that are covered by layers of fine sediment. Mid-ocean ridges form where plates are moving away from each other and have a narrow rift at the center. Seamounts are submerged volcanoes that may rise above the ocean surface to form islands.
5. Guyots and atolls form from islands. When an island sinks and becomes eroded by waves, a flat-topped guyot forms. An atoll is an intermediate stage before the eroding island is completely submerged.
6. The continental shelf, the continental slope, and the continental rise are parts of the continental margin.

Figure 3 The white ridges in this photo are coral reefs of an atoll that formed in the shallow waters around a volcanic island. Erosion is changing the island into a guyot.

Mid-Ocean Ridges

The most prominent features of ocean basins are the *mid-ocean ridges,* which form underwater mountain ranges that run along the floors of all oceans. Mid-ocean ridges rise above sea level in only a few places, such as in Iceland. Mid-ocean ridges form where plates pull away from each other. A narrow depression, or rift, runs along the center of the ridge. Through this rift, magma reaches the sea floor and forms new lithosphere. This new lithosphere is less dense than the old lithosphere. As the new lithosphere cools, it becomes denser and begins to sink as it moves away from the rift. Fault-bounded blocks of crust that form parallel to the ridges as the lithosphere cools and contracts are called *abyssal hills.*

As ridges adjust to changes in the direction of plate motions, they break into segments that are bounded by faults. These faults create areas of rough topography called *fracture zones,* which run perpendicularly across the ridge.

Seamounts

Submerged volcanic mountains that are taller than 1 km are called *seamounts*. Seamounts form in areas of increased volcanic activity called *hot spots.* Seamounts that rise above the ocean surface form oceanic islands. As tectonic plate movements carry islands away from a hot spot, the islands sink and are eroded by waves to form flat-topped, submerged seamounts called *guyots* (GEE OHZ) or *tablemounts*. An intermediate stage in this process, called an *atoll,* is shown in **Figure 3.**

Section 2 Review

Key Ideas

1. **Describe** the three main sections of the continental margins.
2. **Describe** where the boundary between the oceanic crust and the continental crust is located.
3. **Explain** how turbidity currents are related to submarine canyons.
4. **List** four main features of the deep-ocean basins, and describe one characteristic of each feature.
5. **Compare** seamounts, guyots, and atolls.
6. **Explain** the difference between the meanings of the terms *continental margin, continental shelf, continental slope,* and *continental rise.*

Critical Thinking

7. **Making Inferences** The Pacific Ocean is surrounded by trenches, but the Atlantic Ocean is not. In addition, the Pacific Ocean is wider than the Atlantic Ocean, and much of the crust under the Pacific Ocean is very young. Which ocean's abyssal plain has thicker sediments? Explain your answer.
8. **Determining Cause and Effect** If sea level were to fall significantly, what would happen to the continental shelves?

Concept Mapping

9. Use the following terms to create a concept map: *continental margin, deep-ocean basin, continental shelf, continental slope, continental rise, trench, abyssal plain,* and *mid-ocean ridge.*

7. The Atlantic Ocean probably has thicker sediments because its crust is, in general, older, so sediment has had more time to accumulate. It is not surrounded by trenches, which collect sediment that washes down the continental margins. Also, it is smaller than the Pacific Ocean, so more sediment would reach its abyssal plains.
8. The continental shelves would be subject to much more erosion by wind, river water, and ice if sea levels were to fall significantly.
9. The ocean floor has distinct features such as the *continental margin,* which consists of the *continental shelf, continental slope,* and *continental rise*; and the *deep-ocean basin,* which may include *trenches, abyssal plains,* and *mid-ocean ridges.*

Differentiated Instruction

Alternative Assessment

Deep-Sea Tour Have students design a "travel brochure" for an ocean floor vacation tour. Their brochure should include descriptions of key sites they will visit (e.g., the continental margin, submarine canyons, the abyssal plains, mid-ocean ridges, trenches, hydrothermal vents and seamounts). Students may also wish to illustrate their brochures. **LS Verbal/Visual**

SECTION 3

Ocean-Floor Sediments

Key Ideas	Key Terms	Why It Matters
❯ Describe the formation of ocean-floor sediments. ❯ Explain how ocean-floor sediments are classified by their physical composition.	core sample nodule	Products you use every day contain ocean-floor sediments.

Continental shelves and slopes are covered with sediments. Sediments are carried into the ocean by rivers, are washed away from the shoreline by wave erosion, or settle to the ocean bottom when the organisms that created them die. The composition of ocean sediments varies and depends on which part of the ocean floor the sediments form in. The sediments are fairly well sorted by size. Coarse gravel and sand are usually found close to shore because these heavier sediments do not move easily offshore. Lighter particles are suspended in ocean water and are usually deposited at a great distance from shore.

Sources of Deep Ocean–Basin Sediments

Sediments found in the deep-ocean basin, which is beyond the continental margin, are generally finer than those found in shallow water. Samples of the sediments in the deep-ocean basins can be gathered by scooping up sediments or by taking core samples. **Core samples** are cylinders of sediment that are collected by drilling into sediment layers on the ocean floor. **Figure 1** shows a core sample being studied aboard the research vessel *JOIDES Resolution*.

The study of sediment samples shows that most of the sediments in the deep-ocean basins are made of materials that settle slowly from the ocean water above. These materials may come from organic or inorganic sources.

core sample a cylindrical piece of sediment, rock, soil, snow, or ice that is collected by drilling

Figure 1 A scientist studies a core sample that was brought up from the drill aboard the research ship *JOIDES Resolution*.

Section 3

Focus

Overview

This section explains the formation and composition of ocean-floor sediments and how they are studied and classified. The section explains that ocean sediments vary depending on their source and where they are deposited.

Bellringer

Ask students the following question: Where does sediment at the bottom of the ocean come from and what is it like? (Answers may vary but may include rock and mud from rivers and glaciers, and the remains of dead sea creatures. The size of the pieces vary, and they may be either organic or inorganic in origin.) LS Verbal

Motivate

Demonstration GENERAL

Sediments Sinking Show students sediments of various sizes and different shapes. Ask students to predict how the sediments will settle out if suspended in water. Put some sediment of each size and shape in a jar with water and shake the jar. Compare students' predictions with the results. LS Visual/Kinesthetic

Key Resources

Chapter Resource File
- Directed Reading BASIC
- Inquiry Lab: Sediment Loading GENERAL

Technology
- Transparencies
  Bellringer

Differentiated Instruction

Special Education Students

Ocean-Basin Sediments Have students join with a partner. Ask the partners to take turns reading alternate paragraphs quietly aloud. Then, have the students discuss what the paragraph means and draw a simple sketch that goes with the paragraph. When finished, ask partners to share their favorite sketches with the class. LS Verbal

Teach

Demonstration GENERAL

Turbidity Currents and Submarine Canyons Use this demonstration to show students what turbidity currents look like and how they may form submarine canyons. Pour a slurry of mixed sediments (or a mixture of sand, cleaning powder, and water colored with food coloring) through a funnel onto an underwater slope you have constructed in a plastic tub or tank. Then, allow sediments to settle and view the graded bed formed at the base of the slope, which is a model of the continental rise.
LS Visual/Kinesthetic

MISCONCEPTION ALERT

Sediment vs. Sand Students may think most ocean sediments are like the sand found on ocean beaches. Sand is sometimes found on the deep sea floor because of turbidity currents that are caused by earthquakes or underwater landslides. However, most sediments on the deep ocean floor are very fine inorganic and organic particles that settle to the ocean floor from the water above.

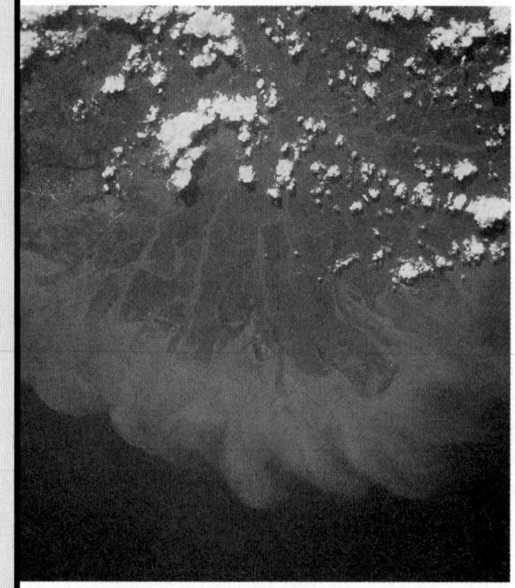

Figure 2 This picture of sediment emptying out of the Mahakam River in Indonesia was taken by astronauts aboard the space shuttle *Columbia*.

Inorganic Sediments

Some ocean-basin sediments are rock particles that were carried from land by rivers. When a river empties into the ocean, the river deposits its sediment load, as shown in **Figure 2.** Most of these sediments are deposited along the shore and on the continental shelf. However, large quantities of these sediments occasionally slide down continental slopes to the ocean floor below. The force of the slide creates powerful turbidity currents that spread the sediments over the continental rise and abyssal plains. Other deep ocean-basin sediments consist of fine particles of rock, including volcanic dust, that have been blown great distances out to sea by the wind. These particles land on the surface of the water, sink, and gradually settle to the bottom of the ocean.

Icebergs also provide sediments that can end up on the ocean basins. As a glacier moves across the land, the glacier picks up rock. The rock becomes embedded in the ice and moves with the glacier. When an iceberg breaks from the glacier, drifts out to sea, and melts, the rock material sinks to the ocean floor.

Even meteorites contribute to deep ocean-basin sediments. Much of a meteorite vaporizes as it enters Earth's atmosphere. The remaining cosmic dust falls to Earth's surface. Because most of Earth's surface is ocean, most meteorite fragments fall into the ocean and become part of the sediments on the ocean floor.

Why It Matters

How Do You Turn Mud into Money?

Oozy mud from underwater may not seem particularly valuable, but ocean sediments are part of a wide variety of familiar products. For example, diatomaceous earth, which comes from the hardened deposits of siliceous oozes, is added to some products for its abrasive qualities. Abrasive qualities are important in such products as toothpaste and metal polishes. Many paints also have diatomaceous earth mixed with them as fine grit.

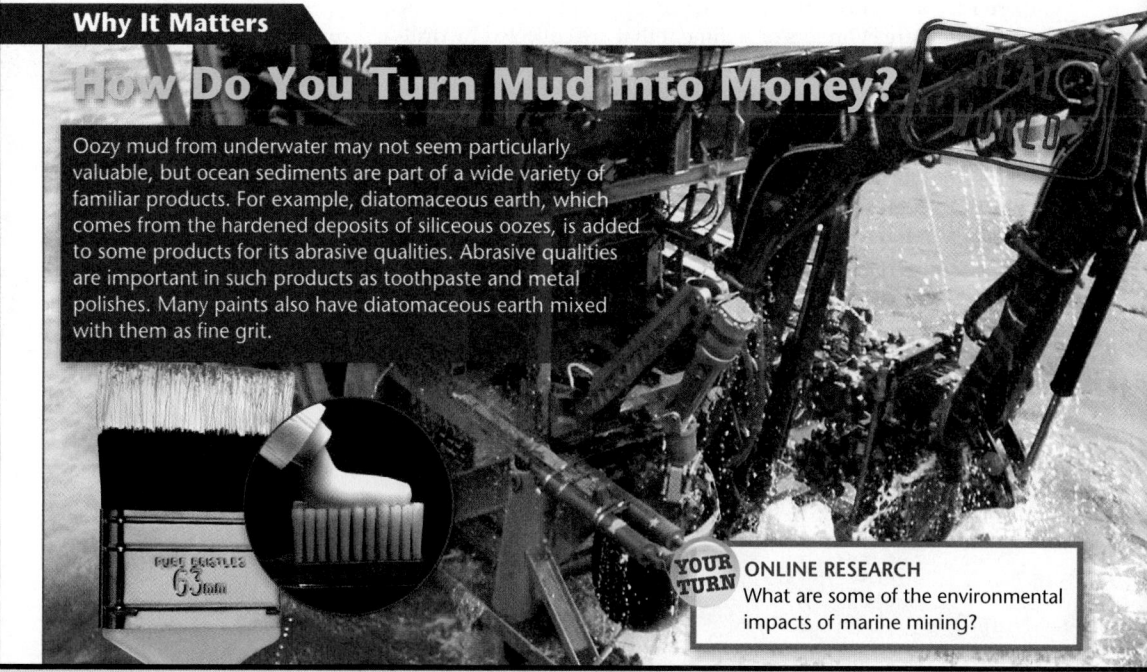

YOUR TURN **ONLINE RESEARCH**
What are some of the environmental impacts of marine mining?

Why It Matters

How Do You Turn Mud into Money?
Diatomaceous earth is a lightweight, white rock that is used for a wide variety of purposes. Swimming pool filters and filters used to separate particles and impurities from alcoholic beverages are made using diatomaceous earth. Diatomaceous earth is a good insulator and is used in blast furnaces. It is also used as a mechanical insecticide and an absorbent for liquids, such as in cat litter.

Answer to Your Turn
Fine sediments can be stirred up into the water column, which could be a problem for organisms that feed by filtering the water in their habitat. Another problem is that certain mining processes could cause nutrients from the deep sea to reach the relatively nutrient-poor surface waters of the ocean, leading to algal blooms and potentially contaminating waters that support commercial fishing industries.

Figure 3 Nodules, such as these mined from the East Pacific Rise, are rich in a variety of minerals.

Math Skills

Ocean-Floor Sediments Ocean-floor sediments are composed of an average of 54% biogenic sediments, 45% Earth rocks and dust, less than 1% precipitation of dissolved materials (nodules and phosphates), and less than 1% of rocks and dust from space. If you collected 10,000 kg of ocean-floor sediment, how many kilograms of each type of ocean-floor sediment would you expect to find?

Biogenic Sediments

In many places on the ocean floor, almost all of the sediments are *biogenic,* meaning that the sediments were originally produced by living organisms. Biogenic sediments are the remains of marine plants, animals, and other organisms. The two most common compounds that make up organic sediments are silica, SiO_2, and calcium carbonate, $CaCO_3$. Silica comes primarily from microscopic organisms called *diatoms* and *radiolarians*. Calcium carbonate comes mostly from the skeletons of tiny organisms called *foraminifera*.

Chemical Deposits

When substances that are dissolved in ocean water crystallize, these materials can form mineral deposits on the ocean floor. Some of these mineral deposits are potato-shaped lumps called **nodules.** Nodules, such as the ones shown in **Figure 3,** are commonly located on the abyssal plains. Nodules are composed mainly of the oxides of manganese, nickel, copper, and iron. Other minerals, such as phosphates, are also carried in the ocean water before they crystallize and form mineral deposits on the ocean floor.

Reading Check **How do nodules form?**

Quick Lab 20 min

Diatoms

Procedure

1. Observe diatoms under a microscope.
2. Sketch what you see. Make sure to note the magnification.

Analysis

1. What characteristics of the diatoms did you observe?
2. Propose one possible function for each of the structures you observed.

nodule a lump of minerals that is made of oxides of manganese, iron, copper, or nickel and that is found in scattered groups on the ocean floor

Math Skills Answer

Amount per source = total amount of sediment × percentage of given source

Biogenic = (10,000 kg × 0.54) = 5,400 kg

Earth rocks and dust = (10,000 kg × 0.45) = 4,500 kg

Dissolved materials = (10,000 kg × 0.01) = < 100 kg

Space rocks and dust = (10,000 kg × 0.01) = < 100 kg

Quick Lab

Skills Acquired

- Observing
- Identifying/Recognizing Patterns
- Analyzing

Materials

- Diatoms
- Microscope

Teacher's Notes: Tell students that diatoms are photosynthetic algae. Diatomaceous earth is the crumbly remains of diatom shells. Diatomaceous earth is used for applications such as paints, polishes, and filters.

Answers to Analysis

1. Answers may vary but should be based on students' sketches. Students may note box-like structures, two-part shells, a golden brown coloration, or that diatoms may be grouped singly or in chains or colonies.
2. Answers may vary. Accept all reasonable answers.

Answer to Reading Check

When chemical reactions take place in the ocean, dissolved substances can crystallize to form nodules that settle to the ocean floor.

Close

Reteaching BASIC

Peer Reviewing Have students work in pairs to write three to five questions about the material in this section. Then, have students use their questions to quiz each other.
LS Interpersonal Co-op Learning

READING TOOLBOX

Spider Maps Lines on spider map may be filled in with the following details: Muds: silt and clay-sized particles of rock, red clay is an example; Ooze: calcareous ooze is made from calcium carbonate, siliceous ooze is made of silicon dioxide

Close, *continued*

Quiz GENERAL

1. What are core samples? (cylinders of sediment collected by drilling into the ocean floor)
2. Are sediments in the deep-ocean basins generally coarse or fine particles? (fine)
3. Where are nodules most commonly located? (on the abyssal plains)

Answers to Section Review

1. Inorganic sediments are rock particles that are carried to the sea by streams, rivers, glaciers, and wind. Biogenic sediments are the remains of marine plants and animals.
2. Icebergs form from glaciers that scour rocks, embedding particles in the ice. Icebergs break off glaciers and float out to sea. When the iceberg melts, any rock materials in the iceberg will sink to the ocean floor.
3. Substances that are dissolved in ocean water can undergo chemical reactions that cause them to crystallize into nodules, which form on the ocean floor.
4. Sediments are classified as muds or oozes. Muds are fine particles of rock. Oozes are muds mixed with at least 30% biogenic material.
5. A mud is sediment composed of fine silt or clay-sized particles.
6. Calcareous ooze is mostly calcium carbonate, whereas siliceous ooze is mostly silicon dioxide.
7. Answers may vary. The presence of volcanic dust indicates that a volcano erupted somewhere on Earth because volcanic dust can be blown great distances.
8. Answers may vary. Possible factors include the expected price of the ore extracted from the nodules; the distribution and density of nodules in any given area; the costs of collecting nodules from the ocean floor; and the cost of extracting ore from the nodules once they are collected.

Answers continued on p. 715A

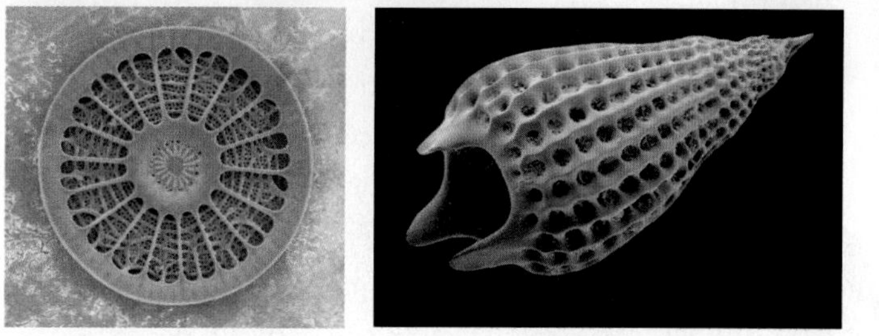

Figure 4 The remains of diatoms (left) and radiolarians (right), both magnified hundreds of times in these photos, are important components of biogenic sediments on the ocean floor.

READING TOOLBOX

Spider Maps
Create a spider map that has two legs and several lines on each leg. Use the map to compare muds and ooze.

Academic Vocabulary
classify (CLAH sih fie) to arrange or divide into categories according to type

SCILINKS.
www.scilinks.org
Topic: Ocean-Floor Sediments
Code: HQX1068

Physical Classification of Sediments

Deep ocean-floor sediments can be classified into two basic types. *Muds* are very fine silt- and clay-sized particles of rock. One common type of mud on the abyssal plains is red clay. Red clay is made of at least 40% clay particles and is mixed with silt, sand, and biogenic material. This clay can vary in color from red to gray, blue, green, or yellow-brown. About 40% of the ocean floor is covered with soft, fine sediment called *ooze*. At least 30% of the ooze is biogenic materials, such as the remains of microscopic sea organisms. The remaining material is fine mud.

Ooze can be classified into two types. *Calcareous ooze* is ooze that is made mostly of calcium carbonate. Calcareous ooze is never found below a depth of 5 km, because at depths between 3 km and 5 km, calcium carbonate dissolves in the deep, cold ocean water. *Siliceous ooze*, which can be found at any depth, is made of mostly silicon dioxide, which comes from the shells of radiolarians and diatoms. Examples of remains of these organisms are shown in **Figure 4.** Most siliceous ooze is found in the cool, nutrient-rich ocean waters around Antarctica because of the abundance of diatoms and radiolarians in that location.

Section 3 Review

Key Ideas

1. **Describe** the formation of two different types of ocean-floor sediments.
2. **Summarize** how icebergs contribute to deep ocean-basin sediments.
3. **Explain** how substances that are dissolved in ocean water travel to the ocean floor.
4. **Explain** how ocean-floor sediments are classified by physical composition.
5. **Describe** how scientists define the word *mud.*
6. **Compare** the compositions of calcareous ooze and siliceous ooze.

Critical Thinking

7. **Making Inferences** What could you infer from a core sample of a layer of sediment that contains volcanic ash and dust?
8. **Applying Ideas** Some businesses have tried to develop methods of extracting nodules from the ocean. Name two factors that businesses should consider when they are determining whether extracting nodules is profitable.

Concept Mapping

9. Use the following terms to create a concept map: *nodule, inorganic sediment, biogenic sediment, diatom, chemical deposit,* and *ocean-floor sediment.*

Differentiated Instruction

Alternative Assessment

Comparing and Contrasting Sediments Have students create a table that compares and contrasts the three types of sediment found on the sea floor: inorganic, biogenic, and chemical.
LS Visual

Why It Matters

Underwater Aliens

WEIRD SCIENCE

Thousands of meters underwater, how can any life exist in the extreme pressure, cold, and darkness? These conditions are as inhospitable to humans as another planet might be. Yet, with ever-improving technologies for exploring the ocean depths, scientists have been discovering underwater creatures that are stranger than science fiction. Peculiar traits of deep-sea organisms represent evolutionary adaptations to the extreme pressure, cold, and darkness of their environment. These discoveries raise new scientific questions, such as did shallow water species colonize the deep ocean or vice versa?

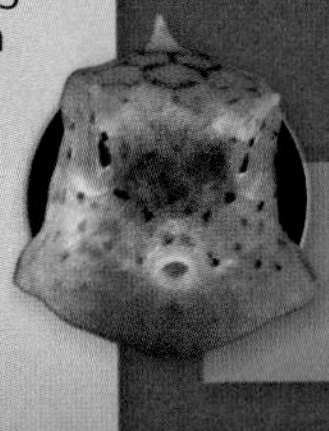

This boxfish is one of the new exotic deep-sea creatures recently discovered by scientists exploring Southeast Asia's Celebes Sea.

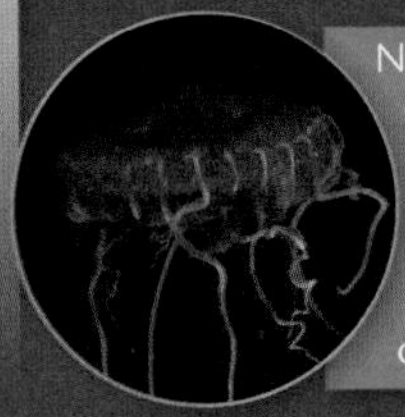

Nicknamed "big red" because of its unusual deep red color, this bizarre new bell-shaped species of jellyfish is a meter in diameter and was discovered in the deep waters off the California coast.

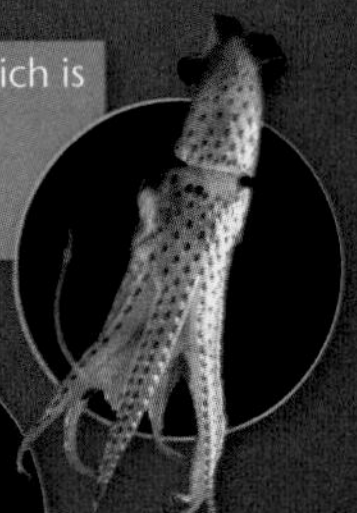

Known for their mismatched eyes, one of which is larger than the other to scope for prey in the deep's darkness, jewel squid live 500 meters beneath the surface of the North Atlantic.

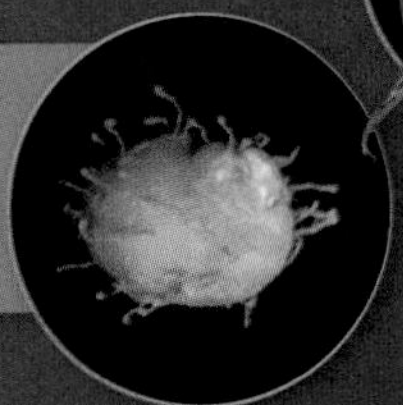

This carnivorous moonsnail lives in the Antarctic deep sea. The polyps, covering its shell, use the moonsnail as transport to food sources.

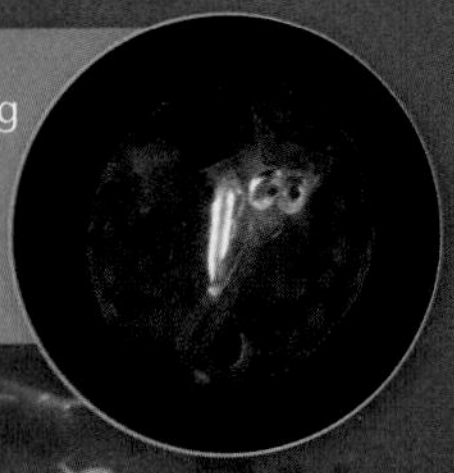

Scientists found this cartoon-like squid among other new species while mapping a deep-sea mountain range in the North Atlantic.

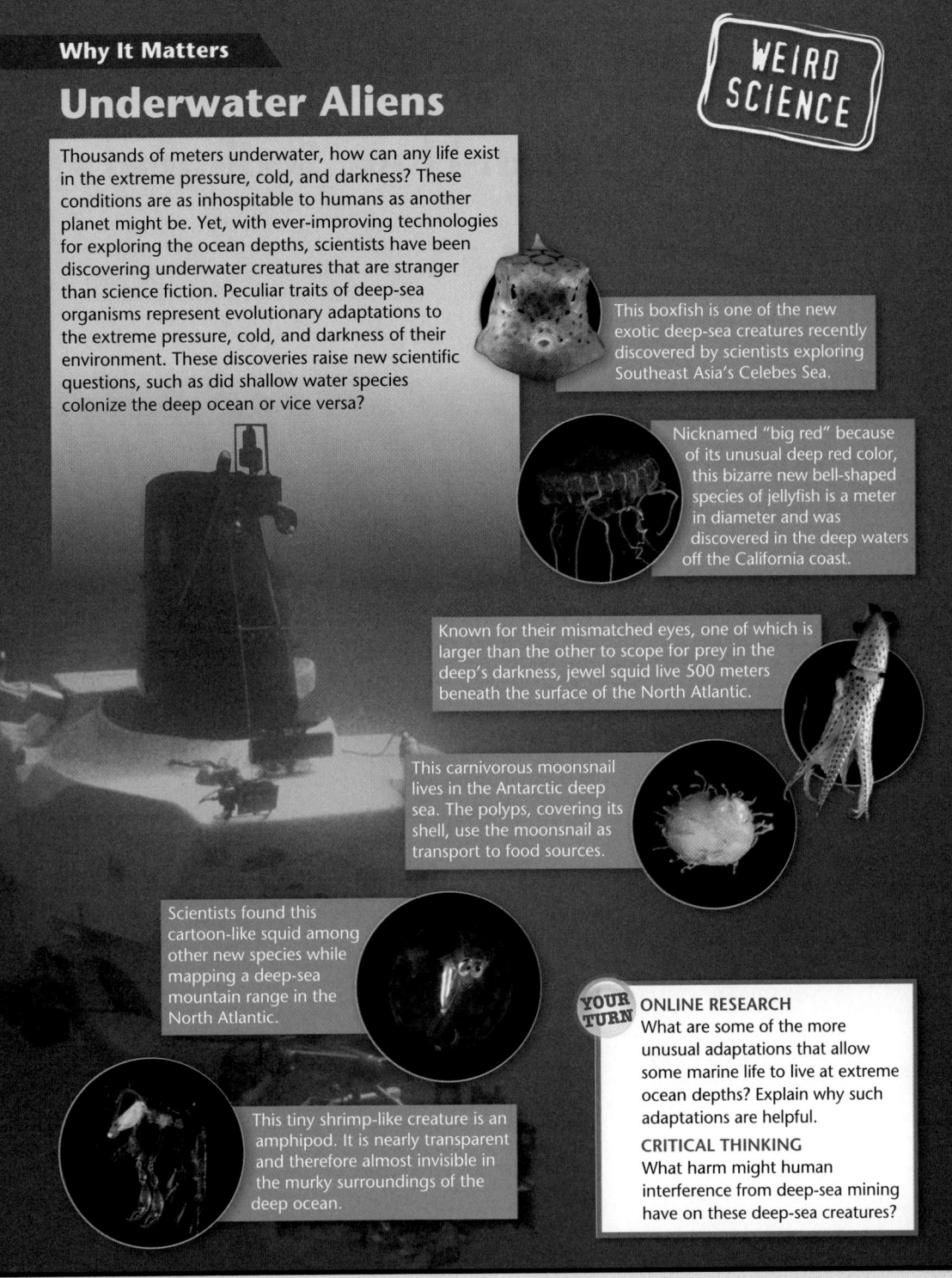

This tiny shrimp-like creature is an amphipod. It is nearly transparent and therefore almost invisible in the murky surroundings of the deep ocean.

YOUR TURN

ONLINE RESEARCH
What are some of the more unusual adaptations that allow some marine life to live at extreme ocean depths? Explain why such adaptations are helpful.

CRITICAL THINKING
What harm might human interference from deep-sea mining have on these deep-sea creatures?

Why It Matters

Underwater Aliens Deep-sea creatures have developed a number of adaptations to survive the harsh environment. The more common adaptations include large eyes, bioluminescence, and a strong sense of smell. Many deep-sea organisms have a body composition with no excess cavities, such as swim bladders, that would collapse under intense pressure. They have expandable stomachs, a large mouth, and an absence of jaws. To hide in the murky depths, deep-sea fish are often transparent, black, silvery, or even red in color. In the absence of red light that occurs at great depth, this keeps them concealed from both predators and prey. There are also barriers to reproduction and bioluminescent light is used to signal potential mates with a specific light pattern. Similarly, chemicals released into the water can attract potential mates with a highly developed sense of smell.

Answers to Your Turn

Online Research Student answers may vary. More unusual adoptions include having extremely long teeth that point inward, which ensures captured prey has little chance of escape, or having huge hinged jaws, which enables an organism to swallow large prey. In some species, such as the deep-sea anglerfish, the males are very small in comparison to females and attach themselves to their mate using hooked teeth, establishing a parasitic relationship for life.

Critical Thinking Disturbing the physical characteristics that these creatures have adapted to may allow other creatures, which live in other areas of the ocean, to colonize the deep sea. Changing environments may lead to an evolutionary disadvantage for those creatures that have adapted to it. For example, light from mining operations may overwhelm the large eyes that have evolved in some creatures.

Skills Practice Lab

Time Required

two 45-minute class periods

Lab Ratings

EASY → HARD

Teacher Preparation
Student Setup
Concept Level
Cleanup

Skills Acquired

- Observing
- Measuring
- Experimenting
- Predicting
- Inferring
- Collecting Data
- Organizing and Analyzing Data

Scientific Methods

In this lab, students will

- Make Observations
- Ask Questions
- Analyze the Results
- Draw Conclusions
- Communicate Results

Materials

The materials listed on this page are enough for groups of two to four students. If soil products with labeled sizes are not available in your area, you can use sieves to separate soil into different sizes. Generally, coarse soil has a diameter of 2.0 to 1.0 mm; medium, 1.0 to 0.5 mm; medium-fine, 0.5 to 0.25 mm; and fine, 0.25 to 0.10 mm, but any divisions of size will work. You may also want to have students measure the diameters of particles in the given samples.

Skills Practice Lab

90 min

Ocean-Floor Sediments

What You'll Do

- **Observe and record** the settling rates of four different sediments.
- **Draw conclusions** about how particle size affects settling rate.
- **Identify** factors that affect settling rate of sediments besides particle size.

What You'll Need

balance, metric
column, clear plastic, 80 cm × 4 cm
cup, paper
pencil, grease
ring stand with clamp
ruler, metric
sieve, 4 mm, 2 mm, 0.5 mm
soil, coarse, medium, medium-fine, and fine grain
stopper, rubber
stopwatch
tape, adhesive
teaspoon
towels, paper
water

Safety

Most of the ocean floor is covered with a layer of sediment that varies in thickness from 0.3 km to more than 1 km. Much of this sediment is thought to have originated on land through the process of weathering. Through erosion, the sediment has made its way to the deep-ocean basins. In this lab, you will use sediment samples of four particle sizes to determine the relationship between the size of particles and the settling rate of the particles in water.

Procedure

1. Take one sample of sediment from each of the following size ranges: coarse, medium, medium-fine, and fine.
2. Plug one end of the plastic column with a rubber stopper, and secure the stopper to the column with tape. Place the column in a vertical position using the ring stand and clamp. Carefully fill the column with water to a level about 5 cm from the top, and allow the water to stand until all large air bubbles have escaped.
3. Use the grease pencil to mark the water level on the column. This will be the starting line.
4. Next, draw a line about 5 cm from the bottom of the column. This will be the finish line.
5. Have a member of your lab group put 1 tsp of the coarse sample into the water column. The other group member should record three time measurements as follows:
   - **a.** Using a stopwatch, start timing when the first particles hit the start line on the column, and stop timing when they reach the finish line. Perform this procedure three times. Record the time for each trial in a table similar to the one shown below.
   - **b.** Next, use the stopwatch to determine how long it takes the last particle in the sample to travel from the start line to the finish line. Perform this procedure three times. Record the time for each trial in your table.

Soil samples	*Trial 1*	*Trial 2*	*Trial 3*	*Average*
Coarse	First time measurment:			
	Second time measurement:			
Medium	First time measurement:			
	Second time measurement:			

6. Determine the average time of the three trials for the first measurement. Do the same for the second measurement. Record the averages.
7. Pour the soil and water from the column into the container provided by your teacher. (Note: Do not pour the soil into the sink.)
8. Refill the plastic column with water up to the original level marked with the grease pencil.
9. Repeat steps 5 through 8 for the remaining sediment sizes. Record the measurements and the averages in your table.
10. With the plastic column filled with water, pour 20 g of unsieved soil into the column, and allow the soil to settle for 5 min. After 5 min, look at the column and record your observations of both the settled sediment and the water. Repeat step 7, and then answer the questions below.

Step 5

Analysis

1. **Organizing Data** Which particles settled fastest? Which particles settled slowest?
2. **Making Comparisons** Compare the settling time of the medium particles with the settling time of the medium-fine particles. Do similar-sized particles fall at the same rate?
3. **Making Inferences** In step 10, why did the water remain slightly cloudy even after most of the particles had settled?
4. **Evaluating Methods** How do the results in step 10 help to explain why the deep-ocean basins are covered with a layer of very fine sediment while areas near the shore are covered with coarse sediment?
5. **Making Predictions** Other than size, what factors do you think would influence the speed at which particles fall in water? Explain your answer.

Extension

Analyzing Predictions Obtain particles of different shapes, such as long, cylindrical grains; flat, disk-shaped grains; round grains; and angular grains. Test the settling times of these grains, and write a brief paragraph that explains how grain shape affects the settling rate of particles in water.

Tips and Tricks

Have students observe the sediments with a magnifying glass or dissecting microscope. You might have students weigh out a given mass of each sediment (or have students weigh their sample) so they can see how the same mass of a given sediment may not have the same density. If possible, leave a column from step 10 set up until the next period. Have students predict whether the water will still be cloudy or if it will have cleared.

Answers to Analysis

1. Students should find that the coarse particles settled fastest. The finest particles settled slowest.
2. Medium-fine particles should settle more slowly than medium particles because of their size.
3. Some very fine particles are still suspended in the water because it takes them more than five minutes to settle to the bottom of the column.
4. Because fine particles remain suspended in the water for a longer time, they can be carried out farther into the deep-ocean regions than coarse particles can. Coarse particles usually settle close to shore.
5. The shape and density of particles also influences their settling rate because these characteristics affect the drag of the particle through the water.

Answer to Extension

Answers may vary but should be based on student data. Flat and disk-shaped particles will take longer to settle than more rounded particles will.

Total Sediment Thickness of Earth's Oceans

Internet Activity ADVANCED

Deep-Sea Sediment Core Samples
Have students visit the Lamont-Doherty Earth Observatory Deep-Sea Sample Repository website to learn about questions scientists have answered or hope to answer by studying deep sea sediment core samples. Have students present their findings to the class. A worksheet designed to direct student research on this topic can be found in the **Chapter Resource File** booklet or by visiting www.thinkcentral.com and entering the keyword **HQXOBAX.**

LS Logical/Verbal

Answers to Map Skills Activity

1. The approximate thickness is about 2,000 m.
2. Two areas with the thickest sediments are 25°N, 95°W (in the Gulf of Mexico), and 20°N, 90°E (off the coast of India and Bangladesh).
3. The amount of sediment in the middle of the ocean is less than the amount of sediment around the continental margins. Near the middle of the oceans, sediment thickness is 500 m or less; near the continental margins, sediment thickness is 1,000 m or more.
4. Major rivers empty into the Gulf of Mexico (the Mississippi) and into the Bay of Bengal (the Ganges/Brahmaputra).
5. The west coast is bordered by a trench. The sediment layer on the west coast is relatively thin all the way up to the coastline.
6. Areas denoted with white spots probably have no valid data on sediment thickness. These areas are predominantly located in the Arctic Circle where the sea is covered with ice. Sampling in those areas may be difficult, if not impossible.

MAPS in Action

Total Sediment Thickness of Earth's Oceans

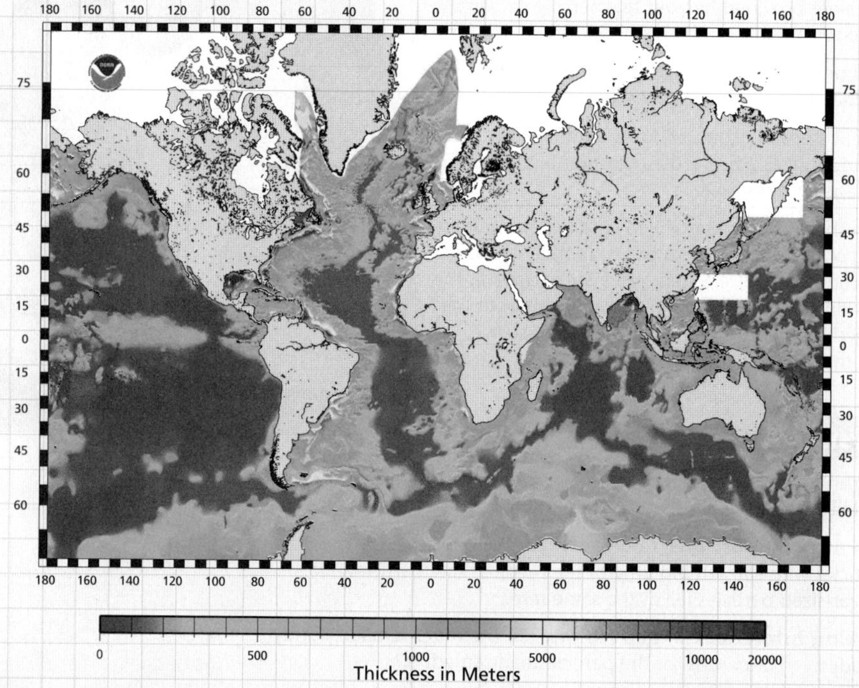

Map Skills Activity

This map shows the total thicknesses of sediments on Earth's ocean floors. Use the map to answer the questions below.

1. **Using a Key** What is the approximate thickness of the sediment located at 45°S and 45°W?
2. **Analyzing Data** Use latitude and longitude to identify two areas that have the thickest sediments.
3. **Comparing Areas** Compare the amount of sediment near the middle of the oceans with the amount of sediment on the continental margins.
4. **Identifying Trends** Rivers deposit massive amounts of sediment when they reach the ocean. Based on this map, at what locations would you expect to find mouths of major rivers?
5. **Inferring Relationships** Which coast of South America—east or west—is most likely bordered by a trench?
6. **Analyzing Relationships** Why does this map contain white spaces even though the key lists no thickness that corresponds with the color white?

Key Resources

Technology

- Transparencies
  119 Total Sediment Thickness of Earth's Oceans

Chapter 23 # Summary

THINK central
SUPER SUMMARY
Keyword: HQXOBAS

Key Ideas | **Key Terms**

Section 1

The Water Planet

- The global ocean can be divided into five major oceans—the Pacific, Atlantic, Indian, Arctic, and Southern Oceans—and many smaller seas.
- Oceanography is the study of the oceans and the seas. Oceanographers study the ocean using research ships, sonar, and submersibles.
- Sonar is a system that uses acoustic signals and echo returns to determine the location of objects or to communicate.

Key Terms:
global ocean, p. 637
sea, p. 637
oceanography, p. 638
sonar, p. 639

Section 2

Features of the Ocean Floor

- Continental margins include the continental shelf, the continental slope, and the continental rise.
- Features of deep-ocean basins include trenches, abyssal plains, mid-ocean ridges, and seamounts.

Key Terms:
continental margin, p. 641
deep-ocean basin, p. 641
trench, p. 643
abyssal plain, p. 643

Section 3

Ocean-Floor Sediments

- Ocean-floor sediments form from inorganic and biogenic materials as well as from chemical deposits.
- Based on physical characteristics, deep ocean-floor sediments are classified as mud or as ooze.

Key Terms:
core sample, p. 645
nodule, p. 647

Chapter Summary

Using THINK central Resources

Super Summary

Have students connect the major concepts in this chapter through an interactive Super Summary. Visit www.thinkcentral.com and type in the keyword **HQXOBAS** to access the Super Summary for this chapter.

Chapter Review

Assignment Guide	
Section	**Questions**
1	1, 2, 3, 5, 8, 10, 11, 19, 24, 29, 32
2	7, 12-15, 18, 22, 25, 31
3	4, 9, 16, 17, 23, 26, 27
1 and 2	30
2 and 3	21, 28
1–3	6, 20

Reading Toolbox

1. Answers will vary but lines may contain the following information: Global Ocean: covers nearly three-fourths of Earth's surface, divided into five major oceans; Sea: smaller than an ocean and may be partially surrounded by land; An example is the Mediterranean Sea

Using Key Terms

2–9. Answers may vary but should show that students understand the definitions of and differences between key terms.

Understanding Key Concepts

10. c
11. d
12. a
13. d
14. a
15. a
16. b
17. a

Short Answer

18. A guyot forms when an island sinks, becoming eroded by waves. A seamount is an underwater mountain that never reaches the ocean surface.

Chapter 23 Review

1. **Spider Map** READING TOOLBOX Create a spider map that has two legs and several lines on each leg. Use the map to compare the global ocean and a sea.

USING KEY TERMS

Use each of the following terms in a separate sentence.

2. *oceanography*
3. *sonar*
4. *core sample*

For each pair of terms, explain how the meanings of the terms differ.

5. *trench* and *abyssal plain*
6. *submersible* and *nodule*
7. *continental margin* and *deep-ocean basin*
8. *oceanography* and *core sample*
9. *mud* and *ooze*

UNDERSTANDING KEY IDEAS

10. A self-propelled, free-moving submarine that is equipped for ocean research is a
a. turbidity.
b. bathysphere.
c. bathyscaph.
d. guyot.
11. A system that is used for determining the depth of the ocean floor is
a. a guyot.
b. radiolarians.
c. a bathysphere.
d. sonar.
12. The parts of the ocean floor that are made up of continental crust are called
a. continental margins.
b. abyssal plains.
c. mid-ocean ridges.
d. trenches.
13. The accumulation of sediments at the base of the continental slope is called the
a. trench.
b. turbidity current.
c. continental margin.
d. continental rise.
14. The deepest parts of the ocean are called
a. trenches.
b. submarine canyons.
c. abyssal plains.
d. continental rises.
15. Large quantities of the inorganic sediment that makes up the continental rise come from
a. turbidity currents.
b. earthquakes.
c. diatoms.
d. nodules.
16. Potato-shaped lumps of minerals on the ocean floor are called
a. guyots. **c.** foraminiferans.
b. nodules. **d.** diatoms.
17. Very fine particles of silt and clay that have settled to the ocean floor are called
a. muds. **c.** guyots.
b. seamounts. **d.** nodules.

SHORT ANSWER

18. What are the differences between a seamount and a guyot?
19. Explain how sonar is used to study the oceans.
20. List three ways that scientists can learn about the deep ocean.
21. How do fine sediments reach the deep-ocean bottom?
22. What effects do deep-ocean trenches have on the sediment thickness of the abyssal plain?
23. List the three main types of ocean-floor sediments, and describe how they are deposited.

19. Sonar uses sound signals and returned echoes to determine the depth of the ocean floor. Depth information from various locations can be compiled to make maps and profiles of the ocean floor.
20. sonar, submersibles, and core samples
21. Turbidity currents can carry sediments hundreds of kilometers out to the deep ocean basins. Volcanic dust can be carried by winds far out to sea and deposited in the deep ocean basins. Fine sediments are also derived from biogenic materials.
22. Abyssal plains surrounded by deep ocean trenches generally have thinner sediment cover.
23. The three main types of sediments are inorganic sediments, biogenic sediments, and chemical deposits. Inorganic sediments are derived from rocks. They can be deposited by rivers that flow into the ocean, by volcanoes that spew dust and ash into the air and out to sea, by icebergs that carry rock particles out to sea, and by meteorites. Biogenic sediments are the deposited remains and waste products of ocean plants and animals. Chemical deposits form when reactions take place in the ocean, causing some substances to crystallize out of the water and settle on the ocean floor.

CRITICAL THINKING

24. Making Comparisons The exploration of the ocean depths has been compared with the exploration of space. What similarities exist between these two environments and the attempts by people to explore them?

25. Making Predictions What may be the eventual fate of seamounts as they are carried along the spreading oceanic crust?

26. Analyzing Ideas A type of fish is known to exist only in one river in the central United States. Explain how the fossilized remains of this fish might become part of the sediments on the ocean floor.

27. Analyzing Relationships Explain how it is possible that scientists have found some red clays on the ocean floor that contain material from outer space.

CONCEPT MAPPING

28. Use the following terms to create a concept map: *deep-ocean basin, continental shelf, mud, ooze, calcareous ooze, siliceous ooze,* and *sediment.*

MATH SKILLS

Math Skills

29. Making Calculations The total area of Earth is approximately 511,000,000 km^2. About 71% of Earth's surface is covered with water. Calculate the area of Earth, in square kilometers, that is covered with water.

WRITING SKILLS

30. Writing from Research Prepare a brief report on the different types of submersibles. Your report should explain the special features of each type of submersible as well as how each type has contributed to oceanographers' knowledge of the oceans.

31. Creative Writing Create an imaginary walking tour of the ocean basins. Your tour should begin at the edge of a continent—perhaps at a beach on the east coast of Florida. Explain exactly what tourists should look for along the continental margin and the ocean floor on their way to the western coast of Africa.

INTERPRETING GRAPHICS

The graph below compares elevations of land and depths of oceans on Earth's surface. Use the graph to answer the questions that follow.

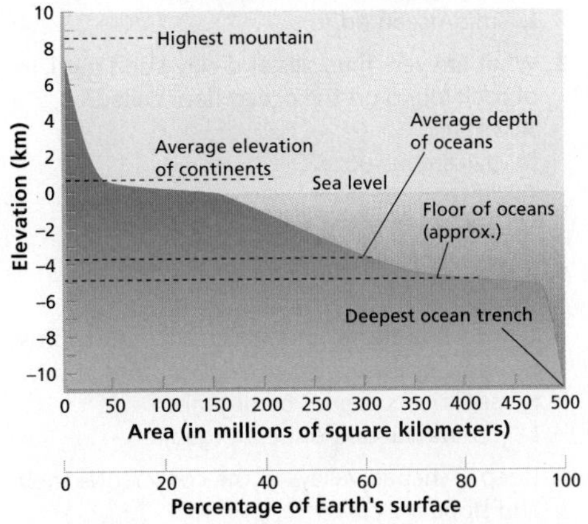

32. What percentage of Earth's surface is covered by land?

33. Which is greater: the elevation of the highest mountain above sea level or the depth of the deepest ocean trench below sea level?

34. Relative to sea level, how many times greater is the average depth of the ocean than the average elevation of land?

35. According to this diagram, how many millions of square kilometers of crust is under ocean water?

Chapter Review

Critical Thinking

24. Both the ocean and space are very harsh environments where humans cannot survive without special equipment because of the extreme temperatures and pressures and the lack of oxygen and light. Thus, exploration requires special methods and/or vehicles. Exploration is often done by robots, which are remotely controlled by humans.

25. Seamounts tall enough to emerge as islands and that are carried along by the spreading of Earth's crust may become atolls and eventually guyots as the crust beneath them subsides. They may eventually become part of a continent at subduction zones, where one tectonic plate collides with another.

26. As the fossil-containing rocks erode and are washed into rivers, the sediments eventually may be carried into the ocean where they may be deposited on the ocean floor.

27. Because most of Earth's surface is water, meteorite fragments often fall into the oceans and become part of the sediments of the ocean floor.

Concept Mapping

28. Answers may vary but should include all of the terms listed. Sample answers appear at the end of this unit on p. 715A.

Math Skills

29. area of Earth covered in water = 511,000,000 km^2 × 0.71 = 363,000,000 km^2

Writing Skills

30. Answers may vary. Accept all reasonable answers.

31. Answers may vary. Accept all reasonable answers.

Interpreting Graphics

32. About 30 percent of Earth's surface is covered by land.

33. The depth of the deepest trench below sea level, which is about 11 km.

34. The average depth of the ocean is about 5 times the average elevation of land. (avg. elevation of land = 0.75 km, avg. depth of ocean = 3.75 km; 3.75 km ÷ 0.75 km = 5)

35. About 340 million km^2 of Earth's surface is underwater.

Estimated Time

To give students practice under more realistic testing conditions, allow them 30 minutes to answer all of the questions in this practice test.

Test Doctor

Question 2 Answer H is correct. Though the features of deep-ocean topography have a greater magnitude than those found on the continents—with the mountains being higher and the plains being flatter in the deep ocean—students can use what they know about continental landforms to arrive at the correct answer. In this case, *plains* are large, flat areas.

Question 6 The correct answer is 178,850,000 km^2. Students should multiply 511,000,000 km^2 by 0.70 to determine the area of Earth that is covered by water. Dividing the result by 2 yields the correct answer.

Question 9 Answer B is the best choice because the passage states that corals and seaweed need sunlight and that algae flourish in the warm, nutrient-rich water.

Chapter 23 Standardized Test Prep

Understanding Concepts

Directions (1–5): For each question, write on a separate sheet of paper the letter of the correct answer.

1. The global ocean is divided into which of the following oceans, in order of decreasing size?
A. Atlantic, Pacific, Arctic, Southern, Indian
B. Arctic, Southern, Indian, Atlantic, Pacific
C. Pacific, Arctic, Indian, Atlantic, Southern
D. Pacific, Atlantic, Indian, Southern, Arctic

2. What is the name for a vast, flat area of a deep-ocean basin?
F. trench
G. seamount
H. abyssal plain
I. mid-ocean ridge

3. What are very fine, silt- and clay-sized particles of rock found on the ocean floor called?
A. muds
B. calcareous ooze
C. siliceous ooze
D. sand

4. The study of deep-ocean sediment samples shows that
F. most of the sediments came from the crust.
G. most of the sediments settled from above.
H. sediments cannot be organic.
I. sediments cannot be inorganic.

5. Deep V-shaped valleys in the continental shelf and slope are called
A. continental rises.
B. seamounts.
C. submarine canyons.
D. turbidity currents.

Directions (6–7): For each question, write a short response.

6. The surface area of Earth is about 511,000,000 km^2. About 70% of the Earth's surface is covered by water and the Pacific Ocean makes up 50% of this amount. Calculate the surface area of Earth that is covered by the Pacific Ocean.

7. What are some of the products made using ocean sediments?

Reading Skills

Directions (8–10): Read the passage below. Then, answer the questions.

Life on a Continental Shelf

While fish, mammals, and other forms of life can be found throughout these ocean waters, most life in the ocean is concentrated near the continental shores. The shallow waters of the continental shelf, which make up less than 10% of the ocean's total surface area, are home to an amazing array of plants, animals, and microscopic organisms.

Organisms such as coral and seaweed can grow on the ocean floor and still receive much needed sunlight that cannot penetrate deeper waters. The sunlight also makes the shallow waters much warmer than deeper abyssal waters. Algae flourishes in these warm, nutrient-rich waters and serves as food for many small ocean organisms. These organisms are in turn eaten by larger organisms. Even humans have become part of the food chain on the shelf. The vast majority of fish caught for human consumption are caught in waters above a continental shelf.

8. Which of the following statements about why humans catch so many fish in the waters over a continental shelf can be inferred from the information in the passage?
F. There are no fish in deeper waters.
G. Fish from deeper waters are inedible.
H. Humans do not have the technological ability to catch fish in deeper ocean waters.
I. There are larger and more varied fish populations over a continental shelf.

9. Which of the following factors was not mentioned in the passage as a factor that influences the concentration of organisms that live over a continental shelf?
A. nutrients
B. salinity
C. sunlight
D. water temperature

10. Why might the waters of a continental shelf have more nutrients than abyssal waters?

Question 11 Answer F is the best choice. Students need to know how sonar is used to correctly answer this question. A sound source dragged behind the boat emits sound waves. These waves travel to the ocean floor. When they strike the ocean floor, they bounce off of it. Some of the waves are lost as they bounce in various directions, though others return to the receiver. A computer can then calculate the time the sound wave took to make its complete journey and plot the depth of the location. When numerous readings are taken, scientists are able to create three dimensional models of the ocean's floor.

Question 12 Full-credit answers should include the following points:
- biologic productivity in the oceans far outstrips the inorganic chemical reactions taking place in the oceans
- biologic organisms are also able to reproduce and thus provide a continuous source of sediment as the organisms die
- biogenic sediment is found mostly in the form of animal remains

Interpreting Graphics

Directions (11–13): For each question below, record the correct answer on a separate sheet of paper.

Base your answer to question 11 on this image, which shows how sonar equipment works.

Studying the Ocean Floor with Sonar

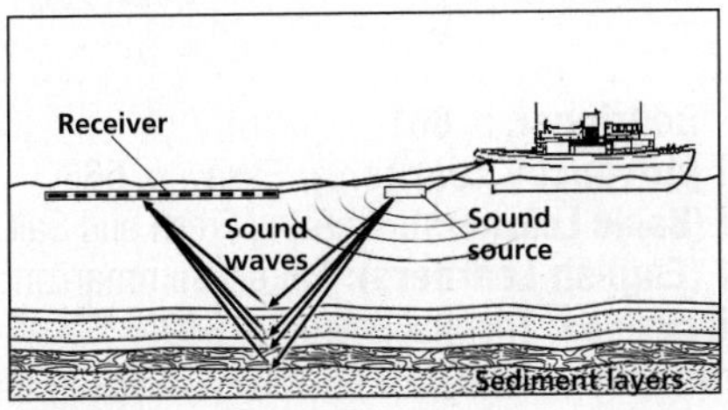

11. Which of the following best summarizes how sound waves are used?

F. A sound source dragged behind the boat emits waves that penetrate the different layers of the sea floor and bounce back to the receiver.

G. A sound source in front of the boat emits waves that penetrate the different layers of the sea floor and then bounce back to the receiver.

H. A receiver dragged behind the boat emits waves that penetrate the different layers of the sea floor and then bounce back to the receiver.

I. A receiver in front of the boat emits waves that penetrate the different layers of the sea floor and then bounce back to the receiver.

Base your answers to questions 12 and 13 on the pie graph below, which shows the composition of ocean-floor sediments.

Composition of Ocean-Floor Sediments

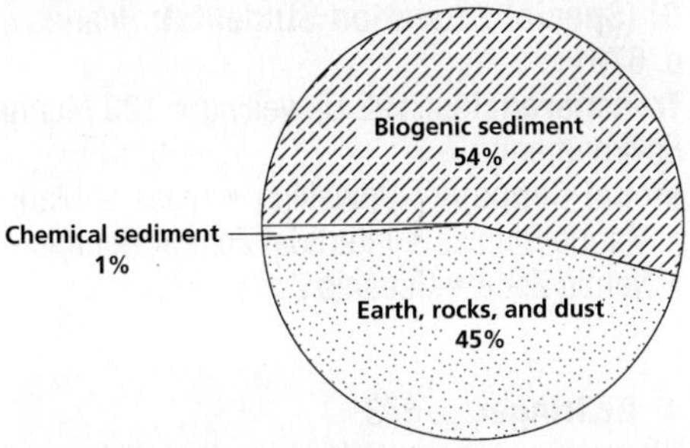

12. Why is there such a large difference between the percentage of biogenic sediment and the percentage of chemical sediment?

13. How did the inorganic materials in the two kinds of inorganic sediment shown on the pie graph above form and become part of the ocean floor?

Test Tip

Before choosing an answer to a question, try to answer the question without looking at the answer choices on the test.

Standardized Test Prep

Using THINK central Resources

State Resources

- For specific resources for your state, visit www.thinkcentral.com and type in the keyword **HSHSTR.**

Answers

Understanding Concepts

1. D
2. H
3. A
4. G
5. C
6. 178,850,000 km^2
7. paint, toothpaste

Reading Skills

8. I
9. B
10. Continental shelf waters have many benefits over deeper ocean waters. The sun makes waters of the shelf rich in plant life. The proximity to land constantly cycles new nutrients into the system by land and river runoff. Upwelling also brings nutrients up from the deeper waters.

Interpreting Graphics

11. F
12. Answers may vary. See Test Doctor for a detailed scoring rubric.
13. Chemical sediment precipitated from the sea water; rocks and dust formed on land and were carried to the ocean by erosion.

Chapter Planner 24 Ocean Water

	Standards	Teach Key Ideas
Chapter Opener, pp. 658–659 (45 min.)	National Science Education Standards	
Section 1 Properties of Ocean Water, pp. 661–668 (45 min.) › Dissolved Gases › Dissolved Solids › Salinity of Ocean Water › Factors That Change Salinity › Temperature of Ocean Water › Density of Ocean Water › Color of Ocean Water	SPSP 4a	■ ◆ **Bellringer,** p. 661 ■ **DI (Advanced Learners):** Essay, p. 663 ■ **DI (Basic Learners):** Freezing Fresh and Salt Water, p. 665 ■ **DI (English Learners):** Paired Summarizing, p. 666 ■ **Discussion:** Thermal Energy, p. 680 ◆ **Transparencies:** 120 Dissolved Gases in the Ocean • 121 Average Surface Salinity of the Global Ocean • 124 Sea Surface Temperatures in August ▲ **Visual Concepts:** Physical Properties of Water • Factors That Affect Salinity • Ocean Surface Temperature Changes • Ocean Temperature Zones
Section 2 Life in the Oceans, pp. 669–672 (45 min.) › Ocean Chemistry and Marine Life › Ocean Environments	SPSP 4a, LS 4c	■ ◆ **Bellringer,** p. 669 ■ **DI (Basic Learners):** Anticipation Guide, p. 669 ■ **DI (Special Education Students):** Hearing Impaired, p. 670 ◆ **Transparencies:** 122 Upwelling • 123 Marine Environments ▲ **Visual Concepts:** Upwelling • Types of Marine Life • Marine Biomes • Intertidal Zone • Benthic Zone • Neritic Zone • Oceanic Zone
Section 3 Ocean Resources, pp. 673–676 (45 min.) › Fresh Water from the Ocean › Mineral and Energy Resources › Food from the Ocean › Ocean-Water Pollution	SPSP 3a, SPSP 4a, LS 4e	■ ◆ **Bellringer,** p. 673 ■ **Discussion:** Fresh Water from Salt Water, p. 673 ■ **DI (Advanced Learners):** Debate, p. 673 ■ **DI (Advanced Learners):** Food from the Ocean, p. 674 ▲ **Visual Concepts:** Saving Our Ocean Resources
Chapter Wrap-Up, pp. 681–685 (90 min.)		**Chapter Summary,** p. 681

See also PowerNotes® Presentations

CHAPTER Fast Track *To shorten instruction because of time limitations, omit Section 2.*

Key

Teacher's Edition ■ | Teaching Transparencies ◆ | Chapter Resource File ● | Online Edition ▲

All resources listed below are also available on the **Teacher One Stop™.**

Why It Matters	Hands-On	Skills Development	Assessment
■ **Chapter Overview,** p. 658 ■ **Using the Figure:** Water of Life, p. 658	**Inquiry Lab:** Testing Temperature and Gauging Gases, p. 659	**Reading Toolbox,** p. 660	
■ **Section Overview,** p. 661 ■ **Using the Figure:** Dissolved Gases, p. 661 **Fresh Water in an Ocean of Salt,** p. 662 ■ **Environmental Connection:** Carbon Dioxide and Sinks, p. 662 ■ **Using the Figure:** Salinity Around the World, p. 664 ■ **Salt Deposits,** p. 664 ■ **Using the Figure:** Thermoclines, p. 666 ■ **Environmental Connection:** Surface-Water Temperature, p. 666 ■ **Using the Figure:** Liquid Density, p. 667	**Quick Lab:** Dissolving Solids, p. 663 ■ **Activity:** Ocean Surface Temperatures, p. 665 **Quick Lab:** Density Factors, p. 667 **Skills Practice Lab:** Ocean Water Density, pp. 678–679 ● **Skills Practice Lab:** The Blue-Green Ocean	**Reading Toolbox:** Key-Term Fold, p. 662 ■ **Skill Builder:** Math, p. 663 **Maps in Action:** Sea Surface Temperatures in August, p. 680	**Reading Check,** p. 663 **Reading Check,** p. 665 **Reading Check,** p. 667 **Section Review,** p. 668 ■ **Reteaching,** p. 667 ■ **Quiz,** p. 667 ■ **DI (Alternative Assessment):** Personal Essay, p. 668 ● **Section Quiz**
■ **Section Overview,** p. 669 ■ **Using the Figure:** Upwelling, p. 670 ■ **Environmental Connection:** Photosynthesis, p. 670	■ **Group Activity:** Poster Project, p. 669	■ **Reading ToolBox:** Comparison Table, p. 671	**Reading Check,** p. 671 **Section Review,** p. 672 ■ **Reteaching,** p. 671 ■ **Quiz,** p. 671 ■ **DI (Alternative Assessment):** Modeling the Ocean, p. 672 ● **Section Quiz**
■ **Section Overview,** p. 673 ■ **Environmental Connection:** Freshwater Sources, p. 674	■ **Activity:** Where's the Oil? p. 674 ● **Inquiry Lab:** Oil Spill!	**Math Skills:** Ocean's Gold, p. 674 ■ **Skill Builder:** Vocabulary, p. 674 **Reading ToolBox:** Analyzing Comparisons, p. 675 ■ ● **Internet Activity:** Aquaculture, p. 675	**Reading Check,** p. 675 **Section Review,** p. 676 ■ **Reteaching,** p. 675 ■ **Quiz,** p. 675 ■ **DI (Alternative Assessment):** Outlining, p. 676 ● **Section Quiz**
Searching for Sunken Treasure, p. 677	■ **Activity:** Ocean Video, p. 681 ■ **Group Activity:** Brine Shrimp, p. 681	▲ **Super Summary** **Standardized Test Prep,** pp. 684–685	**Chapter Review,** pp. 682–683 ● **Chapter Tests**

See also Lab Generator

See also Holt Online Assessment Resources

Chapter Overview

Ocean water is a complex mixture of dissolved gases and solids from different sources. Its composition is affected by a number of factors, such as temperature and evaporation rates. The ocean's dissolved gases and solids are essential to marine life, which, in turn, maintains the chemical balance of ocean water and is supported by nutrients in the water. The oceans are a source of many resources, which are threatened by human pollution.

Using the Figure — GENERAL

Water of Life Ask students to write a paragraph that describes what they see in the image. Have them observe the behavior of the fish in the photo. Ask them to discuss what conditions might be required to support a school of fish both directly and indirectly. (Students may suggest such conditions as the salinity of the water, the temperature, the amount of sunlight, and the availability of food.) **LS Visual/Logical**

Why It Matters

The physical and chemical characteristics of ocean water shape the different ecosystems in the ocean as well as the abundance, location, and availability of resources.

Chapter 24 Ocean Water

Chapter Outline

Virginia Standards of Learning
ES.1.a
ES.1.e
ES.10.a
ES.10.b
ES.10.e

Why It Matters

Oceans are home to thousands of species and play a vital role in Earth's ecology. Important resources, including food and fresh water, come from oceans.

Chapter Correlations — *Virginia Standards of Learning*

ES.1.a volume, area, mass, elapsed time, direction, temperature, pressure, distance, density, and changes in elevation/depth are calculated utilizing the most appropriate tools.
ES.1.e variables are manipulated with repeated trials
ES.10.a physical and chemical changes related to tides, waves, currents, sea level and ice cap variations, upwelling, and salinity variations
ES.10.b importance of environmental and geologic implications
ES.10.e economic and public policy issues concerning the oceans and the coastal zone including the Chesapeake Bay

Inquiry Lab

Central Concept: Students will experiment with the solubility of a liquid at different temperatures.

Teacher's Notes: Remind students to be consistent each time they swirl the soda. Changing the length of time or the vigorousness with which the soda is swirled could affect results.

Materials (per group)
- Cans of soda (2)
- Thermometer
- Beakers, 500 mL (2)
- Stopwatch
- Pencil
- Graph paper

Skills Acquired
- Experimenting
- Observing
- Interpreting Results

Answers to Getting Started
1. As the temperature increases, the soda cannot retain the gas (carbon dioxide) for as long a time.
2. Possible answer: Yes, as water temperature increases, its ability to hold dissolved gases decreases. As water temperature increases, water can dissolve less gas from the atmosphere.

Inquiry Lab Testing Temperature and Gauging Gases

45 min

Open a can of soda at room temperature and a can of chilled soda at the same time. Use a thermometer to measure the temperature of the soda in each can. Pour the soda from each can into a 500 mL beaker, and "swirl" the soda three times. Using a stopwatch, time how long it takes for the "fizziness" in each soda to die down. Return the cold soda to the refrigerator. Repeat the measurements on both sodas at 10 min intervals for the next 40 min. When you have collected all your data, use a pencil to plot your data on graph paper. Your graph should contain two lines: one for the warm soda and one for the cold soda.

Questions to Get You Started

1. Compare the ability of the sodas to retain dissolved gases over time. What is the effect of temperature?
2. Do you think temperature affects the exchange of gases between the ocean and the atmosphere in the same way? Explain your answer.

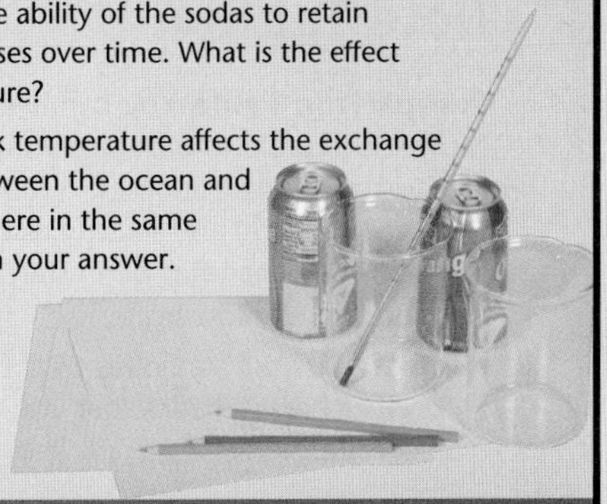

Using THINK central Resources

An online version of this chapter, as well as all the print and multimedia resources that accompany the program are available to registered teachers and their students. Log onto www.thinkcentral.com to access these materials and tools to organize your preparation and student learning.

READING TOOLBOX

FoldNotes

Key-Term Fold Students should create a key-term fold that contains definitions for the twelve key terms in the chapter: salinity, pack ice, thermocline, density, upwelling, plankton, nekton, benthos, benthic zone, pelagic zone, desalination, and aquaculture.

Comparisons

Analyzing Comparisons Sample answers include: First thing: cold water, Second thing: warm water, Similarity or Difference: Gases dissolve more readily in cold water than in warm water, Signal word or phrase: more readily; First thing: polar surface waters, Second thing: tropical surface waters, Similarity or Difference: Polar surface waters are much cooler than tropical surface waters, Signal word or phrase: much cooler

Note Taking

Comparison Table Tables should contain the following information. Petroleum: Resources Included: oil, natural gas, Where found: beneath the ocean floor, Problems involved: pollution from oil spills; Nodules: Resources included: manganese, iron, copper, nickel, Where found: abyssal plains, Problems involved: recovery is expensive and difficult, rights issues; Trace Minerals: Resources included: a variety of minerals, Where found: dissolved in ocean water; Problems involved: extraction too costly

READING TOOLBOX

These reading tools will help you learn the material in this chapter.

FoldNotes

Key-Term Fold A key-term fold can help you learn the key terms in this chapter.

Your Turn Make a key-term fold, as described in **Appendix A.**

1. Write each key term from the Chapter Summary on the front of a tab. The first few terms are shown here.
2. As you read the chapter, write the definition of each term under the appropriate tab.
3. Use this FoldNote to study the key terms.

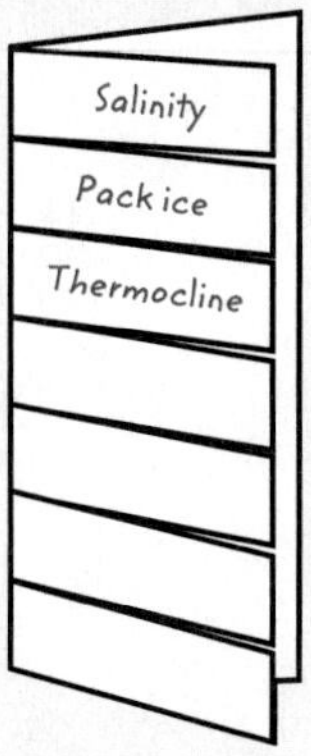

Comparisons

Analyzing Comparisons Comparisons are often signaled in language by the use of a few key words or structures. The words *similar* and *dissimilar* can tell you whether the comparison is focused on similarities or differences. Often, a comparison describes one thing as *greater than, less than,* or ____ *than* another thing in some way.

Your Turn As you read Sections 1 and 2, fill out a table of comparisons like the one below. The sample entry is for the sentence, "The large amount of dissolved solids in ocean water makes it denser than pure fresh water."

First thing	Second thing	Similarity or difference	Signaling word or phrase
ocean water	fresh water	Ocean water is denser than fresh water.	denser

Note Taking

Comparison Table You can use a comparison table to organize your notes as you compare related topics. A table that compares mineral and energy resources found in the ocean has been started for you. It includes the following:

- topics that you are going to compare
- specific characteristics that you are going to compare

Your Turn Make a table like the one below. As you read Section 3, complete your table. Add columns and rows as needed.

	Petroleum	Nodules	Trace minerals
Resources included	oil, natural gas		
Where found			dissolved in ocean water
Problems involved			

For more information on how to use these and other tools, see **Appendix A.**

SECTION 1

Properties of Ocean Water

Key Ideas	Key Terms	Why It Matters
› Describe the chemical composition of ocean water. › Describe the salinity, temperature, density, and color of ocean water.	salinity, thermocline, pack ice, density	Ocean water is a complex mixture of chemicals that supports a vast range of living organisms.

Pure liquid water is tasteless, odorless, and colorless. However, the water in the ocean is not pure. Many solids and gases are dissolved in ocean water. In addition to dissolved substances, small particles of matter and tiny organisms are suspended in ocean water. Ocean water is a complex mixture of chemicals that sustains a variety of plant and animal life. Scientists study various properties of ocean water to understand the complex interactions between the oceans, the atmosphere, and the land.

Dissolved Gases

The two main gases in the atmosphere are nitrogen, N_2, and oxygen, O_2. These two gases are also the main gases dissolved in ocean water. While carbon dioxide, CO_2, is not a major component of the atmosphere, a large amount of this gas is dissolved in ocean water. Other atmospheric gases are also present in ocean water in small amounts.

Ocean water dissolves gases from a variety of sources, as shown in **Figure 1.** Gases may enter ocean water from water in streams and rivers. Some of the gases in ocean water come from volcanic eruptions beneath the ocean. Gases are also released directly into ocean water by organisms that live in the ocean. For example, many plants in the ocean make oxygen as a product of photosynthesis. However, most oxygen in the ocean enters at the surface of the ocean from the atmosphere.

Figure 1 Gases can enter the ocean from streams, volcanoes, organisms, and the atmosphere.

Gases enter the ocean directly from the atmosphere.
Some gases in the ocean come from underwater volcanoes and marine organisms.
Gases enter the ocean from streams and rivers.

Key Resources

Chapter Resource File
- Directed Reading BASIC
- Skills Practice Lab: The Blue-Green Ocean GENERAL

Technology
- Transparencies
  Bellringer
  120 Dissolved Gases in the Ocean

Section 1

Focus

Overview

This section introduces students to the composition of ocean water and describes the sources of the dissolved substances. The section also covers ocean composition, salinity, temperature, density, and color.

Bellringer

Have students list everything they think is found in ocean water. (The list may include such things as dissolved salt, various marine animals, plants, rocks, sand, and dissolved gases.)
LS Logical

Motivate

Using the Figure GENERAL

Dissolved Gases Have students discuss the exchange of gases between ocean water and the atmosphere. Ask students to identify two sources of gases entering the ocean. (the atmosphere and streams and rivers) Ask students to identify two sources of gases from the ocean. (underwater volcanoes and marine organisms) What gases are produced by marine organisms? (carbon dioxide and oxygen during photosynthesis and respiration)
LS Visual

Teach

MISCONCEPTION ALERT

Solubility Trends Because students have learned that gases are more soluble in cooler liquids, they may assume that the same is true of solids. Explain that the solubility trends for solids and gases are generally opposite. Most, though not all, solids become more soluble as water temperature rises, while gases become more soluble as water cools.

Environmental Connection

Carbon Dioxide and Sinks The oceans are an important sink for atmospheric carbon dioxide. As a result, the oceans moderate changes in the concentration of atmospheric carbon dioxide. Ask students what they think might happen if the surface waters of the oceans became warmer. (Dissolved CO_2 would be released into the atmosphere, which would grow warmer because increased CO_2 would trap more thermal energy from the sun. This would probably have a pronounced effect on the global climate system.) **LS Logical/Verbal**

READING TOOLBOX

Key-Term Fold Students may include the following italicized terms in a key-term fold: *carbon sink, sea salts, trace elements, phytoplankton, intertidal zone, sublittoral zone, bathyal zone, abyssal zone, hadal zone, neritic zone, oceanic zone, distillation, freezing, reverse osmosis desalination,* and *nodules.*

SciLinks
www.scilinks.org
Topic: Properties of Ocean Water
Code: **HQX1232**

READING TOOLBOX

Key-Term Fold
As you read this chapter, look for words in italics. These words, while not key terms, are also important. Add them and their definitions to the key-term fold you made at the beginning of the chapter, or make a new key-term fold.

Temperature and Dissolved Gases

The temperature of water affects the amount of gas that dissolves in the water. Gases dissolve more readily in cold water than in warm water. You may have noticed this phenomenon when your glass of soda quickly goes "flat" on a warm day. The soda goes flat quickly because the CO_2 that makes the soda bubbly escapes into the air. But if the soda is kept in the refrigerator, the soda will retain its fizz longer. Because cold water dissolves gases more readily, water at the surface of the ocean in cold regions dissolves larger amounts of gases than water in warm tropical regions does.

Gases can return to the atmosphere from the ocean. If the water temperature rises, smaller amounts of gases will remain dissolved, and the excess gases will be released into the atmosphere. For example, warm equatorial ocean water tends to release CO_2 into the atmosphere, but ocean water at cooler, higher latitudes takes up large amounts of CO_2. Therefore, the ocean and the atmosphere are continuously exchanging gases as water temperature changes.

The Ocean as a Carbon Sink

The global ocean contains more than 60 times as much carbon as the atmosphere does. Dissolved CO_2 may be trapped in the ocean for hundreds to thousands of years. Because of this ability to dissolve and contain a large amount of CO_2, the ocean is commonly referred to as a *carbon sink*. Because gaseous CO_2 affects the atmosphere's ability to trap thermal energy from the sun, the ocean is important in the regulation of climate.

Why It Matters

Fresh Water in an Ocean of Salt

SCIENCE & SOCIETY

Each submarine crewmember needs about 20 liters of water per day. Carrying that much water would take up too much space, so submarines have distillation apparatus.

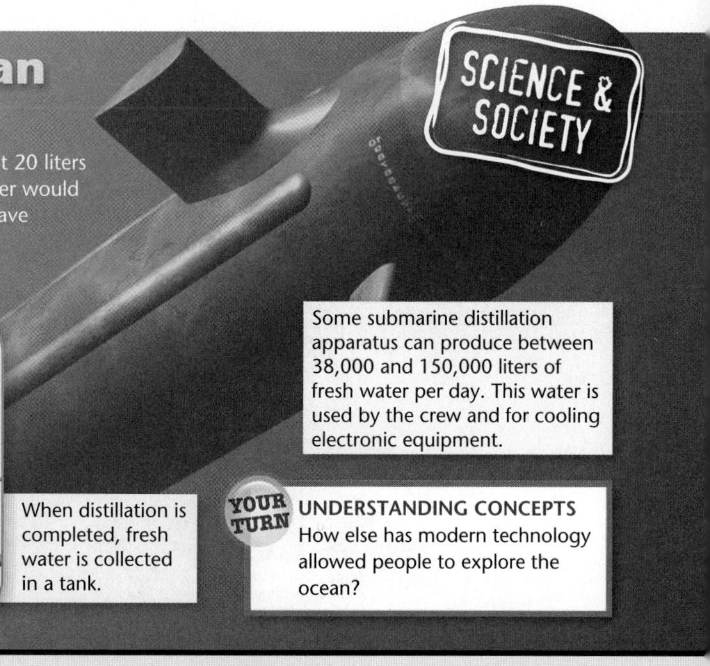

How Distillation Works

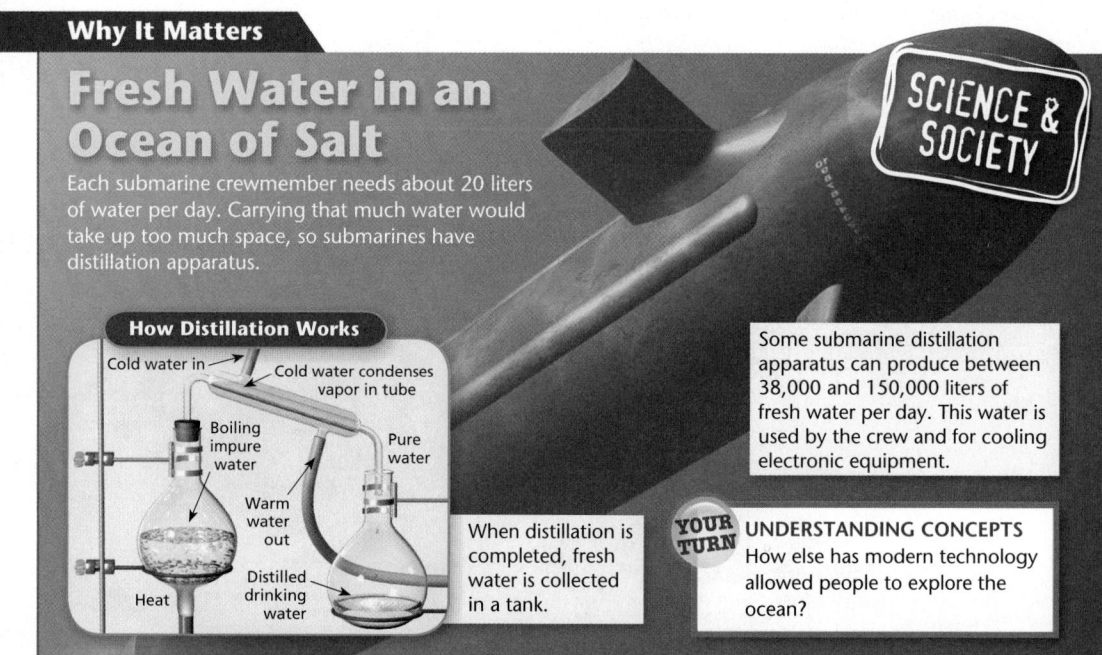

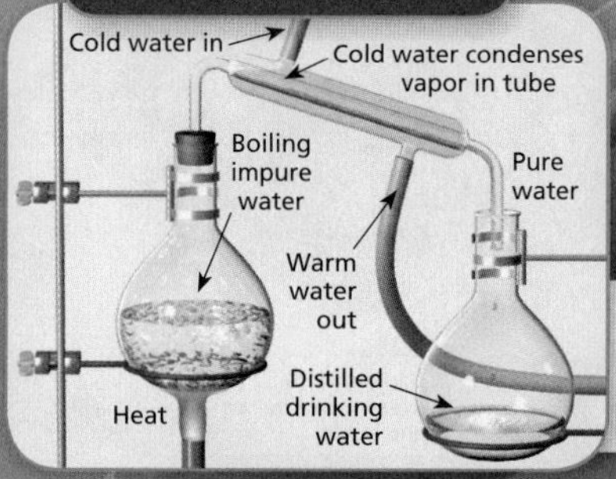

Some submarine distillation apparatus can produce between 38,000 and 150,000 liters of fresh water per day. This water is used by the crew and for cooling electronic equipment.

When distillation is completed, fresh water is collected in a tank.

YOUR TURN UNDERSTANDING CONCEPTS
How else has modern technology allowed people to explore the ocean?

Why It Matters

Fresh Water in an Ocean of Salt Distillation systems on submarines work by heating seawater to its boiling point. When the pure water evaporates, salt and impurities are left. The water vapor is then cooled and collected in large tanks for drinking and other purposes. Modern submarines are also able to generate oxygen for their crew by electrolysis of water. These technologies allow submarines to remain an important tool for exploration and military maneuvers.

Answer to Your Turn
Students may mention how emerging technologies have allowed humans to reach greater depths, remain submerged for longer periods, and explore more rapidly with better propulsion systems.

Figure 2 Dissolved solids make up 3.5% of the mass of ocean water. More than 85% of these dissolved solids are sodium and chlorine.

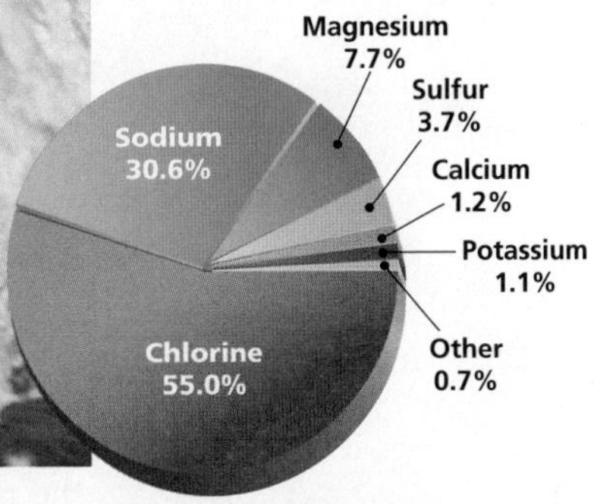

Dissolved Solids

Ocean water is 96.5% pure water, or H_2O. Dissolved solids make up about 3.5% of the mass of ocean water. These dissolved solids, commonly called *sea salts,* give the ocean its salty taste.

Most Abundant Elements

Solids dissolved in ocean water are composed of about 75 chemical elements. The six most abundant elements in ocean water are chlorine, sodium, magnesium, sulfur, calcium, and potassium. The salt halite, which is composed of sodium and chloride ions, makes up more than 85% of the ocean's dissolved solids. The remaining dissolved solids consist of various other salts and minerals, as shown in **Figure 2.** *Trace elements* are elements that exist in very small amounts. Gold, zinc, and phosphorus are some of the trace elements that are found in the ocean.

Sources of Dissolved Solids

Most of the elements that form sea salts come from three main sources: volcanic eruptions, chemical weathering of rock on land, and chemical reactions between sea water and newly formed sea-floor rocks. Each year, rivers carry about 400 billion kilograms of dissolved solids into the ocean. Most of these dissolved solids are salts. As water evaporates from the ocean, salts and other minerals remain in the ocean. Only a small fraction of these salts and minerals are returned to the land in the water that falls as rain and snow during the water cycle.

Reading Check **How do dissolved solids enter the ocean?**
(See Appendix G for answers to Reading Checks.)

Quick Lab

15 min

Dissolving Solids

Procedure

1. Heat 200 mL of water in a beaker over a hot plate until the water is about 60 °C.
2. Dissolve table salt in the water, 1 tsp at a time, until no more salt will dissolve. Record the total amount of salt that dissolves.
3. Dissolve table salt, 1 tsp at a time, into 200 mL of water that has been chilled in the refrigerator to about 5 °C. Record the total amount of salt that dissolves.

Analysis

1. Which water sample dissolved the most salt?
2. Describe what would happen to the dissolved salt in the hot water if the hot water was chilled to 10 °C.

Skill Builder — GENERAL

Math Tell students that 500 g of ocean salts were recovered from a sample of ocean water. Ask them to use the pie chart in the figure on this page to determine the mass of each element in the 500 g sample.
Chlorine: 55.0% = 0.55;
500 g × 0.55 = 275 g
Sodium: 30.6% = 0.306;
500 g × 0.306 = 153 g
Magnesium: 7.7% = 0.077;
500 g × 0.077 = 38.5 g
Sulfur: 3.7% = 0.037;
500 g × 0.037 = 18.5 g
Calcium: 1.2% = 0.012;
500 g × 0.012 = 6 g
Potassium: 1.1% = 0.011;
500 g × 0.011 = 5.5 g
All others: 0.7% = 0.007;
500 g × 0.007 = 3.5 g
LS Visual/Logical

Quick Lab

Skills Acquired
- Observing
- Measuring
- Analyzing

Materials
- Water
- Beaker
- Hot plate
- Table salt

Teacher's Notes: Make sure students stir well after adding each teaspoon of salt. You may want to do this as a demonstration and have students record the amount of salt that dissolved in each solution.

Answers to Analysis
1. The warm water will dissolve more salt than the cold water will.
2. Some salt would precipitate, or settle, out of the solution.

Differentiated Instruction

Advanced Learners

Essay Ask students to write an essay that ties dissolved carbon dioxide in the oceans to atmospheric carbon dioxide, ocean temperature, and climate change. Have them draw diagrams to illustrate the processes described in their essay. **LS Verbal/Visual**

Answer to Reading Check
Dissolved solids enter the oceans from the chemical weathering of rock on land, from volcanic eruptions, and from chemical reactions between sea water and newly formed sea-floor rocks.

MISCONCEPTION ALERT

Salinity of Polar Waters Students may think that only the evaporation of warm ocean water will result in increased salinity. However, the freezing of cold ocean water also increases salinity. This occurs because only the water freezes. The dissolved salts are left behind and increase the salinity of the water that doesn't freeze.

The map on this page shows large areas of highly saline water in the "sun belt," which includes regions of global high pressure located between 30° north and south of the equator. The areas of highly saline waters in polar regions are much smaller—too small to be represented on such a small map.

Using the Figure — GENERAL

Salinity Around the World Ask students to generalize about the location of areas of high salinity and suggest what conditions produce them. (The areas of high salinity on the map are located between 30° north and 30° south of the equator, where temperatures are warm and evaporation rates high.) Answer to caption question: River mouths tend to lower the salinity of nearby ocean waters because river water is fresh water, which is much less saline than ocean water.
LS Visual/Logical

salinity a measure of the amount of dissolved salts in a given amount of liquid

Salinity of Ocean Water

Salinity is a measure of the amount of dissolved salts and other solids in a given liquid. Salinity can be measured by the number of grams of dissolved solids in 1,000 g of ocean water. For example, if 1,000 g of ocean water contained 35 g of solids, the salinity of the sample would be about 35 parts salt per 1,000 parts ocean water. This measurement is written as *salinity* = 35 parts per thousand, or 35‰. Thus, the ocean is about 3.5% salts. However, fresh water is less than 0.1% salt or has a salinity of less than 1‰. Modern instruments measure salinity by recording the conductivity of water, or how easily electricity moves through the water. The higher the salinity of water, the better its conductivity.

Factors That Change Salinity

Precipitation, such as rain and snow, is composed only of fresh water. When ocean surface water evaporates or freezes, only water molecules are removed from the ocean. Dissolved salts and other solids remain behind. Where the rate of evaporation is higher than the rate of precipitation, the salinity of surface water increases. Therefore, in equatorial water, where the rate of precipitation is highest, the salinity is lower than it is in subtropical water, where the rate of evaporation is highest.

Over most of the surface of the ocean, salinity ranges from 33‰ to 36‰. The global ocean has an average salinity of 34.7‰. However, salinity at particular locations can vary greatly, as shown in **Figure 3.** The salinity of the Red Sea, for example, is more than 40‰. The high salinity is due to the hot, dry climate around the Red Sea, which causes high levels of evaporation.

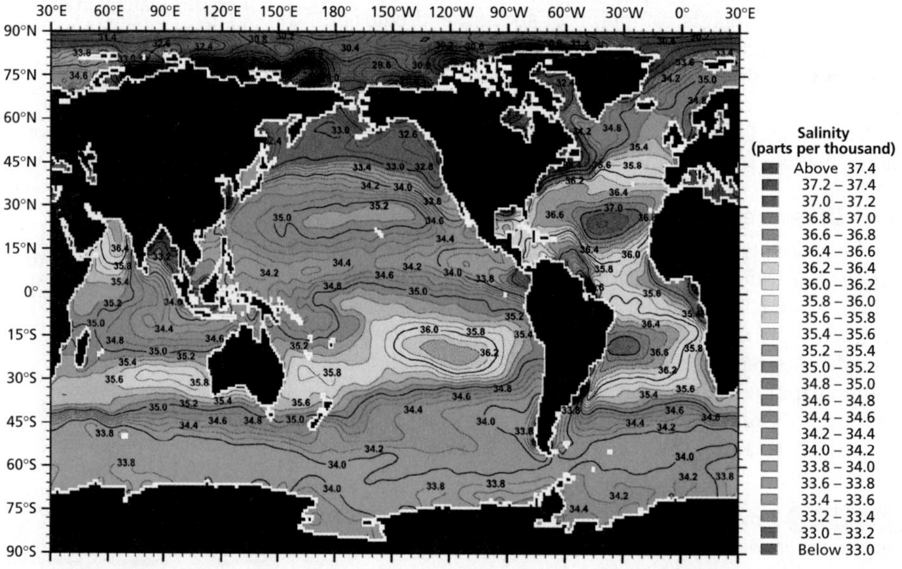

Figure 3 The average surface salinity of the global ocean varies from one location to another. ***What effect do river mouths tend to have on the salinity of the surrounding ocean water?***

Why It Matters

Salt Deposits During the Miocene Epoch, the Straits of Gibraltar were closed off because of moving tectonic plates. Thus, the Mediterranean Sea was cut off from the Atlantic Ocean and completely surrounded by land. Over time, the entire Mediterranean Sea evaporated. This event produced a layer of halite, or rock salt, along the sea floor of this region and caused temperatures to soar to over 50 °C in neighboring landmasses.

Key Resources

Technology
- Transparencies
  121 Average Surface Salinity of the Global Ocean

Figure 4 The surface temperature of tropical ocean water (right) can be as high as 30 °C. However, the surface temperature of polar ocean water (left) is below the freezing point of fresh water.

Temperature of Ocean Water

Like ocean salinity, ocean temperature varies depending on depth and location on the surface of the ocean. The range of ocean temperatures is affected by the amount of solar energy an area receives and by the movement of water in the ocean.

Surface Water

The mixing, by waves and currents, of the ocean's surface water distributes heat down-ward to a depth of 100 to 300 m. Thus, the temperature of this zone of surface water is relatively constant and decreases only slightly as depth increases. However, the temperature of surface water does decrease as latitude increases. Therefore, polar surface water is much cooler than the surface water in the tropics, as explained in **Figure 4.**

The total amount of solar energy that reaches the surface of the ocean is much greater at the equator than in areas near the North and South Poles. In tropical water, an ocean surface temperature of about 30 °C is common. The surface temperature in polar oceans, however, often drops as low as –1.9 °C. Because ocean water freezes at about –1.9 °C, vast areas of sea ice exist in polar oceans. A floating layer of sea ice that completely covers an area of the ocean surface is called **pack ice.** Usually, pack ice is no more than 5 m thick because the ice insulates the water below and prevents it from freezing. In the middle latitudes, the ocean surface temperature varies depending on the seasons. In some areas, the ocean surface temperature may vary by as much as 10 °C and 20 °C between summer and winter.

Reading Check What factors affect the surface temperature of the ocean?

pack ice a floating layer of sea ice that completely covers an area of the ocean surface

Activity GENERAL

Ocean Surface Temperatures Divide the class into groups. Have each group fill a deep plastic tank with room-temperature water. Have students tape a thermometer to the tank so that the bulb is about 5 mm below the surface of the water. Have students aim a heat lamp at the water's surface so that the lamp's light strikes the water at a 90° angle. Leave the lamps on for about 5 minutes. Ask students to check and record the water temperature each minute. Then, have groups repeat the activity using fresh water and placing the lamp so that the light strikes the water's surface at a 30° angle. They should keep all other factors constant, including the lamp's distance from the water's surface. Have them compare data collected in the two trials. Have students graph their data and discuss the differences. (The water should have warmed more significantly in the first trial.) Ask students how this relates to the world's oceans. (Tropical latitudes receive more direct sunlight year round than polar latitudes do.) You might want to do this activity as a demonstration. **LS Kinesthetic/Visual**

Answer to Reading Check

Ocean surface temperatures are affected by the amount of solar energy an area receives and by the movement of water in the ocean.

Differentiated Instruction

Basic Learners

Freezing Fresh and Salt Water Ask students to place 150 mL of water in each of two cups. Have them place 3 teaspoons of table salt in one cup; they should add nothing to the other cup. Have students place the cups in the freezer and check each cup every 20 minutes for one hour. Have them record how long the liquid in each cup took to freeze. Have students make graphs recording the information they collect. In class, start a discussion by asking them which liquid froze first. (The fresh water will freeze before the salt solution does.) **LS Kinesthetic/Visual**

Teach, *continued*

Using the Figure GENERAL

Thermoclines Use the graph of the thermocline on this page to review with students the axes of graphs. Remind them that the vertical axis on this particular graph represents the depth of the ocean in meters, not the decrease in temperature. The water temperature is represented by the horizontal axis, beginning with the lowest temperature to the left. Ask students what the depth range of the surface layer is on the graph. (from 0 m to about 280 m) Ask them the extent of the thermocline layer. (from about 280 m to about 500 m) Have them use the graph to determine the drop in temperature that occurs in the thermocline layer. (The temperature decreases from about 22.5 °C to about 5 °C, for a decline of 17.5 °C.) **LS Visual/Logical**

thermocline a layer in a body of water in which water temperature drops with increased depth faster than it does in other layers

The Thermocline

Because the sun cannot directly heat ocean water below the surface layer, the temperature of the water decreases sharply as depth increases. In most places in the ocean, this sudden decrease in temperature begins close to the surface. The layer in a body of water in which water temperature drops with increased depth faster than it does in other layers is called the **thermocline.**

The thermocline exists because the water near the surface becomes less dense as energy from the sun warms the water. This warm water cannot mix easily with the cold, dense water below. Thus, a thermocline marks the distinct separation between the warm surface water and the cold deep water. Below the thermocline, the temperature of the water continues to decrease, but it decreases very slowly, as shown in **Figure 5.** Changing temperature or shifting currents may alter the depth of the thermocline or cause the thermocline to disappear. Nevertheless, a thermocline is usually present beneath much of the ocean surface.

Deep Water

In the deep zones of the ocean, the temperature of the water is usually about 2 °C. The colder the water is, the denser it is. The density of cold, deep water controls the slow movement of deep ocean currents. This movement occurs when the cold, dense water at the poles sinks and flows beneath warm water toward the equator. Cold, deep ocean water also holds more dissolved gases than warm, shallow ocean water does.

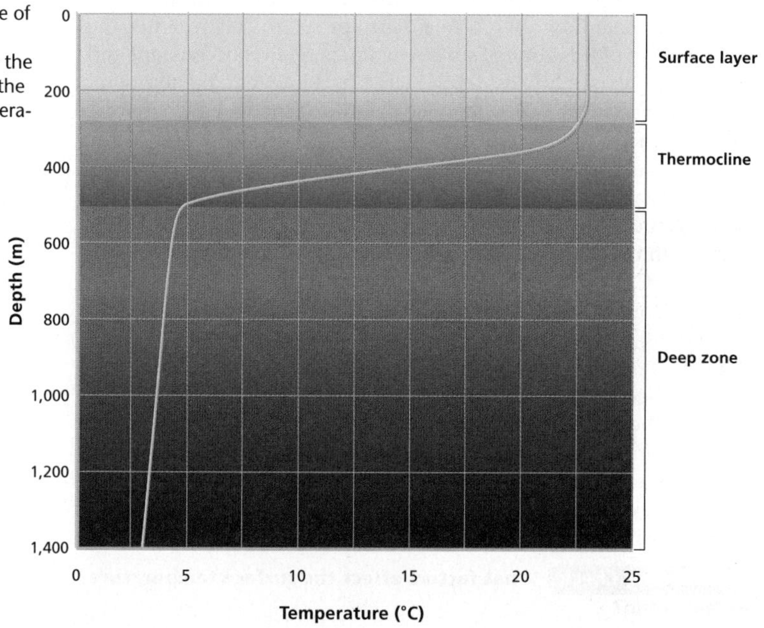

Figure 5 The temperature of ocean water decreases as depth increases. Just below the surface is the thermocline, the area where the water temperature decreases sharply.

Environmental Connection GENERAL

Surface-Water Temperatures Other factors that affect sea surface temperature include surface currents and cold water moving upward. For example, Pacific surface waters along the west coast of the United States stay quite cool all summer in comparison to Atlantic waters at similar latitudes along the east coast of the United States. Invite interested students to do research on surface ocean currents along the coasts of the United States and present their findings in illustrated oral reports to the class. **LS Visual/Verbal**

Differentiated Instruction

English Learners

Paired Summarizing Group students into pairs, and have them read silently about the thermocline. Then, have one student summarize the description of the thermocline. The other student should listen to the retelling, and should point out any inaccuracies or ideas that were left out. Allow students to refer to the text as needed. **LS Verbal/Auditory**

Density of Ocean Water

The mass of a substance per unit volume is that substance's **density.** For example, 1 cm^3 of pure water has a mass of 1 g. So, the density of pure water is 1 g/cm^3. Different liquids have different densities, as shown in **Figure 6.** Two factors affect the density of ocean water: salinity and the temperature of the water. Dissolved solids, which are mainly salts, add mass to the water. The large amount of dissolved solids in ocean water makes it denser than pure fresh water. Ocean water has a density between 1.020 g/cm^3 and 1.029 g/cm^3.

Ocean water becomes denser as it becomes colder and less dense as it becomes warmer. Water temperature usually affects the density of ocean water more than salinity does. Therefore, the densest ocean water is found in the polar regions, where the ocean surface is coldest. This cold, dense water sinks and moves through the ocean basins near the ocean floor.

Reading Check **Explain why ocean water is denser than fresh water.**

Figure 6 This graduated cylinder contains six liquids that have different densities. From top to bottom, the liquids are corn oil, water, shampoo, dish detergent, antifreeze, and maple syrup. ***Which liquid has the lowest density?***

THINK central
INTERACT ONLINE
Keyword: HQXOWAF6

density the ratio of the mass of a substance to the volume of the substance; commonly expressed as grams per cubic centimeter for solids and liquids and as grams per liter for gases

Quick Lab Density Factors

20 min

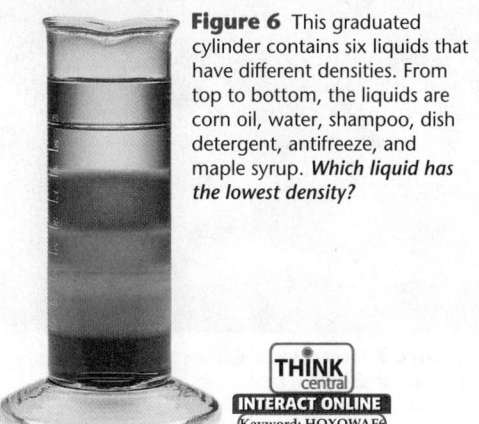

Procedure

1. Fill a deep, clear plastic container half full with room-temperature water.
2. In a 1 L beaker, mix 1/8 cup of table salt, a few drops of red food coloring, and 1 L of room-temperature water. Stir the mixture until the salt is dissolved.
3. Add the red saltwater mixture to the water in the clear plastic container. Record your observations.
4. In the 1 L beaker, mix a few drops of blue food coloring with water that is 8 °C.
5. Slowly add the cold, blue water to the clear plastic container in step 3. Record your observations.

Analysis

1. Describe what happened when you added the red salt water to the fresh water. Which is denser: fresh water or salt water?
2. What happened when you added the cold water to the room-temperature water? Which is denser: cold water or room temperature water?
3. What would you expect to happen if the blue water was heated, instead of cooled?
4. Based on your observations, where would you expect the water in the ocean to be the least dense? the most dense?
5. Describe water layering where a river empties into the ocean.

Quick Lab

Skills Acquired
- Observing
- Interpreting
- Analyzing

Materials
- Clear, plastic container
- Water
- Beaker, 1 L (2)
- Table salt
- Red food coloring
- Blue food coloring

Teacher's Notes: You may want to do this experiment as a demonstration.

Answers to Analysis

1. The salt water sank below the fresh water. Salt water is denser.
2. The cold water sank below the room-temperature water. Cold water is denser.
3. The warm water would float on the room-temperature water, because warm water is less dense.
4. It would be least dense where the water is warm and less saline (near the equator), and most dense where the water is cold and highly saline (near the poles).
5. Fresh water from the river would "float" on the denser ocean water.

Close

Reteaching BASIC

Basic Diagrams Have students create diagrams that illustrate the substances found in the oceans and their sources. **LS Visual**

Quiz GENERAL

1. If polar waters warm, what will happen to their ability to absorb atmospheric carbon dioxide? (It will decrease.)
2. In what part of the ocean are the densest waters located? (near the poles and at the bottom of the ocean)

Using the Figure BASIC

Liquid Density You may want to create a cylinder with six layers as shown in the figure on this page. Ask students whether a layer of water and dissolved salts would come above or below the layer of fresh water. Ask them to explain why. (The salt water would come below the fresh water, because the dissolved salts would add mass to the solution, making it more dense.) Answer to caption question: The least dense liquid is the corn oil at the top of the column. **LS Visual/Logical**

Answer to Reading Check

Ocean water contains dissolved solids (mostly salts) that add mass to a given volume of water. The large amount of dissolved solids in ocean water makes ocean water denser than fresh water.

Close, *continued*

Answers to Section Review

1. Warmer water is less able to dissolve gases than cooler water is.
2. Freezing and evaporation can increase salinity. As water evaporates or freezes, it leaves behind dissolved solids that increase the salinity of the remaining water.
3. Ocean water is a mixture of dissolved solids, such as chlorine and sodium, and gases, such as oxygen, nitrogen, and carbon dioxide.
4. The thermocline is a layer in a body of water in which the temperature drops faster with increased depth than it does in other layers.
5. Ocean water becomes denser as temperature decreases and as salinity increases.
6. Cold, saline, dense water at the poles sinks and flows, as a current, beneath warmer water, toward the equator.
7. When sunlight penetrates the surface of the ocean, the ocean water reflects the blue wavelengths of light. The other colors are absorbed.
8. It varies because the amount of incoming solar radiation varies greatly from season to season in these latitudes.
9. Surface waters in the North Sea are colder. Because cold waters can hold more dissolved gases than warm waters can, more disolved gases would be found in the cold North Sea than in the warm Caribbean waters.
10. If global temperatures increase, the oceans may warm. Warmer waters cannot hold as much CO_2, thus more CO_2 may accumulate in the atmosphere.
11. Because phytoplankton are at the bottom of the food chain, a decrease in phytoplankton will have a negative effect on all ocean animals, and those organisms may decrease in number.
12. The properties of *ocean water* include the amounts of *dissolved gases* and of *dissolved solids,* which is called *salinity,* and which together with *temperature* affects *density.*

Figure 7 Ocean water appears blue as far as 100 m below the surface.

Color of Ocean Water

Have you ever wondered why the ocean appears blue, as shown in **Figure 7**? The color of ocean water is determined by the way it absorbs or reflects sunlight. White light from the sun contains light from all the visible wavelengths of the electromagnetic spectrum. Much of the sunlight penetrates the surface of the ocean and is absorbed by the water. Water absorbs most of the wavelengths, or colors, of visible light. Only the blue wavelengths tend to be reflected. The reflection of this blue light makes ocean water appear blue.

Why Is Ocean Color Important?

Substances or organisms in ocean water, such as phytoplankton, can affect the color of the water. *Phytoplankton* are microscopic plants in the ocean that provide food to many of the ocean's organisms. Phytoplankton absorb red and blue light, but reflect green light. Therefore, the presence and amount of phytoplankton can affect the shade of blue of the ocean.

By studying variations in the color of the ocean, scientists can determine the presence of phytoplankton in the ocean. Because phytoplankton require nutrients, the presence or absence of phytoplankton can indicate the health of the ocean. If the color of an area of the ocean indicates that no phytoplankton are present, a lack of nutrients in the water may be preventing phytoplankton growth.

Academic Vocabulary

affect (uh FEKT) to change; to have an effect on; to influence

Section 1 Review

Key Ideas

1. **Describe** how water temperature affects the ability of the ocean water to dissolve gases.
2. **Summarize** how freezing and evaporation affect salinity.
3. **Describe** the composition of ocean water.
4. **Define** *thermocline.*
5. **Describe** how temperature and salinity affect the density of ocean water.
6. **Explain** how the density of ocean water drives the movement of deep ocean currents.
7. **Explain** why shallow ocean water appears to be blue in color.

Critical Thinking

8. **Making Inferences** Why does the surface temperature of ocean water in middle latitudes vary during the year?
9. **Understanding Relationships** Why would surface water in the North Sea be more likely to contain a high percentage of dissolved gases than surface water in the Caribbean Sea would?
10. **Predicting Consequences** If global temperatures increase, how would this change affect the ability of the ocean to absorb CO_2?
11. **Identifying Relationships** If an area of the ocean has a large decrease in phytoplankton, how would this change affect other ocean organisms? Explain your answer.

Concept Mapping

12. Use the following terms to create a concept map: *ocean water, salinity, temperature, density, dissolved solids,* and *dissolved gas.*

Differentiated Instruction

Alternative Assessment

Personal Essay Have students write a short essay about their experiences with the properties of ocean water, such as salinity and/or temperature. Students may have visited the ocean and tasted the salty water or swam in ocean water of different temperatures. Provide students that have not been to the ocean with photos to compare the color of ocean water in different locations (blue, brown, green). Have students explain what accounts for these color differences.

SECTION 2

Life in the Oceans

ENVIRONMENTAL CONNECTION

Key Ideas	Key Terms	Why It Matters
› Explain how marine organisms alter the chemistry of ocean water. › Explain why plankton can be called *the foundation of life in the ocean.* › Describe the major zones of life in the ocean.	**upwelling** **plankton** **nekton** **benthos** **benthic zone** **pelagic zone**	Variations in sunlight, nutrients, and temperature create different zones in the ocean. These zones are filled with marine organisms especially adapted to the environment.

Most marine organisms depend on two major factors for their survival: sunlight and the essential nutrients available in ocean water. Variations in either of these factors affect the ability of aquatic organisms to survive and flourish.

Ocean Chemistry and Marine Life

The chemistry of the ocean is a balance of dissolved gases and solids that are essential to marine life. Marine organisms help to maintain the chemical balance of ocean water. They do this by removing nutrients and gases from the ocean while returning other nutrients and gases to the ocean. For example, marine organisms, such as the giant kelp shown in **Figure 1**, absorb large amounts of carbon, hydrogen, oxygen, and sulfur. They also absorb other elements, such as nitrogen, phosphorus, and silicon. In addition, marine organisms return nutrients and gases to the ocean. For example, photosynthetic marine plants remove carbon dioxide from ocean water to produce oxygen.

Marine organisms, such as the sea horse shown in **Figure 1**, also help to recycle nutrients in the ocean. During a marine organism's lifetime, the organism absorbs and stores nutrients from the ocean. These nutrients are eventually returned to the water when the organism dies. For example, bacteria in the water digest the remains of dead organisms. The bacteria then release the essential nutrients from the dead organisms into the ocean.

Figure 1 Marine organisms, such as giant kelp and sea horses, help to maintain the balance of dissolved gases and solids in ocean water.

Section 2

Focus

Overview

This section describes life in the oceans and the various environmental zones within the oceans and along the ocean floor. This section discusses how marine life changes the chemistry of sea water, and discusses the importance of plankton.

Bellringer

Ask students to make a list of marine organisms that they are familiar with, and have them identify whether each organism lives on the ocean floor or swims freely through ocean water. (Sample answers: sea-floor dwellers: sea stars, octopuses, sponges; free swimmers: fish, dolphins) **LS Logical**

Motivate

Group Activity — GENERAL

Poster Project Have students read the two paragraphs under the heading "Ocean Chemistry and Marine Life." Then, have students work in groups to create posters with flowcharts that illustrate how marine organisms help maintain the chemical balance of ocean water. Have students prepare prior to the lesson to save time. **LS Visual/Logical**

Key Resources

Chapter Resource File

- Directed Reading BASIC

Technology

- Transparencies
  Bellringer

Differentiated Instruction

Basic Learners

Anticipation Guide Before students read this page, ask them to predict the relationship between ocean chemistry and marine life. Then, ask students to read the page to find out if their predictions were accurate. **LS Verbal/Logical**

Teach

Using the Figure ADVANCED

Upwelling The figure at the top of this page illustrates *prevailing,* or consistent, surface winds that blow parallel to the coastline. This action results in the upwelling of coastal waters. Ask students to consider what might happen if the prevailing winds were to shift and blow more perpendicular to the coastline. (Upwelling would cease.) Ask students how this change would affect marine life in the area. (If upwelling ceases, marine life along the coast will decrease. This decrease would affect industries such as fishing, and the food supply for humans and larger marine organisms.) Answer to caption question: Storms may change the velocity or direction of the prevailing wind, or cause deeper waves that mix the water. Thus, storms may intensify upwelling or temporarily cut it off.
LS Logical

Environmental Connection

Photosynthesis Most organisms derive their energy either directly from photosynthesis or by consuming organisms that engage in photosynthesis. Light is required in order for this process to take place. At best, sunlight can penetrate to a depth of 200 m below the ocean's surface. Thus, most marine organisms can't live too far beneath the ocean surface. Ask students to research some marine organisms that live too far beneath the surface to depend on photosynthesis. Have students present their findings in an illustrated oral report to the class.

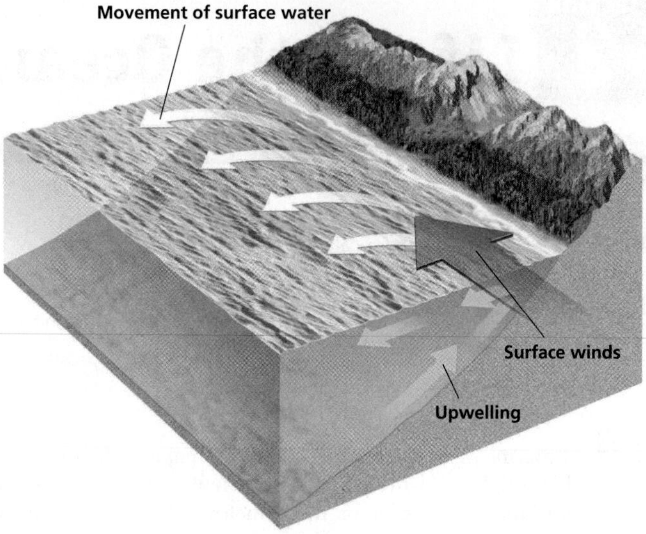

Figure 2 Upwelling is caused by offshore movement of surface water. ***How might stormy weather affect the process of upwelling?***

upwelling the movement of deep, cold, and nutrient-rich water to the surface

plankton the mass of mostly microscopic organisms that float or drift freely in the waters of aquatic (freshwater and marine) environments

nekton all organisms that swim actively in open water, independent of currents

benthos organisms that live at the bottom of oceans or bodies of fresh water

Academic Vocabulary
complex (kahm PLEKS) having many parts or functions

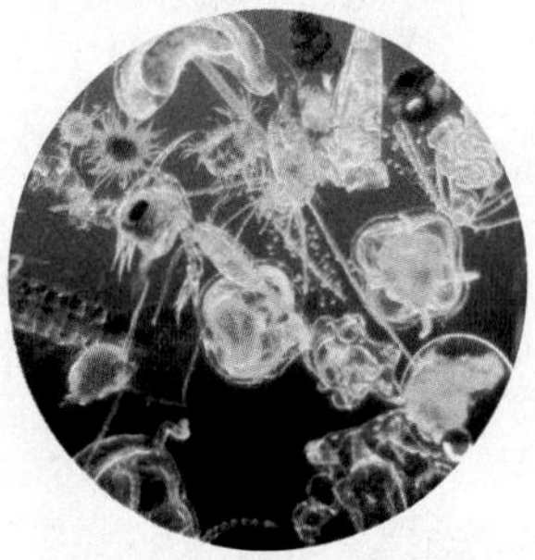

Figure 3 Plankton are so tiny that you need a microscope to see them.

Upwelling

The distribution of life in the ocean depends on the way that life-supporting nutrients cycle in the ocean water. In general, all the elements necessary for life are consumed by organisms near the surface. Elements are then released back into the ocean water when the organisms die, sink to lower depths, and decay. Thus, deep water is a storage area for the nutrients needed for life. These nutrients must, however, return to the surface before most organisms in the ocean can use them.

One way that nutrients return to the surface is through a process called upwelling. **Upwelling** is the movement of deep, cold, and nutrient-rich water to the surface, as shown in **Figure 2.** When the wind blows steadily parallel to a coastline, surface water moves farther offshore. The deep, cold water then rises to replace the surface water that has moved away from the shore.

Marine Food Webs

Because most marine organisms need sunlight as well as nutrients, most marine organisms live in the upper 100 m of water. Free-floating, microscopic organisms, called **plankton,** live within the sunlit zone. Plankton, shown in **Figure 3,** form the base of the complex food webs in the ocean. Plankton are consumed primarily by small marine organisms, which, in turn, become food for larger marine animals. These larger animals fall into two groups. All organisms that swim actively in open water, such as fish, dolphins, and squid, are called **nekton.** The organisms that live on the ocean floor are called **benthos.** Benthos include marine plants and animals, such as oysters, sea stars, and crabs, that live in sunlit, shallow waters.

Differentiated Instruction

Special Education Students

Hearing Impaired Students who have hearing impairments can participate more easily in class discussions if they can see everyone's face. Before beginning a class discussion, ask students to arrange their chairs in a circle, and to talk with their faces unobstructed. Tell the group that, when talking with people who have hearing impairments, they can help the hearing-impaired person understand by always maintaining eye contact. Explain that people who have hearing impairments benefit both from the opportunity to read lips and from meaning they can glean from facial expressions. Furthermore, point out that people who have normal hearing can also better understand others when they have eye contact and can see facial expressions.
LS Interpersonal

Ocean Environments

The ocean can be divided into two basic environments, or zones, as shown in **Figure 4.** These zones are the bottom region, or **benthic zone,** and the upper region, or **pelagic zone.** The amount of sunlight, the water temperature, and the water pressure determine the distribution of marine life within these zones.

benthic zone the bottom region of oceans and bodies of fresh water

pelagic zone the region of an ocean or body of fresh water above the benthic zone

Benthic Zones

The shallowest benthic zone lies between the low-tide and high-tide lines and is called the *intertidal zone*. Shifting tides and breaking waves make this zone a continually changing environment for the marine organisms that flourish there.

Most of the organisms that live in the benthic zone live in the shallow *sublittoral zone*. This continuously submerged zone is located on the continental shelf and is populated by organisms such as sea stars, brittle stars, and sea lilies.

The *bathyal zone* begins at the continental slope and extends to a depth of 4,000 m. Because little or no sunlight reaches this zone, plant life is scarce. Examples of animals that live in the bathyal zone are octopuses, sea stars, and brachiopods.

The *abyssal zone* has no sunlight because it begins at a depth of 4,000 m and extends to a depth of 6,000 m. Organisms that live in the abyssal darkness include sponges and worms.

The *hadal zone* is confined to the ocean trenches, which are deeper than 6,000 m below the surface of the water. This zone is virtually unexplored, and scientists think that life in the hadal zone is sparse.

Reading Check **Which benthic zone has the most marine life? Why?**

READING TOOLBOX

Comparison Table
As you read this page, complete a comparison table for the five benthic zones. Label the rows "Depth," "Sunlight," and "Marine life." See the Reading Toolbox at the beginning of this chapter if you need help getting started.

Figure 4 This diagram shows the classification and locations of marine environments.

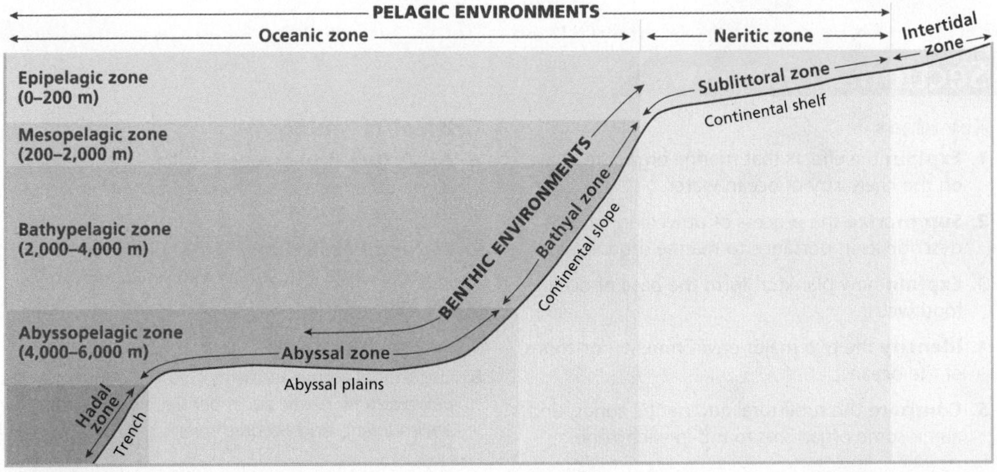

MISCONCEPTION ALERT

The Benthic Zone Students may think that the benthic zone consists only of the deepest part of the ocean, because it runs along the bottom. Explain to students that, although the benthic zone does include areas of extreme depth, it also includes very shallow regions, such as the intertidal and sublittoral zones. The important concept when thinking about the benthic zone is *bottom-dwelling.* The depth of sea water above the sea floor is not important.

Key Resources

Technology
- Transparencies
  122 Upwelling
  123 Marine Environments

READING TOOLBOX

Comparison Table Tables may include the following information: Intertidal Zone: shallow depth, abundant sunlight, some marine life; Sublittoral Zone: shallow depth, abundant sunlight, abundant marine life; Bathyal Zone: depth begins at the continental slope and extends to a depth of 4,000 m, little or no sunlight, plant life is scarce, some animals; Abyssal Zone: depth from 4,000 to 6,000 m, no sunlight, scarce marine life; Hadal Zone: deeper than 6,000 m, no sunlight, sparse marine life

Answer to Reading Check
Most marine life is found in the sublittoral zone. Life in this zone is continuously submerged, but waters are still shallow enough to allow sunlight to penetrate.

Close

Reteaching — BASIC

Peer Reviewing Divide the class into pairs or small groups. Ask each student to write five questions that can be answered after reading the section. Have students use the questions to quiz each other on the information in the section. **LS Interpersonal**

Quiz — GENERAL

1. In what direction must surface winds blow relative to a coastline for upwelling currents to develop? (parallel to the coastline)
2. Why are the sublittoral and neritic oceanic zones important? (Most marine organisms live within these zones.)
3. Which oceanic zone is the least explored? (the hadal)

Close, *continued*

Answers to Section Review

1. Marine organisms help maintain the chemical balance of ocean water. They remove some nutrients and gases from ocean water while returning others to the ocean.
2. Upwelling is a process that brings deep, cold, nutrient-rich waters to the surface. Winds that blow parallel to the coastline cause surface waters to move offshore. Deep water then moves upward to replace the coastal surface waters. The nutrients carried by these deep waters are vital for the survival of organisms that live near the ocean surface.
3. Some types of plankton use sunlight to make their own food. Other organisms that cannot produce their own food eat these organisms.
4. the benthic zone and the pelagic zone
5. The sublittoral zone is the benthic environment that lies along the continental shelf. It is populated by sea stars, brittle stars, and sea lilies. The neritic zone is the pelagic zone that is located above the sublittoral zone. This zone has abundant sunlight, moderate temperatures, and is populated by fish and crustaceans.
6. Answers may vary. Sample answer: Wind currents can cause upwelling, which brings deep water nutrients to the surface, cools the surface waters, and enables more gases to dissolve in the ocean waters.
7. If upwelling decreased, fewer nutrients would reach the surface. Thus, the amount of life would decrease, because organisms depend on deep-water nutrients to live.
8. The *ocean environment* is subdivided into the *benthic zone* and the *pelagic zone,* which contains the *neritic zone* and the *oceanic zone.*

Figure 5 Fish and marine mammals are examples of organisms that live in the pelagic zone.

SCILINKS.
www.scilinks.org
Topic: Marine Life
Code: **HQX0912**

Pelagic Zones

The region of the ocean above the benthic zone is the pelagic zone. The area of the pelagic zone above the continental shelf is called the *neritic zone*. The neritic zone has abundant sunlight, moderate temperatures, and relatively low water pressure, which are ideal factors for marine life. Nekton fill the zone's waters and are the source of much of the fish and seafood that humans eat.

The *oceanic zone* extends into the deep waters beyond the continental shelf. It is divided into four zones, based on depth. The epipelagic zone is the uppermost area of the oceanic zone. It is sunlit and populated by marine life, such as the dolphins shown in **Figure 5.** The mesopelagic, bathypelagic, and abyssopelagic zones occur at increasingly greater depths. The amount of marine life in the pelagic zone decreases as depth increases.

Section 2 Review

Key Ideas

1. **Explain** the effects that marine organisms have on the chemistry of ocean water.
2. **Summarize** the process of upwelling, and describe its importance to marine organisms.
3. **Explain** how plankton form the base of ocean food webs.
4. **Identify** the two major environments, or zones, of the ocean.
5. **Compare** the sublittoral and neritic zones, and name some organisms found in each zone.

Critical Thinking

6. **Analyzing Processes** How can the movement of wind currents alter the chemistry of an area of the ocean?
7. **Making Predictions** How would life in the ocean change if the area of all regions of upwelling decreased?

Concept Mapping

8. Use the following terms to create a concept map: *pelagic zone, neritic zone, benthic zone, ocean environment,* and *oceanic zone.*

Differentiated Instruction

Alternative Assessment

Modeling the Ocean Have groups of students use deep, clear plastic containers to create 3-dimensional models of the benthic and pelagic zones. Have them use clay and sand as needed to develop the model. Models of various marine organisms should be placed in appropriate regions, with toothpicks to place organisms within the pelagic zone, well above the sea floor.
LS Kinesthetic/Visual

SECTION 3

ENVIRONMENTAL CONNECTION

Ocean Resources

Key Ideas	Key Terms	Why It Matters
❯ Describe three important resources of the ocean. ❯ Explain the threat that water pollution poses to marine organisms.	desalination aquaculture	Resources from the ocean include fresh water, minerals, energy, and food.

The ocean supplies humans with a number of natural resources. It is a major source of food and minerals, and it provides a means of transportation. Furthermore, the growth of Earth's population has created new interest in the ocean as a source of fresh water.

Fresh Water from the Ocean

The increasing demand for fresh water, for things such as drinking water, industry, and irrigation, can be met by converting ocean water to fresh water. One way of increasing the freshwater supply is through desalination, as shown in **Figure 1. Desalination** is the extraction of fresh water from salt water. Although desalination may provide needed fresh water, the process is generally costly.

Methods of Desalination

One method of desalination is distillation. During *distillation,* ocean water is heated to remove the salts. Heat causes the liquid water to evaporate and leaves the dissolved salts behind. When the water vapor condenses, the result is pure fresh water. However, the process of evaporating liquid water often requires a large amount of costly heat energy.

desalination a process of removing salt from ocean water

Another method of desalination is *freezing*. When water freezes, the first ice crystals that form do not contain salt. The ice can be removed and melted to obtain fresh water. This process requires about one-sixth of the energy needed for distillation.

Reverse osmosis desalination is a popular method for desalinating ocean water. It includes the use of special membranes that allow water under high pressure to pass through, but block the dissolved salts.

Figure 1 After salt water from the Persian Gulf has undergone desalination, much of the resulting fresh water is stored in these towers in Kuwait.

Section 3

Focus

Overview

This section describes ocean resources and their importance to humans. The section identifies ocean resources, including fresh water, mineral and energy resources, and food. Finally, pollution is discussed as a threat to some of these resources.

Bellringer

Ask students to list as many resources as they can think of that may come from the ocean. Ask students to identify whether the resources they list are renewable or nonrenewable. (Answers may vary. Accept all reasonable responses.) **LS Logical**

Motivate

Discussion GENERAL

Fresh Water from Salt Water Have small groups of students research desalination and outline key points for discussion. Students should present information about the following topics: areas of the world where desalination is used successfully to convert salt water to freshwater; what areas may be likely candidates for desalination; different methods used; costs involved in desalination compared to other methods; how human, plant, and animal life would be affected; any barriers other than cost. **LS Verbal**

Key Resources

Chapter Resource File

- Directed Reading BASIC
- Inquiry Lab: Oil Spill! GENERAL

Technology

- Transparencies
  Bellringer

Differentiated Instruction

Advanced Learners

Debate Have students research and engage in a debate on ocean oil drilling. Have them answer the following questions: What are ocean drilling's effects on the oceans, their marine life, and other resources? What, if any, are the risks to fishing and aquaculture? Can humans continue to drill for offshore oil and expand their efforts to fish and farm the oceans? You may wish to assign students to prepare arguments for and against offshore oil drilling. **LS Logical**

Teach

Activity — Basic

Where's the Oil? Have students use the U.S. Department of Energy Web site or other sources to learn where the world's oil reserves are and how much oil they produce. Ask students to select one region of the world and to mark its oil reserves on a map of the world. Instruct students to create a color key that uses several colors, in which each color represents an amount of oil (in thousands of barrels) produced per day. Students should color each oil reserve area on their map according to the data they collect. Have students compare their regional maps and discuss the world's oil reserves. **LS Visual/Logical**

Math Skills

Answer

$1 × 4,000,000 L/$0.04 = 100,000,000 L; or $1/$0.04 = 25; 25 × 4,000,000 L = 100,000,000 L

Skill Builder — General

Vocabulary Students may have heard the word *petrol* used to mean "oil." However, this usage is misleading, because the Greek root *petra* means "stone" or "rock." The same root is found in *petrify,* meaning "to turn to stone" or "to frighten." It is the Latin root *oleum,* that means "oil." So *petroleum,* literally and appropriately, means "rock oil." **LS Verbal** English Language Learners

Figure 2 Offshore oil rigs, such as this one in the Gulf of Mexico, produce about one-fourth of the world's oil.

Mineral and Energy Resources

Academic Vocabulary
extract (eks TRAKT) to get or draw out something

Salt is one mineral resource that can be obtained from the ocean. Other mineral and energy resources can also be obtained from the ocean. While some valuable minerals are easily extracted from the ocean, others are costly or difficult to extract.

Petroleum

The most valuable resource in the ocean is the petroleum found beneath the sea floor. Offshore oil and natural gas deposits exist along continental margins around the world. About one-fourth of the world's oil is now obtained from offshore wells, such as the one shown in **Figure 2.** As a result of new drilling techniques, oil and gas can be extracted far offshore and from great depths.

Math Skills

Ocean's Gold One cubic kilometer of ocean water contains about 6 kg of gold. If you must process 4 million liters of ocean water to get an amount of gold worth 4¢, how many liters of water would have to be processed to get an amount of gold worth $1?

Nodules

Potato-shaped lumps of minerals, called *nodules,* are found on the abyssal floor of the ocean. Nodules are a valuable source of manganese, iron, copper, nickel, cobalt, and phosphates. However, the recovery of nodules is expensive and difficult because they are located in very deep water. Because country borders are observed only close to land, the question of who has the right to mine minerals from the ocean floor can be difficult to answer.

Trace Minerals

The ocean is also the main source of magnesium and bromine. However, the concentration of most other useful chemicals that are dissolved in the ocean is very small. The extraction of minerals found only in trace amounts is too costly to be practical.

Differentiated Instruction

Advanced Learners

Food from the Ocean Give gifted and talented students a chance to expand their knowledge and to share their information. Ask them to explore common foods that are surprisingly connected to the world's oceans. For example, seaweed is added to ice cream to prevent ice crystals from forming. Have them present the results of their research as an oral report to the class. **LS Verbal/Auditory**

Environmental Connection

Freshwater Sources Present students with a scenario in which the freshwater resources of a coastal community are so polluted that they will be unusable for the next 50 years. Have students discuss alternative sources of water. (Students may suggest bringing in water by boat or truck, producing water by chemical processes, or removing the salt from ocean water.) Use this activity to begin a discussion of conservation and stewardship.

Food from the Ocean

Of all the resources that the ocean supplies, the one in greatest demand is food. Seafood, which is an important source of protein, can be harvested through fishing or through aquaculture.

Fishing

Because fish are a significant food source for people around the world, fishing has become an important industry. But when the ocean is overfished, or overharvested, for a long period of time, fish populations can collapse. A collapsed fish population may damage the ecosystem and threaten the fishing industry. To prevent overharvesting, many governments have passed laws to manage fishing.

Aquaculture

Another way to deal with the high demand for seafood is by farming aquatic life. **Aquaculture** is the raising of aquatic plants and animals for human use or consumption. Catfish, salmon, oysters, and shrimp are already grown on large aquatic farms. Similar methods are used to breed fish and seaweed in ocean farms, such as the one shown in **Figure 3.** A major problem for aquaculturalists is that ocean farms are susceptible to pollution and may themselves be a local source of pollution.

Under the best conditions, an ocean farm can produce more food than an agricultural farm of the same size does. For example, in agriculture, only the top layers of soil can be used. In contrast, ocean farms can use a wide range of depths to produce food. Someday, the nutrient-rich bottom water may be pumped to the surface as a way of fertilizing aquatic farms.

Reading Check **List the benefits and problems of aquaculture.**

READING TOOLBOX

Analyzing Comparisons
As you read about food from the ocean, look for comparisons. Create a comparisons table similar to the one that you started at the beginning of the chapter.

SCILINKS.
www.scilinks.org
Topic: Ocean Resources
Code: **HQX1065**

aquaculture the raising of aquatic plants and animals for human use or consumption

Figure 3 Aquaculture establishments, such as this seaweed farm in Madagascar, provide a reliable, economical source of food.

READING TOOLBOX

Analyzing Comparisons Tables may compare fishing to aquaculture in the areas of food produced, problems, and progress. Sample answer for fishing: a variety of fish are caught, problems include overfishing, and progress is focused on preventing overharvesting. Sample answer for aquaculture: fish raised include catfish and salmon, problems include pollution, progress is focused on using nutrient-rich water to fertilize farms.

Close

Reteaching — BASIC

Summarizing Ask students to list ways in which humans make use of the oceans, and to write a brief summary of the benefits derived from each use. (Answers may vary, but should include desalination to provide fresh water, petroleum to provide energy, minerals for various purposes, and fishing and aquaculture to provide food.) **LS Verbal**

Quiz — GENERAL

1. Why is desalination not widely used as a method of providing fresh water? (because it is expensive)
2. What is the connection between oceans and petroleum? (About 1/4 of the world's oil is obtained from deposits beneath the ocean floor.)
3. Why is aquaculture potentially important to society? (It is an additional food source for the growing human population.)

Answer to the Reading Check
Aquaculture provides a reliable, economical source of food. However, aquatic farms are susceptible to pollution, and they may become local sources of pollution.

Internet Activity — ADVANCED

Aquaculture Several organizations, such as the World Aquaculture Society and Aquaculture for Youth and Youth Educators, have Web sites where students can explore aquaculture in greater depth. Invite students to learn about the latest techniques, issues related to food production, and aquaculture-related projects. Have them report on some aspect of aquaculture that interests them or carry out one of the suggested projects. A worksheet designed to direct student research on this topic can be found in the **Chapter Resource File** booklet or by visiting www.thinkcentral.com and entering the keyword **HQXOWAX.** **LS Interpersonal**

Close, *continued*

Answers to Section Review

1. Distillation involves heating water to cause evaporation and then condensing the vapor to yield pure water. Freezing causes crystals of pure water to form. This ice is collected and melted to yield pure water. In reverse osmosis, sea water is forced through special membranes that let pure water through, but block the salts.
2. Distillation can be expensive because it requires costly energy to heat the water until it evaporates.
3. Answers may vary, but should include two of the following: salt, manganese, iron, copper, nickel, cobalt, phosphates, magnesium, and bromine.
4. petroleum
5. Aquaculture is the raising of aquatic plants and animals for human use and consumption. It is important because it is a reliable, economical source of food.
6. because they are closest to the likely sources of pollution
7. Nodules are normally found in deep waters outside of national boundaries, so there may be problems determining who has the rights to them.
8. Pollution can destroy fish populations, thus destroying the fishing industry.
9. Mercury in the microscopic organisms becomes concentrated in the bodies of marine organisms that eat the microscopic organisms. The concentrated mercury will end up in human bodies when humans eat these larger marine animals.

Figure 4 Pollution can damage the ocean's ecosystem and make seafood unsafe to eat.

Ocean-Water Pollution

The ocean has been used as a dumping ground for many kinds of wastes, including garbage, sewage, and nuclear waste. Until recently, most wastes were diluted or destroyed as they spread throughout the ocean. But the growth of the world population and the increased use of toxic substances have reduced the ocean's ability to absorb wastes and renew itself.

Productive coastal areas and beaches are in the greatest danger of being polluted because they are closest to sources of pollution, as shown in **Figure 4.** Pollution has destroyed clam and oyster beds, sea birds have become tangled in plastic products, and beaches have been closed because of sewage and oil spills.

Besides being found in coastal waters, pollutants can be found in most other areas of the ocean. Traces of mercury, the insecticide DDT, and lead from gasoline have been detected in the ocean. In some areas of the world, concentrations of pollutants are so high that the fish have become unsafe for humans to eat. Recognizing the effects of dumping wastes in the ocean, scientists and governments have been working to reduce pollution. For example, the use of DDT has been banned in the United States and the use of leaded gasoline has been greatly reduced.

Section 3 Review

Key Ideas

1. **Describe** three methods of desalinating ocean water.
2. **Explain** why distillation can be an expensive method of desalination.
3. **List** two important mineral resources in the ocean.
4. **Identify** the most valuable resource that can be obtained from the ocean.
5. **Define** the term *aquaculture,* and explain why aquaculture is important.
6. **Explain** why beaches are especially vulnerable to ocean pollution.

Critical Thinking

7. **Making Inferences** Describe how the mining of nodules may create problems between countries.
8. **Predicting Consequences** How does pollution of the ocean affect the fishing industry?
9. **Analyzing Relationships** How could humans be affected if microscopic marine organisms absorbed small amounts of mercury?

Concept Mapping

10. Use the following terms to create a concept map: *desalination, distillation, freezing, reverse osmosis, petroleum, aquaculture, fishing, salt, ocean resource,* and *pollution.*

10. *Ocean resources* include *petroleum*; food, produced by *fishing* and *aquaculture*, which are threatened by *pollution*; and fresh water, which is produced by *desalination*, in which *salt* is removed from sea water by *distillation*, *freezing*, or *reverse osmosis*

Differentiated Instruction

Alternative Assessment

Outlining Have students practice their note-taking skills by making an outline of this section. Encourage students to use the head structure in the text as a guide and to include details under each entry.

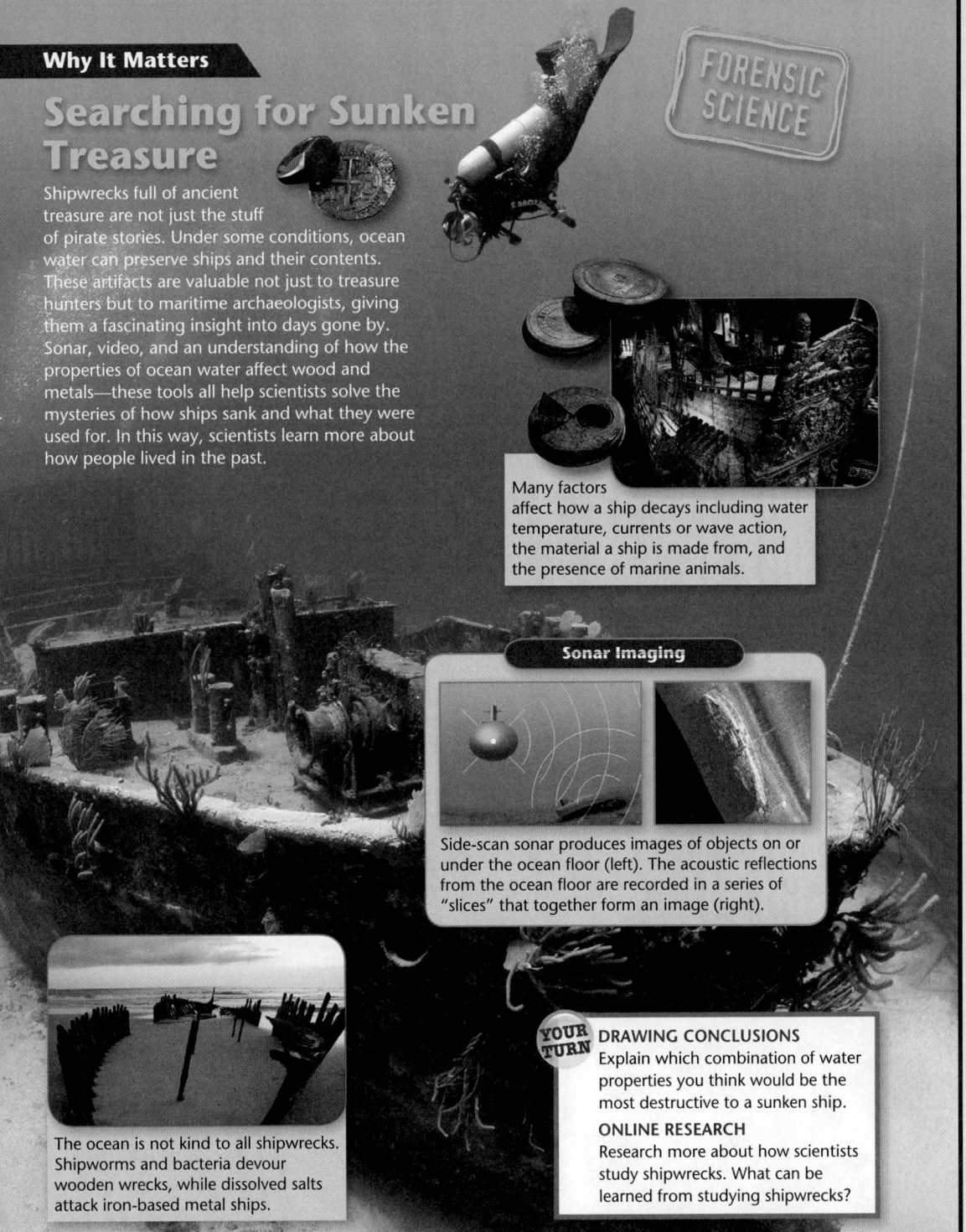

Why It Matters

Searching for Sunken Treasure

Shipwrecks full of ancient treasure are not just the stuff of pirate stories. Under some conditions, ocean water can preserve ships and their contents. These artifacts are valuable not just to treasure hunters but to maritime archaeologists, giving them a fascinating insight into days gone by. Sonar, video, and an understanding of how the properties of ocean water affect wood and metals—these tools all help scientists solve the mysteries of how ships sank and what they were used for. In this way, scientists learn more about how people lived in the past.

Many factors affect how a ship decays including water temperature, currents or wave action, the material a ship is made from, and the presence of marine animals.

Sonar Imaging

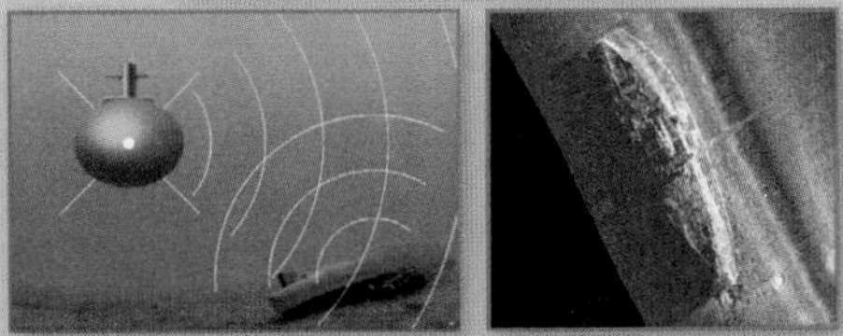

Side-scan sonar produces images of objects on or under the ocean floor (left). The acoustic reflections from the ocean floor are recorded in a series of "slices" that together form an image (right).

The ocean is not kind to all shipwrecks. Shipworms and bacteria devour wooden wrecks, while dissolved salts attack iron-based metal ships.

YOUR TURN

DRAWING CONCLUSIONS
Explain which combination of water properties you think would be the most destructive to a sunken ship.

ONLINE RESEARCH
Research more about how scientists study shipwrecks. What can be learned from studying shipwrecks?

Why It Matters

Searching for Sunken Treasure
Shipwrecks are attractive to archaeologists because they preserve historical information. Sometimes they contain what some would consider to be sunken treasure, for example, gold from the period of European colonization. Underwater archaeology is a sub-discipline of maritime archaeology. Differing ocean conditions can have a powerful effect on the state of a shipwreck. Many factors affect how a ship decays, including water temperature, the material a ship is made from, and the presence of marine animals. Underwater sites are often subject to movement by currents, surf, storm damage, or tidal flows. These factors result in structures becoming uncovered or buried beneath sediments over time. Any exposed structures will eventually be eroded, broken up, and scattered.

Answers to Your Turn

Drawing Conclusions Student answers will vary. The following factors would have a detrimental effect on a shipwreck: salinity, the presence of marine animals, temperature, shallow water and exposure to surface weather conditions at the wreck site, and strong tidal currents at the wreck site

Online Research Student answers will vary. In the right conditions (anaerobic, cold, and dark) shipwrecks provide insight into sediments and organics, such as plants, leather, fabric and wood. Information may be available from these materials as to how they were worked, and they can provide additional knowledge about the crafts, cultures, lifestyles, and technologies of those who built the vessel.

Skills Practice Lab

Time Required
two 45-minute class periods

Lab Ratings
EASY → HARD

Teacher Preparation 1
Student Setup 2
Concept Level 3
Cleanup 1

Skills Acquired
- Observing
- Measuring
- Collecting Data
- Analyzing
- Inferring

Scientific Methods
In this lab, students will
- Make Observations
- Analyze the Results
- Draw Conclusions

Materials
The materials listed on the page are enough for groups of two to four students.

Tips and Tricks
You may want to tell students that the instrument they are making from a straw and clay is called a *hydrometer*. Marking the straw with the grease pencil may be easiest if one student grasps the straw gently just above the water line while another student marks the straw just below the first student's fingers.

Skills Practice Lab

90 min

Ocean Water Density

What You'll Do
- **Measure** the temperature and density of water.
- **Analyze** the effects of temperature and salinity on the density of water.

What You'll Need
beaker, 250 mL
clay, modeling
freezer (optional)
gloves, heat-resistant
graduated cylinder, 100 mL
hot plate
pencil, grease, red
pencil, grease, yellow
ruler, metric
scissors
straw, plastic
table salt
teaspoon
thermometer
water, distilled

Safety

The density of ocean water varies. It is affected by the salinity of the water and the temperature of the water. Furthermore, the salinity of an area of the ocean is affected by the rate of evaporation or freezing and by the addition of fresh water and salts. The temperature of the ocean is determined by the amount of solar radiation that reaches Earth's surface. In this lab, you will observe the effects of temperature and salinity on the density of salt water.

Procedure

1. Make a hydrometer (an instrument used to measure the density of water) by filling 5 cm of one end of a straw with modeling clay.
2. Pour 100 mL of distilled water at room temperature into a glass jar or beaker. Float the straw upright in the jar. If the straw does not float upright, cut off the open end at 1 cm intervals until it floats upright.
3. Use a red grease pencil to mark the water level on the straw. Remove the straw from the water, and draw a continuous line around the straw at the mark.
4. Use a yellow grease pencil to draw lines around the straw at 1 cm intervals above and below the red line. The red line will be used as a reference point.
5. Add 2 tsp of salt to the water, and stir until all the salt has dissolved. Draw a table similar to **Table 1.** Measure the water temperature, and record the measurement in your table.
6. Place the hydrometer in the salt water. In your table, record the density by counting the marks above or below the red line to the water's surface. The higher the hydrometer floats out of the water, the more dense the water.
7. Turn the hot plate on low. Place the beaker of salt water on the hot plate. **CAUTION** Wear heat-resistant gloves.
8. Hold the thermometer in the water. Do not let the thermometer touch the bottom of the beaker.

Step 8

9. When the temperature of the water reaches 25 °C, turn off the hot plate. Immediately place the hydrometer in the water. Record the relative density in your table.

10. Repeat steps 7 to 9, and heat the water until it is 30 °C.

11. Turn the hot plate on high. Heat the salt water until it begins to boil. Boil the water for 5 min. Turn off the hot plate.

12. Place the hydrometer in the water. Draw a table similar to **Table 2.** Measure the density of the water, and record the measurement in your table.

13. Boil the water for another 5 min. Measure and record the density of the water.

14. Repeat step 13. Once the water is cool, measure the amount of water that remains in the beaker.

Temperature (°C)	Density (cm above or below the red line)
25	
30	

Table 1

Minutes of boiling	Density (cm above or below the red line)
5	
10	
15	

Table 2

Analysis

1. **Analyzing Data** In which trial was the water the most dense? In which trial was it the least dense? Explain your answers.
2. **Identifying Trends** As the temperature of water increases, does the density of the water increase or decrease?
3. **Making Inferences** Based on your observations, infer the density of polar ocean water, and compare it with the density of equally saline water near the equator. Explain your answer.
4. **Analyzing Processes** Why did the amount of water in the beaker change? Explain why boiling the water affected its density.
5. **Forming Hypotheses** How would you expect the density of the water to change if the water was frozen instead of boiled? Explain your answer.

Extension

Evaluating Hypotheses Place a beaker of salt water in a freezer until a crust of ice forms. Break up and remove the ice from the water, and record the density of the remaining water. Is the water more or less dense than it was before it was frozen? Explain.

Answers to Analysis

1. The final trial, after step 14, yielded the densest water because the most water had evaporated, leaving a higher percentage of salt in the remaining solution. The least dense water is that at 30 °C, because it is not hot enough to evaporate, but is warmer, and so less dense than the 25 °C water.
2. Density decreases as temperature increases, until the water starts to evaporate as it boils.
3. Because they are colder, polar waters will be denser than equally saline water near the equator.
4. The amount of water changed because some water evaporated as it boiled. The remaining water became more saline because the salt remained behind.
5. If some of the water is converted into ice, the remaining water will become more saline, and thus denser, like the water did when it was boiled. However, the freezing water will be denser than the hot water because cold water is denser than warm water.

Answer to Extension

Denser; the ice contains no salt, so the remaining water contains more salt than before some water froze. In addition, it is cooler than it was before it was frozen.

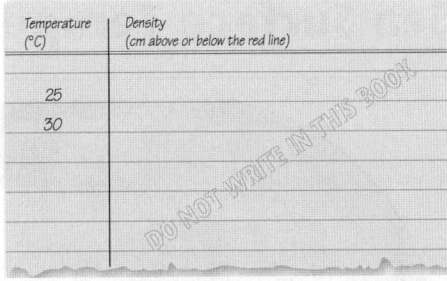

Sea Surface Temperatures in August

Discussion — ADVANCED

Thermal Energy Show students a global solar energy chart (available on the Internet on NASA's Web site and others) and prompt them to identify areas where discrepancies exist between the solar energy map and the sea surface temperature map on this page. Ask them to hypothesize reasons for any discrepancies they find. (Ocean currents may distribute thermal energy in a pattern that differs from the patterns of insolation intensity.)
LS Visual

Answers to Map Skills Activity

1. 20–25 °C
2. Answers may vary, but should include regions where sea surface temperatures are warmest. These are between 0° and 20°S in the western Pacific Ocean and eastern Indian Ocean.
3. Answers may vary. Pack ice is most likely found where sea surface temperatures are coldest—near the North Pole and along the coast of Antarctica.
4. North Africa
5. Answers may vary. Sample answer: I would expect density to increase as surface temperature decreases, except in areas where evaporation is high.
6. Answers may vary. Sample answer: I would expect the water density to increase in December as the water gets colder, provided that the evaporation rate does not change drastically.

MAPS in Action

Sea Surface Temperatures in August

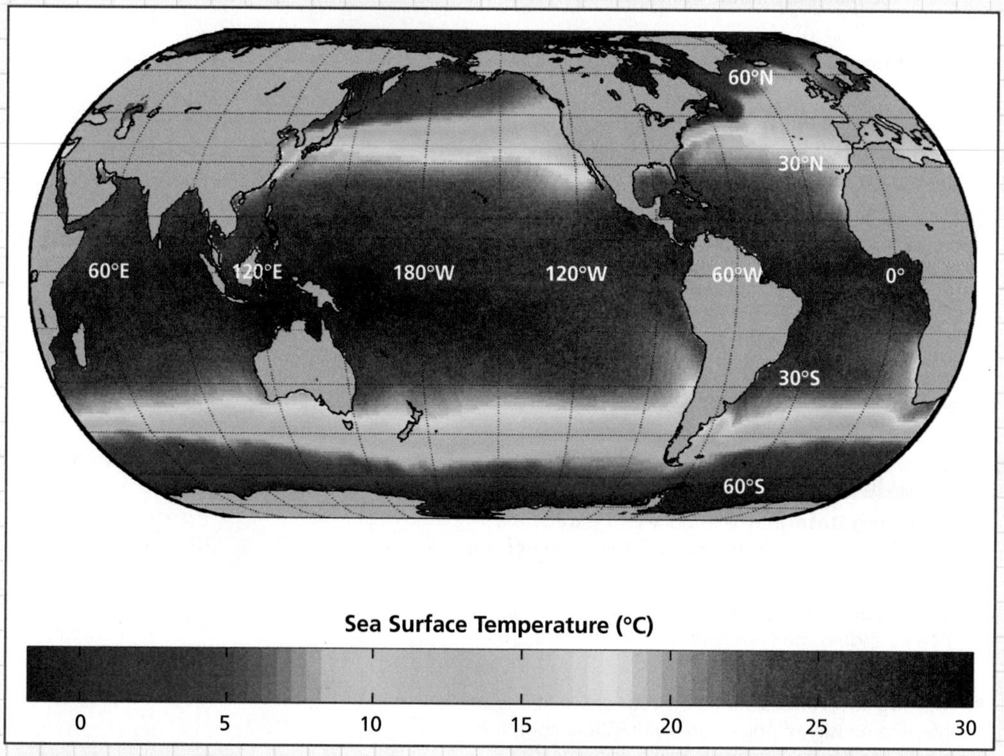

Map Skills Activity

This map shows global sea surface temperatures in the month of August. Latitude is shown in 15° intervals. Longitude is shown in 30° intervals. The latitude of New York City is 41°N 74°W. Use the map to answer the questions below.

1. **Analyzing Data** Estimate the sea surface temperatures off the east coast of Florida.
2. **Identifying Relationships** Identify areas of the globe that receive the most solar energy.
3. **Inferring Relationships** At which locations would you most likely find pack ice?
4. **Making Comparisons** Where would you expect to find higher surface salinity values: off the coast of North Africa or off the coast of the southern tip of South America?
5. **Analyzing Relationships** As latitude increases, surface temperature decreases. How would you expect the density of surface water to change as latitude increases? Explain your answer.
6. **Making Predictions** Off the coast of New York City, would you expect the density of the ocean water to increase or decrease in December, compared with the density of the water in August? Explain.

Key Resources

Technology
- Transparencies
  124 Sea Surface Temperatures in August

Chapter 24 Summary

THINK central
SUPER SUMMARY
Keyword: HQXOWAS

Key Ideas | **Key Terms**

Section 1

Properties of Ocean Water

- Dissolved solids make up 3.5% of the mass of ocean water. Ocean water also contains dissolved gases, such as oxygen, carbon dioxide, and nitrogen.
- Salinity is a measure of the amount of dissolved salts in ocean water. The temperature of ocean water is dependent on depth and latitude. The density of ocean water is dependent on temperature and salinity. The color of ocean water is affected by the presence of phytoplankton.

salinity, p. 664
pack ice, p. 665
thermocline, p. 666
density, p. 667

Section 2

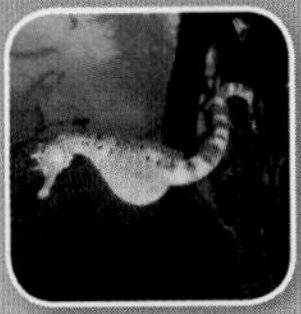

Life in the Oceans

- Marine organisms help to maintain the chemical balance of ocean water by using nutrients for life processes and by returning the nutrients to the water after death.
- Plankton form the base of complex ocean food webs by acting as food for other marine organisms.
- There are two major zones of life in the ocean: benthic and pelagic. Each zone supports different types of organisms.

upwelling, p. 670
plankton, p. 670
nekton, p. 670
benthos, p. 670
benthic zone, p. 671
pelagic zone, p. 671

Section 3

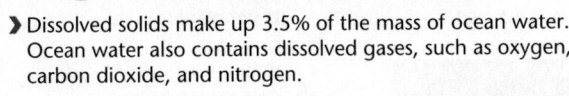

Ocean Resources

- The ocean is valuable as a source of fresh water, minerals, and food.
- Ocean-water pollution threatens both marine organisms and humans by damaging food resources in the ocean.

desalination, p. 673
aquaculture, p. 675

Chapter Summary

Using THINK central Resources

Super Summary
Have students connect the major concepts in this chapter through an interactive Super Summary. Visit www.thinkcentral.com and type in the keyword **HQXOWAS** to access the Super Summary for this chapter.

Activity — GENERAL

Ocean Video Have students work in groups of four or five to produce plans for an animated video or film about the concepts covered in this chapter. Have students prepare a detailed presentation of their plans that they might give to a video producer. The proposal should show how they will cover the concepts using techniques they have seen in films and videos. For example, invite them to create animated characters to narrate the video, and to plan illustrations, graphs, and charts to present the material. Then, have them "pitch" their video to the class. If possible, they should show sketches and samples of visual materials they plan to use, including storyboards. They may want to suggest and play appropriate music and sound effects for various parts of the video.
LS Visual/Auditory

Group Activity — GENERAL

Brine Shrimp Have groups of students gather information from the library or a local aquarium store on raising brine shrimp. Have them culture and raise a batch of brine shrimp by using what they have learned. Ask students to examine the shrimp under a microscope at various developmental stages and to draw what they see. Then, have students produce an exhibit that includes their brine shrimp habitat, drawings, and the information they have gathered. **LS Kinesthetic/Visual**

Chapter Review

Assignment Guide	
Section	**Questions**
1	1, 2, 5, 9–11, 19, 20, 29–31, 34–36
2	3, 6–8, 12–14, 18, 24–28, 32
3	4, 15–17, 21–23, 25, 33

Reading Toolbox

1. Student tables should compare properties of fresh water and ocean water. Sample answer: Fresh water does not taste salty, it is odorless, colorless, has a salinity of less than 1 ppt and a density of 1 g/cm^3; Ocean Water tastes salty, it has a salty odor, it is blue in color, has a salinity of about 35 ppt, and a density between 1.020 g/cm^3 and 1.029 g/cm^3.

Using Key Terms

2–8. Answers may vary but should show that students understand the definitions of and differences between key terms.

Understanding Key Concepts

9. a
10. b
11. d
12. a
13. c
14. a
15. d
16. b
17. c

Chapter 24 Review

1. **Comparison Table** READING TOOLBOX Make a comparison table to describe the similarities and differences between ocean water and pure fresh water.

USING KEY TERMS

Use each of the following terms in a separate sentence.

2. *thermocline*
3. *upwelling*
4. *desalination*

For each pair of terms, explain how the meanings of the terms differ.

5. *salinity* and *density*
6. *plankton* and *nekton*
7. *benthic zone* and *pelagic zone*
8. *upwelling* and *aquaculture*

UNDERSTANDING KEY IDEAS

9. The amount of dissolved salts in ocean water is called the water's
   a. salinity.
   b. nekton.
   c. plankton.
   d. density.
10. When liquid water is warmed, its density
   a. increases.
   b. decreases.
   c. remains the same.
   d. doubles.
11. Although most of the wavelengths of visible light are absorbed by ocean water, the one wavelength that is most often reflected is the color
   a. violet.
   b. green.
   c. yellow.
   d. blue.
12. Drifting marine organisms are known as
   a. plankton.
   b. benthos.
   c. nekton.
   d. sea stars.
13. Marine animals that can swim to search for food and avoid predators are called
   a. phytoplankton.
   b. zooplankton.
   c. nekton.
   d. benthos.
14. Which of the following ocean environments experiences the most change?
   a. intertidal zone
   b. abyssal zone
   c. bathyal zone
   d. neritic zone
15. Which of the following methods is *not* used for producing fresh water by desalination?
   a. distillation
   b. evaporation
   c. reverse osmosis
   d. aquaculture
16. Lumps of minerals on the ocean floor are called
   a. nekton.
   b. nodules.
   c. benthos.
   d. plankton.
17. Aquaculture is another name for
   a. desalination.
   b. distillation.
   c. ocean farming.
   d. rapid temperature changes.

SHORT ANSWER

18. Describe the process of upwelling, and explain its effects on marine life.
19. What are the six most abundant elements that are dissolved in ocean water?
20. How are temperature, salinity, and density related?
21. Describe how an oil spill would affect a fishing industry.
22. List three important resources from the ocean, and describe how they are obtained.
23. What effects does ocean pollution have on humans?

Short Answer

18. Upwelling is a process that brings deep, cold, nutrient-rich waters to the surface. Winds blowing parallel to the coastline cause surface waters to move offshore. Deep water then moves upward to replace the coastal surface waters. The nutrients carried by these deep waters are needed by organisms living near the ocean surface.
19. chlorine, sodium, magnesium, sulfur, calcium, and potassium
20. Density increases as ocean water temperature decreases and/or as salinity increases.
21. Oil is a serious pollutant. Fish become covered in oil and then die. Thus, an oil spill would be harmful to the fishing industry.
22. Answers may vary. Sample answer: Petroleum is obtained by drilling into oil deposits beneath the sea floor. Fish and other foods are acquired by fishing and aquaculture. Salt is obtained by evaporating ocean water.
23. Humans are at the top of the food chain. When humans eat marine organisms that have taken in pollutants, such as mercury, these pollutants enter our bodies and can make us sick.

CRITICAL THINKING

24. Predicting Consequences If climatic conditions over the ocean caused upwelling and wave action to stop, what would happen to marine life? Explain your answer.

25. Identifying Relationships How would a significant and global decrease in sunlight affect plankton and other marine organisms?

26. Applying Concepts If you were to start an aquatic farm, in which zone of marine life would you locate your farm? Explain your answer.

27. Making Inferences When oceanographers first explored the deep-ocean basin along mid-ocean ridges, they discovered a variety of marine life, including sightless crabs. Explain why sightlessness is not a disadvantage to these crabs.

CONCEPT MAPPING

28. Use the following terms to create a concept map: *fishing, marine life, plankton, fish, color, dissolved gas, dissolved solid, desalination, salt, ocean water characteristics,* and *aquaculture.*

MATH SKILLS

Math Skills

29. Using Equations Using the equation *density = mass ÷ volume,* determine the mass of a 3 cm^3 sample of ocean water if the water's density is 1.027 g/cm^3.

30. Making Calculations What percentage of dissolved salts would be present in water that has a salinity of 40‰?

31. Making Calculations A 1,000 g sample of ocean water contains 35 g of dissolved solids. Magnesium makes up 7.7% of the 35 g of dissolved solids. How many grams of magnesium are in the 1,000 g sample of ocean water?

WRITING SKILLS

32. Creative Writing Write a descriptive essay about the deep-ocean waters of the oceanic zone. Your essay should include a description of the marine organisms in this zone, as well as a description of what life is like for these marine organisms.

33. Writing from Research Research the new foods that are being produced through aquaculture and the nations that are investing in this method of farming. Write a short essay that describes these foods, where they are grown, and their nutritional values.

INTERPRETING GRAPHICS

The graph below shows the depths at which different wavelengths of light penetrate ocean water. Use this graph to answer the questions that follow.

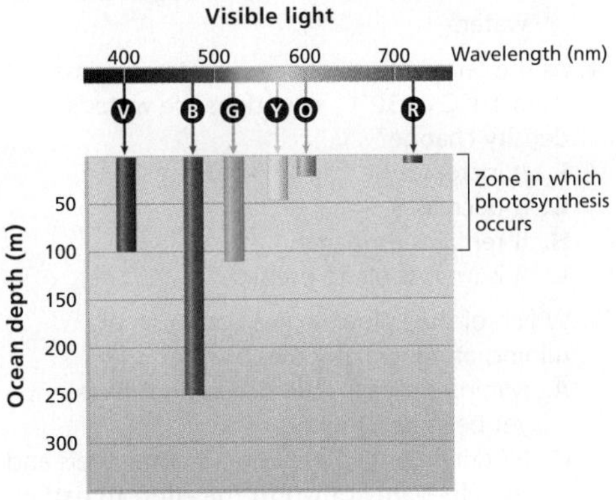

34. Estimate the depth at which yellow light can no longer penetrate ocean water.

35. Which colors can penetrate ocean water to a depth of 50 m?

36. Would an object that is painted red appear red at a depth of 50 m? Explain your answer.

Chapter Review

Critical Thinking

24. Many forms of marine life would die because they would lack the nutrients that are stored in deep water and are supplied by upwelling. This would adversely affect all organisms in the food chain, including humans.

25. Without sunlight, plankton that form the base of food webs in the ocean would die, and so would the small marine life that feeds on them. The larger marine animals would, in turn, lack nourishment and die.

26. In the sublittoral and neritic zones. Organisms that live in these zones are continuously submerged, yet waters are shallow. Sunlight is abundant and temperatures are moderate. These are the most hospitable zones to marine life.

27. Because no sunlight reaches the deep-ocean basin, vision would not be useful to these crabs.

Concept Mapping

28. Answers may vary but should include all of the terms listed. Sample answers appear at the end of this unit on p. 715A.

Math Skills

29. $D = m/v$ can be rearranged to $m = Dv$. So, $m = 1.027\ g/cm^3 \times 3\ cm^3 = 3.081\ g$

30. 40‰ = 40 parts/1000 = 4 parts/100 = 0.04 = 4%

31. 7.7% = 0.077; 35 g × 0.077 = 2.695 g magnesium

Writing Skills

32. Answers may vary. Accept all reasonable answers.

33. Answers may vary. Accept all reasonable answers.

Interpreting Graphics

34. about 50 meters

35. green, blue, and violet

36. No; red wavelengths do not penetrate that deeply, so the object would not look red.

Standardized Test Prep

Estimated Time

To give students practice under more realistic testing conditions, allow them 30 minutes to answer all of the questions in this practice test.

Test Doctor

Question 2 Answer I is correct. Adding fresh water would not remove salt, but it would lower the salt concentration. During *distillation,* answer F, water is heated to remove salt. During *freezing,* answer G, the first ice crystals that form do not contain salt and are removed and melted to obtain fresh water. During *reverse osmosis,* answer H, water is forced, under pressure, through a membrane that allows water, but not salt, to pass through.

Question 9 Answer B is correct. The passage indicates that, normally, weather patterns in the Pacific move from the east to the west. During an El Niño event, this pattern changes. Warm waters move from the west to the east, and bring storms with them. Using their knowledge of geography, students should realize that this pattern pushes these storms toward the United States. Answers A, C, and D contain information that cannot be inferred from the passage.

Chapter 24 Standardized Test Prep

Understanding Concepts

Directions (1–5): For each question, write on a separate sheet of paper the letter of the correct answer.

1. Organisms that live on the ocean floor are called
   A. benthos.
   B. nekton.
   C. plankton.
   D. phytoplankton.

2. Which process cannot be used to remove salt from sea water to make the water safe for drinking?
   F. distillation
   G. freezing
   H. reverse osmosis
   I. adding fresh water

3. The temperature of ocean water is dependent on all of the following except
   A. depth.
   B. the amount of solar energy that the ocean water receives.
   C. water movement.
   D. the number of organisms living in the ocean water.

4. As the temperature of ocean water increases from 10 °C to 30 °C, how does the water's density change?
   F. It increases.
   G. It decreases.
   H. It remains the same.
   I. It is impossible to predict.

5. Which of the following is a barrier to the mining of mineral nodules?
   A. Mining rights for the ocean floor have not yet been determined.
   B. Nodules contain only traces of minerals and therefore are not worth the effort to gather.
   C. Nodules are readily accessible and therefore not valuable.
   D. Nodules primarily contain elements that are dangerous to humans.

Directions (6–7): For each question, write a short response.

6. What is the cause of deep ocean currents?

7. What is the name of the top layer of ocean water that extends to 300 m below sea level?

Reading Skills

Directions (8–10): Read the passage below. Then, answer the questions.

The Effects of El Niño

The interaction between the ocean and the atmosphere can profoundly affect weather conditions. Occurring, on average, every four years and lasting about 18 months, El Niño is one event that triggers global weather changes. El Niño is characterized by changes in wind patterns that allow warmer water from the western Pacific Ocean to surge eastward. Normally, east-to-west winds cause warm water to accumulate in the western Pacific Ocean. During El Niño, the trade winds weaken and warm water shifts east. Sea surface temperatures from the coast of Peru to the equatorial central Pacific rise. The warm water causes the thermocline to sink and contributes to the formation of convective clouds, which cause heavy rains that shift eastward at the same rate as the water. In areas on the western coast of the Pacific Ocean, droughts become common.

8. According to the passage, which of the following statements is not true?
   F. During El Niño, the trade winds weaken and warm water shifts eastward.
   G. El Niño is one event that triggers global weather changes.
   H. An El Niño weather event lasts about two years on average.
   I. An El Niño event leads to the formation of convective clouds that shift eastward.

9. Which of the following statements can be inferred from the passage?
   A. An El Niño event is usually followed by a weather event that moves cold water westward.
   B. The changes caused by El Niño directly affect the weather in the United States.
   C. El Niño causes severe disruptions to international trade and travel.
   D. El Niño weather cycles are a relatively recent phenomenon.

10. During an El Niño weather event, what happens to the thermocline? What effect might this have on upwelling?

Question 11 Answer G is correct. Salt, which is made up of sodium and chloride ions, is the most abundant of dissolved solids in ocean water. The pie graph breaks down solids into their most basic elements, but salt is the most abundant dissolved compound. The scientific name for salt is sodium chloride, which alludes to the elements that compose the substance.

Question 13 Full-credit answers should include the following points:
- nutrients are returned to the surface during upwelling
- an understanding that these nutrients support life near the surface of the ocean
- this may lead to an overgrowth of phytoplankton, which contributes to the "dirtiness"
- a conceptual understanding of how living and natural systems are connected and may affect one another

Interpreting Graphics

Directions (11–13): For each question below, record the correct answer on a separate sheet of paper.

Use the pie graph to answer questions 11 and 12.

Solids Dissolved in Ocean Water

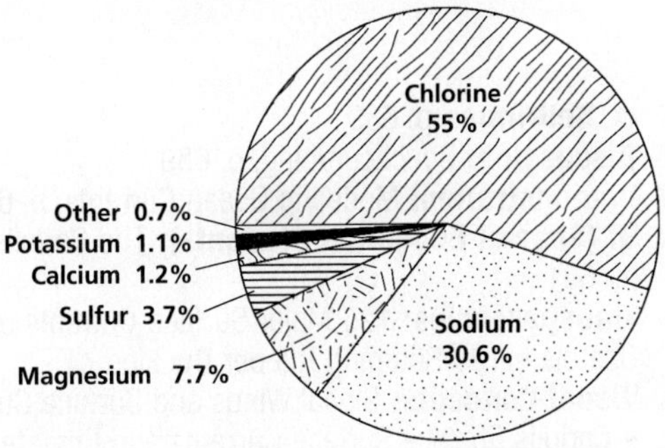

11. The two elements that make up the largest percentage of the dissolved solids combine to make what common solid found in ocean water?
F. sand
G. salt
H. siliceous ooze
I. calcareous ooze

12. Identify the two elements that are most abundant in ocean water. What are the sources of these elements?

The diagram below shows the basic mechanics of upwelling. Use this diagram to answer question 13.

Mechanics of Upwelling

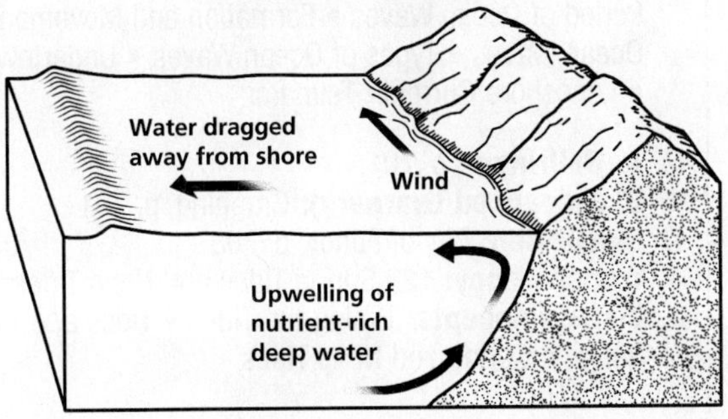

13. During summer months, beaches may sometimes close because of the appearance of large phytoplankton blooms. How might an upwelling contribute to these beach closings during warmer months?

Test Tip

Scan the answer choices for words such as *never* and *always*. Such words are often used in statements that are incorrect because they are too general.

Standardized Test Prep

Using THINK central Resources

State Resources

- For specific resources for your state, visit www.thinkcentral.com and type in the keyword **HSHSTR.**

Answers

Understanding Concepts

1. A
2. I
3. D
4. G
5. A
6. the flow of cold, dense polar water beneath warm water toward the equator
7. the surface layer

Reading Skills

8. H
9. B
10. The thermocline sinks. A deeper thermocline limits the nutrient-rich cold water that is returned by upwelling.

Interpreting Graphics

11. G
12. The two most abundant elements in ocean water are chlorine and sodium. The main sources include volcanic eruptions, the chemical weathering of rock on land, and chemical reactions between sea water and newly formed seafloor rocks.
13. Answers may vary. See Test Doctor for a detailed scoring rubric.

Chapter Planner 25

Movements of the Ocean

	Standards	Teach Key Ideas
Chapter Opener, pp. 686–687 **45 min.**	National Science Education Standards	
Section 1 Ocean Currents, pp. 689–694 **45 min.** ❯ Factors That Affect Surface Currents ❯ Major Surface Currents ❯ Deep Currents	ES 1c	■ ◆ **Bellringer,** p. 689 ■ **Discussion:** Beachcombing, p. 689 ■ **Demonstration:** Modeling Ocean Currents, p. 690 ■ **DI (Special Education Students):** The Coriolis Effect, p. 691 ◆ **Transparencies:** 125 Major Surface Currents of Earth's Oceans • 129 Roaming Rubber Duckies ▲ **Visual Concepts:** Global Winds and Surface Currents • Coriolis Effect • Surface Currents and Climate • Deep Currents • Formation of Deep Ocean Currents
Section 2 Ocean Waves, pp. 695–700 **90 min.** ❯ Wave Energy ❯ Waves and the Coastline ❯ Tsunamis	PS 6a	■ ◆ **Bellringer,** p. 695 ■ **Demonstration:** Student Wave, p. 695 ■ **DI (Basic Learners):** Waves, p. 695 ■ **DI (English Learners):** Anticipation Guide, p. 697 ■ **Discussion:** Water Safety, p. 699 ◆ **Transparencies:** 126 Wave Motion and Wave Energy • 127 The Formation of Breakers ▲ **Visual Concepts:** Anatomy of Ocean Waves • Wave Period of Ocean Waves • Formation and Movement of Ocean Waves • Types of Ocean Waves • Undertow • Longshore Current• Tsunami
Section 3 Tides, pp. 701–704 **45 min.** ❯ The Causes of Tides ❯ Behaviors of Tides ❯ Tidal Variations ❯ Tidal Currents		■ ◆ **Bellringer,** p. 701 ■ **DI (Advanced Learners):** Graphing, p. 701 ■ **Discussion:** Bay of Fundy, p. 703 ◆ **Transparency:** 128 Spring Tides and Neap Tides ▲ **Visual Concepts:** Timing the Tides • Tides and Tidal Range • Spring and Neap Tides
Chapter Wrap-Up, pp. 709–713 **90 min.**		**Chapter Summary,** p. 709

See also PowerNotes® Presentations

CHAPTER Fast Track *To shorten instruction because of time limitations, omit Section 2.*

Key

Teacher's Edition ■ Teaching Transparencies ◆
Chapter Resource File ● Online Edition ▲

All resources listed below are also available on the **Teacher One Stop™.**

Why It Matters	Hands-On	Skills Development	Assessment
■ **Chapter Overview,** p. 686 ■ **Using the Figure:** Sunset Tide, p. 686	**Inquiry Lab:** Creating Currents, p. 687	**Reading Toolbox,** p. 688	
■ **Section Overview,** p. 689 ■ **Using the Figure:** The Ocean Conveyor Belt, p. 691 ■ **Geography Connection:** Research, p. 691 ■ **History Connection:** Gulf Stream Delivery, p. 692 ■ **Biology Connection:** Vertical Ocean Movements, p. 693	**Quick Lab:** Ocean Currents, p. 692 ● **Skills Practice Lab:** Ocean Currents and Water Temperature	■ **Skill Builder:** Vocabulary, p. 692 **Reading Toolbox:** Pyramid, p. 693 **Maps in Action:** Roaming Rubber Duckies, p. 708 ■ ● **Internet Activity:** Beachcomber Tales, p. 708	**Reading Check,** p. 691 **Reading Check,** p. 693 **Section Review,** p. 694 ■ **Reteaching,** p. 693 ■ **Quiz,** p. 693 ■ **DI (Alternative Assessment):** Adventures of a Drop, p. 694 ● **Section Quiz**
■ **Section Overview,** p. 695 ■ **Environmental Connection:** Whitecaps and Climate, p. 697	**Quick Lab:** Waves, p. 697 ■ **Activity:** Wave Refraction in a Tank, p. 698 **Making Models Lab:** Wave Motion, pp. 706–707 ● **Inquiry Lab:** Tsunami	■ **Skill Builder:** Math, p. 696 ■ **Reading ToolBox:** Word Families, p. 698	**Reading Check,** p. 696 **Reading Check,** p. 698 **Section Review,** p. 700 ■ **Reteaching,** p. 699 ■ **Quiz,** p. 699 ■ **DI (Alternative Assessment):** Wave Haikus, p. 700 ● **Section Quiz**
■ **Section Overview,** p. 701 ■ **Using the Figure:** Tidal Bulges, p. 701 ■ **Using the Figure:** Lunar Motions, p. 702 **Spring Spawn,** p. 703		**Math Skills:** Tidal Friction, p. 702 ■ **Reading ToolBox:** Cause and Effect, p. 702	**Reading Check,** p. 702 **Section Review,** p. 704 ■ **Reteaching,** p. 703 ■ **Quiz,** p. 703 ■ **DI (Alternative Assessment):** Making Mobiles, p. 704 ● **Section Quiz**
Monster Waves: Myth or Fact?, p. 705	■ **Activity:** Wave Dioramas, p. 709	▲ **Super Summary** **Standardized Test Prep,** pp. 712–713	**Chapter Review,** pp. 710–711 ● **Chapter Tests**

See also Lab Generator

See also Holt Online Assessment Resources

Chapter Overview

This chapter describes the forces that affect the motion of ocean waters, including winds, Earth's spinning motion, land barriers that affect surface currents, differences in water density, and the gravitational pull of the moon.

Using the Figure GENERAL

Sunset Tide The photo shows a tide coming in at sunset. Tell students that in some places, high tide is 15 m higher than low tide. Ask students to predict what would happen to low-lying features such as harbors, beaches, and rocks if that amount of water came into a bay regularly. (Sample answer: Many features would be covered with water. The energy of so much water could be very destructive.) **LS Visual**

Why It Matters

Ocean currents move heat around the globe. This affects climate on short-term and long-term time scales. Changes to ocean currents can also affect fisheries. Other movements of ocean water, including waves and tides, erode coastlines, damage ships, and can be used as a source of renewable energy.

Chapter 25 Movements of the Ocean

Chapter Outline

1 Ocean Currents
- Factors That Affect Surface Currents
- Major Surface Currents
- Deep Currents

2 Ocean Waves
- Wave Energy
- Waves and the Coastline
- Tsunamis

3 Tides
- The Causes of Tides
- Behavior of Tides
- Tidal Variations
- Tidal Currents

Virginia Standards of Learning
ES.1.b
ES.1.c
ES.2.a
ES.3.b
ES.10.a
ES.10.c

Why It Matters

Both surface currents and deep currents move heat around Earth. This affects climates worldwide.

Chapter Correlations — *Virginia Standards of Learning*

ES.1.b technologies, including computers, probeware, and geospatial technologies, are used to collect, analyze, and report data and to demonstrate concepts and simulate experimental conditions.
ES.1.c scales, diagrams, charts, graphs, tables, imagery, models, and profiles are constructed and interpreted.
ES.2.a science explains and predicts the interactions and dynamics of complex Earth systems.
ES.3.b sun-Earth-moon relationships (seasons, tides, and eclipses)
ES.10.a physical and chemical changes related to tides, waves, currents, sea level and ice cap variations, upwelling, and salinity variations
ES.10.c systems interactions

Inquiry Lab Creating Currents

15 min

Fill a clear cup half full with 3% salt solution, which is dyed red using food coloring. Fill a second cup half full with 10% salt solution, which is dyed blue. Using a dropper, slowly add some of the 10% salt solution to the cup containing the 3% salt solution. Hold the end of the dropper near the edge of the cup, right at the water level. You will need to refill the dropper several times. Observe and record what happens. Repeat the experiment, this time adding some of the 3% salt solution to the cup containing the 10% salt solution.

Questions to Get You Started

1. What is density? Explain how adding salt to water changes the density of the water.
2. Explain your observations. How are your observations related to the movement of ocean water?
3. What other factors might affect the density and movement of ocean water? How could you modify this experiment to investigate a different factor?

Inquiry Lab

Central Concept: Students will experiment to determine how salinity affects the density of water, thereby creating currents in the ocean.

Teacher's Notes: Prepare the salt solutions in advance. The 3% salt solution should be dyed red using food coloring. The 10% salt solution should be dyed blue using food coloring. Remind students that when they are adding one type of salt solution to the other, they should gently drop the water along the side of the cup.

Materials (per group)

- 3% salt solution (dyed red)
- 10% salt solution (dyed blue)
- 2 clear plastic cups
- Dropper

Skills Acquired

- Experimenting
- Observing
- Interpreting Results

Answers to Getting Started

1. Density is the ratio of the mass of a substance to the volume of the substance. Adding salt made the water more dense because there is more mass in the same volume.
2. When the 3% salt solution was added to the 10% solution, a layer of red water sat on top of the blue water. The red water was less dense than the blue water. When the 10% solution was added to the 3% solution, a layer of blue water formed on the bottom of the cup, beneath the red water. The blue water was more dense than the red water. In the ocean, dense water at the surface sinks toward the bottom, creating a vertical current.
3. Answers may vary. Sample answer: Temperature affects the density of water. The experiment could be modified to compare the density of water at different temperatures by dropping warm water into cold water, and then dropping cold water into warm water.

Using THINK central Resources

An online version of this chapter, as well as all the print and multimedia resources that accompany the program are available to registered teachers and their students. Log onto www.thinkcentral.com to access these materials and tools to organize your preparation and student learning.

READING TOOLBOX

Word Families

Tide Students should create a table that contains definitions for the following terms: tidal range, tidal oscillation, tidal current, flood tide, ebb tide, spring tide, neap tide, high tide, low tide, tidal bulge, tidal friction, tidal bore, and tidal pattern. Students should compare their definitions with the ones given in the text.

Cause and Effect

Signal Words Answers may vary. Students' tables should reflect cause-and-effect relationships in Sections 1 and 2. Sample answers include: Cause: trade-wind belts, Effect: currents are pushed westward across the tropical latitudes of all three major oceans, Marker: none; Cause: Earth spins on its axis, Effect: ocean currents and wind belts curve; Marker: as

FoldNotes

Pyramid Answers may vary. Students' pyramids should include information about the three topics on the appropriate sides of the pyramid. Sample answers include: Global Wind Belts: Wind moves water at the ocean's surface. Continental Barriers: Continents deflect and divide surface currents when surface currents flow against them. The Coriolis Effect: It is defined as the curving of the path of water or air due to Earth's rotation. The wind belts and the Coriolis effect cause gyres to form.

READING TOOLBOX

These reading tools will help you learn the material in this chapter.

Word Families

Tide You will soon learn many new terms that contain the word *tide* or *tidal*. Both *tide* and *tidal* come from *tid,* the Old English word for "time." The suffix *-al,* meaning "of" or "like," makes *tidal* an adjective. As you read this chapter, you will see some familiar words combined with *tide* or *tidal,* along with their definitions.

Your Turn As you read Section 3, start a table like the one below. Add all the key terms and italicized words that include either *tide* or *tidal,* and write down the definitions of these terms and words, and compare them to each other.

Term	Definition
tidal current	a horizontal movement of water with the tide, toward and away from the coastline

Cause and Effect

Signal Words Certain words and phrases, called markers, can signal cause-and-effect relationships.

Cause markers	Effect markers
cause	therefore
affect	thus
as a result of	as a result
due to	is an effect of
because	consequently

Sentences can also express cause-and-effect relationships, without using markers.

Your Turn As you read Sections 1 and 2, create a table like the one below. When you find a cause-and-effect relationship, add it to your table.

Cause	Effect	Marker
the uneven heating of the atmosphere	winds	caused by

FoldNotes

Pyramid A pyramid can be used to summarize information in three categories, on the three sides of the pyramid.

Your Turn Create a pyramid, as described in Appendix A.

1. Along one edge of one side of the FoldNote, write "Global Wind Belts."
2. On one edge of another side, write "Continental Barriers."
3. On one edge of the third side, write "The Coriolis Effect."

As you read Section 1, fill in details about the three factors that influence surface currents.

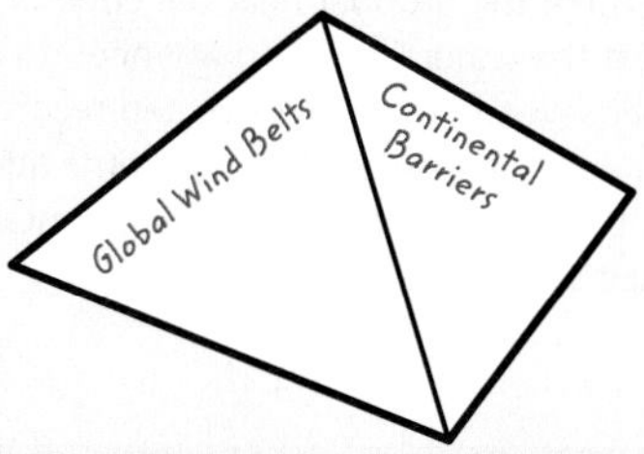

For more information on how to use these and other tools, see **Appendix A.**

SECTION 1
Ocean Currents

Key Ideas	Key Terms	Why It Matters
› Describe how wind patterns, the rotation of Earth, and continental barriers affect surface currents in the ocean. › Identify the major factor that determines the direction in which a surface current circulates. › Explain how differences in the density of ocean water affect the flow of deep currents.	current surface current Coriolis effect gyre Gulf Stream deep current	Spending time near the coast would let you experience the effects of ocean currents on the local climate. Ocean currents have a large impact on climates around the world.

The water in the ocean moves in giant streams called **currents.** Many ocean currents are complex and difficult to trace. Oceanographers identify ocean currents by studying the physical and chemical characteristics of the ocean water. They also identify currents by mapping the path of debris that is dumped or washed overboard from ships, as shown in **Figure 1.** From these data, scientists have mapped a detailed pattern of ocean currents around the world. Scientists place ocean currents into two major categories: surface currents and deep currents.

Factors That Affect Surface Currents

Currents that move at or near the surface of the ocean and are driven by wind are called **surface currents.** Surface currents are controlled by three factors: air currents, Earth's rotation, and the location of the continents.

All surface currents are affected by wind. Wind is caused by the uneven heating of the atmosphere. Variations in air temperature lead to variations in air density and pressure. Colder, denser air sinks and forms areas of high pressure. Air moves away from high-pressure areas to lower pressure areas. This movement gives rise to wind.

Because *wind* is moving air, wind has kinetic energy. The wind passes this energy to the ocean as the air moves across the ocean surface. As energy is transferred from the air to the ocean, the water at the ocean's surface begins to move.

current a horizontal movement of water in a well-defined pattern, such as a river or stream

surface current a horizontal movement of ocean water that is caused by wind and that occurs at or near the ocean's surface

Figure 1 Glass floats, which are used to hold up Japanese fishing nets, have been carried by surface currents from off the coast of Japan to this beach in northwest Hawaii.

Section 1

Focus

Overview

This section identifies factors that affect global surface currents and describes the motions of major surface currents. The section also examines how variations in water density affect the formation of deep-ocean currents.

Bellringer

Ask students to think about movies or pictures they have seen that show an ocean or a beach. Have students list words or phrases that describe the motion of ocean water. (Answers may vary. Students may describe waves, ripples, swells, whitecaps, or tides.)
LS Verbal

Motivate

Discussion GENERAL

Beachcombing Use the figure on the bottom of this page as a starting point for discussion. Ask students to list the kinds of objects they might expect to find on a beach. (Sample answers: shells, driftwood, bottles, seeds, toys, paper cups, rocks, boxes, and seaweed) Ask them where they think these objects came from. (Sample answers: from things living in the sea, from nearby coasts, from boats, or from people who live on the coast) Explain that the motion of ocean currents often deposits floating objects on the shore. **LS Verbal**

Key Resources

Chapter Resource File
- Directed Reading BASIC
- Skills Practice Lab: Ocean Currents and Water Temperature GENERAL

Technology
- Transparencies
  Bellringer

Teach

Demonstration GENERAL

Modeling Ocean Currents Set up an overhead projector. Fill a wide, flat, clear plastic container with water to simulate an ocean. Place the container on the projector and focus as needed. Put a drop of food coloring at one end of the container. Using a straw, blow gently across the water's surface. Have students describe what happens. Students also may draw what they see, both at the surface and below. (Air blown through the straw caused streams of water, just as the wind creates currents in the ocean.) Put a small cup upside down in the center of the model ocean to represent land. Add a drop of food coloring in front of the barrier. Gently blow through the straw and have students describe and draw what happens. Ask what effect a land mass has on the currents. (The currents divide and flow around the barrier.) Repeat with a jar lid placed under the surface. Ask whether the currents always flow in the direction of the wind. (No, sometimes the currents flow in circles around barriers.) **LS Visual**

Global Wind Belts

Global wind belts, such as the trade winds and westerlies shown in **Figure 2,** are a major factor affecting the flow of ocean surface water. The *trade winds* are located just north and south of the equator. In the Northern Hemisphere, the trade winds blow from the northeast. In the Southern Hemisphere, they blow from the southeast. In both hemispheres, trade-wind belts push currents westward across the tropical latitudes of all three major oceans.

The *westerlies* are located in the middle latitudes. In the Northern Hemisphere, westerlies blow from the southwest. In the Southern Hemisphere, they blow from the northwest. Westerlies push ocean currents eastward in the higher latitudes of the Northern and Southern Hemispheres.

Coriolis effect the curving of the path of a moving object from an otherwise straight path due to Earth's rotation

gyre a huge circle of moving ocean water found above and below the equator

Continental Barriers

The continents are another major influence on surface currents. The continents act as barriers to surface currents. When a surface current flows against a continent, the current is deflected and divided.

The Coriolis Effect

As Earth spins on its axis, ocean currents and wind belts curve. The curving of the paths of ocean currents and winds due to Earth's rotation is called the **Coriolis effect.** The wind belts and the Coriolis effect cause huge circles of moving water, called **gyres,** to form.

Figure 3 shows the five main gyres in the ocean. In the Northern Hemisphere, water in the main gyres flows clockwise. In the Southern Hemisphere, water in the main gyres flows counterclockwise.

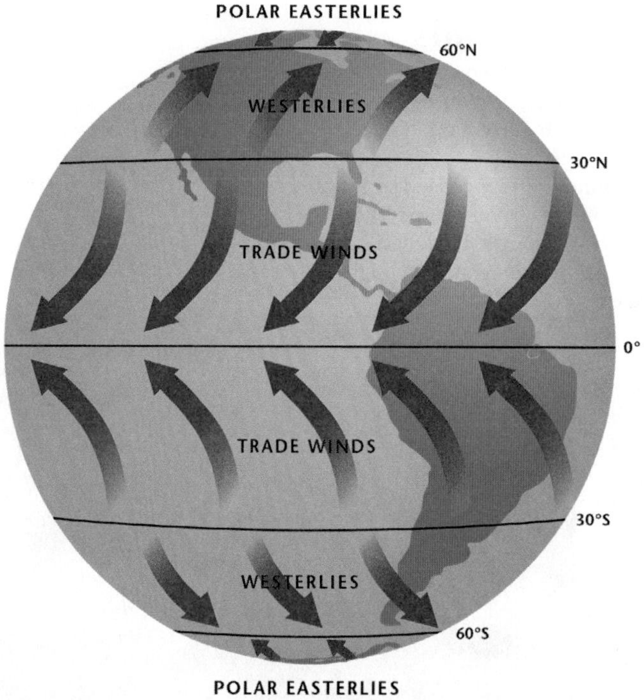

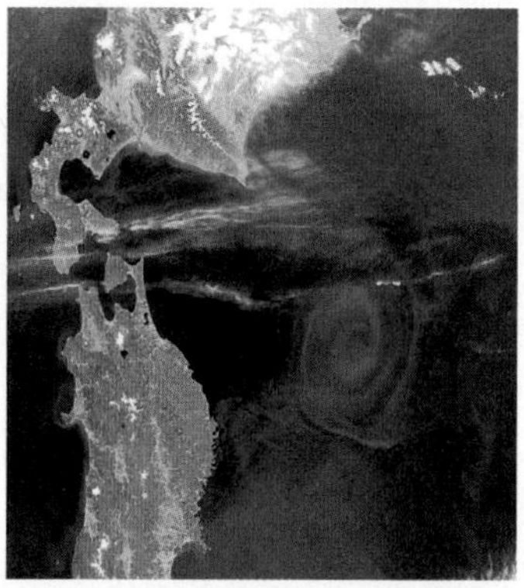

Figure 2 Global winds and the Coriolis effect together drive the surface currents of the oceans in great circular patterns. The photo at the right shows a small gyre in the Pacific Ocean, off the east coast of Japan.

MISCONCEPTION ALERT

Plumbing and the Coriolis Effect Students may think that the way water drains in a circular motion down sinks or in a flushing toilet is related to the Coriolis effect. The rotation of Earth affects large-scale phenomena, such as prevailing winds and ocean currents. However, the deflection is so small that it plays no part in how water moves through household plumbing. Explain that toilets and sinks drain in the directions they do because of the way water is directed into them or pulled away. If water enters in a swirling motion, it will exit with the same swirling pattern.

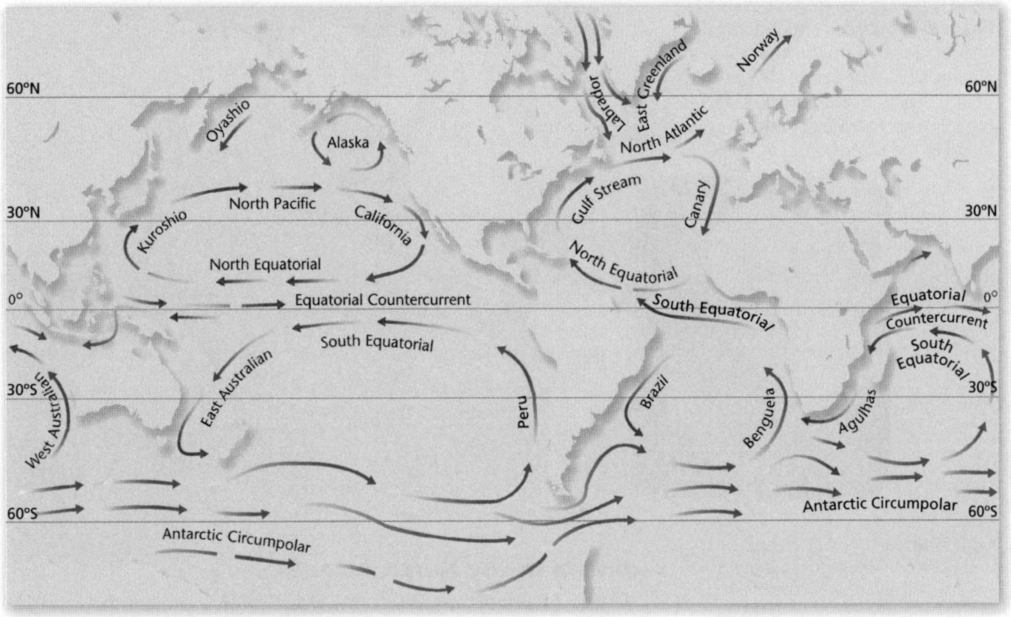

Figure 3 This map shows the major surface currents in the oceans of the world. Warm-water currents are shown in red; cold-water currents are shown in blue.

Major Surface Currents

The major surface currents of the world are shown in **Figure 3.** The major currents in the equatorial region and in the Northern and Southern Hemispheres are described below.

Equatorial Currents

Warm equatorial currents are located in the Atlantic, Pacific, and Indian Oceans. Each of these oceans has two warm-water equatorial currents that move in a westward direction. Between these westward-flowing currents lies a weaker, eastward-flowing current called the *Equatorial Countercurrent*.

Currents in the Southern Hemisphere

In the Southern Hemisphere, the currents in the main gyres move counterclockwise. In the most southerly regions of the oceans, constant westward winds produce the world's largest current, the *Antarctic Circumpolar Current*, also known as *West Wind Drift*. No continents interrupt the movement of this current, which completely circles Antartica and crosses all three major oceans.

The Indian Ocean surface currents follow two patterns. Currents in the southern Indian Ocean follow a circular, counterclockwise gyre. Currents in the northern Indian Ocean are governed by *monsoons*, winds whose directions change seasonally.

Reading Check **What is the world's largest ocean current?** (See Appendix G for answers to Reading Checks.)

Academic Vocabulary

major (MAY juhr) of great importance; large scale

SCILINKS.
www.scilinks.org
Topic: Ocean Currents
Code: **HQX1061**

Using the Figure — General

The Ocean Conveyor Belt Explain that sunlight that shines on the surface of the ocean adds thermal energy to the ocean's surface. Currents help transfer this energy to other regions of the globe. Ask students how the temperature of each water current is indicated on the world map. Note that *warm* means "warmer than surrounding ocean waters." (Warm water currents are shown in red; cold-water currents are shown in blue.) Ask where most of the warm water currents originate. (near the equator) Then, ask students to identify the temperature of currents that flow from the poles. (cold) **LS Visual**

Answer to Reading Check

Because no continents interrupt the flow of the Antarctic Circumpolar Current, also called the *West Wind Drift*, it completely encircles Antarctica and crosses three major oceans and is therefore the world's largest ocean current. All other surface currents are deflected and divided when they meet a continental barrier.

Geography Connection — Advanced

Research Have students research the effect of the Gulf Stream on the climate of the British Isles. Have them compare weather and precipitation with that of a North American location in the same latitude. Ask them to hypothesize what would happen to the climates of these regions if the Gulf Stream passed closer to North America and farther from the British Isles. (The climate of the British Isles would probably be colder with more snow; the North American location would probably be warmer, with more rain.) **LS Verbal**

Key Resources

Technology

- Transparencies
  125 Major Surface Currents of Earth's Oceans

Differentiated Instruction

Special Education Students

The Coriolis Effect Help students understand the Coriolis effect by using a 3-D model of Earth in the form of a globe. Pair a visually impaired student with a sighted partner. Have them place a lump of clay on the equator and another closer to one of the poles. Together they can spin the globe to show how Earth rotates and demonstrate how objects at different points on the globe move at different speeds. **LS Kinesthetic**

Teach, *continued*

Quick Lab

Skills Acquired
- Constructing Models
- Observing
- Analyzing
- Communicating

Materials
- Shallow pan
- Water
- Paper confetti
- Drinking straw

Teacher's Notes: You could substitute pepper grains, talcum powder, or other things that float for the confetti. An aluminum pie pan works well to replace the plate. Students could model the effects of land barriers by using small lumps of clay to model landmasses that deflect currents.

Answers to Analysis
1. Student diagrams may vary but should accurately show the positions of the straw. Arrows should indicate that the water flows in the same direction as the moving air.
2. Surface currents in the ocean are produced by energy transferred to water by the winds, just as the water in the plate received energy from the air that was blown through the straw.

Figure 4 Surface currents in the Atlantic Ocean form the North Atlantic Gyre. The Sargasso Sea results from this pattern of currents. The organisms below are commonly found in the Sargasso Sea.

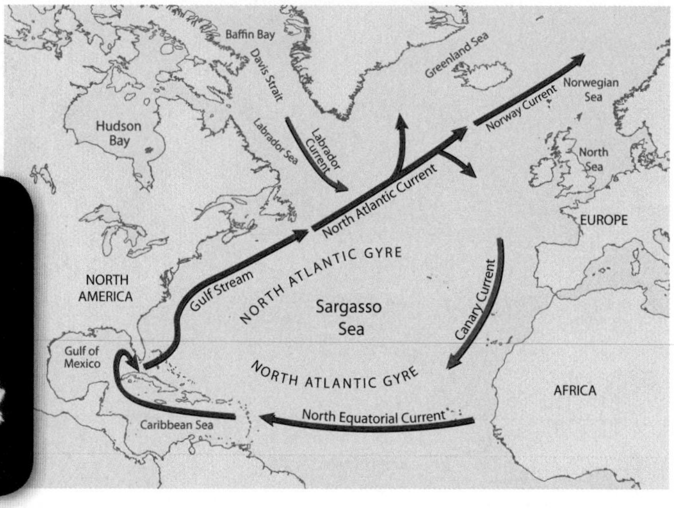

Gulf Stream the swift, deep, and warm Atlantic current that flows along the eastern coast of the United States toward the northeast

Quick Lab — 10 min

Ocean Currents

Procedure
1. Fill a **shallow pan** with **water**.
2. Sprinkle **paper confetti** on the surface of the water.
3. Blow across the surface of the water through a **drinking straw** to produce a clockwise current.
4. Blow through the straw to make a counterclockwise current. Try to make two currents at the same time.

Analysis
1. Draw a diagram of the currents. Draw the straw's positions, and use arrows to show air and water direction.
2. How does this activity relate to what happens in ocean currents?

Currents in the North Atlantic

In the North Atlantic Ocean, warm water moves through the Caribbean Sea and Gulf of Mexico and then north along the east coast of North America in a swift, warm current called the **Gulf Stream.** Farther north, the cold-water Labrador Current, which flows south, joins the Gulf Stream. South of Greenland, the Gulf Stream widens and slows until it becomes a vast, slow-moving warm current known as the *North Atlantic Current.* Near western Europe, the North Atlantic Current splits. One part becomes the Norway Current, which flows northward along the coast of Norway and keeps that coast ice-free all year. The other part is deflected southward and becomes the cool Canary Current, which eventually warms and rejoins the North Equatorial Current.

As **Figure 4** shows, the Gulf Stream, the North Atlantic Current, the Canary Current, and the North Equatorial Current form the North Atlantic Gyre. At the center of this gyre lies a vast area of calm, warm water called the *Sargasso Sea.* The Sargasso Sea is named after *sargassum*, the brown seaweed that floats on the surface of the water in this area. The pattern of winds and currents around the Sargasso Sea concentrates all kinds of floating debris, such as orange peels and plastic cups, in this area.

Currents in the North Pacific

The pattern of currents in the North Pacific is similar to that in the North Atlantic. The warm Kuroshio Current, the Pacific equivalent of the Gulf Stream, flows northward along the east coast of Asia. This current then flows toward North America as the North Pacific Drift. It eventually flows southward along the California coast as the cool California Current.

Skill Builder — GENERAL

Vocabulary Here are three words with Latin roots that students will encounter in ocean study. The term *salinity* comes from *sal*, which means "salt." The term *density* comes from *densus*, which means "thick." The term *turbidity* comes from *turbidus*, which means "disturbed." Ask students to identify how knowing these roots can help them remember the meanings of these terms. **LS Verbal**

History Connection — GENERAL

Gulf Stream Delivery When Benjamin Franklin was deputy postmaster general of the American colonies from 1753 through 1774, mail ships had been making the journey from America to England weeks faster than in the reverse direction. Franklin set out to determine why. He was able to document the motion of the Gulf Stream current. His findings became one of the earliest published charts of North Atlantic ocean currents. Have students find out more about Franklin's maritime observations and report back to the class. **LS Verbal**

Deep Currents

In addition to having wind-driven surface currents, the ocean has **deep currents,** cold, dense currents far below the surface. Deep currents move much more slowly than surface currents do. Deep currents form as cold, dense water of the polar regions sinks and flows beneath warmer ocean water.

The movement of polar waters is a result of differences in density. When water cools, it contracts and the water molecules move closer together. This contraction makes the water denser, and the water sinks. When water warms, it expands and the water molecules move farther apart. The warm water is less dense, so it rises above the cold water. Temperature helps determine density.

Salinity, too, helps determine the density of water. The water in polar regions has high salinity because of the large amount of water frozen in icebergs and sea ice. When water freezes, the salt in the water does not freeze but stays in the unfrozen water. So, unfrozen polar water has a high salt concentration and is denser than water that has a lower salinity. This dense polar water sinks and forms a deep current that flows beneath less dense surface currents, as shown in **Figure 5.**

deep current a streamlike movement of ocean water far below the surface

Antarctic Bottom Water

The temperature of the water near Antarctica is very cold, –2°C. The water's salinity is high. These two factors make the water off the coast of Antarctica the densest and coldest ocean water in the world. This dense, cold water sinks to the ocean bottom and forms a deep current called the *Antarctic Bottom Water*. The Antarctic Bottom Water moves slowly northward along the ocean bottom for thousands of kilometers to a latitude of about 40°N. It takes hundreds of years for the current to make the trip.

Reading Check **Why is Antarctic Bottom Water the densest ocean water in the world?**

READING TOOLBOX

Pyramid
Create a pyramid to compare three examples of currents in the deep ocean: Antarctic Bottom Water, North Atlantic Deep Water, and Turbidity Currents. Be sure to note the similarities and differences among the currents.

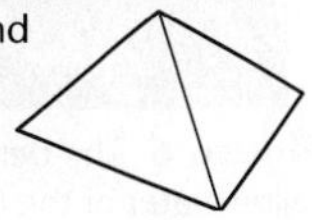

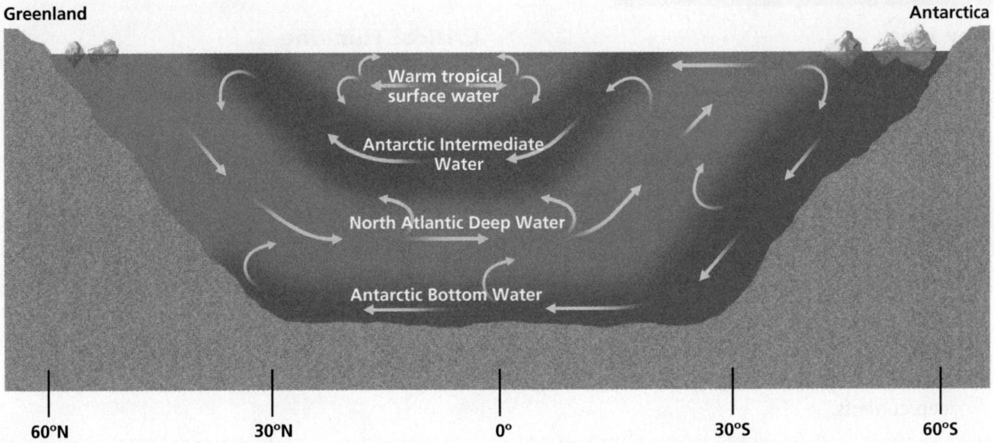

Figure 5 The very dense and highly saline Antarctic Bottom Water travels beneath less dense North Atlantic Deep Water.

READING TOOLBOX

Pyramid Answers may vary. Students' pyramids should include information about the three topics on the appropriate sides of the pyramid. Sample answer: Antarctic Bottom Water: deep, cold, dense current formed by cold Antarctic water (−2 °C) with high salinity sinking to ocean bottom; North Atlantic Deep Water: deep, cold current formed by cold, salty North Atlantic water south of Greenland; Turbidity Currents: strong currents caused by underwater landslides

Close

Reteaching — BASIC

Venn Diagrams Have students work in pairs to construct a Venn diagram that describes the similarities and differences between surface currents and deep currents. Then, have each student write a short summary of what the diagram shows. **LS Visual**

Quiz — GENERAL

1. What three factors control the motion of surface currents? Describe their effects. (1. Prevailing winds transfer energy to the surface to produce surface currents. 2. Earth's rotation causes water currents to curve. 3. Land barriers cause currents to be deflected or divided.)
2. Explain how water density produces deep-ocean currents. (Differences in water temperature and salinity produce differences in density. The denser water sinks and flows beneath surface currents. Sediment from landslides or seismic activity also makes water denser so it flows down slopes on the ocean floor.)

Biology Connection — GENERAL

Vertical Ocean Movements When deeper water moves upward (upwelling), colder, nutrient-rich waters come to the surface. Ask students why deeper waters have more nutrients. (Dying marine organisms fall to the bottom. Decomposition releases nutrients.) Surface water moving downward is known as *downwelling.* It is caused in part by evaporation. Explain that these vertical upward and downward motions of ocean water occur as a constantly moving global system.
LS Verbal/Logical

Answer to Reading Check

Antarctic Bottom Water is very cold. It also has a high salinity. The extreme cold and high salinity combine to make the water extremely dense.

Close, *continued*

Answers to Section Review

1. Uneven heating of Earth's atmosphere produces moving air, or winds. As winds move across the ocean surface, they transfer kinetic energy to the water. This energy drives the horizontal motion of water at the surface.
2. The trade wind belts, located north and south of the equator, push surface currents west across the tropical latitudes of all three major oceans.
3. Westerlies are the wind belt system located in the middle latitudes. They push the currents in an easterly direction.
4. Denser water sinks below less-dense water. This motion of the water is the basis of deep-ocean currents.
5. Temperature, salinity, and turbidity affect the density of water.
6. surface currents: Gulf Stream, Kuroshio Current, Antarctic Circumpolar Current; deep currents: North Atlantic Deep Water, Antarctic Bottom Water
7. Earth's rotation causes the path of ocean currents to curve. If Earth did not rotate, waters would flow in straight paths until they were interrupted by land.
8. Sunlight that shines on the surface of Earth adds thermal energy to the air. Differences in the amount of solar radiation leads to differential heating of Earth's surface. This heating pattern creates winds, which drive surface currents.

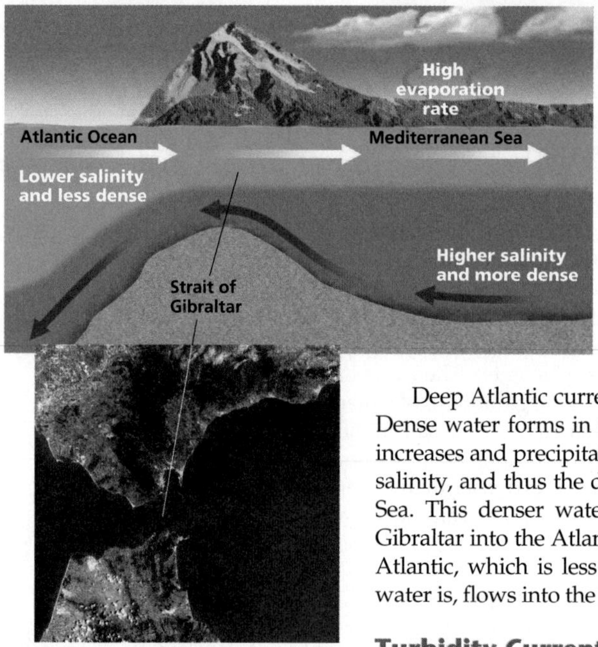

Figure 6 The dense, highly saline water of the Mediterranean Sea forms a deep current as it flows through the Strait of Gibraltar and into the less dense Atlantic Ocean.

North Atlantic Deep Water

In the North Atlantic, south of Greenland, the water is very cold and has a high salinity. This cold, salty water forms a deep current that moves southward under the northward-flowing Gulf Stream. Near the equator, this deep current divides. One part begins to rise, reverse direction, and flow northward again. The rest of the current continues southward toward Antarctica and flows over the colder, denser Antarctic Bottom Water.

Deep Atlantic currents exist near the Mediterranean Sea, too. Dense water forms in the Mediterranean Sea when evaporation increases and precipitation decreases. These changes increase the salinity, and thus the density, of the water of the Mediterranean Sea. This denser water sinks and flows through the Strait of Gibraltar into the Atlantic Ocean. In turn, surface water from the Atlantic, which is less saline and less dense than deep current water is, flows into the Mediterranean Sea, as shown in **Figure 6.**

Turbidity Currents

A turbidity current is a strong current caused by an underwater landslide. Turbidity currents occur when large masses of sediment that have accumulated along a continental shelf or continental slope suddenly break loose and slide downhill. The landslide mixes the nearby water with sediment. The sediment causes the water to become cloudy, or turbid, and denser than the surrounding water. The dense water of the turbidity current moves beneath the less dense, clear water.

Section 1 Review

Key Ideas

1. **Describe** the force that drives most surface currents.
2. **Identify** the winds that affect the surface currents on both sides of the equator.
3. **Identify** the winds that affect the surface currents in the middle latitudes.
4. **Describe** how density affects the flow of deep currents.
5. **List** the factors that affect the density of ocean water.
6. **List** three major surface currents and two major deep currents.

Critical Thinking

7. **Predicting Consequences** Describe how surface currents would be affected if Earth did not rotate.
8. **Identifying Relationships** Explain how the distribution of solar energy around Earth affects ocean surface currents.

Concept Mapping

9. Use the following terms to create a concept map: *ocean currents, surface currents, deep currents, Gulf Stream, North Atlantic Current, Antarctic Bottom Water, gyres,* and *Coriolis effect.*

9. *Ocean currents* can be *deep currents,* such as the *Antarctic Bottom Water,* or *surface currents,* such as the *Gulf Stream* and the *North Atlantic Current,* which are part of a *gyre* that is caused by the *Coriolis effect.*

Differentiated Instruction

Alternative Assessment

Adventures of a Drop Have students write a story about the adventures of a drop of water as it moves through the ocean. They should incorporate what they have learned about the motions of surface and deep-water currents and the factors that affect them. Students may include drawings to illustrate their narratives.
LS Verbal/Visual

SECTION 2

Ocean Waves

Key Ideas	Key Terms	Why It Matters
❯ Describe the formation of waves and the factors that affect wave size. ❯ Explain how waves interact with the coastline. ❯ Identify the cause of destructive ocean waves.	**wave** **wave period** **fetch** **refraction**	Ocean waves, whether small or large, have similar characteristics, which sometimes can cause trouble for people.

A **wave** is a periodic disturbance in a solid, liquid, or gas as energy is transmitted through the medium. One kind of wave is described as the periodic up-and-down movement of water. Such a wave has two basic parts—a *crest* and a *trough*—as shown in **Figure 1.** The crest is the highest point of a wave. The trough is the lowest point between two crests. The *wave height* is the vertical distance between the crest and the trough of a wave. The *wavelength* is the horizontal distance between two consecutive crests or between two consecutive troughs. The **wave period** is the time required for two consecutive wave crests to pass a given point. The speed at which a wave moves is calculated by dividing the wave's wavelength by its period.

$$\textit{wave speed} = \frac{\textit{wavelength}}{\textit{wave period}}$$

wave a periodic disturbance in a solid, liquid, or gas as energy is transmitted through a medium

wave period the time required for identical points on consecutive waves to pass a given point

Wave Energy

The uneven heating of Earth's atmosphere causes pressure differences that make air move. This moving air is called *wind.* Wind then transfers the energy received from the sun to the ocean and forms waves. Small waves, or ripples, form as a result of friction between the moving air and the water. As a ripple receives more energy from the wind, the ripple grows into a larger wave. The longer that the wind blows from a given direction, the more energy that is transferred from the wind to the water and the larger the wave becomes.

The smoothness of the ocean's surface is generally disrupted by many small waves moving in different directions. Because of their large surface area, larger waves receive more energy from the wind than smaller waves do. Thus, larger waves grow larger, and smaller waves die out.

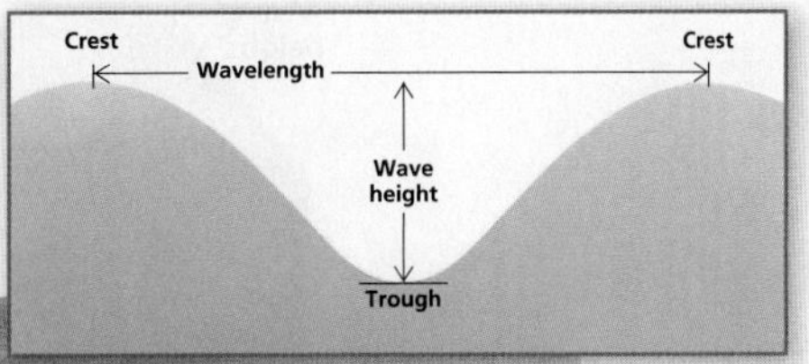

Figure 1 The vertical distance between the crest and the trough of a wave is the wave height.

Section 2

Focus

Overview

This section introduces wave characteristics, explains how waves form, and identifies different types of ocean waves.

Bellringer

Have students list as many words as they can think of that describe the motion of ocean waves. (Answers may vary. Sample answers may include adjectives such as rolling, rocking, bobbing, crashing, breaking, rising and falling, and heaving.) **LS Verbal**

Motivate

Demonstration GENERAL

Student Wave Have 10 to 12 students stand side-by-side at the front of the room. Have them face the same direction and link arms. Tell them that they are going to mimic the motion of an ocean wave. Stand at one end and gently pull the closest student forward and then back. Continue until all the students are in motion. Have the seated students observe. Ask students where the wave energy came from and how far it traveled. (Sample answer: The teacher supplied the energy that pulled the first student. The energy traveled all the way down the line.) Emphasize that waves transfer energy over great distances. **LS Kinesthetic/Visual**

Key Resources

Chapter Resource File
- Directed Reading BASIC
- Inquiry Lab: Tsunami GENERAL

Technology
- Transparencies
  Bellringer

Differentiated Instruction

Basic Learners

Waves Have students create a chart in which they list key words from the text, such as *crest, trough, wave period,* and *wavelength,* and give their meanings. The process of organizing the information into a graphic format will help students process the information visually. Ask students to summarize the main points. **LS Verbal**

Teach

MISCONCEPTION ALERT

Movement of Water Molecules

Students may think that the waves of water breaking on the beach have traveled for many miles before reaching shore. Emphasize that it is only the wave energy or the waveform that moves. Water molecules within a wave actually circulate more or less in place, with little or no forward motion.

Answer to Reading Check

Because waves receive energy from wind that pushes against the surface of the water, the amount of energy decreases as the depth of water increases. As a result, the diameter of the water molecules' circular path also decreases.

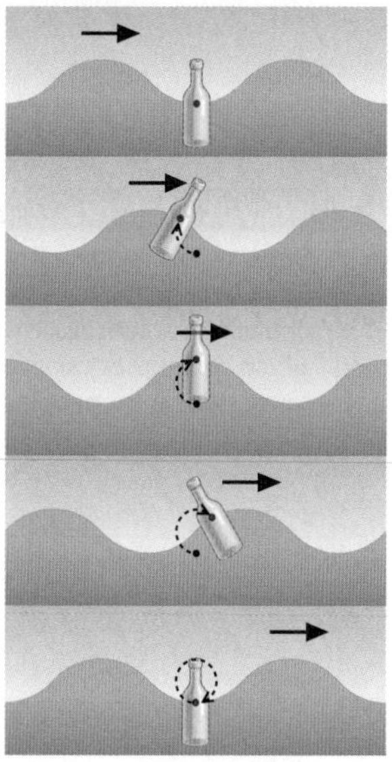

Figure 2 Like the bottle in this diagram, water molecules do not travel horizontally through the water with the wave.

Water Movement in a Wave

Although the energy of a wave moves from water molecule to water molecule in the direction of the wave, the water itself moves very little. This fact can be demonstrated by observing the movement of a bottle floating on the water as a wave passes. The bottle appears to move up and down, but it moves in a circular path, as shown in **Figure 2.** As the wave passes, the bottle moves only a small distance.

As a wave moves across the surface of the ocean, only the energy of the wave, not the water, moves in the direction of the wave. The water molecules within the wave move in a circular motion. During a single wave period, each water particle moves in one complete circle. At the end of the wave period, a circling water particle ends up almost exactly where it started.

As a wave passes a given point, the circle traced by a water particle initially on the surface of the ocean has a diameter that is equal to the height of the wave. Because waves receive their energy from wind pushing against the surface of the ocean, the energy received decreases as the depth of the water increases. As a result, water at various depths receives varying amounts of energy. Thus, the diameter of a water molecule's circular path decreases as the depth of the water increases, as shown in **Figure 3.** Below a depth of about one-half the wavelength, there is almost no circular motion of water molecules.

Reading Check **Why does the diameter of a water molecule's circular path in a wave decrease as depth increases?**

Figure 3 Wave energy decreases as depth increases. As a result, the diameter of a water molecule's circular path in a wave also decreases.

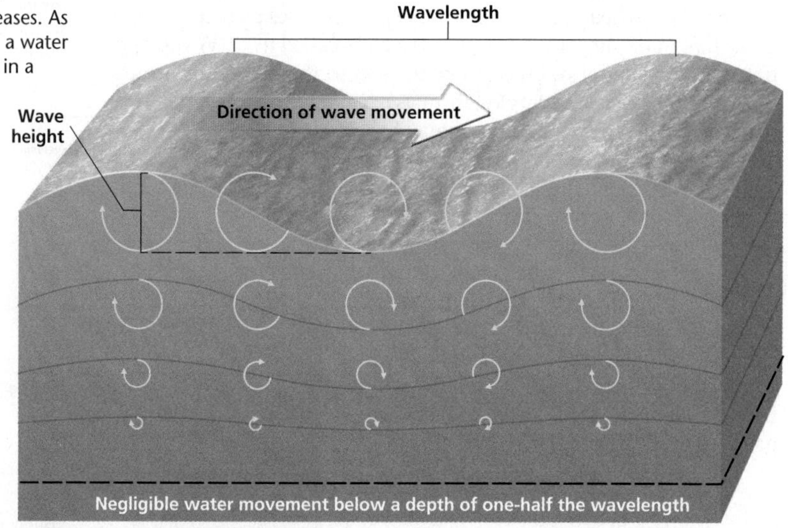

Skill Builder — GENERAL

Math Have students calculate the wave speed of a wave that has a wavelength of 1,530 m and a period of 30 s.

($\mathit{wavespeed} = \dfrac{\mathit{wavelength}}{\mathit{wave\ period}}$

$\mathit{wavespeed} = \dfrac{1{,}530\text{ m}}{30\text{ s}} = 50\text{ m/s}$) **LS Logical**

Key Resources

Technology

- Transparencies
  126 Wave Motion and Wave Energy

Wave Size

Three factors determine the size of a wave. These factors are the speed of the wind, the length of time that the wind blows, and fetch. **Fetch** is the distance that the wind can blow across open water. Very large waves are produced by strong, steady winds blowing across a long fetch.

During a storm, steady high winds can cause some waves to gather enough energy to become very large. Strong, gusty winds, on the other hand, produce choppy water that has waves of various heights and lengths, which may come from various directions. Nevertheless, the size of a wave will increase to only a certain height-to-length ratio before the wave collapses.

On calm days, small, smooth waves move steadily across the ocean's surface. One of a group of long, rolling waves that are of similar size is called a *swell*. Swells move in groups in which one wave follows another. Swells that reach the shore may have formed thousands of kilometers out in the ocean.

Figure 4 Whitecaps, such as the ones shown here off the coast of North Carolina, may form during storms.

fetch the distance that wind blows across an area of the sea to generate waves

Whitecaps

When winds blow the crest of a wave off, *whitecaps* form, as shown in **Figure 4.** Because whitecaps reflect solar radiation, they allow less radiation to reach the ocean. Scientists have been studying how this characteristic may affect climate.

Academic Vocabulary

collapse (kuh LAPS) fall or cave in

Quick Lab: Waves

15 min

Procedure

1. Fill a rectangular pan (40 cm × 30 cm × 10 cm) with water to a depth of 7 cm.
2. Float a cork near the center of the pan. On each side of the pan, mark the location of the cork with a small piece of tape.
3. Hold a spoon in the water at one end of the pan. Carefully move the spoon up and down in the water to make a slow, regular pattern of waves.
4. Observe the movement of the cork for 1 min. Sketch how the cork moves in relation to the waves.
5. Remove the cork from the pan.
6. Use the spoon to make a strong, steady series of waves.
7. Remove the spoon from the pan. Observe what happens when the waves reach the edges of the pan. Write down or sketch what you observe.

Analysis

1. Describe the motion of the cork when a wave passes.
2. How does the cork move relative to the tape on the sides of the pan? Explain your answer.
3. When a wave breaks on the shore, the water is carried in the direction of the wave. Based on your observations in step 4, does this statement contradict your model? Explain your answer.

Quick Lab

Skills Acquired
- Constructing Models
- Experimenting
- Recognizing Patterns
- Interpreting

Materials
- Rectangular pan
- Water
- Cork
- Tape
- Spoon

Teacher's Notes: Another way to make waves is by using a fan or hairdryer set at different speeds. You could also substitute wood blocks for the spoon. If you have a larger tank available, such as an aquarium, you can use fishing sinkers to float several corks at different depths below the water's surface so that students can observe the effect of increasing wave size on the movement of water at different depths.

Answers to Analysis

1. Answers may vary. The cork appears to move slightly forward, then slightly backward about the same distance.
2. The cork stays almost even with the tape, bobbing up and down and moving slightly forward and back. It does not show much movement in the direction of the wave.
3. No, the waves created in the pan resemble waves in deep water instead of waves breaking on a beach. Because the pan is the same depth throughout, the water moves back and forth instead of being carried forward.

Differentiated Instruction

English Learners

Anticipation Guide Before students read this page, ask them to predict what factors determine the size of a wave. Then, ask students to read the page and find out if their predictions were accurate. **LS Logical**

Environmental Connection

Whitecaps and Climate A study by Scripps Institution of Oceanography shows that whitecaps, because they are white, impact climate by reflecting sunlight back into space, thus reducing the amount of warming in ocean water. This effect is especially significant in regions that have high winds and cloudless skies, such as the Arabian Sea and the Indian Ocean. Ask students to find out more about what factors scientists include in their computerized models and report back to the class on some aspect of the study that interests them. **LS Verbal**

Teach, *continued*

Activity — GENERAL

Wave Refraction in a Tank Have individual groups of students investigate the effects of waves in shallow water. Divide the class into small groups. Give each group a clear plastic container or aquarium tank and a bowl or other solid object. Tell students to follow these instructions:

1. Fill the container or tank with a small amount of water.
2. Place the solid object on the bottom at one end. (Make sure students understand that the object represents a piece of land).
3. Direct waves toward the object using a plastic lid or wood block.

Ask students to describe what happens to the wave when it reaches the object. (The wave splits when it touches the object. Part of the wave lags behind and develops a curved front, or bend.) Ask students to name this bending process that occurs in shallow coastal waters. (refraction)

LS Visual/Kinesthetic

READING TOOLBOX

Word Families Students should include the following terms and definitions in their tables: wavelength: the distance between two crests in a row or two troughs in a row; wave height: the distance between the top (crest) and the bottom (trough) of a wave

READING TOOLBOX

Word Families
In this section are several terms that belong to the word family of the key term *wave*. Create a table for these terms, similar to the table described at the beginning of the chapter. Complete your table by writing definitions for these terms in your own words.

Waves and the Coastline

In shallow water near the coastline, the bottom of a wave touches the ocean floor. A wave touches the ocean floor where the depth of the water is about half the wavelength. Contact with the ocean floor causes the wave to slow and eventually break, as shown in **Figure 5.**

Breakers

The height of a wave changes as the wave approaches the coastline. The water involved in the motion of a wave extends to a depth of one-half the wavelength. As the wave moves into shallow water, the bottom of the wave is slowed. The top of the wave, however, continues to move at its original speed. The top of the wave gets farther and farther ahead of the bottom of the wave. Finally, the top of the wave topples over and forms a *breaker*, a foamy mass of water that washes onto the shore. The height of the wave when the wave topples over is one to two times the height of the original wave.

Breaking waves scrape sediments off the ocean floor and move the sediments along the coastline. The waves also erode rocky coastlines. The size and force of breakers are determined by the original wave height, the wavelength, and the steepness of the ocean floor close to the coastline. If the slope of the ocean floor is steep, the height of the wave increases rapidly and the wave breaks with great force. If the coastline slopes gently, the wave rises slowly. The wave spills forward with a rolling motion that continues as the wave advances up the coastline.

Reading Check **As a wave moves into shallow water, what causes the top of the wave to break and topple over?**

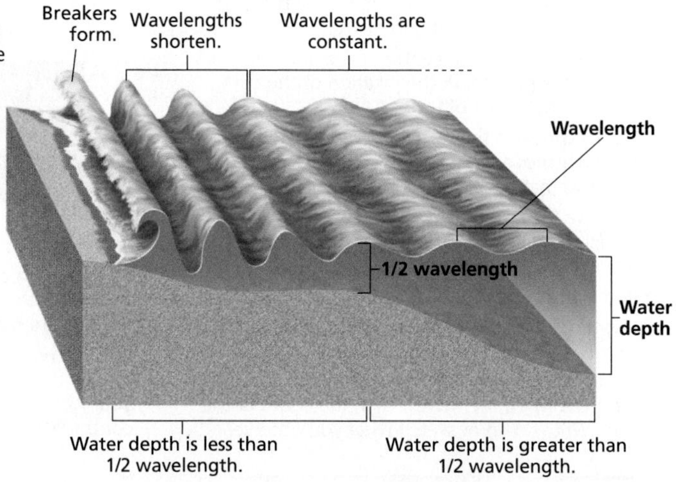

Figure 5 Breakers begin to form as a wave approaches a coastline. As the wave nears the coastline, wave height increases and wavelength decreases.

Answer to Reading Check
Contact with the ocean floor slows down the bottom of the wave but not the top of the wave. Because of the difference in speed between the top and bottom of the wave, the top gets farther ahead of the bottom until the wave becomes unstable and falls over.

Key Resources

Technology
- Transparencies
  127 The Formation of Breakers

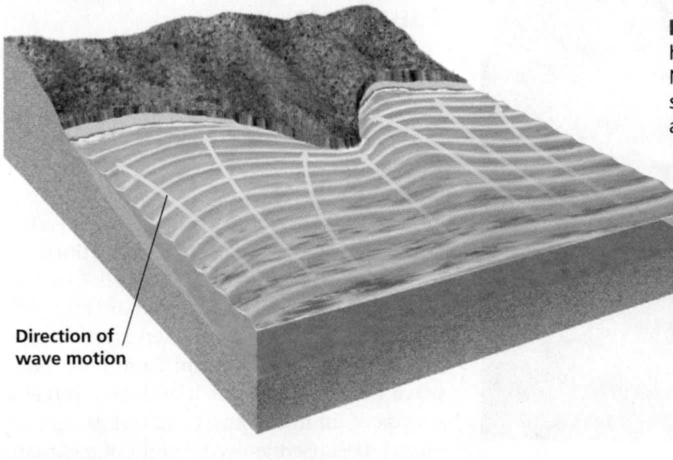

Figure 6 Waves strike the shore head-on as a result of refraction. Notice the waves approaching the shore at an angle. These waves bend as they draw closer to the shore.

Refraction

Most waves approach the coastline at an angle. When a wave reaches shallow water, however, the wave bends. This bending is called refraction. **Refraction** is the process by which ocean waves bend toward the coastline as they approach shallow water. As a wave approaches the coastline, the part of the wave that is in shallower water slows, and the part of the wave that is in deeper water maintains its speed. The wave gradually bends toward the beach and strikes the shore head-on, as shown in **Figure 6.**

refraction the process by which ocean waves bend directly toward the coastline as they approach shallow water

Undertows and Rip Currents

Water carried onto a beach by breaking waves is pulled back into deeper water by gravity. This motion forms an irregular current called an *undertow*. An undertow is seldom strong, and only along shorelines that have steep drop-offs do undertows create problems for swimmers.

The generally weak undertow is often confused with the more dangerous *rip current*. Rip currents form when water from large breakers returns to the ocean through channels that cut through underwater sandbars that are parallel to the beach. Rip currents flow perpendicular to the shore through those channels and may be strong enough to carry a swimmer away from the shore quickly. The presence of rip currents can usually be detected by a gap in a line of breakers or by turbid water—water in which sand has been stirred up by the current.

Longshore Currents

Longshore currents form when waves approach the beach at an angle. Longshore currents flow parallel to the shore. Great quantities of sand are carried by longshore currents. If there is a bay or inlet along the coastline where waves refract, sand will be deposited as the energy of the waves decreases. These sand deposits form low ridges of sand called *sandbars*.

Cultural Awareness — BASIC

Tsunamis The literal translation of tsunami is "harbor wave." This name refers to the fact that these gigantic waves can fill an entire harbor and bury low-lying coastal areas. People all over the world call these waves by their Japanese name. Show the famous Japanese print, Hokusai's "The Great Wave Off Kanagawa," which hangs in the Metropolitan Museum of Modern Art in New York. The print depicts a tsunami off the Japanese coast. Point out that this work has influenced the work of Western impressionist artists such as Monet and Degas.

Homework — ADVANCED

Longshore Currents Have students research and write a report about longshore currents and their effects on the environment. Students may work individually or as a group. Students should consider how wave action shapes beaches and affects other coastal landforms, what human efforts are being made to control the movements of sand and sediment, and why these efforts are being made. The report should show examples of localities that are replenishing beach sand and building sea walls, beach dunes, and jetties. **LS Logical/Verbal**

Discussion — BASIC

Water Safety Ask students to explain what a rip current is and how to identify one. (a strong seaward current created by channels underwater along sandbars or piers; muddy water caused by sand being stirred up, or a gap in a line of breakers) Encourage students to identify ways to protect themselves from these dangerous currents. (Learn to swim. Do not swim alone. If caught in a rip current, swim parallel to the beach until free.) **LS Logical**

Close

Reteaching — BASIC

Learn by Teaching Divide the class into pairs or small groups. Have each pair or group create a presentation for younger students that uses diagrams or demonstrations to explain how wind causes the formation of ocean waves and how waves affect coastlines and erode beaches. **LS Interpersonal**

Quiz — GENERAL

Ask students to write the letter of the best answer to each of the following questions.

1. What characteristic describes the distance between two consecutive wave crests?
   a. wave period
   b. wave height
   c. wavelength
   d. wave speed
2. What causes ocean waves to bend toward the shore as they approach shallow water?
   a. fetch
   b. reflection
   c. rip currents
   d. refraction
3. Which of these factors causes sand to be deposited in ridges called sandbars?
   a. decrease in wave energy
   b. increase in wave height
   c. decrease in wavelength
   d. slope of the ocean floor
4. What type of wave or wave action appears to affect both ocean temperature and global climate?
   a. breakers
   b. swells
   c. tsunamis
   d. whitecaps

Close, *continued*

Answers to Section Review

1. Wave speed equals wavelength divided by wave period.
2. Uneven heating of the atmosphere causes pressure differences that produce moving air, or winds. Waves form when friction between moving air and water causes ripples.
3. Three factors that determine wave size are length of time the wind blows in one direction; the speed of the wind; and the fetch, or distance the wind can blow across open water.
4. Most waves approach the coastline at an angle. As they get closer, the part in shallower water slows, while the part in deeper water keeps its speed. This causes the wave to bend gradually toward the shoreline.
5. Tsunamis are giant waves that are caused by underwater earthquakes, volcanic eruptions, and landslides.
6. Waves touch bottom at about one-half their wavelength. Contact with the ocean floor causes the wave to slow down.
7. No; where a wave breaks depends on original wave height and wavelength, which would vary over time.
8. Whitecaps reflect solar radiation, which allows less radiation to reach the ocean. If less thermal energy is transferred to the water, then there is less heat available to moderate climates along the path of the currents.
9. Two types of *waves* are *tsunamis* and *swells*, which have a constant *wave height*, which is the distance between a *crest* and a *trough*, and form when wind blows across a *fetch*, which may also form *whitecaps*.

Figure 7 The tsunami of 2004 left coastal communities of Sri Lanka in ruins. The tsunami was triggered by an earthquake that had a moment magnitude of 9.0.

SciLinks.
www.scilinks.org
Topic: Tsunamis
Code: **HQX1561**

Tsunamis

The most destructive waves in the ocean are not powered by the wind. *Tsunamis* are giant seismic ocean waves. Most tsunamis are caused by earthquakes on the ocean floor, but some can be caused by volcanic eruptions and underwater landslides. Tsunamis are commonly called *tidal waves*, which is misleading because tsunamis are not caused by tides.

Tsunamis have long wavelengths. In deep water, the wave height of a tsunami is usually less than 1 m, but the wavelength may be as long as 500 km. A tsunami commonly has a wave period of about 1 h and may travel at speeds of up to 890 km/h (as fast as a jet airplane). Because the wave height of a tsunami is so low in the open ocean, a tsunami cannot be felt by people aboard ships.

A Tsunami as a Destructive Force

A tsunami has a tremendous amount of energy. Because its wavelength is so long, the entire depth of the water is involved in the wave motion of a tsunami. All the energy of this mass of water is released against the shore and causes a great deal of destruction, as shown in **Figure 7.** Near the shore, the height of a tsunami greatly increases as the tsunami's speed decreases. As a tsunami approaches the shore, it may reach a height of 30 to 40 m. The arrival of a tsunami may be signaled by the sudden pulling back of the water along the shore. This pulling back occurs when the trough of the tsunami arrives before the crest. If the crest arrives first, a sudden, rapid rise in the water level occurs.

The tsunamis generated by the earthquakes in Chile in 1960 and in the Indian Ocean in 2004 caused widespread destruction. The Chilean tsunami struck the coast of South America and then Hawaii and crossed 17,000 km of ocean to strike Japan.

Section 2 Review

Key Ideas

1. **Explain** how wavelength and wave period can be used to calculate wave speed.
2. **Describe** the formation of waves.
3. **List** three factors that determine the size of a wave.
4. **Explain** why incoming waves refract toward the beach until they strike the shore head-on.
5. **Describe** what factors cause tsunamis.
6. **Explain** why waves slow down in shallow water.

Critical Thinking

7. **Analyzing Processes** Would the breakers on a specific beach always form at the same distance from the shore? Explain your answer.
8. **Predicting Consequences** Explain how whitecaps could affect climate.

Concept Mapping

9. Use the following terms to create a concept map: *wave, wave height, whitecap, trough, crest, fetch, swell,* and *tsunami.*

Differentiated Instruction

Alternative Assessment

Wave Haikus The Japanese poetry form *haiku* is a 3-line poem that has five syllables in the first line, seven syllables in the second line, and five syllables in the last line. Have students write a haiku about waves. Tell them to incorporate what they have learned about how waves form and move. Encourage students to illustrate their work with pen and ink drawings. **LS Verbal**

SECTION

3 Tides

Key Ideas	Key Terms	Why It Matters
❯ Describe how the gravitational pull of the moon causes tides. ❯ Compare spring tides and neap tides. ❯ Describe how tidal oscillations affect tidal patterns. ❯ Explain how the coastline affects tidal currents.	tide tidal range tidal oscillation tidal current	Tides are cyclical and predictable changes in sea level that are important not only to the plants and animals that live along the coast, but to people using the ocean as well.

The periodic rise and fall of the water level in the oceans is called the **tide.** *High tide* is when the water level is highest. *Low tide* is when the water level is lowest. The tide change is most noticeable on the coastline. If you stand on a beach long enough, you can see how the ocean retreats and returns with the tides.

The Causes of Tides

In the late 1600s, Isaac Newton identified the force that causes the rise and fall of tides along coastlines. According to Newton's law of gravitation, the gravitational pull of the moon on Earth and Earth's waters is the major cause of tides. The sun also causes tides, but they are smaller because the sun is so much farther from Earth than the moon is.

As the moon revolves around Earth, the moon exerts a gravitational pull on the entire Earth. However, because the force of the moon's gravity decreases with distance from the moon, the gravitational pull of the moon is stronger on the side of Earth that is nearer the moon. As a result, the ocean on Earth's near side bulges slightly, which causes a high tide within the area of the bulge.

tide the periodic rise and fall of the water level in the oceans and other large bodies of water

At the same time, another tidal bulge forms on the opposite side of Earth. This tidal bulge forms because the solid Earth, which acts as though all its mass were at Earth's center, is pulled more strongly toward the moon than the ocean water on Earth's far side is. The result is a smaller tidal bulge on Earth's far side. **Figure 1** shows the Earth-moon system and the position of the moon in relation to the tidal bulges.

Low tides form halfway between the two high tides. Low tides form because as ocean water flows toward the areas of high tide, the water level in other areas of the ocean drops.

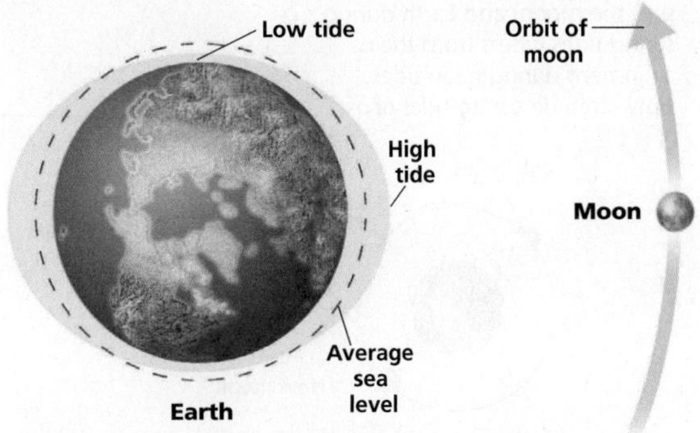

Figure 1 Because of Earth's rotation, most locations in the ocean have two high tides and two low tides daily.

Section 3

Focus

Overview

This section explains how the moon's gravitational pull affects the waters of Earth. The section describes the difference between spring and neap tides and identifies how variations in ocean depth, the shape of ocean basins, and coastline features affect tidal patterns.

Bellringer

Have students answer the following questions: What does the phrase "high and dry" mean? Where do you think this phrase comes from? (Boats anchored near shore during a high tide are left high and dry when the tide goes out.) **LS Intrapersonal**

Motivate

Using the Figure — GENERAL

Tidal Bulges The "circle of water" around the globe in the diagram uses artistic license to illustrate the concept of tidal bulges. The ocean is not really that deep. If it were, it would cover the land masses. At the scale in the figure, however, the tidal bulge would be too small to see if it were not exaggerated. **LS Visual**

Key Resources

Chapter Resource File
- Directed Reading BASIC

Technology
- Transparencies
  Bellringer

Differentiated Instruction

Advanced Learners

Graphing Provide students with a month's time of tidal and moon phase data. Have students graph the tidal data, indicating the time and height of high tide and low tide. Tell students to note the phase of the moon beside the appropriate dates. Have students analyze the data and record how many high and low tides occurred during a 24-hour period. Encourage them to note how the time for the tides vary each day and that the moon's phases correlate with the tidal cycle. **LS Logical**

Teach

Math Skills

Answer

10.8 min × 60 s/min = 648 s
6.5×10^7 years ÷ 6.48×10^2 s = $1.00308642 \times 10^{7-2} = 1.00308642 \times 10^5$ years;
Earth's rotation slows by 1 s in about 100,000 years.

Using the Figure GENERAL

Lunar Motions Ask students to analyze the illustration of spring tides and neap tides. Ask students to identify the phases of the moon that would coincide with the highest tides. (full moon and new moon) Answer to caption question: Spring tides occur twice a month. LS Visual

READING TOOLBOX

Cause and Effect Sample answer: Cause: the gravitational pull of the moon on Earth and its waters, Effect: the tides, Marker: is the major cause; Cause: the gravitational pull of the moon is strongest on the side of Earth that is nearest the moon, Effect: the ocean on Earth's near side bulges slightly, Marker: as a result

Answer to Reading Check

When the tidal range is small, the sun and the moon are at right angles to each other relative to Earth's orbit.

Key Resources

Technology

- Transparencies
  128 Spring Tides and Neap Tides

Math Skills

Tidal Friction As the tidal bulges move around Earth, friction between the water and the ocean floor slows Earth's rotation slightly. Scientists estimate that the average length of a day has increased by 10.8 min in the last 65 million years. How many years does it take for Earth's rotation to slow by 1 s?

Behavior of Tides

Earth rotates on its axis once every 24 h. In that 24 h, the moon moves through about 1/29 of its orbit. Because the moon orbits Earth in the same direction that Earth rotates, all areas of the ocean pass under the moon every 24 h 50 min. As seen from above the North Pole, Earth rotates counterclockwise and the tidal bulges appear to move westward around Earth.

Because there are two tidal bulges, most locations in the ocean have two high tides and two low tides daily. The difference in the levels of the ocean water at high tide and low tide is called the **tidal range.** The tidal range can vary widely from place to place. Because the moon rises about 50 min later each day, the times of high and low tides are also about 50 min later each day.

tidal range the difference in levels of ocean water at high tide and low tide

Spring Tides

The sun's gravitational pull can add to or subtract from the moon's influence on the tides. During the new moon and the full moon, Earth, the sun, and the moon are aligned, as shown in **Figure 2.** The combined gravitational pull of the sun and the moon results in higher high tides and lower low tides. So, the daily tidal range is greatest during the new moon and the full moon. During these two monthly periods, the tides are called *spring tides.*

READING TOOLBOX

Cause and Effect
As you read this section, add the sentences that describe the multiple causes and effects of tides, tidal variations, and tidal currents to the table that you started at the beginning of the chapter.

Neap Tides

During the first-quarter and third-quarter phases of the moon, the moon and the sun are at right angles to each other in relation to Earth, also shown in **Figure 2.** The gravitational forces of the sun and the moon work against each other. As a result, the daily tidal range is small. The tides that occur during this time are called *neap tides.*

Reading Check **Describe the location of the sun and the moon in relation to Earth when the tidal range is small.**

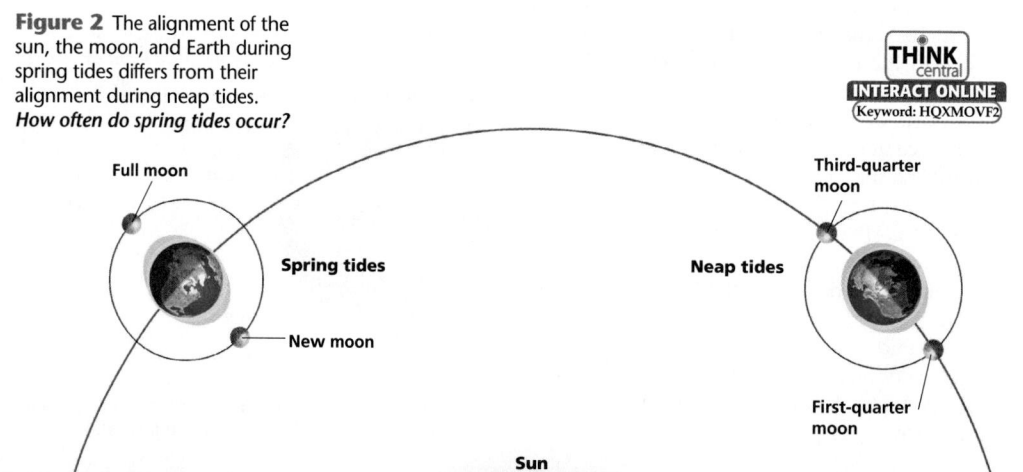

Figure 2 The alignment of the sun, the moon, and Earth during spring tides differs from their alignment during neap tides. *How often do spring tides occur?*

THINK central INTERACT ONLINE (Keyword: HQXMOVF2)

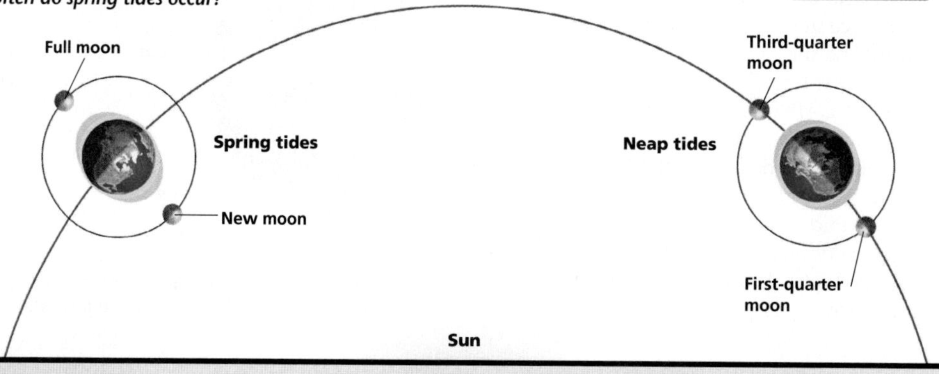

MISCONCEPTION ALERT

Spring Tides Students may think that spring tides have something to do with the season of spring. Emphasize that spring tides occur at all seasons of the year around the time of new and full moons.

Tidal Variations

Although the global ocean is one body of water, continents and irregularities in the ocean floor divide the ocean into several basins. The tidal pattern in an area is greatly influenced by the size, shape, depth, and location of the ocean basin in which the tides occur.

Along the Atlantic coast of the United States, two high tides and two low tides occur each day and have a fairly regular tidal range. Along the shore of the Gulf of Mexico, however, only one high tide and one low tide occur each day. Along the Pacific coast, the tides follow a mixed pattern of tidal ranges. Pacific coast tides commonly have a very high tide followed by a very low tide and then a lower high tide, followed by a higher low tide.

Tidal Oscillations

Tidal patterns are also affected by tidal oscillations. **Tidal oscillations** (TIE duhl AHS uh LAY shunz) are slow, rocking motions of ocean water that occur as the tidal bulges move around the ocean basins. Along straight coastlines and in the open ocean, the effects of tidal oscillations are not very obvious. In some enclosed seas, such as the Baltic and Mediterranean Seas, tidal oscillations reduce the effects of the tidal bulges. As a result, these seas have a very small tidal range. In small basins and narrow bays located off major ocean basins, however, tidal oscillations may amplify the effects of the tidal bulges. An example of the effects of tidal oscillations is shown in **Figure 3.**

Figure 3 A great tidal range of as much as 15 m in the V-shaped Bay of Fundy in Canada is caused by tidal oscillations.

tidal oscillation the slow, rocking motion of ocean water that occurs as the tidal bulges move around the ocean basins

Why It Matters

Spring Spawn

EYE ON THE ENVIRONMENT

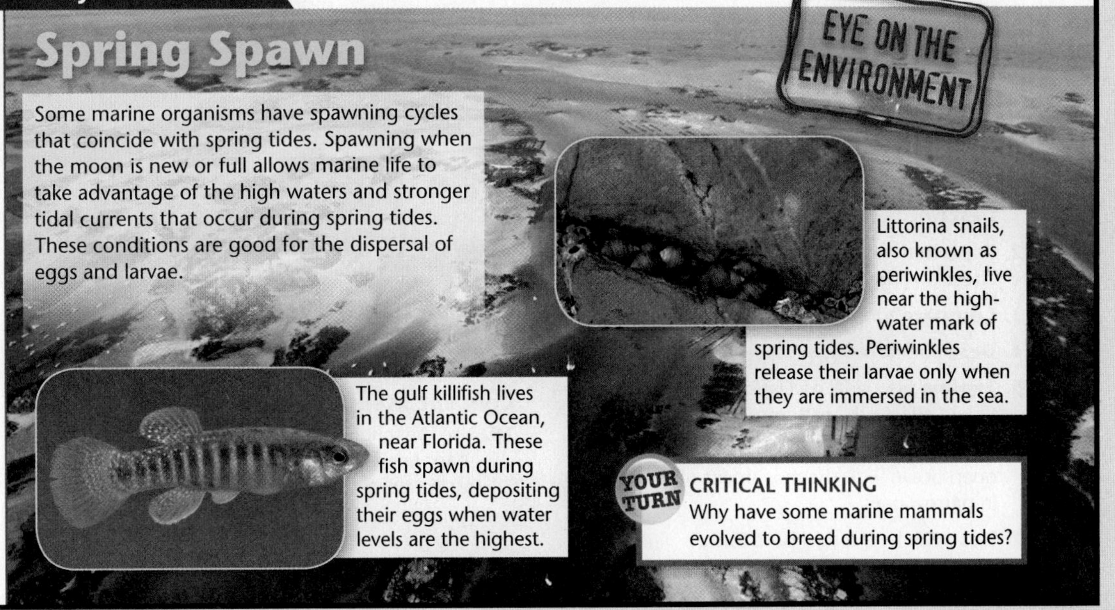

Some marine organisms have spawning cycles that coincide with spring tides. Spawning when the moon is new or full allows marine life to take advantage of the high waters and stronger tidal currents that occur during spring tides. These conditions are good for the dispersal of eggs and larvae.

Littorina snails, also known as periwinkles, live near the high-water mark of spring tides. Periwinkles release their larvae only when they are immersed in the sea.

The gulf killifish lives in the Atlantic Ocean, near Florida. These fish spawn during spring tides, depositing their eggs when water levels are the highest.

YOUR TURN **CRITICAL THINKING**
Why have some marine mammals evolved to breed during spring tides?

Why It Matters

Spring Spawn Gulf killifish (*Fundulus grandis*), are small fish found in along the coast of Florida and Texas. These fish spawn from March to October, laying eggs during spring tides in thick beds of marsh grass. The eggs develop over the next two weeks, exposed to moist, humid air, and hatch at the next spring tide. The common periwinkle (*Littorina littorea)* lives in the intertidal zone of rocky shores. These snails spawn several times a year, releasing eggs during spring tides. Female snails may produce up to 100,000 eggs per year.

Answers to Your Turn

Critical Thinking Some marine mammals have evolved to breed during spring tides to coincide and take advantage of the greater availability of food that becomes available due to marine organisms which spawn during the spring tides.

Discussion — GENERAL

Bay of Fundy Use the two photographs on this page to initiate a discussion about why tides in the Bay of Fundy are among the highest in the world. Explain that the period of the tidal oscillation depends on the basin's length and depth. The rocking movement in the Bay of Fundy coincides with the tides, which drives the water farther into the bay, reinforcing the lunar tide. **LS Logical**

Close

Reteaching — BASIC

Tidal Games Divide the class into pairs. Have students work together to prepare questions, with answers, about causes of tides and tidal patterns. Have them use the questions in a game show style review to study for the section assessment. **LS Auditory/ Interpersonal**

Quiz — GENERAL

Determine whether each of the following statements is true or false. If false, correct the statement to make the statement true.

1. The major cause of tides is the gravitational pull of the sun. (false, moon)
2. When the sun and moon are in line with each other, neap tides occur. (false, spring tides)
3. Movement of tidal waters toward the coast is known as ebb tide. (false, flood tide)

Close, *continued*

Answers to Section Review

1. As the moon revolves around Earth, its gravity exerts a pull on Earth's waters. Two high tidal bulges are created on opposite sides of the planet. Low tides occur in between.
2. The sun contributes to the size of tides by pulling on Earth's waters in the same direction as the moon or in the opposite direction.
3. When the sun and moon pull together in a straight line, high spring tides occur. When the sun and moon are arranged at right angles to each other, their pulls oppose, causing lower neap tides.
4. Variations in the size, shape, depth, and location of the ocean basins with respect to landmasses affect the number of tides, as well as tidal range.
5. In enclosed seas, tidal oscillations reduce the effects of the tidal bulges, producing small tidal range.
6. Tidal currents in open oceans are much smaller than those at the coasts. In narrow bays, tidal oscillations magnify the effects of tidal bulges, producing larger tidal ranges than in the open ocean.
7. Where a river enters an ocean through a long bay, a surge of tidal water may flow upstream in a wave called a *tidal bore.*
8. Where adjacent coastal regions have differences in heights of the tides, ships approaching these coasts must watch out for strong tidal currents. Also, in bays or areas that have narrow coastlines, ships must deal with rapid tidal currents.
9. Answers may vary. Accept all reasonable answers.
10. The moon's gravity produces *tides*, which result in *tidal ranges* that are affected by *spring tides, neap tides, tidal oscillations*, and *tidal currents*, which include *ebb tides* and *flood tides.*

Figure 4 The photo to the right shows a tidal bore in early spring at Turnagain Arm of Cook Inlet, Alaska.

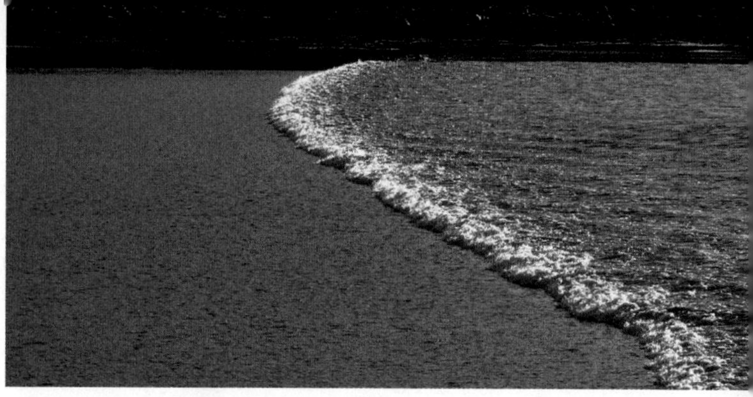

SCILINKS
www.scilinks.org
Topic: Tides
Code: HQX1525

Tidal Currents

tidal current the movement of water toward and away from the coast as a result of the rise and fall of the tides

As ocean water rises and falls with the tides, it flows toward and away from the coast. This movement of the water is called a **tidal current.** When the tidal current flows toward the coast, it is called *flood tide*. When the tidal current flows toward the ocean, it is called *ebb tide*. When there are no tidal currents, the time period between flood tide and ebb tide is called *slack water*.

Tidal currents in the open ocean are much smaller than those at the coastline. Tidal currents are strongest between two adjacent coastal regions that have large differences in the height of the tides. In bays and along other narrow coastlines, tides may create rapid currents. Some tidal currents may reach speeds of 20 km/h.

Where a river enters the ocean through a long bay, the tide may enter the river mouth and create a *tidal bore*, a surge of water that rushes upstream, such as the one shown in **Figure 4.** In some areas, the tidal bore rushes upstream in the form of a large wave, up to 5 m high, that eventually loses energy. The tidal bores in the River Severn in England travel almost 20 km/h and reach as far as 33 km inland.

Academic Vocabulary

energy (EN uhr jee) the capacity to do work

Section 3 Review

Key Ideas

1. **Describe** how the moon causes tides.
2. **Explain** how the sun can influence the moon's effect on tides.
3. **Compare** spring tides and neap tides.
4. **Describe** how ocean basins affect tidal patterns.
5. **Explain** how tidal oscillations in an enclosed sea would affect tidal patterns in that sea.
6. **Compare** the movement of ocean water in the open ocean with the movement of ocean water in narrow bays.
7. **Describe** how a tidal bore forms.

Critical Thinking

8. **Predicting Consequences** Predict where tidal currents may be a concern to ships that are approaching the land.
9. **Identifying Relationships** Describe ways in which tides could be affected if Earth had two moons.

Concept Mapping

10. Use the following terms to create a concept map: *tide, tidal range, spring tide, neap tide, tidal oscillation, tidal current, flood tide,* and *ebb tide.*

Differentiated Instruction

Alternative Assessment

Making Mobiles Have students create mobiles of the sun-Earth-moon system to illustrate how the relationships among these three bodies cause tides to form. Remind them that Earth and the moon spin around a common center of gravity. Have students use these models to explain tides. **LS Kinesthetic**

Why It Matters

Monster Waves: Myth or Fact?

REAL WORLD

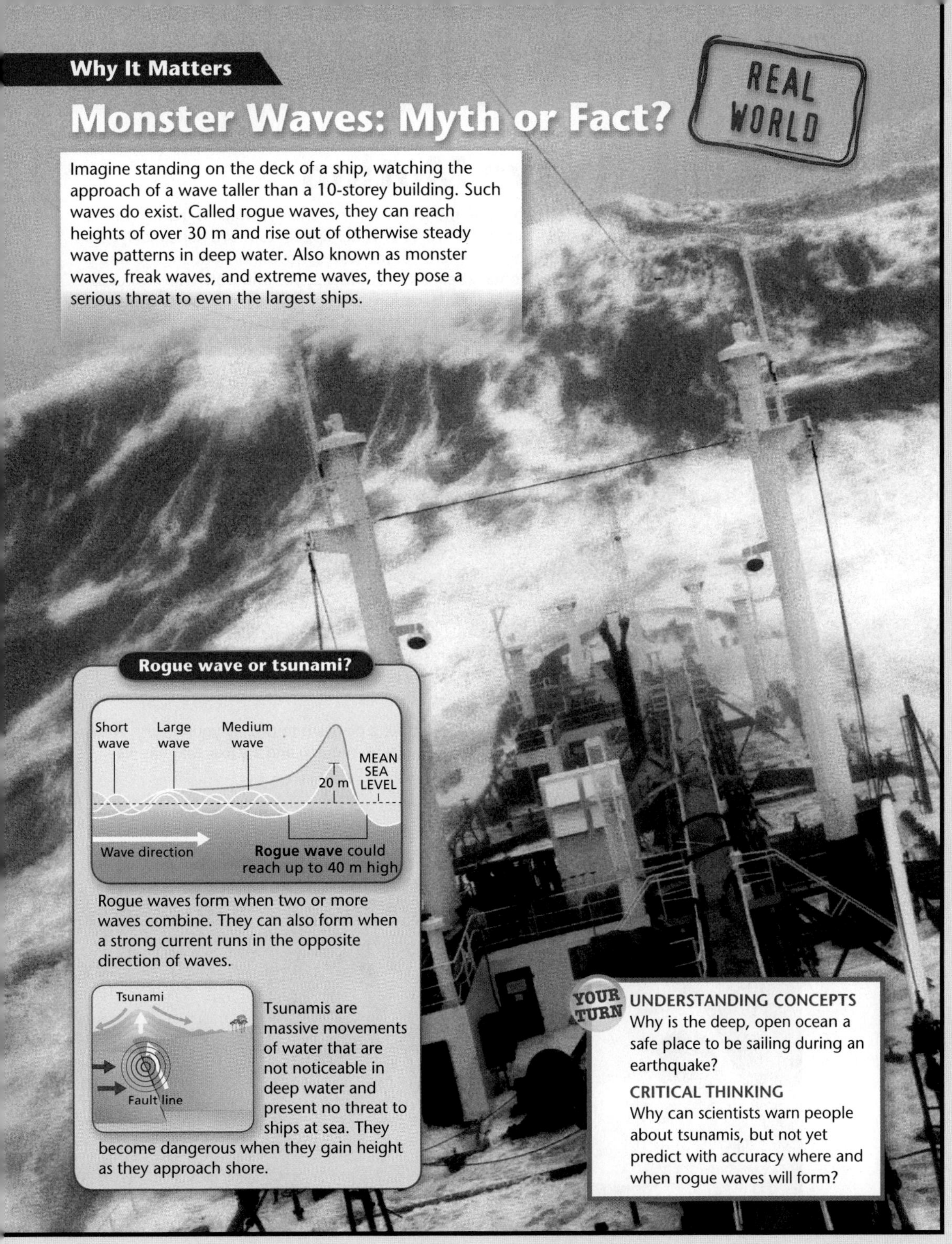

Imagine standing on the deck of a ship, watching the approach of a wave taller than a 10-storey building. Such waves do exist. Called rogue waves, they can reach heights of over 30 m and rise out of otherwise steady wave patterns in deep water. Also known as monster waves, freak waves, and extreme waves, they pose a serious threat to even the largest ships.

Rogue wave or tsunami?

Rogue waves form when two or more waves combine. They can also form when a strong current runs in the opposite direction of waves.

Tsunamis are massive movements of water that are not noticeable in deep water and present no threat to ships at sea. They become dangerous when they gain height as they approach shore.

YOUR TURN

UNDERSTANDING CONCEPTS
Why is the deep, open ocean a safe place to be sailing during an earthquake?

CRITICAL THINKING
Why can scientists warn people about tsunamis, but not yet predict with accuracy where and when rogue waves will form?

Why It Matters

Monster Waves: Myth or Fact? Rogue waves are defined not by overall size, but as waves whose height is more than twice the significant wave height (the mean of the largest third of waves in a wave record). Previously the stuff of mariner's tales, the existence of rogue waves has been identified as a natural ocean phenomenon. The cause of rogue waves is still a matter of active research, and the theory of either common causes or geographic variation is still being developed. Areas of highest predictable risk appear to be where a strong current runs counter to the primary direction of travel of the waves. This is not the full answer though, since this does not explain the existence of all waves that have been detected. It is likely there are several mechanisms that can produce rogue waves coupled with localized variation. For example, waves traveling in the same direction at different speeds may synchronize and merge to form one large wave.

Answers to Your Turn

Understanding Concepts The open ocean is a safe place to be during an earthquake because in deep water tsunamis are typically no more than 1m high and cause no damage. It is only when a tsunami gets close to shore that it gathers height and becomes dangerous.

Critical Thinking Scientists can predict tsunamis by monitoring seismic events. The cause of rogue waves is not as clear or as readily detectable. While a strong current running counter to the primary direction of travel of the waves is one indicator of risk it is not the only set of circumstances that may lead to a rogue wave. Rogue waves are also influenced by changing ocean conditions, such as hurricanes and geographic variation; both of which make prediction even more difficult.

Making Models Lab

Time Required
one 45-minute lab period

Lab Ratings
EASY → HARD

Teacher Preparation 1 of 4 flasks
Student Setup 1 of 4 flasks
Concept Level 2 of 4 flasks
Cleanup 1 of 4 flasks

Skills Acquired
- Experimenting
- Collecting Data
- Organizing and Analyzing Data
- Analyzing Relationships
- Interpreting
- Communicating

Scientific Methods
In this lab, students will
- Make Observations
- Analyze the Results
- Draw Conclusions

Materials
The materials listed are enough for groups of two to four students. You could substitute small wooden beads with a diameter large enough to slip over rope for ties.

Tips and Tricks
You may wish to review graphing techniques with students before they begin this lab.

Making Models Lab

45 min

Wave Motion

The source of wave motion in water is energy, which is generated primarily from wind. Waves of water appear to move horizontally. However, only the energy of the waves moves horizontally; the water moves horizontally very little. In this lab, you will work with two classmates to simulate wave motion and to observe how energy generates wave motion in water. You will also observe the properties of waves.

What You'll Do
- **Model** the movement of waves.
- **Compare** the characteristics of waves when wave speed changes.

What You'll Need
cloth ties, about 50 cm in length (2)
marker
meterstick
paper, 2 m × 1 m
paper, graph
pen or pencil, colored (3)
rope, thin, 2.5 m in length

Procedure

1. Tie one end of the rope securely to the leg of a chair or table.
2. On the large sheet of paper, use the meterstick to draw a grid like the one shown in the illustration on the next page. The vertical axis should be 2 m long, with marks at intervals of 0.25 m. The horizontal axis should be 1 m long, with marks at intervals of 0.125 m.
3. Place the sheet of paper on the floor, and line up the rope along the 2 m line of the grid.
4. To make waves, move the free end of the rope from side to side. (Note: Be sure to maintain a constant motion with the rope.)
5. While one person moves the rope, another person marks the paper where a crest of a wave hits. The third person marks the paper where a trough of a wave hits.
6. On the graph paper, make a diagram to display your results, with an *x* axis that has wavelength (in meters) and a *y* axis that has wave height (in meters).
7. Plot a wave that represents the wave you observed in step 5. Plot the wave height and the wavelength. Indicate the direction of the wave motion.

Step 5

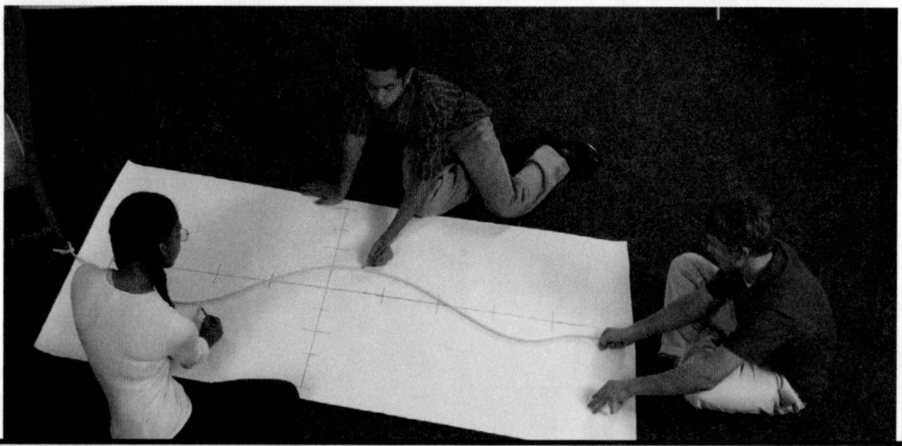

8. Move the rope at a fast speed. Do not change the side-to-side distance that you move the free end of the rope.
9. As soon as a constant motion has been established, repeat step 5. On your diagram, plot a wave that represents the wave you observed when repeating step 5. Use a pen or pencil that is a different color from the color of the first wave plot.
10. Next, generate very small waves. Repeat step 5 and plot the wave, using a third color of pen or pencil.
11. On your diagram, label a crest and a trough on each of the waves you plotted.
12. Use the following formula to calculate the wave speeds of the three waves you plotted, if each wave period is 6 s:

$$wave\ speed = \frac{wavelength}{wave\ period}$$

13. Tie the two pieces of cloth around the middle of the rope, about 15 cm apart.
14. Make waves by moving the end of the rope from side to side. Observe and record the motion of the cloth relative to the motion of the waves.

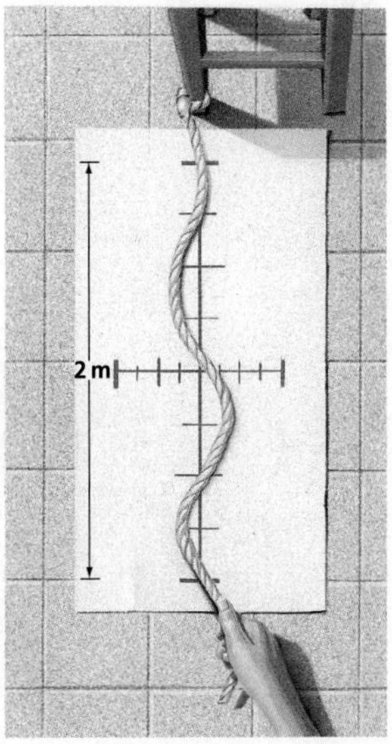

Analysis

1. **Examining Data** How do the waves you plotted differ from each other? If these waves were real water waves, what might be the cause(s) of the differences?
2. **Recognizing Relationships** How is the motion of the rope similar to wave motion in water?
3. **Analyzing Relationships** How does the motion of the cloth differ from the motion of the wave?
4. **Drawing Conclusions** What does the motion of the cloth tell you about wave motion in water?

Extension

Making Comparisons Use a 4 m rope to repeat the investigation. Construct a diagram similar to your first diagram, but extend the *x*-axis to provide room to plot a 4 m length. Observe and plot five waves of varying speeds and heights. Compare waves generated on a 2 m rope with those generated on a 4 m rope. Describe your results. Using 6 s as the wave period for each wave you plot, calculate wave speeds.

Answers to Analysis

1. Answers may vary. Students should note that wave motion in the water varies according to certain wind factors such as strength, fetch, and the length of time the wind blows.
2. The waves created on the rope moved toward the secured end, just as waves move toward the shore. Also, the energy of hand movements determines the speed of the rope motion, just as energy from the wind determines the speed of waves.
3. The ties move from side to side, while the waves move along the rope toward the chair or table leg.
4. As waves pass, the ties move side to side with little forward movement. These motions show that water molecules actually move forward very little as a wave passes.

Answer to Extension

Answers may vary. Students should note that the extra length of the rope enables them to create more varied waveforms in terms of speed and height.

Roaming Rubber Duckies

Internet Activity ADVANCED

Beachcomber Tales Ask students to research how other types of floating objects—from seeds and bottles to toys, hockey equipment, and candy—have helped add to the understanding of ocean currents. Tell them to collect any unusual stories in booklet form and to add their own drawings to illustrate the tales. A worksheet designed to direct student research on this topic can be found in the **Chapter Resource File** booklet or by visiting www.thinkcentral.com and entering the keyword **HQXMOVX.** **LS Verbal/ Visual**

Answers to Map Skills Activity

1. A container ship spilled the bathtub toys in the middle of the North Pacific Ocean on January 10, 1992.
2. 9 months
3. North Equatorial Current
4. The California Current is a cold water current because it is shown in blue on the ocean current map, and because it flows away from the pole but has not yet reached the waters around the Equator.
5. Some of the toys might have floated north past Japan and back toward where they were first dropped.
6. Oyashio Current
7. The toys traveled from January 10, 1992 to July 26, 2003—about 11 years and 6 months, or 4,215 days.

MAPS in Action

Roaming Rubber Duckies

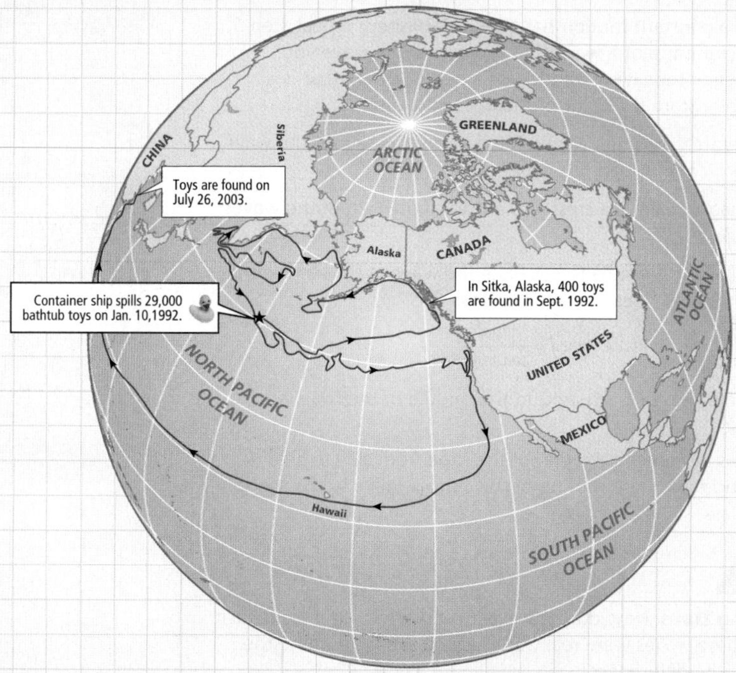

Map Skills Activity

This map shows the estimated route taken by bathtub toys spilled from a cargo ship in the North Pacific Ocean. Use the map to answer the questions below.

1. **Analyzing Data** Describe where the toys started their journey.
2. **Evaluating Data** How long did it take the toys to travel to Sitka, Alaska, by the most direct route?
3. **Identifying Relationships** Compare the map above with the map of the major surface currents in the section entitled "Ocean Currents." Then, name the current that carried the toys past Hawaii.
4. **Evaluating Sources** Is the current that carried the toys along the coast of the western United States cold or warm? Explain your answer.
5. **Predicting Consequences** Predict where the toys might have been located in December 2003 if tracking data were plotted on the map.
6. **Identifying Relationships** What is the name of the current that carried the toys south along the coast of Siberia?
7. **Evaluating Data** How long did it take the toys to travel from the location where they were spilled to their location on the coast of China on July 26, 2003?

Key Resources

Technology

- Transparencies
  129 Roaming Rubber Duckies

Chapter 25

Summary

THINK central SUPER SUMMARY Keyword: HQXMOVS

Key Ideas | **Key Terms**

Section 1

Ocean Currents

- As wind blows, it moves surface water in the ocean in the same direction. Continents deflect and divide surface currents. The Coriolis effect causes surface currents to curve as they flow.
- Surface currents are wind-driven currents.
- Deep currents are produced as dense water near the North and South Poles sinks and moves toward the equator beneath less dense water.

current, p. 689
surface current, p. 689
Coriolis effect, p. 690
gyre, p. 690
Gulf Stream, p. 692
deep current, p. 693

Section 2

Ocean Waves

- Wind is the primary source of wave energy. Wave size is determined by wind speed, by the length of time that wind blows, and fetch.
- As a wave comes into contact with the ocean floor, the wave may undergo refraction or form breakers. Waves near the shoreline can cause currents, such as an undertow and a rip current.
- Tsunamis, which are caused by earthquakes on the ocean floor, volcanic eruptions, and underwater landslides, are giant, destructive waves.

wave, p. 695
wave period, p. 695
fetch, p. 697
refraction, p. 699

Section 3

Tides

- The gravitational pull of the moon is strongest on the side of Earth that is nearer the moon. As a result, the ocean on this side bulges slightly, which causes a high tide within the area of the bulge. At the same time, a smaller tidal bulge forms on the opposite side of Earth.
- Tidal ranges are greatest during spring tides and smallest during neap tides.
- In some enclosed seas, tidal oscillations reduce the effects of tidal bulges, resulting in a very small tidal range. In small basins and narrow bays located off major ocean basins, tidal oscillations may amplify the effects of the tidal bulges.
- Tidal currents are generally small in the open ocean but may create rapid currents in narrow bays along the coastline.

tide, p. 701
tidal range, p. 702
tidal oscillation, p. 703
tidal current, p. 704

Chapter Summary

Using THINK central Resources

Super Summary

Have students connect the major concepts in this chapter through an interactive Super Summary. Visit **www.thinkcentral.com** and type in the keyword **HQXMOVS** to access the Super Summary for this chapter.

Activity — GENERAL

Wave Dioramas Have groups of students create dioramas or models representing the movement of waves, tides, and currents and their effects on coastal areas. Students may have seen representations like these in museums. They can use empty shoeboxes to construct their displays. Those groups that are illustrating tides may create astronomical models. Encourage students to draw a sketch or plan before they start building their model. They can remove the box top to create a large viewing window, and use marking pens, paints, and construction paper to decorate the back and the sides of the shoebox. Students can use pictures cut from magazines or draw typical seashore scenery inside. The setting might also include foreground sand and small rocks to represent a beach. After students finish the background, they can use modeling clay or other art materials to create models of the typical seaside land features. They can also add charts, diagrams, or captions to help viewers interpret their work.
LS Visual

Chapter Review

Assignment Guide	
Section	**Question**
1	1, 2, 3, 6–8, 10–13, 16, 17, 20, 22, 25, 28, 30
2	5, 14, 15, 18, 21, 23, 26, 31
3	4, 9, 19, 24, 27, 32–38
1–3	29

Reading Toolbox

1. Student tables will vary but should include terms such as surface current, deep current, rip currents, longshore currents, tidal currents.

Using Key Terms

2–9. Answers may vary but should show that students understand the definitions of and differences between key terms.

Understanding Key Concepts

10. a 14. d
11. c 15. c
12. c 16. c
13. b 17. b

Short Answer

18. Breakers form as waves approach the coast. As a wave moves into shallow water, the bottom of the wave is slowed. The top of the wave continues at its original speed. The top gets farther ahead of the bottom, until the wave becomes unstable and topples over.
19. A tide is the regular rise and fall of the level of the ocean in response to the gravitational pull of the moon on Earth's waters. This produces two tidal bulges on opposite sides of Earth. Low tides form as ocean waters flow toward the areas of high tide.
20. Ocean surface currents are controlled by global wind patterns; by Earth's spinning motion, which cause the currents to flow in huge circles called *gyres*; and by the location of continents, which act as barriers to the current flow.
21. As waves approach a coast, the part in shallow water slows down. The part that is in deeper water maintains its speed, causing the waves to bend, or refract.
22. Deep currents form as a result of water density differences. The denser water sinks and flows below the less-dense water. Factors that produce these density differences include salt concentration, temperature differences, and turbidity.
23. Uneven heating of the atmosphere produces pressure differences that cause winds. Winds transfer their energy to the ocean water through friction between moving air and the water surface.
24. A tidal bore is a surge of ocean water that rushes upstream through a narrow bay or river mouth.

Critical Thinking

25. The direction of monsoon winds will directly affect the direction in which surface currents flow in the northern part of the Indian Ocean. The surface currents will change direction when winds change direction with the seasons.

Chapter 25 Review

1. **Word Families** Create a table for key terms and italicized words that belong to the word family of the key term *current*. Add the words that are combined with *current* (such as *surface, deep, rip, longshore,* and *tidal*) and their definitions to your table. Combine these words with *current,* and write your own definitions of the new terms. Then compare your definitions with the definitions given in the chapter. READING TOOLBOX

USING KEY TERMS

Use each of the following terms in a separate sentence.

2. *current*
3. *gyre*
4. *tide*
5. *wave*

For each pair of terms, explain how the meanings of the terms differ.

6. *surface current* and *deep current*
7. *Coriolis effect* and *gyre*
8. *fetch* and *refraction*
9. *tidal range* and *tidal oscillation*

UNDERSTANDING KEY IDEAS

10. The water in the ocean moves in giant streams called
    a. currents.
    b. westerlies.
    c. waves.
    d. tides.
11. The effect of Earth's rotation on winds and ocean currents is called the
    a. neap-tide effect.
    b. refraction effect.
    c. Coriolis effect.
    d. tsunami effect.
12. Which of the following currents is the westward warm-water current in the North Atlantic Gyre?
    a. Canary Current
    b. North Atlantic Current
    c. North Equatorial Current
    d. Gulf Stream
13. Deep currents are the result of
    a. the Coriolis effect.
    b. changes in the density of ocean water.
    c. the trade winds.
    d. neap tides.
14. The periodic disturbance in water as energy is transmitted through the water is a
    a. current. **c.** fetch.
    b. breaker. **d.** wave.
15. The highest point of a wave is the
    a. trough. **c.** crest.
    b. period. **d.** length.
16. The distance that a wind blows across an area of the ocean to generate waves is the
    a. trough. **c.** fetch.
    b. sargassum. **d.** wave period.
17. The movement of water toward and away from the coast due to tidal forces is called a
    a. tidal bore.
    b. tidal current.
    c. tidal range.
    d. tidal oscillation.

SHORT ANSWER

18. Describe how a breaker forms.
19. Define *tide,* and explain why tides form.
20. What factors control most ocean surface currents?
21. How does the depth of the ocean affect the shape and speed of a wave?
22. How do deep currents form?
23. Explain how wind is the primary source of wave energy.
24. What is a tidal bore?

CRITICAL THINKING

25. Determining Cause and Effect During winter in the northern Indian Ocean, winds called *monsoons* blow in a direction opposite to the direction that they blow during summer. What effect do these winds have on surface currents?

26. Analyzing Processes Suppose that a retaining wall is built along a shoreline. What will happen to waves as they pass over the retaining wall?

27. Making Inferences Imagine that you are fishing from a small boat anchored off the shore in the Gulf of Mexico. You are lulled to sleep by the gently rocking boat but wake up to find your boat on wet sand. What happened?

28. Making Predictions If Earth rotated in the direction opposite to the direction that it now rotates, what effect would this have on the movement of ocean currents?

CONCEPT MAPPING

29. Use the following terms to create a concept map: *currents, surface currents, trade winds, deep currents, Coriolis effect, wave, breaker, rip current, tide, Antarctic Bottom Water,* and *tidal current.*

MATH SKILLS

30. Applying Quantities The Gulf Stream can move 100 million cubic meters of water per second. The Mississippi River moves 15,400 m^3 of water per second. How many times more water per second does the Gulf Stream move than the Mississippi River does?

31. Making Calculations If a wave has a wavelength of 216 m and a period of 12 s, what is the speed of the wave?

WRITING SKILLS

32. Writing from Research Write a report on the tidal power plant project at La Rance, France. Describe the amount of electricity provided by the project and the impact the project has on the environment of the area.

33. Outlining Topics Create an outline that shows the steps of tide formation. Provide diagrams as needed to illustrate the steps.

INTERPRETING GRAPHICS

The graph below shows the measurements of tides in one location on the Atlantic coast of North America. Use this graph to answer the questions that follow.

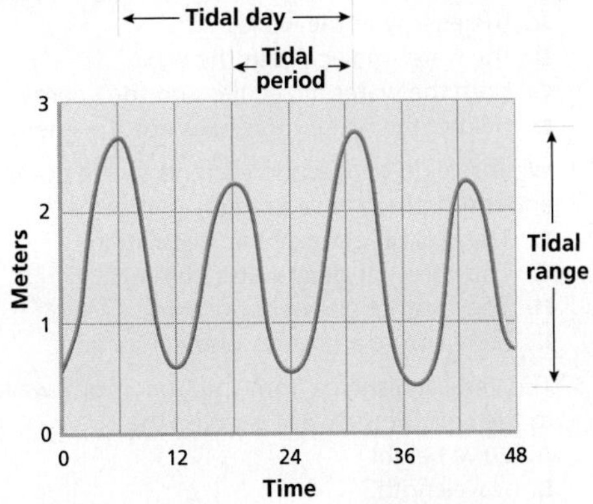

34. How many high tides occur every day in this location?

35. How many hours is the tidal period?

36. How many hours apart are the low tides?

37. What is the average tidal range, in meters?

38. What is the difference in height, in meters, between the first high tide and the second high tide?

Chapter Review

26. Answers may vary. Sample answer: Retaining walls represent a barrier between waves and the shore. The waves are deflected back from the walls onto the adjoining beaches.

27. There is only one high tide and one low tide in the Gulf of Mexico. The boat was anchored offshore during high tide, and the ebb tide swept the waters away from the coast, leaving the boat aground on the sand.

28. If Earth rotated in the opposite direction, both the global wind patterns and the surface currents would be affected. Gyres would flow counterclockwise in the Northern Hemisphere and clockwise in the Southern Hemisphere.

Concept Mapping

29. Answers may vary but should include all of the terms listed. Sample answers appear at the end of this unit on p. 715A.

Math Skills

30. $100{,}000{,}000\ m^3/s \div 15{,}400\ m^3/s = 6{,}494$ times as much water

31. $\textit{wave speed} = \frac{\text{wavelength } (\lambda)}{\text{wave period}}$

$\textit{wave speed} = 216\ m \div 12\ s = 18\ m/s$

Writing Skills

32. Answers may vary. Accept all reasonable answers based upon student research.

33. Answers may vary. Accept all reasonable answers. Outlines should include key steps in the process of tide formation and illustrative diagrams as needed.

Interpreting Graphics

34. 2 high tides daily

35. 12 hours

36. 12 hours

37. 2 meters

38. 0.4 meters

Standardized Test Prep

Estimated Time

To give students practice under more realistic testing conditions, allow them 30 minutes to answer all of the questions in this practice test.

Test Doctor

Question 2 Answer H is correct. The time required for two consecutive wave crests to pass a given point is the wave period. Wave speed is calculated by dividing the wavelength by the wave period. Answers must be given in units of length divided by time, such as meters per second.

Question 3 Answer A is correct. Energy from wind moves the wave across the ocean surface and passes from molecule to molecule as the wave moves horizontally. A water molecule moves in a circle and ends up where it started, but the molecule moves very little, if at all, in the direction of the wave.

Question 4 Answer F is true because when the sun heats Earth's surface, the surface heats the atmosphere above it. This causes winds that circulate air. Answer G is incorrect because convection currents actually help drive deep-water currents. Answer H is incorrect because they redistribute energy globally. Answer I is incorrect because precipitation is not balanced across the Earth's surface.

Chapter 25 Standardized Test Prep

Understanding Concepts

Directions (1–5): For each question, write on a separate sheet of paper the letter of the correct answer.

1. Which of the following factors affects the movement of surface currents?
   A. Earth's rotation on its axis
   B. water salinity
   C. human activity
   D. sea-floor spreading
2. What is the speed of an ocean wave that has 12 s between crests and a wavelength of 216 m?
   F. 6 m/s
   G. 3 km
   H. 18 m/s
   I. 12 m
3. When an ocean wave travels 100 m west, which of the following also travels 100 m west?
   A. the energy in the wave
   B. the water molecules in the wave
   C. both the water molecules and the energy
   D. neither the water molecules nor the energy
4. What role do convection currents in the ocean and atmosphere have in regulating climate?
   F. They set up atmospheric circulation.
   G. They prevent deep-water currents.
   H. They restrict energy to local use.
   I. They ensure a balance of precipitation.
5. The vertical distance from the trough of a wave to the crest of the wave is called the
   A. wave height.
   B. wavelength.
   C. wave speed.
   D. wave distance.

Directions (6–8): For each question, write a short response.

6. What is a main factor that causes the movements of deep-water currents?
7. What happens to the height of a wave as the wave approaches the shore?
8. Most waves are generated by energy that is transferred to water from what?

Reading Skills

Directions (9–11): Read the passage below. Then, answer the questions.

Tsunamis

Tsunamis are the most destructive waves in the ocean. Most tsunamis are caused by earthquakes on the ocean floor, but some can be caused by volcanic eruptions and underwater landslides. Tsunamis are sometimes called *tidal waves*, which is misleading because tsunamis have no connection to tides.

Tsunamis commonly have a wave period of about 1 h and a wave speed of about 890 km/h, which is about as fast as a commercial airplane. By the time a tsunami reaches the shore, the tsunami's height may be 40 m.

Tsunamis can travel thousands of kilometers. One tsunami was triggered by an earthquake off the coast of South America in 1960. The tsunami was so powerful that it crossed the Pacific Ocean and hit the city of Hilo, on the coast of Hawaii, approximately 10,000 km away. The same tsunami then continued and struck Japan.

9. Why is the word "misleading" used to describe the term *tidal waves* in the reading passage?
   F. Tsunamis are really large tides.
   G. Tsunamis can cause extensive damage to coastal areas.
   H. Tsunamis are related to earthquakes.
   I. Tsunamis are not related to tides.
10. Which of the following statements is a fact from the passage?
    A. All tsunamis are caused by earthquakes.
    B. A tsunami can travel as fast as an airplane.
    C. The tsunami of 1960 only struck Japan.
    D. Tsunamis are caused by surface currents.
11. Once triggered, how far can a tsunami travel?
    F. Tsunamis are short-lived and usually dissipate within just a few kilometers.
    G. Tsunamis travel about 100 km before dissipating in the ocean.
    H. Tsunamis travel about 1,000 km before dissipating in the ocean.
    I. Tsunamis can travel thousands of kilometers before dissipating or striking land.

Question 13 Full-credit answers should include the following points:

- students should show an understanding that the moon's gravity, and to a lesser extent the sun's gravity, tugs on the surface of Earth and its waters
- as the moon revolves around Earth, the moon exerts a gravitational pull on Earth's surface and its ocean waters
- two high tidal bulges are created on opposite sides of the planet as the moon's gravity affects Earth. Low tides occur in between these bulges
- because the waters flow more easily they are more affected than the solid Earth is

Question 15 Full-credit answers should include the following points:

- students should use concepts of the differential energy absorption patterns of water and land to explain the observed differences in climate
- an understanding that water heats and cools more slowly than does land
- cities that are located near large bodies of water have fewer temperature variations because of the mediating effect of the water

Interpreting Graphics

Directions (12–15): For each question below, record the correct answer on a separate sheet of paper.

The diagrams below show the Earth, moon, and sun system. Use these diagrams to answer questions 12 and 13.

Effect of Sun and Moon on Earth's Tides

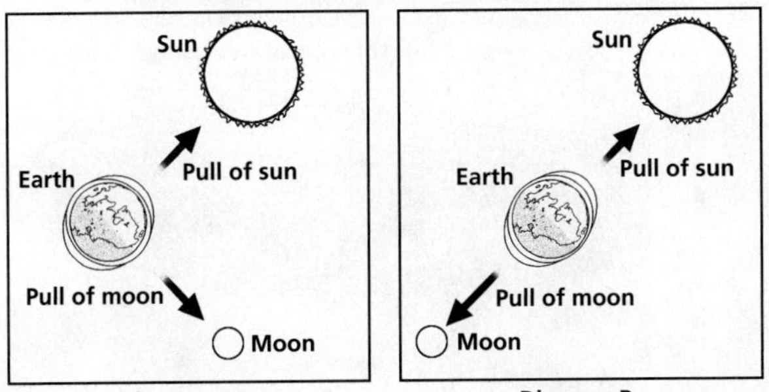

12. What type of tide is produced by the arrangement in Diagram B?
- **A.** spring tide
- **B.** neap tide
- **C.** winter tide
- **D.** weak tide

13. Using the diagrams above, explain how the gravitational effects of astronomical bodies cause tides on Earth.

The climate graphs below combine temperature and precipitation data for San Francisco, California, and Wichita, Kansas. Use these graphs to answer questions 14 and 15.

Average Yearly Weather Data for San Francisco and Wichita

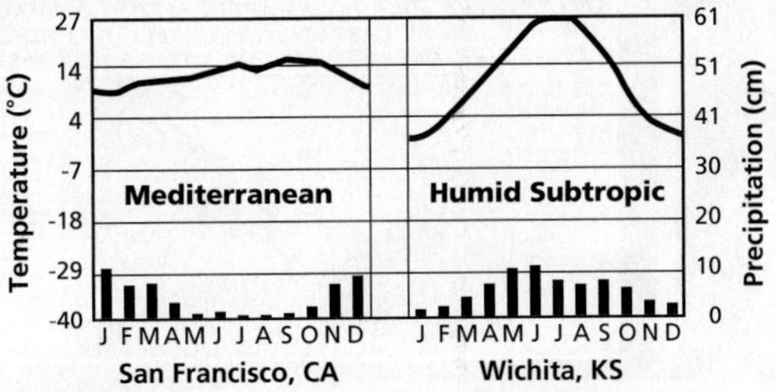

14. Which location shows the most extreme climate variation?
- **F.** Wichita, Kansas shows the most extreme climate variation.
- **G.** San Francisco, California shows the most extreme climate variation.
- **H.** Both climates are equally mild.
- **I.** Both climates are equally variable.

15. How do the locations of these cities and the nearby currents help to explain the differences in their climates?

Test Tip

Allow a few minutes at the end of the test-taking period to check for careless mistakes, such as marking two answers for a single question.

Standardized Test Prep

Using THINK central Resources

State Resources
- For specific resources for your state, visit www.thinkcentral.com and type in the keyword **HSHSTR.**

Answers

Understanding Concepts
1. A
2. H
3. A
4. F
5. A
6. water density differences
7. Its height increases.
8. wind

Reading Skills

9. I
10. B
11. I

Interpreting Graphics

12. A
13. Answers may vary. See Test Doctor for a detailed scoring rubric.
14. F
15. Answers may vary. See Test Doctor for a detailed scoring rubric.

Why It Matters

Oceanography Connections

Remind students that the arrows show broad connections between events, not direct cause-and-effect relationships.

Students often forget that famous scientists were influenced by the social and political events of their time. The following information will help students connect the scientists to the time periods in which they lived.

Donald Redfield Griffin, an American professor of zoology, laid the groundwork for understanding animal echolocation. Griffin studied sensory biophysics, animal navigation, and the acoustic orientation of animals such as bats. In fact, he coined the term *echolocation.* During World War II, Griffin took time away from his professorship at Harvard University to design military equipment, such as cold-weather gear and headphones, based on physiological principles. After the war, he returned to Harvard, where he continued to study animal behavior.

Ferdinand Magellan embodied the curious and relentless spirit of science. He sailed west from Europe, looking for a faster, more efficient trading route to the Spice Islands of Asia. His odyssey became the first successful attempt to circumnavigate the globe. His success provided evidence that Earth is, in fact, a sphere, contrary to the beliefs of many people at the time.

Why It Matters

Oceanography Connectio

Science, technology, and society are closely linked. This flowchart shows just a few of the connections in the history of oceanography.

1918 The first active sonar system is constructed and used.

1000 C.E. Vikings migrated to North America.

1620 Cornelius Drebbel invents first practical submarine.

1859 The first ocean-going ironclad ships are employed by the French.

1519 Magellan and his crew leave Spain to circumnavigate the world.

1912 The RMS *Titanic* strikes an iceberg and sinks.

TITANIC SINKS FOUR HOURS AFTER HITTING ICEBERG;
866 RESCUED BY CARPATHIA, PROBABLY 1250 PERISH;
ISMAY SAFE, MRS. ASTOR MAYBE, NOTED NAMES MISSING

1913 The International Convention for Safety of Life at Sea establishes main shipping routes.

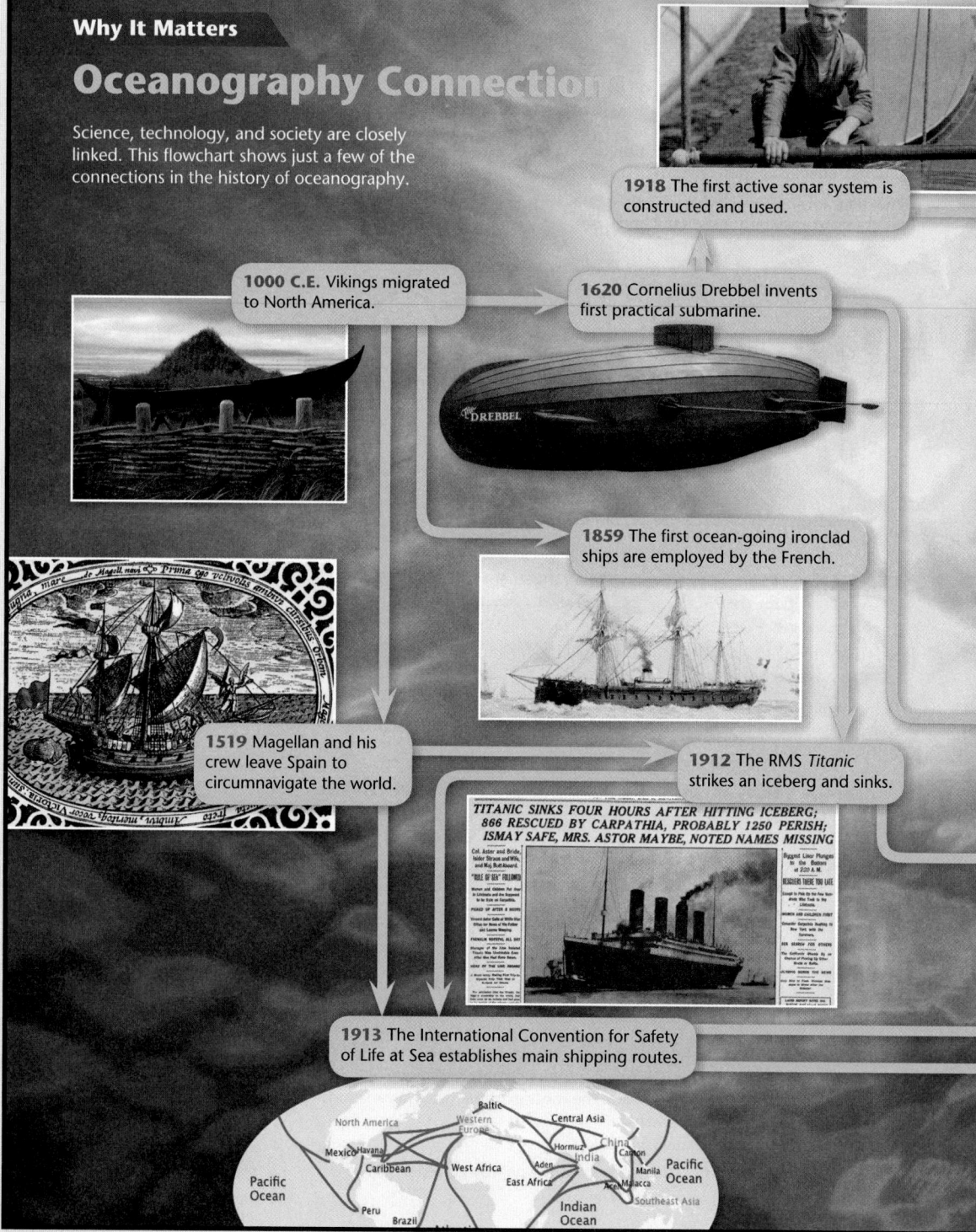

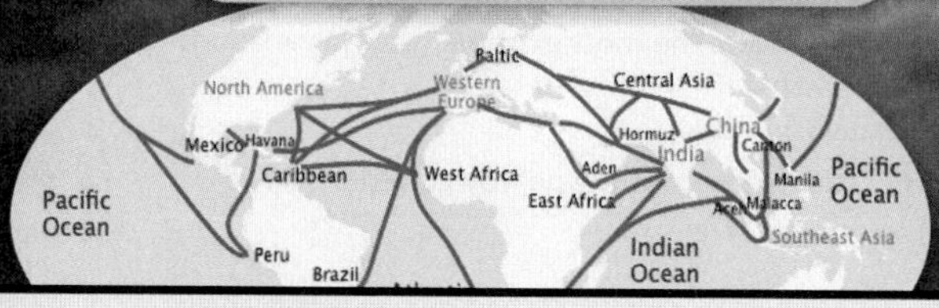

Reading Skill Builder — Basic

Visual Literacy The map at the bottom of the left-hand page shows the most common shipping lanes of the modern world. The shipping lanes were established in the early 20th century and were designed to provide efficient passage between major ports. By proposing specific routes, shipping companies and countries helped to increase the safety of their ships traveling through international waters. Recently, some shipping lanes have been altered slightly to protect the wildlife that inhabit these liquid highways.

HISTORY IN SCIENCE

1939 Sonar is used in World War II to find enemy submarines.

1949 American scientists investigate the use of sonar for medical purposes.

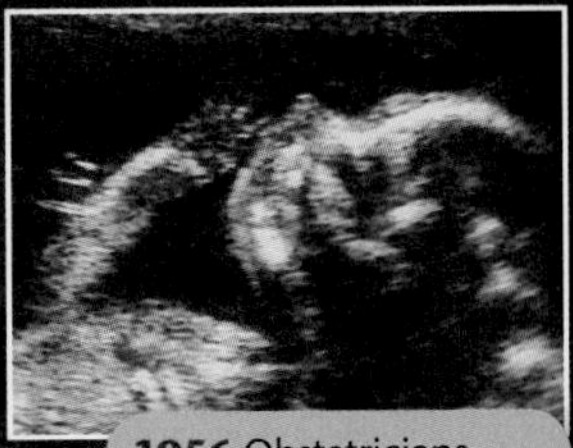

1956 Obstetricians begin to use ultrasound technology.

1947 Scientists suggest that dolphins echolocate.

1939–1945 During WWII, whales are mistakenly identified as submarines.

1964 The submersible *Alvin* is first launched.

2000 Sixteen whales beach themselves in the Bahamas after military low- and mid-frequency sonar tests.

1986 Scientists use *Alvin* to explore the wreckage of the RMS *Titanic.*

2003 North Atlantic shipping lanes are shifted to prevent collisions with Right whales off Canada's coast.

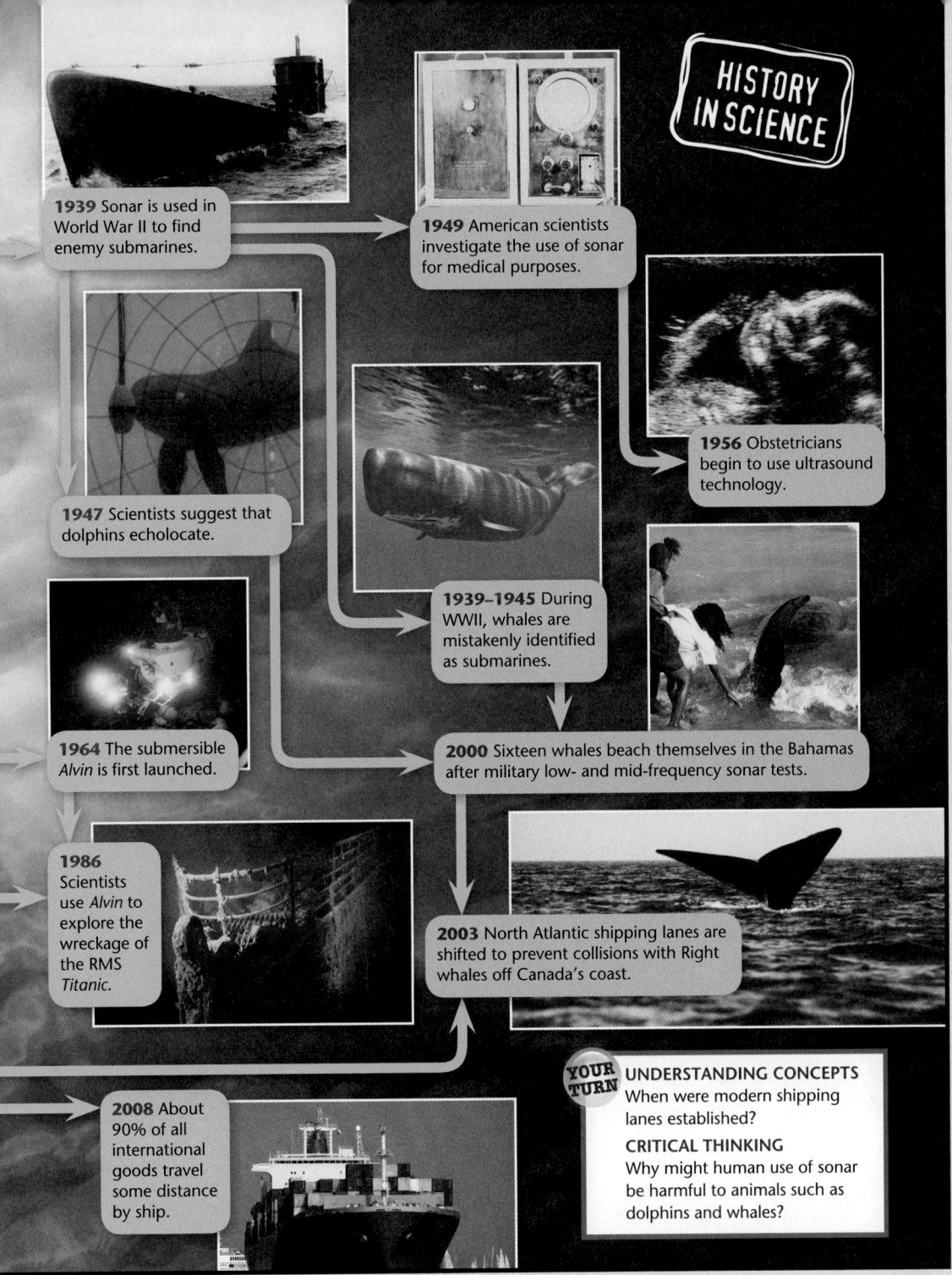

2008 About 90% of all international goods travel some distance by ship.

YOUR TURN

UNDERSTANDING CONCEPTS

When were modern shipping lanes established?

CRITICAL THINKING

Why might human use of sonar be harmful to animals such as dolphins and whales?

Answers to Your Turn

Understanding Concepts The International Convention for Safety of Life at Sea established today's main shipping lanes in 1913.

Critical Thinking Dolphins and whales use a form of sonar to find food and to navigate underwater. By emitting strong sound waves into the water, humans may interrupt the echolocation of these animals. Very loud sonar pulses may also damage the sensitive organs of these animals.

Why It Matters

Medical Sonography In 1949, the American Naval Medical Research Institute performed systematic investigations into the use of medical sonography for diagnostic purposes in humans. In less than 20 years, this technology had been approved for use in obstetrics. Today, most pregnant women in the United States receive an ultrasound image of the fetus as part of regular prenatal care. Other medical uses of sonography include visualizing muscles and other tissues and breaking up kidney and bladder stones.

Why It Matters

The Science of Wartime Scientific advancements seem to go hand in hand with human conflicts. Many benign scientific developments have been used to advance military technologies, and many technologies that were developed during wartime have had practical applications outside the military. For example, sonar and radar were developed during the two World Wars. These technologies have been used outside the military to study weather and to make air travel safer. Similarly, submarines, space craft, and underwater exploration equipment were originally developed for military purposes.

Why It Matters

Safety of Life at Sea In 1912, the RMS *Titanic* struck an iceberg while crossing the North Atlantic Ocean. The damage to the ship caused the ship to sink, and 1,517 people died. As a result, delegates from 13 countries attended the first International Convention for Safety of Life at Sea in London in 1913. The first treaty, signed in 1914, prescribed the number of lifeboats and other emergency equipment, as well as safety procedures, such as continuous radio watches. The treaty also established main shipping routes through the world's oceans.

Answers continued from p. 648

Section Review

9. *Ocean floor sediments* consist of *inorganic sediment* made from rocks and volcanic dust; *biogenic sediment*, which may include the remains of *diatoms*; and *chemical deposits*, such as *nodules*.

Sample Answers to Concept Maps from Chapter Reviews

Chapter 23 The Ocean Basins, p. 655

28.

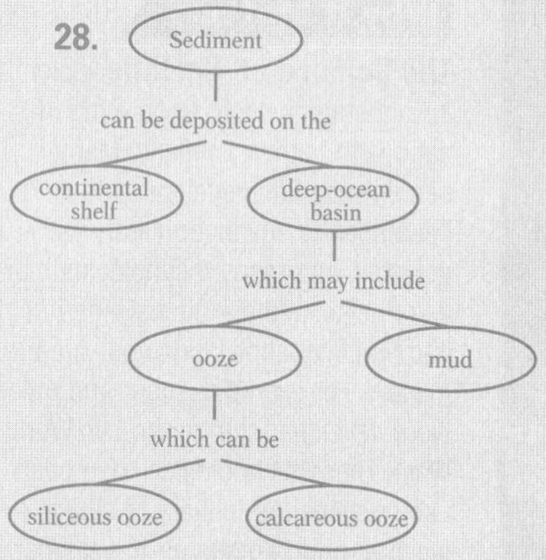

Chapter 24 Ocean Water, p. 683

28.

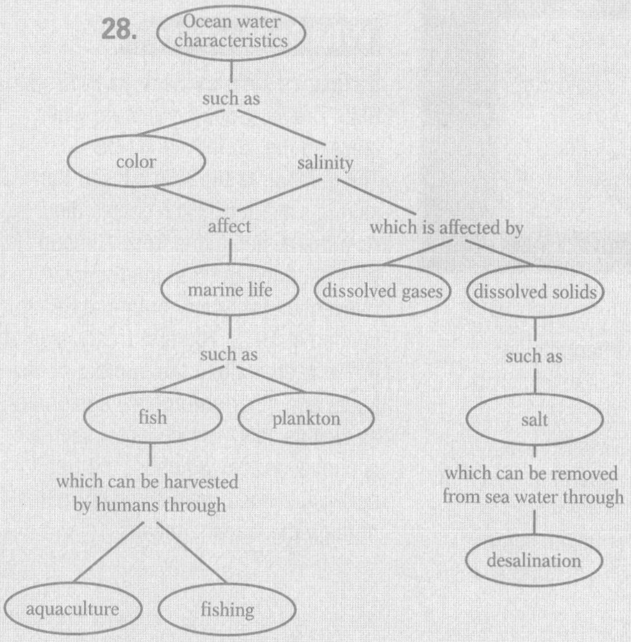

Chapter 25 Movements of the Ocean, p. 711

29.

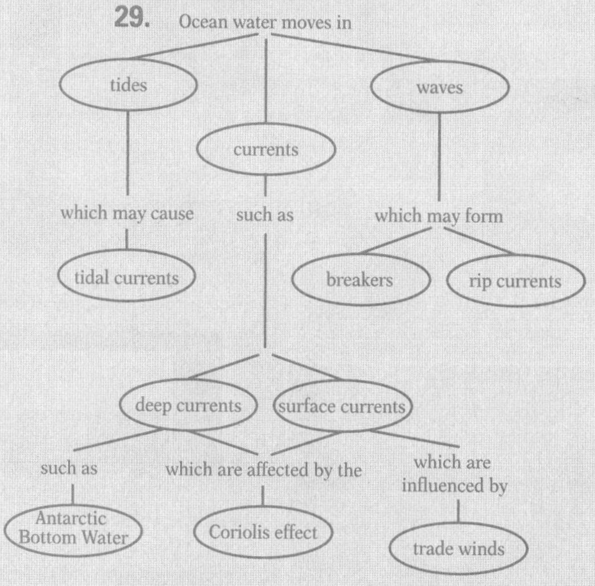

Unit 8 Space

Chapter Planner 26 Studying Space

	Standards	Teach Key Ideas
Chapter Opener, pp. 718–719 **45 min.**	National Science Education Standards	
Section 1 Viewing the Universe, pp. 721–728 **45 min.** ❯ The Value of Astronomy ❯ Characteristics of the Universe ❯ Observing Space ❯ Telescopes ❯ Space-Based Astronomy	SAI 2c, SAI 2d, PS 5a, ES 4a, ES 4b, HNS 3c, SPSP 6b, SPSP 6c, SPSP 6d, UCP 2	■ ◆ **Bellringer,** p. 721 ■ **Discussion:** Galactic Address, p. 722 ■ **Demonstration:** Colors of Light, p. 723 ■ **DI (Special Education Students):** Electromagnetic Spectrum, p. 723 ■ **Demonstration:** Heating with Invisible Light, p. 724 ■ **DI (Struggling Readers):** Paired Summarizing, p. 724 ■ **Debate:** Space Exploration, p. 727 ◆ **Transparencies:** 130 Refracting and Reflecting Telescopes • 135 Light Sources ▲ **Visual Concepts:** Astronomical Unit (AU) • Light-Year • Electromagnetic Spectrum • Refracting and Reflecting Telescopes • Refracting Telescope • Reflecting Telescope • Non-Optical Telescopes • Space Shuttle • Space Station
Section 2 Movements of Earth, pp. 729–736 **135 min.** ❯ The Rotating Earth ❯ The Revolving Earth ❯ Constellations and Earth's Motion ❯ Measuring Time ❯ The Seasons	SAI 2c, SAI 2d, UCP 2	■ ◆ **Bellringer,** p. 729 ■ **Demonstration:** Coriolis Effect, p. 730 ■ **DI (English Learners):** Vocabulary, p. 730 ■ **Discussion:** Comprehension Check, p. 731 ■ **DI (Struggling Readers):** Reading Hint, p. 731 ■ **DI (Special Education Students):** Calendars, p. 732 ■ **Debate:** Daylight Saving Time, p. 734 ◆ **Transparencies:** 131 Earth's Orbit • 132 The Apparent Motion of Constellations • 133 Time Zones • 134 How the Tilt of Earth's Axis Affects Seasons ▲ **Visual Concepts:** Day, Rotation, Period of Rotation • Year, Revolution, Period of Revolution • Calendars • Seasons and Latitude • Solstice and Equinox
Chapter Wrap-Up, pp. 741–745 **90 min.**		**Chapter Summary,** p. 741

See also PowerNotes® Presentations

CHAPTER Fast Track *To shorten instruction because of time limitations, omit the Chapter Lab*

Key

Teacher's Edition ■ | Teaching Transparencies ◆
Chapter Resource File ● | Online Edition ▲

All resources listed below are also available on the **Teacher One Stop™.**

Why It Matters	Hands-On	Skills Development	Assessment
■ **Chapter Overview,** p. 718 ■ **Using the Figure:** Humans in Space, p. 718	**Inquiry Lab:** A Model Telescope, p. 719	**Reading Toolbox,** p. 720	
■ **Section Overview,** p. 721 ■ **Inventing the Telescope,** p. 724 ■ **History Connection:** Seeing the Light, p. 724 ■ **Using the Figure:** Comparing Telescopes, p. 725 ■ **Large Telescopes,** p. 725 **The Interstellar Playlist,** p. 726 ■ **Environmental Connection:** Light Pollution, p. 726 ■ **Math Connection:** Resetting Your Clock, p. 733	■ **Activity:** Descriptive Writing, p. 721 ■ **Group Activity:** Cosmic Timeline, p. 722 ■ **Group Activity:** Splitting Light, p. 723 ■ **Group Activity:** Community Survey, p. 740 ● **Inquiry Lab:** Comet Meets Jupiter ● **Making Models Lab:** Telescopes	**Math Skills:** Astronomical Unit, p. 722 ■ **Skill Builder:** Math, p. 722 ■ ● **Internet Activity:** Space Spinoffs, p. 727 **Reading Toolbox:** Frequency, p. 727 **Maps in Action:** Light Sources, p. 740	**Reading Check,** p. 723 **Reading Check,** p. 725 **Reading Check,** p. 726 **Section Review,** p. 728 ■ **Reteaching,** p. 727 ■ **Quiz,** p. 727 ■ **DI (Alternative Assessment):** Skit, p. 728 ● **Section Quiz**
■ **Section Overview,** p. 729 ■ **History Connection:** It's About Time, p. 732 ■ **Using the Figure:** Time Zone Zigzags p. 733 ■ **Planetary Seasons,** p. 734	■ **Activity:** Role-Playing, p. 729 **Quick Lab:** A Model Pendulum, p. 730 ■ **Activity:** Star Viewers, p. 731 **Quick Lab:** The Angle of the Sun's Rays, p. 735 **Inquiry Lab:** Earth-Sun Motion, pp. 738–739	**Reading Toolbox:** Using Spatial Language, p. 732 ■ ● **Internet Activity:** International Zones, p. 733	**Reading Check,** p. 731 **Reading Check,** p. 733 **Reading Check,** p. 734 **Section Review,** p. 736 ■ **Reteaching,** p. 735 ■ **Quiz,** p. 735 ■ **DI (Alternative Assessment):** Science Fiction Stories, p. 736 ● **Section Quiz**
What Time Is It?, p. 737		▲ **Super Summary** **Standardized Test Prep,** pp. 744–745	**Chapter Review,** pp. 742–743 ■ **DI (Alternative Assessment):** Astronomy Picture Books, p. 741 ● **Chapter Tests**
	See also Lab Generator		See also Holt Online Assessment Resources

Chapter Overview

This chapter describes how scientists study the universe and how telescopes work. It also explains how Earth moves and how the movements are related to timekeeping, calendars, and seasons.

Using the Figure GENERAL

Humans in Space This photo shows an astronaut wearing a spacesuit specially designed for protection and maneuverability while floating in space. The suit enables astronauts to perform experiments and make repairs outside the International Space Station. Ask students what scientists or engineers might study that they could learn about better in space. (Sample answers: the effects of lower gravity, Earth's weather, pollution, medical research, and whether we could manufacture goods in space) **LS Logical**

Why It Matters

NASA has completed over 100 successful shuttle missions, many of which were in support of the construction of the International Space Station. Two shuttles, however, never landed and the crews were lost. In 1986, the *Challenger* space shuttle exploded shortly after takeoff. In 2003, *Columbia* broke apart while returning. Although NASA works to minimize risks, they cannot be eliminated.

Chapter 26 Studying Space

Chapter Outline

1 Viewing the Universe
- The Value of Astronomy
- Characteristics of the Universe
- Observing Space
- Telescopes
- Space-Based Astronomy

2 Movements of Earth
- The Rotating Earth
- The Revolving Earth
- Constellations and Earth's Motion
- Measuring Time
- The Seasons

Virginia Standards of Learning
ES.1.c
ES.3.b
ES.3.d

Why It Matters

In our efforts to study space, we have developed many technologies, from simple telescopes to the International Space Station. Human interest in the regions beyond Earth has impacted life on the surface of the planet, as well as above it, in many ways.

Chapter Correlations

Virginia Standards of Learning

ES.1.c scales, diagrams, charts, graphs, tables, imagery, models, and profiles are constructed and interpreted.
ES.3.b sun-Earth-moon relationships (seasons, tides, and eclipses)
ES.3.d the history and contributions of space exploration

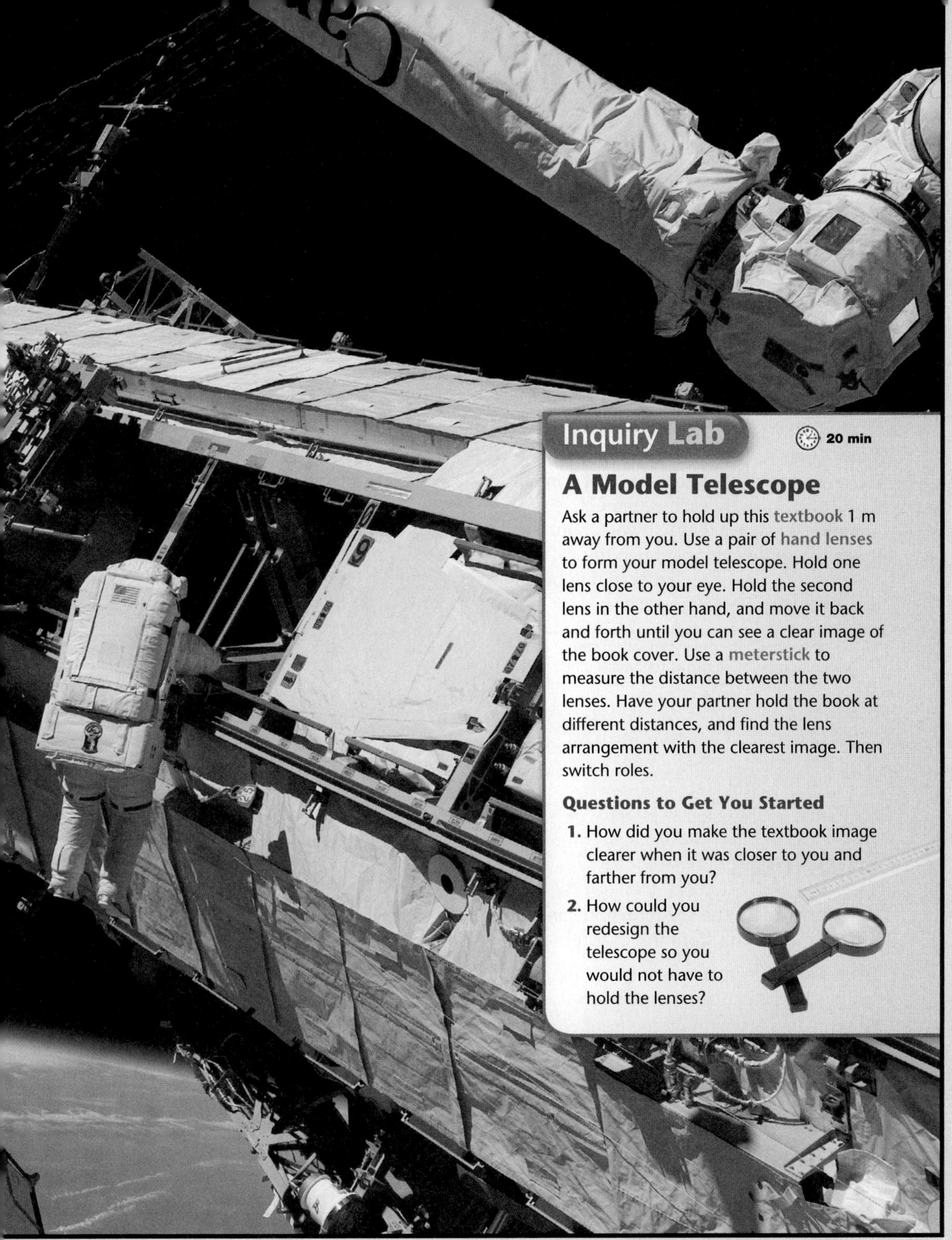

Inquiry Lab

20 min

A Model Telescope

Ask a partner to hold up this textbook 1 m away from you. Use a pair of hand lenses to form your model telescope. Hold one lens close to your eye. Hold the second lens in the other hand, and move it back and forth until you can see a clear image of the book cover. Use a meterstick to measure the distance between the two lenses. Have your partner hold the book at different distances, and find the lens arrangement with the clearest image. Then switch roles.

Questions to Get You Started

1. How did you make the textbook image clearer when it was closer to you and farther from you?
2. How could you redesign the telescope so you would not have to hold the lenses?

Inquiry Lab

Central Concept: Refracting telescopes have been in use for centuries. Students will work with two lenses to form an image. One lens will act as the eyepiece and the other will act as the objective.

Teacher's Notes: This activity connects with optics topics. You may wish to introduce or review the ideas of convex and concave lenses.

Materials (per group)
- Textbook
- Two convex lenses (or magnifying glasses)
- Two lens holders (if needed)
- Meterstick

Skills Acquired
- Making Models
- Measuring

Answers to Getting Started

1. Students should describe how they changed the distances between the two lenses to view the textbook. They may compare the distances they measured when the textbook was close up and far away.
2. Students should propose a way of stabilizing the lenses, probably within an external structure.

Using THINK central Resources

An online version of this chapter, as well as all the print and multimedia resources that accompany the program are available to registered teachers and their students. Log onto www.thinkcentral.com to access these materials and tools to organize your preparation and student learning.

READING TOOLBOX

Frequency

Sample frequency statements from Section 1:

Today, <u>most</u> interest in studying the sky comes from a curiosity to discover what lies within the universe and how the universe changes.

The solar system includes the sun, Earth, the other planets, and <u>many</u> smaller objects such as dwarf planets, asteroids, and comets.

To measure distances in the solar system, astronomers <u>often</u> use astronomical units.

The electromagnetic spectrum is <u>all</u> the wavelengths of electromagnetic radiation.

<u>Every</u> rainbow formed in the sky and <u>any</u> spectrum formed by a prism always has the same colors in the same order.

One problem with using telescopes to detect invisible electromagnetic radiation is that Earth's atmosphere acts as a shield against <u>many</u> forms of electromagnetic radiation.

Atoms and molecules in the atmosphere prevent short wavelengths like gamma rays, X rays, and <u>most</u> ultraviolet rays from reaching Earth's surface.

But the only way to study <u>many</u> forms of radiation is from space.

Crewed spacecraft, or those that carry humans, have <u>never</u> gone beyond Earth's moon.

READING TOOLBOX

These reading tools will help you learn the material in this chapter.

Frequency

Always, Sometimes, Never Many statements include a word that tells you about the frequency of the information in the statement. Examples include words such as *always, sometimes, often,* and *never.* Words such as *some, many,* and *most* are examples of words that tell you about frequency in number.

Your Turn As you read this chapter, record examples of statements that contain frequency words. In each statement, underline the word that tells you about the frequency of the information in the statement or about frequency in number in the statement. Here is one example:

> To measure distances in the solar system, astronomers <u>often</u> use astronomical units.

Describing Space

Using Spatial Language Spatial language is used to describe space and the universe. It can be used to describe

- the shape of objects
- the location of objects
- distance
- orientation
- direction of motion

Your Turn As you read this chapter, complete a table like the one below. Add words or phrases that use spatial language to describe something.

Shape	Location	Distance	Orientation	Direction
spherical	in the core	a long way	vertical	outward
cube	at the North Pole	kilometer	tilt	south

FoldNotes

Key-Term Fold The key-term fold can help you learn key terms from this chapter.

Your Turn Create a key-term fold for Section 1, as described in **Appendix A.**

1. Write one key term on the front of each tab.
2. Write a definition or description for each term under its tab.
3. Use this FoldNote to help you review the key terms.

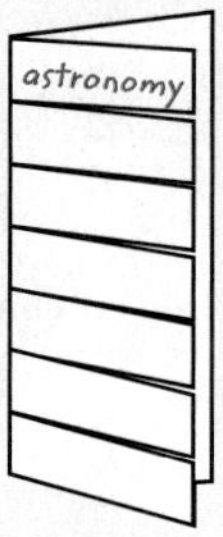

For more information on how to use these and other tools, see **Appendix A.**

Describing Space

Sample lists of words that describe shape, location, distance, orientation, and direction in Section 2 can be found on page 875A.

FoldNotes

The key terms should appear on the front of the tabs of the Key-Term Fold. Each definition should appear under the appropriate tab. The table on page 875A shows key terms and definitions for Section 1.

SECTION 1

Viewing the Universe

Key Ideas	Key Terms	Why It Matters
❯ Describe characteristics of the universe in terms of time, distance, and organization. ❯ Identify the visible and nonvisible parts of the electromagnetic spectrum. ❯ Compare refracting telescopes and reflecting telescopes. ❯ Explain how telescopes for nonvisible electromagnetic radiation differ from light telescopes.	astronomy galaxy astronomical unit electromagnetic spectrum telescope refracting telescope reflecting telescope	Technologies that are developed for space exploration also have spinoffs that allow us to treat illnesses, develop new building materials, predict the weather, and communicate with others around the world.

People studied the sky long before the telescope was invented. For example, farmers observed changes in daylight and the visibility of groups of stars throughout the year to track seasons and to predict floods and droughts. Sailors focused on the stars to navigate through unknown territory. Today, most interest in studying the sky comes from a curiosity to discover what lies within the universe and how the universe changes. This scientific study of the universe is called **astronomy.** Scientists who study the universe are called *astronomers*.

The Value of Astronomy

In the process of observing the universe, astronomers have made exciting discoveries, such as new planets, stars, black holes, and nebulas, such as the one shown in **Figure 1.** By studying these objects, astronomers have been able to learn more about the origin of Earth and the processes involved in the formation of our solar system and other objects in the universe.

Studying the universe is also important for the potential benefits to humans. For example, studies of how stars shine may one day lead to improved or new energy sources on Earth. Astronomers may also learn how to protect us from potential catastrophes, such as collisions between asteroids and Earth. Because of these and other contributions, astronomical research is supported by federal agencies, such as the National Science Foundation and NASA. Private foundations and industry also fund research in astronomy.

astronomy the scientific study of the universe

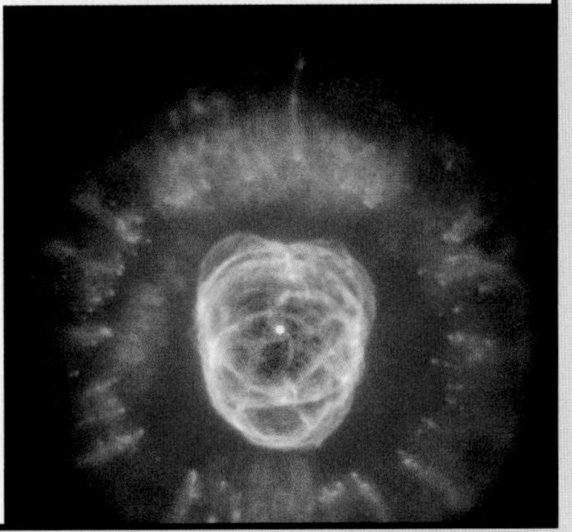

Figure 1 A nebula is a large cloud of gas and dust in space. This nebula is called the Eskimo nebula. It formed as a result of the outer layers of the central star being blown away. Astronomers predict that our sun will reach this state in about 5 billion years.

Section 1

Focus

Overview

This section summarizes the nature of the universe in terms of its size, age, and arrangement; describes the electromagnetic spectrum; and explains various tools astronomers use to study space.

Bellringer

Ask students what comes to mind when they hear about new astronomical discoveries. Have them think about what an astronomer does and then draw a picture, with caption, of an astronomer at work. (Answers may vary.) LS **Visual**

Motivate

Activity GENERAL

Descriptive Writing Have students write a brief essay that compares what they know about ancient astronomy with what they know about present-day space science. Guide students to explain why the sky interested ancient peoples and how celestial bodies and their cycles affected daily lives. Ask students to consider what observations people could make with only their eyes, how modern tools extend knowledge of space, and what benefits space science has for modern societies. LS **Verbal**

Key Resources

Chapter Resource File

- Directed Reading BASIC
  Technology
- Inquiry Lab: Comet Meets Jupiter GENERAL
- Making Models Lab: Telescopes GENERAL

Technology

- Transparencies
  Bellringer

Teach

Group Activity — GENERAL

Cosmic Timeline Help students visualize the time span since the beginning of the universe by making a timeline that corresponds to a 12-month calendar. Hang 12 pieces of paper labeled with the calendar months in order along one wall. Have students brainstorm a list of major events that occurred between the big bang and the present. Students should research when each event occurred. Start with the big bang, 14 billion years ago (bya), as Jan. 1. Other events could include: birth of the solar system, 4.5 bya (Sept. 5); earliest life on Earth, 3.8 bya (Sept. 22); extinction of the dinosaurs, 65.5 million years ago (Dec. 29); appearance of Homo sapiens, 600,000 years ago, (Dec. 31, 11:30 PM). **LS Logical/Kinesthetic** Co-op Learning

Discussion — BASIC

Galactic Address Propose this scenario: "Suppose you want to send a message to an unknown civilization in a different part of the universe. You would probably include your own location in space. Describe your galactic address, starting with your seat in the classroom and expanding outward." (Sample answers: Classroom seat and row, the school name, address, city, state, country, Earth [third planet from the sun], solar system, Milky Way galaxy, the universe) Invite students to create maps that illustrate their descriptions. **LS Verbal**

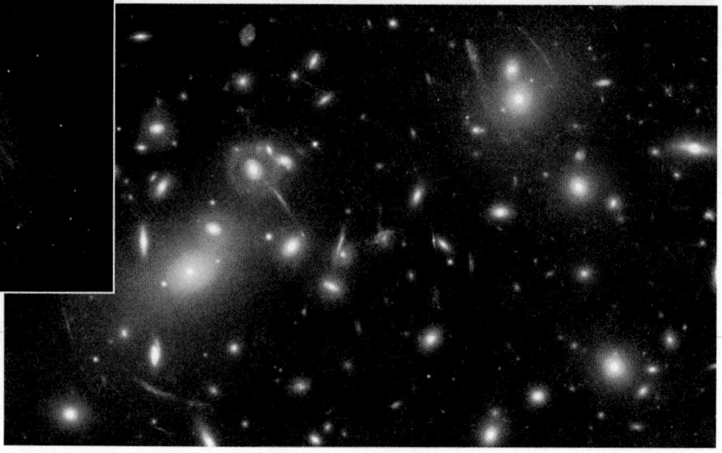

Figure 2 The Whirlpool galaxy, M51 (above), is 31 million light-years from the Milky Way. Abell 2218 (right) is one of the most massive galaxy clusters known. The cluster's mass has distorted the light from even farther objects into the giant arcs shown here.

Characteristics of the Universe

The study of the origin, properties, processes, and evolution of the universe is called *cosmology*. Astronomers have determined that the universe began about 13.7 billion years ago in one giant explosion, called the *big bang*. Since that time, the universe has continued to expand. In fact, it is expanding faster and faster. The universe is very large, and the objects within it are extremely far apart. Telescopes are used to study distant objects. However, astronomers also commonly use computer and mathematical models to study the universe.

Math Skills

Astronomical Unit
An astronomical unit is the average distance between the sun and Earth, or about 150 million km. Venus orbits the sun at a distance of 0.7 AU. Venus is how many kilometers from the sun?

Organization of the Universe

The nearest part of the universe to Earth is our solar system. The solar system includes the sun, Earth, the other planets, and many smaller objects such as dwarf planets, asteroids, and comets. The solar system is part of a **galaxy,** which is a large collection of stars, dust, and gas bound together by gravity. The galaxy in which the solar system resides is called the *Milky Way galaxy*. Beyond the Milky Way galaxy, there are billions of other galaxies, dozens of which are shown in **Figure 2.**

galaxy a collection of stars, dust, and gas bound together by gravity

astronomical unit the average distance between Earth and the sun; approximately 150 million kilometers (symbol, AU)

Measuring Distances in the Universe

Because the universe is so large, the units of measurement used on Earth are too small to represent the distance between objects in space. To measure distances in the solar system, astronomers often use astronomical units. An **astronomical unit** (symbol, AU) is the average distance between Earth and the sun, which is 149,597,870.691 km or about 150 million km.

Astronomers also use the speed of light to measure distance. Light travels at 300,000 km/s. In one year, light travels 9.46×10^{12} km. This distance is known as a *light-year*. Aside from the sun, the closest star to Earth is 4.22 light-years away.

Math Skills

Answer

150,000,000 km × 0.7 AU = 105,000,000 km, or 105 million km

Skill Builder — GENERAL

Math Distances in astronomy are difficult for students to comprehend because the distances are so huge. Have students calculate how far (in km) light travels in one year based on the speed of light (300,000 km/s). Allow them to round their figures. (Answer: 60 s/min × 60 min/h = 3,600 s/h × 24 h/d = 86,400 s/d × 365 d/y = 31,536,000 s/y × 300,000 km/s = 9.4608 × 10^{12} km or 9,461 trillion (9,461,000,000,000) km) Tell them the star Sirius is located 84,321 trillion km from Earth. Have them calculate this distance in light-years. (84,321 trillion km ÷ 9,461 trillion km/ly = 8.91 ly) **LS Logical**

Observing Space

Light enables us to see the world around us and to make observations. When people look at the night sky, they see stars and other objects in space because of the light these objects emit. This visible light is only a small amount of the energy that comes from these objects. By studying other forms of energy, astronomers are able to learn more about the universe. Recall that planets do not emit light. Rather, they reflect the light from stars.

Electromagnetic Spectrum

Visible light is a form of energy that is part of the electromagnetic spectrum. The **electromagnetic spectrum** is all the wavelengths of electromagnetic radiation. Light, radio waves, and X rays are examples of electromagnetic radiation. The radiation is composed of traveling waves of electric and magnetic fields that have fixed wavelengths and therefore fixed frequencies.

electromagnetic spectrum all of the frequencies or wavelengths of electromagnetic radiation

Visible Electromagnetic Radiation

The human eye can see only radiation of wavelengths in the visible light range of the spectrum. When white light passes through a prism, the light is refracted (bent), and a continuous set of colors, as shown in **Figure 3,** results. Every rainbow formed in the sky and any spectrum formed by a prism always has the same colors in the same order. The different colors result because each color of light has a characteristic wavelength that refracts at a different angle when it passes from one medium, such as air, into another, such as a glass prism. For example, the shortest wavelengths of visible light are blue and violet, while the longest wavelengths are orange and red.

Electromagnetic radiation that has wavelengths that are shorter than the wavelengths of violet light or longer than the wavelengths of red light cannot be seen by humans. But these wavelengths can be detected by instruments that are designed to detect electromagnetic radiation that cannot be seen by human eyes. These invisible wavelengths include infrared waves, microwaves, and radio waves (at longer wavelengths than red), as well as ultraviolet rays, X rays, and gamma rays (at shorter wavelengths than blue).

Reading Check **Which type of electromagnetic radiation can be seen by humans?** (See Appendix G for answers to Reading Checks.)

Figure 3 When white light (shown here coming from the upper left) passes from air, through a prism (top right), and then back into air, the light is separated into its different colors.

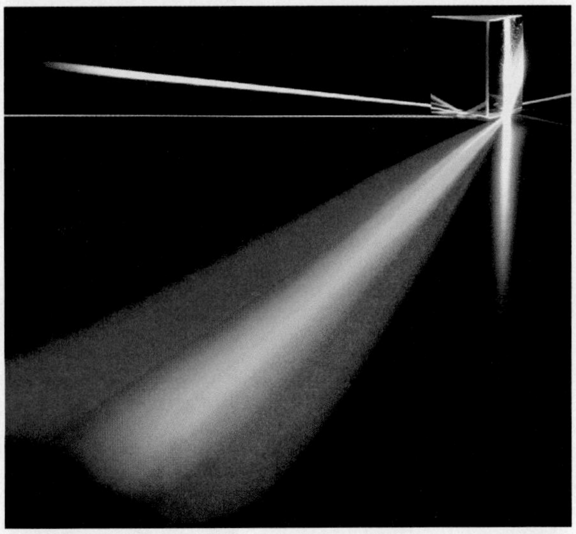

Demonstration — Basic

Colors of Light Shine a flashlight beam onto a white sheet of paper. Put a prism into the path of the beam of light. Turn the prism slightly until the spectrum appears on the paper. Ask students to describe what they see. Ask them which color light seems to bend the most and which color bends the least. (Students should see the colors of the rainbow. The prism bends violet light the most and red light the least.) **LS Visual**

Group Activity — General

Splitting Light Explain that astronomers use an instrument called a *spectrograph* to analyze the light from stars. Spectrographs use prisms or diffraction gratings to break up the light. Students can see the spectrum directly through a diffraction grating cut into 3 cm squares. (You can obtain diffraction grating in sheets or rolls from a science supply house.) Set up a table lamp with the shade removed. Distribute diffraction gratings to students. Darken the room and turn on the lamp. Direct students to look at the light source through the diffraction grating. Tell them to handle the grating by the edges, as oil from their fingers will clog the openings. Have students use crayons or colored pencils to draw the spectra they see. **LS Visual**

Answer to Reading Check

The only kind of electromagnetic radiation the human eye can detect is visible light.

Differentiated Instruction

Special Education Students

Electromagnetic Spectrum Have students draw and color a rainbow in the center of a piece of paper. Then, have them add, in order and in black and white, the wavelengths that are too short or too long to see. Infrared and radio wavelengths should be beyond the red end. Ultraviolet, X-ray, and gamma-ray wavelengths should appear beyond the violet end. **LS Visual/Kinesthetic**

Teach, *continued*

Demonstration GENERAL

Heating with Invisible Light
Demonstrate the thermal properties of infrared radiation by repeating William Herschel's historic experiment. Set up a prism in front of a window so that it breaks white sunlight into a color spectrum. Place three thermometers at different points in the spectrum, one at the violet end, one in the center, and one just beyond the red end. Ask a volunteer to take starting temperatures. Wait at least 5 minutes and take second readings. Ask students what they observe about the temperature data. (There are readings in all parts of the spectrum even in the invisible part beyond the red.) LS **Logical**

History Connection ADVANCED

Seeing the Light Isaac Newton once declared, "If I have seen further, it is by standing on the shoulders of giants." His laws of gravity and motion paved the way to carrying modern spacecraft into orbit. Newton also contributed to understanding the nature of light. His experiments with prisms revealed the spectrum contained in white light, which led to his improvements of the telescope and the particle theory of light. Encourage students to research the contributions of Newton and other "giants," such as James Clerk Maxwell and William Herschel, to our understanding of electromagnetic radiation. Have them make a brief oral report to the class. LS **Verbal**

Invisible Electromagnetic Radiation

If you place a thermometer in any wavelength of the visible spectrum, the temperature reading on the thermometer will rise. In 1800, the scientist William Herschel placed a thermometer just beyond the red end of the visible spectrum. Even though he could not see any light shining on the thermometer, the temperature reading on the thermometer still increased. Herschel had discovered infrared, which means "below the red." Infrared is electromagnetic radiation that has wavelengths that are longer than those of visible light. Other scientists later discovered radio waves, which have even longer wavelengths than infrared.

The ultraviolet wavelengths, which are invisible to humans, are shorter than the wavelengths of violet light. *Ultraviolet* means "beyond the violet." The X-ray wavelengths are shorter than the ultraviolet wavelengths are. The shortest wavelengths are the gamma-ray wavelengths.

Telescopes

Academic Vocabulary
device (di VIES) a piece of equipment made for a specific use

Our eyes can see detail, but some things are too small or too far away to see. Our ability to see the detail of distant objects in the sky began with the Italian scientist Galileo. In 1609, he heard of a device that used two lenses to make distant objects appear closer. He built one of the devices and turned it toward the sky. For the first time, he could see that there are craters on the moon and that the Milky Way is made of stars. Later, Isaac Newton invented another kind of telescope. An example of one of these early devices is shown in **Figure 4.**

telescope an instrument that collects electromagnetic radiation from the sky and concentrates it for better observation

A **telescope** is an instrument that collects electromagnetic radiation from the sky and concentrates it for better observation. While modern telescopes are able to collect and use invisible electromagnetic radiation, the first telescopes that were developed collected only visible light. Telescopes that collect only visible light are called *optical telescopes*. The two types of optical telescopes are refracting telescopes and reflecting telescopes.

Figure 4 An early model of one of the first reflecting telescopes, which was invented by Isaac Newton, can be seen at the Royal Society in London, England.

Why It Matters

Inventing the Telescope Dutch lens-grinder Hans Lippershey is credited with inventing the telescope, which was first used for military purposes. Galileo directed the new instrument, using a combination of concave and convex lenses, at the night sky. Galileo observed the moon and resolved the light of the Milky Way into stars. In 1611, Johannes Kepler built a telescope that combined two convex lenses.

Differentiated Instruction

Struggling Readers

Paired Summarizing Group students into pairs and have them read silently about telescopes. Then, have one student summarize information about reflecting and refracting telescopes. Direct the other student to listen to the retelling and to point out any inaccuracies or ideas that were left out. Allow students to refer to the text as needed. LS **Verbal/Auditory**

Figure 5 Refracting and Reflecting Telescopes

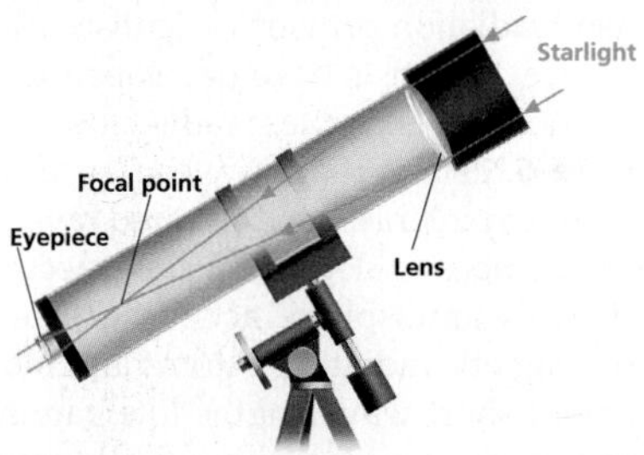

Refracting telescopes use lenses to gather and focus light from distant objects.

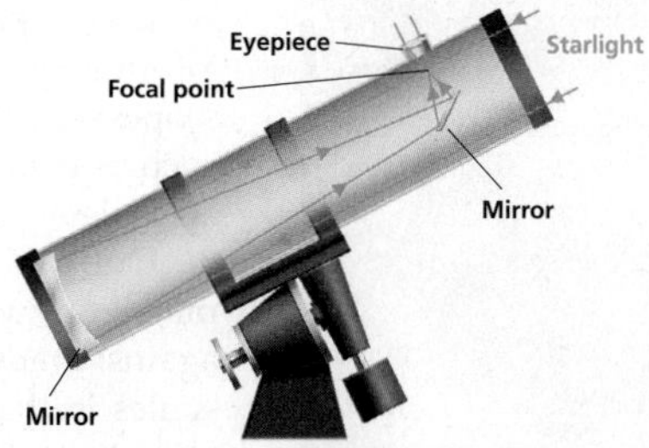

Reflecting telescopes use mirrors to gather and focus light from distant objects.

Refracting Telescopes

Lenses are clear objects shaped to bend light in special ways. The bending of light by lenses is called *refraction*. Telescopes that use a set of lenses to gather and focus light from distant objects are called **refracting telescopes.** Refracting telescopes have an objective lens that bends light that passes through the lens and focuses the light to be magnified by an eyepiece, as shown in **Figure 5.**

One problem with refracting telescopes is that the lens focuses different colors of light at different distances. For example, if an object is in focus in red light, the object will appear out of focus in blue light. Another problem with refracting telescopes is that it is difficult to make very large lenses of the required strength and clarity. The amount of light collected from distant objects is limited by the size of the objective lens.

refracting telescope a telescope that uses a set of lenses to gather and focus light from distant objects

reflecting telescope a telescope that uses a curved mirror to gather and focus light from distant objects

Reflecting Telescopes

In the mid-1600s, Isaac Newton solved the problem of color separation that resulted from the use of lenses. He invented the **reflecting telescope,** which used a curved mirror to gather and focus light from distant objects, as shown in **Figure 5.** When light enters a reflecting telescope, the light is reflected by a large curved mirror to a second mirror. The second mirror reflects the light to the eyepiece, which is a lens that magnifies and focuses the image.

Unlike objective lenses in refracting telescopes, mirrors in reflecting telescopes can be made very large without affecting the quality of the image. Thus, reflecting telescopes can be much larger and can gather more light than refracting telescopes can. The largest reflecting telescopes that can point anywhere in the sky are a pair called the Keck Telescopes in Hawaii and a slightly larger one in the Canary Islands. Each telescope is 10 m in diameter. Astronomers are tentatively planning to build an ELT (Extremely Large Telescope) that would be about 50 m in diameter and an OWL (Overwhelmingly Large Telescope) that would be 100 m in diameter.

Reading Check **What are the problems with refracting telescopes?**

SCILINKS.
www.scilinks.org
Topic: Telescopes
Code: HQX1500

Using the Figure — Basic

Comparing Telescopes Use the pictures of optical telescopes on this page to compare and contrast the features of refracting and reflecting telescopes. Ask students what part of each telescope gathers light. (In refracting telescopes, lenses gather the incoming light. In reflecting telescopes, mirrors gather the light.) Ask students what is similar about how images are focused. (Both telescopes use an eyepiece or lens to focus the image. In the refracting telescope, the first lens bends light toward the eyepiece. In the reflecting telescope, a flat mirror directs the light to the eyepiece.) **LS Visual**

Answer to Reading Check

Images produced by refracting telescopes are subject to distortion because of the ways different colors of visible light are focused at different distances from the lens and because of size limitations on the objective lens.

Why It Matters

Large Telescopes The primary mirrors of the Keck Telescopes are constructed of 36 hexagonal segments. A computer controls the cooperative work of the segments, providing even sharper images than those from the *Hubble Space Telescope*. The OWL project would use a similar mirror design in a telescope about the size of a football field. The likely site for the OWL telescope is the Atacama Desert of Argentina and Chile.

Key Resources

Technology

- Transparencies
  130 Refracting and Reflecting Telescopes

Misconception Alert

Students may think the purpose of a telescope is to magnify distant objects. For astronomers, a telescope's main job is to gather light from distant objects so that they are bright enough to study. As magnifying power doubles, the field of view and surface brightness decrease to 1/4 of the original values. Usually, the Earth's atmosphere instead of the size of the telescope or the eyepiece's magnification limits the amount of detail that is visible. Thus, the ability to detect faint objects is a better indication of usefulness.

Teach, *continued*

Environmental Connection

Light Pollution Sky glow is the brightening of the night sky that occurs when water droplets and dust scatter the large amounts of artificial light produced in urban areas, which profoundly reduces the visibility of stars. Astronomers were first to raise the alarm about this phenomenon. Light pollution not only wastes energy, but also concerns naturalists because it may impact wildlife. Light pollution may produce false signals that disrupt biological rhythms and interfere with the normal behavior patterns of nocturnal animals. For example, migrating bird populations often use the moon and stars to navigate. Artificial light confuses the birds, causing them to fly into buildings and towers. Many animal behaviors in response to light also change their hormonal systems, which can become toxic if overstimulated. Too much exposure to light can even affect human physiology. Invite students to learn more about the consequences of light pollution and ways to reduce this waste by turning down the lights. Have them write letters to community leaders about their concerns. **LS Verbal**

Answer to Reading Check

Scientists launch spacecraft into orbit to detect radiation screened out by Earth's atmosphere and to avoid light pollution and other atmospheric distortions.

Figure 6 Radio telescopes, such as this one (of 27) at the National Radio Astronomy Observatory in New Mexico, provide scientists with information about objects in space.

Telescopes for Invisible Electromagnetic Radiation

Each type of electromagnetic radiation provides scientists with information about objects in space. Scientists have developed telescopes that detect invisible radiation. For example, a radio telescope, such as the one shown in **Figure 6,** detects radio waves. There are also telescopes that detect gamma rays, X rays, and infrared rays.

One problem with using telescopes to detect invisible electromagnetic radiation is that Earth's atmosphere acts as a shield against many forms of electromagnetic radiation. Atoms and molecules in the atmosphere prevent short wavelengths like gamma rays, X rays, and most ultraviolet rays from reaching Earth's surface. Water vapor blocks infrared rays, so ground-based telescopes that are used to study infrared work best at high elevations, where the air is thin and dry. But the only way to study many forms of radiation is from space.

Space-Based Astronomy

While ground-based telescopes have been critical in helping astronomers learn about the universe, valuable information has also come from spacecraft. Spacecraft that contain telescopes and other instruments have been launched to investigate planets, stars, and other distant objects. In space, Earth's atmosphere cannot interfere with the detection of electromagnetic radiation.

Reading Check Why do scientists launch spacecraft beyond Earth's atmosphere?

Why It Matters

The Interstellar Playlist

SCIENCE & SOCIETY

Telescopes gather data from outer space for us to study on Earth. The two Voyager probes carry data in the opposite direction. They carry the Golden Record, which stores 115 images, greetings in 55 languages, sounds from nature, and music from different cultures and eras.

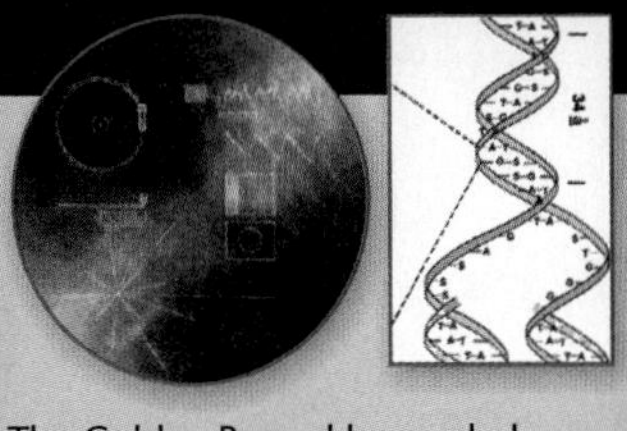

The Golden Record has coded instructions to explain its use and origin. The image at right is one of the images stored on the recording.

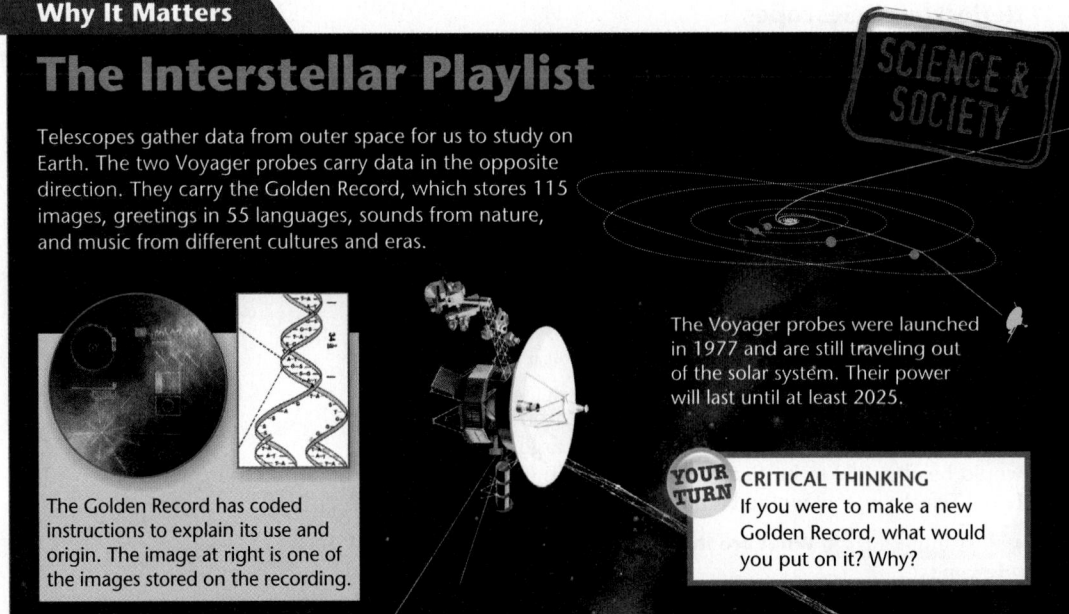

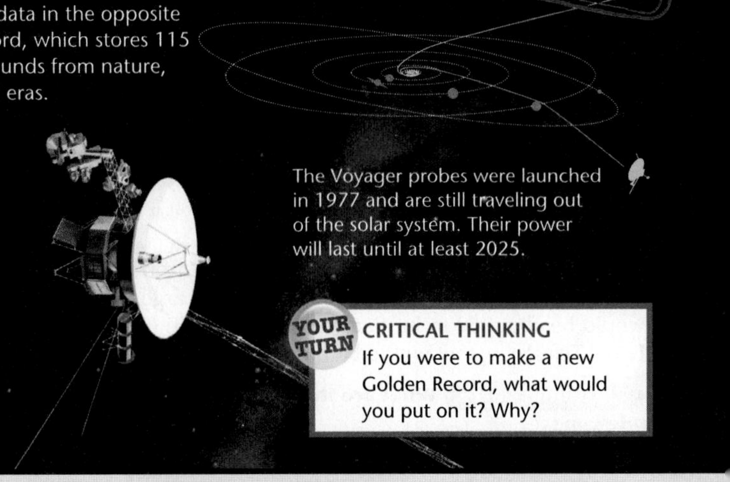

The Voyager probes were launched in 1977 and are still traveling out of the solar system. Their power will last until at least 2025.

YOUR TURN CRITICAL THINKING

If you were to make a new Golden Record, what would you put on it? Why?

Homework

ADVANCED

Space Telescopes and Probes Invite interested students to choose two of the space telescopes or probes discussed in the text and learn more about them. Students may work individually or in pairs and may use library or Internet sources. Students should compare project goals, types of remote-sensing technologies, and the science benefits expected. If either or both of the projects have been completed, students should identify successes and problems. Have them write a report on their findings or make an oral presentation to the class. **LS Verbal** Co-op Learning

Why It Matters

The Interstellar Playlist NASA scientists continue to track and receive communications from the *Voyagers,* which are still traveling out of the solar system at a rate of about 3 AU (450 million kilometers) per year. NASA maintains a web site that commemorates and updates the entire Voyager mission—including visual and audio selections from the Golden Record.

Answer to Your Turn

Critical Thinking Student answers will vary, but likely will reflect visual and audio resources that are more contemporary and/or personal.

Figure 7 The *Hubble Space Telescope* is in orbit around Earth, where the telescope can detect visible and nonvisible electromagnetic radiation without the obstruction of Earth's atmosphere.

Space Telescopes

The *Hubble Space Telescope*, shown in **Figure 7,** is an example of a telescope that has been launched into space to collect electromagnetic radiation from objects in space. Another example, the *Chandra X-ray Observatory,* makes remarkably clear images using X rays from objects in space, such as the remnants of exploded stars. The *Swift* spacecraft detects gamma rays and X rays from explosions and collisions of objects such as black holes. The *Spitzer Space Telescope* detects infrared radiation. The *James Webb Space Telescope* is scheduled to be launched in 2013. When deployed in space, this telescope will be used to detect near- and mid-range infrared radiation from objects in space.

Other Spacecraft

Since the early 1960s, spacecraft have been sent out of Earth's orbit to study other planets. Launched in 1977, the space probes *Voyager 1* and *Voyager 2* investigated Jupiter, Saturn, Uranus, and Neptune. These two spacecraft collected images of these planets and their moons. The *Galileo* spacecraft was in orbit around Jupiter and its moons from 1995 to 2003. This space probe gathered information about the composition of Jupiter's atmosphere and storm systems, which are several times larger than Earth's storm systems. The *Cassini* spacecraft began orbiting Saturn in 2004. In December 2004, the *Huygens* probe detached from the *Cassini* orbiter to study the atmosphere and surface of Titan, Saturn's largest moon. The twin Mars rovers *Spirit*, shown in **Figure 8,** and *Opportunity* landed on Mars in January 2004. They confirmed that water had once been present on Mars. In 2008, the *Phoenix* lander found ice on Mars.

READING TOOLBOX

Frequency
Compare your list of frequency-word statements with the lists made by other students. Add to your list if there are any statements that you missed.

Figure 8 The Mars rover *Spirit* and its twin, *Opportunity*, have transmitted thousands of images of the red planet to scientists on Earth. The mission was originally planned to last only three months, but the rovers continued to operate for several years.

Debate — GENERAL

Space Exploration Some people think that the costs and risks associated with human exploration of space are so great that space missions should be limited to robotic technologies or space probes. Others believe that space is such an important frontier that it would be a mistake to curtail humanity's reach toward the moon, Mars, and the space beyond. Assign students to prepare arguments for and against this public policy issue and stage a classroom debate. LS **Verbal** Co-op Learning

Close

Reteaching — BASIC

Two-Column Notes Organize students into pairs. Have them work together to create a chart that outlines the idea of observing the universe. Have them write main ideas or section heads in the left column and details, examples, or explanations in the right column. Have them use the guide to quiz each other and to study for assessments. LS **Auditory**

Quiz — GENERAL

1. Name the two types of optical telescopes and explain how they differ. (Refracting telescopes use lenses while reflecting telescopes use mirrors to gather light.)
2. How are distances between the stars measured? (in light-years)
3. List the forms of electromagnetic radiation other than visible light. (gamma rays, infrared, radio waves, X rays, microwaves, and ultraviolet radiation) LS **Verbal**

Internet Activity — GENERAL

Space Spinoffs Divide students into small groups and have them identify products of space technology that now have "everyday" applications on Earth. Each group should select products in a specific field, such as weather prediction, medicine, industry, computers, or communications. Have each group create a multimedia presentation to share with the class. A worksheet designed to direct student research on this topic can be found in the **Chapter Resource File** booklet or by visiting www.thinkcentral.com and entering the keyword **HQXSSPX.** LS **Verbal/Visual** Co-op Learning

READING TOOLBOX

Frequency Divide the class into two groups. Have each group take turns writing frequency statements on the board, without any repeats. Continue until all frequency statements are listed.

Close, *continued*

Answers to Section Review

1. The universe began 14 billion years ago, and is organized into solar systems, nebulas of dust and gas, star islands called *galaxies*, and galaxy clusters. Vast distances are measured in astronomical units or light years.
2. visible: continuous color spectrum from violet to red; invisible: radio waves, infrared, microwaves, ultraviolet rays, X rays, and gamma rays
3. Optical telescopes gather visible light. Special telescopes such as radio telescopes detect invisible radiation. Spacecraft and probes study space without interference from Earth's atmosphere.
4. Refracting telescopes use lenses to gather and focus light, while reflecting telescopes use curved mirrors.
5. Optical telescopes make use of lenses or mirrors to gather visible light. Radio telescopes detect radio wave emissions.
6. space telescopes: *Hubble Space Telescope*, *James Webb Space Telescope*, *Chandra X-ray Observatory*; space probes: *Voyager 1* and *2*, *Galileo*, *Cassini-Huygens*
7. The lenses of refracting telescope focus each color differently. Newton's experiments with lenses provided insight into color separation. Concluding that lenses would never give sharp color images, he designed a reflecting telescope.
8. Answers may vary but should show that students have evaluated the pros and cons of human space flight and should take a stand supported by factual information.

Figure 9 Astronaut Doug Wheelock installs a truss that supports a set of solar panels on the International Space Station.

Human Space Exploration

Spacecraft that carry only instruments and computers are described as *robotic*. These spacecraft can explore space and travel beyond the solar system. Crewed spacecraft, or those that carry humans, have never gone beyond Earth's moon.

The first humans went into space in the 1960s. Between 1969 and 1972, NASA landed 12 people on the moon. Now, crewed spaceflights only orbit Earth. Flights, such as those aboard the space shuttles, allow people to release or repair satellites, to perform scientific experiments, or to live and work on the International Space Station, as shown in **Figure 9.**

Eventually, NASA would like to send people to explore Mars. However, such a voyage would be expensive, difficult, and dangerous. The loss of two space shuttles and their crews, the *Challenger* in 1986 and the *Columbia* in 2003, have focused public attention on the risks of human space exploration. NASA is planning first to send astronauts back to the moon.

Spinoffs of the Space Program

Space programs have brought benefits to areas outside the field of astronomy. Satellites in orbit provide information about weather all over Earth. This information helps scientists make accurate weather predictions days in advance. Other satellites broadcast television signals from around the world or allow people to navigate cars and airplanes. Inventing ways to make objects smaller and lighter so that they can go into space has also led to improved electronics. These technological developments have been applied to radios, televisions, and other equipment. Even medical equipment has benefited from space programs. For example, heart pumps have been improved based on NASA's research on the flow of fluids through rockets.

Section 1 Review

Key Ideas

1. **Describe** characteristics of the universe in terms of time, distance, and organization.
2. **Identify** the parts of the electromagnetic spectrum, both visible and invisible.
3. **Explain** how astronomers use electromagnetic radiation to study space.
4. **Compare** reflecting telescopes and refracting telescopes.
5. **Explain** how a radio telescope differs from an optical telescope.
6. **Identify** two examples of space telescopes and two examples of space probes.

Critical Thinking

7. **Identifying Relationships** Using the development of reflecting telescopes as an example, explain how scientific inquiry leads to advances in technology.
8. **Analyzing Processes** Human space exploration is expensive and dangerous. Explain why NASA should or should not continue doing it.

Concept Mapping

9. Use the following terms to create a concept map: *electromagnetic radiation, reflecting telescope, refracting telescope, telescope, probe, astronomy, universe,* Voyager, and Cassini.

9. *Astronomy* is the science of studying the *universe* using *telescopes*, which include *reflecting telescopes*, *refracting telescopes*, and special telescopes that detect other forms of *electromagnetic radiation*; and *probes* such as *Cassini* and *Voyager*.

Differentiated Instruction

Alternative Assessment

Skit Have students present a skit about the history of astronomy. Students should consider how long light takes to travel through space. They should cover naked-eye observations, the invention of telescopes, how electromagnetic radiation brings details into focus, and how space-based astronomy provides a more accurate picture of the universe than was previously obtained. **LS Verbal/Kinesthetic**

SECTION 2
Movements of Earth

Key Ideas	Key Terms	Why It Matters
› Describe two lines of evidence for Earth's rotation. › Explain how the change in apparent positions of constellations provides evidence of Earth's rotation and revolution around the sun. › Summarize how Earth's rotation and revolution provide a basis for measuring time. › Explain how the tilt of Earth's axis and Earth's movement cause seasons.	rotation revolution perihelion aphelion equinox solstice	Earth's rotation and revolution are responsible for natural events such as day and night, weather patterns, and the seasons. We also measure and tell time based on Earth's movements.

Understanding the basic motions of Earth helps scientists understand the motions of other bodies in the solar system and the universe. These movements of Earth are also responsible for the seasons and the changes in weather.

The Rotating Earth

The spinning of Earth on its axis is called **rotation.** Each complete rotation takes one day. The most observable effects of Earth's rotation on its axis are day and night. As Earth rotates from west to east, the sun appears to rise in the east in the morning. The sun then appears to cross the sky and set in the west. At any given moment, the part of Earth that faces the sun experiences daylight. At the same time, the part of Earth that faces away from the sun experiences nighttime.

rotation the spin of a body on its axis

The Foucault Pendulum

In the 19th century, the scientist Jean-Bernard-Leon Foucault provided evidence of Earth's rotation by using a pendulum. He created a long, heavy pendulum that rocks back and forth by attaching a wire to the ceiling and then attaching a weight, called a *bob*, to the wire. Throughout the day, the bob would swing back and forth. The path of the pendulum appeared to change over time. However, it was the floor that was moving while the pendulum's path stayed constant. Because the floor was attached to Earth, one can conclude that Earth rotates. A Foucault pendulum is shown in **Figure 1.**

Figure 1 The 12 ft arc of this Foucault pendulum in Spokane, Washington, appears to change throughout the day. However, the actual path of the pendulum does not change. Instead, it is the floor that moves as Earth rotates under the pendulum.

Section 2

Focus

Overview

This section explains Earth's rotation on its axis and its revolution around the sun. The section also relates Earth's motions to the measurement of time and to the passage of seasons.

Bellringer

Ask students to answer these questions: In what direction did the sun rise this morning? Where is the sun in the sky at noon? In which direction will the sun set tonight? (The sun rose in the east. It is highest in the sky at noon. It will set in the west.) **LS Verbal**

Motivate

Activity GENERAL

Role-Playing Dim the room lights and have one student be the *sun*, standing still and holding an illuminated flashlight. Have another student be *Earth.* Have *Earth* walk around the *sun* while turning counterclockwise. Tell *sun* to keep the flashlight beam pointed at *Earth* as that student moves. Have *Earth* announce "day" when he or she sees the light, and "night" when his or her back is turned to the *sun.* **LS Kinesthetic**

Key Resources

Chapter Resource File
- Directed Reading BASIC

Technology
- Transparencies
  Bellringer

Teach

Demonstration — BASIC

Coriolis Effect Use a turntable to show how objects on a rotating surface are affected by the spinning. Keeping the turntable motionless, roll a marble from the center to the edge. The marble moves in a straight line. Start the turntable moving and release another marble. Ask students how the path changes. (The path of the marble seems to curve as the marble rolls because the turntable is moving.) **LS Visual**

Quick Lab

Skills Acquired
- Collecting data
- Examining events

Materials
- bulletin board paper
- Internet and/or library resources
- markers, different colors
- metric ruler

Teacher's Notes: Students will conduct research individually, and then pairs of students will create *timelines* that consist of 10 milestones in the human exploration of space.

Answers to Analysis
1. Answers will vary depending on which milestones students chose to place on their timelines.
2. Humans have been exploring space since 1957.
3. Sample answer: Humans first used manned suborbital flights and orbital flights to study space. In 1969, humans explored the moon. In recent years, humans have launched probes to study the outer planets, and rovers have explored Mars.

Quick Lab — 30 min

Space Exploration Timeline

Procedure
1. Use the Internet or other library resources to research and identify at least five milestones in the history of space exploration.
2. Compare the five milestones you listed with five milestones listed by a partner.
3. Combine all of your milestones into a single space exploration timeline.

Analysis
1. Did you include the following space-exploration technologies: rockets, space shuttles, space stations; satellites; missions to the moon; rovers, probes?
2. How long has humanity explored space?
3. How has space-exploration technology changed during this time?

The Coriolis Effect

Evidence of the rotation of Earth can also be seen in the movment of ocean surface currents and wind belts. Ocean currents and wind belts do not move in a straight path. The rotation of Earth causes ocean currents and wind belts to be deflected to the right in the Northern Hemisphere. In the Southern Hemisphere, ocean currents and wind belts deflect to the left. This curving of the path of wind belts and ocean currents is caused by Earth's rotation underneath the atmosphere and the sea and is called the *Coriolis effect*.

The Revolving Earth

As Earth spins on its axis, Earth also revolves around the sun. Even though you cannot feel Earth moving, it is traveling around the sun at an average speed of 29.8 km/s. The motion of a body that travels around another body in space is called **revolution.** Each complete revolution of Earth around the sun takes one year, or about 365 ¼ days.

Earth's Orbit

The path that a body follows as it travels around another body in space is called an *orbit*. Earth's orbit around the sun is not quite a circle. Earth's orbit is an ellipse. An *ellipse* is a closed curve whose shape is determined by two points, or *foci,* within the ellipse. In planetary orbits in our solar system, one focus is located deep within the sun. No object is located at the other focus.

Because its orbit is an ellipse, Earth is not always the same distance from the sun. The point in the orbit of a planet at which the planet is closest to the sun is the **perihelion.** The point in the orbit of a planet at which the planet is farthest from the sun is the **aphelion** (uh FEE lee uhn). As shown in **Figure 2**, Earth's aphelion distance is 152 million km. Its perihelion distance is 147 million km.

revolution the motion of a body that travels around another body in space; one complete trip along an orbit

perihelion in the orbit of a planet or other body in the solar system, the point that is closest to the sun

aphelion in the orbit of a planet or other body in the solar system, the point that is farthest from the sun

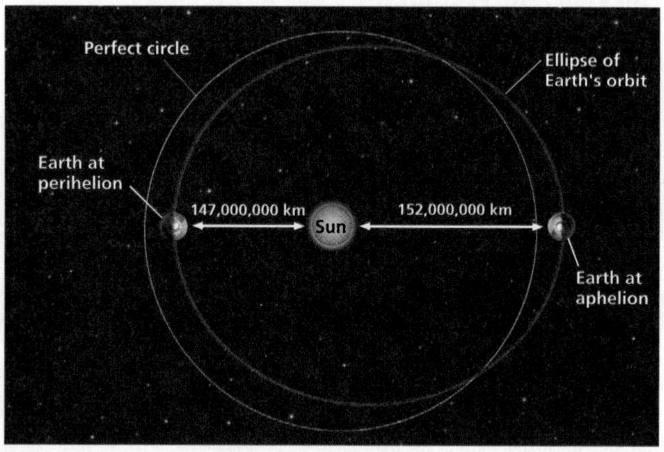

Figure 2 As Earth revolves around its elliptical orbit, the planet is farthest from the sun in July and closest to the sun in January. The elliptical orbit in this illustration has been exaggerated for emphasis.

Key Resources

Technology
- Transparencies
  - 131 Earth's Orbit
  - 132 The Apparent Motion of Constellations

Differentiated Instruction

English Learners

Vocabulary The words *aphelion* and *perihelion* come from the Greek root *-helios*, which means "sun." *Ap-* is a variant of *apo*, which means "away or apart." Thus, the aphelion is the point in a planet's orbit at which the planet is farthest from the sun. *Peri-*, in contrast, means "near." The perihelion is the point in a planet's orbit at which the planet is closest to the sun. **LS Verbal** English Language Learners

Constellations and Earth's Motion

Evidence of Earth's revolution and rotation around the sun can be seen in the motion of constellations. A *constellation* is a group of stars that are organized in a recognizable pattern. In 1930, the International Astronomical Union divided the sky into 88 constellations. Many of the names given to these constellations came from the ancient Greeks more than 2,000 years ago. Taurus, the bull, and Orion, the hunter, are some examples of names from Greek mythology that have been given to constellations.

Evidence of Earth's Rotation

If you gaze at a constellation in the evening sky, you might notice that it appears to be moving in the shape of an arc, as if it were tracing a circle around a fixed point. The apparent change in its position occurs for the same reason that the sun appears to move across the daytime sky. That is, Earth's rotation makes the constellations appear to move in this way.

Evidence of Earth's Revolution

The position of a constellation in the evening sky changes not only because of Earth's rotation but also because of Earth's revolution around the sun. Examine **Figure 3,** which shows the same region of the sky at the same time of night in February and in March. Notice that all the constellations appear lower in the sky in March than they do in February. This change in the position of the constellations is a result of Earth's revolution. As Earth revolves around the sun, the night side of Earth faces in a different direction of the universe. Thus, as Earth moves, different constellations are visible in the night sky from month to month and from season to season.

Reading Check **How does the movement of the constellations provide evidence of Earth's rotation and revolution?**

THINK central
INTERACT ONLINE
(Keyword: HQXSSPF3)

Figure 3 In one month's period, the position of the constellations in the sky seen from Denver, Colorado, at 10 PM change because of the revolution of Earth.

Discussion — BASIC

Comprehension Check Explain that the stars that make up constellations are not necessarily located near each other, but are simply in the same part of the sky. The patterns were devised as a memory aid to help people identify the stars. Ask students why people in ancient cultures wanted to remember the stars. Tell them to think about how constellations change throughout the year. (Answers may vary. Sample answer: Because constellations are visible at different but predictable times of the year, people could anticipate and plan for planting and harvesting seasons and for winter.) **LS Verbal**

Activity — GENERAL

Star Viewers To help students become familiar with star patterns, have them make a star viewer. They will need a cardboard tube, black construction paper, masking tape, and pins of various sizes. Have them select a constellation and find out the names of its main stars. Tell them to put the end of the tube on top of the construction paper and trace a circle the same size as the opening. Have them copy the star pattern on the circle, and use pins to poke holes in the paper for each star. Have them cut out the circle and attach it to the front of the tube with the front of the paper facing the tube. They can hold the tube up to a bright light to view the constellation. **LS Visual**

Answer to Reading Check

Constellations provide two kinds of evidence of Earth's motion. As Earth rotates, the stars appear to change position during the night. As Earth revolves around the sun, Earth's night sky faces a different part of the universe. As a result, different constellations appear in the night sky as the seasons change.

Differentiated Instruction

Struggling Readers

Reading Hint Pair students to practice the "skimming and scanning" technique on the passages about measuring time and calendar formation. Have students brainstorm ways to get the most out of this reading technique, such as looking for italicized words, heads, dates, and captions. First, they can read quickly to identify the main topic, then scan for specific information. They can use the related section review questions as their focus or work together to create an outline to use as a study guide. (English Language Learners)
LS Verbal

Cultural Awareness — BASIC

Constellation Stories Have students identify constellations that people from different cultures saw in the night sky. Then, have students work individually, in pairs, or in small groups to select one constellation to research. Provide star guides and mythology books for reference. Students should identify when and where the constellation appears. Ask them to retell the myth or legend in their own words and to illustrate or act out the story. Have a class storytelling session in which students share their stories. **LS Verbal/Visual/Auditory**

Teach, *continued*

History Connection — GENERAL

It's About Time Calendars are typically based on natural astronomical cycles. Divide the class into small groups and have each group choose a calendar system to research, such as the Mayan, Islamic, Jewish, Gregorian, Aztec, Egyptian, Babylonian, or Chinese systems. Three basic types of calendars have been created: solar calendars designed to match the year, lunar calendars based on the lunar phase cycle, and lunisolar calendars that have months based on the lunar phase cycle with an extra month periodically intercalculated. Have student groups find out the scientific basis of the calendar they chose, interesting facts about its evolution, and its usefulness in helping a society organize its activities. Have them share what they discover with the class. LS Verbal

READING TOOLBOX

Using Spatial Language

Answers will vary. Students may find that it is hard to maintain the meaning of the sentence without using spatial language. They might find themselves using other spatial language to try to bridge the gap. Point out the importance of spatial language for describing the shapes and locations of objects, distance, orientation, and direction of motion.

Figure 4 This is a reconstruction of a 3.6 m stone carving that functioned, in part, as a calendar based on solar and lunar cycles.

Measuring Time

Earth's motion provides the basis for measuring time. For example, the day and year are based on periods of Earth's motion. The day is determined by Earth's rotation on its axis. Each complete rotation of Earth on its axis is one day, which is then divided into 24 hours.

The year is determined by Earth's revolution around the sun. Each complete revolution of Earth around the sun takes 365 ¼ days, or one year.

A month is based on the moon's motion around Earth. A month was originally determined by the period between successive full moons, which is 29.5 days. The word *month* actually comes from the word *moon*. However, the number of full moons in a year is not a whole number. Therefore, a month is now determined as roughly one-twelfth of a year.

Formation of the Calendar

A *calendar* is a system created for measuring long intervals of time by dividing time into periods of days, weeks, months, and years. Many ancient civilizations created versions of calendars based on astronomical cycles. The ancient Egyptians used a calendar based on a solar year. The Babylonians used a 12-month lunar year. The Aztecs, who lived in what is now Mexico, also created a calendar, which is shown in **Figure 4.**

Because the year is about 365 ¼ days long, the extra ¼ day is usually ignored to make the number of days on a calendar a whole number. To keep the calendars on the same schedule as Earth's movements, we must account for the extra time. So, every four years, one day is added to the month of February. Any year that contains an extra day is called a *leap year*.

More than 2,000 years ago, Julius Caesar, of the Roman Empire, revised the calendar so that an extra day every four years was added. His successor, Augustus Caesar, made the extra day come at the end of the shortest month, February. He also made July and August long months with 31 days each.

READING TOOLBOX

Using Spatial Language
How important is spatial language for communicating with people? Choose three sentences in Section 2 that use spatial words or phrases. Try to rewrite each sentence without using the spatial language. Can you do it?

The Modern Calendar

Because the year is not exactly 365 days long, over centuries, the calendar gradually became misaligned with the seasons. In the late 1500s, Pope Gregory XIII formed a committee to create a calendar that would keep the calendar aligned with the seasons. We use this calendar today. In this Gregorian calendar, century years, such as 1800 and 1900, are not leap years unless the century years are exactly divisible by 400. Thus, 2000 was a leap year even though it was a century year. However, 2100, 2200, and 2300 will not be leap years.

Differentiated Instruction

Special Education Students

Calendars Gather several calendars, one for every two students, from a variety of years, including some leap years. Have students sit with a partner, and give each pair a calendar. Read through this page as a group. Have students explore each calendar reference on their individual calendars. LS Verbal

Time Zones

Using the sun as the basis for measuring time, we define noon as the time when the sun is highest in the sky. Because of Earth's rotation, the sun is highest above different locations on Earth at different times of day. Earth's surface has been divided into 24 standard time zones, as shown in **Figure 5**, to avoid problems created by different local times. In each zone, noon is set as the time when the sun is highest over the center of that zone. Earth's circumference equals 360° measured from Earth's center. If you divide 360° by the 24 hours needed for one rotation, you find that Earth rotates at a rate of 15° per hour. Therefore, each of Earth's 24 standard time zones covers about 15°. The time in each zone is one hour earlier than the time in the zone to the east of each zone.

International Date Line

There are 24 standard time zones and 24 h in a day. But there must be some point on Earth's surface where the date changes. The *International Date Line* was established to prevent confusion. The International Date Line is an imaginary line that runs from north to south through the Pacific Ocean. When it is Friday west of the International Date Line, it is Thursday east of the line. The line is drawn so that it does not cut through islands or continents. Thus, everyone living within one country has the same date. Note where the line is drawn between Alaska and Siberia in **Figure 5.**

Reading Check **What is the purpose of the International Date Line?**

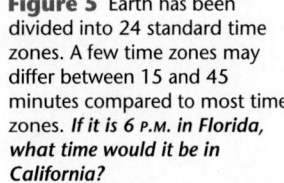

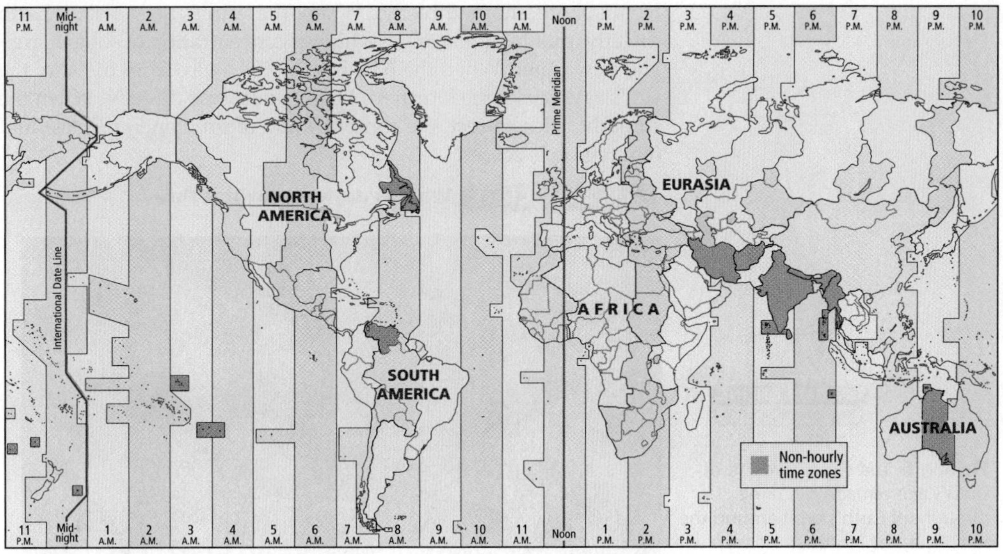

Figure 5 Earth has been divided into 24 standard time zones. A few time zones may differ between 15 and 45 minutes compared to most time zones. ***If it is 6 P.M. in Florida, what time would it be in California?***

Using the Figure — GENERAL

Time Zone Zigzags Explain to students that political borders and other considerations sometimes override the drawing of time zone boundaries strictly on the basis of longitude. Ask students to imagine what it would be like if a time zone line went directly through the middle of your town. Ask students what happens as you move west from one time zone to the next. (As you move west, clock time is one hour earlier.) Answer to caption question: When it is 6 P.M. in Florida, it would be 3 P.M. in California. **LS Visual**

Math Connection — GENERAL

Resetting Your Clock Ask students to use the map of time zones to figure out what time it would be in different parts of the world. If it is 6 A.M. on Tuesday in Beijing, China, what day and time is it in San Francisco, California? (Going east, you move through 8 time zones: 6 A.M. + 8 h = 2 P.M.; When you cross the International Date Line, you lose a day, so it is 2 P.M. on Monday in San Francisco.) If it is 4 P.M. on Saturday in Greenland, what day and time is it in Japan? (Going either east or west, you move through 12 time zones. Going east: 4 P.M. + 12 = 4 A.M. the next day. Going west: 4 P.M. − 12 = 4 A.M. and by crossing the International Date Line, you gain a day, so it is 4 A.M. on Sunday in Japan.) **LS Logical**

Internet Activity — GENERAL

International Zones Invite students to research the evolution of time zones. Students may also investigate what local variations of the time-zone system are used in China, the Middle East, and South Asia. Have students report back to the class on an aspect of this topic that interests them. A worksheet designed to direct student research on this topic can be found in the **Chapter Resource File** booklet or by visiting **www.thinkcentral.com** and entering the keyword **HQXSSPX.** **LS Verbal**

Answer to Reading Check

Because time zones are based on Earth's rotation, as you travel west you eventually come to a location where, on one side of the time zone border, the calendar moves ahead one day. The purpose of the International Date Line is to locate the border so that the transition would affect the least number of people. So that it will affect the least number of people, the International Date Line is in the middle of the Pacific Ocean, instead of on a continent.

Key Resources

Technology

- Transparencies
  133 Time Zones

Teach, *continued*

Debate — General

Daylight Savings Time For thousands of years, many societies based their clocks on local solar time. During World War I, daylight savings time was adopted in an effort to save fuel. Today, the system is followed in more than 70 countries. Some groups object to the practice—for example, farmers must then do chores in the morning darkness. Invite students to offer additional examples and to debate the merits of daylight savings time as a public policy. Assign students to prepare arguments for and against the practice and stage a debate. **LS Verbal/Logical**

Answer to Reading Check

Daylight savings time is an adjustment that is made to standard time by setting clocks ahead one hour to take advantage of longer hours of daylight in the summer months and to save energy.

Why It Matters

Planetary Seasons

Variations in the seasons of other planets are due to axial tilt and how elliptical a planet's orbit is. Venus and Jupiter have axial tilts of about 3° compared with Earth's 23.5°, so their seasonal variations are smaller. Mercury's pattern of rotating three times for every two orbits of the sun produces two week-long seasons. Mars has a more eccentric orbit and a slightly larger axial tilt, so its seasons are different lengths. Uranus's extreme axial tilt of 98° produces seasons that last about 21 years. The coming of spring warmth triggers huge storms in Uranus' atmosphere.

SciLinks
www.scilinks.org
Topic: Seasons
Code: **HQX1363**

Academic Vocabulary
significant (sig NIF uh kahnt) important

Daylight Savings Time

Because of the tilt of Earth's axis, the duration of daylight is shorter in the winter months than in the summer months. During the summer months, days are longer so that the sun rises earlier in the morning when many people are still sleeping. To take advantage of that daylight time, the United States uses *daylight savings time*. Under this system, clocks are set one hour ahead of standard time in March, which provides an additional hour of daylight during the evening. The additional hour also saves energy because the use of electricity decreases. In November, clocks are set back one hour to return to standard time. Countries that are in the equatorial region do not observe daylight savings time because there are not significant changes in the amount of daylight time in the equatorial region. There, daylight is about 12 h every day of the year.

The Seasons

Earth's axis is tilted at 23.5°. As Earth revolves around the sun, Earth's axis always points toward the North Star. Thus, during each revolution, the North Pole sometimes tilts toward the sun and sometimes tilts away from the sun, as shown in **Figure 6.** When the North Pole tilts toward the sun, the Northern Hemisphere has longer periods of daylight than the Southern Hemisphere does. When the North Pole tilts away from the sun, the Southern Hemisphere has longer periods of daylight.

The angle at which the sun's rays strike each part of Earth's surface changes as Earth moves through its orbit. When the North Pole tilts toward the sun, the sun's rays strike the Northern Hemisphere more directly. When the sun's rays strike Earth directly, that region receives a higher concentration of solar energy and is warmer. When the North Pole tilts away from the sun, the sun's rays strike the Northern Hemisphere less directly. When the sunlight is less direct, the concentration of solar energy is less and that region is cooler.

Reading Check **What is daylight savings time?**

THINK central
INTERACT ONLINE
(Keyword: HQXSSPF6)

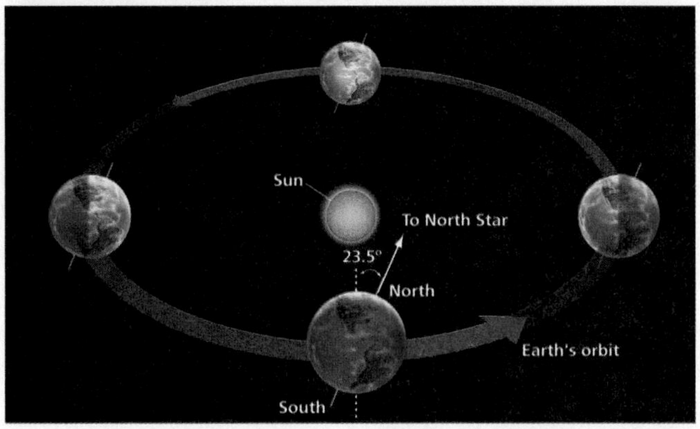

Figure 6 The direction of tilt of Earth's axis remains the same throughout Earth's orbit around the sun. Thus, the Northern Hemisphere receives more direct sunlight during summer months and less direct sunlight during winter months.

MISCONCEPTION ALERT

Seasons Students may believe that seasons are the result of the changing distance between Earth and the sun, with hotter weather occurring in both hemispheres when Earth is closer to the sun. Because Earth's orbit is slightly elliptical in shape, Earth's distance from the sun does vary. But Earth is actually closer to the sun in January and farther from the sun in July, the opposite of what students might expect. Emphasize that the actual cause of seasons is Earth's tilt on its axis. The axial tilt changes the angle at which the sun's rays strike Earth, and also affects the number of daylight hours, resulting in differences in energy and temperatures. In January, when the North Pole is tilted away from the sun, the sun's rays strike the Northern Hemisphere at a low angle, producing colder weather. At the same time, the sun's rays strike the Southern Hemisphere at a higher angle, producing warmer weather. In effect, the seasons are reversed north and south of the equator. **LS Verbal**

Key Resources

Technology

- Transparencies
  134 How the Tilt of Earth's Axis Affects Seasons

Seasonal Weather

Changes in the angle at which the sun's rays strike Earth's surface cause the seasons. When the North Pole tilts away from the sun, the angle of the sun's rays falling on the Northern Hemisphere is low. As a result, the sun's rays spread solar energy over a large area, which leads to lower temperatures. The tilt of the North Pole away from the sun also causes the Northern Hemisphere to experience fewer daylight hours. Fewer daylight hours also means less energy and lower temperatures. Lower temperatures cause the winter seasons. During winter, the Northern Hemisphere tilts away from the sun, and the Southern Hemisphere tilts toward the sun. The sun's rays strike the Southern Hemisphere at a greater angle than they do in the Northern Hemisphere, and there are more daylight hours in the Southern Hemisphere. Therefore, the Southern Hemisphere experiences summer. So, the seasons are caused by the tilt of Earth's axis and not by Earth's distance from the sun.

Equinoxes

The seasons fall and spring begin on days called equinoxes. An **equinox** is the moment when the sun appears to cross the celestial equator. The *celestial equator* is an imaginary line in the sky directly overhead from the equator on Earth. During an equinox, the sun's rays strike Earth at a 90° angle along the equator. The hours of daylight and darkness are approximately equal everywhere on Earth on that day. The *autumnal equinox* occurs on September 22 or 23 of each year and marks the beginning of fall in the Northern Hemisphere. The *vernal equinox* occurs on March 21 or 22 of each year and marks the beginning of spring in the Northern Hemisphere.

equinox the moment when the sun appears to cross the celestial equator

Quick Lab

10 min

The Angle of the Sun's Rays

Procedure

1. Turn the lights down low or off in the classroom.
2. Place a piece of paper on the floor. Using a meterstick, hold a flashlight 1 m above the paper, and shine the light of the flashlight straight down on the piece of paper.
3. Have a partner outline the perimeter of the circle of light cast by the flashlight on the paper. Label the circle "90° angle." Place a clean piece of paper on the floor.
4. At a height of 0.5 m from the floor, shine the light of the flashlight on the paper at an angle. Make sure the distance between the flashlight and the paper is 1 m.
5. Have a partner outline the perimeter of the circle of light cast by the flashlight on the paper. Label the circle "low angle."

Analysis

1. Compare the two circles drawn in steps 3 and 5. Which circle concentrates the light in a smaller area?
2. Which circle would most likely model the sun's rays striking Earth during the summer season?

Close

Reteaching — GENERAL

Evidence Have students develop a cause-and-effect organizer to help them understand the evidence for Earth's motions. Guide them to put Earth's rotation and revolution in the cause boxes and list the different lines of evidence in corresponding effects boxes. Students may work in pairs.
LS Logical Co-op Learning

Quiz — GENERAL

1. How does Earth's axial tilt cause seasonal temperature changes? (At a lower angle, the sun's rays spread over a larger area, reducing their heating effect. At a higher angle, the solar energy is more concentrated.)
2. How are time zones related to Earth's rotation? (Earth's surface was divided along longitude lines into 24 time zones of 15° each. Earth rotates through the longitudes, represented by each time zone, one for each hour, in 24 hours.)
3. What would happen if we did not add an extra day to the solar calendar for leap year? (Because of the extra quarter day in the solar year, over time the calendar would drift out of synch with Earth's motions and be misaligned with the seasons.)

LS Verbal

Quick Lab

Skills Acquired

- Experimenting
- Observing
- Analyzing

Materials

- Piece of paper
- Meterstick
- Flashlight

Teacher's Notes: Make sure that in both steps 2 and 4, students keep the flashlight 1 m from the paper. Students may need to move the piece of paper to the side to draw the circle in step 5.

Answers to Analysis

1. The circle in step 3 concentrates the light in a smaller area.
2. The circle in step 3.

Close, *continued*

Answers to Section Review

1. During different seasons, different constellations appear in the night sky because we see the stars from a different position in Earth's orbit.
2. A Foucault pendulum traces out a changing path because Earth is rotating underneath. Earth's rotation causes wind belts and currents to deflect.
3. Earth's revolution around the sun takes about 365 days. The Earth also spins on its axis every 24 hours. The side that faces the sun has day and the other side has night. The whole lunar cycle takes about four weeks, the basis of our month.
4. The year is actually 365 1/4 days long. In the 1500s the calendar did not match seasons, so leap year was introduced, with an extra day every four years.
5. an additional hour of daylight in the evening; saving energy
6. During summer, half of Earth is tilted toward the sun and during winter that half is tilted away. Regions pointing toward the sun are warmer because daylight lasts longer and the sun's rays are more vertical.
7. Earth is closer to the sun in winter, but the North Pole is tilted away from the sun. The sun's rays strike at a low angle, producing lower winter temperatures in the Northern Hemisphere.
8. During the summer solstice, Earth is located near the aphelion of its orbit, or the farthest distance from the sun.
9. It is hours of daylight and the angle of the sun's rays that cause the seasons, not distance from the sun.
10. If Earth rotated only once a year, one side of the planet would face the sun at all times and the other half of Earth would be in darkness. Because Earth rotates at a rate of 15° of its circumference each hour, we would also not have time measurements dividing the day into 24-hour periods. Earth's rotation on its axis is related to the division of the year into four seasons. If Earth's axis were not tilted at an angle, these seasonal variations would not exist.
11. The movements of *Earth* include its *revolution* around the sun in an *orbit* shaped like an *ellipse* from *perihelion* to *aphelion*; and *rotation* on its axis, which is evidenced by the *Foucault pendulum*, the *Coriolis effect*, and the apparent movement of *constellations.*

Figure 7 In the Northern Hemisphere, the sun appears to follow its highest path across the sky during the summer solstice and its lowest path across the sky during the winter solstice.

solstice the point at which the sun is as far north or as far south of the equator as possible

Summer Solstices

The seasons of summer and winter begin on days called **solstices.** Each year on June 21 or 22, the North Pole's tilt toward the sun is greatest. On this day, the sun's rays strike Earth at a 90° angle along the Tropic of Cancer, which is located at 23.5° north latitude. This day is called the *summer solstice* and marks the beginning of summer in the Northern Hemisphere. *Solstice* means "sun stop" and refers to the fact that in the Northern Hemisphere, the sun follows its highest path across the sky on this day, as shown in **Figure 7,** and then moves lower every day afterward.

The Northern Hemisphere has its most hours of daylight during the summer solstice. The farther north of the equator you are, the longer the period of daylight you have. North of the Arctic Circle, which is located at 66.5° north latitude, there are 24 h of daylight during the summer solstice. At the other extreme, south of the Antarctic Circle, there are 24 h of darkness at that time.

Winter Solstices

By December, the North Pole is tilted to the farthest point away from the sun. On December 21 or 22, the sun's rays strike Earth at a 90° angle along the Tropic of Capricorn, which is located at 23.5° south latitude. This day is called the *winter solstice.* It marks the beginning of winter in the Northern Hemisphere. During the winter solstice, the Northern Hemisphere has the fewest daylight hours. The sun follows its lowest path across the sky. Places that are north of the Arctic Circle then have 24 h of darkness. However, places that are south of the Antarctic Circle have 24 h of daylight at that time.

Section 2 Review

Key Ideas

1. **Explain** how the apparent change of position of constellations over time provides evidence of Earth's revolution around the sun.
2. **Describe** two lines of evidence that indicate that Earth is rotating.
3. **Summarize** how movements of Earth provide a basis for measuring time.
4. **Explain** why today's calendars have leap years.
5. **Identify** two advantages in using daylight savings time.
6. **Explain** how the tilt of Earth's axis and Earth's movements cause seasons.
7. **Identify** the position of Earth in relation to the sun that causes winter in the Northern Hemisphere.
8. **Describe** the position of Earth in relation to the sun during the Northern Hemisphere's summer solstice.

Critical Thinking

9. **Understanding Relationships** How can it be that Earth is at perihelion during wintertime in the Northern Hemisphere?
10. **Predicting Consequences** Explain how measurements of time might differ if Earth rotated on its axis only once per year.

Concept Mapping

11. Use the following terms to create a concept map: *revolution, perihelion, aphelion, rotation, ellipse, orbit, rotation, Foucault pendulum, Coriolis effect, Earth,* and *constellation.*

Differentiated Instruction

Alternative Assessment

Science Fiction Stories Have students write stories in which the evidence for Earth's motions plays a key role in solving a mystery. The key might focus on time zones, seasons, the Coriolis effect, or the apparent movement of constellations. The story must include correct explanations. **LS Verbal**

Why It Matters

What Time Is It?

"Synchronizing your watches" is a surprisingly intricate undertaking. Coordinated Universal Time (UTC), also called civil time, is the time we live by. It is based on Earth's rotation rate. Although the time for a full rotation of Earth is usually expressed as 24 h per day, it is actually 23 h 56 min 4s. As well, Earth's rotation rate is not constant—the moon's gravity is slowing it down. Thus, scientists use atomic clocks to establish International Atomic Time (TAI). Atomic clocks are very precise, because they are based on the vibration rate of atoms. To synchronize UTC with TAI, leap seconds may be added to UTC. Since 1972, 23 leap seconds have been added.

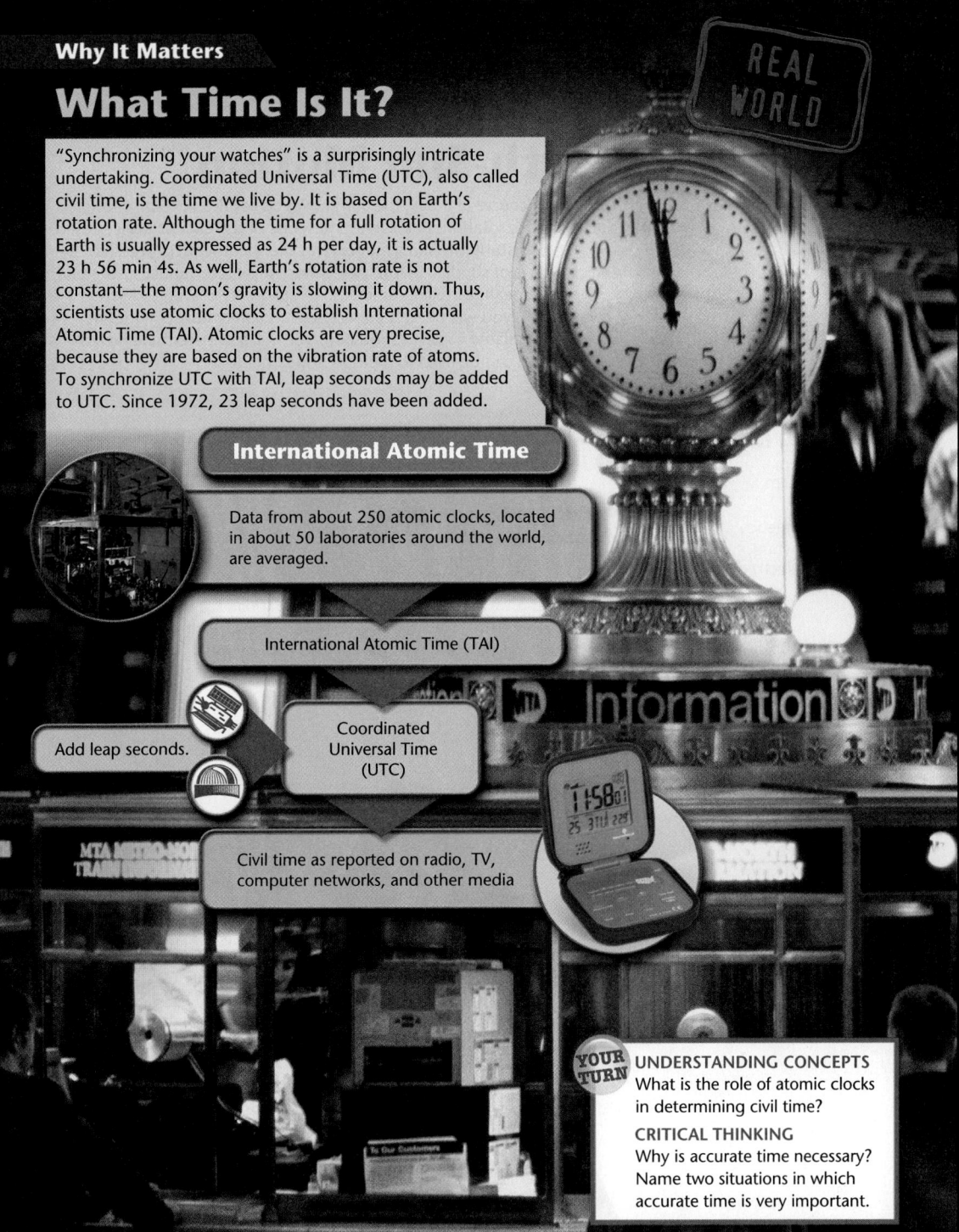

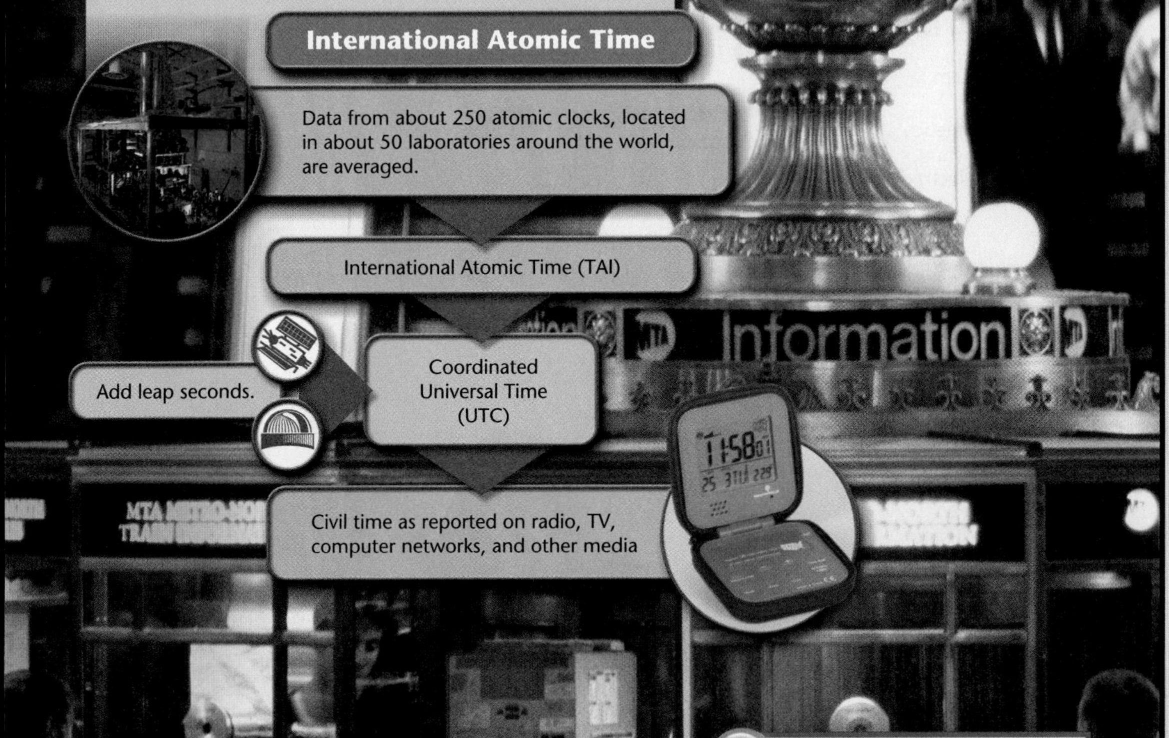
REAL WORLD
International Atomic Time
Data from about 250 atomic clocks, located in about 50 laboratories around the world, are averaged.
International Atomic Time (TAI)
Add leap seconds.
Coordinated Universal Time (UTC)
Information
Civil time as reported on radio, TV, computer networks, and other media

YOUR TURN

UNDERSTANDING CONCEPTS
What is the role of atomic clocks in determining civil time?

CRITICAL THINKING
Why is accurate time necessary? Name two situations in which accurate time is very important.

Why It Matters

What Time is It?

As measured and averaged by the two most sophisticated atomic clocks in the world—one in the United States (in Boulder, Colorado) and the other in France, one second is 9,192,631,770 vibrations of a cesium-133 atom. Data from about 250 less-precise atomic clocks in many other countries are collected monthly by the French International Bureau of Weights and Measures. These data are compared with (and, if necessary, corrected with reference to) the two "master clocks", and the resulting time is called Temps Atomique International (TAI), or International Atomic Time in English. TAI is different from the time experienced and used by us, which is called Temps Universel Coordonne, or Coordinated Universal Time (UTC). Notice that the acronym does not match the English or the French. There are many versions of Universal Time, each with an acronym that begins with UT. The *C* is added to indicate that it is *Coordinated* Universal Time. UTC is time as measured by Earth's rotation, which is very slowly and gradually being slowed by gravitational interaction with the moon. To synchronize TAI with UTC, TAI is adjusted by an additional second—a leap second—approximately every year and a half.

Answers to Your Turn

Understanding Concepts Atomic clocks are used to establish an "absolute" time—a time that is not altered in the way that time as measured by Earth's rotation is altered.

Critical Thinking Answers will vary but should include some notion of the fact that services such as aviation, space missions, military missions, and telecommunications require two or more people or stations to be in contact at specific times.

45 min

Time Required

one 45-minute class period

Lab Ratings

EASY ————————————→ HARD

Teacher Preparation ⚗⚗
Student Setup ⚗
Concept Level ⚗⚗⚗
Cleanup ⚗

Skills Acquired

- Designing Experiments
- Measuring
- Identifying and Recognizing Patterns
- Interpreting
- Organizing and Analyzing Data
- Communicating

Scientific Methods

In this lab, students will
- Ask a Question
- Form and Test a Hypothesis
- Make Observations
- Analyze Results
- Draw Conclusions

Materials

Materials listed are enough for 2 to 3 students to construct the sundial apparatus and measure the movement of Earth. You may wish to make predrilled holes in the wooden board to hold the dowel rod upright, or provide modeling clay so students can change its position. Tell students that another term for a shadow stick is a *gnomon*.

What You'll Do

> **Design** an experiment to measure the movement of Earth.

> **Analyze** the effectiveness of your experimental design.

> **Demonstrate** how shadows can be used to measure time.

What You'll Need

board, wooden,
 20 cm × 30 cm
clock or watch
compass, magnetic
dowel, 30 cm long,
 0.64 cm (¼ inch) diameter
paper, lined
pencil
ruler, metric
tape, masking

Earth-Sun Motion

During the course of a day, the sun moves across the sky. This motion is due to Earth's rotation. In ancient times, one of the earliest devices used by people to study the sun's motion was the shadow stick. The shadow stick is a type of sundial. Before clocks were invented, sundials were one of the only means of telling time.

In this lab, you will use a shadow stick to identify how changes in a shadow are related to Earth's rotation. You will also determine how a shadow stick can be used to measure time.

Ask a Question

❶ How can I measure the movement of Earth?

Form a Hypothesis

❷ With a partner, build a shadow stick apparatus that is similar to the one in the illustration on the following page. Brainstorm with your partner a way in which you can use the apparatus in an experiment to measure the movement of Earth for 30 min. Write a few sentences that describe your design and your hypothesis about how this experiment will measure Earth's motion.

Step ❷

Tips and Tricks

The experiment is best performed on a sunny day. In order to measure the movement of the sun's shadow, students will need to orient the apparatus so that the side with the upright gnomon is toward the south. Once they find north with the compass, students should label the sheet of notebook paper with the proper directions.

Have students present their plan for approval before they begin. One way to proceed would be to use the ruler to record the direction and length of the shadow at 5-minute intervals. If students plan to perform the extension, have them locate a familiar landmark so they can place the apparatus in the same spot each time they use it. Encourage students to graph their data to show how the shadow length changes during the day.

Using Scientific Methods

Test the Hypothesis

3. When you complete your experimental design, have your teacher approve your design before you begin. **CAUTION** Never look directly at the sun.
4. Follow your design to set up and complete your experiment.
5. Take measurements every 5 min, and record this information in a data table.

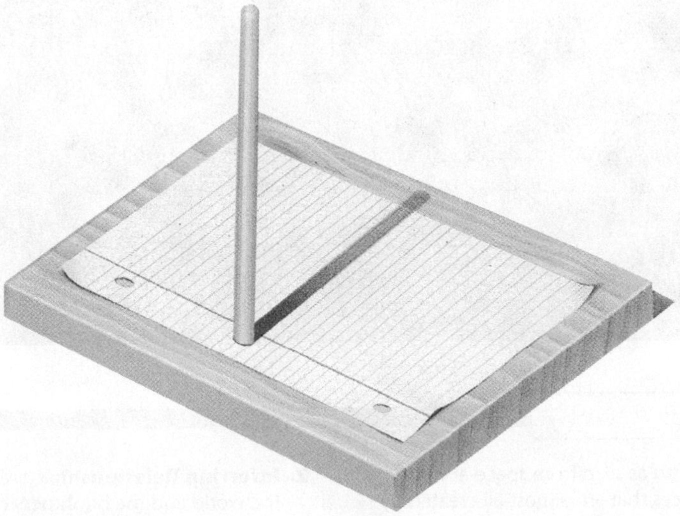

Analyze the Results

1. **Analyzing Data** In what direction did the sun appear to move in the 30 min period?
2. **Evaluating Methods** If you made your shadow stick half as long, would its shadow move the same distance in 30 min? Explain your answer.
3. **Evaluating Methods** Would you make any changes to your experimental design? Explain your answer.

Draw Conclusions

4. **Drawing Conclusions** In what direction does Earth rotate?
5. **Applying Conclusions** How might a shadow stick be used to tell time?

Extension

Evaluating Methods Repeat this lab at different hours of the day. Perform the lab early in the morning, early in the afternoon, and early in the evening. Record the results and any differences that you observe. Explain how shadow sticks can be used to tell direction.

Answers to Analyze the Results

1. The sun appears to move across the sky from east to west while its shadow moves clockwise from west to east.
2. The distance traveled would be unaffected by the length of the stick. This factor is controlled by the rotation of the Earth and the path of the sun across the sky.
3. Answers may vary. Students should evaluate their procedures and suggest appropriate changes.

Answers to Draw Conclusions

4. Earth rotates west to east.
5. Set up a shadow stick to track the movement of the shadow throughout the day. Mark the tip of the shadow line at hourly intervals using a different letter or number for each mark. The shortest shadow represents local noon, when the sunlight comes directly from the south. Once you have a set of measurements for the whole day, mark them permanently so you can use movements of the stick's shadow as a clock to measure time.

Answer to Extension

Use a length of string to make a circle around the shadow stick the length of the shadow in the morning. Place a marker at the point where the shadow reaches. The shadow will get shorter, but eventually it will again touch the tip of the circle. Mark that point. Measure the distance between the two markers to find the halfway point. This is the north-south line. Make a straight line where the arc crosses the circle on each side. This line will be at right angles to the north-south line and will show east-west.

Light Sources

Group Activity GENERAL

Community Survey Conduct a discussion of the environmental effects of light pollution on other organisms as well as the costs in wasted energy. Invite interested students to prepare a survey of the usage patterns of outdoor lights in your community. Identify sources to look for, such as unshielded floodlights and street-lights, lights along bridges that shine into the water, lights along highways, at malls, in housing developments, and in rural areas. Have the survey group document their findings in the form of a map and summary statement of their conclusions. Other students may produce posters to increase public awareness. LS **Visual/Verbal**

Answers to Map Skills Activity

1. Antarctica, Greenland and the Arctic Circle, the Amazon rain forest, northern and central Africa, the mountainous region north of India, and Central Australia
2. India, Northeastern China, Japan, United States, Western Europe, Mexico and Central America, and parts of Southwest Asia
3. Rio de Janeiro, Brazil; Santiago, Chile; Lima, Peru; New York; Canberra and Sidney, Australia; Rabat, Algiers, Tripoli, and Cairo in North Africa; Pretoria in South Africa; Reykjavik in Iceland
4. You can identify the approximate international borders between the United States and Canada and between India and China.

MAPS in Action

Light Sources

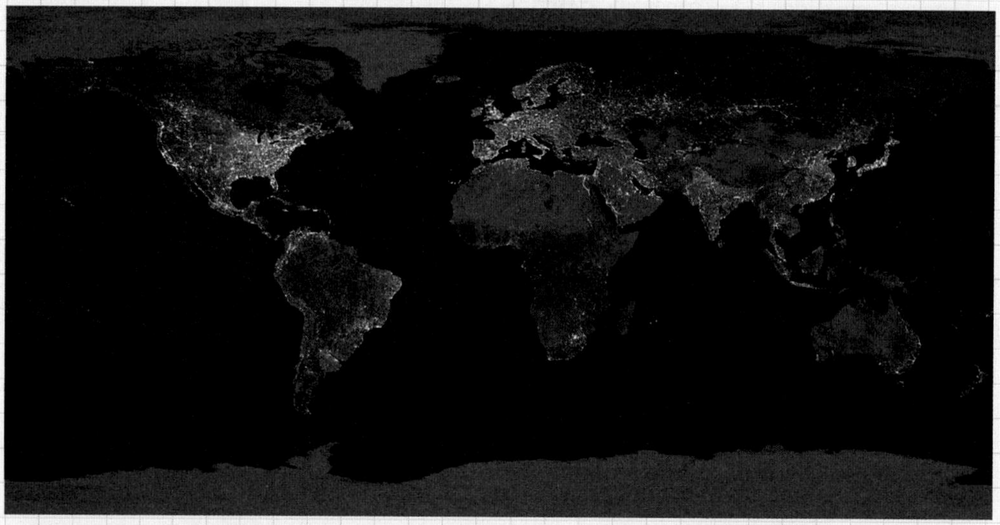

Map Skills Activity

This image of Earth as seen from space at night shows light sources that are almost all created by humans. The image is a composite made from hundreds of nighttime images taken by orbiting satellites. Use the image to answer the questions below.

1. **Comparing Areas** Some climatic conditions on Earth, such as extreme cold, heat, wetness, or a thin atmosphere, make parts of our planet less habitable than other parts. Examples of areas on our planet that do not support large populations include deserts, high mountains, polar regions, and tropical rain forests. Using the image, identify regions of Earth where climatic conditions may not be able to support large human populations.
2. **Inferring Relationships** Using a map of the world and the brightness of the light sources on the image as a key, identify the locations of some of the most densely populated areas on Earth.
3. **Finding Locations** Many large cities are ports on the coastlines of the world's oceans. By using the image, can you look along coastlines and locate light sources that might indicate the sites of large ports? Using a map of the world, name some of these cities.
4. **Inferring Relationships** By looking at the differences in the density of the light sources on the image, can you locate any borders between countries? Identify the countries on both sides of these borders.

Key Resources

Technology

- Transparencies
  135 Light Sources

Chapter 26 # Summary

THINK central SUPER SUMMARY Keyword: HQXSSPS

Key Ideas | **Key Terms**

Section 1

Viewing the Universe

- The universe is about 14 billion years old. It is very large, and objects within it are very far apart. The universe is made up of millions of galaxies, each of which is a large collection of stars, dust, and gases. Some stars, such as our own, include planets and other smaller objects.
- The visible part of the electromagnetic spectrum is visible light. The nonvisible parts include radio waves, microwaves, infrared waves, ultraviolet rays, X rays, and gamma rays.
- Refracting telescopes use lenses to gather and focus light, while reflecting telescopes use curved mirrors to gather and focus light.
- Telescopes for nonvisible electromagnetic radiation are designed to gather and focus nonvisible electromagnetic radiation rather than visible light.

Key Terms

astronomy, p. 721
galaxy, p. 722
astronomical unit, p. 722
electromagnetic spectrum, p. 723
telescope, p. 724
refracting telescope, p. 725
reflecting telescope, p. 725

Section 2

Movements of Earth

- The Foucault pendulum and the Coriolis effect provide evidence of Earth's rotation. As the pendulum swings with a constant motion, the floor beneath it changes position. Wind belts and ocean currents follow a curved, not a straight, path because they are deflected by Earth's rotation.
- The apparent movement of constellations in a circular motion provides evidence of Earth's rotation. The apparent movement from night to night and the change in location in the night sky of constellations from season to season provide evidence of Earth's revolution.
- Movements of Earth provide a basis for measuring time. One revolution of Earth around the sun is equal to one year. One rotation of Earth on its axis is equal to one day.
- The angle of the sun's rays changes throughout the year and leads to seasonal change on Earth.

Key Terms

rotation, p. 729
revolution, p. 730
perihelion, p. 730
aphelion, p. 730
equinox, p. 735
solstice, p. 736

Chapter Summary

Using THINK central Resources

Super Summary

Have students connect the major concepts in this chapter through an interactive Super Summary. Visit www.thinkcentral.com and type in the keyword **HQXSSPS** to access the Super Summary for this chapter.

Differentiated Instruction

Alternative Assessment

Astronomy Picture Books Have students work in small groups to create picture books that will explain to younger children one of the following topics: (1) how scientists study the universe using ground-based observations and telescopes, space telescopes, probes and manned space missions; or (2) how Earth motions are related to time measurement, the calendar, and seasonal change. Provide good models in the form of children's nonfiction books for students to refer to. For students who want to make illustrations using three-dimensional effects, you may want to provide reference materials on paper engineering. Suggest that students plan the contents by making an outline and thumbnail before starting to create the books. Students can draw diagrams to explain concepts and illustrate the books using photos from library sources, from the Internet, or pictures that they have taken themselves of the night sky. Good sources include NASA Web sites. Display the completed picture books in the classroom. **LS Visual/Verbal** Co-op Learning

Chapter Review

Assignment Guide	
Section	**Questions**
1	1, 2, 3, 5, 8, 11, 13, 14, 17, 18, 23, 26, 28, 30
2	4, 6, 7, 9, 10, 12, 15, 16, 19–22, 24, 25, 29, 31–35
1 and 2	27

Reading Toolbox

Key Terms	Sentences
astronomy	Sam said that he wants to study astronomy in college.
galaxy	Earth is part of the Milky Way galaxy.
astronomical unit	Astronomers use astronomical units to measure distances between objects in space.
electromagnetic spectrum	The electromagnetic spectrum includes light, radio waves, and X rays.
telescope	Let's take a better look at that comet with my telescope.
refracting telscope	A refracting telescope is one type of optical telescope.
reflecting telescope	Isaac Newton invented the reflecting telescope in the mid-1600s.

Using Key Terms

2–7. Answers may vary but should show that students understand the definitions of and differences between key terms.

Understanding Key Ideas

8. c **11.** b **14.** c
9. d **12.** d **15.** a
10. b **13.** a **16.** d

Chapter 26 Review

1. Two-Column Notes Use the FoldNote that you made at the beginning of this chapter to study the key terms. See if you know all the definitions. When you have reviewed the terms, use each term in a sentence.

READING TOOLBOX

USING KEY TERMS

Use each of the following terms in a separate sentence.

2. *electromagnetic spectrum*
3. *galaxy*
4. *perihelion*

For each pair of terms, explain how the meanings of the terms differ.

5. *reflecting telescope* and *refracting telescope*
6. *solstice* and *equinox*
7. *rotation* and *revolution*

UNDERSTANDING KEY IDEAS

8. Stars organized into a pattern are
a. perihelions.
b. satellites.
c. constellations.
d. telescopes.

9. Days are caused by Earth's
a. perihelion.
b. aphelion.
c. revolution.
d. rotation.

10. The seasons are caused by
a. Earth's distance from the sun.
b. the tilt of Earth's axis.
c. the sun's temperature.
d. the calendar.

11. Which of the following is a tool that is used by astronomers to study radiation?
a. a computer model
b. a ground-based telescope
c. a Foucault pendulum
d. a calendar

12. Which of the following is evidence of Earth's revolution?
a. a Foucault pendulum
b. the Coriolis effect
c. night and day
d. constellation movement

13. Which of the following forms of radiation can be shielded by Earth's atmosphere?
a. gamma rays
b. radio waves
c. visible light
d. All of the above

14. Which of the following names is not associated with a space telescope?
a. *Hubble*
b. *Chandra*
c. *Cassini*
d. *Spitzer*

15. Which of the following marks the beginning of spring in the Northern Hemisphere?
a. vernal equinox
b. autumnal equinox
c. summer solstice
d. winter solstice

16. Which of the following is evidence of Earth's rotation?
a. a Foucault pendulum
b. day and night
c. the Coriolis effect
d. All of the above

SHORT ANSWER

17. Which two forms of electromagnetic radiation have the shortest wavelengths?

18. What is an advantage of using orbiting telescopes rather than ground-based telescopes?

19. Why does the rotation of Earth require people to establish time zones?

20. What is a leap year, and what purpose does it serve?

21. What line on Earth's surface marks where the date changes?

22. How does the tilt of Earth's axis cause the seasons?

Short Answer

17. X rays and gamma rays

18. Orbiting telescopes are above the distorting effects of Earth's atmosphere and light pollution. They can also study the electromagnetic radiation that does not penetrate our atmosphere.

19. We use Earth's regular rotation around the sun to keep time. Establishing noon as the time when the sun is highest, and dividing Earth into time zones establishes standards that everyone on Earth can use, no matter where they are located.

20. A leap year is any calendar year to which an extra day has been added. The day is added in order to keep the calendar aligned with the seasons over a period of centuries.

21. The International Date Line, which is drawn through the Pacific Ocean.

22. The side of Earth that is tilted toward the sun has longer periods of daylight, receives more concentrated solar radiation at a more vertical angle, and has warmer temperatures. The side that is tilted away from the sun has fewer hours of daylight, receives less concentrated solar radiation at a less direct angle, and has cooler temperatures. Because of Earth's tilt, seasons are reversed north and south of the equator.

CRITICAL THINKING

23. **Evaluating Data** If telescopes had not been developed, how would our knowledge of the universe be different?

24. **Analyzing Ideas** In each time zone, it gets dark earlier on the eastern side of the zone than on the western side. Explain why.

25. **Applying Ideas** How would seasons be different if Earth was not tilted on its axis?

26. **Making Inferences** What limitation of a refracting telescope could be overcome by placing the telescope in space? Explain your answer.

CONCEPT MAPPING

27. Use the following terms to create a concept map: *Galileo, spacecraft, telescope, constellation, rotation, revolution, Foucault pendulum, Coriolis effect, equinox, solstice,* and *astronomy.*

MATH SKILLS

Math Skills

28. **Making Calculations** A certain star is 1.135×10^{14} km away from Earth. If light travels at 9.4607×10^{12} km per year, how long will it take for light from the star to reach Earth?

29. **Applying Quantities** At aphelion, Earth is 152,000,000 km from the sun. At perihelion, the two bodies are 147,000,000 km apart. What is the difference in kilometers between Earth's farthest point from the sun and Earth's closest point to the sun?

WRITING SKILLS

30. **Creative Writing** Imagine that you are the head of a space program that has created the first orbiting telescope. Write a press release that explains to the public why your space agency has spent billions of dollars to build and launch a space telescope.

31. **Communicating Main Ideas** Explain how a Foucault pendulum and the Coriolis effect provide evidence of Earth's rotation.

INTERPRETING GRAPHICS

The diagram below shows the different time zones of the world by looking down at the North Pole. Use the diagram to answer the questions that follow.

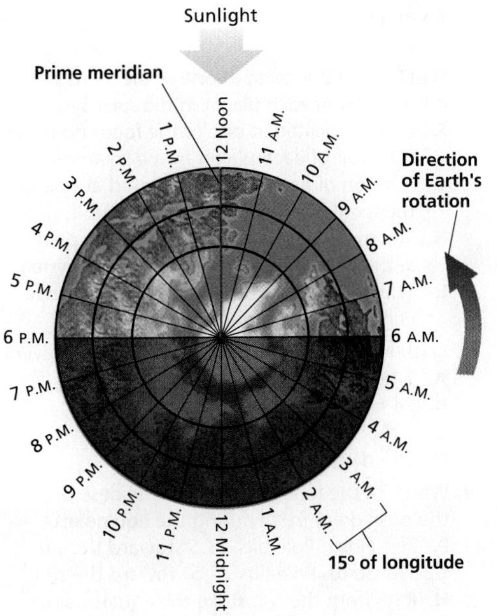

32. If it is 6 P.M. at the prime meridian, what is the time on the opposite side of the world?

33. On the diagram, it is 9 P.M. in Japan and 2 A.M. in Alaska. How many degrees apart are Alaska and Japan?

34. If it is 6 A.M. in Alaska, what time is it in Japan?

35. How many hours are in 120°?

Chapter Review

Critical Thinking

23. Answers may vary. Sample answer: We would be limited to naked-eye observations of the sky and to the interpretations we could make of Earth's motions.
24. Earth rotates in a counterclockwise direction from west to east, exposing the eastern part of each time zone to the sun's light first. The eastern half of the time zone likewise rotates into darkness before the western side does.
25. The sun's rays would strike the northern and southern hemispheres at the same angle throughout the year. Seasonal temperature changes would be minimal and would be related more to distance from the sun.
26. Answers may vary. Sample answers: If the objective lens of a refracting telescope is too large, the lens will sag under its own weight and distort the images. In orbit, the effects of Earth's gravity are less. Larger lenses can be used to view more distant objects without the distortion caused by excess weight.

Concept Mapping

27. Answers may vary but should include all of the terms listed. Sample answers appear at the end of this unit on p. 875B.

Math Skills

28. 1.135×10^{14} km $\div$ 9.4607×10^{12} km/y $= 1.135 \times 10^{(14-12)} \div 9.461$ y $= 0.11997 \times 10^2$ y $=$ 11.997 y, or about 12 y
29. 152,000,000 km − 147,000,000 km = 5,000,000 km

Writing Skills

30. Answers may vary. Accept all reasonable answers.
31. Answers may vary. Accept all reasonable answers.

Interpreting Graphics

32. 6 A.M.
33. 9 P.M. to 2 A.M. = 5 h
$15° \times 5 = 75°$
34. 1 A.M.
35. 120°/15° per hour = 8 h

Estimated Time

To give students practice under more realistic testing conditions, allow them 30 minutes to answer all of the questions in this practice test.

Test Doctor

Question 3 Answer D is correct. Earth makes one complete revolution around the sun every 365.25 days. The other answers do not deal with time markers that involve the sun. Earth rotates on its axis once every 24 hours and rotates 15° every hour, so answers A and B are incorrect. Answer C is incorrect because the moon revolves around Earth about once every month.

Question 10 Answer D is correct. Scientists need to account for the Chandler wobble when using telescopes and when determining the orbit of artificial satellites. Answer A is incorrect because Earth's axis moves constantly, though it takes about 14 months to complete one wobble. Answers B and C are incorrect because these things may cause the wobble to occur, they do not result from the wobble.

Chapter 26 Standardized Test Prep

Understanding Concepts

Directions (1–5): For each question, write on a separate sheet of paper the letter of the correct answer.

1. Earth is closest to the sun at which of the following points in its orbit?
A. aphelion
B. perihelion
C. an equinox
D. a solstice

2. What object is located at one of the focus points for the orbit of each planet in the solar system?
F. Earth is located at one of the focus points in the orbit of each planet in the solar system.
G. A moon of each planet is located at one of the focus points in that planet's orbit.
H. The sun is located at one of the focus points in the orbit of each planet in the solar system.
I. The orbits of the planets do not share any common focus points.

3. Earth revolves around the sun about once every
A. 1 hour.
B. 24 hours.
C. 1 month.
D. 365 days.

4. Which of the following statements describes the position of Earth during the equinoxes?
F. The North Pole tilts 23.5° toward the sun.
G. The South Pole tilts 23.5° toward the sun.
H. Rays from the sun strike the equator at a 90° angle.
I. Earth's axis tilts 90° and points directly at the sun.

5. Which of the following statements about the electromagnetic spectrum is true?
A. It moves slower than the speed of light.
B. It consists of waves of varying lengths.
C. The shortest wavelengths are orange and red.
D. We can only detect waves of visible light.

Directions (6–8): For each question, write a short response.

6. In what year did NASA first land astronauts on the moon?

7. What is the term that describes a spacecraft sent from Earth to another planet?

8. How does the wavelength of gamma rays compare to the wavelength of visible light?

Reading Skills

Directions (9–10): Read the passage below. Then, answer the questions.

The Chandler Wobble

In 1891, an American astronomer named Seth Carlo Chandler, Jr., discovered that Earth "wobbles" as it spins on its axis. This change in the spin of Earth's axis, known as the Chandler wobble, can be visualized if you imagine that Earth is penetrated by an enormous pen at the South Pole. This pen emerges at the North Pole and draws the pattern of rotation of Earth on its axis on a gigantic paper placed directly at the tip of the pen. If Earth did not have a wobble, you would expect the pen to draw a dot as Earth rotated on its axis. Because of the wobble, however, the pen draws a small circle. Over the course of 14 months, the pen will draw a spiral.

While the exact cause of the Chandler wobble is not known, scientists think that it is related to fluctuating pressure at the bottom of the ocean caused by temperature, salinity, and circulation changes. This wobble affects celestial navigation slightly. Because of the wobble, navigators' star charts occasionally are changed to reflect new reference points for the North Pole and South Pole.

9. Because of the Chandler wobble, celestial navigators must occasionally account for new reference points for the poles. Changes in determining the location of the North Pole by using a compass are not required. Why?
F. Compasses point to Earth's magnetic north pole, not Earth's geographic North Pole.
G. Compasses automatically adapt and move with the wobble.
H. The wobble is related to stellar movements.
I. The wobble improves compass accuracy.

10. Which of the following statements can be inferred from the information in the passage?
A. Earth's axis moves once every 14 months.
B. The Chandler wobble prevents the liquid center of Earth from solidifying.
C. The Chandler wobble causes the oceans to move and fluctuate in pressure.
D. To accurately calculate a satellite orbit, scientists must account for the Chandler wobble.

Question 13 Full-credit answers should include the following points:
- students should demonstrate a conceptual understanding that Earth's orbit is elliptical, and the sun is located at one of the foci; the two focal points of the ellipse of Earth's orbit are very close together
- the perihelion marks the closest Earth comes to the sun; the aphelion marks the farthest point Earth moves from the sun
- the solstices mark points at which the tilt of Earth's axis is away from the sun at its maximum angle in the Northern Hemisphere in the winter and is toward the sun at its maximum angle in the Northern Hemisphere in the summer
- during the winter solstice, the sun's rays strike the Tropic of Capricorn in the Southern Hemisphere at a 90° angle; during the summer solstice, the sun's rays strike the Tropic of Cancer in the Northern Hemisphere at a 90° angle
- the perihelion and winter solstice occur close together but are two different events; the same is true of the aphelion and summer solstice

Interpreting Graphics

Directions (11–14): For each question below, record the correct answer on a separate sheet of paper.

The diagram below shows the position of Earth during the four seasons. Use this diagram to answer questions 11 and 12.

Seasons and Tilt

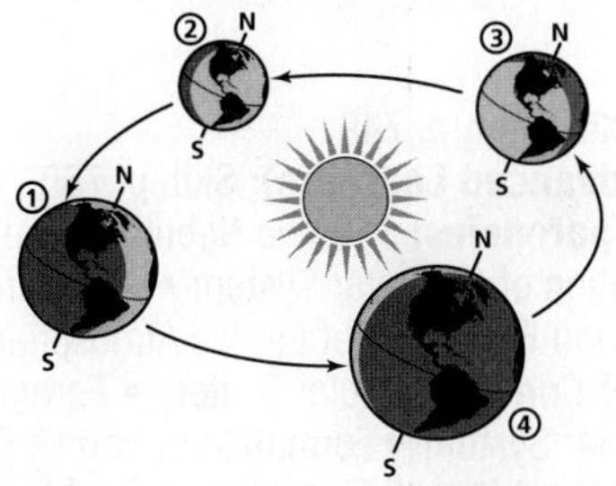

11. The Northern Hemisphere tilts toward the sun during which season?
F. winter
G. spring
H. summer
I. fall

12. The Northern Hemisphere experiences a vernal equinox when it is at which of the following positions on the diagram?
A. position 1
B. position 2
C. position 3
D. position 4

The diagram below shows the dates of specific events in Earth's orbit around the sun. Use this diagram to answer questions 13 and 14.

Orbit of Earth Around the Sun

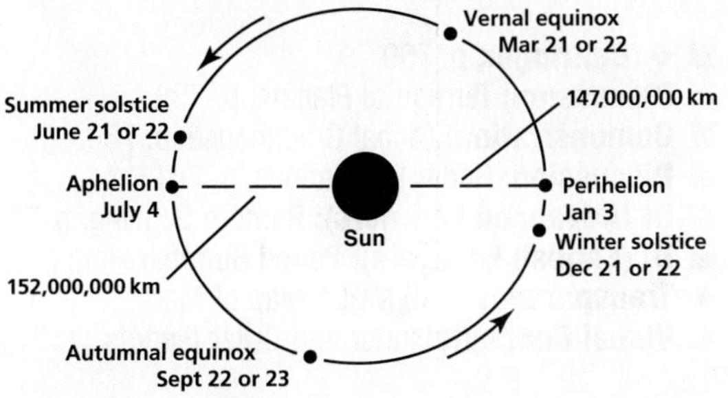

13. Use the diagram to describe the shape of Earth's orbit around the sun, and explain how the solstices differ from the aphelion and perihelion.

14. What is the relationship between Earth and the sun on March 21 or 22? Compare this relationship with the relationship between Earth and the sun on September 22 or 23.

Test Tip

Keep an eye on your time limit. If you begin to run short on time, quickly read the remaining questions to determine which questions might be the easiest for you to answer.

Standardized Test Prep

Using THINK central Resources

State Resources

- For specific resources for your state, visit www.thinkcentral.com and type in the keyword **HSHSTR.**

Answers

Understanding Concepts

1. B
2. H
3. D
4. H
5. B
6. 1969
7. Answers may vary. Correct answers include probes, missions, explorers.
8. Gamma rays have shorter wavelengths.

Reading Skills

9. F
10. D

Interpreting Graphics

11. H
12. B
13. Answers may vary. See Test Doctor for a detailed scoring rubric.
14. On both the vernal and autumnal equinoxes, the tilt of Earth's axis causes sunlight to strike the equator at a 90° angle.

Chapter Planner **27**

Planets of the Solar System

	Standards	Teach Key Ideas
Chapter Opener, pp. 746–747 **45 min.**	National Science Education Standards	
Section 1 Formation of the Solar System, pp. 749–754 **45 min.** ❯ The Nebular Hypothesis ❯ Formation of the Planets ❯ Formation of Solid Earth ❯ Formation of Earth's Atmosphere ❯ Formation of Earth's Oceans	PS 4b, ES 3a, HNS 2a, HNS 2b, UCP 3	■ ◆ **Bellringer,** p. 749 ■ **DI (Advanced Learners):** Skit, p. 750 ◆ **Transparencies:** 136 The Nebular Model of the Formation of the Solar System • 137 Differentiation of Earth and Formation of Earth's Atmosphere ▲ **Visual Concepts:** Solar System • Formation of the Solar System • Formation of Earth's Crust, Mantle, and Core • Formation of Earth's Atmosphere • Ocean Formation
Section 2 Models of the Solar System, pp. 755–758 **45 min.** ❯ Early Models ❯ Kepler's Laws ❯ Newton's Explanation of Kepler's Laws	PS 4b, HNS 2a, HNS 2b, HNS 2c, HNS 3c, UCP 2, UCP 3	■ ◆ **Bellringer,** p. 755 ■ **DI (Special Education Students):** Helping to Remember, p. 757 ◆ **Transparency:** 138 Kepler's Law of Equal Area ▲ **Visual Concepts:** Early Astronomers • Kepler's Law of Planetary Motion • Law of Universal Gravitation • Gravity and Orbit
Section 3 The Inner Planets, pp. 759–764 **90 min.** ❯ Mercury ❯ Venus ❯ Earth ❯ Mars	HNS 2b, UCP 3	■ ◆ **Bellringer,** p. 759 ■ **Discussion:** Terrestrial Planets, p. 759 ■ **Demonstration:** Global Greenhouse, p. 760 ■ **Discussion:** Radar Revelations, p. 761 ■ **DI (Advanced Learners):** Remote Sensing, p. 761 ■ **DI (English Learners):** Paired Summarizing, p. 762 ◆ **Transparency:** 139 MOLA Map of Mars ▲ **Visual Concepts:** Inner and Outer Planets
Section 4 The Outer Planets, pp. 765–772 **45 min.** ❯ Gas Giants ❯ Jupiter ❯ Saturn ❯ Uranus ❯ Neptune ❯ Objects Beyond Neptune ❯ Exoplanets	HNS 2b, UCP 3	■ ◆ **Bellringer,** p. 765 ■ **Demonstration:** Play Ball, p. 765 ■ **DI (English Learners):** Skimming and Scanning, p. 766 ■ **Demonstration:** Gas Storms, p. 767 ■ **Discussion:** What If…?, p. 767 ■ **Discussion:** Saturn's Rings, p. 768 ■ **DI (Special Education Students):** Chart, p. 768 ■ **Demonstration:** Radically Tilted Planet, p. 769 ■ **Discussion:** Composition and Structure, p. 769 ■ **Discussion:** Neptune's Weather, p. 770 ■ **DI (Advanced Learners):** Asking Questions, p. 771 ▲ **Visual Concepts:** Inner and Outer Planets
Chapter Wrap-Up, pp. 777–781 **90 min.**		**Chapter Summary,** p. 777

See also PowerNotes® Presentations

CHAPTER Fast Track

To shorten instruction because of time limitations, omit the Chapter Lab.

Key
Teacher's Edition ■ Teaching Transparencies ◆
Chapter Resource File ● Online Edition ▲

All resources listed below are also available on the Teacher One Stop™.

Why It Matters	Hands-On	Skills Development	Assessment
■ **Chapter Overview,** p. 746 ■ **Using the Figure:** Martian Canyons, p. 746	**Inquiry Lab:** Planetary Distances, p. 747	**Reading Toolbox,** p. 748	
■ **Section Overview,** p. 749 ■ **Using the Figure:** Discussion, p. 750 ■ **Environmental Connection:** Earth's Primitive Atmosphere, p. 752 ■ **Chemistry Connection:** Ocean-Atmosphere Interface, p. 753	■ **Group Activity:** Spinning Nebula, p. 749 **Quick Lab:** Water Planetesimals, p. 751	**Reading Toolbox:** Chain-of-Events Chart, p. 752	**Reading Check,** p. 751 **Reading Check,** p. 753 **Section Review,** p. 754 ■ **Reteaching,** p. 753 ■ **Quiz,** p. 753 ■ **DI (Alternative Assessment):** Cosmic Cartoons, p. 754 ● **Section Quiz**
■ **Section Overview,** p. 755	■ **Activity:** Role Play, p. 755 **Quick Lab:** Ellipses, p. 756	**Reading Toolbox:** Mnemonic, p. 756 ■ **Skill Builder:** Vocabulary, p. 756 **Math Skills:** Law of Periods, p. 757	**Reading Check,** p. 756 **Section Review,** p. 758 ■ **Reteaching,** p. 757 ■ **Quiz,** p. 757 ■ **DI (Alternative Assessment):** Jingles, p. 758 ● **Section Quiz**
■ **Section Overview,** p. 759 ■ **Environmental Connection:** Venus: Earth's Twin, p. 760 ■ **Using the Figure:** Computer Generated Image, p. 761 ■ **Environmental Connection:** Suitable for Life, p. 762	**Making Models Lab:** Crater Analysis, pp. 774–775 ● **Inquiry Lab:** Probing for Information	**Math Skills:** Distance from the Sun, p. 761 ■ **Skill Builder:** Writing, p. 762 ■ ● **Internet Activity:** Life on Mars?, p. 763 **Reading Toolbox:** Word Origins, p. 763 **Maps in Action:** MOLA Map of Mars, p. 776	**Reading Check,** p. 761 **Reading Check,** p. 763 **Section Review,** p. 764 ■ **Reteaching,** p. 763 ■ **Quiz,** p. 763 ■ **DI (Alternative Assessment):** Planetary Base, p. 764 ● **Section Quiz**
■ **Section Overview,** p. 765 ■ **Meteorology Connection:** Lightning Discharge Model, p. 766 ■ **Asteroid Belt,** p. 766 **What Happens When a Comet Hits a Planet?,** p. 767 ■ **Technology Connection:** *Cassini* Mission, p. 768 ■ **History Connection:** Caroline Herschel, p. 769	■ **Group Activity:** To Be or Not to Be a Planet, p. 770 ● **Making Models Lab:** It's a Long Way to Neptune!	**Reading Toolbox:** Word Origins, p. 771 ■ ● **Internet Activity:** Gravitational Microlensing, p. 771	**Reading Check,** p. 766 **Reading Check,** p. 768 **Reading Check,** p. 771 **Section Review,** p. 772 ■ **Reteaching,** p. 771 ■ **Quiz,** p. 771 ■ **DI (Alternative Assessment):** Outer Planets Museum, p. 772 ● **Section Quiz**
New Horizons for Pluto, p. 773 **What's in a Name?,** p.777		▲ **Super Summary** **Standardized Test Prep,** pp. 780–781	**Chapter Review,** pp. 778–779 ● **Chapter Tests**

See also Lab Generator

See also Holt Online Assessment Resources

Chapter Overview

This chapter describes how Earth's solar system formed, the laws that govern the movements of the planets, and how the rocky inner planets differ from the gas giants.

Using the Figure GENERAL

Martian Canyons This photo shows the Valles Marineris, which is a system of canyons located south of the Martian equator. Explain to students that this system of canyons is over 4,000 km long—the coast-to-coast width of the United States on Earth. Point out that in places the canyon is many times deeper than the Grand Canyon. **LS Visual**

Why It Matters

NASA was founded in 1958, and the first U.S. astronaut traveled to space in 1961, just weeks after the former U.S.S.R sent the very first human to space. Future space exploration goals include completing the space station, returning to the moon, and continuing exploration of Mars.

Chapter 27 Planets of the Solar System

Chapter Outline

1 Formation of the Solar System
- The Nebular Hypothesis
- Formation of the Planets
- Formation of Solid Earth
- Formation of Earth's Atmosphere
- Formation of Earth's Oceans

2 Models of the Solar System
- Early Models
- Kepler's Laws
- Newton's Explanation of Kepler's Laws

3 The Inner Planets
- Mercury
- Venus
- Earth
- Mars

4 The Outer Planets
- Gas Giants
- Jupiter
- Saturn
- Uranus
- Neptune
- Objects Beyond Neptune
- Exoplanets

Virginia Standards of Learning

ES.1.c	ES.10.a
ES.3.a	ES.11.a
ES.3.c	ES.11.b
ES.3.d	

Why It Matters

Understanding the formation and the characteristics of our solar system and its planets can help scientists plan missions to study planets and solar systems around other stars in the universe.

Chapter Correlations — *Virginia Standards of Learning*

ES.1.c scales, diagrams, charts, graphs, tables, imagery, models, and profiles are constructed and interpreted.
ES.3.a position of Earth in the solar system
ES.3.c characteristics of the sun, planets and their moons, comets, meteors, and asteroids
ES.3.d the history and contributions of space exploration
ES.10.a physical and chemical changes related to tides, waves, currents, sea level and ice cap variations, upwelling, and salinity variations
ES.11.a scientific evidence for atmospheric composition changes over geologic time
ES.11.b current theories related to the effects of early life on the chemical makeup of the atmosphere

Inquiry Lab

Central Concept: It is difficult to fathom interplanetary distances. Relatively speaking, Mercury, Venus, Earth, and Mars are very close to the Sun, compared with Jupiter, Saturn, Uranus, and Neptune. Here, students will construct a model of our solar system to better understand the relative scale of planetary distances.

Teacher's Notes: Students will likely recognize that the farther from the Sun, the longer distance to complete an orbit. However, the outer planets also move slower, affecting the time it takes to complete an orbit.

Materials (per group)
- Index cards
- Measuring tape

Skills Acquired
- Measuring
- Calculating
- Constructing Models

Answer to Getting Started
The further from the Sun, the longer the orbit, so the longer it would take to complete an orbit.

Inquiry Lab Planetary Distances

20 min

Turn to Appendix E and find the table entitled "Solar System Data." Use the data from the "semimajor axis" row of planetary distances to devise an appropriate scale to model the distances between planets. Then find an indoor or outdoor space that will accommodate the farthest distance. Mark some **index cards** with the name of each planet, use a **measuring tape** to measure the distances according to your scale, and place each index card at its correct location.

Question to Get You Started

How would the distance of a planet from the sun affect the time it takes for the planet to complete one orbit?

Using THINK central Resources

An online version of this chapter, as well as all the print and multimedia resources that accompany the program are available to registered teachers and their students. Log onto www.thinkcentral.com to access these materials and tools to organize your preparation and student learning.

READING TOOLBOX

Word Origins

Planet	Characteristics of Planet	Characteristics of Roman god
Mercury	fastest-moving	speedy messenger of the gods
Venus	brightest object in the night sky (besides Earth's moon)	goddess of love and beauty
Mars	red color	god of war
Jupiter	largest planet	ruler of the Roman gods
Saturn	plethora of moons	god of agriculture
Uranus	third-largest planet; near Saturn and Jupiter	god of the heavens, father of Saturn, grandfather of Jupiter
Neptune	bluish-green color	god of the sea

Mnemonics

Answers will vary. Students' mnemonics should include a word for each planet, with the first letter of each word the same as the first letter of the corresponding planet in the order. An example is shown below.

Mark Viewed Everything Mary Jane Studied Until Now.

READING TOOLBOX

These reading tools will help you learn the material in this chapter.

Word Origins

Names of the Planets The ancient Romans named the five planets that they could see in the night sky after gods from their mythology: Mercury, Venus, Mars, Jupiter, and Saturn. When Uranus and Neptune were discovered, they were also named for Roman gods.

Your Turn Each planet was named for the god in mythology that has something in common with the planet. As you learn about the planets, complete the list of connections between the planets and the Roman gods for which they are named.

Planet	Characteristic of planet	Characteristic of Roman god
Mercury	fastest-moving planet	speedy messenger of the gods
Jupiter	largest planet	ruler of the Roman gods

Mnemonics

Order of the Planets A mnemonic is a sentence or phrase that you can create to help you remember information. For example, the order of the planets from the sun outward is Mercury, Venus, Earth, Mars, Jupiter, Saturn, Uranus, and Neptune. You can use a mnemonic to help you remember this order.

My **V**ery **E**nergetic **M**other **J**ust **S**erved **U**s **N**achos.

Notice that the first letter of each word is the same as the first letter of the corresponding planet in the order.

Your Turn Practice saying this mnemonic to help you learn and remember the order of the planets. Make up a new mnemonic that you could use to remember the order of the planets.

Graphic Organizers

Chain-of-Events Chart Use a chain-of-events chart when you need to remember the steps of a process.

Your Turn As you read Section 1, create a chain-of-events chart that outlines the formation of the solar system. An example has been started at the right.

1. Write the first step of the process in the first frame.
2. Write the next step of the process in the second frame, and use an arrow to show the order of the process.
3. Continue adding frames and arrows until the process for the formation of the solar system is complete.

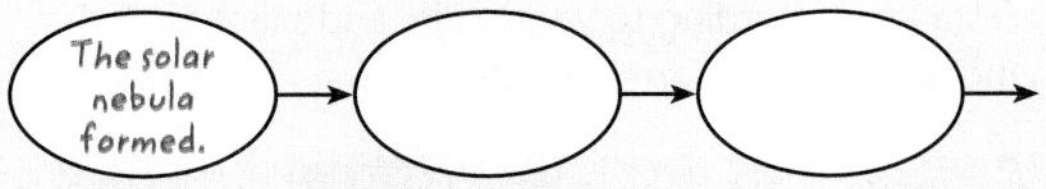

For more information on how to use these and other tools, see **Appendix A**.

Graphic Organizers

Answers may vary, depending on how much detail students include in the chain-of-events chart. Students may include the formation of the sun and the roles of planetesimals and protoplanets in the formation of the inner and outer planets, moons, and dwarf planets.

SECTION 1

Formation of the Solar System

Key Ideas	Key Terms	Why It Matters
› Explain the nebular hypothesis of the origin of the solar system. › Describe how the planets formed. › Describe the formation of the land, the atmosphere, and the oceans of Earth.	solar system planet solar nebula planetesimal	Studying the solar system and its various planets can help us understand our own planet and the changes it has been and is going through.

The **solar system** consists of the sun, the planets, the dwarf planets, and all of the other bodies that revolve around the sun. **Planets** are the primary bodies that orbit the sun. Scientists have long debated the origins of the solar system. In the 1600s and 1700s, many scientists thought that the sun formed first and threw off the materials that later formed the planets. But in 1796, the French mathematician Pierre-Simon, marquis de Laplace, advanced a hypothesis that is now known as the *nebular hypothesis*.

The Nebular Hypothesis

Laplace's hypothesis states that the sun and the planets condensed at about the same time out of a rotating cloud of gas and dust called a *nebula*. Modern scientific calculations support Laplace's hypothesis and help explain how the sun and the planets formed from an original nebula of gas and dust.

Matter is spread throughout the universe. Some of this matter gathers into clouds of dust and gas, such as the one shown in **Figure 1.** Almost 5 billion years ago, the amount of gravity near one of these clouds increased as a result of a nearby supernova or other forces. The rotating cloud of dust and gas from which the sun and planets formed is called the **solar nebula**. Energy from collisions and pressure from gravity caused the center of the solar nebula to become hotter and denser. When the temperature at the center became high enough—about 10,000,000 °C—hydrogen fusion began. A star, which is called the sun, formed. The sun is composed of about 99% of all the matter that was contained in the solar nebula.

solar system the sun and all of the planets and other bodies that travel around it

planet a celestial body that orbits the sun, is round because of its own gravity, and has cleared the neighborhood around its orbital path

solar nebula a rotating cloud of gas and dust from which the sun and planets formed; *also* any nebula from which stars and exoplanets may form

Figure 1 The Orion nebula is about 1,500 light-years from Earth. Scientists study the nebula to learn about the processes that give birth to stars.

Key Resources

Chapter Resource File
- Directed Reading BASIC

Technology
- Transparencies
  Bellringer

Section 1

Focus

Overview

This section describes the formation of the sun and planets of Earth's solar system. The section also describes the origin of the land, atmosphere, and oceans of Earth.

Bellringer

Have students write a list of all of the objects they think make up Earth's solar system. (Student may suggest such objects as planets, moons, the asteroid belt, comets, meteoroids, and the sun.) LS **Verbal**

Motivate

Group Activity — GENERAL

Spinning Nebula Divide the class into groups, and give each group a small plastic container three-quarters full of water, perlite, and a stirring rod. Have each group add perlite to the water, and stir the mixture vigorously. Once the mixture is rotating, have them remove the rod. Have students describe their model solar nebulae. (Answers may vary. Students should notice that most of the material tends to concentrate at the center of the rotating disk. They may notice that the inner parts of the disk move more rapidly than the outer parts do.)
LS **Kinesthetic/Visual**

Teach

Using the Figure GENERAL

Discussion Explain that the explosion of a nearby supernova could have produced a shock wave that led to the collapse of the solar nebula. Ask students "What would cause the center of the solar nebula to become hotter?" (Sample answer: energy from collisions between the particles and the energy released by gravitational contraction) Then, have students summarize the steps that led to the formation of planets. (Sample answers: The accumulation of dust particles formed small planetesimals. Collisions between the planetesimals led to the formation of protoplanets. The protoplanets eventually developed into planets and moons.) **LS Verbal/Visual**

Differentiated Instruction

Advanced Learners

Skit Invite interested students to develop a script about the formation of the solar system and perform it for the rest of the class. Ask students to focus on the differences between the planets that formed close to the developing sun and those that formed in the outer regions of the solar nebula. If there are enough performers, they can assume the roles of the sun, the inner planets, the outer planets, the dwarf planets, and even the debris, such as comets and asteroids, that remained after the formation of the new solar system. **LS Auditory/Kinesthetic**

Formation of the Planets

While the sun was forming in the center of the solar nebula, planets were forming in the outer regions, as shown in **Figure 2.** Small bodies from which a planet originated in the early stages of formation of the solar system are called **planetesimals.** Some planetesimals joined together through collisions and through the force of gravity to form larger bodies called *protoplanets.* The protoplanets' gravity attracted other planetesimals in the solar nebula. These planetesimals collided with the protoplanets and added their masses to the protoplanets.

Eventually, the protoplanets became very large and formed the planets and moons. *Moons* are the smaller bodies that orbit the planets. Planets and moons are smaller and denser than the protoplanets. Some protoplanets were massive enough to become round but not massive enough to clear away other objects near their orbits. These became the dwarf planets.

planetesimal a small body from which a planet originated in the early stages of development of the solar system

Academic Vocabulary

formation (fohr MAY shuhn) the act of giving structure or shape to something

Formation of the Inner Planets

The features of a newly formed planet depended on the distance between the protoplanet and the developing sun. The four protoplanets that became Mercury, Venus, Earth, and Mars were close to the sun. They contained large percentages of heavy elements, such as iron and nickel. These planets lost their less dense gases because, at the temperature of the gases, gravity was not strong enough to hold the gases. Other lighter elements may have been blown or boiled away by radiation from the sun. As the denser material sank to the centers of the planets, layers formed. The less dense material was on the outer part of the planet, and the denser material was at the center. Today, the inner planets have solid surfaces that are similar to Earth's surface. The inner planets are smaller, rockier, and denser than the outer planets.

SciLinks
www.scilinks.org
Topic: Origins of the Solar System
Code: **HQX1087**

Figure 2 The Nebular Model of the Formation of the Solar System

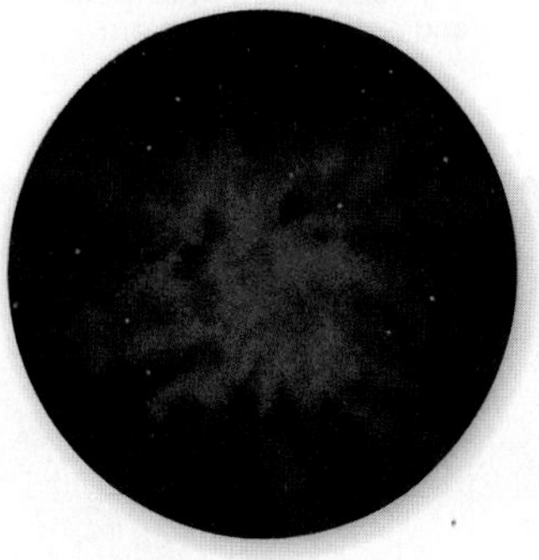

The young solar nebula begins to collapse because of gravity.

As the solar nebula rotates, it flattens and becomes warmer near its center.

Planetesimals begin to form within the swirling disk.

Teaching Tip GENERAL

Connect to Familiar Processes Explain that the solar nebula in which the solar system formed would have spun faster and faster as it contracted. Students may better understand why this happened if you compare it to the rotation of a spinning skater. A skater spins faster with arms folded close to the body (contracted) and slower with arms spread apart. **LS Visual**

Key Resources

Technology

- Transparencies
  136 The Nebular Model of the Formation of the Solar System

Formation of the Outer Planets

Four other protoplanets became Jupiter, Saturn, Uranus, and Neptune. As a group, these outer planets are very different from the small, rocky inner planets. These outer planets formed in the colder regions of the solar nebula. They were far from the sun and therefore were cold. Thus, they did not lose their lighter elements, such as helium and hydrogen, or their ices, such as water ice, methane ice, and ammonia ice.

At first, thick layers of ice surrounded small cores of heavy elements. However, because of the intense heat and pressure in the planets' interiors, the ices melted to form layers of liquids and gases. Today, these planets are referred to as *gas giants* because they are composed mostly of gases, have low density, and are huge planets. Jupiter, for example, has a density of only 24% of Earth's density but a diameter that is 11 times Earth's diameter. Uranus and Neptune are different from Jupiter and Saturn, and are sometimes called *ice giants*.

Pluto—The First Dwarf Planet

From its discovery in 1930, Pluto was known as the ninth planet. However, it is quite unlike the other outer planets, which are gas giants or ice giants. In fact, Pluto is smaller than Earth's moon, and it can be best described as an ice ball that is made of frozen gases and rock. Its orbit is very tilted. Because of its characteristics, many astronomers disagreed with Pluto's classification as a planet.

In 2006, astronomers from around the world revised the definition of *planet*. The new definition includes the first eight familiar planets, but it excludes Pluto. Pluto is part of a new category of solar system bodies called *dwarf planets*.

Reading Check **How is Pluto different from the outer planets?** (See Appendix G for answers to Reading Checks.)

Quick Lab — 5 min

Water Planetesimals

Procedure

1. Use a medicine dropper to place two drops of water about 3 cm apart on a piece of wax paper.
2. Lift one edge of the wax paper so that one drop of water moves toward the other drop until the drops collide.
3. Add a third drop of water to the wax paper. Then, repeat step 2.

Analysis

1. What happened when the water droplets collided?
2. How does this activity model the formation of protoplanets?

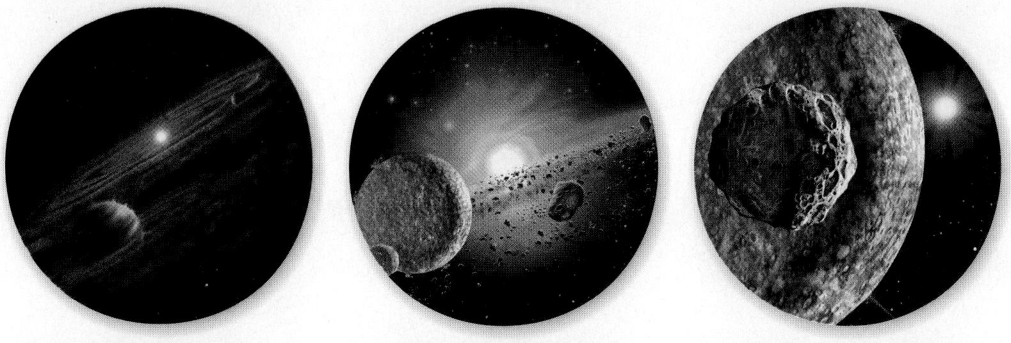

As planetesimals grow, their gravitational pull increases. The largest planetesimals begin to collect more of the gas and dust of the nebula.

Small planetesimals collide with larger ones, and the planets begin to grow.

The excess dust and gas is gradually removed from the solar nebula, which leaves planets around the sun and thus creates a new solar system.

Quick Lab

Skills Acquired
- Constructing Models
- Observing

Materials
- Medicine dropper
- Water
- Wax paper

Teacher's Notes: Students could also use a straightened paper clip to draw the water droplets together. You might point out that the force of attraction in this model is cohesion, or the attractive force between particles of the same substance, while in the solar nebula the attractive force is gravity.

Answers to Analysis

1. They merged to form larger droplets.
2. Answers may vary. Sample answer: Planetesimals grow by clumping together and attracting more matter. Collisions between planetesimals form larger bodies, just as the water droplets do.

Answer to Reading Check

Unlike the outer planets, Pluto is very small and is composed of rock and frozen gas, instead of thick layers of gases.

MISCONCEPTION ALERT

What Happened to Pluto? In the summer of 2006, astronomers from around the world met in Prague (Czech Republic) for the 26th General Assembly of the International Astronomical Union (IAU). At that meeting, the IAU voted on a new definition of *planet*, which includes the first eight planets, but excludes Pluto. Pluto was reclassified as a *dwarf planet*. While students may be familiar with nine planets, which had been the number of planets since soon after the discovery of Pluto in 1930, the decision made by the IAU in 2006 has affected the presentation in this textbook. Pluto, another trans-Neptunian object called Eris, and the asteroid Ceres are the first objects to be named dwarf planets.

Teach, *continued*

MISCONCEPTION ALERT

Gravitational Separation Point out that the layered structure of Earth resulted because accumulated heat caused the early planetary body to become completely molten, or liquid. Only then could gravitational differentiation of the formerly uniform mixture of materials cause them to separate into distinct layers. A solid body cannot be differentiated in this manner. Only later did most of the layers of the planet cool and solidify.

READING TOOLBOX

Chain-of-Events Chart
Answers may vary, depending on how much detail students include in the chain-of-events chart. Students may include the three sources of energy that contributed to Earth's temperature; differentiation and the formation of Earth's layers; the current composition of Earth; the formation of Earth's atmosphere; and the formation of Earth's oceans.

Formation of Solid Earth

When Earth first formed, it was very hot. Three sources of energy contributed to the high temperature on the new planet. First, much of the energy was produced when the planetesimals that formed the planet collided with each other. Second, the increasing weight of Earth's outer layers compressed the inner layers, which generated more energy. Third, radioactive materials that emit high-energy particles were very abundant when Earth formed. When surrounding rocks absorbed the particles, the energy of the particles' motion led to higher temperatures.

READING TOOLBOX

Chain-of-Events Chart
Make a chain-of-events chart. Then, fill in the chart with details about each step of the formation of Earth.

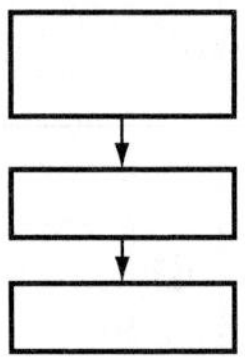

Early Solid Earth

Young Earth was hot enough to melt iron, the most common of the existing heavy elements. As Earth developed, denser materials, such as molten iron, sank to its center, and less dense materials were forced to the outer layers. This process is called *differentiation.* Differentiation caused Earth to form three distinct layers, as shown in **Figure 3.** At the center is a dense *core* that is composed mostly of iron and nickel. Around the core is the very thick layer of iron- and magnesium-rich rock called the *mantle.* The outermost layer of Earth is a thin *crust* of less dense, silica-rich rock. Today, processes that shape Earth, such as plate tectonics, are driven by heat transfer and differences in density.

Present Solid Earth

Eventually, Earth's surface cooled enough for solid rock to form. The solid rock at Earth's surface formed from less dense elements that were pushed toward the surface during differentiation. Earth's surface continued to change as a result of the heat in Earth's interior as well as through impacts and through interactions with the newly forming atmosphere.

Figure 3 Differentiation of Earth

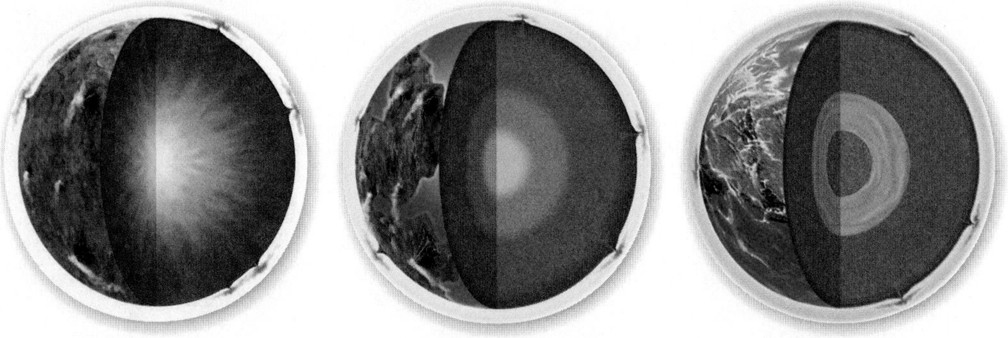

During its early history, Earth cooled to form three distinct layers.

An atmosphere began to form from the water vapor and carbon dioxide released by volcanic eruptions.

Organisms produced oxygen from photosynthesis to create an oxygenated atmosphere.

Environmental Connection

Earth's Primitive Atmosphere Direct students' attention to the illustration of volcanoes on the opposite page. Ask students to consider what volcanic activity has to do with Earth's atmosphere. (Sample answer: After the light gases acquired from the solar nebula escaped Earth's gravity, a new atmosphere composed of carbon dioxide, water vapor, and other gases developed from the eruption of volcanoes on Earth's surface.) You might point out that during the formation of Earth's atmosphere, comets composed of ice and rock debris also plunged into Earth, releasing quantities of water vapor and other gases. Ask students where they think the oxygen in Earth's atmosphere came from. (Sample answer: Initially, it came from the breakdown of water and carbon dioxide by ultraviolet radiation. Then, after life developed, photosynthesizing bacteria and plants produced oxygen as a byproduct of food production.) **LS Verbal**

Formation of Earth's Atmosphere

Like solid Earth, the atmosphere formed because of differentiation. During the original differentiation of Earth, less dense gas molecules, such as hydrogen and helium, rose to the surface. Thus, the original atmosphere of Earth consisted primarily of hydrogen and helium.

Earth's Early Atmosphere

The high concentrations of hydrogen and helium did not stay with Earth's atmosphere. Earth's gravity would have been too weak to hold these gases unless they were very cold. The sun heated the gases enough so that they escaped Earth's gravity. These gases were probably blown away by the solar wind, which might have been stronger at that time than it is today. Also, Earth's magnetic field, which protects the atmosphere from the solar wind, might not have been fully developed.

Outgassing

As Earth's surface continued to form, volcanic eruptions were much more frequent than they are today. The volcanic eruptions released large amounts of gases, mainly water vapor, carbon dioxide, nitrogen, methane, sulfur dioxide, and ammonia, as shown in **Figure 4.** This process, known as *outgassing,* formed a new atmosphere.

The gases released during outgassing interacted with radiation from the sun. The solar radiation caused the ammonia and some of the water vapor in the atmosphere to break down. Most of the hydrogen that was released during this breakdown escaped into space. Some of the remaining oxygen formed *ozone,* a molecule that contains three oxygen atoms. The ozone collected in a high atmospheric layer around Earth and shielded Earth's surface from the harmful ultraviolet radiation of the sun.

Earth's Present Atmosphere

Organisms that could survive in Earth's early atmosphere developed. Some of these organisms, such as cyanobacteria and early green plants, used carbon dioxide during photosynthesis. Oxygen, a byproduct of photosynthesis, was released. So, the amount of oxygen in the atmosphere slowly increased. About 2 billion years ago, the percentage of oxygen in the atmosphere increased rapidly. Since that time, the chemical composition of the atmosphere has been similar to the present composition of the atmosphere, as shown in **Figure 5.**

Reading Check **How did green plants contribute to Earth's present-day atmosphere?**

Figure 4 Earth's early atmosphere formed as volcanic eruptions released nitrogen, N_2; water vapor, H_2O; ammonia, NH_3; methane, CH_4; argon, Ar; sulfur dioxide, SO_2; and carbon dioxide, CO_2.

Figure 5 As Earth's surface changed, the gases in the atmosphere changed. Today, the atmosphere is 78% nitrogen, N_2; 21% oxygen, O_2; and 1% other gases.

Homework — GENERAL

Earth Spheres Posters Have students work in small groups to design a poster around the theme of one of the following Earth spheres: the lithosphere (rock), the atmosphere (air), the hydrosphere (water), and the biosphere (life). Students can use library and Internet resources. **LS Visual**

Chemistry Connection

Ocean-Atmosphere Interface
The formation of the oceans and atmosphere were closely interrelated. UV light disassociated water from the oceans, producing gases that allowed the atmosphere to develop further. Changes in the atmosphere changed ocean chemistry, allowing life to develop. That life produced gases such as free oxygen that altered the atmospheric composition. The increasing concentration of oxygen led to the formation of the protective ozone shield. Thus, a complex feedback system governed changes in both the oceans and atmosphere.

Close

Reteaching — BASIC

Flashcards Have students work in pairs to create flashcards that have drawings and descriptions of the stages in the formation of Earth. Then, students can shuffle the cards and take turns organizing them into chronological order. **LS Logical**

Quiz — GENERAL

1. What process led to the formation of layers in Earth? (differentiation)
2. What process helped form Earth's atmosphere through the release of gases during volcanic eruptions? (outgassing)
3. What is the rotating cloud of dust and gas that formed the solar system called? (solar nebula)

Key Resources

Technology
- Transparencies
  137 Differentiation of Earth and Formation of Earth's Atmosphere

Answer to Reading Check
Green plants release free oxygen as part of photosynthesis, which caused the concentration of oxygen gas in the atmosphere to gradually increase.

Close, *continued*

Answers to Section Review

1. The sun, planets, and other bodies of the solar system formed out of a spinning cloud of gas and dust as a result of collisions and gravitational contraction.
2. Planetesimals are small bodies formed when particles in the nebula stuck together. Protoplanets are larger bodies formed from the planetesimals.
3. through collisions and gravitational attraction of planetesimals and protoplanets
4. Because the outer planets formed far from the hot center of the nebula, they could retain lighter gases that would have escaped at higher temperatures.
5. because the collisions between planetesimals that formed Earth produced heat; because the outer layers of the planet compressed the inner layers, creating heat; and because radioactive elements common in the material of early Earth emitted high-energy particles that heated Earth's rocks
6. As Earth developed, denser materials sank to its center and less dense materials were forced outward. This gave the planet its layered structure. An early atmosphere that consisted of light gases formed, but Earth was too small and too close to the sun to hold them. Large amounts of other gases and water vapor produced by volcanic eruptions and introduced by comets formed a new atmosphere. As Earth cooled further, water vapor condensed and fell as rain, forming oceans. Life began in the oceans. Green plants contributed oxygen to the atmosphere as a byproduct of photosynthesis.
7. The amount of gas in an outer planet is much greater than that in an inner planet because outer planets were too far from the sun to lose their gaseous elements through its radiation. Also, they are more massive, and thus able to hold more gas.
8. because it has abundant liquid water, because it has a moderate temperature, and because it has an ozone layer that shields the surface from harmful ultraviolet radiation
9. The *solar system* formed from the *solar nebula*, within which *planetesimals* joined together to form *protoplanets*, which became *planets*, including the terrestrial planets and the *gas giants*.

Figure 6 Salt from the ocean can be harvested from salt flats, such as this one in Habantota, Sri Lanka.

Formation of Earth's Oceans

Some scientists think that part of Earth's water may have come from space. Early on, icy bodies, such as comets, collided with Earth. Water from these bodies then became part of Earth's atmosphere. As Earth cooled, water vapor condensed to form rain. This liquid water collected on the surface to form the first oceans.

The first ocean was probably made of fresh water. Over millions of years, rainwater fell to Earth and ran over the land, through rivers, and into the ocean. The rainwater dissolved some of the rocks on land and carried those dissolved solids into the oceans. As more dissolved solids were carried to the oceans, the concentration of certain chemicals in the oceans increased. As the water cycled back into the atmosphere through evaporation, some of these chemicals combined to form salts. Over millions of years, water has cycled between the oceans and the atmosphere. Through this process, the oceans have become increasingly salty. Where shallow ocean water has evaporated completely, the salt precipitates and is left behind. This salt may be harvested for human use, as shown in **Figure 6.**

The Ocean's Effects on the Atmosphere

The oceans affect global temperatures in a variety of ways. One way the oceans affect temperature is by dissolving carbon dioxide from the atmosphere. Scientists think that early oceans also affected Earth's early climate by dissolving carbon dioxide. Carbon dioxide in the atmosphere keeps energy from escaping into space and thus helps to heat the atmosphere. Over Earth's long history, the concentration of carbon dioxide has increased and decreased for various periods of time. Thus, at different times in its history, Earth likely has experienced climates that are warmer and cooler than the climates we experience today.

Section 1 Review

Key Ideas

1. **Describe** the nebular hypothesis.
2. **Explain** how planetesimals differ from protoplanets.
3. **Describe** how planets developed.
4. **Explain** why the outer planets are more gaseous than the inner planets.
5. **List** three reasons that Earth was hot when it formed.
6. **Summarize** the process by which the land, atmosphere, and oceans of Earth formed.

Critical Thinking

7. **Identifying Relationships** How does the amount of gas in an outer planet differ from the amount of gas in an inner planet? Explain your answer.
8. **Analyzing Ideas** Explain why Earth is capable of supporting life.

Concept Mapping

9. Use the following terms to make a concept map: *solar system, solar nebula, protoplanet, planetesimal, planet,* and *gas giant.*

Differentiated Instruction

Alternative Assessment

Cosmic Cartoons Have students create a series of cartoon strips that illustrates the steps in the formation of the sun and the inner and outer planets from the solar nebula. Have students use captions to explain what happened at each stage in the process. **LS Visual**

SECTION 2

Models of the Solar System

Key Ideas	Key Terms	Why It Matters
❯ Compare the models of the universe developed by Ptolemy and Copernicus. ❯ Summarize Kepler's three laws of planetary motion. ❯ Describe how Newton explained Kepler's laws of motion.	eccentricity orbital period inertia	We can send people to the moon and rovers to Mars thanks to models of the solar system.

The first astronomers who studied the sky thought that the stars, planets, and sun revolved around Earth. This idea led to the first model of the solar system. However, the model changed as scientists learned more about how the solar system works.

Early Models

More than 2,000 years ago, the Greek philosopher Aristotle suggested an Earth-centered, or *geocentric,* model of the solar system. In this model, the sun, the stars, and the planets revolved around Earth. However, this model did not explain why planets sometimes appeared to move backward in the sky relative to the stars—a pattern called *retrograde motion.*

By 150 CE, the Greek astronomer Claudius Ptolemy (TAHL uh mee) proposed changes to this model. Ptolemy thought that planets moved in small circles, called *epicycles,* as they revolved in larger circles around Earth. These epicycles seemed to explain why planets sometimes appeared to move backward.

In 1543 CE, a Polish astronomer named Nicolaus Copernicus proposed a sun-centered, or *heliocentric,* model of the solar system. In this model, the planets revolved around the sun in the same direction but at different speeds and distances from the sun. Fast-moving planets passed slow-moving planets. Therefore, planets that were slower than Earth appeared to move backward. **Figure 1** compares Ptolemy's and Copernicus's models. Later, the Italian scientist Galileo Galilei observed four moons traveling around the planet Jupiter. This observation indicated that objects can, and do, revolve around objects other than Earth.

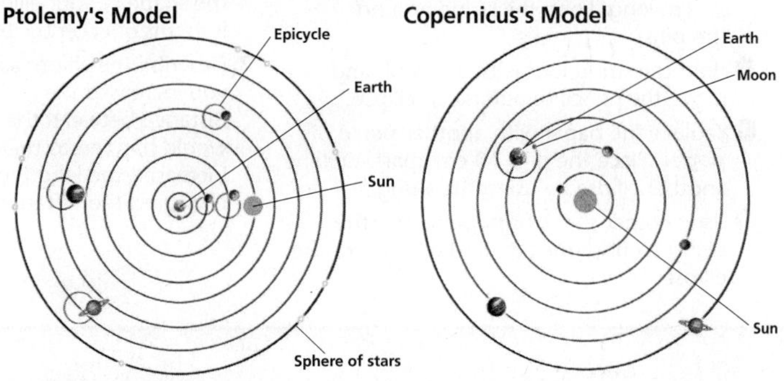

Figure 1 Early Solar System Models Ptolemy's solar system model (left) is Earth-centered and has the planets moving in epicycles around Earth. Copernicus's solar model (right) is heliocentric and has the planets moving at different speeds around the sun.

Section 2

Focus

Overview

This section compares models of the solar system and summarizes the laws of planetary motion.

Bellringer

Ask students to draw a diagram of the solar system and to label all of the parts of the diagram.
LS Verbal

Motivate

Activity — GENERAL

Role Play To help students understand how the planets might appear to move backward, try this activity. Group students into pairs. Have one student in each pair represent Earth, the other Mars. Have them stand next to each other. Ask "Mars" to begin moving forward slowly, while "Earth" observes background objects as "Mars" passes them. Have "Earth" begin moving faster while still looking at the same objects in relation to "Mars." Invite students to report what happens when "Earth" passes "Mars." (Sample answer: "Earth" has to look backward in order to view the objects in relation to its partner.) **LS Kinesthetic/Visual**

Key Resources

Chapter Resource File
- Directed Reading

Technology
- Transparencies
  Bellringer

Teach

READING TOOLBOX

Mnemonic

Answers will vary. Students' mnemonics should help them remember Kepler's laws of planetary motion. Possible answer: Planets LEEAP around (L = law, E = ellipses, EA = equal areas, P = periods).

Skill Builder GENERAL

Vocabulary The word *ellipse* is from the Greek word *elleipsis*. The word *ellipsoid* also derives from this Greek word. The word *eccentricity* is from the Greek *ekkentros*, which is a combination of *ex-* meaning "out of" and *kentron* meaning "center." Thus, *eccentricity* is the extent to which a planet's orbit is elongated, or pulled away from the center. A related word, *eccentric*, is often used to describe people who live their lives outside of the social norms. English Language Learners

LS Verbal

Answer to Reading Check

An ellipse is a closed curve whose shape is defined by two points inside the curve. An ellipse looks like an oval.

READING TOOLBOX

Mnemonic
Create a mnemonic to help you remember the three laws that Kepler developed to explain planetary motion.

SCILINKS.
www.scilinks.org
Topic: Early Astronomers
Code: **HQX0441**

eccentricity the degree of elongation of an elliptical orbit (symbol, *e*)

Kepler's Laws

Twenty years before Galileo used a telescope, the Danish astronomer Tycho Brahe made detailed observations of the positions of the planets. After Tycho's death, one of his assistants, Johannes Kepler, worked with Tycho's observations. His studies led Kepler to develop three laws that explained planetary motion.

Law of Ellipses

Kepler's first law, the *law of ellipses,* states that each planet orbits the sun in a path called an ellipse, not in a circle. An *ellipse* is a closed curve whose shape is determined by two points, or *foci,* within the ellipse. In planetary orbits, one focus is located within the sun. No object is located at the other focus. The combined length of two lines, one from each focus to any one point on the ellipse, would always be the same as the length of two other lines, one from each focus, to any other point on the same ellipse.

Elliptical orbits can vary in shape. Some orbits are elongated ellipses. Other orbit shapes are almost perfect circles. The shape of an orbit can be described by a numerical quantity called *eccentricity.* **Eccentricity** is the degree of elongation of an elliptical orbit (symbol, *e*). Eccentricity is determined by dividing the distance between the foci of the ellipse by the length of the major axis. Therefore, the eccentricity of a circular orbit is $e = 0$. The eccentricity of a type of extremely elongated orbit known as a parabolic orbit is $e = 1$.

Reading Check **Define and describe an ellipse.**

Quick Lab Ellipses

15 min

Procedure

1. Cover a **cork board** with a **piece of paper.** Put **two push pins** into the cork board, 5 cm apart.
2. Tie together the ends of a **string** that is 25 cm long. Loop the string around the pins.
3. Hold the string taut with a **pencil,** and move the pencil to outline an ellipse.
4. Replace the paper with another **piece of paper.** Place the pins 10 cm apart. Outline another ellipse by using the string.
5. Use another **piece of paper.** Loop the string around one pin, and outline another ellipse.

Analysis

1. Which ellipse has an eccentricity closest to 0? Which has an eccentricity closest to 1? Describe the shape of your ellipse in terms of eccentricity.
2. Describe the ellipse as you increased the distance between the foci. Describe what would happen to the ellipse if you increased the length of the string without changing the distance between the foci.

Quick Lab

Skills Acquired
- Constructing Models
- Measuring
- Identifying/Recognizing Patterns

Materials
- Cork board
- Push pins
- Paper
- Pencil
- String

Teacher's Notes: Using graph paper that has 1 cm squares will make measuring easier. Masking tape will hold paper securely to the corkboard and keep it steady while students draw.

Answers to Analysis

1. The ellipse made using only one pin (step 5) has an eccentricity close to 0 and is most like a circle. The ellipse drawn in step 4 has an eccentricity closest to 1 and is least like a circle.
2. As I increased the distance between foci, the ellipses became more elongated. If I increased string length without changing the foci, the ellipse would become larger and more circular.

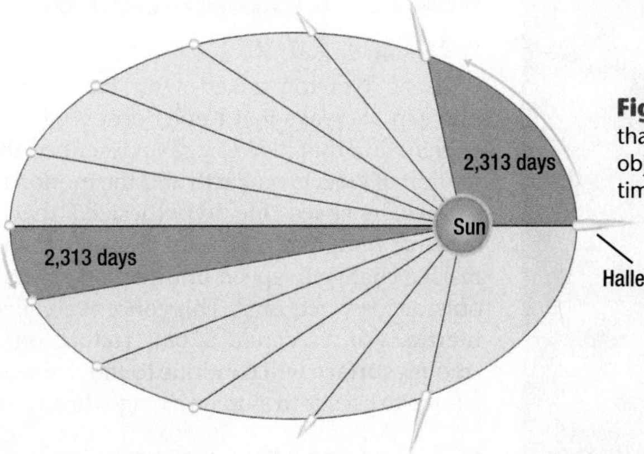

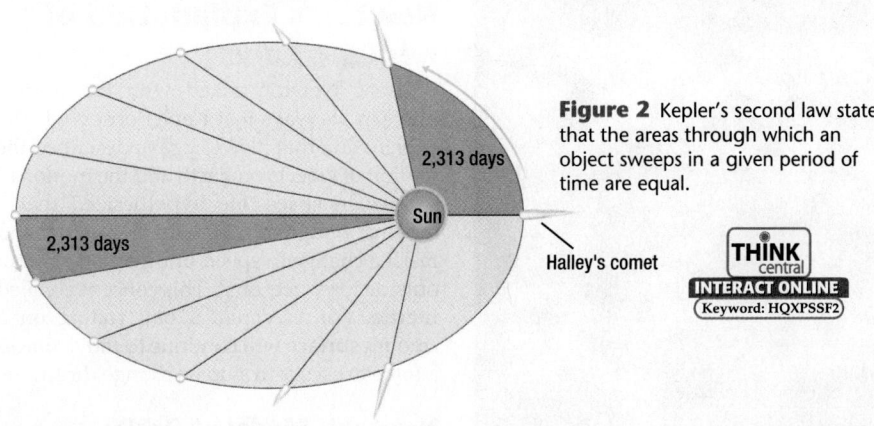

Figure 2 Kepler's second law states that the areas through which an object sweeps in a given period of time are equal.

THINK central
INTERACT ONLINE
(Keyword: HQXPSSF2)

Law of Equal Areas

Kepler's second law, the *law of equal areas,* describes the speed at which objects travel at different points in their orbits. Kepler discovered that Mars moves fastest in its elliptical orbit when it is closest to the sun. He calculated that a line from the center of the sun to the center of an object sweeps through equal areas in equal periods of time. This principle is illustrated in **Figure 2.**

Imagine a line that connects the center of the sun to the center of an object in orbit around the sun. When the object is near the sun, the imaginary line is short. The object moves relatively rapidly, and the line sweeps through a short, wide, pie-shaped sector. When the object is far from the sun, the line is long. However, the object moves relatively slowly when it is far from the sun, and the imaginary line sweeps through a long, thin, pie-shaped sector in the same period. Kepler's second law states that equal areas are covered in equal amounts of time as an object orbits the sun.

Law of Periods

Kepler's third law, the *law of periods,* describes the relationship between the average distance of a planet from the sun and the orbital period of the planet. The **orbital period** is the time required for a body to complete a single orbit. According to Kepler's third law, the cube of the average distance (a) of a planet from the sun is always proportional to the square of the period (p). The mathematical formula that describes this relationship is $K \times a^3 = p^2$, where K is a constant. When distance is measured in astronomical units (AU) and the period is measured in Earth years, $K = 1$ and $a^3 = p^2$.

Scientists can find out how far away the planets are from the sun by using this law, because they can measure the orbital periods by observing the planets. Jupiter's orbital period is 11.9 Earth years. The square of 11.9 is 142. The cubed number that is equal to 142 is 5.2, so Jupiter is 5.2 AU from the sun.

Math Skills

Law of Periods Suppose that scientists discover an asteroid that is 2.0 AU from the sun. If 1 AU = 150 million km, how long would the asteroid's orbital period be in Earth years?

orbital period the time required for a body to complete a single orbit

Math Skills

Answer

$a^3 = p^2$

$a^3 = 2.0 \times 2.0 \times 2.0 = 8.0$

$p^2 = 8.0$; $p = \sqrt{8.0} = 2.8$ y

Close

Reteaching — BASIC

Have students create a Venn diagram to compare the geocentric and heliocentric models of the solar system. Students can use the diagram to study for future assessments. LS **Visual**

Quiz — GENERAL

Determine whether each of the following statements is true or false.

1. A planet moves relatively slower when it is farther from the sun than it does when it is closer to the sun. (true)
2. Kepler's first law states that each planet orbits the sun, not in a circle, but in an ellipse. (true)
3. Kepler's third law states that the square of the average distance of a planet from the sun is proportional to the cube of the orbital period. (false)

Key Resources

Technology

- Transparencies
  138 Kepler's Law of Equal Area

Differentiated Instruction

Special Education Students

Helping to Remember Mnemonics that they create themselves can help students remember scientists' names and accomplishments. Divide the class into groups, and have each team create a mnemonic to help them remember the following people and their accomplishments; Ptolemy, Copernicus, Galileo, Tycho, Kepler, and Newton. Explain that mnemonics can be any word or sentence that is easy to remember. LS **Verbal/Auditory**

Close, *continued*

Answers to Section Review

1. Ptolemy's model was geocentric, with the planets moving in small circles as they revolved in larger circles around Earth. Copernicus's model was heliocentric, showing planets moving around the sun at different speeds and distances.
2. Galileo's observations with the telescope provided support for the heliocentric model because he found smaller objects (Jupiter's moons) that revolved around celestial bodies other than Earth.
3. The orbits are ellipses, with one of two foci located within the sun.
4. The law of equal areas describes the speed at which objects travel at different points in their orbits. Objects move faster when they are closest to the sun. An imaginary line between the two bodies sweeps equal areas in equal amounts of time.
5. The law of periods describes the mathematical relationship between the average distance of a planet from the sun and its orbital period. The cube of the average distance in astronomical units is equal to the square of the planet's orbital period in Earth years, or $a^3 = p^2$.
6. Newton's model showed that the gravitational force that pulls a planet toward the sun combines with the straight-line motion that results from the planet's inertia to cause the planet to move in an elliptical orbit.

Figure 3 Comet Hyakutake, passing only 0.1 AU from Earth, is kept in orbit by the sun's gravitational pull.

Newton's Explanation of Kepler's Laws

Isaac Newton asked why the planets move in the ways that Kepler observed. The explanation that Newton gave described the motion of objects on Earth and the motion of planets in space. He hypothesized that a moving body will remain in motion and resist a change in speed or direction until an outside force acts on it. This concept is called **inertia.** For example, a ball rolling on a smooth surface will continue to move unless a force causes it to stop or change direction.

Newton's Model of Orbits

Because a planet does not follow a straight path, an outside force must cause the orbit to curve. Newton gave this force the name *gravity,* and he realized that this attractive force exists between any two objects in the universe. The gravitational pull of the sun keeps objects, such as the comet shown in **Figure 3,** in orbit around the sun. While gravity pulls an object toward the sun, inertia keeps the object moving forward in a straight line. The sum of these two motions forms the ellipse of a stable orbit.

The farther from the sun a planet is, the weaker the sun's gravitational pull on the planet is. So, the outer planets are not pulled toward the sun as strongly as the inner ones are. As a result, the orbits of the outer planets are larger and are curved more gently, and the outer planets have longer periods of revolution than the inner planets do.

inertia the tendency of an object to resist a change in motion unless an outside force acts on the object

Academic Vocabulary

exist (eg ZIST) to occur or be present

Section 2 Review

Key Ideas

1. **Compare** Ptolemy's and Copernicus's models of the universe.
2. **Identify** the role that Galileo played in developing the heliocentric theory.
3. **Describe** the shape of planetary orbits.
4. **Explain** the law of equal areas.
5. **Summarize** Kepler's third law of planetary orbits.
6. **Describe** how Newton explained Kepler's laws by combining the effects of two forces.

Critical Thinking

7. **Applying Ideas** A comet's orbit is a highly elongated ellipse. So, why does a comet spend so little time in the inner solar system?
8. **Making Comparisons** How did Kepler's explanation of the orbits of planets differ from Newton's explanation?

Concept Mapping

9. Use the following terms to create a concept map: *retrograde motion, geocentric, heliocentric, ellipse, foci, gravity,* and *inertia.*

7. When it is located in the inner region of the solar system, the comet is closer to the sun and moves relatively faster than when it is farther from the sun. Also, a much larger fraction of its orbit is in the outer solar system. Thus, it spends a proportionally shorter time in the inner solar system.
8. Kepler explained his observations of the motions of planets in terms of the elliptical shape of their orbits and the position of the foci. He also described the effects of the sun on the planets' speed at different points in their orbits. Newton supplied the physical causes for what Kepler observed and described: the inertia of planets and gravitational pull of the sun on the planets.

Answers continued on p. 875A

Differentiated Instruction

Alternative Assessment

Jingles Ask students to create an advertising "jingle" for each of Kepler's laws of motion. Each jingle should state the law and describe how to use it. Students may wish to perform their jingles for the class. **LS Auditory**

SECTION 3

The Inner Planets

Key Ideas	Key Terms	Why It Matters
❯ Identify the basic characteristics of the inner planets. ❯ Compare the characteristics of the inner planets. ❯ Summarize the features that allow Earth to sustain life.	**terrestrial planet**	Studying other terrestrial planets helps scientists plan for human travel to, and colonization of, Mars.

The planets closest to the sun are called the *inner planets*. These planets are Mercury, Venus, Earth, and Mars. The inner planets are also called **terrestrial planets,** because they are similar to Earth. These planets consist mostly of solid rock and have metallic cores. The number of moons per planet varies from zero to two. The surfaces of inner planets have bowl-shaped depressions, called *impact craters,* that were caused by collisions of the planets with other objects in space.

terrestrial planet one of the highly dense planets nearest to the sun; Mercury, Venus, Mars, and Earth

Mercury

Mercury, the planet closest to the sun, circles the sun every 88 days. The ancient Romans named the planet after the messenger of the gods, who moved quickly. Mercury rotates on its axis once every 59 days.

Images of Mercury reveal a surface that is heavily cratered, as shown in **Figure 1.** The images also show a line of cliffs hundreds of kilometers long. These cliffs may be wrinkles that developed in the crust when the molten core cooled and shrank.

The absence of a significant atmosphere and the planet's slow rotation contribute to the large daily temperature range on Mercury. During the day, the temperature may reach as high as 427 °C. At night, the temperature may plunge to −173 °C.

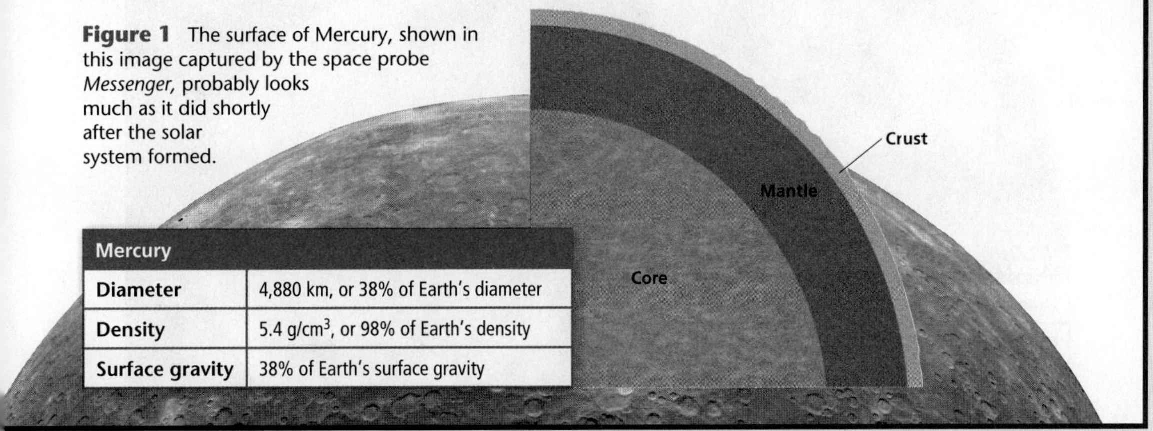

Figure 1 The surface of Mercury, shown in this image captured by the space probe *Messenger,* probably looks much as it did shortly after the solar system formed.

Mercury	
Diameter	4,880 km, or 38% of Earth's diameter
Density	5.4 g/cm^3, or 98% of Earth's density
Surface gravity	38% of Earth's surface gravity

Section 3

Focus

Overview

This section identifies the common and unique characteristics of the inner (terrestrial) planets and summarizes the life-sustaining features of Earth.

Bellringer

Have students write a brief description of the characteristics of Earth. (Answers may vary but should lead to a discussion of characteristics of the planet that are similar to the characteristics of other terrestrial planets.) **LS Verbal/Visual**

Motivate

Discussion GENERAL

Terrestrial Planets Ask students to describe how they think Earth would be different if it were closer to or farther from the sun. (Answers may vary. Students should comment that Earth would be hotter if it were closer to the sun and may be colder if it were farther from the sun.) Use this discussion as a launching point for discussing why the terrestrial planets have unique characteristics. **LS Verbal**

Key Resources

Chapter Resource File
- Directed Reading BASIC
- Inquiry Lab: Probing for Information GENERAL

Technology
- Transparencies
  Bellringer

Teach

Demonstration GENERAL

Global Greenhouse

1. Label two tall plastic tubes or jars "Earth" and "Venus." Use double-sided tape to attach a thermometer to the inside of each container near the top, facing outward. Leave empty space at the base.
2. Place a desk lamp above the model planetary atmospheres. Take a starting temperature reading for each jar.
3. Put a medicine bottle full of vinegar inside the Venus model and drop a twist of paper full of baking soda into the vinegar and wait for the reaction to stop before closing the jar again. Ask students what gas the reaction between the vinegar and baking soda releases into the jar. (carbon dioxide, CO_2)
4. Turn on the light. Have a student record the temperatures of the containers at 5-minute intervals for 30 minutes.
5. Remove the heat source and continue to take readings for another 10 minutes.
6. Examine the data. Have students identify which model was hotter after 30 minutes. (The Venus model will be hotter.) Ask students to compare the temperature changes that occurred in each model. (The model representing Earth's atmosphere cools off faster. Venus, the runaway greenhouse model with additional CO_2, retains the heat much longer.) **LS Logical**

Venus

Venus is the second planet from the sun and has an orbital period of 225 days. However, Venus rotates very slowly, only once every 243 days. In some ways, Venus is Earth's twin. The two planets are of almost the same size, mass, and density. However, Venus and Earth differ greatly in other ways.

Venus's Atmosphere

The biggest difference between Earth and Venus is Venus's atmosphere. Venus's atmospheric pressure is about 90 times the pressure on Earth. The high concentration of carbon dioxide in Venus's atmosphere and Venus's relative closeness to the sun have the strongest influences on surface temperatures. Venus's atmosphere is about 96% carbon dioxide.

Solar energy that penetrates the atmosphere heats the planet's surface. The high concentration of carbon dioxide in the atmosphere blocks most of the infrared radiation from escaping. This type of heating is called a *greenhouse effect*. On Earth, the greenhouse effect warms Earth enough to allow organisms to live on the planet. But the greenhouse effect on Venus makes the average surface temperature 464 °C! This phenomenon is commonly referred to as a *runaway greenhouse effect* and makes Venus's surface temperature the highest known in the solar system.

Venus also has sulfur dioxide droplets in its upper atmosphere. These droplets form a cloud layer that reflects sunlight. The cloud layer reflects the sunlight so strongly that, from Earth, Venus appears to be the brightest object in the night sky, aside from Earth's moon and the sun. Because Venus appears near the sun, Venus is usually visible from Earth only in the early morning or evening. Therefore, Venus is commonly called the *evening star* or the *morning star*.

Academic Vocabulary

phenomenon (fuh NAHM uh NUHN) any fact or event that can be sensed or described scientifically (plural, *phenomena*)

Figure 2 Venus's surface is composed of basalt and granite rocks. However, Venus's dense atmosphere is composed primarily of carbon dioxide.

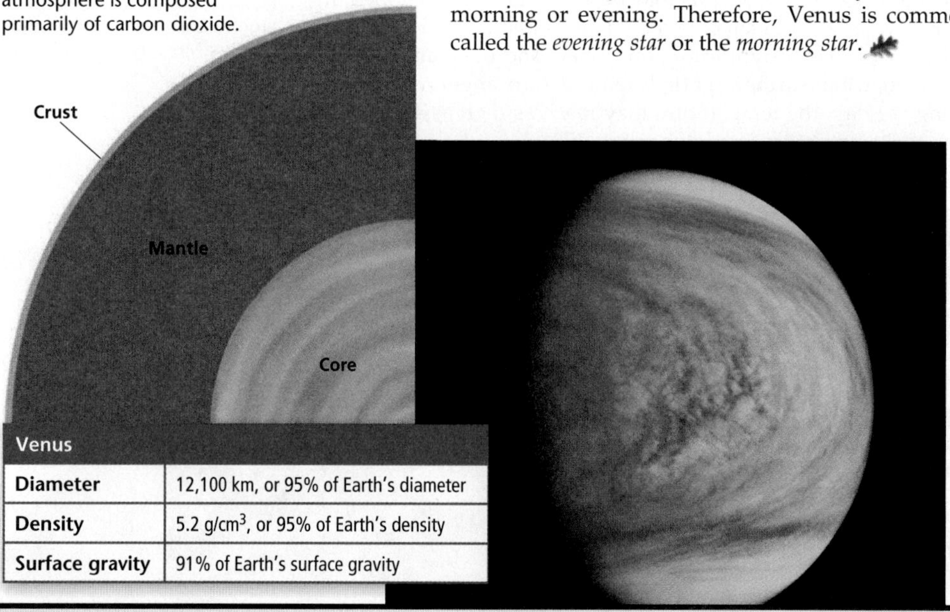

Venus	
Diameter	12,100 km, or 95% of Earth's diameter
Density	5.2 g/cm^3, or 95% of Earth's density
Surface gravity	91% of Earth's surface gravity

Environmental Connection

Venus: Earth's Twin Astronomers have long referred to Venus as "Earth's twin" because the masses, densities, and compositions of the two planets are similar. However, Venus is actually very different from Earth in some ways. Venus's massive atmosphere has caused a runaway greenhouse effect. Venus's atmosphere prevents heat from solar radiation from radiating back into space. As a result, Venus's surface temperature is hot enough to melt lead. Water vapor boils away, so Venus has no oceans. Sulfuric acid makes Venus's upper atmosphere poisonous. The milder greenhouse effect on Earth, however, keeps Earth's temperatures moderate.

One of the most common greenhouse gases on Venus is carbon dioxide (CO_2). On Earth, this compound is present in the atmosphere, but most CO_2 is held in non-atmospheric reservoirs such as the ocean and in rocks. Scientists fear that burning fossil fuels will release too much CO_2 into the atmosphere, causing Earth's surface temperature to rise, which would drastically alter Earth's environment.

Figure 3 The scale of this computer-generated image of the Maat Mons volcano on Venus has been stretched vertically to make the topography look more dramatic. The image has also been color enhanced.

Missions to Venus

In the 1970s, the Soviet Union sent six probes to explore the surface of Venus. The probes survived in the atmosphere long enough to transmit surface images of a rocky landscape. The images showed a smooth plain and some rocks. Other instruments carried by the probes indicated that the surface of Venus is composed of basalt and granite. These two types of rock are also common on Earth.

The United States's *Magellan* satellite orbited Venus for four years in the 1990s before the satellite was steered into the planet to collect atmospheric data. *Magellan* also bounced radio waves off Venus to produce radar images of Venus's surface. The European Space Agency's *Venus Express* orbited Venus between April 2006 and May 2009.

Surface Features of Venus

From the radar mapping produced by *Magellan,* scientists discovered landforms such as mountains, volcanoes, lava plains, and sand dunes. Volcanoes and lava plains are the most common features on Venus. At an elevation of 8 km, the volcano Maat Mons, which is shown in **Figure 3,** is Venus's highest volcano.

The surface of Venus is also somewhat cratered. All the craters are about the same age, and they are surprisingly young. This evidence and the abundance of volcanic features on Venus's surface have led some scientists to speculate that Venus undergoes a periodic resurfacing as a result of massive volcanic activity. Energy inside the planet heats the interior over time, which causes the volcanoes to erupt and cover the planet's surface with lava. However, scientists think that another 100 million years may pass before volcanic activity again covers Venus's surface with lava. Venus's surface is very different from Earth's surface, which is constantly changing because of the motion of tectonic plates.

Reading Check **How is Venus different from Earth?**

Math Skills

Distance from the Sun Earth is about 150 million kilometers from the sun. Venus is 108.2 million kilometers from the sun. How much closer to the sun is Venus than Earth? Express your answer as a percentage.

Using the Figure — Basic

Computer Generated Image
Point out that the vertical scale of this photo of Maat Mons has been exaggerated about 20 times to show clearly the structures and topography of the region around the volcano. The volcanic slope is actually very gentle. Color was added to match the reflectivity of the surface to radar energy. **LS Visual**

Discussion — General

Radar Revelations Invite volunteers to describe the surface features of Venus that have been revealed by radar. (volcanoes, lava flows, mountainous landscape, impact craters, and sand dunes) Ask students to explain why the craters on Venus appear to be in their original condition and almost unaffected by erosion. (The craters are relatively young. There is no surface water to erode them. Also, Venus lacks moving tectonic plates.) **LS Verbal**

Math Skills

Answer
150 million km − 108.2 million km = 41.8 million km ÷ 150 million km = 0.2787. Venus is 28% closer to the sun than Earth is.

Answer to Reading Check
Answers may vary but should address differences in distance from the sun, density, atmospheric pressure and density, and tectonics.

Differentiated Instruction

Advanced Learners

Remote Sensing Venus's dense atmosphere makes viewing its surface difficult. Have students model how radar-imaging probes map a hidden surface.

1. Build a clay terrain model in a box. Do not show the surface to other groups.
2. Label a piece of graph paper with letters in order along the top and numbers in sequence along the left side. Tape the grid on the box.
3. Mark a dowel rod with different colors at 1 cm intervals to use as a probe. Use a pencil to poke a hole in each grid square.
4. Label a new sheet of graph paper with letters and numbers to make a map.
5. Gently insert the probe into the first hole labeled A1 until it hits the surface. On the probe, note the color that is even with the grid. Color the A1 square on the map that color.
6. Repeat step 5 until the entire surface is mapped. **LS Kinesthetic**

Teach, *continued*

Environmental Connection

Suitable for Life Earth is the only planet that has both oceans of liquid water and areas of frozen ice on its surface. The idea that Earth is at the perfect distance from the sun is known as the "Goldilocks" principle. But the composition of Earth's atmosphere may be the key factor. If Earth had a dense atmosphere, Earth could be as hot as Venus; If Earth's atmosphere were thin, like the thin Martian atmosphere, Earth would likely be a rocky ball of ice. Instead, Earth has an oxygen-rich atmosphere that keeps the planet at a comfortable temperature and that protects the surface from harmful radiation. Earth's oceans also prevent the greenhouse effect that warms our planet from getting out of control by dissolving excess CO_2 gas. These environmental conditions make Earth ideally suited to support a complex biosphere.

Cultural Awareness — BASIC

Classical Heritage When early scientists discovered the planets of the solar system, they gave most of them names associated with ancient Western mythology. For example, Mars was the Roman god of war. Have interested students research some ancient myths and legends and explain how the names of the inner and outer planets and some of their moons reflect their characteristics. Students may present their results as an oral or written report. **LS Verbal**

SCILINKS
www.scilinks.org
Topic: Inner Planets
Code: **HQX0798**

Earth

The third planet from the sun is Earth. The orbital period of Earth is 365¼ days, and Earth completes one rotation on its axis every day. Earth has one large moon.

Earth has had an extremely active geologic history. Geologic records indicate that over the last 250 million years, Earth's continents separated from a single landmass and drifted to their present positions. Weathering and erosion have changed and continue to change the surface of Earth.

Water on Earth

Earth's unique atmosphere and distance from the sun allow water to exist in a liquid state. Mercury and Venus are so close to the sun that any liquid water on those planets would boil. The outer planets are so far from the sun that water freezes. Earth is the only planet known to have oceans of liquid water, as shown in **Figure 4.** However, scientists think that Jupiter's moon Europa may have an ocean under its icy crust and that Saturn's moon Enceladus may have underground lakes.

Life on Earth

Scientists theorize that as oceans formed on Earth, liquid water dissolved carbon dioxide from the atmosphere. Because of this process, carbon dioxide did not build up in the atmosphere and solar heat was able to escape. Thus, Earth maintained the moderate temperatures needed to support life. Plants and cyanobacteria contributed free oxygen to the atmosphere. Earth is the only known planet that has the proper combination of water, temperature, and oxygen to support life.

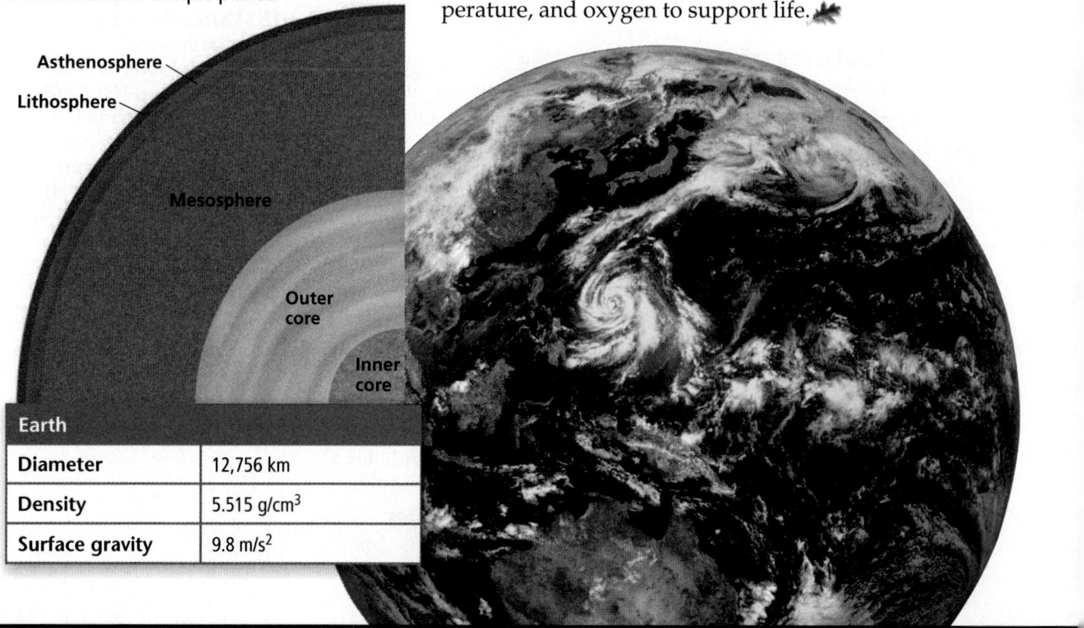

Figure 4 Oceans of water and an atmosphere that can support life make Earth a unique planet.

Earth	
Diameter	12,756 km
Density	5.515 g/cm^3
Surface gravity	9.8 m/s^2

Skill Builder — GENERAL

Writing The terrestrial planets have inspired numerous science fiction tales. For example, Mars was home to Ray Bradbury's *Martian Chronicles.* Venus is often pictured as a steamy jungle. Isaac Asimov wrote a "locked room" mystery located on Mercury. Have interested students share these and other stories with the class. Or, have interested students write a short story or poem set on an inner planet other than Earth. Encourage students to make the planet's physical properties important elements in the story. Students' descriptions of the planets should be consistent with what they have learned. **LS Verbal**

Differentiated Instruction

English Learners

Paired Summarizing Group students into pairs and have them read silently the introductory description of Earth as it might be viewed from elsewhere in our solar system. Then, have one student summarize Earth's characteristics. The other student can listen to the description and make corrections or identify any elements that were left out. Allow students to refer to the text as needed. **LS Auditory**

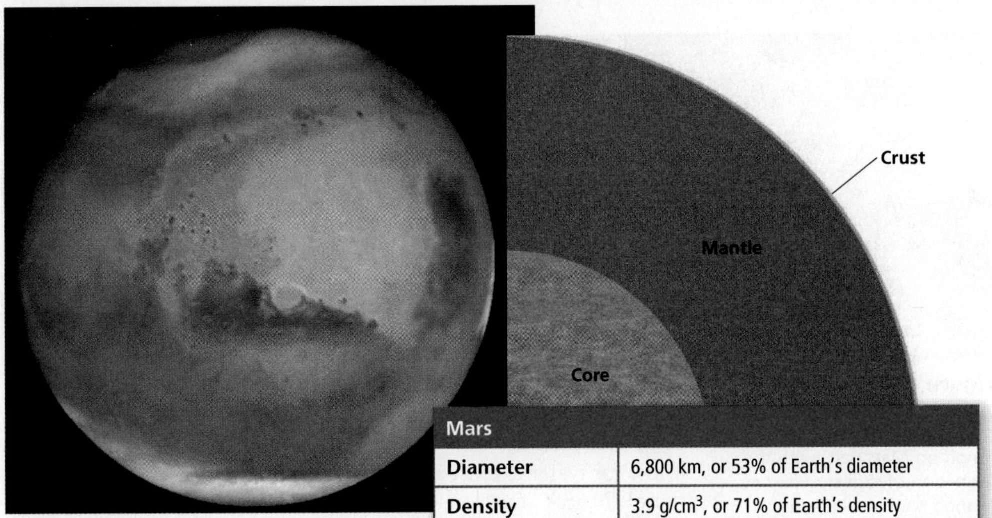

Mars	
Diameter	6,800 km, or 53% of Earth's diameter
Density	3.9 g/cm^3, or 71% of Earth's density
Surface gravity	38% of Earth's surface gravity

Figure 5 Mars is called the *Red Planet* because the oxidized rocks on the planet's surface give the planet a red color.

Mars

Mars, shown in **Figure 5,** is the fourth planet from the sun. At an average distance of about 228 million kilometers from the sun, Mars is about 50% farther from the sun than Earth is. Its orbital period is 687 days, and it rotates on its axis every 24 h 37 min. Because its axis tilts at nearly the same angle that Earth's does, Mars's seasons are much like Earth's seasons.

Mars has been geologically active in its past, which is shown in part by the presence of massive volcanoes. A system of deep canyons also covers part of the surface. Valles Marineris is a series of canyons that is as long as the United States is wide—4,000 km. The canyon is thought to be a crack that formed in the crust as the planet cooled. It was later eroded by water.

Martian Volcanoes

Tharsis Montes is one of several volcanic regions on Mars. Volcanoes in this region are 100 times as large as Earth's largest volcano. The largest volcano on Mars is Olympus Mons, which is nearly 24 km tall. It is three times as tall as Mount Everest. At 550 km across, the base of Olympus Mons is about the size of Nebraska. Scientists think that the volcano has grown so large because Mars has no moving tectonic plates. So, Olympus Mons may have had a magma source for millions of years.

Whether Martian volcanoes are still active is a question scientists have yet to answer. A *Viking* landing craft detected two geological events that produced seismic waves. These events, called *marsquakes,* may indicate that volcanoes on Mars are active.

Reading Check **Why are Martian volcanoes larger than Earth's volcanoes?**

READING TOOLBOX

Word Origins
In English, *Olympus Mons* is "Mount Olympus." Look up *Mount Olympus* to see why it is an appropriate name for this particular formation on Mars.

READING TOOLBOX

Word Origins
Mount Olympus is the tallest mountain in Greece. In Greek mythology, it was the home of the gods. Mount Olympus is an appropriate name for a volcano that is 100 times as large as Earth's largest volcano.

Close

Reteaching — BASIC

Same and Different Organize students into small groups. Have students write questions about the four inner planets based on the section content. Tell students to focus on ways in which the planets are the same and ways they are different. Then, have students join their assigned group and quiz each other using their questions.
LS Auditory

Quiz — GENERAL

Determine whether each of the following statements is true or false. If false, provide the correct word(s) to make the statement true.

1. The biggest differences between Earth and Venus involve mass and density. (false; atmospheric pressure and composition)
2. The surface of Mercury has many craters. (true)
3. Because of the massive geysers on its surface, scientists know that Mars has been geologically active in the past. (false; volcanoes)

LS Verbal

Internet Activity — ADVANCED

Life on Mars? The possibility of liquid water on Mars is important because water is considered essential for life. Some scientists think life may exist in protected niches on Mars. Fossil-like structures and organic chemicals have been found in ancient Martian meteorites. Invite students to research more about the evidence for life on Mars. A worksheet designed to direct student research on this topic can be found in the **Chapter Resource File** booklet or by visiting www.thinkcentral.com and entering the keyword **HQXPSSX**. **LS Verbal/Logical**

Answer to Reading Check
Martian volcanoes are larger than volcanoes on Earth because Mars has no moving tectonic plates. Magma sources remain in the same spot for millions of years and produce volcanic material that builds the volcanic cone higher and higher.

Close, *continued*

Answers to Section Review

1. Mercury lacks a dense atmosphere to hold heat and has a very slow rotational rate.
2. Venus has nearly the same diameter, density, and surface gravity as Earth. Rocks are composed of similar materials. Both are geologically active. Venus has a much denser atmosphere with higher pressure and a much higher surface temperature than Earth's.
3. Earth's distance from the sun, the presence of surface liquid water, moderate surface temperature, and free oxygen in its atmosphere.
4. Mars lacks moving tectonic plates, so volcanoes remain above the magma source for a very long time.
5. Atmospheric pressure and temperature are too low for liquid water to exist on the surface.
6. Answers may vary. Accept all reasonable answers.
7. On Earth, the greenhouse effect warms the planet's surface by absorbing heat radiated by Earth's surface. Because of its large concentration of carbon dioxide (96%), Venus's atmosphere absorbs massive amounts of heat from the surface. This heat makes the average surface temperature of Venus about 464 °C.
8. As the rock on Mars's surface cooled, it shrank and cracked, causing the canyon to form.
9. The *terrestrial planets* include *Mercury*; *Venus*, whose highest volcano is *Maat Mons*; *Earth*, whose surface has *liquid water*; and *Mars*, whose highest volcano is *Olympus Mons*.

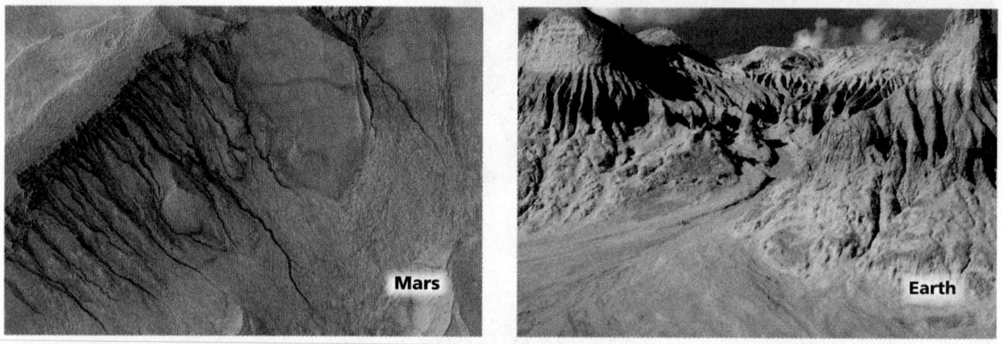

Figure 6 The images above compare the formation of gullies by possible liquid water runoff on Mars (left) with the formation of similar gullies at Mungo National Park in Australia on Earth (right). Mungo National Park is the site of a large lake that dried up more than 10,000 years ago.

Water on Mars

The pressure and temperature of Mars's atmosphere are too low for water to exist as a liquid on Mars's surface. However, several NASA missions—such as the Mars rovers, *Spirit* and *Opportunity,* which landed on Mars in 2004—have found evidence that liquid water did exist on Mars's surface in the past. Mars has many surface features that are characteristic of erosion by water, such as branching paths that look like gullies, as shown in **Figure 6.** Scientists think that other features on Mars might be evidence of vast flood plains produced by a volume of water equal to that of all five of Earth's Great Lakes.

The surface temperature on Mars ranges from 20 °C near the equator during the summer to as low as –130 °C near the poles during the winter. Although most of the water on Mars is trapped in polar icecaps, data from the *Phoenix* lander confirmed in 2008 that water also exists as ice just below the Martian surface. If liquid water were to exist below Mars's surface, the odds of life existing on Mars would dramatically increase. However, no solid evidence of life on Mars has been found.

Section 3 Review

Key Ideas

1. **Explain** why Mercury has such drastically different temperatures during its day and during its night.
2. **Describe** the main ways in which Venus is similar to and different from Earth.
3. **Identify** the aspects that make Earth hospitable for life.
4. **Explain** why Mars's volcanoes became so tall.
5. **Explain** why Mars does not have liquid water on its surface.
6. **Compare** the characteristics of the inner planets.

Critical Thinking

7. **Making Comparisons** Describe the difference between the greenhouse effect on Venus and the greenhouse effect on Earth.
8. **Understanding Relationships** As rock cools, it contracts. How could this fact explain the presence of Valles Marineris on Mars?

Concept Mapping

9. Use the following terms to create a concept map: *Mercury, Venus, Earth, Mars, terrestrial planet, Olympus Mons, liquid water,* and *Maat Mons.*

Differentiated Instruction

Alternative Assessment

Planetary Base Have students work in small groups to plan a permanent colony or base on an inner planet other than Earth. Students may create a model, diagram, or written description. They should include a mission plan that describes the purpose of the development. They should also detail how to protect inhabitants from extremes of temperature, radiation, or other unusual atmospheric conditions and how to provide for personal needs. **LS Interpersonal**

SECTION 4 The Outer Planets

Key Ideas	Key Terms	Why It Matters
❯ Identify the basic characteristics that make the outer planets different from terrestrial planets. ❯ Compare the characteristics of the outer planets. ❯ Explain why Pluto is now considered a dwarf planet.	**gas giant** **Kuiper Belt**	Objects beyond the outer planets hold clues to the origin of the solar system. But sending probes to this region is expensive.

The four planets farthest from the sun are called the *outer planets*. They are separated from the inner planets by a ring of debris called the *asteroid belt*. Jupiter, Saturn, Uranus, and Neptune, which are shown in **Figure 1**, are also called **gas giants** because they are large planets that have deep, massive atmospheres made mostly of gas. Uranus and Neptune have more frozen gases and are also known as ice giants. Usually found past the orbit of Neptune is Pluto. Prior to 2006, Pluto was considered to be the most distant outer planet. However, in August of 2006, Pluto was reclassified as a *dwarf planet*.

Gas Giants

Although the gas giants are much larger and more massive than the terrestrial planets, the gas giants are much less dense than the terrestrial planets. Unlike the terrestrial planets, the gas giants did not lose their original gases during their formation. Their large masses give them a huge amount of gravity, which helps them retain the gases. Each of the gas giants has a thick atmosphere that is made mostly of hydrogen and helium gases. A cloud layer prevents scientists from directly observing more than the topmost part of the atmosphere of the gas giants. But each planet probably has a core made of rock and metals.

Although Saturn's rings may be the most impressive, all four gas giants have ring systems that are made of dust and icy debris that probably came from comets or other bodies.

gas giant a planet that has a deep, massive atmosphere, such as Jupiter, Saturn, Uranus, or Neptune

Figure 1 The four gas giants are much larger than Earth, which is the terrestrial planet shown here at the lower left.

Section 4

Focus

Overview

This section compares characteristics of the outer planets and explains how the outer planets differ from the inner planets. It also explains that Pluto, once considered a planet, is now called a dwarf planet.

Bellringer

Ask students to list what they know about the properties of gases. (Sample answers: no definite shape or volume; atoms have more energy than atoms in solids and liquids; low density; exert pressure and can be compressed)
LS Verbal

Motivate

Demonstration GENERAL

Play Ball Compare the relative sizes of all of the planets in the solar system by using a marble for Mercury, two tennis balls for Earth and Venus, a ping pong ball for Mars, a basketball for Jupiter, a soccer ball for Saturn, and two softballs for Uranus and Neptune. Use a beach ball for the sun. Tell students that sizes are only approximate and not to scale. Ask students which planets are about the same size. (Earth and Venus, Uranus and Neptune) Ask which is the largest and which is the smallest. (largest, Jupiter; smallest, Mercury) **LS Visual/Logical**

Key Resources

Chapter Resource File
- Directed Reading BASIC
- Making Models Lab: It's a Long Way to Neptune! GENERAL

Technology
- Transparencies
  Bellringer

Teach

Meteorology Connection GENERAL

Lightning Discharge Model
During storms on Earth, electric charges build up in the clouds. Lightning flashes between areas of the clouds that have opposite charges. A similar process occurs on Jupiter. To model this effect, use an aluminum pie pan, two large rubber bands, a plastic tumbler, wool fabric, and a foam dinner plate, and follow these instructions:

1. Make a handle by putting a tumbler upside-down in the center of the pie pan. Stretch two rubber bands over the pan and the tumbler to form an “X” to hold the tumbler firmly in place.
2. Place the foam plate on a table and rub it with the fabric vigorously for 2 to 3 minutes.
3. Use the handle to place the aluminum pan onto the foam plate. Lift the pan and plate by the handle. Dim the lights. Slowly touch your finger to the edge of the pie pan.

You may need a few tries to build up the appropriate charge. Ask students to describe what happened. (Sample answers: A spark jumped from the pie pan to the finger. Some students may hear a crackling sound accompanying the spark.) LS **Kinesthetic**

Answer to Reading Check
When Jupiter formed, it did not have enough mass for nuclear fusion to begin.

SC*i*LINKS.
www.scilinks.org
Topic: Outer Planets
Code: HQX1091

Jupiter

Jupiter, shown in **Figure 2,** is the fifth planet from the sun and is by far the largest planet in the solar system. Its mass is more than 300 times that of Earth and is twice that of all the other planets combined. Jupiter's orbital period is almost 12 years. Jupiter rotates on its axis faster than any other planet rotates—once every 9 h 50 min. Jupiter has at least 63 moons, 4 of which are the size of small planets. It also has several thin rings that are made up of millions of particles.

Jupiter's Atmosphere

Hydrogen and helium make up 92% of Jupiter, so Jupiter's composition is much like the sun's. However, when Jupiter formed about 4.6 billion years ago, it did not have enough mass to allow nuclear fusion to begin. So, Jupiter never became a star.

The alternating light and dark bands on its surface make Jupiter unique in our solar system. Orange, gray, blue, and white bands spread out parallel to the equator. The colors suggest the presence of organic molecules mixed with ammonia, methane, and water vapor. Jupiter's rapid rotation causes these gases to swirl around the planet and form the bands. The average temperature of Jupiter's outer atmospheric layers is –160 °C. Jupiter has lightning storms and thunderstorms that are much larger than those on Earth.

Reading Check **Why didn't Jupiter become a star?**

Figure 2 Jupiter is easily identified by its large size and alternating light and dark bands. One of Jupiter's larger moons can be seen in front of the planet.

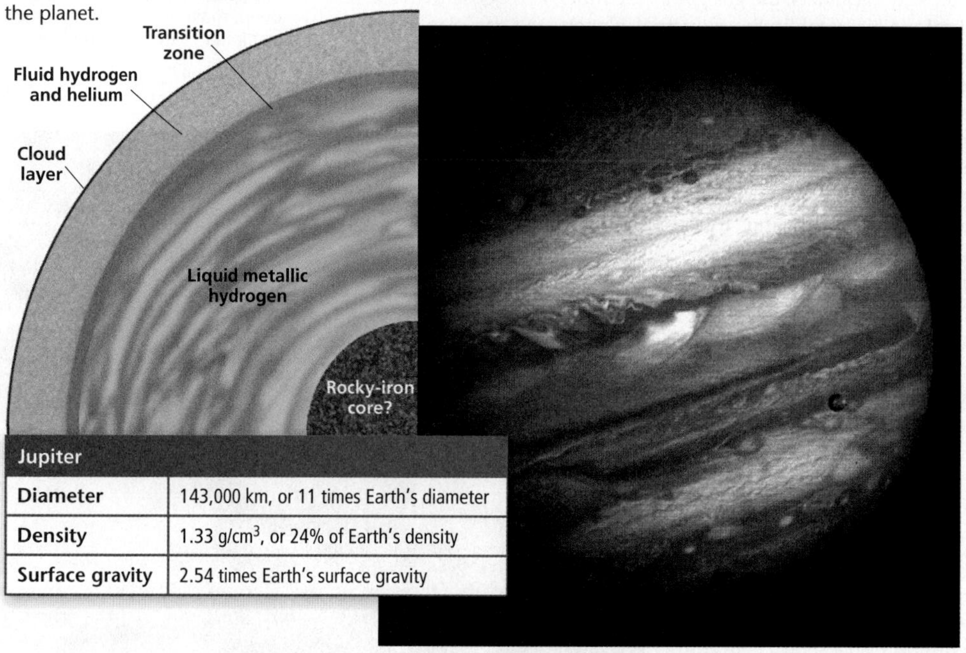

Jupiter	
Diameter	143,000 km, or 11 times Earth's diameter
Density	1.33 g/cm^3, or 24% of Earth's density
Surface gravity	2.54 times Earth's surface gravity

Why It Matters

Asteroid Belt The asteroid belt is a ring of space debris that separates the inner planets from the gas giants. Because there are five to ten distinct asteroid families and mineral types for meteorites, astronomers speculate that a handful of large asteroids may have been shattered by impacts to form the belts we see today.

Differentiated Instruction

English Learners

Skimming and Scanning Pair students to practice the “skimming and scanning” technique while reading the two pages covering Jupiter. Have students brainstorm ways to get the most out of this reading technique, such as looking for italicized words, heads, and captions. First, they can read quickly to identify the main topic, then scan for specific information. Have students work together to make an outline on the topic to use as a study guide. LS **Verbal**

Weather and Storms on Jupiter

Figure 3 Jupiter's Great Red Spot is an ongoing, massive, hurricane-like storm that is about twice the diameter of Earth.

Jupiter's most distinctive feature is its *Great Red Spot,* shown in **Figure 3.** The Great Red Spot is a giant rotating storm, similar to a hurricane on Earth, that has been raging for at least several hundred years. Several other oval spots, or storms, can be seen on Jupiter, although they are usually white. Sometimes, the smaller storms are swallowed up by the larger ones. While storms are common on Jupiter's surface, only a few of the largest storms persist for a long time.

A probe dropped by the *Galileo* spacecraft measured wind speeds of up to 540 km/h on Jupiter. Because winds are caused by temperature differences, scientists have concluded that Jupiter's internal heat affects the planet's weather more than heat from the sun does. From Earth, even using a small telescope, you can see bands of clouds on Jupiter. These bands, which vary depending on latitude, show regions of different wind speeds.

Academic Vocabulary

distinctive (di STINGK tiv) notable, distinguishing

Jupiter's Interior

Jupiter's large mass causes the temperature and pressure in Jupiter's interior to be much greater than they are inside Earth. The intense pressure and temperatures as high as 30,000 °C have changed Jupiter's interior into a sea of liquid, metallic hydrogen. Electric currents in this hot liquid may be the source of Jupiter's enormous magnetic field. Scientists think that Jupiter has a solid, rocky, iron core at its center.

Why It Matters

What Happens When a Comet Hits a Planet?

REAL WORLD

Nobody had ever witnessed a collision between a comet and a planet in all of human history. That changed in 1994 when comet Shoemaker-Levy collided with Jupiter.

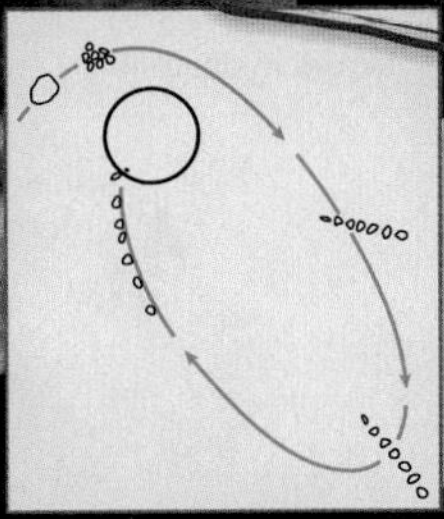

The comet was trapped in July 1992, and its fragments collided two years later.

When it was trapped by Jupiter's gravity, the comet broke into fragments in a formation described as a "string of pearls."

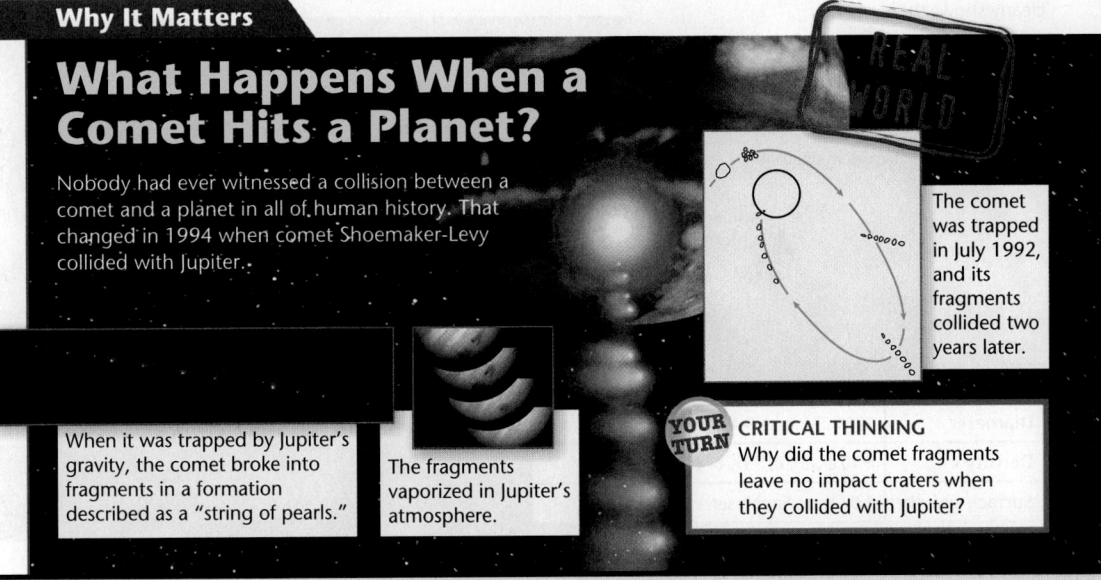

The fragments vaporized in Jupiter's atmosphere.

YOUR TURN

CRITICAL THINKING

Why did the comet fragments leave no impact craters when they collided with Jupiter?

Demonstration — GENERAL

Gas Storms Explain to students that Jupiter's storm systems are similar to hurricanes on Earth. They are produced by vortex-like winds that spin around an area of relative calm. You will need a large glass jar, such as a pasta-sauce jar or a mayonnaise jar. Remove the label by soaking the jar in water. Fill the jar about three-quarters full with water. Add 2 tsp (10 mL) of white vinegar, 1 tsp (5 mL) of dish liquid, and some glitter or food coloring. Screw the cap firmly onto the jar, and hold the jar securely around the middle. Begin to move the jar by using a circular motion to get the contents swirling. Hold the jar so students can observe the motion of the liquids from all sides. Ask students to explain how the pattern that the different liquids make relates to storms on Jupiter. (Sample answer: The swirling water is similar to the violent winds caused by streams of gases, which are represented by the different liquids and the glitter, that move at different speeds and form colored bands.) **LS Visual**

Discussion — GENERAL

What If...? Ask the class to speculate how the solar system might be different if Jupiter had become a star with a larger mass than it now has. (Sample answers: In a binary star system, with two stars that orbit each other, planetary orbits might be unstable; seasonal variations and patterns of night and day would be more complex; atmospheric composition and weather patterns would be more complex.) **LS Verbal/Logical**

Why It Matters

What Happens When a Comet Hits a Planet? This comet is named after its discoverers, Carolyn and Gene Shoemaker and David Levy. The comet broke into 21 discernable pieces, which traveled around the planet until they finally collided with Jupiter. Each "pearl" in the string was approximately 1 km to 5 km in diameter. The reaction from the explosion lasted for a number of weeks, showing how massive a scale the impact was. If the larger fragments from the splintered comet had hit Earth, it would have destroyed all life. If an average sized fragment had hit Earth, probably nothing bigger than bacteria would survive.

Answer to Your Turn

Critical Thinking The comets vaporized in Jupiter's atmosphere and they would not leave a crater in Jupiter's surface of liquid hydrogen.

Teach, *continued*

Discussion

Saturn's Rings Ask students what feature Saturn is especially noted for. (the extensive ring system around its equator) Though they look solid, Saturn's rings are made up of chunks of ice, rock, and dust particles. Ask students where most of the material that makes up this ring system came from. (debris from comets or other rocky bodies) **LS Verbal**

Answer to Reading Check

Saturn and Jupiter are made almost entirely of hydrogen and helium and have rocky iron cores, ring systems, many satellites, rapid rotational periods, and bands of colored clouds.

Saturn

Saturn, shown in **Figure 4,** is the sixth planet from the sun and has an orbital period of 29.5 years. Because it is so far from the sun, Saturn is very cold and has an average cloud-top temperature of −176 °C. Saturn has at least 60 moons, and additional small moons continue to be discovered. Its largest moon, Titan, which has a diameter of 5,150 km, is half the size of Earth.

Saturn, like Jupiter, is made almost entirely of hydrogen and helium and has a rocky, iron core at its center. However, Saturn is much less dense than Jupiter. In fact, Saturn is the least dense planet in the solar system.

Saturn's Bands and Rings

Saturn is known for its rings, which are two times the planet's diameter. While the other gas giants also have rings, Saturn has the most complex and extensive system of rings. The rings are made of billions of dust and ice particles. Most of the ring debris probably came from comets or other bodies.

Like Jupiter, Saturn also has bands of colored clouds that run parallel to its equator. These bands are caused by Saturn's rapid rotation. Saturn rotates on its axis about every 10 h 30 min. This rapid rotation, paired with Saturn's low density, causes Saturn to bulge at its equator and to flatten at its poles.

Scientists are learning more about Saturn and its moons from NASA's *Cassini* spacecraft, which reached Saturn on July 1, 2004. Cassini also carried the European Space Agency's *Huygens* probe, which landed on Titan, Saturn's largest moon.

Reading Check **How is Saturn similar to Jupiter?**

Figure 4 This composite image of Saturn taken from the *Cassini* spacecraft clearly shows the planet's rings.

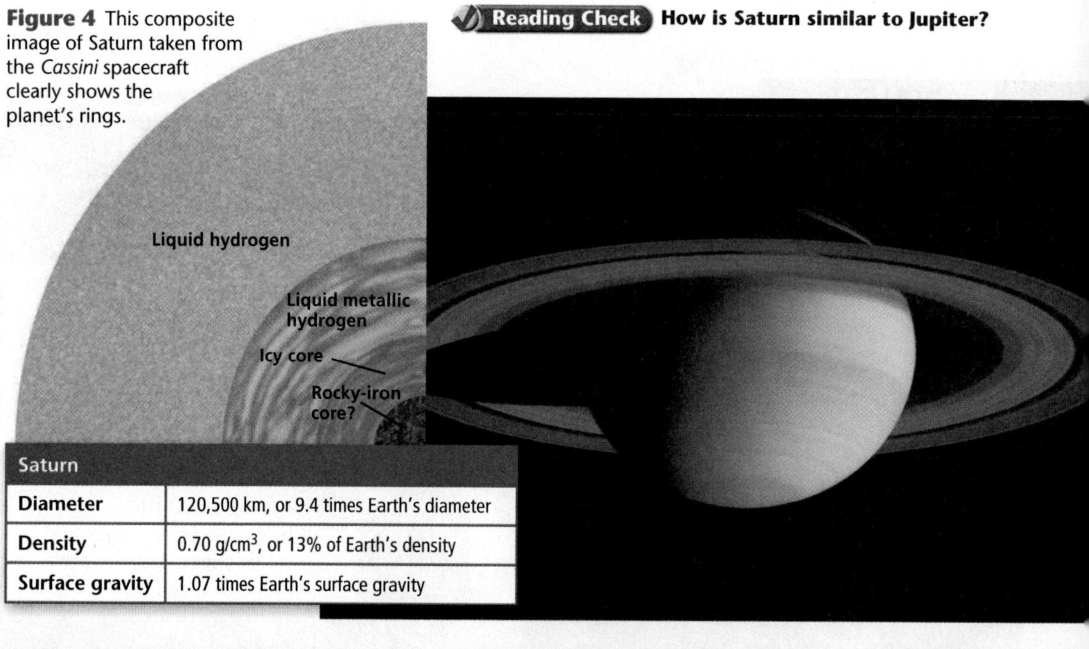

Saturn	
Diameter	120,500 km, or 9.4 times Earth's diameter
Density	0.70 g/cm^3, or 13% of Earth's density
Surface gravity	1.07 times Earth's surface gravity

Technology Connection — ADVANCED

***Cassini* Mission** The *Cassini* mission to Saturn was a joint project of NASA, the European Space Agency (ESA) and the Italian space agency. The *Cassini* orbiter conducted in-depth studies of the planet, its moons, its rings, and its magnetic environment. Have interested students research how the *Huygens* scientific probe and other instruments on board performed their jobs and what information has been collected. Students may present their findings in an oral or written report. **LS Verbal**

Differentiated Instruction

Special Education Students

Chart Help students clarify the similarities and differences between the planets by creating a chart on the board and filling it in as a class. Use these headings for the chart: Number; Order from Sun; Rock or Gas?; Large or Small?; Length of One Day; Length of One Year; Hot or Cold?; Average Daytime Temperature; and Average Nighttime Temperature. **LS Logical**

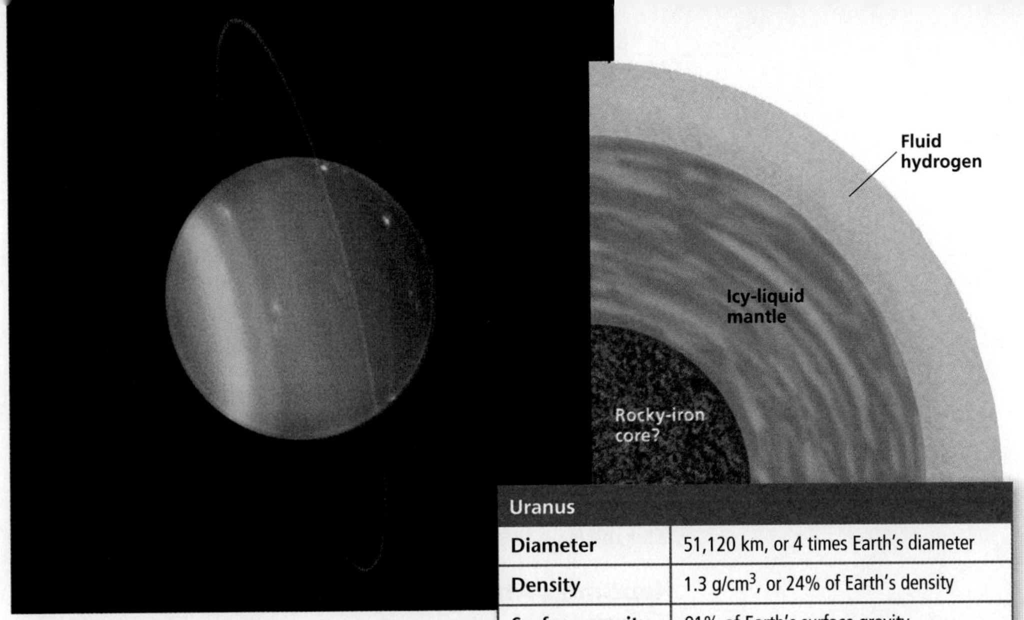

Uranus	
Diameter	51,120 km, or 4 times Earth's diameter
Density	1.3 g/cm^3, or 24% of Earth's density
Surface gravity	91% of Earth's surface gravity

Figure 5 This exaggerated-color image from the *Hubble Space Telescope* shows Uranus, two of its moons, and some of its rings.

Uranus

Uranus, shown in **Figure 5,** is the seventh planet from the sun and the third-largest planet in the solar system. William Herschel discovered Uranus in 1781. Because Uranus is nearly 3 billion kilometers from the sun, Uranus is a difficult planet to study. But the *Hubble Space Telescope* has taken images that show changes in Uranus's atmosphere. Uranus has at least 27 moons and at least 12 thin rings. Its orbital period is almost 84 years.

Uranus's Rotation

The most distinctive feature of Uranus is its unusual orientation. Most planets, including Earth, rotate with their axes perpendicular to their orbital planes as they revolve around the sun. However, Uranus's axis is almost parallel to the plane of its orbit. The rotation rate of Uranus was not discovered until 1986, when *Voyager 2* passed by Uranus. Astronomers were then able to determine that Uranus rotated once about every 17 h.

Uranus's Atmosphere

Like the other gas giants, Uranus has an atmosphere that contains mainly hydrogen and helium. The blue-green color of Uranus indicates that the atmosphere also contains significant amounts of methane. The average cloud-top temperature of Uranus is –214 °C. However, astronomers believe that the planet's temperature is much higher below the clouds. There may be a mixture of liquid water and methane beneath the atmosphere. Scientists also think that the center of Uranus, which has a temperature of approximately 7,000 °C, is a core of rock and melted elements.

Demonstration — GENERAL

Radically Tilted Planet Direct students' attention to the image of Uranus. Ask students to describe the planet's most unusual feature. (The planet is tilted so that it appears to lie on its side.) Tell students that, even though Uranus' axis is almost parallel to the plane of its orbit, its poles do not always point toward the sun. Demonstrate by putting an axis through a sphere of some kind, tilt it as Uranus is tilted, and move the planet around a "sun." Tell students that, because of the tilt, each pole is totally dark for about 21 years out of an orbit of 84 years. Invite students to speculate as to what may have caused this axial tilt. (Perhaps during the period when much of the solar system was bombarded with debris, a large planet-sized object collided with Uranus, knocking the planet on its side.) **LS Visual**

Discussion — BASIC

Composition and Structure Explain that in addition to helium and hydrogen, Uranus' atmosphere apparently also contains organic compounds such as hydrocarbons. Ask students what gives Uranus a blue-green color. (Methane in the atmosphere. The compound absorbs red wavelengths of light, giving the planet a bluish tint.) Invite students to describe what scientists think about the planet's structure. (The planet consists of a cloud layer of fluid hydrogen over a mantle of liquid water, methane, and ammonia, which surrounds a core of rock and metals.) **LS Verbal**

History Connection — ADVANCED

Caroline Herschel Only six planets, including Earth, were known until the eighteenth century. In 1781, amateur astronomer William Herschel made the next discovery: Uranus. His sister Caroline assisted her brother in his hobby of making telescopes and shared his passion for astronomy. Caroline also discovered eight comets, published several astronomical catalogues, and received a gold medal from the Royal Astronomical Society for her research—in an era when women stayed mostly in the home. Invite interested students to learn more about the achievements of this remarkable astronomer, and have them make an oral or written report on their findings. **LS Verbal**

Teach, *continued*

Discussion — GENERAL

Neptune's Weather Point out that Neptune is a very dynamic planet that has giant, hurricane-like storms similar to Jupiter's Great Red Spot. Ask students to name the weather system that *Voyager 2* identified. (the Great Dark Spot) Explain that the Great Dark Spot had disappeared when the *Hubble Space Telescope* was directed at Neptune, but another appeared in the planet's northern hemisphere. Ask students which planet in the solar system is the windiest and what wind speeds have been recorded. (Neptune; 2,000 km/h) Ask students what causes winds on Earth and on Neptune. (Differences in atmospheric temperatures cause differences in pressure. The atmospheric gases move from areas of high pressure to areas of lower pressure.) **LS Verbal**

Group Activity — ADVANCED

To Be or Not to Be a Planet
Many small objects have been discovered in the Kuiper Belt beyond Neptune's orbit. These objects have orbits and other properties that are similar to those of Pluto. In 2006, the International Astronomical Union (IAU) categorized Pluto and another Kuiper-Belt object, named Eris, as dwarf planets. Have interested students research the various IAU resolutions leading up to this reclassification of Pluto, the protests by some astronomers that followed, and the reaction of the general public. Have students prepare short presentations of their findings for the class. **LS Verbal/Logical** Co-op Learning

Neptune

Neptune, shown in **Figure 6,** is the eighth planet from the sun and is similar to Uranus in size and mass. Neptune's orbital period is nearly 164 years, and the planet rotates about every 16 h. Neptune has at least 13 moons and six rings.

The Discovery of Neptune

Neptune's existence was predicted before Neptune was actually discovered. After Uranus was discovered, astronomers noted variations from its calculated orbit. They suspected that the gravity of an unknown planet was responsible for the variation. In the mid-1800s, John Couch Adams, an English mathematician, and Urbain Leverrier, a French astronomer, independently calculated the position of the unknown planet. A German astronomer, Johann Galle, discovered a bluish-green disk where Leverrier had predicted the planet would be. Astronomers named the planet Neptune after the Roman god of the sea.

Neptune's Atmosphere

Data from the *Voyager 2* spacecraft indicate that Neptune's atmosphere is made up mostly of hydrogen, helium, and methane. Neptune's upper atmosphere contains some white clouds of frozen methane. These clouds appear as continually changing bands between the equator and the poles of Neptune.

Images taken by *Voyager 2,* the *Hubble Space Telescope,* and earthbound telescopes indicate that Neptune has an active weather system. Neptune has the solar system's strongest winds, which exceed 1,000 km/h. A storm that is the size of Earth and that is known as the *Great Dark Spot* appeared and disappeared on Neptune's surface. Neptune's average cloud-top temperature is about –225 °C.

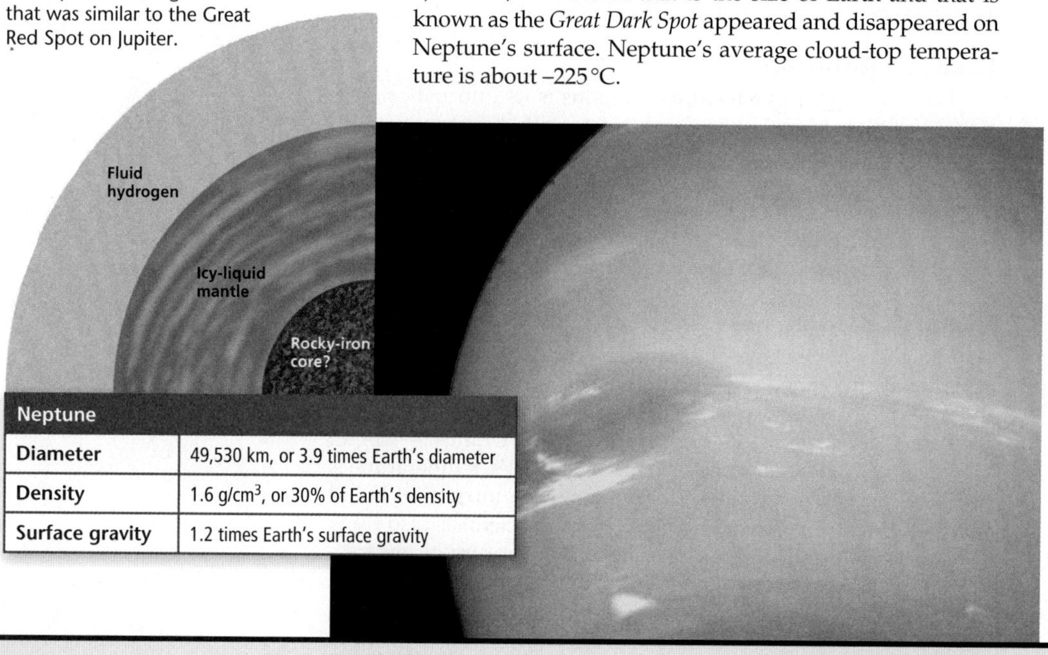

Figure 6 This Great Dark Spot on Neptune was a giant storm that was similar to the Great Red Spot on Jupiter.

Neptune	
Diameter	49,530 km, or 3.9 times Earth's diameter
Density	1.6 g/cm^3, or 30% of Earth's density
Surface gravity	1.2 times Earth's surface gravity

Math Connection

Discovery of Neptune and Pluto The discoveries of Neptune and Pluto were the result of mathematical analysis of irregularities in the motions of Uranus and Neptune, based upon Newton's law of gravitation. In the case of Uranus, English mathematician John Couch Adams and French astronomer Urbain LeVerrier independently calculated not only the orbit, but also the predicted mass, of an unknown object whose gravitational pull was affecting Uranus's orbit. These calculations were the first time Newton's theory of gravitation was used to predict orbital position by observing the effects of a planet's gravity. Later, astronomers searching for an unknown planet that disturbed Uranus's orbit observed Neptune. When Uranus still did not exactly follow its predicted orbit, astronomers began to look for a planet beyond Neptune to explain the data. They found Pluto after a careful search, although it had been predicted erroneously.

Figure 7 This artist drawing illustrates the largest known trans-Neptunian objects. Note that Pluto, once considered one of the nine planets, is not the largest.

Objects Beyond Neptune

Pluto was discovered in 1930. Until 2006, it was known as the ninth planet. Now, it is defined as a dwarf planet. A *dwarf planet* is any object that orbits the sun, is round because of its own gravity, has not cleared the region around its orbit, and is not a satellite of another planet.

Pluto orbits the sun in an unusual elongated and tilted ellipse. Pluto is usually far beyond Neptune, but it is closer to the sun than Neptune is for about 20 years out of its 248-year orbital period. With a diameter of 2,302 km, Pluto is smaller than Earth's moon. Astronomers think that Pluto is made up of frozen methane, rock, and ice and has an average temperature of −235 °C. Infrared images show that Pluto has extensive methane icecaps and a very thin nitrogen atmosphere. It also has three moons, one of which, named Charon (KER uhn), has a diameter more than half that of Pluto.

Kuiper-Belt Objects

In recent years, scientists have discovered hundreds of objects in our solar system beyond Neptune's orbit. These objects are called *trans-Neptunian objects* (TNOs). Some of these TNOs are similar to Pluto in size and composition, as shown in **Figure 7,** but most are simply small chunks of ice. TNOs exist in a region beyond Neptune's orbit called the **Kuiper Belt** (KIE puhr BELT). Scientists think that these bodies are the remnants of material that formed the early solar system.

Like Pluto, Eris, Makemake (MAH kay MAH kay), and Haumea (HAH oo may uh) are trans-Neptunian dwarf planets or *plutoids.* The other large TNOs have not been classified as such, but may eventually be considered as meeting the definition.

Reading Check **Where is the Kuiper Belt located?**

READING TOOLBOX

Word Origins
Eris was a Greek goddess, and Sedna was an Inuit goddess. Quaoar was a god of the Native American Tongva people. Look up these names, and find why they were chosen as names of objects beyond Neptune's orbit.

Kuiper Belt a region of the solar system that starts just beyond the orbit of Neptune and that contains dwarf planets and other small bodies made mostly of ice

READING TOOLBOX

Word Origins
Eris is the Greek goddess of strife and discord. Eris is bigger than Pluto. When Eris was discovered, scientists debated if it should be classified as a planet. In 2006, the International Astronomical Union (IAU) decided that Pluto and Eris are both "dwarf planets." Sedna is the Inuit goddess of the sea. In mythology, her home was the Arctic sea. Appropriatly, Sedna is in the coldest part of our solar system. Quaoar is the Tongva god of creation. According to IAU rules, objects beyond Neptune's orbit are given creation-related mythological names.

Answer to Reading Check
The Kuiper Belt is located beyond the orbit of Neptune.

Close

Reteaching BASIC

Concept Webs Organize students into pairs. Have each pair create a concept web about the gas giants and identify the similarities and differences between the planets. **LS Visual**

Quiz GENERAL

1. Explain how Pluto is similar to the terrestrial planets. (It is smaller and denser than the outer planets, and it is composed of ice and rock.)
2. What do scientists expect to learn by studying exoplanets? (how solar systems form; the general arrangement of solar systems; and possibility of life in other solar systems)

Differentiated Instruction

Advanced Learners

Asking Questions Have students work together to identify questions they have about the solar system. Each student should write up one question, beginning with a summary of what they know about the topic, followed by the question. Have groups choose one question to post on http://quest.nasa.gov/qna. Students should first search the archives and FAQs to make sure that their has not been asked already.
LS Verbal/Interpersonal

Internet Activity ADVANCED

Gravitational Microlensing In 2004, astronomers used a technique first proposed by Albert Einstein to identify exoplanets that orbit distant stars. Gravitational microlensing uses a star or exoplanet as a cosmic lens to magnify and brighten a more distant star lined up behind it. Have interested students report on this technique. A worksheet designed to direct student research on this topic can be found in the **Chapter Resource File** booklet or by visiting www.thinkcentral.com and entering the keyword **HQXPSSX.** **LS Verbal**

Close, *continued*

Answers to Section Review

1. Jupiter is extremely large and has numerous satellites and huge electrical fields. It consists mainly of helium and hydrogen gases; it has very high internal temperatures.
2. All four are extremely large and have massive atmospheres, mainly composed of gases. They are far from the sun and have huge gravity fields, many satellites, and ring systems.
3. Jupiter's Great Red Spot is a giant rotating storm similar to a hurricane on Earth. However, the Great Red Spot is twice the diameter of Earth and has wind speeds of up to 540 km/h.
4. Most planets rotate with their axis nearly perpendicular to the orbital plane, but Uranus's axis is tilted so that its axis is nearly parallel to its orbital plane.
5. Pluto is a dwarf planet made of water and methane ice and rock. The outer planets are very large and are made mostly of hydrogen and helium gases.
6. Located just beyond Neptune's orbit, these small bodies are composed mainly of ice; some are similar in mass to Pluto.
7. Most were detected because of gravitational effects on the stars they orbit, or shifts produced in light coming from those stars; most orbit stars similar to Earth's sun and are larger than Uranus.
8. The compositions of the sun and of the outer planets are similar because all are made mostly of hydrogen and helium.

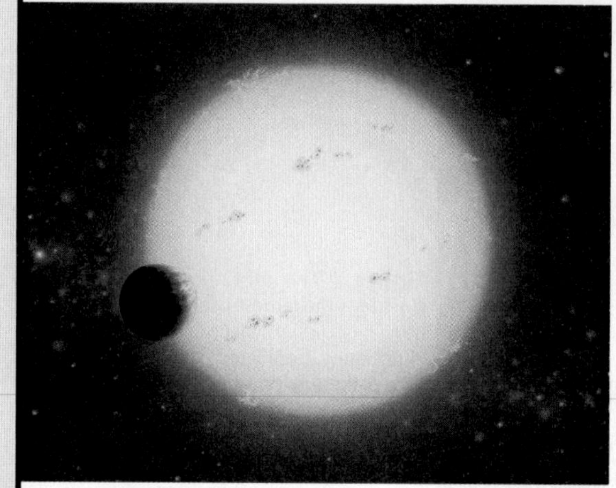

Figure 8 This illustration shows an artist's idea of a Jupiter-sized exoplanet in the foreground. This exoplanet orbits a sun-like star called HD209458, which is located 150 light years from Earth.

Exoplanets

Until the 1990s, all the planets that astronomers had discovered were in Earth's solar system. Since then, however, several hundred planetlike objects have been attributed to stars other than Earth's sun. Because these objects circle stars other than Earth's sun, they are called *exoplanets*. The prefix *exo-* means "outside." **Figure 8** shows an artist's rendition of an exoplanet. Most known exoplanets orbit stars that are similar to Earth's sun. Therefore, the existence of exoplanets leads some scientists to wonder if life could exist in another solar system.

Because of their size and distance, exoplanets have only recently been directly observed with telescopes. Most exoplanets can be detected only because their gravity tugs on stars that they orbit. When scientists study some distant stars, they notice that the light coming from the stars shifts in wavelength. This shifting could be explained by the stars' movement slightly toward and then away from Earth. Scientists know that the gravity of an object that cannot be seen can affect a star's movement. In these cases, that object is most likely an exoplanet that orbits the star.

Most of the exoplanets that have been identified are larger than Uranus, but gradually astronomers are discovering exoplanets that are closer to Earth in mass. One may even be the right temperature to support life as we know it. Many exoplanets, though more massive than Jupiter, are closer to their stars than Mercury is to Earth's sun. From studying these many solar systems, scientists hope to learn more about the formation and basic arrangement of solar systems.

Section 4 Review

Key Ideas

1. **Explain** what makes Jupiter similar to the sun.
2. **Compare** the characteristics of Jupiter, Saturn, Uranus, and Neptune.
3. **Compare** Jupiter's Great Red Spot with weather on Earth.
4. **Describe** the way in which the tilt of the axis of Uranus's rotation is unusual.
5. **Explain** how Pluto differs from the outer planets of the solar system.
6. **Summarize** the features of objects in the Kuiper Belt.
7. **Describe** what scientists know about exoplanets, planetlike objects outside the solar system.

Critical Thinking

8. **Making Comparisons** How are the compositions of the gas giants similar to the composition of the sun?
9. **Making Inferences** Why is Pluto not considered a planet even though Neptune is sometimes farther from the sun than Pluto is?
10. **Evaluating Conclusions** Should scientists reconsider Pluto to be a planet? Explain your answer.

Concept Mapping

11. Use the following terms to create a concept map: *outer planet, Jupiter, Saturn, Uranus, Neptune, Pluto, gas giant, Kuiper Belt,* and *Great Red Spot.*

9. Pluto's elongated orbit takes it into the Kuiper Belt, which Pluto shares with thousands of other objects. Planets do not share their orbits with other objects.
10. Answers may vary. Accept all reasonable answers.
11. The *outer planets* consist of the *gas giants*, which include *Jupiter*, which has a *Great Red Spot*; *Saturn*; *Uranus*; and *Neptune*. *Pluto* is a dwarf planet located in the *Kuiper Belt*.

Differentiated Instruction

Alternative Assessment

Outer Planets Museum Create a mini-space museum around the topic of the outer planets. Have students design displays that feature each of the gas giants, Pluto and the other dwarf planets, the asteroid belt, and the Kuiper Belt. Exhibits should be based on facts about each object and should look as realistic as possible and include explanatory captions.

LS Visual/Kinesthetic

Why It Matters

New Horizons for Pluto

SCIENCE & SOCIETY

The *New Horizons* spacecraft, on its way to Pluto and the nearby region of icy, rocky solar system bodies called the Kuiper Belt, is the fastest traveler in history. However, despite a speed of 75,000 km/h, the craft will take nine years to reach Pluto in 2015. According to Deputy Associate Administrator for NASA's Science Mission Directorate, Dr. Colleen Hartman, "What we know about Pluto could be written on the back of a postage stamp. After this mission, we'll be able to fill textbooks with new information."

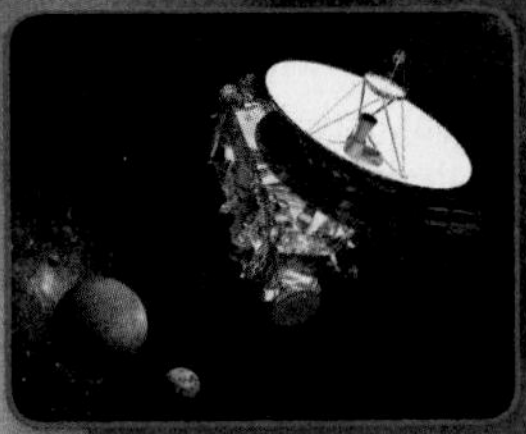

The *New Horizons* spacecraft

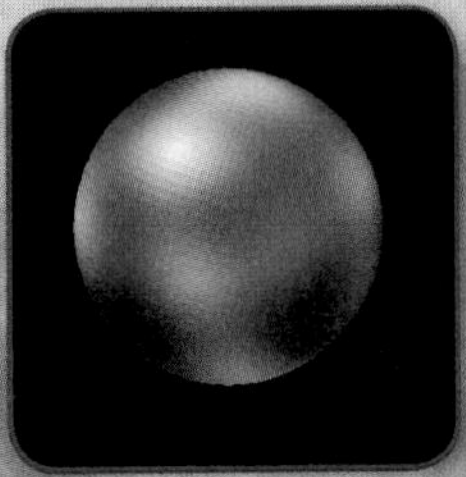

This photo, from 1994, was the first image of Pluto's surface. Taken by the Hubble telescope, it shows 12 distinct surface regions of light and darkness.

The piano-sized craft operates on less power than two 100-watt bulbs. In 2007, it used the gravity of Jupiter to help propel it toward Pluto.

During its Jupiter flyby, *New Horizons* photographed this eruption on Io, one of Jupiter's moons. The volcanic plume rises 320 km above the surface.

YOUR TURN

CRITICAL THINKING
New Horizons was launched when Pluto was still called a planet. Should the mission have been cancelled? Why or why not?

ONLINE RESEARCH
Find out where *New Horizons* is right now.

Why It Matters

New Horizons for Pluto

En route to Pluto, New Horizons had an up-close look at Jupiter and its moons. The speedy spacecraft reached Jupiter in approximately a year and has now long passed the gas giant. New Horizons is the first spacecraft since 1981 to pass Saturn's orbit.

The accuracy for a trip like this is important. The solar system is so large, and New Horizons must travel through a window 800 km across. This is similar to shooting a skeet from Washington and hitting a target in Baltimore.

The spacecraft carries 7 instruments for data collection: a visible and infrared spectrometer, a UV spectrometer, a tool to measure temperature and atmospheric composition, a camera, a solar wind and plasma spectrometer, an energetic particle spectrometer, and a tool to measure space dust. Data gathered is sent back to Earth via radio transmitter. The spacecraft itself will not return to Earth.

Answers to Your Turn

Critical Thinking Answers will vary. Students should include a reasonable explanation of why they think the mission should or should not have been cancelled.

Online Research Answers will vary. Students should use the Internet to locate New Horizons. A record of the spacecraft's travel can be found via www.nasa.gov/newhorizons.

Making Models Lab

Time Required

one 45-minute class period

Lab Ratings

EASY → HARD

Teacher Preparation (1 of 4)
Student Setup (2 of 4)
Concept Level (2 of 4)
Cleanup (3 of 4)

Skills Acquired

- Experimenting
- Collecting Data
- Interpreting Results

Scientific Methods

In this lab, students will
- Make Observations
- Analyze Results
- Communicate Results

Materials

The materials listed are enough for groups of 2 to 4 students. Have students spread newspapers over the work area for easier disposal after completing the lab. Direct students to wrap up the used plaster of Paris mixture in newspaper and toss it into the trash. Tell students not to dispose of plaster in sinks because plaster will clog drains and sinks if it hardens in plumbing fixtures.

Making Models Lab

45 min

Crater Analysis

What You'll Do

- **Create** a model that demonstrates the formation of impact craters.
- **Analyze** how an object's speed and projectile angle affect the impact crater that the object forms on planets and moons.

What You'll Need

marble, large (1)
marbles, small (5)
marker
meter stick
plaster of Paris
protractor
scissors
shoe box
tape, masking
toothpicks (6)
tweezers

Safety

All of the inner planets—Mercury, Venus, Earth, and Mars—have many features in common. They are all made of mostly solid rock and have metallic cores. They have no rings and have from zero to two moons each. And they have bowl-shaped depressions called *impact craters*. Impact craters are caused by collisions between the planets and rocky objects that travel through space. Most of these collisions took place during the formation of the solar system.

Mercury's entire surface is covered with these craters, while very few craters are still evident on the surface of Earth. Many of the moons of the inner and outer planets are also heavily cratered. In this lab, you will experiment with making craters to discover the effect of speed and projectile angle on the way craters form.

Procedure

1. Place the top of a toothpick in the center of a piece of masking tape that is 6 cm long. Fold the tape in half around the toothpick to form a "small flag" and "flagpole." On the flag, write the letter *A*. Repeat this step for the other toothpicks, and label them with the letters *B* through *F*.
2. Mix plaster of Paris with water, according to instructions for making plaster of Paris. Spread your mixture in the bottom of the shoe box. Make your plaster layer about 4 cm thick. The surface should be as smooth as possible.

Step 7

Tips and Tricks

Tell students that hyper-velocity impacts (those at or above 20 km/s) tend to form round craters, despite the projectile's angle when it approaches, as long as the angle is not much below 5°. That is why most craters on planets and moons appear round rather than elliptical.

The book *Craters* produced by the National Science Teachers Association contains a CD disk that has hundreds of images of craters on planets and moons.

The following list describes the craters and the surrounding areas produced in this lab.

Crater A large, deep crater that has very high walls; A great amount of material has splashed out around the crater and may be far from the center of the crater.

Crater B circular crater that has moderately high walls; Some material has splashed out.

Crater C shallow circular crater that has low walls; Little or no visible material was ejected.

Crater D deep, circular crater that has high walls; Much material has splashed out.

Crater E circular crater of moderate depth; One wall is slightly higher than the other. Material that has splashed out of the crater is located more to one side of the lower wall.

Crater F very similar to Crater E

3. Allow the plaster to dry until it is no longer soupy, but not yet rigid.
4. Drop a large marble onto the plaster from a height of 50 cm above the surface. Quickly remove the marble with tweezers, but do not damage the crater that formed. Place flag A next to the crater to label the crater.
5. Repeat step 4 by using a small marble dropped from a height of 50 cm and another small marble dropped from a height of 25 cm. Use the flags to label craters *B* (50 cm drop) and *C* (25 cm drop).
6. Repeat step 4 by using a small marble dropped from a height of 1 m. Label the crater *D*.

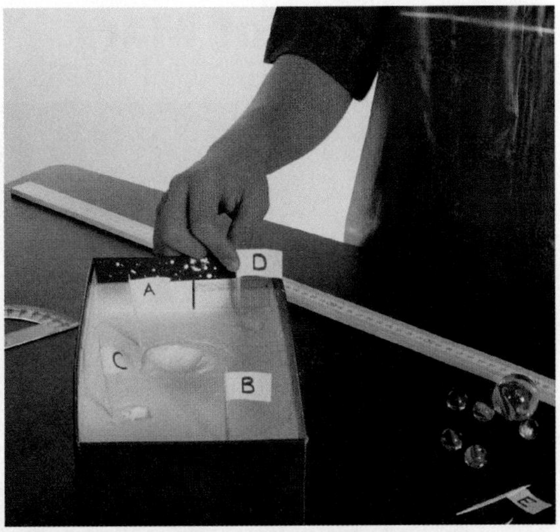

Step 6

7. Using a protractor as a guide, have your partner tilt the box at a 30° angle to the table. Be sure your partner holds the box steady. Then, drop a small marble vertically from a height of 50 cm. Label the crater *E*.
8. Repeat step 7 by using an angle of 45°. Label the crater *F*.
9. Allow the plaster of Paris to harden. Write a description of each crater and the surrounding area.

Analysis

1. **Examining Data** Which crater was formed by the marble that had the highest velocity? What is the effect of velocity on the characteristics of the crater formed?
2. **Explaining Events** Study the shapes of craters B, E, and F. How did the angle of the plaster of Paris affect the shape of the craters that formed?
3. **Making Comparisons** Compare craters A, B, and D. How do they differ from each other? What caused this difference? Is the difference in the masses of the objects a factor? Explain your answer.

Extension

Applying Conclusions Find a map of the surface craters on one of the terrestrial planets. Identify craters that were made by different angles of impact. Label the craters on the diagram, and present your findings to the class.

Answers to Analysis

1. Crater D; a higher velocity impact produces a larger crater that has more material ejected around the crater
2. All three craters are circular. However, the walls of craters E and F are higher on the side of the crater toward which the marble was traveling. No noticeable difference occurred between the craters formed by marbles dropped from different angles.
3. Craters A and D are deeper and have larger diameters. More material was ejected from craters A and D. Also, the material is ejected farther from the craters than the material ejected from crater B was; crater A was formed by a larger object. The difference in mass is a factor because the energy of two objects moving at the same velocity is greater for a more massive object; crater D formed a larger crater due to its greater speed.

Answer to Extension

Answers may vary depending on the maps and the terrestrial planet chosen to investigate. Some students may decide to investigate impacts on Earth. In general, the ejected materials would be thrown preferentially downrange of the impacting objects as was observed in the lab with craters E and F.

MOLA Map of Mars

Answers to Map Skills Activity

1. Elysium Mons is approximately 22° N latitude,140° E longitude.
2. Answers may vary but should include three of the following for below 0: Utopia Planitia, Hellas Planitia, Argyre Planitia, and Valles Marineris; and three of the following for above 0: Tharsis Monte, Olympus Mons, Alba Patera, and Elysium Mons.
3. the south pole
4. Agyre Planitia
5. Olympus Mons is more likely to be a volcano than Hellas Planitia because Olympus Mons is shaped like a mountain and Hellas Planitia is a crater.
6. The distance between Olympus Mons and Ellysium Mons is approximately 280° (or 80°) of longitude.
7. Answers may vary. Sample answers: *Mons* refers to a large isolated mountain, perhaps of volcanic origin; *planitia* is a plain located at a lower elevation than the surrounding terrain.

MAPS *in Action*

MOLA Map of Mars

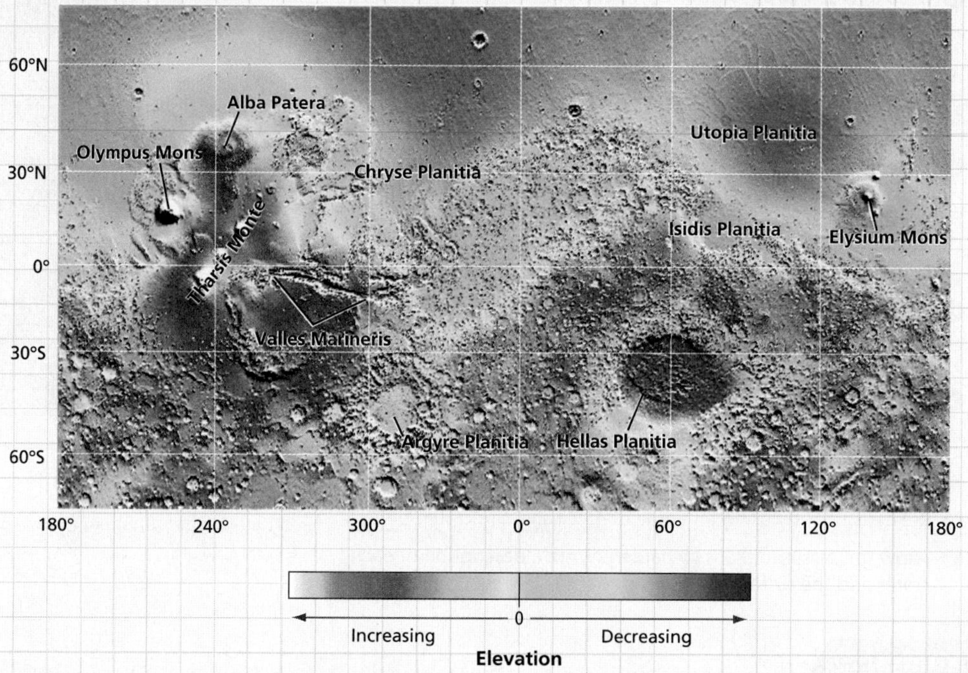

Map Skills Activity

The above map shows the relative elevation of surface features on Mars's surface. The number 0 on the elevation scale marks the average elevation at the equator. This map was created from data collected by the Mars Orbiter Laser Altimeter (MOLA) on the *NASA Mars Global Surveyor*. Use the map to answer the questions below.

1. **Analyzing Data** Estimate the longitude and latitude of Elysium Mons.
2. **Using a Key** Identify three features that have elevations below 0. Identify three features that have elevations above 0.
3. **Comparing Areas** In general, which pole on Mars, the north pole or south pole, has higher elevations?
4. **Using a Key** Which feature, Isidis Planitia or Argyre Planitia, has a higher elevation?
5. **Making Comparisons** Which feature, Hellas Planitia or Olympus Mons, would most likely be a volcano?
6. **Using a Key** Estimate the distance between Olympus Mons and Elysium Mons in degrees of longitude.
7. **Inferring Relationships** Based on what you have learned from the map, what type of features do you think the words *planitia* and *mons* refer to?

Key Resources

Technology

- Transparencies
  139 MOLA Map of Mars

Chapter 27

Summary

THINK central
SUPER SUMMARY
Keyword: HQXPSSS

Key Ideas | **Key Terms**

Section 1

Formation of the Solar System

- The solar system formed from a rotating and contracting region of gas and dust about 5 billion years ago.
- The planets formed from collisions of smaller bodies called *planetesimals*.
- Earth's land and atmosphere formed by differentiation. Oceans formed as water vapor in the atmosphere condensed and fell.

Key Terms:
solar system, p. 749
planet, p. 749
solar nebula, p. 749
planetesimal, p. 750

Section 2

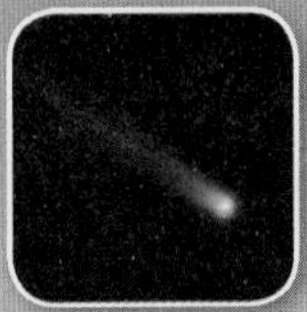

Models of the Solar System

- Ptolemy proposed an Earth-centered model of the universe. Copernicus proposed a sun-centered model.
- Kepler's first law states that orbits of planets are ellipses with the sun at one focus. The second law states that planets closer to the sun travel faster than those farther away. The third law relates a planet's average distance from the sun to the time it takes to make one orbit.
- Newton used the idea of inertia to explain Kepler's laws.

Key Terms:
eccentricity, p. 756
orbital period, p. 757
inertia, p. 758

Section 3

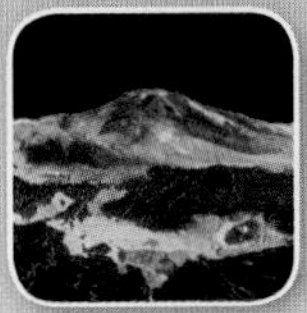

The Inner Planets

- The four inner (terrestrial) planets consist mainly of solid rock. Their surfaces show cratering, and they have metallic cores.
- The terrestrial planets are denser and smaller than the gas giants. Only Earth and Mars have moons. All but Mercury have notable atmospheres.
- Liquid water and an oxygen-enriched atmosphere enable Earth to sustain life.

Key Terms:
terrestrial planet, p. 759

Section 4

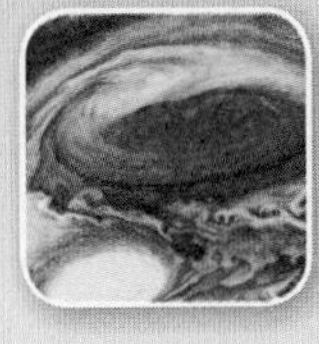

The Outer Planets

- The outer planets lack a solid surface and are much less dense and much larger than the terrestrial planets.
- The outer planets have rings and many moons, as well as atmospheres rich with hydrogen and helium. Unlike the other outer planets, Uranus's axis of rotation is almost parallel to the plane of its orbit.
- Pluto is considered a dwarf planet because astronomers have reclassified objects of the solar system, and Pluto now fits the definition of a dwarf planet.

Key Terms:
gas giant, p. 765
Kuiper Belt, p. 771

Chapter Summary

Using THINK central Resources

Super Summary

Have students connect the major concepts in this chapter through an interactive Super Summary. Visit www.thinkcentral.com and type in the keyword **HQXPSSS** to access the Super Summary for this chapter.

Why It Matters

What's in a Name? At age fifteen, the Danish astronomer Tyge Brahe adopted the Latinized version of his name—Tycho. As is the case with Galileo, Tycho is commonly referred to by his first name alone. Tycho reported his observations of a *supernova*, or explosion of a large star, in 1572. He also compiled the most precise planetary observations of his time by devising the best instruments available before the telescope. Kepler used Tycho's planetary data to develop his Laws of Orbital Motion.

Chapter Review

Assignment Guide	
Section	Question
1	6, 8, 17–20, 24–26, 29
2	2, 9–10, 15, 21–23, 28, 31, 32
3	3, 13, 33, 34
4	4, 11, 12, 14, 16, 27, 35–38
2 and 4	5
3 and 4	1, 7
1–4	30

Reading Toolbox

1. Answers may vary. Students should include in the chain-of-events chart the roles of gravity, solar radiation, and heat and pressure in the planets' interiors in the formation of the different characteristics of the inner and the outer planets.

Using Key Terms

2–8. Answers may vary but should show that students understand the definitions of and differences between the key terms.

Understanding Key Ideas

9. d 12. c 15. c 18. c
10. a 13. c 16. d 19. b
11. a 14. b 17. a

Short Answer

20. Earth's early atmosphere contained mainly water vapor, carbon dioxide, nitrogen, methane, sulfur dioxide, and ammonia from outgassing. Today, Earth's atmosphere contains mainly nitrogen, oxygen, and argon, with some water vapor and carbon dioxide.

Chapter 27 Review

1. **Chain-of-Events Chart** Make a chain-of-events chart to describe why the outer planets have very different characteristics from those of the inner planets. READING TOOLBOX

USING KEY TERMS

Use each of the following terms in a separate sentence.

2. *inertia*
3. *terrestrial planet*
4. *Kuiper Belt*

For each pair of terms, explain how the meanings of the terms differ.

5. *Kuiper belt* and *orbital period*
6. *planet* and *planetesimal*
7. *terrestrial planet* and *gas giant*
8. *solar nebula* and *solar system*

UNDERSTANDING KEY IDEAS

9. Copernicus's model of the solar system is
   a. geocentric. **c.** ethnocentric.
   b. lunocentric. **d.** heliocentric.
10. Kepler's first law states that each planet orbits the sun in a path called a(n)
   a. ellipse. **c.** epicycle.
   b. circle. **d.** period.
11. The most distinctive feature of Jupiter is its
   a. Great Red Spot.
   b. Great Dark Spot.
   c. ring.
   d. elongated orbit.
12. The planet that has an axis of rotation that is almost parallel to the plane of its orbit is
   a. Venus. **c.** Uranus.
   b. Jupiter. **d.** Neptune.
13. The tilt of the axis of Mars is nearly the same as that of
   a. Mercury. **c.** Earth.
   b. Venus. **d.** Jupiter.
14. The planet that rotates faster than any other planet in the solar system is
   a. Earth. **c.** Uranus.
   b. Jupiter. **d.** Venus.
15. Kepler's law that describes how fast planets travel at different points in their orbits is called the law of
   a. ellipses. **c.** equal areas.
   b. equal speeds. **d.** periods.
16. All the outer planets rotate with their axes perpendicular to their orbital planes *except*
   a. Saturn. **c.** Nepture.
   b. Jupiter. **d.** Uranus.
17. The first atmosphere of Earth contained a large amount of
   a. helium. **c.** carbon dioxide.
   b. oxygen. **d.** methane.
18. The hypothesis that states that the sun and the planets developed out of the same cloud of gas and dust is called the
   a. Copernicus hypothesis.
   b. solar hypothesis.
   c. nebular hypothesis.
   d. Galileo hypothesis.
19. In the process of photosynthesis, green plants give off
   a. hydrogen. **c.** carbon dioxide.
   b. oxygen. **d.** helium.

SHORT ANSWER

20. Explain how Earth's early atmosphere differed from Earth's atmosphere today.
21. What is the shape of the planets' orbits?
22. What is Kepler's first law?
23. How did Newton's ideas about the orbits of the planets differ from Kepler's ideas?
24. List three features of Earth that allow it to sustain life.
25. Describe how a planet might form.
26. How did differentiation help to form solid Earth?

21. elliptical
22. Kepler's first law states that planets orbit the sun in curved paths called ellipses, whose shape is determined by two points called foci, one of which is located within the sun.
23. Kepler described the elliptical shape of planetary orbits and the planets' speeds at different points along their orbits. Newton gave the causes of these same orbital motions: the curved elliptical orbital motion is the sum of the straight-line motion of a planet that results from inertia and the attractive force of gravity provided by the sun.
24. the presence of liquid water on the surface, a moderate surface temperature, and free oxygen in the atmosphere
25. Dust particles in a solar nebula stick together to form larger clumps of matter called *planetesimals.* Through collisions caused by motion of the particles and the gravity between them, the planetesimals form larger bodies called *protoplanets.* When protoplanets grow very large, they form bodies called *planets.*
26. When early Earth was molten, denser materials such as iron sank to the center of the planet, and less dense materials were forced to the outer layers through differentiation. This process gave the planet its layered structure of an iron and nickel core surrounded by a thick layer of iron and magnesium-rich rock called the *mantle*, and a less dense, silica-rich crust.

CRITICAL THINKING

27. **Applying Ideas** Suppose astronomers discover that exoplanets orbiting stars similar to Earth's sun have similar compositions to the planets in Earth's solar system. What can the astronomers hypothesize about the formation of those solar systems?
28. **Identifying Trends** If you know the distance from the sun to a planet, what other information can you determine about the orbit of the planet? Explain your answer.
29. **Making Inferences** How would the layers of Earth be different if the planet had never been hotter than it is today?

CONCEPT MAPPING

30. Use the following terms to create a concept map: *solar system, planet, protoplanet, planetesimal, differentiation, core, mantle, crust, geocentric, heliocentric, Aristotle, Ptolemy, Copernicus, ellipse, Earth, terrestrial planet, outer planet, Jupiter, Saturn, gas giant, Kuiper Belt, solar nebula,* and *inner planet.*

MATH SKILLS

Math Skills

31. **Making Calculations** Mercury has a period of rotation equal to 58.67 Earth days. Mercury's period of revolution is equal to 88 Earth days. How many times does Mercury rotate during one revolution around the sun?
32. **Applying Quantities** Uranus's orbital period is 84 years. What is its distance from the sun in astronomical units?
33. **Making Calculations** Venus's orbital period is 225 days. Calculate your age in Venus years.

WRITING SKILLS

34. **Creative Writing** Imagine that you are the first astronaut to land on Mars. In a short essay, describe what you hope and expect to find.
35. **Communicating Main Ideas** Create your own definition for *planet*. Then, write an explanation for why Pluto is or is not a planet.

INTERPRETING GRAPHICS

The graph below shows density in relation to mass for Earth, Uranus, and Neptune. Mass is given in Earth masses. The mass of Earth is equal to 1. Use the graph to answer the questions that follow.

Density Vs. Mass for Earth, Uranus, and Neptune

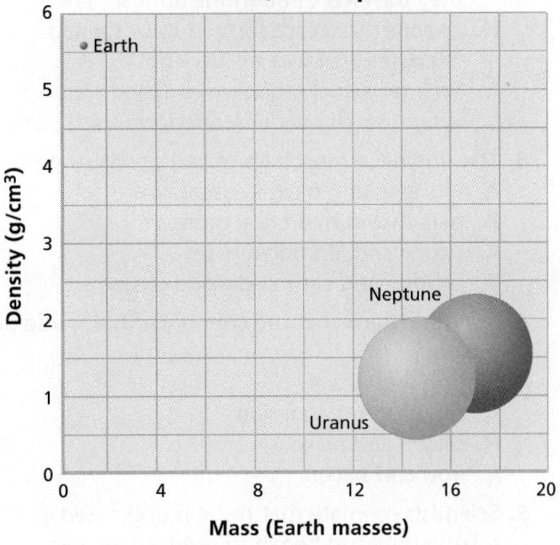

36. Which planet is denser, Uranus or Neptune? Explain your answer.
37. Which planet has the smallest mass?
38. How can Earth be the densest of the three planets even though Uranus and Neptune have so much more mass than Earth does?

Chapter Review

Critical Thinking

27. Answers may vary. Sample answer: Astronomers can hypothesize that the solar system formed in a similar way to how Earth's solar system formed.
28. Answers may vary. Sample answer: If you know the distance of a planet from the sun, you can determine the planet's orbital period. This is done by applying Kepler's law of periods. After converting the distance into astronomical units, cube that number (a^3), and then find the square root of a^3 to obtain the orbital period (p), because $a^3 = p^2$.
29. Answers may vary. Sample answer: If Earth had never been hotter than it is today, the process of differentiation would not have occurred. If Earth had not been in a molten state, substances of different densities would not have separated out into layers. Earth would be more uniform in composition.

Concept Mapping

30. Answers may vary but should include all of the terms listed. Sample answers appear at the end of this unit on p. 875B.

Math Skills

31. 88 days ÷ 58.67 days = 1.5 times
32. $p^2 = a^3$; $p^2 = 84 \times 84 = 7{,}056$; so $a^3 = 7{,}056$. The cube root of 7,056 = 19.18. The average distance of Uranus from the sun is 19 AU.
33. Answers may vary depending on the students' ages. Sample answer: I am exactly 15 years old, so 15 years × 365 days/year = 5475 days ÷ 225 days/Venusian year = 24.3 years. I am 24.3 years old in Venus years.

Writing Skills

34. Answers may vary. Accept all reasonable answers.
35. Answers may vary. Accept all reasonable answers.

Interpreting Graphics

36. Neptune: its density is 1.6 g/cm^3, while Uranus's density is 1.3 g/cm^3.
37. Earth, with a mass of 1
38. Density is mass per unit volume. Both Neptune and Uranus contain more matter than Earth does, so they have more total mass. However, that matter occupies a larger volume than the matter of Earth does, so Earth's density is higher.

Standardized Test Prep

Estimated Time

To give students practice under more realistic testing conditions, allow them 30 minutes to answer all of the questions in this practice test.

Test Doctor

Question 1 Answer C is correct. Protoplanets form before planets do, so answer A is incorrect. A solar nebula is the precursor to a star such as our sun, so answer B is incorrect. Gas giants are the outer planets of the solar system, so answer D is incorrect.

Question 10 Full-credit answers should include the following points:
- the ancient Greeks realized that the stars seem to move as a whole
- the Greeks observed that stars move slowly across the sky each night, and each year, in predictable and regular patterns
- the Greeks believed in a geocentric model of the solar system, in which the planets and sun were thought to revolve around Earth

Question 12 Full-credit answers should include the following points:
- the graphs show that Earth's atmosphere consists of approximately 21% oxygen, whereas Mars has no oxygen in its atmosphere
- Earth obtained oxygen from organisms that used liquid water and carbon dioxide in photosynthesis and released oxygen in the process
- without liquid water, it is unlikely that Mars could currently support photosynthetic organisms
- without photosynthetic organisms, no oxygen could be released into Mars's atmosphere
- some students may mention that it is possible that Mars may have had such organisms in the past

Question 14 The correct answer is 1.5 rotations. Neptune completes its rotation in 16 hours. One day on Earth is 24 hours. Students should determine how many times 16 goes into 24 by dividing 24 by 16. A common mistake that some students may make is to divide 16 by 24 and reach an answer of 2/3 rotations.

Chapter 27 Standardized Test Prep

Understanding Concepts

Directions (1–5): For each question, write on a separate sheet of paper the letter of the correct answer.

1. Small bodies that join to form protoplanets in the early stages of the development of the solar system are
   A. planets.
   B. solar nebulas.
   C. plantesimals.
   D. gas giants.
2. Scientists hypothesize that Earth's first oceans were made of fresh water. How did oceans obtain fresh water?
   F. Water vapor in the early atmosphere cooled and fell to Earth as rain.
   G. Frozen comets that fell to Earth melted as they traveled through the atmosphere.
   H. As soon as icecaps formed, they melted because Earth was still very hot.
   I. Early terrestrial organisms exhaled water vapor, which condensed to form fresh water.
3. The original atmosphere of Earth consisted of
   A. nitrogen and oxygen gases.
   B. helium and hydrogen gases.
   C. ozone and ammonia gases.
   D. oxygen and carbon dioxide gases.
4. Scientists think that the core of Earth is made of molten
   F. iron and nickel.
   G. nickel and magnesium.
   H. silicon and nickel.
   I. iron and silicon.
5. Scientists estimate that the sun originated as a solar nebula and began to produce its own energy through nuclear fusion approximately how many years ago?
   A. 50 million years
   B. 500 million years
   C. 1 billion years
   D. 5 billion years

Directions (6–7): For each question, write a short response.

6. What four planets make up the group known as the inner planets?
7. The Great Red Spot is found on what planet?

Reading Skills

Directions (8–10): Read the passage below. Then, answer the questions.

Movement of the Planets

Imagine that it is the year 200 BCE and that you are an apprentice to a famous Greek astronomer. After many years of observing the sky, the astronomer knows all of the constellations as well as he knows the back of his hand. He shows you how all the stars move together—how the whole sky spins slowly as the night goes on. He also shows you that among the thousands of stars in the sky, some of the brighter ones slowly change their position in relation to the other stars. The astronomer names these stars *planetai,* the Greek word that means "wanderers."

Building on the observations of the ancient Greeks, we now know that the planetai are actually planets, not wandering stars. Because of their proximity to Earth and their orbits around the sun, the planets appear to move relative to the stars.

8. According to the passage, which of the following statements is not true?
   F. It is possible to determine planets in the night sky by the way they move relative to the other stars.
   G. The word *planetai* means "wanderers" in the Greek language.
   H. Some of the earliest astronomers to detect the presence of planets were Roman.
   I. Ancient Greeks were studying astronomy more than 2,200 years ago.
9. What can you infer from the passage about the ancient Greek astronomers?
   A. They were patient and observant.
   B. They knew much more about astronomy than we do today.
   C. They spent all their time counting the number of stars in the sky.
   D. They invented astronomy and were the first people to observe the skies.
10. What did the Greek astronomers note about the movement of stars and constellations?

Interpreting Graphics

Directions (11–14): For each question below, record the correct answer on a separate sheet of paper.

The pie graphs below show the percentages of different gases in the atmospheres of three planets. Use these graphs to answer questions 11 and 12.

Atmospheres of Venus, Earth, and Mars

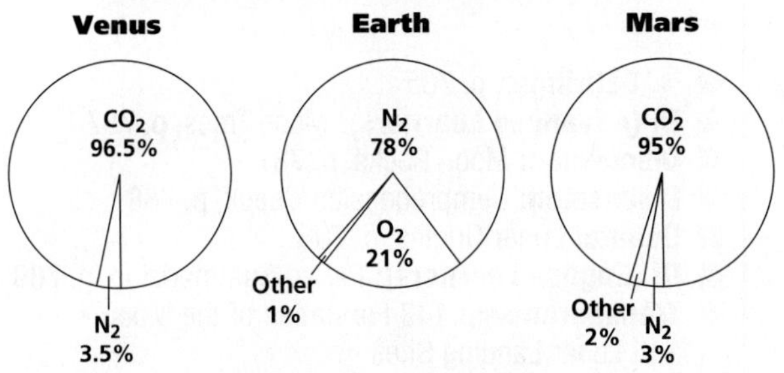

11. What is the percentage of carbon dioxide in the atmosphere of Venus?
F. 3.5%
G. 21%
H. 95%
I. 96.5%

12. Today, Earth's atmosphere includes a large amount of oxygen. Describe how the oxygen in Earth's atmosphere formed, and, using this information, predict the likelihood that Mars will someday have oxygen in its atmosphere.

The table below shows the orbital and rotational periods of the planets in the solar system. Use this table to answer questions 13 and 14.

Planets of the Solar System

Planet	Orbital period	Rotational period
Mercury	88 days	59 days
Venus	225 days	243 days
Earth	365.25 days	23 hours 56 minutes
Mars	687 days	24 hours 37 minutes
Jupiter	12 years	9 hours 50 minutes
Saturn	29.5 years	10 hours 30 minutes
Uranus	84 years	17 hours
Neptune	164 years	16 hours

13. Which planet's day length is nearly the same as Earth's?
A. Mercury
B. Mars
C. Saturn
D. Neptune

14. How many rotations does Neptune complete in one Earth day?

Test Tip

Even if you are sure of the answer to a test question, read all of the answer choices before selecting your response.

Standardized Test Prep

Using THINK central Resources

State Resources

- For specific resources for your state, visit www.thinkcentral.com and type in the keyword **HSHSTR.**

Answers

Understanding Concepts

1. C
2. F
3. B
4. F
5. D
6. Mercury, Venus, Earth, and Mars
7. Jupiter

Reading Skills

8. H
9. A
10. Answers may vary. See Test Doctor for a detailed scoring rubric.

Interpreting Graphics

11. I
12. Answers may vary. See Test Doctor for a detailed scoring rubric.
13. B
14. 1.5 rotations

Chapter Planner 28 Minor Bodies of the Solar System

	Time	Standards	Teach Key Ideas
Chapter Opener, pp. 782–783	45 min.	National Science Education Standards	
Section 1 Earth's Moon, pp. 785–790 › Exploring the Moon › The Lunar Surface › The Interior of the Moon › The Formation of the Moon	45 min.	SAI 2c, SAI 2d, SAI 2f, PS 4b, ES 3a, ST 2c, HNS 2c, HNS 3c, UCP 1, UCP 3	■ ◆ **Bellringer,** p. 785 ■ **DI (Advanced Learners):** Moon Trees, p. 787 ■ **Discussion:** Moon Rocks, p. 787 ■ **Discussion:** Comprehension Check, p. 788 ■ **Debate:** Lunar Origins, p. 788 ■ **DI (English Learners):** Paired Summarizing, p. 789 ◆ **Transparencies:** 140 Formation of the Moon • 145 Lunar Landing Sites ▲ **Visual Concepts:** Satellites • Moon Formation
Section 2 Movements of the Moon, pp. 791–798 › The Earth-Moon System › Eclipses › Phases of the Moon › Tides on Earth	90 min.	SAI 2c, SAI 2d, SAI 2f, PS 4b, ST 2c, HNS 2c, HNS 3c, UCP 1, UCP 3	■ ◆ **Bellringer,** p. 791 ■ **Demonstration:** Synchronous Rotation, p. 792 ■ **DI (Special Education Students):** Orbits, p. 792 ■ **DI (English Learners):** Writing, p. 794 ◆ **Transparencies:** 141 The Earth-Moon System • 142 Solar and Lunar Eclipses • 143 Phases of the Moon • 144 Causes of Tides ▲ **Visual Concepts:** Solar and Lunar Eclipses • Lunar Phases • Tides and Tidal Range
Section 3 Satellites of Other Planets, pp. 799–804 › Moons of Mars › Moons of Jupiter › Moons of Saturn › Moons of Uranus and Neptune › Pluto's Moons › Rings of the Gas Giants	90 min.	SAI 2c, SAI 2d, SAI 2f, PS 4b, ST 2c, HNS 2c, HNS 3c, UCP 1, UCP 3	■ ◆ **Bellringer,** p. 799 ■ **Discussion:** Mythology Connection, p. 799 ■ **DI (Special Education Students):** Mnemonics, p. 801 ■ **Demonstration:** Shepherd Moons, p. 802 ▲ **Visual Concepts:** Moons of Earth and Other Planets
Section 4 Asteroids, Comets, and Meteoroids, pp. 805–810 › Asteroids › Comets › Meteoroids	45 min.	SAI 2c, SAI 2d, SAI 2f, PS 4b, ST 2c, HNS 2c, HNS 3c, UCP 1, UCP 3	■ ◆ **Bellringer,** p. 805 ■ **Discussion:** Asteroid Motions, p. 805 ■ **DI (Advanced Learners):** Comets, p. 807 ▲ **Visual Concepts:** Asteroid Belt • Comets
Chapter Wrap-Up, pp. 815–819	90 min.		**Chapter Summary,** p. 815

CHAPTER Fast Track *To shorten instruction because of time limitations, omit Sections 2 and 3.*

See also PowerNotes® Presentations

Key

Teacher's Edition ■ Teaching Transparencies ◆
Chapter Resource File ● Online Edition ▲

All resources listed below are also available on the **Teacher One Stop™.**

Why It Matters	Hands-On	Skills Development	Assessment
■ **Chapter Overview** p. 782 ■ **Using the Figure:** Asteroids, p. 782	**Inquiry Lab:** Suit Up!, p. 783	**Reading Toolbox,** p. 784	
■ **Section Overview,** p. 785 ■ **Using the Figure:** Research, p. 786 ■ **Using the Figure:** Footprints on the Moon, p. 787	■ **Group Activity:** Moon Rescue, p. 785 **Quick Lab:** Liquid and Solid Cores, p. 788 ● **Making Models Lab:** Crater Eraser	■ **Skill Builder:** Math, p. 786 **Reading Toolbox:** Describing Space, p. 786 **Maps in Action:** Lunar Landing Sites, p. 814 ■ ● **Internet Activity:** Lunar Timeline, p. 814	**Reading Check,** p. 786 **Reading Check,** p. 788 **Section Review,** p. 790 ■ **Reteaching,** p. 789 ■ **Quiz,** p. 789 ■ **DI (Alternative Assessment):** Lunar Picture Book, p. 790 ● **Section Quiz**
■ **Section Overview,** p. 791 ■ **Using the Figure:** Solar Eclipse, p. 793 ■ **Size Is Relative,** p. 793 ■ **Life Science Connection:** Biological Rhythms, p. 795 ■ **Lunar Calendar,** p. 796	■ **Group Activity:** Barycenter, p. 791 ■ **Activity:** Eclipsed, p. 793 **Quick Lab:** Eclipses, p. 794 ■ **Group Activity:** Many Moons, p. 796 ● **Inquiry Lab:** Inconstant Moon	**Reading Toolbox:** Two-Column Notes, p. 792 ■ **Skill Builder:** Vocabulary, p. 797	**Reading Check,** p. 792 **Reading Check,** p. 794 **Reading Check,** p. 797 **Section Review,** p. 798 ■ **Reteaching,** p. 797 ■ **Quiz,** p. 797 ■ **DI (Alternative Assessment):** System Models, p. 798 ● **Section Quiz**
■ **Section Overview,** p. 799 **Early Telescope Images,** p. 800 ■ **Using the Figure:** Geologic Pasts, p. 801 ■ **Environmental Connection:** Hidden Ocean, Hidden Life?, p. 801 ■ **Meteorology Connection:** Titan's Atmosphere, p. 802 ■ **Using the Figure:** Ringmaster, p. 802	■ **Activity:** Planetary Rings, p. 803 **Skills Practice Lab:** Galilean Moons of Jupiter, pp. 812–813	■ ● **Internet Activity:** Martian Moons, p. 800 **Reading Toolbox:** Two-Column Notes, p. 802	**Reading Check,** p. 801 **Reading Check,** p. 803 **Section Review,** p. 804 ■ **Reteaching,** p. 803 ■ **Quiz,** p. 803 ■ **DI (Alternative Assessment):** Satellite Bingo, p. 804 ● **Section Quiz**
■ **Section Overview,** p. 805 ■ **Using the Figure:** Comparing Craters, p. 806 ■ **Environmental Connection:** Target Earth, p. 806 ■ **Using the Figure:** Discussion, p. 807 ■ **Using the Figure:** Oort Cloud Distances, p. 808 ■ **Comet Decay,** p. 808 ■ **Using the Figure:** Leonid Meteor Shower, p. 809		**Reading Toolbox:** Word Origins, p. 806 ■ ● **Internet Activity:** Kuiper Belt Objects, p. 808 **Math Skills:** Matter From Space, p. 809	**Reading Check,** p. 806 **Reading Check,** p. 809 **Section Review,** p. 810 ■ **Reteaching,** p. 809 ■ **Quiz,** p. 809 ■ **DI (Alternative Assessment):** Science Nonfiction, p. 810 ● **Section Quiz**
Dodging Space Debris, p. 811		▲ **Super Summary** **Standardized Test Prep,** pp. 818–819	**Chapter Review,** pp. 816–817 ■ **DI (Alternative Assessment):** Poster Project, p. 815 ● **Chapter Tests**

See also Lab Generator

See also Holt Online Assessment Resources

Chapter Overview

This chapter describes the structure, composition, and movements of Earth's moon. It explains how the moon's orbital motions affect eclipses and tides. The chapter also describes other natural satellites and small bodies in the solar system.

Using the Figure — GENERAL

Asteroids Explain that the majority of asteroids orbit in a belt of debris between the orbits of Mars and Jupiter. Ask students where they think these bodies came from and what clues they might offer about the early solar system. (Sample answer: Asteroids may be the remains of planetesimals that were unable to form a planet due to the effects of Jupiter's gravity. Their composition may be similar to the materials from which the inner planets and many moons formed.) **LS Visual**

Why It Matters

This image is one idea of how an asteroid might look as it moves toward Earth. The largest asteroid on record to pass near Earth is Toutatis. On September 29, 2004, it made its closest pass—just over 1.5 million km away.

Chapter 28 Minor Bodies of the Solar System

Chapter Outline

1 Earth's Moon
- Exploring the Moon
- The Lunar Surface
- The Interior of the Moon
- The Formation of the Moon

2 Movements of the Moon
- The Earth-Moon System
- Eclipses
- Phases of the Moon
- Tides on Earth

3 Satellites of Other Planets
- Moons of Mars
- Moons of Jupiter
- Moons of Saturn
- Moons of Uranus and Neptune
- Pluto's Moons
- Rings of the Gas Giants

4 Asteroids, Comets, and Meteoroids
- Asteroids
- Comets
- Meteoroids

Virginia Standards of Learning
ES.1.b
ES.1.c
ES.3.b
ES.3.c

Why It Matters

Fragments from the formation of the solar system still exist as asteroids, comets, and meteoroids. These objects could demand more than study if they came too close to Earth.

Chapter Correlations — *Virginia Standards of Learning*

ES.1.b technologies, including computers, probeware, and geospatial technologies, are used to collect, analyze, and report data and to demonstrate concepts and simulate experimental conditions.
ES.1.c scales, diagrams, charts, graphs, tables, imagery, models, and profiles are constructed and interpreted.
ES.3.b sun-Earth-moon relationships (seasons, tides, and eclipses)
ES.3.c characteristics of the sun, planets and their moons, comets, meteors, and asteroids

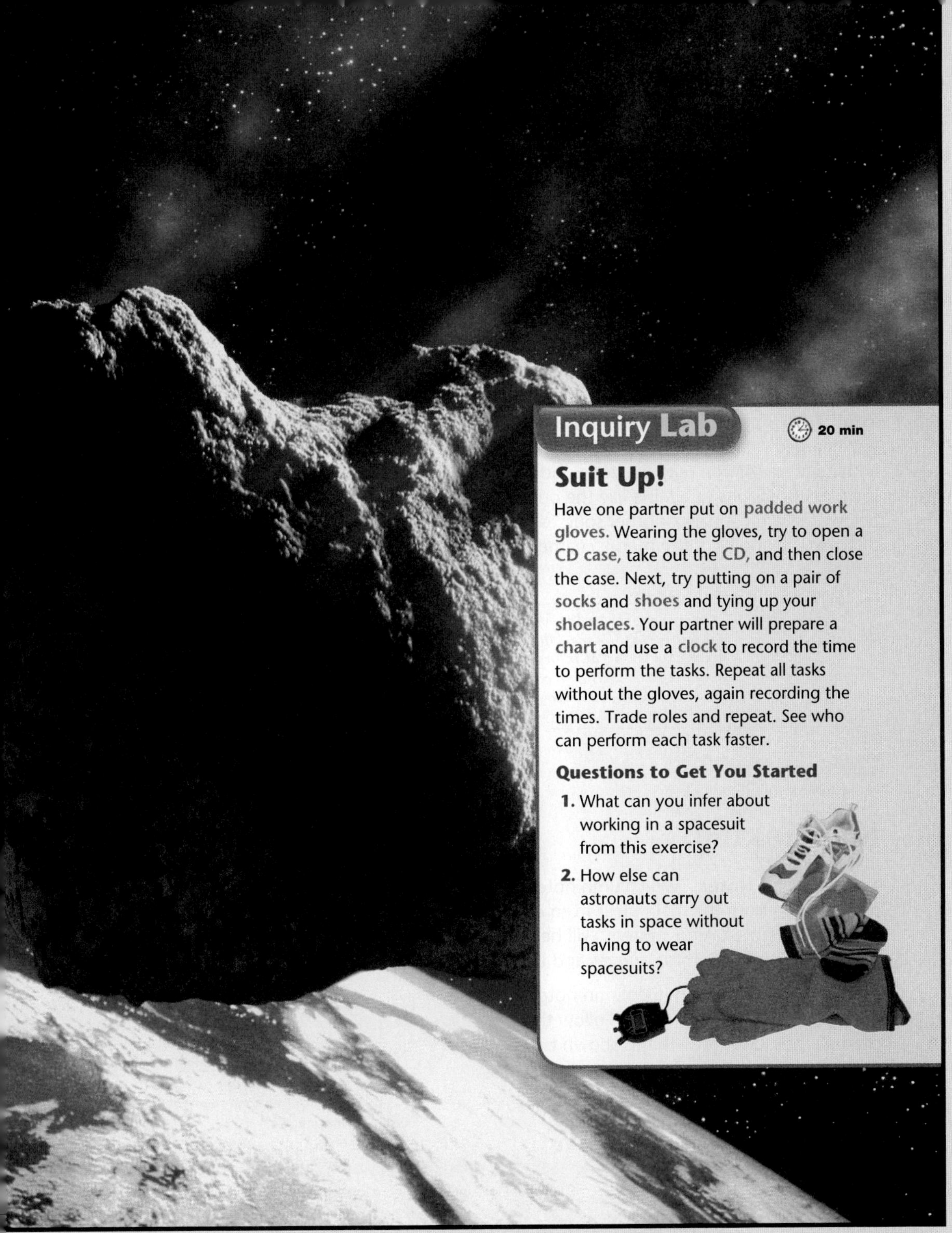

Inquiry Lab

20 min

Suit Up!

Have one partner put on **padded work gloves.** Wearing the gloves, try to open a **CD case,** take out the **CD,** and then close the case. Next, try putting on a pair of **socks** and **shoes** and tying up your **shoelaces.** Your partner will prepare a **chart** and use a **clock** to record the time to perform the tasks. Repeat all tasks without the gloves, again recording the times. Trade roles and repeat. See who can perform each task faster.

Questions to Get You Started

1. What can you infer about working in a spacesuit from this exercise?
2. How else can astronauts carry out tasks in space without having to wear spacesuits?

Inquiry Lab

Central Concept: By trying to conduct familiar activities with gloved hands, students may begin to appreciate the challenges of maneuvering in a spacesuit.

Teacher's Notes: You may wish to ask students to conduct additional tasks, such as assembling or disassembling a simple object.

Materials (per group)
- Padded work gloves
- CD case with CD
- Socks
- Shoes with shoelaces
- Clock

Skills Acquired
- Observing
- Interpreting Models

Answers to Getting Started

1. Answers will vary. Students should note the challenges of working with limited use of their hands.
2. Answers will vary. For example, students may suggest that astronauts could use robotic equipment or other tools.

Using THINK central Resources

An online version of this chapter, as well as all the print and multimedia resources that accompany the program are available to registered teachers and their students. Log onto www.thinkcentral.com to access these materials and tools to organize your preparation and student learning.

READING TOOLBOX

Word Origins

A chart with information on the origins of the largest of each planet's moons (other than Earth's) can be found on page 875A. Students should expand the chart to include all of the moons mentioned in the chapter. Other named moons may be added as well.

Describing Space

Examples from Section 2:

Objects	Words Describing Motion	Meaning of Motion Words
moon	rotate	spin around a central point (an axis)
moon	revolving	travels in a circle around a point
system	orbits	travels in a circle around a point
celestial body	passes through	moves through
moon	comes directly between	moves between
moon	crosses	goes from one side to the other
moon	moves	changes position
moon	go	move

READING TOOLBOX

These reading tools will help you learn the material in this chapter.

Word Origins

Names of Jupiter's Moons The planet Jupiter was named for the king of the gods in Roman mythology. Jupiter's four largest moons are named after characters associated with Jupiter or Zeus (Jupiter's counterpart in Greek mythology): Io, Europa, Ganymede, and Callisto.

Your Turn The moons of many planets were named for characters in mythology and literature. As you read Section 3, add the planets' moons to a table like the one below. Use a dictionary or other sources to discover the origins of the moons' names.

Planet	Moon	Origin of name
Saturn	Titan	In Roman mythology, the sisters and brothers of Chronos (the Greek counterpart of Saturn) were the Titans. (Other moons of Saturn are named after specific Titans.)

Describing Space

Words and Phrases When you describe the motion of objects through space, you use verbs and phrases that modify the verbs. Paying attention to language that describes motion can help you recognize what kind of motion is described.

Your Turn As you read Section 2, make a three-column table like the one below. Add words or phrases that describe the motion of specific objects.

Objects	Words Describing Motion	Meaning of Motion Words
moon	rotate	spin around a central point (an axis)

Note Taking

Two-Column Notes Two-column notes can help you learn the main ideas from each section. This note-taking strategy will help you review information for quizzes and tests.

Your Turn Complete two-column notes for main ideas in Sections 1 and 4. Follow the example from Section 1 that is shown below.

1. Write one main idea in each row in the left column.
2. As you read Sections 1 and 4, add detailed notes and examples in the right column. Be sure to put these details and examples in your own words.

Main Idea	Detail Notes
The lunar surface	• several types of surface features -craters (impact depressions) - rilles (long, deep channels) -ridges (long, narrow rock elevations) -regolith (dust and small rocky fragments) -rocks

For more information on how to use these and other tools, see **Appendix A.**

Note Taking

Answers will vary. Students' two-column notes should include all the key ideas listed on the section opener pages of Sections 1 and 4.

SECTION 1

Earth's Moon

Key Ideas	Key Terms	Why It Matters
❯ List four kinds of lunar surface features. ❯ Describe the three layers of the moon. ❯ Summarize the three stages by which the moon formed.	satellite moon mare crater	The moon is the only body in the solar system besides Earth that humans have visited in person.

A body that orbits a larger body is called a **satellite.** Six of the planets in our solar system have smaller bodies that orbit around them. These natural satellites are also called **moons.** Our moon is Earth's natural satellite.

In 1957, the Soviet Union launched *Sputnik*, which was the first *artificial satellite* launched into space. In 1958, the United States launched its first artificial satellite, which was named *Explorer 1*. Thousands of artificial satellites are now in orbit around Earth, including weather satellites and space telescopes, such as the *Hubble Space Telescope*.

Exploring the Moon

Between 1969 and 1972, the United States sent six spacecraft to the moon as part of the Apollo space program. Apollo astronauts found that the moon's weak gravity affected the way they moved. They discovered that bouncing was more efficient than walking. Apollo astronauts also explored the moon's surface in a variety of specially-designed vehicles, such as the one shown in **Figure 1.**

The moon has much less mass than Earth does, so the gravity on the moon's surface is about one-sixth of the gravity on Earth. As a result, someone who weighs 690 N (newtons) on Earth would weigh about 115 N on the moon. (The person's mass would remain the same.) The gravity at the moon's surface is not strong enough to hold gases, so the moon has no significant atmosphere. Because it has no atmosphere to absorb and transport thermal energy, the moon's surface temperature varies from 134 °C during the day to −170 °C at night.

satellite a natural or artificial body that revolves around a celestial body that is greater in mass

moon a celestial body that revolves around a body that is greater in mass; a natural satellite

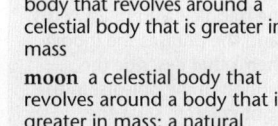

Figure 1 *Apollo 17* astronaut Eugene Cernan explores the lunar surface in a Lunar Roving Vehicle.

Section 1

Focus

Overview

This section describes the moon's surface features and its layers. It also explains the giant impact hypothesis and summarizes how the moon formed.

Bellringer

Ask students to write a paragraph that describes what they know about the moon. (Answers may vary.) LS **Verbal**

Motivate

Group Activity — GENERAL

Moon Rescue Have small groups of students imagine that they are setting up a moon base. Ask groups to make a list of the supplies and materials they would need to build a base for 100 people. Students may wish to organize their group in a way to allow one person to be in charge of identifying resources needed to supply each major need. (Answers may vary but students should provide for the need for temperature control, oxygen, food, water, electricity, exercise, and living quarters.) LS **Logical/Interpersonal**
Co-op Learning

Key Resources

Chapter Resource File

- Directed Reading BASIC
- Making Models Lab: Crater Eraser GENERAL

Technology

- Transparencies
  Bellringer

Teach

Skill Builder GENERAL

Math Use this exercise to help students gain perspective on the enormous distances involved as you teach about the Earth-moon system. Construct a paper model of the Earth-moon system. Write these measurements on the board: Earth's diameter = 12,800 km; Moon's diameter = 3,500 km; Mean distance from Earth to moon = 384,000 km. Select a scale to use. For example, with a 10 cm diameter circle representing Earth, how large must the moon be? (Calculate the conversion factor for the diameters of the two bodies: 12,800 km (Earth) ÷ 3,500 km (moon) = 3.7; rounding up, for any scale model, Earth's diameter must be approximately 4 times larger than the moon's. Divide the size of the Earth model by the scale factor: 10 cm ÷ 4 = 2.5 cm.) Use construction paper to make two paper circles to represent Earth (10 cm) and the moon (2.5 cm). Next, ask how far apart the models must be placed. (If 10 cm = 12,800 km, then 1 cm = 1,280 km; 384,000 km ÷ 1,280 km/cm = 300 cm) Measure out a string 300 cm long to represent this distance. Tape the two circles on a wall with the string between the models. The system model is now to scale for both size and distance. **LS Logical**

Answer to Reading Check

Answers should include two of the following features: maria, highlands, craters, ridges, and rilles.

mare a large, dark area of basalt on the moon (plural, *maria*)

crater a bowl-shaped depression that forms on the surface of an object when a falling body strikes the object's surface or when an explosion occurs

The Lunar Surface

Because *luna* is the Latin word for "moon," any feature of the moon is referred to as *lunar*. Light and dark patches on the moon can be seen with the unaided eye. The lighter areas are rough highlands that are composed of rocks called *anorthosites*. The darker areas are smooth, reflect less light, and are called *maria* (MAHR ee uh). Each dark area is a **mare** (MAHR AY). *Mare* is Latin for "sea." Galileo named these dark areas *maria* because he thought that they looked like Earth's seas. Today, astronomers know that maria are plains of dark, solidified, basaltic lava. These lava plains formed more than 3 billion years ago when lava slowly filled basins that were created by impacts of massive asteroids.

Academic Vocabulary

depression (dee PRESH uhn) an area lower than the surrounding surface

Craters, Rilles, and Ridges

The surface of the moon, shown in **Figure 2,** is covered with numerous bowl-shaped depressions, called **craters.** Most of the moon's craters formed when debris left over from the formation of the solar system struck the moon about 4 billion years ago. Younger craters are characterized by bright streaks, called *rays*, that extend outward from the impact site. Even these younger craters, however, are almost all billions of years old.

Long, deep channels called *rilles* run through the maria in some places. The moon's rilles are thought to be leftover lava channels from the formation of the maria. Some rilles are as long as 240 km. Another surface feature of the moon is ridges. Ridges are long, narrow elevations of rock that rise out of the surface and criss-cross the maria.

READING TOOLBOX

Describing Space
As you read Section 1, make a table like the one described at the beginning of the chapter to describe motion words. In the left column, list objects. In the middle column, list verbs (and the phrases the modify them) that describe the motion of the objects. In the right column, state the meaning of the motion words.

Reading Check **Name two features of the moon.** (See Appendix G for answers to Reading Checks.)

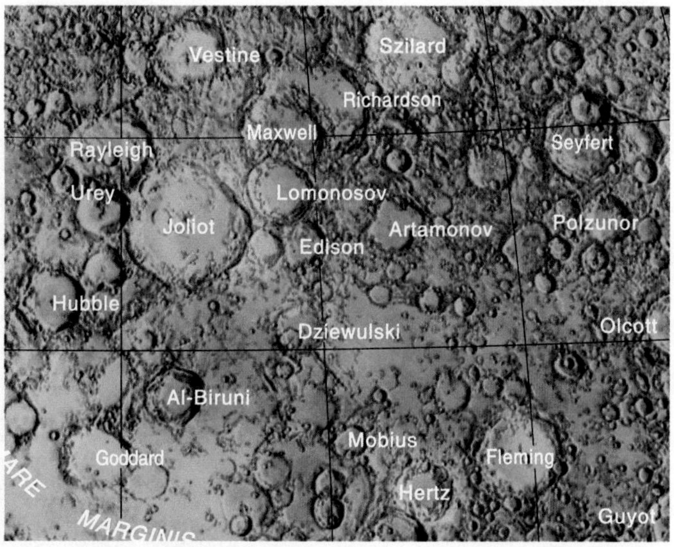

Figure 2 More than 1,500 craters on the moon are named for scientists, scholars, and other noteworthy individuals. The lunar surface also has millions of small, overlapping craters. ***How does the size of a crater relate to the importance of the individual for which it was named?***

Using the Figure GENERAL

Research Invite interested students to learn about the contributions of the scientists and other famous people whose names are used to identify lunar features. For example, the crater Al-Biruni was named for Abū ar-Rayhān Muhammad ibn Ahmad al-Bīrūnī, a Persian astronomer, mathematician, and geographer. The USGS Gazetteer of Planetary Nomenclature on the Internet lists the origin of many other lunar names. Answer to caption question: There is no relationship between crater size and the importance of the individual for which it was named. **LS Logical**

READING TOOLBOX

Describing Space
Students may include over 20 motion words from Section 1 in their charts. Three examples are shown below.

Objects	Words Describing Motion	Meaning of Motion Words
debris	struck	hit with force
laser beams	bounced	hit a surface and sprung back
large object	collided	ran into with force

Figure 3 This footprint from an Apollo astronaut is one of the first marks left on the moon by humans. The footprint is visible because of the fine layer of rock and dust, called *regolith*, that covers the moon's surface.

SciLinks. www.scilinks.org Topic: Earth's Moon Code: HQX0449

Regolith

More meteorites have reached the surface of the moon than have reached Earth's surface because the moon has no atmosphere for protection. Over billions of years, these meteorites crushed much of the rock on the lunar surface into dust and small fragments. Today, almost all of the lunar surface is covered by a layer of dust and rock, called *regolith*. Regolith is shown in **Figure 3.** The depth of the regolith layer varies from 1 m to 6 m.

Lunar Rocks

Many lunar rocks are very similar to rocks on Earth. Lunar rocks, including the one shown in **Figure 4,** contain many of the same elements as Earth's rocks do, but lunar rocks contain different proportions of those elements. Lunar rocks are igneous, and most rocks near the surface are composed mainly of oxygen and silicon. These surface rocks are similar to the rocks in Earth's crust. Rocks from the lunar highlands are light-colored, coarse-grained anorthosites. Highland rocks are rich in calcium and aluminum. Rocks from the maria are fine-grained basalts and contain large amounts of titanium, magnesium, and iron.

Nevertheless, lunar surface rocks have only small amounts of some elements that are common on Earth. Many of these elements have low melting points and may have boiled off early in the moon's history when the moon was still molten. Also, the minerals in lunar rocks do not contain water.

One type of rock that occurs in both maria and the highlands is *breccia*. Lunar breccia contains fragments of other rocks that have been fused together. These breccias formed when meteorites struck the moon. The force of these impacts broke up rocks, and the heat from the impacts partially melted the fragments.

Figure 4 This rock is 4.3 billion to 4.5 billion years old; it is the oldest rock discovered on the moon. The rock's texture indicates that the rock has a complicated history.

Discussion — GENERAL

Moon Rocks Ask students to compare the lunar rocks with rocks found on Earth. For example, are the same kinds of rocks found on both bodies? (Answers may vary. Sample answer: Lunar rocks are almost all igneous, while Earth has sedimentary and metamorphic rocks as well.) How are the composition and structure of moon rocks similar or different from those of Earth's rocks? (Sample answers: Moon rocks are made of the same elements but in different proportions. The lunar samples do not have water in their crystal structure.) **LS Verbal**

Using the Figure — BASIC

Footprints on the Moon Ask students to identify the feature of the lunar environment in which Neil Armstrong's footprints were preserved when he walked on the moon. (the regolith) Have them explain why those first marks left by humans visiting the moon will remain visible for an extremely long time. (The moon lacks water and an atmosphere, which would cause erosion. It also lacks tectonic processes, which also would erase traces of human activity.) **LS Logical**

Differentiated Instruction

Advanced Learners

Moon Trees When *Apollo 14* was launched in January 1971, hundreds of tree seeds orbited in the personal kit of Air Force Colonel Stuart Roosa. The seeds were part of a biological experiment to see whether the trip to the moon would affect the ability of seeds to germinate. Upon their return to Earth, the seeds were planted by the Forest Service throughout the United States as part of the country's bicentennial celebration. Despite the fact that they were exposed to vacuum conditions during decontamination, nearly all of the seeds germinated. The "Moon Trees" remain a living legacy of the space program. No systematic records were kept of all of the plantings, so the Forest Service and NASA are trying to track them down. Have students use the Internet to research Moon Trees and find out if there are any known Moon Trees in your state. Ask students to summarize what they learn in the form of a newspaper article. **LS Verbal**

Teach, *continued*

Quick Lab

Skills Acquired
- Experimenting
- Observing
- Analyzing

Materials
- One uncooked egg
- One hardboiled egg
- One can of solid food
- One can of soup

Teacher's Notes: Use solid foods that are uniform in content, and about the same mass as the soup can, such as a jar of peanut butter or a can of refried beans.

Answers to Analysis
1. The uncooked egg stops first. The can of soup stops first.
2. The object with a solid core would rotate with a more uniform motion. Because of inertia, the liquid would cause the object to wobble slightly.

Answer to Reading Check
The crust of the far side of the moon is thicker than the crust of the near side is. The crust of the far side also consists mainly of mountainous terrain and has only a few small maria.

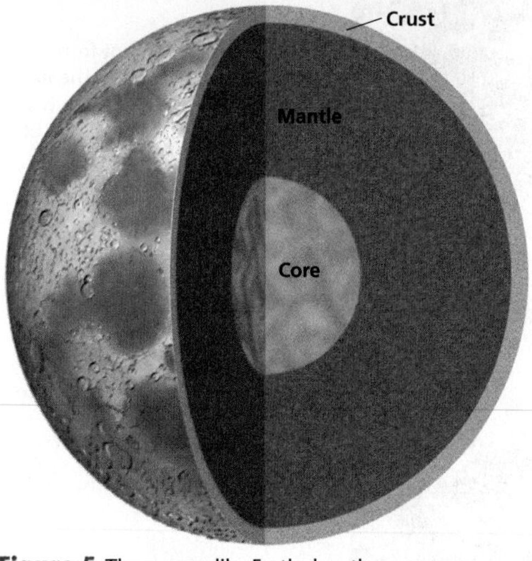

Figure 5 The moon, like Earth, has three compositional layers: the crust, the mantle, and the core.

The Interior of the Moon

Rocks of the lunar surface are about as dense as those on Earth's surface. However, the overall density of the moon is only three-fifths the density of Earth. The difference in overall density indicates that the interior of the moon is less dense than the interior of Earth.

Most of the information about the interior of the moon comes from seismographs that were placed on the moon by the Apollo astronauts. Seismographs recorded numerous weak moonquakes, which are similar to earthquakes. More than 10,000 moonquakes have been detected. Most moonquakes occur in the mantle at a depth that is 10 times deeper than the depth at which most earthquakes occur on Earth. From these moonquakes, scientists learned that the moon's interior is layered, as shown in **Figure 5.**

Quick Lab — 5 min

Liquid and Solid Cores

Procedure
1. Take one uncooked egg and one hardboiled egg. With your thumb and forefinger, spin both eggs.
2. Record the amount of time each egg spins.
3. Lay one can of solid food and one can of soup on their sides, and spin both cans.
4. Record the amount of time each can spins.

Analysis
1. Which egg stopped spinning first? Which can of food stopped spinning first?
2. Which rotates more steadily: an object that has a solid core or an object that has a liquid core? Explain your answer.

The Moon's Crust

One side of the moon always faces Earth. That side is therefore called the *near side*. The other side always faces away from Earth and is called the *far side*. The pull of Earth's gravity during the moon's formation caused the crust on the far side of the moon to become thicker than the crust on the near side. On the near side, the lunar crust is about 60 km thick. On the far side, the lunar crust is up to 100 km thick. Images of the far side show that the far side's surface is mountainous and has only a few small maria. The crust of the far side appears to consist of materials that are similar to those of the rocks in the highlands on the near side.

Reading Check **Name two features of the far side of the moon.**

The Moon's Mantle and Core

Beneath the crust is the moon's mantle. The mantle is thought to be made of rock that is rich in silica, magnesium, and iron. Of the moon's 1,738 km radius, the mantle makes up more than half of that distance and reaches 1,000 km below the crust.

Scientists think that the moon has a small iron core that has a radius of less than 700 km. When laser beams were bounced off small mirrors placed on the moon, scientists discovered that the moon's rotation is not uniform. This non-uniform rotation indicates that the core is neither completely solid nor completely liquid. This characteristic may explain why the moon has almost no overall magnetic field. There are, however, small areas on the moon that exhibit local magnetism.

Discussion GENERAL

Comprehension Check Pose this scenario to students. Suppose someone said that the interior of the moon is very similar to the interior of Earth. Would you agree or disagree with this assessment? (Answers may vary. Sample answer: Like Earth, the moon consists of a thin crust, a mantle and an iron core. However, the moon's overall density is substantially less than that of Earth. No convection currents have been detected in the lunar mantle. The lunar core is also considerably smaller.) LS **Verbal**

Debate ADVANCED

Lunar Origins To gain acceptance, any explanation of lunar origins had to explain these facts: (1) why Earth has such a large moon for its size; (2) why the moon has such a small iron core relative to Earth's; (3) the similarity in oxygen isotopes and trace elements in the two bodies; and (4) the existence of a lava "ocean" on the moon. Invite students to research and debate the merits of the giant impact hypothesis and competing hypotheses on these points. LS **Logical**

The Formation of the Moon

Rocks taken from the moon by Apollo astronauts provided evidence to help astronomers understand the moon's history. Most scientists generally agree that the moon formed in three stages.

The Giant Impact Hypothesis

Most scientists think that the moon's development began when a large object collided with Earth more than 4 billion years ago. This *giant impact hypothesis* states that a Mars-sized body struck Earth early in the history of the solar system. Before the impact, Earth was molten, or heated to an almost liquid state. The collision ejected chunks of Earth's mantle into orbit around Earth. The debris eventually clumped together to form the moon, as shown in **Figure 6.**

Most of the ejected materials came from Earth's silica-rich mantle rather than from Earth's dense, metallic core. This hypothesis explains why moon rocks share many of the chemical characteristics of Earth's mantle. As the material clumped together, it continued to revolve around Earth because of Earth's gravitational pull.

Differentiation of the Lunar Interior

Early in its history, the lunar surface was covered by an ocean of molten rock. Over time, the densest materials moved toward the center of the moon and formed a small core. The least dense materials formed an outer crust. The other materials settled between the core and the outer layer to form the moon's mantle.

Meteorite Bombardment

The outer surface of the moon eventually cooled to form a thick, solid crust over the molten interior. At the same time, debris left over from the formation of the solar system struck the solid surface and produced craters and regolith.

About 3 billion years ago, the number of small objects in the solar system decreased. Less material struck the lunar surface, and few new craters formed. Craters that have rays formed during the most recent meteor impacts. During this stage of lunar development, virtually all geologic activity stopped. Because the moon cooled more than 3 billion years ago, it looks today almost exactly as it did 3 billion years ago. Therefore, the moon is a valuable source of information about the conditions that existed in the solar system long ago.

Figure 6 The First Stage of Moon Formation

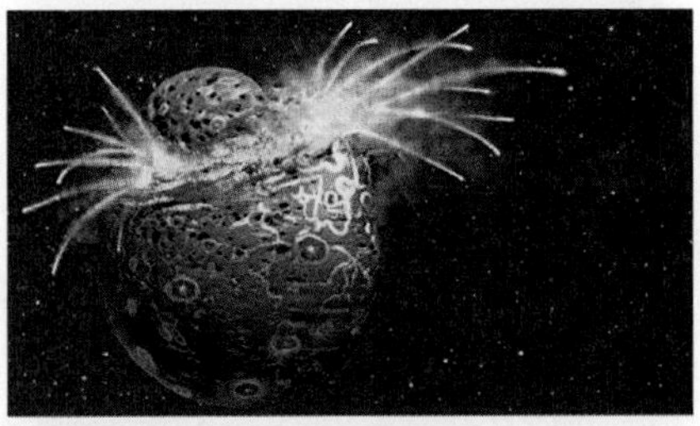

Scientists think that a Mars-sized object collided with Earth and blasted part of Earth's mantle into space.

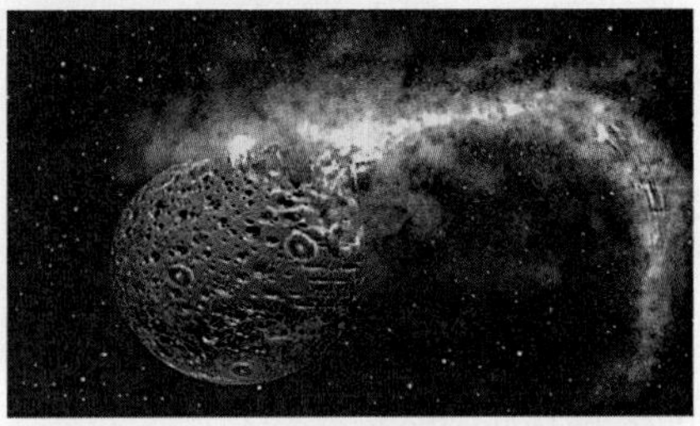

The resulting debris then began to revolve around Earth.

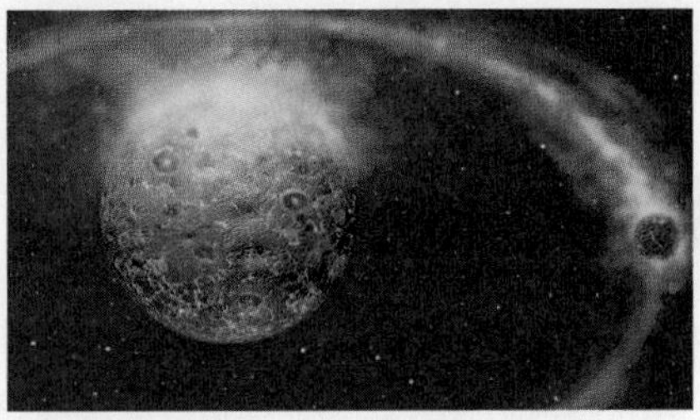

The material eventually joined to form Earth's moon.

Close

Reteaching BASIC

Storyboards Ask students to use a storyboard organizer to sort out the sequence of events in the formation of the moon. Tell them to make sketches that illustrate the steps in the formation process and include an explanatory note with each storyboard.
LS Visual

Quiz GENERAL

1. Describe how the surface features of the far side of the moon compare with those on the near side. (The near side has several large basins filled with lava (maria). The far side has fewer maria and more mountains and craters.)
2. How do scientists know the moon has a layered structure? (Astronauts placed seismographs that have detected weak moonquakes and helped reveal the moon's structure. Observations of the moon's rotation suggest that its core is not completely solid.)
3. How have meteorite impacts affected the surface of the moon? (Impacts have produced numerous craters and pulverized the crust, which covered the surface with a fine layer of dust and rock, and melted together fragments of rock to produce breccias.) **LS Verbal**

Key Resources

Technology
- Transparencies
  140 Formation of the Moon

Differentiated Instruction

English Learners

Paired Summarizing Group students into pairs, and have them read silently about the giant impact hypothesis of the origin of the moon and the events that followed the impact. Then, have one student summarize the stages in the formation of the moon. The other student should listen to the retelling and should point out any inaccuracies or details that were left out. Allow students to refer to the text as needed. **LS**
Auditory Co-op Learning English Language Learners

Close, *continued*

Answers to Section Review

1. Galileo called the smooth dark patches on the lunar surface maria, because he thought they looked like seas.
2. The crust on the far side of the moon is thicker than the crust on the near side is.
3. The maria formed more than 3 billion years ago, when lava filled craters that formed during previous impacts.
4. Many more craters would have been produced and the layer of debris would be much thicker. Some maria may have formed, but they would have been covered with overlapping craters, breccias, and regolith.
5. Breccias are made up of fragments of rocks from the highlands and maria that are cemented by material that was melted and cooled. Breccias formed when the force of impacts broke up existing rocks and heat from the impacts melted some of the fragmented material.
6. Scientists think that the moon formed when a Mars-sized body struck Earth, throwing part of Earth's mantle into orbit. The debris eventually clumped together to form the moon.
7. The pull of Earth's gravity during the moon's formation caused the crust on the far side of the moon to become thicker than the crust on the near side.
8. Sample answer: Impact events formed craters, breccias, and the lunar regolith. Lava flows formed the smooth maria, which filled in many of the largest impact craters.
9. The surface of the *moon* has light areas called *highlands* and dark areas called *maria*, which formed when *craters* formed by *meteorite* impacts filled with *basalt*, which also formed *rilles*.

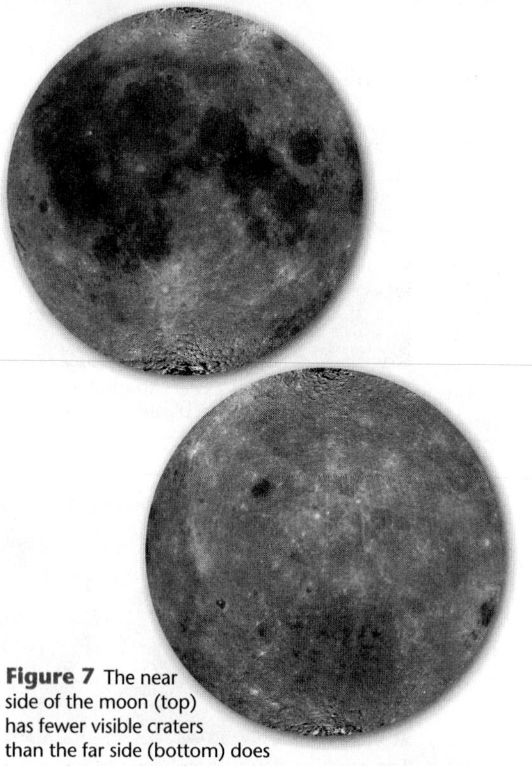

Figure 7 The near side of the moon (top) has fewer visible craters than the far side (bottom) does in part because lava flows on the near side covered many of the impact sites with maria.

Lava Flows on the Moon

After impacts on the moon's surface formed deep basins, lava flowed out of cracks, or *fissures,* in the lunar crust. This lava flooded the crater basins to form maria. The presence of the maria suggests that fissure eruptions once characterized the moon, even though there is no evidence that large active volcanoes have ever been present on the moon.

Because the moon's crust is thinner on the near side than on the far side, much more lava flowed onto the surface on the near side than onto the surface of the far side of the moon. The near side of the moon has several smooth maria, but the far side has few maria and many more craters, as shown in **Figure 7.**

Scientists do not yet know how magma formed in the lunar interior or how the magma reached the surface. There is no evidence of plate tectonics or convection currents in the moon's mantle, so the magma must have formed in some other way. A large amount of energy would have been needed to produce the magma in the upper layers of the moon. Some scientists think this energy may have come from a long period of intense meteorite bombardment. Other scientists think that radioactive decay of materials may have also heated the moon's interior enough to cause magma to form. Scientists agree that the lava flows ended about 3.1 billion years ago, when the interior cooled completely.

Section 1 Review

Key Ideas

1. **Describe** what maria on the surface of the moon look like and how they came to be known as maria.
2. **Compare** the thickness of the moon's crust on the near side with the thickness of the crust on the far side.
3. **Summarize** how and when the maria formed.
4. **Describe** how the surface of the moon would be different today if meteorites had continued to hit it at the same rate as they did 3 billion years ago.
5. **Describe** breccias and how they formed on the moon.
6. **Summarize** how scientists think the moon formed.

Critical Thinking

7. **Analyzing Ideas** Explain how Earth's gravity affected the moon's near side and far side differently.
8. **Making Comparisons** Compare the features of the lunar surface created by lava flows and the features created by impacts.

Concept Mapping

9. Use the following terms to create a concept map: *moon, meteorite, crater, rille, maria, highlands,* and *basalt.*

Differentiated Instruction

Alternative Assessment

Lunar Picture Book Have students create a picture book for younger children that explains the topics in this section, including lunar exploration, the moon's structure, and the origin of the moon. Provide fiction and nonfiction examples for students to use as models.
LS Verbal/Visual

SECTION 2

Movements of the Moon

Key Ideas	Key Terms	Why It Matters
❯ Describe the shape of the moon's orbit around Earth. ❯ Explain why eclipses occur. ❯ Describe the appearance of four phases of the moon. ❯ Explain how the movements of the moon affect tides on Earth.	apogee, perigee, eclipse, solar eclipse, lunar eclipse, phase	Understanding the movements of the moon enables us to predict solar and lunar eclipses as well as low and high tides.

If you looked down on the moon from above its north pole, you would see the moon rotate once on its axis every 27.3 days. However, if you stood on the moon's surface and measured the lunar day by the amount of time between sunrises, you would find that a lunar day is 29.5 Earth days long. This discrepancy is due to the fact that, while the moon is revolving around Earth, Earth and the moon are also revolving around the sun.

The Earth-Moon System

To observers on Earth, the moon appears to orbit Earth. However, if you could observe Earth and the moon from space, you would see that Earth and the moon revolve around each other. Together, they form a single system that orbits the sun.

The mass of the moon is only 1/80 that of Earth. So, the balance point of the Earth-moon system is not halfway between the centers of the two bodies. The balance point is located within Earth's interior because Earth's mass is greater than the moon's mass. This balance point is called the *barycenter*. The barycenter follows a smooth orbit around the sun, as shown in **Figure 1.**

apogee in the orbit of a satellite, the point that is farthest from Earth

perigee in the orbit of a satellite, the point that is closest to Earth

Figure 1 The Earth-moon system.

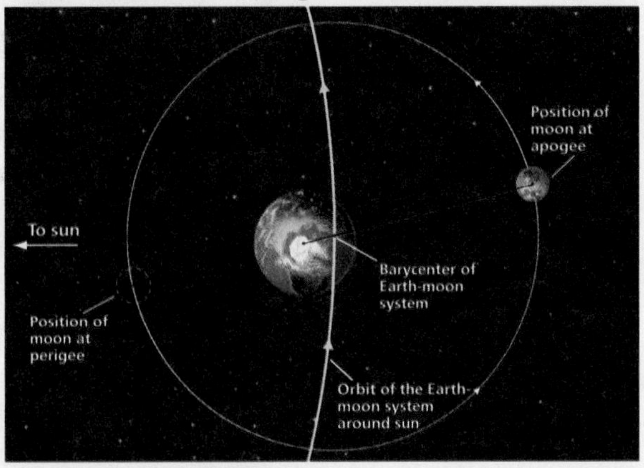

The Moon's Elliptical Orbit

The orbit of the moon around Earth forms an ellipse that is about 5% more elongated than a circle is. Therefore, the distance between Earth and its moon varies over a month's time. When the moon is farthest from Earth, the moon is at **apogee.** When the moon is closest to Earth, the moon is at **perigee.** The average distance of the moon from Earth is 384,000 km.

Section 2

Focus

Overview

This section describes the Earth-moon system, the shape of the moon's orbit, and how the moon's gravity causes tides. The section also explains why eclipses and the phases of the moon occur.

Bellringer

Ask students to create a series of drawings that shows how the moon's appearance changes over several weeks. **LS Visual**

Motivate

Group Activity — GENERAL

Barycenter Have students make a simple model that shows how the Earth-moon system rotates around a common center point. Students should follow these steps: Tie a 30 cm length of string about 3 cm from the end of a pencil. Stick an apple-sized clay ball on the end of the pencil. Mold the clay ball around the string so that the string lies just inside the edge of the ball. Add a grape-sized ball of clay to the other end of the pencil. Holding the model by the end of the string, add small bits of clay to the smaller ball until the whole system is in balance. Ask what the parts of the model represent. (The large ball is Earth, the small ball stands for the moon. The string is located at the balance point, or the barycenter.) **LS Kinesthetic**

Key Resources

Chapter Resource File

- Directed Reading BASIC
- Inquiry Lab: Inconstant Moon GENERAL

Technology

- Transparencies
  Bellringer
  141 The Earth-Moon System

Teach

Demonstration GENERAL

Synchronous Rotation Use a foam ball to represent the moon. Place a dowel rod in the center to form a handle. Mark a series of letters from A to D with a marker or pen at 90° intervals around the face of the ball. Invite a student to sit in a swiveling desk chair a few feet from a desk lamp, which represents the sun. Attach the ball to the armrest of the chair. Slowly turn the chair (Earth), while the seated student observes the view of the moon model. Ask the seated volunteer to report what he or she observes. (The visible part of the ball always remains the same.) Ask the rest of the class what they see and how this differs from what the seated student sees. (Each letter marked on the ball appears in turn as the chair rotates.) Thus, the moon turns once on its axis in the time it takes to complete one orbit, so the same half of the moon always faces Earth. **LS Kinesthetic**

READING TOOLBOX

Two-Column Notes

Students' notes should include all key ideas for Section 2. The first key idea is shown in two-column note form below.

Key Idea	Detail Notes
The shape of moon's orbit around Earth	– orbit forms an ellipse – distance between Earth and moon varies – moon at apogee when farthest from Earth – moon at perigee when closest to Earth

Academic Vocabulary

successive (suhk SES iv) following one after the other; consecutive

Moonrise and Moonset

The moon appears to rise and set at Earth's horizon because of Earth's rotation on its axis. If you were to watch the moon rise or set on successive nights, however, you would notice that it rises or sets approximately 50 minutes later each night. This happens because of both Earth's rotation and the moon's revolution. While Earth completes one rotation each day, the moon also moves in its orbit around Earth. It takes an extra 1/29 of Earth's rotation, or 50 minutes, for the horizon to catch up to the moon.

Lunar Rotation

In addition to orbiting Earth and revolving around the sun, the moon also spins on its axis. The moon rotated rapidly when it formed, but the pull of Earth's gravity has slowed the moon's rate of rotation. The moon now spins very slowly and completes a rotation only once during each orbit around Earth. The moon revolves only once around Earth in about 27.3 days relative to the stars. Because the rotation and the revolution of the moon take the same amount of time, observers on Earth always see the same side of the moon. Therefore, images of the far side of the moon must be taken by spacecraft orbiting the moon.

As the moon orbits Earth, the part of the moon's surface that is illuminated by sunlight changes. The sun's light always illuminates half of the moon and, as shown in **Figure 2**, half the Earth. The near side of the moon is sometimes fully illuminated by the sun. At other times, depending on where the moon is in its orbit, the near side is partly or completely darkened.

READING TOOLBOX

Two-Column Notes
Create two-column notes to review the main ideas for Section 2. Put the main ideas in the left column, and add details and examples in your own words in the right column. Use as a model the two-column notes table that you started at the beginning of the chapter.

Reading Check **Why are we unable to photograph the far side of the moon from Earth?**

Figure 2 The lunar landing module, which was also called *The Eagle*, flew to meet the command module at the end of the *Apollo 11* mission. Seen from this viewpoint, Earth is illuminated from above.

Answer to Reading Check
The far side of the moon is never visible from Earth, because the moon's rotation on its axis and the moon's revolution around Earth take the same amount of time.

Differentiated Instruction

Special Education Students

Orbits To help students understand positions and orbits in the Earth-moon system, have one student pose as the sun, one as Earth, and one as the moon. Ask "Earth" and "moon" to revolve around each other as both revolve around "sun." Have them maintain an orbit with the sun off-center. **LS Kinesthetic**

Figure 3 During a solar eclipse, the shadow of the moon falls on Earth. The distance between Earth and the moon in this diagram is not to scale.

Eclipses

Bodies orbiting the sun, including Earth and its moon, cast long shadows into space. An **eclipse** occurs when one celestial body passes through the shadow of another. Shadows cast by Earth and the moon have two parts. In the inner, cone-shaped part of the shadow, the *umbra*, sunlight is completely blocked. In the outer part of the shadow, the *penumbra*, sunlight is only partially blocked, as shown in **Figure 3.**

Solar Eclipses

When the moon is directly between the sun and part of Earth, the shadow of the moon falls on Earth and causes a **solar eclipse.** During a *total solar eclipse*, the sun's light is completely blocked by the moon. The umbra falls on the area of Earth that lies directly in line with the moon and the sun. Outside the umbra, but within the penumbra, people see a *partial solar eclipse*. The penumbra falls on the area that immediately surrounds the umbra.

The umbra of the moon is too small to make a large shadow on Earth's surface. The part of the umbra that hits Earth during an eclipse, as shown in **Figure 4,** is never more than a few hundred kilometers across. So, a total eclipse of the sun covers only a small part of Earth and is seen only by people in particular parts of Earth along a narrow path. A total solar eclipse also never lasts more than about seven minutes at any one location. A total eclipse will not be visible in the United States until 2017, even though there is a total eclipse somewhere on Earth about every 18 months.

eclipse an event in which the shadow of one celestial body falls on another

solar eclipse the passing of the moon between Earth and the sun; during a solar eclipse, the shadow of the moon falls on Earth

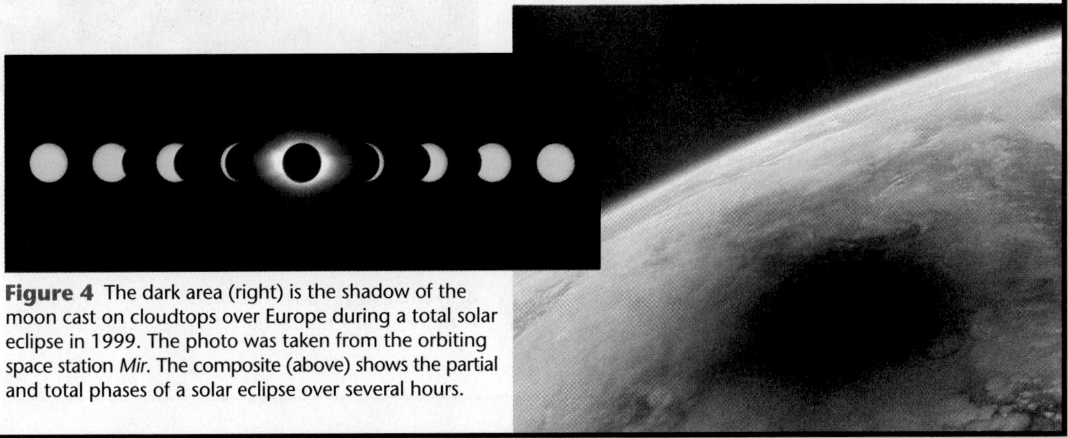
Figure 4 The dark area (right) is the shadow of the moon cast on cloudtops over Europe during a total solar eclipse in 1999. The photo was taken from the orbiting space station *Mir*. The composite (above) shows the partial and total phases of a solar eclipse over several hours.

Using the Figure — BASIC

Solar Eclipse Direct students' attention to the diagram that shows a solar eclipse. Point out that the dark inner shadow or umbra of the moon covers only a very small portion of Earth, sometimes less than 160 km wide. Ask students where people on Earth must be in order to observe a total solar eclipse. (Sample answer: They must be within the area covered by the umbra.) Ask them what observers located within the penumbra will see. (a partial eclipse of the sun) Make sure students understand that the distance between Earth and the moon in this diagram is not to scale. The distance between Earth and its satellite is actually about 60 times the radius of Earth. **LS Visual**

Activity — GENERAL

Eclipsed Demonstrate how a smaller body like the moon can completely block out the light of a larger body like the sun to produce a total eclipse. Provide a coin or small marble for each student. Have them close one eye and look at a distant large object such as a tree by using their open eye. Tell them to hold the coin or marble in front of the open eye and slowly bring it closer until it is directly in front of the eye. As the object nears their faces, the larger object gradually disappears from view. **LS Kinesthetic/Visual**

Key Resources

Technology
- Transparencies
  142 Solar and Lunar Eclipse

Why It Matters

Size is Relative Earth is unusual in the inner solar system in that it has an extremely large companion body. The diameter of the sun is about 400 times greater than the diameter of the moon, but the sun is also roughly 400 times farther away from Earth. The combination of the moon's size and distance from Earth causes the moon to appear roughly the same size as the sun does, and helps explain why eclipses can occur. **LS Verbal**

Teach, *continued*

Quick Lab

Skills Acquired
- Making Models
- Observing
- Analyzing

Materials
- Modeling clay
- Metric ruler
- Sheet of paper
- Penlight

Teacher's Notes: Point out that with a penlight as the light source, the light spreads out to form a cone-shape, whereas the sun's rays are actually parallel.

Answers to Analysis
1. penlight = sun; larger ball = Earth; smaller ball = moon
2. From Earth, it represents a lunar eclipse. From the moon, it represents a solar eclipse.
3. As viewed from Earth, step 4 represents a solar eclipse in which part of Earth is in the moon's shadow. As viewed from the moon, it would represent an eclipse of Earth in which part of Earth passes through the moon's shadow.
4. Answers may vary. Sample answer: It would be more realistic if the models were moving around each other instead of remaining stationary.

Figure 5 The diamond-ring effect produced by a solar eclipse can be stunning for observers on the part of Earth that falls under the moon's shadow.

Effects of Solar Eclipses

During a total solar eclipse, people on the ground are in the moon's umbra. In the areas on Earth's surface under the umbra, the sky becomes as dark as it does at twilight. During this period of darkness, the sunlight that is not eclipsed by the moon shows the normally invisible outer layers of the sun's atmosphere. The last bits of normal sunlight before darkness often glisten like the diamond on a ring and cause what is known as the *diamond-ring effect*. The diamond-ring effect is shown in **Figure 5.** Therefore, many people think that total solar eclipses are very beautiful.

If the moon is at or near apogee when it comes directly between Earth and the sun, the moon's umbra does not reach Earth. If the umbra fails to reach Earth, a ring-shaped eclipse occurs. This type of eclipse is called an *annular eclipse*, because *annulus* is the Latin word for "ring." During an annular eclipse, the sun is never completely blocked out. Instead, a thin ring of sunlight is visible around the outer edge of the moon. The brightness of this thin ring of ordinary sunlight prevents observers from seeing the outer layers of the sun's atmosphere that are visible during a total solar eclipse. An annular eclipse will be visible from the American Southwest on May 20, 2012.

Reading Check **What is one difference between a total solar eclipse and an annular eclipse?**

Quick Lab Eclipses

15 min

Procedure

1. Make two balls from modeling clay, one about 4 cm in diameter and one about 1 cm in diameter.
2. Using a metric ruler, position the balls about 15 cm apart on a sheet of paper, as shown in the photo at right.
3. Turn off any nearby lights. Place a penlight approximately 15 cm in front of and almost level with the larger ball. Shine the light on the larger ball. Sketch your model, and note the effect of the beam of light.
4. Repeat step 3, but reverse the positions of the two balls. You may need to raise the smaller ball slightly to center its shadow on the larger ball. Sketch your model, and again note the effect of the light beam.

Analysis

1. Which planetary bodies do the larger clay ball, the smaller clay ball, and the penlight represent?
2. As viewed from Earth, what event did your model in step 3 represent? As viewed from the moon, what would your model represent?
3. As viewed from Earth, what event did your model in step 4 represent? As viewed from the moon, what would your model represent?
4. In what ways could you modify this activity to more closely model how eclipses occur?

Differentiated Instruction

English Learners

Writing The next total solar eclipse visible from the United States is in 2017. Have students write a poem, story, or spoken word piece that describes what they imagine it would be like to experience a total solar eclipse. Encourage students to use information they learned in this section and to be creative in their writing. Invite students to read their pieces to the class.
LS **Verbal**

Answer to Reading Check

During a total eclipse, the entire disk of the sun is blocked, and the outer layers of the sun become visible. During an annular eclipse, the disk of the sun is never completely blocked out, so the sun is too bright for observers on Earth to see the outer layers of the sun's atmosphere.

Figure 6 During a lunar eclipse, the shadow of Earth falls on the moon. The distance between Earth and the moon in this diagram is not to scale.

Lunar Eclipses

A **lunar eclipse** occurs when Earth is positioned between the moon and the sun and when Earth's shadow crosses the lighted half of the moon. For a total lunar eclipse to occur, the entire moon must pass into Earth's umbra, as shown in **Figure 6.** When only part of the moon passes into Earth's umbra, a *partial lunar eclipse* occurs. The remainder of the moon passes through Earth's penumbra. When the entire moon passes through Earth's penumbra, a *penumbral eclipse* occurs. During a penumbral eclipse, the moon darkens so little that the eclipse is barely noticeable.

lunar eclipse the passing of the moon through Earth's shadow at full moon

A lunar eclipse lasts for several hours. Even during a total lunar eclipse, sunlight is bent around Earth through our atmosphere. Mainly red light reaches the moon, so the totally eclipsed moon appears to have a reddish color, as shown in the middle portion of the composite image in **Figure 7.**

Frequency of Solar and Lunar Eclipses

As many as seven eclipses may occur during a calendar year. Four may be lunar, and three may be solar or vice versa. However, total eclipses of the sun and the moon occur infrequently. Solar and lunar eclipses do not occur during every lunar orbit. This is because the orbit of the moon is not in the same plane as the orbit of Earth around the sun. The moon crosses the plane of Earth's orbit only twice in each revolution around Earth. A solar eclipse will occur only if this crossing occurs when the moon is between Earth and the sun. If this crossing occurs when Earth is between the moon and the sun, a lunar eclipse will occur.

Lunar eclipses are visible everywhere from the dark side of Earth. A total solar eclipse, however, can be seen only by observers in the small path of the moon's shadow as it moves across Earth's lighted surface. A partial solar eclipse can be seen for thousands of kilometers on either side of the path of the umbra.

Figure 7 This composite image shows a total lunar eclipse as seen from Earth over several hours.

Teaching Tip — GENERAL

Connect to Familiar Processes Students may better understand why the moon sometimes has a copper color during a lunar eclipse if you compare the color of the moon with the color of the sky at sunset. Sunsets are red because all of the other colors in sunlight are scattered by dust and molecules in Earth's atmosphere. Only red and orange wavelengths pass through the atmosphere to shed a rosy glow over the early evening sky. The same effect that creates the spectacular shades of red during a sunset also paints the moon a coppery red during a total lunar eclipse. **LS Verbal**

MISCONCEPTION ALERT

Eclipse Frequency Students may think that both a lunar and solar eclipse should happen every month as the moon completes its orbit of Earth. However, the moon is rarely in direct alignment with Earth's orbital plane. Because the moon's orbit is tilted about 5° from the plane of Earth's orbit around the sun, which is called the *ecliptic plane*, the shadows do not fall on Earth. An eclipse can occur only when the moon crosses the ecliptic while it is in the new-moon phase to create a solar eclipse, or in full-moon phase to create a lunar eclipse. This happens only about seven times a year.

Life Science Connection — GENERAL

Biological Rhythms Biologists and zoologists sometimes use eclipses to learn more about the rhythms of living creatures. Totality resembles the arrival of night, and animals and plants respond accordingly. From monitoring the activities of a colony of bats or of fish in coral reefs, researchers study how animals and plants react to the brief moments of darkness.

For example, a team of Polish zoologists observed mammal, bird, and insect behavior from 1954 to 1975 during seven eclipses with different levels of totality. They discovered that insects and birds were influenced the most. Many bird species seemed anxious, stopped singing, and exhibited roosting behaviors. Bees returned to their hives, nocturnal insects such as mosquitoes and moths appeared, and butterflies settled for the night. Invite interested students to learn more about the effects of such events on circadian rhythms of living things and to present their findings in an oral report. **LS Verbal**

Teach, *continued*

Group Activity — GENERAL

Many Moons Collect enough foam balls for each student to have one. Put a lamp without its shade on a stand in the front of the classroom. Distribute the balls and have each student place the point of a pencil into their ball to form a handle. Have students stand in a semicircle facing the light. Tell students to imagine that the ball is the moon. Their bodies represent the spinning Earth. Darken the room lights. Have students turn around counterclockwise slowly, holding the ball level with their heads at arm's length so that the light reflects off the model moon. Tell them to stop every quarter turn to observe the dark portion of the ball. Ask students to compare the positions of the moon model, the light (sun), and their heads (Earth) with the diagram of the moon phases, and explain what causes the different parts of the model moon to light up. **LS Visual/ Kinesthetic**

Why It Matters

Lunar Calendar The period from one new moon to the next is one lunar month. Islamic, Jewish, and other cultures base their calendars on the lunar month. The problem with these calendars is that the lunar year does not contain a whole number of lunar months. It is 11 days short. Different cultures had to find ways of reconciling this difference. Invite interested students to find out more about these calendars and how events are timed according to the lunar phases, or how the calendar has been reconciled. **LS Logical**

Phases of the Moon

phase the change in the illuminated area of one celestial body as seen from another celestial body; phases of the moon are caused by the changing positions of Earth, the sun, and the moon

On some nights, the moon shines brightly enough for you to read a book by its light. But moonlight is not produced by the moon. The moon merely reflects light from the sun. Because the moon is spherical, half of it is always lit by sunlight. As the moon revolves around Earth, however, different amounts of the near side of the moon, which faces Earth, are lighted. Therefore, the apparent shape of the visible part of the moon varies. These varying shapes, lighted by reflected sunlight, are called **phases** of the moon and are shown in **Figure 8.**

When the moon is directly between the sun and Earth, the sun's rays strike only the far side of the moon. As a result, the entire near side of the moon is dark. When the near side is dark, the moon is said to be in the *new-moon* phase. During this phase, no lighted area of the moon is visible from Earth.

Figure 8 Phases of the Moon

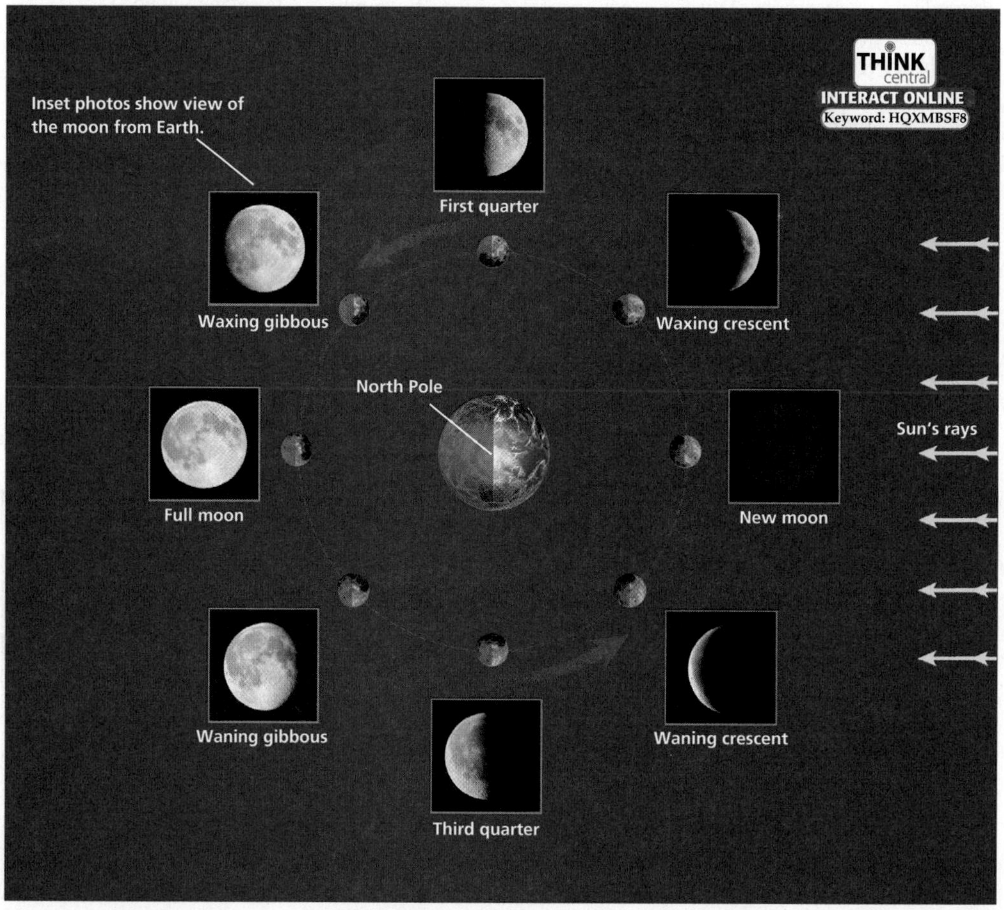

Homework — GENERAL

Moon Watching Invite students to keep a daily moon observation journal for two weeks or more. Students can make naked eye observations or they may use binoculars. Have them record the date and time of their observations, the phase of the moon, and where it appears in the sky. Depending on the phase, students may be able to make observations during daylight hours as well as at night. Have them note the phase, make a picture of what the moon looks like, and list its rising and setting times. Guide students to look for any patterns they observe. **LS Visual**

Key Resources

Technology

- Transparencies
  - 143 Phases of the Moon
  - 144 Causes of Tides

Waxing Phases of the Moon

As the moon continues to move in its orbit around Earth, part of the near side becomes illuminated. When the size of the lighted part of the moon is increasing, the moon is said to be *waxing*. When a sliver of the moon's near side is illuminated, the moon enters its *waxing-crescent* phase.

When the moon has moved through one-quarter of its orbit after the new moon phase, the moon appears to be a semicircle. Half of the near side of the moon is lighted. When a waxing moon becomes a semicircle, the moon enters its *first-quarter* phase. When the lighted part of the moon's near side is larger than a semicircle and still increasing in size, the moon is in its *waxing-gibbous* phase. The moon continues to wax until it appears as a full circle. At *full moon*, Earth is between the sun and the moon. Consequently, the entire near side of the moon is illuminated by the light of the sun.

Waning Phases of the Moon

After the full moon phase, when the lighted part of the near side of the moon appears to decrease in size, the moon is *waning*. When it is waning but the lighted part is still larger than a semicircle, the moon is in the *waning-gibbous* phase. When the lighted part of the near side becomes a semicircle, the moon enters the *third-quarter* phase. When only a sliver of the near side is visible, the moon enters the *waning-crescent* phase. After the waning-crescent phase, the moon again moves between Earth and the sun. The moon once more becomes a new moon, and the cycle of phases begins again.

Before and after a new moon, only a small part of the moon shines brightly. However, the rest of the moon is not completely dark. It shines dimly from sunlight that reflects first off Earth's clouds and oceans and then reflects off the moon. Sunlight that is reflected off Earth is called *earthshine*. The darker part of the moon shown in **Figure 9** is lit by earthshine.

Time from New Moon to New Moon

Although the moon revolves around Earth in 27.3 days, a longer period of time is needed for the moon to go through a complete cycle of phases. The period from one new moon to the next one is 29.5 days. This difference of 2.2 days results from the orbiting of the Earth-moon system around the sun. In the 27.3 days in which the moon orbits Earth, the two bodies move slightly farther along their orbit around the sun. Therefore, the moon must go a little farther to be directly between Earth and the sun. About 2.2 days are needed for the moon to travel this extra distance. The position directly between Earth and the sun is the position of the moon in each new moon phase.

Reading Check **Describe two phases of the waning moon.**

SCILINKS.
www.scilinks.org
Topic: Lunar Cycle
Code: **HQX0887**

Figure 9 The darker portion of this crescent moon is not completely dark because some sunlight is reflected from Earth, to the moon, and back to Earth.

Close

Reteaching — BASIC

Lunar Flipbook Have students create a flipbook about the order of the moon's phases. Students can make drawings based on the text on index cards and label the phases. Stack the cards in order with the new moon on the bottom and attach them with a binder clip so they can flip the cards to view the phases. **LS Visual**

Quiz — GENERAL

1. Explain why the barycenter of the Earth-moon system is not located halfway between the two bodies. (Because Earth is so much more massive than the moon, the balance point is located within Earth's interior.)
2. How does the shape of the lunar orbit cause an annular eclipse? (Because the moon's orbit is elliptical, if the moon is at or near apogee when it passes between Earth and the sun, the moon is too far from Earth for its umbra to reach Earth.)

Answer to Reading Check

When the lighted part of the moon is larger than a semicircle but the visible part of the moon is shrinking, the phase is called *waning gibbous*. When only a sliver of the near side is visible, the phase is called a *waning crescent*.

Skill Builder — GENERAL

Vocabulary The term *crescent* comes from the Latin word *crescere*, which means "to grow." A crescent moon is growing from the dark new-moon phase. The term *gibbous* is derived from the Latin *gibbosus*, which means "humpbacked." A gibbous moon is larger than a quarter moon but smaller than a full moon. The words that describe whether the moon is getting larger or smaller have Germanic roots. *Waxing* comes from the German *wachsen*, which means "to grow." *Waning* comes from the Middle English word *wanen*, which means "to decrease in size." **LS Verbal** English Language Learners

Close, *continued*

Answers to Section Review

1. As Earth completes one rotation each day, the moon also moves in its orbit around Earth. It takes an extra 1/29 of Earth's rotation (or 50 minutes) for Earth's horizon to catch up with the moon.
2. The moon is directly between the sun and Earth, and the cone-shaped inner shadow or umbra of the moon falls on part of Earth.
3. The moon's orbit arond Earth is not in the same plane as Earth's orbit around the sun. A total lunar or solar eclipse occurs only when the moon and Earth are near one of the two crossings of the orbits at the same time.
4. Solar eclipses occur when the moon passes between the sun and Earth. Lunar eclipses occur when Earth is between the sun and the moon and the moon passes through Earth's shadow.
5. The moon is between Earth and the sun.
6. The lighted portion appears to grow larger.
7. Although the moon revolves around Earth in 27.3 days, a longer period of time is needed for the moon to go through a complete cycle of phases. The period from one new moon to the next one is 29.5 days. This difference of 2.2 days is due to the orbiting of the Earth-moon system around the sun.
8. On the near side of Earth, the gravitational force of the moon pulls ocean water toward the moon. The mass of the solid Earth is subject to less gravitational force than the ocean water is. On the far side of Earth, the water is subject to less gravitational force than the solid Earth is. These gravitational differences cause the water on the near side and on the far side of Earth to form two tidal bulges.
9. Observers on Earth always see the same side of the moon because the moon revolves around Earth at the same rate that it rotates on its axis.
10. Lunar eclipses are visible everywhere on the dark side of Earth. Only observers in the narrow path of the moon's shadow see a total solar eclipse as it crosses Earth's lighted surface.

Answers continued on p. 875A

Figure 10 The moon's pull on Earth is greatest at point A, on Earth's near side, and weakest at point C, on Earth's far side. Point B represents Earth's center of mass. Earth's rotation causes two low tides and two high tides each day on most shorelines.

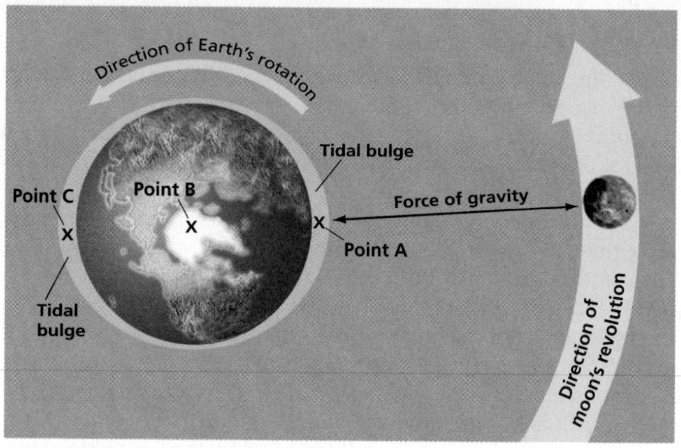

Tides on Earth

Bulges in Earth's oceans, called tidal bulges, form because the moon's gravitational pull on Earth decreases with distance. Thus, the ocean on Earth's near side is pulled toward the moon with the greatest force. The solid Earth, which acts as though all of its mass were its center, experiences less force. The ocean on the far side is subject to less force than the solid Earth is. As shown in **Figure 10,** these differences cause tidal bulges. Because Earth rotates, tides occur regularly at any given point on the surface each day. The sun also causes tides, but they are smaller because the sun is much farther from Earth than the moon is. Twice each month, when the sun, moon, and Earth are almost in line, the gravitational pulls combine to produce especially high tides.

Section 2 Review

Key Ideas

1. **Explain** why the moon rises and sets about 50 minutes later each successive night.
2. **Describe** what causes a total solar eclipse.
3. **Explain** why a lunar eclipse does not occur every time the moon revolves around Earth.
4. **Summarize** how a solar eclipse differs from a lunar eclipse.
5. **Describe** the relative locations of the sun, Earth, and the moon during a new moon phase.
6. **Describe** how the appearance of the moon changes when it is waxing.
7. **Explain** why the moon repeats phases every 29.5 days but completes an orbit in 27.3 days.
8. **Explain** how the moon causes tidal bulges on Earth.

Critical Thinking

9. **Analyzing Ideas** Explain why observers on Earth always see the same side of the moon.
10. **Making Comparisons** Explain why more people see each total lunar eclipse than each total solar eclipse.
11. **Analyzing Relationships** The sun's gravity also affects tides on Earth. Why does the moon have a larger effect on tides than the sun does?

Concept Mapping

12. Use the following terms to create a concept map: *Earth, moon, sun, eclipse, solar eclipse, lunar eclipse, umbra,* and *penumbra.*

Differentiated Instruction

Alternative Assessment

System Models Give groups of students foam balls, modeling clay, dowel rods, pencils, string, paper clips, tape, and poster board. Have them make a model to explain to younger students the phases of the moon, how eclipses occur, or what causes tides. Remind them that Earth and the moon share a common center of gravity. Have each student use the model to explain the process involved. **LS Kinesthetic**

SECTION 3

Satellites of Other Planets

Key Ideas	Key Terms	Why It Matters
❯ Compare the characteristics of the two moons of Mars. ❯ Describe how volcanoes were discovered on Io. ❯ Name one distinguishing characteristic of each of the Galilean moons. ❯ Compare the characteristics of the rings of Saturn with the rings of the other outer planets.	**Galilean moon**	Studying the moons of other planets helps scientists better understand our own moon as well as the forces that have helped to shape the solar system.

Until the 1600s, astronomers thought that Earth was the only planet that had a moon. In 1610, Galileo discovered four moons orbiting Jupiter. He also observed what later were identified as the rings of Saturn. Since the time of Galileo, astronomers have discovered that all of the planets in our solar system except Mercury and Venus have moons. In addition, the gas giants Saturn, Jupiter, Uranus, and Neptune all have rings.

Moons of Mars

Mars has two tiny moons, named Phobos and Deimos. They revolve around Mars relatively quickly. Phobos and Deimos are irregularly shaped chunks of rock and are thought to be captured asteroids. Phobos is 27 km across at its longest, and Deimos is about 15 km across at its longest.

The surfaces of Phobos and Deimos are dark, like maria on Earth's moon. Both moons have many craters. The large number of craters shows that the moons have been hit by many asteroids and comets, and suggests that the moons are fairly old.

Galilean moon any one of the four largest satellites of Jupiter—Io, Europa, Ganymede, and Callisto—that were discovered by Galileo in 1610

Moons of Jupiter

Galileo observed four large moons revolving around Jupiter. Since that discovery was made, scientists have observed dozens of smaller moons around Jupiter. Smaller moons continue to be discovered today. Most of Jupiter's moons have diameters of less than 200 km, but of the largest four, known as the **Galilean moons,** three are bigger than Earth's moon. Until spacecraft flew near the moons, scientists knew little about them. Now, scientists have identified many unique characteristics of the Galilean moons. One of the four Galilean moons is shown in **Figure 1.**

Figure 1 The stormy surface of Jupiter is visible in the background. In the foreground is Io, which orbits Jupiter once every 42 hours.

Section 3

Focus

Overview

This section identifies the distinguishing features of the moons and ring systems of planets in our solar system and describes how space missions have helped us learn more about these objects.

Bellringer

Ask students to write a definition of a moon that identifies the essential characteristics of a moon. (Answers may vary.) Use student responses to assess prior knowledge and encourage deeper thinking. **LS Verbal**

Motivate

Discussion GENERAL

Mythology Connection Have students share what they know about historical origins for names of the planets. Invite interested students to learn more about the names of planetary moons. Students may recognize some lunar names that originated in classical stories. Guide students to explain why a particular moon may be aptly named and why the same name may fit well in a related modern setting. Have students share their findings with the class. **LS Verbal**

Key Resources

Chapter Resource File
- Directed Reading BASIC

Technology
- Transparencies
  Bellringer

Teach

Internet Activity GENERAL

Martian Moons Invite interested students to research the moons of Mars. While the most commonly accepted theory is that they are captured asteroids, some scientists have suggested that the Martian moons could be fragments that formed during the break up of a much larger body that once circled the Red Planet. The nearer moon, Phobos, may eventually spiral in and crash on the planet's surface or be torn apart by gravity. A worksheet designed to direct student research on this topic can be found in the **Chapter Resource File** booklet or by visiting www.thinkcentral.com and entering the keyword **HQXMBSX.**
LS Visual/Auditory

Figure 2 In this image taken by the *Galileo* spacecraft you can see a volcanic eruption on the left side of Io against the background of space.

Academic Vocabulary
extraterrestrial (eks truh tuh RES tree uhl) not of Earth

Io

Io is the innermost of Jupiter's four Galilean moons. An engineer examining images from the *Voyager* spacecraft discovered volcanoes on Io. Io is the first extraterrestrial body on which active volcanoes have been seen. Since the discovery of Io's volcanoes, scientists realize that volcanism is more widespread in the solar system than they had thought. Volcanoes on Io eject thousands of metric tons of material each second. The lava that erupts on Io is much hotter than the lava that erupts on Earth. The temperature of the lava on Io is higher because the lava has more magnesium and iron than lava on Earth does. Plumes of volcanic material on Io reach heights of hundreds of kilometers, as shown in **Figure 2.** Because parts of Io's surface are yellow-red, scientists think that the volcanic material is mostly sulfur and sulfur dioxide.

Io moves inward and outward in its orbit around Jupiter because of the gravitational pull of the other moons of Jupiter. This movement produces differences in gravitational pull on opposite sides of the moon called *tidal forces.* These forces are similar to tides on Earth caused by the pull of the moon. As Io is pulled back and forth, its surface also moves in and out. Calculations show that tidal forces make Io's surface move in and out by 100 m. Heat from the friction caused by this surface flexing results in the melting of the interior of Io and leads to volcanism. Data from the *Galileo* spacecraft show that Io has a giant iron core and may possess a magnetic field. Much of what we know about Jupiter's moons came from information gathered by the *Galileo* spacecraft, which orbited Jupiter from 1995 to 2003.

Why It Matters

Early Telescope Images

To the unaided eye, the only moon visible from Earth is our own. Imagine the surprise about 400 years ago when the Italian scientist and inventor, Galileo Galilei, turned his newly improved telescope to Jupiter and discovered four more moons.

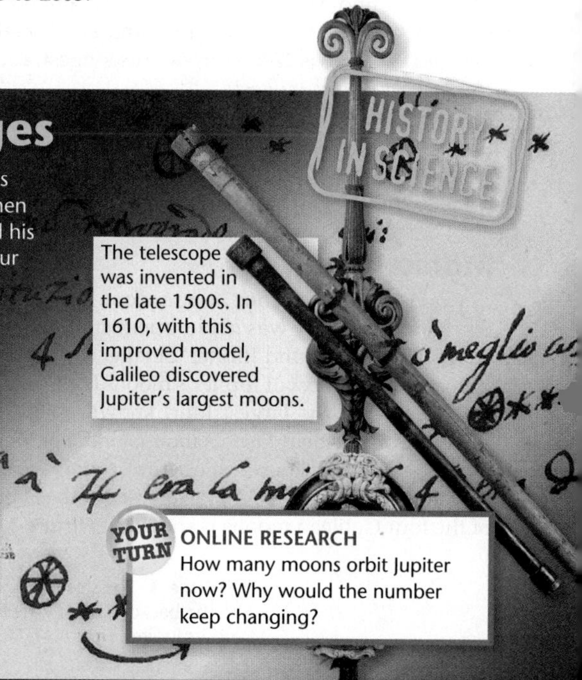

The telescope was invented in the late 1500s. In 1610, with this improved model, Galileo discovered Jupiter's largest moons.

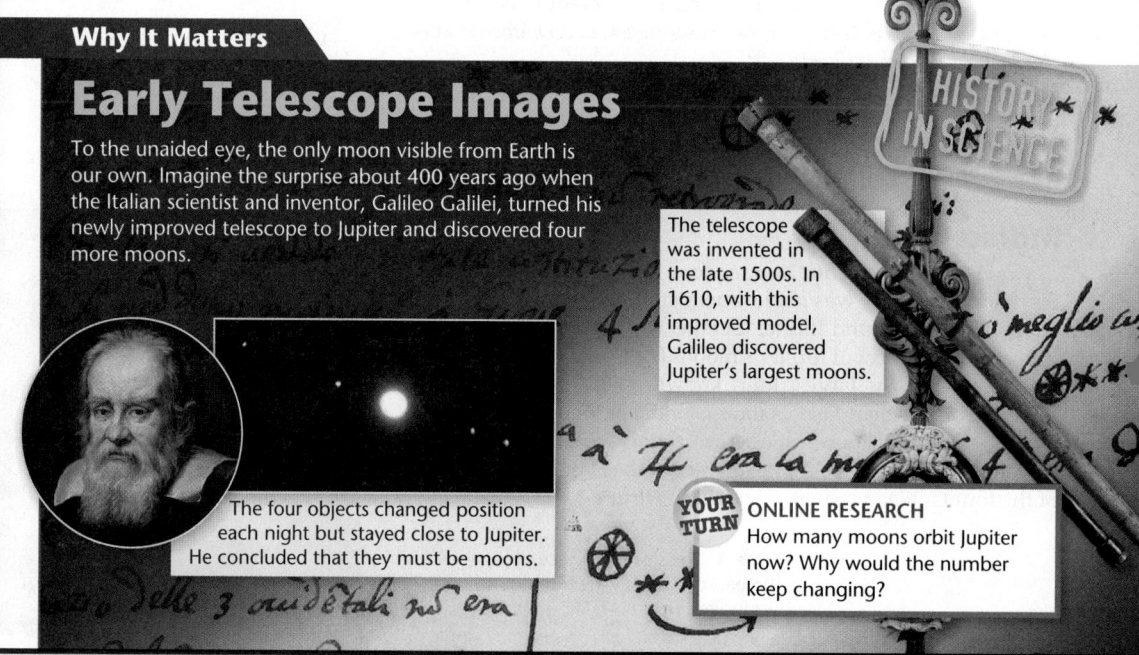

The four objects changed position each night but stayed close to Jupiter. He concluded that they must be moons.

YOUR TURN **ONLINE RESEARCH**
How many moons orbit Jupiter now? Why would the number keep changing?

Why It Matters

Early Telescope Images In 1610, when Galileo turned his telescope toward Jupiter, the planet was second only to the Moon as the brightest object in the night sky. Jupiter's brightness attracted his interest and he noted three "stars" arranged in a line near it. Intrigued, he observed again the next night, only to discover that the "stars" had shifted position. Over a period of eight nights of observation, Galileo determined that there were actually four such objects and that even though their positions changed they remained within Jupiter's sphere of influence. He concluded that these planet-like bodies in orbit around Jupiter must be moons.

Answer to Your Turn

Online Research There are known to be at least 63 moons orbiting Jupiter. This number keeps increasing, however, as our telescopes become more and more powerful.

Europa

Europa is the second closest Galilean moon to Jupiter. Europa is about the size of Earth's moon and it is slightly less dense than Earth's moon. Astronomers think that Europa has a rock core that is covered with a crust of ice that is about 100 km thick. Images of Europa, such as the one shown in **Figure 3,** show cracks in this enormous ice sheet.

Scientists have concluded from observations made from spacecraft that an ocean of liquid water may exist under this blanket of ice. If liquid water exists, simple forms of life could also exist there. Astronomers have no evidence of life on Europa, but many think Europa would be a good place to investigate the possibility of extraterrestrial life.

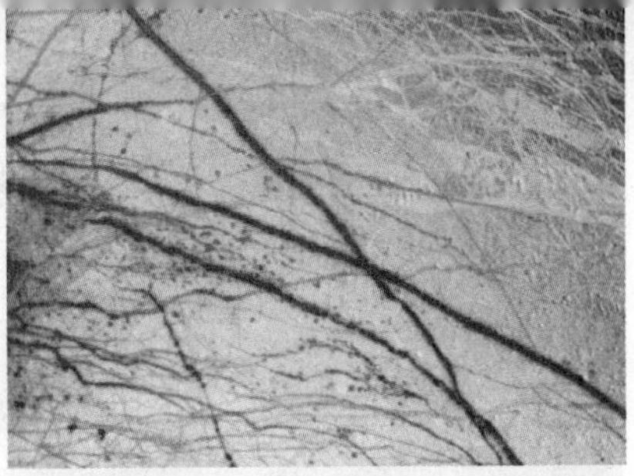

Figure 3 This false-color image of Europa shows immense cracks across its ice sheets.

Ganymede

Ganymede is the third Galilean moon from Jupiter. Ganymede is also the largest moon in the solar system, even larger than the planet Mercury. However, Ganymede has a relatively small mass because it is probably composed mostly of ice mixed with rock.

Images of Ganymede, such as **Figure 4,** show dark, crater-filled areas. Other light areas show marks that are thought to be long ridges and valleys. The *Galileo* spacecraft provided evidence to support the existence of a magnetic field around Ganymede. Ganymede is the only moon in the solar system that is known to have its own magnetic field. This magnetic field is completely surrounded by Jupiter's much more powerful magnetic field.

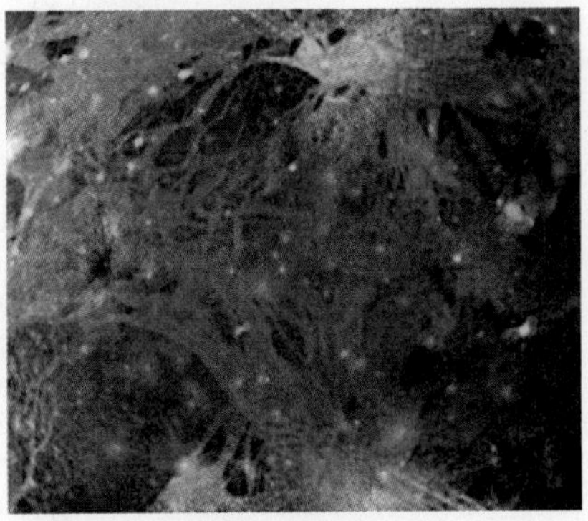

Figure 4 Much of Ganymede's surface is covered with ridges and valleys.

Callisto

Of the four Galilean moons, Callisto is the farthest from Jupiter. Callisto is similar to Ganymede in size, density, and composition. However, Callisto has a much rougher surface than Ganymede does. In fact, Callisto is one of the most densely cratered moons in our solar system.

Like craters on Earth's moon and other bodies in our solar system, craters on Callisto are the result of collisions that occurred early in the history of the solar system. **Figure 5** shows a giant impact basin that is 600 km across and a set of concentric rings that extend about 1,500 km outward in all directions from the crater.

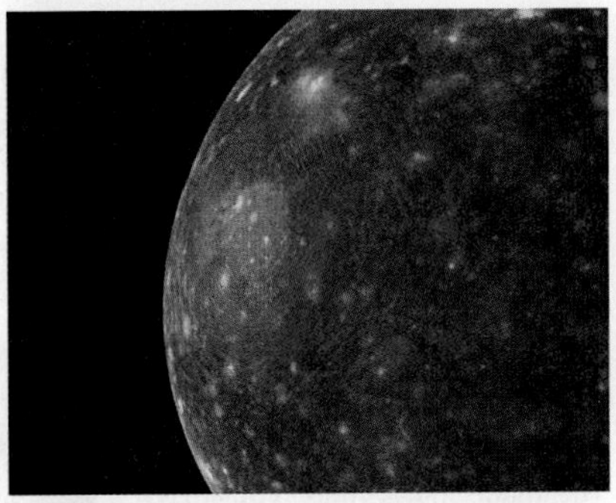

Figure 5 "Ripples" of ice and rock radiate out from this impact crater, called *Valhalla*, on Callisto.

Reading Check **Name one feature of each of the Galilean moons.**

Using the Figure — GENERAL

Geologic Pasts Use the photos of the surfaces of Io, Europa, Ganymede, and Callisto to stimulate a discussion of the diverse geology of Jupiter's moons. Ask students which moon is the most geologically active and why they know that. (Massive volcanoes make Io the most geologically active. Io is continuously being resurfaced as lava flows erase any craters.) Point out that the ice-covered surface of Europa is also remarkably smooth and uncratered. Its craters have been erased, perhaps by liquid water flowing through its cracked surface. Ask students to describe the surface of Ganymede. (It has mountains, ridges, valleys, craters, and dark lava flows.) Explain that some of the grooved features on Ganymede's surface appear to be the result of tectonic processes. Ask students which moon's surface exhibits the most ancient surface features. (Callisto, because its surface is covered by large impact craters from the early days of the solar system.) **LS Visual**

Answer to Reading Check

Io's surface is covered with many active volcanoes. Europa's surface is covered by an enormous ice sheet. Ganymede is the largest moon in the solar system and has a strong magnetic field. Callisto's surface is heavily cratered.

Differentiated Instruction

Special Education Students

Mnemonics Using mnemonic techniques may help students remember the names for the main moons of each planet. Encourage students to invent mnemonic devices for each planet and its main moons. Example 1: Mark phoned Desi (Mars—Phobos, Deimos). Example 2: Judy ignored Eddie Gand's calls (Jupiter—Io, Europa, Ganymede, Callisto). **LS Verbal**

Environmental Connection

Hidden Ocean, Hidden Life? Scientists who are looking for extraterrestrial life are focusing on Jupiter's moon Europa. Oceanographer David Karl has been studying microscopic life in Antarctica, an environment similar to Europa's. Karl hopes to discover ways to sample liquids under frozen ice without contaminating the liquids. This technology could be used to search for signs of life on Europa. Invite students to research the evidence for life on Europa and the biology of microbes in extreme environments on Earth. **LS Auditory/Verbal**

Teach, *continued*

Using the Figure — BASIC

Ringmaster Direct students' attention to the picture of Saturn's family. Have them describe the bodies that make up the Saturn system. (Saturn, the second largest planet in the solar system, is encircled by hundreds of icy rings, one large moon called Titan, and dozens of other moons of various sizes.) Ask students to estimate the relative size of Saturn based on the scale of the image. (Answers may vary but students should realize that Saturn would be extremely large. Students may wish to use butcher paper to try to draw a scale version of the planet.) **LS Visual**

READING TOOLBOX — GENERAL

Two-Column Notes

Two-column notes should include all the key ideas for Section 3. The first key idea is shown in two-column note form below.

Key Idea	Detail Notes
Characteristics of the two moons of Mars	– Phobos and Deimos – irregularly shaped rocks thought to be captured asteroids – revolve around Mars fairly quickly – dark because of plentiful maria

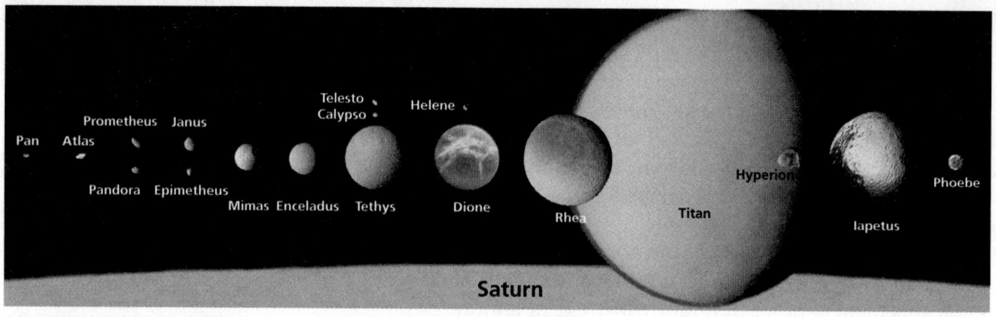

Figure 6 This composite image shows Saturn and many of Saturn's largest moons. The distances of the moons from Saturn and from each other are not to scale.

Moons of Saturn

Saturn has dozens of moons. Most of them are small, icy bodies that have many craters. However, five of Saturn's moons are fairly large. These five moons and many of Saturn's other moons are shown in **Figure 6.**

Titan

Saturn's largest moon, called Titan, has a diameter of more than 5,000 km. Only Jupiter's moon Ganymede is larger. Unlike any of the other moons in our solar system, Titan has a thick atmosphere that is composed mainly of nitrogen. Titan's atmosphere is so thick that hydrocarbon smog conceals most of the surface.

In 2005, the *Huygens* (HIE guhnz) probe, part of the Cassini mission, gathered data about Titan's atmosphere. The information it gathered is giving scientists clues about how Titan and its atmosphere formed. When the probe got below much of the atmosphere's haze, it sent back clear images of the surface, which showed signs of flowing liquid, probably methane. *Cassini* also sent back many images of Titan, an example of which is shown in **Figure 7.**

READING TOOLBOX

Two-Column Notes
Create two-column notes to review the main ideas for Sections 3 and 4. Put the main ideas in the left column, and add details and examples in your own words in the right column. Use as a model the two-column notes table that you started at the beginning of the chapter.

Saturn's Other Moons

Saturn's icy moons resemble Jupiter's icy Galilean moons. Enceladus has erupting geysers and so may have underground water near its surface. For that reason, it may be a better place to look for life than Europa. Saturn's other smaller moons have irregular shapes. Scientists think that many of the smallest moons, such as Janus, were captured by Saturn's gravity.

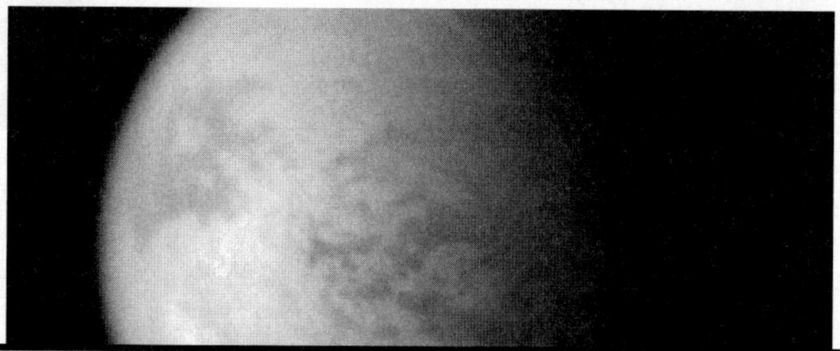

Figure 7 This image of Titan was taken by the Cassini mission in 2008. The image shows Titan in polarized infrared wavelengths by which clouds can be seen in its atmosphere.

Demonstration — GENERAL

Shepherd Moons You will need a rotating stand or turntable. Scatter talcum powder or fine sand on the rotating surface. Explain that the powder represents the chunks of ice that make up planetary rings. Tape two pencils together with their points even to represent the inner moons of the Saturn system. Spin the disk. Lower the pencil points into the powder while spinning the disk. Ask students to describe what happens. (Sample answer: The pencils push the powder aside to clear two paths.) Invite a volunteer to compare the model to how inner moons affect planetary rings. (Sample answer: Moons moving within the rings cause the materials that make up the rings to form separate bands.) **LS Visual**

Meteorology Connection — GENERAL

Titan's Atmosphere The chemistry of Titan's atmosphere appears to be similar to that of Earth's nitrogen atmosphere before living things introduced oxygen and modified it. However, the surface temperature is much colder. On Titan, methane may play the same role as water does on Earth: forming clouds, condensing as rain, and forming oceans on the surface. Studying Titan's atmosphere and surface may give scientists important clues to how life got started on Earth. Invite students to learn more about the Cassini/Huygens mission to Saturn and Titan. **LS Verbal/Auditory**

Moons of Uranus and Neptune

Uranus's four largest moons, Oberon, Titania, Umbriel, and Ariel, were known by the mid-1800s. A fifth, Miranda, was discovered in 1948 and is shown in **Figure 8.** Other much smaller moons have been discovered recently by using spacecraft and orbiting observatories such as the *Hubble Space Telescope*. Astronomers know that Uranus has at least two dozen small moons.

Neptune has at least 13 moons. Triton, a large icy moon, is unusual because it revolves around Neptune in a backward, or *retrograde,* orbit. Some astronomers think that Triton has an unusual orbit because the moon was captured by the gravity of Neptune after forming elsewhere in the solar system and then coming too close to the planet. Triton's diameter is 2,705 km, and the moon has a thin atmosphere.

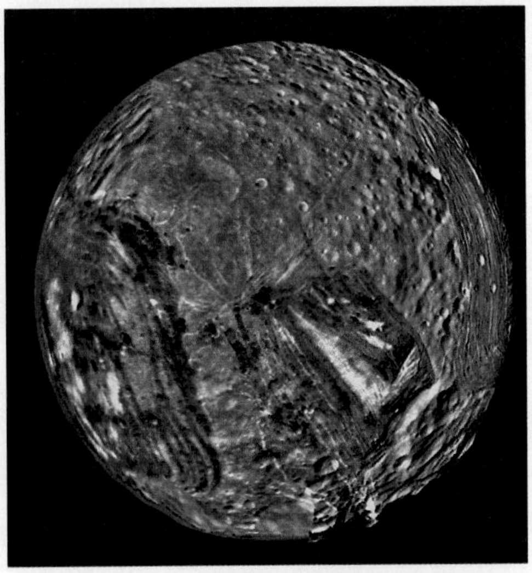

Figure 8 Uranus's moon called Miranda shows intriguing evidence of past geologic activity.

Pluto's Moons

Although Pluto is no longer officially considered a planet, it does have at least three moons. Pluto's largest moon, Charon (KER uhn), is almost half the size of Pluto. In fact, because Pluto and Charon are so similar in mass, they both orbit a common balance point, or *barycenter*, that is located between them. Charon orbits Pluto in 6.4 days, the same length of time as a day on Pluto. Because of these equal lengths, Charon stays in the same place in Pluto's sky. In the same way that one side of Earth's moon always faces Earth, one side of Pluto always faces Charon.

Pluto's other two moons, Hydra and Nix, are much smaller. These moons were discovered in 2005 by astronomers using the *Hubble Space Telescope*. These moons also orbit the barycenter between Pluto and Charon.

Reading Check **Identify two ways Charon is different from other moons.**

SCILINKS.
www.scilinks.org
Topic: Moons of Other Planets
Code: HQX0993

Figure 9 Pluto was discovered in 1930, Charon was discovered in 1978, and two smaller moons, Nix and Hydra, were discovered in 2005. (The spikes of light in the image are effects of the telescope.)

Close

Reteaching — BASIC

Peer Reviewing Divide the class into pairs or small groups. Have each student write five questions that can be answered by using information from the section. Have students use the questions to quiz each other on the section material. **LS Interpersonal**

Quiz — GENERAL

1. What are the names of the moons of Mars? (Phobos and Deimos)
2. What was the role of the Voyager mission in uncovering the secrets of Io's geology? (An engineer scanning images taken of Io discovered erupting volcanoes. Scientists later determined the role of gravitation, including tidal forces.)
3. How is Pluto's largest moon unique? (Charon is unique because it is so close in size to the body that it orbits.)

Answer to Reading Check

Charon is almost half the size of the body it orbits. Charon's orbital period is the same length as Pluto's day, so one side of Pluto always faces its largest moon.

Activity — GENERAL

Planetary Rings Draw a Venn diagram on the board. Label one circle with "Saturn's Rings" and the other with "Rings of Other Gas Giants." Ask students to write words and phrases that describe the differences between the two topics in the outer parts of the two circles. Then, have students list similarities in the area where the two circles overlap. Ask students why the outer planets have ring systems. (Tidal forces close to the gas giants cause planetary rings.) **LS Visual/Verbal**

Close, *continued*

Answers to Section Review

1. Both are small, irregularly shaped bodies that have cratered surfaces and dark regions; Phobos is larger than Deimos.
2. Answers may vary. Sample answer: Io—active volcanoes; Europa—liquid water beneath its icy surface; Ganymede—larger than Mercury; Callisto—heavily cratered
3. by researchers studying the images taken by spacecraft
4. because heat is created in Io's crust by friction caused by the gravitational pull of Jupiter; the heat melts the rocks in the moon's interior.
5. by observatories such as the *Hubble Space Telescope*
6. Triton revolves around Neptune in a backward orbit, which suggests that Triton was "captured" when it got too close to Neptune.
7. Saturn has the most extensive ring system. The other gas giants have much thinner ring systems. Saturn's may be the remains of a comet ripped apart by tidal forces, while Jupiter's may result from particles given off by Io, or debris from meteor collisions. Uranus has a dozen thin rings. Neptune's rings are clumpy and not uniform.
8. Although Ganymede is larger than Mercury, its density is relatively low, which suggests that it may contain mostly ice in its interior rather than rock or iron.
9. Sample answer: Many moons may have formed from materials remaining after the planet they orbit formed, or they may have resulted from collisions. Other moons were captured later. Ring systems appear to result from the break up of comets and moons or from debris left over from collisions.
10. Triton probably retains a thin atmosphere because it is much larger and cooler than Phobos and has sufficient mass to allow its gravity to hold onto the volatile gases.
11. Most planets have *natural satellites*, called *moons*, such as *Mars's* moons *Phobos* and *Deimos*, *Jupiter's Galilean moons*, *Saturn's* moon *Titan*, *Uranus's* moon *Titania*. *Pluto's* largest moon is named *Charon*. Many planets also have *rings* such as those around *Saturn*.

Figure 10 Saturn has the most extensive system of rings in the solar system. The angle at which its rings are visible changes as Saturn orbits the sun.

Rings of the Gas Giants

Saturn's spectacular set of rings, shown in **Figure 10,** was discovered more than 300 years ago. Each of the rings circling Saturn is divided into hundreds of small ringlets. The ringlets are composed of billions of pieces of rock and ice. These pieces range in size from particles the size of dust to chunks the size of a house. Each piece follows its own orbit around Saturn. The ring system of Saturn is very thin.

Originally, astronomers thought that the rings formed from material that was unable to clump together to form moons while Saturn was forming. However, evidence indicates that the rings are much younger than originally thought. Now, most scientists think that the rings are the remains of a large cometlike body that entered Saturn's system and was ripped apart by tidal forces. Particles from the rings continue to spiral into Saturn, but the rings are replenished by particles given off by Saturn's moons.

The other gas giants have rings as well. These rings are relatively narrow. Jupiter's were not discovered until the *Voyager 1* spacecraft flew by Jupiter in 1979. Jupiter has a single, thin ring made of microscopic particles that may have been given off by Io or one of Jupiter's other moons. The particles may also be debris from collisions of comets or meteorites with Jupiter's moons. Uranus also has a dozen thin rings. Neptune's relatively small number of rings are clumpy rather than thin and uniform.

Section 3 Review

Key Ideas

1. **Compare** the characteristics of Phobos and Deimos.
2. **List** the four moons of Jupiter that were discovered by Galileo, and identify one distinguishing characteristic of each.
3. **Describe** how volcanoes were discovered on Io.
4. **Explain** why Io remains volcanically active.
5. **Describe** how the smaller moons of Uranus were discovered.
6. **Explain** why Triton has an unusual orbit.
7. **Compare** the characteristics of Saturn's rings with the rings of the other outer planets.

Critical Thinking

8. **Analyzing Relationships** Explain why scientists think that Ganymede's interior includes ice.
9. **Inferring Relationships** Compare and contrast the way in which moons and ring systems form.
10. **Making Comparisons** Explain why Triton retains an atmosphere while Phobos does not.

Concept Mapping

11. Use the following terms to create a concept map: *moon, ring, Mars, Uranus, Jupiter, Saturn, Phobos, Deimos, Pluto, Galilean moon, natural satellite, Charon, Titania,* and *Titan.*

Differentiated Instruction

Alternative Assessment

Satellite Bingo Have students work in groups to create a bingo game that focuses on the characteristics of the moons of the solar system. Head the columns with the names of moons and identify four distinct features under each name. Use pictures as well as words and phrases to describe the features. Each card should have a different combination of moons and features. Students can play the game using pennies as markers. Four matching features in a row (up, down, or across) wins. **LS Verbal/Kinesthetic**

SECTION 4

Asteroids, Comets, and Meteoroids

Key Ideas	Key Terms	Why It Matters
❯ Describe the physical characteristics of asteroids and comets. ❯ Describe where the Kuiper Belt is located. ❯ Compare meteoroids, meteorites, and meteors. ❯ Explain the relationship between the Oort cloud and comets.	asteroid comet Kuiper Belt Oort cloud meteoroid meteor	Some asteroids are close enough to Earth that they could cause significant damage if one were to strike Earth. For this reason, some scientists keep track of known asteroids and their orbits.

In addition to the sun, the planets, and the planets' moons, our solar system includes millions of smaller bodies. Some of these small bodies are tiny bits of dust or ice that orbit the sun. Other bodies are as big as small moons. Astronomers theorize that these smaller bodies are leftover debris from the formation of the solar system.

Asteroids

The largest of the minor bodies in the solar system are called asteroids. **Asteroids** are fragments of rock that orbit the sun. Astronomers have discovered more than 300,000 asteroids. Millions of asteroids may exist in the solar system. The orbits of asteroids, like those of the planets, are ellipses. The largest known asteroid, Ceres, has a diameter of about 1,000 km. Because it is large enough that gravity has caused it to become round, Ceres is also considered to be a dwarf planet. Two other asteroids are shown in **Figure 1**.

Most asteroids are located in a region between the orbits of Mars and Jupiter known as the *asteroid belt*. This main belt extends from about 299 million to about 598 million kilometers from the sun. However, not all asteroids are located in the main asteroid belt. The closest asteroids to the sun are inside the orbit of Mars, about 224 million kilometers from the sun. The *Trojan asteroids* are concentrated in groups just ahead of and just behind Jupiter as it orbits the sun. In fact, the Trojan asteroids almost share Jupiter's orbit. These asteroids are named for the Trojan and Greek warriors of the famous Trojan War of Greek mythology. Asteroids also exist beyond Jupiter's orbit.

asteroid a small, rocky object that orbits the sun; most asteroids are located in a band between the orbits of Mars and Jupiter

Figure 1 This image of the asteroids Ida (left) and Dactyl (right) were taken by the spacecraft *Galileo* as it passed through the asteroid belt on its way to Jupiter. Ida is 56 km long, and Dactyl is 1.5 km across.

Key Resources

Chapter Resource File
- Directed Reading BASIC

Technology
- Transparencies
  Bellringer

Section 4

Focus

Overview

This section describes characteristics of asteroids, various kinds of meteors, and comets and explains what these small bodies can teach us about the early history of Earth's solar system.

Bellringer

Ask students to write brief descriptions of meteorites, comets, and asteroids or to draw pictures of what these bodies are like. (Answers may vary.) **LS Visual**

Motivate

Discussion — GENERAL

Asteroid Motions Explain that asteroids are essentially large rocks and that they range in size from the size of boulders to the size of a small moon. Ask students to describe where these small objects are located and how they move. (Sample answers: Most orbit the sun in elliptical orbits like the major planets in a ring or belt between the orbits of Mars and Jupiter.) **LS Verbal**

Teach

READING TOOLBOX

Word Origins

Students should include the following information in their chart. Ida: named after a nymph in Greek mythology who lived on Mount Ida; Dactyl: named after Dactyli, the mythical group of people who lived on Mount Ida; Halley's, Hale-Bopp, McNaught, Wild 2, and Tempel 1 comets were all named after the person or people who first saw the comet or who made an important discovery regarding the comet.

Using the Figure GENERAL

Comparing Craters Explain that even if a surface was solid before an impact, when a body is large and fast enough, the ground partially liquefies during impact, forming more complex crater features such as a central peak. Provide photos of craters on the moon or other planets for students to compare with Barringer Meteor Crater. Good sources for images are NASA Web sites or the National Science Teachers Association book about craters. LS **Visual**

Answer to Reading Check

The most common type is made mostly of carbon materials. The second type is made mostly of silicate minerals. Other asteroids are made mostly of metals such as iron and nickel.

Academic Vocabulary

composition (KAHM puh ZISH uhn) the substances that make up an object

SCILINKS.
www.scilinks.org
Topic: Comets, Asteroids, and Meteoroids
Code: **HQX0317**

Composition of Asteroids

The composition of asteroids is similar to that of the inner planets. Asteroids are classified according to their composition into three main categories. The most common of the three types of asteroids is made mostly of carbon materials, which give this type of asteroid a dark color. The second type of asteroid is made of mostly silicate minerals. These asteroids look like Earth rocks. The third, and rarest, type of asteroid is composed of mostly iron and nickel. These asteroids have a shiny, metallic appearance, especially on fresh surfaces.

Many astronomers think that asteroids in the asteroid belt are made of material that was not able to form a planet because of the strong gravitational force of Jupiter. Scientists estimate that the total mass of all asteroids is less than the mass of Earth's moon.

Near-Earth Asteroids

More than a thousand asteroids have orbits that sometimes bring them very close to Earth. These asteroids have wide, elliptical orbits that bring them near Earth's orbit. Thus they are called *near-Earth asteroids*. Near-Earth asteroids make up only a small percentage of the total number of asteroids in the solar system.

Interest in near-Earth asteroids has increased in recent years with the realization that these asteroids could inflict great damage on Earth if they were to strike the planet. Meteor Crater, in Arizona, which is shown in **Figure 2**, formed when a small asteroid that had a diameter of less than 50 m struck Earth about 49,000 years ago. Several recently established asteroid detection programs have begun to track all asteroids whose orbits may approach Earth. By identifying and monitoring these asteroids, scientists hope to predict and possibly avoid future collisions.

READING TOOLBOX

Word Origins
The asteroid Pallas is named after the Greek goddess of wisdom, war, and the arts, Pallas Athena. As you read Section 4, find the origins of the names of asteroids and comets. Add them to the table that you started at the beginning of the chapter.

Reading Check **What are the three types of asteroids by composition?**

Figure 2 Barringer Meteorite Crater, also known simply as Meteor Crater, in Arizona, has a diameter of more than 1 km. Dozens of such craters have resulted from past impacts on Earth, but most craters have eroded or have been covered by sediment.

Environmental Connection

Target Earth Several asteroid groups follow orbits that bring them very close to Earth. Research suggests that terrestrial impacts may seriously disrupt the environment and influence life on Earth. For example, an asteroid that struck 65 million years ago may have played a part in the extinction of the dinosaurs. The rock vaporized when it struck, releasing kinetic energy that blasted a hole in the ocean floor near what is now the Yucatan Peninsula, generated enormous tsunamis, and produced heat waves that created global forest fires. The impact sent a cloud of dust and debris into the atmosphere that remained for months, blocking sunlight and interfering with photosynthesis. This event probably temporarily cooled the climate, caused acid rain, and introduced greenhouse gases. It left behind a chemical signature and impact-melted glass that attest to the projectile's extraterrestrial origin. More than 150 impact craters of various ages have been identified on Earth. Invite interested students to investigate the potential effects of impacts and share their findings in oral reports and presentations. LS **Verbal**

Figure 3 A comet, such as Comet Hale-Bopp consists of a nucleus, a coma, and two tails. The blue streak is the *ion tail,* and the white streak is the *dust tail.*

Comets

Every few years, an object that looks like a star that has a tail is visible in the evening sky. This object is a comet. **Comets** are small bodies of ice, rock, and cosmic dust that follow highly elliptical orbits around the sun. The most famous is Halley's Comet, which passes by Earth every 76 years. It last passed Earth in 1986 and will return in 2061. Every 5 to 10 years, another very bright comet will be visible from Earth. Comet Hale-Bopp, shown in **Figure 3,** was particularly spectacular as it passed Earth in 1997, as was comet McNaught in 2007.

comet a small body of rock, ice, and cosmic dust that follows an elliptical orbit around the sun and that gives off gas and dust in the form of a tail as it passes close to the sun

Composition of Comets

A comet has several parts. The core, or nucleus, of a comet is made of rock, metals, and ice. Cores of comets are commonly between 1 km and 100 km in diameter. A spherical cloud of gas and dust, called the *coma,* surrounds the nucleus. The coma can extend as far as 1 million kilometers from the nucleus. A comet's bright appearance largely results from sunlight reflected by the comet's coma. The nucleus and the coma form the head of the comet. In 2004, the spacecraft *Stardust* flew by a comet named Wild 2. It returned samples from the comet's coma to Earth in 2006. In 2005, the spacecraft, *Deep Impact,* slammed a probe into the nucleus of comet Temple 1. The probe released a plume of dust, giving scientists a look at what a comet's nucleus is made of. The *Rosetta* spacecraft will go into orbit around a comet in 2014 and will drop a lander onto its surface.

The most spectacular parts of a comet are its tails. Tails form when sunlight causes the comet's ice to change to gas. The gas, or ion, tail of a comet streams from the comet's head. The solar wind—electrically charged particles expanding away from the sun—pushes the gas away from the comet's head. Thus, regardless of the direction the comet travels, its ion tail points away from the sun. The comet's second tail is made of dust and curves backward along the comet's orbit. Some comets have tails that are more than 80 million kilometers long.

MISCONCEPTION ALERT

Comet Tails Students may think that comet tails always extend backward in the direction the comet is coming from. The nucleus of a comet is composed of ices, along with bits of dust and rock. The sun's heat makes these ices change directly into gases and produces jets of glowing charged ions—the ion tail. The solar wind pushes these charged particles outward, so that the ion tail always points away from the sun, even as the comet swings around the sun to leave the inner solar system. Some comets also have a second curved tail composed of dust that does point back along the path that the comet has traveled.

Using the Figure GENERAL

Discussion Direct students' attention to the picture of comet Hale-Bopp, one of the most spectacular comets of the last century. Explain that Hale-Bopp is a long-period comet that is believed to have last visited the inner solar system more that 4,000 years ago. No two comets ever look exactly alike. Ask students to describe the basic features of this comet that are visible in the picture. (Sample answer: The comet has a glowing head, or coma, and has both a blue ion tail and a white dust tail.) LS **Visual**

Differentiated Instruction

Advanced Learners

Comets Have students use the NASA website to learn more about one of the comets mentioned in this section. Individually or in groups, have students prepare an informational poster about the comet. The poster should include information about the comet's composition, when it last was and will be again visible from Earth, whether it is thought to have originated in the Kuiper Belt or the Oort cloud, and any recent research on the comet. LS **Verbal/Visual**

Using the Figure GENERAL

Oort Cloud Distances Help students to visualize the vast distances involved with a region of space as far from Earth as the Oort cloud by comparing the distance to a familiar landmark. Tell students that at the scale in which the drawing of the Oort cloud was made, the outer edge of the sphere would be 0.4 km in diameter. Have students identify a landmark or city that is about that distance (about 1/4 mile) from the school. Explain that the diagram would have to be stretched from their school to that landmark for the image to be to scale. LS **Logical**

Internet Activity GENERAL

Kuiper Belt Objects Pluto shares a similar orbit and composition with thousands of other small bodies of rock and ice that travel around the sun in a region called the *Kuiper Belt.* These objects may be among the most primitive objects in the solar system. Invite interested students to research icy Kuiper Belt objects such as Eris, Makemake, Haumea, Sedna, Orcus, Quaoar, and Varuna, and report their findings to the class. A worksheet designed to direct student research on this topic can be found in the **Chapter Resource File** booklet or by visiting www.thinkcentral.com and entering the keyword **HQXMBSX.** LS **Verbal**

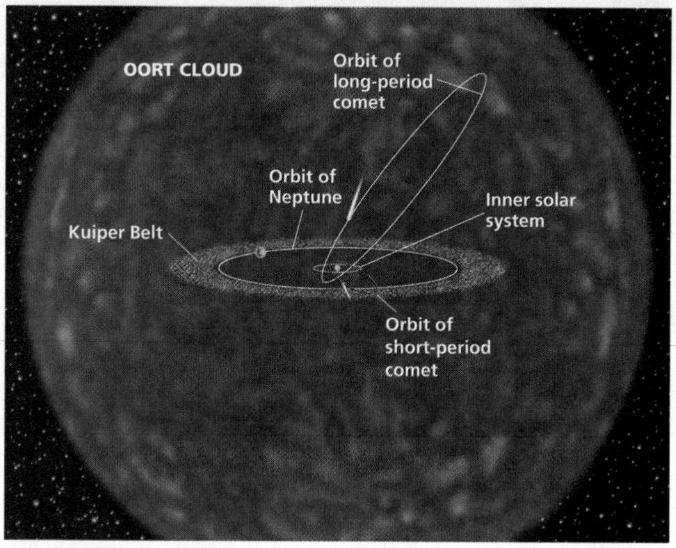

Figure 4 Most comets come from the Oort cloud, a region in the outer solar system that is far beyond the orbit of Neptune.

The Kuiper Belt

Recent advances in technology have allowed scientists to observe thousands of small objects beyond the orbit of Neptune. Most of these objects, including some comets, are from a ring of icy bodies called the **Kuiper Belt** (KIE puhr BELT), which is located just beyond Neptune's orbit. The Kuiper Belt is also illustrated in **Figure 4.** The dwarf planets Pluto and Eris are located in the Kuiper Belt. Several other objects that are candidates for dwarf-planet status also reside in the Kuiper Belt.

Kuiper Belt a region of the solar system that starts just beyond the orbit of Neptune and that contains dwarf planets and other small bodies made mostly of ice

Oort cloud a spherical region that surrounds the solar system, that extends from the Kuiper Belt to almost halfway to the nearest star, and that contains billions of comets

The Oort Cloud

Astronomers think that most comets originate in the Oort cloud, which is illustrated in **Figure 4.** The **Oort cloud** is a spherical cloud of dust and ice that lies far beyond Neptune's orbit and that contains the nuclei of billions of comets. The total mass of the Oort cloud is estimated to be between 10 and 40 Earth masses.

The Oort cloud surrounds the solar system and may reach as far as halfway to the nearest star. Scientists think that the matter in the Oort cloud was left over from the formation of the solar system. Studying this distant matter helps scientists understand the early history of the solar system.

Bodies within the Oort cloud circle the sun so slowly that they take a few million years to complete one orbit. But the gravity of a star that passes near the solar system may cause a comet to fall into a more elliptical orbit around the sun. The orbits of comets that pass by Jupiter may also be changed by Jupiter's gravitational force. If a comet takes more than 200 years to complete one orbit of the sun, the comet is called a *long-period comet*.

Why It Matters

Comet Decay Comets are very fragile bodies. The gas and dust blown off most comets is lost into space. In a natural aging process, some comets simply turn into dark, rocky bodies that resemble asteroids. Many short-lived comets break apart as a result of tidal forces caused by the gravity of large planets or of the sun. The debris trail from a comet's break-up may rain down on the inner planets as meteor showers. If comets are pulled completely from their orbits, they may collide with the sun or with one of the other planets. Comet Shoemaker-Levy 9 broke apart in 1994 and crashed into Jupiter's atmosphere.

Short-Period Comets

Comets called *short-period comets* take less than 200 years to complete one orbit around the sun. In recent years, astronomers have discovered that most short-period comets come from the Kuiper Belt. Some of the comets that originate in the Kuiper Belt have been forced outward into the Oort cloud by Jupiter's gravity. Many comets in the Kuiper Belt are the result of collisions between larger Kuiper-Belt objects there. Halley's comet, which has a period of 76 years, is a short-period comet.

Math Skills

Matter From Space
Astronomers estimate that about 1 million kg of matter from meteoroids falls to Earth each day. Based on this estimate, how many kilograms of matter from meteoroids would fall on Earth in three weeks?

Meteoroids

In addition to relatively large asteroids and comets, very small bits of rock or metal move throughout the solar system. These small, rocky bodies are called **meteoroids.** Most meteoroids have a diameter of less than 1 mm. Scientists think that most meteoroids are pieces of matter that become detached from passing comets. Large meteoroids—more than 1 cm in diameter—are probably the result of collisions between asteroids.

meteoroid a relatively small, rocky body that travels through space

meteor a bright streak of light that results when a meteoroid burns up in Earth's atmosphere

Meteors

Meteoroids that travel through space on an orbit that takes them directly into Earth's path may enter Earth's atmosphere. When a meteoroid enters Earth's atmosphere, friction between the object and the air molecules heats the meteoroid's surface. As a result of this friction and heat, most meteoroids burn up in the atmosphere. As a meteoroid burns up in Earth's atmosphere, the meteoroid produces a bright streak of light called a **meteor.** Meteors are commonly called *shooting stars.* Meteoroids sometimes also vaporize very quickly in a brilliant flash of light called a *fireball*. Observers on Earth may hear a loud noise as a fireball disintegrates.

When a large number of small meteoroids enter Earth's atmosphere in a short period of time, a *meteor shower* occurs. During the most spectacular of these showers, several meteors are visible every minute. A composite photo of a meteor shower is shown in **Figure 5.** Meteor showers occur at the same time each year. This happens because Earth intersects the orbits of comets that have left behind a trail of dust. As these particles burn up in Earth's atmosphere, they appear as meteors streaking across the sky.

Reading Check **What is the difference between a meteor and a meteoroid?**

Figure 5 The straight lines in this composite photo are meteors burning up as they move through Earth's atmosphere.

Math Skills

Answer
1 million kg/d × 7 d/wk × 3 wk = 21,000,000 kg of matter

Close

Reteaching — BASIC

Crater Features Spread newspapers beneath a box lid. Fill the lid about half full with flour. Sprinkle a layer of tempera paint over the flour and smooth the surface. Have students drop a pebble from various heights and then draw the features of the craters that form. **LS Kinesthetic**

Quiz — GENERAL

1. How are asteroids and meteoroids related? (Scientists think most large meteoroids are fragments that break off when asteroids collide.)
2. How are scientists attempting to meet the threat represented by near-Earth asteroids? (They are attempting to monitor and track the positions of these asteroids to predict future collisions.)

Using the Figure — GENERAL

Leonid Meteor Shower The photo of the Leonid meteor shower is a composite of 30 separate 1-min exposures taken over Spain in 2003. The short exposures explain the lack of star trails. The Leonid meteor shower is associated with comet Tempel-Tuttle. The best time to spot meteors is during an annual meteor shower, when Earth passes through a concentration of meteoroids. Meteor showers are named for the constellation from which they appear to originate. Ask students what constellation the Leonid shower was named for. (Leo, the lion.) **LS Visual**

Answer to Reading Check
A meteoroid is a rocky body that travels through space. When a meteoroid enters Earth's atmosphere and begins to burn up, the meteoroid produces a meteor.

Close, *continued*

Answers to Section Review

1. between the orbits of Mars and Jupiter
2. Asteroids are fragments of rock, metals, and carbon that travel in elliptical orbits; they are the largest of the small bodies that orbit the sun.
3. nucleus—a core of rock, metals, and ice; coma—a cloud of gas and dust that surrounds the nucleus; ion tail; and dust tail
4. ion tail—electrically charged particles that point away from the sun; dust tail—debris that curves back along the comet's path
5. Most comets are believed to originate in the Oort cloud.
6. beyond Neptune's orbit
7. A meteoroid is a small body made of rock or metal that travels through space. The streak of light that results when a meteoroid enters an atmosphere is a meteor. A meteoroid that strikes the planetary surface without burning up is a meteorite.
8. The solar wind pushes the gases and particles of the ion tail away from the comet's head so that the gases and particles stream away from the sun.
9. Iron meteorites have a distinctive metallic appearance.

Figure 6 Types of Meteorites

Meteorites

Millions of meteoroids enter Earth's atmosphere each day. A few of these meteoroids do not burn up entirely in the atmosphere because they are relatively large. These meteoroids fall to Earth's surface. A meteoroid or any part of a meteoroid that is left when a meteoroid hits Earth is called a *meteorite*. Most meteorites are small and have a mass of less than 1 kg. However, large meteorites occasionally strike Earth's surface with the force of a large bomb. These impacts leave large impact craters.

Meteorites can be classified into three basic types: stony, iron, and stony-iron. These three types of meteorites are shown in **Figure 6.** *Stony meteorites* are similar in composition to rocks on Earth. Some stony meteorites contain carbon-bearing compounds that are similar to the carbon compounds in living organisms. Although most meteorites are stony, *iron meteorites* are easier to find. Iron meteorites are easier to find because they have a distinctive metallic appearance. This distinctive appearance makes iron meteorites easy to distinguish from common Earth rocks. The third type of meteorites, called *stony-iron meteorites,* contain iron and stone. Stony-iron meteorites are rare.

Astronomers think that almost all meteorites come from collisions between asteroids. The oldest meteoroids may be 100 million years older than Earth and its moon. Therefore, meteorites may provide information about how the early solar system formed.

Some rare meteorites originated on the moon or Mars. Computer simulations have shown that meteorites that hit the moon or Mars can eject rocks that then fall to Earth. Many of these rare meteorites have been found in Antarctica. Finding meteorites in Antarctica is relatively easy because they stand out against the background of snow and ice.

Section 4 Review

Key Ideas

1. **Identify** where the asteroid belt is located in the solar system.
2. **Describe** the physical characteristics of asteroids.
3. **List** the four main parts of a comet, and identify their physical characteristics.
4. **Compare** the ion and dust tails of a comet.
5. **Explain** the relationship between the Oort cloud and comets.
6. **Describe** the location of the Kuiper Belt.
7. **Distinguish** between a meteor, a meteoroid, and a meteorite.

Critical Thinking

8. **Analyzing Relationships** Explain why a comet's ion tail always points away from the sun.
9. **Making Comparisons** Explain how iron meteorites can be distinguished from common rocks of Earth's crust.
10. **Making Comparisons** You find a meteorite on the ground. What kind of meteorite did you most likely find? Describe two steps of its journey from space.

Concept Mapping

11. Use the following terms to create a concept map: *comet, asteroid, Kuiper Belt, Oort cloud, long-period comet, short-period comet,* and *meteoroid.*

10. Answers may vary. Sample answer: Most meteorites are stony, but metallic ones are easier to identify, so it is likely a stony or iron meteorite. Step one: A collision between two asteroids sends a meteoroid hurtling toward the inner solar system. Step two: The meteoroid crosses Earth's orbit, streaks through the atmosphere, and strikes Earth's surface.
11. Minor bodies include *asteroids*; *comets*, such as *short-period comets* that originate in the *Kuiper Belt* and *long-period comets* that originate in the *Oort cloud*; and *meteoroids.*

Differentiated Instruction

Alternative Assessment

Science Nonfiction Have students write a description of a trip through the solar system on one of the minor bodies—for example, the return of a long-lived comet from the Oort cloud to the inner solar system. Students should research their topic to make their stories accurate and entertaining. Have students outline the main points of the story before they begin writing. **LS Verbal**

Why It Matters

Dodging Space Debris

SCIENCE & SOCIETY

The glove that astronaut Edward White lost during the first U.S. spacewalk in 1965 was certainly the fastest-moving glove in history. It circled Earth repeatedly at a speed of 28,000 km/h before burning up in the atmosphere about a month later. The same fate awaits an average of 100 to 200 basketball-sized (or larger) objects each year, as well as innumerable objects 1 cm in size or smaller. NASA calls these objects orbital debris, but their more colorful name is space junk.

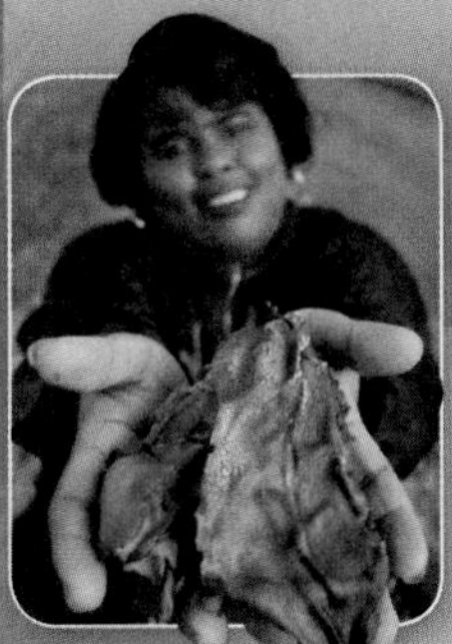

Lottie Williams, in Turley, Oklahoma, was grazed in the shoulder by a lightweight fragment. This is the only known case of a person being struck by space debris.

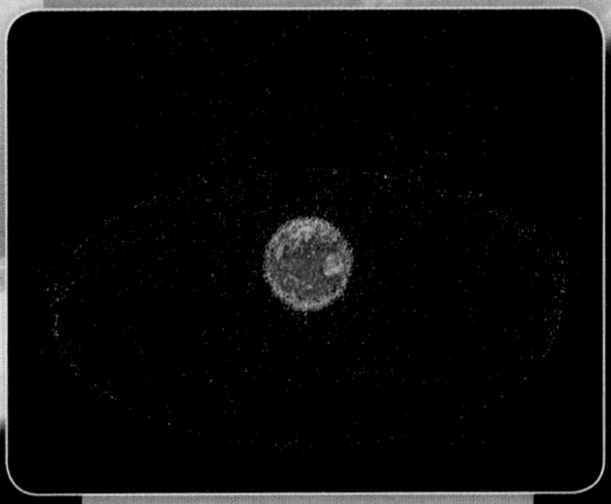

This graphic shows the estimated 100,000-plus pieces of space debris larger than 1 cm. Pieces less than 1 cm number many millions. Most do not survive reentry, so there is little danger to people or property.

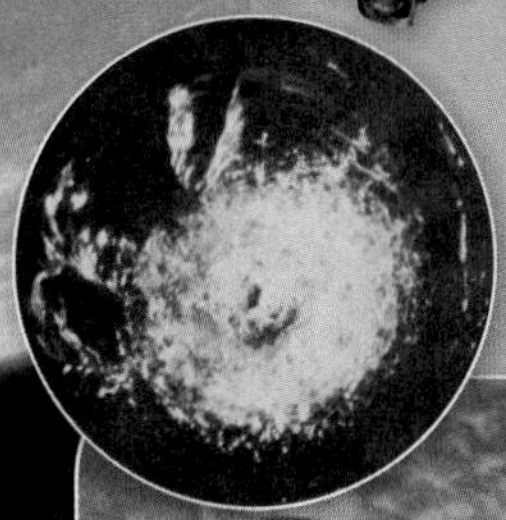

This windshield damage was caused by a 0.2 mm fragment of space debris traveling 3 to 6 km/s—equivalent to the damage from a rifle bullet.

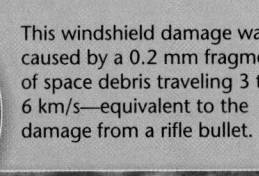

In 1997, this 32 kg pressure sphere and two other items from a Delta II rocket booster landed in Texas. A fourth booster item struck Lottie Williams.

YOUR TURN

UNDERSTANDING CONCEPTS
Even though most pieces of space debris are tiny, why are they an important concern?

CRITICAL THINKING
How can tiny pieces of debris cause such significant damage?

Why It Matters

Dodging Space Debris

Many bodies in the solar system have natural satellites—moons. In addition to our own Moon, Earth has millions of artificial satellites. Only a relatively small number of these are functional objects such as communications devices, space telescopes, and the unfinished International Space Station. Most of them are debris. Some debris has been ejected from piloted orbiters and space stations. Some are dead satellites and rocket parts. But the vast majority is bits and fragments formed by the collisions of pre-existing debris. All space missions must be planned with this debris field in mind. In addition, this debris must be (and is) tracked from Earth to determine when a given object may return to Earth and if its return poses a hazard. On occasion, objects survive the 320-km plummet through Earth's atmosphere. Nearly 60 objects have survived reentry, but there is only one reported case of a person being struck.

Answers to Your Turn

Understanding Concepts Although some pieces of space debris are tiny, they are traveling at very high speeds and can cause significant harm to satellites and other spacecraft and create additional new space junk in the process.

Critical Thinking Although the mass of a piece of space junk may be small, it is traveling at a very high velocity, so the force will be high.

Skills Practice Lab

Time Required
two 45-minute class periods

Lab Ratings
EASY ——— HARD

Teacher Preparation (1 flask)
Student Setup (1 flask)
Concept Level (3 flasks)
Cleanup (1 flask)

Skills Acquired
- Organizing and Analyzing Data
- Identifying and Recognizing Patterns

Scientific Methods
In this lab, students will
- Make Observations
- Test the Hypothesis
- Analyze the Results
- Draw Conclusions

Materials
Students can do this investigation with or without a partner.

Tips and Tricks
You may want to review the use of exponents in recording large numbers. Check student results in step 2 of the procedure, before letting them continue. If they do not calculate p^2 and a^3 carefully, they will arrive at the wrong value for K. Although students may get various values for K, when rounded, these values should be approximately equal to 300.

Skills Practice Lab

90 min

Galilean Moons of Jupiter

What You'll Do
- **Calculate** the value of a constant, K.
- **Explain** how Kepler's law of periods explains orbits of moons of Jupiter.

What You'll Need
calculator
metric ruler

Kepler's third law of motion—the law of periods—explains the relationship between a planet's distance from the sun and the planet's period (the time required to make one revolution around the sun). According to the law of periods, the cube of the average distance of the planet from the sun is proportional to the square of the planet's period. Kepler's third law can be expressed mathematically as $K \times a^3 = p^2$, in which a is the average distance from the sun, p is the period, and K is a constant. Kepler's third law also may be applied to moons orbiting a planet, in which a is the average distance of a moon to the planet and p is the moon's period. In this activity, you will verify that the orbital motions of Jupiter's moons obey Kepler's third law.

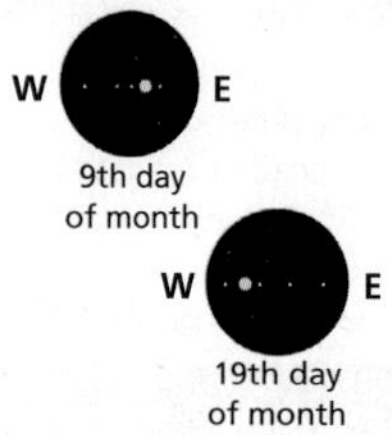

Step 1 The central horizontal band on the chart below represents Jupiter. When a moon's path crosses in front of this band, the moon is in front of the planet. When a moon's path crosses behind this band, the moon is behind Jupiter.

Procedure

1. Two telescope eyepiece views at the left show how Jupiter and its four largest, or Galilean, moons appear through a telescope on Earth at midnight on the 9th and 19th day of a month. Compare these illustrations with the chart below, which shows the path of each moon as it orbits Jupiter during the same month.
   a. List the days when each of Jupiter's moons crosses in front of the planet.
   b. List the days when each of the moons is behind Jupiter.
2. Use the data in the table on the next page to test Kepler's third law. Calculate p^2 and a^3 for each of the planets. Record your results in a table of your own. Then, calculate K for each planet by using Kepler's third law, $K = p^2/a^3$. Record your results in a similar table.
3. Draw Jupiter and its moons as they would appear from Earth at midnight on the 2nd and 26th of the month.

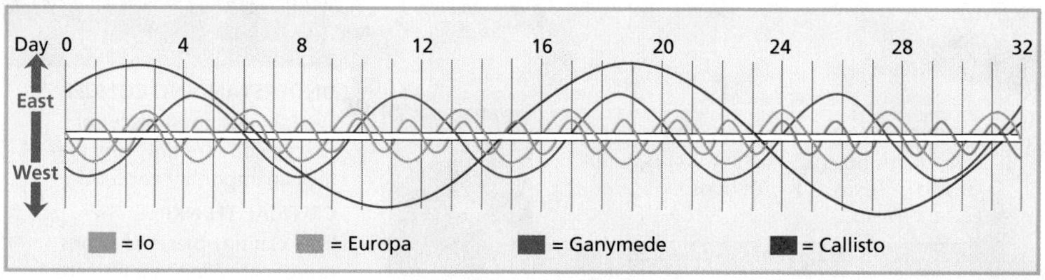

Answers to Procedure
Note: Some student's answers may deviate by one day when the satellite crosses in the middle of a day.

1a. Io: 1, 3, 5, 6, 8, 10, 12, 13, 15, 17, 19, 20, 22, 24, 26, 28, 29, 31; Europa: 0, 3, 7, 10, 14, 17, 21, 24, 28, 31; Ganymede: 6, 13, 20, 27; Callisto: 6, 23

1b. Io: 0, 2, 4, 5, 7, 9, 11, 12, 14, 16, 18, 20, 21, 23, 25, 27, 28, 30; Europa: 1, 5, 8, 12, 16, 19, 23, 26, 30; Ganymede: 2, 9, 16, 23, 31; Callisto: 14, 31

2. Mercury: $a^3 = 0.000195$; $p^2 = 0.058$; $K = 297$.
Venus: $a^3 = 0.00126$; $p^2 = 0.38$; $K = 302$.
Earth: $a^3 = 0.00338$; $p^2 = 1$; $K = 296$.
Mars: $a^3 = 0.01185$; $p^2 = 3.53$; $K = 298$.
Jupiter: $a^3 = 0.47091$; $p^2 = 140.7$; $K = 299$.
Saturn: $a^3 = 2.9058$; $p^2 = 867.9$; $K = 299$.
Uranus: $a^3 = 23.665$; $p^2 = 7{,}022$; $K = 297$.
Neptune: $a^3 = 90.943$; $p^2 = 26{,}798$; $K = 295$.

4 Draw Jupiter's moons on the first day of the month that all four moons are on the same side of the planet. Identify the date.

5 Give a date when only two moons will be visible. Name the two visible moons.

6 Follow each moon's motion on the chart. Find the length of time, in Earth days, required for each moon to orbit Jupiter. To do this, measure the time between two points when the moon is in exactly the same position on the same side of Jupiter. Record your answers in a table with columns for moons, p (in Earth days), a (in mm), p^2, a^3, and K.

Kepler's Third Law

Planet	p (in Earth years)	a (in billions of km)	a^3	p^2	K
Mercury	0.24	0.058			
Venus	0.62	0.108			
Earth	1	0.150			
Mars	1.88	0.228			
Jupiter	11.86	0.778			
Saturn	29.46	1.427			
Uranus	83.8	2.871			
Neptune	163.7	4.497			

7 Measure the scale distance between the maximum outward swing of each moon and the center of Jupiter in millimeters. Record your answers in your table.

8 Square each period measurement, and record the answer in your table. Cube each distance measurement, and record the answer.

9 Use your results to test Kepler's third law. Because $K = p^2/a^3$, divide p^2 by a^3 for each moon to find K. Record your results in your table.

Analysis

1. **Analyzing Events** Will you see all four of Jupiter's largest moons each time you look at Jupiter through a telescope or binoculars? Explain your answer.
2. **Making Inferences** If you look at Jupiter's moons through a telescope, they look like dots. If you had no charts, how could you identify each moon?
3. **Drawing Conclusions** After you solve for K for each moon, study your results. Is K a constant for the moons of Jupiter? Explain your answer.

Extension

Making Calculations Recalculate the values of K for the planets by using astronomical units instead of kilometers. How does this affect the amount of variation in the value of the constant?

3. midnight on the 2nd

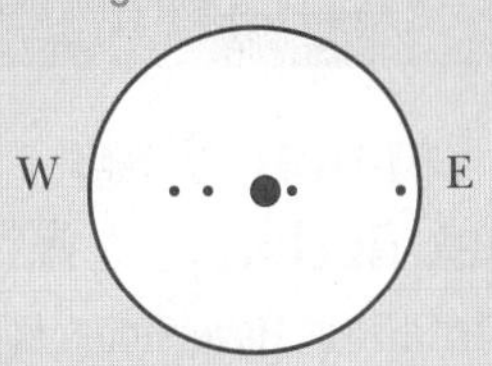

midnight on the 26th

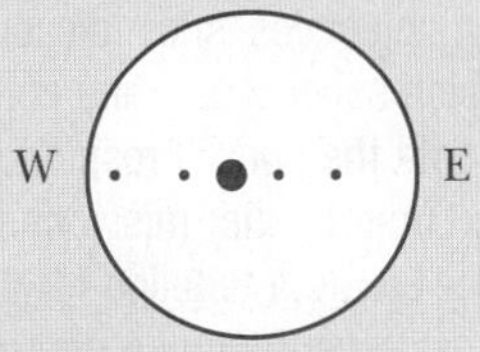

4. the 2nd

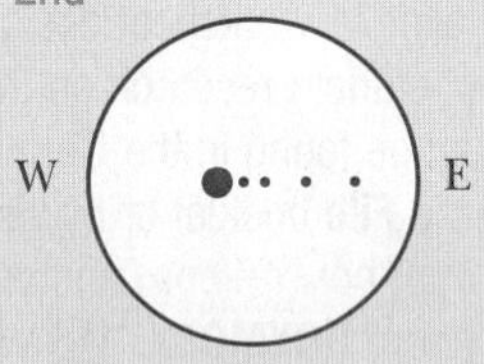

5. 3, 10: Ganymede and Callisto; 14: Europa and Ganymede; 23, 30: Ganymede and Callisto; 31: Io and Europa

6–9. Io: $p = 1.8$ days; $a = 2.5$ mm; $p^2 = 3.24$; $a^3 = 16$; $K = 0.2025$
Europa: 3.6 days; 4 mm; 12.96; 64; 0.2025
Ganymede: 7.4 days; 6.5 mm; 54.76; 27.5; 0.1991
Callisto: 16.5 days; 11 mm; 272.35; 1331; 0.2045

Answers to Analysis

1. No, sometimes a moon will be behind or in front of Jupiter.
2. by observing their maximum outward swing and by determining the periods
3. K is a constant because all the numbers are about equal; average value of $K = 0.20$.

Answer to Extension

The value of K would remain a constant, but when distance is measured in astronomical units that constant would be equal to 1, and $a^3 = p^2$.

Lunar Landing Sites Internet Activity BASIC

Lunar Timeline Have students research the lunar missions shown on the map. They can investigate dates, mission objectives, sites, discoveries, or mission successes. They could also investigate the Lunar Prospector and Selene Lunar Lander missions. Have students create a timeline for these missions. Have them use photos or drawings to illustrate each event on the timeline. A worksheet designed to direct student research on this topic can be found in the **Chapter Resource File** booklet or by visiting www.thinkcentral.com and entering the keyword **HQXMBSX.** **LS Visual**

Answers to Map Skills Activity

1. 8
2. 3
3. three; *Apollo 11* landed near *Surveyor 5,* and *Apollo 12* and *14* landed near *Surveyor 3.*
4. There are no landing sites north of 40°N latitude, south of 40°S latitude, or between 20°S and 30°S latitude.
5. between 5°N and 5°S of the lunar equator
6. maria and craters
7. Sample answer: none, because the radio waves used for communication would be blocked by the moon

MAPS in Action

Lunar Landing Sites

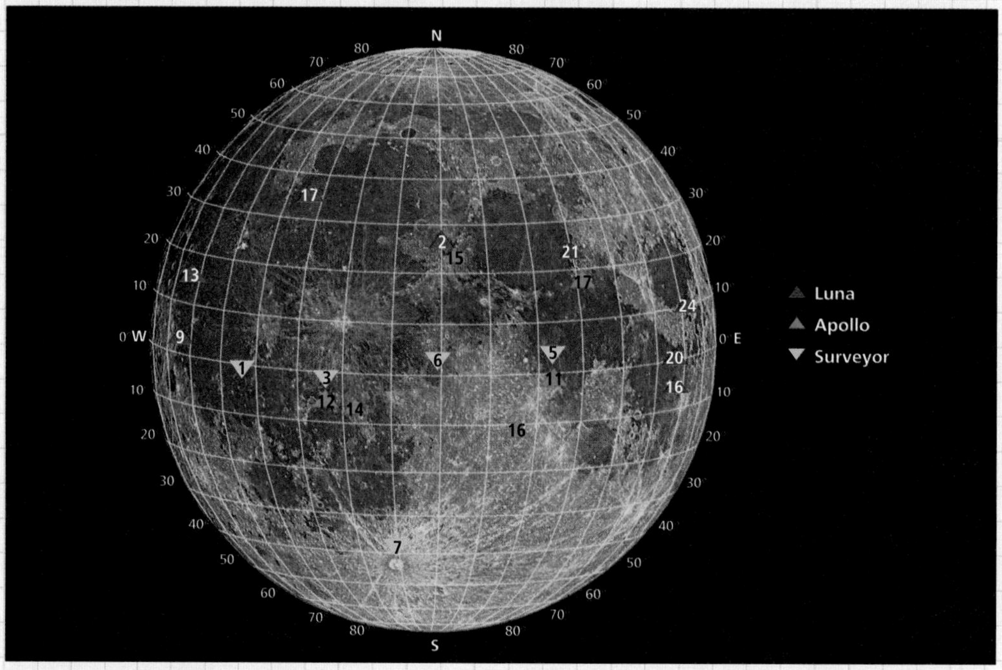

Map Skills Activity

This map shows the surface of the near side of the moon and the landing sites of both lunar missions that had crews and lunar missions that did not have crews. Most Surveyor missions took place before the Apollo missions. The Luna missions were launched by the former Soviet Union. Use the map to answer the questions below.

1. **Using a Key** How many Luna missions landed on the moon?
2. **Using a Key** How many Surveyor missions landed on the moon's southern hemisphere?
3. **Analyzing Data** How many Apollo missions landed close to Surveyor mission landing sites?
4. **Making Comparisons** At which areas of latitude are no landing sites located?
5. **Making Comparisons** In what 10° range of latitude are most landing sites located?
6. **Inferring Relationships** Based on the locations of most landing sites, what surface features do you think interested scientists?
7. **Identifying Trends** The missions to the moon used radio communications. Radio communications require a clear path between the transmitter and receiver. Taking these facts into consideration, how many landing sites would you expect to find on the far side of the moon? Explain your answer.

Key Resources

Technology
- Transparencies
  145 Lunar Landing Sites

Chapter 28

Summary

THINK central
SUPER SUMMARY
Keyword: HQXMBSS

Key Ideas / Key Terms

Section 1

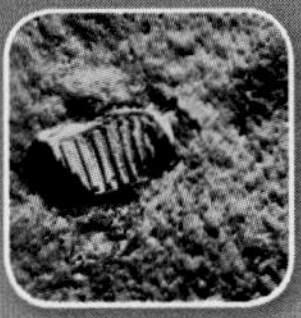

Earth's Moon

- Lunar surface features include maria, craters, rilles, ridges, regolith, and rocks.
- The moon's crust averages about 80 km deep. Extending about 1,000 km below the crust is the rocky mantle, which may be surrounded by a partly solid and partly liquid iron core that is less than 700 km in radius.
- The moon is thought to be a chunk of Earth's early mantle ejected as a result of a giant impact with a Mars-sized body. As the early molten moon cooled, it developed its three layers. Craters and regolith formed from meteorite impacts.

Key Terms:
satellite, p. 785
moon, p. 785
mare, p. 786
crater, p. 786

Section 2

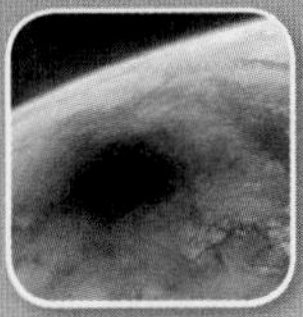

Movements of the Moon

- The shape of the moon's orbit around Earth is an ellipse.
- Eclipses occur when one planetary body passes through the shadow of another.
- The full moon phase shows a fully illuminated moon. Third quarter shows a half-moon (left side lit). New moon is not visible. First quarter shows a half-moon (right side lit).
- Tides result largely from the moon's gravitational pull on Earth.

Key Terms:
apogee, p. 791
perigee, p. 791
eclipse, p. 793
solar eclipse, p. 793
lunar eclipse, p. 795
phase, p. 796

Section 3

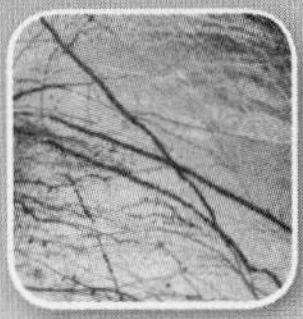

Satellites of Other Planets

- Phobos and Deimos are irregularly shaped with many craters. They revolve around Mars quickly.
- The Voyager spacecraft discovered volcanoes on Io.
- The four Galilean moons of Jupiter are Io (known for its volcanoes), Europa (with an icy coating and possibly liquid water), Ganymede (the largest moon in the solar system), and Callisto (a very densely cratered moon).
- Saturn has many more rings than other planets do.

Key Terms:
Galilean moon, p. 799

Section 4

Asteroids, Comets, and Meteoroids

- Asteroids are large, rocky bodies. Comets are smaller and are made of rock, ice, and dust.
- The Kuiper Belt is located beyond the orbit of Neptune.
- Meteoroids are small rocky bodies. The streak of light made when they burn up in the atmosphere is called a meteor. Any part that reaches the ground is called a meteorite.
- Most comets are thought to originate in the Oort cloud.

Key Terms:
asteroid, p. 805
comet, p. 807
Kuiper Belt, p. 808
Oort cloud, p. 808
meteoroid, p. 809
meteor, p. 809

Chapter Summary

Using THINK central Resources

Super Summary
Have students connect the major concepts in this chapter through an interactive Super Summary. Visit www.thinkcentral.com and type in the keyword **HQXMBSS** to access the Super Summary for this chapter.

Differentiated Instruction

Alternative Assessment

Poster Project Have groups of students create posters about how studying objects such as Earth's moon illuminates the early history of the solar system. Posters could illustrate typical features of the lunar landscape and explain how moon rocks provided insight into lunar origins, or compare the moon's cratered surface with the surfaces of other natural satellites. Other posters might depict what we have learned about the origin of life on Earth from space missions to other moons or how craters throughout the solar system provided clues to mass extinctions, or they may summarize the nature and composition of asteroids, meteorites, and comets or the ancient features preserved in the objects of the Kuiper Belt and Oort cloud. **LS Visual**

Chapter Review

Assignment Guide	
Section	**Questions**
1	2, 3, 10, 11, 18, 19, 24, 26, 27, 33
2	1, 5, 7, 12–14, 20, 25, 28, 30, 31, 34
3	4, 15, 21, 22, 32
4	6, 8, 9, 16, 17, 23, 29, 35–38

Reading Toolbox

1. Two words that describe the motion of all minor bodies of the solar system are *rotate* and *orbit*. When a body rotates, it spins on its axis. When a body orbits, it revolves around a fixed point, often a planet.

Using Key Terms

2–9. Answers may vary but should show that students understand the definitions of and differences between key terms.

Understanding Key Ideas

10. c
11. d
12. a
13. b
14. d
15. a
16. d
17. a

Short Answer

18. Maria formed when lava from the moon's interior slowly filled the basins left behind by prior meteorite impacts.

Chapter 28 Review

1. **Describing Space** Name two words that describe the motion of all minor bodies of the solar system, and explain how the meanings of these words differ. READING TOOLBOX

USING KEY TERMS

Use each of the following terms in a separate sentence.

2. *crater*
3. *mare*
4. *Galilean moon*

For each pair of terms, explain how the meanings of the terms differ.

5. *perigee* and *apogee*
6. *Oort cloud* and *Kuiper Belt*
7. *solar eclipse* and *lunar eclipse*
8. *comet* and *asteroid*
9. *meteoroid* and *meteorite*

UNDERSTANDING KEY IDEAS

10. Dark areas on the moon that are smooth and that reflect little light are called
    a. rilles.
    b. rays.
    c. maria.
    d. breccia.
11. What happened in the most recent stage in the development of the moon?
    a. The densest material sank to the core.
    b. The crust began to break.
    c. Earth's gravity captured the moon.
    d. The number of meteorites hitting the moon decreased.
12. During each orbit around Earth, the moon spins on its axis
    a. 1 time.
    b. about 29 times.
    c. about 27 times.
    d. 365 times.
13. In a lunar eclipse, the moon
    a. casts a shadow on Earth.
    b. is in Earth's shadow.
    c. is between Earth and the sun.
    d. blocks part of the sun from view.
14. When the size of the lighted part of the moon's near side is decreasing, the moon is
    a. full.
    b. waxing.
    c. annular.
    d. waning.
15. Compared with the other moons of Jupiter, the four Galilean moons are
    a. larger.
    b. farther from Jupiter.
    c. lighter.
    d. younger.
16. The main asteroid belt exists in a region between the orbits of
    a. Mercury and Venus.
    b. Earth and Mars.
    c. Venus and Earth.
    d. Mars and Jupiter.
17. Meteorites can provide information about
    a. the composition of the solar system before the planets formed.
    b. the size of Earth.
    c. the destiny of the solar system.
    d. the size of the universe.

SHORT ANSWER

18. Describe how maria formed on the moon.
19. Are craters on the moon caused by volcanism or by impacts with other bodies? Explain your answer.
20. Do total eclipses of the sun occur only at full moons? Explain your answer.
21. Are any moons in the solar system bigger than planets? Explain.
22. Which planets have rings?
23. Which two places in the solar system do comets come from?
24. What is the difference between natural and artificial satellites?

19. Craters on the moon were caused by impacts with other bodies. The circular shape, presence of ejected materials, regolith layer, and texture of lunar rocks provides evidence.
20. no; During the full moon phase, Earth is located between the moon and the sun. Solar eclipses occur only during the new moon when the moon is located between Earth and the sun, and the moon's shadow falls on part of Earth.
21. yes; Both Titan and Ganymede are larger than Mercury.
22. Saturn has the most extensive ring system. Jupiter, Uranus, and Neptune also have rings.
23. Oort cloud and Kuiper Belt
24. A natural satellite is smaller body such as a moon that orbits around a larger body. An artificial satellite is an object launched by humans, such as weather satellites or space observatories.

CRITICAL THINKING

25. Analyzing Relationships If Earth had two moons that traveled on the same orbit and were the same distance from Earth, but formed a 90° angle with Earth, how would Earth's tides be different?

26. Making Inferences How would the craters on the moon be different today if the moon had developed a dense atmosphere that moved as wind and that contained water?

27. Determining Cause and Effect If meteorites had stopped hitting the moon before the outer surface of the moon cooled, how would the moon's surface be different than it is today?

28. Evaluating Information Suppose that the moon spun twice on its axis during each orbit around Earth. How would the study of the moon from Earth be easier than it is currently?

29. Applying Ideas The surfaces of some asteroids reflect only small amounts of light. Other asteroids reflect up to 40% of the light that falls on them. Of what kind of materials would each type of asteroid probably be composed?

CONCEPT MAPPING

30. Use the following terms to create a concept map: *moon, Earth, apogee, perigee, new moon, full moon, waxing, waning, solar eclipse, lunar eclipse, umbra, penumbra,* and *phase.*

MATH SKILLS

Math Skills

31. Making Calculations There are 60 s in 1 min, 60 min in 1 h, 24 h in 1 day, and 365 1/4 days in a year. How many seconds are in a year?

32. Making Calculations The radius of Earth's moon is 1,738 km. The diameter of Neptune's moon Triton is 2,705 km. What percentage of Earth's moon's size is Triton?

WRITING SKILLS

33. Creative Writing Imagine that you want to live on the moon. Describe how you would get your water and how you would acquire food and other supplies.

34. Communicating Ideas Summarize how the moon's gravity and the rotation of Earth cause tides.

INTERPRETING GRAPHICS

The graph below shows the number of near-Earth asteroids discovered each year. Use the graph below to answer the questions that follow.

Near-Earth Asteroid Discoveries

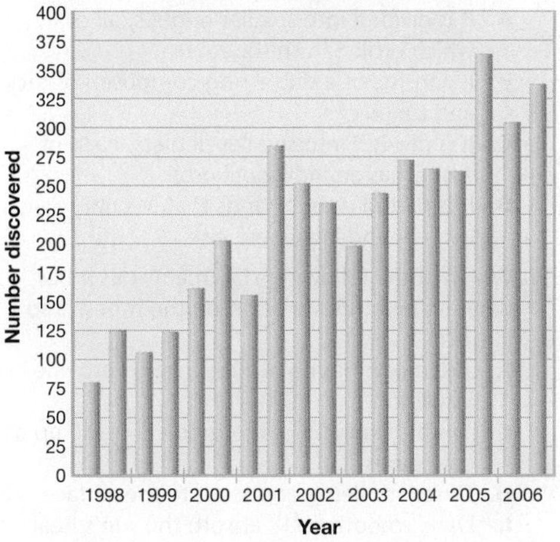

35. Was the rate of discovery of near-Earth asteroids in 2006 higher or lower than the rate in 2005?

36. How many near-Earth asteroids were discovered in the half-year in which the most discoveries were made?

37. Which calendar year had the highest total number of near-Earth asteroid discoveries?

38. What is the total number of near-Earth asteroids discovered in the last three years shown on the graph?

Chapter Review

Critical Thinking

25. Answers may vary. The location and size of the tidal bulges would be different and may not exist at all.

26. If the moon had a dense atmosphere with water, fewer meteorites would have penetrated to reach the surface and many of the craters that formed during the early bombardment period would have been erased by erosion.

27. The moon's surface would be smooth and would not be heavily cratered.

28. If the moon spun on its axis twice in each orbit around Earth, it would present both sides to observers on Earth. We would be able to map what we now think of as the far side of the moon using ordinary telescopes from Earth.

29. The highly reflective asteroids are probably composed mainly of metals such as iron and nickel. Those that reflect only a small amount of light are probably made of rocky materials or carbon.

Concept Mapping

30. Answers may vary but should include all of the terms listed. Sample answers appear at the end of this unit on p. 875B.

Math Skills

31. 60 s/min × 60min/h = 3,600 s/h × 24 h/d = 86,400 s/d × 365.25 d/year = 31,557,600 s/year

32. 1,738 km × 2 = 3,476 km; 2,705 km ÷ 3,476 km = 0.7782 × 100 = 77.82%

Writing Skills

33. Answers may vary. Accept all reasonable answers.

34. Answers may vary. Sample answer: On the near side of Earth, the gravitational force of the moon pulls ocean water toward the moon. The mass of the solid Earth is subject to less gravitational force than the ocean water is. On the far side of Earth, the water is subject to less gravitational force than the solid Earth is. These gravitational differences cause the water on the near side and on the far side of Earth to form two tidal bulges. Rotation causes tides to occur all over Earth.

Interpreting Graphics

35. The overall rate of discovery was higher in 2006.

36. Approximately 360 near-Earth asteroids were discovered in the second half of 2005.

37. 2006

38. Answers may vary. Accept all reasonable answers. The total number of near-Earth asteroids discovered was about 1,790.

Estimated Time

To give students practice under more realistic testing conditions, allow them 30 minutes to answer all of the questions in this practice test.

Test Doctor

Question 1 Answer B is correct. Because the moon has much less mass than Earth does, the moon's surface gravity is about one-sixth the surface gravity of Earth. As a result, a person who weighs 600 newtons (600 N) on Earth would weigh about 100 N on the moon. A person who weighs 360 N on Earth would weigh about 60 N on the moon. Answer A is incorrect because the answer uses one-tenth the gravity of Earth in its math. Answer C is incorrect because the answer uses one-half the gravity of Earth. Answer D is incorrect because the answer uses one-fourth the gravity of Earth.

Question 11 Full-credit answers should include the following points:
- Kuiper Belt objects are usually very small
- the Kuiper Belt was not discovered until the middle of the 20th century because previous technology had not been powerful enough to detect the small objects that populate it
- even with today's advanced technology, scientists speculate that hundreds of Kuiper Belt objects remain undiscovered

Chapter 28 Standardized Test Prep

Understanding Concepts

Directions (1–4): For each question, write on a separate sheet of paper the letter of the correct answer.

1. Because of differences in surface gravity, how much does a person who weighs 360 newtons (360 N) on Earth weigh on the moon?
   A. 36 N **C.** 180 N
   B. 60 N **D.** 90 N
2. The point in the orbit of a satellite at which the satellite is farthest from Earth is the satellite's
   F. apogee.
   G. perigee.
   H. barycenter.
   I. phase.
3. Which of the following statements accurately describes each ring of Saturn?
   A. It is divided into smaller ringlets, all of which orbit Saturn together.
   B. It consists of a single ring composed of rock and ice pieces.
   C. It is divided into smaller ringlets, each of which has an individual orbit.
   D. It is part of a set of rings that are unlike those found anywhere else.
4. Which of the following statements describes why temperature variation on the moon is so large?
   F. The moon has no atmosphere to provide insulation.
   G. The atmosphere of the moon is made up of cold gases.
   H. Gases are dense and close to the surface.
   I. Dark, smooth rocks absorb the sun's heat.

Directions (5–7): For each question, write a short response.

5. Approximately how long does it take the moon to make one orbit around Earth?
6. What are the names of the four moons of Jupiter known as the Galilean moons?
7. When the moon is at its apogee, what part of its shadow cannot reach Earth during an eclipse?

Reading Skills

Directions (8–11): Read the passage below. Then, answer the questions.

Kuiper Belt Objects

To explain the source of short-period comets, or comets that have a relatively short orbit around the sun, the Dutch-American astronomer Gerard Kuiper proposed in 1949 that a belt of icy bodies must lie beyond the orbits of Neptune and Pluto. Kuiper argued that comets were icy planetesimals that formed from the condensation that happened during the formation of our galaxy.

Because the icy bodies are so far from any large planet's gravitational field (30 to 100 AU), they are able to remain on the fringe of the solar system. Some theorists speculate that the large moons Triton and Charon were once independent members of the Kuiper Belt before they were captured by Neptune and Pluto, respectively. These moons and short-period comets have similar physical and chemical properties. Scientists now believe that the Kuiper Belt may be home to thousands of objects that have diameters of more than 100 km.

8. According to the information in the passage, which of the following did Gerard Kuiper think were actually icy planetesimals?
   A. outer planets
   B. comets
   C. moons of every planet
   D. inner planets
9. What two bodies do some scientists believe were once independent Kuiper-Belt objects?
   F. Neptune and Charon
   G. Neptune and Pluto
   H. Triton and Neptune
   I. Triton and Charon
10. What did the moon Triton orbit before it was captured by the gravity of Neptune?
    A. the sun **C.** the solar system
    B. Pluto **D.** Charon
11. Why did it take until the middle of the 20th century for astronomers to discover the presence of the Kuiper Belt?

Question 14 Full-credit answers should include the following points:
- students should demonstrate a conceptual understanding that waxing and waning describe the only the lighted portion of the moon
- during a waxing moon, the lighted portion appears to enlarge each subsequent night. The moon begins to wax after the new moon, when no light is visible
- during a waning moon, the lighted portion appears to shrink each subsequent night. The moon begins to wane after the full moon, when the most light is visible

Question 15 Answer I is correct. Students may recognize the sides of the moon because that the crust is thicker on the right side of the diagram and that there are maria on the left side of the diagram.

Interpreting Graphics

Directions (12–15): For each question below, record the correct answer on a separate sheet of paper.

The diagram below shows the waxing and waning of the moon. Use this diagram to answer questions 12 and 13.

Phases of the Moon in the Northern Hemisphere

12. How would the appearance of the moon in the Southern Hemisphere be different from its appearance in the Northern Hemisphere?
- **F.** The phases of the moon would appear exactly the same.
- **G.** The Southern Hemisphere would see a full moon when the Northern Hemisphere sees a new moon.
- **H.** The moon would wax from left to right instead of from right to left.
- **I.** The Southern Hemisphere would see a waxing moon when the Northern Hemisphere sees a waning moon.

13. What part of the moon is facing Earth during the new moon in stage 1?
- **A.** the near side
- **B.** the far side
- **C.** the north pole
- **D.** the south pole

14. The word *wax* means "to grow larger," while *wane* means "to grow smaller." If the lighted portion of a waxing crescent is the same size as that of a waning crescent, why do you think these terms are used?

The diagram below shows data about the interior structure of the moon. Use this diagram to answer question 15.

Structure of the Moon

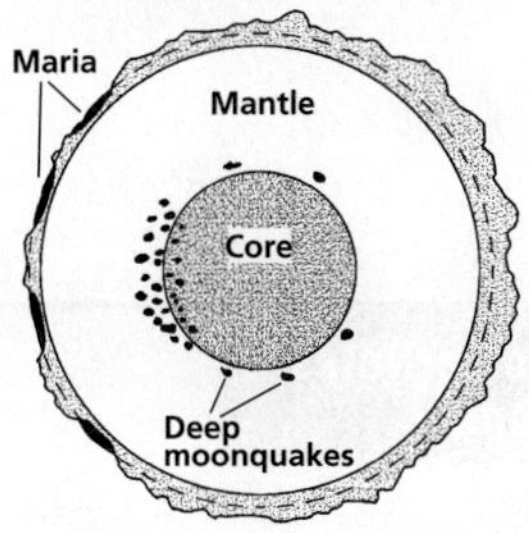

15. Where is the crust of the moon the thickest?
- **F.** at the poles
- **G.** at the equator
- **H.** on the near side
- **I.** on the far side

Test Tip

Test questions are not necessarily arranged in order of difficulty. If you are unable to answer a question, mark it and move on to other questions.

Standardized Test Prep

Using THINK central Resources

State Resources

- For specific resources for your state, visit www.thinkcentral.com and type in the keyword **HSHSTR.**

Answers

Understanding Concepts

1. B
2. F
3. C
4. F
5. about 27.3 days (or one month)
6. Io, Europa, Ganymede, and Callisto
7. the umbra

Reading Skills

8. B
9. I
10. A
11. Answers may vary. See Test Doctor for a detailed scoring rubric.

Interpreting Graphics

12. H
13. A
14. Answers may vary. See Test Doctor for a detailed scoring rubric.
15. I

Chapter Planner 29 The Sun

	Time	Standards	Teach Key Ideas
Chapter Opener, pp. 820–821	45 min.	National Science Education Standards	
Section 1 Structure of the Sun, pp. 823–828 ❯ The Sun's Energy ❯ Mass Changing into Energy ❯ The Sun's Interior ❯ The Sun's Atmosphere	45 min.	PS 5c, PS 5d, ES 4b, ES 4c	■ ◆ **Bellringer,** p. 823 ■ **DI (Basic Learners):** Skit, p. 824 ■ **DI (Special Education Students):** Completing Sentences, p. 826 ◆ **Transparencies:** 146 Nuclear Fusion • 147 The Sun's Interior ▲ **Visual Concepts:** Star Composition • Nuclear Fusion • Structure of the Sun • The Sun's Atmosphere
Section 2 Solar Activity, pp. 829–832 ❯ Sunspots ❯ The Sunspot Cycle ❯ Solar Eruptions ❯ Auroras	45 min.	PS 4e	■ ◆ **Bellringer,** p. 829 ■ **Discussion:** Sunspots, p. 829 ■ **DI (Advanced Learners):** Presentations, p. 830 ◆ **Transparency:** 148 XRT Composite Image of the Sun ▲ **Visual Concepts:** Sunspots
Chapter Wrap-Up, pp. 837–841	90 min.		**Chapter Summary,** p. 837

See also PowerNotes® Presentations

CHAPTER Fast Track

To shorten instruction because of time limitations, omit Section 2.

Key

Teacher's Edition ■	Teaching Transparencies ◆
Chapter Resource File ●	Online Edition ▲

All resources listed below are also available on the Teacher One Stop™.

Why It Matters	Hands-On	Skills Development	Assessment
■ **Chapter Overview,** p. 820 ■ **Using the Figure:** The Explosive Sun, p. 820	**Inquiry Lab:** Making a Spectrum, p. 821	**Reading Toolbox,** p. 822	
■ **Section Overview,** p. 823 ■ **Using the Figure:** Spectra, p. 823 ■ **Solar Life Cycle,** p. 824 ■ **Using the Figure:** Discussion, p. 825 ■ **History Connection:** Reinventing Time and Space, p. 825	**Quick Lab:** Modeling Fusion, p. 825 **Quick Lab:** The Size of Our Sun, p. 826 **Skills Practice Lab:** Energy of the Sun, pp. 834–835 ● **Inquiry Lab:** Solar Cooker ● **Making Models Lab:** Light Fingerprints	■ **Skill Builder:** Math, p. 824 **Reading Toolbox:** Generalizations, p. 824 ■ **Skill Builder:** Vocabulary, p. 827	**Reading Check,** p. 825 **Reading Check,** p. 827 **Section Review,** p. 828 ■ **Reteaching,** p. 827 ■ **Quiz,** p. 827 ■ **DI (Alternative Assessment):** Solar Tales, p. 828 ● **Section Quiz**
■ **Section Overview,** p. 829 ■ **Using the Figure:** Sunspot Cycles, p. 830 **SOHO, So Helpful,** p. 830 ■ **Auroras,** p. 837	■ **Group Activity:** Geomagnetic Storms, p. 831	**Reading Toolbox:** Suffixes, p. 830 ■ ● **Internet Activity:** Solar Activity and Climate, p. 830 ■ **Skill Builder:** Writing, p. 831 **Math Skills:** Magnetic Fields, p. 831 **Maps in Action:** XRT Composite Image of the Sun, p. 836 ■ ● **Internet Activity:** SOHO Images, p. 836	**Reading Check,** p. 831 **Section Review,** p. 832 ■ **Reteaching,** p. 831 ■ **Quiz,** p. 831 ■ **DI (Alternative Assessment):** The Active Sun, p. 832 ● **Section Quiz**
Seasonal Sunlight, p. 833		▲ **Super Summary** **Standardized Test Prep,** pp. 840–841	**Chapter Review,** pp. 838–839 ■ **DI (Alternative Assessment):** Our Daytime Star, p. 837 ● **Chapter Tests**

See also Lab Generator

See also Holt Online Assessment Resources

Chapter Overview

This chapter describes the structure of the sun, how the sun produces energy, and how its activity cycle affects Earth.

Using the Figure GENERAL

The Explosive Sun The outer layers of the sun's atmosphere are extremely volatile and subject to explosive disturbances. Ask students to describe some of the characteristic solar features seen in the photo. (Sample answer: Huge loops and arcs of hot gas are erupting from the surface. Hotter and cooler areas appear on the surface.) Many of these features are associated with the sun's magnetic field. The smallest visible solar surface features—small bubbles of gas called granules—are not visible in this photo. These granules may be as big as the state of Texas and carry energy from below the photosphere. LS **Visual**

Why It Matters

Energy from the sun produces our food and fuel, as well as the ingredients for making products as diverse as drugs, perfumes, dyes, paper, buildings, and clothing.

Chapter 29 The Sun

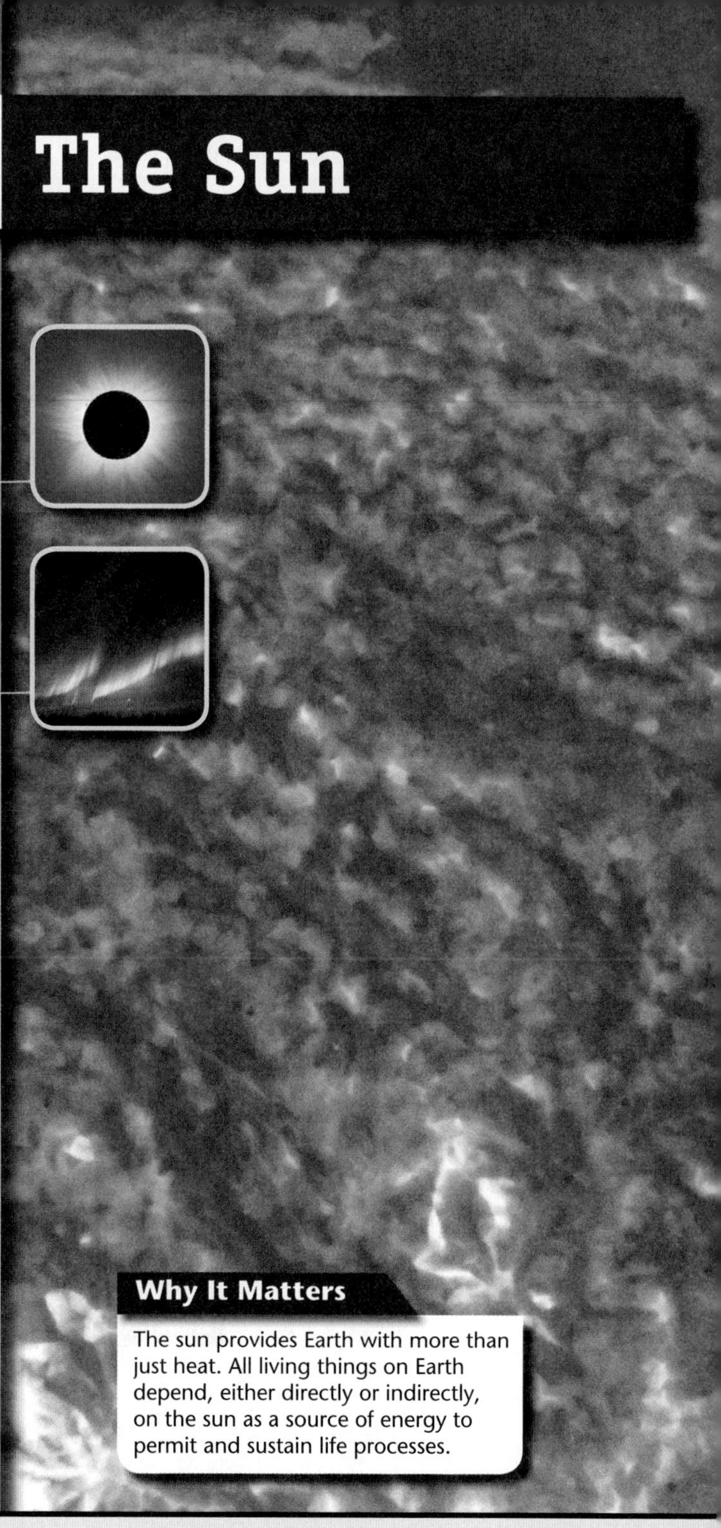

Chapter Outline

Virginia Standards of Learning
ES.1.a
ES.1.c
ES.1.f
ES.3.c

Why It Matters

The sun provides Earth with more than just heat. All living things on Earth depend, either directly or indirectly, on the sun as a source of energy to permit and sustain life processes.

Chapter Correlations — *Virginia Standards of Learning*

ES.1.a volume, area, mass, elapsed time, direction, temperature, pressure, distance, density, and changes in elevation/depth are calculated utilizing the most appropriate tools.
ES.1.c scales, diagrams, charts, graphs, tables, imagery, models, and profiles are constructed and interpreted.
ES.1.f current applications are used to reinforce Earth science concepts
ES.3.c characteristics of the sun, planets and their moons, comets, meteors, and asteroids.

Inquiry Lab — Making a Spectrum

15 min

Fill a **shallow dish** or basin about halfway with **water**. Lean a **flat mirror** against one side of the dish so that the mirror is on an angle. Make sure that part of the mirror is submerged in the water. Darken the classroom, and shine a **flashlight** at the mirror. Observe the reflected image. What do you see?

Questions to Get You Started

1. Why do you see colors even though you started with white light?
2. What would you see if you placed a red filter over the flashlight?

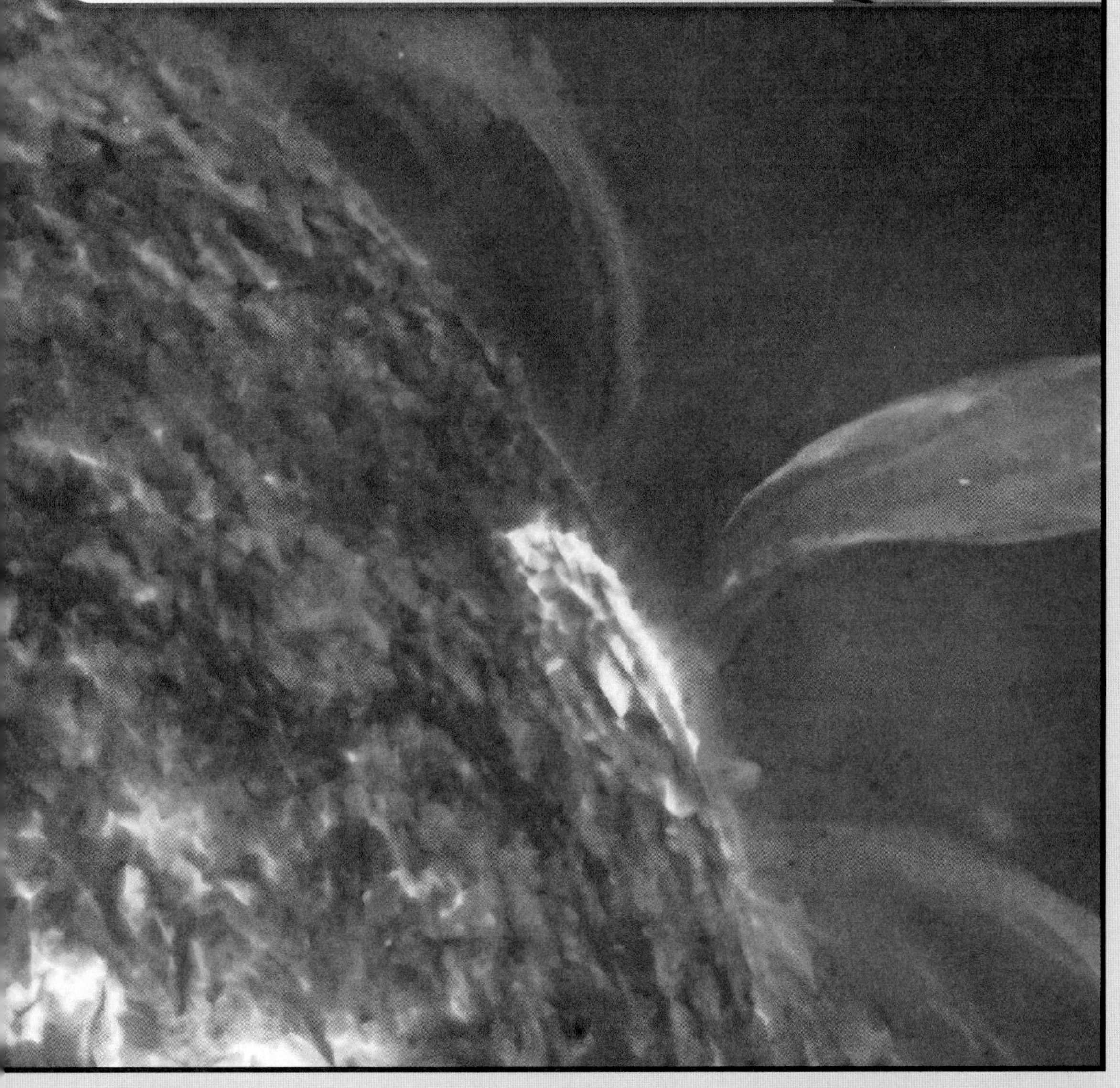

Inquiry Lab

Central Concept: Students will make a model of a prism, and observe how wavelengths of light are separated to form the rainbow of the visible spectrum.

Teacher's Notes: Students should see the spectrum reflected onto the ceiling. If possible, dim classroom lights for easier viewing.

Materials (per group)
- Shallow dish
- Water
- Flat mirror
- Flashlight

Skills Acquired
- Making Models
- Observing

Answers to Getting Started
1. The white light was separated into the different wavelengths, resulting in a rainbow of colors.
2. You would only see red. The other colors would not pass through the filter.

Using THINK central Resources

An online version of this chapter, as well as all the print and multimedia resources that accompany the program are available to registered teachers and their students. Log onto www.thinkcentral.com to access these materials and tools to organize your preparation and student learning.

READING TOOLBOX

Word Parts

Students should include in their charts the key terms *radiative zone* and *convective zone* and the italicized word *convection*. They may also include words from the section such as *massive*, *composition*, *reaction*, *equation*, *formation*, *radiation*, and *transition*.

Generalizations

Students may note several generalizations. One example is shown here.

Sentence	Word or phrase that signals generalization	Why sentence is a generalization
Auroras normally occur between 100 and 1,000 km above Earth's surface.	normally	The statement applies to most, but not all, auroras.

Graphic Organizers

Students should consult Appendix A for tips on making a chain-of-events chart. Their charts should include the three main steps of the process of nuclear fusion: 1) two protons collide, resulting in a proton-neutron pair; 2) another proton combines with the proton-neutron pair, forming a nucleus made up of two protons and one neutron; 3) two nuclei made up of two protons and one neutron collide and fuse.

READING TOOLBOX

These reading tools will help you learn the material in this chapter.

Word Parts

Suffixes The suffix *-ive* changes nouns and verbs to adjectives and adds the meaning "relating or tending to." For example, *supportive* is an adjective formed from the noun *support*. It means "tending to give support." The suffix *-tion* changes verbs to nouns, or nouns to other nouns, and adds the meaning "the act or state of." For example, *connection* is a noun formed from the verb *connect*. It means "the state of joining."

Your Turn Make a table like the one below. In Section 1, there are two key terms with the suffix *-ive* and an italicized word with the suffix *-tion*. Add them to your table, along with other *-ive* or *-tion* words.

Word	Suffix	Related noun or verb	Definition of word
reaction	-tion	react	a response to something

Generalizations

Signal Words Generalizations are statements applied to a large group of things. Generalizations may be signaled by words such as *commonly*, *usually*, *normally*, or *generally*. Sometimes they are signaled by words such as *most*, *mostly*, and *much*, and by phrases such as *in general* and *for the most part*. Many generalizations, however, are not signaled by a word or phrase.

Your Turn As you read Section 2, look for sentences that are generalizations. Make a table like the one below to list the generalizations that you find.

Sentence	Word or phrase that signals generalization	Why sentence is a generalization
Many other solar activities are affected by the sunspot cycle.	many	The statement applies to many, but not all, solar activities.

Graphic Organizers

Chain-of-Events Chart A chain-of-events chart shows the order in which steps occur.

Your Turn As you read Section 1, complete the chain-of-events chart that outlines each step in the process of nuclear fusion.

1. The first step in the process is written in the first box.
2. The second step in the process is written in the second box, and an arrow shows the order of the first and second steps.
3. Continue adding boxes and arrows until the process of nuclear fusion is complete.

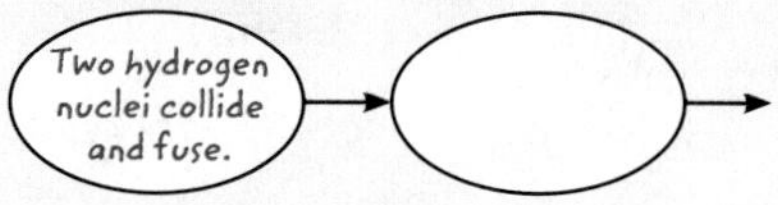

For more information on how to use these and other tools, see **Appendix A.**

SECTION 1 Structure of the Sun

Key Ideas	Key Terms	Why It Matters
❯ Explain how the sun converts matter into energy in its core. ❯ Compare the radiative and convective zones of the sun. ❯ Describe the three layers of the sun's atmosphere.	**nuclear fusion** **radiative zone** **convective zone** **photosphere** **chromosphere** **corona**	Scientists hope that their research will one day result in the technology to create safe, controlled nuclear fusion reactions on Earth, which could then be used as a source of plentiful, reliable energy.

Throughout much of human history, people thought that the sun's energy came from fire. People knew that burning a piece of coal or wood produced energy as heat and light. They assumed that the sun, too, burned some type of fuel to produce its energy. But less than 100 years ago, scientists discovered that the source of the sun's energy is quite different from fire.

The Sun's Energy

The sun appears to the unaided eye as a dazzling, brilliant ball that has no distinct features. Because the sun's brightness can damage your eyes if you look directly at the sun, astronomers look at the sun only through special filters. Astronomers often use other specialized scientific instruments to study the sun.

Composition of the Sun

Scientists break up the sun's light into a spectrum by using a device called a *spectrograph*. Dark lines form in the spectra of stars when gases in the stars' outer layers absorb specific wavelengths of the light that passes through the layers. Because each element produces a unique pattern of spectral lines, astronomers can match the spectral lines of starlight to those of Earth's elements, as shown in **Figure 1**, and identify the elements in the star's atmosphere.

About 75% of the sun's mass is hydrogen, and hydrogen and helium together make up about 99% of the sun's mass. The sun's spectrum reveals, however, that the sun contains traces of almost all other chemical elements.

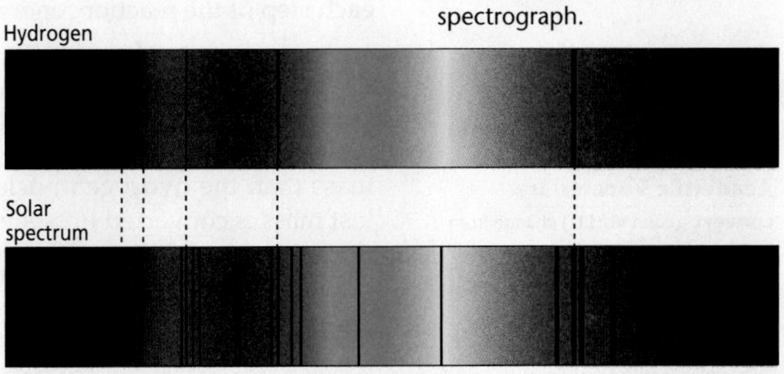

Figure 1 When light passes through hydrogen gas and then through a slit in a prism, dark lines appear in the spectrum. Hydrogen and lines from other elements in the solar spectrum are shown in the bottom spectrograph.

Section 1

Focus

Overview

This section describes the composition of the sun and how the sun produces energy. The section also details the layered structure of the sun and how scientists study the sun.

Bellringer

Have students answer the following questions:

1. What is the sun made of?
2. What does the sun use as a fuel to produce energy?

(Answers may vary but may provide insights into students' misconceptions or may act as a starting point for discussions.)

Motivate

Using the Figure GENERAL

Spectra Point out the dark lines that cross the sun's spectrum in the bottom spectrograph. Explain that astronomers use the pattern of spectral lines present in the light from stars, such as Earth's sun, like a fingerprint to identify what elements are present. **LS Logical/Visual**

Key Resources

Chapter Resource File
- Directed Reading BASIC
- Inquiry Lab: Solar Cooker GENERAL
- Making Models Lab: Light Fingerprints GENERAL

Technology
- Transparencies
  Bellringer

Teach

Skill Builder ADVANCED

Math During the last step of fusion, 26 MeV (megaelectron Volts) of energy are released. 1 MeV equals approximately 1.6×10^{-13} J. Have students calculate how many fusion reactions it would take to release 1 J of energy.
(1 J = 26 (1.6×10^{-13} J) × *N* fusion reactions; *N* fusion reactions = 1 J ÷ (4.16×10^{-12} J) = (10 ÷ 4.16) × 10^{11} = 2.4×10^{11}, or 240,000,000,000 fusion reactions)

Why It Matters

Solar Life Cycle Earth's sun formed about 5 billion years ago when a cloud of interstellar gas began to collapse as a result of its gravity. The gas in the center got hotter and hotter as it absorbed thermal energy that resulted from the kinetic energy of subatomic particles. Eventually, electrons were stripped away from their atoms, and protons (hydrogen nuclei) moved so fast that they collided violently and began the fusion reactions that fuel the sun to this day.

In another 5 billion years, the sun's nuclear furnace will be forced into hotter reactions that fuse helium nuclei to form elements such as carbon. When this happens, the sun will swell in size as its outer shell cools. It will become a red giant that will engulf Mercury, Venus, and perhaps even Earth. When a star uses up the nuclear fuel in its center, it collapses. In this final phase, the sun will shrink in size and become a white dwarf.

Figure 2 In the core of the sun, the nuclei of hydrogen atoms fuse to form helium. The fusion process converts some of the mass into energy.

THINK central
INTERACT ONLINE
(Keyword: HQXSUNF2)

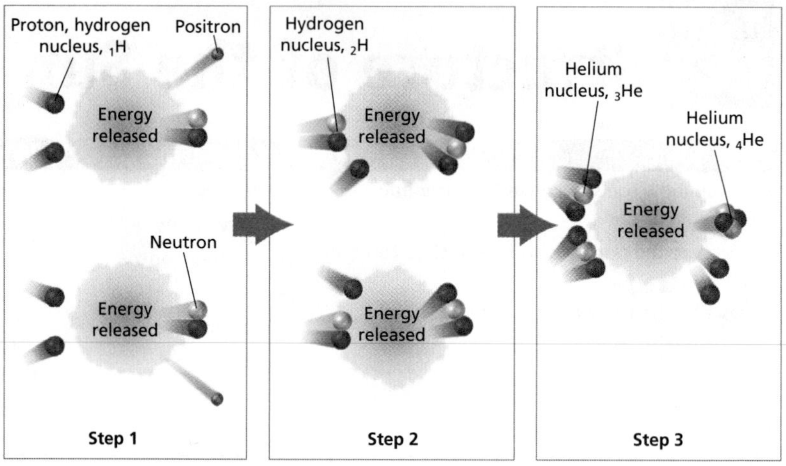

Nuclear Fusion

nuclear fusion the process by which nuclei of small atoms combine to form a new, more massive nucleus; the process releases energy

A powerful atomic process known as nuclear fusion occurs inside the sun. **Nuclear fusion** is the process of combining nuclei of small atoms to form more-massive nuclei. Fusion releases huge amounts of energy. Nuclei of hydrogen atoms are the primary fuel for the sun's fusion. A hydrogen atom, the simplest of all atoms, commonly consists of only one electron and one proton. Inside the sun, however, electrons are stripped from the protons by the sun's intense heat.

Nuclear fusion produces most of the sun's energy and consists of three steps, as shown in **Figure 2.** In the first step, two hydrogen nuclei, or *protons*, collide and fuse. In this step, the positive charge of one of the protons is neutralized as a particle called a *positron* is emitted. As a result, the proton becomes a neutron and the original two protons become a proton-neutron pair. In the second step, another proton combines with this proton-neutron pair to produce a nucleus made up of two protons and one neutron, a rare type of helium. In the third step, two nuclei made up of two protons and one neutron collide and fuse. As this fusion happens, two protons are released. The remaining two protons and two neutrons are fused together as a helium nucleus of the common type. During each step of the reaction, energy is released.

READING TOOLBOX

Generalizations
As you read Section 1, look for sentences that contain generalizations, and list them in a table. Remember that some generalizations are not signaled by a word or phrase.

The Final Product

One of the final products of the fusion of hydrogen in the sun is always a helium nucleus. The helium nucleus has about 0.7% less mass than the hydrogen nuclei that combined to form it do. The lost mass is converted into energy during the series of fusion reactions that forms helium. The energy released during the three steps of nuclear fusion causes the sun to shine and gives the sun its high temperature.

Academic Vocabulary
convert (cohn VUHRT) change from one form to another

READING TOOLBOX

Generalizations
Students may note several generalizations. One example is shown here.

Sentence	Word or phrase that signals generalization	Why it is a generalization
Much of the energy given off from the photosphere is in the form of visible light.	much	The statement applies to much, but not all, of the energy given off from the photosphere.

Differentiated Instruction

For Basic Learners

Skit In small groups, have students develop a brief silent skit to act out the process of nuclear fusion. You may suggest that students use signs or labels to help communicate. Invite students to present their skits to the class. Compare the differences between skits and correct any scientific inaccuracies. LS **Logical/Visual**

Mass Changing into Energy

The sun's energy comes from fusion, and the mass that is lost during fusion becomes energy. In 1905, the physicist Albert Einstein, then an unknown patent-office worker, proposed that a small amount of matter yields a large amount of energy. At the time, the existence of nuclear fusion was unknown. In fact, scientists had not yet discovered the nucleus of the atom. Einstein's proposal was part of his special theory of relativity. This theory included the equation $E = mc^2$. In this equation, E represents energy produced; m represents the mass, or the amount of matter, that is changed; and c represents the speed of light, which is about 300,000 km/s. Einstein's equation can be used to calculate the amount of energy produced from a given amount of matter.

By using Einstein's equation, astronomers were able to explain the huge quantities of energy produced by the sun. The sun changes about 4 million tons of mass into energy every second. Yet this amount of mass is small compared with the total mass of the sun.

During fusion, a type of subatomic particle called a *neutrino* is given off. Neutrinos escape the sun and reach Earth in about eight minutes. Studies of these particles confirm that the sun is fueled by the fusion of hydrogen into helium. One apparatus that collects these particles is shown in **Figure 3.** Elements other than hydrogen can fuse, too. In stars that are hotter than the sun, energy is produced by fusion reactions of the nuclei of carbon, nitrogen, and oxygen.

Reading Check **How did the equation $E = mc^2$ help scientists understand the energy of the sun?** (See Appendix G for answers to Reading Checks.)

Figure 3 In Japan, this giant tank of pure water, which was only partly filled when the photo was taken, captures subatomic particles that fly out of the sun during nuclear fusion.

SCILINKS
www.scilinks.org
Topic: The Sun
Code: **HQX1477**

Quick Lab Modeling Fusion

10 min

Procedure

1. Mark six coins by using a marker or wax pencil. Put a *P* for "proton" on the head side of each coin and an *N* for "neutron" on the tail side of the coins.
2. Place two coins P-side up. These two protons each represent hydrogen's simplest isotope, H. Model the fusion of these two H nuclei by placing them such that their edges touch. When they touch, flip one of them to be N-side up. This flip represents a proton becoming a neutron during fusion. The resulting nucleus, which consists of one proton and one neutron, represents the isotope hydrogen-2, ^{2}H.
3. To model the next step of nuclear fusion, place a third coin, P-side up, against the ^{2}H nucleus from step 2. This forms the isotope helium-3, or ^{3}He.
4. Repeat steps 2 and 3 to form a second ^{3}He nucleus.
5. Next, model the fusion of two ^{3}He nuclei. Move the two ^{3}He nuclei formed in step 3 so that their edges touch. When the two ^{3}He nuclei touch, move two of the protons in the two ^{3}He nuclei away from the other four particles. These four particles form a new nucleus: helium-4, or ^{4}He.

Analysis

1. Large amounts of energy are released when nuclei combine. How many energy-producing reactions did you model?
2. Create a diagram that shows the formation of ^{4}He.

Using the Figure GENERAL

Discussion The light-sensitive detectors in the tank illustrated in the figure on this page were designed to detect subatomic particles called *neutrinos*, that are released during fusion reactions in the sun. Neutrinos were first proposed to help explain how mass is conserved when particles such as protons or neutrons change into other particles during nuclear decay reactions. Review the steps in the fusion process. Ask students: "At which step in this process would these subatomic particles most likely be released?" (During the first step, when a proton spontaneously changes into a neutron.) **LS Logical/Visual**

Answer to Reading Check

Einstein's equation helped scientists understand the source of the sun's energy. The equation explained how the sun could produce huge amounts of energy without burning up.

History Connection ADVANCED

Reinventing Time and Space

Invite interested students to research the life and work of Albert Einstein, whose analysis of space, time, gravity, electromagnetic waves, and matter paved the way for a revolution in physics. Einstein also had a major impact on atomic research as a result of his formula $E = mc^2$. Students may also focus on Einstein's humanitarian and social achievements. Encourage students to share the results of their research with classmates as oral reports, demonstrations, or visual presentations. **LS Verbal/Visual**

Quick Lab

Skills Acquired

- Constructing Models
- Recognizing Patterns

Materials

- Six coins
- Marker or wax pencil

Teacher's Notes: You may wish to have students provide their own coins. This lab can also be performed by using paper circles instead of coins.

Answers to Analysis

1. Five reactions were modeled: the formation of two hydrogen-2 atoms; the formation of two helium-3 atoms; and the formation of one helium-4 atom.
2. Student diagrams may vary but should accurately depict the stages of nuclear fusion.

Key Resources

Technology

- Transparencies
  146 Nuclear Fusion

Teach, *continued*

Quick Lab

Skills Acquired
- Constructing Models
- Measuring
- Analyzing Data
- Communicating

Materials
- Compass
- Butcher paper

Teacher's Notes: In this model, Jupiter will be 1/10 the size of the sun, and Earth will be on the order of 1/110 the size of the sun.

The planets could also be modeled from clay once the paper sun has been drawn to scale.

Sample calculation for step 3: If the diameter of the sun is 20 cm, then the diameter of Earth can be found by solving the equation:
$(1.4 \times 10^9)/(1.3 \times 10^7) = 107.7$
$20 \text{ cm}/107.7 = 0.2 \text{ cm}$

Answers to Analysis

The diameter of the sun's core of 1.75×10^8 km is slightly larger than the diameter of Jupiter (1.4×10^8 km) and over 10 times the diameter of Earth (1.3×10^7 km).

Key Resources

Technology
- Transparencies
  147 The Sun's Interior

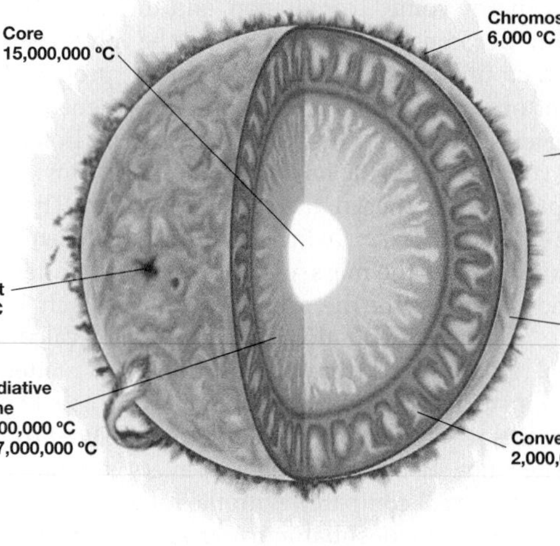

Figure 4 Energy released by fusion reactions in the core slowly works its way through the layers of the sun by the processes of radiation and convection.

Quick Lab — 20 min

The Size of Our Sun

Procedure

1. Using a **compass**, draw a large circle near the edge of a piece of **butcher paper** to represent the sun.
2. Measure the diameter (*D*) of your "sun."
3. Calculate the size of Earth and Jupiter, and compare the sizes with the size of the sun in step 1 by using the following values:
   D (sun) = 1.4×10^9 m
   D (Jupiter) = 1.4×10^8 m
   D (Earth) = 1.3×10^7 m
4. Now, draw Earth and Jupiter to scale on your model.

Analysis

The diameter of the sun's core is about 175,000,000 m. How does the size of the core compare with that of Earth and Jupiter?

The Sun's Interior

Scientists can't see inside the sun. But computer models have revealed what the invisible layers may be like. In recent years, careful studies of motions on the sun's surface have supplied more detail about what is happening inside the sun. The parts of the sun are shown in **Figure 4.**

The Core

At the center of the sun is the core. The core makes up 25% of the sun's total diameter of 1,390,000 km. The temperature of the sun's core is about 15,000,000 °C. No liquid or solid can exist at such a high temperature. The core, like the rest of the sun, is made up entirely of ionized gas. The mass of the sun is 300,000 times the mass of Earth. Because of the sun's large mass, the pressure from the sun's material is so great that the center of the sun is more than 10 times as dense as iron.

The enormous pressure and high temperature of the sun's core cause the atoms to separate into nuclei and electrons. On Earth, atoms generally consist of a nucleus surrounded by one or more electrons. Within the core of the sun, however, the energy and pressure strip electrons away from the atomic nuclei. The nuclei have positive charges, so they tend to push away from each other. But the high temperature and pressure force the nuclei close enough to fuse. The most common nuclear reaction that occurs inside the sun is the fusion of hydrogen into helium.

Differentiated Instruction

Special Education Students

Completing Sentences Have students complete the following sentences to help clarify some of the cause and effect relationships that relate to the structure of the sun:

1—We don't really know what the inside of the sun looks like because (scientists cannot see inside the sun).

2—The layers of the sun are all made of gas because (the sun is too hot for liquids or solids to exist).

3—The center of the sun is more dense than iron because (due to its large mass, the pressure is great).

4—Atoms in the sun's core are different from atoms on Earth because (the energy and pressure at the core strip the electrons away from the atomic nuclei).

The Radiative Zone

Before reaching the sun's atmosphere, the energy produced in the core moves through two zones of the sun's interior. The zone surrounding the core is called the **radiative zone.** The temperature in this zone ranges from about 2,000,000 °C to 7,000,000 °C. In the radiative zone, energy moves outward in the form of electromagnetic waves, or radiation.

radiative zone the zone of the sun's interior that is between the core and the convective zone and in which energy moves by radiation

convective zone the region of the sun's interior that is between the radiative zone and the photosphere and in which energy is carried upward by convection

photosphere the visible surface of the sun

The Convective Zone

Surrounding the radiative zone, comprising the outer 30 percent of the sun, is the **convective zone,** where temperatures are about 2,000,000 °C. Energy produced in the core moves through this zone by convection. *Convection* is the transfer of energy by moving matter. On Earth, boiling water carries energy upward by convection. In the sun's convective zone, hot gases carry energy to the sun's surface. As the hot gases move outward and expand, they lose energy. The cooling gases become denser than the other gases and sink to the bottom of the convective zone. There, the cooled gases are heated by the energy from the radiative zone and rise again. Thus, energy is transferred to the sun's surface as the gases rise and sink.

The Sun's Atmosphere

Surrounding the convective zone is the sun's atmosphere. Although the sun is made of gases, the term *atmosphere* refers to the uppermost region of solar gases. This region has three layers—the photosphere, the chromosphere, and the corona.

The Photosphere

The innermost layer of the solar atmosphere is the **photosphere.** *Photosphere* means "sphere of light." The photosphere is made of gases that have risen from the convective zone. The temperature in the photosphere is about 6,000 °C. Much of the energy given off from the photosphere is in the form of visible light. The layers above the photosphere are transparent, so the visible light is the light that is seen from Earth. A photo of the sun's photosphere is shown in **Figure 5.** The dark spots are cool areas of about 3,800 °C and are called *sunspots.*

Reading Check **What layers make up the sun's atmosphere?**

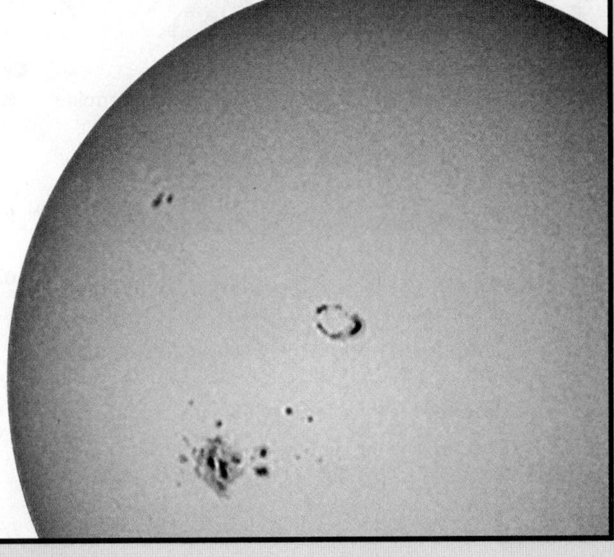

Figure 5 The photosphere is referred to as the sun's surface because this layer is the visible surface of the sun. Sunspots are cooler regions in the photosphere.

Close

Reteaching — BASIC

Diagramming the Sun Have students make a diagram that has six concentric circles. Ask them to label the sun's layers from the core outward to the corona. Underneath the diagram have them summarize the characteristics of each layer. Pairs of students can use their diagrams to quiz each other.
LS Visual/Verbal

Quiz — GENERAL

1. What is the solar wind and in which solar layer does it originate? (The solar wind is a stream of electrically charged particles that flows outward from the corona.)
2. How have scientists learned about the sun's composition and internal structure? (by using devices such as spectrographs, computer models, and spacecraft)
3. What is the source of the sun's energy? (fusion reactions that convert hydrogen nuclei into helium and give off energy in the process)

Skill Builder — GENERAL

Vocabulary The names for the layers of the sun's atmosphere come from the following Greek roots: *chroma* means "color" and *photo* means "pertaining to light." Related scientific terms that students may encounter include *photon, photosynthesis, chromatid,* and *chromatography.* The combining form *-sphere,* from the Greek *sphaira,* meaning "ball," is commonly used to refer to a layer of gas surrounding a planet or star, as in the words *ionosphere* and *atmosphere.*
LS Verbal English Language Learners

Answer to Reading Check
The sun's atmosphere consists of the photosphere, the chromosphere, and the corona.

Close, *continued*

Answers to Section Review

1. The dark lines in spectra show what elements are present in the gases of the star.
2. hydrogen and helium
3. helium nuclei and energy
4. Nuclear fusion consists of a series of reactions in which hydrogen nuclei collide and fuse to form helium nuclei and release other particles. During each step in the process, mass is lost and energy is released.
5. The radiative zone is the region around the sun's core where energy moves in the form of electromagnetic waves. Temperatures range from 2,000,000 °C to 7,000,000 °C. The convective zone is located between the radiative zone and the sun's atmosphere and is where energy moves by convection currents. Temperatures are about 2,000,000 °C.
6. The photosphere is the innermost layer of the sun's atmosphere. Its energy is made of visible light. The outer two layers are thin and transparent. The chromosphere glows with the reddish color of hydrogen. The corona is the extremely hot outermost layer.
7. The corona can be seen during an eclipse because the moon blocks the photosphere's light. As the sky darkens, the corona becomes visible.
8. Answers may vary. Sample answer: Because hydrogen nuclei combine to form helium nuclei during fusion, the amount of hydrogen will decrease over time.
9. Nuclear fusion takes enormous heat and pressure. The core of the sun is the only layer that has the necessary conditions for fusion.
10. Answers may vary. Sample answer: The corona helps prevent most subatomic particles from escaping. If the sun's corona were lost, the solar wind would be much stronger and would bombard Earth and the inner planets with charged particles.
11. The *sun* is composed of several layers, including the *core,* in which *nuclear fusion* of *hydrogen* nuclei forms *helium;* the *radiative zone;* and the *convective zone.*

Figure 6 The corona of the sun becomes visible during a total solar eclipse. The black disk is the silhouette of the moon, which is blocking the photosphere.

The Chromosphere

Above the photosphere lies the **chromosphere,** or color sphere. This is a thin layer of gases that glows with reddish light that is typical of the color given off by hydrogen. The chromosphere's temperature ranges from 6,000°C to 50,000°C. The gases of the chromosphere move away from the photosphere. In an upward movement, gas regularly forms narrow jets of hot gas that shoot outward to form the chromosphere and then fade away within a few minutes. Some of these jets reach heights of 16,000 km.

Spacecraft study the sun from above Earth's atmosphere. These spacecraft can detect small details on the sun. They can also measure wavelengths of light that are blocked by Earth's atmosphere. Movies made from these spacecraft images show how features on the sun rise, change, and sometimes twist.

chromosphere the thin layer of the sun that is just above the photosphere and that glows a reddish color during eclipses

corona the outermost layer of the sun's atmosphere

The Sun's Outer Parts

Just above the chromosphere is a thin zone called the transition region where the temperature rises dramatically. The outermost layer of the sun's atmosphere is the **corona** (kuh ROH nuh), or crown. The corona is a huge region of gas with a temperature above 1,000,000 °C. The corona is not very dense, but its magnetic field can stop most subatomic particles from escaping into space. However, electrons and electrically charged particles called *ions* do stream out into space as the corona expands. These particles make up the *solar wind,* which flows outward from the sun to the rest of the solar system.

The chromosphere and the corona are normally not seen from Earth because the sky during the day is too bright. Occasionally, however, the moon moves between Earth and the sun and blocks out the light of the photosphere. The sky darkens, and the corona becomes visible, as shown in **Figure 6.**

Section 1 Review

Key Ideas

1. **Describe** how scientists use spectra to determine the composition of stars.
2. **Identify** the two elements that make up most of the sun.
3. **Identify** the end products of the nuclear fusion process that occurs in the sun.
4. **Explain** how the sun converts matter into energy in its core.
5. **Compare** the radiative and convective zones of the sun.
6. **Describe** the three layers of the sun's atmosphere.
7. **Explain** why the sun's corona can be seen during an eclipse but not at other times.

Critical Thinking

8. **Making Inferences** Describe whether the amount of hydrogen in the sun will increase or decrease over the next few million years. Explain your reasoning.
9. **Analyzing Ideas** Why does fusion occur in the sun's core but not in other layers?
10. **Predicting Consequences** What might happen to the solar wind if the sun lost its corona?

Concept Mapping

11. Use the following terms to create a concept map: *sun, hydrogen, helium, nuclear fusion, core, radiative zone,* and *convective zone.*

Differentiated Instruction

Alternative Assessment

Solar Tales Have students do a creative writing exercise in which they tell the life story of an atom of hydrogen inside the sun. Student stories should incorporate details about nuclear reactions, the temperatures and forces matter is subjected to in the different layers, and how energy travels within the sun. **LS Verbal**

SECTION 2
Solar Activity

Key Ideas	Key Terms	Why It Matters
❯ Explain how sunspots are related to powerful magnetic fields on the sun. ❯ Compare prominences, solar flares, and coronal mass ejections. ❯ Describe how the solar wind can cause auroras on Earth.	**sunspot** **prominence** **solar flare** **coronal mass ejection** **aurora**	Solar flares and coronal mass ejections can cause geomagnetic storms on Earth that disrupt communications technologies such as radio, television, and cellular telephones.

The gases that make up the sun's interior and atmosphere are in constant motion. The energy produced in the sun's core and the force of gravity combine to cause the continuous rising and sinking of gases. The gases also move because the sun rotates on its axis. Because the sun is a ball of hot gases rather than a solid sphere, not all locations on the sun rotate at the same speed. Places close to the equator on the surface of the sun take 25.3 Earth days to rotate once. Points near the poles take 33 days to rotate once. On average, the sun rotates once every 27 days.

sunspot a dark area of the photosphere of the sun that is cooler than the surrounding areas and that has a strong magnetic field

Sunspots

The movement of gases within the sun's convective zone and the movements caused by the sun's rotation produce magnetic fields. These magnetic fields cause convection to slow in parts of the convective zone. Slower convection causes a decrease in the amount of gas that is transferring energy from the core of the sun to these regions of the photosphere. In some places, the magnetic field is thousands of times stronger than it is in other places. Because less energy is being transferred, these regions of the photosphere are up to 3,000 °C cooler than surrounding regions.

Although they still shine brightly, these cooler areas of the sun appear darker than the areas that surround them do. These cool, dark areas of gas within the photosphere are called **sunspots.** The rest of the photosphere has a grainy appearance called *granulation.* The area around the sunspots shown in **Figure 1** has visible granulation. A large sunspot can have a diameter of more than 100,000 km, which is more than seven times the diameter of Earth.

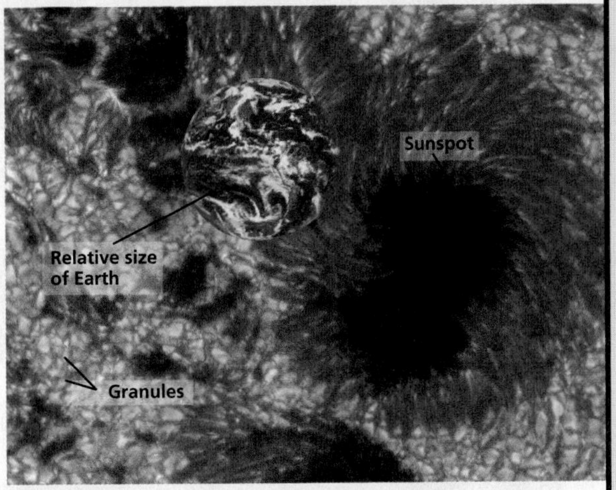

Figure 1 The diameter of this large sunspot is bigger than Earth's diameter. This image also shows the granulation on the sun's surface.

Section 2

Focus

Overview

The section examines the relationship between the sun's magnetic field and sunspots, prominences, coronal mass ejections, and flares, and explains how these solar storms affect the environment around Earth.

Bellringer

Have students answer the following question: "What do you think the 'weather' in the sun's atmosphere is like?" (Answers may vary. Accept all reasonable answers.) **LS Logical**

Motivate

Discussion — GENERAL

Sunspots In 1610, Galileo was among the first to study sunspots in detail when he turned the newly invented telescope toward the sky. Invite students to discuss why these regions appear dark. (They are cooler than hotter, brighter surrounding regions.) Have students use a sheet of paper or a ruler to compare the diameter of Earth shown in the figure to the large sunspot. (At its widest point the sunspot is about 1/3 larger than Earth's diameter.) **LS Verbal/Visual**

Key Resources

Chapter Resource File
- Directed Reading BASIC

Technology
- Transparencies
  Bellringer

Teach

Using the Figure GENERAL

Sunspot Cycles Direct student attention to the graph of the sunspot cycle. Ask them how many sunspot cycles the graph shows. (three) Invite students to create a graph that estimates the sunspot cycle for the next 30 to 35 years. They can use this graph to answer the caption question. Answer to caption question: The next high point will occur in 2011. (Subsequent high points will occur in 2022 and 2033.) **LS Visual/Logical**

READING TOOLBOX

Suffixes Students should add the terms *coronal mass ejection* and *granulation* to their charts.

Why It Matters

SOHO, So Helpful

The Solar and Heliospheric Observatory (SOHO) was a project of the European Space Agency and NASA to study the Sun as well as Sun–Earth interactions. Launched in 1995 and originally designed for only a two-year mission, the mission was extended multiple times. SOHO has also discovered more than 1,000 comets.

Answer to Your Turn

Online Research Answers will vary depending on when you are teaching this chapter.

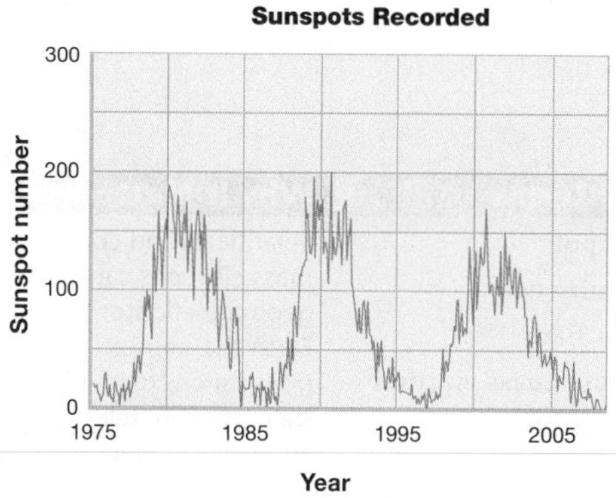

Figure 2 The sunspot cycle lasts an average of 11 years. ***When will the next high point in the cycle occur?***

The Sunspot Cycle

Astronomers have carefully observed sunspots for hundreds of years. Observations of sunspots showed astronomers that the sun rotates. Later, astronomers observed that the numbers and positions of sunspots vary in a cycle that lasts about 11 years.

A sunspot cycle begins when the number of sunspots is very low but begins to increase. Sunspots initially appear in groups about midway between the sun's equator and poles. The number of sunspots increases over the next few years until it reaches a peak of 100 or more sunspots. Then, sunspots at higher latitudes slowly disappear, and new ones appear closer to the sun's equator. **Figure 2** shows that after the peak, the number of sunspots begins to decrease until it reaches a minimum. Another 11-year cycle begins when the number of sunspots begins to increase again.

READING TOOLBOX

Suffixes
In Section 2, one key term and two italicized words contain the suffix *-tion*. Find and add these words to your table.

Solar Eruptions

Many other solar activities are affected by the sunspot cycle. The *solar-activity cycle* is caused by the changing solar magnetic field. This cycle is characterized by increases and decreases in various types of solar activity, including solar eruptions. Solar eruptions are events in which the sun lifts substantial material above the photosphere and emits atomic or subatomic particles. These events include prominences, solar flares, and coronal mass ejections.

Why It Matters

SOHO, So Helpful

On November 4, 2003, the most violent solar flare ever recorded ejected billions of tons of hot gases and particles from the sun's surface at 2,700 km/s. Had Earth been in its direct path, we would have had only 17 hours warning. Without the Solar and Heliospheric Observatory (SOHO), we might not have seen it coming. SOHO images the sun in visible, X-ray, and (as shown here) UV frequencies. Initially planned for two years, the mission has been extended at least three times.

In addition to its sun-related duties, SOHO has discovered more than 1,000 new comets.

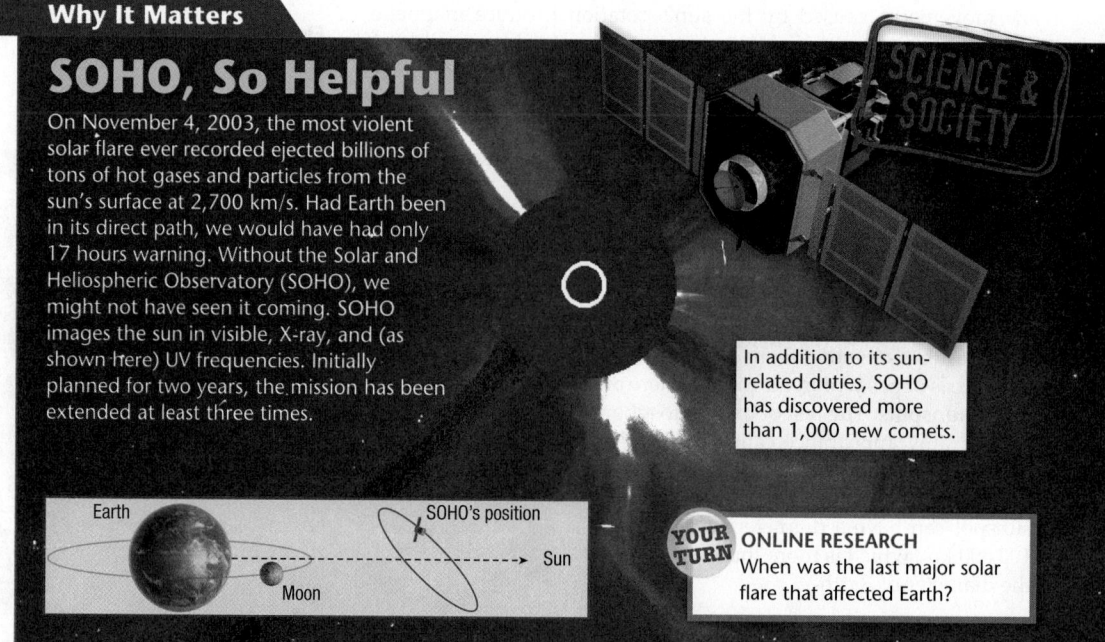

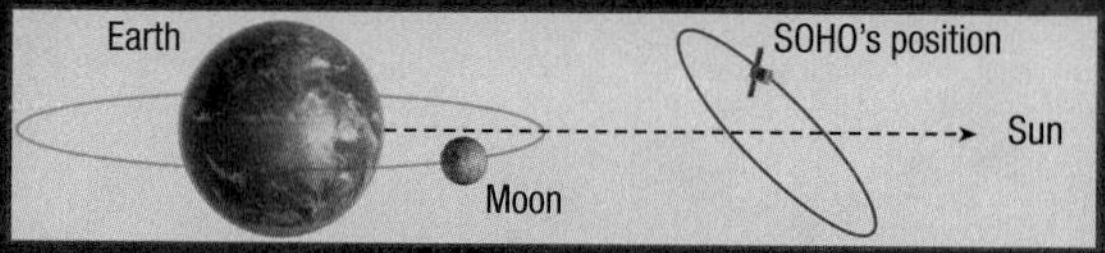

YOUR TURN ONLINE RESEARCH
When was the last major solar flare that affected Earth?

Internet Activity BASIC

Solar Activity and Climate Invite interested students to use the Internet to research the relationship between solar activity levels and climate on Earth. They may investigate the debate over the connection between sunspot activity and climate variations known as the *Medieval Maximum* and the *Little Ice Age*, or the variations in Earth's orbit relative to the sun and changes in solar intensity. A worksheet designed to direct student research on this topic can be found in the **Chapter Resource File** booklet or by visiting www.thinkcentral.com and entering the keyword **HQXSUNX. LS Visual/Verbal/Logical**

Differentiated Instruction

Advanced Learners

Presentations Advanced students may want to learn more about material referred to in the text. Challenge students to explore the frequency, appearances, and other qualities of solar ejections including prominences, solar flares, and coronal mass ejections. Have them create posters or multimedia presentations that show what they find. **LS Visual**

Prominences

The magnetic fields that cause sunspots also create other disturbances in the sun's atmosphere. Great clouds of glowing gases, called **prominences,** form huge arches that reach high above the sun's surface. Each solar prominence follows curved magnetic field lines from a region of one magnetic polarity to a region of the opposite magnetic polarity. Some prominences may last for several weeks, while others may erupt and disappear in hours. The gas in prominences is very hot and is commonly associated with the chromosphere.

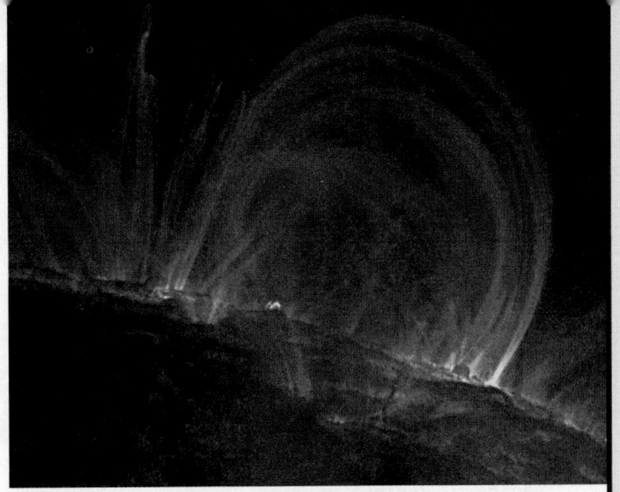

Figure 3 A coronal loop, shown here curving from left to right, can arch more than 500,000 km above the sun's surface.

Solar Flares

The most violent of all solar disturbances is a **solar flare,** a sudden outward eruption of electrically charged particles, such as electrons and protons. The trigger for these eruptions is unknown. However, scientists know that solar flares release the energy stored in the strong magnetic fields of sunspots. This release of energy can lead to the formation of coronal loops, such as the ones shown in **Figure 3.**

Solar flares may travel upward thousands of kilometers within minutes, but few eruptions last more than an hour. During a peak in the sunspot cycle, 5 to 10 solar flares may occur each day. The temperature of the gas in solar flares may reach 20,000,000 °C. Some of the particles from a solar flare escape into space. These particles increase the strength of the solar wind.

prominence a loop of relatively cool, incandescent gas that extends above the photosphere and above the sun's edge as seen from Earth

solar flare an explosive release of energy that comes from the sun and that is associated with magnetic disturbances on the sun's surface

coronal mass ejection coronal gas that is thrown into space from the sun

Coronal Mass Ejections

Particles also escape into space as **coronal mass ejections,** or parts of the corona that are thrown off the sun. As the gusts of particles strike Earth's *magnetosphere*, or the space around Earth that contains a magnetic field, the particles can generate a sudden disturbance in Earth's magnetic field. These disturbances are called *geomagnetic storms*. Although several small geomagnetic storms may occur each month, the average number of severe storms is less than one per year.

Geomagnetic storms have been known to interfere with radio communications on Earth. The high-energy particles that circulate in Earth's outer atmosphere during geomagnetic storms can also damage satellites. They can also lead to blackouts when power lines become overloaded. Not all solar activity is so dramatic, but the activity of the sun affects Earth every day.

Reading Check **How do coronal mass ejections affect communications on Earth?**

Math Skills

Magnetic Fields
Solar magnetic field densities at the sun's poles are 0.001 teslas (T); those near sunspots are up to 0.3 T. How many times the field densities at the poles are field densities near sunspots?

Skill Builder — GENERAL

Writing Have students write a descriptive passage about the spectacular light displays provided by auroras, and include a scientific explanation of how the interaction of the solar wind with Earth's magnetic field and atmospheric gases is responsible for this phenomenon. **LS Verbal**

Math Skills

Answer
(0.3 T) ÷ (0.001 T) = 300; Fields are 300 times more dense near the sunspots.

Close

Reteaching — BASIC

Solar Lingo Have students work in groups to create cards for each key term and italicized word in the section by writing the terms on one side of the card and definitions on the other. Then, have students shuffle the cards and play a game of twenty questions in which teams try to identify the terms on the cards by asking yes-and-no questions. **LS Verbal**

Quiz — GENERAL

1. What is the relationship between solar flares and sunspots? (Solar flares release energy stored in the strong magnetic fields of sunspots.)
2. Describe the role of Earth's magnetic field in causing auroras. (High-energy particles from the solar wind interact with Earth's magnetic field and are trapped by the magnetosphere. These particles strike atoms and gas molecules in the upper atmosphere and cause the molecules to emit light.)

Group Activity — GENERAL

Geomagnetic Storms Have groups of students explore methods of dealing with the effects of geomagnetic storms. Some students could interview experts about how these storms can be predicted. Others could do Internet or library research on the effects of these phenomena on pilots, astronauts, emergency personnel, and others. Other students could prepare posters with safety instructions for the general public. Still others could work on a presentation of their group findings. **LS Interpersonal**
Co-op Learning

Answer to Reading Check
Coronal mass ejections generate sudden disturbances in Earth's magnetic field. The high-energy particles that circulate during these storms can damage satellites, cause power blackouts, and interfere with radio communications.

Close, *continued*

Answers to Section Review

1. The strong magnetic fields of sunspots tend to slow down movement of gases. Slower movement means less energy is transferred between particles, which makes the matter cooler.
2. At the peak of the cycle about 100 or more sunspots occur.
3. During the sunspot cycle, sunspots initially appear in groups about midway between the poles and the equator. After the peak, sunspots at higher latitudes begin to disappear, and new ones appear near middle latitudes.
4. Prominences are larger masses of glowing gases that form arches above the sun's surface. They follow lines of magnetic force and may last several weeks. A solar flare is a violent eruption of electrically charged particles that releases energy stored in the magnetic fields of sunspots. Flares may form coronal loops and travel thousands of kilometers. Eruptions seldom last longer than an hour.
5. Auroras are sheets of light produced by high-energy particles released by the solar wind. These particles excite gases in Earth's upper atmosphere.
6. Sunspots appear darker in contrast with the surrounding regions of the photosphere that are much brighter and hotter.
7. because the sun is made up of gases that do not move as a single unit as solid materials do
8. Patterns of *sunspot* activity are related to the *solar-activity cycle,* which affects solar ejections such as *solar flares, prominences,* and *coronal mass ejections.*

Figure 4 Auroras, such as these over Finland, can fill the entire sky. The different colors in an aurora result from high-energy particles from the sun colliding with atoms of different elements in Earth's atmosphere.

Academic Vocabulary
interaction (IN tuhr AK shuhn) the action or influence between things

aurora colored light produced by charged particles from the solar wind and from the magnetosphere that react with and excite the oxygen and nitrogen of Earth's upper atmosphere; usually seen in the sky near Earth's magnetic poles

SCILINKS.
www.scilinks.org
Topic: Solar Activity
Code: **HQX1413**

Auroras

On Earth, a spectacular effect of the interaction between the solar wind and Earth's magnetosphere is the appearance in the sky of bands of light called **auroras** (aw RAWR uhz). **Figure 4** shows an example of an aurora. Auroras are usually seen close to Earth's magnetic poles because electrically charged particles are guided toward Earth's magnetic poles by Earth's magnetosphere. The electrically charged particles strike the atoms and gas molecules in the upper atmosphere and produce colorful sheets of light. Depending on which pole they are near, auroras are called *northern lights*—or *aurora borealis* (aw RAWR uh BAWR ee AL is)—or *southern lights*—or *aurora australis.*

Auroras normally occur between 100 and 1,000 km above Earth's surface. They are most frequent just after a peak in the sunspot cycle, especially after solar flares occur. Across the northern contiguous United States, auroras are visible about five times per year. In Alaska, however, people can see auroras almost every clear, dark night. Astronauts in orbit can also look down on Earth and see auroras. But Earth is not the only planet that has auroras. Spacecraft have imaged auroras on Jupiter and Saturn.

Section 2 Review

Key Ideas

1. **Explain** why sunspots are cooler than surrounding areas on the sun's surface.
2. **Identify** the number of sunspots that are on the sun during the peak of the sunspot cycle.
3. **Summarize** how the latitude of sunspots varies during the sunspot cycle.
4. **Explain** how prominences are different from solar flares.
5. **Summarize** the cause of auroras on Earth.

Critical Thinking

6. **Identifying Relationships** How can a sunspot be bright but look dark?
7. **Analyzing Ideas** Why doesn't the whole sun rotate at the same rate?

Concept Mapping

8. Use the following terms to create a concept map: *sunspot, prominence, solar flare, solar-activity cycle,* and *coronal mass ejection.*

Differentiated Instruction

Alternative Assessment

The Active Sun Ask students to create a comic strip or poster that explains how electromagnetic radiation and particles from the active sun affect life on Earth. Before they begin the assessment, have them create a concept map or other graphic organizer that includes information about sunspots, the solar activity cycle, auroras, and geomagnetic storms. LS **Logical/Visual**

Why It Matters

Auroras For thousands of years, people have observed auroras with wonder. Eskimos described them as the dancing souls of animals. The Maori of New Zealand believed that they were travelers that had become trapped by ice and cold. Auroras reminded the Finns of magical "fire foxes." The Lakota Sioux associated them with ghost dancers. Encourage student teams to research a folk belief about auroras and then create a children's book based on their choice. LS **Verbal/Visual**
Co-op Learning

Why It Matters

Seasonal Sunlight

Visible light makes up a small fraction of the sun's total energy and is the only part of its energy that your eyes can detect. But this tiny "sliver" of the electromagnetic spectrum helps to feed the world, guide animals on their yearly migrations, and even let you know when it's time to wake up. Earth's green plants and other producers use about 2% of the solar energy that reaches Earth for photosynthesis, generating between 150 and 200 billion tons of organic matter each year. This is the matter that we use for food, fuel, and countless other applications.

Sunlight motivates us to go outside and helps keep our bodies fit. Our skin uses sunlight to make vitamin D, which we need for strong bones and a healthy immune system.

In winter, when there is less natural light available, some people experience seasonal affective disorder (SAD) and use methods known as light therapy to help them cope.

Some migratory animals, such as butterflies and birds, use the sun to help them determine direction when they travel. Fish use patterns of reflected sunlight for the same purpose.

YOUR TURN

UNDERSTANDING CONCEPTS
What are three ways that people depend on sunlight?

CRITICAL THINKING
In what other ways do organisms rely on sunlight?

Why It Matters

Seasonal Sunlight

The sun's infrared (heat) energy provides Earth with warmth and drives atmospheric and hydrospheric systems that help provide and maintain climates suitable for Earth's great diversity of life. Sunlight—energy in the visible band of the sun's electromagnetic spectrum—is specifically responsible for events on Earth as varied as photosynthesis, migration, and circadian rhythms. Earth relies on the sun during the growing season for photosynthesis, which provides the matter and energy that sustains most of the life on the planet.

Sunlight is also directly involved in the manufacture of vitamin D in our skin. Some people need to supplement their vitamin D during darker winter months and some need to use a form of light therapy to treat seasonal affective disorder. Also, the overabundance of artificial light in modern, western society can affect our natural circadian rhythms.

Answers to Your Turn

Understanding Concepts Student answers will vary. Examples include: solar energy, vitamin D, our food, vegetation (thus, indirectly, our shelter), precipitation (solar radiation plays role in the water cycle), warmth, and wind currents (convection currents).

Critical Thinking Student answers will vary. Examples include: photosynthesis, vitamin D, water, and warmth.

Time Required

two 45-minute class periods

Lab Ratings

EASY → HARD

Teacher Preparation

Student Setup

Concept Level

Cleanup

Skills Acquired

- Experimenting
- Measuring
- Collecting Data
- Calculating
- Interpreting Results

Scientific Methods

In this lab, students will

- Analyze Results
- Evaluate Models
- Communicate Results

Materials

The materials listed are enough for groups of 2 or 3 students. You should collect enough similar glass jars for as many groups as plan to do the lab. Pasta sauce jars work well for this purpose. An Erlenmeyer flask with a one-hole stopper can be used instead of a jar if available.

You may want to punch holes in the metal jar lids in advance to save class time. Solar collector jars may be reused with later classes.

Skills Practice Lab

90 min

Energy of the Sun

Objectives

- **Estimate** the sun's energy output.
- **Evaluate** the differences between known values and experimental values.

Materials

aluminum foil, 8 cm × 64 cm
clay, modeling
desk lamp with 100 W bulb
jar, glass, with lid
paint or magic marker, black, flat finish
pencil
ruler, metric
tape, masking
thermometer, Celsius

Safety

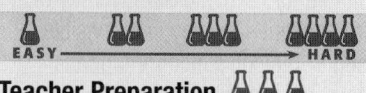

The sun is, on average, 150 million kilometers away from Earth. Scientists use complex astronomical instruments to measure the size and energy output of the sun. However, it is possible to estimate the sun's energy output by using simple instruments and the knowledge of the relationship between the sun's size and its distance from Earth. In this lab, you will collect energy from sunlight and estimate the amount of energy produced by the sun.

Procedure

1. Construct a solar collector in the following way.
   - **a.** Carefully punch a hole in the jar lid, or use a lid that is already prepared by your teacher.
   - **b.** Cut an 8 cm × 64 cm piece of aluminum foil. Place the piece of foil with the shorter (8 cm) edge in front of you. Fold the strip over three times. Then rotate the foil 90°, and fold it over two times. The resulting foil strip is now 2 cm × 8 cm. Wrap the strip snugly around at least half the bulb of the thermometer. Bend the edges out so that they form "wings," as shown in the photo. **CAUTION** Thermometers are fragile. Do not squeeze the bulb of the thermometer too tight or let the thermometer strike any solid object. Bend the remaining foil outward to collect as much sunlight as possible.
   - **c.** Paint the wings black using a marker or flat black paint.
   - **d.** Slip the top of the thermometer through the hole in the jar's lid. On the top and bottom of the lid, mold the clay around the thermometer to hold the thermometer steady. Place the lid on the jar. Adjust the thermometer so that the aluminum-foil wings are centered in the jar. Then, secure the thermometer and clay to the lid with masking tape.
2. Place the solar collector in sunlight. Tilt the jar so that the sun shines directly on the metal wings. Carefully hold the jar in place. You may want to prop the jar up carefully with books.
3. Watch the temperature reading on the thermometer until it reaches a maximum value or until 5 min have elapsed. Record this value. Allow the collector to cool for 2 min.

Tips and Tricks

The wings on the solar collector can be made bigger to exaggerate the temperature differences. A heat lamp bulb can also be used instead of a light bulb. Multiple solar collectors can be built and used to test and compare solar intensities in different conditions.

Make sure that the lab thermometers you are using will fit through the holes in the jar lids and that the holes can easily be plugged with the modeling clay. Another lump of clay or a bookend could be used to prop up the solar collector so that it remains tilted to catch the direct rays of the sun. If it is windy or cool outside, have students set up their experiments indoors on a sunny windowsill. Remind students to allow the thermometer to cool down to room temperature before repeating the experiment with the lamp. (The distance from the lamp to the thermometer has to be about 8 cm for the math to work correctly.)

4. Place the lamp or heat lamp at the end of a table. Remove any reflector or shade from the lamp.
5. Place the collector about 30 cm from the lamp, and turn the collector toward the lamp.
6. Turn on the lamp, and wait 1 min. Then, gradually move the collector toward the lamp in 2 cm increments. Watch the temperature carefully. At each position, let the collector sit until the temperature reading stabilizes. Stop moving the collector when the temperature reaches the maximum temperature that was achieved in sunlight.
7. Once the temperature has stabilized at the same level reached in sunlight, record the distance between the center of the lamp and the thermometer bulb.

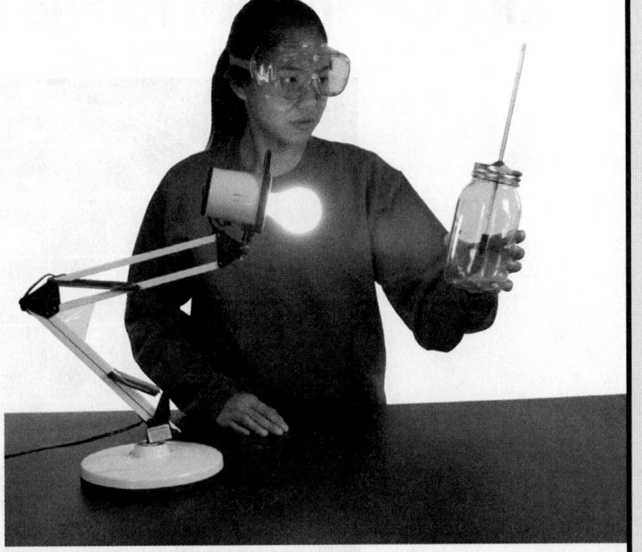

Analysis

1. **Analyzing Results** Because the collector reached the same temperature in both trials, the collector absorbed as much energy from the sun at a distance of 150 million km as it did from the light bulb at the distance that you measured. Using 1.5×10^{13} cm as the distance to the sun, calculate the power of the sun in watts by using the equation that follows. The power of the lamp is equal to the wattage of the light bulb.

$$\frac{power_{sun}}{(distance_{sun})^2} = \frac{power_{lamp}}{(distance_{lamp})^2}$$

2. **Evaluating Models** The sun's power is generally given as 3.7×10^{26} W. Calculate your experimental percentage error by first subtracting your experimental value from the accepted value. Divide this difference by the accepted value, and multiply by 100. Describe two possible sources for your calculated error.

Extension

Evaluating Models How would using a fluorescent bulb instead of an incandescent bulb in the experiment affect the results of the experiment? Explain your answer.

Answers to Analysis

1. Values of student temperature readings and the recorded distances between the center of the lamp and the thermometer bulb may vary. Though answers may vary, calculated values for solar power should be on the order of 3.7×10^{26} watts.
2. Calculated error may vary but should show correct calculations. Possible sources of error in the measurements may include some heat exchange between the jar and the room if the clay plug was affected by heat over time; heat from room lighting; variations in cloud cover affecting solar readings; and variations between the readings obtained for the temperature of the sun and for the incandescent bulb.

Answer to Extension

Answers may vary. The experiment would probably not have worked as well with a fluorescent bulb. Fluorescent bulbs produce light in a different way than incandescent bulbs do, and they do not produce as much thermal energy.

XRT Composite Image of the Sun

Internet Activity GENERAL

SOHO Images The light that humans can see represents only a small fraction of the total electromagnetic spectrum. To study all of the wavelengths of light that are emitted by the sun, scientists need to place observational equipment above Earth's atmosphere. The Solar and Heliospheric Observatory (SOHO), a project of the European Space Agency and NASA, was designed to provide a year-round uninterrupted view of the sun. Have students visit the SOHO Web site and look through the vast archive of solar images. Have them each select an image and use it to construct a map of some aspect of solar activity that interests them. A worksheet designed to direct student research on this topic can be found in the **Chapter Resource File** booklet or by visiting www.thinkcentral.com and entering the keyword **HQXSUNX.** **LS Visual**

Answers to Map Skills Activity

1. approximately −3° south latitude and −21° west longitude
2. The region at 15° north latitude and −15° west longitude has moderate X-ray radiation.
3. The lines of longitude appear to be closer together at the right and left sides of the map because of distortion produced by projecting a curved surface onto a flat map.
4. −15° to −60° longitude
5. at locations that have the color yellow

MAPS in Action

XRT Composite Image of the Sun

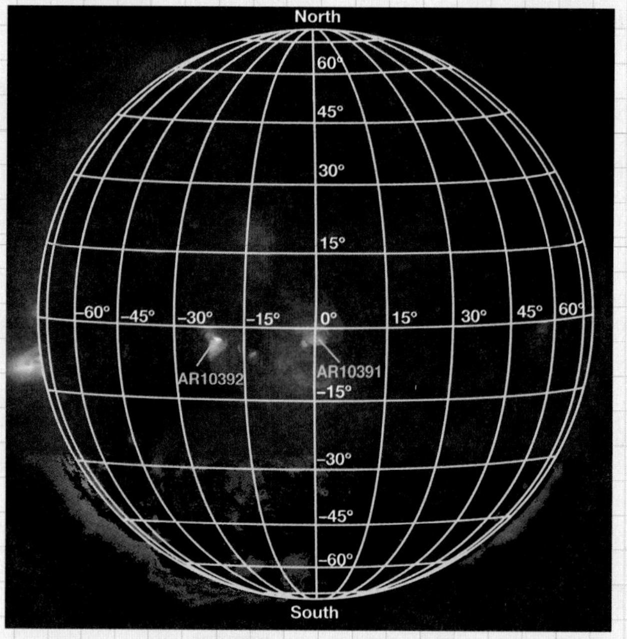

Map Skills Activity

This map is an X-ray telescope (XRT) image of the sun that includes latitude and longitude lines. Yellow represents the strongest X-ray radiation. Red represents moderate X-ray radiation. Black represents the weakest X-ray radiation. Active regions (AR) are numbered. Use the map to answer these questions.

1. **Analyzing Data** What is the latitude and longitude of the active region numbered 10392?
2. **Analyzing Data** How would you describe the intensity of the X-ray radiation in the region at 15° north latitude and –15° west longitude?
3. **Inferring Relationships** Why do the lines of solar longitude appear to be close to each other near the left side and the right side of the map?
4. **Interpreting Data** Dark regions of the corona that are visible in X-ray images are called *coronal holes*. They are the source of the solar wind. What is the range of longitudes covered by the coronal hole in the southwestern quadrant of the map?
5. **Analyzing Relationships** Sunspots emit large amounts of X-ray radiation. Where on this map would you expect to find sunspots?

Key Resources

Technology

- Transparencies
  148 XRT Composite Image of the Sun

Chapter 29

Summary

THINK central
SUPER SUMMARY
Keyword: HQXSUNS

Key Ideas | **Key Terms**

Section 1

Structure of the Sun

- The sun's core converts matter into energy through the process of nuclear fusion. In nuclear fusion, four hydrogen nuclei are combined to form one helium nucleus, releasing much energy.
- Energy produced by nuclear fusion moves from the sun's core through the hotter radiative zone (in the form of electromagnetic waves) and then the cooler convective zone (in the form of gaseous convection currents) before it enters the sun's atmosphere.
- The sun's atmosphere is composed of three layers: the photosphere (the inner layer, but the layer that is visible to us on Earth), the hotter chromosphere, and the much hotter and much larger corona (the outer layer).

nuclear fusion, p. 824
radiative zone, p. 827
convective zone, p. 827
photosphere, p. 827
chromosphere, p. 828
corona, p. 828

Section 2

Solar Activity

- Sunspots are regions of the photosphere that have stronger magnetic fields than the regions that surround them. They are cooler than the surrounding regions because less energy is being transferred to them from the core.
- Prominences are loops of relatively cool gas that extend above the photosphere. They are usually associated with the chromosphere. Solar flares are explosive releases of the energy stored in the magnetic fields of sunspots. Coronal mass ejections cause disturbances in Earth's magnetosphere called geomagnetic storms.
- Auroras are colorful sheets of light that occur in Earth's polar regions when charged particles from the interaction between the solar wind and Earth's magnetosphere collide with atoms and molecules in the atmosphere.

sunspot, p. 829
prominence, p. 831
solar flare, p. 831
coronal mass ejection, p. 831
aurora, p. 832

Chapter Summary

Using THINK central Resources

Super Summary

Have students connect the major concepts in this chapter through an interactive Super Summary. Visit www.thinkcentral.com and type in the keyword **HQXSUNS** to access the Super Summary for this chapter.

Differentiated Instruction

Alternative Assessment

Our Daytime Star Have small groups create models, diagrams, demonstrations, and hands-on activities that will enable them to explain the following concepts to a group of younger children: (1) the nuclear reactions that fuel the sun's energy source, (2) the sun's layered structure, and (3) how the active regions of the sun affect the atmospheric conditions on Earth that make life possible. Caution them to explain all the terms they use, and to include simple directions for doing the activities. If possible, have students present the materials they have created to a local school or community group.
LS Kinesthetic/ Interpersonal

Chapter 29 Review

1. **Chain-of-Events Chart** Create a chain-of-events chart to show how the solar wind interacts with Earth's magnetosphere to form auroras.

READING TOOLBOX

USING KEY TERMS

Use each of the following terms in a separate sentence.

2. *photosphere*
3. *solar flare*
4. *solar wind*
5. *sunspot cycle*

For each pair of terms, explain how the meanings of the terms differ.

6. *chromosphere* and *corona*
7. *photosphere* and *core*
8. *solar flare* and *prominence*
9. *aurora* and *solar wind*

UNDERSTANDING KEY IDEAS

10. According to Einstein's theory of relativity, in the formula $E = mc^2$, the c stands for
    a. corona.
    b. core.
    c. the speed of light.
    d. the length of time.
11. A nuclear reaction in which atomic nuclei combine is called
    a. fission.
    b. fusion.
    c. magnetism.
    d. granulation.
12. The part of the sun in which energy moves from atom to atom in the form of electromagnetic waves is called the
    a. radiative zone.
    b. convective zone.
    c. solar wind.
    d. chromosphere.
13. The number of hydrogen atoms that fuse to form a helium atom is
    a. two.
    b. four.
    c. six.
    d. eight.
14. The part of the sun that is normally visible from Earth is the
    a. core.
    b. photosphere.
    c. corona.
    d. solar nebula.
15. Sunspots are regions of
    a. intense magnetism.
    b. the core.
    c. high temperature.
    d. lighter color.
16. The sunspot cycle repeats about every
    a. month.
    b. 5 years.
    c. 11 years.
    d. 19 years.
17. Sudden outward eruptions of electrically charged particles from the sun are called
    a. prominences.
    b. coronas.
    c. sunspots.
    d. solar flares.
18. Gusts of solar wind can cause
    a. rotation.
    b. magnetic storms.
    c. nuclear fission.
    d. nuclear fusion.
19. *Northern lights* and *southern lights* are other names for
    a. prominences.
    b. auroras.
    c. granulations.
    d. total solar irradiance.

SHORT ANSWER

20. What is the outermost layer of the sun?
21. How is the solar activity cycle related to the sunspot cycle?
22. What is unusual about the magnetic field in a sunspot?
23. From what process does the sun gets its energy? What steps does this process follow?
24. Compare two types of solar activity.
25. Describe the corona, and identify when it is visible from Earth.
26. How does the transfer of energy in the radiative zone differ from the transfer of energy in the convective zone?

Chapter Review

Assignment Guide	
Section	**Questions**
1	2, 4, 6, 7, 10–14, 20, 23, 25–28, 33, 36
2	1, 3, 5, 8, 15–19, 21, 22, 24, 29–32, 34, 35, 37–40
1–2	9

Reading Toolbox

1. Students should consult Appendix A for tips on making a chain-of-events chart. Students' charts should include all steps of the interaction between the solar wind and Earth's magnetosphere that forms auroras.

Using Key Terms

2–9. Answers may vary but should show that students understand the definitions of and differences between key terms.

Understanding Key Ideas

10. c
11. b
12. a
13. b
14. b
15. a
16. c
17. d
18. b
19. b

Short Answer

20. the corona
21. The solar activity cycle is closely linked to changes in the sun's magnetic field. Because sunspots are regions with strong magnetic fields, variations in sunspots affect other disturbances in the sun's atmosphere.
22. Sunspots have magnetic fields that are thousands of times stronger than those in other parts of the photosphere.
23. The sun produces energy through nuclear fusion. In the first step, two hydrogen nuclei (protons) fuse, and one proton changes to a neutron. In step two, another proton joins the nucleus, forming a nucleus made up of one neutron and two protons. In step three, two nuclei from step two collide and fuse. Two protons are released, and a helium nucleus (two protons and two neutrons) is left. Each stage of the process releases energy.
24. Answers may vary. Sample answer: Prominences are huge arches of glowing gases that extend above the sun's surface. Solar flares are sudden eruptions of charged particles that travel upward thousands of kilometers.
25. The corona is the extremely hot outermost layer of the sun's atmosphere. This low-density layer helps prevent atomic particles from escaping into space. The corona becomes visible during a total solar eclipse when the moon blocks the photosphere, and the sky darkens enough for the corona to be seen.
26. In the sun's radiative zone, energy radiates in the form of electromagnetic waves. In the convective zone, hot moving gases carry energy toward the sun's surface. As heated gases move upward and expand, they cool and sink back toward the radiative zone.

CRITICAL THINKING

27. Making Comparisons How is the transfer of energy in a pan of hot water similar to the transfer of energy in the sun's convective zone?

28. Making Comparisons Explain how the radiative zone in the sun is similar to the region between the sun and Earth.

29. Making Predictions Predict what would happen to the number of sunspots if parts of the sun's magnetic field suddenly increased in strength.

30. Drawing Conclusions If Earth's magnetosphere shifted so that solar wind was not deflected toward the poles but was deflected toward the equator, what would happen to the area where auroras are most often visible?

31. Analyzing Relationships Magnetic fields create electric currents that can damage electric power grids and interrupt the flow of electricity. How does this information help explain why strong magnetic storms can knock out power in cities?

32. Predicting Consequences How do scientists predict magnetic storms? List two ways that scientists on Earth could help people prepare for a very large magnetic storm.

CONCEPT MAPPING

33. Use the following terms to create a concept map: *sun, nuclear fusion, core, radiative zone, convective zone, photosphere,* and *corona.*

MATH SKILLS

34. Making Calculations On average, Earth is 1.5×10^8 km from the sun. A coronal mass ejection, or CME, can have a speed of 7×10^6 km/h. At this speed, how long would a CME take to reach Earth?

35. Applying Information A peak of the sunspot cycle occurred in the years 2000–2001. In what years will the next two peaks occur?

WRITING SKILLS

36. Creative Writing Write a short story that describes an imaginary trip to the center of the sun. Describe each layer and zone through which you would pass.

37. Writing from Research Research the northern lights. Write a short travel brochure that describes when and where to go to see the most spectacular and frequent displays of the auroras.

INTERPRETING GRAPHICS

The graph below shows how the latitudes of sunspots vary over time. Use the graph to answer the questions that follow.

Average Daily Sunspot Area

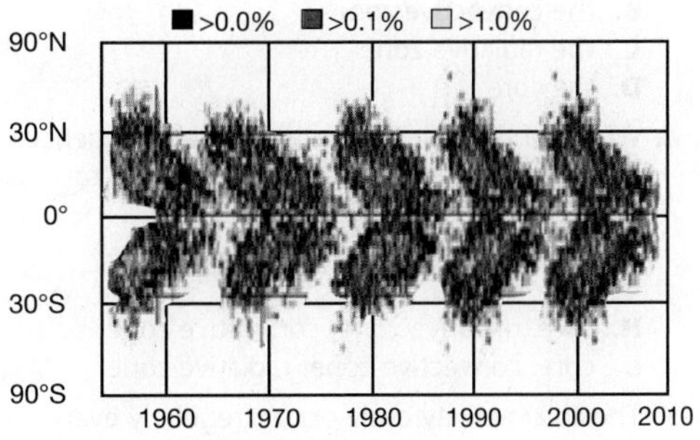

38. How many complete sunspot cycles are illustrated by the graph?

39. How does the range of latitudes of sunspots change over time? How is this change related to the sunspot cycle?

40. According to the graph, how many sunspots were located at the sun's north pole?

Chapter Review

Critical Thinking

27. The transfer of energy in each case involves the movement of matter. In both cases, the matter rises as it is heated from below. As it moves away from the heat source, the matter cools and sinks down toward the heat source again.

28. In both the radiative zone of the sun and in the region of space between the sun and Earth, energy transfers take place by means of electromagnetic waves, or radiation. These waves of energy can travel through both empty space and matter.

29. If parts of the sun's magnetic field suddenly increased in strength, the number of sunspots in those locations would likewise increase.

30. Auroras would be seen more frequently near the equator than near the poles.

31. Strong magnetic storms produce magnetic fields, which in turn produce the electrical currents that can overload power grids and knock out power in cities.

32. Scientists predict the likelihood of magnetic storms by watching for increases in the number of sunspots and related magnetic disturbances such as solar flares. Scientists could encourage individuals to prepare alternate light sources, such as candles and flashlights, that do not depend on the power grids and to expect communications equipment failures. Utilities and power stations should prepare for power surges.

Concept Mapping

33. Answers may vary but should include all of the terms listed. Sample answers appear at the end of this unit on p. 875B.

Math Skills

34. time = distance ÷ speed; time = $(150 \times 10^6 \text{ km}) \div (7 \times 10^6 \text{ km/h}) = 150 \div 7 = 21$ h

35. Peaks in the sunspot cycle occur approximately every 11 years, so 2000 + 11 years = 2011 + 11 = 2022. The next two peaks could be expected in 2011 and 2022.

Writing Skills

36. Answers may vary. Accept all reasonable answers.

37. Answers may vary. Accept all reasonable answers.

Interpreting Graphics

38. Five complete cycles are shown.

39. Sunspots initially appear in groups about midway between the sun's equator and poles. Those spots are gradually replaced by spots closer to the equator. After about 11 years, a new sunspot cycle begins and sunspots begin to appear again midway between the equator and the poles.

40. No sunspots occurred at 90° north latitude.

Standardized Test Prep

Estimated Time

To give students practice under more realistic testing conditions, allow them 30 minutes to answer all of the questions in this practice test.

Test Doctor

Question 3 Answer D is correct. Students should have a conceptual understanding that dense materials are often found in the cores of stellar objects. This is true of Earth and the sun. One reason that the material is so dense at the sun's core is pressure. The enormous pressure exerted on the materials creates a core that scientists believe has a density that is 10 times denser than iron.

Question 6 The convective zone is the best answer. Students may notice a clue in that energy is carried in this part of the sun by the motion of matter. Students should use their understanding of the sun to determine that, unlike other layers of the sun, which move energy by radiation or electromagnetic waves, the convective zone has convection currents, which transfer energy by the rise and fall of moving matter.

Question 12 The correct answer is sunspots. Students should first note the location of the spots. If students notice that these dark spots occur on the sun's surface, they will narrow the range of potential answers to include only surface features. Students should then remember that other surface features, such as solar flares, do not match the description in the question.

Chapter 29 Standardized Test Prep

Understanding Concepts

Directions (1–5): For each question, write on a separate sheet of paper the letter of the correct answer.

1. What is the source of the sun's energy?
   A. nuclear fission reactions that break down massive nuclei to form lighter atoms
   B. nuclear fusion reactions that combine smaller nuclei to form more massive ones
   C. reactions that strip away electrons to form lighter atoms
   D. reactions that strip away electrons to form more massive ones

2. What do electrically charged particles from the sun strike in Earth's magnetosphere to lead to the production of sheets of light known as auroras?
   F. gas molecules
   G. dust particles
   H. water vapor
   I. ice crystals

3. Which layer of the sun has the densest material?
   A. the corona
   B. the convective zone
   C. the radiative zone
   D. the core

4. Which of the following is the correct sequence of layers of the sun's interior, from inner to outer?
   F. convective zone, radiative zone, core
   G. core, corona, photosphere
   H. core, radiative zone, convective zone
   I. core, convective zone, radiative zone

5. The solar activity cycle occurs regularly every
   A. 5 years.
   B. 11 years.
   C. 16 years.
   D. 29 years.

Directions (6–7): For each question, write a short response.

6. In which part of the sun's interior is energy carried to the sun's surface by moving matter?

7. What is the term for the innermost layer of the sun's atmosphere?

Reading Skills

Directions (8–10): Read the passage below. Then, answer the questions.

Studying the Sun

Sunlight that has been focused, especially through a magnifying glass, can produce a great amount of thermal energy—enough to start a fire. Imagine focusing the sun's rays by using a magnifying glass that has a diameter of 1.6 m. The resulting heat could easily melt metal. If a conventional telescope were pointed directly at the sun, some of its parts could melt and become useless.

The McMath-Pierce telescope uses a 1.6-m mirror to produce an image of the sun. First, a flat mirror directs the sun's rays down a long, diagonal shaft to a curved 1.6-m diameter mirror, which is located 50 m underground. This second mirror focuses the sunlight. Because the focal length is so long, the solar image is so large that no part of it is strong enough to melt anything. The focused sunlight is reflected by another flat mirror, which in turn directs the light to an observing room and instrument shaft. This system, while complex, not only protects the sensitive and expensive telescopic equipment but also protects the scientists that use it as well.

8. According to the information in the passage, which of the following statements about solar telescopes is true?
   F. Solar telescopes allow scientists to safely observe the sun.
   G. Solar telescopes do not need mirrors to focus the sun's rays.
   H. All solar telescopes are built 50 m underground.
   I. All solar telescopes are built with a diameter of 1.6 m.

9. Which of the following statements can be inferred from the information in the passage?
   A. Focusing sunlight can help avoid a meltdown.
   B. Unfocused sunlight produces little energy.
   C. A curved mirror can focus sunlight to produce a great amount of thermal energy.
   D. Mirrors greatly increase the intensity and danger of studying sunlight.

10. Why do scientists have to use specialized equipment to study the sun?

Question 13 Full-credit answers should include the following points:
- students should explain that the magnetosphere extends far into space and protects the planet from many of the effects of the solar wind, a stream of ionized particles from the sun's corona
- an example of weakness that students may mention is the fact that there are small gaps in the shield at the poles through which some particles can pass. These particles are responsible for colorful auroras
- students may also mention that radiation from solar flares can generate magnetic storms and may disrupt radio communications, or interfere with power grids

Interpreting Graphics

Directions (11–13): For each question below, record the correct answer on a separate sheet of paper.

The graphic below shows the structure of the sun. Use this diagram to answer questions 11 and 12.

Structure of the Sun

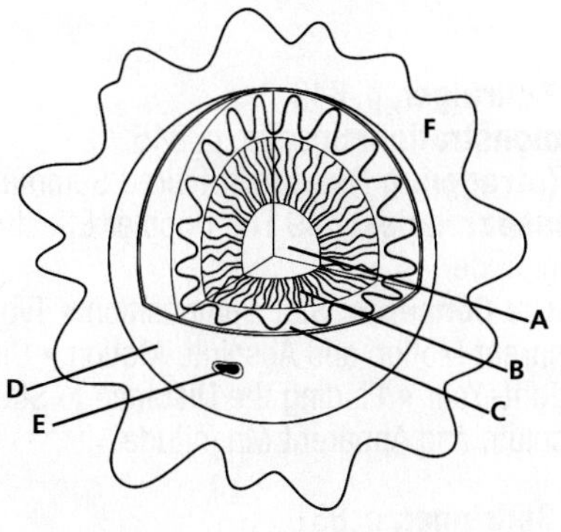

11. Fusion reactions provide power for the stars, such as the sun. In which part of the sun do these fusion reactions take place?

F. layer A
G. layer B
H. layer C
I. layer D

12. What is the term for the dark, cool regions of the sun, which are represented by the letter E on the diagram?

The diagram below shows what happens when Earth's magnetic field interacts with the solar wind. Use this graphic to answer question 13.

Earth's Magnetosphere

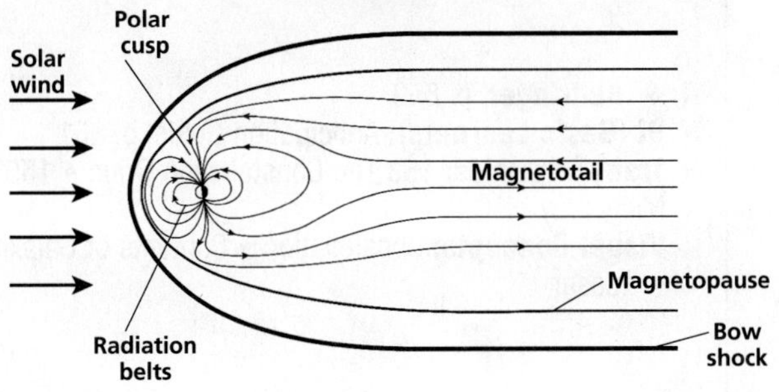

13. How does the solar wind affect humans and other living things on Earth, despite the protection provided by the magnetosphere? Use examples to explain your answer.

Test Tip

Choose the best possible answer for each question, even if you think there is another possible answer that is not given.

Standardized Test Prep

Using THINK central Resources

State Resources

- For specific resources for your state, visit www.thinkcentral.com and type in the keyword **HSHSTR.**

Answers

Understanding Graphics

1. B
2. F
3. D
4. H
5. B
6. the convective zone
7. the photosphere

Reading Skills

8. F
9. C
10. Conventional equipment would be at risk of melting under the intensity of the sun's rays. Scientists' eyesight could also be put at risk by looking directly at the sun.

Interpreting Graphics

11. F
12. sunspots
13. Answers may vary. See Test Doctor for a detailed scoring rubric.

Chapter Planner 30 Stars, Galaxies, and the Universe

	Time	Standards	Teach Key Ideas
Chapter Opener, pp. 842–843	45 min.	National Science Education Standards	
Section 1 Characteristics of Stars, pp. 845–850 ❯ Analyzing Starlight ❯ Stellar Motion ❯ Distances to Stars ❯ Stellar Brightness	45 min.	SAI 2e	■ ◆ **Bellringer,** p. 845 ■ **Demonstration:** Spectra, p. 845 ■ **DI (Struggling Readers):** Paired Summarizing, p. 846 ◆ **Transparencies:** 149 The Doppler Effect • 150 Apparent Magnitude ▲ **Visual Concepts:** Star Composition • Types of Stars • Apparent Motion and Absolute Motion • Circumpolar Stars • Light–Year • Finding the Distance to Stars: Parallax • Absolute and Apparent Magnitude
Section 2 Stellar Evolution, pp. 851–858 ❯ Classifying Stars ❯ Star Formation ❯ The Main-Sequence Stage ❯ Leaving the Main Sequence ❯ The Final Stages of a Sunlike Star ❯ The Final Stages of Massive Stars	90 min.	ES 4b, ES 4c, UCP 3, SAI 2e	■ ◆ **Bellringer,** p. 851 ■ **DI (Special Education Students):** Group Work, p. 853 ■ **Discussion:** Star Mass, p. 853 ■ **Debate:** SETI, p. 855 ■ **DI (English Learners):** Paired Summarizing, p. 855 ◆ **Transparencies:** 151 The Hertzsprung-Russell Diagram • 152 The Life Cycle of Stars ▲ **Visual Concepts:** Classifying Stars • H-R Diagram
Section 3 Star Groups, pp. 859–862 ❯ Constellations ❯ Multiple-Star Systems ❯ Star Clusters ❯ Galaxies ❯ Quasars	45 min.	UCP 1, SAI 2e	■ ◆ **Bellringer,** p. 859 ■ **DI (Basic Learners):** Anticipation Guide, p. 861 ◆ **Transparencies:** 153 The Constellation Orion • 155 The Milky Way ▲ **Visual Concepts:** Constellation • Contents of Galaxies • Quasar
Section 4 The Big Bang Theory, pp. 863–866 ❯ Hubble's Observations ❯ A Theory Emerges ❯ A Universe of Surprises	45 min.	ES 4a, SAI 2e	■ ◆ **Bellringer,** p. 863 ■ **Discussion:** The Expanding Universe, p. 863 ■ **DI (Special Education Students):** Summarizing, p. 864 ◆ **Transparency:** 154 Timeline of the Big Bang ▲ **Visual Concepts:** Red Shift • Universal Expansion • Big Bang Theory
Chapter Wrap-Up, pp. 871–875	90 min.		**Chapter Summary,** p. 871

CHAPTER Fast Track *To shorten instruction because of time limitations, omit Section 1.*

See also PowerNotes® Presentations

Key
Teacher's Edition ■ Teaching Transparencies ◆
Chapter Resource File ● Online Edition ▲

All resources listed below are also available on the **Teacher One Stop™.**

Why It Matters	Hands-On	Skills Development	Assessment
■ **Chapter Overview,** p. 842 ■ **Using the Figure:** Tarantula Nebula, p. 842	**Inquiry Lab:** Color and Temperature, p. 843	**Reading Toolbox,** p. 844	
■ **Section Overview,** p. 845 ■ **The Size of the Sun,** p. 846 ■ **Precession,** p. 847	■ **Activity:** Observing Stars, p. 848 **Quick Lab:** Parallax, p. 849 **Making Models Lab:** Star Magnitudes, pp. 868–869 ● **Skills Practice Lab:** Blackbody Radiation	**Reading Toolbox:** Pattern Puzzle, p. 846 ● ■ **Internet Activity:** Proper Motion of Stars, p. 847	**Reading Check,** p. 847 **Reading Check,** p. 848 **Section Review,** p. 850 ■ **Reteaching,** p. 849 ■ **Quiz,** p. 849 ■ **DI (Alternative Assessment):** Moving Stars, p. 850 ● **Section Quiz**
■ **Section Overview,** p. 851 ■ **Using the Figure:** H-R Diagram, p. 851 ■ **Using the Figure:** Identifying Stars, p. 854 ■ **Physics Connection:** Star Size and Spectra, p. 854 **Where Are Elements Made?,** p. 855 ■ **Using the Figure:** Life Cycles, p. 856 ■ **Physics Connection:** Supernova Physics, p. 857	■ **Group Activity:** Main-Sequence Stars, p. 853	**Math Skills:** Nuclear Fusion, p. 852 **Reading Toolbox:** Scientific Theories vs. Scientific Laws, p. 852 ■ **Skill Builder:** Vocabulary, p. 856	**Reading Check,** p. 853 **Reading Check,** p. 854 **Reading Check,** p. 857 **Section Review,** p. 858 ■ **Reteaching,** p. 857 ■ **Quiz,** p. 857 ■ **DI (Alternative Assessment):** Odd Stars, p. 858 ● **Section Quiz**
■ **Section Overview,** p. 859 ■ **Astronomy Connection:** Identifying a Galaxy from Within, p. 861	■ **Activity:** Constellations, p. 859 ■ **Activity:** Multimedia Project, p. 861 ■ **Group Activity:** Charting the Galaxy, p. 870	**Reading Toolbox:** Everyday Words Used in Science, p. 860 **Maps in Action:** The Milky Way, p. 870	**Reading Check,** p. 860 **Section Review,** p. 862 ■ **Reteaching,** p. 861 ■ **Quiz,** p. 862 ■ **DI (Alternative Assessment):** Modeling Constellations, p. 862 ● **Section Quiz**
■ **Section Overview,** p. 863 ■ **Physics Connection:** New Physics, Old Universe, p. 864	**Quick Lab:** The Expanding Universe, p. 865 ● **Inquiry Lab:** Curving Space-Time	**Reading Toolbox:** Everyday Words Used in Science, p. 866	**Reading Check,** p. 864 **Section Review,** p. 866 ■ **Reteaching,** p. 865 ■ **Quiz,** p. 865 ■ **DI (Alternative Assessment):** Rate of Universal Expansion, p. 866 ● **Section Quiz**
A Cool Telescope, p. 867		▲ **Super Summary** **Standardized Test Prep,** pp. 874–875	**Chapter Review,** pp. 872–873 ■ **DI (Alternative Assessment):** Poster Project, p. 871 ● **Chapter Tests**

See also Lab Generator

See also Holt Online Assessment Resources

Chapter Overview

This chapter describes what stars are and how they evolve. The chapter discusses how to determine a star's temperature, brightness, composition, size, motion, and distance. The chapter also explains star groups and galaxies and describes how each of the structures formed. Finally, the chapter explains the current model for the structure, formation, and evolution of the universe.

Using the Figure GENERAL

Tarantula Nebula The Tarantula Nebula is a gaseous region in the Large Magellanic Cloud, a small galaxy that orbits the Milky Way galaxy. Explain that this particular nebula is called an *emission nebula* because the hot, glowing gases emit light. Ask students what provides the energy for the nebula's gases to emit light. (The high-energy light from bright stars within the nebula causes the gases to emit light.)

Why It Matters

Scientists have gathered much evidence about our universe, but limitless questions remain. Almost all of the universe is made up of substances we know almost nothing about, called dark matter and dark energy.

Chapter 30 Stars, Galaxies, and the Universe

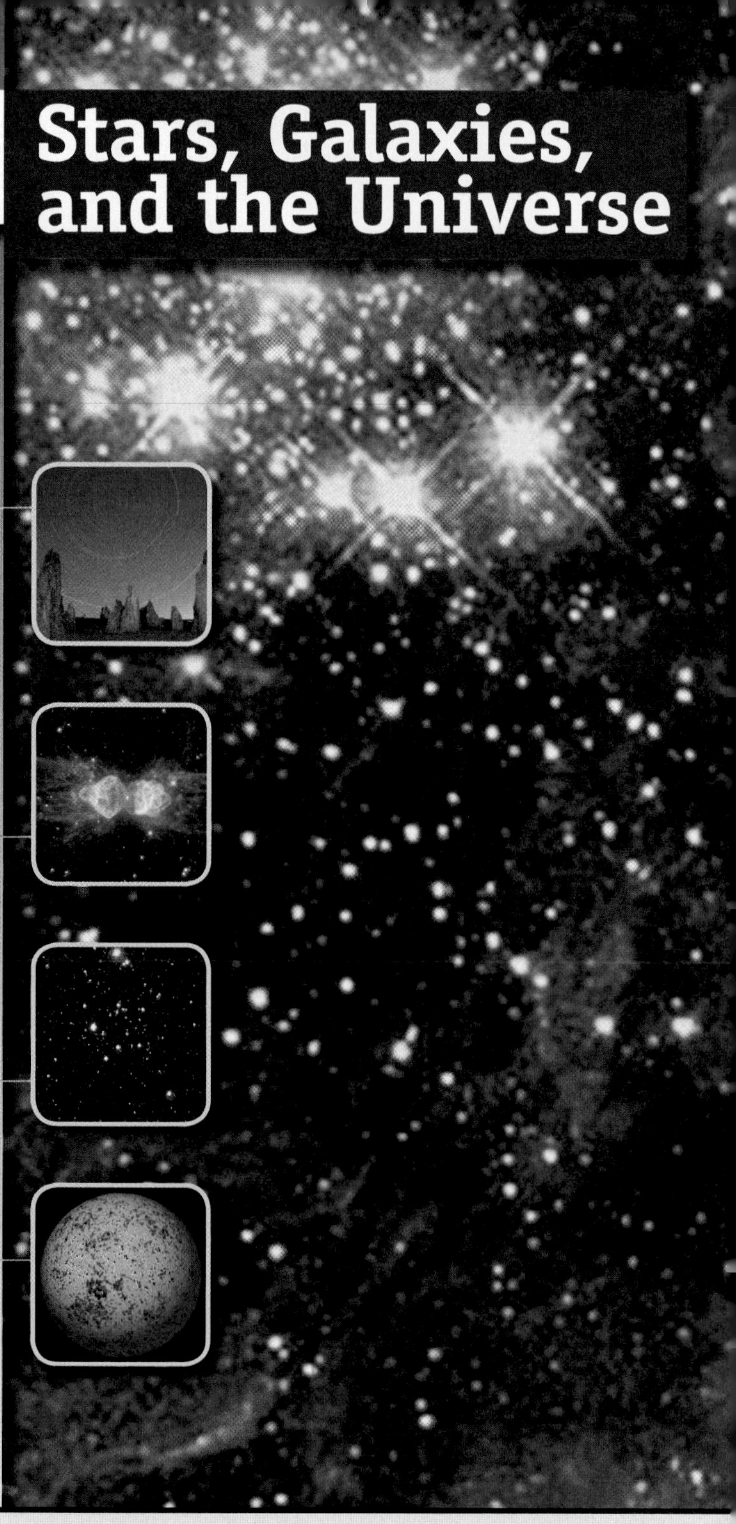

Chapter Outline

1 Characteristics of Stars
- Analyzing Starlight
- Stellar Motion
- Distances to Stars
- Stellar Brightness

2 Stellar Evolution
- Classifying Stars
- Star Formation
- The Main-Sequence Stage
- Leaving the Main Sequence
- The Final Stages of a Sunlike Star
- The Final Stages of Massive Stars

3 Star Groups
- Constellations
- Multiple-Star Systems
- Star Clusters
- Galaxies
- Quasars

4 The Big Bang Theory
- Hubble's Observations
- A Theory Emerges
- A Universe of Surprises

Virginia Standards of Learning
ES.1.c
ES.1.e
ES.1.f
ES.3.d
ES.13.a
ES.13.b

Chapter Correlations

Virginia Standards of Learning

ES.1.c scales, diagrams, charts, graphs, tables, imagery, models, and profiles are constructed and interpreted.
ES.1.e variables are manipulated with repeated trials.
ES.1.f current applications are used to reinforce Earth science concepts.
ES.3.d the history and contributions of space exploration
ES.13.a cosmology including the Big Bang theory
ES.13.b the origin and evolution of stars, star systems, and galaxies.

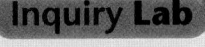

Inquiry Lab

20 min

Color and Temperature

Attach a flashlight bulb to a weak D-cell battery using electrical wire. Record the color of the filament, and carefully touch the bulb to note how warm it feels. Then attach a fully charged D-cell battery to the bulb. Again, record the color of the filament and the warmth of the bulb. Finally, attach a second fully charged D-cell battery, and repeat your observations.

Questions to Get You Started

1. What is the relationship between the color of the filament and the temperature of the bulb?
2. How do you think the color of a star is related to its temperature?

Why It Matters

Our solar system is one small part of the universe. By studying stars and galaxies, we can learn more about the formation and evolution of the universe.

Inquiry Lab

Central Concept: The color of a star gives evidence about how hot its surface is.

Teacher's Notes: Caution students to take care when touching the warm bulb.

Materials (per group)
- Flashlight bulb
- Weak D-cell battery
- Electrical wire
- Two fully charged D-cell batteries

Skills Acquired
- Observing
- Inferring

Answers to Getting Started

1. When the filament is darker and more orange, the bulb is cooler. The brighter and more yellow the filament, the hotter the bulb.
2. Sample answer: The color of a star may be related to the temperature of the star, just like the color of the filament is related to the temperature of the light bulb.

Using THINK central Resources

An online version of this chapter, as well as all the print and multimedia resources that accompany the program are available to registered teachers and their students. Log onto www.thinkcentral.com to access these materials and tools to organize your preparation and student learning.

READING TOOLBOX

Science Terms

Answers will vary. In the first column of their charts, students should write the terms white dwarf, red giant, supergiant, and black hole. In the second column, they should write what they think is the scientific meaning of the term. In the third column, they should write the scientific definition given in the chapter.

Fact, Hypothesis, or Theory?

Sample answer:
The big bang theory explains how the universe was formed. Billions of years ago, all the matter in the universe was compressed into a small area. A large explosion flung matter out from this small area. The matter formed galaxies, and within them stars, planets, and all the other objects in the universe. The matter kept expanding, and keeps expanding to this day. We can observe this when we see that galaxies continue to move apart.

This is a theory because it explains observations and patterns found in nature and can be used to predict other observations and patterns. The big bang is a theory because it is supported by available evidence. If new evidence emerges, the theory may be revised or abandoned.

READING TOOLBOX

These reading tools will help you learn the material in this chapter.

Science Terms

Everyday Words Used in Science Many terms that are used in science are familiar words, taken from everyday speech. Scientists sometimes choose familiar words to describe things that are new, unfamiliar, or difficult to understand.

Your Turn In Section 2, you will learn about the objects listed in the table below. Based on your understanding of the familiar words that make up these terms, explain what you would expect them to mean in a table of your own. After reading Section 2, write the scientific definitions in your table.

Term	What I think it means	Scientific definition
white dwarf		
red giant		
supergiant		
black hole		

Fact, Hypothesis, or Theory?

Scientific Theories A scientific law describes or summarizes a pattern in nature. Scientific theories are sometimes confused with scientific laws, but they are not the same. The following statements apply to scientific theories:

- They explain observations or patterns in nature.
- They can be used to predict other observations or patterns.
- They may be revised or abandoned if reliable evidence contradicts them.

Your Turn In Section 4, the big bang theory is discussed in detail. On a sheet of paper, write "Big Bang Theory" and a definition of this theory. Then write a paragraph explaining why it is a theory.

Note Taking

Pattern Puzzles Pattern puzzles can help you remember information in the correct order. They can also help you review the steps of a process, such as a lab procedure or math solution. Below are the instructions for making a pattern puzzle.

1. Write down the steps of a process on a sheet of paper. Write one step per line.
2. Cut the sheet of paper into strips, with only one step per strip. Shuffle the strips.
3. Put the strips in their proper order. Then check the order in your textbook.

Your Turn As you read Section 2, write down the steps in the life cycle of a main-sequence star in order. If a step is long, divide it into two or three shorter steps. Then cut the steps into strips, shuffle them, and put them in order again. The first two steps are shown below.

- An outside force compresses a nebula.

- Some of the particles of the nebula are pulled toward each other by gravity.

For more information on how to use these and other tools, see **Appendix A.**

Note Taking

Answers may vary. Students should consult Appendix A for tips on making a pattern puzzle. Students' pattern puzzles should accurately represent the steps in the life cycle of a main-sequence star.

SECTION 1

Characteristics of Stars

Key Ideas

- Describe how astronomers determine the composition and temperature of stars.
- Explain why stars appear to move in the sky.
- Describe one way astronomers measure the distances to stars.
- Explain the difference between absolute magnitude and apparent magnitude.

Key Terms

star
Doppler effect
light-year
parallax
apparent magnitude
absolute magnitude

Why It Matters

By analyzing sunlight, scientists discovered the element helium in the sun, a star, even before they found it on Earth. Today, we use helium in high-tech applications as well as in party balloons.

A **star** is a ball of gases that gives off a tremendous amount of electromagnetic energy. This energy comes from nuclear fusion within the star. *Nuclear fusion* is the combination of light atomic nuclei to form heavier atomic nuclei.

As seen from Earth, most stars in the night sky appear to be tiny specks of white light. However, if you look closely at the stars, you will notice that they vary in color. For example, the star Antares shines with a slightly reddish color, the star Rigel shines blue-white, and the star Arcturus shines with an orange tint. Our own star, the sun, is a yellow star.

star a large celestial body that is composed of gas and that emits light

Analyzing Starlight

Astronomers learn about stars primarily by analyzing the light that the stars emit. Astronomers direct starlight through *spectrographs*, which are devices that separate light into different colors, or wavelengths. Starlight passing through a spectrograph produces a display of colors and lines called a *spectrum*. There are three types of spectra: *emission*, or bright-line; *absorption*, or dark-line; and *continuous*.

All stars have *dark-line spectra*—bands of color crossed by dark lines where the color is diminished, as shown in **Figure 1.** A star's dark-line spectrum reveals the star's composition and temperature.

Stars are made up of different elements in the form of gases. While the inner layers of a star's photosphere are very hot, the outer layers are somewhat cooler. Elements in the outer layers absorb some of the light radiating from lower in the photosphere. Because different elements absorb different wavelengths of light, scientists can study the elements that make up a star, and find out from them how hot the star is by studying its spectrum.

Figure 1 The solar spectrum is shown here with each colored section on a new band.

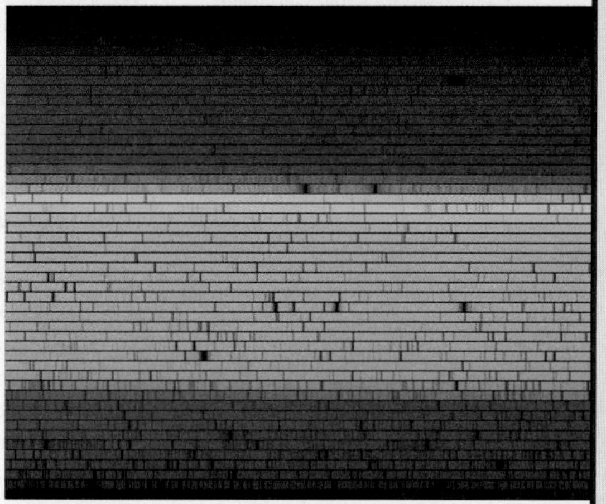

Key Resources

Chapter Resource File

- Directed Reading BASIC
- Skills Practice Lab: Blackbody Radiation GENERAL

Technology

- Transparencies Bellringer

Section 1

Focus

Overview

This section explains how light is used to determine the chemical composition and temperature of a star's surface, the apparent motion of stars due to Earth's motion, and the parallax method of measuring a star's distance.

Bellringer

Have students write down the names of stars that they are familiar with. (Sample answers: North Star [Polaris], Rigel, Betelgeuse, Antares, Sirius, Vega, Alpha Centauri) LS **Verbal**

Motivate

Demonstration GENERAL

Spectra Darken the room and place a hydrogen discharge tube into a power source. Turn on the power source, have students look at the light through diffraction gratings. Turn off the power, use heat-resistant gloves to remove the hydrogen tube, and insert a neon spectrum tube. Repeat the demonstration. Ask students how the lines from the two gases differ. (Hydrogen produces violet, dark blue, blue-green, and red lines; neon produces green, yellow, and orange lines.) Explain that the emission lines are produced from hot gases and that each element produces a unique combination of colors. LS **visual**

Teach

MISCONCEPTION ALERT

Stellar Composition The composition of a star is based not on materials deep within the star but on the spectra of substances in the star's photosphere. The photosphere, the region of the star that emits the light we see, is considered the star's surface. The term "surface," when applied to a star, does not mean a solid region. Like all parts of a star, the surface is made up of gas or plasma. Because the material in the photosphere is cooler than the material underneath, the atoms of the photosphere will absorb certain colors of light from the continuous spectrum of light that comes through the photosphere, producing the characteristic absorption spectrum.

READING TOOLBOX

Pattern Puzzle

Answers may vary. Students should consult Appendix A for tips on making a pattern puzzle. Students' pattern puzzles should accurately represent the steps used by scientists to determine the elements that make up a star.

Classification of Stars

Color	Surface temperature (°C)	Examples
Blue	above 30,000	10 Lacertae
Blue-white	10,000–30,000	Rigel, Spica
White	7,500–10,000	Vega, Sirius
Yellow-white	6,000–7,500	Canopus, Procyon
Yellow	5,000–6,000	sun, Capella
Orange	3,500–5,000	Arcturus, Aldebaran
Red	less than 3,500	Betelgeuse, Antares

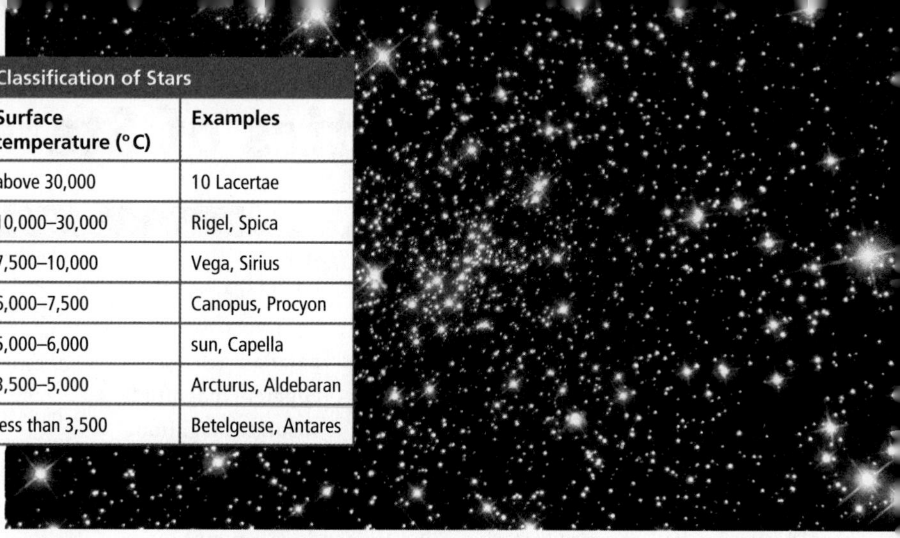

Figure 2 Stars in the sky show tinges of different colors, which reveal the temperatures of the stars' surfaces. Blue stars shine with the hottest temperatures, and red stars shine with the coolest.

The Compositions of Stars

Every chemical element has a characteristic spectrum in a given range of temperatures. The colors and lines in the spectrum of a star indicate the elements that make up the star. Through spectrum analysis, scientists have learned that stars are made up of the same elements that compose Earth. But while the most common element on Earth is oxygen, the most common element in stars is hydrogen. Helium is the second most common element in stars. Elements such as carbon, oxygen, and nitrogen, usually in small quantities, make up most of the remaining one percent or so of the mass of stars.

READING TOOLBOX

Pattern Puzzle

Make a pattern puzzle that outlines the steps used by scientists to determine the elements that make up a star. Follow the instructions for making a pattern puzzle, given at the beginning of the chapter. See Appendix A for further instructions.

The Temperatures of Stars

The surface temperature of a star is indicated by its color, as shown in **Figure 2.** Most star temperatures range from 2,800 °C to 24,000 °C, although some are hotter. Generally, blue stars have an average surface temperature of 35,000 °C. Red stars are the coolest, with average surface temperatures of 3,000 °C. Yellow stars, such as the sun, have surface temperatures of about 5,500 °C.

The Sizes and Masses of Stars

Stars also vary in size and mass. The smallest stars are slightly bigger than Jupiter, about one-seventh the size of our sun. Most stars are smaller and less massive than the sun. The sun, a medium-sized star, has a diameter of about 1,390,000 km. Some giant stars have diameters that are 1,000 times the sun's diameter. Most of the stars you can see in the night sky are medium-sized stars that are similar in size to our sun.

Many stars also have about the same mass as the sun, though some stars may be significantly more or less massive. Stars that are very dense may have more mass than the sun and still be much smaller than the sun. Less-dense stars may have a larger diameter than the sun has but still have less mass than the sun.

Differentiated Instruction

Struggling Readers

Paired Summarizing Group students into pairs and have them read this page silently. Then, have one student summarize information about the composition, temperatures, sizes, and masses of stars. The other student should listen to the retelling and point out any inaccuracies or ideas that were left out. **LS Verbal/Auditory**

Why It Matters

The Size of the Sun Help students to understand how large a distance 1,390,000 km is by noting that Earth's diameter is about 12,700 km. Thus, if nearly 110 Earths were placed end to end they would extend from one side of the sun to the other. More than 1 million Earths would be needed to fill a volume equal to that of the sun.

Stellar Motion

Two kinds of motion are associated with stars—actual motion through space and apparent motion across the night sky. Because stars are so far from Earth, their actual motion can be measured only with high-powered telescopes and specialized spacecraft. Apparent motion on any given night, on the other hand, is much more noticeable.

Apparent Motion of Stars

The *apparent motion* of stars, or motion as it appears from Earth, is caused by the movement of Earth. By aiming a camera at the sky and leaving the shutter open for a few hours, you can photograph the apparent motion of the stars. The curves of light in **Figure 3** record the apparent motion of stars in the northern sky. The circular trails make it seem as though the stars are moving counterclockwise around a central star called Polaris, or the North Star. The circular pattern is caused by the rotation of Earth on its axis. Polaris, which is not a very bright star, is almost directly above the North Pole, and thus the star does not appear to move much.

Earth's revolution around the sun causes the stars to appear to move in a second way. Stars located on the side of the sun opposite Earth are obscured by the sun. As Earth orbits the sun, however, different stars become visible during different seasons. The visible stars appear slightly to the west at a given time every night. Each night, most stars appear a small distance farther across the sky than they were at the same time the night before. After many months, some stars may finally disappear below the western horizon.

Reading Check **Why does Polaris appear to remain stationary in the night sky?** (See Appendix G for answers to Reading Checks.)

SCILINKS.
www.scilinks.org
Topic: Stars
Code: HQX1448

Figure 3 Stars appear as curved trails in this long-exposure photograph. These trails result from the rotation of Earth on its axis.

Internet Activity — ADVANCED

Proper Motion of Stars Explain to students that a star's actual motion is divided into two components: its radial motion, which is the amount a star moves toward or away from Earth along the observer's line of sight; and its proper motion, which is the amount a star moves in the plane of the sky. Proper motion varies with how close the star is to Earth and how fast it is actually moving. Have students use the Internet to research the topic of proper motion for stars. Have them note the speeds at which some stars actually move, how far those stars are from Earth, and how much they move relative to the background sky as a result of their speed and distance. Have students present their findings in a written report or oral presentation. A worksheet designed to direct student research on this topic can be found in the **Chapter Resource File** booklet or by visiting www.thinkcentral.com and entering the keyword **HQXSTGX.**
LS Verbal

Answer to Reading Check

Polaris is almost exactly above the pole of Earth's rotational axis, so Polaris moves only slightly around the pole during one rotation of Earth.

Cultural Awareness — BASIC

Earth's Rotation The idea that the apparent motion of stars results from Earth's rotation was suggested as long ago as the fourth century BCE, by a Greek scholar named Heraclides (hair RAH kli deez). However, Aristotle's belief that Earth could not move, and therefore neither rotated nor traveled through the heavens, prevailed over Western classical and medieval thinking. The concept of Earth's rotation was renewed, along with the notion that Earth revolved around the sun, in the early sixteenth century CE by Nicolaus Copernicus.

Why It Matters

Precession Earth wobbles around its rotational axis much as a top does. This process, called *precession*, causes the North Pole to point at different parts of the northern sky, so that Polaris is not always the "pole star." Other stars that have been "the north star" include Vega, Thuban, and Deneb. During most of the 26,000-year precession cycle, no bright stars are situated above the North Pole.

Teach, *continued*

Activity — ADVANCED

Observing Stars Explain that the location of circumpolar stars in the sky depends on the observer's location on Earth. When standing at the North Pole, all of the stars in the sky are circumpolar, but as a person moves south, more and more of the stars seen from the Northern Hemisphere disappear for a time beneath the horizon. At the equator, all stars rise above the eastern horizon and set in the west. Polaris makes a small circular path above and below the northern horizon. Students can gain a better sense of which stars appear at different latitudes by performing the following exercise. Have students draw sketches of the northern half of Earth and the position of Polaris with respect to the North Pole. Have students draw an observer at different latitudes on Earth, and then have them show where Polaris will appear above the observer's horizon. Students should then show that the angle between Polaris and the northern horizon is equal to the angle of northern latitude of the observer. **LS Logical**

Answer to Reading Check

Starlight is shifted toward the red end of the spectrum when the star is moving away from the observer.

Key Resources

Technology
- Transparencies
  149 The Doppler Effect

Math Skills

Space Exploration beyond the Solar System Proxima Centauri, the nearest star outside the solar system, lies 4.2 light-years from the sun. Our fastest spacecraft travel at about 58,000 km/h. At this speed, how long would it take a spacecraft to reach Proxima Centauri? What does your calculation tell you about humanity's ability to travel to another solar system using current technology?

Doppler effect an observed change in the frequency of a wave when the source or observer is moving

Academic Vocabulary

occur (uh KUHR) happen

THINK central
INTERACT ONLINE
(Keyword: HQXSTGF4)

Circumpolar Stars

Some stars are always visible in the night sky. These stars never pass below the horizon in either their nightly or annual movements. In the Northern Hemisphere, the movement of these stars makes them appear to circle Polaris, the North Star. These circling stars are called *circumpolar stars*. The stars of the Little Dipper are circumpolar for most observers in the Northern Hemisphere. For a person at the North Pole, all visible stars are circumpolar. The farther the observer moves from the North Pole toward the equator, the fewer circumpolar stars the observer will be able to see.

Actual Motion of Stars

Most stars have several types of *actual motion*. First, they move across the sky, which can be seen only for the closest stars. Second, they may revolve around another star. Third, they either move away from or toward our solar system.

From a star's spectrum, astronomers can learn more about how that star is moving in space toward or away from Earth. The spectrum of such a star appears to shift, as shown in **Figure 4.** The apparent shift in the wavelength of light emitted by a light source moving toward or away from an observer is called the **Doppler effect.** The colors in the spectrum of a star moving toward Earth are shifted slightly toward blue. This shift, called *blue shift*, occurs because the light waves from a star appear to have shorter wavelengths as the star moves toward Earth.

A star moving away from Earth has a spectrum that is shifted slightly toward red. This shift, called *red shift*, occurs because the wavelengths of light appear to be longer. Distant galaxies all have red-shifted spectra, which indicates that all these galaxies are moving away from Earth.

Reading Check **What causes starlight to shift toward the red end of the spectrum?**

Figure 4 The light from a star is shifted based on the star's movement in relationship to Earth. For example, light from stars that are moving away from Earth is shifted slightly toward the red end of the spectrum.

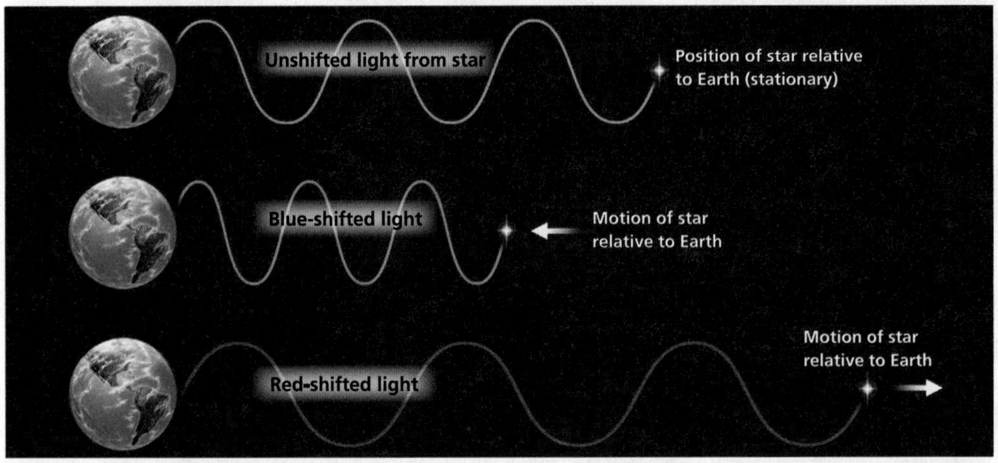

Answer to Math Skills Activity

1. 58,000 km/h × 24 h = 1,392,000 km/day × 365 days = 508,080,000 km/year; 1 light-year = 10,000,000,000,000 km × 4.2 = 42,000,000,000,000/508,080,000 = 82,664 years
2. Sample answer: Using our present spacecraft technology, we could not attempt to travel to objects as distant as Proxima Centauri.

Distances to Stars

Because space is so vast, distances between the stars and Earth are measured in light-years. A **light-year** is the distance that light travels in one year. Because the speed of light is 300,000 km/s, light travels about 9.46 trillion km in one year. The light you see when you look at a star left that star sometime in the past. Light from the sun, for example, takes about 8 minutes to reach Earth. The sun is therefore 8 light-minutes from Earth. When we witness an event on the sun, such as a solar flare, the event actually took place about 8 minutes before we saw it.

Apart from the sun, the star nearest Earth is Proxima Centauri. This star is 4.2 light-years from Earth, nearly 300,000 times the distance from Earth to the sun. Polaris is about 430 light-years from Earth. When you look at Polaris, you see the star the way it was 430 years ago.

For relatively close stars, scientists can determine a star's distance by measuring **parallax,** the apparent shift in a star's position when viewed from different locations. As Earth orbits the sun, observers can study the stars from different perspectives, as shown in **Figure 5.** As Earth moves halfway around its orbit, a nearby star will appear to shift slightly relative to stars that are farther from Earth. The closer the star is to Earth, the larger the shift will be. Using this method from a spacecraft, astronomers measured the distance to about a million stars within 1,000 light-years of Earth.

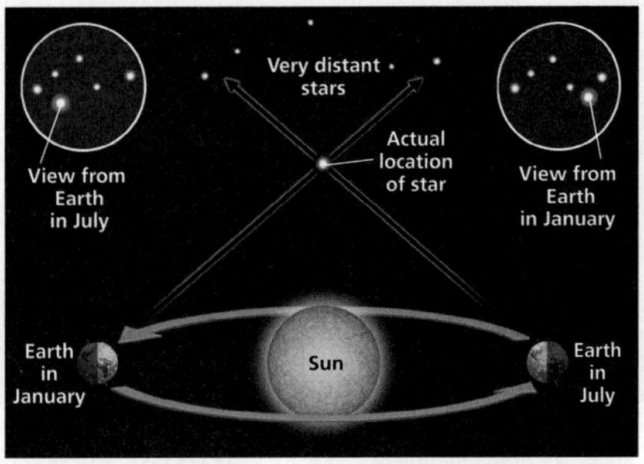

Figure 5 Observers on Earth see nearby stars against those in the distant background. The movement of Earth causes nearby stars to appear to move.

light-year the distance that light travels in one year

parallax an apparent shift in the position of an object when viewed from different locations

Quick Lab — Parallax

15 min

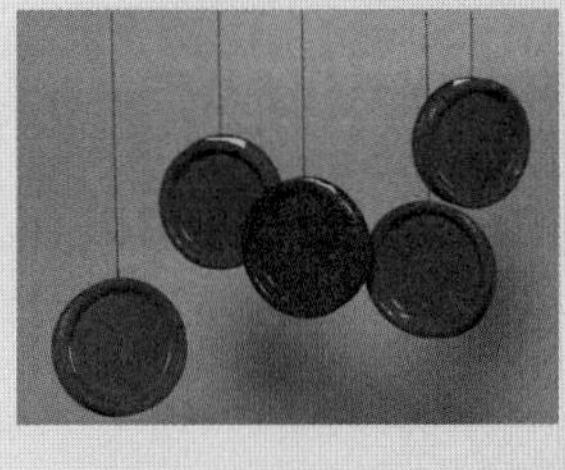

Procedure

1. Use a metric ruler and scissors to cut five 1 m lengths of thread. Use masking tape to tape one end of each piece of thread to the edge of a paper plate. Each plate should have the same diameter. One plate should be red, and four should be blue.
2. Stand on a ladder, and tape the free end of each piece of thread to the ceiling at various heights. Place the threads 30 cm apart in a staggered pattern. Hang the plates in a location that allows the widest field of view and movement.
3. Stand directly in front of and facing the red plate at a distance of several meters.
4. Close one eye, and sketch the position of the red plate in relation to the blue plates.
5. Take several steps back and to the right. Repeat step 4.
6. Take several more steps and make another sketch.
7. Repeat step 6.

Analysis

1. Compare your drawings. Did the red plate change position as you viewed it from different locations? Explain your answer.
2. What results would you expect if you continued to repeat step 6? Explain your answer.
3. If you noted the positions of several stars by using a powerful telescope, what would you expect to observe about their positions if you saw the same stars six months later? Explain.

Close

Reteaching — Basic

Star Temperatures and Colors Create cards that have circles colored red, orange, yellow, yellow-white (pale yellow), white, blue-white (pale blue), and blue. Mix these cards up and have students place these "stars" in the correct order from coolest to hottest. **LS Visual/Logical**

Quiz — General

1. What color are the hottest stars? (blue)
2. What causes a star's spectrum to be blue-shifted? (the Doppler effect acting on light from a star that is moving toward the observer)
3. What are stars that never set below the horizon called? (circumpolar stars)

Quick Lab

Skills Acquired

- Observing
- Interpreting

Materials

- Metric ruler
- Scissors
- Thread
- Masking tape
- Paper plates (one red, four blue)
- Ladder

Teacher's Notes: You may want to hang the plates from the ceiling to save time.

Answers to Analysis

1. yes; The red plate appeared to shift to the side relative to the blue plates. The shift was less extreme when the observer was farther away.
2. Eventually the red plate would not appear to shift relative to the blue plates. This would happen once the observer was far enough away.
3. Closer stars would have shifted the most relative to the background, while more distant stars would have shifted less.

Close, *continued*

Answers to Section Review

1. Dark lines in a star's spectrum tell which substances are present at the star's surface. The color of the star's light indicates its surface temperature.
2. The sun is an average star, so most stars share its general size and mass characteristics. However, very dense stars may have more mass than the sun but be much smaller. Less-dense stars may have larger diameters but have less mass.
3. Earth rotates toward the east, so that objects in the sky appear to move in the opposite direction (to the west).
4. Distances are described in terms of how far light will travel in a given time. The speed of light is 300,000 km/s. A light-minute is how far light travels in a minute. A light-year is how far light travels in a year.
5. Parallax is used to measure distances to stars that are close to Earth. When Earth has moved to the opposite side of the sun in six months, the stars will appear to have shifted slightly. The greater the shift is, the closer the star is.
6. Apparent magnitude is how bright a star appears from Earth. Absolute magnitude is the star's actual brightness if the star were a standard distance from Earth.
7. Stars appear to move in circles around points in the sky above Earth's poles, in a direction opposite Earth's rotational direction.
8. In one year, Earth will have returned to roughly the same position it had when the first measurement was made, so no parallax shift will be observed.
9. The closer star would appear to be brighter.
10. A *star* is described in terms of distance from Earth, which is measured in *light-years*; brightness, which is measured in terms of *apparent magnitude*, which is how bright it appears to be, and *absolute magnitude*, which is how bright it would be at a standard distance; and motion, in which the *Doppler effect* causes a shift in the wavelength of light, either away from Earth, which is called a *red shift*, or toward Earth, which is called a *blue shift*.

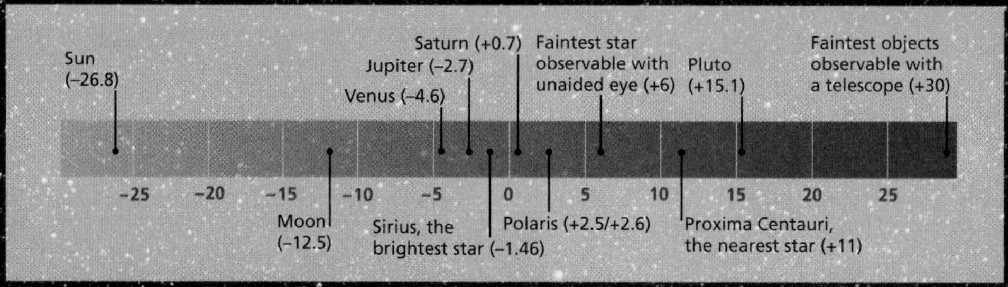

Figure 6 The sun, which has an apparent magnitude of −26.8, is the brightest object in our sky. All other objects appear dimmer in the sky, so their apparent magnitudes are higher on the scale.

Stellar Brightness

More than 3 billion stars can be seen through telescopes on Earth. Of these, only about 6,000 are visible without a telescope. Billions more stars can be observed from Earth-orbiting telescopes, such as the *Hubble Space Telescope*. The visibility of a star depends on its brightness and its distance from Earth. Astronomers use two scales to describe the brightness of a star.

apparent magnitude the brightness of a star as seen from the Earth

absolute magnitude the brightness that a star would have at a distance of 32.6 light-years from Earth

The brightness of a star as it appears to us on Earth is called the star's **apparent magnitude.** The apparent magnitude of a star depends on both how much light the star emits and how far the star is from Earth. The lower the number of the star on the scale shown in **Figure 6**, the brighter the star appears to observers on Earth. The true brightness, or **absolute magnitude,** of a star is how bright the star would appear if all the stars were at a standard, uniform distance from Earth. The brighter a star actually is, the lower the number of its absolute magnitude.

Section 1 Review

Key Ideas

1. **Describe** what astronomers analyze to determine the composition and surface temperature of a star.
2. **Compare** the mass of the sun with the masses of most other stars in the universe.
3. **Explain** why, as you observe the night sky over time, stars appear to move westward across the sky.
4. **Describe** the units used to measure the distance to stars in terms of whether their starlight takes minutes or years to reach Earth.
5. **Describe** the method astronomers use to measure the distance to stars that are less than 1,000 light-years from Earth.
6. **Explain** the difference between apparent magnitude and absolute magnitude.

Critical Thinking

7. **Identifying Relationships** How does the movement of Earth affect the apparent movement of stars in the sky?
8. **Analyzing Ideas** Why is it better for astronomers to measure parallax by observing every six months instead of observing every year?
9. **Understanding Relationships** If two stars have the same absolute magnitude, but one of the stars is farther from Earth than the other one, which star would appear brighter in the night sky?

Concept Mapping

10. Use the following terms to create a concept map: *star, apparent magnitude, red shift, Doppler effect, light-year, absolute magnitude,* and *blue shift.*

Differentiated Instruction

Alternative Assessment

Moving Stars Have students create a series of posters or a computer model that shows how the stars in a chosen constellation will move over time. The models should show how the constellation looks after several 100,000-year periods have passed. **LS Kinesthetic/Logical**

Key Resources

Technology

- Transparencies
  150 Apparent Magnitude

SECTION 2

Stellar Evolution

Key Ideas	Key Terms		Why It Matters
❯ Describe how a protostar becomes a star. ❯ Explain how a main-sequence star generates energy. ❯ Describe the evolution of a star after its main-sequence stage.	**main sequence** **nebula** **giant** **white dwarf**	**nova** **neutron star** **pulsar** **black hole**	Theories of stellar evolution help us to predict the age of our sun, as well as when it will stop shining. In fact, there's nothing to worry about.

Because a typical star exists for billions of years, astronomers will never be able to observe one star throughout its entire lifetime. Instead, they have developed theories about the evolution of stars by studying stars in different stages of development.

Classifying Stars

Plotting the surface temperatures of stars against their *luminosity*, or the total amount of energy they give off each second, reveals a consistent pattern. The graph that illustrates this pattern is the *Hertzsprung-Russell diagram*, or *H-R diagram*, a simplified version of which is shown in **Figure 1.** The graph is named for Ejnar Hertzsprung and Henry Norris Russell, the astronomers who discovered the pattern nearly 100 years ago.

Astronomers plot the highest temperatures on the left and the highest luminosities at the top. The temperature and luminosity for most stars fall within a band that runs diagonally through the middle of the H-R diagram. This band, which extends from cool, dim, red stars at the lower right to hot, bright, blue stars at the upper left, is known as the **main sequence.** Stars within this band are called *main-sequence stars* or *dwarfs.* The sun is a main-sequence star.

main sequence the location on the H-R diagram where most stars lie; it has a diagonal pattern from the lower right to the upper left

Figure 1 The Hertzsprung-Russell Diagram

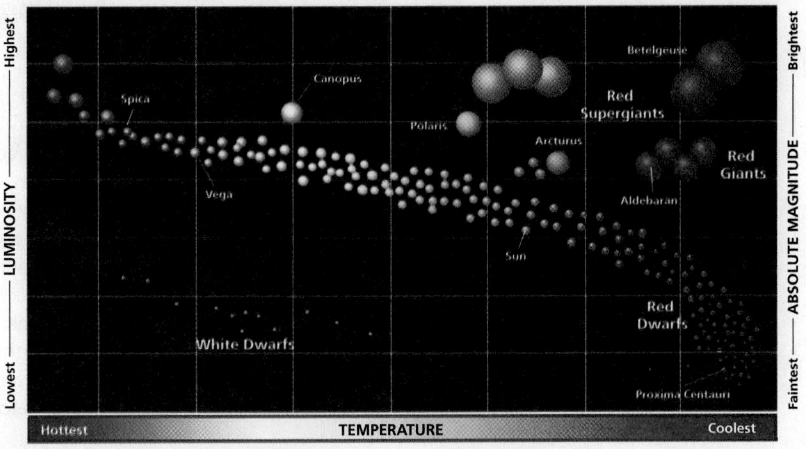

Section 2

Focus

Overview

This section explains how stars are classified and how they form and evolve. The section also describes how stars generate energy and describes the final stages of massive stars.

Bellringer

Have students write down two or three characteristics of stars that they might expect to change as the star ages. (Sample answers: the size of the star, surface color and temperature, brightness, and interior composition) **LS Logical**

Motivate

Using the Figure GENERAL

H-R Diagram Have students examine the Hertzsprung-Russell diagram and note what properties vary along the horizontal and vertical axes. Ask students what stars are hottest and brightest. (blue stars) Point out that the more massive stars at the upper left end of the H-R diagram convert fuel faster than the low-mass stars in the lower right do, so the more massive stars go through their life cycle more rapidly. **LS Visual/Logical**

Key Resources

Chapter Resource File
- Directed Reading BASIC

Technology
- Transparencies
  Bellringer
  151 The Hertzsprung-Russell Diagram

Teach

MISCONCEPTION ALERT

False Color Photographs Many photographs of distant astronomical objects, notably nebulae and galaxies, are reproduced in false colors. This is most commonly done when the object has been observed in a part of the electromagnetic spectrum other than visible light. In order to reproduce the image as a visible photograph with the proper contrast, areas of different intensities are assigned colors that visually convey the information effectively.

Math Skills

Answer

percent of mass radiated = (3.6 million metric tons/s ÷ 545 million metric tons/s) × 100 = (3.6/545) × 100 = 0.66%; 60 s/min × 60 min/h × 24 h/day × 365 days/y = 3.2×10^7 s/y; 3.6×10^6 metric tons/s × 3.2×10^7 s/y = 1.2×10^{14} metric tons/y

READING TOOLBOX

Scientific Theories vs. Scientific Laws

Sample answer: Newton's law of universal gravitation states that all objects in the universe attract each other through gravitational force. Newton's law of universal gravitation is a law and not a theory because it has been verified many times, and there is little chance that scientists will uncover new evidence that would cause them to revise or discard this law.

Figure 2 The Eagle Nebula is a region in which star formation is currently taking place. This false-color image of a small part of the Eagle Nebula was captured by the *Hubble Space Telescope*.

READING TOOLBOX

Scientific Theories vs. Scientific Laws

On a sheet of paper, write the name and definition of the law given on this page. Explain why it is a law, not a theory.

nebula a large cloud of gas and dust in interstellar space; a region in space where stars are born

Math Skills

Nuclear Fusion The sun converts nearly 545 million metric tons of hydrogen to helium every second. In the process, approximately 3.6 million metric tons of that hydrogen mass are changed into energy and radiated into space. What percentage of the converted hydrogen is changed into radiated energy? If the sun loses 3.6 million metric tons of mass per second, how many metric tons of mass will it lose in one year?

Star Formation

A star begins in a **nebula** (NEB yu luh), a cloud of gas and dust, such as the one shown in **Figure 2.** A nebula commonly consists of about 70% hydrogen, 28% helium, and 2% heavier elements. When an outside force, such as the explosion of a nearby star, compresses the cloud, some of the particles move close to each other and are pulled together by gravity. Alternatively, the collapse may start randomly, without an identifiable force.

According to Newton's *law of universal gravitation,* all objects in the universe attract each other with a force that increases as the mass of any object increases or as the distance between the objects decreases. Thus, as gravity pulls particles closer together, the attraction on each other increases. This pulls more nearby particles toward an area of increasing mass. As more particles come together, dense regions of matter build up within the nebula.

Protostars

As gravity makes these dense regions more compact, any spin the region has is greatly amplified. The shrinking, spinning region begins to flatten into a disk that has a central concentration of matter called a *protostar*. Gravitational energy is converted into heat energy as more matter is pulled into the protostar. This heat energy causes the temperature of the protostar to increase.

The protostar continues to contract and increase in temperature for several million years. Eventually, the gas becomes so hot that its electrons are stripped from their parent atoms. The nuclei and free electrons move independently, and the gas is then considered a separate state of matter called *plasma.* Plasma is a hot, ionized gas that has an equal number of free-moving positive ions and electrons.

Teaching Tip — GENERAL

Connect to Prior Knowledge To help students understand why a nebula spins faster to form a protostar, have them visualize an ice skater spinning. At first, the skater has his or her arms extended outward while spinning slowly. Then, by pulling the arms inward, the skater begins to spin faster. As gravity pulls particles toward the nebula's center (like a skater pulling in his or her arms), the circular motion around the center increases.

Why It Matters

The Messier Catalogue The term "nebula" originally referred to any object in the night sky that was vaguely defined and cloudlike. The first serious investigation of these objects was conducted by French astronomer Charles Messier. While searching for comets in the mid-eighteenth century, Messier noticed objects that appeared hazy, like comets, but which did not change position. By 1784, Messier had published a description of 103 "nebulae," most of which are now known as galaxies.

The Birth of a Star

Temperature continues to increase in a protostar to about 10,000,000 °C. At this temperature, nuclear fusion begins. *Nuclear fusion* is a process that occurs when extremely high temperature and pressure cause less-massive atomic nuclei to combine to form more-massive nuclei and, in the process, release enormous amounts of energy. The onset of fusion marks the birth of a star. Once nuclear fusion begins in a star, the process can continue for billions of years.

A Delicate Balancing Act

As gravity increases the pressure on the matter within the star, the rate of fusion increases. In turn, the energy radiated from fusion reactions heats the gas inside the star. The outward pressures of the radiation and the hot gas resist the inward pull of gravity. The stabilizing effect of these forces is shown in **Figure 3.** This equilibrium makes the star stable in size. A main-sequence star maintains a stable size as long as the star has an ample supply of hydrogen to fuse into helium.

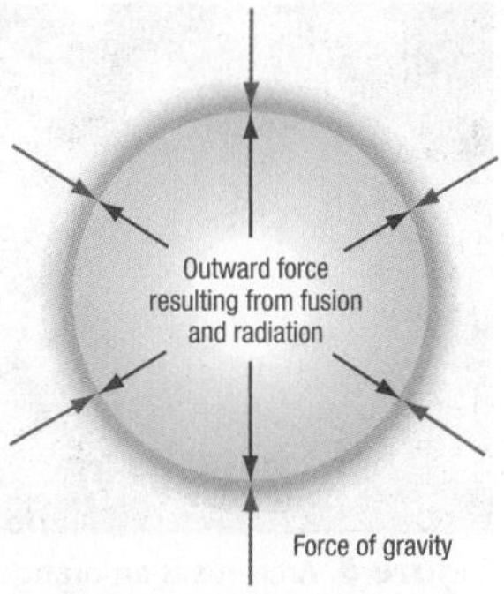

Figure 3 Stellar equilibrium is achieved when the inward force of gravity is balanced by the outward pressure from fusion and radiation inside the star.

Reading Check **How does the pressure from fusion and hot gas interact with the force of gravity to maintain a star's stability?**

The Main-Sequence Stage

The second and longest stage in the life of a star is the main-sequence stage. During this stage, energy continues to be generated in the core of the star as hydrogen fuses into helium. Fusion releases enormous amounts of energy. For example, when only 1 g of hydrogen is converted into helium, the energy released could keep a 100 W light bulb burning for more than 200 years.

A star that has a mass about the same as the sun's mass stays on the main sequence for about 10 billion years. More-massive stars, on the other hand, fuse hydrogen so rapidly that they may stay on the main sequence for only 10 million years. Because the universe is about 14 billion years old, massive stars that formed long ago have long since left the main sequence. Less massive stars, which are at the bottom right of the main sequence on the H-R diagram, are thought to be able to exist for hundreds of billions of years.

The stages in the life of a star cover an enormous period of time. Scientists estimate that over a period of almost 5 billion years, the sun, shown in **Figure 4,** has converted only 5% of its original hydrogen nuclei into helium nuclei. After another 5 billion years, though, with 10% of the sun's original hydrogen converted, the rate of fusion in the core will decrease significantly, causing the sun's temperature and luminosity to change. Then the sun will move off the main sequence.

READING TOOLBOX

Compare Make a table that compares the life span and energy output of a blue giant star with the life span and energy output of the sun. Then answer the following questions using your data: Which star is more likely to have life on one or more of the planets that orbit it? Why?

Figure 4 Our sun is a yellow dwarf star. It is located in the diagonal band of main-sequence stars on the H-R diagram.

Discussion — GENERAL

Star Mass The mass of the material in a protostar determines what class of star will ultimately form. Have students look at the figure at the top of the page. Ask what would happen if a large amount of matter were in the protostar. (The gravitational force will be greater.) Ask how equilibrium is maintained in a more massive star. (More energy is produced within the star, so a greater outward pressure from radiation balances the greater inward pull of gravity.) Ask students what would happen if the mass of the protostar were smaller. (The gravitational force will be less. Less radiant energy will be needed and produced to balance the force of gravity.) Point out that nuclear fusion can occur only at pressures and temperatures equal to or greater than a certain minimum. This is why certain massive bodies, like the planet Jupiter, are not stars. **LS Visual**

Answer to Reading Check

The forces balance each other and keep the star in equilibrium. As gravity increases the pressure on the matter within a star, the rate of fusion increases. This increase in fusion causes a rise in gas pressure. As a result, the energy from the increased fusion and gas pressure generates outward pressure that balances the force of gravity.

Group Activity — ADVANCED

Main-Sequence Stars Separate students into small groups. Have each group research the properties and lifetimes of each class of main-sequence star. One student should research the range of masses for each class of star. Another should research the spectral classification system based on stellar colors and temperatures. A third student should learn how long the stars remain on the main sequence before entering more evolved stages. Each member should present his or her findings in a short written or oral report or as a poster. **LS Verbal/Logical**

Differentiated Instruction

Special Education Students

Group Work Divide the class into small groups and assign one student who has behavior issues to be the "writer" for each group. Have each group read the section and summarize the most important idea for each of the section's subheadings. The writers should record the chosen ideas and each group should share its findings with the class.

Teach, *continued*

Answer to Reading Check
Giants and supergiants appear in the upper-right part of the H-R diagram.

Using the Figure — BASIC

Identifying Stars Have students study the image of the constellation Orion. Ask why the blue-white stars in Orion are bright. (Blue-white stars are very hot and may be very luminous.) Ask why the red star Betelgeuse at the upper left of Orion is bright. (Betelgeuse is a red supergiant, so its size makes it very luminous.) Point out that the red object near the bottom of the photograph is the large Orion nebula, an emission nebula where stars are forming. Answer to caption question: The temperature of Betelgeuse, an orange-red star, is lower than that of the sun, a yellow star. LS **Visual**

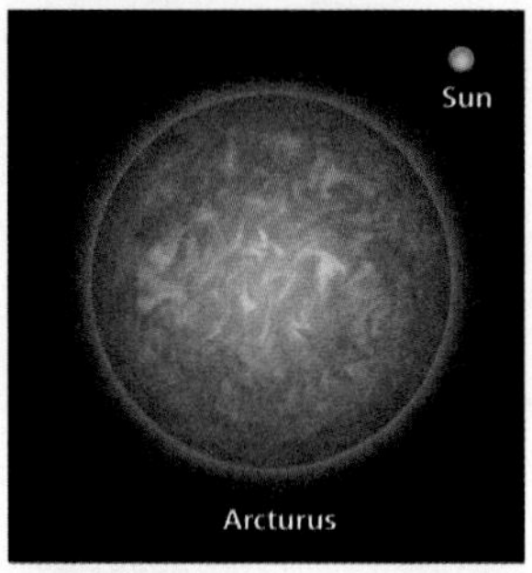

Figure 5 Arcturus is an orange giant that is about 23 times larger than the sun. Despite being about 1,000°C cooler than the sun, Arcturus gives off more than 100 times as much light as the sun does because it has so much surface area.

Leaving the Main Sequence

A star enters its third stage when about 20% of the hydrogen atoms within its core have fused into helium atoms. The core of the star begins to contract under the force of its own gravity. This contraction increases the temperature in the core. As the helium core becomes hotter, it transfers energy into a thin shell of hydrogen surrounding the core. This energy causes hydrogen fusion to continue in the shell of gas. The on-going fusion of hydrogen radiates large amounts of energy outward, which causes the outer shell of the star to expand greatly.

Giant Stars

A star's shell of gases grows cooler as it expands. As the gases in the outer shell become cooler, their glow becomes reddish. These large, red stars are known as **giants** because they are larger than main-sequence stars of the same surface temperature.

Because of their large surface areas, giant stars are bright. Giants, such as the star Arcturus shown in **Figure 5,** are 10 or more times larger than the sun. Stars that contain about as much mass as the sun will become giants. As they become larger, more luminous, and cooler, they move off the main sequence. Giant stars are above the main sequence on the H-R diagram.

giant a very large and bright star whose hot core has used most of its hydrogen

Supergiants

Main-sequence stars that are more massive than the sun will become larger than giants in their third stage. These highly luminous stars are called *supergiants*. These stars appear along the top of the H-R diagram. Supergiants are often at least 100 times larger than the sun. Betelgeuse, the large, orange-red star shown in **Figure 6,** is one example of a supergiant. Located in the constellation Orion, Betelgeuse is 1,000 times larger than the sun.

Though such supergiant stars make up only a small fraction of all the stars in the sky, their high luminosity makes the stars easy to find in a visual scan of the night sky. However, despite the high luminosity of supergiants, their surfaces are relatively cool.

Reading Check **Where are giants and supergiants found on the H-R diagram?**

Figure 6 If the sun were replaced by the red supergiant Betelgeuse, the surface of this star would be farther out than Jupiter's orbit. ***How does the temperature of Betelgeuse compare with that of the sun?***

Physics Connection — GENERAL

Star Size and Spectra The absorption spectrum of a star is a ready indicator of whether the star is a main-sequence dwarf, a giant, or a supergiant. The atoms in the denser dwarf stars collide more often, causing a broadening of absorption lines. Collisions are less frequent in giant and supergiant stars, so the lines are thinner. Thus, the thickness of the absorption lines indicates the evolutionary stage of the star. Have students research how spectra are used to determine the size and temperature of stars. Have them present findings as a written or oral report or as a poster project. LS **Verbal**

The Final Stages of a Sunlike Star

In the evolution of a medium-sized star, fusion in the core will stop after the helium atoms have fused into carbon and oxygen. With energy no longer available from fusion, the star enters its final stages.

Planetary Nebulas

As the star's outer gases drift away, the remaining core heats these expanding gases. The gases appear as a *planetary nebula,* a cloud of gas that forms around a sunlike star that is dying. Some of these clouds may form a simple sphere or ring around the star. However, many planetary nebulas form more-complex shapes. For example, the Ant nebula has a double-lobed shape, as shown in **Figure 7.**

Figure 7 The Ant nebula is a planetary nebula that is located more than 3,000 light-years from Earth in the southern constellation Norma.

White Dwarfs

As a planetary nebula disperses, gravity causes the remaining matter in the star to collapse inward. The matter collapses until it cannot be pressed further together. A hot, extremely dense core of matter—a **white dwarf**—is left. White dwarfs shine for billions of years before they cool completely.

White dwarfs are in the lower left of the H-R diagram. They are hot but dim. These stars are very small, about the size of Earth. As white dwarfs cool, they become fainter. This is the final stage in the life cycle of many stars.

white dwarf a small, hot, dim star that is the leftover center of an old sunlike star

Why It Matters

Where Are Elements Made?

To live on the moon or Mars, people will need a reliable supply of oxygen. Fortunately, both places have plenty of oxygen in their rocks and soil. But oxygen atoms were first created in the hearts of stars, along with almost all other matter.
About 20% of the air you breathe is oxygen, O2.
Supernovas such as 1987A, shown here, create all the atoms in the universe, except for hydrogen and helium.
YOUR TURN
CRITICAL THINKING
How can there be oxygen in lunar rocks and soil?

MISCONCEPTION ALERT

Planetary Nebulae While a planetary nebula is a true nebula (that is, a region of gas or dust, and not a distant grouping of stars), it has nothing to do with planets. The name has been handed down from the time these objects were first discovered. When observed through a small telescope, many planetary nebulae looked like dim, greenish, fuzzy disks, which is how distant large planets like Uranus and Neptune appeared through the same telescopes. The similarity in appearance to planets gave rise to the name "planetary" nebula.

Debate — Advanced

SETI Have interested students research and debate the advantages and disadvantages of the SETI program. Arguments in favor are the potential for increased knowledge and information exchange that could arise from the discovery of life on other worlds. Arguments against SETI are siphoning of resources away from more pressing research, the long time periods required for signals to travel through space, and the possibility that information may be missed.
LS Verbal/Logical

Differentiated Instruction

English Learners

Paired Summarizing Group students into pairs, and have them read silently about white dwarfs. Then, have one student summarize how white dwarfs form, what properties they have, and how they ultimately evolve. The other student should listen to the retelling and should point out any inaccuracies or ideas that were left out. Allow students to refer to the text as needed. **LS Verbal** English Language Learners

Why It Matters

Where Are Elements Made? With the exception of hydrogen and helium, all the matter in the universe originates in the life cycle of stars. All of the oxygen in the universe, including the oxygen we breathe, is forged in high-mass stars that become supernovas.

Answer to Your Turn

Critical Thinking Answers will vary. Sample answer: The oxygen would not be gaseous O_2, but as oxides of various other elements, such as silicon (SiO_2).

Teach, *continued*

Homework — GENERAL

Star Remnants Have students research when the first white dwarf and neutron star were discovered, who made the discoveries, and by what means the discoveries were made. Students may present their findings in a short written report. **LS Verbal**

Using the Figure — BASIC

Life Cycles Have students study the figure and then ask what causes the difference between the upper and lower paths. (The mass of the original nebula determines how massive the stars that form from it will be, and thus which evolutionary path the stars will undergo.) Point out that massive stars also go through several supergiant stages as fusion takes place in the carbon core and, in the more massive stars, in the various shells of heavier material. In the largest stars, the shells are like the layers of an onion, with the lighter outer shell producing material to fuel the shell below it. **LS Visual/Logical**

Key Resources

Technology

- Transparencies
  152 The Life Cycle of Stars

Novas and Supernovas

Some white dwarf stars are part of binary star systems. If a white dwarf revolves around a red giant, the gravity of the very dense white dwarf may capture loosely held gases from the red giant. As these gases accumulate on the surface of the white dwarf, pressure begins to build up. This pressure may cause large explosions, which release energy and stellar material into space. Such an explosion is called a **nova.**

nova a star that suddenly becomes brighter

A nova may cause a star to become many thousands of times brighter than it normally is. However, within days, the nova begins to fade to its normal brightness. Because these explosions rarely disrupt the stability of the binary system, the process may start again and a white dwarf may become a nova several times.

A white dwarf star in a binary system may also become a *supernova*, a star that has such a tremendous explosion that it blows itself apart. Unlike an ordinary nova, a white dwarf can sometimes accumulate so much mass on its surface that gravity overwhelms the outward pressure. The star collapses and becomes so dense that the outer layers rebound and explode outward. Supernovas are thousands of times more violent than novas. The explosions of supernovas completely destroy the white dwarf star and may destroy much of the red giant.

SCILINKS
www.scilinks.org
Topic: How Stars Evolve
Code: HQX0764

The Final Stages of Massive Stars

Stars that have masses of more than 8 times the mass of the sun may produce supernovas without needing a secondary star to fuel them. In 1054, Chinese astronomers saw a supernova so bright that it was seen during the day for more than three weeks. At its peak, the supernova radiated an amount of energy that was equal to the output of about 400 million suns.

Life Cycle of Stars

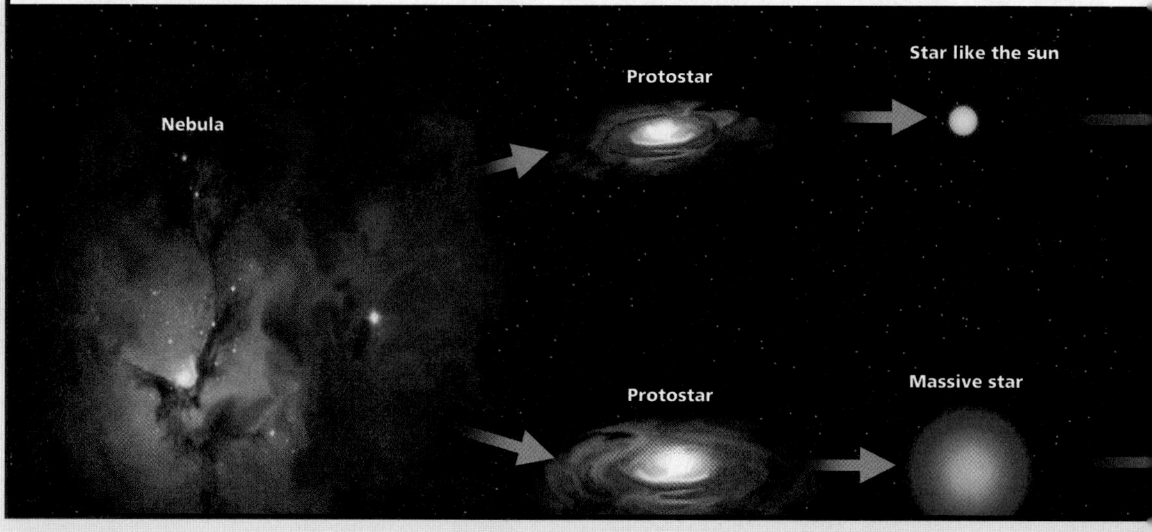

Skill Builder — GENERAL

Vocabulary The terms *nova*, *supernova*, and *nebula* are among the few pure Latin terms commonly used in astronomy. *Nova* is Latin for "new" and was applied to the bright stars that would suddenly appear in the night sky and fade after a few days. Because the process that causes novas to brighten was not understood, they were believed to be new stars. The prefix *super-* means "above" or "greater than," suggesting that these bright appearances were new stars with even greater brilliance. *Nebula* is the Latin word for "cloud." **LS Verbal**

Supernovas in Massive Stars

While only a small percentage of white dwarfs become supernovas, massive stars become supernovas as part of their life cycle, which is shown in **Figure 8.** After the supergiant stage, these stars contract with a gravitational force that is much greater than that of small-mass stars. The collapse produces such high pressures and temperatures that nuclear fusion begins again. This time, carbon atoms in the core of the star fuse into heavier elements such as oxygen, magnesium, or silicon.

Fusion continues until the core is almost entirely made of iron. Because iron has a very stable nuclear structure, fusion of iron into heavier elements takes energy from the star rather than giving off energy. Having used up its supply of fuel, the core begins to collapse under its own gravity. Energy released as the core collapses is transferred to the outer layers of the star, which explode outward with tremendous force. Within a few minutes, the energy released by the supernova may surpass the amount of energy radiated by a sunlike star over its entire lifetime.

Academic Vocabulary

structure (STRUHK chuhr) the arrangement of the parts of a whole; a whole that is built or put together from parts

Reading Check **What causes a supergiant star to explode as a supernova?**

Neutron Stars

Stars that contain about 8 or more times the mass of the sun do not become white dwarfs. After a star explodes as a supernova, the core may contract into a very small but incredibly dense ball of neutrons, called a **neutron star.** A single teaspoon of matter from a neutron star would have a mass of 2×10^{30} kilograms (a 2 followed by 30 zeroes). A neutron star that has more mass than the sun may have a diameter of only about 20 km but may emit the same amount of energy as 100,000 suns. Neutron stars rotate very rapidly.

neutron star a star that has collapsed under gravity to the point that the electrons and protons have smashed together to form neutrons

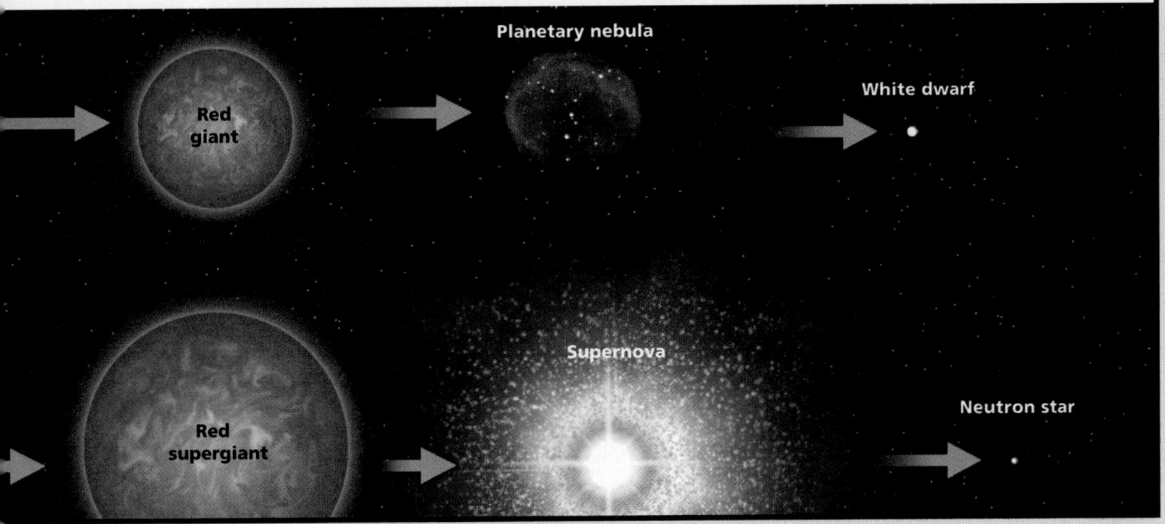

Figure 8 A star the mass of the sun becomes a white dwarf near the end of its life cycle. A more massive star may become a neutron star.

Answer to Reading Check

As supergiants collapse because of gravitational forces, fusion begins and continues until the supply of fuel is used up. The core begins to collapse under its own gravity and causes energy to transfer to the outer layers of the star. The transfer of energy to the outer layers causes the explosion.

Close

Reteaching — BASIC

Stellar Evolution On the board, write the words *red giant, main sequence, nebula, white dwarf, protostar,* and *planetary nebula.* Have students write these words on a sheet of paper and place each term in the correct order from earliest event to latest event. (From earliest to latest: nebula, protostar, main sequence, red giant, planetary nebula, white dwarf) **LS Logical**

Quiz — GENERAL

Determine whether each of the following statements is true or false.

1. Red stars are hotter and more luminous than blue stars. (false)
2. The force of gravity pulling a star's gases inward is balanced by the outward forces of gas pressure and radiation produced from fusion. (true)

Physics Connection — ADVANCED

Supernova Physics Supernovas are difficult to observe because they involve massive stars or massive close binary-star systems, both of which are relatively rare. Also, the supernova stage of a star represents a relatively short part of a star's life. The best-studied supernova is the event 1987A, a Type II (single massive star) supernova that occurred in the Large Magellanic Cloud, a small galaxy that orbits the Milky Way galaxy. Because the exploding star was relatively close and technology was available to study it, scientists obtained information about the physics of a supernova. One observation involved measuring the number of neutrinos—highly energetic and nearly massless particles that barely interact with matter—while the supernova was brightening. The two dozen neutrinos that were detected confirmed theoretical predictions about the nuclear processes that take place during a supernova. Have interested students research the various types of supernovas and the physical properties of each type. Students may present their findings in a written report or oral presentation. **LS Verbal**

Close, *continued*

Answers to Section Review

1. Gravity causes the gas and dust of a nebula to concentrate, flatten, and spin. The gas and dust become hotter as gravitational energy converts to thermal energy. The hydrogen nuclei at the center of the nebula undergo fusion, and the compact center of the nebula becomes a star.
2. During the fusion process, the tremendous pressure at the center of the star causes hydrogen nuclei to fuse and release energy as electromagnetic radiation.
3. The equilibrium between the inward force of gravity and the outward pressure from fusion and radiation makes the star stable in size.
4. Nuclear fusion in a main-sequence star takes place entirely within the star's core. In a giant star, fusion takes place in a shell of matter surrounding the core.
5. A star leaves the main sequence as hydrogen core fusion gives way to hydrogen shell fusion around the core. This causes the outer part of the star to expand and cool, so that the star becomes a giant.
6. When a white dwarf draws matter from its companion star, the pressure may cause an explosion.
7. Only very massive stars have enough mass in their dense cores to prevent light or matter from escaping when the star dies.

Figure 9 This pulsar, located in the heart of the Crab nebula, is still surrounded by the remains of a supernova explosion that took place less than 1,000 years ago.

pulsar a rapidly spinning neutron star that emits pulses of radio and optical energy

black hole an object so massive and dense that even light cannot escape its gravity

Pulsars

Some neutron stars emit a beam of radio waves that sweeps across space like a lighthouse light beam sweeps across water. Because we detect pulses of radio waves every time the beam sweeps by Earth, these stars are called **pulsars.** For each pulse we detect, we know that the star has rotated within that period. Newly formed pulsars, such as the one shown in **Figure 9,** are commonly surrounded by the remnants of a supernova. But most known pulsars are so old that these remnants have long since dispersed and have left behind only the spinning star.

Black Holes

Some massive stars produce leftovers too massive to become stable neutron stars. If the remaining core of a star contains more than 3 times the mass of the sun, the star may contract further under its greater gravity. The force of the contraction crushes the dense core of the star and leaves a **black hole.** The gravity of a black hole is so great that nothing, not even light, can escape it.

Because black holes do not give off light, locating them is difficult. But a black hole can be observed by its effect on a companion star. Matter from the companion star is pulled into the black hole. Just before the matter is absorbed, it swirls around the black hole. The gas becomes so hot that X rays are released. Astronomers locate black holes by detecting these X rays. Scientists then try to find the mass of the object that is affecting the companion star. Astronomers conclude that a black hole exists only if the companion star's motion shows that a massive, invisible object is present nearby.

Section 2 Review

Key Ideas

1. **Explain** the steps that the gas in a nebula goes through as it becomes a star.
2. **Describe** the process that generates energy in the core of a main-sequence star.
3. **Explain** how a main-sequence star like the sun is able to maintain a stable size.
4. **Describe** how nuclear fusion in a main-sequence star is different from nuclear fusion in a giant star.
5. **Describe** how a star similar to the sun changes after it leaves the main-sequence stage of its life cycle.
6. **Describe** what causes a nova explosion.
7. **Explain** why only very massive stars can form black holes.
8. **Describe** two types of supernovas.

Critical Thinking

9. **Identifying Relationships** How do astronomers conclude that a supergiant star is larger than a main-sequence star of the same temperature?
10. **Analyzing Ideas** Why would an older main-sequence star be composed of a higher percentage of helium than a young main-sequence star?
11. **Compare and Contrast** Why does temperature increase more rapidly in a more massive protostar than in a less massive protostar?
12. **Analyzing Ideas** How can astronomers detect a black hole if it is invisible to an optical telescope?

Concept Mapping

13. Use the following terms to create a concept map: *main-sequence star, nebula, supergiant, white dwarf, planetary nebula, black hole, supernova, protostar, giant, pulsar,* and *neutron star.*

8. A supernova may occur when a white dwarf accumulates matter from its larger companion star, and the star collapses and pushes matter outward in an explosive supernova. A supernova also may occur when a massive star whose core consists of iron that cannot fuse and produce energy to counter the weight of overlying layers collapses inward, and matter is pushed outward in a powerful explosion.
9. The supergiant star is much brighter, so it must have a larger surface area.
10. Hydrogen fusion produces helium; so older stars will have fused more of their initial hydrogen supply into helium.

Answers continued on p. 845A

Differentiated Instruction

Alternative Assessment

Odd Stars Have students research the behavior of Wolf-Rayet stars and blue stragglers to learn how their evolution differs from the pattern of stellar evolution for a low-mass star. Students should note how each star's initial mass affects the unusual ways in which it evolves. Have students present their findings as a written report or oral presentation. **LS Logical**

SECTION 3

Star Groups

Key Ideas	Key Terms	Why It Matters
❯ Describe the characteristics that identify a constellation. ❯ Describe the three main types of galaxies. ❯ Explain how a quasar differs from a typical galaxy.	constellation galaxy quasar	People have used the stars for thousands of years to help them navigate and to know when to plant crops.

When you look into the sky on a clear night, you see what appear to be individual stars. These visible stars are only some of the trillions of stars that make up the universe. Most of the ones we see are within 100 light-years of Earth. However, in the constellation Andromeda, there is a hazy region that is actually a huge collection of stars, gas, and dust. This region is more than two million light-years from Earth. It is the farthest one can see with the unaided eye.

Constellations

By using a star chart and observing carefully, you can identify many star groups that form star patterns or regions. Although the stars that make up a pattern appear to be close together, they are not all the same distance from Earth. In fact, they may be very distant from one another, as shown in **Figure 1**.

If you look at the same region of the sky for several nights, the positions of the stars in relation to one another do not appear to change. Because of the tremendous distance from which the stars are viewed, they appear fixed in their patterns. For more than 3,000 years, people have observed and recorded these patterns. These patterns of stars and the region of space around them are called **constellations.**

constellation one of 88 regions into which the sky has been divided in order to describe the locations of celestial objects; a group of stars organized in a recognizable pattern

Dividing Up the Sky

In 1930, astronomers around the world agreed upon a standard set of 88 constellations. The stars of these constellations and the regions around them divide the sky into sectors. Just as you can use a road map to locate a particular town, you can use a map of the constellations to locate a particular star. Star charts can be found in Appendix F.

Figure 1 The Constellation Orion

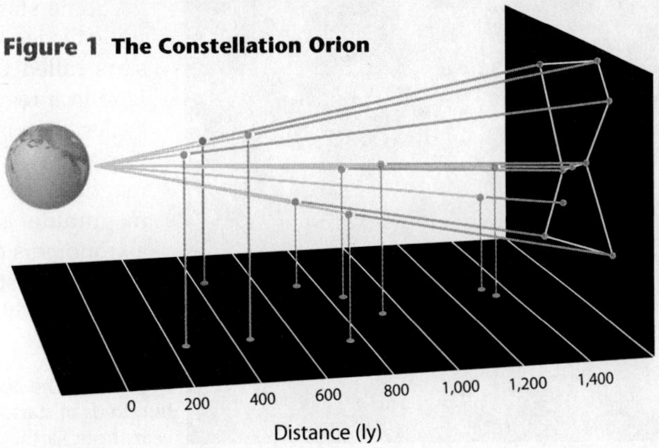

Section 3

Focus

Overview

This section describes groupings of stars, including constellations, star clusters, and galaxies. Types of galaxies and quasars are also discussed.

Bellringer

Ask students what they think a constellation is. (Sample answer: a group of stars that form a pattern) Have students write down the names of five constellations. (Sample answers: Ursa Major, Canis Major, Scorpius, Orion, Taurus, Pegasus, Gemini, Leo, Virgo, and Sagittarius) **LS Verbal**

Motivate

Activity GENERAL

Constellations Have each student choose a constellation and research its name; its history, paying particular attention to the role of the constellation in agriculture, navigation, and cultural rituals; and its significance for cultures other than Greek or Roman. Students may present their findings as a written or oral report, a poster project, a skit, a poem, or a song. **LS Verbal/Visual**

Key Resources

Chapter Resource File
- Directed Reading BASIC

Technology
- Transparencies
  Bellringer
  153 The Constellation Orion

Teach

READING TOOLBOX

Everyday Words Used in Science

Sample answer:

Yes, I think the term *globular cluster* accurately describes a large group of stars globbed together. I think that *open cluster* sort of describes the object it represents. It is *open* because it is loose, not tightly packed together, but *open* also has other meanings.

Answer to Reading Check

More than 50% of all stars similar to the sun are in multiple-star systems.

MISCONCEPTION ALERT

Changing Constellations Remind students that, because stars have their own motion, they will move toward or away from each other over thousands of years. Many constellations we see today will not be recognizable in 30,000 years.

READING TOOLBOX

Everyday Words Used in Science

The word *glob* means "a rounded clump." Based on what you know about the words *glob, open,* and *cluster,* do you think *globular cluster* and *open cluster* accurately describe the objects they represent? Why or why not?

Multiple-Star Systems

Stars are not always solitary objects isolated in space. When two or more stars are closely associated, they form multiple-star systems. *Binary stars* are pairs of stars that revolve around each other and are held together by gravity. In systems where the two stars have similar masses, the center of mass, or *barycenter*, will be somewhere between the stars. If one star is more massive than the other, the barycenter will be closer to the more massive star.

Multiple-star systems sometimes have more than two stars. In such a star system, two stars may revolve rapidly around a common barycenter, while a third star revolves more slowly at a greater distance from the pair. Astronomers estimate that more than half of all sunlike stars are part of multiple-star systems.

Reading Check **What percentage of stars similar to the sun are in multiple-star systems?**

Academic Vocabulary

association (uh SOH see AY shuhn) a connection or combination

Star Clusters

Sometimes, nebulas collapse to form groups of hundreds or thousands of stars, called clusters. *Globular clusters* have a spherical shape and can contain up to one million stars. An *open cluster*, such as the one shown in **Figure 2,** is loosely shaped and rarely contains more than a few hundred stars.

galaxy a collection of stars, dust, and gas bound together by gravity

Galaxies

A large-scale group of stars, gas, and dust that is bound together by gravity is called a **galaxy.** Galaxies are the major building blocks of the universe. A typical galaxy, such as the Milky Way galaxy in which we live, has a diameter of about 100,000 light-years and may contain more than 200 billion stars. Astronomers estimate that the universe contains hundreds of billions of galaxies.

Distances to Galaxies

Some stars allow astronomers to find distances to the galaxies that contain the stars. For example, giant stars called *Cepheid* (SEF ee id) *variables* brighten and fade in a regular pattern. Most Cepheids have regular cycles that range from 1 to 100 days. The longer a Cepheid's cycle is, the brighter the star's visual absolute magnitude is. By comparing the Cepheid's absolute magnitude and the Cepheid's apparent magnitude, astronomers calculate the distance to the Cepheid variable. This distance, in turn, tells them the distance to the galaxy in which the Cepheid is located.

Figure 2 The open cluster M50 is made up of hundreds of stars. It is located about 3,000 light-years from Earth.

Cultural Awareness

The Pleiades The open cluster known as the *Pleiades*, which can be seen in the constellation Taurus during the Northern Hemisphere winter months, has long been one of the most recognizable star clusters in the sky. It is so close that its brightest stars can be seen individually, though overall it gives the impression of being a nebulous object. It is even classified in Charles Messier's catalogue of nebulae as *M45*.

Nearly every culture that has looked at the night sky has made some reference to the Pleiades. To the Greeks, they were the seven daughters of Atlas and Pleione. Early Hindus believed they were the Krittikas, the six nurses of the god of war. Different tribes of Aborigines in Australia assign different meanings to the stars, so that the cluster represents ancestral women, kangaroos, gum trees, and the realm of the dead. The Navajo called them the *Flint Boys*, who were raised to the heavens by the sky god. For the Inuit, the stars are called *Aggiattaat* and represent dogs that chased away a polar bear that threatened humanity. When the Aztecs viewed the Pleiades, the busy cluster reminded them of the market place.

Figure 3 The three main types of galaxies are spiral (left), elliptical (center), and irregular (right).

Types of Galaxies

In studying galaxies, astronomers found that galaxies could be classified by shape into the three main types shown in **Figure 3.** The most common type of large galaxy, called a *spiral galaxy*, has a nucleus of bright stars and flattened arms that spiral around the nucleus. The spiral arms consist of billions of young stars, gas, and dust. Some have a straight bar of stars that runs through the center. These galaxies are called *barred spiral galaxies*.

Galaxies of the second type vary in shape from nearly spherical to very elongated, like a stretched-out football. These galaxies are called *elliptical galaxies*. They are extremely bright in the center and do not have spiral arms. Elliptical galaxies have few young stars and contain little dust and gas.

The third type of galaxy, called an *irregular galaxy*, has no particular shape. These galaxies usually have low total masses and are fairly rich in dust and gas. Irregular galaxies make up only a small percentage of the total number of observed galaxies.

The Milky Way

If you look into the night sky, you may see what appears to be a cloudlike band that stretches across the sky. Because of its milky appearance, this part of the sky is called the Milky Way. We see this band of stars when looking through the dense plane of our own galaxy.

The *Milky Way galaxy* is a spiral galaxy in which the sun is one of hundreds of billions of stars. Each star orbits around the center of the Milky Way galaxy. It takes the sun about 225 million years to complete one orbit around the galaxy.

Two irregular galaxies, the Large Magellanic Cloud and Small Magellanic Cloud, are our closest neighbors. Even so, these galaxies are each more than 170,000 light-years away from Earth. Within 5 million light-years of the Milky Way are about 30 other galaxies. These galaxies and the Milky Way galaxy are collectively called the *Local Group*.

SCILINKS.
www.scilinks.org
Topic: Galaxies
Code: **HQX0632**

Activity — GENERAL

Multimedia Project Have students research the three basic classes of galaxies. Students may wish to show the differences between the classes of galaxies by using drawings, photographs, or video footage. Have students display their projects in the classroom. **LS Visual**

Close

Reteaching — BASIC

Galaxy Types Draw examples or paste photographic reproductions of various galaxies onto flashcards. Show the cards in quick succession to students, and have students indicate whether the galaxy on the card is spiral, barred spiral, elliptical, or irregular. You may choose to separate the class into teams and let them compete to see who can answer most accurately and quickly. **LS Logical**

Astronomy Connection — ADVANCED

Identifying a Galaxy from Within Because Earth is part of the Milky Way galaxy, it is impossible for us to say for certain what the galaxy looks like from an outside point of view. Dust in the center of the galaxy obscures the view of the spiral arms opposite our solar system. This area is gradually being explored by monitoring forms of nonvisible electromagnetic energy. Recent data suggest that the Milky Way, long thought to be a "twin" of the spiral galaxy M31, is actually a barred spiral galaxy.

Differentiated Instruction

Basic Learners

Anticipation Guide Before students read about the types of galaxies, ask them to predict the difference between spiral, barred spiral, elliptical, and irregular galaxies. Then, ask students to read silently the first half of the page to find out if their predictions were accurate. **LS Verbal**

Close, *continued*

Quiz — GENERAL

1. How does a constellation differ from a star cluster? (A constellation is an arrangement of stars into a pattern as seen from Earth at a particular time. A star cluster is a group of stars located near each other that formed when a nebula collapsed.)
2. What type of galaxy has flattened arms that extend outward from a central nucleus? (a spiral galaxy)
3. What type of galaxy has no particular shape and is rich in dust and gas from which new stars form? (an irregular galaxy)

Answers to Section Review

1. A constellation is a group of stars organized into a recognizable pattern that occupies one of 88 regions into which the sky has been divided. Although the stars may appear close together, they are different distances from Earth.
2. spiral, elliptical, and irregular
3. It is a spiral galaxy, because it has flattened arms that spiral around a bright nucleus of stars.
4. A quasar is a very bright feature in some galaxies that produces large amounts of energy and has the appearance of a bright star. Typical galaxies do not emit such intense radio signals.
5. The pattern of stars in a constellation is based on the way they appear against the sky. To a viewer, the stars all appear to be in a plane the same distance from Earth along the line of sight, even though they are different distances from Earth.

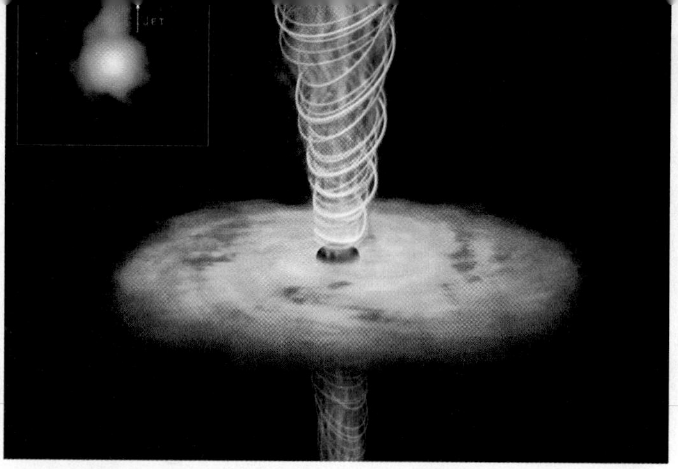

Figure 4 The jets of gas projected from a quasar can extend for more than 100,000 light-years. Quasars are too distant to be clearly photographed. The image shown is an artist's rendition of a quasar. The smaller inset is an actual image taken by the *Chandra X-Ray Observatory.*

Quasars

quasar quasi-stellar radio source; a very luminous object that produces energy at a high rate

Discovered in 1963, quasars used to be the most puzzling objects in the sky. Viewed through an optical telescope, a quasar appears as a point of light, almost in the same way that a small, faint star would appear. The word **quasar** is a shortened term for *quasi-stellar radio source*. The prefix *quasi-* means "similar to," and the word *stellar* means "star." Quasars are not related to stars, but quasars are related to galaxies. Some quasars project a jet of gas, as shown in **Figure 4.**

Astronomers have discovered quasars that are located in the center of galaxies far from Earth. In fact, quasars are among the most distant objects that have been observed from Earth. Galaxies that have quasars in them differ from other galaxies in that the quasars are very bright. The large amount of energy emitted from such a small volume could be explained by the presence of a supermassive black hole. One theory is that these supermassive black holes originated from stellar black holes and have grown larger by continuing to absorb matter. Some scientists think that supermassive black holes at galactic centers influence the structure of galaxies and their evolution.

Section 3 Review

Key Ideas

1. **Identify** the characteristics of a constellation.
2. **List** the three basic types of galaxies.
3. **Describe** the Milky Way galaxy in terms of galaxy types.
4. **Describe** the difference between a typical galaxy and a quasar.

Critical Thinking

5. **Identifying Relationships** Explain how stars can form a constellation when seen from Earth but can still be very far from each other.
6. **Making Calculations** The sun orbits the center of the Milky Way galaxy every 225 million years. How many revolutions has the sun made since the formation of Earth 4.6 billion years ago?
7. **Analyzing Ideas** Why are the constellations that are seen in the winter sky different from those seen in the summer sky?

Concept Mapping

8. Use the following terms to create a concept map: *galaxy, elliptical galaxy, Milky Way galaxy, irregular galaxy, barred spiral galaxy,* and *spiral galaxy.*

6. $(4.6 \times 10^9 \text{ y})/(2.25 \times 10^8 \text{ y/revolution}) = 20.4$ revolutions
7. Earth is on the opposite side of the sun during winter, so Earth faces a different part of the universe during night in the winter.
8. A *galaxy* may be an *elliptical galaxy*; an *irregular galaxy*; or a *spiral galaxy*, such as the *Milky Way galaxy*, which may be a *barred spiral galaxy*.

Differentiated Instruction

Alternative Assessment

Modeling Constellations Have students create a clay or plaster model that shows the actual relative positions of the stars in a chosen constellation. Students will need to scale the model so that the great distances between stars are manageable. **LS Kinesthetic/Logical**

SECTION 4
The Big Bang Theory

Key Ideas	Key Terms	Why It Matters
❯ Explain how Hubble's discoveries led to an understanding that the universe is expanding. ❯ Summarize the big bang theory. ❯ List evidence for the big bang theory.	**cosmology** **big bang theory** **cosmic background radiation**	Studying the origin, structure, and future of the universe helps us better understand our origins and our place in the universe.

The study of the origin, structure, and future of the universe is called **cosmology.** Cosmologists, or people who study cosmology, are concerned with processes that affect the universe as a whole. Like the parts found within it, the universe is always changing. While some astronomers study how planets, stars, or galaxies form and evolve, a cosmologist studies how the entire universe formed and tries to predict how it will change in the future.

Like all scientific theories, theories about the origin and evolution of the universe must constantly be tested against new observations and experiments. Many current theories of the universe began with observations made less than 100 years ago.

cosmology the study of the origin, properties, processes, and evolution of the universe

Hubble's Observations

Just as the light from a single star can be used to make a stellar spectrum, scientists can also use the light given off by an entire galaxy to create the spectrum for that galaxy. In the early 1900s, finding the spectrum of a galaxy could take the whole night, or even several nights. Although collecting new spectra was very time consuming, the astronomer Edwin Hubble used these galactic spectra to uncover new information about our universe.

Measuring Red Shifts

Near the end of the 1920s, Hubble found that the spectra of galaxies, except for the few closest to Earth, were shifted toward the red end of the spectrum. By examining the amount of red shift, he determined the speed at which the galaxies were moving away from Earth. Hubble found that the most distant galaxies showed the greatest red shift and thus were moving away from Earth the fastest.

Many distant galaxies are shown in **Figure 1.** Modern telescopes that have electronic cameras can take images of hundreds of spectra per hour. These spectra all confirm Hubble's original findings.

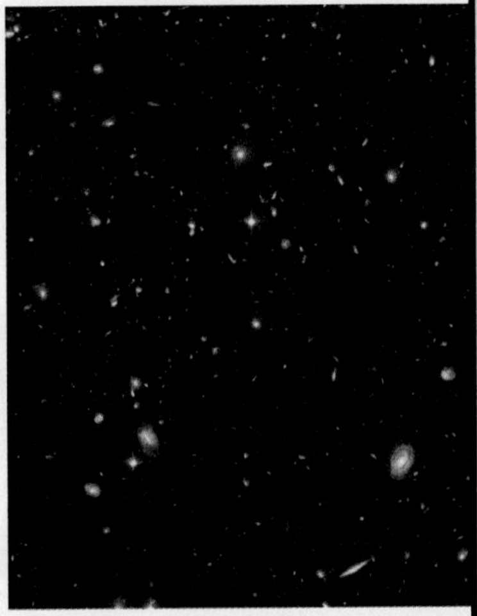

Figure 1 This image from the *Hubble Space Telescope* shows hundreds of galaxies. These galaxies all have large red shifts, so they are moving away from Earth very fast.

Focus

Overview

This section describes how cosmologists study processes that affect the universe as a whole and explains current theories about the origin of the universe.

Bellringer

Ask students how they think the universe formed. (Answers may vary.)
LS Logical/Verbal

Motivate

Discussion GENERAL

The Expanding Universe Ask students to recall how the Doppler effect relates to light from a moving object. Ask how they could tell if all galaxies were moving toward the observer. (The light from all galaxies would be shifted toward the blue end of the spectrum.) Ask how they could tell if all galaxies were moving away from the observer. (The light from all galaxies would be shifted toward the red end of the spectrum.) Ask students to explain which condition corresponds to an expanding universe, and why. (a red shift; All galaxies moving away from the observer and each other would indicate that the space between them was growing larger, and therefore the universe was expanding.) **LS Visual**

Key Resources

Chapter Resource File
- Directed Reading BASIC
- Inquiry Lab: Curving Space-Time GENERAL

Technology
- Transparencies
  Bellringer

Teach

MISCONCEPTION ALERT

Expanding Space-Time Students may think the expansion of the universe is simply a matter of the volume of space increasing. Point out that the situation is more complicated. According to the theory of general relativity, which provides the modern description for gravitation, the three spatial dimensions and time are treated as related and inseparable dimensions. To help simplify the process, it is easier for students to think of space in terms of just two spatial dimensions, like a sheet of paper, and then use these in conjunction with time. The expanding universe for this model does resemble a ball or balloon that is getting larger in time, which corresponds to the radius of the ball. The change in space occurs only on the ball's surface.

Answer to Reading Check

All matter and energy in the early universe was compressed into a small volume at an extremely high temperature until the temperature cooled and all of the matter and energy was forced outward in all directions.

Key Resources

Technology

- Transparencies
  154 Timeline of the Big Bang

Figure 2 Like raisins in expanding cake batter, the farther galaxies are from each other, the faster they move away from each other.

THINK central
INTERACT ONLINE
(Keyword: HQXSTGF2)

The Expanding Universe

Imagine a raisin cake rising in a kitchen oven. If you were able to sit on one raisin, you would see all the other raisins moving away from you. Raisins that are farther away in the dough when it begins rising move away faster because there is more cake between you and them and because the whole cake is expanding. The situation is similar with galaxies and the universe, as shown in **Figure 2.** By using Hubble's observations, astronomers were able to determine that the universe was expanding.

A Theory Emerges

Although cosmologists have proposed several different theories to explain the expansion of the universe, the current and most widely accepted is the big bang theory. The **big bang theory** states that billions of years ago, all the matter and energy in the universe was compressed into an extremely small volume. If you trace the expanding universe back in time, all matter would have been close together at one point in time. About 14 billion years ago, a sudden event called the *big bang* sent all of the matter and energy outward in all directions.

big bang theory the theory that all matter and energy in the universe was compressed into an extremely small volume that 13 to 15 billion years ago exploded and began expanding in all directions

As the universe expanded, some of the matter gathered into clumps that evolved into galaxies. Today, the universe is still expanding, and the galaxies continue to move apart from one another. This expansion of space explains the red shift that we detect in the spectra of galaxies. **Figure 3** shows a timeline of events following the big bang.

By the mid-20th century, almost all astronomers accepted the big bang theory. An important discovery in the 1960s finally convinced most of the remaining scientists that a sudden event, the big bang, had taken place.

Reading Check **What does the big bang theory tell us about the early universe?**

Figure 3 A Big Bang Timeline

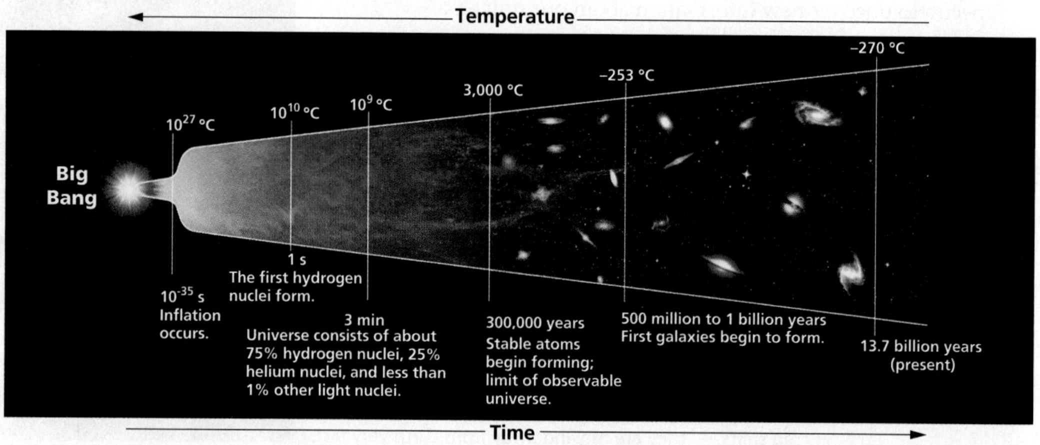

Physics Connection ADVANCED

New Physics, Old Universe Cosmology is an evolving and theoretical science. Many discoveries were made in just the last century. These discoveries include Einstein's work on general relativity and the quantum mechanical model for atomic and subatomic matter. More radical physics such as string theory, "brane" (membrane) theory, and multiple universes are part of cosmology. Have students research previous scientific models of the universe leading to the current model. Have them present their findings in a written report or oral presentation. **LS Verbal**

Differentiated Instruction

Special Education Students

Summarizing To help students identify important information, use this summarizing technique. As a group, read a paragraph. Ask a volunteer to summarize the paragraph in one sentence. Adjust the sentence so it is a good summary sentence. Have students write the sentence. Continue until all paragraphs have been read and summarized, and guide students to use the sentences when they study. **LS Verbal**

Quick Lab — The Expanding Universe

15 min

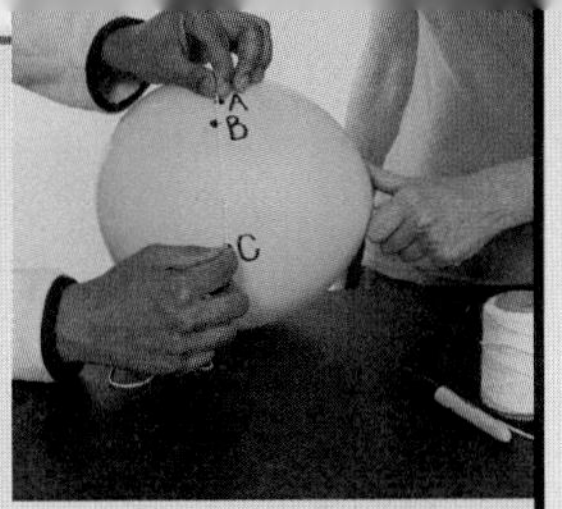

Procedure

1. Use a marker to make 3 dots in a row on an uninflated balloon. Label them "A," "B," and "C." Dot B should be closer to A than dot C is to B.
2. Blow the balloon up just until it is taut. Pinch the balloon to keep it inflated, but do not tie the neck.
3. Use string and a ruler to measure the distances between A and B, B and C, and A and C.
4. With the balloon still inflated, blow into the balloon until its diameter is twice as large.
5. Measure the distances between A and B, B and C, and A and C. For each set of dots, subtract the original distances measured in step 3 from the new distances. Then, divide by 2, because the balloon is about twice as large. This calculation will give you the rate of change for each pair of dots.
6. Repeat steps 4 and 5.

Analysis

1. Did the distance between A and B, between B and C, or between A and C show the greatest rate of change?
2. Suppose dot A represents Earth and that dots B and C represent galaxies. How does the rate at which galaxies are moving away from us relate to how far they are from Earth?

Cosmic Background Radiation

In 1965, researchers using radio telescopes detected **cosmic background radiation,** or low levels of energy evenly distributed throughout the universe. Astronomers concluded that this background radiation formed shortly after the big bang.

cosmic background radiation radiation uniformly detected from every direction in space; considered a remnant of the big bang

The universe soon after the big bang would have been very hot and would have cooled to a great extent by now. The energy of the background radiation has a temperature of only about 3 °C above *absolute zero,* the coldest temperature possible. Because absolute zero is about –273 °C, the cosmic background radiation's temperature is about 270 °C below zero.

Like any theory, the big bang theory must continue to be tested against each new discovery about the universe. But the big bang theory has been well tested, and any changes are likely to be modifications of the general concept.

Ripples in Space

Maps of cosmic background radiation over the whole sky look very smooth. But on satellite maps that show where temperatures differ from the average background temperature, "ripples" become apparent, as shown in **Figure 4.** These ripples are irregularities in the cosmic background radiation, which were caused by small fluctuations in the distribution of matter in the early universe. The ripples are thought to indicate the first stages in the formation of the universe's first galaxies.

Figure 4 This display is shown on half a globe that represents the sky as seen from Earth orbit. The temperature difference between the red spots and the blue spots is only 2/10,000 °C.

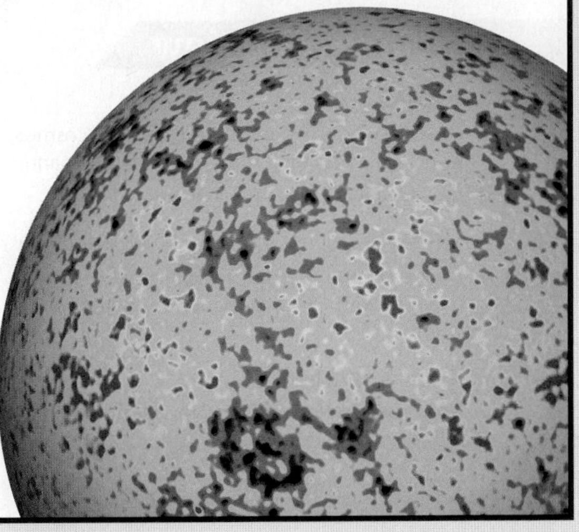

Close

Reteaching — BASIC

Timeline Have students create a timeline that indicates the major events in the development of the big bang model of the universe. Allow students to refer to the text as needed. **LS Logical**

Quiz — GENERAL

1. What indicates that the universe is expanding? (Almost all galaxies have spectra that are shifted toward the red end of the spectrum and thus are moving away from Earth and each other at a rate that increases with distance.)
2. Why is cosmic background radiation important to cosmological research? (Cosmic background radiation indicates that the universe has cooled over the last 14 billion years, and thus provides support for an initially hot, compact, outwardly-expanding universe.)
3. Why is dark matter an important concept? (Most matter that holds the universe together by gravity is invisible. Dark matter helps account for the estimated mass of the universe.)

Quick Lab

Skills Acquired

- Observing
- Interpreting

Materials

- Marker
- Balloon
- String
- Ruler

Teacher's Notes: Be sure that students do not overinflate the balloon. Adhesive paper dots may be used instead of ink dots. To extend the lab, repeat steps 4 and 5 and chart or graph the different rates of change and physical changes in distance.

Answers to Analysis

1. The distance between A and C showed the greatest rate of change.
2. The faster a galaxy moves away from Earth, the farther the galaxy is from Earth.

READING TOOLBOX

Everyday Words Used in Science

Sample answer:

I thought *dark matter* might be matter with a dark color, but it is actually matter that has gravity but does not give off light. I was not sure about *dark energy*, since energy isn't something that you can really see. Dark energy might be a force that opposes gravity, but little is known about it.

Close, *continued*

Answers to Section Review

1. The spectra of light from most galaxies were Doppler-shifted toward the red end, indicating that these galaxies were moving away from our galaxy.
2. All of the matter and energy in the universe was compressed into an extremely small volume that, about 13 to 15 billion years ago, exploded and began expanding in all directions.
3. cosmological red shifts, cosmic background radiation, and "ripples" in space
4. Only about 4% of matter and energy is visible.
5. The uneven distribution of matter in the early universe has caused subtle temperature ripples to form in the cosmic background radiation.
6. Because the universe is expanding outward, galaxies move away from each other on the large scale, even if galaxies within a group locally move toward each other. As a result, the spectra of all galaxies will show a cosmological red shift, not a blue shift. This effect is greater for more distant galaxies.
7. The observations of distant galaxies indicate that those galaxies are accelerating outward. The concept of dark energy is needed to help account for this acceleration.
8. Evidence for the *big bang theory* is found in the presence of *cosmic background radiation*, by the *red shift* in the spectra of *galaxies*, and the concepts of *dark energy* and *dark matter*.

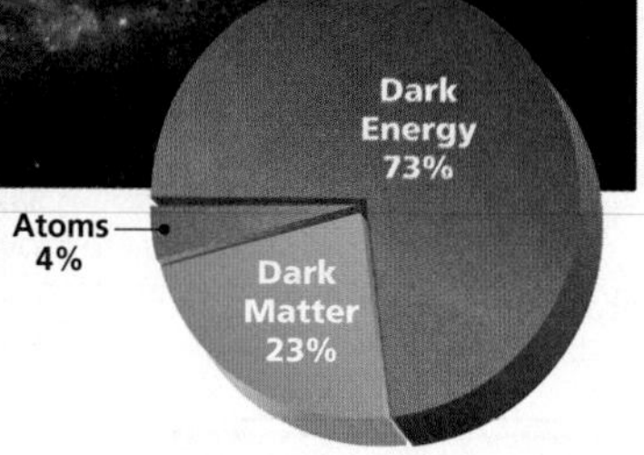

Figure 5 Normal matter may make up only a small portion of the universe.

A Universe of Surprises

Recent data based on the ripples in the cosmic background radiation and studies of the distance to supernovas found in ancient galaxies have forced astronomers to rethink some of the theories about what makes up the universe. Astronomers now think that the universe is made up of more mass and energy than they can currently detect.

Dark Matter

Surprisingly, analyzing the ripples in the cosmic background radiation suggests that the kinds of matter that humans, the planets, the stars, and the matter between the stars are made of makes up only 4% of the universe, as shown in **Figure 5.** Another 23% of the universe is made up of a type of matter that does not give off light but that has gravity that we can detect. Because this type of matter does not give off light, it is called *dark matter*.

SciLinks

www.scilinks.org
Topic: Big Bang
Code: **HQX0146**

READING TOOLBOX

Everyday Words Used in Science

How would you define *dark matter* and *dark energy?* Compare your definitions with those on this page.

Dark Energy

Another surprise is that most of the universe is composed of something that we know almost nothing about. The unknown material is called *dark energy*, and scientists think that it acts as a force that opposes gravity. Recent evidence suggests that distant galaxies are farther from Earth than current theory would indicate. So, many scientists conclude that some form of undetectable dark energy is pushing galaxies apart. Because of dark energy, the universe is not only expanding, but the rate of expansion also seems to be accelerating.

Section 4 Review

Key Ideas

1. **Describe** how red shifts were used by cosmologists to determine that the universe is expanding.
2. **Summarize** the big bang theory.
3. **List** evidence that supports the big bang theory.
4. **Compare** the amount of visible matter in the universe with the total amount of matter and energy.

Critical Thinking

5. **Inferring Relationships** How did the distribution of matter in the early universe affect how we are able to detect cosmic background radiation today?
6. **Evaluating Theories** Use the big bang theory to explain why scientists do not expect to find galaxies that have large blue shifts.
7. **Identifying Relationships** Why do observations made of distant galaxies indicate that dark energy exists?

Concept Mapping

8. Use the following terms to create a concept map: *cosmic background radiation, dark energy, red shift, dark matter, big bang theory,* and *galaxies.*

Differentiated Instruction

Alternative Assessment

Rate of Universal Expansion Have students research the Hubble constant, which is a measure of both the speed at which the universe expands and the age of the universe. Students should note why the value of this "constant" has changed, how stellar evolution limits the value that it can have, and how the Hubble constant relates to the big bang theory and the current "dark-energy" model of the universe. Students should present their findings in a written or oral report or poster project. **LS Verbal/Logical**

Why It Matters

A Cool Telescope

WEIRD SCIENCE

Every year, over 100 researchers brave the coldest, windiest place on Earth to use a special telescope that looks deep inside Earth. Why? This special telescope, called IceCube, is searching for hints of the origins of the universe. Pure, deep Antarctic ice provides the perfect observatory for detecting subatomic particles called neutrinos that reach Earth from far across space.

The average depth of an IceCube hole is nearly 2.5 km below the surface. These holes are drilled using hot water, producing approximately 750,000 L of melted ice in the process. It took about 57 hours to drill IceCube's first hole.

YOUR TURN

UNDERSTANDING CONCEPTS
What is the telescope IceCube designed to do?

CRITICAL THINKING
How might life at a research station on Antarctica be similar to, and different from, life on the International Space Station?

Why It Matters

A Cool Telescope

Stars in the final stages of their lives, as well as other deep-space celestial events, emit subatomic particles. Some are familiar, such as protons and photons, which are relatively easy to detect. Others, such as neutrinos, have no charge, virtually no mass, and rarely interact with matter. Although extremely difficult to do, astronomers have developed methods of detecting neutrinos, including with the unusual telescope IceCube.

Instead of looking into space to find particles that originated in the stars, IceCube searches down, through Earth itself. Cables carry special detectors nearly 2,500 m below the Antarctic surface, where no light or other type of radiation can interfere with the neutrino research.

IceCube consists of over 4,000 sensors designed to detect particles that result from neutrino collisions. Scientists will then determine the directions from which the neutrinos came, and how much energy each carried, thus giving some insight into the origins and development of the universe.

Answers to Your Turn

Understanding Concepts It is designed to detect neutrinos, subatomic particles that reach Earth from space.

Critical Thinking Similarities: harsh climate, isolated, very few people, limited space (other answers possible); Differences: not weightless in Antarctica, can still breathe the air and go outside, may see wildlife in Antarctica (other answers possible)

Making Models Lab

Time Required
one 45-minute class period

Lab Ratings

EASY → HARD

Teacher Preparation 2
Student Setup 1
Concept Level 2
Cleanup 1

Skills Acquired
- Experimenting
- Collecting Data
- Organizing and Analyzing Data
- Interpreting
- Identifying and Recognizing Patterns

Scientific Methods
In this lab, students will
- Make Observations
- Analyze the Results
- Draw Conclusions

Materials
The materials listed on the page are enough for groups of two students. Be sure the paraffin bricks are new and smooth on all sides. If the light from the bulbs appears to be weak, replace the batteries.

Making Models Lab

45 min

What You'll Do
- **Construct** a model photometer and two model stars.
- **Demonstrate** how distance affects the brightness of stars.
- **Explain** how color is related to the temperature of stars.

What You'll Need
aluminum foil, 12 cm × 12 cm
batteries, AA (3)
desk lamp with incandescent bulb
flashlight bulbs, 3-volt (2)
paraffin, 12 cm × 6 cm bricks (2)
rubber band, large
ruler, metric
tape, electrical
wire, plastic-coated with stripped ends, 15 cm
wire, plastic-coated with stripped ends, 20 cm

Safety

Star Magnitudes

Among other things, astronomers study the brightness, or magnitude, of stars. Except for the sun, stars are very faint and visible only at night. Thus, their brightness must be measured with a device called a *photometer* or, more recently, a CCD (charge-coupled device). An astronomical photometer consists of a surface that is sensitive to light and a device that measures the amount of light that reaches the surface. Photometers can also be used to compare the colors of different light sources. In this lab, you will determine the effect of distance on brightness and the relationship between temperature and color.

Procedure

1. Construct two flashlights:
   a. Arrange the bulbs and batteries as shown in the figure below. Using electrical tape, attach the wires to the batteries and bulbs. The bulbs should be on. If they are not on, study the illustration again and make adjustments.
   b. Tape the flashlight arrangements together so that they can be moved. Be sure to leave the wires loose at the negative ends of the batteries so that you can turn your flashlights on and off.
2. Construct a model photometer by folding the aluminum foil in half with the shiny side facing out, and placing it between two paraffin bricks. Hold the pieces together using a rubber band.
3. Place the two flashlights about 2 m apart on a table. Place the photometer between them with the largest sides of the bricks facing each flashlight bulb, as shown in the figure below.
4. Turn on both flashlights, and turn off all room lights.
5. Move the photometer until both sides are equally bright. Measure the distance, in centimeters, from each flashlight bulb to the center of the photometer. Record these measurements.

Step 1

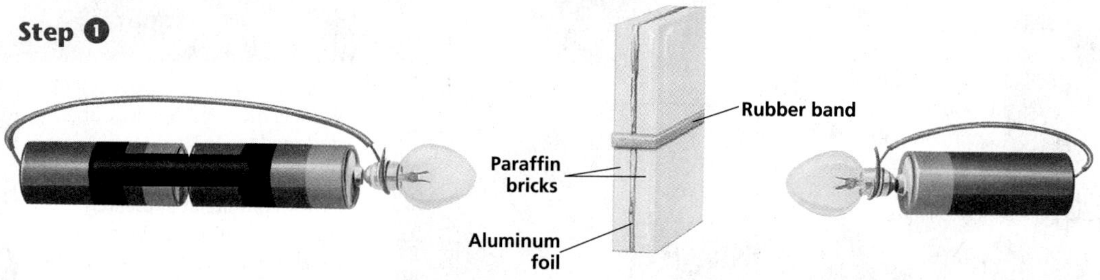

Tips and Tricks
Students should be sure that the foil blocks off any light leaking between the paraffin bricks. This lab can be performed effectively on an overcast day, though the outside light will have a noticeably different color from that of unfiltered sunlight on a clear day. Be sure students are comparing light from only two sources, and that no other light is interfering with the observations.

6. Square the distances you recorded in step 5. Record these values.
7. Incandescent light bulbs have filaments that emit light at a temperature that is much cooler than the sun's surface. Place the photometer between the desk lamp and a window on a bright day. Sunlight coming through a window will be the same color as the sunlight outdoors. Turn off any fluorescent ceiling lighting, and turn on the desk lamp.
8. Compare the color differences between the paraffin sides of your photometer.
9. Darken the room once again, and compare the colors of the bulb powered by one battery with the colors of the bulb powered by two batteries.

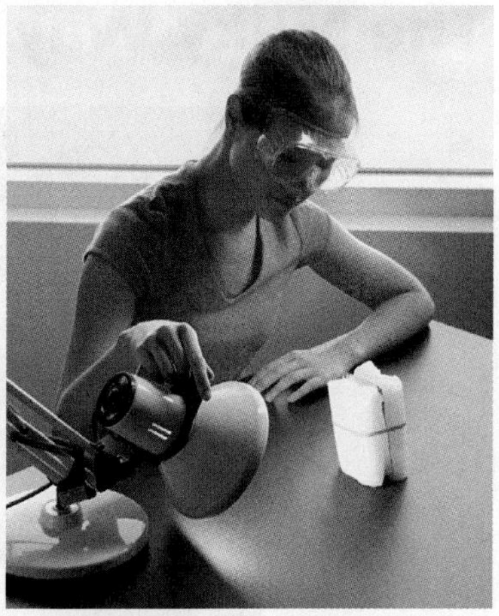
Step 8

Analysis

1. **Analyzing Data** The ratio of the square of the distances you calculated in step 6 is equal to the ratio of the brightnesses of the bulbs. What is the ratio of the square of the distance of the two-battery flashlight to that of the one-battery flashlight? What does this information tell you about the relationship between the brightness of the two flashlights?
2. **Drawing Conclusions** Based on the results of the investigation, would you expect a white star to be hotter or cooler than a yellow star?
3. **Applying Conclusions** Using your knowledge of the spectrum, would you expect a white star to be hotter or cooler than an orange star? Predict whether a blue star is hotter or cooler than a white star. Also, predict whether a red star is hotter or cooler than an orange star.

Extension

Explaining Observations Find an incandescent bulb controlled by a dimmer. Watch the color of the light as it fades. Does it become more yellow or more white? Explain why.

Answers to Analysis

1. Answers should be close to 2:1. The brightness of the flashlight with two batteries is twice as great as the brightness of the flashlight with one battery.
2. The white star is brighter and uses more energy in a given time. This means that a white star is hotter than a yellow star is.
3. A white star is hotter than an orange star. A blue star is hotter than a white star. A red star is cooler than an orange star. (Temperature increases as light progresses from red to blue.)

Answer to Extension

As the light fades, it becomes more yellow. This is because the filament of the bulb is cooler when less current passes through it, and the light associated with this decreased temperature is redder.

The Milky Way

Group Activity GENERAL

Charting the Galaxy Divide the class into groups of two or three students and have them research those portions of the Milky Way's arms whose contents are well-identified, such as a segment of the Perseus arm that contains a number of prominent stars. Each group should create a map of their section, labeling the largest and/or brightest stars, star clusters, and nebulae. Have each group present its chart and explain the details to the class. LS **Visual**

Answers to Map Skills Activity

1. 90,000 to 100,000 ly
2. 15,000 to 20,000 ly
3. The Orion Spur branches off of the Sagittarius Arm.
4. The solar system is located within the Orion Spur.
5. They spread out and become less dense than the center. Single arms tend to branch into multiple arms.
6. It is rotating clockwise.

MAPS in Action

The Milky Way

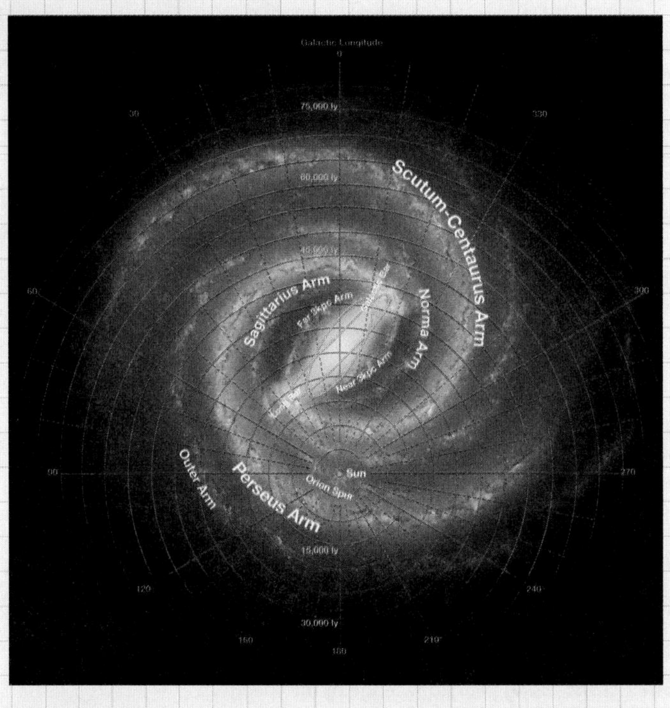

Map Skills Activity

The map above shows what astronomers think the Milky Way galaxy looks like. Because of Earth's position within the galaxy, scientists must hypothesize what our galaxy looks like from a perspective outside of the galaxy. They must also form a hypothesis about the shape and location of those spiral arms that are obscured by either the galactic core or other spiral arms that are closer to Earth. Use the map to answer the questions below.

1. **Using a Key** What is the approximate distance from one edge of the Milky Way to the other edge?
2. **Analyzing Data** What is the approximate width of the galactic core through its long axis?
3. **Inferring Relationships** How are the Sagittarius Arm and the Orion Spur related to each other?
4. **Identifying Locations** In which feature of the galaxy is the solar system located?
5. **Identifying Trends** What happens to the arms of the Milky Way as they radiate outward from the center of the galaxy?
6. **Evaluating Data** As shown on this map, the Milky Way is a barred spiral galaxy with two major arms each attached to opposite ends of the galactic core. Considering the shape of these arms, in which direction is the galaxy rotating when viewed from this perspective?

Key Resources

Technology

- Transparencies
  155 The Milky Way

Chapter 30 Summary

SUPER SUMMARY
Keyword: HQXSTGS

Key Ideas | **Key Terms**

Section 1

Characteristics of Stars

- To determine its composition and surface temperature, astronomers study a star's spectrum.
- Stars appear to move in the sky because of the Earth's rotational movement.
- Astronomers measure the distance to stars using the distance light travels in one year (the light-year) and the apparent shift in a star's position when viewed from different locations (parallax).
- Apparent magnitude is a star's brightness as it appears to us on Earth. Absolute magnitude is its true brightness if all stars were at a standard, uniform distance from Earth.

Key Terms

star, p. 845
Doppler effect, p. 848
light-year, p. 849
parallax, p. 849
apparent magnitude, p. 850
absolute magnitude, p. 850

Section 2

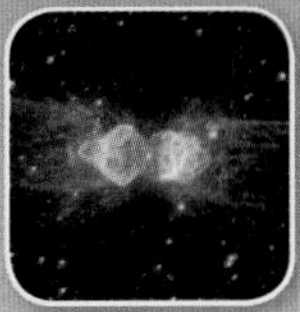

Stellar Evolution

- A protostar becomes a star when its hydrogen begins to fuse to form helium.
- Main-sequence stars generate energy through hydrogen fusion.
- Sunlike stars may become planetary nebulas and then white dwarfs. Massive stars may become supernovas and then neutron stars, pulsars, or black holes.

Key Terms

main sequence, p. 851
nebula, p. 852
giant, p. 854
white dwarf, p. 855
nova, p. 856
neutron star, p. 857
pulsar, p. 858
black hole, p. 858

Section 3

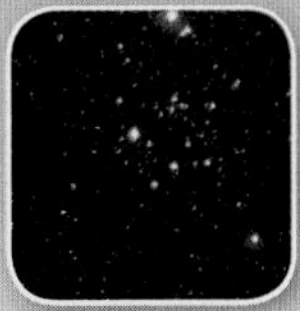

Star Groups

- A constellation contains a recognizable star pattern and can be used to locate celestial objects.
- The three types of galaxies are spiral, elliptical, and irregular.
- Quasars are very bright, distant galaxies that are thought to have enormous black holes in their centers.

Key Terms

constellation, p. 859
galaxy, p. 860
quasar, p. 862

Section 4

The Big Bang Theory

- Hubble found that the spectra of galaxies are red-shifted, indicating they are moving away from Earth and from each other.
- The big bang theory states that, about 14 billion years ago, all matter and energy in the universe was compressed into an extremely small volume that began to expand in all directions.
- Evidence for the big bang theory includes red shifts, cosmic background radiation, and ripples in space.

Key Terms

cosmology, p. 863
big bang theory, p. 864
cosmic background radiation, p. 865

Chapter Summary

Using THINK central Resources

Super Summary

Have students connect the major concepts in this chapter through an interactive Super Summary. Visit **www.thinkcentral.com** and type in the keyword **HQXSTGS** to access the Super Summary for this chapter.

Differentiated Instruction

Alternative Assessment

Poster Project Have students create a poster that shows the different classes of stars and their properties, as well as the types of star clusters or regions in galaxies in which different stars are most likely to be located. Posters should show the changing composition and physical evolution of the star. **LS Logical**

Chapter Review

Assignment Guide	
Section	**Questions**
1	2, 9, 11, 13, 15, 17, 23–25, 31
2	12, 14, 16, 18, 19, 26, 27, 34–36
3	5–7, 20, 30, 33
4	3, 4, 8, 10, 21, 22, 28
1–3	29
2 and 3	1, 32

READING TOOLBOX

Reading Toolbox

1. Sample answer: Newton's law of universal gravitation is a scientific certainty. On the other hand, the big bang theory cannot be proven beyond the shadow of a doubt. Much evidence supports the big bang theory, but new evidence may cause scientists to revise it in some way.

Using Key Terms

2–8. Answers may vary but should show that students understand the definitions of and differences between key terms.

Understanding Key Ideas

9. b
10. d
11. a
12. c
13. d
14. c
15. d
16. a
17. a

Chapter 30 Review

1. **Scientific Theories vs. Scientific Laws** As you review Newton's law of universal gravitation and the big bang theory, think about why one is a law and the other is a theory. Write a paragraph to explain your thoughts about this. READING TOOLBOX

USING KEY TERMS

Use each of the following terms in a separate sentence.

2. *light-year*
3. *cosmology*
4. *big bang theory*

For each pair of terms, explain how the meanings of the terms differ.

5. *constellation* and *cluster*
6. *spiral galaxy* and *elliptical galaxy*
7. *galaxy* and *quasar*
8. *cosmic background radiation* and *red shift*

UNDERSTANDING KEY IDEAS

9. The most common element in most stars is
   a. oxygen. **c.** helium.
   b. hydrogen. **d.** sodium.
10. Cosmic background radiation
    a. is very hot.
    b. is blue-green.
    c. comes from supernovas.
    d. comes almost equally from all directions.
11. Stars appear to move in circular paths through the sky because
    a. Earth rotates on its axis.
    b. Earth orbits the sun.
    c. the stars orbit Polaris.
    d. the Milky Way is a spiral galaxy.
12. A nebula begins the process of becoming a protostar when the nebula
    a. develops a red shift.
    b. changes color from red to blue.
    c. begins to shrink and increases its spin.
    d. explodes as a nova.
13. The brightest star in the night sky is
    a. Polaris.
    b. Mars.
    c. Arcturus.
    d. Sirius.
14. A main-sequence star generates energy by fusing
    a. nitrogen into iron.
    b. helium into carbon.
    c. hydrogen into helium.
    d. nitrogen into carbon.
15. Which of the following choices lists the colors of stars from hottest to coolest?
    a. red, yellow, orange, white, blue
    b. orange, red, white, blue, yellow
    c. yellow, orange, red, blue, white
    d. blue, white, yellow, orange, red
16. The heaviest element formed in the core of a star is
    a. iron.
    b. carbon.
    c. helium.
    d. nitrogen.
17. The change in position of a nearby star as seen from different points on Earth's orbit compared with the position of a faraway star is called
    a. parallax.
    b. blue shift.
    c. red shift.
    d. a Cepheid variable.

SHORT ANSWER

18. Describe what scientists think will happen to the sun in the next 5 billion years.
19. How can a black hole be detected if it is invisible?
20. How does a galaxy that contains a quasar differ from an ordinary galaxy?
21. What evidence indicates that the universe is expanding?
22. How does the presence of cosmic background radiation support the big bang theory?

Short Answer

18. The sun will enter a red giant stage, becoming larger and cooler.
19. The X-rays emitted by material being pulled into the black hole provide a clue as to the black hole's whereabouts. The source of the material is usually a companion star, so by studying the motion of that star, the mass of the invisible object can be determined and compared to the mass necessary for a star to become a black hole.
20. Galaxies that have quasars at their centers are very bright because of the large amount of energy emitted by the quasar.
21. The red shift of the spectra of all galaxies indicates that the universe is expanding. All galaxies are moving away from the Milky Way and from each other at a rate that increases with distance.
22. The cosmic background radiation indicates that the universe was once much more compact and much hotter, and that it expanded, cooling in the process. This is the behavior predicted by the big bang theory.

CRITICAL THINKING

23. Inferring Relationships If the spectrum of a star indicates that the star shines with red light, what is the approximate surface temperature of the star?

24. Analyzing Ideas Why are different constellations visible during different seasons?

25. Analyzing Ideas Explain why Polaris is considered to be a very significant star even though it is not the brightest star in Earth's sky.

26. Making Comparisons Why does energy build up more rapidly in a massive protostar than in a less massive one?

27. Analyzing Ideas Explain why an old main-sequence star is made of a higher percentage of helium than a young main-sequence star is.

28. Analyzing Ideas If all galaxies began to show blue shifts, what would this change indicate about the fate of the universe?

CONCEPT MAPPING

29. Use the following terms to create a concept map: *galaxy, star, black hole, white dwarf, neutron star, giant, spiral galaxy, supergiant, elliptical galaxy, planetary nebula, main sequence, irregular galaxy,* and *protostar.*

MATH SKILLS

Math Skills

30. Making Calculations The Milky Way galaxy has about 200 billion stars. If only 10% of an estimated 125 billion galaxies thought to exist in the universe were as large as the Milky Way, how many total stars would be in those galaxies?

31. Making Calculations Given that the nearest star is about 4 light-years from Earth and a light-year is about 10,000,000,000,000 km, how many years would it take to travel to the nearest star if your spaceship goes 100 times faster than a car traveling 100 km/h?

WRITING SKILLS

32. Creative Writing Imagine that you are navigating through the galaxy and seeing many kinds of objects. Write a brief tour article for a magazine that describes your trip.

33. Writing from Research Use the Internet and library resources to research the function of constellations in ancient cultures. Write a short essay describing three different ways that ancient cultures used constellations.

INTERPRETING GRAPHICS

The graph below shows the relationship between a star's age and mass. Use the graph to answer the questions that follow.

Relationship Between Age and Mass of a Star

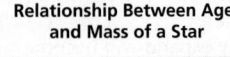

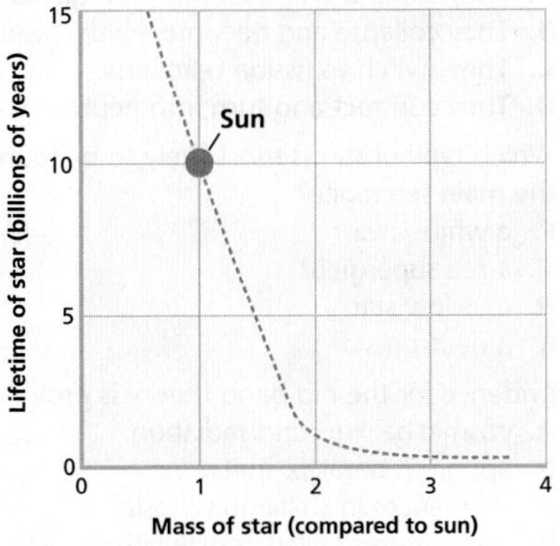

34. Which star would live longer, a star that has half the mass of the sun or a star that has 2 times the mass of the sun?

35. Approximately how long would a main-sequence star that has a mass about 1.5 times that of our sun live?

36. If the mass of the sun was reduced by one-half, approximately how much longer would the sun live than it would with its current mass?

Chapter Review

Critical Thinking

23. The approximate surface temperature is less than 3,500 °C.

24. During each season, Earth is at a different position relative to the sun. Thus, in each season, the night sky faces a different direction from the sun, and therefore different constellations are viewed.

25. Polaris is almost directly over Earth's North Pole and does not appear to move around the North Pole, as do the other stars. Polaris is bright enough that it can be used to find true north.

26. More mass equals more potential gravitational energy. As the mass clumps together, the gravitational energy increases, which causes even more mass to accumulate.

27. A young main-sequence star has just begun the core fusion process by which it converts hydrogen to helium, whereas an old main-sequence star has been converting hydrogen to helium for a long time. Therefore, the older star contains more helium.

28. A universal blue shift in the spectra of galaxies would indicate that all galaxies were moving toward each other, and therefore the universe would be contracting.

Concept Mapping

29. Answers may vary but should include all of the terms listed. Sample answers appear at the end of this unit on p. 875B.

Math Skills

30. total number of stars = number of stars in Milky Way × percentage of Milky-Way sized galaxies × number of galaxies; total number of stars = $(2.00 \times 10^{11}$ stars/galaxy$) \times (0.10) \times (1.25 \times 10^{11}$ galaxies$)$; total number of stars = 2.5×10^{21} stars, or 2,500,000,000,000,000,000,000 stars

31. time of travel = (number of light years × length of light-year)/ speed of vehicle; time of travel = $[(4 \text{ ly} \times 10^{13} \text{ km/ly})/(100 \times 100 \text{ km/h})] \times (1 \text{ d}/24 \text{ h}) \times (1 \text{ y}/365.25 \text{ d}) = [(4 \times 10^{13} \text{ km})/10^4 \text{ km/h}] \times (1 \text{ y}/8{,}766 \text{ h}) = 4.6 \times 10^5$ y, or 460,000 y

Writing Skills

32. Answers may vary. Accept all reasonable answers.

33. Answers may vary. Accept all reasonable answers.

Interpreting Graphics

34. a star with half the mass of the sun

35. 5 billion years

36. more than 5 billion years longer

Standardized Test Prep

Estimated Time

To give students practice under more realistic testing conditions, allow them 30 minutes to answer all of the questions in this practice test.

Test Doctor

Question 2 Answer I is correct. Answer F is incorrect because the composition of stars does not indicate their motion. Answer G is incorrect because these circular trails are evidence of Earth's motion, not the motion of the stars. Color separation alone does not reveal motion, so answer H is incorrect.

Question 4 Answer H is correct, because typical yellow stars are the most likely to be found on the main sequence. Answer F is incorrect. White dwarf stars evolve after the main sequence stage from a star with a sunlike mass. Answer G is incorrect because red supergiants evolve after the main sequence stage. Answer I is incorrect because neutron stars are the result of a red supergiant star that has experienced a supernova.

Question 10 Answer C is correct. Students should multiply the distance light travels in one second (300,000 km/s) by 60. Then, they should multiply the total by 8 minutes. The true average distance between Earth and sun is approximately 149,500,000 km.

Chapter 30 Standardized Test Prep

Understanding Concepts

Directions (1–5): For each question, write on a separate sheet of paper the letter of the correct answer.

1. What accounts for different stars being seen in the sky during different seasons of the year?
   A. stellar motion around Polaris
   B. Earth's rotation on its axis
   C. Earth's revolution around the sun
   D. position north or south of the equator
2. How do stellar spectra provide evidence that stars are actually moving?
   F. Dark-line spectra reveal a star's composition.
   G. Long-exposure photos show curved trails.
   H. Light separates into different wavelengths.
   I. Doppler shifts occur in the star's spectrum.
3. What happens to main-sequence stars like the sun when energy from fusion is no longer available?
   A. They expand and become supergiants.
   B. They collapse and become white dwarfs.
   C. They switch to fission reactions.
   D. They contract and turn into neutron stars.
4. Which type of star is most likely to be found on the main sequence?
   F. a white dwarf
   G. a red supergiant
   H. a yellow star
   I. a neutron star
5. Evidence for the big bang theory is provided by
   A. cosmic background radiation.
   B. apparent parallax shifts.
   C. differences in stellar luminosity.
   D. star patterns called constellations.

Directions (6–8): For each question, write a short response.

6. What type of galaxy has no identifiable shape?
7. What is the collective name for the Milky Way galaxy and a cluster of approximately 30 other galaxies located nearby?
8. What is the name for stars that seem to circle around Polaris and never dip below the horizon?

Reading Skills

Directions (9–11): Read the passage below. Then, answer the questions.

DISCOVERING GALAXIES

Today, we know that Copernicus was right: the stars are very far from Earth. In fact, stars are so distant that a new unit of length—the light-year—was created to measure their distance. A light-year is a unit of length equal to the distance that light travels through space in 1 year. Because the speed of light through space is about 300,000 km/s, light travels approximately 9.46 trillion kilometers in one year.

Even after astronomers figured out that stars were far from Earth, the nature of the universe was hard to understand. Some astronomers thought that our galaxy, the Milky Way, included every object in space. In the early 1920's, Edwin Hubble made one of the most important discoveries in astronomy. He discovered that the Andromeda galaxy, which is the closest major galaxy to our own, was past the edge of the Milky Way. This fact confirmed the belief of many astronomers that the universe is larger than our galaxy.

9. Why was Edwin Hubble's discovery important?
   F. Hubble's discovery showed scientists that the universe was smaller than previously thought.
   G. Hubble showed that the Andromeda galaxy was larger than the Milky Way galaxy.
   H. Hubble's discovery showed scientists that the universe was larger than our own galaxy.
   I. Hubble showed that all of the stars exist in two galaxies, Andromeda and The Milky Way.
10. Because the sun and Earth are close together, the distance between the sun and Earth is measured in light-minutes. A light-minute is the distance light travels in 1 minute. The sun is about 8 light-minutes from Earth. What is the approximate distance between the sun and Earth?
   A. 2,400,000 km
   B. 18,000,000 km
   C. 144,000,000 km
   D. 1,000,000,000 km
11. Why might scientists use light-years as a measurement of distance between stars?

Question 12 Full-credit answers should include the following points:

- the diagrams show that the individual stars move at different rates and in different directions from one another
- constellations are arbitrary human distinctions. The stars within constellations move along individual paths, not as a group as many ancient civilizations thought they did
- the familiar patterns that stars form in Earth's sky change slowly over time as the stars that comprise the patterns move relative to each other
- star movement may take thousands of years to become apparent

Question 15 Full-credit answers should include the following points:

- the star in the table with the closest temperature to the sun in most likely Capella
- a star's temperature can be determined by its color. Stars that have similar colors share a common temperature range
- Capella is a yellow star like the sun and thus it is the most likely to have a temperature similar to that of the sun

Interpreting Graphics

Directions (12–15): For each question below, record the correct answer on a separate sheet of paper.

The diagram below shows a group of stars called the Big Dipper moving over a period of 200,000 years. Use this diagram to answer question 12.

Changing Shape of the Big Dipper over Time

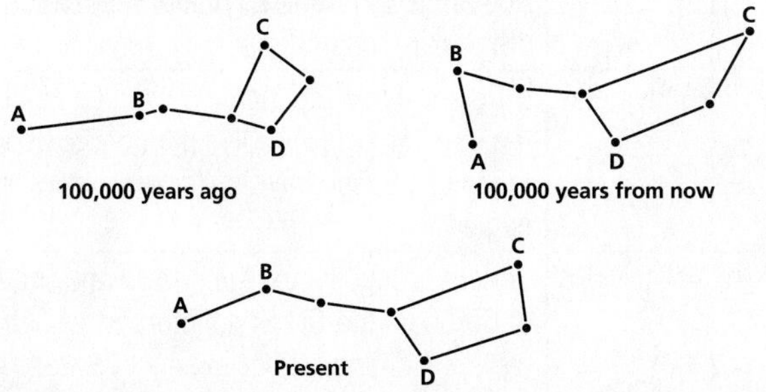

12. What does this series of drawings demonstrate about the individual stars in such a star group?

The table below shows data about several well-known stars. Distance is given in light-years. Use this table to answer questions 13 through 15.

Stellar Characteristics

Name	Color	Magnitude	Distance
Arcturus	orange	0.0	36.8 ly
Betelgeuse	red	0.5	400 ly
Canopus	yellow-white	−0.6	310 ly
Capella	yellow	0.1	42.2 ly
Mintaka	blue-violet	2.2	915 ly
Rigel	blue-white	0.2	800 ly
Sirius	white	−1.4	8.6 ly
Vega	white	0.0	25.3 ly

13. Which star has the brighest apparent magnitude as seen from Earth?
F. Rigel
G. Betelgeuse
H. Mintaka
I. Sirius

14. Which of these stars is the coolest?
A. Arcturus
B. Betelgeuse
C. Mintaka
D. Vega

15. Which star most likely has a temperature that is similar to the temperature of our sun? Explain how you are able to determine this information.

Test Tip

If you are unsure of an answer, eliminate the answers that you know are wrong before choosing your answer.

Standardized Test Prep

Using THINK central Resources

State Resources

- For specific resources for your state, visit www.thinkcentral.com and type in the keyword **HSHSTR.**

Answers

Understanding Concepts

1. C
2. I
3. B
4. H
5. A
6. irregular galaxy
7. the local group
8. circumpolar stars

Reading Skills

9. H
10. C
11. Light-years can express vast distances in compact form. When expressing distance between stars, using light-years is easier and more efficient than using kilometers.

Interpreting Graphics

12. Answers may vary. See Test Doctor for a detailed scoring rubric.
13. I
14. B
15. Answers may vary. See Test Doctor for a detailed scoring rubric.

Answers continued from p. 720

Describing Space

Shape	Location	Distance	Orientation	Direction
axis	the ceiling	not always the same distance	faces the sun	west to east
curving	Earth	152 million km	faces away from the sun	east
circle	Northern Hemisphere	147 million km	to the right	west
ellipse	Southern Hemisphere		to the left	back and forth
curve	underneath the atmosphere		faces in a different direction	stayed constant
shape	underneath the sea		tilts toward the sun	in a straight path
	within the ellipse		tilts away from the sun	around the sun
	in our solar system			around another body

FoldNotes

Key Term	Definition
astronomy	the scientific study of the universe
galaxy	a collection of stars, dust, and gas bound together by gravity
astronomical unit	the average distance between Earth and the sun; approximately 150 million kilometers (symbol, AU)
electromagnetic spectrum	all of the frequencies or wavelengths of electromagnetic radiation
telescope	an instrument that collects electromagnetic radiation from the sky and concentrates it for better observation
refracting telescope	a telescope that uses a set of lenses to gather and focus light from distant objects
reflecting telescope	a telescope that uses a curved mirror to gather and focus light from distant objects

Answers continued from p. 758

Section Review

9. The *geocentric* model of the solar system was replaced by the *heliocentric* model that accounts for apparent *retrograde motion*, and that describes how planets travel in orbits that are governed by the laws of *gravity* and *inertia* and that have the shape of *ellipses* that have two *foci*.

Answers continued from p. 784

Word Origins

Planet	Moon	Origin of name
Mars	Phobos	a Greek word that means "fear"; alternately described as an attendant or messenger of the Roman god Mars or as one of the horses that drew Mars' chariot
Jupiter	Ganymede	a Trojan prince; abducted by Jupiter to become the cupbearer of the Olympian gods; he was taken to Olympus by Jupiter disguised as an eagle
Saturn	Titan	In Roman mythology, the sisters and brothers of Chronos (the Greek counterpart of Saturn) were the Titans. (Other moons of Saturn are named after specific Titans.)
Uranus	Titania	queen of the fairies; a character in William Shakespeare's *A Midsummer Night's Dream*
Neptune	Triton	messenger of the deep; son of Poseidon, Greek god of the sea

Answers continued from p. 798

Section Review

11. The moon has a larger effect on the tides than the sun does because the moon is so much closer to the Earth than the sun is.

12. As *Earth* and the *moon* orbit the *sun*, their shadows may fall on one another producing an *eclipse* that is either a *solar eclipse*, in which the shadow of the moon falls on Earth, or a *lunar eclipse*, in which the moon passes through Earth's shadow; the shadows have two parts, the inner *umbra* and the outer *penumbra*.

Answers continued from p. 858

Section Review

11. Because more mass increases the gravitational force exerted on gases.

12. A black hole emits X-rays.

13. Gases in a *nebula* contract to form a hot *protostar*, which may become a *main-sequence star*, which may evolve into a *giant* star, which may form a *planetary nebula*, until all that is left is a *white dwarf*, or into a *supergiant* star, which may explode in a *supernova* and leave behind a *black hole* or a *neutron star*, which may become a *pulsar*.

Sample Answers to Concept Maps from Chapter Reviews

Chapter 26 Studying Space, p. 743

27.

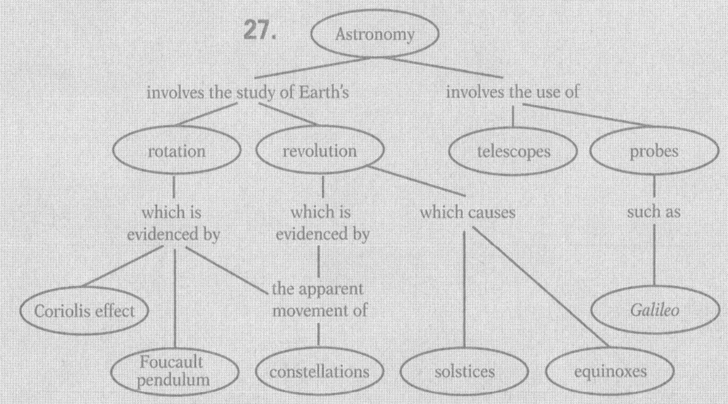

Chapter 28 Minor Bodies of the Solar System, p. 817

30.

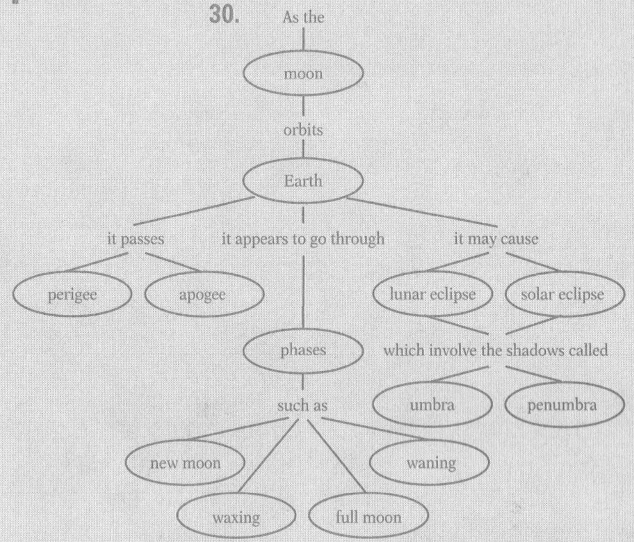

Chapter 27 Planets of the Solar System, p. 779

30.

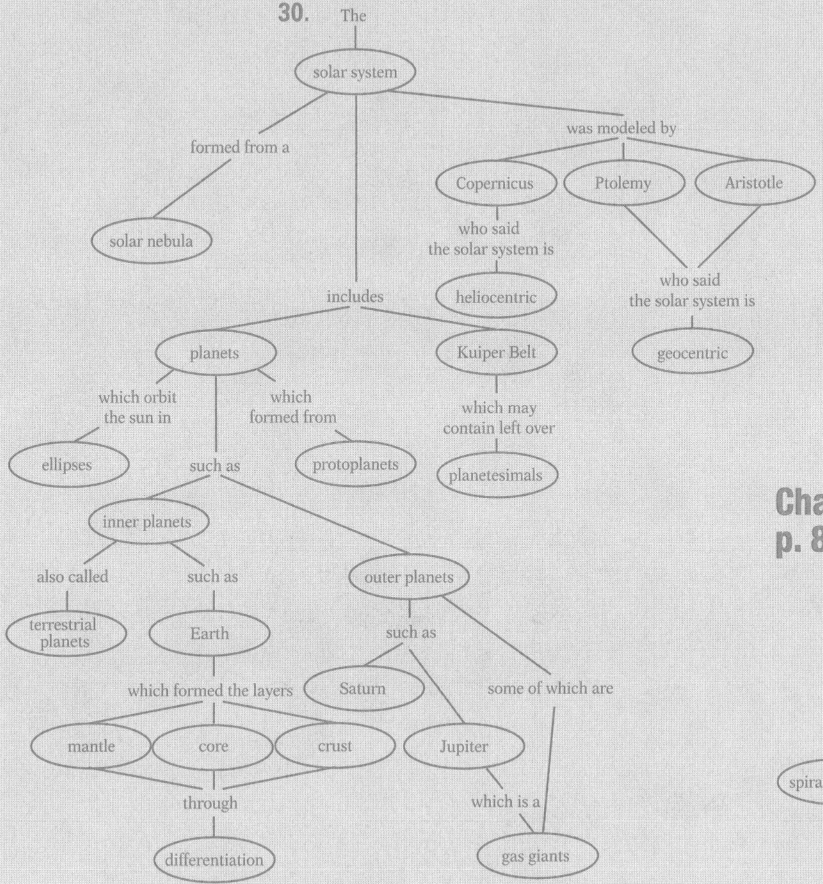

Chapter 29 The Sun, p. 839

33.

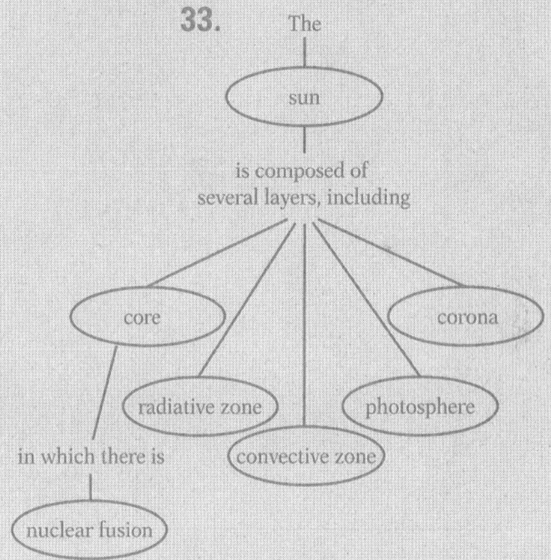

Chapter 30 Stars, Galaxies, and the Universe, p. 873

29.

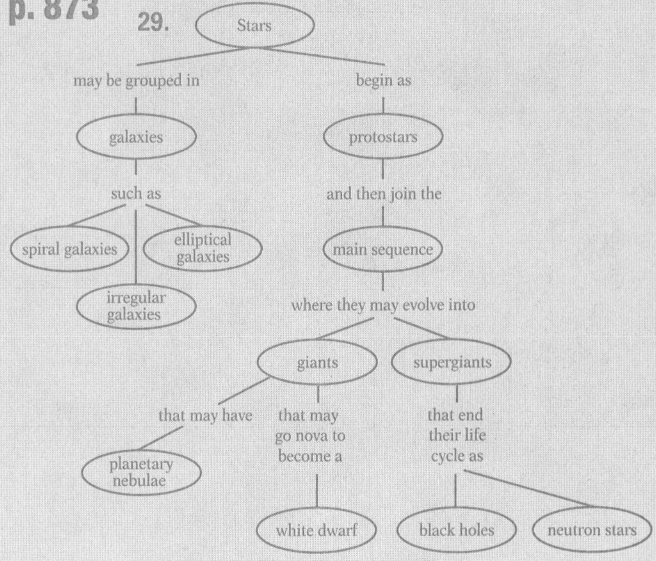

Virginia Close-Up

Virginia's tumultuous geologic past resulted in the natural beauty that can be seen in this photo of Sharp Top Mountain and Abbott Lake in the Blue Ridge Mountains.

VA

Science Standards of Learning Curriculum Framework

ES.7 c); ES.8 a); ES.9 d); ES.9 f); ES.10 d); ES.11 d)

Virginia's Place on Earth

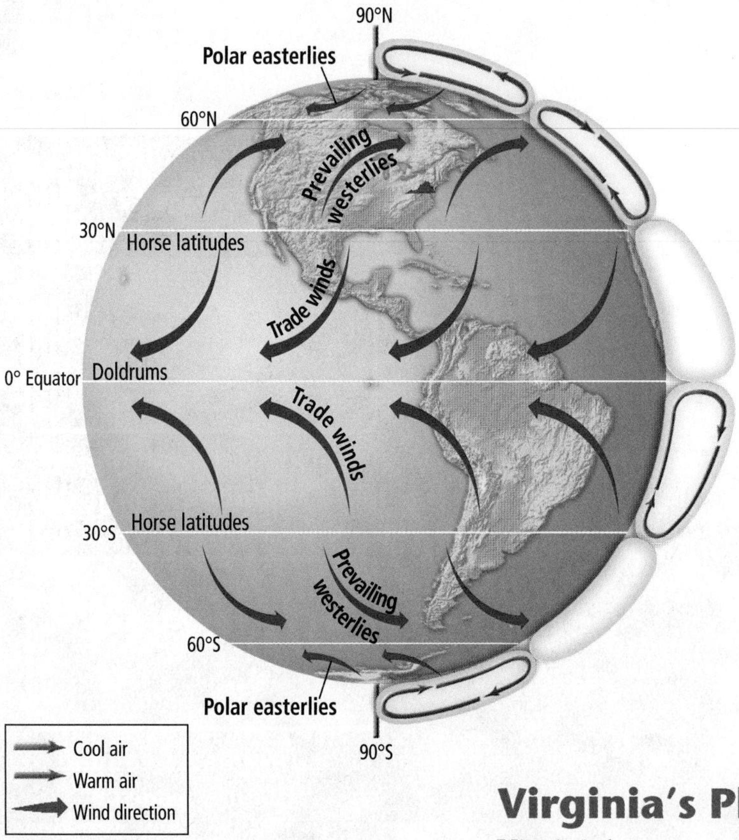

Figure 1 Virginia (colored red) is located between 36°31′ and 39°37′ north latitude. Winds in these latitudes blow from west to east. Make a copy of the drawing above. In the white oval areas on the map, draw the convection cells that were left out. Use a pencil to indicate warm air and a pen to indicate cool air.

In this book, you have learned about the physical processes that work in Earth's atmosphere, hydrosphere, and geosphere. On the following pages, you will learn how these physical processes affect Virginia.

Virginia's Place in the Atmosphere

As you can see in **Figure 1**, Virginia is located in the Northern Hemisphere, above 30°N latitude. This location puts Virginia within the prevailing westerlies wind belt, which means that the winds in Virginia generally blow from the west. Virginia's local wind circulation patterns are influenced by the mountains that lie along the western edge of the state and by the Atlantic Ocean, which lies at the eastern edge. As a result, surface winds may come from different directions.

Virginia's Place in the Hydrosphere

Virginia's eastern edge meets the Atlantic Ocean to form a coastline that is about 180 km long and includes Chesapeake Bay. The ocean is a major influence on Virginia. An ocean current called the *Gulf Stream* flows from southwest to northeast along Virginia's coast. This wide, fast-moving current carries warm water along the coast and influences the climate, particularly in eastern Virginia, by warming the air in coastal areas. Most rivers in Virginia, including the Potomac, Rappahannock, York, James, Chowan, and Roanoke Rivers, flow southeast to the Chesapeake Bay. The New, Tennessee, and Big Sandy Rivers in southwestern Virginia, however, flow into the Tennessee and Ohio River Basins and eventually into the Gulf of Mexico.

Figure 2 Warm water from the tropics is transported along the Atlantic coast of Virginia by the Gulf Stream. Can you label the Gulf Stream, its direction of flow, and its temperature on the map?

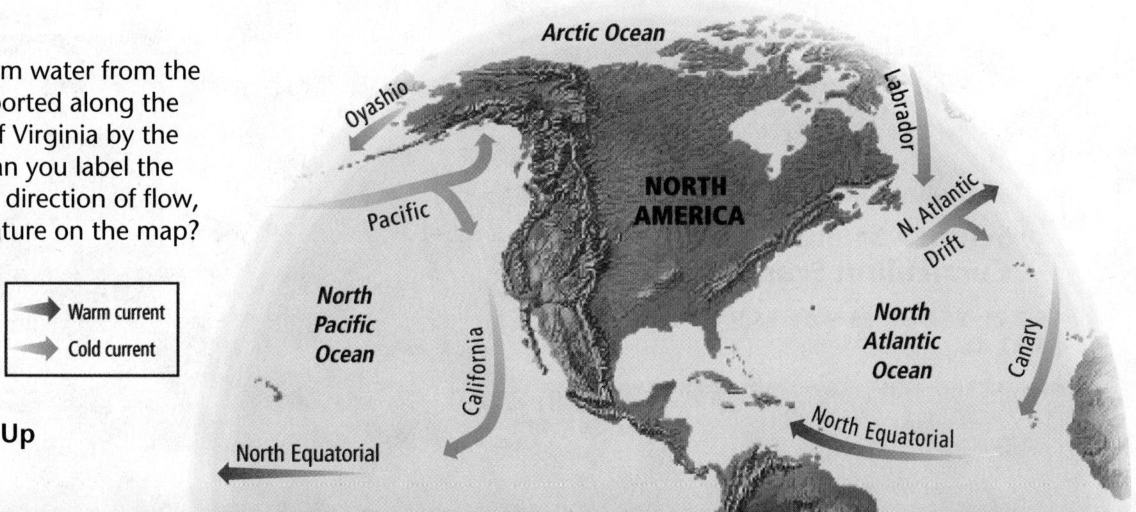

Virginia's Place in the Geosphere

As shown in **Figure 3,** Virginia is located on the North American plate away from any active tectonic plate boundaries. This was not always the case, however. Violent continental landmass collisions that happened about 480 million years ago created the Appalachian Mountains, which run through western Virginia from southwest to northeast. The Blue Ridge Mountains were formed during three uplift phases, between about one billion years ago and 300 million years ago. Mount Rogers in the Blue Ridge Mountains, shown in **Figure 4,** is the highest point in the state. The lowest point in the state is sea level, which occurs along the Atlantic coastline. The 1,746 m difference in elevation between Mount Rogers and sea level emphasizes the range of elevations that occur in Virginia.

Reading Check **In which direction do winds generally blow over Virginia? Why?** (See Appendix G for answers to Reading Checks.)

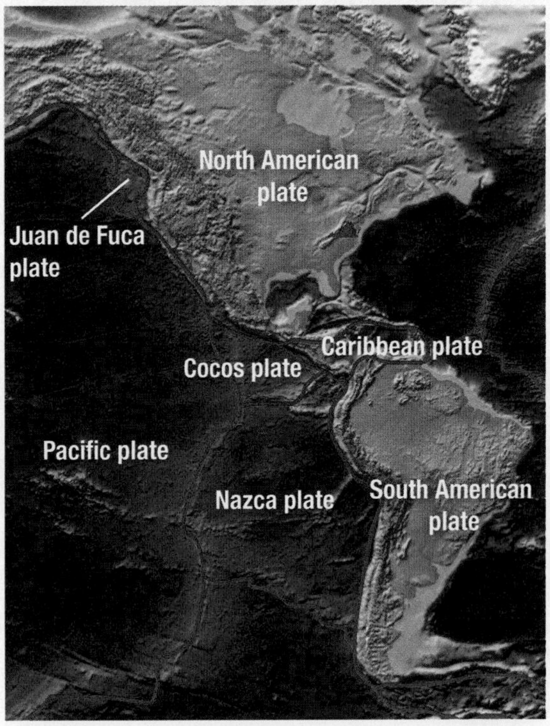

Figure 3 Virginia (colored red) is located on the North American plate and is not significantly affected by tectonic activities at plate boundaries.

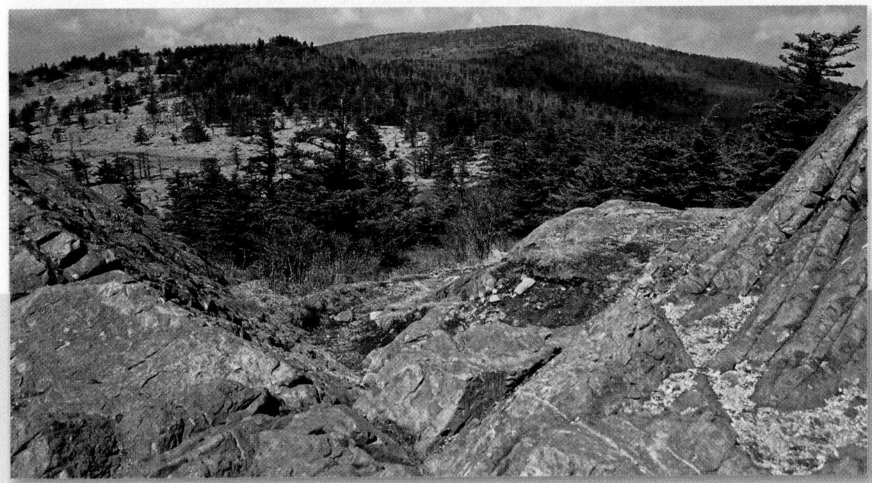

Figure 4 The highest point in Virginia is Mount Rogers (left) at 1,746 m. The lowest point is sea level, in places such as Virginia Beach (below).

Rainfall and Climate in Virginia

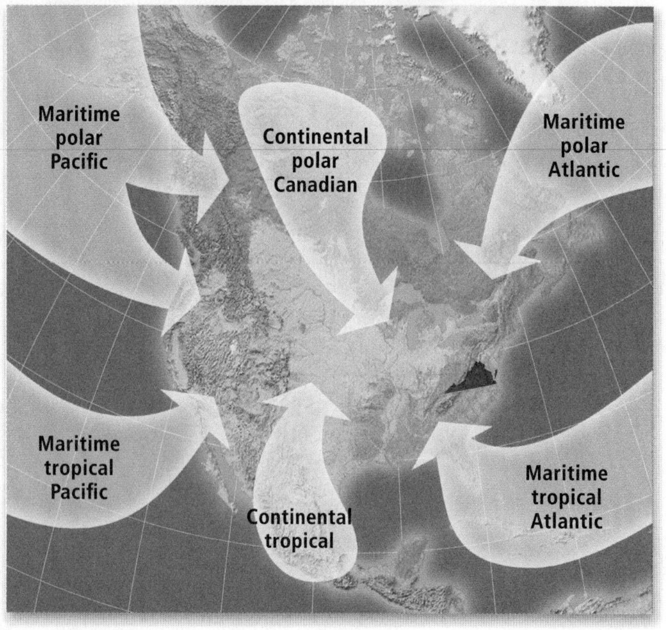

Figure 1 The two air masses that most directly affect the climate of Virginia are the maritime tropical Atlantic air mass and the continental polar Canadian air mass.

Virginia has one of the most varied climates of any eastern state. Virginia's climate is affected by its latitude, its proximity to the Atlantic Ocean, and its rivers. In addition, the mountains along Virginia's western border protect much of the state from the cold, dry air of the continental polar Canadian air mass that sweeps southeastward across the United States in the winter. The Gulf Stream and maritime tropical Atlantic air mass from the southern Atlantic Ocean contribute to the mild winter temperatures and to winter precipitation patterns. The two air masses that most directly affect Virginia's climate are shown in **Figure 1**.

Rainfall in Virginia

Virginia has no distinct wet and dry seasons, and rainfall varies with location. Virginia's rainfall is mostly the result of the warm maritime tropical Atlantic air mass and the Atlantic Ocean. Southern parts of Virginia tend to receive the most rain, particularly along the Atlantic coast, as shown in **Figure 2.** Much of this rain is carried by tropical storms such as hurricanes, which can release a large percentage of Virginia's annual rainfall in a single storm. The driest areas of Virginia are the New River and Shenandoah River valleys.

Figure 2 There can be a considerable difference between the amounts of rainfall on Virginia's Atlantic coast (below) and in the Shenandoah Valley (right).

Rain-Shadow Zones

The elevation map of Virginia, **Figure 3,** shows that mountains cover the western edge of the state. These are the Appalachian Mountains, which also extend into West Virginia, Kentucky, and North Carolina. The Appalachian Mountains create rain-shadow zones that affect precipitation rates in the state.

In a rain shadow, large amounts of precipitation fall on the side of the mountains that the winds are blowing from, while very little precipitation falls on the opposite side. The prevailing westerly winds carry moist air from the interior of the continent toward the Appalachian Mountains. As the air rises up the mountains, it cools and loses the moisture as precipitation in the form of rain or snow. This leaves a dry zone to the east, on the other side of the Appalachians. In addition, the Gulf Stream can bring warm, moist air and precipitation from the east to Virginia. When this happens, rain is deposited on the eastern side of the Blue Ridge Mountains. The result is bands of higher rainfall along the western Appalachians and eastern Blue Ridge Mountains, and dry rain-shadow zones along the New River and Shenandoah River valleys between the two ranges. **Figure 4** shows moist air getting pushed up, over the Blue Ridge Mountains.

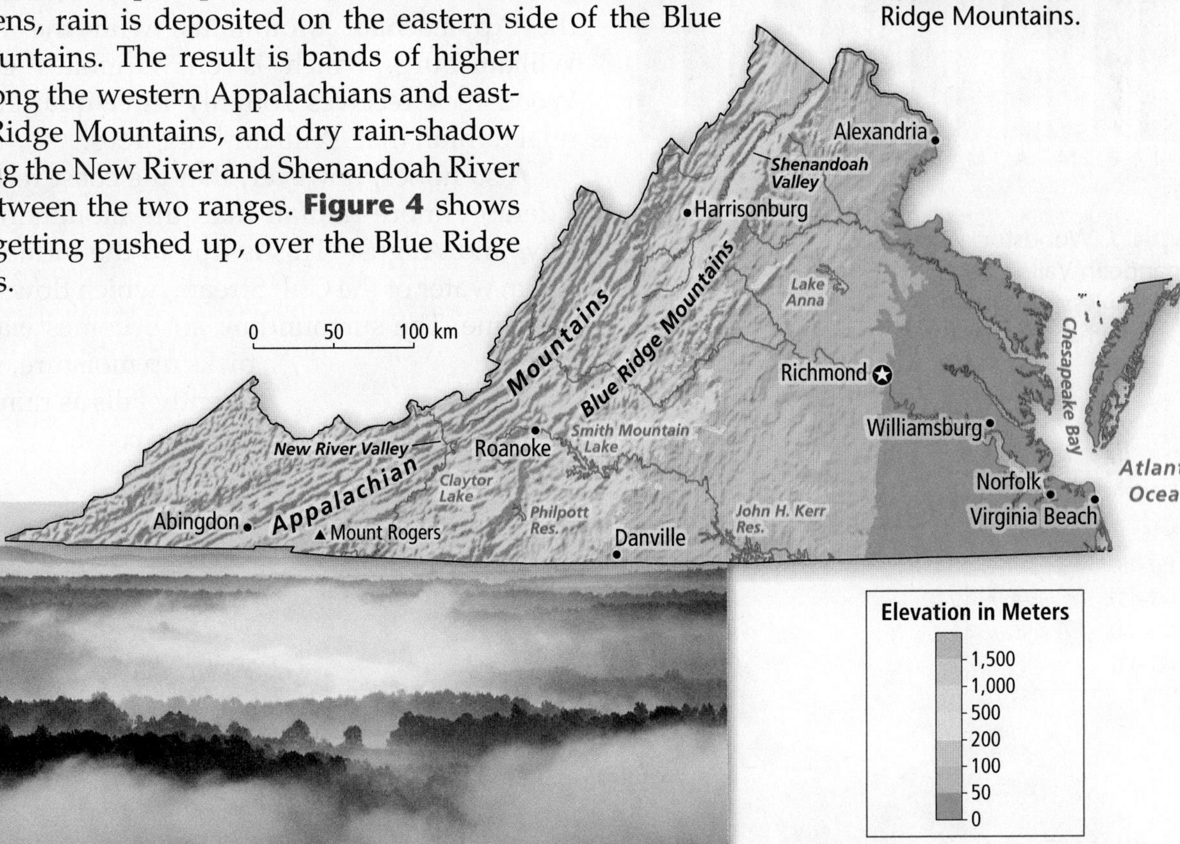

Figure 3 This map shows Virginia's topography. A rain-shadow zone exists between the Appalachian and Blue Ridge Mountains.

Figure 4 Clouds conform to the contours of the Blue Ridge Mountains. When the air meets the mountains, the air rises and cools, and rain or snow falls in the mountains.

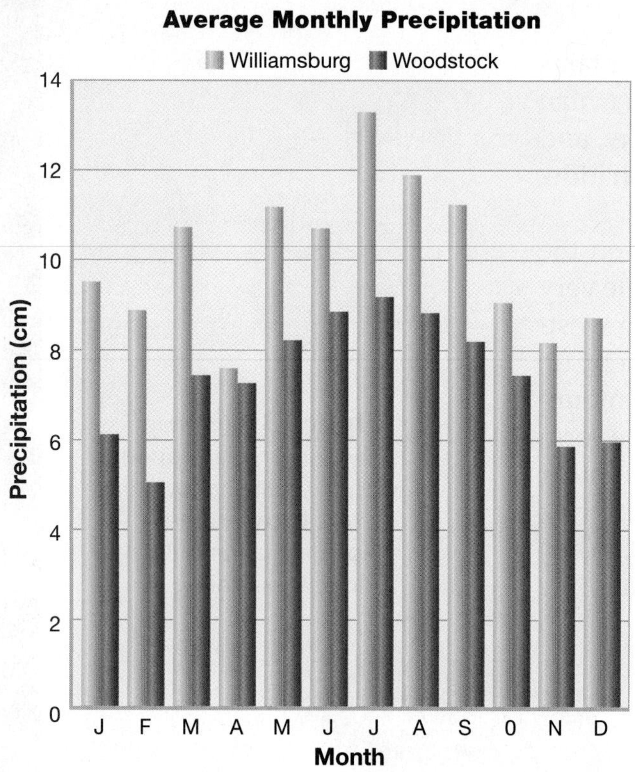

Graph 1 Woodstock, in the Shenandoah Valley, receives a great deal less precipitation than Williamsburg.

Annual Precipitation

Virginia's average annual precipitation, shown in **Figure 5,** includes rain, snow, sleet, and hail. Across the state, average annual precipitation ranges from less than 100 cm to more than 150 cm. Notice that there is a relationship between Virginia's topography, which is shown in Figure 3, and average annual precipitation. Notice that the lowest amounts of precipitation fall in the mountains in western Virginia. This is because they are in the rain shadow of part of the Appalachian Mountains that lie to the west, in the state of West Virginia.

Rainfall differences across Virginia are highlighted in **Graph 1.** This graph compares the rainfall in Woodstock, which is in the rain shadow of the Appalachian Mountains, with the rainfall in Williamsburg, which is on Virginia's east coast. Woodstock receives roughly three-quarters the annual rainfall that Williamsburg does.

Also notice, however, that the coast receives considerably more rainfall than the mountains in June, July, and August. This is due to the influence of the warm water of the Gulf Stream, which flows along the coastline. The surrounding air becomes warmer and picks up moisture, which frequently falls as rain along the Atlantic coast.

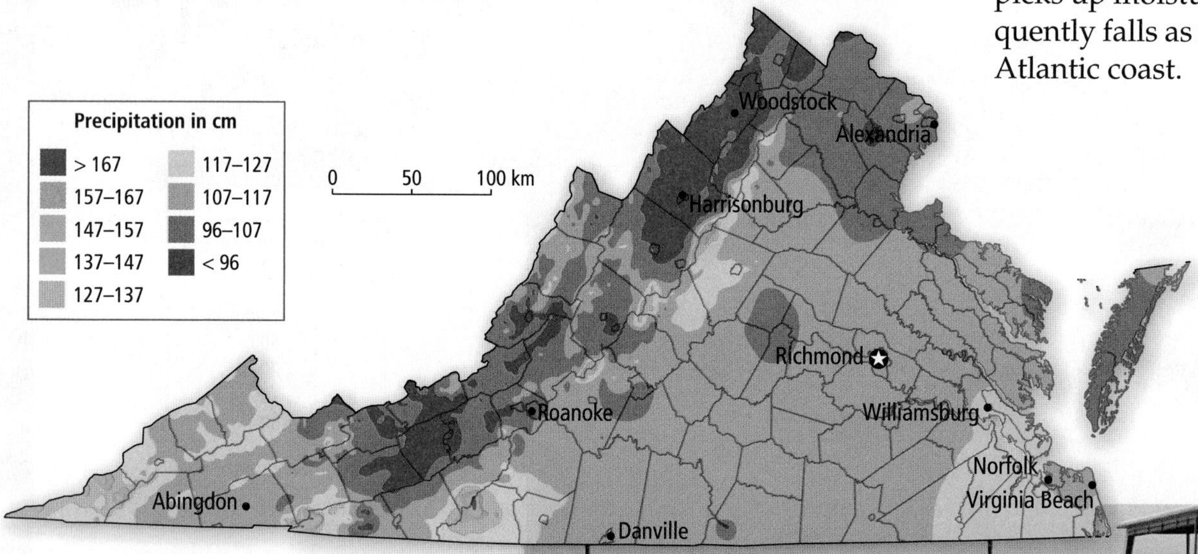

Figure 5 This map shows the average annual precipitation in Virginia. Alexandria (right) receives most of its rain during the summer.

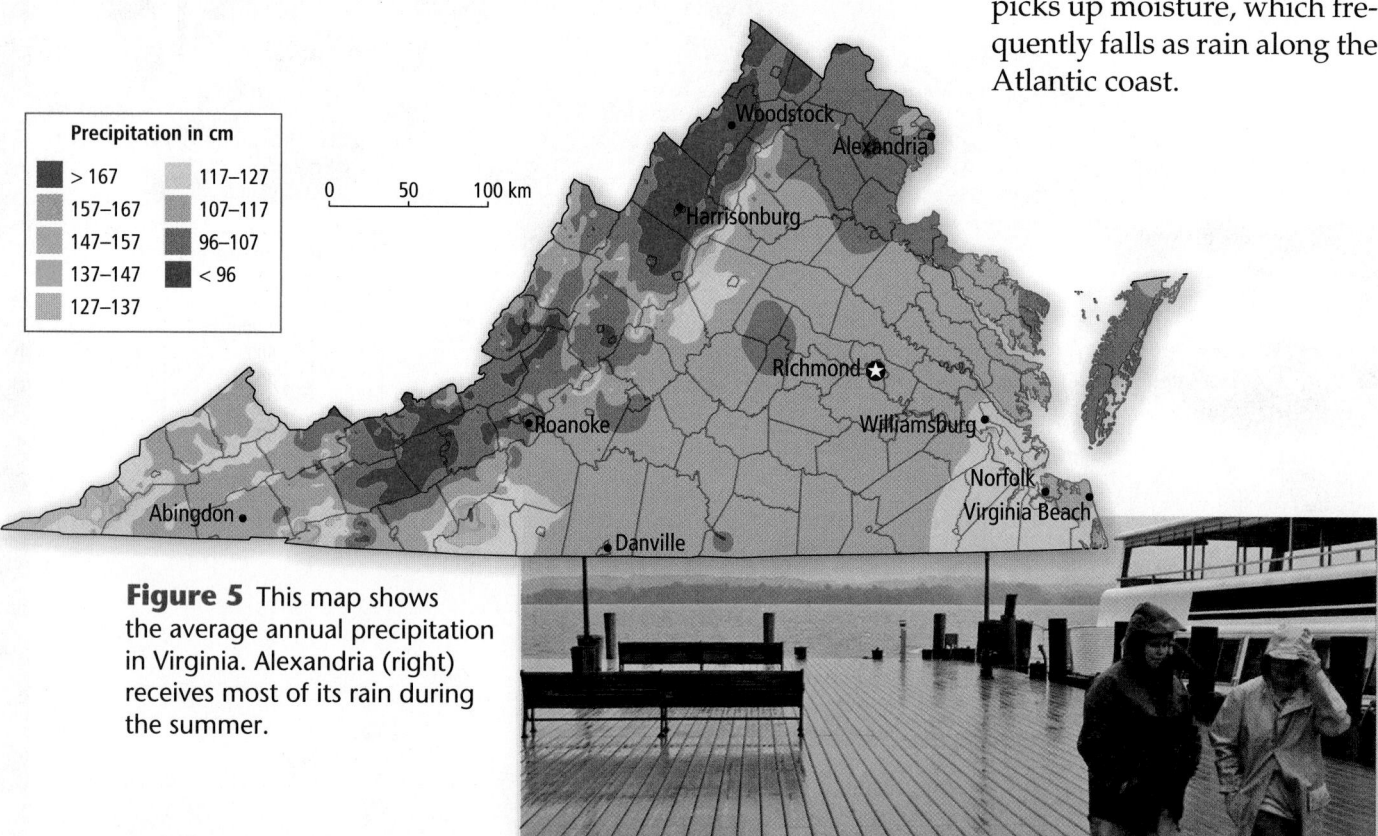

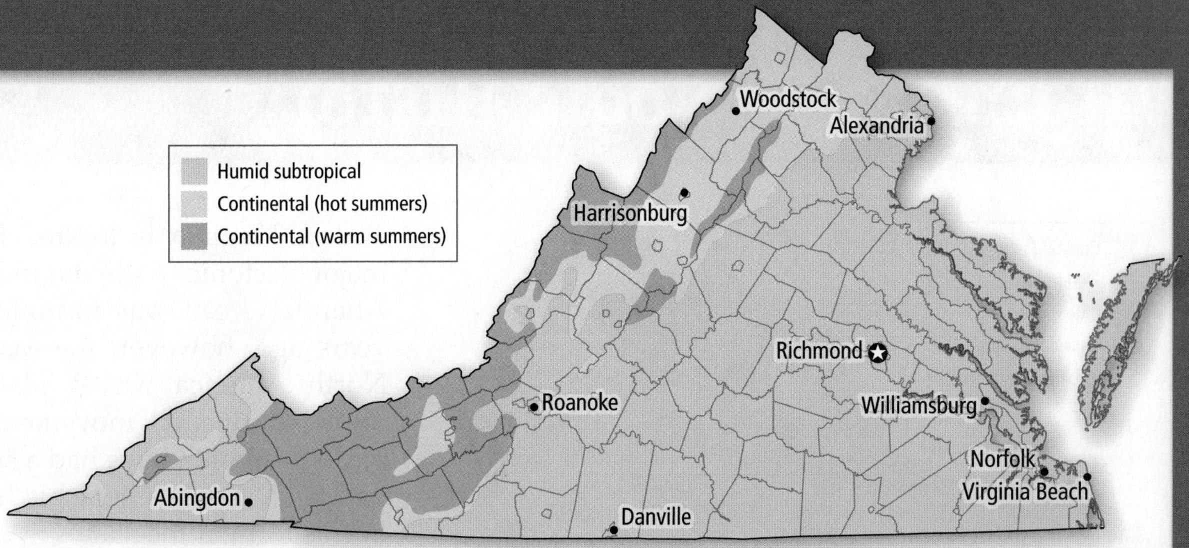

Figure 6 Most of Virginia has a humid subtropical climate. The mountainous western part of Virginia experiences a more continental type of climate.

Climate Zones in Virginia

As you can see in **Figure 6,** most of Virginia has a humid subtropical climate, with warm, humid summers and cool, wet winters. The warmest part of Virginia is along the Atlantic coast. This area is warmed by the Gulf Stream, which keeps it from experiencing particularly cold winter temperatures. Virginia's mountainous western region has a cooler continental climate, with greater temperature variations between the seasons. The mountainous region is likely to experience snow, which is typically carried in from the northwest by the cold continental polar Canadian air mass. The climatic variations within the state provide Virginians with the opportunity to enjoy a variety of outdoor activities throughout the year, as shown in **Figure 7.**

Despite Virginia's regional climatic differences, winter temperatures throughout most of the state seldom drop below freezing, and summers are fairly hot, averaging from 23 °C to 26 °C. This provides Virginia with a long growing season. The last frost of winter usually occurs in April, and the first frost in autumn usually does not occur until October. The Virginia coast can experience a slightly longer growing season, due to its more temperate climate.

Reading Check How does the Gulf Steam affect Virginia's climate?

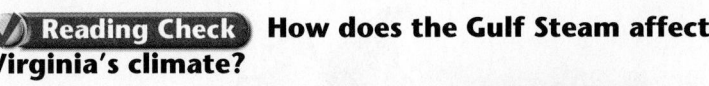

Figure 7 Virginia's climate zones allow its residents to enjoy a variety of outdoor activities.

Courtesy National Park Service; ©PBimages/Alamy; ©Bill Curtsinger/National Geographic/Getty Images

Virginia's Geologic History

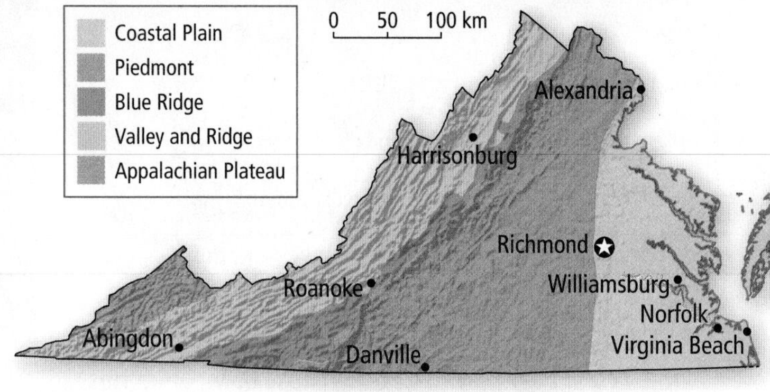

Figure 1 Virginia's landscape is divided into five geologic provinces. Can you label the Appalachian Mountains and Blue Ridge Mountains using this map?

Today, Virginia is located far from any major tectonic plate boundary. As the Atlantic Ocean was forming 200 million years ago, however, the eastern coast of North America was a plate boundary. Thus, continental movement and ocean-basin formation have had a significant impact on Virginia's geologic history. These events formed the state's five distinct geologic provinces: the Coastal Plain, the Piedmont, the Blue Ridge, the Valley and Ridge, and the Appalachian Plateau, shown in **Figure 1**.

An Early History of Virginia

The geologic map of Virginia in **Figure 2** shows rocks that date from 1.4 billion years ago to the present. Virginia's natural history began around 2 billion years ago. Island terranes that had formed during the Archaean Eon combined to form the core of a continent called *Laurentia.* Over time, a variety of large and small terranes were added to Laurentia as a result of plate movement. These accreted terranes enlarged Laurentia and formed the base of the North American craton and the Precambrian Canadian Shield.

As you learn about important events in Virginia's geologic history, you may want to refer to the geologic time scale in Chapter 9.

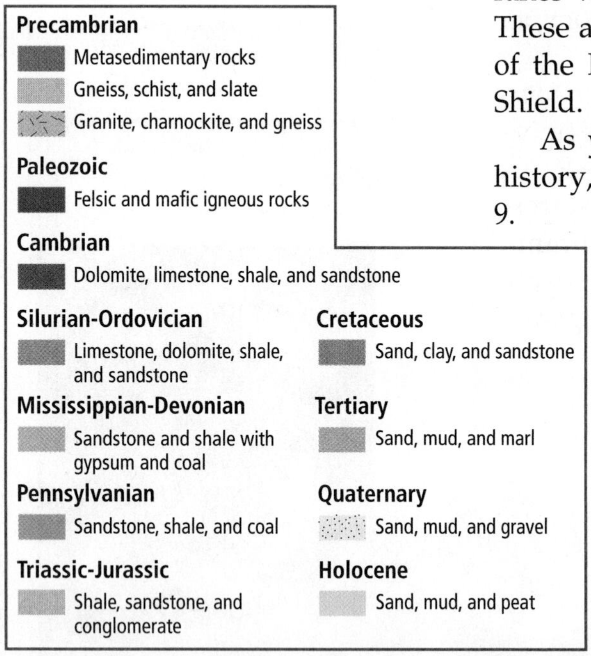

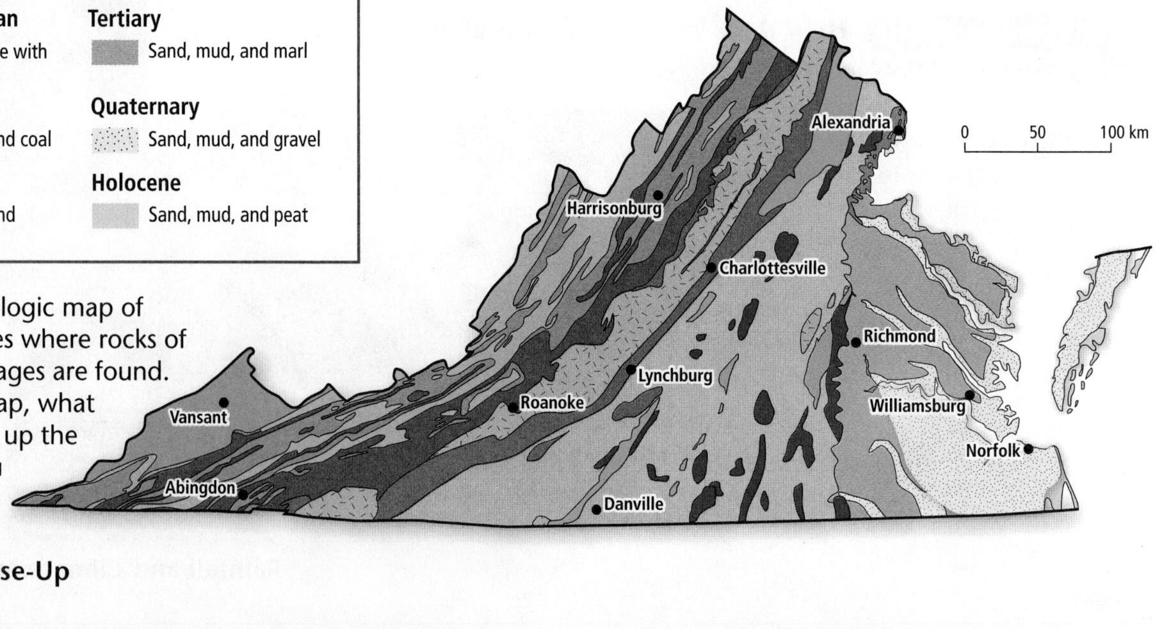

Figure 2 This geologic map of Virginia shows places where rocks of different types and ages are found. According to the map, what kinds of rocks make up the Appalachian Plateau geologic province?

Eastern North America Begins

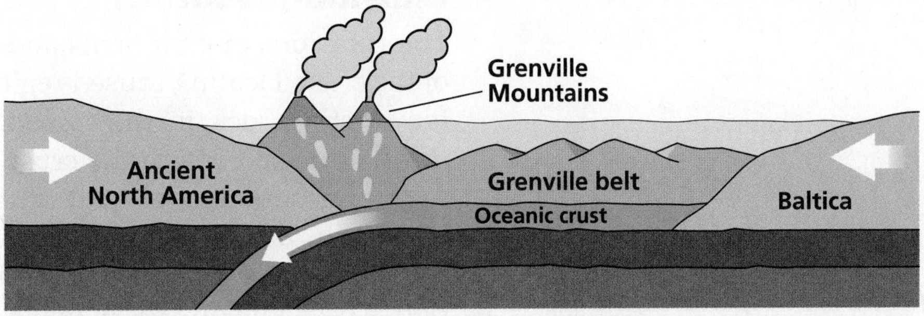

Figure 3 As the ancient continents of North America and Baltica collided 1 billion years ago, the Grenville Mountains formed.

More than 1 billion years ago, ancient North America collided with other early continents. These collisions crumpled the continental crust, forming mountain ranges. One key event in the development of the North American continent was the Grenville mountain-building event, shown in **Figure 3.** Between 1.3 billion and 1 billion years ago, sediment that had been eroding off the eastern edge of Laurentia was caught between colliding continents and was thrust onto the eastern edge of ancient North America. This resulted in the formation of the Grenville Mountains, which were an enormous mountain range that ran from present-day northern Mexico to Labrador, Canada.

Virginia Begins

Around 1 billion years ago, the southeastern margin of Laurentia collided with the core of what would become South America. The collision deformed and metamorphosed the basement rock of the Western Blue Ridge. This rock, shown in **Figure 4,** is the oldest rock in Virginia and is mainly granite and gneiss. It is exposed in the Shenandoah Valley. Around the same time, the early cores of East Antarctica, Australia, India, Europe, and Africa also collided with North America and South America to form a supercontinent called *Rodinia*.

Figure 4 This gneiss, which can be seen near Mary's Rock Tunnel in the Blue Ridge Mountains, is more than 1 billion years old.

Blue Ridge Plutons

The collisions of continents and terranes caused intense heating of the crust. Heating caused regional metamorphism that affected the existing rock in the region. In addition, large amounts of magma formed inside the crust. The magmatic activity resulted in the formation of several plutons. The basaltic rock of Afton Mountain and the volcanic deposits of the Mount Rogers Formation, in south-central Virginia, formed during this time period. These igneous rocks make up the basement of the modern Blue Ridge Mountains.

Figure 5 The supercontinent Rodinia included almost all of Earth's landmasses.

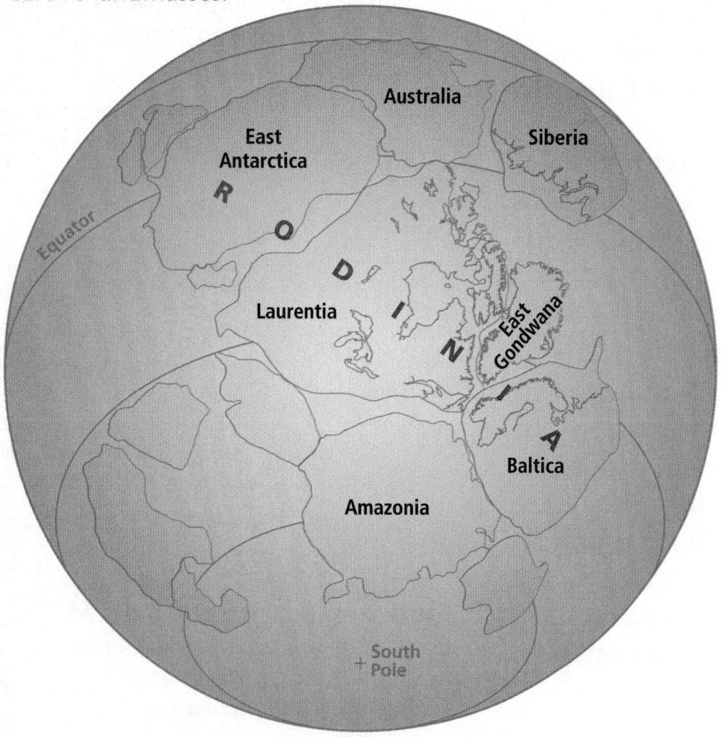

Breakup of Rodinia

The exact arrangement of the cratons that made up Rodinia is still unknown. Scientists think that Laurentia was located at the center of Rodinia, as shown in **Figure 5.** Around 600 million years ago, however, intense heat and volcanism caused Rodinia to begin to break apart. The basaltic lava shown in **Figure 6** erupted in association with the breakup of Rodinia. Also, the Iapetus Ocean, which was the predecessor of today's Atlantic Ocean, began to open up, as shown in **Figure 7,** and the edge of North America became a passive margin. This new margin was located approximately where the Blue Ridge Mountains are today. By about 550 million years ago, the separation of North America from other landmasses was complete. The continental margin began to sink below sea level, and sediments were deposited on the subsiding margin. The area that is now Virginia was located south of the equator and had a tropical climate.

Reading Check **Where is the oldest rock in Virginia found? What is its origin?**

Figure 6 Evidence of basaltic lava flows from about 580 million years ago can be seen at Hawksbill Mountain, west of Charlottesville.

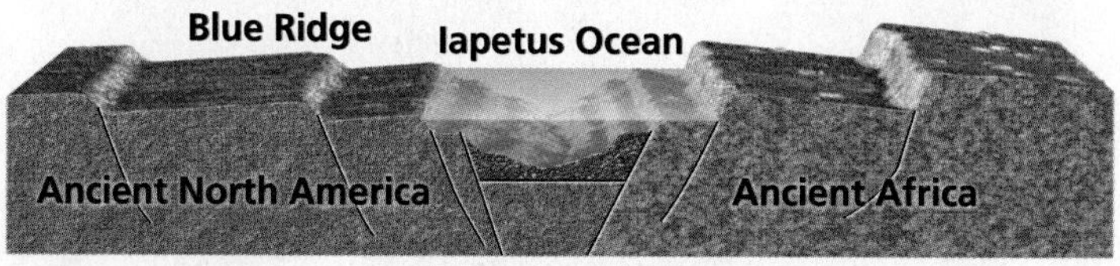

Figure 7 As Rodinia broke up, the Iapetus Ocean formed between North America and the ancient African and European continents.

A Middle History of Virginia

Virginia's topography is dominated by features that formed during several mountain-building events in the Paleozoic and Mesozoic Eras. These mountain-building events resulted from collisions between continents. The formation of the Appalachian Mountain Range is a central feature of this mountain building.

Continental Collisions

Around 450 million years ago, the Iapetus Ocean began to close again as the African plate approached the North American plate. As the continents drew closer, the oceanic plate began to subduct beneath the North American plate. Volcanic island chains formed on the North American plate between the continents.

Between 400 million and 330 million years ago, several collisions occurred between the North American plate and smaller exotic terranes, as shown in **Figure 8.** These collisions led to several uplifts and the eventual formation of the Taconic Mountains and Acadian Mountains. Coastal carbonate deposits were squeezed and uplifted onto the North American continent. The volcanic mountains that formed as a result of subduction in the Iapetus Ocean were also uplifted onto the North American continent. The Iapetus Ocean narrowed as the North American and African continents collided, and the smaller terranes were thrust over the North American plate. The rocks of these terranes, shown in **Figure 9,** can still be seen in parts of Virginia.

Between collisions of terranes, the highlands eroded and the basins filled with sediment. Carbonates, such as limestone and dolomite, formed in the Valley and Ridge province and the Appalachian Plateau province. Evaporite deposits of gypsum and salt also formed because of the hot, dry climate.

Figure 8 Around 400 million years ago, collisions occurred between ancient North America and the Chopawamsic/Arvonia and Avalon terranes.

Figure 9 These rocks in Prince William Forest National Park, near Fredericksburg, were once part of exotic terranes that collided with ancient North America.

Figure 10 Coal seams like this can be found in western Virginia.

Coal Formation

Because plates carrying continental crust are always moving, Virginia has not always occupied its current location. Virginia was located much closer to the equator 300 million years ago. As a result, its climate was warmer, and western parts of the state were covered by vast swamps filled with scaly trees called *lycophytes*. Some of these lycophytes grew to be 35 m tall. As temperature and sea level rose and fell during the next several million years, the massive mountains of Virginia eroded and buried the swampy forests beneath sediment. The sediment eventually became sandstone and shale, and the buried vegetation became the coal seams that are found today in the Allegheny Plateau. One of these coal seams is shown in **Figure 10.** Within these coal seams are some of the world's only fossils of the huge lycophytes that once covered much of North America.

The Appalachian Mountains

Between 325 million and 280 million years ago, ancient northern Africa collided with the eastern coast of ancient North America. This collision completed the formation of the supercontinent Pangaea, which you learned about in Chapter 10. Compression of the rocks where the continents collided caused folding and faulting of the Valley and Ridge province, and thrust the Blue Ridge rocks westward. These rocks were pushed up and over the Valley and Ridge rocks, forming the Blue Ridge Mountains. The compression also caused the folding and metamorphism of rocks, as well as the formation of igneous intrusions, in what is now the Piedmont province. This uplift is known as the *Alleghenian Orogeny* and resulted in the formation of the Appalachian Mountains, which are shown in **Figure 11.**

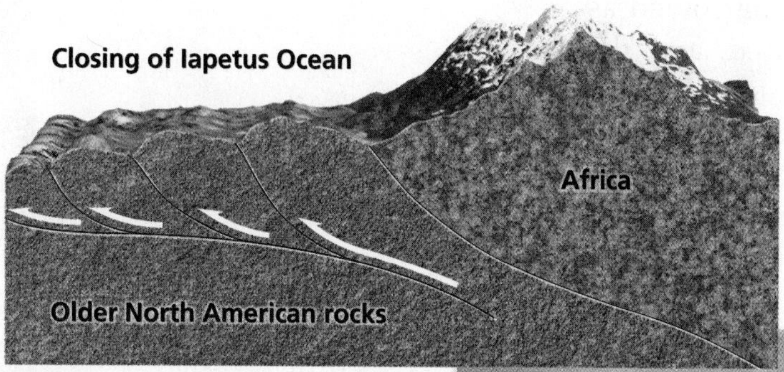

Figure 11 The Appalachian Mountains, including McAfee's Knob, formed during the late Paleozoic Era.

Figure 12 Today, the Atlantic Ocean forms the eastern boundary of Virginia.

Formation of the Atlantic Ocean

Between 250 million and 200 million years ago, Pangaea split into two major continents—Laurasia and Gondwanaland—and the Atlantic Ocean began to open. The tensional stress along the boundary between the two continents caused rift basins to open along the east coast of North America. As the newly formed Appalachian Mountains began to erode, sediment was deposited in the rift basins. The Culpeper Basin in northern Virginia is one of the basins that formed during this time.

Around 200 million years ago, the rifting that had formed the Atlantic Ocean had reached a stage in which lava from the mantle had begun to form new sea floor between the continents. Sea-floor spreading began in the Atlantic Ocean between 180 million and 160 million years ago. The Atlantic Ocean, shown in **Figure 12,** continues to undergo sea-floor spreading along the Mid-Atlantic Ridge.

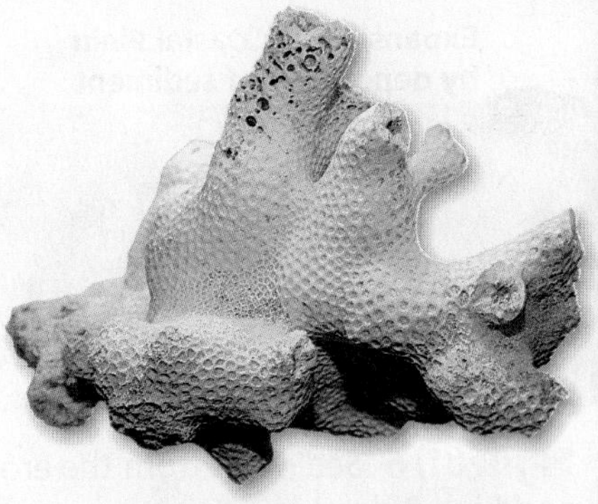

Figure 13 Coral reefs were once present in Virginia.

Fossils of the Paleozoic and Mesozoic Eras

Some of the earliest fossils in Virginia are fossils of worm-like creatures that lived about 500 million years ago. Fossils of marine plants and animals tell us that warm, shallow seas covered much of Virginia between mountain-building events. The state's fossil record includes trilobites that lived on the muddy Cambrian sea floor and brachiopods that are found in Ordovician limestone and sandstone. More fossils of marine life, including evidence of coral reefs shown in **Figure 13,** are found in rocks formed as the Taconic Mountains eroded during the Silurian Period. The sedimentary rock in the Piedmont province is particularly rich in fossils, including dinosaurs, plants, and fish.

Between 250 million and 210 million years ago, dinosaurs lived in Virginia. As shown in **Figure 14,** their tracks became fossilized in the rocks of the Culpeper Basin near the Blue Ridge Mountains.

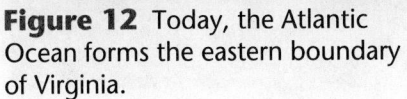

Figure 14 About 208 million years ago, therapod dinosaurs roamed the Culpeper Basin in northern Virginia.

The Recent History of Virginia

About 150 million years ago, the east coast of North America became a passive margin. Since then, the east coast of Virginia has been shaped as a result of the accumulation of sediment from the eroding Appalachian Mountains and sea-level changes. Over time, sediment has accumulated on the sea floor of the Atlantic Ocean and on the subsiding continental margin.

Figure 15 East-flowing rivers, such as the Roanoke River, formed during the Mesozoic and Cenozoic Eras.

Development of the Coastal Plain

The erosion of the Appalachian Mountains continued into the Cenozoic Era. Rivers like the Roanoke River, shown in **Figure 15,** carried the sediment from the eroding mountains eastward toward the coast. Sea level rose and fell repeatedly during the Cenozoic Era, in part because of the expansion and melting of continental glaciers. When sea level was high, the eastern part of the state was covered by ocean water. Layers of sediment, rich in marine fossils, were deposited in the shallow sea. When sea level was low, sandy deposits of eroded material from the western mountains accumulated on the low-lying coastal areas. As a result, the Coastal Plain province developed eastward, as shown in **Figure 16.**

Figure 16 Sediment from the eroding Appalachian and Blue Ridge Mountains was carried eastward and accumulated to form the coastal plains of Virginia.

The Fall Line

Virginia's *Fall Line* is a zone where the resistant metamorphic and igneous rocks of the Piedmont province transition to the softer sedimentary rocks of the Coastal Plain province. The Fall Line has played an important part in Virginia's history. Rivers west of the Fall Line contain numerous rapids and waterfalls, which made navigating them very difficult for early settlers. This is why cities like Richmond, shown in **Figure 17,** occur along the Fall Line.

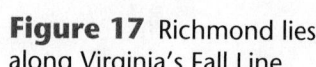

Figure 17 Richmond lies along Virginia's Fall Line.

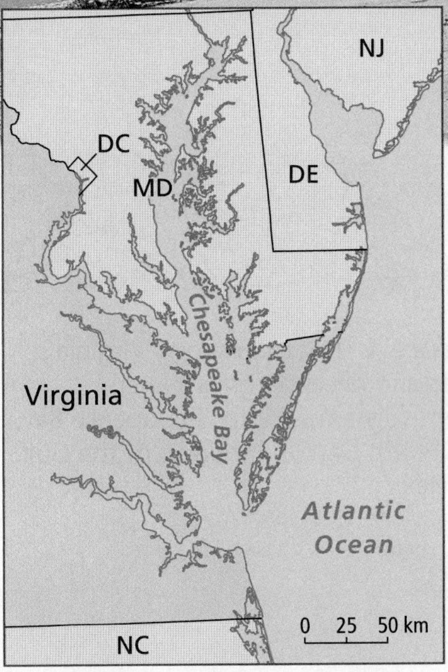

Figure 18 Chesapeake Bay is a natural estuary and acts as an important shipping lane for Virginia.

Formation of Chesapeake Bay

It is hard to imagine Virginia without Chesapeake Bay, shown in **Figure 18.** With 11,400 km^2 of area, Chesapeake Bay is the largest estuary in the United States. It is used by ships traveling to and from Virginia and Maryland, and it is popular with sailors and anglers. Although affected by pollution, it is still rich with plant and animal life. But 18,000 years ago, it did not exist.

When glaciers advanced across much of North America, sea level dropped dramatically. As water froze into massive ice sheets, the Atlantic Ocean fell by approximately 100 m, exposing the continental shelf. The Susquehanna River, fortified by runoff from the Potomac, Patuxent, Rappahannock, and James Rivers, carved a valley across the exposed shelf as it flowed past Cape Charles and out to the Atlantic Ocean. When the glaciers began to melt, sea level began to rise. By 15,000 years ago, the continental shelves were again covered with water. By 6,000 years ago, the ancient river valley had flooded, creating Chesapeake Bay.

Reading Check **How did Virginia's coastal plains extend eastward during the Cenozoic Era?**

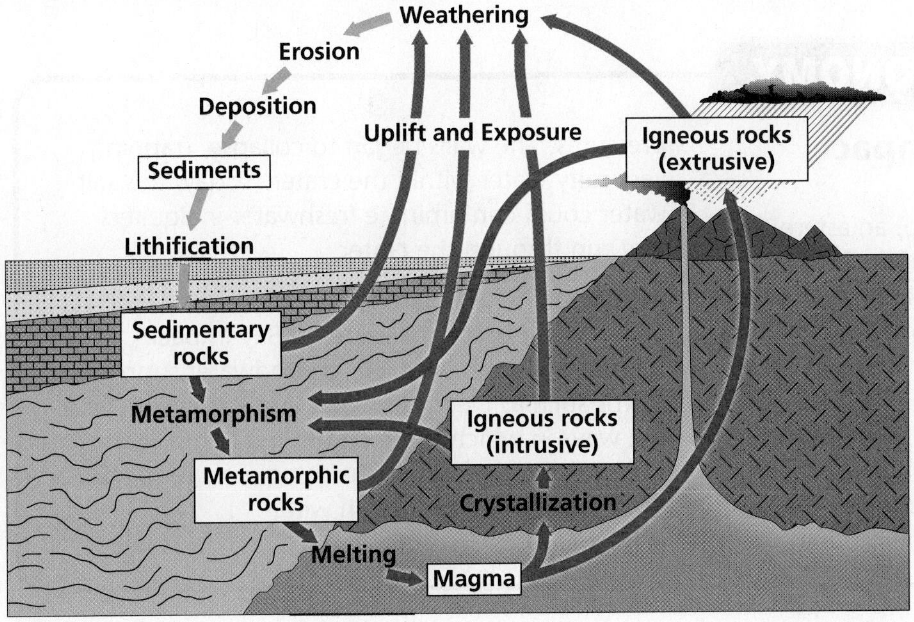

Figure 19 Virginia is made up of igneous, metamorphic, and sedimentary rock. This diagram of the rock cycle shows those geologic forces and processes that formed Virginia's rocks.

Virginia's Natural Resources

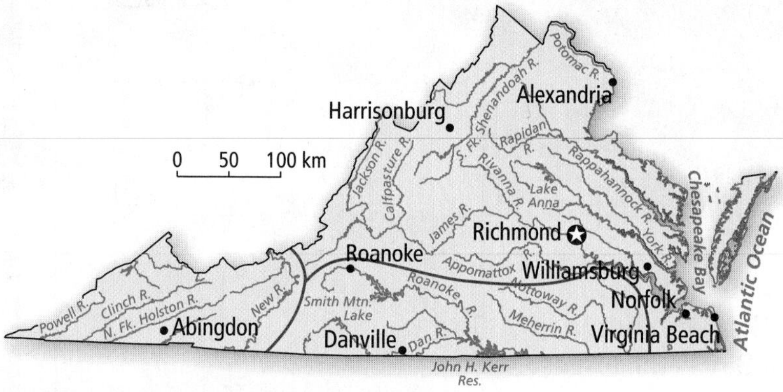

Figure 1 This map shows Virginia's lakes and rivers. Virginia's rivers eventually empty into Chesapeake Bay, the North Carolina sounds, or the Gulf of Mexico.

Virginia is rich in natural resources. Some of these resources are renewable, while others are nonrenewable. Wise management of nonrenewable resources is necessary for Virginians to maintain their present lifestyle.

Water Resources

Virginia's fresh water flows through its lakes, rivers, and streams, shown in **Figure 1.** These valuable water resources, which include Virginia's coastal waters and watersheds, must be protected and restored. All Virginians have a responsibility to conserve and protect their water resources. The state government has been involved in developing public policies and dealing with economic issues associated with protecting the Virginia coast.

The Chesapeake 2000 Agreement, which was agreed to by several states, including Virginia, and the U.S. government, is a commitment to protect and restore the Chesapeake Bay watershed and the ecosystem associated with it. With its agreement, Virginia became committed to several objectives. These objectives include providing a meaningful outdoor experience in the bay area for all students who live in the watershed and providing all students with the opportunity to participate in local restoration and protection projects through their schools.

Connection to ASTRONOMY

The Chesapeake Bay Impact Structure

Approximately 35 million years ago, an asteroid or a comet struck the floor of the Atlantic Ocean off the eastern Virginia coastline. This area is now the Cape Charles area of the Chesapeake Bay. The two km–wide object excavated a crater that was 19 km wide and 6.5 km deep. During the past 35 million years, the crater has been covered by more than 300 m of sediment and is largely hidden beneath the waters of Chesapeake Bay. Over time, the crater walls were no longer able to withstand the pressures. The walls began to collapse, trapping very salty water within the crater. Today, this salt water could contaminate freshwater in aquifers that run through the crater.

Research Investigate reasons why salt water trapped within the Chesapeake Bay Impact Structure is a threat to the groundwater supply of towns such as Newport News and Poquoson. Find out ways in which these communities are seeking alternatives to groundwater in aquifers to meet their requirements for fresh water.

Surface Water

Surface water in Virginia meets most of the state's water requirements. **Graph 2** summarizes water use in Virginia. As you can see, mining and other industries use more than three-quarters of Virginia's surface-water resources. About two-thirds of Virginians get their drinking water from surface water.

Surface water can be found across the state in its nine major river systems, 450 lakes, and 1,600 springs. The James, York, Rappahannock, and Potomac Rivers drain almost two-thirds of Virginia. Although most of Virginia's rivers drain into Chesapeake Bay and the North Carolina sounds, rivers in the westernmost part of the state eventually drain into the Gulf of Mexico.

While fresh water is abundant in Virginia, its quality is affected in some areas by pollution from farms and urban runoff that contaminate freshwater with substances such as fertilizers, pesticides, and animal waste. Today, state agencies monitor water quality along more than 27,000 km of streams.

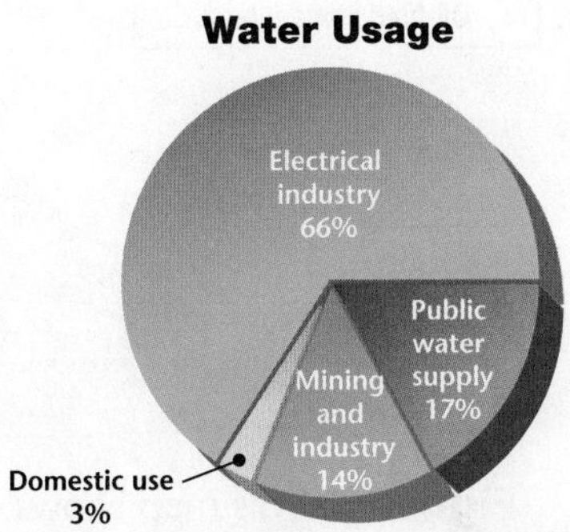

Graph 2 Most of the surface water in Virginia is used for electricity generation.

Groundwater

Although Virginians get most of their water from rivers and lakes, one-third of the water that is used in Virginia comes from groundwater. A significant amount of water percolates through the soil into natural groundwater storage basins, called *aquifers*. The major aquifers in Virginia are shown on the map in **Figure 2.** In these aquifers, the groundwater can dissolve minerals, which are sometimes deposited in caverns as stalagmites and stalactites, and carry them downstream. Unfortunately, pollutants, such as pesticides and fertilizers from runoff, can also be transported by groundwater.

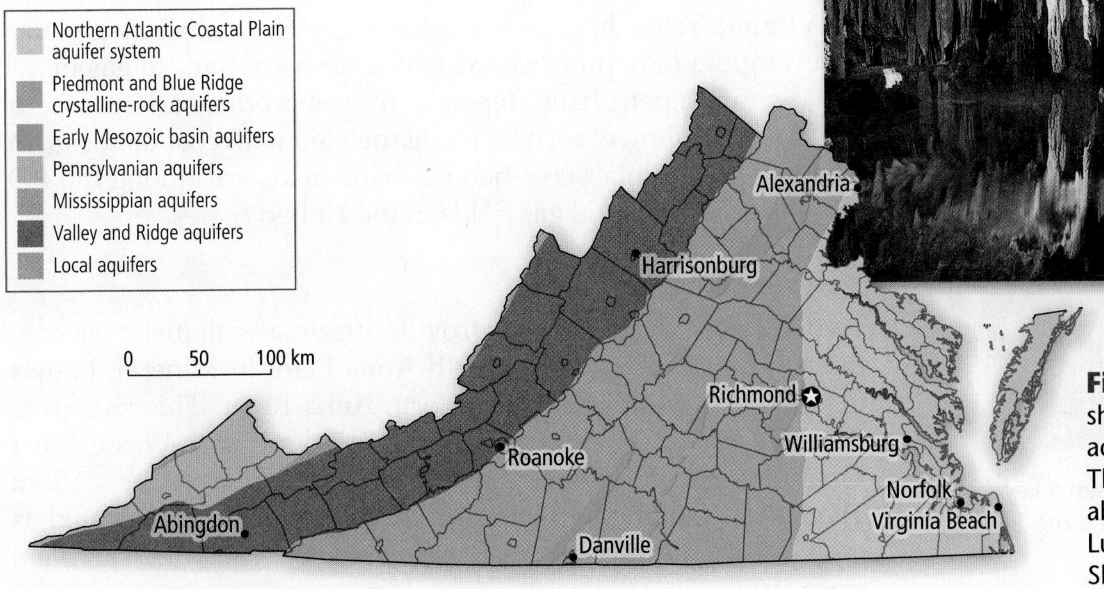

Figure 2 This map shows the major aquifers in Virginia. The stalagmites above formed in Luray Caverns in the Shenandoah Valley.

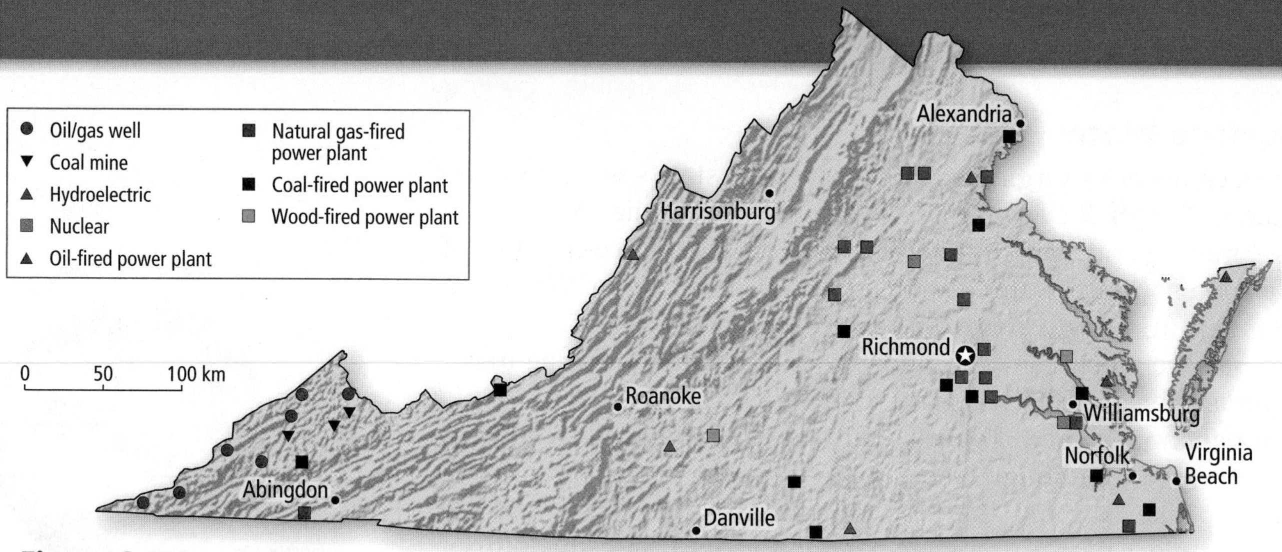

Figure 3 This map shows Virginia's energy resources and sources of electricity.

Energy Resources

Virginians need fuel, heat, and electricity to maintain their modern lifestyle. Most of this energy comes from nonrenewable energy resources. Because Virginia only produces about half of the energy it consumes, alternative energy resources will become increasingly important.

Coal and Natural Gas

A map of Virginia's energy resources and major power stations is shown in **Figure 3.** Most of Virginia's energy comes from coal, with about half of its electricity being generated by coal-fired power plants. Coal has been an important part of Virginia's economy since it was first mined near Richmond in the 1700s. Most of the coal comes from the Appalachian coal beds in southwestern Virginia, where mining began in the 1880s. Today, the state is responsible for 5% of the coal production east of the Mississippi River. An example of the large amount of coal that moves through Virginia can be seen in **Figure 4.**

Virginia relies heavily on natural gas for electricity generation. Virginia only produces a small amount of natural gas in association with petroleum deposits. It does produce another form of natural gas, however, which is associated with coal deposits. In fact, two of Virginia's coal-bed methane fields are among the 100 top-producing natural gas fields in the United States.

Figure 4 Coal has been a key resource in Virginia since the 1800s.

Nuclear Energy

Two nuclear power stations provide Virginia with just over one-third of its electricity. The North Anna Plant in Mineral, Louisa County, was named after the North Anna River. This river was dammed to form the Lake Anna reservoir and Waste Heat Treatment Facility, which provide cooling water for the station. The Surry Plant, named after the county in which it is located, is on a 3.4 km² site near Williamsburg and has been in operation since 1972.

Hydroelectric Energy

Virginia generates little hydroelectric energy. Only about 1% of its energy needs are met by this resource. There are two *pumped storage* facilities, at Bath County and Smith Mountain Lake, shown in **Figure 5.** These facilities have storage basins above and below the turbines. When demand is low, excess electricity is used to pump water up, into the top basin. When demand is high, the water is released to generate more electricity. Pumped storage helps to keep enough energy in the grid during peak times and is used with intermittent sources, such as wind power and solar power.

Figure 5 Pumped-storage hydroelectric facilities, such as this one at Smith Mountain Lake, help to provide a reliable flow of electricity.

Wind and Solar Energies

Virginia produces little wind energy but has a program to encourage its use. According to the state's energy plan, there is the potential for 1,950 wind farms. The best locations for wind turbines are along the Atlantic coast and on the mountains in the western part of the state.

Solar energy is another renewable resource whose use is growing in Virginia. There are a few small facilities, such as the one in Cape Charles, shown in **Figure 6.** Virginia's energy plan includes the potential for significant solar power. Together, wind and solar energies could help the state reduce its dependence on fossil fuels.

Figure 6 Renewable energy in Virginia includes this wind turbine at James Madison University (right) and a photovoltaic solar array at the Sustainable Technology Park in Cape Charles (below).

Table 1

Virginia's Nonfuel Mineral Products	
clay	kyanite
crushed stone	limestone
dimension stone	rutile
dolostone	salt
feldspar	sand and gravel
Fuller's earth	shale
gemstones	slate
granite	titanium
ilmenite	vermiculite
iron oxide pigments	zirconium

Mineral Resources

Historically, Virginia has had a diverse mining industry. **Table 1** lists some of Virginia's nonfuel mineral-resource products. Specimens of some of the minerals that are mined in Virginia are shown in **Figure 7.**

Crushed Stone

Crushed stone is by far the largest nonfuel mineral-resource product in Virginia. Most of the crushed stone is used for fill or concrete in construction or for road building. Sources of crushed stone include limestone, dolostone, sandstone, quartzite, granite, gneiss, basalt, and marble. Limestone and dolostone, which were deposited during the Ordovician Period, are mined to make lime, which is used in cement and for manufacturing steel, paper, and chemicals.

Sand and Gravel

Sand and gravel are used mostly in the construction industry. Together, they are Virginia's second largest nonfuel mineral-resource product. Sand and gravel are mined throughout the state. However, most mining occurs in the Coastal Plain province, where thick layers of sediment were deposited from the Cretaceous through the Quaternary Periods.

Titanium and Zirconium

Virginia is the second largest producer of both titanium and zirconium in the United States. Like other common metallic elements, titanium and zirconium do not occur in pure form in Earth's crust. They commonly occur in combination with other elements in certain minerals. Titanium is extracted from heavy mineral sand and is used as a pigment for paint and in sunscreen, paper, and other products. Ilmenite and rutile are the most common sources of titanium. These minerals are extracted from Pliocene beach sands in Dinwiddie County, along with minerals that contain zirconium. Zirconium is used to make ceramics.

Hematite

Turquoise

Amethyst (quartz)

Barite

Figure 7 These specimens represent just some of the minerals that are mined in Virginia.

Feldspar

Virginia is the second largest producer of feldspar in the United States. Anorthosite, an intrusive igneous rock that consists almost entirely of plagioclase feldspar, is mined in Hanover County and used to produce alumina. Alumina is used as a strengthening agent in glass and fiberglass manufacturing. Feldspar that is mined in Amherst County is used as aggregate.

Kyanite

The only kyanite mine in North America is located on the Whispering Creek Anticline in Buckingham County, shown in **Figure 8.** The kyanite is found in quartzite, which is metamorphosed volcanic and sedimentary rock that formed during the Ordovician Period. Kyanite is made up of aluminum and silicon, and it remains stable at very high temperatures. For this reason, it is mainly used to produce furnace bricks and other high-temperature ceramics. It is also used for making abrasives, brake shoes, cookware, and other products. Virginia exports kyanite around the world, particularly to Europe, Latin America, and the Pacific Rim.

Figure 8 Virginia is the only producer of kyanite in North America.

Iron Oxide Pigment

For centuries, people have used iron oxide as a pigment. It provides color to products such as paint, crayons, chalk, and bricks. Today, iron oxide pigment is produced in only four U.S. states. In Virginia, it is extracted from Cambrian rock in open-pit mines, such as the one shown in **Figure 9,** in Pulaski and Wythe Counties. Different ores are used to create various colors of pigments. Hematite is used for red, limonite and goethite are used for yellow and brown, siderite is used for brown and red, and magnetite is used for black.

Reading Check **Name three energy resources and two mineral-resource products in Virginia.**

Figure 9 Colorful Cambrian rocks, rich in iron ore, are mined for pigment in Hiawassee, Pulaski County.

Natural Hazards in Virginia

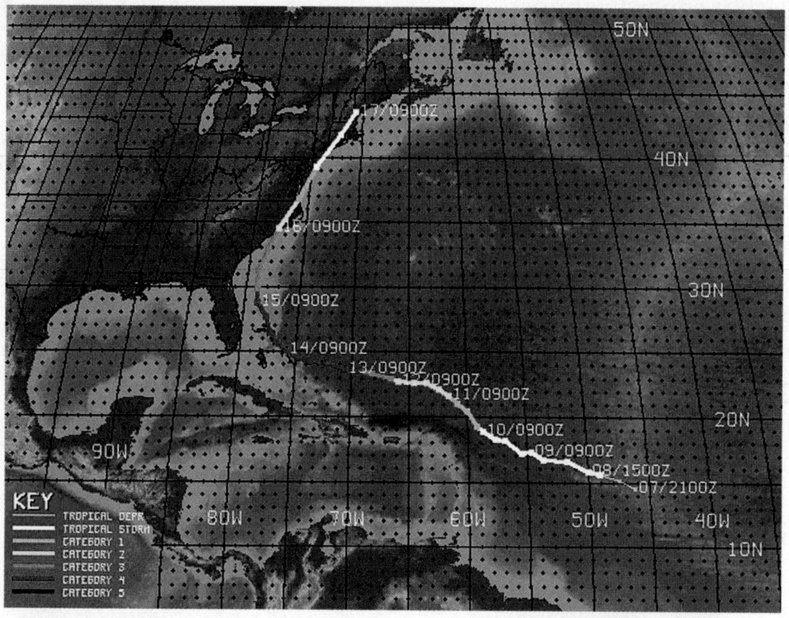

Figure 1 This is the path of Hurricane Floyd, which slammed into coastal Virginia in 1999. The colors indicate hurricane intensity along its path.

Location, topography, and geological history make Virginia prone to certain natural hazards. Hurricanes can hit the coastal areas, heavy rains can cause floods and landslides, tornadoes can rip across the state, and even earthquakes can happen from time to time. Erosion along Virginia's coastline and rising sea level also pose significant threats.

Hurricanes

Hurricanes have historically struck Virginia in August and September. Hurricanes form in areas of very low pressure over the tropical waters of the Atlantic Ocean. As a hurricane approaches North America, it moves north into the band of prevailing westerly winds. As a result, most hurricanes are moving northward when they hit Virginia. The track of Hurricane Floyd is shown in **Figure 1.**

Hurricanes that hit Virginia can dump over 80 cm of rain in a matter of hours and can account for up to 40% of the state's total annual rainfall. Rain and powerful winds can be very destructive, as you can see in the photos of the damage caused by Hurricane Isabel in **Figure 2.** Prior to using satellite technology, it was difficult to tell where hurricanes were forming. Today, meteorologists can use satellite photos to determine hurricane formation, and the paths they are likely to take, five days in advance.

Figure 2 In 2003, Hurricane Isabel's powerful winds caused extensive damage in Alexandria.

Tornadoes

Tornadoes are extremely powerful, short-lived severe storms. Their rapidly-spinning winds develop into a distinctive funnel shape. A waterspout, which is a tornado that forms over water, is shown in **Figure 3.**

An average of seven tornadoes touch down in Virginia each year. Heat and humidity in July can fuel tornadoes, but most are fairly weak. Although fewer tornadoes form in late spring and autumn, these tornadoes are more likely to be powerful and destructive storms.

The worst tornado in Virginia's history ripped through Chesterfield County in 1993, killing four people and injuring 238, and causing over $47 million in damage. More recently, several tornadoes swept through southeastern Virginia during one day in April 2008, injuring over 200 people.

Figure 3 Tornadoes, like this waterspout that travelled across the James River, are a yearly occurrence in Virginia.

Flooding

The effects of flooding can range from minor damage to major disasters. In any case, flooding is a serious hazard in Virginia. There are four types of flooding that occur in Virginia. Coastal flooding occurs when strong winds, such as the winds from a hurricane, push water onto the shore. About 60% of the floods in Virginia can be directly attributed to hurricane rainfall. Urban flooding happens when water builds up on non-porous surfaces, such as pavement, and cannot run off because of insufficient drainage. Flash flooding is the deadliest type of flooding because of its sudden development. Flash flooding is the result of heavy rain that falls too fast to be absorbed into the ground. Finally, river flooding is the result of heavy rainfall or multiple flash floods that overflow small streams and rivers. Examples of flood damage can be seen in **Figure 4.**

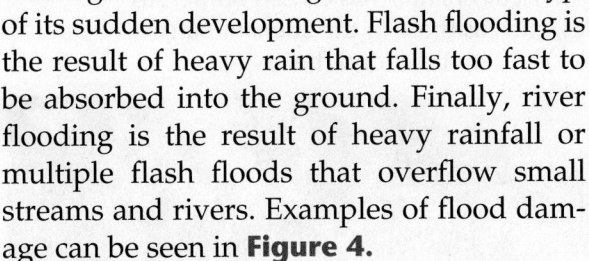

Figure 4 Hurricane Isabel caused the Potomac River to overflow, flooding the streets of Alexandria (above). The fast-moving water carried a lot of sediment, which is evident in the photo taken in Lewisetta (left).

Earthquakes

As you have read, Virginia is located far from any tectonic plate boundaries and is relatively stable tectonically. However, Virginia is home to many ancient faults, so there is a moderate earthquake risk. There are two seismic zones in Virginia. One is on the New River in Giles County. The other extends from Richmond through Charlottetown, and on to the Blue Ridge Mountains. While most earthquakes do not cause serious damage, significant earthquakes do occur. On August 23, 2011, a magnitude 5.8 earthquake shook northern Virginia and Washington, D.C., causing damage in both places. The earthquake was centered near Mineral, Louisa County.

Landslides

Landslides are a common occurrence whenever the terrain has steep slopes made of loose, or unconsolidated, sediment. Landslides are most commonly triggered in Virginia by heavy rainfall. The heavy rainfall associated with hurricanes can cause small, disruptive slumping or very destructive landslides, as shown in **Figure 5.** For example, rain from Hurricane Camille in 1969 triggered hundreds of debris flows, mostly in Nelson and Rockbridge Counties. These debris flows killed 114 people and washed away or buried 900 buildings and 100 bridges.

Figure 5 Heavy rainfall has caused numerous landslides, such as these in the Shenandoah Valley (left) and in Richmond (below).

Coastal Erosion

Virginia's Atlantic coastline is in the Coastal Plain province, which is made up of sandy material that has eroded from the mountains to the west. This material is easily washed away by wave action, particularly during violent storms. Much of Virginia's coastline is considered to be at moderate or high risk from coastal erosion. **Figure 6** shows the areas that are most severely affected and the kinds of damage that coastal erosion can cause.

Water speeds up when it is forced around solid structures, such as foundations or bridge footings. Fast-moving water carries more sediment than slow-moving water, so areas around solid structures are susceptible to scouring, which can cause bridges and buildings to sink or collapse. Different methods have been used to try to prevent the process of coastal erosion. No method, however, has been found to be completely effective in stopping this process.

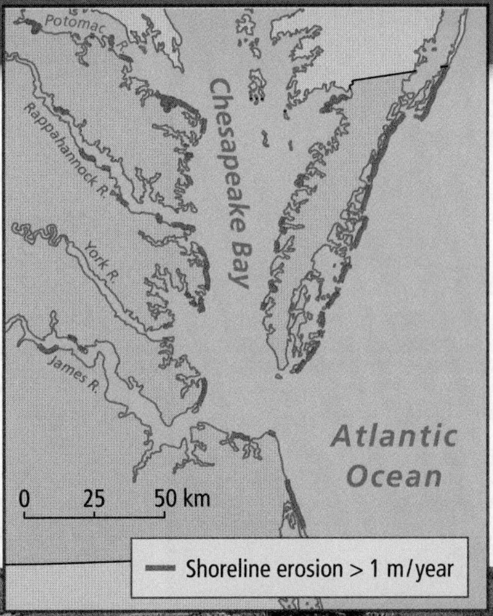

Figure 6 The map above shows the areas that are most at risk from coastal erosion along the Atlantic and Chesapeake Bay shorelines. The photo of Cedar Island shows just how invasive coastal erosion can be.

Sea-Level Rise

Virginia has a submergent shoreline, which means that its coast is in the process of being submerged. Sea level has risen about 9 m over the last 6,000 years, and continues to rise at a rate of 1.4 mm per year. Evidence indicates that global warming is increasing the rate at which glacial ice is melting around the world. As glacial ice melts, sea level rises. As a point of reference, if all the glacial ice in the world melted, sea level would rise about 70 m. More modest rises, which are widely predicted, would flood much of the low-lying land around Chesapeake Bay and along the Atlantic Coast, as you can see in **Figure 7.** Reducing the effects of climate change caused by human activities may slow this hazard.

Reading Check **Name three natural hazards that Virginians may face.**

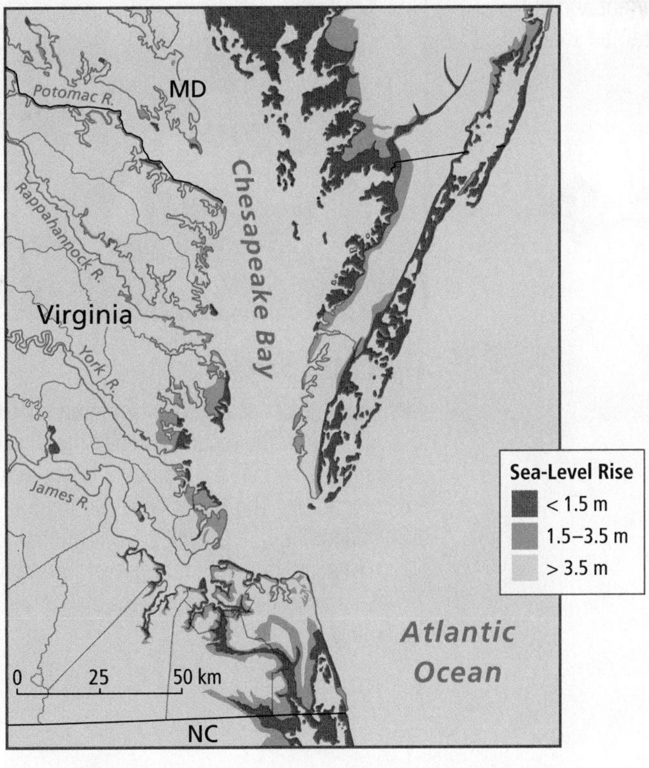

Figure 7 This map shows areas that would be flooded if sea level rose by 1.5 m (red) and 3.5 m (green).

Inquiry Lab

Time Required
one 45-minute class period

Lab Ratings
EASY → HARD

Teacher Preparation 3 of 4
Student Setup 1 of 4
Concept Level 3 of 4
Cleanup 4 of 4

Skills Acquired
- Constructing Models
- Observing
- Measuring
- Collecting Data
- Analyzing Models
- Interpreting Models

Scientific Methods
In this lab, students will
- Form a Hypothesis
- Test the Hypothesis
- Analyze the Results
- Draw Conclusions

Materials
The materials listed are enough for one lab group. Equipment and bulk materials, however, can be shared among groups.

Safety

Inquiry Lab

45 min

Materials
beaker, 600 mL (2)
beaker, 1,000 mL (2)
charcoal, activated
clay, powdered
decaying plant matter
gravel
hammer and nail, small
hand lens
laundry detergent
pH test strips
ring stand with ring
sand
scissors
soda bottle, plastic, 2 L
spoon, plastic (2)
vinegar
water, 2,000 mL

Safety

Clean Up Your Act

When you wash dishes, the bathroom sink, your clothes, or a car, you wash them with water. But have you ever wondered how water gets clean? Filtration is a common method of removing various pollutants from water. Cities in Virginia, such as Richmond and Norfolk, use filtration systems to produce high-quality drinking water. Filtration requires very little energy—gravity pulls water down through the layers of filter material. In this lab, you will see how well this energy-efficient method works to clean samples of polluted water. You will test water samples that contain decaying plant matter, powdered clay, vinegar, and laundry detergent.

Form a Hypothesis

1. Form a hypothesis about whether and how filtration will clean each of the four pollutants from the water. Predict whether the pollutant will be completely, partially, or not removed. Then, use the steps below to test your hypothesis.

Test the Hypothesis

2. Put on your apron, gloves, and goggles. Using scissors, carefully cut the bottom out of the empty soda bottle.
3. Carefully punch four or five small holes through the plastic cap of the bottle using a small nail and a hammer. Screw the plastic cap onto the bottle.
4. Turn the bottle upside down, and set its neck in the ring of a ring stand, as shown on the next page. Put a handful of gravel into the inverted bottle. Add a layer of activated charcoal, followed by thick layers of sand and gravel. Place a 600-mL beaker under the neck of the bottle.
5. Fill two 1,000-mL beakers with 1,000 mL of clean water. Set one beaker aside to serve as the control. Add three or four spoonfuls of each of the following pollutants to the other beaker: decaying plant matter, powdered clay, household vinegar, and laundry detergent.

Tips and Tricks

Varying the thickness of the layers can contribute to a variation in the results. Specify the thickness of each layer so that the results between groups are comparable. The layers could be the following dimensions: 7 cm of gravel, 2.5 cm of charcoal, 10 cm of sand, and 10 cm of gravel. You may adjust the layers according to your class size or the size of the bottles.

For variation, try different sizes of gravel or different textures of sand. Both will affect how many particles travel through the filter. If you place a few drops of food coloring in the water, students can watch the progress of the water as it passes through the filter.

You may decide that it is easier and safer for you to perform steps 2 and 3, cutting the soda bottles and punching the holes, before class.

6. Copy the table below into a notebook, and record your observations for each beaker in the columns labeled "Before cleaning."
7. Observe the color of the water in each beaker.
8. Use a hand lens to examine the water for visible particles.
9. Smell the water, and note any unusual odor.
10. Stir the water in each beaker rapidly with a plastic spoon, and check for suds. Use a different spoon for each sample.
11. Use a pH test strip to find the pH of the water in each beaker.
12. Gently stir the clean water, and then pour half of it through the filtration device into one of the 600-mL collection beakers.
13. Observe the water in the collection beaker for color, particles, odors, suds, and pH. Be patient. It may take several minutes for the water to travel through the filtration device. Record your observations in the column labeled "After filtration (clean water)" in your table.
14. Repeat steps 12 and 13 using the polluted water. Record your observations in the column labeled "After filtration (polluted water)" in your table.

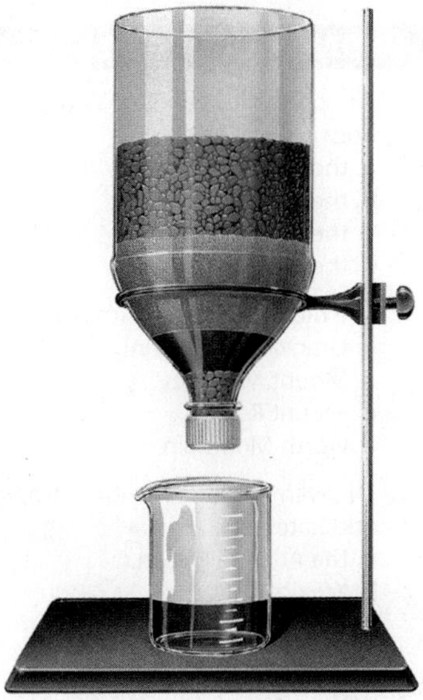

Results Table				
	Before cleaning (clean water)	Before cleaning (polluted water)	After filtration (clean water)	After filtration (polluted water)
Color				
Particles				
Odor				
Suds				
pH				

Analysis and Conclusion

1. How did the color of the polluted water change after filtration? Did the color of the clean water change?
2. Did the filtration method remove all of the visible particles from the polluted water? How do you know?
3. Did any suds form in the "After filtration (polluted water)" step? Explain.
4. How much did the pH of the polluted water change?
5. How did the final pH of the polluted water compare to the pH of the clean water before filtering?

Extension

Applying Your Data
Determine sources of clean water in your community. Gather and analyze data that show the amount of clean water in supply and how that water is consumed. You may want to organize your data into graphs and tables.

Answers to Analysis and Conclusion

1. Sample answer: The filtered water was lighter in color than the unfiltered water. However, the water was still not as clear as the clean water. The color of the clean water stayed about the same.
2. Sample answer: No, the filtration method did not remove all of the particles from the polluted water. Many of the particles passed through the filter, but there were fewer particles than before the filtration.
3. Some suds were present because not all of the detergent was removed by filtration.
4. The pH of the water changed slightly.
5. The final pH of the polluted water was not the same as that of the clean water. After the polluted water was filtered, its pH was still slightly more acidic than that of the clean water.

Answer to Extension

Students' answers will vary depending on the community in which they live. Student data should show the amount of clean water that is in supply in aquifers, lakes, streams, or reservoirs. Student data on water consumption can include residential use, industrial use, or agricultural use. Students may want to organize their data for water consumption in a circle graph or bar graph.

Close-Up Review

Understanding Key Ideas

1. d
2. c
3. a
4. d
5. d
6. b
7. a
8. b
9. c
10. b

Short Answer

11. The Gulf Stream carries warm water along the coast and influences the climate, particularly in eastern Virginia, by warming the coastal air.
12. Virginia is located near the middle of the North American plate, so it is not near any active plate boundaries.
13. Coastal areas of Virginia receive more rainfall because the Appalachian Mountains to the west of Virginia cause a rain-shadow effect in western Virginia and because the warm water of the Gulf Stream causes rain along the Atlantic coast.
14. Two factors that affect Virginia's climate are the state's latitude and its proximity to the Atlantic Ocean.
15. Compression of the rocks where continents collided caused folding and faulting of the Valley and Ridge province, and thrust the Blue Ridge rocks westward. These rocks were pushed up and over the Valley and Ridge rocks, forming the Blue Ridge Mountains.
16. During the Ice Age, the Susquehanna River carved a valley across the exposed continental shelf. When the glaciers began to melt, sea level rose and the continental shelf became covered with water. The ancient river valley flooded and Chesapeake Bay formed.
17. Most of the coal beds in Virginia are located in southwestern Virginia.
18. The best locations in Virginia for wind turbines are along the Atlantic coast and in the western mountainous regions, where winds are the most consistent.

Close-Up Review

UNDERSTANDING KEY IDEAS

1. The prevailing winds in Virginia generally blow from
a. the north.
b. the south.
c. the east.
d. the west.

2. The highest point in Virginia is
a. Grenville Mountain.
b. Mount McKinley.
c. Mount Rogers.
d. North Mountain.

3. The warm air of a maritime tropical air mass originates in
a. the Atlantic Ocean.
b. Mexico.
c. the Pacific Ocean.
d. Canada.

4. Which of the following does NOT affect rainfall in Virginia?
a. hurricanes
b. the Gulf Stream
c. a maritime tropical air mass
d. a maritime polar air mass

5. Which of the following types of rock is the oldest found in Virginia?
a. limestone
b. marble
c. slate
d. gneiss

6. About 2 billion years ago, Virginia was part of
a. Gondwanaland.
b. Laurentia.
c. Grenville.
d. Pangaea.

7. The most abundant energy resource in Virginia is
a. coal.
b. natural gas.
c. peat.
d. oil.

8. The renewable energy source that provides about 2% of Virginia's electricity is
a. wind power.
b. hydroelectric power.
c. solar power.
d. geothermal power.

9. Which of the following statements about tornadoes in Virginia is false?
a. Most tornadoes occur during the summer.
b. The worst tornado season on record was in 1993.
c. Tornadoes bring as much as 40% of Virginia's annual rainfall.
d. The most powerful tornadoes occur in late spring and autumn.

10. The most valuable nonfuel mineral-resource product in Virginia is
a. sand and gravel.
b. crushed stone.
c. coal.
d. titanium.

SHORT ANSWER

11. Describe the major influence of the Gulf Stream on Virginia.

12. Describe Virginia's geologic location.

13. Explain why coastal areas of Virginia receive more rainfall than most areas inland.

14. Name two factors that affect Virginia's climate.

15. Briefly describe how the Blue Ridge Mountains formed.

16. Explain how Chesapeake Bay formed.

17. Where are most of the coal beds in Virginia found?

18. Where are the best locations in Virginia to erect wind turbines? Why?

19. Explain how the rain-shadow effect alters precipitation patterns in Virginia.

20. How will climate change affect coastal areas of Virginia?

19. The moisture from the interior of the continent condenses as the air rises over the Appalachians Mountains to the west of Virginia. As the air goes up, it cools and drops its moisture as precipitation. This precipitation pattern leaves a dry zone to the east, along Virginia's western border.
20. Rising sea level could cause flooding of much of the low-lying land around Chesapeake Bay and along the Atlantic coast.

Critical Thinking

21. Around 300 million years ago, the massive mountains of Virginia eroded and buried the swampy forests that once covered the state under sediment. The sediment eventually became sandstone and shale, and the vegetation underneath became huge coal seams. During the Cenozoic Era, the erosion of the Appalachian Mountains provided sediment that was deposited alternatively with limestone from a shallow sea to form the Coastal Plain.

CRITICAL THINKING

21. Making Comparisons Compare the way in which sedimentation created coal beds in southwestern Virginia and sandy shores in the Coastal Plain.

22. Analyzing Relationships Explain the relationship between glaciation and Chesapeake Bay.

23. Analyzing Ideas Explain why coal, oil, and natural gas are considered to be nonrenewable resources.

24. Making Inferences Describe two effects that global warming may have on the Virginia coastline.

CONCEPT MAPPING

25. Use the following terms to create a concept map: *energy resources, hydroelectric, solar, oil and natural gas, solar panels, renewable resources, wind, dams, nonrenewable resources,* and *wind farms.*

MATH SKILLS

Math Skills

26. Making Calculations Rising sea level is responsible for Chesapeake Bay's submergent shoreline. Over a period of 6,000 years, the shoreline has risen 9 m. On average, how many millimeters did sea level rise per year during this period?

WRITING SKILLS

27. Writing from Research Research Virginia's potential as a producer of one of the following energy resources: hydroelectric energy, solar energy, and wind energy. Consider arguments for and against the construction of pumped-storage hydroelectric facilities, solar arrays, or wind turbines in different locations. Write a paragraph that summarizes the best location(s) for the energy resource you chose. Write another paragraph that looks at the costs and the effects on the environment of constructing a renewable energy facility of your choice.

INTERPRETING GRAPHICS

The pie graph below shows Virginia's total electricity generation based on fuel type in 2008. The total amount of electricity generated was 5,893,000 GW·h (gigawatt-hours). Use this pie graph to answer the questions that follow.

Energy Sources for Electricity

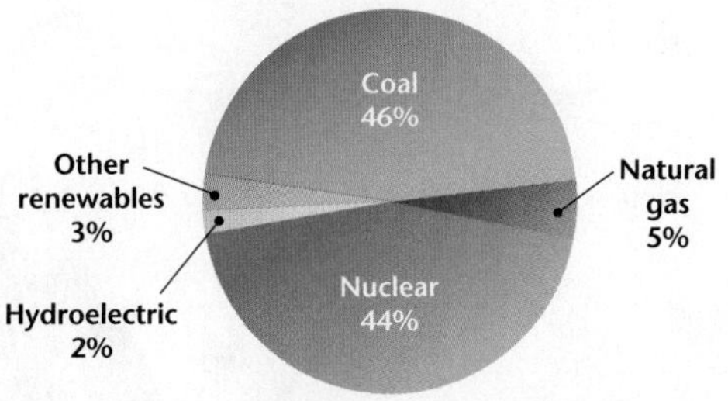

28. Name the fuel type that was used most to generate electricity in Virginia in 2008.

29. Which sector on this graph would Virginia's solar power be part of? Why?

30. How many gigawatt-hours of electricity were generated by nuclear energy in Virginia in 2008?

31. How many gigawatt-hours of electricity were generated from renewable energy resources? Explain your answer.

Close-Up Review

22. During periods of glacial advance, sea level dropped and the continental shelf became eroded by rivers, causing formation of deep river valleys. During periods of glacial retreat, the ice melted and sea level rose. As sea level rose, the continental shelf flooded and the coastline of Chesapeake Bay formed.

23. Coal, oil, and natural gas are considered nonrenewable resources because they take millions of years to form, and they are used more rapidly than they can be replaced.

24. Answers may vary. Sample answer: Global warming could result in increased coastal erosion and the flooding of the low-lying areas along Chesapeake Bay and the Atlantic coast.

Concept Mapping

25. Answers may vary but should include all of the terms listed. A sample answer appears below.

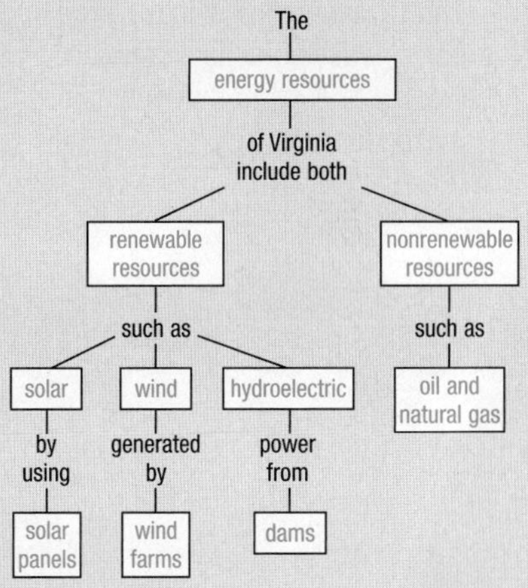

Math Skills

26. 9 m × 1,000 mm/m = 9,000 mm; 9,000 mm ÷ 6,000 years = 1.5 mm/year

Writing Skills

27. Answers may vary. Accept all reasonable answers.

Interpreting Graphics

28. Coal was used the most.

29. Solar power is derived from solar energy, which is a renewable resource. Therefore, it is part of the "Other renewables" category.

30. Nuclear energy = 44%; $\frac{44}{100} \times 5{,}893{,}000$ GW•h = 2,592,920 GW•h.

31. 2% (hydroelectric) + 3% (other renewables) = 5% of electricity from renewable resources.

Therefore, $\frac{5}{100} \times 5{,}893{,}000$ GW•h = 294,650 GW•h.

Maps in Action

Answers to Map Skills Activity

1. The smallest watershed in Virginia is the Yadkin watershed.
2. Roanoke is located in the Roanoke watershed.
3. Answers may vary. Sample answer: The names of the watersheds seem to be based on the names of large or important rivers within the watersheds.
4. Answers may vary. Sample answer: The most densely populated regions of Virginia are the areas around Arlington and Alexandria (in the Potomac watershed), Richmond (in the James watershed), and Norfolk (in the James watershed). The watershed that I think has the greatest risk of potential for pollution as a result of being densely populated is the James watershed.
5. Rainfall runoff can transport pollutants from the ground surface into flooded streams and rivers that flow for miles into Chesapeake Bay. Runoff from streets, parking lots, and other impervious structures in urban areas can flow into storm drains, washing pollutants into streams and rivers that flow into Chesapeake Bay.

MAPS in Action

Watershed Map of Virginia

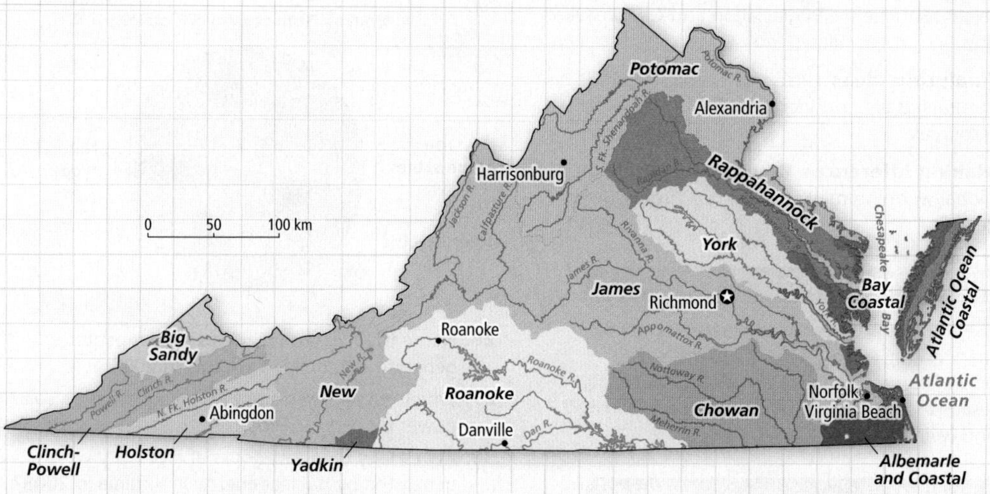

Map Skills Activity

This map shows the major watersheds in Virginia. Each watershed is indicated by a different color. Use the map to answer the questions below.

1. **Analyzing Data** Which watershed is the smallest watershed in Virginia?
2. **Analyzing Data** Which watershed includes the city of Roanoke?
3. **Inferring Relationships** What do you think the names of these watersheds are based on?
4. **Identifying Relationships** A major contributing factor to watershed pollution is population density. Which watershed do you think has the greatest risk of pollution due to a densely populated area?
5. **Analyzing Relationships** How can different types of pollutants, such as fertilizers, pesticides, and animal waste, pollute Chesapeake Bay even though the sources of the pollutants may be hundreds of miles from the bay?

Why It Matters

Not So Dismal Anymore

The Great Dismal Swamp—it sounds like something worth avoiding, and, a few years ago, it was! Today, thanks to conservation efforts, this swamp in southeast Virginia is being rejuvenated. Although it was drained and extensively logged in the 1700s, it is now a national wildlife refuge and an important habitat for many species of animals and plants.

Lake Drummond is located in the center of the swamp and supplies water to the wetlands surrounding it. It is the largest natural lake in Virginia, with a surface area of about 13 km². However, its maximum depth is only 2 m!

The Great Dismal Swamp is home to a variety of animals, such as black bears. It also supports numerous plant species, such as this log fern, or *Dryopteris celsa*—one of the rarest American ferns.

This swamp is one of the few places on Earth where peat is currently forming. Peat bogs act as carbon reservoirs, which are important to the carbon cycle.

YOUR TURN

CRITICAL THINKING
Explain why the Great Dismal Swamp is important.

WRITING IN SCIENCE
Research other efforts to protect or restore important ecosystems in Virginia.

Why It Matters

The Great Dismal Swamp

Conservation and restoration of habitats, such as the Great Dismal Swamp, are becoming more and more important as the human population increases and takes over many existing habitats. The Great Dismal Swamp was drained in the 1700s and logged extensively for its Atlantic white cedar. Both Tupelo-bald cypress and Atlantic white-cedar once dominated the area. However, the logging destroyed the populations of these trees. Red maples have taken over the area due to logging practices, extensive draining, and lack of forest fires.

While the Great Dismal Swamp provides habitat for many species of plants and animals, three rare plants deserve special mention. The dwarf trillium is a small, flowering plant that is located in the northwestern section of the swamp. The dwarf trillium blooms briefly each year for only two weeks in March. Silky camellia is a flower that grows on the hardwood ridges and in the northwestern corner of the swamp. The log fern, or *Dryopteris celsa*, is one of the rarest American ferns. It is more common in the Great Dismal Swamp than anywhere else.

Answers to Your Turn

Understanding Concepts The Great Dismal Swamp is an important habitat for many species of animals and plants. It is also an important carbon reservoir, as a result of peat formation.

Writing in Science Answers may vary. Accept all reasonable answers.

Reference

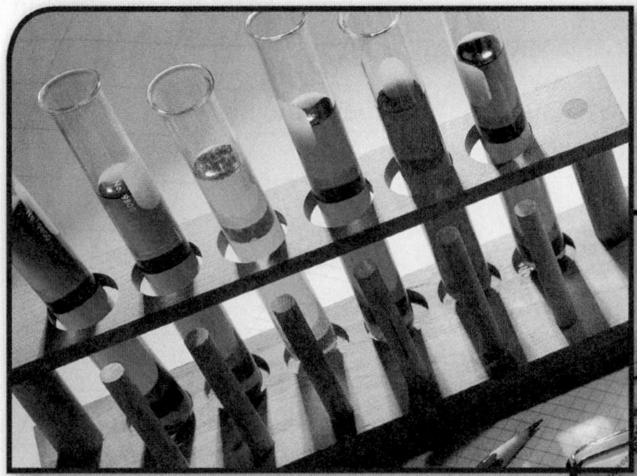

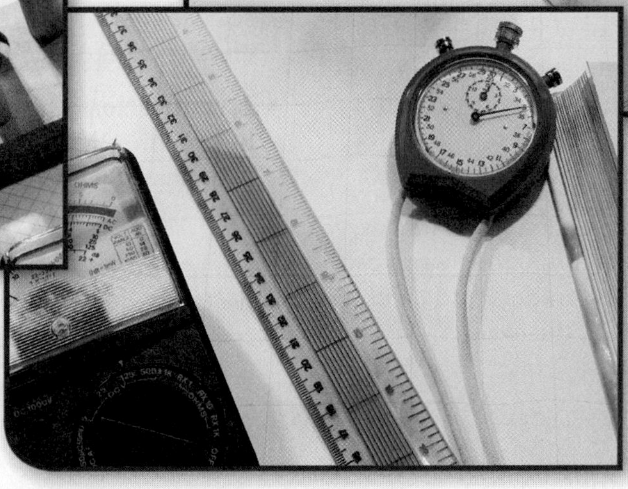

Reading Toolbox Overview

Science textbooks can be hard to read because you have to learn new words and new ideas. The Reading Toolbox page at the beginning of each chapter in this book contains tools that can help you get the most out of your reading. Each of the sections on these pages is designed to help you analyze words, language, or ideas.

Analyzing Words

Analyzing Words tools will help you learn and understand specific words or phrases in a chapter.

- **FoldNotes** The key-term fold will help you learn the key terms in the chapter. Instructions for making a key-term fold are on page 884.
- **Science Terms** This tool will help you understand how the common meanings of words can differ from the scientific meanings. A table of everyday words used in science can be found on page 894.
- **Word Parts** If you understand the meanings of the prefixes, suffixes, or word roots, you can understand many science terms. A table of word parts used in science terms is on page 896.
- **Word Origins** Learning the origin of words and phrases used in science can help you remember the word.
- **Word Families** Because similar words can be grouped together into word families, understanding one word can help you understand all of the words in the family.

Analyzing Language

Analyzing Language tools will help you discover connections between ideas and specific kinds of language.

- **Analogies, Comparisons, and Cause and Effect** These tools help you understand the relationship between various words and phrases.
- **Generalizations, Making Predictions, Frequency, and Finding Examples** These tools help you identify language that can key you into when generalizations or predictions are being made, how often something occurs, and when an example is being used.
- **Fact, Hypothesis, or Theory?; Describing Time and Space; Reading Equations; and Word Problems** These tools can help you understand language that is used to describe science concepts and mathematical language.
- **Classification** This tool will help you understand how language is used to organize items.
- **Mnemonics** A mnemonic is a useful study tool to help you remember related words.

Analyzing Ideas

Analyzing Ideas tools will help you organize ideas and create materials that you can use to study.

- **Note Taking** These tools are various methods for taking notes while you read. For details about note-taking methods, see pages 879–883.
- **FoldNotes** There are various types of FoldNotes that you can make to help you learn information. Instructions for making FoldNotes can be found on pages 884–887.
- **Graphic Organizers** These tools are a visual way of showing relationships between ideas. Information on how to create various types of graphic organizers can be found on pages 888–893.

Note Taking

It is important to organize the information that you learn while you are reading a chapter so that you can use those notes to study for your tests. There are many ways to take notes. Each of these note-taking methods is a way to create a clear summary of the key points that you will need to remember for exams.

Comparison Table

A comparison table is useful when you want to compare the characteristics of two or more topics in science. Organizing information in a table helps you compare several topics at one time. In a table, all topics are described in terms of the same list of characteristics, which helps you make a thorough comparison.

1. **Create Table** Draw as many columns and rows as you need to compare the topics of interest, as shown below.
2. **Identify Topics** In the top row, write the topics that you want to compare.
3. **Identify Characteristics** In the left-column, write the general characteristics that you want to compare. As you read the chapter, fill in the characteristics for each topic in the appropriate boxes.

	Solid	Liquid	Gas	Plasma
Definite volume	yes	yes	no	no
Definite shape	yes	no	no	no
Possible changes of state	melting, sublimation	freezing, evaporation	condensation	

Practice

1. Make a comparison table to compare apples, oranges, and broccoli. Compare the following characteristics: color, shape, fruit or vegetable, and vitamins contained.

Outlining

Outlining is one of the most widely used methods for taking notes. A well-prepared outline can be an effective tool for understanding, comprehending, and achieving success on tests. Most outlines follow the same structure. This textbook is organized in such a way that you can easily outline the important ideas in a chapter or section.

1. **List Main Ideas** List main ideas or topics first. Each topic can be a section title and is listed after a Roman numeral.
2. **Add Major Points** Add major points that give you important information about the topic. Each major point will appear in red type in the section. You should add the points to your outline following capitalized letters.
3. **Add Subpoints** Add subpoints that describe parts of the major points. The first subpoint should be the green heading that appears after the red main topic. Subpoints should be added after numerals in your outline.
4. **Include Supporting Details** Finally, add supporting details for each subpoint. Pick important details from the text that follow the green headings. Add the details to your outline following lower-case letters.

II. Igneous Rock
    A. The Formation of Magma
        1. Partial Melting
            a. minerals melt at different temperatures
            b. magma composition changes
        2. Fractional Crystallization
            a. minerals freeze at different temperatures
            b. crystallization removes minerals from magma

Practice

1. Outline one of the sections in the chapter that you are currently covering in class.

Pattern Puzzles

You can use pattern puzzles to help you remember information in the correct order. Pattern puzzles are not just a tool for memorization. They can also help you better understand a variety of scientific processes, from the steps used to solve a mathematical conversion to the procedure used to write a lab report. Pattern puzzles are useful tools to practice and to review before tests. They also work very well in problem solving.

1. **Write Steps** In your own words, write down the steps of a process on a sheet of paper. Write one step per line, and do not number the steps. You should divide longer steps into two or three shorter steps.
2. **Separate Steps** Cut the sheet of paper into strips with only one step per strip of paper. Shuffle the strips of paper so that they are out of sequence.
3. **Reorganize Steps** Place the strips in their proper sequence. Confirm the order of the process by checking your text or your class notes.

How to determine the density of a mineral

- Place the mineral on a balance beam.
- Read and record the mass indicated by the balance, in grams.
- Place the mineral in a graduated cylinder with a given volume of water.
- Subtract the difference in volume, and record the difference, in cubic centimeters.
- Divide the mass by the volume to find the density.

- Place the mineral in a graduated cylinder with a given volume of water.
- Place the mineral on a balance beam.
- Divide the mass by the volume to find the density.
- Read and record the mass indicated by the balance, in grams.
- Subtract the difference in volume, and record the difference, in cubic centimeters.

Practice

1. Create a pattern puzzle that describes the steps that you take during one of your favorite activities (for example, baking cookies, writing a short story, playing a song on the guitar, or scoring a soccer goal). See if a friend can put the pieces of your puzzle in the correct order.

Summarizing

Summarizing is a simple method of taking notes in which you restate what you read in your own words. A summary is simply a brief restatement of a longer passage. Summarizing is a useful way to take notes because it helps you focus on the most important ideas. You can use your notes when you are reviewing for a test so that you can study all of the main points without having to reread the entire chapter.

1. **Identify Main Ideas** Identify the main idea in a paragraph by reading completely through the paragraph. Sometimes, the first or last sentence of a paragraph states the main idea directly. Key-idea sentences may also be used as the main idea.

2. **Create Summary Statement** Write a short statement that expresses the main idea. It is best to use complete sentences. You can use abbreviations as long as you will remember later what they mean. You may be able to summarize more than one paragraph in a single statement. In other cases, you may need more than one sentence to summarize a paragraph. Skip a couple of lines, and then repeat these first two steps for each paragraph in the section or chapter that you are reading.

3. **Include Additional Notes** Add important notes or facts in the lines in between your summary statements. Read the text in Section 4 of Chapter 6 that follows the heading "Nonfoliated Rocks." The heading, "Nonfoliated Rocks," is too simple to be a summary statement because it does not tell you what nonfoliated rocks are nor any of their characteristics. On the other hand, you don't need to include any of the information about the Parthenon in your summary. A good summary for this text is given below.

Nonfoliated rocks do not have bands or aligned minerals.

The rock they come from contains mainly grains of only one mineral, which are usually round or square.

Quartzite and marble are common nonfoliated rocks.

Practice

1. Summarize the first paragraph of this page.

Two-Column Notes

Two-column notes can be used to learn and review definitions of vocabulary terms or details of specific concepts. One strategy for using two-column notes is to organize main ideas and their details. The two-column method of review is great for preparing for quizzes or tests. Cover the information in the right-hand column with a sheet of paper, and after reciting what you know, uncover the notes to check your answers.

1. **Make Table** Divide a blank sheet of paper into two columns. Label the left-hand column "Main idea" and the right-hand column "Detail notes."
2. **Identify Main Ideas** Identify the main ideas. Key ideas are listed at the beginning of each section. However, you should decide which ideas to include in your notes. Key words can include boldface terms as well as any other terms that you may have trouble remembering. Questions may include those that the author has asked or any questions that your teacher may have asked during class.
3. **Add Main Ideas** In the right-hand column, write the main ideas as questions, key words, or a combination of both. The table below shows some of the main ideas from sections 1 and 2 of Chapter 1, "Introduction to Earth Science."
4. **Create Detail Notes** Do not copy ideas from the book or waste time writing in complete sentences. Summarize your ideas using by phrases that are easy to understand and remember. Decide how many details you need for each main idea, and include that number to help you focus on the necessary information.
5. **Include Detail Notes** Write the detail notes in the right-hand column. Be sure to list as many details as you designated in the main-idea column.

Main idea	Detail notes
Branches of Earth science (3 important details)	• natural science—observation and experimentation • four branches—geology, oceanography, meteorology, astronomy • branches of science overlap (environmental science)
Scientific methods (4 important details)	• ask a question • form a hypothesis • test the hypothesis • draw conclusions

Practice

1. Make your own two-column notes using the periodic table. Include in the details the symbol and the atomic number of each of the following elements.
   a. neon
   b. oxygen
   c. copper
   d. calcium
   e. lead
   f. sodium

FoldNotes

FoldNotes are a useful study tool that you can use to organize concepts. One FoldNote focuses on a few main concepts. By using a FoldNote, you can learn how concepts fit together. FoldNotes are designed to make studying concepts easier so that you can remember the ideas for tests.

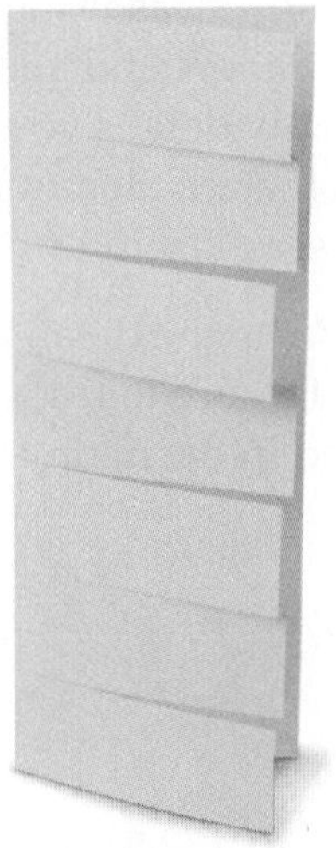

Key-Term Fold

A key-term fold is useful for studying definitions of key terms in a chapter. Each tab can contain a key term on one side and its definition on the other. Use the key-term fold to quiz yourself on the definitions of the key terms in a chapter.

1. Fold a **sheet of lined notebook paper** in half from left to right.
2. Using **scissors,** cut along every third line from the right edge of the paper to the center fold to make tabs.

Booklet

A booklet is a useful tool for taking notes as you read a chapter. Each page of the booklet can contain a main topic from the chapter. Write details of each main topic on the appropriate page to create an outline of the chapter.

1. Fold a **sheet of paper** in half from left to right. Then, unfold the paper.
2. Fold the sheet of paper in half again from the top to the bottom. Then, unfold the paper.
3. Refold the sheet of paper in half from left to right.
4. Fold the top and bottom edges to the center crease.
5. Completely unfold the paper.
6. Refold the paper from top to bottom.
7. Using **scissors,** cut a slit along the center crease of the sheet from the folded edge to the creases made in step 4. Do not cut the entire sheet in half. Unfold the paper.
8. Fold the sheet of paper in half from left to right. While holding the bottom and top edges of the paper, push the bottom and top edges together so that the center collapses at the center slit. Fold the four flaps to form a four-page book.

Double-Door Fold

A double-door fold is useful when you want to compare the characteristics of two topics. The double-door fold can organize characteristics of the two topics side by side under the flaps. Similarities and differences between the two topics can then be easily identified.

1. Fold a **sheet of paper** in half from the top to the bottom. Then, unfold the paper.
2. Fold the top and bottom edges of the paper to the center crease.

Four-Corner Fold

A four-corner fold is useful when you want to compare the characteristics of four topics. The four-corner fold can organize the characteristics of the four topics side by side under the flaps. Similarities and differences between the four topics can then be easily identified.

1. Fold a **sheet of paper** in half from top to bottom. Then, unfold the paper.
2. Fold the top and bottom of the paper to the crease in the center of the paper.
3. Fold the paper in half from side to side. Then, unfold the paper.
4. Using **scissors,** cut the top flap creases made in step 3 to form four flaps.

Layered Book

A layered book is a useful tool for taking notes as you read a chapter. The four flaps of the layered book can summarize information into four categories. Write details of each category on the appropriate flap to create a summary of the chapter.

1. Lay one **sheet of paper** on top of **another sheet.** Slide the top sheet up so that 2 cm of the bottom sheet is showing.
2. Holding the two sheets together, fold down the top of the two sheets so that you see four 2 cm tabs along the bottom.
3. Using a **stapler,** staple the top of the FoldNote.

Pyramid

A pyramid provides a unique way for taking notes. The three sides of the pyramid can summarize information into three categories. Use the pyramid as a tool for studying information in a chapter.

1. Place a **sheet of paper** in front of you. Fold the lower left-hand corner of the paper diagonally to the opposite edge of the paper.
2. Cut off the tab of paper created by the fold (at the top).
3. Open the paper so that it is a square. Fold the lower right-hand corner of the paper diagonally to the opposite corner to form a triangle.
4. Open the paper. The creases of the two folds will have created an X.
5. Using **scissors,** cut along one of the creases. Start from any corner, and stop at the center point to create two flaps. Use **tape** or **glue** to attach one of the flaps on top of the other flap.

Table Fold

A table fold is a useful tool for comparing the characteristics of two or three topics. In a table fold, all topics are described in terms of the same characteristics so that you can easily make a thorough comparison.

1. Fold a **piece of paper** in half from the top to the bottom. Then, fold the paper in half again.
2. Fold the paper in thirds from side to side.
3. Unfold the paper completely. Carefully trace the fold lines by using a pen or pencil.

Tri-Fold

A tri-fold is a useful tool that helps you track your progress. By organizing the chapter topic into what you know, what you want to know, and what you learn, you can see how much you have learned after reading a chapter.

1. Fold a piece a paper in thirds from the top to the bottom.
2. Unfold the paper so that you can see the three sections. Then, turn the paper sideways so that the three sections form vertical columns.
3. Trace the fold lines by using a **pen** or **pencil.** Label the columns "Know," "Want," and "Learn."

Three-Panel Flip Chart

A three-panel flip chart is useful when you want to compare the characteristics of three topics. The three-panel flip chart can organize the characteristics of the three topics side by side under the flaps. Similarities and differences between the three topics can then be easily identified.

1. Fold a **piece of paper** in half from the top to the bottom.
2. Fold the paper in thirds from side to side. Then, unfold the paper so that you can see the three sections.
3. From the top of the paper, cut along each of the vertical fold lines to the fold in the middle of the paper. You will now have three flaps.

Two-Panel Flip Chart

A two-panel flip chart is useful when you want to compare the characteristics of two topics. The two-panel flip chart can organize the characteristics of the two topics side by side under the flaps. Similarities and differences between the two topics can then be easily identified.

1. Fold a **piece of paper** in half from the top to the bottom.
2. Fold the paper in half from side to side. Then, unfold the paper so that you can see the two sections.
3. From the top of the paper, cut along the vertical fold line to the fold in the middle of the paper. You will now have two flaps.

Graphic Organizers

Graphic Organizers are a way to draw or map concepts. Graphic Organizers can show simply how concepts are connected, when steps occur in a process, or how events are related. When you outline a concept using Graphic Organizers, you will understand the concept better and have a study tool that you can use later.

Concept Map

Concept maps are useful when you are trying to identify how several ideas are connected to a main concept. Concept maps may be based on vocabulary terms or on main topics from the text. As you read about science, look for terms that can be organized in a concept map.

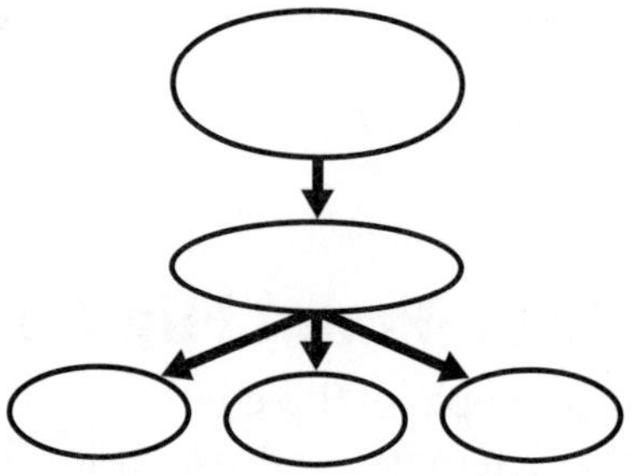

How to Make a Concept Map

1. **Main Ideas** Identify main ideas from the text. Write the ideas as short phrases or single words.
2. **Main Concepts** Select a main concept. Place this concept at the top or center of a piece of paper.
3. **More Ideas** Place other ideas under or around the main concept based on their relationship to the main concept. Draw a circle around each idea.
4. **Connections** Draw lines between the concepts. Add linking words to connect the ideas.

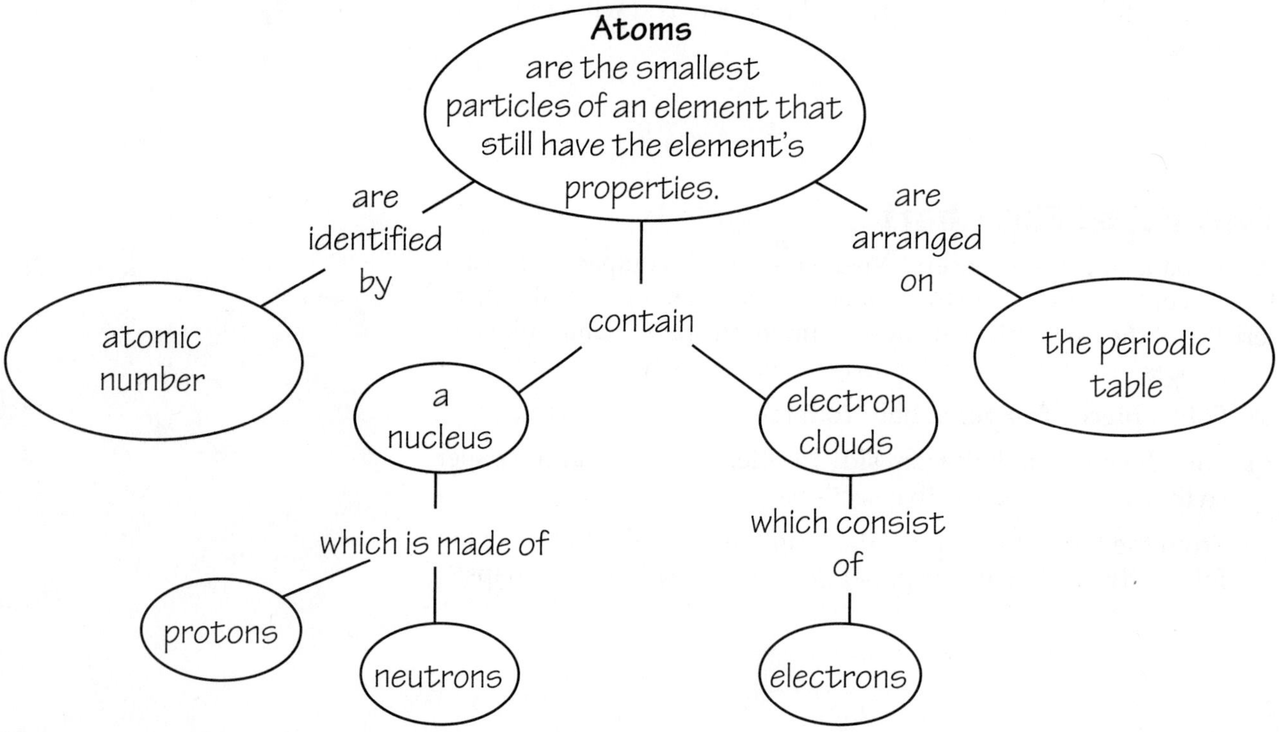

Flow Chart

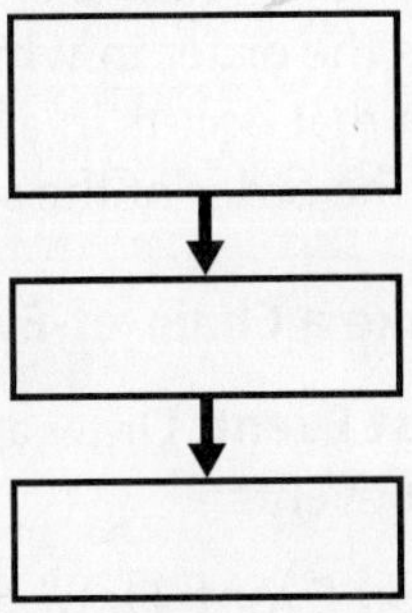

Science is full of processes. A flow chart shows the steps that a process takes to get from one point to another point. Timelines and cycles are examples of the kinds of information that can be organized well in a flow chart. As you read, look for information that is described in steps or in a sequence, and draw a process chart that shows the progression of the steps or sequence.

How to Make a Flow Chart

1. **Box First Step** Draw a box. In the box, write the first step of a process or cycle.
2. **Add Next Step** Under the box, draw another box, and draw an arrow to connect the two boxes. In the second box, write the next step of the process.
3. **Add More Steps** Continue adding boxes until each step of the process or cycle is written in a box. For cycles only, draw an arrow to connect the last box and the first box.

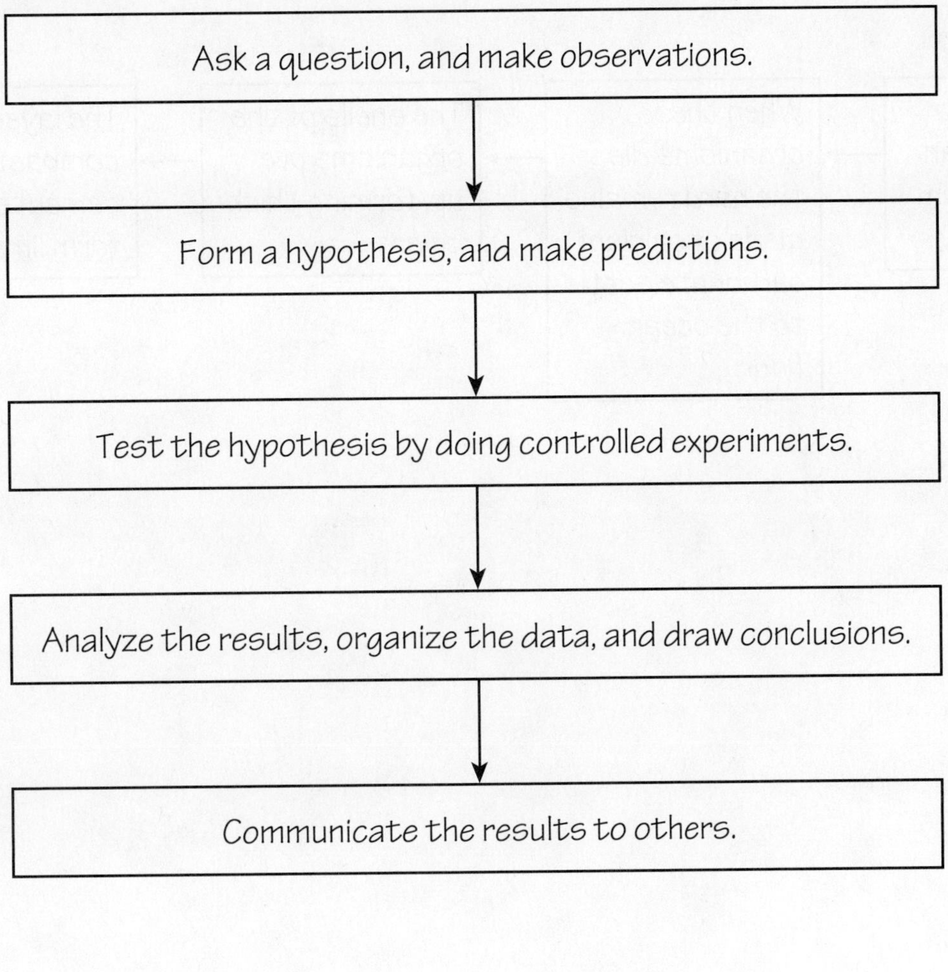

Ask a question, and make observations.
Form a hypothesis, and make predictions.
Test the hypothesis by doing controlled experiments.
Analyze the results, organize the data, and draw conclusions.
Communicate the results to others.

APPENDIX A

Chain-of-Events Chart

When to Use a Chain-of-Events Chart

A chain-of-events chart is similar to a flow chart. A chain-of-events chart shows the order in which steps occur. As you read, look for information that occurs in a sequence, and draw a chain-of-events chart that shows the order of the sequence.

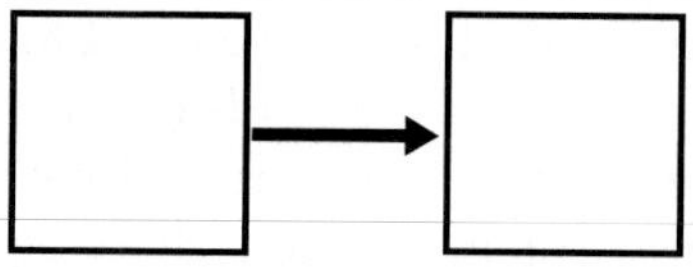

How to Make a Chain-of-Events Chart

1. **Box First Event** Draw a box. In the box, write the first event of a chain of events.
2. **Add Next Event** Draw another box to the right of the first box. Draw an arrow to connect the two boxes. In the second box, write the next event in the timeline.
3. **Add More Events** Continue adding boxes until each step of the chain of events is written in a box.

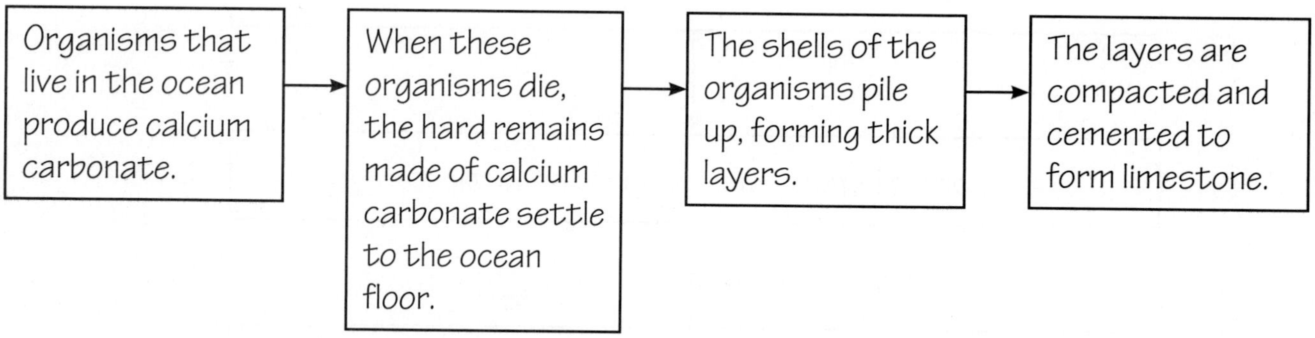

Cause-and-Effect Map

A cause-and-effect map is a useful tool for illustrating a specific type of scientific process. Use a cause-and-effect map when you want to describe how, when, or why one event causes another event. As you read, look for events that are either causes or results of other events, and draw a cause-and-effect map that shows the relationships between the events.

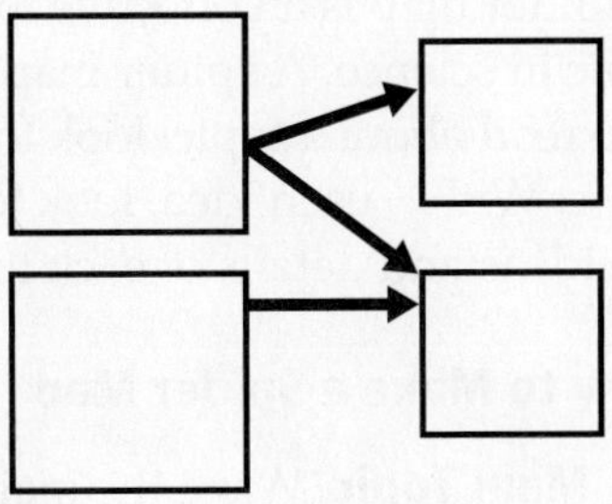

How to Make a Cause-and-Effect Map

1. **Cause Box** Draw a box, and write a cause in the box. You can have as many cause boxes as you want. The diagram shown here is one example of a cause-and-effect map.
2. **Effect Boxes** Draw another box to the right of the cause box to represent an effect. You can have as many effect boxes as you want. Draw arrows from each cause box to the appropriate effect boxes.
3. **Descriptions** In the cause boxes, explain the process that makes up the cause. In the effect boxes, write a description of the effect or details about the effect.

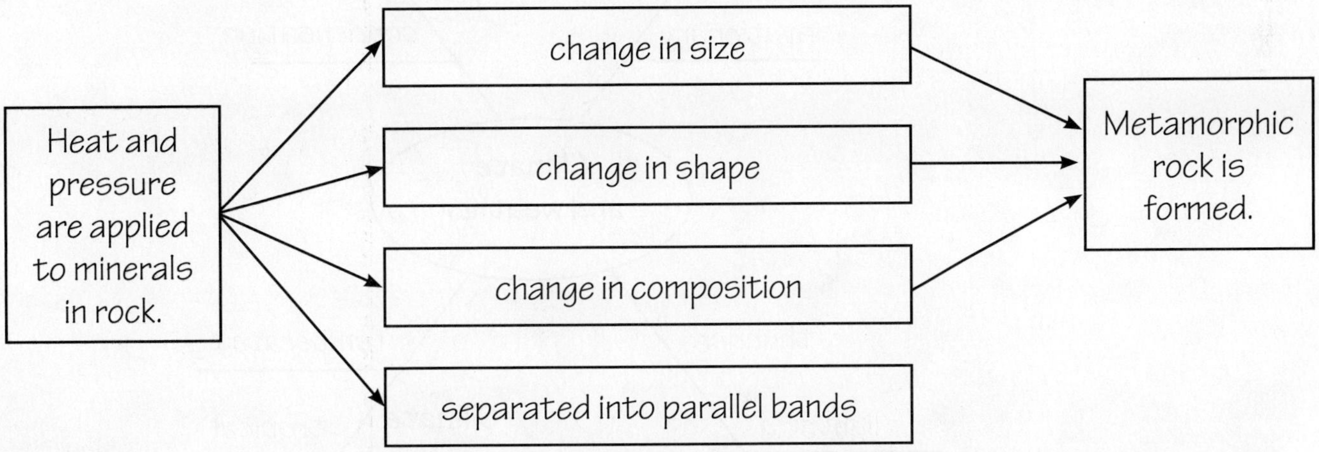

Spider Map

A spider map is an effective tool for classifying the details of a specific topic in science. A spider map divides a topic into ideas and details. As you read about a topic, look for the main ideas or characteristics of the topic. Within each idea, look for details. Use a spider map to organize the ideas and details of each topic.

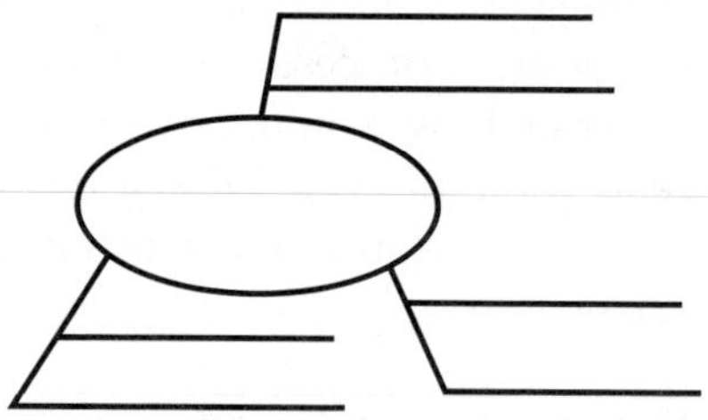

How to Make a Spider Map

1. **Main Topic** Write the main topic in the center of your paper. Draw a circle around the topic.
2. **Main Ideas** From the circle, draw legs to represent the main ideas or characteristics of the topic. Draw as many legs as you want. Write an idea or characteristic along each leg.
3. **Details** From each leg, draw horizontal lines. As you read the chapter, write details about each idea on the idea's horizontal lines. To add more details, make the legs longer and add more horizontal lines.

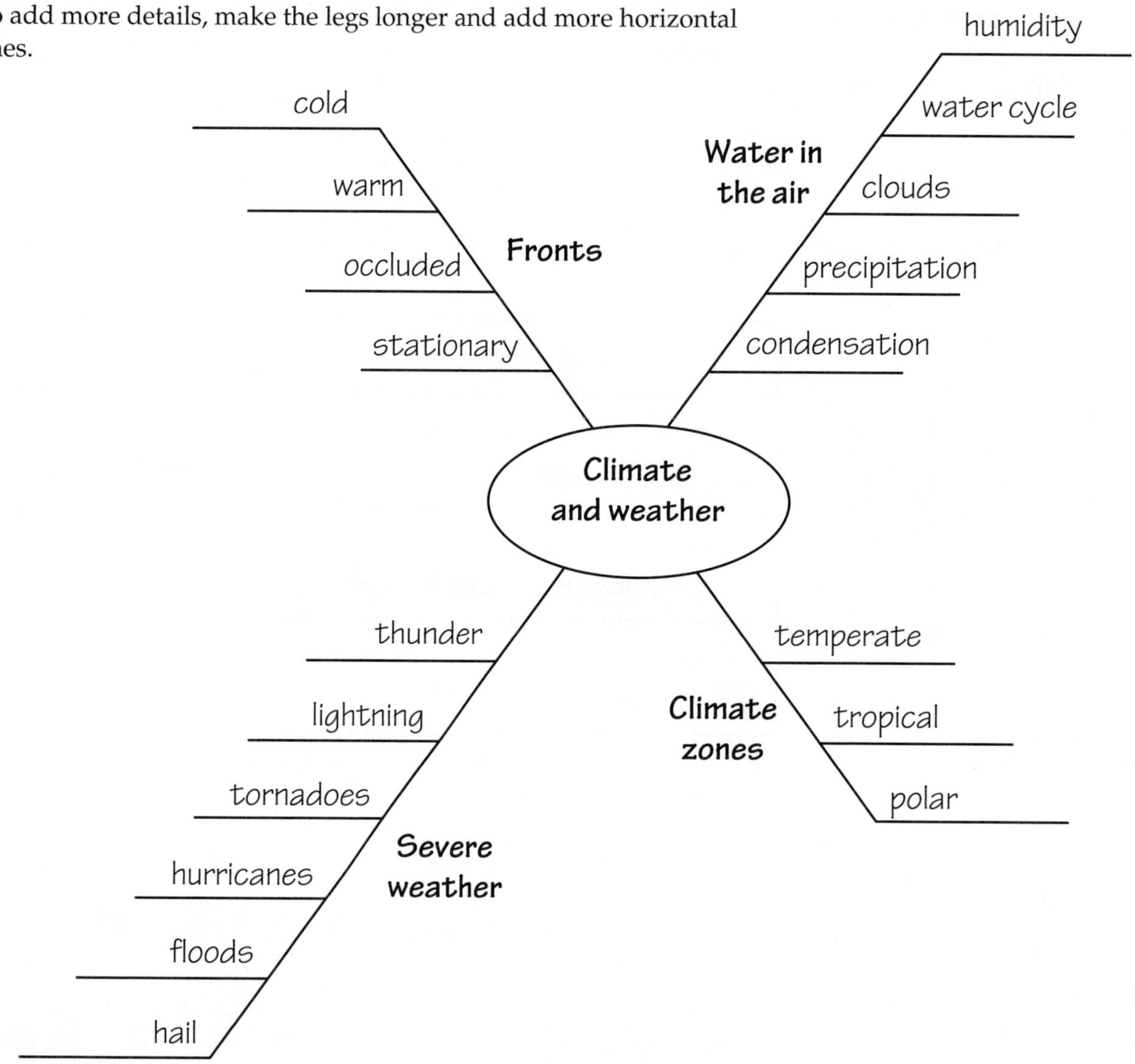

Venn Diagram

A Venn diagram is a useful tool for comparing two or three topics in science. A Venn diagram shows which characteristics that the topics share and which characteristics are unique to each topic. Venn diagrams are ideal when you want to illustrate relationships in a pair or small group of topics. As you read, look for topics that have both shared and unique characteristics, and draw a Venn diagram that shows how the topics are related.

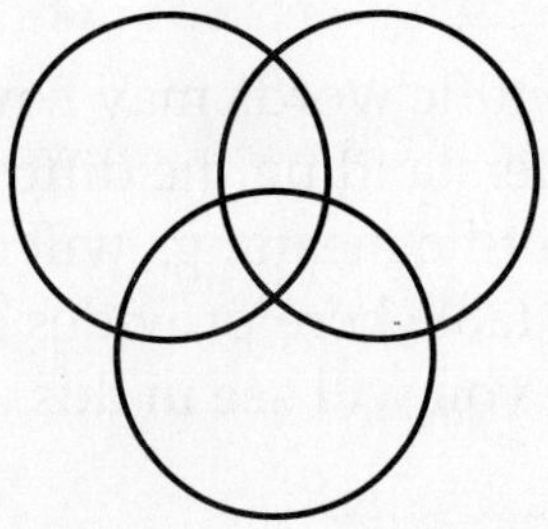

How to Make a Venn Diagram

1. **Circles** Draw overlapping circles. Draw one circle for each topic, and make sure that each circle partially overlaps the other circles.
2. **Main Topics** In each circle, write a topic that you want to compare with the topics in the other circles.
3. **Shared Characteristics** In the areas of the diagram where circles overlap, write the characteristics that the topics in the overlapping circles share.
4. **Unique Characteristics** In the areas of the diagram where circles do not overlap, write the characteristics that are unique to the topic of the particular circle.

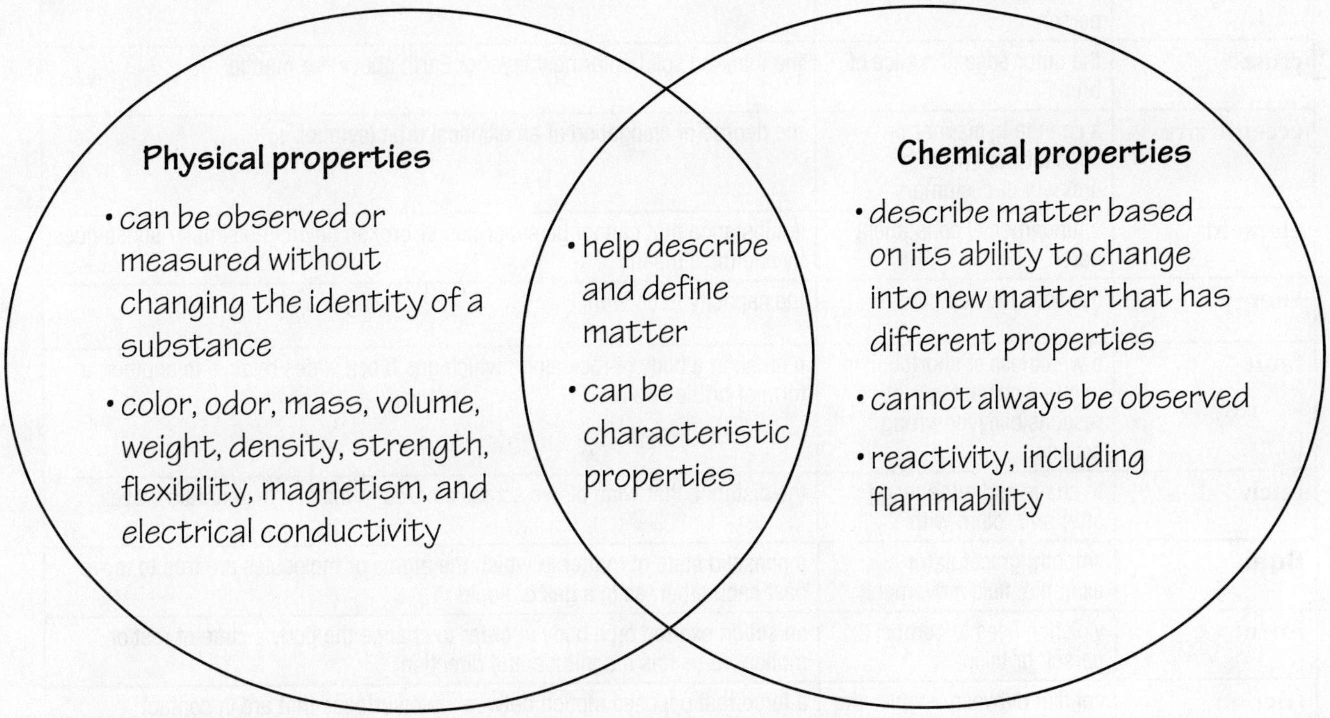

Physical properties
• can be observed or measured without changing the identity of a substance
• color, odor, mass, volume, weight, density, strength, flexibility, magnetism, and electrical conductivity
• help describe and define matter
• can be characteristic properties
Chemical properties
• describe matter based on its ability to change into new matter that has different properties
• cannot always be observed
• reactivity, including flammability

Everyday Words Used in Science

Scientific words may have common meanings that you already know. Understanding the difference between everyday meanings and scientific meanings will help you develop a scientific vocabulary. The table here provides common and scientific meanings for words that you will see in this textbook.

Word	Common meaning	Scientific meaning
abrasion	a spot, such as on the skin, that has been scraped or worn away	the grinding and wearing away of rock surfaces through the mechanical action of other rock or sand particles
atmosphere	general mood of the social environment	a mixture of gases that surrounds a planet, moon, or other celestial body
carbonation	full of carbon dioxide, as in soda water	the conversion of a compound into a carbonate
concentration	the act of focusing one's attention on something	the amount of a particular substance in a given quantity of a mixture, solution, or ore
condensation	the droplets of liquid on the outside of a glass or window	the change of state from a gas to a liquid
conservation	protection of something	the preservation and wise use of natural resources
creep	a crawling motion; an annoying or disgusting person	the slow downhill movement of weathered rock material
crust	the outer edge of a slice of bread	the thin and solid outermost layer of Earth above the mantle
eccentricity	a change in manner or conduct from what is ordinary or customary	the degree of elongation of an elliptical orbit (symbol, *e*)
element	a fundamental constituent part	a substance that cannot be separated or broken down into simpler substances by chemical means
energy	the ability to be active	the capacity to do work
fault	a weakness or shortcoming in one's character; responsibility for wrong actions	a break in a body of rock along which one block slides relative to another; a form of brittle strain
fetch	to chase and retrieve; go after and return with	the distance that wind blows across an area of the sea to generate waves
fluid	smooth; graceful (for example, fluid movement)	a nonsolid state of matter in which the atoms or molecules are free to move past each other, as in a gas or liquid
force	violence used to compel a person or thing	an action exerted on a body in order to change the body's state of rest or motion; force has magnitude and direction
friction	conflict between people who have opposing views	a force that opposes motion between two surfaces that are in contact
gas	short for gasoline; a liquid fuel used by vehicles, such as cars and buses	a form of matter that does not have a definite volume or shape

Word	Common meaning	Scientific meaning
gravity	seriousness (for example, the gravity of the situation)	a force of attraction between objects that is due to their masses and that decreases as the distance between the objects increases
inertia	resistance to change	the tendency of an object to resist a change in motion unless an outside force acts on the object
kettle	a metal pot used for cooking or boiling water	a bowl-shaped depression in a glacial drift deposit
legend	a person who has done great deeds; an old story of such deeds	a list of map symbols and their meanings
mass	a quantity of material that has an unspecified shape	a measure of the amount of matter in an object
matter	a subject of concern or topic of discussion	anything that has mass and takes up space
mineral	a substance required by animals or plants for proper development	a natural, usually inorganic solid that has a characteristic chemical composition, an orderly internal structure, and a characteristic set of physical properties
model	a miniature representation of a larger object	a pattern, plan, representation, or description designed to show the structure or workings of an object, system, or concept
motion	movement	an object's change in position relative to a reference point
organic	an organism or object produced without the use of synthetic drugs, fertilizers, or hormones	a covalently bonded compound that contains carbon, excluding carbonates and oxides
period	a punctuation mark used to indicate the end of a sentence	a unit of geologic time that is longer than an epoch but shorter than an era
phase	a distinguishable stage in a cycle	the change in the illuminated area of one celestial body as seen from another celestial body
pressure	the burden of mental stress	the amount of force exerted per unit area of a surface
product	something available for sale (for example, a computer product)	a substance that forms in a chemical reaction
relief	a lessening of pain or discomfort; aid given in time of trouble	the difference between the highest and lowest elevations in a given area; the variations in elevation of a land surface
revolution	the overthrow of one government and the substitution with another (for example, the American Revolution)	the motion of a body that travels around another body in space; one complete trip along an orbit
solution	the answer to a problem	a homogeneous mixture throughout which two or more substances are uniformly dispersed
star	a person who is highly celebrated in a particular field	a large celestial body that is composed of gas and that emits light
table	a piece of furniture that has a flat, horizontal surface	an orderly arrangement of data
theory	an assumption based on limited knowledge	a system of ideas that explains many related observations and is supported by a large body of evidence acquired through scientific investigation
volume	a measure of how loud a sound is	a measure of the size of a body or region in three-dimensional space

Analyzing Science Terms

You can unlock the meaning of an unfamiliar science term by analyzing its word parts. Many parts of scientific words carry a meaning that derives from Latin or Greek. The parts of words listed below provide clues to the meanings of many science terms.

Word part or root	Meaning	Application
a-	not, without	abiotic
astr-, aster-	star	astronomy
bar-, baro-	weight, pressure	barometer
batho-, bathy-	depth	batholith, bathysphere
circum-	around	circum-Pacific, circumpolar
-cline	lean, slope	anticline, syncline
-duct-	to lead, draw	conduction
eco-	environment	ecology, ecosystem
epi-	on	epicenter
ex-, exo-	out, outside of	exosphere, exfoliation, extrusion
geo-	earth	geode, geology, geomagnetic
-graph	write, writing	seismograph
hydro-	water	hydrosphere
hypo-	under	hypothesis
iso-	equal	isoscope, isostasy, isotope
-lith, -lithic	stone	Neolithic, regolith
-log-	study	ecology, geology, meteorology
magn-	great, large	magnitude
mar-	sea	marine
meta-	among, change	metamorphic, metamorphism
-meter	to measure	thermometer, spectrometer
micro-	small	microquake
-morph, -morphic	form, shape	metamorphic
nebula-	mist, cloud	nebula
neo-	new	Neolithic
paleo-	old	paleontology, Paleozoic
ped-, pedo-	ground, soil	pediment
per-	through	permeable
peri-	around	perigee, perihelion
seism-, seismo-	shake, earthquake	seismic, seismograph
sol-	sun	solar, solstice
spectro-	look at, examine	spectroscope, spectrum
-sphere	ball, globe	geosphere, lithosphere
strati-, strato-	spread, layer	stratification, stratovolcano
terra-	earth, land	terracing, terrane
thermo-	heat	thermosphere, thermometer
top-, topo-	place	topographic
trop-, tropo-	turn, respond to	tropopause, troposphere

Math Skills

Fractions

Fractions represent numbers that are less than 1. In other words, fractions are a way of using numbers to represent a part of a whole. For example, if you have a pizza with 8 slices and you eat 2 of the slices, you have 6 out of the 8 slices, or $\frac{6}{8}$, of the pizza left. The top number in the fraction is called the *numerator*. The bottom number is called the *denominator*.

There are special rules for adding, subtracting, multiplying, and dividing fractions. **Figure 1** summarizes these rules.

Figure 1 Basic Operations for Fractions

	Rule and example
Multiplication	$\left(\frac{a}{b}\right)\left(\frac{c}{d}\right)=\left(\frac{ac}{bd}\right)$ $\left(\frac{2}{3}\right)\left(\frac{4}{5}\right)=\frac{8}{15}$
Division	$\frac{a}{b}\div\frac{c}{d}=\frac{\left(\frac{a}{b}\right)}{\left(\frac{c}{d}\right)}=\frac{ad}{bc}$ $\frac{2}{3}\div\frac{4}{5}=\frac{\left(\frac{2}{3}\right)}{\left(\frac{4}{5}\right)}=\frac{(2)(5)}{(3)(4)}=\frac{10}{12}$
Addition and subtraction	$\frac{a}{b}\pm\frac{c}{d}=\frac{ad\pm bc}{bd}$ $\frac{2}{3}-\frac{4}{5}=\frac{(2)(5)-(3)(4)}{(3)(5)}=-\frac{2}{15}$

Practice

1. Perform the following calculations:

a. $\frac{7}{8}+\frac{1}{3}=$

b. $\frac{7}{8}\times\frac{1}{3}=$

c. $\frac{7}{8}\div\frac{1}{3}=$

d. $\frac{7}{8}-\frac{1}{3}=$

Percentages

Percentages are the same as other fractions except that in a percentage the whole (or the number in the denominator) is considered to be 100. Any percentage, $x\%$, can be read as x out of 100. For example, if you completed 50% of an assignment, you completed $\frac{50}{100}$, or $\frac{1}{2}$, of the assignment.

Percentages can be calculated by dividing the part by the whole. Your calculator displays a decimal value when it solves a division problem that has an answer that is less than 1. The decimal value can be written as a fraction. For example, 0.45 can be written as the fraction $\frac{45}{100}$.

An easy way to calculate a percentage is to divide the part by the whole and then multiply by 100. This multiplication moves the decimal point two positions to the right and gives you the number that would be over 100 in a fraction. So, $0.45 = 45\%$.

Try this example:

> You scored 73 out of 92 problems on your last exam. What was your percentage score?

First, divide the part by the whole to get a decimal value. The fraction $\frac{73}{92} = 0.7935$, which is equal to $\frac{79.35}{100}$.

Then, multiply by 100 to find the percentage: $0.7935 \times 100 = 79.35\%$.

Practice

1. The mass of the oxygen atom in a water molecule is 16.00 u. A water molecule has a total molar mass of 18.01 u. What percentage of the mass of water is made up of oxygen?
2. A candy bar contains 14 g of fat. The total fat contains 3.0 g of saturated fat and 11 g of unsaturated fat. What percentage of the fat is saturated? What percentage is unsaturated?

Exponents

An exponent is a number that is a superscript to the right of another number. The best way to explain how an exponent works is with an example. In the value 5^4, 4 is the exponent on 5. The number with its exponent means that 5 is multiplied by itself 4 times.

$$5^4 = 5 \times 5 \times 5 \times 5 = 625$$

Exponent are powers.

You will frequently hear exponents referred to as *powers*. Using this terminology, one could read the above equation as *five to the fourth power equals 625.* Keep in mind that any number raised to the zero power is equal to 1. Also, any number raised to the first power is equal to itself:

$$5^1 = 5$$

Figure 2 summarizes the rules for dealing with exponents.

Figure 2 Rules for Dealing with Exponents

	Rule	Example
Zero power	$x^0 = 1$	$7^0 = 1$
First power	$x^1 = x$	$6^1 = 6$
Multiplication	$(x^n)(x^m) = x^{(n+m)}$	$(x^2)(x^4) = x^{(2+4)} = x^6$
Division	$\frac{x^n}{x^m} = x^{(n-m)}$	$\frac{x^8}{x^2} = x^{(8-2)} = x^6$
Exponents that are fractions	$x^{1/n} = \sqrt[n]{x}$	$4^{1/3} = \sqrt[3]{4} = 1.5874$
Exponents raised to a power	$(x^n)^m = x^{nm}$	$(5^2)^3 = 5^6 = 15,625$

Roots are the opposite of exponents.

The symbol for a square root is $\sqrt{\ }$. The value underneath this symbol is equal to a number times itself. It is also possible to have roots other than the square root. For example, $\sqrt[3]{x}$ is a cube root, which means that if you multiply some number, n, by itself 3 times, you will get the number x, or $x = n \times n \times n$.

We can turn our example of $5^4 = 625$ around to solve for the fourth root of 625.

$$\sqrt[4]{625} = 5$$

Taking the nth root of a number is the same as raising that number to the power of $1/n$. Therefore, $\sqrt[4]{625} = 625^{1/4}$.

Use a calculator to solve exponents and roots.

You can solve problems involving exponents and roots easily by using a scientific calculator. Many calculators have dedicated keys for squares and square roots. But what do you do if you want to find other powers, such as cubes and cube roots? Most scientific calculators have a key with a caret symbol, (^), that is used to enter exponents. If you type in "5^4" and hit the equals sign or the enter key, the calculator will display the answer 625.

Many scientific calculators have a key with the symbol $\sqrt[x]{\ }$ that you can use to enter roots. When using this key, enter the root first. To solve the problem of the fourth root of 625, you would type "4 $\sqrt[x]{\ }$ 625," and the calculator would return the answer 5. If your calculator does not have the root key, you may be able to enter the root as a fraction if your calculator has a key that allows you to enter fractions. In this case you would use the exponent key and the fraction key to enter "625^ $\frac{1}{4}$." If your calculator does not have a fraction key, you can enter the decimal equivalent of the fractional exponent to find the root. Instead of entering $\frac{1}{4}$ as the exponent, enter "625^0.25," because 0.25 is equal to $\frac{1}{4}$.

Practice

1. Perform the following calculations:

a. $9^1 =$

b. $(3^3)^5 =$

c. $\frac{2^8}{2^2} =$

d. $(14^2)(14^3) =$

e. $11^0 =$

f. $6^{1/6} =$

Order of Operations

Use the following phrase to remember the correct order for long mathematical problems: *Please Excuse My Dear Aunt Sally*. This phrase stands for "Parentheses, Exponents, Multiplication, Division, Addition, Subtraction." **Figure 3** summarizes these rules.

Figure 3 Order of Operations

Step	Operation
1	**Parentheses** Simplify groups inside parentheses. Start with the innermost group, and work out.
2	**Exponents** Simplify all exponents.
3	**Multiplication and Division** Perform multiplication and division in order from left to right.
4	**Addition and Subtraction** Perform addition and subtraction in order from left to right.

Try the following example:

$$4^3 + 2 \times [8 - (3 - 1)] = ?$$

1. Simplify the operations inside parentheses. Begin with the innermost parentheses:

$$(3 - 1) = 2$$
$$4^3 + 2 \times [8 - 2] = ?$$

Move on to the next-outer brackets:

$$[8 - 2] = 6$$
$$4^3 + 2 \times 6 = ?$$

2. Simplify all exponents:

$$4^3 = 64$$
$$64 + 2 \times 6 = ?$$

3. Perform multiplication:

$$2 \times 6 = 12$$
$$64 + 12 = ?$$

4. Solve the addition problem:

$$64 + 12 = 76$$

Practice

1. $2^3 \div 2 + 4 \times (9 - 2^2) =$
2. $\dfrac{2 \times (6 - 3) + 8}{4 \times 2 - 6} =$

Geometry

Shapes are a useful way to model many objects and substances studied in science. For example, many of the properties of a wheel can be understood by using a perfect circle as a model.

Therefore, knowing how to calculate the area or the volume of certain shapes is a useful skill in science. Equations for the area and volume of several geometric shapes are provided in **Figure 4.**

Figure 4 Geometric Areas and Volumes

Geometric shape	Useful equations
Rectangle 	$area = lw$
Circle 	$area = \pi r^2$ $circumference = 2\pi r$
Triangle 	$area = \frac{1}{2}bh$
Sphere 	$surface\ area = 4\pi r^2$ $volume = \frac{4}{3}\pi r^3$
Cylinder 	$volume = \pi r^2 h$
Rectangular box 	$surface\ area = 2(lh + lw + hw)$ $volume = lwh$

Practice

1. A cylinder has a diameter of 14 cm and a height of 8 cm. What is the cylinder's volume?
2. Calculate the surface area of a 4 cm cube.
3. Will a sphere with a volume of 76 cm^3 fit in a rectangular box that is 7 cm × 4 cm × 10 cm?

Algebraic Rearrangements

Often in science, you will need to determine the value of a variable from an equation written as an algebraic expression.

Algebraic expressions contain constants and variables. *Constants* are numbers that you know and that do not change, such as 2, 3.14, and 100. *Variables* are represented by letters, such as x, y, a, and b. Variables in equations are unspecified quantities and are also called the *unknowns*.

An algebraic expression contains one or more of the four basic mathematical operations: addition, subtraction, multiplication, and division. Constants, variables, or terms made up of both constants and variables can be involved in the basic operations.

Solve for the variable.

To find the value of some variable, you need to simplify the expression by rearranging the equation. Ideally, after you have finished rearranging the equation, you will end up with a simple equation that tells you the value of the variable.

To get from a complicated equation to a simpler one, you need to isolate the variable on one side of the equation. You can do so by performing the same operations on both sides of the equation until the variable is alone. Because both sides of the equation are equal, if you do the same operation on both sides of the equation, the results will still be equal.

Look at the following simple problem:

$$\boxed{8x = 32}$$

In this equation, you need to solve for the variable x. You can add, subtract, multiply, or divide anything to or from one side of an equation as long as you do the same thing to the other side of the equation. In this case, we need to get rid of the 8 so that the x is by itself. If we divide both sides by 8, we have this equation:

$$\frac{8x}{8} = \frac{32}{8}$$

The 8s on the left side of the equation cancel each other out, and the fraction $\frac{32}{8}$ can be reduced to give the whole number 4.

$$x = 4$$

Next, consider the following equation:

$$x + 2 = 8$$

Remember that you can add or subtract the same quantity from each side. To isolate x, you need subtract 2 from each side:

$$x + 2 - 2 = 8 - 2$$
$$x + 0 = 6$$
$$x = 6$$

Now, consider one more equation:

$$-3(x - 2) + 4 = 29$$

One way to solve this more complicated expression is to follow the order of operations in reverse order to isolate x. First, subtract the 4.

$$-3(x - 2) + 4 - 4 = 29 - 4$$
$$-3(x - 2) = 25$$

Now, divide by –3.

$$\frac{-3(x - 2)}{-3} = \frac{25}{-3}$$

$$x - 2 = -8.3$$

Now, only the expression that was inside the parentheses remains on the left side of the equation. You can find the value of x by adding 2 to both sides of the equation.

$$x - 2 + 2 = -8.3 + 2$$
$$x = -6.3$$

Practice

1. Rearrange each of the following equations to give the value of the variable indicated with a letter:
   a. $8x - 32 = 128$
   b. $6 - 5(4a + 3) = 26$
   c. $-2(3m + 5) = 14$
   d. $\left[8\frac{(8 + 2z)}{32}\right] + 2 = 5$
   e. $\frac{(6b + 3)}{3} - 9 = 2$

Scientific Notation

Often, scientists deal with very large or very small quantities. For example, in one second, about 3,000,000,000,000,000,000 electrons' worth of charge pass through a standard light bulb; and the ink required to make the dot over an *i* in this textbook has a mass of about 0.000000001 kg.

Obviously, it is very time-consuming to read and write such large and small numbers. It is also easy to lose track of the zeros and make an error when doing calculations with numbers that have many zeros. Powers of the number 10 are used to keep track of the zeros in large and small numbers. Numbers that are expressed as some power of 10 multiplied by another number with only one digit to the left of the decimal point are said to be written in *scientific notation.*

Use exponents to write large numbers.

Study the positive powers of 10 shown in **Figure 5.** The number of zeros corresponds to the exponent to the right of the 10. The number for 10^4 is 10,000; it has 4 zeros.

But how can you use the powers of 10 to simplify large numbers such as the number of electron-sized charges passing through a light bulb? The number 3,000,000,000,000,000,000 can be written as 3 × 1,000,000,000,000,000,000. To write the large number as an exponent, count the zeros—there are 18 zeros. Therefore, the exponent is 10^{18}. So, 3,000,000,000,000,000,000 can be expressed as 3×10^{18} in scientific notation.

Use exponents to write small numbers.

Now, you know how to simplify really large numbers, but how do you simplify really small numbers, such as 0.000000001? To simplify numbers that are less than 1, use negative exponents.

Next, study the negative powers of 10. To determine the exponent that you need to use, count the number of decimal places that you must move the decimal point to the right so that only one digit is to the left of the decimal point. To simplify the mass of the ink in the dot on an *i*, 0.000000001 kg, you must move the decimal point 9 decimal places to the right for the numeral 1 to be on the left side of the decimal point. In scientific notation, the mass of the ink is 1×10^{-9} kg.

Figure 5 Powers of 10

Power of 100	Decimal equivalent
10^4	10,000
10^3	1,000
10^2	100
10^1	10
10^0	1
10^{-1}	0.01
10^{-2}	0.001
10^{-3}	0.0001

Use scientific notation to write any number.

Values that have more than one nonzero number can also be written using scientific notation. For example, 5,943,000,000 is 5.943×10^9 when expressed in scientific notation. The number 0.0000832 is 8.32×10^{-5} when expressed in scientific notation.

When you use scientific notation in calculations, follow the rules for using exponents in calculations. When you multiply two numbers expressed in scientific notation, add the exponents, as shown below.

$$(4 \times 10^5) \times (2 \times 10^3) = [(4 \times 2) \times 10^{(5+3)}] = 8 \times 10^8$$

When you divide two numbers expressed in scientific notation, subtract the exponents.

Practice

1. Rewrite the following values using scientific notation:
   a. 12,300,000 m/s
   b. 0.0000000000045 kg
   c. 0.0000653 m
   d. 55,432,000,000,000 s
   e. 273.15 K
   f. 0.00062714 kg

SI

One of the most important parts of scientific research is being able to communicate your findings to other scientists. Today, scientists need to be able to communicate with other scientists all around the world. They need a common language in which to report data. If you do an experiment in which all of your measurements are in pounds and you want to compare your results to those of a French scientist whose measurements are in grams, you will need to convert all of your measurements. For this reason, the *Système International d'Unités*, or SI, was created in 1960.

You are probably accustomed to measuring distance in inches, feet, and miles. Most of the world, however, measures distance in centimeters (cm), meters (m), and kilometers (km). The meter is the official SI unit for measuring distance. **Figure 6** lists the SI units for some common measurements.

Prefixes are used to indicate quantities.

Notice that centi*meter* and kilo*meter* each contain the word *meter*. When dealing with SI units, you frequently use the base unit, in this case the meter, and add a prefix to indicate that the quantity that you are measuring is a multiple of that unit. Most SI prefixes indicate multiples of 10. For example, the centimeter is 1/100 of a meter. Any SI unit with the prefix *centi-* will be 1/100 of the base unit. A centigram is 1/100 of a gram.

Figure 6 Some SI Units

Quantity	Unit name	Symbol
Length	meter	m
Mass	kilogram	kg
Time	second	s
Temperature	kelvin	K
Amount of substance	mole	mol
Electric current	ampere	A
Pressure	pascal	Pa
Volume	cubic meters	m^3

Figure 7 Some SI Prefixes

Prefix	Symbol	Exponential factor
giga-	G	10^9
mega-	M	10^6
kilo-	k	10^3
hecto-	h	10^2
deka-	da	10^1
deci-	d	10^{-1}
centi-	c	10^{-2}
milli-	m	10^{-3}
micro-	μ	10^{-6}
nano-	n	10^{-9}
pico-	p	10^{-12}
femto-	f	10^{-15}

How many meters are in a *kilo*meter? The prefix *kilo-* indicates that the unit is 1,000 times the base unit. A kilometer is equal to 1,000 meters. Multiples of 10 make dealing with SI values much easier than values such as feet or gallons. To convert from feet to miles, you must remember a large conversion factor, 1.893939×10^{-4} miles per foot. To convert from kilometers to meters, you need to look only at the prefix to know that you will multiply by 1,000.

Figure 7 lists possible prefixes and their meanings. When working with a prefix, simply take the unit symbol and add the prefix symbol to the front of the unit symbol. For example, the symbol for *kilometer* is written "km."

Practice

1. Convert each value to the requested units:
   a. 0.035 m to decimeters
   b. 5.24 m^3 to cubic centimeters
   c. 13,450 g to kilograms

Significant Figures

Significant figures indicate the precision of a value. You can use the rules in the following list to determine the number of significant figures in a reported value. After you have reviewed the rules, use **Figure 8** to check your understanding of the rules. Cover up the second column of the table, and try to determine how many significant figures each number has.

You can use a few rules to determining the number of significant figures in a measurement.

1. All nonzero digits are significant.

   Example 1,246 (four significant figures, shown in red)

2. Any zeros between significant digits are also significant.

   Example 1,206 (four significant figures)

3. If the value does not contain a decimal point, any zeros to the right of a nonzero digit are not significant.

   Example 1,200 (two significant figures)

4. Any zeros to the right of a significant digit and to the left of a decimal point are significant.

   Example 1,200. (four significant figures)

5. If a value has no significant digits to the left of a decimal point, any zeros to the right of the decimal point and to the left of a nonzero digit are not significant.

   Example 0.0012 (two significant figures)

6. If a measurement is reported that ends with zeros to the right of a decimal point, those zeros are significant.

   Example 0.1200 (four significant figures)

If you are adding or subtracting two measurements, your answer can have only as many decimal positions as the value with the least number of decimal places. The final answer in the following problem has five significant figures. It has been rounded to two decimal places because 0.04 g has only two significant figures.

$$\begin{array}{r} 134.050\text{ g} \\ -0.04\text{ g} \\ \hline 134.01\text{ g} \end{array}$$

Figure 8 Significant Figures

Measurement	Number of significant figures	Rule
12,345	5	1
2,400 cm	2	3
305 kg	3	2
2,350. cm	4	4
234.005 K	6	2
12.340	5	6
0.001	1	5
0.002450	4	5 and 6

When you multiply or divide measurements, your final answer can have only as many significant figures as the value with the least number of significant figures. Examine the following multiplication problem.

$$\begin{array}{r} 12.0\text{ cm}^2 \\ \times 0.04\text{ cm} \\ \hline 0.5\text{ cm}^3 \end{array}$$

The final answer has been rounded to one significant figure because 0.04 cm has only one. When performing both types of operations (addition/subtraction and multiplication/division), round the result after you complete each type of operation, and round the final result.

Practice

1. Determine the number of significant figures in each of the following measurements:
   a. 65.04 mL
   b. 564.00 m
   c. 0.007504 kg
   d. 1,210 K
2. Perform each of the following calculations, and report your answer with the correct number of significant figures and units:
   a. 0.004 dm + 0.12508 dm
   b. 340 m ÷ 0.1257 s
   c. 40.1 kg × 0.2453 m^2
   d. 1.03 g – 0.0456 g

Graphing Skills

Line Graphs

Usually, in laboratory experiments, you will control one variable and see how changes in that variable affect another variable. Line graphs can show these relationships clearly. Suppose that you want to determine the rate of a plant's growth by measuring the growth of a plant over time. In this experiment, you would control the time intervals at which the plant height is measured. Thus, time is the *independent variable*. The change in the height of the plant that you measure depends on the time interval that you choose. So, plant height is the *dependent variable*. The table in **Figure 1** shows some sample data from an experiment that measured the rate of plant growth.

When you make a line graph, always plot the independent variable on the x-axis. For the plant-height experiment, the axis will be labeled "Time (days)." Remember to include the units in your axis label. Pick a range for your graph that is just large enough to enter all of your data points. From the data in **Figure 1,** you can see that plant height was measured over 35 days. Therefore, the x-axis should have a range of 0 days to 35 days.

Plot the dependent variable on the y-axis. In this case, the y-axis is labeled "Plant height (cm)" and has a range from 0 cm to 5 cm.

When you draw the axes for your graph, you want to use as much of the available space as possible. You should label the grid marks for each axis at intervals that evenly divide up the data range. In the graph in **Figure 2,** the y-axis has grid marks at intervals of 1, and the x-axis has grid marks at intervals of 5. Notice that the interval of the grid marks on the x-axis is not the same interval at which the data were measured.

Think of your graph as a grid with lines running horizontally from the y-axis and vertically from the x-axis. To plot a point, find the x-value for that point on the x-axis. Follow the vertical line from the x-axis until it intersects the horizontal line from the y-axis at the corresponding y-value. At the intersection of these two lines, place your point. After you have plotted all of your data points, connect each point with a straight line. **Figure 2** shows a line graph of the data in **Figure 1.**

Figure 1 Data for Plant Growth Versus Time

Time (days)	Plant height (cm)
0	1.43
7	2.16
14	2.67
21	3.25
28	4.04
35	4.67

Figure 2 Line Graph for Plant Growth Versus Time

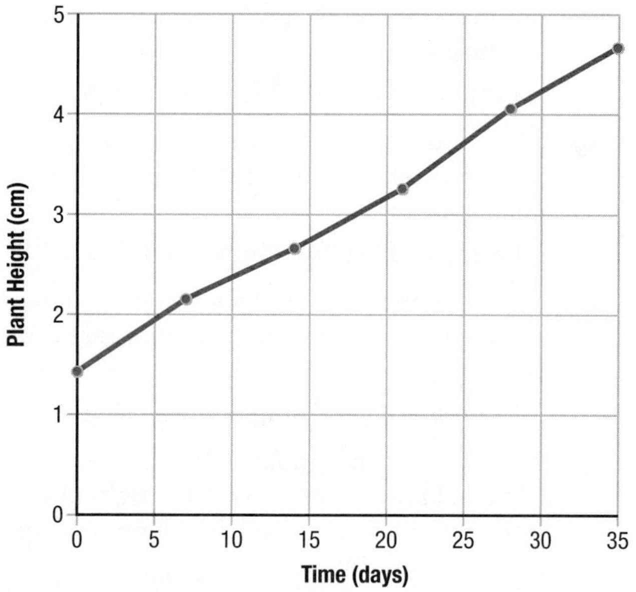

Practice

1. Create a line graph of the data below.

Time (days)	Plant height (cm)
0	1.46
7	2.67
14	3.89
21	4.82

2. Compare the graph you made with **Figure 9.** What can you conclude about the two groups of plants?

Scatter Plots

Some groups of data are best represented in a graph called a *scatter plot.* Scatter plots are often used to find trends, or general patterns, in data. A scatter plot is similar to a line graph. The data points are plotted on the graph that has an x-axis and a y-axis, but each point is not connected with a line. Instead, a straight best-fit line is drawn through the data points to show the overall trend. A best-fit line is a single, smooth line that represents all of the data points without necessarily going through all of them. To find a best-fit line, pick a line that is equidistant from as many data points as possible. Examine the graph in **Figure 3.**

Figure 3

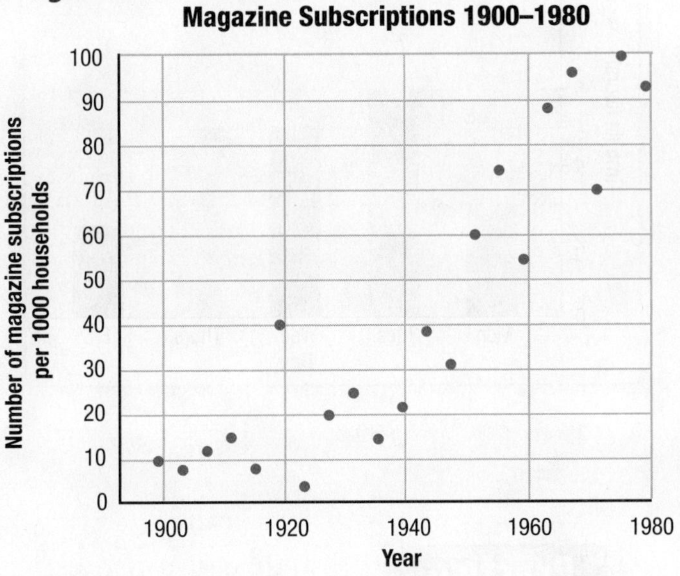

Figure 4

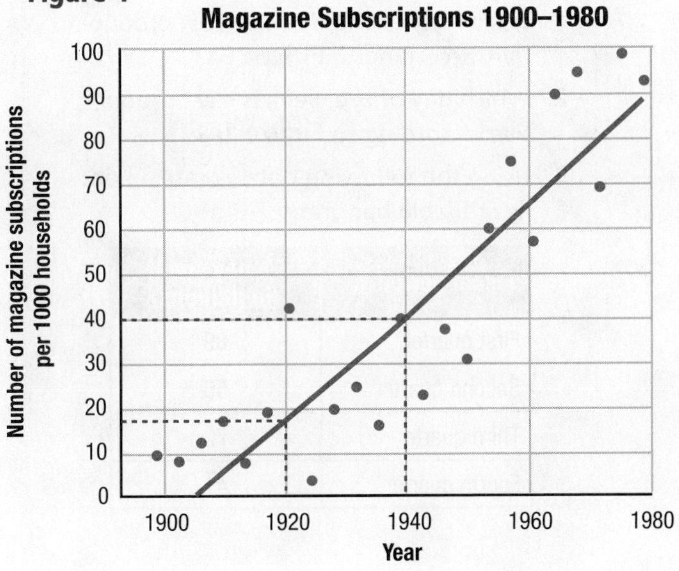

If we connected all of the data points with lines, the lines would create a zigzag pattern. It would be hard to see the general pattern in the data. But if we find a best-fit line, we can see a trend more clearly. The trend in a scatter plot depends on the data. The best-fit line in **Figure 4** shows that magazine subscriptions increased.

If you pick two points on the best-fit line, you can estimate the line's slope. The slope will tell you the average rate of increase in magazine subscriptions. By using the dotted lines in **Figure 4,** you can estimate the data point for 1940 as 18 magazine subscriptions per 1,000 households and for 1960 as 42 magazine subscriptions per 1,000 households. The slope is (42 subscriptions – 18 subscriptions) divided by (1960 – 1940). The slope tells you that there is an increase of 24 subscriptions per 1,000 households every 20 years.

Practice

1. Create a scatter plot, and draw a best-fit line for the data below.

Year	Magazine subscriptions per 1,000 households
1918	17
1931	15
1942	42
1954	36
1967	64
1980	73
1992	60
2008	70

2. What does the best-fit line represent?
3. If these data are from a different city than the data in **Figure 4,** what conclusions could you draw about the two cities?

Bar Graphs

Bar graphs should be used for noncontinuous data. They make it easy to compare data quickly when you have one value for multiple items. You can see from **Figure 5** that Jupiter has the largest radius and Mercury has the smallest radius. You could easily arrange the planets in order of size.

Figure 5

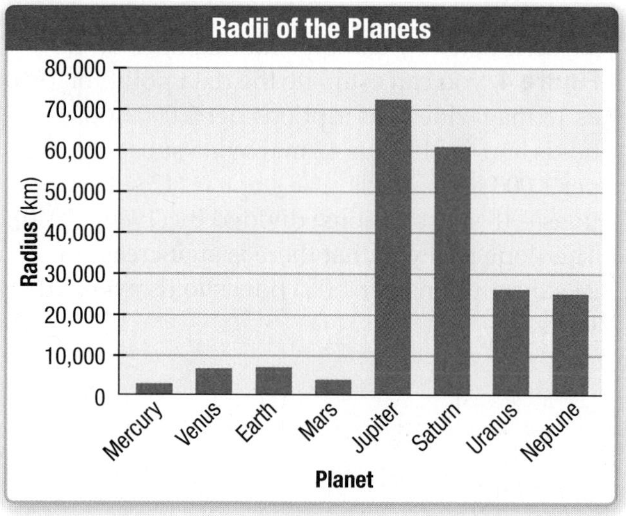

Choosing the scale of a bar graph will make identifying trends in the data easier. Examine **Figure 6** below.

Figure 6

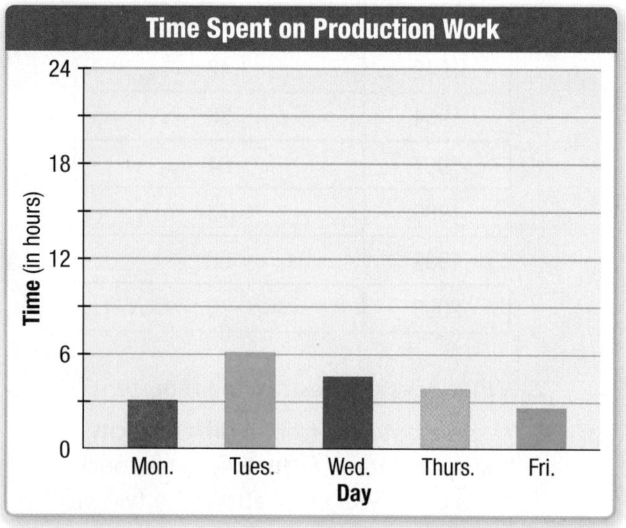

The data are represented accurately in **Figure 6,** but you cannot draw conclusions quickly. Remember that when you create a graph, you want the graph to be as clear as possible. The same data are graphed in **Figure 7,** but the range and scale of the y-axis are smaller than they are in **Figure 6.** The trend in the data is much easier to see in **Figure 7.**

Figure 7

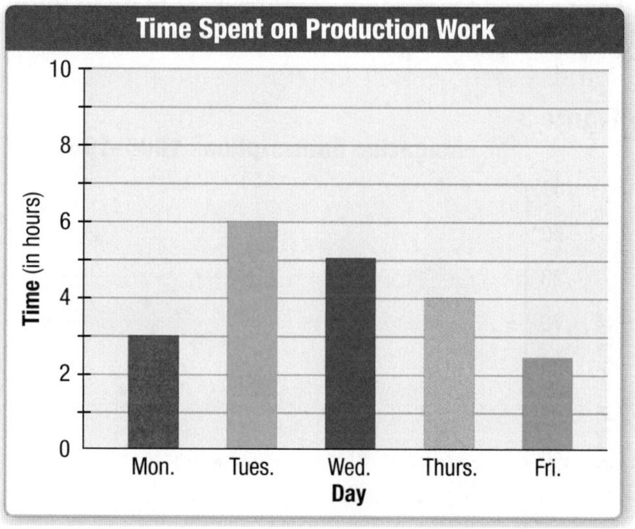

Practice

1. Which day of the week is most productive, according to **Figure 14**?
2. Which day of the week is least productive, according to **Figure 14**?
3. Using the following data, create an easily readable bar graph.

Fiscal period	Money spent (in millions)
First quarter	89
Second quarter	56
Third quarter	72
Fourth quarter	41

Pie Graphs

Pie graphs are an easy way to visualize how parts make up a whole. Often, pie graphs are made from percentage data, such as the data in **Figure 8.**

To create a pie graph, begin by drawing a circle. Because percentages represent parts of 100, imagine dividing the circle into 100 equal parts. Then, you need to figure out how much of the pie each part takes up. It is easiest to start with the largest piece. To graph the data in **Figure 8,** you would start with the data for oxygen. Half of the circle equals 50 parts, so you know that 46% will be slightly less than half of the pie. Shade a piece that is less than half, and label it "Oxygen." Continue making pie pieces for each element until the entire pie graph has been filled. Each element should be a different color to make the graph easy to read as the pie graph in **Figure 9** shows.

You can also use a protractor to construct a pie graph. This method is especially helpful when your data cannot be converted into simple percentages. First, convert the percentages to degrees by dividing each number by 100 and multiplying that result by 360. Next, draw a circle, and make a vertical mark across the top of the circle. Use a protractor to measure the largest angle from your table. Mark this angle along the circumference. For example, 32.9% would be 118° because $32.9/100 = 0.329$ and $0.329 \times 360 = 118$.

Figure 8 Composition of Earth's Crust

Element	Percentage of Earth's crust
Oxygen	46%
Silicon	28%
Aluminium	8%
Iron	6%
Calcium	4%
Sodium	2%
Magnesium	2%
Potassium	2%
Titanium	1%
All remaining elements	1%

To create the next pie piece, measure a second angle from the second mark to make a third mark along the circumference. Continue measuring the angles for each segment until all of your slices are measured. Draw lines from the marks to the center of the circle, and label each slice.

Figure 9 Composition of Earth's Crust

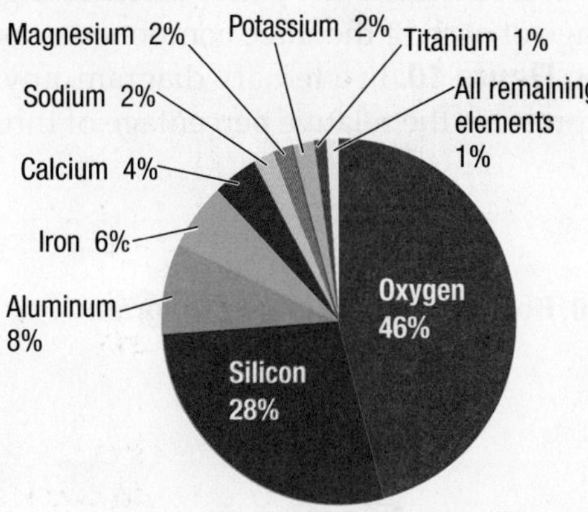

Practice

1. Use the data below to make a pie graph.

Kind of land use	Percentage of total land
Grassland and rangeland	29
Wilderness and parks	13
Urban	7
Wetlands and deserts	4
Forest	30
Cropland	17

2. If humans use half of forests and grasslands, as well as all croplands and urban areas, how much of the total land do humans use?

Ternary Diagrams

Ternary graphs, or ternary diagrams, show three variables on the same plot. Earth scientists use ternary diagrams to show composition of rocks and minerals and the physical states of rock material. The most common use of ternary diagrams is to represent the relative percentage of three components, such as three minerals or three elements.

The composition of any point on a ternary diagram can be described by first determining the percentage of each of the three components, as shown in **Figure 10.** In a ternary diagram, any point represents the relative percentage of three components: A, B, and C. The three components must always add up to 100%. In other words, the total composition of the mineral or rock represented by a given point on a ternary diagram is a combination of A, B, and C, so that

$$x\%\ A + y\%\ B + z\%\ C = 100\%$$

Readings of composition are stated as % A, % B, and % C. For example, the point in the diagram below has a composition of 40% A, 50% B, and 10% C. In most ternary diagrams, areas of the triangle are given names so that scientists can identify a rock or mineral by its name, rather than by its composition.

Figure 10 How to Read a Ternary Diagram

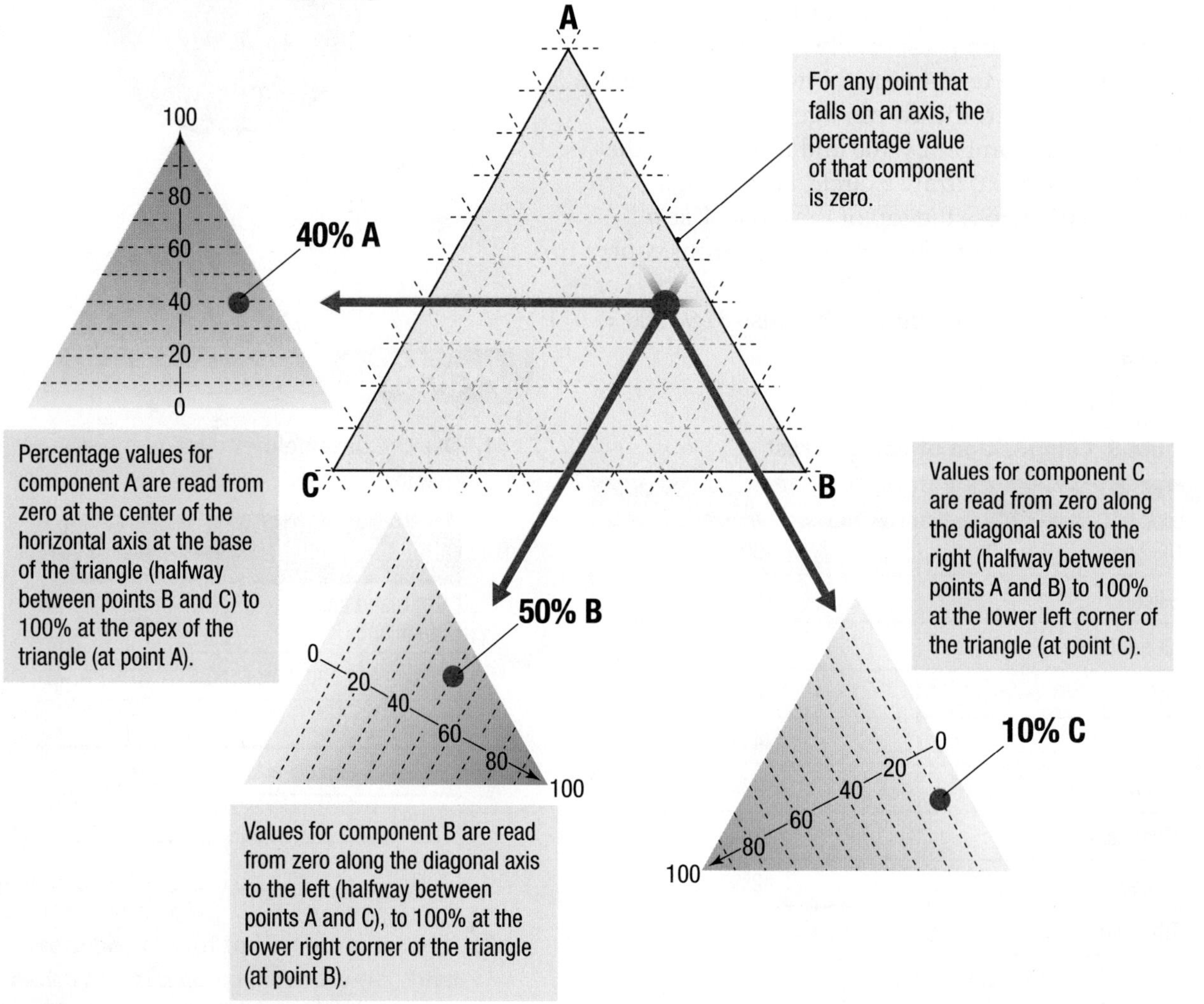
A
B
C
For any point that falls on an axis, the percentage value of that component is zero.
40% A
100
80
60
40
20
0
Percentage values for component A are read from zero at the center of the horizontal axis at the base of the triangle (halfway between points B and C) to 100% at the apex of the triangle (at point A).
50% B
0
20
40
60
80
100
Values for component B are read from zero along the diagonal axis to the left (halfway between points A and C), to 100% at the lower right corner of the triangle (at point B).
10% C
0
20
40
60
80
100
Values for component C are read from zero along the diagonal axis to the right (halfway between points A and B) to 100% at the lower left corner of the triangle (at point C).

Chemistry Skills Refresher

Atoms and Elements

Every object in the universe is made up of particles of matter. Matter is anything that has mass and takes up space. An element is a substance that cannot be separated into simpler substances by chemical means. Elements cannot be separated in this way because each element consists of only one kind of atom. An atom is the smallest unit of an element that maintains the properties of that element.

Atomic Structure Atoms are made up of small particles called *subatomic particles*. The three major types of subatomic particles are **electrons, protons,** and **neutrons** as shown in **Figure 1.** Electrons have a negative electrical charge, protons have a positive charge, and neutrons have no electrical charge. The protons and neutrons are packed close to one another and form the **nucleus.** The protons give the nucleus a positive charge. The electrons of an atom are located in a region around the nucleus known as an **electron cloud.** The negatively charged electrons are attracted to the positively charged nucleus.

Figure 1 Atomic Structure

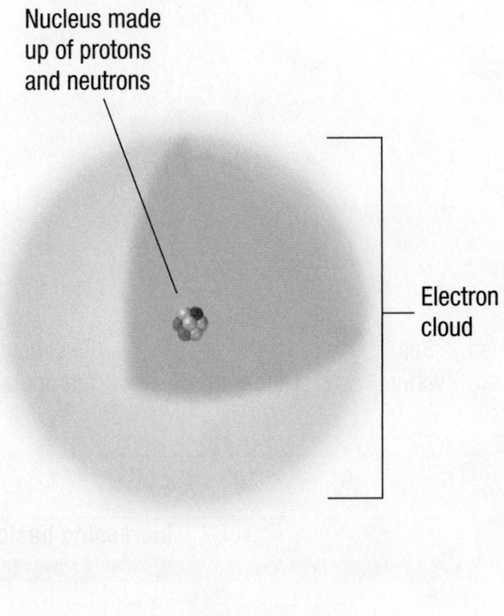

Atomic Number To help in the identification of elements, scientists have assigned an **atomic number** to each kind of atom. The atomic number is equal to the number of protons in the atom. Atoms that have the same number of protons are all of the same element. An uncharged, or electrically neutral, atom has an equal number of protons and electrons. Therefore, the atomic number is also equal to the number of electrons in an uncharged atom. The number of neutrons, however, can vary for a given element. Atoms that have different numbers of neutrons but are of the same element are called **isotopes.**

Periodic Table of the Elements In a periodic table, the elements are arranged in order of increasing atomic number. Each element in the table is found in a separate box. In each horizontal row of the table, each element has one more electron and one more proton than the element to its left. Each row of the table is called a **period.** Changes in chemical properties across a period correspond to changes in the elements' electron arrangements. Each vertical column of the table, known as a **group,** contains elements that have similar properties. The elements in a group have similar chemical properties because they have the same number of electrons in their outer energy level. For example, the elements helium, neon, argon, krypton, xenon, and radon all have similar properties and are known as the noble gases.

Molecules and Compounds

When the atoms of two or more elements are joined chemically, the resulting substance is called a **compound.** A compound is a new substance that has properties different from those of the elements that compose it. For example, water, H_2O, is a compound formed when atoms of hydrogen, H, and oxygen, O, combine. The smallest complete unit of a compound that has all of the properties of that compound is called a **molecule.**

Chemical Formulas

A chemical formula indicates the elements that make up a compound. The chemical formula also indicates the relative number of atoms of each element present. For example, the chemical formula for water is H_2O, which indicates that each water molecule consists of two atoms of hydrogen and one atom of oxygen.

Chemical Equations

A chemical reaction occurs when a chemical change takes place. (During a chemical change, new substances that have new properties form.) A chemical equation is a useful way of describing a chemical reaction by means of chemical formulas. The equation indicates the substances that react and the products. For example, when carbon and oxygen combine, they can form carbon dioxide. The equation for this reaction is as follows:

$$C + O_2 \longrightarrow CO_2$$

Acids, Bases, and pH

An ion is an atom or group of atoms that has an electrical charge because it has lost or gained one or more electrons. When an acid, such as hydrochloric acid, HCl, is mixed with water, the acid separates into ions. An acid is a compound that produces hydrogen ions, H^+, in water. The hydrogen ions then combine with a water molecule to form a hydronium ion, H_3O^+. A solution that contains hydronium ions is an acidic solution. A base, on the other hand, is a substance that produces hydroxide ions, OH^-, in water.

To determine whether a solution is acidic or basic, scientists measure pH. **pH** is a measure of how many hydronium ions are in solution. The pH scale ranges from 0 to 14. The middle point, pH = 7, is neutral, neither acidic nor basic. Acids have a pH of less than 7; bases have a pH of more than 7. The lower the number is, the stronger the acid is. The higher the number is, the stronger the base is. **Figure 2** shows the pH of some common substances.

Figure 2 pH Measurements of Some Common Substances

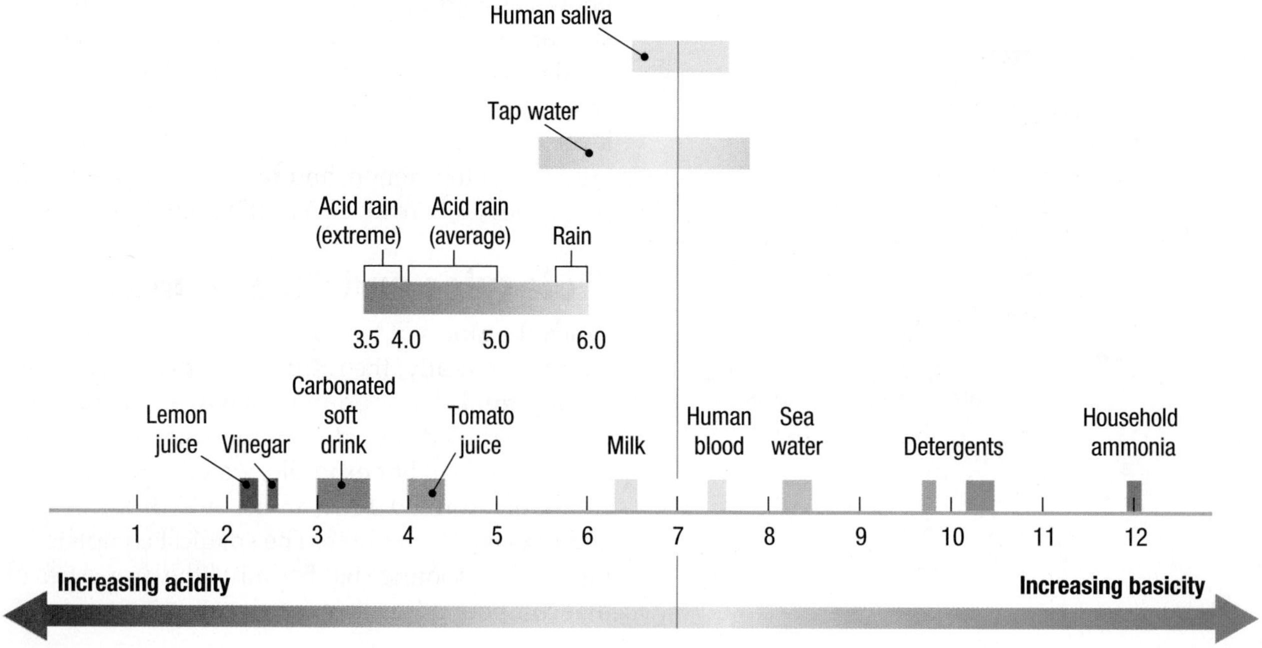

Physics Skills Refresher

Mass
All matter has mass. Mass is the amount of matter that makes up an object. For example, Earth is made of a very large amount of matter and therefore has a large mass. An object's mass can be changed only by changing the amount of matter in the object.

Weight
Weight is different from mass. Weight is a measure of the gravitational force that is exerted on an object. Objects that have large mass are heavier than objects that have a small mass, even if the objects are the same size.

Density
The mass per unit of volume of a substance is density. Thus, a material's density is the amount of matter it has in a given space. To find density, both mass and volume must be measured. Density is calculated by using the following equation:

$$density = \frac{mass}{volume}$$

Density is expressed in units of mass over units of volume. Most commonly, density is expressed as grams per cubic centimeter (g/cm^3) or as kilograms per cubic meter (kg/m^3).

The density of a particular substance is always the same at a given temperature and pressure. The density of one substance is usually different from the density of other substances. Therefore, density is a useful property for identifying substances.

Concentration
A measure of the amount of one substance that is dissolved in another substance is concentration. The substance that is dissolved is the solute. The substance that dissolves another substance is the solvent. Concentration is calculated by using the following equation:

$$concentration = \frac{mass\ of\ solute}{volume\ of\ solvent}$$

Concentration is expressed as mass of solute divided by volume of solvent. Most commonly, concentration is expressed as grams per milliliter (g/mL) or as kilograms per liter (kg/L).

Forces
In science, a force is simply a push or a pull. All forces have both magnitude and direction. Force is expressed using a unit called a newton (N). All forces are exerted by one object on another object.

More than one force can be exerted on an object at the same time. The net force is the force that results from combining all the forces exerted on an object. When forces are in the same direction, net force is calculated by using the following equation:

$$net\ force = force\ A + force\ B$$

When forces are in the opposite direction, net force is calculated by using the following equation:

$$net\ force = force\ A - force\ B$$

Pressure
The force exerted over a given area is pressure. Pressure can be calculated by using the following equation:

$$pressure = \frac{force}{area}$$

The SI unit for pressure is the pascal (Pa). Other common units of pressure include bars and atmospheres.

Speed
The rate at which an object moves is its speed. Speed depends on the distance traveled and the time taken to travel that distance. Speed is calculated by using the following equation:

$$speed = \frac{distance}{time}$$

The SI unit for speed is meters per second (m/s). Other units commonly used to express speed are kilometers per hour, feet per second, and miles per hour.

Velocity

The speed of an object in a particular direction is velocity. Speed and velocity are not the same, even though they are calculated using the same equation. Velocity must include a direction, so velocity is described as speed in a certain direction. For example, the speed of a plane that is traveling south at 600 km/h is 600 km/h. The velocity of a plane that is traveling south at 600 km/h is 600 km/h south.

Velocity can also be thought of as the rate of change of an object's position. An object's velocity remains constant only if its speed and direction don't change. Therefore, constant velocity occurs only along a straight line.

Acceleration

The rate at which velocity changes is called acceleration. Acceleration can be calculated by using the following equation:

$$acceleration = \frac{final\ velocity - starting\ velocity}{time\ it\ takes\ to\ change\ velocity}$$

Velocity is expressed in meters per second (m/s), and time is expressed in seconds (s). Therefore, acceleration is expressed in meters per second per second (m/s/s), or meters per second squared (m/s^2).

Inertia

The tendency of an object to resist any change in motion is called *inertia*. Because of inertia, an object at rest will remain at rest until something causes it to move. A moving object continues to move at the same speed and in the same direction unless something acts on it to change its speed or direction.

Momentum

The property of a moving object that is equal to the product of the object's mass and velocity is momentum. Momentum is calculated by using the following equation:

$$momentum = mass \times velocity, \text{ or } p = mv$$

The SI unit for momentum is kilograms multiplied by meters per second (kg•m/s). When a moving object hits another object, some or all of the momentum of the first object is transferred to the other object. If only some of the momentum is transferred, the rest of the momentum stays with the first object.

Thermodynamics

The study of the behavior of the flow of energy in natural systems is thermodynamics. The laws of thermodynamics describe some of the basic truths of how energy behaves in the universe. Many Earth processes involve the flow of energy through the Earth system.

The First Law of Thermodynamics This law is often called the Law of Conservation of Energy. Simply stated, this law states that energy can be changed from one form to another but that it cannot be created or destroyed. Energy constantly changes from one form to another, but the total amount of energy available in the universe is constant.

The Second Law of Thermodynamics This law states that in all energy exchanges, if no energy enters or leaves the system, the potential energy of the new state will always be less than that of the initial state. In other words, no form of energy converts entirely to another form of energy without losing some energy as heat. So, the entropy of an isolated system always increases as time increases. Entropy is a measure of disorder, or randomness, of energy and matter.

The Third Law of Thermodynamics This law states that if all of the thermal motion of molecules, or kinetic energy, were removed from a system, a temperature called absolute zero would be reached. Absolute zero is in a temperature of 0 Kelvin or –273.15 degrees Celsius.

$$\text{absolute zero} = 0\ K = -273.15\ °C$$

Technology Skills

Using Search Engines

The World Wide Web is filled with information on almost any topic imaginable. Search engines make it possible to sort through this vast amount of information to find what you need.

A search engine is software that you use to search for Web pages by using keywords. Some search engines let you search huge databases that cover large portions of the Web. Other search engines may search a limited but more focused range of pages, such as the pages on a single Web site or journal articles in a specific subject area.

Although the scope of search engines may differ, most search engines work in a similar way. For example, consider Scirus, a search engine that searches for scientific information. You can access Scirus by entering the Web address *www.scirus.com* into the address bar of your Web browser, as **Figure 1** shows.

Figure 1 Address Bar of Web Browser

Once you are on the Scirus home page, you will see a search box. To find information on a specific topic, type into the search box keywords that you think are most likely to target the web pages about that topic. Then, click on the Search button to start the search. For example, if you are researching black holes, you would type the keywords "black hole." The search engine will return a list of pages containing those keywords. You can then click on the links to visit the pages that seem most promising for your research goals.

Use the help pages to improve your searches.

Although all search engines work in a similar way, they are all slightly different. To make your searches more effective on a particular site, look at the site's help page or advanced search page for helpful tips and advanced search options.

If you search a broad topic, you may get too many Web sites in your search results. The help page or advanced search page can also help you determine the best way to narrow your search so that you will find a more manageable number of Web sites. For example, these pages may allow you to select other keywords to include or exclude from your search, tell you where to look for the keywords on Web pages, and tell you what types of Web sites to include in the search. Suppose that you wanted to find only Web pages that contain information about neutrinos and black holes. You could use the advanced search page to help narrow your results, as **Figure 2** shows.

Figure 2 Advanced Search Page

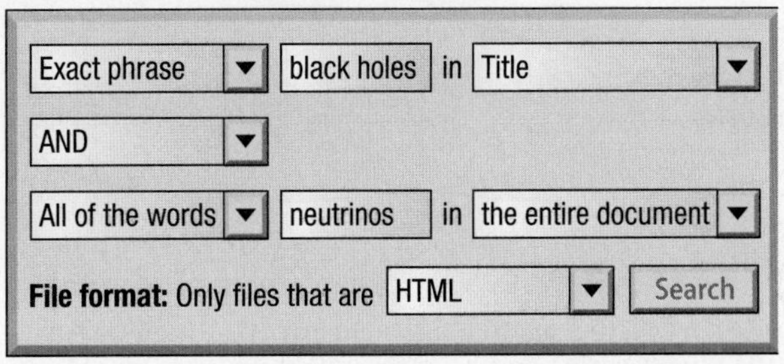

Check the reliability of Web sites.

When you visit a site to find factual information, remember to check the source of the information. Anyone can post information on the Internet, but the information does not have to be correct. Usually, government and educational institutions are reliable sources of information; personal Web sites may not contain accurate information.

Practice

1. Use an Internet search engine to find information about gamma rays. List three Web sites, and discuss how reliable each one might be.

APPENDIX B

How Search Engines Work

Most search engines rely on Boolean logic. Boolean logic uses three words—*AND, OR,* and *NOT*—to define the relationships between topics. These three words, known as *Boolean operators*, can be used to make very effective searches.

Use the AND operator to find multiple terms.

When you use the AND operator between two search terms, both of the terms must be present in the results. For example, to find Web pages that contain both the words *work* and *power*, you would enter both search terms, as **Figure 3** shows. The shaded area of the Venn diagram in **Figure 3** represents the results of this search.

Figure 3 Search Results Using AND

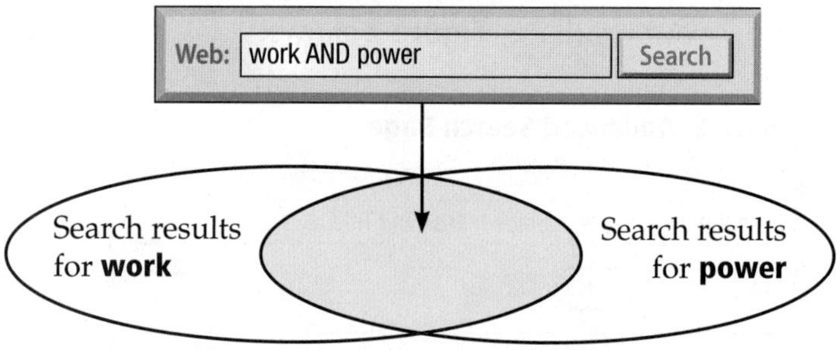

Note that the AND operator is in all capital letters. Some search engines require that you use all capital letters to distinguish the operators from the search terms.

Use the OR operator to find either term.

When you use the OR operator between two search terms, the results should show pages that contain either one or both of the terms. If you use the OR operator, your search result will have more Web pages, as the shaded area in **Figure 4** shows.

Figure 4 Search Results Using OR

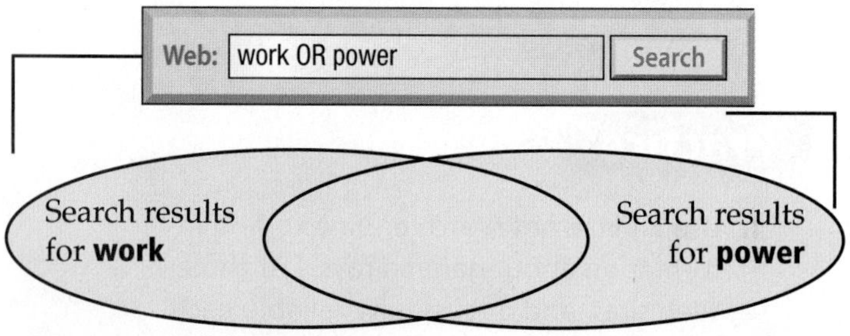

Use the NOT operator to exclude a term.

When you use the NOT operator before a word, your search results should not contain that term. This operator will help you narrow your search by excluding a certain set of Web pages that commonly have the word of the topic that you are looking for. **Figure 5** shows a Venn diagram of the search results for the search "work NOT power."

Figure 5 Search Results Using NOT

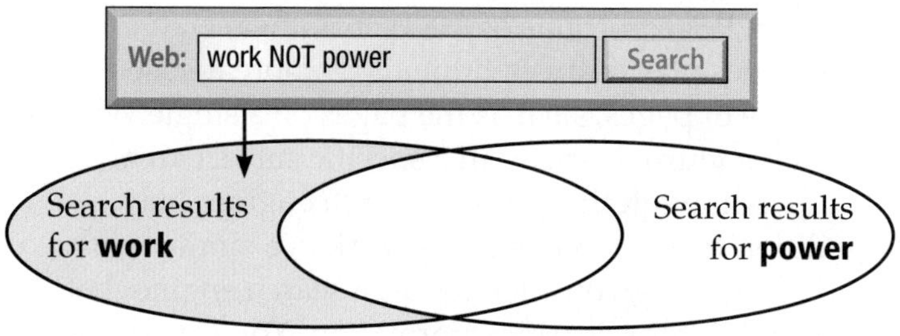

Using more than one Boolean operator will make your searches more specific. For example, to find Web sites that contain information about work and power, but not electricity, you would search "work AND power NOT electricity."

Some search engines do not support the direct use of Boolean operators. You may have to go to the advanced search page to do Boolean searches. Many advanced search pages allow you to fill in search fields that are similar to the Boolean operators, as **Figure 6** shows.

Figure 6 Search Fields and Boolean Operators

Advanced search field	Boolean operator
All of the words	AND
Any of the words	OR
None of the words	NOT

Practice

1. Write a Boolean search query to find Web pages that must contain the word *rock* and either the word *sedimentary* or the word *metamorphic.*
2. Draw a Venn diagram to represent the search query that you wrote in item 1.

Technology in the Library

Libraries are one of the best places to find highly reliable reference materials, such as encyclopedias, dictionaries, and nonfiction books. Printed materials are often subject to editing and peer review, unlike much of the information on the Internet. Libraries also have books, magazines, newspapers, and journals that may not be available on the Internet or are expensive to access.

If you do not have a specific source in mind, the best place to start your library research is the library's catalog. Most libraries now have systems for searching their catalogs by computer. So, searching the catalog is similar to using a search engine on the Web. When you are doing a library search, you should specify whether the keywords are for a subject, a title, or an author.

Once you have the results of a catalog search, you will need to know where to find the books that come up in your search results. Most libraries use one of two classification systems—the Library of Congress system or the Dewey decimal system. Whichever system your library uses, you should write down the call numbers for the books that you want to find from your catalog search. Then, use a map or directory of the library to find the books.

Both classification systems organize nonfiction books by subject, as **Figure 7** and **Figure 8** show. Most large libraries use the Library of Congress system, whereas many smaller libraries use the Dewey decimal system.

Figure 7 Dewey Decimal System

Number on book binding	Subject
000–099	General works
100–199	Philosophy and psychology
200–299	Religion
300–399	Social studies
400–499	Language
500–599	Pure sciences
600–699	Technology
700–799	Arts
800–899	Literature
900–999	History

Figure 8 Library of Congress Classification System

Letter on book binding	Subject
A	General works
B	Philosophy, psychology, and religion
C–F	History
G–H	Geography and social sciences (e.g., anthropology)
J	Political science
K	Law
L	Education
M	Music
N	Fine arts
P	Literature
Q	Science
R	Medicine
S	Agriculture
T	Technology
U–V	Military and naval science
Z	Bibliography and library science

Practice

1. What system does your school library use to classify books?
2. List three magazines or journals in your school or local library that could contain current information on scientific research.
3. Name the title and call number for a book on science.

Scientific Methods

Scientists gain new knowledge and understanding of the natural world by using scientific methods. These methods are sometimes presented in a series of ordered steps. However, there is no single scientific method. The steps may be done in a different order, or certain steps may be repeated in some scientific investigations.

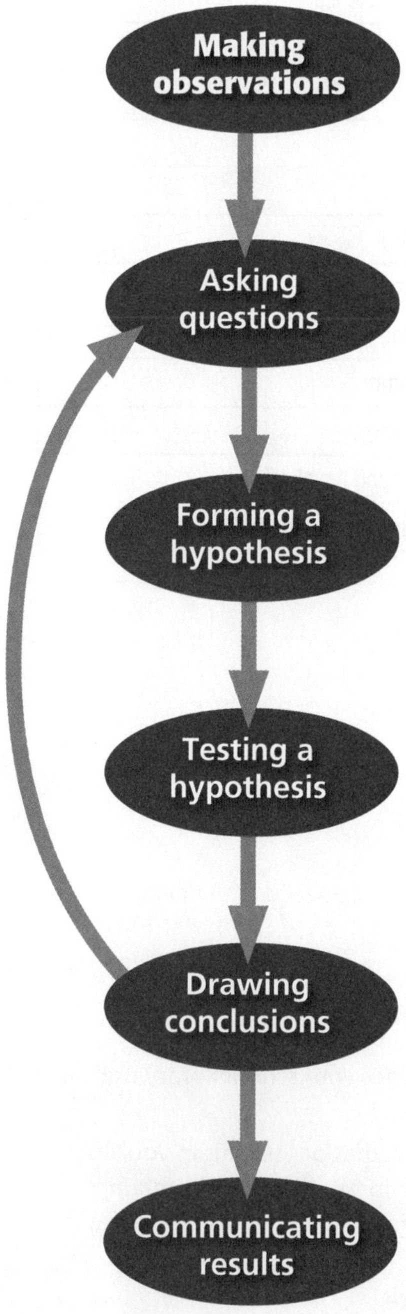

Making Observations Observing objects and events in the natural world is an important step in any scientific method. Observation is usually the starting point of any scientific study. You also make observations when doing experiments. It is important to keep detailed records of observations so that you can accurately remember them.

Asking Questions Careful observations eventually lead to questions. A good question should be specific and should serve as the focus for the entire investigation.

Forming a Hypothesis A hypothesis is a possible explanation or answer to your question. You do not know whether a hypothesis is the right answer until it is tested. You should be able to test your hypothesis to determine whether it is true or false. You should make predictions about what you think will happen if your hypothesis is true and what will happen if your hypothesis is false. These predictions can help you design an experiment to test the hypothesis.

Testing a Hypothesis Once you have a question, a hypothesis, and a set of predictions, you are ready to do an experiment to test the hypothesis. You should design your experiment to be as simple as possible, and you should consider which variables you want to control. Your design should also include plans about what instruments and materials you will use and how you will analyze the data that you collect.

Drawing Conclusions After you finish an experiment, you will determine whether your hypothesis is correct by examining your results. You may evaluate your hypothesis by seeing if your original predictions were correct. If your results do not support your hypothesis, they may lead you to ask more questions. You may need to form a new hypothesis, make new predictions, and perform a new or modified version of your experiment.

Communicating Results If you carry out an investigation that provides new information, you should publish your results. Others who read about your investigation may try to understand how you drew your conclusions. They may try your experiment to see if they get the same results or use your results to form new hypotheses and do new experiments.

Conducting Experiments

Many scientific experiments try to determine a cause-and-effect relationship—"When *A* happens, *B* happens." The *A* and the *B* in this relationship are variables, or changing quantities. The variable that you change intentionally in an experiment is called the *independent variable* and, in this case, is *A*. The *dependent variable*, *B*, changes in response to the changes in the independent variable.

Suppose that your experiment is seeking to answer the following question: "What happens to the rate of crystal formation when the temperature of the solution changes?" In this case, temperature would be the independent variable, and the rate of crystal formation would be the dependent variable. You would change the temperature and then measure the resulting change in rate. When you graph your results, independent variables are represented on the *x*-axis, and dependent variables are represented on the *y*-axis.

Make observations in the lab.

You should write down any observations that you make during an experiment, along with any data that you collect. Record the characteristics of the materials that you use, the conditions during your experiment, any changes that occur, and anything that you think might be relevant to the experiment. These observations will help you when you are reporting your results. They can also help you figure out why your experimental results may not be what you expected. Usually, a pen is used to record your observations in a lab notebook because people reading the notes later can be sure that you did not change your notes after the experiment.

Avoid measurement pitfalls.

One common error in taking measurements results from parallax. *Parallax* is an apparent shift in position caused by a change in viewing angle. To avoid parallax errors, always line up your eyes with the part of the measurement scale that you are reading.

Another common measurement error is recording the wrong units of measurement. Always check the instrument to make sure that you know which units it uses, and record those units.

Taking Measurements

It is important to note the limits of the tools that you use to collect data. The exactness of a measurement is called *precision*, and it is determined by the instrument that you use. Precision is reflected in the number of significant figures. When you record measurements, you should use the correct number of significant figures. Usually, instruments with a digital readout give you the correct number of significant figures. So, you can record the measurement exactly as you see it on the instrument. When you need to read the measurement from a scale on an instrument, you should record as many digits as are marked on the scale and estimate one more digit beyond that.

Measure volume with a graduated cylinder.

You should use a graduated cylinder when you need precise measurements of volume.

1. Place the graduated cylinder on a flat, level surface.
2. Make sure that you are at eye level with the surface of the liquid.
3. Read the mark closest to the liquid level. Because most liquids climb slightly up the glass walls of a graduated cylinder, they produce a curved surface called a *meniscus*, shown in **Figure 1.** You should always take volume readings from the bottom of the meniscus.

Tip Holding a piece of white paper behind the graduated cylinder can make the meniscus easier to see.

Figure 1 Meniscus in a Graduated Cylinder

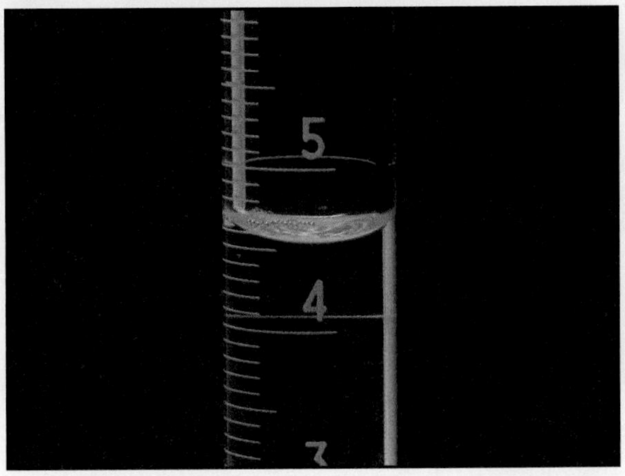

Measure mass with a balance.

A triple-beam balance, shown in **Figure 2,** can measure mass to a precision of 0.01 g.

1. Make sure that the balance is properly "zeroed." First, make sure that the balance is on a level surface. Then, slide all of the slider weights to zero. Turn the zero adjustment knob until the pointer is in line with the zero at the center of the arrow.
2. Place the object to be measured on the pan. **CAUTION** Never place chemicals or hot objects directly on the balance pan.
3. To determine the total mass of the object, add the readings from all three beams.
4. Move the largest slider weight to the right along the beam until the balance tips. Then, move the slider back one notch so that the beam tips back the other way. Repeat this step for the next-largest slider weight. Then, move the smallest slider weight to the right until the pointer points to the zero on the right end.
5. If you are measuring solid chemicals, start by putting a piece of weighing paper on the pan. Record the mass of the weighing paper. Then, place the chemical on the weighing paper. Measure the total mass of the chemical and paper. Then, subtract the mass of the paper to determine the mass of the chemical alone. You may use a similar method for measuring the mass of a liquid in a container.

Tip If you want to use a specified amount of a substance, move the sliders to the right by the amount of mass that you want to obtain. The balance will tip. Slowly add the substance until the balance points to zero.

Figure 2 Triple-Beam Balance

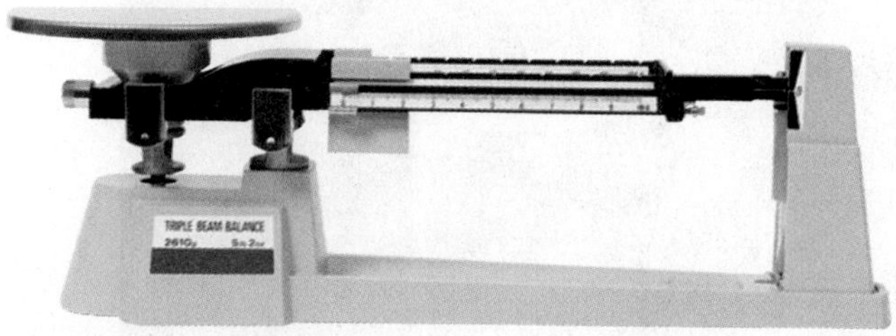

Measure temperature with a thermometer.

Digital thermometers and bulb thermometers are often used in the lab. Bulb thermometers consist of a column of liquid—either mercury or colored alcohol—in a glass tube, as shown in **Figure 3.** As the liquid heats up, it expands, so the column of liquid rises up the tube.

1. To measure temperature with a digital thermometer, immerse the probe in the liquid or touch it to an object. Wait for the digital readout to stabilize, and then record the temperature. Make sure that the thermometer is set to the desired scale (Celsius or Fahrenheit).
2. To measure temperature with a bulb thermometer, put the thermometer in the liquid to be measured. Wait for the level of liquid inside the thermometer to stabilize.
3. With your eyes level with the top of the liquid inside the thermometer, take the reading on the scale next to the column of liquid. Pay attention to the scale on the thermometer. The smallest unit marked on a bulb thermometer is usually 1 °C. These markings are close together, so you can only estimate half a unit between marks, or 0.05 °C.

CAUTION A glass thermometer can break if it hits a solid object or overheats. In addition to producing broken glass, the liquid inside will spill. If a mercury thermometer should ever break, immediately notify your teacher or another adult. Let your teacher clean up the spill. Do not touch the mercury. Because mercury is a hazardous substance, mercury thermometers are rarely used in class laboratories.

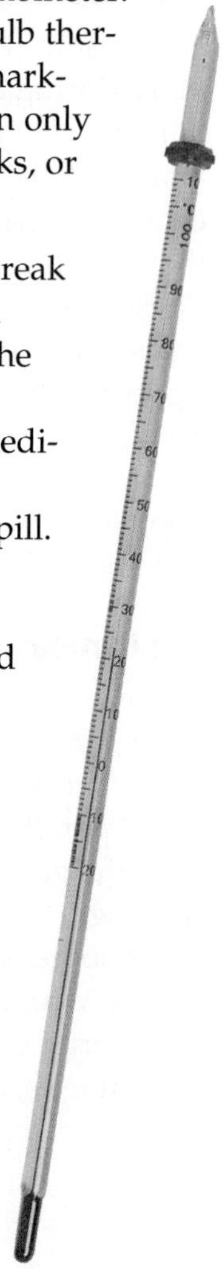

Figure 3 Alcohol Thermometer

Communicating Scientific Results

Whether you are writing a laboratory report for your teacher or submitting a paper to a scientific journal, you should use a similar structure to report the results of an experiment. Your lab report should contain enough information so that others can use it to reproduce your experiment and compare their results to yours. Laboratory reports should contain the same basic parts.

Start with a title.

Choose a title that clearly conveys the nature of the experiment. The title could describe the subject, the hypothesis, or the result. If you are doing an experiment from a lab manual, this title could be the same as the title of the experiment given in the manual.

Include background information.

The background section should briefly explain why your experiment is important. State the question that your experiment is trying to answer. You could also include a description of the initial observations that led you to the question. Sometimes, the background section includes the basic principles that you will use when you analyze your experiment.

State your hypothesis.

This section should state your hypothesis and your predictions of what will happen if the hypothesis is true and what will happen if the hypothesis is false. Your hypothesis is what you think will happen in the experiment. Often, a hypothesis is written as an "If . . . then" statement. The independent variable, or variable that you will change, should follow the "If" in the statement. The effect on the dependent variable should follow the "then" in the statement. Suppose that you want to find out if adding salt to water changes the boiling temperature of water. You would change the amount of salt that you add to water and measure the temperature at which the water boils. So, the amount of salt would be your independent variable, and the boiling temperature would be your dependent variable. Your hypothesis statement could be "If salt is added to water, the temperature at which water boils will increase."

List your materials before you start your experiment.

To make sure that you have everything that you need for your experiment, list all of the equipment and other supplies that you use in the experiment. For experiments taken from a lab manual, these materials are usually listed in the manual.

Describe the procedure that you used.

Detailed steps that describe exactly how you did your experiment are included in the procedure. Include details about how you set up the equipment, how you took your measurements, and what analysis or calculations you did with your data after collecting it. Your description should be detailed enough that someone else could reproduce the experiment exactly as you did it. If you are doing an experiment from a lab manual, you should write the steps in your own words and note anything that you did that was different from the procedure in the manual.

Record your observations, data, and analysis.

You should list all of the data you collected and show the results of any analysis or calculations that you performed with the data. It is often useful to present data or other results using tables or graphs. Also, include any observations that you made that might be relevant to your conclusions. Some experiments in lab manuals list specific questions that you should answer in your analysis.

End the report with your conclusions.

In your conclusions, you should discuss whether or not your experiment supports your original hypothesis. Remember that your experiment may not support your hypothesis. You can still explain why you think that the experiment did not turn out the way that you expected. You can also present a new or modified hypothesis and briefly describe additional experiments that could be done if you were to continue or expand your investigation. Some experiments in lab manuals list specific questions that you should answer in your conclusions.

Mapping Expeditions

Journey to Red River

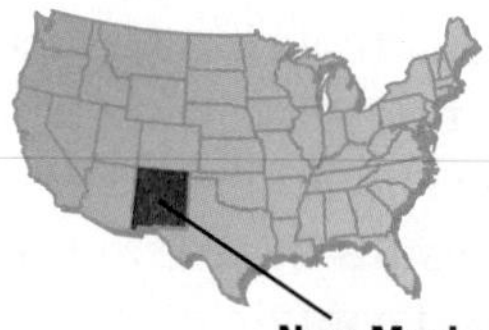

Materials
compass, magnetic, with degree markings (optional)
ruler, metric

How do you get from one place to another when you don't know the route? Whether you are planning a trip on foot or by car or boat, a map can be very handy. The ability to read a map can help you reach your destination quickly and safely and can help you avoid becoming disoriented and lost.

The topographic map on the facing page shows the area around Red River, New Mexico. Imagine that you are traveling to Red River to do some camping, hiking, and sightseeing. Study the map for a few moments, and note the locations of roads, creeks, hills, and other features. Then, answer the questions below.

1. Red River lies in northeastern New Mexico near the Colorado border. The magnetic declination in Red River is about 13°E. Draw a diagram that shows how you would adjust a magnetic compass to determine true north in Red River. Why is distinguishing true north from geomagnetic north important?
2. You set up a tent at Mallette Campground. If you walk in a straight line from your campsite to the cemetery at the base of Graveyard Canyon, how far will you walk? Show your work.
3. You decide to hike from St. Edwin Chapel to location A. What is your elevation at location A? How much higher than your starting point is your destination? (Elevations on the map are given in feet.)
4. Notice that the road in the lower-right corner of the map winds back and forth to make a series of hairpin turns. Why did the road designers build the road this way?
5. Most United States Geological Survey maps, including this one, were created in the early 1960s. Like most towns, Red River has changed in the last few decades. Which features of the map might not reflect how Red River looks today? Which features are probably still accurate?

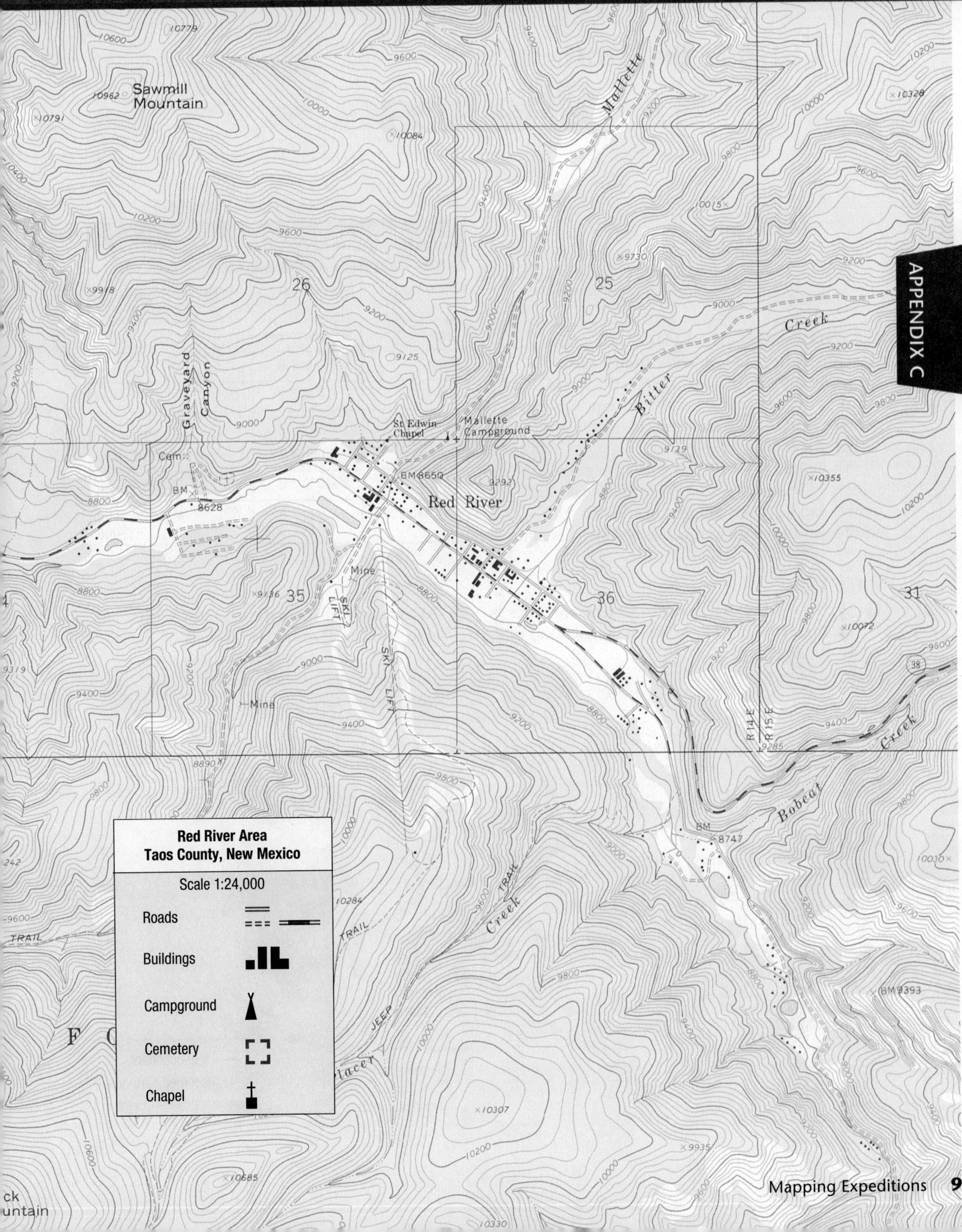
Red River Area
Taos County, New Mexico
Scale 1:24,000
Roads
Buildings
Campground
Cemetery
Chapel
Sawmill Mountain
Graveyard Canyon
Mallette
Bitter Creek
St Edwin Chapel
Mallette Campground
Red River
Cem
BM 8628
BM 8650
Mine
SKI LIFT
Bobcat Creek
BM 8747
BM 9393
TRAIL
JEEP
Creek
Placer
R 14 E
R 15 E
26
25
35
36
31
38

A Case of the Tennessee Shakes

Materials
road map of Tennessee

Did you know that almost 10,000 earthquakes occur every day? In fact, an earthquake likely is occurring right now somewhere in the world. Fortunately, less than 2% of the earthquakes that seismographs record are strong enough to do serious damage.

You might think that scientists are most interested in strong earthquakes. But weak earthquakes can tell a seismologist (a scientist who studies earthquakes) as much as strong ones can.

Earthquake Frequency (based on observations since 1900)

Descriptor	Magnitude	Average occurring annually
Great	8.0 and higher	1
Major	7.0 to 7.9	18
Strong	6.0 to 6.9	120
Moderate	5.0 to 5.9	800
Light	4.0 to 4.9	about 6,200
Minor	3.0 to 3.9	about 49,000
Very minor	2.0 to 2.9 1.0 to 1.9	about 365,000 about 29,200,000

Part 1

1. Examine the map below. Which tectonic plates are involved in most earthquakes that occur in North America?

2. At tectonic plate boundaries, most earthquake epicenters are densely distributed, or closely packed. Why do most earthquakes occur along tectonic plate boundaries?

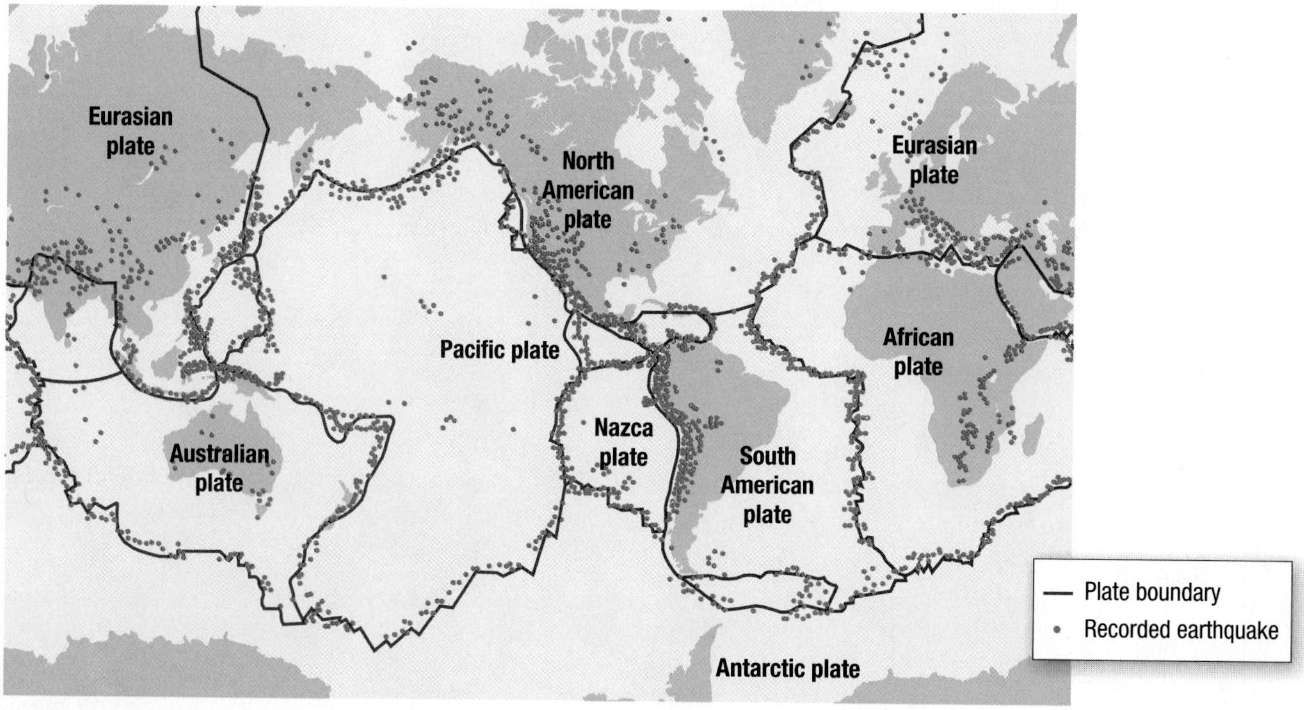

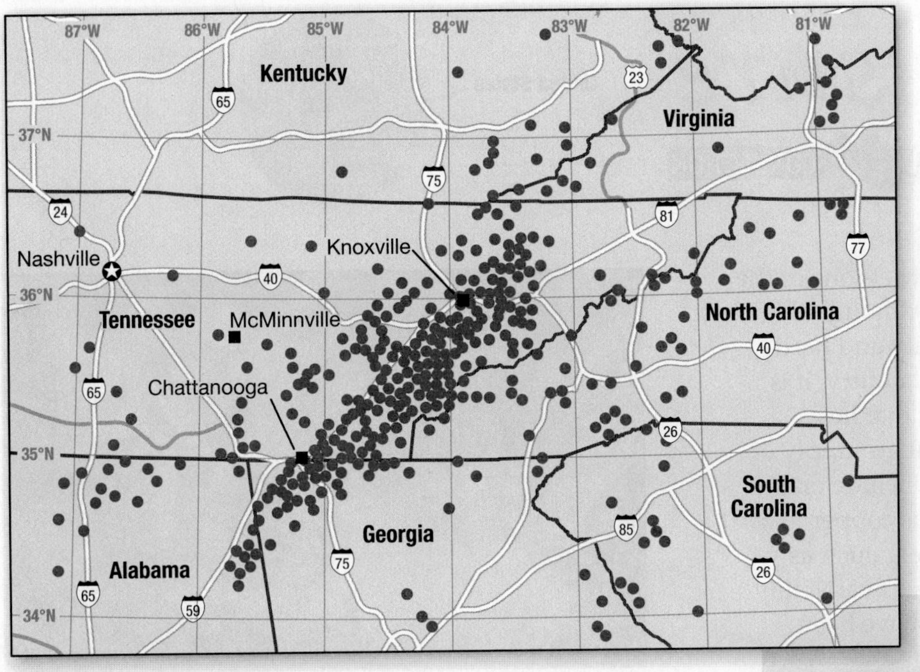

Each dot on this map represents the epicenter of an earthquake. Most of these earthquakes, which occurred over a 20-year period, were too weak to be felt by people.

3. Some earthquakes, however, occur in the interior of the United States, which is far from any plate boundary. Propose a hypothesis that explains these earthquakes.

Part 2

The map above shows the epicenters of earthquakes in eastern Tennessee. However, Tennessee is far from any plate boundary. Some scientists think that the earthquakes in this region are the result of an ancient fault that has been reactivated. Other scientists think that a new fault zone is forming in eastern Tennessee. If they are correct, eastern Tennessee may experience a major earthquake in this zone.

1. Use the map to describe the location of the eastern Tennessee seismic zone (ETSZ) in terms of longitude and latitude.
2. Name at least two major cities that are located in the ETSZ. How could a major earthquake affect these cities?
3. Two nuclear power plants are located in the ETSZ. Imagine that a company has plans to build a plant near McMinnville, Tennessee. The United States Geological Survey has hired you to advise this company about the risk of a major earthquake. Briefly describe what you would say in a letter to the company. Explain your reasoning as clearly as possible.

By using trench excavations, seismologist Karl Mueller can study sediments across the New Madrid fault in Tennessee to estimate the dates and magnitudes of past earthquakes.

Buried *Treasure*

ENVIRONMENTAL CONNECTION

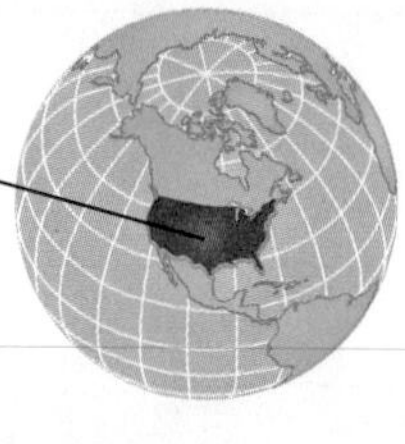

By many standards, the United States is one of the wealthiest countries in the world. Although this wealth is largely due to the ingenuity and hard work of the people who live in the country, it is also due to good fortune. The crust that lies beneath the United States holds a huge supply of natural resources. These resources include ores that contain precious metals, such as copper, silver, and gold, as well as fossil fuels, such as petroleum, coal, and natural gas. The availability and distribution of these resources have been important in shaping U.S. history.

This worker in California cuts through steel, an iron alloy, at 2,000 °F!

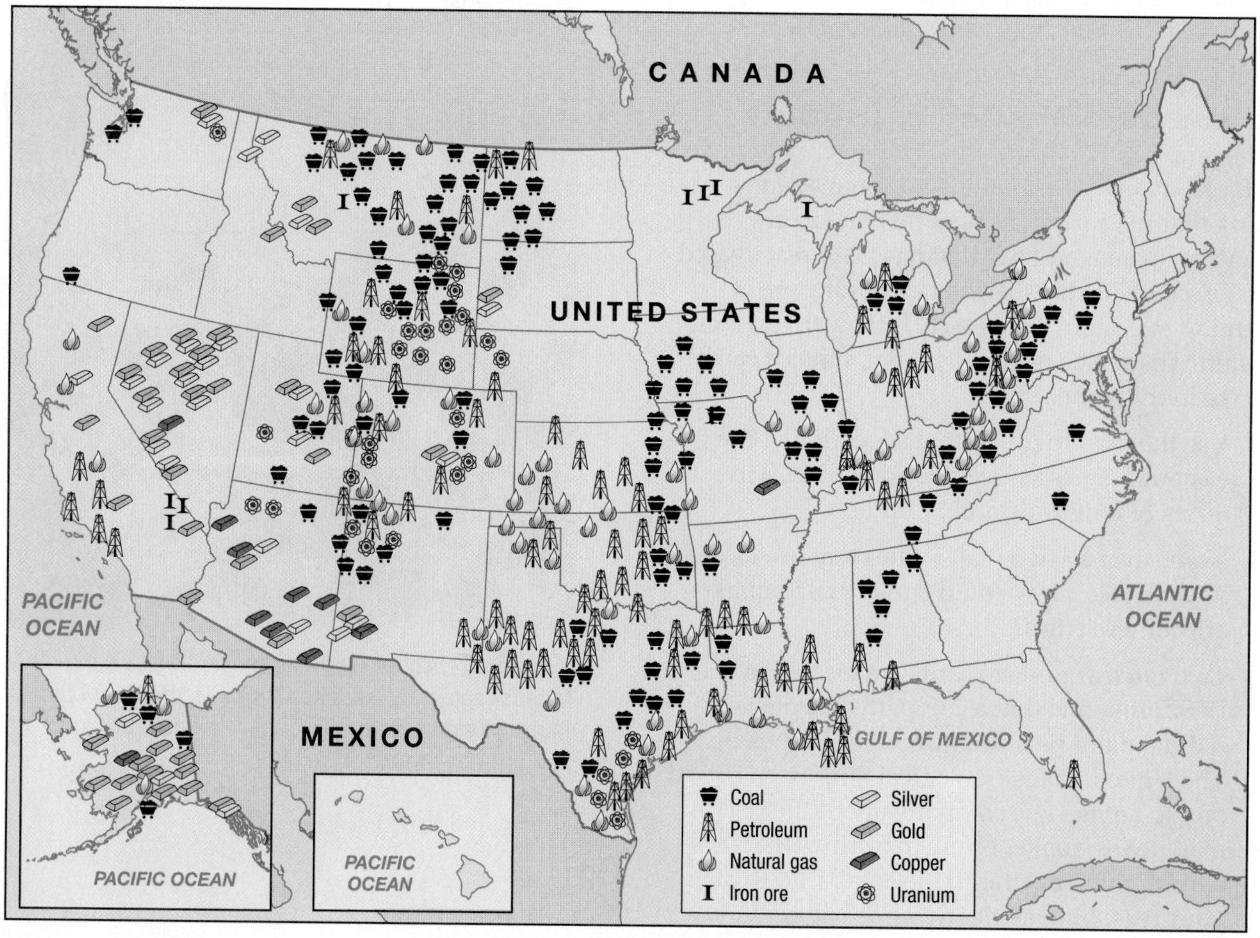

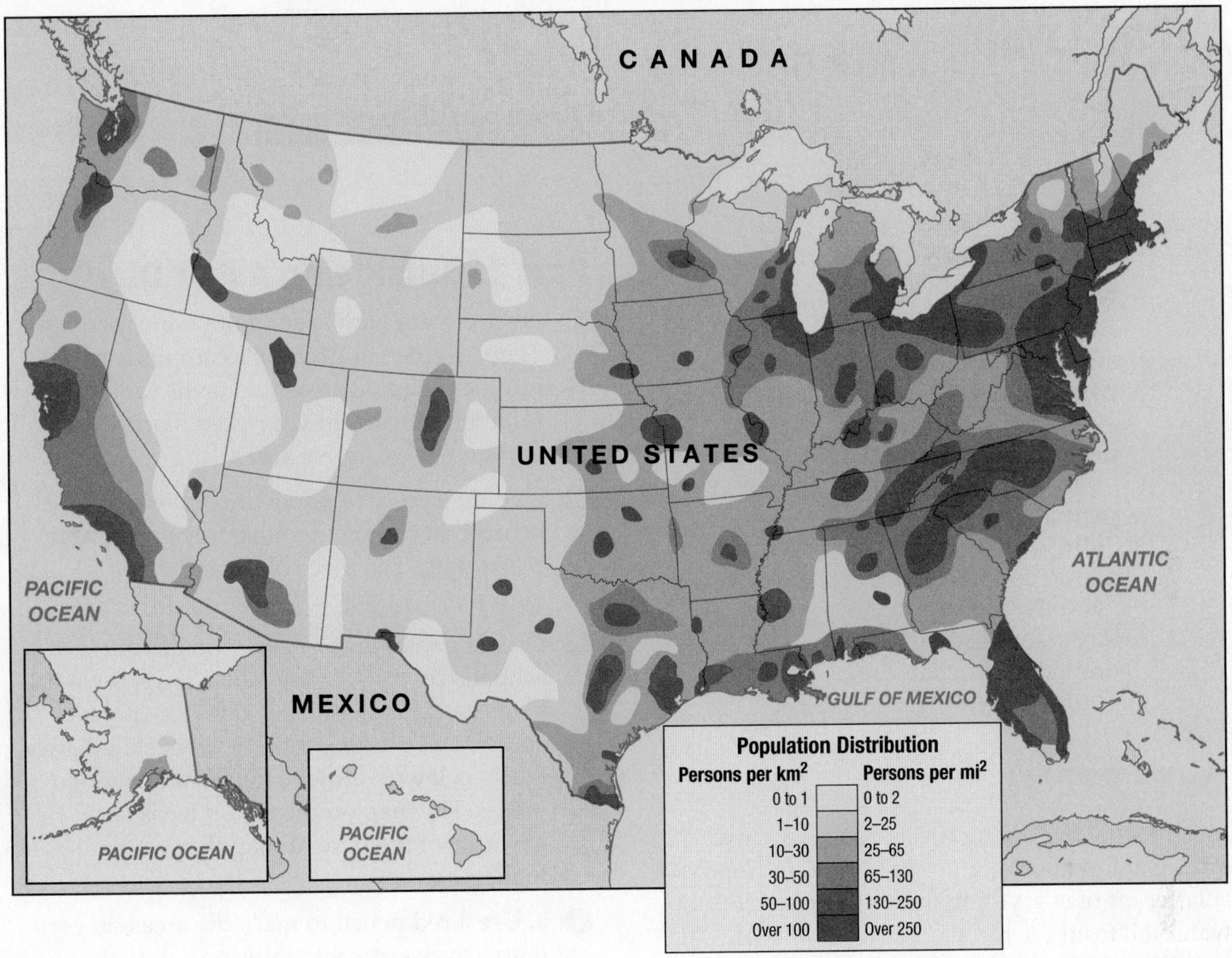

1. Find your state on the map of natural resources on the previous page. What resources are produced in your state?
2. Look at the locations of the various resources. Which resources are commonly located near each other? Why do certain resources commonly occur together?
3. When tectonic plates collide, pockets of hot magma may come into contact with cooler, solid rock. Using what you know about plate tectonics and the ways in which minerals form, describe why California has more iron-ore deposits than Nebraska does.
4. Describe the conditions that existed in the United States millions of years ago and that resulted in the formation of the modern petroleum and natural-gas deposits.
5. Compare the map on this page with the map on the previous page. What areas have both high concentrations of people and a large reserve of natural resources? What areas have many people but few resources? How could resources be transported to areas in which they are needed?
6. Using these two maps, would you say that most cities have grown up in places in or near which there are natural resources? Why or why not? What other factors could have influenced the location of cities?
7. Imagine that you work for a company that builds electrical equipment made primarily of copper. Why might southern Arizona be a good place to locate a new plant? What might be a disadvantage of locating your plant there?

What Comes Down Must Go...WHERE?

ENVIRONMENTAL CONNECTION

Materials
- cardboard, about 23 cm × 33 cm
- paper, about 23 cm × 33 cm
- pencils, red, blue, and purple
- permanent marker, fine-tipped
- plastic bag, reclosable, about 23 cm × 33 cm
- scissors
- umbrella, raincoat, or other rain gear

Imagine looking out your classroom window during a downpour. Billions of tiny raindrops splatter off of everything in sight. Streams of water fall from the roof and form dozens of puddles and streams on the ground. These miniature lakes and rivers swirl together, and tiny torrents carry away leaves, bits of trash, and other debris. A day or two later, the ground outside looks completely dry. Where did all of the water go?

In this activity, you will create a map of your school. After observing the type of ground cover and the slope of the terrain at various locations, you will predict whether rainwater will collect or run off at those locations. You will also look for possible sources of pollution and places where erosion might occur. Later, you will go outside in the rain and find out whether your predictions are correct.

Part 1: Outside on a Fair Day

1. Form a team with several of your classmates. Then, divide your school's campus into the number of equal areas that is the same as the number of teams in your class. Each team will work on one campus area.
2. Cut out a piece of paper and a piece of cardboard that fit exactly into a large reclosable plastic bag. The piece of paper will be your map.
3. On the paper, map one section of your school's campus. Include buildings, paved areas (such as sidewalks, outdoor sports courts, and parking lots), and vegetated areas (such as lawns, athletic fields, and wooded areas). The map on the next page is an example of the type of map that you will make.
4. **a.** Use a red pencil to mark the areas on your map. Draw arrows to indicate a downhill slope. Use a narrow arrow to indicate a steep slope and a wider arrow to indicate a gradual slope. Use circles to indicate flat areas.

b. Use a blue pencil to draw arrows and circles that indicate where you think surface water may collect or flow during a steady rain. These areas may include low-lying areas, the roofs of buildings, gutters, and drainage ditches.

c. Use a purple pencil to mark the locations that you think might contribute pollution to the runoff. (These areas may include parking lots that contain oil stains or places where trash is usually found on the ground, such as near a dumpster.)

5 Seal your map and the piece of cardboard in the reclosable bag. When you are outside in the rain, use a permanent marker to write your observations on the outside of the bag.

Part 2: Outside During a Steady Rain

6 Dress appropriately, and go outside. Using the marker, write on your plastic-covered map the places where water collects and runs. In places where water moves along the ground, use arrows to show the water's direction. Use the letter *P* to mark the locations of pollutants that you observe in the water. Use the letter *E* to mark the locations where erosion seems to be occurring. (Look for soil or natural debris that is being washed along by moving water.)

Part 3: Back in the Classroom

7 Discuss your predictions for some of the locations. Were your predictions correct? How do you explain differences between your predictions and your observations?

8 Was the pollution that you observed suspended load, bed load, or dissolved load? Explain how there may have been pollution that you could not observe.

9 Explain how erosion on your school's campus could affect the erosion and deposition that occurs downstream from the campus.

10 Assemble the maps from your class into a single map of your school's campus. In your opinion, does most of the rainfall at your school become groundwater or runoff? Where does runoff go when it leaves your school's campus? Your school is probably part of a larger, local watershed. Find out what stream or other body of water the surface runoff in your area empties into.

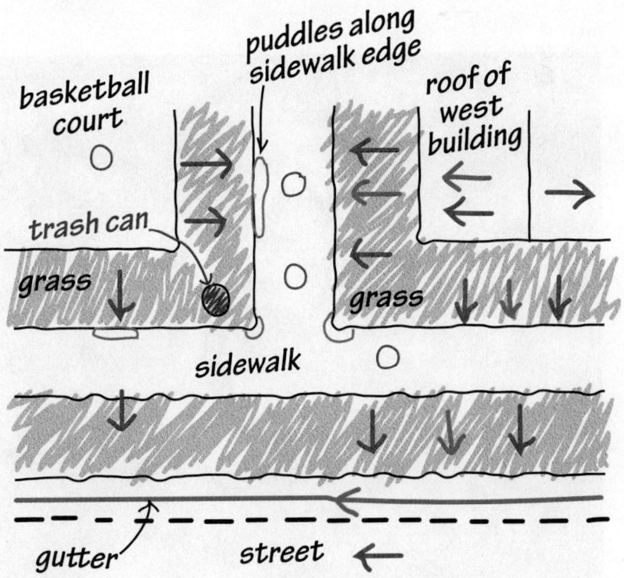

Where the hippos Roam

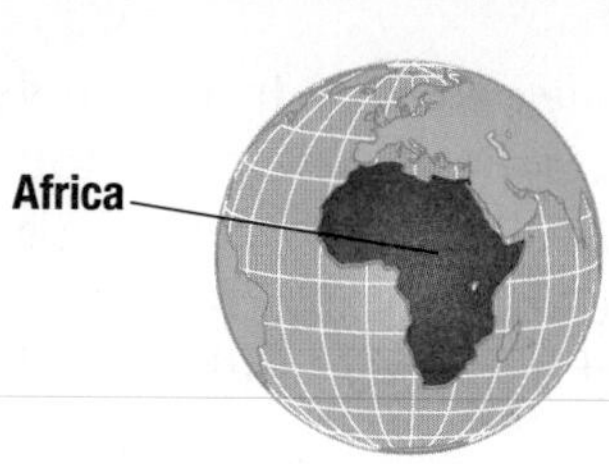

ENVIRONMENTAL CONNECTION

Materials
pencils, assorted colors
ruler, metric

Millions of years ago, ancestors of modern crocodiles lurked in the shallow waters of lakes and other bodies of water. Like their current descendents, they hunted fish and other animals. If you could travel back in time to visit one of those lakes, you might see the ancestors of today's hippopotamuses there, too. Antelopes might browse along the edges of the lake, and rodents of various sizes might scurry back and forth.

When paleontologists examine the fossil of a prehistoric organism, they may discover clues about the organism's life. They may also answer questions about the organism's environment: Was the area hot or cold? Was it humid or dry? Then, by putting all of these clues together, the paleontologists may be able to learn a little more about how organisms and environments change over time.

Unfortunately, studying a fossil site is no easy task! Discoveries of complete organisms are rare. More often, a paleontologist may find a few teeth scattered over a very large area. In such cases, keeping track of where the fossils were found is very important. In this activity, you will use the data from a fossil site to create a map of fossil locations at that site. Then, you will draw some conclusions about the past environment, or *paleoenvironment*, at that location.

The animals that lived near lakes millions of years ago probably had lives similar to the lives of animals that live near lakes today.

Location of Fossil Teeth

Layer	Hippos	Rodents	Crocodiles	Bovids*
A	B11, C6, D3, I15, J10, L7, M6		C14, F7, G13, I3, L13, 02	
B	F2, J3, K1, K2	B10, B11, F13	H2, I7, K2, N5, N7	G14
C		B3, C10, D1, H8, M9, N4		A5, A6, E2, E4, E14, H7, H8, H12, K4, M1, N15

*Bovids are antelopes and other such animals.

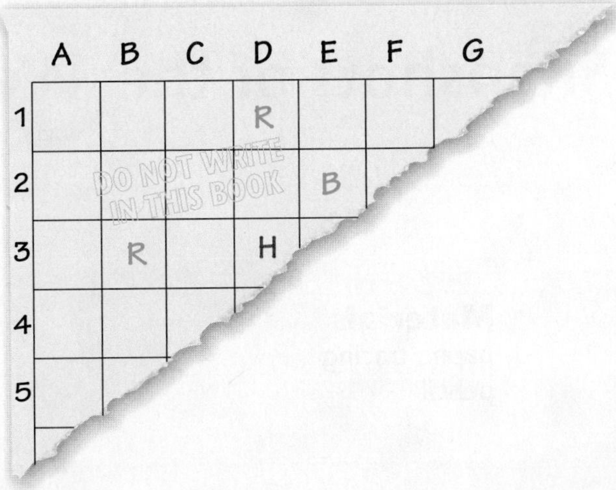

The table above shows the locations of fossils that were found spread out over 22,500 m^2. A team of paleontologists decided that this site, which measured 150 m × 150 m, was too large to work on all at once. So, the paleontologists decided to create a grid of 10 m squares. Starting in the northwest corner of the site, they labeled the squares from west to east with the letters *A–O*. Then, they numbered the squares 1–15 from north to south. Thus, each fossil could be labeled with a letter and a number that would identify where the fossil was found. For example, A1 would signify the 10 m × 10 m square in the northwest corner of the site, and O15 would signify the square in the southeast corner.

1. Create a map of the fossil site by drawing a grid similar to the one described above. The scale should be 1 cm = 10 m. Use letters to label across the top edge of the grid, and use numbers to label down the left edge of the grid. For each fossil, place a letter (*H* for a hippo fossil, *R* for a rodent fossil, *C* for a crocodile fossil, and *B* for a bovid fossil) in the square that corresponds to where the fossil was found. Use pencil color to represent the different layers of sediment, and make a key that shows which layer each color represents.
2. From the distribution of fossils in the layer of sediment just below the surface layer, what part of this site might have been under water? Explain your answer, and devise a way to show that area on your map.
3. Describe how the environment at this site changed over time.
4. One team member wished to search this site for fossils of dry-climate plants. Which layer or layers would most likely yield fossils of such plants? Explain your answer.
5. One paleontologist suggested that tectonic uplift had raised the area's elevation over time and thus caused the climate to change. A second paleontologist thought that the area had probably lost elevation over time. With which scientist do you agree? Explain your answer.

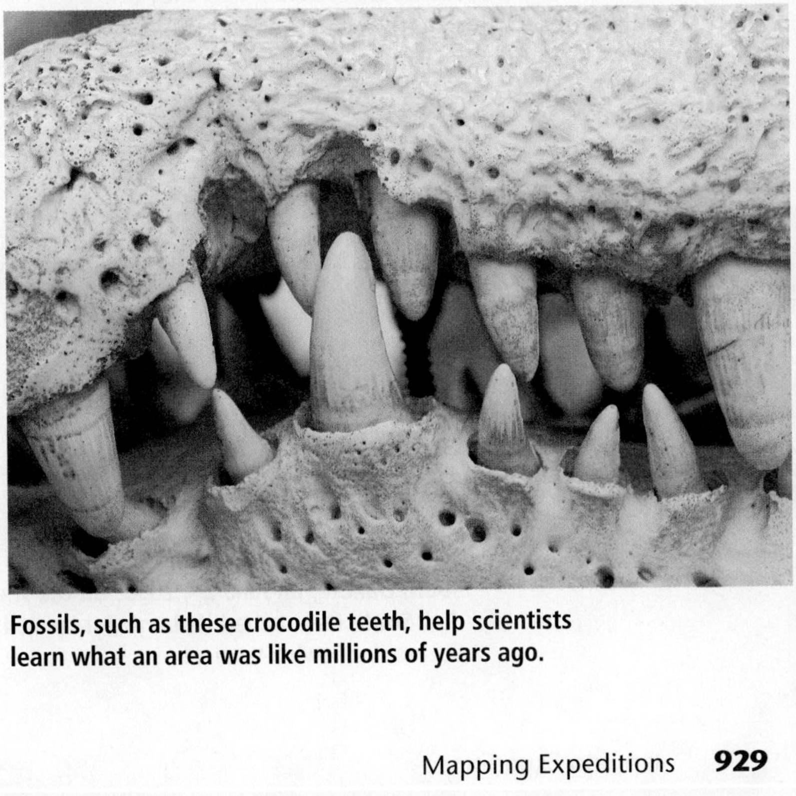

Fossils, such as these crocodile teeth, help scientists learn what an area was like millions of years ago.

Snapshots of the Weather

Materials
paper, tracing
pencil

From looking at a weather map, you might get the impression that the clouds, fronts, and other features shown are standing still. However, weather patterns change constantly, and a weather map can show only what is happening at one particular instant. For this reason, meteorologists rely on a sequence of maps to make predictions about local weather.

In this activity, you will analyze a sequence of weather maps. The maps were taken from a daily newspaper and show weather patterns that occurred in the United States during a 4-day period. You will note what information the maps show and do not show, and you will make a few predictions based on your observations.

1. Look carefully at the maps on the next page. What weather information do they show? Now, look at the weather symbols in the Reference Tables section of Appendix E. What information is not included on these maps? Why might a newspaper exclude certain types of information on daily weather maps?
2. Why would a newspaper that serves only a specific geographic region publish the weather for the entire continental United States?
3. Describe how the weather patterns in your location changed during the 4-day period shown.
4. During what season do you think this 4-day period occurred? Explain your answer.
5. Trace the outline of one weather map on a separate piece of paper, but do not include any information on the map. Predict the locations of the fronts on the day following this 4-day period. Note the locations of the fronts on your new map.
6. Predict the temperature and precipitation patterns that occur in your location on the day following this 4-day period.

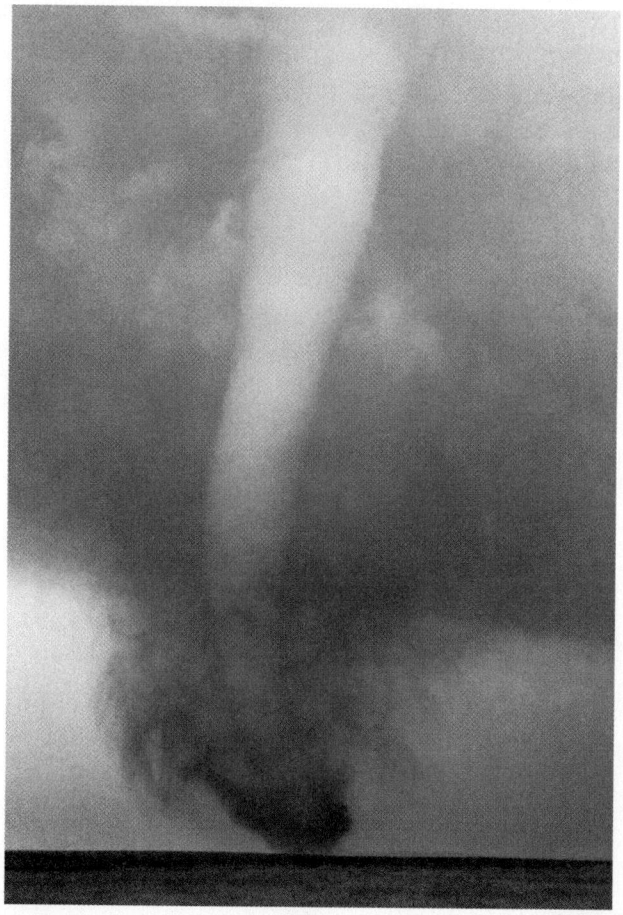

This tornado twisted through Manchester, South Dakota, on June 24, 2003. On the same day, South Dakota had its largest recorded outbreak of twisters ever!

APPENDIX C

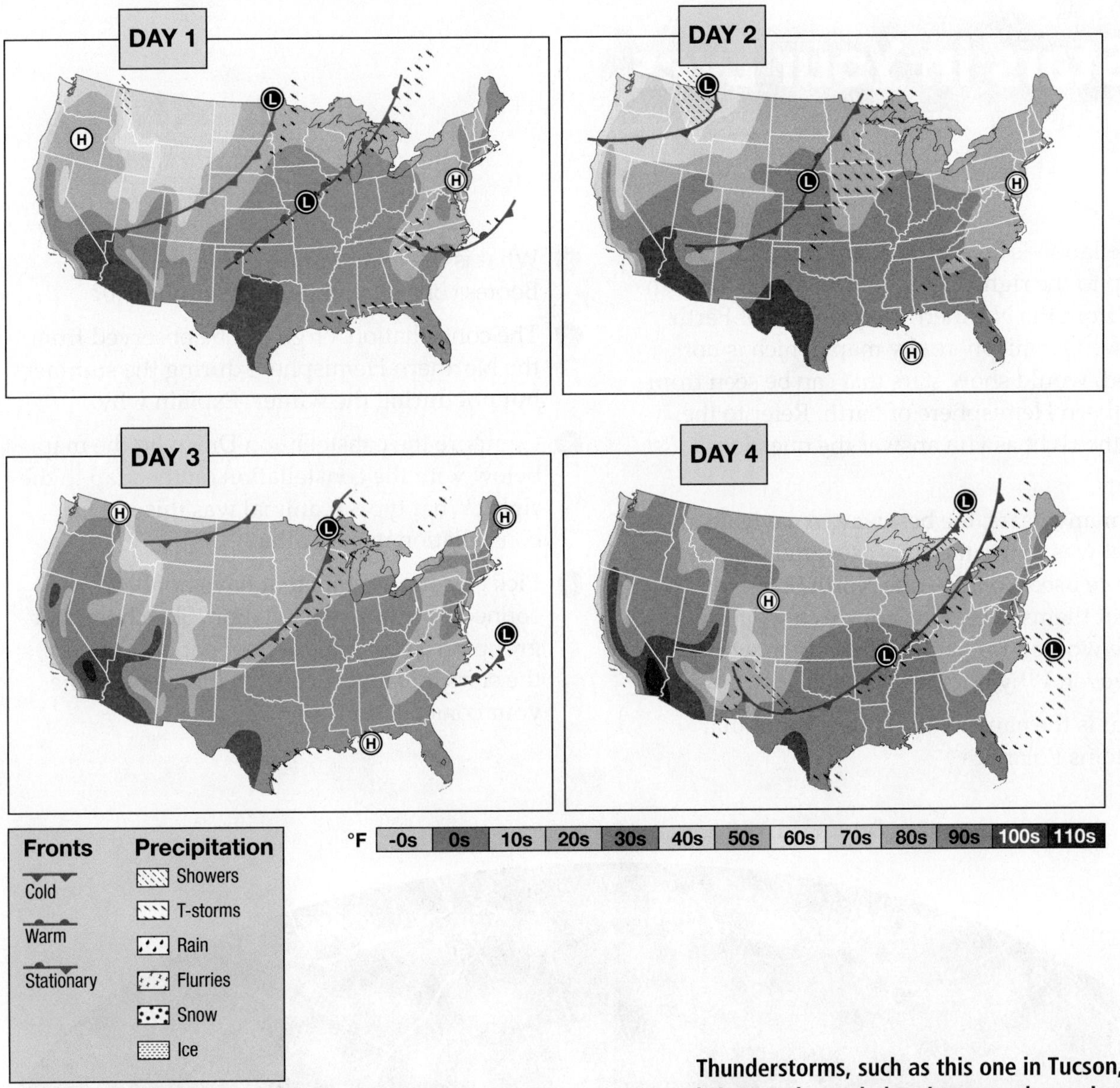

Thunderstorms, such as this one in Tucson, Arizona, bring much-needed moisture to dry regions.

Stars in Your Eyes

A constellation is an arbitrary grouping of stars. The map to the right shows constellations that can be seen from the Northern Hemisphere of Earth. A Southern Hemisphere sky map, which is not provided, would show stars that can be seen from the Southern Hemisphere of Earth. Refer to the map to the right as you answer the questions below.

1. For many years, the best way to navigate at night was to use the stars as a guide. Many people used Polaris—the North Star—to orient themselves. This approach would not have worked for people all over the world, however. Why not?
2. What is the name of the constellation that contains Polaris?
3. What is the temperature of the star in the Bootes constellation, with magnitude 0?
4. The constellation Virgo can be observed from the Northern Hemisphere during the summer but not during the winter. Explain why.
5. Compare the constellation Draco on the map below with the constellation on the map to the right. What type of animal was this constellation named after?
6. Pick a group of stars that have not been connected into a constellation. Sketch the star group on a separate piece of paper. Connect the stars into a new constellation, and name your constellation.

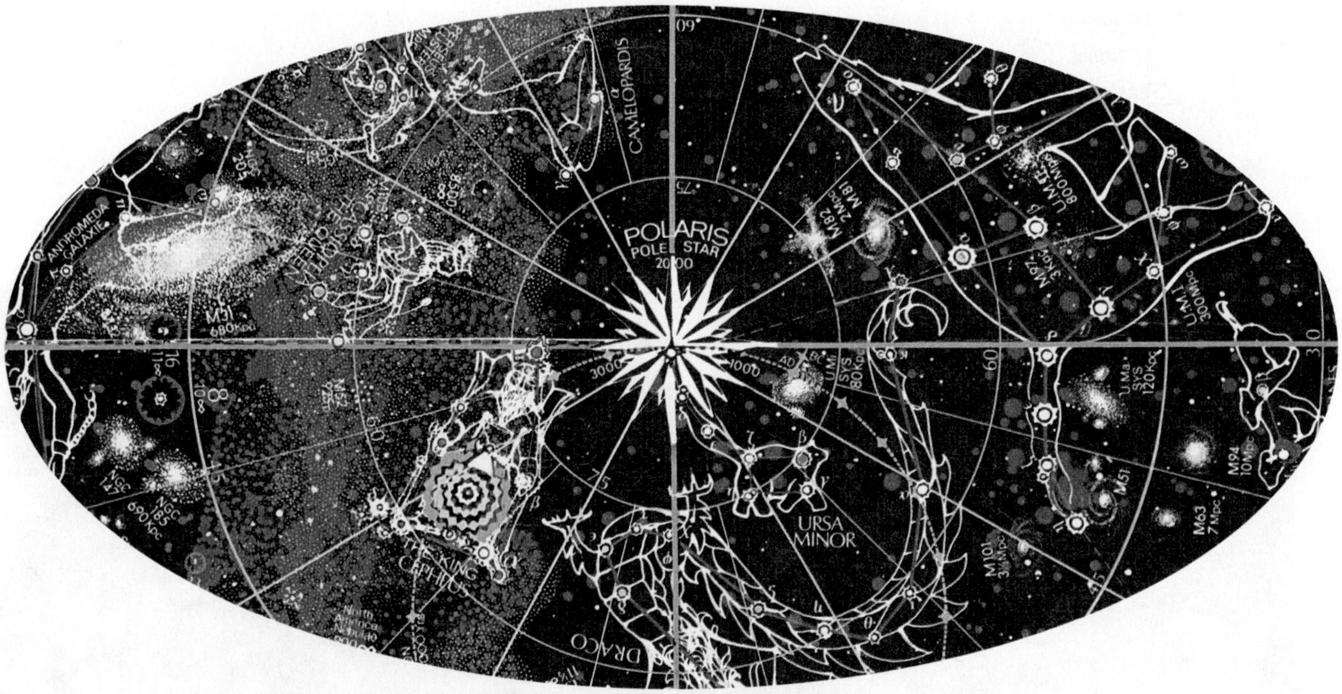

People, such as Sumerians, Greeks, Chinese, and Egyptians, have been grouping stars into constellations like these for thousands of years.

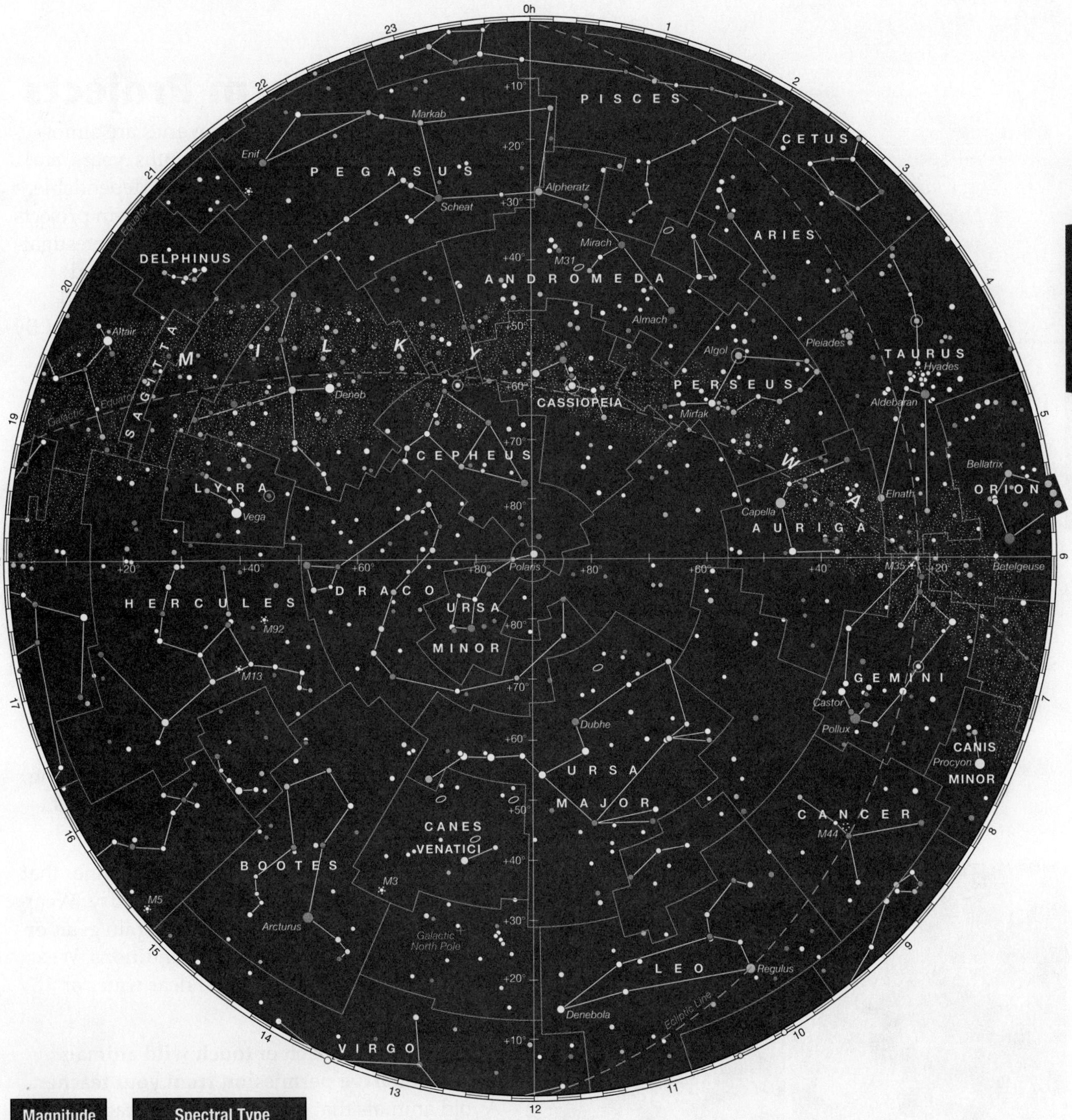

Magnitude Scale
- 0
- 1
- 2
- 3
- 4
- 5

Spectral Type

Temperature (K)	
50,000–25,000	O-B
11,000	A
7,500	F
6,000	G
5,000	K
3,500	M

- Variable star
- Open cluster
- Globular cluster
- Galaxy
- Constellation boundary

There are 88 constellations recognized by modern astronomers. The Northern Hemisphere sky map shows those that can be seen from the Northern Hemisphere of Earth.

Long-Term Projects

Introducing Long-Term Projects

Scientific investigations that lead to important discoveries are almost never short term. Usually, these investigations last months, years, and even decades before results are considered complete and dependable. Investigations in Earth science are no exception. The long-term projects included in this section will give you practical experience in investigating Earth science the way that Earth scientists do—over extended periods of time. You will observe changes over time, keep detailed records of your observations, and draw conclusions from your data. By following these steps, you will learn firsthand what it is like to be an Earth scientist.

Safety First!

Many of the long-term projects require you to make field trips to an observation site or to conduct your activities outdoors. Advance planning is essential. You should plan carefully for these investigations and should be certain that you are aware of the safety guidelines that must be followed. The following are general guidelines for fieldwork and lab work.

Conducting Fieldwork

Find out about on-site hazards before setting out. Determine whether there are poisonous plants or dangerous animals where you are going, and know how to identify them. Also, find out about other hazards, such as steep or slippery terrain.

Wear protective clothing. Dress in a manner that will keep you warm, comfortable, and dry. Wear sunglasses, sunscreen, a hat, gloves, rain gear, or other gear to suit local weather conditions. Wear waterproof shoes if you will be near water or mud.

Do not approach or touch wild animals unless you have permission from your teacher. Avoid animals that may sting, bite, scratch, or otherwise cause injury.

Do not touch wild plants or pick wildflowers without permission from your teacher. Many wild plants can cause irritation or can be toxic, and many are protected by law. Never taste a wild plant.

Do not wander away from the group. Do not go beyond where you can be seen or heard. Travel with a partner at all times.

Report any hazards or accidents to your teacher immediately. Even if an incident seems unimportant, tell your teacher about it.

Consider the safety of the ecosystem that you will be visiting as well as your own safety. Do not remove anything from a field site without your teacher's permission. Stay on trails when possible to avoid trampling delicate vegetation. Never leave garbage behind at a field site. Strive to leave natural areas just as you find them.

Conducting Lab Work

Be aware of safety hazards. Any field or lab exercises in which there are known safety hazards will include safety cautions and icons to identify specific hazards. By being aware of safety concerns, you may avoid accidents. Know where safety equipment and emergency exits are located so that you are prepared in the event of an emergency.

Do not engage in inappropriate behavior. Most laboratory accidents are caused by carelessness, lack of attention, or inappropriate behavior. Always be aware of your surroundings, and pay attention to safety cautions.

Be neat. Keep your work area free of unnecessary clutter. Tie back loose hair and loose articles of clothing. Do not wear dangling jewelry or open-toed shoes in the lab. Never eat or drink in the laboratory.

Clean your lab station when your lab time is over. Before leaving the lab, clean up your work area. Put away all equipment and supplies, and dispose of chemicals and other materials as directed by your teacher. Turn off water, gas, and burners, and unplug electrical equipment. Wash your hands with soap and water after working on any lab.

For additional information about safety in the lab and in the field, refer to the Lab and Field Safety section in the front of this book. Don't take any chances with safety!

What safety concerns are being ignored in this photograph?

Long-Term Project 1

Positions of Sunrise and Sunset

Duration
8 or 9 months

Objectives

- **Observe and record** the positions of sunrise and sunset once per month.
- **Graph and analyze** collected data that describe the positions of sunrise and sunset.
- **Predict** the positions of sunrise and sunset for 3 or 4 months.

Materials
compass, magnetic
glue
paper
paper, graph
pen
pencil
poster board
scissors
twist tie (or pipe cleaner)

Safety

You are probably aware that the sun rises in the east and sets in the west each day. What may not be obvious to you is that the positions of sunrise and sunset along the horizon differ from day to day in a specific pattern. As the positions of sunrise and sunset change, the amount of sunlight that an area receives also changes. In this investigation, you will observe the changes in the sun's position along the horizon at sunrise and at sunset. You will be making two observations on or near the 21st of each month for approximately 8 or 9 months (depending on the schedule of your school year).

Procedure

1. Construct the bearing chart before taking any measurements. Copy the bearing chart from the next page onto a piece of paper.
2. Glue your copy of the chart to a piece of poster board. When the glue is dry, trim away the excess poster board.
3. Wrap the center of a twist tie once around the center of a pencil. Poke the ends of the twist tie through the center of the bearing chart to make a pointer for your chart.

The sun appears to rise and set at different positions relative to landmarks, such as these skyscrapers in Los Angeles, California.

4. On a cloudless morning just before sunrise, place the bearing chart on a level spot where no buildings or trees block your view of sunrise and sunset. **CAUTION** Although sunlight is less intense at sunrise and sunset, you should never stare at the sun for extended periods of time.

5. Use the magnetic compass to determine the direction of north. Set the bearing chart so that 0° is pointing north and 180° is pointing south. (Note: Have the chart face the same direction for every observation, even months from now.) Try to align an edge of the chart with some permanent object near your observation point.

Step 1 Copy the chart below on a separate piece of paper, and use it to construct your bearing chart.

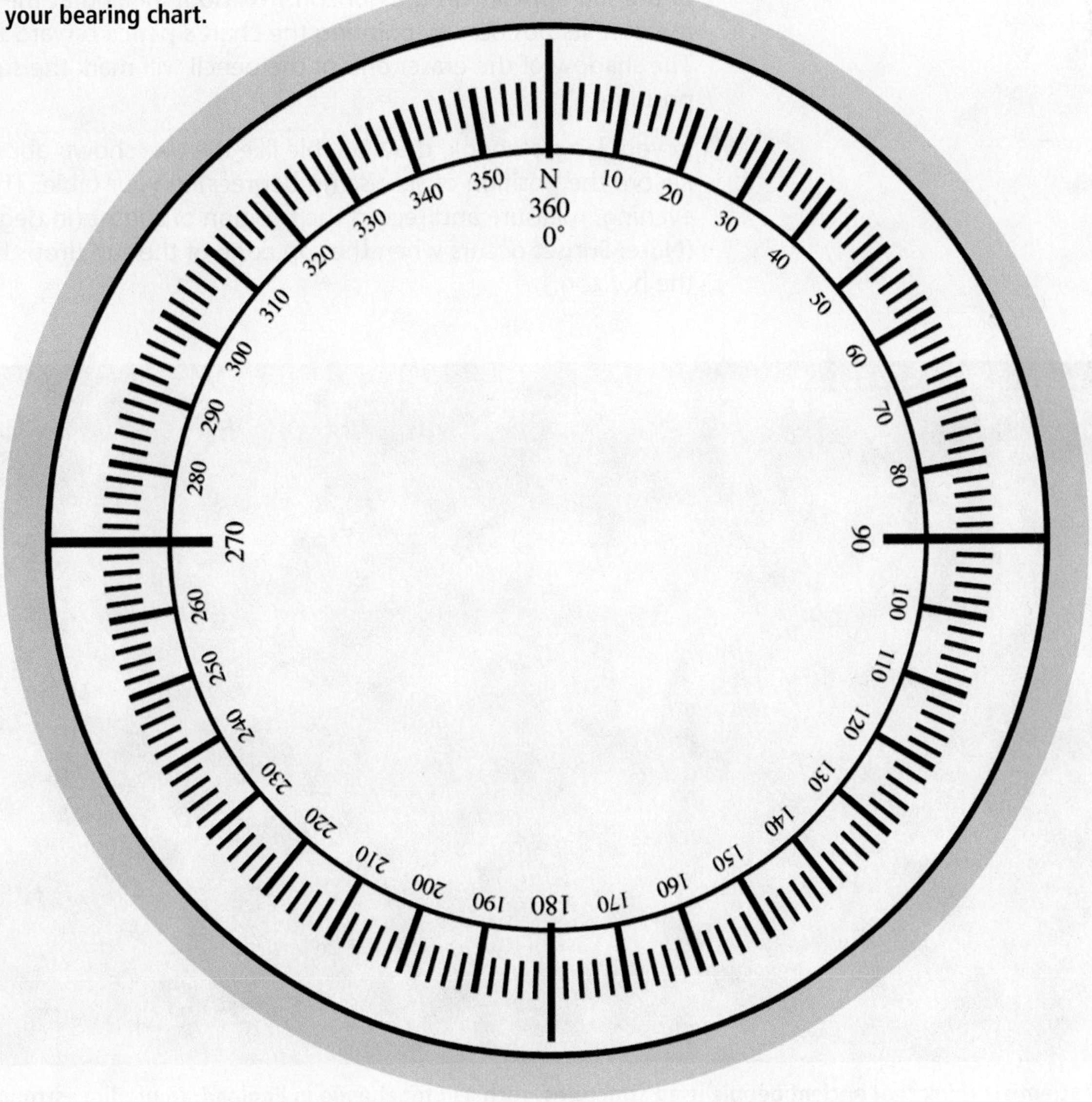

Long-Term Project 1, *continued*

Step 7

Date	Position of sunrise (in degrees)	Position of sunset (in degrees)

6. When the bearing chart is in place and properly aligned, measure the position of sunrise. (Note: Sunrise occurs at the instant the top of the sun appears on the horizon.) Without looking at the sun, measure its position by pointing the chart's pencil toward the sun. The shadow of the eraser end of the pencil will mark the sun's position.

7. In your lab notebook, draw a table like the one shown above. Record the position of sunrise (in degrees) in your table. That evening, measure and record the position of sunset (in degrees). (Note: Sunset occurs when the top edge of the sun drops below the horizon.)

Many scientists think that ancient people used structures, such as Stonehenge in England, to predict astronomical occurrences and to determine the timing of solstices and equinoxes.

Step 9

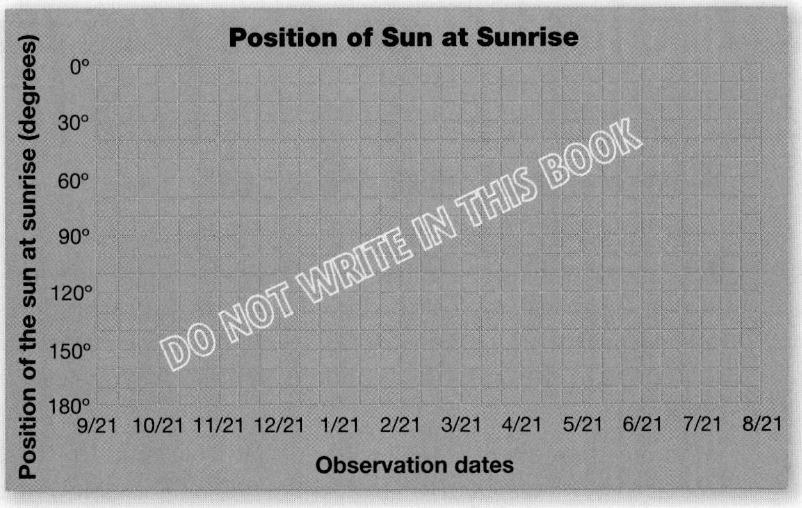

8. Repeat steps 6 and 7 on the same date each month. (Note: On the equinoxes, the sun will rise due east and set due west. On the solstices, the sunrise and sunset will be shifted from these directions. The amount of the maximum shift will depend on the observer's latitude.)

9. On a sheet of graph paper, prepare a graph similar to the one shown above. Label the graph's *y*-axis, which represents the position (in degrees) of the sun at sunrise, from 0° to 180°. The position of 90° will be in the center of the *y*-axis scale. The *x*-axis represents observation dates. Next, make a graph on which to plot the position of the sun at sunset. Label the *y*-axis of this graph from 180° to 360°.

10. On each graph, connect the points by drawing a smooth line. Estimate the positions of points between the plotted points.

Analysis

1. **Analyzing Data** On which date does the sun appear to follow the highest path across the sky? What happens to the length of daylight during this season?
2. **Analyzing Data** On which date does the sun appear to follow the lowest path across the sky? What happens to the length of daylight during this season?
3. **Analyzing Results** On which dates are the positions of the sun at sunrise and again at sunset about 180° apart? Those dates mark the beginning of which seasons?
4. **Describing Events** What general statement can you make about the pattern of sunrise and sunset according to the graphs?
5. **Forming a Hypothesis** Expand your graph to include the predicted position of the sun in June and July. Describe the pattern that you predicted.

Extension

Evaluating Hypotheses
Use the process described in the investigation to chart the positions of sunrise and sunset for the months of June and July. How do your observations compare with your prediction?

Making Comparisons
Use the same process to chart the positions of the moon at moonrise and moonset. Refer to an almanac when you choose the times at which you will make measurements. Do the positions of sunrise and sunset correlate to those of moonrise and moonset? What can you conclude from your observations?

Long-Term Project 2 ENVIRONMENTAL CONNECTION

Duration
2 weeks

Objectives
- **Count and record** the number of particulates in the air over a 2-week period.
- **Analyze** how wind direction and particulate source are related.

Materials
compass, magnetic
microscope
microscope slides (8 or more)
paper, graph
pencil, grease
petroleum jelly
slide box
tape, masking or packaging, or rubber bands

Safety

Air-Pollution Watch

When certain types of pollutants are present in high concentrations, they threaten the general health and well-being of humans. Some substances that can be air pollutants include dust and smoke particles, pollen, mold spores, and waste gases. If these tiny particles remain suspended in the air for long periods of time, they are called *particulates.*

Wind direction affects the number of particulates in the air. If there is a source of particulates in an area, there will be a large number of particulates in the air when the wind blows from the direction of that source. There will be fewer particulates in the air when the wind blows from the direction opposite the source.

In this investigation, you will collect and view a few types of particulates. You will collect particulates from an outdoor site every day for 2 weeks. Then, you will examine those particulates.

Procedure

1. Select a collection site in an open area, such as a large field or pasture, where the wind can blow past the site from every direction.
2. Locate a four-sided post, such as a 4 in. × 4 in. fence post, that is firmly driven into the ground. Try to choose a post whose top is at least 1 m above ground level. If there are no fences in your area, look for another four-sided structure that you could use.

Haze and smog are common in large cities, such as Los Angeles, California.

Step 3

Day	Date	Wind direction	Slide direction	Number of particulates 1	2	3	4	5	Total
1			N						
			S						
			E						
			W						

3. Use a compass to establish north, south, east, and west directions from the post's location. Determine the direction from which the wind is blowing by watching objects, such as a flag, move in the wind. Record the wind direction and the date in a table like the one shown above.
4. Look for any phenomena that may affect air quality, such as smoke-stacks or heavy traffic. Record these observations and the day's weather conditions.
5. Use a grease pencil to mark on the back of each microscope slide the direction that the slide will face when placed on the post. Place each slide on the appropriate side of the post.
6. Use tape or rubber bands to attach the slides to the post, as shown on the lower-right side of this page. Use your finger to spread a thin, even film of petroleum jelly on one side of each slide.
7. Return to the site the following day. Remove the slides. Place each slide carefully in the slide box. (Note: Do not touch the greased surface.)

Step 6

Long-Term Project 2, *continued*

8. Place new slides on the post, and record the wind direction and weather conditions.
9. Examine each slide under the microscope at 100×. Focus on one section that you have chosen at random. Count the number of particulates that you observe in the section. Record this number in column 1 of your table.
10. Move the slide, and examine another section that you have chosen at random. Count the number of particulates in this section. Record this number in column 2 of your table.
11. Repeat step 10 three more times so that you have a total of five observations per slide. Record the total number of particulates counted in the five sections.
12. Repeat steps 7 through 11 each weekday for 2 weeks.
13. When you have finished examining the slides and recording your results, total the number of particulates counted for each of the wind directions.
14. Using the data in your table, construct a bar graph. On the *y*-axis, plot the total number of particulates obtained in the past 5 days. On the *x*-axis, plot the day and wind direction. A sample graph is shown on the next page.

Step 9

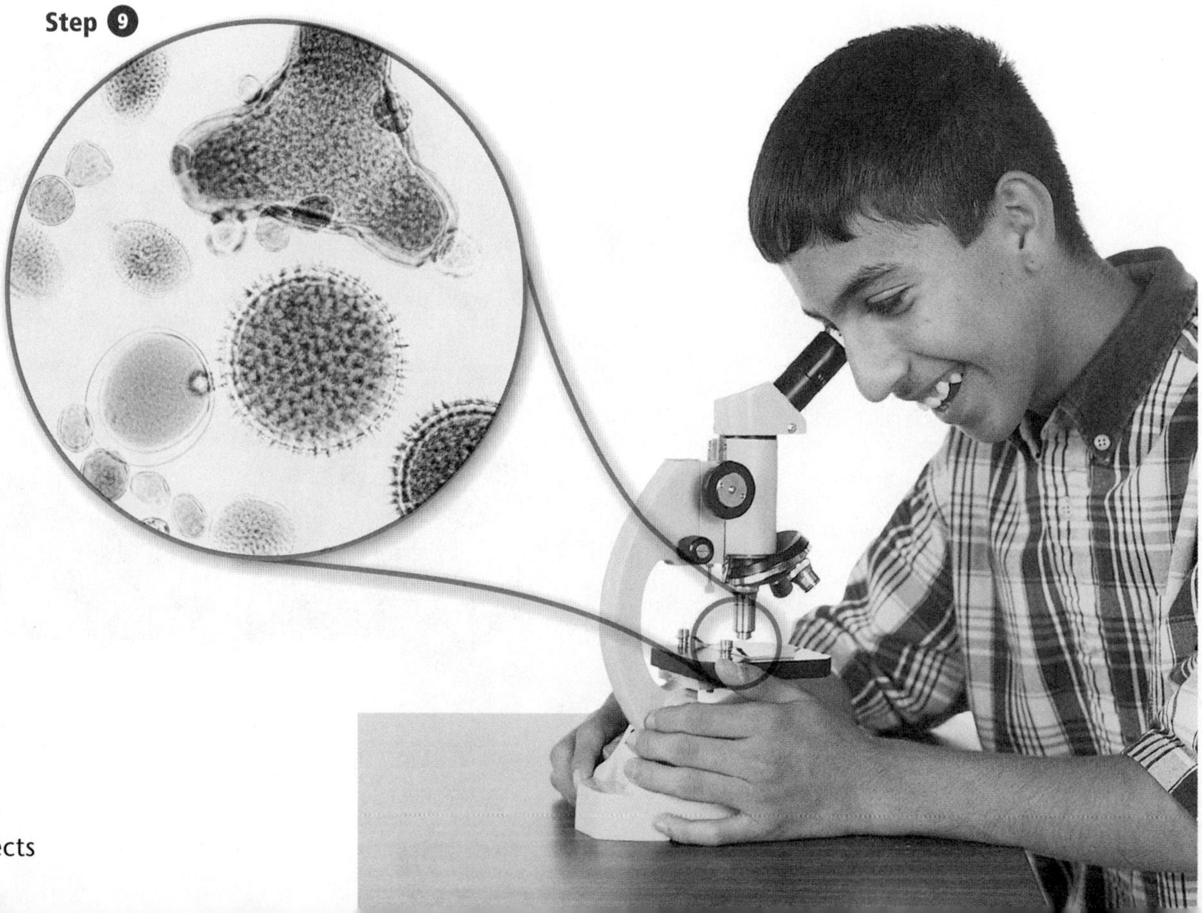

Step 14

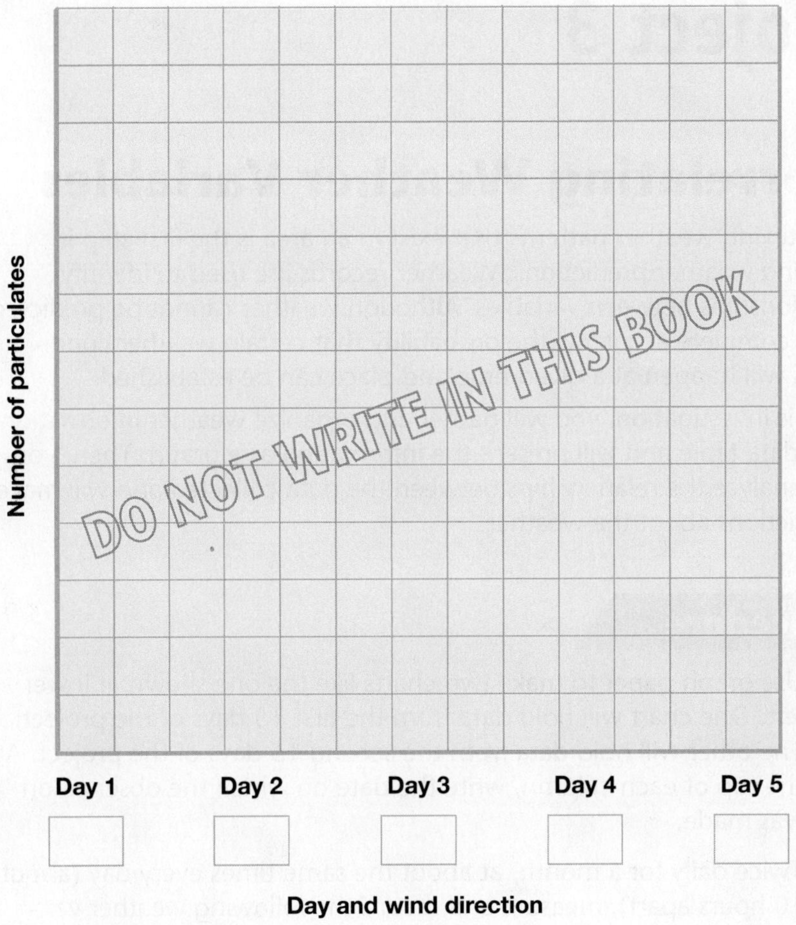

Analysis

1. **Analyzing Results** For your location, did any one wind direction or group of wind directions result in more particulates than any other direction or directions did?
2. **Interpreting Information** What are possible sources of these particulates?
3. **Applying Conclusions** What would your results likely be if you set up this investigation near a populated urban area?
4. **Evaluating Methods** Did weather conditions have any effect on your results? Explain your answer.
5. **Graphing Data** Construct a second graph that uses data from all 10 days on which you collected samples. How does this graph differ from your previous graph?
6. **Identifying Patterns** Did you see a different pattern in the data when you plotted data from more than 5 days? Explain your answer.

Extension

Research Use the library or the Internet to research common particulates. Use your research to identify common particulates on several of the slides from this investigation. Which particulates are most common in your area? Explain why these particulates are most common.

Long-Term Project 3

Duration
1 month

Objectives

- **Measure and record** weather variables twice every day.
- **Predict** weather conditions based on data that you collected.

Materials
aneroid barometer or barograph
compass, magnetic
paper, graph
thermometer, Celsius

Safety

Correlating Weather Variables

Identifying weather patterns that exist in an area is the first step in making weather predictions. Weather records are used to identify relationships between variables. Although weather cannot be predicted with complete accuracy, the probability that certain weather conditions will happen at a given time and place can be established.

In this investigation, you will gather and organize weather information in a data table and will present the information as a graph. Then, you will analyze the relationships between the data collected and will make predictions about the weather.

Procedure

1. Use graph paper to make two charts like the one shown at lower left. One chart will hold data from the first 15 days of the project. The other will hold data from the second 15 days of the project. At the top of each column, write the date on which the observation was made.
2. Twice daily for a month, at about the same times every day (about 10 hours apart), measure and record the following weather variables: temperature (°C), barometric pressure (mb), wind direction, cloud cover, and weather conditions. The chart on the following page explains how to measure and record these variables.
3. Use the month's data to make two graphs. Do so by connecting the points for temperature with one smooth line and the points for pressure with a second smooth line.

Step 1

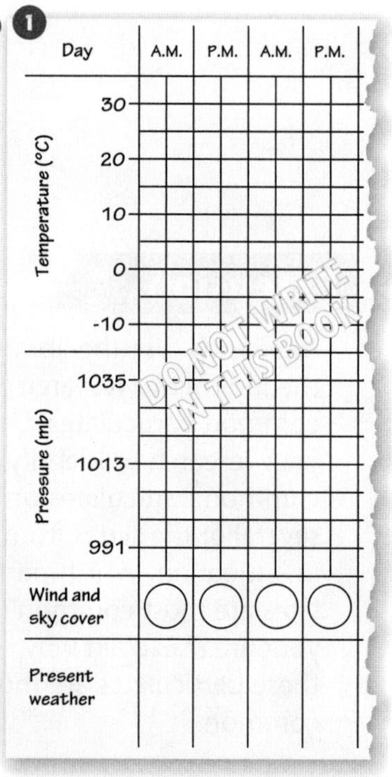

How to Measure Weather Variables	
Weather variable	**How to measure and record the variable**
Temperature	Place a thermometer where it is in the shade and is not exposed to precipitation. Wait at least 3 min, and then read the temperature. Plot a point for that temperature on your chart.
Barometric pressure	Using a barometer, record the barometric pressure to the nearest tenth of a millibar. If your barometer is calibrated in "inches of mercury," change inches to millibars by using the Barometric Conversion Scale at right. Plot a point for the barometric pressure.
Wind direction	Determine the wind direction by using a weather vane or by observing objects moved by the wind. Wind direction is named according to the direction from which the wind blows. Use a compass to help determine direction. Using the symbols shown in the Table of Weather Symbols in the Reference Tables section of Appendix E of this book, record wind direction on the circles at the bottom of your chart.
Cloud cover	Estimate the amount of sky that is covered by clouds. Using the symbols shown in the Table of Weather Symbols in the Reference Tables section of Appendix E of this book, shade the circles at the bottom of your chart.
Weather conditions	Observe the present weather conditions. Using the Table of Weather Symbols in the Reference Tables section of Appendix E of this book, draw in your chart the symbol that most accurately indicates the weather conditions.

Step 2

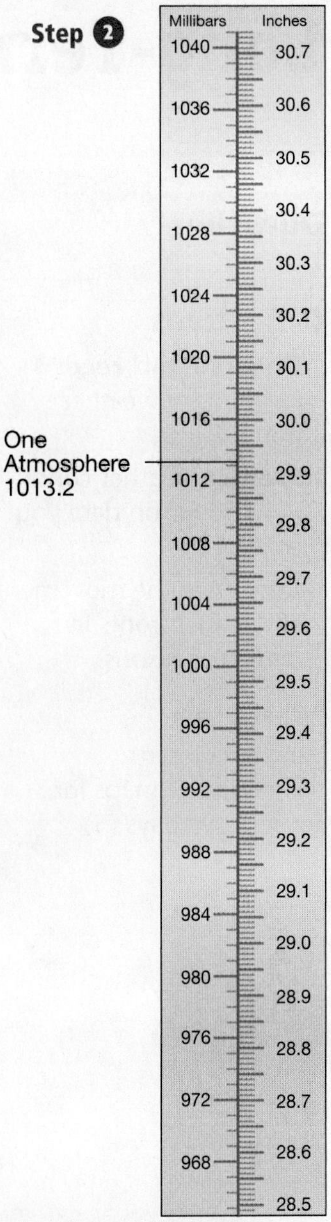

Analysis

1. **Evaluating Data** According to your graph, on how many days was the temperature falling? On how many days was the barometric pressure falling?
2. **Identifying Patterns** Of the days that had falling temperature, how many had rising barometric pressure?
3. **Inferring Relationships** In general, what is the relationship between temperature and pressure?
4. **Analyzing Results** What sky cover and wind direction are generally associated with falling barometric pressure?
5. **Interpreting Results** What weather conditions are generally associated with high barometric pressure? with low barometric pressure?
6. **Drawing Conclusions** How do the relationships between certain weather variables help you predict the weather?
7. **Evaluating Methods** Which weather variables are most useful in predicting precipitation?

Extension

Research Find out what the normal temperature, pressure, and precipitation are for your area during the time period in which you recorded your data. Do your observations match the normal conditions for that time period? How can you explain differences between your observations and the normal conditions?

Long-Term Project 4

Duration

1 week

Objectives

- **Observe and record** locations of weather fronts.
- **Predict** weather conditions based on data you collected.
- **Compare** the movement of weather fronts in different seasons.

Materials

pencils, colored
daily weather maps for consecutive days (5)

Weather Forecasting

The National Weather Service collects data from hundreds of weather stations located around the world. Daily newspapers summarize this weather data in the form of national weather maps. The data include temperature, precipitation, cloud cover, and barometric pressure. The patterns produced by the data allow meteorologists to identify weather fronts and to provide information about weather conditions around the globe.

In this investigation, you will use a series of daily weather maps to track the movements of weather systems in the winter months. Then, you will use these data to predict weather conditions.

Procedure

1. Find a local or national newspaper that prints a daily weather map from the National Weather Service. You may also use the Internet to find daily weather maps.
2. Cut out or print out the map, and write on it the date that it represents.
3. Make a data table similar to the sample table shown at the bottom of this page.
4. Fill in your table with the information from the weather map.
5. Make at least one copy of the blank weather map on the third page of this exercise.

Step 3

	Week 1 (winter)					Week 2 (spring)		
	1	2	3	4	5	1	2	3
Temperature								
Barometric pressure								
Barometric trend (R = rising; F = falling; S = steady)								
Wind direction								
Cloud cover (C=clear; CL=cloudy; PC=partly cloudy; O=overcast)								
Present weather (rain, sleet, snow, etc.)								
Prediction								

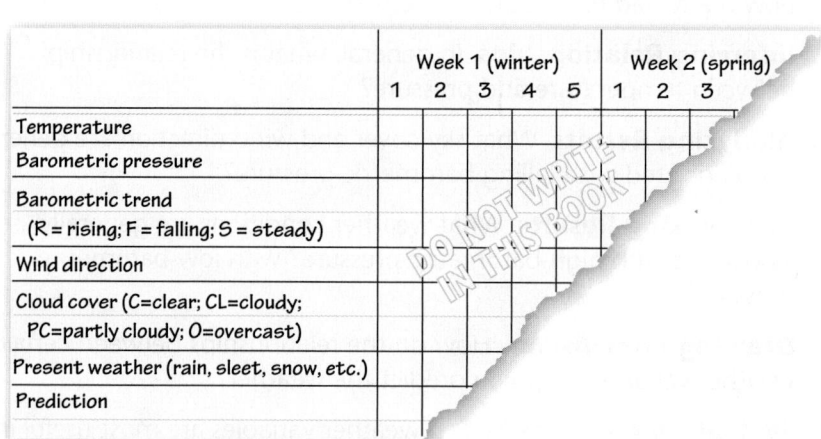

A meteorologist from the National Weather Service tracks the path of a hurricane in the Gulf of Mexico.

6. On your copy of the map, put an *L* at any locations where low-pressure centers are shown on the daily weather map that you collected in step 1. Circle the *Ls* with a colored pencil, and label each circle with the date.

7. Put an *H* on your map at the locations of any high-pressure centers. Circle the *Hs* with a second colored pencil, and label each circle with the date.

8. Repeat steps 1–7, but use four consecutive daily weather maps that follow the first day's map, and reuse your data table and weather map. For each symbol, use the same colors that you used for the first day's map.

9. Draw arrows to connect the daily positions of each high-pressure center and of each low-pressure center.

10. Use the formula below to calculate the average velocity (in kilometers per day) of each high-pressure center and each low-pressure center. The average velocity equals the total distance traveled divided by the number of days traveled, or

$$\text{average velocity} = \frac{\text{total distance traveled}}{\text{number of days}}$$

Long-Term Project 4, *continued*

Step 5

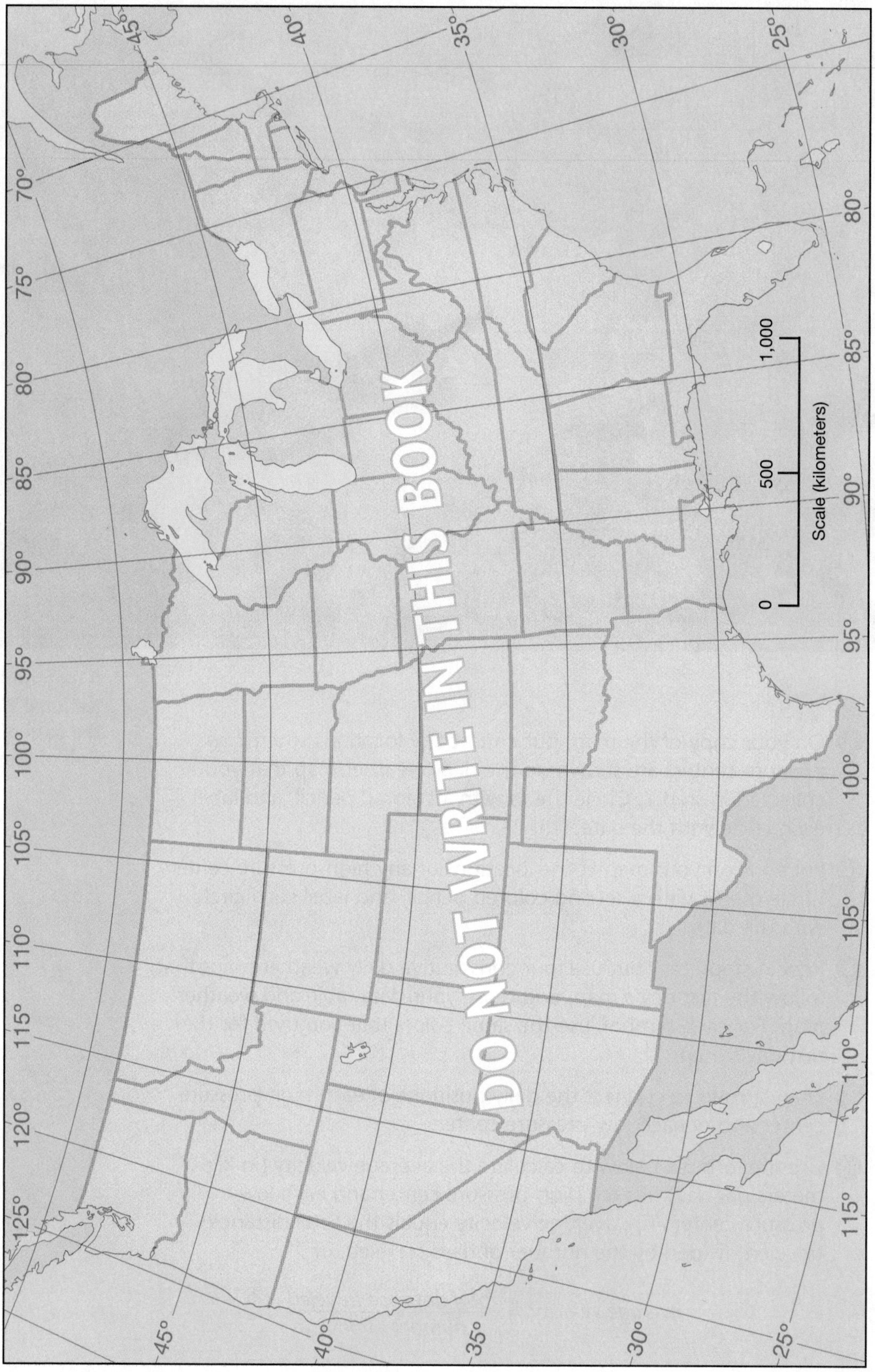

Many hurricane-prone areas have established evacuation routes to help people reach safety before a hurricane hits. This man is boarding up windows in his house to prepare for an imminent hurricane.

Analysis

1. **Analyzing Data** Generally, in which direction do the pressure centers over the United States move?
2. **Analyzing Results** From your calculations, what is the average rate of movement (in kilometers per day) of low- and high-pressure centers in winter?
3. **Making Predictions** Predict where the low- and high-pressure centers will be located on the day following the date of the last map in your series.
4. **Forming a Hypothesis** Refer to your series of daily weather maps to predict the weather for your hometown on the sixth day of the series. Write a forecast with your predictions of weather conditions.
5. **Evaluating Predictions** Was your prediction about the locations of the low- and high-pressure centers from question 3 accurate? Explain why or why not.
6. **Evaluating Hypotheses** Compare your weather prediction with the daily weather map for the appropriate day. Check the accuracy of your prediction. What factors could have caused errors in your prediction?
7. **Explaining Events** Describe the general weather conditions associated with regions of low and high atmospheric pressure.

Extension

Designing Experiments In the spring, repeat the entire investigation. What is the average rate of movement (in kilometers per day) of low- and high-pressure centers in the spring? Compare the rate of movement of pressure systems during spring and winter.

Long-Term Project 5

ENVIRONMENTAL CONNECTION

APPENDIX D

Duration

6 months (October 1 to April 1)

Objectives

- **Record** temperature and precipitation data for eight regions.
- **Graph and analyze** climate features for eight regions.
- **Classify** regions by using two climate classification systems.

Materials

almanac
atlas
paper, graph
rain gauge (optional)
thermometer (optional)
weather reports, daily

Safety

Comparing Climate Features

A graph of the monthly temperatures and amounts of precipitation for a region is called a *climatograph.* Climatographs can be used to compare the climates of different areas or to classify an area's climate.

In this investigation, you will use climate data to compare your local climate with the climates of other regions of the United States. You will keep a daily temperature and precipitation log. You will record data every day from the first day of October until the first day of April. You will then compare your graphed data with information about the world's climates. You will use this comparison to develop a conclusion about the type of climate that your location has.

Procedure

1. Listen to or watch a daily weather report for your area, or find this information in a daily newspaper or on the Internet. You may also keep your own records by using a thermometer and a rain gauge.
2. Beginning on the first day of October, keep a daily record of the high and low temperatures and of the amount of precipitation that occurs. During winter, snow should be melted before determining the amount of precipitation (in centimeters).

Rain gauges collect precipitation for scientists to measure.

3. Calculate the average temperature for each day by dividing the sum of the day's high and low temperatures by 2. Record this information.

4. At the end of each month, record the average monthly temperature given by the weather report, or calculate the average monthly temperature by dividing the sum of the daily averages by the number of days in the month. Also, record the total monthly precipitation given by the weather report.

5. Use the Internet or an almanac to look up climate data for your town or city and for seven other cities in the United States. Select one city from each of the following regions: New England, the Gulf Coast, the Midwest, the Southwest, the Pacific Northwest, the interior of Alaska, and the Hawaiian Islands.

6. Look up the average monthly temperatures and precipitation for your town or city and for each city that you chose. Record these data in a table.

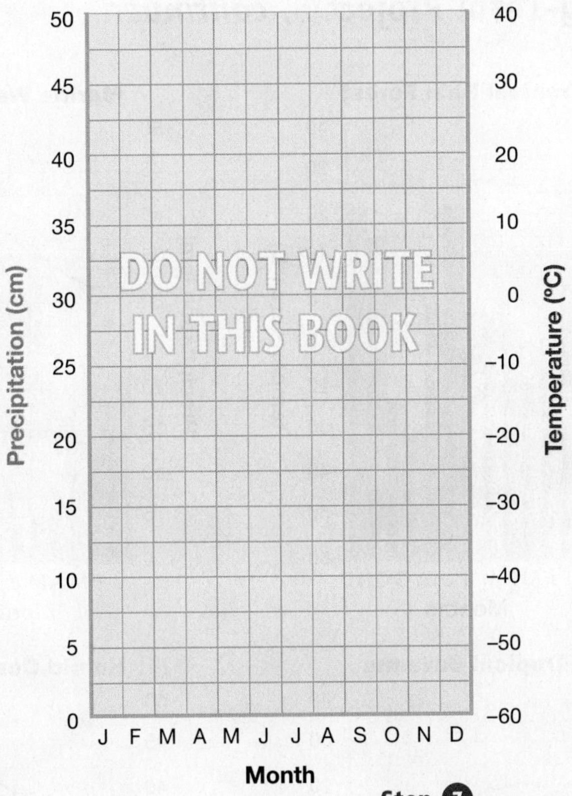

Step 7

7. On your graph paper, make eight copies of the blank climatograph shown on the upper-right side of this page.

8. Label each blank climatograph with the name of one of the seven cities. Label the eighth climatograph with the name of your town or city.

9. If you recorded temperature and precipitation in English (American) units, such as degrees Fahrenheit or inches, convert your measurements to SI units, such as degrees Celsius or centimeters. Use the SI Conversions table in Appendix E of this book to convert English units to SI units.

10. For each of the eight locations, plot the average temperature for January by placing a dot in the center of the square that is located in the column representing January and in the row representing that average temperature.

11. Using the same method, plot the average precipitation for January.

12. Repeat steps 10 and 11 for each month's data for each location. Then, connect the temperature points in order of consecutive months to form a line, and shade the columns from 0 up to the recorded precipitation amount for each month.

Long-Term Project 5, *continued*

Tropical Rain Forest

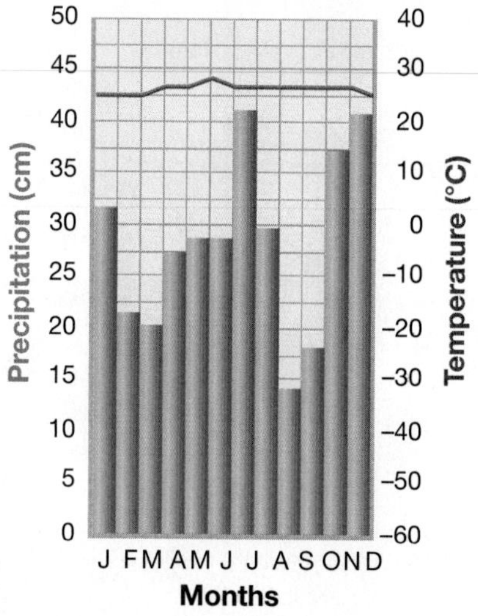

Marine West Coast

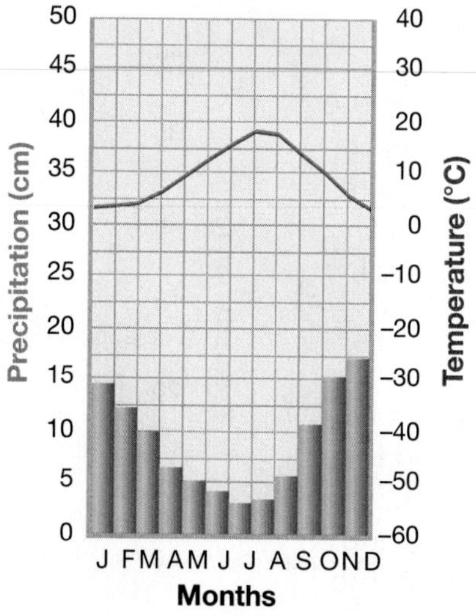

Subarctic

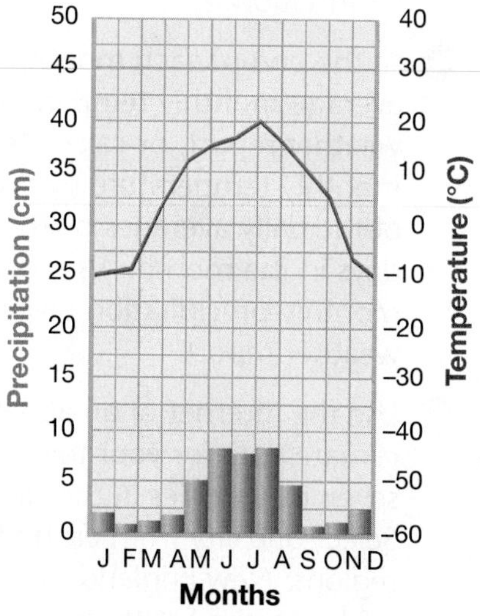

Tropical Savanna

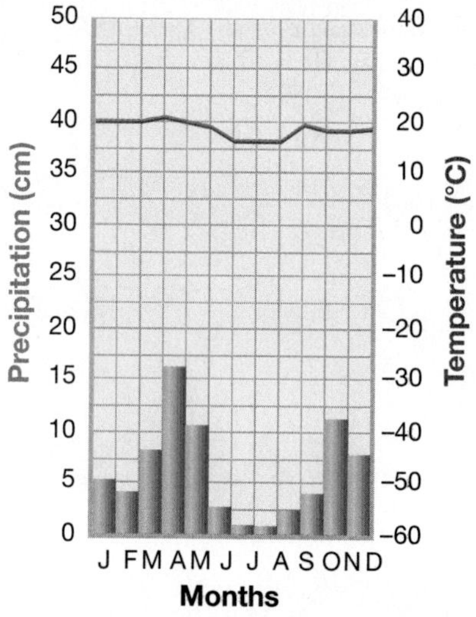

Humid Continental

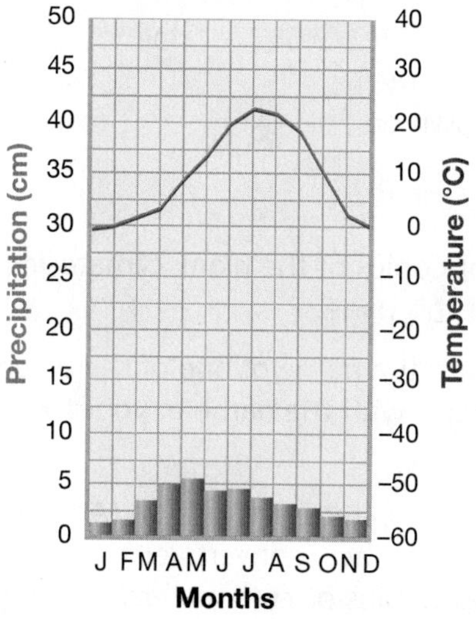

Mediterranean

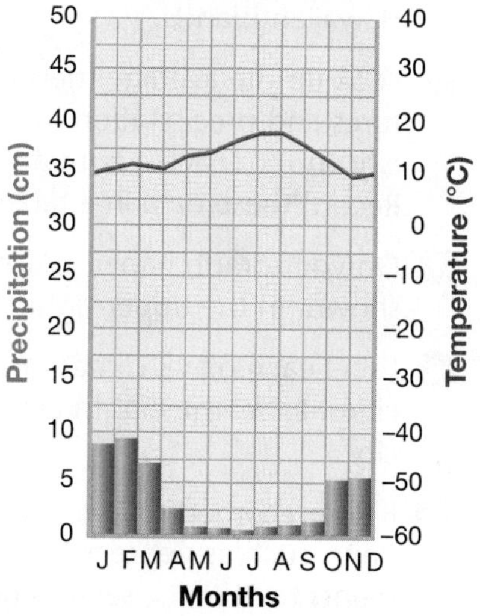

Tropical Desert

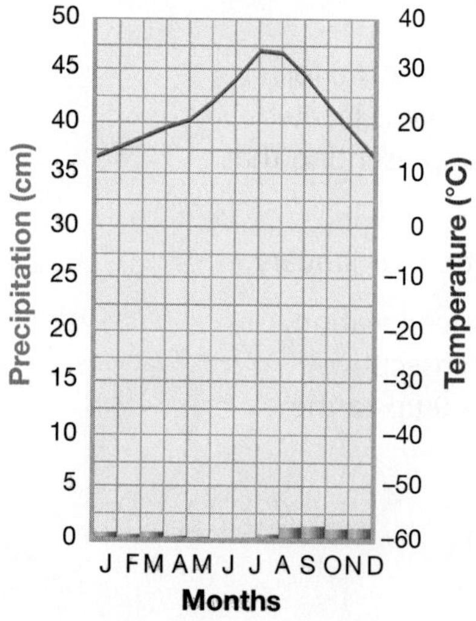

Tundra

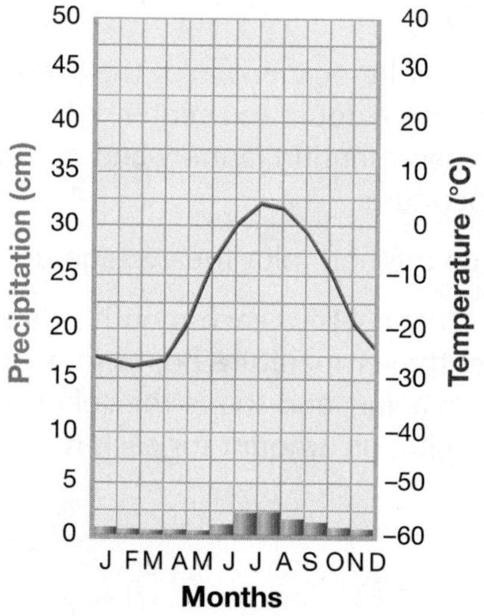

Although rain forests and deserts may have similar latitudes, the amount of precipitation that rain forests receive differs greatly from the amount that deserts receive.

Analysis

1. **Making Comparisons** Compare each of the climatographs of your seven chosen U.S. cities with the sample climatographs on the previous page. Identify the climate type or types for each location that you selected. What features of each climatograph helped you classify each region?
2. **Analyzing Results** Use the climatograph for your area to classify your regional climate. What features of your climatograph helped you identify the climate type?
3. **Examining Data** Compare the average temperatures and precipitation amounts for your location that you collected to the values that you obtained from the Internet or an almanac. Do you think that this year's climate data are typical for your region? Explain your answer.
4. **Classifying Information** How would each of the climatographs, including the one for your region, fit into the climate classification system outlined in the chapter entitled "Climate"?
5. **Evaluating Methods** In this investigation, you compared climates by looking at average precipitation and temperature. What other factors might affect the climate of an area? Give examples of each factor.

Extension

Making Comparisons
Bermuda is a small island in the Atlantic Ocean. Bermuda is at about the same latitude as St. Louis, Missouri, which lies in the middle of a continent. In which of the two locations does the temperature vary least from month to month? Explain the cause of the temperature pattern in the location that has the more moderate pattern.

Long-Term Project 6

Duration
8 months

Objectives

- **Observe** the position of Mars in the night sky for 8 months.
- **Graph** the apparent movement of Mars through the night sky.
- **Identify** changes in the relative positions of Earth and Mars.

Materials

celestial sphere model (optional)
compass, magnetic
constellation charts
flashlight
metric ruler

Planetary Motions

While observing the evening sky over a period of time, you might have noticed that some objects look like stars but do not maintain fixed positions relative to the celestial sphere. These objects are the planets. As viewed from Earth at various times during the year, the patterns in the planets' motions differ from the patterns that you might expect.

In this investigation, you will observe the planet Mars in the night sky on the 1st and 15th of each month over a period of 8 months. Then, you will use your observations to draw conclusions and make predictions about planetary motion.

Procedure

1. Obtain data on the positions of Mars in the night sky throughout the last year from an astronomical yearbook or from the Internet. Astronomical yearbooks can be found at most libraries.
2. Check the Internet, an almanac, or the weather section of a newspaper to find the time of night that Mars will be visible in your area.
3. Copy the star chart on the third and fourth pages of this lab onto a separate piece of paper.
4. Practice measuring angular distance by using the method shown at the bottom of this page. Always use the same hand when measuring angular distance. To have confidence in the accuracy of your measurements, you may need to practice measuring angular distance for a few days or weeks before beginning this lab.

Step 4

Estimating Angular Distance in Degrees

Hold your hand at arm's length.

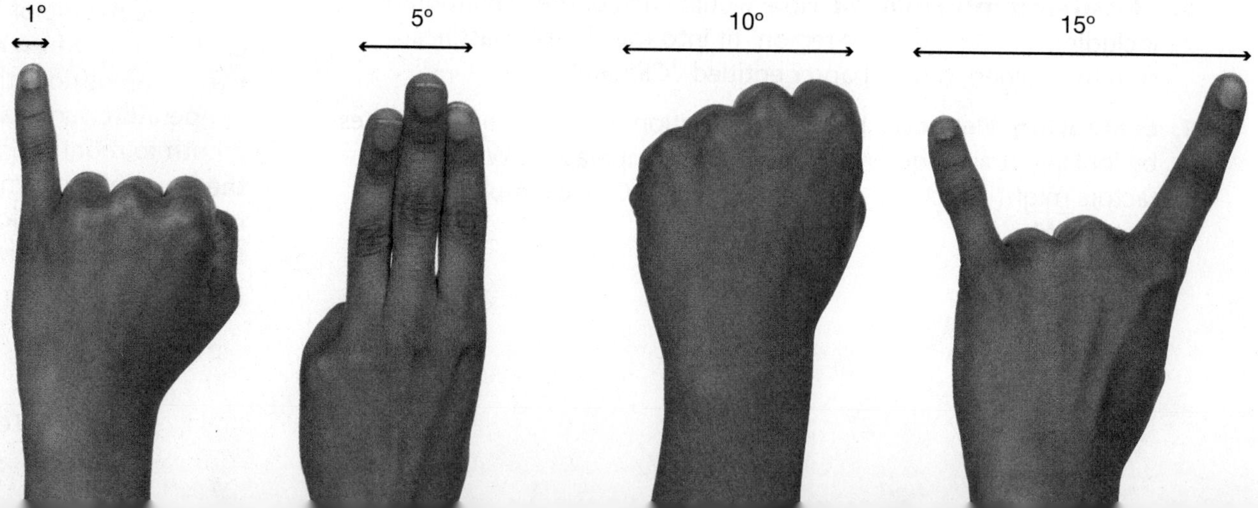

In 2003, Mars was closer to Earth than it had been for about 60,000 years.

5 On the 1st and 15th of each month, go at night to an area that gives you a clear view of the eastern, southern, and western skies. (Note: If the skies are not clear on the 1st and 15th, make observations as close to these dates as possible.)

6 At the same time each night, locate Mars in the night sky. Mars will have a dull red appearance.

7 Use your magnetic compass to position yourself facing south, and observe the position of Mars relative to the background stars.

8 Choose a constellation. Use the method illustrated at the bottom of the previous page to estimate Mars's angular distance (in degrees) from the constellation.

9 On your star chart, locate the constellation from which you measured Mars's angular distance. Draw Mars in the appropriate position relative to the constellation, and label the planet's position with the date.

10 Compare the apparent brightness of Mars with that of the background stars. Record your observation on a separate sheet of paper.

11 Repeat steps 6–10 on the 1st and 15th of each month for the next 8 months.

12 After each observation, draw an arrow from Mars's previous position to the position that you just observed. The progression of arrows will show Mars's apparent path.

Long-Term Project 6, *continued*

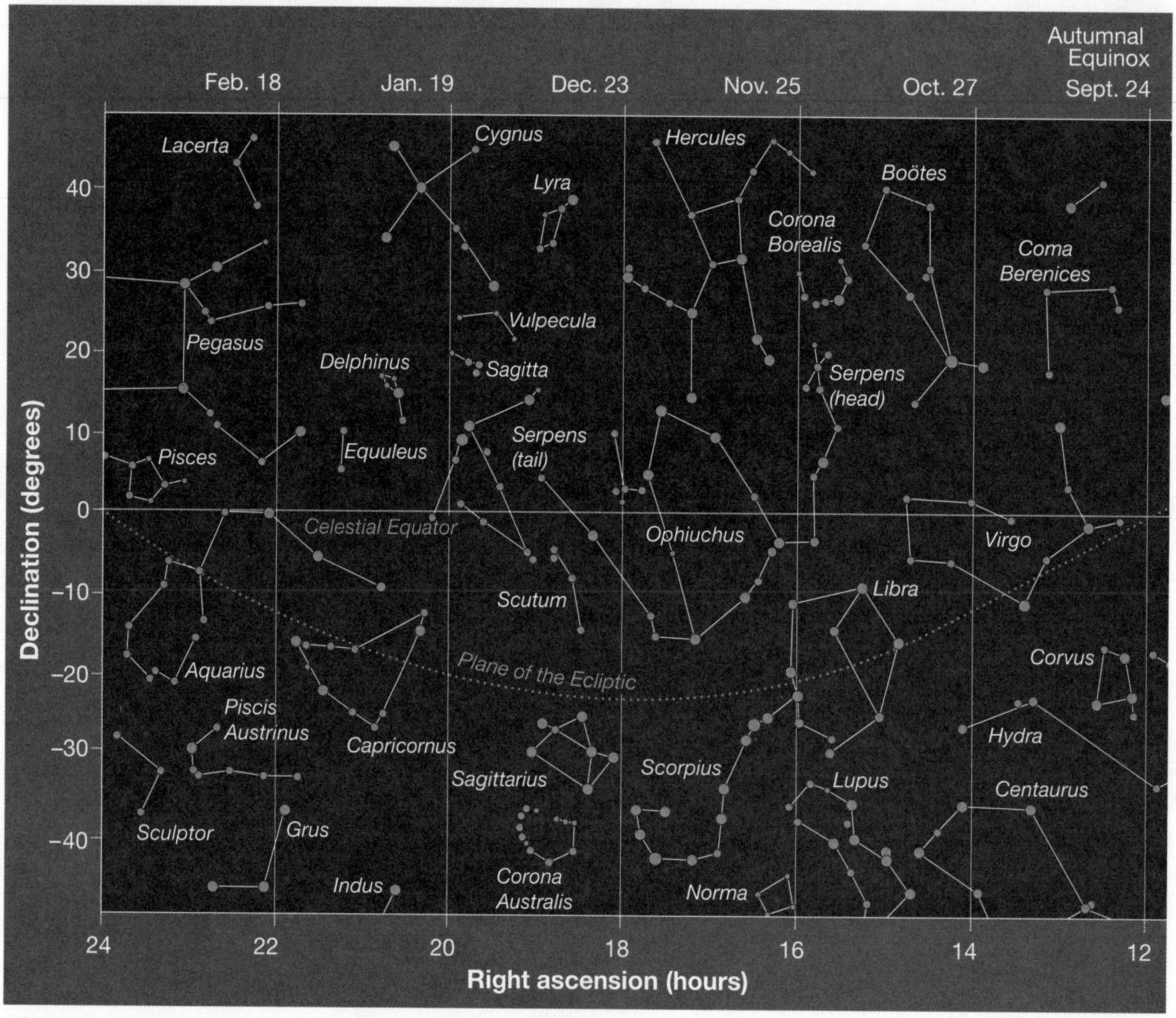

Step 3

Analysis

1. **Examining Data** In which months does Mars appear highest in the night sky? lowest in the night sky?
2. **Evaluating Results** In which direction does Mars appear to move across the sky? At any point during the year, does Mars appear to deviate from this apparent path?
3. **Making Predictions** In one year from today, will Mars be in the same position that it is in today? Explain.
4. **Drawing Conclusions** From your observations of the apparent brightness of Mars at different times of the year, what can you infer about the distance between Mars and Earth? Explain your answer.

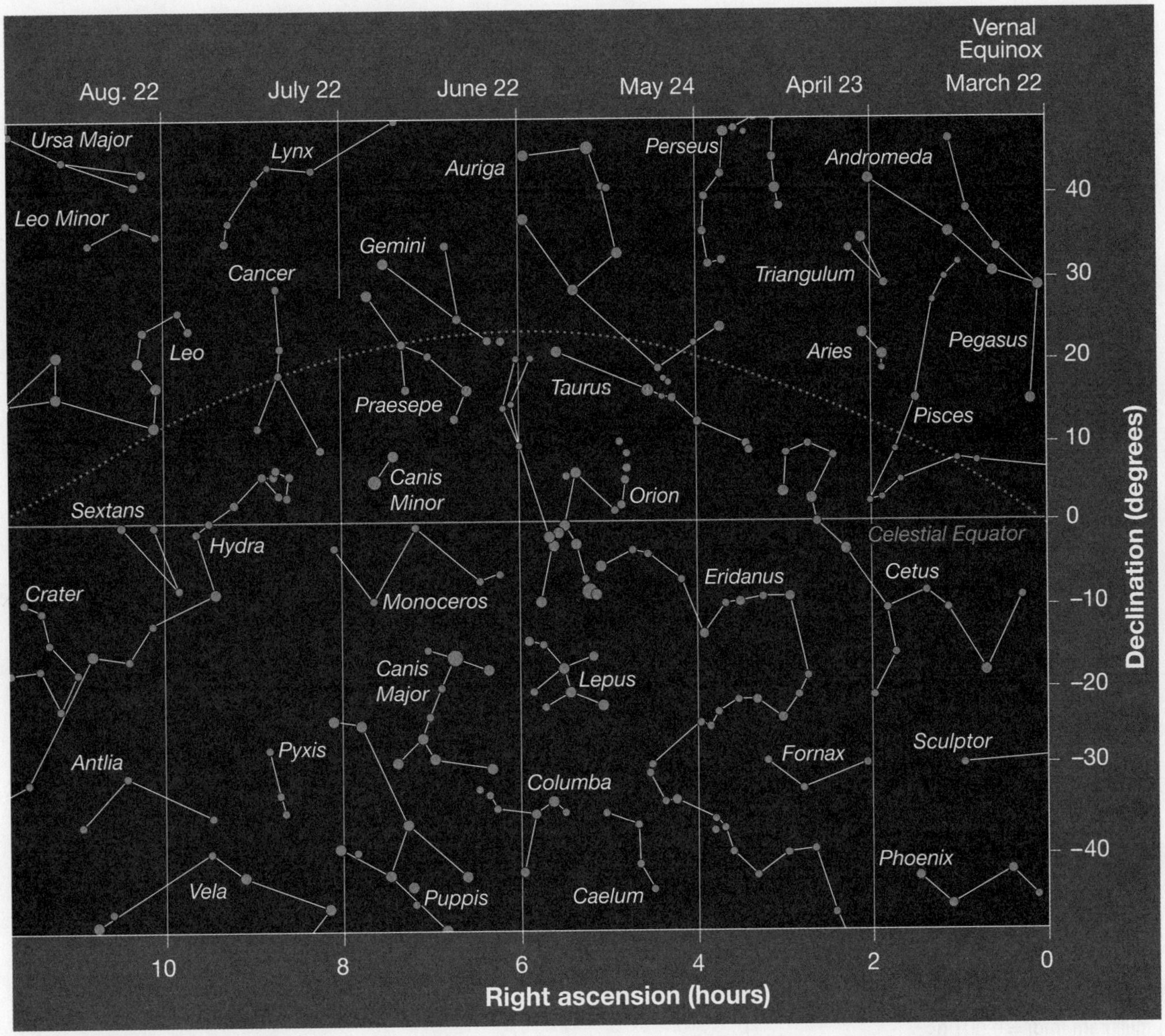

Extension

Evaluating Predictions In the Analysis section of this investigation, you predicted the position of Mars in one year. Use the Internet or library to research where astronomers predict Mars will be in one year. Was your prediction accurate? Explain why or why not.

Evaluating Hypotheses Repeat this investigation, but measure the positions of another planet, such as Venus, over the course of 8 months. Write a brief essay that explains how the paths of Mars and Venus differ.

REFERENCE TABLES

SI Conversions

The metric system is used for making measurements in science. The official name of this system is the Système Internationale d'Unités, or International System of Measurements (SI).

SI Units	From SI to English	From English to SI
Length		
kilometer (km) = 1,000 m	1 km = 0.62 mile	1 mile = 1.609 km
meter (m) = 100 cm	1 m = 3.28 feet	1 foot = 0.305 m
centimeter (cm) = 0.01 m	1 cm = 0.394 inch	1 inch = 2.54 cm
millimeter (mm) = 0.001 m	1 mm = 0.039 inch	
micrometer (µm) = 0.000 001 m		
nanometer (nm) = 0.000 000 001 m		
Area		
square kilometer (km^2) = 100 hectares	1 km^2 = 0.386 square mile	1 square mile = 2.590 km^2
hectare (ha) = 10,000 m^2	1 ha = 2.471 acres	1 acre = 0.405 ha
square meter (m^2) = 10,000 cm^2	1 m^2 = 10.765 square feet	1 square foot = 0.093 m^2
square centimeter (cm^2) = 100 mm^2	1 cm^2 = 0.155 square inch	1 square inch = 6.452 cm^2
Volume		
liter (L) = 1,000 mL = 1 dm^3	1 L = 1.06 fluid quarts	1 fluid quart = 0.946 L
milliliter (mL) = 0.001 L = 1 cm^3	1 mL = 0.034 fluid ounce	1 fluid ounce = 29.577 mL
microliter (µL) = 0.000 001 L		
Mass		* Equivalent weight at Earth's surface
kilogram (kg) = 1,000 g	1 kg = 2.205 pounds*	1 pound* = 0.454 kg
gram (g) = 1,000 mg	1 g = 0.035 ounce*	1 ounce* = 28.35 g
milligram (mg) = 0.001 g		
microgram (µg) = 0.000 001 g		
Energy		
British Thermal Units (BTU)	1 BTU = 1,055.056 joules	1 joule = 0.00095 BTU
Temperature		

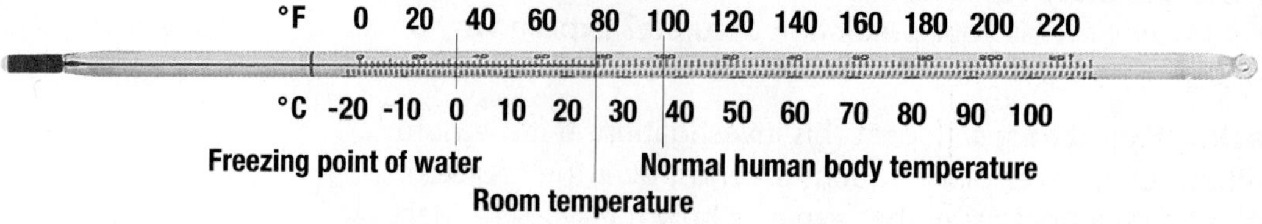

Conversion of Fahrenheit to Celsius:
$°C = \frac{5}{9}(°F - 32)$

Conversion of Celsius to Fahrenheit:
$°F = \frac{9}{5}(°C) + 32$

Mineral Uses

Metallic Minerals

Mineral and chemical formula	Location of economically important deposits	Important uses
Chalcopyrite, $CuFeS_2$	Chile, U.S., and Indonesia	electrical and electronic products, wiring, telecommunications equipment, industrial machinery and equipment
Chromite, $FeCr_2O_4$	South Africa, Kazahkstan, and India	production of stainless steel, alloys, and metal plating
Galena, PbS	Australia, China, and U.S.	batteries, ammunition, glass and ceramics, and X-ray shielding
Gold, Au	South Africa, U.S., and Australia	computers, communications equipment, spacecraft, jet engines, dentistry, jewelry, and coins
Ilmenite, $FeTiO_3$	Australia, South Africa, and Canada	jet engines; missile components; and white pigment in paints, toothpaste, and candy
Magnetite, Fe_3O_4	China, Brazil, and Australia	steelmaking
Uraninite, UO_2	Canada and Australia	fuel in nuclear reactors and manufacture of radioisotopes

Nonmetallic Minerals

Mineral and chemical formula	Location of economically important deposits	Important uses
Barite, $BaSO_4$	China, India, and U.S.	weighting agent in oil well drilling fluids, automobile paint primer, and X-ray diagnostic work
Borax, $Na_2B_4O_7 \bullet 10H_2O$	Turkey, U.S., and Russia	glass, soaps and detergents, agriculture, fire retardants, and plastics and polymer additives
Calcite, $CaCO_3$	China, U.S., and Russia	cement, lime production, crushed stone, glassmaking, chemicals, and optics
Diamond, C	Australia, Democratic Republic of the Congo, and Russia	jewelry, cutting tools, drill bits, and manufacture of computer chips
Fluorite, CaF_2	China, Mexico, and South Africa	hydrofluoric acid, steelmaking, water fluoridation, solvents, manufacture of glass, and enamels
Gypsum, $CaSO_4 \bullet 2H_2O$	U.S., Iran, and Canada	wallboard, building plasters, and manufacture of cement
Halite, NaCl	U.S., China, and Germany	chemical production, human and animal nutrition, highway deicer, and water softener
Sulfur, S	Canada, U.S., and Russia	sulfuric acid, fertilizers, gunpowder, and tires
Kaolinite, $Al_2Si_2O_5(OH)_4$	U.S., Uzbehkistan, and Czech Republic	glossy paper and whitener and abrasive in toothpaste
Orthoclase, $KAlSi_3O_8$	Italy, Turkey, and U.S.	glass, ceramics, and soaps
Quartz, SiO_2	U.S., Germany, and France	glass, computer chips, ceramics, abrasives, and water filtration
Talc, $Mg_3Si_4O_{10}(OH)_2$	China, U.S., and Republic of Korea	ceramics, plastics, paint, paper, rubber, and cosmetics

Guide to Common Minerals

This table is used in the chapter lab for the chapter entitled "Minerals of Earth's Crust."

	Luster		Hardness	Cleavage	Fracture	Color/opacity
Nonmetallic; light color	glassy to pearly	Scratches glass	6	two cleavage planes at nearly right angles		various colors but often white or pink; opaque
	glassy		6	two cleavage planes at 86° and 94°		colorless, white, pink, or various colors; translucent to opaque
	glassy and waxy		7	no cleavage	conchoidal fracture	various colors; transparent to opaque
	glassy		6.5–7	no cleavage	conchiodal to irregular fracture	olive green; transparent to translucent
	glassy	Does not scratch glass	2.5–3	three cleavage planes at right angles		colorless to gray; transparent to opaque
	glassy		3	three cleavage planes at 75° and 105°		colorless or white and may be tinted; transparent to opaque
	glassy, pearly, or silky		1–2.5	one perfect cleavage plane	conchoidal and fibrous fracture	white, pink, or gray to colorless; transparent to opaque
	pearly to waxy		1	one cleavage plane		white to green; opaque
	glassy or pearly		2–2.5	one cleavage plane		colorless to light gray or brown; translucent to opaque
	glassy		4	eight cleavage planes (octahedral)		green, yellow, purple, and other colors; transparent to translucent
	glassy		4.5–5	no cleavage	conchiodal to irregular fracture	green, blue, violet, brown, or colorless; translucent to opaque
	silky		3.5–4	no cleavage	irregular, splintery fracture	green; translucent to opaque
Nonmetallic; dark color	glassy and silky	Scratches glass	5–6	two cleavage planes at 56° and 124°		dark green, brown, or black; translucent to opaque
	resinous and glassy		6.5–7.5	no cleavage	irregular fracture	dark red or green; transparent to opaque
	pearly and glassy	Does not scratch glass	2.5–3	one cleavage plane		black to dark brown; translucent to opaque
	metallic to earthy		1–2	one cleavage plane		black to gray; opaque
Metallic	metallic or earthy	Does not scratch glass	5.5–6.5	no cleavage	irregular fracture	reddish brown to black; opaque
	metallic		2.5	three cleavage planes at right angles		lead gray; opaque
	metallic	Scratches glass	5–6	two cleavage planes at 56° and 124°		iron black; opaque
	metallic		6–6.5	no cleavage	conchoidal to irregular fracture	brass yellow; opaque

Streak	Specific gravity	Other properties	Mineral name and chemical formula
white	2.6	prismatic, columnar, or tabular crystals	orthoclase, $KAlSi_3O_8$
blue-gray to white	2.6 to 2.7	striations	plagioclase, (Na, Cl)(Al, Si)$_4O_8$
white	2.65	six-sided crystals	quartz, SiO_2
white to pale green	3.2 to 3.3	stubby, prismatic crystals	olivine, $(Mg, Fe)_2SiO_4$
white	2.2	cubic crystals and salty taste	halite, NaCl
white	2.7	may produce double image when you look through it	calcite, $CaCO_3$
white	2.2 to 2.4	thin layers and flexible	gypsum, $CaSO_4 \bullet 2H_2O$
white	2.7 to 2.8	soapy feel and thin scales	talc, $Mg_3Si_4O_{10}(OH)_2$
white	2.7 to 3	thin sheets	muscovite, $KAl_2Si_3O_{10}(OH)_2$
white	3.2	fluorescent under UV light; cubic and six-sided crystals	fluorite, CaF_2
white or pale red-brown	3.1	six-sided crystals	apatite, $Ca_5(OH, F, Cl)(PO_4)_3$
emerald green	4	fibrous, radiating aggregates or circular, banded structure	malachite, $CuCO_3 \bullet Cu(OH)_2$
pale green or white	3.2	six-sided crystals	hornblende, $(Ca, Na)_{2\text{-}3}(Mg, Fe, Al)_5 Si_6(Si, Al)_2O_{22}(OH)_2$
white	4.2	12- or 24-sided crystals	garnet, $Fe_3Al_2(SiO_4)_3$
white to gray	2.7 to 3.2	thin, flexible sheets	biotite, $K(Mg, Fe)_3AlSi_3O_{10}(OH)_2$
black to dark green	2.3	greasy feel, soft, and flaky	graphite, C
red to red-brown	5.25	granular masses	hematite, Fe_2O_3
lead gray to black	7.4 to 7.6	very heavy	galena, PbS
black to dark green	5.2	8- or 12-sided crystals; may be magnetic	magnetite, Fe_3O_4
greenish black	5	cubic crystals	pyrite, FeS_2

Guide to Common Rocks

This table is used in the chapter lab for the chapter entitled "Rocks."

Rock class	Grain size	Description	Rock class	Rock name
Made of crystals	Coarse grained	mostly light in color; shades of pink, gray, and white are common	igneous	granite
		dark in color; commonly black and white; heavy heft	igneous	gabbro
		foliated; layers of different minerals give a banded appearance	metamorphic	gneiss
		foliated; contains abundant amount of quartz, and may contain garnet; flaky minerals	metamorphic	schist
		nonfoliated; reacts with acid	metamorphic	marble
	Fine grained	usually light in color; many holes and spongy appearance; may float in water	igneous	pumice
		light to dark in color; glassy luster; conchoidal fracture	igneous	obsidian
		dark in color; may ring like a bell when struck with a hammer	igneous	basalt
		fine grained; foliated; cleaves into thin, flat plates	metamorphic	slate
Made of rock particles	Coarse grained	coarse-grained particles, more than 2 mm; rounded pebbles; some sorting; clay and sand are visible	sedimentary	conglomerate
		well-preserved fossils are common; can be scratched with a knife; many colors but usually white-gray; reacts with acid	sedimentary	limestone
		cube-shaped crystals; commonly colorless; does not react with acid	sedimentary	halite
	Medium grained	1/16 to 2 mm grains; mostly quartz fragments; surface feels sandy	sedimentary	sandstone
	Fine grained	soft and porous; commonly white or buff color	sedimentary	chalk
		microscopic grains; clay composition; smooth surface; hardened mud appearance	sedimentary	shale

Radiogenic Isotopes and Half-Life

Unstable isotopes, called *radiogenic isotopes* or *radioactive isotopes,* decay to form different isotopes called *daughter isotopes.* Each radiogenic isotope breaks down at a predictable rate, called its *half-life,* into a daughter isotope. Because of this predictable decay pattern, radiogenic isotopes are used to determine numeric dates for rocks. The table below describes several common radiometric dating methods.

Radiometric dating method	How it works	Parent isotope	Daughter isotope	Half-life	Effective dating range
Argon-argon dating ($^{39}Ar/^{40}Ar$)	Comparison made between ^{39}Ar and ^{40}Ar in a sample specially irradiated to form ^{39}Ar; ^{39}Ar is equivalent to ^{40}K in potassium-argon dating.	potassium-40, ^{40}K irradiated to form argon-39, ^{39}Ar	argon-40, ^{40}Ar	1.25 billion years	10,000 to 4.6 billion years
Fission track dating	Tracks of damage created by charged particles from radioactive decay that pass through a mineral's crystal lattice are counted under an electron microscope.	uranium, U	ultimately, lead, Pb, but also several other daughter isotopes	not applicable	500 years to 1 billion years
Potassium-argon dating ($^{40}K/^{40}Ar$)	Comparison is made between the amount of ^{40}K and amount of ^{40}Ar; over time, ^{40}K decreases and ^{40}Ar increases.	potassium-40, ^{40}K	argon-40, ^{40}Ar	1.25 billion years	50,000 to 4.6 billion years
Radiocarbon dating ($^{14}C/^{12}C$)	Comparison is made between the amount of ^{14}C in organic matter and the amount of ^{12}C; ^{12}C remains constant over time, and ^{14}C breaks down.	carbon-14, ^{14}C	nitrogen-14, ^{14}N	5,730 years	$<$70,000 years
Rubidium-strontium dating ($^{87}Rb/^{87}Sr$)	Comparison made between the ratio of $^{87}Sr/^{86}Sr$ and the ratio of $^{87}Rb/^{86}Sr$ to find the amount of ^{87}Sr formed by radioactive decay.	rubidium-87, ^{87}Rb	strontium-87, ^{87}Sr	48.1 billion years	10 million to 4.6 billion years
Thorium-lead dating ($^{232}Th/^{208}Pb$)	Comparison made between amount of ^{232}Th and the ratio of $^{208}Pb/^{204}Pb$; ^{232}Th breaks into ^{208}Pb, and ^{204}Pb remains constant.	thorium-232, ^{232}Th	lead-208, ^{208}Pb	14.0 billion years	$>$200 million years
Uranium-lead dating ($^{235}U/^{207}Pb$)	Comparison made between amount of ^{235}U and the ratio of $^{207}Pb/^{204}Pb$; ^{235}U breaks into ^{207}Pb, and ^{204}Pb remains constant.	uranium-235, ^{235}U	lead-207, ^{207}Pb	704 million years	10 million to 4.6 billion years
Uranium-lead dating ($^{238}U/^{206}Pb$)	Comparison made between amount of ^{238}U and the ratio of $^{206}Pb/^{204}Pb$; ^{238}U breaks into ^{206}Pb, and ^{204}Pb remains constant.	uranium-238, ^{238}U	lead-206, ^{206}Pb	4.5 billion years	10 million to 4.6 billion years

Topographic and Geologic Map Symbols

Topographic Map Symbols		Geologic Map Symbols

Topographic Map Symbols

Elevation markers

Contour lines	
Index contour lines	100
Depression contour lines	
Water elevation	9600
Spot elevation	x 9136

Boundaries

National	
State	
County, parish, municipal	
Township, precinct, town	
Incorporated city, village, or town	
National or state reservation	
Small park, cemetery, airport, etc.	
Land grant	

Buildings and Structures

Buildings	
School	
Church	
Cemetery	† cem
Barn and warehouse	
Wells (non-water)	○ oil ○ gas
Open-pit mine, quarry, or prospect	
Tunnel	
Benchmark	⊗BM △8025
National Park	
Campsite	
Bridge	

Roads and Railroads

Divided highway	
Road	
Trail	
Railroad	

Geologic Map Symbols

Sedimentary Rocks

Breccia	
Conglomerate	
Dolomite	
Limestone	
Mudstone	
Sandstone	
Siltstone	
Shale	

Igneous and Metamorphic Rocks

Extrusive	
Intrusive	
Metamorphic	

Features

River	
Water well	water
Spring	
Lake	
Glacier

Contour Map

This map is used in the chapter lab for the chapter entitled "Models of the Earth."

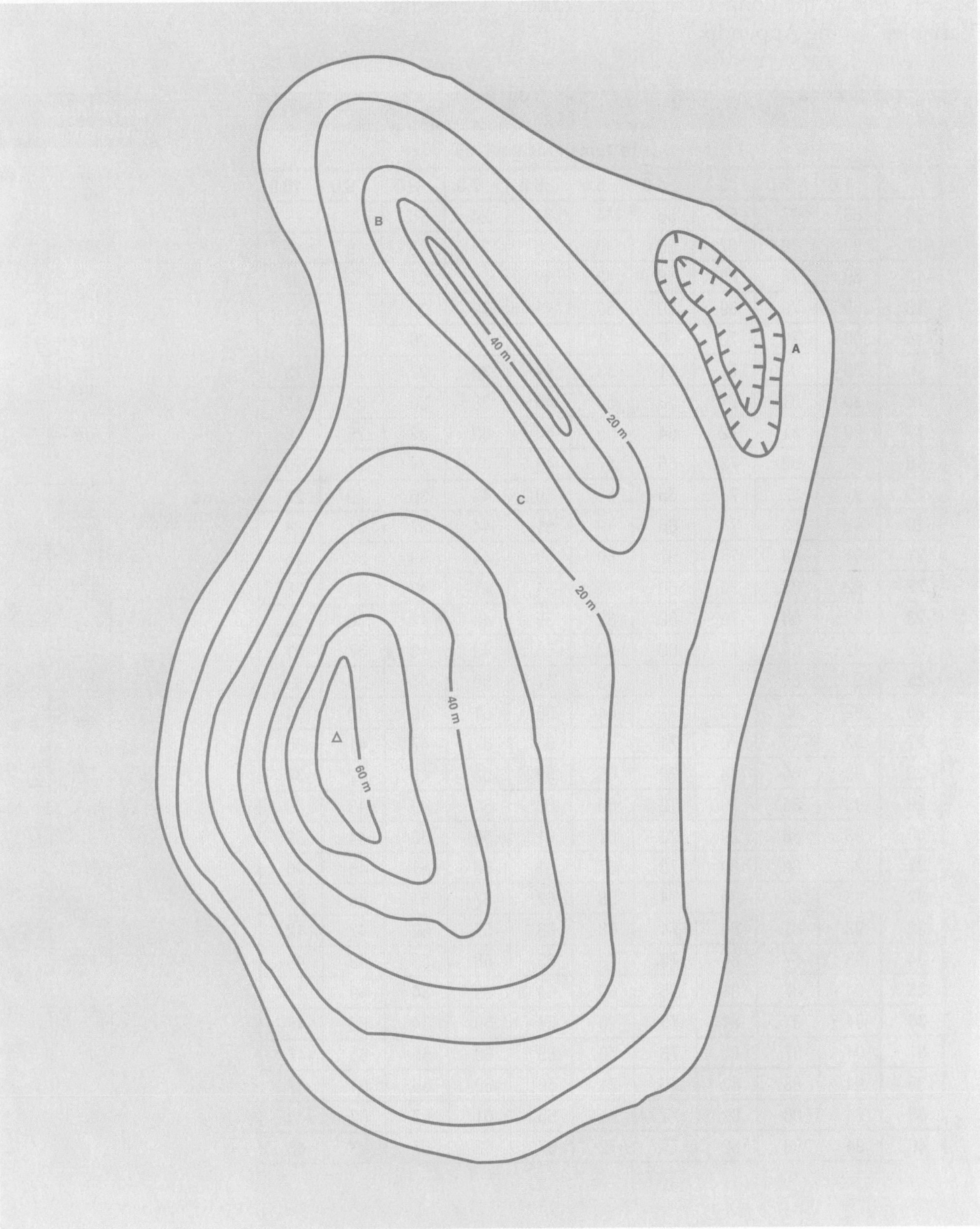

Humidity and Air Pressure

The Relative Humidity table below is used in the chapter lab for the chapter entitled "Water in the Atmosphere." The Barometric Conversion Scale is used in the Long-Term Project entitled "Correlating Weather Variables" in the Appendix.

Relative Humidity (%)

Dry-bulb temperature (°C)	Difference in temperature (°C)									
	1.0	**2.0**	**3.0**	**4.0**	**5.0**	**6.0**	**7.0**	**8.0**	**9.0**	**10.0**
10	88	77	66	55	44	34	24	15	6	—
11	89	78	67	56	46	36	27	18	9	—
12	89	78	68	58	48	39	29	21	12	—
13	89	79	69	59	50	41	32	23	15	7
14	90	79	70	60	51	42	34	26	18	10
15	90	80	71	61	53	44	36	27	20	13
16	90	81	71	63	54	46	38	30	23	15
17	90	81	72	64	55	47	40	32	25	18
18	91	82	73	65	57	49	41	34	27	20
19	91	82	74	65	58	50	43	36	29	22
20	91	83	74	66	59	51	44	37	31	24
21	91	83	75	67	60	53	46	39	32	26
22	92	83	76	68	61	54	47	40	34	28
23	92	84	76	69	62	55	48	42	36	30
24	92	84	77	69	62	56	49	43	37	31
25	92	84	77	70	63	57	50	44	39	33
26	92	85	78	71	64	58	51	46	40	34
27	92	85	78	71	65	58	52	47	41	36
28	93	85	78	72	65	59	53	48	42	37
29	93	86	79	72	66	60	54	49	43	38
30	93	86	79	73	67	61	55	50	44	39
31	93	86	80	73	67	61	56	51	45	40
32	93	86	80	74	68	62	57	51	46	41
33	93	87	80	74	68	63	57	52	47	42
34	93	87	81	75	69	63	58	53	48	43
35	94	87	81	75	69	64	59	54	49	44
36	94	87	81	75	70	64	59	54	50	45
37	94	87	82	76	70	65	60	55	51	46
38	94	88	82	76	71	66	60	56	51	47
39	94	88	82	77	71	66	61	57	52	48
40	94	88	82	77	72	67	62	57	53	48

Barometric Conversion Scale

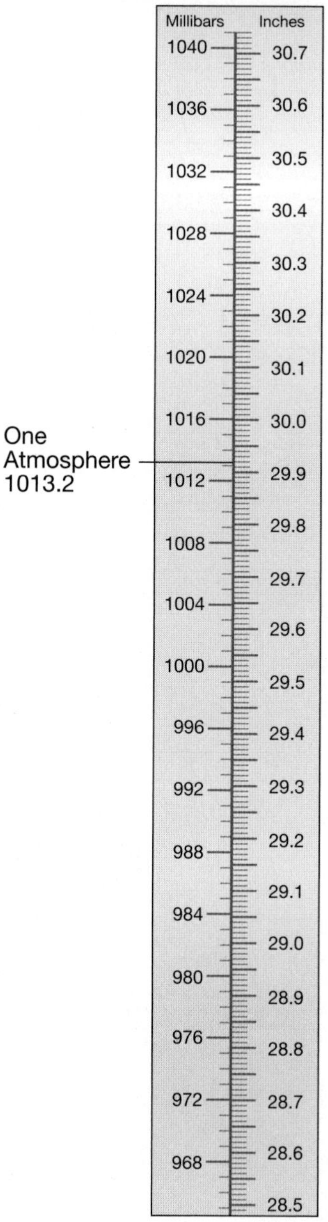

Weather Map of the United States

This map is used in the chapter lab for the chapter entitled "Weather."

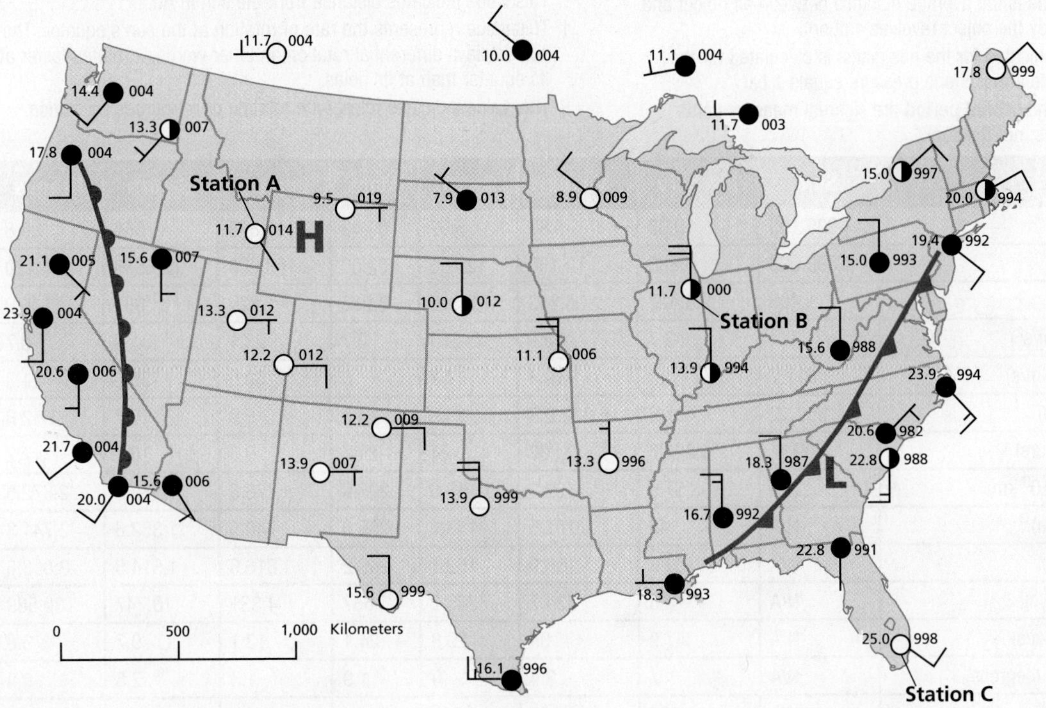

Weather Map Symbols

This chart is used in the Long-Term Project entitled "Weather Forecasting."

Cloud cover (fraction of sky covered)	◯ Clear	◔ $\frac{1}{8}$	◔ Scattered	◑ $\frac{3}{8}$	◑ $\frac{4}{8}$
	◑ $\frac{5}{8}$	◕ Broken	◕ $\frac{7}{8}$	● Overcast ⊗ Obscured	Ⓜ No data
Wind speed (knots)	⊙ Calm	1 to 2	3 to 7	8 to 12	13 to 17
	18 to 22	23 to 27	48 to 52	73 to 77	103 to 107
Wind direction	North	Northeast	East	Southeast	
	South	Southwest	West	Northwest	
Weather conditions	Drizzle	Fog	Hail	Haze	Rain Shower
	Freezing rain	Smoke	Snow	Thunderstorm	Hurricane Tropical storm

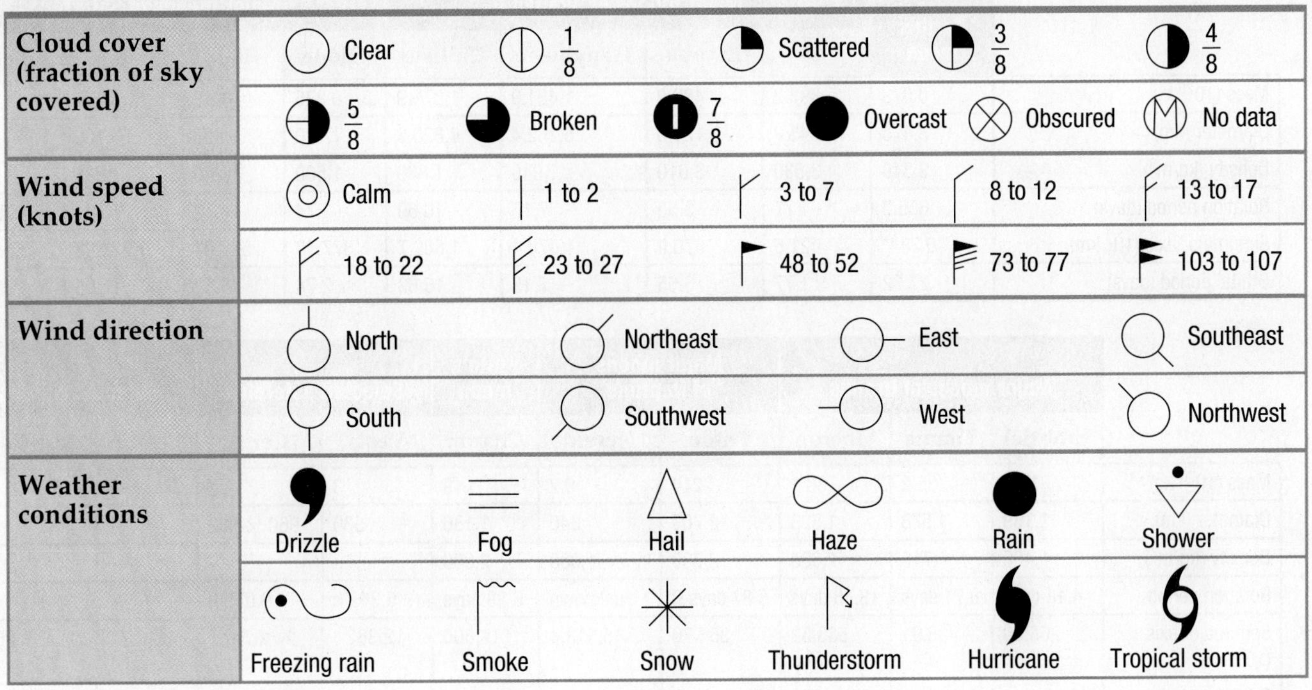

Solar System Data

Notes

The **semimajor axis** is the average distance between an object and its primary (the body the object revolves around).

Surface gravity indicated for the gas giants is calculated for the altitude at which the atmospheric pressure equals 1 bar.

Rotation period and **orbital period** are sidereal measurements (relative to the stars, not the sun).

* This value indicates distance from the sun in AU.

† This value represents the rate of rotation at the sun's equator. The sun displays differential rotation; in other words, it rotates faster at its equator than at its poles.

R This value indicates retrograde rotation or retrograde revolution.

	Sun	Mercury	Venus	Earth	Mars	Jupiter	Saturn	Uranus	Neptune
Mass (10^{24} kg)	1,989,100	0.33	4.87	5.97	0.642	1,899	568	86.8	102
Diameter (km)	1,390,000	4,880	12,100	12,756	6,800	143,000	120,535	51,120	49,530
Density (kg/m^3)	1,408	5,427	5,243	5,515	3,933	1,326	687	1,270	1,638
Surface gravity (m/s^2)	274	3.7	8.9	9.8	3.7	23.1	9	8.7	11
Escape velocity (km/s)	617.7	4.3	10.4	11.2	5	59.5	35.5	21.3	23.5
Rotation period (h)	609.12	1,407.6	5,832.5 R	23.9	24.6	9.9	10.7	17.2 R	16.1
Length of day (hours)	609.6†	4,222.6	2,802	24	24.7	9.9	10.7	17.2	16.1
Semimajor axis (10^6 km)	N/A	57.9	108.2	149.6	227.9	778.6	1,433.5	2,872.5	4,495.1
Perihelion (10^6 km)	N/A	46	107.5	147.1	206.6	740.5	1,352.6	2,741.3	4,444.5
Aphelion (10^6 km)	N/A	69.8	108.9	152.1	249.2	816.6	1,514.5	3,003.6	4,545.7
Orbital period (days)	N/A	88	224.7	365.2	687	4,331	10,747	30,589	59,800
Orbital velocity (km/s)	N/A	47.9	35	29.8	24.1	13.1	9.7	6.8	5.4
Orbital inclination (degrees)	N/A	7	3.4	0	1.9	1.3	2.5	0.8	1.8
Orbital eccentricity	N/A	0.205	0.007	0.017	0.094	0.049	0.057	0.046	0.011
Axial tilt (degrees)	7.25	0.01	2.6	23.5	25.2	3.1	26.7	82.2	28.3
Mean surface temperature (°C)	6,073	167	464	15	–65	–110	–140	–195	–200
Global magnetic field?	yes	yes	no	yes	no	yes	yes	yes	yes

	Earth's moon	Major moons of Jupiter				Major moons of Saturn			
		Io	Europa	Ganymede	Callisto	Dione	Rhea	Titan	Iapetus
Mass (10^{20} kg)	0.073	893.2	480.0	1,481.9	1,075.9	0.375	11.0	1,345.5	15.9
Diameter (km)	3,475	3,643.2	3,121.6	5,262.4	4,820.6	1,120	1,528	5,150	1,436
Density (kg/m^3)	3,340	3,530	3,010	1,940	1,830	1,500	1,240	1,881	1,020
Rotation period (days)	655.7	1.77	3.55	7.15	16.69	2.74	4.52	15.95	79.33
Semimajor axis (10^3 km)	0.384*	421.6	670.9	1,070.4	1,882.7	377.40	527.04	1,221.83	3,561.3
Orbital period (days)	27.32	1.77	3.55	7.15	16.69	2.74	4.52	15.95	79.33

	Major moons of Uranus			Major moons of Neptune		Pluto's moon	Selected asteroids		Selected comets	
	Umbriel	Titania	Oberon	Triton	Nereid	Charon	Vesta	Ceres	Chiron	Hale-Bopp
Mass (10^{20} kg)	11.7	35.2	30.1	214	0.2	19	3	8.7	—	—
Diameter (km)	1,169	1,578	1,523	2,707	340	1,186	530	960 × 932	—	—
Density (kg/m^3)	1,400	1,710	1,630	2,050	1,000	2,000	—	—	—	—
Rotation period	4.14 days	8.71 days	13.46 days	5.87 days R	unknown	6.39 days	5.342 h	9.075 h	—	—
Semimajor axis (10^3 km)	266.30	435.91	583.52	354.76	5,513.4	19,600	2.362 *	2.767 *	13.7 *	250 *
Orbital period	4.14 days	8.71 days	13.46 days	5.87 days R	360.14 days	6.39 days	3.63 y	4.60 y	50.7 y	4,000 y

REFERENCE MAPS

Topographic Provinces of North America

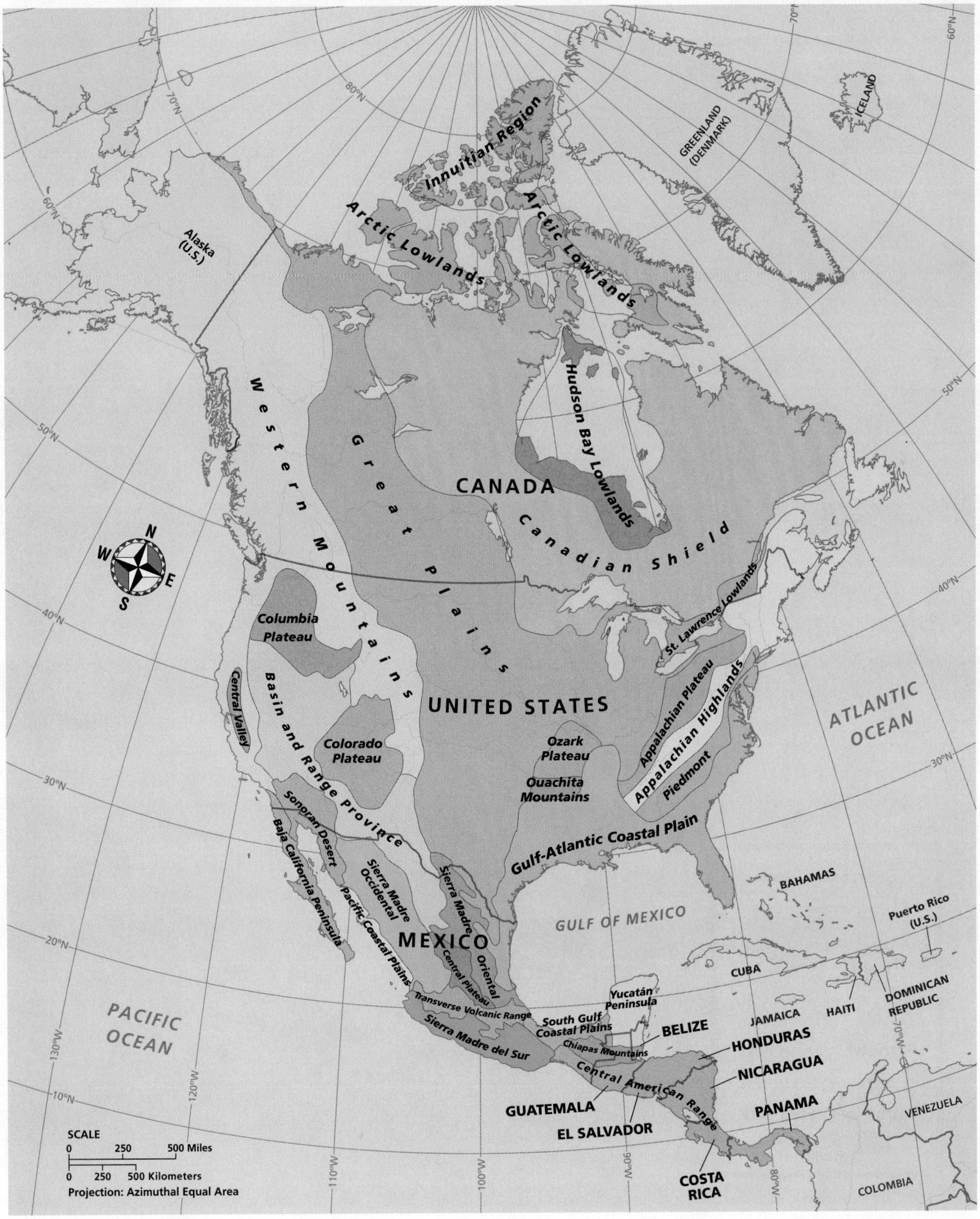

Geologic Map of North America

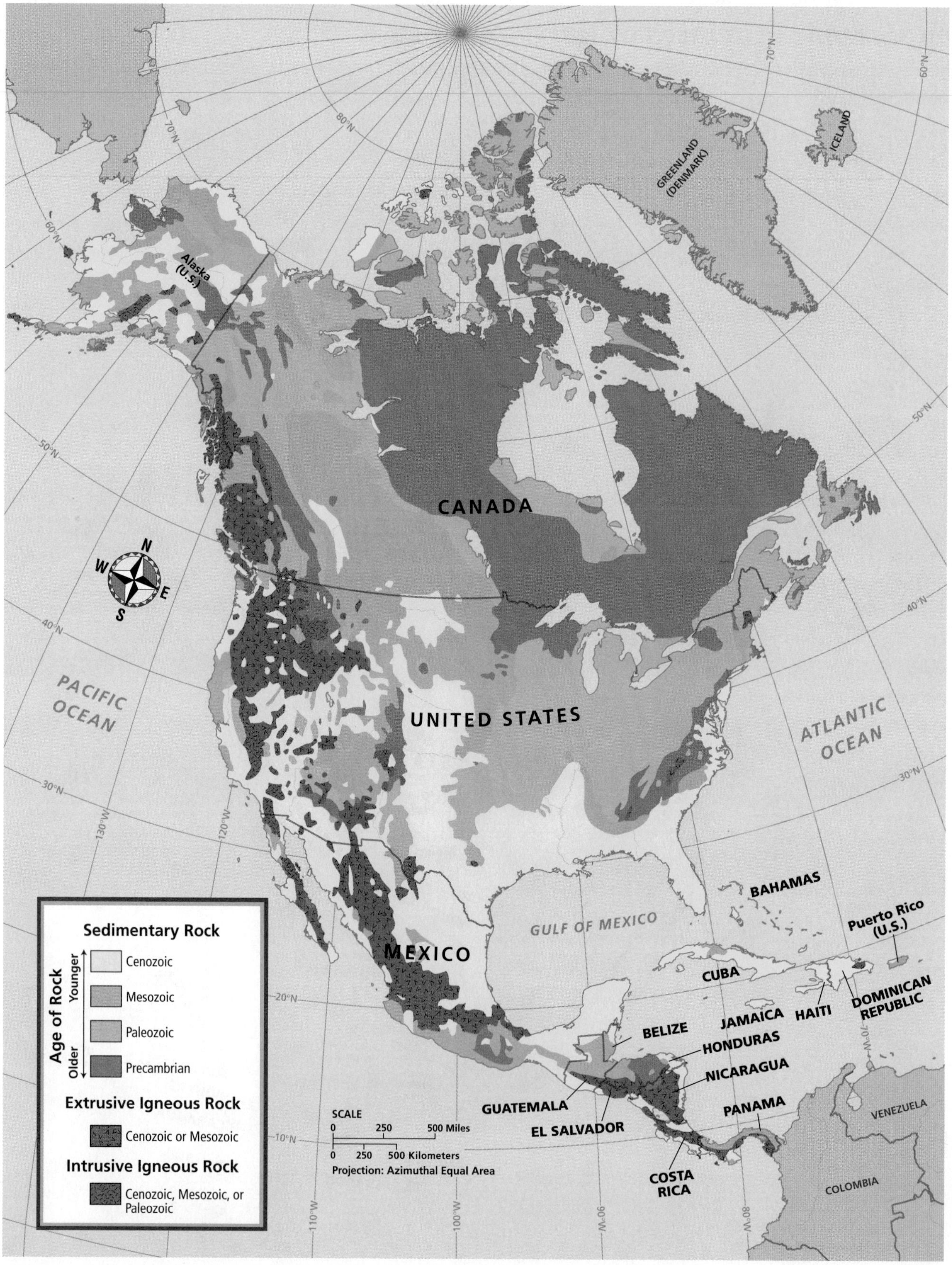

Mineral and Energy Resources of North America

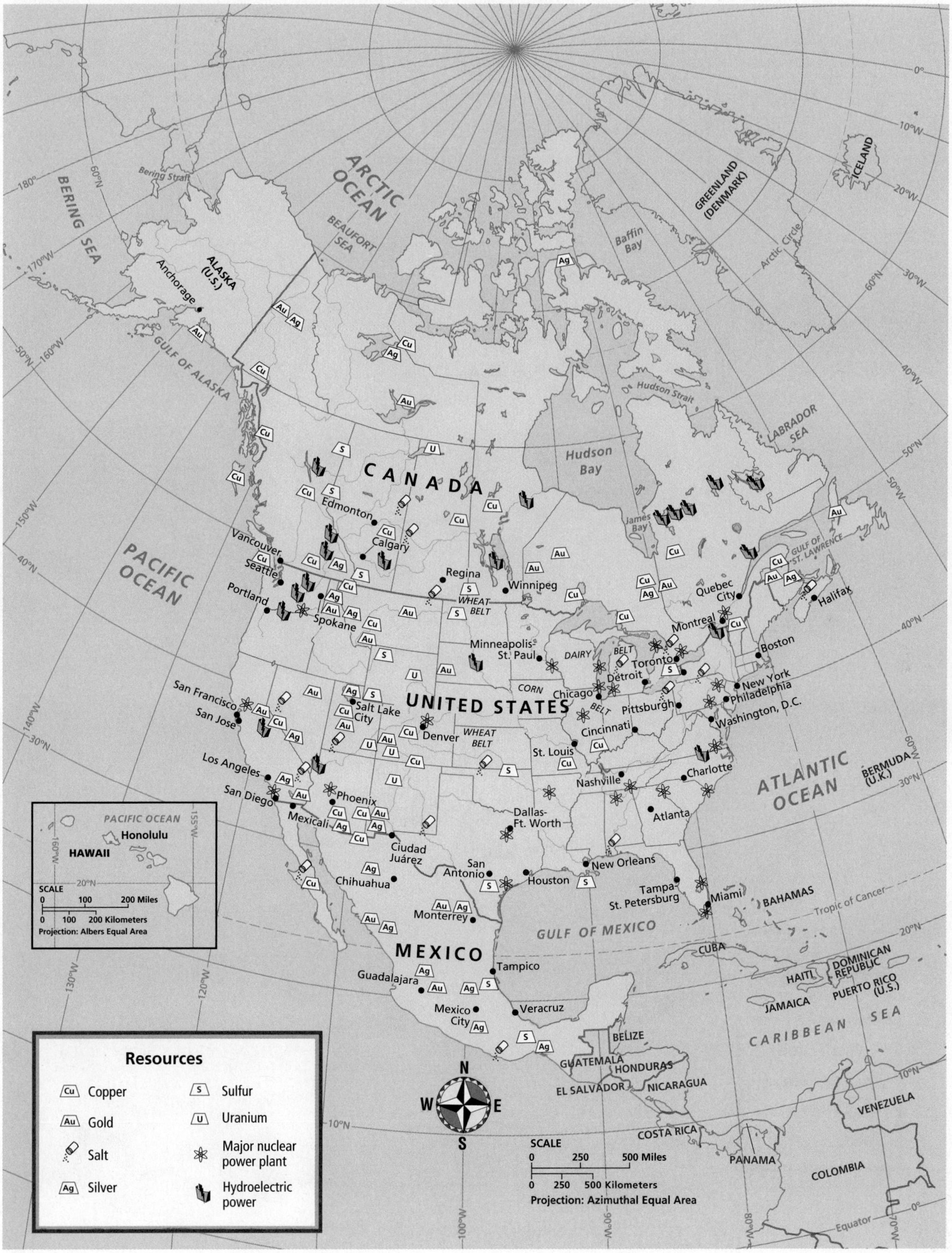

Fossil Fuel Deposits of North America

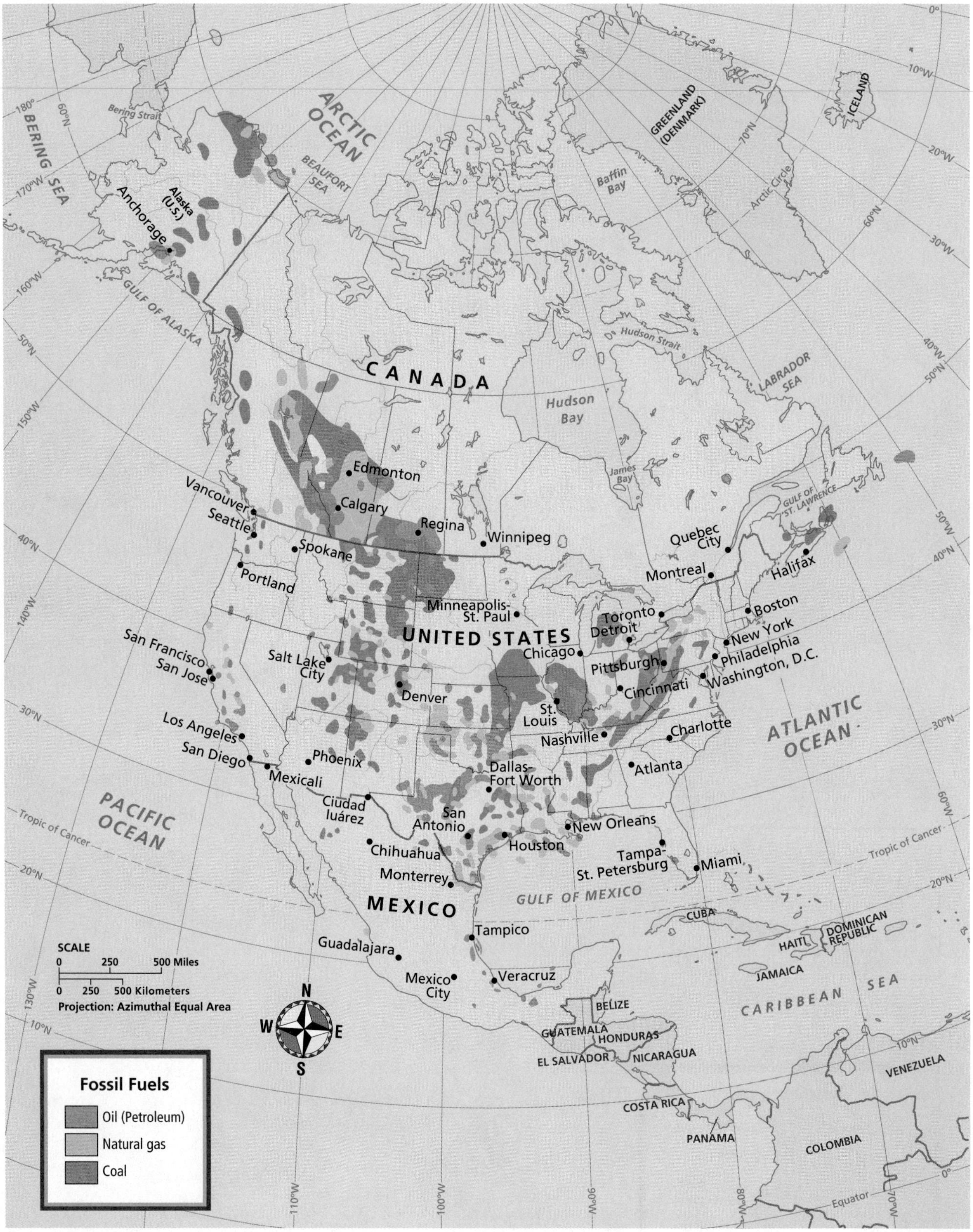

Topographic Maps of the Moon

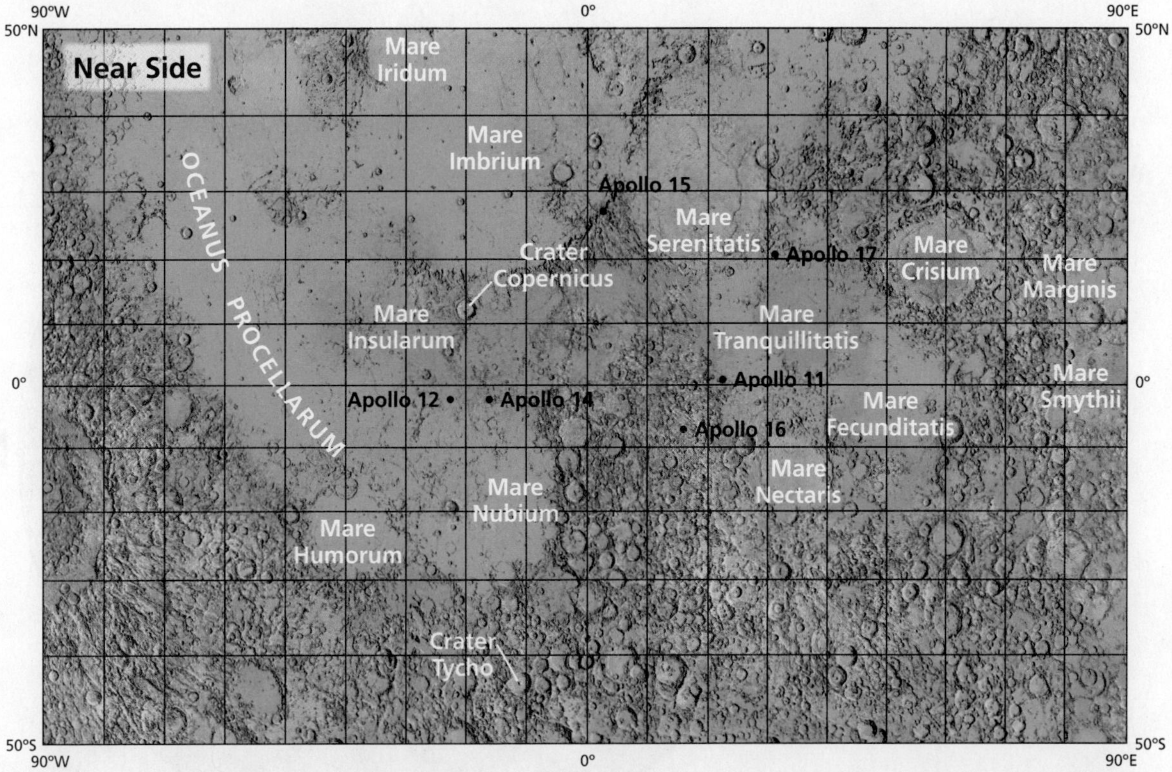

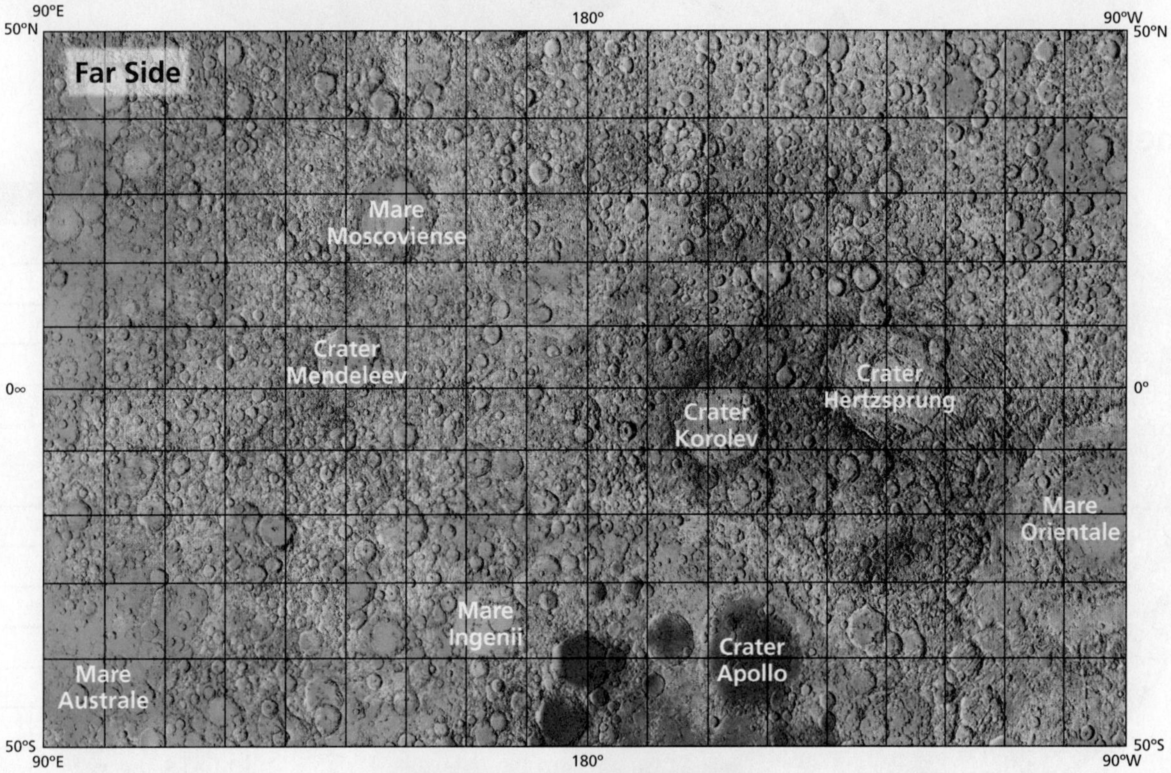

● Apollo landing sites

Color-coded topography key

Star Charts for the Northern Hemisphere

Spring

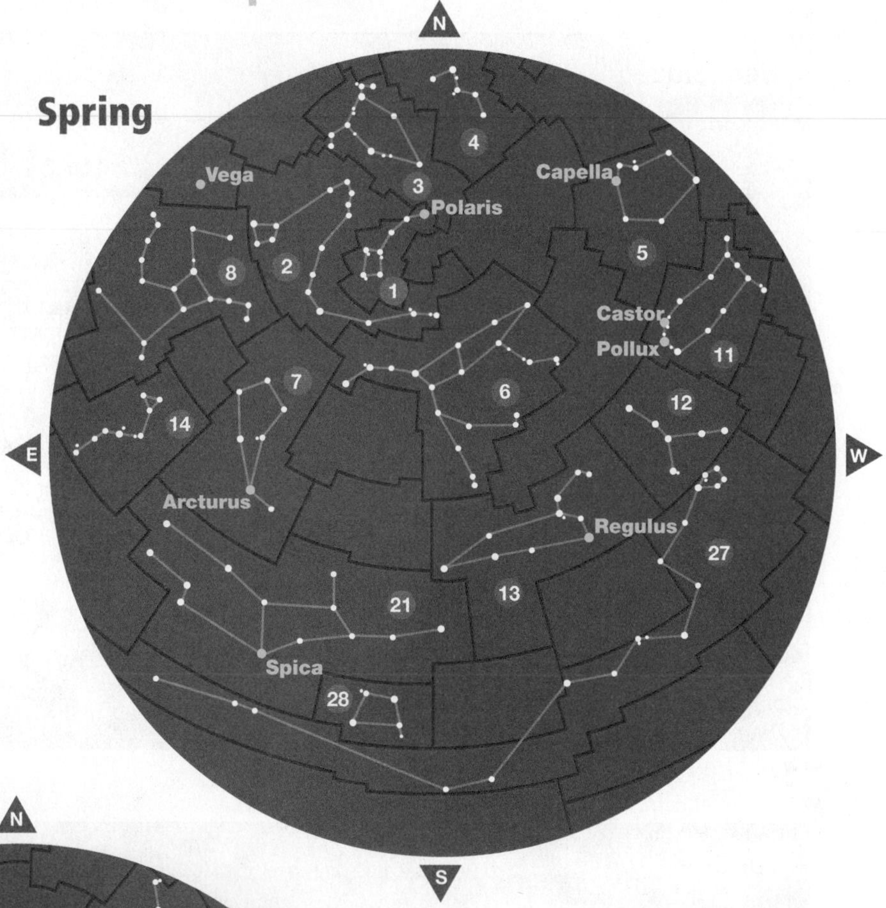

Summer

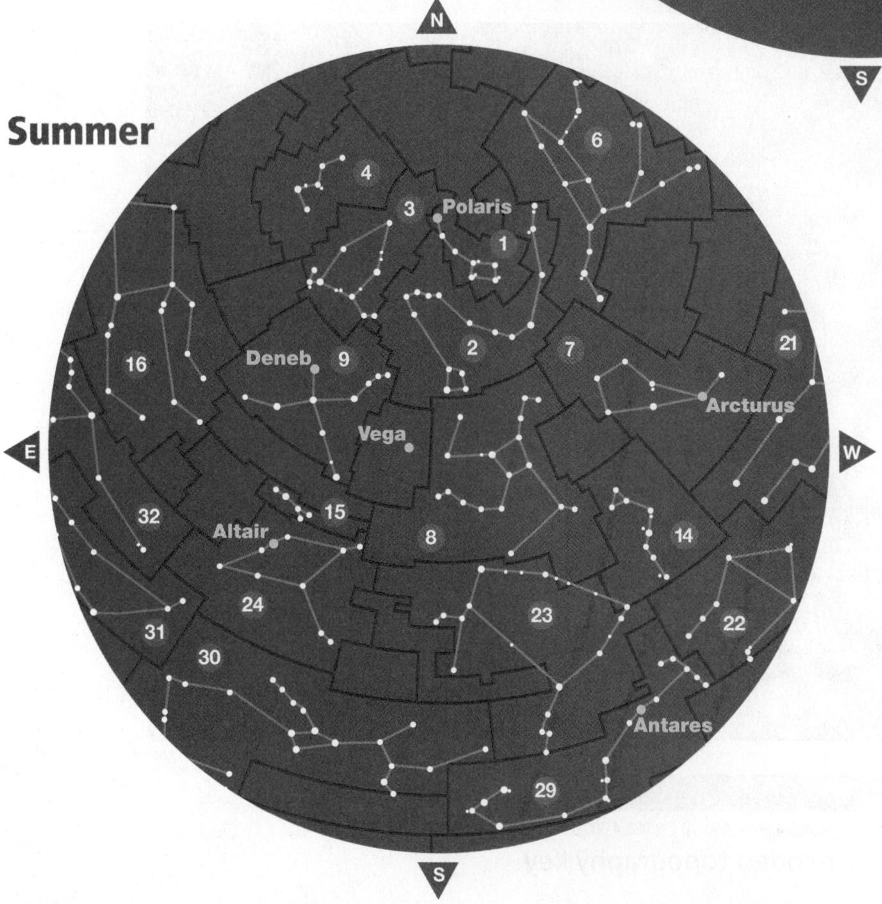

Constellations	
1	Ursa Minor
2	Draco
3	Cepheus
4	Cassiopeia
5	Auriga
6	Ursa Major
7	Boötes
8	Hercules
9	Cygnus
10	Perseus
11	Gemini
12	Cancer
13	Leo
14	Serpens
15	Sagitta
16	Pegasus
17	Pisces

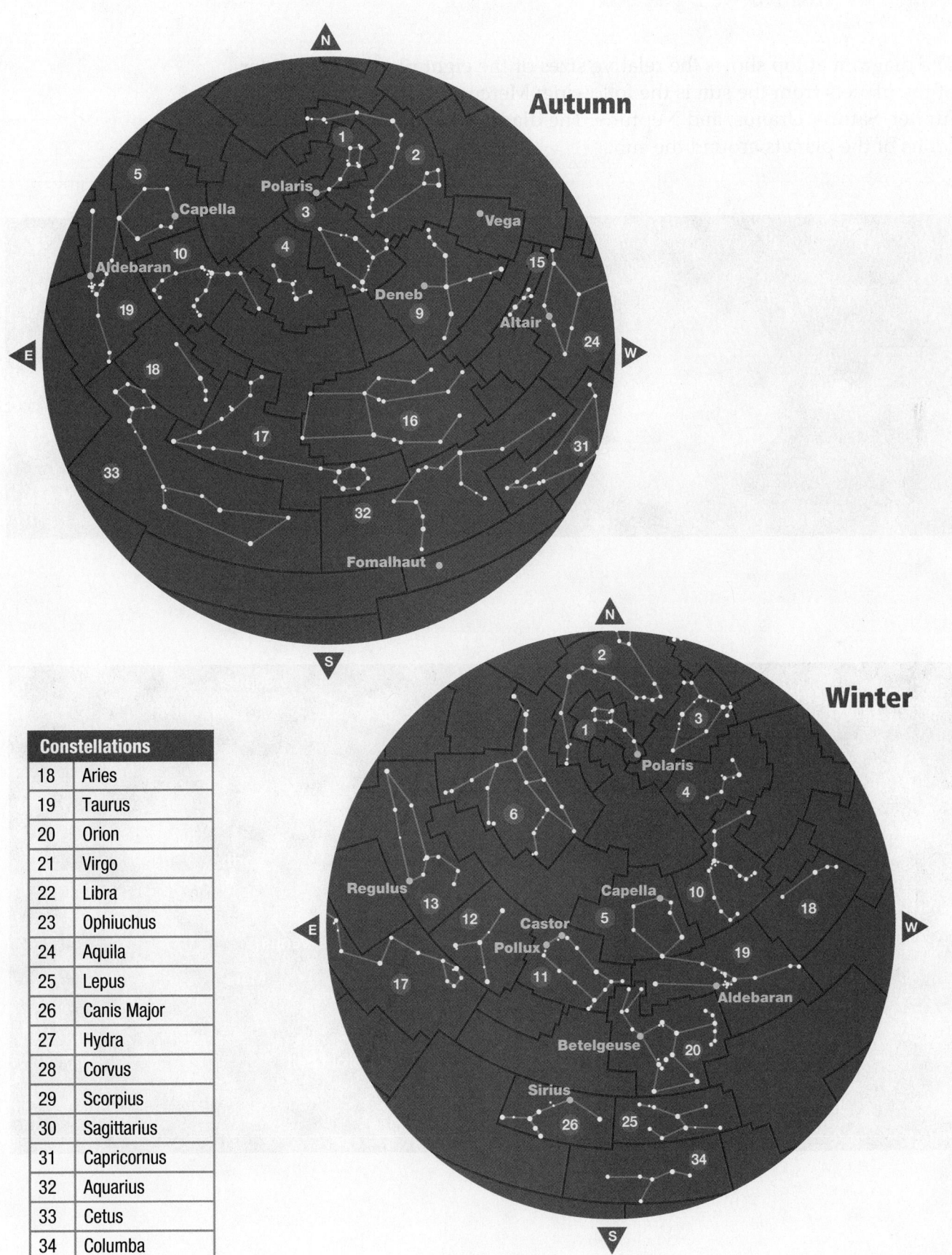

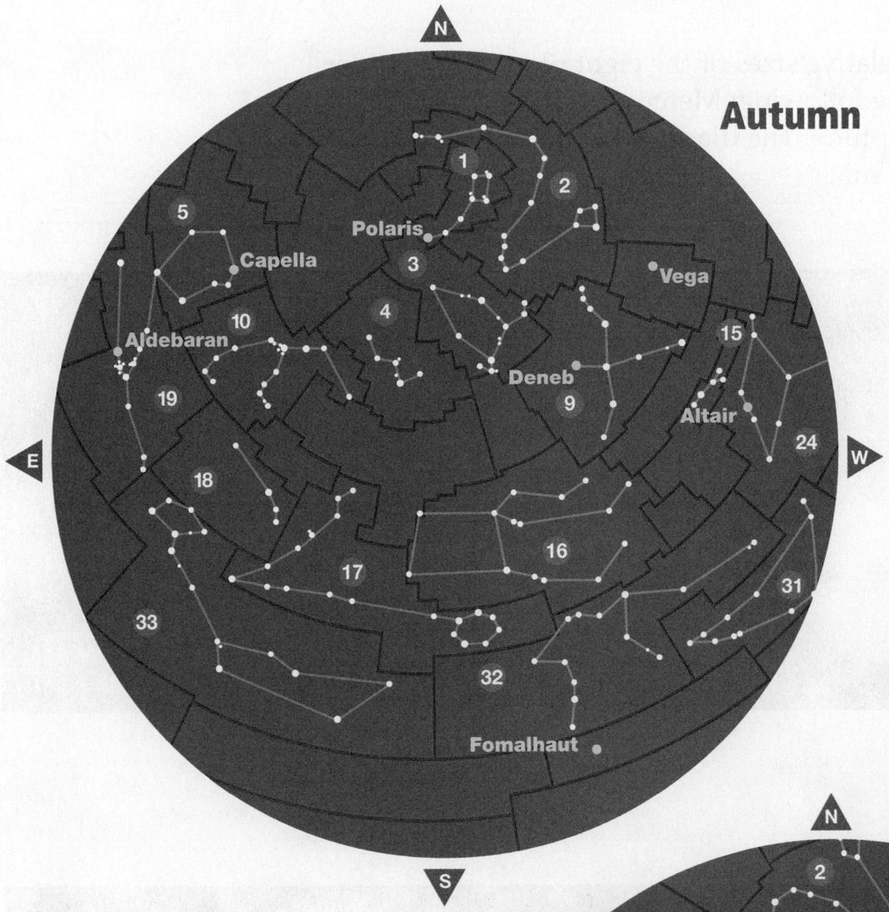

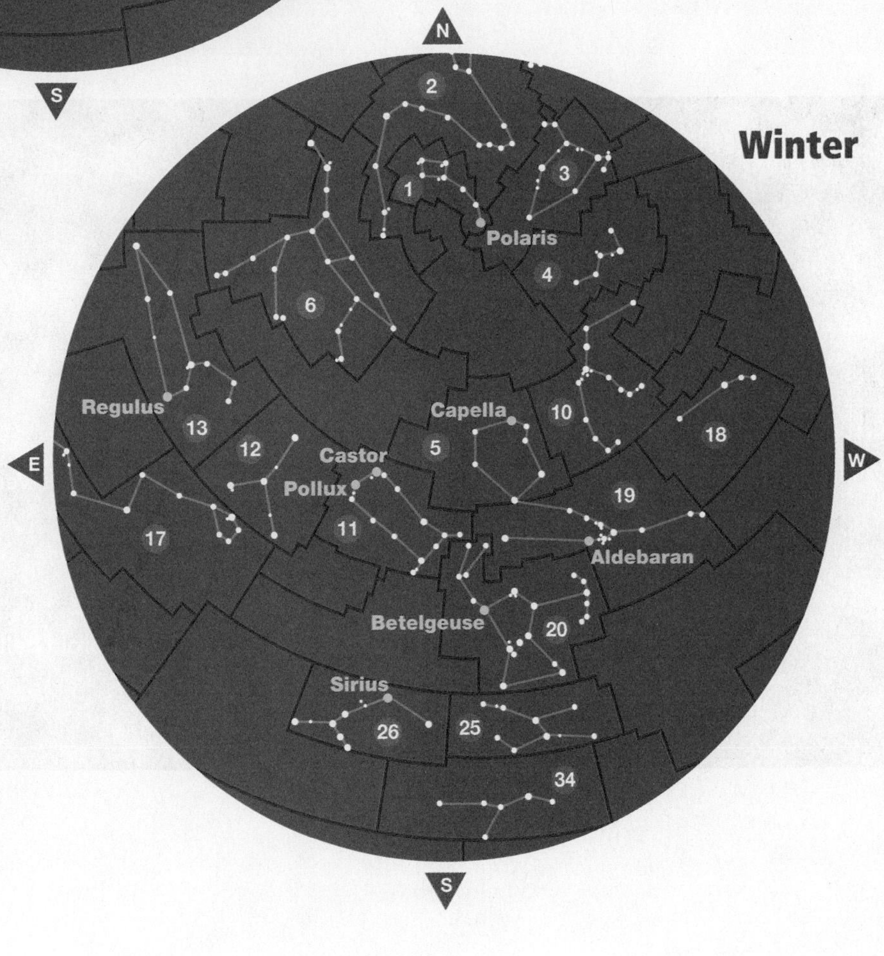

Constellations	
18	Aries
19	Taurus
20	Orion
21	Virgo
22	Libra
23	Ophiuchus
24	Aquila
25	Lepus
26	Canis Major
27	Hydra
28	Corvus
29	Scorpius
30	Sagittarius
31	Capricornus
32	Aquarius
33	Cetus
34	Columba

Maps of the Solar System

The diagram at top shows the relative sizes of the eight planets. The order of the planets from the sun is the following: Mercury, Venus, Earth, Mars, Jupiter, Saturn, Uranus, and Neptune. The diagrams at bottom show the orbits of the planets around the sun.

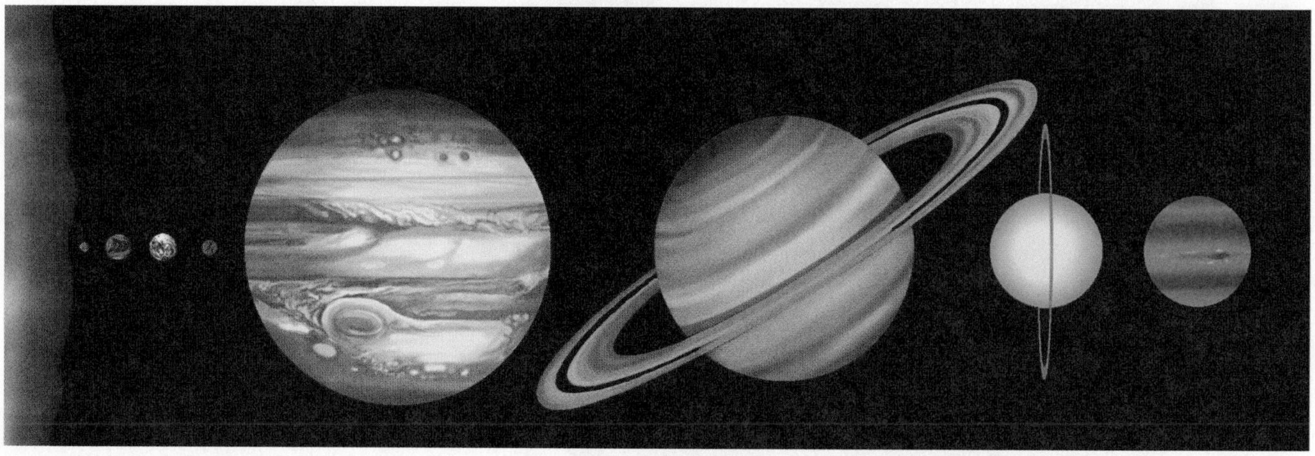

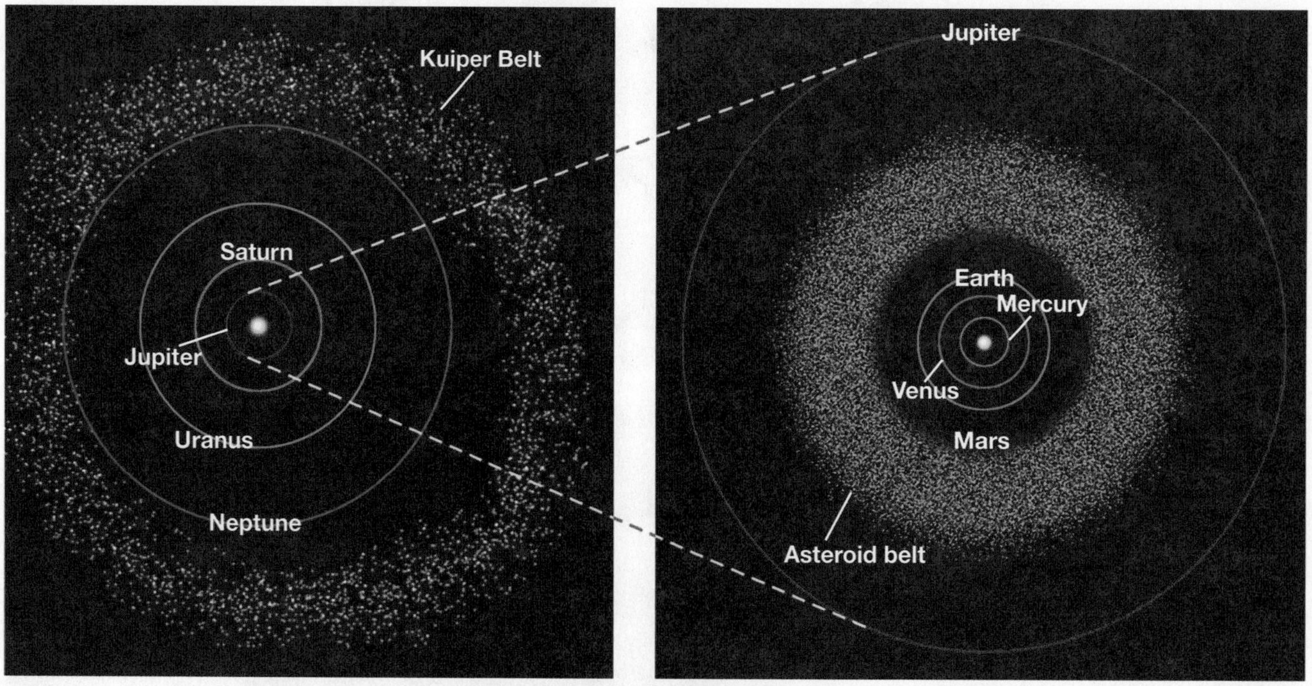

Answers to Reading Checks

Chapter 1

Page 7: Meteorologists use information gathered by satellites, radar, and other technologies on factors such as wind speed, temperature, and rainfall to create weather maps.

Page 10: Observations may lead to interesting scientific questions and may help scientists formulate reasonable and testable hypotheses.

Page 13: Answers may vary but should include three of the following types of models: physical models, graphic models, conceptual models, computer models, and mathematical models.

Page 14: Scientists present the results of their work at professional meetings and in scientific journals.

Chapter 2

Page 30: Indirect observations are the only means available for exploring Earth's interior at depths too great to be reached by drilling.

Page 34: Dust and rock come to Earth from space, while hydrogen atoms in the atmosphere enter space from Earth.

Page 36: An energy budget is the total distribution of energy to, from, and between Earth's various spheres.

Page 38: soil and plants

Page 42: The amount of matter and energy in an ecosystem can supply a population of a given size, and no larger. This maximum population is the carrying capacity of the ecosystem.

Chapter 3

Page 58: because the equator is the only parallel that divides Earth into halves

Page 62: Because both the parallels and the meridians are equally spaced straight lines on a cylindrical projection, the parallels and meridians form a grid.

Page 65: by using a graphic scale, or a printed line divided into proportional parts that represent units of measure; a fractional scale, in which a ratio shows how distance on Earth relates to distance on a map; or a verbal scale, which expresses scale in sentence form

Page 69: Water moves from areas of higher elevation to areas of lower elevation. Because the V shape points toward higher elevation, it points upstream.

Page 71: Scientists create soil maps to classify, map, and describe soils.

Chapter 4

Page 89: The atomic number is the number of protons in an atom's nucleus. The mass number is the sum of the number of protons and the number of neutrons in an atom. The unified atomic mass unit is used to express the mass of subatomic particles or atoms.

Page 95: Atoms form chemical bonds by transferring electrons or by sharing electrons.

Page 97: The oxygen atom has a larger and more positively charged nucleus than the hydrogen atoms do. As a result, the oxygen nucleus pulls the electrons from the hydrogen atoms closer to it than the hydrogen nuclei pull the shared electrons from the oxygen. This unequal attraction forms a polar-covalent bond.

Chapter 5

Page 113: Nonsilicate minerals never contain compounds of silicon bonded to oxygen.

Page 114: The building block of the silicate crystalline structure is a four-sided structure known as the silicon-oxygen tetrahedron, which is one silicon atom surrounded by four oxygen atoms.

Page 119: The strength and geometric arrangement of the bonds between the atoms that make up a mineral's internal structure determine the hardness of a mineral.

Page 121: Chatoyancy is the silky appearance of some minerals in reflected light. Asterism is the appearance of a six-sided star when a mineral reflects light.

Chapter 6

Page 137: As magma cools and solidifies, minerals crystallize out of the magma in a specific order that depends on their melting points.

Page 141: Fine-grained igneous rock forms mainly from magma that cools rapidly; coarse-grained igneous rock forms mainly from magma that cools more slowly.

Page 143: A batholith is an intrusive structure that covers an area of at least 100 km^2. A stock covers an area of less than 100 km^2.

Page 147: Three groups of clastic sedimentary rock are conglomerates and breccias, sandstones, and shales.

Page 149: Graded bedding is a type of stratification in which different sizes and types of sediments settle to different levels.

Page 152: The high pressures and temperatures that result from the movements of tectonic plates may cause chemical changes in the minerals.

Chapter 7

Page 168: Water creates ore deposits by eroding rock and releasing minerals, and by carrying the mineral fragments and depositing them in streambeds.

Page 173: Cap rock is a layer of impermeable rock at the top of an oil- or natural gas-bearing formation through which fluids cannot flow.

Page 174: As neutrons strike neighboring nuclei, the nuclei split and release additional neutrons that strike other nuclei and cause the chain to continue.

Page 179: Answers may vary but should include three of the following: geothermal, solar, hydroelectric, and biomass.

Page 182: The use of fossil fuels affects the environment when coal is mined from the surface, which destroys the land. When fossil fuels are burned, they affect the environment by creating air pollution.

Chapter 8

Page 202: Hutton reasoned that the extremely slow-working forces that changed the land on his farm had also slowly changed the rocks that make up Earth's crust. He concluded that large changes must happen over a period of millions of years.

Page 204: Because ripple marks form at the top of a rock layer, scientists can use the orientation of the ripple marks to determine which direction was "up" when the rock layers formed.

Page 208: Varves are like tree rings in that varves are laid down each year. Thus, counting varves can reveal the age of sedimentary deposits.

Page 211: An isotope that has an extremely long half-life will not show significant or measurable changes in a young rock. In a very old rock, an isotope that has a short half-life may have decayed to the point at which too little of the isotope is left to give an accurate age measurement. So, the estimated age of the rock must be correlated to the dating method used.

Page 215: A trace fossil is fossilized evidence of past animal movement, such as tracks, footprints, borings, or burrows, that can provide information about prehistoric life.

Chapter 9

Page 229: You would find fossils of extinct animals in older layers of a geologic column.

Page 234: Earth is approximately 4.6 billion years old.

Page 236: Answers may vary but should include three of the following: trilobites, brachiopods, jellyfish, worms, snails, and sponges.

Page 240: Answers may vary but could include *Archaeopteryx*, pterosaurs, *Apatosaurus*, and *Stegosaurus*.

Page 243: During ice ages, water from the ocean was frozen as ice on the continents, so the amount of liquid water in the seas decreased and sea level fell.

Chapter 10

Page 261: Many scientists rejected Wegener's hypothesis because the mechanism that Wegener suggested was physically impossible.

Page 263: New sea floor forms as magma rises to fill the rift that forms when two plates pull apart at a divergent boundary.

Page 265: The symmetrical magnetic patterns in sea-floor rocks show that rock formed at one place (at a ridge) and then broke apart and moved away from the center in opposite directions.

Page 268: Scientists use the locations of earthquakes, volcanoes, trenches, and mid-ocean ridges to outline tectonic plates.

Page 270: Collisions at convergent boundaries can happen between two oceanic plates, between two continental plates, or between one oceanic plate and one continental plate.

Page 273: When denser lithosphere sinks into the asthenosphere, the asthenosphere must move out of the way. As the asthenosphere moves, it drags or pushes on other parts of the lithosphere, which causes movement.

Page 276: As a plate subducts beneath another plate, islands and other land features on the subducting plate are scraped off the subducting plate and become part of the overriding plate.

Page 279: The continents Africa, South America, Antarctica, and Australia formed from Gondwanaland. The subcontinent of India was also part of Gondwanaland.

Chapter 11

Page 295: Tension and shear stress can both pull rock apart.

Page 297: limbs and hinges

Page 299: A thrust fault is a type of reverse fault in which the fault plane is at a low angle relative to the surface.

Page 303: The Himalayas are growing taller because the two plates are still colliding and causing further compression of the rock, which further uplifts the mountains.

Page 305: Answers may include three of the following: folded mountains, fault-block mountains, dome mountains, and volcanic mountains.

Chapter 12

Page 321: Rayleigh waves cause the ground to move in an elliptical, rolling motion. Love waves cause rock to move side-to-side and perpendicular to the direction the waves are traveling.

Page 322: The speed of seismic waves changes as they pass through different layers of Earth.

Page 327: Moment magnitude is more accurate for larger earthquakes than the Richter scale is. Moment magnitude is directly related to rock properties and so is more closely related to the cause of the earthquake than the Richter scale is.

Page 331: Scientists think that stress on a fault builds up to a critical point and is then released as an earthquake. Seismic gaps are areas in which no earthquakes have happened in a long period of time and thus are likely to be under a high amount of stress.

Chapter 13

Page 347: The denser plate of oceanic lithosphere subducts beneath the less dense plate of continental lithosphere.

Page 349: As the lithosphere moves over the mantle plume, older volcanoes move away from the mantle plume. A new hot spot forms in the lithosphere above the mantle plume as a new volcano begins to form. In addition, a long plume can produce several volcanoes at once.

Page 352: The faster the rate of flow is and the higher the gas content is, the more broken up and rough the resulting cooled lava will be.

Page 355: A caldera may form when a magma chamber empties or when large amounts of magma are discharged, causing the ground to collapse.

Chapter 14

Page 374: Two types of mechanical weathering are ice wedging and abrasion. Ice wedging is caused by water that seeps into cracks in rock and freezes. When water freezes, it expands and creates pressure on the rock, which widens and deepens cracks. Abrasion is the grinding away of rock surfaces by other rocks or sand particles. Abrasive agents may be carried by gravity, water, and wind.

Page 376: Two effects of chemical weathering are changes in the chemical composition and changes in the physical appearance of a rock.

Page 380: Fractures and joints in a rock increase surface area and allow weathering to occur more rapidly.

Page 385: Large amounts of rainfall and high temperatures cause thick soils to form in both tropical and temperate climates. Tropical soils have thin A horizons because of the continuous leaching of topsoil. Temperate soils have three thick layers, because leaching of the A horizon in temperate climates is much less than leaching of the A horizon in tropical climates.

Page 388: Dust storms may form during droughts when the soil is made dry and loose by lack of moisture and wind-caused sheet erosion carries it away in clouds of dust. If all of the topsoil is removed, the remaining subsoil will not contain enough nutrients to raise crops.

Page 391: Landslides are masses of loose rock combined with soil that suddenly fall down a slope. A rockfall consists of rock falling from a steep cliff.

Page 393: When a mountain is no longer being uplifted, weathering and erosion wear down its jagged peaks to low, featureless surfaces called *peneplains.*

Chapter 15

Page 408: Precipitation is any form of water that falls to Earth from the clouds, including rain, snow, sleet, and hail.

Page 413: A river that has meanders probably has a low gradient.

Page 417: Floods can be controlled indirectly through forest and soil conservation measures that reduce or prevent runoff, or directly by building artificial structures, such as dams, levees, and floodways, to redirect water flow.

Chapter 16

Page 433: The two zones of groundwater are the zone of saturation and the zone of aeration.

Page 434: The depth of a water table depends on topography, aquifer permeability, the amount of rainfall, and the rate at which humans use the groundwater.

Page 437: Ordinary springs occur where the ground surface drops below the water table. An artesian spring occurs where groundwater flows to the surface through natural cracks in the overlying caprock.

Page 441: A natural bridge may form when two sinkholes form close to each other. The bridge is the uncollapsed rock between the sinkholes.

Chapter 17

Page 456: Continental glaciers exist only in Greenland and Antarctica.

Page 460: A moving glacier forms a cirque by pulling blocks of rock from the floor and walls of a valley and leaving a bowl-shaped depression.

Page 463: A drumlin is a long, low, tear-shaped mound of till.

Page 464: Eskers form when meltwater from receding continental glaciers flows through ice tunnels and deposits long, winding ridges of gravel and sand.

Page 468: The sea level was up to 140 m lower than it is now.

Chapter 18

Page 484: Moisture makes soil heavier, so the soil sticks and is more difficult to move. Therefore, erosion happens faster in dry climates.

Page 486: Barchan dunes are crescent shaped; transverse dunes form linear ridges.

Page 490: Answers should include three of the following: sea cliffs, sea caves, sea arches, sea stacks, wave-cut terraces, and wave-built terraces.

Page 495: As sea levels rise over a flat coastal plain, the shoreline moves inland and isolates dunes from the old shoreline. These dunes become barrier islands.

Chapter 19

Page 514: Transpiration increases the amount of water vapor in the atmosphere.

Page 517: An aneroid barometer contains a sealed metal container that has a partial vacuum.

Page 519: The lower region of the thermosphere is called the *ionosphere.*

Page 525: Deserts are colder at night than other areas are because the air in deserts contains little water vapor that can absorb heat during the day and release heat slowly at night.

Page 528: They flow in opposite directions from each other, and they occur at different latitudes.

Chapter 20

Page 544: When the air is very dry and the temperature is below freezing, ice and snow change directly into water vapor by sublimation.

Page 546: Dew is liquid moisture that condenses from air on cool objects when the air is nearly saturated and the temperature drops. Frost is water vapor that condenses as ice crystals onto a cool surface directly from the air when the dew point is below freezing.

Page 550: The source of energy that warms the air and leads to cloud formation is solar energy that is reradiated as heat by Earth's surface. As the process continues, latent heat released by the condensation may allow the clouds to expand beyond the condensation level.

Page 553: because cirrus clouds form at very high altitudes where air temperature is low

Page 557: Doppler radar measures the location, direction of movement, and intensity of precipitation.

Chapter 21

Page 573: a continental tropical air mass

Page 577: The air of an anticyclone sinks and flows outward from a center of high pressure. The air of a midlatitude cyclone rotates toward the rising air of a central low-pressure region.

Page 579: over warm tropical seas

Page 584: A barometer is used to measure atmospheric pressure.

Page 589: Areas of precipitation are marked by using colors or symbols.

Page 590: Meteorologists compare models because different models are better at predicting different weather variables. If information from two or more models matches, scientists can be more confident of their predictions.

Chapter 22

Page 607: Waves, currents, and other water motions continually replace warm surface waters with cooler water from the ocean depths, which keeps the surface temperature of the water from increasing rapidly.

Page 608: The temperature of land increases faster than that of water because the specific heat of land is lower than that of water, and thus the land requires less energy to heat up than the water does.

Page 612: marine west coast, humid continental, and humid subtropical

Page 616: Scientists use computer models to incorporate as much data as possible to sort out the complex variables that influence climate and to make predictions about climate.

Page 618: Climate change influences humans, plants, and animals. It also affects nearby climates, sea level, and precipitation rates.

Chapter 23

Page 638: Oceanographers study the physical characteristics, chemical composition, and life-forms of the ocean.

Page 642: Trenches; broad, flat plains; mountain ranges; and submerged volcanoes are part of the deep-ocean basins.

Page 647: When chemical reactions take place in the ocean, dissolved substances can crystallize to form nodules that settle to the ocean floor.

Chapter 24

Page 663: Dissolved solids enter the oceans from the chemical weathering of rock on land, from volcanic eruptions, and from chemical reactions between sea water and newly formed sea-floor rocks.

Page 665: Ocean surface temperatures are affected by the amount of solar energy an area receives and by the movement of water in the ocean.

Page 667: Ocean water contains dissolved solids (mostly salts) that add mass to a given volume of water. The large amount of dissolved solids in ocean water makes ocean water denser than fresh water.

Page 671: Most marine life is found in the sublittoral zone. Life in this zone is continuously submerged, but waters are still shallow enough to allow sunlight to penetrate.

Page 675: Aquaculture provides a reliable, economical source of food. However, aquatic farms are susceptible to pollution, and they may become local sources of pollution.

Chapter 25

Page 691: Because no continents interrupt the flow of the Antarctic Circumpolar Current, also called the *West Wind Drift*, it completely encircles Antarctica and crosses three major oceans and is therefore the world's largest ocean current. All other surface currents are deflected and divided when they meet a continental barrier.

Page 693: Antarctic Bottom Water is very cold. It also has a high salinity. The extreme cold and high salinity combine to make the water extremely dense.

Page 696: Because waves receive energy from wind that pushes against the surface of the water, the amount of energy decreases as the depth of water increases. As a result, the diameter of the water molecules' circular path also decreases.

Page 698: Contact with the ocean floor slows down the bottom of the wave but not the top of the wave. Because of the difference in speed between the top and bottom of the wave, the top gets farther ahead of the bottom until the wave becomes unstable and falls over.

Page 702: When the tidal range is small, the sun and the moon are at right angles to each other relative to Earth's orbit.

Chapter 26

Page 723: The only kind of electromagnetic radiation the human eye can detect is visible light.

Page 725: Images produced by refracting telescopes are subject to distortion because of the ways different colors of visible light are focused at different distances from the lens and because of size limitations on the objective lens.

Page 726: Scientists launch spacecraft into orbit to detect radiation screened out by Earth's atmosphere and to avoid light pollution and other atmospheric distortions.

Page 731: Constellations provide two kinds of evidence of Earth's motion. As Earth rotates, the stars appear to change position during the night. As Earth revolves around the sun, Earth's night sky faces a different part of the universe. As a result, different constellations appear in the night sky as the seasons change.

Page 733: Because time zones are based on Earth's rotation, as you travel west you eventually come to a location where, on one side of the time zone border, the calendar moves ahead one day. The purpose of the International Date Line is to locate the border so that the transition would affect the least number of people. So that it will affect the least number of people, the International Date Line is in the middle of the Pacific Ocean, instead of on a continent.

Page 734: Daylight savings time is an adjustment that is made to standard time by setting clocks ahead one hour to take advantage of longer hours of daylight in the summer months and to save energy.

Chapter 27

Page 751: Unlike the outer planets, Pluto is very small and is composed of rock and frozen gas, instead of thick layers of gases.

Page 753: Green plants release free oxygen as part of photosynthesis, which caused the concentration of oxygen gas in the atmosphere to gradually increase.

Page 756: An ellipse is a closed curve whose shape is defined by two points inside the curve. An ellipse looks like an oval.

Page 761: Answers may vary but should address differences in distance from the sun, density, atmospheric pressure and density, and tectonics.

Page 763: Martian volcanoes are larger than volcanoes on Earth because Mars has no moving tectonic plates. Magma sources remain in the same spot for millions of years and produce volcanic material that builds the volcanic cone higher and higher.

Page 766: When Jupiter formed, it did not have enough mass for nuclear fusion to begin.

Page 768: Saturn and Jupiter are made almost entirely of hydrogen and helium and have rocky-iron cores, ring systems, many satellites, rapid rotational periods, and bands of colored clouds.

Page 771: The Kuiper Belt is located beyond the orbit of Neptune.

Chapter 28

Page 786: Answers should include two of the following features: maria, highlands, craters, ridges, and rilles.

Page 788: The crust of the far side of the moon is thicker than the crust of the near side is. The crust of the far side also consists mainly of mountainous terrain and has only a few small maria.

Page 792: The far side of the moon is never visible from Earth, because the moon's rotation on its axis and the moon's revolution around Earth take the same amount of time.

Page 794: During a total eclipse, the entire disk of the sun is blocked, and the outer layers of the sun become visible. During an annular eclipse, the disk of the sun is never completely blocked out, so the sun is too bright for observers on Earth to see the outer layers of the sun's atmosphere.

Page 797: When the lighted part of the moon is larger than a semicircle but the visible part of the moon is shrinking, the phase is called *waning gibbous.* When only a sliver of the near side is visible, the phase is called a *waning crescent*.

Page 801: Io's surface is covered with many active volcanoes. Europa's surface is covered by an enormous ice sheet. Ganymede is the largest moon in the solar system and has a strong magnetic field. Callisto's surface is heavily cratered.

Page 803: Charon is almost half the size of the body it orbits. Charon's orbital period is the same length as Pluto's day, so only one side of Pluto always faces its largest moon.

Page 806: The most common type is made mostly of carbon materials. The second type is made mostly of silicate minerals. Other asteroids are made mostly of metals such as iron and nickel.

Page 809: A meteoroid is a rocky body that travels through space. When a meteoroid enters Earth's atmosphere and begins to burn up, the meteoroid produces a meteor.

Chapter 29

Page 825: Einstein's equation helped scientists understand the source of the sun's energy. The equation explained how the sun could produce huge amounts of energy without burning up.

Page 827: The sun's atmosphere consists of the photosphere, the chromosphere, and the corona.

Page 831: Coronal mass ejections generate sudden disturbances in Earth's magnetic field. The high-energy particles that circulate during these storms can damage satellites, cause power blackouts, and interfere with radio communications.

Chapter 30

Page 847: Polaris is almost exactly above the pole of Earth's rotational axis, so Polaris moves only slightly around the pole during one rotation of Earth.

Page 848: Starlight is shifted toward the red end of the spectrum when the star is moving away from the observer.

Page 853: The forces balance each other and keep the star in equilibrium. As gravity increases the pressure on the matter within a star, the rate of fusion increases. This increase in fusion causes a rise in gas pressure. As a result, the energy from the increased fusion and gas pressure generates outward pressure that balances the force of gravity.

Page 854: Giants and supergiants appear in the upper right part of the H-R diagram.

Page 857: As supergiants collapse because of gravitational forces, fusion begins and continues until the supply of fuel is used up. The core begins to collapse under its own gravity and causes energy to transfer to the outer layers of the star. The transfer of energy to the outer layers causes the explosion.

Page 860: More than 50% of all stars similar to the sun are in multiple-star systems.

Page 864: All matter and energy in the early universe was compressed into a small volume at an extremely high temperature until the temperature cooled and all of the matter and energy was forced outward in all directions.

Glossary • Glosario

A

abrasion (uh BRAY zhuhn) the grinding and wearing away of rock surfaces through the mechanical action of other rock or sand particles (374)

abrasion proceso por el cual las superficies de las rocas se muelen o desgastan por medio de la acción mecánica de otras rocas y partículas de arena (374)

absolute age (AB suh LOOT AYJ) the numeric age of an object or event, often stated in years before the present, as established by an absolute-dating process, such as radiometric dating (207)

edad absoluta la edad numérica de un objeto o suceso, que suele expresarse en cantidad de años antes del presente, determinada por un proceso de datación absoluta, tal como la datación radiométrica (207)

absolute humidity (AB suh LOOT hyoo MID uh tee) the mass of water vapor per unit volume of air that contains the water vapor; usually expressed as grams of water vapor per cubic meter of air (545)

humedad absoluta la masa de vapor de agua por unidad de volumen de aire que contiene al vapor de agua; normalmente se expresa por metro cúbico de aire (545)

absolute magnitude (AB suh LOOT MAG nuh TOOD) the brightness that a star would have at a distance of 32.6 light-years from Earth (850)

magnitud absoluta el brillo que una estrella tendría a una distancia de 32.6 años luz de la Tierra (850)

abyssal plain (uh BIS uhl PLAYN) a large, flat, almost level area of the deep-ocean basin (643)

llanura abisal un área amplia, llana y casi plana de la cuenca oceánica profunda (643)

acid precipitation (AS id pree SIP uh TAY shuhn) precipitation, such as rain, sleet, or snow, that contains a high concentration of acids, often because of the pollution of the atmosphere (378)

precipitación ácida precipitación tal como lluvia, aguanieve o nieve, que contiene una alta concentración de ácidos debido a la contaminación de la atmósfera" (378)

adiabatic cooling (AD ee uh BAT ik KOOL ing) the process by which the temperature of an air mass decreases as the air mass rises and expands (550)

enfriamiento adiabático el proceso por medio del cual la temperatura de una masa de aire disminuye a medida que ésta se eleva y se expande (550)

advective cooling (ad VEK tiv KOOL ing) the process by which the temperature of an air mass decreases as the air mass moves over a cold surface (551)

enfriamiento advectivo el proceso por medio del cual la temperatura de una masa de aire disminuye a medida que ésta se mueve sobre una superficie fría (551)

air mass (ER MAS) a large body of air throughout which temperature and moisture content are similar (571)

masa de aire un gran volumen de aire, cuya temperatura y cuyo contenido de humedad son similares en toda su extension (571)

albedo (al BEE doh) the fraction of solar radiation that is reflected off the surface of an object (523)

albedo porcentaje de la radiación solar que la superficie de un objeto refleja (523)

alluvial fan (uh LOO vee uhl FAN) a fan-shaped mass of rock material deposited by a stream when the slope of the land decreases sharply; for example, alluvial fans form when streams flow from mountains to flat land (415)

abanico alluvial masa de materiales rocosos en forma de abanico, depositados por un arroyo cuando la pendiente del terreno disminuye bruscamente; por ejemplo, los abanicos aluviales se forman cuando los arroyos fluyen de una montaña a un terreno llano (415)

alpine glacier (AL PIEN GLAY shuhr) a narrow, wedge-shaped mass of ice that forms in a mountainous region and that is confined to a small area by surrounding topography; examples include valley glaciers, cirque glaciers, and piedmont glaciers (456)

glaciar alpino una masa de hielo angosta, parecida a una cuña, que se forma en una región montañosa y que está confinada a un área pequeña por la topografía que la rodea; los glaciares de valle, los circos glaciares y los glaciares de pie de monte son algunos ejemplos de esto (456)

anemometer (AN uh MAHM uht uhr) an instrument used to measure wind speed (584)

anemómetro un instrumento que se usa para medir la rapidez del viento (584)

aphelion (uh FEE lee uhn) in the orbit of a planet or other body in the solar system, the point that is farthest from the sun (730)

afelio en la órbita de un planeta u otros cuerpos en el sistema solar, el punto que está más lejos del Sol (730)

apogee (AP uh JEE) in the orbit of a satellite, the point that is farthest from Earth (791)

apogeo en la órbita de un satélite, el punto en el que el satélite está más alejado de la Tierra (791)

apparent magnitude (uh PER uhnt MAG nuh TOOD) the brightness of a star as seen from Earth (850)

magnitud aparente el brillo de una estrella como se percibe desde la Tierra (850)

aquaculture (AHK wuh KUHL chuhr) the raising of aquatic plants and animals for human use or consumption (675)

acuacultura el cultivo de plantas y animales acuáticos para uso o consumo humano (675)

aquifer (AHK wuh fuhr) a body of rock or sediment that stores groundwater and allows the flow of groundwater (431)

acuífero un cuerpo rocoso o sedimento que almacena agua subterránea y permite que fluya (431)

arête (uh RAYT) a sharp, jagged ridge that forms between cirques (460)

cresta una cumbre puntiaguda e irregular que se forma entre circos glaciares (460)

artesian formation (ahr TEE zhuhn fawr MAY shuhn) a sloping layer of permeable rock sandwiched between two layers of impermeable rock and exposed at the surface (437)

formación artesiana capa inclinada de rocas permeables que está en medio de dos capas de rocas impermeables y expuesta en la superficie (437)

asteroid (AS tuhr OYD) a small, rocky object that orbits the sun; most asteroids are located in a band between the orbits of Mars and Jupiter (805)

asteroide un objeto pequeño y rocoso que se encuentra en órbita alrededor del Sol; la mayoría de los asteroides se ubican en una banda entre las órbitas de Marte y Júpiter (805)

asthenosphere (as THEN uh SFIR) the solid, plastic layer of the mantle beneath the lithosphere; made of mantle rock that flows very slowly, which allows tectonic plates to move on top of it (31, 267)

astenosfera la capa sólida y plástica del manto, que se encuentra debajo de la litosfera; está formada por roca del manto que fluye muy lentamente, lo cual permite que las placas tectónicas se muevan en su superficie (31, 267)

astronomical unit (AS truh NAHM i kuhl YOON it) the average distance between Earth and the sun; approximately 150 million kilometers (symbol, AU) (722)

unidad astronómica la distancia promedio entre la Tierra y el Sol; aproximadamente 150 millones de kilómetros (símbolo: UA) (722)

astronomy (uh STRAHN uh mee) the scientific study of the universe (7, 721)

astronomía el estudio científico del universo (7, 721)

atmosphere (AT muhs FIR) a mixture of gases that surrounds a planet, moon, or other celestial body (35, 513)

atmósfera una mezcla de gases que rodea un planeta, una luna, u otras cuerpos celestes (35, 513)

atmospheric pressure (AT muhs FIR ik PRESH uhr) the force per unit area that is exerted on a surface by the weight of the atmosphere (516)

presión atmosférica la fuerza por unidad de área que el peso de la atmósfera ejerce sobre una superficie (516)

atom (AT uhm) the smallest unit of an element that maintains the chemical properties of that element (88)

átomo la unidad más pequeña de un elemento que conserva las propiedades químicas de ese elemento (88)

aurora (aw RAWR uh) colored light produced by charged particles from the solar wind and from the magnetosphere that react with and excite the oxygen and nitrogen of Earth's upper atmosphere; usually seen in the sky near Earth's magnetic poles (832)

aurora luz de colores producida por partículas con carga del viento solar y de la magnetosfera, que reaccionan con los átomos de oxígeno y nitrógeno de la parte superior de la atmósfera de la Tierra y los excitan; normalmente se ve en el cielo cerca de los polos magnéticos de la Tierra (832)

B

barometer (buh RAHM uht uhr) an instrument that measures atmospheric pressure (584)

barómetro un instrumento que mide la presión atmosférica (584)

barrier island (BAR ee uhr IE luhnd) a long ridge of sand or narrow island that lies parallel to the shore (495)

isla barrera un largo arrecife de arena o una isla angosta ubicada paralela a la costa (495)

basal slip (BAY suhl SLIP) the process that causes the ice at the base of a glacier to melt and the glacier to slide (457)

deslizamiento basal el proceso que hace que el hielo de la base de un glaciar se derrita y que éste se deslice (457)

beach (BEECH) an area of the shoreline that is made up of deposited sediment (491)

playa un área de la costa que está formada por sedimento depositado (491)

benthic zone (BEN thik zohn) the bottom region of oceans and bodies of fresh water (671)

zona bentónica la región del fondo de los océanos y de las masas de agua dulce (671)

benthos (BEN THAHS) organisms that live at the bottom of oceans or bodies of fresh water (670)

benthos organismos que viven en el fondo de los océanos o de las masas de agua dulce (670)

big bang theory (BIG BANG THEE uh ree) the theory that all matter and energy in the universe was compressed into an extremely small volume that 13 billion to 15 billion years ago exploded and began expanding in all directions (864)

teoría del Big Bang la teoría que establece que toda la materia y la energía del universo estaban comprimidas en un volumen extremadamente pequeño que explotó hace aproximadamente 13 a 15 mil millones de años y empezó a expandirse en todas direcciones (864)

biomass (BIE oh MAS) plant material, manure, or any other organic matter that is used as an energy source (179)

biomasa materia vegetal, estiércol o cualquier otra materia orgánica que se usa como fuente de energía (179)

biosphere (BIE oh SFIR) the part of Earth where life exists; includes all of the living organisms on Earth (35)

biosfera la parte de la Tierra donde existe la vida; comprende todos los seres vivos de la Tierra (35)

black hole (BLAK HOHL) an object so massive and dense that even light cannot escape its gravity (858)

hoyo negro un objeto tan masivo y denso que ni siquiera la luz puede salir de su campo gravitacional (858)

body wave (BAHD ee WAYV) in geology, a seismic wave that travels through the body of a medium (320)

onda interna en geología, una onda sísmica que se desplaza a través del cuerpo de un medio (320)

Bowen's reaction series (BOH inz ree AK shuhn SIR eez) the simplified pattern that illustrates the order in which minerals crystallize from cooling magma according to their chemical composition and melting point (137)

serie de reacción de Bowen el patrón simplificado que ilustra el orden en que los minerales se cristalizan a partir del magma que se enfría, de acuerdo con su composición química y punto de fusion (137)

braided stream (BRAYD uhd STREEM) a stream or river that is composed of multiple channels that divide and rejoin around sediment bars (414)

corriente anastomosada una corriente o río compuesto por varios canales que se dividen y se vuelven a encontrar alrededor de barreras de sedimento (414)

C

caldera (kal DER uh) a large, circular depression that forms when the magma chamber below a volcano partially empties and causes the ground above to sink (355)

caldera una depresión grande y circular que se forma cuando se vacía parcialmente la cámara de magma que hay debajo de un volcán, lo cual hace que el suelo se hunda (355)

carbonation (KAHR buh NAY shuhn) the conversion of a compound into a carbonate (377)

carbonación la transformación de un compuesto a un carbonato (377)

carrying capacity (KAR ee ing kuh PAS i tee) the largest population that an environment can support at any given time (42)

capacidad de carga la población más grande que un ambiente puede sostener en cualquier momento dado (42)

cavern (KAV uhrn) a natural cavity that forms in rock as a result of the dissolution of minerals; also a large cave that commonly contains many smaller, connecting chambers (440)

caverna una cavidad natural que se forma en la roca como resultado de la disolución de minerales; también, una gran cueva que generalmente contiene muchas cámaras más pequeñas comunicadas entre sí (440)

cementation (SEE men TAY shuhn) the process in which minerals precipitate into pore spaces between sediment grains and bind sediments together to form rock (145)

cementación el proceso en el cual los minerales se precipitan entre los poros de granos de sedimento y unen los sedimentos para formar rocas (145)

Cenozoic Era (SEN uh ZOH ik ER uh) the current geologic era, which began 65.5 million years ago; also called the *Age of Mammals* (242)

era Cenozoica la era geológica actual, que comenzó hace 65.5 millones de años; también llamada *Edad de los Mamíferos* (242)

chemical sedimentary rock (KEM i kuhl SED uh MEN tuhr ee RAHK) sedimentary rock that forms when minerals precipitate from a solution or settle from a suspension (146)

roca sedimentaria química roca sedimentaria que se forma cuando los minerales precipitan a partir de una solución o se depositan a partir de una suspension (146)

chemical weathering (KEM i kuhl WETH uhr ing) the process by which rocks break down as a result of chemical reactions (376)

desgaste químico el proceso por medio del cual las rocas se fragmentan como resultado de reacciones químicas (376)

chromosphere (KROH muh SFIR) the thin layer of the sun that is just above the photosphere and that glows a reddish color during eclipses (828)

cromosfera la delgada capa del Sol que se encuentra justo encima de la fotosfera y que resplandece con un color rojizo durante los eclipses (828)

cirque (SUHRK) a deep and steep bowl-like depression produced by glacier erosion (460)

circo una depresión profunda y empinada, con forma de tazón, producida por erosión glaciar (460)

cirrus cloud (SIR uhs KLOWD) a feathery cloud that is composed of ice crystals and that has the highest altitude of any cloud in the sky (553)

nube cirro una nube liviana formada por cristales de hielo, la cual tiene la mayor altitud de todas las nubes en el cielo (553)

clastic sedimentary rock (KLAS tik SED uh MEN tuhr ee RAHK) sedimentary rock that forms when fragments of preexisting rocks are compacted or cemented together (147)

roca sedimentaria clástica roca sedimentaria que se forma cuando los fragmentos de rocas preexistentes se unen por compactación o cementación (147)

cleavage (KLEEV IJ) in geology, the tendency of a mineral to split along specific planes of weakness to form smooth, flat surfaces (118)

exfoliación en geología, la tendencia de un mineral a agrietarse a lo largo de planos débiles específicos y formar superficies lisas y planas (118)

climate (KLIE muht) the weather conditions in an area over a long period of time (605)

clima las condiciones del tiempo en un área durante un largo período de tiempo (605)

climatologist (KLIE muh TAHL uh jist) a scientist who gathers data to study and compare past and present climates and to predict future climate change (615)

climatólogo un científico que recopila datos para estudiar y comparar los climas del pasado y del presente y para predecir cambios climáticos en el futuro (615)

cloud (KLOWD) a collection of small water droplets or ice crystals suspended in the air, which forms when the air is cooled and condensation occurs (549)

nube un conjunto de pequeñas gotitas de agua o cristales de hielo suspendidos en el aire, que se forma cuando el aire se enfría y ocurre condensación (549)

cloud seeding (KLOWD SEED ing) the process of introducing freezing nuclei or condensation nuclei into a cloud in order to cause rain to fall (558)

sembrado de nubes el proceso de introducir núcleos congelados o núcleos de condensación en una nube para producir lluvia (558)

coalescence (KOH uh LE suhns) the formation of a larger droplet by the combination of smaller droplets (556)

coalescencia la formación de una gota más grande al combinarse gotas más pequeñas (556)

cold front (KOHLD FRUHNT) the front edge of a moving mass of cold air that pushes beneath a warmer air mass like a wedge (575)

frente frío el borde del frente de una masa de aire frío en movimiento que empuja por debajo de una masa de aire más caliente como una cuña (575)

comet (KAHM it) a small body of ice, rock, and cosmic dust that follows an elliptical orbit around the sun and that gives off gas and dust in the form of a tail as it passes close to the sun (807)

cometa un cuerpo pequeño formado por hielo, roca y polvo cósmico que sigue una órbita elíptica alrededor del Sol y que libera gas y polvo, los cuales forman una cola al pasar cerca del Sol (807)

compaction (kuhm PAK shuhn) the process in which the volume and porosity of a sediment is decreased by the weight of overlying sediments as a result of burial beneath other sediments (145)

compactación el proceso en el que el volumen y la porosidad de un sedimento disminuyen por efecto del peso al quedar el sedimento enterrado debajo de otros sedimentos superpuestos (145)

compound (KAHM POWND) a substance made up of atoms of two or more different elements joined by chemical bonds (93)

compuesto una sustancia formada por átomos de dos o más elementos diferentes unidos por enlaces químicos (93)

condensation (KAHN duhn SAY shuhn) the change of state from a gas to a liquid (408)

condensación el cambio de estado de gas a líquido (408)

condensation nucleus (KAHN duhn SAY shuhn NOO klee uhs) a solid particle in the atmosphere that provides the surface on which water vapor condenses (549)

núcleo de condensación una partícula sólida en la atmósfera que proporciona la superficie en la que el vapor de agua se condensa (549)

conduction (kuhn DUHK shuhn) the transfer of energy as heat through a material (526)

conducción la transferencia de energía en forma de calor a través de un material (526)

conservation (KAHN suhr VAY shuhn) the preservation and wise use of natural resources (183)

conservación la preservación y el uso inteligente de los recursos naturales (183)

constellation (KAHN stuh LAY shuhn) one of 88 regions into which the sky has been divided in order to describe the locations of celestial objects; a group of stars organized in a recognizable pattern (859)

constelación una de las 88 regiones en las que se ha dividido el cielo con el fin de describir la ubicación de los objetos celestes; un grupo de estrellas organizadas en un patrón reconocible (859)

contact metamorphism (KAHN TAKT MET uh MAWR FIZ uhm) a change in the texture, structure, or chemical composition of a rock due to contact with magma (152)

metamorfismo de contacto un cambio en la textura, estructura o composición química de una roca debido al contacto con el magma (152)

continental drift (KAHN tuh NENT'l DRIFT) the hypothesis that a single large landmass broke up into smaller landmasses to form the continents, which then drifted to their present locations; the movement of continents (259)

deriva continental la hipótesis de que una sola masa de tierra se dividió en masas de tierra más pequeñas para formar los continentes, los cuales se fueron a la deriva hasta terminar en sus ubicaciones actuales; el movimiento de los continentes (259)

continental glacier (KAHN tuh NENT'l GLAY shuhr) a massive sheet of ice that may cover millions of square kilometers, that may be thousands of meters thick, and that is not confined by surrounding topography (456)

glaciar continental una enorme capa de hielo que puede cubrir millones de kilómetros cuadrados, tener un espesor de miles de metros y que no está confinada por la topografía que la rodea (456)

continental margin (KAHN tuh NENT'l MAHR jin) the shallow sea floor that is located between the shoreline and the deep-ocean bottom (641)

margen continental el suelo marino poco profundo que se ubica entre la costa y el fondo profundo del océano (641)

contour line (KAHN TOOR LIEN) a line that connects points of equal elevation on a map (68)

curva de nivel una línea en un mapa que une puntos que tienen la misma elevación (68)

convection (kuhn VEK shuhn) the movement of matter due to differences in density that are caused by temperature variations; can result in the transfer of energy as heat (526)

convección el movimiento de la materia debido a diferencias en la densidad que se producen por variaciones en la temperatura; puede resultar en la transferencia de energía en forma de calor (526)

convective zone (kuhn VEK tiv ZOHN) the region of the sun's interior that is between the radiative zone and the photosphere and in which energy is carried upward by convection (827)

zona convective la región del interior del Sol que se encuentra entre la zona radiactiva y la fotosfera y en la cual la energía se desplaza hacia arriba por convección (827)

convergent boundary (kuhn VUHR juhnt BOWN duh ree) the boundary between tectonic plates that are colliding (270)

límite convergente el límite entre placas tectónicas que chocan (270)

core (KAWR) the central part of Earth below the mantle; also the center of the sun (30)

núcleo la parte central de la Tierra, debajo del manto; también, el centro del Sol (30)

core sample (KAWR SAM puhl) a cylindrical piece of sediment, rock, soil, snow, or ice that is collected by drilling (645)

muestra de sondeo un fragmento de sedimento, roca, suelo, nieve o hielo que se obtiene taladrando (645)

Coriolis effect (KAWR ee OH lis e FEKT) the curving of the path of a moving object from an otherwise straight path due to Earth's rotation (527, 690)

efecto de Coriolis la desviación de la trayectoria recta que experimentan los objetos en movimiento debido a la rotación de la Tierra (527, 690)

corona (kuh ROH nuh) the outermost layer of the sun's atmosphere (828)

corona la capa externa de la atmósfera del Sol (828)

coronal mass ejection (KAWR uh nuhl MAS ee JEK shuhn) coronal gas that is thrown into space from the sun (831)

eyección de masa coronal gas coronal que el Sol expulsa al espacio (831)

cosmic background radiation (KAHZ mik BAK GROWND RAY dee AY shuhn) radiation uniformly detected from every direction in space; considered a remnant of the big bang (865)

radiación cósmica de fondo radiación que se detecta de manera uniforme desde todas las direcciones en el espacio; se considera un resto del Big Bang (865)

cosmology (kahz MAHL uh jee) the study of the origin, properties, processes, and evolution of the universe (863)

cosmología el estudio del origen, propiedades, procesos y evolución del universo (863)

covalent bond (koh VAY luhnt BAHND) a bond formed when atoms share one or more pairs of electrons (97)

enlace covalente un enlace formado cuando los átomos comparten uno o más pares de electrons (97)

crater (KRAY tuhr) a bowl-shaped depression that forms on the surface of an object when a falling body strikes the object's surface or when an explosion occurs; a similar depression around the central vent of a volcano or geyser (786)

crater una depresión con forma de tazón, que se forma sobre la superficie de un objeto cuando un cuerpo en caída impacta sobre ésta o cuando se produce una explosión; una depresión similar alrededor de la chimenea de un volcán o géiser (786)

creep (KREEP) the slow downhill movement of weathered rock material (392)

arrastre el movimiento lento y descendente de materiales rocosos desgastados (392)

crevasse (kruh VAS) in a glacier, a large crack or fissure that results from ice movement (458)

grieta en un glaciar, una fractura o fisura grande debida al movimiento del hielo (458)

crust (KRUHST) the thin and solid outermost layer of Earth above the mantle (30)

corteza la capa externa, delgada y sólida de la Tierra, que se encuentra sobre el manto (30)

crystal (KRIS tuhl) a solid whose atoms, ions, or molecules are arranged in a regular, repeating pattern (114)

cristal un sólido cuyos átomos, iones o moléculas están ordenados en un patrón regular y repetitivo (114)

cumulus cloud (KYOO myoo luhs KLOWD) a low-level, billowy cloud that commonly has a top that resembles cotton balls and a dark bottom (553)

nube cúmulo una nube esponjada ubicada en un nivel bajo, cuya parte superior normalmente parece una bola de algodón y es obscura en la parte inferior (553)

current (KUHR uhnt) in geology, a horizontal movement of water in a well-defined pattern, such as a river or stream; the movement of air in a certain direction (689)

corriente en geología, un movimiento horizontal de agua en un patrón bien definido, como por ejemplo, un río o arroyo; el movimiento del aire en una cierta dirección (689)

D

deep current (DEEP KUHR uhnt) a streamlike movement of ocean water far below the surface (693)

corriente profunda un movimiento del agua del océano que es similar a una corriente y ocurre debajo de la superficie (693)

deep-ocean basin (DEEP OH shuhn BAYS uhn) the part of the ocean floor that is under deep water beyond the continental margin and that is composed of oceanic crust and a thin layer of sediment (641)

cuenca oceánica profunda la parte del fondo del océano que está bajo aguas profundas más allá del margen continental y que se compone de corteza oceánica y una delgada capa de sedimento (641)

deflation (dee FLAY shuhn) a form of wind erosion in which fine, dry soil particles are blown away (484)

deflación una forma de erosión del viento en la que se mueven partículas de suelo finas y secas (484)

deformation (DE fawr MAY shuhn) the bending, tilting, and breaking of Earth's crust; the change in the shape of rock in response to stress (293)

deformación el proceso de doblar, inclinar y romper la corteza de la Tierra; el cambio en la forma de una roca en respuesta a la tension (293)

delta (DEL tuh) a fan-shaped mass of rock material deposited at the mouth of a stream; for example, deltas form where streams flow into the ocean at the edge of a continent (415)

delta un depósito de materiales rocosos en forma de abanico ubicado en la desembocadura de un río; por ejemplo, los deltas se forman en el lugar donde las corrientes fluyen al océano en el borde de un continente (415)

density (DEN suh tee) the ratio of the mass of a substance to the volume of the substance; commonly expressed as grams per cubic centimeter for solids and liquids and as grams per liter for gases (120, 667)

densidad la relación entre la masa de una sustancia y su volumen; comúnmente se expresa en gramos por centímetro cúbico para los sólidos y líquidos, y como gramos por litro para los gases (120, 667)

dependent variable (dee PEN duhnt VER ee uh buhl) in an experiment, the factor that changes as a result of manipulation of one or more other factors (the independent variables) (11)

variable dependiente en un experimento, el factor que cambia como resultado de la manipulación de uno o más factores (las variables independientes) (11)

desalination (DEE SAL uh NAY shuhn) a process of removing salt from ocean water (410, 673)

desalación (o desalinización) un proceso de remoción de sal del agua del océano (410, 673)

dew point (DOO POYNT) at constant pressure and water vapor content, the temperature at which the rate of condensation equals the rate of evaporation (545)

punto de rocío a presión y contenido de vapor de agua constantes, la temperatura a la que la tasa de condensación es igual a la tasa de evaporación (545)

differential weathering (DIF uhr EN shuhl WETH uhr ing) the process by which softer, less weather resistant-rocks wear away at a faster rate than harder, more weather-resistant rocks do (379)

desgaste diferencial el proceso por medio cual las rocas más blandas y menos resistentes al clima se desgastan a una tasa más rápida que las rocas más duras y resistentes al clima (379)

discharge (dis CHAHRJ) the volume of water that flows within a given time (412)

descarga el volumen de agua que fluye en un tiempo determinado (412)

divergent boundary (die VUHR juhnt BOWN duh ree) the boundary between two tectonic plates that are moving away from each other (269)

límite divergente el límite entre dos placas tectónicas que se están separando una de la otra (269)

dome mountain (DOHM MOWN tuhn) a circular or elliptical, almost symmetrical elevation or structure in which the stratified rock slopes downward gently from the central point of folding (305)

domo una elevación o estructura circular o elíptica, casi simétrica, en la cual la roca estratificada se encuentra en una ligera pendiente hacia abajo a partir del punto central de plegamiento (305)

Doppler effect (DAHP luhr e FEKT) an observed change in the frequency of a wave when the source or observer is moving (848)

efecto Doppler un cambio que se observa en la frecuencia de una onda cuando la fuente o el observador está en movimiento (848)

dune (DOON) a mound of wind-deposited sand that moves as a result of the action of wind (485)

duna un montículo de arena depositada por el viento que se mueve como resultado de la acción de éste (485)

E

Earth science (UHRTH SIE uhns) the scientific study of Earth and the universe around it (5)

ciencias de la Tierra el estudio científico de la Tierra y del universo que la rodea (5)

earthquake (UHRTH KWAYK) a movement or trembling of the ground that is caused by a sudden release of energy when rocks along a fault move (319)

terremoto un movimiento o temblor del suelo causado por una liberación súbita de energía que se produce cuando las rocas ubicadas a lo largo de una falla se mueven (319)

eccentricity (EK sen TRIS uh tee) the degree of elongation of an elliptical orbit (symbol, *e*) (756)

excentricidad el grado de alargamiento de una órbita elíptica (símbolo: *e*) (756)

eclipse (i KLIPS) an event in which the shadow of one celestial body falls on another (793)

eclipse un suceso en el que la sombra de un cuerpo celeste cubre otro cuerpo celeste (793)

ecosystem (EE koh SIS tuhm) a community of organisms and their abiotic environment (41)

ecosistema una comunidad de organismos y su ambiente abiótico (41)

El Niño (el NEEN yoh) the warm-water phase of the El Niño–Southern Oscillation; a periodic occurrence in the eastern Pacific Ocean in which the surface-water temperature becomes unusually warm (609)

El Niño la fase caliente de la Oscilación Sureña "El Niño"; un fenómeno periódico que ocurre en el océano Pacífico oriental en el que la temperatura del agua superficial se vuelve más caliente que de costumbre (609)

elastic rebound (ee LAS tik REE BOWND) the sudden return of elastically deformed rock to its undeformed shape (319)

rebote elástico ocurre cuando una roca deformada elásticamente vuelve súbitamente a su forma no deformada (319)

electromagnetic spectrum (ee LEK troh mag NET ik SPEK truhm) all of the frequencies or wavelengths of electromagnetic radiation (521, 723)

espectro electromagnético todas las frecuencias o longitudes de onda de la radiación electromagnética (521, 723)

electron (ee LEK TRAHN) a subatomic particle that has a negative charge (88)

electron una partícula subatómica que tiene carga negative (88)

element (EL uh muhnt) a substance that cannot be separated or broken down into simpler substances by chemical means; all atoms of an element have the same atomic number (87)

elemento una sustancia que no se puede separar o descomponer en sustancias más simples por medio de métodos químicos; todos los átomos de un elemento tienen el mismo número atómico (87)

elevation (EL uh VAY shuhn) the height of an object above sea level (67)

elevación la altura de un objeto sobre el nivel del mar (67)

epicenter (EP i SENT uhr) the point on Earth's surface directly above an earthquake's starting point, or focus (320)

epicentro el punto de la superficie de la Tierra que queda justo arriba del punto de inicio, o foco, de un terremoto (320)

epoch (EP uhk) a subdivision of geologic time that is longer than an age but shorter than a period (232)

época una subdivisión del tiempo geológico que es más larga que una edad pero más corta que un período (232)

equinox (EE kwi NAHKS) the moment when the sun appears to cross the celestial equator (735)

equinoccio el momento en que el Sol parece cruzar el ecuador celeste (735)

era (IR uh) a unit of geologic time that includes two or more periods (232)

era una unidad de tiempo geológico que incluye dos o más períodos (232)

erosion (ee ROH zhuhn) a process in which the materials of Earth's surface are loosened, dissolved, or worn away and transported from one place to another by a natural agent, such as wind, water, ice, or gravity (387)

erosion un proceso por medio del cual los materiales de la superficie de la Tierra se aflojan, disuelven o desgastan y son transportados de un lugar a otro por un agente natural, como el viento, el agua, el hielo o la gravedad (387)

erratic (er RAT ik) a large rock transported from a distant source by a glacier (462)

errática una piedra grande transportada de una fuente lejana por un glacial (462)

esker (ES kuhr) a long, winding ridge of gravel and coarse sand deposited by glacial meltwater streams (464)

esker una cumbre larga y con curvas, compuesta por grava y arena gruesa depositada por corrientes de aguas glaciares (464)

estuary (ES tyoo er ee) an area where fresh water from rivers mixes with salt water from the ocean; the part of a river where the tides meet the river current (494)

estuario un área donde el agua dulce de los ríos se mezcla con el agua salada del océano; la parte de un río donde las mareas se encuentran con la corriente del río (494)

evapotranspiration (ee VAP oh TRAN spuh RAY shuhn) the total loss of water from an area, which equals the sum of the water lost by evaporation from the soil and other surfaces and the water lost by transpiration from organisms (408)

evapotranspiración la pérdida total de agua de un área, igual a la suma del agua perdida por evaporación del suelo y otras superficies, y el agua perdida debido a la transpiración de los organismos (408)

evolution (EV uh LOO shuhn) the process of change by which new species develop from preexisting species over time (233)

evolución el proceso de cambio por el cual se desarrollan nuevas especies a partir de especies preexistentes a lo largo del tiempo (233)

extrusive igneous rock (eks TROO siv IG nee uhs RAHK) rock that forms from the cooling and solidification of lava at Earth's surface (141)

roca ígnea extrusiva roca que se forma a partir del enfriamiento y la solidificación de la lava en la superficie de la Tierra (141)

F

fault (FAWLT) a break in a body of rock along which one block slides relative to another; a form of brittle strain (299)

falla una grieta en un cuerpo rocoso a lo largo de la cual un bloque se desliza respecto a otro; una forma de tensión quebradiza (299)

fault zone (FAWLT ZOHN) a region of numerous, closely spaced faults (324)

zona de fallas una región donde hay muchas fallas, las cuales están cerca unas de otras (324)

fault-block mountain (FAWLT BLAHK MOWN tuhn) a mountain that forms where faulting breaks Earth's crust into large blocks, which causes some blocks to drop down relative to other blocks (305)

montaña de bloque de falla una montaña que se forma cuando una falla rompe la corteza de la Tierra en grandes bloques, lo cual hace que algunos bloques se hundan respecto a otros bloques (305)

felsic (FEL sik) describes magma or igneous rock that is rich in feldspars and silica and that is generally light in color (142, 351)

félsico término que describe un tipo de magma o roca ígnea que es rica en feldespatos y sílice y generalmente tiene un color claro (142, 351)

fetch (FECH) the distance that wind blows across an area of the sea to generate waves (697)

alcance la distancia que el viento sopla en un área del mar para generar olas (697)

floodplain (FLUD PLAYN) an area along a river that forms from sediments deposited when the river overflows its banks (416)

llanura de inundación un área a lo largo de un río formada por sedimentos que se depositan cuando el río se desborda (416)

focus (FOH kuhs) the location within Earth along a fault at which the first motion of an earthquake occurs (320)

foco el lugar dentro de la Tierra a lo largo de una falla donde ocurre el primer movimiento de un terremoto (320)

fog (FAWG) water vapor that has condensed very near the surface of Earth because air close to the ground has cooled (554)

niebla vapor de agua que se ha condensado muy cerca de la superficie de la Tierra debido al enfriamiento del aire próximo al suelo (554)

fold (FOHLD) a form of ductile strain in which rock layers bend, usually as a result of compression (297)

pliegue una forma de tensión dúctil en la cual las capas de roca se curvan, normalmente como resultado de la compression (297)

folded mountain (FOHLD uhd MOWNT uhn) a mountain that forms when rock layers are squeezed together and uplifted (304)

montaña de plegamiento una montaña que se forma cuando las capas de roca se comprimen y se eleven (304)

foliation (FOH lee AY shuhn) the metamorphic rock texture in which mineral grains are arranged in planes or bands (153)

foliación la textura de una roca metamórfica en la que los granos de mineral están ordenados en planos o bandas (153)

food web (FOOD WEB) a diagram that shows the feeding relationships between organisms in an ecosystem (43)

red alimenticia un diagrama que muestra las relaciones de alimentación entre los organismos de un ecosistema (43)

fossil (FAHS uhl) the trace or remains of an organism that lived long ago, most commonly preserved in sedimentary rock (213)

fósil los indicios o los restos de un organismo que vivió hace mucho tiempo, comúnmente preservados en las rocas sedimentarias (213)

fossil fuel (FAHS uhl FYOO uhl) a nonrenewable energy resource formed from the remains of organisms that lived long ago; examples include oil, coal, and natural gas (171)

combustible fósil un recurso energético no renovable formado a partir de los restos de organismos que vivieron hace mucho tiempo; algunos ejemplos incluyen el petróleo, el carbón y el gas natural (171)

fracture (FRAK chuhr) in geology, a break in a rock, which results from stress, with or without displacement, including cracks, joints, and faults; also the manner in which a mineral breaks along either curved or irregular surfaces (118)

fractura en geología, un rompimiento en una roca, que resulta de la tensión, con o sin desplazamiento, incluyendo grietas, fisuras y fallas; también, la forma en la que se rompe un mineral a lo largo de superficies curvas o irregulares (118)

G

galaxy (GAL uhk see) a collection of stars, dust, and gas bound together by gravity (722, 860)

galaxia un conjunto de estrellas, polvo y gas unidos por la gravedad (722, 860)

Galilean moon (GAL uh LEE uhn MOON) any one of the four largest satellites of Jupiter—Io, Europa, Ganymede, and Callisto—that were discovered by Galileo in 1610 (799)

satélite galileano cualquiera de los cuatro satélites más grandes de Júpiter (Io, Europa, Ganímedes y Calisto) que fueron descubiertos por Galileo en 1610 (799)

gas giant (GAS JIE uhnt) a planet that has a deep, massive atmosphere, such as Jupiter, Saturn, Uranus, or Neptune (765)

gigante gaseoso un planeta con una atmósfera masiva y profunda, como por ejemplo, Júpiter, Saturno, Urano o Neptuno (765)

gemstone (JEM STOHN) a mineral, rock, or organic material that can be used as jewelry or an ornament when it is cut and polished (169)

piedra preciosa un mineral, roca o material orgánico que se puede usar como joya u ornamento cuando se corta y se pule (169)

geologic column (JEE uh LAHJ ik KAHL uhm) an ordered arrangement of rock layers that is based on the relative ages of the rocks and in which the oldest rocks are at the bottom (229)

columna geológica un arreglo ordenado de capas de rocas que se basa en la edad relativa de las rocas y en el cual las rocas más antiguas están al fondo (229)

geology (jee AHL uh jee) the scientific study of the origin, history, and structure of Earth and the processes that shape Earth (6)

geología el estudio científico del origen, la historia y la estructura del planeta Tierra y los procesos que le dan forma (6)

geosphere (JEE oh sfir) the mostly solid, rocky part of Earth; extends from the center of the core to the surface of the crust (35)

geosfera la capa de la Tierra que es principalmente sólida y rocosa; se extiende desde el centro del núcleo hasta la superficie de la corteza terrestre (35)

geothermal energy (JEE oh THUHR muhl EN uhr jee) the energy produced by heat within Earth (177)

energía geotérmica la energía producida por el calor del interior de la Tierra (177)

giant (JIE uhnt) a very large and bright star whose hot core has used most of its hydrogen (854)

gigante una estrella muy grande y brillante que tiene un núcleo caliente que ha usado la mayor parte de su hidrógeno (854)

glacial drift (GLAY shuhl DRIFT) the rock material carried and deposited by glaciers (462)

deriva glacial el material rocoso que es transportado y depositado por los glaciares (462)

glacier (GLAY shuhr) a large mass of moving ice (455)

glaciar una masa grande de hielo en movimiento (455)

global ocean (GLOH buhl OH shuhn) the body of salt water that covers nearly three-fourths of Earth's surface (637)

océano global la masa de agua salada que cubre cerca de tres cuartas partes de la superficie de la Tierra (637)

global warming (GLOH buhl WAWRM ing) a gradual increase in average global temperature (619)

calentamiento global un aumento gradual de la temperatura global promedio (619)

gradient (GRAY dee uhnt) the change in elevation over a given distance (412)

gradiente el cambio en la elevación a lo largo de una distancia determinada (412)

greenhouse effect (GREEN HOWS e FEKT) the warming of the surface and lower atmosphere of Earth that occurs when carbon dioxide, water vapor, and other gases in the air absorb and reradiate infrared radiation (524)

efecto invernadero el calentamiento de la superficie terrestre y de la parte más baja de la atmósfera, el cual se produce cuando el dióxido de carbono, el vapor de agua y otros gases del aire absorben radiación infrarroja y la vuelven a irradiar (524)

groundwater (GROWND WAWT uhr) the water that is beneath Earth's surface (431)

agua subterránea el agua que está debajo de la superficie de la Tierra (431)

Gulf Stream (GULF STREEM) the swift, deep, and warm Atlantic current that flows along the eastern coast of the United States toward the northeast (692)

corriente del Golfo la corriente rápida, profunda y cálida del océano Atlántico que fluye por la costa este de los Estados Unidos hacia el noreste (692)

gyre (JIER) a huge circle of moving ocean water found above and below the equator (690)

giro un círculo enorme de agua oceánica en movimiento que se encuentra debajo del ecuador (690)

H

half-life (HAF LIEF) the time required for half of a sample of a radioactive isotope to break down by radioactive decay to form a daughter isotope (210)

vida media el tiempo que se requiere para que la mitad de una muestra de un isótopo radiactivo se descomponga por desintegración radiactiva y forme un isótopo hijo (210)

headland (HED LAND) a high and steep formation of rock that extends out from shore into the water (490)

promontorio una formación rocosa alta y empinada que se extiende de la costa hacia el agua (490)

horizon (huh RIE zuhn) a horizontal layer of soil that can be distinguished from the layers above and below it; also a boundary between two rock layers that have different physical properties (384)

horizonte una capa horizontal de suelo que puede distinguirse de las capas que están por encima y por debajo de ella; también, un límite entre dos capas de roca que tienen propiedades físicas distintas (384)

horn (HAWRN) a sharp, pyramid-like peak that forms because of the erosion of cirques (460)

cuerno un pico puntiagudo en forma de pirámide que se forma debido a la erosión de los circos (460)

hot spot (HAHT SPAHT) a volcanically active area of Earth's surface, commonly far from a tectonic plate boundary (349)

mancha caliente un área volcánicamente activa de la superficie de la Tierra que comúnmente se encuentra lejos de un límite entre placas tectónicas (349)

humus (HYOO muhs) dark, organic material formed in soil from the decayed remains of plants and animals (384)

humus material orgánico obscuro que se forma en la tierra a partir de restos de plantas y animales en descomposición (384)

hurricane (HUHR i KAYN) a severe storm that develops over tropical oceans and whose strong winds of more than 120 km/h spiral in toward the intensely low-pressure storm center (579)

huracán tormenta severa que se desarrolla sobre océanos tropicales, con vientos fuertes que soplan a más de 120 km/h y que se mueven en espiral hacia el centro de presión extremadamente baja de la tormenta (579)

hydroelectric energy (HIE DROH ee LEK trik EN uhr jee) electrical energy produced by the flow of water (179)

energía hidroeléctrica energía eléctrica producida por el flujo del agua (179)

hydrolysis (hie DRAHL i sis) a chemical reaction between water and another substance to form two or more new substances; a reaction between water and a salt to create an acid or a base (377)

hidrólisis una reacción química entre el agua y otras sustancias para formar dos o más sustancias nuevas; una reacción entre el agua y una sal para crear un ácido o una base (377)

hydrosphere (HIE droh SFIR) the portion of Earth that is water (35)

hidrosfera la porción de la Tierra que es agua (35)

hypothesis (hie PAHTH uh sis) a testable idea or explanation that leads to scientific investigation (10)

hipótesis una idea o explicación que conlleva a la investigación científica y que se puede probar (10)

I

ice age (IES AYJ) a long period of climatic cooling during which the continents are glaciated repeatedly (467)

edad de hielo un largo período de enfriamiento del clima, durante el cual los continentes se ven repetidamente sometidos a la glaciación (467)

igneous rock (IG nee uhs RAHK) rock that forms when magma cools and solidifies (139)

roca ígnea una roca que se forma cuando el magma se enfría y se solidifica (139)

independent variable (IN di PEN duhnt VER ee uh buhl) in an experiment, the factor that is deliberately manipulated (11)

variable independiente el factor que se manipula deliberadamente en un experimento (11)

index fossil (IN DEKS FAHS uhl) a fossil that is used to establish the age of a rock layer because the fossil is distinct, abundant, and widespread and the species that formed that fossil existed for only a short span of geologic time (216)

fósil guía un fósil que se usa para establecer la edad de una capa de roca debido a que puede diferenciarse bien de otros, es abundante y está extendido; la especie que formó ese fósil existió sólo por un corto período de tiempo geológico (216)

inertia (in UHR shuh) the tendency of an object to resist a change in motion unless an outside force acts on the object (758)

inercia la tendencia de un objeto a resistir un cambio en el movimiento a menos que actúe una fuerza externa sobre el objeto (758)

intensity (in TEN suh tee) in Earth science, the amount of damage caused by an earthquake (328)

intensidad en las ciencias de la Tierra, la cantidad de daño causado por un terremoto (328)

internal plastic flow (in TUHR nuhl PLAS tik FLOH) the process by which glaciers flow slowly as grains of ice deform under pressure and slide over each other (457)

flujo plástico interno el proceso por medio del cual los glaciares fluyen lentamente a medida que los granos de hielo se deforman por efecto de la presión y se deslizan unos sobre otros (457)

intrusive igneous rock (in TROO siv IG nee uhs RAWK) rock formed from the cooling and solidification of magma beneath Earth's surface (141)

roca ígnea intrusiva una roca formada a partir del enfriamiento y solidificación del magma debajo de la superficie terrestre (141)

ion (IE AHN) an atom, radical, or molecule that has gained or lost one or more electrons and has a negative or positive charge (96)

ion un átomo, radical o molécula que ha ganado o perdido uno o más electrones y que tiene una carga negativa o positiva (96)

ionic bond (ie AHN ik BAHND) the attractive force between oppositely charged ions, which form when electrons are transferred from one atom to another (96)
enlace iónico la fuerza de atracción entre iones con cargas opuestas, que se forman cuando se transfieren electrones de un átomo a otro (96)

isogram (IE soh GRAM) a line on a map that represents a constant or equal value of a given quantity (66)
isograma una línea en un mapa que representa un valor constante o igual de una cantidad dada (66)

isostasy (ie SAHS tuh see) a condition of gravitational and buoyant equilibrium between Earth's lithosphere and asthenosphere (293)
isostasia una condición de equilibrio gravitacional y flotante entre la litosfera y la astenosfera de la Tierra (293)

isotope (IE suh TOHP) one of two or more atoms that have the same number of protons (atomic number) but different numbers of neutrons (atomic mass) (89)
isótopo uno de dos o más átomos que tienen el mismo número de protones (número atómico) pero diferente número de neutrones (masa atómica) (89)

J

jet stream (JET STREEM) a narrow band of strong winds that blow in the upper troposphere (529)
corriente en chorro un cinturón delgado de vientos fuertes que soplan en la parte superior de la troposfera (529)

K

karst topography (KAHRST tuh PAHG ruh fee) a type of irregular topography that is characterized by caverns, sinkholes, and underground drainage and that forms on limestone or other soluble rock (442)
topografía de karst una tipo de topografía irregular que se caracteriza por cavernas, depresiones y drenaje subterráneo y que se forma en piedra caliza o algún otro tipo de roca soluble (442)

kettle (KET'l) a bowl-shaped depression in a glacial drift deposit (464)
marmita una depresión con forma de tazón en un depósito de deriva glaciar (464)

Kuiper Belt (KIE puhr BELT) a region of the solar system that starts just beyond the orbit of Neptune and that contains dwarf planets and other small bodies made mostly of ice (771, 808)
cinturón de Kuiper una región del Sistema Solar que comienza justo después de la órbita de Neptuno y que contiene planetas enanos y otros cuerpos pequeños formados principalmente de hielo (771, 808)

L

lagoon (luh GOON) a small body of water separated from the sea by a low, narrow strip of land (169)
laguna una masa pequeña de agua separada del mar por una tira de tierra baja y angosta (169)

landform (LAND FAWRM) a physical feature of Earth's surface (393)
accidente geográfico una característica física de la superficie terrestre (393)

latent heat (LAYT'nt HEET) the heat energy that is absorbed or released by a substance during a phase change (543)
calor latente la energía calorífica que es absorbida o liberada por una sustancia durante un cambio de fase (543)

latitude (LAT uh TOOD) the angular distance north or south from the equator; expressed in degrees (57)
latitud la distancia angular hacia el norte o hacia el sur del ecuador; se expresa en grados (57)

lava (LAH vuh) magma that flows onto Earth's surface; the rock that forms when lava cools and solidifies (346)
lava magma que fluye a la superficie terrestre; la roca que se forma cuando la lava se enfría y se solidifica (346)

law of crosscutting relationships (LAW UHV KRAWS KUHT ing ri LAY shuhn SHIPS) the principle that a fault or body of rock is younger than any other body of rock that it cuts through (206)
ley de las relaciones entrecortadas el principio que establece que una falla o cuerpo rocoso siempre es más joven que cualquier otro cuerpo rocoso que atraviese (206)

law of superposition (LAW UHV soo puhr puh ZISH uhn) the principle that a sedimentary rock layer is older than the layers above it and younger than the layers below it if the layers are not disturbed (203)
ley de la sobreposición el principio de que una capa de roca sedimentaria es más vieja que las capas que se encuentran arriba de ella y más joven que las capas que se encuentran debajo de ella si las capas no han sido alteradas (203)

legend (LEJ uhnd) a list of map symbols and their meanings (65)
leyenda una lista de símbolos de un mapas y sus significados (65)

light-year (LIET YIR) the distance that light travels in one year; about 9.46 trillion kilometers (849)
año luz la distancia que viaja la luz en un año; aproximadamente 9.46 trillones de kilómetros (849)

lithosphere (LITH oh SFIR) the solid, outer layer of Earth that consists of the crust and the rigid upper part of the mantle (31, 267)

litosfera la capa externa y sólida de la Tierra que está formada por la corteza y la parte superior y rígida del manto (31, 267)

lode (LOHD) a mineral deposit within a rock formation (168)

veta un depósito mineral que se encuentra dentro de una formación rocosa (168)

loess (LOH ES) fine-grained sediments of quartz, feldspar, hornblende, mica, and clay deposited by the wind (488)

loess sedimentos de grano fino de cuarzo, feldespato, horneblenda, mica y arcilla depositados por el viento (488)

longitude (LAHN juh TOOD) the angular distance east or west from the prime meridian; expressed in degrees (58)

longitud la distancia angular hacia el este o hacia el oeste del primer meridiano; se expresa en grados (58)

longshore current (LAWNG SHAWR KUHR uhnt) a water current that travels near and parallel to the shoreline (492)

corriente de ribera una corriente de agua que se desplaza cerca de la costa y paralela a ella (492)

lunar eclipse (LOO nuhr i KLIPS) the passing of the moon through Earth's shadow at full moon (795)

eclipse lunar el paso de la Luna frente a la sombra de la Tierra cuando hay luna llena (795)

luster (LUHS tuhr) the way in which a mineral reflects light (118)

brillo la forma en que un mineral refleja la luz (118)

M

mafic (MAF ik) describes magma or igneous rock that is rich in magnesium and iron and that is generally dark in color (142, 351)

máfico término que describe un tipo de magma o roca ígnea que es rica en magnesio y hierro y generalmente tiene un color oscuro (142, 351)

magma (MAG muh) liquid rock produced under Earth's surface; igneous rocks are made of magma (345)

magma roca líquida producida debajo de la superficie terrestre; las rocas ígneas están hechas de magma (345)

magnitude (MAG nuh TOOD) a measure of the strength of an earthquake (327)

magnitud una medida de la intensidad de un terremoto (327)

main sequence (MAYN SEE kwuhns) the location on the H-R diagram where most stars lie; it has a diagonal pattern from the lower right (low temperature and luminosity) to the upper left (high temperature and luminosity) (851)

secuencia principal la ubicación en el diagrama H-R donde se encuentran la mayoría de las estrellas; tiene un patrón diagonal de la parte inferior derecha (baja temperatura y luminosidad) a la parte superior izquierda (alta temperatura y luminosidad) (851)

mantle (MAN tuhl) in Earth science, the layer of rock between Earth's crust and core (30)

manto en las ciencias de la Tierra, la capa de roca que se encuentra entre la corteza terrestre y el núcleo (30)

map projection (MAP proh JEK shuhn) a flat map that represents a spherical surface (62)

proyección cartográfica un mapa plano que representa una superficie esférica (62)

mare (MAH RAY) a large, dark area of basalt on the moon (plural, *maria*) (786)

mar lunar una gran área oscura de basalto en la Luna (786)

mass extinction (MAS ek STINGK shuhn) an episode during which large numbers of species become extinct (239)

extinción masiva un episodio durante el cual grandes cantidades de especies se extinguen (239)

mass movement (MAS MOOV muhnt) the movement of a large mass of sediment or a section of land down a slope (391)

movimiento masivo el movimiento hacia abajo por una pendiente de una gran masa de sedimento o una sección de terreno (391)

matter (MAT uhr) anything that has mass and takes up space (87)

materia cualquier cosa que tiene masa y ocupa un lugar en el espacio (87)

meander (mee AN duhr) one of the bends, twists, or curves in a low-gradient stream or river (413)

meandro una de las vueltas, giros o curvas de un arroyo o río de bajo gradiente (413)

mechanical weathering (muh KAN i kuhl WETH uhr ing) the process by which rocks break down into smaller pieces by physical means (373)

desgaste mecánico el proceso por medio del cual las rocas se rompen en pedazos más pequeños mediante medios físicos (373)

meridian (muh RID ee uhn) any semicircle that runs north and south around Earth from the geographic North Pole to the geographic South Pole; a line of longitude (58)

meridiano cualquier semicírculo que va de norte a sur alrededor de la Tierra, del Polo Norte geográfico al Polo Sur geográfico; una línea de longitud (58)

mesosphere (MES oh SFIR) literally, the "middle sphere"; the strong, lower part of the mantle between the asthenosphere and the outer core (31); *also* the coldest layer of the atmosphere, between the stratosphere and the thermosphere, in which temperature decreases as altitude increases (519)

mesosfera literalmente, la "esfera media"; la parte fuerte e inferior del manto que se encuentra entre la astenosfera y el núcleo externo (31); *también*, la capa más fría de la atmósfera que se encuentra entre la estratosfera y la termosfera, en la cual la temperatura disminuye al aumentar la altitud (519)

Mesozoic Era (MES oh ZOH ik ER uh) the geologic era that lasted from 251 million to 65.5 million years ago; also called the Age of Reptiles (239)

era Mesozoica la era geológica que comenzó hace 251 millones de años y terminó hace 65.5 millones de años; también llamada Edad de los Reptiles (239)

metamorphism (MET uh MAWR FIZ uhm) the process in which one type of rock changes into metamorphic rock because of chemical processes or changes in temperature and pressure (151)

metamorfismo el proceso en el que un tipo de roca cambia a roca metamórfica debido a procesos químicos o cambios en la temperatura y la presión (151)

meteor (MEET ee uhr) a bright streak of light that results when a meteoroid burns up in Earth's atmosphere (809)

meteoro un rayo de luz brillante que se produce cuando un meteoroide se quema en la atmósfera de la Tierra (809)

meteoroid (MEET ee uhr OYD) a relatively small, rocky body that travels through space (809)

meteoroide un cuerpo rocoso relativamente pequeño que viaja en el espacio (809)

meteorology (MEET ee uhr AHL uh jee) the scientific study of Earth's atmosphere, especially in relation to weather and climate (7)

meteorología el estudio científico de la atmósfera de la Tierra, sobre todo en lo que se relaciona al tiempo y al clima (7)

microclimate (MIE kroh KLIE mit) the climate of a small area (614)

microclima el clima de un área pequeña (614)

middle-latitude climate (MID'l LAT uh TOOD KLIE muht) a climate that has an average maximum temperature below 18 °C in the coldest month and an average minimum temperature above 10 °C in the warmest month (612)

clima de latitud media un clima que tiene una temperatura promedio máxima de 18 °C en el mes más frío y una temperatura promedio mínima de 10 °C en el mes más caliente (612)

mid-latitude cyclone (MID LAT uh TOOD SIE KLOHN) an area of low pressure that is characterized by rotating wind that moves toward the rising air of the central low-pressure region; the motion is counterclockwise in the Northern Hemisphere (576)

ciclón de latitud media un área de baja presión caracterizada por la presencia de viento en rotación que se desplaza hacia el aire ascendente de la región central de baja presión; en el hemisferio norte, el movimiento se produce en sentido contrario al de las manecillas del reloj (576)

mid-ocean ridge (MID OH shuhn RIJ) a long, undersea mountain chain that has a steep, narrow valley at its center, that forms as magma rises from the asthenosphere, and that creates new oceanic lithosphere (sea floor) as tectonic plates move apart (262)

dorsal oceánica una larga cadena submarina de montañas que tiene un valle empinado y angosto en el centro, se forma a medida que el magma se eleva a partir de la astenosfera y produce una nueva litosfera oceánica (suelo marino) a medida que las placas tectónicas se separan (262)

Milankovitch theory (MUH lan KOH vich THEE uh ree) the theory that cyclical changes in Earth's orbit and in the tilt of Earth's axis occur over thousands of years and cause climatic changes (469)

teoría de Milankovitch la teoría que establece que los cambios cíclicos en la órbita de la Tierra y en la inclinación de su eje se producen a lo largo de miles de años y provocan cambios climáticos (469)

mineral (MIN uhr uhl) a natural, usually inorganic solid that has a characteristic chemical composition, an orderly internal structure, and a characteristic set of physical properties (111)

mineral un sólido natural, normalmente inorgánico, que tiene una composición química característica, una estructura interna ordenada y propiedades físicas y químicas características (111)

mineralogist (MIN uhr AL uh jist) a person who examines, analyzes, and classifies minerals (117)

mineralólogo una persona que examina, analiza y clasifica los minerales (117)

mixture (MIKS chuhr) a combination of two or more substances that are not chemically combined (98)

mezcla una combinación de dos o más sustancias que no están combinadas químicamente (98)

Mohs hardness scale (MOHZ HAHRD nis SKAYL) the standard scale against which the hardness of minerals is rated (119)

escala de dureza de Mohs la escala estándar que se usa para clasificar la dureza de un mineral (119)

molecule (MAHL i KYOOL) a group of atoms that are held together by chemical forces (93)

molécula un conjunto de átomos que se mantienen unidos por acción de las fuerzas químicas (93)

monsoon (mahn SOON) a seasonal wind that blows toward the land in the summer, bringing heavy rains, and that blows away from the land in the winter, bringing dry weather (609)

monzón viento estacional que sopla hacia la tierra en el verano, ocasionando fuertes lluvias, y que se aleja de la tierra en el invierno, ocasionando tiempo seco (609)

moon (MOON) a celestial body that revolves around a body that is greater in mass; a natural satellite (785)

luna un cuerpo celeste que gira alrededor de un cuerpo que tiene mayor masa; un satélite natural (785)

moraine (moh RAYN) a landform that is made from unsorted sediments deposited by a glacier (463)

morrena un accidente geográfico que se forma a partir de varios tipos de sedimentos depositados por un glaciar (463)

mountain range (MOWN tuhn RAYNJ) a series of mountains that are closely related in orientation, age, and mode of formation (301)

cinturón de montañas una serie de montañas que están íntimamente relacionadas en orientación, edad y modo de formación (301)

N

nebula (NEB yu luh) a large cloud of gas and dust in interstellar space; a region in space where stars are born (852)

nebulosa una nube grande de gas y polvo en el espacio interestelar; una región en el espacio donde las estrellas nacen (852)

nekton (NEK tuhn) all organisms that swim actively in open water, independent of currents (670)

necton todos los organismos que nadan activamente en las aguas abiertas, de manera independiente de las corrientes (670)

neutron (NOO TRAHN) a subatomic particle that has no charge and that is located in the nucleus of an atom (88)

neutrón una partícula subatómica que no tiene carga y que está ubicada en el núcleo de un átomo (88)

neutron star (NOO TRAHN STAHR) a star that has collapsed under gravity to the point that the electrons and protons have smashed together to form neutrons (857)

estrella de neutrones una estrella que se ha colapsado debido a la gravedad hasta el punto en que los electrones y protones han chocado unos contra otros para formar neutrones (857)

nodule (NAHJ OOL) a lump of minerals whose composition differs from the composition of the surrounding sediment or rock; also a lump of minerals that is made of oxides of manganese, iron, copper, or nickel and that is found in scattered groups on the ocean floor (647)

nódulo un bulto de minerales que tienen una composición diferente a la de los sedimentos o rocas de los alrededores; también, un bulto de minerales compuesto por óxidos de manganeso, hierro, cobre o níquel y que se encuentra en grupos esparcidos en el fondo del océano (647)

nonfoliated (NAHN FOHL ee ayt id) the metamorphic rock texture in which mineral grains are not arranged in planes or bands (154)

no foliada la textura de una roca metamórfica en la que los granos de mineral no están ordenados en planos ni bandas (154)

nonrenewable resource (NAHN ri NOO uh buhl REE SAWRS) a resource that forms at a rate that is much slower than the rate at which the resource is consumed (171)

recurso no renovable un recurso que se forma a una tasa que es mucho más lenta que la tasa a la que se consume (171)

nonsilicate mineral (NAHN SIL i kit MIN uhr uhl) a mineral that does not contain compounds of silicon and oxygen (113)

mineral no-silicato un mineral que no contiene compuestos de sílice y oxígeno (113)

nova (NOH vuh) a star that suddenly becomes brighter (856)

nova una estrella que súbitamente se vuelve más brillante (856)

nuclear fission (NOO klee uhr FISH uhn) the process by which the nucleus of a heavy atom splits into two or more fragments; the process releases neutrons and energy (174)

fisión nuclear el proceso por medio del cual el núcleo de un átomo pesado se divide en dos o más fragmentos; el proceso libera neutrones y energía (174)

nuclear fusion (NOO klee uhr FYOO zhuhn) the process by which nuclei of small atoms combine to form a new, more massive nucleus; the process releases energy (176, 824)

fusión nuclear el proceso por medio del cual los núcleos de átomos pequeños se combinan y forman un núcleo nuevo con mayor masa; el proceso libera energía (176, 824)

O

observation (AHB zuhr VAY shuhn) the process of obtaining information by using the senses; the information obtained by using the senses (10)

observación el proceso de obtener información por medio de los sentidos; la información que se obtiene al usar los sentidos (10)

occluded front (uh KLOOD id FRUHNT) a front that forms when a cold air mass overtakes a warm air mass and lifts the warm air mass off the ground and over another air mass (576)

frente ocluido un frente que se forma cuando una masa de aire frío supera a una masa de aire caliente y la levanta del suelo por encima de otra masa de aire (576)

oceanography (OH shuh NAHG ruh fee) the scientific study of the ocean, including the properties and movements of ocean water, the characteristics of the ocean floor, and the organisms that live in the ocean (6, 638)

oceanografía el estudio científico del océano, incluyendo las propiedades y los movimientos del agua, las características del fondo y los organismos que viven en él (6, 638)

Oort cloud (AWRT KLOWD) a spherical region that surrounds the solar system, that extends from the Kuiper Belt to almost halfway to the nearest star, and that contains billions of comets (808)

nube de Oort una región esférica que rodea al Sistema Solar, que se extiende desde el cinturón de Kuiper hasta la mitad del camino hacia la estrella más cercana y contiene miles de millones de cometas (808)

orbital period (AWR buh tuhl PIR ee uhd) the time required for a body to complete a single orbit (757)

período de órbita el tiempo que se requiere para que un cuerpo complete una órbita (757)

ore (AWR) a natural material whose concentration of economically valuable minerals is high enough for the material to be mined profitably (167)

mena un material natural cuya concentración de minerales con valor económico es suficientemente alta como para que el material pueda ser explotado de manera rentable (167)

organic sedimentary rock (awr GAN ik SED uh MEN tuhr ee RAHK) sedimentary rock that forms from the remains of plants or animals (146)

roca sedimentaria orgánica roca sedimentaria que se forma a partir de los restos de plantas o animales (146)

oxidation (AHKS i DAY shuhn) the process by which a metallic element combines with oxygen (376)

oxidación el proceso por medio del cual un elemento metálico se combina con oxígeno (376)

ozone (OH ZOHN) a gas molecule that is made up of three oxygen atoms (515)

ozono una molécula de gas que está formada por tres átomos de oxígeno (515)

P

P wave (PEE WAYV) a primary wave, or compression wave; a seismic wave that causes particles of rock to move in a back-and-forth direction parallel to the direction in which the wave is traveling; P waves are the fastest seismic waves and can travel through solids, liquids, and gases (321)

onda P una onda primaria u onda de compresión; una onda sísmica que hace que las partículas de roca se muevan en una dirección de atrás hacia delante en forma paralela a la dirección en que viaja la onda; las ondas P son las ondas sísmicas más rápidas y pueden viajar a través de sólidos, líquidos y gases (321)

pack ice (PAK IES) a floating layer of sea ice that completely covers an area of the ocean surface (665)

manto de hielo marino una capa flotante de hielo marino que cubre completamente un área de la superficie del océano (665)

paleomagnetism (PAY lee oh MAG nuh TIZ uhm) the study of the alignment of magnetic minerals in rock, specifically as it relates to the reversal of Earth's magnetic poles; *also* the magnetic properties that rock acquires during formation (263)

paleomagnetismo el estudio de la alineación de los minerales magnéticos en la roca, específicamente en lo que se relaciona con la inversión de los polos magnéticos de la Tierra; también, las propiedades magnéticas que la roca adquiere durante su formación (263)

paleontology (PAY lee uhn TAHL uh jee) the scientific study of fossils (213)

paleontología el estudio científico de los fósiles (213)

Paleozoic Era (PAY lee OH ZOH ik ER uh) the geologic era that followed Precambrian time and that lasted from 542 million to 251 million years ago (236)

era Paleozoica la era geológica que vino después del período Precámbrico; comenzó hace 542 millones de años y terminó hace 251 millones de años (236)

Pangaea (pan JEE uh) the supercontinent that formed 300 million years ago and that began to break up 200 million years ago (278)

Pangea el supercontinente que se formó hace 300 millones de años y que comenzó a separarse hace 200 millones de años (278)

Panthalassa (PAN thuh LAH suh) the single, large ocean that covered Earth's surface during the time the supercontinent Pangaea existed

Panthalassa el único gran océano que cubría la superficie de la Tierra cuando existía el supercontinente Pangea

parallax (PAR uh LAKS) an apparent shift in the position of an object when viewed from different locations (849)

paralaje un cambio aparente en la posición de un objeto cuando se ve desde lugares distintos (849)

parallel (PAR uh LEL) any circle that runs east and west around Earth and that is parallel to the equator; a line of latitude (57)

paralelo cualquier círculo que va hacia el Este o hacia el Oeste alrededor de la Tierra y que es paralelo al ecuador; una línea de latitud (57)

peer review (PIR ri VYOO) the process in which experts in a given field examine the results and conclusions of a scientist's study before that study is accepted for publication (14)

evaluación de pares el proceso en el cual los expertos en un campo dado examinan los resultados y las conclusiones de un estudio científico antes de aceptar su publicación (14)

pelagic zone (pi LAJ ik ZOHN) the region of an ocean or body of fresh water above the benthic zone (671)

zona pelágica la región de un océano o una masa de agua dulce sobre la zona bentónica (671)

perigee (PER i JEE) in the orbit of a satellite, the point that is closest to Earth (791)

perigeo en la órbita de un satélite, el punto que está más cerca de la Tierra (791)

perihelion (PER i HEE lee uhn) in the orbit of a planet or other body in the solar system, the point that is closest to the sun (730)

perihelio en la órbita de un planeta u otros cuerpos en el sistema solar, el punto que está más cerca del Sol (730)

period (PIR ee uhd) a unit of geologic time that is longer than an epoch but shorter than an era (232)

período una unidad de tiempo geológico que es más larga que una época pero más corta que una era (232)

permeability (PUHR mee uh BIL uh tee) the ability of a rock or sediment to let fluids pass through its open spaces, or pores (432)

permeabilidad la capacidad de una roca o sedimento de permitir que los fluidos pasen a través de sus espacios abiertos o poros (432)

phase (FAYZ) in astronomy, the change in the illuminated area of one celestial body as seen from another celestial body; phases of the moon are caused by the changing positions of Earth, the sun, and the moon (796)

fase en astronomía, el cambio en el área iluminada de un cuerpo celeste según se ve desde otro cuerpo celeste; las fases de la Luna se producen como resultado de los cambios en la posición de la Tierra, el Sol y la Luna (796)

photosphere (FOHT oh SFIR) the visible surface of the sun (827)

fotosfera la superficie visible del Sol (827)

placer deposit (PLAS uhr dee PAHZ it) a deposit that contains a valuable mineral that has been concentrated by mechanical action (168)

yacimiento de aluvión un yacimiento que contiene un mineral valioso que se ha concentrado debido a la acción mecánica (168)

planet (PLAN it) a celestial body that orbits the sun, is round because of its own gravity, and has cleared the neighborhood around its orbital path (749)

planeta un cuerpo celeste que orbita alrededor del Sol, es redondo debido a su propia fuerza de gravedad y ha despejado los alrededores de su trayectoria orbital (749)

planetesimal (PLAN i TES i muhl) a small body from which a planet originated in the early stages of development of the solar system (750)

planetesimal un cuerpo pequeño a partir del cual se originó un planeta en las primeras etapas de desarrollo del Sistema Solar (750)

plankton (PLANGK tuhn) the mass of mostly microscopic organisms that float or drift freely in the waters of aquatic (freshwater and marine) environments (670)

plancton la masa de organismos casi microscópicos que flotan o se encuentran a la deriva en aguas (dulces y marinas) de ambientes acuáticos (670)

plate tectonics (PLAYT tek TAHN iks) the theory that explains how large pieces of the lithosphere, called *plates*, move and change shape (267)

tectónica de placas la teoría que explica cómo las grandes partes de litosfera, denominadas placas, se mueven y cambian de forma (267)

polar climate (POH luhr KLIE muht) a climate that is characterized by average temperatures that are near or below freezing; typical of polar regions (613)

clima polar un clima caracterizado por temperaturas cercanas o inferiores al punto de congelación; típico de las regiones polares (613)

polar easterlies (POH luhr EES tuhr leez) prevailing winds that blow from east to west between 60° and 90° latitude in both hemispheres (528)

vientos polares del este vientos preponderantes que soplan de este a oeste entre los 60° y los 90° de latitud en ambos hemisferios (528)

porosity (poh RAHS uh tee) the percentage of the total volume of a rock or sediment that consists of open spaces (431)

porosidad el porcentaje del volumen total de una roca o sedimento que está formado por espacios abiertos (431)

Precambrian time (pree KAM bree uhn TIEM) the interval of time in the geologic time scale from Earth's formation to the beginning of the Paleozoic era, from 4.6 billion to 542 million years ago (234)

período Precámbrico el intervalo en la escala de tiempo geológico que abarca desde la formación de la Tierra hasta el comienzo de la era Paleozoica; comenzó hace 4,600 millones de años y terminó hace 542 millones de años (234)

precipitation (pree SIP uh TAY shuhn) any form of water that falls to Earth's surface from the clouds; includes rain, snow, sleet, and hail (408, 555)

precipitación cualquier forma de agua que cae de las nubes a la superficie de la Tierra; incluye a la lluvia, nieve, aguanieve y granizo (408, 555)

prominence (PRAHM uh nuhns) a loop of relatively cool, incandescent gas that extends above the photosphere and above the sun's edge as seen from Earth (831)

protuberancia una espiral de gas incandescente y relativamente frío que, vista desde la Tierra, se extiende por encima de la fotosfera y la superficie del Sol (831)

proton (PROH TAHN) a subatomic particle that has a positive charge and that is located in the nucleus of an atom; the number of protons in the nucleus is the atomic number, which determines the identity of an element (88)

protón una partícula subatómica que tiene una carga positiva y que está ubicada en el núcleo de un átomo; el número de protones que hay en el núcleo es el número atómico, y éste determina la identidad del elemento (88)

pulsar (PUHL SAHR) a rapidly spinning neutron star that emits pulses of radio and optical energy (858)

pulsar una estrella de neutrones que gira rápidamente y emite pulsaciones de energía radioeléctrica y óptica (858)

pyroclastic material (PIE roh KLAS tik muh TIR ee uhl) fragments of rock that form during a volcanic eruption (352)

material piroclástico fragmentos de roca que se forman durante una erupción volcánica (352)

Q

quasar (KWAY ZAHR) quasi-stellar radio source; a very luminous object that produces energy at a high rate; quasars are thought to be the most distant objects in the universe (862)

cuasar fuente de radio cuasi-estelar; un objeto muy luminoso que produce energía a una gran velocidad; se piensa que los cuasares son los objetos más distantes del universo (862)

R

radar (RAY DAHR) **ra**dio **d**etection **a**nd **r**anging, a system that uses reflected radio waves to determine the velocity and location of objects (585)

radar detección y exploración a gran distancia por medio de ondas de radio; un sistema que usa ondas de radio reflejadas para determinar la velocidad y ubicación de los objetos (585)

radiative zone (RAY dee ay tiv ZOHN) the zone of the sun's interior that is between the core and the convection zone and in which energy moves by radiation (827)

zona radiactiva la zona del interior del Sol que se encuentra entre el núcleo y la zona de convección y en la cual la energía se mueve por radiación (827)

radiometric dating (RAY dee oh MET rik DAYT ing) a method of determining the absolute age of an object by comparing the relative percentages of a radioactive (parent) isotope and a stable (daughter) isotope (209)

datación radiométrica un método para determinar la edad absoluta de un objeto comparando los porcentajes relativos de un isótopo radiactivo (precursor) y un isótopo estable (hijo) (209)

radiosonde (RAY dee oh SAHND) a package of instruments that is carried aloft by a balloon to measure upper atmospheric conditions, including temperature, dew point, and wind velocity (585)

radiosonda un conjunto de instrumentos que se colocan en un globo para medir condiciones de la atmósfera superior, como la temperatura, el punto de rocío y la velocidad del viento (585)

recycling (ree SIE kling) the process of recovering valuable or useful materials from waste or scrap; the process of reusing some items (183)

reciclar el proceso de recuperar materiales valiosos o útiles de los desechos o de la basura; el proceso de reutilizar algunas cosas (183)

reflecting telescope (ri FLEKT ing TEL uh SKOHP) a telescope that uses a curved mirror to gather and focus light from distant objects (725)

telescopio reflector un telescopio que utiliza un espejo curvo para captar y enfocar la luz de objetos lejanos (725)

refracting telescope (ri FRAKT ing TEL uh SKOHP) a telescope that uses a set of lenses to gather and focus light from distant objects (725)

telescopio refractante un telescopio que utiliza un conjunto de lentes para captar y enfocar la luz de objetos lejanos (725)

refraction (ri FRAK shuhn) the process by which ocean waves bend directly toward the coastline as they approach shallow water (699)

refracción el proceso por medio del cual las olas oceánicas se curvan directamente hacia la costa a medida que se acercan a agua poco profunda (699)

regional metamorphism (REE juhn uhl MET uh MAWR FIZ uhm) a change in the texture, structure, or chemical composition of a rock due to changes in temperature and pressure over a large area, generally as a result of tectonic forces (152)

metamorfismo regional un cambio en la textura, estructura o composición química de una roca debido a cambios en la temperatura y presión en un área extensa, generalmente como resultado de la acción de fuerzas tectónicas (152)

relative age (REL uh tiv AYJ) the age of an object in relation to the ages of other objects (202)

edad relativa la edad de un objeto en relación con la edad de otros objetos (202)

relative humidity (REL uh tiv hyoo MID uh tee) the ratio of the amount of water vapor in the air to the amount of water vapor needed to reach saturation at a given temperature (546)

humedad relativa la proporción de la cantidad de vapor de agua que hay en el aire respecto a la cantidad de vapor de agua que se necesita para alcanzar la saturación a una temperatura dada (546)

relief (ri LEEF) the difference between the highest and lowest elevations in a given area; the variations in elevation of a land surface (68)

relieve la diferencia entre las elevaciones más altas y las más bajas en un área dada; las variaciones en elevación de una superficie de terreno (68)

remote sensing (ri MOHT SENS ing) the process of gathering and analyzing information about an object without physically being in touch with the object (61)

teledetección el proceso de recopilar y analizar información acerca de un objeto sin estar en contacto físico con el objeto (61)

renewable resource (ri NOO uh buhl REE SAWRS) a natural resource that can be replaced at the same rate at which the resource is consumed (177)

recurso renovable un recurso natural que puede reemplazarse a la misma tasa a la que se consume (177)

revolution (REV uh LOO shuhn) the motion of a body that travels around another body in space; one complete trip along an orbit (730)

revolución el movimiento de un cuerpo que viaja alrededor de otro cuerpo en el espacio; un viaje completo a lo largo de una órbita (730)

rifting (RIFT ing) the process by which Earth's crust breaks apart; can occur within continental crust or oceanic crust (275)

fracturación el proceso por medio del cual la corteza de la Tierra se fractura; puede producirse dentro de la corteza continental u oceánica (275)

rock cycle (RAHK SIE kuhl) the series of processes in which rock forms, changes from one type to another, is destroyed, and forms again by geologic processes (136)

ciclo de las rocas la serie de procesos por medio de los cuales una roca se forma, cambia de un tipo a otro, se destruye y se forma nuevamente por procesos geológicos (136)

rotation (roh TAY shuhn) the spin of a body on its axis (729)

rotación el giro de un cuerpo alrededor de su eje (729)

S

S wave (ES WAYV) a secondary wave, or shear wave; a seismic wave that causes particles of rock to move in a side-to-side direction perpendicular to the direction in which the wave is traveling; S waves are the second-fastest seismic waves and can travel only through solids (321)

onda S una onda secundaria u onda rotacional; una onda sísmica que hace que las partículas de roca se muevan en una dirección de lado a lado, en forma perpendicular a la dirección en la que viaja la onda; las ondas S son las segundas ondas sísmicas en cuanto a velocidad y únicamente pueden viajar a través de sólidos (321)

salinity (suh LIN uh tee) a measure of the amount of dissolved salts in a given amount of liquid (664)

salinidad una medida de la cantidad de sales disueltas en una cantidad determinada de líquido (664)

saltation (sal TAY shuhn) the movement of sand or other sediments by short jumps and bounces that is caused by wind or water (483)

saltación el movimiento de la arena u otros sedimentos por medio de saltos pequeños y rebotes debido al viento o al agua (483)

satellite (SAT'l IET) a natural or artificial body that revolves around a celestial body that is greater in mass (785)

satélite un cuerpo natural o artificial que gira alrededor de un cuerpo celeste que tiene mayor masa (785)

scale (SKAYL) the relationship between the distance shown on a map and the actual distance (65)

escala la relación entre la distancia que se muestra en un mapa y la distancia real (65)

sea (SEE) a large, commonly saline body of water that is smaller than an ocean and that may be partially or completely surrounded by land; also a subdivision of an ocean (637)

mar una gran masa de agua, generalmente salada, que es más pequeña que un océano y que puede estar parcial o totalmente rodeada de tierra; también, una subdivisión de un océano (637)

sea-floor spreading (SEE FLAWR SPRED ing) the process by which new oceanic lithosphere (sea floor) forms when magma rises to Earth's surface at mid-ocean ridges and solidifies, as older, existing sea floor moves away from the ridge (263)

expansión del suelo marino el proceso por medio del cual se forma nueva litósfera oceánica (suelo marino) cuando el magma sube a la superficie de la Tierra en las dorsales oceánicas y se solidifica, a medida que el antiguo suelo marino existente se aleja de la dorsal oceánica (263)

seismic gap (SIEZ mik GAP) an area along a fault where relatively few earthquakes have occurred recently but where strong earthquakes are known to have occurred in the past (331)

brecha sísmica un área a lo largo de una falla donde han ocurrido relativamente pocos terremotos recientemente, pero donde se sabe que han ocurrido terremotos fuertes en el pasado (331)

seismogram (SIEZ muh GRAM) a tracing of earthquake motion that is recorded by a seismograph (325)

sismograma una traza del movimiento de un terremoto registrada por un sismógrafo (325)

seismograph (SIEZ muh GRAF) an instrument that records vibrations in the ground (325)

sismógrafo un instrumento que registra las vibraciones en el suelo (325)

shadow zone (SHAD oh ZOHN) an area on Earth's surface where no direct seismic waves from a particular earthquake can be detected (322)

zona de sombra un área de la superficie de la Tierra donde no se detectan ondas sísmicas directas de un determinado terremoto (322)

sheet erosion (SHEET ee ROH zhuhn) the process by which water flows over a layer of soil and removes the topsoil (388)

erosión laminar el proceso por medio del cual el agua fluye sobre el suelo y remueve la capa superior de éste (388)

silicate mineral (SIL i kit MIN uhr uhl) a mineral that contains a combination of silicon and oxygen and that may also contain one or more metals (112)

mineral silicato un mineral que contiene una combinación de silicio y oxígeno y que también puede contener uno o más metales (112)

silicon-oxygen tetrahedron (SIL i KAHN AHKS i juhn TE truh HEE druhn) the basic unit of the structure of silicate minerals; a silicon ion chemically bonded to and surrounded by four oxygen ions (114)

tetraedro de sílice-oxígeno la unidad fundamental de la estructura de los minerales silicatos: un ion de silicio unido químicamente a cuatro iones de oxígeno, los cuales lo rodean (114)

sinkhole (SINGK HOHL) a circular depression that forms when rock dissolves, when overlying sediment fills an existing cavity, or when the roof of an underground cavern or mine collapses (441)

depresión una depresión circular que se forma cuando la roca se funde, cuando el sedimento suprayacente llena una cavidad existente, o al colapsarse el techo de una caverna o mina subterránea (441)

soil (SOYL) a loose mixture of rock fragments and organic material that can support the growth of vegetation (383)

suelo una mezcla suelta de fragmentos de roca y material orgánico en la que puede crecer vegetación (383)

soil profile (SOYL PROH FIEL) a vertical section of soil that shows the layers, or horizons (384)

perfil del suelo una sección vertical de suelo que muestra las capas u horizontes (384)

solar eclipse (SOH luhr i KLIPS) the passing of the moon between Earth and the sun; during a solar eclipse, the shadow of the moon falls on Earth (793)

eclipse solar el paso de la Luna entre la Tierra y el Sol; durante un eclipse solar, la sombra de la Luna cae sobre la Tierra (793)

solar energy (SOH luhr EN uhr jee) the energy received by Earth from the sun in the form of radiation (178)

energía solar la energía que la Tierra recibe del Sol en forma de radiación (178)

solar flare (SOH luhr FLER) an explosive release of energy that comes from the sun and that is associated with magnetic disturbances on the sun's surface (831)

erupción solar una liberación explosiva de energía que proviene del Sol y que se asocia con disturbios magnéticos en la superficie solar (831)

solar nebula (SOH luhr NEB yuh luh) a rotating cloud of gas and dust from which the sun and planets formed; *also* any nebula from which stars and exoplanets may form (749)

nebulosa solar una nube de gas y polvo en rotación a partir de la cual se formaron el Sol y los planetas; también, cualquier nebulosa a partir de la cual se pueden formar estrellas y exoplanetas (749)

solar system (SOH luhr SIS tuhm) the sun and all of the planets and other bodies that travel around it (749)

Sistema Solar el Sol y todos los planetas y otros cuerpos que se desplazan alrededor de él (749)

solifluction (SAHL uh FLUHK shuhn) the slow, downslope flow of soil saturated with water in areas surrounding glaciers at high elevations (392)

soliflucción el flujo lento y descendente de suelo saturado con agua en áreas que rodean glaciares a altas elevaciones (392)

solstice (SAHL stis) the point at which the sun is as far north or as far south of the equator as possible (736)

solsticio el punto en el que el Sol está tan lejos del ecuador como es posible, ya sea hacia el norte o hacia el sur

solution (suh LOO shuhn) a homogeneous mixture throughout which two or more substances are uniformly dispersed (98)

solución una mezcla homogénea en la cual dos o más sustancias se dispersan de manera uniforme (98)

sonar (SOH NAHR) **so**und **n**avigation **a**nd **r**anging, a system that uses acoustic signals and returned echoes to determine the location of objects or to communicate (639)

sonar navegación y exploración por medio del sonido; un sistema que usa señales acústicas y ondas de eco que regresan para determinar la ubicación de los objetos o para comunicarse (639)

specific heat (spuh SIF ik HEET) the quantity of heat required to raise a unit mass of homogeneous material 1 K or 1 °C in a specified way, given constant pressure and volume (608)

calor específico la cantidad de calor que se requiere para aumentar una unidad de masa de un material homogéneo 1 K ó 1° C de una manera especificada, dados un volumen y una presión constantes (608)

star (STAHR) a large celestial body that is composed of gas and that emits light; the sun is a typical star (845)

estrella un cuerpo celeste grande que está compuesto de gas y emite luz; el Sol es una estrella típica (845)

station model (STAY shuhn MAHD'l) a pattern of meteorological symbols that represents the weather at a particular observing station and that is recorded on a weather map (588)

estación modelo el modelo de símbolos meteorológicos que representan el tiempo en una estación de observación determinada y que se registra en un mapa meteorológico (588)

stationary front (STAY shuh NER ee FRUHNT) a front of air masses that moves either very slowly or not at all (576)

frente estacionario un frente de masas de aire que se mueve muy lentamente o que no se mueve (576)

strain (STRAYN) any change in a rock's shape or volume caused by stress; deformation (296)

tensión cualquier cambio en la forma o volumen de una roca causado por el estrés; deformación (296)

stratosphere (STRAT uh SFIR) the layer of the atmosphere that lies between the troposphere and the mesosphere and in which temperature increases as altitude increases; contains the ozone layer (519)

estratosfera la capa de la atmósfera que se encuentra entre la troposfera y la mesosfera y en la cual la temperatura aumenta al aumentar la altitud; contiene la capa de ozono (519)

stratus cloud (STRAT uhs KLOWD) a gray cloud that has a flat, uniform base and that commonly forms at very low altitudes (552)

nube estrato una nube gris que tiene una base plana y uniforme y que comúnmente se forma a altitudes muy bajas (552)

streak (STREEK) the color of a mineral in powdered form (118)

veta el color de un mineral en forma de polvo (118)

stream load (STREEM LOHD) the materials other than the water that are carried by a stream (412)

carga de un arroyo los materiales que lleva un arroyo, además del agua (412)

stress (STRES) in geology, the amount of force per unit area that acts on a rock (295)

estrés en geología, la cantidad de fuerza por unidad de área que se ejerce sobre una roca (295)

sublimation (SUHB luh MAY shuhn) the process in which a solid changes directly into a gas (the term is sometimes also used for the reverse process) (544)

sublimación el proceso por medio del cual un sólido se transforma directamente en un gas (en ocasiones, este término también se usa para describir el proceso inverso) (544)

sunspot (SUHN SPAHT) a dark area of the photosphere of the sun that is cooler than the surrounding areas and that has a strong magnetic field (829)

mancha solar un área oscura en la fotosfera del Sol que es más fría que las áreas que la rodean y que tiene un campo magnético fuerte (829)

supercontinent cycle (soo puhr KAHN tuh nuhnt SIE kuhl) the process by which supercontinents form and break apart over millions of years (278)

ciclo de los supercontinentes el proceso por medio del cual los supercontinentes se forman y se separan a lo largo de millones de años (278)

supercooling (SOO puhr KOOL ing) a condition in which a substance is cooled below its freezing point, condensation point, or sublimation point without going through a change of state (556)

superfrío una condición en la que una sustancia se enfría por debajo de su punto de congelación, punto de condensación o punto de sublimación sin pasar por un cambio de estado (556)

surface current (SUHR fis KUHR uhnt) a horizontal movement of ocean water that is caused by wind and that occurs at or near the ocean's surface (689)

corriente superficial un movimiento horizontal del agua del océano que es producido por el viento y que ocurre en la superficie del océano o cerca de ella (689)

surface wave (SUHR fis WAYV) in geology, a seismic wave that travels along the surface of a medium and that has a stronger effect near the surface of the medium than it has in the interior (320)

onda superficial en geología, una onda sísmica que se desplaza a lo largo de la superficie de un medio, cuyo efecto es más fuerte cerca de la superficie del medio que en el interior de éste (320)

system (SIS tuhm) a set of particles or interacting components considered to be a distinct physical entity for the purpose of study (33)

sistema un conjunto de partículas o componentes que interactúan unos con otros, el cual se considera una entidad física independiente para fines de estudio (33)

T

telescope (TEL uh SKOHP) an instrument that collects electromagnetic radiation from the sky and concentrates it for better observation (724)

telescopio un instrumento que capta la radiación electromagnética del cielo y la concentra para mejorar la observación (724)

terrane (tuh RAYN) a piece of lithosphere that has a unique geologic history and that may be part of a larger piece of lithosphere, such as a continent (276)

macizo autóctono un fragmento de litosfera que tiene una historia geológica única y que puede formar parte de un fragmento de litosfera mayor, como por ejemplo, un continente (276)

terrestrial planet (tuh RES tree uhl PLAN it) one of the highly dense planets nearest to the sun; Mercury, Venus, Mars, and Earth (759)

planeta terrestre uno de los planetas muy densos que se encuentran más cerca del Sol; Mercurio, Venus, Marte y la Tierra (759)

theory (THEE uh ree) a system of ideas that explains many related observations and is supported by a large body of evidence acquired through scientific investigation (15)

teoría un sistema de ideas que explica muchas observaciones relacionadas y que está respaldado por una gran cantidad de pruebas obtenidas mediante la investigación científica (15)

thermocline (THUHR moh KLIEN) a layer in a body of water in which water temperature drops with increased depth faster than it does in other layers (666)

termoclina una capa en una masa de agua en la que, al aumentar la profundidad, la temperatura del agua disminuye más rápido de lo que lo hace en otras capas (666)

thermometer (thuhr MAHM uht uhr) an instrument that measures and indicates temperature (583)

termómetro un instrumento que mide e indica la temperatura (583)

thermosphere (THUHR moh SFIR) the uppermost layer of the atmosphere, in which temperature increases as altitude increases; includes the ionosphere (519)

termosfera la capa más alta de la atmósfera, en la cual la temperatura aumenta a medida que la altitud aumenta; incluye la ionosfera (519)

thunderstorm (THUHN duhr STAWRM) a usually brief, heavy storm that consists of rain, strong winds, lightning, and thunder (578)

tormenta eléctrica una tormenta fuerte y normalmente breve que consiste en lluvia, vientos fuertes, relámpagos y truenos (578)

tidal current (TIED'l KUHR uhnt) the movement of water toward and away from the coast as a result of the rise and fall of the tides (704)

corriente de marea el movimiento del agua hacia la costa y de la costa hacia el mar, como resultado del ascenso y descenso de las mareas (704)

tidal oscillation (TIED'l AHS uh LAY shuhn) the slow, rocking motion of ocean water that occurs as the tidal bulges move around the ocean basins (703)

oscilación de las mareas el movimiento lento y mecedor del agua del océano que se produce cuando los abultamientos de marea se mueven alrededor de las cuencas oceánicas (703)

tidal range (TIED'l RAYNJ) the difference in levels of ocean water at high tide and low tide (702)

rango de marea la diferencia en los niveles del agua del océano entre la marea alta y la marea baja (702)

tide (TIED) the periodic rise and fall of the water level in the oceans and other large bodies of water (701)

marea el ascenso y descenso periódico del nivel del agua en los océanos y otras masas grandes de agua (701)

till (TIL) unsorted rock material that is deposited directly by a melting glacier (462)

arcilla glaciárica material rocoso desordenado que deposita directamente un glaciar que se está derritiendo (462)

topography (tuh PAHG ruh fee) the size and shape of the land surface features of a region, including its relief (67)

topografía el tamaño y la forma de las características de una superficie de terreno, incluyendo su relieve (67)

tornado (tawr NAY doh) a destructive, rotating column of air that has very high wind speeds and that may be visible as a funnel-shaped cloud (582)

tornado una columna destructiva de aire en rotación cuyos vientos se mueven a velocidades muy altas y que puede verse como una nube con forma de embudo (582)

trace fossil (TRAYS FAHS uhl) a fossilized mark that formed in sedimentary rock by the movement of an animal on or within soft sediment (215)

fósil traza una marca fosilizada que se formó en una roca sedimentaria por el movimiento de un animal sobre sedimento blando o dentro de éste (215)

trade winds (TRAYD WINDZ) prevailing winds that blow from east to west from 30° latitude to the equator in both hemispheres (528)

vientos alisios vientos prevalecientes que soplan de este a oeste desde los 30° de latitud hacia el ecuador en ambos hemisferios (528)

transform boundary (TRANS FAWRM BOWN duh ree) the boundary between tectonic plates that are sliding past each other horizontally (271)

límite de transformación el límite entre placas tectónicas que se están deslizando horizontalmente una sobre otra (271)

trench (TRENCH) a long, narrow, and steep depression that forms on the ocean floor as a result of subduction of a tectonic plate, that runs parallel to the trend of a chain of volcanic islands or the coastline of a continent, and that may be as deep as 11 km below sea level; also called an *ocean trench* or a *deep-ocean trench* (643)

fosa submarina una depresión larga, angosta y empinada que se forma en el fondo del océano debido a la subducción de una placa tectónica; corre paralela al curso de una cadena de islas montañosas o a la costa de un continente; y puede tener una profundidad de hasta 11 km bajo el nivel del mar; también denominada *fosa oceánica* o *fosa oceánica profunda* (643)

tributary (TRIB yoo TER ee) a stream that flows into a lake or into a larger stream (411)

afluente un arroyo que fluye a un lago o a otro arroyo más grande (411)

tropical climate (TRAHP i kuhl KLIE muht) a climate characterized by high temperatures and heavy precipitation during at least part of the year; typical of equatorial regions (611)

clima tropical un clima caracterizado por temperaturas altas y precipitación fuerte durante al menos una parte del año; típico de las regiones ecuatoriales (611)

troposphere (TROH poh SFIR) the lowest layer of the atmosphere, in which temperature drops at a constant rate as altitude increases; the part of the atmosphere where weather conditions exist (518)

troposfera la capa inferior de la atmósfera, en la que la temperatura disminuye a una tasa constante a medida que la altitud aumenta; la parte de la atmósfera donde se dan las condiciones del tiempo (518)

tsunami (tsoo NAH mee) a giant ocean wave that forms after a volcanic eruption, submarine earthquake, or landslide (329)

tsunami una ola gigante del océano que se forma después de una erupción volcánica, terremoto submarino o desprendimiento de tierras (329)

U

unconformity (UHN kuhn FAWRM uh tee) a break in the geologic record created when rock layers are eroded or when sediment is not deposited for a long period of time (205)

disconformidad una ruptura en el registro geológico, creada cuando las capas de roca se erosionan o cuando el sedimento no se deposita durante un largo período de tiempo (205)

uniformitarianism (YOON uh FAWRM uh TER ee uhn IZ uhm) a principle that geologic processes that occurred in the past can be explained by current geologic processes (201)

uniformitarianismo un principio que establece que es posible explicar los procesos geológicos que ocurrieron en el pasado en función de los procesos geológicos actuales (201)

upwelling (UHP WEL ing) the movement of deep, cold, and nutrient-rich water to the surface (670)

surgencia el movimiento de las aguas profundas, frías y ricas en nutrientes hacia la superficie (670)

V

varve (VAHRV) a pair of sedimentary layers (one coarse, one fine) that is deposited in an annual cycle, commonly in glacial lakes, and that can be used to determine absolute age (208)

varva un par de capas sedimentarias (una gruesa y otra fina) que se deposita en un ciclo anual. Esto ocurre comúnmente en lagos glaciares , y que puede usarse para determinar la edad absoluta (208)

ventifact (VEN tuh FAKT) any rock that is pitted, grooved, or polished by wind abrasion (485)

ventifacto cualquier roca que es marcada, estriada o pulida por la abrasión del viento (485)

volcanism (VAHL kuh NIZ uhm) any activity that includes the movement of magma toward or onto Earth's surface (346)

volcanismo cualquier actividad que incluye el movimiento de magma hacia la superficie de la Tierra o sobre ella (346)

volcano (vahl KAY noh) a vent or fissure in Earth's surface through which magma and gases are expelled (346)

volcán una chimenea o fisura en la superficie de la Tierra a través de la cual se expulsan magma y gases (346)

W

warm front (WAWRM FRUHNT) the front edge of an advancing warm air mass that replaces colder air with warmer air (576)

frente cálido el borde del frente de una masa de aire caliente en movimiento que reemplaza al aire más frío (576)

water cycle (WAWT uhr SIE kuhl) the continuous movement of water between the atmosphere, the land, and the oceans (407)

ciclo del agua el movimiento continuo del agua entre la atmósfera, la tierra y los océanos (407)

water table (WAWT uhr TAY buhl) the upper surface of underground water; the upper boundary of the zone of saturation (433)

capa freática el nivel más alto del agua subterránea; el límite superior de la zona de saturación (433)

watershed (WAWT uhr SHED) the area of land that is drained by a river system (411)

cuenca hidrográfica el área del terreno que es drenada por un sistema de ríos (411)

wave (WAYV) a periodic disturbance in a solid, liquid, or gas as energy is transmitted through a medium (695)

onda una perturbación periódica en un sólido, líquido o gas que se transmite a través de un medio en forma de energía (695)

wave period (WAYV PIR ee uhd) the time required for identical points on consecutive waves to pass a given point (695)

período de onda el tiempo que se requiere para que puntos idénticos de ondas consecutivas pasen por un punto dado (695)

weathering (WETH uhr ing) the natural process by which atmospheric and environmental agents, such as wind, rain, and temperature changes, disintegrate and decompose rocks (373)

meteorización el proceso natural por medio del cual los agentes atmosféricos o ambientales, como el viento, la lluvia y los cambios de temperatura, desintegran y descomponen las rocas (373)

westerlies (WES tuhr leez) prevailing winds that blow from west to east between 30° and 60° latitude in both hemispheres (528)

vientos del oeste vientos preponderantes que soplan de oeste a este entre 30° y 60° de latitud en ambos hemisferios (528)

white dwarf (WIET DWAWRF) a small, hot, dim star that is the leftover center of an old sunlike star (855)

enana blanca una estrella pequeña, caliente y tenue que es el centro sobrante de una estrella vieja parecida al Sol (855)

wind vane (WIND VAYN) an instrument used to determine the direction of the wind (584)

veleta un instrumento que se usa para determinar la dirección del viento (584)

Index

Note: Page references followed by *f* refer to figures. Page references followed by *t* refer to tables.

A

B

C

E

F

G

H

INDEX

Q

R

U

V

Photo Credits

COVER PHOTOS: cover (tl), NASA/Peter Arnold, Inc.; cover (tr), Pacific Stock/SuperStock; cover (bl), Tim Fitzharris/Minden Pictures/Getty Images; cover (br), Jim Reed/CORBIS;

FRONTMATTER: title page (r), Jim Reed/CORBIS; title page (cr), Tim Fitzharris/Minden Pictures/Getty Images; title page (cr), Pacific Stock/SuperStock; title page (l), NASA/Peter Arnold, Inc.; vii (b), Richard Sisk/Panoramic Images/NGSimages.com; viii (l), Layne Kennedy/CORBIS; ix (t), Stuart Westmoreland/Getty Images; x (b), Jim Wark/Airphoto; xi (t), Ralph A. Clevenger/CORBIS; xii (t), Chris Noble/Getty Images; xiii (b), Craig Tuttle/CORBIS; xiv (b), Jean-Charles Cuillandre/Canada-france-Hawaii Telescope/SPL/Photo Researchers, Inc.; xv (t), NOAO/AURA/NSF; xvii (b), HMH/Victoria Smith Photo; xix (t), PatitucciPhoto/Aurora; xxi (b), Sam Dudgeon/Harcourt; xxii (b), HMH/Victoria Smith;

UNIT ONE: 1 (cr), Terry Donnelly & Mary Liz Austin Photography; 1 (bl), Steve Bloom Images; 1 (br), National Geophysical Data Center/National Oceanic and Atmospheric Administration/Department of Commerce; 2-3 (all), Terry Donnelly & Mary Liz Austin Photography; 2 (t), Roger Ressmeyer/CORBIS; 2 (b), NASA; 3 (t), HMH/Victoria Smith; 5, Danny Lehman/CORBIS; 6 (r), Bryan and Cherry Alexander Photography; 6 (c), Roger Ressmeyer/CORBIS; 6 (bl), Roger Ressmeyer/CORBIS; 7 (bkgd), Bill Stevenson / Stock Connection/Aurora Photo; 7 (bl), ©Tate,London 2008; 7 (bl), Tate,London/Art Resource; 7 (br), AP Images; 8, Dr. Howard B. Bluestein; 9 (br), CSIRO/Simon Fraser/SPL/Photo Researchers, Inc.; 9 (bl), ©Michael Sewell/Peter Arnold, Inc.; 11, NASA; 12 (b), HMH/Andy Christiansen; 12 (tr), HMH/Sam Dudgeon; 12 (tc), HMH/Sam Dudgeon; 12 (tl), HMH/Sam Dudgeon; 13 (r), NASA/JPL/NIMA; 13 (l), Kuni/AP/Wide World Photos; 14, Ric Francis/AP/Wide World Photos; 15 (br), Courtesy of Los Alamos National Laboratories; 15 (cr), Dr. David A. Kring; 15 (cl), V. L. Sharpton/LPI; 15 (bl), Aventurier Patrick/Gamma; 16, Tony Waltham/Robert Harding World Imagery/CORBIS; 17 (bkgd), Eberhard Hummel/zefa/Corbis; 17 (cl), NASA/JPL-Caltech/Cornell University; 17 (tr), www.robovolc.dees.unict.it; 17 (cr), courtesy of DepthX/NASA; 17 (bl), Coneyl Jay / Photo Researchers,Inc.; 18 (b), HMH; 21, NASA; 21 (t), Roger Ressmeyer/CORBIS; 27, HMH/Victoria Smith; 27 (b), Bob Krist; 27 (c), Bernhard Lang/The Image Bank/Getty Images; 27 (t), Getty Images/PhotoDisc; 28-29 (all), Steve Bloom Images; 29 (bl), Getty Images/PhotoDisc; 33 (inset), Stuart Westmorland/CORBIS; 33 (inset), Stuart Westmorland/CORBIS; 33 (bkgd), Douglas Faulkner; 34 (r,l), HMH/Andy Christiansen; 35, Darrell Gulin/CORBIS; 37, Bernhard Lang/The Image Bank/Getty Images; 40, Pam Ostrow/Index Stock Imagery, Inc.; 41, Martin Harvey/Gallo Images/CORBIS; 42 (t), Raymond Gehman/CORBIS ; 42 (bkgd), Solarfilma; 42 (br), Sigmar Metusalemsson; 42 (bl), Robert Simmon,SSAI/NASA GSFC; 44, Bob Krist; 45 (bkgd, t), Peter Essick/Aurora Photos; 45 (bkgd, b), John W. Warden/Stock Connection/Aurora Photos; 45 (c), Rick Rosenthal/Getty Images; 45 (r), Jacqueline Windh Photography; 46, HMH/Peter Van Steen; 47, HMH/Andy Christiansen; 48, Provided by the SeaWiFS Project, NASA/Goddard Space Flight Center and ORBIMAGE/NASA/Seawifs; 49 (b), Bob Krist; 49 (c), Bernhard Lang/The Image Bank/Getty Images; 49 (t), Getty Images/PhotoDisc; 54-55 (all), National Geophysical Data Center/National Oceanic and Atmospheric Administration/Department of Commerce; 54 (b), Nathan Wier/Getty Images; 54 (c), Christopher Cormack/CORBIS; 54 (t), Layne Kennedy/CORBIS; 55, HMH/Victoria Smith; 59 (tl), Layne Kennedy/CORBIS; 59 (bkgd), Corey Rich/Aurora; 59 (bl), Peter Casolino/Alamy; 59 (bc), www.geocaching.com; 59 (br), Courtesy of Garmin; 61 (bl), Christopher Cormack/CORBIS; 64 (inset), Rand McNally; 64 (bl), Courtesy U.S. Geological Survey; 65 (t), Ohio Department of Transportation; 66 (tl), Bill Frymire/Masterfile; 68 (tl), Nathan Wier/Getty Images; 68 (l), HMH/Victoria Smith Photo; 70 (t), Courtesy U.S. Geological Survey; 71 (br), National Conservation Resource Service; 71 (bl), National Conservation Resource Service; 72 (tl), Image courtesy NSSTC Lightning Team; 73 (bkgd), NASA/CORBIS; 73 (l), Stephen Alvarez/Getty Images; 73 (c), Courtesy Marcus Gary, photo by Art Palmer; 73 (cr), Alex Webb/Magnum Photos; 73 (tr), NASA; 74 (b), HMH/Victoria Smith Photo; 74 (t), HMH/Victoria Smith Photo; 74 (c), HMH/Victoria Smith Photo; 76 (t), Courtesy U.S. Geological Survey; 77 (bl), Nathan Wier/Getty Images; 77 (cl), Christopher Cormack/CORBIS; 77 (tl), Layne Kennedy/CORBIS;

UNIT TWO: 83 (cr), Steve Allen/PictureQuest; 83 (l), Richard Price/Getty Images; 83 (br), Lester Lefkowitz/CORBIS; 84 (b), Steve Chen/CORBIS; 85, HMH/Victoria Smith Photo; 86-87 (all), Steve Allen/PictureQuest; 93 (br), Tony Freeman/PhotoEdit; 93 (bc,bl), Andrew Lambert Photography/Photo Researchers, Inc.; 95 (tr), Steve Chen/CORBIS; 95 (bkgd), Diavik Diamond Mines, Inc.,photo by Jiri Hermann; 95 (bl), Lew Robertson/Corbis; 95 (br), Marvvy!/Corbis; 96 (inset), Bruce Dale/National Geographic Image Collection; 97 (tr), HMH/Charlie Winters; 98 (tl), Craig Aurness/CORBIS; 99 (bkgd), NASA; 99 (l), Chuck Pefley/IPN; 99 (b), Harrison Shull/Getty Images; 99 (r), Yasuhide Fumoto/Getty Images; 99 (r, inset), Reuters/Corbis; 101 (cr), HMH/Victoria Smith; 103 (bl), Steve Chen/CORBIS; 108 (b), Mark Schneider/Visuals Unlimited/Getty Images; 108 (t), Mark Schneider/Visuals Unlimited/Getty Images; 108-109 (all), Richard Price/Getty Images; 109, HMH/Victoria Smith Photo; 112 (cl), Charles D. Winters/Photo Researchers, Inc.; 112 (bkgd), Scott Stulberg/Getty Images; 112 (bl), Steve Gschmeissner/Photo Researchers, Inc.; 112 (br), Royalty Free/CORBIS; 112 (l), Breck P. Kent/Animals Animals/Earth Scenes; 112 (c), Visuals Unlimited/CORBIS; 112 (r), Denise J. Mayes/University of Delaware; 113 (anhydrite), Geoff Tompkinson/SPL/Photo Researchers, Inc.; 113 (gypsum), Grace Davies Photography; 113 (flourite), Paul Silverman/Fundamental Photographs; 113 (halite), Stonetrust, Inc.; 113 (corundum), Colin Keates/Dorling Kindersley, Courtesy of the Natural History Museum, London; 113 (galena), Colin Keates/Dorling Kindersley, Courtesy of the Natural History Museum, London; 113 (hematite), Dr. John D. Cunningham/Visuals Unlimited/Alamy; 113 (copper), E. R. Degginger/Photo Researchers, Inc.; 113 (silver), Colin Keates/Dorling Kindersley, Courtesy of the Natural History Museum, London; 113 (calcite), Mark Schneider/Visuals Unlimited/Getty Images; 113 (dolomite), Charles D. Winters/Photo Researchers, Inc.; 113 (pyrite), Editorial Image, LLC/Alamy; 116 (tr), Breck P. Kent; 116 (tc), Jose Manuel Sanchez Calvate/CORBIS; 116 (tl), Mark A. Schneider/Photo Researchers, Inc.; 117 (bl), G. Tompkinson/Photo Researchers, Inc.; 117 (br), Mark Schneider/Visuals Unlimited/Getty Images; 118 (bl), Tom Pantages Photography; 118 (bl), José Manuel Sanchis Calvete/CORBIS; 118 (talc), Mark Schneider/Visuals/Getty Images; 118 (platinum), Harry Taylor/Dorling Kindersley; 121 (inset), HMH/Victoria Smith; 121 (tr), Mark A. Schneider/Photo Researchers, Inc.; 121 (cr), Mark A. Schneider/Photo Researchers, Inc.; 122, Paul Silverman/Fundamental Photographs, NYC; 123 (bkgd), HMH/Victoria Smith Photo; 123 (tl), David Trilling/CORBIS; 123 (c), Photodisc/Alamy; 123 (bl), Corbis Premium RF/Alamy; 123 (b), Beth McElhaney; 123 (tr), HMH/Victoria Smith Photo; 124 (b), HMH/Victoria Smith Photo; 132-133 (all), Worldwide Picture Library/Alamy; 132 (b), Adam Crowley/Photodisc Green/gettyimages; 132 (bl), Russell Wood; 132 (cr), Breck P. Kent; 132 (t), Brand X Photos/Alamy Photos; 132 (cl), sciencephotos/Alamy; 133, HMH/Victoria Smith Photo; 135 (c), Astrid & Hans-Frieder Michler/SPL/Photo Researchers, Inc.; 135 (l), Breck P. Kent; 135 (br), Breck P. Kent/Animals Animals/Earth Scenes; 136 (bl), Breck P. Kent; 136 (t), Joyce Photographics/Photo Researchers, Inc.; 136 (br), Breck P. Kent; 138, Brand X Photos/Alamy Photos; 140 (b), HMH/Andy Christiansen; 141 (obsidian), G. R. Roberts/Natural Sciences Image Library (NSIL) of New Zealand; 141 (porphyritic), Breck P. Kent; 141 (rhyolite), Breck P. Kent; 141 (pumice), Tony Liley/Alamy; 141 (granite), sciencephotos/Alamy; 142 (tr inset), HMH/Victoria Smith; 142 (tr), Paul Harris/Getty Images/Stone; 142 (tl inset), Breck P. Kent; 142 (tl), James Sparshatt/CORBIS; 143 (t), Mark Schneider/Visuals Unlimited/Getty Images; 144, Richard Sisk/Panoramic Images/NGSimages.com; 145 (b), Mark Schneider/Visuals Unlimited/Getty Images; 147 (sandstone), Copyright Dorling Kindersley; 147 (breccia, conglomerate), Breck P. Kent; 147 (shale), Gary Ombler/Dorling Kindersley; 149 (r), Bernhard Edmaier/Photo Researchers, Inc.; 149 (l), Russell Wood; 150, Tom Wagner/CORBIS SABA; 151 (br), Joyce Photographics/Photo Researchers, Inc.; 151 (slate), Harry Taylor/Dorling Kindersley; 152 (bl), DEA/A.Rizzi/Getty Images; 152 (bkgd), Zak Warters/Alamy; 152 (bl ruby), GIA; 152 (cr), International School of Gemology; 152 (br), International School of Gemology; 153 (br), Galen Rowell/CORBIS; 153 (bl), Breck P. Kent; 154 (inset), HMH/Andy Christiansen; 154 (t), Adam Crowley/Photodisc Green/gettyimages; 155 (bkgd), U.S. Department of Energy ; 155 (r), U.S. Department of Energy ; 155 (l), David Frazier/The Image Works; 156 (b), Sam Dudgeon/Harcourt; 158, Ohio Department of Natural Resources, Division of Geological Survey; 159 (b), Adam Crowley/Photodisc Green/gettyimages; 159 (Sec. 3), Russell Wood; 159 (Sec. 2), Breck P. Kent; 159 (Sec. 1), Brand X Photos/Alamy Photos; 159 (Sec. 2, l), sciencephotos/Alamy; 164-165 (all), Lester Lefkowitz/CORBIS; 164 (t), H. David Seawell/CORBIS; 164 (c), Macduff Everton/CORBIS; 164 (c), Bob Krist; 164 (b), Jose Fuste Raga/CORBIS; 165, HMH/Victoria Smith Photo; 168 (br), Neal Mishler/Getty Images/Photographer's Choice; 170, H. David Seawell/CORBIS; 171, Macduff Everton/CORBIS; 172 (peat), DK Limited/CORBIS; 172 (lignite), Scientifica/Visuals Unlimited/Getty Images; 172 (coal), Mark Schneider/Visuals Unlimited/Getty Images; 172 (anthracite), Mark Schneider/Visuals Unlimited/Getty Images; 176, Roger Ressmeyer/CORBIS; 177, Bob Krist; 178, HMH/Andy Christiansen; 180, Stefan Schott/Panoramic Images; 181, Peter Essick/Aurora; 182, John Lovretta/The Hawk Eye/AP/Wide World Photos; 183 (t), Jose Fuste Raga/CORBIS; 183 (bkgd), EMPA; 183 (bl), San Mateo County/RecycleWorks; 183 (br), AP IMAGES/John Bazemore; 184 (t), Photodisc/gettyimages; 185 (bkgd), Reuters/CORBIS; 185 (br), Car Culture/CORBIS; 185 (golf cart), Sunray; 185 (bus), U. S. Department of Agriculture; 185 (hybrid), AP IMAGES/Dirk Lammers; 185 (air car), AP IMAGES/Sipa Press; 189 (4), Jose Fuste Raga/CORBIS; 189 (3), Bob Krist; 189 (2), Macduff Everton/CORBIS; 189 (1), H. David Seawell/CORBIS; 194 (300 B.C.E.), Wustmann/dpa/CORBIS; 194 (8000 B.C.E.); Paul Thompson/Alamy; 194 (1200 B.C.E.), Erich Lessing/Art Resource, NY; 194 (1751), Hulton Archive/Getty Images; 194 (t), Ludek Pesek/Photo Researchers, Inc.; 194 (1882), SSPL/The Image Works; 194 (1849), Copyright Dorling Kindersley; 194 (1824), Patrice Tourenne/Getty Images; 194-195 (all), Alvis Upitis/Getty Images; 195 (1935), Robert Cameron/Getty Images; 195 (2007), Artifex; 195 (1855), SuperStock; 195 (1859), From Pennsylvania Historical and Museum Commission,Drake Well Museum Collection,Titusville,PA; 195 (1886), Mercedes Benz USA; 195 (1928), U.S. Department of Energy ; 195 (1970s), Owen Franken/CORBIS; 195 (2006), Nick Ut/AP Images;

UNIT THREE: 197 (cr), James L. Amos/Photo Researchers, Inc.; 197 (l), Annie Griffiths Belt/CORBIS; 197 (br), John Gurche; 198 (t), Tom Bean/CORBIS; 198 (c), Pat O'Hara/CORBIS; 198 (b), James L. Amos/Photo Researchers, Inc.; 198-199 (all), Mark E. Gibson/CORBIS; 199, HMH/Victoria Smith Photo; 201 (r), Tom Bean/CORBIS; 201 (l), CORBIS; 202, Tom Bean/CORBIS; 204 (tl), Christian Hass; 204 (tr), Wayne G. Lawler/Photo Researchers, Inc.; 204 (tc), Bernhard Edmaier/Photo Researchers, Inc.; 207, Alan Smith/Getty Images/Stone; 208 (l), Bruce Molnia/Terra Photo Graphics; 208 (r), Pat O'Hara/CORBIS; 209 (bkgd), AFP/Getty Images; 209 (bl), AP IMAGES/Czarek Sokolowski; 210, HMH/Victoria Smith; 210 (t), HMH/Sam Dudgeon; 210 (all), HMH/Sam Dudgeon; 212, James King-Holmes/SPL/Photo Researchers, Inc.; 213, Annie Griffiths Belt/CORBIS; 214 (log), Bernhard Edmaier/Photo Researchers, Inc.; 214 (mammoth), Bettmann/CORBIS; 214 (tar), Nick Ut/AP/Wide World Photos; 214 (amber), Layne Kennedy/CORBIS; 214 (mummy), Patrick Landmann/Getty Images; 215 (gastrolith), Francios Gohier/Photo Researchers, Inc.; 215 (coprolite), Sinclair Stammers/SPL/Photo Researchers, Inc.; 215 (mold), G. R. Roberts/Natural Sciences Image Library (NSIL) of New Zealand; 215 (leaf), Layne Kennedy/CORBIS ; 216, James L. Amos/Photo Researchers, Inc.; 217 (cr), Momatiuk-Eastcott/CORBIS; 217 (b), SR Brantley/U. S. Geological Survey; 217 (bkgd), George D. Lepp/CORBIS; 218, HMH/Victoria Smith; 219, HMH/Victoria Smith; 219 (t), HMH/Victoria Smith; 220, Courtesy, Ohio Department of Natural Resources, Division of Geological Survey; 221 (t), Tom Bean/CORBIS; 221 (c), Pat O'Hara/CORBIS;

221 (b), James L. Amos/Photo Researchers, Inc.; 226-227 (all), John Gurche; 226 (t), Jonathan Blair/CORBIS; 226 (c), John Reader/SPL/Photo Researchers, Inc.; 226 (b), Stuart Westmorland/CORBIS; 227, HMH/Victoria Smith Photo; 230, Jonathan Blair/CORBIS; 232, Reuters New Media Inc./CORBIS; 234 (bkgd), Chase Studio/Photo Researchers, Inc.; 234 (bl), J. William Schopf; 234 (bc), Dennis Kunkel Microscopy, Inc.; 235, John Reader/SPL/Photo Researchers, Inc.; 236, James L. Amos/CORBIS; 237, 238, Kaj R. Svensson/SPL/Photo Researchers, Inc.; 239 (bc), Joe Tucciarone/SPL/Photo Researchers, Inc.; 239 (bl), Chris Butler/SPL/Photo Researchers, Inc.; 240 (b), James L. Amos/CORBIS; 240 (t), Doug Henderson; 241, Sue Ogrocki/Reuters; 242, Stuart Westmorland/CORBIS; 243 (bl), Jeff Gage/Florida Museum of Natural History; 243 (br), Wardene Weiser/Bruce Coleman, Inc.; 244, Bettmann/CORBIS; 245 (t), Louie Psihoyos/CORBIS; 245 (cr), Courtesy of Smithsonian Institution; 245 (b), Courtesy of Smithsonian Institution; 245 (cl), Louie Psihoyos/CORBIS; 247, Jonathan Blair/CORBIS; 249 (b), Stuart Westmorland/CORBIS; 249 (c), John Reader/SPL/Photo Researchers, Inc.; 249 (t), Jonathan Blair/CORBIS;

UNIT FOUR: 255 (cr), Stuart Westmoreland/Getty Images; 255 (b), NASA; 256-257 (all), Mats Wibe Lund; 256 (t), British Antarctic Survey/SPL/Photo Researchers, Inc.; 256 (c), Jacques Descloitres. MODIS Land Rapid Response Team, NASA/GSFC; 256 (b), Y. Arthus-B./Peter Arnold, Inc.; 257, HMH/Victoria Smith Photo; 259 (bl), The Granger Collection, New York.; 260 (inset), Natural History Museum/University of Oslo, Norway; 261 (inset), British Antarctic Survey/SPL/Photo Researchers, Inc.; 261 (b), Galen Rowell/CORBIS; 262 (t), P. Hickey/Woods Hole Oceanographic Institute; 264 (bkgd), Loukas Hapsis / Aurora; 264 (br), NASA; 264 (bl), NASA; 266 (t), Courtesy of Dr. Donald Prothero; 269 (tl), NASA; 270 (br), Jacques Descloitres. MODIS Land Rapid Response Team, NASA/GSFC; 271 (tr), Tom Bean/CORBIS; 273 (br), HMH/Victoria Smith; 275 (b), Y. Arthus-B./Peter Arnold, Inc.; 277 (cr), Michael Dick/Animals Animals/Earth Scenes; 281 (bkgd), Todd Korol/Getty Images; 281 (bl), Gen Nishino/Getty Images; 281 (tr), Science Source/Photo Researchers, Inc.; 281 (mine), Victor Rojas/WPN; 281 (underground), Peter Bowater/Photo Researchers, Inc.; 281 (chalcopyrite), E.R. Degginger/Photo Researchers, Inc.; 281 (inset phone), Todd Korol/Getty Images; 281 (nugget), Kaj R. Svensson/Photo Researchers, Inc.; 282 (b), HMH/Victoria Smith; 283 (tr), HMH/Victoria Smith; 285 (b), Y. Arthus-B./Peter Arnold, Inc.; 285 (cr), Jacques Descloitres. MODIS Land Rapid Response Team, NASA/GSFC; 285 (tl), British Antarctic Survey/SPL/Photo Researchers, Inc.; 290-291 (all), Roger Ressmeyer/CORBIS; 290 (t), Jeremy Woodhouse/Getty Images; 290 (b), Kim Westerskov/Getty Images/Stone; 291, HMH/Victoria Smith Photo; 294, Jeremy Woodhouse/Getty Images; 296 (b), HMH/Andy Christiansen; 296 (t), Tom Brownold Photography; 297, Bill Bachman; 298 (bkgd), Eric Draper/Aurora; 298 (br), Valley Giants Cam, photo by Thomas A. Kasper; 298 (bl), James S. Aber; 298 (b), PatitucciPhoto/Aurora; 300, Lloyd Cluff/CORBIS; 301, Jeremy Woodhouse/Pixelchrome; 303 (b), Alexander Stewart/Getty Images; 303 (t), Kim Westerskov/Getty Images; 304 (valley), Bob Krist/CORBIS; 304 (colorado), George H. H. Huey/CORBIS; 304 (sierra), Russ Bishop; 305, Photodisc Green/gettyimages; 305 (arkansas), Zephyr Picture/Index Stock Imagery, Inc.; 305 (appalachian), James P. Blair/National Geographic Image Collection; 305 (dome), Alan Schein Photography/CORBIS; 306, Harvey Lloyd/Getty Images; 307 (bkgd), © NASA/Science Source/Photo Researchers, Inc.; 307 (t), NASA; 307 (cr), U. S. Geological Survey; 307 (b), Falk Amelung; 307 (b, inset), Michael T. Sedam/CORBIS; 308 (b), HMH/Victoria Smith Photo; 310, Institute of Geological and Nuclear Sciences; 311 (b), Kim Westerskov/Getty Images; 311 (t), Jeremy Woodhouse/Getty Images; 316-317 (all), Tom Wagner/CORBIS SABA; 316 (t), Yann Arthus Bertrand/CORBIS; 316 (b), Michael S. Yamashita/CORBIS; 317, Sam Dudgeon/Harcourt; 321 (inset), Jonathan Burnett/Photo Researchers, Inc.; 321 (bl), AP IMAGES/LaRepublica Newspaper; 321 (c), Courtesy U.S. Geological Survey; 321 (r), NASB; 324 (tl), Yann Arthus Bertrand/CORBIS; 325 (bl), Reuters/CORBIS; 326 (br), HMH/Sam Dudgeon; 327 (br), Michael S. Yamashita/CORBIS; 329 (br), Reuters/CORBIS; 330 (t), Samuel Zuder/laif/Aurora; 333 (bkgd), Marilyn Shea, Professor of Psychology, University of Maine at Farmington; 333 (bl), James Stevenson / Dorling Kindersley; 333 (bc), Kent Anderson/ Incorporated Research Institutions for Seismology; 333 (br), Justin Sullivan/Getty Images; 336, Global Seismic Hazard Assessment Program; 337 (bl), Reuters/CORBIS; 337 (cl), Michael S. Yamashita/CORBIS; 337 (tl), Yann Arthus Bertrand/CORBIS; 342-343 (all), Gavriel Jecan/CORBIS; 342 (t), Jacques Descloitres, MODIS Rapid Response Team, NASA/GSFC; 342 (b), Gary Braasch/CORBIS; 343, HMH/Victoria Smith Photo; 347 (br), Barry Tessman/National Geographic Image Collection; 348 (tl), James Watt/Animals Animals/Earth Scenes; 348 (bkgd), Annette Soumillard/Hemis/CORBIS; 348 (bl), Charles O'Rear/CORBIS; 349 (cl), Jacques Descloitres, MODIS Rapid Response Team, NASA/GSFC; 350 (t), Bill Ross/CORBIS; 351 (bl), Stuart Westmoreland/Getty Images; 352 (tr), David Muench/CORBIS; 352 (tc), J. D. Griggs/CORBIS; 352 (tl), Gary Braasch/CORBIS; 353 (bl), Michael Yamashita/CORBIS; 353 (br), Juerg Alean, Switzerland/www.stromboli.net; 353 (cr), Robert Patrick/Corbis Sygma; 353 (bkgd), Gary Braasch/CORBIS; 354 (br), Japack Company/CORBIS; 354 (cl), Yann Arthus-Bertrand/CORBIS; 354 (cr), Mike Zens/CORBIS; 356 (tl), Roger Ressmeyer/CORBIS; 357 (bkgd), Courtesy U.S. Geological Survey; 357 (tl), Courtesy U.S. Geological Survey; 357 (cl), Chuck Pefley/Getty Images; 357 (bl), Courtesy U.S. Geological Survey; 359 (tr), Koji Sasahara/AP/Wide World Photos; 361 (bl), Gary Braasch/CORBIS; 361 (tl), Jacques Descloitres, MODIS Rapid Response Team, NASA/GSFC; 366-367 (all), Frans Lanting/CORBIS; 366 (132 c.e.), USGS; 366 (1880), SSPL / The Image Works; 366 (1897), SPL /Photo Researchers,Inc.; 366 (1851), Alain Compost/BIOS/Peter Arnold; 366 (1916); Jackson School of Geology, University of Texas, Austin; 366 (1921), Patrick Ray Dunn/Alamy; 366 (1936, earth), American Museum of Natural History; 366 (1936), Photo Courtesy of B.A.Bolt; 367 (1900), Zephyr/Photo Researchers, Inc.; 367 (79 B.C.E.), Roger Ressmeyer/CORBIS; 367 (1960), Courtesy U.S. Geological Survey; 367 (1967-1968), Courtesy U.S. Geological Survey; 367 (1912), Jim Sugar/CORBIS; 367 (1985), Jacques Langevin/CORBIS SYGMA; 367 (1986), Krafft/Explorer/Photo Researchers, Inc.; 367 (1991), Alberto Garcia/Corbis; 367 (1986), UN Photo/WPN; 367 (2006), AP Images/Aaron Favila;

UNIT FIVE: 369 (cr), Mark Laricchia/CORBIS ; 369 (l), Joseph Van Os/Getty Images/The Image Bank; 369 (br), Mark J. Terrill/AP/Wide World Photos; 370-371 (all), Mark Laricchia/CORBIS; 370 (t), Adam Hart-Davis/SPL/Photo Researchers, Inc.; 370 (c), Richard Hamilton Smith/CORBIS; 370 (c), Jeff Vanuga/USDA/NRCS; 370 (b), Galen Rowell/CORBIS; 371, Sam Dudgeon/Harcourt; 373, Stephen Ingram/Animals Animals/Earth Scenes; 374 (tr), SuperStock; 375 (br), HMH/Victoria Smith; 375 (tr), W. Perry Conway/CORBIS; 375 (tl), Layne Kennedy/CORBIS; 376 (br), Kevin Fleming/CORBIS; 378 (tr), Adam Hart-Davis/SPL/Photo Researchers, Inc.; 379 (br), Tom Till/Getty Images; 381 (tc), Joen Iaconetti/Bruce Coleman, Inc.; 381 (tl), Bettman/CORBIS; 382 (tl), Richard Hamilton Smith/CORBIS; 383 (bl), Jeff Vanuga/USDA/NRCS; 388 (tr), Yann Arthus-Bertrand/CORBIS; 389 (tr), Jason Hawkes/CORBIS; 389 (bkgd), Scott W. Smith/Animals Animals/Earth Scenes; 389 (br), Michael Thompson/Animals Animals/Earth Scenes; 389 (bl), Rachel Rosen; 390 (tr), Keren Su/CORBIS; 390 (tl), Jim Richardson/CORBIS; 390 (tc), Photo by Tim McCabe, USDA NRCS; 391 (bl), Handout/Malacanang/Reuters/CORBIS; 391 (br), AFP/Getty Images; 392 (br), CORBIS; 393 (tr), Steve Terrill/CORBIS; 393 (tl), Galen Rowell/CORBIS; 394 (t), Robert Frerck/Odyssey/Chicago; 395 (bkgd), Chris Selby/Alamy; 395 (cl), AP IMAGES/Nick Ut; 395 (c), Sandy Huffaker/Getty Images; 395 (tr), Thomas Kitchin & Victoria Hurst/Getty Images; 396 (b), HMH/Victoria Smith; 397 (tr), HMH/Victoria Smith; 399 (bl), Galen Rowell/CORBIS; 399 (cl), Jeff Vanuga/USDA/NRCS; 399 (cl), Richard Hamilton Smith/CORBIS; 399 (tl), Adam Hart-Davis/SPL/Photo Researchers, Inc.; 404-405 (all), Jim Wark; 404 (b), Marli Bryant Miller Photography; 404 (t), Annie Reynolds/PhotoLink/gettyimages; 404 (c), Harald Sund/Getty Images; 405, HMH/Victoria Smith Photo; 407 (bl), Annie Reynolds/PhotoLink/gettyimages; 409 (cr), Brad Wrobleski/Masterfile; 409 (tr), Mark Taylor/Warren Photographic/Bruce Coleman, Inc.; 410 (tl), Peter Turnley/CORBIS; 412 (br), Rich Reid/National Geographic Image Collection; 412 (bl), Nancy Simmerman/Getty Images; 413 (tl), Harald Sund/Getty Images; 414 (tr), Jim Wark/Airphoto; 415 (bl), Jim Wark/Airphoto; 415 (br), Marli Bryant Miller Photography; 416 (tl), Kevin R. Morris/CORBIS; 416 (bkgd), Manor Photography/Alamy; 417 (b), AP IMAGES/Bill Feig; 419 (bkgd), Li Ming/Imaginechina/ZUMA; 419 (c), Jiang Zhang/Color China/ZUMA; 419 (b), Jeffrey A. Austin /ZUMA; 419 (t), Keren Su/CORBIS; 420 (bl), HMH/Victoria Smith; 421 (cr, tr), HMH/Victoria Smith; 423 (cl), Harald Sund/Getty Images; 423 (tl), Annie Reynolds/PhotoLink/gettyimages; 423 (b), Marli Bryant Miller Photography; 428-429 (all), Joseph Van Os/Getty Images; 428 (b), Peter Essick/Aurora; 428 (t), Peter Bowater/Alamy; 429, HMH/Victoria Smith Photo; 432, HMH/Victoria Smith; 435, Charles River Watershed Association; 436, Tom Bean/CORBIS; 437 (b), Peter Bowater/Alamy; 437 (t), Peter Bowater/Alamy; 439 (bl), Peter Essick/Aurora; 439 (inset), Martyn F. Chillmaid/SPL/Photo Researchers, Inc.; 440 (t), Adam Woolfitt/CORBIS; 440 (bkgd), ©Richard Weiss/Peter Arnold, Inc.; 440 (c), Robert and Linda Mitchell; 440 (b), Robert and Linda Mitchell; 440 (bl), John R. MacGregor/Peter Arnold, Inc.; 441 (b), Natural Bridge Caverns; 441 (t), Bettmann/CORBIS; 442, Keren Su/CORBIS; 443 (bkgd), RealImage/Alamy; 443 (bc), Bettmann/CORBIS; 443 (bl), Chris Bell; 443 (br), Peter Titmuss/Alamy; 444, 445, HMH/Victoria Smith; 446 (t), U. S. Geological Survey; 447 (b), Peter Essick/Aurora; 447 (t), Peter Bowater/Alamy; 452-453 (all), Andrew Wenzel/Masterfile; 452 (t), Jim Brandenburg/Minden Pictures; 452 (c), Scott T. Smith/CORBIS; 452 (b), Astrid & Hanns-Frieder Michler/SPL/Photo Researchers, Inc.; 453, HMH/Victoria Smith Photo; 455 (b), Kevin R. Morris/CORBIS; 456 (tr), Hanne & Jens Eriksen/Nature Picture Library; 456 (tl), Jim Wark/Airphoto; 458 (tr), Jim Brandenburg/Minden Pictures; 458 (l), Ralph A. Clevenger/CORBIS; 459, Mark Burnett/Photo Researchers, Inc.; 461 (br), HMH/Victoria Smith; 461 (tr), G. R. Roberts/Natural Sciences Image Library (NSIL) of New Zealand; 464 (t), Galen Rowell/CORBIS; 465 (tr), Scott T. Smith/CORBIS; 465 (bkgd), Adam Bacher/Aurora; 465 (b), Vladimir Mikhalenko; 465 (br), Ramin Talaie/CORBIS; 467 (bkgd), George D. Lepp/CORBIS; 470 (tl), Astrid & Hanns-Frieder Michler/SPL/Photo Researchers, Inc.; 471 (bkgd), Paul Ward; 471 (tl), Tom Vogelmann; 471 (r), Wayne P. Armstrong, Palomar College; 471 (cl), Mauri S Pelto; 471 (bl), Wayne P. Armstrong, Palomar College; 472 (br), HMH/Victoria Smith; 473 (tr), HMH/Victoria Smith; 473 (b), Sam Dudgeon/Harcourt; 475 (bl), Astrid & Hanns-Frieder Michler/SPL/Photo Researchers, Inc.; 475 (cl), Scott T. Smith/CORBIS; 475 (tl), Jim Brandenburg/Minden Pictures; 480-481, Nicole Duplaix/National Geographic Image Collection; 480 (t), Mark J. Terrill/AP/Wide World Photos; 480 (c), David Welling; 480 (b), Tami Chappell/Reuters; 481, HMH/Victoria Smith; 483, Mark J. Terrill/AP/Wide World Photos; 484, Jonathan Blair/CORBIS; 487 (b), HMH/Andy Christiansen; 487 (t), John Warden/Getty Images/Stone; 488, Walter H. Hodge/Peter Arnold, Inc.; 489, David Welling; 490 (tl), Jeff Foott/Tom Stack & Associates; 490 (br, inset), J Marshall - Tribaleye Images/Alamy; 491 (br), John S. Shelton ; 491 (tc), Breck P. Kent; 491 (bl), G. R. Roberts/Natural Sciences Image Library (NSIL) of New Zealand; 495 (t), Aerial by Caudell; 495 (bkgd), Pelamis Wave Power; 496, Robert Sullivan/AFP/Getty Images; 497 (bkgd), Corbis/Inmagine; 497 (cl), Cary Wolinsky/Aurora; 497 (cr), Peter Mross/Aurora; 497 (b), Georg Gerster/Photo Researchers, Inc.; 498, HMH; 499 (b), HMH/Sam Dudgeon; 499 (c), HMH/Sam Dudgeon; 499 (t), HMH/Sam Dudgeon; 500, Joost Van der Sanden, Canada Centre for Remote Sensing/Natural Resources Canada, RADARSAT image: 1999 Canadian Space Agency; 501 (c), David Welling; 501 (t), Mark J. Terrill/AP/Wide World Photos; 501 (b), Robert Sullivan/AFP/Getty Images; 506-507 (all), Image Source/Corbis; 506 (tr), The Granger Collection, New York; 506 (1790), The Granger Collection, New York; 506 (1935-1938), The Granger Collection, New York; 506 (1837), The Granger Collection, New York; 506 (1831), The Granger Collection, New York; 506 (1730s), Studio Eye/Corbis; 506 (1916), The Granger Collection, New York; 506 (1620), Mary Evans Picture Library/The Image Works; 507 (1900), Dewitt Jones/Corbis; 507 (2000), Donovan Reese /Getty Images; 507 (2004), Kristy-Anne Glubish/Design Pics/Corbis; 507 (800 B.C.E.), George Steinmetz/Corbis; 507 (312 B.C.E.), Marco Scataglini/Alamy; 507 (1954), Tom Brakefield/Corbis; 507 (1935), Jeff Vanuga/NRCS; 507 (2008), USDA NRCS;

UNIT SIX: 509 (cr), Charles Doswell III/Getty Images; 509 (l), Getty Images/Taxi; 509 (br), Theo Allofs/CORBIS; 510-511 (all), Kevin Kelly/Getty Images; 510 (b), NASA/Photo Researchers, Inc.; 510 (c), Jeremy Woodhouse/Photodisc/Getty; 510 (t), Wolfgang

Kaehler/CORBIS; 511, HMH/Victoria Smith Photo; 515 (br), Royalty Free/CORBIS; 515 (tl), Roger Ressmeyer/CORBIS ; 515 (tr), Wolfgang Kaehler/CORBIS; 515 (bl), Carol Hughes; Gallo Images/CORBIS; 516 (tl), Didrik Johnck/CORBIS; 516 (tr), Chris Noble/Stone/Getty Images; 517, HMH/Andy Christiansen; 519, NASA/CORBIS; 520, Martin Thomas/Reuters NewMedia Inc./ CORBIS; 521 (infrared), NOAO/SPL/Photo Researchers, Inc.; 521 (ultraviolet), SOHO/ESA/NASA; 521 (visible), NASA/JIAS/SPL/Photo Researchers, Inc.; 521 (x-ray), NASA/JIAS/SPL/Photo Researchers, Inc.; 521 (radio), NRAO/AUI/NSF; 522 (b), Tim Boyle/Getty Images; 523, Jeremy Woodhouse/Photodisc/Getty; 529, NASA/ Photo Researchers, Inc.; 530, Charles Benes/Index Stock Imagery, Inc.; 531 (bkgd), Design Pics Inc./Alamy; 531 (l), Morgan David de Lossy/CORBIS; 531 (tr), Pekka Parviainen/Photo Researchers, Inc.; 531 (c), Marko Mikkila; 531 (cr), Mark Duffy/Alamy; 532 (b), HMH/Andy Christiansen; 534, NASA; 535 (b), NASA/Photo Researchers, Inc.; 535 (c), Jeremy Woodhouse/Photodisc/Getty; 535 (t), Wolfgang Kaehler/CORBIS; 540-541 (all), Charles Doswell III/Getty Images; 540 (c), Michael S. Yamashita/CORBIS; 540 (b), Gary W. Carter/CORBIS; 540 (t), Paul Zahl/National Geographic Image Collection; 541, HMH/Victoria Smith Photo; 544 (bkgd), Craig Aurness/CORBIS; 544 (br), David Vintiner/CORBIS; 544 (bl), Jon Hicks/CORBIS; 546 (tr), Paul Zahl/National Geographic Image Collection; 547 (b), Breck Kent/Animals Animals/Earth Scenes; 548 (tl), Graham Neden/Ecoscene/CORBIS; 550 (br), Michael S. Yamashita/CORBIS; 551 (t), Beth Wald/Aurora; 553 (tr), Gary Braasch/CORBIS; 553 (tl), Royalty Free/CORBIS; 554 (tl), Charles O'Rear/CORBIS; 555 (bc), Gary W. Carter/CORBIS; 555 (bl), Darrell Gulin/CORBIS; 556 (b), Ted Kinsman/Photo Researchers, Inc.; 557 (t), Gene Rhoden/Weatherpix; 558 (tl), Jim Brandenburg/Minden Pictures; 560 (br), HMH/Victoria Smith; 561 (tr), HMH/Victoria Smith; 563 (bl), Gary W. Carter/CORBIS; 563 (cl), Michael S. Yamashita/CORBIS; 563 (t), Paul Zahl/ National Geographic Image Collection; 568-569 (all), Getty Images/ Taxi; 568 (t), Benjamin Lowy/CORBIS; 568 (c), A & J Verkaik/ CORBIS; 568 (b), NASA; 569, HMH/Victoria Smith Photo; 571, NOAA; 572, Rick Doyle/CORBIS; 574, Benjamin Lowy/Corbis; 578, A & J Verkaik/CORBIS; 580 (c), CIMSS/NOAA; 580 (b), Smiley N. Pool/ Dallas Morning News/CORBIS; 581 (b), ROBERT GALBRAITH/Reuters/CORBIS; 581 (cr), Brian Collins/USGS; 581 (tr), David J. Phillip/AP Images; 582 (tl), Howard B. Bluestein/Photo Researchers, Inc.; 582 (inset), Jim Reed/CORBIS; 583, Jonathan Blair/CORBIS; 584 (b), HMH/Victoria Smith; 584 (t), Philippe Giraud/CORBIS SYGMA ; 585 (bkgd), RF123; 585 (tl), Direccao dos Servicos Meteorologicos e Geofisicos; 586 (t), NASA; 587, Courtesy World Meteorological Organization; 589 (t), Courtesy, The Weather Channel; 590, Jim Reed/CORBIS; 592, H. David Seawell/ CORBIS; 593 (bkgd), Dale O'Dell/Veer/Getty; 593 (bl), Michael S. Yamashita/CORBIS; 593 (br), John Tinning/Frank Lane Picture Agency/CORBIS; 593 (bc), ON PAGE CREDIT; 594 (b), HMH; 597 (4), Jim Reed/CORBIS; 597 (2), A & J Verkaik/CORBIS; 597 (1), Benjamin Lowy/CORBIS; 597 (3), NASA; 599 (bkgd), Kim Morris/ZUMA; 599 (tr), Gene Rhoden/weatherpix; 599 (cl), Gary Gardiner/ZUMA; 599 (b), Southern Stock/Brand X/CORBIS; 599 (cr), Tulsa World/WPN; 602-603 (all), Theo Allofs/CORBIS; 602 (t), Wolfgang Kaehler/CORBIS; 602 (c), Bryan and Cherry Alexander Photography; 602 (b), Wendy Stone/CORBIS; 603, HMH/Victoria Smith Photo; 605 (br), Andrea Pistolesi/Getty Images; 605 (bl), Wolfgang Kaehler/CORBIS; 609 (bl), Reuters NewMedia, Inc./ CORBIS; 609 (br), Indranil Mukherjee/AFP/Getty Images; 613 (tl), Bryan and Cherry Alexander Photography; 616 (tl), Bojan Brecelj/ CORBIS; 616 (inset), Simon Fraser/Photo Researchers, Inc.; 616 (bkgd), Arctic-Images/CORBIS; 618 (tr), Yann Arthus-Bertrand/ CORBIS; 620 (bl), Wendy Stone/CORBIS; 620 (tl), Wendy Stone/ CORBIS; 621 (bkgd), Norbert Rosing/Getty Images; 621 (t), Johnny Johnson/Getty Images; 621 (r), Ralph Lee Hopkins/Getty Images; 621 (bl), NASA; 621 (br), NASA; 622 (b), Victoria Smith/ Harcourt; 625 (cl), Bryan and Cherry Alexander Photography; 625 (tl), Wolfgang Kaehler/CORBIS; 630 (tr), Kunsthistorisches Museum, Vienna,Austria/ Bridgeman Art Library; 630 (1654), Alamy; 630 (1783), The Gallery Collection/CORBIS; 630 (1930), Hulton-Deutsch Collection/CORBIS; 630 (1887), Bettmann/ CORBIS; 630 (1935), Bettmann/CORBIS; 630 (1943), Jim Reed/ CORBIS; 630 (1946), Gabe Palmer/CORBIS; 630 (2007), Robin Nelson/ZUMA; 630-631 (all), Anthony Redpath/CORBIS; 631 (1939), The Dmitri Baltermants Collection/CORBIS; 631 (1926), Bettmann/CORBIS; 631 (1957), Bettmann/CORBIS; 631 (1946), Bettmann/CORBIS; 631 (1960), AP IMAGES/NASA; 631 (2002), NASA; 631 (2005), NASA; 631 (1988), National Oceanic and Atmospheric Administration/Department of Commerce; 631 (1969), Reuters/CORBIS; 631 (2005), National Oceanic and Atmospheric Administration/Department of Commerce;

UNIT SEVEN: 633 (cr), Tom Stewart/CORBIS; 633 (l), G. R. Roberts/Natural Sciences Image Library (NSIL) of New Zealand; 633 (br), Craig Tuttle/CORBIS; 634-635 (all), Jeffrey L. Rotman/ CORBIS; 634 (t), Ocean Drilling Program - Texas A&M University; 634 (c), B. Tanaka/Getty Images/Taxi; 634 (b), Tom McHugh/ Photo Researchers, Inc.; 635, HMH/Victoria Smith Photo; 638 (l, br), Ocean Drilling Program - Texas A&M University; 639 (ship), National Oceanic and Atmospheric Administration/Department of Commerce; 640 (inset), David Shale/naturepl.com; 640 (tl), Alexis Rosenfeld/SPL/Photo Researchers, Inc.; 644, B. Tanaka/ Getty Images/Taxi; 645, Ocean Drilling Program - Texas A&M University; 646 (b), Courtesy Stephen Morris, Experimental Nonlinear Physics Group, University of Toronto; 646 (bkgd), Nautilus Mining; 646 (bc), Rob Cousins/Alamy; 646 (bl), Brian North/ Alamy; 647 (nodules), Tom McHugh/Photo Researchers, Inc.; 647 (bkgd), Darryl Torckler/Getty Images/Stone; 647 (nodules), Tom McHugh/Photo Researchers, Inc.; 648 (r), Andrew Syred/ SPL/Photo Researchers, Inc.; 648 (l), Jim Zuckerman/CORBIS; 649 (bkgd), Science Source/Photo Researchers, Inc.; 649 (red jelly), AP IMAGES/Ocean Geographic Magazine through WHOI/ ISSP,Michael Aw,HO; 649 (t), AP IMAGES/Ocean Geographic Magazine through WHOI/ISSP,Michael Aw,HO; 649 (larval squid), AP IMAGES/Dr. Ross Hopcroft, University of Alaska through WHOI/ ISSP/HO; 649 (moonsnail), Katrin Linse/British Antarctic Survey; 649, David Shale; 649 (bl, cr), David Shale; 651, HMH/Victoria Smith; 652, NGDC/NOAA; 653 (c), B. Tanaka/Getty Images/Taxi; 653 (t), Ocean Drilling Program - Texas A&M University; 658-659 (all), David Hall/seaphotos.com; 658 (t), Sean Davey/AllSport/Getty Images; 658 (c), David Hall/seaphotos.com; 658 (b), Chris Hellier/ CORBIS; 659, Sam Dudgeon/Harcourt; 662 (bkgd), Snaprender/ Alamy Images; 663 (tl), Sean Davey/AllSport/Getty Images; 665 (tr), Craig Tuttle/CORBIS; 665 (tl), Tom Stewart/CORBIS; 667 (br), HMH/Victoria Smith; 667 (tc), HMH/Sam Dudgeon; 668 (tl), Lawson Wood/CORBIS; 669 (bl), David Hall/seaphotos.com; 670 (bl), IQ3d/Bruce Coleman, Inc.; 672 (tr), Craig Tuttle/CORBIS; 673 (bl), Steve Raymer/National Geographic Image Collection; 674 (tr), Bohemian Nomad Picturemakers/CORBIS; 675 (b), Chris Hellier/ CORBIS; 676 (tl), Simon Fraser/SPL/Photo Researchers, Inc.; 677 (bkgd), Stephen Frink/CORBIS; 677 (b), John Daniels/Alamy; 677 (tr), David Noble/Alamy; 677 (tr, inset), Victor R. Boswell Jr./ National geographic/Getty Images; 677 (cr), NOAA/NURC-Uconn 677 (t), Richard T. Nowitz/CORBIS; 678 (bl), HMH/Victoria Smith; 680, Courtesy of N.R. Nalli, NOAA/NESDIS, Washington, D.C.; 681 (tl), Sean Davey/AllSport/Getty Images; 681 (bl), Chris Hellier/ CORBIS; 681 (cl), David Hall/seaphotos.com; 686-687 (all), Chris Walsh/IFA Bilderteam/Jupiterimages; 686 (c), Darrell Wong; 686 (t), Jonathan Blair/CORBIS; 686 (b), Paul A. Souders/CORBIS; 687, Sam Dudgeon/Harcourt; 689 (bl), Jonathan Blair/CORBIS; 690 (br), Provided by the SeaWiFS Project, NASA/Goddard Space Flight Center, and ORBIMAGE; 692 (inset), Peter David/Natural Visions; 694 (cl), M-SAT LTD/Photo Researchers, Inc.; 695 (bl), Jack Fields/CORBIS; 697 (br), HMH/Victoria Smith; 697 (tr), Darrell Wong; 699 (tr), G. R. Roberts/Natural Sciences Image Library (NSIL) of New Zealand; 700 (inset), Connie Rica/CORBIS; 700 (tl), John Stanmeyer/VII/AP/Wide World Photos; 703 (cl), Paul A. Souders/CORBIS; 703 (tl), Buddy Mays/CORBIS; 703 (bkgd), V. Mouchel/MAXPPP /ZUMA; 703 (br), Sally Morgan / Ecocsene; 703 (bl), Department of Biological and Environmental Sciences,Samford University; 704 (tl), Bruce M. Herman/Photo Researchers, Inc.; 705 (bkgd), Karsten Petersen; 706 (b), HMH/Victoria Smith; 709 (cl), Darrell Wong; 709 (tl), Jonathan Blair/CORBIS; 709 (bl), Paul A. Souders/CORBIS; 714-715 (all), Stephen Frink/zefa/Corbis; 714 (1000 C.E.), Wolfgang Kaehler/Alamy; 714 (1859), London Art Archive/Alamy; 714 (1620), ©London Photos-Homer Sykes/ Alamy; 714 (1519), North Wind Picture Archives/ Alamy; 714 (t), Naval Historical Foundation; 714 714 (1912), The Granger Collection, New York; 715 (1939), The Granger Collection, New York; 715 (1944), James L. Amos/Corbis; 715 (1949), R. Ludwig Turner and the Ludwig Family; 715 (2008), Kos Picture Source/Alamy; 715 (2003), Carl D. Walsh/Aurora Photos; 715 (1964), Emory Kristof and Alvin Chandler/National Geographic Image Collection; 715 (1986), Emory Kristof/National Geographic Image Collection; 715 (1967), Vincenzo Lombardo/Getty Images; 715 (1939-1945), Denis Scott/Corbis; 715 (2000), Tim Aylen/ AP Images;

UNIT EIGHT: 717 (cr), NASA; 717 (l), NASA/Gemini Observatory, GMOS Team; 717 (br), Fred Espenak; 718-719 (all), Stocktrek Images/Getty Images; 718 (b), Visuals Unlimited/CORBIS; 718 (t), Jean-Charles Cuillandre/Canada-france-Hawaii Telescope/ SPL/Photo Researchers, Inc.; 719, HMH/Victoria Smith Photo; 721 (bl), NASA; 722 (tl), Jean-Charles Cuillandre/Canada-france-Hawaii Telescope/SPL/Photo Researchers, Inc.; 722 (tr), NASA; 723 (br), Alfred Pasieka/SPL/Photo Researchers, Inc.; 724 (br), Michael Freeman/CORBIS; 726 (tl), Glen Alison/PhotoDisc Green/ gettyimages; 726 (bkgd), NASA; 726 (bl), NASA; 726 (dna), ©Jon Lomberg; 727 (br), NASA-JPL; 727 (tl, bl), NASA; 728 (t), NASA; 729, Visuals Unlimited/CORBIS; 732 (tl), Gianni Dagli Orti/ CORBIS; 735 (br), HMH/Andy Christiansen; 737 (bkgd), Atlantide Phototravel/CORBIS; 737 (cl), The National Institute of Standards and Technology; 737 (br), HMH/Victoria Smith Photo; 738 (br), HMH/Peter Van Steen; 740 (t), C. Mayhew & R. Simmon/NASA/ GSFO; 741 (tl), Jean-Charles Cuillandre/Canada-france-Hawaii Telescope/SPL/Photo Researchers, Inc.; 743, Visuals Unlimited/ CORBIS; 746-747 (all), Denis Scott/CORBIS; 746 (t), Royal Observatory, Edinburgh/SPL/Photo Researchers, Inc.; 746 (c), NASA/SPL/Photo Researchers, Inc.; 746 (b), CORBIS; 746 (b), Ctein /Getty Images; 747, HMH/Victoria Smith Photo; 749 (bl), Royal Observatory, Edinburgh/SPL/Photo Researchers, Inc.; 754 (tl), Lindsay Hebberd/CORBIS; 756 (br), HMH/Victoria Smith; 758 (t), Ctein/Getty Images; 759 (b), JPL/NASA; 760 (br), NASA/SPL/ Photo Researchers, Inc.; 761 (tl), NASA/SPL/Photo Researchers, Inc.; 762 (br), ESA/PLI/CORBIS; 763 (t), NASA; 764 (tr), Gordon Garradd/Photo Researchers, Inc.; 764 (tl), NASA; 765 (bl), Kevin Kelley/Getty Images; 766 (br), NASA; 767 (tr), CORBIS; 767 (bkgd), Science Source/Photo Researchers, Inc.; 767 (bl), NASA; 767 (bc), NASA; 768 (br), NASA/JPL/Space Science Institute; 769 (tl), Lawrence Sromovsky, University of Wisconsin-Madison,Keck Observatory; 770 (br), JPL/NASA; 771, Wikipedia based on a NASA image; 772 (tl), Lynette R. Cook; 773 (bkgd), www. launchphotography.com; 773 (tr), NASA; 773 (tl), NASA; 773 (bl), NASA; 774 (b), HMH/Victoria Smith; 775 (tr), HMH/Victoria Smith; 776 (tc), NASA/SPL/Photo Researchers, Inc.; 777 (b), CORBIS; 777 (bl), NASA/SPL/Photo Researchers, Inc.; 777 (t), Royal Observatory, Edinburgh/SPL/Photo Researchers, Inc.; 777 (cl), Ctein /Getty Images; 782 (t), NASA; 782 (c), CNES/GAMMA; 782 (c), Galileo Project/JPL/NASA; 782 (b), Wally Pacholka/ AstroPics.com; 783, HMH/Victoria Smith Photo; 785, NASA; 786 (b), Courtesy U.S. Geological Survey; 787 (b), NASA; 787 (t), NASA; 790 (b,t), USGS; 792, NASA; 793 (br), CNES/GAMMA; 793 (bl), Detlev van Ravenswaay/Photo Researchers Inc.; 794 (t), Royalty Free/CORBIS; 794 (b), HMH/Victoria Smith; 795 (b), Dr. Fred Espenak/Photo Researchers, Inc.; 796, NASA; 796 (moons), John Bova/Photo Researchers, Inc.; 797, John Sanford/Photo Researchers, Inc.; 799, NASA/JPL/University of Arizona; 800 (b), Galileo Project/JPL/NASA; 800 (bc), AstronomyOnline.org; 800 (br), Scala /Art Resource, NY; 800 (bl), Galleria Palatina,Palazzo Pitti,Florence,Italy/Bridgeman Art Library; 800 (bkgd), Special Collection Library, University of Michigan; 801 (t), Galileo Project/ JPL/NASA; 801 (b,c), NASA; 802 (t,b), NASA; 803 (b), Dr. R. Albrecht, ESA/ESO Space Telescope European Coordinating Facility; NASA ; 803 (t), NASA; 803, NASA, ESA, H. Weaver (JHU/APL), A. Stern (SwRI), and the HST Pluto Companion Search Team; 804 (t), NASA; 805, NASA; 806, Getty Images/PhotoDisc; 809, Juan Carlos Casado; 810 (b), Ken Nichols/Institute of Meteorites; 810 (c), Breck P. Kent/Animals Animals/Earth Scenes; 810 (t), E.R. Degginger/Bruce Coleman, Inc.; 811 (bkgd), NASA; 811 (r), NASA; 811 (tl), Tulsa World; 811 (cl), NASA; 811 (b), Enver Essop; 814, NASA; 815 (4), Wally Pacholka/AstroPics.com; 815 (3), Galileo Project/JPL/NASA; 815 (2), CNES/GAMMA; 815 (1), NASA; 820-821 (all), SOHO/ESA/NASA; 820 (t), Fred Espenak; 820 (b), Pekka Parviainen/Photo Researchers, Inc.; 821, HMH/ Victoria Smith Photo; 825 (b), HMH/Andy Christiansen; 825 (t), Kamioka Observatory, ICRR (Institute for Cosmic Ray Research), The University of Tokyo; 827 (inset), NOAO/AURA/NSF; 827 (b),

John Chumack/Photo Researchers, Inc.; 828, Fred Espenak; 829 (inset), Getty Images/Photodisc; 829 (bl), The Institute for Solar Physics, The Royal Swedish Academy of Sciences; 830 (bkgd), NASA; 830 (br), SOHO (ESA & NASA); 831, M. Aschwanden et al. (LMSAL), TRACE, NASA ; 832, Pekka Parviainen/Photo Researchers, Inc.; 833 (bkgd), Bill Barksdale/CORBIS; 833 (cl), Craig Hammelln/CORBIS; 833 (cr), Najlah Feanny/CORBIS; 833 (br), Gary Carter/CORBIS; 834, 835 HMH; 836, SAO, NASA, JAXA, NAOJ; 837 (t), Fred Espenak; 837 (b), Pekka Parviainen/Photo Researchers, Inc.; 839, NASA; 842-843 (all), Stocktrek/CORBIS; 842 (1), Grant Faint/Getty Images; 842 (2), NASA The Heritage Hubble Team; 842 (3), NASA/WMAP Science Team; 842 (4), S. Kohle,T. Credner, et al; 843, HMH/Victoria Smith Photo; 845 (b), N.A.Sharp, NOAO/NSO/Kitt Peak FTS/AURA/NSF; 846 (t), NASA/Hubble Heritage Team; 847 (b), Grant Faint/Getty Images; 849 (inset), HMH/Victoria Smith; 850 (bkgd), Roger Ressmeyer/CORBIS; 852 (tr), NASA; 853 (b), ©Arthur Morris/CORBIS; 853 (l), Biodisc/Visuals Unlimited/Getty Images; 854 (br), Matthew Spinelli; 855 (tr), NASA The Heritage Hubble Team; 855 (bl), NASA; 855 (br), Catherine Karnow/CORBIS; 858 (tl), NASA; 860 (b), S. Kohle,T. Credner, et al; 861 (tc), NOAO/Photo Researchers, Inc.; 861 (tr), Royal Observatory, Edinburgh/AATB/SPL/Photo Researchers, Inc.; 861 (tl), NASA/Gemini Observatory, GMOS Team; 862 (tr), NASA/CXC/A.Siemiginowska et al.; Illustration: CXC/M.Weiss ; 863 (br), NASA; 865 (br), NASA/WMAP Science Team; 865 (tr), HMH/Victoria Smith; 866 (tl), NASA and Hubble Heritage Team; 867 (bkgd), IceCube/NSF; 867 (cl), IceCube/NSF; 867 (c), IceCube/NSF; 869 (tr), HMH/Victoria Smith; 870 (t), Courtesy NASA/JPL-Caltech; 871 (cl), NASA The Heritage Hubble Team; 871 (tl), Grant Faint/Getty Images; 871 (bl), NASA/WMAP Science Team; 871 (cl), S. Kohle,T. Credner, et al;

APPENDIX: 920 (b), HMH/Victoria Smith; 920 (bkgd), David Muench/CORBIS; 921 (all), USGS; 923 (r), Karl Mueller/University of Colorado/AP/Wide World Photos; 924 (tr), David McNew/Getty Images/NewsCom; 927 (b), HMH/Victoria Smith; 928 (b), Chris Johns/Getty Images/National Geographic; 929 (b), Greg Dimijian/Photo Researchers, Inc.; 930 (br), A.T. Willett/Alamy Photos; 931 (b), A.T. Willett/Alamy Photos; 932 (b), Courtesy Earth and Sky; 934 (b), HMH ; 935 (br), Photodisc Green/Getty Images; 935 (tr), David Young-Wolff/PhotoEdit; 936 (b), Digital Image copyright 2006 Larry Brownstein/PhotoDisc; 938 (b), David Gallant/CORBIS; 940-941 (b), Robert Landau/CORBIS; 941 (br), HMH/Victoria Smith; 942 (br), HMH/Daniel Schaefer; 944 (b), A & J Verkaik/CORBIS; 947 (t), Hillery Smith/AP/Wide World Photos; 949 (t), Michael Wirtz/Philadelphia Inquirer/NewsCom; 950 (b), Tony Freeman/PhotoEdit; 953 (r), Paul Wakefield/Getty Images/Stone; 953 (l), Galen Rowell/CORBIS; 954 (b), HMH; 954 (b), HMH; 954 (b), HMH; 954 (b), HMH; 955 (tl), Stocktrek/CORBIS; 955 (tr), WallyPacholka/AstroPics.com;

Staff Credits

The people who contributed to this edition of ***Holt McDougal Earth Science*** are listed below. They represent design, editorial, marketing, multimedia, and production.

Wesley M. Bain, Kelly Ballew, Kimberly Barr, Angela Beckmann, Sara Butler, Soojinn Choi, Clarissa Cochran, Lorraine Cooper, Lana Cox, Eddie Dawson, Juliet Dervin, Michelle Dike, Lydia Doty, Sam Dudgeon, Holly Everett, Jenevieve Eyre, Leigh Ann García, Diana Goetting, Kristin Hay, Tim Hovde, John Koonz, Denise Mahoney, Stuart McKenzie, Ivonne Mercado, Richard Metzger, Erin Miller, Jessica Mraz, Ali Nagib, Mercedes Newman, David Parisotto, Bill Rader, Sara Rider, Jeff Robinson, Karen Ross, Tara Ross, Beth Sample, Kay Selke, Susan Skinner, Chris Smith, Victoria Smith, Kim Soriano, Sherry Sprague, Jeannie Taylor, Bob Tucek, Kira J. Watkins, and Nadyne Wood.